*The Consumer Credit and Sales
Legal Practice Series*

CONSUMER ARBITRATION AGREEMENTS

Enforceability and Other Topics

Fifth Edition With CD-Rom

F. Paul Bland, Jr.
Leslie A. Bailey
Michael J. Quirk
Richard H. Frankel
Jonathan Sheldon

National Consumer Law Center
77 Summer Street, 10th Floor   Boston, MA 02110
www.consumerlaw.org

with the Public Justice Foundation
www.publicjustice.net

About NCLC The National Consumer Law Center, a nonprofit corporation founded in 1969, assists consumers, advocates, and public policy makers nationwide who use the powerful and complex tools of consumer law to ensure justice and fair treatment for all, particularly those whose poverty renders them powerless to demand accountability from the economic marketplace. For more information, go to www.consumerlaw.org.

Ordering NCLC Publications Order securely online at www.consumerlaw.org, or contact Publications Department, National Consumer Law Center, 77 Summer Street, Boston, MA 02110, (617) 542-9595, FAX: (617) 542-8028, e-mail: publications@nclc.org. [Effective Summer 2008:7 Winthrop Sq., Boston, MA 02110.]

Training and Conferences NCLC participates in numerous national, regional, and local consumer law trainings. Its annual fall conference is a forum for consumer rights attorneys from legal services programs, private practice, government, and nonprofit organizations to share insights into common problems and explore novel and tested approaches that promote consumer justice in the marketplace. Contact NCLC for more information or see our web site.

Case Consulting Case analysis, consulting and co-counseling for lawyers representing vulnerable consumers are among NCLC's important activities. Administration on Aging funds allow us to provide free consulting to legal services advocates representing elderly consumers on many types of cases. Massachusetts Legal Assistance Corporation funds permit case assistance to advocates representing low-income Massachusetts consumers. Other funding may allow NCLC to provide very brief consultations to other advocates without charge. More comprehensive case analysis and research is available for a reasonable fee. See our web site for more information at www.consumerlaw.org.

Charitable Donations and Cy Pres Awards NCLC's work depends in part on the support of private donors. Tax-deductible donations should be made payable to National Consumer Law Center, Inc. For more information, contact Suzanne Cutler of NCLC's Development Office at (617) 542-8010 or scutler@nclc.org. NCLC has also received generous court-approved *cy pres* awards arising from consumer class actions to advance the interests of class members. For more information, contact Robert Hobbs (rhobbs@nclc.org) or Rich Dubois (rdubois@nclc.org) at (617) 542-8010.

Comments and Corrections Write to the above address to the attention of the Editorial Department or e-mail consumerlaw@nclc.org.

About This Volume This is the Fifth Edition of *Consumer Arbitration Agreements* with a 2007 companion CD-Rom. The Fifth Edition and 2007 CD-Rom supersede all prior editions, supplements, and CDs, which should all be discarded. Continuing developments can be found in periodic updates to this volume and in NCLC REPORTS.

Cite This Volume As National Consumer Law Center, Consumer Arbitration Agreements (5th ed. 2007).

Attention
> *This publication is designed to provide authoritative information concerning the subject matter covered. Always use the most current edition and supplement, and use other sources for more recent developments or for special rules for individual jurisdictions. This publication cannot substitute for the independent judgment and skills of an attorney or other professional. Non-attorneys are cautioned against using these materials to conduct a lawsuit without advice from an attorney and are cautioned against engaging in the unauthorized practice of law.*

Copyright © 2007 by National Consumer Law Center, Inc.
All Rights Reserved

ISBN-13 978-1-60248-018-6 (this volume)
ISBN-10 1-60248-018-4 (this volume)
ISBN 0-943116-10-4 (Series)

Library of Congress Control Number 2007939771

About the Authors

F. Paul Bland, Jr. is a staff attorney at Public Justice (formerly Trial Lawyers for Public Justice), handling precedent-setting complex civil litigation. He has argued and won more than twenty reported decisions from federal and state courts, including the U.S. Courts of Appeal for the Fourth, Fifth, Eighth and Ninth Circuits, and California, Florida, Maryland, Washington State and West Virginia high courts. He is a co-author of the prior four editions of this title and of numerous articles. He is a past co-chair of the National Association of Consumer Advocates, and the 2006 recipient of the Vern Countryman Award. His role in challenging mandatory arbitration clauses led to his being named the 2002 San Francisco Trial Lawyer of the Year and the 2001 Maryland Trial Lawyer of the Year. He formerly was a plaintiffs' class action and libel defense attorney in Baltimore and Chief Nominations Counsel to the U.S. Senate Judiciary Committee.

Leslie A. Bailey is the Brayton-Baron Attorney at Public Justice, focusing on consumers' rights, including fighting abusive mandatory arbitration clauses and federal preemption defenses; civil rights, including disability rights and prisoners' rights; and challenges to court secrecy orders. Her successful briefs to state high courts include in *Scott v. Cingular Wireless*, 161 P.3d 1000 (Wash. 2007) (class action ban in consumer contract is unconscionable) and *Sweeney v. Savings First Mortgage, LLC*, 879 A.2d 1037 (Md. 2005) (federal mortgage lending law does not preempt state law limiting mortgage broker fees). She has been a featured speaker on mandatory arbitration, opposing confirmation of arbitration awards in debt collection cases, and other consumers' rights issues, and has authored several articles on fighting class action bans and confirmation of arbitration awards in debt collection cases.

Michael J. Quirk is an associate with Williams Cuker Berezofsky in Philadelphia, where he represents consumers, workers, and toxic exposure victims. He was formerly an Equal Justice Works Fellow and staff attorney with Public Justice, where his work focused primarily on fighting mandatory arbitration abuses. He has represented plaintiffs making successful challenges to mandatory arbitration provisions before the U.S. Court of Appeals for the Ninth Circuit in *Tamayo v. Brainstorm USA*, the New Jersey Supreme Court in *Muhammad v. County Bank of Rehoboth Beach, Del.*, and the Mississippi Supreme Court in *Sanderson Farms, Inc. v. Gatlin*. He is co-author of the first four editions of *Consumer Arbitration Agreements*, and has written several articles on mandatory arbitration and other consumer rights issues.

Richard H. Frankel is a teaching fellow in the Appellate Litigation Clinic at the Georgetown University Law Center. He is formerly the Goldberg-Saladoff Fellow at Public Justice, where he worked extensively on consumer protection and civil rights issues, including litigating class actions, fighting mandatory arbitration abuse, challenging the reach of federal preemption, stopping class action abuse, and fighting court secrecy.

Jonathan Sheldon is an NCLC staff attorney focusing on automobile fraud, deceptive practices law and other consumer law topics since 1976. Previously he was a staff attorney with the Federal Trade Commission. His publications include the four prior editions of this title, *Automobile Fraud*, *Unfair and Deceptive Acts and Practices*, *Consumer Warranty Law*, *Consumer Class Actions*, and *Repossessions*.

Acknowledgments: The authors thank Carlene McNulty of the North Carolina Justice Center for contributing appendix material and AAA, JAMS, and NAF for granting copyright permission to reprint their arbitration rules. We are particularly grateful to Eric Secoy for editorial supervision; Katherine Hunt for editorial assistance; Shannon Halbrook for production assistance; Shirlron Williams for assistance with cite checking; Allen Agnitti for research assistance and cite checking, Xylutions for typesetting services; Mary McLean for indexing; and Neil Fogarty of Law Disks for preparing the CD-Rom.

PUBLIC JUSTICE
AMERICA'S PUBLIC INTEREST LAW FIRM

JOIN US & CONTRIBUTE

The Public Justice Foundation, a non-profit 501(c)(3) membership organization, supports Public Justice's cutting-edge litigation and educates the public about the issues it addresses. Through annual membership dues, special gifts, and other support, our members make justice possible. Many take on active roles, serve as cooperating counsel, become active in their states, and network with public interest organizations on our behalf. Some of the benefits of annual membership include:

PUBLIC JUSTICE
Our newsletter updates members on our litigation and important developments in the legal world.

E-LERTS
Our *Public Justice E-lerts* inform members by email of breaking news and important activities as they happen.

WEB SITE
Download key briefs, decisions and other materials at www.publicjustice.net

NETWORKING
Attend our annual events and meetings across the country and network with leading attorneys committed to the public interest.

TRIAL LAWYER OF THE YEAR AWARD
Nominate candidates and meet the finalists and winners of this prestigious award.

VOLUNTEER
Members can volunteer for key committees, serve as state coordinators, or serve as cooperating counsel when appropriate.

PRIDE
The number one benefit cited by our members is the tremendous pride they feel in being associated with Public Justice and its 25 year history of making a difference. Once you have become a member, we encourage you to provide a link to Public Justice on your firm's home page, noting that you are a proud supporter.

SUPPORT PUBLIC JUSTICE

Join us as a member with a tax-deductible gift. You may choose to join as an individual at any of our membership levels, or, you may want to consider a gift from your firm that covers each of your attorneys as members at the $250 level or above:

- ○ $250 General
- ○ $500 Supporting
- ○ $1,000 Sustaining
- ○ $2,500 Advocate
- ○ $5,000 Benefactor
- ○ $10,000 Patron

- ○ $100 Associate (limited to non-lawyers, lawyers in practice less than 5 years, professors, and government and legal service lawyers)
- ○ $25 Student (year of graduation _____)

Make a special gift to our 25ᵀᴴ Anniversary Campaign for Public Justice, with a tax-deductible gift at the following level:

- ○ $10,000 (A generous Board member will match gifts from individuals or firms that have never given at this level before. Also benefits below.)
- ○ $5,000 (Donors at this level will receive special recognition on the Public Justice web site with a hot link to their firm's web site, in addition to the recognition listed below.)
- ○ $2,500 (Donors at this level will receive a limited edition sterling silver Public Justice lapel pin, and recognition throughout the year in both the newsletter and on a traveling plaque displayed at all events.)
- ○ $1,000   ○ $500   ○ $250   ○ Other

NAME _____

FIRM/ORGANIZATION _____

ADDRESS _____

CITY   STATE   ZIP

PHONE   FAX   EMAIL

REFERRED BY _____

○ Check enclosed (made out to the **Public Justice Foundation**)
○ Charge my   ○ AmEX   ○ Visa   ○ MCard

CARD NUMBER   EXP

DATE   SEC. CODE

Send this form to: Public Justice Foundation • 1825 K Street, NW #200, Washington, DC 20006
Fax (202) 232-7203   Email: publicjustice@publicjustice.net

What Your Library Should Contain

The Consumer Credit and Sales Legal Practice Series contains 17 titles, updated annually, arranged into four libraries, and designed to be an attorney's primary practice guide and legal resource in all 50 states. Each manual includes a CD-Rom allowing pinpoint searches and the pasting of text into a word processor.

Debtor Rights Library

2006 Eighth Edition (Two Volumes), 2007 Supplement, and 2007 CD-Rom, Including Law Disks' 2007 Bankruptcy Forms

Consumer Bankruptcy Law and Practice: the definitive personal bankruptcy manual, from the initial interview to final discharge, including consumer rights when a company files for bankruptcy. The eighth edition and supplement fully incorporate the 2005 Act in the text and include such practice aids as a redlined Code, Interim Rules, a date calculator, over 150 pleadings and forms, initial forms software, means test data, and a client questionnaire and handout.

2004 Fifth Edition, 2007 Supplement, and 2007 CD-Rom

Fair Debt Collection: the basic reference, covering the Fair Debt Collection Practices Act and common law, state statutory and other federal debt collection protections. Appendices and companion CD-Rom contain sample pleadings and discovery, the FTC Commentary, *all* FTC staff opinion letters, and summaries of reported and unreported cases.

2007 Second Edition with CD-Rom

Foreclosures: covers VA, FHA, Fannie Mae, subprime, other workout agreements, remedies against abusive servicers, rights to stave off foreclosure and to deal with tax liens, and tactics after the foreclosure sale.

2005 Sixth Edition, 2007 Supplement, and 2007 CD-Rom

Repossessions: a unique guide to motor vehicle and mobile home repossessions, threatened seizures of household goods, statutory liens, and automobile lease and rent-to-own default remedies.

2006 Third Edition, 2007 Supplement, and 2007 CD-Rom

Student Loan Law: collection harassment; closed school, disability, and other discharges; tax intercepts, wage garnishment, and offset of social security benefits; repayment plans, consolidation loans, deferments, and non-payment of loan based on school fraud.

2004 Third Edition, 2007 Supplement, and 2007 CD-Rom

Access to Utility Service: consumer rights as to regulated and unregulated utilities, including telecommunications, terminations, billing errors, low-income payment plans, utility allowances in subsidized housing, LIHEAP, and weatherization.

Credit and Banking Library

2007 Sixth Edition with CD-Rom

Truth in Lending: detailed analysis of *all* aspects of TILA, the Consumer Leasing Act, and the Home Ownership and Equity Protection Act (HOEPA). Appendices and the CD-Rom contain the Acts, Reg. Z, Reg. M, and their Official Staff Commentaries, numerous sample pleadings, rescission notices, and two programs to compute APRs.

2006 Sixth Edition, 2007 Supplement, and 2007 CD-Rom

Fair Credit Reporting: the key resource for handling any type of credit reporting issue, from cleaning up blemished credit records to suing reporting agencies and creditors for inaccurate reports. Covers credit scoring, privacy issues, identity theft, FACTA, the Credit Repair Organizations Act, state credit reporting and repair statutes, and common law claims.

National Consumer Law Center ■ (617) 542-9595 ■ FAX (617) 542-8028 ■ publications@nclc.org
Order securely online at www.consumerlaw.org

2005 Third Edition, 2007 Supplement, and 2007 CD-Rom

Consumer Banking and Payments Law: covers checks, electronic transfers and direct deposits, money orders, credit, debit, payroll, and stored value cards, and banker's right of setoff. Also extensive treatment of electronic records and signatures.

2005 Third Edition, 2007 Supplement, and 2007 CD-Rom

The Cost of Credit: Regulation, Preemption, and Industry Abuses: a one-of-a-kind resource detailing state and federal regulation of consumer credit in all 50 states, federal usury preemption, explaining credit math, and how to challenge excessive credit charges and credit insurance.

2005 Fourth Edition, 2007 Supplement and 2007 CD-Rom

Credit Discrimination: analysis of the Equal Credit Opportunity Act, Fair Housing Act, Civil Rights Acts, and state credit discrimination statutes, including reprints of all relevant federal interpretations, government enforcement actions, and numerous sample pleadings.

Consumer Litigation Library

2007 Fifth Edition with CD-Rom

Consumer Arbitration Agreements: successful approaches to challenge arbitration agreements' enforceability, the interrelation of the Federal Arbitration Act and state law, class actions in arbitration, collections via arbitration, the right to discovery, and other topics.

2006 Sixth Edition, 2007 Supplement, and 2007 CD-Rom

Consumer Class Actions: makes class litigation manageable even for small offices, including numerous sample pleadings, class certification memoranda, discovery, class notices, settlement materials, and much more. Includes a detailed analysis of the Class Action Fairness Act, class arbitration, and other topics.

2007 CD-Rom with Index Guide: ALL pleadings from ALL NCLC Manuals, including Consumer Law Pleadings Numbers One through Thirteen

Consumer Law Pleadings on CD-Rom: over 1300 notable recent pleadings from all types of consumer cases, including predatory lending, foreclosures, automobile fraud, lemon laws, debt collection, fair credit reporting, home improvement fraud, student loans, and lender liability. Finding aids pinpoint desired pleading in seconds, ready to paste into a word processor.

Deception and Warranties Library

2004 Sixth Edition, 2007 Supplement, and 2007 CD-Rom

Unfair and Deceptive Acts and Practices: the only practice manual covering all aspects of a deceptive practices case in every state. Special sections on automobile sales, the federal racketeering (RICO) statute, unfair insurance practices, and the FTC Holder Rule.

2007 Third Edition with CD-Rom

Automobile Fraud: examination of title law, odometer tampering, lemon laundering, sale of salvage and wrecked cars, undisclosed prior use, prior damage to new cars, numerous sample pleadings, and title search techniques.

2006 Third Edition, 2007 Supplement, and 2007 CD-Rom

Consumer Warranty Law: comprehensive treatment of new and used car lemon laws, the Magnuson-Moss Warranty Act, UCC Articles 2 and 2A, mobile home, new home, and assistive device warranty laws, FTC Used Car Rule, tort theories, car repair and home improvement statutes, service contract and lease laws, with numerous sample pleadings.

NCLC's CD-Roms

Every NCLC manual includes a companion CD-Rom with pop-up menus, Internet-style navigation, bonus pleadings, hard-to-find agency interpretations and other practice aids. All pleadings are in Word format to be copied into a word processor.

December 2007 CD-Rom

Consumer Law in a Box: combines *all* documents and software from 17 other NCLC CD-Roms. Quickly pinpoint a document from thousands found on the CD through keyword searches and Internet-style navigation, links, bookmarks, and other finding aids.

National Consumer Law Center ■ **(617) 542-9595** ■ **FAX (617) 542-8028** ■ **publications@nclc.org**
Order securely online at www.consumerlaw.org

Other NCLC Publications for Lawyers

issued 24 times a year — **NCLC REPORTS** covers the latest developments and ideas in the practice of consumer law.

2007 First Edition with Companion Web Site — **Bankruptcy Basics: A Step-by-Step Guide for Pro Bono Attorneys, General Practitioners, and Legal Services Offices:** provides everything attorneys new to bankruptcy need to file their first case, with a companion web site that contains software, sample pleadings, and other practice aids that greatly simplify handling a bankruptcy case.

2006 Second Edition with CD-Rom — **The Practice of Consumer Law: Seeking Economic Justice:** contains an essential overview to consumer law and explains how to get started in a private or legal services consumer practice. Packed with invaluable sample pleadings and practice pointers for even experienced consumer attorneys.

2007 First Edition with CD-Rom — **Foreclosure Prevention Counseling: Preserving the American Dream:** explains how to obtain a workout, with advice specifically tailored for Fannie Mae, Freddie Mac, subprime, FHA-insured, VA, and Rural Housing Service loans. The book also includes homeowner strategies for reducing and prioritizing debt and options after the sale.

2007 Second Edition with CD-Rom — **STOP Predatory Lending: A Guide for Legal Advocates:** provides a roadmap and practical legal strategy for litigating predatory lending abuses, from small loans to mortgage loans. How to analyze the documents, spot issues, raise legal claims, select defendants, and even how to craft a community response.

National Consumer Law Center Guide Series

are books designed for consumers, counselors, and attorneys new to consumer law:

2006 Edition — **NCLC Guide to Surviving Debt:** a great overview of consumer law. Everything a paralegal, new attorney, or client needs to know about debt collectors, managing credit card debt, whether to refinance, credit card problems, home foreclosures, evictions, repossessions, credit reporting, utility terminations, student loans, budgeting, and bankruptcy.

2006 Edition — **NCLC Guide to the Rights of Utility Consumers:** explains consumer rights concerning electric, gas, and other utility services: shut off protections, rights to restore terminated service, bill payment options, weatherization tips, rights to government assistance, and much more.

2006 Edition — **NCLC Guide to Consumer Rights for Domestic Violence Survivors:** provides practical advice to help survivors get back on their feet financially and safely establish their economic independence.

First Edition — **NCLC Guide to Mobile Homes:** what consumers and their advocates need to know about mobile home dealer sales practices and an in-depth look at mobile home quality and defects, with 35 photographs and construction details.

First Edition — **Return to Sender: Getting a Refund or Replacement for Your Lemon Car:** find how lemon laws work, what consumers and their lawyers should know to evaluate each other, investigative techniques and discovery tips, how to handle both informal dispute resolution and trials, and more.

> Visit **www.consumerlaw.org** to order securely online or for more information on all NCLC manuals and CD-Roms, including the full tables of contents, indices, listings of CD-Rom contents, and **web-based searches of the manuals' full text**.

National Consumer Law Center ■ (617) 542-9595 ■ FAX (617) 542-8028 ■ publications@nclc.org
Order securely online at www.consumerlaw.org

Finding Aids and Search Tips

The Consumer Credit and Sales Legal Practice Series presently contains seventeen volumes, twelve supplements, and seventeen companion CD-Roms—all constantly being updated. The Series includes over 10,000 pages, 100 chapters, 100 appendices, and over 1200 pleadings, as well as hundreds of documents found on the CD-Roms, but not found in the books. Here are a number of ways to pinpoint in seconds what you need from this array of materials.

Internet-Based Searches

www.consumerlaw.org — **Electronically search every chapter and appendix of all seventeen manuals and their supplements:** go to www.consumerlaw.org/keyword and enter a case name, regulation cite, or other search term. You are instantly given the book names and page numbers of any of the NCLC manuals containing that term, with those hits shown in context.

www.consumerlaw.org — **Current indexes, tables of contents, and CD-Rom contents for all seventeen volumes** are found at www.consumerlaw.org. Just click on *The Consumer Credit and Sales Legal Practice Series* and scroll down to the book you want. Then click on that volume's index, contents, or CD-Rom contents.

Finding Material on NCLC's CD-Roms

Consumer Law in a Box CD-Rom — **Electronically search all seventeen NCLC CD-Roms,** including thousands of agency interpretations, all NCLC appendices and over 1200 pleadings: use Acrobat's search button* in NCLC's *Consumer Law in a Box* (this two-CD-Rom set is free to set subscribers) to find every instance that a keyword appears on any of our seventeen CD-Roms. Then, with one click, go to that location to see the full text of the document.

CD-Rom accompanying this volume — **Electronically search the CD-Rom accompanying this volume,** including pleadings, agency interpretations, and regulations. Use Acrobat's search button* to find every instance that a keyword appears on the CD-Rom, and then, with one click, go to that location on the CD-Rom. Or just click on subject buttons until you navigate to the document you need.

Finding Pleadings

Consumer Law Pleadings on CD-Rom and Index Guide — **Search five different ways for the right pleading from over 1200 choices:** use the *Index Guide* accompanying *Consumer Law Pleadings on CD-Rom* to search for pleadings by type, subject, publication title, name of contributor, or contributor's jurisdiction. The guide also provides a summary of the pleading once the right pleading is located. *Consumer Law Pleadings on CD-Rom* and the *Consumer Law in a Box CD-Rom* also let you search for all pleadings electronically by subject, type of pleading, and by publication title, giving you instant access to the full pleading in Word and/or PDF format once you find the pleading you need.

Using This Volume to Find Material in All Seventeen Volumes

This volume — **The Quick Reference** at the back of this volume lets you pinpoint manual sections or appendices where over 1000 different subject areas are covered.

---

* Users of NCLC CD-Roms should become familiar with Search, a powerful Acrobat tool, distinguished from Find, another Acrobat feature that is less powerful. The Acrobat 5 Search icon is a pair of binoculars with paper in the background, while the Find icon is a pair of binoculars without the paper. Acrobat 6, 7, and 8 use one icon, a pair of binoculars labeled Search, that opens a dialog box with search options.

Contents

Contents xi

CD-Rom Contents xxiii

Chapter 1   Preliminary Issues 1

Chapter 2   Threshold Issues for Challenges to Arbitration Clauses 13

Chapter 3   The Federal Arbitration Act, State Laws, and Preemption 29

Chapter 4   When the FAA's Enforcement of Arbitration Clause Conflicts with Another Federal Statute 55

Chapter 5   Formation of Agreement to Arbitrate 91

Chapter 6   Unconscionability and Other Contract Law Defenses to Arbitration Clauses 117

Chapter 7   Arbitration Clause's Applicability to Particular Claims or Parties 171

Chapter 8   Waiver of Right to Compel Arbitration 203

Chapter 9   Constitutional Challenges to Mandatory Arbitration Clauses 219

Chapter 10 Arbitration of Claims on a Classwide Basis 223

Chapter 11 Judicial Review and Effect of the Arbitration Award 231

Chapter 12 Creditor's Use of Arbitration to Collect Consumer Debts 255

Appendix A	Federal Statutes	275
Appendix B	Arbitration Service Provider Rules	281
Appendix C	Sample Discovery	359
Appendix D	Brief Requesting Discovery As to Arbitrability	389
Appendix E	Briefs on Arbitration Costs, Damage Limitations, and Unconscionability	393
Appendix F	Briefs on Unconscionability of Arbitration Clauses Restricting Class Actions	447
Appendix G	Brief on Magnuson-Moss Warranty Act's Prohibition of Predispute Binding Arbitration Clauses	487
Appendix H	Brief on Arbitration Service Provider Bias	497
Appendix I	Brief on Waiver and on Bankruptcy Court Discretion to Deny Arbitration	521
Appendix J	Brief Advocating Switching to Service Provider Capable of Administering Class Arbitration	531
Appendix K	Sample Response and Counterclaim in Arbitration Action to Collect a Consumer Debt	537
Appendix L	Brief Opposing Confirmation of Collector's Arbitration Award	541
Appendix M	AAA and NAF Documents, Additional Briefs, Other Resources Found Only on the CD-Rom	551
	Index	559
	Quick Reference to Consumer Credit and Sales Legal Practice Series	573
	About the Companion CD-Rom	589

Contents

CD-Rom Contents xxiii

Chapter 1   Preliminary Issues

1.1 Scope of This Manual. 1
1.2 Predispute Binding Arbitration Agreement Defined 3
1.3 Why Many Consumers Try to Avoid Predispute Binding Arbitration 4
    1.3.1 Introduction 4
    1.3.2 Limitations on Class Actions. 5
    1.3.3 Concerns About Arbitrators' Impartiality. 6
    1.3.4 Secrecy in Arbitration. 8
    1.3.5 Limitations on Discovery 9
    1.3.6 Arbitration Fees. 9
    1.3.7 Other Concerns 10
1.4 Corporations Avoid Binding Arbitration When It Applies to Them 11
1.5 Serious Flaws with Studies Allegedly Showing Benefits of Consumer
    Arbitration. 11

Chapter 2   Threshold Issues for Challenges to Arbitration Clauses

2.1 Introduction. 13
2.2 Who Decides Challenges to an Arbitration Clause—Courts or Arbitrators? 13
2.3 Jurisdictional Issues. 14
    2.3.1 When Federal Jurisdiction Exists over Actions to Compel Arbitration
          Under the FAA 14
          2.3.1.1 Overview. 14
          2.3.1.2 Diversity Jurisdiction over Claims Subject to Arbitration. 15
          2.3.1.3 Federal Question Jurisdiction over Claims Subject to Arbitration . . 16
    2.3.2 Parallel Proceedings in State and Federal Courts. 18
    2.3.3 Venue. 19
2.4 Right to Discovery Relating to Enforceability of Arbitration Clause 20
    2.4.1 Introduction. 20
    2.4.2 Precedent Upholding Right to Discovery 20
    2.4.3 Discovery Serves Public Policy Goals 22
2.5 Right for a Jury to Decide If Arbitration Agreement Is Enforceable 22
2.6 Appeal from Judicial Orders Relating to Arbitration. 24
    2.6.1 FAA Section 16 24
    2.6.2 Orders Compelling Arbitration Are Appealable When the District Court
          Issues an Order Dismissing All Claims 25
    2.6.3 Pendent Jurisdiction 27
    2.6.4 Broader Appealability of State Court Arbitration Orders. 27

Chapter 3 — The Federal Arbitration Act, State Laws, and Preemption

- 3.1 Introduction to the Federal Arbitration Act and Its Policy Favoring Arbitration Agreements ... 29
  - 3.1.1 General ... 29
  - 3.1.2 External Limitations on the FAA's Policy Favoring Enforcement of Arbitration Clauses ... 30
  - 3.1.3 Clarification of the FAA's Policy Favoring the Enforceability of Arbitration Clauses ... 30
- 3.2 FAA Preemption of State Law ... 31
  - 3.2.1 FAA Preemption of State Laws That Limit the Enforceability of Arbitration Clauses ... 31
    - 3.2.1.1 Introduction ... 31
    - 3.2.1.2 When State Law Singles Out Arbitration Clauses for Less Favored Treatment ... 32
    - 3.2.1.3 When State Law Effectively Prohibits Arbitration Without Explicitly Mentioning It ... 33
    - 3.2.1.4 No FAA Preemption When Arbitration Inconsistent with Effective Vindication of State Law Rights ... 34
      - 3.2.1.4.1 Claims for "Public" Injunctive Relief ... 34
      - 3.2.1.4.2 Effective Vindication of Any Statutory Claim ... 34
  - 3.2.2 Limited FAA Preemption of State Procedural Law ... 35
    - 3.2.2.1 Introduction ... 35
    - 3.2.2.2 The FAA Generally Does Not Preempt State Procedural Rules Addressing Enforcement of Arbitration Agreements ... 35
    - 3.2.2.3 FAA Procedural Provisions, by Their Own Language, Apply Only to Federal Court Actions ... 35
    - 3.2.2.4 State Law, Not the FAA, Governs Motions to Vacate and Confirm in State Court ... 36
  - 3.2.3 FAA Preemption and Substantive State Laws Not Aimed at Restricting Arbitration ... 37
    - 3.2.3.1 General ... 37
    - 3.2.3.2 Whether Federal or State Law Applies to Questions of Contract Formation, Validity, and Enforceability ... 37
    - 3.2.3.3 Whether the FAA Preempts State Consumer Protection Laws That Do Not Target Arbitration Clauses ... 38
      - 3.2.3.3.1 Overview ... 38
      - 3.2.3.3.2 Cases Rejecting Preemption Argument ... 39
      - 3.2.3.3.3 Cases Finding Preemption ... 40
  - 3.2.4 FAA Preemption and State Laws Regulating the Conduct Of Private Arbitrators and Arbitration Services ... 41
- 3.3 Statutory and Contractual Limits to the FAA's Application and Preemptive Effect ... 41
  - 3.3.1 Introduction ... 41
  - 3.3.2 The FAA Only Applies to Transactions Involving Interstate Commerce ... 42
    - 3.3.2.1 The FAA Virtually Always Applies ... 42
    - 3.3.2.2 Even If the FAA Does Not Apply, Most States Enforce Arbitration Agreements on Similar Terms ... 43
  - 3.3.3 Parties May Contract to Have State Law Displace the FAA with Respect to the Arbitrability of Disputes ... 44
  - 3.3.4 Exception for State Regulation of the Business of Insurance ... 45
    - 3.3.4.1 General ... 45
    - 3.3.4.2 Is a State Law One Enacted for the Purpose of Regulating Insurance? ... 46

Contents

     3.3.4.3 Does State Insurance Law Restrict the Enforceability of Arbitration Agreements? 46
 3.4 Courts Determine an Arbitration Clause's Enforceability Under *State* Contract Law Principles, *With One Big Exception* 47
  3.4.1 Introduction 47
  3.4.2 State Contract Law Governs the Question of Whether an Agreement to Arbitrate Was Formed 48
  3.4.3 State Law Determines Whether a Contract Defense Applicable to an Arbitration Clause Bars the Clause's Enforceability 49
  3.4.4 Agreement to Arbitrate "Arbitrability Disputes" Does Not Displace Right Under FAA to Judicial Determination As to Existence and Enforceability of Arbitration Clause 50
  3.4.5 One Big Exception: FAA Determines Severability, Requires *Arbitrator* to Decide Validity of General Contract Provisions 52

Chapter 4 **When the FAA's Enforcement of Arbitration Clause Conflicts with Another Federal Statute**

 4.1 Introduction 55
 4.2 FAA's Per Se Inconsistency with Specified Federal Statutes 55
  4.2.1 Standard for Determining Whether a Federal Statute Prohibits or Restricts Use of Arbitration 55
   4.2.1.1 General 55
   4.2.1.2 Does Arbitration Allow Vindication of Statute's Purpose? 56
   4.2.1.3 Specific Examples 56
  4.2.2 The Magnuson-Moss Warranty Act 58
   4.2.2.1 Introduction 58
   4.2.2.2 The Text and Structure of the Act 58
   4.2.2.3 The Act's Legislative History 59
   4.2.2.4 The Act's Implementing Regulations 59
   4.2.2.5 Case Law Relating to Arbitration and the Act 60
    4.2.2.5.1 Numerous federal and state courts hold that Magnuson-Moss prohibits binding arbitration 60
    4.2.2.5.2 Case law finding binding arbitration permissible under Magnuson-Moss, and a critique of this holding 61
   4.2.2.6 Debunking Argument That Magnuson-Moss Claims Are Subject to "Formal" Arbitration As Distinct from "Informal" Procedures Under the Act 64
    4.2.2.6.1 Introduction 64
    4.2.2.6.2 Supreme Court views arbitration as informal 64
    4.2.2.6.3 Other courts find arbitration to be informal 64
   4.2.2.7 The Act Prevents Use of Arbitration Agreements in Only Certain Consumer Transactions 66
   4.2.2.8 Binding Arbitration Clauses, When Permitted, Must Still Comply with the Act's Provisions Concerning Disclosures and Tie-Ins 67
    4.2.2.8.1 Introduction 67
    4.2.2.8.2 Arbitration requirement must be disclosed in written warranties 67
    4.2.2.8.3 Significance of disclosure requirement 68
    4.2.2.8.4 Does disclosure requirement extend to service contracts and extended warranties? 69
    4.2.2.8.5 Does Magnuson-Moss Act prohibit merchant's designation of arbitration service provider? 69
  4.2.3 Claims Asserted in Bankruptcy 70

Consumer Arbitration Agreements

	4.2.3.1 Introduction	70
	4.2.3.2 Conflict Between Bankruptcy Code and FAA	70
	4.2.3.3 *Zimmerman*, the 1984 Amendments, and Subsequent Case Law	70
	4.2.3.4 Court Need Not Require Arbitration of Core Matters	71
	4.2.3.5 Application to Consumer Cases	73
	4.2.3.6 Non-Core Matters Subject to Arbitration	75
	4.2.3.7 Confirmed Plan Can Bar Enforcement of Arbitration Clause	76
4.3	Arbitration Clauses That Explicitly Limit Consumers' Statutory Rights	76
	4.3.1 General Principles	76
	4.3.1.1 Arbitration Clause Cannot Limit Federal Statutory Right	76
	4.3.1.2 Statutory Remedies Serve Three Functions	77
	4.3.2 Limitations on Specific Statutory Rights	78
	4.3.2.1 Introduction	78
	4.3.2.2 Arbitration Clauses That Limit Statutory Right to Attorney Fees and Costs	79
	4.3.2.3 When Arbitration, But Not Statute, Applies Loser Pays Rule	79
	4.3.2.4 Limits on Statutory Right to Punitive Damages	80
	4.3.2.5 Limits on Statutory Right to Proceed As a Class	81
	4.3.2.6 Limits on Statutory Right to Injunctive Relief	83
	4.3.2.7 Shortening of a Statute of Limitation	84
4.4	High Arbitration Fees *Effectively* Prevent Vindication of Statutory Rights	84
	4.4.1 Introduction	84
	4.4.2 The Supreme Court's Decision in *Randolph*	85
	4.4.3 When Are Arbitration Charges Inconsistent with Federal Statute?	86
	4.4.3.1 When Charges Exceed Those for a Court Action	86
	4.4.3.2 When Charges Deter Pursuit of Statutory Claims	87
	4.4.4 Does Reimbursement of Fees to a Prevailing Consumer Cure the Problem?	88
4.5	When a Party's One-Sided Control Over the Arbitration Process Prevents Effective Vindication of Statutory Rights	89

Chapter 5 — Formation of Agreement to Arbitrate

5.1	No Presumption That Arbitration Agreement Is Formed	91
5.2	Assent to Arbitration Agreement Is Required	92
	5.2.1 Introduction	92
	5.2.2 Express Assent	92
	5.2.2.1 Assent by Signature	92
	5.2.2.2 Forged Signatures and Fraud in the Factum	95
	5.2.2.3 Electronic Assent	95
	5.2.3 Implied Assent Based on Conduct or Reliance	96
	5.2.3.1 Overview	96
	5.2.3.2 Notice Requirement	96
	5.2.3.3 Action Sufficient to Signify Acceptance Is Required	98
	5.2.4 Lack of Capacity to Assent	101
5.3	Illusory Agreements and the Requirement of Consideration	101
5.4	Language of Arbitration Clause Must Be Clear and Unambiguous	103
5.5	Waiver of Right to Jury Trial Must Be Knowing and Voluntary	105
	5.5.1 Introduction to the Doctrine	105
	5.5.2 The Doctrine and FAA Preemption	106
	5.5.3 Examples of Application of the Doctrine	107
	5.5.4 Application of the Doctrine to Waiver of Statutory Rights	108
	5.5.5 Cases Rejecting the Doctrine	109
5.6	Arbitration Clauses Sent Unilaterally After Agreement Reached	109
	5.6.1 Introduction	109

Contents

        5.6.2 Arbitration Clause Unilaterally Added After Agreement Is Consummated . 110
        5.6.3 Final Agreement Not Reached Until After Purchase Is Delivered 111
  5.7 Legal Enforceability of Arbitration Clauses Added to Contracts Via Bill
      Stuffers 112
        5.7.1 Introduction 112
        5.7.2 Does the Original Agreement Allow the Addition of an Arbitration
                Clause? 112
                5.7.2.1 Cases Holding That "Change-in-Terms" Provisions Do Not
                         Allow the Addition of an Arbitration Clause 112
                5.7.2.2 Card Issuers' Responses to Cases Invalidating Bill Stuffers 114
                      5.7.2.2.1 Contracts Permitting Issuers to Add New Terms 114
                      5.7.2.2.2 The Delaware Legislation 114

Chapter 6   **Unconscionability and Other Contract Law Defenses to Arbitration Clauses**

  6.1 Introduction 117
  6.2 General Unconscionability Standards 119
  6.3 Relationship Between Procedural and Substantive Unconscionability 120
  6.4 Procedural Unconscionability 122
        6.4.1 Contracts of Adhesion—Enough in Some States, Merely a Factor in
                Others 122
        6.4.2 Surprise As a Factor in Procedural Unconscionability 124
        6.4.3 Meaningful Choice As a Factor 128
  6.5 Substantively Unconscionable Arbitration Provisions 130
        6.5.1 Introduction 130
        6.5.2 Excessive Fees and Costs 130
                6.5.2.1 Demonstrating That the Arbitration Fees Will, in Fact, Be
                         Excessive 130
                6.5.2.2 AAA Fees for Consumer Cases 132
                6.5.2.3 NAF Fees for Consumer Cases 135
                6.5.2.4 Varying Approaches As to Who Pays the Fees 135
                6.5.2.5 Precedent Regarding Unconscionable Arbitration Fees 136
        6.5.3 One-Way or Non-Mutual Arbitration Clauses Are Often Unconscionable . . 137
                6.5.3.1 Introduction 137
                6.5.3.2 Non-Mutuality Rendering Clause Unconscionable Distinguished
                         from Non-Mutuality Creating Lack of Consideration for
                         Agreement 137
                6.5.3.3 Cases Finding Non-Mutuality to Be Unconscionable 137
                6.5.3.4 Cases Not Finding Non-Mutuality to Be Unconscionable 139
                6.5.3.5 Non-Mutual Clauses That Appear to Be Mutual 140
                6.5.3.6 Non-Mutual Appeal Rights Rendering Clause Unconscionable . . . 141
        6.5.4 Clauses That Strip Statutory Remedies 141
                6.5.4.1 Limitation on Damages 141
                6.5.4.2 Limitation on Attorney Fees 143
                6.5.4.3 Limitation on Injunctive and Equitable Relief 143
                6.5.4.4 Shortened Statute of Limitations 143
                6.5.4.5 High Arbitration Fees Accentuate Problem of Remedy Stripping
                         Provisions 144
        6.5.5 Class Action Bans Embedded in Arbitration Clauses 144
                6.5.5.1 General 144
                6.5.5.2 Courts Finding That Class Action Bans Are Exculpatory Because
                         of the Small Size of Claims 145

	6.5.5.3	Courts Finding That Class Action Bans Are Exculpatory Based On Other Factors	148
	6.5.5.4	Courts Finding That Class Action Bans Are Unconscionably One-Sided	148
	6.5.5.5	Courts Upholding Class Action Bans	149
	6.5.5.6	Class Action Bans Imposed After a Class Action Has Been Filed	150
	6.5.5.7	FAA Does Not Preempt State Law of Unconscionability from Striking Down Class Action Bans	150
6.5.6	Inconvenient Venue for Arbitration	151
6.5.7	Bias of Arbitrator or Arbitration Mechanism	153
	6.5.7.1	General	153
	6.5.7.2	Bias Challenges to the National Arbitration Forum	155
	6.5.7.3	Defenses to Bias Allegations	156
6.5.8	Secrecy Provisions	156
	6.5.8.1	Introduction	156
	6.5.8.2	Cases Finding Mandatory Confidentiality to Be Unconscionable	157
	6.5.8.3	Cases Finding Mandatory Confidentiality Not to Be Unconscionable	159
6.5.9	Loser Pays Rules	159

6.6 Remedies When Part, or Parts, of an Arbitration Clause Are Unconscionable... 160
    6.6.1 Introduction... 160
    6.6.2 Party That Drafted Unconscionable Clause Should Not Receive Court's Assistance... 160
    6.6.3 Interdependent Aspects of Arbitration Clause Should Not Be Severed.... 163
6.7 Miscellaneous Contract Defenses Other Than Unconscionability... 165
    6.7.1 Fraud in the Inducement Related to the Arbitration Clause Itself... 165
    6.7.2 Impossibility, Infancy, Undue Influence, Breach of Covenant of Good Faith, and Other Common Law Contract Defenses... 166
    6.7.3 State Statutes That Regulate Contract Terms... 166
    6.7.4 Was the Arbitration Agreement Conditional, Rescinded, or Superseded?... 167
        6.7.4.1 "Yo-Yo" Sales and Other Condition Precedent Contracts... 167
        6.7.4.2 TIL Rescission and Other Three-Day Rights to Cancel... 167
        6.7.4.3 Document Containing Arbitration Clause Is Superseded by Later Document or Does Not Survive Termination of the Contract... 168

Chapter 7   Arbitration Clause's Applicability to Particular Claims or Parties

7.1 Introduction... 171
7.2 General Standards of Interpretation... 171
7.3 Whether Particular Claims Fall Within an Arbitration Clause... 173
    7.3.1 General... 173
    7.3.2 Application to Issues of Arbitrability... 175
    7.3.3 Application to Tort and Statutory Claims... 177
    7.3.4 Arbitration Clause Does Not Apply to Consumer's Self-Help Remedies... 182
    7.3.5 The Temporal Scope of an Arbitration Provision... 182
    7.3.6 Whether an Arbitration Clause in One Contract Applies to Claims Arising from an Earlier or Later Contract Between the Same Parties... 185
    7.3.7 When Some Claims Are Within the Arbitration Clause's Scope and Some Are Not... 186
7.4 Application of an Arbitration Agreement to a Non-Signatory... 187
    7.4.1 General... 187
    7.4.2 Equitable Estoppel... 189
        7.4.2.1 Overview... 189
        7.4.2.2 Equitable Estoppel When a Non-Signatory Seeks to Enforce the Arbitration Agreement... 190

Contents

	7.4.2.3 Equitable Estoppel When a Signatory Seeks to Enforce the Arbitration Agreement Against a Non-Signatory	193
	7.4.3 Third Party Beneficiaries	194
	7.4.4 Agency	196
	7.4.5 Treatment of Common Third Party Relationships	198
	7.4.6 Affinity Group Members	199
	7.4.7 Specific Types of Claims	200
	7.4.7.1 Wrongful Death Claims	200
	7.4.7.2 Claims Arising Out of Mistreatment in Nursing Homes	200
	7.4.7.3 Debt Collection Claims Involving MBNA Contracts When MBNA Is Not a Party to the Proceeding	201
	7.4.8 Enforcement Agencies and Contempt Proceedings	202
7.5	Can the Terms of the Arbitration Clause Be Satisfied?	202

Chapter 8   Waiver of Right to Compel Arbitration

8.1	Introduction	203
8.2	Does Court or Arbitrator Decide Whether There Is a Waiver?	204
8.3	Arguments That Litigation Conduct Constituted Waiver of the Right to Compel Arbitration	205
	8.3.1 Filing of a Suit As Waiver	205
	8.3.2 Waiver by Delay in Enforcing the Arbitration Provision	207
	8.3.2.1 Factors When Evaluating If a Party's Delay Constitutes Waiver	207
	8.3.2.2 Delaying Actions Found to Constitute Waiver	209
	8.3.2.3 Delaying Actions Found Not to Constitute Waiver	212
	8.3.2.4 Unsuccessful Defenses to Waiver Arguments Based Upon Delay	213
8.4	Breach of Arbitration Clause's Provisions As Waiver	213
	8.4.1 Overview	213
	8.4.2 Breach of an Arbitration Clause's Covenant of Good Faith	214
	8.4.3 Breach of an Arbitration Clause's Provisions for Payment of Forum Costs	215
8.5	Prejudice As a Requirement or Factor to Establish Waiver	215
8.6	Defenses to Waiver Based Upon Contract Terms or Arbitral Rules	217

Chapter 9   Constitutional Challenges to Mandatory Arbitration Clauses

9.1	Right to Jury Trial	219
	9.1.1 When Private Parties Agree to Waive the Right	219
	9.1.2 When State Requires Waiver of Right	219
9.2	Equal Protection in Selection of Arbitrator	220
9.3	Improper Delegation of Power	220
9.4	Due Process	220

Chapter 10   Arbitration of Claims on a Classwide Basis

10.1	Introduction	223
10.2	The Supreme Court's Ruling in *Green Tree Financial Corp. v. Bazzle*	224
	10.2.1 Arbitrator Decides Class Action Issues by Applying State Law When Contract Is Arguably Silent Regarding Class Claims	224
	10.2.2 The Facts and Holding of *Bazzle*	224
	10.2.3 *Bazzle's* Likely Implications for Consumers	224
	10.2.4 Cases Following Bazzle's Holding	225
10.3	Critique of Pre-*Bazzle* Cases Holding That the FAA Presumptively Prohibits Arbitration of Class Claims	225
	10.3.1 Overview	225

Consumer Arbitration Agreements

10.3.2 Absence of Statutory Support for *Champ's* Presumption Against Arbitration of Class Claims	226
10.3.3 Seventh Circuit Precedent Also Undermined *Champ*.	226
10.3.4 Consolidation Distinguished from Class Actions	226
10.4 State Court Approaches to Arbitration of Class Claims	227
10.4.1 Lower Federal Court Precedent Is Not Controlling on State Courts	227
10.4.2 State Cases Following Pre-*Bazzle* Federal Approach.	227
10.4.3 State Cases Allowing Arbitration of Class Claims	227
10.5 When Arbitration Clause Expressly Prohibits Class Claims in Arbitration or Court	228

Chapter 11 Judicial Review and Effect of the Arbitration Award

11.1 Introduction	231
11.1.1 Effect of Arbitration Award	231
11.1.2 This Chapter Applies Only to Binding Arbitration	232
11.2 Procedure to Confirm, Vacate, or Modify an Award	232
11.2.1 The Proper Court	232
11.2.2 Does State or Federal Law Apply?	233
11.2.3 Strict Timing Requirements	234
11.2.3.1 Short Period to Vacate or Modify an Award	234
11.2.3.2 Longer Period to Confirm an Award	235
11.2.3.3 Barriers to Vacating an Award at the Confirmation Hearing	236
11.2.4 Can the Parties, by Contract, Alter the Nature of Judicial Review?	236
11.2.4.1 Contract Cannot Limit Court's Power to Vacate or Modify an Award	236
11.2.4.2 Arbitration Agreements That Increase the Scope of Judicial Review	236
11.2.5 Appeals of Trial Court Review of Arbitration Award	237
11.3 Grounds to Modify or Correct an Award	237
11.4 Grounds to Vacate Based on Defects in the Arbitration Process	238
11.4.1 General	238
11.4.2 When Arbitrators Exceed Their Powers or There is No Arbitration Agreement	238
11.4.3 Arbitrator's Evident Partiality or Corruption	240
11.4.3.1 General.	240
11.4.3.2 California Statutes Requiring Disclosures by Arbitrators.	241
11.4.3.3 *Ex Parte* Communications	242
11.4.4 Arbitrator's Refusal to Postpone the Hearing or to Hear Evidence or Other Misbehavior	242
11.4.5 Award Procured by Corruption, Fraud, or Undue Means	242
11.5 Vacating an Award Based on Its Merits.	243
11.5.1 General	243
11.5.2 Manifest Disregard of the Law	243
11.5.2.1 General.	243
11.5.2.2 When Arbitrator Does Not Explain the Decision	245
11.5.2.3 A Different Standard for Statutory Claims?	245
11.5.3 Must Courts Insure Arbitration Decision Is Consistent with Public Policy?	246
11.5.4 Arbitrary and Capricious Awards.	247
11.5.5 Can the Court Re-Examine Evidence?	247
11.6 Arbitral Immunity	248
11.7 Protecting the Arbitrator's Punitive Damages Award	248
11.7.1 Introduction	248

Contents

    11.7.2 Is a Challenge to a Punitive Damage Award Timely and Brought in the Correct Court? 249
    11.7.3 Does the Award Exceed the Arbitrator's Powers?................. 249
      11.7.3.1 Introduction... 249
      11.7.3.2 Does the Arbitration Agreement Limit the Arbitrator's Authority to Award Punitive Damages? 249
      11.7.3.3 Do the Rules of the Arbitration Service Provider Limit The Arbitrator's Authority to Award Punitive Damages?.......... 250
      11.7.3.4 Does State Law Limit the Arbitrator's Authority to Award Punitive Damages?..................................... 250
        11.7.3.4.1 Few state laws limit punitive damages in arbitration... 250
        11.7.3.4.2 FAA preempts state law limitations on punitive damages 251
        11.7.3.4.3 Do general state law limits on punitive damages apply in arbitration?................................ 251
    11.7.4 Has the Arbitrator Disregarded the Law or Facts? 252
    11.7.5 Does a Punitive Damages Award Violate Public Policy? 252
    11.7.6 Due Process Challenges to Punitive Damages Award 252
  11.8 Arbitration and Issue or Claim Preclusion 253
    11.8.1 Introduction 253
    11.8.2 Arbitration's Preclusive Effect on Subsequent Court Proceeding 253
    11.8.3 Preclusive Effect of Arbitration or Court Ruling on Subsequent Arbitration 253

Chapter 12 **Creditor's Use of Arbitration to Collect Consumer Debts**

  12.1 How Collection Using Arbitration Works 255
  12.2 Options After Receiving a Notice of Arbitration........................... 256
    12.2.1 Introduction 256
    12.2.2 Objecting to Arbitration When No Agreement to Arbitrate Exists...... 257
    12.2.3 Seeking a Stay of Arbitration 257
    12.2.4 Participating in the Arbitration Proceeding 258
      12.2.4.1 Introduction... 258
      12.2.4.2 Filing a Response...................................... 258
      12.2.4.3 Requesting a Hearing 258
      12.2.4.4 Risk That Consumer Will Be Ordered to Pay Creditor's Arbitration and Attorney Fees 258
      12.2.4.5 Can the Consumer Avoid Costs Under the MBNA Clause?..... 259
  12.3 Filing Counterclaims Against the Creditor in Court or in Arbitration......... 259
  12.4 Seeking to Vacate the Award... 259
    12.4.1 Introduction 259
    12.4.2 Timeliness.. 260
    12.4.3 Applicable Law, Jurisdiction, and Venue.......................... 260
    12.4.4 Grounds for Vacating an Award in a Debt Collection Case 261
      12.4.4.1 Introduction... 261
      12.4.4.2 When Arbitration Award Not Binding on the Consumer....... 261
      12.4.4.3 Lack of Notice of the Arbitration Proceeding 263
      12.4.4.4 Lack of a Required In-Person Hearing..................... 263
      12.4.4.5 Failure to Follow the Arbitration Agreement or Arbitration Service Provider Rules 263
      12.4.4.6 Arbitrator Improperly Selected........................... 264
      12.4.4.7 Arbitration Award Is Contrary to the Law or Facts 264
      12.4.4.8 Arbitrator Bias... 264
      12.4.4.9 Inconvenient Venue 264
  12.5 Opposing Confirmation of the Award 265

Consumer Arbitration Agreements

12.5.1 Introduction	265
12.5.2 The Confirmation Process	265
12.5.3 Lack of Arbitration Agreement or Defective Arbitration Proceeding As Grounds to Oppose Confirmation	266
12.5.3.1 General	266
12.5.3.2 Time Period to Vacate Does Not Start Running When Notice of Award Is Defective or Not Sent	266
12.5.3.3 Time Limits May Not Apply to Challenges to the Existence or Enforceability of the Arbitration Agreement	267
12.5.3.4 Creditor's Failure to Produce Arbitration Agreement and Any Applicable Assignment	269
12.5.4 Effect on Confirmation When Consumer Objects to, or Fails to Participate in, Arbitration	269
12.5.5 Defects in the Form of the Confirmation Proceeding	270
12.5.5.1 Creditor's Petition to Confirm Is Untimely	270
12.5.5.2 Creditor Filed Petition to Confirm in the Wrong Court	271
12.5.5.3 Seeking an Amount in Excess of the Award	271
12.5.5.4 Other Requirements for Confirmation	271
12.6 What If a Default Has Already Been Entered in the Confirmation Proceeding?	272
12.7 Affirmative Challenges to Debt Collection Practices Related to the Arbitration	272
12.7.1 Potential Defendants	272
12.7.2 Practices Subject to Challenge	272
12.7.3 The Federal Fair Debt Collection Practices Act	273
12.7.4 State Law Claims	273
12.7.5 Must the Consumer's Debt Harassment Claim Be Sent to Arbitration?	273
12.7.6 Preclusive Effect of Creditor's Arbitration Action on Debt	274
12.8 Government Enforcement Action Against Using Arbitration for Collection	274

Appendix A Federal Statutes

A.1 The Federal Arbitration Act	275
A.2 Other Federal Statutes	278
A.2.1 Limits on Arbitration Involving Military Personnel	278
A.2.2 Limits on Arbitration Involving Car Dealers and Their Franchisors	279

Appendix B Arbitration Service Provider Rules

B.1 The American Arbitration Association	281
B.1.1 Commercial Arbitration Rules and Mediation Procedures (Including Procedures for Large, Complex Commercial Disputes)	281
B.1.2 Supplementary Procedures for Consumer-Related Disputes	292
B.1.3 Class Arbitrations	295
B.1.3.1 Policy on Class Arbitrations	295
B.1.3.2 Supplementary Rules for Class Arbitrations	295
B.1.4 Disclosures for California Consumer Cases	298
B.1.4.1 Consumer-Related Disputes Filing Form—California	298
B.1.4.2 Ethics Standards for Neutral Arbitrators in Contractual Arbitration in California: Fact Sheet	299
B.1.4.3 Business Advisory of Consumer Case Disclosures	300
B.1.4.4 Consumer Statistics	301
B.1.4.5 Affidavit for Waiver of Fees—California	302
B.1.4.6 Demand for Arbitration—California Employment-Related Disputes	303
B.1.5 Consumer Due Process Protocol	304
B.2 The National Arbitration Forum	321

Contents

	B.2.1 Code of Procedure and Fee Schedule	321
	B.2.2 Consumer and Employee Arbitration Rights	340
B.3	JAMS	340
	B.3.1 Streamlined Arbitration Rules and Procedures	340
	B.3.2 Comprehensive Arbitration Rules and Procedures	347
	B.3.3 Class Action Procedures	354
	B.3.4 Policy on Consumer Arbitrations Pursuant to Pre-Dispute Clauses	356
	B.3.4.1 Minimum Standards of Procedural Fairness	356
	B.3.4.2 Disclosures for California Consumer Arbitrations	356

Appendix C Sample Discovery

C.1	Interrogatories and Document Requests Directed to Credit Card Issuer	359
C.2	Discovery Directed to Credit Card Issuers	360
	C.2.1 Interrogatories	360
	C.2.2 Document Requests	361
	C.2.3 Additional Document Requests and Interrogatories	362
	C.2.4 Notice of Deposition	365
	C.2.5 Subpoena for Document Production to National Arbitration Forum	367
	C.2.6 Second Subpoena for Document Production to National Arbitration Forum	369
C.3	Discovery Directed to Auto Financer	373
	C.3.1 Interrogatories	373
	C.3.2 Document Requests	375
	C.3.3 Request for Admissions	376
C.4	Interrogatories Directed to Car Dealer	377
C.5	Discovery Directed to Pay Day Loan Company	379
C.6	Discovery Directed to Payday Lender	380
	C.6.1 First Set of Interrogatories and Document Requests	380
	C.6.2 Second Set of Interrogatories and Document Requests	383
C.7	Document Request Directed to Auto Title Pawn Company	386

Appendix D Brief Requesting Discovery As to Arbitrability ... 389

Appendix E Briefs on Arbitration Costs, Damage Limitations, and Unconscionability

E.1	Opening Brief Focusing on Unconscionability Based on Cost (Leeman)	393
E.2	Reply Brief Focusing on Unconscionability Based on Cost (Leeman)	406
E.3	Brief Focusing on Unconscionability Based on Limitation of Remedies and Cost (Sanderson Farms)	413
E.4	Brief Focusing on Unconscionability Based on Lack of Mutuality, Limitation of Rights, and Cost (Scovill)	432

Appendix F Briefs on Unconscionability of Arbitration Clauses Restricting Class Actions

F.1	Opening Brief Focusing on Unconscionability Based on Class Action Ban (Insight)	447
F.2	Briefs on Unconscionability of Class Action Ban (Scott)	455
	F.2.1 Plaintiffs' Opening Brief	455
	F.2.2 Plaintiffs' Reply Brief	468
	F.2.3 Plaintiffs' Supplemental Brief	474

Consumer Arbitration Agreements

    F.2.4 Plaintiff's Response to Industry Amicus Brief 480

Appendix G   Brief on Magnuson-Moss Warranty Act's Prohibition of Predispute Binding Arbitration Clauses 487

Appendix H   Brief on Arbitration Service Provider Bias 497

Appendix I   Brief on Waiver and on Bankruptcy Court Discretion to Deny Arbitration 521

Appendix J   Brief Advocating Switching to Service Provider Capable of Administering Class Arbitration 531

Appendix K   Sample Response and Counterclaim in Arbitration Action to Collect a Consumer Debt 537

Appendix L   Brief Opposing Confirmation of Collector's Arbitration Award 541

Appendix M   AAA and NAF Documents, Additional Briefs, Other Resources Found Only on the CD-Rom

    M.1 Introduction 551
    M.2 American Arbitration Association Materials 551
    M.3 National Arbitration Forum Materials 553
    M.4 Reprints of Arbitration Agreements 556
    M.5 Statutes and Standards Concerning Arbitration 556
    M.6 Pleadings 556
    M.7 Materials Regarding Impact on Consumers of Arbitration Requirement 556

Index 559

Quick Reference to Consumer Credit and Sales Legal Practice Series ... 573

About the Companion CD-Rom 589

CD-Rom Contents

How to Use/Help
CD-Rom Text Search (Adobe Acrobat 5 and 6)
Searching NCLC Manuals
Ten-Second Tutorial on Adobe Acrobat 5
Two-Minute Tutorials on Adobe Acrobat 5 and 6
    Navigation: Bookmarks
    Disappearing Bookmarks?
    Navigation Links
    Navigation Arrows
    Navigation: "Back" Arrow
    Adobe Acrobat Articles
    View-Zoom-Magnification: Making Text Larger
    Full Screen vs. Bookmark View
    Copying Text in Adobe Acrobat
    How to Copy Only One Column
    Printing
    Other Sources of Help
Microsoft Word Files
About This CD-Rom
How to Install Adobe Acrobat Reader, with Search
Finding Aids for NCLC Manuals: What Is Available in the Books

Statutes/Standards
Federal Arbitration Act (FAA) (Appendix A.1)
Other Federal Statutes (Appendix A.2)
Letter from NADA to Congress Indicating Support for Voluntary Arbitration Act
California Statutes Regulating Arbitration Service Providers
    Cal. Civ. Proc. Code § 1281.9 (West)
    Cal. Civ. Proc. Code § 1281.92 (West)
    Cal. Civ. Proc. Code § 1281.96 (West)
    Cal. Civ. Proc. Code § 1284.3 (West)
California Ethics Standards for Arbitrators
N.M. Stat. Ann. § 44-7A (Michie) (significantly amends revised Uniform Arbitration Act to restrict "disabling civil dispute clauses")
Fair Bargaining State Model Act
National Consumer Law Center State Model Acts

AAA, NAF, JAMS Rules
American Arbitration Association (AAA) Commercial Arbitration Rules and Mediation Procedures (Appendix B.1.1)
AAA Supplementary Procedures for Consumer-Related Disputes (Appendix B.1.2)
AAA Supplementary Rules for Class Arbitrations (Appendix B.1.3)

Consumer Arbitration Agreements
    AAA Disclosures for California Consumer Cases (Appendix B.1.4)
    AAA Consumer Due Process Protocol (Appendix B.1.5)
    National Arbitration Forum (NAF) Code of Procedure (Appendix B.2.1)
    NAF Consumer and Employee Arbitration Rights (Appendix B.2.2)
    JAMS Streamlined Arbitration Rules and Procedures (Appendix B.3.1)
    JAMS Comprehensive Arbitration Rules and Procedures (Appendix B.3.2)
    JAMS Class Action Procedures (Appendix B.3.3)
    JAMS Policy on Consumer Arbitrations, Minimum Standards of Procedural Fairness (Appendix B.3.4.1)
    JAMS Policy on Consumer Arbitrations, Disclosures for California Consumer Arbitrations (Appendix B.3.4.2)
    Links to AAA, NAF, and JAMS Web Sites

Pleadings

Discovery
    Interrogatories and Document Requests Directed to Credit Card Issuer (MD) (Appendix C.1)
    Interrogatories Directed to Credit Card Issuer (AL) (Appendix C.2.1)
    Document Requests Directed to Credit Card Issuer (AL) (Appendix C.2.2)
    Additional Document Request and Interrogatories Directed to Credit Card Issuer (AL) (Appendix C.2.3)
    Notice of Deposition to Credit Card Issuer (AL) (Appendix C.2.4)
    Subpoena for Document Production to NAF (AL) (Appendix C.2.5)
    Second Subpoena for Document Production to NAF (AL) (Appendix C.2.6)
    Interrogatories Directed to Auto Financier (CT) (Appendix C.3.1)
    Document Requests Directed to Auto Financier (CT) (Appendix C.3.2)
    Requests for Admissions Directed to Auto Financier (CT) (Appendix C.3.3)
    First Set of Interrogatories Directed to Car Dealer (FL) (Appendix C.4)
    Interrogatories, Document Requests, and Requests for Admissions Directed to Pay Day Loan Company (AL) (Appendix C.5)
    First Set of Interrogatories and Document Requests Directed to Check Cashing Companies (NC) (Appendix C.6.1)
    Second Set of Interrogatories and Document Requests Directed to Check Cashing Companies (NC) (Appendix C.6.2)
    Document Request Directed to Auto Title Pawn Company (FL) (Appendix C.7)

Affidavits Filed by Attorneys for Consumer
    Sullivan v. QC Financial Servicers, Inc.—Affidavit of Edward F. Sherman Regarding Importance of the Class Action Remedy

Briefs
    Requesting Discovery on Arbitration Clauses Enforceability
        Hager v. Check Into Cash (NC)—Plaintiff's Motion Requesting Discovery as to Arbitration Enforceability (Appendix D)
        Kucan v. Advance America (NC)—Plaintiff's Motion Requesting Discovery on Arbitration Enforceability (Appendix D)
    Relationship of FAA to Federal Bankruptcy Code
        Hill v. MBNA America Bank—Amicus Brief Arguing That Bankruptcy Code Supersedes FAA
        Lewallen v. Green Tree Servicing—Brief on Waiver and on Bankruptcy Court Discretion to Deny Arbitration (Appendix I)
        Mintze v. American General Finance, Inc.—Brief Arguing Bankruptcy Code Supersedes FAA
    Relationship of FAA to Magnuson-Moss Act

CD-Rom Contents

Abela v. General Motors Corp.—Petition for *Certiorari* Concerning Interrelationship of Magnuson-Moss Warranty Act and FAA (Appendix G)

Abela v. General Motors Corp.—Interrelationship of Magnuson-Moss Warranty Act and the FAA

California Disclosure Requirements and the FAA

Jevne v. Superior Court—California's Statutory Ethics Rules Not Preempted Either by the Securities Exchange Act or the FAA

Method of Arbitration Clause Consummation

Luke v. Baptist Medical Center-Princeton—Employee Refused to Sign Arbitration Clause and Informed Employer Repeatedly That She Refused to Be Bound or to Waive Her Rights

McDougle v. Silvernell—Arbitration Clause Unilaterally Added to Agreement After the Agreement Has Been Consummated

Ting v. AT & T—Class Action Seeking Relief Against Use of Arbitration Clause Based on Unconscionability in the Formation of the Agreement and in the Terms of the Arbitration Agreement

Wells v. Chevy Chase Bank—Arbitration Clause Added As a "Bill Stuffer"; Unconscionability Based on "Loser Pays Rule," Excessive Arbitration Fees, and Denial of Class Action Remedy

Wells v. Chevy Chase Bank—Reply Brief

Who Decides Unconscionability—Court or Arbitrator

Nagrampa v. MailCoups, Inc.—Unconscionability Based on Venue and Costs of AAA Arbitration

Nagrampa v. MailCoups—Reply Brief

Nagrampa v. MailCoups, Inc.—Petition for Rehearing Before the Ninth Circuit Concerning Who Determines Unconscionability, the Arbitrator or the Court

Bias of Designated Arbitrator or Arbitration Service Provider

BDO Seidman L.L.P. v. Hottle—Arbitration Clause Unenforceable When Owners Resolve Disputes Between the Firm and Its Employees

McQuillan v. Check 'N' Go of North Carolina—Memorandum of Law in Opposition to Defendants' Motion to Compel Arbitration, Arguing That Limitation on Class Actions Is an Illegal Exculpatory Clause That Violates Public Policy and Is Unconscionable, and That Arbitration Requirement Forces Consumers to Appear Before a Biased Forum (NAF Arbitration) (Appendix H)

Cost

Boghos v. Certain Underwriters at Lloyd's—Unconscionability Based on Non-Mutuality and Cost Requirements

Boghos v. Certain Underwriters at Lloyd's—Appellate Brief on Unconscionability of Costs of Arbitration and Insurer's Consent to Court Jurisdiction

Green Tree Financial Corp. v. Randolph—High Arbitration Fees Thwart Vindication of Statutory Rights

Leeman v. Cook's Pest Control—Unconscionability Based on High Cost of Arbitration (Appendix E.1)

Leeman v. Cook's Pest Control—Reply Brief (Appendix E.2)

Nagrampa v. MailCoups, Inc.—Unconscionability Based on Venue and Costs of AAA Arbitration

Nagrampa v. MailCoups—Reply Brief

Consumer Arbitration Agreements

>*Nagrampa v. MailCoups, Inc.*—Petition for Rehearing Before the Ninth Circuit Concerning Who Determines Unconscionability, the Arbitrator or the Court
>*Sanderson Farms, Inc. v. Austin*—Brief to the Mississippi Supreme Court—Unconscionability Based on Limitation of Remedies and Cost (Appendix E.3)
>*Sanderson Farms, Inc. v. Gatlin*—Unconscionability Based on High Arbitration Costs and Waiver Based on Company's Breach of the Arbitration Agreement
>*Sanderson Farms, Inc. v. Gatlin*—Supplemental Authority to Appellee's Brief
>*Wells v. Chevy Chase Bank*—Arbitration Clause Added As a "Bill Stuffer"; Unconscionability Based on "Loser Pays Rule," Excessive Arbitration Fees, and Denial of Class Action Remedy
>*Wells v. Chevy Chase Bank*—Reply Brief

Limits on Remedies and Non-Mutuality
>*Boghos v. Certain Underwriters at Lloyd's*—Appellate Brief on Unconscionability of Costs of Arbitration and Insurer's Consent to Court Jurisdiction
>*Cavalier Manufacturing, Inc. v. Jackson*—Whether Limit on Punitive Damages Makes Arbitration Clause Unenforceable
>*Eastman v. Conseco Finance Servicing Corporation*—FAA Preemption of State Consumer Protection Laws and Non-Mutual Arbitration Clause That Bars Class Actions, Injunctive Relief, and Punitive Damages
>*Scoville v. WSYX/ABC*—Appellate Brief Claiming Unconscionability Based on Limitation of Remedies, Lack of Mutuality, and Cost (Appendix E.4)

Limits on Class-Wide Arbitration
>*Discover Bank v. Superior Court*—Unconscionability Based on Ban on Class Actions (Appendix F.1, 4th ed.)
>*Discover Bank v. Superior Court*—Reply Brief (Appendix F.2, 4th ed.)
>*Eastman v. Conseco Finance Servicing Corporation*—FAA Preemption of State Consumer Protection Laws and Non-Mutual Arbitration Clause That Bars Class Actions, Injunctive Relief, and Punitive Damages
>*Fiser v. Dell*—Amicus Brief Addressing Whether Corporations Can Prohibit Class Actions in Arbitration or in Court
>*Leonard v. Terminix*—Arbitration Clause That Effectively Bars Class Actions
>*Muhammad v. County Bank of Rehoboth Beach*—Brief in Support of Motion for Leave to File Interlocutory Appeal, Arguing That Ban on Class Actions and Limitation on Discovery Make Arbitration Clause Unconscionable
>*Muhammad v. County Bank of Rehoboth Beach*—Brief on the Merits
>*Muhammad v. County Bank of Rehoboth Beach*—Amicus Brief of New Jersey Attorney General
>*Schnuerle v. Insight Communications*—Opening Brief on Unconscionability Based on Class Action Ban (Appendix F.1)
>*Scott v. Cingular Wireless*—Opening Brief on Unconscionability Based on Limitation of Class Action Remedy (Appendix F.2.1)
>*Scott v. Cingular Wireless*—Reply Brief (Appendix F.2.2)
>*Scott v. Cingular Wireless*—Supplemental Brief (Appendix F.2.3)

CD-Rom Contents

>>*Scott v. Cingular Wireless*—Petitioner's Response to Amicus Briefs Supporting Respondent (Appendix F.2.4)
>>*Scott v. Cingular Wireless*—Motion for Discretionary Review—Unconscionability Based on Limitation of Class Action Remedy
>
>*Distant Venue*
>>*Nagrampa v. MailCoups, Inc.*—Unconscionability Based on Venue and Costs of AAA Arbitration
>>*Nagrampa v. MailCoups*—Reply Brief
>>*Nagrampa v. MailCoups, Inc.*—Petition for Rehearing Before the Ninth Circuit Concerning Who Determines Unconscionability, the Arbitrator or the Court
>
>*Unconscionability—General*
>>*American General Finance, Inc. v. Branch*—Unconscionability
>
>*Switching to Service Provider Capable of Administering Class Arbitration*
>>*Betts v. Fastfunding*—Motion Arguing That, As NAF Is Unwilling to Administer Class Arbitration, Court Should Assign Different Arbitrator (Appendix J)
>
>*Waiver*
>>*Raymond James Financial Services, Inc. v. Saldukas*—Prejudice Not Required to Establish That Other Party Waived Right to Compel Arbitration
>>*Lewallen v. Green Tree Servicing*—Brief on Waiver and on Bankruptcy Court Discretion to Deny Arbitration (Appendix I)
>
>*Arbitration As a Creditor Collection Device*
>>*Karnette v. Wolpoff & Abramson*—Brief Opposing Debt Collector's Ability to Compel Arbitration
>>*Strunk v. MBNA*—Brief Opposing Confirmation As to Debt Collector's Arbitration Award (Appendix L)
>
>*Other*
>>*Bautisa v. Star Cruises & Norwegian Cruise Line, Ltd.*—Arbitration Clause Requiring Arbitration in Philippines Unenforceable As Against Public Policy
>
>Link to additional pleadings from Public Justice (www.publicjustice.net)

Information About American Arbitration Association (AAA), National Arbitration Forum (NAF)

>Deposition of Arbitrator for AAA, NAF (Sept. 2006)
>
>*American Arbitration Association (AAA)*
>>Letter from AAA Regarding Calculation of Administrative Fees
>>Transcript of a Hearing in the U.S. District Court for the Southern District of New York, Relating to a Motion to Compel AAA to Provide Certain Information (Nov. 18, 2004)
>>AAA Federal Tax Return Form 990 for the Year 2000
>>AAA's Documents in Its AT & T File (AAA000001 to AAA000115): Correspondence between AT & T and AAA, and notes by AAA employees relating to their relationship with AT & T, including AT & T hiring AAA to help set up its arbitration program
>
>*Affidavits of AAA Officers*
>>Affidavits Indicating Hours and Hourly Rates in AAA Arbitrations (Feb. 27, 2004)
>>Affidavit: AAA Conflict of Interest (Sept.–Oct., 2002)

Consumer Arbitration Agreements

> Affidavit of Christine Newhall, Vice President, Case Administration of the AAA, on April 18, 2001 (AAA 000309-311): Arbitrator charges in Indiana and fee waivers
> Affidavit of Frank Zotto, Vice President, Case Administration of the AAA, on June 25, 2001 (AAA 000452-454): Fees and waivers
> Affidavit of Frank Zotto, Vice President, Case Administration of the AAA, on June 28, 2001 (AAA 000387-389): Application of consumer rules, Denver arbitrator charges
> Affidavit of Frank Zotto, Vice President, Case Administration of the AAA, on July 9, 2001 (AAA 000119-122): Application of consumer rules, Chicago arbitrator charges
> Affidavit of Chris Heelan, Vice President of Finance of the AAA, on August 1, 2001 (AAA 000116-118): Waivers under consumer and commercial rules
> Affidavit of Frank Zotto, Vice President, Case Administration of the AAA, on August 15, 2001 (AAA 000188-189): Fees, arbitrator costs in Ohio, and waivers
> Affidavit of Chris Heelan, Vice President of Finance of the AAA, on August 28, 2001 (AAA 000218-219): Fee waivers
> Affidavit of Chris Heelan, Vice President of Finance of the AAA, on September 18, 2001 (AAA 000220-222): Fee waivers
> Affidavit of Frank Zotto, Vice President, Case Administration of the AAA, on September 18, 2001 (AAA 000223-224): Fee waivers
> Affidavit of Frank Zotto, Vice President, Case Administration of the AAA, on September 4, 2001 (AAA 000225-228): Application of consumer rules, Chicago arbitrator charges, fee waivers
> Affidavit of Frank Zotto, Vice President, Case Administration of the AAA, on October 4, 2001 (AAA 000478-480): Filing fees and arbitrator charges for Virginia, North Carolina, Maryland, and D.C.
> Affidavit of Chris Heelan, Vice President of Finance of the AAA, on October 5, 2001 (AAA 000517-519): Fee waivers

Depositions of AAA Officers
> Deposition of Gerald Strathmann (Aug. 18, 2004)—Applicability of AAA Rules to *Scott v. Cingular Wireless* Arbitration
> Deposition of Molly Bargenquest on December 16, 2003
> Deposition of Frank Zotto, Vice President, Case Administration of the AAA, on October 4, 2001: Fee waivers
> Deposition of Chris Heelan, Vice President of Finance of the AAA, on October 4, 2001: Fee waivers
> Deposition of Christine Newhall, Vice President, Case Administration of the AAA, on October 4, 2001: Information available on AAA's computers and in its files to track cases

Letters from AAA Notifying Household Finance and Counsel of Arbitration Rejection

National Arbitration Forum (NAF)
> Sample Response and Counterclaim to Arbitration Action to Collect a Consumer Debt (Appendix K)
> Public Citizen, *How Credit Card Companies Ensnare Consumers* (Sept. 2007)
> McQuillan *Brief and Related NAF Exhibits*
>> *McQuillan v. Check 'N'Go of North Carolina, Inc.*, Memorandum of Law in Opposition to Defendants' Motion to Compel Arbitration, North Carolina Superior Court (Appendix H)
>> Affidavit of Richard Fisher, Dated August 6, 2005, Indicating NAF's Failure to Appear for a Deposition (McQuillan Ex. 14)

CD-Rom Contents

Deposition of Edward Anderson Taken in *Toppings* Concerning the Workings of NAF (McQuillan Ex. 15)

Deposition of Edward Anderson taken in *Hubbert v. Dell* Concerning the Workings of NAF (McQuillan Ex. 16)

Affidavit of Paul Bland Dated August 8, 2005, with Exhibits, Concerning NAF Marketing to Corporations and Other Aspects of NAF (McQuillan Ex. 17)

Letter from Brown to Banks, January 14, 1999, Concerning NAF Marketing to Corporations (McQuillan Ex. 18)

Letter from Haydock to Kaplinsky, Concerning NAF Marketing to Corporations (McQuillan Ex. 19)

Affidavit of Geist, Concerning NAF Marketing to Corporations (McQuillan Ex. 20)

NAF Advertisement Labeled "Professionals and the National Arbitration Forum" (McQuillan Ex. 21)

NAF News Release Listing "Lenders Adopting Forum Agreements" (McQuillan Ex. 22)

Duhl Affidavit Discussing NAF Bias (McQuillan Ex. 25)

Pomponio Affidavit Discussing NAF Bias (McQuillan Ex. 26)

Excerpts of Clinton Walker Deposition Discussing NAF Marketing to Corporations (McQuillan Ex. 27)

California Superior Court Decision in *Klussman v. Cross-Country Bank*, Discussing NAF's Lack of Compliance with California Law Requiring NAF to Make Certain Disclosures (McQuillan Ex. 29)

Baxter and Raymond Affidavit Discussing Questionable NAF Procedures (McQuillan Ex. 30)

Curtis Affidavit Discussing Questionable NAF Procedures (McQuillan Ex. 31)

Perry Affidavit Discussing Questionable NAF Procedures (McQuillan Ex. 32)

Maese Affidavit Discussing Questionable NAF Procedures (McQuillan Ex. 33)

Faulkner Affidavit Discussing Questionable NAF Procedures (McQuillan Ex. 34)

DeSalvo Affidavit Discussing Questionable NAF Procedures (McQuillan Ex. 36)

Other *McQuillan* Exhibits (*Consumer Impact* section)

Affidavits Indicating Hours and Hourly Rates in AAA Arbitrations (Feb. 27, 2004)

Deposition of Edward Anderson (Sept. 29, 2003)

Complaint alleging NAF violates California Disclosure Law

NAF solicitation listing "Lenders Adopting Forum Agreements" and "Information Resources," a list of lenders and lender counsel considered by NAF to be its clients

A letter from Curtis Brown, Director of Development of the NAF, encouraging Richard Shephard, General Counsel of Saxon Mortgage (a subsidiary of Meritech), to add arbitration language to Saxon's contracts

A letter from Leif Stennes of the NAF to Richard Shephard, General Counsel of Saxon Mortgage, encouraging him to use the NAF as his arbitration provider

A letter from Ed Anderson, Managing Director of the NAF, to Richard Shephard, General Counsel of Saxon Mortgage, chastising him for invoking the rules of "the other guys" (referring to the American

Arbitration Association) in his arbitration agreement and encouraging him to redraft the agreement

The NAF Fee Schedule (in effect on March 1, 1996)

The NAF "Starter Kit"—This pamphlet is sent to companies by the NAF, which encourages them to "plan now [and ensure] no lawsuits, no exorbitant legal fees, no court delays, no irrational jury verdicts" by including "a simple clause—an arbitration clause—in every contract." The kit includes sample arbitration clauses for standard business, employment, and credit contracts, as well as consumer credit contracts.

An NAF marketing document entitled "All Arbitration is Not the Same," indicating the differences between the NAF and the American Arbitration Association (AAA)—for instance, in the NAF "consolidation [is] permitted only with agreement of all parties" whereas the rules in other forums are silent as to consolidation, and in the NAF the failure of a party to respond to a claim results in admission of the claim whereas in other forums there is a mandatory hearing even if the other party does not respond

An NAF marketing document that begins by describing the NAF as "The Alternative to the Million Dollar Lawsuit"

A letter from Curtis Brown, Vice President and General Counsel of the NAF, to Robert Banks, encouraging him to use arbitration because it eliminates class actions and "will make a positive impact on the bottom line"

A letter from Roger Haydock, Director of Arbitration of the NAF, to Alan Kaplinsky, encouraging him to use arbitration to resolve Y2K class actions and characterizing the plaintiff's bar as the "class action" bar

NAF Advertisement in *Corporate Counsel* stating, "Arbitration can save up to 66% of your collection costs"

Letters from Charles DiSalvo, Martin Glasser, and the Hon. Thomas McHugh, indicating that they have become aware that they are listed by the NAF in a federal court filing as neutral arbitrators for NAF but that NAF's representations to the court are not true—that in fact they have never agreed to arbitrate for the NAF

Answers to interrogatories from First U.S.A. Bank in the case, *Bownes v. First USA Bank*, in the Circuit Court of Montgomery County, Ala., indicating in a chart on the final page that First USA prevailed in 98% of almost 20,000 bank/cardmember arbitrations that had proceeded to a final resolution

NAF marketing document summarizing the NAF Code of Procedure and stating benefits of the NAF such as limited awards, cost control, "little or no discovery," confidentiality, and loser pays provisions requiring consumers to pay the corporation's attorney fees

Interview of Ed Anderson in *Metropolitan Corporate Counsel*, including observations by Anderson that arbitration can reduce the possibility of punitive damages and extensive discovery; also that arbitration agreements can include "loser pays" provisions

July 16, 2001, deposition of Ed Anderson, Managing Director of the NAF, in *Toppings v. Meritech*—deposition includes information about Anderson's previous involvement as a shareholder of Equilaw, a wholly owned subsidiary of NAF, at the same time he was counsel for ITT Financial, a company that used NAF arbitration and also discusses arbitrator selection, arbitration fees, and the NAF Code of Procedure

CD-Rom Contents

- Letter dated October 20, 1997, from Ed Anderson, Managing Director of the NAF, to an undisclosed recipient, urging this person to put arbitration agreements in his/her contracts and stating that "there is no reason for your clients to be exposed to the costs and risks of the jury system"
- Article by Alan Kaplinsky entitled "Excuse Me, but Who's the Predator?" discussing ways in which "banks can use arbitration clauses as a defense"—Kaplinsky is listed by the NAF as one of its "Information Resources" on a document it sends to corporate counsel (listed above)
- A legal memorandum from NAF counsel to undisclosed recipients, regarding "Arbitration and Class Actions in Financing," concluding that "Forum Arbitrations may not be consolidated into class actions unless all parties consent"
- Professor Michael Giest's study of NAF arbitrator bias in the Internet Corporation for Assigned Names and Numbers (ICANN) process, entitled "Fair.com? An Examination of the Allegations of Systematic Unfairness in the ICANN UDRP" (UDRP is the Uniform Domain Name Dispute Resolution Policy)—study finds that complainants win in arbitration before the NAF nearly 83% of the time, due primarily to the fact that "despite claims of impartial random case allocation as well as a large roster of 131 panelists, the majority of NAF single panel cases are actually assigned to little more than a handful of panelists"; the study also mentions the NAF's marketing strategy of sending out a newsletter highlighting cases in which complainants have won in arbitration (see DomainNews articles referenced below)
- Articles from DomainNews, the news service of the National Arbitration Forum, highlighting cases in which a high-profile complainant won a domain name dispute in arbitration—examples include "Master of Domains: metallica.org," "Rose Bowl Kicks out Squatter," and "Johnny Unitas Wins Another One"
- Letter brief from TLPJ to the California Supreme Court in *Mercuro v. Superior Court*, opposing NAF's request for depublication of that case on the grounds that the case involves an issue of continuing public interest and that the court in *Mercuro* correctly characterized the NAF as being subject to repeat player bias
- Amicus brief filed by NAF in the U.S. District Court (N.D. Tex.) in *Marsh v. First USA Bank*—the NAF brief is filed on behalf of neither side but makes the same arguments as the defendant in that case: namely, that "arbitration is pro-consumer," that arbitration is important in the modern economy, that arbitration provisions should be enforced, and that the NAF is not a biased forum
- June 1, 1994, deposition of Ed Anderson in *ITT Commercial Finance v. Wangerin*, demonstrating the connection between the NAF and Equilaw, Inc., the decision of ITT (where Anderson was employed) to use Equilaw for arbitration, and Mr. Anderson's involvement as a shareholder of Equilaw
- Declaration Concerning Debtor's Schedules filed in U.S. Bankruptcy Court in 1994 by Ed Anderson on behalf of Equilaw and indicating that at that time Mr. Anderson was director, officer, and major shareholder of Equilaw
- November 27, 2002, deposition of Ed Anderson, Managing Director of the NAF, in *Ebarle v. Household Retail Services*—deposition includes discussion of NAF's solicitations comparing NAF and AAA, NAF's arbitrator selection process, the application of NAF rules where they conflict with the language in the parties' contract, and NAF's relationship with Household

Consumer Arbitration Agreements

Other Material on Impact of Arbitration on Consumers

McQuillan *Brief and Related Exhibits*

    McQuillan v. Check 'N' Go of North Carolina, Inc., Memorandum of Law in Opposition to Defendants' Motion to Compel Arbitration, North Carolina Superior Court (Appendix H.1)

    Compilation of Payday Lending Contracts Showing Consumer Lack of Choice (McQuillan Ex. 7)

    Weir Affidavit of August 5, 2005, Detailing the Readability of the Arbitration Clause (McQuillan Ex. 9)

    Rossman Affidavit of July 15, 2005, Indicating the Impact of the Arbitration Clause Limiting Class Actions (McQuillan Ex. 10)

    Series of Affidavits Indicating That Arbitration Clause and Requirement for Individual Appearance Before an Arbitrator Makes Litigation Impractical (McQuillan Exs. 11a–11i)

    Series of Affidavits Indicating Impracticality for Legal Aid Offices to Handle the Consumer's Dispute (McQuillan Exs. 12a–12d)

    Illustrative List of Arbitration Court Decisions (McQuillan Ex. 38)

    Other *McQuillan* Exhibits (NAF section)

Letter to Mr. Phil Goldsmith from opposing counsel representing Beneficial, indicating that Beneficial will opt for AAA arbitration and suggesting a resolution of the dispute, which Beneficial counsel indicates would be in the consumer's best interest because "in my experience . . . arbitration through the AAA can be quite expensive, especially for your client"

Transcript of November 7, 2002, H & R Block conference call discussing judicial ruling's effect on H & R Block, indicating that, for years after arbitration agreement went into effect, exposure to liability would be largely eliminated

Letter: Law Firm Solicits Car Dealers for Arbitration Services

Unreported Decisions

Barajas v. PHP, Clearinghouse No. 51,778D (D. Ariz. Nov. 6, 1997)

Cheatham v. Air System Engineering Co., Clearinghouse No. 51,969 (Cal. Super. Ct. Apr. 30, 1997)

Commonwealth v. Metro Chrysler-Plymouth Jeep-Eagle, Inc., Clearinghouse No. 52,028 (Pa. Commw. Ct. 1997)

Discover v. Shea, Clearinghouse No. 53,553 (N.J. Super. Ct. Law Div. Oct. 26, 2001)

Gutierrez v. Auto West, No 317755 (Cal Superior Ct, July 21, 2005)

Harris v. Montgomery Catalog Sales, Clearinghouse No. 52,505 (Ala. Cir. Ct. May 21, 1999), *aff'd sub nom. Alabama Catalog Sales v. Harris*, 794 So. 2d 312 (Ala. 2000)

Hong v. First Alliance Mortgage Co., Clearinghouse No. 52,122 (Cal. Super. Ct. Dec. 3, 1997)

Horenstein v. Mortgage Market, (D. Ore., Jan. 11, 1999)

Mirza v. National Standard Mortgage Corp., Clearinghouse No. 52,514 (N.Y. City Ct. Apr. 28, 1999)

Nefores v. Branddirect Marketing, Inc., Clearinghouse No. 53,552 (Ohio C.P. Richland County Jan. 28, 2002)

Neighbors v. Lynn Hickey Dodge, Clearinghouse No. 51,616B (Okla. Ct. App. Aug. 6, 1996) Op. La. Att'y Gen. No. 98-380, Clearinghouse No. 53,554, at 2 (Mar. 28, 1999)

Williams v. Showmethemoney Check Cashers, Clearinghouse No. 52,500 (Ark. Cir. Ct. Aug. 26, 1999), *aff'd on related grounds*, 342 Ark. 112, 27 S.W.3d 361 (Ark. 2000)

Woods v. Harris Financial Recovery, No. C04-1836C (W.D. Wash. Jan. 24, 2005)

CD-Rom Contents

Text of Arbitration Agreements
    Creditors Only
        Creditors, Banks, Employers, Health Care Plans, Communications Service Providers, Others

Consumer Arbitration Agreements Appendices on CD-Rom
    Table of Contents
    Appendix A, Federal Statutes
    Appendix B, Arbitration Service Provider Rules
    Appendix C, Sample Discovery
    Appendix D, Brief Requesting Discovery As to Arbitrability
    Appendix E, Briefs on Arbitration Costs, Damage Limitations, and Unconscionability
    Appendix F, Briefs on Unconscionability of Arbitration Clauses Restricting Class Actions
    Appendix G, Brief on Magnuson-Moss Warranty Act's Prohibition on Predispute Binding Arbitration Clauses
    Appendix H, Brief on Arbitration Service Provider Bias
    Appendix I, Brief on Waiver and on Bankruptcy Court Discretion to Deny Arbitration
    Appendix J, Brief Advocating Switching to Service Provider Capable of Administering Class Arbitration
    Appendix K, Sample Response and Counterclaim in Arbitration Action to Collect a Consumer Debt
    Appendix L, Brief Opposing Confirmation of Collector's Arbitration Award
    Appendix M, AAA and NAF Documents, Additional Briefs, Other Resources Found Only on the CD-Rom
    Index
    Quick Reference to the *Consumer Credit and Sales Legal Practice Series*
    What Your Library Should Contain

Word Files on CD-Rom
    Complaints
    Discovery
    Affidavits Filed by Attorneys for Consumer
    Briefs

Search This Manual
    Search This Manual's Appendices, Plus All Other Documents on This CD-Rom
    Limit Search Only to the Current File You Are Using on the CD-Rom
    Search Chapters and Appendices of This Manual
    Summary Contents of This Manual
    Table of Contents of This Manual
    Index of This Manual
    CD-Rom Contents for This Manual
    Contents of Other NCLC Manuals

Other NCLC Publications
    Descriptions of Other Publications
    Searching NCLC Publications
    What Your Library Should Contain
    Quick Reference to the *Consumer Credit and Sales Legal Practice Series*
    Free Consumer Education Brochures

Consumer Arbitration Agreements

NCLC Resources, About This CD-Rom
About NCLC
consumerlaw.org
Unreported Cases
Consumer Law Weblinks
Disclaimer Regarding Pleadings
Licenses and Copyright
About Law Disks

Chapter 1 Preliminary Issues

1.1 Scope of This Manual

This manual covers one of the most active areas of consumer litigation today: the enforceability of arbitration agreements entered into before any dispute has arisen between the parties, which force consumers to submit future legal claims to binding arbitration. This manual focuses on how consumers can avoid being forced into arbitration in some situations, and instead retain their constitutional right to litigate their claims in court.

The manual surveys current theories and selected case law. Comprehensiveness is beyond the scope of this or any publication, not only because new cases are reported on a weekly basis, but also because of the great variation in arbitration clauses and in the underlying transactions.

The remainder of this preliminary chapter defines the phrase "predispute binding arbitration agreement," and discusses some of the reasons why many consumers resist being compelled to submit their claims to binding arbitration.

Chapter 2, *infra*, examines a number of threshold issues involved when challenging arbitration clauses. Section 2.1, *infra*, addresses how arguments against arbitration clauses arise procedurally; § 2.2, *infra*, addresses whether particular types of challenges to arbitration clauses should be addressed by courts or arbitrators; § 2.3, *infra*, addresses jurisdictional issues that arise in the enforcement of arbitration clauses; § 2.4, *infra*, addresses when consumers may seek discovery on the validity of arbitration clauses; § 2.5, *infra*, addresses when consumers may demand a jury trial in order to decide whether an arbitration agreement is enforceable; and § 2.6, *infra*, addresses appeals from orders granting or denying motions to compel arbitration.

Chapter 3, *infra*, addresses the principal substantive provision of the Federal Arbitration Act (FAA): that predispute arbitration clauses are enforceable. Section 3.2, *infra*, details the preemptive scope and effect of the FAA, as that statute has been held to override and nullify a variety of state limitations on binding arbitration.[1] Section 3.3, *infra*, addresses limitations of the applicability of the FAA, which include that the FAA does not extend to transactions that do not involve interstate commerce. Section 3.4, *infra*, explains that generally applicable state contract law governs whether an agreement to arbitrate exists, and explores whether such an agreement runs afoul of generally applicable contract defenses such as unconscionability.

Chapter 4, *infra*, describes conflicts between the FAA's authorization of predispute binding arbitration clauses and other federal statutes. Section 4.2, *infra*, discusses authorities indicating that claims under a limited number of federal statutes may never be forced into arbitration, and discusses the standard for determining if predispute binding arbitration is generally precluded by a statute. Subsections 4.2.2 and 4.2.3, *infra*, detail authorities holding that claims under the Magnuson-Moss Warranty Act and in bankruptcy proceedings, respectively, are not subject to predispute binding arbitration clauses.

While claims under most federal remedial statutes generally may be the subject of binding predispute arbitration clauses, some such clauses contain serious flaws peculiar to their language or operation, and thus run afoul of the federal statutes. Section 4.3, *infra*, examines authorities holding that arbitration clauses which *explicitly* prevent consumers from receiving relief that is provided by statute are not enforceable. Section 4.4, *infra*, examines authorities holding that arbitration clauses which operate to *effectively* prevent consumers from vindicating their statutory rights—such as arbitration clauses that impose prohibitive costs—will not be enforced.

Chapter 5, *infra*, reviews some of the issues that frequently arise with respect to whether an agreement to arbitrate has actually been formed.

Chapter 6, *infra*, analyzes generally applicable contract defenses to predispute binding arbitration clauses—most particularly the prohibition against unconscionable contracts—and provides numerous illustrations of situations in which such defenses have been successful.

Chapter 7, *infra*, reviews arguments about the scope of arbitration clauses, including the question of whether a party who has not signed an arbitration clause may enforce the clause, and the question of whether an arbitration clause may be enforced against a consumer who has not signed it. Chapter 8, *infra*, examines situations in which a party

---

[1] For a comprehensive and well-reasoned critique of the doctrine of FAA preemption and a discussion of the harms to consumers and workers resulting from the loss of state regulation in this area, see David S. Schwartz, *Correcting Federalism Mistakes in Statutory Interpretation: The Supreme Court and the Federal Arbitration Act,* 67 Law & Contemp. Probs. 5 (2004).

waives its right to compel arbitration by suing the other party, by delaying moving to enforce the arbitration clause, or by some similar action. Chapter 9, *infra*, reviews the constitutional challenges that have been made to arbitration clauses, though very few of these have been successful.

Chapter 10, *infra*, addresses the complex issues that arise concerning arbitration on a classwide basis.

Chapter 11, *infra*, addresses the effect of an arbitration award, the procedure to confirm an award, and the limited scope of judicial review to vacate or modify an arbitration award, including an award of punitive damages for the consumer. The chapter also examines the effect of an arbitration award on a subsequent court or arbitration proceeding.

Chapter 12, *infra*, examines the growing practice of creditors, particularly credit card issuers, to utilize arbitration to collect on their consumer debts. It explains how the process works, and sets out consumer strategies to respond to the threat of arbitration or to the actual proceeding and an action to confirm such an award.

There are several ways to search for cases, keywords, and other terms found in the manual's chapters and appendices. Besides the detailed table of contents and the index, NCLC offers a unique web-based text search feature which covers this manual and all our other manuals. The search engine is located at www.consumerlaw.org. Clicking on "Keyword Search" brings up a screen that allows the user to search for any term, phrase, or combination of terms in NCLC's manuals. The search can be confined to a single manual, or can be extended to all of NCLC's manuals. The search engine will indicate the pages in the manual where the term or phrase appears.

This function not only rapidly locates the discussion of a particular topic, but is also an excellent way to find out where a particular case, statute, or regulation is discussed in NCLC's manuals. The search instructions explain how to use wildcards and how to search for phrases, one term that is near another term, for either of two terms, and for one term that is not on the same page as another term.

This manual's appendices provide useful primary source materials, all of which are also available on the CD-Rom accompanying this manual. The CD-Rom allows users to search the appendices and to copy and paste them into a word-processing document. Appendix A, *infra*, reprints the Federal Arbitration Act and also federal statutes that limit the enforceability of arbitration involving military personnel and between car dealers and their franchisors. Appendix B, *infra*, reprints the rules from the three major consumer arbitration service providers, including fee information. Appendix C, *infra*, consists of various sets of discovery regarding the enforceability of arbitration agreements.

Appendices D through I, *infra*, are sample briefs dealing with the enforceability of arbitration agreements. Appendix D, *infra*, is a brief requesting discovery as to arbitrability, Appendix E, *infra*, contains briefs on arbitration costs, damage limitations and unconscionability, and Appendix F, *infra*, contains briefs on the unconscionability of arbitration clauses restricting class actions. Appendix G, *infra*, is a brief on the Magnuson-Moss Warranty Act's prohibition of predispute binding arbitration clauses, Appendix H, *infra*, is a brief on arbitration service provider bias, and Appendix I, *infra*, is a brief on waiver and on bankruptcy court discretion to deny arbitration.

Appendix J, *infra*, is a brief advocating switching an arbitration to an arbitration service provider capable of administering class arbitration. Appendices K and L, *infra*, are sample materials seeking to prevent the use of arbitration to collect on a consumer debt. Appendix K, *infra*, is consumer's response and counterclaim to an arbitration proceeding initiated by a credit card debt purchaser. Appendix L, *infra*, is a brief opposing confirmation of a collector's arbitration award. Appendix M, *infra*, details material found on the CD-Rom accompanying this manual but not found in the appendices. This information is also briefly summarized below.

All of these appendices, the index, and the table of contents are included on the CD-Rom accompanying this manual. The material is provided in Adobe Acrobat (PDF) format. This format allows users to perform key word searches across the whole CD-Rom, and to use Internet-style links, buttons, forward and backward searches, bookmarks, and the like to quickly pinpoint relevant material. The material then can be easily pasted into a word-processing document.

In addition, the CD-Rom contains a number of briefs and other material not found in the appendices. The additional briefs and also the briefs, discovery, and other pleadings found in the appendices are all presented in both PDF format and Microsoft Word format, thus facilitating their transfer to a word-processing document for editing and use.

The CD-Rom also includes affidavits, depositions, correspondence, and tax returns from the American Arbitration Association (AAA), dealing in part with costs of arbitration with AAA, waiver of certain fees, and AAA's relationship to certain high-volume users of AAA's services. As well, the CD-Rom includes a number of documents pertaining to the National Arbitration Forum (NAF), collected by attorneys around the country in an attempt to show that the NAF is biased in favor of corporations and other repeat users.

Additional information found only on the CD-Rom includes California and New Mexico statutes limiting arbitration agreements, and California rules requiring disclosures about arbitration and imposing standards as to arbitrators. The CD-Rom also contains copies of over one hundred arbitration agreements used by creditors and other corporations.

A comment is also appropriate about the cases and authorities cited in this manual. While the focus of this manual is on predispute binding arbitration agreements in the consumer context, arbitration clauses have been the subject of extensive litigation in other contexts. A rapidly growing number of employers require their employees to sign arbitration agreements,[2] for example, and many of those clauses have led to litigation with respect to their interaction with a variety of federal civil rights and employment statutes.[3] Similarly, a growing number of medical care providers require patients to sign arbitration clauses as a condition of receiving medical care, and those provisions have also given rise to quite a bit of litigation.[4] This manual will cite and discuss a number of these and other non-consumer court decisions involving arbitration, because the principles that they establish about such subjects as the FAA, the formation of arbitration agreements, and the defenses to arbitration agreements are generally applicable in the consumer setting. For instance, much of the pro-consumer case law relating to prohibitively expensive mandatory arbitration clauses arises from doctrines first articulated in employment law cases.

Certain documents are included in this manual and cited by a "Clearinghouse" number. With some exceptions, these documents are found on the CD-Rom accompanying this manual. These documents can also be obtained from the Sargent Shriver National Center on Poverty Law (formerly known as the National Clearinghouse for Legal Services, Inc.). Cases of special interest to low-income advocates, including unpublished cases, are frequently cited by a "Clearinghouse" number. Current case pleadings are available on the organization's website, www.povertylaw.org.

Summaries are available to the general public. Subscribers can download the full text. Website subscription fees are currently $25 per month or $200 per year. For older pleadings, call the Sargent Shriver National Center on Poverty Law at (312) 263-3830. A minimal copying and delivery fee will be charged.

1.2 Predispute Binding Arbitration Agreement Defined

There are a wide variety of alternative dispute resolution (ADR) mechanisms, one of which is arbitration. There are also a variety of types of arbitration. Most of the controversy and thus litigation involves mandatory predispute binding arbitration agreements. When this manual refers to "mandatory arbitration" or "arbitration clauses," those phrases are used as a shorthand for mandatory predispute binding arbitration agreements.

"Predispute arbitration agreement" refers to a contractual provision, agreed to in advance of any dispute or claim, which requires a party to take any claims that may later arise to arbitration instead of to court. This is distinct from postdispute arbitration, in which two parties who have an existing dispute agree after the dispute arises to submit that dispute to arbitration. Many of the concerns voiced by consumer advocates with respect to predispute arbitration are greatly reduced in the setting of postdispute arbitration, and some courts have expressed a similar sentiment.[5] Most significantly consumers, unlike corporations, rarely have access to counsel when they enter into transactions and therefore are unlikely to focus on the significance of waiving their future access to the public court system when no dispute has yet arisen.[6]

---

2 *See* Leslie Kaufman & Anne Underwood, *Sign or Hit the Street*, Newsweek, June 30, 1997, at 48 (noting that employers such as ITT, JC Penny, Brown & Root, and Renaissance hotels have adopted arbitration systems for employment disputes); Michael A. Verespej, *Sidestepping Court Costs*, Industry Wk., Feb. 2, 1998, at 68 (more than 400 employers, with a combined 4.5 million employees, have subscribed to some form of alternative dispute resolution for employment claims, mostly within the past two years).

There is also extensive academic commentary on arbitration in the employment context. *See, e.g.*, Harry T. Edwards, *Where Are We Heading with Mandatory Arbitration of Statutory Claims in Employment?*, 16 Ga. St. U. L. Rev. 293 (1999); Geraldine Szott Mohr, *Arbitration and the Goals of Employment Discrimination Law*, 56 Wash. & Lee L. Rev. 395 (1999); Stephen J. Ware, *Default Rules from Mandatory Rules: Privatizing Law Through Arbitration*, 83 Minn. L. Rev. 703, 719–725 (1999).

3 *See, e.g.*, Circuit City Stores v. Adams, 532 U.S. 105, 121 S. Ct. 1302, 149 L. Ed. 2d 234 (2001); Floss v. Ryan's Family Steak Houses, Inc., 211 F.3d 306, 313 (6th Cir. 2000); Desiderio v. Nat'l Assoc. of Sec. Dealers, 191 F.3d 198 (2d Cir. 1999) (Title VII); Jones v. Fujitsu Network Communications, Inc., 81 F. Supp. 2d 688, 693 (N.D. Tex. 1999) (Family Medical Leave Act); Little v. Auto Steigler, 29 Cal. 4th 1064, 130 Cal. Rptr. 2d 892, 63 P.3d 979 (2003); Armendariz v. Found. Health Psychcare Services, Inc., 24 Cal. 4th 83, 106, 99 Cal. Rptr. 745, 6 P.3d 669 (2000).

4 *See, e.g.*, Broemmer v. Abortion Services, 173 Ariz. 148, 840 P.2d 1013 (Ariz. 1992); Buckner v. Tamarin, 119 Cal. Rptr. 2d 489 (Ct. App. 2002); Obstetrics & Gynecologists Wixted, Flanagan & Robinson v. Pepper, 101 Nev. 105, 693 P.2d 1259 (1985); Sanchez v. Sirmons, 121 Misc. 2d 249, 467 N.Y.S.2d 757 (Sup. Ct. 1983).

5 *E.g.*, Armendariz v. Found. Health Psychcare Services, Inc., 24 Cal. 4th 83, 99 Cal. Rptr. 2d 745, 6 P.3d 669 (2000).

"We emphasize at the outset that our general endorsement of the Cole [v. Burns Int'l Sec. Services, 105 F.3d 1465 (D.C. Cir. 1997)] requirements [that arbitrators must be neutral, and be able to provide for all types of relief that would otherwise be available in court, among other things] occurs in the particular context of mandatory employment arbitration agreements, in order to ensure that such agreements are not used as a means of effectively curtailing an employee's FEHA [Fair Employment and Housing Act] rights. These requirements would generally not apply in situations in which an employer and an employee knowingly and voluntarily enter into an arbitration agreement *after* a dispute has arisen. In those cases, employees are free to determine what trade-offs between arbitral efficiency and formal procedural protections best safeguard their statutory rights." Armendariz, 24 Cal. 4th at 103 n.8 (emphasis added); *see also* United States Senate Committee on Banking, Housing & Urban Affairs, Summary of the Predatory Lending Consumer Protection Act of 2002, *available at* http://banking.senate.gov/pss/predlend/summary.htm (seeking to prohibit use of predispute arbitration clauses in high-cost home mortgages, but preserving option of postdispute arbitration agreements).

6 *See* Statement of Federal Loan Mortgage Corp., Freddie

In "binding arbitration" the arbitrator is empowered to issue a final, binding ruling on the merits of a suit, subject only to the sharply limited judicial review provided by the FAA or state law.[7] It is this combination of a consumer's loss of virtually all access to the public court system within the context of form contracts of adhesion, where there is little if any meaningful consent by consumers, that gives rise to what one commentator called the "anti-democratic consequences of mandatory arbitration."[8]

Mediation differs from arbitration in that a mediator attempts to facilitate an agreement between the parties while an arbitrator actually decides the case. Mediation does not prevent the consumer from bringing an action in court. Texas's deceptive acts and practices (UDAP) statute, for example, was amended in 1995 to provide for mandatory mediation, upon either party's motion, of UDAP suits seeking less than $15,000 in economic damages.[9] This mediation is not binding on the consumer.

1.3 Why Many Consumers Try to Avoid Predispute Binding Arbitration

1.3.1 Introduction

One of the more troubling trends for consumers today is the increased use of binding arbitration clauses in consumer credit and sales agreements. These clauses are fast becoming as common in consumer contracts as merger clauses and implied warranty disclaimers, and arbitration is spreading rapidly.[10]

Creditors and merchants favor binding arbitration for a number of reasons and, in almost every case, these are reasons why the consumer will want to avoid binding arbitration.[11] The main reason corporations want to arbitrate disputes is that arbitration often sharply reduces companies' exposure to large damage awards, even when the companies engage in widespread patterns of egregious wrongdoing. As one commentator has observed:

> [A]rbitration clauses that provide slanted processes or limited remedies undermine the efficiency goal of personal injury law. A powerful contracting party can impose inadequate arbitration systems on countless potential plaintiffs. By doing so, it can reduce the anticipated cost of its accidents significantly and thereby decrease the

---

Mac Promotes Consumer Choice with New Subprime Mortgage Arbitration Policy (Dec. 4, 2003), *available at* www.freddiemac.com/cgi-bin/printme/print_page.cgi?fileName=consumer_120403 ("[T]here exists the greater likelihood that borrowers may be unaware that they are agreeing to be bound by this [arbitral] dispute resolution mechanism."); Linda J. Demain & Deborah Hensler, *"Volunteering" to Arbitrate Through Predispute Arbitration Clauses: The Average Consumer's Experience*, 67 Law & Contemp. Probs. 55, 73–74 (2004) ("Given the lack of information available to consumers in predispute arbitration clauses, and the difficulty of obtaining and deciphering these clauses, it is likely that most consumers only become aware of what rights they retain and what rights they have waived after disputes arise."); Christine Reilly, *Achieving Knowing and Voluntary Consent in Pre-Dispute Mandatory Arbitration Agreements at the Contracting Stage of Employment*, 90 Cal. L. Rev. 1203, 1225 (2002) (empirical research demonstrates that employees "do not understand the remedial and procedural consequences of consenting to arbitration" and that "[v]ery few are aware of what they are waiving"); *see also* Paul D. Carrington & Paul Y. Castle, *The Revocability of Contract Provisions Controlling Resolution of Future Disputes Between the Parties*, 67 Law & Contemp. Probs. 207, 218 (2004).

7 For a discussion of the scope of judicial review under the FAA, see Chapter 11, *infra*.

8 Richard C. Reuben, *Democracy and Dispute Resolution: The Problem of Arbitration*, 67 Law & Contemp. Probs. 279, 309–318 (2004).

9 Tex. Bus. & Com. Code Ann. § 17.5051 (Vernon).

10 *See, e.g.*, Karl E. Neudorfer, *Defining Due Process Down: Punitive Awards and Mandatory Arbitration of Securities Disputes*, 15 Ohio St. J. on Disp. Resol. 207 (1999) ("Customer agreements that do not contain boilerplate language requiring that all disputes be submitted to arbitration are now the exception to the rule. As a result, in the new era, arbitration is suddenly everywhere." (footnotes omitted)); *Arbitration: Happy Endings Not Guaranteed*, Bus. Wk., Nov. 20, 2000 ("Since 1995, cases filed with the American Arbitration Association, one of several arbitrators available, have increased dramatically. . . ."); David Hechler, *ADR Finds True Believers*, The Nat'l L. J., July 2, 2001 ("[M]ost of the organizations that collect ADR data report substantial increases in recent years. For example, of the cases filed between 1996 and 2000 with the American Arbitration Association, mediations and arbitrations combined almost tripled."); Robert W. Snarr, Jr., *No Cash 'til Payday: The Payday Lending Industry*, Federal Reserve Bank of Philadelphia Compliance Corner (First Quarter 2002), *available at* www.phil.frb.org/src/srcinsights/srcinsights/a1cc1.html (noting that use of mandatory arbitration clauses appears to be "standard operating procedure among payday lenders and banks that partner with payday lenders to originate payday loans"); *see also* Jean R. Sternlight & Elizabeth Jensen, *Using Arbitration to Eliminate Consumer Class Actions: Efficient Business Practice or Unconscionable Abuse?*, 67 Law & Contemp. Probs. 75 (2004) ("If one looks at the form contracts she receives regarding her credit card, cellular phone, land phone, insurance policies, mortgage, and so forth, most likely, the majority of those contracts include arbitration clauses, and many of those include prohibitions on class actions." (footnote omitted)).

11 The points made in this section are presented as background information that consumer advocates should consider in determining whether to resist arbitration, *not* as arguments that should be made in court to resist arbitration in particular cases. It is fairly clear that broad arguments against the institution of arbitration will nearly always fail. *See, e.g.*, Rollins, Inc. v. Foster, 991 F. Supp. 1426, 1436 (M.D. Ala. 1998) ("Foster's argument goes to the adequacy of arbitration proceedings as compared to civil proceedings. This type of argument has been routinely rejected by federal courts as grounds for invalidating an arbitration clause.").

deterrent effect of tort law.[12]

Therefore, no less an authority than the Office of the Comptroller of the Currency has observed that mandatory arbitration clauses "have been associated with abusive lending practices."[13]

Arbitration involves the loss of a number of rights and procedural protections that some consumers may wish to retain. "[U]nlike a judge, an arbitrator is neither publicly chosen nor publicly accountable."[14] Arbitrators in most commercial arbitration cases are not required to give a reasoned explanation of the result.[15] Arbitrators need not follow rules of evidence.[16] There is some empirical evidence indicating that arbitrators tend to be less familiar than judges with recent cases and developments in the law.[17] One of the leading corporate proponents of forced arbitration has openly stated that arbitration strips consumers of familiar protections: "Arbitration materially changes the dispute resolution rules that consumers and borrowers are accustomed to: there is no right to a jury trial, pre-hearing discovery is limited, class actions are eliminated and appeals are severely circumscribed."[18]

1.3.2 Limitations on Class Actions

The vast majority of arbitration clauses in use in consumer contracts throughout the United States explicitly prohibit consumers from bringing or participating in class actions. In addition, the rules of one of the most widely used arbitration service providers, the National Arbitration Forum, bar consumers from bringing or participating in class actions in cases handled by that company.[19]

The loss of any class action remedy is often a grievous blow to consumer rights. As the United States Supreme Court and many other courts have repeatedly recognized, the class action offers individuals with small claims their only realistic opportunity to receive justice.[20] There are some indications that many lenders have adopted arbitration clauses precisely for the purpose of avoiding all class actions, and at least one arbitration service provider has

---

12 Elizabeth G. Thornburg, *Contracting with Tortfeasors: Mandatory Arbitration Clauses and Personal Injury Claims,* 67 Law & Contemp. Probs. 253, 271 (2004).

13 Office of the Comptroller of the Currency, Administrator of National Banks, Guidelines for National Banks to Guard Against Predatory and Abusive Lending Practices, OCC Advisory Letter 2003-2, at 2, 3 (Feb. 21, 2003).

14 Cole v. Burns Int'l Sec. Services, 105 F.3d 1465, 1476 (D.C. Cir. 1997); *see also* Elizabeth G. Thornburg, *Contracting with Tortfeasors: Mandatory Arbitration Clauses and Personal Injury Claims*, 67 Law & Contemp. Probs. 253, 272 (2004) ("The public nature of litigation, and its status as a function of government, is a way in which society enunciates its values, and in which it creates and enforces the rules that govern primary behavior. From the standpoint of the legal system, arbitration can eliminate the ability of courts to perform this declarative function.").

15 *See* Paul D. Carrington & Paul H. Haagen, *Contract and Jurisdiction*, 1996 Sup. Ct. Rev. 331, 347, 348.

16 *See* Davis v. Prudential Sec., 59 F.3d 1186, 1190 (11th Cir. 1995).

17 *See* Cole v. Burns Int'l Sec. Services, 105 F.3d 1465, 1478 (D.C. Cir. 1997).

18 Alan S. Kaplinsky & Mark J. Levin, *Anatomy of An Arbitration Clause: Drafting and Implementation Issues Which Should Be Considered By A Consumer Lender*, 1113 Prac. L. Inst. Corp. L. Prac. Course Handbook 655, 657 (1999).

The Rand Institute for Civil Justice has also concluded that mandatory arbitration has been adopted by some businesses to limit verdicts on behalf of consumers and thereby reduce the incentives for consumer attorneys to take cases. Eric Moller, Elizabeth Rolph & Patricia Ebener, Rand Inst. for Civil Justice, Private Dispute Resolution in the Banking Industry 6–8, 12, 13, 32 (1993); *see also* Alan S. Kaplinsky & Mark J. Levin, *Alternative to Litigation Attracting Consumer Financial Services Companies*, Consumer Fin. Services L. Rep., 1102 Prac. L. Inst. Corp. 845, 847 (1999) (arguing that banks might find arbitration preferable to litigation because, "perhaps most importantly . . . it eliminates irrational jury verdicts").

19 *See* Lockman v. J.K. Harris & Co., L.L.C., 2007 WL 734951, at *2 n.1 (W.D. Ky. Mar. 6, 2007).

In *Lockman*, a plaintiff sought to amend a claim to provide for class action treatment in arbitration. The court noted that: "The arbitrator denied that request on the grounds that the National Arbitration Forum's procedural rules do not provide jurisdiction over unnamed persons. . . ." *Id.* at *2. In other words, *Lockman* makes clear that the actual practice of NAF arbitrators is to look first and only at NAF's own rules, and then to decide questions about the possibility of class action treatment automatically in favor of the defendant. The *Lockman* court further noted that NAF's policy in this respect is not uniform among arbitration firms: "Unlike the American Arbitration Association, which apparently amended its rules in response to the [United States Supreme Court's holding in Green Tree Financial Corp. v. Bazzle, 539 U.S. 444, 451–452 (2003) that an arbitrator must decide whether the parties' contract permits class arbitration], the National Arbitration Forum does not permit class arbitration and advertises that fact." *Lockman*, 2007 WL 734951, at *2 n.1 (citing Robert S. Safi, *Beyond Unonscionability: Preserving the Class Mechanism Under State Law in the Era of Consumer Arbitration*, 83 Tex. L. Rev. 1715, 1737 (2005)). In addition, the National Arbitration Forum has regularly advertised to potential corporate clients that it will not permit individuals to bring class actions before it. See Exhibits to Plaintiffs' Brief in *McQuillan v. Check 'N Go*, included on the CD-Rom accompanying this manual.

20 *See, e.g.*, Amchem Products Inc. v. Windsor, 521 U.S. 591, 138 L. Ed. 2d 689, 117 S. Ct. 2231, 2246 (1997); Phillips Petroleum Co. v. Shutts, 472 U.S. 797, 809, 86 L. Ed. 2d 628, 105 S. Ct. 2965 (1985); *see also* Ting v. AT & T, 182 F. Supp. 2d 902 (N.D. Cal. 2002), aff'd in part and rev'd in part, 319 F.3d 1126 (9th Cir. 2003); Arenson v. Whitehall Convalescent & Nursing Home, 164. F.R.D. 659, 666 (N.D. Ill. 1996); Fogie v. Rent-A-Center, 867 F. Supp. 1398, 1404 (D. Minn. 1993); Leonard v. Terminix Int'l Co., 854 So. 2d 529 (Ala. 2002); Fletcher v. Sec. Pac. Nat'l Bank, 23 Cal. 3d 442, 591 P.2d 51, 57 (1979); Mandel v. Household Bank, 129 Cal. Rptr. 2d 380 (Ct. App. 2003); Eshaghi v. Hanley Dawson Cadillac Co., 214 Ill. App. 3d 995, 574 N.E.2d 760, 766 (1991); Streich v. Am. Family Mut. Ins. Co., 399 N.W.2d 210, 218 (Minn. Ct. App. 1987); King v. Club Med, Inc. 76 A.D.2d 123, 430 N.Y.S.2d 65, 68 (1980); 4 Herbert Newberg, *Newberg on Class Actions* § 21.01, at 21–23 (3d ed. 1992).

advertised its services to companies on the basis that it will not permit consumers to proceed on a class action basis.[21]

1.3.3 Concerns About Arbitrators' Impartiality

There are a number of different private arbitration companies who compete to be selected by corporations in their standard form contracts with consumers and employees. Arbitration work is often very lucrative, and arbitrators know that if they rule against a corporate defendant too frequently or too generously (from the standpoint of that corporation), they will lose the work.

There is also some empirical evidence and a good deal of commentary suggesting that arbitrators have a tendency to favor "repeat player" clients.[22] In the consumer law context, the repeat player will generally be the corporate defendant. One cause of this repeat player bias may be that many arbitrators compete to be selected by corporations, and if they rule against a corporate defendant too frequently or too generously (from the standpoint of that defendant), they may lose the business account of that corporation.[23]

One recent study of mandatory arbitration in managed care cases in California, for example, found a small number of cases in which an arbitrator awarded a plaintiff more than one million dollars against a health maintenance organization (HMO).[24] In each instance, that was the only HMO case that the arbitrator ever handled,[25] suggesting that every time an arbitrator entered a substantial verdict against an HMO, the arbitrator was unable to get any further work from HMOs in the state.

In the last few months, there have also been two publicly disclosed episodes of arbitrators who were handling cases for the National Arbitration Forum (NAF) being blackballed after ruling for consumers against NAF's most prominent client, MBNA Bank. The first episode is described in the deposition of Harvard Law Professor Elizabeth Bartholet, taken on September 26, 2006, by a lawyer challenging NAF as being biased in a consumer case against Gateway Computers.[26] Professor Bartholet had served as an independent contractor arbitrator for NAF, until she resigned. Her deposition describes how she was blackballed by a credit card company after she ruled against it in a single arbitration. At the time that the credit card company decided to block her from hearing any more cases involving itself, she was scheduled to hear a number of other consumer cases. NAF sent out letters to the consumers falsely stating that she would no longer be the arbitrator in their cases, because she had a scheduling conflict. The professor, however, did not have a scheduling conflict; instead, NAF had sent out this explanation to conceal the fact that in reality she had been blackballed by a lender who did not like how she ruled in a past case.

The second recent disclosure came in an article written by Richard Neely, a former justice of the West Virginia Supreme Court of Appeals, in the September/October 2006 issue of *The West Virginia Lawyer*.[27] After retiring from the bench, Justice Neely was approached by NAF to serve as one of its independent contractor arbitrators, and he agreed to do so. He reported that when he did not award a bank the full amount of attorney fees it asked for, that he found

---

21 *See* Brief of *Amicus Curiae* Trial Lawyers for Public Justice, the American Association of Retired Persons, the Association of Trial Lawyers of America, and the National Association of Consumer Advocates in Support of Appellees, Baron v. Best Buy Co., 260 F.3d 625 (11th Cir. 2001) (includes as an attachment such a letter from an arbitration service provider) (reproduced on the CD-Rom accompanying this manual); *see also* Alan S. Kaplinsky & Mark J. Levin, *Excuse Me, But Who's the Predator?*, Bus. L. 739 (May/June 1988) (encouraging banks to use arbitration as a "defense" against class actions and class action lawyers).

22 Cole v. Burns Int'l Sec. Services, 105 F.3d 1465, 1476 D.C. Cir. 1997); Mercuro v. Super. Ct., 116 Cal. Rptr. 2d 671 (Ct. App. 2002); Lisa B. Bingham, *Employment Arbitration: The Repeat Player Effect*, 1 Emp. Rts. & Emp. Pol'y J. 189 (1997) (study finding that employees recover a lower percentage of their claims in repeat player cases than in non-repeat player cases); Paul D. Carrington & Paul Y. Castle, *The Revocability of Contract Provisions Controlling Resolution of Future Disputes Between the Parties*, 67 Law & Contemp. Probs. 207, 218 (2004); David S. Schwartz, *Enforcing Small Print to Protect Big Business: Employee and Consumer Rights Claims in an Age of Compelled Arbitration*, 1997 Wis. L. Rev. 33, 60, 61; Jean R. Sternlight, *Panacea or Corporate Tool?: Debunking the Supreme Court's Preference for Binding Arbitration*, 74 Wash. U. L.Q. 637, 684, 685 (1996); James L. Guill & Edward A. Slavin, Jr., *Rush to Unfairness: The Downside of ADR*, Judges' J., Summer 1989, at 8.

23 *See* Kirby Behre, *Arbitration: A Permissible Or Desirable Method for Resolving Disputes Involving Federal Acquisition and Assistance Contracts?*, 16 Pub. Cont. L.J. 66 (1986) (discussing possibility "that an arbitrator will make a decision with an eye toward his role in future disputes involving one or both of the parties—that is, an arbitrator's decision might be influenced by the desire for future employment by the parties"); Ellen Dannin, *Employers Can Just About Bank on Winning in Arbitration*, Los Angeles Times, Dec. 24, 2000 ("Arbitrators are hired by private parties. They know that whether they get picked to work in the next case may depend on how their current case is decided. They also know that most employees will only be involved in one case, but the odds are that an employer will be involved in others."); James L. Guill & Edward A. Slavin, Jr., *Rush Unfairness: The Downside of ADR*, Judges' J., Summer 1989, at 8, 11 (1989) ("[A]n arbitrator's decision might be influenced by the desire for future employment by the parties.... Some arbitrators openly solicit work. They write to parties noting their availability, sometimes enclosing samples of their awards." (citations omitted)).

24 Marcus Nieto & Margaret Hosel, Arbitration in California Managed Health Care Systems 22, 23 (2000).

25 *Id.*

26 This deposition transcript is included on the CD-Rom accompanying this manual.

27 Richard Neely, *Arbitration and the Godless Bloodsuckers*, The W. Va. Law. 12 (Sept/Oct. 2006).

himself barred from handling any more cases involving that bank. He explained that banks, as "professional litigants," can make use of their superior knowledge of arbitrators' past decisions to help ensure that their cases are heard by NAF arbitrators who will rule in their favor.

In addition to the possibility that individual arbitrators may be blackballed, there are many indications that private arbitration companies are subject to financial pressures if they irritate corporate clients. One recent action by a major arbitration provider exemplifies this issue:

> Declaring that contractual restrictions on class suits are "inappropriate," JAMS announced in 2004 that it would start to "ensure fairness" by ignoring such prohibitions and letting class arbitrations go forward. But then Citibank, Discover Card and American Express fought back, writing JAMS out of their arbitration accords. Within months, JAMS reversed itself....[28]

While many arbitration service providers are very secretive about the identity and background of their arbitrators, a good deal of anecdotal evidence indicates that they are disproportionately drawn from lawyers who specialize in representing large corporations.

A September 2007 report by Public Citizen, *The Arbitration Trap, How Credit Card Companies Ensnare Consumers*,[29] examines issues of repeat player bias. Among the report's findings are that:

- 99.6% of NAF cases are brought by creditors, not consumers;
- 94.7% of awards were in favor of businesses;
- In California the top five NAF arbitrators handled on average 1000 cases each and ruled for businesses almost 97% of the time;
- The highest-volume NAF arbitrator issued as many as sixty-eight awards in a single day, in which he awarded every penny the creditor sought in all sixty-eight cases. On his six busiest days, when he issued 332 awards, businesses sought $3,432,919 and he awarded $3,432,919;
- Arbitrators ruling for consumers are blackballed;
- Excessive fees are charged for a written decision and for other aspects of the arbitration; and
- Consumer attorneys are frustrated by NAF's failure to follow its own procedures and seeming pro-business bias in case administration.

In binding arbitration consumers lose the right to have a jury decide their claims. Juries often sympathize with a victimized consumer, and so access to a jury may be the difference between winning and losing the case. More critically, in many consumer cases the potential of a jury trial and jury verdict is critical in convincing the defendant to settle before trial. Arbitrators, on the other hand, typically handle disputes between two businesses, and are most frequently drawn from law firms that largely represent corporate defendants. While most arbitration service providers are quite secretive about the identity and background of their arbitrators, there is some evidence that arbitrators are overwhelmingly older white men.[30] Furthermore, they often are unfamiliar with consumer protection laws, and may be unsympathetic to consumers.[31] As one commentator concluded: "Sending a case to arbitration not only deprives the claimant of a jury trial but also deprives society of the jury's role as enunciator of behavioral norms."[32]

Some commentators have also suggested that arbitrators—who may tend to look for split-the-difference compromises of the sort that work well in many types of commercial disputes—are not effective in enforcing legal rights. "[T]here is inherent in the institutions of private dispute resolution an endemic disinclination to enforce legal rights rigorously."[33] The California Supreme Court recently expounded on this point:

> [C]ourts and juries are viewed as more likely to adhere to the law and less likely than arbitrators to "split the difference" between the two sides, thereby lowering damages awards for plaintiffs. See Haig, *Corporate Counsel's Guide: Development Report on Cost-Effective Management of Corporate Litigation* (July 1999) 610 PLI/Lit. 177, 186–187 ["a company that believes it has a

---

28 *See* Eric Berkowitz, *Is Justice Served*, Los Angeles Times Magazine, Oct. 22, 2006; *see also* Justin Scheck, *JAMS Reverses Class Action Policy; Under Corporate Pressure, It Agrees To Enforce Exclusion Clauses*, The Recorder 1 (Mar. 11, 2005).

29 Available on the CD-Rom accompanying this manual and also at www.citizen.org/documents/Final_wcover.pdf.

30 *See* Gen. Accounting Office, Employment Discrimination: How Registered Representatives Fare in Discrimination Disputes 2 (1994) ("We estimate that most of the NYSE New York Arbitrators (about 89 percent of 726 at the end of 1992) are white men, averaging 60 years of age.").

31 A prominent academic has thus concluded that "the [Supreme] Court's espousal of largely unregulated and unregulable mandatory arbitration appears likely to harm the poorest and least educated members of society." Jean Sternlight, *Panacea or Corporate Tool?: Debunking the Supreme Court's Preference for Binding Arbitration*, 74 Wash. U. L.Q. 637, 683, 684 (1996).

32 Elizabeth G. Thornburg, *Contracting with Tortfeasors: Mandatory Arbitration Clauses and Personal Injury Claims*, 67 Law & Contemp. Probs. 253, 273 (2004).

33 Paul D. Carrington & Paul H. Haagen, *Contract and Jurisdiction*, 1996 Sup. Ct. Rev. 331, 346; *see also* Gregory T. Higgins & William D. O'Connell, *Mediation Arbitration Square Off: The Majority of In-House Counsel Surveyed Prefer Mediation to Binding Arbitration, A Significant Change from Three Years Ago*, The Nat'l L. J., Mar. 24, 1997 (" 'Arbitrators or mediators are perceived as having the sole goal to compromise a result rather than determine whether a party wins or loses,' commented one participant, who added, 'Some disputes must be resolved in a win/lose posture due to potential damage exposure; ADR is seen as a "split the baby" process with no legal integrity and thus clients fear to use it.' ").

strong legal and factual position may want to avoid arbitration, with its tendency to 'split the difference,' in favor of a judicial forum where it may be more likely to win a clear-cut victory"]....[34]

While little public data is available about consumer arbitration some evidence in the context of civil rights and medical malpractice claims finds that arbitrators tend to make smaller awards to individual plaintiffs than do courts or juries.[35] There is also empirical evidence in the context of medical malpractice/insurance coverage indicating that arbitrators are roughly twenty times more likely than judges to grant summary judgment to defendants.[36] Finally, some anecdotal evidence indicates that arbitrators are far more likely to rule for credit card companies than consumers.[37]

1.3.4 Secrecy in Arbitration

Arbitration also largely takes place in secret, with most arbitration clauses and the rules of most arbitration providers requiring that all parties to a dispute keep all facts about both the dispute and the arbitrator's resolution of the dispute "confidential." In addition, "[a]rbitrators have no obligation to the court to give their reasons for an award,"[38] and it is common for arbitrators to provide no written explanation for their decisions.[39] Even when arbitrators do produce written decisions, "arbitrators' decisions are not intended to have precedential effect even in arbitration (unless given that effect by contract), let alone in the courts."[40]

This secrecy tends to reduce the ability of consumer attorneys to effectively represent their clients.[41] It also undermines the public function of litigation. "By closing off access to proceedings, eliminating judicial precedent, and allowing parties to write their own laws, we compromise society's role in setting the terms of justice."[42] Secrecy also makes it harder to evaluate whether a given arbitration service provider is exhibiting bias in favor of corporate defendants or not.[43] One federal court has given a concrete illustration of the social significance of such a confidentiality provision:

> The implications of such secrecy to society are troubling. Among many others, they mean that if consumers obtain determinations that a particular AT & T practice is unlawful, they are prohibited from alerting other consumers. Since the AAA does not require the arbitrator to state reasons for the award and does not provide a public record of

---

34 Armendariz v. Found. Health Psychcare Services, Inc., 24 Cal. 4th 83, 99 Cal. Rptr. 2d 745, 6 P.3d 669 (2000).

35 *See* Armendariz v. Found. Health Psychcare Services, Inc., 24 Cal. 4th 83, 99 Cal. Rptr. 2d 745, 6 P.3d 669 (2000) ("the amount awarded [in arbitration] is on average smaller") (citing David S. Schwartz, *Enforcing Small Print to Protect Big Business: Employee and Consumer Claims in an Age of Compelled Arbitration*, 1997 Wis. L. Rev. 33, 60, 61)); Marcus Nieto & Margaret Hosel, Arbitration in California Managed Health Care Systems 21 (2000) ("Large medical malpractice awards are less common in arbitration than in jury trials. In 1999, medical malpractice awards under $100,000 were 17 percent of the total awards in the court system and 45 percent of the awards in arbitration cases. Nationally, 27 percent of the cases litigated in courts received awards over $1 million, while only 6 percent of patients in arbitration cases received more than $1 million.").

36 *See* Marcus Nieto & Margaret Hosel, Arbitration in California Managed Health Care Systems 18 (2000).

37 Carolyn E. Mayer, *Win Some, Lose Rarely? Arbitration Forum's Rulings Called One-Sided*, Wash. Post, Mar. 1, 2000.

38 United Steelworkers of Am. v. Enter. Wheel & Car Corp., 363 U.S. 593, 598, 4 L. Ed. 2d 1424, 80 S. Ct. 1358 (1960).

39 *See* Paul D. Carrington & Paul H. Haagen, *Contract and Jurisdiction*, 1996 Sup. Ct. Rev. 331, 397, 398; *see also* Richard C. Reuben, *Democracy and Dispute Resolution: Systems Design and the New Workplace*, 10 Harv. Negot. L. Rev. 11 (2005) ("[T]ransparency and rationality are not essential valves of arbitration. Arbitrators are generally not required to articulate reasons for their decisions in the form of written opinions, effectively precluding substantively judicial review of arbitral awards. Moreover, arbitrators do not have to make their decisions according to rules of law. . . ." (footnotes omitted)).

40 IDS Life Ins. Co. v. SunAmerica Life Ins. Co., 136 F.3d 537, 543 (7th Cir. 1998).

41 *See* Marcus Nieto & Margaret Hosel, Arbitration in California Managed Health Care Systems 22 (2000) ("[P]laintiffs in California health care claims generally do not have information about arbitrators' decision records before selecting a neutral arbitrator. In contrast, health care plans do have information about the win-lose decisions of arbitrators. This information gap may favor health care plans."); Jean Sternlight, *Panacea or Corporate Tool?: Debunking the Supreme Court's Preference for Binding Arbitration*, 74 Wash. U. L.Q. 637, 683, 684 (1996) ("[A] consumer's attorney often relies on public information gained from other lawsuits to build her own claims of negligent or intentional misconduct. Repeat-player companies can gain similar information through private channels. Thus, by requiring private arbitration the company may again deprive the consumer of certain relief she might have obtained through litigation." (citations omitted)).

42 Jean Sternlight, *Panacea or Corporate Tool?: Debunking the Supreme Court's Preference for Binding Arbitration*, 74 Wash. U. L.Q. 637, 695 (citations omitted); *see also* Elizabeth G. Thornburg, *Contracting with Tortfeasors: Mandatory Arbitration Clauses and Personal Injury Claims*, 67 Law & Contemp. Probs. 253, 272 (2004); *Arbitration: Happy Endings Not Guaranteed*, Bus. Wk., Nov. 20, 2000 ("[E]ven when both sides walk away 'winners,' the public may lose by failing to hear about cases that involve product safety, anticompetitive behavior, or intellectual-property theft. But privacy is part of arbitration's appeal to companies. 'Companies don't have to worry about disputes showing up in the paper,' said William K. Slate II, AAA's president and CEO.").

43 *E.g.*, Elizabeth Rolph, Erik Moller & John E. Rolph, *Arbitration Agreements in Health Care: Myths and Reality*, 60 Law & Contemp. Probs. 153, 158 (1997) ("The effects of private, binding arbitration are even more difficult to determine. Some organizations that use arbitration agreements have conducted internal evaluations, but the data necessary for a broad-based, non-proprietary evaluation are widely dispersed, private, and often well guarded. Consequently, few studies of private arbitration have been undertaken. . . .").

arbitrator rulings, this confidentiality provision means that a contract that affects seven million Californians will be interpreted largely without public scrutiny. This puts AT & T in a vastly superior legal posture since as a party to every arbitration, it will know every result and be able to guide itself and take legal positions accordingly, while each class member will have to operate in isolation and largely in the dark.[44]

1.3.5 Limitations on Discovery

One of the most compelling advantages of an arbitration proceeding for a creditor or merchant is that it sharply limits the consumer's ability to engage in discovery.[45] One prominent arbitration provider has advertised to potential corporate clients that it provides individuals with "little or no discovery" in arbitration.[46] The scope of discovery permitted is left to the discretion of the arbitrator, and most arbitrators will only permit depositions to be taken if doing so is necessary to preserve the testimony of key witnesses who will be unable to testify in person at the arbitration hearing.[47] Often a company is as concerned with public exposure of the nature of its practices as it is with a monetary verdict. Restrictions on discovery also mean that consumers cannot determine if a practice is part of a more general pattern. Not only is this critical information in any case seeking punitive damages, but it can also result in an individual case expanding into a class action. Limiting discovery in a case to basic document production only also makes it difficult for individual consumers to prove their individual claims.[48]

While a number of courts have shown little concern for many arbitrators' practice of sharply limiting the discovery available to individual plaintiffs, some courts have displayed a greater sensitivity to the impact of this practice. In the *Armendariz* case, for example, the California Supreme Court held that arbitration clauses will not be enforced in statutory employment civil rights cases unless they provide "discovery sufficient to adequately arbitrate [the employee's] statutory claim, including access to essential documents and witnesses."[49] Creditors already have available from their own files all of the information they need to proceed. Consumers, on the other hand, often need information held by the creditor to prove their case.

1.3.6 Arbitration Fees

In *Circuit City Stores, Inc. v. Adams*, Justice Kennedy asserted (without citation to any evidence in the record or to any other authority) that "[a]rbitration agreements allow parties to avoid the costs of litigation," and opined that this "benefit . . . may be of particular importance" in litigation involving "smaller sums of money than disputes concerning commercial contracts," such as employment cases.[50] Experienced consumer lawyers will recognize that, from the consumer's standpoint, Justice Kennedy's notion of cheap arbitration being a benefit is often more of a statement of aspiration (at best) than an accurate reflection of empirical reality.

Corporations often fall into one of two categories: those who adopt arbitration clauses principally as a means of banning class actions, and those who adopt arbitration clauses for perceived advantages in responding to individual cases. Corporations in the first category often (but not always) agree to pay most (and sometimes nearly all) of the costs of arbitration. (There are many circumstances in which there is less to these offers than meets the eye, however, and consumer lawyers must pay close attention to the details of those arrangements.)

---

44 Ting v. AT & T, 182 F. Supp. 2d 902, 932 (N.D. Cal. 2002).

In affirming the holding of the trial court that this confidentiality provision was unconscionable, the Ninth Circuit reiterated that such confidentiality provisions contribute to an unfair repeat-player effect: by imposing a "gag order," the court said, "AT & T has placed itself in a far superior legal posture by ensuring that none of its potential opponents have access to precedent while, at the same time, AT & T accumulates a wealth of knowledge on how to negotiate the terms of its own unilaterally crafted contract." Ting v. AT & T, 319 F.3d 1126, 1152 (9th Cir. 2003).

45 *See* Edward Brunet, *Questioning the Quality of Alternative Dispute Resolution*, 62 Tul. L. Rev. 1, 12, 13 (1987); Mark E. Budnitz, *Arbitration of Disputes Between Consumers and Financial Institutions: A Serious Threat to Consumer Protection*, 10 Ohio St. J. on Disp. Resol. 267, 283, 284 (1995); Paul D. Carrington & Paul H. Haagen, *Contract and Jurisdiction*, 1996 Sup. Ct. Rev. 331, 348.

46 *See* Exhibits to Plaintiffs' Brief in *McQuillan v. Check 'N Go*, included on the CD-Rom accompanying this manual.

47 *See* David S. Schwartz, *Enforcing Small Print to Protect Big Business: Employee and Consumer Rights Claims in an Age of Compelled Arbitration*, 1997 Wis. L. Rev. 33, 46, 47.

48 Jean Sternlight, *Panacea or Corporate Tool?: Debunking the Supreme Court's Preference for Binding Arbitration*, 74 Wash. U. L.Q. 637, 683, 684 (1996) ("One way defendants can decrease a consumer's expected return is to prevent the consumer from engaging in adequate discovery. Because the consumer will be more needful of discovery than will the company, which maintains the relevant records and has continuing access to the decisionmakers, even a seemingly neutral restriction on discovery will affect consumers adversely." (citations omitted)).

49 Armendariz v. Found. Health Psychcare Services, Inc., 24 Cal. 4th 83, 106, 99 Cal. Rptr. 745, 6 P.3d 669 (2000).

The *Armendariz* safeguards regarding discovery were extended to the arbitration of claims involving unwaivable public rights in a recent California Supreme Court case. Little v. Auto Steigler, 29 Cal. 4th 1064, 130 Cal. Rptr. 2d 892, 63 P.3d 979 (2003).

In a similar vein, one federal court has refused to enforce an arbitration clause that limited the time for hearings and limited post-hearing briefs. *See* Gourley v. Yellow Transp., L.L.C., 178 F. Supp. 2d 1196 (D. Colo. 2001).

50 532 U.S. 105, 121 S. Ct. 1302, 1313, 149 L. Ed. 2d 234 (2001).

For corporations in the second category, however, consumers often find that a significant disadvantage of arbitration compared to a court action is the hefty cost of filing fees and arbitrators' hourly charges that are often imposed upon consumers. The consumer may have to pay all or part of the filing fees, and the hourly or daily rate for the arbitrators themselves is quite high.

> I ... think that some courts still subscribe to the fond, but misguided, view that employment arbitration is invariably quick and cheap. The simple truth is it just ain't necessarily so. When we researched the subject in connection with the appeal in Cole [v. Burns], we found that ... JAMS/Endispute arbitrators charged an average of $400 per hour, but fees of $500 or $600 per hour were not uncommon. CPR Institute for Dispute Resolution estimated arbitrators' fees of $250–$350 per hour and fifteen to forty hours of arbitrator time in a typical employment case results in total arbitrators' fees of $3,750 to $14,000 in an "average" case.... I was recently told of a case in which a private mediator billed the parties $25,000 *for one day of work!*[51]

Judicial filing fees are often less (or can be waived if the consumer proceeds *in forma pauperis*). Most importantly, consumers do not have to pay an hourly rate to have a judge hear their case. In arbitration, however, it is even possible that the consumer will have to pay all or part of the fees of several arbitrators.[52]

The costs of arbitration are often particularly high when the arbitrators are former judges. As one commentator has noted:

> The current system provides no limitation on the arbiters' fees, as well as other charges that the providers may demand from the public. Even if fees were publicly disclosed in advance, there is a glaring anomaly in that many retired judges or lawyers are obtaining hourly fees of $350 or more for their arbitration services, as compared with much lower salaries for many attorneys or the full-time court judges who handle heavy dockets of every kind of litigation.[53]

The upshot is that high arbitration costs favor companies and harm consumers by deterring valid claims. As one state court stated in a recent consumer case, requiring consumers to pay filing fees and arbitration costs that are often much more than the amount of the consumers' actual claims effectively deters consumers from bringing these claims at all, and thus represents "the antithesis of access to justice."[54]

1.3.7 Other Concerns

Another consequence of arbitration is that the FAA provides the consumer with a sharply circumscribed ability to appeal the decision maker's erroneous interpretation of the law.[55] This lack of oversight often effectively allows arbitrators to ignore state or federal consumer protection statutes and judicial precedent.

Many corporations also tack on unfair provisions to their arbitration clauses that are not inherent to the idea of arbitration, but that further rig the system against individuals. For example, some corporations impose "loser pays

---

51 Harry T. Edwards, *Where Are We Heading With Mandatory Arbitration of Statutory Claims in Employment?*, 16 Ga. St. U. L. Rev. 293, 306, 307 (1999) (emphasis added) (citations omitted); *see also* Elizabeth Rolph, Erik Moller & Laura Peterson, Rand Inst. for Civil Justice, Escaping the Courthouse 1, 44 (1994) (concluding, based on a study of ADR in Los Angeles, that arbitration fees "usually greatly exceed those levied by the courts"); Paul D. Carrington & Paul H. Haagen, *Contract and Jurisdiction*, 1996 S. Ct. Rev. 331, 384 ("The AAA charges an administrative fee for its services that is generally higher than court filing fees, and ... most [arbitrators] must be paid by the parties, sometimes at handsome hourly rates."); Frederick L. Miller, *Arbitration Clauses in Consumer Contracts; Building Barriers to Consumer Protection*, 78 Mich. B.J. 302, 303 (1999) ("Courts are subsidized; arbitration forums are not. Filing fees for commercial cases (which include cases brought by consumers) at the AAA start at $500, for claims under $10,000, and go up from there. Additional administrative fees are charged for each day of arbitration. The arbitrators themselves charge an hourly fee.... The AAA may require a party to deposit in advance sums of money to cover anticipated arbitrators' fees or administrative costs. Failure to pay fees and charges in full may result in suspension or termination of the arbitration proceeding."); Dennis Nolan, *Labor and Employment Arbitration: What's Justice Got to Do With It?*, 53 Disp. Resol. J. 40, 47, 48 (1998) ("[S]haring the arbitrator's fees and expenses might prove an insurmountable barrier for the putative grievant. Even a relatively simple case can cost several thousand dollars; a complicated case could easily run several times that. Few grievants can afford that much of a commitment, even if an arbitrator could order reimbursement in the event the grievant prevails."); Beth E. Sullivan, *The High Cost of Efficiency: Mandatory Arbitration in the Securities Industry*, 26 Fordham Urb. L.J. 311, 331, 332 (1999) ("[W]ith arbitration filing and administration fees totaling thousands of dollars per case, and hourly rates ranging from $200–$700, arbitration can be extremely expensive for plaintiffs, especially in more complex cases, and particularly in light of the fact that plaintiffs are almost always required to pay at least half of the costs. As such, an out-of-work plaintiff facing a 'deep pocket' defendant may be severely disadvantaged.").

52 *See* § 4.4, *infra* (further discussion of the fees imposed in arbitration).

53 Harold Brown, *Alternative Dispute Resolution: Realities and Remedies*, 30 Suffolk U. L. Rev. 743, 760 (1997).

54 Mendez v. Palm Harbor Homes, Inc., 111 Wash. App. 446, 461, 45 P.3d 594 (2002); *see also* Lelouis v. W. Directory Co., 230 F. Supp. 2d 1214 (D. Or. 2001) (employment case) ("The higher cost of arbitration—at least from the plaintiff's perspective—also is significant because it is another example of how this arbitration agreement is slanted to favor [the corporation's] interests at the employee's expense.").

55 *See* Ch. 11, *infra*.

rules" to discourage individuals from bringing claims; some corporations insert provisions into arbitration clauses that strip individuals of substantive statutory rights; and some corporations require people to arbitrate their claims in inconvenient locations far across the country. The enforceability of these sorts of provisions is discussed in both Chapters 4 and 6, *infra*.

1.4 Corporations Avoid Binding Arbitration When It Applies to Them

Evidence of corporations' true motivations in requiring binding arbitration is demonstrated by their reactions when forced to arbitrate claims they would otherwise bring in court. Franchised car dealers were so upset by having to arbitrate disputes with their franchisors that they approached Congress to obtain an exemption from the FAA.[56] The dealers complained to Congress that manufacturers were able to exploit the dealers by using a superior bargaining position.

Similarly, a recent study looked at whether corporations include arbitration clauses in their contracts with other companies. Only eleven percent of contracts had such a requirement, indicating that corporations do not view arbitration as an efficient substitute for court litigation.[57]

1.5 Serious Flaws with Studies Allegedly Showing Benefits of Consumer Arbitration

The industry has paid for or cites various studies that allegedly support the merits of consumer arbitration. These studies are all of questionable value. One report often cited is *Outcomes of Arbitration: An Empirical Study of Consumer Lending Cases*, commissioned by the law firm of Wilmer, Cutler, Pickering, Hale and Dorr, L.L.P., with funding provided by the American Bankers Association.[58] This study has been the subject of extensive criticism.

Although the study purports to examine the merits of arbitration as compared to litigation, the study does not examine outcomes for comparable cases in litigation. The report does not measure the differences between decisions from juries versus those from arbitrators, the comparative size of monetary awards for litigation as opposed to arbitration, or the size of arbitration fees and costs compared to court costs. No effort is made to consider the relative merits for consumers of a class action compared with individual arbitration.

The study considers that consumer claimants prevailed if the case was dismissed per claimant request or party agreement. The study also considers the consumer to have prevailed if the consumer recovered any monetary amount, even if it was far less than that being sought or if no amount was awarded, when the arbitrator merely states that the consumer prevailed.

The limited data set is of special note. The study considered 226 cases filed by consumers, disregarding more than 100,000 filed by corporations against consumers during the same four-year period. The study thus systematically excludes over 99% of the cases. The report also never examined why more than 99% of the cases were filed by corporations, or considered the impediments facing consumers when filing for arbitration.

The report examines an even smaller subset of these 226 cases—only 29, an essentially meaningless sample—to measure consumer satisfaction with arbitration. Additionally, of those who said they were satisfied with the outcome of their arbitration proceedings, it is not known in which of those cases the company agreed to pay all arbitration costs and in which cases they did not. The conclusions drawn from the study's already loaded survey questions were also highly dubious. For example, the study assumed that consumers who did not retain a legal representative found the process "straightforward enough not to require the assistance of legal representation." The question does not explore the reason why consumers did not have legal representation, such as cost or lack of familiarity with arbitration proceedings. Even more telling was what these twenty-nine respondents or other potential litigants were not asked. For example, no attempt was made to measure how many consumers gave up pressing their rights when they could not resort to a court process.

Another study of arbitration, the Harris Interactive study,[59] conducted for the U.S. Chamber of Commerce's Institute for Legal Reform, only involves parties who voluntarily chose arbitration, not those who were forced by an adhesive consumer contract to arbitrate their disputes. Even then, only twenty percent of the respondents in the study had entered into contracts with arbitration agreements, the balance agreeing to arbitration after the dispute had arisen. Thus the sample is ill-suited to say anything about manda-

---

56 *See* 15 U.S.C. § 1226 (reprinted in Appx. A, *infra*); *cf.* Arciniaga v. Gen. Motors Corp., 460 F.3d 231 (2d Cir. 2006) (dealer did not meet the definition of a franchisee and thus was forced to arbitrate its dispute).

57 Theodore Eisenberg & Geoffrey P. Miller, Cornell Legal Studies Research Paper Series, The Flight from Arbitration: An Empirical Study of Ex Ante Arbitration Clauses in Publicly-Held Companies' Contracts (Aug. 30, 2006), *available at* http://ssrn.com/abstract=927423.

58 Ernst & Young, L.L.P., Outcomes of Arbitration: An Empirical Study of Consumer Lending Cases (Nov. 30, 2004), *available at* www.arb-forum.com.

59 Harris Interactive, Arbitration: Simpler, Cheaper, and Faster Than Litigation (Apr. 6, 2005), *available at* www.institutefor legalreform.org/issues/docload.cfm?docId=489.

tory consumer arbitration—it excluded ninety-eight percent of the arbitrations that were originally in its sample and were of special relevance to consumer arbitration. The study also does not examine how many people with valid claims were discouraged from pursuing them because of the arbitration requirement, nor does it consider cases in which consumers with very small claims were forced to arbitrate. The study does not compare arbitration and litigation in any manner more objective than relying upon individuals' opinions.

A California Dispute Resolution Institute study[60] concludes that more data is necessary and that it cannot make conclusions based on the information it had. The information the study had was skewed because it considered only voluntary reporting. Moreover, the study appears to exclude collection actions brought by creditors against consumers and any arbitrations from the National Arbitration Forum, a lightning rod concerning the fairness of consumer arbitration. The overwhelming number of arbitrations had no prevailing party listed. Other inadequacies of the data prevented the study from saying anything meaningful.

In comparison to these studies is a September 2007 report by Public Citizen, *The Arbitration Trap, How Credit Card Companies Ensnare Consumers*.[61] In addition to investigating individual cases, the report analyzes in detail California data disclosing information on arbitration outcomes. Among the report's findings are that:

- 99.6% of NAF cases are brought by creditors, not consumers;
- 94.7% of awards were in favor of businesses;
- In California the top five NAF arbitrators handled on average 1000 cases each and ruled for businesses almost 97% of the time;
- The highest-volume NAF arbitrator issued as many as sixty-eight awards in a single day, in which he awarded every penny the creditor sought in all sixty-eight cases. On his six busiest days, when he issued 332 awards, businesses sought $3,432,919 and he awarded $3,432,919;
- Arbitrators ruling for consumers are blackballed;
- Excessive fees are charged for a written decision and for other aspects of the arbitration; and
- Consumer attorneys are frustrated by NAF's failure to follow its own procedures and seeming pro-business bias in case administration.

---

60 Cal. Dispute Resolution Inst., Consumer & Employment Arbitration: A Review of Website Data Posted Pursuant to Section 1281.96 of the Code of Civil Procedure (Aug. 2004), *available at* www.mediate.com/cdri/cdri_print_Aug_6.pdf.

61 Available on the CD-Rom accompanying this manual and also at www.citizen.org/documents/Final_wcover.pdf.

Chapter 2   Threshold Issues for Challenges to Arbitration Clauses

2.1 Introduction

This chapter lays the procedural framework for challenging arbitration clauses. A consumer may challenge the enforceability of an arbitration clause at any point at which a corporation is attempting to enforce the clause. Generally, challenges arise in three ways.

First, in cases initiated by the consumer against the corporation, the corporate defendant may respond to the complaint by filing a motion to compel arbitration under an arbitration clause in the contract. In opposing the motion to compel arbitration the consumer may make any applicable arguments related to the enforceability of the clause, including arguing that the consumer is not required to arbitrate certain claims under federal law (see Chapter 4, *infra*); that no arbitration agreement was formed (see Chapter 5, *infra*); that the arbitration clause is unconscionable or otherwise invalid under state contract law (see Chapter 6, *infra*); that the dispute is not within the scope of the clause (see Chapter 7, *infra*); or that the defendant waived the right to compel arbitration (see Chapter 8, *infra*).

Second, in cases in which a corporation initiates an arbitration proceeding against the consumer (for example, in a debt collection case), the consumer may seek a stay of arbitration and ask a court to determine whether the arbitration clause is enforceable.

Third, if the corporation obtains an arbitration award against the consumer, and no court has previously determined that the consumer is bound by an enforceable arbitration clause, the consumer can contest the validity of the clause in a motion to vacate the award or in opposing confirmation of the award. This process is discussed generally in Chapter 11, *infra*, and specifically with regard to debt collection cases in Chapter 12, *infra*.

2.2 Who Decides Challenges to an Arbitration Clause—Courts or Arbitrators?

Depending upon the facts of a particular case, there may be a wide variety of grounds available for resisting the enforcement of a given arbitration agreement. In addition to the question of what legal rules apply to a given type of legal challenge to an arbitration agreement, however, there is also a second question: who is to decide in the first instance whether a particular argument bars the enforcement of an arbitration clause in regards to a particular dispute—a court or an arbitrator?[1]

According to several United States Supreme Court decisions, and numerous other decisions following the Supreme Court's lead, many issues related to the enforceability of arbitration agreements are to decided by arbitrators in the first instance, rather than by courts. For many other issues, however, the law is clear that courts, rather than arbitrators, are to decide them in the first instance. There are also sharp splits in authority on other topics, with courts disagreeing whether courts or arbitrators should decide various issues in the first instance.

This issue is explored at some length with respect to a nearly every type of challenge to the enforcement of arbitration agreements that this manual covers. This section will merely introduce the issue, and indicate where more extensive discussion of it may be found in the manual.

In trying to decide what issues are for a court to decide and what issues are for an arbitrator to decide, many parties try to find a guide in the United States Supreme Court's statement that "gateway disputes about whether parties are bound by a given dispute" are generally for courts to decide.[2] In actual practice, however, this vague phrase seems to have created more disputes than it has resolved. Different courts' ideas of what is a "gateway dispute" diverge quite a bit (as do parties' ideas on the point), and consumer lawyers would be well advised to examine the case law on various types of challenges rather than to assume that they will be able to tell whether an issue is for a court or an arbitrator on whether it "feels" like a "gateway dispute" or not.

Section 3.4, *infra*, for example, is entitled "Courts Determine an Arbitration Clause's Enforceability Under State

---

1   This issue is often, if not always, a question of federal law, and state laws that differ from federal law are preempted and overridden. *See* § 3.2, *infra*.
2   Howsam v. Dean Witter Reynolds, Inc., 537 U.S. 79, 84, 123 S. Ct. 588, 154 L. Ed. 2d 491 (2002).

Contract Law Principles, *with One Big Exception.*" As the section goes on to explain, the "one big exception" is the so-called separability principle that the United States Supreme Court first enunciated in *Prima Paint, Corp. v. Flood & Conklin Manufacturing Co.*[3] and later expanded in *Buckeye Check Cashing, Inc. v. Cardegna.*[4] Under this principle, when a party challenges the validity of an entire contract that has an arbitration clause on any ground other than whether the parties assented to the contract,[5] the Federal Arbitration Act (FAA) makes the arbitration clause severable from the rest of the contract so that the parties must arbitrate their challenges to the rest of the contract.[6] When a party challenges the arbitration clause itself, however, rather than the broader contract in which it is embedded, those challenges are for courts to decide.[7]

When there is no dispute as to the existence of a valid arbitration clause, but there is a dispute as to whether a given type of claim falls within the scope of that arbitration clause, that dispute over "arbitrability" is normally one for a court to decide in the first instance, unless the parties have explicitly and clearly agreed that the arbitrator should decide that dispute.[8]

There are some disputes relating to the enforcement of arbitration clauses that are not only to be decided by courts, rather than arbitrators, but are actually be decided by juries under section 4 of the FAA. As § 2.5, *infra*, discusses, these disputes generally involve factual disputes over whether parties did or did not enter into an agreement to arbitrate (such as disputes over whether one party's signature is a forgery) and are only available when the party challenging the existence of an agreement can produce some kind of threshold evidence to substantiate its denial that there is a contract.[9] Some but not all states have analogous procedures for jury trials of such disputes.

There are also significant disputes as to whether a court or an arbitrator should decide disputes about whether an arbitration clause is enforceable when it allegedly violates some federal statute by stripping parties of their rights under that statute. There is a great deal of case law on both sides of the issue, with some courts holding, based upon language in the United States Supreme Court's decision in *Pacificare Health Systems, Inc. v. Book*,[10] that these issues are for the arbitrator to decide and with other courts holding that *Pacificare* only applies to situations in which it is ambiguous and unclear as to whether an arbitration clause actually strips parties of statutory rights, and that courts (and not arbitrators) may decide the enforceability of arbitration clauses that clearly strip parties of those rights.[11]

Another situation in which the "who decides" issue arises involves challenges to the enforcement of arbitration clauses based upon the notion that a party has waived its right to invoke an arbitration clause by engaging in extensive litigation activity in court. As § 8.2., *infra*, describes, there is a cryptic sentence in a United States Supreme Court decision[12] that some parties argue suggests that all waiver challenges to the enforcement of an arbitration clause should be decided by arbitrators. Notwithstanding that language, however, § 8.2, *infra*, goes on to demonstrate that the majority of courts have held that it is proper for courts to decide challenges to the enforcement of arbitration clauses based upon a party's waiver of its right to compel arbitration through its litigation activity in court, but it is for arbitrators to decide waiver arguments based upon activity in arbitration.

Finally, as § 10.2, *infra*, discusses, after the United States Supreme Court's decision in *Green Tree Financial Corp. v. Bazzle*,[13] it is clear that an arbitrator—rather than a court—should decide whether a contract permits a case to proceed on a class action basis in arbitration when the contract does not explicitly address the issue.

2.3 Jurisdictional Issues

2.3.1 When Federal Jurisdiction Exists over Actions to Compel Arbitration Under the FAA

2.3.1.1 Overview

Section 4 of the Federal Arbitration Act (FAA) allows an aggrieved party to file a petition in federal court to compel arbitration of a dispute. The statute states:

---

3 388 U.S. 395, 87 S. Ct. 1801, 18 L. Ed. 2d 1270 (1967).
4 546 U.S. 440, 126 S. Ct. 1204, 163 L. Ed. 2d 1038 (2006).
5 *Buckeye*, 546 U.S. at 444 n.1.
  Extensive additional authorities for the proposition that courts, not arbitrators, decide whether parties have consented to arbitration are discussed in § 5.1, *infra*.
6 *See* § 3.4.5, *infra*.
7 Section 6.1, *infra*, includes numerous citations to court decisions that have in part or in full struck down arbitration clauses based upon unconscionability challenges to the arbitration clauses themselves. More particularly, § 6.5.5, *infra*, discusses court decisions that have struck down contractual terms embedded in arbitration clauses that ban parties from bringing or participating in class actions.
8 *See* §§ 3.4.4, 7.3.2, *infra* (discussing First Options of Chicago, Inc. v. Kaplan, 514 U.S. 938, 115 S. Ct. 1920, 131 L. Ed. 2d 985 (1995)).
9 Authorities demonstrating that courts, rather than arbitrators, decide disputes involving fraud in the factum are discussed in § 5.2.2.2, *infra*.

10 537 U.S. 79, 123 S. Ct. 588, 154 L. Ed. 2d 491 (2002).
11 *See* §§ 4.3.1.1, 4.3.2.4, *infra*.
12 Howsam v. Dean Witter Reynolds, Inc., 537 U.S. 79, 123 S. Ct. 588, 590, 154 L. Ed. 2d 491 (2002) (quoting Moses H. Cone Mem'l Hosp. v. Mercury Constr. Corp., 460 U.S. 1, 24, 25, 103 S. Ct. 927, 74 L. Ed. 2d 765 (1983)).
13 539 U.S. 444, 123 S. Ct. 2402, 156 L. Ed. 2d 414 (2003).

> A party aggrieved by the alleged failure, neglect or refusal of another to arbitrate under a written agreement for arbitration may petition any United States district court which, save for such agreement, would have jurisdiction under Title 28, in a civil action or in admiralty of the subject matter of a suit arising out of the controversy between the parties, for an order directing that such arbitration proceed in the manner provided for in such agreement.[14]

Although section 4 of the FAA provides an independent federal cause of action to compel arbitration, it does not itself confer federal subject matter jurisdiction.[15] There must be diversity of citizenship or some other basis for federal jurisdiction before a federal court can entertain a section 4 petition.[16] Consequently, when a consumer brings a state court action, the defendant cannot remove the question of the enforceability of the arbitration agreement to federal court simply by invoking section 4 of the FAA.[17] The mere fact that a dispute involves interstate commerce is not sufficient to permit a party to bring an action to compel arbitration in federal court. The FAA's preemption of state arbitration law does not create such federal jurisdiction.[18]

Nor does arbitration-related behavior appear to create personal jurisdiction. Rather, in assessing whether an arbitrator has personal jurisdiction, one court has held that courts should examine the parties' activities giving rise to the dispute itself, rather than confining their examination to only the parties' activities connected with the arbitration process.[19]

2.3.1.2 Diversity Jurisdiction over Claims Subject to Arbitration

Courts have permitted parties to proceed in federal court with a petition to compel arbitration when there was diversity of citizenship, even when a second co-defendant in the state court action was not diverse.[20] This unfortunate rule permits a defendant shopping for a federal forum to manufacture diversity jurisdiction by purposely omitting non-diverse parties to the state-court lawsuit, and then using an ensuing federal court order compelling arbitration to enjoin the non-diverse parties from proceeding in state court.[21]

For petitions to compel arbitration brought under section 4 of the FAA, the $75,000 amount in controversy requirement for federal court diversity jurisdiction is measured by the amount of the potential arbitration award in the underlying dispute that the petitioner seeks to have arbitrated.[22] The party attempting to establish diversity jurisdiction has the burden to show that the amount in controversy is satisfied.[23] Thus, when arbitration rules prohibit the award

---

14 9 U.S.C. § 4.
15 Moses H. Cone Mem'l Hosp. v. Mercury Constr. Corp., 460 U.S. 1, 26 n.32, 103 S. Ct. 927, 74 L. Ed. 2d 765 (1983); Discover Bank v. Vaden, 396 F.3d 366, 368 (4th Cir. 2005); America's Moneyline, Inc. v. Coleman, 360 F.3d 782, 784 (7th Cir. 2004); Perpetual Sec., Inc. v. Tang, 290 F.3d 132, 136 (2d Cir. 2002) (FAA's provisions for judicial review do not confer jurisdiction); U.S. Bank v. Strand, 2002 WL 31973836, at *3 (D. Or. Sept. 19, 2002) ("A petition under [the FAA] to compel or stay arbitration must be brought in state court unless some other basis for federal jurisdiction exists, such as diversity of citizenship or assertion of a claim in admiralty."); Associates Hous. Fin., L.L.C. v. Young, 2001 WL 34043450 (D. Or. Aug. 10, 2001) (FAA does not give rise to an independent basis for federal jurisdiction and, when a case does not meet the jurisdictional amount and thus there is no diversity jurisdiction, court dismissed a petition to compel arbitration).
16 Moses H. Cone Mem'l Hosp. v. Mercury Constr. Corp., 460 U.S. 1, 26 n.32, 103 S. Ct. 927, 74 L. Ed. 2d 765 (1983).
17 See Moses H. Cone Mem'l Hosp. v. Mercury Constr. Corp., 460 U.S 1, 103 S. Ct. 927, 74 L. Ed. 2d 765 (1982); Rio Grande Underwriters, Inc. v. Pitts Farms Inc., 276 F.3d 683 (5th Cir. 2001); Snap-on tools Corp. v. Mason, 18 F.3d 1261 (5th Cir. 1994); Gen. Elec. Capital Corp. v. Haymer, 151 F. Supp. 2d 753 (S.D. Miss. 2001); cf. Am. Bankers Life Assurance Co. of Fla. v. Evans, 319 F.3d 907, 908 (7th Cir. 2003) (the FAA "does not grant independent federal question jurisdiction"); Bank One v. Shumake, 281 F.3d 507 (5th Cir. 2002) (holding that FAA does not abrogate tribal exhaustion doctrine and does not allow federal court to divest tribal court of jurisdiction over claims arising out of consumer credit transactions on Choctaw Reservation); U.S. Bank v. Strand, 2002 WL 31973836, at *3 (D. Or. Sept. 19, 2002) ("A petition under [the FAA] to compel or stay arbitration must be brought in state court unless some other basis for federal jurisdiction exists, such as diversity of citizenship or assertion of a claim in admiralty.").
18 Rio Grande Underwriters, Inc. v. Pitts Farms Inc., 276 F.3d 683 (5th Cir. 2001).

19 See Sole Resort, S.A. v. Allure Resorts Mgmt., L.L.C., 450 F.3d 100 (2d Cir. 2006).
20 See, e.g., MS Dealer Serv. Corp. v. Franklin, 177 F.3d 942 (11th Cir. 1999); First Franklin Fin. Corp. v. McCollum, 144 F.3d 1362, 1363 (11th Cir. 1998).
21 We Care Hair Dev., Inc. v. Engen, 180 F.3d 838, 844 (7th Cir. 1999) ("Once the district court determined that the arbitration clauses were valid, it did not abuse its discretion in enjoining appellants from proceeding in the state court lawsuit.").
22 America's Moneyline, Inc. v. Coleman, 360 F.3d 782, 786–787 (7th Cir. 2004); Woodmen of the World Life Ins. Soc'y v. Manganaro, 342 F.3d 1213, 1216–1217 (10th Cir. 2003); Am. Bankers Life Assurance Co. of Fla. v. Evans, 319 F.3d 907, 909 (7th Cir. 2003); We Care Hair Dev., Inc. v. Engen, 180 F.3d 838, 841 (7th Cir. 1999) ("[I]t is the stakes of the arbitration and not the possible state court award that control."); Doctor's Associates, Inc. v. Hamilton, 150 F.3d 157, 160–161 (2d Cir. 1998) (holding that courts must "look through to the possible award resulting from the desired arbitration" in determining the amount in controversy); Webb v. Investacorp, 89 F.3d 252, 256 n.1 (5th Cir. 1996); Jumara v. State Farm Ins. Co., 55 F.3d 873, 877 (3d Cir. 1995); Delta Fin. Corp. v. Paul D. Comanduras & Associates, 973 F.2d 301, 304 (4th Cir. 1992); Associates Hous. Fin., L.L.C. v. Young, 2001 WL 34043450, at *3 (D. Or. Aug. 10, 2001); Gen. Elec. Capital Corp. v. Haymer, 151 F. Supp. 2d 753 (S.D. Miss. 2001); Wheat, First Sec., Inc. v. Green, 1992 WL 515343, at *2 (N.D. Ga. Mar. 17, 1992) ("the amount of the underlying arbitration claim determines the amount in controversy"); S.J. Groves & Sons Co. v. Am. Arbitration Ass'n, 452 F. Supp. 121, 123 (D. Minn. 1978).
23 See, e.g., Woodmen of the World Life Ins. Soc'y v. Manganaro, 342 F.3d 1213, 1216–1217 (10th Cir. 2003); Am. Bankers Life

of punitive damages, these damages cannot be considered in computing the amount in controversy.[24] Likewise, when a class action defendant attempts to enforce an arbitration clause that prohibits class claims, the amount in controversy for purposes of federal jurisdiction over the arbitration motion is the value of the *individual* claim the defendant seeks to have arbitrated.[25] As a result, an interesting wrinkle develops when the defendant in a class action lawsuit files a federal petition to compel arbitration and names only the putative class representatives, rather than the entire class, as respondents to the petition. Especially when the class action defendant seeks to establish the amount in controversy requirement by alleging that the cost of any classwide injunctive relief in the underlying class action would exceed $75,000, the defendant must show that an injunction limited *only* to the named class representatives would exceed that amount, because the class representatives are the only individuals whom the defendant seeks to force into arbitration.[26] Consequently, when facing a class action defendant's petition to compel individualized arbitrations, consumer advocates may have an effective argument at their disposal to challenge the existence of federal diversity jurisdiction.

When a party brings a motion to vacate an arbitration award, the amount in controversy for purposes of diversity jurisdiction is determined by the amount requested in the motion to vacate filed in court, not the amount actually awarded in the arbitration.[27] The amount requested in the motion to vacate usually will be identical to either the amount awarded or the amount sought in arbitration, because that amount will be what the party is seeking to vacate or restore. As a result, even though the cases involving motions to vacate arbitration awards require examination of the amount requested in pleadings filed in court, those cases are consistent with the cases addressing the determination of the amount in controversy in motions to compel arbitration because, in both, the amount in controversy is determined by the amount at stake in the underlying arbitration.[28]

Assurance Co. of Fla. v. Evans, 319 F.3d 907, 909 (7th Cir. 2003).

24 Am. Bankers Life Assurance Co. of Fla. v. Evans, 319 F.3d 907, 909 (7th Cir. 2003); *see also* We Care Hair Dev., Inc. v. Engen, 180 F.3d 838, 841 (7th Cir. 1999) ("[I]t is the stakes of the arbitration and not the possible state court award that control."); Associates Hous. Fin., L.L.C. v. Young, 2001 WL 34043450, at *3 (D. Or. Aug. 10, 2001).

25 America's Moneyline, Inc. v. Coleman, 360 F.3d 782, 786–787 (7th Cir. 2004).

26 *See* Republic Bank & Trust Co. v. Kucan, 2007 WL 2376927, at *5 (4th Cir. Aug. 21, 2007) (looking only to the cost of an injunction against the three named respondents and questioning "whether the cost of complying with an injunction involving only three borrowers could amount to more than $75,000").

27 *See* § 11.2.1, *infra*.

28 *See, e.g.*, Sirotsky v. N.Y. Stock Exch., 347 F.3d 985, 989 (7th Cir. 2003) ("the amount in controversy in a suit challenging an arbitration award includes the matter at stake in the arbitration").

2.3.1.3 Federal Question Jurisdiction over Claims Subject to Arbitration

As explained above, section 4 of the FAA does not on its own create federal question jurisdiction over a petition to compel arbitration. Instead, the party seeking arbitration must find some other source of federal jurisdiction. One way that parties attempt to invoke federal jurisdiction is by arguing that the underlying dispute they seek to arbitrate raises a federal question, for example when the underlying dispute involves securities violations or employment discrimination. However the federal courts are split as to whether jurisdiction is determined by looking at the underlying dispute that the petition to compel arbitration is attempting to send to arbitration, or whether federal jurisdiction is determined solely by the allegations in the petition itself. This question has significant implications for the scope of federal jurisdiction over section 4 petitions. Because the dispute raised by the petition invariably will be a contractual one raising questions of state contract law—that is, whether the parties have entered into a valid and enforceable agreement to arbitrate—a rule establishing that jurisdiction must be determined solely on the petition itself essentially means that there will almost never be federal question jurisdiction, and that a court can hear a section 4 petition only if the parties are diverse, or it arises out of a maritime contract or collective bargaining agreement.[29]

A majority of courts have held that jurisdiction must be determined by the allegations in the petition itself, and that the federal nature of the underlying dispute that the petitioner seeks to send into arbitration does not establish federal question jurisdiction.[30] Those courts rely on several

---

29 *See, e.g.*, Discover Bank v. Vaden, 366 F.3d 366, 369 (4th Cir. 2005) (stating that such a rule means that "federal question jurisdiction will never form the basis of a court's subject matter jurisdiction to hear a § 4 petition"); Smith Barney, Inc. v. Sarver, 108 F.3d 92, 94 (6th Cir. 1997) (finding no federal question jurisdiction under section 4 because "[t]he rights asserted by Smith Barney in this case are based simply on an interpretation of the contract to arbitrate, as opposed to the actual merits of the underlying substantive claims").

30 *See, e.g.*, Smith Barney, Inc. v. Sarver, 108 F.3d 92, 94 (6th Cir. 1997) ("[T]he Federal Arbitration Act does not supply an independent basis for federal jurisdiction, nor does the federal nature of the underlying claims."); Westmoreland Capital Corp. v. Findlay, 100 F.3d 263 (2d Cir. 1996) (finding that section 4 requires jurisdiction from some source other than a federal question in the underlying dispute, such as diversity of citizenship or admiralty claims); Prudential-Bache v. Fitch, 966 F.2d 981, 986–989 (5th Cir. 1992); Klein v. Drexel Burnham Lambert, Inc., 717 F. Supp. 319 (E.D. Pa. 1990); Drexel Burnham Lambert, Inc. v. Valenzuela Bock, 696 F. Sup. 957 (S.D.N.Y. 1988); *see also* Blue Cross of Cal., Inc. v. Anesthesia Care Associates Med. Group, Inc., 187 F.3d 1045, 1050, n.5 (9th Cir. 1999) ("We recognize that there is a substantial body of case law which holds that the existence of a federal question in the underlying dispute is not sufficient to create subject matter jurisdiction over a petition to compel arbitration under § 4 of the

rationales to support their conclusion. First, they have held that relying solely on the petition is consistent with the well-pleaded complaint rule, which would be undermined by looking beyond the petition to the federal nature of the underlying dispute.[31] Second, they have held that it makes little sense to examine what is at issue in the underlying dispute when deciding whether federal jurisdiction exists over a petition to compel arbitration because whether a valid arbitration agreement exists is a contractual question that is entirely separate from the underlying dispute, raises no issue of federal law, and requires no interpretation or analysis of the federal right at issue in the underlying dispute.[32] Third, they have relied on the statutory structure of the FAA in finding that jurisdiction must be determined by the allegations in the petition itself. Several courts have noted that whether federal jurisdiction exists over petitions to confirm or vacate an arbitration award is determined on the basis of the petition itself, and that adopting a contrary rule when interpreting section 4 would lead to the "bizarre" outcome that a federal court would have jurisdiction to order arbitration under section 4, but would lack jurisdiction to confirm or vacate the arbitration award after the arbitration is complete.[33] Additionally, although these courts have acknowledged that the language of section 4, which states that federal courts have jurisdiction to compel arbitration of disputes "which save for such agreement [to arbitrate]" they would have jurisdiction over in a civil action, suggests that courts should look to the underlying dispute, they have held that this language was inserted to overturn an old common law rule that an agreement to arbitrate "ousts" the court of jurisdiction over a dispute, and to establish that federal courts could compel arbitration of disputes properly before them.[34] Finally, several courts adopting or urging adoption of this rule have noted that requiring courts to examine the underlying dispute is unwise as a policy matter because it forces the court to address important questions of the merits of the case at the jurisdictional stage, because the merits of the dispute often will turn on whether a federal issue is presented in the case.[35] Consequently, under the majority rule, federal question jurisdiction will be present in a section 4 petition to compel arbitration only in very narrow circumstances, such as when the arbitration clause is part of a maritime contract governed by federal admiralty law, or when the arbitration is contained in a labor agreement governed by the federal Labor Management Relations Act.[36] Otherwise, a federal court will be able to entertain a section 4 petition only if there is diversity jurisdiction.

The Fourth and Eleventh Circuits, in contrast, have rejected this view and hold that federal question jurisdiction exists over a section 4 petition to compel arbitration if the underlying dispute sought to be arbitrated presents an issue of federal law.[37] In *Discover Bank v. Vaden*, the Fourth Circuit relied heavily on the "save for" language of section 4 and rejected the view that this language was intended simply to repudiate the old common law "ouster" rule.[38] It also held that the majority rule, which would essentially eliminate federal question jurisdiction over petitions to compel arbitration, was inconsistent with section 4's reference to compelling arbitration of all disputes that a court would have jurisdiction over under Title 28 of the United States Code, which includes the federal question statute, 28 U.S.C.

FAA."); Kasap v. Folger Nolan Fleming & Douglas, Inc., 166 F.3d 1243, 1246–1247 (D.C. Cir. 1999) (noting that the "clear weight of authority" holds that a court cannot examine the underlying dispute to determine whether federal question jurisdiction exists); Minor v. Prudential Sec., Inc., 94 F.3d 1103, 1106 (7th Cir. 1996) (same); *cf.* Cmty. State Bank v. Strong, 485 F.3d 597, 613–635 (11th Cir. 2007) (Marcus, J., concurring) (acknowledging that Eleventh Circuit precedent required the court to look to the federal nature of the underlying dispute, but arguing that such a rule was ill-conceived and advocating a rule that assesses jurisdiction on the basis of the petition itself).

31 *See, e.g., Westmoreland Capital Corp.*, 100 F.3d at 268–269; *Fitch*, 966 F.2d at 988; *Valenzuela Bock*, 696 F. Supp. at 963–964; *see also Cmty. State Bank*, 485 F.3d at 616–622 (Marcus, J., concurring) (arguing that looking through to the underlying dispute violates the well-pleaded complaint rule).

32 *See Fitch*, 966 F.2d at 988 ("The petition does not ask the court to address any issues of federal law (other than the FAA, which does not provide a basis for federal jurisdiction) in deciding whether the arbitration clause is enforceable."); *Valenzuela Bock*, 696 F. Supp. at 963 ("In petitions to compel arbitration, the only issue is generally whether the parties have entered into a binding agreement to arbitrate that covers the dispute. The interpretation of the federal right at stake is generally not implicated in the dispute before the court until the time of arguments to confirm or vacate the award."); *see also Cmty. State Bank*, 485 F.3d at 618–619 (Marcus, J., concurring) ("[The] essential elements of a § 4 petition make out a simple contract enforcement claim, nothing more. Most assuredly they do not raise a federal question.").

33 *Westmoreland Capital Corp.*, 100 F.3d at 268; *see Valenzuela Bock*, 696 F. Supp. at 963 ("The interest of the federal court in determining whether the arbitration award was entered in manifest disregard of the federal law . . . would seem to be far greater than the federal interest in seeing that the claims could be arbitrated.").

34 *See, e.g., Westmoreland Capital Corp.*, 100 F.3d at 268 & n.6; *Fitch*, 966 F.2d at 987–988; *Valenzuela Bock*, 696 F. Supp. at 961–963. *But see* Discover Bank v. Vaden, 396 F.3d 366, 369 n.2 (4th Cir. 2005) (rejecting this reading of section 4 as "historically inaccurate").

35 *See, e.g., Cmty. State Bank*, 485 F.3d at 634 (Marcus, J., concurring) ("[a]s we noted in the majority opinion, determining whether Strong's claims-to-be-arbitrated arise under federal law would require us to provide some answer to the very legal and factual questions that form the parties' underlying dispute"); *Valenzuela Bock*, 696 F. Supp. at 964 n.6.

36 *See Valenzuela Bock*, 696 F. Supp. at 964–965.

37 *See* Cmty. State Bank v. Strong, 485 F.3d 597 (11th Cir. 2007); Discover Bank v. Vaden, 396 F.3d 366 (4th Cir. 2005); *see also* Rio Grande Underwriters, Inc. v. Pitts Farms, Inc., 276 F.3d 683, 685 (5th Cir. 2001) (stating that jurisdiction exists under section 4 "only when the underlying civil action would otherwise be subject to the court's federal question jurisdiction").

38 Discover Bank v. Vaden, 396 F.3d 366, 369–370 & n.2 (4th Cir. 2005).

§ 1331.[39] Finally, *Vaden* concluded that the majority rule was unduly restrictive and that there was no basis for eliminating federal question jurisdiction as a basis for jurisdiction under section 4.[40]

Even in those jurisdictions where courts will examine the underlying dispute when evaluating a petition to compel arbitration, the dispute must present a *substantial* question of federal law to establish federal jurisdiction.[41] This requirement means that the federal law claim must not be "so patently without merit as to justify ... the court's dismissal for want of jurisdiction."[42] Thus, for example, the Second Circuit has held that a party may not invoke federal question jurisdiction based entirely on a due process argument that was resoundingly rejected under established precedent.[43]

2.3.2 Parallel Proceedings in State and Federal Courts

Occasionally federal courts will be asked to stay related state court proceedings while considering a petition to compel arbitration or, alternatively, to abstain from examining the motion to compel until the state court proceedings are completed. These issues sometimes arise in class action cases when some, but not all, of the class members are covered by arbitration clauses, and the defendant moves to compel arbitration of the claims of those class members who are covered by the arbitration clauses at the same time that the certification of the class is proceeding in state court.[44] In such a situation the Seventh Circuit has said that the federal court should abstain from exercising jurisdiction, by staying the federal action seeking to compel arbitration pending the outcome of the state court case, rather than enjoining the state proceeding and compelling arbitration.[45] In this way the federal court can retain jurisdiction over the case "in case the state court action does not meet its anticipated end."[46]

However, in a similar situation (though not one involving a class action), the Sixth Circuit declined to abstain from exercising jurisdiction over a motion to compel arbitration when the state court was simultaneously addressing the issue of whether the contract had been induced by fraud.[47]

In this case the court upheld a lower court decision to issue an injunction staying the state court action, holding that the injunction did not violate the Anti-Injunction Act[48] because it was "necessary to protect the final judgment of the district court" on the issue of the validity of the arbitration clause.[49] On the other hand, one district court refused to enjoin a related state-court action following a finding that the arbitration clause was unenforceable on the grounds that doing so would violate the Anti-Injunction Act.[50]

Abstention may be appropriate, however, when a state court defendant, instead of moving to compel arbitration in the state court action, files a separate section 4 petition in federal court for tactical litigation reasons. If a state court defendant believes that it has a better chance of succeeding in compelling arbitration in a federal forum than in a state forum, when faced with a lawsuit filed in state court, it may attempt to compel arbitration by filing a section 4 petition in federal court and staying the state court proceedings rather than by seeking to compel arbitration in state court. Although courts do not typically abstain in favor of concurrent state court proceedings, a court may abstain from hearing the federal arbitration petition if it was filed for vexatious or forum shopping purposes.[51] Several courts have abstained when a state court defendant's federal petition to compel arbitration was motivated by a desire to forum shop.[52] A party's intent to forum shop may be shown when, for example, the state court defendant chooses not to first move to compel arbitration in state court or waits until it appears that it will receive an unfavorable result in state court before

---

39 *Id.* at 370.
40 *Id.* at 372.
41 Greenberg v. Bear, Stearns & Co., 220 F.3d 22, 25 (2d Cir. 2001) (citation omitted).
42 Perpetual Sec., Inc. v. Tang, 290 F.3d 132, 137 (2d Cir. 2002).
43 *Id.* at 138, 139.
44 *See, e.g.*, CIGNA HealthCare of St. Louis, Inc. v. Kaiser, 294 F.3d 849 (7th Cir. 2002).
45 *Id.* at 851.
46 *Id.* at 851, 852 (citation omitted).
47 Great Earth Co. v. Simons, 288 F.3d 878, 886–888 (6th Cir. 2002); *see also* United Serv. Prot. Corp. v. Lowe, 354 F. Supp. 2d 651, 656–658 (S.D. W. Va. 2005) (declining to abstain in favor of parallel state court proceedings on arbitration).

48 28 U.S.C. § 2283 (forbidding federal courts from granting injunctions to stay state court proceedings except under narrow circumstances).
49 Great Earth Co. v. Simons, 288 F.3d 878, 894 (6th Cir. 2002).
50 United Serv. Prot. Corp. v. Lowe, 354 F. Supp. 2d 651, 659 (S.D. W. Va. 2005).
51 *See, e.g.*, Moses H. Cone Mem'l Hosp. v. Mercury Constr. Corp., 460 U.S. 1, 17 n.20, 103 S. Ct. 927, 74 L. Ed. 2d 765 (1983) (noting that a factor to consider in deciding to abstain is "the vexatious or reactive nature of either the federal or the state litigation").
52 *See, e.g.*, Morgan Stanley Dean Witter Reynolds, Inc. v. Gekas, 309 F. Supp. 2d 652, 658–659 (M.D. Pa. 2004) (abstaining when federal petition raised the specter of forum-shopping); Cigna Healthcare of St. Louis, Inc. v. Kaiser, 181 F. Supp. 2d 914, 926 n.13 (N.D. Ill. 2002) (abstaining from hearing federal petition to compel arbitration when state-court defendant rushed to federal court instead of moving to compel arbitration in state court), *aff'd as modified*, 294 F.3d 849, 853 (7th Cir. 2002) (affirming district court's decision to abstain in part because the federal plaintiff had avoided filing a motion to compel arbitration in the state court proceeding); *cf.* Citifinancial Corp. v. Harrison, 453 F.3d 245 (5th Cir. 2006) (noting that, as a "matter of respect and institutional orderliness, if not jurisdiction," a district court should shy away from addressing matters before, or staying the proceedings of, another district court when it appears that a party is seeking to forum shop among judges in the same court). *See generally* Jean R. Sternlight, *Forum Shopping for Arbitration Decisions: Federal Courts' Use of Antisuit Injunctions Against State Courts*, 147 U. Pa. L. Rev. 91 (1998).

filing its petition in federal court. One court, however, has rejected the argument that a federal petition to compel arbitration, designed to bypass state court proceedings, constitutes a vexatious litigation tactic, reasoning that the FAA creates a federal cause of action and that a party should not be penalized for invoking it.[53]

Parties attempting to keep such cases in state court may argue that the *Rooker-Feldman* doctrine, which bars lower federal courts from reviewing state court judgments, prevents district courts from considering petitions to compel arbitration while related proceedings are going forward in state court.[54] Under the *Rooker-Feldman* doctrine a party cannot obtain federal court review of a state court ruling on an arbitration motion, whether the party seeking review does so directly, or indirectly by asserting a due process violation based on the state court's ruling.[55] However at least one court has held that, because the right to compel arbitration exists independently under the FAA, such a motion is separate from any state court analysis of the arbitrability of the dispute, and therefore the *Rooker-Feldman* doctrine does not apply.[56] On the other hand, if the state court has actually ruled on a similar motion to compel arbitration, the federal court may find the two proceedings to be so "inextricably entwined" that the *Rooker-Feldman* doctrine applies and the federal court will decline jurisdiction.[57] The Supreme Court, however, recently narrowed the scope of the *Rooker-Feldman* doctrine in *Exxon Mobil Corp. v. Saudi Basic Industries Corp.*,[58] and so consumers may face greater hurdles in attempting to use the *Rooker-Feldman* doctrine to forestall federal actions to compel arbitration.

2.3.3 Venue

Many arbitration clauses specify the location in which the arbitration is to take place. In situations in which a location is specified, motions to compel arbitration brought under section 4 of the FAA can be dismissed for improper venue if brought in a district court outside the venue chosen in the arbitration agreement. This provision limits the ability of a party seeking to compel arbitration from shopping for a favorable forum.[59] Section 4 states that, if a court is satisfied that a valid arbitration agreement exists, it shall require the parties to arbitrate "in accordance with the terms of the agreement."[60]

Section 4 also states that the arbitration proceedings "shall be within the district in which the petition for an order directing such arbitration is filed."[61] Courts have interpreted these two provisions to mean that, when an arbitration agreement specifies a particular venue, only the district court that covers the venue selected in the agreement can compel arbitration.[62] If a party files a section 4 petition to

---

53 *See* Bank One v. Boyd, 288 F.3d 181, 186 (5th Cir. 2002) (finding nothing improper with federal petition to compel arbitration because the FAA explicitly provides parties to an arbitration agreement with a federal cause of action).

54 *See, e.g.*, Pieper v. Am. Arbitration Ass'n, Inc., 336 F.3d 458, 464 (6th Cir. 2003); Am. Reliable Ins. Co. v. Stillwell, 336 F.3d 311, 316, 317 (4th Cir. 2003); Zurich Am. Ins. Co. v. Super. Ct., 326 F.3d 816 (7th Cir. 2002).

55 *See, e.g., Pieper*, 336 F.3d at 460, 461 (finding that *Rooker-Feldman* bars federal court's consideration of due process challenge to state court order compelling arbitration); *Stillwell*, 336 F.3d at 316, 317 (finding no federal jurisdiction over arbitration motion when party completed filing of federal action after state court had ruled on arbitration motion in underlying case).

56 Zurich Am. Ins. Co. v. Super. Ct., 326 F.3d 816, 822 (7th Cir. 2002) ("But Zurich's federal claim arises under the Federal Arbitration Act (FAA) and would exist even if the state court had determined the duty to defend or arbitrability issues in Zurich's favor or if these issues had never been before it. The federal claim does not therefore seek to set aside the state court's orders and does not depend on a determination that the court erred.").

57 *See* Gayfer Montgomery Fair Co. v. Austin, 222 F. Supp. 2d 1292 (M.D. Ala. 2002).

58 544 U.S. 280, 125 S. Ct. 1517, 161 L. Ed. 2d 454 (2005).

59 *See, e.g.*, Snyder v. Smith, 736 F.2d 409, 419 (7th Cir. 1984) (holding that allowing a party to file a motion to compel arbitration in any district and therefore to avoid the agreed-upon forum "could lead to the parties racing to different courthouses to obtain what each thinks is the most convenient forum for it, in disregard of its contractual obligations"), *overruled on other grounds by* Felzen v. Andreas, 134 F.3d 873 (7th Cir. 1998).

60 9 U.S.C. § 4.

61 9 U.S.C. § 4.

62 *See, e.g.*, Ansari v. Qwest Communications Corp., 414 F.3d 1214, 1219–1220 (10th Cir. 2005) ("where the parties agreed to arbitrate in a particular forum, only a district court in that forum has authority to compel arbitration under § 4"); Inland Bulk Transfer Co. v. Cummins Engine Co., 332 F.3d 1007, 1018 (6th Cir. 2003); Mgmt. Recruiters Int'l Inc. v. Bloor, 129 F.3d 851, 854 (6th Cir. 1997); Merrill Lynch, Pierce, Fenner & Smith, Inc. v. Lauer, 49 F.3d 323, 328 (7th Cir. 1995) ("a district court lacks authority to compel arbitration in other districts, or in its own district if another has been specified for arbitration"); Econo-Car Int'l, Inc. v. Antilles Car Rental, Inc., 499 F.2d 1391, 1394 (3d Cir. 1974); Prof'l Transp., Inc. v. Am. Cas. Co. of Reading, Pa., 2007 WL 30554 (S.D. Ind. Jan. 3, 2007); Vertucci v. Orvis, 2006 WL 1688078, at *4 (D. Conn. May 30, 2006); Sinclair Broad. Group, Inc. v. Interep Nat'l Radio Sales, Inc., 2005 WL 1000086, at *4 (D. Md. Apr. 28, 2005); Sea Spray Holdings, Ltd. v. Pali Fin. Group, Inc., 269 F. Supp. 2d 356, 363 (S.D.N.Y. 2003); Roe v. Gray, 165 F. Supp. 2d 1164, 1173 (D. Colo. 2001); M.C. Constr. Corp. v. Gray Co., 17 F. Supp. 2d 541, 548 (W.D. Va. 1998); Dempsey v. George S. May Int'l Co., 933 F. Supp. 72, 75–76 (D. Mass. 1996); Federated Rural Elec. Ins. Co. v. Nationwide Mut. Ins. Co., 874 F. Supp. 1204, 1210 (D. Kan. 1995); Haluska v. RAF Fin. Corp., 875 F. Supp. 825, 828 (N.D. Ga. 1994). *But see* Textile Unlimited, Inc. v. A. BMH & Co., 240 F.3d 781, 783 (9th Cir. 2001) (permitting district court to compel arbitration in its district and to ignore the forum selection clause); Dupuy-Busching Gen. Agency, Inc. v. Ambassador Ins. Co., 524 F.2d 1275, 1276, 1278 (5th Cir. 1975) (allowing district court to compel arbitration outside district in accordance with the forum-selection clause); Legacy Wireless Services, Inc. v. Human Capital, L.L.C., 314 F. Supp. 2d 1045, 1058 (D. Or.

compel arbitration in a district court outside the chosen venue, the court can either dismiss the petition for improper venue, stay the proceedings, or transfer the case to the proper court.[63]

2.4 Right to Discovery Relating to Enforceability of Arbitration Clause

2.4.1 Introduction

Courts have refused to enforce arbitration clauses in numerous cases when specific evidence showed that the particular clauses at issue should not be enforced under the circumstances of those cases. While general or abstract attacks upon the entire idea of arbitration will virtually never prevail, parties who document specific flaws with an arbitration clause may defeat particularly unfair or illegal arbitration clauses.[64]

When facts or evidence relating to the enforceability of an arbitration clause are in the possession of the party attempting to enforce the arbitration clause, the party resisting enforcement has a right to pursue those facts and evidence in discovery. When the enforceability of an arbitration clause turns upon a factual question, discovery is available just as it is for other factual disputes.

2.4.2 Precedent Upholding Right to Discovery

A number of courts have upheld the right of parties to take discovery of factual matters relating to the enforceability of arbitration clauses. In *Wrightson v. ITT Financial Services*, for example, a Florida district court of appeals held that "[o]n remand, the trial court is directed to afford the parties a reasonable opportunity to conduct discovery for the limited purpose of determining the validity of the arbitration agreements under state law."[65]

In *Berger v. Cantor Fitzgerald Securities*, similarly, a federal district court concluded that arbitration could not be compelled until the plaintiff was given the opportunity to pursue discovery:

> Discovery is needed before defendants' motion may be decided, as it should help to clarify several disputed issues of fact that may or may not give rise to special circumstances rendering the U-4 arbitration agreement unenforceable.... Given the Supreme Court's statement in *Gilmer* that claims of special circumstances such as coercion, fraud, or unequal bargaining power are "best left for resolution in specific cases," 500 U.S. at 33, 111 S. Ct. at 1656, further development of the factual record is warranted.[66]

A New York state trial court reached the same conclusion in granting a consumer plaintiff's motion to compel answers to her discovery motions:

> [T]he plaintiff served a demand for document discovery on the defendant which the defendant refused to answer. The discovery sought by the plaintiff pertains to matters such as the impartiality of [the National Arbitration Forum], the relationship between NAF and the defendant, and

---

2004) (same); Indian Harbor Ins. Co. v. Global Transp. Sys., Inc., 197 F. Supp. 2d 1, 3–4 (S.D.N.Y. 2002) (same).

63 Cont'l Cas. Co. v. Am. Nat'l Ins. Co., 417 F.3d 727, 733 (7th Cir. 2005) (affirming district court's dismissal for improper venue); Prof'l Transp., Inc. v. Am. Cas. Co. of Reading, Pa., 2007 WL 30554 (S.D. Ind. Jan. 3, 2007) (transferring action to the district court encompassing the designated arbitration venue); Vertucci v. Orvis, 2006 WL 1688078, at *4 (D. Conn. May 30, 2006) (holding that court can stay proceedings under § 3 of the FAA even if it cannot compel arbitration under § 4); Sinclair Broad. Group, Inc. v. Interep Nat'l Radio Sales, Inc., 2005 WL 1000086, at *4 (D. Md. Apr. 28, 2005) (when party moves to compel arbitration in district not encompassing the designated forum, the court "may either dismiss the case, stay the proceedings, or transfer the action to the appropriate federal district court"); Sea Spray Holdings, Ltd. v. Pali Fin. Group, 269 F. Supp. 2d 356, 363 (S.D.N.Y. 2003) (holding that a court lacking authority to compel arbitration outside its district pursuant to § 4 nonetheless may stay proceedings under § 3 if the court determines that the dispute is "referable to arbitration" elsewhere); M.C. Constr. Corp. v. Gray Co., 17 F. Supp. 2d 541, 548 (W.D. Va. 1998) (same); Optopics Laboratories Corp. v. Nicholas, 947 F. Supp. 817, 825 (D.N.J. 1996) (transferring venue); Dempsey v. George S. May Int'l Co., 933 F. Supp. 72, 76 (D. Mass. 1996) (transferring case to district in the forum specified in the arbitration agreement); Federated Rural Elec. Ins. Co. v. Nationwide Mut. Ins. Co., 874 F. Supp. 1204, 1210 (D. Kan. 1995) (transferring venue to forum specified in arbitration agreement); Messing v. Rosenkrantz, 872 F. Supp. 539, 542 (N.D. Ill. 1995) (staying proceedings).

64 See, e.g., Rhode v. E & T Investments, Inc., 6 F. Supp. 2d 1322, *summary judgment granted in part, denied in part*, 29 F. Supp. 2d 1298 (M.D. Ala. 1998) ("The court finds that Plaintiff's allegations are insufficient to show that the arbitration clauses are unconscionable.... 'A party cannot rely on an abstract principle or theory of unfairness of a bargain to make a case for unconscionability; it must still be gauged by the actual circumstances of the case, and not in the abstract.' "); Rainbow Inv. v. Super Eight Motels, Inc., 973 F. Supp. 1387, 1389, 1390 (M.D. Ala. 1997) (parties must present the court with evidentiary facts that show grounds for revoking an arbitration agreement).

65 Wrightson v. ITT Fin. Services, 617 So. 2d 334, 336 (Fla. Dist. Ct. App. 1993); *see also* Harrison v. Toyota, 2002 WL 533478 (Ohio Ct. App. Apr. 10, 2002).

However, disputes as to the *existence* of an agreement are for the fact finder, and thus a court may deny a motion to stay on the basis that there was no agreement to arbitrate, without allowing further discovery on the issue. *See* Giltner v. Mitchell, 2002 WL 31387032, at *3 (Ohio Ct. App. Oct. 23, 2002).

66 Berger v. Cantor Fitzgerald Sec., 942 F. Supp. 963, 966 (S.D.N.Y. 1996) (referring to Gilmer v. Interstate/Johnson Lane Corp., 500 U.S. 20, 111 S. Ct. 1647, 114 L. Ed. 2d 26 (1991)).

defendant's alleged conduct inconsistent with the bona fides of the arbitration clause. "It is well settled that there shall be full disclosure of all evidence, or information leading to evidence, that is material and necessary in the prosecution or defense of an action regardless of the burden of proof. . . ." (*In re Matthews*, 266 A.D.2d 290, 698 N.Y.S.2d 509; *Northway Eng'g v. Felix Indus.*, 77 N.Y.2d 322, 567 N.Y.S.2d 634, 569 N.E.2d 437.) In view of the authority reviewed above establishing that an arbitration clause governed by the FAA may be set aside on sufficient grounds such as unconscionability, the court finds that the plaintiff has demonstrated her entitlement to the discovery sought from the defendant.[67]

One federal court held that discovery is particularly important in cases involving bias challenges:

> In order to discharge its obligation to assure there is a valid arbitration agreement, the Court agrees discovery is necessary on the Toppings' challenges to the Agreement. The Court believes additional factual development is warranted particularly, without limitation, on both the issues of unconscionability and the impartiality and other challenges to the NAF as the chosen arbitral forum.[68]

An Ohio court has held that when an arbitration clause is vaguely worded or lacking in specific details the parties are entitled to discovery regarding the validity of the clause.[69] The Alabama Supreme Court has held that discovery on arbitrability is allowed in rare circumstances when the party opposing arbitration is virtually unable to obtain the necessary evidence except through discovery.[70]

Courts also have rejected the suggestion that parties may not take depositions relating to the issue of arbitrability "without first demonstrating to the court some extraordinary need therefore."[71] Even courts that have prescribed summary procedures for motions to compel arbitration have stated that such motions should be decided based upon "affidavits, pleadings, *discovery* and stipulations."[72] Still other courts have noted that discovery was taken on arbitrability issues, without questioning the propriety of doing so.[73]

The Supreme Court's decision in *Green Tree Financial Corp.-Alabama v. Randolph* can also be seen as an invitation for consumers to conduct discovery on the enforceability of an arbitration clause. The decision places the burden on the consumer to present evidence of the amount of the arbitration fees and their impact on the consumer's ability to vindicate her statutory rights.[74] If that is the case, the consumer must be given the opportunity to develop such evidence. The Third Circuit has drawn precisely that lesson from the *Randolph* case:

> Without some discovery, albeit limited to the narrow issue of the estimated costs of arbitration and the claimant's ability to pay, it is not clear how a claimant could present information on the costs of arbitration as required by *Green Tree* and how the defendant could meet its burden to rebut the claimant's allegation that she cannot afford to share the cost.[75]

---

67 Hayes v. County Bank, 185 Misc. 2d 414, 713 N.Y.S.2d 267, 270 (Sup. Ct. 2000), aff'd, 286 A.D.2d 371 (2001).
68 Toppings v. Meritech Mortgage Services, Inc., 140 F. Supp. 2d 683, 685 (S.D. W. Va. 2001).
69 Brunke v. Ohio State Home Services, Inc., 2007 WL 1805026, at *3 (Ohio Ct. App. June 25, 2007).
70 *Ex parte* Horton Family Hous., Inc., 882 So. 2d 838, 841–842 (Ala. 2003) (allowing party opposing arbitration to take limited discovery).
71 Int'l Union of Elec., Radio & Mach. Workers v. Westinghouse Elec. Corp., 48 F.R.D. 298, 300, 301 (S.D.N.Y. 1969). *But see Ex parte* Greenstreet, Inc., 806 So. 2d 1203 (Ala. 2001) ("if the party opposing a properly supported motion to compel arbitration desires discovery, that party must present a factually based predicate before a right to conduct discovery regarding matters that could invalidate the agreement to arbitrate arises").
72 Jack B. Anglin Co. v. Tipps, 842 S.W.2d 266, 269 (Tex. 1992) (emphasis added).
73 CIGNA HealthCare of St. Louis, Inc. v. Kaiser, 294 F.3d 849, 955 (7th Cir. 2002) ("[a]s far as we can tell, discovery relating to the state court judge's resolution of the issue of arbitrability is complete"); Duffield v. Robertson Stephens & Co., 144 F.3d 1182 (9th Cir. 1998) (noting that the district court "allowed extensive discovery on the securities industry's arbitration system"); McLaughlin Gormley King Co. v. Terminix Int'l Co., 105 F.3d 1192, 1193 (8th Cir. 1997) (affirming trial court "order freezing resolution of the parties' dispute pending discovery pertinent to the issue of arbitrability"); Hooters of Am., Inc. v. Phillips, 39 F. Supp. 2d 582, 591 (D.S.C. 1998) ("The court concluded that in order for Phillips to respond properly to the § 3 and § 4 motions, she was entitled to limited discovery relative to the circumstances surrounding the making of the alleged arbitration agreement. The court authorized limited discovery in the form of interrogatories, requests to produce and five depositions."), aff'd, 173 F.3d 933 (4th Cir. 1999).
74 *See* § 4.4.2, *supra*.
75 Blair v. Scott Specialty Gases, 283 F.3d 595, 609 (3d Cir. 2002); *accord* Livingston v. Associates Fin., Inc., 2001 U.S. Dist. LEXIS 8678, at *10–*11 (N.D. Ill. June 25, 2001) ("While this Court is extremely doubtful that Plaintiffs, in the case *sub judice*, will ultimately be able to prove the likelihood that they will be saddled with prohibitive costs, the Court recommends that they at least be allowed limited discovery into this arena, or the Supreme Court's burden of proof enunciated in *Green Tree* becomes a nullity. The Court recommends, however, that such discovery be strictly limited to the likely costs that Plaintiffs will incur in this particular case if Plaintiffs are compelled to arbitrate, as well as procedures regarding the waiving of fees and costs. Discovery requests shall not include requests for general statistical information, because such information is irrelevant as to Plaintiffs' costs in this specific case. In sum, while cognizant that Plaintiffs should not be allowed to embark on a fishing expedition, this Court believes they should at least be given a fighting chance to prove prohibitive costs with respect to the

Courts will also permit parties attempting to compel arbitration to take discovery of consumers resisting arbitration.[76]

In addition, Uniform Commercial Code (UCC) section 2-302(2) requires that, when a party challenges a contract provision as unconscionable, "the parties shall be afforded a reasonable opportunity to present evidence as to its commercial setting, purpose and effect to aid the court in making the determination." It is fundamental that the opportunity to present evidence means little without the power to develop that evidence through discovery.[77]

Only a few courts have refused to permit parties to take discovery related to arbitrability.[78]

2.4.3 Discovery Serves Public Policy Goals

In addition to helping litigants in particular cases resist mandatory arbitration, discovery also provides policymakers and the public with an otherwise rare glimpse at the workings of mandatory arbitration. The major arbitration service providers all require that the facts about a dispute in arbitration and the resolution of such dispute be kept confidential. Accordingly, it is generally very hard for consumer advocates or regulators to test the degree to which arbitrators tend to favor one set of actors over another.

Discovery from a case in Alabama state court recently revealed, however, that out of nearly 20,000 arbitration actions brought to a conclusion between First USA Bank and its credit card holders, First USA prevailed in all but eighty-seven of the cases (a success rate of 99.6%).[79] This fact, which made headlines and was extensively discussed in a United States Senate Judiciary Committee hearing on mandatory arbitration, would never have become public if it had not been unearthed in discovery by the Alabama plaintiff.

2.5 Right for a Jury to Decide If Arbitration Agreement Is Enforceable

Few consumers resisting attempts to enforce arbitration agreements request that the court submit factual disputes to a jury. This approach is surprising because juries may be more sympathetic to the consumer's plight than a court wishing to remove a case from its docket by sending it to arbitration.

Section 4 of the Federal Arbitration Act (FAA) gives a party to an arbitration agreement the right, when a case meets federal jurisdictional requirements, to go to federal court to obtain an order requiring the other party to arbitrate the dispute.[80] But section 4 also gives the consumer or other party resisting the arbitration clause the right to:

> [D]emand a jury trial of such issue, and upon such demand the court shall make an order referring the issue or issues to a jury in the manner provided by the Federal Rules of Civil Procedure or may specially call a jury for that purpose. If the jury find that no agreement in writing for arbitration was made or that there is no default in proceeding thereunder, the proceeding shall be dismissed.[81]

In interpreting this provision of section 4, the Third Circuit has held that the jury trial provision should be construed liberally and that a trial should be denied only if there is no genuine dispute over the validity of the arbitration agreement. The court stated that:

> Before a party to a lawsuit can be ordered to arbitrate and thus be deprived of a day in court, there should be an express, unequivocal agreement to that effect. If there is doubt as to whether such an agreement exists, the matter, upon a proper and timely demand, should be submitted to a jury. Only when there is no genuine issue of fact concerning the formation of the agreement should the court decide as a matter of law that the parties did or did not enter into such an agreement.[82]

---

specific statutory right at issue. The total costs, of course, are not just the administrative fee, but include all fees associated with arbitration, including (but not limited to) the arbitrator's fees and expenses."); *see also* Higgs v. Warranty Group, 2007 WL 2034376, at *10 (S.D. Ohio July 11, 2007) (deciding to hold evidentiary hearing on whether the costs of arbitration rendered arbitration clause unconscionable).

For a good example of a consumer using discovery to show the prohibitive cost of arbitration, see Ting v. AT & T, 182 F. Supp. 2d 902, 933, 934 (N.D. Cal. 2002).

76 *E.g.*, H & S Homes, L.L.C. v. McDonald, 823 So. 2d 627 (Ala. 2001) (vendor permitted to take discovery of consumer's claim that he had been a minor when he signed the contract, that the mobile home was not "necessary," and that he had sought to avoid the contract upon becoming an adult).

77 *Cf.* Higgs v. Warranty Group, 2007 WL 2034376, at *10 (S.D. Ohio July 11, 2007) (deciding to hold evidentiary hearing on whether the costs of arbitration rendered arbitration clause unconscionable).

78 *E.g.*, Bank One v. Lake, 2002 WL 663788 (5th Cir. Apr. 5, 2002) (table); Bank One v. Harris, 2001 U.S. Dist. LEXIS 9615 (S.D. Miss. Jan. 2, 2001), *aff'd*, 2002 U.S. App. LEXIS 7756 (5th Cir. Apr. 5, 2002) (table).

79 *See* Carole E. Mayer, *Win Some, Lose Rarely? Arbitration Forum's Rulings Called One-Sided*, Wash. Post, Mar. 1, 2000.

80 9 U.S.C. § 4; *see also* Spahr v. Secco, 330 F.3d 1266, 1269 n.4 (10th Cir. 2003).

81 9 U.S.C. § 4.
Notably, although FAA section 4 provides these rights for a party opposing an independent motion to compel arbitration, section 3 does not explicitly enumerate these procedural rights for a party opposing a motion to stay an existing case. *See, e.g.*, Maestle v. Best Buy Co., 800 N.E.2d 7, 11 (Ohio 2003) (evidentiary hearing not required for motion to stay brought pursuant to 9 U.S.C. § 3); Household Realty Corp. v. Rutherford, 2004 WL 1077369 (Ohio Ct. App. May 14, 2004) (holding that section 3 does not mandate evidentiary hearing on existence of arbitration agreement).

82 Par-Knit Mills, Inc. v. Stockbridge Fabrics Co., 636 F.2d 51, 54 (3d Cir. 1980) (footnote omitted).

Other courts have reached similar conclusions.[83] Of course, the party opposing arbitration must demand a jury trial in order to be entitled to one pursuant to the statute. In addition, the consumer must present a prima facie case sufficient to demonstrate the factual dispute. This requirement may be met by "[a]n unequivocal denial that the agreement had been made, accompanied by supporting affidavits ... in most cases [this] should be sufficient to require a jury determination on whether there had in fact been a meeting of the minds."[84] Although the FAA's jury trial provision is procedural, and therefore states are not bound to follow it,[85] some states also provide for evidentiary hearings or jury trials with respect to limited issues regarding the formation of an agreement to arbitrate.[86]

States, however, are not governed by the FAA, and many states do not provide for jury trials on disputed issues of contract formation but instead provide for expedited bench evidentiary hearings.[87] Having a judge decide disputed factual questions is consistent with section 2-302 of the Uniform Commercial Code, which refers to a "court as a matter of law" determining unconscionability, after a presentation of evidence as to the commercial setting, purpose, and effect of the clause. Consequently, while some issues as to the enforceability of the agreement may be matters of fact for a jury, others may be matters of law for a judge. Other states, however, have statutes like the FAA that do provide for a

---

83 *See, e.g.*, Am. Int'l Specialty Lines Ins. Co. v. Elec. Data Sys. Corp., 347 F.3d 665, 671 (7th Cir. 2003) (holding that a trial is required only if the dispute over the validity of the arbitration agreement is "fairly contestable"); Jackman v. Jackman, 2006 WL 3792109, at *2 (D. Kan. Dec. 21, 2006) (stating that a party must produce some evidence in order to obtain a jury trial on arbitrability); Barbieri v. K-Sea Transp. Corp., 2006 WL 3751215, at *9 (E.D.N.Y. Dec. 19, 2006) (ordering bench trial to determine whether parties agreed to arbitrate when the plaintiff submitted evidence creating a genuine dispute of fact as to whether he was fraudulently induced to enter the agreement, whether he acted under duress, and whether the agreement was unconscionable); McCord v. Am. Gen. Life & Accident Ins. Co., 1999 U.S. Dist. LEXIS 4482, at *8–*9 (E.D. Pa. Mar. 22, 1999) ("If there is doubt as to whether an express, unequivocal agreement to arbitrate exists, the matter, upon a proper and timely demand should be submitted to a jury. Only when there is no genuine issue of fact concerning the formation of the agreement should the court decide as a matter of law that the parties did or did not enter into such an agreement."); The Bergquist Co. v. Sunroc Corp., 777 F. Supp. 1236 (E.D. Pa. 1991); Pyle v. Wells Fargo Fin., 2004 WL 2065652, at *4 (Ohio Ct. App. Sept. 16, 2004) (requiring trial on arbitrability when a dispute of fact existed over the validity of the arbitration agreement); Benson v. Spitzer Mgmt., Inc., 2004 WL 2002503, at *4 (Ohio Ct. App. Sept. 9, 2004) (reversing trial court when "the trial court failed to hold a hearing to determine whether there was a legitimate challenge to the validity of the arbitration clause"); *see also* Omaha Cold Storage Terminals, Inc. v. Patterson, 733 N.W.2d 219 (Neb. Ct. App. 2007) (ordering jury trial when the dispute concerning the validity of the parties' arbitration agreement required "almost uniformly factual determinations").

84 Par-Knit Mills, Inc. v. Stockbridge Fabrics Co., 636 F.2d 51, 55 (3d Cir. 1980); *see also* Wheat, First Sec., Inc. v. Green, 993 F.2d 814, 818 (11th Cir. 1993) (party seeking jury trial must unequivocally deny that an agreement to arbitrate was reached and must offer some evidence to substantiate the denial); Jackman v. Jackman, 2006 WL 3792109, at *2 (D. Kan. Dec. 21, 2006) (stating that a party must produce some evidence in order to obtain a jury trial on arbitrability); Barbieri v. K-Sea Transp. Corp., 2006 WL 3751215, at *9 (E.D.N.Y. Dec. 19, 2006) (finding that plaintiff's affidavit contesting the formation of the arbitration agreement created a genuine dispute of fact and ordering a bench trial on whether the parties agreed to arbitrate); Battels v. Sears Nat'l Bank, 365 F. Supp. 2d 1205, 1215–1216 (M.D. Ala. 2005) (denying request for jury trial when there was no genuine issue of fact concerning the formation of the arbitration agreement); Lawrence v. Household Bank (SB), 343 F. Supp. 2d 1101, 1111 (M.D. Ala. 2004) (denying request for jury trial in the absence of sufficient evidence to put the making of the arbitration clause in dispute); Castro v. Higginbotham, 2007 WL 1849086 (Ohio Ct. App. June 28, 2007) ("[W]here a party challenges the validity or existence of an arbitration agreement, R.C. 2711.03 requires the trial court to conduct a hearing."). *But see* LeGere v. New Millennium Homes, Inc., 2003 WL 23018774, at *2 (Mich. Ct. App. Dec. 23, 2003) (holding that party resisting arbitration must meet a "threshold evidentiary showing" before it can obtain a jury trial under the FAA).

85 *See* § 3.2.2, *supra*.

86 *See, e.g.*, Premiere Auto. Group, Inc. v. Welch, 794 So. 2d 1078 (Ala. 2001) ("[T]he trial court had before it conflicting evidence, in the form of affidavits, as to the execution of the agreements. The appropriate method of resolving this conflict is a jury trial limited to the issue whether Welch entered an arbitration agreement with Premiere and/or with AmSouth."); *Ex parte* Meadows, 782 So. 2d 277 (Ala. 2000) (directing the trial court to conduct a jury trial as to whether the plaintiff signed a contract, when the plaintiff produced an affidavit and an opinion from a handwriting expert that he had not signed the contract); Omaha Cold Storage Terminals, Inc. v. Patterson, 733 N.W.2d 219 (Neb. Ct. App. 2007) (holding that Nebraska's arbitration statute permits jury trials to resolve disputes concerning the formation of an agreement to arbitrate); Maestle v. Best Buy Co., 800 N.E.2d 7, 11 (Ohio 2003) (noting similarities between Ohio's arbitration statute and Section 4 of the FAA); Castro v. Higginbotham, 2007 WL 1849086 (Ohio Ct. App. June 28, 2007) ("[W]here a party challenges the validity or existence of an arbitration agreement, R.C. 2711.03 requires the trial court to conduct a hearing."); Brunke v. Ohio State Home Services, Inc., 2007 WL 1805026 (Ohio Ct. App. June 25, 2007) (noting that Ohio's arbitration statute requires a hearing on a motion to compel arbitration); Pyle v. Wells Fargo Fin., 2004 WL 2065652, at *3–*4 (Ohio Ct. App. Sept. 16, 2004) (holding that Ohio's arbitration statute, like Section 4 of the FAA, allows a party resisting arbitration to seek a trial on arbitrability).

87 *See* Estate of Blanchard v. Cent. Park Lodges (Tarpon Springs), Inc., 805 So. 2d 6 (Fla. Dist. Ct. App. 2001) ("If there are disputed issues regarding the making of the agreement, the court must summarily hear and determine the issue in an expedited evidentiary hearing."); Jalis Constr., Inc. v. Mintz, 724 So. 2d 1254 (Fla. Dist. Ct. App. 1999); LeGere v. New Millennium Homes, Inc., 2003 WL 23018774, at *1 (Mich. Ct. App. Dec. 23, 2003) (holding that Michigan law provides for summary bench hearing on genuine fact disputes); *see also* Higgs v. Warranty Group, 2007 WL 2034376, at *10 (S.D. Ohio July 11, 2007) (deciding to hold evidentiary hearing on whether the costs of arbitration rendered arbitration clause unconscionable).

jury trial.[88] Additionally, when an arbitration clause calls for application of the FAA, some state courts have applied federal law concerning the right to an evidentiary hearing or jury trial.[89]

2.6 Appeal from Judicial Orders Relating to Arbitration

2.6.1 FAA Section 16

Section 16 of the Federal Arbitration Act (FAA) establishes a detailed set of procedural rules governing the availability of appeals from federal district court orders relating to arbitration.[90] Section 16(a) *permits* appeals from: district court orders refusing to stay litigation in favor of arbitration under section 3 of the Act;[91] orders denying petitions to compel arbitration under section 4 of the Act;[92] orders confirming or denying confirmation of arbitration awards;[93] orders modifying, correcting, or vacating arbitration awards;[94] interlocutory orders sustaining in whole or in part injunctions against arbitration;[95] and any other order with respect to arbitration that is a "final decision."[96] When section 16(a) applies and an order regarding arbitration *is* appealable, the federal circuit courts are split over whether the appeal divests the district court of jurisdiction to proceed while the appeal is ongoing, with the majority holding that it does.[97] A party may forfeit its right to appeal under section 16 if it does not take an interlocutory appeal of the court's arbitration ruling and instead waits for completion of proceedings in the trial court—if such delay is prejudicial to the opposing party.[98] Although a party generally does not waive its appellate rights by declining to take an interlocutory appeal, because the purpose of section 16's automatic appeal provisions is to streamline the judicial process and avoid unnecessary litigation of a case that might be subject to arbitration, a party's failure to take an immediate appeal and to wait for litigation to run its course before appealing would, if prejudicial to the opposing party, defeat the purpose of the statute and therefore justify forfeiture of the party's appellate rights.[99]

Although section 16 generally permits appeals from orders denying motions to compel arbitration, at least two federal circuit courts, the D.C. Circuit and the Tenth Circuit, have held that it does not allow appeals when the claim for arbitration is not based on a written agreement to arbitrate between the parties.[100] Section 16 permits parties to appeal an order "refusing a stay of any action under section 3" of the FAA, as well as of any order "denying a petition to order arbitration under section 4" of the FAA.[101] Section 3, in

---

88 *See, e.g.*, Ohio Rev. Code Ann. § 2711.03(B) (West); Omaha Cold Storage Terminals, Inc. v. Patterson, 733 N.W.2d 219 (Neb. Ct. App. 2007) (holding that Nebraska's arbitration statute, which requires that disputes concerning the formation of an arbitration agreement be "forthwith and summarily tried" did not preclude the plaintiff from obtaining a jury trial).

89 *See, e.g.*, LeGere v. New Millennium Homes Inc., 2003 WL 23018774, at *1–*2 (Mich. Ct. App. Dec. 23, 2003) (applying FAA based on contract's choice of law provision); Household Realty Corp. v. Rutherford, 2004 WL 1077369, at *9 (Ohio Ct. App. May 14, 2004) (applying FAA, not Ohio procedural rule alleged to require evidentiary hearing, based on arbitration clause's choice of law provision).

90 9 U.S.C. § 16 (reprinted in Appendix A.1, *infra*).

91 9 U.S.C. § 16(a)(1)(A).
Even preliminary orders with respect to arbitration, such as a refusal to stay litigation to allow the parties to conduct discovery as to the validity of the arbitration agreement, are immediately appealable under this statute, even though no final ruling with respect to arbitration may have been made. *See, e.g.*, Madol v. Dan Nelson Auto. Group, 372 F.3d 997, 998–999 (8th Cir. 2004) (district court order refusing to stay litigation to allow parties to conduct limited discovery was immediately appealable).

92 9 U.S.C. § 16(a)(1)(B).
93 9 U.S.C. § 16(a)(1)(D).
94 9 U.S.C. § 16(a)(1)(E).
95 9 U.S.C. § 16(a)(2).
96 9 U.S.C. § 16(a)(3).
97 *Compare* Ehleiter v. Grapetree Shores, Inc., 482 F.3d 207, 215 n.6 (3d Cir. 2007) (agreeing with those courts that have found that an appeal of an order denying a motion to compel arbitration automatically stays proceedings in the district court); McCauley v. Halliburton Energy Services, Inc., 413 F.3d 1158, 1160 (10th Cir. 2005) (district court lacks the power to proceed while the appeal is pending); Blinco v. GreenTree Servicing, Inc., 366 F.3d 1249, 1252 (11th Cir. 2004) (same); Bombardier v. Nat'l R.R. Passenger Corp., 2002 WL 3181924, at *1 (D.C. Cir. Dec. 12, 2002) (district court could not proceed with discovery while the appeal of the district court's order denying the motion to compel arbitration was pending) *and* Combined Energies v. CCI, Inc., 495 F. Supp. 2d 142 (D. Me. 2007) (court lacked the power to continue after party appealed order denying motion to stay litigation and compel arbitration) *with* Motorola Credit Corp. v. Uzan, 388 F.3d 39 (2d Cir. 2004) (litigation can continue in district court while order denying arbitration is appealed) *and* Britton v. Co-op Banking Group, 916 F.2d 1405 (9th Cir. 1990) (same).

98 Franceschi v. Hosp. Gen. San Carlos, Inc., 420 F.3d 1 (1st Cir. 2005) ("failure to promptly appeal a denial of arbitration will[,] if prejudicial to the opposing party, operate to forfeit the demanding party's right to arbitration"); Cargill Ferrous Int'l v. Sea Phoenix MV, 325 F.3d 695, 700 (5th Cir. 2003); John Morrell & Co. v. United Food & Commercial Workers Int'l Union, 37 F.3d 1302, 1303 n.3 (8th Cir. 1994); Cotton v. Sloane, 4 F.3d 176, 180 (2d Cir. 1993); *cf. In re* Tyco Int'l Sec. Litig., 422 F.3d 41, 46 (1st Cir. 2005) (party waived right to arbitrate by failing to take timely appeal pursuant to 9 U.S.C. § 16(a)(1) of order denying arbitration). *But see* Clark v. Merrill Lynch, Pierce, Fenner & Smith, Inc., 924 F.2d 550, 553 (4th Cir. 1991) (party does not forfeit appeal rights by failing to take interlocutory appeal).

99 *See* Franceschi v. Hosp. Gen. San Carlos, Inc., 420 F.3d 1 (1st Cir. 2005); Colon v. R.K. Grace & Co., 358 F.3d 1, 4 & n.2 (1st Cir. 2003).

100 *In re* Universal Serv. Fund Tel. Billing Practice Litig., 428 F.3d 940 (10th Cir. 2005); DSMC v. Convera Corp., 349 F.3d 679, 683–684 (D.C. Cir. 2003).

101 9 U.S.C. § 16(a)(1)(A)–(B).

turn, requires "an agreement in writing for such arbitration,"[102] and section 4 requires a "written agreement" to arbitrate.[103] Thus, for example, the D.C. and Tenth Circuits have held that a party may not appeal an order denying a motion to arbitrate based on principles of equitable estoppel, because equitable estoppel arises when one party seeks to compel another party to arbitrate by virtue of its conduct, in the absence of any written agreement between the two.[104] The Second Circuit, however, has rejected this view and holds that an order denying a motion to compel arbitration based on equitable estoppel principles is appealable.[105]

At the same time, section 16(b) *prohibits* appeals from: federal district court orders granting stays under section 3 of the Act in favor of arbitration;[106] and orders compelling arbitration under section 4 of the Act.[107] However, section 16(b)'s prohibitions may be overridden when a district court judge certifies an order for appeal under section 1292 of the federal jurisdiction statute.[108] Section 16(b)'s prohibitions do not preclude appellate review altogether, but they do require parties to proceed through arbitration to resolve the merits of their claims before they can appeal the threshold determination of whether their claims are properly subject to arbitration in the first place.[109]

2.6.2 Orders Compelling Arbitration Are Appealable When the District Court Issues an Order Dismissing All Claims

Although section 16(a)(1)(B) makes an order compelling arbitration and staying litigation non-appealable, the Supreme Court in *Green Tree Financial Corp.-Alabama v. Randolph*, held that a district court order compelling arbitration and dismissing all claims with prejudice (rather than issuing a stay) is appealable as a "final decision" under section 16(a)(3).[110] The Supreme Court's unanimous holding in *Randolph* that district court orders compelling arbitration and dismissing all claims are immediately appealable is significant for consumers because it recognizes the availability of appeals in at least some cases in which consumers file suit on their claims and defendants raise arbitration as a defense to avoid court proceedings. Lower federal courts have followed *Randolph* in holding that orders dismissing all claims and compelling arbitration are immediately appealable.[111] In addition, several federal courts since *Randolph* have held that arbitration orders dismissing the plaintiff's claims *without prejudice* are final orders that are immediately appealable.[112] Likewise, in actions brought under section 4 of the FAA solely for the purpose of seeking to compel arbitration, an order compelling arbitration is final and immediately appealable.[113] Some states have applied similar rules in allowing immediate appeals of an order compelling arbitration when the order finally disposes of all claims.[114]

---

102 9 U.S.C. § 3.
103 9 U.S.C. § 4.
104 *In re* Universal Serv. Fund Tel. Billing Practice Litig., 428 F.3d 940 (10th Cir. 2005); DSMC v. Convera Corp., 349 F.3d 679, 683–684 (D.C. Cir. 2003).
105 *See* Ross v. Am. Express Co., 478 F.3d 96 (2d Cir. 2007).
106 9 U.S.C. § 16(b)(1).
107 9 U.S.C. § 16(b)(2).
108 9 U.S.C. § 16(b).
109 *See, e.g.*, Am. Int'l Specialty Lines Ins. Co. v. Elec. Data Sys. Corp., 347 F.3d 665, 669 (7th Cir. 2003) (party did not waive its right to challenge the validity of the arbitration clause by complying with order compelling arbitration and then challenging the arbitrator's decision); Napleton v. Gen. Motors Corp., 138 F.3d 1209, 1214 (7th Cir. 1998); McCarthy v. Providential Corp., 122 F.3d 1242, 1245 (9th Cir. 1997) ("We stress again that we are not precluding review of the district court's order compelling arbitration; we are merely postponing it until the arbitration proceeding has run its course."); Gammaro v. Thorp Consumer Discount Co., 15 F.3d 93, 95 (8th Cir. 1994) (dismissing appeal pursuant to Section 16(b) "without prejudice to later timely appeal").

110 531 U.S. 79, 121 S. Ct. 513, 148 L. Ed. 2d 373 (2000).
111 *See, e.g.*, Circuit City Stores, Inc. v. Mantor, 417 F.3d 1060, 1062 (9th Cir. 2005) (order compelling arbitration and dismissing claims was appealable); Carbajal v. H & R Block Tax Services, 372 F.3d 903, 904 (7th Cir. 2004) (order dismissing action outright and compelling arbitration was appealable); Lloyd v. Hovensa, L.L.C., 369 F.3d 263, 268 (3d Cir. 2004) (dismissal with prejudice was immediately appealable); Am. Heritage Life Ins. Co. v. Orr, 294 F.3d 702 (5th Cir. 2002) (when district court "closed" the case and compelled arbitration, this was functionally equivalent to "dismissing" the case and was a final order under the *Randolph* standard).
112 *See* Municipality of San Juan v. Corporacion para el Fomento Economico de la Ciudad Capital, 415 F.3d 145, 148 (1st Cir. 2005) (dismissal without prejudice appealable); Hill v. Rent-A-Center, Inc., 398 F.3d 1286, 1288 (11th Cir. 2005) (finding district court's dismissal without prejudice appealable because it disposed of the entire case and left no part of it pending before the court); Blair v. Scott Specialty Gases, 283 F.3d 595, 599–602 (3d Cir. 2002); Salim Oleochemicals, Inc. v. M/V Shropshire, 278 F.3d 90, 93 (2d Cir. 2002); Employers Ins. of Wausau v. Bright Metal Specialties, Inc., 251 F.3d 1316, 1322 (11th Cir. 2001) (order compelling arbitration and dismissing claims was appealable even though it did not specify whether the dismissal was with or without prejudice); Interactive Flight Technologies, Inc. v. Swiss Air Transp. Co., 249 F.3d 1177, 1179 (9th Cir. 2001) (recognizing that *Randolph* overturns earlier Ninth Circuit precedent).
113 *See, e.g.*, Great Earth Companies v. Simons, 288 F.3d 878, 885 (6th Cir. 2002) (holding that when action is brought solely to compel arbitration, arbitration order is a final order disposing of all claims); Clarendon Am. Ins. Co. v. Kings Reinsurance Co., 241 F.3d 131, 134 (2d Cir. 2001) (holding that arbitration order in case filed under FAA solely for purpose of obtaining order was immediately appealable despite pending state court action on related contract claims; framing federal action as an "independent" proceeding).
114 Dusold v. Porta-John Corp., 807 P.2d 526, 529 (Ariz. Ct. App. 1990) (allowing immediate appeal when the trial court compelled arbitration and dismissed all claims pursuant to Rule 12A(b)(1)); Childers v. Advanced Found. Repair, Ltd. P'ship,

§ 2.6.2 Consumer Arbitration Agreements

Before *Randolph*, a majority of federal circuit courts had held that a district court order dismissing a case in favor of arbitration was appealable only when arbitration was the sole issue presented to the district court ("independent proceedings"), and that a dismissal was not appealable when parties had asserted additional claims or issues beyond whether or not a dispute should be arbitrated ("embedded proceedings").[115] As most consumer cases are embedded proceedings in which arbitration is raised as a defense, the pre-*Randolph* majority rule prohibited consumers from immediately appealing arbitration orders because such orders were deemed interlocutory regardless of whether the district court issued a stay or instead dismissed all claims. By rejecting these decisions which made the distinction between independent and embedded proceedings the determining factor for immediate appealability, the Supreme Court in *Randolph* has interpreted section 16 to enable consumers to take an immediate appeal and obtain a final arbitrability determination before going to arbitration in those cases in which the federal district court dismisses all claims with prejudice in its order.[116]

The *Randolph* decision also recognized, however, that section 16(b)(1) would have prohibited an appeal if the district court had entered a stay of litigation instead of dismissing all claims.[117] The availability of an immediate appeal in such cases may turn on whether a court's order staying litigation pending arbitration is functionally a final order, even if it is styled as a stay of litigation. For example, when the district court stays the litigation solely to await the outcome of the arbitration for purposes of confirming the arbitration award but otherwise has no remaining action to take in the case, then the district court's order is functionally a final dismissal of all claims and thus immediately appealable.[118] However, a district court's order administratively closing or dismissing a case is not a final order disposing of all claims for purposes of appeal under section 16(b)(1) because it is simply an administrative tool to remove the case from the court's docket rather than a total closure of the case.[119] When a district court orders arbitration without specifying whether it is staying or dismissing proceedings, at least one federal circuit court has rejected a party's attempt to take a direct appeal.[120] Consumer lawyers should be aware of the procedural difference between a stay of litigation and a dismissal of all claims with prejudice.

Notwithstanding *Randolph*'s holding that orders compelling arbitration and dismissing all claims are immediately appealable, federal circuit courts have disagreed over whether, with respect to motions to stay litigation pending arbitration brought under section 3 of the FAA, a district court actually has discretion to dismiss an action after compelling arbitration, or whether it is required by the terms of the statute to enter a stay. Because dismissals are imme-

---

193 S.W.3d 897 (Tex. 2006) (allowing immediate appeal of order compelling arbitration when the trial court dismissed the case "in its entirety").

115 *See, e.g.*, Seacoast Motors of Salisbury, Inc. v. Chrysler Corp., 143 F.3d 626, 628, 629 (1st Cir. 1998); Napleton v. Gen. Motors Corp., 138 F.3d 1209, 1212 (7th Cir. 1998); McCarthy v. Providential Corp., 122 F.3d 1242, 1244 (9th Cir. 1997); Pisgah Contractors, Inc v. Rosen, 117 F.3d 133, 136 (4th Cir. 1997); Altman Nursing, Inc. v. Clay Capital Corp., 84 F.3d 769, 771 (5th Cir. 1996); Gammaro v. Thorp Consumer Discount Co., 15 F.3d 93, 95 (8th Cir. 1994).

All of these cases have been overruled in part by Green Tree Fin. Corp.-Ala. v. Randolph, 531 U.S. 79, 121 S. Ct. 513, 148 L. Ed. 2d 373 (2000).

116 *See Randolph*, 531 U.S. at 86, 87; *see also* Lloyd v. Hovensa, L.L.C., 369 F.3d 263, 268 (3d Cir. 2004) (dismissal with prejudice was immediately appealable).

117 *Randolph*, 531 U.S. at 87 n.2; *see also* Citifinancial Corp. v. Harrison, 453 F.3d 245 (5th Cir. 2006) (no right to appeal order staying proceedings under 9 U.S.C. § 3); Dees v. Billy, 394 F.3d 1290, 1294 (9th Cir. 2005) (order staying litigation and compelling arbitration, even when accompanied by an order administratively closing the case, was not immediately appealable); Comanche Indian Tribe of Okla. v. 49, L.L.C., 391 F.3d 1129, 1132–1133 (10th Cir. 2004) (finding order staying litigation and compelling arbitration not immediately appealable); Mire v. Full Spectrum Leasing, 389 F.3d 163, 167 (5th Cir. 2004) (order to stay arbitration and requiring administrative closure of the case file was not immediately appealable); Apache Bohai Corp. v. Texaco China, 330 F.3d 307 (5th Cir. 2003) (holding that district court order staying proceedings in favor of arbitration is not appealable under FAA § 16); ATAC Corp. v. Arthur Treacher's, Inc., 280 F.3d 1091, 1099 (6th Cir. 2002) (same).

118 Am. Int'l Specialty Life Ins. Co. v. Elec. Data Sys. Corp., 347 F.3d 665, 668 (7th Cir. 2003) ("[I]f *all* the judge is retaining jurisdiction for is to allow the arbitrator's award to be confirmed without need for the filing of a separate lawsuit, the order to arbitrate is final . . . and therefore immediately appealable."); Cap Gemini Ernst & Young, U.S., L.L.C. v. Nackel, 346 F.3d 360 (2d Cir. 2003) (allowing appeal of order compelling arbitration and staying litigation solely to allow the parties to seek confirmation of an arbitration award, but holding in the future that, in such circumstances, the court should officially dismiss all claims in order for its order to be appealable); *see also* Am. Heritage Life Ins. Co. v. Orr, 294 F.3d 702 (5th Cir. 2002) (when district court "closed" the case and compelled arbitration this was functionally equivalent to "dismissing" the case and was a final order under the *Randolph* standard).

119 Citifinancial Corp. v. Harrison, 453 F.3d 245 (5th Cir. 2006) (an administrative dismissal is not a "final decision" under the FAA); Dees v. Billy, 394 F.3d 1290, 1294 (9th Cir. 2005) (order staying litigation and compelling arbitration, even when accompanied by an order administratively closing the case, was not immediately appealable); Mire v. Full Spectrum Leasing, 389 F.3d 163, 167 (5th Cir. 2004) (administrative closure of case was not a final order giving rise to a right to immediate appeal); S. La. Cement, Inc. v. Van Aalst Bulk Handling, B.V., 383 F.3d 298, 302 (5th Cir. 2004); Penn W. Associates, Inc. v. Cohen, 371 F.3d 118, 128 (3d Cir. 2004); ATAC Corp. v. Arthur Treacher's, Inc., 280 F.3d 1091, 1099 (6th Cir. 2002); Lehman v. Revolution Portfolio, Inc., 166 F.3d 389, 392 (1st Cir. 1999); Fla. Ass'n for Retarded Citizens, Inc. v. Bush, 246 F.3d 1296, 1298 (11th Cir. 2001).

120 Bushley v. Credit Suisse First Boston, 360 F.3d 1149, 1153 (9th Cir. 2004) (rejecting joint appeal of order requiring arbitration before alternative forum).

diately appealable and stays are not, how courts resolve this question will significantly affect the ability of litigants to immediately appeal orders compelling arbitration. Section 3 of the FAA states that if a dispute is arbitrable, then the court "shall on application of one of the parties stay the trial of the action until such arbitration has been had in accordance with the terms of the agreement."[121] Although section 3 uses mandatory language the majority of circuits, both before and after *Randolph*, have held that a district court has discretion to deny a motion to stay pending arbitration and instead to dismiss all claims.[122] A minority of circuits have interpreted section 3's language strictly and held that a district court is required to issue a stay if the dispute is arbitrable, and lacks the authority to enter a dismissal.[123]

2.6.3 Pendent Jurisdiction

Appellate courts may also exercise pendent jurisdiction to review orders compelling arbitration. The Second Circuit has held that pendent jurisdiction over an arbitration order is appropriate when the questions raised by the primary appeal and the arbitration appeal are closely related, finding immediate review to be consistent with section 16's goal of greater procedural efficiency.[124] On the other hand, the Seventh Circuit has held that section 16's prohibition of appeals from orders enforcing arbitration precludes the exercise of pendent jurisdiction over such orders.[125] This split of authority stems from differing interpretations of section 16's general purpose.

2.6.4 Broader Appealability of State Court Arbitration Orders

Rules regarding appeals from arbitration orders may be more favorable to consumers in the state courts than they are in federal court under section 16 of the FAA.[126] For example, courts in some states will allow a party to take an immediate appeal of an order compelling arbitration, whether it is styled as a stay of litigation or a dismissal of claims.[127] Conversely, some states prohibit parties from

---

121 9 U.S.C. § 3.
122 *See* Choice Hotels Int'l, Inc. v. BSR Tropicana Resort, Inc., 252 F.3d 707, 709–710 (4th Cir. 2001) ("Notwithstanding the terms of § 3, however, dismissal is a proper remedy when all of the issues presented in a lawsuit are arbitrable."); Green v. Ameritech Corp., 200 F.3d 967, 973 (6th Cir. 2000) ("The weight of authority clearly supports dismissal of the case when all of the issues raised in the district court must be submitted to arbitration."); Bercovitch v. Baldwin Sch., Inc., 133 F.3d 141, 156 & n.21 (1st Cir. 1998) (remanding to the district court to decide whether to dismiss or stay, depending upon whether all issues before the court are arbitrable); Alford v. Dean Witter Reynolds, Inc., 975 F.2d 1161, 1164 (5th Cir. 1992); Sparling v. Hoffman Const. Co., 864 F.2d 635, 638 (9th Cir. 1988); *see also* Halford v. Deer Valley Home Builders, Inc., 2007 WL 1229339 (M.D. Ala. Apr. 25, 2007) (court had authority to issue dismissal rather than stay); Gilchrist v. CitiFinancial Services, Inc., 2007 WL 177821, at *4 (M.D. Fla. Jan. 19, 2007) (same); Dale v. Comcast Corp., 453 F. Supp. 2d 1367, 1378 (N.D. Ga. 2006) (same); Lewis Tree Serv., Inc. v. Lucent Tech., Inc., 239 F. Supp. 2d 332, 340 (S.D.N.Y. 2002) (finding all claims arbitrable and dismissing action); Reynolds v. Halliburton, 217 F. Supp 2d 756, 758 (E.D. Tex. 2002) (same).
123 *See* Lloyd v. Hovensa, L.L.C., 369 F.3d 263, 268–271 (3d Cir. 2004); Adair Bus Sales, Inc. v. Blue Bird Corp., 25 F.3d 953, 955 (10th Cir. 1994); *see also* Brooks v. The Finish Line, Inc., 2006 WL 1129376 (M.D. Tenn. Apr. 26, 2006). *But cf.* Armijo v. Prudential Ins. Co., 72 F.3d 793, 796–797 (10th Cir. 1995) (district court can enter a dismissal if the party seeking arbitration requests a dismissal rather than a stay).
124 Freeman v. Complex Computing Co., 119 F.3d 1044, 1050 (2d Cir. 1997) ("we do not think that Congress has demonstrated any interest in interfering with a judicially-created doctrine that has served to conserve judicial resources and save time and work for litigants").
125 IDS Life Ins. Co. v. SunAmerica, Inc., 103 F.3d 524, 528 (7th Cir. 1996), *aff'd in part, vacated in part*, 136 F.3d 537 (7th Cir. 1998) (prudential considerations of pendent jurisdiction are outweighed by "Congress's emphatically expressed support for facilitating arbitration in order to effectuate private ordering and lighten the caseload of the federal courts").
126 For a discussion of why state procedural rules at variance with the provisions of section 16 of the FAA are not preempted, see § 3.2.2.3, *supra*.
127 *See, e.g.,* Phillips Constr. Co. v. Cowart Iron Works, Inc., 299 S.E.2d 538, 540 (Ga. 1983) (recommending that trial courts certify all orders granting or denying stays of litigation in favor of arbitration; acknowledging but declining to adopt contrary federal rule); Peach v. CIM Ins. Corp., 816 N.E.2d 668, 671 (Ill. App. Ct. 2004) (holding that an order compelling arbitration is injunctive in nature and therefore immediately appealable); Onni v. Apartment Inv. & Mgmt. Co., 801 N.E.2d 586, 590–591 (Ill. App. Ct. 2003) (granting appeal of order compelling arbitration and vacating order for lack of a reasoned basis); Atkins v. Rustic Woods Partners, Inc., 525 N.E.2d 551, 554–555 (Ill. App. Ct. 1988) (holding that compelling arbitration is analogous to ordering an injunction and therefore is appealable); Chesterfield Mgmt., Inc. v. Cook, 655 N.E.2d 98, 99 (Ind. Ct. App. 1996) (recognizing right of appeal from trial court order refusing to stay arbitration); Evansville-Vanderburgh Sch. Corp. v. Evansville Teachers Ass'n, 494 N.E.2d 321, 322–324 (Ind. Ct. App. 1986); Horsey v. Horsey, 620 A.2d 305, 311 (Md. 1993) ("an order compelling the parties before the trial court to submit their dispute to arbitration, thereby denying all relief sought in the trial court and terminating the action there, is a final appealable judgment"); Neubauer v. Household Fin. Corp., 2002 WL 31771287, at *2 (Ohio Ct. App. Dec. 12, 2002) ("An order which *grants or denies* a stay of the proceedings pending arbitration is a final appealable order and may be reviewed by this court." (emphasis added)); Okla. Oncology & Hematology, P.C. v. U.S. Oncology, Inc., 160 P.3d 936, 942–943 (Okla. 2007) (holding that an order compelling arbitration is final and appealable because it leaves nothing for the district court to do, notwithstanding the contrary rule under the FAA); Gilliand v. Chronic Pain Associates, 904 P.2d 73 (Okla. 1995); *see also* Brennan v. Gen. Accident Fire & Life Ins. Co., 453 A.2d 356, 357 (Pa. Super. Ct. 1982) (holding that an order compelling arbitration under the Pennsylvania Arbitration Act is appealable, but that an order compelling "common law arbitration" is not appealable).

immediately appealing any order relating to arbitration and thus would not allow a merchant to appeal a trial court's order refusing to compel arbitration until after litigation on the merits is completed.[128] When arbitration disputes arise in state court proceedings, parties should thus look to state procedural rules defining the finality of judgments and delineating the circumstances in which interlocutory appeals may be taken in order to determine the availability and timing of appeals from arbitration orders. This principle includes orders to which section 2 of the FAA provides the substantive rule of decision.

---

[128] *See, e.g.*, Bush v. Paragon Products, Inc., 997 P.2d 882, 887–888 (Or. Ct. App. 2000) (state law does not establish appellate jurisdiction over interlocutory order refusing to enforce contractual arbitration clause); Belmont Constructors, Inc. v. Lyondell Petrochemical Co., 896 S.W.2d 352, 355 (Tex. App. 1995) (trial court order denying arbitration under the federal act does not fall within any exception to the prohibition of interlocutory appeals). *But see* Eddings v. S. Orthopedic & Musculoskeletal Associates, 555 S.E.2d 649 (N.C. Ct. App. 2001) ("an order denying arbitration is immediately appealable because it involves a substantial right—the right to arbitrate a claim—which may be lost if appeal is delayed"), *rev'd on other grounds*, 569 S.E.2d 645 (N.C. 2002).

Chapter 3 The Federal Arbitration Act, State Laws, and Preemption

3.1 Introduction to the Federal Arbitration Act and Its Policy Favoring Arbitration Agreements

3.1.1 General

The Federal Arbitration Act[1] (FAA) creates a general rule of contract enforcement and a set of procedural rules that together have been found to manifest a "liberal federal policy favoring arbitration agreements."[2] Section 2 of the Act provides that arbitration clauses are "valid, irrevocable, and enforceable, save upon such grounds as exist at law or in equity for the revocation of any contract."[3] This provision makes contractual arbitration agreements generally enforceable as a matter of federal law, while also leaving various limitations on their enforceability arising under both federal[4] and state[5] laws.[6]

To give effect to this general enforceability rule, the FAA also enacts a set of procedural rules for federal courts to use in enforcing arbitration agreements,[7] as well as rules for courts to apply in confirming or vacating an arbitration award.[8]

Section 2 of the Act and its enforceability rule apply to most claims brought by consumers and other litigants in state court as well as federal court,[9] and to most statutory claims as well as common law claims.[10] Written[11] arbitration clauses are generally enforceable, even if they force deceptive practices act,[12] RICO,[13] or other consumer protection claims to be arbitrated.[14] The Supreme Court has

---

1 9 U.S.C. §§ 1–16.
2 Moses H. Cone Mem'l Hosp. v. Mercury Constr. Corp., 460 U.S. 1, 24, 103 S. Ct. 927, 74 L. Ed 2d 765 (1983).
3 9 U.S.C. § 2.
   The text of the FAA, 9 U.S.C. §§ 1–16, is included as Appendix A.1, *infra*.
4 *See* Ch. 4, *infra*.
5 *See* Ch. 6, *infra*.
6 *See generally* Perry v. Thomas, 482 U.S. 483, 492 n.9, 107 S. Ct. 2520, 96 L. Ed. 2d 426 (1987) (describing FAA's rule of enforceability and its limitations).
7 *See* 9 U.S.C. §§ 3–7, 16; *see also* § 3.2.2, *infra*.
8 *See* 9 U.S.C. §§ 9–12; *see also* § 3.2.2.4, *infra*.
9 Southland Corp. v. Keating, 465 U.S. 1, 104 S. Ct. 852, 79 L. Ed. 2d 1 (1984).
   As noted in § 3.3.2, *infra*, however, the FAA does not apply to state claims involving a contract that does not memorialize a transaction involving interstate commerce.
10 Gilmer v. Interstate/Johnson Lane Corp., 500 U.S. 20, 111 S. Ct. 1647, 114 L. Ed. 2d 26 (1991); Shearson/American Express, Inc. v. McMahon, 482 U.S. 220, 107 S. Ct. 2332, 96 L. Ed. 2d 185 (1987); Mitsubishi Motors Corp. v. Soler Chrysler-Plymouth, Inc., 473 U.S. 614, 105 S. Ct. 3346, 87 L. Ed. 2d 444 (1985).
   As noted in Ch. 4, *infra*, however, there are authorities holding that the FAA does not apply to claims arising from a limited number of federal statutes, such as the Magnuson-Moss Warranty Act.
11 One California court has interpreted the phrase "written agreement" in the California Arbitration Act, which mirrors the FAA, to exclude oral arbitration agreements and oral modifications to written arbitration agreements. *See* Magness Petroleum Co. v. Warren Res. of Cal., Inc., 103 Cal. App. 4th 901, 127 Cal. Rptr. 2d 159 (2002).
12 Ommani v. Doctor's Associates, Inc., 789 F.2d 298 (5th Cir. 1986) (Tex. law); Garber v. Sir Speedy, Inc., 930 F. Supp. 267 (N.D. Tex. 1995), *aff'd*, 91 F.3d 137 (5th Cir. 1996); Coonly v. Rotan Mosle, Inc., 630 F. Supp. 404 (W.D. Tex. 1985); Flower World of Am., Inc. v. Wenzel, 122 Ariz. 319, 594 P.2d 1015 (Ct. App. 1978); Value Car Sales, Inc. v. Bouton, 608 So. 2d 860 (Fla. Dist. Ct. App. 1992); J & K Cement Constr., Inc. v. Montalbano Builders, Inc., 119 Ill. App. 3d 663, 456 N.E.2d 889 (1983); Greenleaf Eng'g & Constr. Co. v. Teradyne, Inc., 15 Mass. App. Ct. 571, 447 N.E.2d 9 (1983); Bennett v. Shearson Lehman-American Express, Inc., 168 Mich. App. 80, 423 N.W.2d 911 (1987); Rodgers Builders, Inc. v. McQueen, 76 N.C. App. 16, 331 S.E.2d 726 (1985); Stern v. Prudential Fin., Inc., 2003 WL 1848279 (Pa. C.P. Feb. 4, 2003), *rev'd*, 836 A.2d 953 (Pa. Super. Ct. 2003); Southwest Health Plan, Inc. v. Sparkman, 921 S.W.2d 355 (Tex. App. 1996); Emerald Tex., Inc. v. Peel, 920 S.W.2d 398 (Tex. App. 1996); Garmo v. Dean, Witter, Reynolds, Inc., 101 Wash. 2d 585, 681 P.2d 253 (1984).
13 Shearson/American Express, Inc. v. McMahon, 482 U.S. 220, 107 S. Ct. 2332, 96 L. Ed. 2d 185 (1987); Hill v. Gateway 2000 Inc., 105 F.3d 1147 (7th Cir. 1987); Bellizan v. Easy Money of La., Inc., 2002 WL 1066750 (E.D. La. May 29, 2002), *vacated in part*, 2002 WL 1611648 (E.D. La. July 19, 2002).
14 *See* Mitsubishi Motors Corp. v. Soler-Chrysler Plymouth, Inc., 473 U.S. 614, 105 S. Ct. 3346, 87 L. Ed. 2d 444 (1985) (antitrust claims involving international transactions); Dean Witter Reynolds, Inc. v. Byrd, 470 U.S. 213, 105 S. Ct. 1238, 84 L. Ed. 2d 158 (1985); Kuehner v. Dickinson & Co., 84 F.3d 316 (9th Cir. 1996) (securities claims); Fluehmann v. Associated Fin. Ser-

held that the FAA applies to most consumer transactions.[15]

This chapter sets forth in greater detail: (1) the FAA's effect in preempting and saving from preemption different types of state laws;[16] (2) some limited circumstances in which the FAA does not apply, meaning that state law governs all questions concerning arbitration;[17] and (3) when the FAA does apply, the important role of courts in applying state contract law to determine whether arbitration clauses are in fact enforceable.[18] But before analyzing these issues, the chapter first examines the growing number of instances in which legislative and other enactments are imposing explicit restrictions on the ability of companies to impose binding mandatory arbitration against consumers and other parties.

3.1.2 External Limitations on the FAA's Policy Favoring Enforcement of Arbitration Clauses

Notwithstanding the FAA's general policy favoring the enforceability of arbitration agreements, over time there have been increasing numbers of legislative and other enactments that *dis*favor or restrict arbitration under specific types of contracts. While these enactments disfavoring arbitration are addressed in various places throughout this manual, a non-exhaustive list of such enactments is provided here to illustrate the growing public sentiment against binding mandatory arbitration in consumer and other types of adhesive contractual relationships:

- *Consumer loans to military servicemembers and their dependents*: Congress in 2006 expressly prohibited lenders from imposing arbitration clauses on service members and their dependents;[19]
- *Car dealer contracts with manufacturers*: At the request of car dealer lobbyists, Congress has expressly prohibited automotive manufacturers from requiring car dealers to arbitrate;[20]
- *Express consumer warranty agreements*: Numerous courts have held that Congress's express prohibition against binding informal dispute settlement mechanisms in the Magnuson-Moss Warranty Act prohibits companies from requiring consumers to submit express warranty disputes to binding arbitration;[21]
- *Contracts involving parties in bankruptcy*: Numerous federal courts have held that Congress's enactment of the Bankruptcy Code creates an exclusive forum for resolving core bankruptcy claims in certain cases, thereby prohibiting resort to private arbitration;[22]
- *Insurance policies under the law of some states*: Many courts have held that Congress's enactment of the McCarran-Ferguson Act[23] "reverse preempts" the FAA as it would apply to insurance contracts, thereby allowing enforcement of state laws that prohibit enforcement of arbitration clauses in insurance policies;[24] and
- *Subprime mortgage loans purchased or securitized by Fannie Mae or Freddie Mac*: Although these prohibitions do not have the force of law and thus cannot be enforced by consumers, both the Federal National Mortgage Association (Fannie Mae) and the Federal Home Loan and Mortgage Corp. (Freddie Mac) have enacted policies prohibiting the inclusion of mandatory arbitration clauses in home mortgage loans that they purchase from lenders.[25]

3.1.3 Clarification of the FAA's Policy Favoring the Enforceability of Arbitration Clauses

It is sometimes said that the FAA embodies a policy in favor of arbitration. This statement is not accurate. Rather, the FAA embodies a policy in favor of enforcing agreements to arbitrate, when such an agreement exists.[26]

---

vices, 2002 WL 500564 (D. Mass. Mar. 29, 2002) (TILA claims).

15 Allied-Bruce Terminix Companies v. Dobson, 513 U.S. 265, 115 S. Ct. 834, 130 L. Ed. 2d 753 (1995).

16 *See* § 3.2, *infra*.

17 *See* § 3.3, *infra*.

18 *See* § 3.4, *infra*.

19 10 U.S.C. § 987(f)(4).

20 15 U.S.C. § 1226.

21 15 U.S.C. § 2310(a)(3); *see also* § 4.2.2, *infra*.

22 *See* § 4.2.3, *infra*.

23 15 U.S.C. § 1012(b).

24 *See* § 3.3.4, *infra*.

For a listing of state laws that prohibit arbitration clauses in insurance policies, see § 3.3.4.3, *infra*.

25 *See* Fed. Nat'l Mortgage Ass'n, Frequently Asked Questions: Predatory Lending Practices, *available at* www.fanniemae.com/faq/faq6.jhtml?p=FAQ (last updated July 7, 2006) (visited Aug. 21, 2007); Fed. Home Loan & Mortgage Corp., Freddie Mac Promotes Consumer Choice With New Subprime Mortgage Arbitration Policy, *available at* www.freddiemac.com/news/archives/ afford_housing/2003/consumer_120403.html (Dec. 4, 2003).

26 The basis of this policy is a matter of some dispute. Justice Stevens has written:

> Times have changed. Judges in the 19th century disfavored private arbitration. The 1925 Act was intended to overcome that attitude, but a number of this Court's cases decided in the last several decades have pushed the pendulum far beyond a neutral attitude and endorsed a policy that strongly favors private arbitration. The strength of that policy preference has been echoed in the recent Court of Appeals opinions on which the Court relies. In a sense, therefore the Court is standing on its own shoulders when it points to those cases....

Circuit City v. Adams, 532 U.S. 105, 121 S. Ct. 1302, 1318, 149 L. Ed. 2d 234 (2001) (Stevens, J., dissenting) (citations omitted).

The FAA was not enacted to force parties into arbitration, but to enforce voluntary agreements between parties to arbitrate certain specified disputes. The Supreme Court has instructed that "arbitration is simply a matter of contract between parties; it is a way to resolve disputes—but only those disputes—that the parties have agreed to submit to arbitration."[27] This rule is rooted in the FAA's legislative history:

> The legislative history of the Act establishes that the purpose behind its passage was to ensure judicial enforcement of privately made agreements to arbitrate. We therefore reject the suggestion that the overriding goal of the Arbitration Act was to promote the expeditious resolution of claims. The Act . . . does not mandate the arbitration of all claims, but merely the enforcement . . . of privately negotiated arbitration agreements.[28]

Matters the parties have not agreed to arbitrate need not be arbitrated.[29] The purpose of the FAA is only "to reverse the longstanding judicial hostility to arbitration agreements that had existed at English common law and had been adopted by American courts, and to place arbitration agreements on the same footing as other contracts."[30] Indeed, "a party will suffer irreparable harm if compelled to arbitrate in the absence of any agreement to do so."[31]

Accordingly, the FAA policy in favor of enforcing arbitration clauses does not come into play in determining whether an agreement to arbitrate exists.[32] To the contrary, the question of whether parties have entered into an agreement to arbitrate is resolved through application of state contract law principles that govern the formation of any contractual agreement.[33] "[T]he policy favoring arbitration cannot displace the necessity for a voluntary agreement to arbitrate."[34] To apply the policy in favor of enforcing arbitration clauses to the question of whether an agreement to arbitrate exists "would permit the presumption to displace the fundamental rule that parties can be required to arbitrate only that which they have agreed to arbitrate."[35]

In addition to state law governing contract formation, the FAA explicitly saves from preemption state law "grounds as exist at law or in equity for the revocation of any contract."[36] Thus, state law principles concerning fraud, waiver, duress, and unconscionability provide grounds for invalidating arbitration clauses covered by the FAA.[37]

3.2 FAA Preemption of State Law

3.2.1 FAA Preemption of State Laws That Limit the Enforceability of Arbitration Clauses

3.2.1.1 Introduction

The preemptive effect of the Federal Arbitration Act (FAA) has been a source of considerable controversy. As one commentator recently argued: "FAA preemption is nothing more or less than procedural regulation of state courts, and . . . Congress lacks the power to regulate procedures in state courts. In short, FAA preemption is unconstitutional."[38] Nonetheless, the fact that the FAA preempts certain state laws that are deemed hostile to arbitration agreements is well established as a matter of substantive federal law that is applicable in federal and state courts alike.[39]

The FAA's preemptive effect arises out of the Supremacy Clause of Article VI of the Constitution, which provides that state laws must give way when they conflict with federal laws. Although the Supreme Court has recognized that "the FAA contains no express preemption provision, nor does it reflect a congressional intent to occupy the entire field of

---

27 First Options of Chicago, Inc. v. Kaplan, 514 U.S. 938, 943, 115 S. Ct. 1920, 1924, 131 L. Ed. 2d 985 (1995); accord Howsam v. Dean Witter Reynolds, 537 U.S. 79, 123 S. Ct. 588, 591, 154 L. Ed. 2d 491 (2002).

28 Dean Witter Reynolds, Inc. v. Byrd, 470 U.S. 213, 219, 105 S. Ct. 1238, 1242, 84 L. Ed. 2d 158 (1985).

29 Howsam v. Dean Witter Reynolds, Inc., 537 U.S. 79, 123 S. Ct. 588, 591, 154 L. Ed. 2d 491 (2002); AT & T Technologies, Inc. v. Communications Workers of Am., 475 U.S. 643, 648, 106 S. Ct. 1415, 1418, 89 L. Ed. 2d 648 (1986).

30 Gilmer v. Interstate/Johnson Lane Corp., 500 U.S. 20, 24, 111 S. Ct. 1647, 1651, 114 L. Ed. 2d 26 (1991).

31 GTFM v. TKN Sales, Inc., 2000 WL 364871, at *2 (S.D.N.Y. Apr. 7, 2000), rev'd on other grounds, 257 F.3d 235 (2d Cir. 2001); Mount Ararat Cemetery v. Cemetery Workers & Greens Attendants Union, 975 F. Supp. 445, 446, 447 (E.D.N.Y. 1997); Spear, Leeds & Kellogg v. Cent. Life Assurance Co., 879 F. Supp. 403 (S.D.N.Y. 1995), rev'd on other grounds, 85 F.3d 21 (2d Cir. 1996); see also Zimring v. Coinmach Corp., 2000 U.S. Dist. LEXIS 18221, at *4 (S.D.N.Y. Dec. 14, 2000) (citing Mount Ararat Cemetery on this issue).

32 Carson v. Giant Food, Inc., 175 F.3d 325, 329 (4th Cir. 1999); Va. Carolina Tools, Inc. v. Int'l Tool Supply, Inc., 984 F.2d 113, 117 (4th Cir. 1993); Badie v. Bank of Am., 67 Cal. App. 4th 779, 790, 79 Cal. Rptr. 2d 273, 280 (1998); Curtis G. Testerman Co. v. Buck, 340 Md. 569, 580, 667 A.2d 649, 654, 665 (1995).

33 See First Options of Chicago, Inc. v. Kaplan, 514 U.S. 938, 944, 115 S. Ct. 1920, 131 L. Ed. 2d 985 (1995).

34 Victoria v. Super. Ct., 40 Cal. 3d 734, 739, 222 Cal. Rptr. 1, 710 P.2d 833 (1985).

35 Hendrick v. Brown & Root, Inc., 50 F. Supp. 2d 527, 538 (E.D. Va. 1999).

36 9 U.S.C. § 2.

37 See, e.g., BancOne Acceptance Corp. v. Hill, 367 F.3d 426, 431, 432 (5th Cir. 2004) (holding that FAA does not preempt state unconscionability law); In re Media Arts Group, 116 S.W.3d 900, 906 (Tex. App. 2003) (FAA does not preempt state waiver law).

38 David S. Schwartz, The Federal Arbitration Act and the Power of Congress over State Courts, 83 Or. L. Rev. 541, 542 (2004).

39 See, e.g., Allied-Bruce Terminix Companies v. Dobson, 513 U.S. 265, 281, 115 S. Ct. 834, 130 L. Ed. 2d 753 (1995).

arbitration,"[40] the Supreme Court has held that state laws are preempted under the FAA when they interfere with the Act's underlying policy goals.[41] Congress's primary purposes in enacting the FAA were to "reverse the longstanding judicial hostility to arbitration that had existed at English common law and had been adopted by American courts," and to "place arbitration agreements upon the same footing as other contracts."[42] In light of these legislative purposes, the United States Supreme Court has held that the FAA preempts two primary and distinct types of state laws that it has found to interfere with the enforcement of arbitration agreements.[43]

3.2.1.2 When State Law Singles Out Arbitration Clauses for Less Favored Treatment

When the FAA applies, courts may not invalidate arbitration agreements under state laws that single out arbitration clauses for suspect status by prohibiting or imposing unique obstacles to their enforcement. In *Doctor's Associates, Inc. v. Casarotto*,[44] the Supreme Court held that the FAA preempted a Montana statute that conditioned the enforcement of arbitration clauses upon their compliance with unique disclosure requirements, including that they be capitalized, underlined, and presented on the first page of a document.[45] The Court specifically held that "[c]ourts may not . . . invalidate arbitration agreements under state laws applicable *only* to arbitration provisions," because the FAA "precluded states from singling out arbitration provisions for suspect status, requiring instead that such provisions be placed upon the same footing as other contracts."[46] As Montana's arbitration-specific disclosure requirements conflicted with the FAA's goal of placing arbitration clauses on the same footing as other contractual terms, the Supreme Court held that the Montana law was preempted.

In light of *Casarotto*, numerous courts have struck down state laws that prohibit or impose unique obstacles to the enforcement of arbitration clauses. For example, a California appellate court held that the FAA preempts a state statute governing real estate purchases that imposes point-size and bold-font requirements on arbitration clauses in real estate contracts.[47] The FAA's policy of placing arbitration clauses on the "same footing" as other contractual clauses, prohibits states from singling out these clauses for restrictive or disfavored treatment.

In what may be a narrow exception to this general preemption rule, a Texas appeals court has held that the FAA does not preempt a state statute requiring a *court*'s approval of the transfer of rights to structured settlement payments. In *Rapid Settlements, Ltd. v. BHG Structured Settlements, Inc.*,[48] the court held that the FAA did not preempt this state law requirement for a judicial determination because (1) the statute did not prohibit inclusion of an arbitration clause in such a transfer agreement and (2) the statute "requires prior court approval of the transfer agreement, not the arbitration clause, and therefore is not pre-empted by the FAA."[49] The reasoning of this decision seems to be consistent with the Supreme Court cases applying the FAA inasmuch as the court approval requirement is a condition precedent to the *formation* of a contract, and once the contract is formed the arbitration agreement is valid.

States also remain free to enforce laws specifically governing arbitration if those laws do not interfere with enforcement of arbitration agreements.[50] For example, state legislatures have enacted laws restricting arbitration agreements in ways that may avoid federal preemption. For example, an Illinois statute relating to home repair requires the contractor to advise the consumer of the arbitration requirement and to explain to the consumer that the con-

---

40 Volt Info. Sciences, Inc. v. Bd. of Trustees, 489 U.S. 468, 477, 109 S. Ct. 1248, 103 L. Ed. 2d 488 (1989).
41 *Id.*
42 Equal Employment Opportunity Comm'n v. Waffle House, Inc., 534 U.S. 279, 289, 122 S. Ct. 754, 151 L. Ed. 2d 755 (2002) (quoting Gilmer v. Interstate/Johnson Lane Corp., 500 U.S. 20, 23, 111 S. Ct. 1647, 114 L. Ed. 2d 26 (1991)).
43 For discussion of a third type of preempted state contract law rule concerning the relationship between an arbitration clause and the contract in which it appears, see § 3.4.5, *infra*.
44 517 U.S. 681, 116 S. Ct. 1652, 134 L. Ed. 2d 902 (1996).
45 *Id.*, 517 U.S. at 683.
46 *Id.*, 517 U.S. at 687.
47 *See* Hedges v. Carrigan, 117 Cal. App. 4th 578, 583 (2004); *see*

also Am. Fin. Services Ass'n v. Burke, 169 F. Supp. 2d 62 (D. Conn. 2001) (FAA preempts state statute prohibiting arbitration clauses in high cost mortgage loan agreements); Cent. Jersey Freightliner, Inc. v. Freightliner Corp., 987 F. Supp. 289, 300 (D.N.J. 1997) (FAA preempts franchise statute requiring proof of option of franchise without arbitration clause); Basura v. U.S. Home Corp., 98 Cal. App. 4th 1205, 120 Cal. Rptr. 2d 328 (2002) (FAA preempts state statute barring arbitration of home defect claims); Allen v. World Inspection Network Int'l, Inc., 911 A.2d 484, 490 (N.J. Super. Ct. App. Div. 2006) (FAA preempts franchise statute requiring proof of option for franchise without arbitration clause); Hubert v. Turnberry Homes, L.L.C., 2006 WL 2843449, at *6 (Tenn. Ct. App. Oct. 4, 2006) (FAA preempts statute requiring separate signature for arbitration clause in home construction contract); *In re* Nexion Health at Humble, Inc., 173 S.W.3d 67 (Tex. 2005) (FAA preempts provision of Texas Arbitration Act requiring signature of party's counsel to arbitration clauses in personal injury cases).

For cases holding or stating that a blanket prohibition against arbitration for particular types of claims is preempted, see Allied-Bruce Terminix Companies v. Dobson, 513 U.S. 265, 115 S. Ct. 834, 130 L. Ed. 2d 753 (1995); Washburn v. Beverly Enterprises-Georgia, L.L.C., 2006 WL 3404804, at *3 (S.D. Ga. Nov. 14, 2006); Leslie v. U.S. Home Corp., 2002 Cal. App. Unpub. LEXIS 3778, at *7–*8 (Cal. Ct. App. Feb. 21, 2002).
48 2006 WL 2622382 (Tex. App. Sept. 14, 2006).
49 *Id.* at *2.
50 *See, e.g.*, Buzas Baseball, Inc. v. Salt Lake Trappers, Inc., 925 P.2d 941, 952–953 (Utah 1996) (holding that FAA does not preempt Utah Arbitration Act provision allowing party that successfully defends arbitration award against judicial challenge to recover attorney fees incurred in challenge).

sumer can make a counter-offer excluding the arbitration clause.[51] Failure to comply is an unfair trade practice, leading to a potential damage remedy.[52] There is a good argument that this provision is not preempted because the arbitration agreement is still enforceable even if the contractor fails to comply. Instead, the arbitration provision could be enforceable, but the contractor could be liable for damages. Nevertheless, another provision of the Illinois statute makes null and void any clause not accepted or rejected by the consumer.[53]

3.2.1.3 When State Law Effectively Prohibits Arbitration Without Explicitly Mentioning It

Even if a state law does not explicitly single out arbitration clauses for disfavored treatment, the FAA may still preempt the state law if it effectively prohibits enforcement of all arbitration clauses for particular types of claims. In *Southland Corp. v. Keating*,[54] the Supreme Court held that the FAA preempted the general anti-waiver provision of California's Franchise Investment Law because it was construed definitively by the California courts to prohibit arbitration of claims arising under the state statute. Although the state statute's anti-waiver provision did not single out arbitration clauses from other contractual waivers of rights, the Supreme Court still held that its blanket prohibition of the arbitration of claims conflicted with the FAA and therefore was preempted.[55] The Supreme Court found that, in enacting the FAA, "Congress intended to foreclose state legislative attempts to undercut the enforceability of arbitration agreements."[56]

Several years later, the Supreme Court reaffirmed *Southland* by holding in *Perry v. Thomas*[57] that the FAA preempted an anti-waiver provision in California's Labor Code covering wage and hour claims, after the provision was likewise construed to prohibit arbitration. In reaffirming *Southland*'s preemption holding, *Perry* explained that, under the FAA, "[a] state-law principle that takes its meaning precisely from the fact that a contract to arbitrate is at issue," is preempted.[58]

In light of *Southland* and *Perry*, numerous federal and state courts have held that the FAA preempts a variety of state laws that effectively prohibit arbitration of entire categories of claims. For example, in *Saturn Distribution Corp. v. Paramount Saturn, Ltd.*,[59] the Fifth Circuit held that the FAA preempts a state motor vehicle franchise statute's provision giving an administrative agency exclusive jurisdiction over franchisee claims, because it undercut the enforcement of private agreements to arbitrate these disputes.[60] Similarly the Michigan Court of Appeals in an unpublished opinion has held that the FAA preempts the anti-waiver provisions of Michigan's Consumer Protection Act, Retail Installment Sales Act, and Mobile Home Warranty Act to the extent those provisions barred all arbitration of claims under those respective statutes.[61] The Supreme Court's *Southland* and *Perry* decisions thus appear for the foreseeable future to prevent states from using generally applicable anti-waiver rules as a bar to enforcement of arbitration clauses for entire categories of claims.[62]

At least one federal court has gone further than the United States Supreme Court in finding that the FAA preempts a state law rule restricting waivers of jury trial rights, even though it did not impose a complete bar against arbitration. In *Merrill Lynch, Pierce, Fenner & Smith, Inc. v. Coe*,[63] the district court addressed *dictum* in a state supreme court opinion suggesting that a "knowing and intelligent waiver" standard should apply to all contracts waiving jury trial rights, including arbitration agreements.[64] The federal court

---

51 815 Ill. Comp. Stat. § 513/15.1.
52 815 Ill. Comp. Stat. § 513/30.
53 815 Ill. Comp. Stat. § 513/15.1(c).
54 465 U.S. 1, 104 S. Ct. 852, 79 L. Ed. 2d 1 (1984).
55 *Id.*, 465 U.S. at 15, 16.
56 *Id.*, 465 U.S. at 16.
57 482 U.S. 483, 107 S. Ct. 2520, 96 L. Ed. 2d 426 (1987).
58 *Id.*, 482 U.S. at 492 n.9.
59 326 F.3d 684 (5th Cir. 2003).
60 *Id.* at 687.
61 LeGere v. New Millennium Homes, Inc., 2003 WL 23018774, at *3 (Mich. Ct. App. Dec. 23, 2003); *see also* Dahiya v. Talmidge Int'l Ltd., 931 So. 2d 1163 (La. Ct. App. 2006) (holding that Louisiana statute prohibiting all forum selection clauses in employment contracts conflicts with, and thus is preempted by, the FAA); *cf.* Jim Walter Homes, Inc. v. Saxton, 880 So. 2d 428 (Ala. 2003) (holding that FAA preempts state statute barring predispute arbitration clauses, even when statute might fall within contractual choice of law clause adopting state law); Wis. Auto Title Loans, Inc. v. Jones, 714 N.W.2d 155 (Wis. 2006) (discussing, without deciding, whether FAA would preempt Wisconsin Consumer Act provision prohibiting self-help repossession by car lender and requiring judicial process to the extent this provision might bar arbitration of repossession claims). *But see* Global Travel Mktg., Inc. v. Shea, 908 So. 2d 392, 397 (Fla. 2005) (holding that FAA does not preempt Florida public policy principle prohibiting children from waiving any of their litigation rights as it would apply to arbitration clause because this principle also applies to provisions unrelated to arbitration and thus "is not peculiar to arbitration agreements").
62 For additional cases holding that the FAA preempts state anti-waiver rules that would prohibit all arbitration, see Ashley River Properties I, L.L.C. v. Ashley River Properties II, L.L.C., 2006 WL 4037137 (S.C. Cir. Ct. Oct. 18, 2006) (state statute prohibiting contractual waiver of trial court's jurisdiction is preempted to the extent it bars enforcement of arbitration agreement); Rosenberg v. Bluecross Blueshield of Tenn., Inc., 2006 WL 3455209, at *19 (Tenn. Ct. App. Nov. 29, 2006) (state consumer protection act preempted to extent its anti-waiver provision prohibits waiver of judicial forum); *In re* Border Steel, Inc., 2007 Tex. App. LEXIS 5014, at *12 (Tex. App. June 28, 2007) (Texas Labor Code's anti-waiver rule preempted to extent it would prohibit enforcement of arbitration agreements).
63 313 F. Supp. 2d 603 (S.D. W. Va. 2004).
64 *Id.* at 612 (citing State *ex rel.* Dunlap v. Berger, 567 S.E.2d 265, 277 (W. Va. 2002)).

found that this state law rule would be preempted because it necessarily imposes heightened requirements on arbitration clauses.[65] It is notable that the state law rule at issue neither applied exclusively to arbitration clauses, as in *Casarotto*, nor prohibited enforcement of arbitration clauses, as in *Southland*. The district court's preemption finding thus sweeps more broadly than any decision of the Supreme Court applying the FAA.

3.2.1.4 No FAA Preemption When Arbitration Inconsistent with Effective Vindication of State Law Rights

3.2.1.4.1 Claims for "Public" Injunctive Relief

Despite the foregoing, the California Supreme Court has crafted an exception to FAA preemption, holding in 1999 and again in 2003 that the state legislature may restrict a private arbitration agreement when it inherently conflicts with a public statutory purpose that transcends private interests.[66] In the earlier case, *Broughton v. CIGNA Healthplans*, the court found that the arbitration agreement would have prevented an individual from acting as a private attorney general and seeking injunctive relief on behalf of the public at large under a state UDAP statute. The court thought it would be perverse if the FAA allowed individuals to vitiate, through arbitration, substantive policies provided by state legislation to protect the public at large (as opposed to just the single litigant before the court).[67]

Soon after the California Supreme Court issued its decision in *Broughton*, one federal district court held that the FAA preempts *Broughton*'s interpretation of the state statute as allowing the prohibition of the arbitration of these claims.[68] Though this decision created a split between state and federal courts applying California law and the FAA, the California Supreme Court recently reiterated its position that the FAA permits a state to create a cause of action for public injunctive relief that is not amenable to resolution through private arbitration in *Cruz v. PacifiCare Health Systems, Inc.*[69]

3.2.1.4.2 Effective Vindication of Any Statutory Claim

Likewise, the FAA does not preempt a state law rule that invalidates an arbitration clause whose specific terms and conditions (as opposed to the general requirement of arbitration itself) would prevent parties from effectively vindicating their state law statutory rights. Just as the FAA gives way to substantive federal statutes by allowing courts to invalidate arbitration clauses whose prohibitive terms would prevent a party from vindicating their rights under those statutes,[70] courts also have held that the FAA does not compel enforcement of an arbitration clause whose terms would prevent parties from effectively vindicating their *state law* statutory claims. In *Armendariz v. Foundation Health Psychare Services, Inc.*,[71] the California Supreme Court held that arbitration clauses that would prevent employees from vindicating claims under the state's anti-discrimination statute by limiting remedies, denying adequate discovery, failing to provide for a written opinion, or imposing forum costs in excess of court costs were unenforceable as a matter of state statutory law.[72] More recently, the United States Court of Appeals for the First Circuit held in *Kristian v. Comcast Corp.*[73] that provisions in a cable television service provider's arbitration clause barring classwide claims by consumers and awards of attorney fees were unenforceable because they prevented consumers from vindicating their federal *and state* statutory rights.[74]

In striking down arbitration clause terms that prevent parties from effectively vindicating their state law statutory claims, these courts are recognizing a state law defense to arbitration that is neither preempted by the FAA *nor compelled by cases recognizing a federal law statutory rights defense to arbitrability*. This latter point is made clear in a Sixth Circuit case that rejected a consumer's assertion of a state law statutory rights defense on the grounds that no court in the state had ever recognized such a defense and that federal statutory rights cases were not controlling authority.[75] However, as the concurring opinion in this case also makes clear, there is nothing in federal law under the FAA or otherwise that *prevents* a state court from recognizing this state law statutory rights defense to enforcement of prohibitive arbitration clause terms.[76]

Finally, when a state law limits creditor remedies more generally, and does not single out arbitration, then the state law may not be preempted even if it has the effect of limiting

---

65 *Id.* at 615.
66 Broughton v. CIGNA Healthplans, 21 Cal. 4th 1066, 90 Cal. Rptr. 2d 334, 988 P.2d 67 (1999); *see also* Cruz v. PacifiCare Health Sys., Inc., 30 Cal. 4th 303, 133 Cal. Rptr. 2d 58, 66 P.3d 1157 (2003) (reaffirming the principle that claims for injunctive relief under a private attorney general statute are not subject to arbitration).
67 Broughton v. CIGNA Healthplans, 21 Cal. 4th 1066, 90 Cal. Rptr. 2d 334, 988 P.2d 67 (1999).
68 *See* Arriaga v. Cross Country Bank, 163 F. Supp. 2d 1189, 1199, 1200 (S.D. Cal. 2001) ("although the public injunctive relief available under Section 17200 might be evidence that the state legislature did not want this type of claim to go to arbitration, unless Congress declares otherwise, that determination will not be enough to make the arbitration clause unenforceable").
69 *See* Cruz v. PacifiCare Health Sys., Inc., 30 Cal. 4th 303, 133 Cal. Rptr. 2d 58, 66 P.3d 1157 (2003).
70 *See* Green Tree Fin. Corp.—Alabama v. Randolph, 531 U.S. 79, 90, 121 S. Ct. 513, 148 L. Ed. 2d 373 (2000).
71 6 P.3d 669 (Cal. 2000).
72 *Id.* at 682–689.
73 446 F.3d 25 (1st Cir. 2006).
74 *Id.* at 52–61 ("Finally, the societal goals of federal *and state* antitrust laws will be frustrated because of the 'enforcement gap' created by the de facto liability shield." (emphasis added)).
75 Stutler v. T.K. Constructors, Inc., 448 F.3d 343 (6th Cir. 2006).
76 *Id.* (Moore, J., concurring).

arbitration clauses. A good example is an amendment to the Uniform Arbitration Act that New Mexico enacted in 2001, which limits "disabling civil dispute clauses" in consumer transactions, such as clauses which require a forum that is less convenient, more costly, or more dilatory than a court action; that limit the consumer's ability to discover evidence; and that limit the consumer's ability to pursue a claim as a class.[77]

3.2.2 Limited FAA Preemption of State Procedural Law

3.2.2.1 Introduction

In addition to section 2, providing for the enforcement of agreements to arbitrate, the FAA also has a number of procedural provisions. For example, sections 16(b)(1) and 16(b)(2) prohibit appeals of most interlocutory orders directing arbitration to proceed or staying litigation.[78] By contrast, FAA section 16(a)(1)(B) permits immediate appeals of orders denying motions to compel arbitration. Thus, with a few exceptions, the FAA establishes a one-way right of appeal: a party attempting to compel arbitration has an immediate right of appeal if it loses, but a party opposing arbitration does not.

Many states have different laws relating to procedural questions such as appealability. For example, some states permit a party resisting arbitration to immediately appeal an order compelling arbitration and staying the litigation.[79] Some states also do not permit the immediate appeal of orders denying motions to compel arbitration.[80] Accordingly, there has been a good deal of litigation over the question of whether the FAA's procedural provisions preempt contrary state law. While the law is not unanimous on the point, the great weight of authority is against preemption, unless the state procedural law (a) is aimed at disfavoring arbitration, and is not a generally applicable rule; or (b) would result in a different outcome regarding the validity of an arbitration clause in state court than would apply in federal court.

3.2.2.2 The FAA Generally Does Not Preempt State Procedural Rules Addressing Enforcement of Arbitration Agreements

The Supreme Court's rulings relating to FAA preemption have not extended to procedural matters. The Supreme Court has held that "[t]here is no federal policy favoring arbitration under a certain set of procedural rules. . . ."[81] When the dissent in *Southland Corp. v. Keating* suggested that the majority's preemption holding would extend two of the FAA's procedural provisions to the state courts, the majority expressly disavowed the charge.[82]

While the Supreme Court has thus disclaimed an intention to extend FAA preemption to state procedural law, it has established two general principles of FAA preemption that would appear to apply to all state laws (whether procedural or substantive). The first principle is that "Congress would not have wanted state and federal courts to reach different outcomes about the validity of arbitration in different cases."[83] Thus a state may not adopt a procedural rule that would bar the enforcement of arbitration clauses in state court, if those clauses would be valid and enforceable in federal court.

The second principle is that states may not promulgate laws "applicable only to arbitration provisions" that would invalidate arbitration agreements.[84] Thus state procedural laws that single out arbitration for adverse treatment will not be enforced.

3.2.2.3 FAA Procedural Provisions, by Their Own Language, Apply Only to Federal Court Actions

Courts should be reluctant to find that the FAA's procedural provisions preempt state law, because the FAA's central procedural provisions on their face apply exclusively in federal court. For example, section 4 of the Act states that:

> A party aggrieved by the alleged failure, neglect, or refusal of another to arbitrate under a written agreement for arbitration may petition any United States district court which, save for such agreement, would have jurisdiction under Title 28, in a civil action or in admiralty of the subject matter of a suit arising out of the controversy between the parties, for an order directing that such arbitration

---

77 2001 N.M. Laws 227, § 5 (codified at N.M. Stat. § 44-7A-5) (2001 N.M. Laws 227 adopted the Uniform Arbitration Act with amendments).
78 9 U.S.C. § 16(b)(1), (2).
79 *See, e.g.*, Simmons Co. v. Deutsche Fin. Services Corp., 243 Ga. App. 85, 532 S.E.2d 436 (2000); Horsey v. Horsey, 329 Md. 392, 620 A.2d 305 (1993).
80 Bush v. Paragon Prop., Inc., 165 Or. App. 700, 997 P.2d 882 (2000) (en banc); Belmont Constructors, Inc. v. Lyondell Petrochemical Co., 896 S.W.2d 352 (Tex. App. 1995).

81 Volt Info. Sciences, Inc. v. Bd. of Trustees, 489 U.S. 468, 476, 109 S. Ct. 1248, 1254, 103 L. Ed. 2d 488 (1989).
82 Southland Corp. v. Keating, 465 U.S. 1, 16 n.10, 104 S. Ct. 852, 861 n.10, 79 L. Ed. 2d 1 (1984).
83 Allied-Bruce Terminix Companies v. Dobson, 513 U.S. 265, 272, 115 S. Ct. 834, 838, 130 L. Ed. 2d 753 (1995).
84 Doctor's Associates, Inc. v. Casarotto, 517 U.S. 681, 682, 116 S. Ct. 1652, 1653, 134 L. Ed. 2d 902 (1996).

proceed in the manner provided for in such agreement.[85]

Similarly, section 16(b)(2), which prohibits appeals of interlocutory orders "directing arbitration to proceed" explicitly refers to section 4 which, as quoted above, applies only in federal court.[86] Likewise, section 16(b)(1), which prohibits appeals of orders staying litigation under section 3 of the FAA, is limited by the latter's application to proceedings brought "in any of the courts of the United States."[87]

Accordingly, it is not surprising that a host of courts have begun with the presumption that states are free to apply their own rules of judicial procedure in cases litigated in their own courts.[88] Thus, most courts have held that state procedural law governing which types of orders relating to arbitration may be appealed is not preempted even when federal law is to the contrary.[89]

Similarly, the California Supreme Court has held that a state procedural rule providing for a stay of arbitration proceedings when a related case is pending in litigation is not preempted by the FAA regardless of whether the parties specifically contracted to follow the state law.[90] The California Supreme Court held that the California Arbitration Act provision was neutral as between arbitration and litigation because it gave courts discretion to stay either type of proceeding to avoid duplication of proceedings and inconsistency in outcome. In doing so, the court held that the state statute "does not contravene the letter or the spirit of the FAA."[91]

Finally, at least one appellate court has held that the FAA's standards for vacating an arbitration award do not preempt state standards.[92] The rationales for this holding, while similar to those underpinning the decisions addressing pre-arbitration orders, are set forth separately in the following subsection.

3.2.2.4 State Law, Not the FAA, Governs Motions to Vacate and Confirm in State Court

Section 2 of the FAA, regarding the enforceability of arbitration agreements, generally preempts state laws limiting that enforceability. But other sections of the FAA may not preempt state law. The most important examples are the FAA sections governing vacating and confirming awards. States have their own procedures and standards for those actions, generally patterned after the Uniform Arbitration Act or the revised Uniform Arbitration Act. When there is independent federal jurisdiction to bring an action in federal court, the FAA will govern motions to vacate or confirm an award. But when the action is brought in state court, state law presumptively applies.[93]

A state's standards for vacating and confirming an award obviously can have an impact on arbitration proceedings. While they do not prevent the arbitration from proceeding, they do affect the enforceability of the arbitrator's award. Nevertheless, the FAA generally has been found not to preempt these standards. For example, an appellate court has

---

85 9 U.S.C. § 4.
86 9 U.S.C. § 16(b)(2).
87 9 U.S.C. § 3.
88 S. Cal. Edison Co. v. Peabody W. Coal Co., 194 Ariz. 47, 51, 997 P.2d 769, 773 (Ariz. 1999); Cronus Investments, Inc. v. Concierge Services, L.L.C., 35 Cal. 4th 376, 25 Cal. Rptr. 3d 540, 187 P.3d 217 (2005); Rosenthal v. Great W. Fin. Sec. Corp., 14 Cal. 4th 394, 58 Cal. Rptr. 2d 875, 926 P.2d 1061, 1068 n.6 (1996); Siegel v. Prudential Ins. Co., 67 Cal. App. 4th 1270, 79 Cal. Rptr. 726, 734 (1998); Collins v. Prudential Ins. Co., 752 So. 2d 825, 828, 829 (La. 2000); Xaphes v. Mowry, 478 A.2d 299, 301 (Me. 1984); Weston Sec. Corp. v. Aykanian, 46 Mass. App. Ct. 72, 703 N.E.2d 1185, 1188, 1189 (1998); Greenpoint Credit, L.L.C. v. Reynolds, 151 S.W.3d 868, 873 n.3 (Mo. Ct. App. 2005); Reilly v. Sands Bros. & Co., 803 N.Y.S.2d 385 (Sup. Ct. 2005); Trombetta v. Raymond James Fin. Services, Inc., 907 A.2d 550, 565 (Pa. Super. Ct. 2006); Jack B. Anglin Co. v. Tipps, 842 S.W.2d 266, 272 (Tex. 1992). *But see In re Palacios*, 221 S.W.3d 564, 565 (Tex. 2006) (favorably citing *Tipps* for proposition that state courts applying FAA follow state procedural rules but noting that "[i]t is important for federal and state law to be as consistent as possible in this area, because federal and state courts have concurrent jurisdiction to enforce the FAA." (citation omitted)); *In re* D. Wilson Constr. Co., 196 S.W.3d 774 (Tex. 2006) (holding that FAA's and Texas arbitration statute's appeal rules *both* apply in state court unless conflict preempts the latter, inviting state legislature to harmonize state with federal law).
89 Simmons Co. v. Deutsche Fin. Services Corp., 243 Ga. App. 85, 532 S.E.2d 436 (2000) (FAA § 16 does not preempt Georgia's procedural rule permitting appeals of trial court orders compelling arbitration); Wells v. Chevy Chase Bank, 363 Md. 232, 768 A.2d 620 (2001); Bush v. Paragon Properties, 165 Or. App. 700, 997 P.2d 882 (2000) (FAA § 16 does not preempt Oregon law barring appeals of trial court orders denying motions to compel arbitration); Belmont Constructors, Inc. v. Lyondell Petrochemical Co., 896 S.W.2d 352 (Tex. App. 1995). *But see* Dakota Wesleyan Univ. v. HPG Int'l, Inc., 1997 SD 30, 560 N.W.2d 921 (1997) (FAA § 16 preempted state law that would have permitted an appeal from an order compelling arbitration).
90 Cronus Investments, Inc. v. Concierge Services, L.L.C., 35 Cal. 4th 376, 187 P.3d 217, 25 Cal. Rptr. 3d 540 (2005); *cf.* Volt Info. Sciences, Inc. v. Bd. of Trustees, 489 U.S. 468, 109 S. Ct. 1248, 103 L. Ed. 2d 488 (1989) (holding that same state procedural rule not preempted when parties contracted to follow state law).
91 Cronus Investments, Inc. v. Concierge Services, L.L.C., 35 Cal. 4th 376, 187 P.3d 217, 25 Cal. Rptr. 3d 540 (2005); *see also* Rambus, Inc. v. Hynix Semiconductor, Inc., 2007 WL 18829, at *14–*15 (Cal. Ct. App. Jan. 3, 2007) (following *Cronus*, applying California stay provision in case involving international commerce governed by 9 U.S.C. §§ 201–208); N. Slope Borough v. Hydropro, Inc., 2000 WL 35509009 (Alaska Super. Ct. June 2000) (holding that Alaska arbitration statute provision allowing stay of arbitration pending related judicial proceedings is not preempted).
92 Trombetta v. Raymond James Fin. Services, Inc., 970 A.2d 550 (Pa. Super. Ct. 2006); *see also* MBNA Am. Bank v. Straub, 815 N.Y.S.2d 450 (Civ. Ct. 2006) (questioning FAA's preemption of state law rules for confirming arbitration awards).
93 *See* Trombetta v. Raymond James Fin. Services, 907 A.2d 550 (Pa. Super. Ct. 2006).

upheld a California law requiring *vacatur* of any award issued by an arbitrator who violates the state's disclosure requirements for arbitrators. The state action does not undermine the enforceability of the arbitration agreement but presupposes that the arbitration agreement has been enforced and the arbitration has been held.[94]

More recently, Pennsylvania's intermediate court of appeals held that the FAA does not preempt that state's rules for confirming and vacating arbitration awards.[95] In *Trombetta v. Raymond James Financial Services, Inc.*, the court found that the United States Supreme Court's decisions applying the FAA supported the conclusion that "pre-emption will not be used to eviscerate state procedural arbitration rules *when such rules have no effect on the enforceability of the underlying agreement.*"[96] The court found further support for this conclusion in both the plain language of the FAA's judicial review provisions, which address proceedings in *federal* courts, and in the Constitution's federalism principles that "have never been understood to confer upon Congress the ability to require the states to govern according to Congress' instructions."[97]

Despite the broad constitutional considerations discussed in *Trombetta*, it is important to emphasize the fact that the state law provisions at issue concerning *vacatur* or arbitration awards were, by the court's own admission, "strikingly similar" to those in the FAA.[98] Whether the same finding against preemption would apply in a case involving radically divergent *vacatur* standards from those in the FAA remains to be seen.

3.2.3 FAA Preemption and Substantive State Laws Not Aimed at Restricting Arbitration

3.2.3.1 General

While the Supreme Court now has held on several occasions that the FAA preempts state laws that target or are triggered by the very presence of an arbitration clause, the question remains whether this principle represents the full scope of preemption under the Act or whether it might preempt other types of state laws as well. This question arises either implicitly or explicitly in at least two different contexts. The first involves the FAA's application of general principles of contract law to arbitration clauses and whether that contract law is itself the product of state or federal law. The second involves whether the FAA preempts state statutes that govern some types of contracts (such as franchise agreements or consumer loans) but not others, when this law would regulate some feature of an arbitration clause *other than the bare requirement of arbitration*. The Supreme Court's interpretations of the FAA and its underlying policies strongly suggest that state law is not preempted and should be applied in either case.

A number of lower federal courts, however, have taken a far more expansive view of FAA preemption as displacing almost all state laws that could affect the provisions of arbitration clauses. Consumer advocates should be aware of the existence of these rulings and should also understand how they may be vulnerable to challenge.

3.2.3.2 Whether Federal or State Law Applies to Questions of Contract Formation, Validity, and Enforceability

Section 2 of the FAA states that contractual agreements to arbitrate covered by the Act "shall be valid, irrevocable, and enforceable, save upon such grounds as exist at law or in equity for the revocation of any contract."[99] In *Perry v. Thomas*,[100] the Supreme Court explained how section 2 delineates the boundary between federal law and state law with regard to the regulation of arbitration clauses:

> [T]he text of § 2 provides the touchstone for choosing between state-law principles and the principles of federal common law envisioned by the passage of [the FAA]: An agreement to arbitrate is valid, irrevocable, and enforceable, *as a matter of federal law*, "save upon such grounds as exist at law or in equity for the revocation of *any* contract." Thus, state law, whether of legislative or judicial origin, is applicable *if* that law arose to govern issues concerning the validity, revocability, and enforceability of contracts generally.[101]

The Supreme Court has subsequently reiterated on numerous occasions that state contract law applies to arbitration clauses under the FAA.[102]

In light of these holdings, many courts have held that state law rules limiting the enforcement of non-negotiable or one-sided contract provisions apply to arbitration clauses,

---

94 Ovitz v. Schulman, 35 Cal. Rptr. 3d 117 (Ct. App. 2005).
95 Trombetta v. Raymond James Fin. Services, Inc., 907 A.2d 550 (Pa. Super. Ct. 2006).
96 *Id.* at 567 (emphasis added).
97 *Id.* at 568–569.
98 *Id.* at 564.
99 9 U.S.C. § 2.
100 482 U.S. 483, 107 S. Ct. 2520, 96 L. Ed. 2d 426 (1987).
101 482 U.S. at 492 n.9 (citations omitted).
102 *See, e.g.*, Doctor's Associates, Inc. v. Casarotto, 517 U.S. 681, 686, 687, 116 S. Ct. 1652, 134 L. Ed. 2d 902 (1996) ("Repeating our observation in *Perry*, the text of § 2 declares that state law may be applied '*if* that law arose to govern issues concerning the validity, revocability, and enforceability of contracts generally.'"); First Options of Chicago, Inc. v. Kaplan, 514 U.S. 938, 944, 115 S. Ct. 1920, 131 L. Ed. 2d 985 (1995) ("When deciding whether the parties agreed to arbitrate a certain matter ..., courts generally ... should apply ordinary state-law principles that govern the formation of contracts.").

and that is consistent with the FAA.[103] Thus, numerous state supreme courts have held that a state law rule of unconscionability prohibiting adhesive contracts that ban class actions for small-value claims because such clauses are unreasonably one-sided or exculpatory can apply to arbitration clauses that expressly ban class actions without being preempted by the FAA.[104]

Despite these cases and the Supreme Court's repeated holdings that state contract law applies to arbitration clauses under the FAA, some federal courts have proceeded as though the Act federalizes *all* law governing arbitration clauses.[105] The Third Circuit, for example, has held that the common law doctrine of mutuality (recognized in some, but not all, states) can never apply to arbitration clauses under the FAA as a matter of "substantive federal law."[106] Similarly, the Ninth Circuit has held that the FAA federalizes the common law contract doctrine of waiver.[107] In the latter case, the application of federal common law may not have made a great difference, because the court adopted waiver standards closely resembling those applicable under most state law.[108] Still, these decisions could diminish, if not eviscerate, the important role that the FAA preserves for state law in ensuring the fairness of arbitration agreements by applying the same rules of law to them that apply to other contracts.

The response to federal court rulings like *Harris* and *Sovak*, which use the FAA to federalize all contract law that applies to arbitration clauses, lies first and foremost in the Supreme Court's decisions interpreting the FAA. The Supreme Court held in *Volt Information Sciences, Inc. v. Board of Trustees*[109] that the FAA does not evince Congress's intent to occupy the entire field of arbitration.[110] Instead, state statutory and common law concerning the validity, revocability, and enforceability of contracts applies to arbitration clauses just as it does to other contracts.[111] Therefore, challenges to the enforcement of arbitration clauses based on unconscionability, waiver, consideration, mutuality, duress, or any other general contract law doctrine are governed by state law, even when the FAA applies to the arbitration clause.

3.2.3.3 Whether the FAA Preempts State Consumer Protection Laws That Do Not Target Arbitration Clauses

3.2.3.3.1 Overview

The Supreme Court has made clear that the FAA preempts any state law that is specifically targeted at arbitration and that the Act preserves enforcement of state statutory and common law that applies to contracts generally. These two precepts, however, do not cover the entire universe of state laws that might ever apply to the provisions of arbitration clauses. For example, a state consumer protection statute may contain a prohibition against exculpatory clauses in consumer lending contracts. The prohibition could be triggered if a lender drafts its mandatory arbitration clause to prohibit the arbitrator from awarding compensatory damages. This state law plainly does not fall within the bounds of FAA preemption recognized by the Supreme Court because it does not single out arbitration clauses and it does not take effect based solely on the presence of an arbitration clause. At the same time, it is not a law that governs the validity and enforceability of *all* contracts and so, arguably, it could be said to fall outside the FAA's savings provision for general contract law.

There are strong arguments that this state law would not be preempted under the Supreme Court's interpretations of

---

103 *See, e.g.*, Henderson v. Lawyers Title Ins. Corp., 843 N.E.2d 152 (Ohio 2006) (FAA does not preempt state insurance law rule invalidating arbitration clause when parties agreed to "standard" policy terms, and arbitration clauses were not deemed to be standard industry practice); Wis. Auto Title Loans, Inc. v. Jones, 714 N.W.2d 155 (Wis. 2006) (application of state's law of unconscionability to invalidate consumer arbitration clause creating one-sided obligation to arbitrate is not preempted by the FAA).

104 *See, e.g.*, Discover Bank v. Super. Ct., 36 Cal. 4th 148, 172, 113 P.3d 1100 (2005); Kinkel v. Cingular Wireless, L.L.C., 857 N.E.2d 250, 262 (Ill. 2006); Scott v. Cingular Wireless, L.L.C., 161 P.3d 1000, 1008 (Wash. 2007); *see also* Shroyer v. New Cingular Wireless Services, Inc., 2007 U.S. App. LEXIS 19560, at *36–*45 (9th Cir. Aug. 17, 2007) (summarizing cases, rejecting preemption argument).

105 *See* Charles Davant IV, *Tripping on the Threshold: Federal Courts' Failure to Observe Controlling State Law under the Federal Arbitration Act*, 51 Duke L.J. 521 (2001) (critique of this tendency among federal courts).

106 *See* Harris v. Green Tree Fin. Corp., 183 F.3d 173, 180 (3d Cir. 1999) (citing federal court holdings and concluding that "[t]his substantive federal law stands for the proposition that parties to an arbitration agreement need not equally bind each other with respect to an arbitration agreement if they provided each other with consideration beyond the promise to arbitrate"). *But see* Alexander v. Anthony Int'l, Ltd. P'ship, 341 F.3d 256, 264–265 (3d Cir. 2003) (applying state contract law in determining whether arbitration clause is unconscionable).

107 *See* Sovak v. Chugai Pharm. Co., 280 F.3d 1266, 1270 (9th Cir. 2002) ("We further conclude that waiver of the right to compel arbitration is a rule for arbitration such that the FAA controls.... Accordingly, the FAA, and not Illinois law, supplies the standard of waiver."). *But see* Shroyer v. New Cingular Wireless Services, Inc., 2007 U.S. App. LEXIS 19560, at *36–*45 (9th Cir. Aug. 17, 2007) (rejecting argument that FAA preempts state law of unconscionability).

108 Sovak v. Chugai Pharm. Co., 280 F.3d 1266, 1270 (9th Cir. 2002) ("In order to prevail, Sovak must show (1) Cook had knowledge of its existing right to compel arbitration; (2) Cook acted inconsistently with that existing right; and (3) he suffered prejudice from Cook's delay in moving to compel arbitration.").

109 489 U.S. 468, 109 S. Ct. 1248, 103 L. Ed. 2d 488 (1989).

110 489 U.S. at 477; *see* § 3.2.2, *supra*.

111 Perry v. Thomas, 482 U.S. 483, 492 n.9, 107 S. Ct. 2520, 96 L. Ed. 2d 426 (1987).

the FAA and under basic principles of federal preemption law. As the FAA does not expressly preempt state law and does not occupy the entire field of law regarding arbitration,[112] preemption only arises under the FAA through the doctrine of implied conflict preemption. Implied conflict preemption arises either when it is "impossible for a private party to comply with both state and federal requirements . . . or where state law 'stands as an obstacle to the accomplishment and execution of the full purposes and objectives of Congress.' "[113] As there is no serious argument that it would be impossible for a lender to draft an arbitration clause that complies with a state rule against exculpatory contracts, the determinative question is whether the application of that state rule to an exculpatory provision in an arbitration clause would frustrate or pose an obstacle to the underlying policies and objectives of Congress in enacting the FAA.

Because preemption constitutes a radical intrusion on state power, the Supreme Court has repeatedly applied a strong presumption *against* preemption that can only be overcome by clear evidence of Congress's purposes that would prohibit enforcement of the state law at issue.[114] The Supreme Court has on numerous occasions identified the policies and objectives animating Congress's enactment of the FAA, most recently explaining that the purpose of the Act was " 'to reverse the longstanding judicial hostility to arbitration agreements that had existed at English common law and had been adopted by American courts, and *to place arbitration agreements on the same footing as other contracts.*' "[115]

Because a state consumer protection statute's anti-exculpatory rule does not evince hostility towards arbitration and does not treat arbitration clauses differently from other contracts, a party asserting preemption under the FAA should not be able to overcome the strong presumption against preemption of such a state law.

3.2.3.3.2 Cases Rejecting Preemption Argument

The Wisconsin Supreme Court has found that United States Supreme Court precedent "strongly suggests that the Wisconsin Consumer Act would not be preempted [by the FAA] were the U.S. Supreme Court to address the issue."[116] But the Wisconsin court stopped short of resolving this issue because it held that the consumer arbitration clause in the case before it was unconscionable under general contract law regardless of the state's consumer protection statute.[117] Furthermore, a finding that the state law *is* preempted and the arbitration clause's exculpatory provision must be enforced would *itself* frustrate the FAA's purposes by placing the arbitration clause on a *different* footing from all other consumer loan contracts (in which exculpatory provisions would be illegal).[118] Simply put, the FAA was never intended to allow businesses to impose requirements other than arbitration itself that would be illegal under *any* state law.

Another opinion recognizing the limited scope of FAA preemption described herein is *Mitchell v. American Fair Credit Association, Inc.*[119] In *Mitchell*, the California Court of Appeal held that a credit services organization's arbitration clause was not enforceable against consumers because the clause was added in a contract amendment that consumers did not sign, thereby violating the state Credit Services Act's signature requirement. When faced with the defendant's argument that the FAA preempted this state statute because it was not "generally applicable" to every term of every contract in existence, the Court rejected the argument and squarely held that the FAA does not preempt the Credit Services Act's signature requirement because it does not single out the arbitration clause for disfavored treatment or treat the clause any differently than any other amended

---

112 Volt Info. Sciences, Inc. v. Bd. of Trustees, 489 U.S. 468, 477, 109 S. Ct. 1248, 103 L. Ed. 2d 488 (1989).

113 English v. Gen. Elec. Co., 496 U.S. 72, 79, 110 S. Ct. 2270, 110 L. Ed. 2d 65 (1990) (quoting Hines v. Davidowitz, 312 U.S. 52, 67, 61 S. Ct. 399, 85 L. Ed. 581 (1941)).

114 *See, e.g.*, Lorillard Tobacco Co. v. Reilly, 533 U.S. 525, 121 S. Ct. 2402, 2414, 150 L. Ed. 2d 532 (2001); Cal. Div. of Labor Standards v. Dillingham Constr., N.A., 519 U.S. 316, 325, 117 S. Ct. 832, 136 L. Ed. 2d 791 (1997) (in a field of traditional state regulation, we "work on the assumption that the historic police powers of the States are not to be superseded by the Federal Act unless that [is] the clear and manifest purpose of Congress"); Medtronic v. Lohr, 518 U.S. 470, 485, 116 S. Ct. 2240, 135 L. Ed. 2d 700 (1996); Metro. Life Ins. Co. v. Massachusetts, 471 U.S. 724, 740, 105 S. Ct. 2380, 85 L. Ed. 2d 728 (1985).

115 Equal Employment Opportunity Comm'n v. Waffle House, Inc., 534 U.S. 279, 122 S. Ct. 754, 761, 151 L. Ed. 2d 755 (2002) (emphasis added) (quoting Gilmer v. Interstate/Johnson Lane Corp., 500 U.S. 20, 24, 111 S. Ct. 1647, 114 L. Ed. 2d 26 (1991)); *see also* Doctor's Associates, Inc. v. Casarotto, 517 U.S. 681, 687, 116 S. Ct. 1652, 134 L. Ed. 2d 902 (1996) ("By enacting § 2, we have several times said, Congress precluded States from singling out arbitration provisions for suspect status, requiring instead that such provisions be placed 'upon the same footing as other contracts.' " (quoting Scherk v. Alberto-Culver Co., 417 U.S. 506, 511, 94 S. Ct. 2449, 41 L. Ed. 2d 270 (1974)); Prima Paint Corp. v. Flood & Conklin Mfg. Co., 388 U.S. 395, 404 n.12, 87 S. Ct. 1801, 18 L. Ed. 2d 1270 (1967) ("the purpose of Congress [in enacting the FAA] was to make arbitration agreements as enforceable as other contracts, but not more so").

116 Wis. Auto Title Loans, Inc. v. Jones, 714 N.W.2d 155 (Wis. 2006); *see also* Coady v. Cross Country Bank, Inc., 729 N.W.2d 732, 748 (Wis. Ct. App. 2007) (following *Wis. Auto Title Loans*).

117 *Wis. Auto Title Loans*, 714 N.W.2d at 178; *see also Coady*, 729 N.W.2d at 748.

118 *Cf.* Shroyer v. New Cingular Wireless Services, L.L.C., 2007 U.S. App. LEXIS 19560, at *35 (9th Cir. Aug. 17, 2007) (applying the rule finding adhesive class-action waivers unconscionable to arbitration clauses furthers FAA's purpose of placing these clauses on the same footing as other contracts).

119 99 Cal. App. 4th 1345, 122 Cal. Rptr. 2d 193 (2002).

consumer credit contract term.[120] Although the court recognized that the Credit Services Act's signature requirement was "not universal" among all contracts or contract terms, the court also recognized that this fact is not determinant for purposes of FAA preemption.[121]

Similarly, a federal district court rejected an FAA preemption challenge and upheld a Georgia statute governing payday loan contracts which provides that contractual exclusions of remedies, such as the right to participate in a class action, shall be considered evidence of unconscionability. In *Bankwest, Inc. v. Baker*,[122] the court found that this consumer protection statute provision was consistent with general state public policy and did not conflict with the FAA.[123] In addressing cases holding that a ban on class claims does not render an arbitration clause unconscionable, the court found that none of those cases prevented courts from considering such a ban as one element of a multi-factor unconscionability analysis.[124] The court's finding that this consumer protection statute did not conflict with the FAA and therefore was not preempted further supports the argument that subject-specific statutes are not per se preempted.

3.2.3.3.3 Cases Finding Preemption

Despite the overwhelming arguments against preemption of non-universal and nondiscriminatory state laws, several federal courts of appeal have held that the FAA preempts an analogous type of state statute. To redress the imbalance in bargaining power that exists in most franchise relationships, many states have enacted statutes granting certain rights to local franchise owners in their dealings with national franchisors. These state statutes typically prohibit the national franchisor from requiring the local franchisee to travel out of state to resolve any legal dispute. Once again, this type of state law does not target arbitration, but applies the same rule to contracts involving adjudication and arbitration alike. Still, a number of federal circuit courts have held that these laws are preempted simply because they apply only to *some* contracts (franchise agreements) and therefore do not fall within the FAA's savings clause for *generally applicable* contract law.[125] These courts are in effect holding that the FAA preempts *all* state laws *except* those that fall within the Act's savings clause.[126] A number of federal district and state courts have followed these decisions in holding that the FAA preempts state laws prohibiting distant-venue requirements for franchise operators, despite the fact that these laws do not in any way disfavor arbitration.[127]

Building on these franchise cases adopting an unnecessarily broad view of FAA preemption, the Ninth Circuit has held that the FAA preempts any application of California's Consumer Legal Remedies Act (CLRA) to an arbitration clause in a consumer contract.[128] The court held that the FAA preempts the CLRA's provisions that would have struck down the terms of a telephone company's arbitration clause banning punitive damages awards and class action relief to consumers because the CLRA applies only to consumer contracts and therefore is not a law of general applicability.[129] The Court proceeded to hold, however, that these same contract provisions were illegal under state common law unconscionability principles, which the FAA does not preempt.[130] The identical effect of the state's general and consumer-specific rules against exculpatory contracts calls into question the validity of the court's holding that the FAA preempts the latter.

---

120 99 Cal. App. 4th at 1357, 1358.
121 99 Cal. App. 4th at 1359.
122 324 F. Supp. 2d 1333 (N.D. Ga. 2004).
123 *Id.* at 1354.
124 *Id.* at 1354 n.22.
125 *See* Saturn Distribution Corp. v. Paramount Saturn, Ltd., 326 F.3d 684 (5th Cir. 2003) (holding that the Texas Motor Vehicle Board does not have exclusive jurisdiction over disputes between franchisors and franchisees in the motor vehicle industry, but that if it did, this regulation would be preempted by the FAA); Bradley v. Harris Research, Inc., 275 F.3d 884 (9th Cir. 2001); OPE Int'l Ltd. P'ship v. Chet Morrison Contractors, Inc., 258 F.3d 443 (5th Cir. 2001); KKW Enterprises, Inc. v. Gloria Jean's Gourmet Coffees Franchising Corp., 184 F.3d 42 (1st Cir. 1999); Doctor's Associates, Inc. v. Hamilton, 150 F.3d 157 (2d Cir. 1998); *see also* Mgmt. Recruiters Int'l, Inc. v. Bloor, 129 F.3d 851, 856 (6th Cir. 1997) (suggesting in dictum that, if state statute did require in-state dispute resolution, FAA would preempt its application to franchise agreement's arbitration clause); *cf.* Lim v. Offshore Specialty Fabricators, Inc., 404 F.3d 898, 906–907 (5th Cir. 2005) (holding that Chapter 2 of FAA governing international arbitration agreements preempts Louisiana Labor Code provision prohibiting choice-of-forum and choice-of-law clauses in all employment contracts).
126 *See, e.g., Bradley*, 275 F.3d at 890 ("Section 20040.5 applies only to forum selection clauses and only to franchise agreements; it therefore does not apply to 'any contract.' We accordingly reject the Bradleys' argument and hold that § 20040.5 is preempted by the FAA.").
127 *See, e.g.,* S & G Elec., Inc. v. Normant Sec. Group, Inc., 2007 WL 210517, at *5–*6 (E.D. Pa. Jan. 24, 2007) (FAA preempts state law prohibiting contractors or subcontractors from contracting to litigate or arbitrate out of state); Allen v. World Inspection Network, Inc., 911 A.2d 484, 492–493 (N.J. Super. Ct. App. Div. 2006) (FAA preempts state franchisee protection statute's prohibition against distant-venue clauses); B & S Ltd., Inc. v. Elephant & Castle Int'l, Inc., 906 A.2d 511, 520 (N.J. Super. Ct. Ch. Div. 2006) (same); Ashley River Properties I, L.L.C. v. Ashley River Properties II, L.L.C., 2006 WL 4037137 (S.C. Cir. Ct. Oct. 18, 2006) (FAA preempts state anti-forum selection clause rule as it would apply to provision requiring arbitration in another state).
128 *See* Ting v. AT & T, 319 F.3d 1126, 1147–1148 (9th Cir. 2003).
129 *Id.* at 1148.
130 *Id.* at 1152; *see also* Discover Bank v. Super. Ct., 36 Cal. 4th 148, 113 P.3d 1100 (2005) (waiver of class arbitration in consumer contract of adhesion was unconscionable; state law provision banning class action waivers in consumer contracts not preempted by FAA); Mandel v. Household Bank (Nev.), 105 Cal. App. 4th 75, 129 Cal. Rptr. 380 (2003) (consumer arbitration clause banning class action claims is unconscionable).

The fact that a state law does not fall within the FAA's savings clause would only compel a finding of preemption if the FAA was a field-preemption statute, which it is not. As the Supreme Court has squarely held that the FAA does not preempt the entire field of state laws pertaining to arbitration, a court must do more than discuss the savings clause before it can find that a state law is preempted.[131] A court must find that the state law would frustrate the FAA's underlying purpose of making arbitration agreements generally enforceable by placing them on the same footing as other contracts. As state franchisee protection statutes prohibiting out-of-state forum selection do not prevent parties from agreeing to arbitrate and do not treat arbitration agreements differently from other forum selection clauses, these laws do not conflict with the FAA and its underlying policy goals and should not be preempted. Despite the contrary case law, parties should continue vigorously to oppose preemption arguments regarding state laws that are enacted to protect specifically identified classes of parties, such as consumers, who have little or no contractual bargaining power.

3.2.4 FAA Preemption and State Laws Regulating the Conduct Of Private Arbitrators and Arbitration Services

Because of the large number of consumer and other cases brought by individual litigants that are being forced into arbitration, some states have started to enact laws designed to provide greater fairness in the arbitration process by regulating the conduct of the private arbitrators who decide cases and the private arbitration services that employ them. For example, California has enacted laws creating ethical standards for private arbitrators and imposing disclosure requirements on private arbitrators who decide cases within the state.[132] Notably, the California Ethics Standards apply to arbitrators themselves, and not to contractual arbitration agreements. Thus they address a different subject matter than that which has previously been found to give rise to preemption under the FAA.

Nevertheless, state and federal courts have split over whether California's Ethics Standards for arbitrators are preempted. In *Jevne v. Superior Court*,[133] a California court of appeals held that the FAA does not preempt the Ethics Standards because they are not antagonistic to the arbitration process.[134] As the Standards do not automatically invalidate arbitration clauses and do not single out these clauses by conditioning their enforcement upon special notice requirements, the court in *Jevne* held that they are not preempted. By contrast, in *Mayo v. Dean Witter Reynolds, Inc.*,[135] a federal district court held that the FAA preempts California's Ethics Standards because the Standards imposed different procedures than those set out in the parties' arbitration agreement and the FAA gave either party the right to enforce that agreement according to its terms.[136] The federal court in *Mayo* further found that violation of the Standards could not invalidate an arbitration clause because the Standards apply only to arbitration clauses.[137]

When rulings on these issues arising in securities industry cases were appealed, both the United States Court of Appeals for the Ninth Circuit and the California Supreme Court did not decide whether the FAA preempts the California Ethics Standards. Instead, both courts held that the federal Securities Exchange Act preempts the California Ethics Standards as they would apply to cases involving claims under that Act.[138]

The split of authority over whether the FAA preempts California's Ethics Standards for arbitrators is important because the ability of states to regulate the arbitration process for greater fairness hangs in the balance. Under the federal district court's opinion in *Mayo*, a company could avoid any state regulation by drafting an arbitration clause that provides to the contrary and then arguing that the FAA gives it the right to enforce the clause as written. As the FAA itself does not establish independent federal law standards governing arbitrator neutrality or cost-allocation or any number of other important procedural matters, this broad preemption rule would leave consumers with little or no protection against companies that try to enforce unfair and one-sided arbitration clauses.

3.3 Statutory and Contractual Limits to the FAA's Application and Preemptive Effect

3.3.1 Introduction

This section discusses a small number of statutory and contractually based limitations on or exceptions to the FAA's scope. Of the exceptions to the FAA's application discussed in each of the following subsections, only the one involving

---

131 Volt Info. Sciences, Inc. v. Bd. of Trustees, 489 U.S. 468, 477, 109 S. Ct. 1248, 103 L. Ed. 2d 488 (1989).
132 *See* Cal. Civ. Proc. Code § 1281.85 (West); Judicial Council of California, Ethics Standards for Neutral Arbitrators in Contractual Arbitration, *available at* www.courtinfo.ca.gov/rules/appendix/appdiv6.pdf (effective July, 2002).
133 6 Cal. Rptr. 3d 542 (Ct. App. 2003), *aff'd*, 35 Cal. 4th 935, 28 Cal. Rptr. 3d 685, 111 P.3d 954 (2005).
134 *Id.*, 6 Cal. Rptr. 3d at 551, 552.
135 258 F. Supp. 2d 1097 (N.D. Cal. 2002).
136 *Id.* at 1114.
137 *Id.* at 1116.
138 *See* Credit Suisse First Boston Corp. v. Grunwald, 400 F.3d 1119, 1136–1137 (9th Cir. 2005); Jevne v. Super. Ct., 35 Cal. 4th 935, 28 Cal. Rptr. 3d 685, 111 P.3d 954, 958 (2005).

insurance policy disputes and "reverse preemption" of the FAA[139] has been found to prohibit arbitration in a meaningful number of cases. Nonetheless, each of these exceptions is addressed for the sake of comprehensiveness.

3.3.2 The FAA Only Applies to Transactions Involving Interstate Commerce

3.3.2.1 The FAA Virtually Always Applies

The FAA applies to any contract "evidencing a transaction involving commerce,"[140] commerce being defined in the FAA as interstate commerce.[141] If the FAA were not to apply, then enforceability of an arbitration agreement would depend on state law. This distinction could be significant because state law in a number of jurisdictions places more limits on the enforceability of arbitration agreements than does the FAA.

However, the United States Supreme Court has construed the FAA so broadly that it applies to almost every conceivable economic transaction involving a consumer or worker. In two decisions, the second of which was issued per curiam without oral argument, the Supreme Court held that the FAA's "involving commerce" requirement covers all transactions within Congress's constitutional power to regulate interstate commerce.[142] The Court made it clear that, in the FAA, the phrase "involving commerce" is functionally equivalent to "affecting commerce," meaning that the FAA applies as broadly as possible to any contract within Congress's Commerce Clause power.[143]

The more recent of these two decisions, *Citizens Bank v. Alafabco, Inc.*,[144] overturns a number of state decisions, mostly from Alabama, that had utilized various standards to determine whether a transaction involved interstate commerce.[145] The Supreme Court rejected tests that consider whether the individual transaction at issue, taken by itself, has a substantial effect on interstate commerce.[146] Instead, the issue is whether the type of economic activity involved in the transaction in the aggregate can be said to involve interstate commerce.[147]

The Supreme Court has criticized the Alabama Supreme Court's reliance in the arbitration context on the limited interpretation of interstate commerce in *United States v. Lopez*, a 1995 United States Supreme Court decision.[148] *Lopez* found no authority under the Commerce Clause for Congress to enact a law criminalizing gun possession near a school. In *Citizens Bank*, the Court found the *Lopez* ruling immaterial to the issue of Congress's Commerce Clause authority in relation to the FAA's regulation of *economic* activity.[149]

After *Allied-Bruce* and *Citizens Bank*, a consumer will be hard-pressed to show that a transaction does not affect or involve interstate commerce. Many courts have followed the Supreme Court's lead and found that a wide variety of consumer transactions involve interstate commerce, and thus fall within the scope of the FAA.[150]

---

139 See § 3.3.4, infra.
140 9 U.S.C. § 2.
141 9 U.S.C. § 1.
142 Citizens Bank v. Alafabco, Inc., 539 U.S. 52, 123 S. Ct. 2037, 156 L. Ed. 2d 46 (2003); Allied-Bruce Terminix Companies, Inc. v. Dobson, 513 U.S. 265, 115 S. Ct. 834, 130 L. Ed. 2d 753 (1995).
143 Citizens Bank v. Alafabco, Inc., 539 U.S. 52, 123 S. Ct. 2037, 156 L. Ed. 2d 46 (2003); Allied-Bruce Terminix Companies, Inc. v. Dobson, 513 U.S. 265, 115 S. Ct. 834, 130 L. Ed. 2d 753 (1995); *see also* State of Wisconsin v. Ho-Chunk Nation, 478 F. Supp. 2d 1093, 1100–1101 (W.D. Wis. 2007) (holding that FAA's application to matters involving commerce applies to Indian commerce, including tribe's gaming compact with a state).
144 Citizens Bank v. Alafabco, Inc., 539 U.S. 52, 123 S. Ct. 2037, 156 L. Ed. 2d 46 (2003).
145 See, e.g., Liberty Nat'l Life Ins. Co. v. Douglas, 826 So. 2d 806 (Ala. 2002) (employment as an insurance agent); *Ex parte* Kampis, 826 So. 2d 819 (Ala. 2002); *Ex parte* Learakos, 826 So. 2d 782 (Ala. 2001); Alternative Fin. Solutions v. Colburn, L.L.C., 821 So. 2d 981 (Ala. 2001); Tefco Fin. Co. v. Green, 793 So. 2d 755 (Ala. 2001); Sisters of the Visitation v. Cochran Plastering Co., 775 So. 2d 759 (Ala. 2000).
146 This narrower view of interstate commerce was espoused in Sisters of the Visitation v. Cochran Plastering Co., 775 So. 2d 759 (Ala. 2000).
147 Citizens Bank v. Alafabco, Inc., 539 U.S. 52, 123 S. Ct. 2037, 156 L. Ed. 2d 46 (2003).
148 United States v. Lopez, 514 U.S. 549, 115 S. Ct. 1624, 131 L. Ed. 2d 626 (1995).
149 Citizens Bank v. Alafabco, Inc., 539 U.S. 52, 123 S. Ct. 2037, 2041, 156 L. Ed. 2d 46 (2003).
150 Am. Fin. Services Ass'n v. Burke, 169 F. Supp. 2d 62 (D. Conn. 2001) (lenders "are multistate commercial concerns with headquarters outside the State of Connecticut, some of the loans are processed outside the State of Connecticut, many of the loans are funded wholly or in part by investment sources from outside Connecticut, and the loans are often resold to secondary lenders in a national market for mortgage agreements"); *In re* Knepp, 229 B.R. 821 (Bankr. N.D. Ala. 1999) (automobile sale); Keene v. Hayden, 2007 Ala. LEXIS 40, at *4–*5 (Ala. Mar. 9, 2007) (real estate sale); Southtrust Bank v. Bowen, 2006 WL 3530655, at *4–*5 (Ala. Dec. 8, 2006) (mortgage); Cavalier Mfg., Inc. v. Jackson, 823 So. 2d 1237 (Ala. 2001) (mobile home sale); Thompson v. Skipper Real Estate Co., 729 So. 2d 287 (Ala. 1999) (sale of real estate); Coastal Ford, Inc. v. Kidder, 694 So. 2d 1285 (Ala. 1997) (as used truck had actually traveled in interstate commerce, contract for sale of the truck involved interstate commerce); *Ex parte* Gates, 675 So. 2d 371 (Ala. 1996) (sale of mobile home); Lopez v. Home Buyers Warranty Corp., 670 So. 2d 35 (Ala. 1995) (home owners' warranty agreement constituted a transaction which involved interstate commerce); Basura v. U.S. Home Corp., 98 Cal. App. 4th 1205 (2002) (sale of newly constructed residential housing); Warren-Guthrie v. Health Net, 84 Cal. App. 4th 804, 101 Cal. Rptr. 2d 260 (2000) (health insurance contract involved interstate commerce); Duggan v. Zip Mail Services, Inc., 920 S.W.2d 200 (Mo. Ct. App. 1996) (employment contract involved interstate

Nevertheless, a party wishing to invoke the FAA should provide evidence that interstate commerce is implicated.[151] The burden of proof, minimal though it is, still should fall on the party wishing to invoke the FAA.[152] A small number of courts have continued to find on occasion that contracts made in purely local transactions do not satisfy the interstate commerce requirement, so that the FAA does not apply.[153] Whether or not these decisions correctly apply Supreme Court precedent, they are few and far between and do not in any event provide a meaningful basis for resisting the FAA's application in the vast majority of cases.

3.3.2.2 Even If the FAA Does Not Apply, Most States Enforce Arbitration Agreements on Similar Terms

If the FAA does not apply to an arbitration agreement, the agreement may or may not be enforceable under state law. There are several situations in which state law may refuse to enforce an arbitration agreement that the FAA would have enforced. So long as the FAA does not apply, state law may prohibit or sharply restrict the enforceability of arbitration agreements generally.[154] State law may require the arbitration agreement to meet certain disclosure or other requirements for it to be effective.[155] A particular state statute, such as the Texas deceptive practices statute, may explicitly prohibit any agreement requiring that claims under that statute be resolved by arbitration.[156] Finally, a state court may find that arbitration is inconsistent with a particular state statutory right.[157]

---

commerce); Kelley v. Benchmark Homes, Inc., 250 Neb. 367, 550 N.W.2d 640 (1996) (home owners' warranty agreement constituted a transaction which involved interstate commerce); Tong v. S.A.C. Capital Mgmt., L.L.C., 835 N.Y.S.2d 881, 888 (N.Y. Sup. Ct. 2007) (stock broker's employment contract); In re FirstMerit Bank, 52 S.W.3d 749 (Tex. 2001) (mobile home lending contract "relates to interstate commerce"); In re L & L Kempwood Associates, 9 S.W.3d 125 (Tex. 1999); Neatherlin Homes, Inc. v. Love, 2007 WL 700996, at *2 (Tex. App. Mar. 8, 2007) (home construction contract); Palm Harbor Homes, Inc. v. McCoy, 944 S.W.2d 716 (Tex. App. 1997) (mobile home sale in which home manufactured, sold, and installed in same state); see also Gayfer Montgomery Fair Co. v. Austin, 870 So. 2d 683 (Ala. 2003) (employment contract with department store); Wolff Motor Co. v. White, 869 So. 2d 1129 (Ala. 2003) (tow truck used to move cars interstate); Potts v. Baptist Health Sys., Inc., 853 So. 2d 194 (Ala. 2002) (medical employment contract); Fid. Nat'l Title Ins. Co. v. Jericho Mgmt., Inc., 722 So. 2d 740 (Ala. 1998); Levitan v. Fanfare Media Works, Inc., 2003 WL 21028339 (Cal. Ct. App. May 8, 2003) (employment contract with media company); Frizzell Constr. Co. v. Gatlinburg, 9 S.W.3d 79 (Tenn. 1999) (contract to build hotel involved interstate commerce). But see Terminix Int'l Co. v. Stabbs, 930 S.W.2d 345 (Ark. 1996) (Arkansas arbitration law applies to home termite inspection agreement); Wools v. Super. Ct., 127 Cal. App. 4th 197, 212–214 (2005) (holding that FAA does not apply to transaction to renovate single-family home due to lack of nexus with interstate commerce and therefore does not preempt state statute requiring arbitration provisions in contracts for work on residential property to satisfy certain disclosure requirements); In re Godt, 28 S.W.3d 732, 737 (Tex. App. 2000) (attorney-client retainer agreement was not shown to relate to interstate commerce); Marina Cove Condo. Owners Ass'n, 109 Wash. App. 230, 34 P.2d 870 (2001) (defects in a condominium complex do not involve interstate commerce because the condominiums were constructed, marketed and sold within Washington, the owners live in Washington, and the warranty was offered by a Washington corporation).

151 See Sisters of the Visitation v. Cochran Plastering Co., 775 So. 2d 759 (Ala. 2000); Jim Burke Auto., Inc. v. Beavers, 674 So. 2d 1260 (Ala. 1996) (when seller offered no arguments or evidence in the trial court indicating that contract for the sale of an automobile involved interstate commerce, Alabama Supreme Court did not apply FAA and refused to compel arbitration); Broughton v. CIGNA Healthplans, 21 Cal. 4th 1066, 90 Cal. Rptr. 2d 334, 988 P.2d 67 (1999); Stewart Title Guarantee Co. v. Mack, 945 S.W.2d 330 (Tex. App. 1997).

152 Ex parte Kampis, 826 So. 2d 819 (Ala. 2002); Alternative Fin. Solutions v. Colburn, L.L.C., 821 So. 2d 981 (Ala. 2001).

153 See, e.g., Ark. Diagnostic Ctr., Prof'l Ass'n v. Tahiri, 2007 Ark. LEXIS 345, at *15–*17 (Ark. May 31, 2007) (doctor's employment contract); Baronoff v. Kean Dev. Co., 818 N.Y.S.2d 421 (Sup. Ct. 2006) (housing renovation contract); Satomi Owners Ass'n v. Satomi, L.L.C., 159 P.3d 460, 467–468 (Wash. Ct. App. 2007) (condominium development contract).

154 See, e.g., Ala. Code § 8-1-41(3) (all written predispute arbitration agreements invalid and unenforceable); Ark. Code Ann. § 16-108-201 (Uniform Arbitration Act provision that arbitration clause is enforceable does not apply to personal injury or tort claims, or to employer-employee disputes); Ga. Code Ann. § 9-9-1 (state arbitration code provision that arbitration clause is enforceable does not apply to consumer transactions, to employment terms or conditions, or to personal injury claims); Ind. Code § 24-4.5-3-104 (arbitration clauses in consumer loan agreements not enforceable); Iowa Code § 679A.1 (limiting arbitration in contracts of adhesion and limiting applicability to tort claims); Kan. Stat. Ann. § 5-401 (Uniform Arbitration Act provision that arbitration clause is enforceable does not apply to personal injury or tort claims, or to employer-employee disputes); Mo. Rev. Stat. § 435.350 (Uniform Arbitration Act provision that arbitration clause is enforceable does not apply to contracts of adhesion, to insurance, or to new home warranties); Mont. Code Ann. § 27-5-114 (no arbitration of personal injury claims, small consumer transactions, or insurance claims); Neb. Rev. Stat. § 25-2601 (Uniform Arbitration Act provision that arbitration clause is enforceable does not apply to personal injury claims, to claims under fair employment act, or to insurance claims); N.Y. Gen. Bus. Law § 399-c (McKinney) (prohibiting arbitration agreements in purchase of consumer goods); Tex. Civ. Prac. & Rem. Code Ann. § 171.001(b) (Vernon) (consumer arbitration agreement unenforceable if not signed by consumer's attorney).

155 See Cal. Bus. & Prof. Code § 7191 (West) (disclosure of arbitration agreements in work on specified residential property); Mo. Rev. Stat. § 435.460; Mont. Code Ann. § 27-5-114(4) (repealed 1997); Neb. Rev. Stat. § 25-2602.02; S.C. Code Ann. § 15-48-10; Vt. Stat. Ann. tit. 12, § 5652.

156 See Tex. Bus. & Com. Code Ann. § 17.42 (Vernon); see also Alaska Stat. § 9.43.10; Cal. Bus. & Prof. Code § 7191 (West) (disclosure of arbitration agreements in work on specified residential property); Mont. Code Ann. § 31-1-723 (prohibiting arbitration agreements in payday loan transactions).

157 E.g., Showmethemoney Check Cashers, Inc. v. Williams, 342

In most states, however, it appears that state law favors the enforcement of mandatory arbitration clauses on more or less the same basis as the FAA.[158] Thus, in one case in which a court held that the FAA did not apply, the court nonetheless compelled enforcement of the arbitration clause, finding: "While the distinctive procedural apparatus and presumption of arbitrability of the FAA would fall away, [the plaintiff] would still be required under the law of contract to arbitrate in accordance with the clause."[159] The Third Circuit reached the same result in an employment case concerning the exemption in the FAA for workers in interstate transportation: a court found that, although the employee did fall within that exemption, her claims could still be forced into arbitration under state law.[160]

3.3.3 Parties May Contract to Have State Law Displace the FAA with Respect to the Arbitrability of Disputes

The FAA's application to a transaction or case also can be limited by the terms of a contract, particularly by a choice of law clause that displaces the FAA with the arbitration law of a particular state.[161] As with the "involving commerce" requirement, however, this limitation does not provide a basis for any significant number of consumers to avoid arbitration. This is because the argument depends entirely on the terms of a contract *drafted by the party seeking arbitration*. Because the party that imposed the arbitration requirement also controls any choice-of-law clause, it will be an exceptional case, typically involving a serious drafting error, when a contract's choice-of-law clause prevents enforcement of its arbitration clause. Nevertheless, this argument is addressed for the benefit of those few cases in which it might apply.

Consumer contracts often include choice-of-law provisions specifying that a particular state's law will govern the agreement. In that case, it can be argued that the choice-of-law provision also applies to a binding arbitration clause in the agreement, meaning that state law, not the FAA, governs the arbitration agreement. For example, in *Volt Information Sciences, Inc. v. Board of Trustees*, the United States Supreme Court found that the phrase "the contract shall be governed by the law of the place where the Project is located" meant that California rules as to arbitration had been selected, not the federal rules.[162]

The Supreme Court stated in *Volt* that the parties can choose to enter into an arbitration agreement specifying that state law will apply to the arbitration, not the FAA.[163] A number of courts have subsequently held that contracting parties have chosen state law over the FAA in particular contracts.[164] State arbitration rules can be selected by the parties as long as application of state rules does not undermine the goals and policies of the FAA. In *Volt*, the state rules would stay arbitration pending the outcome of related cases, and this rule was found not to undermine the federal act.[165] On the other hand, the California Supreme Court has been more specific that a choice-of-law provision can determine the arbitration procedures, but cannot affect the enforceability of the arbitration clause under section 2 of the FAA.[166]

In other cases, however, the United States Supreme Court and other courts have held that a contract's general choice-of-law clause applies to the underlying merits of the parties' dispute but does not displace the FAA. In *Mastrobuono v. Shearson Lehman Hutton, Inc.*,[167] for example, the Court held that a contract's choice-of-law clause did not displace

---

Ark. 112, 119, 27 S.W. 3d 361, 365 (Ark. 2000) ("The Federal Arbitration Act and the laws of other jurisdictions do not restrict the scope of arbitration as we do in this state. Under Arkansas law, certain matters are not arbitrable, regardless of the language used in an arbitration agreement.").

158 *E.g.*, ASW Allstate Painting & Constr. Co. v. Lexington Ins. Co., 188 F.3d 307 (5th Cir. 1999) ("There is a strong presumption in Texas public policy favoring arbitration and upholding the parties' intentions, which is similar to the federal policy of ensuring the enforceability, according to their terms, of private agreements to arbitrate."); Armendariz v. Found. Health Psychare Services, Inc., 24 Cal. 4th 83, 99 Cal. Rptr. 2d 745, 6 P.3d 669 (2000) ("California law, like federal law, favors enforcement of valid arbitration agreements . . . under California law, as under federal law, an arbitration agreement may only be invalidated for the same reasons as other contracts.").

159 Chappel v. Lab. Corp. of Am., 232 F.3d 719, 725 (9th Cir. 2000) (footnote omitted).

160 Palcko v. Airborne Express, Inc., 372 F.3d 588 (3d Cir. 2004) ("[W]e conclude that the District Court erred in holding that Palcko's exemption status under section 1 of the FAA preempts the enforcement of the arbitration agreement under Washington state law.").

161 *See, e.g.*, Volt Info. Sciences, Inc. v. Bd. of Trustees, 489 U.S. 468, 109 S. Ct. 1248, 103 L. Ed. 2d 488 (1989) (holding that FAA does not preempt California arbitration rules applicable pursuant to contract's choice of law clause).

162 *Id.*; *see also In re* Knepp, 229 B.R. 821 (Bankr. N.D. Ala. 1999); Mirza v. Nat'l Standard Mortgage Corp., Clearinghouse No. 52,514 (N.Y. City Ct. Apr. 28, 1999) (New York choice of law provision in mortgage agreement ousted applicability of Federal Arbitration Act) (text of this decision is also available on the CD-Rom accompanying this manual); Ghanem v. Am. Greetings Corp., 2003 WL 22510663, at *4 (Ohio Ct. App. Nov. 6, 2003) (FAA does not preempt Ohio arbitration law adopted in parties' contract); BDO Seidman v. Miller, 949 S.W.2d 858 (Tex. App. 1997). *But see In re* L & L Kempwood Associates, 9 S.W.3d 125 (Tex. 1999).

163 Volt Info. Sciences, Inc. v. Bd. of Trustees, 489 U.S. 468, 479, 109 S. Ct. 1248, 1256, 103 L. Ed. 2d 488 (1989).

164 *See, e.g.*, Specialty Healthcare Mgmt., Inc. v. St. Mary Parish Hosp., 220 F.3d 650 (5th Cir. 2000) (parties selected Louisiana law over FAA).

165 *Volt*, 489 U.S. at 479.

166 Broughton v. CIGNA Healthplans, 21 Cal. 4th 1066, 90 Cal. Rptr. 2d 334, 988 P.2d 67 (1999) (citing Doctor's Associates, Inc. v. Casarotto, 517 U.S. 681, 116 S. Ct. 1652, 134 L. Ed. 2d 902 (1996)).

167 514 U.S. 52, 115 S. Ct. 1212, 131 L. Ed. 2d 76 (1995).

the FAA with New York arbitration law, which would have prohibited arbitration of a claim for punitive damages.[168] Lower federal courts have subsequently reached similar conclusions and applied the FAA despite a contract's inclusion of a general choice-of-law clause.[169]

Of course, if the binding arbitration provision explicitly refers to the FAA, and the transaction involves interstate commerce, the FAA will govern the arbitration agreement. But if the party seeking to compel arbitration has drafted a contract that indicates a choice of state law, and if that choice-of-law provision appears to apply to the arbitration provision, the principle that contracts should be interpreted against their drafters should apply to make that choice-of-law provision effective. The FAA says that arbitration should be enforced so long as the parties voluntarily submitted their claims to arbitration. Thus, the parties should be able to voluntarily submit claims to arbitration governed by standards other than those of the FAA.[170]

3.3.4 Exception for State Regulation of the Business of Insurance

3.3.4.1 General

Even when interstate commerce is involved, state law may restrict arbitration of insurance policy disputes notwithstanding the FAA. The federal McCarran-Ferguson Act prohibits federal regulation of insurance practices to the extent that such regulations would invalidate, impair, or supersede state law enacted for the purpose of regulating the business of insurance, unless the federal law explicitly relates to the business of insurance.[171] The FAA does not explicitly relate to the business of insurance.[172] Consequently, if a state statute regulating the business of insurance limits the enforceability of an arbitration provision, the FAA conflicts with the state statute and, therefore, state law, not the FAA, determines whether the arbitration provision is enforceable.[173]

There are two issues to analyze in determining whether state law limits the enforceability of an arbitration agreement as to insurance claims. The first is whether the state statute is one enacted for the purpose of regulating the business of insurance. If it is, then the second issue to consider is whether the statute restricts the enforceability of arbitration agreements.

---

168 *Id.*, 514 U.S. at 958.
169 *See, e.g.*, Action Industries, Inc. v. Fid. & Guar. Co., 358 F.3d 337, 343 (5th Cir. 2004); Azammi, Ltd. P'ship v. Mitchell Gold Co., 2007 U.S. Dist. LEXIS 38231, at *6–*7 (W.D. Tex. May 25, 2007).
170 Volt Info. Sciences, Inc. v. Bd. of Trustees, 489 U.S. 468, 109 S. Ct. 1248, 103 L. Ed. 2d 488 (1989); *see also* Engalla v. Permanente Med. Group, 15 Cal. 4th 951, 64 Cal. Rptr. 2d 843, 938 P.2d 903 (1997); BDO Seidman v. Miller, 949 S.W.2d 858 (Tex. App. 1997). *But cf.* Mastrobuono v. Shearson Lehman Hutton, Inc., 514 U.S. 52, 115 S. Ct. 1212, 131 L. Ed. 2d 76 (1995).
171 15 U.S.C. § 1012(b); *see also* United States Dep't of the Treasury v. Fabe, 508 U.S. 491, 113 S. Ct. 2202, 124 L. Ed. 2d 449 (1993).
172 *See* Standard Sec. Life Ins. Co. of N.Y. v. West, 267 F.3d 821, 823 (8th Cir. 2001) (noting agreement of parties that FAA does not specifically relate to business of insurance); Am. Bankers Ins. Co. v. Crawford, 757 So. 2d 1125 (Ala. 1999); Smith v. Pacificare Behavioral Health of Cal., Inc., 93 Cal. App. 4th 139, 154, 113 Cal. Rptr. 2d 140, 151 (2001) (noting agreement of parties that FAA does not specifically relate to business of insurance); Cox v. Woodmen of the World Ins. Co., 556 S.E.2d 397, 400 (S.C. Ct. App. 2001) (same); Little v. Allstate Ins. Co., 167 Vt. 171, 705 A.2d 538 (1997).
173 Standard Sec. Life Ins. Co. of N.Y. v. West, 267 F.3d 821 (8th Cir. 2001); Quackenbush v. Allstate Ins. Co., 121 F.3d 1372 (9th Cir. 1997) (insurance statute prohibiting insurance liquidator from being compelled to arbitrate disputes prevails over FAA); Stephens v. Am. Int'l Ins. Co., 66 F.3d 41 (2d Cir. 1995); Mut. Reinsurance Bureau v. Great Plains Mut. Ins. Co., 969 F.2d 931 (10th Cir. 1992); Balaban-Zilke v. Cigna Healthcare of Cal., Inc., 2003 WL 21228038 (Cal. Ct. App. May 28, 2003); Ciccarelli v. Blue Cross of Cal., 2003 WL 150045 (Cal. Ct. App. Jan. 22, 2003); Imbler v. PacifiCare of Cal., Inc., 103 Cal. App. 4th 567, 126 Cal. Rptr. 2d 715 (2002); Pagarigan v. Super. Ct., 102 Cal. App. 4th 1121, 126 Cal. Rptr. 2d 124 (2001); Smith v. Pacificare Behavioral Health of Cal., Inc., 93 Cal. App. 4th 139, 158, 161, 162, 113 Cal. Rptr. 2d 140, 154, 156, 157 (2001); Allen v. Pacheco, 71 P.3d 375 (Colo. 2003); Love v. Money Tree, Inc., 614 S.E.2d 47, 50 (Ga. 2005); Cont'l Ins. Co. v. Equity Residential Properties Trust, 255 Ga. App. 445, 565 S.E.2d 603 (2002); Friday v. Trinity Universal of Kan., 262 Kan. 347, 939 P.2d 869 (1997); *In re* Kepka, 178 S.W.3d 279 (Tex. App. 2005); Little v. Allstate Ins. Co., 167 Vt. 171, 705 A.2d 538 (1997); Kruger Clinic Orthopaedics v. Regence Blueshield, 138 P.3d 936 (Wash. 2006) (state statute and regulation prohibiting binding arbitration clauses in contracts between insurers and health providers is deemed a regulation of insurance that McCarran-Ferguson Act saves from FAA preemption); *see also* Davister Corp. v. United Republic Life Ins. Co., 152 F.3d 1277 (10th Cir. 1998); Munich Am. Reinsurance Co. v. Crawford, 141 F.3d 585 (5th Cir. 1998); Murff v. Prof'l Med. Ins. Co., 97 F.3d 289 (8th Cir. 1996); Towe, Hester & Erwin, Inc. v. Kan. City Fire & Marine Ins. Co., 947 P.2d 594 (Okla. Civ. App. 1997) (while recognizing that Oklahoma law, which limits arbitration in insurance, would oust the FAA, the dispute in that case between an insurance company and its employees did not relate to insurance); Cox v. Woodmen of the World Ins. Co., 556 S.E.2d 397 (S.C. Ct. App. 2001) (South Carolina's anti-arbitration insurance provision not preempted by FAA but provision does not apply to fraternal benefits association). *But see* Goshawk Dedicated Ltd. v. Portsmouth Settlement Co. I, Inc., 466 F. Supp. 2d 1293, 1304–1305 (N.D. Ga. 2006) (holding that FAA chapter 2 supersedes McCarran-Ferguson Act with regard to international contracts); Pinnoak Res., L.L.C. v. Certain Underwriters at Lloyd's of London, 394 F. Supp. 2d 821 (S.D. W. Va. 2005) (discussing split of authority over whether McCarran-Ferguson Act reverse preempts chapter 2 of FAA governing international arbitration agreements, without resolving issue).

3.3.4.2 Is a State Law One Enacted for the Purpose of Regulating Insurance?

A number of state statutes limit the enforceability of arbitration agreements but do not specifically mention insurance.[174] Instead, these are laws of general application that apply to insurance and most other forms of commerce. The question is whether such statutes are state laws enacted for the purpose of regulating insurance, thereby triggering application of the McCarran-Ferguson Act.[175]

For example, an Alabama statute provides that agreements to submit controversies to arbitration may not be enforced.[176] That statute does not mention insurance and the Alabama courts have found that the statute is not one regulating the business of insurance and thus does not supersede the FAA under McCarran-Ferguson.[177]

On the other hand, a statute need not be enacted solely for the purpose of regulating insurance in order to qualify. For example, a number of states have enacted the Uniform Arbitration Act but have explicitly stated that the provision concerning the enforceability of arbitration agreements does not apply to insurance or to certain lines of insurance.[178] Such an exemption is a state enactment for the purpose of regulating insurance.[179]

Likewise, a state law need not directly regulate the insurer-insured relationship so long as that law has a substantial effect on this relationship. Thus the Washington Supreme Court has held that a statute and regulation barring binding arbitration clauses in contracts between insurers and healthcare providers would "strengthen the reliability of the carrier's promises to its insureds and thereby 'regulat[e] the business of insurance' within the meaning of the McCarran-Ferguson Act."[180] This state statute and regulation prohibiting binding arbitration clauses therefore was not preempted by the FAA.

3.3.4.3 Does State Insurance Law Restrict the Enforceability of Arbitration Agreements?

Even if a state statute regulates the business of insurance, it will not displace the applicability of the FAA if it does not restrict the enforceability of arbitration agreements. If the statute does not, there is no conflict with the FAA, and the FAA continues to apply.[181] State insurance law does not preempt the field but only supersedes federal law that is inconsistent with it.[182]

A number of states clearly restrict the enforceability of arbitration agreements concerning certain lines of insurance. For example: Kentucky prohibits predispute arbitration clauses in automobile liability policies;[183] and Louisiana, Mississippi, South Carolina, Tennessee, Virginia, and West Virginia forbid arbitration clauses in uninsured motorist policies.[184] In Nevada, arbitration clauses in motor vehicle insurance policies are not enforceable and group health insurance beneficiaries can opt out of an arbitration provision.[185] California's Knox-Keene Act imposes disclosure

---

174 See § 3.2.1, supra.
175 For the most recent Supreme Court discussion about whether a statute "regulates the business of insurance," see UNUM Life Ins. Co. v. Ward, 526 U.S. 358, 119 S. Ct. 1380, 143 L. Ed. 2d 462 (1999).
176 Ala. Code § 8-1-41.
177 Am. Bankers Ins. Co. v. Crawford, 757 So. 2d 1125 (Ala. 1999); see also Clayton v. Woodmen of the World Life Ins. Soc'y, 981 F. Supp. 1447 (M.D. Ala. 1997); Celtic Life Ins. Co. v. McLendon, 814 So. 2d 222 (Ala. 2001); cf. Hart v. Orion Ins. Co., 453 F.2d 1358 (10th Cir. 1971); Hamilton Life Ins. Co. v. Republic Nat'l Life Ins. Co., 408 F.2d 606 (2d Cir. 1969); Triton Lines, Inc. v. S.S. Mut. Underwriting Ass'n, 707 F. Supp. 277, 279 (S.D. Tex. 1989) (dealing with interrelationship of Texas insurance code and state deceptive practices statute); Am. Int'l Group, Inc. v. Siemens Bldg. Technologies, Inc., 881 So. 2d 7 (Fla. Dist. Ct. App. 2004) (McCarran-Ferguson Act does not cover generally applicable common law). But see In re Knepp, 229 B.R. 821 (Bankr. N.D. Ala. 1999).
178 Ark. Code Ann. § 16-108-201; Ga. Code Ann. § 9-9-1 (arbitration statute significantly different than the Uniform Arbitration Act); Kan. Stat. Ann. § 5-401; Mo. Rev. Stat. § 435.350; Mont. Code Ann. § 27-5-111; Neb. Rev. Stat. § 25-2601; Okla. Stat. tit. 15, § 802; S.C. Code Ann. § 15-48-10(b)(4).
179 Standard Sec. Life Ins. Co. of N.Y. v. West, 267 F.3d 821 (8th Cir. 2001); Mut. Reinsurance Bureau v. Great Plains Mut. Ins. Co., 969 F.2d 931 (10th Cir. 1992); Love v. Money Tree, Inc., 614 S.E.2d 47, 50 (Ga. 2005); Friday v. Trinity Universal of Kan., 939 P.2d 869 (Kan. 1997); Harley v. Sayas, 2006 WL 4037577 (S.C. Cir. Ct. June 21, 2006) (applying state arbitration statute's insurance exclusion to variable life insurance policy); see also Cox v. Woodmen of the World Ins. Co., 556 S.E.2d 397, 401, 402 (S.C. Ct. App. 2001) (holding that provision of South Carolina Arbitration Act exempting any insured or insurance policy beneficiary is an insurance regulation that McCarran-Ferguson Act saves from preemption by the FAA, but finding that provision does not apply to defendant as a fraternal benefits association). But see In re Northwestern Corp. v. Nat'l Union Fire Ins. Co., 321 B.R. 120, 126–127 (Bankr. D. Del. 2005) (holding that private coverage dispute in which insurer resists arbitration under its own clause does not implicate state's interest in regulating insurance business, despite state arbitration statute's provision exempting insurance claims from its coverage); Little v. Allstate Ins. Co., 167 Vt. 171, 705 A.2d 538 (1997).
180 Kruger Clinic Orthopaedics v. Regence Blueshield, 138 P.3d 936, 941 (Wash. 2006).
181 See Miller v. Nat'l Fid. Ins. Co., 588 F.2d 185 (5th Cir. 1979) (no law in Georgia insurance code is impaired by the Federal Arbitration Act); Flach v. Clarendon Nat'l Ins. Co., 2004 WL 5042294, at *2 n.1 (M.D. Fla. Apr. 8, 2004) (plaintiff fails to cite any Florida law governing the insurance business that stands in conflict with the FAA).
182 Humana v. Forsyth, 525 U.S. 299, 119 S. Ct. 710, 142 L. Ed. 2d 753 (1999).
183 Ky. Rev. Stat. Ann. § 304.20-050 (West).
184 La. Rev. Stat. Ann. § 22:1406(D)(5) (arbitration optional for the consumer); Miss. Code Ann. § 83-11-109; S.C. Code Ann. § 38-77-200; Tenn. Code Ann. § 56-7-1206(c); Va. Code Ann. § 38.2-2206(H); W. Va. Code § 33-6-31(g).
185 Nev. Rev. Stat. §§ 690B.017 (motor vehicle insurance), 695C.267 (health insurance).

requirements for arbitration provisions in health maintenance organization contracts.[186] Likewise, Colorado's Health Care Availability Act seeks to ensure that arbitration clauses in health insurance policies are voluntary by requiring specific language and use of bold-faced ten-point type.[187] Similarly, Texas law requires health insurance providers to comply with specific disclosure requirements to be able to enforce arbitration clauses against patients.[188] Similarly, the state of Washington ensures that an insurer's use of an arbitration clause does not shut off another party's access to judicial remedies by making such arbitration nonbinding: "carriers may not require alternative dispute resolution to the exclusion of judicial remedies," but "may require alternative dispute resolution prior to judicial remedies."[189] The Washington Supreme Court has construed this provision to prohibit insurers from enforcing binding arbitration clauses.[190] More generally, South Dakota voids arbitration agreements in insurance policies,[191] and Wisconsin requires that arbitration clauses be approved by the insurance commissioner.[192]

A number of states also have amended their Uniform Arbitration Act to specify that arbitration agreements are enforceable *except as to insurance claims*.[193] Although there is some ambiguity in such provisions, the clear legislative intent is to prohibit the enforceability of arbitration agreements involving insurance claims.[194] Similarly, a state insurance commissioner, acting under authority of insurance law, could prohibit the use of arbitration clauses relating to a particular line of insurance or could refuse to approve use of an insurance policy that contained an arbitration clause.

Sometimes the issue of whether state insurance law does or does not limit arbitration can become quite complex. An old Massachusetts statute prohibits any agreement to deprive the courts of Massachusetts of jurisdiction against the insurer.[195] A more recent statute indicates arbitration provisions are enforceable except in collective bargaining agreements.[196] The First Circuit, while recognizing the effect of the McCarran-Ferguson Act if the state insurance statute did in fact limit arbitration, found that the older insurance statute did not limit arbitration clauses because arbitration does not deprive the courts of Massachusetts of jurisdiction over a matter.[197] In any event, the court found that the more recent, non-insurance statute prevails.[198]

3.4 Courts Determine an Arbitration Clause's Enforceability Under *State* Contract Law Principles, With One Big Exception

3.4.1 Introduction

Many corporate defendants urge courts to recognize that the Federal Arbitration Act (FAA) applies to a given arbitration clause and to a given case as if the FAA resolved all of the relevant issues. In fact, the FAA leaves to state law the two principal issues involved in the vast majority of litigation over arbitration clauses—whether an agreement to arbitrate has been formed,[199] and whether any generally applicable state contract doctrine bars the enforcement of the arbitration agreement.[200]

However, in one particular situation, the FAA does determine the enforceability of an arbitration clause *irrespective of state contract law*.[201] When a party challenges the validity of an entire contract that includes an arbitration clause based on fraudulent or unlawful provisions that do not relate to the arbitration clause, the Supreme Court has held, in *Prima Paint, Corp. v. Flood & Conklin Manufac-*

---

186 *See* Smith v. Pacificare Behavioral Health of Cal., Inc., 93 Cal. App. 4th 139, 158, 161, 162, 113 Cal. Rptr. 2d 140, 154, 156, 157 (2001) (holding that FAA does not preempt Knox-Keene Act's restrictions on arbitration); *see also* Ogle v. Pacificare Life & Health Ins. Co., 2007 WL 615596 (Cal. Ct. App. Mar. 1, 2007) (same); Balaban-Zilke v. CIGNA Healthcare of Cal., Inc., 2003 WL 21228038, at *4 (Cal. Ct. App. May 28, 2003) (same).
187 Colo. Rev. Stat. § 13-64-603; *see* Allen v. Pacheco, 71 P.3d 375, 383, 384 (Col. 2003).
188 Tex. Civ. Prac. & Rem. Code Ann. § 74.451(a) (Vernon).
189 Wash. Admin. Code 284-43-322(4).
190 Kruger Clinic Orthopaedics v. Regence Blueshield, 138 P.3d 936, 941 (Wash. 2006).
191 S.D. Codified Laws § 21-25A-3.
192 Wis. Stat. § 631.85.
193 Ark. Code Ann. § 16-108-201; Ga. Code Ann. § 9-9-1 (arbitration statute significantly different than the Uniform Arbitration Act); Kan. Stat. Ann. § 5-401; Mo. Rev. Stat. § 435.350; Mont. Code Ann. § 27-5-111; Neb. Rev. Stat. § 25-2601; Okla. Stat. tit. 15, § 802; S.C. Code Ann. § 15-48-10(b)(4).
194 McKnight v. Chicago Title Ins. Co., 358 F.3d 854, 858 (11th Cir. 2004); Standard Sec. Life Ins. Co. of N.Y. v. West, 267 F.3d 821 (8th Cir. 2001); Mut. Reinsurance Bureau v. Great Plains Mut. Ins. Co., 969 F.2d 931 (10th Cir. 1992); Am. Health & Life Ins. Co. v. Heyward, 272 F. Supp. 2d 578, 582 (D.S.C. 2003); Love v. Money Tree, Inc., 614 S.E.2d 47, 50 (Ga. 2005); Friday v. Trinity Universal of Kan., 939 P.2d 869 (Kan. 1997); *see also* Cox v. Woodmen of the World Ins. Co., 556 S.E.2d 397, 401, 402 (S.C. Ct. App. 2001) (holding that provision of South Carolina Arbitration Act exempting any insured or insurance policy beneficiary from arbitration is an insurance regulation that McCarran-Ferguson saves from preemption by the FAA, but finding that provision does not apply to defendant as a fraternal benefits association).
195 Mass. Gen. Laws ch. 175, § 22.
196 Mass. Gen. Laws ch. 251, § 1.
197 DiMercurio v. Sphere Drake Ins., PLC, 202 F.3d 71 (1st Cir. 2000).
198 *Id.*
199 For a discussion of issues frequently litigated in connection with the question of whether an agreement to arbitrate exists, see Chapter 5, *infra*.
200 For a discussion of such state contract doctrines, see Chapter 6, *infra*.
201 This exception to the general application of state contract law is discussed more fully at § 3.4.5, *infra*.

turing Co.[202] and *Buckeye Check Cashing, Inc. v. Cardegna*,[203] that the FAA makes the arbitration clause severable from the rest of the contract thus requiring parties to arbitrate their challenges to the other provisions. The FAA's severability rule applies notwithstanding state contract law under which certain types of illegal provisions would otherwise invalidate an entire contract, including its arbitration clause.[204]

Even this severability rule, however, only applies to questions concerning the validity of agreed-upon contract provisions, but not to questions of assent to a contract containing an arbitration clause, which courts themselves resolve applying state contract law principles.[205]

3.4.2 State Contract Law Governs the Question of Whether an Agreement to Arbitrate Was Formed

Arbitration may only be compelled if the parties to a contract have consented to arbitrate their claims.[206] Accordingly, under "the FAA a court must decide whether an agreement to arbitrate exists before it may order arbitration."[207] In *Sandvik AB v. Avent International Corp.*,[208] the Third Circuit wrote that "before arbitration could be ordered, the district court had to be certain that there was an agreement to arbitrate."[209] In a recent Seventh Circuit case, Judge Easterbrook also strongly endorsed idea that "courts, rather than arbitrators, usually determine whether the parties have agreed to arbitrate," and adopted the holding of *Sandvik*:

> The approach of *Sandvik* and *Sphere Drake* is sound, for a person who has not consented (or authorized an agent to do so on his behalf) can't be

packed off to a private forum. Courts have jurisdiction to determine their jurisdiction not only out of necessity (how else would jurisdictional disputes be resolved?) but also because their authority depends on statutes rather than the parties' permission. Arbitrators lack a comparable authority to determine their own authority because there is a non-circular alternative (the judiciary) and because the parties do control the existence and limits of an arbitrator's power. No contract, no power.[210]

Under Pennsylvania law, similarly, "the threshold question of whether a party agreed to arbitrate a dispute is a jurisdictional question that must be decided by a court."[211] Numerous courts have refused to compel arbitration when they concluded that the parties had not agreed to arbitrate their claims.[212]

In deciding whether an agreement to arbitrate was formed, the Supreme Court has instructed the courts to look to state law governing the formation of contracts.[213] Ac-

---

202 388 U.S. 395, 87 S. Ct. 1801, 18 L. Ed. 2d 1270 (1967).
203 546 U.S. 440, 126 S. Ct. 1204, 163 L. Ed. 2d 1038 (2006).
204 *Id.*, 546 U.S. at 446.
205 *See id.*, 546 U.S. at 444 n.1.
206 *See* § 3.1.2, *supra*.
207 Sandvik AB v. Avent Int'l Corp., 220 F.3d 99, 107 (3d Cir. 2000); *see also* Stout v. Byrider, 228 F.3d 709 (6th Cir. 2000) ("When asked by a party to compel arbitration under a contract, a federal court must determine whether the parties agreed to arbitrate the dispute at issue."); Coady v. Ashcraft & Gerel, 223 F.3d 1, 8 (1st Cir. 2000) ("The question whether the parties agreed to arbitrate certain matters was for the court to decide."); McCreary v. Liberty Nat'l Life, 6 F. Supp. 2d 920 (N.D. Miss. 1998) ("[B]efore arbitration can be compelled, the court must first determine whether the parties actually agreed to arbitrate their dispute.").
208 220 F.3d 99 (3d Cir. 2000); *see also* Petals Factory Outlet of Del., Inc. v. EWH & Associates, 90 Md. App. 312, 600 A.2d 1170, 1173 (1992) ("where the parties are . . . in disagreement on the very question whether there exists an agreement to arbitrate the subject matter of the dispute, the resolution of the question is for the court").
209 *Sandvik*, 220 F.3d at 106.
210 Sphere Drake Ins. Ltd. v. All Am. Ins. Co., 256 F.3d 587, 591 (7th Cir. 2001).
211 Smith v. Cumberland Group, Ltd., 455 Pa. Super. 276, 687 A.2d 1167, 1171 (1997).
212 *See, e.g.,* Sec. Watch, Inc. v. Sentinel Sys., Inc., 176 F.3d 369 (6th Cir. 1999); Diskin v. J.P. Stevens & Co., 836 F.2d 47 (1st Cir. 1987); Coastal Indus., Inc. v. Automatic Steam Products Corp., 654 F.2d 375 (5th Cir. 1981); Supak & Sons Mfg. Co. v. Pervel Indus., Inc., 593 F.2d 135 (4th Cir. 1979); N & D Fashions, Inc. v. DHJ Indus., Inc., 548 F.2d 722 (8th Cir. 1976); Long v. Fid. Water Sys., Inc., 2000 U.S. Dist. LEXIS 7827 (N.D. Cal. May 26, 2000); Hendrick v. Brown & Root, Inc., 50 F. Supp. 2d 527 (E.D. Va. 1999); *Ex parte* Pointer, 714 So. 2d 971 (Ala. 1997); Crown Pontiac, Inc. v. McCarrell, 695 So. 2d 615 (Ala. 1997); Badie v. Bank of Am., 67 Cal. App. 4th 779, 79 Cal. Rptr. 2d 273 (1998); Curtis G. Testerman Co. v. Buck, 340 Md. 569, 667 A.2d 649 (1995); *see also* Baychar, Inc. v. Frisby Technologies, Inc., 230 F. Supp. 2d 75 (D. Me. 2001) ("Based on the federal policy liberally favoring arbitration, most questions are left to the jurisdiction of an arbitrator. One question, however, exists outside this federal policy, and remains within the purview of the courts: whether or not the parties actually agreed to arbitrate the dispute in the first place."); Specht v. Netscape Communications Corp., 150 F. Supp. 2d 585 (S.D.N.Y. 2001), *aff'd*, 306 F.3d 17 (2d Cir. 2002) ("The first stage of the analysis—whether a contract was formed—is a question of state law."); Toppings v. Meritech Mortgage Services, Inc., 140 F. Supp. 2d 683, 685 (S.D. W. Va. 2001); Estate of Blanchard v. Cent. Park Lodges (Tarpon Springs), Inc., 805 So. 2d 6 (Fla. Dist. Ct. App. 2001) ("When the 'party opposing arbitration disputes the existence or validity of the agreement to arbitrate, the trial court must resolve that issue as a part of its consideration of the motion seeking to compel arbitration.'"); Hill v. Ray Carter Auto Sales, Inc., 745 So. 2d 1136, 1138 (Fla. Dist. Ct. App. 1999); J.M. Davidson, Inc. v. Webster, 128 S.W.3d 223 (Tex. 2003) (whether an agreement imposes a duty on the parties to arbitrate a dispute is a matter of contract interpretation and, thus, a question of law for the court).
213 First Options of Chicago, Inc. v. Kaplan, 514 U.S. 938, 115 S. Ct. 1920, 131 L. Ed. 2d 985 (1995) ("When deciding whether

cordingly, courts regularly turn to state law in resolving these questions.[214]

3.4.3 State Law Determines Whether a Contract Defense Applicable to an Arbitration Clause Bars the Clause's Enforceability

The FAA states that arbitration clauses are enforceable "save upon grounds as exist at law or in equity for the revocation of any contract."[215] The Supreme Court has stated that arbitration clauses can be voided under state law, but only on grounds that would apply generally to any contract provision.[216] The FAA does set limits on how state law can regulate arbitration. But within those limits, state law applies to determine an arbitration clause's validity.[217]

Despite the "liberal federal policy favoring arbitration agreements," *Green Tree Fin. Corp.—Alabama v. Randolph*, 531 U.S. 79, 81 (2000), state law is not entirely displaced from federal arbitration analysis. Under [FAA] § 2, "state law, whether of legislative or judicial origin, is applicable *if* that law arose to govern issues concerning the validity, revocability, and enforceability of contracts generally." *Perry v. Thomas*, 482 U.S. 483, 492 n.9 (1987) (emphasis in original).[218]

Even courts that have rejected unconscionability arguments against particular arbitration clauses have done so based upon analysis of applicable state law.[219]

This principle means that not only state common law, but also state statutory law regulating contracts should apply. For example, New Mexico in 2001 enacted an amendment to its Uniform Arbitration Act which limits "disabling civil dispute clauses" in consumer transactions, such as clauses which require a forum that is less convenient, more costly, or more dilatory than a court action; that limit the consumer's ability to discover evidence; and that limit the consumer's ability to pursue a claim as a class.[220]

Because compliance with state law is a prerequisite to enforcement of arbitration clauses, it follows that courts rather than arbitrators determine whether an arbitration

---

the parties agreed to arbitrate a certain matter . . . courts generally . . . should apply ordinary state-law principles that govern the formation of contracts."); *see also* W.M. Schlosser Co. v. Sch. Bd., 980 F.2d 253, 259 (4th Cir. 1992) ("Section 2 [of the FAA] dictates the effect of a contractually agreed-upon provision, but it does not displace state law on the general principles governing the formation of the contract itself."); Casteel v. Clear Channel Broad., 254 F. Supp. 2d 1081, 1087 (W.D. Ark. 2003) ("It is for the court to decide whether an agreement to arbitrate is valid. . . . The validity of an arbitration agreement is determined by reference to state law."); Baychar, Inc. v. Frisby Tech., Inc., 2001 U.S. Dist. LEXIS 11037 (D. Me. July 26, 2001) ("when determining whether the parties agree to arbitrate, federal courts utilize general state law principles of contract law"); Myers v. MBNA Am., 2001 WL 965063, at *3 (D. Mont. Mar. 20, 2001) ("[T]here is no federal law of contracts. State law *must* supply the laws and tests to determine whether an arbitration clause is a binding contract."); The Money Place v. Barnes, 349 Ark. 411, 413, 78 S.W.3d 714 (Ark. 2002).

214 *E.g.*, Bailey v. Fed. Nat'l Mortgage Ass'n, 209 F.3d 740 (D.C. Cir. 2000) (D.C. law); *In re* Taylor, 260 B.R. 548, 559 (Bankr. M.D. Fla. 2000) ("the United States Supreme Court has interpreted the phrase 'such grounds as exist in law or in equity for the revocation of any contract' to stand for the proposition that state law controls any inquiry into fraud, duress or unconscionability in procuring an arbitration clause"); Badie v. Bank of Am., 67 Cal. App. 4th 779, 79 Cal. Rptr. 2d 273 (1998) (Cal. law); Quigley v. KPMG Peat Marwick, LLP, 330 N.J. Super. 252, 749 A.2d 405 (Super. Ct. App. Div. 2000) ("[I]n determining whether the parties have agreed to arbitrate, state law contract principles apply."); Frizzell Constr. Co. v. Gatlinburg, 9 S.W.3d 79 (Tenn. 1999) (Tenn. law).

215 9 U.S.C. § 2.

216 Doctor's Associates, Inc. v. Casarotto, 517 U.S. 681, 116 S. Ct. 1652, 134 L. Ed. 2d 902 (1996); *see also* Shearson/American Express, Inc. v. McMahon, 482 U.S. 220, 107 S. Ct. 2332, 96 L. Ed. 2d 185 (1987); Baychar, Inc. v. Frisby Technologies, Inc., 230 F. Supp. 2d 75 (D. Me. 2002) (presumption of arbitrability does not come into play until "the Court finds that the parties have agreed to arbitrate a claim").

The Third Circuit has in the past stood this doctrine on its head, indicating that general state rules as to the enforceability of contract terms do not apply to arbitration clauses. Instead federal law should determine the unconscionability of an arbitration provision, not the state's law as to unconscionability. *See* Harris v. Green Tree Fin. Corp, 183 F.3d 173 (3d Cir. 1999).

Hopefully, other courts will reject this patently wrong interpretation. *See* First Options of Chicago, Inc. v. Kaplan, 514 U.S. 938, 115 S. Ct. 1920, 131 L. Ed. 2d 985 (1995) (courts "should apply ordinary state-law principles that govern the formation of contracts"); Discover Bank v. Super. Ct., 36 Cal. 4th 148, 113 P.3d 1100 (2005) (waiver of class arbitration in consumer contract of adhesion was unconscionable; state law provision banning class action waivers in consumer contracts not preempted by FAA).

217 *See, e.g.*, Alexander v. Anthony Int'l, Ltd. P'ship, 341 F.3d 256, 264 (3d Cir. 2003) ("But a court, before directing the parties to proceed with this favored method of dispute resolution, must still ascertain whether the parties entered a valid agreement to arbitrate. We are to look to the relevant state law of contracts in making this determination." (citation omitted)).

218 Ticknor v. Choice Hotels Int'l, Inc., 265 F.3d 931, 936 (9th Cir. 2001).

219 *See, e.g.*, Bess v. Check Express, 294 F.3d 1298 (11th Cir. 2002) (finding clause conscionable under Alabama law); DiMercurio v. Sphere Drake Ins., PLC, 202 F.3d 71, 81 (1st Cir. 2000) (finding clause conscionable under Massachusetts law); We Care Hair Dev., Inc. v. Engen, 180 F.3d 838, 843 (7th Cir. 1999) (finding clause conscionable under Illinois law); Barker v. Golf U.S.A., Inc., 154 F.3d 788, 793 (8th Cir. 1998) (finding clause conscionable under Oklahoma law); Discover Bank v. Super. Ct., 36 Cal. 4th 148, 113 P.3d 1100 (2005) (waiver of class arbitration in consumer contract of adhesion was unconscionable; state law provision banning class action waivers in consumer contracts not preempted by FAA).

220 2001 N.M. Laws 227, § 5 (codified at N.M. Stat. § 44-7A-5) (2001 N.M. Laws 227 adopted the Uniform Arbitration Act with amendments).

clause is valid and enforceable.[221] Thus, even the Alabama Supreme Court, among the most pro-arbitration courts in the United States, has stated: " 'Where the attack is addressed to the arbitration clause itself, as opposed to the contract as a whole, the court, and not the arbitrator, resolves the issue.' Thus, the threshold 'issue of unconscionability of an *arbitration clause* is a question for the court and not the arbitrator.' "[222] Likewise, the Texas Supreme Court, which at one time required arbitration of challenges to arbitration clauses based on substantive unconscionability,[223] has clarified that courts (not arbitrators) must decide whether an arbitration clause is unconscionable.[224] Appellate courts thus will reverse a trial court decision that fails to conduct an inquiry into the conscionability of the arbitration clause.[225]

3.4.4 Agreement to Arbitrate "Arbitrability Disputes" Does Not Displace Right Under FAA to Judicial Determination As to Existence and Enforceability of Arbitration Clause

Some businesses have been attempting to avoid the FAA's requirement for a judicial determination as to the existence and validity of an agreement to arbitrate by drafting clauses that require arbitration of disputes over "arbitrability." This argument should not succeed because the FAA and long-standing judicial interpretations of the Act recognize that arbitration is *solely* the product of a contract between parties and, therefore, a court must first determine for itself whether an agreement to arbitrate exists, whether the agreement is enforceable, and whether the agreement covers the parties' particular dispute *before* it can order parties into arbitration.[226]

Section 4 of the FAA empowers courts to compel arbitration of disputes only "upon being satisfied that the making of the arbitration agreement is not in issue."[227] Section 2 of the Act provides that contractual arbitration agreements shall be enforceable "save upon such grounds as exist at law or in equity for the revocation of any contract."[228] In *Prima Paint Corp. v. Flood & Conklin Manufacturing Co.*,[229] the Supreme Court held that, although a claim of fraud in the inducement of a contract containing an arbitration clause can be subject to arbitration, a court must resolve any claim of fraud in the inducement of the arbitration clause itself before the clause may be enforced and arbitration required under the FAA. The Supreme Court explained:

> This position is consistent with the [FAA's] statutory scheme. As the "saving clause" in § 2 indicates, the purpose of Congress in 1925 was to make arbitration agreements as enforceable as

---

221 *See, e.g.*, Nagrampa v. Mailcoups, Inc., 469 F.3d 1257, 1264 (9th Cir. 2006) (en banc) ("When the crux of the complaint is not the invalidity of the contract as a whole, but rather the arbitration provision itself, then the federal courts must decide whether the arbitration provision is invalid and unenforceable under 9 U.S.C. § 2 of the FAA."); Muhammad v. County Bank of Rehoboth Beach, 912 A.2d 88, 96 (N.J. 2006) ("Those class-arbitration waivers, based on their location and subject matter, are part of the arbitration agreements, and not part of the contracts as a whole. As such, we are empowered to address this challenge.").

222 Am. Gen. Fin., Inc. v. Branch, 793 So. 2d 738 (Ala. 2000) (citations omitted); *accord* Anderson v. Ashby, 2003 WL 21125998 (Ala. May 16, 2003) (court decides unconscionability claims even when contract says that questions of arbitrability are for the arbitrator); *see also* Barker v. Golf U.S.A., Inc., 154 F.3d 788, 791 (8th Cir. 1998) (court, not arbitrator, must decide unconscionability claims "that go to the making of the arbitration agreement itself"); Plaskett v. Bechtel Int'l, 243 F. Supp. 2d 334, 339 (D. V.I. 2003) ("The Court applies general contract principles of territorial law in determining whether an arbitration agreement is enforceable.... A term of an arbitration agreement that is unconscionable is unenforceable."); Prevot v. Phillips Petroleum Co., 133 F. Supp. 2d 937 (S.D. Tex. 2001) (procedural unconscionability "claims are for the Court to decide when they relate specifically to the arbitration clause"); Haga v. Martin Homes, Inc., 1999 WL 254530 (Ohio Ct. App. Apr. 19, 1999) (consumers "are not required to prove through arbitration proceedings the arbitration provision is unconscionable," this issue was for the trial court), *aff'd in part, rev'd in part*, 2000 WL 1133267 (Ohio Ct. App. Aug. 4, 2000).

223 *See, e.g., In re* Oakwood Mobile Homes, Inc., 987 S.W.2d 571, 573 (Tex. 1999).

224 *See In re* Halliburton Co., 80 S.W.3d 566, 572 (Tex. 2002).

225 *See* Burden v. Check Into Cash of Ky., 267 F.3d 483 (6th Cir. 2001); Chapman & Villaire v. King Motor Co. of S. Fla., 833 So. 2d 820 (Fla. Dist. Ct. App. 2002); Pulte Home Corp. v. Smith, 823 So. 2d 305 (Fla. Dist. Ct. App. 2002); Battle v. Bill Swad Chevrolet, Inc., 746 N.E.2d 1167 (Ohio Ct. App. 2000).

226 *See, e.g.*, Casteel v. Clear Channel Broad., Inc., 254 F. Supp. 2d 1081, 1087 (W.D. Ark. 2003) ("It is for the court to decide whether an agreement to arbitrate is valid."); Curtis v. Olson, 837 So. 2d 1155, 1156, 1157 (Fla. Dist. Ct. App. 2003) (court must determine validity and scope of agreement before it can order parties to arbitrate); Allstate Ins. Co. v. Stinebaugh, 374 Md. 631, 824 A.2d 87 (2003) (court's role in deciding motion to compel arbitration is to determine "[i]s there an agreement to arbitrate the subject matter of a particular dispute?"); Brown v. Anderson, 102 S.W.3d 245, 248 (Tex. App. 2003) (court must determine existence and scope of agreement to arbitrate).

Note, however, that when a party has already insisted post-dispute that an arbitrator should decide arbitrability, she cannot then turn around and question the arbitrator's ruling on the basis that the arbitrator had no power to determine the arbitrability question. *See* Poweragent Inc. v. Elec. Data Sys. Corp., 358 F.3d 1187 (9th Cir. 2004).

227 9 U.S.C. § 4.

228 9 U.S.C. § 2.

229 388 U.S. 395, 403–404, 87 S. Ct. 1801, 18 L. Ed 2d 1270 (1967).

other contracts, *but not more so*. To immunize an arbitration agreement from judicial challenge on the ground of fraud in the inducement would be to elevate it over other forms of contract—a situation inconsistent with the "saving clause."[230]

A court therefore must resolve a party's challenges to the making or validity of an arbitration clause before it can order a case into arbitration.[231] As there can be no arbitration without the existence of a valid agreement, a party should not be able to evade this core requirement of the FAA simply by drafting its arbitration clause so that it covers disputes over arbitrability.

Some parties seeking to compel arbitration have recently begun arguing that an opposing party's challenges to the validity of an arbitration clause, including the claim that an arbitration clause is unconscionable, can be forced into arbitration based on the Supreme Court's decision in *First Options of Chicago, Inc. v. Kaplan*.[232] In *First Options*, it was undisputed that there was a valid arbitration agreement between a stock trade clearing firm and an investment company wholly owned by the Kaplans. But the parties disagreed, first, over whether the *scope* of the arbitration clause was broad enough to cover a claim by the clearing firm to recover the investment company's debts from the company's owners and, second, over whether a court or an arbitrator should resolve the first dispute over the scope of the arbitration agreement.[233] In answering the second question, *First Options* held that a court ordinarily should decide whether a particular dispute is covered by an arbitration clause but also stated that the parties may, by "clear and unmistakable language," allow an arbitrator to make this arbitrability determination.[234] Because *First Options* involved only the question of whether a court or an arbitrator should determine the scope of a valid arbitration clause, the court had no occasion to revisit *Prima Paint*'s holding that a court must first pass on the existence and validity of an arbitration clause before it can order parties into arbitration under the FAA.

Nor did the Supreme Court have occasion to revisit this holding of *Prima Paint* in two recent decisions recognizing that the FAA reserves certain procedural and contractual *interpretation* questions for arbitrators. In *Howsam v. Dean Witter Reynolds, Inc.*,[235] the Court held that an arbitrator must decide whether a party's claims were timely filed within the limitations period set out in the procedural rules adopted in an arbitration clause. In so holding, *Howsam* recognized that "a gateway dispute about whether the parties are bound by a given arbitration clause raises a 'question of arbitrability' for a court to decide."[236] Likewise the Court's holding in *PacifiCare Health Systems, Inc. v. Book*,[237] that an arbitrator has to decide whether a contract term prohibiting arbitral awards of punitive damages would bar claims for treble RICO damages, involved strictly a matter of contract interpretation and therefore does not limit a court's authority to decide the separate question of whether an arbitration agreement is valid and enforceable as a matter of state contract law.

Consumers opposing a business's motion to compel arbitration should be prepared to respond to the argument that *First Options* requires them to arbitrate their challenges to the existence or validity of the arbitration clause. The response should be that *First Options* addresses whether a court or an arbitrator should resolve an "arbitrability" dispute over the *scope* of an arbitration clause, a dispute that only requires interpretation of an admittedly valid arbitration clause.[238] Even in such instances, *First Options* held that the issue is presumptively for a court to decide but may be turned over to an arbitrator by clear and explicit contractual language. *First Options* did not involve, and therefore does not address, claims challenging the very existence and validity of an arbitration clause.[239] Therefore, based on the earlier decision in *Prima Paint*, these claims must be de-

---

230 388 U.S. at 404 n.12 (emphasis added).
231 *See* Spahr v. Secco, 330 F.3d 1266, 1273 (10th Cir. 2003) (holding that the question of whether an arbitration clause was unenforceable because the party who signed it was mentally incompetent at the time of signing places the "making" of the agreement to arbitrate at issue, and therefore falls under section 4 of the FAA); Matterhorn, Inc. v. NCR Corp., 763 F.2d 866, 867 (7th Cir. 1985) ("[A]lthough section 4 . . . speaks only of challenges to 'the making' of the agreement to arbitrate, the term has been held to encompass any challenge to the validity of the agreement, even if there is no disagreement that it was 'made.' ").
232 514 U.S. 938, 115 S. Ct. 1920, 131 L. Ed 2d 985 (1995).
233 514 U.S. at 940, 941.
234 514 U.S. at 944, 945.
235 537 U.S. 79, 123 S. Ct. 588, 154 L. Ed. 2d 491 (2002).
236 537 U.S. at 84.
237 538 U.S. 401, 123 S. Ct. 1531, 155 L. Ed. 2d 578 (2003).
238 *See, e.g.*, Wilson v. Wells Fargo Fin. Acceptance, Inc., 2003 WL 1877336 (M.D. Tenn. Apr. 9, 2003) (holding that, under *Howsam*, the question of whether parties' claims are covered by the arbitration clause is for the arbitrator when the parties' contract "clearly and unmistakably" states that questions of scope are for the arbitrator; holding further that the arbitrator should decide any questions of contract ambiguity concerning the scope of the arbitration clause); Bahuriak v. Bill Kay Chrysler Plymouth, Inc., 786 N.E.2d 1045, 1050 (Ill. App. Ct. 2003) (under FAA and state law, clause providing for arbitration of arbitrability disputes gives arbitrator authority to decide scope of valid arbitration clause).
239 This differentiation between challenges to the scope of a valid arbitration agreement and challenges to the existence of such an agreement defines the boundaries of the "liberal federal policy favoring arbitration" under the FAA. *See, e.g.*, Equal Employment Opportunity Comm'n v. Waffle House, Inc., 534 U.S. 279, 122 S. Ct. 754, 764, 151 L. Ed 2d 755 (2002) ("Because the FAA is at bottom a policy guaranteeing the enforcement of private contractual arrangements, we look first to whether the parties agreed to arbitrate a dispute, not to general policy goals, to determine the scope of the agreement." (citation omitted)); Moses H. Cone Mem'l Hosp. v. Mercury Constr. Corp., 460 U.S. 1, 24, 103 S. Ct. 927, 74 L. Ed 2d 765 (1983) ("The Arbitration Act establishes that . . . any doubts concerning the

cided by a court as a precondition to the court's authority to order arbitration under the FAA.[240]

The Fifth Circuit has articulated the logic of this position in a case in which the defendant argued that the plaintiff had rejected its offer of a purchase agreement by not providing all necessary signatures to the agreement and, thus, that there was never any contract between the parties.[241] The court held that the question of the formation of a contract containing an arbitration agreement was for the court, even when the parties had clearly signed the arbitration clause:

> [W]here the very existence of an agreement is challenged, ordering arbitration could result in an arbitrator deciding that no agreement was ever formed. Such an outcome would be a statement that the arbitrator *never* had any authority to decide the issue. A presumption that a signed document represents an agreement could lead to this untenable result. We therefore conclude that where a party attacks the very existence of an agreement, as opposed to its continued validity or enforcement, the courts must first resolve that dispute.[242]

This statement is a nice common-sense summation of the conclusion reached by *First Options* and *Prima Paint*: when the question is whether a contract containing an arbitration clause was ever formed in the first place, the court must step in to answer that question.[243]

3.4.5 One Big Exception: FAA Determines Severability, Requires Arbitrator *to* Decide Validity of General Contract Provisions

The Supreme Court has created a narrow, but important, exception to the FAA's application of state contract law. When a contract contains an arbitration clause, and a party challenges the validity of the entire contract based on fraudulent or unlawful provisions that do not relate to arbitration, the Supreme Court has held that the FAA makes the arbitration clause severable thus requiring the parties to arbitrate these issues.

In *Prima Paint, Corp. v. Flood & Conklin Manufacturing Co.*,[244] the Supreme Court held that, although a court could decide a claim of fraudulent inducement of the arbitration clause itself,[245] the FAA requires that the parties arbitrate a claim that the contract as a whole was fraudulently induced.[246] The Supreme Court found that the FAA made the arbitration clause severable from the rest of the contract, *regardless of whether state contract law provided for severability*.[247]

Subsequently, in *Buckeye Check Cashing, Inc. v. Cardegna*,[248] the Supreme Court reaffirmed *Prima Paint* and extended its holding to require parties to arbitrate a claim that a payday loan contract's usurious interest provision rendered the entire contract (including its arbitration clause) void *ab initio*. In reversing the Florida Supreme Court's holding that state contract law prohibited severing or preserving any part of an illegal contract that was void at its inception, the Supreme Court in *Buckeye* held that *Prima Paint* had "rejected application of state severability rules to the arbitration agreement *without discussing* whether the challenge at issue would have rendered the contract void or voidable."[249] Thus, in this one instance, the FAA preempts even generally applicable state contract law as it would apply to determine the severability of an arbitration clause from the contract in which it appears.

Although it is important to understand the *Prima Paint* and *Buckeye* decisions in assessing the arguments that are available for challenging an arbitration clause, the severability rule theses cases apply is fairly narrow. As *Buckeye* itself recognized, this severability rule for challenges to the *validity* of contract provisions does not necessarily apply to challenges to the *formation* of contracts with arbitration clauses, as questions of assent to different provisions may not be divisible.[250] *Buckeye* thus leaves in place the numer-

---

scope of arbitrable issues should be resolved in favor of arbitration.").

240 *See, e.g.*, Prevot v. Phillips Petroleum Co., 133 F. Supp. 2d 937, 939 (S.D. Tex. 2001) (holding post-*First Options* that court must decide whether or not arbitration clause is unconscionable even when clause provides for arbitration of arbitrability disputes); Anderson v. Ashby, 873 So. 2d 168 (Ala. 2003) (same); Am. Gen. Fin., Inc. v. Branch, 793 So. 2d 738, 748 (Ala. 2000) (same). *But see* Bell v. Cendant Corp., 293 F.3d 563, 567, 568 (2d Cir. 2002) (holding that "arbitrate arbitrability" clause requires arbitrator to determine scope of arbitration agreement; stating in dictum that arbitrator could also determine validity of underlying arbitration agreement); Berkley v. H & R Block E. Tax Services, Inc., 30 S.W.3d 341, 344 (Tenn. Ct. App. 2000) (citing *First Options* in support of holding that challenge to enforceability of arbitration clause must be arbitrated when clause so provides).

241 Will-Drill Res., Inc. v. Samson Res. Co., 352 F.3d 211 (5th Cir. 2003).

242 *Id.* at 219.

243 For a case in which an arbitrator determined that he had no power to hear a case because the consumer had never actually agreed to the contract containing the arbitration clause, and thus dismissed the arbitration proceeding, see McIntyre v. Household Bank, 2004 WL 1088228 (N.D. Ill. May 14, 2004) (denying bank's motion to continue staying litigation pending arbitration when the arbitrator had determined that there was no valid contract and thus no valid agreement to arbitrate).

244 388 U.S. 395, 87 S. Ct. 1801, 18 L. Ed. 2d 1270 (1967).
245 *Id.*, 388 U.S. at 403–404.
246 *Id.*
247 *Id.*, 388 U.S. at 402–403.
248 546 U.S. 440, 126 S. Ct. 1204, 163 L. Ed. 2d 1038 (2006).
249 *Id.*, 546 U.S. at 446 (emphasis in original).
250 *Id.*, 546 U.S. at 444 n.1.

ous federal circuit court decisions holding that courts, not arbitrators, decide questions concerning *assent* to a contract containing an arbitration clause.[251]

Likewise, and perhaps most importantly, *Buckeye* does not disturb *Prima Paint*'s recognition that courts (not arbitrators) must resolve challenges to the making or validity of an arbitration clause itself.[252] Thus, federal and state courts have continued after *Buckeye* to decide for themselves whether an arbitration clause is unconscionable or otherwise unenforceable, even when some parts of an unconscionability argument may also apply to the whole contract, so long as "the crux of the complaint is not the invalidity of the contract as a whole, but rather the arbitration provision itself."[253]

---

251 *Id.* (citing Spahr v. Secco, 330 F.3d 1266 (10th Cir. 2003); Sphere Drake Ins. Ltd. v. All Am. Ins. Co., 256 F.3d 587 (7th Cir. 2001); Sandvik AB v. Advent Int'l Corp., 220 F.3d 99 (3d Cir. 2000); Chastain v. Robinson-Humphrey Co., 957 F.2d 851 (11th Cir. 1992)).

252 *Buckeye*, 546 U.S. at 445 (quoting *Prima Paint*, 388 U.S. at 403–404).

253 Nagrampa v. Mailcoups, Inc., 469 F.3d 1257, 1264 (9th Cir. 2006) (en banc); *see also* Muhammad v. County Bank of Rehoboth Beach, 912 A.2d 88, 96 (N.J. 2006) ("Those class-arbitration waivers, based on their location and subject matter, are part of the arbitration agreements, and not part of the contracts as a whole. As such, we are empowered to address this challenge.").

Chapter 4   When the FAA's Enforcement of Arbitration Clause Conflicts with Another Federal Statute

4.1 Introduction

Claims under federal statutes generally are subject to mandatory arbitration when there is a valid agreement to arbitrate such a claim. The Supreme Court has held that claims under a variety of statutes (including RICO, the antitrust statutes, the Age Discrimination in Employment Act, and the Truth In Lending Act) may be the subject of mandatory binding predispute arbitration clauses. The Supreme Court has recognized three types of exceptions to this general rule, however.

First, claims under some federal statutes may be precluded from all predispute binding arbitration. While the Supreme Court has not yet identified any statutes that fall within this category, Congress in recent years has enacted several bills that expressly prohibit enforcement of arbitration clauses. In addition, the lower federal and state courts have identified several statutes that explicitly or implicitly limit the use of arbitration. Section 4.2.1, *infra*, discusses the standards that the Supreme Court has set forth to use to identify such statutes. Section 4.2.2, *infra*, discusses authorities which indicate that when a written warranty is offered under the Magnuson-Moss Warranty Act, claims may not be subject to predispute binding arbitration. Section 4.2.3, *infra*, discusses whether claims involving the United States Bankruptcy Code may be forced into arbitration.

Second, even if a claim under a federal statute may properly be subject to predispute binding arbitration, the arbitration system at issue must still permit the consumer to obtain the full range of remedies provided by that statute. Arbitration clauses that explicitly circumscribe statutory remedies have repeatedly been found unenforceable, as is described in § 4.3, *infra*.

Third, arbitration clauses will not be enforced if the arbitration system at issue, while not explicitly limiting a statutory right, nevertheless by its operation prevents the effective vindication of rights under a federal statute. Section 4.4, *infra*, addresses the question whether high arbitration fees restrict the effective vindication of statutory claims, therefore making the arbitration requirement unenforceable.

4.2 FAA's Per Se Inconsistency with Specified Federal Statutes

4.2.1 Standard for Determining Whether a Federal Statute Prohibits or Restricts Use of Arbitration

4.2.1.1 General

Consumers who oppose a defendant's attempt to compel arbitration of their federal statutory claims face formidable, but not necessarily insurmountable, obstacles in arguing that the statute giving rise to their claims prohibits some or all arbitration. The party seeking access to court bears the burden of demonstrating that Congress intended to prohibit a waiver of judicial remedies.[1] This burden is a heavy one that a party cannot satisfy merely by pointing to Congress's provision of a judicial forum under a statute without identifying something more which indicates Congress's intent to restrict or prohibit resort to private arbitration.[2]

Several recently enacted federal laws contain express prohibitions against mandatory arbitration clauses that prevent courts from ordering parties to certain types of disputes into arbitration. First, Congress has prohibited lenders from enforcing arbitration clauses against consumers who are military servicemembers or their dependents.[3] This prohi-

---

1 Gilmer v. Interstate/Johnson Lane Corp., 500 U.S. 20, 26, 111 S. Ct. 1647, 114 L. Ed. 2d 26 (1991); Shearson/American Express, Inc. v. McMahon, 482 U.S. 220, 227, 107 S. Ct. 2332, 96 L. Ed. 2d 185 (1987).

2 *Gilmer*, 500 U.S. at 29 ("Gilmer also argues that compulsory arbitration is improper because it deprives claimants of the judicial forum provided for in the [Age Discrimination in Employment Act]. Congress, however, did not explicitly preclude arbitration or other nonjudicial resolution of claims, even in its recent amendments to the ADEA.").

3 10 U.S.C. § 987(f)(4) ("Arbitration. Notwithstanding section 2 of title 9, or any other Federal or State law, rule, or regulation, no agreement to arbitrate any dispute involving the extension of consumer credit shall be enforceable against any covered member or dependent of such a member, or any person who was a covered member or dependent of that member when the agreement was made.").

bition expressly supersedes the Federal Arbitration Act. Second, and ironically, Congress has exempted car *dealers* from mandatory predispute arbitration clauses in their contracts with automotive manufacturers by requiring *postdispute* consent.[4] Congress thus is showing an increasing willingness to place limits on the FAA's policy favoring arbitration.

Although federal policy favoring the enforcement of arbitration agreements colors the inquiry into statutory restrictions on the use of arbitration,[5] the Supreme Court has explained repeatedly that arbitration of federal statutory claims is a matter of congressional intent which the Federal Arbitration Act alone does not resolve:

> Just as it is the congressional policy manifested in the Federal Arbitration Act that requires courts liberally to construe the scope of arbitration agreements covered by that Act, it is the congressional intent expressed in some other statute on which the courts must rely to identify any category of claims as to which agreements to arbitrate will be held unenforceable.[6]

Thus, "[l]ike any other statutory directive, the Arbitration Act's mandate may be overridden by a contrary congressional command."[7] The focal point for federal policy with regard to arbitration of federal statutory claims therefore is the statute which gives rise to a particular claim.

Prohibitions or restrictions on the use of arbitration need not be explicit in the text of a statute. The Supreme Court has emphasized that "[i]f Congress did intend to limit or prohibit waiver of a judicial forum for a particular claim, such an intent 'will be deducible from [the statute's] text *or* legislative history *or* from an inherent conflict between arbitration and the statute's underlying purposes.' "[8] Congress's intent to preserve a claimant's access to the courts thus may be inferred despite the absence of a plain statement in Congress's enactment of a statute. What is more, this inference may arise out of the text and structure of the Act itself, the Act's legislative history, *or* the underlying purposes of the Act, and need not be drawn from all of these sources.

4.2.1.2 Does Arbitration Allow Vindication of Statute's Purpose?

But the courts will not routinely find that a federal statute prohibits enforcement of arbitration agreements. Even when a statute serves a strong congressional purpose, claims under that statute may often be subject to mandatory arbitration out of the belief that arbitration will serve the purposes of the particular statute as well as a court proceeding. When a statute's remedial scheme is intended both to address individual grievances and to further important social policy goals, courts generally presume that either a judicial or an arbitral forum can fulfill each of these goals.[9]

The corollary to this principle is that an agreement to arbitrate a federal statutory claim is *not* enforceable if submission of that claim to an arbitral forum *does* prevent the consumer from effectively vindicating their rights under the statutory cause of action. If the litigant cannot effectively vindicate a statutory cause of action through arbitration, there is a conflict between arbitration and the federal statute's underlying purposes, and the arbitration clause is therefore unenforceable.[10] An arbitration provision which solely offers an alternative forum cannot strip the consumer of rights under a federal statute or in any way conflict with the terms or purposes of that statute.[11]

4.2.1.3 Specific Examples

Courts examining claims under a variety of federal statutes have concluded that Congress intended to prohibit predispute binding arbitration of such claims. A substantial body of case law has interpreted the Magnuson-Moss Warranty Act[12] to prohibit warrantors from forcing consumers to resolve their disputes through binding arbitration.[13] Likewise, courts have held that the federal Bankruptcy Code's creation of an exclusive forum for certain bankruptcy-related matters gives the bankruptcy judge discretion to avoid enforcement of private arbitration agreements.[14]

---

4 15 U.S.C. § 1226(a)(2) ("Notwithstanding any other provision of law, whenever a motor vehicle franchise contract provides for the use of arbitration to resolve a controversy arising out of or relating to such contract, arbitration may be used to settle such controversy only if after such controversy arises all parties to such controversy consent in writing to use arbitration to settle such controversy.").

5 *Gilmer*, 500 U.S. at 26.

6 Mitsubishi Motors Corp. v. Soler Chrysler-Plymouth, Inc., 473 U.S. 614, 627, 105 S. Ct. 3346, 87 L. Ed. 2d 444 (1985).

7 *McMahon*, 482 U.S. at 226; *see also Gilmer*, 500 U.S. at 26 ("all statutory claims may not be appropriate for arbitration").

8 Shearson/American Express, Inc. v. McMahon, 482 U.S. 220, 226, 107 S. Ct. 2332, 96 L. Ed. 2d 185 (1987) (citation omitted) (emphasis added) (quoting Mitsubishi Motors Corp. v. Soler Chrysler-Plymouth, Inc., 473 U.S. 614, 628, 105 S. Ct. 3346, 87 L. Ed. 2d 444 (1985)).

9 *Mitsubishi Motors*, 473 U.S. at 628 ("By agreeing to arbitrate a statutory claim, a party does not forgo the substantive rights afforded by the statute; it only submits to their resolution in an arbitral, rather than a judicial, forum."); *accord Gilmer*, 500 U.S. at 26 (same).

10 *See* § 4.3, *infra*.

11 Graham Oil Co. v. ARCO Products Co., 43 F.3d 1244 (9th Cir. 1994); *see also* Spinetti v. Serv. Corp. Int'l, 324 F.3d 212 (3d Cir. 2003); Morrison v. Circuit City Stores, Inc., 317 F.3d 646 (6th Cir. 2003) (en banc); Paladino v. Avnet Computer Technologies, Inc., 134 F.3d 1054 (11th Cir. 1998).

12 15 U.S.C. §§ 2301–2312.

13 *See* § 4.2.2, *infra*.

14 *See* § 4.2.3, *infra*.

While these two statutes and the bodies of case law that have developed around them are addressed more fully in separate sections of this chapter, the following is a summary of other statutes that particular courts have found to prohibit mandatory arbitration of consumer or employee claims.

In *Alexander v. U.S. Credit Management, Inc.*,[15] the federal district court held that consumers asserting claims under the Credit Repair Organizations Act (CROA)[16] could not be forced into arbitration because of the statute's provision invalidating "[a]ny waiver by any consumer of any protection provided by or any right of the consumer under this title."[17] The Court found that this provision prohibited waivers of a consumer's "right to sue" under the Act,[18] and that the text and legislative history of the Act demonstrated that "a right to sue is a right to sue in a court of law."[19]

Arguments that statutes prohibit mandatory arbitration have succeeded more frequently, although not very frequently, in employment cases. At one time, the Ninth Circuit stood alone in holding, in *Duffield v. Robertson Stephens & Co.*, that the 1991 Civil Rights Act prohibits employers from using predispute arbitration agreements that require employees to waive their right to bring future Title VII claims in court as a condition of employment.[20] However, the Ninth Circuit sitting en banc overruled *Duffield*, holding that Congress did not intend for Title VII claims to be exempt from arbitration.[21]

In *Pram Nguyen v. City of Cleveland*,[22] a federal district court applied a similar analysis in holding that predispute contracts making submission of claims to arbitration a condition of employment were inconsistent with the purposes of the anti-retaliation provision of the False Claims Act (FCA).[23] The court in *Pram Nguyen* treated the *qui tam* relator plaintiff as an agent of the federal government and found the Act's provision of federal jurisdiction to be a protection whose waiver could not be compelled by a private employer.[24] The court also noted that the conflict between mandatory arbitration and the FCA's protection of whistleblowers precluded arbitration even though the Act's text and legislative history were silent on arbitration.[25]

In addressing another employment law issue involving the rights of returning military servicemembers to be reinstated to their jobs, two federal district courts (one of which was subsequently reversed) have held that the Uniformed Services Employment and Reemployment Rights Act of 1994 (USERRA)[26] prohibits employers from enforcing arbitration clauses against returning servicemen and women who are asserting claims for reinstatement to their pre-active duty jobs.[27] These courts have found that USERRA's provision stating that it "supercedes any ... contract ... that reduces, limits, or eliminates in any manner any right or benefit provided by this chapter[,] including the establishment of additional prerequisites to the exercise of any such right,"[28] bars enforcement of contracts requiring arbitration as an "additional prerequisite to the exercise of plaintiff's rights."[29]

---

15 384 F. Supp. 2d 1003 (N.D. Tex. 2005).
16 15 U.S.C. §§ 1679–1679i.
17 *Alexander*, 384 F. Supp. 2d at 1009 (quoting 15 U.S.C. § 1679f(a)).
18 *Id.* at 1011–1012.
19 *Id.* at 1016. *But see* Rex v. CSA-Credit Solutions of Am., Inc., 2007 U.S. Dist. LEXIS 46498, at *25 (W.D. Mich. June 27, 2007) ("In consideration of these Supreme Court cases [addressing other statutes], this Court cannot conclude that Congress intended claims under the CROA to be nonarbitrable.").
20 Duffield v. Robertson Stephens & Co., 144 F.3d 1182 (9th Cir. 1998).
21 Equal Employment Opportunity Comm'n v. Luce, Forward, Hamilton & Scripps, 345 F.3d 742 (9th Cir. 2003) (en banc).
    The Court's opinion in *Luce, Forward* brings the Ninth Circuit into line with the vast majority of other federal courts on the issue of Title VII arbitration. *See, e.g.*, Weeks v. Harden Mfg. Corp., 291 F.3d 1307 (11th Cir. 2002) ("We see no reason to depart from our own precedent, the mandate of the Supreme Court, and the holdings of almost every other circuit to find that compulsory arbitration agreements constitute an unlawful employment practice."); Desiderio v. Nat'l Ass'n of Sec. Dealers, Inc., 191 F.3d 198, 203, 204 (2d Cir. 1999) (text of 1991 Act unambiguously permits predispute binding arbitration of Title VII claims); Rosenberg v. Merrill Lynch, Pierce, Fenner & Smith, Inc., 170 F.3d 1 (1st Cir. 1999) (neither the text nor legislative history of the 1991 Civil Rights Act prohibits predispute binding arbitration); Koveleskie v. SBC Capital Markets, Inc., 167 F.3d 361, 365 (7th Cir. 1999) (text of 1991 Act unambiguously permits predispute arbitration of Title VII claims).

22 121 F. Supp. 2d 643 (N.D. Ohio 2000).
23 31 U.S.C. § 3730(h).
24 *Pram Nguyen*, 121 F. Supp. 2d at 646, 647 ("given the policies of the FCA, an employee who brings a claim against his employers as relator on behalf of the federal government should not be forced by unequal bargaining power to accept a forum demanded as a condition of employment by the very party on which he informed"). *But see also* United States v. Bankers Ins. Co., 245 F.3d 315 (4th Cir. 2001) (holding that government's FCA claims may be forced into arbitration pursuant to arbitration clause in contract drafted by government agency); Oldroyd v. Elmira Sav. Bank, 134 F.3d 72, 77, 78 (2d Cir. 1998) (rejecting claim that whistleblower protection provision of Financial Institutions Reform, Recovery, and Enforcement Act (FIRREA) precludes arbitration of claims).
25 *Pram Nguyen*, 121 F. Supp. 2d at 647.
    "Thus, while this Court does not find that the plain text of the whistleblower statute or the legislative history clearly demonstrate Congress's intention to except whistleblower retaliation claims from the Arbitration Act, it does find that a conflict exists between arbitration and the underlying purposes of the FCA." *Id.*
26 38 U.S.C. §§ 4301–4334.
27 *See* Lopez v. Dillard's, Inc., 382 F. Supp. 2d 1245 (D. Kan. 2005); Garrett v. Circuit City Stores, Inc., 338 F. Supp. 2d 717 (N.D. Tex. 2004), *rev'd*, 449 F.3d 672 (5th Cir. 2006).
28 38 U.S.C. § 4302(b).
29 *See, e.g.*, Lopez v. Dillard's, Inc., 382 F. Supp. 2d 1245 (D. Kan. 2005). *But see* Garrett v. Circuit City Stores, Inc., 449 F.3d 672, 677 (5th Cir. 2006) (holding that failure of USERRA to mention

One of these district court opinions was subsequently reversed on appeal by the Fifth Circuit, which held that USERRA prohibits waivers only of substantive rights, not forum-selection rights.[30] The Fifth Circuit's opinion seems to require a clear statement by Congress expressly prohibiting enforcement of arbitration clauses before a court will recognize any conflict between a statute creating substantive rights and the FAA.[31] The Fifth Circuit's ruling in the face of USERRA's broad and clear anti-waiver language demonstrates how difficult it can be for plaintiffs, at least in some courts, to argue that a federal statute prohibits arbitration.

In *Adkins v. Labor Ready, Inc.*, the Fourth Circuit recently determined that employment claims brought under the Fair Labor Standards Act (FLSA) are arbitrable, because there is no inherent conflict between the FLSA and the FAA.[32] The Court based its decision almost entirely on the similarities between the FLSA and the Age Discrimination in Employment Act, which the Supreme Court found in *Gilmer* did not conflict with the FAA.[33] Courts addressing a wide variety of other federal statutes likewise have rejected arguments that these statutes prohibit arbitration of claims.[34]

Finally, although this does not involve an express or implied statutory prohibition of arbitration clauses, the Federal Trade Commission has exercised its regulatory authority in at least one instance to persuade a major home building company, KB Home, to enter into a consent decree barring the company from imposing arbitration clauses against consumers.[35]

4.2.2 The Magnuson-Moss Warranty Act

4.2.2.1 Introduction

The federal Magnuson-Moss Warranty Act[36] permits warrantors to require that consumers resort to informal dispute resolution mechanisms to resolve their claims arising under the Act, but specifies that these mechanisms must be nonbinding, and that consumers retain the right to go to court to assert their claims. The text of the Act appears to explicitly prohibit binding informal dispute resolution procedures and guarantees consumers access to the courts to resolve their claims. Statements in the legislative history likewise demonstrate that the Act's sponsors understood that claimants would retain access to the courts. In light of this evidence, a number of courts have rejected warrantors' motions to compel binding arbitration and have held that the Magnuson-Moss Warranty Act only permits nonbinding arbitration of consumer claims. But a number of courts, including two federal circuit courts, have come to the opposite conclusion.

Although the party seeking access to court must demonstrate Congress's intent to prohibit a waiver of access to court, this burden is not meant to be prohibitive. The Supreme Court has explained that arbitration of federal statutory claims is a matter of congressional intent which the Federal Arbitration Act alone does not resolve.[37] "Like any other statutory directive, the Arbitration Act's mandate may be overridden by a contrary congressional command."[38] Congress's intent to carve out an exception to the policies of the Arbitration Act need not be explicit.[39] Congress's intent to preserve claimants' access to court thus may simply be inferred from the text, history, and underlying purposes of the Magnuson-Moss Act. The inference that Congress intended to preserve claimants' access to court is properly drawn because Magnuson-Moss places extensive restrictions on the use of informal dispute resolution procedures.

4.2.2.2 The Text and Structure of the Act

The Magnuson-Moss Warranty Act sets out specific requirements for disclosures, duties, remedies, and procedures relating to warranties on consumer products, creating an unqualified right of access to the courts for consumers claiming breach of warranty. "[A] consumer who is damaged by the failure of a supplier, warrantor, or service contractor to comply with an obligation under this title or under a written warranty, implied warranty, or service contract, may bring suit for damages and other legal and

---

arbitration or the FAA defeats argument that statute prohibits mandatory arbitration).

30 Garrett v. Circuit City Stores, Inc., 449 F.3d 672, 677–679 (5th Cir. 2006).

31 *Id.* at 677 ("[t]he text of [38 U.S.C.] § 4302(b) is not a clear expression of Congressional intent concerning the arbitration of servicemembers' employment disputes").

32 Adkins v. Labor Ready, Inc., 303 F.3d 496, 506 (4th Cir. 2002).

33 *Id.*

34 *See, e.g.*, Equal Employment Opportunity Comm'n v. Woodmen of the World Life Ins. Soc'y, 479 F.3d 561, 569–570 (8th Cir. 2007) (Title VII claims by employee intervening in EEOC enforcement action); Terrebone v. K-Sea Transp. Corp., 477 F.3d 271, 284–285 (5th Cir. 2007) (addressing claims under the Jones Act, 46 U.S.C. § 688, governing rights of injured seamen); Vanvels v. Betten, 2007 U.S. Dist. LEXIS 7003, at *14 (W.D. Mich. Jan. 31, 2007) (claims on behalf of employee benefits plan governed by Employee Retirement Income Savings Act); Qwest Communications Corp. v. Ansari, 2007 U.S. Dist. LEXIS 4576, at *10–*11 (D.D.C. Jan. 23, 2007) (claims under Federal Communications Act); Barbieri v. K-Sea Transp. Corp., 2006 WL 3751215, at *6 (E.D.N.Y. Dec. 19, 2006) (Jones Act claim).

35 *See* Kemba J. Dunham, *KB Home May Be Fined by FTC for Curbing Buyers' Right to Sue*, Wall St. J., July 12, 2005, at D5.

36 15 U.S.C. §§ 2301–2312.

37 Mitsubishi Motors Corp. v. Soler Chrysler-Plymouth, Inc., 473 U.S. 614, 627, 105 S. Ct. 3346, 87 L. Ed. 2d 444 (1985).

38 Shearson/American Express, Inc. v. McMahon, 482 U.S. 220, 226, 107 S. Ct. 2332, 96 L. Ed. 2d 185 (1987).

39 *Id.* (citation omitted).

equitable relief."[40] While Magnuson-Moss also permits warrantors to use informal dispute resolution procedures, the Act makes such procedures a nonbinding pre-litigation exhaustion requirement rather than a substitute for litigation:

> One or more warrantors may establish an informal dispute settlement procedure which meets the requirements of the Commission's rules under paragraph (2). If—
> (A) a warrantor establishes such a procedure,
> (B) such procedure, and its implementation, meets the requirements of such rules; and
> (C) he incorporates in a written warranty a requirement that the consumer resort to such procedure *before pursuing any legal remedy under this section respecting such warranty*,
>
> then (i) the consumer may not commence a civil action (other than a class action) under subsection (d) of this section unless he *initially resorts to such procedure*. . . . In any civil action arising out of a warranty obligation and relating to a matter considered in such a procedure, any decision in such procedure shall be admissible in evidence.[41]

In placing restrictions on the use of alternative dispute resolution, Magnuson-Moss both embraces adjudication after exhaustion of informal proceedings and establishes that the decision reached in the proceedings only constitutes relevant evidence for courts to consider. The Act's plain language thus strongly supports the conclusion that binding arbitration of written warranty claims is prohibited.[42]

4.2.2.3 The Act's Legislative History

The legislative history of the Magnuson-Moss Warranty Act provides further support for the argument that Congress intended to ban the use of binding arbitration clauses in written warranties. Congressman Moss, the named sponsor of the Act, explained in floor remarks that these provisions allow an opportunity for private dispute resolution, without limiting a warranty claimant's ultimate right to a judicial resolution:

> First, the bill provides the consumer with an economically feasible private right of action so that when a warrantor breaches his warranty or service contract obligations, the consumer can have effective redress. Reasonable attorney's fees and expenses are provided for the successful consumer litigant, and the bill is further refined so as to place a minimum extra burden on the courts by requiring as *a prerequisite to suit* that the purchaser give the [warrantor] reasonable opportunity to settle the dispute out of court, including the use of a fair and formal dispute settlement mechanism. . . .[43]

The House report accompanying this legislation further states that "[a]n adverse decision in any informal dispute settlement proceeding would not be a bar to a civil action on the warranty involved in the proceeding."[44]

4.2.2.4 The Act's Implementing Regulations

The Magnuson-Moss Warranty Act contains an express delegation of authority to the Federal Trade Commission (FTC) to make rules governing informal proceedings[45] and the FTC has promulgated such regulations.[46] The FTC rules are entitled to considerable judicial deference.[47]

FTC Rule 703 establishing minimum standards that warrantors must follow in any informal dispute settlement procedure specifically provides that such a procedure *cannot* be binding on the consumer.[48] Rule 703 applies to *any* informal dispute settlement procedure which is incorporated into the terms of a written warranty,[49] and the FTC in promulgating Rule 703 was very explicit that the Rule prohibits binding arbitration as a warranty condition: "reference within the written warranty to any binding, non-judicial remedy is prohibited by the Rule and the Act."[50]

The FTC reiterated this ban in 1999 after a three-year review of its Magnuson-Moss rules:[51]

> The Commission examined the legality and the merits of mandatory binding arbitration clauses in written consumer product warranties when it pro-

---

40 15 U.S.C. § 2310(d)(1).
41 15 U.S.C. § 2310(a)(3) (emphasis added).
42 The discussion of the Magnuson-Moss Warranty Act and binding arbitration herein does not apply to state law claims for breach of *oral* warranties, which fall outside the scope of the federal Act's relevant provisions. *See, e.g.,* Richardson v. Palm Harbor Homes, Inc., 254 F.3d 1321, 1325 (11th Cir. 2001) ("the Act's preference for nonbinding dispute resolution, arguably to the exclusion of binding arbitration, expressly applies only to dispute-resolution mechanisms for which *written* warranties provide as a prerequisite to suit").
43 119 Cong. Rec. 972 (1973) (statement of Rep. Moss).
44 H.R. Rep. No. 93-1107, at 41 (1974), *reprinted in* 1974 U.S.C.C.A.N. 7702, 7723.
45 15 U.S.C. § 2310(a)(2) ("The Commission shall prescribe rules setting forth minimum requirements for any informal dispute settlement procedure which is incorporated into the terms of a written warranty to which any provision of this title applies.").
46 16 C.F.R. § 703.
47 *See generally* Chevron U.S.A., Inc. v. Natural Res. Def. Council, Inc., 467 U.S. 837, 104 S. Ct. 2778, 81 L. Ed. 2d 694 (1984).
48 *See* 16 C.F.R. § 703.5(j); *see also* 16 C.F.R. § 703.5(g)(1) (consumers must be informed that they can pursue legal remedies if they are dissatisfied with the resolution of the informal dispute settlement procedure).
49 *See* 16 C.F.R. § 703.1(e).
50 *See* 40 Fed. Reg. 60,168, 60,211 (Dec. 31, 1975).
51 Final Action Concerning Review of Interpretations of Magnuson-Moss Warranty Act § C(2), 64 Fed. Reg. 19,700, 19,708 (Apr. 22, 1999).

mulgated Rule 703 in 1975. Although several industry representatives at that time had recommended that the Rule allow warrantors to require consumers to submit to binding arbitration, the Commission rejected that view as being contrary to the Congressional intent.

The Commission based this decision on its analysis of the plain language of the Warranty Act. Section 110(a)(3) of the Warranty Act provides that if a warrantor establishes an IDSM that complies with Rule 703 and incorporates that IDSM in its written consumer product warranty, then "(t)he consumer may not commence a civil action (other than a class action) * * * *unless he initially resorts to such procedure*." (Emphasis added.) This language clearly implies that a mechanism's decision cannot be legally binding, because if it were, it would bar later court action. The House Report supports this interpretation by stating that "(a)n adverse decision in any informal dispute settlement proceeding would not be a bar to a civil action on the warranty involved in the proceeding."[fn69] In summarizing its position at the time Rule 703 was adopted, the Commission stated:

> The Rule does not allow (binding arbitration) for two reasons. First * * * Congressional intent was that decisions of section 110 Mechanisms not be legally binding. Second, even if binding Mechanisms were contemplated by section 110 of the Act, the Commission is not prepared, at this point in time, to develop guidelines for a system in which consumers would commit themselves, at the time of product purchase, to resolve any difficulties in a binding, but nonjudicial proceeding. *The Commission is not now convinced that any guidelines which it set out could ensure sufficient protection for consumers.* (Emphasis added.)[fn70]

Based on its analysis, the Commission determined that "reference within the written warranty to any binding, non-judicial remedy is prohibited by the Rule and the Act."[fn71] The Commission believes that this interpretation continues to be correct.[fn72] Therefore, the Commission has determined not to amend section 703.5(j) to allow for binding arbitration. Rule 703 will continue to prohibit warrantors from including binding arbitration clauses in their contracts with consumers that would require consumers to submit warranty disputes to binding arbitration.

fn 69 House Report (to accompany H.R. 7917), H. Report, No. 93-1107, 93d Cong., 2d Sess. 41 (1974). [*Ed. note: reprinted in* 1974 U.S.C.C.A.N. 7702, 7723.]

fn 70 40 Fed. Reg. 60168, 60210 (1975). The Commission noted, however, that warrantors are not precluded from offering a binding arbitration option to consumers *after* a warranty dispute has arisen. 40 Fed. Reg. 60168, 60211 (1975).

fn 71 40 Fed. Reg. 60168, 60211 (1975).

fn 72 At least one federal district court has upheld the Commission's position that the Warranty Act does not intend for warrantors to include binding arbitration clauses in written warranties on consumer products. Wilson v. Waverlee Homes, Inc., 954 F. Supp. 2d 1530 (M.D. Ala. 1997). The court ruled that a mobile home warrantor could not require consumers to submit their warranty dispute to binding arbitration based on the arbitration clauses in the installment sales and financing contracts between the consumers and the dealer who sold them the mobile home. The court noted that a contrary result would enable warrantors and the retailers selling their products to avoid the requirements of the Warranty Act simply by inserting binding arbitration clauses in sales contracts. *Id.* at 1539–1540.

4.2.2.5 Case Law Relating to Arbitration and the Act

4.2.2.5.1 *Numerous federal and state courts hold that Magnuson-Moss prohibits binding arbitration*

For a number of years, reported federal court decisions were unanimous in holding that the Magnuson-Moss Warranty Act prohibits binding arbitration requirements imposed by warrantors on consumers.[52] Although several of these decisions have been overturned by subsequent federal appellate rulings,[53] a number of federal and state courts alike continue to hold that Magnuson-Moss claims cannot be subject to predispute binding arbitration clauses.[54]

---

52 *See, e.g.*, Raesley v. Grand Hous., Inc., 105 F. Supp. 2d 562 (S.D. Miss. 2000), *overruled by* Walton v. Rose Mobile Homes, L.L.C., 298 F.3d 470 (5th Cir. 2002); Wilson v. Waverlee Homes, Inc., 954 F. Supp. 1530 (M.D. Ala.), *aff'd*, 127 F.3d 40 (11th Cir. 1997), *overruled by* Davis v. S. Energy Homes, Inc., 305 F.3d 1268 (11th Cir. 2002).

53 *See* § 4.2.2.5.2, *infra*.

54 *See* Higgs v. The Warranty Group, 2007 WL 2034376, at *8 (S.D. Ohio July 11, 2007); Rickard v. Teynor's Homes, Inc., 279 F. Supp. 2d 910, 921 (N.D. Ohio 2003); Browne v. Kine Tyson's Imports, Inc., 190 F. Supp. 2d 827, 831 (E.D. Va. 2002); Pitchford v. Oakwood Mobile Homes, Inc., 124 F. Supp. 2d 958, 963–964 (W.D. Va. 2000); Koons Ford of Baltimore, Inc. v. Lobach, 919 A.2d 722, 735–737 (Md. 2007); Parkerson v. Smith, 817 So. 2d 529 (Miss. 2002); Tucker v. Ford Motor Co., 2007 Va. Cir. LEXIS 24, at *29–*30 (Va. Cir. Ct. Feb. 1, 2007); Philylaw v. Platinum Enterprises, Inc., 54 Va. Cir. 364 (2001); *see also* Simpson v. MSA of Myrtle Beach, Inc., 644 S.E.2d 663, 673 (S.C. 2007) (holding that arbitration clause provision covering breach of express warranty claims violates public policy and thus is unconscionable under *state* law).

In *Browne v. Kline Tysons Imports, Inc.*,[55] a federal district court held that Magnuson-Moss "prohibits binding arbitration of a claim arising under a written warranty because any informal dispute procedure proffered by a warrantor cannot be final."[56] *Browne* held that 15 U.S.C. § 2310(a)(1) establishes the Act's policies with regard to out-of-court dispute resolution procedures and that 15 U.S.C. § 2310(d)(1) requires that such procedures be non-binding by allowing consumers to bring actions in federal court after exhausting the warrantor's informal dispute settlement procedures.[57] The court further found that this interpretation of the Act was supported by the FTC's regulations which echo the statutory language and mandate that consumers retain access to the courts.[58]

Similarly, in *Pitchford v. Oakwood Mobile Homes, Inc.*,[59] the court denied a mobile home seller's motion to compel arbitration and held that "there can be no agreement at the time of sale to enter into binding arbitration on a written warranty."[60] The *Pitchford* court found both that the clear intent of Magnuson-Moss was to encourage alternative dispute resolution without depriving parties of their right of access to the courts, and that the FTC's regulations prohibiting binding dispute resolution procedures are entitled to judicial deference.[61]

In *Parkerson v. Smith*,[62] a majority of the Mississippi Supreme Court embraced the reasoning of these federal decisions and likewise held that Magnuson-Moss prohibits all binding arbitration of disputes arising under the Act. The court in *Parkerson* found that "Congress intended to preserve for consumers the right to bring suit for breach of written or implied warranties" and therefore that "the Magnuson-Moss Warranty Act has superceded the FAA in regard to breach of consumer warranties, and binding arbitration cannot be compelled . . . without contravening the purposes of the Act."[63]

Subsequently, in *Rickard v. Teynor's Homes, Inc.*,[64] the federal district court found that the FTC's interpretation of Magnuson-Moss to prohibit binding arbitration was reasonable, entitled to deference, and consistent with the pro-consumer policy goals of Magnuson-Moss.[65] In so holding, the court in *Rickard* relied heavily on the analysis of Magnuson-Moss set forth in the dissenting opinion of the Chief Justice of the Fifth Circuit in *Walton v. Rose Mobile Homes, L.L.C.*[66]

More recently, in *Koons Ford of Baltimore, Inc. v. Lobach*,[67] Maryland's highest court joined these other federal and state courts in holding that Magnuson-Moss prohibits binding arbitration. While echoing these other courts in finding that the plain language of the Act and the FTC's interpretation of it support this conclusion,[68] the Maryland Court of Appeals also focused on the Act's legislative history and its enactment against a backdrop presumption in case law and the Congressional record that binding arbitration of statutory claims was prohibited.[69] Finally, the court relied on logic and common sense in so construing the statute, finding that "[i]t would be inconsistent with common sense, and the MMWA's pro-consumer approach, to hold that Congress intended for consumers to retain their ability to pursue a civil action, but did not intend to bar the use of binding arbitration that would constitute a substitute for litigation."[70]

Finally, in *Simpson v. MSA of Myrtle Beach, Inc.*,[71] the South Carolina Supreme Court effectively joined these courts in prohibiting binding arbitration under Magnuson-Moss by holding that "the inclusion of the MMWA in the scope of the arbitration clause is unenforceable as a matter of policy."[72] Although the court seems to have applied state law in holding that the arbitration clause's coverage of Magnuson-Moss claims "is an unconscionable and unenforceable violation of public policy,"[73] the result is the same as in those cases applying federal law to prohibit binding arbitration of these claims.

4.2.2.5.2 Case law finding binding arbitration permissible under Magnuson-Moss, and a critique of this holding

Two federal circuit courts have now held that Magnuson-Moss does not prohibit warrantors from imposing binding

---

55 190 F. Supp. 2d 827 (E.D. Va. 2002).
56 *Id*. at 831.
57 *Id*. at 830, 831; *see also* Koons Ford of Baltimore, Inc. v. Lobach, 919 A.2d 722, 735 (Md. 2007) (finding that Congress expressly intended to preclude binding arbitration of claims).
58 Browne v. Kline Tysons Imports, Inc., 190 F. Supp. 2d 827, 831 (E.D. Va. 2002); *see also* Higgs v. The Warranty Group, 2007 WL 2034376, at *8 (S.D. Ohio July 11, 2007) (holding that FTC reasonably construed statute to prohibit binding arbitration); *Koons Ford*, 919 A.2d at 735 (FTC regulations further support conclusion that Congress prohibited binding arbitration); Tucker v. Ford Motor Co., 2007 Va. Cir. LEXIS 24, at *29–*30 (Va. Cir. Ct. Feb. 1, 2007).
59 124 F. Supp. 2d 958 (W.D. Va. 2000).
60 *Id*. at 965; *see also* Philyaw v. Platinum Enterprises, Inc., 54 Va. Cir. 364 (Va. Cir. Ct. 2001) (denying used car dealer's motion to compel arbitration of buyers' breach of express warranty claims, finding *Pitchford*'s interpretation of Magnuson-Moss Act persuasive).
61 124 F. Supp. 2d at 963, 964.
62 817 So. 2d 529 (Miss. 2002).
63 *Id*. at 534.

64 279 F. Supp. 2d 910 (N.D. Ohio 2003).
65 *Id*. at 920–926.
66 *Id*. at 921 (*citing* Walton v. Rose Mobile Homes, L.L.C., 298 F.3d 470, 486 (King, C.J. dissenting)).
67 919 A.2d 722 (Md. 2007).
68 *Id*. at 935.
69 *Id*. at 736–737.
70 *Id*. at 737.
71 644 S.E.2d 663 (S.C. 2007).
72 *Id*. at 673.
73 *Id*.

§ 4.2.2.5.2   Consumer Arbitration Agreements

arbitration requirements on consumers. In *Walton v. Rose Mobile Homes, L.L.C.*,[74] a divided panel of the Fifth Circuit held that Magnuson-Moss does not preclude binding arbitration. *Walton* reached this conclusion after finding that the text of Magnuson-Moss does not explicitly address arbitration, that the statutory reference to "informal dispute settlement procedure[s]" does not extend to arbitration, that the legislative history of Magnuson-Moss was inconclusive on this point, that binding arbitration was consistent with the underlying purposes of the Act, and that the FTC's regulations were not entitled to deference because the Act does not empower the FTC to ban arbitration.[75] In an extensive dissenting opinion, Chief Judge King of the Fifth Circuit argued that the textual ambiguity of Magnuson-Moss with regard to binding arbitration compelled courts to defer to the FTC's interpretation that the Act prohibited binding arbitration.[76]

In *Davis v. Southern Energy Homes, Inc.*,[77] the Eleventh Circuit joined the Fifth Circuit in holding that Magnuson-Moss does not preclude enforcement of binding arbitration clauses in written warranties.[78] *Davis* held that the Magnuson-Moss Act's explicit regulation of informal dispute settlement procedures does not demonstrate Congress's intent to preclude binding arbitration, that the Act's legislative history was inconclusive on this point, that binding arbitration would not conflict with the Act's underlying purposes, and that the FTC's prohibition of binding arbitration was not a reasonable construction of the Act because it relied on an interpretation of statutory provisions that the Supreme Court had rejected under other statutes.[79] Therefore, the Eleventh Circuit held that claims for breach of a written warranty arising under Magnuson-Moss may be subject to binding arbitration.[80] Several federal and state courts before and after these decisions have adopted similar interpretations that Magnuson-Moss permits binding arbitration of claims arising under the Act.[81]

Although several recent state court decisions have simply followed *Walton* and *Davis* without any independent analysis,[82] one of the earlier state court decisions holding that binding arbitration is permissible under Magnuson-Moss serves to highlight the vulnerabilities of the opinions adopting this position. In *Southern Energy Homes, Inc. v. Lee*,[83] a divided Alabama Supreme Court originally denied a mobile home manufacturer's motion to compel arbitration of the buyers' written warranty claims and adopted then prevailing federal court interpretations of Magnuson-Moss with respect to such claims.[84] Soon thereafter, however, the court in *Southern Energy Homes, Inc. v. Ard*[85] used a change of one member in the court's composition to reverse *Lee*'s interpretation of Magnuson-Moss. Instead, without further explanation, the court adopted the *Lee* dissent as the opinion of the court and held that the manufacturer of a mobile home could compel binding arbitration of buyers' claims for breach of written warranty.[86] To reach this conclusion the *Ard* majority/*Lee* dissent relies on numerous debatable interpretations of federal law.

First, by averring that "the text of the Magnuson-Moss Act does not expressly preclude arbitration[,]"[87] the *Lee* dissent transforms the United States Supreme Court's holdings that a statute's intent to preclude mandatory arbitration need only be "discernible" or "deducible" into a plain statement requirement that has no basis in federal law.

---

74 298 F.3d 470 (5th Cir. 2002).
75 *Id*. at 475–478.
76 *Id*. at 480–492 (King, C.J., dissenting).
77 305 F.3d 1268 (11th Cir. 2002).
78 *But see also* Cunningham v. Fleetwood Homes of Ga., 253 F.3d 611 (11th Cir. 2001) (holding that Magnuson-Moss prohibits warrantor from enforcing arbitration clause not included in warranty based on Act's "one document rule"); § 4.2.2.8.2, *infra* (addressing one document rule).
79 305 F.3d at 1274–1280.
80 *Id*. at 1280.
81 *See, e.g.*, Pack v. Damon Corp., 320 F. Supp. 2d 545 (E.D. Mich. 2004); S. Energy Homes, Inc. v. Ard, 772 So. 2d 1131 (Ala. 2000); S. Energy Homes, Inc. v. Lee, 732 So. 2d 994 (Ala. 1999) (See, J., dissenting) (opinion adopted by majority of the court in *Ard*); Stacy David, Inc. v. Consuegra, 845 So. 2d 303 (Fla. Dist. Ct. App. 2003) (noting authority holding that Magnuson-Moss permits binding arbitration); Borowiec v. Gateway 2000, Inc., 808 N.E.2d 957 (Ill. 2004); Walker v. DaimlerChrysler Corp., 856 N.E.2d 90, 95–99 (Ind. Ct. App. 2006); Daimler Chrysler Corp. v. Yaeger, 818 N.E.2d 527, 535–538 (Ind. Ct. App. 2004), *transfer granted and opinion vacated*, 831 N.E.2d 744 (Ind. 2005); Howell v. Cappaert Manufactured Hous., Inc., 819 So. 2d 461 (La. Ct. App. 2002) (split panel decision holding by 2–1 vote that Magnuson-Moss permits binding arbitration); Abela v. Gen. Motors Corp., 677 N.W.2d 325 (Mich. 2004); McDaniel v. Gateway Computer Corp., 2004 WL 2260497, at *3–*4 (Ohio Ct. App. Sept. 24, 2004); *In re* Am. Homestar of Lancaster, Inc., 50 S.W.3d 480 (Tex. 2001); *cf. Ex parte* Homes of Legend, Inc., 831 So. 2d 13 (Ala. 2002) (denying writ of *mandamus*, discussing without deciding whether trial court's order requiring use of informal dispute settlement mechanism under Magnuson-Moss constitutes an arbitration order).
82 Borowiec v. Gateway 2000, Inc., 808 N.E.2d 957, 970 (Ill. 2004); Abela v. Gen. Motors Corp., 677 N.W.2d 325, 327, 328 (Mich. 2004).
83 732 So. 2d 994 (Ala. 1999).
84 *Id*. at 999, 1000.
85 772 So. 2d 1131 (Ala. 2000).
86 *Id*. at 1135; *see also* S. Energy Homes, Inc. v. McCray, 788 So. 2d 882 (Ala. 2000) (affirming *Ard*); *In re* Am. Homestar of Lancaster, Inc., 50 S.W.3d 480 (Tex. 2001) (holding that Magnuson-Moss permits binding arbitration, relying heavily on reasoning of Alabama Supreme Court in *Ard*).
87 *Lee*, 732 So. 2d at 1008 (See, J., dissenting); *see also* Walton v. Rose Mobile Homes, L.L.C., 298 F.3d 470, 475 (5th Cir. 2002); Walker v. DaimlerChrysler Corp., 856 N.E.2d 90, 96–97 (Ind. Ct. App. 2006) ("Here, Congress has not spoken directly as to the permissibility of mandatory binding arbitration."); *In re* Am. Homestar of Lancaster, Inc., 50 S.W.3d 480, 487 (Tex. 2001) ("neither the Magnuson-Moss Act nor the FTC regulations mention arbitration or the FAA").

More fundamentally, the *Lee* dissent misapplies the holding of *Gilmer v. Interstate/Johnson Lane Corp.*[88] regarding the effect of informal *public* administrative proceedings on arbitration requirements to the very different context of Magnuson-Moss's regulation of *private* dispute resolution.[89] The issue before the Supreme Court in *Gilmer* was whether the requirement under the Age Discrimination in Employment Act[90] (ADEA) that parties use informal public procedures established by the Equal Employment Opportunity Commission (EEOC) served to prohibit all private arbitration of ADEA claims. The Supreme Court held that it did not because informal conciliation by the EEOC "suggests that out-of-court dispute resolution, such as arbitration, is consistent with the statutory scheme established by Congress."[91] By contrast, the question under Magnuson-Moss is whether the Act's explicit limitations on privately administered informal dispute resolution procedures apply to regulate the use of arbitration. Under the reasoning of *Gilmer*, Magnuson-Moss should be found to prohibit binding arbitration. While the ADEA's requirement of informal dispute resolution is entirely consistent with binding arbitration, Magnuson-Moss, by its express terms, makes *all* informal dispute resolution procedures nonbinding. The *Lee* dissent and its progeny thus ignore crucial differences between Magnuson-Moss and the statutory scheme at issue in *Gilmer*.

Furthermore, the *Lee* dissent's discussion of Magnuson-Moss's legislative history is not persuasive. The *Lee* dissent dismisses as irrelevant the House Report's statement that claimants retain the right to bring a civil action after any informal proceeding, contending that the report "does not expressly deal with arbitration."[92] Once again, this plain statement requirement ignores the Supreme Court's holdings that the intent of Congress to restrict private use of arbitration may be *deducible* from a statute's legislative history and the requirement relies on an erroneous differentiation between arbitration and other informal dispute resolution procedures.

The *Lee* dissent and several of its progeny also draw a mistaken analogy between the legislative history of the Magnuson-Moss Act and that of the Securities Act, which the Supreme Court addressed in *Shearson/American Express, Inc. v. McMahon*.[93] In *McMahon*, the Supreme Court noted that Congress had favorably discussed anti-arbitration precedent regarding Securities Act claims but had done so "without enacting into law any provision remotely addressing that subject."[94] Therefore, the Supreme Court found that this legislative history did not support the interpretation that the Securities Act prohibits arbitration. Under Magnuson-Moss, in contrast, the committee report and sponsor's floor statements noting that consumers would retain access to court corresponded with the enactment of section 2310(a)(3). This legislative history therefore does support the conclusion that Magnuson-Moss prohibits binding arbitration. In any case, discussions of the legislative history of *other* statutes do not answer the question of whether Congress intended to prohibit binding arbitration under Magnuson-Moss.

Finally, the Alabama Supreme Court's rejection of the Federal Trade Commission's interpretation of Magnuson-Moss to prohibit binding arbitration, despite the deference that is generally accorded an agency's interpretation of the statute that it is charged with administering, also involves a misapplication of United States Supreme Court precedent.[95] In addition, the *Lee* dissent cites a string of decisions rejecting anti-arbitration arguments that are based *solely* on a statute's provision of a judicial forum,[96] while ignoring the additional Magnuson-Moss provisions requiring that all informal dispute resolution proceedings be nonbinding.

More recently, the Indiana Court of Appeals followed these decisions allowing binding arbitration under Magnuson-Moss and rejecting the FTC's contrary conclusions based on similarly erroneous findings.[97] First, the Indiana court likewise erroneously held that the statute's provision of a judicial forum and its restrictions on informal dispute settlement mechanisms not only did not expressly apply to arbitration, *but could not reasonably be construed to do so* under the deferential standard applied to agency interpretations of statutory provisions.[98]

Second, the Indiana court further erred in finding that the FTC's factual conclusion, reached in 1975 and reaffirmed in 1999, that binding arbitration would not adequately protect consumers under this statute was barred by unsubstantiated statements in intervening Supreme Court decisions addressing arbitration of other types of consumer claims.[99]

---

88 500 U.S. 20, 111 S. Ct. 1647, 114 L. Ed. 2d 26 (1991).
89 *See* S. Energy Homes, Inc. v. Lee, 732 So. 2d 994, 1008 (Ala. 1999) (See, J., dissenting); *see also In re* Am. Homestar of Lancaster, Inc., 50 S.W.3d 480, 487 (Tex. 2001).
90 29 U.S.C. §§ 621–634.
91 *Gilmer*, 500 U.S. at 29.
92 *Lee*, 732 So. 2d at 1009 (See, J., dissenting); *see also* Davis v. S. Energy Homes, Inc., 305 F.3d 1268, 1275, 1276 (11th Cir. 2002); *In re* Am. Homestar of Lancaster, Inc., 50 S.W.3d 480, 488 (Tex. 2001).
93 482 U.S. 220, 107 S. Ct. 2332, 96 L. Ed. 2d 185 (1987).
94 *McMahon*, 482 U.S. at 237.
95 *See* § 4.2.2.4, *supra*.
96 *See* S. Energy Homes, Inc. v. Lee, 732 So. 2d 994, 1010, 1011 (Ala. 1999); *see also* Walton v. Rose Mobile Homes, L.L.C., 298 F.3d 470, 474–476 (5th Cir. 2002); Davis v. S. Energy Homes, Inc., 305 F.3d 1268, 1277–1279 (11th Cir. 2002); Walker v. DaimlerChrysler Corp., 856 N.E.2d 90, 97–98 (Ind. Ct. App. 2006). *But see Walton*, 298 F.3d at 480–492 (King, C.J., dissenting) (arguing that FTC's interpretation is entitled to judicial deference).
97 *See* Walker v. DaimlerChrysler Corp., 856 N.E.2d 90, 97–98 (Ind. Ct. App. 2006).
98 *Id.*
99 *Id.* at 98 (quoting Allied-Bruce Terminix Companies v. Dobson, 513 U.S. 265, 279, 115 S. Ct. 834, 130 L. Ed. 2d 753 (1995)).

§ 4.2.2.6   *Consumer Arbitration Agreements*

Thus, although a considerable number of courts have rejected the argument that Magnuson-Moss prohibits binding arbitration, upon close scrutiny the reasoning of these decisions is vulnerable to challenge.

4.2.2.6 Debunking Argument That Magnuson-Moss Claims Are Subject to "Formal" Arbitration As Distinct from "Informal" Procedures Under the Act

4.2.2.6.1 Introduction

Warrantors' arguments in favor of requiring binding arbitration of Magnuson-Moss claims often attempt to erect a distinction between "more formal" binding arbitration and the informal dispute resolution procedures which the Act explicitly regulates. These arguments run head first into a vast body of case law spanning the enactment of Magnuson-Moss which describes arbitration proceedings as informal and indeed exalts this informality as both a primary benefit to parties and the very basis for the existence of federal and state policies favoring arbitration. In light of this bedrock understanding of arbitration as informal, courts should not differentiate between arbitration and the "informal dispute settlement procedures" that Magnuson-Moss (MMWA) requires to be nonbinding. As one federal district court held, "[a]ny informal dispute settlement procedure under the MMWA must be a non-binding mechanism, which serves as a prerequisite, and not a bar, to relief in court."[100]

4.2.2.6.2 Supreme Court views arbitration as informal

The Supreme Court for almost half a century has characterized private arbitration proceedings as informal in contradistinction to adjudication procedures in court. More than a decade before the enactment of Magnuson-Moss, the Court distinguished private commercial arbitration from litigation based on its informal nature: "There the choice is between the adjudication of cases or controversies in courts with established procedures or even special statutory safeguards on the one hand and *the settlement of them in the more informal arbitration tribunal on the other.*"[101] The Supreme Court echoed this assessment at around the time when Congress was contemplating passage of Magnuson-Moss:

> [T]he fact-finding process in arbitration usually is not equivalent to judicial fact-finding. The record of the arbitration proceeding is not as complete; the usual rules of evidence do not apply; and rights and procedures common to civil trials, such as discovery, compulsory process, cross-examination, and testimony under oath are often severely limited or unavailable. . . . *Indeed, it is the informality of arbitral procedure that enables it to function as an efficient, inexpensive, and expeditious means for dispute resolution.*[102]

The well-established conception of arbitration proceedings as inherently informal by the time the Magnuson-Moss Act was enacted in 1974 should inform the understanding that Congress included arbitration among the informal dispute resolution procedures that the Act requires to be nonbinding.

Although the tone animating the differentiation between labor arbitration and commercial arbitration in *Warrior & Gulf Navigation* and *Gardner-Denver* has subsequently been softened, the Supreme Court continues to refer to private arbitration proceedings as informal and to trumpet arbitration's informal nature as a benefit to parties. In *Mitsubishi Motors Corp. v. Soler Chrysler-Plymouth, Inc.*,[103] for example, the Court authorized private arbitration for the resolution of many types of statutory claims because a party who agrees to arbitrate "trades the procedures and opportunity for review of the court room for the simplicity, informality, and expedition of arbitration."[104] The Court went a step further in *Gilmer* by holding that ADEA claims are subject to mandatory arbitration because "[t]he EEOC . . . is directed to pursue '*informal methods* of conciliation, conference, and persuasion,' 29 U.S.C. § 626(b), which suggests that *out-of-court dispute resolution, such as arbitration,* is consistent with the statutory scheme established by Congress."[105] By treating informal proceedings, out-of-court dispute resolution, and arbitration as interchangeable, *Gilmer* undercuts the argument that Magnuson-Moss's prohibition of binding informal dispute resolution procedures has no application to warrantors' use of arbitration.

4.2.2.6.3 Other courts find arbitration to be informal

The contention that arbitration proceedings are "formal," and therefore not affected by Magnuson-Moss's regulation of informal dispute resolution proceedings, is supported by two recent decisions from the Fifth and Eleventh Circuits.[106]

---

100 Browne v. Kline Tysons Imports, Inc., 190 F. Supp. 2d 827, 831 (E.D. Va. 2002). *But see* Davis v. S. Energy Homes, Inc., 305 F.3d 1268 (11th Cir. 2002); Walton v. Rose Mobile Homes, L.L.C., 298 F.3d 470 (5th Cir. 2002).

101 United Steelworkers of Am. v. Warrior & Gulf Navigation Co., 363 U.S. 574, 578, 80 S. Ct. 1347, 4 L. Ed. 2d 1409 (1960) (emphasis added).

102 Alexander v. Gardner-Denver Co., 415 U.S. 36, 57, 94 S. Ct. 1011, 39 L. Ed. 2d 147 (1974) (citations omitted) (emphasis added).

103 473 U.S. 614, 105 S. Ct. 3346, 87 L. Ed. 2d 444 (1985).

104 *Mitsubishi Motors,* 473 U.S. at 628; *see also* Gilmer v. Interstate/Johnson Lane Corp., 500 U.S. 20, 31, 111 S. Ct. 1647, 114 L. Ed. 2d 26 (1991) (quoting *Mitsubishi Motors* for the proposition that securities industry arbitration proceedings are not as extensive as federal court procedures).

105 *Gilmer,* 500 U.S. at 29 (emphasis added).

106 Davis v. S. Energy Homes, Inc., 305 F.3d 1268 (11th Cir. 2002);

But these two decisions run counter to a vast body of case law from other courts, characterizing arbitration as an informal mechanism for resolving disputes. Numerous courts have recognized that the very purpose of arbitration is to provide informal dispute resolution proceedings.[107] Procedural informality has long been trumpeted as a primary virtue of arbitration,[108] and is often identified as the very basis for federal and state legislation creating a general public policy in favor of arbitration as a mechanism for resolving disputes.[109] It would be a drastic departure from longstanding principles of arbitration law to treat arbitration proceedings as "formal" in order to exempt them from the requirements of Magnuson-Moss.

Courts have repeatedly characterized private arbitration as "informal" in order to differentiate it from formal adjudication in the courts.[110] The informal nature of arbitration arises out of its dispensation with various procedural requirements of public adjudication.[111] Although arbitration

---

Walton v. Rose Mobile Homes, L.L.C., 298 F.3d 470 (5th Cir. 2002).

107 *See, e.g.*, Liberty Mut. Fire Ins. Co. v. Mandile, 192 Ariz. 216, 963 P.2d 295, 299 (Ct. App. 1998); May Constr. Co. v. Thompson, 20 S.W.3d 345, 352 n.1 (Ark. 2000) ("the underlying reason for arbitration is to allow an informal and fast resolution of the parties' disputes without the formality of the court system"); Fireman's Fund Ins. Companies v. Bugailiskis, 278 Ill. App. 3d 19, 662 N.E.2d 555, 558 (1996); Firmin v. Garber, 353 So. 2d 975, 977 (La. 1977) ("[t]he object of arbitration is the speedy disposition of differences through informal procedures without resort to court action"); Schmidt v. Midwest Family Mut. Ins. Co., 426 N.W.2d 870, 874 (Minn. 1988) ("providing a speedy, informal, and relatively inexpensive procedure for resolving controversies [is the] raison d'etre of arbitration"); Roggio v. Nationwide Mut. Ins. Co., 66 N.Y.2d 260, 496 N.Y.S.2d 404, 487 N.E.2d 261, 263 (1985) (describing arbitration's "objective of providing an efficient, informal mechanism for recovery of benefits").

108 Swift Indus., Inc. v. Botany Indus., Inc., 466 F.2d 1125, 1129 n.10 (3d Cir. 1972) ("[f]ederal courts have recognized that one of the primary virtues of the arbitration is its procedural informality"); Ballantine Books, Inc. v. Capital Distrib. Co., 302 F.2d 17, 21 (2d Cir. 1962) ("among the virtues of arbitration which presumably have moved the parties to agree upon it are speed and informality"); Pisciotta v. Shearson Lehman Bros., Inc., 629 A.2d 520, 525 (D.C. 1993) ("[p]arties select arbitration, and are encouraged to do so, because of the 'manifold' advantages such proceedings offer, i.e.: [speed and economy], informality, the possibility of coordination with other modes of conciliation"); Just Pants v. Wagner, 247 Ill. App. 3d 166, 617 N.E.2d 246, 249 (1993) ("arbitration proceedings are valued for their informality and their expedient resolution of disputes").

109 *See, e.g.*, Forsythe Int'l, S.A. v. Gibbs Oil Co., 915 F.2d 1017, 1022 (5th Cir. 1990) ("As a speedy and informal alternative to litigation, arbitration resolves disputes without confinement to many of the procedural and evidentiary strictures that protect the integrity of formal trial. . . . The informal nature of arbitration proceedings effectuates the national policy favoring arbitration. . . ."); New Eng. Energy, Inc. v. Keystone Shipping Co., 855 F.2d 1, 3 (1st Cir. 1988) ("[t]he Federal Arbitration Act, 9 U.S.C. §§ 1–14, was passed to ensure that courts would honor the contractual agreements of parties who choose to resolve their disputes by means of informal arbitration procedure"); Soc'y of Am. Foresters v. Renewable Natural Res. Found., 114 Md. App. 224, 689 A.2d 662, 669 (1997) (complaint for relief from arbitrator's ruling on legal issue would "thwart the legislative purpose of arbitration as an informal, expeditious, and final resolution of disputes"); Lickteig v. Alderson, Ondov, Leonard & Sween, P.A., 556 N.W.2d 557, 562 (Minn. 1996) ("[t]he general policy of Minnesota is to encourage arbitration as a speedy, informal, and relatively inexpensive procedure for resolving controversies").

110 *See, e.g.*, Telum, Inc. v. E.F. Hutton Credit Corp., 859 F.2d 835, 838 (10th Cir. 1988); Hart v. Orion Ins. Co., 453 F.2d 1358, 1361 (10th Cir. 1971) ("arbitration differs radically from litigation, and one who chooses it must be content with its informalities and looser approximations"); Bakers Union Factory No. 326 v. ITT Cont'l Baking Co., 749 F.2d 350, 353 (6th Cir. 1984) ("[t]he policy in favor of the finality of arbitration is but one part of a broader goal of encouraging *informal, i.e., nonjudicial*, resolution of labor disputes" (emphasis added)); Saturn Constr. Co. v. Premier Roofing Co., 238 Conn. 293, 680 A.2d 1274, 1277 (1996) ("arbitration is an informal proceeding designed, in part, to avoid the complexities of litigation"); Marino v. Tagaris, 395 Mass. 397, 480 N.E.2d 286, 289 (1985) ("arbitration enables the disputants to interact in an informal, private situation as opposed to the more public, accusatory form of litigation"); Am. Ins. Co. v. Messinger, 43 N.Y.2d 184, 401 N.Y.S.2d 36, 371 N.E.2d 798, 803 (1977) ("the arbitration forum necessarily imports acceptance of the more summary, informal and less structured procedures which characterize arbitration as compared with judicial litigation"); Aetna Cas. & Sur. Co. v. Grabbert, 590 A.2d 88, 92 (R.I. 1991) ("[p]arties contract to use arbitration as an expeditious and informal means of private dispute resolution, thereby avoiding litigation in courts").

111 *See, e.g.*, Local 1545, United Mine Workers v. Inland Steel Coal Co., 876 F.2d 1288, 1296 (7th Cir. 1989); Bayamon Can Co. v. Congreso de Uniones Industriales, 843 F.2d 65, 66 (1st Cir. 1988) ("[T]he award in this case is hardly a model of erudition. But then again this is not atypical of the kind of informal proceeding the parties bargain for when they agree to labor arbitration. . . ."); Greenblatt v. Drexel Burnham Lambert, Inc., 763 F.2d 1352, 1360 (11th Cir. 1985) ("arbitrable factfinding is generally not procedurally equivalent to judicial factfinding"); Piggly Wiggly Operators' Warehouse, Inc. v. Piggly Wiggly Operators' Warehouse Indep. Truck Drivers Union, Local No. 1, 611 F.2d 580, 583 (5th Cir. 1980) ("[c]ustomarily, an arbitration hearing is informal; either or both parties may not be represented by counsel, evidence is submitted without regard to the strictures of judicial rules and no transcript of the testimony is made"); United Elec. Radio & Mach. Workers v. Honeywell, Inc., 522 F.2d 1221, 1228 (7th Cir. 1975) ("notions of res judicata are less suited to the informal process of industrial arbitration than to the litigation process"); Clairol, Inc. v. Enertrac Corp., 44 Conn. App. 506, 690 A.2d 418, 422 (1997) ("[t]his relaxation of strict evidentiary rules is both necessary and desirable because arbitration is an informal proceeding designed, in part, to avoid the complexities of litigation"); Gordon Sel-Way, Inc. v. Spence Bros., Inc., 438 Mich. 488, 475 N.W.2d 704, 709 (1991) ("[b]y narrowing the grounds upon which an arbitration decision may be invaded, the court rules preserve the efficiency and reliability of arbitration as an expedited, efficient, and informal means of private dispute resolution"); Town of Silver City v. Silver City Police Officers Ass'n, 115 N.M. 628, 857 P.2d 28, 32 (N.M. 1993) (de novo review of arbitration award would "frustrate the purpose of arbitration,

proceedings typically follow some set of rules, the mere existence of procedural rules does not alter the fundamentally informal nature of arbitration.[112] Likewise, the fact that some forms of alternative dispute resolution may be even more informal than arbitration does not affect the prevailing characterization of arbitration as an informal dispute settlement mechanism.[113]

The prevailing conception of arbitration proceedings as informal is perhaps best captured in a recent Seventh Circuit decision. In holding that the felony conviction of a labor arbitrator while proceedings are pending does not invalidate the arbitrator's subsequent award, the Seventh Circuit explained that:

> A contrary rule would encourage losing parties to an arbitration to conduct a background check on arbitrators, looking for dirt—a particularly questionable undertaking because arbitrators, unlike judges, are not subjected to background checks when appointed. *It is another example of the lesser formality, and concomitant relaxation of due process norms, of arbitration in comparison to adjudication.*[114]

4.2.2.7 The Act Prevents Use of Arbitration Agreements in Only Certain Consumer Transactions

In those jurisdictions in which courts agree with the conclusion that binding arbitration agreements are not allowed for claims under the Magnuson-Moss Warranty Act for breach of explicit written warranties,[115] merchants are prevented from using arbitration agreements in many types of consumer transactions. Manufacturers typically provide written warranties on virtually all new consumer products, from cars and mobile homes to appliances and electronic equipment. Retailers who sell these new goods to consumers may add their own written warranties as well, although frequently these merchants attempt to disclaim that they are making warranties, and instead tell the consumer to rely solely on the manufacturer's written warranties.

When a consumer purchases used goods, the remainder of the manufacturer's written warranty or an implied warranty may still apply, and the consumer cannot be required to arbitrate warranty disputes with the manufacturer. More typically in the purchase of used cars and other used goods, the consumer's dispute is with the dealer selling the goods to the consumer. In some such circumstances, the dealer will offer a written warranty. In that case, an attendant arbitration agreement will violate Magnuson-Moss.

More commonly, the dealer offers no written warranty, but state law provides that the dealer offers implied warranties in the transaction or the dealer may sell an extended warranty (also called a service contract). The Magnuson-Moss Warranty Act provides a private right of action for breach of such implied warranties or extended warranties,[116] and the issue is then whether a merchant who only provides implied warranties or sells an extended warranty can include a binding arbitration requirement in the sales agreement.

The Act's rules as to informal dispute settlement procedures only apply if a written warranty is provided, so the analysis must be different than when a written warranty is provided. Courts may find the inclusion of an arbitration agreement not automatically inconsistent with the Magnuson-Moss Act.[117] This conclusion still begs the question whether the congressional intent behind the Magnuson-Moss Act in encouraging a practical remedial scheme for small consumer warranty disputes is inconsistent with an arbitration mechanism that prevents class actions, refuses to award attorney fees to a prevailing consumer, or that as-

---

which seeks to further judicial economy by providing a quick, informal, and less costly alternative to the judicial resolution of disputes"); Westminster Constr. Corp. v. PPG Indus., Inc., 119 R.I. 205, 376 A.2d 708, 710 (1977) (reasoned arbitral opinion requirement would "undermine the very purpose of arbitration, which is to provide a relatively quick, efficient, and informal means of private dispute settlement"); Dane County v. Dane County Union Local 65, 210 Wis. 2d 267, 565 N.W.2d 540, 545 (Ct. App. 1997) ("preclusion doctrines may be less suited to the informality of the arbitration process").

112 *See, e.g.,* Benjamin v. Traffic Executive Ass'n E. Railroads, 869 F.2d 107, 109 (2d Cir. 1989) ("[b]oth parties set up informal procedural rules to govern the arbitration proceeding"); Int'l Chem. Workers Union, Local No. 566 v. Mobay Chem. Corp., 755 F.2d 1107, 1114 (4th Cir. 1985) (Sprouse, J., dissenting) ("Arbitration is not restricted by the formal rules of procedure that bind courts. Certain basic rules of decision-making, however, must be observed even under the most informal dispute resolution procedure...."); Columbine Valley Constr. Co. v. Bd. of Directors, 626 P.2d 686, 693 (Colo. 1981) ("The requirement of the arbitrator's oath lends dignity to the arbitration proceeding without impairing its basic informality.").

113 *See* Beard v. Mt. Carroll Mut. Fire Ins. Co., 203 Ill. App. 3d 724, 561 N.E.2d 116, 118 (1990) ("[T]he salutary purposes for permitting an informal mechanism to resolve disputes finally and expeditiously are served here by limiting judicial intercession in the decision of the arbitrators. Although such agreements may call for less formal proceedings than arbitrations, both provide a contractual method for settling questions in a less complicated and expensive manner than through court adjudication...." (internal quotation marks omitted)); Penn Cent. Corp. v. Consol. Rail Corp., 56 N.Y.2d 120, 451 N.Y.S.2d 62, 436 N.E.2d 512, 516 (1982) ("[T]he courts have recognized a basic distinction between appraisal and arbitration. Although both contemplate a non-judicial and informal resolution of a dispute by a third party, the prevailing practice in appraisal is more informal....").

114 United Transp. Union v. Gateway W. Ry. Co., 284 F.3d 710 (7th Cir. 2002) (Posner, J.) (emphasis added).

---

115 The term "written warranty" is defined at 15 U.S.C. § 2301(6). *See* National Consumer Law Center, Consumer Warranty Law § 2.2.3 (3d ed. 2006 and Supp.).
116 15 U.S.C. § 2310(d)(1).
117 *See* Rhode v. E & T Investments, Inc., 6 F. Supp. 2d 1322 (M.D. Ala. 1998); Boyd v. Homes of Legend, Inc., 981 F. Supp. 1423 (M.D. Ala. 1997), *remanded on jurisdictional grounds*, 188 F.3d 1294 (11th Cir. 1999).

sesses high arbitration costs to the consumer.[118] This type of conflict is examined in § 4.3, *infra*.

4.2.2.8 Binding Arbitration Clauses, When Permitted, Must Still Comply with the Act's Provisions Concerning Disclosures and Tie-Ins

4.2.2.8.1 Introduction

In jurisdictions where courts permit binding arbitration of written warranty disputes, the arbitration agreement still must comply with Magnuson-Moss Warranty Act disclosure requirements[119] and prohibitions concerning tie-ins.[120] In addition, Magnuson-Moss tie-in prohibitions relate not only to written, but also to *implied* warranties,[121] while its disclosure requirements apply both to written warranties and to *service contracts*.[122] Magnuson-Moss, being a federal statute, is not preempted by the Federal Arbitration Act (FAA), and compliance with these requirements is not inconsistent with FAA requirements.

The precise application of these requirements to arbitration clauses is unclear because case law is sparse and Federal Trade Commission (FTC) regulations do not directly address this issue, which is not surprising considering that the FTC maintains that Magnuson-Moss prohibits binding arbitration.[123] Why specify how to disclose a requirement that the FTC has already prohibited?

This section examines three issues: whether an arbitration requirement must be disclosed in a written warranty, whether such a requirement must be disclosed in an extended warranty or service contract, and whether a company offering a written or implied warranty may designate the name of the arbitration service provider, or whether such a designation is a prohibited tie-in. If a court determines that written warranty disputes are not subject to binding arbitration, then the first issue described above is largely moot. But even if written warranty disputes are not subject to arbitration, the Magnuson-Moss provisions still apply to regulate whether an arbitration requirement must be disclosed in a *service contract* and whether a merchant can designate the name of an arbitration service provider to resolve a dispute relating to *implied* warranties.

4.2.2.8.2 Arbitration requirement must be disclosed in written warranties

The Eleventh Circuit, in *Cunningham v. Fleetwood Homes of Georgia, Inc.*,[124] and cases that follow it, hold that a warrantor cannot compel arbitration of written warranty claims when the arbitration requirement was not disclosed in the written warranty. Because written warranties (and service contracts) often do not contain the arbitration agreement, this ruling is of great importance in warranty litigation, and requires a detailed look at the holdings of both *Cunningham* and subsequent decisions.

The Magnuson-Moss Warranty Act states:

> In order to improve the adequacy of information available to consumers, prevent deception, and improve competition in the marketing of consumer products, any warrantor warranting a consumer product to a consumer by means of a written warranty shall, to the extent required by rules of the Commission, fully and conspicuously disclose in simple and readily understood language the terms and conditions of such warranty.[125]

The FTC rules require that that certain terms be clearly and conspicuously disclosed "in a single document in simple and readily understood language."[126] This single document requirement is significant, because it means the arbitration clause cannot be included in another document, but must be disclosed in the actual written warranty document.

The Eleventh Circuit has found that the FTC's "comprehensive disclosure requirements . . . are an integral, if not the central, feature of the Act." Accordingly, *Cunningham* holds that a warrantor's attempt to force a consumer into arbitration when the arbitration requirement is not disclosed in the warranty itself "contravenes the text, legislative history, and purpose of the Magnuson-Moss Warranty Act. . . . Compelling arbitration on the basis of an arbitration agreement that is not referenced in the warranty presents an inherent conflict with the Act's purpose of providing clear and concise warranties to consumers."[127]

One of the FTC's specific disclosure requirements is "the availability of an informal dispute settlement mechanism."[128] *Cunningham* also notes two other FTC rules that require disclosure "of what the warrantor will do in the event of a defect, malfunction or failure to conform to the written warranty,"[129] and of a "step by step explanation of

---

118 *But see* Boyd v. Homes of Legend, Inc., 981 F. Supp. 1423 (M.D. Ala. 1997) (legislative intent to encourage Magnuson-Moss litigation concerning implied warranty claims cannot override the FAA), *remanded on jurisdictional grounds*, 188 F.3d 1294 (11th Cir. 1999).
119 15 U.S.C. § 2302(a).
120 15 U.S.C. § 2302(c).
121 15 U.S.C. § 2302(c).
122 15 U.S.C. § 2306(b).
123 *See* § 4.2.2.4, *supra*.
124 253 F.3d 611 (11th Cir. 2001).
125 15 U.S.C. § 2302(a).
126 16 C.F.R. § 710.3(a).
127 Cunningham v. Fleetwood Homes of Ga., Inc., 253 F.3d 611, 621 (11th Cir. 2001); *see also* Harnden v. Ford Motor Co., 408 F. Supp. 2d 300 (E.D. Mich. 2004).
128 16 C.F.R. § 703.2(b)(1); *see also* 16 C.F.R. § 701.3(a)(6).
129 16 C.F.R. § 701.3(a)(3).

the procedure which the consumer should follow in order to obtain performance of any warranty obligation."[130] Based on these disclosure requirements and the Congressional purpose, *Cunningham* finds that any arbitration requirement must be disclosed in the same document as the written warranty.

Relevant to *Cunningham's* continuing viability is the decision's refusal to go along with the FTC's position that arbitration requirements in written warranties must be nonbinding, because they are a form of informal dispute settlement mechanism, which must be nonbinding.[131] *Cunningham* disagrees: the FTC requirement does not force arbitration to be nonbinding. Arbitration is not a type of informal dispute settlement mechanism, at least in the context of the FTC requirement that such mechanisms be nonbinding.

Despite this finding, *Cunningham* states that arbitration requirements must be disclosed just like informal dispute settlement mechanisms. In other words, in looking at the purposes of the Magnuson-Moss Warranty Act and the FAA, *Cunningham* takes a middle ground: even though arbitration is not a type of informal dispute settlement mechanism as to the *nonbinding requirement*, the Congressional and FTC intent is that it must be *disclosed* like an informal dispute settlement mechanism. The fact that *Cunningham* adopts this middle stance means its holding should not be seen as inconsistent with decisions which find arbitration not to be a type of informal dispute settlement mechanism for purposes of the nonbinding requirement.

With the exception of courts in Alabama, every court considering this issue has adopted the *Cunningham* approach.[132] That Alabama is the one exception is particularly strange because one would expect the Eleventh Circuit's interpretation of the interplay of two federal statutes to be binding on courts within the Eleventh Circuit. But an Alabama federal court and the Alabama Supreme Court have refused to follow *Cunningham*,[133] and in the case of the Alabama Supreme Court even overturned its prior decision in *In Re Thicklin*,[134] which had followed *Cunningham*.

These Alabama decisions rest on some questionable reasoning. First they argue that no FTC rule explicitly requires disclosure of an arbitration requirement in the written warranty—hardly surprising because the FTC's position is that the Magnuson-Moss Act prohibits binding arbitration of written warranty disputes.[135] Second, they argue that the single document requirement is unnecessary, and that disclosure of the arbitration requirement is not that important to the consumer—even though the FTC Magnuson-Moss rules require all disclosures be made in a single document,[136] and that the arbitration requirement is critical to the consumer's ability to enforce the warranty. Third, they argue that *Cunningham* has been overruled by the later Eleventh Circuit decision in *Davis*,[137] which holds that Magnuson-Moss does not prohibit arbitration of warranty disputes. But *Cunningham* reaches the same conclusion, and still decides that the arbitration requirement must be disclosed in the warranty. Finally, the FTC's failure to more explicitly amend its rules to require disclosure of the arbitration requirement evinces the FTC's intent that an arbitration requirement need not be disclosed. But the FTC has not changed its position that binding arbitration of written warranty claims is prohibited, so it would be illogical for the FTC to amend its disclosure rules.

4.2.2.8.3 Significance of disclosure requirement

Mobile home manufacturers and other warrantors often avail themselves of arbitration agreements found in dealers' contracts. *Cunningham*, and cases that follow it, require that this arbitration requirement also be found in the manufacturer's written warranty. It may not even be sufficient for the manufacturer to disclose in its warranty the bare fact that the consumer is bound by an arbitration clause that is found elsewhere.[138] Instead, the manufacturer should coordinate with the dealer so that the manufacturer describes the dealer's arbitration clause in its written warranty.

A manufacturer or seller's attempt to achieve the converse—for example by placing the arbitration clause *only* in the warranty or other warranty-related documents—may not work. For starters, if the arbitration clause in the warranty only requires arbitration of claims under the written warranty, then it does not prevent the consumer from litigating in court claims based on an implied warranty or other legal claims.[139]

The manufacturer is also vulnerable if it puts the arbitration clause not in the written warranty itself but in the owner's manual. The consumer typically does not see the owner's manual until after consummation of the transaction, nor does the consumer's reading of the owner's manual indicate assent to its terms. The seller may even have

---

130 16 C.F.R. § 701.3(a)(5).
131 *See* § 4.2.2.4, *infra*.
132 Harnden v. Ford Motor Co., 408 F. Supp. 2d 300 (E.D. Mich. 2004); DaimlerChrysler Corp. v. Matthews, 848 A.2d 577 (Del. Ch. Ct. 2004); Tropical Ford, Inc. v. Major, 882 So. 2d 476 (Fla. Dist. Ct. App. 2004); Manly v. Daimler Chrysler Corp., Clearinghouse No. 55,633 (Mich. Cir. Ct. Aug. 30, 2005).
133 Patriot Mfg., Inc. v. Dixon, 399 F. Supp. 2d 1298 (S.D. Ala. 2005); Patriot Mfg., Inc. v. Jackson, 2005 WL 3086668 (Ala. Nov. 18, 2005).
134 824 So. 2d 723, 729 (Ala. 2002).

135 *See* § 4.2.2.4, *infra*.
136 16 C.F.R. § 701.3(a).
137 Davis v. S. Energy Homes, Inc., 305 F.3d 1268 (11th Cir. 2002).
138 *But see* Adkins v. Palm Harbor Homes, 157 F. Supp. 2d 1256 (M.D. Ala. 2001) (speculating, but not holding, that mere reference may be sufficient), *aff'd*, 2002 U.S. App. LEXIS 12972 (11th Cir. Apr. 29, 2002).
139 *See, e.g.*, Lyles v. Pioneer Hous. Sys., Inc., 858 So. 2d 226 (Ala. 2003).

difficulty proving that the consumer ever saw the owner's manual. Courts may find an arbitration clause in an owner's manual to have no effect on the consumer's claims, even claims relating to the written warranty.[140] Moreover the single document requirement may mean that the arbitration provision must be disclosed in the written warranty, not the owner's manual.

If the arbitration clause is found only in a written warranty that the consumer receives after purchasing the item, one can argue that the consumer has not agreed to such a term. But courts find that a consumer bringing a claim under the written warranty ratifies that warranty's provisions.[141]

Magnuson-Moss disclosure requirements apply only to written warranties. The Act does not require disclosure of an arbitration clause when a written warranty is not offered,[142] and at least one court has found that the failure to disclose the arbitration clause in the written warranty only prevents the arbitration of written warranty disputes, and not other legal claims.[143]

4.2.2.8.4 Does disclosure requirement extend to service contracts and extended warranties?

Consumers are often sold service contracts or extended warranties. Magnuson-Moss disclosure provisions relating to written warranties do not apply to such contracts, but there are other Magnuson-Moss disclosure requirements that apply to service contracts. A company can enter "into a service contract with the consumer in addition to or in lieu of a written warranty if such contract fully, clearly, and conspicuously discloses its terms and conditions in simple and readily understood language."[144] One of the terms and conditions that should be disclosed is the requirement to resort to binding arbitration instead of to a court proceeding, just as such a condition must be disclosed in a written warranty.

The Magnuson-Moss Warranty Act authorizes the Federal Trade Commission (FTC) to prescribe by rule the manner and form in which the terms and conditions of service contracts are to be fully, clearly, and conspicuously disclosed, but the FTC has not issued such regulations. Nevertheless, the statute makes it clear that service contracts must fully disclose their terms whether or not specific standards have been set by the FTC.[145]

If a court decides that under Magnuson-Moss an arbitration requirement must be disclosed in the service contract it will have significant implications. A service contract company would not be able to rely on an arbitration agreement between the consumer and the seller, if it is not also disclosed in the service contract. Additionally, putting the arbitration agreement only in the service contract would not be sufficient because the consumer typically does not even see the service contract until weeks after its purchase, if even then. Service contracts are rarely provided at the time of sale, particularly when a financial penalty applies to cancel the service contract when it is eventually delivered to the consumer. Attorneys should note whether the consumer is able to cancel the service contract with no financial obligation upon receipt of the actual service contract weeks later. At least one court has found such a unilaterally imposed arbitration requirement unenforceable when it was contained in a service contract only provided weeks later to the consumer.[146]

If a service contract is regulated by a state as insurance, this classification will pose additional issues. On the one hand, the Magnuson-Moss Warranty Act may not apply, and then neither would the Act's disclosure requirements.[147] On the other hand, because of the operation of the federal McCarran-Ferguson Act, states have the authority to limit binding arbitration in insurance transactions and a number of states have done so, at least for certain lines of insurance.[148]

4.2.2.8.5 Does Magnuson-Moss Act prohibit merchant's designation of arbitration service provider?

The Magnuson-Moss Warranty Act states that the warrantor cannot "condition his written or implied warranty of such product on the consumer's using, in connection with such product, any article or service (other than article or service provided without charge under the terms of the warranty) which is identified by brand, trade, or corporate name."[149] Congress was concerned that warrantors would diminish the "free" aspect of a warranty by conditioning its coverage on the consumer's use of a designated product or service, whose price would be in excess of the price available elsewhere in the marketplace, or when the quality of the service or good would not be adequate.[150]

---

140 *See, e.g., Ex parte* Cain, 838 So. 2d 1020 (Ala. 2002); S. Energy Homes, Inc. v. Hennis, 776 So. 2d 105 (Ala. 2000).
141 *See* Lyles v. Pioneer Hous. Sys., Inc., 858 So. 2d 226 (Ala. 2003); *see also* S. Energy Homes, Inc. v. Kennedy, 774 So. 2d 540 (Ala. 2000).
142 Lewis v. Conseco Fin. Corp., 848 So. 2d 920 (Ala. 2002) (when party's representation did not constitute a written warranty, Magnuson-Moss rules regarding binding arbitration clauses do not apply); Huegel v. Mifflin Constr. Co., 796 A.2d 350 (Pa. Super. Ct. 2002) (same).
143 Stevens v. Phillips, 852 So. 2d 123 (Ala. 2002) (Magnuson-Moss one-document rule is not applicable when party's claims are not for breach of written warranty).
144 15 U.S.C. § 2306(b).
145 15 U.S.C. § 2306(b).
146 *See* Paul v. Timco, Inc., 811 A.2d 948 (N.J. Super. Ct. App. Div. 2002).
147 *See* National Consumer Law Center, Consumer Warranty Law § 2.3.8.3 (3d ed. 2006 and Supp.).
148 *See* § 3.3.4, *supra*.
149 15 U.S.C. § 2302(c).
150 *See* National Consumer Law Center, Consumer Warranty Law § 2.4.1 (3d ed. 2006 and Supp.).

This tie-in prohibition should apply when the warrantor conditions the consumer's ability to obtain relief on the consumer's paying to use a particular arbitration service provider. (If there is no charge for the arbitration, this provision does not apply.)

Warrantors typically designate the service provider by name, such as the American Arbitration Association (AAA) or National Arbitration Forum (NAF), forcing the consumer to pay their fee structure and obtain the level of service offered by those organizations in enforcing the warranty. This restriction prevents the consumer from selecting an alternative arbitration provider who may charge less or offer more enforcement of warranty rights.

Unlike certain Magnuson-Moss provisions that apply only to written warranties, this tie-in provision explicitly applies to written or *implied* warranties. Consequently it applies even when a written warranty is not offered, and when the seller only provides implied warranties, as is often the case with many car dealers or other merchants.

The Magnuson-Moss Act, being a federal statute, is not preempted by the Federal Arbitration Act (FAA). Moreover compliance with this prohibition is not inconsistent with FAA requirements. Instead it only means that the parties must agree on an arbitrator, rather than the consumer being forced to use an arbitration service provider selected by the warrantor.

4.2.3 Claims Asserted in Bankruptcy

4.2.3.1 Introduction

The United States Bankruptcy Code provides for one forum to resolve all disputes affecting the administration of a party's bankruptcy estate, with the goal of swift adjudication and access to the courts.[151] For this reason most courts have held that, even when the parties have signed an arbitration agreement, if the issue under dispute is a "core issue" in the bankruptcy proceeding, the bankruptcy court has discretion in determining whether to stay the proceeding pending the resolution of arbitration.[152] This section examines case law resolving the potential conflict between the Bankruptcy Code and the Federal Arbitration Act (FAA) and highlights the crucial distinction between core and non-core proceedings in resolving this conflict.

4.2.3.2 Conflict Between Bankruptcy Code and FAA

The centralization of all bankruptcy claims in one forum, unhampered by concurrent proceedings in other forums, is a "fundamental tenet of bankruptcy law."[153] Furthermore, by staying all other proceedings upon filing for bankruptcy, the court protects the rights of creditors who would be prejudiced if the limited assets of a bankrupt estate were used to pay outside costs, such as those associated with arbitration.[154]

On the other hand, the Federal Arbitration Act requires that, when a valid and enforceable arbitration agreement exists, courts must halt their proceedings while an arbitrator determines the rights of the parties to the arbitration agreement.[155] Some courts have held that this general rule applies in the bankruptcy courts as well,[156] based on the strong federal presumption in favor of enforcing valid arbitration agreements.[157] "Thus, when one party to an arbitration agreement seeks to enforce arbitration against a debtor who has filed for protection under the Bankruptcy Code, the federal courts face a dilemma."[158] The federal courts have not come to a consensus on the solution.

4.2.3.3 *Zimmerman*, the 1984 Amendments, and Subsequent Case Law

In *Zimmerman v. Continental Airlines, Inc.* the Third Circuit, the first circuit court to address this conflict, found that bankruptcy courts had the "sound discretion"—original and exclusive jurisdiction—to determine if arbitration should be stayed in order to protect the debtor.[159] In 1984, however, Congress amended the Bankruptcy Code and

---

151 Bankruptcy Reform Act of 1978, Pub. L. No. 95-598, 92 Stat. 2549 (codified at 11 U.S.C. and in scattered sections of 28 U.S.C); *see also In re* Hemphill Bus Sales, Inc., 259 B.R. 865 (Bankr. E.D. Tex. 2001); *In re* Slipped Disc, Inc., 245 B.R. 342, 344 (Bankr. N.D. Iowa 2000); *In re* Trident Shipworks, Inc., 243 B.R. 130, 132 (Bankr. M.D. Fla. 1999).

152 *See* 28 U.S.C. § 157(b)(1) (defining the scope of bankruptcy judges' discretion).

153 Fred Neufeld, *Enforcement of Contractual Arbitration Agreements Under the Bankruptcy Code*, 65 Am. Bankr. L.J. 525, 525 (1991); *see also* MBNA Am. Bank v. Hill, 436 F.3d 104, 108 (2d Cir. 2006) ("bankruptcy policy exerts an inexorable pull towards centralization") (quoting *In re* U.S. Lines, 197 F.3d at 640); *In re* U.S. Lines, Inc., 197 F.3d 631, 640 (2d Cir. 1999) (one of the primary purposes of bankruptcy "effectuated by Sections 362 and 105 of the Code" is to "allow the bankruptcy court to centralize all disputes concerning property of the debtor's estate so that reorganization can proceed efficiently, unimpeded by uncoordinated proceedings in other arenas") (quoting Shugrue v. Air Line Pilots Ass'n Int'l (*In re* Ionosphere Clubs, Inc.), 922 F.2d 984, 989 (2d Cir. 1990)).

154 *See In re* Slipped Disc, Inc., 245 B.R. 342, 344 (Bankr. N.D. Iowa 2000); *In re* Knepp, 229 B.R. 821 (Bankr. N.D. Ala. 1999).

155 9 U.S.C. § 3.

156 *See In re* Knepp, 229 B.R. 821 (Bankr. N.D. Ala. 1999).

157 *See* § 3.2, *supra*.

158 Mette Kurth, *An Unstoppable Mandate and an Immovable Policy: The Arbitration Act and the Bankruptcy Code Collide*, 43 UCLA L. Rev. 999, 1000 (1996).

159 Zimmerman v. Cont'l Airlines, Inc., 712 F.2d 55 (3d Cir. 1983) (Bankruptcy Code "impliedly modifies" the FAA).

scaled back the bankruptcy courts' control by providing for original but not exclusive jurisdiction over certain matters.[160] Congress also returned some non-core matters to the district courts' jurisdiction by providing for the opportunity for a trial de novo in district court of non-core proceedings initially heard in bankruptcy court.[161]

These amendments led the Third Circuit in *Hays & Co. v. Merrill Lynch, Pierce, Fenner & Smith, Inc.* to modify its holding in *Zimmerman* by limiting bankruptcy court discretion in non-core matters.[162] The Third Circuit reasoned that, as to non-core matters, a trial in bankruptcy court followed by a possible challenge to the bankruptcy court's recommended findings of fact and conclusions of law and a subsequent trial de novo in the district court could be less expedient than proceeding by arbitration.

More recently in *In re Mintze*,[163] the Third Circuit narrowed the range of cases in which *Zimmerman* and *Hays* would have recognized a bankruptcy court's discretion to deny arbitration by holding that the bankruptcy court may only deny arbitration of core claims asserting rights granted by the Bankruptcy Code itself.[164] The Third Circuit in *Mintze* reversed a bankruptcy court's denial of arbitration of a debtor's Truth In Lending Act claims and other claims arising under federal and state consumer protection statutes that were raised as objections to a lender's proof of claim.[165] The Third Circuit found that it was of no matter whether these statutory claims were core or non-core because the only claims that could create a conflict between arbitration and bankruptcy law justifying a denial of arbitration were those arising under the Bankruptcy Code.[166]

However, many cases continue to uphold the bankruptcy court's broad authority to exercise its sound discretion.[167] Most recently, statutory developments as well as certain pro-arbitration decisions by the Supreme Court[168] have led courts in *non-core* matters to shift discretionary power away from the bankruptcy courts and towards mandatory enforcement of arbitration agreements.[169]

4.2.3.4 Court Need Not Require Arbitration of Core Matters

If the consumer's claim concerns a *core proceeding*, many courts hold that the bankruptcy court has wide discretion to determine if the arbitration should be stayed.[170] The Bank-

---

160 Bankruptcy Amendments and Federal Judgeship Act of 1984, Pub. L. No. 98-353, 98 Stat. 333; *see* National Consumer Law Center, Consumer Bankruptcy Law and Practice § 13.2 (8th ed. 2006).

161 Under the jurisdictional scheme, virtually all bankruptcy matters are immediately referred by the district court to the bankruptcy court, which is a "unit" of the district court. 28 U.S.C. § 151. If the proceeding is a non-core proceeding, the bankruptcy judge may not enter a final judgment or order unless the parties consent. 28 U.S.C. § 157(c)(1), (2). If the parties do not consent, the bankruptcy judge will issue proposed findings of fact and conclusions of law. Any party may object to the proposed findings and conclusions, in which case the matter will be heard de novo in the district court. 28 U.S.C. § 157(c)(1), (2).

162 *See* Hays & Co. v. Merrill Lynch, Pierce, Fenner & Smith, Inc., 885 F.2d 1149 (3d Cir. 1989) (when an adversary proceeding involves a non-core matter, court lacks discretion to deny enforcement of arbitration absent showing that text, legislative history, or purpose of Bankruptcy Code conflicts with arbitration of the matter in question); *see also In re* Nat'l Gypsum Co., 118 F.3d 1056, 1067 (5th Cir. 1997) ("[W]e refuse to find . . . an inherent conflict [between the Bankruptcy Code and FAA] based solely on the jurisdictional nature of a bankruptcy proceeding."); *cf. In re* Guild Music Corp., 100 B.R. 624 (Bankr. D.R.I. 1989) (court retains discretion to decline to enforce arbitration even as to non-core matters).

163 434 F.3d 222 (3d Cir. 2006).

164 *Id.* at 231–232.

165 *Id.* at 231.

166 *Id.* at 231–232.

167 *See, e.g., In re* Slipped Disc, Inc., 245 B.R. 342 (Bankr. N.D. Iowa 2000); *see also* Jeffrey T. Ferriell, *Core Proceedings in Bankruptcy Court*, 56 UMKC L. Rev. 47 (1987); Fred Neufeld, *Enforcement of Contractual Arbitration Agreements Under the Bankruptcy Code*, 65 Am. Bankr. L.J. 525, 545 (1991) (providing a circuit-by-circuit analysis of the recent cases and finding that: "A review of the current state of the law at the district court and bankruptcy court level shows that the bankruptcy courts have been reluctant to relinquish control over proceedings involving the debtor or the property of the estate.").

168 *See* Shearson/American Express, Inc. v. McMahon, 482 U.S. 220, 107 S. Ct. 2332, 96 L. Ed. 2d 185 (1987) (in determining whether the FAA preempts other federal statutes, the party arguing against arbitration must show that Congress intended to preclude a waiver of judicial remedies in the particular statute at issue).

This standard is discussed in § 4.2.1.1, *supra*. This test, known as the "*McMahon* test" or "*McMahon* standard," has been adopted by a number of courts in resolving the conflict between the Bankruptcy Code and the FAA. *See, e.g., In re* Nat'l Gypsum Co., 118 F.3d 1056, 1064–1069 (5th Cir. 1997).

169 *See* § 4.2.3.6, *infra*.

170 *See, e.g., In re* Elec. Mach. Enterprises, Inc., 479 F.3d 791, 796 (11th Cir. 2007) (noting that bankruptcy court may decide core proceeding if enforcement of arbitration agreement "would inherently conflict with the underlying purposes of the Bankruptcy Code"); MBNA Am. Bank v. Hill, 436 F.3d 104, 108 (2d Cir. 2006) (bankruptcy court has discretion to deny arbitration of core claim when "arbitration of the claim would 'necessarily jeopardize' the objectives of the Bankruptcy Code"); *In re* White Mountain Mining Co., L.L.C. v. Congelton, L.L.C., 403 F.3d 164, 169–170 (4th Cir. 2005) (recognizing bankruptcy court's discretion to deny arbitration of core dispute even in case under FAA Chapter 2 governing international arbitration agreements); *In re* Gandy, 299 F.3d 489, 495 (5th Cir. 2002) (bankruptcy court may "decline to stay a proceeding whose underlying nature derives exclusively from the provisions of the Bankruptcy Code"); *In re* U.S. Lines, Inc., 197 F.3d 631, 641 (2d Cir. 1999) ("[i]t was within the bankruptcy court's discretion to refuse to refer the declaratory judgment proceedings, which it properly found to be core, to arbitration"); Selcke v. New Eng. Ins. Co., 995 F.2d 688, 691 (7th Cir. 1993) ("[e]ven broadly worded arbitration clauses are assumed not to extend to claims that arise out of the provisions of the bankruptcy law

§ 4.2.3.4 Consumer Arbitration Agreements

ruptcy Code gives examples of core proceedings but does not explicitly define the phrase "core proceeding."[171] One judge explained the category as follows:

> If the proceeding involves a right created by the federal bankruptcy law, it is a core proceeding; for example, an action by the trustee to avoid a preference. If the proceeding is one that would arise only in bankruptcy, it is also a core proceeding; for example, the filing of a proof of claim or an objection to the discharge of a particular debt. If the proceeding does not invoke a substantive right created by the federal bankruptcy law and is one that could exist outside of bankruptcy it is not a core proceeding [although] it may be related to the bankruptcy because of its potential effect.[172]

If the court determines that the proceeding involves a core bankruptcy matter and that enforcement of the arbitration agreement would conflict with the purposes of the Bankruptcy Code, the bankruptcy court may exercise discretion to decide whether the matter should be sent to arbitration.[173] In using its discretion, bankruptcy courts consistently rely upon the following three factors: (1) the degree to which the nature and extent of litigation and evidence would make the judicial forum preferable to arbitration, (2) the extent to which special expertise is necessary to resolve the dispute, and (3) the extent to which the bankruptcy court can more efficiently and economically resolve the dispute without depleting estate assets.[174]

Another factor given considerable weight is that bankruptcy courts can more appropriately consider the interests of creditors who are not a party to the arbitration agreement and who would likely be precluded from participating in the arbitration forum.[175] Other relevant factors may include the identity of the persons comprising the arbitration panel and their track record in resolving disputes; the stage of the arbitration at the time of the bankruptcy filing and the

---

itself"); *In re* Am. Freight Sys., Inc., 164 B.R. 341, 347 (D. Kan. 1994) ("The teachings of *Hays & Co.* are not applicable to an adversary proceeding involving a core matter."); *In re* FRG, 115 B.R. 72, 74, 75 (E.D. Pa. 1990); *In re* Northwestern Corp. v. Nat'l Union Fire Ins. Co. of Pittsburgh, 321 B.R. 120, 123 (Bankr. D. Del. 2005); Lucas v. Cash 'N Advance, Inc. (*In re* Lucas), 312 B.R. 407, 409–410 (Bankr. D. Nev. 2004); *In re* Hemphill Bus Sales, Inc., 259 B.R. 865 (Bankr. E.D. Tex. 2001); *In re* Spectrum Info. Technologies, Inc., 183 B.R. 360, 363 (Bankr. E.D.N.Y. 1995) ("[E]specially with respect to core proceedings, . . . arbitration should not triumph over the specific jurisdiction bestowed upon the bankruptcy courts under the Bankruptcy Code." (citing cases)); *In re* Sacred Heart Hosp., 181 B.R. 195, 202 (Bankr. E.D. Pa. 1995) ("[A]s to core proceedings, this court may exercise its full panoply of discretion . . . in determining whether to refer a proceeding before it to arbitration."); *In re* Glen Eagle Square, Inc., 1991 Bankr. LEXIS 1422 (Bankr. E.D. Pa. May 1, 1991) (holding that the court retained discretion to order arbitration of core proceedings because "they impact upon the Debtor's relationship with its entire body of creditors"). *But see In re* James P. Barkman, Inc., 170 B.R. 321, 323 n.1 (Bankr. E.D. Mich. 1994) ("For purposes of determining whether Congress intended to carve out an exception to § 3 of the Arbitration Act, the core/non-core distinction would seem to be of only indirect significance.").

171 *See* 28 U.S.C. § 157(b)(2).

172 *In re* Jotan, Inc., 232 B.R. 503, 506 (Bankr. M.D. Fla. 1999) (citing *In re* Wood, 825 F.2d 90, 97 (5th Cir. 1987)); *see also In re* Elec. Mach. Enterprises, Inc., 479 F.3d 791 (11th Cir. 2007); *In re* White Mountain Mining Co., L.L.C. v. Congelton, L.L.C., 403 F.3d 164, 169 (4th Cir. 2005) ("Core proceedings include, for example, 'matters concerning the administration of the estate' and the 'allowance or disallowance of claims against the estate.'" (citing 28 U.S.C. § 157(b)(2)(A)); *In re* Slipped Disc, Inc., 245 B.R. 342, 345 (Bankr. N.D. Iowa 2000) ("[w]hen the issues to be arbitrated do not implicate . . . some other substantive right created in the Bankruptcy Code, the issues are non-core and suitable for arbitration, even if they arise in a § 157(b) core proceeding"); Fred Neufeld, *Enforcement of Contractual Arbitration Agreements under the Bankruptcy Code*, 65 Am. Bankr. L.J. 525, 528 (1991) ("A core proceeding has been defined as one involving a right created by federal bankruptcy law and which would only arise in bankruptcy. . . . A non-core proceeding is defined as a civil proceeding which could have been brought in a federal or state court in the absence of a bankruptcy petition.").

For a more detailed discussion of bankruptcy court jurisdiction, see National Consumer Law Center, Consumer Bankruptcy Law and Practice Ch. 13 (8th ed. 2006).

173 If the proceeding involves both core and non-core matters, the bankruptcy court is more likely to exercise discretion when the core bankruptcy claims predominate. *See In re* Gandy, 299 F.3d 489 (5th Cir. 2002).

174 *See, e.g., In re* White Mountain Mining Co., L.L.C. v. Congelton, L.L.C., 403 F.3d 164, 170 (4th Cir. 2005) (upholding bankruptcy court's findings that arbitration of allegation that cash advance to debtor was loan would make it difficult for debtor to attract funding, would undermine creditors' and other parties' confidence, and would impose added costs on the estate); *In re* First Alliance Mortgage Co., 280 B.R. 246 (C.D. Cal. 2002) (arbitration of class truth in lending and unfair and deceptive practices claims against debtor mortgage lender would deplete estate assets and negatively impact creditors); Lucas v. Cash 'N Advance, Inc. (*In re* Lucas), 312 B.R. 407, 409–410 (Bankr. D. Nev. 2004) (finding debtor's TILA claims to raise core issues as counterclaims to a proof of claim but enforcing arbitration clause because of nominal amounts at stake); *In re* Hicks, 285 B.R. 317 (Bankr. W.D. Okla. 2002) (arbitration agreement requiring creditor to pay costs for only first day of arbitration will significantly impact bankruptcy estate and creditors because proceeding on debtor's Truth in Lending Act rescission claim likely to last more than one day); *In re* Hemphill Bus Sales, Inc., 259 B.R. 865 (Bankr. E.D. Tex. 2001); *In re* Trident Shipworks, Inc., 243 B.R. 130, 133 (Bankr. M.D. Fla. 1999); *In re* Spectrum Info. Technologies, Inc., 183 B.R. 360 (Bankr. E.D.N.Y. 1995); *In re* Bicoastal Corp., 111 B.R. 999 (Bankr. M.D. Fla. 1990); *In re* Edgerton, 98 B.R. 392 (Bankr. N.D. Ill. 1989).

175 *See, e.g., In re* White Mountain Mining Co., L.L.C. v. Congelton, L.L.C., 403 F.3d 164, 170 (4th Cir. 2005); *In re* Larocque, 283 B.R. 640 (Bankr. D.R.I. 2002); *In re* Hemphill Bus Sales, Inc., 259 B.R. 865 (Bankr. E.D. Tex. 2001). *But see* MBNA Am. Bank v. Hill, 436 F.3d 104, 109–110 (2d Cir. 2006) (reversing bankruptcy court's denial of arbitration for claims asserted after bankruptcy was closed, finding that "arbitration would not interfere with or affect the distribution of the estate").

likelihood that further arbitration proceedings will delay the administration of the bankruptcy estate; whether the party seeking to enforce the arbitration clause has filed a proof of claim in the debtor's bankruptcy; and interpretation of the congressional intent underlying the federal bankruptcy statutes giving rise to a possible irreconcilable conflict.[176] In general, courts use their discretion to hold that core matters should be resolved in the bankruptcy court and not in arbitration.[177]

The United States Court of Appeals for the Third Circuit, however, departed from this substantial body of authority by holding that a bankruptcy court only has discretion to deny arbitration of a party's core claims *if those claims arise under provisions of the Bankruptcy Code itself.*[178] The Third Circuit reversed two lower court opinions denying arbitration of a debtor's core claims objecting to a creditor's proof of claim based on violations of the Truth In Lending Act and other federal and state consumer protection statutes.[179] While not taking issue with the lower courts' treatment of these statutory claims as involving a core bankruptcy proceeding, the Third Circuit held that requiring arbitration could only conflict with the Bankruptcy Code's underlying purposes when claims arose from the Code itself: "Mintze has failed to raise any statutory claims that were created by the Bankruptcy Code. With no bankruptcy issue to be decided by the Bankruptcy Court, we cannot find an inherent conflict between arbitration . . . and the underlying purposes of the Bankruptcy Code."[180]

The Third Circuit's ruling in *Mintze* almost immediately came under fire for adopting a formalistic test that fails to account for how the Bankruptcy Code's underlying purposes may be implicated when *any* claim in a core proceeding, regardless of its source, is split off from the bankruptcy case for separate arbitral resolution. One bankruptcy court has found that *Mintze* adopted a "somewhat strained interpretation of 'bankruptcy issue' given the context of the ongoing chapter 13 plan," and quoted secondary authority criticizing *Mintze*'s finding as " 'overly simplistic.' "[181]

4.2.3.5 Application to Consumer Cases

The core/non-core distinction generally favors the resolution of consumer claims in the bankruptcy court rather than by arbitration.[182] For example, an action seeking to enforce the rescission of a home mortgage under the Truth in Lending Act may be brought as an adversary proceeding filed within a bankruptcy case and will be treated as a core proceeding.[183]

Likewise, claims and defenses of all types asserting violations of consumer protection statutes or based on common law theories may be filed as an objection to a creditor's proof of claim in a consumer bankruptcy case. Claims asserted in this manner involve the administration of the debtor's bankruptcy case[184] and are likely to be retained by the bankruptcy

---

176 *See In re* Gandy, 299 F.3d 489, 499 (5th Cir. 2002) (filing of proof of claim by party in adversary proceeding invoked "peculiar powers of the bankruptcy court"); *In re* Hemphill Bus Sales, Inc., 259 B.R. 865 (Bankr. E.D. Tex. 2001); *In re* Slipped Disc, Inc., 245 B.R. 342, 345, 346 (Bankr. N.D. Iowa 2000) (relying on the following factors: expediency of court versus arbitration in resolving the dispute; whether special expertise is necessary; the impact on creditors who were not parties to the arbitration agreement; and whether arbitration "threatens assets of the estate"); *In re* Jotan, Inc., 232 B.R. 503, 507 (Bankr. M.D. Fla. 1999) (determining that, in some cases, ordering arbitration might hamper the "ability [of the debtor] . . . to proceed to sell certain assets of their business without worry as to arbitrating claims"); *In re* Day, 208 B.R. 358, 370 (Bankr. E.D. Pa. 1997) ("Deferring allowance of the claims to arbitration would likely result in delays of several months before we would be able to rule on confirmation and thus significantly delay the progress of these cases.").

177 *See In re* Hemphill Bus Sales, Inc., 259 B.R. 865 (Bankr. E.D. Tex. 2001); *In re* Spectrum Info. Technologies, Inc., 183 B.R. 360 (Bankr. E.D.N.Y. 1995) (and cases cited therein); *In re* Guild Music Corp., 100 B.R. 624 (Bankr. D.R.I. 1989); *see also In re* Trident Shipworks, Inc., 243 B.R. 130, 133 (Bankr. M.D. Fla. 1999). *Compare* Zimmerman v. Cont'l Airlines, Inc., 712 F.2d 55 (3d Cir. 1983) *with* Hays & Co. v. Merrill Lynch, Pierce, Fenner & Smith, Inc., 885 F.2d 1149 (3d Cir. 1989).

178 *In re* Mintze, 434 F.3d 222, 231–232 (3d Cir. 2006).

179 *Id.* at 231.

180 *Id.* at 231–232.

181 *In re* Merrill, 343 B.R. 1 (Bankr. D. Me. 2006) (quoting Jacob Aaron Esher, *Arbitration and Judicial Discretion: The Circuits are Split*, Norton Bankr. L. Advisor, May 2006, at 6, 9–10); *see also In re* Brown, 354 B.R. 591, 601 (D.R.I. 2006) (finding that *Mintze* approach in which bankruptcy courts are afforded discretion to deny arbitration only if proceeding derives from bankruptcy law is inconsistent with intent of Federal Arbitration Act to "place arbitration agreements on the same footing as other contracts").

182 Consumer claims are generally raised in an "adversary proceeding," which is a lawsuit within the bankruptcy case initiated by the filing of an adversary complaint. An adversary proceeding is subject to procedural rules almost identical to the Federal Rules of Civil Procedure. *See* Fed. R. Bankr. P. 7001–7087.
    For a more detailed discussion of adversary proceedings, see National Consumer Law Center, Consumer Bankruptcy Law and Practice Ch. 13 (8th ed. 2006).

183 Such an action involves a "determination of the validity, extent or priority of liens." 28 U.S.C. § 157(b)(2)(K); *see In re* Brown, 354 B.R. 591 (D.R.I. 2006) (affirming bankruptcy court's exercise of discretion to deny arbitration of core proceeding involving TILA rescission claim); *In re* Larocque, 283 B.R. 640 (Bankr. D.R.I. 2002) (resolution of TILA rescission claim will determine whether mortgage lender treated as secured or unsecured creditor in chapter 13 case). *But see In re* Arellano, 2007 WL 1746246 (Bankr. D.N.M. June 14, 2007) (adversary proceeding brought to determine validity, extent, or priority of mortgage lien based entirely on state and federal non-bankruptcy law was not core proceeding; court lacked discretion to deny referral to arbitration).
    For a discussion of litigating a Truth in Lending Act claim in bankruptcy, see National Consumer Law Center, Consumer Bankruptcy Law and Practice § 13.4.4 (8th ed. 2006).

184 An objection to a proof of claim is a core proceeding because it involves the "allowance or disallowance of claims against the

court despite the creditor's attempt to enforce an arbitration clause.[185] On the other hand, when the consumer is bringing a claim against a defendant who has not submitted a proof of claim, or when a consumer claim is not brought as an objection to a creditor's proof of claim, the result may be different.[186]

Some courts have wrongly concluded that a claim objection proceeding in which truth in lending or other consumer protection causes of action are asserted is not a core proceeding because the consumer claims do not derive from bankruptcy law.[187] These courts improperly focus on the derivation of the legal claims rather than on the nature of the proceeding itself. Non-bankruptcy law is often applied exclusively by bankruptcy courts in determining whether a creditors' claim should be allowed and this reliance on applicable non-bankruptcy law does not transform the proceeding into a non-core matter.[188] Because a claim objection proceeding is unique to bankruptcy law and can arise only in a bankruptcy case, it is a core proceeding irrespective of whether the objection itself is grounded in non-bankruptcy law.[189] On this point, the Fifth Circuit has stated:

> A claim against the estate is instituted by filing a proof of claim as provided by the bankruptcy rules. The filing of the proof invokes the special rules of bankruptcy concerning objections to the claim, estimation of the claim for allowance purposes, and the rights of the claimant to vote on the proposed distribution. Understood in this sense, a claim filed against the estate is a core proceeding because it could arise only in the context of bankruptcy. Of course, the state-law right underlying the claim could be enforced in a state court proceeding absent the bankruptcy, but the nature of the state proceeding would be different from the nature of the proceeding following the filing of a proof of claim.[190]

In addition, an arbitration clause should not prevent a bankruptcy court from resolving creditor abuses involving the bankruptcy process itself, such as violations of the automatic stay and discharge injunction, as these proceedings are clearly core proceedings and directly implicate the purposes of the Bankruptcy Code.[191] Such proceedings also may not fall within the scope of the arbitration agreement.[192]

---

estate" and may include "counterclaims by the estate against persons filing claims against the estate." 28 U.S.C. § 157(b)(2)(B), (C); *see In re* Hicks, 285 B.R. 317 (Bankr. W.D. Okla. 2002) (debtor's objection to lender's secured claim is core proceeding); *In re* Pate, 198 B.R. 841 (Bankr. S.D. Ga. 1996) (TILA adversary proceeding filed in response to creditor's proof of claim in chapter 13 case is core proceeding based on 28 U.S.C. § 157(b)(2)(C)).

185 *See In re* Serv. Marine Indus., Inc., 2000 U.S. Dist. LEXIS 16580 (E.D. La. Nov. 3, 2000) (staying the bankruptcy proceeding to allow the creditor to arbitrate the objection to its claim would prejudice the rights of all the other creditors and delay the administration of the debtor's bankruptcy); *cf.* Lucas v. Cash 'N Advance, Inc. (*In re* Lucas), 312 B.R. 407 (Bankr. D. Nev. 2004) (TIL counterclaim to proof of claim is a core proceeding, but court in its discretion does not use that as basis to avoid arbitration clause but does so on other grounds). *But see In re* Dawsey, 2007 WL 1140358 (Bankr. M.D. Ala. Apr. 16, 2007) (adversary proceeding in which TILA claims asserted as counterclaims to creditor's proof of claim referred to arbitration); *In re* Cooley, 362 B.R. 514 (Bankr. N.D. Ala. 2007) (core proceeding asserting TILA claims by way of recoupment to creditor's proof of claim referred to arbitration because debtor's claims not derived from bankruptcy law and therefore enforcement of arbitration does not present conflict with Bankruptcy Code).

186 *In re* Dixon, 2007 WL 703612 (Bankr. M.D. Ala. Mar. 5, 2007) (finding that adversary proceeding asserting state law claims against mobile home lender which had not filed proof of claim for deficiency in debtor's bankruptcy case was not core proceeding); Brown v. Ocwen Fed. Bank, 311 B.R. 702 (Bankr. E.D. Pa. 2004); *see also In re* Gardner, 2006 WL 3735942 (Bankr. N.D. Ala. Dec. 14, 2006) (concluding that arbitration of TILA action filed after chapter 13 plan confirmation and which did not seek to reduce creditor's claim would not delay or interfere with debtor's confirmed plan).

187 *E.g., In re* Rozell, 357 B.R. 638 (Bankr. N.D. Ala. 2006).

188 Section 502(b) of the Bankruptcy Code mandates a procedure for bankruptcy courts to determine the amount and allowance of claims if an objection to the claim is filed. It provides that "the court, after notice and hearing, shall determine the amount of such claim . . . and shall allow such claim in such amount." 11 U.S.C. § 502(b); *see also* Fed. R. Bankr. P. 3007.

The bankruptcy court may disallow the claim if it is "unenforceable against the debtor" based on the contract between the parties or "applicable law." 11 U.S.C. § 502(b)(1).

189 *In re* Martinez, 2007 WL 1174186 (Bankr. S.D. Tex. Apr. 19, 2007) (rejecting argument that objection to creditor's claim based solely on TILA and state law is non-core proceeding).

190 *In re* Wood, 825 F.2d 90, 97 (5th Cir. 1987) (internal quotations omitted).

191 *See In re* Merrill, 343 B.R. 1 (Bankr. D. Me. 2006) (court exercised discretion to deny motion to compel arbitration of stay violation claim); *In re* Startec Global Communications Corp., 300 B.R. 244, 253, 254 (D. Md. 2003) (declining to order arbitration of stay violation proceeding on basis that "the automatic stay is the single most important protection afforded to debtors by the Bankruptcy Code"), *stayed pending appeal,* 303 B.R. 605 (D. Md. 2004) (court noted that arbitrability was "an open question"); *In re* Cavanaugh, 271 B.R. 414 (Bankr. D. Mass. 2001) (debtor's claim for violation of the automatic stay derives exclusively from the Bankruptcy Code); *In re* Grant, 281 B.R. 721 (Bankr. S.D. Ala. 2000) (bankruptcy court's inherent power to enforce its own orders must be upheld over arbitration clause). *But see* MBNA Am. Bank v. Hill, 436 F.3d 104 (2d Cir. 2006) (distinguishing facts from other cases in which appellate courts have affirmed bankruptcy court discretion to refuse to stay proceedings pending arbitration; court noted that debtor's estate had been fully administered before stay violation proceeding was heard by the bankruptcy court and that debtor therefore no longer required protection of Bankruptcy Code's automatic stay).

192 *In re* Startec Global Communications Corp., 300 B.R. 244, 253, 254 (D. Md. 2003) (arbitration clause referring to claims arising out of or connected with prepetition agreement did not encompass alleged violations of court orders or postpetition agreements), *stayed pending appeal,* 303 B.R. 605 (D. Md. 2004) (court noted that arbitrability was "an open question").

One court has held that the unique grant of jurisdiction to bankruptcy courts over stay-violation proceedings establishes that Congress intended to preclude a waiver of remedies under the Bankruptcy Code for such violations.[193]

However, the Second Circuit has held that, even in cases alleging violations of the automatic bankruptcy stay, the bankruptcy court's discretion to deny arbitration is limited and arbitration must be allowed when the claim is asserted after the bankruptcy case is completed and there are no longer any ongoing proceedings with which arbitration could interfere.[194]

And, in a departure from prior precedent, the Third Circuit in *In re Mintze*[195] reversed the bankruptcy court's exercise of discretion to refuse to compel arbitration of an adversary proceeding in a chapter 13 case which sought to enforce the debtor's rescission of her home mortgage based on violations of the Truth in Lending Act. The *Mintze* panel concluded that the core/non-core distinction was not dispositive and that the bankruptcy court lacked discretion to adjudicate the claims asserted by the debtor in the core proceeding because the claims did not derive precisely from the Bankruptcy Code and instead involved the application of separate federal and state consumer protection statutes.[196]

The opinion is troubling from a procedural standpoint because the court erroneously applied a de novo standard of review rather than a clearly erroneous or abuse of discretion standard. More significantly, the *Mintze* court misapplied the *McMahon* "inherent conflict" analysis[197] by narrowly focusing on the legal basis for the claims in the core proceeding and ignoring the role of the proceeding in relation to the overall bankruptcy case and the Code's goal of centralized jurisdiction over property of the estate. Adversary proceedings typically involve legal claims that are based solely or primarily on non-bankruptcy law, but that factor is not determinative of whether the proceeding may be inextricably intertwined with other matters involving the bankruptcy estate or the administration of the bankruptcy case. In *Mintze*, adjudication of the adversary proceeding in an arbitration forum presented a clear conflict with the Code's jurisdictional scheme because the proceeding concerned matters central to the chapter 13 case, such as confirmation of the debtor's chapter 13 plan and related matters concerning priority of creditor claims and the amount of distributions to unsecured creditors. The Third Circuit panel in *Mintze* refused to recognize this conflict and instead placed undue emphasis on the lack of a "bankruptcy issue."

4.2.3.6 Non-Core Matters Subject to Arbitration

If the dispute involves a non-core matter, on the other hand, the courts are much more likely to follow the reasoning of *Hays* that a bankruptcy court "should enforce [an arbitration] clause unless that effect would seriously jeopardize the objectives of the [Bankruptcy] Code."[198] As one court explained:

> [A]ny conflict between the Bankruptcy Code, which favors centralization of disputes concerning a debtor's estate, and the [Federal] Arbitration Act, which advocates a decentralized approach to dispute resolution, is lessened in non-core proceedings which are unlikely to present a conflict sufficient to override by implication the presumption in favor of arbitration.... In sum, bankruptcy courts must generally stay non-core proceedings in favor of arbitration. Core proceedings implicate more pressing bankruptcy concerns.[199]

Bankruptcy courts must generally stay non-core proceedings in favor of arbitration.[200]

---

193 *In re* Cavanaugh, 271 B.R. 414 (Bankr. D. Mass. 2001).
    The *Cavanaugh* court relied upon *In re* Gruntz, 202 F.3d 1074 (9th Cir. 2000), which held that bankruptcy courts have final authority to determine the application and scope of the automatic stay, making bankruptcy stay orders immune from collateral attack by state courts.
194 MBNA Am. Bank v. Hill, 436 F.3d 104, 109–110 (2d Cir. 2006).
195 434 F.3d 222 (3d Cir. 2006).
196 *Id.* at 231–232 (3d Cir. 2006) ("Mintze has failed to raise any statutory claims that were created by the Bankruptcy Code. With no bankruptcy issue to be decided by the Bankruptcy Court, we cannot find an inherent conflict between arbitration of Mintze's federal and state consumer protection issues and the underlying purposes of the Bankruptcy Code."); *see also In re* Herrington, 2007 WL 2318135 (Bankr. E.D. Pa. Aug. 8, 2007) (determining based on *Mintze* that bankruptcy court lacked discretion to deny enforcement of arbitration agreement in core proceeding raising TILA and UDAP claims).
197 *See* § 4.2.3.3, *supra*.
198 Hays & Co. v. Merrill Lynch, Pierce, Fenner & Smith, Inc., 885 F.2d 1149, 1161 (3d Cir. 1989); *see also In re* Crysen/Montenay Energy Co., 226 F.3d 160 (2d Cir. 2000) ("[T]he presumption in favor of arbitration generally will trump the lesser interest of bankruptcy courts in adjudicating non-core proceedings which are unlikely to present a conflict sufficient to override by implication the presumption in favor of arbitration."); *In re* U.S. Lines, Inc., 197 F.3d 631 (2d Cir. 1999) (same); *In re* Nat'l Gypsum Co., 118 F.3d 1056, 1065 (5th Cir. 1997) (stating that the *Hays* standard for non-core matters is now "universally accepted"); *In re* Cooker Restaurant Corp., 292 B.R. 308 (S.D. Ohio 2003); *In re* Northwestern Corp. v. Nat'l Union Fire Ins. Co. of Pittsburgh, 321 B.R. 120, 122 (Bankr. D. Del. 2005); Lucas v. Cash 'N Advance, Inc. (*In re* Lucas), 312 B.R. 407 (Bankr. D. Nev. 2004); Brown v. Ocwen Fed. Bank, 311 B.R. 702 (Bankr. E.D. Pa. 2004); *In re* Teu Holdings, Inc., 287 B.R. 26 (Bankr. D. Del. 2002); *In re* Slipped Disc, Inc., 245 B.R. 342 (Bankr. N.D. Iowa 2000); *In re* Jotan, Inc., 232 B.R. 503 (Bankr. M.D. Fla. 1999). *But see* Fred Neufeld, *Enforcement of Contractual Arbitration Agreements under the Bankruptcy Code*, 65 Am. Bankr. L.J. 525 (1991) (providing a circuit-by-circuit analysis and concluding that *Hays* remains the "minority view").
199 *In re* Crysen/Montenay Energy Co., 226 F.3d 160, 166 (2d Cir. 2000); *see also In re* Slipped Disk, Inc., 245 B.R. 342, 345 (Bankr. N.D. Iowa 2000) (citing *In re* Pisgah Contractors, Inc., 215 B.R. 679 (W.D.N.C. 1995)).
200 *In re* Crysen/Montenay Energy Co., 226 F.3d 160 (2d Cir.

§ 4.2.3.7 Confirmed Plan Can Bar Enforcement of Arbitration Clause

The order confirming a chapter 13 plan is binding upon the debtor and all creditors, and is res judicata as to all issues which could have been raised in opposition to confirmation.[201] After confirmation, no creditor may take actions that are inconsistent with the plan.[202]

The binding effect of a bankruptcy reorganization plan led one court to recently conclude that a plan which expressly provided that the bankruptcy court would retain jurisdiction to "adjudicate" a pending adversary proceeding precluded one of the parties from enforcing an arbitration agreement after the plan was confirmed.[203] The court found that the party had actively participated in the plan confirmation process and could have protected its right to arbitrate by objecting to the plan. Consumers seeking to litigate claims in an adversary proceeding filed within a chapter 13 bankruptcy may wish to include a specific provision in the plan providing that the claims raised in the adversary proceeding are to be determined by the bankruptcy court.[204]

4.3 Arbitration Clauses That *Explicitly* Limit Consumers' Statutory Rights

4.3.1 General Principles

4.3.1.1 Arbitration Clause Cannot Limit Federal Statutory Right

It is axiomatic that an arbitration agreement that prevents a consumer from obtaining relief under a federal statutory claim is unenforceable because it conflicts with the legislature's purpose in enacting the statute. The concept that an arbitration clause may not limit a consumer's statutory rights follows from a premise that the United States Supreme Court has repeatedly set forth:

> We have held that federal statutory claims may be the subject of arbitration agreements that are enforceable pursuant to the FAA because the agreement only determines the choice of forum. "In these cases we recognized that '[b]y agreeing to arbitrate a statutory claim, a party does not forgo the substantive rights afforded by the statute; it only submits to their resolution in an arbitral, rather than a judicial, forum.'"[205]

The California Supreme Court recently summarized the extent of the consensus on this point as follows: "The principle that an arbitration agreement may not limit statutorily imposed remedies such as punitive damages and attorney fees appears to be undisputed."[206] Therefore, an arbitration clause that prevents a party from effectively vindicating her federal statutory rights should not be enforced.[207] Some courts have also refused to enforce arbitration clauses that barred consumers from vindicating their rights under state statutes.[208]

2000); *In re* U.S. Lines, Inc., 197 F.3d 631 (2d Cir. 1999). *But see In re* Caldor, Inc., 217 B.R. 121 (Bankr. S.D.N.Y. 1998).

To the extent that an arbitration agreement is binding on the debtor, courts have held that it is similarly binding on the bankruptcy trustee. *See, e.g.*, Hays & Co. v. Merrill Lynch, Pierce, Fenner & Smith, Inc., 885 F.2d 1149, 1153 (3d Cir. 1989).

201 11 U.S.C. § 1327(a); *In re* Harvey, 213 F.3d 318 (7th Cir. 2000); *In re* Anderson, 179 F.3d 1253 (10th Cir. 1999); Corbett v. MacDonald Moving Services, Inc., 124 F.3d 82 (2d Cir. 1997); *In re* Ivory, 70 F.3d 73 (9th Cir. 1995); *see also* National Consumer Law Center, Consumer Bankruptcy Law and Practice § 12.11 (8th ed. 2006).

202 *In re* Talbot, 124 F.3d 1201 (10th Cir. 1997).

203 Ernst & Young, L.L.P. v. Baker O'Neal Holdings, Inc., 304 F.3d 753, 756 (7th Cir. 2002) ("[creditor's] right to arbitrate is superceded by the terms of the confirmed plan").

Although the case involved a business reorganization plan under chapter 11, as the court's holding is based on the binding effect of confirmed bankruptcy plans, it is applicable in chapter 13 cases.

204 Sample chapter 13 plans can be found in Appendix G, National Consumer Law Center, Consumer Bankruptcy Law and Practice (8th ed. 2006).

205 Equal Employment Opportunity Comm'n v. Waffle House, Inc., 534 U.S. 279, 122 S. Ct. 754, 770 n.10, 151 L. Ed. 2d 755 (2002) (quoting Mitsubishi Motors Corp. v. Soler Chrysler-Plymouth, Inc., 473 U.S. 614, 628, 105 S. Ct. 3346, 87 L. Ed. 2d 444 (1985) and Gilmer v. Interstate/Johnson Lane Corp., 500 U.S. 20, 26, 111 S. Ct. 1647, 114 L. Ed. 2d 26 (1991)).

206 Armendariz v. Found. Health Psychcare Services, Inc., 24 Cal. 4th 83, 103, 99 Cal. Rptr. 2d 745, 6 P.3d 669 (2000).

207 Walker v. Ryan's Family Steak Houses, Inc., 400 F.3d 370 (6th Cir. 2005); McMullen v. Meijer, Inc., 355 F.3d 485, 491, 492 (6th Cir. 2004); Safranek v. Copart, Inc., 379 F. Supp. 2d 927, 930 (N.D. Ill. 2005) ("[O]nly those agreements that do not undermine the statutory scheme are enforceable."); Booker v. Robert Half Int'l, Inc., 315 F. Supp. 2d 94, 104 (D.D.C. 2004). *But see* Faber v. Menard, Inc., 367 F.3d 1048, 1052 (8th Cir. 2004) ("Questions about remedy do not affect the validity of the agreement to arbitrate.")

208 *See* Mayard-Paul v. The Mega Life & Health Ins. Co., 2001 U.S. Dist. LEXIS 22256 (S.D. Fla. Dec. 21, 2001) ("the Court finds the arbitration clause unenforceable due to its conflict with

The Southern District of New York has held that "contractual clauses purporting to mandate arbitration of statutory claims as a condition of employment are enforceable only if the arbitration preserves the substantive protections and remedies afforded by the statute."[209] The Eleventh Circuit, in *Paladino v. Avnet Computer Technologies, Inc.*,[210] has found similarly that a binding arbitration agreement that nominally applied to all of an employee's claims should be interpreted as not applying to a claim under an employment discrimination statute because the arbitration clause only allowed the arbitrator to award damages for breach of contract, and not damages for statutory claims. The rule is that if the arbitrator cannot provide relief under the legal claim relied upon by an individual employee or consumer, the arbitration clause cannot be enforced to cover such a claim.[211]

A handful of courts have refused to entertain such arguments, however. The Eighth Circuit, for example, recently held that courts may not consider challenges to the enforceability of arbitration clauses based on provisions limiting damages. The court reasoned that such challenges should only be considered by the arbitrator, not a court:

> At this juncture, our jurisdiction extends only to determine whether a valid agreement to arbitrate exists, not to determine whether public policy conflicts with the remedies provided in the arbitration clause. . . . Whether a prospective waiver of punitive damages violates the public policy underlying RICO's treble damages provision is a matter for the arbitrators in the first instance when fashioning an appropriate remedy if a RICO claim is proven to the arbitrators' satisfaction, and we express no views on the issue at this time. We are limited to determining whether the matter is arbitrable. We hold that it is.[212]

Notwithstanding these exceptions, most courts will not enforce arbitration clauses that limit statutory remedies. Those trying to enforce such clauses in these courts often argue that the offending contract language should not be grounds for refusing to enforce the arbitration clause because it may be remedied through informal means. Courts generally will not permit a party to save an otherwise illegal arbitration provision by contacting the arbitration service provider and directing the provider to interpret the provision in a manner that will render it legal:

> A solution proposed by AT & T, that it would notify the AAA of the true meaning of the Legal Remedies Provisions, does not save the Provisions for a number of reasons. It would require the court to ignore a violation of law based on a representation in court that AT & T would not seek to take advantage of the violation. It is not at all clear how AT & T would respond or how this representation would work out in practice. It would be very unfair to the class because in deciding whether to pursue a claim, the class would assume they were limited by the Legal Remedies Provisions and not by some side agreement between AT & T and the AAA.[213]

Similarly, some parties attempting to enforce arbitration clauses argue that such illegal limitations on remedies are of no consequence, as the arbitrator will necessarily ignore them because they are contrary to law. Courts will not accept this defense, however, as it disregards basic arbitration law, which confines arbitrators to the contract which creates their power.[214]

4.3.1.2 Statutory Remedies Serve Three Functions

Remedies that accompany federal consumer legislation serve three functions. They compensate the injured consumer. They also deter merchant misconduct (see, for example, the provisions for injunctive relief under a number of statutes, for punitive damages under the Equal Credit Opportunity Act and Fair Credit Reporting Act, and for class actions providing up to $500,000 in statutory damages for disclosure violations under the Fair Debt Collection Practices Act, Truth in Lending Act, Consumer Leasing Act, and Home Ownership and Equity Protection Act).

Florida law on attorney's fees"); Martinez v. Master Prot. Corp., 12 Cal. Rptr. 3d 663, 671–672 (Ct. App. 2004) (finding clause unconscionable based on limitations of statutory rights); Harper v. Ultimo, 7 Cal. Rptr. 3d 418, 423 (Ct. App. 2003) (same); Blankfeld v. Richmond Health Care, Inc., 902 So. 2d 296, 298–299 (Fla. Dist. Ct. App. 2005); Presidential Leasing, Inc. v. Krout, 896 So. 2d 938, 941–942 (Fla. Dist. Ct. App. 2005); Romano *ex rel.* Romano v. Manor Care, Inc., 861 So. 2d 59, 63 (Fla. Dist. Ct. App. 2003). *But see* Richmond Healthcare, Inc. v. Digati, 878 So. 2d 388, 390 (Fla. Dist. Ct. App. 2004) (loss of statutory right of access to court is not grounds for revoking arbitration clause).

209 De Gaetano v. Smith Barney, Inc., 983 F. Supp. 459, 469 (S.D.N.Y. 1997).
210 134 F.3d 1054 (11th Cir. 1998).
211 *See* §§ 4.3.2, 4.4, *infra* (setting out a large number of cases in which courts have refused to enforce arbitration clauses that stripped consumers of substantive statutory rights).
212 Larry's United Super, Inc. v. Dean Werries, 253 F.3d 1083, 1086 (8th Cir. 2001); *see also* Faber v. Menard, Inc., 367 F.3d 1048, 1052 (8th Cir. 2004) ("Questions about remedy . . . do not affect the validity of the agreement to arbitrate."); Hawkins v. Aid Ass'n for Lutherans, 338 F.3d 801, 807 (7th Cir. 2003) (same).

As to Paladino v. Avnet Computer Technologies, Inc., 134 F.3d 1054, 1062 (11th Cir. 1998) and Graham Oil Co. v. Arco Products Co., 43 F.3d 1244, 1248, 1249 (9th Cir. 1994), the Eighth Circuit stated: "In large part, those cases are distinguishable, and to the extent they are not distinguishable, we choose not to follow them now." Larry's United Super, Inc. v. Dean Werries, 253 F.3d 1083, 1086 (8th Cir. 2001).

213 Ting v. AT & T, 182 F. Supp. 2d 902, 926 (N.D. Cal. 2002).
214 *Id.*

Third, certain statutory remedies (for example, attorney fees and costs, minimum damages, and class actions) make it practical for consumers to enforce statutory violations, even those that involve minimal consumer injury. Relevant to this last function, the Supreme Court has stated that an arbitration clause may be set aside if the proceedings "in the contractual forum will be so gravely difficult and inconvenient that [the resisting party] will for all practical purposes be deprived of his day in court."[215]

When an arbitration provision deprives a consumer of a statutory remedy, all three purposes of the remedy must be considered in order to determine if the arbitral forum, which lacks this remedy, will serve the statute's purposes as effectively as would a judicial forum, when that remedy is available. The Supreme Court, in *Mitsubishi Motors Corp. v. Soler Chrysler-Plymouth, Inc.*, stated that if an arbitration clause waives the plaintiff's "right to pursue statutory remedies for antitrust violations, we would have little hesitation in condemning the agreement as against public policy."[216] The same Court stated, "so long as the prospective litigant effectively may vindicate [her] statutory cause of action in the arbitral forum, the statute will continue to serve both its remedial and deterrent function."[217] The clear implication is that if the consumer cannot effectively vindicate a statutory cause of action in arbitration, the arbitration clause is ineffective.

4.3.2 Limitations on Specific Statutory Rights

4.3.2.1 Introduction

The rest of this subsection examines case law that finds that limitations in arbitration on specific statutory remedies conflict with the purposes of the underlying statute. While each remedy will be analyzed separately, in practice the consumer should present the court with all the limitations and barriers to the consumer's access to a resolution of the dispute, including all limitations on remedies and also high arbitration costs.[218] Note also the discussion in § 6.5.4, *infra*, concerning whether a limitation on remedies is unconscionable.[219]

This subsection deals primarily with limitations on *federal* statutory remedies. A similar analysis should apply to limitations on state statutory remedies that serve important state policy concerns.[220] A state may restrict a private arbitration agreement when it inherently conflicts with a public statutory purpose that transcends private interests. It would be perverse if the FAA allowed individuals to vitiate through arbitration substantive rights afforded by state legislation meant to protect the public at large.[221] In any event, such a limitation should be unconscionable.[222] Therefore, cases in which courts refuse to enforce arbitration clauses for denying effective vindication of state statutory claims are also included in this chapter.

If a court finds a conflict between a federal statute and the arbitration clause, the court must then decide whether to reform the arbitration clause to eliminate the conflict or whether to simply refuse to enforce the arbitration clause. Most courts find that all parts of an arbitration clause are interdependent, and that offending parts should not be severed but the whole clause thrown out.[223] A more detailed discussion of the doctrine of severability is provided in § 6.6, *infra*.

---

215 M/S Bremen v. Zapata Off-Shore Co., 407 U.S. 1, 18, 92 S. Ct. 1907, 32 L. Ed. 2d 513 (1972) (quoted approvingly in Mitsubishi Motors Corp. v. Soler Chrysler-Plymouth, Inc., 473 U.S. 614, 105 S. Ct. 3346, 87 L. Ed. 2d 444 (1985)).

216 Mitsubishi Motors Corp. v. Soler Chrysler-Plymouth, Inc., 473 U.S. 614, 637 n.19, 105 S. Ct. 3346, 87 L. Ed. 2d 444 (1985).

217 *Id.*, 473 U.S. at 637.

218 *See* Margaret M. Harding, *The Redefinition of Arbitration by Those with Superior Bargaining Power*, 1999 Utah L. Rev. 857, 914 ("If a party is going to successfully challenge, on the basis of public policy, the enforceability of an agreement to arbitrate because it restricts remedies available by statute, it must make clear to the court that the challenge is neither premised on the unsuitability of the subject matter for arbitration, nor on the inadequacy of 'pure arbitration.' Rather, the argument must be based on the arbitrability of the statutory claim under the rules applicable to the particular arbitration.").

219 *See, e.g.,* Stirlen v. Supercuts, Inc., 51 Cal. App. 4th 1519, 60 Cal. Rptr. 2d 138 (1997); Powertel, Inc. v. Bexley, 743 So. 2d 570 (Fla. Dist. Ct. App. 1999); Samuel Williston, Treatise on the Law of Contracts § 18.13 (Richard A. Lord ed., 4th ed. 1998).

220 *See* Cruz v. PacifiCare Health Sys., Inc., 30 Cal. 4th 303, 133 Cal. Rptr. 2d 58, 66 P.3d 1157 (2003); Broughton v. CIGNA Healthplans, 21 Cal. 4th 1066, 90 Cal. Rptr. 2d 334, 988 P.2d 67 (1999); Blankfeld v. Richmond Health Care, Inc., 902 So. 2d 296, 299 (Fla. Dist. Ct. App. 2005) ("We now clarify that holding a contractual provision unenforceable because it defeats the remedial provisions of a [state] statute, and is thus contrary to public policy, is distinct from finding unconscionability.").

221 *See* Cruz v. PacifiCare Health Sys., Inc., 30 Cal. 4th 303, 133 Cal. Rptr. 2d 58, 66 P.3d 1157 (2003); Broughton v. CIGNA Healthplans, 21 Cal. 4th 1066, 90 Cal. Rptr. 2d 334, 988 P.2d 67 (1999).

222 *See* § 6.5, *infra*.

223 Paladino v. Avnet Computer Technologies, Inc., 134 F.3d 1054 (11th Cir. 1998); Graham Oil Co. v. ARCO Products Co., 43 F.3d 1244 (9th Cir. 1994). *But see* Graham v. Scissor-Tail, Inc., 28 Cal. 3d 807, 831, 171 Cal. Rptr. 604, 623 P.2d 165 (1981) (holding that in light of the "strong public policy of this state in favor of resolving disputes by arbitration," offending clause regarding non-neutral arbitrator should be severed from the agreement, but the remainder of the clause enforced); Saika v. Gold, 49 Cal. App. 4th 1074, 1082, 56 Cal. Rptr. 2d 922 (1996) (severing clause that allowed either party a trial de novo if the arbitration award exceeded $250,000, but upholding remainder of the agreement and enforcing arbitration award of $350,000 based on that agreement); Beynon v. Garden Grove Med. Group, 100 Cal. App. 3d 698, 712, 713, 161 Cal. Rptr. 146 (1980) (severing paragraph of arbitration agreement allowing health care provider to reject unacceptable arbitration award and request re-arbitration; otherwise upholding the agreement).

4.3.2.2 Arbitration Clauses That Limit Statutory Right to Attorney Fees and Costs

An essential element of the Truth in Lending Act and other federal consumer legislation is the provision requiring courts to award attorney fees to a prevailing consumer (but not to a prevailing creditor). This statutory provision, more than any other, makes enforcement of disclosure requirements in the statute practical. Not only does it make private litigation practical, but it deters creditors from improperly contesting meritorious claims. Otherwise, creditors with deep legal pockets could overwhelm any attempt by a consumer to press an action.[224]

Consequently, arbitration agreements that require each party to bear its own attorney fees and costs, regardless of which party prevails, are fundamentally in conflict with the congressional intent underlying many federal consumer statutes. Such an arbitration provision is unenforceable.[225] When an arbitration clause does not provide for an award of attorney fees, but does not explicitly forbid the arbitrator from awarding attorney fees, however, "there is no reason to believe that [a consumer] will be unable to vindicate effectively his rights under [federal consumer statutes] in arbitration."[226] It is important for parties facing arbitration clauses to differentiate between clauses that clearly and explicitly limit their statutory remedies and those that arguably may or may not limit their remedies. In the former case, in which a clause clearly bars an arbitrator from awarding a statutory remedy, the court itself must determine whether the clause is unenforceable because it violates the plaintiff's statutory rights.[227] In the latter case, in which the clause is ambiguous, the question is one of contract interpretation that is for the arbitrator to decide.[228]

4.3.2.3 When Arbitration, But Not Statute, Applies Loser Pays Rule

Some arbitration clauses contain a "loser pays rule" that requires non-prevailing consumer plaintiffs to pay the attorney fees and expenses of the prevailing defendant. These loser pays provisions often have the effect of substantially rewriting the attorney fee provisions of the consumer protection statute involved, which only authorizes attorney fees and costs for a prevailing consumer, not for a prevailing defendant. Such arbitration clauses should not be enforceable. As § 6.5.9, *infra*, discusses, these loser pays provisions may also be unconscionable.

Nearly every major consumer protection statute provides that a prevailing plaintiff shall recover attorney fees, but that a defendant shall recover attorney fees only if the plaintiffs' claims are frivolous. Such statutes include the Truth in Lending Act, the Fair Debt Collection Practices Act, the Fair Credit Reporting Act, and the Equal Credit Opportunity Act.[229]

In the related context of civil rights statutes, which also provide remedies for individuals wronged by more powerful corporations, the Supreme Court in *Christiansburg Garment Co. v. Equal Employment Opportunity Commission* enunciated the rationale behind this rule: "To take the further step of assessing attorney's fees against plaintiffs simply because they do not finally prevail would substantially add to the risks inherent in most litigation and would undercut the efforts of Congress to promote the vigorous enforcement of the provisions of Title VII."[230] This rationale has been used

---

224 Graham Oil Co. v. ARCO Products Co., 43 F.3d 1244 (9th Cir. 1994).
225 Kristian v. Comcast Corp., 446 F.3d 25, 52–53 (1st Cir. 2006) ("[T]he ban on the recovery of attorney's fees and costs in the arbitration agreements would burden Plaintiffs here with prohibitive arbitration costs, preventing Plaintiffs from vindicating their statutory rights in arbitration."); Alexander v. Anthony Int'l, Ltd. P'ship, 341 F.3d 256, 267 (3d Cir. 2003) (Virgin Islands Wrongful Discharge Act); Safranek v. Copart, Inc., 379 F. Supp. 2d 927, 934–935 (N.D. Ill. 2005) (arbitration clause provision barring Title VII claimant from recovering attorney fees violates statute, is severed from clause); *see* Graham Oil Co. v. ARCO Products Co., 43 F.3d 1244 (9th Cir. 1994) (Petroleum Marketing Practices Act); Gourley v. Yellow Transp., L.L.C., 178 F. Supp. 2d 1196 (D. Colo. 2001) (agreement denying attorney fees violates public policy); Horenstein v. Mortgage Mkt., Inc., 1999 U.S. Dist. LEXIS 21463 (D. Or. Jan. 11, 1999) (employment case); DeGaetano v. Smith Barney, Inc., 983 F. Supp. 459 (S.D.N.Y. 1997); Broughton v. CIGNA Healthplans, 21 Cal. 4th 1066, 90 Cal. Rptr. 2d 334, 988 P.2d 67 (1999) (indicating that restriction of UDAP attorney fees and costs was inconsistent with statutory intent, and agreement construed so such fees could be recovered); Maciejewski v. Alpha Sys. Lab, Inc., 73 Cal. App. 4th 1372, 87 Cal. Rptr. 2d 390 (1999) (limitation on attorney fees was unconscionable), *review granted, opinion superseded*, 89 Cal. Rptr. 2d 834, 986 P.2d 170 (Cal. 1999), *vacated*, 101 Cal. Rptr. 2d, 11 P.3d 954 (Cal. 2000); Stirlen v. Supercuts, Inc., 51 Cal. App. 4th 1519, 60 Cal. Rptr. 2d 138 (1997) (same); Holt v. O'Brien Imports of Ft. Myers, Inc., 862 So. 2d 87, 90 (Fla. Dist. Ct. App. 2003); Romano *ex rel.* Romano v. Manor Care, Inc., 861 So. 2d 59, 63 (Fla. Dist. Ct. App. 2003). *But see* Faber v. Menard, Inc., 367 F.3d 1048, 1055 (8th Cir. 2004) (clause denying attorney fees to ADEA claimant enforced; arbitrator decides remedial issue); Hawkins v. Aid Ass'n for Lutherans, 338 F.3d 801, 807 (7th Cir. 2003) (same).
226 Sarver v. Trans Union, L.L.C., 264 F. Supp. 2d 691, 693 (N.D. Ill. 2003); *see* Johnson v. Long John Silver's Restaurants, Inc., 320 F. Supp. 2d 656, 669 (M.D. Tenn. 2004), *aff'd*, 414 F.3d 583 (6th Cir. 2005); Cash in Advance of Fla., Inc. v. Jolley, 612 S.E.2d 101, 104 (Ga. Ct. App. 2005).
227 *See* Safranek v. Copart, Inc., 379 F. Supp. 2d 927, 934 (N.D. Ill. 2005).
228 PacifiCare Health Sys., Inc. v. Book, 538 U.S. 401, 406–407, 123 S. Ct. 1531, 155 L. Ed. 2d 578 (2003); Safranek v. Copart, Inc., 379 F. Supp. 2d at 933–934 (N.D. Ill. 2005); Johnson v. Long John Silver's Restaurants, Inc., 320 F. Supp. 2d 656, 669 (M.D. Tenn. 2004), *aff'd*, 414 F.3d 583 (6th Cir. 2005).
229 1 Alba Conte, Attorney Fee Awards § 5.01, at 266 n.1 (1993).
230 Christiansburg Garment Co. v. Equal Employment Opportunity

to deny claims for fees by prevailing defendants in Truth in Lending Act claims,[231] and in state consumer protection act claims.[232]

When an arbitration clause imposes a loser pays rule, it directly interferes with the congressional intent in enacting these laws, and thus the arbitration clause should be unenforceable.[233] It must be noted, however, that the Eleventh Circuit has rejected this conclusion and has enforced an arbitration clause that included a loser pays provision.[234]

4.3.2.4 Limits on Statutory Right to Punitive Damages

A number of statutes, such as the Fair Credit Reporting Act and the Equal Credit Opportunity Act, explicitly provide for punitive damages. By providing a statutory right for punitive damages instead of minimum statutory damages (such as under the Truth in Lending Act), Congress indicated that violations of these statutes are serious matters of public policy, and that such violations must be deterred to protect the public. The Alabama Supreme Court has set out a powerful rationale for this rule:

> We hold that a predispute arbitration clause that forbids an arbitrator from awarding punitive damages is void as contrary to the public policy of this State—to protect its citizens in certain legislatively prescribed actions from wrongful behavior and to punish the wrongdoer. If parties to an arbitration agreement waive an arbitrator's ability to award punitive damages, the door will open wide to rampant fraudulent conduct with few, if any, legal repercussions.[235]

If an arbitration agreement restricts the ability to award punitive damages under one of these statutes, the agreement conflicts with the statute's purposes and must not be enforced.[236] In the civil rights context, analogously, courts have recognized that the threat of punitive damages is crucial to the enforcement of anti-discrimination statutes, and that arbitration clauses which bar such punitive damages conflict with those statutes and are unenforceable.[237]

Nonetheless, several federal courts have enforced arbitration clauses despite their explicit bans on awards of punitive damages that were provided by statute. In *Hadnot v. Bay, Ltd.*,[238] the Fifth Circuit held that an employer's arbitration clause provision denying punitive damages to a Title VII claimant was unenforceable, but could be severed so that the remainder of the arbitration clause was enforceable.[239] In

---

Comm'n, 434 U.S. 412, 422, 98 S. Ct. 694, 700, 54 L. Ed. 2d 648 (1978).

231 Postow v. OBA Fed. Sav. & Loan Ass'n, 627 F.2d 1370, 1387, 1388 (D.C. Cir. 1980).

232 *See* National Consumer Law Center, Unfair and Deceptive Acts and Practices § 8.8.10.3 (6th ed. 2004 and Supp.).

233 *Cf.* Alexander v. Anthony Int'l, Ltd. P'ship, 341 F.3d 256, 268, 269 (3d Cir. 2003) (finding provision requiring losing party in employment discrimination case to pay all arbitrator fees and costs unconscionable); Presidential Leasing, Inc. v. Krout, 896 So. 2d 938, 942 (Fla. Dist. Ct. App. 2005) (used-car sale dealer's arbitration clause requiring consumer to pay dealer's attorney fees and cost *win or lose* held unenforceable for preventing consumer from vindicating rights under Florida Deceptive and Unfair Trade Practices Act).

234 *See* Musnick v. King Motor Co., 325 F.3d 1255 (11th Cir. 2003); *cf.* Johnson v. Long John Silver's Restaurants, Inc., 320 F. Supp. 2d 656, 669 (M.D. Tenn. 2004) (when employer's arbitration clause is ambiguous as to whether non-prevailing Fair Labor Standards Act claimant must pay company's attorney fees, court holds that ambiguity is matter of contract interpretation for arbitrator to resolve), *aff'd*, 414 F.3d 583 (6th Cir. 2005).

235 Cavalier Mfg., Inc. v. Jackson, 823 So. 2d 1237, 1248 (Ala. 2001).

236 Kristian v. Comcast Corp., 446 F.3d 25, 48 (1st Cir. 2006) ("[T]he conflict on the award of treble damages between the arbitration agreements and the federal antitrust statutes, and the non-waivability of treble damages in the federal antitrust context, indicate that Plaintiffs should prevail on their vindication of statutory rights claim."); Graham Oil Co. v. ARCO Products Co., 43 F.3d 1244 (9th Cir. 1994); Armendariz v. Found. Health Psychcare Services, Inc., 24 Cal. 4th 83, 99 Cal. Rptr. 2d 745, 6 P.3d 669 (2000) ("The principle that an arbitration agreement may not limit statutorily imposed remedies such as punitive damages and attorney fees appears to be undisputed."); Kinney v. United HealthCare Services, Inc., 70 Cal. App. 4th 1322, 83 Cal. Rptr. 2d 348 (1999); Stirlen v. Supercuts, Inc., 51 Cal. App. 4th 1519, 60 Cal. Rptr. 2d 138 (1997); Blankfeld v. Richmond Health Care, Inc., 902 So. 2d 296, 298–299 (Fla. Dist. Ct. App. 2005) (arbitration clause provision requiring heightened "clear and convincing evidence" standard for awarding punitive and exemplary damages renders clause unenforceable as against public policy for violating nursing home patient's state statutory rights); Powertel, Inc. v. Bexley, 743 So. 2d 570 (Fla. Dist. Ct. App. 1999); Samuel Williston, Treatise on the Law of Contracts § 18.13 (Richard A. Lord ed., 4th ed. 1998). *But see* Herrington v. Union Planters Bank, 113 F. Supp. 2d 1026 (S.D. Miss. 2000) (arbitration clause enforceable despite waiver of punitive damages in Truth in Savings Act action), *aff'd*, 265 F.3d 1059 (5th Cir. 2001) (table).

237 *See* Alexander v. Anthony Int'l, Ltd. P'ship, 341 F.3d 256, 267 (3d Cir. 2003); Ingle v. Circuit City Stores, Inc., 328 F.3d 1165, 1178, 1179 (9th Cir. 2003); Derrickson v. Circuit City Stores, Inc., 1999 U.S. Dist. LEXIS 21100, 81 Fair Empl. Prac. Cas. (BNA) 1533, 1538 (D. Md. Mar. 19, 1999) ("Punitive damages and back pay are powerful deterrents to employers who might otherwise discriminate on the basis of race. The failure of the Circuit City arbitration provision to provide those remedies shields Circuit City from the full force of Section 1981 and prevents Plaintiff from effectively vindicating her rights."), *aff'd sub nom.* Johnson v. Circuit City Stores, Inc., 203 F.3d 821 (4th Cir. 2000) (table); Harper v. Ultimo, 7 Cal. Rptr. 3d 418, 421, 422 (Ct. App. 2003); Romano *ex rel.* Romano v. Manor Care, Inc., 861 So. 2d 59, 63 (Fla. Dist. Ct. App. 2003).

238 344 F.3d 474 (5th Cir. 2003).

239 *Id.* at 478; *see also* Booker v. Robert Half Int'l, Inc., 413 F.3d 77, 85 (D.C. Cir. 2005) (affirming district court opinion severing punitive damages ban from employer's arbitration clause, enforcing remainder of clause as applied to state statutory employment discrimination claims).

Hawkins v. Aid Association for Lutherans,[240] the Seventh Circuit enforced an arbitration clause in a fraternal benefit society's policy document despite its remedy-stripping provisions, based on the court's holding that questions concerning the availability of remedies do not relate to arbitrability and therefore should be decided by the arbitrator rather than by the court. Although this holding represents a minority opinion among courts, consumer advocates in the Seventh Circuit should be aware of the holding. The better reasoned majority rule is that arbitrators do not have power to rewrite contracts, are constrained by remedy-stripping provisions, and therefore cannot enable parties to effectively vindicate their statutory claims for punitive damages and other remedies when such provisions are involved.

Racketeer Influenced and Corrupt Organizations Act (RICO) treble damage awards, in which the congressional intent is primarily to compensate the victim rather than to create a deterrent effect, should be distinguished from punitive damages.[241] The Supreme Court found no plausible private attorney general role under RICO,[242] and so the Court found no inherent conflict between plaintiffs being forced to arbitrate RICO claims and that statute's underlying purposes,[243] at least so long as the arbitrator could award treble damages. The most recent case on this issue is *PacifiCare Health Systems, Inc. v. Book*, in which the Supreme Court determined that the very question of whether an arbitration clause that limits punitive damages does actually prevent an arbitrator from awarding treble damages under RICO is for the arbitrator, not the court, to decide.[244] In that case, the Court noted that the real dispute concerned the parties' intent in using the word "punitive," given that this term may not encompass RICO damages, which are generally remedial in nature.[245] As it would be impermissible for the Court to speculate that the arbitrator would interpret the agreement to deny treble damages, the Court sent the contract interpretation issue to the arbitrator for resolution.[246]

Similarly, at least one federal court has found that an arbitration clause containing a limitation on "punitive damages" does not foreclose treble damages for antitrust claims under the Clayton Act, and thus that such a clause is enforceable.[247]

Another exception is when the award of punitive damages is pursuant to a common law tort claim.[248] The FAA may preempt the policies underlying state common law, while it does not preempt a federal policy to award punitive damages as explicitly provided by a federal statute.

4.3.2.5 Limits on Statutory Right to Proceed As a Class

Businesses usually draft arbitration clauses so that they expressly prohibit consumers from bringing class actions to enforce their rights under federal or state law.[249] Consumer plaintiffs have had some success in challenging these arbitration clauses on the ground that class actions are necessary for the effective enforcement of federal statutory rights, although a number of courts have also rejected this argument. This latter result occurs because some courts do not find the right to bring an action on a classwide basis to be a substantive right under the statute, when the statute does not explicitly create such a right. It is important for advocates to understand the decisions accepting and rejecting challenges to the validity of class action waivers.

An increasing number of courts have put the formalistic procedure/substance distinction aside and focused instead on the role of class actions in enabling consumers to effectively vindicate statutory rights. Foremost among these is the First Circuit. In *Kristian v. Comcast Corp.*,[250] the First Circuit held that an arbitration clause that barred consumers from seeking classwide relief for their small-value antitrust claims was unenforceable because it would prevent them from effectively vindicating these federal and state law statutory claims.[251]

In so holding, the First Circuit relied heavily on a factual record produced by the plaintiffs containing affidavits from antitrust practitioners showing that the up-front cost to litigate these price-fixing claims would be in the hundreds of thousands of dollars, while the individual relief available was at best several hundred dollars.[252] The First Circuit identified this factual record in distinguishing several cases from other circuits where courts upheld class arbitration bans as they would have applied to different types of consumer claims.[253] The lesson to be learned from *Kristian* and the cases it distinguished is that parties challenging enforcement of an arbitration clause that bans class claims

---

240 338 F.3d 801, 807 (7th Cir. 2003).
241 Shearson/American Express, Inc. v. McMahon, 482 U.S. 220, 107 S. Ct. 2332, 96 L. Ed. 2d 185 (1987).
242 *Id.*
243 *Id.*
244 PacifiCare Health Sys., Inc. v. Book, 538 U.S. 401, 123 S. Ct. 1531, 155 L. Ed. 2d 578 (2003).
245 *Id.*, 538 U.S. at 405–407.
246 *Id.*, 538 U.S. at 407.
247 Inv. Partners v. Glamour Shots, 298 F.3d 314 (5th Cir. 2002).
248 *See* Mastrobuono v. Shearson Lehman Hutton, Inc., 514 U.S. 52, 115 S. Ct. 1212, 131 L. Ed. 2d 76 (1995) (implying that a party can contract away a punitive damages claim under state law in the securities context, with no discussion of the enforceability of such a waiver if the remedy is either part of a federal statutory scheme or would be unconscionable).
249 For discussion of federal and state law governing *whether* an arbitration clause allows for class action proceedings, see § 9.4, *infra*. The instant section focuses solely on the legal effect of arbitration clauses that do not allow class-based claims.
250 446 F.3d 25 (1st Cir. 2006).
251 *Id.* at 61.
252 *Id.* at 57–58.
253 *Id.* at 57–59.

§ 4.3.2.5 Consumer Arbitration Agreements

must bear their burden of *proving*, rather than merely asserting, that this ban would be effectively exculpatory in a given case.

Likewise, in *Discover Bank v. Superior Court*,[254] the California Supreme Court held that an adhesive consumer contract banning class actions in cases involving small-value claims would be unconscionable *or contrary to public policy* because it would be effectively exculpatory.[255]

Courts most often have addressed class action prohibitions in the context of federal statutory enforcement of claims under the Truth in Lending Act (TILA).[256] TILA's provisions outline specific relief that is available to plaintiffs through class action enforcement.[257] In *Lozada v. Dale Baker Oldsmobile, Inc.*,[258] a federal district court recognized that "the remedial purposes of TILA are substantially defeated or impaired" when arbitration clauses prohibit enforcement through class actions.[259] The court in *Lozada* did not rest its decision on this finding however, but instead proceeded to hold that the arbitration clause and its class action prohibition were unconscionable under state contract law for denying the classwide statutory remedies that were available under state consumer protection law.[260]

Similarly, in an employment discrimination case brought under Title VII and a state civil rights statute, the Ninth Circuit followed state law in holding that an employer's arbitration clause was unconscionable in part because it barred employees from seeking class relief.[261] The Ninth Circuit found that this provision was unenforceable because it shielded the employer from certain statutory claims while providing no corresponding benefit to employees.[262]

Two federal courts of appeal, however, have rejected the argument that class actions are necessary for effective consumer enforcement of TILA. In *Johnson v. West Suburban Bank*,[263] the Third Circuit reversed the district court and held that arbitration allows for effective enforcement of TILA claims even when class actions are not available and that the Act's specific class action remedies may be waived because of the availability of individual relief to consumer plaintiffs.[264] The Eleventh Circuit made the same ruling with regard to TILA in deciding *Randolph v. Green Tree Financial Corp.* on remand from the Supreme Court.[265] A number of courts are starting to apply the reasoning of *Johnson* and *Randolph* to other federal and state statutes, and are finding that these acts also do not create an absolute right for consumers or workers to bring a class action in court.[266] As

---

254 36 Cal. 4th 148 (2005).

255 *Id.* at 166 ("Agreements to arbitrate may not be used to harbor terms, conditions and practices that undermine public policy." (citation omitted)); *see also* Whitney v. Alltel Communications, Inc., 173 S.W.3d 300, 314 (Mo. Ct. App. 2005) ("Such a requirement, if found to bar [class] actions such as this, would effectively strip consumers of the protections afforded to them under the Merchandising Practices Act and unfairly allow companies like Alltel to insulate themselves from the consumer protection laws of this State. This result would be unconscionable *and in direct conflict with the legislature's declared public policy as evidenced by the Merchandising Practices Act* and similar statutes." (emphasis added)).

256 15 U.S.C. §§ 1601–1666j.

257 15 U.S.C. § 1640(a)(2)(B) (providing classwide damages awards of up to the lesser of $500,000 or one percent of the creditor's net worth).

258 91 F. Supp. 2d 1087 (W.D. Mich. 2000).

259 *Id.* at 1104, 1105; *see also* Ting v. AT & T, 182 F. Supp. 2d 902, 926, 927 (N.D. Cal. 2002) (holding that explicit ban on class actions in telephone company's consumer arbitration clause is contrary to public policy under California's Consumer Legal Remedies Act, Cal. Civ. Code § 1780(a) (West), and therefore is unenforceable and void), *aff'd in part and rev'd in part*, 319 F.3d 1126 (9th Cir. 2003); Schwartz v. Alltel Corp., 2006 Ohio App. LEXIS 3280 (Ohio Ct. App. June 29, 2006) (in holding arbitration clause banning class claims under Ohio's Consumer Sales Practices Act unconscionable, finding that "[b]y eliminating a consumer's right to proceed through a class action, the arbitration clause directly hinders the consumer protection purposes of the CSPA.").

260 Lozada v. Dale Baker Oldsmobile, Inc., 91 F. Supp. 2d at 1105.

261 Circuit City Stores, Inc. v. Ingle, 328 F.3d 1165, 1176 (9th Cir. 2003).

262 *Id.* at 1175, 1176.

263 225 F.3d 366 (3d Cir. 2000).

264 *Id.* at 369, 377.

For a detailed study that takes issue with the *Johnson* decision for exalting the federal policy favoring arbitration enforcement over the policy guaranteeing plaintiffs the ability to effectively enforce their statutory rights, see Richard B. Cappalli, *Arbitration of Consumer Claims: The Sad Case of Two-Time Victim Terry Johnson or Where Have You Gone Learned Hand?*, 10 B.U. Pub. Int. L. J. 366, 414, 415 (2001). Cappalli characterizes *Johnson v. W. Suburban Bank* as a "case study in consumer victimization by a federal appellate panel" and an "astoundingly bad decision." *Id.* at 366.

265 Randolph v. Green Tree Fin. Corp., 244 F.3d 814 (11th Cir. 2001); *see also* Bowen v. First Family Fin. Services, Inc., 233 F.3d 1331, 1338 (11th Cir. 2000) (holding in putative class action that Equal Credit Opportunity Act, 15 U.S.C. §§ 1691–1691f, does not create non-waivable right to litigate TILA claims in court); Fluemann v. Associated Fin. Services, 2002 WL 500564 (D. Mass. Mar. 29, 2002) ("Although class actions are clearly within the contemplation of [TILA], the law does not expressly confer upon borrowers a right to commence them or suggest a congressional intent to exempt putative class action claims from binding arbitration clauses.").

266 *See, e.g.*, Adkins v. Labor Ready, Inc., 303 F.3d 496, 506 (4th Cir. 2002) (finding that arbitration clause waives right of individual workers to proceed as class under federal Fair Labor Standards Act); Discover Bank v. Cook, 2005 WL 1514034, at *4–*5 (M.D. Ala. June 27, 2005) (following *Randolph*, Fair Credit Billing Act (FCBA) does not create non-waivable class action right); Battels v. Sears Nat'l Bank, 365 F. Supp. 2d 1205, 1216 (M.D. Ala. 2005) (same, applying Truth in Lending Act (TILA) and FCBA); Lawrence v. Household Bank (SB), 343 F. Supp. 2d 1101, 1112 (M.D. Ala. 2004) (same, applying TILA); Taylor v. Citibank USA, 292 F. Supp. 2d 1333, 1340, 1341 (M.D. Ala 2003) (federal FCBA does not create non-waivable right to bring class action); Pitchford v. AmSouth Bank, 285 F. Supp. 2d 1286, 1291, 1292 (M.D. Ala. 2003) (Equal Credit Opportunity Act does not create non-waivable class action right); O'Quin v. Verizon Wireless, 256 F. Supp. 2d 512, 519

is discussed in Ch. 10, *infra*, however, there remains the possibility that classwide relief may be available in arbitration.

Despite these anti-consumer decisions, these same courts in other contexts not involving arbitration clauses have looked with disfavor on corporate practices intended to eliminate the right of consumers to participate in class actions. For example, in *Weiss v. Regal Collections*,[267] the Third Circuit held that a defendant cannot stave off a class action by making offers of judgment to named plaintiffs and thereby deprive the putative class of representation.[268] In so holding, the court recognized that representative actions were fundamental to the Fair Debt Collection Practices Act's[269] enforcement scheme and that, "[l]acking this mechanism, meritorious FDCPA claims might go unredressed because the awards in an individual case might be too small to prosecute an individual action."[270]

These cases rejecting arguments against arbitration based solely on the unavailability of classwide relief highlight the importance of identifying all of the ways in which a particular arbitration clause may prohibit consumers from effectively enforcing their statutory rights. Consumer plaintiffs may still be able to demonstrate that a prohibition of class actions coupled with excessive arbitration fees or a contractual damages limitation renders their federal statutory rights effectively unenforceable.[271]

While most cases discussed herein address arbitration clauses that ban class actions prospectively, some companies have gone a step further by imposing clauses *after a putative class action is filed* that retroactively eliminate the right to participate in the pending case. In these cases, courts have been much more vigilant in protecting the rights of putative class members to bring their claims as a class by holding that Federal Rule of Civil Procedure 23 itself prohibits the defendant from making communications to putative class members that would undermine their existing claims without the court's approval and oversight. In *In re Currency Conversion Fee Antitrust Litigation*,[272] the federal court held that Federal Rule of Civil Procedure 23 prohibited the defendants' imposition of a retroactive arbitration clause banning class actions against putative class members because "they sought to eliminate putative class members' rights in this litigation."[273] Courts in these types of cases thus seem to recognize that the availability of the class action procedure is of significant value to consumers and other putative class members.

4.3.2.6 Limits on Statutory Right to Injunctive Relief

When a federal statute explicitly provides for injunctive relief, and the consumer seeks this relief, can that claim be forced into arbitration? As set forth in § 4.3.1, *supra*, arbitration of statutory claims may only be required when it can provide effective relief for those claims. Consequently, when an arbitration clause or the rules of an arbitration service provider rule out injunctive relief as a consumer remedy, then an action seeking injunctive relief cannot be forced into arbitration.[274]

The closer question is when an arbitration clause and service provider's rules allow the consumer to seek injunctive relief in arbitration. Is such relief a viable remedy? Can arbitrators issue injunctive relief and is it the same relief as that ordered by a court? The answer principally will depend upon the type of injunctive relief that is sought.

Perhaps the most detailed discussion of an arbitration mechanism's ability to provide injunctive relief is the California Supreme Court's 1999 decision in *Broughton*.[275] The court discussed the difficulty an arbitrator would encounter monitoring an injunction and issuing subsequent orders. The court in particular found that private arbitration could not provide the type of equitable relief that the California legislature had intended in passing the Consumer Legal

---

(M.D. La. 2003) (Louisiana's Unfair Trade Practices Act does not create any right to bring class action); Gras v. Associates First Capital Corp., 786 A.2d 886 (N.J. Super. Ct. App. Div. 2001) (finding arbitration clause prohibiting class actions enforceable in case involving consumer claims under New Jersey's Consumer Fraud Act); Auto Nation USA Corp. v. Leroy, 105 S.W.3d 190 (Tex. App. 2003) (same, under Texas Finance Code); *see also* Sagal v. First USA Bank, 69 F. Supp. 2d 627 (D. Del. 1999) (pre-*Johnson* decision holding that lender's arbitration clause is enforceable in TILA case despite unavailability of class action device).

267 Weiss v. Regal Collections, 385 F.3d 337 (3d Cir. 2004).
268 *Id.* at 345.
269 15 U.S.C. § 1692.
270 Weiss v. Regal Collections, 385 F.3d at 345 (3d Cir. 2004).
271 An alternative approach for consumers would be to argue that questions concerning the propriety of a class action ban do not involve arbitrability issues and therefore should be decided by an arbitrator. *See, e.g.*, Hawkins v. Aid Ass'n for Lutherans, 338 F.3d 801, 807 (7th Cir. 2003).

272 *In re* Currency Conversion Fee Antitrust Litig., 361 F. Supp. 2d 237 (S.D.N.Y. 2005).
273 *Id.* at 254; *see also* Carnegie v. H & R Block, Inc., 687 N.Y.S.2d 528, 531–532 (N.Y. Sup. Ct. 1999) (making defendant's retroactive arbitration clause only enforceable on an *opt-in* basis against putative consumer class members).
274 Lozada v. Dale Baker Oldsmobile, Inc., 91 F. Supp. 2d 1087 (W.D. Mich. 2000); Broughton v. CIGNA Healthplans, 21 Cal. 4th 1066, 90 Cal. Rptr. 2d 334, 988 P.2d 67 (1999); Stirlen v. Supercuts, Inc., 51 Cal. App. 4th 1519, 60 Cal. Rptr. 2d 138 (1997); Holt v. O'Brien Imports of Fort Myers, Inc., 862 So. 2d 87, 89 (Fla. Dist. Ct. App. 2003); *see also* Simitar Entm't, Inc. v. Silva Entm't, Inc., 44 F. Supp. 2d 986 (D. Minn. 1999) (refusing to compel arbitration of statutory claims when the statute provides injunctive relief but arbitrator lacked power to provide such relief, as this "would amount to a de facto waiver of the substantive rights that are afforded by state and Federal law").
275 Broughton v. CIGNA Healthplans, 21 Cal. 4th 1066, 90 Cal. Rptr. 2d 334, 988 P.2d 67 (1999).

Remedies Act, which allows an individual to seek injunctive relief on behalf of a large number of consumers, acting as a private attorney general.

Such an injunction is for the benefit of the general public and not for the resolution of a private dispute. The legislature did not intend injunctive relief under a private attorney general type of statute to be subject to arbitration. In that situation, arbitration of an injunctive action is inconsistent with the legislative intent and cannot be enforced.[276]

The California Supreme Court has since reaffirmed its ruling in *Broughton*, and has extended its holding rejecting arbitration for Consumer Legal Remedies Act public injunction actions to private attorney general actions under California's Business and Professions Code section 17200.[277] However, the Court made it clear that it is only claims for injunctive relief that are not subject to arbitration; claims under section 17200 for restitution and disgorgement are functionally equivalent to damages claims, and are arbitrable.[278]

The result in *Broughton* and *Cruz* can be distinguished from *Gilmer*, in which an employee had argued before the Supreme Court that Age Discrimination in Employment Act (ADEA) claims need not be submitted to arbitration. The employee reasoned that arbitration does not further the purposes of the ADEA, because it does not provide for equitable relief.[279] The Supreme Court responded that in the arbitration at issue, the arbitrator had the power to fashion equitable relief and such relief was not restricted by the rules of the arbitration mechanism.[280] In addition, the Court pointed out that the Equal Employment Opportunity Commission can intervene at any time, stop the individual action, and instead bring its own action in court seeking equitable relief.[281]

4.3.2.7 Shortening of a Statute of Limitation

An important part of a federal statutory right is the statute of limitations. Congress weighs competing factors in establishing a time period within which the consumer must bring a claim. If the arbitration procedure requires the consumer to bring the claim in a much shorter period, this limitation in effect forecloses certain consumers from bringing a federal statutory claim that they could otherwise bring. As such, shorter limitations periods conflict with the federal statute, and cannot be enforced.[282]

4.4 High Arbitration Fees *Effectively* Prevent Vindication of Statutory Rights

4.4.1 Introduction

Arbitration clauses that expressly or explicitly prevent consumers from vindicating their rights under consumer protection statutes are not enforceable.[283] An arbitration clause is also unenforceable even if it does not explicitly

---

276 *Id.*
   One federal court has pronounced *Broughton*'s reasoning "persuasive" and adopted it. Gray v. Conseco, Inc., 2000 U.S. Dist. LEXIS 14821 (C.D. Cal. Sept. 29, 2000).
   Another federal court has concluded that the California Supreme Court erred in the *Broughton* case, however, and that federal law preempts any California law that would ban arbitration of certain statutory claims. Arriaga v. Cross County Bank, 163 F. Supp. 2d 1189 (S.D. Cal. 2001).
277 Cruz v. PacifiCare Health Sys., Inc., 30 Cal. 4th 303, 133 Cal. Rptr. 2d 58, 66 P.3d 1157 (2003).
278 *Id.*
279 Gilmer v. Interstate/Johnson Lane Corp., 500 U.S. 20, 111 S. Ct. 1647, 114 L. Ed. 2d 26 (1991).
280 *Id.*; *see also* Stewart Agency, Inc. v. Robinson, 855 So. 2d 726, 728 (Fla. Dist. Ct. App. 2003) (car buyer's claims under Florida Deceptive and Unfair Trade Practices Act are subject to arbitration when clause allows arbitrator to enter award with injunctive or declaratory component to it).
281 Gilmer v. Interstate/Johnson Lane Corp., 500 U.S. 20, 111 S. Ct. 1647, 114 L. Ed. 2d 26 (1991).
282 Parilla v. IAP Worldwide Services, VI, Inc., 368 F.3d 269, 277, 278 (3d Cir. 2004) (employer's clause requiring employee to provide notice of discrimination claims within thirty days is unconscionable); Alexander v. Anthony Int'l, Ltd. P'ship, 341 F.3d 256, 266, 267 (3d Cir. 2003) (same); Circuit City Stores, Inc. v. Ingle, 328 F.3d 1165, 1175 (9th Cir. 2003) (employer's one-year limitations period is unconscionable for unreasonably shortening applicable statutory period); Circuit City Stores, Inc. v. Adams, 279 F.3d 889, 894 (9th Cir. 2002) (arbitration clause that "imposes a strict one year statute of limitations on arbitrating claims . . . would deprive [the employee] of the benefit of the continuing violation doctrine available in FEHA suits"); Graham Oil Co. v. ARCO Products Co., 43 F.3d 1244 (9th Cir. 1994); Bailey v. Ameriquest Mortgage Co., 2002 U.S. Dist. LEXIS 1343 (D. Minn. Jan. 23, 2002) ("By shortening the limitations period to one year and failing to provide for greater liability for a willful violation, the arbitration agreement denies plaintiffs 'access to a remedy Congress made available to ensure violations of the statute are effectively remedied and deterred.' " (quoting Perez v. Globe Airport Sec. Services Inc., 253 F.3d 1280 (11th Cir. 2001)); *In re* Managed Care Litig., 132 F. Supp. 2d 989, 1000, 1001 (S.D. Fla. 2000) ("Additionally, the one year statute of limitations raises grave concerns that Dr. Porth's statutory claims will not be adjudicated appropriately in an arbitration forum."; refusing to compel arbitration with respect to Dr. Porth's statutory claims, though compelling arbitration with respect to his common law claims despite the limitations issue), *rev'd on other grounds sub nom.* PacifiCare Health Sys., Inc. v. Book, 538 U.S. 401 (2003); *see also* Stirlen v. Supercuts, Inc., 51 Cal. App. 4th 1519, 60 Cal. Rptr. 2d 138 (1997) (time limitation is unconscionable). *But see* Kristian v. Comcast Corp., 446 F.3d 25, 43–44 (1st Cir. 2006) (holding that validity and effect of arbitration clause provision shortening statutory limitations period are questions for arbitrator, not court, to resolve).
283 *See* § 4.3, *supra*.

limit a statutory right, if its operation effectively achieves the same result. The United States Supreme Court has authorized mandatory arbitration for statutory claims, but only "so long as the prospective litigant *effectively* may vindicate [her] statutory cause of action in the arbitral forum."[284]

High arbitration fees can be an enormous impediment to a consumer pursuing a statutory claim. This section will examine the conflict between a statutory remedial scheme and an arbitration mechanism that imposes high fees. The section must be read in conjunction with § 6.5.2, *infra*, which discusses when high arbitration fees render an arbitration clause unconscionable. If high fees are assessed to arbitrate a federal claim, the consumer can argue both that the fees conflict with the federal statute and that they make the clause unconscionable. If high fees are assessed to arbitrate a state statutory claim, however, the consumer should rely on an unconscionability argument or another argument that would apply to any contract term, such as the argument that the term is unenforceable as against public policy.

This section should also be read in conjunction with the other sections in this chapter which deal with the other ways in which an arbitration clause may conflict with a federal statute. When both high fees and restrictions on remedies are present, it is important to present these impediments together, because it may be the totality of impediments that makes the arbitral forum inadequate to resolve federal statutory claims.[285]

In reviewing a given consumer statute and a given arbitration clause, it is also important to emphasize the remedial scheme of the consumer legislation. In many cases, Congress intended that consumers be able to enforce their rights even though the monetary size of their claim is small. High arbitration costs in comparison with the costs of a court proceeding may frustrate this purpose.

4.4.2 The Supreme Court's Decision in Randolph

In *Green Tree Financial Corp.-Alabama v. Randolph*,[286] the United States Supreme Court examined for the first time the potential effect of arbitration fees on a plaintiff's enforcement of federal statutory rights through arbitration. *Randolph* addressed whether an arbitration clause that is silent as to the payment of arbitration fees would, without any additional evidence of costs that might be borne, prevent a plaintiff from effectively vindicating her Truth In Lending Act claim through arbitration. While reiterating the baseline principle that "claims arising under a statute designed to further important social policies may be arbitrated . . . 'so long as the prospective litigant effectively may vindicate [her] statutory cause of action,' "[287] *Randolph* narrowly held that an arbitration contract's silence as to payment of costs alone does not render it unenforceable.[288]

Randolph's holding was based on the complete absence of an evidentiary record concerning the costs that the plaintiff would be required to pay. Indeed, the court acknowledged that "[i]t may well be that the existence of large arbitration costs could preclude a litigant such as Randolph from effectively vindicating her federal statutory rights in the arbitral forum."[289]

Thus, in order to challenge enforcement of an arbitration clause on the basis of excessive costs, consumer plaintiffs enforcing federal statutory rights should present (in addition to any relevant contractual provisions) evidence identifying the particular arbitration service provider to be used in their case, the provider's fee requirements for the type of claim presented, and the defendant's practices with regard to arbitration fees. Nothing in *Randolph* would prevent a court from prohibiting arbitration of federal statutory claims in the face of such evidence. Many courts applying *Randolph* have rejected challenges when plaintiffs did not produce much evidence of excessive fees, however.[290]

In some cases, courts have read the *Randolph* decision as having much greater significance than would be justified by the actual holding of the case, and have instead read it as a signal that arbitration clauses are to be favored in nearly every circumstance. On remand, the circuit court took the Supreme Court's holding in *Randolph* to be a broader statement of the need to favor arbitration: "According to the Supreme Court, the last time this case was before us, we made the mistake of giving too little weight to the FAA's pro-consumer policy. We decline to make the same mistake again."[291] Similarly, another circuit court has held that *Randolph* requires parties resisting arbitration to meet an elevated burden of "concrete" proof.[292]

---

284 Mitsubishi Motors Corp. v. Soler Chrysler-Plymouth, Inc., 473 U.S. 614, 637, 105 S. Ct. 3346, 87 L. Ed. 2d 444 (1985) (emphasis added); *see* Green Tree Fin. Corp.-Ala. v. Randolph, 531 U.S. 79, 121 S. Ct. 513, 521, 148 L. Ed. 2d 373 (2000) (quoting *Mitsubishi*).

285 Wood v. Cooper Chevrolet, Inc., 102 F. Supp. 2d 1345 (N.D. Ala. 2000) ("Given the limits imposed on plaintiffs for recovery, if plaintiffs are bound to arbitrate and required to pay arbitration costs, it simply doesn't make good financial sense for plaintiffs to file suit to protect their TILA rights.").

286 531 U.S. 79, 121 S. Ct. 513, 148 L. Ed. 2d 373 (2000).

287 531 U.S. at 90 (quoting Gilmer v. Interstate/Johnson Lane Corp., 500 U.S. 20, 28, 111 S. Ct. 1647, 114 L. Ed. 2d 26 (1991) (internal quotation marks omitted)).

288 531 U.S. at 90–92.

289 *Id.*

290 *E.g.*, Gruber v. Louis Hornick & Co., 2003 WL 21222541 (S.D.N.Y. May 23, 2003) (citing *Randolph*, then holding that the record before it "is inadequate for the Court to conclude that even the higher fee schedule would constitute a barrier to the vindication of plaintiff's rights").

291 Randolph v. Green Tree Fin. Corp., 244 F.3d 814, 818, 819 (11th Cir. 2001).

292 MicroStrategy, Inc. v. Lauricia, 268 F.3d 244 (4th Cir. 2001).

4.4.3 When Are Arbitration Charges Inconsistent with Federal Statute?

4.4.3.1 When Charges Exceed Those for a Court Action

Several courts have offered an easy to administer bright line test to determine when arbitration fees are sufficiently large to undermine statutory rights. These employment cases hold that arbitration fees may not exceed those that an individual would face in court. The California Supreme Court, for example, has held:

> Accordingly, consistent with the majority of jurisdictions to consider this issue, we conclude that when an employer imposes mandatory arbitration as a condition of employment, the arbitration agreement or arbitration process cannot generally require the employee to bear any type of expense that the employee would not be required to bear if he or she were free to bring the action in court.[293]

The Ninth Circuit has repeatedly embraced and applied this aspect of California law.[294] The D.C. Circuit, similarly, has held that "it is unacceptable to require [an employee] to pay arbitrators' fees, because such fees are unlike anything that he would have to pay to pursue his statutory claims in court."[295] The Ninth Circuit recently agreed, finding that a provision requiring an employee to split the arbitrator's fees with the employer "alone would render an arbitration agreement unenforceable."[296]

The idea that arbitration clauses that require individuals to split the fees necessarily violate statutory rights is not limited to the employment setting. With respect to ERISA plans, the Eighth Circuit has applied a Department of Labor regulation forbidding fee splitting for arbitration clauses:

> [W]hen a plan such as the one here provides for mandatory arbitration before allowing a claimant to initiate a civil action, it may not carry a presumption of cost-splitting. To hold otherwise would permit a plan to limit claims by merely adding an expensive appellate process to its claims procedure before allowing a claimant to initiate a civil action.[297]

Quite a few courts have rejected any kind of categorical approach, however.[298] Consumer advocates will have to research the law in their jurisdiction before advancing this argument.

---

293 Armendariz v. Found. Health Psychcare Services, Inc., 24 Cal. 4th 83, 110, 111, 99 Cal. Rptr. 2d 745, 6 P.3d 669 (2000).

   Subsequently, California courts have made it clear that this rule applies to "any statute enacted 'for a public reason,' " and not merely the specific statutes at issue in the *Armendariz* case. Mercuro v. Super. Ct., 96 Cal. App. 4th 167, 116 Cal. Rptr. 2d 671 (2002); *cf.* Little v. Auto Stiegler, Inc., 63 P.3d 979 (Cal. 2003) (applying rule to certain common law claims).

294 *See, e.g.*, Circuit City Stores, Inc. v. Ingle, 328 F.3d 1165, 1177, 1178 (9th Cir. 2003); Ting v. AT & T, 319 F.3d 1126 (9th Cir. 2003); Circuit City Stores, Inc. v. Adams, 279 F.3d 889 (9th Cir. 2002). *But see* Marshall v. John Hine Pontiac, 287 F. Supp. 2d 1229, 1234 (S.D. Cal. 2003) (issue of which costs each party must bear is a matter of contract construction, not grounds for invalidating the contract).

295 Cole v. Burns Int'l Sec. Services, 105 F.3d 1465, 1484 (D.C. Cir. 1997); *see also* Gourley v. Yellow Transp., L.L.C., 178 F. Supp. 2d 1196 (D. Colo. 2001) (refusing to enforce an arbitration agreement that "requires Plaintiffs to share the costs of arbitration"); Lelouis v. W. Directory Co., 230 F. Supp. 2d 1214 (D. Or. 2001) ("The better approach is that taken by the California Supreme Court in *Armendariz*, which 'places the cost of arbitration on the party that imposes it.' "); Ball v. SFX Broad., Inc., 165 F. Supp. 2d 230 (N.D.N.Y. 2001) ("[I]t is sufficient for an employee seeking to avoid arbitration to show a likelihood that he or she will be responsible for significant arbitrators' fees, or other costs which would not be incurred in a judicial forum. Such a showing is sufficient to demonstrate that the challenged arbitration agreement does not provide an effective mechanism for the vindication of statutory rights."); *cf.* Op. La. Att'y Gen. No. 98-380, Clearinghouse No. 53,554, at 2 (Mar. 28, 1999) ("Although it is clear that consumer credit lenders may utilize and enforce an arbitration agreement, it is questionable whether the costs of arbitration may exceed those costs specifically enumerated as allowable in the Louisiana Consumer Credit Law.") (text of this opinion is also available on the CD-Rom accompanying this manual).

   The D.C. Circuit has subsequently narrowed *Cole* by holding that employee plaintiffs may be assessed arbitral forum fees other than filing fees or arbitrator's fees (such as fees for reasonable administrative expenses) and may be billed fees for non-statutory claims. *See* LaPrade v. Kidder, Peabody & Co., 246 F.3d 702 (D.C. Cir. 2001).

   The *Cole* case has also been narrowly interpreted in a subsequent D.C. Circuit case to apply only to statutory claims. In Brown v. Wheat First Sec., Inc., 257 F.3d 821 (D.C. Cir. 2001) the court rejected the claim that *Cole* extends to common law claims. The court opined that state common law claims (unlike the federal statutory claims at issue in *Cole*) were preempted by the FAA and concluded that "the proposed extension of *Cole* would significantly alter the terms of the Federal Arbitration Act, imposing a serious procedural limit on a wide (but unpredictable) range of arbitration claims, all without the slightest signal from Congress." *Id.* at 826.

296 Circuit City Stores, Inc. v. Adams, 279 F.3d 889, 894 (9th Cir. 2002); *see also* Circuit City Stores, Inc. v. Mantor, 335 F.3d 1101 (9th Cir. 2003); Ingle v. Circuit City Stores, Inc., 328 F.3d 1165 (9th Cir. 2003); Ferguson v. Countrywide Credit Indus., Inc., 298 F.3d 778 (9th Cir. 2002).

297 Bond v. Twin Cities Carpenters Pension Fund, 307 F.3d 704, 797 (8th Cir. 2002).

298 Blair v. Scott Specialty Gases, 283 F.3d 595 (3d Cir. 2002) ("Blair would have us hold that the mere existence of a fee-splitting provision in an agreement would satisfy the claimant's burden to prove the likelihood of incurring prohibitive costs under *Green Tree*, 530 U.S. at 92. We decline to do so. It would be inconsistent with *Green Tree* and would run counter to the strong federal preference for arbitration and the liberal policy regarding arbitration."); *see also* Faber v. Menard, Inc., 367 F.3d 1048, 1053 (8th Cir. 2004); Bradford v. Rockwell Semiconductor Sys., Inc., 238 F.3d 549 (4th Cir. 2001); Rosenberg v. Merrill Lynch, Pierce, Fenner & Smith, Inc., 170 F.3d 1

4.4.3.2 When Charges Deter Pursuit of Statutory Claims

Other courts look to determine whether arbitral fees deter an individual from pursuing statutory claims. One court has suggested, for example, that an arbitration agreement should not be enforced if the arbitration fees may curtail or bar the consumer's access to an arbitral forum to resolve a truth in lending claim.[299]

A growing number of federal circuit courts use this same approach in employment discrimination cases. These courts hold that it is impractical to expect an employee to pay half of the potential costs of thousands of dollars that arbitration of the claim would entail, and that therefore such arbitration is not an acceptable forum to enforce the employee's statutory rights.[300] In *Shankle*, a Tenth Circuit case, the arbitration agreement allowed the employer to advance all the arbitration fees. The employee would be liable for half the fees, but the fees could be deducted from the employee's recovery, if the employee prevailed. The court held that this arrangement was not sufficient to make the arbitration forum a practical one for resolution of the employee's statutory rights.[301] Similarly, the Third Circuit held in an employment case that a provision requiring the losing party to pay all of the arbitrator's fees would be unenforceable, even though the employee was not guaranteed to be subject to these costs, because the mere prospect of these costs could deter her from vindicating her statutory rights.[302]

Not all courts agree. Some courts require evidence of both the likely arbitration fees and the specific plaintiff's inability to pay those fees.[303] Thus, when an arbitration clause requires a statutory claimant to pay substantial arbitration fees but the defendant subsequently offers to pay these fees, these courts have held that the arbitration clause should be enforced because it no longer would prevent vindication of the plaintiff's statutory claims.[304]

> Other circuits have found that the possibility that a plaintiff may be required to pay arbitration fees is not, by itself, a sufficient reason to invalidate an agreement to arbitrate Title VII claims at the outset of an action because the arbitral panel may not in fact require the plaintiff to pay fees and, if a plaintiff believes that excessive fees have been levied against him or her, judicial review of the imposition of the fees is available after arbitration.[305]

Like the Eighth Circuit in *Faber*, the Seventh Circuit has also held that a party challenging an arbitration clause based on excessive costs must show not only what those costs would be but also that he or she exhausted any fee waiver procedure that the arbitration service provides.[306] Finally, the Sixth Circuit has held that cases recognizing a cost-based defense to arbitration clauses involving claims under *federal* statutes are not controlling as to cases involving claims under *state* statutes, where states may craft their own rules.[307]

(1st Cir. 1999); Koveleskie v. SBC Capital Markets, Inc., 167 F.3d 361 (7th Cir. 1999); Taylor v. Citibank USA, 292 F. Supp. 2d 1333, 1341, 1342 (M.D. Ala. 2003) (following *Bradford*, focusing on aggregate difference between costs of arbitration and court proceedings).

299 Camacho v. Holiday Homes, Inc., 167 F. Supp. 2d 892 (W.D. Va. 2001) (consumer plaintiff had "successfully demonstrated that the arbitration clause precludes her from effectively vindicating the rights afforded her by the [Truth in Lending Act] because the arbitral forum is financially inaccessible to her"); *see also* Rhode v. E & T Investments, Inc., 6 F. Supp. 1322 (M.D. Ala. 1998) (expressing concern in a long footnote that the consumer's responsibility to pay part of the American Arbitration Association fees would conflict with the underlying policy of the Magnuson-Moss Warranty Act, which was enacted to provide consumers practical remedies for breaches of warranty).

300 Equal Employment Opportunity Comm'n v. Woodmen of the World Life Ins. Soc'y, 479 F.3d 561, 567 (8th Cir. 2007) ("Excessive arbitration costs can make an arbitration agreement unconscionable because a litigant does not face fees for the decision-maker similar to arbitration costs when she proceeds in federal court."); Alexander v. Anthony Int'l, Ltd. P'ship, 341 F.3d 256, 269, 270 (3d Cir. 2003); Spinetti v. Serv. Corp. Int'l, 324 F.3d 212 (3d Cir. 2003); Morrison v. Circuit City Stores, Inc., 317 F.3d 646 (6th Cir. 2003) (en banc); Shankle v. B-G Maint. Mgmt. of Colo., Inc., 163 F.3d 1230 (10th Cir. 1999); Paladino v. Avnet Computer Technologies, Inc., 134 F.3d 1054 (11th Cir. 1998); *see also* Giles v. City of New York, 41 F. Supp. 2d 308 (S.D.N.Y. 1999).

The court's holding in *Paladino* that an arbitration clause was unenforceable when it required an employee to pay half of the arbitration fees has subsequently been rejected by that same court, however. *See* Perez v. Globe Airport Sec. Services, Inc., 253 F.3d 1280 (11th Cir. 2001) ("The *Paladino* court also concluded the agreement at issue was unenforceable in part because it did not require the employer to advance the costs of arbitration. [citation omitted] The Supreme Court recently held the opposite; the absence of a provision specifying which party must advance the arbitration fees and costs does not render the agreement unenforceable. *See* [Green Tree Fin. Corp.-Ala. v. Randolph, 121 S. Ct. 513, 521, 522 (2000).] The Court's decision in *Green Tree* does not cast doubt on the continuing vitality of the primary holding in *Paladino*.").

301 Shankle v. B-G Maint. Mgmt. of Colo., Inc., 163 F.3d 1230 (10th Cir. 1999).

302 Parilla v. IAP Worldwide Services, VI, Inc., 368 F.3d 269, 284, 285 (3d Cir. 2004). *But see* Pitchford v. AmSouth Bank, 285 F. Supp. 2d 1286, 1293 (M.D. Ala. 2003) (upholding similar clause).

303 *See, e.g.*, Faber v. Menard, Inc., 367 F.3d 1048, 1053 (8th Cir. 2004).

304 *See, e.g.*, Equal Employment Opportunity Comm'n v. Woodmen of the World Life Ins. Soc'y, 479 F.3d 561, 567 (8th Cir. 2007).

305 Arakawa v. Japan Network Group, 56 F. Supp. 2d 349, 354 (S.D.N.Y. 1999) (citing Koveleskie v. SBC Capital Markets, Inc., 167 F.3d 361, 366 (7th Cir. 1999) and Rosenberg v. Merrill Lynch, Pierce, Fenner & Smith, Inc., 170 F.3d 1, 16 (1st Cir. 1999)).

306 *See* James v. McDonald's Corp., 417 F.3d 672, 679 (7th Cir. 2005).

307 Stutler v. T.K. Constructors, Inc., 448 F.3d 343 (6th Cir. 2006).

4.4.4 Does Reimbursement of Fees to a Prevailing Consumer Cure the Problem?

An arbitration procedure that reimburses all arbitration costs to the consumer if the consumer prevails may still conflict with the congressional purpose in enacting a statute. As noted in § 6.5.2.2, *infra*, arbitration clauses incorporating the rules of the American Arbitration Association (which permit such reimbursements) have frequently been found to be unconscionable despite such provisions, and the same result should prevail in statutory challenges to high arbitral fees. Requiring the consumer to assemble and risk thousands of dollars in the hope of prevailing on the claim will discourage many consumers from enforcing their statutory rights. This procedure is certainly not the equivalent of a judicial procedure in which filing fees are minimal, and which an attorney will often take on a contingency fee basis, with the consumer fronting little or no money. The Seventh Circuit thus has held that the availability of reimbursement of arbitration costs or judicial review of the costs imposed after the fact is inadequate to protect claimants who may be deterred by these costs from prosecuting their statutory claims in the first place.[308] Some courts have rejected challenges to the expense of arbitration clauses, however, when the arbitration service provider had rules that permitted indigent consumers to request a waiver of fees.[309]

Even if the arbitration mechanism does not require the consumer to pay costs up front, the very threat that consumers will have to pay large fees unless they prevail will be enough to discourage many consumer claims that Congress intended to encourage. Such is the case even when an arbitration mechanism requires a non-prevailing consumer to pay only half of the arbitration costs, particularly if the amount in controversy is small compared to the potential liability for arbitration charges.[310] Even though a prevailing consumer is not affected by this provision, the risk may be enough to deter the prosecution of meritorious claims.

A consumer with a meritorious claim must evaluate the benefits and risks of proceeding with a claim in arbitration. Non-prevailing consumers' liability for high fees will be enough to discourage some claims that would otherwise be brought before a court and in which the consumer would have prevailed. While it may be legitimate for an arbitration mechanism to deter frivolous or bad faith claims, it is quite different to deter claims that sometimes would and sometimes would not prevail.[311]

The Truth in Lending Act (TILA), for example, was very carefully crafted so that the prevailing consumer was awarded fees and costs, but no amount is awarded to a prevailing creditor. To do so would have deterred consumers from bringing disclosure violation cases, in which recovery is relatively small.

An arbitration mechanism that requires a non-prevailing consumer to pay charges of several thousand dollars effectively deters consumers with meritorious TILA claims from exercising their statutory rights. To be consistent with TILA's statutory intent, the arbitration mechanism should only assess fees and charges if the consumer's claim is found to be frivolous or in bad faith.

The D.C. Circuit has set out a clear rule that, in an employment discrimination case, the plaintiff cannot be required to pay any arbitrator fees ever, win or lose.[312] Filing fees can be reviewed in relation to what a consumer would pay in a court action, but a plaintiff enforcing statutory rights cannot be required to pay for the arbitrator.

> Indeed, we are unaware of any situation in American jurisprudence in which a beneficiary of a federal statute has been required to pay for the services of a judge assigned to hear her or his case. Under *Gilmer*, arbitration is supposed to be a reasonable substitute for a judicial forum. Therefore, it would undermine Congress's intent to prevent employees who are seeking to vindicate statutory rights from gaining access to a judicial forum and then require them to pay for the services of an arbitrator when they would never be required to pay for a judge in court.[313]

---

308 *See* James v. McDonald's Corp., 417 F.3d 672, 679 n.4 (7th Cir. 2005) ("Ms. James maintains that she can not afford to pursue arbitration in the first instance. A review of the allocation of costs conducted after the arbitration would be of little help to her.").

309 *See, e.g.*, Hale v. First USA Bank, 2001 U.S. Dist. LEXIS 8045 (S.D.N.Y. June 19, 2001).

310 Cole v. Burns Int'l Sec. Services, 105 F.3d 1465 (D.C. Cir. 1997).

311 *See* Cal. Teachers Ass'n v. State, 20 Cal. 4th 327, 84 Cal. Rptr. 2d 425, 975 P.2d 622 (1999); *see also* Martinez v. Master Prot. Corp., 12 Cal. Rptr. 3d 663, 671 (Ct. App. 2004) (employer's belated offer to pay all arbitration costs is ineffective because "the mere inclusion of the costs provision in the arbitration agreement produces an unacceptable chilling effect"). *But see* Johnnie's Homes, Inc. v. Holt, 790 So. 2d 956 (Ala. 2001) ("Although the record contains evidence indicating Melvin would have to pay a $2000 fee to have his claims arbitrated and evidence indicating he has a limited financial capacity, this evidence—standing alone—is not enough to persuade us to rule in Melvin's favor.... Some arbitration provisions permit the arbitrator to order the other party to pay all the fees or to pay a partial amount, depending on who wins and depending on the financial condition of the claimant.... Therefore, Melvin has failed to show that general contract defenses should prohibit the enforcement of the arbitration provision against him." (citation omitted)).

312 Cole v. Burns Int'l Sec. Services, 105 F.3d 1465 (D.C. Cir. 1997).

313 *Id.* at 1484.

4.5 When a Party's One-Sided Control Over the Arbitration Process Prevents Effective Vindication of Statutory Rights

Just as high forum costs can prevent a consumer from enforcing her statutory rights in arbitration even when all remedies are nominally available, contract terms which allow one party to retain control over the rules and procedures for arbitration can likewise prevent a consumer from enforcing her statutory rights. For example, the Sixth Circuit held in an employment case that an arbitration clause granting an employer exclusive control over who is chosen for a list of potential arbitrators rendered arbitration an ineffective substitute for a judicial forum.[314] Therefore, the Sixth Circuit held that the employee's Title VII claims were not subject to this provision.[315] More recently, the Sixth Circuit affirmed the district court's decision in *Walker*, holding that an employer's mandatory arbitration system effectively denied employees an opportunity to vindicate their statutory claims because (1) the arbitration service was largely controlled by the employer, whose business provided 42% of the service's revenues; (2) the service was biased in favor of industry defendants; (3) the employer exercised an extremely controlling influence over the pools from which arbitrators were selected; and (4) the arbitration rules imposed severe restrictions on the employees' ability to take discovery to prove their claims.[316]

---

314 McMullen v. Meijer, Inc., 355 F.3d 485, 494 (6th Cir. 2004).

315 *Id.*; *see also* Walker v. Ryan's Family Steak Houses, Inc., 400 F.3d 370 (6th Cir. 2005) (finding clause under which arbitration service provider allowed employer to 1) modify rules, 2) eliminate class action provision, and 3) control selection of arbitrators ineffective for vindication of employee's Fair Labor Standards Act claims).

316 *See* Walker v. Ryan's Family Steak Houses, Inc., 400 F.3d 370, 385–387 (6th Cir. 2005).

Chapter 5 Formation of Agreement to Arbitrate

5.1 No Presumption That Arbitration Agreement Is Formed

A court should not compel arbitration unless it (not an arbitrator) has first determined that an agreement to arbitrate exists under the generally applicable contract law of the state whose law governs the question.[1] The Federal Arbitration Act (FAA) was not enacted to force parties into arbitration, but to enforce parties' voluntary agreements to arbitrate certain specified disputes. "Arbitration is simply a matter of contract between parties; it is a way to resolve disputes—but only those disputes—that the parties have agreed to submit to arbitration."[2]

The FAA provides that a court may compel arbitration only "upon being satisfied that the making of the agreement or the failure to comply therewith is not at issue."[3] Thus, the FAA policy in favor of enforcing arbitration clauses does not come into play in determining *whether* an agreement to arbitrate exists.[4] In *Equal Employment Opportunity Commission v. Waffle House, Inc.*,[5] the United States Supreme Court explicitly rejected the suggestion that the pro-arbitration policy of the FAA should be considered in determining whether the parties to a contract agreed to arbitrate the dispute at issue. The Court stated that "we look first to whether the parties agreed to arbitrate a dispute, not to general policy goals, to determine the scope of the agreement." Lower courts have applied this holding in a variety of contexts.[6] For example, a California appellate court recently held that a plaintiff who was representing a putative class that included consumers who had signed an arbitration clause, but who was not herself bound by the clause, could not be required to arbitrate her claims.[7]

It follows that the burden is on the party seeking to compel arbitration (or to confirm an arbitration award) to prove that a valid agreement to arbitrate was formed, and failure to produce an agreement is grounds for denial of the motion.[8] If there is no agreement to arbitrate, any award

---

1 See § 3.4.2, *supra*.
2 First Options of Chicago, Inc. v. Kaplan, 514 U.S. 938, 943, 115 S. Ct. 1920, 1924, 131 L. Ed. 2d 985 (1995); *see also* AT & T Technologies, Inc. v. Communications Workers of Am., 475 U.S. 643, 648–649, 106 S. Ct. 1415, 89 L. Ed. 2d 648 (1986) ("[A]rbitration is a matter of contract and a party cannot be required to submit to arbitration any dispute which he has not so agreed to submit.... This axiom recognizes the fact that arbitrators derive their authority to resolve disputes only because the parties have agreed in advance to submit such grievances to arbitration." (internal citations omitted)).
3 9 U.S.C. § 4.
4 BCS Ins. Co. v. Wellmark, Inc., 410 F.3d 349 (7th Cir. 2005); Fleetwood Enterprises, Inc. v. Gaskamp, 280 F.3d 1069 (5th Cir. 2002) ("[T]his federal policy favoring arbitration does not apply to the determination of whether there is a valid agreement to arbitrate between the parties; instead '[o]rdinary contract principles determine who is bound.' "); Carson v. Giant Food, Inc., 175 F.3d 325, 329 (4th Cir. 1999); Riley Mfg. Co. v. Anchor Glass Container Corp., 157 F.3d 775 (10th Cir. 1998); Va. Carolina Tools, Inc. v. Int'l Tool Supply, Inc., 984 F.2d 113, 117 (4th Cir. 1993); Gourley v. Yellow Transp., L.L.C., 178 F. Supp. 2d 1196 (D. Colo. 2001); Lanier Worldwide, Inc. v. Clouse, 875 So. 2d 292 (Ala. 2003) ("The courts are not to twist the language of the contract to achieve a result that is favored by federal policy but contrary to the interest of the parties.") (internal citations omitted); San Francisco Unified Sch. Dist. v. Keenan & Associates, 2007 WL 1417419 (Cal. Ct. App. May 15, 2007); Lopez v. Charles Schwab & Co., 118 Cal. App. 4th 1224, 13 Cal. Rptr. 3d 544 (2004); Badie v. Bank of Am., 67 Cal. App. 4th 779, 790, 79 Cal. Rptr. 2d 273, 280 (1998); Victoria v. Super. Ct., 40 Cal. 3d 734, 739, 222 Cal. Rptr. 1, 710 P.2d 833 (1985) ("[T]he policy favoring arbitration cannot displace the necessity for a voluntary agreement to arbitrate."); Curtis G. Testerman Co. v. Buck, 340 Md. 569, 580, 667 A.2d 649, 654, 665 (1995); Sears Roebuck & Co. v. Avery, 593 S.E.2d 424, 428 (N.C. Ct. App. 2004) ("Public policy [favoring arbitration] does not come into play unless a court finds that the parties entered into an enforceable agreement to arbitrate."); Maestle v. Best Buy Co., 2005 WL 1907282, at *5 (Ohio Ct. App. Aug. 11, 2005) ("When there is a question as to whether a party has agreed to an arbitration clause, there is a presumption against arbitration."); In Re Kellogg Brown & Root, Inc., 166 S.W.3d 732 (Tex. 2005); *In re* Media Arts Group, Inc., 116 S.W.3d 900, 906 (Tex. App. 2003) ("Therefore, while the FAA preempts application of state law that would render an existing arbitration agreement unenforceable, it does not preempt application of state law to determine the existence of an arbitration agreement.").
5 534 U.S. 279, 122 S. Ct. 754, 151 L. Ed. 2d 755 (2002).
6 *See* Ch. 7, *infra*.
7 Lee v. S. Cal. Univ. for Prof'l Studies, 148 Cal. App. 4th 782, 786 (2007).
8 *See, e.g.*, Spaces, Inc. v. RPC Software, Inc., 2007 WL 675505 (D. Kan. Mar. 1, 2007) (holding that the party seeking to compel arbitration "bears the initial summary-judgment-like burden of establishing that it is entitled to arbitration," and holding that competing affidavits on the issue of whether the parties agreed to arbitration created a genuine issue of material fact."); Newman v. Hooters of Am., Inc., 2006 WL 1793541, at *2 (M.D.

issued by an arbitrator is a nullity.[9] The question of whether an agreement to arbitrate ever was formed is for the court to decide, not the arbitrator; if there never was an agreement to arbitrate, there is no right to force the matter before an arbitrator.[10] Moreover the question of whether an arbitration agreement exists must be determined under state law.[11] As one court explained, "the FAA does not apply until the existence of an enforceable arbitration agreement is established under state law principles involving formation, revocation, and enforcement of contracts generally."[12] Finally, under many state arbitration laws if the existence of an agreement to arbitrate is in dispute a court is required to conduct a hearing in order to satisfy itself that an agreement does exist before compelling the parties to arbitrate their claims.[13]

5.2 Assent to Arbitration Agreement Is Required

5.2.1 Introduction

As with any contract, an arbitration clause is only enforceable if there is an offer and it is accepted: in other words, if both parties assent.[14] If a company fails to demonstrate that a consumer assented in some way to arbitration, the arbitration clause should not be enforced.[15] Parties who do not assent to a contract containing an arbitration clause are generally not bound by such a clause.[16] A party seeking to avoid arbitration may request a jury trial on the issue of assent.[17]

5.2.2 Express Assent

5.2.2.1 Assent by Signature

"Assent must be manifested by something. Ordinarily, it is manifested by a signature."[18] In general, a party that signs an arbitration clause, as with any other agreement, is deemed to have assented to it, even if the party later claims she did not intend to agree to arbitration.[19] However, courts

---

Fla. June 28, 2006) ("Under Defendant's reasoning, if Plaintiff began working, then she must have executed an Arbitration Agreement. This Court will not rely on 'if, then' scenarios and reverse factual inferences to establish the existence of a contract.").

9 MCI Telecommunications Corp. v. Exalon Indus., Inc., 138 F.3d 426, 430 (1st Cir. 1998) ("[S]ection 12, as well as section 2 and the other enforcement provisions of the FAA, do not come into play unless there is a written agreement to arbitrate."); Buczek v. Trans Union L.L.C., 2006 WL 3666635, at *2 (S.D. Fla. Nov. 9, 2006) (dismissing consumer's argument that debt had been eliminated by arbitration award, when the agreement with the creditor had not provided for arbitration; award was "of no force and effect").

10 See Sanford v. MemberWorks, Inc., 483 F.3d 956 (9th Cir. 2007) (vacating order compelling arbitration and remanding for determination of whether contract was formed, after arbitrator found no contract existed but still issued award); Sandvik AB v. Advent Int'l Corp., 220 F.3d 99 (3d Cir. 2000); Par-Knit Mills, Inc. v. Stockbridge Fabrics Co., Ltd., 636 F.2d 51 (3d Cir. 1980); Stephens v. TES Franchising, 2002 WL 1608281 (D. Conn. July 10, 2002) (court uses ordinary contract law to interpret ambiguity concerning whether contract actually requires arbitration); Ex parte Mountain Heating & Cooling, 867 So. 2d 1112 (Ala. 2003) (same).

11 See, e.g., First Options of Chicago, Inc. v. Kaplan, 514 U.S. 938, 115 S. Ct. 1920, 131 L. Ed. 2d 985 (1995); Wash. Mut. Fin. Group, L.L.C. v. Bailey, 364 F.3d 260, 264 (5th Cir. 2004); Hawkins v. Aid Ass'n for Lutherans, 338 F.3d 801, 806 (7th Cir. 2003) ("Whether the parties agreed to arbitrate is a matter of state contract law."); Hightower v. GMRI, 272 F.3d 239 (4th Cir. 2001); Specht v. Netscape Communications Corp., 150 F. Supp. 2d 585 (S.D.N.Y. 2001), aff'd, 306 F.3d 17 (2d Cir. 2002); Jubert v. Cent. Mich. Univ., 2003 WL 288984 (Mich. Ct. App. Feb. 7, 2003); In Re Kellogg Brown & Root, Inc., 166 S.W.3d 732 (Tex. 2005).

12 Lopez v. Charles Schwab & Co., 118 Cal. App. 4th 1224, 1229 (2004).

13 See, e.g., Molina v. Ponksy, 2005 WL 3219720 (Ohio Ct. App. Dec. 1, 2005) (when home owner denied agreeing to arbitration with mortgage lender, trial court abused discretion by failing to satisfy itself that valid arbitration agreement existed before compelling arbitration, under Ohio law providing that courts shall stay an action pending arbitration "upon being satisfied that the issue involved in the action is referable to arbitration under an agreement in writing").

See § 2.5, supra, for a discussion of the right to a jury trial to decide whether an arbitration clause exists.

14 When no offer is made or an offer is withdrawn, no agreement to arbitrate can come into existence. See, e.g., Lopez v. Charles Schwab & Co., 13 Cal. Rptr. 3d 544, 550, 551 (Ct. App. 2004) (brokerage firm's withdrawal of offer for account negates existence of any agreement, despite broker's subsequent conduct).

15 S. Energy Homes, Inc. v. Hennis, 776 So. 2d 105 (Ala. 2000).

16 See § 7.4, infra.

17 See § 2.5, supra.

18 S. Energy Homes, Inc. v. Hennis, 776 So. 2d 105, 108 (Ala. 2000); see also Gold v. Deutsche Aktiengesellschaft, 365 F.3d 144, 149 (2d Cir. 2004); Morales v. Rent-A-Center, Inc., 306 F. Supp. 2d 175, 181 (D. Conn. 2003); Brown v. Dorsey & Whitney, LLP, 267 F. Supp. 2d 61, 81 (D.D.C. 2003); Ex parte Cain, 2002 WL 1302532 (Ala. June 14, 2002); W.K. v. Farrell, 853 N.E.2d 728 (Ohio Ct. App. 2006) (employee's failure to read arbitration agreement she signed does not negate her assent to arbitration).

19 See, e.g., Gardner v. Randall Mortgage Services, Inc., 2007 WL 1432047 (S.D. Ohio May 14, 2007) (consumer in predatory lending case deemed to have read and understood arbitration clause she signed even though she was rushed through the signing, and not given a copy of the papers she had signed); Butcher v. Total Bally Fitness, 2003 WL 1785027, at *6 (Ohio Ct. App. Apr. 3, 2003) (holding that a signature alone signifies assent, because "the parties to an agreement should be able to rely on the fact that affixing a signature which acknowledges one has read, understood, and agrees to be bound by the terms of an agreement means what it purports to mean"); Neatherlin Homes, Inc. v. Love, 2007 WL 700996 (Tex. App. Mar. 8, 2007) (enforcing arbitration clause signed by consumer despite her argument that "they hid from me the fact that I was agreeing

have found exceptions to this rule in extreme cases, holding that a consumer who has "no meaningful opportunity to read or know the contents of the arbitration provisions" cannot be deemed to have assented to arbitration.[20]

By the same reasoning, absent other manifestation of assent,[21] if the party seeking to enforce an arbitration clause cannot prove that the other party signed it, then the arbitration clause should not be binding under basic contract principles.[22] For example, if the party seeking to avoid arbitration denies signing the agreement, and the other party cannot produce an agreement, then the clause should not be enforced unless there is other evidence of assent.[23] As an Iowa federal court explained: "The calculus changes significantly when it is undisputed that the party seeking to avoid arbitration has not signed any contract requiring arbitration. Under these circumstances, there is no presumption of validity that would trigger the court's duty to compel arbitration."[24]

Likewise, if an arbitration clause provides a space for the consumer's signature or initials, and the consumer did not sign in that space, then the arbitration provision is not enforceable.[25] If the consumer crosses out the arbitration clause before signing, this action should be sufficient to reject the clause.[26] However refusal to sign may not be sufficient to manifest rejection in some cases. For example, if the clause by its terms indicates that continued employment will indicate acceptance of an employer's arbitration clause, some courts may hold that an employee is bound by the clause despite her refusal to sign.[27]

Even if the consumer signs the arbitration clause, if the other party does not sign it the provision may not be enforceable.[28] For example, an arbitration provision in the buyer's order may not be not enforceable if the buyer's order states that it is not valid unless signed by the dealer, and the dealer fails to sign the buyer's order.[29] However the agree-

---

to arbitration and giving up my right to a jury trial"); *In re Media Arts Group, Inc.*, 116 S.W.3d 900, 908 (Tex. App. 2003).

In contrast, at least one court has held that a party that did not sign a written agreement may revoke voluntary verbal consent to arbitration. Liberty Mut. Ins. Co v. Mandaree Pub. Sch. Dist. No. 36, 2006 WL 3030136 (D.N.D. Oct. 23, 2006).

20 *E.g.*, Chrzanowski v. S.D.S. Autos, Inc., 13 Fla. L. Weekly Supp. 975 (No. 16-2005-CA-005434, July 21, 2006); Montgomery v. Brumos Motor Cars, Inc., 13 Fla. L. Weekly Supp. 979 (No. 16-2005-CA-005709, July 21, 2006).

The court also may have based its holding in part on the fact that the buyer's order signed by the consumers did not contain an arbitration clause, and indicated that it was the "entire agreement" between the parties. See § 5.6.3, *infra*.

21 See § 5.2.3, *infra*.

22 Crown Pontiac, Inc. v. McCarrell, 695 So. 2d 615 (Ala. 1997); *see also* Moses.com Sec., Inc. v. Comprehensive Software Sys., Inc., 263 F.3d 783 (8th Cir. 2001) (refusing to enforce an arbitration clause when the parties did not sign or agree to a final contract: although an arbitration clause had been included in early drafts of the contract, the district court's holding that the question of arbitration was still open to negotiation was not clearly erroneous); Kaplan v. First Options of Chicago, Inc., 19 F.3d 1503 (3d. Cir. 1994), *aff'd*, 514 U.S. 938 (1995); Chastain v. Robinson-Humphrey Co., 957 F.2d 851, 855 (11th Cir. 1992); Maguire Products, Inc. v. Comet Automation Sys., Inc., 2006 WL 2381454 (S.D. Ohio Aug. 16, 2006) (denying motion to compel arbitration when moving party provided only unsigned draft of arbitration clause, and opposing party presented evidence that it had not assented to arbitration); Rivera v. Clark Melvin Sec. Corp., 59 F. Supp. 2d 297 (D. P.R. 1999); S. Energy Homes, Inc. v. Harcus, 754 So. 2d 622 (Ala. 1999) (vacating order compelling arbitration and remanding to determine whether consumers really agreed to arbitration by ratification or other means when they did not sign the arbitration agreement); *Ex parte* Cain, 838 So. 2d 1020 (Ala. 2002) (consumers who accepted repairs pursuant to a warranty agreement were not bound by an arbitration clause in a separate agreement with the same company, which they had not signed); *cf.* Paul v. Merit Constr., Inc., 2007 WL 1836879 (Tenn. Ct. App. June 27, 2007) (arbitration clause in contract presented to subcontractors midway through work not enforceable when subcontractors did not sign). *But see* Banks v. Mitsubishi Motors Credit of Am., Inc., 156 Fed. Appx. 710, 711 (5th Cir. 2005) (compelling consumer to arbitrate claims despite car dealer's failure to produce any signed arbitration agreement, based solely on affidavit claiming that consumer "could not have" bought a car without signing an arbitration agreement).

23 Spaces, Inc. v. RPC Software, Inc., 2007 WL 675505 (D. Kan. Mar. 1, 2007) (when neither party had a copy of the signed document in its files, holding that competing affidavits created a genuine issue of material fact and that the party seeking to compel arbitration had failed to meet its burden of proving the existence of an agreement to arbitrate).

24 Owen v. MBPXL Corp., 173 F. Supp. 2d 905, 923 (N.D. Iowa 2001).

25 *See, e.g.*, Spears v. DaimlerChrysler Corp., No. 04CV62918 (Ohio Ct. Com. Pl. 2005) (arbitration clause void when buyer signed bottom of contract indicating her acceptance of initialed terms but did not initial next to the arbitration provision).

26 *See, e.g.*, Gen. Steel Corp. v. Collins, 196 S.W.3d 18 (Ky. Ct. App. 2006) (arbitration clause in building contract not enforceable when buyer had crossed out clause in its entirety before signing).

27 Omni Hotels Mgmt. Corp. v. Bayer, 2007 WL 1493878 (5th Cir. May 21, 2007); Hardin v. First Cash Fin. Services, Inc., 465 F.3d 470 (10th Cir. 2006).

28 *In re* Knepp, 229 B.R. 821 (Bankr. N.D. Ala. 1999); Premiere Chevrolet, Inc. v. Headrick, 748 So. 2d 891 (Ala. 1999); Med Ctr. Cars, Inc. v. Smith, 727 So. 2d 9 (Ala. 1998); Basura v. U.S. Home Corp., 98 Cal. App. 4th 1205, 120 Cal. Rptr. 2d 328 (2002) (seller's failure to initial arbitration clauses mandates factual inquiry as to whether the seller intended to be bound by those agreements); *cf.* Copeland v. KB Homes, 2004 WL 1778949 (N.D. Tex. Aug. 4, 2004) (employer's failure to initial arbitration clause in employment provision as required by its express terms constituted failure to satisfy condition precedent to the formation of a contract to arbitrate); Flanary v. Carl Gregory Dodge of Johnson City, L.L.C., 2005 WL 1277850 (Tenn. Ct. App. May 31, 2005) (fact that car dealer did not sign arbitration agreement raises genuine issue of material fact as to whether there was mutuality with respect to the agreement to arbitrate).

29 Premiere Chevrolet, Inc. v. Headrick, 748 So. 2d 891 (Ala. 1999); Med Ctr. Cars, Inc. v. Smith, 727 So. 2d 9 (Ala. 1998); *cf.* Jonessee v. Burlington Mitsubishi, 2007 WL 528047 (N.J. Super. Ct. App. Div. Feb. 22, 2007) (consumer who had signed

ment may be enforceable despite the dealer's failure to sign, as long as the dealer's conduct signifies intent to be bound.[30] It remains unenforceable though when the two parties later sign a consumer credit agreement or lease, if that later document does not contain an arbitration provision.[31]

The issue of whether an unsigned arbitration clause can be incorporated by reference into a contract signed by the consumer is an issue of state law. Some courts allow an unsigned document to be incorporated into a signed document as long as the signed paper specifically refers to the unsigned document.[32] Other courts are careful not to enforce arbitration clauses in these circumstances unless the incorporated document is delivered to the consumer. For example, a North Carolina appellate court held that an account holder was not bound by an arbitration clause in a bank services agreement, even though he had executed a signature card that incorporated the agreement by reference, when the bank had not delivered a copy of the bank services agreement to him until after he commenced litigation and he was unaware of the arbitration clause.[33] Still other courts enforce arbitration clauses incorporated by reference even if the only document signed by the consumer makes no mention of arbitration.[34]

Even if the consumer signs the arbitration clause, it may be unenforceable. For example, a Louisiana court recently refused to enforce an arbitration clause that had been signed by a consumer when the arbitration clause provided that it "is executed contemporaneously with, and becomes part of, the Retail Installment of Sales Contract," and no retail installment sales contract had subsequently been executed between the parties.[35] The court held that an arbitration agreement that "attempted to incorporate by reference a document and a transaction that did not exist at any time" between the parties could not be enforced.[36]

If the consumer signs an acknowledgment, but not an agreement to be bound by the terms of an arbitration clause, the clause should likewise be unenforceable. For example, the Supreme Court of Hawaii recently held that an employee who signed an acknowledgment verifying merely that he had *received* an employee handbook was not bound by an arbitration clause in the handbook.[37] The court explained:

> Douglass merely acknowledged his receipt and understanding of the items presented to him. He never expressed assent to the terms contained in those items, except for those terms expressly stating that the policies in the Handbook did "not create a contract," were to be treated as "guidelines," and were presented for "information only." The acknowledgment which Douglass signed makes no mention of the arbitration provision contained in the Handbook, nor sufficiently informs him that the Handbook contains terms to which he is contractually obligating himself. Nothing in the acknowledgment form that Douglass signed suggests to us that he was entering into an arbitration agreement.[38]

However courts have been more willing to enforce arbitration clauses when employees acknowledged that they were *bound* by the terms in the handbook,[39] even in cases when the employees argue they never received a copy of the handbook.[40] For example, a federal court in West Virginia recently held that an employee was bound by an arbitration clause he signed, even though the agreement stated that "neither this Agreement nor the Dispute Resolution Rules and Procedures form a contract of employment."[41] The court held that an arbitration agreement had been formed, regardless of whether a contract of employment had been formed.[42]

In some cases, courts may find that non-signatories assented to arbitration when they were acting jointly with a signatory or were third-party beneficiaries of the contract. This issue is discussed in § 7.4, *infra*.

---

agreement to participate in court run arbitration, but who later brought a claim in court, could not be compelled to arbitrate by car dealer which had never signed the arbitration agreement).

30 See § 5.2.3, *infra*, for a discussion of action sufficient to indicate implied assent.

31 Premiere Chevrolet, Inc. v. Headrick, 748 So. 2d 891 (Ala. 1999); Med Ctr. Cars, Inc. v. Smith, 727 So. 2d 9 (Ala. 1998).
See § 6.7.4, *infra*, for a discussion of cases in which a contract containing an arbitration clause is superseded by a new contract.

32 *See, e.g.*, Metro. Life Ins. Co. v. Glisson, 295 F.3d 1192, 1193–1194 (11th Cir. 2002) (Ala. law) (if a paper is attached to a signed paper and any language in the signed paper serves to "identify the papers as related," the attached paper is considered incorporated by reference); Jureczki v. Banc One Tex., 252 F. Supp. 2d 368 (S.D. Tex.) (an unsigned paper can be incorporated by reference if the language in the signed document specifically and "plainly refers to another writing"), *aff'd*, 75 Fed. Appx. 272 (5th Cir. 2003); Harby v. Wachovia Bank, 172 Md. App. 415, 915 A.2d 462 (2007) (enforcing arbitration clause when guardian of minor had signed "signature card" referencing acceptance of terms in separate document).

33 Kennedy v. Branch Banking & Trust Co., 165 N.C. App. 275 (2004) (table) (text available at 2004 WL 1491197).

34 Dufrene v. HBOS Mfg., Ltd. P'ship, 872 So. 2d 1206 (La. Ct. App. 2004) (separate arbitration agreement was incorporated by reference into a sales agreement even though the sales agreement, which was the only document signed by the seller, made no mention of arbitration agreement).

35 Easterling v. Royal Manufactured Hous., Inc., 963 So. 2d 399 (La. Ct. App. 2007).

36 *Id.* at 408.

37 Douglass v. Pflueger Haw., Inc., 135 P.3d 129 (Haw. 2006).

38 *Id.* at 141; *see also* Gourley v. Yellow Transp. L.L.C., 178 F. Supp. 2d 1196 (D. Colo. 2001).

39 *E.g.*, Carlisle v. CitiMortgage, Inc., 2007 WL 1557411 (E.D. Mo. May 25, 2007); Armstrong v. Associates Int'l Holding Corp., 2006 WL 2707431 (N.D. Tex. Sept. 20, 2006).

40 *E.g.*, Lindgren v. Pub. Storage, Inc., 2007 WL 1406917 (D. Or. May 7, 2007); Nudelman v. Int'l Rehabilitation Associates, Inc., 2006 WL 3098009 (E.D. Pa. Oct. 30, 2006).

41 Captain D's, L.L.C. v. McClenathan, 2006 WL 3409757, at *3 (S.D. W. Va. Nov. 27, 2006).

42 *Id.*

5.2.2.2 Forged Signatures and Fraud in the Factum

Fraud in the execution of a contract, or "fraud in the factum," occurs when one party's misrepresentation of the character or an essential term of the contract induces conduct that appears to be a manifestation of assent.[43] It is "the sort of fraud that procures a party's signature to an instrument without knowledge of its true nature or contents."[44] As the California Supreme Court has explained:

> To make out a claim of fraud in the execution, it must be remembered, plaintiffs must show their apparent assent to the contracts—their signatures on the client agreements—is negated by fraud so fundamental that they were deceived as to the basic character of the documents they signed and had no reasonable opportunity to learn the truth.[45]

For example, there is no assent if the consumer reasonably relied upon misrepresentations and could not read the agreement herself;[46] if the arbitration clause was deliberately or inadvertently hidden or left off the document containing the signature page;[47] if the signature was forged or obtained by fraud; or if the document on which the consumer's signature is found may have been altered since the signature was placed there.[48]

Because fraud in the factum arguably means that the consumer never assented, and that therefore no agreement to arbitrate was formed, this type of challenge should be resolved by a court rather than by an arbitrator.[49]

5.2.2.3 Electronic Assent

Arbitration agreements are increasingly being presented to consumers electronically. The rules as to the formation of such electronic arbitration agreements are the same as for paper ones—the agreement is not binding unless properly formed under state law. Assent to the terms of an electronic agreement is not signified by a written signature, but by some other action specifically expressing assent, such as clicking a button on a website. But mutual assent must still be demonstrated.[50]

One type of electronic agreement is called "click-wrap." The full agreement is presented on the computer screen and the consumer cannot proceed further in making a purchase, downloading software, or otherwise completing the transaction without first clicking a button stating "I agree" or similar language. Courts have found such click-wrap agreements to be valid.[51]

Another type of electronic agreement is called "browse-wrap." With these kinds of agreements, the consumer is not required to take a specific action to agree to the terms before proceeding with the transaction. Instead, a notice (which can be of varying degrees of conspicuousness) is provided on the website, stating that the actual terms of the agreement are found elsewhere on that or some other website. To review the terms, the consumer must click on one or more buttons, but the consumer is allowed to complete the transaction without clicking on those buttons. Such a contract is of suspect validity.[52] Providing a notice that the terms of the

---

43 Rosenthal v. Great W. Fin. Sec. Corp., 14 Cal. 4th 394, 420–423, 58 Cal. Rptr. 2d 875, 926 P.2d 1061 (Cal. 1996) (quoting Restatement (Second) of Contracts § 163, cmts. a & c (1981)).

44 Langley v. Fed. Deposit Ins. Corp., 484 U.S. 86, 93, 108 S. Ct. 396, 98 L. Ed. 2d 340 (1987).

45 Rosenthal v. Great W. Fin. Sec. Corp., 14 Cal. 4th 394, 425, 58 Cal. Rptr. 2d 875, 926 P.2d 1061 (1996).

46 *See, e.g.*, Cancanon v. Smith Barney, Harris, Upham & Co., 805 F.2d 998 (11th Cir. 1986) (plaintiffs with no knowledge of English entitled to trial on issue of whether their signatures were forged or "furtively obtained"); *Rosenthal*, 14 Cal. 4th at 427; Jones v. Adams Fin. Services, 71 Cal. App. 4th 831, 84 Cal. Rptr. 2d 151 (1999) (refusing to enforce arbitration clause when partially blind senior citizen with dementia had been allegedly tricked into signing mortgage documents she could not see). *But cf.* Gardner v. Randall Mortgage Services, Inc., 2007 WL 1432047 (S.D. Ohio May 14, 2007) (enforcing arbitration clause against consumer who later claimed she had no opportunity to review the terms, and was never given copies of documents she had signed).

47 Gustavsson v. Wash. Mut. Bank, 850 So. 2d 570 (Fla. Dist. Ct. App. 2003) (no assent when a faxed signature card and bank account agreement did not include the back of the signature card which included a reference to the disclosure statement and arbitration agreement); Evangelistic Outreach Ctr. v. Gen. Steel Corp., 640 S.E.2d 840 (N.C. Ct. App. 2007) (refusing to enforce arbitration clause on back of faxed agreement when party denied seeing back of the agreement); Britt v. May Davis Group, Inc., 641 S.E.2d 417 (N.C. Ct. App. 2007) (table) (same). *But see* Le Gere v. New Millennium Homes, 2003 WL 23018774 (Mich. Ct. App. Dec. 23, 2003) (enforcing arbitration without an evidentiary hearing despite consumer's testimony that mobile home dealer hid the arbitration clause from his view during the signing).

48 Walter Indus., Inc. v. McMillan, 804 So. 2d 1081 (Ala. 2001).

49 *See* Buckeye Check Cashing, Inc. v. Cardegna, 546 U.S. 440, 126 S. Ct. 1204, 1208 n.1, 163 L. Ed. 2d 1038 (2006) (holding that challenges to the underlying legality of a contract containing an arbitration clause must be decided by an arbitrator, but emphasizing that the Court was not addressing the "issue of whether any agreement... was ever concluded," such as "whether a party ever signed a contract, whether the signor lacked authority to commit the principal, and whether the signor lacked the capacity to assent" (internal citations omitted)).

See § 2.2, *supra*, for a discussion of which challenges courts decide and which ones arbitrators decide.

50 *See* Specht v. Netscape Communications, 306 F.3d 17 (2d Cir. 2002) (downloading software is not consent when the user was not given adequate notice of the terms and conditions of the download).

51 *See, e.g., id.*; Bar-Ayal v. Time Warner Cable, 2006 WL 2990032, at *8–*13 (S.D.N.Y. Oct. 16, 2006); Siebert v. Amateur Athletic Union, 422 F. Supp. 2d 1033 (D. Minn. 2006); *In re* RealNetworks, Inc. Privacy Litig., 2000 U.S. Dist. LEXIS 6584 (N.D. Ill. May 8, 2000); Hotmail Corp. v. Van Money Pie, Inc., 1998 U.S. Dist. LEXIS 10729 (N.D. Cal. Apr. 6, 1998).

52 *See* Specht v. Netscape Communications, 306 F.3d 17 (2d Cir. 2002); Pollstar v. Gigmania, Ltd., 170 F. Supp. 2d 974 (E.D.

agreement are available to be read does not equate with some action taken by the consumer to actually indicate assent to those terms.

5.2.3 Implied Assent Based on Conduct or Reliance

5.2.3.1 Overview

Besides a signature, a party's assent to a contract may be manifested in other ways, such as through conduct that is consistent with an agreement to be bound by contractual terms. However, before finding implied assent, two conditions need to be satisfied. First, there must be sufficient evidence that the offer was communicated: that the party was adequately notified of the term. Second, the party must have taken action that is sufficient to indicate assent. The burden is on the party seeking to enforce arbitration to show that the term was communicated and accepted.

5.2.3.2 Notice Requirement

Implied assent does not apply unless the party attempting to enforce the arbitration clause demonstrates that the other party received actual or constructive notice of the term and did not reject the offered term.[53] Courts should look at two factors when determining whether notice was sufficient: first, whether notice of the arbitration clause was delivered to the consumer or employee, and second, whether the content of the notice was sufficient to make an average person aware that she would become bound by the clause.

Thus, when an employer fails to present sufficient evidence to demonstrate that an employee was aware that by continuing to come to work every day she was assenting to arbitration, courts have refused to enforce arbitration clauses against employees who continued their employment.[54] Absent proof of effective notice, actions taken by the consumer or employee cannot be construed as manifesting assent.[55]

A Pennsylvania federal court held that a corporation had failed to show that one of its customers was bound by any agreement to arbitrate, when the plaintiff claimed he had no knowledge that such an agreement existed. The court explained that the corporation's evidence was insufficient to establish notice:

> In its attempt to establish that plaintiff indeed was aware of the subscriber agreement and the arbitration provisions contained therein, defendant offers a boilerplate subscriber agreement and evidence of a policy for all Comcast technicians to hand this boilerplate agreement to all consumers prior to service installation.... I conclude that there is insufficient evidence of a clear and unmistakable agreement between these two parties.... The existence of a policy to hand the subscriber agreement to all consumers does not constitute proof of actual notice to this particular plaintiff.[56]

Similarly, a federal court in Iowa refused to enforce an arbitration clause against an employee who testified that he never received the policy containing the clause, when the employer failed to prove that it had delivered the policy.[57] The court examined in great detail the evidence submitted by the employer, and found it insufficient to satisfy the burden of proof.[58]

Disputes as to whether an arbitration clause was communicated are very fact specific; faced with habit and practice testimony by an employer, a court may be more likely to enforce an arbitration clause against an employee who does not recall assenting to it[59] than against one who testifies that she rejected the term[60] or that she is certain she never received it.

For example, a Massachusetts federal court recently held that an employee had sufficient notice of an arbitration clause, given that the employer had submitted extensive testimony and documentation indicating that she had been

---

Cal. 2000); DeFontes v. Dell Computers Corp., 2004 WL 253560, at *6–*8 (R.I. Super. Ct. Jan. 29, 2004) (following *Specht*, finding that consumer had not assented to browse-wrap arbitration clause); *cf.* Acher v. Fujitsu Network Communications, Inc., 354 F. Supp. 2d 26 (D. Mass. 2005) (employee not bound by arbitration clause posted on employer's website).

53 *See, e.g.*, Higgs v. The Warranty Group, 2007 WL 2034376, at *2–*3 (S.D. Ohio July 11, 2007) (consumers who never received limited warranty containing arbitration clause "could not have assented to its terms by failing to return the document").

54 *See, e.g.*, Acher v. Fujitsu Network Communications, Inc., 354 F. Supp. 2d 26 (D. Mass. 2005) (arbitration clause in employer's new policy not binding on employee when corporation could not prove that employee ever received notice of new policy "circulated" to employees). *But see* Johnson v. Long John Silver's Restaurants, Inc., 320 F. Supp. 2d 656 (M.D. Tenn. 2004) (finding implied-in-fact agreement to arbitrate, despite employee's testimony that he was not aware of arbitration clause in employment contract and employer's inability to produce agreement signed by employee, when employer's testimony that it always required employees to sign agreement convinced court it was "more likely than not" that employee had assented), *aff'd*, 414 F.3d 583 (6th Cir. 2005).

55 Alltel Corp. v. Sumner, 203 S.W.3d 77 (Ark. 2005) (wireless company's arbitration clause not binding on consumer when company submitted affidavit setting forth its general procedures but could not adequately prove that the clause was given to that particular consumer).

56 Schwartz v. Comcast Corp., 2006 WL 3251092 (E.D. Pa. Nov. 8, 2006).

57 Owen v. MBPXL Corp., 173 F. Supp. 2d 905 (N.D. Iowa 2001).

58 *Id.* at 921–925.

59 Johnson v. Long John Silver's Restaurants, Inc., 320 F. Supp. 2d 656 (M.D. Tenn. 2004), *aff'd*, 414 F.3d 583 (6th Cir. 2005).

60 Steve Owren, Inc. v. Connolly, 877 So. 2d 918 (Fla. Dist. Ct. App. 2004).

given the information packet containing the term.[61] The court explained:

> [Plaintiff] does not dispute that she signed the Agreement, and does not even directly deny that she received the Policy. Instead, she submitted an affidavit stating that she cannot "recall" whether she was ever given a copy.... That is not sufficient, under the circumstances, to rebut defendants' overwhelming evidence that she did, in fact, have actual knowledge of the Policy and its terms.[62]

Credit card issuers have frequently attempted to add arbitration clauses to credit card contracts by enclosing them in "bill stuffers" mailed to cardholders. Courts evaluating the facts of various cases have come to differing conclusions about the circumstances under which these bill stuffers can provide sufficient notice.[63] In such cases, courts often rely on the "mailbox rule," holding that sufficient evidence that a document was mailed to an accurate address creates a rebuttable presumption that the notice was received.[64]

A mere statement by a bank representative without personal knowledge that the term was delivered is not sufficient evidence. In one case, for example, a court refused to enforce an arbitration clause when the bank offered only vague, generalized testimony to show that the arbitration clause was actually mailed to consumers:

> What Conseco fails to recognize, however, is the method of establishing that proper mailing took place.... [The card issuer's witness] does not claim that she was the person who mailed the notice. Nor does she attest to the procedures followed in the regular course of operations to ensure proper addressing and mailing of notices. Instead, she reaches conclusions about the mailing without indicating that she has any personal knowledge of any of procedures that were followed, and she says nothing about how addresses were selected for use in the mailing, what Conseco's records showed [the card holder's] address to be at the time, or what procedures were followed to ensure that all cardholders received notice. Further, [the card issuer's witness's] declaration does not establish that it was Conseco's routine practice to note in a cardholder's file if and when mail was returned unopened or undeliverable or if and when the cardholder sent correspondence to the company. Without such evidence, the Court can not apply the presumption of delivery.[65]

In addition, even if the mailbox presumption applies, it can be rebutted by evidence that the employee or consumer never received the arbitration clause in the mail. For example, a federal court in Ohio recently held that an employer had failed to meet its burden of showing that the plaintiff-employee had ever received or read a new dispute resolution term that it claimed had been mailed to all employees.[66] The court explained that the sworn, uncontradicted statement by the employee that he never received the materials was sufficient to rebut the mailbox presumption.[67] Absent proof of notice, the fact that the employee had continued to work for the employer was insufficient proof of assent to arbitration. As the court explained:

> NCR contends that Stepp accepted the arbitration agreement . . . by continuing in his employment with NCR and by accepting future promotions, pay increases, bonuses, and other benefits. Both of these "forms of acceptance" were set forth in the informational brochure distributed to him and

---

61 Boateng v. Gen. Dynamics Corp., 473 F. Supp. 2d 241 (D. Mass. 2007).
62 *Id.* at 249.
63 The legal validity of bill stuffers is discussed in § 5.7, *infra*.
64 *See, e.g.*, Discover Bank v. Vaden, 2007 WL 1695758, at *9 (4th Cir. June 13, 2007) (enforcing arbitration clause, when cardholder's "only evidence that she did not receive it is her own statement that she did not, and mere denial is insufficient to rebut the presumption of receipt"); Capone v. Elec. Boat Corp., 2007 WL 1520112 (D. Conn. May 18, 2007); Johnston v. Arrow Fin. Services, 2006 WL 2710663 (N.D. Ill. Sept. 15, 2006) (consumer's testimony that she "did not recall" receiving arbitration agreement "is simply not sufficient to rebut the presumption that Capitol One mailed Customer Agreements containing valid arbitration clauses").
65 Kennedy v. Conseco Fin Corp., 2000 WL 1760943, at *4 (N.D. Ill. Nov. 30, 2000); *see also* Acher v. Fujitsu Network Communications, Inc., 354 F. Supp. 2d 26 (D. Mass. 2005) (company's assertion that policy containing arbitration clause was circulated to all employees insufficient to meet burden of proof when employee testified he had never received policy).
66 Stepp v. NCR Corp., 2007 WL 1964890 (S.D. Ohio July 9, 2007).
67 *Id.* at *6–*7; *see also* Galle v. MBNA Bank, 2006 WL 839531 (S.D. Miss. Mar. 28, 2006) (denying MBNA's motion to compel when the account was transferred to MBNA from another creditor and the cardholder denied having received an arbitration amendment or any other materials from MBNA after the transfer, and finding "no evidence that Galle voluntarily and knowingly waived his right to access to the courts").

However, other courts have refused to credit this kind of testimony. *See, e.g.*, Tickanen v. Harris & Harris, Ltd., 2006 WL 3365788 (E.D. Wis. Oct. 20, 2006) (noting that, while the consumers had disputed the competency of the corporation's evidence, they "fail to submit any personal evidence disputing that they received any of the documents"); Rivera v. AT & T Corp., 420 F. Supp. 2d 1312, 1320 (S.D. Fla. 2006) ("In response to AT & T's evidence that it mailed a CSA to Plaintiffs which never returned to AT & T, Plaintiffs simply state that they never received the CSA. This is insufficient."); *In re* Am. Express Merchants Litig., 2006 WL 662341, at *9 (S.D.N.Y. Mar. 16, 2006) (appeal pending) ("[a]lthough plaintiffs deny having received the amendments, this self-serving assertion is insufficient to rebut the presumption of mailing" when the creditor presented evidence that mailings were normal business practice); Hoefs v. CACV of Colo., L.L.C., 365 F. Supp. 2d 69, 72–74 (D. Mass. 2005) (cardholder failed to rebut mailbox presumption).

other employees. The potential defect in NCR's argument is that there is every reason to think that Stepp would have performed in an identical fashion even had he not been made aware of [the arbitration clause].[68]

Likewise the Ninth Circuit recently held that posting a revised contract containing an arbitration clause did not give consumers adequate notice such that their continued use of the company's services constituted acceptance.[69] The court explained:

> Parties to a contract have no obligation to check the terms on a periodic basis to learn whether they have been changed by the other side. . . . Even if Douglas's continued use of Talk America's service could be considered assent, such assent can only be inferred after he received proper notice of the proposed changes.[70]

In addition to proving delivery, the party seeking to enforce an arbitration clause must also demonstrate that the content of the notice was sufficient to make an average person aware that she would become bound by the clause. For instance, while notice sent via e-mail is not necessarily ineffective, courts have refused to enforce arbitration agreements imposed via e-mail when the arbitration clause was downplayed or easy to miss.[71] Thus a Massachusetts federal court recently refused to enforce an arbitration clause that had been sent to employees via e-mail, when the employer failed to prove that the plaintiff-employee had received and read the e-mail.[72] The court further noted: "There was nothing in the email heading that would have compelled an employee to open it. . . . It did not announce that the message was important and affected employee rights. . . . Even assuming Hudyka received and read the [e-mail], it did not clearly advise him that arbitration was mandatory. . . ."[73] Likewise, an Oregon appellate court refused to enforce an arbitration clause sent by Comcast in a bill stuffer to subscribers.[74] The court explained that there was insufficient evidence that the consumers had received notice of the new term:

> Inaction *might* constitute acceptance, but whether it does or not in any particular case depends on that case's facts and circumstances. . . . The record contains an example of the type of "bill stuffer" reportedly sent to cable subscribers, and the context in which it was sent. Those documents support the inference that a subscriber could easily have continued using Comcast's service without ever being aware of the arbitration clause.[75]

In some lawsuits, consumers have introduced marketing evidence establishing that very few consumers would ever detect particular bill stuffers (particularly if they are buried among a number of advertisements, or if they are written in impenetrable legalese).[76] The preeminent example of the use of such evidence is *Ting v. AT & T*, the consumers conducted extensive discovery, hired experts, and presented a compelling case that AT & T's bill stuffer was intended by AT & T *not* to be read and was not in fact read or understood by the overwhelming majority of customers.[77]

5.2.3.3 Action Sufficient to Signify Acceptance Is Required

Even if the party seeking to enforce arbitration can demonstrate that the offer of arbitration was received, there is no assent unless the other party somehow signified their acceptance. The question of what type of action (or in some cases, inaction) may be sufficient to manifest assent must be resolved on a fact-specific basis. In the employment context, for example, the D.C. Circuit held that a court cannot find that an individual has agreed to arbitration merely by failing to object to another party's assertion of an agreement:

> Fannie Mae's principal claim is that Mr. Bailey agreed to the new arbitration policy because he did not positively reject it. This is a *non sequitur*. Even if we accepted the premise . . . it would not follow that Mr. Bailey's failure to reject a proposal, without more, evidenced his assent to be bound.[78]

---

68 Stepp v. NCR Corp., 2007 WL 1964890, at *5 (S.D. Ohio July 9, 2007).
69 Douglass v. United States Dist. Ct., 2007 WL 2069542 (9th Cir. July 18, 2007); *see also* Al-Safin v. Circuit City Stores, Inc., 394 F.3d 1254, 1260 (9th Cir. 2005) (former employee did not have constructive notice of arbitration clause adopted after his employment was terminated, and no consideration existed for his purported acceptance of the term).
70 Douglass v. United States Dist. Ct., 2007 WL 2069542, at *1 (9th Cir. July 18, 2007).
71 *See, e.g.*, Campbell v. Gen. Dynamics, 407 F.3d 546, 558 (1st Cir. 2005) (employer's mass e-mail adding arbitration clause not binding on employee when e-mail "undersold significance" of new policy and "omitted the critical fact that it contained a mandatory arbitration agreement"); Carfagno v. ACE, Ltd., 2005 WL 1523530 (D.N.J. June 28, 2005) (no formation of arbitration agreement through e-mail requiring employees to link to webpage to sign employment handbook when signature link appeared on top of page and arbitration clause could only be found by scrolling downward).
72 Hudyka v. Sunoco, Inc., 474 F. Supp. 2d 712 (E.D. Pa. 2007).
73 *Id.* at 716–717.
74 Martin v. Comcast of California/Colorado/Florida/Oregon, Inc., 146 P.3d 380 (Or. Ct. App. 2006).
75 *Id.* at 388–339.
76 *See, e.g.*, Opening Brief of Appellants, Wells v. Chevy Chase Bank, at 5–7 (reproduced on the CD-Rom accompanying this manual).
77 182 F. Supp. 2d 902 (N.D. Cal. 2002).
78 Bailey v. Fed. Nat'l Mortgage Ass'n, 209 F.3d 740 (D.C. Cir. 2000); *see also* Hendrick v. Brown & Root, Inc., 50 F. Supp. 2d 527, 535 (E.D. Va. 1999) (the waiver of a vested right to a judicial resolution can never be inferred from silence).

Likewise, the Supreme Court of Mississippi recently refused to enforce an arbitration clause against a consumer who continued to use her checking accounts after the bank sent her a new "signature card" with an arbitration clause that indicated that the arbitration provision would take effect upon continued use of the accounts, when the consumer did not sign the new card.[79] The court held that, because the signature cards the consumer had originally executed had *not* contained an arbitration clause, and she had not executed new cards with arbitration clauses, the new arbitration clause could not be enforce against her. In so holding, the court explained: "Submitting to arbitration means giving up the right to file a lawsuit in a court of competent jurisdiction. Waiving that right requires more than implied consent. . . . We find absolutely no evidence that either of the Rogerses voluntarily and knowingly waived their right to access to the courts."[80]

However, some courts have held that an employee who receives an employer's document providing that she will become bound by an arbitration clause if she keeps working, and who then continues working in her job, is deemed to have given assent to those terms regardless of whether she signed any document accepting the term.[81] Similarly, a consumer's continuing use of a product or service, such as a credit card, after receiving notice of contractual terms may be deemed evidence of the consumer's assent to those terms.[82]

Likewise performance under the contract can manifest intent to be bound by its terms. On such ground the Alabama Supreme Court enforced an arbitration clause between a vendor and lessor despite the fact that the agreement in which the clause was included expressly required written acceptance by the vendor and the vendor had never confirmed acceptance in writing.[83] The court held that subsequent performance under the contract manifested acceptance by the vendor.[84] Similarly courts have enforced arbitration clauses contained in nursing home admission contracts, despite the failure of a nursing home representative to sign the admission contract, when the nursing home indicated its assent by admitting the resident and performing the contract terms.[85]

A party's assent to an arbitration clause may also be inferred from the party's reliance on accompanying terms appearing in the same contract as the clause. For example, a consumer who asserts claims based on rights under a contract or who alleges breach of a contract will ordinarily be deemed to be bound by *all* of the contract's terms,

---

79 Union Planters Bank v. Rogers, 912 So. 2d 116 (Miss. 2005).
80 *Id.* at 119; *see also* Stone v. Memberworks, Inc., 2003 WL 21246771, at *3–*5 (Cal. Ct. App. May 30, 2003) (finding no agreement to arbitrate when document was mailed but not signed, and there was no preexisting relationship between the parties). See discussion of the voluntary, knowing, and intelligent doctrine in § 5.5, *infra*.
81 *E.g.*, Hardin v. First Cash Fin. Services, Inc., 465 F.3d 470 (10th Cir. 2006); Berkley v. Dillard's, Inc., 450 F.3d 775 (8th Cir. 2006) (employee who refused to sign arbitration clause assented to arbitration by continuing employment, when clause so provided); Caley v. Gulfstream Aerospace Corp., 428 F.3d 1359, 1374–1376 (11th Cir. 2005) (employees accepted new arbitration provision by continuing employment, when provision stated that no signature was required and that continuation of employment would constitute acceptance); Marino v. Dillard's, Inc., 413 F.3d 530 (5th Cir. 2005); May v. Higbee Co., 372 F.3d 757, 764 (5th Cir. 2004); Circuit City Stores, Inc. v. Najd, 294 F.3d 1104 (9th Cir. 2002) (failure of an employee to opt out of an arbitration clause equals assent when the circumstances made clear the significance of the employee's silence); Armstrong v. Associates Int'l Holding Corp., 2006 WL 2707431 (N.D. Tex. Sept. 20, 2006); Johnson v. Long John Silver's Restaurants, Inc., 320 F. Supp. 2d 656, 664–665 (M.D. Tenn. 2004) (employee whose conduct during course of employment indicated he was aware of arbitration clause in contract "could have quit working if he did not want to arbitrate his claims"), *aff'd*, 414 F.3d 583 (6th Cir. 2005); *In re* Dallas Peterbilt, Ltd., 196 S.W.3d 161 (Tex. 2006); *cf.* George v. LeBeau, 455 F.3d 92 (2d Cir. 2006) (employment contract, including arbitration clause, valid despite having expired, when no new contract was negotiated and employee continued to work). *But see* Holland v. Trav Corp., 2007 WL 778874 (Cal. Ct. App. Mar. 16, 2007) (employee did not manifest assent by renewing employment contract when employee had previously opted out of arbitration clause, and new contract did not clearly require arbitration for continuing employees); *cf.* Foss v. Circuit City Stores, Inc., 477 F. Supp. 2d 230 (D. Me. 2007) (employee's continuing to work after reaching age of majority was not sufficient to constitute ratification of arbitration clause).
82 *See, e.g.*, Kurz v. Chase Manhattan Bank USA, 319 F. Supp. 2d 457, 465, 466 (S.D.N.Y. 2004); Taylor v. Citibank USA, 292 F. Supp. 2d 1333, 1338 (M.D. Ala. 2003).
83 Lanier Worldwide, Inc. v. Clouse, 875 So. 2d 292 (Ala. 2003).
84 *Id.* at 296; *see also* Bradford v. Robert Peltier Nissan Pontiac, 2007 WL 865685 (E.D. Tex. Mar. 15, 2007) (enforcing arbitration clause in purchase order that expressly required seller's signature, despite fact that seller never signed, when seller signified acceptance of terms by releasing title); McMahan v. Rizza Chevrolet, Inc., 2006 WL 2560883, at *2 (N.D. Ill. Aug. 31, 2006) (enforcing clause when dealer did not sign, indicated its assent to be bound by "attach[ing] the [arbitration] Agreement to the purchase documents signed by both parties"); Consol. Res. Healthcare Fund I, Ltd. v. Fenelus, 853 So. 2d 500 (Fla. Dist. Ct. App. 2003) (when nursing home representative failed to sign the admission contract, arbitration clause contained in the contract was nonetheless valid when both parties had performed according to terms of contract and thus indicated assent to its terms); Integrated Health Services of Green Briar, Inc. v. Lopez-Silvaro, 827 So. 2d 338 (Fla. Dist. Ct. App. 2002) (same); Dodge of Winter Park, Inc. v. Morly, 756 So. 2d 1085 (Fla. Dist. Ct. App. 2000) (enforcing arbitration clause against car buyer even though dealer failed to sign it); Dufrene v. HBOS Mfg., Ltd. P'ship, 872 So. 2d 1206 (La. Ct. App. 2004) (enforcing separate arbitration agreement executed contemporaneously with sales contract against buyers of mobile home, despite fact that seller did not sign arbitration agreement and signed sales contract did not incorporate arbitration clause by reference).
85 Consol. Res. Healthcare Fund I, Ltd. v. Fenelus, 853 So. 2d 500 (Fla. Dist. Ct. App. 2003); Integrated Health Services of Green Briar, Inc. v. Lopez-Silvaro, 827 So. 2d 338 (Fla. Dist. Ct. App. 2002).

including its arbitration clause.[86] However, a party alleging breach of a contract separate from the contract containing the arbitration clause should not thereby become subject to arbitration.[87]

The question of whether a consumer's actions manifest assent to arbitration frequently arises in the context of arbitration clauses added to credit card agreements through bill stuffers. Some of these arbitration clauses by their own terms apply only to cardholders who continue to use the credit card after a certain date.[88] Even if the clause does not specifically so provide, card issuers often argue that the consumer's continued use of a credit card indicates assent.[89]

If use of the card after receiving notice constitutes assent, a cardholder who has *not* used the card after receiving notice of the arbitration clause should *not* be bound by it.[90] Equally, a consumer whose card privileges were revoked before the arbitration clause was added should not be bound by the clause. According to at least one court, a consumer who continued to pay off an outstanding balance after she received the change in terms notice, but did not use the card after that date, may not be bound by the agreement.[91] However a federal court in Illinois found that a consumer was bound by the arbitration clause in his contract with the credit card company even though he had never used the card. The court held that the question of whether the consumer was bound was for the arbitrator because the court's only inquiry should be whether he "was a party to an agreement which contains a facially valid arbitration clause."[92]

Courts should also be careful to ensure that any use of the card after the term was added was authorized. A few courts have enforced arbitration clauses even when there is insufficient evidence that the consumer used the card. In one particularly egregious case a court enforced an arbitration clause in a credit card agreement without any evidence that the consumer had assented to the term; while the court noted that the card had been used, and that "the use of the cards amounts to acceptance of the terms of the cardholder agreement," there was no proof that the consumer in question had *himself* used the card.[93]

In many debt collection cases the creditor or debt buyer attempting to compel arbitration or confirm an arbitration award is not the company with whom the consumer originally executed the credit card agreement. In such cases the court should require additional proof of assent to arbitrate. A Mississippi federal court recently rejected a creditor's proof of agreement as insufficient.[94] The court explained: "There must be an unbroken chain of assent from the signatures of the plaintiffs on the agreement providing for changes by assent through the clause requiring arbitration. The defendants have not met their burden."[95]

As one federal court analyzed the situation, under the general law of contracts, "an offeror has no power to cause the silence of the offeree to operate as an acceptance when the offeree does not intend it to do so."[96] In the context of a credit card bill stuffer, this principle meant the following:

> MBNA proposed the Arbitration Section as a change in the terms of the parties' relationship that would be effective unless rejected by the card holder. In other words, MBNA skipped offer and

---

86 *See, e.g.*, Wash. Mut. Fin. Group, L.L.C. v. Bailey, 364 F.3d 260, 267 (5th Cir. 2004) (holding that non-signatory's assertion of rights under home loan agreement binds claimant to arbitration clause); Jim Walter Homes, Inc. v. Saxton, 880 So. 2d 428 (Ala. 2003) (party alleging breach cannot disavow contract's arbitration clause); God's Battalion of Prayer Pentecostal Church, Inc. v. Miele Associates, LLP, 845 N.E.2d 1265 (N.Y. 2006) (church bound by arbitration clause in contract it did not sign, when it alleged breach of contract containing clause). *But see* Homes of Legend, Inc. v. Spraldin, 2003 WL 23096489 (Ky. Ct. App. Dec. 31, 2003) (mobile home buyer suing for breach of contract not bound by unsigned arbitration clause in limited warranty that was delivered with mobile home after purchase agreement was executed, when buyer never acknowledged receipt of the warranty and received no benefit under it); *cf.* Springhill Nursing Homes, Inc. v. McCurdy, 898 So. 2d 694 (Ala. 2004) (party did not indicate assent to arbitration clause in written contract by suing for breach of implied contract).

87 *See* Masteller v. Champion Mobile Home Builders, Inc., 723 N.W.2d 561 (S.D. 2006) (suit for "breach of warranty" failed to establish consent to arbitration, when plaintiffs sued based on warranty in purchase agreement and had never assented to arbitration clause in warranty delivered after purchase was complete).

88 *See, e.g.*, Battels v. Sears Nat'l Bank, 365 F. Supp. 2d 1205 (M.D. Ala. 2005); MBNA Am. Bank v. Engen, 2005 WL 1754169 (Wash. Ct. App. July 25, 2006).

89 *See* Ragan v. AT & T Corp., 824 N.E.2d 1183 (Ill. App. Ct. 2005) (cardholder did not opt out of new arbitration clause sent in bill stuffer).

90 *E.g.*, Perry v. FleetBoston Fin. Corp., 2004 WL 1508518, at *4 (E.D. Pa. July 6, 2004) (cardholders who did not continue to use their cards not bound by arbitration clause in bill stuffer even though clause by its terms did not require continued use to be effective).

91 Shea v. Household Bank, 105 Cal. App. 4th 85, 129 Cal. Rptr. 2d 387 (2003).

92 McIntyre v. Household Bank, 216 F. Supp. 2d 719 (N.D. Ill. 2002).

93 Fahey v. U.S. Bank, 2006 WL 2850529, at *2 (E.D. Mo. Sept. 29, 2006).

94 Robertson v. J.C. Penney Co., 484 F. Supp. 2d 561 (S.D. Miss. 2007).

95 *Id.* at 565; *see also* West v. Household Life Ins. Co., 867 N.E.2d 868 (Ohio Ct. App. 2007) (affirming trial court's denial of motion to compel arbitration, when arbitration clause was between "lender" and "borrower" but did not specify that Household was the lender, and Household did not claim that illegible signature on form was that of its employee or agent).

For a more detailed discussion of the proof of assent to arbitration that should be required in debt collection cases, see § 12.4.4.2, *infra*.

96 Myers v. MBNA Am., 2001 U.S. Dist. LEXIS 11900, at *8 (D. Mont. Mar. 28, 2001) (quoting Joseph M. Perillo, Corbin on Contracts § 3.18, at 407, 408 (1993 & Supp. Fall 2000)); *see also* Badie v. Bank of Am., 67 Cal. App. 4th 779, 79 Cal. Rptr. 2d 273 (1998).

went straight to acceptance. Myers did not perform an act and did not forego the performance of an act.[97]

Finally, in some states, arbitration clauses imposed unilaterally on cardholders via bill stuffers are invalid as a matter of law, regardless of whether the cardholder continued to use the card.[98]

In one recent unusual case, the Supreme Court of Alabama upheld an amendment sent by customers to a pest control company which stipulated that any arbitration must be agreed to post-dispute and must be nonbinding, and that any future amendments to the contract had to be in writing and signed by both the consumer and a representative of the company.[99] The court held that this amendment was valid, and not unilaterally imposed, as it was sent along with a renewal payment rather than in the middle of the duration of an existing contract. Because the company continued to provide its services after receiving the amendment, the court deemed that it had assented to the changed terms.[100]

5.2.4 Lack of Capacity to Assent

If a consumer is alleged to lack the mental capacity to assent to a contract, then the arbitration clause in any contract to which the consumer is a party cannot take effect until the court determines whether the consumer had sufficient capacity to enter into an enforceable agreement.[101] In cases in which the individual completely lacked capacity to assent, the court may find that an agreement was never formed.[102] In cases in which the individual had the capacity to assent, but is partially incapacitated or a minor, the court may conclude that a contract was formed, but that the individual has a defense to its enforcement.[103]

5.3 Illusory Agreements and the Requirement of Consideration

In order to be valid, a contract requires consideration. As one court explained:

> Consideration consists of a promise to do something that a party is under no legal obligation to do or to forbear from doing something he has a legal right to do. Restatement (Second) of Contracts §§ 73, 74, at 179, 185 (1981). Furthermore, a promise must be binding. When a promise puts no constraints on what a party may do in the future—in other words, when a promise, in reality, promises nothing—it is illusory, and it is not consideration.[104]

In general, if both parties agree to submit claims to arbitration, this constitutes sufficient consideration.[105] However if a consumer or employee agrees to give up her right to bring a claim in court, but the other party reserves the right to pursue its claims in court, some courts hold that such a contract lacks consideration, and that this lack of mutuality is enough to void the arbitration clause and render it unenforceable as a matter of contract law.[106] The Arkansas

---

97 Myers v. MBNA Am., 2001 U.S. Dist. LEXIS 11900, at *8 (D. Mont. Mar. 28, 2001).
98 *See, e.g.*, Myers v. MBNA Am., 2001 WL 965063 (D. Mont. Mar. 20, 2001) (consumer's silence not acceptance of new arbitration term); Badie v. Bank of Am., 79 Cal. Rptr. 2d 273 (Cal. Ct. App. 1998) (arbitration clause could not be unilaterally added to credit card contract pursuant to change-in-terms provision in original contract); Discover Bank v. Shea, 827 A.2d 358 (N.J. Super. Ct. Law Div. 2001) (bill stuffer adding arbitration clause to credit card contract not effective under New Jersey law). *But see* Joseph v. MBNA Am. Bank, 775 N.E.2d 550, 553 (Ohio Ct. App. 2002) (collecting cases upholding MBNA's bill stuffer).
  See § 5.7, *infra*, for a discussion of the legality of bill stuffers.
99 Cook's Pest Control, Inc. v. Rebar, 852 So. 2d 730 (Ala. 2002).
100 *Id.*
101 *See* § 2.5, *supra*.
102 *See, e.g.*, Foss v. Circuit City Stores, Inc., 477 F. Supp. 2d 230 (D. Me. 2007) (when employee was under 18 at time of entering into employment agreement containing arbitration clause, and continuing to work after reaching age of majority did not constitute ratification, finding that "the Agreement never came into existence between Foss and Circuit City"); Covenant Health & Rehab. of Picayune, Ltd. P'ship v. Lambert, 2006 WL 3593437, at *3–*4 (Miss. Ct. App. Dec. 12, 2006) (remanding for determination of whether patient admitted to nursing home was competent to sign admission agreement, and thus whether arbitration agreement came into existence).
103 *See* § 6.4.4, *infra*.
104 Heye v. Am. Gold Corp., 80 P.3d 495, 499 (N.M. Ct. App. 2003).
105 *See, e.g.*, Captain D's, L.L.C. v. McClenathan, 2006 WL 3409757, at *4 (S.D. W. Va. Nov. 27, 2006) (refusing to require additional consideration, and noting that "it is well-established that an employer's agreement to be bound by the arbitration process constitutes sufficient consideration to support an agreement to arbitrate an employee's claims"); McCollum v. Tenet Healthcare Corp., 2006 WL 3373096, at *3 (D.S.C. Nov. 20, 2006) ("Continued employment can constitute sufficient consideration to render an agreement to arbitrate binding.... The Defendant's agreement to submit to arbitration is also adequate consideration.").
106 Hull v. Norcom, Inc., 750 F.2d 1547 (11th Cir. 1985) (N.Y. law) (may now be limited by Sablosky v. Edward S. Gordon Co., 73 N.Y.2d 133, 538 N.Y.S.2d 13 (1989)); Gonzalez v. W. Suburban Imports, Inc., 411 F. Supp. 2d 970 (N.D. Ill. 2006) (there was no mutuality of obligation under an arbitration agreement between an automobile dealership and buyers; thus the agreement lacked consideration and was unenforceable when the agreement exempted from arbitration nearly every claim that could have been brought by the dealership against the buyers); Lopez v. Plaza Fin. Co., 1996 U.S. Dist. LEXIS 5566 (N.D. Ill. Apr. 25, 1996); Stirlen v. Supercuts, Inc., 51 Cal. App. 4th 1519, 60 Cal. Rptr. 2d 138 (1997) (arbitration agreement did not possess even a modicum of bilaterality); Saika v. Gold, 49 Cal. App. 4th 1074, 56 Cal. Rptr. 2d 922 (1996) (doctor-patient arbitration agreement which allowed either party to disregard the results of the arbitration and litigate in the courts when the arbitration award exceeded $25,000 was unenforceable because it tilted the play-

Supreme Court recently joined the ranks of such courts. After first noting that "it is state law that must be considered to determine an obligation of mutuality," the court held that a non-mutual arbitration clause "does not constitute a valid enforceable agreement."[107] The court went on to comment that these one-way clauses are inconsistent with the claims made by the supporters of arbitration:

> The laudable policy behind enforcing arbitration agreements is the belief that they provide a less expensive, more expeditious means of settling litigation and relieving congested court dockets. However, they should not be used as a shield against litigation by one party while simultaneously reserving solely to itself the sword of a court action.[108]

Even courts that find non-mutual arbitration agreements enforceable may question what consideration the consumer has received in a side agreement that only sets out a requirement that the consumer, but not the merchant, arbitrate claims.[109] For example, some sellers or creditors present the arbitration agreement as a document separate from the sales or credit agreement, and the goods or credit obtained is thus not consideration for the arbitration agreement.[110]

In addition, if an arbitration agreement is subject to change by one party without the consent of the other, it may be viewed as illusory and not effective. For example, in one employment case the company retained the right to modify, supplement, or delete provisions at any time without notice. The court found that the agreement was illusory because the employer had not promised anything.[111]

Similarly, there may be no consideration for a contract when the consumer is required to enter into an arbitration agreement not with the company but with an arbitration service provider. In the employment context, companies sometimes require individuals to enter into an arbitration agreement not with the employer itself but with a particular arbitration provider, such as Employment Dispute Services, Inc. (EDS). In a case in which EDS's part of the bargain was promising to provide an arbitration mechanism pursuant to

---

ing field in favor of the doctor and made arbitration virtually illusory as far as the patient was concerned); Douglass v. Pflueger Haw., Inc., 135 P.3d 129 (Haw. 2006) (arbitration clause in employment contract unenforceable for lack of consideration); Vassilkova v. Woodfield Nissan, 830 N.E.2d 619, 626 (Ill. App. Ct. 2005) (separate arbitration agreement in car sales transaction was illusory and unenforceable for lack of consideration when car dealer retained right to pursue its claims in court: "[w]e hold that where the agreement to arbitrate is itself a separate document, purporting to bind each party to the arbitration agreement, but subsequently creates a total exclusion of one party's obligation to arbitrate, the obligation to arbitrate is illusory and unenforceable"); Fireman's Fund Ins. Companies v. Bugailiskis, 278 Ill. App. 3d 19, 662 N.E.2d 555 (1996); Neighbors v. Lynn Hickey Dodge, Clearinghouse No. 51,616B (Okla. Civ. App. Aug. 6, 1996) (text of this decision is also available on the CD-Rom accompanying this manual); see also Solovay, Foley & Ignatin, Using Arbitration in Commercial Disputes § 3.015[2] (Matthew Bender: Business Law Monograph 1984). But see Cook v. River Oaks Hyundai, Inc., 2006 WL 931685 (N.D. Ill. Apr. 5, 2006) (distinguishing Vassilkova and Gonzales because the arbitration agreement at issue was not a stand-alone contract and because the defendant had identified several types of claims that it might have for which it might be compelled into arbitration).

107 Showmethemoney Check Cashers, Inc. v. Williams, 342 Ark. 112, 121, 27 S.W.3d 361 (Ark. 2000); accord Casteel v. Clear Channel Broad., 254 F. Supp. 2d 1081 (W.D. Ark. 2003); Cash in a Flash Check Advance of Ark., L.L.C. v. Spencer, 348 Ark. 459, 74 S.W.3d 600 (Ark. 2002); The Money Place, L.L.C. v. Barnes, 339 Ark. 411, 78 S.W.3d 714 (Ark. 2002).

108 Showmethemoney Check Cashers, Inc., 342 Ark. at 121.

109 See Pitchford v. Oakwood Mobile Homes, Inc., 124 F. Supp. 2d 958 (W.D. Va. 2000).

110 Id.

111 Gourley v. Yellow Transp., L.L.C., 178 F. Supp. 2d 1196 (D. Colo. 2001) ("Plaintiffs point out that the Arbitration Agreement is contained in the Employee Handbook. That Handbook repeatedly states that the Handbook is not a contract and is in no way binding on Defendant. Plaintiffs therefore argue that any 'contract' is illusory at best. I agree."); see also Dumais v. Am. Golf Corp., 299 F.3d 1216 (10th Cir. 2002); Hooters of Am., Inc. v. Phillips, 173 F.3d 933 (4th Cir. 1999); Brennan v. Bally Total Fitness, 198 F. Supp. 2d 377 (S.D.N.Y. 2002); Diaz v. Arapahoe (Burt) Ford, Inc., 68 F. Supp. 2d 1193 (D. Colo. 1999); Cheek v. United Healthcare of the Mid-Atlantic, 835 A.2d 656, 662, 663 (Md. 2003); Salazar v. Citadel Communications Corp., 90 P.3d 466 (N.M. 2004) (arbitration clause not binding on employee when it was part of employee handbook that employer retained unilateral right to amend without notice); Sears Roebuck & Co. v. Avery, 593 S.E.2d 424, 432, 433 (N.C. Ct. App. 2004); Heye v. Am. Gold Corp., 80 P.3d 495, 500 (N.M. Ct. App. 2003) ("The agreement, in essence, gives AGC unfettered discretion to terminate arbitration at any time, while binding Plaintiff to arbitration. AGC remains free to selectively abide by its promise to arbitrate; the promise, therefore, is illusory."); In re Jobe Concrete Products, Inc., 2003 WL 21757512 (Tex. App. July 31, 2003) (no agreement to arbitrate was formed when employer retained unilateral right to amend, modify, or terminate occupational injury plan containing arbitration clause); In re C & H News Co., 2003 WL 131770 (Tex. App. Jan. 16, 2003); cf. Al-Safin v. Circuit City Stores, Inc., 394 F.3d 1254, 1259–1260 (9th Cir. 2005) (provision allowing company to unilaterally modify rules and procedures governing arbitration "almost at will" substantively unconscionable under Washington law); J.M. Davidson v. Webster, 49 S.W.3d 507 (Tex. App. 2001). But see Caley v. Gulfstream Aerospace Corp., 428 F.3d 1359, 1373–1374 (11th Cir. 2006) (arbitration clause in Gulfstream's employment contract not illusory when agreement can be unilaterally modified "only on notice," and corporation is bound by the version of the agreement in place at the time of the claim); Taylor v. Citibank USA, 292 F. Supp. 2d 1333, 1339, 1340 (M.D. Ala. 2003); Holloman v. Circuit City Stores, Inc., 894 A.2d 547 (Md. 2006) (arbitration clause in Circuit City's employment contract not illusory under Cheek when agreement can be unilaterally modified by corporation on a single day each year upon providing thirty-day written notice to employees); cf. Battels v. Sears Nat'l Bank, 365 F. Supp. 2d 1205 (M.D. Ala. 2005) (arbitrator, not court, must decide claim that change-of-terms provision makes contract illusory).

its rules, but EDS retained the right to unilaterally change those rules or terminate the entire agreement, a court found that EDS had provided no consideration and that the contract was therefore illusory.[112] Because the contract was illusory, it was not binding on the individual employee.[113] Similarly, when an arbitration clause is part of a document in which the drafter explicitly disavows the intention of creating a binding contract, the clause is not enforceable against either party.[114]

However the fact that the clause permits the drafting party (or a third party) to unilaterally change its terms may not automatically make the clause illusory. For example, a Maryland appellate court recently held that an arbitration agreement was not illusory when the bank was required to give the consumer at least thirty days notice before any change would take effect.[115] Likewise, a federal court in New Mexico recently held that a contract containing an arbitration clause which provides that one party may terminate the entire agreement—as opposed to the arbitration clause—is not illusory.[116]

Many jurisdictions do not find that a non-mutual arbitration agreement lacks consideration—they find that other aspects of the contract provide sufficient consideration for the contract to be binding.[117] In these jurisdictions, unconscionability may be the only ground on which to challenge a lack of mutuality. For a discussion of the growing number of cases striking down arbitration clauses that require the consumer, but not the merchant, to arbitrate disputes as unconscionable, see § 6.5.3, *infra*. For a discussion of courts that treat illusory contracts as an unconscionability issue, see § 6.4.8, *infra*.

5.4 Language of Arbitration Clause Must Be Clear and Unambiguous

Because arbitration is a matter of consent, when the language of an arbitration clause does not actually *require* consumers to submit their claims to arbitration, courts will not compel arbitration.[118] Moreover, a generally applicable body of contract law in most jurisdictions provides that contractual clauses purporting to waive constitutional rights must be clear and unambiguous.

This doctrine has been applied to arbitration clauses because, by agreeing to arbitration, parties waive their right under the Seventh Amendment to a jury trial. When determining the scope of an arbitration clause (as opposed to determining whether an arbitration agreement exists), the Supreme Court has held that "[c]ourts should not assume that the parties agreed to arbitrate arbitrability unless there is clea[r] and unmistak[able] evidence that they did so."[119]

---

112 Penn v. Ryan's Family Steak Houses, Inc., 269 F.3d 753 (7th Cir. 2001); *see also* Walker v. Ryan's Family Steak Houses, Inc., 400 F.3d 370 (6th Cir. 2005); Floss v. Ryan's Family Steak Houses, Inc., 211 F.3d 306 (6th Cir. 2000); State *ex rel.* Sylor v. Wilkes, 613 S.E.2d 914 (W. Va. 2005). *But see* Hill v. PeopleSoft U.S.A., Inc., 412 F.3d 540 (4th Cir. 2005) (arbitration clause in employment contract not illusory even though employer retained unilateral right to change it, without notice; separate "Internal Dispute Solution" policy provided for binding arbitration).

113 Penn v. Ryan's Family Steak Houses, Inc., 269 F.3d 753 (7th Cir. 2001); *see also* Floss v. Ryan's Family Steak Houses, Inc., 211 F.3d 306 (6th Cir. 2000).

114 *See* Hubner v. Cutthroat Communications, Inc., 80 P.3d 1256, 1261, 1262 (Mont. 2003).

115 Harby v. Wachovia Bank, 172 Md. App. 415, 915 A.2d 462 (2007).

116 Thompson v. THI of N.M. at Casa Arena Blanca, 2006 WL 4061187 (D.N.M. Sept. 12, 2006).

117 *See* Harris v. Green Tree Fin. Corp, 183 F.3d 173 (3d Cir. 1999); Doctors' Associates v. Distajo, 66 F.3d 438 (2d Cir. 1995) (consideration sufficient when one-sided nature of the clause was clear and apparently bargained for); Wilson Elec. Contractors, Inc. v. Minnotte Contracting Corp., 878 F.2d 167 (6th Cir. 1989); Dorsey v. H.C.P. Sales, Inc., 46 F. Supp. 2d 804 (N.D. Ill. 1999); Goodwin v. Ford Motor Credit Co., 970 F. Supp. 1007 (M.D. Ala. 1997); Design Benefit Plans, Inc. v. Enright, 940 F. Supp. 200 (N.D. Ill. 1996); W.L. Jorden & Co. v. Blythe Indus., Inc., 702 F. Supp. 282 (N.D. Ga. 1988); *In re* Pate, 198 B.R. 841 (Bankr. S.D. Ga. 1996); *Ex parte* Smith, 736 So. 2d 604 (Ala. 1999); *Ex parte* Parker, 730 So. 2d 168 (Ala. 1999); Grubb & Ellis Co. v. Bello, 19 Cal. App. 4th 231, 23 Cal. Rptr. 2d 281 (1993); Sablosky v. Edward S. Gordon Co., 73 N.Y.2d 133, 538 N.Y.S.2d 513, 535 N.E.2d 643 (1989); Ishmael v. Dutch Hous. Inc., 1997 Ohio App. LEXIS 3974 (Ohio Ct. App. Aug. 13, 1997); Lackey v. Green Tree Fin. Corp., 330 S.C. 388, 498 S.E.2d 898 (Ct. App. 1998).

118 *See, e.g.*, Hudyka v. Sunoco, Inc., 474 F. Supp. 2d 712 (E.D. Pa. 2007) (refusing to compel arbitration when the "language describing the arbitration process is permissive and not imperative, suggesting that the employee has the option of resolving claims by arbitration or by resort to the courts"); Van Jackson v. Check 'N Go of Ill., Inc., 193 F.R.D. 544 (N.D. Ill. 2000) ("[A] mere mention of arbitration in a contract does not mean that the parties are ruled out of court. The arbitration clauses here do not provide for mandatory arbitration, but for arbitration at the election of 'you [plaintiff] or us [defendants].' ... An elective arbitration clause does not *require* the plaintiffs to submit to arbitration. They may choose their own forum. That is what 'elective' means."); Allstate Ins. v. Suarez, 833 So. 2d 762 (Fla. 2002) (per curiam) (appraisal clause in a home owners' policy was not clearly an arbitration agreement, and thus plaintiffs were not required to arbitrate their claims); Wells v. Chevy Chase Bank, 768 A.2d 620, 630 (Md. 2001) (cardholder cannot be compelled to arbitrate dispute when language of clause requires arbitration only "if necessary"); *cf.* W. Nat'l Mut. Ins. Co. v. Lennes (*In re* Workers' Compensation Refund), 46 F.3d 813, 819 (8th Cir. 1995); Triarch Indus., Inc. v. Crabtree, 158 S.W.3d 772 (Mo. 2005) (when contract gave corporation the right to choose either arbitration or litigation, corporation lost right to compel arbitration after commencing litigation). *But see* Adcock v. Adams Homes, 906 So. 2d 924 (Ala. 2005) (despite language stating that parties "may" request arbitration, holding that arbitration was mandatory—though not binding—when interpretation of arbitration as optional would be illogical and inconsistent with other provisions); Celtic Life Ins. Co. v. McLendon, 814 So. 2d 222 (Ala. 2001).

119 First Options of Chicago, Inc. v. Kaplan, 514 U.S. 938, 944, 115

A number of lower state and federal courts have adopted this "clear and unmistakable" requirement when determining whether the parties have agreed to arbitration.[120] The Third Circuit, for example, has stated that any agreement to arbitrate must be "express" and "unequivocal."[121] Texas courts likewise require that language expressing intent to arbitrate be "express, plain, clear, and certain."[122]

In *Badie v. Bank of America*, a California appeals court held that "absent a clear agreement to submit disputes to arbitration or some other form of ADR, we cannot infer that the right to a jury trial has been waived."[123] This conclusion was required by the fundamental nature of the right to a jury trial:

> In order to be enforceable, a contractual waiver of the right to a jury trial must be clearly apparent in the contract and its language must be unambiguous and unequivocal, leaving no room for doubt as to the intentions of the parties. . . . In light of the importance of the jury trial in our system of jurisprudence, any waiver thereof should appear in clear and unmistakable form. Where it is doubtful whether a party has waived his or her constitutionally-protected right to a jury trial, the question should be resolved in favor of preserving that right.[124]

In the same vein, the New York Court of Appeals has held:

> It is settled that a party will not be compelled to arbitrate and, thereby, to surrender the right to resort to the courts, absent "evidence which affirmatively establishes that the parties expressly agreed to arbitrate their disputes." . . . The agreement must be clear, explicit and unequivocal . . . and must not depend upon implication or subtlety. . . .[125]

An Ohio Court of Appeals has similarly held that an arbitration clause characterized by "pervasive ambiguity" cannot be enforced.[126]

The Ninth Circuit has also derived such a clarity requirement from the terms of certain civil rights statutes:

> Any bargain to waive the right to a judicial forum for civil rights claims, including those covered by the ADA, in exchange for employment or continued employment must at the least be express: the choice must be explicitly presented to the employee and the employee must explicitly agree to waive the specific right in question. That did not occur in the case before us.[127]

Furthermore, as with any contract, ambiguities in a purported agreement to arbitrate should be construed against the drafter.[128]

S. Ct. 1920, 131 L. Ed. 2d 985 (1995); *cf.* Wright v. Universal Maritime Serv. Corp., 525 U.S. 70, 80, 119 S. Ct. 391, 142 L. Ed. 2d 361 (1998) (holding in a collective bargaining case that "the right to a federal forum is of sufficient importance to be protected against less-than-explicit union waiver").

120 *See, e.g.*, McLaughlin Gormley King Co. v. Terminix Int'l Co., 105 F.3d 1192, 1194 (8th Cir. 1997) ("In this case, neither the arbitration clause nor any other provision in the 1984 contract between Terminix and MGK clearly and unmistakably evidenced the parties' intent to give the arbitrator power to determine arbitrability."); Hudyka v. Sunoco, Inc., 474 F. Supp. 2d 712, 716 (E.D. Pa. 2007) ("Agreements to arbitrate in Pennsylvania are upheld only where it is clear that the parties have agreed to arbitrate their disputes—employment and otherwise—in a clear an unmistakeable manner."); DiLucente Corp. v. Pa. Roofing Co., 440 Pa. Super. 450, 456–457, 655 A.2d 1035, 1038 (1995) ("When parties agree to arbitration in a clear and unmistakeable manner, the court will make every reasonable effort to favor such agreements.").

121 Par-Knit Mills, Inc. v. Stockbridge Fabrics Co., 636 F.2d 51, 54 (3d Cir. 1980); *see also* McCord v. Am. Gen. Life & Accident Ins. Co., 1999 U.S. Dist. LEXIS 4482, at *10 (E.D. Pa. Mar. 22, 1999) ("In the case *sub judice*, there is simply no express or unequivocal agreement between plaintiff and American General to arbitrate as required by our Court of Appeals in *Par-Knit*.").

122 Bates v. MTH Homes-Texas, Ltd. P'ship, 177 S.W.3d 419 (Tex. App. 2005) (construction defects disclosure notice making reference to arbitration does not constitute agreement to arbitrate).

123 67 Cal. App. 4th 779, 804, 79 Cal. Rptr. 2d 273, 290 (1998) (internal citations omitted).

124 *Id.*; *see also* Jubert v. Cent. Mich. Univ., 2003 WL 288984 (Mich. Ct. App. Feb. 7, 2003) (university's procedures "did not put plaintiff on notice that [by taking certain actions] she was conclusively waiving her right to litigate her discrimination claims in a judicial forum").

125 Waldron v. Goddess, 61 N.Y.2d 181, 473 N.Y.S.2d 136 (1984) (citations omitted); *see also* Marlene Indus. Corp. v. Carnac Textiles, Inc., 45 N.Y.2d 327, 408 N.Y.S.2d 410, 413 (1978) ("[P]arties to a commercial transaction will not be held to have chosen arbitration as the forum for the resolution of their disputes in the absence of an express, unequivocal agreement to that effect; absent such an explicit commitment neither party may be compelled to arbitrate."); Grovesteen v. N.Y. State Pub. Employees Fed'n, 265 A.D.2d 784, 697 N.Y.S.2d 392 (1999).

A New Jersey court recently followed suit, in Grasser v. United Healthcare Corp., 778 A.2d 521 (N.J. Super. Ct. App. Div. 2001) ("[A]ny such waiver and agreement to arbitrate claims under New Jersey's statutory Law Against Discrimination must be explicit and must refer specifically to arbitration of termination disputes and claims of LAD violations. Our courts will not indulge an assumption that an employee would probably know, or should know, that vague or non-specific language is intended to include termination disputes and/or LAD violations.").

126 Jones v. Fred Martin Motor Co., 2002 Ohio App. LEXIS 516 (Ohio Ct. App. Feb. 13, 2002).

127 Nelson v. Cyprus Bagdad Copper Corp., 119 F.3d 756, 762 (9th Cir. 1997).

128 *E.g.*, Luke v. Gentry Realty, Ltd., 96 P.3d 291 (Haw. 2004) (refusing to stay proceedings pending arbitration when scope of arbitration provision was unclear); Bucks Orthopaedic Surgery Associates v. Ruth, 2007 WL 1544649 (Pa. Super. Ct. May 30, 2007) (when contract called for "binding" arbitration but also permitted the exercise of "judicial remedies," this ambiguity would be read not to require binding arbitration; vacating decision confirming arbitration award); *cf.* Cavalier Mfg., Inc. v. Clarke, 862 So. 2d 634 (Ala. 2003) (when two conflicting arbitration clauses were executed contemporaneously, compel-

Similarly, language in a contract *referring* to an arbitration agreement cannot take the place of an arbitration agreement itself. Thus, a California appellate court recently held that, when a real estate contract contains language advising buyers of the rights they are giving up by agreeing to a separate arbitration provision—but the contract contains no separate arbitration provision—the parties cannot be compelled to arbitrate their claims.[129]

Likewise, even if an arbitration clause unambiguously and unequivocally requires binding arbitration, the terms and procedures under which arbitration must proceed are still unclear if the consumer is required to sign multiple arbitration clauses with conflicting terms. A New Jersey court refused to order arbitration when the parties had executed two contracts containing "conflicting descriptions of the manner and procedure which would govern the arbitration proceedings."[130] However the mere absence of specific rules or procedures for arbitration may not be sufficient to invalidate the clause for vagueness.[131]

A few courts have rejected the concept that a waiver of the right to a jury trial in an arbitration clause must be clear and unmistakable.[132]

5.5 Waiver of Right to Jury Trial Must Be Knowing and Voluntary

5.5.1 Introduction to the Doctrine

As explained above, many courts have held that, because an arbitration clause waives constitutional rights, it must be clear and unambiguous in order to be enforceable. Related to this requirement is a generally applicable state law doctrine that provides that a party does not waive a constitutional right unless that waiver is made knowingly and voluntarily.[133] The existence of this doctrine of general application is very well established.[134] Nevertheless, there are a number of cases in which courts have held that parties

---

ling arbitration under terms of clause more favorable to the consumer); Holland v. Trav Corp., 2007 WL 778874, at *8 (Cal. Ct. App. Mar. 16, 2007) (refusing to compel employee who had renewed employment based on arbitration clause in contract that required arbitration for "new employees").

129 Villacreses v. Molinari, 132 Cal. App. 4th 1223 (2005).

130 Rockel v. Cherry Hill Dodge, 847 A.2d 621, 623 (N.J. Super. Ct. App. Div. 2004). *But cf.* Harbor Vill. Home Ctr., Inc. v. Thomas, 882 So. 2d 811 (Ala. 2003) (when three conflicting arbitration clauses were executed, compelling arbitration under terms of clause most favorable to corporation); Cavalier Mfg., Inc. v. Clarke, 862 So. 2d 634 (Ala. 2003) (when two conflicting arbitration clauses were executed contemporaneously, compelling arbitration under terms of clause more favorable to the consumer).

131 *See* Villar v. Mut. Prot. Trust, 2007 WL 1519788, at *6 (Cal. Ct. App. May 25, 2007) ("That the parties' agreement to arbitrate does not refer to or incorporate specific arbitral rules does not preclude its enforcement."); Leslie v. U.S. Home Corp., 2002 WL 244817, at *2 (Cal. Ct. App. Feb. 21, 2002) (compelling arbitration despite acknowledgment that arbitration provisions were "not entirely clear as to what specific procedures should govern the arbitration," when "general intention to submit to arbitration is clearly demonstrated").

132 *E.g.,* Snowden v. Checkpoint Check Cashing, 290 F.3d 631 (4th Cir. 2002); Bank One v. Harris, 2001 U.S. Dist. LEXIS 9615 (S.D. Miss. Jan. 2, 2001), *aff'd,* 2002 U.S. App. LEXIS 7756 (5th Cir. 2002) (table).

133 *See* Samukai v. Emily Fisher Charter Sch. of Advanced Studies, 2007 WL 316449 (D.N.J. Jan. 30, 2007) (arbitration clause not a knowing and voluntary waiver of judicial remedies unless it is clear and unambiguous).

134 *E.g.,* Fuentes v. Shevin, 407 U.S. 67, 95, 92 S. Ct. 1983, 32 L. Ed. 2d 556 (1972) ("a waiver of constitutional rights in any context must, at the very least, be clear"); Finch v. Vaughn, 67 F.3d 909 (11th Cir. 1995) ("[w]aivers of constitutional rights not only must be voluntary but must be knowing, intelligent acts done with sufficient awareness of relevant circumstances and likely consequences"); Erie Telecommunications, Inc. v. City of Erie, 853 F.2d 1084, 1096 (3d Cir. 1988) ("constitutional rights, like rights and privileges of lesser importance, may be contractually waived where the facts and circumstances surrounding the waiver make it clear that the party foregoing its rights has done so of its own volition, with full understanding of the consequences of its waiver"); K.M.C. Co. v. Irving Trust Co., 757 F.2d 752, 756 (6th Cir. 1985) ("Those cases in which the validity of a contractual waiver of jury has been in issue have overwhelmingly applied the knowing and voluntary standard"); First Union Nat'l Bank v. United States, 164 F. Supp. 2d 660 (E.D. Pa. 2001) ("[C]ourts do not uphold jury trial waivers lightly and the burden of proving that a waiver was done both knowingly and intelligently falls upon the party seeking enforcement of a waiver of a jury trial clause."); In re Hannie, 3 Cal. 3d 520, 526, 90 Cal. Rptr. 742, 476 P.2d 110 (1970) ("[w]aivers of constitutional and statutory rights must be voluntary . . . and knowing, intelligent acts done with sufficient awareness of the relevant circumstances and likely consequences" (citations omitted)); In re Laura H., 8 Cal. App. 4th 1689, 1695, 11 Cal. Rptr. 2d 285, 288 (1992) ("a waiver [of a constitutional right] must be knowing and intelligent"); Bess v. DirecTV, Inc., 815 N.E.2d 455, 461 (Ill. App. Ct. 2004) (remanding case when trial court decided unconscionability issue but failed to address consumer's alternative argument that she had not voluntarily and knowingly waived her right to a trial by jury); In re Gilliland, 103 S.E.2d 807, 811 (N.C. 1958) ("It is a general rule, since the right of trial by jury is highly favored, that waivers of the right are always strictly construed and are not to be lightly inferred or extended by implication, whether with respect to a civil or criminal case. There can be no presumption of a waiver of trial by jury where such a trial is provided for by law. Thus, in the absence of an express agreement or consent, a waiver of the right to a jury trial will not be presumed or inferred. Indeed, every reasonable presumption should be made against its waiver.").

attempting to enforce arbitration agreements have no duty to explain or specifically disclose the existence of an arbitration clause, even when it is fairly clear that the party waiving its right did not understand the effect of the agreement.[135]

Section 5.5.2, *infra*, explains that the state law doctrine of voluntary, knowing, and intelligent waiver should not be preempted by the Federal Arbitration Act (FAA). Section 5.5.3, *infra*, discusses a number of cases which apply this doctrine to arbitration clauses and find the clauses therefore ineffective. While most of the case law applying the voluntary, knowing, and intelligent requirement to arbitration clauses does not arise in the consumer law context, the principles should be equally applicable. Section 5.5.4, *infra*, discusses cases involving knowing and voluntary waivers of the right to a judicial forum when that forum is guaranteed by the particular statute under which the plaintiff is bringing the claim. And finally, § 5.5.5, *infra*, discusses cases rejecting the imposition of a knowing, voluntary, and intelligent standard in arbitration cases.

5.5.2 The Doctrine and FAA Preemption

The FAA does not permit states to single out arbitration clauses for treatment that is more restrictive than the treatment accorded to other types of contractual provisions.[136]

Thus, for example, courts have regularly rejected arguments that arbitration clauses must be in larger type than other contract provisions.

Parties attempting to enforce arbitration agreements often argue that waivers of the right to trial by jury may be *un*knowing and *in*voluntary, because the FAA preempts state law that might apply the knowing and voluntary waiver standard to arbitration clauses.[137] But the FAA only preempts state laws that single out arbitration clauses for discriminatory treatment; it does not preempt generally applicable state law contract doctrines.[138] The doctrine that waivers of constitutional rights must be knowing and voluntary is not aimed specifically against arbitration clauses, but is merely a generally applicable rule of law that treats arbitration clauses the same as it treats other such contractual provisions. Therefore, it should not be preempted under the FAA.

Nonetheless, some courts have held that a state law requirement of a knowing and voluntary waiver of the right to a jury trial is preempted by the FAA when applied to arbitration clauses. In *Merrill Lynch, Pierce, Fenner & Smith, Inc. v. Coe*, for example, the district court found that this heightened consent standard would be preempted, even though it did not apply exclusively to arbitration clauses, because it "necessarily imposes heightened requirements on 'agreements to go to arbitration.'"[139] Although *Coe*'s finding of preemption was not compelled by United States Supreme Court case law, advocates making arguments based on the knowing and voluntary waiver standard need to be aware of its implications.

---

135 *E.g.*, Adams v. Merrill Lynch, Pierce, Fenner & Smith, Inc., 888 F.2d 696, 701 (10th Cir. 1989) (defendant had no duty to specifically disclose that there was an arbitration provision included within the customer agreement); Pierson v. Dean, Witter, Reynolds, Inc., 742 F.2d 334, 339 (7th Cir. 1984) (no duty to explain terms); Greene v. Chase Manhattan Auto. Fin. Corp., 2003 WL 22872102 (E.D. La. Dec. 3, 2003) (obvious placement of arbitration clause weighed in favor of assent); Brown v. Dorsey & Whitney, LLP, 267 F. Supp. 2d 61, 82 (D.D.C. 2003) (defendant has no duty to ensure that plaintiff understands meaning of the phrase "dispute resolution policy"); Rogers v. Brown, 986 F. Supp. 354 (M.D. La. 1996) (defendant has no duty to explain arbitration provision); McCarthy v. Providential Corp., 1994 U.S. Dist. LEXIS 10122, at *15–*16 (N.D. Cal. July 18, 1994) (no duty to explain arbitration clause to senior citizens); Meyers v. Univest Home Loan, Inc., 1993 U.S. Dist. LEXIS 11333 (N.D. Cal. Aug. 4, 1993); Federowicz v. Snap-on Tools Corp., 1992 U.S. Dist. LEXIS, at *8–*9 (E.D. Pa. Mar. 10, 1992) (no special duty to explain the arbitration provision); Bender v. Smith Barney, Harris Upham & Co., 789 F. Supp. 155, 159 (D.N.J. 1992); Brener v. Becker Paribas, Inc., 628 F. Supp. 442, 445, 446 (S.D.N.Y. 1985) ("it is conclusively presumed that an individual who signs a contract knows its contents and assents to them"); *In re* Brown, 311 B.R. 702 (Bankr. E.D. Pa. 2004) (defendants had no duty to explain arbitration clause to elderly, sick plaintiffs); First Family Fin. Services v. Rogers, 736 So. 2d 553 (Ala. 1999) ("when a competent adult, having the ability to read and understand an instrument, signs a contract, he will be held to be on notice of all the provisions contained in that contract, including an arbitration provision, and will be bound thereby"); Patrick Home Ctr., Inc. v. Karr, 730 So. 2d 1171 (Ala. 1999) (no legal duty to point out or explain the arbitration provision).

136 *See* § 3.2, *supra*.

137 For an argument that holding arbitration clauses to a lower standard than jury waiver clauses is permitted by the Constitution, see Andrew M. Kepper, *Contractual Waiver of Seventh Amendment Rights: Using the Public Rights Doctrine to Justify a Higher Standard of Waiver for Jury-Waiver Clauses than for Arbitration Clauses*, 91 Iowa L. Rev. 1345 (2006).

138 *See* § 3.2, *supra*.

139 313 F. Supp. 2d 603, 615 (S.D. W. Va. 2004); *see also* Battels v. Sears Nat'l Bank, 365 F. Supp. 2d 1205 (M.D. Ala. 2005) (to hold that bill stuffer gave insufficient notice that arbitration provision was being added to cardholder agreement would contravene FAA's prohibition against singling out arbitration clauses for suspect status); Dabney v. Option One Mortgage Corp., 2001 U.S. Dist. LEXIS 4949 (E.D. Pa. Apr. 19, 2001) ("An inquiry into whether a party entered an agreement knowingly and voluntarily is inconsistent with the FAA and federal law."); *cf.* Choice v. Option One Mortgage Corp., 2003 WL 22097455, at *8–*10 (E.D. Pa. May 13, 2003) (asserting that, unlike generally applicable defenses such as fraud and duress, "invalid waiver is not a recognized legal ground for the revocation of contracts, and thus, is not sufficient to avoid enforcement of an arbitration agreement" and distinguishing precedent requiring voluntary, knowing, and intelligent waiver of constitutional rights on ground arbitration does not require parties to waive constitutional rights but rather "merely provides an alternative forum").

See also the discussion of preemption in § 3.2.1.2, *supra*.

5.5.3 Examples of Application of the Doctrine

In *Kloss v. Edward D. Jones & Co.*, the Montana Supreme Court reaffirmed the essential right to a jury trial and the need for a meaningful waiver of that right.[140] The plaintiff in the case, Alice Kloss, a ninety-five-year-old widow, sought damages caused by her stockbroker's wrongful conduct. In response, the brokerage firm filed a motion to compel arbitration based on a provision in the contract that Kloss had signed when establishing a living trust account with the broker's firm. In a concurrence signed by five judges, Justice Nelson relied on the Montana Constitution and argued that mandatory consumer arbitration agreements, such as those typically used by stockbrokers, unconstitutionally foreclose consumers' rights of access to courts and to a jury trial. Thus these agreements must be "rigorously examined" by the courts to ensure that the parties really understand the significance of the waiver of jury trial.[141] In this case, Justice Nelson found, Kloss had not knowingly and intelligently waived her right, and the clause was therefore unenforceable.[142]

In *Broemmer v. Abortion Services of Phoenix*, a twenty-one-year-old pregnant woman earning less than $100 a week was, at a time of "considerable confusion and emotional and physical turmoil for her," given a stack of three forms to complete.[143] The court also noted that "[t]he clinic did not explain the purpose of the form to plaintiff and did not show whether plaintiff was required to sign the form or forfeit treatment."[144] Under these circumstances, the Arizona Supreme Court concluded that "there was no conspicuous or explicit waiver of the fundamental right to a jury trial or any evidence that such rights were knowingly, voluntarily and intelligently waived."[145]

The Nevada Supreme Court reached the same result using a similar analysis in *Obstetrics & Gynecologists Wixted, Flanagan & Robinson v. Pepper*.[146] In that case, as in *Broemmer*, the medical malpractice plaintiff "did not remember receiving any information regarding the terms of the arbitration agreement," and it appeared that "the agreement was never explained to respondent."[147] Accordingly, the court held that the patient had not given "informed consent to the agreement and . . . no meeting of the minds occurred."[148] Although the *Pepper* court did not use the knowing, voluntary, and intelligent rubric, its use of the phrase "informed consent" appears to embody the same sort of requirement.

A third medical malpractice case to follow this line of reasoning is *Sanchez v. Sirmons*.[149] In *Sanchez*, a New York court noted that the patient viewing the consent form at issue "could easily be misled" into believing that she was consenting only to a surgical procedure, and not to an arbitration clause.[150] The court also noted that the arbitration clause was not pointed out or explained to the patient, and that the patient was naturally preoccupied with her impending surgery. Accordingly, the court refused "to compel arbitration in the case at bar because it has not been demonstrated that the petitioner made an informed and knowledgeable waiver of her constitutional right to trial by jury."[151]

The Alabama Supreme Court, similarly, has stated:

> [A]ny arbitration agreement is a waiver of a party's right under Amendment VII of the United States Constitution to a trial by jury and, regardless of the federal courts' policy favoring arbitration, we find nothing in the FAA that would permit such a waiver unless it is made knowingly, willingly, and voluntarily.[152]

The Alabama Supreme Court's application of this constitutional waiver standard, however, does not necessarily make it much easier for consumers to resist enforcement of arbitration clauses. In a subsequent case, the court held that the knowing, voluntary, and intelligent waiver standard was satisfied when "a competent adult, having the ability to read and understand an instrument, signs a contract" and therefore he "will be held to be on notice of all the provisions contained in that contract and will be bound thereby."[153]

Some courts have gone even further, holding that individuals are held to what they sign even when they lack the ability to read or understand the agreement. In *Estate of Etting v. Regents Park at Aventura, Inc.*, a Florida court enforced a nursing home's arbitration clause against a

---

140 310 Mont. 123, 54 P.3d 1 (2002).
141 *Id.*, 310 Mont. at 140.
142 *Id.*, 310 Mont. at 144. The majority opinion rests its decision to invalidate the clause on unconscionability rather than unconstitutionality grounds.
  See also Galle v. MBNA Am. Bank, 2006 WL 839531 (S.D. Miss. Mar. 28, 2006) (denying MBNA's motion to compel arbitration when the account was transferred to MBNA from another creditor and the cardholder denied having received an arbitration amendment or any other materials from MBNA after the transfer, and finding "no evidence that Galle voluntarily and knowingly waived his right to access to the courts"); Union Planters Bank v. Rogers, 912 So. 2d 116, 119 (Miss. 2005).
143 Broemmer v. Abortion Services, 173 Ariz. 148, 149, 840 P.2d 1013, 1014 (Ariz. 1992).
144 *Id.*, 840 P.2d at 1017.
145 *Id.*
146 101 Nev. 105, 693 P.2d 1259, 1261 (1985); *see also* Lucas v. Cash 'N Advance, Inc., 312 B.R. 407 (Bankr. D. Nev. 2004).
147 Obstetrics & Gynecologists Wixted, Flanagan & Robinson v. Pepper, 101 Nev. 105, 693 P.2d 1259, 1261 (1985).
148 *Id.*
149 121 Misc. 2d 249, 467 N.Y.S.2d 757 (Sup. Ct. 1983).
150 121 Misc. 2d at 253–254.
151 121 Misc. 2d at 252.
152 Allstar Homes, Inc. v. Waters, 711 So. 2d 924, 929 (Ala. 1998).
153 Jim Walter Homes, Inc. v. Saxton, 880 So. 2d 428 (Ala. 2003); *see also* Kisner v. Bud's Mobile Homes, 2007 WL 686734 (S.D. Miss. Mar. 3, 2007).

woman who had been legally blind when she signed it.[154] The court held that, because the woman had not been prevented from reading the contract by the nursing home, it was binding on her.[155]

A case requiring a stricter waiver standard is *In re Turner Brothers Trucking Co.*[156] In this personal injury case, the functionally illiterate plaintiff was presented an arbitration clause by a company representative "who did not understand the agreement," "in an environment where there was no opportunity to read and understand, even if [the plaintiff] was literate."[157] Although the case was decided upon grounds of procedural unconscionability rather than contract formation, the court refused to enforce the clause because the "evidence fully supports the trial court's conclusion that [the plaintiff] did not knowingly consent to the contract to compel arbitration of his personal injury claim."[158]

The Sixth Circuit has adopted a slightly different standard, taking into account not only whether the arbitration clause contained an explicit waiver but also the educational level of the employee and whether the circumstances under which the contract was presented made it unlikely the employee would realize he was relinquishing important rights.[159]

While cases addressing the question of whether the agreement was voluntary (as opposed to knowing) appear to be more unusual, at least one court has invalidated an arbitration agreement on the grounds that, because the employee was "recovering from a back injury and taking medication . . . [and] believed that he had no meaningful choice to signing the Agreement," the employee "cannot be said to have voluntarily agreed to arbitration."[160]

5.5.4 Application of the Doctrine to Waiver of Statutory Rights

The cases discussed to this point in this section either explicitly or apparently required the showing of a knowing and voluntary waiver because arbitration entails the loss of the constitutional right to a jury trial. Some other courts have found that a knowing and voluntary waiver is required when an arbitration clause would require an individual to arbitrate a claim arising under a statute that provides a judicial remedy.

In *Kummetz v. Tech Mold, Inc.*, for example, the Ninth Circuit held that there was "no knowing waiver" of an employee's right to a judicial forum for statutory claims when the "Acknowledgment" document the employee signed contained "no *explicit* reference to arbitration or waiver of right to sue."[161] The Court went on to state that "[o]nly if Tech Mold had specifically called Kummetz's attention to the arbitration clause in the Booklet would the clause suffice in the face of the uninformative Acknowledgment."[162] Some other courts have followed the Ninth Circuit's adoption of this standard.[163]

In *Prudential Insurance Co. v. Lai*, likewise, the Ninth Circuit held that "Congress intended there to be at least a knowing agreement to arbitrate employment disputes before an employee may be deemed to have waived the comprehensive statutory rights, remedies and procedural protections prescribed in Title VII and related state statutes."[164] The Ninth Circuit's adoption of a voluntary, knowing standard for civil rights claims has been rejected by some other courts, however, and the law appears to differ from one jurisdiction to the next.[165] New Jersey courts have adopted

---

154 *See, e.g.*, Estate of Etting v. Regents Park at Aventura, Inc., 891 So. 2d 558, 558 (Fla. Dist. Ct. App. 2004).

155 *Id.* at 558; *see also* McKenzie Check Advance of Miss., L.L.C. v. Hardy, 866 So. 2d 446, 455 (Miss. 2004) (finding knowing, voluntary, and intelligent waiver when consumers were literate, had an opportunity to read the contract, and the arbitration clause was printed in large, bold face, and capitalized letters); *In re* Jobe Concrete Products, Inc., 2003 WL 21757512 (Tex. App. July 31, 2003) (agreement to arbitrate not valid despite employee's signature, when employee could not read English and employer retained unilateral right to modify terms of plan containing arbitration clause).

156 8 S.W.3d 370 (Tex. App. 1999).

157 *Id.* at 376. *But see* Bill Heard Chevrolet Corp. v. Wilson, 877 So. 2d 15 (Fla. Dist. Ct. App. 2004) (consumers bound by arbitration clause they signed despite trial court's finding of "mutual mistake" based on evidence that consumers had relied on "imperfect understanding of arbitration" by representative of car dealership).

158 8 S.W.3d 370 (Tex. App. 1999).

159 Walker v. Ryan's Family Steak Houses, Inc., 400 F.3d 370 (6th Cir. 2005).

160 Garza Nunez v. Weeks Marine, Inc., 2007 WL 2008105, at *7 (E.D. La. July 5, 2007).

161 152 F.3d 1153, 1155 (9th Cir. 1988); *see also* Douglass v. Pflueger Haw., Inc., 135 P.3d 129, 141 (Haw. 2006) (applying *Kummetz* to hold that employee had not assented to arbitration merely by signing acknowledgment of employee handbook containing arbitration clause, when the handbook itself did "not constitute an employment contract").

162 *Kummetz*, 152 F.3d at 1156.

163 *E.g.*, Cooper v. MRM Inv. Co., 199 F. Supp. 2d 771, 775 (M.D. Tenn. 2002) (holding in Title VII context that "although mandatory arbitration is presumed valid, the waiver of any rights (substantive or procedural) must be both knowing and clear"); Penn v. Ryan's Family Steakhouses, Inc., 95 F. Supp. 2d 940, 955 (N.D. Ind. 2000) ("In this setting, where an individual waives his right to a judicial forum in a pre-dispute arbitration agreement such as the Agreement entered into between EDS and Mr. Penn, this court agrees with the Ninth Circuit's heightened standard of ensuring that a waiver of that judicial forum be at the very least knowing, and/or voluntary."), *aff'd on other grounds*, 269 F.3d 753 (7th Cir. 2001).

164 42 F.3d 1299, 1304 (9th Cir. 1994); *see also* Renteria v. Prudential Ins. Co., 113 F.3d 1104 (9th Cir. 1997).

165 *Compare* Rosenberg v. Merrill Lynch, Pierce, Fenner & Smith, Inc., 170 F.3d 1 (1st Cir. 1999) (not adopting the Ninth Circuit's knowing and voluntary standard, but nonetheless holding that it was "inappropriate to enforce" an arbitration clause with which the employee was not "familiar" in light of the New York Stock

a similar approach for state statutory claims.[166]

5.5.5 Cases Rejecting the Doctrine

Other courts have rejected the concept of applying the knowing and voluntary waiver standard to arbitration clauses.[167] For example, the Fourth Circuit has held that:

Nor does the fact that the appellees waived their right to a jury trial require the court to evaluate the agreement to arbitrate under a more demanding standard. It is clear that a party may waive her right to adjudicate disputes in a judicial forum. Similarly, the right to a jury trial attaches in the context of judicial proceedings after it is determined that litigation should proceed before a court. Thus, the "loss of right to a jury trial is a necessary and fairly obvious consequence of an agreement to arbitrate." *Pierson v. Dean Witter, Reynolds, Inc.*, 742 F.2d 334, 339 (7th Cir. 1984). We therefore conclude that the district court erred in finding that the appellees did not knowingly and voluntarily waive their right to a jury trial.[168]

5.6 Arbitration Clauses Sent Unilaterally After Agreement Reached

5.6.1 Introduction

In quite a few cases, the fine print that contains an arbitration clause is not communicated to the consumer until after the consumer is irrevocably bound to the agreement. For example, the consumer might sign an agreement to purchase a vehicle. When the car arrives a week later, there is a written warranty in the glove compartment that includes an arbitration agreement, which the consumer may not notice until much later. This scenario is discussed in § 5.6.2, *infra*.

In other cases, the product is delivered to the consumer, contingent on the consumer accepting the terms sent with the product, one of which is the arbitration agreement. For example, the consumer may place a telephone order for a product. When the product arrives it bears a conspicuous notice outside the box indicating that the purchase is subject to terms included in the box, and that the consumer should return the item if the terms are not acceptable. This scenario is discussed in § 5.6.3, *infra*.

In addition § 5.7, *infra*, considers a third possibility, in which the consumer has an ongoing relationship with the company (such as with a credit card issuer or a telephone service provider), and the original agreement allows the

---

Exchange Rules and other matters) *with* Haskins v. Prudential Ins. Co., 230 F.3d 231, 239 (6th Cir. 2000) (holding that "absent a showing of fraud, duress, mistake, or some other ground upon which a contract may be voided, a court must enforce a contractual agreement to arbitrate," and finding that this rule "is superior to the standards set forth in *Rosenberg* and *Lai* because it does not plainly ignore long-standing rules of contract law").

166 *See* Samukai v. Emily Fisher Charter Sch. of Advanced Studies, 2007 WL 316449 (D.N.J. Jan. 30, 2007) (arbitration clause that "makes no mention of statutory claims" nor "reflect[s] a general understanding of the types of claims being waived" invalid because not a clear and unambiguous waiver of statutory rights, and thus not knowing and voluntary); Garfunkel v. Morristown Obstetrics & Gynecology Associates, 773 A.2d 665, 667 (N.J. 2001) (arbitration clause providing that "any controversy arising out of, or relating to, this Agreement or the breach thereof, shall be settled by arbitration" too ambiguous to constitute waiver of statutory rights under state discrimination laws); Grasser v. United Healthcare Corp., 778 A.2d 521 (N.J. Super. Ct. App. Div. 2001) (refusing to enforce an arbitration clause when the defendant did not meet its burden of demonstrating a knowing and binding waiver by the plaintiff of his right to maintain suit); Quigley v. KPMG Peat Marwick, L.L.P., 330 N.J. Super. 252, 269, 270, 749 A.2d 405, 415 (Super. Ct. App. Div. 2000) (when employee signed arbitration clause before a right to jury trial was provided for the particular type of statutory claim at issue, the "plaintiff did not knowingly and voluntarily waive his right to a trial by jury on his statutory remedies" as that right arose subsequently).

167 *See, e.g.,* Caley v. Gulfstream Aerospace Corp., 428 F.3d 1359, 1372 (11th Cir. 2006) ("general contract principles govern the enforceability of arbitration agreements, [and] no heightened 'knowing and voluntary' standard applies, even when the covered claims include federal statutory claims generally involving a jury trial right"); Deluca v. Bear Stearns & Co., 175 F. Supp. 2d 102 (D. Mass. 2001) (rejecting an individual's claim that she was not bound by an arbitration agreement; "In the absence of fraud, a person who signs a written agreement is bound by its terms whether she reads and understands them or not."); Lloyd v. MBNA Am. Bank, 2001 WL 194300 (D. Del. Feb. 22, 2001) ("Plaintiff argues that he did not knowingly and intentionally waive his right to a jury trial because notification of the Arbitration Section was buried among other 'junk mail' documents. However, the inconspicuousness of an arbitration clause does not provide a basis to invalidate an agreement to arbitrate."), *aff'd,* 27 Fed. Appx. 82 (3d Cir. 2002); Melena v. Anheuser-Busch, Inc., 847 N.E.2d 99 (Ill. 2006) ("knowing and voluntary" standard not necessary because loss of the constitutional right to a jury trial is an obvious consequence of agreeing to arbitration); Holloman v. Circuit City Stores, Inc., 894 A.2d 547, 595–596 (Md. 2006) (rejecting employee's argument that she had not knowingly and voluntarily waived her constitutional right to a jury trial, on grounds that the employee had signed a clause that clearly foreclosed her access to the courts); Gras v. Associates First Capital Corp., 786 A.2d 886 (N.J. Super. Ct. App. Div. 2001) (noting that plaintiffs claimed that agreements were unenforceable because they did not knowingly waive their rights, then concluding: "[W]e reject any claim that plaintiffs did not know what they were signing. The documents in question were presented to them, albeit, in a stack of documents; however, that standing alone provides no basis for refusing enforcement."); *cf.* Neatherlin Homes, Inc. v. Love, 2007 WL 700996 (Tex. App. Mar. 8, 2007) (enforcing arbitration clause signed by consumer despite her argument that "they hid from me the fact that I was agreeing to arbitration and giving up my right to a jury trial").

168 Sydnor v. Conseco Fin. Servicing Corp., 252 F.3d 302, 307 (4th Cir. 2001).

§ 5.6.2   *Consumer Arbitration Agreements*

company to change the terms of the agreement, with the consumer's continued use of the company's services taken to signify the consumer's assent to any changes in terms.

5.6.2 Arbitration Clause Unilaterally Added After Agreement Is Consummated

When there is a final agreement between the parties and the company sends the consumer the arbitration clause after that agreement has been made, the legal result should be clear. An arbitration clause should not be enforceable when it is unilaterally presented to the consumer after the agreement has been reached. An arbitration clause is a material term that cannot be unilaterally added by one party after both parties have agreed upon terms for a binding contract unless the original contract so specifies.[169]

Thus, in a case involving a life insurance policy, a federal court held that a consumer was not bound by an arbitration clause that was sent to the plaintiff after she had signed the application, when the application did not mention the arbitration clause.[170] The court emphasized that: "There was no notice, no discussion, and no negotiation of the arbitration endorsement, circumstances, which in this court's view, hardly signify either agreement or waiver. The arbitration endorsement is therefore not enforceable, and this matter may proceed in this court."[171]

Likewise, an arbitration clause found only in a written warranty sent to a mobile home purchaser after the sale had been completed should not be enough to require the consumer to arbitrate claims not based on the written warranty.[172] It is not part of the terms of the parties' agreement, because the consumer did not receive the warranty before completing the transaction, and thus did not signify assent to the warranty terms.

In *Supak & Sons Manufacturing Co. v. Pervel Industries, Inc.*,[173] the parties reached an oral agreement by telephone. During the conversation, no mention was made of any arbitration agreement. The seller subsequently sent a "confirmation form" that included an arbitration clause. Applying section 2-207 of the Uniform Commercial Code (UCC), the Fourth Circuit held that "[w]hen a written confirmation form contains terms in addition to those reached in the oral sales contract between merchants and the party receiving the form does not make timely objection, then the additional terms become part of the contract unless they 'materially alter' it."[174] The court concluded that the arbitration clause was a material term. "Moreover, courts of last resort of both states [New York and North Carolina] have held that the addition of an arbitration clause constitutes a per se material alteration of the contract. . . . Thus, under the law of either state, the arbitration clause did not become part of the contract."[175]

The Fifth Circuit reached the same conclusion on similar facts in *Coastal Industries, Inc. v. Automatic Steam Products Corp.*[176] "By requiring evidence of an express agreement before permitting the inclusion of an arbitration provision into the contract, a court protects the litigant who will be unwillingly deprived of a judicial forum in which to air his grievance or defense."[177] Many other courts have come to this conclusion,[178] as have a number of scholarly

---

169   See § 5.7, *infra*, for a discussion of arbitration clauses added pursuant to change-in-terms provisions.
170   McCreary v. Liberty Nat'l Life, 6 F. Supp. 2d 920 (N.D. Miss. 1998).
171   *Id.* at 920.
172   *See, e.g.*, S. Energy Homes, Inc. v. Hennis, 776 So. 2d 105 (Ala. 2000); S. Energy Homes, Inc. v. Kennedy, 774 So. 2d 540 (Ala. 2000); Homes of Legend, Inc. v. Spraldin, 2003 WL 23096489 (Ky. Ct. App. Dec. 31, 2003) (refusing to enforce arbitration clause contained in limited warranty delivered with mobile home after purchase agreement was executed when buyer had never received any benefits from warranty); St. Romain v. Cappaert Manufactured Hous., Inc., 903 So. 2d 1186 (La. Ct. App. 2005) (refusing to enforce arbitration clause in an unsigned owner registration card placed inside a drawer in the mobile home, when the card conditioned activation of a limited warranty on consent to arbitration and the buyer had never activated the warranty); Masteller v. Champion Mobile Home Builders, Inc., 723 N.W.2d 561 (S.D. 2006).

173   593 F.2d 135 (4th Cir. 1979).
174   593 F.2d at 136; *see also* Rogers v. Dell Computer Corp., 127 P.3d 560 (Okla. 2005) (record insufficient for determination of whether, under U.C.C., arbitration clause in "terms and conditions" document included with already purchased computer is a new proposed term upon which assent was not conditioned).
175   Supak & Sons Mfg. Co. v. Pervel Indus., Inc., 593 F.2d 135, 136 (4th Cir. 1979) (citations omitted).
176   Coastal Indus., Inc. v. Automatic Steam Products Corp., 654 F.2d 375 (5th Cir. 1981).
177   *Id.* at 379.
178   *See* Diskin v. J.P. Stevens & Co., 836 F.2d 47 (1st Cir. 1987) (similar facts and same holding as in *Supak & Sons*); N & D Fashions, Inc. v. DHJ Indus., Inc., 548 F.2d 722, 727 (8th Cir. 1976) ("[W]e cannot say on this record that the District Court was clearly erroneous in holding that the arbitration provision in DHJ's acknowledgement form was a 'material alteration.' "); J & C Dyeing, Inc. v. Drakon, Inc., 1994 U.S. Dist. LEXIS 15194, at *6, *8 (S.D.N.Y. Oct. 20, 1994) ("[I]t is clear that an arbitration clause is a material addition which can become part of a contract only if it is expressly assented to by both parties."; "Although Drakon did not object to the arbitration clause, the mere retention of confirmation slips without any additional conduct indicative of a desire to arbitrate cannot bind Drakon, for it does not rise to the level of assent required to bind parties to arbitration provisions." (citation omitted)); DeMarco Cal. Fabrics, Inc. v. Nygard Int'l, Ltd., 1990 U.S. Dist. LEXIS 3842, at *7 (S.D.N.Y. Apr. 9, 1990) ("provision for arbitration is 'clearly a proposed additional term' to the parties' agreement which 'materially alters' the agreement"); Universal Plumbing & Piping Supply, Inc. v. John C. Grimberg Co., 596 F. Supp. 1383, 1385 (W.D. Pa. 1984) (similar facts and same holding as in *Supak & Sons*) ("Other courts have held that an arbitration

commentators.[179]

In addition, a number of courts deciding unrelated issues have held that arbitration clauses are material terms to a contract.[180] Only the Second Circuit and the Alabama Supreme Court have diverged from this consensus, holding that arbitration clauses are not material terms and permitting their unilateral addition to already formed contracts, in at least certain special circumstances.[181]

5.6.3 Final Agreement Not Reached Until After Purchase Is Delivered

Courts may reach a different conclusion when a product is delivered to the consumer and there is notice that the purchase is not final unless the consumer accepts the terms of the purchase included inside the product's box.[182] The seller may characterize the transaction as not consummated until the buyer reviews the product and the terms of the sale,

---

clause is a material alteration requiring the parties' assent."); Fairfield-Noble Corp. v. Pressman-Gutman Co., 475 F. Supp. 899, 903 (S.D.N.Y. 1979) ("Thus, arbitration was a term 'additional to or different from' those agreed upon. As such, the arbitration provision, unilaterally inserted by the defendant, was a material alteration of the contract and accordingly did not become a part thereof."); Duplan Corp. v. W.B. Davis Hosiery Mills, Inc., 442 F. Supp. 86 (S.D.N.Y. 1977) (similar facts and same holding as in *Supak & Sons*); Valmont Indus., Inc. v. Mitsui & Co. (U.S.A.), 419 F. Supp. 1238, 1240 (D. Neb. 1976) (same); John Thallon & Co. v. M & N Meat Co., 396 F. Supp. 1239 (E.D.N.Y. 1975) (same) ("[T]he arbitration clause and the correlative forfeiture by plaintiff of its right to trial by jury in the courts, 'alter[ed] the original bargain' and involved an 'element of unreasonable surprise.' " (citations omitted)); Windsor Mills, Inc. v. Collins & Aikman Corp., 25 Cal. App. 3d 987, 995, 101 Cal. Rptr. 347, 352 (1972) ("[I]t is clear that a provision for arbitration inserted in the acceptance or confirmation of an offer to purchase goods 'materially alters' the offer."); Abshire v. Belmont Homes, 896 So. 2d 277, 285 (La. Ct. App. 2005) (arbitration clause executed after mobile home purchase was executed was not part of agreement when "plaintiffs did not need to sign the arbitration agreement in order to take delivery of their mobile home" and "there is no evidence that the arbitration agreement was part of the consideration of the original purchase agreement"); Marlene Indus. Corp. v. Carnac Textiles, Inc., 45 N.Y.2d 327, 408 N.Y.S.2d 410 (1978) ("[T]he inclusion of an arbitration agreement materially alters a contract for the sale of goods.... [B]y agreeing to arbitrate a party waives in large part many of his normal rights under the procedural and substantive law of the State, and it would be unfair to infer such a significant waiver on the basis of anything less than a clear indication of intent." (citation omitted)); Licitra v. Gateway, Inc., 189 Misc. 2d 721 (Civ. Ct. 2001); Frances Hosiery Mills, Inc. v. Burlington Indus., Inc., 285 N.C. 344, 204 S.E.2d 834, 842 (1974) ("Beyond question, [the addition of an arbitration clause] would be a material alteration of [the contract]."); Henderson v. Lawyers Title Ins. Corp., 843 N.E.2d 152 (Ohio 2006) (arbitration clause in title insurance policy not binding on insureds when insureds did not receive copy of policy in time to reject term, and arbitration clauses are not a usual and customary term of title insurance policies); Rogers v. Dell Computer Corp., 138 P.3d 826 (Okla. 2005) (insufficient facts to determine whether arbitration clause contained in click-wrap agreement either sent to customers who ordered computers with an acknowledgment of purchase or shipped with computers was part of contract at time of formation or was additional term not accepted under U.C.C.); Just Born, Inc. v. Stein Hall & Co., 59 Pa. D. & C.2d 407 (C.P. 1971) (similar facts and same holding as *Supak & Sons*); Stanley-Bostitch, Inc. v. Regenerative Envtl. Equip. Co., 697 A.2d 323, 329 (R.I. 1997) ("We are of the opinion that a provision compelling a party to submit to binding arbitration materially alters the terms of the parties' agreement."); *cf.* Gen. Steel Corp. v. Collins, 196 S.W.3d 18 (Ky. Ct. App. 2006) (arbitration clause in building contract not enforceable when buyer had crossed out clause in its entirety before signing).

179 *See* 2 Richard A. Lord, Williston on Contracts § 6:22, at 208, 209 (4th ed. 1991) ("It is now generally recognized that an arbitration provision contained in an acceptance or confirmation constitutes a material alteration although, again, if the trade is one in which arbitration provisions are the norm, the provision might nevertheless become part of the contract as one not unfairly surprising or causing hardship."); Gregory M. Travalio, *Clearing the Air After the Battle: Reconciling Fairness and Efficiency in a Formal Approach to U.C.C. Section 2-207*, 33 Case W. Res. L. Rev. 327, 334 (1983) ("Whether the arbitration provision becomes part of the contract depends upon its materiality. As courts in most jurisdictions would consider such a term material, it probably would not become part of the contract.").

180 *See, e.g.*, Weddington Productions, Inc. v. Flick, 60 Cal. App. 4th 793, 815, 71 Cal. Rptr. 2d 265, 280 (1998) (finding that no enforceable licensing contract existed when the parties had not agreed upon "such material terms as . . . whether the license would contain an arbitration clause or whether the right to jury trial would be preserved, etc."); Bolingbrook Park Dist. v. National-Ben Franklin Ins. Co., 96 Ill. App. 3d 26, 420 N.E.2d 741, 744 (1981) (one reason given for enforcing an arbitration clause was that it "is a material term of the contract"); Boston Teachers Union v. Sch. Comm., 372 Mass. 617, 363 N.E.2d 492, 493 (1977) (one reason given for enforcing arbitration clause was that "it was a material term of these agreements that alleged violations must be submitted to grievance procedures with ultimate disposition through grievance arbitration").

181 *See* Aceros Prefabricados, S.A. v. Tradearbed, Inc., 282 F.3d 92 (2d Cir. 2002) (arbitration clause was not a material alteration to contract between two sophisticated commercial entities, when arbitration clauses are standard in the industry and did not surprise the party objecting to arbitration); McDougle v. Silvernell, 738 So. 2d 806 (Ala. 1999).

182 *See* Hill v. Gateway 2000 Inc., 105 F.3d 1147 (7th Cir. 1997) (arbitration agreement binding when the consumer orders a product over the telephone, the product can be returned within thirty days, and the product arrives with an arbitration agreement included in the papers inside the box; Levy v. Gateway 2000, 33 U.C.C. Rep. Serv. 2d 1060 (N.Y. Sup. Ct. 1997) (arbitration provision included with mail-ordered product is integrated into sales agreement); *cf.* Higgs v. Auto. Warranty Corp. of Am., 134 Fed. Appx. 828 (6th Cir. 2005) (enforcing arbitration when arbitration clause was sent as part of "accept-or-return" service warranty after consumer paid for service and consumer did not exercise option to reject warranty within specified time period); Brower v. Gateway 2000, 246 A.D.2d 246, 676 N.Y.S.2d 569 (1998) (no procedural unconscionability in putting arbitration agreement in the computer box).

and accepts the product. The seller will argue that, if the terms are not agreeable, the consumer should return the product.

In this situation, courts take differing views. For example, some courts have held that it is impractical to place all contract terms on the outside of a box and that, even if money has already been paid for a product, it is permissible to add an arbitration agreement as long as it is clear that the purchase is still conditioned on the consumer accepting the terms found inside the box.[183] One court held that a consumer could be compelled to arbitrate her claims even if the terms and conditions were *not* in the box. In *Schafer v. AT & T Wireless Services, Inc.*, the court held that, because the box stated that "use of the service indicates acceptance" of the terms and conditions in a Welcome Guide in the box, the consumer assented to terms and conditions—including the arbitration clause—by activating her cell phone service.[184] The court held that whether the consumer actually received the terms and conditions was "irrelevant" because she had the opportunity to call and request them.[185] Other courts find that additional terms included inside the box are not binding on the consumer when the seller did not make it clear that the sale was conditioned on the consumer accepting the additional terms.[186]

This issue should generally be irrelevant for consumer products in which the arbitration clause is found in the product warranty contained inside the product's box. The Magnuson-Moss Warranty Act prohibits such arbitration clauses in written warranties, and they should be unenforceable at least on that ground.[187]

5.7 Legal Enforceability of Arbitration Clauses Added to Contracts Via Bill Stuffers

5.7.1 Introduction

In the last few years, a great many credit card issuers and other merchants have attempted to create binding arbitration agreements with their customers by inserting a notice to that effect in a monthly billing statement ("bill stuffer"), stating either that this provision is a change of terms, as authorized in the master agreement, or that the fact that the consumer continues to use the credit card or other service is evidence that the consumer agrees to the change in terms. Some courts have enforced arbitration clauses which were sent out to consumers as bill stuffers,[188] but the better reasoned decisions refuse to enforce such agreements, on a variety of grounds. This section analyzes this case law that finds such agreements unenforceable as a matter of law.[189]

5.7.2 Does the Original Agreement Allow the Addition of an Arbitration Clause?

5.7.2.1 Cases Holding That "Change-in-Terms" Provisions Do Not Allow the Addition of an Arbitration Clause

Credit card agreements typically contain a provision allowing the card issuer to change the terms, such as to increase the interest rate or other fees over time. Card issuers use such provisions to justify sending consumers an arbitration agreement as part of a bill stuffer, arguing that the arbitration agreement is just another change in terms.

The leading case examining whether a credit card agreement's change-in-terms provision permits the addition of an arbitration agreement is the California Court of Appeals decision in *Badie v. Bank of America*. The court ruled that a credit card issuer cannot impose binding arbitration on its cardholders via a notice sent with the monthly statement, even if the card holders had initially agreed that "all terms

---

183 Hill v. Gateway 2000, Inc., 105 F.3d 1147 (7th Cir. 1997); ProCD, Inc. v. Zeidenberg, 86 F.3d 1447 (7th Cir. 1996).
184 Schafer v. AT & T Wireless Services, Inc., 2005 WL 850459 (S.D. Ill. Apr. 1, 2005).
185 *Id.* at *4–*5.
186 Klocek v. Gateway, Inc., 104 F. Supp. 2d 1332 (D. Kan. 2000).
187 See § 4.2.2, *supra*.

188 *See, e.g.*, Battels v. Sears Nat'l Bank, 365 F. Supp. 2d 1205 (M.D. Ala. 2005); Kurz v. Chase Manhattan Bank USA, 319 F. Supp. 2d 457, 465 (S.D.N.Y 2004) (Del. law); Bank One v. Harris, 2001 U.S. Dist. LEXIS 9615 (S.D. Miss. Jan. 2, 2001), *aff'd*, 2002 U.S. App. LEXIS 7756 (5th Cir. 2002) (table); Goetsch v. Shell Oil Co., 197 F.R.D. 574 (W.D.N.C. 2000); Herrington v. Union Planters Bank, 113 F. Supp. 2d 1026 (S.D. Miss. 2000), *aff'd*, 265 F.3d 1059 (5th Cir. 2001) (table); Marsh v. First USA Bank, 103 F. Supp. 2d 909 (N.D. Tex. 2000); Sagal v. First USA Bank, 69 F. Supp. 2d 627 (D. Del. 1999), *aff'd*, 254 F.3d 1078 (3d Cir. 2001); Stiles v. Home Cable Concepts, 994 F. Supp. 1410 (M.D. Ala. 1998) (stuffer agreement is enforceable); Perry v. Beneficial Nat'l Bank USA, No. CV 97-218 (Ala. Cir. Ct. May 19, 1998); Williams v. Direct Cable TV, No. CV-97-009, 1 Consumer Fin. Serv. Law Rep., Issue 6, at 6 (Ala. Cir. Ct. Aug. 13, 1997) (arbitration agreement enforceable when credit card agreement allowed issuer to change terms of agreement, and card issuer mailed change requiring arbitration, but gave card holders the right to opt out of arbitration provision); Hutcherson v. Sears Roebuck & Co., 793 N.E.2d 886, 899, 900 (Ill. App. Ct. 2003) (Ariz. law); *see also* Hawkins v. Aid Ass'n for Lutherans, 338 F.3d 801, 806 (7th Cir. 2003) (Wis. law) (fraternal benefit society can change its rules to require arbitration); Woodmen of the World Life Ins. Soc'y v. Harris, 740 So. 2d 362 (Ala. 1999) (fraternal benefit society can change its rules to require arbitration).
189 The factual issue of whether a consumer has received notice of a term sent in a bill stuffer is discussed in § 5.2.3.2, *supra*. The related factual issue of whether a consumer who continues to use the credit card or service after receiving the bill stuffer has manifested assent is discussed in § 5.2.3.3, *supra*.

are subject to change."[190] Essentially, the court found that the arbitration clause was a newly *added* term rather than a change to a term that was already in the agreement, and thus was not authorized by the initial agreement. The court found that a "bill-stuffer" imposed change in terms that takes away the right to a jury trial is fundamentally different than a change in the interest rate, late charges, or other card terms.[191]

Other courts have reached similar conclusions.[192] For example, a federal court has stated:

> Defendants argue that the insertion of the arbitration clause and subsequent modification of it was authorized by the "Change of Terms" provision in [the consumer's] original credit card application. However, the provision is reasonably construed as allowing [the credit card issuer] to terminate its agreement, change the credit limit or change financial terms of the account. It cannot be reasonably construed as explicitly allowing the insertion of an arbitration clause.[193]

Another federal court enunciated a similar rationale:

> The section headings of the original Agreement show that the scope of the Agreement is confined to the basis of the bargain between a credit card company and a credit card holder: the credit limit and payment. The amendment requiring arbitration is not foreshadowed in the original Agreement. . . .
>
> If MBNA's argument that Myers "agreed" to arbitration when she agreed to allow MBNA to amend the Agreement were accepted, there would be no reason to stop at arbitration. MBNA could "amend" the Agreement to include a provision taking a security interest in Myer's home or requiring Myers to pay a penalty if she failed to convince three friends to sign up for MBNA cards. Such provisions were as much within the agreement of the parties at the outset of their relationship as the arbitration provision.[194]

Similarly, the North Carolina Court of Appeals held that Sears could not add a new contract term concerning arbitration to its service agreement for credit card customers pursuant to a change of terms clause. In *Sears Roebuck & Co. v. Avery*[195] the court held that Sears could not create an arbitration agreement using the change of terms clause in an agreement that did not address arbitration or dispute resolution, because this alteration was not a "change" of existing terms, and was not within the reasonable expectation of customers. The court concluded that such a broad power to rewrite the existing contract would render the contract illusory, and held that Sears could not compel its customers to arbitrate their claims.[196]

If a creditor purchased an account from another creditor with whom the consumer originally contracted and attempts to enforce an arbitration clause in a contract from that purchased account, the purchasing creditor has the burden of showing that any change-of-terms provision in the original contract permits it, as the assignee, to add an arbitration clause. A federal court in Texas recently refused to enforce an arbitration clause that had been allegedly added to a credit card agreement by the assignee of the account, on grounds that the assignee had failed to meet this burden.[197] In denying the motion to compel arbitration, the court explained:

> Citibank claims that Poulson accepted the arbitra-

---

190 67 Cal. App. 4th 779, 79 Cal. Rptr. 2d 273 (1998).
    The consumer's complaint and two trial briefs in the case are included in National Consumer Law Center, Consumer Law Pleadings No. 1, Ch. 1 (Cumulative CD-Rom and Index Guide).
191 Badie v. Bank of Am., 67 Cal. App. 4th 779, 79 Cal. Rptr. 2d 273 (1998).
192 *E.g.*, Stone v. Golden Wexler & Sarnese, Prof'l Corp., 341 F. Supp. 2d 189, 198 (E.D.N.Y. 2004) (Va. law) (following *Badie*, and holding that: "[To interpret the bank's change-of-terms provision as permitting the addition of an arbitration clause] would permit the Bank to add terms to the Customer Agreement without limitation as to the substance or nature of such new terms. There is nothing to suggest that plaintiff intended to give such unlimited power to the Bank, or that the law would sanction such a grant."); Myers v. MBNA Am., 2001 U.S. Dist. LEXIS 11900 (D. Mont. Mar. 28, 2001); Long v. Fid. Water Sys., Inc., 2000 U.S. Dist. LEXIS 7827 (N.D. Cal. May 24, 2000); Sears Roebuck & Co. v. Avery, 593 S.E.2d 424, 429, 430 (N.C. Ct. App. 2004) (Ariz. law) (following *Badie*); Discover Bank v. Shea, 827 A.2d 358 (N.J. Super. Ct. Law Div. 2001); Maestle v. Best Buy Co., 2005 WL 1907282 (Ohio Ct. App. Aug. 11, 2005) (following *Badie*, when change-in-terms provision referenced only other kinds of terms, and original contract contained no dispute resolution clause); *see also* Union Planters Bank v. Watson, 2000 Ala. LEXIS 546 (Ala. Dec. 15, 2000), *opinion withdrawn, aff'd without opinion*, 794 So. 2d 1094 (Ala. Apr. 6, 2001); *cf.* Avedon Eng'g, Inc. v. Seatex, 126 F.3d 1279 (10th Cir. 1997) (state law determines whether an unsigned statement requiring binding arbitration should be incorporated into the signed contract between the two parties). *But see In re Am. Express Merchants Litig.*, 2006 WL 662341, at *8 (S.D.N.Y. Mar. 16, 2006) (appeal pending) (change-in-terms provision in merchant contract "rendered the arbitration amendment at issue a reasonable addition to the original contracts").
193 Long v. Fid. Water Sys., Inc., 2000 U.S. Dist. LEXIS 7827, at *9 (N.D. Cal. May 24, 2000).
194 Myers v. MBNA Am., 2001 WL 965063, at *8, *14–*15. (D. Mont. Mar. 28, 2001); *see also* Perry v. FleetBoston Fin. Corp., 2004 WL 1508518, at *4 (E.D. Pa. July 6, 2004) ("The Change in Terms provision is reasonably limited to terms previously contemplated by the original agreement, so long as cardholders do not accept the unilateral change by continuing to use their cards. Otherwise, credit card holders would find themselves in an Orwellian nightmare, trapped in agreements that can be amended unilaterally in ways they never envisioned.").
195 593 S.E.2d 424 (N.C. Ct. App. 2004).
196 *Id.* at 432–433.
    For other examples of illusory contracts, see § 5.3, *supra*.
197 Poulson v. Trans Union L.L.C., 406 F. Supp. 2d 744 (E.D. Tex. 2005).

tion provision because she did not send a notice opting out of the agreement when Citibank sent her the change in terms. Citibank's argument is premised on its ability to change the account terms at will by notifying the account holder.... Citibank, however, has failed to produce Poulson's agreement with Sears and therefore cannot show that Poulson's original agreement with Sears allowed Citibank, as Sears's assignee, to modify the terms of the agreement by sending such a notice.... Because Citibank has not shown that it had the right to change Poulson's account terms by sending a notice and requiring an opt-out letter, Poulson's alleged failure to opt out of the arbitration provision does not suffice as consent to arbitrate.[198]

5.7.2.2 Card Issuers' Responses to Cases Invalidating Bill Stuffers

5.7.2.2.1 Contracts Permitting Issuers to Add New Terms

To evade the holding of *Badie* and its progeny, some credit card issuers have rewritten their change of terms provisions to purportedly authorize the lender to add new terms to the contract as well as change any existing terms. Initially, it should be noted that this action should have little practical import. The rewritten change in terms provision will only apply to new customers, and not those who already have credit card agreements that contain the old change in terms provision.

In addition, there is another problem with such broad change in terms provisions. There is a serious question as to whether a bank can enforce a contract against a consumer that essentially says "we can change our agreement or add terms to it in the future without any limitation whatsoever and you agree at the outset to those changes without knowing what they will be." To allow a bank to change *any* aspect of its relationship to its card holders with mere notice would conflict with the bank's duty of good faith and fair dealing and would also open up the card agreement to challenge for being so one-sided as to be an illusory contract.[199]

5.7.2.2.2 The Delaware Legislation

In addition the credit card industry has pushed for protective state legislation. The Delaware Banking and Financial Services Amendments of 1999 attempt to legalize the use of bill stuffer arbitration agreements.[200] The statute purports to allow banks to amend their agreements "in any respect" whether the change was originally contemplated by the parties or is integral to their relationship, as long as the agreement does not otherwise provide. New terms may be added. It explicitly allows the addition of an arbitration requirement or "other matters of any kind whatsoever."

The statute does not require consumer assent, and applies even to terminated accounts and those who do not continue to use their cards. No notice requirement is specified, but notice is allowed in any mailing to the consumer. The statute apparently only provides a way for the consumer to opt out of a change in terms if it relates to a change in interest rates, and not to the creation of an arbitration requirement.[201]

Delaware banks have attempted to use this provision not only in dealing with Delaware consumers, but have also tried to export the impact of this legislation to other states where their cardholders reside, with varying results. A New Jersey court considering this provision refused to enforce arbitration delivered in a credit card bill stuffer even though the credit card agreement specified that Delaware law applied in interpreting the contract. The court refused to apply Delaware law allowing unlimited change in terms because it violated New Jersey public policy.[202] However, an Ohio court applied the Delaware statute to a contract between a Delaware bank and its Ohio customers, finding that the statute "expressly permits banks to amend credit card agreements to add arbitration clauses."[203]

Of course, even in jurisdictions upholding bill stuffers as a valid means of adding arbitration clauses to contracts, the credit card issuer should still be required to prove that it

---

198 *Id.* at 747.
199 *See, e.g.*, Gourley v. Yellow Transp., L.L.C., 178 F. Supp. 2d 1196, 1202, 1203 (D. Colo. 2001) ("Yellow Cab simultaneously attempts to bind the employee to the Arbitration Agreement as written, while withholding the power to interpret, modify, rescind or supplement its terms unilaterally. Plaintiffs would be both irretrievably bound and at the Defendant's mercy, while Defendants are bound to nothing. Such terms in a contract render it illusory, as it binds one party without binding the other."); *see also* § 5.3, *supra*.
200 Del. Code Ann. tit. 5, § 952; *see also* 1999 Utah Laws 180 (defining "change" and "term" and authorizing use of bill stuffers to change terms).
201 Del. Code Ann. tit. 5, § 952(b)(2).
  At least one court has upheld an arbitration clause sent to a cardholder as a bill stuffer when the credit card company, while not required to do so by the Delaware law applicable to the contract, permitted the cardholder to opt out of the new term. Johnson v. Chase Manhattan Bank USA, 784 N.Y.S.2d 921 (Sup. Ct. 2004), *aff'd*, 13 A.D.3d 322 (2004).
202 Discover Bank v. Shea, 827 A.2d 358 (N.J. Super. Ct. Law Div. 2001).
203 Joseph v. MBNA Am. Bank, 148 Ohio App. 3d 660, 775 N.E.2d 550 (2002); *see also* Jaimez v. MBNA Am. Bank, 2006 WL 470587 (D. Kan. Feb. 27, 2006); Mackey v. MBNA Am. Bank, 343 F. Supp. 2d 966 (W.D. Wash. 2004); Kurz v. Chase Manhattan Bank USA, 319 F. Supp. 2d 457, 465 (S.D.N.Y. 2004) (applying Delaware statute, enforcing bill stuffer amendment); Johnson v. Chase Manhattan Bank USA, 784 N.Y.S.2d 921 (Sup. Ct. 2004), *aff'd*, 13 A.D.3d 322 (2004).

reasonably informed the cardholder of the new term.[204] Furthermore, if a credit card agreement specifies a procedure for the card issuer to use in changing terms, it must follow that procedure in order for the change to be effective. In at least one case, a court found that insufficient evidence had been submitted to show that the contract had been properly amended.[205]

---

[204] See § 5.2.3.2, supra.

[205] Blue Cross & Blue Shield of Ala. v. Woodruff, 803 So. 2d 519 (Ala. 2001); Mattingly v. Hughes Electronics Corp., 810 A.2d 498 (Md. Ct. Spec. App. 2002), aff'd sub nom. DirecTV v. Mattingly, 829 A.2d 626 (Md. 2003).

Chapter 6 Unconscionability and Other Contract Law Defenses to Arbitration Clauses

6.1 Introduction

Section 2 of the Federal Arbitration Act (FAA) states that arbitration clauses are enforceable "save upon such grounds as exist at law or in equity for the revocation of any contract."[1] The Supreme Court has stated that arbitration clauses may be voided under state law, but only on grounds that would generally apply to any contract provision.[2] When general state contract law principles of conscionability lead to the invalidation of an arbitration clause, therefore, that is not preempted by the FAA.[3] This chapter reviews state law theories that provide for the revocation of any contract, and that therefore may be applied to invalidate an arbitration agreement.

Unconscionability is one of the grounds that exist for the revocation of any contract. An arbitration provision may be struck down if it is unconscionable.[4] "Because unconscionability is a defense to contracts generally and does not single out arbitration clauses for special scrutiny, it is also a valid reason not to enforce an arbitration agreement under the FAA."[5] Unconscionability is an extremely fertile issue for consumers confronted by particularly one-sided or unfair arbitration clauses, as quite a few courts have refused to enforce all or part of particular arbitration clauses on the grounds that they were unconscionable.[6] These courts have

---

1 9 U.S.C. § 2.
   The text of the FAA, 9 U.S.C. §§ 1–16, is included as Appendix A.1, *infra*.
2 Doctor's Associates, Inc. v. Casarotto, 517 U.S. 681, 116 S. Ct. 1652, 134 L. Ed. 2d 902 (1996); *see also* Shearson/American Express, Inc. v. McMahon, 482 U.S. 220, 107 S. Ct. 2332, 96 L. Ed. 2d 185 (1987).
3 Ingle v. Circuit City Stores, Inc., 328 F.3d 1165 (9th Cir. 2003) (noting that argument that FAA preempts state unconscionability law actually imposes an impermissibly higher standard on arbitration agreements than on other contracts); Ticknor v. Choice Hotels Int'l, Inc., 265 F.3d 931 (9th Cir. 2001) ("The arbitration clause in the Franchise Agreement was unenforceable as unconscionable under Montana law, which was not preempted by the Federal Arbitration Act.").
   There are a particularly large number of decisions holding that the FAA does not preempt state law holding that bans on class actions embedded in arbitration clauses are unconscionable. These cases are discussed in detail in § 6.5.5, *infra*.
4 *See* Doctor's Associates, Inc. v. Casarotto, 517 U.S. 681, 116 S. Ct. 1652, 134 L. Ed. 2d 902 (1996); Vimar Seguros y Reaseguros, S.A. v. M/V Sky Reefer, 515 U.S. 528, 555, 556, 115 S. Ct. 2322, 132 L. Ed. 2d 462 (1995) (O'Connor, J., concurring); *see also* Stirlen v. Supercuts, Inc., 51 Cal. App. 4th 1519, 60 Cal. Rptr. 2d 138 (1997).
5 Circuit City Stores, Inc. v. Adams, 279 F.3d 889, 895 (9th Cir. 2002).
6 *See, e.g.*, Dale v. Comcast Corp., 498 F.3d 1216 (11th Cir. 2007); Shroyer v. New Cingular Wireless Services, Inc., 2007 WL 2332068 (9th Cir. Aug. 17, 2007); Davis v. O'Melveny & Myers, 485 F.3d 1066 (9th Cir. 2007); Net Global Mktg., Inc. v. Dialtone, Inc., 217 Fed. Appx. 598 (9th Cir. 2007) (unpublished); Nagrampa v. MailCoups, Inc., 469 F.3d 1257 (9th Cir. 2006) (en banc); Al-Safin v. Circuit City Stores, Inc., 394 F.3d 1254 (9th Cir. 2005); Iberia Credit Bureau, Inc. v. Cingular Wireless, 379 F.3d 169 (5th Cir. 2004) (one wireless phone company's arbitration clause was unconscionable, two others' clauses were not); Banc One Acceptance Corp. v. Hill, 367 F.3d 426 (5th Cir. 2004); Alexander v. Anthony Int'l, Ltd. P'ship, 341 F.3d 256 (3d Cir. 2003); Ingle v. Circuit City Stores, Inc., 328 F.3d 1165 (9th Cir. 2003); Ting v. AT & T, 319 F.3d 1126 (9th Cir. 2003); Murray v. United Food & Commercial Workers Int'l Union, 289 F.3d 297 (4th Cir. 2002); Circuit City Stores, Inc. v. Adams, 279 F.3d 889 (9th Cir.); Ticknor v. Choice Hotels Int'l, Inc., 265 F.3d 931 (9th Cir. 2001); Shankle v. B-G Maint. Mgmt. of Colo., Inc., 163 F.3d 1230 (10th Cir. 1999); Cooper v. QC Fin. Services, Inc., 2007 WL 974100 (D. Ariz. Mar. 30, 2007); Bragg v. Linden Research, Inc., 487 F. Supp. 2d 593 (E.D. Pa. 2007); Geoffrey v. Wash. Mut. Bank, 484 F. Supp. 2d 1115 (S.D. Cal. 2007); Hollings v. Debt Relief of Am., 479 F. Supp. 2d 1099 (D. Neb. 2007); Riensche v. Cingular Wireless L.L.C., 2006 WL 3827477 (W.D. Wash. Dec. 27, 2006); Doerhoff v. Gen. Growth Properties, Inc., 2006 WL 3210502 (W.D. Mo. Nov. 6, 2006); Skirchak v. Dynamics Research Corp., 432 F. Supp. 2d 175 (D. Mass. 2006); Dunham v. Envtl. Chem. Corp., 2006 WL 2374703 (N.D. Cal. Aug. 16, 2006); Lowden v. T-Mobile, USA, Inc., 2006 WL 1009279 (W.D. Wash. Apr. 13, 2006); Sprague v. Household Int'l, 473 F. Supp. 2d 966 (W.D. Mo. June 15, 2005); Plattner v. Edge Solutions, Inc., 2004 WL 1575557 (N.D. Ill. May 27, 2004); Garrett v. Hooters-Toledo, 295 F. Supp. 2d 774, 777 (N.D. Ohio 2003); Wilcox v. Valero Ref. Co., 256 F. Supp. 2d 687 (S.D. Tex. 2003); Plaskett v. Bechtel Int'l, 243 F. Supp. 2d 334 (D. V.I. 2003); Torrance v. Aames Funding Corp., 242 F. Supp. 2d 862 (D. Or. 2002); Luna v. Household Fin. Corp., 236 F. Supp. 2d 1166 (W.D. Wash. 2002); Brennan v. Bally Total Fitness, 198 F. Supp. 2d 377 (S.D.N.Y. 2002); Lelouis v. W. Directory Co., 230 F. Supp. 2d 1214 (D. Or. 2001); Geiger v. Ryan's Family Steak Houses, Inc., 134 F. Supp. 2d 985 (S.D. Ind. 2001); Prevot v. Phillips

Petroleum Co., 133 F. Supp. 2d 937 (S.D. Tex. 2001); Lozada v. Dale Baker Oldsmobile, Inc., 91 F. Supp. 2d 1087 (W.D. Mich. 2000); Nicholson v. Labor Ready, Inc., 1997 U.S. Dist. LEXIS 23494 (N.D. Cal. May 23, 1997); *In re* Knepp, 229 B.R. 821 (Bankr. N.D. Ala. 1999); Anderson v. Ashby, 873 So. 2d 168 (Ala. 2003); Leonard v. Terminix Int'l Co., 854 So. 2d 529 (Ala. 2002); Harold Allen's Mobile Home Factory Outlet, Inc. v. Butler, 825 So. 2d 779 (Ala. 2002); Am. Gen. Fin., Inc. v. Branch, 793 So. 2d 738 (Ala. 2000); Gentry v. Super. Ct., 2007 WL 2445122 (Cal. Aug. 30, 2007); Discover Bank v. Super. Ct., 30 Cal. Rptr. 3d 76, 113 P.3d 1100 (Cal. 2005); Little v. Auto Stiegler, Inc., 29 Cal. 4th 1064, 63 P.3d 979 (2003); Armendariz v. Found. Health Psychcare Services, Inc., 24 Cal. 4th 83, 99 Cal. Rptr. 2d 745, 6 P.3d 669 (2000); Graham v. Scissor-Tail, Inc., 28 Cal. 3d 807, 171 Cal. Rptr. 604, 623 P.2d 165 (1981); Firchow v. Citibank (S.D.), 2007 WL 64763 (Cal. Ct. App. Jan. 10, 2007) (unpublished); Higgins II v. Super. Ct., 140 Cal. App. 4th 1238, 45 Cal. Rptr. 3d 293 (2006); Aral v. Earthlink, 36 Cal. Rptr. 3d 229 (Ct. App. 2006); Nyulassy v. Lockheed Martin Corp., 16 Cal. Rptr. 3d 296 (Ct. App. 2004); Martinez v. Master Prot. Corp., 12 Cal. Rptr. 3d 663 (Ct. App. 2004); Abramson v. Juniper Networks, Inc., 115 Cal. App. 4th 638, 9 Cal. Rptr. 3d 422 (2004); Torigian v. Michael Cadillac, Inc., 2003 WL 21246609 (Cal. Ct. App. May 29, 2003); Fittante v. Palm Springs Motors, Inc., 105 Cal. App. 4th 708, 129 Cal. Rptr. 2d 659 (2003); O'Hare v. Mun. Res. Consultants, 132 Cal. Rptr. 2d 116 (Ct. App. 2003); Szetela v. Discover Bank, 118 Cal. Rptr. 2d 862 (Ct. App. 2003); Mercuro v. Super. Ct., 96 Cal. App. 4th 167, 116 Cal. Rptr. 2d 671 (2002); Flores v. Transamerica Homefirst, Inc., 113 Cal. Rptr. 2d 376 (Ct. App. 2001); Bolter v. Super. Ct., 87 Cal. App. 4th 900, 104 Cal. Rptr. 2d 888 (2001); McCoy v. Super. Ct., 104 Cal. Rptr. 2d 504 (Ct. App. 2001) (unpublished); Pinedo v. Premium Tobacco, Inc., 85 Cal. App. 4th 774, 102 Cal. Rptr. 2d 435 (2000); Villa Milano Homeowners Ass'n v. Il Davorge, 84 Cal. App. 4th 819, 102 Cal. Rptr. 2d 1 (2000); Shubin v. William Lyon Homes, Inc., 84 Cal. App. 4th 1041, 101 Cal. Rptr. 2d 390 (2000), *opinion withdrawn*, 2001 Cal. LEXIS 1552 (Cal. Mar. 14, 2001); Stirlen v. Supercuts, Inc., 51 Cal. App. 4th 1519, 60 Cal. Rptr. 2d 138 (1997); Patterson v. ITT Consumer Fin. Corp., 14 Cal. App. 4th 1659, 18 Cal. Rptr. 2d 563 (1993); Worldwide Ins. Group v. Klopp, 603 A.2d 788 (Del. Super. Ct. 1992); Palm Beach Motor Cars Ltd., Inc. v. Jeffries, 885 So. 2d 990 (Fla. Dist. Ct. App. 2004); Powertel, Inc. v. Bexley, 743 So. 2d 570 (Fla. Dist. Ct. App. 1999); Kinkel v. Cingular Wireless, L.L.C., 857 N.E.2d 250 (Ill. 2006); Bess v. DirecTV, Inc., 2007 WL 2013613 (Ill. App. Ct. July 10, 2007); Ballard v. Southwest Detroit Hosp., 119 Mich. App. 814, 327 N.W.2d 370 (1982); Pitts v. Watkins, 905 So. 2d 553 (Miss. 2005); E. Ford, Inc. v. Taylor, 826 So. 2d 709 (Miss. 2002); State *ex rel.* Vincent v. Schneider, 194 S.W.3d 853 (Mo. 2006); Whitney v. Alltel Communications, Inc., 173 S.W.3d 300 (Mo. Ct. App. 2005); Swain v. Auto Services, Inc., 128 S.W.3d 103 (Mo. Ct. App. 2003); Iwen v. U.S. W. Direct, 293 Mont. 512, 977 P.2d 989 (1999); D.R. Horton, Inc. v. Green, 96 P.3d 1159 (Nev. 2004); Burch v. Second Judicial Dist. Ct., 49 P.3d 647 (Nev. 2002); Muhammad v. County Bank of Rehobeth Beach, 912 A.2d 88 (N.J. 2006); Teleserve Sys., Inc. v. MCI Telecommunications Corp., 230 A.D.2d 585, 659 N.Y.S.2d 659 (1997); Williams v. Aetna Fin. Co., 83 Ohio St. 3d 464, 700 N.E.2d 859 (1998); Taylor Bldg. Corp. of Am. v. Benfield, 860 N.E.2d 1058 (Ohio Ct. App.), *appeal allowed*, 859 N.E.2d 556 (Ohio 2006); Schwartz v. Alltel Corp., 2006 WL 2243649 (Ohio Ct. App. June 29, 2006); Olah v. Ganley Chevrolet, Inc., 2006 WL 350204 (Ohio Ct. App. Feb. 16, 2006); Small v. HCF of Perrysburg, 823 N.E.2d 19 (Ohio Ct. App. 2004); Eagle v. Fred Martin Motor Co., 809 N.E.2d 1161 (Ohio Ct. App. 2004); O'Donoghue v. Smythe, Cramer Co., 2002 WL 1454074 (Ohio Ct. App. July 3, 2002); Myers v. Terminix Int'l Co., 91 Ohio Misc. 2d 41, 697 N.E.2d 227 (Ct. Com. Pl. 1998); Vasquez-Lopez v. Beneficial Or., Inc., 152 P.3d 940 (Or. Ct. App. 2007); Thibodeau v. Comcast Corp., 912 A.2d 874 (Pa. Super. Ct. 2006); McNulty v. H & R Block, 843 A.2d 1267 (Pa. Super. Ct. 2004); Carll v. Terminix Int'l Co., 793 A.2d 921 (Pa. Super. Ct. 2002); Zak v. Prudential Prop. & Cas. Ins. Co., 713 A.2d 681 (Pa. Super. Ct. 1998); Taylor v. Butler, 142 S.W. 3d 277 (Tenn. 2004), *cert. denied*, 125 S. Ct. 1304 (2005); Brown v. Tenn. Title Loans, Inc., 2006 WL 2842788 (Tenn. Ct. App. Feb. 26, 2007); Olshan Found. Repair Co. v. Ayala, 180 S.W.3d 212 (Tex. App. 2005); *In re* Turner Bros. Trucking Co., 8 S.W.3d 370 (Tex. App. 1999); Sosa v. Paulos, 924 P.2d 357 (Utah 1996); Scott v. Cingular Wireless, 161 P.3d 1000 (Wash. 2007); Zuver v. Airtouch Communications, Inc., 153 Wash. 2d 293, 103 P.3d 753 (2004); Adler v. Fred Lind Manor, 153 Wash. 2d 331, 103 P.3d 773 (2004); Mendez v. Palm Harbor Homes, Inc., 45 P.3d 594 (Wash. 2002); Toppings v. Meritech Mortgage Services, 569 S.E.2d 149 (W. Va. 2002); West Virginia *ex rel.* Dunlap v. Berger, 567 S.E.2d 265 (W. Va. 2002); Arnold v. United Companies Lending Corp., 204 W. Va. 229, 511 S.E.2d 854 (1998); Wis. Auto Title Loans, Inc. v. Jones, 714 N.W.2d 155 (Wis. 2006); Coady v. Cross Country Bank, 729 N.W.2d 732 (Wis. Ct. App. 2007).

7 *E.g.*, Coleman v. Prudential-Bache Sec., Inc., 802 F.2d 1350, 1351 (11th Cir. 1986) ("There is nothing inherently unfair or oppressive about arbitration clauses."); Griffen v. Alpha Phi Alpha, Inc., 2007 WL 707364 (E.D. Pa. Mar. 2, 2007) (arguments that arbitration is per se unconscionable are inconsistent with the law in favor of arbitration).

8 Khan v. Parsons Global Services, Ltd., 480 F. Supp. 4 327 (D.D.C. 2007).

not found that arbitration clauses are unconscionable in general; such a finding would be plainly contrary to the Federal Arbitration Act.[7]

Instead, as the following sections make clear, courts will only find arbitration clauses to be unconscionable when some aspect of their language, or some circumstance surrounding their making or their contemplated implementation, renders them particularly unfair. As a practical matter, many of the grounds for striking down an arbitration clause as inconsistent with a federal statute, which are discussed in Ch. 4, *supra*, overlap with the grounds for finding an arbitration clause unconscionable.

Consequently, when a case's underlying claim is federal, a consumer should argue both that the clause requiring the federal claim to be arbitrated conflicts with the federal statute and that the clause is unconscionable. When the underlying claim is based solely on state law the consumer should focus on whether the clause requiring the claim to be arbitrated is unconscionable. It should be noted that there is authority limiting the unconscionability defense to domestic contracts, and holding that it does not apply to claims under the New York Convention on the Recognition and Enforcement of Foreign Arbitral Awards.[8]

It is also important to distinguish between a claim that the arbitration clause is unconscionable and a claim that the whole contract is unconscionable. While the court will determine the former, a line of cases indicates that the arbitrator should be the one to determine the unconscionability of the whole contract.[9]

6.2 General Unconscionability Standards

The doctrine of unconscionability is found in Uniform Commercial Code (UCC) Articles 2 and 2A covering the sale or lease of goods, and is also found in a number of consumer credit, deceptive acts or practices (UDAP), and other statutes. Courts will also adopt those unconscionability concepts for use in other types of transactions. However, as noted in § 3.2.1.2, *supra*, some courts have held that the FAA preempts any state statute that does not apply to all contracts. Given that the UCC does not apply to all contracts, even in cases involving the sale of goods, consumer attorneys might be well advised to rely upon the common law doctrine of unconscionability rather than the UCC doctrine of unconscionability.

A number of state law doctrines for refusing to enforce a contract are similar to the doctrine of unconscionability. For example, a court may strike down an arbitration clause as against public policy or on related grounds.[10] This subsection will treat all of these doctrines as synonymous with unconscionability.

Unconscionability and these related doctrines provide particularly effective grounds for challenging arbitration agreements that are drafted in a manner that is particularly unfair.[11] The court must determine if the provision is unconscionable; the arbitrator does not make this determination.[12] The consumer should have an opportunity to present evidence as to the commercial setting, purpose, and effect of the arbitration provision.[13]

In some cases, such as arbitration clauses that explicitly limit consumer remedies in ways that undermine consumer protection statutes,[14] the substantive unconscionability of a clause may be identified from the face of the clause itself. However, with respect to many other types of unconscionability challenges such as challenges based upon either cost or bias arguments, significant discovery may be necessary to develop an adequate factual record.[15]

It is also important to note that unconscionability is typically judged at the time of contracting. Accordingly, many courts have been unwilling to permit defendants and arbitration service providers to defeat an unconscionability argument by rewriting the arbitration rules after a challenge has been made.[16]

The court then considers all aspects of the challenged terms in the arbitration clause (or sometimes the entire clause): how it was negotiated and its substantive terms. Based on all factors, the court must decide if the terms and the clause are unconscionable.

---

9 This issue is discussed extensively in § 3.4.5, *supra*. *See also* Madol v. Dan Nelson Auto. Group, 372 F.3d 997 (8th Cir. 2004) (rejecting unconscionability challenge aimed at "the transactions as a whole from start to finish" when the consumers "did not make any discernable arguments to the magistrate judge that go to the making of the arbitration agreement itself"); Sydnor v. Conseco Fin. Servicing Corp., 252 F.3d 302 (4th Cir. 2001); Benoay v. Prudential-Bache Sec., Inc., 805 F.2d 1437 (11th Cir. 1986); Coleman v. Prudential-Bache Sec., Inc., 802 F.2d 1350 (11th Cir. 1986); Russell v. Performance Toyota, 826 So. 2d 719, 726 (Miss. 2002); *see also* Wright v. SFX Entm't, Inc., 2001 U.S. Dist. LEXIS 1000 (S.D.N.Y. Feb. 7, 2001); Boseinger v. Phillips Plastic Corp., 57 F. Supp. 2d 986, 993 (S.D. Cal. 1999) (claims of duress relating to the contract as a whole); Dale v. Prudential-Bache Sec., Inc., 719 F. Supp. 1164, 1169 (E.D.N.Y. 1989) (claim of fraudulent inducement, duress, or unconscionability must be determined by the arbitrator); Brener v. Becker Paribas Inc., 628 F. Supp. 442, 446 (S.D.N.Y. 1985) (claims concerning duress, unconscionability, coercion, or confusion in signing should be determined by an arbitrator).

10 *See* Cruz v. PacifiCare Health Sys., Inc., 30 Cal. 4th 303, 133 Cal. Rptr. 2d 58, 66 P.3d 1157 (2003); Broughton v. CIGNA Healthplans, 21 Cal. 4th 1066, 90 Cal. Rptr. 2d 334, 988 P.2d 67 (1999). *But see* Sears Termite & Pest Control, Inc. v. Robinson, 883 So. 2d 153 (Ala. 2003) (court may not extend unconscionability analysis to include public policy considerations without stepping on the toes of the legislature).

11 *See* §§ 6.5.2 (discussing cases holding that arbitration clauses that impose excessive fees and costs upon individuals are unconscionable), 6.5.3 (discussing cases holding that arbitration clauses that are one-sided and non-mutual and which thereby favor the stronger party are unconscionable), 6.5.4 (discussing cases holding that arbitration clauses that strip individuals of statutory remedies are unconscionable), *infra*.

12 *See, e.g.*, Banc One Acceptance Corp. v. Hill, 367 F.3d 426, 430, 431 (5th Cir. 2004); Prevot v. Phillips Petroleum Co., 133 F. Supp. 2d 937, 939 (S.D. Tex. 2001); Anderson v. Ashby, 873 So. 2d 168 (Ala. 2003) (issue of unconscionability is for the court even when the agreement says that the arbitrator decides questions of arbitrability); Am. Gen. Fin., Inc. v. Branch, 793 So. 2d 738 (Ala. 2000); Haga v. Martin Homes, Inc., 1999 Ohio App. LEXIS 1740 (Ohio Ct. App. Apr. 19, 1999); West Virginia *ex rel.* Dunlap v. Berger, 567 S.E.2d 265, 271 (W. Va. 2002). *But see* Smith v. Gateway, 2002 WL 1728615 (Tex. App. July 26, 2002) (whether terms are substantively unconscionable is issue for the arbitrator, not the court).

13 Haga v. Martin Homes, Inc., 1999 Ohio App. LEXIS 1740 (Ohio Ct. App. Apr. 19, 2002); *see also* Montrosse v. Conseco Fin. Servicing Corp., 2000 U.S. Dist. LEXIS 20792 (S.D. W. Va. Dec. 20, 2000) ("[T]he court concludes that, at least with respect to plaintiff's claims of unconscionability, adhesion, and public policy, evidence must be taken before these matters can be resolved.").

14 *See* § 4.3.2, *supra*.

15 *See* § 2.4, *supra* (discussing the right to take discovery).

16 *See* § 6.6, *infra*.

6.3 Relationship Between Procedural and Substantive Unconscionability

Most courts will examine both procedural and substantive unconscionability—that is, the nature of the negotiation and the disclosure of the arbitration terms, and the fairness of the terms themselves. While most courts require some showing of both procedural *and* substantive unconscionability,[17] the two factors are often treated as playing against one another in a sliding scale relationship. The California Supreme Court, for example, has stated that "the more substantively oppressive the contract term, the less evidence of procedural unconscionability is required to come to the conclusion that the term is unenforceable, and vice versa."[18] In a number of other jurisdictions, a similar doctrine is set forth in slightly different terms: when contracts are procedurally objectionable because they are adhesive or oppressive, courts will be more likely to find that the contract is unenforceable in general. For example, some courts will note that the arbitration clause is found in a standard form adhesion contract to which the consumer has no power to negotiate terms,[19] and will therefore conclude that a careful examination of the actual terms of the arbitration agreement is required. The court will then examine the substantive terms, and its determination as to unconscionability will turn on its examination of those substantive terms.[20] A significant number of important decisions relating to procedural unconscionability can also be found in the area of employment law.[21]

A number of corporations have adopted an ostensible "opt out" strategy to take advantage of the common statement that both procedural and substantive unconscionability must be proven to establish that a contract term is unconscionable and unenforceable. Under this strategy, businesses offer consumers a limited opportunity to opt out of an arbitration clause, and then argue that this opt-out option means that the contract is not a take-it-or-leave-it contract of adhesion,[22] and is therefore not procedurally unconscionable. They then argue that as a given arbitration provision is not procedurally unconscionable, no part of it may be struck down as substantively unconscionable, no matter how unfair a given provision may be. A number of courts have accepted this line of reasoning, enforcing arbitration clauses, at least in part, because of the presence of opt-out provisions.[23]

---

17 *E.g.*, Equal Employment Opportunity Comm'n v. Woodmen of the World Life Ins. Soc'y, 2007 WL 702758 (8th Cir. Mar. 9, 2007) (Neb. law) (both procedural and substantive unconscionability are required); Skirchak v. Dynamics Research Corp., 432 F. Supp. 2d 175 (D. Mass. 2006) ("[T]o establish unconscionability a plaintiff must demonstrate both a lack of meaningful choice about whether to accept the provision in question, and that the disputed provisions were so one-sided as to be oppressive." (internal quotations and citations omitted)); Storie v. Household Int'l, Inc. 2005 WL 3728718 (D. Mass. Sept. 22, 2005) ("The test is a conjunctive one; that is, a plaintiff must prove *both* substantive *and* procedural unconscionability to prevail on this theory." (citation omitted)); Sprague v. Household Int'l, 473 F. Supp. 2d 966 (W.D. Mo. June 15, 2005) ("a court will not find an arbitration agreement unconscionable unless both aspects of unconscionability are present"); Murphy v. Courtsey Ford, L.L.C., 944 So. 2d 1131, 1134 (Fla. Dist. Ct. App. 2006) ("[t]o invalidate a contract under Florida law, a court must find that the contract is both procedurally and substantively unconscionable"); Doyle v. Fin. Am., L.L.C., 173 Md. App. 370, 918 A.2d 1266 (2007) ("The prevailing view is that [procedural and substantive unconscionability] must both be present in order for a court to exercise its discretion to refuse to enforce a contract or clause under the doctrine of unconscionability.") (citation omitted); Ball v. Ohio State Home Services, Inc., 2006 WL 2485193 (Ohio Ct. App. Aug. 30, 2006) ("[a] party seeking to invalidate an arbitration clause on grounds of unconscionability must establish that the provision is both procedurally and substantively unconscionable"); Wis. Auto Title Loans, Inc. v. Jones, 714 N.W.2d 155, 164 (Wis. 2006) ("For a contract or a contract provision to be declared invalid as unconscionable, the contract or contract provision must be determined to be both procedurally and substantively unconscionable.").

18 Armendariz v. Found. Health Psychcare Services, Inc., 24 Cal. 4th 83, 114, 99 Cal. Rptr. 2d 745, 6 P.3d 669 (2000).

Numerous other jurisdictions embrace this same rule. *E.g.*, Sprague v. Household Int'l, 473 F. Supp. 2d 966 (W.D. Mo. June 15, 2005); Wis. Auto Title Loans, Inc. v. Jones, 714 N.W.2d 155, 165, 171 (Wis. 2006) ("Even if the arbitration provision is procedurally unconscionable, it may be enforced if it is not substantively unconscionable."; however, "[t]he more substantive unconscionability present, the less procedural unconscionability is required, and vice versa.").

19 *See* Powertel, Inc. v. Bexley, 743 So. 2d 570 (Fla. Dist. Ct. App. 1999).

20 *See* Zawikowski v. Beneficial Nat'l Bank, 1999 U.S. Dist. LEXIS 514 (N.D. Ill. Jan. 7, 1999) (the adhesive nature of the contract is not enough, the consumer must also show that the arbitration provision itself is oppressive); West Virginia *ex rel.* Dunlap v. Berger, 567 S.E.2d 265, 273 n.4 (W. Va. 2002).

21 *See, e.g.*, Brennan v. Bally Total Fitness, 198 F. Supp. 2d 377 (S.D.N.Y. 2002) (finding procedural unconscionability when employer "used high pressure tactics," "gave the employees no more than fifteen minutes to review a sixteen-page single-spaced document," and employee plaintiff "was an unrepresented, single mother who was then pregnant with twins, and lacked other adequate means of support").

22 The legal significance of a contract being a contract of adhesion is discussed in § 6.4.1, *infra*.

23 *See, e.g.*, Davidson v. Cingular Wireless L.L.C., 2007 WL 896349 (E.D. Ark. Mar. 23, 2007) (arbitration clause not procedurally unconscionable, in part, because plaintiff had not exercised option to reject the arbitration agreement); Hicks v. Macy's Dep't Stores, Inc., 2006 WL 2595941 (N.D. Cal. Sept. 11, 2006) (arbitration clause is not procedurally unconscionable, given that the plaintiff had the opportunity to opt out, so the court does not need to reach issue of whether class action ban is substantively unconscionable); Tsadilas v. Providian Nat'l Bank, 13 A.D.3d 190, 786 N.Y.S.2d 478 (2004) ("The arbitration provision alone is not unconscionable because plaintiff had the opportunity to opt out without any adverse consequences."); Johnson v. Chase Manhattan Bank USA, 784 N.Y.S.2d 921 (Sup. Ct. 2004) (table) (text available at 2004 WL 413213) ("The allegations, however, bear no relation to the facts. The Arbitration Agreement was not presented on a 'take or leave it'

There are a number of indications that this opt-out ploy may not succeed in many situations, however. The biggest problem for businesses relying on this ploy is that a rapidly increasing number of courts have held that parties need not prove procedural unconscionability for a court to strike down a class action ban, and that substantive unconscionability is adequate.[24] This trend holds particularly true for contract terms that are effectively exculpatory. As the California Supreme Court has found, "a finding of procedural unconscionability is not required to invalidate a class arbitration waiver if that waiver implies unwaivable statutory rights."[25] Other courts have refused to give weight to opt-out provisions which were burdened by limitations and conditions.[26]

In a few jurisdictions particularly egregious circumstances surrounding the negotiation of an arbitration clause may be enough for a court to find the arbitration clause unconscionable, without reference to the actual terms of the agreement. While such a finding is relatively infrequent, a handful of courts have refused to enforce arbitration agreements involving extreme procedural unconscionability, such as when the clause was presented on a take-it-or-leave-it basis, the clause was buried deep within a confusing multipage document, and the contract was in a language unfamiliar to the consumers.[27]

In an extreme case a court has found unconscionability when a patient was asked to sign a standard form printed agreement as the patient was being whisked into surgery, without being orally informed about the arbitration provision buried within the standard form.[28]

Nonetheless, it must be stressed that in most states it is necessary to prove both procedural *and* substantive unconscionability, and counsel for consumers would be well advised to provide the court with evidence and arguments relating to both sets of issues. This advice is particularly valid in states in which a contract is procedurally unconscionable when it has been drafted by the more powerful party and imposed upon the weaker party on a take-it-or-leave-it basis.[29] As such contracts compose the majority of

---

basis. It permits plaintiff the opportunity to opt out of arbitration, and to still continue using his Chase USA credit card without the requirement that 'any claim or dispute' be arbitrated."), *aff'd*, 13 A.D.3d 322, 786 N.Y.S.2d 302 (2004); *cf.* Omstead v. Dell, Inc., 473 F. Supp. 2d 1018 (N.D. Cal. Feb. 13, 2007) (arbitration clause not unconscionable when it gave the plaintiffs a minimum twenty-one-day rescission option, rather than imposing the arbitration provision on a "take it or leave it" basis).

24 *See, e.g.*, Dale v. Comcast Corp., 498 F.3d 1216, 1220 n.5 (11th Cir. 2007) ("The subscribers also argue on appeal that the class action waiver is procedurally unconscionable. We do not address this argument since we conclude infra that the clause is substantively unconscionable and thus unenforceable as a matter of law."); Batory v. Sears, Roebuck & Co., 456 F. Supp. 2d 1137 (D. Ariz. 2006) (substantive unconscionability alone is enough to strike a provision); Covenant Health Rehab. of Picayune v. Brown, 949 So. 2d 732 (Miss. 2007) (even though arbitration contract is not procedurally unconscionable, provision banning punitive damages and waiving liability for criminal acts of individuals is unconscionable and stricken); Vasquez-Lopez v. Beneficial Or., Inc., 152 P.3d 940, 948 (Or. Ct. App. 2007) ("[B]oth procedural and substantive unconscionability are relevant, although only substantive unconscionability is absolutely necessary."); Scott v. Cingular Wireless, 160 Wash. 2d 843, 854 n.4, 161 P.3d 1000, 1006 n.4 (Wash. 2007) (finds "it unnecessary to address plaintiffs' claims of procedural unconscionability" after holding that the defendant's class action ban was substantively unconscionable); Adler v. Fred Lind Manor, 103 P.2d 773 (Wash. 2004) ("[S]ubstantive unconscionability alone can support a finding of unconscionability.").

25 Gentry v. Super. Ct., 42 Cal. 4th 443, 64 Cal. Rptr. 3d 773, 165 P.3d 556 (2007).

26 Massie v. Ralph's Grocery Co., 2007 WL 1395580 (Cal. Ct. App. May 14, 2007) (opt-out right did not eliminate procedural unconscionability when employees were given only vague information about how to opt out and when employees would have to opt out of a bonus plan after working towards it for nearly a year); Firchow v. Citibank (S.D.), 2007 WL 64763 (Cal. Ct. App. Jan. 10, 2007) (unpublished) (arbitration clause procedurally unconscionable, notwithstanding limited "opt out" provision).

Also, to the extent that marketing experts or other data, combined with the testimony of the consumers in the case, can demonstrate that such "choices" are not meaningful because the "option" is presented in a manner designed to ensure that consumers are not aware of it, many courts may not give much weight to such language. For an example of a factual record developed using marketing experts for this purpose, see Ting v. AT & T, 182 F. Supp. 2d 902, 911, 912 (N.D. Cal. 2002), *aff'd with respect to unconscionability*, 319 F.3d 1126 (9th Cir. 2003).

27 Barajas v. PHP, Clearinghouse No. 51,778D (D. Ariz. Nov. 6, 1997) (text of this decision is also available on the CD-Rom accompanying this manual); *see also* Al-Safin v. Circuit City Stores, Inc., 394 F.3d 1254 (9th Cir. 2005) ("In Washington, a contract generally may be invalid based on either substantive or procedural unconscionability."); Banc One Acceptance Corp. v. Hill, 367 F.3d 426, 431, 432 (5th Cir. 2004) (applying Mississippi contract law, clause stricken entirely due to procedural unconscionability); Wilcox v. Valero Ref. Co., 256 F. Supp. 2d 687, 691 n.1 (S.D. Tex. 2003) (same, applying Texas law).

28 Sosa v. Paulos, 924 P.2d 357 (Utah 1996). *But see* Jim Burke Auto., Inc. v. Murphy, 739 So. 2d 1084 (Ala. 1999) (the fact that consumer had no ride home from dealership did not make contract unconscionable).

29 *E.g.*, Ting v. AT & T, 319 F.3d 1126 (9th Cir. 2003); Flores v. Transamerica Homefirst, Inc., 93 Cal. App. 4th 846, 113 Cal. Rptr. 2d 376 (2001); McNulty v. H & R Block, 843 A.2d 1267, 1273 (Pa. Super. Ct. 2004) ("no meaningful choice" prong met when "[t]he contract in question is a classic example of an adhesion contract").

In some cases, however, courts have struck down substantively illegal arbitration clauses even when the contract was not adhesive. *See* O'Donoghue v. Smythe Cramer Co., 2002 WL 1454074 (Ohio Ct. App. July 3, 2002) (refusing to enforce an arbitration clause that required consumer to pay more in arbitration fees than it was possible for the consumer to recover, given limitations of liability clause, even though there was no evidence that the clause was presented on a take-it-or-leave-it basis); *see also* Nyulassy v. Lockheed Martin Corp., 16 Cal. Rptr. 3d 296, 306 (Ct. App. 2004) ("[Y]ou can show procedural unconscionability by a showing of adhesion, but it is not the only way. There will be cases . . . where procedural unconscio-

consumer contracts in the United States—most consumer contracts are drafted by the merchant or business, and the standard form's terms may not be rewritten for an individual consumer—most courts will require some kind of additional evidence of procedural or substantive unconscionability before they will refuse to enforce a contract.[30] In most circumstances and in most jurisdictions it is far easier to prove that an arbitration clause is procedurally unconscionable than to prove that it is substantively unconscionable and, while counsel for consumers generally need to pay attention to proving both elements, greater attention usually must be spent on establishing substantive unconscionability.

6.4 Procedural Unconscionability

6.4.1 Contracts of Adhesion—Enough in Some States, Merely a Factor in Others

The phrase "contract of adhesion" is defined differently from state to state. In California it describes "a standard-form contract, drafted by the party with superior bargaining power, which relegates to the other party the option of either adhering to its terms without modification or rejecting the contract entirely."[31]

Some other states impose a much heavier burden upon consumers, however, before accepting that a contract is adhesive. One court applying Michigan law has stated, for example, that "[a] contract is an adhesion contract only if the party agrees to the contract because he has no meaningful choice to obtain the desired goods or services elsewhere."[32] In Louisiana, similarly, the state Supreme Court held that an arbitration clause that was in very small font in a standard form contract was not a contract of adhesion, because the arbitration clause applied mutually to both parties and because there was no inequality in bargaining power.[33] An Indiana court of appeals has gone so far as to hold that an arbitration clause was not adhesive when a party did "not allege that they entered into the Contract unwillingly or without knowledge of its terms."[34] In Missouri, the Supreme Court held that consumers "cannot simply allege that a pre-printed contract is a contract of adhesion and offer no other proof on the matter," requiring additional factors for a finding of procedural unconscionability.[35]

In California the mere fact that a contract is a contract of adhesion is sufficient to render it procedurally unconscionable.[36] Courts applying the law of several different states similarly have found procedural unconscionability based on the factual circumstances surrounding a contract of adhesion.[37] In New Jersey, the Supreme Court has held:

---

nability is obvious without the need to establish that the contract is one of adhesion." (citation omitted)).

30 See Faber v. Menard, Inc., 367 F.3d 1048, 1053 (8th Cir. 2004) ("Faber did not have the ability to negotiate and change particular terms in the form contract. Mere inequality in bargaining power does not make the contract automatically unconscionable, however.... This disparity of bargaining power nevertheless calls for careful scrutiny of the substance of the contract."); Storie v. Household Int'l, Inc., 2005 WL 3728718 (D. Mass. Sept. 22, 2005) ("Under Massachusetts law, even if an agreement is a contract of adhesion, it is not necessarily unconscionable.").

31 Circuit City Stores, Inc. v. Adams, 279 F.3d 889, 893 (9th Cir. 2002); see also Dunham v. Envtl. Chem. Corp., 2006 WL 2374703 (N.D. Cal. Aug. 16, 2006) ("[B]ecause the employment agreements were: (1) drafted by [the employer]; (2) standardized contracts; and (3) presented on a take or leave it basis, the Court thus finds that the Arbitration Agreement is a contract of adhesion."); Aral v. Earthlink, Inc., 134 Cal. App. 4th 544, 35 Cal. Rptr. 3d 229 (2005) ("In the present case, the terms of the agreement were presented on a 'take or leave it' basis either through installation of the software or through materials included in the package mailed with the software with no opportunity to opt out. This is quintessential procedural unconscionability.").

32 Veal v. Orkin Exterminating Co., 2001 U.S. Dist. LEXIS 4846, at *7 (W.D. Mich. Apr. 9, 2001); see also Cooper v. MRM Inv. Co., 367 F.3d 493, 500 (6th Cir. 2004) ("A contract is not adhesive merely because it is a standardized form offered on a take-it-or-leave-it basis.... Tennessee courts decline to find arbitration provisions adhesive where the consumer fails to prove that refusal to sign would cause some detriment other than not being able to buy from the particular merchant (such as not being able to obtain the goods or services elsewhere)."); Fid. Nat'l Corp. v. Blakely, 305 F. Supp. 2d 639, 644 (S.D. Miss. 2003); Montrosse v. Conseco Fin. Servicing Corp., 2000 U.S. Dist. LEXIS 20792 (S.D. W. Va. Dec. 20, 2000) ("An adhesion contract is generally defined as one 'drafted unilaterally by a business enterprise and forced upon an unwilling and often unknowing public for services that cannot readily be obtained elsewhere.'"); Hottel v. BDO Seidman, L.L.P., 846 A.2d 862 (Conn. 2004) (contract not adhesive when "[T]he plaintiff does not claim that the contract language is in any way deceptive, or that the defendants used high pressure tactics in the formation of the contract."); Lovey v. Regence Blueshield of Idaho, 72 P.3d 877, 883 (Idaho 2003).

33 Aguillard v. Auction Mgmt. Corp., 908 So. 2d 1 (La. 2005).

34 Roddie v. N. Am. Manufactured Homes, Inc., 851 N.E.2d 1281 (Ind. Ct. App. 2006).

35 State ex rel. Vincent v. Schneider, 194 S.W.3d 853 (Mo. 2006).

36 Circuit City Stores, Inc. v. Adams, 279 F.3d 889, 893 (9th Cir. 2002); see also Siordia v. Circuit City Stores, Inc., 2005 WL 1368083 (9th Cir. June 9, 2005) (employment contract is procedurally unconscionable under California law because it is a contract of adhesion); ACORN v. Household Int'l, 211 F. Supp. 2d 1160, 1168 (N.D. Cal. 2002); Mercuro v. Super. Ct., 96 Cal. App. 4th 167, 116 Cal. Rptr. 2d 671 (2002) ("Procedural unconscionability turns on adhesiveness—a set of circumstances in which the weaker or 'adhering' party is presented a contract drafted by the stronger party on a take it or leave it basis."); Flores v. Transamerica Homefirst, Inc., 93 Cal. App. 4th 846, 113 Cal. Rptr. 2d 376 (2001) ("A finding of a contract of adhesion is essentially a finding of procedural unconscionability.").

37 Banc One Acceptance Corp. v. Hill, 367 F.3d 426, 431 (5th Cir. 2004) (finding procedural unconscionability under Mississippi law based on the "relative position of the parties, the nature of

It is sufficient to note that the arbitration agreement is in a consumer contract of adhesion where Delta, as a financial institution, possessed superior bargaining power and was the more sophisticated party in the transaction. . . . Although that level of procedural unconscionable does not, by itself, render the arbitration unenforceable, it must be taken into account as we turn to the "public interests affected by the contract."[38]

In a number of jurisdictions, however, it is not enough to establish procedural unconscionability to show that a contract is adhesive.[39] While this factor may not be enough on its own, however, it is still often seen by courts as being sufficient for the court to view the substantive terms of a contract between a corporation and a consumer with "considerable skepticism."[40]

The Ohio Supreme Court finds that an arbitration provision in a standard form consumer credit agreement "engenders more reservations" than arbitration agreements found in collective bargaining agreements, brokerage account agreements, or in commercial settings. While most such agreements come with a presumption in favor of their enforcement, the adhesive nature of the consumer credit agreement substantially weakens this presumption.[41] Other courts also find that when the arbitration clause is found in a standard form adhesion contract to which the consumer has no power to negotiate terms, a careful examination of the actual terms of the arbitration agreement is required.[42] A number of courts have looked at the "take-it-or-leave-it" prong with a practical eye, and have rejected formalistic defense arguments that did not recognize the true nature of this sort of situation.[43] Some courts have even found that it is a factor in procedural unconscionability if one party is not represented by counsel.[44]

Consumer lawyers may be wise to *prove*—not merely allege—this point to avoid the risk that a court will refuse to assume that a standard form contract is a contract of adhesion.[45] In many instances, defendants will agree to stipulate

---

the contract at issue, and the appearance and placement of the arbitration clause"); Alexander v. Anthony Int'l, Ltd. P'ship, 341 F.3d 256, 265 (3d Cir. 2003) (procedural unconscionability "is generally satisfied if the agreement constitutes a contract of adhesion"); D.R. Horton, Inc. v. Green, 96 P.3d 1159 (Nev. 2004) ("A clause is procedurally unconscionable when a party lacks a meaningful opportunity to agree to the clause terms . . . because of unequal bargaining power, as in an adhesion contract. . . ."). *But see* Lovey v. Regence Blueshield of Idaho, 72 P.3d 877, 883 (Idaho 2003) ("[A]n adhesion contract cannot be held procedurally unconscionable simply because there was no bargaining over the terms.").

38 Delta Funding Corp. v. Harris, 912 A.2d 104 (N.J. 2006) (citations omitted).
39 Bawer v. Chase Bank, USA, 2007 WL 1072133 (D. Or. Jan. 23, 2007) (contract is not procedurally unconscionable merely because it is a contract of adhesion).
40 Simpson v. MSA of Myrtle Beach, Inc., 2006 WL 4388016 (S.C. Mar. 26, 2007).
41 Williams v. Aetna Fin. Co., 83 Ohio St. 3d 464, 700 N.E.2d 859 (1998).

In Wisconsin Auto Title Loans, Inc. v. Jones, 714 N.W.2d 155, 159–160 (Wis. 2006), the court found procedural unconscionability based on the following factors: "Wisconsin Auto . . . was in the business of providing loans[;] . . . was experienced in drafting such loan agreements; . . . was in a position of substantially greater bargaining power . . .; the borrower was indigent and in need of cash; and the loan agreement was an adhesion contract presented to the borrower on a take-it-or-leave-it basis.").

In Schwartz v. Alltel Corp., 2006 WL 2243649 (Ohio Ct. App. June 29, 2006), similarly, the court stated:

Primarily we note the inherent disparity of the bargaining position of Schwartz and Alltel. Schwartz, a consumer, contracted with Alltel, a multi-billion dollar corporation, for the purchase of a cellular telephone and service. Though we are unaware of how often Schwartz engaged in contracts of this nature, it is clear that for Alltel, this was a common occurrence. Additionally, when Schwartz expressed interest in the advertised deal, an Alltel employee presented him with Alltel's pre-printed form.

42 *See* Powertel, Inc. v. Bexley, 743 So. 2d 570 (Fla. Dist. Ct. App. 1999); Sosa v. Paulos, 924 P.2d 357, 362 (Utah 1996).
43 *E.g.*, Bragg v. Linden Research, Inc., 2007 WL 1549013 (E.D. Pa. May 30, 2007) (arbitration clause in take-or-leave-it contract is procedurally unconscionable even though the plaintiff was an experienced attorney, because he never had an opportunity to use his lawyering skills to affect the adhesion contract); Cooper v. QC Fin. Services, Inc., 2007 WL 974100 (D. Ariz. Mar. 30, 2007) (it does not change the adhesive nature of a contract that an employer gave an more time to consider whether or not to sign the contract, because the additional time did not alter the take-it-or-leave-it basis of contract).
44 Taylor Bldg. Corp. of Am. v. Benfield, 860 N.E.2d 1058 (Ohio Ct. App.), *appeal allowed*, 859 N.E.2d 556 (Ohio 2006). *But see* Ball v. Ohio State Home Services, Inc., 861 N.E.2d 553 (Ohio Ct. App. 2006) (lack of counsel is not dispositive).
45 *See, e.g.*, Griffen v. Alpha Phi Alpha, Inc., 2007 WL 707364 (E.D. Pa. Mar. 2, 2007) (no evidence in the record that plaintiff attempted to negotiate the terms of the contract); Thompson v. THI of N.M. at Casa Arena Blanca, 2006 WL 4061187 (D.N.M. Sept. 12, 2006) (nursing home arbitration clause not procedurally unconscionable when plaintiff did not attempt to prove that he had attempted to negotiate out of the arbitration clause); Watts v. Pac. Window Products, Inc., 2007 WL 987872 (Cal. Ct. App. Apr. 4, 2007) (contract not adhesive because there is no evidence that the plaintiffs tried to negotiate arbitration clause out of the contract); Gainesville Health Care Ctr., Inc. v. Weston, 857 So. 2d 278, 285 (Fla. Dist. Ct. App. 2003) (finding preprinted nursing home admission clause not procedurally unconscionable due to lack of evidence that it was non-negotiable); Sikes v. Ganley Pontiac Honda, Inc., 2004 WL 67224 (Ohio Ct. App. Jan. 15, 2004) ("Here, there is no evidence in the record that the purchase agreement, including the arbitration clause, was presented to Sikes on a 'take-it-or-leave-it' basis."); *see also* Lopez v. Ernie Haire Ford, Inc., 2007 WL 486616 (Fla. Dist. Ct. App. Feb. 16, 2007) (no procedural unconscionability when plaintiffs negotiated changes to the agreement and thus demonstrably did not lack negotiating power); Orkin Exterminating Co. v. Petsch, 872 So. 2d 259 (Fla. Dist. Ct. App. 2004) (arbitration clause not procedurally unconscionable when consumer offered no evidence that "he was forced to take the

that a given contract was not negotiable—it is, in fact, generally true in consumer contracts, and many companies do not want to go through discovery to prove something that they cannot seriously deny. If a defendant will not stipulate to this fact, however, a consumer attorney must establish through a request for admission, an interrogatory, or by deposition that the company does not allow and has never allowed a consumer to reject or rewrite the arbitration clause. Even when an arbitration clause is not ostensibly proffered on a take-it-or-leave-it basis, alert courts may still recognize it as such from its context. A good example comes from a recent Ohio case:

> The arbitration clause does contain a sentence that provides that admission is not conditioned on agreement to the clause. However, the same clause states that any "controversy, dispute, disagreement or claim," of a resident "shall be settled exclusively by binding arbitration." Further, and most important, the bold print directly above the signature lines states that[,] by signing the agreement, the parties agree to arbitrate their disputes and that the parties agree to the terms of the agreement "in consideration of the facility's acceptance of and rendering services to the resident." The residents or their representatives are provided no means by which they may reject the arbitration clause. Accordingly, we believe that the resident or representative is, by signing the agreement that is required for admission, for all practical purposes being required to agree to the arbitration clause.[46]

6.4.2 Surprise As a Factor in Procedural Unconscionability

Another factor considered by many courts in evaluating whether a given contract provision is procedurally unconscionable is whether the party challenging the term was likely to be (and was in fact) surprised to learn of the term. Accordingly, a number of courts have noted that the lack of conspicuousness of the arbitration provision itself can contribute to procedural unconscionability.[47] Courts note that in automotive sales and lease transactions it is also typical for dealers to hurry consumers through the paperwork process, offering no opportunity to read the documents, and sometimes not even providing copies of the paperwork at the time of signing.[48]

A Missouri federal court, for example, has found procedural unconscionability in a case in which a lender "presented the Arbitration Rider to the Plaintiffs in circumstances that discouraged careful consideration and critical thinking, and [where the lender] rushed the Plaintiffs through the process of signing the documents."[49] Courts have also found procedural unconscionability in cases in which consumers were buried in a blizzard of paper. One California court recently commented on such a situation:

> As for the surprise component, the [documents containing the contract] are 70 pages long and the arbitration clause appears on pages 67 to 68. The arbitration clause was decidedly well buried in a heap of paper. To top it off, at the same time that the purchasers received copies of the [documents] they most likely received a thick stack of additional documents. . . . In short, it is unlikely the arbitration clause popped right out to the purchasers' attention. . . .[50]

In Texas, however, such pressure is not sufficient to establish procedural unconscionability.[51] Texas courts seem to require

---

contract with Orkin on a 'take it or leave it basis' "); Wilson v. Mike Steven Motors, Inc., 111 P.3d 1076 (Kan. Ct. App. 2005) (table) (text available at 2005 WL 1277948) (consumer failed to prove that a contract was adhesive; "While automobile dealers may routinely use the form provided by their trade associations, the record does not reflect that Dealer would have missed the sale if [the consumer] had balked at signing the separate arbitration agreement.").

46 Small v. HCF of Perrysburg, Inc., 159 Ohio App. 3d 66, 823 N.E.2d 19 (2004).

47 See Banc One Acceptance Corp. v. Hill, 367 F.3d 426, 431 (5th Cir. 2004) (addressing "placement of the arbitration clause relative to the rest of the contract," in finding procedural unconscionability); Powertel, Inc. v. Bexley, 743 So. 2d 570 (Fla. Dist. Ct. App. 1999) (arbitration clause inserted in among various bill stuffers); D.R. Horton, Inc. v. Green, 96 P.3d 1159 (Nev. 2004); see also Net Global Mktg., Inc. v. Dialtone, Inc., 217 Fed. Appx. 598 (9th Cir. 2007) (the fact that the clause was adhesive and hidden was sufficient to meet California's test for surprise); Bragg v. Linden Research, Inc., 2007 WL 1549013 (E.D. Pa. May 30, 2007) (arbitration clause procedurally unconscionable, in part, when it was "buried . . . in a lengthy paragraph under the benign heading 'GENERAL PROVISIONS' "); Geoffrey v. Wash. Mut. Bank, 484 F. Supp. 2d 1115 (S.D. Cal. 2007) (procedural unconscionability found (in part) with clause embedded in small font dense print, on a signature card of a sort that does not usually contain substantive contract terms); Bradberry v. T-Mobile USA, Inc., 2007 WL 1241936 (N.D. Cal. Apr. 27, 2007) (class action ban procedurally unconscionable when it was not mentioned in documents given to consumer when he bought cell phone service, and only appeared in terms and conditions fine print brochure referenced in sales documents); Janda v. T-Mobile USA, Inc., 2006 WL 708936 (N.D. Cal. Mar. 17, 2006) (surprise present when arbitration clause appeared in fine print on page 49 of the 60-page contract); Sosa v. Paulos, 924 P.2d 357, 362 (Utah 1996).

48 See Lozada v. Dale Baker Oldsmobile, Inc., 91 F Supp. 2d 1087 (W.D. Mich. 2000).

49 Sprague v. Household Int'l, 473 F. Supp. 2d 966 (W.D. Mo. 2005).

50 Villa Milano Homeowners Ass'n v. Il Davorge, 84 Cal. App. 4th 819, 829, 102 Cal. Rptr. 2d 1 (2000); see also Sutton's Steel & Supply, Inc. v. Bellsouth Mobility, Inc., 776 So. 2d 589 (La. Ct. App. 2000) ("[T]he clause is on Bell South's standard form and is in exceedingly small print. Furthermore, Bell South presented no evidence to show that the plaintiffs were even in a position to bargain over the arbitration provisions in question.").

51 Fleetwood Enterprises, Inc. v. Gaskamp, 280 F.3d 1069 (5th Cir.

evidence of actual surprise, such as when an employer imposes an arbitration clause *after* suit has been filed, in order to find procedural unconscionability.[52]

The issue of surprise is inherently a fact specific one, and consumer lawyers would be well advised to build as full a factual record as possible about the manner in which an arbitration clause was communicated to their clients. First, when applicable, consumer attorneys should produce testimony from their clients demonstrating that they did not know that they were waiving their constitutional rights. In addition, when applicable, consumer attorneys should produce testimony from their clients or other witnesses about any factors that reduced the likelihood that the consumers would read or understand the arbitration clause, for example, that they were rushed through signing at a closing or that they were urged by a salesperson not to bother going through all the fine print.

Some courts, at least, will be less sympathetic to such arguments when they are advanced by well-heeled persons. In one recent case, for example, a federal court made this point strongly:

> Plaintiffs claim they were rushed into signing the agreements and were refused a fair opportunity to read the agreements.... Plaintiffs argue that they were never given a copy of the agreement and that arbitration was never mentioned or explained.... This argument is not well-taken. Plaintiffs were loan officers earning over $100,000 per year.[53]

In addition, consumer attorneys in significant cases would be well advised to build a factual record establishing that the consumer's failure to read a given arbitration clause was reasonable under the circumstances of a case. If the clause is densely written in "legalese," for example, a consumer attorney might consider retaining a "readability" expert to run some tests to determine if the clause is likely to be comprehensible to people with the level of education of a given consumer.[54] In other cases, marketing experts might review communications relating to an arbitration clause and point out any serious problems which would be likely to greatly reduce consumer awareness of the arbitration clause. In some instances, a company's own records may establish that a company drafted a communication about an arbitration clause with the express goal of ensuring that many consumers would not understand it. In *Ting v. AT & T*, for example, a federal court essentially found that the defendant had not wanted its customers to notice the arbitration clause:

> AT & T was concerned that if its customers focused on the Legal Remedies Provisions, they might become concerned, less likely to perceive detariffing as a non-event and possibly defect. As a high ranking member on the detariffing team stated: "I don't want them to tell customers that now individual contracts need to be established with customers and pay attention to the details [sic]." (Pls.' Ex. 132-1.) While presenting the CSA as a non-event may have helped AT & T retain its customers, it also made customers less alert to the fact that they were being asked to give up important legal rights and remedies.[55]

Similarly, some companies do in-house studies to determine how many of their customers read information that is mailed to them in various forms, and those studies may provide very important information to consumers resisting arbitration clauses on the grounds that they are procedurally unconscionable. In the *Ting* case, for example, the court placed great weight on such studies: "AT & T's own research found that only 30% of its customers would actually read the entire [customer service agreement containing the arbitration clause] and 10% of its customers would not read it at all. AT & T's research also found that 1/4 of the class would not open the separate mailing."[56] In significant cases, such as large class actions, parties may even consider hiring pollsters to commission surveys of consumers. In the *Ting* case, for example, the plaintiffs hired a well-known polling firm who conducted a survey that "concluded that

---

2002) ("[A]llegations of misrepresentations and pressure to sign the documents quickly... are insufficient to establish unconscionability. And while there may be imbalance in the relative sophistication of the parties, this imbalance is insufficient on its own to render the agreement unconscionable. The only cases under Texas law in which an agreement was found procedurally unconscionable involve situations in which one of the parties appears to have been incapable of understanding the agreement." (citation omitted)).

52 *See* Wilcox v. Valero Ref. Co., 256 F. Supp. 2d 687, 691, 692 (S.D. Tex. 2003).

53 Cook v. All State Home Mortgage, Inc., 2006 WL 2252538 (N.D. Ohio Aug. 7, 2006); *see also* Nissan World L.L.C. v. Mkt. Scan Info. Sys., Inc., 2007 WL 1657350 (D.N.J. June 5, 2007) (no procedural unconscionability when plaintiffs own ten multi-million dollar car dealerships and are very sophisticated); *In re* Olympus Healthcare Group, Inc., 2006 WL 28547900 (Bankr. D. Del. Oct. 6, 2006) (rejecting unconscionability challenge when complaining party: "[W]as a sophisticated business entity, operating several large medical and rehabilitative health facilities in Connecticut and Massachusetts, and employing as many as 1600 persons. It undoubtedly had access to legal counsel to assist with drafting and negotiating the form of the Program Agreement, as well as understanding its terms and conditions."); Villar v. Mut. Prot. Trust, 2007 WL 1519788 (Cal. Ct. App. May 25, 2007) (agreement not procedurally unconscionable, when plaintiff was a sophisticated doctor with actual knowledge of clearly set forth arbitration provision).

54 *Cf.* Geiger v. Ryan's Family Steak Houses, Inc., 134 F. Supp. 2d 985, 999 (S.D. Ind. 2001) ("We have major doubts that a typical high school graduate would be able to read the multiple documents provided to her at her interview, comprehend the Arbitration Agreement and the [arbitration firm's] Rules well enough to formulate questions as to their substance, and ask those questions during that interview.").

55 Ting v. AT & T, 182 F. Supp. 2d 902, 911, 912 (N.D. Cal. 2002), *aff'd with respect to unconscionability*, 319 F.3d 1126 (9th Cir. 2003).

56 *Id.*, 182 F. Supp. 2d at 930.

the vast majority of class members had either not opened or not read" the defendant's consumer service agreement containing the arbitration clause.[57] While the court did not accept the conclusions of this survey in their entirety, it "could not ignore the clear trend of these answers, which indicate that people are unlikely to read solicitations received in the mail, even if from AT & T. Nor could I ignore their consistency with the results of AT & T's research."[58]

Some courts have also noted that consumers cannot realistically be handed five print contracts that refer to other documents, and then be expected to go research the details of those other documents:

> Here is the oppression: The inability to receive full relief is artfully hidden by merely referencing the Better Business Bureau rules, and not attaching those rules to the contract for the customer to sign. The customer is forced to go to another source to find out the full import of what he or she is about to sign—and must go to that effort prior to signing.[59]

Similar facts gave rise to a finding of procedural unconscionability in a Florida case:

> [T]he organization of the contract provisions; the exceptionally small size of the type of the provision alerting the customer to the terms on the back of the agreement; the lack of initials on the back page of the agreement; and the customary practice of employees in *not* calling attention to the provisions on the back of the form all provide evidence that Motor cars actively discouraged and/or prevented the purchaser from knowing and understanding the disputed contract terms.[60]

In *Higgins v. Superior Court*,[61] five orphaned siblings sued home owners, who had originally taken them in after their parents died, then later expelled them after the home had been completely rebuilt to accommodate the siblings as part of a home renovation reality television show. The siblings sued the television network and producers of the show as well, who responded by filing a motion to compel arbitration pursuant to a clause in a release agreement executed by the siblings. The court found that the agreement was procedurally unconscionable when it was a standardized twenty-four-page, single-spaced, take-it-or-leave-it contract that was drafted by defendants who had far superior bargaining power and when the undistinguishable arbitration clause was buried in the "miscellaneous" section of the contract. The court noted: "There is nothing in the Agreement that brings the reader's attention to the arbitration provision[,] . . . initialing is not required for the arbitration provision."[62] In addition, the court found that the eldest sibling, upon signing the agreement at the behest of the caretaker home owners, "did not understand" the "complex legal terms" contained in the document, nor did he "know what an arbitration agreement was[,] . . . its significance or the legal consequences that could flow from signing it."[63] Finally, "[the siblings] were given only five to ten minutes before [the home owners] asked [them] to sign the Agreement."[64]

In another recent case, a federal court held that an arbitration clause was adopted in a procedurally unconscionable manner when, among other things, it was communicated to employees primarily through e-mail.[65]

Similarly, an Ohio Court of Appeals recently detected procedural unconscionability when an arbitration clause was communicated in an unenlightening manner:

> The form itself contained small, hard-to-read print and contained margin-to-margin boilerplate, contractual language. As stated above, Alltel placed the arbitration provision at the very bottom of the back side of the agreement, without calling any attention to the provision.[66]

Nonetheless, a number of courts have also held that the mere fact that an arbitration clause was included in fine print is not enough to render it procedurally unconscionable.[67]

---

57 *Id.* at 912.
58 *Id.*
59 Harper v. Ultimo, 7 Cal. Rptr. 3d 418, 422 (Ct. App. 2003); *see also* Eagle v. Fred Martin Motor Co., 809 N.E.2d 1161, 1178 (Ohio Ct. App. 2004) (arbitration clause procedurally unconscionable, in part, because the clause "was on a preprinted form and did not contain specific details concerning the arbitration process. . . . [T]he clause in this case merely makes a reference to the NAF Code of Procedure and a website and address.").
60 Palm Beach Motor Cars Ltd., Inc. v. Jeffries, 885 So. 2d 990 (Fla. Dist. Ct. App. 2004); *see also* Cooper v. QC Fin. Services, Inc., 2007 WL 974100 (D. Ariz. Mar. 30, 2007) (one factor in finding procedural unconscionability was that "No explanation of the arbitration provision was provided to Plaintiff.").
61 45 Cal. Rptr. 3d 293 (Cal. Ct. App. 2006).
62 *Id.* at 297.
63 *Id.* at 298.
64 *Id.* at 299.
65 Skirchak v. Dynamics Research Corp., Inc., 432 F. Supp. 2d 175, 180 (D. Mass. 2006) ("DRC's use of email as the primary means to inform employees about the implementation of such a drastic change in policies governing the disposition of employee grievances created significant notice problems such that the plaintiffs cannot be held to have knowingly agreed to waive their right to pursue class actions.").
66 Schwartz v. Alltel Corp., 2006 WL 2243649 (Ohio Ct. App. June 29, 2006).
67 *See, e.g.*, Harris v. Green Tree Fin. Corp, 183 F.3d 173 (3d Cir. 1999); Mason v. Praxair, Inc., 2006 WL 2385360 (W.D. Ky. Aug. 16, 2006) (not unconscionable for an employer to falsely tell a prospective employee that an arbitration clause did not apply to her when the written contract itself provided that verbal statements were not binding on terms of the contract); Smart v. Bob Wilson Dodge Inc., 2006 WL 1037113, at *2–*3 (M.D. Fla. Apr. 19, 2006) (finding that an arbitration provision within a motor vehicle retail sales order is not procedurally unconscionable when "[t]he arbitration provision at issue is located directly above the Plaintiff's signature, under a bold, capitalized

§ 6.4.2

Furthermore, courts may be less sympathetic to a consumer who has ample opportunity to read an agreement but who later complains that he or she was surprised that an arbitration provision was in the agreement.[68] But, even then, courts will give special consideration to the important nature of the

---

heading entitled 'ACKNOWLEDGMENTS,' " and is written "in the same sized print as the majority of other provisions . . . in unambiguous language"); Lawrence v. Household Bank (SB), 397 F. Supp. 2d 1332, 1335–1336 (M.D. Ala. 2005) (finding an arbitration clause in a credit card agreement was not unconscionable under Nevada law when: (1) the arbitration clause is "included in the main body of the document," (2) "the word 'ARBITRATION' is written in bold, capital letters, (3) "the end of the arbitration clause explicitly states, in bold, capital letters that the parties will not have the right to litigate claims before a judge or jury, (4) the defendant Bank made no representations downplaying the significance of the arbitration clause, and (5) the arbitration clause did not contain "a hefty penalty provision for failing to arbitrate, nor did [it] require each party to pay equally for the cost of arbitration"); "the evidence in the record does not establish procedural unconscionability with regard to the arbitration agreements," when "[t]he plaintiff set forth no evidence regarding her education, financial status, access to legal counsel, or the availability of other banks or lending institutions."); First Fid. Nat'l Corp. v. Blakely, 305 F. Supp. 2d 639, 643 (S.D. Miss. 2003); *see also* Lowden v. T-Mobile, USA, Inc., 2006 WL 1009279, at *4–*5 (W.D. Wash. Apr. 13, 2006) (finding an arbitration agreement in a cell phone service contract not procedurally unconscionable, "despite the adhesive nature of these agreements"); New S. Fed. Sav. Bank v. Anding, 414 F. Supp. 2d 636 (S.D. Miss. 2005) ("The [consumers] admit, however, that they did not lack the ability to read and/or understand the agreement. They do not accuse [the bank] of preventing them from carefully reading the agreement."); Storie v. Household Int'l, Inc., 2005 WL 3728718 (D. Mass. Sept. 22, 2005) ("The facts as alleged do not show that the Arbitration Rider was riddled with improprieties in its formation, was hidden or obscured in a prolix form, or that it otherwise had the potential for unfair surprise. Nor do the plaintiffs allege that they had insufficient time to consider the agreement or any other procedural deficiency."). *But see* Stone v. Memberworks, 2003 WL 21246771 (Cal. Ct. App. May 30, 2003) (surprise established by small font and lack of emphasis on arbitration clause); Sutton's Steel & Supply, Inc. v. Bellsouth Mobility, Inc., 776 So. 2d 589 (La. Ct. App. 2000) (arbitration clause in standard form with very small print unenforceable when company showed no evidence that plaintiffs were able to bargain over the provision).

68 *See* Cooper v. MRM Inv. Co., 367 F.3d 493, 504 (6th Cir. 2004) (rejecting procedural unconscionability argument when party failed to demonstrate lack of opportunity to understand contract terms); Wash. Mut. Fin. Group, L.L.C. v. Bailey, 364 F.3d 260, 265 (5th Cir. 2004) (party has obligation to read or have contract read to him); Hill v. Gateway 2000, Inc., 105 F.3d 1147 (7th Cir. 1997) (enforcing binding arbitration provision against consumers who purchased a computer by telephone when consumers had thirty days to read and reject the terms of the company's agreement by returning the computer); Davidson v. Cingular Wireless, L.L.C., 2007 WL 896349 (E.D. Ark. Mar. 23, 2007) (no surprise when arbitration clause is in print the same size as the rest of the contract; plaintiff had time to consider the arbitration provision; and plaintiff agreed to two more arbitration clauses since filing suit); Kisner v. Bud's Mobile Homes, 2007 WL 686734 (S.D. Miss. Mar. 3, 2007) ("There is no evidence of disparity in sophistication and/or bargaining power, and it is clear to the Court that the arbitration provision signed by the plaintiffs was easily readable and understandable."); *In re* Olympus Healthcare Group, Inc., 2006 WL 28547900 (Bankr. D. Del. Oct. 6, 2006) (no procedural unconscionability when: "[The arbitration agreement] appears in the same type face and font as all other terms and provisions of the Agreement. It is not concealed or printed in small print or on the reverse side of the contract."); Murphy v. Courtesy Ford, 944 So. 2d 1131 (Fla. Dist. Ct. App. 2006) (arbitration clause not procedurally unconscionable when it was signed by the buyer, was in the same typeface as other provisions of the agreement, and thee was no indication that the dealership actively discouraged or prevented the buyer from knowing and understanding the arbitration clause); Covenant Health Rehab. of Picayune v. Brown, 949 So. 2d 732 (Miss. 2007) (because arbitration provision was under a boldface title in print the same size as the rest of the contract, it was not procedurally unconscionable); Motsinger v. Lithia Rose-FT, Inc., 156 P.3d 156, 167 (Or. Ct. App. 2007) (no procedural unconscionability when there was no deception, and when plaintiff had plenty of time to review the contract); *see also In re* Universal Serv. Fund Tel. Billing Practices Litig., 300 F. Supp. 2d 1107, 1126 (D. Kan. 2003); Stout v. J.D. Byrider, 50 F. Supp. 2d 733 (N.D. Ohio 1999), *aff'd*, 228 F.3d 709 (6th Cir. 2000); Zawikowski v. Beneficial Nat'l Bank, 1999 U.S. Dist. LEXIS 514 (N.D. Ill. Jan. 7, 1999); Golenia v. Bob Baker Toyota, 915 F. Supp. 201 (S.D. Cal. 1996) (arbitration provision enforced against employee when he failed to read employment agreement); Sloan v. McQueen, 2006 WL 2383256 (Ala. Aug. 18, 2006) (defendant's failure to discuss, disclose, or explain an arbitration clause was not grounds for finding that it was unconscionable or fraudulent); Green Tree Fin. Corp. v. Vintson, 753 So. 2d 497 (Ala. 1999) (when contract conspicuously referred to arbitration provisions within the agreement, consumers could have read the provisions and cannot argue that they had not agreed to it); Rosenthal v. Great W. Fin. Sec. Corp., 14 Cal. 4th 394, 58 Cal. Rptr. 2d 875, 926 P.2d 1061 (1996) (unreasonable reliance on another's misrepresentation caused by failure to read a written agreement before signing it is an insufficient basis for avoiding arbitration); Crippen v. Cent. Valley RV Outlet, Inc., 124 Cal. App. 4th 1159, 22 Cal. Rptr. 3d 189 (2004) ("Nor does the form of the document itself show procedural unconscionability. The arbitration Addendum was not set in small type or hidden in a prolix form. It was printed on a separate page, in ordinary type, with 'Arbitration Addendum' at the top, and was signed separately by plaintiff."); Fonte v. AT & T Wireless Services, Inc., 903 So. 2d 1019 (Fla. Dist. Ct. App. 2005) ("although the arbitration clause was somewhat buried, page 38 of a 40-page booklet, Fonte received ample notice to review the Terms and Conditions of her Service Agreement with AT & T"); Gainesville Health Care Ctr., Inc. v. Weston, 857 So. 2d 278, 285, 286 (Fla. Dist. Ct. App. 2003); Lovey v. Regence Blueshield of Idaho, 72 P.3d 877, 884 (Idaho 2003); Hutcherson v. Sears Roebuck & Co., 793 N.E.2d 886, 892, 893 (Ill. App. Ct. 2003); Lear v. Rusk Indus., Inc., 2002 WL 31716383 (Ohio Ct. App. Dec. 4, 2002) (plaintiffs did not take advantage of a three-day rescission period and therefore have no plausible argument that agreement was procedurally unconscionable); Haga v. Martin Homes, Inc., 2000 Ohio App. LEXIS 3576 (Ohio Ct. App. Aug. 4, 2000) (finding contract to be conscionable when consumers "were given ample opportunity to read, question and review the purchase agreement," and consumers "remember seeing the arbitration provision in bold face"); EZ Pawn Corp. v. Mancias, 934 S.W.2d 87 (Tex. 1996) (it is presumed that a party who has an opportunity to read an arbitration agreement, and then signs it, knows its contents).

rights being waived and whether their waiver is within the consumer's normal expectations.[69] As the Nevada Supreme Court found in finding an arbitration clause in a home-purchase contract procedurally unconscionable, "even if any home purchasers noticed and read the arbitration provision, . . . they would not be put on the notice that they were agreeing to forgo important rights under state law."[70] An Ohio court of appeals similarly has held that "[f]or even had [the consumer] read the arbitration clause thoroughly, nothing on the face of the clause could have put her on notice of excessive, prohibitive costs associated with the arbitration."[71]

The ability of a consumer to read English is also sometimes a factor in proving the surprise element of procedural unconscionability. In *Prevot v. Phillips Petroleum Co.*, for example, the court found:

> In this case, the Plaintiffs were illiterate in that they did not speak and hence could not read English. The contracts they signed were in English. They were not given a translation of the agreements and testified that they were pressured into signing them. Under the circumstances, the Court concludes that the arbitration agreements are procedurally unconscionable.[72]

Courts will also consider the consumer's ability to understand the disputed contract terms.[73] Some courts look to other facts that render persons vulnerable, even when they do speak English: "When Mrs. Small signed the agreement, she was under a great deal of stress. The agreement was not explained to her; she did not have an attorney present. Mrs. Small did not have any particularized legal expertise, and was 69 years old on the date the agreement was signed."[74]

The issue of what weight to place upon the sophistication of the consumer is one that divides different states, however. One Texas appellate court held that an arbitration agreement was procedurally unconscionable as applied to a functionally illiterate man,[75] but the Alabama Supreme Court has held that a consumer "cannot avoid enforcement of [an] arbitration provision merely on the basis that he could not read what he was signing."[76] Similarly, the Fifth Circuit, applying Mississippi law, found that illiterate borrowers could not demonstrate procedural unconscionability when they failed to have the lender's agent read the arbitration clause to them.[77]

6.4.3 Meaningful Choice As a Factor

Another issue often considered in determining whether a contract is procedurally unconscionable is whether a consumer could have obtained the good or service from some other business without having to agree to the objectionable term. In some cases, courts have held that contracts are enforceable when the plaintiff could have obtained the good or service without agreeing to the term.[78] Some courts have

---

69 *See* Ingle v. Circuit City Stores, Inc., 328 F.3d 1165 (9th Cir. 2003) (fact that employee had three days in which to consider the terms of the arbitration agreement was irrelevant to the question of procedural unconscionability when one party had greater bargaining power and contract was non-negotiable); Nelson v. Cyprus Bagdad Copper Corp., 119 F.3d 756 (9th Cir. 1997) (employment discrimination case in which arbitration agreement found in employee rights handbook); Garrett v. Hooters-Toledo, 295 F. Supp. 2d 774, 784 (N.D. Ohio 2003); *In re* Knepp, 229 B.R. 821 (Bankr. N.D. Ala. 1999); Badie v. Bank of Am., 67 Cal. App. 4th 779, 79 Cal. Rptr. 2d 273 (1998); D.R. Horton, Inc. v. Green, 96 P.3d 1159 (Nev. 2004); *cf.* Circuit City Stores, Inc. v. Najd, 294 F.3d 1104 (9th Cir. 2002) (when Circuit City employee was given thirty days in which to opt out of the arbitration agreement, agreement was not procedurally unconscionable); Circuit City Stores, Inc. v. Ahmed, 283 F.3d 1198 (9th Cir. 2002) (same).

70 D.R. Horton, Inc. v. Green, 96 P.3d 1159, 1164 (Nev. 2004); *see also* Dunham v. Envtl. Chem. Corp., 2006 WL 2374703 (N.D. Cal. Aug. 16, 2006) (one factor in finding procedural unconscionability is that the rules of the American Arbitration Association themselves were never provided to an employee). *But see* Sikes v. Ganley Pontiac Honda, Inc., 2004 WL 67224 (Ohio Ct. App. Jan. 15, 2004) ("Sikes cites no authority supporting her proposition that the arbitration clause is required to relay all of the above information to be enforceable. To the contrary, courts have consistently held that an arbitration clause does not have to include the specific costs.").

71 Eagle v. Fred Martin Motor Co., 809 N.E.2d 1161, 1178 (Ohio Ct. App. 2004).

72 Prevot v. Phillips Petroleum Co., 133 F. Supp. 2d 937, 940, 941 (S.D. Tex. 2001); *see also* Vasquez-Lopez v. Beneficial Or., Inc., 210 Or. App. 553, 152 P.3d 940 (2007) (arbitration clause was procedurally unconscionable when it was a contract of adhesion and drafted in English (which the plaintiffs did not read and could not understand)).

73 *See* Powertel, Inc. v. Bexley, 743 So. 2d 570 (Fla. Dist. Ct. App. 1999); Sosa v. Paulos, 924 P.2d 357, 362 (Utah 1996).

74 Small v. HCF of Perrysburg, Inc., 159 Ohio App. 3d 66, 823 N.E.2d 19 (2004).

75 *In re* Turner Bros. Trucking Co., 8 S.W.3d 370 (Tex. App. 1999); *see also* Am. Heritage Life Ins. v. Lang, 2002 WL 32074883 (N.D. Miss. July 16, 2002) (refusing to enforce arbitration agreement against illiterate consumer).

76 Johnnie's Homes, Inc. v. Holt, 790 So. 2d 956, 961 (Ala. 2001); *see also* Mitchell Nissan, Inc. v. Foster, 775 So. 2d 138 (Ala. 2000) ("Foster cannot avoid his contractual obligation by now asserting that he could not read the contract or understand it.").

77 Wash. Mut. Fin. Group, L.L.C. v. Bailey, 364 F.3d 260, 265 (5th Cir. 2004).

78 *See, e.g.*, Cooper v. MRM Inv. Co., 367 F.3d 493, 500 (6th Cir. 2004) (Tenn. law); Sherr v. Dell, Inc., 2006 WL 2109436 (S.D.N.Y. July 27, 2006) ("Plaintiff has not met his burden. Under the circumstances, plaintiff could have chosen not to enter into the Agreement with defendant. He could have chosen to buy a computer from another company."); Veal v. Orkin Exterminating Co., 2001 U.S. Dist. LEXIS 4846 (W.D. Mich. Apr. 9, 2001) ("Plaintiffs have presented no evidence that they had no meaningful choice to obtain pest control services elsewhere. Accordingly, it does not appear that this Agreement suffered from procedural unconscionability."); Lovey v. Regence Blueshield of Idaho, 72 P.3d 877, 883 (Idaho 2003); Russell v. Performance Toyota, 826 So. 2d 719, 726 (Miss. 2002) ("[T]here were numerous car dealerships in Tupelo and

even treated this lack of choice as a prerequisite to a finding of unconscionability and refused to find arbitration clauses to be unconscionable unless the plaintiff proves that she could not obtain the good or service from other sources.[79] In one particularly extreme case, a court held that a plaintiff had a meaningful choice not to sign arbitration clause, and therfore that the clause was not procedurally unconscionable, when it was theoretically possible for the man to have driven his elderly and infirm wife to a long-term care facility sixty miles away from their home which would not have required that he sign an oppressive arbitration clause.[80] Numerous other courts have disagreed, however, and have held that a contract can be procedurally unconscionable even when an individual might have received the same good or service from some other source.[81]

Given this backdrop, consumer lawyers should spend time and effort to prove this fact when possible. In *American General Finance, Inc. v. Branch*,[82] the plaintiffs built up a substantial factual record to establish that all but two subprime lenders in the consumer's home city required borrowers to agree to arbitration clauses and, thus, "the market was virtually closed to consumers seeking comparable financing without agreeing to arbitration provisions." This showing helped the plaintiffs win the first ruling ever from the Alabama Supreme Court that an arbitration clause was unconscionable.

It will not always be necessary to prove that nearly all companies in a field have such objectionable clauses, however, and at least one court has found that this element is present when a far smaller percentage of companies have such clauses:

> Here, the class members' lack of a meaningful choice with respect to the Legal Remedies Provisions satisfies the "oppression" prong of procedural unconscionability. Residential long distance carriers who service two-thirds of the California market all provide substantially similar dispute resolution provisions which include mandatory arbitration and limitations on damages. Finding a carrier who did not contain such a provision was not easy.[83]

Numerous other courts have held in consumer and employment cases alike that a party challenging a company's arbitration clause can establish procedural unconscionability by showing that it is difficult to find an alternative supplier or employer that does not also require arbitration.[84] In employment cases, courts have split over whether a take-it-or-leave-it offer, in which an employee is forced to choose between a job and resisting an arbitration clause, is procedurally unconscionable based on lack of *meaningful* choice without regard to whether other jobs are available.[85]

Memphis and Russell was not by any means coerced to do business with Performance Toyota.").

79 *See, e.g.*, Cooper v. MRM Inv. Co., 367 F.3d 493, 500 (6th Cir. 2004) (Tenn. law); McCabe v. Dell, Inc., 2007 WL 1434972 (C.D. Cal. Apr. 12, 2007) (arbitration clause enforceable under Texas law because "Texas law requires a 'lack of alternatives' to be present before a court will deem a contract procedurally unconscionable.... At the time of Plaintiff's purchase, there were competitors offering a very similar product without the imposition of an arbitration provision."); Battle v. Nissan Motor Acceptance Corp., 2007 WL 1095681 (E.D. Wis. Mar. 9, 2007) (no procedural unconscionability, because: "Like any car purchaser, she could have walked out and taken her business elsewhere, both for the car and for the dealer."); Griffen v. Alpha Phi Alpha, Inc., 2007 WL 707364 (E.D. Pa. Mar. 2, 2007) (no procedural unconscionability, in part, because: "The Court cannot say whether [plaintiff] did or did not have the opportunity to join another Fraternity if this provision was unacceptable to him."); Sherr v. Dell, Inc., 2006 WL 2109436 (S.D.N.Y. July 27, 2006) ("Plaintiff has not met his burden. Under the circumstances, plaintiff could have chosen not to enter into the Agreement with defendant. He could have chosen to buy a computer from another company."); Veal v. Orkin Exterminating Co., 2001 U.S. Dist. LEXIS 4846 (W.D. Mich. Apr. 9, 2001) ("Plaintiffs have presented no evidence that they had no meaningful choice to obtain pest control services elsewhere. Accordingly, it does not appear that this Agreement suffered from procedural unconscionability."); Lovey v. Regence Blueshield of Idaho, 72 P.3d 877, 883 (Idaho 2003); Russell v. Performance Toyota, 826 So. 2d 719, 726 (Miss. 2002) ("[T]here were numerous car dealerships in Tupelo and Memphis and Russell was not by any means coerced to do business with Performance Toyota.").

80 Thompson v. THI of N.M. at Casa Arena Blanca, 2006 WL 4061187 (D.N.M. Sept. 12, 2006).

81 *See* Davis v. O'Melveny & Myers, 485 F.3d 1066 (9th Cir. 2007) (rejecting "argument that the availability of other employment can defeat a claim of procedural unconscionability when an employee is faced with a 'take it or leave it' condition of employment"; citing Nagrampa v. MailCoups, Inc., 469 F.3d 1257 (9th Cir. 2006) (en banc)); Geoffrey v. Wash. Mut. Bank, 484 F. Supp. 2d 1115 (S.D. Cal. 2007) (availability in the marketplace of substitute services alone cannot defeat a claim of procedural unconscionability); Hoffman v. Cingular Wireless, L.L.C., 2006 U.S. Dist. LEXIS 79067 (S.D. Cal. Oct. 26, 2006) (the availability of market alternatives does not preclude finding that Cingular's arbitration provision is procedurally unconscio-

nable); Winig v. Cingular Wireless, L.L.C., 2006 WL 2766007 (N.D. Cal. Sept. 27, 2006) (it does not eliminate procedural unconscionability that the consumer could have gotten cell phone service from another company).

82 793 So. 2d 738 (Ala. 2000).

83 Ting v. AT & T, 182 F. Supp. 2d 902, 929 (N.D. Cal. 2002) (footnote omitted); *see* ACORN v. Household Int'l, 211 F. Supp. 2d 1160, 1169 (N.D. Cal. 2002) (finding lack of meaningful choice based on limited credit histories and modest income levels of consumer plaintiffs); Kloss v. Edward D. Jones & Co., 310 Mont. 123, 54 P.3d 1 (Mont. 2002) (finding procedural unconscionability based on lack of meaningful choice in the investment brokerage community).

84 *See, e.g.*, Alexander v. Anthony Int'l, Ltd. P'ship, 341 F.3d 256, 266 (3d Cir. 2003) (noting plaintiffs' "at best, very narrow options for other employment"); Wilcox v. Valero Ref. Co., 256 F. Supp. 2d 687, 691 (S.D. Tex. 2003) (noting employee's "limited alternatives, other than accepting" arbitration clause).

85 *See, e.g.*, Garrett v. Hooters-Toledo, 295 F. Supp. 2d 774, 784 (N.D. Ohio 2003) (finding procedural unconscionability when employer told waitress to sign arbitration clause or else "she

6.5 Substantively Unconscionable Arbitration Provisions

6.5.1 Introduction

This section examines various grounds for finding the terms of the arbitration clause itself to be substantively unconscionable. The section identifies the more prominent grounds. However, courts have identified a remarkable number of other factors in various contexts.[86] Parties will usually not get far, however, with challenges that are based upon differences between arbitration and court that are intrinsic to the less formal nature of arbitration.[87]

While each issue is examined separately, the combination of a number of suspect terms can render a clause unconscionable when a court might not reach the same conclusion based on finding only one suspect term. Moreover, the stronger the case for procedural unconscionability, the more powerful the argument that the terms of the agreement are substantively unconscionable.

6.5.2 Excessive Fees and Costs

6.5.2.1 Demonstrating That the Arbitration Fees Will, in Fact, Be Excessive

The United States Supreme Court held in *Green Tree Financial Corp.-Alabama v. Randolph* that an arbitration clause will not be held to violate the Truth in Lending Act because of the risk of prohibitive fees, when the consumer opposing arbitration failed to establish an adequate evidentiary record demonstrating that the arbitration fees would in fact be prohibitive.[88] Consequently, as a matter of practice, consumers should seek clarification as to their potential liability for arbitration filing fees and the cost of the arbitrator(s). If the arbitration clause specifies an arbitration service provider such as the American Arbitration Association, which has several different sets of rules, which set of rules will apply in this case?[89] What filing fees must a consumer pay to the arbitration service provider (such as the American Arbitration Association or the National Arbitration Forum) to initiate the arbitration? What are the hourly rates for arbitrators used by these arbitration service providers in the geographic area where the case will be arbitrated?[90] How many hours must an arbitrator typically spend

---

could not work another shift"). *But see* Carter v. Countrywide Credit Indus., Inc., 362 F.3d 294, 301 (5th Cir. 2004) ("An employer may make precisely such a take-it-or-leave-it offer to its at-will employees." (citation omitted)).

86 Additional factors cited by some courts as evidence of unconscionability, for example, include arbitration clauses that are unusually broad in scope and application, and arbitration clauses that place excessive limitations upon an individual's right to take discovery. *See* Am. Gen. Fin., Inc. v. Branch, 793 So. 2d 738 (Ala. 2000) (breadth of scope and application); Armendariz v. Found. Health Psychcare Services, Inc., 24 Cal. 4th 83, 99 Cal. Rptr. 2d 745, 6 P.3d 669 (2000) (limits on discovery).

Also, one court has held an arbitration clause to be unconscionable that allowed an employer to unilaterally modify the contract at any time and that barred the employee from proceeding in court with a pending sexual harassment claim against the company. Brennan v. Bally Total Fitness, 198 F. Supp. 2d 377 (S.D.N.Y. 2002). Another court held an arbitration clause to be unconscionable when the plaintiff would be required to pay any and all fees, including those associated with administration costs, attorney fees, and cost of litigation, if the plaintiff avoids or challenges either the "grievance resolution process" or an award therefrom. Covenant Health Rehab. of Picayune v. Brown, 949 So. 2d 732, 739 (Miss. 2007).

In *Olah v. Ganley Chevrolet, Inc.*, 2006 WL 350204 (Ohio Ct. App. Feb. 16, 2006), a court found substantively unconscionable an arbitration clause that says "arbitration procedures are simpler and more limited than rules applicable in court" and "arbitrator decisions are as enforceable as any court order," because these statements were misleading and incomplete. *Id.* at *5. The court held that the initial statement "fail[s] to provide accurate information about the arbitration process, it also fails to describe the type of arbitration forum plaintiffs will be bound to participate in and it fails to clearly explain how arbitration is 'simpler and more limited.'" *Id.* at *4. The court held that the second statement "fails to mention that the burdens are different for each party in the appeal process" and is incomplete insofar as "[a]rbitration decisions are generally subject to a very narrow and strict appeal process." *Id.* at *4–*5. As the court explained, "[o]verturning an arbitration award on appeal is more difficult than an ordinary civil appeal from a judgment in a court of law." *Id.* at *5.

87 *See, e.g.*, Jones v. Titlemax of Ga., Inc., 2006 WL 562189 (N.D. Ga. Mar. 7, 2006) (finding an arbitration provision was not substantively unconscionable by virtue of a rules clause that directed the arbitrator not to apply federal or state rules of civil procedure or evidence, when such rules "traditionally have not been applied to arbitrations"); New S. Fed. Sav. Bank v. Anding, 414 F. Supp. 2d 636 (S.D. Miss. 2005) (arbitration clause not substantively unconscionable because it waived a consumer's right to a jury trial).

88 Green Tree Fin. Corp.-Alabama v. Randolph, 531 U.S. 79, 121 S. Ct. 513, 148 L. Ed. 2d 373 (2000); *see also* Sydnor v. Conseco Fin. Servicing Corp., 252 F.3d 302 (4th Cir. 2001).

89 *See, e.g.*, Bess v. Check Express, 294 F.3d 1298 (11th Cir. 2002) ("First, although the district court discussed the fees and costs set forth under various rules of the AAA, it specifically found that there is no uniform set of AAA rules and that the arbitration clause failed to specify which set of rules were applicable. The district court could not have made any findings about Colburn's costs without finding which set of rules, and concomitantly, which set of fees and costs applied to the dispute. . . . For these reasons, any discussion of Colburn's potential costs under the AAA rules necessarily is based on speculation and cannot provide an adequate basis for concluding that her costs likely would be prohibitively expensive.").

90 Too many consumer counsel overlook this point. As explained in further detail later in this subsection, it is quite common for consumer attorneys to put evidence before courts of the filing fees to be paid to the arbitration service provider (such as AAA, JAMS, or NAF), but not to introduce evidence of the fees likely to be charged by the arbitrators themselves. This mistake

(counting preparation time, hearings, time spent on discovery, and deciding motions) to resolve a case like this case?[91] Are there other fees, such as room rentals or travel fees, that the consumer is likely to have to pay? Will the fees be waived because of the consumer's indigency? If so, will just the filing fee be waived, or also the much larger hourly fees for the arbitrator? Will fees be assessed to the losing party only? What retainer must the consumer pay up front? The key to any arbitration fee challenge is a thorough presentation to the court of admissible evidence establishing the actual fees and charges likely to be involved and whether the consumer is in fact liable for those charges.

After the *Randolph* case, being able to prove these answers (or the fact that the arbitration service provider will not provide these answers) is crucial in most jurisdictions for a consumer to prevail on the argument that the arbitration agreement should not be enforced due to excessive charges.[92] The failure to put such evidence before the court is often fatal to consumers' efforts to avoid compelled arbitration.[93] Consumers should also demonstrate to the court through sworn testimony that the amount of the fees

---

is significant for at least two reasons: (a) in the vast majority of cases, the filing fees are much smaller than the arbitrators' fees, and thus a number of courts have been given serious misimpressions about the total cost of arbitration, and (b) several arbitration service providers are willing in certain circumstances to waive or reduce the filing fees but are unwilling, in general, to waive or reduce the fees of the arbitrators themselves.

91 This proof may require an affidavit from experienced counsel describing the usual and expected length of an arbitration hearing for this kind of case, and describing the sorts of witnesses likely to be called and the likely length of their testimony.

92 At least one court has found that arbitration clauses which are prohibitively costly are unenforceable under *Randolph*, even when the clauses are not unconscionable. In Murphy v. Mid-West Nat'l Life Ins. Co. of Tenn., 78 P.3d 766 (Idaho 2003), the court held that an arbitration clause was neither procedurally nor substantively unconscionable, but was nonetheless unenforceable. "[T]he district court found that the cost of the arbitrator, plus the costs of witnesses and attorney fees was at a minimum $2,500 and that the Murphys could not afford that amount. That determination is supported by the record. Effectively the arbitration agreement in this case turns the purposes of arbitration upside down. It is an expensive alternative to litigation that precludes the Murphys from pursuing the claim." 78 P.3d at 768.

93 *See, e.g.*, Faber v. Menard, Inc., 367 F.3d 1048, 1054 (8th Cir. 2004) ("Faber has not provided the evidence necessary to estimate the length of the arbitration and the corresponding amount of arbitrators' fees (e.g., sophistication of the issues, average daily or hourly arbitrator costs in the region). He has also failed to provide evidence of his particular financial situation."); Livingston v. Associates Fin., Inc., 339 F.3d 553, 557 (7th Cir. 2003) ("[T]he Livingstons have not offered any specific evidence of arbitration costs that they may face in this litigation, prohibitive or otherwise, and have failed to provide any evidence of their inability to pay such costs, even though the district court permitted discovery on that very question."); Jaimez v. MBNA Am. Bank, 2006 WL 470587 (D. Kan. Feb. 27, 2006) (rejecting cost challenge to arbitration clause when the lender promised to pay any arbitration fees or costs that would exceed the costs if the case were filed in state court); Storie v. Household Int'l, Inc., 2005 WL 3728718, at *10 n.9 (D. Mass. Sept. 23, 2005) ("Because plaintiffs . . . have not presented *any* evidence as to the costs of arbitration in their case or their ability to afford it, the question of whether the terms of the Arbitration Rider are substantively oppressive to plaintiffs would seem to be more theoretical than real."); Kotch v. Clear Channel Broad., Inc., 2004 WL 483502 (S.D. Fla. Mar. 8, 2004) ("Kotch has failed to put forward evidence that he is unable to pay any arbitration fees that may be imposed as part of the arbitration process, or that he is even likely to bear such fees."); Gruber v. Louis Hornick & Co., 2003 WL 21222541 (S.D.N.Y. May 23, 2003) (rejecting a cost-based challenge when the plaintiff had not submitted evidence about AAA's fee schedule or that she would be unable to pay any fees incurred); Owner-Operator Indep. Drivers Ass'n, Inc. v. Swift Transp. Co., 288 F. Supp. 2d 1033 (D. Ariz. 2003) ("[T]he plaintiffs have not cited the Court to any evidence establishing that any such costs that might reasonably be incurred would in fact be prohibitive to the affected plaintiffs."); Fluehmann v. Associates Fin. Services, 2002 WL 500564, at *9 (D. Mass. Mar. 29, 2002) ("In the instant case, the plaintiff has presented no evidence that she would be saddled with arbitration costs that she cannot afford."); Cavalier Mfg., Inc. v. Jackson, 2001 Ala. LEXIS 115 (Ala. Apr. 13, 2001) (rejecting a cost-based challenge to an arbitration clause when "the record contains no information about how much arbitration would cost the plaintiffs"); Fleetwood Enterprises, Inc. v. Bruno, 784 So. 2d 277 (Ala. 2000) ("Bruno claims that the agreements, assuming they are valid, are unconscionable because, she says, she cannot afford to pay arbitration fees. This bare allegation, without substantial evidence to support it, cannot defeat the appellants' motion to compel arbitration."); Stewart Agency, Inc. v. Robinson, 855 So. 2d 726, 728, 729 (Fla. Dist. Ct. App. 2003) ("There is nothing to show that the expense of arbitration is greater than the expense of litigating the issues or would prevent the appellee from vindicating her statutory rights."); Roddie v. N. Am. Manufactured Homes, Inc., 851 N.E.2d 1281 (Ind. Ct. App. 2006) ("there is no evidence of the potential cost to the Roddies of arbitration"); Doyle v. Fin. Am., L.L.C., 173 Md. App. 370, 918 A.2d 1266 (2007) ("no evidence was presented by appellants to demonstrate the excessive costs of the arbitration forum"); Handler v. Southerland Custom Builders, Inc., 2006 WL 2441673 (Ohio Ct. App. Aug. 24, 2006) ("[H]omeowners here did not provide the trial court with any detail beyond the comparative costs of the initial fees. Consequently, their assertion that the cost of arbitration is prohibitive when compared to the cost of litigating in the Common Pleas Court is purely speculative."); Motsinger v. Litia Rose-FT, Inc., 156 P.3d 156, 162 (Or. Ct. App. 2007) ("plaintiff has offered no evidence of the likely costs of arbitration nor the potential impact of those costs here . . . [therefore] we reject plaintiff's argument"); *In re* Standard Meat Co., 2007 WL 730660, at *4 (Tex. App. Mar. 9, 2007) ("Here, [plaintiff] brought no evidence to the trial court showing that the expenses are unconscionable in her situation."); Walters v. A.A.A. Waterproofing, Inc., 85 P.3d 389, 393 (Wash. Ct. App. 2004) ("Walters has not shown that the costs of arbitrating his claim are prohibitive."), *review granted*, 108 P.3d 1227 (Wash. 2005); *see also* Williams v. CIGNA Fin. Advisors Inc., 197 F.3d 752 (5th Cir. 1999); Dobbins v. Hawk's Enterprises, 198 F.3d 715 (8th Cir. 1999) (refusing to find fees unconscionable when consumer never explored whether fees could be waived); Arakawa v. Japan Network Group, 56 F. Supp. 2d 349 (S.D.N.Y. 1999) (arbitration agreement enforced

prevents the consumer from pursuing the arbitration—that the consumer in fact has no ability to pay whatever fee is required or that it will be an excessive hardship, preventing the consumer from pursuing the arbitration.[94] One court has even suggested that a plaintiff must supplement her sworn testimony as to her ability to pay these fees with documentary material such as tax returns, bank statements, and the like.[95] Some courts have focused not on the ability of plaintiffs to pay arbitration fees, however, but upon the relationship of those fees to the amount at issue.[96]

The fees required to arbitrate even relatively small consumer disputes are often prohibitively high. The amount of these fees and how they are assessed varies not only among the different arbitration service providers (and among different individual arbitrators associated with a given arbitration service provider), but from year to year, as arbitration service providers have repeatedly restructured their fees and operations to respond to case law finding their fees to be unconscionable.

It is important to recognize that the filing fees—which typically go to the forum, such as the AAA, National Arbitration Forum (NAF), or JAMS—do not cover the fees paid directly to the arbitrators themselves. These latter fees tend to be much larger and are much less likely to be waived. As one federal court has noted, "the initial filing fee is far from the only cost involved in the arbitration."[97] One problem with quantifying arbitral fees, however, is that, while the filing fee can be ascertained with some precision at the outset of the case, the arbitrator's fee cannot. Arbitrators charge by the hour for preparation, research and conducting hearings, and it is impossible to predict with certainty how long it will take any given arbitrator to prepare for a case.[98] Additionally, different arbitrators charge widely varying hourly rates.[99] Accordingly, as one federal court has noted, "[i]t is impossible to establish the exact amount [the consumer] would have to pay because the arbitrator sets the amount after the arbitration has been initiated."[100]

Consumer attorneys must strive to fill in the gaps as much as possible, however. Consumers can usually obtain data from arbitration service providers as to the range of fees charged by arbitrators in a given area and the average fees charged by those arbitrators. In one case, for example, a federal court found that American Arbitration Association arbitrators in San Francisco charged an average of $1899 per day for arbitration hearings.[101] When such gaps are filled, at least one court has looked at the expected cost to plaintiff not only in absolute terms but also in comparison to the price of a trial.[102]

6.5.2.2 AAA Fees for Consumer Cases

At present, the American Arbitration Association (AAA) assesses a variety of fees during the course of an arbitration. For claims under $75,000, the AAA's "Consumer Rules," promulgated in February of 2002, may apply.[103] In its promotional materials, and in its vigorous litigation support for corporate defendants whose arbitration clauses have been challenged, the AAA stresses that under its Consumer

---

when not clear how large fees would be or whether plaintiff would be required to pay any portion of it); *Ex parte* Foster, 758 So. 2d 516 (Ala. 1999) (no showing consumer attempted to obtain waiver of fees as allowed by arbitration service provider's rules); Green Tree Fin. Corp. v. Wampler, 749 So. 2d 409 (Ala. 1999) (insufficient showing of financial impact of fees).

94 *See* Williams v. CIGNA Fin. Advisors Inc., 197 F.3d 752 (5th Cir. 1999) (former employee who now makes well over $100,000 a year did not demonstrate burden of paying $3000 in fees); Green Tree Fin. Corp. v. Wampler, 749 So. 2d 409 (Ala. 1999) (insufficient showing of financial impact of fees).

95 *See* Blair v. Scott Specialty Gases, 283 F.3d 595 (3d Cir. 2002); *see also* Lowden v. T-Mobile, USA, Inc., 2006 WL 1009279, at *9 (W.D. Wash. Apr. 13, 2006) (carrying the burden of showing the likelihood that arbitration would be prohibitively expensive "requires production of 'specific information' about the party's personal finances and the prospective arbitration fees" (citation omitted)).

96 *E.g.*, McNulty v. H & R Block, 843 A.2d 1267, 1274 (Pa. Super. Ct. 2004) ("This arbitration clause requires a consumer to pay $50.00 in the hopes of receiving, at most, $37.00. . . . [T]his is a situation where the costs of arbitration, minimal though they may seem, work to preclude the individual presentation of claims."); *see also* Taylor Bldg. Corp. of Am. v. Benfield, 860 N.E.2d 1058 (Ohio Ct. App.) (significant undisclosed costs substantively unconscionable in home construction contract, when "they create a chilling effect"), *appeal allowed*, 859 N.E.2d 556 (Ohio 2006); Sikes v. Ganley Pontiac Honda, Inc., 2004 WL 67224 (Ohio Ct. App. Jan. 15, 2004) (rejecting unconscionability challenge to an arbitration clause when the arbitral fees did not exceed the amount sought in the complaint).

97 Phillips v. Associates Home Equity Services, Inc., 179 F. Supp. 2d 840, 846 (N.D. Ill. 2001).

98 Camacho v. Holiday Homes, Inc., 167 F. Supp. 2d 892 (W.D. Va. 2001) (under AAA rules, arbitration fees are shared "for a minimum of one full day for hearings, plus the arbitrator's additional preparation and research time before and after the hearing").

99 *Id.* ("the arbitration fee . . . typically ranges between $100 and $300 per hour").

100 *Id.* at 897 n.4; *see also* Phillips v. Associates Home Equity Services, Inc., 179 F. Supp. 2d 840 (N.D. Ill. 2001) ("Phillips has made a reasonable, good faith effort to estimate her arbitration costs with assistance from the AAA, and without actually going through arbitration and receiving a final bill, we see no way for her to provide a more precise showing of her costs than she has done here.").

101 Ting v. AT & T, 182 F. Supp. 2d 902 (N.D. Cal. 2002), *aff'd*, 319 F.3d 1126 (9th Cir. 2003); *see also* Appx. M, *infra* (summaries of affidavits from AAA officials setting out their arbitrators' average daily rates in several different cities) (reproduced on the CD-Rom accompanying this manual).

102 Vasquez-Lopez v. Beneficial Or., Inc., 152 P.3d 940, 952 (Or. Ct. App. 2007) (estimate that arbitration will cost $1000 is not only "high in the absolute sense," but also "high in comparison to a trial," and therefore sufficiently onerous to deter vindication of plaintiff's claim).

103 The AAA's Consumer Rules are included as Appendix B.1.2, *infra*.

Rules the consumer need only pay $375 ($125 for claims under $10,000) for an arbitration of her claims. What the AAA does not stress, however, is how skeletal the $375 arbitration process is. Essentially, the Consumer Rules provide the consumer with an opportunity to submit a letter to an arbitrator "briefly" explaining the dispute for resolution. The company may then respond, and then the arbitrator is to rule. The arbitration under the AAA's Consumer Rules provides the consumer with no ability to require an in-person hearing with the arbitrator, although it does permit the consumer to receive a telephone hearing.

Many consumers' claims exceed $75,000, however, such as in many mortgage cases. In addition, some consumers want to have an in-person hearing on a case, with the ability to present evidence and appear in person. Consumers in these situations who are parties to an arbitration clause specifying the AAA's rules must pursue the arbitration under the AAA's Commercial Rules.[104] The initial filing fee is $500 or more, depending on the size of the claim. There is a daily hearing fee of $150 per party, with the added possibility of a daily room rental fee of $150 per party, certain administrative fees, plus compensation for the arbitrator at a rate of between $100 and $450 an *hour* (depending on the area). The arbitrator's hourly compensation accrues not only for in-hearing time, but also for "study" time. These hourly charges for the arbitrator can become quite hefty when time must be expended on discovery disputes, motions practice, and scheduling conferences. Moreover, the rules for certain disputes call for three arbitrators. An estimated amount for all of these fees is often billed in advance, usually half to each party.

A number of courts have recently struck down arbitration clauses on the grounds that the fees imposed by the AAA's Commercial Rules are prohibitive. In one consumer case involving the AAA's Commercial Rules, for example, a federal court found:

> Under [the Commercial] Rules, the costs of arbitration are likely to be staggering; Popovich has submitted an unrebutted affidavit from an AAA-certified arbitrator that the cost is likely to be as much as $48,000 and perhaps as high as $126,000. Popovich himself has averred, unsurprisingly, that costs in that range would be prohibitive, and McDonald's has not disputed that claim.[105]

Those seeking to enforce arbitration clauses frequently argue that no arbitration clause invoking the AAA's rules may ever be held to be prohibitively expensive because the AAA's rules supposedly incorporate various safeguards against excessive fees. Recently, however, several courts have held that the AAA's rules do not provide adequate protection against excessive arbitral fees. In *Phillips v. Associates Home Equity Services, Inc.*, for example, the court stated:

> [D]efendants argue that the AAA's Commercial Rules contain certain safeguards to protect Philips against incurring exorbitant costs. These arguments are unavailing.... [D]efendants note that the arbitrator at his or her discretion can assess all expenses to one party at the conclusion of the case. But that is nothing more than an argument that there exists some possibility that Philips ultimately may not have to bear a prohibitively expensive portion of the arbitration costs.[106]

As another federal court has found: "However, even if the initial $2000 in administrative fees were waived and deferred, [the consumer] has demonstrated the additional costs of the arbitration process itself amount to an insurmountable financial barrier to her.... The parties stipulate that these fees are not subject to waiver or deferral for 'extreme hardship.' "[107]

The court explained:

> The [AAA Commercial Rules] permit the initiating party to apply for a waiver, reduction or deferral (complete or partial) of these administra-

---

104 The AAA's Commercial Rules are included as Appendix B.1.1, *infra*.

105 Popovich v. McDonald's Corp., 189 F. Supp. 2d 772, 778 (N.D. Ill. 2002); *see also* Dunham v. Envtl. Chem. Corp., 2006 WL 2374703 (N.D. Cal. Aug. 16, 2006) ("The Commercial Rules would require [the employee] to pay half of the arbitrator's expenses, a fee not usually associated with litigation. As such, the cost-sharing provision of the Chemical Rules is clearly unconscionable...."); Arnold v. Goldstar Fin. Sys., Inc., 2002 WL 1941546, at *11 (N.D. Ill. Aug. 22, 2002) (after extensive analysis of fees under AAA's Commercial Rules, the court states that "plaintiffs have shown a genuine likelihood that they would incur prohibitive costs in arbitration"); Mendez v. Palm Harbor Homes, Inc., 111 Wash. App. 446, 471, 45 P.3d 594, 607 (2002) ("[W]e conclude that Mr. Mendez has made a sufficient showing that the anticipated filing and administrative costs of AAA arbitration would be prohibitively high. The costs have the practical effect of preventing Mr. Mendez from pursuing his statutory claims."); *cf.* Spinetti v. Serv. Corp. Int'l, 324 F.3d 212 (3d Cir. 2003) (affirming district court holding that arbitration fees were proven to be prohibitive under the AAA's rules in employment case); Cooper v. MRM Inv. Co., 199 F. Supp. 2d 771 (M.D. Tenn. 2002) (same).

106 Phillips v. Associates Home Equity Services, Inc., 179 F. Supp. 2d 840, 846–847 (N.D. Ill 2001) (citation omitted); *see also* Higgins v. Super. Ct., 140 Cal. App. 4th 1238, 1254, 45 Cal. Rptr. 3d 293, 305 (2006) ("Additional elements of substantive unconscionability are found in the provision barring only petitioners from seeking appellate review of the arbitrator's decision and, at least insofar as it could impact petitioners' statutory claims, the provision requiring arbitration in accordance with the rules of the American Arbitration Association, which provide that arbitration costs are to be borne equally by the parties."); Vasquez-Lopez v. Beneficial Or., Inc., 152 P.3d 940, 952 (Or. Ct. App. 2007) (not only is the estimate of $1000 in expenses high in the absolute sense, but also high in comparison to a trial, and therefore unconscionable).

107 Camacho v. Holiday Homes, Inc., 167 F. Supp. 2d 892, 897 (W.D. Va. 2001).

tive fees due to "extreme hardship." The AAA's accounting department determines which claimant should be afforded "extreme hardship" status. There are no formal standards that govern the accounting department's determination. In practice, the complete waiver of a fee is extremely rare; partial deferral is the usual response when hardship is established. The arbitrator may assess the losing party any deferred fee as part of the arbitrator's final award. . . .

[The consumer] could not recover those fees, unless she ultimately prevailed on her claim. Even if she prevailed, however, [the consumer] does not have $2,000 to pay the fees in the first place, and she has no collateral with which she could obtain a sufficient loan. Though [the consumer] may apply for fee deferral or reduction due to "extreme hardship," the parties stipulate that waiver of fees is extremely rare in practice. The AAA does not provide formal standards for granting hardship, and its accounting department actually determines who is afforded "extreme hardship" status.[108]

Other courts, however, have found that the AAA's rules relating to arbitral fees are adequate to protect consumers against excessive fees. In *Dabney v. Option One Mortgage Corp.*, for example, the court held:

The Court concludes that the Arbitration Agreement is not unenforceable because any risk of Plaintiff bearing such costs is speculative. The AAA rules submitted by Plaintiff and incorporated into the Arbitration Agreement contain safeguards protecting Plaintiffs from inordinately high arbitration costs. Specifically, the AAA rules provide the filing and administrative fees may be reduced in cases of extreme hardship and are subject to final apportionment by the arbitrator.[109]

On February 11, 2002, after several of the foregoing decisions were handed down in which AAA arbitration clauses were not enforced by the courts because they required consumers or employees to pay excessive fees, the AAA issued a press release announcing new rules. This press release states, among other things:

Changes to Fees for Consumer Cases: Currently, consumers pay only $125 towards the arbitrator's fee for consumer cases under $10,000, a fee that has been in place since July 1999. The remaining fee of $625, paid by the business, represents the other half of the arbitrator's fee and a $500 administrative fee.

Beginning March 1, 2002, where a consumer's claim is between $10,000 and $75,000, the consumer will only be responsible for one-half of the arbitrator's fee, capped at a maximum of $375. The business will pay the $750 administrative fee and the remaining balance of the arbitrator's fee. For all cases under $75,000, the fees paid by the consumer are fully refundable if the dispute is settled before the arbitrator takes any action.

Availability of Pro Bono Arbitrators: In addition to the caps of $125 and $375 for arbitrator fees in cases below $10,000 and $75,000 respectively, thousands of arbitrators from the AAA panel have volunteered to serve pro bono in appropriate cases. These arbitrators have met the high standards for admission to the AAA panel and have completed the Association's arbitrator training.

Hardship Provisions: For many years, the Association has had a process where parties could request a waiver or deferral of the AAA's fees based on financial hardship. That process has now been formalized with guidelines to make the process clearer. In every case filed with the AAA, any party may apply for a hardship fee reduction, waiver or denial. The guidelines, based on 200% of the Federal Poverty Guidelines, along with other relevant financial data, will be used in assessing all applications.

It is not yet clear what effect these changes will have, but it appears that the AAA has shifted a much heavier portion of the costs of arbitration from consumers to businesses. At least some courts have enforced arbitration clauses that relied upon these consumer rules because of the changes.[110]

---

108 *Id*. at 894; *cf.* Ball v. SFX Broad., Inc., 165 F. Supp. 2d 230, 240 n.10 (N.D.N.Y. 2001) ("[Defendants] assert that 'the AAA is the place for Ms. Christopher to make her costs argument. The AAA's National Rules for the Resolution of Employment Disputes provide that "the AAA may, in the event of extreme hardship on any party, defer or reduce the administrative fees" '. . . . This argument is rejected. The mere fact that Christopher might possibly obtain some relief from the significant fees described above does not prohibit the conclusion that she has shown the 'likelihood' of incurring such fees, as required by the Supreme Court's Green Tree decision." (citation omitted)).

109 2001 U.S. Dist. LEXIS 4949, at *9 (E.D. Pa. Apr. 19, 2001) (footnote, citations omitted); *see also* New S. Fed. Sav. Bank. v. Anding, 414 F. Supp. 2d 636 (S.D. Miss. 2005) ("[T]he Fifth Circuit enforces arbitration provisions where the parties agree to arbitrate pursuant to the AAA's Commercial Arbitration rules, including cases where one party objects to the alleged high costs of arbitration."); Lovey v. Regence Blueshield of Idaho, 72 P.3d 877 (Idaho 2003) (arbitration costs not prohibitive or unconscionable because the plaintiff will be reimbursed for those fees if she prevails). *But see* Dombrowski v. Gen. Motors Corp., 318

F. Supp. 2d 850 (D. Ariz. 2004) (finds AAA clause not to be unconscionable, with no reasoning or discussion).

110 *E.g.*, Wilks v. The Pep Boys, 241 F. Supp. 2d 860, 866 (M.D. Tenn. 2003) (noting that the AAA's rules changes were possibly influenced by the concerns expressed by some courts, and holding that the rules were not unconscionable as applied to these plaintiffs).

6.5.2.3 NAF Fees for Consumer Cases

There is also a growing body of litigation relating to the fees charged by the National Arbitration Forum (NAF). NAF is a much less transparent organization than the American Arbitration Association, and its fees are harder to determine. For one thing, NAF's fee structure includes multiple fees for various litigation events, and NAF also insists upon broad protective orders with respect to most discovery it provides.

Nonetheless, a recent Ohio case developed a substantial factual record about NAF's fees, and the court held that those fees were unconscionable in the setting of a consumer dispute. The court's discussion of the NAF's complex and obscure fee structure is instructive:

> Ms. Eagle asserts that her damages are at least $75,000. Under the NAF Code of Procedure's fee schedule a claim of $75,000 or higher is labeled a "Large Claim." "Large Claims" carry higher fees than "Common Claims," which are claims under $75,000. To file a claim between $75,000 and $100,000, the claimant is required to pay a filing fee of $750 plus an additional one percent of the excess over $75,000. Additionally, Ms. Eagle brings to our attention a number of Large Claim fees that she also asserts are excessive. Some of these fees include the following: (1) $75 for a single subpoena request; (2) $150 for each discovery order; (3) $100 for a continuance request; (4) $2,500 for a document hearing, or $1,500 for an initial participatory hearing session; (5) at least $1,250 to submit a post-hearing brief; (6) a fee for an objection to the request equal to as much as the cost of the original request; and (7) between $1,000 and $1,250 for a written findings of facts, conclusions of law, or reasons for an award. Ms. Eagle asserts that a conservative estimation of the fees she would likely have to incur for an in-person arbitration with a written opinion would range between $4,200 and $6,000. We note that there are additional fees associated with the NAF arbitration, such as fees for a request for reopening or reconsideration, and other procedural fees that may be assessed by the NAF as well. *Suffice it to say that, for virtually every piece of documentation requested by a party, a corresponding fee exists.*[111]

The car dealer responded that the high arbitration fees were not significant, because the NAF might waive such fees. The court of appeals noted that no such waiver was possible in cases involving claims of more than $75,000, and that even in smaller cases that waivers were entirely contingent and discretionary.[112] In any case, the court concluded that the possibility of fee waivers would not rescue the clause:

> Assuming arguendo that the NAF Code of Procedure Rules actually provided for a mandatory full waiver of both Common and Large Claim fees, the fact that the rules would provide for such a guaranteed waiver for indigent claimants is ultimately irrelevant. Practically speaking, such arbitration costs would serve to deter even low-income persons who do not qualify for indigent status, as well. That a consumer such as Ms. Eagle, a primary caregiver for one child and who more recently made approximately $20,000 per year, would be willing and able to expend on a conservative scale between $4,000 and $6,000 on arbitration fees and costs, is highly doubtful.[113]

6.5.2.4 Varying Approaches As to Who Pays the Fees

Who pays these fees varies not only by the rules of the arbitration service provider, but by the arbitration agreement itself. Sometimes, the consumer can apply to the arbitration service provider (such as the American Arbitration Association or the National Arbitration Forum) through procedures analogous to *in forma pauperis* to seek a waiver of all or some of these charges.[114] But, in general, there are several ways that the arbitration charges can be assessed, with various additional combinations possible (for example, the consumer pays the filing fee and the merchant pays the arbitrators' fees):

- Each party pays half of the total estimated cost of the arbitration up front;
- The merchant pays all required up-front charges, but the consumer must pay half eventually;
- Each party must pay half of the estimated cost of the arbitration up front, and the non-prevailing party must reimburse the other party for those charges;
- The merchant advances the up-front charges and the non-prevailing party eventually is liable for all charges; or
- The merchant pays all charges.

---

111 Eagle v. Fred Martin Motor Co., 809 N.E.2d 1161, 1176 (Ohio Ct. App. 2004) (footnotes omitted). *But see* Stenzel v. Dell, Inc., 870 A.2d 133 (Me. 2005) ("Because an NAF arbitrator can award a successful Dell customer the fees and costs of arbitration, [the consumer plaintiffs] have not established the likelihood of incurring prohibitively expensive costs by proceeding through the NAF's procedures.").

112 Eagle v. Fred Martin Motor Co., 809 N.E.2d 1161, 1177 (Ohio Ct. App. 2004).

113 *Id.*

114 As set forth in § 6.5.2.2, *supra*, however, several courts have found serious fault with the American Arbitration Association's rules for the waiver or deferral of fees. In February of 2002, though, the AAA revamped those procedures somewhat, providing that deferrals or waivers would be available to any consumer whose income was less than two hundred percent of the federal poverty guidelines.

Obviously, arbitration may not be practical if the consumer is obligated to pay $1000 in arbitration fees to recover $500. Many consumers also cannot afford to pay $1000 up front, even if that amount will be reimbursed to the consumer if she prevails. In addition, even if the consumer need not put up anything in advance, the risk of a $1000 or larger fee if the consumer does not prevail may deter many valid consumer claims.[115] In short, any system, short of the merchant paying all fees all the time, raises questions of fairness.

6.5.2.5 Precedent Regarding Unconscionable Arbitration Fees

A growing number of courts have considered potentially high arbitration fees as a factor in finding an arbitration agreement unconscionable.[116] In arguing that the absolute size of the fees is unconscionable, it is also relevant whether the arbitration clause provides consumers with any idea that they must pay various types of fees or of the size of fees they will in fact become obligated to pay, or whether the costs that will be assessed are beyond consumers' expectations.[117] Also persuasive on this issue are cases which find that high fees conflict with the purposes of federal statutes.[118]

---

115 *See, e.g.*, Mercuro v. Super. Ct., 96 Cal. App. 4th 167, 116 Cal. Rptr. 2d 671 (2002) (giving no weight to a company's offer to front arbitration costs, because the individual "could wind up paying the entire cost of the arbitration, including the arbitrator's fee, should he lose").

116 *See* Alexander v. Anthony Int'l, Ltd. P'ship, 341 F.3d 256, 269, 270 (3d Cir. 2003) (requiring employee to pay costs ranging from $800 to $1000 a day for arbitration "effectively denied [the employees] for recompense for the [employer's] alleged misconduct, resulting in an unfair advantage for their former employer.... We therefore must find that the 'loser pays' provision is unconscionable as to these particular plaintiffs."); Ting v. AT & T, 319 F.3d 1126 (9th Cir. 2003); Circuit City Stores, Inc. v. Adams, 279 F.3d 889 (9th Cir. 2002); Bragg v. Linden Research, Inc., 487 F. Supp. 2d 593, 609–610 (E.D. Pa. 2007) (when shared costs of arbitration impose costs greater than filing a complaint in state or federal court upon the consumer, agreement is rendered substantively unconscionable); Jones v. Household Realty Corp., 2003 WL 23750601 (S.D. Ohio Dec. 17, 2003) (when arbitration clause would require low-income plaintiffs to pay between $3000 and $4000 to have their claims heard, it is unenforceable because it "would deter a substantial number of similarly situated persons from attempting to vindicate their statutory rights in the arbitral forum"); Torrance v. AAMES Funding Corp., 242 F. Supp. 2d 862 (D. Or. 2002); Pitchford v. Oakwood Mobile Homes, Inc., 124 F. Supp. 2d 958 (W.D. Va. 2000) (arbitration fees of several thousand dollars are so unfair as to make the arbitration agreement unconscionable; fees serve to bar rather than provide a means for an economical solution to controversies); *In re* Knepp, 229 B.R. 821 (Bankr. N.D. Ala. 1999) (arbitration unconscionable when it would cost the consumer initially anywhere from $500 to $7000, plus daily costs of hundreds of dollars, to arbitrate a dispute and the consumer, being in bankruptcy, could not afford that amount); Little v. Auto Stiegler, Inc., 29 Cal. 4th 1064, 63 P.3d 979 (2003) (arbitration clause requiring employee to pay half of fees was unconscionable); Wilson v. Bally Total Fitness Corp., 2003 WL 21398324 (Cal. Ct. App. June 18, 2003); Pinedo v. Premium Tobacco, Inc., 85 Cal. App. 4th 774, 102 Cal. Rptr. 2d 435 (2000) (one factor cited in finding an arbitration clause unconscionable is that it required an employee to front all fees in the arbitration); Ramirez v. Circuit City Stores, Inc., 90 Cal. Rptr. 2d 916 (Ct. App. 1999), *review granted and opinion superseded*, 94 Cal. Rptr. 2d 1, 995 P.2d 137 (Cal. 2000); Maciejewski v. Alpha Sys. Lab, 87 Cal. Rptr. 2d 390 (Ct. App.), *review granted and opinion superseded*, 89 Cal. Rptr. 2d 834, 986 P.2d 170 (Cal. 1999), *vacated and transferred*, 101 Cal. Rptr. 2d 198, 11 P.3d 954 (Cal. 2000); Patterson v. ITT Consumer Fin. Corp., 14 Cal. App. 4th 1659, 18 Cal. Rptr. 2d 563 (1993); Murphy v. Mid-West Nat'l Life Ins. Co. of Tenn., 78 P.3d 766 (Idaho 2003) (arbitration clause requiring insured to pay at least $2500 to have a claim heard was unconscionable; it "is an expensive alternative to litigation that precludes the Murphys from pursuing the claim"); State *ex rel.* Vincent v. Schneider, 194 S.W.3d 853 (Mo. 2006) ("It is unconscionable to have a provision in an arbitration clause that puts all fees for arbitration on the consumer. This is particularly true when the cost-shifting terms could work to grant one party immunity from legitimate claims on the contract."); D.R. Horton, Inc. v. Green, 96 P.3d 1159 (Nev. 2004) ("[T]he district court properly considered Horton's failure to disclose potential arbitration costs in examining the asymmetrical effects of the provision. We ... conclude that the arbitration provision was also substantively unconscionable."); Brower v. Gateway 2000, 246 A.D.2d 246, 676 N.Y.S.2d 569 (1998) ($4000 fee, only $2000 of which would be refunded if the consumer prevailed); Licitra v. Gateway, Inc., 189 Misc. 2d 721, 734 N.Y.S.2d 389 (Civ. Ct. 2001) (outlining the National Arbitration Forum's arbitration fees and concluding that "[i]t is obvious that these costs can make arbitration not a viable alternative for many consumers"); Williams v. Aetna Fin. Co., 83 Ohio St. 3d 464, 700 N.E.2d 859 (1998); O'Donoghue v. Smythe, Cramer Co., 2002 WL 145074 (Ohio Ct. App. July 3, 2002) (when limitation of liability clause limits recovery to $265 and arbitration fees are at least $500, clause is unconscionable); Myers v. Terminix Int'l Co., 91 Ohio Misc. 2d 41, 697 N.E.2d 277 (Ct. Com. Pl. 1998) (fees not only excessive, but not disclosed to the consumer in the original arbitration agreement); *see also* Sosa v. Paulos, 924 P.2d 357 (Utah 1996) (unconscionable if consumer must pay the other side's attorney fees and costs if the consumer does not recover at least half of the damages sought in the arbitration). *But see* Am. Heritage Life Ins., Co. v. Orr, 294 F.3d 702 (5th Cir. 2002); Gary v. Rent-A-Center W., Inc., 2007 WL 283035 (D. Or. Jan. 24, 2007) (arbitration contract requiring plaintiff to pay half of the arbitration costs not unconscionable); Raasch v. NCR Corp., 254 F. Supp. 2d 847 (S.D. Ohio 2003) (arbitration clause not unconscionable); Rollins, Inc. v. Foster, 991 F. Supp. 1426 (M.D. Ala. 1998) (high fees could lead to an unconscionability finding, but not justified based on the facts of this case); Commercial Credit Corp. v. Leggett, 744 So. 2d 890 (Ala. 1999) (not unconscionable when the consumer must pay $125, the other party then pays for the first day of the arbitrator's time, and the losing party pays all remaining fees).

117 *See* Myers v. Terminix Int'l Co., 91 Ohio Misc. 2d 41, 697 N.E.2d 277 (Ct. Com. Pl. 1998) (fees not only excessive, but not disclosed to the consumer in the original arbitration agreement).

118 *See* Morrison v. Circuit City Stores, Inc., 317 F.3d 646 (6th Cir. 2003) (en banc) (striking cost-splitting provision from employer's arbitration clause for interfering with enforcement of plain-

On the other hand, determination of the conscionability of high fees in a consumer context should not be influenced by courts' determination that similar fees are conscionable when a dispute between two business litigants is submitted to arbitration.[119] But even in a commercial case, a court has found a filing fee of $4000 plus one-half of one percent of the amount claimed to be unconscionable, because this fee bore no reasonable relation to the arbitration forum's administrative expenses.[120]

6.5.3 One-Way or Non-Mutual Arbitration Clauses Are Often Unconscionable

6.5.3.1 Introduction

A number of arbitration clauses are not mutual: the consumer must arbitrate claims, but the lender or merchant can resort to judicial or non-judicial remedies. For example, the arbitration provision may require that the consumer's disputes be submitted to binding arbitration, but reserve the right for the creditor to engage in self-help repossession or foreclosure without first submitting the dispute to binding arbitration. Other provisions allow the creditor to file a judicial collection action even though consumers must arbitrate their disputes. In other clauses, companies have tried to retain a unilateral right to modify or opt out of an obligation to arbitrate any particular claim, when they so chose.[121] Such clauses may indicate that most corporations do not actually favor mandatory arbitration as a method of effective dispute resolution with respect to disputes in which they are interested.[122]

6.5.3.2 Non-Mutuality Rendering Clause Unconscionable Distinguished from Non-Mutuality Creating Lack of Consideration for Agreement

The argument that non-mutual remedies render the clause unconscionable is different than the argument that the lack of mutuality means there is no consideration, and thus that the contract is unenforceable. Even if a court finds that other aspects of the agreement provide sufficient consideration for the non-mutual arbitration clause,[123] consumers may—and should—still raise the question of whether the clause is unconscionable.[124]

6.5.3.3 Cases Finding Non-Mutuality to Be Unconscionable

A number of cases find such one-sided clauses, coupled with the typical procedural aspects of a consumer negotiation, make the arbitration agreement unconscionable.[125] The

---

tiff's Title VII rights); Shankle v. B-G Maint. Mgmt. of Colo., Inc., 163 F.3d 1230 (10th Cir. 1999) (impractical to expect an employee to pay half of the potential thousands of dollars in arbitration costs that arbitration of the claim would entail, which means that arbitration is not an acceptable forum to enforce the employee's statutory rights); Paladino v. Avnet Computer Technologies Inc., 134 F.3d 1054 (11th Cir. 1998) (arbitration ruled invalid when employee may be liable for at least half of the "hefty" cost of arbitration with the American Arbitration Association); Cole v. Burns Int'l Sec. Services, 105 F.3d 1465 (D.C. Cir. 1997) (employee could not be required to agree to arbitrate statutory claims as a condition of employment if the arbitration agreement required him to pay all or part of the arbitrator's fees or expenses; fees ranging from $500 to $1000 or more per day would be prohibitively expensive for employee and would be unlike anything he would have to pay to pursue his statutory claims in court).

119 See Doctor's Associates, Inc. v. Jabush, 89 F.3d 109 (2d Cir. 1996); Doctor's Associates, Inc. v. Stuart, 85 F.3d 975 (2d Cir. 1996).

120 Teleserve Sys., Inc. v. MCI Telecommunications Corp., 230 A.D.2d 585, 659 N.Y.S.2d 659 (1997).

121 See, e.g., Taylor v. Douglas Butler Auto Sales, 142 S.W.3d 277 (Tenn. 2004); *In re* Palm Harbor Homes, Inc., 129 S.W.3d 636 (Tex. App. 2003).

122 See, e.g., *Arbitration: Happy Endings Not Guaranteed*, Bus.

Week, Nov. 20, 2000 ("[A]s companies come to grips with the possibility of expensive delays and unfavorable verdicts etched in stone, they may find a trip to court doesn't look so bad after all."); Gregory T. Higgins & William D. O'Connell, *Mediation, Arbitration Square Off: The Majority of In-House Counsel Surveyed Prefer Mediation to Binding Arbitration, A Significant Change from Three Years Ago*, The Nat'l L.J., Mar. 24, 1997.

123 See, e.g., Cook v. River Oaks Hyundai, Inc., 2006 WL 931685, at *2–*3 (N.D. Ill. Apr. 5, 2006) (granting motion to compel arbitration when the arbitration agreement was "supported by the consideration for the Purchase Order Agreement," and the defendants promise to arbitrate "some specified class of claims," was sufficient consideration); see also § 5.3, *supra*.

124 See, e.g., Ameriquest Mortgage Co. v. Bentley, 2002 WL 31664283, at *6 (Ala. Nov. 27, 2002) (holding that employee lost right to argue unconscionability of non-mutual clause by only raising lack of consideration as an issue at the trial court; two issues are separate and independent).

125 Circuit City Stores, Inc. v. Adams, 279 F.3d 889 (9th Cir. 2002) (holding an arbitration clause unconscionable when "[t]he provision does not require Circuit City to arbitrate its claims against employees"); Geoffrey v. Wash. Mut. Bank, 484 F. Supp. 2d 1115 (S.D. Cal. 2007) (a contract requiring consumer to pay to vindicate federal rights granted under Electronic Funds Transfer Act is substantively unconscionable); Batory v. Sears, Roebuck & Co., 456 F. Supp. 2d 1137, 1140 (D. Ariz. 2006) (an employment contract arbitration clause substantively unconscionable when it required employee, but not employer, to arbitrate all claims); Casteel v. Clear Channel Broad., 254 F. Supp. 2d 1081 (W.D. Ark. 2003); Nicholson v. Labor Ready, Inc., 1997 U.S. Dist. LEXIS 23494 (N.D. Cal. May 23, 1997); Northcom, Ltd. v. James, 694 So. 2d 1329 (Ala. 1997) (subsequently largely overturned by Alabama cases cited in § 6.5.3.4, *infra*); The Money Place, L.L.C. v. Barnes, 349 Ark. 411, 78 S.W.3d 714 (Ark. 2002); Cash in a Flash Check Advance of Ark., L.L.C. v. Spencer, 348 Ark. 459, 74 S.W. 3d 600 (Ark. 2002); Williams v. Showmethemoney Check Cashers, Inc., Clearinghouse No. 52,500 (Ark. Cir. Ct. Aug. 26, 1999) (text of this decision is also available on the CD-Rom accompanying this manual), *aff'd on related grounds*, 342 Ark. 112, 27 S.W.3d

§ 6.5.3.3 Consumer Arbitration Agreements

leading case is the decision of the West Virginia Supreme Court of Appeals in *Arnold v. United Companies Lending Corp.*[126] In *Arnold*, a "national corporate lender" and unsophisticated consumers signed a contract that included an arbitration clause.[127] The clause required the consumers to submit any claims they might have to arbitration, but permitted the lender to go to court to collect the debt owed.[128] The court described this arrangement as the sort of deal that might be reached by a rabbit and a fox, and held that it unreasonably favored the lender:

> United Lending's acts or omissions could seriously damage the Arnolds, yet the Arnolds' only recourse would be to submit the matter to binding arbitration. At the same time, United Lending's access to the courts is wholly preserved in every conceivable situation where United Lending would want to secure judicial relief against the Arnolds.[129]

The court concluded that this agreement was unconscionable and unenforceable.[130]

The Tennessee Supreme Court followed *Arnold* in a case in which a used car dealer's arbitration clause reserved the dealer's right to repossess or to collect the debt through a court action. In *Taylor v. Douglas Butler Auto Sales*,[131] the court examined case law on both sides of this issue, followed *Arnold*, and held that this one-sided arbitration clause was "unreasonably favorable to City Auto and oppressive to Taylor."[132]

The California Supreme Court similarly held in *Armendariz v. Foundation Health Psychcare Services, Inc.* that:

> Given the disadvantages that may exist for plaintiffs arbitrating disputes, it is unfairly one-sided for an employer with superior bargaining power to impose arbitration on the employee as plaintiff but not to accept such limitations when it seeks to prosecute a claim against the employee, without at least some reasonable justification for such one-sidedness based on "business realities". . . . Without reasonable justification for this lack of mutuality, arbitration appears less as a forum for neutral dispute resolution and more as a means of maximizing employer advantage. Arbitration was not intended for this purpose.[133]

---

361 (Ark. 2000); Pinedo v. Premium Tobacco, Inc., 85 Cal. App. 4th 774, 102 Cal. Rptr. 2d 435 (2000) (arbitration clause held to be unconscionable, in part because it only addressed claims that would normally be raised by employees and not employers); Kinney v. United HealthCare Services, Inc., 70 Cal. App. 4th 1322, 83 Cal. Rptr. 2d 348 (1999); Stirlen v. Supercuts, Inc., 51 Cal. App. 4th 1519, 60 Cal. Rptr. 2d 138 (1997); Hong v. First Alliance Mortgage Co., Clearinghouse No. 52,122 (Cal. Super. Ct. Dec. 3, 1997) (text of this decision is also available on the CD-Rom accompanying this manual); Iwen v. U.S. W. Direct, 293 Mont. 512, 977 P.2d 989 (1999); Burch v. Second Judicial Dist. Ct., 49 P.3d 647 (Nev. 2002); Williams v. Aetna Fin. Co., 83 Ohio St. 3d 464, 700 N.E.2d 859 (1998); Taylor v. Douglas Butler Auto Sales, 142 S.W.3d 277 (Tenn. 2004); Brown v. Tenn. Title Loans, Inc., 2006 WL 2842788 (Tenn. Ct. App. Feb. 26, 2007) (arbitration agreement unconscionable that "require[d] Plaintiffs to arbitrate any and all claims they may have against Defendant," but allowed defendant to "file a lawsuit and refuse to arbitrate any claim based on Plaintiffs' failure to do the one thing they agreed to do in the contract, i.e., pay a certain amount by a specified date"); Arnold v. United Companies Lending Corp., 204 W. Va. 229, 511 S.E.2d 854 (1998); *see also* Siordia v. Circuit City Stores, Inc., 2005 WL 1368083 (9th Cir. June 9, 2005) (contract that requires employee to arbitrate claims "but makes no similar provision that Circuit City's claims be arbitrated" is substantively unconscionable); Iberia Credit Bureau, Inc. v. Cingular Wireless, 379 F.3d 169 (5th Cir. 2004) (Centennial Wireless's arbitration clause was unconscionable because it was one-sided and non-mutual: it required all of the company's consumers to arbitrate their claims but did not require the company to do so; the court did not enforce the arbitration clauses of two other wireless companies that did require mutual arbitration); Palm Beach Motor Cars Ltd., Inc. v. Jeffries, 885 So. 2d 990 (Fla. Dist. Ct. App. 2004) ("Where one party is bound to arbitration of its claims but the other is not, there can be substantive unconscionability."); Greenpoint Credit, L.L.C. v. Reynolds, 151 S.W.3d 868 (Mo. Ct. App. 2005) (court held that "the part of the contract that limited [the borrower's] access to state courts while permitting Green Point access [was] unconscionable and unenforceable."); Wis. Auto Title Loans, Inc. v. Jones, 714 N.W.2d 155 (Wis. 2006). *But see* McCabe v. Dell, Inc., 2007 WL 1343972, at *3 (C.D. Cal. Apr. 12, 2007) (upholds provision because defendant has presented reasonable justification for non-mutual arbitration provision—namely, that arbitration offers a low cost, fair forum near plaintiff's home—and because this contract is for a consumer non-essential good instead of an employment contract).

126 204 W. Va. 229, 511 S.E.2d 854 (1998).
127 *Id.*, 511 S.E.2d at 861.
128 *Id.*, 511 S.E.2d at 858.

129 *Id.*, 511 S.E.2d at 861; *see also* ACORN v. Household Int'l, Inc., 211 F. Supp. 2d 1160 (N.D. Cal. 2002); O'Hare v. Mun. Res. Consultants, 132 Cal. Rptr. 2d 116 (Ct. App. 2003); Simpson v. Grimes, 849 So. 2d 740, 749 (La. Ct. App. 2003); Taylor v. Douglas Butler Auto Sales, 142 S.W.3d 277, 286 (Tenn. 2004); *In re* Palm Harbor Homes, Inc., 129 S.W.3d 636, 645, 646 (Tex. App. 2003); West Virginia *ex rel*. Dunlap v. Berger, 567 S.E.2d 265, 280 n.12 (W. Va. 2002).
130 *Arnold*, 511 S.E.2d at 862.
131 142 S.W.3d 277 (Tenn. 2004).
132 *Id.* at 286.
133 Armendariz v. Found. Health Psychcare Services, Inc., 24 Cal. 4th 83, 117, 118, 99 Cal. Rptr. 2d 745, 6 P.3d 669 (2000); *see also* Fitz v. NCR Corp., 13 Cal. Rptr. 3d 88, 104, 105 (Ct. App. 2004); Martinez v. Master Prot. Corp., 12 Cal. Rptr. 3d 663, 669, 670 (Ct. App. 2004); Abramson v. Juniper Networks, Inc., 9 Cal. Rptr. 3d 422, 443, 444 (Ct. App. 2004); Jaramillo v. JH Real Estate Partners, Inc., 3 Cal. Rptr. 3d 525, 535, 536 (Ct. App. 2004) (finding landlord's arbitration clause covering only personal injury claims to be substantively unconscionable for applying exclusively to tenant's claims). *But see* Dunham v. Envtl. Chem. Corp., 2006 WL 2374703 (N.D. Cal. Aug. 16, 2006) (when employee was required to arbitrate all of her claims but the employer reserved the right to go to court to pursue certain injunctive claims that it might have, such as breach of a secrecy agreement, the arbitration clause was unreasonably one-sided and therefore unconscionable and unenforceable); Wis. Auto Title Loans, Inc. v. Jones, 714 N.W.2d 155 (Wis. 2006) (one-sided arbitration provision in loan agree-

The California Supreme Court clarified in *Armendariz* that it was not holding that a one-way arbitration clause was lacking in consideration. "We conclude, rather, that in the context of an arbitration agreement imposed by the employer on the employee, such a one-sided term is unconscionable."[134] In California, at least, it is not necessary that a contract be completely non-mutual for it to be unconscionable, so long as "the agreement exempts from arbitration the claims [the company] is most likely to bring against [individuals]."[135]

The Ninth Circuit has subsequently followed *Armendariz* in holding that an employer's arbitration clause is presumptively unconscionable under California law if it covers only the employee's claims.[136] In *Ingle v. Circuit City Stores, Inc.*,[137] the Ninth Circuit further found that the employer's arbitration clause would be non-mutual and one-sided even if its terms did not explicitly say so because "the possibility that Circuit City would initiate an action against one of its employees is so remote," that the "lucre of the arbitration agreement flows one way: the employee relinquishes rights while the employer generally reaps the benefits of arbitrating its employment disputes."[138] Based on this finding, the Ninth Circuit in *Ingle* concluded that arbitration clauses between employers and individual employees bore a rebuttable presumption of substantive unconscionability in all cases.[139]

An extreme version of a non-mutual one-sided arbitration clause is one that is illusory. As § 5.3, *supra*, explains, a number of courts have refused to enforce illusory arbitration clauses on the grounds that they are insufficient to form an agreement or contract in the first place. In addition, several other courts have held that illusory contracts are unconscionable and unenforceable for that reason as well.[140]

6.5.3.4 Cases Not Finding Non-Mutuality to Be Unconscionable

A number of courts, on the other hand, particularly in Alabama, have found this one-sidedness not to be enough to make an arbitration clause unconscionable.[141] Even the

---

ment, requiring indigent borrower to arbitrate all claims while lender remained free to enforce its rights in court, was unconscionable).

One federal court purportedly applying California law ignored the *Armendariz* case, however, and (citing two cases from other states) held that, "even when one party alone has the option of compelling arbitration, courts have not found the arbitration clause to be unconscionable." Arriaga v. Cross Country Bank, 163 F. Supp. 2d 1189 (S.D. Cal. 2001). Another federal court purportedly applying California law implicitly distinguished *Armendariz* on the basis that it applied only to employment contracts, and not to contracts for a "consumer non-essential good." McCabe v. Dell, Inc., 2007 WL 1434972, at *3 (C.D. Cal. Apr. 12, 2007). *McCabe* also relied on defendant's contention that arbitration offered the plaintiff a fair, low cost, "consumer friendly forum" forum. *Id.*

134 *Armendariz*, 24 Cal. 4th at 118; *accord* Flores v. Transamerica Homefirst, Inc., 93 Cal. App. 4th 846, 113 Cal. Rptr. 2d 376 (2001); Kinney v. United Healthcare Services, Inc., 70 Cal. App. 4th 1322, 83 Cal. Rptr. 2d 348 (1999); Stirlen v. Supercuts, Inc., 51 Cal. App. 4th 1519, 60 Cal. Rptr. 2d 138 (1997).

135 Mercuro v. Super. Ct., 96 Cal. App. 4th 167, 176, 116 Cal. Rptr. 2d 671 (2002); *see also* Higgins v. Super. Ct., 45 Cal. Rptr. 3d 293 (Ct. App. 2006) (contract was unconscionable when it provided for arbitration for the weaker party but the right to go to court for the stronger party); Flores v. Transamerica Homefirst, Inc., 93 Cal. App. 4th 846, 855, 113 Cal. Rptr. 2d 376, 383 (2001) ("As a practical matter, by reserving to itself the remedy of foreclosure, Homefirst has assured the availability of the only remedy it is likely to need.").

136 Ferguson v. Countrywide Credit Indus., Inc., 298 F.3d 778, 783, 784 (9th Cir. 2002); Circuit City Stores v. Adams, 279 F.3d 889, 893, 894 (9th Cir. 2002).

137 328 F.3d 1165 (9th Cir. 2003).

138 *Id.* at 1174.

139 *Id.* at 1174, 1175.

140 *E.g.*, Net Global Mktg., Inc. v. Dialtone, Inc., 217 Fed. Appx. 598 (9th Cir. Jan. 9, 2007) ("The effect of Dialtone's unilateral right to modify the arbitration clause is that it could, for example, craft precisely the sort of asymmetrical arbitration agreement that is prohibited under California law as unconscionable."); Geoffrey v. Wash. Mut. Bank, 484 F. Supp. 2d 1115 (S.D. Cal. 2007) (agreement that permits bank to unilaterally and without notice change the terms is substantively unconscionable).

141 Edwards v. Hovensa, L.L.C., 2007 WL 2200473 (3d Cir. Aug. 2, 2007); Bess v. Check Express, 294 F.3d 1298, 1301 (11th Cir. 2002) (fact that lender may litigate while borrower must arbitrate does not by itself render clause unconscionable); Harris v. Green Tree Fin. Corp, 183 F.3d 173 (3d Cir. 1999) (inequality of bargaining power not reason enough to invalidate arbitration agreement); Battle v. Nissan Motor Acceptance Corp., 2007 WL 1095681, at *4 (E.D. Wis. Mar. 9, 2007) (upholding a non-mutual one-sided arbitration clause when there is adequate consideration for the clause in other provisions of the contract); New S. Fed. Sav. Bank v. Anding, 414 F. Supp. 2d 636 (S.D. Miss. 2006) ("[A]n arbitration clause is not unenforceable solely because it is one-sided. . . . One-sidedness is a factor a court may consider in determining whether an arbitration clause is substantively unconscionable. . . ." (citations omitted)); Miller v. Equifirst Corp. of WV, 2006 WL 2571634, at *14 (S.D. W. Va. Sept. 5, 2006) (considering a retention of right of access to judicial forum for foreclosure and bankruptcy claims "is not so inherently unfair and one-sided as to render the arbitration agreements unenforceable on those grounds"); Fid. Nat'l Corp. v. Blakely, 305 F. Supp. 2d 639, 643 (S.D. Miss. 2003); Owner-Operator Indep. Drivers Ass'n, Inc. v. Swift Transp. Co., 288 F. Supp. 2d 1033, 1039, 1040 (D. Ariz. 2003); Torrance v. Aames Funding Corp., 242 F. Supp. 2d 862 (D. Or. 2002) (reserving foreclosure claims for court justified on the basis of business realities; clause struck down on other unconscionability grounds); Pick v. Discover Fin. Services, Inc., 2001 U.S. Dist. LEXIS 15777 (D. Del. Sept. 28, 2001) ("mutuality is not a requirement of a valid arbitration clause, provided that the underlying contract is supported by consideration"); Hale v. First USA Bank, 2001 U.S. Dist. LEXIS 8045 (S.D.N.Y June 19, 2001); Pridgen v. Green Tree Fin. Servicing Corp., 88 F. Supp. 2d 655 (S.D. Miss. 2000); Gray v. Conseco, Inc., 2000 U.S. Dist. LEXIS 14821 (C.D. Cal. Sept. 29, 2000) (holding that a non-mutual arbitration clause is conscionable because "this Court is compelled to follow the approach taken by the

Alabama Supreme Court has stated, however, that "the absence of mutuality of remedy is still relevant in an unconscionability analysis," and has deemed a one-way provision to be an indicium of unconscionability.[142]

6.5.3.5 Non-Mutual Clauses That Appear to Be Mutual

In response to case law finding lack of mutuality to be unconscionable, creditors may try to draft their arbitration provisions to give the appearance of binding both sides to arbitrate. The practical effect of the clause though is not to bind the creditor.

For example, a clause might state that either party may invoke binding arbitration. Then, if the creditor is sued, it can require that the matter be arbitrated. On the other hand, until the debtor invokes the arbitration clause, the creditor can continue to file collection actions in court. Virtually all collection actions are disposed of by default judgment, meaning the debtor never requests removal to arbitration. Creditors may be so confident that they can continue to bring actions in court despite the debtor's ability to remove the case to arbitration that the creditor may reserve the right to collect attorney fees and court costs if a collection action is brought in court, and the consumer does not elect arbitration.[143]

Another way of avoiding mutuality problems is to state that all multi-party claims, such as class actions, are to be sent to arbitration. No creditor collection actions are ever brought as a class action, but consumer claims often are. Similarly, the arbitration agreement may specify that actions over a certain amount, such as $25,000, must go to arbitration. This provision would apply to almost all class actions, but not to the creditor's collection actions. A related ploy is to require that all disputes above the small claims jurisdictional limit be sent to arbitration. This provision allows the creditor to continue to use small claims court as a collection mill.[144]

Courts are willing to look beneath the surface of an arbitration agreement to determine if in fact the merchant as a practical matter will arbitrate its disputes, or whether the arbitration provision allows the merchant essentially to avoid the requirement.[145] An unconscionability finding is based on whether a clause is oppressive in practice, even if it superficially appears to be even-handed.

In *Ingle v. Circuit City Stores, Inc.*, the Ninth Circuit recently articulated a rule that all arbitration clauses between employers and employees are rebuttably presumed to be substantively unconscionable because of the likelihood that only the employee will bring claims to arbitration.[146] It remains to be seen whether this very broad rule will be adopted by other courts.

---

majority of courts out of deference to the federal policy favoring arbitration"); Goodwin v. Ford Motor Credit Co., 970 F. Supp. 1007 (M.D. Ala. 1997); Jim Walter Homes, Inc. v. Saxton, 880 So. 2d 428 (Ala. 2003); Walter Indus., Inc. v. McMillan, 804 So. 2d 1081 (Ala. 2001); Green Tree Fin. Corp. v. Vintson, 753 So. 2d 497 (Ala. 1999); Green Tree Fin. Corp. v. Wampler, 749 So. 2d 409 (Ala. 1999); *Ex parte* Perry, 744 So. 2d 859 (Ala. 1999); *Ex parte* McNaughton, 728 So. 2d 592 (Ala. 1998); Villar v. Mut. Prot. Trust, 2007 WL 1519788, at *8 (Cal. Ct. App. May 25, 2007) ("limited exceptions to the obligation to arbitrate are justified by a legitimate commercial need"); Rains v. Found. Health Sys. Life & Health, 23 P.3d 1249 (Colo. Ct. App. 2001); Crawford v. Results Oriented, Inc., 548 S.E.2d 342 (Ga. 2001); Conseco Fin. Servicing Corp. v. Wilder, 47 S.W.3d 335 (Ky. Ct. App. 2001) ("there is no inherent reason to require that the parties have equal arbitration rights"); McKenzie Check Advance v. Hardy, 866 So. 2d 446, 452, 453 (Miss. 2004); State *ex rel.* Vincent v. Schneider, 194 S.W.3d 853 (Mo. 2006) ("The contract will not be invalidated for lack of mutuality of obligation of the arbitration clause."); Motsinger v. Litia Rose-FT, Inc., 156 P.3d 156, 167 (Or. Ct. App. 2007) ("[T]he exception from mandatory arbitration for foreclosure contained within the . . . arbitration agreement, in and of itself, does not render the arbitration agreement presumptively unconscionable under Pennsylvania law."); DEX Media, Inc. v. Nat. Mgmt. Services, Inc., 150 P.3d 1093, 1100 (Or. Ct. App. 2007) (one-sided, non-mutual contract not unconscionable under Colorado law); Salley v. Option One Mortgage Corp., 925 A.2d 115, 128 (Pa. 2007) (finding a facial business justification for excepting foreclosures from arbitration, as the safeguards preserved benefit both lender and borrower); Lackey v. Green Tree Fin. Corp., 330 S.C. 388, 498 S.E.2d 898 (Ct. App. 1998); *In re* FirstMerit Bank, 52 S.W.3d 749 (Tex. 2001); Walters v. AAA Waterproofing, Inc., 85 P.3d 389, 393, 394 (Wash. Ct. App. 2004), *review granted*, 108 P.3d 1227 (Wash. 2005); *see also* Choice v. Option One Mortgage Corp., 2003 WL 22097455 (E.D. Pa. May 13, 2003) (one-sided, non-mutual contract is not unconscionable under Pennsylvania law, as the Third Circuit has predicted that law in Harris v. Green Tree Fin. Corp., 183 F.3d 173 (3d Cir. 1999)); Stenzel v. Dell, Inc., 870 A.2d 133 (Me. 2005) (one-sided, non-mutual contract is not unconscionable under Texas law); Neatherlin Homes, Inc. v. Love, 2007 WL 700996, at *6 (Tex. App. Mar. 8, 2007) ("The agreement's provision allowing Neatherlin to retain the option to use judicial or non-judicial relief in certain circumstances did not make either the consideration for the underlying contract, or the promises to arbitrate any disagreements, illusory.")

142 Am. Gen. Fin., Inc. v. Branch, 793 So. 2d 738, 749 (Ala. 2000); *see also* Potts v. Baptist Health Sys., Inc., 2002 WL 31845929, at *11 (Ala. Dec. 20, 2002) (finding that the "type and degree of inequality of contractual provisions" is an important factor in an unconscionability analysis).

143 *See* Zawikowski v. Beneficial Nat'l Bank, 1999 U.S. Dist. LEXIS 514 (N.D. Ill. Jan. 7, 1999) (finding no problems with non-mutuality because the consumer still has the right to invoke arbitration).

144 *But see* Lozano v. AT & T Wireless, 216 F. Supp. 2d 1071, 1075 (clause that sends claims over small claims limit to arbitration not substantively unconscionable).

145 *See* Pitchford v. Oakwood Mobile Homes, Inc., 124 F. Supp. 2d 958 (W.D. Va. 2000). *But see* Zawikowski v. Beneficial Nat'l Bank, 1999 U.S. Dist. LEXIS 514 (N.D. Ill. Jan. 7, 1999) (finding no problems with non-mutuality because the consumer still has the right to invoke arbitration).

146 Ingle v. Circuit City Stores, Inc., 328 F.3d 1165 (9th Cir. 2003).

6.5.3.6 Non-Mutual Appeal Rights Rendering Clause Unconscionable

Some courts have also struck down arbitration clauses that include one-way appeals provisions that effectively insure that the merchant will be the only party to bring appeals. In *Worldwide Insurance Group v. Klopp*, for example, the Delaware Supreme Court found that an arbitration clause that only permitted appeals of high awards would only benefit the insurance company and not the insured:

> It is the insurer who, generally, would be dissatisfied with a high award. The policy provision thus presents an "escape hatch" to the insurer for avoidance of high arbitration awards, whether or not the award was fair and reasonable. However, the insured, who would tend to be dissatisfied with a low award, is barred from appealing such an award. . . .[147]

In light of this one-sided procedure, the court held that the arbitration clause at issue was against public policy, and therefore unconscionable, and refused to enforce it.[148] The California courts have also reached the same conclusion as to such provisions.[149]

A Pennsylvania appellate court reached the same conclusion in another case involving a one-way appeals provision, setting out a powerful analysis of the economic reality of the matter:

> In this case, the clause is completely unconscionable. It allows the insurer to obtain a trial when the claimant or insured obtains an arbitration award of any significant amount but binds the claimant or insured to the amount of the arbitration award when the claimant or insured is awarded nothing or a minuscule amount. Appellee suggests that the clause is fair because "either party" can appeal if the award is over $15,000. This suggestion ignores the reality of the effect of the clause. It allows the insurance company the unfettered right to a trial whenever an award is made in favor of a claimant or insured while a losing claimant or insured is bound by his award. The clause so clearly favors the insurer over the claimant or insured that it is repugnant to notions of due process, equal protection, justice and fair play.[150]

6.5.4 Clauses That Strip Statutory Remedies

6.5.4.1 Limitation on Damages

One factor in determining whether a clause is unconscionable is whether it requires consumers to give up legal remedies.[151] For example, an arbitration clause that expressly limits the merchant's liability to actual damages can lead to a finding of substantive unconscionability, because it shields the merchant from punitive damages.[152]

---

147 Worldwide Ins. Group v. Klopp, 603 A.2d 788, 791 (Del. 1992).
148 603 A.2d at 791, 792.
149 *See* Little v. Auto Stiegler, Inc., 29 Cal. 4th 1064, 130 Cal. Rptr. 2d 892, 63 P.3d 979 (2003); Higgins v. Super. Ct., 140 Cal. App. 4th 1238, 1253–1254, 45 Cal. Rptr. 3d 293, 305 (2006); Fittante v. Palm Springs Motors, Inc., 105 Cal. App. 4th 708, 129 Cal. Rptr. 2d 659 (2003).
150 Zak v. Prudential Prop. & Cas. Ins. Co., 713 A.2d 681, 684 (Pa. Super. Ct. 1998).
151 Lowden v. T-Mobile, USA, Inc., 2006 WL 1009279, at *4–*5 (W.D. Wash. Apr. 13, 2006) (finding limitations with respect to punitive and exemplary damages substantively unconscionable "because they deprive Plaintiffs of the means to effectively vindicate their rights under the CPA" and "they are effectively one-sided" when, despite being "nominally mutual, the Court cannot imagine a scenario in which Defendant would ever seek punitive damages, under the CPA or otherwise, against its individual customers"); Alterra Healthcare Corp. v. Linton, 953 So. 2d 574, 578 (Fla. Dist. Ct. App. 2007) (arbitration clauses capping noneconomic damages and waiving punitive damages are void as against public policy expressed in the Assisted Living Facilities Act); Alterra Healthcare Corp. v. Bryant, 937 So. 2d 263, 266 (Fla. Dist. Ct. App. 2006) (same); SA-PG Ocala, L.L.C. v. Stokes, 935 So. 2d 1242 (Fla. Dist. Ct. App. 2006) (arbitration clause limiting various types of damages violated the state nursing home act and thus violated the public policy of the state); Covenant Health Rehab. of Picayune, Ltd. P'ship v. Brown, 949 So. 2d 732, 739 (Miss. 2007) (finding provisions that limited liability and waived criminal damages unenforceable); *see* Torrance v. Aames Funding Corp., 242 F. Supp. 2d 862 (D. Or. 2002); Stirlen v. Supercuts, Inc., 51 Cal. App. 4th 1519, 60 Cal. Rptr. 2d 138 (1997); Powertel, Inc. v. Bexley, 743 So. 2d 570 (Fla. Dist. Ct. App. 1999); Carll v. Terminix Int'l Co., 793 A.2d 921 (Pa. Super. Ct. 2002); West Virginia *ex rel.* Dunlap v. Berger, 567 S.E.2d 265 (W. Va. 2002); Samuel Williston, Treatise on the Law of Contracts § 18:13 (Richard A. Lord ed., 4th ed. 1998); *see also* Broughton v. CIGNA Healthplans, 21 Cal. 4th 1066, 90 Cal. Rptr. 2d 334, 988 P.2d 67 (1999) (striking down a limitation on a state statutory remedy as against public policy).
152 *See* Hadnot v. Bay, Ltd., 344 F.3d 474, 478 n.14 (5th Cir. 2003) ("[T]he Agreement's ban on punitive and exemplary damages is unenforceable in a Title VII case."); Circuit City Stores, Inc. v. Adams, 279 F.3d 889 (9th Cir. 2002) (holding an arbitration clause unconscionable when the agreement limits the relief available to employees; "Under the [agreement], the remedies are limited to injunctive relief, up to one year of back pay and up to two years of front pay, compensatory damages, and punitive damages in an amount up to the greater of the amount of back pay and front pay awarded or $5,000."); Ting v. AT & T, 182 F. Supp. 2d 902 (N.D. Cal. 2002), *aff'd in relevant part*, 319 F.3d 1126 (9th Cir. 2003); Hausmaninger Benoe Lang Alford & Geselowitz, CPAs, Inc. v. Paychex, Inc., 2002 WL 1839273, at *3 (Cal. Ct. App. Aug. 12, 2002) ("the limitations on remedies in the contract are against public policy and render the arbitration clause unenforceable"); Pinedo v. Premium Tobacco, Inc., 85 Cal. App. 4th 774, 102 Cal. Rptr. 2d 435 (2000) (arbitration clause held to be unconscionable, in part because it barred employee from recovering damages that were provided under employment statutes); Kinney v. United HealthCare Ser-

In two recent cases, the Alabama Supreme Court has held that a provision in an arbitration contract immunizing a party from liability for punitive damages is substantively unconscionable. In *Cavalier Manufacturing, Inc. v. Jackson*, the Alabama Supreme Court stated:

> We hold that a predispute arbitration clause that forbids an arbitrator from awarding punitive damages is void as contrary to the public policy of this State—to protect its citizens in certain legislatively prescribed actions from wrongful behavior and to punish the wrongdoer. If parties to an arbitration agreement waive any arbitrator's ability to award punitive damages, the door will open wide to rampant fraudulent conduct with few, if any, legal repercussions.[153]

In *Ex parte Thicklin*, similarly, the court stated: "[I]t violates public policy for a party to contract away its liability for punitive damages, regardless whether the provision doing so was intended to operate in an arbitral or judicial forum. Thus, enforcement of this portion of the arbitration agreement violates public policy, and its enforcement would be unconscionable."[154] Even if the arbitration clause nominally prevents both sides from obtaining punitive damages, as a practical matter, the restriction only applies to the consumer's ability to obtain such an award, because merchants never recover such damages from consumers.[155]

Similarly, the West Virginia Supreme Court of Appeals recently ruled that an arbitration clause in a merchant's consumer contracts which prohibited awards of punitive damages was substantively unconscionable.[156] In so holding, the state supreme court recognized that this rule was consistent with a well-established body of general state law prohibiting exculpatory provisions in contracts of adhesion.[157]

The same is the case for an arbitration agreement that limits the type of actual damages that a plaintiff can recover.[158] On the other hand, an arbitration agreement may not be unconscionable just because the consumer seeks treble damages, when the arbitrator has the authority to award such damages.[159] Also, a California court has held that limitations on damages are not so one-sided as to shock the conscience when an arbitrator ruled in favor of the defendants, and plaintiff was not entitled to any of the remedies she sought.[160] Because plaintiff did not claim on appeal that she was precluded from presenting her case to the arbitration panel, nor did she challenge the arbitration award on any other ground, the limitation on damages did not produce a harsh result.[161]

In the wake of the United States Supreme Court's decision in *Pacificare v. Book*, however, a number of courts have refused to consider unconscionability challenges to arbitration clauses that stripped individuals of statutory rights. These courts have held that the arbitrator, rather than a court, should consider the validity of these challenges.[162]

---

vices, Inc., 70 Cal. App. 4th 1322, 83 Cal. Rptr. 2d 348 (1999); Stirlen v. Supercuts, Inc., 51 Cal. App. 4th 1519, 60 Cal. Rptr. 2d 138 (1997); Powertel, Inc. v. Bexley, 743 So. 2d 570 (Fla. Dist. Ct. App. 1999); Carll v. Terminix Int'l Co., 793 A.2d 921 (Pa. Super. Ct. 2002) (arbitration clause prohibiting direct, indirect, special, incidental, consequential, exemplary or punitive damages is unconscionable); West Virginia *ex rel.* Dunlap v. Berger, 567 S.E.2d 265 (W. Va. 2002) (arbitration clause prohibiting award of punitive damages is unconscionable); Samuel Williston, Treatise on the Law of Contracts § 18:13 (Richard A. Lord ed., 4th ed. 1998). *But see* Brennan v. Bally Total Fitness, 198 F. Supp. 2d 377 (S.D.N.Y. 2002) (not unconscionable for arbitration clause to bar employee from pursuing certain damage remedies, capping certain damage awards, and shortening the limitations period); Veal v. Orkin Exterminating Co., 2001 U.S. Dist. LEXIS 4846 (W.D. Mich. Apr. 9, 2001) ("The fact that the arbitration provision prohibits the recovery of exemplary, treble, liquidated, or punitive damage does not of itself render the contract substantively unreasonable."); *In re* Standard Meat Co., 2007 WL 730660, at *4 (Tex. App. Mar. 9, 2007) (when arbitration agreement limits remedy based on "missing the proper caption," and when party stipulates that the complained-of provision will not be enforced, court need not address the complaint).

153 Cavalier Mfg., Inc. v. Jackson, 823 So. 2d 1237, 1248 (Ala. 2001).

154 *Ex parte* Thicklin, 824 So. 2d 723 (Ala. 2002); *see also* Alterra Healthcare Corp. v. Linton, 953 So. 2d 574, 578 (Fla. Dist. Ct. App. 2007) ("The arbitrability of statutory claims rests on the assumption that the arbitration clause permits relief equivalent to that available via the courts. An arbitration clause is thus unenforceable if its provisions deprive the plaintiff of the ability to obtain meaningful relief for alleged statutory violations."); Simpson v. MSA of Myrtle Beach, Inc., 644 S.E.2d 663, 671 (S.C. 2007) ("[T]his provision is an unconscionable waiver of statutory rights, and therefore, unenforceable."). *But see also* Sears Termite & Pest Control, Inc. v. Robinson, 883 So. 2d 153 (Ala. 2003) (arbitration clause limiting consumer's damages to $250,000 is not unconscionable).

155 *See* Powertel, Inc. v. Bexley, 743 So. 2d 570 (Fla. Dist. Ct. App. 1999); Samuel Williston, Treatise on the Law of Contracts § 18:13 (Richard A. Lord ed., 4th ed. 1998).

156 West Virginia *ex rel.* Dunlap v. Berger, 567 S.E.2d 265 (W. Va. 2002).

157 *Id.* at 274–276.

158 *See, e.g.*, Carll v. Terminix Int'l Co., 793 A.2d 921 (Pa. Super. Ct. 2002) (prohibition of awards of direct, indirect, special, incidental, consequential, exemplary, or punitive damages renders arbitration clause unconscionable).

159 Stehli v. Action Custom Homes, Inc., 1999 Ohio App. LEXIS 4464 (Ohio Ct. App. Sept. 24, 1999); *cf.* Oblix, Inc. v. Winiecki, 2003 WL 1964193 (N.D. Ill. Apr. 24, 2003) (arbitration clause is enforceable despite cap on damages recovery because cap is trumped by incorporation of arbitration rules that guarantee all remedies that would be available in court).

160 Watts v. Pac. Window Products, Inc., 2007 WL 987872, at *5 (Cal. Ct. App. Apr. 4, 2007).

161 *Id.*

162 *See, e.g.*, Terminix Int'l Co. v. Palmer Ranch Ltd. P'ship, 432 F.3d 1327 (11th Cir. 2005) (challenge to the legality of contract term stripping one party of substantive statutory rights and remedies should be decided by the arbitrator rather than a court.

6.5.4.2 Limitation on Attorney Fees

A limitation on statutory attorney fees and costs has also been found to be unconscionable or against public policy.[163] The unconscionability argument is somewhat weaker when the arbitrator has the authority to award fees to a prevailing consumer, but does not usually do so.[164] On the other hand, if an award of attorney fees to a prevailing consumer is mandatory under a statute, then providing discretion to the arbitrator to decide whether or not to award those fees could lead to an unconscionability finding.

6.5.4.3 Limitation on Injunctive and Equitable Relief

An arbitration clause that restricts a consumer's ability to seek injunctive or other equitable relief can be found unconscionable, particularly when the right to that relief is explicitly granted by state statute.[165] The same can be said about an arbitration clause or arbitration rule that appears to allow injunctive relief. Even if the arbitrator nominally has authority to order injunctive relief, arbitration is not an appropriate forum for an action involving a "public injunction" under a state statute permitting representative actions.[166]

Arbitration is not a suitable forum for an action seeking injunctive relief when it is being sought under a deceptive practices (UDAP) statute and the consumer is acting as a private attorney general on behalf of the public at large. In California, for example, the state legislature did not intend injunctive relief under a private attorney general statute to be subject to arbitration.[167]

6.5.4.4 Shortened Statute of Limitations

Some arbitration agreements or the rules of certain arbitration service providers require that the consumer's claim be brought to arbitration within a set period of time, or the claim is forfeited. This period of time may be substantially shorter than the applicable limitations period for bringing the action in court. Such a limitation has been found to be unconscionable.[168] Even if a provision shortening the limitations period would not affect the outcome in a given case, such a provision may still render an arbitration clause unenforceable because "unconscionability is determined on the basis of the circumstances at the time of contract formation, and whether the agreement was reasonable then."[169] Even when a provision shortening the limitations period is not unconscionable, it may nonetheless be argued in some cases to be illegal under state law.[170]

The Third Circuit has carved out a more nuanced position on this issue. It has held that, in general, parties may contract to shorten limitations periods, but has held that "such a time period must still be reasonable."[171] In the context of an

---

163 Alexander v. Anthony Int'l, Ltd. P'ship, 341 F.3d 256 (3d Cir. 2003) (provisions barring punitive damages and limiting attorney fees were "one-sided in the extreme and unreasonably favorable to" the employer, and were substantively unconscionable); Lowden v. T-Mobile, USA, Inc., 2006 WL 1009279, at *8 (W.D. Wash. Apr. 13, 2006) (finding a limitation on attorney fees substantively unconscionable when such prohibition undermines a specific statutory entitlement for such fees); Broughton v. CIGNA Healthplans, 21 Cal. 4th 1066, 90 Cal. Rptr. 2d 334, 988 P.2d 67 (1999); Matthews-Deaton v. El Torito Restaurants, Inc., 2006 WL 2349557 (Cal. Ct. App. Aug. 15, 2006) (striking as unenforceable a provision that stripped an employee of her right to receive attorney fees); Maciejewski v. Alpha Sys. Lab, Inc., 87 Cal. Rptr. 2d 390 (Ct. App. 1999), *vacated*, 11 P.3d 954 (Cal. 2000); Stirlen v. Supercuts, Inc., 51 Cal. App. 4th 1519, 60 Cal. Rptr. 2d 138 (1997); Delta Funding Corp. v. Harris, 912 A.2d 104 (N.J. 2006) ("To the extent that this provision in Harris's consumer contract would prevent her from recovering discretionary attorney's fees and costs under RESPA, it is unconscionable.").

164 Stehli v. Action Custom Homes, Inc., 1999 Ohio App. LEXIS 4464 (Ohio Ct. App. Sept. 24, 1999).

165 Lozada v. Dale Baker Oldsmobile, Inc., 91 F. Supp. 2d 1087 (W.D. Mich. 2000); Stirlen v. Supercuts, Inc., 51 Cal. App. 4th 1519, 60 Cal. Rptr. 2d 138 (1997); Powertel, Inc. v. Bexley, 743 So. 2d 570 (Fla. Dist. Ct. App. 1999); Samuel Williston, Treatise on the Law of Contracts § 18:13 (Richard A. Lord ed., 4th ed. 1998).

166 Broughton v. CIGNA Healthplans, 21 Cal. 4th 1066, 90 Cal. Rptr. 2d 334, 988 P.2d 67 (1999).

167 *Id.*

168 Davis v. O'Melveny & Myers, 485 F.3d 1066 (9th Cir. 2007) ("forcing employees to comply with a strict one-year limitations period for employment-related statutory claims is oppressive in a mandatory arbitration clause"); Nyulassy v. Lockheed Martin Corp., 16 Cal. Rptr. 3d 296, 308 (Ct. App. 2004) (arbitration clause that shortened the plaintiff's limitations period from four years to 180 days was "substantively unconscionable"); Martinez v. Master Prot. Corp., 12 Cal. Rptr. 3d 663 (Ct. App. 2004) ("The shortened limitations period provided by FireMaster's arbitration agreement is unconscionable and insufficient to protect its employees' right to vindicate their statutory rights."); Wilson v. Bally Total Fitness Corp., Inc., 2003 WL 21398324 (Cal. Ct. App. June 18, 2003) ("[A]s to the nonwaivable statutory claims at issue, the provision [shortening the limitations period] is contrary to public policy because the Agreement compels employees to arbitrate such claims while depriving them of significant remedies they would normally enjoy."); Stirlen v. Supercuts, Inc., 51 Cal. App. 4th 1519, 60 Cal. Rptr. 2d 138 (1997); *see also* Al-Safin v. Circuit City Stores, Inc., 394 F.3d 1254 (9th Cir. 2005) (provision in arbitration clause that shortened limitations period for employment claims to 180 days was unconscionable); Siordia v. Circuit City Stores, Inc., 2005 WL 1368083 (9th Cir. June 9, 2005) (arbitration clause that "imposes a strict one year statute of limitations" is substantively unconscionable).

169 Lelouis v. W. Directory Co., 230 F. Supp. 2d 1214, 1221 (D. Or. 2001).

170 *But see* Ting v. AT & T, 319 F.3d 1126 (9th Cir. 2003) (holding that a state statute prohibiting the waiver of protections such as the statute of limitations was preempted by the FAA).

171 Alexander v. Anthony Int'l, Ltd. P'ship, 341 F.3d 256, 266 (3d Cir. 2003).

employment dispute, the Third Circuit held that a limitations period of only thirty days was "clearly unreasonable and unduly favorable to" the employer.[172]

6.5.4.5 High Arbitration Fees Accentuate Problem of Remedy Stripping Provisions

When considering whether limitations on remedies are unconscionable, the consumer should also point out any requirement that the consumer pay hefty arbitration costs.[173] One aspect of the unconscionability of a limitation on remedies is that it makes consumer litigation impractical. The high cost of arbitration fees aggravates the impact of restrictions on remedies when those restrictions also make consumer litigation uneconomical (for example, limits on attorney fees, class actions, and punitive damages). All these limits taken together mean that the merchant has effectively insulated itself from liability under state consumer protection laws, while providing the consumer with no opportunity to bargain to retain such a right.[174]

6.5.5 Class Action Bans Embedded in Arbitration Clauses

6.5.5.1 General

Class action proceedings are often necessary for consumers to sustain an economically viable cause of action when their individual claims against a merchant or lender are for small sums of money.[175] When businesses use arbitration clauses in their standard form contracts of adhesion to secure a waiver of consumers' rights to bring class action claims, there is a serious concern that the businesses are abusing their superior bargaining power to bring about an effective waiver of liability for their unlawful conduct.

Courts have held or stated that class action bans embedded in arbitration clauses are unconscionable and unenforceable in the context of particular cases in numerous jurisdictions, including federal courts applying the laws of Arizona, California, Georgia, Florida, Massachusetts, Michigan, Oregon, and Washington, and state courts applying the laws of Alabama, California, Illinois, Missouri, New Jersey, Ohio, Oregon, Pennsylvania, Washington, West Virginia, and Wisconsin.[176]

The vast majority of courts to consider the issue have held that challenges alleging unconscionability, and thus challenging the enforceability of class action bans embedded in arbitration clauses, are to be evaluated by courts, and not arbitrators. In *Dale v. Comcast Corp.*, for example, the Eleventh Circuit stated that the issue presented "is whether the Arbitration Provision's class action waiver is unconscio-

---

172 *Id.*
173 *See* § 6.5.2.4, *supra*.
174 *See* Powertel, Inc. v. Bexley, 743 So. 2d 570 (Fla. Dist. Ct. App. 1999); Samuel Williston, Treatise on the Law Contracts § 18:13 (Richard A. Lord ed., 4th ed. 1998).
175 For a discussion of judicial authority recognizing the economic necessity of class action proceedings, see §§ 6.5.5.2, 6.5.5.3, *infra*.
176 *See* Dale v. Comcast Corp., 498 F.3d 1216 (11th Cir. 2007) (Ga. law); Shroyer v. New Cingular Wireless Services, Inc., 2007 WL 2332068 (9th Cir. Aug. 17, 2007) (Cal. law); Al-Safin v. Circuit City Stores, Inc., 394 F.3d 1254 (9th Cir. 2005) (Cal. law); Tamayo v. Brainstorm USA, 154 Fed. Appx. 564 (9th Cir. 2005); Ingle v. Circuit City Stores, Inc., 328 F.3d 1165 (9th Cir. 2003) (Cal. law); Ting v. AT & T, 319 F.3d 1126, 1152 (9th Cir. 2003) (Cal. law); Oestreicher v. Alienware Corp., 2007 WL 2302490 (N.D. Cal. Aug. 10, 2007); Brazil v. Dell Inc., 2007 WL 2255296 (N.D. Cal. Aug. 3, 2007); Creighton v. Blockbuster, 2007 WL 1560626 (D. Or. May 25, 2007); Bradberry v. T-Mobile USA, Inc., 2007 WL 1241936 (N.D. Cal. Apr. 27, 2007); Cooper v. QC Fin. Serv., Inc., 2007 WL 974100, at *10 (D. Ariz. Mar. 30, 2007); Skirchak v. Dynamics Research Corp., 432 F. Supp. 2d 175, 181 (D. Mass. 2006); Riensche v. Cingular Wireless, L.L.C., 2006 WL 3827477 (W.D. Wash. Dec. 27, 2006); Doerhoff v. Gen. Growth Properties, Inc., 2006 WL 3210502, at *6 (W.D. Mo. Nov. 6, 2006); Winig v. Cingular Wireless, L.L.C., 2006 WL 2766007 (N.D. Cal. Sept. 27, 2006); Wong v. T-Mobile U.S.A., 2006 WL 2042512 (E.D. Mich. July 20, 2006); Lowden v. T-Mobile, USA, Inc., 2006 WL 1009279 (W.D. Wash. Apr. 13, 2006); Janda v. T-Mobile USA, Inc., 2006 WL 708936 (N.D. Cal. Mar. 17, 2006); Sprague v. Household Int'l, 473 F. Supp. 2d 966 (W.D. Mo. 2005); Luna v. Household Fin. Corp., III, 236 F. Supp. 2d 1166, 1178–1179 (W.D. Wash. 2002); Comb v. PayPal, Inc., 218 F. Supp. 2d 1165 (N.D. Cal. 2002); ACORN v. Household Int'l, Inc., 211 F. Supp. 2d 1160 (N.D. Cal. 2002); Lozada v. Dale Baker Oldsmobile, Inc., 91 F. Supp. 2d 1087, 1105 (W.D. Mich. 2000); Gentry v. Super. Ct., 64 Cal. Rptr. 3d 773, 788, 165 P.3d 556, 571 (Cal. 2007); Discover Bank v. Super. Ct., 36 Cal. 4th 148, 161, 113 P.3d 1100, 1108–1109 (Cal. 2005); *In re* Cingular Cases, 2007 WL 93229 (Cal. Ct. App. Jan. 16, 2007); Merritt v. Cingular Wireless, L.L.C., 2006 WL 2744357 (Cal. Ct. App. Sept. 27, 2006); Cable Connection, Inc. v. DirecTV, Inc., 143 Cal. App. 4th 207, 49 Cal. Rptr. 3d 187 (2006); Cohen v. DirecTV, Inc., 142 Cal. App. 4th 1442, 48 Cal. Rptr. 3d 813 (2006); Aral v. Earthlink, Inc., 134 Cal. App. 4th 544, 36 Cal. Rptr. 3d 229 (2005); Szetela v. Discover Bank, 97 Cal. App. 4th 1094, 1101, 118 Cal. Rptr. 2d 862, 868 (2002); Powertel, Inc. v. Bexley, 743 So. 2d 570, 576 (Fla. Dist. Ct. App. 1999); Reuter v. Davis, 2006 WL 3743016, at *4 (Fla. Cir. Ct. Dec. 12, 2006); Kinkel v. Cingular Wireless, L.L.C., 223 Ill. 2d 1, 42, 857 N.E.2d 250, 275 (Ill. 2006); Whitney v. Alltel Communications, Inc., 173 S.W.3d 300, 309 (Mo. Ct. App. 2005); Muhammad v. County Bank of Rehoboth Beach, 189 N.J. 1, 21, 912 A.2d 88, 100 (2006); Schwartz v. Alltel Corp., 2006 WL 2243649, at *6 (Ohio Ct. App. June 29, 2006); Eagle v. Fred Martin Motor Co., 157 Ohio App. 3d 150, 178, 809 N.E.2d 1161, 1183 (Ohio Ct. App. 2004); Vasquez-Lopez v. Beneficial Or., Inc., 210 Or. App. 553, 567, 152 P.3d 940, 948 (2007); Thibodeau v. Comcast Corp., 912 A.2d 874, 885 (Pa. Super. Ct. 2006); Scott v. Cingular Wireless, 160 Wash. 2d 843, 854 n.4, 161 P.3d 1000, 1006 n.4 (Wash. 2007); State *ex rel.* Dunlap v. Berger, 211 W. Va. 549, 562–563, 567 S.E.2d 265, 278–279 (W. Va. 2002); Coady v. Cross Country Bank, 729 N.W.2d 732 (Wis. Ct. App. 2007). *See generally* Pamela MacLean, *Class Action Waivers Hit a Wall*, Nat'l L.J., Aug. 27, 2007 (noting the "definite trend" of courts striking class action bans as unconscionable).

nable under Georgia law and thus unenforceable as a matter of law," and held that "because the subscribers' unconscionability argument places in issue the enforceability of the Arbitration Provision itself, we may decide the issue."[177] In *Muhammad v. County Bank of Rehoboth Beach*,[178] the defendant argued that the enforceability of a ban on class actions that would limit the ability of the arbitrator to conduct the case is a question for the arbitrator and not the court. The court flatly rejected that argument, and held that because the "class-arbitration waivers . . . are part of the arbitration agreements, and not part of the contracts as a whole," the court was "empowered to address this challenge."[179] The court then struck down the class action ban under New Jersey law.[180] Numerous other courts have agreed with these conclusions and have held that challenges to the enforceability of class action bans are to be decided by courts and not arbitrators.[181]

It is beyond the scope of this manual to offer a detailed or thorough discussion of choice-of-law principles. Practitioners should be aware, however, that many corporations have sought to avoid the impact of state laws that strike down class action bans by including provisions in their contracts that select the law of some jurisdiction that would enforce the class action ban. Some courts have upheld such choice-of-law terms and enforced class action bans embedded in arbitration clauses in reliance upon them.[182] Many other courts have disagreed, however, and have held that when the contract law of a state where a consumer lives would strike down a class action ban, a choice-of-law term selecting the law of a state that would enforce the class action ban violates a fundamental policy of the consumer's state and should be disregarded.[183]

As noted in § 6.5.5.5, *infra*, however, a large number of courts have rejected the argument that a prohibition of consumer class actions by itself renders an arbitration clause substantively unconscionable.

6.5.5.2 Courts Finding That Class Action Bans Are Exculpatory Because of the Small Size of Claims

The district court in *Ting* held that the ban on class actions amounted to an exculpatory clause. It based its conclusion upon an evidentiary record that included the complaints from previous consumer class actions filed against AT & T, declarations from the lawyers who brought those cases stating that the claims would have been economically infeasible to prosecute on an individual basis, and records showing that past administrative actions by the Federal Communications Commission did not provide for effective enforcement of individual damages claims by consumers.[184] By producing an extensive factual record on the effects of the particular arbitration clause provisions at issue, the plaintiffs in *Ting* succeeded in having the clause struck down based, in part, upon the district court's finding that AT & T was "rewriting substantially the legal landscape on which its customers must contend."[185]

---

177 Dale v. Comcast Corp., 498 F.3d 1216, 1218 n.2 (11th Cir. 2007).
178 912 A.2d 88 (N.J. 2006).
179 *Id.* at 96.
180 *Id.* at 100–101.
181 Kristian v. Comcast Corp., 446 F.3d 25, 55 (1st Cir. 2006) (noting that "[b]ecause the denial of class arbitration in the pursuit of antitrust claims has the potential to prevent Plaintiffs from vindicating their statutory rights, Plaintiffs present a question of arbitrability" for a court to decide, and striking class action ban on grounds that consumer antitrust plaintiffs could not vindicate their rights absent a class action); Cooper v. QC Fin. Services, Inc., 2007 WL 974100 (D. Ariz. Mar. 30, 2007) (court has jurisdiction to consider challenge to class action ban included in an arbitration clause); Vasquez-Lopez v. Beneficial Or., Inc., 210 Or. App. 553, 152 P.3d 940, 947–948 (2007) ("The trial court, properly considering the issues raised in plaintiffs' complaint as well as its response to the motion to compel arbitration, properly concluded that the challenge to the arbitration agreement was distinct from the challenges to the substantive provisions of the contract. For that reason, the court did not err in deciding the validity of the arbitration rider instead of staying proceedings while the arbitrator decided it.").
182 *See, e.g.,* Homa v. Am. Express Co., 2007 WL 1585168 (D.N.J. May 31, 2007) (rejecting the argument that a class-arbitration ban is unconscionable under New Jersey law, because the court enforced a Utah choice-of-law provision and found that class action bans are acceptable under Utah law); Omstead v. Dell, Inc., 473 F. Supp. 2d 1018 (N.D. Cal. Feb. 13, 2007) (Texas law (which permits class action bans) governs over California law in case involving allegations of sales of defective computers); Spann v. Am. Express Travel Related Services Co., 2006 WL 2516431 (Tenn. Ct. App. Aug. 30, 2006) (holding that the class action ban embedded in arbitration clause was acceptable under Utah law).
183 *E.g.,* Tamayo v. Brainstorm USA, 154 Fed. Appx. 564 (9th Cir. 2005) ("[t]o the extent that Ohio law would enforce the class-action waiver at issue . . . it would be contrary to California public policy and thus not applicable"); Oestreicher v. Alienware Corp., 2007 WL 2302490 (N.D. Cal. Aug. 10, 2007) ("Because Florida law is contrary to California's fundamental policy, and because California has a materially greater interest in the litigation, the court will apply California law to determine whether the arbitration clause is enforceable."); Brazil v. Dell Inc., 2007 WL 2255296 (N.D. Cal. Aug. 3, 2007); Doerhoff v. Gen. Growth Properties, Inc., 2006 WL 3210502 (W.D. Mo. Nov. 6, 2006) ("application of New York law in this case would be contrary to the fundamental policy of Missouri"); Klussman v. Cross Country Bank, 134 Cal. App. 4th 1283, 36 Cal. Rptr. 3d 728 (2005) ("Delaware's approval of class action waivers, especially in the context of a 'take it or leave it' arbitration clause is contrary to fundamental public policy of California."); Coady v. Cross Country Bank, 729 N.W.2d 732 (Wis. Ct. App. 2007) (refusing to enforce Delaware choice-of-law provision in lending contract because it would bar consumers from asserting claims under the Wisconsin Consumer Protection Act, and striking down class action ban as unconscionable under Wisconsin law).
184 Ting v. AT & T, 182 F. Supp. 2d 902, 917–920, 931 (N.D. Cal. 2002).
185 *Id.* at 938.

A California appellate court has reached a similar conclusion, finding that an arbitration clause that banned class actions was effectively one-sided (as this prohibition only took rights from consumers, not the company) and would create "virtual immunity" for the company.[186] The court also commented how this provision would eliminate the deterrent effect of class actions:

> [I]t also serves as a disincentive for Discover to avoid the type of conduct that might lead to class action litigation in the first place. By imposing this clause on its customers, Discover has essentially granted itself a license to push the boundaries of good business practices to their furthest limits, fully aware that relatively few, if any, customers will seek legal remedies.... The potential for millions of customers to be overcharged small amounts without an effective method of redress cannot be ignored.... This is not only substantively unconscionable, it violates public policy by granting Discover a "get out of jail free" card while compromising important consumer rights.[187]

In *Discover Bank v. Superior Court*, the court held as follows:

> Class action and arbitration waivers are not, in the abstract, exculpatory clauses. But because, as discussed above, damages in consumer cases are often small and because "[a] company which wrongfully exacts a dollar from each of millions of customers will reap a handsome profit," ... "the class action is often the only effective way to halt and redress such exploitation."

As the Washington Supreme Court held in *Scott v. Cingular Wireless L.L.C.*: "[T]he class action waiver is unconscionable because it effectively denies large numbers of consumers the protection of Washington's Consumer Protection Act (CPA) ..., and because it effectively exculpates Cingular from liability for a whole class of wrongful conduct. It is therefore, unenforceable."[188]

In *Muhammad v. County Bank of Rehoboth Beach*,[189] the New Jersey Supreme Court held that: "[T]he class-arbitration waiver in this consumer contract is unenforceable. Such a waiver would be unconscionable whether applied in a lawsuit or in arbitration."

First, the *Muhammad* court noted that "[t]he difficulty lies in the fact that [the plaintiff's] individual consumer-fraud case involves a small amount of damages, rendering individual enforcement of her rights, and the rights of her fellow consumers, difficult if not impossible. In such circumstances a class-action waiver can act effectively as an exculpatory clause."[190] As a further indication that *Muhammad* applies only to cases involving small claims, the same day that it was released, that court issued a second opinion holding that a ban on class actions would not be unconscionable in the setting of a case involving claims for over $100,000 for an individual.[191]

In *Leonard v. Terminix International Co.*, similarly, the Alabama Supreme Court found that by "foreclosing the Leonards from an attempt to seek practical redress through a class action and restricting them to a disproportionately expensive individual arbitration," the defendants had essentially closed the door of justice to these consumers.[192]

The same reasoning animated *West Virginia ex rel. Dunlap v. Berger*,[193] in which the West Virginia Supreme Court of Appeals held that an arbitration clause which effectively barred class actions under state law was unconscionable. "In Mr. Dunlap's case, the total of $8.46 in insurance damages that Friedman's added to his purchase by Friedman's is precisely the sort of small dollar/high volume (alleged) illegality that class action claims and remedies are effective in addressing."[194] The court also noted that:

> [I]n the contracts of adhesion that are so commonly involved in consumer and employment transactions, permitting the proponent of such a contract to include a provision that prevents an aggrieved party from pursuing class action relief would go a long way toward allowing those who commit illegal activity to go unpunished, undeterred, and unaccountable.[195]

A Missouri appellate court held in *Whitney v. All-Tel Communications* that a class action ban was unconscionable because of its exculpatory effect:[196]

> An average person would not reasonably expect that a dispute like the one at issue would be required to be resolved through arbitration on an individual case by case basis. Such a requirement, if found to bar actions such as this, would effectively strip consumers of the protections afforded to them under the Merchandising Practices Act and unfairly allow companies like Alltel to insu-

---

186 Szetela v. Discover Bank, 97 Cal. App. 4th 1094, 118 Cal. Rptr. 2d 862 (2002); *see also* Stern v. Cingular Wireless, 453 F. Supp. 2d 1138, 1148–1149 (C.D. Cal. 2006) ("Although styled as a mutual prohibition on class actions, the likelihood of defendants bringing a class action against their wireless customers is vanishingly small.... The class action waiver is thus unconscionable under California law and should not be enforced." (internal citation omitted)).
187 *Szetela*, 97 Cal. App. 4th at 1101.
188 161 P.3d 1000, 1003 (Wash. 2007).
189 912 A.2d 88 (N.J. 2006).
190 *Id.* at 99.
191 Delta Funding Corp. v. Harris, 912 A.2d 104 (N.J. 2006).
192 Leonard v. Terminix Int'l Co., 2002 WL 31341084, at *8 (Ala. Oct. 18, 2002).
193 567 S.E.2d 265 (W. Va. 2002).
194 *Id.* at 278.
195 *Id.* at 278, 279.
196 Whitney v. All-Tel Communications, 173 S.W.3d 300 (Mo. Ct. App. 2005).

late themselves from the consumer protection laws of this State. This result would be unconscionable and in direct conflict with the legislature's declared policy....[197]

Similarly, in *Powertel, Inc. v. Bexley*,[198] a Florida appellate court struck down an arbitration clause in a cellular telephone service provider's contract with its consumers in part because it would prohibit class actions, and focused upon the small size of the claims at issue:

> Class litigation provides the most economically feasible remedy for the kind of claim asserted here. The potential claims are too small to litigate individually, but collectively they might amount to a large sum of money. The prospect of class litigation ordinarily has some deterrent effect on a manufacturer or service provider, but that is absent here. By requiring arbitration of all claims, Powertel has precluded the possibility that a group of its customers might join together to seek relief that would be impractical for any of them to obtain alone.[199]

Many other courts have agreed with this conclusion.[200]

---

[197] *Id.* at 314.

[198] 743 So. 2d 570 (Fla. Dist. Ct. App. 1999).

[199] *Id.* at 576.

The U.S. Court of Appeals for the Eleventh Circuit has recognized that *Powertel* correctly states the rule of law in Florida. In Rollins, Inc. v. Garrett, 2006 WL 1024166 (11th Cir. Apr. 19, 2006), the court stated that, "[u]nder Florida law, a consumer contract that prohibits class arbitration is unconscionable because it 'preclude[s] the possibility that a group of its customers might join together to seek relief that would be impractical for any of them to obtain alone.' " (quoting *Powertel*). *See also* BellSouth Mobility L.L.C. v. Christopher, 819 So. 2d 171, 173 (Fla. Dist. Ct. App. 2002) (arbitration clause substantively unconscionable when, among other factors, it removes exposure to class action suit even if class treatment may be warranted).

[200] *See, e.g.*, Chung Wing Wong v. T-Mobile USA, Inc., 2006 WL 2042512 (E.D. Mich. July 20, 2006) ("Whether the right to a class action is a substantive or procedural one, it is certainly necessary for the effective vindication of statutory rights, at least under the facts of this case. Defendant makes much of the fact that it contributes toward plaintiffs' arbitration costs, but in order for arbitration to be feasible, the amount at issue must also exceed the value in time and energy required to arbitrate a claim. Defendant is alleged to have bilked its customers out of millions of dollars, though only a few dollars at a time. Plaintiff's damages are a paltry $19.74, hardly enough to make arbitration worthwhile. Class actions were designed for situations just like this. The [Michigan Consumer Protection Act's] class action mechanism is essential to the effective vindication of its statutory cause of action."); Lowden v. T-Mobile, USA, Inc., 2006 WL 1009279, at *5–*6 (W.D. Wash. Apr. 13, 2006) (finding class action waivers substantively unconscionable because "the class action prohibitions deprive Plaintiffs of the means to effectively vindicate their rights under the CPA"); Stern v. Cingular Wireless Corp., 453 F. Supp. 2d 1138, 1149 (C.D. Cal. 2006) ("the class action waiver 'operate[s] effectively as [an] exculpatory contract clause' that functions to exempt defendants from responsibility of wrongdoing") (citing Discover Bank v. Super. Ct., 113 P.3d 1100, 1108 (Cal. 2005)); Skirchak v. Dynamics Research Corp., Inc., 432 F. Supp. 2d 175, 181 (D. Mass. 2006) (an arbitration agreement that eliminates the right to a class-wide proceeding may have "the 'substantial' effect of contravening the principle behind class action policies and 'chilling the effect of protection of interests common to a group.' . . . Requiring employees prospectively to waive their statutory rights to sue in order to obtain or maintain their employment is utterly inconsistent with the FLSA's purpose of protecting the class of employees that possesses the least bargaining power in the workforce. . . . In this case, the imposition of a waiver of class action provision thereby circumscribes the legal options of these employees, who may be unable to incur the expense of individual pursuing their claims. In this respect, the class action waiver is not only unfair to DRC employees, but also removes any incentive for DRC to avoid the type of conduct that might lead to class action litigation in the first instance. The class action clause is therefore substantively unconscionable); Sprague v. Household Int'l, 473 F. Supp. 2d 966 (W.D. Mo. 2005) ("The prohibition of class actions, including class actions in arbitration, operates not only to deprive many individual defendants of an effective remedy, but also to eliminate any disincentive for Household to avoid the kind of harmful behavior that would form the basis of a class action lawsuit. Accordingly, the prohibition of class actions 'weighs heavily in favor of a finding of substantive unconscionability.' (citation omitted)); Schwartz v. Alltel Corp., 2006 WL 2243649 (Ohio Ct. App. June 29, 2006) (a ban on class actions was unconscionable because, "[b]y prohibiting its customers from filing suit as a class, Alltel prevents the cost effective use of class action litigation that can end abusive practices by large corporations in those instances in which individual claims are ineffective"); Eagle v. Fred Martin Motor Co., 809 N.E.2d 1161, 1183 (Ohio Ct. App. 2004) ("by expressly eliminating a consumer's right to proceed through a class action . . . the arbitration clause directly hinders the consumer protection purposes of the [Ohio Consumer Sales Practices Act]"); Vasquez-Lopez v. Beneficial Or., Inc., 210 Or. App. 553, 152 P.3d 940, 950 (2007) (class action ban would, if enforced, exculpate the lender from liability: "[T]he opportunity that the class action ban denies to borrowers is, in many instances, a crucial one, without which many meritorious claims would simply not be filed."); Thibodeau v. Comcast Corp., 912 A.2d 874, 885 (Pa. Super. Ct. 2006) ("It is only the class action vehicle which makes small consumer litigation possible. Consumers joining together as a class pool their resources, share the costs and efforts of litigation and make redress possible. Should the law require consumers to litigate or arbitrate individually, defendant corporations are effectively immunized from redress of grievances."); *cf.* Eastman v. Conseco Fin. Servicing Corp., 2002 WL 1061856, at *3 (Wis. Ct. App. May 29, 2002) (certifying to state supreme court the question whether an arbitration clause permitted class actions in arbitration; "The arbitrator's authority to grant class-wide relief is very significant in this case. Because each individual plaintiff suffered less than $200 actual damage, the cost and inconvenience of separate actions would result in no recovery for most plaintiffs and substantial unjust enrichment to Conseco, assuming the plaintiffs' claims have merit. While arbitration is preferred in most circumstances because it is less expensive and more simple than court proceedings, it is probably more difficult and more expensive than small claims actions.").

6.5.5.3 Courts Finding That Class Action Bans Are Exculpatory Based On Other Factors

Courts striking down class action bans have focused on the fact that class action bans are effectively exculpatory, for a variety of reasons. Some courts have focused only on the issue addressed in the previous section—that class action bans may be exculpatory in some cases because of the small size of individual claims. A few courts have focused so heavily on this point that they have refused to follow precedents striking down class action bans on the grounds that the dollar values of the claims at issue in those cases were somewhat larger than the amounts at issue in the earlier cases, and the courts presumed that class action bans would not be exculpatory in these cases involving larger amounts.[201] While there are obviously quite a few cases in which the facts—including the magnitude of individual claims—make it clear that individual litigation is feasible,[202] and thus that a ban on class actions is not effectively exculpatory, arguably some of the courts that have focused narrowly on the magnitude of the claim to the exclusion of all other factors have missed the broader nature of the issue. As the California Supreme Court held in rejecting an argument that a class action ban was enforceable because the claims could well be in the thousands of dollars for some plaintiffs:

> [T]he above quoted passage in *Discover Bank* was not intended to suggest that consumer actions involving miniscule amounts of damages were the only actions in which class actions would not be enforced. Rather, *Discover Bank* was an application of a more general principle that although "[c]lass action and arbitration waivers are not, in the abstract, exculpatory clauses" ... such a waiver can be exculpatory in practical terms because it can make it very difficult for those injured by unlawful conduct to pursue a legal remedy.[203]

A number of courts have recognized that there are many circumstances in which the vast majority of consumers will never realize that they have any claim or cause of action on their own, and that unless they become part of a class action they will never have an opportunity to effectively vindicate their claims. As the Illinois Supreme Court has explained:

> The typical consumer may feel that such a charge is unfair, but only with the aid of an attorney will the consumer be aware that he or she may have a claim that is supported by law, and only with the aid of an attorney will such a consumer be able to make the merits of such a claim apparent in arbitration or litigation.[204]

The New Jersey Supreme Court, similarly, has held:

> Moreover, without the availability of a class-action mechanism, many consumer fraud victims may never realize that they may have been wronged. As commentators have noted, often consumers do not know that a potential defendant's conduct is illegal. When they are being charged an excessive interest rate or a penalty for check bouncing, for example, few know or even sense that their rights are being violated.[205]

In a particular case there may be other factors that cause a class action ban to be exculpatory. In the wage and hour employment setting, for example, the California Supreme Court has noted that a ban on class actions might bar individuals from bringing cases because of the potential for retaliation against persons who sue their employer.[206] Accordingly, the stronger precedent suggests that what renders a given class action ban exculpatory will depend upon a variety of factors, and cannot be judged merely by the dollar value of the claims or some other single simple test.

6.5.5.4 Courts Finding That Class Action Bans Are Unconscionably One-Sided

As noted in § 6.5.3, *supra*, a substantial number of courts have struck down as unconscionable arbitration clauses that were either explicitly or effectively one-sided and non-

---

201 *E.g.*, McCabe v. Dell, Inc., 2007 WL 1434972 (C.D. Cal. Apr. 12, 2007) (refusing to follow Discover Bank v. Super. Ct., 113 P.3d 1100 (Cal. 2005), because claims at issue involved $700, rather than $29); Omstead v. Dell, Inc., 473 F. Supp. 2d 1018 (N.D. Cal. Feb. 13, 2007) (holding that the limited policy against class action bans in California did not apply when the amount of damages at issue is not "small"). *But see* Massie v. Ralph's Grocery S., 2007 WL 1395580 (Cal. Ct. App. May 14, 2007) (*Discover Bank* applied and governs, even though claims of individuals could exceed $4000).
202 *E.g.*, Delta Funding Corp. v. Harris, 189 N.J. 28, 912 A.2d 104 (2006) (class arbitration waiver was enforceable and not unconscionable because the plaintiff had adequate incentives to pursue her individual claim (she was seeking substantial individual damages, was at risk of losing her house, and was seeking relief under statutes which provided for attorney fees and costs to prevailing plaintiffs)).
203 Gentry v. Super. Ct., 42 Cal. 4th 443, 64 Cal. Rptr. 3d 773, 165 P.3d 556 (2007).
204 Kinkel v. Cingular Wireless, L.L.C., 306 Ill. Dec. 157, 857 N.E.2d 250 (Ill. 2006).
205 Muhammad v. County Bank of Rehobeth Beach, 912 A.2d 88 (N.J. 2006); *see also* Gentry v. Super. Ct., 42 Cal. 4th 443, 64 Cal. Rptr. 3d 773, 165 P.3d 556 (2007) ("some individual employees may not sue because they are unaware that their legal rights have been violated"); Eastman v. Conseco Fin. Servicing Corp., 2002 WL 1061856, at *3 (Wis. Ct. App. May 29, 2002) (certifying to state supreme court the question whether an arbitration clause permitted class actions in arbitration; "Unless class action is authorized, many plaintiffs will be unaware of the allegedly illegal activities and will not commence any proceedings.")
206 Gentry v. Super. Ct., 42 Cal. 4th 443, 64 Cal. Rptr. 3d 773, 165 P.3d 556 (2007).

mutual. In evaluating the enforceability of class action bans, a number of courts have concluded that this body of law striking down one-sided clauses applies to this area as well. The Ninth Circuit for example, applying California contract law, has held that an express class action ban in AT & T's consumer arbitration clause was substantively unconscionable because it was effectively one-sided, as it applied only against consumers.[207] "Although styled as a mutual prohibition on representative or class actions, it is difficult to envision the circumstances under which the provision might negatively impact Discover [Bank], because credit card companies typically do not sue their customers in class action lawsuits."[208] An Oregon appellate court used particularly pointed language to make this point, stating that a class action ban, though nominally mutual, was truly one-sided: "We are reminded of the observation by a character in an Anatole France novel that the majestic equality of the laws forbid[s] rich and poor alike to sleep under the bridges, to beg in the streets, and to steal their bread."[209] A number of other courts have adopted this same reasoning.[210]

6.5.5.5 Courts Upholding Class Action Bans

A very large number of courts have upheld contracts including class action bans. As noted in § 4.3.2.5, *supra*, many of these decisions rejected challenges to the class action bans on the grounds that the bans supposedly violated various federal statutes. Several of the courts that have held that class action bans were unconscionable have distinguished these decisions involving federal statutes as being inapposite to the issue of unconscionability. Nonetheless, it is also true that quite a few of the decisions upholding class action bans have done so on the ground that class action bans are not exculpatory and are not unconscionable under state law.[211]

---

207 Ting v. AT & T, 319 F.3d 1126, 1150 (9th Cir. 2003).
208 Discover Bank v. Super. Ct., 30 Cal. Rptr. 3d 76, 86, 113 P.3d 1100 (Cal. 2005).
209 Vasquez-Lopez v. Beneficial Or., Inc., 210 Or. App. 553, 152 P.3d 940, 949–950 (2007) (internal citation omitted).
210 *E.g.*, Lowden v. T-Mobile, USA, Inc., 2006 WL 1009279, at *5–*6 (W.D. Wash. Apr. 13, 2006) ("although the class action limitations . . . are nominally mutual, they are effectively one-sided because there is no conceivable set of facts under which T-Mobile would bring a class action against its customers"); Sprague v. Household Int'l, 473 F. Supp. 2d 966 (W.D. Mo. 2005) ("Although the Arbitration Rider's prohibition of class actions applies to both parties, the prohibition is one-sided in its practical effect. Companies such as Household rarely seek to sue a class of their customers."); Powertel v. Bexley, 743 So. 2d 570 (Fla. Dist. Ct. App. 1999) ("This is an advantage that inures only to Powertel."); Scott v. Cingular Wireless L.L.C., 161 P.3d 1000, 1008 (Wash. 2007) (recognizing that corporation's class action ban "effectively prevents one party to the contract, the consumer, from pursuing valid claims").
211 *See, e.g.*, Snowden v. CheckPoint Check Cashing, 290 F.3d 631 (4th Cir. 2002); Ornelas v. Sonic-Denver T, Inc., 2007 WL 274738 (D. Colo. Jan. 29, 2007) (enforcing class action ban); Barrer v. Chase Bank, 2007 WL 1072133 (D. Or. Jan. 23, 2007) (upholding class action ban under Oregon law, although it is notable that this case predates Vasquez-Lopez v. Beneficial Or., Inc., 210 Or. App. 553, 152 P.3d 940, 950 (2007)); Rivera v. AT & T Corp., 420 F. Supp. 2d 1312 (S.D. Fla. 2006) ("the Eleventh Circuit has held that arbitration agreements precluding class-action relief are valid and enforceable" (citations omitted)); Chalk v. T-Mobile USA, Inc., 2006 WL 2599506 (D. Or. Sept. 7, 2006) (same as *Barrer*); Sherr v. Dell, Inc., 2006 WL 2109436 (S.D.N.Y. July 27, 2006) (rejecting position of California Supreme Court, holding that a class action waiver was not unconscionable); Forness v. Cross Country Bank, Inc., 2006 WL 726233 (S.D. Ill. Mar. 20, 2006) (class action waiver provision not unconscionable); *In re* Am. Express Merchants Litig., 2006 WL 662341 (S.D.N.Y. Mar. 16, 2006) (appeal pending) (finding a collective action waiver in a credit card acceptance agreement between merchants and American Express was not unconscionable, when forcing merchants to arbitrate their anti-trust claims individually would not "impose such punishing costs as to preclude vindication in that forum"); Taylor v. Citibank USA, 292 F. Supp. 2d 1333, 1344 (M.D. Ala. 2003) ("Although Taylor and his lawyers may be unwilling to litigate this case due to the fact that it may not provide them with enough financial incentive to justify their efforts, this court cannot conclude that either the Plaintiff or his attorneys are so lacking in economic incentive to warrant a finding that the Bank's class action prohibition is unconscionable." (footnote omitted)); Pick v. Discover Fin. Services, Inc., 2001 U.S. Dist. LEXIS 15777 (D. Del. Sept. 28, 2001) ("[I]t is generally accepted that arbitration clauses are not unconscionable because they preclude class actions."); Edelist v. MBNA Am. Bank, 790 A.2d 1249 (Del. Super. Ct. 2001) ("The surrender of that class action right was clearly articulated in the arbitration amendment. The court finds nothing unconscionable about it and finds the bar on class actions enforceable."); Hayes v. County Bank, 26 A.D.3d 465 (N.Y. 2006) (fact that the arbitration provision effectively precluded class actions did not render the provision unconscionable); Spann v. Am. Express Travel Related Services Co., 2006 WL 2516431 (Tenn. Ct. App. Aug. 30, 2006) (Utah law) (class action ban not unconscionable); *see also* Iberia Credit Bureau, Inc. v. Cingular Wireless, 379 F.3d 169 (5th Cir. 2004) (La. law) (holding that arbitration clauses that barred consumers from bringing or participating in class actions were not unconscionable); Billups v. Bankfirst, 294 F. Supp. 2d 1265 (M.D. Ala. 2003) (arbitration clause that barred card holder from utilizing class action procedures was not unconscionable under Alabama law because she was bringing a claim under a fee-shifting statute); Gipson v. Cross Country Bank, 294 F. Supp. 2d 1251 (M.D. Ala. 2003) (even applying Alabama law, a ban on class actions is not unconscionable when it is possible that consumers will receive fees pursuant to a fee-shifting statute); Forrest v. Verizon Communications, Inc., 805 A.2d 1007 (D.C. 2002) (forum selection clause in case not involving an arbitration clause that had the effect of banning class actions was not unreasonable); Wilson v. Mike Steven Motors, Inc., 111 P.3d 1076 (Kan. Ct. App. 2005) (table) (text available at 2005 WL 1277948) (same, under Kansas law); Stenzel v. Dell, Inc., 870 A.2d 133 (Me. 2005) (arbitration clause that banned class actions not unconscionable under Texas law); Tsadilas v. Providian Nat'l Bank, 13 A.D.3d 190, 786 N.Y.S.2d 478 (2004) ("Under New York law, a contractual proscription against class actions . . . is neither unconscionable nor violative of public policy." (citations, internal quotations deleted)).

Also it should be noted that some of the cases that have struck down class action bans under the specific facts before them have done so on theories that would uphold class action bans in general. Some courts have held or suggested that while class action bans may be unconscionable in cases involving causes of action that do not provide for statutory fee shifting, class action bans may not be unconscionable in cases in which the plaintiffs' cause of action does include a fee shifting provision.[212] Many of the courts that have struck down class action bans, in the decisions cited in the preceding sections, disagree with this reasoning,[213] and courts are sharply split on the importance of fee shifting provisions. Similarly, there are several cases in which courts have enforced class action bans on the theory that most (if not all) of the earlier cases striking down class action bans also involved other unconscionable provisions, and that the class action ban by itself was not sufficient to be unconscionable.[214]

6.5.5.6 Class Action Bans Imposed After a Class Action Has Been Filed

Although most cases addressing waiver of the right to bring a class action have treated it as an issue of substantive unconscionability, the manner in which such a waiver is obtained may also raise procedural unconscionability issues. A New York state trial court, for example, held that a defendant could not use an arbitration clause that it inserted into its loan contracts *after* a class action suit was filed in order to induce a waiver from putative class members, unless the members were actually made aware of the pending class action.[215] The court in *Carnegie* framed this problem as an issue of class action management under the state rules of civil procedure, but the abuse of superior bargaining power to obtain an unknowing opt-out from an existing class action might also be addressed as an issue of procedural unconscionability.

6.5.5.7 FAA Does Not Preempt State Law of Unconscionability from Striking Down Class Action Bans

In § 3.2.3, *supra*, there is an extensive discussion of how unconscionability challenges to arbitration clauses are not preempted by the Federal Arbitration Act (FAA), so long as they are based upon generally applicable principles of state law and do not treat arbitration clauses less favorably than other contract terms. There are a number of cases that particularly discuss the issue of FAA preemption as it applies to unconscionability challenges to class action bans, however, and this issue is repeatedly raised by defendants. Thus far the vast majority of courts to consider the argument that the FAA preempts unconscionability challenges to class action bans have rejected that argument. Perhaps the most cogent and thorough analysis of this issue was provided by the Washington Supreme Court in *Scott v. Cingular Wireless*:

> Congress simply requires us to put arbitration clauses on the same footing as other contracts, not make them the special favorites of the law. See 9 U.S.C. § 2. As we held above, contracts that effectively exculpate their drafter from liability under the CPA for broad categories of liability are not enforceable in Washington, even if they are embedded in an arbitration clause. The arbitration clause is irrelevant to the unconscionability.
>
> Class action waivers have very little to do with arbitration. Clauses that eliminate causes of action, eliminate categories of damages, or otherwise strip away a party's right to vindicate a wrong do not change their character merely because they are found within a clause labeled "Arbitration." At least based on the briefing before us, we see no reason why the purposes of favoring individual arbitration would not equally favor class-wide arbitration. *Cf. Kinkel*, 223 Ill.2d at 19, 306 Ill. Dec. 157, 857 N.E.2d 250 ("Cingular cites many sources demonstrating that encouraging arbitration is, indeed, a strong federal objective, but offers no authority for the claim that individual arbitration, rather than class arbitration, is favored.").
>
> The FAA favors arbitration, not exculpation. As the United States Supreme Court has noted, arbitration can be a perfectly appropriate place for individuals to vindicate legislative policy, "so long as the prospective litigant effectively may vindicate its statutory cause of action in the arbitral forum." *Mitsubishi Motors Corp. v. Soler Chrysler-Plymouth, Inc.*, 473 U.S. 614, 637, 105 S. Ct. 3346, 87 L. Ed. 2d 444 (1985). But this clause prevents the use of arbitration to vindicate a broad range of statutory CPA rights. We join those courts that have found that striking a class action waiver in an arbitration clause does not

---

212 *See, e.g.*, Dale v. Comcast Corp., 498 F.3d 1216 (11th Cir. 2007).

213 Vasquez-Lopez v. Beneficial Or., Inc., 210 Or. App. 553, 152 P.3d 940, 950 (2007) (rejecting lender's argument that availability of attorney fees made individual arbitration sufficiently feasible, and noted that "the possibility of state [enforcement] action cannot reliably serve as a substitute for private actions").

214 Davidson v. Cingular Wireless, L.L.C., 2007 WL 896349 (E.D. Ark. Mar. 23, 2007) (ban on class actions not unconscionable when it is not burdened with other remedy-stripping provisions or when plaintiff could have rejected the clause).

215 *See* Carnegie v. H & R Block, Inc., 180 Misc. 2d 67, 687 N.Y.S.2d 528 (Sup. Ct. 1999); *see also* H & R Block v. Haese, 82 S.W.3d 331 (Tex. App. 2000) (affirming order prohibiting defendant from enforcing arbitration clause as it would apply retroactively to claims in consumer class action filed prior to clause's promulgation).

violate the FAA. *E.g., Discover Bank*, 36 Cal. 4th at 165–166, 30 Cal. Rptr. 3d 76, 113 P.3d 1100; *Kinkel*, 223 Ill. 2d at 19, 306 Ill. Dec. 157, 857 N.E.2d 250.[216]

In *Discover Bank*, similarly, the California Supreme Court rejected the defendant's claim of FAA preemption. Among other points, the court noted that the issue of class action bans had not been considered by Congress when it enacted the FAA:

> [T]he FAA is silent on the matter of class actions and class action arbitration. Indeed, not only is classwide arbitration a relatively recent development, but class action litigation for damages was for the most part unknown in federal jurisdictions at the time the FAA was enacted in 1925. . . . The Congress that enacted the FAA therefore can not be said to have contemplated the issues before us.[217]

The California Supreme Court also explained that the state law at issue was not targeted at arbitration clauses, and thus did not raise the kinds of concerns involved in cases in which the FAA has been found to preempt state law:

> In the present case, the principle that class action waivers are, under certain circumstances, unconscionable as unlawfully exculpatory is a principle of California law that does not specifically apply to arbitration agreements, but to contracts generally. In other words, it applies equally to class action litigation waivers in contracts without arbitration agreements as it does to class arbitration waivers in contracts with such agreements.[218]

The Illinois Supreme Court, similarly, has indicated that state laws that would strike a class action ban embedded in an arbitration clause are not preempted so long as the same result would apply to a class action ban found in a contract that did not contain an arbitration clause:

> The authorities relied upon by Cingular stand for the proposition that under federal law, a class action waiver cannot be found unconscionable on grounds that apply only to arbitration clauses. We agree with Cingular that such a finding is expressly preempted by the FAA. Plaintiff, however, does not argue that the class action waiver is unconscionable solely because it is contained in an arbitration clause. Her claim, therefore, is not expressly preempted by federal law.[219]

The Illinois Supreme Court went on to reject an argument that the FAA implicitly preempts state laws that prohibit class action bans, in part on the grounds that the United States Supreme Court has acknowledged that class actions are permitted in arbitration.

> We, therefore, reject Cingular's claim of conflict preemption. The FAA does not require state courts, when applying state law to a question of the enforceability of a particular contract, to necessarily reach an outcome that encourages individual arbitration. Further, class arbitration cannot be in conflict with the FAA when the Supreme Court has recognized the arbitrability of class claims.[220]

Only a very small number of courts, by contrast, have yet stated (even in dicta) that the FAA preempts state contract laws from being applied to class action bans.[221]

6.5.6 Inconvenient Venue for Arbitration

The arbitration clause or arbitration rules may specify where the arbitration is to take place. Inconvenience of the venue is another grounds for finding an arbitration clause unconscionable.[222] In one case, the arbitration provision specified arbitration through "the National Arbitration Fo-

---

216 Scott v. Cingular Wireless L.L.C., 161 P.3d 1000, 1008 (Wash. 2007).
217 Discover Bank v. Super. Ct., 36 Cal. 4th 148, 30 Cal. Rptr. 3d 76, 88–89, 113 P.3d 1100 (2005).
218 *Id.*, 30 Cal. Rptr. 3d at 89.
219 Kinkel v. Cingular Wireless L.L.C., 223 Ill. 2d 1, 857 N.E.2d 250, 262 (2006).
220 *Id.* (citing Green Tree Fin. Corp. v. Bazzle, 539 U.S. 444, 123 S. Ct. 2402, 156 L. Ed. 2d 414 (2003)).
221 *See* Schultz v. AT & T Wireless Services, Inc., 376 F. Supp. 2d 685, 691 (N.D. W. Va. 2005); Pyburn v. Bill Heard Chevrolet, 63 S.W.3d 351, 365 (Tenn. Ct. App. 2001).
222 Nagrampa v. MailCoups, Inc., 469 F.3d 1257, 1289–1290 (9th Cir. 2006) (en banc); Comb v. PayPal, 218 F. Supp. 2d 1165, 1176, 1177 (N.D. Cal. 2002); Stone v. Memberworks, 2003 WL 21246771 (Cal. Ct. App. May 30, 2003); Patterson v. ITT Consumer Fin. Corp., 14 Cal. App. 4th 1659, 18 Cal. Rptr. 2d 563 (1993); *see also* Wrightson v. ITT Fin. Services, Clearinghouse No. 47,962 (Fla. Dist. Ct. App. 1993) (text of this decision is also available on the CD-Rom accompanying this manual); Brown v. Karemor Int'l, Inc., 1999 Tenn. App. LEXIS 249 (Tenn. Ct. App. Apr. 19, 1999) (Tennessee franchisee must arbitrate claims against franchisor in Nevada); *cf.* Taylor Bldg. Corp. of Am. v. Benfield, 860 N.E.2d 1058 (Ohio Ct. App.) (requiring Ohio resident to travel to Kentucky for arbitration violates state statute governing construction contracts), *appeal allowed*, 859 N.E.2d 556 (Ohio 2006). *But see* G.C. & K.B. Investments, Inc. v. Wilson, 326 F.3d 1096 (9th Cir. 2003) (upholding forum selection clause sending parties to "AAA office nearest region where franchisor was located"; holding that arbitration should be compelled in the location to which the franchisor had moved (Louisiana) rather than where the franchisor had been located at the time of the contract (California)); Bragel v. Gen. Steel Corp., 2006 WL 4536019 (Mass. Super. Ct. July 28, 2006) (upholding arbitration clause specifying Colorado as venue for arbitration when Colorado is home state of party who wrote the arbitration agreement); *cf.* Doctor's Associates, Inc. v. Stuart, 85 F.3d 975 (2d Cir. 1996) (arbitration clause not unconscionable when Illinois franchisee required to travel to either Connecticut or Florida to arbitrate claims against franchisor).

rum, Minneapolis, Minnesota." Even if a consumer inquired at the time the contract was signed where the arbitration would in fact take place, the consumer would not be provided a definite location. NAF rules provide for arbitration within the federal judicial district where the arbitration agreement was signed, unless the parties agree otherwise. Consumers might view the clause specifying "National Arbitration Forum, Minneapolis, Minnesota" as such an agreement specifying Minneapolis. These facts helped the court to find the arbitration provision was unconscionable.[223]

In *Aral v. Earthlink, Inc.*,[224] similarly, a California court of appeals held that the forum selection clause in an Internet service contract, providing all actions would be brought in Georgia, was unreasonable as applied to a putative class action of California residents' claims. The court held that "a forum selection clause that requires a consumer to travel 2,000 miles to recover a small sum is not reasonable."[225] It went on to state that, "[t]o expect any or all of [the consumers] to travel to Georgia in order to obtain redress [on individual claims of $40 or $50] on a case-by-case basis, whether in a courthouse or in an arbitration hearing room, would be unreasonable as a matter of law."[226]

One Virginia state trial court judge has succinctly set forth an explanation of why such clauses are unconscionable:

> Obviously, the arbitration provision effectively eliminates any remedy for consumers. The clause precludes access to courts. The only dispute mechanism allowed—binding arbitration—is purely illusory. Common sense dictates that retail purchasers such as the Philyaws could not afford the time and expense to go to Los Angeles to arbitrate a claim arising from a used car sale in Virginia. In essence, the consumers have paid valuable consideration for a set of warranties but unwittingly have signed away all realistic relief in the event of a dispute about the warranties.[227]

Another court invalidated a provision in an arbitration clause that required California franchisees to arbitrate their claims in Utah when this was not what the franchisees would have expected: "When petitioners first purchased their Chem-Dry franchises in the early 1980s Harris was headquartered in California, and the franchise agreement did not contain an arbitration provision. Thus, they never anticipated Harris would relocate its headquarters to Utah and mandate that all disputes be litigated there."[228] Another court has voiced similar concerns in the course of an opinion directing the parties to attempt to agree upon a more "suitable" forum: "[T]he court believes that there may be something inherently wrong and unfair in setting the venue for an arbitration in a distant city, when the amount in issue is a relatively small amount. This effectively deprives consumers of the opportunity to have their claims heard."[229]

These concerns are particularly pronounced when they arise in the context of cases involving small sums of money and significant arbitration fees. As one federal district court held:

> [T]he arbitration clause is substantively unconscionable because the estimated travel costs for plaintiff—when considered in tandem with the likely costs of arbitration—are prohibitive in light of [the consumer plaintiff's] financial difficulties. [The consumer] has fulfilled his burden of showing that he cannot afford the $1,300 to $2,500 in travel and arbitration costs that he would likely incur if forced to travel from Illinois to New York to arbitrate his claim. Because [the consumer] is in severe financial straights—and because his claim is worth less than $5,000—the forum selection

---

223 Patterson v. ITT Consumer Fin. Corp., 14 Cal. App. 4th 1659, 18 Cal. Rptr. 2d 563 (1993); *see also* Bragg v. Linden Research, Inc., 487 F. Supp. 2d 593, 610 (E.D. Pa. 2007) (arbitration clause held to be unconscionable, in part because it required arbitration in San Francisco over relatively small amounts when customers number in the millions and reside throughout the country); Pinedo v. Premium Tobacco, Inc., 85 Cal. App. 4th 774, 102 Cal. Rptr. 2d 435 (2000) (arbitration clause held to be unconscionable, in part because it required the employee to arbitrate in Oakland); Wrightson v. ITT Fin. Services, Clearinghouse No. 47,962 (Fla. Dist. Ct. App. 1993) (text of this decision is also available on the CD-Rom accompanying this manual). *But see* Doctor's Associates, Inc. v. Stuart, 85 F.3d 975 (2d Cir. 1996) (not unconscionable to require an Illinois company to go to Florida or Connecticut to arbitrate).
224 36 Cal. Rptr. 3d 229 (Ct. App. 2005).
225 *Id.* at 241.
226 *Id.* at 242.
227 Philyaw v. Platinum Enterprises, 54 Va. Cir. 364, 2001 WL 112107, at *3 (Va. Cir. Ct. Jan. 9, 2001); *see also* Nagrampa v. MailCoups, Inc., 469 F.3d 1257, 1290 (9th Cir. 2006) (en banc) ("[t]he forum selection provision has no justification other than as a means of maximizing an advantage" over franchisees).
228 Bolter v. Super. Ct., 87 Cal. App. 4th 900, 909, 104 Cal. Rptr. 2d 888 (2001).
229 Bank v. Worldcom, Inc., 2002 WL 171629, at *3 (N.Y. Sup. Ct. Jan. 24, 2002); *see also* De Ornellas v. Aspen Square Mgmt, Inc., 295 F. Supp. 2d 753, 766 (E.D. Mich. 2003) (provision permitting the defendant to designate any venue for arbitration "could place the plaintiffs at great disadvantage and may prevent the vindication of the plaintiffs' rights"); Hagedorn v. Veritas Software Corp., 250 F. Supp. 2d 857, 862 (S.D. Ohio 2002) (provision in arbitration agreement requiring lifelong Ohio resident employee to participate in mandatory arbitration proceedings in San Francisco was unduly burdensome and unconscionable); Comb v. PayPal, 218 F. Supp. 2d 1165, 1177 (N.D. Cal. 2002) ("Limiting venue to PayPal's backyard appears to be yet one more means by which the arbitration clause serves to shield PayPal from liability instead of providing a neutral forum in which to arbitrate disputes."); Swain v. Auto Services, Inc., 128 S.W.3d 103, 108 (Mo. Ct. App. 2003) ("[T]he selection of Arkansas as the venue for arbitration is unexpected and unconscionably unfair. An average consumer purchasing a car in Missouri would not reasonably expect that any disputes arising under the service plan accompanying the car would have to be resolved in another state.").

clause effectively precludes plaintiff from bringing his claim.[230]

6.5.7 Bias of Arbitrator or Arbitration Mechanism

6.5.7.1 General

Under the FAA, bias in the arbitration mechanism is ground for overturning an arbitration award.[231] A number of courts have held that if the arbitrator or arbitration mechanism is biased, this bias can also be a factor in determining that the arbitration clause is unconscionable and unenforceable.

The leading case for this proposition is *Graham v. Scissor-Tail, Inc.*,[232] in which the California Supreme Court found unconscionable an arbitration clause that would provide for a musicians' union to arbitrate disputes involving union members. The court held that "a contractual party may not act in the capacity of arbitrator—and a contractual provision which designates him to serve in that capacity is to be denied enforcement on the grounds of unconscionability."[233] It is unconscionable because "irrespective of any proof of actual bias or prejudice, the law presumes that a party to a dispute cannot have that disinterestedness and impartiality necessary to act in a judicial or quasi-judicial capacity regarding that controversy."[234]

In addition, the court went on, a person cannot serve as arbitrator if, even though he is not a party to the contract, his "interests are so allied with those of [a] party [to the contract] that, for all practical purposes, he is subject to the same disabilities which prevent the party himself from serving."[235] Concluding that the designated arbitrator was not in a position to arbitrate with the required degree of "disinterestedness and impartiality," the court declined to enforce the arbitration provision before it.[236]

Similarly, the Fourth Circuit struck down as unconscionable an arbitration clause that "placed control over the selection of the single arbitrator for employment disputes in the hands of his employer."[237]

The West Virginia Supreme Court of Appeals has also declared unconscionable an arbitration clause that permitted a lender to designate the decision maker, when the arbitration provider was compensated on a case-volume fee system.[238] The reason was that "the decision maker's income as an arbitrator is dependent on continued referrals from the creditor," and thus the arrangement "so impinges on neutrality and fundamental fairness that it is unconscionable and unenforceable under West Virginia law."[239] The court cited its earlier opinion in *West Virginia ex rel. Dunlap v. Berger*, in which it stated: "We observe that neutrality in the selection and composition of any forum or tribunal is essential to the legal validity of contractual provisions providing for dispute resolution mechanisms, particularly when such provisions are placed in contracts of adhesion like the one signed by Mr. Dunlap."[240] A California court of appeal expressed a similar concern in *Mercuro v. Superior Court*, holding unconscionable an arbitration clause in part because of concerns over repeat-player bias with the National Arbitration Forum.[241]

In an employment case, a federal district court in Indiana found an arbitration clause to be unconscionable when "there is a strong potential for bias in the selection of the arbitration panel."[242] First, the court noted that the arbitration firm had a strong incentive to favor the party who wrote the contract naming (and thus sending business to) the arbitration firm: "EDSI thus clearly has an incentive to maintain its contractual relationship with Ryan's and other such business partners while applicants or employees . . . have no leverage, having been presented with the arrangement on a take-it-or-leave-it basis."[243] Second, the court

---

230 Plattner v. Edge Solutions, Inc., 2004 WL 1575557, at *1 (N.D. Ill. May 27, 2004); *see also* Nagrampa v. MailCoups, Inc., 469 F.3d 1257, 1290 n.13 (9th Cir. 2006) (en banc) (requiring arbitration of plaintiff's claim in Boston, when plaintiff resides in California, had the effect of increasing the cost to, and burden on, plaintiff so as to be prohibitive, when costs of proceeding would have resulted in plaintiff overdrawing her bank account).
231 9 U.S.C. § 10.
   This statutory provision relates to the constitutional due process requirement that parties be given access to unbiased decision makers. *See* Aetna Life Ins. Co. v. Lavoie, 475 U.S. 813, 824, 106 S. Ct. 1580, 89 L. Ed. 2d 823 (1986); Morrissey v. Brewer, 408 U.S. 471, 485, 486, 92 S. Ct. 2593, 33 L. Ed. 2d 484 (1972); *see also* State *ex rel.* Vincent v. Schneider, 194 S.W.3d 853, 859 (Mo. 2006) (appointment of a biased arbitrator violates Missouri statutory law).
   Courts have also held that arbitrators are required to disclose in advance any possible conflicts of interest to the parties. *See* Sanko S.S. Co., Ltd. v. Cook Indus., Inc. 495 F.2d 1260, 1264 (2d Cir. 1973); Barcon Associates, Inc. v. Tri-County Asphalt Corp., 86 N.J. 179, 430 A.2d 214, 220 (1981).
232 28 Cal. 3d 807, 171 Cal. Rptr. 604, 623 P.2d 165 (1981).
233 *Id.*, 623 P.2d at 177.
234 *Id.*, 623 P.2d at 175.
235 *Id.*, 623 P.2d at 177.
236 *Id.*, 623 P.2d at 178.
237 Murray v. United Food & Commercial Workers Union, 289 F.3d 297, 303 (4th Cir. 2002); *see also* State *ex rel.* Vincent v. Schneider, 194 S.W.3d 853, 859 (Mo. 2006) (striking down provision of arbitration that granted the president of local home builders' association, who was also the president of defendant, sole power to select arbitrator).
238 Toppings v. Meritech Mortgage Services, Inc., 569 S.E.2d 149 (W. Va. 2002).
239 *Id.* at 149.
240 West Virginia *ex rel.* Dunlap v. Berger, 211 W. Va. 549, 567 S.E.2d 265, 280 n.12 (2002).
241 Mercuro v. Super. Ct., 116 Cal. Rptr. 2d 671 (Ct. App. 2002).
242 Geiger v. Ryan's Family Steak Houses, Inc., 134 F. Supp. 2d 985, 995 (S.D. Ind. 2001).
243 *Id.*

noted that the arbitration firm had the power and opportunity to act upon any bias it might have:

> EDSI also retains full authority to select both the Rules for arbitration as well as the pools of potential arbitrators. Such power in the face of the potential for bias on the part of EDSI in favor of employers such as Ryan's renders it unlikely that applicants/employees will participate in an unbiased forum.[244]

The outer limit of what a court may tolerate with respect to incentives for arbitral bias was probably reached by the Connecticut Supreme Court in *Hottle v. BDO Seidman, L.L.P.*[245] In that case, the court enforced an arbitration clause against a former employee for an accounting firm even though it "authorize[d] an arbitration panel consisting solely of directors and partners of" the accounting firm. As illustrative of the reasoning that led to this improbable result, the court concluded that the sum of money involved was too small to trigger concerns of bias:

> The plaintiff asserts, as an example, that were he to prevail on his contractual claim for $300,000, each of the 250 partners of the partnership would bear an average loss of $1200. Even if we were to assume that this is true, although we agree that $1200 is not an insignificant sum of money, we cannot say that it constitutes so substantial an interest that the law should presume, in advance of arbitration, that the partners acting as arbitrators "cannot have [the] disinterestedness and impartiality necessary to acting judicial or quasi-judicial capacity regarding the controversy."[246]

At least one other court has reached the opposite conclusion with respect to this idiosyncratic clause, however.[247]

A number of other courts have struck down arbitration clauses involving grievous issues of arbitrator bias without specifying any particular doctrinal grounds, such as unconscionability.[248] Still other courts have found a different doctrinal ground for refusing to compel arbitration in settings in which the arbitrators' neutrality was compromised: that biased arbitration is not really arbitration. The Fourth Circuit has refused to enforce an arbitration award in an employment contract when the rules of an arbitration procedure were "crafted to ensure a biased decision maker."[249]

In particular, the court pointed out that the employer need not file an answer to the employee's claim; only the employee must provide a list of witnesses; the arbitrators are selected from a list chosen by the employer; only the employer can expand the scope of the arbitration; only the employer can seek summary judgment; only the employer can record the proceedings; only the employer can appeal in certain situations; and only the employer can cancel the agreement to arbitrate. The Fourth Circuit rescinded the agreement on the basis that the employer had breached its obligation to specify a fair mechanism and violated its duty of good faith.[250]

In another recent case, the Missouri Supreme Court held that it was unconscionable for one party to have sole power to select the arbitrator:

> Relators argue that the arbitration clause is uncon-

---

244 *Id.*; *cf.* Walker v. Ryan's Family Steak Houses, 400 F.3d 370 (6th Cir. 2005) (statutory, rather than unconscionability, case; "[Arbitration firm] is clearly a for-profit business, and Ryan's annual fee accounted for over 42% of [the arbitration firm's] gross income in 2002. Given the symbiotic relationship between Ryan's and [the arbitration firm], Ryan's effectively determines the three pools of arbitrators, thereby rendering the arbitral forum fundamentally unfair to claimants who are applicants or employees.").

245 846 A.2d 862 (Conn. 2004).

246 *Id.* at 877 (citation omitted).

247 Buhrer v. BDO Seidman, L.L.P., 16 Mass. L. Rptr. 551 (Mass. Super. Ct. 2003) ("[T]he financial interests of the arbitrators are identical to those of the defendant; this is clearly inequitable and unjust.").

248 *See* McMullen v. Meijer, Inc., 355 F.3d 485 (6th Cir. 2004) ("[Clause] grants one party to the arbitration unilateral control over the pool of potential arbitrators. This procedure prevents [this arbitration system] from being an effective substitute for a judicial forum because it inherently lacks neutrality."); Hudson v. Chicago Teachers Union Local No. 1, 743 F.2d 1187 (7th Cir. 1984), *aff'd*, 475 U.S. 292 (1986) (arbitrator not independent when she was to be picked by and paid by union); Walker v. Ryan's Family Steak Houses, Inc., 289 F. Supp. 2d 916, 924 (M.D. Tenn. 2003) ("The most compelling reason that the EDSI forum is fundamentally unable to provide an effective substitute for the judicial forum is that EDSI both exercises control over the pool of potential arbitrators and relies on the favor of its employer-clients for its livelihood."), *aff'd*, 400 F.3d 370 (6th Cir. 2005); Cross & Brown Co. v. Nelson, 4 A.D.2d 501, 167 N.Y.S.2d 573, 575 (1957) (not enforcing an arbitration agreement between a real estate broker and his employer because it appointed the employer's Board of Directors as arbitrator; this contravened the "well-recognized principle of 'natural justice' that a man may not be a judge in his own cause"); Ditto v. RE/MAX Preferred Properties, Inc., 861 P.2d 1000 (Okla. Civ. App. 1993) (when only one party had a voice in selection of arbitrators, clause would not be enforced); Bd. of Educ. v. W. Harley Miller, Inc., 160 W. Va. 473, 236 S.E.2d 439, 443 (W. Va. 1977) (finding exclusive control over selection of arbitrators by one party inherently inequitable).

249 Hooters of Am., Inc. v. Phillips, 173 F.3d 933 (4th Cir. 1999).
The Fourth Circuit has subsequently cautioned that the *Hooters* precedent must be limited to its facts, however. *See* Sydnor v. Conseco Fin. Servicing Corp., 252 F.3d 302, 306 (4th Cir. 2001) ("The egregiously unfair arbitration rules in *Hooters*, however, provide only a limited departure from the general rule that arbitrators decide questions of fairness regarding arbitration proceedings.... Arbitration is not inherently unconscionable, and *Hooters* does not give a federal court license to make a 'full-scale assault' on arbitration....").

250 Hooters of Am., Inc. v. Phillips, 173 F.3d 933 (4th Cir. 1999).
The Fourth Circuit's approach—that the arbitration system at issue was so biased that it did not even qualify as arbitration and thus could not be compelled—was very similar to that taken in Cheng-Canindan v. Renaissance Hotel Associates, 50 Cal. App. 4th 676, 57 Cal. Rptr. 2d 867 (1996).

scionable because it gives the President of the Home Builder Association . . ., which happens to be the president of McBride, the sole discretion to choose the arbitrator. . . . Even if the president of the Home Builder Association of Greater St. Louis was not also the president of McBride, this portion of the arbitration provision would be unconscionable. It requires that an individual in a position of bias be the sole selector of an arbitrator, who must be unbiased.[251]

While the foregoing discussion demonstrates that many courts will refuse to enforce an arbitration clause that is structured in such a way as to give the arbitrator a significant incentive to favor one party, in other cases a determination of unconscionability based on the arbitration service provider's bias may be a fact-specific one. As § 2.4, *supra*, establishes, the consumer is entitled to discovery from the service provider to determine whether the arbitration should be compelled. A determination of unconscionability due to bias will also be made more readily if a particularly strong showing has been made of procedural unconscionability, or if bias appears in combination with other issues of substantive unconscionability.[252]

6.5.7.2 Bias Challenges to the National Arbitration Forum

In the consumer context, many litigants have challenged as unconscionable any arbitration clause which designates the National Arbitration Forum (NAF) as the arbitration service provider. The NAF was involved in the cases of *Toppings v. Meritech Mortgage Services, Inc.*[253] and *Mercuro v. Superior Court*[254] discussed in the preceding section, for example. Nonetheless some other courts have not yet accepted these arguments.[255] While the *Toppings* and *Mercuro* courts focused on structural factors, consumers challenging the NAF's neutrality have accumulated a number of pieces of evidence of NAF's bias.

Interrogatory answers filed in litigation in a case in Alabama state court offer some insight into NAF's track record in consumer cases. Out of nearly 20,000 cases that resulted in a final decision, NAF ruled for the credit card issuer First USA Bank in all but eighty-seven cases—a success rate of about 99.6%.[256] One of NAF's principals essentially told the *Washington Post* that these statistics are not significant, because the cases were largely collections cases in which one would expect a bank to win 99.6% of cases,[257] but others disagree.

A good discussion of bias on the part of the NAF, a for-profit entity offering arbitration services with a modest staff entirely located in Minneapolis, is found in two recent briefs arguing that consumers should not be required to arbitrate their claims before the NAF.[258] The briefs point to NAF's marketing literature, which highlights the advantage creditors will have in their relationship with consumers if they sign up with NAF. NAF solicitation letters to would-be clients promise to eliminate class actions for companies who join up with it, and coach creditors on how they can reduce their liabilities to consumers and eliminate class actions by signing up with NAF.[259] NAF marketing letters also promise to limit the consumer's recovery to the original claim, to limit consumers to "little or no discovery," and not to issue injunctive relief.[260]

The briefs also argue that past NAF actions and the past employment history of NAF personnel also display pro-

---

251 State *ex rel.* Vincent v. Schneider, 194 S.W.3d 853 (Mo. 2006).

252 *See* Mercuro v. Super. Ct., 96 Cal. App. 4th 167, 116 Cal. Rptr. 2d 671 (2002) ("We too are not prepared to say without more evidence the 'repeat player effect' is enough to render an arbitration agreement unconscionable. However, given the low threshold of substantive unconscionability in this case, we find the lack of mutuality as to arbitrable claims together with the disadvantages to the employee in using NAF as the arbitration provider renders the Countrywide arbitration agreement substantively unconscionable.").

253 569 S.E.2d 149 (W. Va. 2002).

254 96 Cal. App. 4th 167, 116 Cal. Rptr. 2d 671 (2002).

255 *See* Miller v. Equifirst Corp. of WV, 2006 WL 2571634, at *14 (S.D. W. Va. Sept. 5, 2006) ("Plaintiffs' speculative arguments in this case that the NAF is biased and its rules will not result in the appointment of an unbiased arbitrator represent little more than general antipathy to arbitration which both the United States Supreme Court and the Fourth Circuit have rejected." (internal citation omitted)); Lloyd v. MBNA Am. Bank, 2001 U.S. Dist. LEXIS 8279 (D. Del. Feb. 22, 2001) ("Plaintiff offers no persuasive evidence that the National Arbitration Forum is anything but neutral and efficient."), *aff'd*, 2002 WL 21932 (3d Cir. Jan. 7, 2002) (table); Bank One v. Harris, 2001 U.S. Dist. LEXIS 9615 (S.D. Miss. Jan. 2, 2001) ("[T]he rules governing the conduct of NAF arbitrations belie defendants' speculation that suspected bias by the NAF has any realistic potential for affecting decisions of arbitrators in NAF arbitrations."); Marsh v. First USA Bank, 103 F. Supp. 2d 909 (N.D. Tex. 2000) (holding that the NAF arbitration clause would be enforced, rejecting plaintiff's extensive bias arguments); *see also* Hale v. First USA Bank, 2001 U.S. Dist. LEXIS 8045 (S.D.N.Y. June 19, 2001); Vera v. First USA Bank, 2001 U.S. Dist. LEXIS 9052 (D. Del. Apr. 19, 2001).

256 Carolyn E. Mayer, *Win Some Lose Rarely? Arbitration Forum's Rulings Called One-Sided*, Wash. Post, Mar. 1, 2000.

257 *Id.*

258 *See* Petition of Plaintiffs and of Defendant Salmons Agency to Docket Certified Questions, Toppings v. Meritech Mortgage Services, Inc., No. 011984 (W. Va. Dec. 4, 2001).

 This petition and the reply brief, along with a description of the exhibits thereto, are included on the CD-Rom accompanying this manual. Additional evidence is discussed in a letter submitted by Trial Lawyers for Public Justice to the Working Group on Consumer Protection of the National Association of Insurance Commissioners. This letter is also included on the CD-Rom accompanying this manual.

259 *See* Petition of Plaintiffs and of Defendant Salmons Agency to Docket Certified Questions, Toppings v. Meritech Mortgage Services, Inc., No. 011984 (W. Va. Dec. 4, 2001) (available on the CD-Rom accompanying this manual).

260 *Id.*

creditor bias. As noted above, a handful of courts have rejected challenges to the NAF, however, though substantial litigation is still pending.

6.5.7.3 Defenses to Bias Allegations

Those seeking to compel arbitration in the face of charges of arbitral bias frequently make arguments suggesting that the courts may not consider bias claims at all. In particular, they argue that bias may not be considered until after the conclusion of arbitration, and several courts have accepted this argument.[261]

A second argument they make is that those resisting arbitration should not be permitted to challenge arbitration service providers such as the NAF, no matter how strong the evidence of bias is with respect to these companies. According to this argument, the individual arbitrators, rather than arbitration service providers, are the actual "decision makers." Arbitrators are not employees of the arbitration service providers but more akin to independent contractors. As such, arbitrators are not subject to the control of a service provider. Therefore, even if an arbitration service provider was biased, that bias would have no impact on the impartiality of, or "taint," the individual arbitrators who actually decide the disputes. Several courts have accepted some version of this argument.[262] The Sixth Circuit, however, has flatly rejected it: "When the process used to select the arbitrator is fundamentally unfair, as in this case, the arbitral forum is not an effective substitute for a judicial forum, and there is no need to present separate evidence of bias or corruption in the particular arbitrator selected."[263]

In addition, those defending arbitration often argue that an arbitrator may not be challenged based upon the appearance or potential for a conflict of interest and that only actual conflicts of interest may serve as grounds for a successful challenge.[264] In any case, for these reasons or others, a number of courts have rejected bias challenges to various arbitration service providers.[265]

Similarly, the First Circuit found that the New York Stock Exchange's (NYSE's) arbitration mechanism passed scrutiny. The court pointed to the following factors in reaching this conclusion: the NYSE is not comprised primarily of securities companies; the federal Securities and Exchange Commission regulates the NYSE's arbitration provisions; most of its arbitrators are not from the securities industry, and do not have industry links; the consumer has unlimited challenges for cause and one preemptory challenge; the mechanism does not limit the relief available; fees and costs usually are awarded to a prevailing consumer; and fees are not excessive.[266]

6.5.8 Secrecy Provisions

6.5.8.1 Introduction

Arbitration is generally a less transparent system than the civil justice system: "When parties waive litigation in favor of the arbitral forum, they also commonly waive the openness of the courts for the secrecy of arbitration."[267] As Ch. 3, *supra*, explains, however, the Federal Arbitration Act has been repeatedly held to override challenges to arbitration clauses that are based on the nature of arbitration in general. Nonetheless, a number of courts have embraced challenges to clauses that go further and incorporate broad gag orders or secrecy provisions. Many predispute arbitration agreements contain clauses mandating confidentiality,[268] while

---

261 *See* Aviall, Inc. v. Ryder Sys., Inc., 110 F.3d 892, 895 (2d Cir. 1997); Miller v. Equifirst Corp. of WV, 2006 WL 2571634, at *14 (S.D. W. Va. Sept. 5, 2006); Vera v. First USA Bank, 2001 U.S. Dist. LEXIS 9052 (D. Del. Apr. 19, 2001).

262 *E.g.*, MCI Telecommunications Corp. v. Matrix Communications Corp., 135 F.3d 27, 35, 36 (1st Cir. 1998) ("substantial relationship" between an arbitration service provider and a party is immaterial, because there was no claim of bias against the individual arbitrator); Bank One v. Coates, 125 F. Supp. 2d 819, 835 (S.D. Miss. 2001) ("the rules governing the conduct of NAF arbitrations belie defendant's speculation that suspected bias by the NAF has any realistic potential for affecting decisions of arbitrators in NAF arbitrations"), *aff'd*, 2002 WL 663804 (5th Cir. Apr. 5, 2002) (table).

263 McMullen v. Meijer, Inc., 355 F.3d 485, 494 n.7 (6th Cir. 2004).

264 *See* Lifecare Int'l, Inc. v. CD Med., Inc., 68 F.3d 429, 433 (11th Cir. 1995) ("the mere appearance of bias or partiality is not enough to set aside an arbitration award").

265 *E.g.*, Malone v. Bechtel Int'l, Inc., 2002 U.S. Dist. LEXIS 1112

(D. V.I. Jan. 22, 2002) (arbitration clause that bars residents of the U.S. Virgin Islands and Puerto Rico from serving as arbitrators does not establish bias); Phillips v. Associates Home Equity Services, Inc., 179 F. Supp. 2d 840 (N.D. Ill. 2001) ("Phillips provides no evidence that the AAA, one of the country's leading non-for-profit dispute resolution organizations, is on defendants' payroll or any other evidence of actual bias on the part of the AAA."); LLT Int'l, Inc. v. MCI Telecommunications Corp., 18 F. Supp. 2d 349, 354 (S.D.N.Y. 1998) (declining to give credence to repeat-player impact; "LLT's assertion that the AAA forum is biased because MCI is a big company with many disputes decided by arbitration does not even succeed in showing the 'mere appearance of bias' "); Rains v. Found. Health Sys. Life & Health, 23 P.3d 1249 (Colo. Ct. App. 2001) (AAA "safeguards" rendered enforceable a contract that permitted the defendant to select all three possible arbitrators, from whom the consumer must then select one).

266 Rosenberg v. Merrill Lynch, Pierce, Fenner & Smith, Inc., 170 F.3d 1 (1st Cir. 1999).

267 *See* Laurie Kratky Dore, *Public Courts Versus Private Justice: It's Time to Let Some Sun Shine in on Alternative Dispute Resolution*, 81 Chi.-Kent L. Rev. 463, 482–483 (2006).

268 *See, e.g.*, Ting v. AT & T, 319 F. Supp. 2d 902, 931 (N.D. Cal. 2002) (confidentiality provision requiring that any arbitration remain confidential); Torrance v. Aames Funding Corp., 242 F. Supp. 2d 862, 875 (D. Or. 2002) (clause stating that "[b]orrower and lender agree that the arbitration proceedings are confidential"); ACORN v. Household Int'l, Inc., 211 F. Supp. 2d 1160, 1171 (N.D. Cal. 2002) (agreement stated that "award shall be kept confidential"); Zuver v. Airtouch Communications, Inc.,

many others incorporate confidentiality by reference to arbitral rules.[269] The rules of most major dispute resolution organizations—including the American Arbitration Association, JAMS, and the National Arbitration Forum—have been drafted to contain confidentiality provisions.[270] For instance, the American Arbitration Association's Employment Arbitration Rules and Procedures state that: "The arbitrator shall maintain the confidentiality of the arbitration and shall have the authority to make appropriate rulings to safeguard that confidentiality, unless the parties agree otherwise or the law provides to the contrary."[271]

There is not unanimous support, however, for the proposition that the secrecy of arbitration is a bad thing. The ability to keep proceedings secret is touted as a selling point for arbitration,[272] and certain courts have declared that parties seeking to maintain confidentiality should seek resolution through arbitration rather than in court.[273]

6.5.8.2 Cases Finding Mandatory Confidentiality to Be Unconscionable

Several courts have held that confidentiality provisions in mandatory arbitration agreements are substantively unconscionable, typically on the grounds that such provisions confer an advantage on repeat players such as lenders, employers, and service providers.[274] According to these courts, facially neutral confidentiality provisions disproportionately favor repeat participants who have firsthand knowledge of how prior arbitrations against them have fared. In contrast one-shot participants like employees and consumers cannot access or utilize such arbitral precedent.[275] Not only does confidentiality conceal the advantages it bestows on repeat players, it prevents the public scrutiny that would help to mitigate those advantages.[276]

The Ninth Circuit found a confidentiality clause unconscionable as between a consumer and AT & T, when the clause was presented to the consumer in the form of a contract of adhesion sent to millions of customers.[277] The court held that the consequences of a confidentiality clause would provide AT & T with a decisive advantage in arbitration: "[I]f the company succeeds in imposing a gag order, plaintiffs are unable to mitigate the advantages inherent in being a repeat player."[278] The court went on to state that "AT & T has placed itself in a far superior legal posture by ensuring that none of its potential opponents have access to precedent while, at the same time, AT & T accumulates a wealth of knowledge on how to negotiate the terms of its own unilaterally crafted contract."[279] In a later Ninth Circuit case in the employment context, the court made similar points:

> Such restrictions would prevent an employee from contacting other employees to assist in litigating (or arbitrating) an employee's case. An inability to mention even the existence of a claim to current or former O'Melveny employees would handicap if not stifle an employee's ability to investigate and engage in discovery.[280]

Similar points were made by a federal district court in Missouri:

> The Court finds that the confidentiality provision in Household's arbitration agreement is unconscionable. As other courts have concluded, the provision ensures that Household reaps the advantages of repeatedly appearing before the same group of arbitrators, while consumers do not.... Although it appears that Household has had related disputes with consumers in the past, the

---

103 P.3d 753, 764 n.9 (Wash. 2004) (stating that "[a]ll arbitration proceedings, including settlements and awards, under the Agreement will be confidential").

269 *See, e.g.*, Parilla v. IAP Worldwide Services VI, Inc., 368 F.2d 269, 272 (3d Cir. 2004) (arbitration agreement incorporating confidentiality by reference to rules of American Arbitration Association); *see also* Llewellyn Joseph Gibbons, *Private Law, Public "Justice": Another Look at Privacy, Arbitration, and Global E-Commerce*, 15 Ohio St. J. on Disp. Resol. 769, 777 (2000) (describing sources of arbitration privacy).

270 *E.g.*, Am. Arbitration Ass'n, Employment Arbitration Rules & Procedures Rule 23, *available at* www.adr.org/sp.asp?id= 28481; JAMS Streamlined Arbitration Rules & Procedures Rule 23 (reprinted in Appx. B.3.1, *infra*); National Arbitration Forum Code of Procedure Rule 4 (reprinted in Appx. B.2.1, *infra*).

271 *See* Am. Arbitration Ass'n, Employment Arbitration Rules & Procedures Rule 23, *available at* www.adr.org/sp.asp?id= 28481.

272 *E.g.*, Global Arbitration & Mediation Serv., GAMS Confidentiality Policy, *available at* www.globalarbitrationmediation.com/gams_confidentiality_policy.shtml ("We at GAMS appreciate that confidentiality is one of the key reasons businesses select arbitration or mediation to resolve disputes. Your privacy is important to us. The proprietary information of your business is important to us as well. We will do everything possible to keep your business matters as confidential as possible.").

273 Baxter Int'l, Inc. v. Abbott Laboratories, 297 F.3d 544, 548 (7th Cir. 2002) (closed arbitration presents "a sure path to dispute resolution with complete confidentiality"); Union Oil Co. of Cal. v. Leavell, 220 F.3d 562, 568 (7th Cir. 2000) ("People who want secrecy should opt for arbitration.").

274 *E.g.*, Ting v. AT & T, 319 F.3d 1126, 1152 (9th Cir. 2003); Torrance v. Aames Funding Corp., 242 F. Supp. 2d 862, 875 (D.

Or. 2002); Luna v. Household Fin. Corp. III, 236 F. Supp. 2d 1166, 1181 (W.D. Wash. 2002); Acorn v. Household Int'l, Inc., 211 F. Supp. 2d 1160, 1172 (N.D. Cal. 2002); Zuver v. Airtouch Communications, Inc., 103 P.3d 753, 765 (Wash. 2004); *see also* Bragg v. Linden Research, Inc., 487 F. Supp. 2d 593, 610 (E.D. Pa. 2007) (confidentiality of arbitration provision supported a finding of unconscionability).

275 Laurie Kratky Dore, *Public Courts Versus Private Justice: It's Time to Let Some Sun Shine in on Alternative Dispute Resolution*, 81 Chi.-Kent L. Rev. 463, 502–503 (2006).

276 *Bragg*, 487 F. Supp. 2d at 610; *Acorn*, 211 F. Supp. 2d at 1172.

277 Ting v. AT & T, 319 F.3d 1126, 1134 (9th Cir. 2003).

278 *Id.* at 1152.

279 *Id.*

280 Davis v. O'Melveny & Myers, 485 F.3d 1066 (9th Cir. 2007).

Plaintiffs will not have access to the details of those proceedings—for example, to see how fees and waiver requests have been handled or to determine whether an agreement to arbitrate is even wise, given the track record of Household's success during arbitration. But for this litigation, Plaintiffs would never have known that Household could not arbitrate before the AAA, yet Household would have that information because of prior arbitrations with the AAA. In addition, Household has not explained why these confidentiality agreements provide any real benefit, much less a comparable benefit, to the consumer. As repeat players, Household is the obvious beneficiary of any attempt to obscure the process.[281]

Other federal district courts have similarly held confidentiality clauses unconscionable because of the advantage they grant repeat players.[282] Despite the facial neutrality of confidentiality clauses, these courts have found the enforcement of those clauses to disproportionately favor the company over the consumer.[283]

Several courts have also considered the claim that confidentiality clauses are unconscionable because of the wider public interest at issue.[284] In *Ting*, the district court stated:

> The implications of such secrecy to society are troubling. Among many others, they mean that if consumers obtain determinations that a particular AT & T practice is unlawful, they are prohibited from alerting other consumers. Since the AAA does not require the arbitrator to state reasons for the award and does not provide a public record of arbitrator rulings, this confidentiality provision means that a contract that affects seven million Californians will be interpreted largely without public scrutiny. This puts AT & T in a superior legal posture since as a party to every arbitration it will know every result and be able to guide itself and take legal positions accordingly, while each class member will have to operate in isolation and largely in the dark.[285]

However, while the district court's ruling in *Ting* was upheld on appeal, the Ninth Circuit made no similar statement concerning the effect of confidentiality on the public interest and future controversies. Similarly, in *Torrance v. Aames Funding Corp.*, while the plaintiffs "contend[ed] that [the] clause is unconscionable because consumer fraud is a public interest problem that should be aired in a fair and open proceeding," the district court did not reach the issue.[286]

On the other hand, the Washington Supreme Court held that the advantages conferred by confidentiality "undermines [the] employee's confidence in the fairness and honesty of the arbitration process and thus, potentially discourages that employee from pursuing a valid discrimination claim."[287] The court held that the confidentiality agreement was unconscionable not only because of a public interest in open proceedings, but also because it served "no purpose other than to tilt the scales of justice in favor of the employer."[288] Thus, while no court has held a confidentiality clause unconscionable solely on public interest grounds, such grounds may provide evidence of an advantage so unfair that it is unconscionable.

---

281 Sprague v. Household Int'l, 473 F. Supp. 2d 966 (W.D. Mo. 2005).

282 Torrance v. Aames Funding Corp., 242 F. Supp. 2d 862, 875 (D. Or. 2002) (defendant stands in a vastly superior legal posture with respect to its borrowers due to the secrecy of individual proceedings); Luna v. Household Fin. Corp. III, 236 F. Supp. 2d 1166, 1180 (W.D. Wash. 2002) ("[T]he confidentiality clause is facially neutral. However, its application disproportionately favors Household. The advantages repeat participants possess over 'one time' participants in arbitration proceedings are widely recognized in legal literature and by federal courts."); ACORN v. Household Int'l, Inc., 211 F. Supp. 2d 1160, 1172 (N.D. Cal. 2002) ("The secrecy provisions of the arbitration agreements both affect the outcomes of individual arbitrations and clearly favor Defendants. They do so by reinforcing the advantages Defendants already possess as repeat participants in the arbitration process."); Zuver v. Airtouch Communications, Inc., 103 P.3d 753, 775 (Wash. 2004) ("The effect of the provision here benefits only Airtouch. As written, the provision hampers an employee's ability to prove a pattern of discrimination or to take advantage of findings in past arbitrations. Moreover, keeping past findings secret undermines an employee's confidence in the fairness and honesty of the arbitration process and thus, potentially discourages that employee from pursuing a valid discrimination claim."); *see also* Bragg v. Linden Research, Inc., 487 F. Supp. 2d 593, 610 (E.D. Pa. 2007) (arbitration clause unconscionable in part because: "[I]f the company succeeds in imposing a gag order on arbitration proceedings, it places itself in a far superior legal posture by ensuring that none of its potential opponents have access to precedent while, at the same time, the company accumulates a wealth of knowledge on how to negotiate the terms of its own unilaterally crafted contract. The unavailability of arbitral decisions could also prevent potential plaintiffs from obtaining the information needed to build a case of intentional misconduct against a company."); *cf.* Cole v. Burns Int'l Sec. Services, 105 F.3d 1465, 1477 (D.C. Cir. 1997) ("[W]hile a lack of public disclosure of arbitration awards is acceptable in the collective bargaining process . . . in the context of individual statutory claims, a lack of public disclosure may systematically favor companies over individuals.").

283 Luna v. Household Fin. Corp. III, 236 F. Supp. 2d 1166, 1180 (W.D. Wash. 2002).

284 Torrance v. Aames Funding Corp., 242 F. Supp. 2d 862, 875 (D. Or. 2002); Ting v. AT & T, 182 F. Supp. 2d 902, 932 (N.D. Cal. 2002).

285 Ting v. AT & T, 182 F. Supp. 2d 902, 932 (N.D. Cal. 2002).

286 Torrance v. Aames Funding Corp., 242 F. Supp. 2d 862, 875 (D. Or. 2002).

287 Zuver v. Airtouch Communications, Inc., 103 P.3d 753, 765 (Wash. 2004).

288 *Id.*

6.5.8.3 Cases Finding Mandatory Confidentiality Not to Be Unconscionable

In contrast to the courts that have found confidentiality clauses unconscionable in contracts of adhesion, other courts have concluded that confidentiality and secrecy provisions are not grounds for a finding of unconscionability.[289] In addition several commentators have criticized courts that have found confidentiality to be unconscionable for supposedly violating the FAA's prohibition against singling out arbitration for heightened scrutiny.[290]

In *Iberia Credit Bureau, Inc. v. Cingular Wireless L.L.C.*, the Fifth Circuit held that while a confidentiality requirement may be more favorable to one party, it does not rise to the level of unconscionability.[291] The court viewed "the plaintiffs' attack on the confidentiality provision" as "in part, an attack on the character of arbitration itself."[292] "[P]art of the point of arbitration is that one 'trades the procedures and opportunity for review of the courtroom for the simplicity, informality, and expedition of arbitration.'"[293] The court also concluded that confidentiality provisions are not only potentially harmful to consumers, but also to repeat players,[294] and thereby are not so one-sided as to be unconscionable.

In *Parilla v. IAP Worldwide Services VI, Inc.*, the Third Circuit concluded that concern about the impact of a confidentiality clause on other claimants in subsequent proceedings is not sufficient to find the clause unconscionable.[295] Because both parties have the same rights and restraints under confidentiality provisions, "and there is nothing inherent in confidentiality itself that favors one party vis-a-vis the other in the dispute resolution process," confidentiality is not unconscionable.[296] "This concern has to do[] not with unfairness between contracting parties. . . . Moreover, we do not perceive the potential for confidentiality in arbitrations as posing a substantial threat to employees' future ability to prove a case under these statutes."[297] Therefore, these courts have found confidentiality provisions neither unconscionable as applied to the instant arbitration nor unconscionable as violations of public policy.[298]

6.5.9 Loser Pays Rules

Arbitration clauses that require non-prevailing plaintiffs to pay the defendants' attorneys fees (a "loser pays rule") may conflict with certain consumer protection statutes. These rules are surprisingly common, and the Executive Director of the National Arbitration Forum (NAF) told a corporate counsel magazine that NAF has adopted a loser pays rule as a means of achieving tort reform:

> Editor: Another goal of Civil Justice Reform is to impose a penalty on commencing litigation as a way to extort a settlement of a frivolous claim. Civil Justice Reform advocates have proposed a "loser pays" rule to counter such tactics.
>
> Anderson: The rules of the National Arbitration Forum allows the arbitrator to award the prevailing party the cost of the arbitration including attorneys' fees. The rules of the other major arbitration administrators have similar provisions. The economics of dispute resolution by arbitration are entirely different from the economics of bringing lawsuits. There is no such thing as a "no risk" arbitration for either side.[299]

One court has addressed what the NAF's loser pays rule with respect to arbitration fees means to consumers:

> The NAF Code could not only result in the consumer-claimant losing the action, but also in the imposition of an award of fees double the expenses the consumer already incurred in filing the

---

[289] Iberia Credit Bureau, Inc. v. Cingular Wireless L.L.C., 379 F.3d 159, 176 (5th Cir. 2004); Lloyd v. Hovensa, L.L.C., 369 F.3d 263, 275 (3d Cir. 2004); Parilla v. IAP Worldwide Services VI, Inc., 368 F.3d 269, 281 (3d Cir. 2004).

[290] Laurie Kratky Dore, *Public Courts Versus Private Justice: It's Time to Let Some Sun Shine in on Alternative Dispute Resolution*, 81 Chi.-Kent L. Rev. 463, 504 n.10 (2006); *see also* Kelly Thompson Cochran & Eric J. Mogilnicki, *Current Issues in Consumer Arbitration*, 60 Bus. Law. 785, 788 (2005) (arguing that treating confidentiality clauses with more scrutiny may trigger federal preemption concerns); Michael G. McGuinness & Adam J. Karr, *California's "Unique" Approach to Arbitration: Why This Road Less Traveled Will Make All the Difference on the Issue of Preemption Under the Federal Arbitration Act*, 1 J. Disp. Resol. 61 (2005) (arguing that the FAA should preempt the use of the unconscionability doctrine as backdoor bias against arbitration); Susan Randall, *Judicial Attitudes Toward Arbitration and the Resurgence of Unconscionability*, 52 Buff. L. Rev. 185, 194 (arguing that courts are circumventing the FAA "through expansive, arbitration-specific uses of unconscionability" and calling for a restrained use of unconscionability doctrine to avoid preemption).

[291] *See* Iberia Credit Bureau, Inc. v. Cingular Wireless L.L.C., 379 F.3d 159, 175 (5th Cir. 2004) ("While the confidentiality requirement is probably more favorable to the cellular provider than to its customer, the plaintiffs have not persuaded us that the requirement is so offensive as to be invalid.").

[292] Iberia Credit Bureau, Inc. v. Cingular Wireless L.L.C., 379 F.3d 159, 175 (5th Cir. 2004).

[293] *Id.* at 176 (quoting Mitsubishi Motors Corp. v. Soler Chrysler-Plymouth, Inc., 473 U.S. 614, 628, 105 S. Ct. 3346, 87 L. Ed. 2d 444 (1985)).

[294] *Id.* at 176 ("We note as well that the creation of precedent—one of the plaintiffs' main concerns—can cut both ways, since precedent can be helpful or harmful, depending on the decision.").

[295] Parilla v. IAP Worldwide Services VI, Inc., 368 F.3d 269, 290–291 (3d Cir. 2004).

[296] *Id.*; *cf.* Iberia Credit Bureau, Inc. v. Cingular Wireless L.L.C., 379 F.3d 159, 175 (5th Cir. 2004) ("Confidentiality can be desirable to customers in some circumstances.").

[297] *Parilla*, 368 F.3d at 280–281.

[298] *Id.*, 368 F.3d at 281.

[299] *Do an LRA: Implement Your Own Civil Justice Reform Program NOW*, Metro. Corp. Couns., Aug. 2001.

NAF arbitration. This is another example of the economics of the arbitration process potentially having a "chilling effect" on the consumer's rights.[300]

Section 4.3.2.3, *supra*, notes that loser pays rules are likely to discourage most consumers from pursuing their claims, and that loser pays rules for consumers are contrary to the statutory schemes of most consumer protection statutes. For the same reasons, such loser pays rules will render arbitration clauses unconscionable in many jurisdictions.

In *Sosa v. Paulos*, the Utah Supreme Court considered an arbitration provision requiring a medical malpractice plaintiff to pay the litigation costs of the doctor if the patient "wins less than half the amount of damages sought in arbitration."[301] The court held "that this provision is substantively unconscionable on its face," and stated: "We find no precedent in law for the award of attorney fees to the loser in malpractice arbitration, and we hold that such a contractual term embedded in a negotiated agreement is not only substantively unconscionable but against public policy."[302] A sharply contrary view has been voiced by the Eleventh Circuit, however.[303] An Ohio appellate court has added a powerful explanation of why such a rule is unconscionable:

> On review of the arbitration clause and the arguments of the parties, we find troubling the fact that the prevailing party is entitled to attorney fees. Typically, attorney fees are not awarded to the prevailing party in a civil action unless ordered by the court (such as following a finding of frivolous conduct). Though the prevailing party may be the resident or the representative, individuals may be discouraged from pursuing claims because, in addition to paying their attorney and, pursuant to the arbitration clause, the costs of arbitration, they may be saddled with the facility's costs and attor-

ney fees. Such a burden is undoubtedly unconscionable.[304]

One troubling new trend is that some corporations are adding provisions to arbitration clauses that would require consumers to pay the corporation's attorney fees if the consumer brings a challenge in court to the enforceability of an arbitration clause. While this kind of provision would seem to be unenforceable under all of the authorities cited above with respect to "loser pays rule," at least one court has enforced such a term.[305]

6.6 Remedies When Part, or Parts, of an Arbitration Clause Are Unconscionable

6.6.1 Introduction

It is common for a corporate defendant who has drafted an unconscionable arbitration clause, and who faces court scrutiny of the clause, to ask the court to rewrite the arbitration clause so that it will be enforceable. A number of consumer lawyers who have challenged blatantly illegal portions of arbitration clauses have received roughly the following response from the corporate defendant: "We will agree to jettison the most extreme elements of the arbitration clause, and we ask the court to enforce the remainder of the clause." While this sort of request has met with mixed success in the courts, the better rule is that courts should not rewrite unconscionable arbitration clauses to give their drafters the benefits they sought.

6.6.2 Party That Drafted Unconscionable Clause Should Not Receive Court's Assistance

The Supreme Court has said that the "primary purpose" of the FAA is to ensure "that private agreements to arbitrate are enforced according to their terms."[306] Thus, if an agreement to arbitrate cannot be enforced according to its terms, a court should refuse to enforce it. When a corporation drafts

---

300 Licitra v. Gateway, Inc., 189 Misc. 2d 721, 735 N.Y.S.2d 289 (Civ. Ct. 2001).
301 Sosa v. Paulos, 924 P.2d 357, 362 (Utah 1996).
302 *Id.*; *see also* Matthews-Deaton v. El Torito Restaurants, Inc., 2006 WL 2349557 (Cal. Ct. App. Aug. 15, 2006) (a contract provision permitting prevailing employer to recover attorney fees from an employee violated a California statute and was unenforceable); Taylor Bldg. Corp. of Am. v. Benfield, 860 N.E.2d 1058 (Ohio Ct. App.) (loser-pays-attorney-fees provision in construction contract an "example[] of the substantive unfairness of the terms in [a] contract"), *appeal allowed*, 859 N.E.2d 556 (Ohio 2006); Delta Funding Corp. v. Harris, 912 A.2d 104 (N.J. 2006) (if arbitrator were to interpret contract as creating a loser pays provision, that would impose upon the consumer a risk that "is unconscionable in that it is a deterrent to the vindication of her statutory rights").
303 Musnick v. King Motor Co., 325 F.3d 1255 (11th Cir. 2003); *see also* Mazotas v. Home Comfort Now, L.L.C., 2007 WL 586903 (Conn. Super. Ct. Feb. 1, 2007) (upholding arbitration agreement under which loser pays because "since the clause requires that the selected arbitrator be 'neutral,' . . . a finding of unconscionability cannot be made").

304 Small v. HCF of Perrysburg, 159 Ohio App. 3d 66, 823 N.E.2d 19 (2004).
305 *See* Kahn v. Option One Mortgage Corp., 2006 WL 156942 (E.D. Pa. Jan. 18, 2006) (upholding an arbitration clause in a mortgage loan contract providing that, "[i]f either party, you or we, fails to submit to arbitration following a proper demand to do so, that party shall bear all costs and expenses, including reasonable attorney's fees, incurred by the other party compelling arbitration."; the court, pursuant to the terms of the arbitration agreement, awarded defendant the costs and expenses of compelling arbitration).
306 Volt Info. Sciences, Inc. v. Bd. of Trustees, 489 U.S. 468, 479, 109 S. Ct. 1248, 103 L. Ed. 2d 488 (1989).

an unenforceable contract of adhesion it is not the responsibility of a court to supply the legal acumen to rewrite the contract, and thereby find a legal way for the drafter to enjoy the otherwise unobtainable results it sought. As a comment to the Restatement (Second) of Contracts states, "a court will not aid a party who has taken advantage of his dominant bargaining power to extract from the other party a promise that is clearly so broad as to offend public policy by redrafting the agreement so as to make a part of the promise enforceable."[307]

As one federal court has noted, permitting defendants to rewrite arbitration clauses whenever they are found to be unconscionable or illegal would encourage defendants to draft clauses that are as draconian as possible:

> [I]f I were to accept defendant's proposal [to pay the plaintiff's share of the costs of arbitration and to drop the provision of the clause shortening the period for limitations], employers would have no incentive to ensure that a coerced arbitration agreement is fair to both sides. Instead, the employer could write a one-sided agreement that favors the employer, and then make the bare minimum modifications necessary to obtain the court's approval.[308]

A California Court of Appeals has also held that it is fundamentally unfair to allow a party to rewrite an arbitration clause after litigation begins.

> [I]t strikes us as woefully unfair to allow Homefirst at this late date—after a dispute has arisen and after the reverse mortgage has terminated—to refute the unconscionable aspects of the arbitration agreement which Homefirst itself drafted and from which Homefirst stood to benefit over the life of the loan.[309]

A Florida appellate court has similarly refused to allow a defendant to rewrite an arbitration clause that contained an illegal provision barring a prevailing plaintiff from receiving her attorney fees under Title VII.[310] In addition, the South Carolina Supreme Court has held that "the general principle in this State that is that it is not the function of the court to rewrite contracts for parties," and that "the intent of the parties is best achieved by severing the arbitration clause in its entirety rather than 'rewriting' the contract by severing multiple unenforceable provisions."[311] While the court "generally would encourage severability of an unconscionable provision," the arbitration agreement at issue was not "a proper candidate for the application of this remedy."[312]

One increasingly common tactic is for defendants to draft a prohibitively expensive arbitration clause, but then to reverse course during litigation and offer to pay all or some of the arbitration fees if a consumer brings a particularly aggressive challenge to the validity of the fee arrangement. This behavior is particularly common in appellate settings or in trial courts when defendants perceive that the court is leaning against them. A Florida state appellate court has rejected such an offer, holding that a corporation may not mend an unenforceable arbitration clause during litigation by offering to pay all costs.[313] Another federal court refused to allow a defendant to "voluntarily pay" the costs of arbitration, noting that "the fairness of a contract must be viewed as of the time the contract was formed" and "this court may not rewrite the contract for the parties."[314]

The Sixth Circuit has recently identified a "federal policy" that courts should not rewrite or otherwise fix arbitration clauses containing illegal terms:

> To sever the costs and fees provision and force the employee to arbitrate a Title VII claim despite the employer's attempt to limit the remedies available would reward the employer for its actions and fail to deter similar misconduct by others.... Under

---

307 Restatement (Second) of Contracts § 184 cmt. b (1981).
308 Lelouis v. W. Directory Co., 230 F. Supp. 2d 1214, 1225 (D. Or. 2001).
309 Flores v. Transamerica Homefirst, Inc., 93 Cal. App. 4th 846, 857, 113 Cal. Rptr. 2d 376 (2001); *see also* Bragg v. Linden Research, Inc., 487 F. Supp. 2d 593, 612 (E.D. Pa. 2007) ("The Court declines to rewrite the agreement, at Linden's request, to save an unconscionable arbitration provision which Linden itself drafted and now seeks to enforce."); Covenant Health Rehab. of Picayune v. Brown, 949 So. 2d 732 (Miss. 2007) (dissent) ("The majority's excision of unconscionable sections results in this Court re-writing a contract which favors a goal of the nullifying party; and undeserved reward for unconscionable conduct.").

A different but related tactic was at issue in Stern v. Cingular Wireless Corp., 453 F. Supp. 2d 1138 (C.D. Cal. 2006). When plaintiff, who entered into a contract with AT & T Wireless, sued, defendant argued that Cingular's arbitration provision—not AT & T's—controlled. *See id.* at 1144. The court held that as procedural and substantive unconscionability are properly evaluated as of the time of contract formation, the operable arbitration clause was that entered into by plaintiff and AT & T. *Id.* While Cingular did not attempt to rewrite the arbitration contract in response to the instant litigation, its attempt to substitute a different version of the arbitration agreement shared the same purpose.
310 Flyer Printing Co. v. Hill, 805 So. 2d 829 (Fla. Dist. Ct. App. 2001).
311 Simpson v. MSA of Myrtle Beach, Inc., 644 S.E.2d 663, 673–674 (S.C. 2007).
312 *Id.* at 674 n.9.
313 Flyer Printing Co. v. Hill, 805 So. 2d 829 (Fla. Dist. Ct. App. 2001) ("Flyer Printing points out that it offered to pay all the costs of arbitration notwithstanding the language of the agreement. Hill rejected this unilateral offer to amend the agreement, however, and we are not authorized to remake the parties contract."); *cf.* Livingston v. Associates Fin., Inc., 2002 WL 31101669 (N.D. Ill. Sept. 18, 2002) (when defendant offered to pay all costs of arbitration "to the extent [the arbitration costs] exceed[] the costs plaintiffs would incur in litigation in federal court," such offer was too vague and nebulous to solve the problem of excessive arbitral fees).
314 Lelouis v. W. Directory Co., 230 F. Supp. 2d 1214, 1224, 1225 (D. Or. 2001).

the contrary approach, an employer will not be deterred from routinely inserting such a deliberately illegal clause into the arbitration agreement it mandates for its employees if it knows that the worst penalty for such illegality is the severance of the clause after the employee has litigated the matter...."[315]

A number of courts have also refused to rewrite arbitration clauses that had one or more unconscionable or otherwise unenforceable provisions.[316]

In some cases, a corporation's arbitration clause cannot be enforced as written. In *Martinez v. Master Protection Corp.*, for example, the arbitration clause designated an arbitration firm (the American Arbitration Association) that refused to administer the arbitration because the corporation violated the firm's due process protocols.[317] The trial court effectively rewrote the clause, however, and required arbitration before another arbitrator. The court of appeals, however, held that it was improper to rewrite the clause: "If an arbitration agreement designates an exclusive arbitral forum . . ., and arbitration in that forum is not possible, courts may not compel arbitration in an alternate forum by appointing substitute arbitrators. . . ."[318]

Other courts, however, have substantially rewritten arbitration clauses that were illegal or unenforceable in part, and then proceeded to compel arbitration. For example, the Eighth Circuit has held that, if an arbitration agreement has a single unenforceable provision (a prohibition on the recovery of punitive damages) but also has a severability clause, then the objectionable provision would be stricken but the remainder of the agreement would be preserved.[319]

---

315 Cooper v. MRM Inv. Co., 367 F.3d 493, 512 (6th Cir. 2004).

316 Alexander v. Anthony Int'l, Ltd. P'ship, 341 F.3d 256, 271 (3d Cir. 2003) ("The cumulative effect of such illegality prevents us from enforcing the arbitration agreement. Because the sickness has infected the trunk, we must cut down the entire tree."); Ingle v. Circuit City Stores, Inc., 328 F.3d 1165 (9th Cir. 2003); Hooters of Am., Inc. v. Phillips, 173 F.3d 933, 940 (4th Cir. 1999) (when the improper provisions of an arbitration clause are "by no means insubstantial," the Court "therefore permit[ed the employee] to cancel the agreement and thus Hooters' suit to compel arbitration must fail'"); Paladino v. Avnet Computer Technologies, Inc., 134 F.3d 1054, 1058 (11th Cir. 1998) ("the presence of an unlawful provision in an arbitration agreement may serve to taint the entire arbitration agreement, rendering the agreement completely unenforceable, not just subject to judicial reformation"); Graham Oil Co. v. ARCO Products Co., 43 F.3d 1244, 1249 (9th Cir. 1994) ("Our decision to strike the entire clause rests in part upon the fact that the offensive provisions clearly represent an attempt by ARCO to achieve through arbitration what Congress has expressly forbidden. . . . Such a blatant misuse of the arbitration procedure serves to taint the entire clause."); Bragg v. Linden Research, Inc., 487 F. Supp. 2d 593, 612 (E.D. Pa. 2007) ("The arbitration clause before the Court is simply not one where a single term may be stricken to render the agreement conscionable."); Underwood v. Chef Francisco/Heinz, 200 F. Supp. 2d 475, 481 (E.D. Pa. 2002) ("When faced with situations similar to the one before us, other courts have declined to enforce the entire agreement rather than severing or reforming the offending clause."); Browne v. Kline Tysons Imports, Inc., 190 F. Supp. 2d 827, 832 (E.D. Va. 2002) ("The Court finds [altering a provision in an arbitration clause] to be an impermissible attempt to rewrite the contract at issue."); Popovich v. McDonald's Corp., 189 F. Supp. 2d 772, 779 (N.D. Ill. 2002); Gourley v. Yellow Transp., L.L.C., 178 F. Supp. 2d 1196 (D. Colo. 2001) (not allowing defendant to jettison three offending provisions of arbitration clause); Geiger v. Ryan's Family Steak Houses, Inc., 134 F. Supp. 2d 985, 992 (S.D. Ind. 2001) ("The original EDSI Rules formed the basis of the contract between EDSI and the Plaintiffs and are at the heart of Plaintiffs' allegations of invalidity of the alleged contractual relationship. . . . EDSI and Ryan's attempts to change the rules a month-and-a-half after the close of discovery on this motion does not alter our analysis. . . ."); Anderson v. Ashby, 873 So. 2d 168, 179 (Ala. 2003) (the entire arbitration provision is unconscionable and unenforceable when there are multiple unconscionable provisions); Nyulassy v. Lockheed Martin Corp., 16 Cal. Rptr. 3d 296 (Ct. App. 2004); SA-PG-Ocala, L.L.C. v. Stokes, 935 So. 2d 1242, 1243 (Fla. Dist. Ct. App. 2006) (provisions stripping nursing home patients of the right to obtain certain types of damages "served to taint the entire agreement and rendered the arbitration agreement completely unenforceable"); Schaefer v. Allstate Ins. Co., 590 N.E.2d 1242 (Ohio 1992) (striking entire arbitration clause, not rewriting it);

see also Al-Safin v. Circuit City Stores, Inc., 394 F.3d 1254 (9th Cir. 2005) (holding that, because an arbitration agreement was permeated with multiple unconscionable provisions, the entire agreement was unenforceable and the unconscionable provisions would not be severed); Plattner v. Edge Solutions, Inc., 2004 WL 1575557, at *1 (N.D. Ill. May 27, 2004) ("[T]he court cannot rewrite the arbitration clause to compel arbitration in a forum not contemplated by the parties when the contract was executed."); Wilson v. Bally Total Fitness Corp., Inc., 2003 WL 21398324, at *5 (Cal. Ct. App. June 18, 2003) ("While Bally offered to modify the Agreement to pay all arbitration expenses, Wilson never accepted the offer and the trial court correctly concluded that Bally's offer was 'too little, too late.'"); Mercuro v. Super. Ct., 96 Cal. App. 4th 167, 116 Cal. Rptr. 2d 671 (2002) ("Here, we reach the same conclusion as did the *Armendariz* court. The Countrywide arbitration agreement is unenforceable because it is permeated with unconscionability and illegality and it cannot be cured by merely extirpating the offending provisions—we would have to rewrite the contract which we lack the power to do."); Flores v. Transamerica Homefirst, Inc., 93 Cal. App. 4th 846, 113 Cal. Rptr. 2d 376 (2001) ("In the present case, we are likewise faced with an arbitration agreement in which no single provision can be stricken to remove the unconscionable taint."); Presidential Leasing, Inc. v. Krout, 896 So. 2d 938 (Fl. Dist. Ct. App. 2005) ("The presence of an unlawful provision in an arbitration agreement may serve to taint the entire arbitration agreement, rendering the agreement completely unenforceable.").

317 12 Cal. Rptr. 3d 663 (Ct. App. 2004);

318 12 Cal. Rptr. 3d at 674 (citation omitted).

319 Gannon v. Circuit City Stores, Inc., 262 F.3d 677 (8th Cir. 2001); *see also* Hadnot v. Bay, Ltd., 344 F.3d 474 (5th Cir. 2003) (striking as illegal provision barring punitive damages, but severing that provision and enforcing the rest of the arbitration clause); Spinetti v. Serv. Corp. Int'l, 324 F.3d 212 (3d Cir. 2003) (striking illegal provisions of arbitration contract and referring the case to arbitration); Great Earth Companies Inc. v. Simons, 288 F.3d 878 (6th Cir. 2002) (enforcing arbitration clause and severing provision that required arbitration to take

The court relied upon Missouri contract law that enforced severability clauses and "the FAA's policy favoring the enforcement of arbitration agreements."[320] There was a strong dissent in the case:

> This case does not involve a procedural provision or a minor term of any sort. It involves a term that guts a major substantive remedy that Congress and the Missouri legislature chose to provide to employees. It is a term that seeks to drastically change the substantive law (in favor of the employer) that is to be applied in the arbitration process that definitely is not minor.[321]

Other courts have placed weight upon belated offers to pay arbitral fees,[322] or have appointed new arbitrators when the clause could not be enforced with the arbitrators set forth in the contract.[323] Some other courts have even suggested that, whenever the arbitration system set forth in a contract is prohibitively expensive, courts should nonetheless compel the plaintiff to enter into arbitration, strike the cost sharing provision, and rewrite the contract to order the defendant to pay the costs associated with arbitration.[324]

6.6.3 Interdependent Aspects of Arbitration Clause Should Not Be Severed

Many courts have held that all parts of an arbitration clause are interdependent and that offending parts should thus not be severed, but the whole clause thrown out.[325] For

---

place in New York); Cooper v. QC Fin. Services, 2007 WL 974100 (D. Ariz. Mar. 30, 2007) (preserving arbitration agreement while severing clause containing class action ban); Safranek v. Copart, Inc., 379 F. Supp. 2d 927 (N.D. Ill. 2005) ("Given the strong federal policy favoring arbitration, and the ability of courts to sever unenforceable provisions of otherwise valid agreements, the best course in this case is to sever the portion of the arbitration clause stating that each party shall bear its own costs with respect to attorney's fees."); De Ornellas v. Aspen Square Mgmt, Inc., 295 F. Supp. 2d 753 (E.D. Mich. 2003) (striking provisions limiting employees' right to recover attorney fees, requiring employees to share the costs of arbitration, and permitting the employer to pick the venue for arbitration, but nonetheless enforcing the remainder of the clause and compelling arbitration); Smith v. Beneficial Ohio, Inc., 284 F. Supp. 2d 875 (S.D. Ohio 2003) (court severed a provision requiring a plaintiff to pay half of the costs of arbitration); Matthews-Deaton v. El Torito Restaurants, Inc., 2006 WL 2349557 (Cal. Ct. App. Aug. 15, 2006) (severing unenforceable provisions in an arbitration clause that stripped individuals of their right to receive attorney fees, charged excessive fees for arbitration, and enforced the remainder of the arbitration agreement); Jones v. Humanscale Corp., 130 Cal. App. 4th 401, 29 Cal. Rptr. 3d 881 (2005) (court severed a provision that allowed the arbitrator to split the fees and expenses between the parties); Alterra Healthcare v. Linton, 953 So. 2d 574, 579 (Fla. Dist. Ct. App. 2007) (striking a limitation on punitive damages while enforcing the remainder of the arbitration clause when severability clause existed); Fonte v. AT & T Wireless Services, Inc., 903 So. 2d 1019 (Fla. Dist. Ct. App. 2005) ("We find the void provision prohibiting any award of attorney's fees can be severed without affecting the intent of the parties to arbitrate."); Covenant Health Rehab. of Picayune, Ltd. P'ship v. Brown, 949 So. 2d 732, 741–742 (Miss. 2007) (striking five separate provisions of arbitration agreement as unconscionable, but enforcing remaining three provisions of agreement); Russell v. Performance Toyota Inc., 826 So. 2d 719 (Miss. 2002) (if a provision in an arbitration clause shortening the limitations period is illegal, it will be stricken and the remainder of the agreement enforced); Swain v. Auto Services, Inc., 128 S.W.3d 103 (Mo. Ct. App. 2003) (striking provision requiring arbitration in a convenient forum, but enforcing the rest of the arbitration clause).

320 Gannon v. Circuit City Stores, Inc., 262 F.3d 677, 683 (8th Cir. 2001).
321 *Id.* at 684 (Vietor, J., dissenting).
322 Equal Employment Opportunity Comm'n v. Woodmen of the World Ins. Soc'y, 2007 WL 702758 (8th Cir. Mar. 9, 2007) (rejecting challenge to cost of arbitration clause, when "Woodmen has agreed to waive the fee-splitting provision and pay the arbitrator's fees in full"); Jones v. Household Realty Corp., 2003 WL 23750601 (S.D. Ohio Dec. 17, 2003) (when company offered to pay all costs of arbitration, notwithstanding clause that placed half of the costs on the consumer, the court enforced the arbitration agreement); *see* Sydnor v. Conseco Fin. Servicing Corp., 252 F.3d 302, 306 (4th Cir. 2001) (apparently accepting as resolving the fees issue that "[a]ppellant has also represented to this court its willingness to pay arbitration fees arising from this dispute"); First Family Fin. Services, Inc. v. Sanford, 203 F. Supp. 2d 662, 667 (N.D. Miss. 2002); Fluehmann v. Associates Fin. Services, 2002 WL 500564 (D. Mass. Mar. 29, 2002).
323 Harold Allen's Mobile Home Factory Outlet, Inc. v. Butler, 825 So. 2d 779 (Ala. 2002) (holding that an arbitration clause giving the company the sole power to appoint the arbitrator was unconscionable, but then directing the trial court to appoint a new arbitrator); State *ex rel.* Vincent v. Schneider, 194 S.W.3d 853 (Mo. 2006) (when arbitration clause unconscionably provided one party the sole power to select an arbitrator, the court was to appoint another arbitrator); *In re* FirstMerit Bank, 52 S.W.3d 749 (Tex. 2001) (suggesting that if the arbitration clause in a case specifies a prohibitively expensive arbitrator, then instead of striking the clause the trial court should "choose an alternative set of arbitrators" pursuant to § 5 of the F.A.A.).
324 *See* Gooden v. Vill. Green Mgmt Co., 2002 WL 31557689 (D. Minn. Nov. 15, 2002) (severs provision of arbitration agreement requiring individual to pay costs, requires defendant to pay all the costs); Livingston v. Associates Fin., Inc., 2001 U.S. Dist. LEXIS 8678, at *13 (N.D. Ill. June 25, 2001); Giordano v. Pep Boys—Manny, Moe & Jack, Inc., 2001 U.S. Dist. LEXIS 5433, at *5–*6 (E.D. Pa. Mar. 29, 2001).
325 Graham Oil Co. v. ARCO Products Co., 43 F.3d 1244 (9th Cir. 1994); *see also* Hooters of Am., Inc. v. Phillips, 173 F.3d 933 (4th Cir. 1999) (rescinding the whole arbitration agreement); Paladino v. Avnet Computer Technologies, Inc., 134 F.3d 1054 (11th Cir. 1998); Gonzalez v. Hughes Aircraft Employees Fed. Credit Union, 70 Cal. App. 4th 468, 83 Cal. Rptr. 2d 763, *review granted and opinion superseded*, 85 Cal. Rptr. 2d 843, 978 P.2d 1 (Cal.), *review dismissed*, 91 Cal. Rptr. 2d 622, 990 P.2d 504 (Cal. 1999); Stirlen v. Supercuts, Inc., 51 Cal. App. 4th 1519, 60 Cal. Rptr. 2d 138 (1997). *But see* Fuller v. Pep Boys—Manny, Moe & Jack of Del., Inc., 88 F. Supp. 2d 1158, 1162, 1163 (D. Colo. 2000) (severing provision imposing excessive fees and enforcing the remainder of the clause); Jones v. Fujitsu Network

example, the Alabama Supreme Court has refused to allow a trial court to reform the arbitration agreement—the agreement stands as written or must be overturned.[326]

Still other courts have steered a middle course. In the *Armendariz* case, the California Supreme Court held that a state statute required that it invalidate the entire agreement only when it is "permeated" by unconscionability.[327] The court found that the instant agreement was so permeated:

> In this case, two factors weigh against severance of the unlawful provisions. First, the arbitration agreement contains more than one unlawful provision; it has both an unlawful damages provision and an unconscionably unilateral arbitration clause. Such multiple defects indicate a systematic effect to impose arbitration on an employee not simply as an alternative to litigation, but as an inferior forum that works to the employer's advantage.... Second, in the case of the agreement's lack of mutuality, such permeation is indicated by the fact that there is no single provision a court can strike or restrict in order to remove the unconscionable taint from the agreement. Rather, the court would have to, in effect, reform the contract, not through severance or restriction, but by augmenting it with additional terms.[328]

In *Lowden v. T-Mobile, USA, Inc.*,[329] similarly, the court found severance inappropriate, and the arbitration agreement as a whole unenforceable when unconscionable provisions " 'taint' or 'pervade' the entire arbitration agreement . . . or reveal an 'insidious pattern' of seeking to tip the scales unfairly." The court found the instant agreement unenforceable:

> The Court finds that these arbitration agreements are tainted with substantive unconscionability and that they cannot be enforced. Although some of the provisions are not so one-sided as to be offending, the unconscionable provisions reveal a pattern of attempting to deprive Defendant's customers of a way to enforce their rights against Defendant in a meaningful way. The fact that these are consumer claims brought for individually small sums of money makes the damages limitations, class action prohibitions, and the attorneys' fees limitation in Plaintiff['s] agreement unconscionable to the point of tainting these entire arbitration agreements with unconscionability. These provisions also threaten the strong public policy of protecting consumers in Washington State. This "fundamental unfairness" renders these entire agreements substantively unconscionable and therefore unenforceable.

In *Pitchford v. Oakwood Mobile Homes*, the court made a distinction between "severing" and "blue-penciling" that might be important for plaintiffs trying to argue that an entire arbitration clause, not just a portion of the clause, is unenforceable.[330] In Virginia, argues the court, "courts will look to the intent of the parties to determine severability of clauses or provisions, [but] they will not 'blue pencil' a contract to make it enforceable."[331] The difference between the two is that severing allows courts to treat independent clauses independently, whereas blue-penciling implies actual editing of interdependent sections to "fix" the contract. In *Pitchford*, the court ultimately struck down the entire contract because it was precluded by the Magnuson-Moss Warranty Act, and because there was no one severable section dealing with warranty issues:

> The structure and nature of the Arbitration Agreement indicate that all parts contemplate interdependence. Based on the drafting of the contract on its face, severability is unavailable because there is no particular clause or provision that could be treated independently to cure the conflict with the Magnuson-Moss Act. To the contrary, in order to cure the problems with the Arbitration Agreement, the court would be forced to edit the agreement in one of two ways: the court would have to remove all reference to the warranty or remove all reference to the fact that the arbitration must be binding. As noted above, this form of blue penciling is precisely what Virginia courts consistently have refused to engage in. The court sees the wisdom of the refusal to rewrite the contract between the parties because to do so would be to wreak potential havoc with basic contractual principles, such as mutual assent.[332]

The Fifth Circuit has reached the same conclusion:

Communications, Inc., 81 F. Supp. 2d 688, 693 (N.D. Tex. 1999) (same).

326 Universal Underwriters Life Ins. Co. v. Dutton, 736 So. 2d 564 (Ala. 1999).

327 Armendariz v. Found. Health Psychcare Services, Inc., 24 Cal. 4th 83, 99 Cal. Rptr. 2d 745, 6 P.3d 669 (2000).

328 24 Cal. 4th at 124 (footnotes omitted); *see also* Little v. Auto Stiegler, Inc., 63 P.3d 979 (Cal. 2003) (following *Armendariz*).
   The Ninth Circuit recently followed *Armendariz* and refused to sever "objectionable provisions [that] pervade[d] the entire contract." Circuit City Stores, Inc. v. Adams, 279 F.3d 889 (9th Cir. 2002).

329 2006 WL 1009279, at *9 (W.D. Wash. Apr. 13, 2006).

330 Pitchford v. Oakwood Mobile Homes, 124 F. Supp. 2d 958 (W.D. Va. 2000).

331 *Id.* at 965.

332 *Id.* at 966; *see also* Browne v. Kline Tysons Imports, Inc., 190 F. Supp. 2d 827, at *11, *12 (E.D. Va. 2002) (when Magnuson-Moss would prohibit binding arbitration, severance of binding provision of arbitration clause would be an "impermissible attempt to rewrite the contract"); Torigian v. Michael Cadillac, Inc., 2003 WL 21246609 (Cal. Ct. App. May 29, 2003) (court would not sever unlawful provisions but struck the entire clause when "[t]he court would have to add language" to correct illegalities; "The courts do not have the power to make such reforms.").

[T]he offensive provision here is the sentence in which the customer, but not Centennial, is required to arbitrate. Saving the clause would require not that we excise an invalid excrescence and then send the pared-down contract to arbitration but that we redraft the contract to add important new material—a duty on Centennial's part to arbitrate. The severability clause cannot accomplish the needed repair.[333]

6.7 Miscellaneous Contract Defenses Other Than Unconscionability

6.7.1 Fraud in the Inducement Related to the Arbitration Clause Itself

Courts will enforce an arbitration agreement even when the agreement is part of a contract that involved fraud in the inducement. That is, when a consumer intends to sign a contract, and there is no misrepresentation as to the arbitration provision, disputes as to what the other side said to induce the consumer to sign the contract may not be sufficient to invalidate the arbitration provision.[334] One court has even extended this rule to a setting in which a party boasted that its perceived advantage in arbitration would help to further its overall fraudulent scheme.[335]

Courts will not require parties to arbitrate, however, if there were misrepresentations about the nature of the arbitration provision itself.[336] In fact, at least one state supreme court has held that a party (in this case, an illiterate borrower) has the right to a jury trial on the question of whether an arbitration clause was fraudulently induced.[337] Such misrepresentation may be found when the merchant enters into an arbitration agreement with the knowledge that it would breach the requirement of an expeditious arbitration.[338] Fraudulent concealment of an arbitration clause can also defeat the clause's enforceability, as when a salesman rushes elderly consumers through the execution of various documents, not disclosing the existence of the arbitration agreement.[339]

But the Alabama Supreme Court has ruled that the consumer must provide substantial evidence of fraud in the inducement of the arbitration clause to avoid arbitration.[340] It is not enough to say that the consumer was rushed through the contracting process, without an opportunity to study the arbitration clause, particularly if the consumer was capable of reading the contract and inquiring into its contents, entered into the agreement voluntarily, and the wording of

---

333 Iberia Credit Bureau, Inc. v. Cingular Wireless L.L.C., 379 F.3d 159, 171 (5th Cir. 2004); *see also* Batory v. Sears, Roebuck & Co., 456 F. Supp. 2d 1137, 1141 (D. Ariz. 2006) (when one party is contractually bound to arbitrate while the other is not, the agreement cannot be saved by limiting or severing the offending provision, and the court refused to enforce the agreement as a whole).

334 Prima Paint Corp. v. Flood & Conklin Mfg. Co., 388 U.S. 395, 87 S. Ct. 1801, 18 L. Ed. 2d 1270 (1967); Harris v. Green Tree Fin. Corp, 183 F.3d 173 (3d Cir. 1999); Ferro Corp. v. Garrison Indus., 142 F.3d 926 (6th Cir. 1998); Rollins, Inc. v. Foster, 991 F. Supp. 1426 (M.D. Ala. 1998); Haynsworth v. Lloyd's of London, 933 F. Supp. 1315 (S.D. Tex. 1996), *aff'd*, 121 F.3d 956 (5th Cir. 1997); Nuclear Elec. Ins. v. Cent. Power & Light Co., 926 F. Supp. 428 (S.D.N.Y. 1996); Gouger v. Bear, Stearns & Co., 823 F. Supp. 282 (E.D. Pa. 1993) (if the claim of fraud in the inducement pertains to the contract generally, the court is unable to adjudicate it); Green Tree Fin. Corp. v. Wampler, 749 So. 2d 409 (Ala. 1999); *Ex parte* Perry, 744 So. 2d 859 (Ala. 1999); Anniston Lincoln Mercury Dodge v. Conner, 720 So. 2d 898 (Ala. 1998); *Ex parte* Lorance, 669 So. 2d 890 (Ala. 1995); Rosenthal v. Great W. Fin. Sec. Corp., 14 Cal. 4th 394, 58 Cal. Rptr. 2d 875, 926 P.2d 1061 (1996); Britz, Inc. v. Alfa-Laval Food & Dairy Co., 34 Cal. App. 4th 1085, 40 Cal. Rptr. 2d 700 (1995); Lee v. Heftel, 81 Haw. 1, 911 P.2d 721 (Haw. 1996); Dacres v. John Deere Ins. Co., 548 N.W.2d 576 (Iowa 1996) (because plaintiff's allegations of fraud in the inducement went to the entire agreement, they were properly determined by the arbitrators); ABM Farms, Inc. v. Woods, 81 Ohio St. 3d 498, 692 N.E.2d 574 (1998); Pepe Int'l Dev. Co. v. Pub Brewing Co., 915 S.W.2d 925 (Tex. App. 1996); *see also* Jay M. Zitter, Annotation, *Claim of Fraud in Inducement of Contract as Subject to Compulsory Arbitration Clause Contained in Contract*, 11 A.L.R.4th 774 (1982 and Supp. 1996). *But see* Fouquette v. First Am. Nat'l Sec., Inc., 464 N.W.2d 760 (Minn. Ct. App. 1991) (fraud in the inducement may make an arbitration agreement unenforceable if a party can use that as a basis to rescind the entire agreement; the party may not rescind just the arbitration provision); Shaffer v. Jeffery, 915 P.2d 910 (Okla. 1996); City of Blaine v. John Coleman Hayes & Associates, Inc., 818 S.W.2d 33 (Tenn. Ct. App. 1991).

One federal district court went so far as to hold that, under *Prima Paint*, a court could not consider claims of fraudulent inducement even when the plaintiff alleged that the arbitration clause was used to shield a scheme to defraud. Arriaga v. Cross Country Bank, 163 F. Supp. 2d 1189 (S.D. Cal. 2001).

335 Garten v. Kurth, 265 F.3d 136 (2d Cir. 2001).

336 *See* Am. Heritage Life Ins. Co. v. Lang, 321 F.3d 533 (5th Cir. 2003); Doctor's Associates, Inc. v. Distajo, 107 F.3d 126 (2d Cir. 1997); Torrance v. Aames Funding Corp., 242 F. Supp. 2d 862, 868, 869 (D. Or. 2002); *Ex parte* Perry, 744 So. 2d 859 (Ala. 1999); Engalla v. Permanente Med. Group Inc., 15 Cal. 4th 951, 64 Cal. Rptr. 2d 843, 938 P.2d 903 (1997); Rosenthal v. Great W. Fin. Sec. Corp., 14 Cal. 4th 394, 58 Cal. Rptr. 2d 875, 926 P.2d 1061 (1996); Palm Harbor Homes, Inc. v. McCoy, 944 S.W.2d 716 (Tex. App. 1997) (to avoid arbitration, a fraudulent inducement claim must focus specifically on the negotiation and acceptance of the arbitration provision in a contract, not on the contract as a whole); *see also* Sydnor v. Conseco Fin. Servicing Corp., 252 F.3d 302 (4th Cir. 2001).

337 Anderson v. Ashby, 2003 WL 21125998, at *16–*17 (Ala. May 16, 2003).

338 *See* Engalla v. Permanente Med. Group Inc., 15 Cal. 4th 951, 64 Cal. Rptr. 2d 843, 938 P.2d 903 (1997).

339 Pagter v. First Alliance Mortgage Co., No. CV766996 (Cal. Super. Ct. Dec. 12, 1997); *see also* Braga v. VMR Capital Markets, U.S., 2002 Cal. App. LEXIS 1622 (Cal. Ct. App. Feb. 13, 2002); Hong v. First Alliance Mortgage Co., Clearinghouse No. 52,122 (Cal. Super. Ct. Dec. 3, 1997) (text of this decision is also available on the CD-Rom accompanying this manual).

340 *Ex parte* Perry, 744 So. 2d 859 (Ala. 1999).

§ 6.7.2 Consumer Arbitration Agreements

the arbitration clause was clear.[341] Moreover a Texas court has held that, in the absence of affirmative fraud or deception about an arbitration clause, a seller's failure to disclose the existence of an arbitration clause may not itself be a UDAP violation, nor did it vitiate the arbitration clause.[342]

6.7.2 Impossibility, Infancy, Undue Influence, Breach of Covenant of Good Faith, and Other Common Law Contract Defenses

Section 2 of the Federal Arbitration Act states that arbitration clauses are enforceable "save upon such grounds as exist at law or in equity for the revocation of any contract."[343] Any grounds to revoke a contract will apply if appropriate. For example, the Supreme Court itself has cited duress.[344] Other examples would include incapacity or minority, undue influence, impossibility or mistake, frustration, and breach of the covenant of good faith and fair dealing.[345] A Texas court of appeals recently made a rare finding that an arbitration clause was unenforceable for duress when a trial court found that an employer withheld salary, due for work already performed, from an employee who was "afraid she would be unable to meet her financial obligations without her regular compensation and benefits," unless the employee signed an arbitration clause.[346] In many states, standard form boilerplate or adhesion contracts can be challenged under informed consent or reasonable expectation principles, and this challenge should provide a basis to invalidate an arbitration provision as well.[347] One additional defense involves agreements that were formed but are voidable due to infancy or partial incapacity.[348]

6.7.3 State Statutes That Regulate Contract Terms

Challenges to an arbitration provision need not rest on common law theories. A state statute regulating contract terms may invalidate an arbitration provision, as long as the statute applies to the arbitration provision in the same way it would to any other consumer contract term.[349] State law may apply to arbitration provisions if that law governs issues concerning the validity, revocability, and enforceability of contracts generally.[350] Thus, a state statute may regulate an arbitration provision if it applies to all contract terms and requires such contract terms to be readable, in plain English, written in the language spoken during the transaction, in a certain size type, or in some standard format.

One type of state statute that applies equally to arbitration provisions and other aspects of the contract are a state unfair and deceptive acts and practices (UDAP) statute. An arbitration provision is susceptible to a state UDAP challenge that the provision is unfair or deceptive, just as any other contract provision may be unfair or deceptive. An example of a UDAP complaint challenging an arbitration provision, and the subsequent trial briefs in that case, are found on the CD-Rom accompanying another NCLC manual.[351]

An extremely interesting example of a state statute of general applicability that would regulate arbitration agreements is found in New Mexico's 2001 enactment of a variation of the Uniform Arbitration Act. The statute limits "disabling civil dispute clauses" in consumer transactions, such as clauses which require a forum that is less convenient, more costly, or more dilatory than a court action, that limit the consumer's ability to discover evidence, or that limit the consumer's ability to pursue a claim as a class.[352]

Finally, the Louisiana attorney general has issued an opinion that the costs under an arbitration agreement cannot

---

341 *Id.*; *see also* Brown v. Dorsey & Whitney, L.L.P., 267 F. Supp. 2d 61 (D.D.C. 2003) (rejecting claim of fraudulent inducement based on failure to affirmatively disclose fact that arbitration clause was in series of papers signed by employee).
342 Palm Harbor Homes, Inc. v. McCoy, 944 S.W.2d 716 (Tex. App. 1997).
343 9 U.S.C. § 2.
344 Doctor's Associates, Inc. v. Casarotto, 517 U.S. 681, 116 S. Ct. 1652, 134 L. Ed. 2d 902 (1996); *see also* Casteel v. Clear Channel Broad., 254 F. Supp. 2d 1081 (Ark. 2003) (striking down clause because plaintiff employees were under extreme duress when signing, in that their managers were standing over them). *But see* Simpkins v. New Century Volkswagen, 2002 WL 31648747 (Cal. Ct. App. Nov. 25, 2002) (withholding paychecks until agreement signed did not constitute duress).
345 *See* Chase v. Blue Cross, 42 Cal. App. 4th 1142, 50 Cal. Rptr. 2d 178 (1996); *see also* Provencio v. WMA Sec., 125 Cal. App. 4th 1028, 23 Cal. Rptr. 3d 524 (2005) (court refused to enforce arbitration clause when defendant was no longer a member of the National Association of Securities Dealers, a precondition to contract's arbitration requirement).
346 *In re* RLS Legal Solutions, L.L.C., 156 S.W.3d 160 (Tex. App. 2005).
347 *Cf.* Brown v. KFC Nat'l Mgmt. Co., 82 Haw. 226, 921 P.2d 146 (Haw. 1996) (arbitration agreement that is "adhesive" is unenforceable only if (1) contract is the result of coercive bargaining between parties of unequal bargaining strength and (2) contract unfairly limits the obligations and liabilities of, or otherwise unfairly gives advantages to, stronger party); Buraczynski v. Eyring, 919 S.W.2d 314 (Tenn. 1996) (court's conclusion that arbitration agreements between physician and patients were contracts of adhesion was not determinative of enforceability of the agreements; agreements contained no unconscionable or oppressive terms and therefore were enforceable).
348 Stroupes v. Finish Line, Inc., 2005 WL 5610231 (E.D. Tenn. Mar. 16, 2005) (infancy makes contract voidable).
349 Doctor's Associates, Inc. v. Casarotto, 517 U.S. 681, 116 S. Ct. 1652, 134 L. Ed. 2d 902 (1996).
350 *Id.*; Perry v. Thomas, 482 U.S. 483, 107 S. Ct. 2520, 96 L. Ed. 2d 426 (1987).
351 National Consumer Law Center, Consumer Law Pleadings No. 1, Ch. 1 (Cumulative CD-Rom and Index Guide).
352 2001 N.M. Laws 227, § 5 (codified at N.M. Stat. § 44-7A-5) (2001 N.M. Laws 227 adopted the Uniform Arbitration Act with amendments).

exceed the costs enumerated as allowable under the Louisiana Consumer Credit Law.[353] For example, a requirement that a non-prevailing consumer pay all or even half of the arbitration costs may be contrary to Louisiana's credit law. This approach may also be applicable in other states whose credit statute limits those charges that may be assessed to a consumer debtor.

It should be noted, however, that merchants may have a strong argument that such state statutes may be preempted to the extent they might apply to arbitration clauses. The strength and reach of this argument is addressed in detail in Ch. 3, *supra*.

6.7.4 Was the Arbitration Agreement Conditional, Rescinded, or Superseded?

6.7.4.1 "Yo-Yo" Sales and Other Condition Precedent Contracts

A condition precedent contract is one that is not effective until a specified condition occurs. A condition subsequent contract is one that is effective, subject to being undone if a specified condition later occurs.

For example, assume a consumer enters into a condition precedent contract with a dealer to purchase a car that does not become effective until the financing goes through. If financing does not go through, the consumer never owned the car and the contract was never effective. In a condition subsequent sale, the dealer will have turned over title to the consumer and there is an agreement that, if the financing falls through, the consumer must return title to the dealer.

In a condition precedent transaction, no contract was ever consummated when the condition precedent does not occur and an arbitration clause that was part of that contract is not effective.[354] In that case, if the consumer wants to bring a tort or deceptive practices (UDAP) claim against the dealer for misrepresenting that the deal would go through, that claim can be brought in court because the arbitration clause never went into effect.[355]

The result may be different if the consumer brings a claim on the contract, simultaneously claiming that the contract is in effect and that the arbitration provision in the contract is not. For example, when a company rescinds a contract pursuant to a condition subsequent and the consumer brings an action on that contract, claiming it should still be in effect, a court has found that the consumer cannot simultaneously seek to avoid arbitration by claiming that the arbitration clause in the same agreement has been rescinded.[356]

6.7.4.2 TIL Rescission and Other Three-Day Rights to Cancel

The Truth in Lending Act (TILA) provides a right to rescind a special subset of credit agreements by sending a rescission notice within three days.[357] In addition, every state and a Federal Trade Commission rule provide a three-day right to cancel certain door-to-door sales,[358] and there are other examples of state and federal legislation providing consumers with the right to cancel contracts under specified conditions.

If a contract is canceled, its terms are no longer effective, including the arbitration requirement. Nevertheless, typically the creditor or other merchant does not agree that the contract is canceled, and litigation ensues to determine whether in fact the contract as a whole, including the arbitration clause has been canceled. The Supreme Court has stated that the decision is for the arbitrator, not the court, when the litigation relates to whether a contract as a whole is void (as opposed to whether just the arbitration clause is void).[359] In that case before the Court, the consumer argued that a usurious and illegal contract was void *ab initio*, and thus the arbitration clause was also void. The Court ruled that this attack on the contract as a whole is for the arbitrator to determine, not the court.[360]

---

353 Op. La. Att'y Gen. No. 98-380, Clearinghouse No. 53,554 (Mar. 28, 1999) (text of this opinion is also available on the CD-Rom accompanying this manual).

354 *See* Will-Drill Res., Inc. v. Samson Res. Co., 352 F.3d 211, 215, 220 (5th Cir. 2003) (finding that party's allegation that not all necessary parties signed agreement goes to very existence of any contract and therefore must be resolved by a court before court can order arbitration); Easterling v. Royal Manufactured Hous., Inc., 2007 WL 1611138 (La. Ct. App. June 6, 2007) (signed arbitration clause that by its terms is incorporated into sales installment contract is not enforceable given that sales installment contract was never executed). *But see* Jenson v. Quik, Int'l, 820 N.E.2d 462 (Ill. 2004) (franchisee must arbitrate claim for rescission of contract, alleging failure to comply with registration provision of state franchise disclosure act).

355 *Ex parte* Payne, 741 So. 2d 398 (Ala. 1999).

356 Celtic Life Ins. Co. v. McLendon, 814 So. 2d 222 (Ala. 2001).

357 *See* National Consumer Law Center, Truth in Lending Ch. 6 (5th ed. 2003 and Supp.).

358 *See* National Consumer Law Center, Unfair and Deceptive Acts and Practices § 5.8.2 (6th ed. 2004 and Supp.).

359 Buckeye Check Cashing, Inc. v. Cardegna, 126 S. Ct. 1204 (2006).

360 *See also* Thompson v. Irwin Home Equity Corp., 300 F.3d 88 (1st Cir. 2002) (TILA rescission case); Large v. Conseco Fin. Servicing Corp., 292 F.3d 49 (1st Cir. 2002) (same); Anderson v. Delta Funding Corp., 316 F. Supp. 2d 554, 562, 563 (N.D. Ohio 2004) (same); Bertram v. Beneficial Consumer Discount Co., 286 F. Supp. 2d 453, 459 (M.D. Pa. 2003) (same); Fluehmann v. Associates Fin. Services, 2002 WL 500564 (D. Mass. Mar. 29, 2002) (same); Arellano v. Household Fin. Corp. III, 2002 WL 221604 (N.D. Ill. Feb. 13, 2002) (same); Phillips v. Associates Home Equity Services, Inc., 179 F. Supp. 2d 840 (N.D. Ill. 2001) (same); Livingson v. Associates Fin. Inc., 2001 U.S. Dist. LEXIS 8678 (N.D. Ill. June 22, 2001) (same); Dorsey

§ 6.7.4.3 Consumer Arbitration Agreements

On the other hand, if a contract's rescission or cancellation is not in dispute, then the arbitration clause is also canceled and the consumer need not arbitrate any subsequent litigation unrelated to the effectiveness of the consumer's cancellation.[361] While rescission not subject to dispute is less common in consumer litigation, it can occur, such as when the consumer cancels within the three-day period, or if the creditor fails to challenge the consumer's allegation that the creditor's truth in lending (TIL) disclosure was defective. For example, the creditor may not challenge the validity of a consumer's TIL rescission, but only the tender amount. Or the creditor may not dispute the right to rescind under TIL, but insists on conditional rescission. In such cases, a consumer's claims should not be forced into arbitration because there is no dispute that the transaction has been automatically rescinded.

Thus, in *Chapman*,[362] the creditor had marked the note rescinded and did not dispute the consumer's claim that the consumer had rescinded the note within the three-day rescission period. As the contract was clearly rescinded, the court had no problem finding that its terms became void, and the arbitration clause thus became unenforceable.[363]

Moreover, some arbitration clauses exclude from their scope litigation relating to the enforcement of self-help remedies (for example, repossession or non-judicial foreclosures). If the arbitration clause can be interpreted as excluding litigation relating to the self-help remedy of cancellation or rescission, then it will be for the court to determine the effectiveness of the consumer's cancellation.[364]

Finally, the claim that a mortgage has been rescinded pursuant to TILA is often raised in a consumer's bankruptcy proceeding, and there are strong arguments that a bankruptcy judge has discretion to resolve whether the rescission is effective. Courts often hold that a bankruptcy court has discretion in a "core" proceeding to hear a dispute, and not to refer it to arbitration.[365] As a claim for TILA rescission is generally considered a core bankruptcy proceeding,[366] the claim should be heard by the bankruptcy court, and not by an arbitrator.[367]

6.7.4.3 Document Containing Arbitration Clause Is Superseded by Later Document or Does Not Survive Termination of the Contract

In general an arbitration clause may remain enforceable even if the contract in which it was contained has expired or been terminated.[368] However, there are exceptions. For example, if the terminated contract that contained an arbitration clause has been superseded by a new agreement that does not contain an arbitration clause, the clause cannot be enforced. In addition, if the cause of action does not arise out of the expired or terminated contract, or accrued after the contract expired, the dispute may not fall within the scope of the clause.[369]

In many consumer transactions, the consumer must sign a series of documents. Sometimes the arbitration clause appears in some of the documents, but not in the final, integrated agreement. This omission may provide a basis on which to challenge the arbitration clause. For example, motor vehicle sales finance statutes and retail installment sales acts often require that the installment sale be evidenced by a writing that contains all the agreements of the parties with reference to the subject matter of the sale.[370] Similarly, when the arbitration clause is found in a proposed agreement but not in the final agreement, the clause is not enforceable.[371]

Thus, if a car dealer places an arbitration agreement in the sales order or other preliminary document but not in the final installment sales agreement, the arbitration agreement is not

---

v. H.C.P. Sales, Inc., 46 F. Supp. 2d 804 (N.D. Ill. 1999); Gen. Motors Acceptance Corp. v. Johnson, 354 Ill. App. 3d 885, 822 N.E.2d 30 (Ill. App. Ct. 2004) (rescission under state statute).

361 *See* Large v. Conseco Fin. Servicing Corp., 292 F.3d 49, 55 (1st Cir. 2002) (distinguishing between cases in which "the creditor acknowledges that the right of rescission is available or because the appropriate decision maker has so determined" from cases in which "a lender disputes a borrower's purported right to rescind." Only in the latter case must the arbitrator decide whether the conditions for rescission have been met); Chapman v. Mortgage One Corp., 359 F. Supp. 2d 831 (E.D. Mo. 2005).

362 Chapman v. Mortgage One Corp., 359 F. Supp. 2d 831 (E.D. Mo. 2005).

363 *Id.*; *see also* DeGrezia v. Super. Ct., 106 Cal. App. 4th 1278 (2003) (question whether party rescinded insurance policy is for arbitrator, but finding of rescission requires return of case to court).

364 *See* Franklin v. Hartland Mortgage Centers, Inc., 2001 WL 726986 (N.D. Ill. June 28, 2001).

365 *See* § 4.2.3, *supra*.

366 Such an action involves a "determination of the validity, extent or priority of liens." 28 U.S.C. § 157(b)(1)(K).

For a discussion of litigating a Truth in Lending claim in bankruptcy, see National Consumer Law Center, Consumer Bankruptcy Law and Practice § 13.4.4 (8th ed. 2006).

367 *See* § 4.2.3.5, *supra*.

368 *See, e.g.*, Goshawk Dedicated Ltd. v. Portsmouth Settlement Co. I, 466 F. Supp. 2d 1293, 1300 (N.D. Ga. 2006) ("[I]t is well-settled that an arbitration clause may be enforced after the *termination* of a contract.... As the Supreme Court has reasoned, an arbitration provision may survive the termination of a contract because it is a 'structural provision' that relates to remedies and dispute resolution, and not an obligation concerning performance.").

369 *See* Rockwood Automatic Mach., Inc. v. Lear Corp., 13 Misc. 3d 1219(A), 831 N.Y.S.2d 349 (N.Y. Sup. Ct. 2006) (table) (text available at 2006 WL 2882348) (holding that dispute arising out of expired contract is arbitrable and analyzing United States Supreme Court precedent).

See § 7.3.5, *infra*, for a discussion of this scope issue.

370 *See, e.g.*, Mich. Comp. Laws §§ 492.112(a), 566.302.

371 *See* Aceros Prefabricados, S.A. v. Tradearbed, Inc., 2001 U.S. Dist. LEXIS 3445 (S.D.N.Y. Mar. 28, 2001), *vacated*, 282 F.3d 92 (2d Cir. 2002).

part of the final transaction and is not binding on the consumer.[372] The sales order is not the installment sales agreement, and the final agreement does not contain an arbitration clause. Consequently the final terms of the parties' agreement do not include an arbitration requirement.

Likewise, a payday loan borrower should not be bound by an arbitration clause that appears only in a previous agreement she signed if subsequent agreements executed with the lender do not contain such a clause.[373]

This result should apply even if the arbitration clause in the sales order explicitly states it applies to the installment sales agreement. State installment sales acts typically either explicitly or implicitly require that the parties execute a single, comprehensive installment agreement, without side agreements or riders.[374] This single document requirement may also be found in state unfair and deceptive acts and practices (UDAP) regulations or other state legislation. The attempt to put the arbitration clause in a side agreement runs afoul of this single document rule.[375]

In addition, an integration or merger clause in the final contract itself may be enough to void an arbitration agreement found in a side document. Such integration clauses often state that the agreement is the full, final, and only agreement between the parties.[376] Even without a merger clause, if it is clear that the original contract containing the arbitration clause was superseded by a new contract that does not have an arbitration clause, the court should not enforce the clause.[377]

By the same token, even if an arbitration clause is included in what purports to be the only agreement between the parties, this does not necessarily mean that a consumer who brings a claim based on a preexisting agreement is bound by the clause. The Seventh Circuit recently held that a dispute regarding a franchise agreement was not subject to an arbitration clause contained in a subsequent e-commerce agreement, even though the latter agreement provided that it was the "entire" agreement between the parties.[378] The court reasoned that the two agreements addressed distinct obligations and that the plaintiff's claims arose under the agreement that did not have an arbitration clause.[379]

Courts may reach a different result in a non-consumer context in which no state law requires that the final contract contain all the terms in a single document, and the final contract refers to another document that contains an arbitration requirement.[380] In addition, although courts may strike down an arbitration clause not found in the final, binding contract, they may allow the arbitration clause in the final contract to refer elsewhere for the specific terms of the arbitration requirement. For example, courts often enforce arbitration clauses that incorporate by reference the rules of the selected arbitration provider.[381]

In general assignment of the contract to a third party does not terminate the arbitration agreement contained in the original contract. Thus a consumer suing the corporation with

---

372 Rugumbwa v. Betten Motor Sales, 136 F. Supp. 2d 729 (W.D. Mich. 2001); *see also* Colorama Paints & Equip. v. Akzo Nobel Coatings, Inc., 2007 WL 129057 (D. P.R. Jan. 12, 2007) (arbitration clause not enforceable when it appeared in first agreement, but not second renewal agreement); Treadaway v. Damon Corp., 2003 WL 24091983 (E.D. Mich. Dec. 23, 2003) (arbitration clause in purchase agreement not signed by buyer of mobile home unenforceable when parties subsequently signed new purchase agreement providing for right to sue in court); Sanford v. H.A.S., Inc., 136 F. Supp. 2d 1215 (M.D. Ala. 2001) (arbitration clause in vehicle financing contract that was rescinded and replaced by subsequent financing contract lacking an arbitration clause was not binding on purchaser). *But see* Flores v. Jewels Mktg. & Agribusiness, 2007 WL 2022042 (E.D. Cal. July 9, 2007) (arbitration clause in marketer-grower agreement not superseded by release that did not expressly terminate previous agreement).

373 *See, e.g.*, Smith v. Steinkamp, 318 F.3d 775, 778 (7th Cir. 2003) (rejecting the argument that if the consumer signs one contract containing an arbitration clause and another contract without the clause, the arbitration agreement applies to both contracts).

374 *See, e.g.*, Cal. Civ. Code § 2985.8 (West) (leasing); Wash. Rev. Code § 63.14.040; Kroupa v. Sunrise Ford, 77 Cal. App. 4th 835, 92 Cal. Rptr. 2d 42 (1999); Commonwealth v. Metro Chrysler-Plymouth Jeep-Eagle, Inc., Clearinghouse No. 52,028 (Pa. Commw. Ct. 1997) (text of this decision is also available on the CD-Rom accompanying this manual); Kenworthy v. Bolin, 17 Wash. App. 650, 564 P.2d 835 (1977); *see also* Ohio Rev. Code Ann. § 1317.02 (West). *But see* Scott v. Forest Lake Chrysler-Plymouth-Dodge, 611 N.W.2d 346 (Minn. 2000) (contingency clause need not be included in retail installment contract despite single document rule); *see also* Sharlow v. Wally McCarthy Pontiac-GMC Trucks-Hyundai, Inc., 2000 U.S. App. LEXIS 15627 (8th Cir. July 6, 2000) (following *Scott*).

375 Rugumbwa v. Betten Motor Sales, 136 F. Supp. 2d 729 (W.D. Mich. 2001); Lozada v. Dale Baker Oldsmobile, Inc., 197 F.R.D. 321 (W.D. Mich. 2000).

376 *See, e.g.*, Montgomery v. Brumos Motor Cars, Inc., 13 Fla. L. Weekly Supp. 979 (July 21, 2006) (refusing to enforce arbitration clause presented to car buyers after they had already negotiated terms and signed retail buyer's order that purported to be the "entire agreement" and that did not contain an arbitration clause); Chrzanowski v. S.D.S. Autos, Inc., 13 Fla. L. Weekly Supp. 975 (July 21, 2006) (same).

377 *See, e.g.*, WFC Commodities Corp. v. Linnco Futures Group, Inc., 1998 WL 834374 (N.D. Ill. Nov. 25, 1998) (denying motion to compel arbitration when earlier contracts required arbitration but later contracts sued upon did not).

378 Suburban Leisure Ctr., Inc. v. AMF Bowling Products, Inc., 468 F.3d 523 (7th Cir. 2006).

379 *Id.* at 527; *see also* United States Small Bus. Admin. v. Chimicles, 447 F.3d 207 (3d Cir. 2006) (in action brought by SBA to enforce subscription agreements, SBA could not enforce arbitration clause in agreement between limited partners because contracts were not sufficiently related).

380 *See, e.g.*, R.J. O'Brien & Associates v. Pipkin, 64 F.3d 257, 260 (7th Cir. 1995) (holding that individual registering as a commodity futures associate with the National Futures Association (NFA), who agrees to be bound by NFA rules, is bound by the NFA's arbitration requirement).

381 *See Ex parte* Dan Tucker Auto Sales, Inc., 718 So. 2d 33, 36 (Ala. 1998) (contract may incorporate by reference an arbitration provision in another document; in this case, the contract incorporated the AAA Commercial Rules).

which it originally contracted may be bound by the clause and compelled to arbitrate her claim, even though no continuing contractual obligation exists between the parties.[382]

Finally, at least one court has held that an *oral* agreement modifying a written agreement to arbitrate is not enforceable. In *Magness Petroleum Co. v. Warren Resources of California, Inc.*, the court held that when a written arbitration agreement specified the AAA as the parties' arbitral forum, but the parties had orally agreed afterwards to use JAMS instead, the oral modification was not a "written agreement" under the terms of the Federal Arbitration Act, and thus was not enforceable.[383]

---

[382] *See, e.g.*, Goshawk Dedicated Ltd. v. Portsmouth Settlement Co. I, 466 F. Supp. 2d 1293, 1300 (N.D. Ga. 2006) ("[I]t is well-settled that an arbitration clause may be enforced after the *termination* of a contract. . . . Because the effect of a novation is to terminate the old agreement and to substitute or create one that is entirely new, the well-established rule that contractual termination does not extinguish an agreement to arbitrate thus applies with equal force in the context of novation." (citations and internal quotations omitted)).

[383] 103 Cal. App. 4th 901, 127 Cal. Rptr. 2d 159 (2002).

Chapter 7 Arbitration Clause's Applicability to Particular Claims or Parties

7.1 Introduction

The previous two chapters addressed how to determine whether an arbitration agreement between two parties has been formed and, if so, whether it is enforceable. This chapter addresses the interpretation and scope of a valid and enforceable arbitration agreement. Specifically, this chapter addresses (1) whether an arbitration clause covers a particular claim or dispute,[1] and (2) whether and when an arbitration clause covers a party that is not a signatory to the arbitration agreement.[2]

7.2 General Standards of Interpretation

"Arbitration is a matter of contract and a party cannot be required to submit to arbitration any dispute which he has not agreed so to submit."[3] The Supreme Court has said: "[W]e look first to whether the parties agreed to arbitrate a dispute, not to general policy goals, to determine the scope of the agreement."[4]

Because arbitration is a matter of contract, the intent of the parties governs whether a dispute is arbitrable.[5] That intent is determined according to general principles of contract interpretation.[6] "[I]t is the language of the contract that defines the scope of disputes subject to arbitration."[7]

Because the parties' intent defines the meaning of an arbitration agreement, a consumer cannot be forced to arbitrate claims that the consumer did not agree to arbitrate, even if it would be more efficient to do so.[8] The Supreme Court has held that the purpose of the Federal Arbitration Act (FAA) is to require arbitration only when the parties agree to it, not to further economy in conflict resolution.[9]

If the intent of the parties is clear as to whether a particular party or dispute is included within or excluded from an arbitration clause, then the question whether to order arbitration is a simple matter of giving effect to the parties' clearly expressed intent. More difficult questions arise when the language of the arbitration clause is ambiguous. In such circumstances parties seeking to compel arbitration often will rely on the "federal policy" favoring arbitration.[10] In *Moses H. Cone Memorial Hospital v. Mercury Construction Corp.*, the Supreme Court first identified a "federal policy favoring arbitration" and determined that "any doubts concerning the scope of arbitrable issues should be resolved in favor of arbitration."[11] Although the

---

1 *See* § 7.3, *infra*.
2 *See* § 7.4, *infra*.
3 AT & T Technologies, Inc. v. Communications Workers of Am., 475 U.S. 643, 648, 106 S. Ct. 1415, 1418, 89 L. Ed. 2d 648 (1986); *accord* Equal Employment Opportunity Comm'n v. Waffle House, Inc., 534 U.S. 279, 122 S. Ct. 754, 151 L. Ed. 2d 755 (2002); Technosteel, L.L.C. v. Beers Constr. Co., 271 F.3d 151 (4th Cir. 2001).
4 Equal Employment Opportunity Comm'n v. Waffle House, Inc., 534 U.S. 279, 294, 122 S. Ct. 754, 151 L. Ed. 2d 755 (2002); Mitsubishi Motors Corp. v. Soler Chrysler-Plymouth, Inc., 473 U.S. 614, 87 L. Ed. 2d 444, 105 S. Ct. 3346 (1985).
5 Equal Employment Opportunity Comm'n v. Waffle House, Inc., 534 U.S. 279, 289, 122 S. Ct. 754, 151 L. Ed. 2d 755 (2002); Bridas S.A.P.I.C. v. Gov't of Turkmenistan, 345 F.3d 347, 355 (5th Cir. 2003) (the reach of an arbitration clause depends on the parties' intent); Ryan Warranty Services, Inc. v. Welch, 694 So. 2d 1271 (Ala. 1997); Dusold v. Porta-John Corp., 807 P.2d 526, 530 (Ariz. Ct. App. 1990); *cf.* Allstate Ins. Co. v. Martinez, 833 So. 2d 761 (Fla. 2002) (holding that appraisal language in Allstate's contract could not be held to constitute formal arbitration, as this result could not have been in the contemplation of the parties when signing the agreement.).
6 Welborn Clinic v. Medquist, Inc., 301 F.3d 634, 639 (7th Cir. 2002) ("Whether an issue is subject to arbitration is a simple matter of contract interpretation.").
7 Equal Employment Opportunity Comm'n v. Waffle House, Inc., 534 U.S. 279, 289, 122 S. Ct. 754, 151 L. Ed. 2d 755 (2002); *see also* Bridas S.A.P.I.C. v. Gov't of Turkmenistan, 345 F.3d 347, 355 (5th Cir. 2003) (stating that the intent of the contracting parties often will be expressed in the contract language).
8 Dean Witter Reynolds, Inc. v. Byrd, 470 U.S. 213, 105 S. Ct. 1238, 84 L. Ed. 2d 158 (1985).
9 *Id.*; *see also* Broughton v. CIGNA Healthplans, 21 Cal. 4th 1066, 90 Cal. Rptr. 2d 334, 988 P.2d 67 (1999) (requiring court to hear plea for injunctive relief and arbitrator to hear plea for damages concerning the same claim).
10 Moses H. Cone Mem'l Hosp. v. Mercury Constr. Corp., 460 U.S. 1, 24–25, 103 S. Ct. 927, 74 L. Ed. 2d 765 (1983) (establishing "federal policy favoring arbitration"); *see also* Volt Info. Sciences, Inc. v. Bd. of Trustees, 489 U.S. 468, 475–476, 109 S. Ct. 1248, 103 L. Ed. 2d 488 (1989) (same).
11 Moses H. Cone Mem'l Hosp. v. Mercury Constr. Corp., 460 U.S. 1, 24–25, 103 S. Ct. 927, 74 L. Ed. 2d 765 (1983).

171

statement in that case was mere *dicta* and in no way relevant to the case's outcome, that *dicta* has been cited by numerous courts, and it has now become a generally accepted interpretation of the FAA.

Although companies are fond of relying heavily on the presumption favoring arbitration, there are many cases in which the presumption either is inapplicable or is not determinative. First, there are several types of disputes as to which the presumption does not apply at all. For example, the presumption applies only to the types of disputes that an arbitration clause covers. It does not apply to whether an arbitration clause binds non-signatory parties to a dispute.[12] Nor should it, because to apply the presumption to non-signatories would be to presume the existence of the contractual relationship which gives rise to the obligation to arbitrate. The policy favoring arbitration also does not apply to the issue of whether a court or an arbitrator must decide whether a matter must be submitted to arbitration. The Supreme Court has stated that the question of whether a dispute is arbitrable is one that is presumptively for the Court to decide, absent clear and unmistakable evidence that the parties intended for an arbitrator to decide it.[13] Thus the federal policy favoring arbitration is limited to determining whether an ambiguous arbitration clause encompasses a dispute between two parties that have agreed to a valid and enforceable arbitration clause.

Even when the federal policy favoring arbitration does apply, it does not mandate sending every dispute between contracting parties to arbitration.[14] Courts "do not override the clear intent of the parties, or reach a result inconsistent with the plain text of the contract, simply because the policy favoring arbitration is implicated."[15] In other words, courts must give effect to the parties' intent, even if that means resolving the dispute in court rather than in arbitration.[16]

Additionally, the fact that the contract law of many states requires interpreting ambiguous language against the drafter—which in most consumer cases will be the party seeking to enforce the arbitration clause—may temper the force of the federal policy favoring arbitration. The Supreme Court and other courts have indicated that ambiguous provisions in standard form agreements should be subject to state law rules for construing ambiguities against a contract's drafter.[17] This rule may conflict with the federal policy favoring arbitration, and courts must decide which principle to apply. Given that the purpose of the FAA "was to make arbitration agreements as enforceable as other contracts, but not more so,"[18] applying the general state law

---

12 Becker v. Davis, 491 F.3d 1292, 1298 (11th Cir. 2007); Comer v. Micor, Inc., 436 F.3d 1098, 1104 n.11 (9th Cir. 2006) ("The question here is not whether a particular issue is arbitrable, but whether a particular *party* is bound by the arbitration agreement. Under these circumstances, the liberal federal policy regarding the scope of arbitrable issues is inapposite."); InterGen N.V. v. Grina, 344 F.3d 134, 150 (1st Cir. 2003); Westmoreland v. Sadoux, 299 F.3d 462, 465 (5th Cir. 2002); Fleetwood Enterprises, Inc. v. Gaskamp, 280 F.3d 1069, 1073 (5th Cir. 2002) (refusing to apply policy favoring arbitration to determination as to whether or not a party was bound by the arbitration clause); McCarthy v. Azure, 22 F.3d 351, 355 (1st Cir. 1994) ("The federal policy, however, does not extend to situations in which the identities of the parties who have agreed to arbitrate is unclear."); Washburn v. Beverly Enterprises-Georgia, Inc., 2006 WL 3404084, at *5–*6 (S.D. Ga. Nov. 14, 2006) (stating that "neither the FAA nor any other federal policy favors arbitration for parties who have not contractually bound themselves to arbitrate their disputes" and distinguishing the determination of what claims fall within the scope of an arbitration agreement with which parties may be bound by an arbitration agreement (internal quotation omitted)); County of Contra Costa v. Kaiser Found. Health Plan, Inc., 47 Cal. App. 3d 237, 245 (1996) ("Even the strong public policy in favor of arbitration does not extend to those who are not parties to an arbitration agreement. . . ."); *In re* Merrill Lynch, Pierce, Fenner & Smith, Inc., 195 S.W.3d 807 (Tex. App. 2006) ("the strong presumption favoring arbitration does not arise until a person seeking to compel arbitration proves that a valid arbitration agreement exists").

13 *See* § 7.3.2, *infra*.

14 *See* Harvey v. Joyce, 199 F.3d 790, 793 (5th Cir. 2000) ("A finding that the scope of the arbitration clause is vague does not automatically catapult the entire dispute into arbitration."); Coors Brewing Co. v. Molson Breweries, 51 F.3d 1511, 1516 (10th Cir. 1995) (stating that the Supreme Court "did not proclaim that all disputes between parties who include an arbitration clause in their contracts are subject to arbitration"); *see also* Siefert v. U.S. Home Corp., 750 So. 2d 633, 638 (Fla. 1999) ("not every dispute that arises between contracting parties should be subject to arbitration").

15 Equal Employment Opportunity Comm'n v. Waffle House, Inc., 534 U.S. 279, 294, 122 S. Ct. 754, 151 L. Ed. 2d 755 (2002).

16 *See* BCS Ins. Co. v. Wellmark, Inc., 410 F.3d 349, 352 (7th Cir. 2005); *see also* Albert M. Higley Co. v. N/S Corp., 445 F.3d 861, 863 (6th Cir. 2006); Alticor, Inc. v. Nat'l Union Fire Ins. Co., 411 F.3d 669, 673 (6th Cir. 2005); Welborn Clinic v. Medquist, Inc., 301 F.3d 634, 639 (7th Cir. 2002) ("Despite this strong pro-arbitration tilt, agreements must not be construed so broadly as to force arbitration of claims that the parties never agreed to submit to arbitration."); Gravillis v. Coldwell Banker Residential Brokerage Co., 49 Cal. Rptr. 3d 531, 538 (Ct. App. 2006) ("there is no policy in favor of arbitrating a dispute the parties did not agree to arbitrate"); Northwest Chrysler Plymouth v. DaimlerChrysler Corp., 168 S.W.3d 693, 696 (Mo. Ct. App. 2005) ("Standing alone, a public policy favoring arbitration is not enough to extend the application of an arbitration clause far beyond its intended scope.").

17 *See* Mastrobuono v. Shearson Lehman Hutton, Inc., 514 U.S. 52, 115 S. Ct. 1212, 131 L. Ed. 2d 76 (1995); Karnette v. Wolpoff & Abramson, L.L.P., 444 F. Supp. 2d 640, 647 (E.D. Va. 2006); Caldwell v. KFC Corp., 958 F. Supp. 962 (D.N.J. 1997); *In re* Grant, 281 B.R. 721 (Bankr. S.D. Ala. 2000); Victoria v. Super. Ct., 710 P.2d 833, 838–839 (Cal. 1985); Mayhew v. Benninghoff, 53 Cal. App. 4th 1365, 62 Cal. Rptr. 2d 27 (1997); Seifert v. U.S. Home Corp., 750 So. 2d 633 (Fla. 1999); Luke v. Gentry Realty, Ltd., 96 P.3d 261, 269 (Haw. 2004); Barrett v. McDonald Investments, Inc., 870 A.2d 146, 151–152 (Me. 2005).

18 Prima Paint Corp. v. Flood & Conklin Mfg. Co., 388 U.S. 394, 404 n.12, 87 S. Ct. 1801, 18 L. Ed. 2d 1270 (1967); *see also* Stone v. Doerge, 328 F.3d 343, 345 (7th Cir. 2003) ("Nothing in the Federal Arbitration Act overrides normal rules of con-

rule of interpreting ambiguous contracts against the drafter to arbitration clauses appears to be more faithful to the FAA's purposes than creating a special rule for arbitration agreements that requires interpreting ambiguities in favor of arbitration. Nevertheless, courts have differed when deciding which rule to apply.[19] Also, even in jurisdictions that have held that federal policy favoring arbitration trumps general state law rules of contract interpretation, the state law rule interpreting ambiguous contracts against the drafter may apply if the contract includes a choice-of-law provision designating that state law governs.[20]

7.3 Whether Particular Claims Fall Within an Arbitration Clause

7.3.1 General

In general whether a particular dispute falls within the scope of an arbitration clause is a matter of contractual interpretation. Thus the specific wording of an arbitration clause will be important in determining whether a particular dispute falls within its scope. Based on the specific wording of the arbitration clause, courts have tended to divide arbitration clauses into two categories: (a) general, broadly written clauses, and (b) narrowly written clauses that are tied to specific disputes.[21] The more broadly written the arbitration clause, the more likely it is that it applies to a particular dispute.[22]

Courts have reached some consensus regarding whether particular commonly-used language denotes a broad or narrow arbitration clause, but have differed as to the reach of other language. Although an arbitration clause's specific language may differ from contract to contract, there are certain phrases that commonly appear in standard form arbitration clauses. These include arbitration clauses covering disputes "arising out of" or "arising under" the contract, disputes "arising out of or related to" the contract, and disputes "arising out of or in connection with" the contract. Arbitration clauses using "arising out of or related to" language will be given a broad construction.[23] The same is

---

tractual interpretation; the Act's goal was to put arbitration on a par with other contracts and eliminate any vestige of old rules disfavoring arbitration.").

19 *Compare* Karnette v. Wolpoff & Abramson, L.L.P., 444 F. Supp. 2d 640, 647 (E.D. Va. 2006) ("Notwithstanding the federal policy favoring arbitration, the rule of *contra proferentem* applies to arbitration clauses just as to other contractual terms."); Caldwell v. KFC Corp., 958 F. Supp. 962, 973–974 (D.N.J. 1997); Victoria v. Super. Ct., 710 P.2d 833, 838–839 (Cal. 1985); Parfi Holding, AB v. Mirror Image Internet, Inc., 817 A.2d 149, 156 (Del. 2002) ("The policy that favors alternate dispute resolution mechanisms, such as arbitration, does not trump basic principles of contract interpretation."); Seifert v. U.S. Home Corp., 750 So. 2d 633 (Fla. 1999) (resolving ambiguities in arbitration agreement against the drafter); Luke v. Gentry Realty, Ltd., 96 P.3d 261, 269 (Haw. 2004) (same) *and* Barrett v. McDonald Investments, Inc., 870 A.2d 146, 151–152 (Me. 2005) (same) *with* ING Fin. Partners v. Johansen, 446 F.3d 777, 779 (8th Cir. 2006) ("the construction of an agreement to arbitrate is governed by the Federal Arbitration Act unless an agreement expressly provides that state law should govern"); Kristian v. Comcast Corp., 446 F.3d 25, 35 (1st Cir. 2006) ("Where the federal policy favoring arbitration is in tension with the tenet of *contra proferentem* for adhesion contracts, and there is a scope question at issue, the federal policy favoring arbitration trumps the state contract law tenet."); MedCam, Inc. v. MCNC, 414 F.3d 972, 975 (8th Cir. 2005); Wagner v. Stratton Oakmont, Inc., 83 F.3d 1046 (9th Cir. 1996) ("We interpret the contract by applying general state law principles of contract interpretation, while giving due regard to the federal policy in favor of arbitration by resolving ambiguities as to the scope of arbitration in favor of arbitration."); Roby v. Corp. of Lloyd's, 996 F.2d 1353, 1361 (2d Cir. 1993) (resolving ambiguities in favor of arbitration); Cornell v. Harmony Homes, Inc., 2007 WL 38132, at *3 (D. Colo. Jan. 4, 2007) *and* Allen v. Pacheco, 71 P.3d 375, 380–381 (Colo. 2003).

20 *See* ING Fin. Partners v. Johansen, 446 F.3d 777, 779 (8th Cir. 2006) ("the construction of an agreement to arbitrate is governed by the Federal Arbitration Act unless an agreement expressly provides that state law should govern").

One quite helpful decision, given the frequency of choice-of-law provisions in consumer contracts designating Delaware law, is the Delaware Supreme Court's decision in Parfi Holding, AB v. Mirror Image Internet, Inc., 817 A.2d 149 (Del. 2002). In that case the court acknowledged the liberal policy favoring arbitration, but also concluded that "[t]he policy that favors alternate dispute resolution mechanisms, such as arbitration, does not trump basic principles of contract interpretation." *Id.* at 156; *see also* Karnette v. Wolpoff & Abramson, L.L.P., 444 F. Supp. 2d 640, 647 (E.D. Va. 2006) (applying Delaware choice-of-law clause and choosing to interpret ambiguous arbitration clause against the drafter notwithstanding the federal policy favoring arbitration).

21 *See, e.g.*, Cummings v. Fedex Ground Package Sys., Inc., 404 F.3d 1258, 1261 (10th Cir. 2005); Simon v. Pfizer, 398 F.3d 765, 775 (6th Cir. 2005); Louis Dreyfus Negoce S.A. v. Blystad Shipping & Trading Inc., 252 F.3d 218, 224 (2d Cir. 2001); Snyder v. Belmont Homes, Inc., 899 So. 2d 57, 62 (La. Ct. App. 2005).

22 *Simon*, 398 F.3d at 775; *Snyder*, 899 So. 2d at 62.

23 Prima Paint Corp. v. Flood & Conklin Mfg. Co., 388 U.S. 395, 406, 87 S. Ct. 1801, 18 L. Ed. 2d 1270 (1967); Carbajal v. H & R Block Tax Services, Inc., 372 F.3d 903, 905 (7th Cir. 2004); Welborn Clinic v. Medquist, Inc., 301 F.3d 634, 639 (7th Cir. 2002); Ford v. NYLCare Health Plans of Gulf Coast, Inc., 141 F.3d 243, 250 n.7 (5th Cir. 1998); Pennzoil Exploration & Prod. Co. v. Ramco Energy Ltd., 139 F.3d 1061, 1067 (5th Cir. 1998); Collins & Aikman Products, Co. v. Bldg. Sys., Inc., 58 F.3d 16, 20 (2d Cir. 1995); Sharifi v. Aamco Transmissions, Inc., 2007 WL 1944371 (N.D. Tex. June 28, 2007); Kisner v. Bud's Mobile Homes, 2007 WL 686734, at *3 (S.D. Miss. Mar. 3, 2007); S & G Elec., Inc. v. Normant Sec. Group, 2007 WL 210517 (E.D. Pa. Jan. 24, 2007); JP Morgan Chase Bank v. Lott, 2007 WL 30271, at *4 (S.D. Miss. Jan. 3, 2007); Winterwood Farm, L.L.C. v. JER, Inc., 327 F. Supp. 2d 34, 39–40 (D. Me. 2004); AmSouth Bank v. Dees, 847 So. 2d 923, 932 (Ala. 2002); Siefert v. U.S. Home Corp., 750 So. 2d 633, 638 (Fla. 1999); Lovey v. Regence Blueshield of Idaho, 72 P.3d 877, 886 (Idaho 2003); Smith v. Captain D's, L.L.C., 2007 WL 1704349 (Miss. June 14, 2007); Aiken v. World Fin. Corp. of S.C., 644 S.E.2d

true for arbitration clauses using "arising out of or in connection with" language.[24] Courts, however, have disagreed over how to treat "arising under" or "arising out of" language that does not include the additional "related to" or "in connection with" language. Some courts have construed such language as forming a narrow arbitration clause.[25] Other courts, however, have found no difference between the two and have interpreted "arising under" and "arising out of" broadly.[26]

Depending on the particular jurisdiction, a broad clause will be applied to claims that are collateral to the contract containing the arbitration provision as long as the claims bear a "significant relationship" to the contract,[27] "touch matters covered by the contract,"[28] implicate the parties' rights under the contract or matters of contract construction,[29] or have their "origin or genesis" in the contract.[30] A broad arbitration clause, however, does not have unlimited reach and will not apply to claims that are unrelated to or substantially attenuated from the contract containing the arbitration clause.[31] For example, a court held that a broad arbitration clause in a consumer's automobile buyer order did not require arbitration of the consumer's claim that the dealer's unsolicited pre-purchase offer of credit violated the Fair Credit Reporting Act.[32]

Narrowly written clauses, by contrast, do not cover claims that are not clearly encompassed by the contract.[33] Thus,

---

705, 708 n.2 (S.C. 2007); Neatherlin Homes, Inc. v. Love, 2007 WL 700996, at *4 (Tex. App. Mar. 8, 2007); *cf.* Alexander v. U.S. Credit Mgmt., Inc., 384 F. Supp. 2d 1003 (N.D. Tex. 2005) (whether language indicates a broad or narrow arbitration clause depends on context and the surrounding language).

24 MedCam, Inc. v. MCNC, 414 F.3d 972, 975 (8th Cir. 2005); Jackman v. Jackman, 2006 WL 3792109 (D. Kan. Dec. 21, 2006); Wood v. Pentex Res., Ltd. P'ship, 458 F. Supp. 2d 355, 373 (S.D. Tex. 2006); Best Concrete Mix Corp. v. Lloyd's of London Underwriters, 413 F. Supp. 2d 182, 188 (E.D.N.Y. 2006).

25 Pennzoil Exploration & Prod. Co. v. Ramco Energy Ltd., 139 F.3d 1061, 1067 (5th Cir. 1998); Tracer Research Corp. v. Nat'l Envtl. Services Co., 42 F.3d 1292, 1295 (9th Cir. 1994); McCarthy v. Azure, 22 F.3d 351, 358 (1st Cir. 1994) (reading narrowly a clause requiring arbitration of disputes "arising under" the agreement); Wood v. Pentex Res., Ltd. P'ship, 458 F. Supp. 2d 355, 373 (S.D. Tex. 2006); AmSouth Bank v. Dees, 847 So. 2d 923, 932 (Ala. 2002) (holding that a narrow clause will not cover matters collateral to the agreement); Am. Bankers Life Assurance Co. v. Rice Acceptance Co., 709 So. 2d 1188, 1190–1191 (Ala. 1998); Siefert v. U.S. Home Corp., 750 So. 2d 633, 637 (Fla. 1999); MS Credit Ctr., Inc. v. Horton, 926 So. 2d 167, 176 (Miss. 2006) ("Broad arbitration clauses govern disputes 'related to' or 'connected with' a contract, and narrow arbitration language requires arbitration of disputes that directly 'arise out of' a contract.").

26 JLM Indus., Inc. v. Stolt-Nielsen SA, 387 F.3d 163, 172 (2d Cir. 2004) (giving broad construction to clause requiring arbitration of any and all disputes "arising out of" the agreement); Highlands Wellmont Health Network, Inc. v. John Deere Health Plan, Inc., 350 F.3d 568, 578 (6th Cir. 2003); Battaglia v. McKendry, 233 F.3d 720, 727 (3d Cir. 2000) (arbitration clauses covering disputes "arising under" or "arising out of" the contract are generally given a broad construction); Gregory v. Electro-Mechanical Corp., 83 F.3d 382, 386 (11th Cir. 1996); Sweet Dreams Unlimited, Inc. v. Dial-A-Mattress Int'l, Ltd., 1 F.3d 639, 642 (7th Cir. 1993); Higgs v. The Warranty Group, 2007 WL 2034376, at *3 (S.D. Ohio July 11, 2007); Alexander v. U.S. Credit Mgmt., Inc., 384 F. Supp. 2d 1003 (N.D. Tex. 2005) (whether "arising out of" language is given a broad or narrow construction depends on the totality of circumstances); Northwest Chrysler Plymouth v. DaimlerChrysler Corp., 168 S.W.3d 693, 696 n.2 (Mo. Ct. App. 2005).

27 Pennzoil Exploration & Prod. Co. v. Ramco Energy Ltd., 139 F.3d 1061, 1067–1068 (5th Cir. 1998); J.J. Ryan & Sons v. Rhone Poulenc Textiles, S.A., 863 F.3d 315, 321 (4th Cir. 1988) (broad arbitration clause covers disputes that have "a significant relationship to the contract"); Kisner v. Bud's Mobile Homes, 2007 WL 686734, at *3 (S.D. Miss. Mar. 3, 2007); Wood v. Pentex Res., Ltd. P'ship, 458 F. Supp. 2d 355, 373 (S.D. Tex. 2006); Siefert v. U.S. Home Corp., 750 So. 2d 633, 638, 642 (Fla. 1999); Lovey v. Regence Blueshield of Idaho, 72 P.3d 877, 886 (Idaho 2003); Aiken v. World Fin. Corp. of S.C., 644 S.E.2d 705, 708 (S.C. 2007).

28 Fazio v. Lehman Bros., 340 F.3d 386, 395 (6th Cir. 2003); P & P Indus., Inc. v. Sutter Corp., 179 F.3d 861 (10th Cir. 1999); Simula, Inc. v. Autoliv, Inc., 175 F.3d 716, 721 (9th Cir. 1999); Griffen v. Alpha Phi Alpha, Inc., 2007 WL 707364, at *7 (E.D. Pa. Mar. 2, 2007); Parfi Holding, AB v. Mirror Image Internet, Inc., 817 A.2d 149, 155 (Del. 2002) ("touch on" contract rights or performance); Smith v. Captain D's, L.L.C., 2007 WL 1704349 (Miss. June 14, 2007); MS Credit Ctr., Inc. v. Horton, 926 So. 2d 167, 176 (Miss. 2006).

29 Cummings v. Fedex Ground Package Sys., Inc., 404 F.3d 1258, 1261 (10th Cir. 2005); Louis Dreyfus Negoce S.A. v. Blystad Shipping & Trading Inc., 252 F.3d 218, 224 (2d Cir. 2001); Parfi Holding, AB v. Mirror Image Internet, Inc., 817 A.2d 149, 156 n.23 (Del. 2002); Snyder v. Belmont Homes, Inc., 899 So. 2d 57, 62 (La. Ct. App. 2005) (holding that a broad clause covers a claim that "has its roots" in the contract).

30 Sweet Dreams Unlimited, Inc. v. Dial-A-Mattress Int'l, Ltd., 1 F.3d 639, 642 (7th Cir. 1993).

31 *See, e.g.*, Parfi Holding, AB v. Mirror Image Internet, Inc., 817 A.2d 149, 151 (Del. 2002) ("[T]he arbitration provision, no matter how broadly drafted, can reach only the claims within the scope of the contract, and the fiduciary duty claims here are beyond that scope.").

32 Hyde v. RDA, Inc., 389 F. Supp. 2d 658, 664 (D. Md. 2005) (finding that Fair Credit Reporting Act (FCRA) claim did not bear any significant relationship to the automobile contract and that the transaction giving rise to the FCRA claim was separate and independent from the transaction involving the arbitration agreement); *see also* Ford v. NYLCare Health Plans of Gulf Coast, Inc., 141 F.3d 243, 251 (5th Cir. 1998) (holding that a doctor's false advertising claim against health maintenance organization (HMO) was not related to contract between doctor and HMO covering the performance of medical services); Coors Brewing Co. v. Molson Breweries, 51 F.3d 1511, 1516 (10th Cir. 1995) (finding that antitrust claim based on market behavior was not related to parties' licensing agreement); Parfi Holding, AB v. Mirror Image Internet, Inc., 817 A.2d 149, 151 (Del. 2002) (finding breach of fiduciary duty claim unrelated to contract containing arbitration clause).

33 Cummings v. Fedex Ground Package Sys., Inc., 404 F.3d 1258, 1261 (10th Cir. 2005); Louis Dreyfus Negoce S.A. v. Blystad Shipping & Trading Inc., 252 F.3d 218, 224 (2d Cir. 2001) (with a narrow clause a claim is arbitrable if it "is on its face within

"[w]here the arbitration clause is narrow, a collateral matter generally will be beyond its purview."[34] For instance, those courts that have construed "arising under" language narrowly have limited its reach to claims relating to the interpretation and performance of the contract itself.[35] Additionally, when an arbitration clause by its terms applies only to specific types of claims, it should not be extended to other types of claims.[36] If the arbitration agreement's scope includes only particular statutory claims, then other statutory claims will not be subject to arbitration, even if they arise from the same facts as those giving rise to claims that are subject to arbitration.[37] Courts should not ignore specific exclusions identified in arbitration clauses. If an arbitration clause states that it does not apply to Magnuson-Moss written warranty claims, for example, then those claims need not be arbitrated, even though other claims must be.[38] Similarly, when a company excludes certain types of claims from arbitration in order to ensure that it can bring its own affirmative claims against the consumer in court, the exclusion also applies to consumer claims against the company that cover that same subject matter. For example, when a mortgagor drafted an arbitration clause to exclude actions to repossess property, a home owner's counterclaim against the mortgagor for wrongful repossession and related fraud was not covered by the arbitration clause.[39]

7.3.2 Application to Issues of Arbitrability

Often the first question that arises when parties disagree over the scope of an arbitration agreement is whether a court or an arbitrator should resolve whether the parties agreed to arbitrate their dispute. In other words, the first scope question is whether the agreement covers disputes over arbitrability. Notwithstanding the federal policy favoring arbitration, the question of whether an arbitration clause covers a particular dispute is presumptively for a court to decide.[40] The Supreme Court has stated that "a gateway dispute about whether the parties are bound by a given arbitration clause raises a 'question of arbitrability' for a court to decide. . . . Similarly, a disagreement about whether an arbitration clause in a concededly binding contract applies to a particular type of controversy is for the court."[41] Thus a court

---

the purview of the clause"); Balandran v. Labor Ready, Inc., 22 Cal. Rptr. 3d 441 (Ct. App. 2004) (agreement to arbitrate disputes arising out of employment does not apply to pre-employment discrimination claims alleging a failure to hire on the basis of gender).

34 Cummings v. Fedex Ground Package Sys., Inc., 404 F.3d 1258, 1261 (10th Cir. 2005); see Louis Dreyfus Negoce S.A. v. Blystad Shipping & Trading Inc., 252 F.3d 218, 224 (2d Cir. 2001); AmSouth Bank v. Dees, 847 So. 2d 923, 932 (Ala. 2002) (collateral matters fall outside a narrow arbitration clause).

35 Tracer Research Corp. v. Nat'l Envtl. Services Co., 42 F.3d 1292, 1295 (9th Cir. 1994); Wood v. Pentex Res., Ltd. P'ship, 458 F. Supp. 2d 355, 373 (S.D. Tex. 2006); AmSouth Bank v. Dees, 847 So. 2d 923, 932 (Ala. 2002); Am. Bankers Life Assurance Co. v. Rice Acceptance Co., 709 So. 2d 1188, 1190–1191 (Ala. 1998). But see Int'l Brotherhood of Elec. Workers Local 21 v. Ill. Bell Tel. Co., 491 F.3d 685 (7th Cir. 2007) (finding that arbitration clause covering all disputes regarding the interpretation or performance of the contract to be a broad arbitration clause).

36 United States Small Bus. Admin. v. Chimicles, 447 F.3d 207, 210 (3d Cir. 2006) (clause that was limited to enforcing provisions of partnership agreement and actions brought by private limited partners did not cover claims by other parties); Cummings v. Fedex Ground Package Sys., Inc., 404 F.3d 1258 (10th Cir. 2005) (arbitration clause covering disputes arising out of termination of agreement did not cover claims of breach of implied agreements unrelated to termination); Bratt Enterprises, Inc. v. Noble Int'l Ltd., 338 F.3d 609 (6th Cir. 2003) (refusing to compel arbitration of breach of contract claims when arbitration clause was limited to disputes over amounts included on a balance sheet); Welborn Clinic v. Medquist, Inc., 301 F.3d 634, 640 (7th Cir. 2002) (arbitration clause limited to disputes over invoice amounts did not apply to other billing disputes); Paladino v. Avnet Computer Tech., Inc., 134 F.3d 1054 (11th Cir. 1998) (construing contract as being limited only to contractual claims); Nat'l League of Junior Cotillions v. Porter, 2007 WL 1741278 (W.D.N.C. June 14, 2007) (when claims for injunctive relief were specifically excluded from arbitration agreement, they could be brought in court); Ryan Warranty Services, Inc. v. Welch, 694 So. 2d 1271 (Ala. 1997) (when arbitration agreement related to costs, did not apply to dispute as to whether consumer had breached the agreement); Okla. Oncology & Hematology, Prof'l Corp. v. U.S. Oncology, Inc., 160 P.3d 936 (Okla. 2007) (arbitration clause regarding disputes over subsequent changes to the contract does not require arbitration of disputes arising out of the contract or relating to performance).

37 Simon v. Pfizer, 398 F.3d 765, 774–777 (6th Cir. 2005); see also Cummings v. Fedex Ground Package Sys., Inc., 404 F.3d 1258 (10th Cir. 2005) (arbitration clause covering disputes arising out of termination of agreement did not cover claims of breach of implied agreements unrelated to termination).

38 Gossett v. HBL, L.L.C., 2006 WL 1328757 (D.S.C. May 11, 2006); see also Boyd v. Homes of Legend, 981 F. Supp. 1423 (M.D. Ala. 1997) (holding that breach of warranty claims against home manufacturer were not encompassed in purchase contract with home dealer); Wilson v. Waverlee Homes, Inc., 954 F. Supp. 1530 (M.D. Ala. 1996); cf. Dell, Inc. v. Muniz, 163 S.W.3d 177 (Tex. App. 2005) (consumer's claims were not based on written warranty, and thus were not excluded from arbitration clause).

39 See Sadler v. Green Tree Servicing, L.L.C., 2005 WL 2464208 (W.D. Mo. Oct. 5, 2005), vacated and remanded on other grounds, 466 F.3d 623 (8th Cir. 2006); Greenpoint Credit, L.L.C. v. Reynolds, 151 S.W.3d 868, 875–876 (Mo. Ct. App. 2005).

40 First Options of Chicago, Inc. v. Kaplan, 514 U.S. 938, 944–945, 115 S. Ct. 1920, 131 L. Ed. 2d 985 (1995); Goldman Sachs & Co. v. Becker, 2007 WL 1982790, at *3 (N.D. Cal. July 2, 2007) ("The usual presumption in favor of arbitration is reversed when deciding the issue of whether a particular dispute is arbitrable. Where parties did not agree to submit the question of arbitrability to the arbitrator, the court should decide the question independently.").
This issue of "who decides" also is discussed in § 2.2, supra.

41 Howsam v. Dean Witter Reynolds, Inc., 537 U.S. 79, 84, 123 S. Ct. 588, 154 L. Ed. 2d 491 (2002) (citations omitted).

should determine whether an arbitration clause applies to a particular controversy,[42] just as the court would decide whether a clause is binding on a party in the first place.[43]

Despite the general presumption that courts should decide questions of arbitrability, the Supreme Court has held that disputes concerning the scope of an arbitration clause may be referred to arbitration when a valid arbitration clause clearly and unmistakably states that an arbitrator shall decide such issues. In *First Options of Chicago, Inc. v. Kaplan*,[44] the Supreme Court recognized the presumption that that questions concerning arbitrability are decided by a court, but recognized that they may be referred to arbitration if there is clear and unmistakable evidence that the parties agreed to arbitrate disputes about arbitrability.[45]

The Court in *First Options* stated that:

> Courts should not assume that the parties agreed to arbitrate arbitrability unless there is "clea[r] and unmistakeabl[e]" evidence that they did so.... [T]he law treats silence or ambiguity about the question "*who* (primarily) should decide arbitrability" differently from the way it treats silence or ambiguity about the question "*whether* a particular merits-related dispute is arbitrable because it is within the scope of a valid arbitration agreement"—for in respect to this latter question the law reverses the presumption.[46]

Thus, if an arbitration clause is silent or ambiguous as to arbitrability disputes, those disputes should be decided by a court, even if the parties agreed to submit other disputes to arbitration.[47] But arbitrability questions will be sent to an arbitrator when a contract specifically so designates.[48] The intent to send arbitrability disputes to an arbitrator, however, must be expressed "clearly and unmistakably."[49] Thus a generally worded general arbitration clause, even one that is broadly written, may not always be sufficient to demonstrate such intent.[50] Some courts have held that when an arbitration clause incorporates the rules of a particular arbitration provider, and when those rules require arbitrability to be decided by an arbitrator, arbitrability disputes will be sent to an arbitrator even if the rules themselves were not explicitly listed in the arbitration agreement.[51] However when the scope of an arbitration clause is limited to specific disputes and arbitrability disputes are not specifically mentioned in the agreement, incorporation of an arbitration provider's rules may not suffice to send arbitrability questions to an arbitrator.[52]

---

42 AT & T Technologies, Inc. v. Communications Workers of Am., 475 U.S. 643, 106 S. Ct. 1415, 89 L. Ed. 2d 648 (1986); Atkinson v. Sinclair Ref. Co., 370 U.S. 238, 82 S. Ct. 1318, 8 L. Ed. 2d 462 (1962).

43 *See also* John Wiley & Sons, Inc. v. Livingston, 376 U.S. 543, 84 S. Ct. 909, 11 L. Ed. 2d 898 (1964).

44 514 U.S. 938, 115 S. Ct. 1920, 131 L. Ed. 2d 985 (1995).

45 *Id.*

46 *Id.* at 944–945 (citations omitted).

47 Int'l Brotherhood of Elec. Workers Local 21 v. Ill. Bell Tel. Co., 491 F.3d 685, 687 (7th Cir. 2007) ("Unless the parties clearly provide otherwise, the question of arbitrability is properly decided by a court, not the arbitrator."); Sarhank Group v. Oracle Corp., 404 F.3d 657, 661 (2d Cir. 2005) ("As arbitrability is not arbitrable in the absence of the parties' agreement, the district court was required to determine whether Oracle had agreed to arbitrate."); Morton v. Polivchak, 931 So. 2d 935 (Fla. Dist. Ct. App. 2006).

48 Sadler v. Green Tree, Servicing, L.L.C., 466 F.3d 623 (8th Cir. 2006); Nazar v. Wolpoff & Abramson, L.L.P., 2007 WL 528753 (D. Kan. Feb. 15, 2007); Pest Mgmt., Inc. v. Langer, 96 Ark. App. 220 (2006).

49 *First Options*, 514 U.S. at 944.

50 *See, e.g.*, Smith v. Microskills San Diego, Ltd. P'ship, 63 Cal. Rptr. 3d 368 (Ct. App. 2007) (holding that contract stating that any dispute relating to "the validity, enforceability or scope of this Arbitration Provision" did not deprive the court of jurisdiction to determine arbitrability). *But see* Alliance Bernstein Inv. Research & Mgmt., Inc. v. Schaffran, 445 F.3d 121, 125 (2d Cir. 2006) (arbitration agreement covering "all disputes" between the parties covered arbitrability disputes); Bell v. Cendant, 293 F.3d 563 (2d Cir. 2002) (employment case; when arbitration clause is very broad, *any* questions of the scope or applicability of the arbitration clause should be decided by the arbitrator).

51 *See* Terminix Int'l Co. v. Palmer Ranch Ltd. P'ship, 432 F.3d 1327, 1332 (11th Cir. 2005) (holding that contract incorporating American Arbitration Association (AAA) rules required sending arbitrability disputes to arbitrator); Contec Corp. v. Remote Solution Co., Ltd., 398 F.3d 205, 210 (2d Cir. 2005) (same); Nazar v. Wolpoff & Abramson, L.L.P., 2007 WL 528753, at *4 (D. Kan. Feb. 15, 2007) (same); Brake Masters Sys., Inc. v. Gabbay, 78 P.3d 1081, 1087–1088 (Ariz. Ct. App. 2003); Dream Theater, Inc. v. Dream Theater, 21 Cal. Rptr. 3d 322, 329–330 (Ct. App. 2004); Morrell & Co. v. Lehr Constr. Corp., 287 A.D.2d 257, 730 N.Y.S.2d 709 (2001). *But see* Washburn v. Beverly Enterprises-Georgia, Inc., 2006 WL 3404804, at *1 (S.D. Ga. Nov. 14, 2006) (refusing to send arbitrability dispute to arbitrator, even though arbitration clause incorporated the rules of the National Arbitration Forum, when the plaintiff alleged that he was not competent to enter into the arbitration agreement); Diesselhorst v. Munsey Bldg., L.L.P, 2005 WL 327532, at *3–*4 (D. Md. Feb. 9, 2005) (incorporation of the AAA rules by reference does not rise to the level of "clear and unmistakable evidence" that the parties intended to have an arbitrator decide threshold issues of arbitrability).

52 James & Jackson, L.L.C. v. Willie Gary, L.L.C., 906 A.2d 796, 80–81 (Del. 2006) (incorporation of arbitration provider rules did not constitute clear and unmistakable evidence of an intent to submit arbitrability disputes to an arbitrator when the arbitration clause reserved the parties' right to go to court for certain types of disputes); Burlington Res. & Oil Co. v. Palmer Ranch Ltd. P'ship, 2007 WL 2332661 (Tex. App. Aug. 16, 2007) (holding that when arbitration agreement was limited to "audit disputes," incorporation of AAA rules was not clear and unmistakable evidence of an intent to send arbitrability questions to an arbitrator).

7.3.3 Application to Tort and Statutory Claims

While tort and statutory claims are not automatically excluded from arbitration,[53] nor are parties automatically required to arbitrate all tort and statutory claims simply because they signed a contract containing an arbitration clause.[54] Broadly worded arbitration clauses often will be read to encompass tort and statutory claims.[55] An arbitration clause, if drafted using broad enough language, need not explicitly list all the different tort and statutory claims that it is intended to cover.[56] Rather, if the universe of arbitrable claims described by the general language of the agreement includes tort or statutory claims, then such claims are arbitrable.[57]

Even when a contract contains a broad arbitration clause, however, the tort or statutory claim must bear a significant relationship to the contract to be arbitrable. At a minimum, the claim must refer to or require construction of some portion of the contract in order to relate to the contract.[58] A tort claim may not be arbitrable unless it is so interwoven with the contract containing the arbitration clause that it could not stand alone.[59]

In other words, a tort or statutory claim is not arbitrable if it is independent of the contract. While stating that general standard is easy, whether a particular claim is "independent" of the contract is not always apparent, and courts have formulated different guidelines to help assess how closely related a tort claim is to the contract containing the arbitration clause. One common test holds that a tort claim is independent of the underlying contract if it arises from a breach of a duty created by law that is generally owed to others beside the contracting parties.[60] In other words, if the

---

53 Gregory v. Electro-Mechanical Corp., 83 F.3d 382, 384 (11th Cir. 1996) ("The law is clear that tort claims and claims other than breach of contract are not automatically excluded from a contractual arbitration clause."); Garfinkel v. Morristown Obstetrics & Gynecology Associates, Prof'l Ass'n, 773 A.2d 665 (N.J. 2001) ("As a general rule, courts have construed broadly worded arbitration clauses to encompass tort as well as contract claims.").

54 Coors Brewing Co. v. Molson Breweries, 51 F.3d 1511, 1516 (10th Cir. 1995) ("[not] all disputes between parties who include an arbitration clause in their contracts are subject to arbitration"); Siefert v. U.S. Home Corp., 750 So. 2d 633, 638 (Fla. 1999) ("not every dispute that arises between contracting parties should be subject to arbitration").

55 Simula, Inc. v. Autoliv, Inc., 175 F.3d 716, 721 (9th Cir. 1999); Housh v. Dinovo Inv., Inc., 2003 WL 1119526, at *7 (D. Kan. Mar. 7, 2003) (reading arbitration clause covering "all controversies" to include tort claims); McBurney v. The GM Card, 869 A.2d 586, 591 (R.I. 2005) (libel claim against creditor fell within scope of arbitration clause); Hou-Scape, Inc. v. Lloyd, 945 S.W.2d 202 (Tex. App. 1997).

56 See, e.g., Brown v. ITT Consumer Fin. Corp., 211 F.3d 1217 (11th Cir. 2000).

New Jersey, however, appears to have adopted a different rule. In Garfinkel v. Morristown Obstetrics & Gynecology Associates, Prof'l Ass'n, 773 A.2d 665 (N.J. 2001), the New Jersey Supreme Court found that a generally worded arbitration clause did not require arbitration of the plaintiff's statutory employment discrimination claims because the clause did not state, at a minimum, that statutory claims were covered by the clause. Id. at 672. The court based its holding on the state's strong public policy of protecting workers against unlawful discrimination as well as on the principle that a party should not be presumed to have waived the ability to seek judicial review of statutory rights absent clear evidence. Id. at 669–672. Subsequent decisions, however, suggest that this rule is limited to employment discrimination claims. See Alfano v. BDO Seidman, L.L.P., 925 A.2d 22 (N.J. Super. Ct. App. Div. 2007) (limiting Garfinkel to employment discrimination cases and finding that general arbitration clause covered plaintiff's state law RICO claims).

57 Simon v. Pfizer, 398 F.3d 765, 775 (6th Cir. 2005) (stating that, with a broadly worded arbitration clause, "only an express provision excluding a specific dispute, or the most forceful evidence of a purpose to exclude the claim from arbitration will remove the dispute from consideration by the arbitrators");

JLM Indus., Inc. v. Stolt-Nielsen S.A., 387 F.3d 163, 172–173 (2d Cir. 2004) (broadly worded arbitration clause required arbitration of Sherman Act antitrust claim); Anders v. Hometown Mortgage Services, Inc., 346 F.3d 1024 (11th Cir. 2003); Bender v. A.G. Edwards & Sons, Inc., 971 F.2d 698 (11th Cir. 1992); Webb v. MBNA Am. Bank, 2006 WL 618186, at *2 (E.D. Ark. Mar. 10, 2006) (broad arbitration agreement covered plaintiff's Fair Debt Collection Practices Act claim); Pitchford v. AmSouth Bank, 285 F. Supp. 2d 1286 (M.D. Ala. 2003); Hou-Scape, Inc. v. Lloyd, 945 S.W.2d 202 (Tex. App. 1997); cf. ING Fin. Partners v. Johansen, 446 F.3d 777, 779–780 (8th Cir. 2006) (NASD rules that required consent for arbitration of statutory employment discrimination claims were read not to preclude arbitration of such claims pursuant to a general pre-dispute binding arbitration clause that did not specifically identify employment discrimination claims as being subject to arbitration).

58 Fazio v. Lehman Bros., 340 F.3d 386, 395 (6th Cir. 2003); Ford v. NYLCare Health Plans of Gulf Coast, Inc., 141 F.3d 243, 251 (5th Cir. 1998); Higgs v. The Warranty Group, 2007 WL 2034376, at *3 (S.D. Ohio July 11, 2007); Hersman, Inc. v. Fleming Companies, 19 F. Supp. 2d 1282 (M.D. Ala. 1998), aff'd, 180 F.3d 271 (11th Cir. 1999); AmSouth Bank v. Dees, 847 So. 2d 923, 932 (Ala. 2002); Dusold v. Porta-John Corp., 807 P.2d 526, 530 (Ariz. Ct. App. 1990); Seifert v. U.S. Home Corp., 750 So. 2d 633, 638 (Fla. 1999); Lovey v. Regence Blueshield of Idaho, 72 P.3d 877, 887 (Idaho 2003); Rhodes v. Amega Mobile Home Sales, Inc., 186 S.W.3d 793, 798 (Mo. Ct. App. 2006); Northwest Chrysler Plymouth v. DaimlerChrysler Corp., 168 S.W.3d 693, 696 (Mo. Ct. App. 2005); see also Hendrick v. Brown & Root, Inc., 50 F. Supp. 2d 527 (E.D. Va. 1999); Stacy David, Inc. v. Consuegra, 845 So. 2d 303 (Fla. Dist. Ct. App. 2003); cf. Green Tree Fin. Corp. v. Vintson, 753 So. 2d 497 (Ala. 1999) (tort claims that closely relate to the contract are covered by arbitration clause); Porter v. Money Tree Fin. Corp., 2001 Tenn. App. LEXIS 873 (Tenn. Ct. App. Nov. 28, 2001) (tort claim in this case was directly related to a contract provision).

59 Ford v. NYLCare Health Plans of Gulf Coast, Inc., 141 F.3d 243 (5th Cir. 1998); Sharifi v. Aamco Transmissions, Inc., 2007 WL 1944371, at *3 (N.D. Tex. June 28, 2007); Rhodes v. Amega Mobile Home Sales, Inc., 186 S.W.3d 793 (Mo. Ct. App. 2006).

60 Dusold v. Porta-John Corp., 807 P.2d 526, 531 (Ariz. Ct. App.

complained-of actions would give rise to a tort whether or not a contractual relationship existed between the parties, then the dispute is not related to the agreement and not arbitrable. But if the contract places the parties in a relationship giving rise to duties not imposed by law, then a claim for a breach of those duties is subject to arbitration.[61]

Under this standard, courts have held that various types of tort and statutory claims fall outside the scope of a generally worded arbitration clause.[62] For example, the Delaware Supreme Court has held that a claim brought by minority shareholders against a corporation for breach of fiduciary duty was not arbitrable because the claim was for a breach of a legal obligation rather than a contractual obligation created by the parties' underwriting agreement.[63] A claim against a lender for misappropriating a consumer's personal information was not covered by an arbitration clause dealing with the lending relationship between the two parties.[64] Similarly, an arbitration clause in a contract for the sale of an automobile did not apply to tort claims that the automobile was defectively designed.[65] Some courts have suggested that consumers' tort claims for debt collection harassment are independent of the consumer's credit agreement.[66] In all these cases the courts relied on the fact that the defendants' actions violated duties imposed by law and thus were independent of the contract containing the arbitration clause.

Although a tort or statutory claim may be arbitrable if the claim requires "reference to" the contract, merely showing a factual connection between the contract and the tort claim will not always be sufficient to bring the claim within the scope of the arbitration clause. A claim is arbitrable only if the parties must reference the contract in order to establish an element of the claim or the basis for the legal duty at issue.[67] The true test is whether the claim and the contract are *legally* distinct rather than *factually* distinct.[68] Thus several courts have found tort claims to fall outside the

---

1990); Parfi Holding, AB v. Mirror Image Internet, Inc., 817 A.2d 149, 151 (Del. 2002); Seifert v. U.S. Home Corp., 750 So. 2d 633 (Fla. 1999); King Motor Co. of Ft. Lauderdale v. Jones, 901 So. 2d 1017, 1019–1020 (Fla. Dist. Ct. App. 2005); Lovey v. Regence Blueshield of Idaho, 72 P.3d 877, 887 (Idaho 2003); Northwest Chrysler Plymouth v. DaimlerChrysler Corp., 168 S.W.3d 693 (Mo. Ct. App. 2005); *see also* Ford v. NYLCare Health Plans of Gulf Coast, Inc., 141 F.3d 243, 250 (5th Cir. 1998) (suggesting similar rule).

61 Dusold v. Porta-John Corp., 807 P.2d 526, 531 (Ariz. Ct. App. 1990); Seifert v. U.S. Home Corp., 750 So. 2d 633 (Fla. 1999).

62 *See, e.g.*, Coors Brewing Co. v. Molson Breweries, Inc., 51 F.3d 1511, 1516 (10th Cir. 1995) (licensing agreement between two brewers did not require arbitration of antitrust claim because the licensing agreement was legally irrelevant to the claim); Tracer Research Corp. v. Nat'l Envtl. Services Co., 42 F.3d 1292 (9th Cir. 1994) (claim for misappropriation of trade secrets arose from legal duty that was independent of the parties' licensing agreement and was not subject to arbitration); AIG Fin. Advisors, Inc. v. Yim, 2007 WL 1827138 (D. Nev. June 22, 2007) (tort claim against investment advisor for misappropriation of client funds was not related to the underlying agreement); *Ex parte* Discount Foods, Inc., 711 So. 2d 992 (Ala. 1998) ("The parties' arbitration provision, although broad, cannot be construed to encompass intentional torts of the parties that are separate and distinct from the dealings that gave rise to the signing of the document containing the arbitration provision in the first place."); Dusold v. Porta-John Corp., 807 P.2d 526, 531 (Ariz. Ct. App. 1990); Smith v. Mircoskills San Diego, Ltd. P'ship, 63 Cal. Rptr. 3d 608 (Ct. App. 2007) (arbitration agreement in student loan contract did not require student to arbitrate misrepresentation claim brought against educational institution because the contract for financing the student's education was unrelated to the actions taken by the educational institution); Seifert v. U.S. Home Corp., 750 So. 2d 633 (Fla. 1999) (plaintiff's tort claim against home manufacturer for failing to warn of known risks from defective design arose from a legal duty existing independently of the contract and therefore was not subject to arbitration); Smith v. Captain D's, L.L.C., 2007 WL 1704349 (Miss. June 14, 2007) (employee's sexual assault and rape claims against manager bore no connection to her employment agreement); Rhodes v. Amega Home Sales, Inc., 186 S.W.3d 793 (Mo. Ct. App. 2006) (products liability claim against mobile home manufacturers for excessive levels of formaldehyde did not require reference to the purchase contract and was not subject to arbitration).

63 Parfi Holding, AB v. Mirror Image Internet, Inc., 817 A.2d 149 (Del. 2002).

64 King Motor Co. of Ft. Lauderdale v. Jones, 901 So. 2d 1017, 1019–1020 (Fla. Dist. Ct. App. 2005) (invasion of privacy claim brought by consumer against auto dealer not covered by arbitration clause in auto purchase agreement because consumer's tort claims arose from a separate, extra-contractual legal duty and could survive independently of the contract); Nefores v. Branddirect Mktg., Inc., Clearinghouse No. 53,552 (Ohio Ct. Com. Pl. Jan. 28, 2002) (text of this decision is also available on the CD-Rom accompanying this manual); *see also* Rogers-Dabbs Chevrolet-Hummer, Inc. v. Blakeney, 950 So. 2d 170, 177 (Miss. 2007) (claim of misappropriation of personal identity through forgery was not related to the underlying contract); Aiken v. World Fin. Corp. of S.C., 644 S.E.2d 705, 709 (S.C. 2007) (claim of identity theft was not arbitrable because it was not a foreseeable consequence of a consumer finance agreement that the finance company's employees would misappropriate the plaintiff's personal identity information).

65 Northwest Chrysler Plymouth v. DaimlerChrysler Corp., 168 S.W.3d 693 (Mo. Ct. App. 2005)

66 *See* Green Tree Servicing Corp. v. Fisher, 162 P.3d 944 (Okla. Civ. App. 2007); Chassereau v. Global-Sun Pools, Inc., 644 S.E.2d 718, 720 (S.C. 2007) ("We believe a reasonable person would not have foreseen and would not have expected (and ought not to expect) Global-Sun employees to commit acts historically associated with the common law tort of outrage in seeking to collect an overdue debt."). *But see* Pridgen v. Green Tree Fin. Servicing Corp., 88 F. Supp. 2d 655 (S.D. Miss. 2000) (debt collection harassment claim is within scope of arbitration clause).

67 *See, e.g.*, Ford v. NYLCare Health Plans of the Gulf Coast, Inc., 141 F.3d 243, 252 (5th Cir. 1998) (finding that doctor's false advertising claim not covered by their contractual arbitration clause because the existence of the contract was "legally irrelevant" to his claim).

68 Parfi Holding, AB v. Mirror Image Internet, Inc., 817 A.2d 149, 156–157 (Del. 2002); Aiken v. World Fin. Corp. of S.C., 644 S.E.2d 705, 709 (S.C. 2007) (claims which are factually related to but legally distinct from the contract fall outside the scope of the arbitration clause).

scope of a contractual arbitration clause even when the underlying complaint references the contract, or when the contract provides factual support for the plaintiff's claims.[69]

Similarly, the fact that the tort would not have occurred but for the contractual relationship is insufficient to bring a tort claim within the scope of a contractual arbitration provision, because the duty giving rise to the tort claim can be created by law even if the contractual relationship establishes the context in which the tort occurs.[70] This rule is a sensible one, because it often will be the case that the parties to a tort dispute would not have interacted absent a preexisting contractual relationship. Applying a "but for" test to determine whether a claim falls within a contractual arbitration clause would reach too broadly and sweep many independent claims within an arbitration clause simply because two parties entered into a contractual relationship. Indeed, the South Carolina Supreme Court recently recognized that if the existence of the contractual relationship as a "but for" cause of the tort were enough, then the arbitration clause would cover virtually "every dispute imaginable" between the parties, regardless of whether the claim arose from duties created by law or by contract.[71] Other courts, however, interpret an arbitration agreement's scope more broadly and hold that tort claims are arbitrable if they "aris[e] from the same set of operative facts" as covered in the contract.[72]

Another helpful test looks at whether a breach of the underlying contract is a necessary element of the tort claim. If the cause of action would still exist even if the parties fully performed their contractual obligations, then a court may be more likely to find that it falls outside the scope of the arbitration clause.[73] This test ensures that not all torts are sent into arbitration, but only those claims that in reality are contract claims dressed up as tort claims in an attempt to evade arbitration.[74]

Some courts also consider whether the tort claim would exist if the complained-of actions had injured a non-contracting third party instead of a contracting party.[75] If it is simply a "fortuitous" circumstance that the injured party happened to be the contracting party, then the claim is independent of the contract and not subject to arbitration.[76] For example, the Florida Supreme Court found that a tort claim against a home builder for failing to warn about defects and dangerous conditions in a home it constructed fell outside the scope of the parties' arbitration clause because the builder owed the same duty to any third party that it owed to the home owner.[77] Another court noted that

---

69 Ford v. NYLCare Health Plans of Gulf Coast, Inc., 141 F.3d 243, 251 (5th Cir. 1998) (fact that the contract might be relevant evidence did not bring the plaintiff's false advertising claim within the scope of the arbitration clause); Northwest Chrysler Plymouth v. DaimlerChrysler Corp., 168 S.W.3d 693, 697 (Mo. Ct. App. 2005). *But see* Fazio v. Lehman Bros., 340 F.3d 386, 395 (6th Cir. 2003) (tort claim fell within the scope of the arbitration clause because the claim required describing the contractual arrangement between the parties).

70 Tracer Research Corp. v. Nat'l Envtl. Services Co., 42 F.3d 1292, 1295 (9th Cir. 1994) (fact that the contract is a "but for" cause of the tort is not determinative); Dusold v. Porta-John Corp., 807 P.2d 526, 531 (Ariz. Ct. App. 1990); Seifert v. U.S. Home Corp., 750 So. 2d 633, 638 (Fla. 1999); Aiken v. World Fin. Corp. of S.C., 644 S.E.2d 705, 709 (S.C. 2007); *cf.* R.J. Griffin & Co. v. Beach Club II Homeowners Ass'n, 384 F.3d 157, 162 (4th Cir. 2004) (applying the same rule to hold that a non-party to the arbitration clause was not compelled to arbitrate under principles of estoppel). *But see* Snyder v. Belmont Homes, Inc., 899 So. 2d 57, 62 (La. Ct. App. 2005) (tort claims involving presence of toxic mold in home were arbitrable, even though the tort claim did not arise from the home purchase agreement, because the facts giving rise to the tort claim would not have occurred "but for" the agreement).

71 Aiken v. World Fin. Corp. of S.C., 644 S.E.2d 705, 708 (S.C. 2007).

72 CD Partners, L.L.C. v. Grizzle, 424 F.3d 795, 800 (8th Cir. 2005); Fazio v. Lehman Bros., 340 F.3d 386, 395 (6th Cir. 2003) (tort claim arbitrable when the claim required a factual reference to the contract); Ingstad v. Grant Thornton, L.L.P., 2006 WL 3751204, at *5 (D.N.D. Dec. 19, 2006).

73 *See* Telecom Italia, SPA v. Wholesale Telecom Corp., 248 F.3d 1109, 1114–1115 (11th Cir. 2001) (noting that the court had in the past compelled arbitration on the theory that the tort claim would never have arisen had the defendant honored the contract); Ford v. NYLCare Health Plans of the Gulf Coast, Inc., 141 F.3d 243, 252 (5th Cir. 1998) (false advertising claim was unrelated to the contract because the plaintiff "clearly would suffer the same injuries regardless of the agreement or a breach thereof"); H.S. Gregory, G.E. v. Electro-Mechanical Corp., 83 F.3d 382, 385 (11th Cir. 1996); Fridl v. Cook, 908 S.W.2d 507, 513 (Tex. App. 1995).

74 *Ford*, 141 F.3d at 250.

75 Coors Brewing Co. v. Molson Breweries, Inc., 51 F.3d 1511, 1515–1516 (10th Cir. 1995) (brewing company was not required to arbitrate an antitrust claim against another brewer by virtue of the fact that they entered into a licensing agreement); Parfi Holding, AB v. Mirror Image Internet, Inc., 817 A.2d 149, 156 n.24 (Del. 2002); Siefert v. U.S. Home Corp., 750 So. 2d 633, 641 (Fla. 1999) (claims against home builder for breach of its duty to warn of known dangerous conditions and defective design were not covered by contractual arbitration clause because the allegations would give rise to claims by anyone, not just the contracting parties); *see also In re* Weekley Homes, Ltd. P'ship, 180 S.W.3d 127, 132 (Tex. 2005) (personal injury claims against home repair company were not related to the repair contract because the plaintiff's claim was no different "from what any bystander might assert," but compelling arbitration on other grounds).

76 Coors Brewing Co. v. Molson Breweries, Inc., 51 F.3d 1511, 1516 (10th Cir. 1995); Seifert v. U.S. Home Corp., 750 So. 2d 633, 641 (Fla. 1999).

77 Seifert v. U.S. Home Corp., 750 So. 2d 633, 641 (Fla. 1999) ("These allegations rely on obligations that would extend to anyone, third parties as well as the Sieferts, who might be injured by U.S. Home's tortious conduct. Indeed, it appears to be entirely fortuitous that it was Mr. Seifert, and not a guest or someone else in the house, who was injured as a result of the alleged neglect by U.S. Home."); *see also* Terminix Int'l Co. v. Michaels, 668 So. 2d 1013 (Fla. Dist. Ct. App. 1996) (arbitration clause did not apply to a consumer's claim against a pest control company for its failure to warn of the dangerous nature of its chemical product, even though the company sprayed the

this limitation on the scope of arbitration agreements is necessary to avoid the "absurd results" that would ensue from sending tort claims into arbitration that are unrelated to the contract containing the arbitration clause.[78]

Finally, some courts employ a foreseeability test, holding that an arbitration clause does not apply to torts that are not a foreseeable result of the underlying contractual relationship.[79] Courts have not defined with precision which types of claims are foreseeable. The Eleventh Circuit has held that a dispute is foreseeable if it "occurs as a fairly direct result of the performance of contractual duties."[80] The South Carolina Supreme Court has held that it was not foreseeable when a consumer entered into a loan agreement with a finance company that the company's employees would misappropriate his personal information.[81]

Thus whether a particular tort or statutory claim falls within the scope of an arbitration clause is a fact specific inquiry that turns on the subject matter of the contract, the specific tort or statutory duties that the parties seek to enforce, and the specific language of the arbitration provision. Merely determining the category of tort claim being asserted (for example, fraudulent inducement or negligence) will not determine whether a claim is arbitrable. For example, courts sometimes have found that claims brought under state unfair or deceptive practices (UDAP) laws fall outside the scope of the contract's arbitration clause and at other times have found that such claims relate to the contract and therefore are arbitrable.[82] The same is true for claims of fraud or fraudulent inducement.[83] Arguably fraudulent in-

---

consumer's residence pursuant to a contract between those parties); *cf.* Sears Authorized Termite & Pest Control, Inc. v. Sullivan, 816 So. 2d 603 (Fla. 2002) (negligence claim against pest company for failing to control spiders did fall within the scope of a contractual arbitration clause).

Similarly, the Tenth Circuit noted that two parties to a sales agreement would not have to arbitrate a claim that one assaulted the other because it would be irrelevant whether the assault victim was the contracting party or an unrelated third party. *See* Coors Brewing Co., 51 F.3d at 1516.

78 *Coors Brewing Co.*, 51 F.3d at 1516 (refusing to compel arbitration of antitrust claim between brewers simply because they entered into a licensing agreement and holding that accepting the defendant's argument would mean that "*every brewer in America* except Coors may bring an antitrust action against Molson" (emphasis in original)).

79 *See* Telecom Italia, SPA v. Wholesale Telecom Corp., 248 F.3d 1109, 1116 (11th Cir. 2001) (looking to "whether the tort or breach in question was an immediate, foreseeable result of the performance of contractual duties"); Aiken v. World Fin. Corp. of S.C., 644 S.E.2d 705, 709 (S.C. 2007) ("[T]his Court will refuse to interpret any arbitration agreement as applying to outrageous torts that are unforeseeable to a reasonable consumer in the context of normal business dealings.").

80 *Telecom Italia, SPA*, 248 F.3d at 1116.

81 *Aiken*, 644 S.E.2d at 708–709 (consumer's identity theft claim fell outside the scope of a contractual arbitration clause); *see also* Chassereau v. Global-Sun Pools, Inc., 644 S.E.2d 718 (S.C. 2007) (finding claims of harassment, defamation, and intentional infliction of emotional distress committed by pool company's employees were not a foreseeable result of consumer's contract to purchase an above-ground swimming pool).

82 I Sports v. IMG Worldwide, Inc., 813 N.E.2d 4, 9 (Ohio Ct. App. 2004) (suggesting that plaintiff's deceptive trade practices claim did not rely on the terms of the underlying agreement); Decision Control Sys., Inc. v. Personnel Cost Control, Inc., 787 S.W.2d 98 (Tex. App. 1990) (UDAP claim not covered by contractual arbitration clause); *see also* Feinstein v. BDS Remodeling Services, L.L.C., 2005 WL 704290 (N.J. Super. Ct. App. Div. Mar. 21, 2005) (arbitration provision "only applies to claims arising from the contract itself and not to statutory claims or claims stemming from the relationship and conduct of the parties involved"). *But see* Genesco, Inc. v. T. Kakiuchi & Co., 815 F.2d 840 (2d Cir. 1987) (finding fraud and unfair competition claims arbitrable, but holding that a tortious interference claim based on a bribe of an executive of a contracting party was not related to the underlying agreement); Higgs v. The Warranty Group, 2007 WL 2034376, at *4 (S.D. Ohio July 11, 2007) (UDAP claim subject to arbitration); Winterwood Farm, L.L.C. v. JER, Inc., 327 F. Supp. 2d 34, 39–40 (D. Me. 2004) (UDAP claim arbitrable); Stout v. J.D. Byrider, 50 F. Supp. 2d 733 (N.D. Ohio 1999) (UDAP claim is one arising under the contract), *aff'd*, 228 F.3d 709 (6th Cir. 2000); McCarthy v. Providential Corp., 1994 U.S. Dist. LEXIS 10122 (N.D. Cal. July 18, 1994) ("relating to loan documents" covers Truth in Lending and UDAP claims); Rodgers Builders, Inc. v. McQueen, 76 N.C. App. 16, 331 S.E.2d 726 (1985) (UDAP claims subject to arbitration); Kline v. Oak Ridge Builders, Inc., 102 Ohio App. 3d 63, 656 N.E.2d 992 (1995) (clause requiring arbitration when claim arises out of or relates to construction contract applied to consumer's UDAP claim); Shadduck v. Christopher J. Kaclik, Inc., 713 A.2d 635 (Pa. Super. Ct. 1998) (UDAP claim against construction company related to construction contract and was subject to arbitration); Flanary v. Carl Gregory Dodge of Johnson City, L.L.C., 2005 WL 1277850 (Tenn. Ct. App. May 31, 2005) (claim that auto dealer charged consumer unfair fee in violation of the Tennessee Consumer Protection Act related to the contract and was subject to arbitration); Porter v. Money Tree Fin. Corp., 2001 Tenn. App. LEXIS 873 (Tenn. Ct. App. Nov. 28, 2001) (UDAP claim in this case was directly related to a contract provision); Jack B. Anglin Co. v. Tipps, 842 S.W.2d 266 (Tex. 1992) (UDAP claim closely related to breach of contract claim); Emerald Tex., Inc. v. Peel, 920 S.W.2d 398 (Tex. App. 1996) (compelling arbitration of UDAP claim but noting that arbitration is not required when the UDAP claim is "completely independent" of the contract); Merrill Lynch, Pierce, Fenner & Smith v. Wilson, 805 S.W.2d 38 (Tex. App. 1991).

83 Davis v. Becker, 491 F.3d 1292 (11th Cir. 2007) (claim that documents used to create the trust when unfair and unsuitable were unrelated to trust agreement covering trust investments); Liberty Fin., Inc. v. Carson, 793 So. 2d 702 (Ala. 2000); Am. Bankers Life Assurance Co. v. Rice Acceptance Co., 709 So. 2d 1188 (Ala. 1998) (fraud claim did not relate to the performance of the contract); Carl Gregory Chrysler-Plymouth, Inc. v. Barnes, 700 So. 2d 1358 (Ala. 1997) (claim of forgery on separate document not subject to arbitration; Smith v. Microskills San Diego, Ltd. P'ship, 63 Cal. Rptr. 3d 608 (Ct. App. 2007) (arbitration clause in student loan agreement with financing company did not require arbitration of misrepresentation and unfair competition claims against the school); Simpson v. Grimes, 849 So. 2d 740 (La. Ct. App. 2003) (claim of forgery on separate document not covered by broad arbitration clause), *abrogated on other grounds by* Aguillard v. Austin Mgmt.

ducement claims should not be covered by an arbitration clause because they relate to actions taken to induce a party to sign a contract rather than on performance of the contract itself, but most courts have not taken that view.[84] With respect to defamation claims, whether they must be submitted to arbitration often will depend on whether the statements at issue are related to the underlying agreement, or whether the statements' truth or falsity hinges on whether there was a breach of the underlying agreement.[85] When an arbitration clause does cover a particular tort or statutory claim it also covers whether that claim gives rise to punitive damages.[86]

In the context of employment-related torts, courts have held that an arbitration agreement in an employment contract generally will apply to any claim of unlawful harassment, discrimination, or wrongful discharge, including public policy, contract, or statutory claims.[87] However one court has held that an arbitration clause in an employment contract did not reach an employee's claim that she was raped and assaulted by her manager.[88] A federal district court in New Mexico has found that an arbitration agreement that specified it would apply to discrimination and unlawful harassment claims did not apply to the plaintiff's claims for intentional infliction of emotional distress.[89]

Even when a claim falls within the scope of an arbitration agreement, arbitration is not required unless a party invokes the arbitration provision. Thus, one court has allowed a case to go forward in litigation despite an arbitration clause that allows either party to proceed to arbitration. Because neither party had filed an arbitration claim, the arbitration clause does not require removal of the case from court.[90]

Although courts have not employed any hard and fast rule as to whether or not particular tort claims are arbitrable, they generally seem less inclined to force parties into arbitration when a plaintiff brings intentional tort claims or alleges particularly outrageous conduct.[91] Thus courts have found

---

Corp., 908 So. 2d 1 (La. 2005); Rogers-Dabbs Chevrolet-Hummer, Inc. v. Blakeney, 950 So. 2d 170, 177 (Miss. 2007) (fraud claims arising out of forged signature were not subject to arbitration). *But see* Highlands Wellmont Health Network, Inc. v. John Deere Health Plan, Inc., 350 F.3d 568, 578 (6th Cir. 2003); Welborn Clinic v. Medquist, Inc., 301 F.3d 634, 639 (7th Cir. 2002) (when contract includes "arising out of or relating to" language, the clause can be read to include "all manner of claims tangentially related to the agreement, including claims of fraud, misrepresentation, and other torts involving both contract formation and performance"; in this case, because the clause did not contain such broad language, the court did not construe it to cover tort claims not arising out of the contract); Battaglia v. McKendry, 233 F.3d 720, 725–727 (3d Cir. 2000) (fraud claims arbitrable); Gregory v. Electro-Mechanical Corp., 83 F.3d 382, 386 (11th Cir. 1996) (fraudulent inducement claims subject to arbitration); Sweet Dreams Unlimited, Inc. v. Dial-A-Mattress Int'l, Ltd., 1 F.3d 639, 643 (7th Cir. 1993) (claims of fraudulent inducement subject to arbitration); Genesco, Inc. v. T. Kakiuchi & Co., 815 F.2d 840 (2d Cir. 1987) (finding fraud and unfair competition claims arbitrable, but holding that a tortious interference claim based on a bribe of an executive of a contracting party was not related to the underlying agreement); Higgs v. The Warranty Group, 2007 WL 2034376, at *3 (S.D. Ohio July 11, 2007); Sharifi v. Aamco Transmissions, Inc., 2007 WL 1944371 (N.D. Tex. June 28, 2007) (fraud claims arbitrable); Ingstad v. Grant Thornton, L.L.P., 2006 WL 3751204, at *5 (D.N.D. Dec. 19, 2006); Serra Chevrolet, Inc. v. Hock, 891 So. 2d 844 (Ala. 2004) (claim of fraudulent alteration of auto lease was related to the lease and was subject to arbitration); Coastal Ford, Inc. v. Kidder, 694 So. 2d 1285 (Ala. 1997) (claim that auto dealer fraudulently misrepresented mileage of used truck related to auto agreement and was subject to arbitration); Lovey v. Regence Blueshield of Idaho, 72 P.3d 877, 886 (Idaho 2003) (fraud claims arbitrable); Pierman v. Green Tree Fin. Servicing Corp., 933 P.2d 955 (Okla. Civ. App. 1997) (claims of fraudulent misrepresentation in financing agreement were subject to arbitration); Shadduck v. Christopher J. Kaclik, Inc., 713 A.2d 635 (Pa. Super. Ct. 1998) (fraudulent misrepresentation claim against construction company related to construction contract and was subject to arbitration); *see also* Prima Paint Corp. v. Flood & Conklin Mfg. Co., 388 U.S. 395, 87 S. Ct. 1801, 18 L. Ed. 2d 1270 (1967) (holding that broad arbitration clause could apply to fraudulent inducement claims).

84 *But see* Decision Control Sys., Inc. v. Personnel Cost Control, Inc., 787 S.W.2d 98 (Tex. App. 1990) (plaintiff's UDAP claims did not relate to the contract because the illegal conduct occurred prior to the formation of the contract).

85 Kruse v. AFLAC Int'l, 458 F. Supp. 2d 375 (E.D. Ky. 2006) (defamation dispute was arbitrable because "the alleged defamatory statements were also made in relation to the plaintiff's service in an employment capacity"); McMahon v. RMS Electronics, 618 F. Supp. 189, 192 (S.D.N.Y. 1985) (defamation claims relating to certain statements fell within the arbitration clause, and that claims relating to other statements fell outside the arbitration clause); Nardi v. Povich, 2006 WL 2127714, at *4–*5 (N.Y. Sup. Ct. July 31, 2006) (agent could enforce arbitration clause with respect to defamation claims that pertained to the plaintiff's employment agreement); I Sports v. IMG Worldwide, Inc., 813 N.E.2d 4, 9 (Ohio Ct. App. 2004) (defamation claims were unrelated to contract).

86 Morton v. Polivchak, 931 So. 2d 935 (Fla. Dist. Ct. App. 2006).

87 *See generally* Gilmer v. Interstate/Johnson Lane Corp., 500 U.S. 20, 111 S. Ct. 1647, 114 L. Ed. 2d 26 (1991) (employment discrimination claims can be subject to arbitration)

88 Smith v. Captain D's, L.L.C., 2007 WL 1704349 (Miss. June 14, 2007) ("We find that a claim of sexual assault neither pertains to nor has a connection with [plaintiff's] employment.").

89 Dumais v. Am. Golf Corp., 150 F. Supp. 2d 1182, 1192 (D.N.M. 2001), *aff'd on other grounds*, 299 F.3d 1216 (10th Cir. 2002); *see also* Scaglione v. Kraftmaid Cabinetry, Inc., 2002 WL 31812941 (Ohio Ct. App. Dec. 13, 2002) (tortfeasor/victim relationship is inherently separate from the employer/employee relationship). *But see* Sharifi v. Aamco Transmissions, Inc., 2007 WL 1944371 (N.D. Tex. June 28, 2007) (finding intentional infliction of emotional distress claims arbitrable because they arose out of fraud claims that were subject to arbitration).

90 Fernandes v. Ramsey Nissan, 2005 WL 3148228 (N.J. Super. Ct. App. Div. Nov. 28, 2005); *cf.* Okla. Oncology & Hematology, Prof'l Corp. v. U.S. Oncology, Inc., 160 P.3d 936 (Okla. 2007) (because dispute resolution clause included both judicial and arbitral remedies, the parties were not required to submit to arbitration).

91 *Ex parte* Discount Foods, Inc., 711 So. 2d 992 (Ala. 1998) ("The parties' arbitration provision, although broad, cannot be construed to encompass intentional torts of the parties that are

claims like assault,[92] identity theft,[93] forgery,[94] and unlawful harassment in connection with a debt collection[95] to be unrelated to contracts containing arbitration clauses.

Finally, in addition to challenging the scope of a contractual arbitration clause as it relates to a tort or statutory claim, it is also worth investigating relevant state law, as several states have adopted statutory restrictions on the types of claims subject to arbitration, and some have even prohibited arbitration of tort claims altogether.[96] Although the Federal Arbitration Act (FAA) likely preempts these statutes,[97] in cases not governed by the FAA they provide a basis for excluding from arbitration tort claims that otherwise would fall within the scope of a contractual arbitration clause. Moreover, even in cases governed by the FAA, it is possible that if an arbitration clause also includes a specific choice-of-law provision providing that the contract and arbitration provision are governed by state law, then the state law restrictions on arbitration may apply.[98]

7.3.4 Arbitration Clause Does Not Apply to Consumer's Self-Help Remedies

Consumers have a number of self-help remedies available to them that should not be affected by an arbitration clause. Under the Uniform Commercial Code consumers can reject goods, revoke acceptance, and withhold payments.[99] Consumers can also cancel certain contracts within three days by sending in a notice.[100]

No court permission is required to take these actions, and it makes no sense to require the consumer to arbitrate self-help actions that the law provides as a statutory right. In addition, a careful reading of the arbitration agreement will typically indicate that there is not even an argument that these actions are covered by the agreement's language. Some arbitration agreements exempt self-help remedies, and others apply to "disputes." There is no dispute involved in the use of a self-help remedy. The law allows consumers to take certain actions in certain situations. Such consumers are not disputing anything, but merely exercising their rights. After they exercise the right, there may be a dispute over the legal effect of such action, and that dispute may be subject to an arbitration clause.

7.3.5 The Temporal Scope of an Arbitration Provision

It is important to examine not just the substantive scope of an arbitration clause, but its temporal scope as well. An arbitration clause, even a broadly worded one, typically will not be applied to claims arising from conduct occurring *before* the contract containing the arbitration clause was

---

separate and distinct from the dealings that gave rise to the signing of the document containing the arbitration provision in the first place.").

92 Smith v. Captain D's, L.L.C., 2007 WL 1704349 (Miss. June 14, 2007) ("We find that a claim of sexual assault neither pertains to nor has a connection with [plaintiff's] employment."); *see also* Coors Brewing Co. v. Molson Breweries, 51 F.3d 1511, 1516 (10th Cir. 1995) ("[I]f two small business owners execute a sales contract including a general arbitration clause, and one assaults the other, we would think it elementary that the sales contract did not require the victim to arbitrate the tort claim because the tort claim is not related to the sales contract.").

93 King Motor Co. of Ft. Lauderdale v. Jones, 901 So. 2d 1017, 1019–1020 (Fla. Dist. Ct. App. 2005) (invasion of privacy claim brought by consumer against auto dealer not covered by arbitration clause in auto purchase agreement because consumer's tort claims arose from a separate, extra-contractual legal duty and could survive independently of the contract); Nefores v. Branddirect Mktg., Inc., Clearinghouse No. 53,552 (Ohio Ct. Com. Pl. Jan. 28, 2002) (text of this decision is also available on the CD-Rom accompanying this manual); Aiken v. World Fin. Corp. of S.C., 644 S.E.2d 705, 709 (S.C. 2007) (claim of identity theft was not arbitrable because it was not a foreseeable consequence of a consumer finance agreement that the finance company's employees would misappropriate the plaintiff's personal identity information).

94 Carl Gregory Chrysler-Plymouth, Inc. v. Barnes, 700 So. 2d 1358 (Ala. 1997) (claim of forgery on separate document not subject to arbitration); Simpson v. Grimes, 849 So. 2d 740 (La. Ct. App. 2003) (claim of forgery on separate document not covered by broad arbitration clause), *abrogated on other grounds by* Aguillard v. Austin Mgmt. Corp., 908 So. 2d 1 (La. 2005); Rogers-Dabbs Chevrolet-Hummer, Inc. v. Blakeney, 950 So. 2d 170, 177 (Miss. 2007) (claim of misappropriation of personal identity through forgery was not related to the underlying contract).

95 Chassereau v. Global-Sun Pools, Inc., 644 S.E.2d 718, 720 (S.C. 2007) ("We believe a reasonable person would not have foreseen and would not have expected (and ought not to expect) Global-Sun employees to commit acts historically associated with the common law tort of outrage in seeking to collect an overdue debt.").

96 *See, e.g.*, Ark. Code Ann. § 16-108-201(b)(2) (excluding from arbitration "personal injury and tort matters, employer-employee disputes," and insurance disputes); Ga. Code Ann. § 9-9-2(c) (precluding arbitration of medical malpractice claims, insurance claims, claims relating to consumer finance loans, claims relating to contracts for the sale of consumer goods, unfair business practices claims, and future claims related to personal bodily injury and wrongful death); Iowa Code § 679A.1(2) (stating that tort claims are not arbitrable unless so provided in a separate writing executed by the parties); Kan. Stat. Ann. § 5-401(c) (excluding from arbitration tort, employment, and insurance claims); Tex. Civ. Prac. & Rem. Code Ann. § 171.002(c) (Vernon) (stating that personal injury claims are not arbitrable unless the parties, on advice of counsel, agree to arbitrate them and that agreement is signed by both the parties and their attorneys).

97 *See* Ch. 3, *supra*.

98 *See* § 3.3.3, *supra*. *But see* Housh v. Dinovo Inv., Inc., 2003 WL 1119526 (D. Kan. Mar. 7, 2003) (contract with Kansas choice-of-law provision did not incorporate Kansas' statutory restriction on the arbitration of tort claims).

99 *See* National Consumer Law Center, Consumer Warranty Law Ch. 8 (3d ed. 2006 and Supp.).

100 *See* § 6.7.4.2, *supra*.

signed.[101] In *Security Watch, Inc. v. Sentinel Systems, Inc.*, the Sixth Circuit was faced with two consecutive agreements, only the second of which contained a arbitration clause.[102] Although the court noted that the arbitration clause was "very broad in scope," it held that "this breadth of scope does not extend over time" to encompass debt accrued under the first agreement, and held that the clause was "essentially forward-looking."[103] The court reasoned that a party seeking to apply an arbitration agreement retroactively bears a heavy burden of proof because it is "nonsensical to suggest that [plaintiffs] simply would abandon [their] established rights to litigate disputes arising under the [earlier agreement]."[104]

Several courts have taken this approach to retroactive clauses and refused to apply arbitration clauses to prior claims when the party seeking to compel arbitration failed to show that the arbitration agreement was intended to cover earlier claims.[105] This case law may be inspired in part by law in other contexts addressing the fundamental unfairness of retroactive rules.[106] On the other hand, when the language of an arbitration clause clearly covers conduct which occurred before the arbitration provision was signed, some courts have found that the consumer must arbitrate the dispute even if it is based on conduct which occurred before the consumer signed the agreement.[107]

While arbitration clauses generally will not cover actions arising *before* the signing of the contract, how and when arbitration clauses apply to actions occurring *after* the expiration of the agreement raises thornier questions. Some contracts are time-limited by their express terms, as are some arbitration clauses. In such circumstances several courts have refused to compel arbitration when the events giving rise to the claim occurred after the defined time-period had elapsed.[108] By the same token, however, when an

---

101 Becker v. Davis, 2007 WL 1988551, at *7 (11th Cir. July 11, 2007) (arbitration clause in trust agreements did not require arbitration of breach of fiduciary duty claims arising from transactions occurring before the trust agreements were executed); Sec. Watch, Inc. v. Sentinel Sys., Inc., 176 F.3d 369 (6th Cir. 1999); Biddeford Internet Corp. v. Verizon New Eng., Inc., 456 F. Supp. 2d 165 (D. Me. 2006); Hyde v. RDA, Inc., 389 F. Supp. 2d 658, 662–663 (D. Md. 2005) (arbitration clause in automobile financing agreement requiring arbitration of claims relating to the purchase of the vehicle did not apply to plaintiff's Fair Credit Reporting Act claims arising from pre-purchase credit offer); In re Universal Serv. Fund Tel. Billing Practices Litig., 300 F. Supp. 2d 1107 (D. Kan. 2003) (agreement to arbitrate disputes relating to the contract does not apply to disputes arising before the contract was signed); Hendrick v. Brown & Root, Inc., 50 F. Supp. 2d 527 (E.D. Va. 1999); Balandran v. Labor Ready, Inc., 22 Cal. Rptr. 3d 441 (Ct. App. 2004) (agreement to arbitrate disputes arising out of employment does not apply to pre-employment discrimination claims alleging a failure to hire on the basis of gender); Stinger v. Ultimate Warranty Corp., 829 N.E.2d 735, 737–738 (Ohio Ct. App. 2005) (arbitration clause in warranty agreement does not apply to claims prior to finalization of the warranty); *cf.* Bess v. Check Express, 294 F.3d 1298 (11th Cir. 2002) (remanding case to district court to determine on what date consumer signed the arbitration clause, because without date court cannot determine whether clause covered the transaction that was the subject of the parties' dispute); Harley v. Sayas, 2006 WL 4037577, at *5 (S.C. Ct. Com. Pl. June 21, 2006) (refusing to compel arbitration "as to claims which arose prior to the execution of the arbitration agreement").
102 Sec. Watch, Inc. v. Sentinel Sys., Inc., 176 F.3d 369, 372–374 (6th Cir. 1999).
103 *Id.* at 373.
104 *Id.*
105 Long v. Fid. Water Sys., Inc., 2000 U.S. Dist. LEXIS 7827 (N.D. Cal. May 24, 2000) ("Even assuming [the consumer] is deemed to have agreed to the arbitration provision, defendants offer no justification for holding that he agreed to arbitrate acts that occurred before the effective date of that agreement."); Hendrick v. Brown & Root, Inc., 50 F. Supp. 2d 527, 537 (E.D. Va. 1999) (an arbitration agreement "may not be used to reach back to cover disputes arising before the agreement was executed, unless such pre-existing disputes are brought within the scope of the clause"); Paul v. Timco, Inc., 811 A.2d 948 (N.J. Super. Ct. App. Div. 2002) (arbitration clause included in agreement sent to plaintiff months after transaction cannot apply to transaction without evidence of plaintiff's clear acceptance of arbitration); Stinger v. Ultimate Warranty Corp., 829 N.E.2d 735, 737–738 (Ohio Ct. App. 2005) (arbitration clause in warranty agreement does not apply to claims prior to finalization of the warranty).
106 *See, e.g.*, Gen. Motors Corp. v. Romein, 503 U.S. 181, 191, 112 S. Ct. 1105, 1112, 117 L. Ed. 2d 328 (1992) ("Retroactive legislation presents problems of unfairness that are more serious than those posed by prospective legislation because it can deprive citizens of legitimate expectations and upset settled transactions.").
107 *See In re* Universal Serv. Fund Tel. Billing Practices Litig., 300 F. Supp. 2d 1107 (D. Kan. 2003) (clause applied "regardless of the date of accrual of such claim"); Arriaga v. Cross Country Bank, 163 F. Supp. 2d 1189 (S.D. Cal. 2001) (applying an arbitration provision in a later agreement to a dispute that arose under the former agreement, based on the breadth of the language of the arbitration clause); Southtrust Bank v. Bowen, 959 So. 2d 624 (Ala. 2006) (counterclaim alleging fraud in connection with promissory note was covered by arbitration clause in a subsequent agreement between the parties stating that it applied to all disputes arising from the contract "or otherwise"); *see also* Wirdzek v. Monetary Mgmt. of Cal., Inc., 1999 WL 688100 (E.D. Cal. May 25, 1999) (applying an arbitration provision in a later agreement to a dispute that arose under a former agreement); Zawikowski v. Beneficial Nat'l Bank, 1999 U.S. Dist. LEXIS 514 (N.D. Ill. Jan. 7, 1999) (same).
108 *See* Klay v. All Defendants, 389 F.3d 1191, 1202–1203 (11th Cir. 2004); Smith v. Steinkamp, 318 F.3d 775, 778 (7th Cir. 2003) (when contract failed to reference future events, claims occurring after the expiration of the contract were not subject to arbitration); Cornell v. Harmony Homes, Inc., 2007 WL 38132 (D. Colo. Jan. 4, 2007) (employment contract that by its terms only went through December 2002 did not apply to employment discrimination claim arising in 2004, even though the plaintiff continued to work for the defendant after December 2002); Heseman v. Hensler, 2005 WL 941362 (Cal. Ct. App. Apr. 22, 2005) (arbitration clause in employment application required applicant to raise any dispute in arbitration within six months of the application date; dispute arising more than six months after the application was not subject to arbitration).

§ 7.3.5   *Consumer Arbitration Agreements*

arbitration clause clearly states that it survives termination of the agreement it will apply to post-termination claims.[109] That a contract applies to claims that occur after the termination of the contract does not necessarily mean that all post-termination disputes are subject to arbitration. If the claims do not relate to the underlying contract containing the arbitration clause, they should still fall outside the scope of the arbitration clause under normal contract interpretation principles.[110]

Whether post-expiration claims must be arbitrated is less clear when the contract containing an arbitration clause does not incorporate express time limits. Some courts have held that post-expiration claims are not arbitrable in such circumstances. An Oklahoma appellate court recently held that a consumer's claim against a loan servicing company for harassment in connection with a collection of a debt was not arbitrable because the harassment occurred after the debt was discharged in bankruptcy and no longer due.[111] The court held that the discharge of the debt terminated the loan contract and that, as a consequence, the creditor's actions "occurred *subsequent* to the contract's termination, and which did not arise as a *natural consequence* of the contract."[112] Also the Seventh Circuit has held that an arbitration clause in a consumer's payday loan agreement did not apply to claims arising out of future loans because the original loan contract had expired.[113]

Similarly, some courts have held that when a contract between two parties expires, and the parties subsequently resume business without re-incorporating the provisions of the prior contract (including the arbitration clause), arbitration of disputes arising from the subsequent relationship is not required.[114]

Other courts, however, have held that an arbitration clause generally survives the termination of the contract.[115] It is not clear whether the arbitration clause survives indefinitely, or only for a "reasonable" time after the termination of the contract. One court found that claims arising from events which "followed on the heels" of the agreement were arbitrable, but suggested that they might not be arbitrable if they occurred a significant time after the expiration of the agreement.[116] In the employment area a court has required arbitration of employment disputes occurring after the termination of the written employment agreement if the employee continued to work for the employer, reasoning that the employee's decision to continue to work for the employer extended the terms of the employment agreement, including the arbitration clause.[117] Finally, one court has held that the question whether an arbitration agreement has expired and therefore does not apply to the plaintiff's claims is a question that must be decided by an arbitrator rather than a court.[118]

The United States Supreme Court has given some guidance regarding the survival of arbitration clauses following the termination of the contract in the context of collective

---

109   DEX Media, Inc. v. Nat'l Mgmt. Services, Inc., 150 P.3d 1093, 1097 (Or. Ct. App. 2007); *see also* Riegelsperger v. Siller, 150 P.3d 764 (Cal. 2007) (arbitration clause between doctor and patient that covered all those who treated patient "now or in the future" required arbitration of medical malpractice claims arising from treatment for a separate medical condition than the one leading to the treatment under which the contract originated).

110   *Cf.* Riley Mfg. Co. v. Anchor Glass Container Corp., 157 F.3d 775, 781 (10th Cir. 1998) (for a dispute to be considered as "arising under" a previous agreement, it must relate to events which occurred in part while the agreement was still in effect or involve rights which vested or accrued during the life of the contract); DEX Media, Inc. v. Nat'l Mgmt. Services, Inc., 150 P.3d 1093, 1097 (Or. Ct. App. 2007) (interpreting arbitration clause that explicitly applied to claims occurring after termination of the contract to apply to such claims "as long as [they] relate[] to the Agreement").

111   Green Tree Servicing, L.L.C. v. Fisher, 162 P.3d 944 (Okla. Civ. App. 2007); *see also* Gitgood v. Howard-Pontiac-GMC, Inc., 57 P.3d 875 (Okla. Civ. App. 2002) (automobile buyer's trespass action against seller for repossessing her car arose after the termination of the sales agreement and was not arbitrable).

112   *Green Tree Servicing, L.L.C.*, 162 P.3d at 948.

113   *See* Smith v. Steinkamp, 318 F.3d 775, 778 (7th Cir. 2003) (when contract failed to reference future events claims occurring after the expiration of the contract were not subject to arbitration); *see also* Kaplan v. First Options of Chicago, Inc., 19 F.3d 1503 (3d Cir. 1994) (arbitration was not required because the agreement with the arbitration clause was terminated prior to the occurrence of the action forming the basis of the plaintiff's claim), *aff'd*, 514 U.S. 938 (1995).

114   Nissan N. Am., Inc. v. Jim M'Lady Oldsmobile, 307 F.3d 601 (7th Cir. 2002); Colorama Paints & Equip., Inc., 2007 WL 129057, at *2–*3 (D. P.R. Jan. 12, 2007).

115   *See, e.g.*, Sweet Dreams Unlimited, Inc. v. Dial-A-Mattress Int'l, Ltd., 1 F.3d 639, 643–644 (7th Cir. 1993) (an arbitration clause lives on for a reasonable time after the termination of the agreement); Goshawk Dedicated Ltd. v. Portsmouth Settlement Co. I, 466 F. Supp. 2d 1293, 1300 (N.D. Ga. 2006) ("[I]t is well-settled that an arbitration clause may be enforced after the *termination* of a contract. . . . As the Supreme Court has reasoned, an arbitration provision may survive the termination of a contract because it is a 'structural provision' that relates to remedies and dispute resolution, and not an obligation concerning performance.").

116   Sweet Dreams Unlimited, Inc. v. Dial-A-Mattress Int'l, Ltd., 1 F.3d 639, 643–644 (7th Cir. 1993) (suggesting that a claim occurring six months after the expiration of the contract might come too late to be covered by the contract's arbitration clause).

117   *See* George v. LeBeau, 455 F.3d 92 (2d Cir. 2006); *see also* Signavong v. Volt Mgmt. Corp., 2007 WL 1813845 (W.D. Wash. June 21, 2007) (one-month gap between temporary employee's first work assignment and second work assignment was insufficient to terminate arbitration clause contained in contract that she signed for her first assignment, and that a dispute arising from the second assignment was subject to arbitration). *But see* Cornell v. Harmony Homes, Inc., 2007 WL 38132 (D. Colo. Jan. 4, 2007) (employment contract that by its terms only went through December 2002 did not apply to employment discrimination claim arising in 2004, even though the plaintiff continued to work for the defendant after December 2002).

118   Rockwood Automatic Mach., Inc. v. Lear Corp., 13 Misc. 3d 1219, 831 N.Y.S.2d 349 (Sup. Ct. 2006).

bargaining agreements. In that context the Supreme Court adopted a presumption that disputes arising out of a contractual relationship are arbitrable, even if they occur after termination of the contract.[119] The Court however later clarified in *Litton Financial Printing Division v. National Labor Relations Board* that the presumption applies only to disputes "arising out of the contract" and held that a post-expiration grievance arises under the contract only if (1) it involves facts or occurrences that arose before the contract expired; (2) the action infringes rights that accrued or vested during the agreement; or (3) the rights at issue would survive expiration of the agreement under normal contract principles.[120] The Court has not ruled on whether these principles apply outside of the context of collective bargaining agreements, and lower courts have gone in different directions on that question.[121]

7.3.6 Whether an Arbitration Clause in One Contract Applies to Claims Arising from an Earlier or Later Contract Between the Same Parties

Another issue that relates to both the substantive and temporal scope of arbitration agreements is whether an arbitration agreement contained in one contract applies to claims arising out of a second contract between the same parties (whether entered into before, after, or contemporaneously with the first contract).[122] Generally, unless the agreement with the arbitration clause specifically references the other contract, the arbitration agreement should not apply to disputes arising out of the other contract.[123] This is true even if the two contracts are closely intertwined.[124] Thus if the first contract does not contain an arbitration clause, but a second contract does have such a clause relating to disputes under the second contract, the arbitration clause does not apply to disputes relating to the earlier contract.[125] For example, a clause in a subsequent contract that requires arbitration of disputes relating to "this agreement" does not require arbitration of claims relating to the original agreement signed by the parties.[126] This rule applies even if the second contract containing an arbitration clause also contains a merger clause indicating that it constitutes the entire agreement between the parties.[127] However, if the

---

119 Nolde Bros. v. Local No. 358, Bakery & Confectionery Workers Union, 430 U.S. 243, 253–255, 97 S. Ct. 1067, 51 L. Ed. 2d 300 (1977).
120 Litton Fin. Printing Div. v. Nat'l Labor Relations Bd., 501 U.S. 190, 205–206, 111 S. Ct. 2215, 115 L. Ed. 2d 177 (1991).
121 *Compare, e.g.*, Sweet Dreams Int'l, Inc., 1 F.3d 639, 643–644 (applying the *Nolde Bros.* presumption without discussing *Litton Fin. Printing Div.*) *and* Rockwood Automatic Mach., Inc. v. Lear Corp., 13 Misc. 3d 1219, 831 N.Y.S.2d 349 (Sup. Ct. 2006) (holding that the *Nolde Bros.* presumption should apply to ordinary commercial disputes and that the limitations of *Litton Fin. Printing Div.* are limited to the collective bargaining arena) *with* Klay v. All Defendants, 389 F.3d 1191, 1203 (11th Cir. 2004) (applying *Litton Fin. Printing Div.*); Nissan N. Am., Inc. v. Jim M'Lady Oldsmobile, Inc., 307 F.3d 601 (7th Cir. 2002) (applying *Litton Fin. Printing Div.* to commercial dispute); Riley Mfg. Co. v. Anchor Glass Container Corp., 175 F.3d 775, 781 (10th Cir. 1998) (same) *and* Cornell v. Harmony Homes, Inc., 2007 WL 38132 (D. Colo. Jan. 4, 2007) (same).
122 *See, e.g.*, Klay v. All Defendants, 389 F.3d 1191, 1201 (11th Cir. 2004) ("Because arbitration can only be compelled when the subject of the dispute has been agreed to be settled by arbitration, having one contract that contains a broad arbitration agreement does not necessarily mean that arbitration can be compelled when the subject of the dispute arises from a second contract which does not have an arbitration clause.").
123 Suburban Leisure Ctr., Inc. v. AMF Bowling Products, Inc., 468 F.3d 523, 526–527 (8th Cir. 2006) (arbitration clause in contract for delivery and installation of products sold by licensee did not apply to dispute arising out of agreement for the promotion and sale of products); United States Small Bus. Admin. v. Chimicles, 447 F.3d 207 (3d Cir. 2006) (arbitration clause in one agreement did not require arbitration of dispute arising out of separate agreement); Alticor, Inc. v. Nat'l Union Fire Ins. Co., 411 F.3d 669 (6th Cir. 2005); Bouriez v. Carnegie Mellon Univ., 359 F.3d 292, 295 (3d Cir. 2004) ("A dispute that arises under one agreement may be litigated notwithstanding an arbitration clause in a second agreement, even where the two agreements are closely intertwined."); Rosenblum v. Travelbuys.com Ltd., 299 F.3d 657 (7th Cir. 2002) (arbitration clause in employment agreement did not require arbitration of dispute arising out of separate acquisition agreement between the parties); Seaboard Coast Line R.R. Co. v. Trailer Train Co., 690 F.2d 1343 (11th Cir. 1982); Colorama Paints & Equip., Inc. v. Akzo Nobel Coatings, Inc., 2007 WL 129057, at *2 (D. P.R. Jan. 12, 2007) ("we may not compel arbitration on the assumption that the parties meant for the written arbitration clause to apply with equal force to the second distribution agreement"); Goodrich Cargo Sys. v. Aero Union Corp., 2006 WL 3708065 (N.D. Cal. Dec. 14, 2006) (arbitration clause in second agreement did not apply to dispute arising out of first agreement); Chapman v. Mortgage One Corp., 359 F. Supp. 2d 831, 833–834 (E.D. Mo. 2005); Cho v. Haw. Nissan, Inc., 113 P.3d 223 (Haw. 2005) (table); Rhodes v. Amega Mobile Home Sales, Inc., 186 S.W.3d 793 (Mo. Ct. App. 2006) (home purchaser's claim based on warranty agreement was not subject to arbitration based on arbitration clause in sales contract); Smith v. Grand Imports, Ltd., Cause No. 22062-00533 (Mo. Cir. Ct. Aug 7, 2006), *reprinted at* www.consumerlaw.org/unreported; Sloan Fin. Group, Inc. v. Beckett, 583 S.E.2d 325 (N.C. Ct. App. 2003), *aff'd*, 593 S.E.2d 583 (N.C. 2004) (table); Woodhaven Homes, Inc. v. Alford, 143 S.W.3d 202 (Tex. App. 2004).
124 *See* Bouriez v. Carnegie Mellon Univ., 359 F.3d 292, 295 (3d Cir. 2004) ("A dispute that arises under one agreement may be litigated notwithstanding an arbitration clause in a second agreement, even where the two agreements are closely intertwined.").
125 Verizon Advanced Data, Inc. v. Frognet, Inc., 2006 WL 2373265 (S.D. Ohio Aug. 14, 2006); Haga v. Martin Homes, Inc., 2000 WL 1133267 (Ohio Ct. App. Aug. 4, 2000) (arbitration clause in one contract does not apply to disputes based on different contract).
126 Alticor, Inc. v. Nat'l Union Fire Ins. Co., 411 F.3d 669 (6th Cir. 2005).
127 *See* § 6.7.4, *supra*.

second contract contains a broadly worded arbitration clause, a claim based on the first contract (with no arbitration clause) may be subject to arbitration if it is "related to" the second contract.[128]

The same rules apply when the first contract contains an arbitration clause, and the dispute between the parties pertains to a second contract with no arbitration clause. Generally arbitration of those claims is not required.[129] For example, when a home buyer rescinds an original mortgage contract containing an arbitration agreement and subsequently agrees to a new mortgage contract that does not contain an arbitration clause, the second agreement does not revive the terms, including the arbitration clause, of the first agreement.[130] However when a party signs an arbitration clause that explicitly applies to future claims it may cover claims arising from disputes relating to subsequent contracts or agreements between the same parties, even if the subsequent agreements do not include separate arbitration clauses.[131]

7.3.7 When Some Claims Are Within the Arbitration Clause's Scope and Some Are Not

Sometimes certain claims fall outside the scope of an arbitration agreement and other claims come within its scope. In this situation, a court could theoretically require that all claims be arbitrated, that all claims be litigated, or that two separate proceedings go forward: an arbitration of claims subject to the arbitration agreement and a judicial proceeding resolving claims that are not subject to the agreement.[132]

Of course, the parties can always waive their arbitration agreement and consolidate the whole case in the judicial proceeding, or agree to arbitrate the whole case. But when they do not agree, the issue that arises—when certain claims are subject to arbitration and certain claims are not—is whether a party can require that all claims be arbitrated or, conversely, whether a party can insist that none of the claims be arbitrated.

The Supreme Court in *Dean Witter Reynolds, Inc. v. Byrd*[133] held that when some claims fall within an arbitration clause and other claims fall outside it, only the arbitrable claims must be arbitrated and that parties are not required to arbitrate their other claims. According to the *Byrd* Court, even if sending all claims to arbitration would be the most efficient or effective procedure, the purpose of the Federal Arbitration Act is not to further economy in conflict resolution but to require arbitration whenever the parties agree to be bound by arbitration.[134] The converse also is true; the court cannot force the non-arbitrable claims into arbitration because it would run counter to the parties' intent. In *Byrd*, therefore, litigation of the non-arbitrable federal law claim was allowed to proceed. Likewise, when one claim is specifically governed by an arbitration clause and the other is not, the second cannot be subject to arbitration even if the two arise from a common nucleus of facts, unless the two claims are "substantially identical."[135] Claims are not substantially identical if they are legally independent or if they depend upon different legal standards.[136]

Even though the FAA does not permit courts to force non-arbitrable claims into arbitration, courts retain the discretion to either stay the non-arbitrable claims pending resolution of the arbitrable claims in arbitration, or allow the non-arbitrable claims to go forward in litigation while the arbitration proceeds.[137] In exercising that discretion, there is a "heavy presumption . . . that the arbitration and the lawsuit will each proceed in due course,"[138] and therefore

---

128 Drews Distrib. v. Silicon Gaming, Inc., 245 F.3d 347, 350–351 (4th Cir. 2001); Sinclair Broad. Group, Inc. v. Interep Nat'l Radio Sales, Inc., 2005 WL 1000086, at *3 (D. Md. Apr. 28, 2005); Southtrust Bank v. Bowen, 959 So. 2d 624 (Ala. 2006) (counterclaim alleging fraud in connection with promissory note was covered by arbitration clause in a subsequent agreement between the parties stating that it applied to all disputes arising from the contract "or otherwise").

129 *See* Smith v. Steinkamp, 318 F.3d 775 (7th Cir. 2003) (arbitration clause signed at time of original payday loan was not applicable to future payday loans taken by the same borrowers, because these were separate transactions); Nissan N. Am., Inc. v. Jim M'Lady Oldsmobile, 307 F.3d 601, 604 (7th Cir. 2002); Colorama Paints & Equip., Inc. v. Akzo Nobel Coatings, Inc., 2007 WL 129057 (D. P.R. Jan. 12, 2007).

130 Chapman v. Mortgage One Corp., 359 F. Supp. 2d 831, 833–834 (E.D. Mo. 2005); *see also* Breakie v. Ivonyx Group Serv., Inc., 2003 WL 1440098 (Mich. Ct. App. Mar. 20, 2003) (dispute over settlement agreement was not subject to arbitration even though the parties had originally signed an arbitration clause, because the settlement agreement superseded that first contract).

131 Riegelsperger v. Siller, 150 P.3d 764 (Cal. 2007) (arbitration clause between doctor and patient that covered all those who treated patient "now or in the future" required arbitration of medical malpractice claims arising from treatment for a separate medical condition than the one leading to the treatment under which the contract originated).

132 *See* Welborn Clinic v. Medquist, Inc., 301 F.3d 634, 641, 642 (7th Cir. 2002).

133 470 U.S. 213, 105 S. Ct. 1238, 84 L. Ed. 2d 158 (1985).

134 *Id.*; *see also* Broughton v. CIGNA Healthplans, 21 Cal. 4th 1066, 90 Cal. Rptr. 2d 334, 988 P.2d 67 (1999) (requiring court to hear plea for injunctive relief and arbitrator to hear plea for damages concerning the same claim).

135 Simon v. Pfizer, 398 F.3d 765, 774–777 (6th Cir. 2005).

136 *See id.* at 777.

137 Klay v. All Defendants, 389 F.3d 1191, 1204 (11th Cir. 2004) (affirming denial of stay); Coors Brewing Co. v. Molson Breweries, 51 F.3d 1511, 1518 (10th Cir. 1995); Nissan World, L.L.C. v. Mkt. Scan Info. Sys., Inc., 2007 WL 1657350 (D.N.J. June 5, 2007); Captain D's, L.L.C. v. McClenathan, 2006 WL 3409757 (S.D. W. Va. Nov. 27. 2006) (declining to stay non-arbitrable claims); Alfano v. BDO Seidman, L.L.P., 925 A.2d 22 (N.J. Super. Ct. App. Div. 2007).

138 Dean Witter Reynolds, Inc. v. Byrd, 470 U.S. 213, 225, 105 S. Ct. 1238, 84 L. Ed. 2d 158 (1985) (White J., concurring).

courts should ordinarily refuse to stay proceedings and should allow the non-arbitrable claims to proceed if litigation is feasible.[139] Factors affecting whether a court should grant or deny a stay include (1) the risk of inconsistent rulings if the litigation were to proceed because of the likelihood that the arbitration will resolve the disputed issues in the litigation; (2) whether the arbitrable issues are factually inseparable from the non-arbitrable claims; and (3) the prejudice that would result from delaying the litigation.[140]

Although the vast majority of arbitration disputes will be subject to the FAA, in non-FAA cases, state law may dictate different results. For example, courts in both New Jersey and Colorado have found that in cases involving both arbitrable and non-arbitrable claims, judicial economy warrants consolidating all the claims together in court.[141] A court in Texas has taken the opposite approach, finding that, when non-arbitrable claims are inextricably intertwined with arbitrable ones, all claims should be submitted to arbitration.[142] A California statute states that when a party to an arbitration proceeding also is a party to litigation against a third party, the court may either (1) join all claims and parties in a single court proceeding; (2) join some arbitrable claims into the court proceeding; (3) stay the litigation claims pending arbitration, or (4) stay the arbitration in favor of the litigation.[143]

7.4 Application of an Arbitration Agreement to a Non-Signatory

7.4.1 General

A valid, enforceable arbitration agreement generally will require arbitration of disputes between the signatories to the agreement. However legal disputes not only arise between signatories, but also may arise between a signatory and one or more non-signatories to the arbitration agreement. This section addresses whether, and under what circumstances, a non-signatory can be subject to an arbitration clause. Such issues arise in two contexts. One is when a signatory to an arbitration agreement sues a non-signatory, and the non-signatory seeks to compel arbitration of the dispute. The second is when a signatory-defendant seeks to enforce an arbitration clause against a non-signatory plaintiff. In other words, first, can a non-signatory enforce an arbitration clause and second, can a non-signatory be bound by an arbitration clause? Often the analysis used to determine whether a non-signatory can enforce an arbitration clause will be the same used to determine whether a non-signatory can be bound by an arbitration clause. As explained in the following sections, courts in some situations are less likely to enforce an arbitration clause against a non-signatory than in favor of a non-signatory.

Because arbitration is a matter of contract, it should be compelled only when it is consistent with the intent of the contracting parties. Parties generally intend that the contracts they sign apply only to the parties enumerated in the agreement. Consequently the general rule is that a non-party to an arbitration agreement is neither bound by the arbitration agreement nor has the right to enforce the arbitration agreement. With respect to the former, "[i]t goes without saying that a contract cannot bind a non-party."[144] Similarly, a non-party to the arbitration agreement generally lacks the authority to enforce the arbitration agreement against a signatory to the contract.[145]

There are several exceptions to this general rule that may bring non-signatories within the scope of a contractual arbitration clause. Because arbitration is a matter of contract, ordinary principles of contract and agency determine

---

139 Klay v. All Defendants, 389 F.3d 1191, 1204 (11th Cir. 2004).
140 Volkswagen of Am., Inc. v. Sud's of Peoria, Inc., 474 F.3d 966 (7th Cir. 2007); Waste Mgmt., Inc. v. Residuos Industriales Multiquim, S.A. de C.V., 372 F.3d 339, 344 (5th Cir. 2004); AgGrow Oils, L.L.C. v. Nat'l Union Fire Ins. Co., 242 F.3d 777, 783 (8th Cir. 2001); Coors Brewing Co. v. Molson Breweries, 51 F.3d 1511, 1518 (10th Cir. 1995); St. Paul Fire & Marine Ins. Co. v. La Firenza, L.L.C., 2007 WL 2010759, at *3 (M.D. Fla. July 6, 2007); AIG Fin. Advisors, Inc. v. Yim, 2007 WL 1827138 (D. Nev. June 22, 2007); Verizon Advanced Data, Inc. v. Frognet, Inc., 2006 WL 2373265 (S.D. Ohio Aug. 14, 2006); Gossett v. HBL, L.L.C., 2006 WL 1328757 (D.S.C. May 11, 2006) (non-arbitrable claim was stayed pending arbitration); Parfi Holding, AB v. Mirror Image Internet, Inc., 817 A.2d 149 (Del. 2002).
141 Grohn v. Sisters of Charity Health Services, 960 P.2d 722 (Colo. Ct. App. 1998) (holding that when arbitrable and non-arbitrable claims are inextricably intertwined, so that it is difficult to separate out the claims and resolve them independently, then none of the claims should be resolved by arbitration); Garfinkel v. Morristown Obstetrics & Gynecology Associates, Prof'l Ass'n, 773 A.2d 665 (N.J. 2001); cf. Framan Mech., Inc. v. Lakeland Reg'l High Sch. Bd. of Educ., 2005 WL 2877923, at *2 (N.J. Super. Ct. App. Div. Nov. 3, 2005) (noting that it is possible for interrelated disputes to be divided between court and arbitration).
142 See In re Prudential Sec., Inc., 159 S.W.3d 279, 283–284 (Tex. App. 2005) ("Although Lynda's original claims are grounded in legal theories distinct from the claims she brings as assignee under the contract Ned signed, they are factually intertwined and subject to the arbitration provision.").
143 Cal. Civ. Proc. Code § 1281.2(c) (West).
144 Equal Employment Opportunity Comm'n v. Waffle House, Inc., 534 U.S. 279, 294, 122 S. Ct. 754, 151 L. Ed. 2d 755 (2002); see also, e.g., Bridas S.A.P.I.C. v. Gov't of Turkmenistan, 345 F.3d 347, 353 (5th Cir. 2003) ("In order to be subject to arbitral jurisdiction, a party must generally be a signatory to a contract containing an arbitration clause."); Universal Underwriters Life Ins. Co. v. Dutton, 736 So. 2d 564 (Ala. 1999); First Family Fin. Services, Inc. v. Rogers, 736 So. 2d 553 (Ala. 1999); Flores v. Evergreen at San Diego, Inc., 148 Cal. App. 4th 581, 587, 55 Cal. Rptr. 3d 823 (2007) ("Generally, a person who is not a party to an arbitration agreement is not bound by it.").
145 See Britton v. Co-op Banking Group, 4 F.3d 742, 744 (9th Cir. 1993); Ex parte Isbell, 708 So. 2d 571, 577 (Ala. 1997).

whether a non-party to the agreement nonetheless can enforce it or be bound by it.[146] Courts have recognized several contract and agency theories for applying arbitration clauses to non-parties, including (1) equitable estoppel, (2) third-party beneficiary, (3) agency, (4) incorporation by reference of the contract containing the arbitration clause, (5) assignment, and (6) alter ego.[147] The sections below address some of the most commonly applied exceptions.

However, these exceptions are just that, and courts should allow "a nonsignatory to invoke an arbitration agreement only in rare circumstances."[148] Unless one of these doctrines applies, the mere fact that a non-signatory and a signatory share a close relationship—such as husband and wife or parent and child—often will not be sufficient to subject the non-signatory to the arbitration clause.[149] For example, the Fifth Circuit held that the children of mobile home owners could not be forced to arbitrate their personal injury claims against the mobile home manufacturer, even though the children's parents agreed to arbitrate their own claims.[150] A different result may be reached, however, when a child is an intended beneficiary of a parent's contract and courts in those situations have found that a child can be bound by an arbitration clause signed by the parent.[151] Also a consumer may not be bound by an arbitration agreement when the consumer only signed the financing agreement, and another consumer signed the sales agreement that contained the arbitration clause.[152]

If none of the above exceptions apply consumers should be able avoid the explicit language of the arbitration clause by bringing a court action against an individual or company not named in the arbitration clause. Indeed, courts have allowed plaintiffs to avoid arbitration of claims against a non-signatory in such circumstances.[153]

The specific language of the arbitration clause at issue also may affect a court's willingness to extend an arbitration clause to cover non-parties. When an arbitration clause specifically mentions the parties subject to the arbitration clause by name, courts appear less inclined to interpret the agreement to cover non-parties or to apply one of the

---

146 *See, e.g.*, Zurich Am. Ins. Co. v. Watts Indus., Inc., 417 F.3d 682, 687 (7th Cir. 2005); Bridas S.A.P.I.C. v. Gov't of Turkmenistan, 345 F.3d 347, 356 (5th Cir. 2003); E.I. DuPont de Nemours & Co. v. Rhone Poulenc, 269 F.3d 187, 195–197 (3d Cir. 2001); Thomson-CSF, S.A. v. Am. Arbitration Ass'n, 64 F.3d 773, 776 (2d Cir. 1995); Alliance Title Co. v. Boucher, 25 Cal. Rptr. 3d 440, 444 (Ct. App. 2005); Mohamed v. Auto Nation USA Corp., 2002 WL 31429859, at *4 (Tex. App. Oct. 31, 2002) ("[A]n entity that was not a party to the arbitration agreement may not enforce the agreement's provisions unless that non-signatory entity falls into an exception, recognized under general equitable or contract law, that would allow such enforcement.").

147 *See, e.g., Bridas*, 347 F.3d at 356; *E.I. DuPont de Nemours & Co.*, 269 F.3d at 195–197; *Thomson-CSF, S.A.*, 64 F.3d at 776.

148 Westmoreland v. Sadoux, 299 F.3d 462, 465 (5th Cir. 2002).

149 *Ex parte* Dickinson, 711 So. 2d 984 (Ala. 1998) (signature of husband did not bind wife); Flores v. Evergreen at San Diego, Inc., 148 Cal. App. 4th 581, 587, 55 Cal. Rptr. 3d 823 (2007) (signature of husband did not bind wife); Snyder v. Belmont Homes, Inc., 899 So. 2d 57, 64 (La. Ct. App. 2005) (refusing to compel arbitration of child's claim on the basis of arbitration clause signed by parents because under state law, a child is not bound by parent's contract); Finney v. Nat'l Health Care Corp., 193 S.W.3d 393 (Mo. Ct. App. 2006) (daughter who signed nursing home agreement on behalf of her mother was not required to arbitrate wrongful death claims because only claims on behalf of her mother, rather than her own personal claims, were subject to arbitration); *In re* Kepka, 178 S.W.3d 279 (Tex. App. 2005) (wife who signed arbitration agreement with nursing home as legal representative of her husband was not required to arbitrate wrongful death claim that was personal to her and was not brought in her representative capacity). *But see* Fluehmann v. Assoc. Fin. Services, 2002 WL 500564 (D. Mass. Mar. 29, 2002) (finding wife bound by husband's signature on mortgage documents because wife "exploited or benefited from" the contract); Garrison v. Super. Ct., 132 Cal. App. 4th 253, 264, 33 Cal. Rptr. 3d 350 (2005) (noting that spouses can bind one another under California law); Hansford v. Cappaert Manufactured Hous., 911 So. 2d 901, 905 (La. Ct. App. 2005) (husband's signature on mobile home purchase agreement bound wife to arbitration clause because "the buyers of the home were presumably husband and wife"); Le Gere v. New Millenium Homes, 2003 WL 23018774, at *5 (Mich. Ct. App. Dec. 23, 2003) (non-signatory wife acting jointly with signatory husband in mobile home purchase assented to be bound by arbitration clause in purchase contained in the purchase agreement).

150 Fleetwood Enterprises, Inc. v. Gaskamp, 280 F.3d 1069 (5th Cir. 2002); *see also* Costanza v. Allstate Ins. Co., 2002 WL 31528447, at *7 (E.D. La. Nov. 12, 2002); Accomazzo v. CEDU Educ. Services, Inc., 15 P.3d 1153, 1156 (Idaho 2000); Snyder v. Belmont Homes, Inc., 899 So. 2d 57, 64 (La. Ct. App. 2005) (refusal to compel arbitration of child's claim on the basis of arbitration clause signed by parents because under state law a child is not bound by parent's contract).

151 *See* Global Travel Mktg., Inc. v. Shea, 908 So. 2d 392 (Fla. 2005) (non-signatory child's claims were arbitrable when parent signed arbitration clause on behalf of the child); Hojnowski v. Vans Skate Park, 901 A.2d 381 (N.J. 2006) (arbitration clause signed by parent on behalf of child was enforceable as to claims brought by child); *In re* Weekley Homes, Ltd. P'ship, 180 S.W.3d 127 (Tex. 2005).

152 Sikes v. Ganley Pontiac Honda, 2001 WL 1075726 (Ohio Ct. App. Sept. 13, 2001).

153 *See* Sarhank Group v. Oracle Corp., 404 F.3d 657, 662 (2d Cir. 2005); Klay v. All Defendants, 389 F.3d 1191, 1201–1202 (11th Cir. 2004); Sadler v. Green Tree Servicing, L.L.C., 2005 WL 2464208 (W.D. Mo. Oct. 5, 2005), *vacated and remanded on other grounds*, 466 F.3d 623 (8th Cir. 2006); Jim Burke Auto., Inc. v. McGrue, 826 So. 2d 122 (Ala. 2002); Oakwood Mobile Homes, Inc. v. Godsey, 824 So. 2d 713 (Ala. 2001); Monsanto Co. v. Benton Farm, 813 So. 2d 867 (Ala. 2001); Equifirst Corp. v. Ware, 808 So. 2d 1 (Ala. 2001); Parkway Dodge, Inc. v. Yarbrough, 779 So. 2d 1205 (Ala. 2000); Med Ctr. Cars, Inc. v. Smith, 727 So. 2d 9 (Ala. 1998); Hansford v. Cappaert Manufactured Hous., 911 So. 2d 901, 906 (La. Ct. App. 2005) (consumer who signed arbitration clause with housing manufacturer was not required to arbitrate claim brought against housing retailer when retailer was not identified in the agreement); *cf.* Tittle v. Enron Corp., 463 F.3d 410 (5th Cir. 2006) (arbitration clause between insurer and insureds did not apply to disputes between the insureds).

above-listed exceptions.[154] However, if an arbitration clause is written more generally to apply to disputes between "the parties," then the agreement will cover non-signatory parties when contract and agency principles require it.[155]

Although courts agree that under the Federal Arbitration Act (FAA) state contract law determines whether the parties have formed a valid agreement to arbitrate,[156] they have not reached agreement regarding whether state contract law or federal common law determines the applicability of an arbitration clause to a non-party.[157] Some courts have held that non-signatory questions are determined exclusively by federal law,[158] some have held that federal law governs, but that state law provides helpful guidance,[159] some have suggested that state law applies,[160] and some have simply applied state law without addressing whether state or federal law applies.[161] In any event federal and state law will often be similar enough that the choice of law will not affect the outcome.[162]

7.4.2 Equitable Estoppel

7.4.2.1 Overview

Courts sometimes find that a party not mentioned in the arbitration agreement can still enforce the agreement based on the doctrine of equitable estoppel. Estoppel applies when a party attempts to hold the opposing party to the terms of the agreement while simultaneously trying to avoid the agreement's arbitration clause.[163] The principle underlying estoppel is equity, namely that it would be unfair to allow a party to enforce one part of the agreement but not to be bound by another part of the same agreement. The rules for applying equitable estoppel differ based on whether a signatory seeks to enforce an arbitration clause against a signatory to the agreement or whether a signatory to the agreement seeks to enforce the agreement against a non-signatory. The specific differences between the two are described in more detail below, but courts generally are more reluctant to apply equitable estoppel in the latter circumstance than in the former, because "[i]t is one thing to permit a non-signatory to relinquish his right to a jury trial, but quite another to compel him to do so."[164]

---

154 Pullen v. Victory Woodwork, Inc., 2007 WL 1847633, at *3 (E.D. Cal. June 27, 2007) (contract that explicitly governed the rights of the contractor and the owner could not be enforced by a subcontractor); P.L. Services, Ltd. P'ship v. Millenium Constr., Inc., 328 F. Supp. 2d 245 (D. P.R. 2004); Boyd v. Homes of Legend, Inc., 981 F. Supp. 1423 (M.D. Ala. 1997), *remanded on jurisdictional grounds*, 188 F.3d 1294 (11th Cir. 1999), *abrogated on other grounds by* Davis v. S. Energy Homes, Inc., 305 F.3d 1268 (11th Cir. 2002); Wilson v. Waverlee Homes, Inc., 954 F. Supp. 1530, 1534 (M.D. Ala.), *aff'd*, 127 F.3d 40 (11th Cir. 1997); Parkway Dodge, Inc. v. Yarbrough, 779 So. 2d 1205 (Ala. 2000); *see also* Progressive Cas. Ins. Co. v. C.A. Reaseguradora Nacional de Venezuela, 991 F.2d 42, 47–48 (2d Cir. 1993) (a contract that identifies specific parties may be limited to those parties, but a contract that uses the term "parties" generically will not exclude non-signatories); *cf.* InterGen N.V. v. Grina, 344 F.3d 134, 146 (1st Cir. 2003) ("the law requires 'special clarity' to support a finding that the contracting parties intended to confer a benefit on a third party"; arbitration clause limited to defined buyer and seller did not evince an intent to benefit other parties).

155 *See, e.g.*, Progressive Cas. Ins. Co. v. C.A. Reaseguradora Nacional de Venezuela, 991 F.2d 42, 47–48 (2d Cir. 1993) (a contract that identifies specific parties may be limited to those parties, but a contract that uses the term "parties" generically will not exclude non-signatories).

156 *See* § 3.4.2, *supra*.

157 *See* J.P. Morgan Chase & Co. v. Conegie *ex rel.* Lee, 2007 WL 2028926 (5th Cir. July 26, 2007) (recognizing divergent decisions); Wood v. Pentex Res., Ltd. P'ship, 458 F. Supp. 2d 355, 361 (S.D. Tex. 2006) (recognizing uncertainty on the issue).

158 R.J. Griffin & Co. v. Beach Club II Homeowners Ass'n, 384 F.3d 157, 160 n.1 (4th Cir. 2004); Wash. Mut. Fin. Group, L.L.C. v. Bailey, 364 F.3d 260, 267 n.6 (5th Cir. 2004); Chew v. KPMG, L.L.P., 407 F. Supp. 2d 790, 800 n.10 (S.D. Miss. 2006); Alliance Title Co. v. Boucher, 25 Cal. Rptr. 3d 440, 443 (Ct. App. 2005) ("The question presented, then, is whether defendant, a nonsignatory to the June 5, 2003 employment agreement, can rely on it to compel plaintiff to arbitrate his claims. Under the United States Arbitration Act, that question is answered not by state law, but by the federal substantive law of arbitrability."); *In re* Kellogg, Brown & Root, Inc., 166 S.W.3d 732, 738–739 (Tex. 2005) (holding that federal law governs whether a non-signatory is bound by an arbitration clause).

159 Flink v. Carlson, 856 F.2d 44, 45 (8th Cir. 1988).

160 Fleetwood Enter., Inc. v. Gaskamp, 269 F.3d 1069, 1074–1075 (5th Cir. 2002); Ervin v. Nokia, Inc., 812 N.E.2d 534, 541–543 (Ill. App. Ct. 2004) (applying Illinois law and rejecting broader federal rule); *In re* Weekley Homes, 180 S.W.3d 127, 131–132 (Tex. 2005) ("We apply state law while endeavoring to keep it as consistent as possible with federal law.").

161 *See, e.g.*, Trippe Mfg. Co. v. Niles Audio Corp., 401 F.3d 529, 532–533 (3d Cir. 2005) (N.Y. law); R.J. Griffin & Co. v. Beach Club II Homeowners Ass'n, Inc., 384 F.3d 157, 164–166 (4th Cir. 2004) (stating that federal law governs but applying South Carolina law to determine third-party beneficiary status); E.I. DuPont de Nemours & Co. v. Rhone Poulenc Fiber & Resin Intermediates, S.A.S., 269 F.3d 187, 195–197 (3d Cir. 2001) (Del. law); Siebert v. Amateur Athletic Union of the United States, Inc., 422 F. Supp. 2d 1033, 1039 (D. Minn. 2006) (looking to state law and applying Minnesota law).

162 *See, e.g.*, J.P. Morgan Chase & Co. v. Conegie *ex rel.* Lee, 2007 WL 2028926 (5th Cir. July 26, 2007) (finding that principles of estoppel bound non-party to arbitration agreement under both federal and Mississippi law).

163 *See, e.g.*, R.J. Griffin & Co. v. Beach Club II Homeowners Ass'n, 384 F.3d 157, 161 (4th Cir. 2004).

164 Bridas, S.A.P.I.C. v. Gov't of Turkmenistan, 345 F.3d 347, 361 (5th Cir. 2003); Merrill Lynch Inv. Managers v. Optibase, Ltd., 337 F.3d 125, 131 (2d Cir. 2003) (noting the distinction between a willing non-signatory and unwilling non-signatory); E.I. Dupont de Nemours & Co. v. Rhone Poulenc Fiber & Resin Intermediates, 269 F.3d 187 (3d Cir. 2001); MAG Portfolio Consultant, GMBH v. Merlin Biomed Group, 268 F.3d 58 (2d Cir. 2001); Wood v. Pentex Res., Ltd. P'ship, 458 F. Supp. 2d 355 (S.D. Tex. 2006); Bensara v. Marciano, 92 Cal. App. 4th 991 (2001).

Even when the doctrine of estoppel might otherwise apply, two federal circuit courts have held that equitable estoppel cannot form the basis for a petition to compel arbitration under section 4 of the Federal Arbitration Act (FAA). In *DSMC Inc. v. Convera Corp.*,[165] the District of Columbia Circuit held that, under section 4, a party may only compel arbitration when there has been an alleged failure to arbitrate "under a written agreement to arbitrate."[166] Because equitable estoppel applies only in the absence of a written agreement to arbitrate between the parties to the dispute (because one of the parties to the dispute is not a party to the contract containing the arbitration agreement), the court held that the doctrine does not fit within the framework of the FAA.[167] The Tenth Circuit reached the same conclusion in *In re Universal Service Fund Telephone Billing Practices Litigation*, in which it held that sections 3 and 4 of the FAA apply only to "written agreements" to arbitrate, and therefore excludes attempts to compel arbitration on estoppel grounds.[168] The Second Circuit, however, has rejected the view of these two circuits and held that the doctrine of equitable estoppel is fully consistent with the FAA.[169]

Additionally one court in Pennsylvania has held that Pennsylvania law does not recognize equitable estoppel as a basis for bringing a non-signatory within the scope of a contractual arbitration clause.[170] This decision, however, appears fairly unique, and consumer advocates should generally assume that the doctrine of equitable estoppel applies in some form in their respective jurisdictions.

7.4.2.2 Equitable Estoppel When a Non-Signatory Seeks to Enforce the Arbitration Agreement

When a non-signatory defendant seeks to compel arbitration against a signatory plaintiff, estoppel will apply in two circumstances. First, estoppel applies when "the signatory to a written agreement containing an arbitration clause must rely on the terms of the agreement in asserting claims against the non-signatory."[171] A claim relies on the contract if it makes reference to the contract, presumes the existence of the contract, or attempts to hold the non-signatory party to the terms of the contract.[172] In other words, if a signatory

---

165 DSMC Inc. v. Convera Corp., 349 F.3d 679 (D.C. Cir. 2003).
166 Id. at 683 (quoting 9 U.S.C. § 4); see also In re Universal Serv. Fund Tel. Billing Practice Litig., 428 F.3d 940, 942–944 (10th Cir. 2005) (holding that sections 3 and 4 of the FAA apply only to written arbitration agreements).
167 See DSMC Inc. v. Convera Corp., 349 F.3d 679 (D.C. Cir. 2003) ("What we do decide is that an effort to compel arbitration in such circumstances on the basis of equitable estoppel does not fall within Section 4 of the FAA."); see also In re Universal Serv. Fund Tel. Billing Practice Litig., 428 F.3d 940, 942–944 (10th Cir. 2005) (holding that equitable estoppel is not based on a written agreement to arbitrate and therefore does not fall within the rubric of sections 3 and 4 of the FAA).
168 In re Universal Serv. Fund Tel. Billing Practice Litig., 428 F.3d 940, 942–944 (10th Cir. 2005).
169 Ross v. Am. Express Co., 478 F.3d 96 (2d Cir. 2007).
170 Salkin v. MasterCard Int'l, Inc., 77 Pa. D & C.4th 39, 45–46 (Pa. C.P. 2005).
171 Grigson v. Creative Artists Agency, L.L.C., 210 F.3d 524, 527 (5th Cir. 2000); see Am. Bankers Ins. Group, Inc. v. Long, 453 F.3d 623 (4th Cir. 2006) (signatory consumer); CD Partners, L.L.C. v. Grizzle, 424 F.3d 795, 800 (8th Cir. 2005); Brantley v. Republic Mortgage Ins. Co., 424 F.3d 392, 395–396 (4th Cir. 2005); InterGen N.V. v. Grina, 344 F.3d 134, 145 (1st Cir. 2003); Choctaw Generation Ltd. P'ship v. Am. Home Assurance Co., 271 F.3d 403 (2d Cir. 2001) (estoppel applies if the claims "are intertwined with the agreement that the estopped party has signed"); E.I. Dupont de Nemours & Co. v. Rhone Poulenc Fiber & Resin Intermediates, 269 F.3d 187, 199–200 (3d Cir. 2001) (estoppel applies if "the claims [are] intimately founded in and intertwined with the underlying contract obligations"); MS Dealer Serv. Corp. v. Franklin, 177 F.3d 942 (11th Cir. 1999), on remand to 1999 WL 495912 (N.D. Ala. July 9, 1999); Vertucci v. Orvis, 2006 WL 1688078, at *5 (D. Conn. May 30, 2006) (holding that, when plaintiff signed contract with a law firm to help repair negative entries on his credit report, equitable estoppel required plaintiff to arbitrate claims that individual attorneys at the firm misused the plaintiff's credit information because such claims were "intertwined" with the underlying contract containing the arbitration clause); Jureczki v. Banc One Texas, 252 F. Supp. 2d 368 (S.D. Tex. 2003), aff'd, 75 Fed. Appx. 272 (5th Cir. 2003); Boyd v. Homes of Legend, Inc., 981 F. Supp. 1423, 1432–1434 (M.D. Ala. 1997) (finding estoppel theory inapplicable to the facts of the case), remanded on jurisdictional grounds, 188 F.3d 1294 (11th Cir. 1999), abrogated on other grounds by Davis v. S. Energy Homes, Inc., 305 F.3d 1268 (11th Cir. 2002); Roberson v. Money Tree, 954 F. Supp. 1519 (M.D. Ala. 1997) (forced-placed insurer can benefit from arbitration provision); Staples v. Money Tree, Inc., 936 F. Supp. 856 (M.D. Ala. 1996); Usina Costa Pinto S.A. Acucar E Alcool v. Louis Dreyfus Sugar Co., 933 F. Supp. 1170 (S.D.N.Y. 1996); In re Knepp, 229 B.R. 821 (Bankr. N.D. Ala. 1999); Ex parte Napier, 723 So. 2d 49 (Ala. 1998); Ex parte Isbell, 708 So. 2d 571 (Ala. 1997)); Alliance Title Co. v. Boucher, 25 Cal. Rptr. 3d 440 (Ct. App. 2005); Luke v. Gentry Realty, Ltd., 96 P.3d 261, 268 (Haw. 2004) ("[A] signatory to an arbitration agreement is estopped from refusing to arbitrate claims against a nonsignatory when the signatory's claims are intertwined with, rather than independent of, the arbitration clause.").
172 Brantley v. Republic Mortgage Ins. Co., 424 F.3d 392, 395–396 (4th Cir. 2005); R.J. Griffin & Co. v. Beach Club II Homeowners Ass'n, Inc., 384 F.3d 157, 164–165 (4th Cir. 2004); In re Humana Inc. Managed Care Litig., 285 F.3d 971 (11th Cir. 2002), rev'd on other grounds sub nom. PacifiCare Health Sys. Inc. v. Book, 538 U.S. 401 (2003); Choctaw Generation Ltd. P'ship v. Am. Home Assurance Co., 271 F.3d 403 (2d Cir. 2001); E.I. Dupont de Nemours & Co. v. Rhone Poulenc Fiber & Resin Intermediates, 269 F.3d 187, 199–200 (3d Cir. 2001); Grigson v. Creative Artists Agency, 210 F.3d 524 (5th Cir. 2000); MS Dealer Serv. Corp. v. Franklin, 177 F.3d 942 (11th Cir. 1999), on remand to 1999 U.S. Dist. LEXIS 10662 (N.D. Ala. July 9, 1999); Thomson-CSF, S.A. v. Am. Arbitration Ass'n, 64 F.3d 773, 779 (2d Cir. 1995); Sunkist Soft Drinks, Inc. v. Sunkist Growers, Inc., 10 F.3d 753 (11th Cir. 1993); Letizia v. Prudential Bache Sec., Inc., 802 F.2d 1185 (9th Cir. 1986); Mundi v. Union Sec. Life Ins. Co., 2007 WL 1574871 (E.D. Cal. May 30, 2007); Kirsh v. Finova Group, Inc., 2007 WL

consumer sues on the contract, then the consumer also is bound by the contract's arbitration clause.

In this sense, the standard for estoppel is similar to the standards that courts employ in determining whether tort and statutory claims fall within the scope of an arbitration clause, and those standards may be helpful in determining whether estoppel applies to a particular claim.[173] As with tort claims, when the consumer's claim does not depend on, or can stand independently of, the contract containing the arbitration agreement, then equitable estoppel should not apply.[174] Also, estoppel ordinarily will not apply simply because of a factual connection between the contract and the claims asserted, or because the claim "touch[es] matters" covered by the contract.[175] The mere fact that the signatory receives benefits from the contract is insufficient to warrant estoppel.[176] Additionally, if there are two agreements and the arbitration clause only appears in one, for estoppel to apply the consumer's claims must be based on the contract containing the arbitration clause, and not on the other agreement.[177] Finally, some jurisdictions will refuse to apply equitable estoppel, even when the consumer is suing on the contract, if the party seeking to compel arbitration has not detrimentally relied on the consumer's actions.[178]

The similarity between the standard for estoppel and the standard for compelling arbitration of tort claims generally

---

1574551 (D.S.C. May 30, 2007); JP Morgan Chase Bank v. Lott, 2007 WL 30271, at *5 (S.D. Miss. Jan. 3, 2007) (automobile fraud claims against bank based on bank's failure to inform the buyer of a preexisting lien were related to agreement and that arbitration was required); Vertucci v. Orvis, 2006 WL 1688078, at *5 (D. Conn. May 30, 2006) (holding that, when plaintiff signed contract with a law firm to help repair negative entries on his credit report, equitable estoppel required plaintiff to arbitrate claims that individual attorneys at the firm misused the plaintiff's credit information because such claims were "intertwined" with the underlying contract containing the arbitration clause); *In re* Currency Conversion Fee Antitrust Litig., 265 F. Supp. 2d 385 (S.D.N.Y. 2003); *In re* Kellogg, Brown & Root, Inc., 166 S.W.3d 732, 740–741 (Tex. 2005); Neatherlin Homes, Inc. v. Love, 2007 WL 700996 (Tex. App. Mar. 8, 2007); *In re* Merrill Lynch, Pierce, Fenner & Smith, Inc., 195 S.W.3d 807 (Tex. App. 2006) (holding that a signatory cannot seek to hold a non-signatory accountable under the contract but also avoid the contractual requirement of arbitration). *But see* I Sports v. IMG Worldwide, Inc., 813 N.E.2d 4, 9 (Ohio Ct. App. 2004) (finding no estoppel because "although I Sports' claims may be dependent upon establishing APE's breach of the agreement, I Sports does not need to rely on the terms of the agreement in asserting its claims").

173 *See* § 7.3.3, *supra*.
174 Brantley v. Republic Mortgage Ins. Co., 424 F.3d 392, 395–396 (4th Cir. 2005) (mortgage insurer could not rely on equitable estoppel to compel consumer to arbitrate Fair Credit Reporting Act claims on the basis of an arbitration contract between the consumer and a mortgage lender when the plaintiff's claims against the insurer were unconnected to the contract); Klay v. All Defendants, 389 F.3d 1191, 1201–1202 (11th Cir. 2004); *In re* Humana Inc. Managed Care Litig., 285 F.3d 971 (11th Cir. 2002), *rev'd on other grounds sub nom.* PacifiCare Health Sys. Inc. v. Book, 538 U.S. 401 (2003); Hill v. GE Power Sys., Inc., 282 F.3d 343 (5th Cir. 2002) (plaintiff's claim did not rely on the express terms of the agreement); Kisner v. Bud's Mobile Homes, 2007 WL 686734, at *6 (S.D. Miss. Mar. 3, 2007) (estoppel inapplicable when consumer's breach of warranty claims against mobile home dealer not related to contract with mobile home seller); Heller v. Deutsche Bank AG, 2005 WL 665052, at *5 (E.D. Pa. Mar. 17, 2005) (plaintiff's claims against bank for marketing and selling an illegal tax shelter strategy were not subject to arbitration because they were independent of any underlying agreement, as "plaintiffs would still have an independent right to recover on their claims against the Deutsche Bank defendants even if the BDO agreement were declared invalid"); Boyd v. Homes of Legend, Inc., 981 F. Supp. 1423 (M.D. Ala. 1997) (estoppel did not require consumer to arbitrate breach of warranty claims against mobile home manufacturer because the claims were not related to contract containing arbitration clause that the consumer signed with the home dealer), *remanded on jurisdictional grounds*, 188 F.3d 1294 (11th Cir. 1999), *abrogated on other grounds by* Davis v. S. Energy Homes, Inc., 305 F.3d 1268 (11th Cir. 2002); Wilson v. Waverlee Homes, Inc., 954 F. Supp. 1530, 1536 (M.D. Ala. 1996) (same), *aff'd*, 127 F.3d 40 (11th Cir. 1997); Matei v. Alioto, 2005 WL 15439 (Cal. Ct. App. Jan. 3, 2005); *In re* Kellogg, Brown & Root, Inc., 166 S.W.3d 732, 740–741 (Tex. 2005) (*quantum meruit* claim not subject to arbitration because it arises independently of the underlying contract); Holcim (Tex.) Ltd. P'ship v. Humboldt Wedag, Inc., 211 S.W.3d 796, 804 (Tex. App. 2006); Merrill Lynch Trust Co. v. Alaniz, 159 S.W.3d 162, 170–171 (Tex. App. 2004) (claim brought by settlers of trust alleging that trustees breached their fiduciary duty by engaging in self-dealing did not depend on the underlying contract); Brown v. Anderson, 102 S.W.3d 245 (Tex. App. 2003). *But see* N. Am. Ins. Co. v. Moore, 2002 WL 31050995, at *3 (N.D. Miss. Aug. 26, 2002) (non-signatory insurer can compel arbitration of insured's claims because those claims are "intertwined" with insured's state court claims against the defendant who signed the arbitration clause), *aff'd*, 2003 WL 21418113 (5th Cir. June 10, 2003) (table).

175 Wachovia Bank v. Schmidt, 445 F.3d 662, 770 (4th Cir. 2006) ("it is far from clear whether a close factual connection between claims and a contract is sufficient in itself to estop a signatory from denying the applicability of the contract's arbitration clause"); Hill v. GE Power Sys., Inc., 282 F.3d 343, 349 (5th Cir. 2002).

176 Wachovia Bank v. Schmidt, 445 F.3d 662, 671 (4th Cir. 2006) ("The fact that a signatory receives benefits from a contract is therefore insufficient, in and of itself, to estop it from asserting that a nonsignatory is not entitled to invoke the contract's arbitration clause.").

177 S. Energy Homes, Inc. v. Kennedy, 774 So. 2d 540 (Ala. 2000); *see also* Mundi v. Union Sec. Life Ins. Co., 2007 WL 1574871, at *12 (E.D. Cal. May 30, 2007); *see also* Carriage Homes v. Channell, 777 So. 2d 83 (Ala. 2000); *In re* Kellogg, Brown & Root, Inc., 166 S.W.3d 732, 740–741 (Tex. 2005) (as applied in action seeking to compel arbitration against non-signatory, arbitration clause in construction subcontract did not require arbitration of claims involving parties higher up in the contracting chain who had not signed an arbitration agreement).

178 *See, e.g.*, Peach v. CIM Ins. Co., 816 N.E.2d 668, 674 (Ill. App. Ct. 2004); Ervin v. Nokia, Inc., 812 N.E.2d 534, 543 (Ill. App. Ct. 2004); *see also* Grigson v. Creative Artists Agency, L.L.C., 210 F.3d 524, 528 (5th Cir. 2000) ("Of course, detrimental reliance is one of the elements for the usual application of equitable estoppel.").

suggests that courts have overreached in applying arbitration clauses to non-signatory defendants by functionally eviscerating the distinction between signatory and non-signatory parties. If estoppel applies whenever the underlying claims relate to the contract, then the only claims to which estoppel does not apply are those that would fall outside the scope of the arbitration clause anyway. In other words, the courts' current interpretation of equitable estoppel suggests that non-signatories can enforce an arbitration clause whenever a signatory can enforce an arbitration clause, thus eliminating any distinction between non-signatories and signatories. Consequently there is some reason to believe that whether a party "relies" on a contract for purposes of non-signatory estoppel should be construed more narrowly than whether a claim has a significant relationship to the contract for purposes of determining if a dispute between two signatories falls within the scope of the contract's arbitration clause.[179] In fact, even if the two standards are very similar doctrinally, courts sometimes have appeared more reluctant to apply an arbitration clause to a non-party on estoppel grounds than to find that a particular tort claim falls outside the scope of an arbitration clause.[180]

Second, equitable estoppel applies "when the signatory to the contract containing an arbitration clause raises allegations of substantially interdependent and concerted misconduct by both the nonsignatory and one or more of the signatories to the contract."[181] Similarly, estoppel likely will apply if the plaintiff's claims against the non-signatory defendant are "inherently inseparable" from claims against the signatory defendant.[182] The Eleventh Circuit has retreated from applying this factor as a basis for estoppel, however, and has held that estoppel will apply only if the signatory's claim depends on the contract.[183] Other courts have held that estoppel can apply when a "sufficiently close" relationship exists between a signatory and a non-signatory, but have offered little guidance as to what makes a particular relationship "sufficiently close."[184]

The mere fact that the consumer sues one party that is a signatory to the agreement and another that is a non-signatory to the agreement is not sufficient on its own for the claims to be "substantially interdependent" for estoppel purposes.[185] Generally a plaintiff must alleges something

---

179 *See, e.g.*, Hill v. GE Power Sys., Inc., 282 F.3d 343, 349 (5th Cir. 2002) (estoppel does not apply simply because the claim touches on the contract containing the arbitration clause).

180 For example, whereas courts have commonly found that fraudulent inducement claims fall within the scope of a contractual arbitration clause even though the fraudulent statements relate to events prior the formation of the contract, see § 7.3.3., *supra*, in Bouriez v. Carnegie Mellon Univ., 359 F.3d 292, 295 (3d Cir. 2004), the Third Circuit refused to apply equitable estoppel to the plaintiff's claim of fraudulent inducement. *See also* InterGen N.V. v. Grina, 344 F.3d 134, 145 (1st Cir. 2003) (misrepresentation claims were not contractual claims and therefore estoppel did not apply to require arbitration of those claims); *cf.* Thomas v. Redman Manufactured Homes, Inc., 244 F. Supp. 2d 1295 (M.D. Ala. 2003) (equitable estoppel principles cannot be used by one non-signatory defendant to compel arbitration against another non-signatory defendant).

181 Westmoreland v. Sadoux, 299 F.3d 462, 466–467 (5th Cir. 2002) (a non-signatory can enforce an arbitration clause "when the signatory to the contract raises allegations of substantially interdependent and concerted misconduct by both the nonsignatory and one or more of the signatories to the contract"); Grigson v. Creative Artists Agency, L.L.C., 210 F.3d 524, 527 (5th Cir. 2000); MS Dealer Serv. Corp. v. Franklin, 177 F.3d 942, 947 (11th Cir. 1999) (allowing a non-signatory to compel arbitration when "the relationship between the signatory and nonsignatory defendants is sufficiently close that only by permitting the nonsignatory to invoke arbitration may evisceration of the underlying arbitration agreement between the parties be avoided"); JP Morgan Chase Bank v. Lott, 2007 WL 30271, at *5 (S.D. Miss. Jan. 3, 2007) (estoppel applied to automobile fraud claims against bank, which was a non-signatory to the underlying auto sale agreement, because the plaintiff alleged a conspiracy between the bank and the auto dealer); Ingstad v. Grant Thornton, L.L.P., 2006 WL 3751204, at *6 (D.N.D. Dec. 19, 2006) (applying estoppel when plaintiff alleged a conspiracy between the signatory defendant and the non-signatory defendant); Orcutt v. Kettering Radiologists, Inc., 199 F. Supp. 2d 746, 752–753 (S.D. Ohio 2002); S. Energy Homes, Inc. v. Gary, 774 So. 2d 521 (Ala. 2000) (when claims must be arbitrated against one defendant, and claims against other defendant are inextricably intertwined with claims against first defendant, then case should proceed in arbitration against both defendants; this holding may be overruled by Jim Burke Auto., Inc. v. McGrue, 826 So. 2d 122 (Ala. 2002)); Luke v. Gentry Realty, Ltd., 96 P.3d 261, 267 (Haw. 2004); *In re* Merrill Lynch, Pierce, Fenner & Smith, Inc., 195 S.W.3d 807 (Tex. App. 2006) (equitable estoppel applies to claims brought against a non-signatory "where the signatory of the contract containing an arbitration clause raises allegations of substantially interdependent and concerted misconduct by both the nonsignatory and one or more of the signatories to the contract").

182 Estoppel can apply when claims are "inherently inseparable" from claims against signatory party. Hill v. GE Power Sys., Inc., 282 F.3d 343, 348 (5th Cir. 2002); *Ex parte* Napier, 723 So. 2d 49, 53–54 (Ala. 1998); Rowe v. Exline, 63 Cal. Rptr. 3d 787 (Ct. App. 2007); Alliance Title Co. v. Boucher, 25 Cal. Rptr. 3d 440, 443–444 (Ct. App. 2005).

183 *In re* Humana Inc. Managed Care Litig., 285 F.3d 971, 976 (11th Cir. 2002) ("The plaintiff's actual dependence on the underlying contract in making out the claim against the nonsignatory defendant is therefore always the *sine qua non* of an appropriate situation for applying equitable estoppel."), *rev'd on other grounds sub nom.* PacifiCare Health Sys. Inc. v. Book, 538 U.S. 401 (2003); *cf.* Grigson v. Creative Artists Agency, L.L.C., 210 F.3d 524, 527–528 (5th Cir. 2000) (noting that equitable estoppel is more likely to be applied when both factors are present rather than just a single factor). *But cf.* Davis v. Becker, 491 F.3d 1292 (11th Cir. 2007) (applying equitable estoppel on the basis of allegations of conspiracy between a signatory defendant and a non-signatory defendant without discussing *Humana*).

184 CD Partners, L.L.C. v. Grizzle, 424 F.3d 795, 798–799 (8th Cir. 2005); Thomson-CSF, S.A. v. Am. Arbitration Ass'n, 64 F.3d 773, 776 (2d Cir. 1995); County of Contra Costa v. Kaiser Found. Health Plan, Inc., 47 Cal. App. 3d 237, 242 (1996).

185 *See, e.g.*, Boyd v. Homes of Legend, Inc., 981 F. Supp. 1423, 1434 (M.D. Ala. 1997) (allegations of separate or parallel misconduct by a signatory and a non-signatory defendant is insufficient to warrant estoppel and that the plaintiff must allege

akin to a conspiracy between the signatory and non-signatory defendants for estoppel to apply.[186]

However, even when a consumer does not allege substantially interdependent conduct, if the consumer sues both a signatory and a non-signatory, the non-signatory can seek a stay of the court proceeding pending the outcome of the arbitration with the other defendant even if it cannot compel arbitration of the claims against it.[187] Thus, consumer advocates should be careful in deciding which defendants to sue even if they are confident that equitable estoppel does not apply.

Even if the elements of estoppel are satisfied, application of estoppel is not mandatory, but rests in the court's discretion.[188] In determining how to exercise its discretion, courts may balance the relative equities of the parties, and may also choose to examine whether the consumer is bringing a claim against a signatory to the agreement in addition to the non-signatory. If the signatory party is not or will not be involved in the arbitration proceeding, then courts may be less likely to find that equitable estoppel applies.[189]

7.4.2.3 Equitable Estoppel When a Signatory Seeks to Enforce the Arbitration Agreement Against a Non-Signatory

The doctrine of equitable estoppel also may apply to bind non-signatory consumers to an arbitration clause. Because courts understandably are more reluctant to bind a non-signatory to an arbitration agreement than to permit a non-signatory to enforce an arbitration agreement, more restrictive standards apply when a party seeks to use estoppel to force a non-signatory into arbitration. Equitable estoppel applies *against* a non-signatory only if the non-signatory seeks to exploit or obtain a direct benefit from the contract containing the arbitration clause.[190] An indirect or tangential benefit is insufficient to give rise to equitable estoppel.[191] The benefit must flow directly from the rights created by the agreement, and not simply from the fact that a contractual relationship exists.[192] If the non-signatory's claim can stand independently of the contract, even if the parties would not have interacted but for the existence of the contract containing the arbitration clause, then equitable estoppel does

---

a conspiracy or other concerted misconduct), *remanded on jurisdictional grounds*, 188 F.3d 1294 (11th Cir. 1999), *abrogated on other grounds by* Davis v. S. Energy Homes, Inc., 305 F.3d 1268 (11th Cir. 2002); *In re* Hartigan, 107 S.W.3d 684, 691–692 (Tex. App. 2003) (plaintiff's allegation that signatory and non-signatory defendants contributed "both individually and severally" to the plaintiff's injuries did not demonstrate concerted misconduct for purposes of estoppel).

186 *See, e.g.,* Becker v. Davis, 491 F.3d 1292 (11th Cir. 2007) (finding estoppel when the plaintiff alleged a conspiracy between the defendants); JP Morgan Chase Bank v. Lott, 2007 WL 30271, at *5 (S.D. Miss. Jan. 3, 2007); Ingstad v. Grant Thornton, L.L.P., 2006 WL 3751204, at *5 (D.N.D. Dec. 19, 2006).

187 *See* § 7.3.7, *supra.*

188 *In re* Humana Inc. Managed Care Litig., 285 F.3d 971, 976 (11th Cir. 2002), *rev'd on other grounds sub nom.* PacifiCare Health Sys. Inc. v. Book, 538 U.S. 401 (2003); Hill v. GE Power Sys., Inc., 282 F.3d 343 (5th Cir. 2002) (district court did not abuse its discretion in denying estoppel even though the elements of estoppel were satisfied); Grigson v. Creative Artists Agency, L.L.C., 210 F.3d 524, 528 (5th Cir. 2000).

189 *In re* Humana Inc. Managed Care Litig., 285 F.3d 971 (11th Cir. 2002), *rev'd on other grounds sub nom.* PacifiCare Health Sys. Inc. v. Book, 538 U.S. 401 (2003); MS Dealer Serv. Corp. v. Franklin, 177 F.3d 942 (11th Cir. 1999), *on remand to* 1999 U.S. Dist. LEXIS 10662 (N.D. Ala. July 9, 1999); *see also* Hansford v. Cappaert Manufactured Hous., 911 So. 2d 901 (La. Ct. App. 2005) (arbitration clause between consumer and housing manufacturer did not require arbitration of claim between consumer and housing retailer).

190 Am. Bankers Ins. Group, Inc. v. Long, 453 F.3d 623 (4th Cir. 2006); Comer v. Micor, Inc., 436 F.3d 1098, 1101 (9th Cir. 2006) (plaintiff's ERISA claim against investment advisor for breach of fiduciary duty did not seek any benefit from the investment contracts between the ERISA plan trustees and the investment advisor); R.J. Griffin & Co. v. Beach Club II Homeowners Ass'n, Inc., 384 F.3d 157, 164–165 (4th Cir. 2004) (estoppel does not apply because plaintiff's claims were based on duties created by law, not by contract); Bridas, S.A.P.I.C. v. Gov't of Turkmenistan, 345 F.3d 347, 361–362 (5th Cir. 2003); E.I. Dupont de Nemours & Co. v. Rhone Poulenc Fiber & Resin Intermediates, 269 F.3d 187, 201–202 (3d Cir. 2001) (equitable estoppel did not apply because there was no evidence that the non-signatory embraced the agreement or received any direct benefit from it); Am. Bureau of Shipping v. Tencara Shipyard S.P.A., 170 F.3d 349, 353 (2d Cir. 1999); Wood v. Pentex Res., Ltd. P'ship, 458 F. Supp. 2d 355, 366 (S.D. Tex. 2006); Best Concrete Mix Corp. v. Lloyd's of London Underwriters, 413 F. Supp. 2d 182, 187 (E.D.N.Y. 2006); Peltz v. Sears, Roebuck & Co., 367 F. Supp. 2d 711, 719 (E.D. Pa. 2005) (non-signatory may be equitably estopped from avoiding arbitration when it "knowingly exploits" the contract containing the arbitration agreement); Boucher v. Alliance Title Co., 25 Cal. Rptr. 3d 440, 444 (Ct. App. 2005); Snyder v. Belmont Homes, Inc., 899 So. 2d 57, 63–64 (La. Ct. App. 2005) (equitable estoppel did not apply when non-signatory did not benefit from the contract containing an arbitration clause); *In re* Kellogg, Brown & Root, Inc., 166 S.W.3d 732, 739 (Tex. 2005); *In re* Merrill Lynch, Pierce, Fenner & Smith, Inc., 195 S.W.3d 807 (Tex. App. 2006).

191 Zurich Am. Ins. Co. v. Watts Indus., Inc., 417 F.3d 682, 688 (7th Cir. 2005) (fact that agreement may have resulted in lower insurance premiums was too indirect to warrant estoppel); Bouriez v. Carnegie Mellon Univ., 359 F.3d 292, 295 (3d Cir. 2004); Thomson-CSF, S.A. v. Am. Arbitration Ass'n, 64 F.3d 773, 778–779 (2d Cir. 1995) (equitable estoppel did not apply when non-signatory only sought an indirect market-based benefit from the contract); Phoenix Companies v. Abrahamsen, 2006 WL 2847812 (S.D.N.Y. Sept. 28, 2006); *In re* Merrill, Lynch, Pierce, Fenner & Smith, Inc., 195 S.W.3d 807 (Tex. App. 2006) (equitable estoppel did not apply when non-signatory's interests were not "strictly derivative" of a signatory's interests).

192 MAG Portfolio Consultant, GMBH v. Merlin Biomed Group, 268 F.3d 58, 61 (2d Cir. 2001) (estoppel does not apply if the benefit results from "the contractual relation of the parties to an agreement" and not from the agreement itself); Coots v. Wachovia Sec., Inc., 304 F. Supp. 2d 694, 699 (D. Md. 2003) (benefit is indirect if it "flows as a result of contract formation").

not apply.[193] Similarly, equitable estoppel does not apply if the non-signatory's legal claims derive from a legal duty created by law rather than by the contract containing the arbitration clause.[194] That the claims are factually related to the contract or would not have occurred absent the existence of a contractual relationship is irrelevant; what is relevant is whether the legal duty at issue derives from the contract.[195]

In evaluating whether a non-signatory seeks a direct benefit from the contract, some courts analyze the legal claims that the non-signatory asserts in litigation. Other courts, however, examine whether the non-signatory received contractual benefits during the life of the contract. A Texas court has held that even if the non-signatory's litigation claims are unrelated to the contract, estoppel still applies if the non-signatory received direct benefits from the performance of the contract.[196] In doing so, the court noted that other courts had examined the benefits received by a party during the life of the contract in applying estoppel, even if they had not adopted an explicit standard to that effect.[197] It remains unclear whether courts outside of Texas will explicitly adopt this additional basis for applying estoppel against a non-signatory party.

Finally, unlike in the situation in which a non-signatory seeks to compel a signatory into arbitration under an estoppel theory, the fact that the non-signatory may have a close relationship or engaged in concerted misconduct with a signatory party is insufficient to estop a non-signatory from avoiding the arbitration clause.[198]

7.4.3 Third Party Beneficiaries

A non-party can also be subject to an arbitration clause if that party is a third party beneficiary of the contract containing the arbitration agreement.[199] Whether a party is a third-party beneficiary is determined according to ordinary contract law principles. Merely receiving contractual benefits is not sufficient to bring a third party within the scope of an arbitration clause.[200] At a minimum, the party alleging

---

193 R.J. Griffin & Co. v. Beach Club II Homeowners Ass'n, Inc., 384 F.3d 157, 164–165 (4th Cir. 2004) (home owners' association's claims against builder for negligence and breach of warranty arose out of legal duties independent of the contract and were not subject to arbitration on an estoppel theory); Bouriez v. Carnegie Mellon Univ., 359 F.3d 292, 295 (3d Cir. 2004) (investor's claim of misrepresentation regarding funding for particular project did not relate to the project agreement); InterGen N.V. v. Grina, 344 F.3d 134, 145 (1st Cir. 2003) (equitable estoppel did not apply because misrepresentation claims were unrelated to the contract); Datatreasury Corp. v. Wells Fargo & Co., 490 F. Supp. 2d 756 (E.D. Tex. 2007) (tax fraud claims unrelated to underlying contract); Chew v. KPMG, L.L.P., 407 F. Supp. 2d 790, 800 (S.D. Miss. 2006); In re Kellogg, Brown & Root, Inc., 166 S.W.3d 732, 740–741 (Tex. 2005); In re Merrill Lynch, Pierce, Fenner & Smith, Inc., 195 S.W.3d 807 (Tex. App. 2006) (investment firm's defamation claims against brokerage firm were independent of the contract containing the arbitration clause and arbitration was not required); see also Comer v. Micor, Inc., 436 F.3d 1098, 1101 (9th Cir. 2006) (plaintiffs' ERISA claim against investment advisor for breach of fiduciary duty did not seek any benefit from the investment contracts between the ERISA plan trustees and the investment advisor). But see Pullen v. Victory Woodwork, Inc., 2007 WL 1847633, at *3 (E.D. Cal. June 27, 2007) (applying estoppel); Griffen v. Alpha Phi Alpha, Inc., 2007 WL 707364, at *7 (E.D. Pa. Mar. 2, 2007) (fraternity pledge's personal injury claim arose from fraternity contract and applying estoppel).

194 R.J. Griffin & Co. v. Beach Club II Homeowners Ass'n, Inc., 384 F.3d 157, 164–165 (4th Cir. 2004); San Francisco Unified Sch. Dist. v. Keenan & Associates, 2007 WL 1417419, at *10 (Cal. Ct. App. May 15, 2007) (estoppel did not apply to a breach of fiduciary duty claim because the duty was created by law rather than by the contract); In re Kellogg, Brown & Root, Inc., 166 S.W.3d 732, 740–741 (Tex. 2005) (quantum meruit claim not arbitrable because the claim is independent of the contract).

195 R.J. Griffin & Co. v. Beach Club II Homeowners Ass'n, Inc., 384 F.3d 157, 163–165 (4th Cir. 2004); San Francisco Unified Sch. Dist. v. Keenan & Associates, 2007 WL 1417419, at *10 (Cal. Ct. App. May 15, 2007).

196 See Wood v. Penntex Res., Ltd. P'ship, 458 F. Supp. 2d 355, 366–373 (S.D. Tex. 2006) (applying Weekley Homes and holding that receiving benefits during the life of the contract can satisfy the elements of estoppel); In re Weekley Homes, 180 S.W.3d 127, 132–133 (Tex. 2005).

197 Weekley Homes, 180 S.W.3d at 132–133 nn.29–32.

198 Bridas S.A.P.I.C. v. Gov't of Turkmenistan, 345 F.3d 347, 360 (5th Cir. 2003) ("a signatory may not estop a nonsignatory from avoiding arbitration regardless of how closely affiliated the nonsignatory is with another signing party"); E.I. Dupont de Nemours & Co. v. Rhone Poulenc Fiber & Resin Intermediates, 269 F.3d 187, 201–202 (3d Cir. 2001) (interrelatedness of claims does not allow application of equitable estoppel against a non-signatory to an arbitration agreement); MAG Portfolio Consultant, GMBH v. Merlin Biomed Group L.L.C., 268 F.3d 58, 62 (2d Cir. 2001); Thomson-CF, SA v. Am. Arbitration Ass'n, 64 F.3d 773, 779 (2d Cir. 1995); Chew v. KPMG, L.L.P., 407 F. Supp. 2d 790, 801 (S.D. Miss. 2006); In re Merrill Lynch, Pierce, Fenner & Smith, Inc., 195 S.W.3d 807 (Tex. App. 2006).

199 J.P. Morgan Chase & Co. v. Conegie ex rel. Lee, 2007 WL 2028926 (5th Cir. July 26, 2007) (third-party beneficiary was required to arbitrate claims arising from nursing home admission agreement); Cont'l Cas. Co. v. Am. Nat'l Ins. Co., 417 F.3d 727, 733–734 (7th Cir. 2005) (third-party beneficiary could enforce arbitration agreement); In re Palm Harbor Homes, 195 S.W.3d 672 (Tex. 2006) (non-signatory home manufacturer could require plaintiff to arbitrate claims against it when the agreement explicitly stated that it was intended to benefit the manufacturer); see Global Travel Mktg., Inc. v. Shea, 908 So. 2d 392 (Fla. 2005) (waiver of liability and arbitration provision signed by parent on behalf of child was enforceable as to claims brought by child); Hojnowski v. Vans Skate Park, 901 A.2d 381 (N.J. 2006) (arbitration clause signed by parent on behalf of child was enforceable as to claims brought by child); LSB Fin. Services, Inc. v. Harrison, 2000 WL 35508810 (N.C. Super. Ct. Feb. 16, 2000) (enforcing arbitration clause against third-party beneficiary).

200 Bridas S.A.P.I.C. v. Gov't of Turkmenistan, 345 F.3d 347, 362 (5th Cir. 2003); InterGen N.V. v. Grina, 344 F.3d 134, 147 (1st Cir. 2003) ("a benefiting third party is not necessarily a third party beneficiary"); San Francisco Unified Sch. Dist. v. Keenan & Associates, 2007 WL 1417419, at *4–*6 (Cal. Ct. App. May 15, 2007).

third-party beneficiary status (either for itself or the opposing party) must show that the parties to the agreement specifically intended to confer the benefits of the agreement on the non-signatory when they signed the arbitration agreement.[201] That a party was not enumerated in the agreement and that the consumer had no reason to suspect that the party would be covered often should be evidence enough to defeat a third-party beneficiary argument.[202] Moreover, even if a non-signatory is a third-party beneficiary, a dispute is not arbitrable unless it arises from the third party's status as a beneficiary to the contract.[203]

While a third-party beneficiary is entitled to enforce an arbitration clause against a signatory to the contract conferring beneficiary status, it is less certain that an arbitration clause can be enforced *against* a third-party beneficiary. Generally, while a third-party beneficiary is entitled to certain benefits under the contract, a beneficiary is not a promisor, does not oblige itself to perform under the contract by virtue of its beneficiary status, and is not responsible for a breach of the contract.[204] Indeed, a third-party benefi-

---

201 Brantley v. Republic Mortgage Ins. Co., 424 F.3d 392, 396–397 (4th Cir. 2005) (no third-party beneficiary); R.J. Griffin & Co. v. Beach Club II Homeowners Ass'n, Inc., 384 F.3d 157, 164–165 (4th Cir. 2004) (same); Bridas S.A.P.I.C. v. Gov't of Turkmenistan, 345 F.3d 347, 362 (5th Cir. 2003) (no third-party beneficiary); E.I. Dupont de Nemours & Co. v. Rhone Poulenc Fiber & Resin Intermediates, 269 F.3d 187, 195 (3d Cir. 2001); Gibson v. Wal-Mart Stores, Inc., 181 F.3d 1163, 1170 n.3 (10th Cir. 1999); Housh v. Dinovo Inv., Inc., 2003 WL 1119526, at *5 (D. Kan. Mar. 7, 2003) (employee could not enforce arbitration clause signed by employer because the agreement did not evince any intent to benefit the employee); Boyd v. Homes of Legend, Inc., 981 F. Supp. 1423 (M.D. Ala. 1997), *remanded on jurisdictional grounds*, 188 F.3d 1294 (11th Cir. 1999), *abrogated on other grounds by* Davis v. S. Energy Homes, Inc., 305 F.3d 1268 (11th Cir. 2002); *see also In re* Palm Harbor Homes, 195 S.W.3d 672 (Tex. 2006) (non-signatory home manufacturer could require plaintiff to arbitrate claims against it when the agreement explicitly stated that it was intended to benefit the manufacturer).

202 *See* Brantley v. Republic Mortgage Ins. Co., 424 F.3d 392, 396–397 (4th Cir. 2005) (mortgage insurer was not third party beneficiary of contract between consumer and mortgage lender because the contract made no reference to the insurer or otherwise evinced any intent to benefit the insurer); R.J. Griffin & Co. v. Beach Club II Homeowners Ass'n, Inc., 384 F.3d 157, 164–165 (4th Cir. 2004); Bridas S.A.P.I.C. v. Gov't of Turkmenistan, 345 F.3d 347, 362 (5th Cir. 2003) (failure to identify beneficiary in the contract showed that party was not a third-party beneficiary); InterGen N.V. v. Grina, 344 F.3d 134, 146 (1st Cir. 2003) ("the law requires 'special clarity' to support a finding that the contracting parties intended to confer a benefit on a third party"; arbitration clause limited to defined buyer and seller did not evince an intent to benefit other parties); McCarthy v. Azure, 22 F.3d 351, 362 (1st Cir. 1994) (a company's employees and agents were not third-party beneficiaries of contract signed by the company and therefore could not enforce the company's arbitration clause); Pack v. Damon Corp., 320 F. Supp. 2d 545 (E.D. Mich. 2004), *rev'd in part on other grounds*, 434 F.3d 810 (6th Cir. 2006); Housh v. Dinovo Inv., Inc., 2003 WL 1119526, at *5 (D. Kan. Mar. 7, 2003) (employee could not enforce arbitration clause signed by employer because the agreement did not evince any intent to benefit the employee); Boyd v. Homes of Legend, Inc., 981 F. Supp. 1423 (M.D. Ala. 1997) (finding third party beneficiary theory inapplicable to the facts of the case), *remanded on jurisdictional grounds*, 188 F.3d 1294 (11th Cir. 1999), *abrogated on other grounds by* Davis v. S. Energy Homes, Inc., 305 F.3d 1268 (11th Cir. 2002); Monsanto Co. v. Benton Farm, 813 So. 2d 867 (Ala. 2001); *Ex parte* Gray, 686 So. 2d 250 (Ala. 1996) (salesman can enforce arbitration agreement entered into by dealership employing the salesperson); Smith v. Microskills San Diego, Ltd. P'ship, 63 Cal. Rptr. 3d 368 (Ct. App. 2007) (third-party beneficiary must be "explicitly identified"); City of Hope v. Cave, 102 Cal. App. 4th 1356, 126 Cal. Rptr. 2d 283 (2002); Everett v. Dickinson & Co., 929 P.2d 10, 14 (Colo. Ct. App. 1996) ("Significantly, the language does not to refer to the introducing broker, which omission we regard as purposeful and from which we can reasonably infer that the parties did not intend that the introducing broker be a beneficiary of the arbitration clause."); Dan Wiebold Ford, Inc. v. Universal Computer Consulting Holding, Inc., 127 P.3d 138 (Idaho 2005); Ervin v. Nokia, Inc., 812 N.E.2d 534, 540–541 (Ill. App. Ct. 2004); *see also* J.P. Morgan Chase & Co. v. Conegie *ex rel.* Lee, 2007 WL 2028926 (5th Cir. July 26, 2007) (nursing home patient was third-party beneficiary of contract that was signed for the purpose of providing nursing care to the patient).

203 E.I. Dupont de Nemours & Co. v. Rhone Poulenc Fiber & Resin Intermediates, 269 F.3d 187, 197–198 (3d Cir. 2001) (third-party beneficiary not bound by arbitration clause because claims for misrepresentation, while arising from the contract, do not arise from the party's beneficiary status); Indus. Elec. Corp. v. iPower Distrib. Group, Inc., 215 F.3d 677, 680 (7th Cir. 2000) (third-party beneficiary non-signatory was not compelled to arbitrate claim because the claims did not arise out of the contract from which it derived its third-party status); Oakwood Mobile Homes, Inc. v. Godsey, 824 So. 2d 713 (Ala. 2001); Equifirst Corp. v. Ware, 808 So. 2d 1 (Ala. 2001); *see also* Crayton v. Conseco Fin. Corp., 237 F. Supp. 2d 1325 (M.D. Ala. 2002) (finding no third party beneficiary status when mobile home purchaser took over financing a mobile home which was in the process of being repossessed from another consumer; even though original contract had contained an arbitration clause, purchaser did not have to arbitrate her claims because her claims were brought under her separate financing agreement with Conseco to take over the first consumer's account); Fluehmann v. Associates Fin. Services, 2002 WL 500564 (D. Mass. Mar. 29, 2002); UBS Fin. Services, Inc. v. Johnson, 943 So. 2d 118 (Ala. 2006); Ballard Services, Inc. v. Conner, 807 So. 2d 519 (Ala. 2001); Greenpoint Credit, L.L.C. v. Reynolds, 151 S.W.3d 868, 874 (Mo. Ct. App. 2005) (non-signatory was not required to arbitrate claims when there was no evidence that contract containing the arbitration clause intended to benefit the non-signatory); Beser v. Miller, 785 N.Y.S.2d 625, 626 (App. Div. 2004) (holding that arbitration clause did not apply to non-signatory petitioner because "[t]here is no evidence establishing that the parties to the brokerage agreement intended petitioner to be bound by the arbitration clause therein and no evidence that petitioner intended to be so bound"); *In re* FirstMerit Bank, 52 S.W.3d 749 (Tex. 2001).

204 *See, e.g.*, Comer v. Micor, 436 F.3d 1098, 1102 (9th Cir. 2006) ("A third party beneficiary might in certain circumstances have the power to sue under a contract; it certainly cannot be *bound* to a contract that it did not sign or otherwise assent to."); Flink v. Carlson, 856 F.2d 44, 46 (8th Cir. 1988) (non-party could not

ciary may not even be aware of the contract conferring beneficiary status, let alone aware of his or her status as a beneficiary. Thus there is a strong argument that requiring a party to submit unwillingly to an arbitration clause in a contract that it did not sign, simply because it happened to be a fortuitous beneficiary of some of the contract's terms, is inconsistent with general contract principles and would be unfair to the beneficiary party.

Nevertheless, several courts have held or indicated that a third-party beneficiary can be bound by a contract containing an arbitration clause when the claims the beneficiary asserts arise out of the contract.[205] In particular courts seem more willing to require a third-party beneficiary to submit claims to arbitration is when a parent signs a contract containing an arbitration agreement on behalf of a child.[206]

7.4.4 Agency

Principles of agency also may subject a non-signatory to an arbitration clause in appropriate circumstances. Salespersons and other employees may argue that they are agents of a merchant or creditor that is a party to an arbitration agreement. As agents of the party that has the right to compel arbitration, they may argue that they also have the right to require that a dispute be arbitrated. Also, defendants often will seek to compel consumers to arbitrate claims by arguing that the signatory party was acting as their agent. Agency questions frequently arise in cases involving elder abuse at nursing homes, as it is often the case that the patient did not sign the admission contract, but that a close family member signed the agreement on the patient's behalf. This section briefly addresses how agency law applies in the arbitration context.

A non-signatory may be subject to an arbitration clause under normal agency principles. Initially, courts will not assume that one party is acting as an agent of another. Rather, courts apply a presumption of independent status, and the party asserting the existence of an agency relationship bears the burden of proof.[207] Indeed, courts sometimes may require very specific evidence of an agency relationship, such as a signature from the principal on the contract as well as the agent, or some other explicit manifestation of an agency relationship.[208]

An agency relationship cannot be created by conduct of the agent alone. There must be some conduct by the principal demonstrating the principal's assent to the agency relationship.[209] This principle may be helpful in nursing home abuse cases when a family member signs an admission agreement on behalf of the patient. Often the patient who is admitted to the nursing home (and against whom the home seeks to compel arbitration) will lack the capacity to manifest his or her assent to the creation of an agency relationship between themselves and the party signing the admission agreement on the patient's behalf.[210]

Once an agency relationship is established, the next question is whether the principal and the agent are subject to the arbitration agreement. Generally a contract signed by an agent of a principal is binding on the principal. Thus courts have found that non-signatory principals are entitled to enforce arbitration agreements signed by their agents,[211] and that non-signatory principals are bound by arbitration agreements signed by their agents.[212]

---

be required to arbitrate under a third-party beneficiary theory because "mere status as a third-party beneficiary (or receipt of benefits) does not bind the beneficiary to perform duties imposed by the contract"); Wood v. Penntex Res., Ltd. P'ship, 458 F. Supp. 2d 355, 373 n.3 (S.D. Tex. 2006) (noting that, under Texas law, a third-party beneficiary is not a promisor and stating that "[t]hird-party beneficiary estoppel does not apply because the doctrine applies to allow a nonparty to enforce the contract under certain circumstances, but not to impose obligations against a third-party that has not sought to enforce its terms").

205 J.P. Morgan Chase & Co. v. Conegie ex rel. Lee, 2007 WL 2028926 (5th Cir. July 26, 2007) (third party beneficiary was required to arbitrate claims arising from nursing home admission agreement); E.I. Dupont de Nemours & Co. v. Rhone Poulenc Fiber & Resin Intermediates, 269 F.3d 187, 197–199 (3d Cir. 2001) (holding that third-party beneficiary is required to arbitrate if the beneficiary's claims arise out of the contract containing the arbitration clause and creating third-party-beneficiary status); Ballard Services, Inc. v. Conner, 807 So. 2d 519 (Ala. 2001); Colonial Sales-Lease-Rental, Inc. v. Target Auction & Land Co., 735 So. 2d 1161 (Ala. 1999); Westendorf v. Gateway 2000, Inc., 2000 Del. Ch. LEXIS 54 (Del. Ch. Ct. Mar. 16, 2000), aff'd, 763 A.2d 92 (Del. 2000); Terminix Int'l Co. v. Ponzio, 693 So. 2d 104 (Fla. Dist. Ct. App. 1997); Greenpoint Credit, L.L.C. v. Reynolds, 151 S.W.3d 868, 874 (Mo. Ct. App. 2005); Beser v. Miller, 785 N.Y.S.2d 625, 626 (App. Div. 2004); LSB Fin. Services, Inc. v. Harrison, 2000 WL 35508810 (N.C. Super. Ct. Feb. 16, 2000); In re FirstMerit Bank, 52 S.W.3d 749 (Tex. 2001); Nationwide of Bryan v. Dyer, 969 S.W.2d 518 (Tex. App. 1998).

206 See Global Travel Mktg., Inc. v. Shea, 908 So. 2d 392 (Fla. 2005) (waiver of liability and arbitration provision signed by parent on behalf of child was enforceable as to claims brought by child); Hojnowski v. Vans Skate Park, 901 A.2d 381 (N.J. 2006) (arbitration clause signed by parent on behalf of child was enforceable as to claims brought by child).

207 See Bridas S.A.P.I.C. v. Gov't of Turkmenistan, 345 F.3d 347, 356–358 (5th Cir. 2003).

208 Id.

209 See Mariner Health Care, Inc. v. Ferguson, 2006 WL 1851250, at *4–*5 (N.D. Miss. June 30, 2006); Flores v. Evergreen at San Diego, L.L.C., 148 Cal. App. 4th 581, 587–588, 55 Cal. Rptr. 3d 823 (2007); Pagarigan v. Libby Care Ctr., Inc., 120 Cal. Rptr. 2d 892 (Ct. App. 2002).

210 Pagarigan v. Libby Care Ctr., Inc., 120 Cal. Rptr. 2d 892 (Ct. App. 2002).

211 See Chew v. KPMG, L.L.P., 407 F. Supp. 2d 790, 799 (S.D. Miss. 2006) ("Based on the agency relationship between DB Alex. Brown and Deutsche Bank, the Court finds that Deutsche Bank may also enforce the subject arbitration agreement at least as to the claims asserted by the Chew trust.").

212 Bridas S.A.P.I.C. v. Gov't of Turkmenistan, 345 F.3d 347, 357 (5th Cir. 2003) ("If Turkmenneft indeed signed the JVA in its capacity as the Government's agent the Government would be

In contrast to a principal, an agent generally can neither enforce nor be bound by an arbitration agreement that it signed on behalf of a principal.[213] An agent is normally not liable under a contract executed on behalf of the principal.[214] Thus, in cases in which a consumer signs a contract with a company containing an arbitration clause, although the company has the right to enforce the contract's arbitration clause that right does not necessarily extend to the company's employees, absent any intent by the parties to allow the employees to enforce the arbitration clause.[215] As a result a non-party agent can enforce an arbitration agreement only if equitable estoppel or some other contract doctrine that operates independently of the principal-agency relationship applies.[216]

However, if the contract reflects an intent to protect the agents as well as the principal, then agents may be able to enforce the arbitration clause against the consumer. Following this reasoning, a number of courts have allowed employees or salesmen to enforce arbitration clauses that were signed by their employer.[217] One court has suggested that a broad arbitration clause will protect agents as well as principals.[218] Even when the contract brings agents within the scope of the arbitration clause, a party cannot deny its status as an agent and then rely on an agency theory to compel arbitration.[219] Additionally, an arbitration agreement that by its terms covers the company's agents does not protect the company's principal if the contract was not signed on behalf of the principal.[220] Thus a company should not be permitted to enforce an arbitration clause by claiming to be an agent when it is in fact a principal.[221]

Even when an agent is subject to an arbitration clause, the claims must relate to the agent's behavior as an agent in order for the arbitration clause to apply.[222] When the dispute

---

bound by the JVA's arbitration requirement."); Sinclair Broad. Group v. Interep Nat'l Radio Sales, Inc., 2005 WL 1000086, at *3 (D. Md. Apr. 28, 2005) (principal bound by arbitration clause signed by agent with apparent authority to act on behalf of principal); Garrison v. Super. Ct., 132 Cal. App. 4th 253, 264 33 Cal. Rptr. 3d 350 (2005); Alfano v. BDO Seidman, L.L.P., 925 A.2d 22 (N.J. Super. Ct. App. Div. 2007); *see also* Viola v. Dep't of Managed Health Care, 133 Cal. App. 4th 299, 34 Cal. Rptr. 3d 626 (2005) (an employer, acting as agent of its employees, has implied authority to agree to binding arbitration of malpractice claims arising under a health services plan it negotiates as part of an employee benefits package).

213 Westmoreland v. Sadoux, 299 F.3d 462, 466–467 (5th Cir. 2002) ("[A] nonsignatory cannot compel arbitration merely because he is an agent of one of his signatories."); Britton v. Co-op Banking Group, 4 F.3d 742 (9th Cir. 1993) (agent was not entitled to enforce arbitration clause); Flink v. Carlson, 856 F.2d 44, 46 (8th Cir. 1988) ("Signing an arbitration agreement as agent for a disclosed principal is not sufficient to bind the agent to arbitrate claims against him personally."); Usina Costa Pinto S.A. Acucar E Alcool v. Louis Dreyfus Sugar Co., 933 F. Supp. 1170, 1178 (S.D.N.Y. 1996); Koechli v. BIP Int'l, Inc., 870 So. 2d 940, 944 (Fla. Dist. Ct. App. 2004); I Sports v. IMG Worldwide, Inc., 813 N.E.2d 4, 11 (Ohio Ct. App. 2004).

214 *See* Westmoreland v. Sadoux, 299 F.3d 462, 466–467 (5th Cir. 2002); Clausen v. Watlow Elec. Mfg. Co., 242 F. Supp. 2d 877, 882–883 (D. Or. 2002); Luke v. Gentry Realty, Ltd., 96 P.3d 261, 267–268 (Haw. 2004).

215 McCarthy v. Azure, 22 F.3d 351, 357 (1st Cir. 1994) (suggesting that employees can enforce an arbitration clause signed by an employer only when the contractual language demonstrates an intent to benefit both the employer and employee alike); Housh v. Dinovo Inv., Inc., 2003 WL 1119526, at *5 (D. Kan. Mar. 7, 2003) (employee could not enforce arbitration clause signed by employer).

216 Westmoreland v. Sadoux, 299 F.3d 462, 466–467 (5th Cir. 2002); Britton v. Co-op Banking Group, 4 F.3d 742, 747–748 (9th Cir. 1993); Luke v. Gentry Realty, Ltd., 96 P.3d 261, 268 (Haw. 2004) ("A nonsignatory may not invoke an arbitration clause merely because of its status as an agent of one of the signatories. If the claim(s) against the nonsignatory are independent of the agreement in which the arbitration clause appears, then the nonsignatory agent may not invoke the arbitration clause.").

217 *See* Pritzger v. Merrill Lynch Pierce Fenner & Smith, 7 F.3d 1110, 1121 (3d Cir. 1993); Roby v. Corp. of Lloyd's, 996 F.2d 1353, 1360 (2d Cir. 1993) (finding agents and employees protected by arbitration agreement signed by their principal); Arnold v. Arnold Corp., 920 F.2d 1269, 1282 (6th Cir. 1990) (same); Letzia v. Prudential Bache Sec., Inc., 802 F.2d 1185, 1187 (9th Cir. 1986) (same); Vertucci v. Orvis, 2006 WL 1688078, at *5 (D. Conn. May 30, 2006) (applicability of arbitration clause is not affected "simply because Plaintiff has sued the individual defendants rather than Lexington itself"); Staples v. Money Tree, Inc., 936 F. Supp. 856 (M.D. Ala. 1996) (same); Messing v. Rosenkrantz, 872 F. Supp. 539, 541 (N.D. Ill. 1995) (agent can enforce and/or be bound by arbitration clause); Sterns v. Phillips, 852 So. 2d 123 (Ala. 2002) (salesman can enforce arbitration agreement when he or she stands "in the shoes" of the employer or principal); Monsanto Co. v. Benton Farm, 813 So. 2d 867 (Ala. 2001) (same); *Ex parte* Gray, 686 So. 2d 250 (Ala. 1996) (salesman can enforce arbitration agreement entered into by dealership employing the salesperson); Westra v. Marcus & Millichap Real Estate Inv. Brokerage Co., 28 Cal. Rptr. 3d 752 (Ct. App. 2005). *But see* Boyd v. Homes of Legend, Inc., 981 F. Supp. 1423 (M.D. Ala. 1997) (mobile home dealers were not agents of manufacturer and therefore manufacturer could not enforce dealer's arbitration clause, *remanded on jurisdictional grounds*, 188 F.3d 1294 (11th Cir. 1999), *abrogated on other grounds by* Davis v. S. Energy Homes, Inc., 305 F.3d 1268 (11th Cir. 2002); Jenkens & Gilchrist v. Riggs, 87 S.W.3d 198 (Tex. App. Sept. 17, 2002) (finding attorney not to be the agent of client (with whom the other party had arbitration agreement) because client was not vicariously liable for the conduct of the attorney).

218 Qutby v. Nagda, 817 So. 2d 952, 958 (Fla. Dist. Ct. App. 2002) ("broad arbitration clauses [are] intended to obligate signatories to the agreement to arbitrate disputes brought not only against the principal, but claims made against the principal's agents").

219 *See, e.g.*, Peach v. CIM Ins. Corp., 816 N.E.2d 668, 672–673 (Ill. App. Ct. 2004); Ervin v. Nokia, Inc., 812 N.E.2d 534, 540 (Ill. App. Ct. 2004).

220 Carriage Homes v. Channell, 777 So. 2d 83 (Ala. 2000).

221 *See id.*

222 Kruse v. AFLAC Int'l, 458 F. Supp. 2d 375 (E.D. Ky. 2006) (allowing defendant to enforce arbitration clause when defendant was "sued because of actions he took or did not take in his capacity as an employee or agent of AFLAC"); Rowe v. Exline, 63 Cal. Rptr. 3d 787, 793 (Ct. App. 2007) ("California courts do

does not relate to the agent's conduct in its capacity as an agent the arbitration clause does not apply.[223] Equally significant, a party's status as an agent is insufficient to bring a party within the scope of an arbitration clause if the dispute concerns conduct by the agent in the agent's individual capacity. In such circumstances the agent is neither bound by, nor entitled to enforce, the arbitration clause.[224]

7.4.5 Treatment of Common Third Party Relationships

In addition to the exceptions outlined above to the rule that non-signatories are not subject to an arbitration agreement, a non-signatory also can be subject to an arbitration clause in a few other circumstances. Specifically, an assignee of a contract generally has the same rights under the contract as the assignor, and courts have allowed assignees to take advantage of arbitration clauses in assigned contracts.[225] Also, parties can incorporate by reference a contract signed by other parties containing an arbitration clause.[226] However incorporating the arbitration clause into a new contract does not enlarge or expand the scope of the clause, and so if the clause in the earlier contract was limited to particular claims or parties, it likely will have the same limitations in the subsequent contract.[227] Moreover, with regard to surety contracts that incorporate an arbitration

---

recognize, however, that a nonsignatory sued as an *agent* of a signatory may enforce an arbitration agreement."); Hirschfeld Products, Inc. v. Mirvish, 88 N.Y.2d 1054, 1056 (1996); Nardi v. Povich, 2006 WL 2127714, at *4–*5 (N.Y. Sup. Ct. July 31, 2006) (agent could enforce arbitration clause with respect to defamation claims that pertained to the plaintiff's employment agreement); Merrill Lynch Trust Co. v. Alaniz, 159 S.W.3d 162, 168–169 (Tex. App. 2004) (agent could not enforce arbitration clause when claims were unrelated to the agent's conduct).

223 InterGen v. Grina, 344 F.3d 134, 148 (1st Cir. 2003) (agent could not enforce arbitration clause that applied to disputes relating to purchasing order when the parties failed to establish that an agency relationship existed with respect to the execution of the purchase orders); Britton v. Co-op Banking Group, 4 F.3d 742, 747–748 (9th Cir. 1993); Goodrich Cargo Sys. v. Aero Union Group, 2006 WL 3708065 (N.D. Cal. Dec. 14, 2006); Bensara v. Marciano, 92 Cal. App. 4th 987 (2001) (when one corporate president sued another for defamation, arbitration clause in licensing agreement between the two corporations did not apply); Merrill Lynch Trust Co. v. Alaniz, 159 S.W.3d 162, 168–169 (Tex. App. 2004) (agent could not enforce arbitration clause when claims were unrelated to the agent's conduct).

224 McCarthy v. Azure, 22 F.3d 351, 356, 359–361 (1st Cir. 1994) (business executive who signed arbitration agreement in his official capacity was not required to arbitrate claims asserted against him individually); Kaplan v. First Options of Chicago, Inc., 19 F.3d 1503 (3d Cir. 1994) (arbitration clause did not apply to claims arising out of agent's actions as an individual), *aff'd*, 514 U.S. 938 (1995); Flink v. Carlson, 856 F.2d 44, 46 (8th Cir. 1988) (signing as agent is not sufficient to bind agent to arbitrate claims against the agent personally); Housh v. Dinovo Inv., Inc., 2003 WL 1119526, at *3 (D. Kan. Mar. 7, 2003); Clausen v. Watlow Elec. Mfg. Co., 242 F. Supp. 2d 877, 883 (D. Or. 2002) ("Plaintiff's claims are individual claims: Plaintiff does not allege that he is entitled to prevail because of his relationship with Datatronix."); Liberty Communications, Inc. v. MCI Telecommunications Corp., 733 So. 2d 571 (Fla. Dist. Ct. App. 1999) (contract signed by individual in corporate capacity did not require arbitration of claims brought in his individual capacity); Finney v. Nat'l Health Care Corp., 193 S.W.3d 393 (Mo. Ct. App. 2006) (daughter who signed nursing home agreement on behalf of her mother was not required to arbitrate wrongful death claims because only claims on behalf of her mother, rather than her own personal claims, were subject to arbitration); Suttle v. Decesare, 2001 Ohio App. LEXIS 3030 (Ohio Ct. App. July 5, 2001) (arbitration agreement running to corporation does not benefit corporation president individually); Teramar v. Rodier Corp., 531 N.E.2d 721 (Ohio Ct. App. 1987) (company president not personally bound by arbitration clause signed in franchise agreement); Harley v. Sayas, 2006 WL 4037577, at *5 (S.C. Ct. Com. Pl. June 21, 2006); *In re* Kepka, 178 S.W.3d 279, 293 (Tex. App. 2005) (agent who signed nursing home admission agreement in representative capacity was not required to arbitrate individual claims). *But see* Rowe v. Exline, 63 Cal. Rptr. 3d 787 (Ct. App. 2007) (agent can be bound); Levitan v. Fanfare Media Works, Inc., 2003 WL 21028339 (Cal. Ct. App. May 8, 2003) (when corporate president sued for acts done in corporate capacity, he was entitled to enforce arbitration clause signed by company); Koechli v. BIP Int'l, Inc., 870 So. 2d 940, 944 (Fla. Dist. Ct. App. 2004).

225 Galbraith v. Resurgent Capital Services, 2006 WL 2990163 (E.D. Cal. Oct. 19, 2006) (allowing successor-in-interest to enforce arbitration clause); Goodwin v. Ford Motor Credit Co., 970 F. Supp. 1007 (M.D. Ala. 1997); Ocwen Loan Servicing, L.L.C. v. Washington, 939 So. 2d 6 (Ala. 2006) ("As a general rule, an assignee stands in the shoes of the assignor and may enforce an arbitration agreement entered into between the assignor and another party."); Universal Underwriters Life Ins. Co. v. Dutton, 736 So. 2d 564 (Ala. 1999); Nissan Motor Acceptance Corp. v. Ross, 703 So. 2d 324 (Ala. 1997); *see also* Hoefs v. CACV of Colo., L.L.C., 365 F. Supp. 2d 69, 74–75 (D. Mass. 2005) (consumer was required to arbitrate claim against non-signatory assignee when the contract explicitly provided for enforcement by assignees); *cf.* Stromberg Sheet Metal Works, Inc. v. Wash. Gas Energy Sys., Inc., 448 F. Supp. 2d 64 (D.D.C. 2006); Green Tree Fin. Corp. v. Channell, 825 So. 2d 90 (Ala. 2002) (when assignee could not take advantage of arbitration clause in one document between consumer and dealer, it could still take advantage of arbitration clause found in the installment sales agreement); Ill. Farmers Ins. Co. v. Glass Serv. Co., 683 N.W.2d 792, 803 (Minn. 2004) ("Thus, if Farmers had the right to demand no-fault arbitration against individual policyholders, it will also have that right against Glass Service as assignee of the policyholders' claims against Farmers."). *But cf.* Cheatham v. Air Sys. Eng'g Co., Clearinghouse No. 51,969 (Cal. Super. Ct. Apr. 30, 1997) (the text of this decision is also available on the CD-Rom accompanying this manual); Mohamed v. Auto Nation USA Corp., 89 S.W.3d 830 (Tex. App. 2002) (barring non-signatory from enforcing arbitration clause when it failed to present sufficient evidence showing that it was a successor-in-interest to the signatory party).

226 *See, e.g.*, Goodrich Cargo Sys. v. Aero Union Group, 2006 WL 3708065 (N.D. Cal. Dec. 14, 2006).

227 *Cf.* Progressive Cas. Ins. Co. v. C.A. Reaseguradora Nacional de Venezuela, 991 F.2d 42, 47–48 (2d Cir. 1993) (a contract that identifies specific parties may be limited to those parties, but a contract that uses the term "parties" generically will not exclude non-signatories).

clause between the principal parties, the guarantor is not bound by the arbitration agreement unless the surety contract specifically incorporates the arbitration provision, rather than the underlying contract generally.[228]

On the other hand, some relationships are not sufficiently close to permit a non-signatory to enforce an arbitration clause. A manufacturer,[229] credit insurer,[230] forced-placed insurer,[231] a mortgage insurer,[232] or service contract company[233] will have difficulty piggy-backing on the dealer's arbitration agreement with the consumer.[234] Typically, a parent corporation-subsidiary relationship also is not sufficient to allow one to enforce an arbitration clause signed by the other.[235] A number of decisions also find that a corporation's arbitration clause does not cover claims against its president or principal.[236] Additionally, an attorney cannot rely on an arbitration clause contained in a settlement agreement between a client and a third party when the client then sues its attorney for malpractice arising out of the attorney's legal representation in the dispute resolved by the settlement.[237] However, ERISA plan members may be bound by an arbitration agreement signed by the plan if their claims relate to the terms of the plan.[238]

7.4.6 Affinity Group Members

With the growing popularity of both arbitration and affinity groups, which consumers join to receive goods and services, sometimes the arbitration clause may be found not in an individual agreement with the consumer but in the merchant's master agreement with the affinity group. In such cases courts might utilize a different standard than they would if the clause was in a contract seen and signed by the consumer.

For example, the Supreme Court has said that when a collective bargaining agreement specifies arbitration of certain claims, any language granting waiver of a judicial forum for federal discrimination claims must be "clear and unmistakable" in order for individuals to be bound by that

---

228 AgGrow Oils, L.L.C. v. Nat'l Union Fire Ins. Co., 242 F.3d 777 (8th Cir. 2001); Grunstad v. Ritt, 106 F.3d 201 (7th Cir. 1997). *But see* St. Paul Fire & Marine Ins. Co. v. La Firenza, L.L.C., 2007 WL 2010759 (M.D. Fla. July 6, 2007) (incorporating arbitration clause into surety agreement without specific reference).

229 Kisner v. Bud's Mobile Homes, 2007 WL 686734, at *6–*7 (S.D. Miss. Mar. 3, 2007); Adkins v. Palm Harbor Homes, Inc., 157 F. Supp. 2d 1256 (M.D. Ala. 2001); Boyd v. Homes of Legend, Inc., 981 F. Supp. 1423 (M.D. Ala. 1997), *remanded on jurisdictional grounds*, 188 F.3d 1294 (11th Cir. 1999), *abrogated on other grounds by* Davis v. S. Energy Homes, Inc., 305 F.3d 1268 (11th Cir. 2002); Wilson v. Waverlee Homes, Inc., 954 F. Supp. 1530 (M.D. Ala.), *aff'd*, 127 F.3d 40 (11th Cir. 1997); Monsanto Co. v. Benton Farm, 813 So. 2d 867 (Ala. 2001); Parkway Dodge, Inc. v. Yarborough, 779 So. 2d 1205 (Ala. 2000); Carriage Homes v. Channell, 777 So. 2d 83 (Ala. 2000); S. Energy Homes, Inc. v. Kennedy, 774 So. 2d 540 (Ala. 2000); Universal Underwriters Life Ins. Co. v. Dutton, 736 So. 2d 564 (Ala. 1999); *Ex parte* Isbell, 708 So. 2d 571 (Ala. 1997); *Ex parte* Martin, 703 So. 2d 883 (Ala. 1996); Hansford v. Cappaert Manufactured Hous., 911 So. 2d 901, 905 (La. Ct. App. 2005); Rhodes v. Amega Mobile Home Sales, Inc., 186 S.W.3d 793 (Mo. Ct. App. 2006); *see* Pack v. Damon Corp., 320 F. Supp. 2d 545 (E.D. Mich. 2004), *rev'd in part on other grounds*, 434 F.3d 810 (6th Cir. 2006).

230 In re Knepp, 229 B.R. 821 (Bankr. N.D. Ala. 1999); Universal Underwriters Life Ins. Co. v. Dutton, 736 So. 2d 564 (Ala. 1999); First Family Fin. Services, Inc. v. Rogers, 736 So. 2d 553 (Ala. 1999). *But see* Staples v. Money Tree, Inc., 936 F. Supp. 856 (M.D. Ala. 1996); *Ex parte* Napier, 723 So. 2d 49 (Ala. 1998) (seller of physical damage insurance on mobile home).

231 *Ex parte* Jones, 686 So. 2d 1166 (Ala. 1996). *But see* Roberson v. Money Tree, 954 F. Supp. 1519 (M.D. Ala. 1997); *Ex parte* Napier, 723 So. 2d 49, 51–52 (Ala. 1998).

232 Brantley v. Republic Mortgage Ins. Co., 424 F.3d 392 (4th Cir. 2005).

233 *But see* MS Dealer Serv. Corp. v. Franklin, 177 F.3d 942 (11th Cir. 1999) (claims against service contract company were based on the contract containing arbitration clause and were based on interdependent misconduct between dealer signing contract and service contract company), *on remand to* 1999 U.S. Dist. LEXIS 10662 (N.D. Ala. July 9, 1999).

234 *Cf.* Spector v. Toys "R" Us, Inc., 784 N.Y.S.2d 924 (Sup. Ct. 2004) (company cannot rely on arbitration clause contained in agreement between two other parties when the agreement is not implicated in the dispute), *aff'd on other grounds*, 12 A.D.3d 358, 784 N.Y.S.2d 153 (2004).

235 Zurich Am. Ins. Co. v. Watts Indus., Inc., 417 F.3d 682, 688 (7th Cir. 2005); *cf.* Am. Int'l Specialty Lines Ins. Co. v. Elec. Data Sys. Corp., 347 F.3d 665, 669–671 (7th Cir. 2003) (a subsidiary may be covered by agreement of parent if the language of agreement expresses such an intent); Thomson-CSF, S.A. v. Am. Arbitration Ass'n, 64 F.3d 773, 777 (2d Cir. 1995); Goldman Sachs & Co. v. Becker, 2007 WL 1982790, at *4 (N.D. Cal. July 2, 2007) (shareholder not bound by arbitration clause signed by corporation). *But see* Nefores v. Branddirect Mktg., Inc., 2002 WL 31057387 (Ohio Ct. App. Sept. 14, 2002) (corporate parent can enforce subsidiary's agreement).

236 McCarthy v. Azure, 22 F.3d 351, 356, 359–361 (1st Cir. 1994) (business executive who signed arbitration agreement in his official capacity was not required to arbitrate claims asserted against him individually); Suttle v. Decesare, 2001 Ohio App. LEXIS 3030 (Ohio Ct. App. July 5, 2001) (arbitration agreement running to corporation does not benefit corporation president individually); Teramar v. Rodier Corp., 531 N.E.2d 721 (Ohio Ct. App. 1987) (company president not personally bound by arbitration clause signed in franchise agreement); *see also* Putnam Lovell NBF Group v. Conlon, 2005 WL 1513128 (D. Conn. June 22, 2005) (corporate parent not automatically bound by arbitration agreement entered into by wholly-owned subsidiary); Levitan v. Fanfare Media Works, Inc., 2003 WL 21028339 (Cal. Ct. App. May 8, 2003) (when corporate president sued for acts done in corporate capacity, he was entitled to enforce arbitration clause signed by company); County of Contra Costa v. Kaiser Found. Health Plan, Inc., 47 Cal. App. 3d 237, 243 (1996) (general partner can be bound by an arbitration clause entered into by the partnership).

237 *See* Matei v. Alioto, 2005 WL 15439 (Cal. Ct. App. Jan. 3, 2005).

238 Vanvels v. Betten, 2007 WL 329048 (W.D. Mich. Jan. 31, 2007).

agreement.[239] The same principle might apply to agreements with affinity groups. On the other hand, an association suing on behalf of members that have signed arbitration clauses may not be able to maintain its action in court rather than in arbitration.[240]

7.4.7 Specific Types of Claims

7.4.7.1 Wrongful Death Claims

Non-signatory issues arise with some regularity in the context of wrongful death claims. An arbitration clause may be implicated when the decedent's death occurred as a result of some contractual relationship, such as a wrongful death claim arising out of abusive treatment at a nursing home, or out of medical malpractice by a physician. In such cases the decedent may have signed a contract with an arbitration clause, or a representative of the decedent may have signed the contract on the decedent's behalf, and the wrongful death defendant attempts to use the contract to compel arbitration of the survivor's wrongful death claim. Courts have split over whether the survivor's claim is subject to arbitration based on an arbitration clause signed by the decedent or by the survivor as a representative of the decedent.[241]

Those courts that have declined to compel arbitration typically have relied on the fact that a wrongful death claim does not belong to the decedent but is a separate cause of action that attaches to the survivor.[242] Because the wrongful death claim is distinct to the survivor, the fact that the decedent or a close relative of the decedent may have signed an arbitration clause is immaterial.[243] Similarly, even if the plaintiff signed the arbitration clause on behalf of the decedent, the plaintiff is not bound to arbitrate because the plaintiff has only consented to arbitrate claims brought in his representative capacity, and the wrongful death claim is one that accrues to the plaintiff personally.[244] Moreover, an arbitration clause that applies to the decedent's heirs does not compel a different result because a wrongful death plaintiff is suing in her own capacity, not as an heir to the decedent, and cannot be an heir to his or her own claims.[245]

Conversely, those courts that have held that wrongful death claims can be arbitrated appear to have held either that the wrongful death claim was derivative of any claim of the decedent under relevant state law,[246] that arbitration clauses that apply to a decedent's heirs are broad enough to encompass a survivor's claim,[247] or that the claim was arbitrable because it was brought by the survivor as executor of the decedent's estate, rather than by the survivor in his or her personal capacity.[248]

7.4.7.2 Claims Arising Out of Mistreatment in Nursing Homes

Non-signatory issues also arise in claims involving mistreatment of patients at nursing homes or elder care facilities. In many cases the patient did not sign the admission agreement containing the arbitration clause when first en-

---

239 Wright v. Universal Mar. Serv. Corp., 525 U.S. 70, 119 S. Ct. 391, 142 L. Ed. 2d 361 (1998); *see also* Baton Rouge Oil & Chem. Workers Union v. ExxonMobil Corp., 289 F.3d 373 (5th Cir. 2002) (refusing to read collective bargaining agreement to compel arbitration of wrongful termination claim by probationary worker because arbitration would create conflict with separate provision in agreement that allowed termination of such workers "at will").
240 Med. Soc'y of State of N.Y. v. Oxford Health Plans, Inc., 790 N.Y.S.2d 79, 80 (App. Div. 2005).
241 *Compare* Briarcliff Nursing Home, Inc. v. Turcotte 894 So. 2d 661, 663 (Ala. 2004) (requiring arbitration); Herbert v. Super. Ct., 169 Cal. App. 3d 718, 727 (1985) (requiring arbitration); Allen v. Pacheco, 71 P.3d 375 (Colo. 2003) (requiring arbitration) *and* Cleveland v. Mann, 942 So. 2d 108 (Miss. 2006) (requiring arbitration) *with* Wasburn v. Beverly Enterprises-Georgia, Inc., 2006 WL 2404804, at *6 (S.D. Ga. Nov. 14, 2006) (arbitration not required); Goliger v. AMS Properties, Inc., 123 Cal. App. 4th 374, 377 (2004) (daughter who signed admission agreement did not sign away right to bring wrongful death action); Finney v. Nat'l Health Care Corp., 193 S.W.3d 393 (Mo. Ct. App. 2006) (daughter who signed nursing home agreement on behalf of her mother was not required to arbitrate wrongful death claim that accrued to her personally, because only claims on behalf of her mother were subject to arbitration) *and In re* Kepka, 178 S.W.3d 279 (Tex. App. 2005).
242 Washburn v. Beverly Enterprises-Georgia, Inc., 2006 WL 3404804, at *6 (S.D. Ga. Nov. 14, 2006) (plaintiff brings these claims in her individual capacity, not in her capacity as administrator of decedant's estate); Goliger v. AMS Properties, Inc., 123 Cal. App. 4th 374, 377 (2004); Finney v. Nat'l Health Care Corp., 193 S.W.3d 393 (Mo. Ct. App. 2006) ("The wrongful death claim does not belong to the deceased or even to decedent's estate...."); *In re* Kepka, 178 S.W.3d 279, 294 (Tex. App. 2005) ("Wrongful-death claims are personal to the statutory beneficiaries who assert the claims, and recovery for those claims does not benefit the estate."); *cf.* Peltz v. Sears, Roebuck & Co., 367 F. Supp. 2d 711 (E.D. Pa. 2005) (claim under a state survivor statute, rather than a wrongful death claim, was subject to arbitration based on agreement signed on behalf of the decedent).
243 *See* Washburn v. Beverly Enterprises-Georgia, Inc., 2006 WL 3404804, at *6 (S.D. Ga. Nov. 14, 2006); Finney v. Nat'l Health Care Corp., 193 S.W.3d 393 (Mo. Ct. App. 2006).
244 *In re* Kepka, 178 S.W.3d 279 (Tex. App. 2005); *see* Washburn v. Beverly Enterprises-Georgia, Inc., 2006 WL 3404804, at *6 (S.D. Ga. Nov. 14, 2006) (wrongful death claim was not subject to arbitration because plaintiff brought the claim in her individual capacity and not in her capacity as administrator of the decedent's estate); Goliger v. AMS Properties, Inc., 123 Cal. App. 4th 374, 377 (2004).
245 *See In re* Kepka, 178 S.W.3d 279, 295–296 (Tex. App. 2005).
246 *See* Cleveland v. Mann, 942 So. 2d 108, 118–119 (Miss. 2006).
247 *See* Allen v. Pacheco, 71 P.3d 375, 378–381 (Colo. 2003) (broad arbitration clause that included claims by heirs applied to wrongful death claim brought by spouse because the state's wrongful death act defined "heirs" to include a spouse).
248 Briarcliff Nursing Home, Inc. v. Turcotte, 894 So. 2d 661, 663 (Ala. 2004).

tering the facility, because they often lack the capacity to do so. Instead, a close family member or friend typically signs the arbitration agreement on the patient's behalf. In a subsequent lawsuit arising out of mistreatment, the nursing home often will argue that the arbitration clause applies, even though it was never signed by the patient. The nursing homes make two primary arguments: (1) that the signatory was acting as the agent of the patient, and therefore the patient is bound by the arbitration agreement; and (2) that the signatory was acting under statutory authority to make binding decisions regarding nursing home care, and those decisions include being able to bind the patient to an arbitration clause. These arguments have met with only limited success.

As to the first argument, California courts have held that a family member's signature on a nursing home admission agreement is not binding on the patient under agency principles unless the family member was acting under a durable power of attorney.[249] Other courts have held that the family member's act of signing the admission agreement did not create an agency relationship because the law requires conduct by the *principal* demonstrating assent to the agency relationship. When such conduct was absent, the court refused to bind the patient to the admission agreement's arbitration clause.[250]

As to the second argument, most courts have held that even when state statutes authorize individuals to make health care decisions for family members, whether to submit future disputes to binding arbitration is not a health care decision, and therefore the surrogate's statutory authority does not extend to agreements to arbitrate.[251]

7.4.7.3 Debt Collection Claims Involving MBNA Contracts When MBNA Is Not a Party to the Proceeding

A specific issue that has arisen more than once involves whether a non-signatory debt collector can invoke an arbitration clause in MBNA's credit agreement with a consumer if MBNA is not a party to the proceeding. MBNA's credit agreement, at least the one in present use, applies to debt collectors when the collector is named as a co-defendant with MBNA. While this provision may apply to a debt collector who is a co-defendant,[252] it does not apply to a debt collector who is sued individually, without MBNA being a co-defendant.[253]

Collectors may also argue that they are covered by another part of the MBNA agreement, which says that the arbitration clause applies to MBNA's agents. Faced with this conflict between a specific clause that applies the arbitration requirement only to collectors who are co-defendants and another clause that applies more generally to agents, at least one court has found that the more specific language controls. Thus debt collectors, whether or not they are agents of MBNA, are excluded from the arbitration clause unless MBNA also is a co-defendant.[254] Courts, however, have differed as to whether MBNA's arbitration clause requires an arbitrator to decide whether debt collectors can enforce the clause.[255]

---

249 *See* Flores v. Evergreen at San Diego, L.L.C., 55 Cal. Rptr. 3d 823, 827–828 (Ct. App. 2007) (husband could not bind wife when power of attorney was executed after the husband signed the admission agreement); Hogan v. Country Villa Health Services, 55 Cal. Rptr. 3d 450 (Ct. App. 2007) (daughter's signature on nursing home agreement bound the mother to arbitrate when the daughter had power of attorney); Garrison v. Super. Ct., 33 Cal. Rptr. 3d 850 (Ct. App. 2005) (daughter's actions under power of attorney bound parent to arbitration agreement signed by daughter); Pagarigan v. Libby Care Ctr., Inc., 120 Cal. Rptr. 2d 892 (Ct. App. 2002) (patient not bound when there was no power of attorney).

250 Mariner Health Care, Inc. v. Ferguson, 2006 WL 1851250, at *3–*7 (N.D. Miss. June 30, 2006); Mariner Healthcare, Inc. v. King, 2006 WL 1716863 (N.D. Miss. June 19, 2006); Mariner Healthcare, Inc. v. Green, 2006 WL 1626581 (N.D. Miss. June 7, 2006); Flores v. Evergreen at San Diego, L.L.C., 55 Cal. Rptr. 3d 823, 827–828 (Ct. App. 2007); Goliger v. AMS Properties, Inc., 123 Cal. App. 4th 374, 377 (2004); Pagarigan v. Libby Care Ctr., Inc., 120 Cal. Rptr. 2d 892 (Ct. App. 2002); Buckner v. Tamarin, 98 Cal. App. 4th 140, 119 Cal. Rptr. 2d 489 (2002) (fact that patient had signed medical arbitration agreement compelling arbitration of all claims arising out of doctor's treatment and care did not waive right of adult daughters to sue for medical malpractice; *see also* Grenada Living Ctr., L.L.C. v. Coleman, 2007 WL 2128392, at *3 (Miss. July 26, 2007) (signature of family member did not bind patient when patient was mentally competent and never expressly designated the family member as an agent).

251 Mariner Health Care, Inc. v. Ferguson, 2006 WL 1851250, at *5 (N.D. Miss. June 30, 2006); Mariner Healthcare, Inc. v. King, 2006 WL 1716863 (N.D. Miss. June 19, 2006); Flores v. Evergreen at San Diego, L.L.C., 55 Cal. Rptr. 3d 823, 832–833 (Ct. App. 2007); Blankfield v. Richmond Health Care, Inc., 902 So. 2d 296, 300 (Fla. Dist. Ct. App. 2005); Covenant Health & Rehab. of Picayune, Ltd. P'ship v. Estate of Lambert, 2006 WL 3593437, at *3 (Miss. Ct. App. Dec. 12, 2006). *But see* J.P. Morgan Chase & Co. v. Conegie *ex rel.* Lee, 2007 WL 2028926 (5th Cir. July 26, 2007); Covenant Health Rehab. of Picayune, Ltd. P'ship v. Brown, 949 So. 2d 732 (Miss. 2007) (under Mississippi law, surrogate had the authority to sign an arbitration agreement as part of making health care decisions for a family member).

252 *See* Feil v. MBNA, 417 F. Supp. 2d 1214 (D. Kan. 2006).

253 Bontempo v. Wolpoff & Abramson, L.L.P., 2006 WL 3040905 (W.D. Pa. Oct. 24, 2006); Karnette v. Wolpoff & Abramson, L.L.P., 444 F. Supp. 2d 640 (E.D. Va. 2006).

254 Bontempo v. Wolpoff & Abramson, L.L.P., 2006 WL 3040905 (W.D. Pa. Oct. 24, 2006); Karnette v. Wolpoff & Abramson, L.L.P., 444 F. Supp. 2d 640 (E.D. Va. 2006).

255 *Compare* Nazar v. Wolpoff & Abramson, L.L.P., 2007 WL 528753 (D. Kan. Feb. 15, 2007) (sending question to arbitrator) *with Karnette*, 444 F. Supp. 2d at 643–644 (deciding that arbitrability was a question for the court).

7.4.8 Enforcement Agencies and Contempt Proceedings

While a consumer's claim against a creditor or merchant may be subject to an arbitration clause, an administrative agency's enforcement action against that creditor or merchant is not subject to the arbitration agreement entered into by the consumer.[256] The same result applies even if the agency seeks monetary relief for an individual who has signed an arbitration agreement.[257] When an agency files a case in its own name both in the public interest and on behalf of an individual, that action need not be submitted to arbitration even when the individual must submit her claim to arbitration.[258] However, if a consumer intervenes in an agency proceeding, the consumer may be required to arbitrate his or her individual claims even if the agency is not required to arbitrate its claims.[259]

Consequently, a state attorney general or the Federal Trade Commission can bring an action in court against a company and recover restitution or damages for individual consumers even when those consumers signed arbitration agreements.[260] Nor does the existence of an arbitration clause prevent the consumer from complaining to an agency and asking the agency to resolve the matter.[261] And a consumer who does complain need not submit claims to arbitration, even if a government agency is pursuing the claim. The consumer can instead wait and benefit from any resolution of the agency's claim in court.[262]

Applying the logic of *Waffle House*, one court has held that a private litigant who sues as a private attorney general seeking public injunctive relief may not be subject to arbitration even when suing on behalf of a class of consumers who have signed arbitration clauses and even though the action is not brought by a public entity.[263]

Contempt proceedings, even those initiated by an individual subject to an arbitration clause, are not covered by such clauses. The court is the real party in interest and the court is not subject to the arbitration agreement. For example, this issue arose in bankruptcy court when a debtor brought an adversary proceeding against a creditor for violating a bankruptcy court's automatic stay and discharge orders.[264] Although the two parties had a written contract containing an arbitration clause, the court said that the aggrieved party in this matter was the court itself, and that because it had never signed the arbitration agreement, the claim could not be forced into arbitration.

7.5 Can the Terms of the Arbitration Clause Be Satisfied?

Under certain circumstances, courts may refuse to enforce an arbitration clause when it is impossible for the terms of the arbitration clause to be satisfied. If the terms of the arbitration clause cannot be met by the parties as a result of changed factual circumstances, the arbitration clause as written cannot be complied with and therefore does not apply to disputed claims. For instance, some courts have indicated that an arbitration clause that incorporates the rules of the National Association of Securities Dealers does not require arbitration if one of the parties to the dispute is not a "person" within the meaning of the NASD rules such that the NASD would refuse to arbitrate the claim if brought before that tribunal.[265]

---

256 Equal Employment Opportunity Comm'n v. Waffle House, Inc., 534 U.S. 279, 122 S. Ct. 754, 151 L. Ed. 2d 755 (2002). *But see* Ropp v. 1717 Capital Mgmt. Co., 2004 WL 93945 (D. Del. Jan. 14, 2004) (refusing to apply *Waffle House* beyond the employment context to a securities matter).

257 Equal Employment Opportunity Comm'n v. Waffle House, Inc., 543 U.S. 279, 122 S. Ct. 754, 151 L. Ed. 2d 755 (2002).

258 *Id.*; *see also* State ex rel. Hatch v. Cross Country Bank, Inc., 703 N.W.2d 562 (Minn. Ct. App. 2005).

259 *See* Equal Employment Opportunity Comm'n v. Woodmen of the World Life Ins. Co., 479 F.3d 561, 567–570 (8th Cir. 2007); Equal Employment Opportunity Comm'n v. Hooters of Am., Inc., 2007 WL 64163 (W.D.N.Y. Jan. 9, 2007); Equal Employment Opportunity Comm'n v. Rappaport, Hertz, Cherson & Rosenthal, 273 F. Supp. 2d 260, 264–265 (E.D.N.Y. 2003). *But see* Equal Employment Opportunity Comm'n v. Physician Services, P.S.C., 425 F. Supp. 2d 859, 861–862 (E.D. Ky. 2006) (intervenor in Equal Employment Opportunity Commission proceeding was not required to arbitrate her own claims).

260 *See* State ex rel. Hatch v. Cross Country Bank, Inc., 703 N.W.2d 562 (Minn. Ct. App. 2005).

261 Gilmer v. Interstate/Johnson Lane Corp., 500 U.S. 20, 111 S. Ct. 1647, 114 L. Ed. 2d 26 (1991) (while individual must arbitrate Age Discrimination in Employment Act claim, the individual is still free to file charges with the Equal Employment Opportunity Commission).

262 Equal Employment Opportunity Comm'n v. Circuit City Stores, Inc., 285 F.3d 404 (6th Cir. 2002).

263 Latterell v. Cross Country Bank, 2004 WL 928246 (Cal. Ct. App. Apr. 30, 2004).

264 *In re* Grant, 281 B.R. 721 (Bankr. S.D. Ala. 2000).

The court in *Grant* also noted that allowing an arbitrator to resolve a contempt claim would result in an erosion of the court's power, and would undermine the Bankruptcy Code. *Id.* at 725. For more information on the relationship between arbitration and the Bankruptcy Code, see § 4.2.3, *supra*.

265 *See, e.g.*, Burns v. N.Y. Life Ins. Co., 202 F.3d 616 (2d Cir. 2000) (refusing to compel arbitration under clause designating NASD because no party to the dispute was a person within the meaning of NASD rules); Provencio v. WMA Sec., Inc., 23 Cal. Rptr. 3d 524 (Ct. App. 2005). *But see* Reddam v. KPMG L.L.P., 457 F.3d 1054 (9th Cir. 2006) (NASD's refusal to hear arbitration under arbitration clause designating NASD rules did not render arbitration clause unenforceable); Alfano v. BDO Seidman, L.L.P., 925 A.2d 22 (N.J. Super. Ct. App. Div. 2007) (arbitration clause designating NASD rules was still enforceable even though no parties to the dispute were "persons" under NASD rules). *But cf.* ING Fin. Partners v. Johansen, 446 F.3d 777, 779–780 (8th Cir. 2006) (NASD rules that required consent for arbitration of statutory employment discrimination claims were read not to preclude arbitration of such claims pursuant to a general predispute binding arbitration clause that did not specifically identify employment discrimination claims as being subject to arbitration).

Chapter 8   Waiver of Right to Compel Arbitration

8.1 Introduction

The question of when a party has waived its right to compel arbitration has proven to be controversial among courts in several respects. First, there is a significant debate as to when this question is one to be decided by courts, and when it is one to be decided by arbitrators.[1] Second, there is some tension—not always directly recognized—present in the case law as to the extent to which this issue is governed by federal law as opposed to normal principles of state contract law.

Because "arbitration is simply a matter of contract between the parties,"[2] to which ordinary principles of contract law generally apply, a party may waive its right to compel arbitration.[3] The usual contract law test for determining whether a party has waived a right is whether the party acted inconsistently with a known right, and numerous courts have applied this formulation to claims that a party waived the right to arbitrate.[4]

Courts have overlaid at least some rules of federal law over the normal principles of state law that would apply to other contracts, however, such as holding that the Federal Arbitration Act (FAA) creates a presumption against finding a waiver of the contractual right to arbitrate.[5] The relation-

---

1   See § 8.2, *infra*.
2   First Options of Chicago, Inc. v. Kaplan, 514 U.S. 938, 943, 944, 115 S. Ct. 1920, 131 L. Ed. 2d 985 (1995).
3   Welborn Clinic v. Medquist, Inc., 301 F.3d 634, 637 (7th Cir. 2002) ("Like any other contractual right, the right to arbitrate a claim may be waived."); Mourik Int'l B.V. v. Reactor Services Int'l, Inc., 182 F. Supp. 2d 599, 604 (S.D. Tex. 2002) ("Whether Mourik waived its right to compel arbitration is an issue squarely determined by state law."); Levitan v. Fanfare Media Works, Inc., 2003 WL 21028339, at *6 (Cal. Ct. App. May 8, 2003) (California's common law waiver analysis escapes preemption by the FAA because waiver rules are "generally applicable" to all contracts, within the meaning of the FAA); Brendsel v. Winchester Constr. Co., 392 Md. 601, 898 A.2d 472 (2006) ("because the right to arbitration pursuant to the Federal or Uniform Arbitration Act arises from contract, it may be waived like most other contractual rights"); Blackburn v. Citifinancial, Inc., 2007 WL 927222 (Ohio Ct. App. Mar. 29, 2007) ("arbitration, as with any other contractual right, may be waived").
4   See, e.g., United Computer Sys., Inc. v. AT & T Corp., 298 F.3d 756 (9th Cir. 2002); Barker v. Golf U.S.A., Inc., 154 F.3d 788, 793 (8th Cir. 1998); PPG Indus., Inc. v. Webster Auto Parts, Inc., 128 F.3d 103, 107 (2d Cir. 1997); N. Cent. Constr., Inc. v. Siouxland Energy & Livestock Co-op., 232 F. Supp. 2d 959 (N.D. Iowa 2002); Pa. Life Ins. Co. v. Simoni, 641 N.W.2d 807 (Iowa 2002); In re Bruce Terminix Co., 988 S.W.2d 702, 704 (Tex. 1998).

   Although perhaps it should go without saying, a party generally cannot argue for a finding of waiver based on *its own conduct* in filing a case in court. See, e.g., McCann v. New Century Mortgage Corp., 2003 WL 21246040, at *3 (Ohio Ct. App. May 29, 2003) ("First, the appellant argues that she has waived her right to arbitration by filing litigation in a court of law and thus she must proceed with litigation of her claims in court. While appellant has chosen not to elect arbitration of the issues, she cannot waive Wells Fargo's right to arbitration. . . .").
   Similarly, a party's opposition to an arbitration motion does not, when the opposition fails, result in a waiver of that party's right *to participate* in the later arbitration of its own claims. See Kalai v. Gray, 109 Cal. App. 4th 768, 773–777 (2003).
5   Moses H. Cone Mem'l Hosp. v. Mercury Constr. Corp., 460 U.S. 1, 24, 25, 103 S. Ct. 927, 74 L. Ed. 2d 765 (1983) ("The Arbitration Act establishes that, as a matter of federal law, any doubts concerning the scope of arbitrable issues should be resolved in favor of arbitration, whether the problem at hand is the construction of the contract language itself or an allegation of waiver, delay, or a like defense to arbitrability."); *accord* Mitsubishi Motors Corp. v. Soler Chrysler-Plymouth, Inc., 473 U.S. 614, 626, 105 S. Ct. 3346, 87 L. Ed. 2d 444 (1985) (quoting *Moses*); Sovak v. Chugai Pharm. Co., 280 F.3d 1266, 1270 (9th Cir. 2002) (holding that FAA's presumption makes waiver a question of federal law, but applying common law waiver standards); Lyster v. Ryan's Family Steak Houses, Inc., 239 F.3d 939, 945 (8th Cir. 2001); Walker v. J.C. Bradford & Co., 938 F.2d 575, 577 (5th Cir. 1991); Connelly Mgmt., Inc. v. N. Am. Indem., N.V., 486 F. Supp. 2d 558 (D.S.C. 2007) (in light of FAA presumption, waiver not to be lightly inferred); Gordon v. Dadante, 2007 WL 949657 (N.D. Ohio Mar. 29, 2007) (waiver issue is "a matter of federal substantive law"); Citifinancial Corp. v. Peoples, 2007 WL 1454441 (Ala. May 18, 2007) (in light of strong presumption created by FAA, "the party opposing arbitration bears a heavy burden, and waiver is not lightly to be inferred" (citations omitted)); MS Credit Ctr., Inc. v. Horton, 926 So. 2d 167, 179 (Miss. 2006) ("waiver of arbitration is not a favored finding and there is a presumption against it"); Getz Recycling, Inc. v. Watts, 71 S.W.3d 224, 229 (Mo. Ct. App. 2002) (same); Blackburn v. Citifinancial, Inc., 2007 WL 927222 (Ohio Ct. App. Mar. 29, 2007) ("Because of the strong public policy in favor of arbitration, the heavy burden of proving waiver over the right to arbitration is on the party asserting a waiver." (citations omitted)); Neatherlin Homes, Inc. v. Love, 2007 WL 700996 (Tex. App. Mar. 8, 2007) ("There is a strong

ship of these two bodies of law has been the subject of some confusion.[6] Among other controversies, courts are divided as to whether the FAA creates a requirement that the party claiming that there has been a waiver of the right to arbitrate must establish that it suffered prejudice due to the actions of the other party (something that a party is not required to prove when claiming waiver of other contract rights).[7]

8.2 Does Court or Arbitrator Decide Whether There Is a Waiver?

As noted in § 2.2, *supra*, a recurring question in all manner of challenges to arbitration clauses is whether a particular challenge should be heard by a court or an arbitrator. On its face, the Supreme Court seemingly resolved this question in favor of the arbitrator in *Howsam v. Dean Witter Reynolds, Inc.*, in which the Court held that the category of issues to be left to courts does not include matters such as " 'allegation[s] of waiver, delay, or a like defense to arbitrability.' "[8] Several courts have since used this language from *Howsam* to hold that allegations that a party waived its right to compel arbitration are a procedural question that should be resolved by the arbitrator.[9] The categorization of waiver as a procedural issue for the arbitrator to resolve had also been adopted by several courts prior to the *Howsam* decision.[10]

Upon a closer review, however, it appears that the ostensibly broad language in *Howsam* was likely intended only to refer to allegations that a party waived its right to arbitrate based upon actions taken in arbitration, and not based upon actions taken in court. Many courts have reached this conclusion.[11] These decisions are consistent with the rule that generally applied before *Howsam* was decided.[12]

---

presumption against waiver under the FAA.").

6 *Compare* Sovak v. Chugai Pharm. Co., 280 F.3d 1266, 1270 (9th Cir. 2002) ("Accordingly, the FAA, and not Illinois law, supplies the standard of waiver.") *with* Levitan v. Fanfare Media Works, Inc., 2003 WL 21028339, at *6 (Cal. Ct. App. May 8, 2003) ("[W]e conclude that the state waiver principles that were invoked by the trial court escaped preemption by the FAA because they are generally applicable to contracts, within the meaning of the FAA.") *and In re* Media Arts Group, 116 S.W.3d 900, 906 (Tex. App. 2003) ("Therefore, while the FAA preempts application of state law that would render an existing arbitration agreement unenforceable, it does not preempt application of state law to determine the existence of an arbitration agreement.").

7 *See* § 3.2, *supra*.

8 Howsam v. Dean Witter Reynolds, Inc., 537 U.S. 79, 123 S. Ct. 588, 590, 154 L. Ed. 2d 491 (2002) (quoting Moses H. Cone Mem'l Hosp. v. Mercury Constr. Corp., 460 U.S. 1, 24, 25, 103 S. Ct. 927, 74 L. Ed. 2d 765 (1983)).

9 *See* Pro Tech Indus., Inc. v. URS Corp., 377 F.3d 868, 872 (8th Cir. 2004); Nat'l Am. Ins. Co. v. Transamerica Occidental Life Ins. Co., 328 F.3d 462 (8th Cir. 2003); RMES Communications, Inc. v. Qwest Bus. Gov't Services, Inc., 2006 WL 1183173, at *4–*5 (D. Colo. May 2, 2006) (arguments of waiver due to litigation activity are for the arbitrator under *Howsam*); Bellevue Drug Co. v. Advance PCS, 333 F. Supp. 2d 318, 324–325 (E.D. Pa. 2004) (finding that waiver is presumptively for the arbitrator to decide but then reaching the waiver question); Housh v. Dinovo Investments, Inc., 2003 WL 1119526 (D. Kan. Mar. 7, 2003); Woodland Ltd. v. Wulff, 868 A.2d 860, 865 (D.C. 2005) ("Even though the question of waiver in this case will turn on the degree and nature of appellants' participation in the court proceeding and—to that extent—considerations of efficiency might favor resolution by trial court, we think that the parties broad agreement to arbitrate 'any dispute arising under or related to' the Reed Smith partnership agreement dictates that this question incidental to their dispute about ownership of the Woodland shares under that agreement be submitted to the arbitrator."); Guam Hous. & Urban Renewal Auth. v. Pac. Super. Enter. Corp., 2004 Guam 22, ¶ 40 (Guam 2004) (applying *Howsam* to send waiver question to the arbitrator); Int'l River Ctr. v. Johns-Manville Sales Corp., 861 So. 2d 139, 144 (La. Ct. App. 2003) (applying *Howsam* to conclude that, for arbitration agreements governed by a state statute similar to the FAA, "waiver is reserved for the arbitrator to decide"); *cf.* Ansari v. Qwest Communications Corp., 414 F.3d 1214, 1220 (10th Cir. 2005) ("We do not address waiver in this appeal. It is presumed that the arbitrator will address any allegations concerning waiver.").

10 *See* Bell v. Cendant Corp., 293 F.3d 563 (2d Cir. 2002); Dean Witter Reynolds, Inc. v. McDonald, 758 So. 2d 539, 542 (Ala. 1999) ("matters of 'procedural arbitrability,' such as whether a party seeking arbitration has waived its right to arbitration by failing to comply with procedural requirements set forth in the arbitration agreement, are for the arbitrator to decide").

11 *See, e.g.,* Marie v. Allied Home Mortgage, Inc., 402 F.3d 1, 3–4 (1st Cir. 2005) (rejecting the argument that waiver must be decided by an arbitrator post-*Howsam* and holding that waiver is still an issue for the court to decide); Tristar Fin. Ins. Agency, Inc. v. Equicredit Corp. of Am., 97 Fed. Appx. 462, 464 (5th Cir. 2004) (applying *Howsam* and holding that "[c]ontracting parties would expect the court to decide whether one party's conduct before the court waived the right to arbitrate"); Ocwen Loan Servicing, L.L.C. v. Washington, 939 So. 2d 6 (Ala. 2006) (holding that allegation of waiver based on conduct during litigation was for the court to decide); *see also* Ehleiter v. Grapetree Shores, Inc., 482 F.3d 207, 217–218 (3d Cir. 2007) ("Finding persuasive the First Circuit's analysis in Marie v. Allied Home Mortgage, 402 F.3d 1 (1st Cir. 2005), one of the first post-*Howsam/Green Tree* cases that has squarely addressed the issue before us, we conclude that the Supreme Court did not intend its pronouncements in *Howsam* and *Green Tree* to upset the 'traditional rule' that courts, not arbitrators, should decide the question of whether a party has waived its right to arbitrate by activity litigating the case in court."); Reid Burton Constr. Co. v. Carpenters Dist. Council of S. Colo., Inc., 535 F.2d 598, 603–604 (10th Cir. 1976) (pre-*Howsam* case in which court ruled that equitable defenses based on conduct occurring in court should be decided by a court rather than by an arbitrator); Khan v. Parsons Global Services, Ltd., 480 F. Supp. 2d 327, 332 (D.D.C. 2007) ("Because this type of determination is one concerning the arbitrability of a claim, the issue of waiver of right to arbitrate should be decided by the Court, not an arbitrator, according to federal law."); Bahuriak v. Bill Kay Chrysler Plymouth, Inc., 337 Ill. App. 3d 714, 786 N.E.2d 1045 (2003) (post-*Howsam* case in which the court holds that questions of arbitrability were for the arbitrator under the contract terms, but then proceeds to analyze waiver as an issue for the court).

12 *See* S & R Co. of Kingston v. Latona Trucking, Inc., 159 F.3d

Both the text of the FAA and the rationale underlying the *Howsam* decision provide support for the argument that questions of waiver generally should be decided by the court rather than by the arbitrator. Section 4 of the FAA permits a court to order arbitration only "upon being satisfied that the making of the arbitration agreement *or the failure to comply therewith* is not in issue."[13] Similarly, section 3 of the FAA authorizes a court to stay litigation and enforce an arbitration agreement only if the party seeking arbitration "is not in default in proceeding with such arbitration."[14] Because an allegation that a party waived its right to arbitrate necessarily means that the party has defaulted or failed to comply with the arbitration agreement, waiver should thus be decided by a court.[15]

In addition to arguments based upon the statutory language, courts holding that allegations of waiver based on litigation activity are properly for courts rather than arbitrators to decide have done so for a host of valid policy and procedural concerns. Several courts have held, for example, that allegations of waiver based on a party's judicial conduct should be decided by a court based on both the court's comparative expertise (an important consideration in *Howsam*) in evaluating the effect of judicial conduct,[16] and on the court's inherent power to control its own docket and to punish unfair litigation tactics.[17] Other reasons that courts should retain the power to decide the waiver issue are that waiver is generally unconnected to the merits of the underlying dispute, and that it would be inefficient to remove a case from the judicial system and send it to an arbitrator to decide whether previous judicial activity requires returning the case back to the court that just sent it to arbitration.[18]

When the conduct allegedly constituting waiver occurred in arbitration rather than in court, or involved the failure to comply with the arbitration provider's rules, then there seems to be little question but that the arbitrator is in the best position to decide whether waiver has taken place.[19]

8.3 Arguments That Litigation Conduct Constituted Waiver of the Right to Compel Arbitration

8.3.1 *Filing of a Suit As Waiver*

A number of courts have held that a creditor who sues a consumer on a contract acts inconsistently with its right to compel arbitration and thus may waive such right.[20] Other

---

80, 83 (2d Cir. 1998); N & D Fashions, Inc. v. DHJ Indus., Inc., 548 F.2d 722 (8th Cir. 1976) (default based on active litigation "is a question for determination by courts"); Provident Bank v. Kabas, 141 F. Supp. 2d 310, 316 (E.D.N.Y. 2001).

13 9 U.S.C. § 4 (emphasis added).
14 9 U.S.C. § 3.
15 *See, e.g.*, Marie v. Allied Home Mortgage, Inc., 402 F.3d 1, 11–13 (1st Cir. 2005); N & D Fashions, Inc. v. DHJ Indus., Inc., 548 F.2d 722, 728–729 (8th Cir. 1976); Rugumbwa v. Betten Motor Sales, 136 F. Supp. 2d 729, 734 (W.D. Mich. 2001) (waiver implicated the validity of the arbitration clause and thus was for the court to decide); *cf.* Doctor's Associates, Inc. v. Distajo, 66 F.3d 438, 455 (2d Cir. 1995) (noting that the court has "equated a waiver of the right to arbitrate with a 'default in proceeding with such arbitration' under § 3" of the FAA); Engalla v. Permanente Med. Group, Inc., 15 Cal. 4th 951, 982, 64 Cal. Rptr. 2d 843, 938 P.2d 903 (1997) (non-FAA case holding that, when waiver argument concerns whether a valid arbitration clause exists at all, the issue is for the court).
16 *See* Marie v. Allied Home Mortgage, Inc., 402 F.3d 1, 13 (1st Cir. 2005); *see also* Engalla v. Permanente Med. Group, Inc., 15 Cal. 4th 951, 982, 64 Cal. Rptr. 2d 843, 938 P.2d 903 (1997) (pre-*Howsam* decision holding that waiver should be decided by the court). *But see* Nat'l Am. Ins. Co. v. Transamerica Occidental Life Ins. Co., 328 F.3d 462, 466 (8th Cir. 2003) (sending allegation of waiver based on judicial conduct to arbitrator).
17 Marie v. Allied Home Mortgage, Inc., 402 F.3d 1, 13 (1st Cir. 2005); *see also* Doctor's Associates, Inc. v. Distajo, 66 F.3d 438, 456 n.12 (2d Cir. 1995) (noting that courts' previous decisions "to rule on the waiver issue, rather than to refer the question to the arbitrators, could have been explained as exercises of the federal courts' inherent power to deal with abusive litigation tactics in their courtrooms"); Reid Burton Constr. Co. v. Carpenters Dist. Council of S. Colo., Inc., 535 F.2d 598, 603–604 (10th Cir. 1976) (holding that courts should decide allegations of waiver based on judicial conduct because "[t]o hold otherwise would unnecessarily hamper a court's control of its proceedings").
18 Marie v. Allied Home Mortgage, Inc., 402 F.3d 1, 13 (1st Cir. 2005).
19 *See, e.g.*, Pro Tech Indus., Inc. v. URS Crop., 377 F.3d 868, 872 (8th Cir. 2004) (finding that allegation that party waived right to arbitrate by making an untimely request for arbitration under the arbitration agreement was for the arbitrator to decide, because "arbitrators are the experts about the meaning of their own rules, and are comparatively better able to interpret and apply them than courts"); RMES Communications, Inc. v. Qwest Bus. Gov't Services, Inc., 2006 WL 1183173 (D. Colo. May 2, 2006) (holding that the question of whether a party's pre-litigation activity waived the right to arbitrate was for the arbitrator to decide).
20 *See* United Computer Sys., Inc. v. AT & T Corp., 298 F.3d 756 (9th Cir. 2002) (finding that first two prongs of the three-part waiver analysis were satisfied by the filing of a state court complaint, but ultimately holding that no prejudice had resulted from the filing and thus there was no waiver); Multicare Physicians & Rehab. Group, Prof'l Corp. v. Wong, 2006 WL 2556584 (Conn. Super. Ct. Aug. 15, 2006) (party waived right to compel arbitration by filing complaint in court asserting a number of arbitrable claims); Getz Recycling, Inc. v. Watts, 71 S.W.3d 224, 229 (Mo. Ct. App. 2002) ("There is no question that Getz acted inconsistently with its right to arbitrate, given that it first initiated suit for breach of contract, replevin, etc. in Jackson County."); Framan Mech., Inc. v. Lakeland Reg'l High Sch. Bd. of Educ., 2005 WL 2877923, at *1 (N.J. Super. Ct. App. Div. Nov. 3, 2005) (filing of complaint seeking "substantive resolution" of party's claims waived right to demand arbitration); Blackburn v. Citifinancial, Inc., 2007 WL 927222 (Ohio Ct. App. Mar. 29, 2007) ("by actively pursuing litigation in lieu of arbitration by filing a complaint to enforce its contractual rights under the note, Citifinancial has waived its own arbitration clause"); Elite Home Remodeling, Inc. v. Lewis, 2007 WL 730072 (Ohio Ct. App.

courts have used a more demanding phrase, insisting that a party must "substantially invoke the litigation process" to have waived the right to invoke an arbitration clause, and a great deal of case law involves disputes over what behavior does or does not constitute "substantially invoking the litigation process."[21]

One factor in determining whether a party has substantially invoked the machinery of the courtroom may be whether a party has learned something in litigation in the civil justice system that it might not have learned in arbitration. For example, in rejecting a plaintiff's motion to compel arbitration after the plaintiff had the chance to observe its opponent's legal theories, the California Supreme Court explained that " '[t]he courtroom may not be used as a convenient vestibule to the arbitration hall so as to allow a party to create his own unique structure combining litigation and arbitration.' "[22]

Other courts have focused on the fact that parties who file suit in court are undermining the purpose of arbitration of bringing efficiency to dispute resolution. The Seventh Circuit, for example, recognizes a presumption that a party's initiation of litigation waives the right to arbitrate because "selection of a forum in which to resolve a legal dispute should be made at the earliest possible opportunity in order to economize on the resources, both public and private, consumed in dispute resolution."[23] Thus, if an arbitration agreement requires both sides to arbitrate disputes, and one party ignores the arbitration agreement and sues on the contract, a number of courts have held that the party filing the lawsuit has waived the right to remove the whole case to arbitration.[24] Some courts have reached the same result, but given as their reason that the party bringing a lawsuit in the face of an arbitration agreement has breached its contractual promise to arbitrate and thereby lost its right to compel arbitration.[25]

On the other hand, a party generally does not waive the right to arbitrate a dispute merely by threatening to litigate.[26]

Mar. 12, 2007) ("Elite filed the complaint against Lewis, thereby waiving their right to arbitrate."); Checksmart v. Morgan, 2003 WL 125130, at *4 (Ohio Ct. App. Jan. 16, 2003) ("We are guided by *Mills* [v. Jaquar-Cleveland Motors, Inc.], wherein the institution of a lawsuit was an action inconsistent with the party's right to arbitrate."); *cf. In re* Citigroup Global Markets, Inc., 200 S.W.3d 742 (Tex. App. 2006) (when corporation removed lawsuit to federal court, seeking to have it resolved before multi-district litigation panel, it expressly waived its right to invoke the arbitration clause). *But see* Liberty Chevrolet, Inc. v. Rainey, 791 N.E.2d 625, 630 (Ill. App. Ct. 2003) ("There is simply no bright-line rule that, merely by filing a complaint, a plaintiff waives the right to demand arbitration of the issues raised by the complaint.").

21 Duferco Steel Inc. v. Kalisti, 121 F.3d 321, 326 (7th Cir. 1997); Worldsource Coil Coating, Inc. v. McGraw Constr. Co., 946 F.2d 473, 477 (6th Cir. 1991) (Ill. law) (finding waiver of right to arbitrate based on moving party's filing of a state court action seeking preliminary and permanent injunctions and compensatory and punitive damages); Palm Harbor Homes, Inc. v. Crawford, 689 So. 2d 3 (Ala. 1997) (manufacturer waives right to arbitrate breach of warranty claims by substantially invoking litigation process); Christensen v. Dewor Developments, 33 Cal. 3d 778, 191 Cal. Rptr. 8, 661 P.2d 1088 (1983) (denying motion to compel arbitration by party who filed suit, amended complaint after *demurrer*, voluntarily dismissed own claims, and filed motion the day before a hearing on the adequacy of the complaint); Harsco Corp. v. Crane Carrier Co., 701 N.E.2d 1040, 1044 (Ohio Ct. App. 1997) (noting in dictum that "a plaintiff's waiver may be effected by filing suit"); Mills v. Jaguar-Cleveland Motors, Inc., 430 N.E.2d 965, 967 (Ohio Ct. App. 1980); *see also* Cabinetree of Wis., Inc. v. Kraftmaid Cabinetry, Inc., 50 F.3d 388, 390, 391 (7th Cir. 1995) ("We have said that invoking judicial process is *presumptive* waiver."). *But see* Louis Dreyfus Negoce S.A. v. Blystad Shipping & Trading, Inc., 252 F.3d 218, 229 (2d Cir. 2001) (finding no waiver when party filed suit eight days before commencing arbitration and no litigation activity took place beyond parties' initial assertion of claims); Williams v. Healthalliance Hospitals, Inc., 158 F. Supp. 2d 156, 161 (D. Mass. 2001) (finding no waiver when plaintiff sought arbitration before filing litigation complaint and complaint included arbitration request if agreement was found to be applicable).

22 Christensen v. Dewor Developments, 33 Cal. 3d 778, 784, 191 Cal. Rptr. 8, 661 P.2d 1088 (1983) (quoting DeSapio v. Kohlmeyer, 35 N.Y.2d 402, 362 N.Y.S.2d 843, 321 N.E.2d 770, 773 (1974)).

23 Cabinetree of Wis., Inc. v. Kraftmaid Cabinetry, Inc., 50 F.3d 388, 391 (7th Cir. 1995); *see also* Welborn Clinic v. Medquist, Inc., 301 F.3d 634, 637 (7th Cir. 2002) ("Litigating a claim is clearly inconsistent with any perceived right to arbitration; we do not want parties to forum shop, taking a case to the courts and then, if things go poorly there, abandoning their suit in favor of arbitration.").

24 Chattin v. Cape May Greene, Inc., 216 N.J. Super. 618, 524 A.2d 841 (Super. Ct. App. Div. 1987), *aff'd*, 124 N.J. 520, 591 A.2d 943 (1991); Sears Roebuck & Co. v. Avery, 593 S.E.2d 424, 435 (N.C. Ct. App. 2004) (Ariz. law); *see also In re* S & R Co., 159 F.3d 80 (2d Cir. 1998); Connelly Mgmt., Inc. v. N. Am. Indem., N.V., 486 F. Supp. 2d 558 (D.S.C. 2007) (by resisting discovery in other lawsuits, and by suing in several other jurisdictions, party has acted inconsistently with its right to arbitrate); Marble Slab Creamery, Inc. v. Wesic, Inc., 823 S.W.2d 436 (Tex. App. 1992) (franchisor waived right to compel arbitration when it filed its application for compulsory arbitration one month before trial and when franchisee had filed an answer and counterclaims, taken part in depositions, and responded to discovery); Smith, Annotation, *Defendant's Participation in Action as Waiver of Right to Arbitration of Dispute Involved Therein*, 98 A.L.R.3d 767 (1980 and Supp. 1996). *But see* Liberty Chevrolet, Inc. v. Rainey, 791 N.E.2d 625 (Ill. App. Ct. 2003) (auto company's filing of complaint against consumer did not constitute waiver of right to compel arbitration of consumer's counterclaim); Nationwide of Bryan v. Dyer, 969 S.W.2d 518 (Tex. App. 1998); J.J. Andrews, Inc. v. Midland, 164 Wis. 2d 215, 474 N.W.2d 756 (Ct. App. 1991) (contractor who filed suit in court did not waive right to pursue arbitration against home owners; Wisconsin law does not require that a request for arbitration be made before a suit is commenced, and it does not require a plaintiff to reserve the right to arbitrate in the pleadings in order to avoid waiver).

25 Triarch Indus., Inc. v. Crabtree, 158 S.W.3d 772, 775–777 (Mo. 2005).

26 Inlandboatmens Union of the Pac. v. Dutra Group, 279 F.3d 1075, 1084 (9th Cir. 2002); Doctor's Associates, Inc. v. Distajo,

One court has also found that repossessing a vehicle does not waive the right to arbitrate the consumer's dispute.[27] Similarly, a party's filing suit on one claim may not constitute waiver of its right to compel arbitration of other related or unrelated claims.[28] A company waives its right to arbitrate when it brings a complaint against a consumer, and then seeks to non-suit that complaint and force the consumer's counterclaim into arbitration.[29]

It should be noted that the case law relating to the filing of lawsuits may not apply to other types of non-judicial proceedings. For instance, in *Russell v. Performance Toyota, Inc.*, the Supreme Court of Mississippi determined that an automobile dealership's act of repossessing and reselling the pickup truck that was the subject of a fraud dispute did not constitute a waiver of its right to compel arbitration, as this act did not qualify as the institution of a legal proceeding in court.[30] Furthermore, a party may go to court to obtain a provisional remedy, such as a temporary restraining order or preliminary injunction, without necessarily waiving its right to arbitrate the same general matter, so long as there is no evidence of significant delay or prejudice to the other party.[31]

8.3.2 Waiver by Delay in Enforcing the Arbitration Provision

8.3.2.1 Factors When Evaluating If a Party's Delay Constitutes Waiver

A number of courts have held that a party acts inconsistently with its right to arbitrate if it waits too long to move to compel arbitration after litigation has commenced.[32] In class action litigation, for example, a defendant must promptly move to compel arbitration in order to preserve its arbitration rights as to the entire class; it is not entitled to wait for class certification to be granted before seeking to compel the entire class into arbitration.[33]

---

107 F.3d 126, 132 (2d Cir. 1997).

27 Muhammad v. Serpentini, 2006 WL 2192096 (Ohio Ct. App. Aug. 3, 2006).

28 *See* Ivax Corp. v. B. Braun of Am., Inc., 286 F.3d 1309 (11th Cir. 2002) (defendant's prior suit against plaintiff's accounting firm to enforce separate agreement did not waive right to enforce parties' arbitration agreement); Gingiss Int'l, Inc. v. Bormet, 58 F.3d 328, 332 (7th Cir. 1995) (holding that party's prior prosecution of breach of contract claims in state court was not a waiver of its right to compel arbitration of federal Lanham Act claims); Fid. Nat'l Corp. v. Blakely, 305 F. Supp. 2d 639, 642 (S.D. Miss. 2003) (finding no waiver when party filed suit on claims excluded from arbitration clause but sought to compel arbitration of covered counterclaims); Federico v. Charterers Mut. Assurance Ass'n, Ltd., 158 F. Supp. 2d 565, 575 (E.D. Pa. 2001) ("The fact that Charterers participated in the underlying lawsuit is irrelevant to the question of waiver because Charterers was not a party to that litigation and, moreover, Federico has failed to establish that the underlying suit involved an arbitrable issue."); Liberty Chevrolet, Inc. v. Rainey, 791 N.E.2d 625 (Ill. App. Ct. 2003) (filing of complaint may not constitute waiver if changed circumstances make waiver inappropriate); *see also* Bischoff v. DirecTV, Inc., 180 F. Supp. 2d 1097, 1113 (C.D. Cal. 2002) (defendant's litigation and settlement in class action not involving plaintiff does not give rise to waiver of arbitration right as against plaintiff); Arriaga v. Cross Country Bank, 163 F. Supp. 2d 1189, 1201 (S.D. Cal. 2001) (same); Pa. Life Ins. Co. v. Simoni, 641 N.W.2d 807, 813 (Iowa 2002) ("[T]he claims made by Penn Life against the agents were not subject to the arbitration clause. Therefore, we do not think the company's filing of the present lawsuits was 'inconsistent with the right to arbitration.'" (citation omitted)). *But see* Grumhaus v. Comerica Sec., Inc., 223 F.3d 648, 652 (7th Cir. 2000) (holding that prior litigation of conversion, unjust enrichment, and constructive fraud claims waives right to arbitrate negligence, breach of duty, and securities law claims when all arose out of the "same issue," the liquidation of certain stocks); Schonfeldt v. Blue Cross of Cal., 2002 WL 4771 (Cal. Ct. App. Jan. 2, 2002) (holding that insurer's prior prosecution of reimbursement action in state court waives right to arbitrate insured's malicious prosecution and other tort claims based on the insurer's conduct in the prior litigation).

29 Grossinger N. Autocorp, Inc. v. Auysh, 2005 WL 4006535 (Ill. App. Ct. Nov. 18, 2005).

30 Russell v. Performance Toyota, Inc., 826 So. 2d 719 (Miss. 2002); *see also* Stern v. Prudential Fin., Inc., 2003 WL 1848279, at *4 (Pa. C.P. Feb. 4, 2003) (holding that defendant's alleged oral communication that plaintiff would not be bound by the arbitration agreement was not enough to evidence waiver, because it did not constitute " 'undisputed acts or language so inconsistent with a purpose to stand on the contract provisions as to leave no opportunity for a reasonable inference to the contrary.' " (citation omitted)), *rev'd*, 836 A.2d 953 (Pa. Super. Ct. 2003).

31 Simms v. NPCK Enterprises, Inc., 109 Cal. App. 4th 233, 134 Cal. Rptr. 2d 557 (2003); *see also* Citifinancial Corp. v. Peoples, 2007 WL 1454441 (Ala. May 18, 2007) (when lender brought non-judicial foreclosure that involved no litigation, it did not waive its right to arbitrate); *In re* Media Arts Group, 116 S.W.3d 900, 908, 909 (Tex. App. 2003) (finding no waiver based on agent's predispute representation that business-owners never enforced their arbitration clause).

32 *In re* Tyco Int'l Sec. Litig., 422 F.3d 41, 44 (1st Cir. 2005) ("an arbitration provision has to be invoked in a timely manner or the option is lost"); Grapetree Shores, Inc. v. Ehleiter, 2006 WL 889230, at *8 (D. V.I. Mar. 24, 2006) (four-year delay in seeking arbitration plus extensive pre-trial activity constituted waiver); AFD Fund v. Hinton, 2004 WL 2296983, at *3 (N.D. Tex. Oct. 13, 2004) (party waived right to arbitrate when it did not move to compel arbitration until three weeks before trial date, four months after summary judgment motion was filed, and two years after litigation was commenced); Rugumbwa v. Betten Motor Sales, 136 F. Supp. 2d 729 (W.D. Mich. 2001); Palm Harbor Homes, Inc. v. Crawford, 689 So. 2d 3 (Ala. 1997); Sobremonte v. Super. Ct., 61 Cal. App. 4th 980, 72 Cal. Rptr. 2d 43 (1998); Woodall v. Green Tree Fin. Servicing Corp., 755 So. 2d 681 (Fla. Dist. Ct. App. 1999). *But see* Thompson v. Skipper Real Estate Co., 729 So. 2d 287 (Ala. 1999); Dudenhefer v. Auto. Prot. Corp., 695 So. 2d 550 (La. Ct. App. 1997).

33 *In re* Currency Conversion Fee Antitrust Litig., 361 F. Supp. 2d 237, 257–258 (S.D.N.Y. 2005).

While waiver is not simply a function of the passage of time,[34] courts typically consider the delay between the initiation of litigation and a party's request for arbitration as one of several factors that are relevant to the waiver determination.[35] As delay alone may not establish prejudice to the non-moving party, courts look for additional evidence of prejudice, such as "lost evidence, duplication of efforts, use of discovery methods that are unavailable in arbitration, or litigation of substantial issues going to the merits."[36]

---

[34] See, e.g., Creative Solutions Group, Inc. v. Pentzer Corp., 252 F.3d 28, 32 (1st Cir. 2001) (" 'Waiver is not to be lightly inferred, and mere delay in seeking [arbitration] without some resultant prejudice to a party cannot carry the day.' " (citations omitted)); Peltz v. Sears, Roebuck & Co., 367 F. Supp. 2d 711 (E.D. Pa. 2005) (no waiver from seven-month delay in seeking arbitration when opposing party was not prejudiced); DeGroff v. Mascotech Forming Technologies—Ft. Wayne, Inc., 179 F. Supp. 2d 896, 913 (N.D. Ind. 2001) ("a delay in instituting arbitration as a result of participation in EEOC proceedings is insufficient to constitute waiver"); Green v. W.R.M. & Associates, Ltd., 174 F. Supp. 2d 459, 464 (N.D. Miss. 2001) ("the Greens have failed to show that they were 'materially prejudiced' by the [thirteen-month] delay"); Provident Bank v. Kabas, 141 F. Supp. 2d 310, 316 (E.D.N.Y. 2001) ("Neither the passage of time, standing alone, nor the incurring of legal expenses inherent in litigation, without more, are sufficient to support a finding of waiver."); Media Edge v. W.B. Doner, Inc., 112 F. Supp. 2d 383, 385 (S.D.N.Y. 2000) ("Given that other factors contributed to plaintiff's ten-month delay [in moving to compel arbitration], this lapse of time is not of itself enough to infer waiver."); Goldsmith v. Pinez, 84 F. Supp. 2d 228, 234 (D. Mass. 2000) (finding two-year delay between filing of suit and motion to compel arbitration not conclusive as to waiver because litigation had been stayed for one of the two years and neither party had yet taken discovery); MS Credit Ctr., Inc. v. Horton, 926 So. 2d 167, 180 (Miss. 2006) ("a party who seeks to compel arbitration after a long delay will not ordinarily be found to have waived the right where there has been no participation in, or advancement of, the litigation process"); Homes of Legend, Inc. v. McNiel, 2004 WL 2404336, at *2 (Tex. App. Oct. 28, 2004) ("Length of delay alone is not a basis for inferring waiver.").

[35] Ehleiter v. Grapetree Shores, Inc., 482 F.3d 207 (3d Cir. 2007) (although delay alone is not sufficient to constitute a waiver of right to arbitrate, a four-year delay is such a long period that it is a heavy factor in support of finding a waiver); In re Tyco Int'l Sec. Litig., 422 F.3d 41, 44 (1st Cir. 2005) (one party's unilateral demand to delay or stay arbitration until after the outcome of the party's criminal trial created waiver); Republic Ins. Co. v. PAICO Receivables, L.L.C., 383 F.3d 341 (5th Cir. 2004) (examining extent of pre-trial activity, time and expenses incurred, and failure to timely assert right to arbitrate in assessing prejudice); Kelly v. Golden, 352 F.3d 344, 350 (8th Cir. 2003) (noting more than a year's delay from complaint to motion for arbitration); PPG Indus., Inc. v. Webster Auto Parts, Inc., 128 F.3d 103, 107 (2d Cir. 1997) (examining lapse of time, amount of litigation activity, and proof of prejudice); Hoxworth v. Blinder, Robinson & Co., 980 F.2d 912, 925 (3d Cir. 1992) (eleven-month delay combined with participation in numerous pre-trial proceedings constituted waiver); Grapetree Shores, Inc. v. Ehleiter, 2006 WL 889230, at *8 (D. V.I. Mar. 24, 2006) (four-year delay in seeking arbitration plus extensive pre-trial activity constituted waiver); In re Currency Conversion Fee Antitrust Litig., 361 F. Supp. 2d 237, 257–258 (S.D.N.Y. 2005) (examining time elapsed, the amount of litigation and discovery already completed, and evidence of prejudice); AFD Fund v. Hinton, Inc., 2004 WL 2296983, at *2–*3 (N.D. Tex. Oct. 13, 2004); Perry v. Sonic Graphic Sys., Inc., 94 F. Supp. 2d 623, 625 (E.D. Pa. 2000) (examining timeliness, extent of litigation on the merits, notice to opposing party, extent of motion practice, moving party's assent to pre-trial orders, and extent of discovery); MS Credit Ctr., Inc. v. Horton, 926 So. 2d 167, 180 (Miss. 2006) (delay of eight months plus participation in litigation process sufficient to constitute waiver); Pass Termite & Pest Control v. Walker, 904 So. 2d 1030, 1035 (Miss. 2004) (waiver when defendant waited 237 days after complaint was filed before seeking arbitration and, in the interim, participated in litigation and proceeded with discovery); Getz Recycling, Inc. v. Watts, 71 S.W.3d 224, 229–231 (Mo. Ct. App. 2002) (four-month delay, plus efforts to seek interim injunctive relief from the court, created prejudice); Reis v. Peabody Coal Co., 935 S.W.2d 625, 631 (Mo. Ct. App. 1996) (two-year delay plus "pre-trial maneuvering" constituted waiver).

[36] Kelly v. Golden, 352 F.3d 344, 349 (8th Cir. 2003) (finding waiver when party had repeatedly urged court to resolve the entire dispute on the merits); Hoxworth v. Blinder, Robinson & Co., 980 F.2d 912, 926–927 (3d Cir. 1992); Com-Tech Assoc. v. Computer Assoc. Int'l, Inc., 938 F.2d 1574, 1578 (2d Cir. 1991) ("To permit litigants to exercise their contractual rights at such a late date, after they have deliberately chosen to participate in costly and extended litigation would defeat the purpose of arbitration: that disputes be resolved with dispatch and minimum expense."); Smith v. IMG Worldwide, Inc., 360 F. Supp. 2d 681, 687 (E.D. Pa. 2005) (waiver found when party engaged in extensive motions practice, requested and provided discovery, and obtained discovery not available in arbitration); Simitar Entm't, Inc. v. Silva Entm't, Inc., 44 F. Supp. 2d 986, 991 n.3 (D. Minn. 1999); Ocwen Loan Servicing, L.L.C. v. Washington, 939 So. 2d 6 (Ala. 2006) (costs expended responding to pre-trial motions constituted prejudice); O'Keefe Architects, Inc. v. CED Constr. Partners, Ltd., 944 So. 2d 181 (Fla. 2006) (mere delay does not constitute a waiver of the right to compel arbitration, the party must also participate in litigation); Getz Recycling, Inc. v. Watts, 71 S.W.3d 224, 229–231 (Mo. Ct. App. 2002) (four-month delay, plus efforts to seek interim injunctive relief from the court, created prejudice); Reis v. Peabody Coal Co., 935 S.W.2d 625, 631 (Mo. Ct. App. 1996); Moose v. Versailles Condo. Ass'n, 614 S.E.2d 418, 422 (N.C. Ct. App. 2005) ("A party may be prejudiced if, for example, it is forced to bear the burden and expenses of a lengthy trial; evidence helpful to a party is lost because of delay in seeking of arbitration; a party's opponent takes advantage of judicial discovery procedures not available in arbitration; or by reason of delay, a party has taken steps in litigation to its detriment or expended significant amounts of money thereupon."); see also Rugumbwa v. Betten Motor Sales, 136 F. Supp. 2d 729 (W.D. Mich. 2001) (mag.) (finding waiver based on defendant's failure to raise arbitration either in answer, joint status report, or amended answer, as well as defendant's filing of summary judgment motion on the merits and taking of substantial discovery after first requesting arbitration; the defendant apparently had not itself been aware of the arbitration clause until well into the litigation, to which the magistrate judge responded: "The court is troubled by defendant's contention that it did not discover the arbitration clause found in its own 'sales order' forms until after it filed its answer."); Evans v. Accent Manufactured Homes, Inc., 575 S.E.2d 74 (S.C. Ct. App. 2003) (finding that "[a] party seeking to establish waiver must show prejudice through an undue

Additionally, moving to compel arbitration after filing a motion for summary judgment or otherwise seeking to have a court decide the merits of the dispute constitutes prejudice because, otherwise, a party would be allowed two bites at the apple.[37] Parties claiming waiver of arbitration should treat this issue as one on which they bear the burden of proof in demonstrating both delay *and* prejudice, when required, through production of evidence.[38] The Fourth Circuit has held that the party opposing arbitration not only bears a "heavy burden of proving waiver," but also that the "proof must be concrete, not merely speculative."[39] However, courts seem to require less evidence of prejudice when the party seeking arbitration has purposely engaged in delaying tactics.[40]

8.3.2.2 Delaying Actions Found to Constitute Waiver

A number of courts have held that a party generally cannot seek to compel arbitration after submitting arguments on the merits of the case to a court.[41] So, for example, bringing a motion to dismiss or seeking summary judgment is inconsistent with arbitration and waives the right to arbitrate the dispute.[42]

Likewise, a merchant's filing of a bad faith bankruptcy to avoid litigation, and subsequent filing of a counterclaim in the litigation, are inconsistent with the right to arbitrate, and constitute a waiver of that right.[43] Other actions that may constitute waiver include filing an answer, withdrawing a motion to compel arbitration and answering a complaint without referring to the right to compel arbitration, asserting a counterclaim, moving for a continuance, and failing to timely request arbitration.[44]

---

burden caused by delay in demanding arbitration," and that " '[m]ere inconvenience to an opposing party is not sufficient' " to make such a showing; in this case the court did find waiver, based on the defendant's use of discovery not allowable in arbitration as well as the discovery costs imposed on the plaintiff).

37 Baker v. Stevens, 114 P.3d 580, 584 (Utah 2005); *see also* Hoxworth v. Blinder, Robinson & Co., 980 F.2d 912, 926 (3d Cir. 1992) (prejudice turns on the degree to which the party seeking arbitration has contested the merits of the underlying claim in court); Gordon v. Dadante, 2007 WL 949657 (N.D. Ohio Mar. 29, 2007) (when party attempted to litigate issues in front of court, it would be "grossly inequitable" to allow it to later take those issues to arbitration after the court issued "decisions [that] did not suit it"); Reis v. Peabody Coal Co., 935 S.W.2d 625, 631 (Mo. Ct. App. 1996) (finding waiver when party waited until after losing motion for summary judgment before filing for arbitration).

38 *See* MicroStrategy, Inc. v. Lauricia, 268 F.3d 244, 251, 252 (4th Cir. 2001) (holding that party asserting waiver failed to carry its burden of proving that opponent obtained discovery through litigation that it could not have obtained in arbitration; court applied holding of Green Tree Financial Corp.-Alabama v. Randolph, 531 U.S. 79, 121 S. Ct. 513, 148 L. Ed. 2d 373 (2000), on proof of arbitration costs to issue of waiver); Green v. W.R.M. & Associates, 174 F. Supp. 2d 459, 463 (N.D. Miss. 2001) ("a party alleging waiver of arbitration must carry a heavy burden"); Robinson v. Daimler Chrysler Corp., 2004 WL 1393768, at *2 (Mich. Ct. App. June 22, 2004) ("A party arguing that waiver occurred bears a heavy burden of proof."); Homes of Legend, Inc. v. McNiel, 2004 WL 2404336, at *2 (Tex. App. Oct. 28, 2004) (no waiver when party failed to prove prejudice beyond simply showing delay).

39 MicroStrategy, Inc. v. Lauricia, 268 F.3d 244 (4th Cir. 2001) (citations omitted).

40 *In re* Tyco Int'l Ltd. Sec. Litig., 422 F.3d 41, 46 & n.5 (1st Cir. 2005) (requiring only a "modicum of prejudice" when the defendant had engaged in dilatory behavior); Ocwen Loan Servicing, L.L.C. v. Washington, 939 So. 2d 6 (Ala. 2006) (costs expended responding to pre-trial motions constituted prejudice when defendant's actions were motivated by forum shopping).

41 Grumhaus v. Comerica Sec., Inc., 223 F.3d 648, 651 (7th Cir. 2000); Woodall v. Green Tree Fin. Servicing Corp., 755 So. 2d 681 (Fla. Dist. Ct. App. 1999); Atkins v. Rustic Woods Partners, 171 Ill. App. 3d 373, 525 N.E.2d 551, 555 (1988) ("submitting substantive issues to the court for determination manifests an intent to abandon the right to arbitrate"); Cox v. Howard, Weil, Labouisse, Friedrichs, Inc., 619 So. 2d 908, 914 (Miss. 1993) (waiver found after party sought summary judgment); Harsco Corp. v. Crane Carrier Co., 701 N.E.2d 1040, 1044 (Ohio Ct. App. 1997); Mills v. Jaguar-Cleveland Motors, Inc., 430 N.E.2d 965, 967 (Ohio Ct. App. 1980) ("Failure to move for a stay, coupled with responsive pleadings, will constitute a defendant's waiver."); Baker v. Stevens, 114 P.3d 580, 584 (Utah May 31, 2005).

42 Karnette v. Wolpoff & Abramson, L.L.P., 444 F. Supp. 2d 640 (E.D. Va. 2006); *cf.* Smay v. E.R. Steubner, Inc., 864 A.2d 1266, 1278 (Pa. Super. Ct. 2004) (acceptance of judicial process includes a party's failure to raise the arbitration issue promptly, a party's engagement in discovery, and a party waiting until it receives adverse rulings on pre-trial motions before raising arbitration). *But see* Pack v. Damon Corp., 320 F. Supp. 2d 545 (E.D. Mich. 2004) (no waiver when summary judgment motion accompanied by request to remove to arbitration), *rev'd in part on other grounds*, 434 F.3d 810 (6th Cir. 2006).

43 Sedillo v. Campbell, 5 S.W.3d 824 (Tex. App. 1999).

44 Lewallen v. Green Tree Servicing, L.L.C., 487 F.3d 1085 (8th Cir. 2007) (lender waived its right to compel arbitration by not raising the issue when bankrupt debtor filed an objection to a proof of claim, asked the bankruptcy court to reject those objections and dispose of the debtor's claims on their merits, served discovery requests on the debtor, and waited eleven months before moving to compel arbitration); Ehleiter v. Grapetree Shores, Inc., 482 F.3d 207 (3d Cir. 2007) (when party engaged in extensive discovery and substantial non-merits motion practice, these were significant factors in finding a waiver of the right to compel arbitration); Republic Ins. Co. v. PAICO Receivables, L.L.C., 383 F.3d 341, 345 (5th Cir. 2004) (finding waiver when party answered counterclaims, "conducted full-fledged discovery," took depositions, moved for summary judgment, and filed "numerous other motions"); Kelly Golden, 352 F.3d 344, 349, 350 (8th Cir. 2003) (year's delay and significant litigation of the merits of the case support finding of waiver); Navieros Inter-Americanos, S.A. v. M/V Vasilia Express, 120

§ 8.3.2.2 Consumer Arbitration Agreements

Similarly, if certain defendants file motions to compel arbitration, but one fails to do so, that defendant may have waived its right to compel arbitration.[45] A defendant may also waive the right to arbitrate a claim by excessively delaying the arbitration process.[46]

Courts are especially apt to find a waiver of the right to arbitrate when there has already been extensive discovery

---

F.3d 304, 315, 316 (1st Cir. 1997) (defendant's month-long participation in litigation up until eve of trial, during which parties "scrambled to prepare for trial, incurring expenses that would not have been occasioned by preparing for an arbitration," establishes waiver of right to arbitrate); Hoxworth v. Blinder, Robinson & Co., 980 F.2d 912, 925 (3d Cir. 1992) (litigating for eleven months and participating in numerous pre-trial proceedings constituted waiver); S & H Contractors, Inc. v. A.J. Taft Coal Co., 906 F.2d 1507, 1514 (11th Cir. 1990) (when a party delayed eight months and engaged in merits and non-merits motion practice and took several depositions, it waived its right to compel arbitration); Van Ness Townhouses v. Mar Indus. Corp., 862 F.2d 754, 759 (9th Cir. 1988) (waiver when defendant chose "to litigate actively the entire matter—including pleadings, motions, and approving a pre-trial conference order—and did not move to compel arbitration until more than two years after [plaintiffs] brought the action"); Nat'l Found. for Cancer Research v. A.G. Edwards & Sons, 821 F.2d 772, 775 (D.C. Cir. 1987) (court found waiver when the defendant "had invoked the litigation machinery" by, *inter alia*, filing an answer without asserting arbitration as an affirmative defense, requesting documents and deposing plaintiff's witnesses, opposing plaintiff's motion to amend its complaint, and moving for summary judgment); Price v. Drexel, Burnham Lambert, Inc., 791 F.2d 1156 (5th Cir. 1986) (court found waiver when defendant litigated for seventeen months and participated in extensive discovery before demanding arbitration); S. Broward Hosp. Dist. v. MedQuist, Inc., 2007 WL 1041684 (D.N.J. Mar. 30, 2007) (party waived its right to compel arbitration by filing seven motions and answering the complaint prior to filing its motion to compel arbitration); *In re* Currency Conversion Antitrust Litig., 361 F. Supp. 2d 237, 257–258 (S.D.N.Y. 2005) (delay of several years in seeking arbitration, along with extensive discovery taken by defendant, supported finding of waiver); Snelling & Snelling, Inc. v. Reynolds, 140 F. Supp. 2d 1314, 1322 (M.D. Fla. 2001) (defendant's filing of answer to complaint, participation in court-ordered mediation, taking and responding to discovery, are "acts inconsistent with the intent to arbitrate" and give rise to waiver of right); Rugumbwa v. Betten Motor Sales, 136 F. Supp. 2d 729 (W.D. Mich. 2001); Ocwen Loan Servicing, L.L.C. v. Washington, 939 So. 2d 6 (Ala. 2006) (waiver occurred when defendant did not seek arbitration until after it unsuccessfully sought to remove case to federal court and transfer it into federal multi-district litigation); Voyager Life Ins. Co. v. Hughes, 2001 Ala. LEXIS 466, at *5–*9 (Ala. Dec. 21, 2001) (defendant's filing of answers to plaintiff's four amended or restated complaints, pursuit of cross-claim, filing of third-party indemnity actions, conduct and participation in discovery, and filing of motions to dismiss and consolidate over four years of litigation constitute waiver of right to arbitrate); Aviation Data, Inc. v. Am. Express Travel Related Services Co., 152 Cal. App. 4th 1522, 62 Cal. Rptr. 3d 396 (2007) (when company engaged in substantial litigation to have class action settlement approved by court, and settlement was later discovered to have been approved based upon misrepresentations to court, the company could not invoke the arbitration clause against subsequent plaintiffs because it had already "indisputably made use of the judicial process"); Pitkin v. Fid. Nat'l Title Ins. Co., 2002 WL 462506 (Cal. Ct. App. Mar. 27, 2002) (finding waiver based on defendant's failure to plead arbitration as affirmative defense, filing of cross-complaint seeking declaration of parties' rights under insurance policy, taking of discovery including depositions against plaintiffs, and filing of nineteen motions *in limine* between parties framing issues for trial); Coastal Systems Dev., Inc. v. Bunnell Found., 2007 WL 982438 (Fla. Dist. Ct. App. Apr. 4, 2007) (company waived its right to invoke arbitration clause when it did not seek to compel arbitration until two years into litigation, answered the other party's complaint, asserted counterclaims, and proceeded with discovery, before seeking to compel arbitration); Marine Envtl. Partners, Inc. v. Johnson, 863 So. 2d 423, 427 (Fla. Dist. Ct. App. 2003) (when a party defends on the merits by answering the complaint without demanding arbitration, a waiver is deemed to have occurred); Griffis v. Branch Banking & Trust Co., 268 Ga. App. 588, 602 S.E.2d 307 (2004) (finding waiver when defendants asserted a multicount counterclaim, engaged in extensive discovery, and waited nine months before asserting their right to arbitration); Phil Wooden Homes v. Ladwig, 262 Ga. App. 792, 586 S.E.2d 697 (2003) (finding waiver when defendants asserted a counterclaim and engaged in extensive discovery before asserting their right to arbitration); Cencula v. Keller, 152 Ill. App. 3d 754, 757, 504 N.E.2d 997 (1987) (defendant's filing of fact-based answer to complaint waives later right to compel arbitration); NSC v. Borders, 317 Md. 394, 564 A.2d 408 (1989) (litigation to the point of trial on the merits constitutes a waiver of arbitration); Commonwealth Equity v. Messick, 152 Md. App. 381, 831 A.2d 1144 (2003) (defendants filed arbitration by filing answers, participating in discovery, and waiting until eve of trial for arbitration); RTKL v. Four Villages, 95 Md. App. 135, 620 A.2d 351 (1993) (defendants waived arbitration by filing cross claims, participating in discovery, and waiting five years to demand arbitration); Robinson v. Daimler Chrysler Corp., 2004 WL 1393768, at *3 (Mich. Ct. App. June 22, 2004) (waiver found when defendant filed a counterclaim, defended motions, deposed witnesses, and waited until six months after the completion of discovery to move to compel arbitration); Cox v. Howard, Weil, Labouisse, Friedrichs, Inc., 619 So. 2d 908, 914 (Miss. 1993) (waiver when party sought summary judgment, requested two continuances, and sought various types of discovery); Reis v. Peabody Coal Co., 935 S.W.2d 625, 631 (Mo. Ct. App. 1996) (two-year delay plus unsuccessful summary judgment motion constituted waiver); GE Lancaster Investments, L.L.C. v. Am. Exp. Tax & Bus., 920 A.2d 850 (Pa. Super. Ct. 2007) (when party litigated pre-complaint discovery in fraud case—knowing that if it was able to prevail on those issues, it would prevail in the litigation—and then filed an answer to the complaint, it waived its right to compel arbitration); Sedillo v. Campbell, 5 S.W.3d 824 (Tex. App. 1999); Cent. Nat'l Ins. Co. v. Lerner, 856 S.W.2d 492 (Tex. App. 1993). *But see Ex parte* Smith, 736 So. 2d 604 (Ala. 1999) (answer had been filed, but no discovery initiated); Greenpoint v. Reynolds, 151 S.W.3d 868, 876 (Mo. Ct. App. 2005) (no waiver when party filed counterclaim that was excluded from the scope of the arbitration clause).

45 Palm Harbor Homes, Inc. v. Crawford, 689 So. 2d 3 (Ala. 1997).
46 Engalla v. Permanente Med. Group, Inc., 15 Cal. 4th 951, 64 Cal. Rptr. 2d 843, 938 P.2d 903 (1997). *But see Ex parte* Smith, 736 So. 2d 604 (Ala. 1999) (delay justified because merchant was waiting for consumer to obtain counsel).

through the judicial process.[47] These courts find that the moving party's ability to use litigation to obtain discovery that is not available in arbitration makes the subsequent removal of the case to arbitration prejudicial to the non-moving party[48] or, alternatively, that prolonged discovery proceedings can be unduly costly, and thus prejudicial, to the non-moving party.[49]

One principle related to waiver is that a party may forfeit its right to appeal a denial of a motion to compel arbitration if it does not take advantage of its right to take an immediate interlocutory appeal and instead waits for the completion of proceedings in the trial court.[50] Because 9 U.S.C.

---

[47] *See, e.g.*, PPG Indus., Inc. v. Webster Auto Parts, Inc., 128 F.3d 103, 109 (2d Cir. 1997) (finding prejudice to non-moving party when opponent obtained answers to interrogatories and subpoena); Cabinetree of Wis., Inc. v. Kraftmaid Cabinetry, Inc., 50 F.3d 388, 391 (7th Cir. 1995) (finding waiver when moving party presented no plausible reason for waiting until after discovery to move for arbitration); Connelly Mgmt., Inc. v. N. Am. Indem., N.V., 486 F. Supp. 2d 558 (D.S.C. 2007) (by resisting discovery in other lawsuits, and by suing in several other jurisdictions, party has acted inconsistently with its right to arbitrate); Smith v. IMG Worldwide, Inc., 360 F. Supp. 2d 681, 687 (E.D. Pa. 2005) (waiver found when party engaged in extensive motions practice, assented to court orders, requested and provided discovery, and obtained discovery not available in arbitration); Snelling & Snelling, Inc. v. Reynolds, 140 F. Supp. 2d 1314, 1322 (M.D. Fla. 2001); Perry v. Sonic Graphic Sys., Inc., 94 F. Supp. 2d 623, 625 (E.D. Pa. 2000) (finding waiver based in part on parties' extensive written discovery and defendant's deposition of plaintiff); Voyager Life Ins. Co. v. Hughes, 2001 Ala. LEXIS 466, at *5–*9 (Ala. Dec. 21, 2001); Sobremonte v. Super. Ct., 61 Cal. App. 4th 980, 994, 995, 72 Cal. Rptr. 2d 43 (1998) (finding waiver when moving party enjoyed the "advantage of judicial discovery procedures not available in arbitration"); MS Credit Ctr., Inc. v. Horton, 926 So. 2d 167 (Miss. 2006) (lenders waived their right to compel arbitration when they engaged in the litigation process for eight months by consenting to a scheduling order, engaging in written discovery, and conducting deposition of borrower, before asserting the right to arbitration); Pass Termite & Pest Control v. Walker, 904 So. 2d 1030, 1035 (Miss. 2004) (waiver when defendant waited 237 days after complaint was filed before seeking arbitration and, in the interim, participated in litigation and proceeded with discovery); Moose v. Versailles Condo. Ass'n, 614 S.E.2d 418, 422–423 (N.C. Ct. App. 2005) (waiver found when defendant obtained discovery and then moved to compel arbitration in order to prevent plaintiff from receiving any discovery); Evans v. Accent Manufactured Homes, Inc., 575 S.E.2d 74 (S.C. Ct. App. 2003) (finding waiver when the defendant "availed itself of discovery tools unavailable in arbitration," thus "obtaining information from [plaintiff] it might not have been able to otherwise obtain," and also necessitating plaintiff's own costly pursuit of discovery); *cf.* Neatherlin Homes, Inc. v. Love, 2007 WL 700996 (Tex. App. Mar. 8, 2007) (no waiver when discovery sent was minimal, no depositions had taken place, and party had not filed any dispositive motions).

[48] Republic Ins. Co. v. PAICO Receivables, L.L.C., 383 F.3d 341, 347 (5th Cir. 2004) (finding prejudice when party sought discovery not available in arbitration); PPG Indus., Inc. v. Webster Auto Parts, Inc., 128 F.3d 103, 109 (2d Cir. 1997) ("We have held that sufficient prejudice to sustain a finding of waiver exists when a party takes advantage of pre-trial discovery not available in arbitration."); Stifel, Nicolaus & Co. v. Freeman, 924 F.2d 157, 159 (8th Cir. 1991) ("[p]rejudice may result from . . . use of discovery methods unavailable in arbitration"); *In re* Currency Conversion Fee Antitrust Litig., 2005 WL 1427400, at *4 (S.D.N.Y. June 20, 2005); Smith v. IMG Worldwide, Inc., 360 F. Supp. 2d 681, 687 (E.D. Pa. 2005) (waiver found when party engaged in extensive motions practice, requested and provided discovery, and obtained discovery not available in arbitration); Provident Bank v. Kabas, 141 F. Supp. 2d 310, 316 (E.D.N.Y. 2001) (listing "proof of prejudice, including taking advantage of pre-trial discovery not available in arbitration," among factors to be considered in waiver determination); Robinson v. Daimler Chrysler Corp., 2004 WL 1393768, at *3 (Mich. Ct. App. June 22, 2004) (waiver found when defendant filed a counterclaim, defended motions, deposed witnesses, and waited until six months after the completion of discovery to try to compel arbitration); *cf.* Walker v. J.C. Bradford & Co., 938 F.2d 575, 578 n.30 (5th Cir. 1991) (suggesting that waiver would occur if a party took discovery of "items that would not be discoverable in arbitration proceedings"). *But see* MicroStrategy, Inc. v. Lauricia, 268 F.3d 244, 251 (4th Cir. 2001) (rejecting waiver argument based on defendant's discovery requests in litigation when plaintiff "made no effort to establish what discovery would or would not be available to in an arbitration proceeding"); Lewis Tree Serv., Inc. v. Lucent Technologies Inc., 239 F. Supp. 2d 332 (S.D.N.Y. 2002) (holding that discovery on the issue of the scope of the arbitration clause, rather than on the merits of the claim, did not constitute waiver).

[49] *See, e.g.*, Republic Ins. Co. v. PAICO Receivables, L.L.C., 383 F.3d 341, 347 (5th Cir. 2004) (finding prejudice when opposing party incurred significant litigation costs resulting from failure to timely move to compel arbitration); Kelly v. Golden, 352 F.3d 344, 350 (8th Cir. 2003) (finding prejudice based on costs, delay incurred in year of litigation prior to motion for arbitration); *In re* Currency Conversion Fee Antitrust Litig., 2005 WL 1427400, at *4 (S.D.N.Y. June 20, 2005); Smith v. IMG Worldwide, Inc., 360 F. Supp. 2d 681, 687 (E.D. Pa. 2005); AFD Fund v. Hinton, Inc., 2004 WL 2296983, at *3 (N.D. Tex. Oct. 13, 2004) (finding that expenses and attorney fees incurred to file motion for summary judgment and prepare for trial constituted prejudice); N. Cent. Constr., Inc. v. Siouxland Energy & Livestock Co-op., 232 F. Supp. 2d 959 (N.D. Iowa 2002); Robinson v. Daimler Chrysler Corp., 2004 WL 1393768, at *3 (Mich. Ct. App. June 22, 2004) (waiver found when defendant filed a counterclaim, defended motions, deposed witnesses, and waited until six months after the completion of discovery to try to compel arbitration); Moose v. Versailles Condo. Ass'n, 614 S.E.2d 418, 422–423 (N.C. Ct. App. 2005) (finding prejudice when opposing party had already spent more than $32,000 in legal fees); Rhodes v. Benson Chrysler-Plymouth, Inc., 2007 WL 816811 (S.C. Ct. App. Mar. 19, 2007) (finding waiver of right to compel arbitration when parties exchanged written interrogatories and requests to produce, took five depositions, and "completed virtually all discovery" before defendant moved to compel arbitration); Evans v. Accent Manufactured Homes, Inc., 575 S.E.2d 74 (S.C. Ct. App. 2003); Baker v. Stevens, 114 P.3d 580, 584 (Utah 2005).

[50] Franceschi v. Hosp. Gen. San Carlos, Inc., 420 F.3d 1 (1st Cir. 2005) ("failure to promptly appeal a denial of arbitration will[,] if prejudicial to the opposing party, operate to forfeit the demanding party's right to arbitration"); Cargill Ferrous Int'l v. Sea Phoenix MV, 325 F.3d 695, 700 (5th Cir. 2003); John Morrell & Co. v. United Food & Commercial Workers Int'l Union, 37 F.3d 1302, 1303 n.3 (8th Cir. 1994); Cotton v. Sloane,

§ 16(a)(1)(B) makes denials of orders compelling arbitration immediately appealable in order to streamline the judicial process and avoid unnecessary litigation of a case that might be subject to arbitration, a party's failure to take an immediate appeal and to wait for litigation to run its course before appealing would, if prejudicial to the opposing party, defeat the purpose of the statute.[51]

Finally, a court should find that a party waives its contractual right to compel arbitration if the party has taken the position in litigation that it is not bound by the contract in which the arbitration clause appears. A defendant should not be able to enforce an arbitration clause while denying that it ever entered into a binding contract with the plaintiff. As the First Circuit explained in a commercial case:

> Vasilia complains of self-inflicted wounds. Vasilia denied it had a valid charter with Navieros up until the eve of trial. It then switched positions, admitted the validity of the charter party, and sought to invoke arbitration under the charter party. We agree with the district court that this conduct amounted to a waiver.[52]

8.3.2.3 Delaying Actions Found Not to Constitute Waiver

A company has been found not to have waived its right to arbitrate a dispute just because it did not promptly respond to a consumer's letter requesting that the matter be arbitrated.[53] Another court has ruled that answering a complaint and asking for a jury trial does not waive the right to arbitrate when the defendant simultaneously requested that the case be removed to arbitration.[54] Courts also may find a defendant's limited defense of a consumer's claim (for example, filing a motion to dismiss or initiating limited discovery) not to act as a waiver of the right to arbitrate.[55] Filing a counterclaim of a type that is excluded from the scope of the arbitration agreement is not inconsistent with the right to arbitrate.[56]

One court has held that even "remarkably aggressive" litigation activities in court will not waive a company's right to insist on arbitration, when the litigation was "primarily directed to claims unrelated to those asserted" in the case in which the company was trying to compel arbitration.[57]

---

4 F.3d 176, 180 (2d Cir. 1993); *see also In re* Tyco Int'l Sec. Litig., 422 F.3d 41, 46 (1st Cir. 2005) (party waived right to arbitrate by failing to take timely appeal pursuant to 9 U.S.C. § 16(a)(1) of order denying arbitration). *But see* Clark v. Merrill Lynch, Pierce, Fenner & Smith, Inc., 924 F.2d 550, 553 (4th Cir. 1991) (party does not forfeit appeal rights by failing to take interlocutory appeal).

51 *See* Franceschi v. Hosp. Gen. San Carlos, Inc., 420 F.3d 1 (1st Cir. 2005); *see also* Colon v. R.K. Grace & Co., 358 F.3d 1, 4 & n.2 (1st Cir. 2003).

52 Navieros Inter-Americanos, S.A. v. M/V Vasilia Express, 120 F.3d 304, 316 (1st Cir. 1997). *But see* Saint Agnes v. PacifiCare, 8 Cal. Rptr. 3d 517 (Cal. 2003) (mere filing of a lawsuit, even a lawsuit seeking to declare the entire contract void ab initio, does not indicate a waiver of the right to compel arbitration; waiver can only be evidenced by the actual litigation of the merits of any arbitrable issues).

53 *In re* Oakwood Mobile Homes, Inc., 987 S.W.2d 571 (Tex. 1999); *see also* Williamson v. Pub. Storage, Inc., 2004 WL 491058 (D. Conn. Mar. 1, 2004) (finding no waiver when defendant notified plaintiff of intent to seek arbitration one month after complaint was filed); Provident Bank v. Kabas, 141 F. Supp. 2d 310, 318 (E.D.N.Y. 2001) ("[D]efendants sought enforcement of the parties' agreement to arbitrate shortly after the Bank commenced litigation. There was no obligation to seek any 'preemptive' arbitration prior to commencement of this lawsuit. In short, there was no waiver of the right to arbitrate the parties' dispute.").

54 Sloan v. Nat'l Healthcorp., Ltd. P'ship, 2006 WL 2516403 (Tenn. Ct. App. Aug. 30, 2006).

55 *See* Sovak v. Chugai Pharm. Co., 280 F.3d 1266, 1269, 1270 (9th Cir. 2002) (no waiver based on defendant's motion to dismiss second amended complaint when plaintiff failed to show prejudice); Dumont v. Saskatchewan Gov't Ins., 258 F.3d 880, 886, 887 (8th Cir. 2001) (no waiver based on defendant's motion to dismiss, which referred to intent to seek arbitration); Walker v. J.C. Bradford & Co., 938 F.2d 575, 577 (5th Cir. 1991) (defendant's thirteen-month delay, during which it removed complaint to federal court and served interrogatories on plaintiffs, did not establish waiver); Reidy v. Cyberonics, Inc., 2007 WL 496679 (S.D. Ohio Feb. 8, 2007) ("though Defendant removed this case to federal court, filed an answer, and engaged in discovery, Defendant's actions do not rise to the level of substantial participation in litigation"); Peltz v. Sears, Roebuck & Co., 367 F. Supp. 2d 711 (E.D. Pa. 2005) (no waiver from seven-month delay in seeking arbitration when opposing party was not prejudiced); Wisch v. Freedom Yachts, Inc., 2004 WL 3048759 (D. Conn. Dec. 31, 2004); Bellevue Drug Co. v. Advance PCS, 333 F. Supp. 2d 318, 325–326 (E.D. Pa. 2004) (delay of ten months and filing of motion to dismiss that did not address the merits did not constitute waiver); Owner-Operator Indep. Drivers Ass'n, Inc. v. Swift Transp. Co., 288 F. Supp. 2d 1033, 1035 (D. Ariz. 2003) (party's alternative argument for directed verdict made in tandem with motion for arbitration does not give rise to waiver of arbitration right); Fid. Nat'l Title Ins. Co. v. Jericho Mgmt., Inc., 722 So. 2d 740 (Ala. 1998); Redemptorists v. Coulthard, 145 Md. App. 116, 801 A.2d 1104 (2002) (mere filing of motion to dismiss for lack of jurisdiction not a waiver of arbitration); Ill. Farmers Ins. Co. v. Glass Serv. Co., 683 N.W.2d 792, 800 (Minn. 2004) (company's initial decision to participate in litigation and to contest opposing party's right to arbitrate and to initiate consolidated arbitration did not constitute waiver because the company's opposition was jurisdictional in nature and did not attack the merits of the opposing party's position); Harsco Corp. v. Crane Carrier Co., 701 N.E.2d 1040, 1047 (Ohio Ct. App. 1997) (no waiver based on filing of answer to complaint, conduct of limited discovery and depositions); *In re* Medallion, Ltd., 70 S.W.3d 284 (Tex. App. 2002) (no waiver based on limited discovery, participation in mediation, entering into agreed order regarding existence of settlement).

56 Greenpoint v. Reynolds, 151 S.W.3d 868, 876 (Mo. Ct. App. 2005); *cf.* Republic Ins. Co. v. PAICO Receivables, L.L.C., 383 F.3d 341, 345 (5th Cir. 2004) ("a party only invokes the judicial process to the extent it litigates a specific claim it subsequently seeks to arbitrate").

57 MicroStrategy, Inc. v. Lauricia, 268 F.3d 244 (4th Cir. 2001);

Likewise, a defendant's participation in administrative proceedings or delay to await the conclusion of those proceedings has been held not to constitute a waiver of the right to arbitrate.[58] Participating in settlement negotiations after a lawsuit is filed, or participating in or awaiting settlement results from a class action that may encompass the claims allegedly subject to arbitration, has been held insufficient to establish waiver.[59]

Finally, a court might not find waiver in a particular case simply because the facts of the case do not seem quite as bad as in a previous case in the same jurisdiction in which the court did find waiver. This reliance on analogy and the distinctions between different sets of facts, rather than on any particular legal test, can lead to disturbing results. For example, in one Texas case the court of appeals determined that there was no waiver by an employer who: had filed its motion to compel only ninety days before a set trial date (and over a year after the lawsuit was originally filed); had paid a jury fee; had engaged the employee in discovery including the taking of depositions and identification of experts; and had obtained a scheduling order for the upcoming trial.[60] The court's holding was based entirely on the fact that the Fifth Circuit had not found waiver in several cases in which the facts indicated even greater participation in the judicial process than in this case.[61]

8.3.2.4 Unsuccessful Defenses to Waiver Arguments Based Upon Delay

Some defendants have sought to argue that they have preserved and not waived the right to compel arbitration by asserting arbitration as an affirmative defense in their answer, but a number of courts have held that such an assertion will not excuse a defendant's delay in filing for arbitration.[62] Like any other affirmative defense, the failure to raise arbitration as such in an answer to a complaint can constitute waiver.[63]

Similarly, several courts have held that a defendant cannot justify delay in asserting arbitration on the ground that the law was uncertain whether the underlying claim could be subject to arbitration.[64]

8.4 Breach of Arbitration Clause's Provisions As Waiver

8.4.1 Overview

With consumer advocates enjoying more and more success in striking down unfair arbitration clauses, some businesses are changing tactics by drafting clauses that look fair on their face regarding cost and arbitrator selection, and then completely disregarding those provisions as soon as a dispute arises. There is a strong argument in these cases that the defendant's failure to comply with the terms of its own arbitration clause supports a judicial determination that the defendant thereby waived or defaulted on the right to require arbitration. For example, a party who refuses a demand for arbitration cannot later turn around and seek to enforce the arbitration clause when the opposing party files suit in court.[65]

---

see also Saint Agnes v. PacifiCare, 8 Cal. Rptr. 3d 517 (Cal. 2003) (mere filing of a lawsuit, even a lawsuit seeking to declare the entire contract void ab initio, does not indicate a waiver of the right to compel arbitration; waiver can only be evidenced by the actual litigation of the merits of any arbitrable issues).

58 Marie v. Allied Home Mortgage, Inc., 402 F.3d 1, 15–16 (1st Cir. 2005) (employer did not waive right to arbitrate by waiting for the outcome of Equal Employment Opportunity Commission (EEOC) proceedings before moving to compel arbitration, especially because the EEOC, as a non-party to the arbitration clause, cannot be bound to arbitrate); Brown v. ITT Consumer Fin. Corp., 211 F.3d 1217, 1223 (11th Cir. 2000) (employer's participation in EEOC proceedings does not constitute waiver of right to compel arbitration); DeGroff v. Mascotech Forming Technologies—Fort Wayne, Inc., 179 F. Supp. 2d 896, 913 (N.D. Ind. 2001) (no waiver for failure to invoke arbitration during EEOC proceedings); Roberson v. Clear Channel Broad., Inc., 144 F. Supp. 2d 1371, 1374, 1375 (S.D. Fla. 2001) (same); Goldsmith v. Pinez, 84 F. Supp. 2d 228, 235 (D. Mass. 2000) (finding defendant's failure to move for arbitration before completion of Securities Exchange Commission proceedings not to constitute waiver).

59 Walker v. J.C. Bradford, Inc., 938 F.2d 575, 578 (5th Cir. 1991) (holding that attempts at settlement are not inconsistent with the right to arbitrate); Dickinson v. Heinold Sec., Inc., 661 F.2d 638, 641 (7th Cir. 1981).

60 Brown v. Anderson, 102 S.W.3d 245 (Tex. App. Mar. 6, 2003).

61 *Id.*

The Fifth Circuit seems particularly unsympathetic to waiver arguments. *See, e.g.*, Gulf Guar. Life Ins. Co. v. Connecticut, 304 F.3d 476, 484 (5th Cir. 2002) ("This court has... recognized that, even where a party takes substantial steps toward litigation of the arbitral dispute, or participates substantially in litigation procedures, it ordinarily will not waive the right to arbitrate.").

62 *In re* Currency Conversion Fee Antitrust Litig., 2005 WL 1427400, at *4 (S.D.N.Y. June 20, 2005); Robinson v. Daimler Chrysler Corp., 2004 WL 1393768, at *3 (Mich. Ct. App. June 22, 2004) (waiver found even though defendant raised arbitration as an affirmative defense in its answer).

63 Ocwen Loan Servicing, L.L.C. v. Washington, 939 So. 2d 6 (Ala. 2006) (waiver occurred when defendant removed state-court complaint to federal court and filed answer that did not assert right to arbitration); MS Credit Ctr., Inc. v. Horton, 926 So. 2d 167, 180 (Miss. 2006); *see also* Nat'l Found. for Cancer Research v. A.G. Edwards & Sons, 821 F.2d 772, 775 (D.C. Cir. 1987) (court found waiver when the defendant "had invoked the litigation machinery" by, *inter alia*, filing an answer without asserting arbitration as an affirmative defense).

64 Robinson v. Daimler Chrysler Corp., 2004 WL 1393768, at *3 (Mich. Ct. App. June 22, 2004).

65 *See, e.g.*, Brown v. Dillard's, Inc., 430 F.3d 1004, 1009–1010 (9th Cir. 2005) ("Dillard's breached its agreement with Brown by refusing to participate in the arbitration proceeding Brown initiated. Having breached the agreement, Dillard's cannot now enforce it."); *In re* Tyco Int'l Sec. Litig., 422 F.3d 41, 46 (1st Cir. 2005) ("Schwartz should not be allowed to reject the Tyco

The Federal Arbitration Act itself makes a party's compliance with the terms of the arbitration clause at issue a precondition to the clause's enforcement. When a party brings an independent action to enforce an arbitration clause in federal court under the FAA, the court shall issue an arbitration order only "upon being satisfied that the making of the agreement *or the failure to comply therewith* is not in issue."[66] Likewise, when a party raises arbitration as a defense to litigation of a claim in federal court, the court may stay the litigation and order arbitration only when there is an "agreement in writing for such arbitration" and "the applicant for the stay *is not in default in proceeding with such arbitration.*"[67] Thus, a party's continuing compliance with the particular arbitration clause should be a necessary precondition to a court's ability to enforce that clause under the FAA.[68]

8.4.2 Breach of an Arbitration Clause's Covenant of Good Faith

While the case law is sparse on whether a party's failure to comply with the terms of an arbitration clause constitutes a waiver, several decisions offer strong support for this waiver argument. The U.S. Court of Appeals for the Fourth Circuit, for example, held in *Hooters of America, Inc. v. Phillips*[69] that a party cannot compel arbitration after it has been found to have breached its duty under the arbitration clause to promulgate arbitration rules in good faith. *Hooters* first squarely rejected the argument that judicial review of an arbitration clause is limited to the circumstances of contract formation, finding instead that courts should resolve any asserted grounds for revocation of an arbitration clause.[70] The court then held that, by designing a one-sided arbitration system, the defendant in this employment discrimination case breached its contractual duty to establish dispute resolution rules and its contractual obligation of good faith.[71] Rather than repair the defendant's breach by referring the case to arbitration under neutral rules, the Fourth Circuit struck down the arbitration clause and allowed the plaintiff to bring her discrimination claims in court.[72]

In *Tri-Star Petroleum Co. v. Tipperary Corp.*, a Texas appellate court reached a similar conclusion in denying enforcement of an arbitration agreement after finding that one party's misconduct in arbitration rose to the level of a material breach of the agreement.[73] Based on factual findings that the defendant had "engaged in a conscious effort to exclude Tipperary and the Intervenors from knowledge of and access to [the arbitrator]," "exercised undue influence over the role of [the arbitrator] as a neutral arbitrator," and, in fact, had engaged the arbitrator "in the capacity as its own accounting firm,"[74] the court concluded that this misconduct rose to the level of a material breach and that material breach is a grounds for a party to revoke an arbitration clause.[75] *Tri-Star Petroleum* squarely rejected the argument that arbitration clauses can only be revoked for defects in contract formation, holding instead that one party's material breach allows the opposing party to contest the existence of a binding agreement.[76]

An analogous ruling by the California Supreme Court in *Engalla v. Permanente Medical Group*[77] shows that a waiver argument is appropriate when a party completely disregards the requirements of its own arbitration agreement, even in actions that started out in arbitration. The issue in *Engalla* was whether a party's dilatory conduct in the course of arbitration proceedings may be so contrary to the contractual right to arbitrate as to constitute a waiver of that right. More specifically, a health maintenance organization engaged in repeated delays after a terminally ill patient submitted a claim for arbitration—first in its processing of the claim, then in drawing out the process of appointing party arbitrators, then again in drawing out the appointment of a neutral arbitrator, and finally in the scheduling of depositions—all

---

demand for arbitration, stand idle, then submit a motion to compel arbitration after Tyco has been required to commence a court proceeding following the AAA's dismissal of its demand for arbitration."); Aberdeen Golf & Country Club v. Bliss Constr., Inc., 932 So. 2d 235, 240 (Fla. Dist. Ct. App. 2005) ("the owner's refusal to initiate mediation as a precondition to arbitration and to comply with the duty to make progress payments instead of terminating the contract could be deemed a voluntary and intentional relinquishment of the known right to arbitration"); *see also* Reis v. Peabody Coal Co., 935 S.W.2d 625, 630–631 (Mo. Ct. App. 1996) (finding that party waived right to compel arbitration of fraud and punitive damages claims when the party previously argued that the arbitrator lacked authority to decide those claims). *But see* Ill. Farmers Ins. Co. v. Glass Serv. Co., 683 N.W.2d 792, 800 (Minn. 2004) (finding that a company did not waive its right to arbitrate by opposing arbitration in court when the opposition was on jurisdictional grounds rather than on the merits).

66 9 U.S.C. § 4 (emphasis added).
67 9 U.S.C. § 3 (emphasis added).
68 Although FAA sections 3 and 4 are not worded identically, courts have construed these two provisions to impose substantially the same rule that parties who breach or default under an arbitration clause lose their right to enforce the clause. *See, e.g.,* Sink v. Aden Enterprises, Inc., 352 F.3d 1197, 1200, 1201 (9th Cir. 2003); *cf.* Ill. Farmers Ins. Co. v. Glass Serv. Co., 683 N.W.2d 792, 799 (Minn. 2004) (no waiver when party did not breach the contract or fail to perform a condition precedent of the contract).
69 173 F.3d 933 (4th Cir. 1999).
70 *Id.* at 938.
71 *Id.* at 940.
72 *Id.* ("Given Hooters' breaches of the arbitration agreement and Phillips' desire not to be bound by it, we hold that rescission is the proper remedy.").
73 Tri-Star Petroleum Co. v. Tipperary Corp., 107 S.W.3d 607 (Tex. App. 2003).
74 *Id.* at 616–623 (findings of fact regarding material breach).
75 *Id.* at 612–616 (conclusion of law that material breach is basis for revoking arbitration clause).
76 *Id.* at 613.
77 938 P.2d 903 (Cal. 1997).

while the patient was nearing death.[78] As there had been no trial court determination on the issue of waiver, the California Supreme Court remanded the question, but not before advising the trial court of its own conclusion that "the evidence of Kaiser's course of delay, reviewed extensively above, which was arguably unreasonable or undertaken in bad faith, may provide sufficient grounds for a trier of fact to conclude that Kaiser has in fact waived its arbitration agreement."[79]

8.4.3 Breach of an Arbitration Clause's Provisions for Payment of Forum Costs

In *Sanderson Farms, Inc. v. Gatlin*,[80] the Mississippi Supreme Court applied a similar waiver analysis to a poultry production company's breach of its contractual promise to pay half the costs of arbitration in a dispute with an individual chicken farmer. When the farmer commenced arbitration, the company refused to pay any of the $2750 filing fees that were billed by the American Arbitration Association, thereby leaving the farmer to pay these fees plus additional costs totaling at least $11,000 before he could have a hearing on his claims.[81] The Mississippi Supreme Court held that this behavior was a breach of the parties' arbitration agreement, that the breach resulted in a waiver of the company's right to compel arbitration, and that arbitration statutes (including the FAA) empower courts to make these findings rather than simply order parties into (or back into) arbitration.[82]

The U.S. Court of Appeals for the Ninth Circuit recently issued a similar holding. In *Sink v. Aden Enterprises, Inc.*,[83] the Ninth Circuit held that a party that was obligated to pay all forum costs under an arbitration clause, but failed to do so, was in default.[84] Having found that the defendant-employer defaulted by materially breaching the arbitration clause, the Ninth Circuit held that the defendant could not compel the plaintiff to return the case to arbitration.[85] The court explained that any contrary ruling that allowed a defaulting party to return to arbitration would be a license for abuse by defendants:

> Accepting Aden's reading of the FAA would also allow a party refusing to cooperate with arbitration to indefinitely postpone litigation. Under Aden's interpretation, the sole remedy available to a party prejudiced by default would be a court order compelling a return to arbitration. The same offending party could then default a second time, and the prejudiced party's sole remedy, again, would be another order compelling arbitration. This cycle could continue, resulting in frustration of the aggrieved party's attempts to resolve its claims.[86]

Overall, the cases show that the applicability of the state contract law doctrine of waiver under the Federal Arbitration Act may serve as a powerful tool for consumers by providing an escape hatch when a defendant is found to have abused the arbitration process in order to maximize its own advantage.[87]

8.5 Prejudice As a Requirement or Factor to Establish Waiver

As noted in § 8.1, *supra*, courts have differed over the extent to which allegations that a party has waived its right to arbitrate are to be governed by normal principles of state contract law, or are rather governed by an overlay of law from the Federal Arbitration Act. Because contract law in most states does not require any showing of prejudice to establish waiver of a normal contract right (a showing of

---

78 *Id.* at 910–914.
79 *Id.* at 924; *see also* Sink v. Aden Enterprises, Inc., 352 F.3d 1197, 1201 (9th Cir. 2003) ("[The FAA's] purpose is not served by requiring a district court to enter an order returning parties to arbitration upon the motion of a party that is already in default of arbitration.").
80 848 So. 2d 828 (Miss. 2003).
81 *Id. But see* Gulf Guar. Life Ins. Co. v. Connecticut, 304 F.3d 476, 483 (5th Cir. 2002) (defendant attempted to veto the selection of a third arbitrator by the arbitrators chosen by the parties; refused to move forward with arbitration; and took active steps to prevent arbitration; "[S]uch allegations regarding [defendant's] participation in the dispute over the composition of the arbitration panel do not indicate sufficient overt acts evincing a desire by to litigate, instead of arbitrate, the . . . dispute that would constitute waiver of [defendant's] contractual right to arbitrate.").
82 Sanderson Farms, Inc. v. Gatlin, 848 So. 2d 828 (Miss. 2003) (citing 9 U.S.C. § 3). *But see* Welborn Clinic v. Medquist, Inc., 301 F.3d 634 (7th Cir. 2002) (company's failure to follow the explicit dispute resolution steps outlined in its contract, including providing both written notice to its clients of an alleged failure to pay an invoice and any specific information supporting that allegation, did not support the client's claim of waiver, because these steps were not conditions precedent to arbitration).

83 352 F.3d 1197 (9th Cir. 2003).
84 *Id.* at 1199, 1200.
85 *Id.* at 1201.
86 *Id.*
87 *See generally* Russell Evans, Note, *Engalla v. Permanente Medical Group, Inc.: Can Arbitration in Employment Contracts Survive a "Fairness" Analysis?*, 50 Hastings L.J. 635 (1999).
  "[W]here procedural unfairness is successfully linked to claims of fraud, waiver, or unconscionability, as alleged in *Engalla*, traditional deference to arbitration and the usual presumption of arbitrability may be overcome." *Id.* at 653. "The Court's examination of the arbitral process, rather than agreement formation, and its focus on procedural deficiencies imply that minimum levels of 'fairness' must be present in the operation of all arbitration systems." *Id.* at 636.

§ 8.5 Consumer Arbitration Agreements

prejudice is generally a requirement of estoppel, but not waiver),[88] a number of courts have held that prejudice is not a required element to establish that a party has waived its right to compel arbitration.[89]

A majority of federal circuits have taken the other side, however, and held that a showing of prejudice is required to establish a waiver of the right to arbitrate.[90] Arguments attacking these cases as poorly reasoned are contained in the brief of appellees in *Raymond James Financial Services v. Saldukas*, found on the CD-Rom accompanying this manual. Some other courts have even permitted parties who filed suit to compel arbitration of the claims on which they had sued when the opposing party could not demonstrate that the preliminary litigation proceedings had caused them prejudice.[91]

A few courts have invented in-between rules on this topic. For example, some courts have suggested that, in those jurisdictions requiring prejudice, prejudice need only be shown if the allegation of waiver is based solely on undue delay and need not be shown if the allegation of waiver is based on the express acts of the opposing party.[92]

---

88 *See, e.g.,* Royal Air Properties, Inc. v. Smith, 333 F.2d 568, 571 (9th Cir. 1964) ("[N]o detriment to a third party is required for waiver, it is unilaterally accomplished."); City of Glendale v. Coquat, 52 P.2d 1178, 1180 (Ariz. 1935) ("[W]aiver depends upon what one himself intends to do, regardless of the attitude assumed by the other party, whereas estoppel depends rather upon what the other party has done. Waiver does not necessarily imply that the other party has been misled to his prejudice...."); Cole v. Colo. Springs Co., 381 P.2d 13, 17 (Colo. 1963); Best Place, Inc. v. Penn Am. Ins. Co., 920 P.2d 334, 353 (Haw. 1996) ("Waiver encompasses either an express or implied voluntary and intentional relinquishment of a known and existing right. Waiver is essentially unilateral in character, focusing only upon the acts and conduct of the insurer. Prejudice ... or detrimental reliance is *not* required." (citation omitted)); Brown v. State Farm Mut. Auto. Ins. Co., 776 S.W.2d 384, 387 (Mo. 1989); Farm Bureau Mut. Auto. Ins. Co. v. Houle, 102 A.2d 326, 330 (Vt. 1954) ("A waiver does not necessarily imply that one has been misled to his prejudice or into an altered position."); Potesta v. U.S.F. & G. Co., 504 S.E.2d 135, 143 (W. Va. 1998); *see also* Cabinetree of Wis., Inc. v. Kraftmaid Cabinetry, Inc., 50 F.3d 388, 390 (7th Cir. 1995) ("[I]n ordinary contract law, a waiver normally is effective without proof of consideration or detrimental reliance. E. Allen Farnsworth, *Contracts* § 8.5 (2d ed. 1990); 3A Arthur Linton Corbin, *Corbin on Contracts* § 753 (1960)....").

89 Grumhaus v. Comerica, Inc., 223 F.3d 648, 652 (7th Cir. 2000) (rejecting argument for prejudice as an element of waiver); St. Mary's Med. Ctr. of Evansville, Inc. v. Disco Aluminum Products Co., 969 F.2d 585 (7th Cir. 1992); Worldsource Coil Coating, Inc. v. McGraw Const. Co., 946 F.2d 473, 479 (6th Cir. 1991) ("Unless authorized by contract, submission of arbitrable issues in a judicial proceeding constitutes a waiver of the right to compel arbitration regardless of the prejudice to the other party."); Nat'l Found. for Cancer Research v. A.G. Edwards & Sons, Inc., 821 F.2d 772 (D.C. Cir. 1987); Raymond James Fin. Services, Inc. v. Saldukas, 896 So. 2d 707, 711 (Fla. 2005) (prejudice not required); Blackburn v. Citifinancial, Inc., 2007 WL 927222 (Ohio Ct. App. Mar. 29, 2007) ("Ohio law does not absolutely require a finding of prejudice to waive a contractual right.").

90 *See In re* Tyco Int'l Sec. Litig., 422 F.3d 41, 44 (1st Cir. 2005) (requiring show of prejudice); Cargill Ferrous Int'l v. Highgate MV, 70 Fed. Appx. 759, 760 (5th Cir. 2003); United Computer Sys., Inc. v. AT & T Corp., 298 F.3d 756 (9th Cir. 2002) (requiring show of prejudice); Subway Equip. Leasing Corp. v. Forte, 169 F.3d 324, 326 (5th Cir. 1999) (prejudice required); Leadertex, Inc. v. Morganton Dyeing & Finishing Corp., 67 F.3d 20, 26 (2d Cir. 1995); S & H Contractors, Inc. v. A.J. Taft Coal Co., 906 F.2d 1507, 1514 (11th Cir. 1990); Rush v. Oppenheimer & Co., 779 F.2d 885 (2d Cir. 1985) (prejudice required); Carcich v. Rederie A/B Nordie, 389 F.2d 692, 696 (2d Cir. 1968) (prejudice required); *In re* Bruce Terminix Co., 988 S.W.2d 702, 704 (Tex. 1998) (prejudice required).

91 *Cf.* United Computer Sys., Inc. v. AT & T Corp., 298 F.3d 756 (9th Cir. 2002) (finding no waiver when United's request for damages and a jury trial never got past the pleading stage, and thus did not cause prejudice to AT & T); MicroStrategy, Inc. v. Lauricia, 268 F.3d 244, 246, 247, 254 (4th Cir. 2001) (holding that employer did not waive right to arbitrate employee's federal statutory claims by engaging in "remarkably aggressive" litigation strategy wherein employer filed multiple declaratory judgment actions against employee seeking to absolve itself of liability under these statutes, because employee failed to demonstrate that she had been prejudiced); Louis Dreyfus Negoce S.A. v. Blystad Shipping & Trading, Inc., 252 F.3d 218, 229 (2d Cir. 2000) (granting motion to compel arbitration submitted by party one week after it had filed suit in London on the same claims); Roe v. Gray, 165 F. Supp. 2d 1164, 1176, 1177 (D. Colo. 2001) (holding that consumer plaintiff's filing of suit in Colorado does not waive his contractual right to compel defendant credit card issuer to arbitrate in North Carolina); Goldsmith v. Pinez, 84 F. Supp. 2d 228, 235 (D. Mass. 2000) (granting Securities Act plaintiffs' motion for stay pending arbitration when litigation-related delays and procedural rulings were found not to have prejudiced the defendant, while emphasizing the "unusual context of this litigation"); Simms v. NPCK Enterprises, Inc., 109 Cal. App. 4th 233, 134 Cal. Rptr. 2d 557 (2003) ("[S]uing on an arbitrable claim does not per se result in waiver of plaintiffs' right to compel arbitration.... '[T]he court must [also] be satisfied ... that the objecting party was prejudiced by such action.'" (citations omitted)); Benedict v. Pensacola Motor Sales, Inc., 846 So. 2d 1238, 1241 (Fla. Dist. Ct. App. 2003) (requiring showing of prejudice in order to avoid "hypertechnical application of the law in a manner that would allow substantive determinations to be made based on the sequence of pleadings rather than on the merits of the claims"; finding no prejudice when appellee filed an answer to appellant's complaint but then filed a motion to compel arbitration twenty-eight days later), *disapproved by* Raymond James Fin. Services, Inc. v. Saldukas, 896 So. 2d 707 (Fla. 2005) (showing of prejudice not required in order to show waiver); Liberty Chevrolet, Inc. v. Rainey, 791 N.E.2d 625, 630 (Ill. App. Ct. 2003) (finding that consumer's filing of counterclaim constituted changed circumstances making auto company's filing of complaint against consumer insufficient to constitute waiver in the absence of prejudice); Keystone Tech. Group, Inc. v. Kerr Group, Inc., 824 A.2d 1223, 1226 (Pa. Super. Ct. 2003) ("Under Pennsylvania law, a party does not waive its right to compel arbitration by filing a complaint."); Bank One Del. v. Mitchell, 70 Pa. D. & C.4th 353, 370 (C.P. 2005), *aff'd*, 897 A.2d 512 (Pa. Super. Ct. 2006) (table).

92 Beverly Hills Dev. Corp. v. George Wimpey of Fla., Inc., 661 So. 2d 969 (Fla. Dist. Ct. App. 1995).

8.6 Defenses to Waiver Based Upon Contract Terms or Arbitral Rules

In some instances companies have attempted to protect themselves from unwittingly waiving their right to arbitrate by inserting clauses into their arbitration agreements stating that the companies' institution of, or participation in, litigation shall not be considered a waiver of the right to arbitrate.[93] Courts, however, have expressed skepticism of such provisions and have held that they do not prevent a court from finding that a party waived its right to compel arbitration.[94] Such contractual provisions have been rejected because a district court's authority to determine that a party waived its right to arbitrate through judicial activity derives from its inherent authority to control its docket, which cannot be limited by a contract between the parties to litigation.[95] Additionally, enforcing such provisions would sanction abuse of the judicial process and would waste scarce judicial resources by permitting parties to test the waters of litigation before seeking to compel arbitration and thereby to waste scarce judicial resources.[96]

Similarly, the American Arbitration Association's Commercial Arbitration Rules R-48(a) states that "[n]o judicial proceeding by a party relating to the subject matter of the arbitration shall be deemed a waiver of the party's right to arbitrate." But the existence of a contract to arbitrate and the enforceability of an arbitration agreement is a judicial question that cannot be decided by the arbitrator.[97] A court is thus not bound by the arbitrator service provider's rules defining what is or is not a waiver of the arbitration agreement.[98]

---

[93] *See, e.g.*, Republic Ins. Co. v. PAICO Receivables, Inc., 383 F.3d 341, 348 (5th Cir. 2004) (company's clause stated: "The institution and maintenance of an action for judicial relief, the pursuit of provisional or ancillary remedies or other remedies provided for in this Agreement or the Related Settlement Documents shall not be deemed a waiver of a party's right to demand arbitration or continue arbitration."); Rugumbwa v. Betten Motor Sales, 136 F. Supp. 2d 729, 734 (W.D. Mich. 2001) (arbitration clause used American Arbitration Association's Rule that stated: "No judicial proceeding by a party relating to the subject matter of the arbitration shall be deemed a waiver of the party's right to arbitrate.").

[94] Republic Ins. Co. v. PAICO Receivables, L.L.C., 383 F.3d 341, 348 (5th Cir. 2004); S & R. Co. of Kingston v. Latona Trucking, Inc., 159 F.3d 80, 85 (2d Cir. 1998) ("Accordingly, we hold that the presence of a 'no waiver' clause does not alter the ordinary analysis undertaken to determine if a party has waived its right to arbitration."); *see also* Rugumbwa v. Betten Motor Sales, 136 F. Supp. 2d 729, 734 (W.D. Mich. 2001) (finding waiver despite American Arbitration Association's no-waiver rule).

[95] Republic Ins. Co. v. PAICO Receivables, L.L.C., 383 F.3d 341, 348 (5th Cir. 2004) ("The inclusion of a 'no-waiver' clause does not eliminate the district court's inherent power to control its docket.").

[96] Republic Ins. Co. v. PAICO Receivables, L.L.C., 383 F.3d 341, 348 (5th Cir. 2004); S & R Co. of Kingston v. Latona Trucking, Inc., 159 F.3d 80, 85 (2d Cir. 1998); Home Gas Corp. v. Walter's of Hadley, Inc., 532 N.E.2d 681, 685 (Mass. 1989).

[97] *See* § 8.2, *supra*.

[98] Rugumbwa v. Betten Motor Sales, 136 F. Supp. 2d 729 (W.D. Mich. 2001).

Chapter 9 Constitutional Challenges to Mandatory Arbitration Clauses

9.1 Right to Jury Trial

9.1.1 When Private Parties Agree to Waive the Right

Mandatory binding predispute arbitration clauses require parties to forego their right to trial by jury. That right is protected by the Seventh Amendment to the United States Constitution, and by the constitutions of nearly all of the states. Nonetheless, the overwhelming majority of courts to consider the matter have held that the enforcement of arbitration clauses is constitutional,[1] either because the courts find that the consumer's waiver of the right to a jury trial does not involve any state action,[2] or because the Seventh Amendment "does not 'confer the right to a trial, but only the right to have a jury hear the case once it is determined that the litigation should proceed before a court,' "[3] or because any constitutional right to a jury trial is waived "when a competent adult, having the ability to read and understand an instrument, signs a contract."[4]

Moreover, when a state constitutional protection of the right to a jury trial restricts or imposes heightened standards on the enforcement of arbitration clauses governed by the Federal Arbitration Act (FAA),[5] some courts have held that the FAA preempts the state constitutional provisions.[6]

9.1.2 When State Requires Waiver of Right

Courts do sometimes strike down state statutes which *require* that claims be resolved by binding arbitration.[7] In *Mattos v. Thompson*, the Pennsylvania Supreme Court held that a statutorily imposed mandatory arbitration system for medical malpractice claims was unconstitutional.[8] The court held that there was nothing unconstitutional per se about the concept of state-required mandatory arbitration, but that the system was administered in a way that gave rise to "unconscionable" and "oppressive" delays.[9]

In *Simon v. St. Elizabeth Medical Center*, an Ohio court held that a state statute requiring medical malpractice plaintiffs to submit their claims to nonbinding arbitration was an

---

1 *See, e.g.*, Rollings v. Thermodyne Indus., Inc., 910 P.2d 1030, 1034 (Okla. 1996) ("Most states, however, which have considered the question of constitutionality have upheld arbitration statutes.").

2 *See, e.g.*, Perpetual Sec. v. Tang, 290 F.3d 132, 137–140 (2d Cir. 2002).

For an analysis of similar holdings, see Jean R. Sternlight, *Rethinking the Constitutionality of the Supreme Court's Preference for Binding Arbitration: A Fresh Assessment of Jury Trials, Separation of Powers, and Due Process Concerns*, 72 Tul. L. Rev. 1, 11 (1997). Professor Sternlight offers an interesting intellectual critique of these holdings: "By expressing and applying a preference for binding arbitration over litigation, the Court is directly countering the Constitution's guarantees of due process of law in all courts, to a life-tenured judge and jury trial in appropriate matters brought in federal court." *Id.* at 10 (footnote omitted); *see also* Jean R. Sternlight, *Mandatory Binding Arbitration and the Demise of the Seventh Amendment Right To A Jury Trial*, 16 Ohio St. J. on Disp. Resol. 669 (2001).

For a discussion of whether waiver of a jury trial right must be "knowing and voluntary," see § 5.5, *supra*.

3 McKenzie Check Advance of Miss., L.L.C. v. Hardy, 866 So. 2d 446, 455 (Miss. 2004) (quoting Bank One v. Coates, 125 F. Supp. 2d 819, 834 (S.D. Miss. 2001)).

4 Jim Walter Homes, Inc. v. Saxton, 880 So. 2d 428, 431 (Ala. 2003) (internal quotation omitted); *see also* In re Currency Conversion Fee Antitrust Litig., 265 F. Supp. 2d 385, 414 (S.D.N.Y. 2003) ("A plaintiff is deemed to have forgone the right to a jury trial under the Seventh Amendment as a result of entering into an agreement to arbitrate certain matters."); *cf.* Viola v. Dep't of Managed Health Care, 133 Cal. App. 4th 299, 34 Cal. Rptr. 3d 626 (2005) (employer acting as agent of its employees in negotiation of health plan has implied authority to waive employees' right to jury trial).

5 9 U.S.C. §§ 1–16.

6 *See, e.g.*, Merrill Lynch, Pierce, Fenner & Smith, Inc. v. Coe, 313 F. Supp. 2d 603, 615 (S.D. W. Va. 2004); *see also* § 3.2, *supra*.

7 Such claims are very often dependent on the state constitution's language concerning the right to jury trial. In states where the right has not been adopted, a consumer will most likely not be able to bring a constitutional challenge to such a statute. *See, e.g.*, GTFM, L.L.C. v. TKN Sales, Inc., 257 F.3d 235 (2d Cir. 2001) (Minnesota statute requiring foreign corporations to submit certain claims against sales representatives to arbitration was not unconstitutional, because the Seventh Amendment does not apply to the states, and claims would be brought under state law (even though they would almost certainly be removed to the federal courts on the basis of diversity of citizenship)).

8 Mattos v. Thompson, 491 Pa. 385, 421 A.2d 190 (1980).

9 491 Pa. at 396, 421 A.2d at 195, 196.

unconstitutional burden on the right to a jury trial under the state constitution, when the prevailing party in the arbitration could introduce the decision of the arbitrator into evidence.[10] Likewise the Florida Supreme Court, in *Nationwide Mutual Fire Insurance Co. v. Pinnacle Medical, Inc.*, held that a statute requiring medical providers to arbitrate certain claims against automobile insurers violated the providers' right of access to the courts under the Florida Constitution.[11]

In *Lisanti v. Alamo Title Insurance of Texas*, the New Mexico Court of Appeals found unconstitutional a section of the state's title insurance law which mandated compulsory arbitration of title insurance disputes of one million dollars or less.[12] The court held that, by making arbitration compulsory, the law violated the parties' right to trial by jury as guaranteed by the state and federal constitutions. The opinion was based on a common law understanding of the right to trial by jury as it existed during the New Mexico territorial period when, the court held, "contract actions seeking money damages were routinely tried to juries."[13] Because all of the plaintiffs' claims were contractual, and the plaintiffs sought only monetary damages, the common law right to trial by jury prevailed.

On the other hand, some courts have held that states may statutorily impose a mandatory arbitration requirement on claims that did not exist at common law. That is because in some states the constitutional right to a jury trial only applies to claims that existed at common law.[14] In addition, at least one court has held that a state statute requiring arbitration of fee disputes between attorneys is constitutional, because attorney fees have always been under the regulatory jurisdiction of the state bar.[15]

9.2 Equal Protection in Selection of Arbitrator

A creative attempt to challenge the constitutionality of an arbitration clause was made in *Smith v. American Arbitration Association, Inc.*[16] In that case, the plaintiff argued (among other things) that the defendant's action in striking the only woman on a list of fifteen possible arbitrators, thus guaranteeing an all-male arbitration panel, violated the Equal Protection Clause. The Seventh Circuit rejected this claim, holding that the AAA is a private body that does not operate as a state actor:

> Arbitration is a private self-help remedy. The American Arbitration Association is a private organization selling a private service to private parties who are under no legal obligation to agree to arbitrate their disputes or, if they decide to use arbitration to resolve disputes, to use the services of the Association, which is not the only provider of such services. When arbitrators issue awards, they do so pursuant to the disputants' contract—in fact the award is a supplemental contract obligating the losing party to pay the winner. The fact that the courts enforce these contracts, just as they enforce other contracts, does not convert the contracts into state or federal action and so bring the equal protection clause into play.[17]

9.3 Improper Delegation of Power

In cases involving municipalities, at least one court has indicated that giving power to an arbitration panel to decide disputes may be an improper delegation of power to a private body. In *County of Riverside v. Superior Court*, the California Supreme Court held that a statute requiring cities and counties to submit economic disputes arising during negotiations with city police and firefighters' unions to binding arbitration is an unconstitutional delegation of municipal functions to a private body by the legislature.[18] The court found the statute also violated the California Constitution by depriving counties of their power to control county employee compensation.[19]

9.4 Due Process

Courts generally reject a claim that an arbitration award is not enforceable because the arbitration proceeding lacked due process.[20] This argument typically arises in the context of an arbitrator's punitive damages award. Courts find that the arbitration proceeding itself involves no state action.[21]

---

10 Simon v. St. Elizabeth Med. Ctr., 355 N.E.2d 903, 908 (Ohio Ct. Com. Pl. 1976).

11 Nationwide Mut. Fire Ins. Co. v. Pinnacle Med., Inc., 753 So. 2d 55 (Fla. 2000).

12 Lisanti v. Alamo Title Ins. of Tex., 35 P.3d 989 (N.M. Ct. App. 2001), aff'd, 55 P.3d 962 (N.M. 2002).

13 *Lisanti*, 35 P.3d at 992.

14 See State Farm Mut. Auto Ins. Co. v. Broadnax, 827 P.2d 531 (Colo. 1992); Reed v. Farmers Ins. Group, 188 Ill. 2d 168, 720 N.E.2d 1052 (Ill. 1999).

15 Shinko v. Lobe, 813 N.E.2d 669 (Ohio 2004).

16 233 F.3d 502 (7th Cir. 2000).

17 *Id.* at 507 (citation omitted).

18 County of Riverside v. Super. Ct., 30 Cal. 4th 278, 132 Cal. Rptr. 2d 713, 66 P.3d 718 (2003). *But see* Shinko v. Lobe, 813 N.E.2d 669 (Ohio 2004) (state statute's requirement that attorney-fee disputes be arbitrated does not amount to the creation of an unauthorized tribunal).

19 County of Riverside v. Super. Ct., 30 Cal. 4th 278, 132 Cal. Rptr. 2d 713, 66 P.3d 718 (2003).

20 Davis v. Prudential Sec., Inc., 59 F.3d 1186 (11th Cir. 1995); Hadelman v. Deluca, 274 Conn. 442, 876 A.2d 1136 (2005); Medvalusa Health Programs, Inc. v. Memberworks, Inc., 273 Conn. 634 (2005).

21 Smith v. Am. Arbitration Ass'n, 233 F.3d 502 (7th Cir. 2000); Davis v. Prudential Sec., Inc., 59 F.3d 1186 (11th Cir. 1995); Fed. Deposit Ins. Corp. v. Air Fla. Sys., Inc., 822 F.2d 833 (9th

Courts generally also find that court confirmation of a private arbitration proceeding is not sufficient state action to trigger due process considerations.[22] Courts are even less sympathetic to due process arguments when made by the party who drafted a standard form contract that requires arbitration. The merchant, having chosen the process to adjudicate a dispute, is not in any position to challenge the fairness of that process.[23]

Cir. 1987); Elmore v. Chicago & Ill. Midland Ry. Co., 782 F.2d 94 (7th Cir. 1986); Cremin v. Merrill Lynch Pierce Fenner & Smith, 957 F. Supp. 1460 (N.D. Ill. 1997); Int'l Ass'n of Heat & Frost Insulators & Asbestos Workers Local Union 42 v. Absolute Envtl. Services, Inc., 814 F. Supp. 392, 402 (D. Del. 1993); Medvalusa Health Programs, Inc. v. Memberworks, Inc., 273 Conn. 634 (2005).

22 Smith v. Am. Arbitration Ass'n, 233 F.3d 502 (7th Cir. 2000); Davis v. Prudential Sec., Inc., 59 F.3d 1186 (11th Cir. 1995);

Medvalusa Health Programs, Inc. v. Memberworks, Inc., 273 Conn. 634 (2005); *see also* Cremin v. Merrill Lynch Pierce Fenner & Smith, 957 F. Supp. 1460 (N.D. Ill. 1997); United States v. Am. Soc'y of Composers, Authors & Publishers, 708 F. Supp. 95 (S.D.N.Y. 1989).

23 Davis v. Prudential Sec., Inc., 59 F.3d 1186 (11th Cir. 1995).

Chapter 10 Arbitration of Claims on a Classwide Basis

10.1 Introduction

An increasingly prominent issue in current consumer litigation concerns the availability of class action procedures when businesses impose mandatory arbitration clauses on their consumer customers. Businesses are aggressively arguing that the arbitration clauses in their standard form contracts automatically prevent consumers from asserting claims on a classwide basis, either in court or through arbitration.[1] As the California Supreme Court has noted, this practice has the potential to undermine altogether the ability of many consumers to effectively vindicate their legal rights:

> It is common knowledge that arbitration clauses frequently appear in standardized contracts of adhesion. A primary consideration that has led courts to uphold such clauses, despite the adhesive nature of the contract, is the belief that arbitration is not oppressive and does not defeat the reasonable expectations of the parties. If, however, an arbitration clause may be used to insulate the drafter of an adhesive contract from any form of class proceeding, *effectively foreclosing many individual claims*, it may well be oppressive and may defeat the expectations of the non-drafting party.[2]

Despite the widely recognized need for class action procedures to enforce the legal rights of plaintiffs whose individual claims involve relatively small sums of money,[3] some courts have required consumer plaintiffs to arbitrate claims even after holding that arbitration would not allow the plaintiffs to assert class-based claims.

A court addressing a defendant's motion to compel arbitration in a case filed as a putative class action will likely face arguments concerning the parties' respective rights to arbitrate under their contract and to bring claims on a classwide basis under controlling state or federal law. Generally, arbitration clauses are either silent regarding class proceedings or else, as is occurring with greater frequency, the clauses expressly prohibit class actions. If an arbitration clause is silent, or at least does not squarely prohibit class proceedings, the Supreme Court has held that the question of whether plaintiffs may arbitrate class-based claims is for the arbitrator to decide as a matter of state law.[4] When arbitration clauses expressly prohibit class actions, courts have either enforced the arbitration clauses as written and prohibited class actions[5] or else have struck down the arbitration clause (or at least the class action ban) as unconscionable under applicable state law.[6] While many, although not all, federal courts have been willing to enforce arbitration clauses even after finding that they prohibit class actions, several state courts have taken different approaches. At the same time, many courts are just now addressing these issues for the first time.

---

1 For an extensive discussion of this problem, the underlying policy concerns, and existing case law relating to arbitration and class actions, see Jean R. Sternlight, *As Mandatory Binding Arbitration Meets the Class Action, Will the Class Action Survive?*, 42 Wm. & Mary L. Rev. 1 (2000).

2 Keating v. Super. Ct., 645 P.2d 1192, 1207 (Cal. 1982) (citation omitted) (emphasis added), *rev'd on other grounds sub nom.* Southland Corp. v. Keating, 465 U.S. 1 (1984); *see also* Furgason v. McKenzie Check Advance of Ind., Inc., 2001 U.S. Dist. LEXIS 2725 (S.D. Ind. Jan. 3, 2001) ("The inability of a plaintiff to pursue relief on behalf of a class in a case challenging the legality of a relatively modest payday loan agreement is likely to have a significant practical effect on the ability of a consumer to obtain relief authorized by federal statutes.").

3 *See, e.g.,* Amchem Products, Inc. v. Windsor, 521 U.S. 591, 617, 117 S. Ct. 2231, 138 L. Ed. 2d 689 (1998); Phillips Petroleum Co. v. Shutts, 472 U.S. 797, 809, 105 S. Ct. 2965, 86 L. Ed. 2d 628 (1985) (recognizing that individual plaintiffs' $100 claims must be pooled in class action because individual claims would be uneconomical); Eisen v. Carlisle & Jacqueline, 417 U.S. 156, 161, 94 S. Ct. 2140, 40 L. Ed. 2d 732 (1974) (recognizing that antitrust claim for damages of $70 realistically must proceed either as class action or not at all).

4 Green Tree Fin. Corp. v. Bazzle, 539 U.S. 444, 123 S. Ct. 2402, 156 L. Ed. 2d 414 (2003) (plurality opinion).

5 Jenkins v. First S. Cash Advance of Ga., 400 F.3d 868 (11th Cir. 2005).

6 *See, e.g.,* Ting v. AT & T, 182 F. Supp. 2d 902 (N.D. Cal. 2002), *aff'd in relevant part*, 319 F.3d 1126 (9th Cir. 2003); Leonard v. Terminix Int'l Co., 854 So. 2d 529 (Ala. 2002); Discover Bank v. Super. Court, 113 P.3d 1100 (Cal. 2005); *see also* § 6.5.5, *supra*.

10.2 The Supreme Court's Ruling in *Green Tree Financial Corp. v. Bazzle*

10.2.1 Arbitrator Decides Class Action Issues by Applying State Law When Contract Is Arguably Silent Regarding Class Claims

In *Green Tree Financial Corp. v. Bazzle*,[7] the United States Supreme Court held that an arbitrator, not a court, must make decisions regarding class proceedings when an arbitration clause does not squarely state whether or not they are permissible. As this case is the first time that the Supreme Court has discussed the interrelationship among arbitration clauses, the FAA, and the right of parties to bring class claims, the continuing validity of much of the pre-*Bazzle* lower court case law may be called into question. What follows is a brief examination of the *Bazzle* case and decision, an analysis of *Bazzle*'s likely implications, and an overview of the preexisting and developing lower court case law relating to these issues.

10.2.2 The Facts and Holding of *Bazzle*

Bazzle came to the Supreme Court as two consolidated cases. The first case involved a state trial court's certification of a class in advance of ordering arbitration, and the second involved an order by the same arbitrator who, while hearing the first case, certified a second class in the aftermath of the trial court's order.[8] The South Carolina Supreme Court affirmed both class certification orders and both subsequent awards on the merits to the plaintiff classes, holding that the defendant's arbitration clause did not expressly prohibit class-based claims in arbitration and that these claims were permissible under state law.[9]

The United States Supreme Court granted review to determine the effect of the FAA on the state court's ruling. The Supreme Court first held that the state court was correct in applying state law to determine whether the arbitration clause permitted class claims: "THE CHIEF JUSTICE believes that Green Tree is right; indeed, that Green Tree is so right that we should ignore *the fact that state law, not federal law, normally governs such matters....*"[10] The Supreme Court then held that decisions regarding class proceedings involve contract interpretation questions in the absence of contract language explicitly addressing these issues, and that these issues must be decided by the arbitrator because neither party was disputing the validity of the arbitration clause.[11] As the Court found that it was not clear whether the arbitrator had ever made an independent ruling on these issues, it vacated the state court's ruling and remanded the case with an order for the arbitrator to decide whether class proceedings were available under the contract.[12]

10.2.3 *Bazzle*'s Likely Implications for Consumers

The Supreme Court's ruling in *Bazzle* is significant and likely to be helpful to consumers for several reasons. First, by allowing the arbitrator to determine whether class proceedings were permissible under Green Tree's arbitration clause, the Supreme Court necessarily rejected the holdings of several lower federal courts and the arguments of many corporate defendants that the FAA itself presumptively prohibits class proceedings.[13] By granting the arbitrator discretion to decide class action issues when the FAA applies, the Court puts to rest once and for all the proposition that the FAA prohibits or restricts class proceedings.

Second, by holding that the availability of class proceedings in the face of an unclear arbitration clause is a question of state law, rather than federal law, the Supreme Court allows consumers to rely upon contract law and other bodies of state law that often work to protect the weaker parties when adhesive contracts are involved, as they are in most consumer cases.[14]

---

7 539 U.S. 444, 123 S. Ct. 2402, 156 L. Ed. 2d 414 (2003) (plurality opinion).

8 123 S. Ct. at 2405, 2406.

9 *Id.* (describing holding in Green Tree Fin. Corp. v. Bazzle, 569 S.E.2d 349 (S.C. 2002)).

10 *Id.*, 123 S. Ct. at 2406 (emphasis added); *see also id.*, 123 S. Ct. at 2408 (Stevens, J., concurring); *id.*, 123 S. Ct. at 2411 (Thomas, J., dissenting) (arguing that FAA does not apply in state court).

11 *Id.*, 123 S. Ct. at 2407; *see also* Brennan v. ACE INA Holdings, Inc., 2002 WL 1804918 (E.D. Pa. Aug. 1, 2002) (arbitrator must resolve parties' dispute over availability of class arbitration); *cf.* Gilkey v. Cent. Clearing Co., 202 F.R.D. 515, 522, 523 (E.D. Mich. 2002) (holding that mere existence of arbitration clauses does not preclude consideration of class certification issues); Bond v. Fleet Bank, 2002 WL 31500393, at *6–*7 (D.R.I. Oct. 10, 2002) (same). *But see* Wong v. First Union Nat'l Bank, 69 Pa. D. & C.4th 516 (C.P. 2004) (post-*Bazzle* decision holding that it is for the court to decide whether an arbitration can proceed on a classwide basis).

12 *Bazzle*, 123 S. Ct. at 2408.

13 *See, e.g.*, Champ v. Siegel Trading Co., 55 F.3d 269, 271 (7th Cir. 1995) ("absent a provision in the parties' arbitration agreement providing for class treatment of disputes, a district court has no authority to certify class arbitration"); Furgason v. McKenzie Check Advance of Ind., Inc., 2001 U.S. Dist. LEXIS 2725 (S.D. Ind. Jan. 3, 2001) (payday loan case, following *Champ* in barring class claims in arbitration).

14 *See, e.g.*, Green Tree Fin. Corp. v. Bazzle, 569 S.E.2d 349 (S.C. 2002) (holding that contract's ambiguity regarding class proceedings should be resolved against party that drafted the contract).

Third, by holding that state law applies to these questions of contract interpretation, the *Bazzle* decision strengthens the argument that state law regarding contractual unconscionability applies when a corporate defendant's arbitration clause explicitly bans class claims. If state law controls the proper *interpretation* of arbitration clause provisions, then state law is also more likely appropriate to determine the *validity* and *enforceability* of these provisions.

10.2.4 Cases Following Bazzle's *Holding*

Since the Supreme Court decided *Bazzle*, several courts have followed suit in holding that questions concerning class claims must be resolved by the arbitrator when an arbitration clause does not directly address these issues.[15] In *Pedcor Management Co. v. National Personnel of Texas*,[16] the Fifth Circuit found that a commercial reinsurer's policy was silent regarding class claims, and therefore vacated the district court's order certifying a class for arbitration, holding that *Bazzle* dictated that the arbitrator must resolve disputes over the availability of classwide relief under such a contract.[17]

In *Genus Credit Management Corp. v. Jones*,[18] the court held that an arbitrator must determine whether an arbitration clause that prohibited the plaintiff from serving as a "representative plaintiff" in a class action "lawsuit" permitted or prohibited class arbitration. The arbitrator determined that the clause's prohibition on class action "lawsuits" did not bar class actions in arbitration, and the district court affirmed the arbitrator's decision.[19]

Similarly, the Texas Supreme Court recently applied *Bazzle* in holding that a group of former clients could ask an arbitrator for class certification of their claims relating to a lawyer's fee agreement. In *In re Wood*,[20] the court rejected the defendant's attempt to distinguish *Bazzle* by claiming that the arbitration service rules "then in effect" under the contract did not provide for class-based claims, and found instead that the interpretation of what rules applied was for the arbitrator to determine.[21] Courts have applied the reasoning of *Bazzle* to questions of consolidation as well as to that of class actions.[22]

10.3 Critique of Pre-*Bazzle* Cases Holding That the FAA Presumptively Prohibits Arbitration of Class Claims

10.3.1 Overview

Prior to the Supreme Court's ruling in *Bazzle*, the prevailing view among federal courts regarding the effect of arbitration agreements on plaintiffs who assert class-based claims was stated in the Seventh Circuit's decision in *Champ v. Siegel Trading Co.*[23] *Champ* held that an arbitration clause that was silent as to the availability of class proceedings prohibited all class claims because, under the FAA, "absent a provision in the parties' arbitration agreement providing for class treatment of disputes, a district court has no authority to certify class arbitration."[24] Although *Bazzle*'s holding regarding the applicability of state law and the authority of the arbitrator to decide these issues effectively overrules *Champ*, parties might still need to rebut arguments

---

15 *See, e.g.*, Rollins, Inc. v. Garrett, 2006 WL 1024166, at *1 (11th Cir. Apr. 19, 2006) (unpublished) ("When a contract is silent as to whether it prohibits class arbitration, the arbitrator, rather than the court, must resolve the issue as a matter of state law."); Pedcor Mgmt. Co. v. Nat'l Personnel of Tex., 343 F.3d 355 (5th Cir. 2003); Genus Credit Mgmt. Corp. v. Jones, 2006 WL 905936 (D. Md. Apr. 6, 2006); Veliz v. Cintas Corp., 2005 WL 1048699, at *5 (N.D. Cal. May 4, 2005); Ramirez v. Cintas Corp., 2005 WL 659984, at *10–*11 (N.D. Cal. Mar. 22, 2005) (holding that an arbitrator must decide if an arbitration clause that is silent on class actions permits class arbitrations); Garcia v. DirecTV, Inc., 9 Cal. Rptr. 3d 190, 195–196 (Ct. App. 2004); Bess v. DirecTV, Inc., 815 N.E.2d 455, 460 (Ill. App. Ct. 2004); *In re* Wood, 140 S.W.3d 367 (Tex. 2004). *But see* Wong v. First Union Nat'l Bank, 69 Pa. D. & C.4th 516 (C.P. 2004) (post-*Bazzle* decision holding that it is for the court to decide whether an arbitration can proceed on a classwide basis).

16 343 F.3d 355 (5th Cir. 2003).

17 *Id.* at 359, 360; *see also* Garcia v. DirecTV, Inc., 9 Cal. Rptr. 3d 190, 195, 196 (Ct. App. 2004) (reversing state trial court's finding that classwide arbitration was permitted).

18 2006 WL 905936 (D. Md. Apr. 6, 2006).

19 *See id.* at *3.

20 140 S.W.3d 367 (Tex. 2004).

21 *Id.* at 369, 370.

22 *See, e.g.*, Certain Underwriters at Lloyd's London v. Westchester Fire Ins. Co., 489 F.3d 580 (3d Cir. 2007); Employers Ins. Co. of Wausau v. Century Indem. Co., 443 F.3d 573, 577 (7th Cir. 2006) (holding that the "question whether an arbitration agreement forbids consolidated arbitration is a procedural one, which the arbitrator should resolve"); Pedcor Mgmt. Co. v. Welfare Benefit Plan, 343 F.3d 355, 363 (5th Cir. 2003) (stating in dictum that *Bazzle* likely overruled a previous Fifth Circuit decision holding that a court should determine whether an arbitration clause permits consolidation); *In re* Allstate Ins. Co., 2006 WL 2289999, at *1 (S.D.N.Y. Aug. 8, 2006); Blimpie Int'l, Inc. v. Blimpie of the Keys, 371 F. Supp. 2d 469, 473–474 (S.D.N.Y. 2005) (whether arbitration can be consolidated is a question for the arbitrator after *Bazzle*); Yuen v. Super. Court, 121 Cal. App. 4th 1133, 18 Cal. Rptr. 3d 127 (2004) (same); *see also* Shaw's Supermarkets, Inc. v. United Food & Commercial Workers Union Local 791, 321 F.3d 251 (1st Cir. 2003) (holding, pre-*Bazzle*, that whether or not to consolidate arbitration proceedings was a procedural question to be decided by arbitrator); *cf.* Birmingham News Co. v. Horn, 901 So. 2d 27, 55 (Ala. 2004) (finding that arbitration panel did not exceed its authority in deciding to consolidate disputes).

23 55 F.3d 269 (7th Cir. 1995).

24 *Id.* at 271.

relying on *Champ* until courts expressly recognize that it is effectively overturned.

10.3.2 Absence of Statutory Support for Champ's Presumption Against Arbitration of Class Claims

The court in *Champ* had no basis for presuming that the silence of the arbitration clause before it amounted to a "negotiated risk/benefit allocation" which included a deliberate waiver of classwide proceedings.[25] Faced with the complete absence of federal statutes addressing these issues, *Champ* simply analogized to findings of other federal courts of appeal regarding arbitration and consolidation of claims without examining either the propriety of these decisions or the important differences between class actions and case consolidation.[26] *Bazzle*'s holding that, in the absence of express contractual direction, questions regarding the availability of such proceedings raise questions of contract interpretation to be decided under state law, and that these questions are for arbitrators to decide, effectively overrules the Seventh Circuit's decision in *Champ* to decide these questions itself as matters of federal common law.

10.3.3 Seventh Circuit Precedent Also Undermined Champ

Although a majority of federal circuit courts have previously held that courts should not consolidate the claims of different parties before sending cases to arbitration absent express contractual authorization,[27] there is contrary authority on this point. Indeed, the Seventh Circuit itself rejected this rule with regard to consolidation in *Connecticut General Life Insurance Co. v. Sun Life Assurance Co. of Canada*.[28] *Connecticut General Life* not only undermines the foundation of *Champ*'s holding on class actions, but also offers strong arguments that would support a rule *permitting* the certification of plaintiff classes in arbitration.

> [T]he same considerations of adjudicative economy that argue in favor of consolidating closely related court cases argue for consolidating closely related arbitrations. . . . [P]arties to a contract generally aim at obtaining sensible results in a sensible way. . . . To have the identical dispute litigated before different arbitration panels is a formula for duplication of effort and a fertile source, in this case, of disputes over esoteric issues in the law of res judicata.[29]

These same concerns apply with at least equal force to many consumer class actions, particularly those arising out of a merchant's standard form contract, and individual arbitrations would be duplicative and would create the risk that consumers with identical claims could receive substantially varying results. *Connecticut General Life*, by allowing consolidation of claims for arbitration in the absence of express statutory or contractual authorization, thus further calls into question the continuing validity of the Seventh Circuit's earlier holding in *Champ*.

10.3.4 Consolidation Distinguished from Class Actions

Because a majority of federal circuit courts have held that courts may not consolidate claims for arbitration absent express contractual authorization,[30] an additional basis for opposing adoption of *Champ*'s holding regarding class actions is the tenuousness of the analogy between case consolidation and class actions. Professor Sternlight has argued persuasively that *Champ*'s analogy is inapt for several reasons.[31]

First, and perhaps foremost, consolidation only arises after individual claims have been filed, whereas many times plaintiffs file cases as class actions precisely *because* their individual claims are too small to justify filing separately.[32] Thus only in the latter case is the procedural device necessary for effective enforcement of the claimants' legal rights.

Furthermore, class action treatment of consumer claims would entail a lesser intrusion on standard form contractual

---

25 Champ v. Siegel Trading Co., 55 F.3d 269, 275 (7th Cir. 1995).
26 *Id.*
27 *See* Gov't of the United Kingdom v. Boeing Co., 998 F.2d 68, 69 (2d Cir. 1993); Am. Centennial Ins. Co. v. Nat'l Cas. Co., 951 F.2d 107, 108 (6th Cir. 1991); Baesler v. Cont'l Grain Co., 900 F.2d 1193, 1195 (8th Cir. 1990); Protective Life Ins. Corp. v. Lincoln Nat'l Life Ins. Corp., 873 F.2d 281, 282 (11th Cir. 1989) (per curiam); Del E. Webb Constr. v. Richardson Hosp. Auth., 823 F.2d 145, 150 (5th Cir. 1987); Weyerhauser Co. v. W. Seas Shipping Co., 743 F.2d 635, 637 (9th Cir. 1984).
28 210 F.3d 771, 776 (7th Cir. 2000) (Posner, C.J.); *see also* New Eng. Energy, Inc. v. Keystone Shipping Co., 855 F.2d 1, 5 (1st Cir. 1988) (holding that arbitration contract's silence on consolidation does not supersede state arbitration statute, which is apparently enforceable in federal court, allowing court to consolidate individual claims for arbitral resolution); Ill. Farmers Ins. Co. v. Glass Serv. Co., 683 N.W.2d 792, 805–806 (Minn. 2004) (holding that, under state law, a court can order a consolidated arbitration when the contract is silent on the matter; in deciding whether to order consolidation, the court should balance the efficiencies of consolidation against the potential prejudice to the parties resulting from consolidation).
29 *Conn. Gen. Life*, 210 F.3d at 774–776.
30 No court has yet addressed whether any of these cases prohibiting consolidation of arbitrated claims remains good law in light of the Supreme Court's holding in *Bazzle* that class action questions are for arbitrators, not courts, to decide.
31 *See* Jean R. Sternlight, *As Mandatory Binding Arbitration Meets the Class Action, Will the Class Action Survive?*, 42 Wm. & Mary L. Rev. 1 (2000).
32 *Id.* at 86.

agreements than would consolidation of claims in business relationships involving separately negotiated contracts.[33]

Finally, consolidation may be ordered by an arbitrator, even in the face of judicial abdication, because all parties to the disputes are present in arbitration, whereas constitutional due process concerns might at least arguably limit the authority of private arbitrators to certify classes of absentee plaintiffs in the absence of ongoing judicial involvement with the case.[34]

10.4 State Court Approaches to Arbitration of Class Claims

10.4.1 Lower Federal Court Precedent Is Not Controlling on State Courts

State courts are not bound by lower federal court precedent on questions concerning the permissibility of class claims in arbitration. Although federal courts prior to *Bazzle* justified their refusal to permit class-based claims in arbitration by citing to the command of section 4 of the FAA that arbitration be enforced "in accordance with the terms of the agreement,"[35] section 4 by its express terms applies only in federal court and does not bind state courts to follow the same procedural rules.[36] In *Bazzle*, by contrast, the Supreme Court's holding turned on the allocation of authority between courts and arbitrators under section 2 of the FAA which, unlike section 4, has been held to apply in state court cases.[37]

10.4.2 State Cases Following Pre-*Bazzle* Federal Approach

A number of state courts have found earlier lower federal court rulings to be persuasive authority and have embraced the pre-*Bazzle* federal approach and held that class-based claims cannot go forward in arbitration absent explicit contractual or statutory authorization.[38] These decisions are vulnerable to challenge for the same reasons that *Champ v. Siegel Trading Co.* itself is vulnerable, and should be open to reconsideration in light of the United States Supreme Court's recent ruling in *Bazzle*.

10.4.3 State Cases Allowing Arbitration of Class Claims

Numerous other state courts have departed from earlier lower federal court precedent, however, and have attempted to preserve plaintiffs' right to proceed as a class in the face of contractual duties to arbitrate. The leading state court authority for the proposition that arbitration is not a barrier to classwide relief for plaintiffs is the California Supreme Court's decision in *Keating v. Superior Court*.[39]

The *Keating* court noted the critical function performed by class actions in eliminating repetitious litigation and preserving claims for small sums of money in cases arising out of standard form contracts of adhesion, and expressed concern that businesses might be able to insulate themselves from liability by using arbitration to prohibit plaintiffs from bringing claims on a classwide basis.[40] *Keating* also noted that California law explicitly authorized courts to consolidate claims going to arbitration; explained that class certification would be less intrusive on the arbitration process than would consolidation; and concluded that "[w]here . . . gross unfairness would result from the denial of opportunity to proceed on a classwide basis, then an order structuring arbitration on that basis would be justified."[41] *Keating*'s holdings regarding the value of class action procedures and the need to preserve them in the face of a defendant's arbitration rights under the FAA should survive the United States Supreme Court's holding in *Bazzle* that the permissibility of class claims in arbitration turns on state law questions of contract interpretation.

In describing the procedures to be employed in a classwide arbitration, however, *Keating* recognized a need for judicial involvement in determinations relating to class certification, notice to absentee class members, and adequacy of representation in the event of a settlement or dismissal, while demanding that courts allow arbitrators to make all merits-related determinations.[42] It is unclear how much of this part of *Keating*'s holding survives *Bazzle* because the latter case requires an arbitrator, rather than a court, to determine whether class proceedings are available. *Keating* and the state court cases that follow its holding may therefore be limited to the proposition that class proceedings are permissible in arbitration as a matter of state law, with

---

33 *Id.* at 86, 87 (quoting Keating v. Super. Ct., 645 P.2d 1192, 1208, 1209 (Cal. 1982)).
34 *Id.* at 87, 88.
35 9 U.S.C. § 4.
36 *See generally* § 3.2.2.3, *supra*.
37 *See, e.g.,* Southland Corp. v. Keating, 465 U.S. 1, 104 S. Ct. 852, 79 L. Ed. 2d 1 (1984) (holding that section 2 of the FAA applies in state court, but recognizing bases for distinguishing sections 3 and 4). *But see also* Green Tree Fin. Corp. v. Bazzle, 539 U.S. 444, 123 S. Ct. 2402, 2411, 156 L. Ed. 2d 414 (2003) (Thomas, J., dissenting) (arguing that none of the FAA applies in state court cases).
38 *See, e.g.,* Med Ctr. Cars, Inc. v. Smith, 727 So. 2d 9, 20 (Ala. 1998); Stein v. Geonerco, Inc., 17 P.3d 1266, 1271 (Wash. Ct. App. 2001).

39 645 P.2d 1192 (Cal. 1982), *rev'd on other grounds sub nom.* Southland Corp. v. Keating, 465 U.S. 1 (1984).
40 *Id.,* 645 P.2d at 1206, 1207.
41 *Id.,* 645 P.2d at 1209.
42 *Id.*

Bazzle providing the basis for allocating authority between courts and arbitrators under the FAA.[43]

Several state courts, most but not all in California, have followed *Keating*'s holding that class certification may be appropriate in certain arbitrations. In *Dickler v. Shearson Lehman Hutton, Inc.*,[44] Pennsylvania's intermediate appellate court reversed a trial court ruling in a case involving claims by a putative class of securities buyers against their broker and remanded the case for a determination of whether class certification in advance of arbitration would be appropriate.[45]

Dickler, unlike *Keating*, identified no generally applicable statutory authority recognizing classwide arbitration proceedings and acknowledged that the arbitration contract before it did not explicitly address such proceedings.[46] Relying instead on a Pennsylvania Supreme Court decision which had allowed classwide arbitration under a statute governing claims against the state,[47] *Dickler* interpreted the private securities broker's contract referring "any controversy" to arbitration as allowing classwide arbitration in order to "serve the dual interest of respecting and advancing contractually agreed upon arbitration agreements while allowing individuals who believe they have been wronged to have an economically feasible route to get injunctive relief from large institutions employing adhesion contracts."[48]

Numerous California intermediate appellate court decisions have also ordered trial courts to make determinations necessary for classwide arbitration proceedings, following *Keating*.[49] A California intermediate appellate court reaffirmed *Keating* in the face of a preemption challenge, holding that the Federal Arbitration Act does not preempt state decisional authority allowing classwide arbitration.[50] The court concluded that classwide arbitration furthers the FAA's policy goal of enforcing arbitration agreements, then differentiated federal cases on the grounds that section 4 of the federal act does not apply in state court and that California law provides the authority for classwide arbitration which was found lacking in the federal cases. Finally the court noted that section 4 of the FAA has not conclusively been determined to prohibit classwide arbitration in any event.[51]

Although the case involved consolidation of arbitrations rather than class actions, in *Illinois Farmers Insurance Co. v. Glass Service Co.*,[52] the Minnesota Supreme Court held that a court has the discretion to order a consolidated arbitration when the arbitration clause does not expressly prohibit it.[53] The court explicitly rejected the federal line of cases holding that arbitration agreements must be rigidly enforced according to their terms and therefore cannot be consolidated in the absence of express language in the contract permitting it.[54] The court instead held that, in determining whether to consolidate arbitration proceedings, the district court should balance the efficiency gains from consolidation against the potential prejudice to the parties.[55]

10.5 When Arbitration Clause Expressly Prohibits Class Claims in Arbitration or Court

Finally, when an arbitration clause expressly prohibits class actions, the question arises whether such a clause is valid and enforceable. The Supreme Court's opinion in *Bazzle* should not interfere with a court's authority to determine the validity of such clauses under state law prohibiting the enforcement of unconscionable contracts. *Bazzle* expressly differentiates between an arbitrator's authority to interpret an enforceable arbitration clause and a court's authority to determine whether the clause is enforceable against the parties in the first place.[56] Furthermore, *Bazzle*'s holding that questions of contract interpretation concerning

---

43 *See, e.g.*, Garcia v. DirecTV, 9 Cal. Rptr. 3d 190, 195, 196 (Ct. App. 2004) (applying *Bazzle* rather than *Keating*).
44 596 A.2d 860 (Pa. Super. Ct. 1991).
45 *Id.* at 867.
46 *Id.* at 865.
47 *See* Stevenson v. Commonwealth Dep't of Revenue, 413 A.2d 667 (Pa. 1980).
48 Dickler v. Shearson Lehman Hutton, Inc., 596 A.2d 860, 867 (Pa. Super. Ct. 1991); *see also* Wong v. First Union Nat'l Bank, 69 Pa. D. & C.4th 516 (C.P. 2004) (post-*Bazzle* decision holding that it is for the court to decide whether an arbitration can proceed on a classwide basis).
49 *See* Blue Cross of Cal. v. Super. Ct., 78 Cal. Rptr. 2d 779 (Ct. App. 1998) (remanding for trial court to determine whether class proceedings are appropriate); Izzi v. Mesquite Country Club, 231 Cal. Rptr. 315 (Ct. App. 1986) (remanding for development of record relevant to class certification determination); Gainey v. Occidental Land Research, 231 Cal. Rptr. 249 (Ct. App. 1986) (restoring members to plaintiff class that trial court had excluded before ordering arbitration); Lewis v. Prudential Bache Sec., Inc., 225 Cal. Rptr. 69 (Ct. App. 1986) (ordering trial court to make class certification and notice determinations, select arbitrators).
50 Blue Cross of Cal. v. Super. Ct., 78 Cal. Rptr. 2d 779, 781 (Ct. App. 1998).
51 *Id.* at 793.
 While these decisions are still good law for the proposition that the FAA does not preclude states from allowing class claims in arbitration, the United States Supreme Court's decision in *Bazzle* may also modify these decisions by holding that under section 2 of the FAA state courts must allow arbitrators to decide class-related issues.
52 Ill. Farmers Ins. Co. v. Glass Serv. Co., 683 N.W.2d 792 (Minn. 2004).
53 *Id.* at 805–807.
54 *Id.* at 806.
55 *Id.*
56 Green Tree Fin. Corp. v. Bazzle, 539 U.S. 444, 123 S. Ct. 2402, 2407, 156 L. Ed. 2d 414 (2003) (decisions for courts include "certain gateway matters, such as whether the parties have a valid arbitration agreement at all or whether a concededly binding arbitration clause applies to a certain type of controversy").

class proceedings are questions of state law[57] provides additional support for the argument that questions of contract validity are also to be decided under state law.

Consistent with these arguments, numerous courts have held as a matter of state law that arbitration clauses expressly banning class claims by consumers are unconscionable and therefore unenforceable.[58] In *Ting v. AT & T*,[59] for example, the federal district court held that AT & T's arbitration clause for long distance telephone customers was unconscionable in part because it deprived consumers of the right to bring or participate in class action proceedings.[60] At the same time, though, the court recognized that AT & T would have been free to require arbitration had it not attempted to take away important substantive and procedural rights of consumers.[61] Decisions like this one holding that contractual class action bans are illegal in certain cases, while recognizing the general enforceability of arbitration clauses, thus provide additional support for the argument that class action proceedings are permissible under the FAA without regard to the existence of an express contractual directive authorizing such proceedings.

---

57 *Id.*
58 See cases discussed in § 6.5.5, *supra*.
59 182 F. Supp. 2d 902 (N.D. Cal. 2002), *aff'd in relevant part*, 319 F.3d 1126 (9th Cir. 2003).
60 *Id.*, 182 F. Supp. 2d at 931; *see also* Jenkins v. First S. Cash Advance of Ga., 400 F.3d 868 (11th Cir. 2005); Leonard v. Terminix Int'l Co., 854 So. 2d 529 (Ala. 2002) (holding that arbitration clause's ban on class actions is unconscionable); Discover Bank v. Super. Court, 113 P.3d 1100 (Cal. 2005); Mandel v. Household Bank, 105 Cal. App. 4th 75, 129 Cal. Rptr. 2d 380 (2003).
61 *Ting,* 182 F. Supp. 2d at 938, 939.

Chapter 11 Judicial Review and Effect of the Arbitration Award

11.1 Introduction

11.1.1 Effect of Arbitration Award

An arbitration proceeding is a private matter arranged by contract, and the parties to the contract agree to be bound by the arbitration award. When a party does not comply with the award, there is a breach of contract, and the other party has an action to enforce the contract. The Federal Arbitration Act (FAA) and state arbitration law, wishing to expedite resolution of disputes over arbitration awards, establish an alternative statutory procedure to enforce and review arbitration awards. The procedure gives great deference to the arbitrator's decision and requires a party challenging that award to act quickly.

This statutory procedure allows a party to ask a trial court to "confirm" the award, which converts the arbitration award into a final judgment enforceable like any other court judgment. Until an award is confirmed it does *not* have the effect of a judgment, and a party cannot use post-judgment remedies to collect on the award, such as wage garnishment and judgment liens.

Confirmation is almost automatic unless there is a defect in the confirmation application or the other party succeeds in vacating or modifying the award—and the grounds to vacate or modify an award are severely limited. A party has a short time period to bring an independent action to vacate or modify an award or, subject to similar significant time constraints, may seek to vacate or modify the award in the confirmation proceeding. A party can seek to either vacate or modify an award, or the party can seek both remedies in the alternative.[1]

If a court modifies the award it will then confirm the award as modified. But if the court vacates the award the court will not conduct an independent trial on the matter, but will remand the matter back to arbitration. The FAA provides that, if an award is vacated, the court in its discretion may direct the arbitrators to hold a rehearing.[2] This provision creates at least a plausible argument that, if the decision is vacated, the court could determine that the case instead proceed to court. The Supreme Court has held, however, that under the Labor Management Relations Act[3] the appropriate remedy after a court vacates an arbitration award is to remand the case for further arbitration proceedings.[4]

If a party loses an action to modify the award, the court confirms the award.[5] If a party brings an affirmative action to vacate and the action fails, typically the other party must still seek to confirm the award. Unlike a motion to modify, defeating a motion to vacate in most states is not the same as winning a motion to confirm.[6] The best practice is usually to seek to confirm the award in the same action that the other party seeks to vacate it. The procedures to confirm, vacate, or modify an award are examined in § 11.2, *infra*.

Section 11.3, *infra* considers the limited grounds to modify or correct an award. The FAA and state statutes also delineate grounds to vacate an award but, as described in § 11.4, *infra*, those grounds are also very limited and relate only to the adequacy of the arbitration process, and not to whether the award itself comports with the law or the facts. Although not mentioned by the arbitration statutes, courts identify several very narrow situations in which a party can challenge the arbitrator's legal interpretations or fact finding, as set out in § 11.5, *infra*.

Special issues arise when a creditor seeks to collect a consumer debt using an arbitration proceeding. Chapter 12, *infra*, examines the nature of that proceeding, and also the consumer's options to enjoin or participate in the arbitration proceeding, and to vacate or resist confirmation of an award resulting from such a proceeding.

Because it is difficult to challenge confirmation of an award directly, some litigants instead sue the arbitrator or arbitration service provider, seeking damages for those persons' failure to properly conduct the arbitration. But the

---

1 Unif. Arbitration Act § 13(c) (1955); Unif. Arbitration Act § 24(c) (2000).
2 9 U.S.C. § 10(a)(5).
3 29 U.S.C. § 185.
4 *See* Major League Baseball Players Ass'n v. Garvey, 532 U.S. 504, 511, 121 S. Ct. 1724, 149 L. Ed. 2d 740 (2001) (per curiam).
5 *See* § 11.3, *infra*.
6 MBNA Am. Bank v. Mackey, 343 F. Supp. 2d 966 (W.D. Wash. 2004). *But see* Mass. Gen. Laws ch. 251, § 12(d) (if application to vacate is denied, the court shall confirm the award).

doctrine of arbitral immunity generally protects the arbitrator and arbitration service provider, as detailed in § 11.6, *infra*.

The difficulty in overturning an arbitration award is a double-edged sword for corporations. On the one hand, it makes it difficult for consumers to vacate or modify an award even when the arbitrator ignores consumer protection legislation. On the other hand, it makes it difficult for the corporation to challenge an arbitrator's decision to award punitive damages. The ability of a corporation to challenge a punitive damages award favoring the consumer is detailed at § 11.7, *infra*.

Finally, an arbitration award can also have an impact on subsequent litigation. Just as a court proceeding may be res judicata or may collaterally estop determinations in a subsequent proceeding, so may an arbitration award. Section 11.8, *infra*, considers the effect of an arbitration award on a subsequent court proceeding or arbitration.

11.1.2 This Chapter Applies Only to Binding Arbitration

The procedures to vacate, modify, or confirm an award detailed in this chapter apply only to binding arbitration agreements. For example, informal dispute resolution procedures complying with the Federal Trade Commission's Magnuson-Moss Warranty Act rules or many state lemon laws are not binding on the consumer. The warrantor cannot confirm the award in court, and the dissatisfied consumer's remedy is not to seek to vacate the dispute resolution award. Instead, the consumer brings a new action in court.

A similar result should apply to arbitration awards made by the Internet Corporation for the Assigned Names and Numbers (ICANN), which operates a private dispute resolution system that allows domain name registrants to file actions in court before, during, or after an arbitration proceeding. As such, FAA or other procedures to modify, vacate, or confirm an award are not applicable.[7]

11.2 Procedure to Confirm, Vacate, or Modify an Award

11.2.1 The Proper Court

There are very narrow grounds to establish federal court jurisdiction for an action to confirm, vacate, or modify an arbitration award. The action must present an independent basis for federal jurisdiction other than the FAA—even though the FAA specifies federal court procedures to be used to confirm, vacate or modify an award, those FAA provisions do not establish, on their own, federal court jurisdiction to pursue such a proceeding.[8]

Moreover, the fact that the underlying claims decided by the arbitration involve questions of federal law does not suffice to establish federal question jurisdiction. The request for review is not of the federal claims, but of the arbitrator's actions in the arbitration proceeding.[9] Some courts, however, hold that a federal question exists when the matter presented for judicial review is whether the arbitrator disregarded applicable federal law. In that situation, when the specific issue to be reviewed is the disregard of federal law, as opposed to arbitrator bias or procedural mistakes, the court may be provided with federal jurisdiction.[10]

Otherwise, federal court jurisdiction must be based on diversity, labor relations, or maritime subject matter jurisdiction. In computing the amount in controversy required to establish federal diversity jurisdiction, the amount at stake is neither the amount at issue in the underlying litigation nor the amount of the arbitration award. What is determinative is the amount at stake in the judicial review action, that is, the monetary difference depending on whether the judicial action is successful or not. When a plaintiff brings an action to vacate an award and seek a new arbitration because the award is inadequate, diversity jurisdiction is based on the

---

7 Dluhos v. Strasberg, 321 F.3d 365 (3d Cir. 2003).

8 *See* Southland Corp. v. Keating, 465 U.S. 1, 15 n.9, 104 S. Ct. 852, 79 L. Ed. 2d 1 (1984) ("While the Federal Arbitration Act creates federal substantive law requiring parties to honor arbitration agreements, it does not create any independent federal question jurisdiction under 28 U.S.C. § 1331 or otherwise."); Moses H. Cone Mem'l Hosp. v. Mercury Constr. Corp., 460 U.S. 1, 103 S. Ct. 927, 74 L. Ed. 2d 765 (1983); *see also* Perpetual Sec., Inc. v. Tang, 290 F.3d 132, 136 (2d Cir. 2002); Kasap v. Folger Nolan Fleming & Douglas, Inc., 166 F.3d 1243, 1245, 1246 (D.C. Cir. 1999) (applying *Southland* to reject claim of federal jurisdiction to consider motion to vacate arbitration award based solely on section 10 of the FAA); Baltin v. Alaron Trading Corp., 128 F.3d 1466, 1469 (11th Cir. 1997); Garrett v. Merrill Lynch, Pierce, Fenner & Smith, Inc., 7 F.3d 882 (9th Cir. 1993).

9 Perpetual Sec., Inc. v. Tang, 290 F.3d 132, 139 (2d Cir. 2002); Greenberg v. Bear, Stearns & Co., 220 F.3d 22, 25 (2d Cir. 2000); Kasap v. Folger Nolan Fleming & Douglas, Inc., 166 F.3d 1243 (D.C. Cir. 1999); Westmoreland Capital Corp. v. Findlay, 100 F.3d 263 (2d Cir. 1996); Ford v. Hamilton Investments, Inc., 29 F.3d 255 (6th Cir. 1994); Goodman v. CIBC Oppenheimer & Co., 131 F. Supp. 2d 1180 (C.D. Cal. 2001). *But see* Biscanin v. Merrill Lynch & Co., 407 F.3d 905, 907 (8th Cir. 2005) ("assum[ing] for the sake of argument that a claim of manifest disregard of federal law could endow the federal court with subject-matter jurisdiction").

10 *See* Luong v. Circuit City Stores, Inc., 368 F.3d 1109 (9th Cir. 2004) (motion to vacate based on arbitrator's alleged manifest disregard of the federal Americans with Disabilities Act); Greenberg v. Bear, Stearns & Co., 220 F.3d 22, 25 (2d Cir. 2000) (petition for review based on arbitrator's alleged manifest disregard of federal Securities Exchange Act granted); Barbara v. N.Y. Stock Exch., Inc., 99 F.3d 49 (2d Cir. 1996); Minor v. Prudential Sec., Inc., 94 F.3d 1103 (7th Cir. 1996). *But cf.* Kasap v. Folger Nolan Fleming & Douglas, Inc., 166 F.3d 1243 (D.C. Cir. 1999).

additional amount the plaintiff is seeking, not on the amount of the award.[11] If the defendant seeks to vacate an arbitration award for the plaintiff that is for less than $75,000, there is no diversity jurisdiction.[12] Of course, in an action to confirm the amount of the award is at issue and should determine the diversity amount.

If there is no basis for federal jurisdiction, an action to modify, vacate, or confirm an award must be brought in state court. State arbitration law generally specifies that venue is proper in a trial court of the county where the arbitration hearing was held. Otherwise, venue is proper in a trial court in the county where the adverse party resides or does business.[13]

The FAA specifies that an application to *vacate or modify* an award be made in the federal court for the district where the arbitration award was made.[14] Actions to *confirm* the award can be brought in the court specified by agreement; if there is no agreement, then in the federal court for the district where the arbitration award was made.[15] The Supreme Court has held that these are permissive venue rules, allowing parties to move for post-arbitration judicial determinations in any federal court in which venue is proper under the general venue statute.[16]

When a creditor brings an action to confirm an arbitration award to collect on a debt, additional venue issues arise, including compliance with the Fair Debt Collection Practices Act and with state deceptive practices standards. These statutory standards may restrict proper venue of the confirmation proceeding to the county of the consumer's residence. Because the UAA requires that the confirmation hearing be held in the county where the arbitration was held, the creditor would have to have brought the arbitration proceeding in that county, if venue to confirm the award is to be proper. More on this issue is found in § 12.5.5.2, *infra*.

11.2.2 Does State or Federal Law Apply?

There is much confusion as to what law applies to a motion to vacate, modify, or confirm an award—the FAA or state law. On the one hand, the FAA's provisions regarding judicial review by their own language apply only to actions in federal court,[17] and every state has enacted statutes governing judicial review of arbitration actions in state courts.[18] On the other hand, it is clear that FAA section 2 preempts any attempt by state law to limit the enforceability of an *agreement* to arbitrate. Less clear is what effect the FAA has on state laws that limit the enforceability of an arbitration *award*. The Supreme Court has made it clear that the FAA does not occupy the field and preempt all state laws on the subject, and only preempts a state law if there is a conflict, that is, if the state law is an obstacle to the Congressional purpose.[19]

In the rare consumer arbitration case in which federal court review of the award is based upon federal subject matter jurisdiction, the FAA's procedures and substantive standards for judicial review clearly apply. In the less rare consumer case in which federal court review is based on diversity jurisdiction, the FAA's *procedures* as to review should clearly apply, but a number of courts have held that state law standards govern the *substance* of the review, as long as those standards are at least as protective of the arbitration award as the FAA.[20]

The typical action to confirm, vacate, or modify an award in a consumer case is brought in state court, and state law should govern the procedures and substance of that action.[21] But it is an open question to what extent the FAA preempts any such procedures or standards that conflict with the FAA. Most likely to be preempted are those that allow for less deference to the arbitrator's award or less deference to the arbitration agreement than the FAA. In general it will be state courts who will be making the determination as to whether the FAA preempts state law, and these courts are far from uniform in either recognizing or resolving these issues.

---

11 Theis Research, Inc. v. Brown & Bain, 400 F.3d 659, 662 (9th Cir. 2005); Sirotsky v. N.Y. Stock Exch., 347 F.3d 985, 989 (7th Cir. 2003).
12 Baltin v. Alaron Trading Corp., 128 F.3d 1466 (11th Cir. 1997); Ford v. Hamilton Investments, Inc., 29 F.3d 255 (6th Cir. 1994).
13 Unif. Arbitration Act § 27 (2000); Unif. Arbitration Act § 18 (1955).
14 9 U.S.C. §§ 10, 11.
15 9 U.S.C. § 9.
16 Cortez Byrd Chips, Inc. v. Harbert Constr. Co., 529 U.S. 193, 120 S. Ct. 1331, 1334, 146 L. Ed. 2d 171 (2000).
17 9 U.S.C. §§ 10, 11.
  9 U.S.C. § 9 concerning confirmation of awards is less clear.

18 Virtually every state has enacted a version of the Uniform Arbitration Act (1955) and twelve have enacted a version of the revised Uniform Arbitration Act (2000).
19 Volt Info. Sciences, Inc. v. Bd. of Trustees, 489 U.S. 468, 476, 109 S. Ct. 1248, 1254, 103 L. Ed. 2d 488 (1989).
20 Penn Va. Oil & Gas Corp. v. CNX Gas Co, L.L.C., 2007 WL 593578 (W.D. Va. Feb. 22, 2007); M & L Power Services, Inc. v. Am. Networks Int'l, 44 F. Supp. 2d 134 (D.R.I. 1999); Flexible Mfg. Sys. Pty. Ltd. v. Super Products Corp., 874 F. Supp. 247 (E.D. Wis. 1994).
21 Siegel v. Prudential Ins. Co. of Am., 67 Cal. App. 4th 1270 (1998); Trombetta v. Raymond James Fin. Services, 907 A.2d 550 (Pa. Super. Ct. 2006); *see also* Consol. Rail Corp. v. Del. & Hudson Ry. Co., 867 F. Supp. 25 (D.D.C. 1994); Armendariz v. Found. Health Psychcare Services, Inc., 24 Cal. 4th 83 (2000); Ovitz v. Schulman, 35 Cal. Rptr. 3d 117 (Ct. App. 2005); Sloan Elec. v. Prof'l Realty & Dev. Corp., 819 N.E.2d 37, 44 (Ill. App. Ct. 2004); MBNA Am. Bank v. Rogers, 838 N.E.2d 475 (Ind. Ct. App. 2005); D Enterprises Contracting Corp. v. Lexington-Fayette Urban County Gov't, 134 S.W.3d 558 (Ky. 2004); NCO Portfolio Mgmt., Inc. v. Lewis, 2007 WL 2229251 (Ohio Ct. App. Aug. 6, 2007); Warbington Constr., Inc. v. Franklin Landmark, L.L.C., 66 S.W.3d 853 (Tenn. Ct. App. 2001); § 3.2.2.4, *supra*. *But see* Birmingham News Co. v. Horn, 901 So. 2d 27 (Ala. 2004) (FAA applies, not unique Alabama law that provides very limited grounds for review); Hecla Mining Co. v. Bunker Hill Co., 617 P.2d 861 (Idaho 1980); Edward D. Jones & Co. v. Schwartz, 969 S.W.2d 788 (Mo. Ct. App. 1998); Dowd v. First Omaha Sec. Corp., 495 N.W.2d 36 (Neb. 1993).

Some state courts even assume that the FAA governs actions in state court to confirm or review an arbitration award.[22]

There should be less chance that the FAA preempts state procedures than state substantive review standards. The Supreme Court has held that "[t]here is no federal policy favoring arbitration under a certain set of procedural rules."[23] In that case, state law allowed a stay of the arbitration pending resolution of a related court case, and the Court found that state law was not preempted by the FAA. State courts thus are likely to find "procedural"—and thus not subject to preemption—much of the state procedures for judicial review of an arbitration agreement.[24] For example, while the FAA requires that an action to vacate an award be brought within ninety days, state law could provide for 100, 200, or even 300 days, because this difference is procedural and not substantive.

In addition, state standards similar to or more protective of arbitration awards than the federal standards may escape preemption.[25] For example, some state appellate courts hold that awards cannot be vacated for manifest disregard of the law, which is a federal ground for vacating an award.[26] That determination is more protective of the award than the federal standard and is unlikely to be preempted.[27]

Some state statutes or courts create their own judicial grounds for *vacatur*. For example, in Illinois a court may vacate an arbitration award "where a gross error of law or fact appears on the award's face, or where the award fails to dispose of all matters properly submitted to the arbitrator."[28] A California statute requires *vacatur* when the arbitrator fails to disclose certain information.[29] State courts have found no preemption when the state standards are intended to make arbitration a fairer process, which is consistent with the Congressional purpose.[30]

The key question may be whether a state standard creates a standard of judicial review that has the effect of limiting the arbitration agreement's enforceability. Thus the FAA is likely to preempt a state statute that provides for de novo review of the law or the facts.

Virtually every state has adopted a version of the 1956 Uniform Arbitration Act (UAA), drafted by the National Conference of Commissioners on Uniform State Laws (NCCUSL). In 2000, NCCUSL issued a revised Uniform Arbitration Act (revised UAA), enacted so far in twelve states (Alaska, Colorado, Hawaii, Nevada, New Jersey, New Mexico, North Carolina, North Dakota, Oregon, Oklahoma, Utah, and Washington), and introduced in 2007 in the New York and District of Columbia legislatures. Individual state laws often vary from the standard provisions of the UAA or revised UAA, and practitioners should become familiar with their own statutes and case law.

11.2.3 Strict Timing Requirements

11.2.3.1 Short Period to Vacate or Modify an Award

In most cases, actions to vacate or modify an award must be brought *immediately* after an award is issued. If, instead, a dissatisfied party waits to defend the prevailing party's attempt to confirm the award, the dissatisfied party may lose the ability to challenge the award.

The FAA, the UAA, and the revised UAA require a party to apply to vacate or modify an arbitration award within ninety days after delivery of a copy of the award to that party (the FAA standard is actually three months). The party opposing a motion to vacate on timeliness grounds has the burden of establishing the delivery date,[31] and there may be issues as to whether the delivery itself was proper, thus extending the time period.[32] In addition, equitable tolling may apply to the time limit for moving to vacate an arbitration award.[33] Under the UAA and revised UAA when the party's application to vacate alleges corruption, fraud, or undue means, the application must be made within ninety days after such grounds are known or should have been known.[34]

---

22 *See, e.g.*, RSG Caulking & Waterproofing, Inc. v. J.P. Morgan Chase & Co., 831 N.Y.S.2d 350 (Sup. Ct. 2006); Siemens Transp. P'ship P.R., S.E. v. Redondo Perini Joint Venture, 824 N.Y.S.2d 758 (Sup. Ct. 2006).

23 Volt Info. Sciences, Inc. v. Bd. of Trustees, 489 U.S. 468, 476, 109 S. Ct. 1248, 1254, 103 L. Ed. 2d 488 (1989).

24 *See* Trombetta v. Raymond James Fin. Services, 907 A.2d 550 (Pa. Super. Ct. 2006) (suggesting that standards of review of an arbitration award are procedural, and thus less likely to be subject to federal preemption).

25 Siegel v. Prudential Ins. Co. of Am., 67 Cal. App. 4th 1270 (1998); Trombetta v. Raymond James Fin. Services, 907 A.2d 550 (Pa. Super. Ct. 2006).

26 Siegel v. Prudential Ins. Co. of Am., 67 Cal. App. 4th 1270 (1998); 3D Enterprises Contracting Corp. v. Lexington-Fayette Urban County Gov't, 134 S.W.3d 558 (Ky. 2004); *see also* Warbington Constr., Inc. v. Franklin Landmark, L.L.C., 66 S.W.3d 853 (Tenn. Ct. App. 2001) (rejecting the manifest disregard of the law standard in that state).

27 Siegel v. Prudential Ins. Co. of Am., 67 Cal. App. 4th 1270 (1998).

28 Sloan Elec. v. Prof'l Realty & Dev. Corp., 819 N.E.2d 37, 44 (Ill. App. Ct. 2004) (arbitrator made gross error of law by awarding damages in summary judgment without evidentiary hearing).

29 *See* § 11.4.3.2, *infra*.

30 Ovitz v. Schulman, 35 Cal. Rptr. 3d 117 (Ct. App. 2005).

31 MBNA v. Barben, 111 P.3d 663 (Kan. Ct. App. 2005) (burden not met when award could not possibly have been delivered to absent party on date of arbitration proceeding in which default award was entered).

32 This is examined in some detail in § 12.5.3.2, *infra*.

33 Bauer v. Carty & Co., 2005 WL 948641, at *4 (W.D. Tenn. Mar. 9, 2005); *cf.* Pfannenstiel v. Merrill Lynch Pierce Fenner & Smith, 477 F.3d 1155 (10th Cir. 2007) (facts of the case did not justify equitable estoppel).

34 Unif. Arbitration Act §§ 12, 13 (1956); Unif. Arbitration Act §§ 23, 24 (2000).

While ninety days is the usual standard, individual states vary the time period to vacate. California law provides for one-hundred days.[35] In Arizona, a party seeking to *modify* an arbitration award must do so within ninety days, but no similar statute of limitations exists for motions to *set aside* the award in its entirety.[36] Other states' laws impose shorter time limits within which a party must move to vacate. Connecticut and Massachusetts provide only thirty days to vacate an award;[37] Michigan allows only twenty-one days.[38]

Private parties often seek to confirm an award after the time limit to vacate has expired. The question then arises whether the other party can still bring a motion to vacate in that confirmation proceeding. Although most courts say no,[39] a minority of courts allow motions to vacate to be made in response to a confirmation proceeding even after the time limits have expired.[40] More significantly, a growing number of courts say that challenges to the existence or enforceability of the arbitration agreement go to the court's jurisdiction, and can be raised even after the deadline. This latter ground is examined in some detail in § 12.5.3, *infra*.

11.2.3.2 Longer Period to Confirm an Award

There are longer deadlines to apply to confirm an award, although there is significant confusion as to what those deadlines are. The FAA states that a party "may" seek to confirm an award in federal court within one year of that award,[41] and federal courts come to differing views as to whether the one-year period must be strictly complied with.[42]

Because the typical consumer arbitration award can only be confirmed in state court,[43] state timing rules should apply,[44] and these are even less clear than the FAA's rules. Neither the UAA nor the revised UAA establish time limits to confirm an award. The drafters of the revised UAA rejected the FAA's one-year time limit, opting instead for the general statute of limitations for the filing and execution of a judgment in a state.[45] An Indiana appellate court has decided to use the FAA's one-year time period when the Indiana arbitration procedures (based on the UAA) do not specify a time limit, even though the general limitations period to collect a debt in Indiana is much longer.[46] A federal court interpreting District of Columbia law used the District's three year limitation period for actions for which a limitation is not otherwise specially prescribed.[47]

On the other hand, nonconforming amendments to the UAA in some states do specify a time period for award confirmation. For example, California has a four-year limit.[48] Connecticut, New York, and Ohio have one-year limits.[49]

As with the FAA, there is also an issue whether those time periods are mandatory. For example, one court found the Ohio limit not mandatory, and instead used its discretion whether to allow the action, considering the length of the delay, the reason for the delay, and the prejudice to the other party.[50]

If a party waits too long and the court refuses to confirm the award because of the delay, then the award will not have the force of a court judgment.[51] Nevertheless, the arbitration award still exists, and in some states that party can initiate a common law proceeding to enforce the arbitration award as it would enforce any other contract. Some state courts have found that, unless a statute or the arbitration agreement indicates that confirmation is the only way to enforce the award, a party can enforce the award though a common law action.[52] One would expect that there would be more de-

---

35 Cal. Civ. Proc. Code § 1288 (West).
36 Ariz. Rev. Stat. Ann. § 12-1512; Morgan v. Carillon Investments, Inc., 109 P.3d 82 (Ariz. 2005).
37 Conn. Gen. Stat. § 52-417; Mass. Gen. Laws ch. 251, § 12.
38 Mich. Ct. R. 3.602(J)(2).
39 *See, e.g.*, Kutch v. State Farm Mut. Auto. Ins. Co., 960 P.2d 93 (Colo. 1998); MBNA Am. Bank v. Leslie, 2005 WL 2277252 (Conn. Super. Ct. Aug. 25, 2005); MBNA Am. Bank v. Swartz, 2006 WL 1071523 (Del. Ch. Ct. Apr. 13, 2006); Walter A. Brown Inc. v. Moylan, 509 A.2d 98 (D.C. 1986); Broward County Paraprofessional Ass'n v. Sch. Bd. of Broward County, 406 So. 2d 1252, 1253 (Fla. Dist. Ct. App. 1981); MBNA Am. Bank v. Tackleson, 720 N.W.2d 192 (Iowa Ct. App. 2006); Local 589, Amalgamated Transit Union v. Mass. Bay Transp. Auth., 491 N.E.2d 1053 (Mass. App. Ct. 1986); MBNA Am. Bank v. Belleslie, 2005 Mont. Dist. LEXIS 1119 (Mont. Dist. Ct. Apr. 26, 2005); MBNA Am. Bank v. Hart, 710 N.W.2d 125 (N.D. 2006); MBNA Am. Bank v. Cooper, 2006 WL 1519640 (Ohio Ct. App. June 5, 2006); Burst v. MBNA Am. Bank, 2005 Tex. App. LEXIS 3461 (Tex. App. May 5, 2005), *review granted* (Tex. Feb. 24, 2006); MBNA Am. Bank v. Miles, 164 P.3d 164 (Wash. Ct. App. 2007).
40 *See* Paul Allison v. Minkin Storage of Omaha, Inc., 452 F. Supp. 573 (D. Neb. 1978); Riko Enterprises, Inc. v. Seattle Supersonics Corp., 357 F. Supp. 521 (S.D.N.Y. 1973); Milwaukee Police Ass'n v. City of Milwaukee, 285 N.W.2d 119 (Wis. 1979).
41 9 U.S.C. § 9.
42 *Compare* Photopaint Technologies, L.L.C. v. Smartlens Corp., 335 F.3d 152 (2d Cir. 2003) (strict compliance) *and* Consol. Rail Corp. v. Del. & Hudson Ry. Co., 867 F. Supp. 25 (D.D.C. 1994) (strict compliance) *with* Sverdrup Corp. v. WHC Constructors, Inc., 989 F.2d 148 (4th Cir. 1993) *and* Val-U Constr. Co. of S.D. v. Rosebud Sioux Tribe, 146 F.3d 573 (8th Cir. 1998).
43 *See* § 11.2.1, *supra*.
44 *See* § 11.2.2, *supra*.
45 Unif. Arbitration Act § 22 cmt. 2 (2000).
46 MBNA Am. Bank v. Rogers, 838 N.E.2d 475 (Ind. Ct. App. 2005).
47 Consol. Rail Corp. v. Del. & Hudson Ry. Co., 867 F. Supp. 25 (D.D.C. 1994).
48 Cal. Civ. Proc. Code § 1288 (West).
49 Conn. Gen. Stat. § 52-417; N.Y. C.P.L.R. 7510 (McKinney); Ohio Rev. Code Ann. § 2711.09 (West); *see also* MBNA Am. Bank v. Terry, 2006 WL 513952 (Ohio Ct. App. Mar. 3, 2006).
50 *See* NCO Portfolio Mgmt., Inc. v. Lewis, 2007 WL 2229251 (Ohio Ct. App. Aug. 6, 2007).
51 *See* Photopaint Technologies, L.L.C. v. Smartlens Corp., 335 F.3d 152 (2d Cir. 2003).
52 Spearhead Constr. Corp. v. Bianco, 665 A.2d 86 (Conn. App. Ct. 1995); Krystoff v. Kalama Land Co., Ltd., 965 P.2d 142 (Haw.

fenses available to the party opposing enforcement in such a common law action than there are in a statutory action to confirm.

11.2.3.3 Barriers to Vacating an Award at the Confirmation Hearing

The fact that the time limit to confirm an award is significantly longer than that to vacate or modify an award has important practical consequences. A dissatisfied party should seek to vacate or modify an award immediately, instead of waiting to respond to the other party's attempt to confirm the award. It may be that many grounds to vacate an award can only be raised in the confirmation proceeding if the other party brings the confirmation proceeding within the time limits specified to vacate or modify an award.

Of course, there are certain circumstances in which a party can vacate or modify an award even after the ninety-day or other applicable period. The period runs from when the party receives notice of an arbitration award. If the notice is never received, or that notice is defective, the ninety-day period does not start running.[53] In addition an increasing number of cases find the time deadline to vacate does not apply when a party challenges the existence or enforceability of the arbitration agreement.[54] Moreover, the ninety-day period concerns actions to vacate or modify the award, not actions challenging defects in the confirmation proceeding itself, such as that the confirmation proceeding is not timely, that there is no jurisdiction to confirm the award in federal court, or that the proceeding is in the wrong venue.[55]

11.2.4 Can the Parties, by Contract, Alter the Nature of Judicial Review?

11.2.4.1 Contract Cannot Limit Court's Power to Vacate or Modify an Award

The Second Circuit has stated in the most clear-cut terms that parties to an arbitration agreement cannot eliminate judicial review of the award, while still seeking court review to confirm the award.[56] In other words, when one party seeks to confirm an award, the other party must have the rights set out by statute and case law to vacate or modify that award. While the Second Circuit noted that there are conflicting views as to whether the parties can contract to expand judicial review,[57] parties cannot contract to eliminate judicial review. Courts interpreting state arbitration statutes reach similar results.[58] Although parties cannot eliminate judicial review entirely, the Tenth Circuit recently held that the parties can agree to dispense with appellate court review of the trial court's review of the arbitration award,[59] as long as the waiver of appellate review is clear and unequivocal.[60]

11.2.4.2 Arbitration Agreements That Increase the Scope of Judicial Review

The federal courts of appeal are split over whether the FAA permits parties to contract for a heightened level of judicial review of the merits of an arbitration award. Such an agreement might allow judicial review of all errors of law, as to whether the award was supported by evidence, or de novo judicial review.[61] This split among the federal circuit courts is expected to be resolved by the United States Supreme Court in 2008, because certiorari was granted on this issue in *Hall Street Associates, L.L.C. v. Mattel*.[62]

The First, Third, Fourth, and Fifth Circuits consider heightened review to be a legitimate area for contractual modification, allowing the agreement to override the review standards set out in the FAA.[63] The First Circuit however has stated that, in light of the "strong federal policy requiring limited judicial review," any displacement of the FAA's judicial review standards can only be achieved by clear contractual language.[64]

Ct. App. 1998); Cent. Collection v. Gettes, 584 A.2d 689 (Md. 1991); Beall v. Bd. of Trade of Kan. City, 148 S.W. 386 (Mo. Ct. App. 1912); Jones v. John A. Johnson & Sons, 129 N.Y.S.2d 479 (N.Y. Sup. Ct. 1954); Warren Found. Assoc. v. Warren City Bd. of Educ., 18 Ohio St. 3d 170 (1985); MBNA Am. Bank v. Canfora, 2007 WL 2318095 (Ohio Ct. App. Aug. 15, 2007); *see also* Consol. Rail Corp. v. Del. & Hudson Ry. Co., 867 F. Supp. 25 (D.D.C. 1994).

53 *See* § 5.3.2, *infra*.
54 *See* § 5.3.3, *infra*.
55 *See* § 5.5, *infra*.
56 Hoeft v. MVL Group, Inc., 343 F.3d 57 (2d Cir. 2003).
57 *See* § 11.2.4.2, *infra*.
58 *See* Alterra Healthcare Corp. v. Bryant, 937 So. 2d 263 (Fla. Dist. Ct. App. 2006); VoiceStream Wireless Corp. v. U.S. Communications, Inc., 912 So. 2d 34 (Fla. Dist. Ct. App. 2005); Van Duren v. Rzasa-Ormes, 2007 WL 1853988 (N.J. Super. Ct. App. Div. June 29, 2007).
59 Mactec, Inc. v. Gorelick, 427 F.3d 821, 824 (10th Cir. 2005); *see also* Van Duren v. Rzasa-Ormes, 2007 WL 1853988 (N.J. Super. Ct. App. Div. June 29, 2007).
60 Mactec, Inc. v. Gorelick, 427 F.3d 821, 824 (10th Cir. 2005); Bowen v. Amoco Pipeline Co., 254 F.3d 925 (10th Cir. 2001).
61 *See* Nat'l Arbitration Forum, Code of Procedure, Rule 5(O) (court may decide if arbitrator properly applied applicable law).
62 127 S. Ct. 2875 (2007); *see also* Brief for Petitioner, Hall St. Associates, L.L.C. v. Mattel, 2007 WL 2197585 (U.S. July 27, 2007).
63 *See* P.R. Tel. Co. v. U.S. Phone Mfg., 427 F.3d 21 (1st Cir. 2005); Roadway Package Sys., Inc. v. Kayser, 257 F.3d 287 (3d Cir. 2001); Hughes Training, Inc. v. Cook, 254 F.3d 588 (5th Cir. 2001); Syncor Int'l Corp. v. McLeland, 1997 WL 452245 (4th Cir. Aug. 11, 1997); Gateway Technologies, Inc. v. MCI Telecommunications Corp., 64 F.3d 993 (5th Cir. 1995).
64 P.R. Tel. Co. v. U.S. Phone Mfg., 427 F.3d 21 (1st Cir. 2005) (choice-of-law provision providing that arbitration would be conducted in accordance with Puerto Rico law, which provides that arbitration awards can be reviewed for legal error, was not

In contrast, the Ninth and Tenth Circuits hold that parties cannot contractually modify or displace the FAA's provisions governing judicial *vacatur*,[65] and the Seventh and Eighth Circuits have issued opinions indicating they are likely to agree.[66] These courts find that contract modification of judicial review conflicts with the FAA because the Act's limited judicial review standards "manifest a legislative intent to further the federal policy favoring arbitration by preserving the independence of the arbitration process."[67]

The typical consumer case to vacate or confirm an award will be brought in state court and it will be the state courts that will determine, under state law, whether the agreement can expand the nature of the judicial review of the arbitration award.[68] These state courts will not feel bound by federal court rulings interpreting the FAA.[69]

California courts for instance consistently hold that the standard of judicial review cannot be expanded.[70] Illinois, Michigan, North Dakota, and Pennsylvania courts have reached the same conclusion.[71] The Ohio Supreme Court assumes that the standard for review cannot be expanded and decided to sever the offending clause rather than find the arbitration agreement to be unenforceable.[72]

11.2.5 Appeals of Trial Court Review of Arbitration Award

Motions to confirm, vacate, or modify an award are brought before a trial court, whether in federal or state court. Appellate court review of these trial court decisions will involve de novo review of the trial court's legal conclusions, while the appellate court will accept the trial court's findings of fact unless clearly erroneous.[73]

11.3 Grounds to Modify or Correct an Award

Federal and state law allow a dissatisfied party to ask a court to modify or correct an award, which means asking the court change the size or nature of the award. The Uniform Arbitration Act (UAA) and revised UAA explicitly state that, if the court agrees to modify the award, the court shall then confirm the award as modified. If the court refuses to modify the award, then the court shall confirm the award as issued.[74] In neither case does the matter go back to the arbitrator or require a separate confirmation proceeding.

The Federal Arbitration Act (FAA), UAA, and revised UAA provide the following grounds on which a court can modify an arbitration award, on application of a party:

1. When there was an evident miscalculation of figures or an evident mistake in the description of any person, thing, or property referred to in the award;
2. When the arbitrators have awarded upon a matter not submitted to them; and
3. When the award is imperfect in matter or form not affecting the merits of the controversy.[75]

There is minor variation in language among the FAA, UAA, and revised UAA. In the first ground, the FAA requires the miscalculation or mistake to be "material" and the revised UAA specifies that the miscalculation be "mathematical." Under the FAA, the second ground applies only when the matter not submitted affects the merits of the decision. Under the UAA and revised UAA, modification for that ground only applies if the correction does not affect the merits of the decision upon the matter submitted.

---

sufficient to supplant the FAA's standards for *vacatur*).

65 *See* Kyocera v. Prudential-Bache Trade Services, Inc., 341 F.3d 987 (9th Cir. 2003); Bowen v. Amoco Pipeline Co., 254 F.3d 925, 933 (10th Cir. 2001) (construing Taft-Hartley Act, but looking to the FAA for guidance).
66 Chicago Typographical Union No. 16 v. Chicago Sun-Times, Inc., 935 F.2d 1501, 1504–1505 (7th Cir. 1991); UHC Mgmt. Co. v. Computer Sciences Corp., 148 F.3d 992, 997–998 (8th Cir. 1998).
67 *See* Bowen v. Amoco Pipeline Co., 254 F.3d 925, 933 (10th Cir. 2001).
68 Trombetta v. Raymond James Fin. Services, 907 A.2d 550 (Pa. Super. Ct. 2006); *see also* Siegel v. Prudential Ins. Co. of Am., 67 Cal. App. 4th 1270 (1998).
69 *See* Trombetta v. Raymond James Fin. Services, 907 A.2d 550 (Pa. Super. Ct. 2006); *see also* Crowell v. Downey Cmty. Hosp. Found., 95 Cal. App. 4th 730, 739, 115 Cal. Rptr. 2d 810, 817 (2002) (reaching a different conclusion than the Ninth Circuit had at the time (see Lapine Tech. Corp. v. Kyocera Corp., 130 F.3d 884, 888 (9th Cir. 1997), which was not overruled until after *Crowell* was decided)).
70 Cable Connection, Inc. v. DIRECTV, Inc., 143 Cal. App. 4th 207 (2006); Crowell v. Downey Cmty. Hosp. Found., 95 Cal. App. 4th 730, 739, 115 Cal. Rptr. 2d 810, 817 (2002).
71 *See* Chicago SouthShore & S. Bend R.R. v. N. Ind. Commuter Transp. Dist., 682 N.E.2d 156 (Ill. App. Ct. 1997), *rev'd on other grounds*, 703 N.E.2d 7 (Ill. 1998); Brucker v. McKinlay Transp. Inc., 557 N.W.2d 536 (Mich. 1997); John T. Jones Constr. Co. v. City of Grand Forks, 665 N.W.2d 698 (N.D. 2003); Trombetta v. Raymond James Fin. Services, 907 A.2d 550 (Pa. Super. Ct. 2006).
72 Ingazio v. Clear Channel Broad., Inc., 113 Ohio St. 3d 276 (2007).

73 First Options of Chicago, Inc. v. Kaplan, 514 U.S. 938, 115 S. Ct. 1920, 131 L. Ed. 2d 985 (1995); *see also* Aldred v. Avis Rent-A-Car, 2007 WL 2110720 (11th Cir. July 24, 2007); Am. Laser Vision, Prof'l Ass'n v. The Laser Vision Inst., L.L.C., 487 F.3d 255 (5th Cir. 2007); Hudson v. Conagra Poultry Co., 484 F.3d 496 (8th Cir. 2007); Three S Del., Inc. v. DataQuick Info. Sys., Inc., 2007 WL 2004454 (4th Cir. July 12, 2007); McCarthy v. Citigroup Global Markets, Inc., 463 F.3d 87 (1st Cir. 2006); Roehl v. Ritchie, 147 Cal. App. 4th 338 (2007).
74 Unif. Arbitration Act § 13 (1956); Unif. Arbitration Act § 24 (2000).
75 9 U.S.C. § 11; Unif. Arbitration Act § 13 (1956); Revised Unif. Arbitration Act § 24 (2000).

The purpose of a modification or correction is not to change the arbitrator's legal conclusions or fact finding, but to conform the award to the arbitrator's intent in issuing the award.[76] For example, a court may not modify an arbitration award by adding attorney fees to its judgment confirming the award, when the arbitrator declined to award attorney fees.[77] Instead the party challenging the intent of the award should seek judicial review to vacate the award. But, as described in §§ 11.4 and 11.5, *infra*, grounds to vacate an award are also quite narrow.

11.4 Grounds to Vacate Based on Defects in the Arbitration Process

11.4.1 General

The FAA, UAA, and revised UAA enumerate limited grounds upon which a court may vacate an arbitration award. All of these grounds concern the nature of the arbitration process, and not the correctness of the arbitrator's rulings of law or fact.

The FAA provides the following four grounds:

1. The award was procured by corruption, fraud, or other undue means (see § 11.4.5, *infra*);
2. Arbitrator partiality or corruption or misconduct (see § 11.4.3, *infra*);
3. The arbitrators exceeded their powers (see § 11.4.2, *infra*); or
4. The arbitrators refused to postpone a hearing upon sufficient cause, refused to hear evidence, or otherwise improperly conducted the hearing (see § 11.4.4, *infra*).[78]

The UAA adopts the same four grounds and adds a fifth:

5. There was no arbitration agreement and the party participated in the hearing, if at all, under protest.[79]

The revised UAA adopts the above five grounds, and also adds a sixth ground:

6. The arbitration was conducted without proper notice.[80]

The FAA implicitly includes the fifth ground because, if there is no arbitration agreement, then the arbitrators exceeded their powers.[81] Both the FAA and the UAA implicitly include the sixth ground because, if the proceeding was conducted without proper notice, then the award was procured by undue means.

The party contesting an arbitration award must produce evidence that would support a court finding that the award satisfies one of these grounds for *vacatur*.[82] Because these enumerated grounds for judicial *vacatur* of an arbitrator's award are fairly narrow, a considerable burden is placed on a party challenging the arbitration decision.[83] The limited nature of judicial review has been deemed necessary to further arbitration's policy goals of efficient dispute resolution and avoidance of litigation.[84]

11.4.2 When Arbitrators Exceed Their Powers or There is No Arbitration Agreement

The court may vacate an award when the arbitrators exceeded their powers or when they failed to render a decision in the matter.[85] Arbitration is a matter of contract, and the arbitrator's powers emanate from that contract. There is no federal or state policy favoring arbitration of claims that the parties have not agreed to arbitrate, because an arbitrator's powers are solely the product of the parties' agreement.[86] Thus arbitrators exceed their powers when they arbitrate a matter when one party objects to the arbitration and there is no enforceable arbitration agreement. The determination whether the arbitrator exceeded his powers is made by the reviewing court de novo.[87]

Of course, if a party participates in the arbitration that party must object to the arbitrator's authority at the start of the arbitration.[88] Doing so preserves the right to dispute the validity of the arbitration clause in a later court proceed-

---

76 9 U.S.C. § 11; Unif. Arbitration Act § 13(b) (1956).
77 Kosty v. S. Shore Harbour Cmty. Ass'n, Inc., 2006 WL 2042385, at *4 (Tex. App. July 20, 2006).
78 9 U.S.C. § 10.
79 Unif. Arbitration Act § 12(a) (1955).
80 Unif. Arbitration Act § 23(a) (2000).
81 *See* First Options of Chicago, Inc. v. Kaplan, 514 U.S. 938, 115 S. Ct. 1920, 131 L. Ed. 2d 985 (1995).

82 *See, e.g.,* Dawahare v. Spencer, 210 F.3d 666, 669 (6th Cir. 2000) (moving party "must establish specific facts that indicate improper motives on the part of the arbitrator"); Scott v. Prudential Sec., Inc., 141 F.3d 1007, 1015 (11th Cir. 1998); Middlesex Mut. Ins. Co. v. Levine, 675 F.2d 1197, 1202 (11th Cir. 1982) (alleged impartiality must be "direct, definite and capable of demonstration rather than remote, uncertain and speculative").
83 *See, e.g.,* Willemijn Houdstermaatschappij, B.V. v. Standard Microsystems, Inc., 103 F.3d 9, 12 (2d Cir. 1997) ("[t]he showing required to avoid summary confirmation of an arbitration award is high"); Conoco, Inc. v. Oil, Chem. & Atomic Workers Int'l Union, 26 F. Supp. 2d 1310, 1316 (N.D. Okla. 1998).
84 *See* Willemijn Houdstermaatschappij, B.V. v. Standard Microsystems, Inc., 103 F.3d 9, 12 (2d Cir. 1997).
85 9 U.S.C. § 10(a)4); Unif. Arbitration Act § 12(a)(3) (1956); Unif. Arbitration Act § 23(a)(4) (2000).
86 *See* § 3.1, *supra*.
87 MBNA v. Boata, 2007 WL 2089678 (Conn. July 31, 2007).
88 *See, e.g.,* Garner v. MBNA Am. Bank., 2006 WL 2354939 (N.D. Tex. Aug. 14, 2006); MBNA Am. Bank v. Felton, 2004 WL 2898632 (Conn. Super. Ct. Nov. 8, 2004).

ing.[89] Courts find that objection before the arbitrator is sufficient and that it is not necessary for the consumer to bring a collateral court proceeding challenging the arbitrator's authority.[90]

Because arbitration is a matter of contract, and thus consent, there is no presumption that an arbitration agreement was formed, and no policy in favor of enforcing arbitration, until and unless a court finds that there is an agreement to arbitrate.[91] Therefore an award can be vacated as beyond the arbitrator's powers if the other party cannot produce evidence sufficient for the court to conclude that an arbitration agreement does indeed exist.[92] The same result should apply when the court finds the arbitration agreement unenforceable. Even if a court previously held that an agreement to arbitrate was enforceable, and that the consumer must submit to arbitration, this issue may be reviewable again via a motion to vacate the award.[93]

When certain claims are subject to arbitration, but not other claims, the arbitrator can only issue an award based on the claims within the arbitrator's authority.[94] Courts have also declined to enforce arbitration awards which involve parties who were outsiders to the underlying arbitration agreement or which grant relief that the arbitrator was not authorized to award.[95] Likewise, an arbitration award may be subject to *vacatur* for exceeding the arbitrator's power when the arbitrator was not selected in accordance with the parties' contractual provisions for designating an arbitrator.[96]

Parties sometimes argue that an arbitrator exceeded the scope of her authority if she failed to apply applicable law, or failed to apply it "correctly." However, courts have generally held that arbitrators do not exceed their powers by disregarding arguably applicable law.[97] This is the case even when the arbitration agreement states that the arbitrator must follow the law.[98]

A court may vacate an arbitration award when it was imperfectly executed so that a "mutual, final, and definite award upon the subject matter submitted was not made."[99] The Seventh Circuit has held that this provision comes into play when an award is incomplete or indefinite, but an alleged inconsistency in the arbitrator's resolution of the

---

89 *See* Unif. Arbitration Act § 12(a)(5) (1956); Unif. Arbitration Act § 23(a)(5) (2000); *see also* MBNA Am. Bank v. Barben, 111 P.3d 663 (Kan. Ct. App. 2005) (table) (text available at 2005 WL 1214244).

90 Holcim (Tex.) Ltd. P'ship v. Humbolt Wedag, Inc., 211 S.W.3d 796 (Tex. App. 2006).

91 *See* § 3.1, *supra*.

92 Unif. Arbitration Act § 12(a)(5) (1956); Unif. Arbitration Act § 23(a)(5) (2000); *see also* MBNA Am. Bank v. Credit, 132 P.3d 898 (Kan. 2006); *cf.* AT & T Technologies, Inc. v. Communications Workers of Am., 475 U.S. 643, 106 S. Ct. 1415, 89 L. Ed. 2d 648 (1986).

93 *See* Martinez v. Master Prot. Corp., 118 Cal. App. 4th 107 (2004).

94 Geneva Sec., Inc. v. Johnson, 138 F.3d 688, 692 (7th Cir. 1998) (vacating arbitrator's award when arbitrator considered multiple claims and decision did not distinguish between those that were eligible and ineligible for arbitration).

95 Spero Elec. Corp. v. Int'l Brotherhood of Elec. Workers Local Union No. 1377, 439 F.3d 324 (6th Cir. 2006) (vacating arbitrator's ruling on grounds that it did not draw its essence from collective bargaining agreement); 187 Concourse Assoc. v. Fishman, 399 F.3d 524 (2d Cir. 2005) (in labor case, arbitrator exceeded authority under collective bargaining agreement by ordering worker reinstated despite finding that employer "had no option but to terminate" worker); Pa. Power Co. v. Int'l Brotherhood of Elec. Workers Local Union No. 272, 276 F.3d 174, 179 (3d Cir. 2001) (in labor relations case, vacating award of retirement benefits to employees when arbitrator recognized that contractual precondition to award had not been established); Lindland v. U.S. Wrestling Ass'n, Inc., 227 F.3d 1000, 1003, 1004 (7th Cir. 2000) (vacating arbitration award that itself had vacated an earlier arbitrator's ruling when governing statute did not authorize arbitral *vacatur*); Agco v. Anglin, 216 F.3d 589, 594 (7th Cir. 2000) (vacating award on claims against third party to wholesale finance agreement because agreement's arbitration clause was limited in application to parties to that contract); Thomason v. Citigroup Global Markets Inc., 2006 WL 149046 (D. Utah Jan. 18, 2006) (vacating arbitration award that purported to bind previously dismissed party); O'Flaherty v. Belgum, 115 Cal. App. 4th 1044 (2004). *But cf. In re* Int'l Brotherhood of Elec. Workers Local 1593 & Dakota Gasification Co., 362 F. Supp. 2d 1135 (D.N.D. 2005) (arbitrator did not exceed scope of authority by ruling on an issue not presented to him when both parties mentioned the issue in their briefs); Sooper Credit Union v. Sholar Group Architects, Prof'l Corp., 113 P.3d 768 (Colo. 2005) (arbitrator did not exceed power authorized under state law when he clarified and corrected internally inconsistent award).

96 *See* Brook v. Peak Int'l Ltd., 169 F. Supp. 2d 641, 645 (W.D. Tex. 2001) ("arbitrators are without power to arbitrate a dispute when they are not chosen in accordance with the parties' arbitration agreement"), *rev'd*, 294 F.3d 668 (5th Cir. 2002) (party failed to object properly and waived right to do so); Martinez v. Master Prot. Corp., 118 Cal. App. 4th 107 (2004); *see also* Alan v. Super. Ct., 111 Cal. App. 4th 217 (2003).

97 *See, e.g.*, Three S Del., Inc. v. DataQuick Info. Sys., Inc., 2007 WL 2004454 (4th Cir. July 12, 2007); Wise v. Wachovia Sec., Inc., 450 F.3d 265, 269 (7th Cir. 2006) ("[I]n the typical arbitration, . . . the issue for the court is not whether the contract interpretation is incorrect or even wacky but whether the arbitrators had failed to interpret the contract at all."); Brentwood Med. Associates v. United Mine Workers, 396 F.3d 237 (3d Cir. 2005) (arbitrator did not exceed authority by basing award in part on non-existent language attributed to collective bargaining agreement, despite express provision in agreement prohibiting arbitrator from modifying terms, when conclusion was nonetheless supported by a rational interpretation of the agreement); Int'l Union of Operating Engineers Local 139 v. J.H. Findorff & Son, Inc., 393 F.3d 742 (7th Cir. 2004) (arbitrator did not exceed authority by disregarding plain language of agreement); Penn Va. Oil & Gas Corp. v. CNX Gas Co, L.L.C., 2007 WL 593578 (W.D. Va. Feb. 22, 2007); Long John Silver's Restaurants, Inc. v. Cole, 409 F. Supp. 2d 682 (D.S.C. 2006); Meyer v. McGee, 125 P.3d 1060 (Haw. 2006).

98 *See* Cable Connection, Inc. v. DIRECTV, Inc., 143 Cal. App. 4th 207 (2006); Marsch v. Williams, 23 Cal. App. 4th 238 (1994); Pac. Gas & Elec. Co. v. Super. Ct., 15 Cal. App. 4th 576 (1993).

99 9 U.S.C. § 10(a)(4).

issues presented is not grounds for *vacatur*.[100] The Seventh Circuit confirmed an award that it found to be "so incomprehensible that three years later the judges and the parties are still trying to figure it out," based on the conclusion that section 10's "requirements of finality and definiteness are ones more of form than of substance."[101]

11.4.3 Arbitrator's Evident Partiality or Corruption

11.4.3.1 General

Upon application of a party to the arbitration a court can vacate an arbitration decision when there was evident partiality or corruption in the arbitrators.[102] Parties attacking an arbitration award on the basis of arbitral bias "must establish specific facts that indicate improper motives on the part of the arbitrator" and that the "alleged impartiality [is] direct, definite, and capable of demonstration."[103] The party should demonstrate the extent and character of the arbitrator's personal interest, the directness of the relationship, the connection of that relationship to the arbitrator, and the proximity in time between the relationship and the arbitration proceeding.[104]

The Supreme Court holds that "any tribunal permitted by law to try cases and controversies not only must be unbiased but also must avoid even the appearance of bias."[105] In *Commonwealth Coatings*, the Court vacated an award on the basis of arbitral bias when the arbitrator had previously worked as a consultant for one of the parties, but had failed to disclose this relationship to the opposing party.[106] Although the majority in *Commonwealth Coatings* did not require arbitrators to satisfy the federal judiciary's standards for neutrality, the Court did require arbitrators to disclose substantial business relationships with the parties before them.[107]

The Second, Fifth, and Sixth Circuits have all recently addressed the question of what constitutes "evident partiality." The Second Circuit held that, when an arbitrator knows of a potential conflict, a failure to either investigate or disclose an intention not to investigate is indicative of evident partiality.[108] Subjective good faith is not the test. Once the arbitrator was aware that a nontrivial conflict of interest might exist, there is a duty to investigate or disclose. Other circuit courts also require the arbitrator to disclose potential conflicts.[109]

The Fifth Circuit recently interpreted *Commonwealth Coatings* as indicating that an award may not be vacated because of a trivial or insubstantial prior relationship between the arbitrator and the parties to a proceeding, finding the relationship in the case before it to be too slender to demonstrate bias.[110] Other circuit courts also have been unreceptive to bias challenges based solely on the financial interests of an individual arbitrator outside the particular case being decided.[111] In addition, the Seventh Circuit has found that an arbitrator's felony conviction while the arbitration proceedings are pending does not establish evident

---

100 *See* IDS Life Ins. Co. v. Royal Alliance Associates, Inc., 266 F.3d 645, 651 (7th Cir. 2001) (Posner, J.).

101 *Id.* at 648, 650; *cf.* Hart Surgical, Inc. v. Ultracision, Inc., 244 F.3d 231, 235 (1st Cir. 2001) (without discussing *vacatur* grounds, holding that parties can obtain judicial review of arbitrator's liability determination before arbitrator decides damages by structuring agreement to provide for bifurcated arbitration proceedings).

102 9 U.S.C. § 10(a)(2); Unif. Arbitration Act § 12(a)(2) (1956); Unif. Arbitration Act § 23(a)(2) (2000).

103 Three S Del., Inc. v. DataQuick Info. Sys., Inc., 2007 WL 2004454 (4th Cir. July 12, 2007); Dawahare v. Spencer, 210 F.3d 666, 669 (6th Cir. 2000) (rejecting bias challenge based on discrepancy between relief sought and that awarded to prevailing party); Nationwide Mut. Ins. Co. v. Home Ins. Co., 278 F.3d 621, 626 (6th Cir. 2002); Harter v. Iowa Grain Co., 220 F.3d 544, 553 (7th Cir. 2000); Scott v. Prudential Sec., Inc., 141 F.3d 1007, 1015 (11th Cir. 1998); *see also* Thomason v. Citigroup Global Markets Inc., 2006 WL 149046 (D. Utah Jan. 18, 2006) (speculation that arbitrator was biased in favor of party because of party's potential influence over arbitrator's ability to receive future legal work insufficient to show evident partiality); RDC Golf of Fla. I, Inc. v. Aposoplicas, 925 So. 2d 1082 (Fla. Dist. Ct. App. 2006) (impression of partiality must be "reasonable" and based on credible evidence, rather than speculative).

104 Three S Del., Inc. v. DataQuick Info. Sys., Inc., 2007 WL 2004454 (4th Cir. July 12, 2007).

105 Commonwealth Coatings Corp. v. Cont'l Cas. Co., 393 U.S. 145, 150, 89 S. Ct. 337, 21 L. Ed. 2d 301 (1968).

106 393 U.S. at 147, 148; *see also* Univ. Commons-Urbana, Ltd. v. Universal Constructors Inc., 304 F.3d 1331 (11th Cir. 2002).

107 393 U.S. at 150, 152 (White, J., concurring).

108 Applied Indus. Materials Corp. v. Ovalar Makine Ticaret Ve Sanayi, A.S., 2007 WL 1964955 (2d Cir. July 9, 2007).

109 *See, e.g.*, Univ. Commons-Urbana, Ltd. v. Universal Constructors Inc., 304 F.3d 1331 (11th Cir. 2002) (arbitrator's failure to disclose fact that he had represented a co-defendant during the course of arbitration, and had met with the president of a corporation with an interest in the dispute during the course of arbitration, necessitated a remand to the district court for an evidentiary hearing to determine potential bias); Olson v. Merrill Lynch, Pierce, Fenner & Smith, Inc., 51 F.3d 157, 159 (8th Cir. 1995) (arbitrator's failure to disclose that he was vice president and chief financial officer of company that does substantial underwriting business for one of the parties creates impression of bias showing "evident impartiality"); Schmitz v. Zilvetti, 20 F.3d 1043, 1046, 1048 (9th Cir. 1994) (arbitrator's failure to disclose his law firm's extensive representation of the defendant's parent company creates reasonable impression of bias; arbitrator's professed lack of knowledge does not mitigate failure to disclose).

110 Positive Software Solutions, Inc. v. New Century Mortgage Corp., 476 F.3d 278 (5th Cir. 2006).

111 *See, e.g.*, Harter v. Iowa Grain Co., 220 F.3d 544, 555 (7th Cir. 2000) (fact that arbitrator has acted as grain buyer in other transactions does not establish bias against seller in arbitration case); Scott v. Prudential Sec., Inc., 141 F.3d 1007, 1015, 1016 (11th Cir. 1998) (rejecting bias challenge in collections case based on arbitrators' outside work in the collections business).

corruption or partiality and is not grounds for vacating the subsequent award.[112]

In the Sixth Circuit case, the parties had agreed to tripartite arbitration, in which each party selects one arbitrator (usually an industry expert) and those two arbitrators together appoint a third, neutral arbitrator.[113] The losing party sought to vacate the award on grounds that the arbitrator selected by the other party had ongoing contact with that party, including social contacts that were not disclosed. The Sixth Circuit, noting that only a plurality of Justices in *Commonwealth Coating* had endorsed the "appearance of bias" standard for *vacatur*, declined to apply that standard to an arbitration in which both parties, commercial entities, had agreed to submit their claims to "panel members who are involved in the business of insurance."[114]

Other circuit courts have similarly found that certain relationships are inevitable in arbitrations between two large commercial entities, in which parties purportedly seek the expertise of decision makers with extensive experience in the fields out of which their disputes arise.[115] One circuit court thus recently held that two large commercial entities are free to draft their arbitration agreements to provide for the selection of partisan arbitrators and that, in such cases, a party must demonstrate actual prejudice in order to obtain judicial *vacatur* based on arbitral bias.[116]

Several creditors have recently adopted the tactic of bringing arbitration actions against tens of thousands of consumers to collect on credit card debts. This practice raises issues of repeat player bias when the list of potential arbitrators is selected by the same arbitration service provider (in these cases the National Arbitration Forum (NAF)), and it is the creditor that selects the NAF for this lucrative arrangement. NAF thus has a financial incentive to please the creditor—or the creditor will select a different arbitration service provider for tens of thousands of cases. Therefore NAF has a financial incentive to select arbitrators who will rule for the creditor and to blackball those who rule for the consumer. In turn, arbitrators learn that their employment is dependent on their ruling for the creditor.

When two commercial entities are involved in an arbitration, and one of them has appeared more frequently before the arbitration service provider than the other, courts may be reluctant to find a repeat player bias.[117] But a very different situation is presented when one creditor has filed tens of thousands of arbitrations with a particular service provider and the consumer only one involving that service provider. This form of repeat player bias is examined in more detail elsewhere in this manual.[118]

11.4.3.2 California Statutes Requiring Disclosures by Arbitrators

California law requires arbitrators to make certain disclosures to the parties participating in the arbitration, including any relationships the arbitrator has with the parties or with the attorneys for the parties.[119] California law also specifies that the court "shall" vacate an award if the arbitrator fails to make a disclosure of a ground for disqualification of which the arbitrator was then aware.[120]

This provision is interpreted as requiring a court to vacate an award whenever an arbitrator fails to make the disclosures required by state law.[121] The party seeking to vacate the award need not prove that the undisclosed information would have led a reasonable person to question the arbitrator's impartiality.[122] Nor does that party have to show that

---

112 *See* United Transp. Union v. Gateway W. Ry. Co., 284 F.3d 710 (7th Cir. 2002) (Posner, J.) (finding in Railway Labor Act case that arbitrator's "criminal violation of federal tax law was unrelated to the grievances that he was asked to arbitrate, and there is no suggestion that his violation would have inclined him in favor of (or, for that matter, against) the union").

113 Nationwide Mut. Ins. Co. v. Home Ins. Co., 429 F.3d 640 (6th Cir. 2005).

114 *Id.* at 645–646.

115 Univ. Commons-Urbana, Ltd. v. Universal Constructors Inc., 304 F.3d 1331, 1340 (11th Cir. 2002) ("[F]amiliarity due to confluent areas of expertise does not indicate bias. Rather, so long as the previous interactions do not represent part of an ongoing business relationship, it may be an asset, since 'an arbitrator's experience in an industry, far from requiring a finding of partiality, is one of the factors that can make arbitration a superior means of resolving disputes.' " (citation omitted)); Nationwide Mut. Ins. Co. v. Home Ins. Co., 278 F.3d 621, 627 (6th Cir. 2002) ("[T]he arbitration agreement states that the panel members would be active members of the insurance industry. As a result, the parties should have expected that the business interests of the arbitrators might become entangled with those of the parties."); Harter v. Iowa Grain Co., 220 F.3d 544, 555 (7th Cir. 2000); The Andersons, Inc. v. Horton Farms, Inc., 166 F.3d 308, 329 (6th Cir. 1998); Scott v. Prudential Sec., Inc., 141 F.3d 1007, 1016 (11th Cir. 1998).

116 Delta Mine Holding Co. v. AFC Coal Properties, Inc., 280 F.3d 815, 821, 822 (8th Cir. 2001).

117 *See* LLT Int'l, Inc. v. MCI Telecommunications Corp., 18 F. Supp. 2d 349, 354 (S.D.N.Y. 1998) (rejecting bias challenge based on larger company's repeated appearance before American Arbitration Association arbitrators as source of ongoing business, finding "repeat player" allegation not to create even the appearance of bias, let alone actual bias); *see also* Hoffman v. Cargill, Inc., 236 F.3d 458, 463 (8th Cir. 2001) (reversing district court's *vacatur* based on "fundamental unfairness" of proceedings, while noting that record does not sustain allegation that National Grain & Feed Association systematically favors buyers over sellers in conducting arbitrations); *cf.* The Andersons, Inc. v. Horton Farms, Inc., 166 F.3d 308, 329 (6th Cir. 1998) (fact that arbitrator and one party to dispute are members of industry association does not establish bias against party in industry that is not a member of the association).

118 *See* § 6.5.7, *supra*.

119 *See* Cal. Civ. Proc. Code § 1281.9 (West).

120 Cal. Civ. Proc. Code § 1286.2(a)(6) (West).

121 Ovitz v. Schulman, 35 Cal. Rptr. 3d 117 (Ct. App. 2005); Int'l Alliance of Theatrical Stage Employees Local No. 16 v. Laughon, 118 Cal. App. 4th 1380 (2004).

122 Int'l Alliance of Theatrical Stage Employees Local No. 16 v. Laughon, 118 Cal. App. 4th 1380 (2004).

the arbitrator was in fact biased—only that the arbitrator was required to disclose information that the statute defines as possibly creating an impression of bias, and that information was not disclosed.[123]

The California Supreme Court recently held that, as applied to arbitration of investor disputes, California's ethics standards for neutral arbitrators are preempted by federal rules promulgated by the National Association of Securities Dealers (NASD) under the Securities Exchange Act.[124] However, a California appellate court has held that the provision of the California law requiring *vacatur* of any award issued by an arbitrator who violates the state's disclosure requirements for arbitrators is *not* preempted by the FAA.[125] The court held that the California law is not inconsistent with the purpose of the FAA because by its terms it "does not undermine the enforceability of arbitration agreements" and indeed "presupposes that the arbitration agreement has been enforced and the arbitration held."[126] The court further held that the California law helps further the FAA's purpose of encouraging arbitration by increasing public confidence in the process, and thus is not preempted.[127]

11.4.3.3 *Ex Parte* Communications

A common source of allegations of arbitral bias or misconduct is the arbitrator's involvement in undisclosed *ex parte* communications with a party. The party moving for *vacatur* must demonstrate prejudice that resulted from the arbitrator's *ex parte* conduct.[128] Disclosure of *ex parte* communications has been held to obviate prejudice that might otherwise have occurred.[129] On the other hand, a court may vacate an award when the arbitrator failed to disclose such communications with a party.[130]

11.4.4 Arbitrator's Refusal to Postpone the Hearing or to Hear Evidence or Other Misbehavior

Upon proper application, a court may vacate an arbitration decision when the arbitrator is guilty of misconduct in refusing to postpone the hearing upon sufficient cause shown, or when the arbitrator refuses to hear evidence pertinent and material to the controversy, or when the arbitrator otherwise engages in misbehavior by which the rights of any party are prejudiced.[131] Although arbitration proceedings generally are not governed by the federal or state rules of evidence, courts have vacated arbitration awards when arbitrators refused to consider relevant evidence.[132] Likewise, an arbitrator's failure to grant a continuance that was necessary for a party to present a defense has been deemed misconduct warranting judicial *vacatur*.[133]

11.4.5 Award Procured by Corruption, Fraud, or Undue Means

A court may vacate an award upon application of any party to the arbitration when the award was procured by corruption, fraud, or undue means.[134] Parties moving for *vacatur* on these grounds generally must establish by clear and convincing evidence that the requisite misconduct occurred, that the misconduct was not discoverable with due diligence before or during the arbitration, and that the misconduct was material to an issue in the arbitration.[135]

---

123 *Id. But cf.* Hayden v. Robertson Stephens, Inc., 150 Cal. App. 4th 360 (2007) (no requirement to disclose relationship with uninvolved affiliate of one of the parties).

124 Jevne v. Super. Ct. (JB Oxford Holdings, Inc.), 28 Cal. Rptr. 3d 685 (Cal. 2005).

125 Ovitz v. Schulman, 35 Cal. Rptr. 3d 117 (Ct. App. 2005).

126 *Id.* at 134.

127 *Id.*

128 Nationwide Mut. Ins. Co. v. Home Ins. Co., 278 F.3d 621, 627 (6th Cir. 2002) (meeting between arbitrator and party representative did not give rise to inference of partiality); Mut. Fire, Marine & Inland Ins. Co. v. Norad Reinsurance Co., 868 F.2d 52, 57 (3d Cir. 1989) (evidence of arbitrator's *ex parte* investigation of facts does not establish prejudice to moving party).

129 Polin v. Kellwood Co., 103 F. Supp. 2d 238, 263 (S.D.N.Y. 2000); Nationwide Mut. Ins. Co. v. The Home Ins. Co., 90 F. Supp. 2d 893, 902 (S.D. Ohio 2000).

130 *See* Valrose Maui, Inc. v. Maclyn Morris, Inc., 105 F. Supp. 2d 1118, 1123 (D. Haw. 2000); Flexsys Am., Ltd. P'ship v. United Steelworkers of Am. Local Union No. 12610, 88 F. Supp. 2d 600, 602 (S.D. W. Va. 2000).

131 9 U.S.C. § 10(a)(3); Unif. Arbitration Act § 12(a)(4) (1956); Unif. Arbitration Act § 23(a)(3) (2000).

132 Tempo Shain Corp. v. Bertek, Inc., 120 F.3d 16, 20 (2d Cir. 1997) (vacating award when arbitrator excluded evidence as cumulative which the court found to be probative); Gulf Coast Indus. Workers Union v. Exxon Co., U.S.A., 70 F.3d 847, 850 (5th Cir. 1995) (vacating award based on finding that arbitrator misled party into withholding evidence by stating that equivalent evidence was already in record and then issuing decision based on failure to present the withheld evidence). *But see* Prestige Ford v. Ford Dealer Computer Services, 324 F.3d 391 (5th Cir. 2003) (arbitrator considered request to admit evidence, but determined it would not be admitted); Nationwide Mut. Ins. Co. v. Home Ins. Co., 278 F.3d 621, 625 (6th Cir. 2002) (arbitrators did not engage in misconduct by denying discovery to party on issue of arbitration cost allocation when party had opportunity to review opposing party's submissions and submit objections); Meyer v. McGee, 125 P.3d 1060 (Haw. 2006) (arbitrator not guilty of misconduct for failure to consider evidence, when arbitrator had discretion to reopen hearing but was not required to do so).

133 Floyd Co. Bd. of Educ. v. EUA Cogenex Corp., 19 F. Supp. 2d 735, 736, 737 (E.D. Ky. 1998), *rev'd*, 198 F.3d 245 (6th Cir. 1999) (table) (text available at 1999 U.S. App. LEXIS 29692).

134 9 U.S.C. § 10(a)(1); Unif. Arbitration Act § 12(a)(1) (1956); Unif. Arbitration Act § 23(a)(1) (2000).

135 Bonar v. Dean Witter Reynolds, Inc., 835 F.2d 1378, 1383 (11th Cir. 1988); LaFarge Conseils et Etudes, S.A. v. Kaiser Cement,

Even when an award is attributable to fraud or misconduct, the award will be enforced if the party could have discovered it and brought it to the arbitrator's attention before the award was issued.[136]

Courts have emphasized the "award . . . procured by" language of the statute in holding that the existence of fraud or misconduct is not sufficient for *vacatur* unless there is a nexus with the arbitrator's award.[137] Thus a party's concealment of evidence is not grounds for *vacatur* when the concealment does not prevent the arbitrator from reaching the issue to which the evidence would have been material.[138] On the other hand, the Eleventh Circuit found the nexus or materiality requirement to be satisfied when it vacated an award in which the arbitrator's opinion reflected the influence of expert witness testimony that the arbitrator would not have heard had the witness not committed perjury in establishing his qualifications.[139]

The Idaho Supreme Court has also affirmed a lower court's decision vacating its earlier confirmation of an arbitration award when a non-party with standing to challenge the award presented evidence that the arbitration itself was a "sham" in which the parties had engaged solely to circumvent county requirements. The court held that the parties had committed a "fraud on the court" and that the lower court had properly set aside its order confirming the arbitration award.[140]

Challenges to arbitration awards based on "undue means" have been rare. Courts have held that the listing of undue means with fraud and misconduct imports a bad faith requirement which might exclude certain ordinary procedural errors as a basis for judicial *vacatur*.[141]

11.5 Vacating an Award Based on Its Merits

11.5.1 General

The Federal Arbitration Act (FAA), Uniform Arbitration Act (UAA), and revised UAA do not list any grounds to vacate an arbitration award based on its merits. Nevertheless, dicta in Supreme Court decisions recognizes the availability of some judicial review of the merits of arbitral awards[142] and, as described below, this has led the federal appeals courts to develop standards as to when an award can be vacated on the merits. These standards only provide very narrow opportunities to vacate an award on the merits,[143] and certain state courts do not even recognize any bases to vacate an award on the merits.[144]

11.5.2 Manifest Disregard of the Law

11.5.2.1 General

The Supreme Court in *First Options* states that a court can set aside an award only in very unusual circumstances, one of which being "manifest disregard of the law."[145] Never-

---

791 F.2d 1334, 1339 (9th Cir. 1986).

136 *See, e.g., LaFarge Conseils*, 791 F.2d at 1339 (upholding award when losing party failed to subpoena allegedly falsified documents during arbitration proceedings); *see also* Delta Mine Holding Co. v. AFC Coal Properties, Inc., 280 F.3d 815, 821 (8th Cir. 2001) (finding waiver of arbitral bias challenge based on failure to raise allegation before arbitration panel).

137 Forsythe Int'l, S.A. v. Gibbs Oil Co. of Tex., 915 F.2d 1017, 1022 (5th Cir. 1990) (holding fraud was immaterial because arbitrator had so declared); Conoco, Inc. v. Oil, Chem. & Atomic Workers Int'l Union, 26 F. Supp. 2d 1310, 1320 (N.D. Okla. 1998).

138 Forsythe Int'l, S.A. v. Gibbs Oil Co. of Tex., 915 F.2d 1017, 1022 (5th Cir. 1990) (holding fraud was immaterial because arbitrator had so declared); Conoco, Inc. v. Oil, Chem. & Atomic Workers Int'l Union, 26 F. Supp. 2d 1310, 1320 (N.D. Okla. 1998).

139 Bonar v. Dean Witter Reynolds, Inc., 835 F.2d 1378, 1383 (11th Cir. 1988).

140 Campbell v. Kildew, 115 P.3d 731 (Idaho 2005).

141 Am. Postal Workers Union v. United States Postal Serv., 52 F.3d 359, 362 (D.C. Cir. 1995) ("undue means" under the FAA is "limited to an action *by a party* that is equivalent in gravity to corruption or fraud, such as a physical threat to an arbitrator or other improper influence"); Shearson Hayden Stone, Inc. v. Liang, 493 F. Supp. 104, 108 (N.D. Ill. 1980) (finding context of section 10 to imply a bad faith requirement whereby the alleged insufficiency of evidence supporting an award does not constitute "undue means"), *aff'd*, 653 F.2d 310 (7th Cir. 1981); *see also* Nat'l Cas. Co. v. First State Ins. Group, 430 F.3d 492 (1st Cir. 2005) (refusal by one party to produce evidence does not invalidate award, when arbitrator offered that party a choice between producing the documents or having an inference drawn from a refusal to produce them).

142 *See, e.g.,* First Options of Chicago, Inc. v. Kaplan, 514 U.S. 938, 942, 115 S. Ct. 1920, 131 L. Ed. 2d 985 (1995) (recognizing "manifest disregard of the law" as basis for vacating arbitration award); Wilko v. Swan, 346 U.S. 427, 436, 74 S. Ct. 182, 98 L. Ed. 168 (1953) (failure of arbitrators to decide Securities Act claim in accordance with statute would be grounds for *vacatur* if failure were clear).

143 *See, e.g., First Options*, 514 U.S. at 942 ("the court will set aside [an arbitrator's] decision only in very unusual circumstances"); Baravati v. Josephthal, Lyon & Ross, 28 F.3d 704, 706 (7th Cir. 1994) ("[j]udicial review of arbitration awards is tightly limited"); Lattimer-Stevens Co. v. United Steelworkers of Am. Dist. 27, 913 F.2d 1166, 1169 (6th Cir. 1990) ("When courts are called on to review an arbitrator's decision, the review is very narrow; one of the narrowest standards of judicial review in all of American jurisprudence.").

144 *See, e.g.,* Siegel v. Prudential Ins. Co. of Am., 67 Cal. App. 4th 1270 (1998); Warbington Constr., Inc. v. Franklin Landmark, L.L.C., 66 S.W.3d 853 (Tenn. Ct. App. 2001) (declining to adopt manifest disregard of the law and public policy as bases for reviewing arbitration awards).

145 First Options of Chicago, Inc. v. Kaplan, 514 U.S. 938, 942, 115 S. Ct. 1920, 131 L. Ed. 2d 985 (1995) (citing Wilko v. Swan, 346 U.S. 427, 436, 74 S. Ct. 182, 98 L. Ed. 168 (1953)); *see also* Ga. Code Ann. § 9-9-13(b)(5) (explicitly listing manifest disregard of the law as grounds to vacate an award).

theless, the Supreme Court has not provided additional guidance as to the meaning of "manifest disregard." The federal circuit courts uniformly agree that manifest disregard of the law is a much stricter standard than mere misinterpretation of the law,[146] but there is not uniformity as to what the standard is.

The Seventh Circuit's manifest disregard standard is that an arbitration award cannot direct a party to violate the law or exceed their powers under the arbitration agreement.[147] Most other circuit courts find that there is manifest disregard if the arbitrators knew of a governing legal principle, yet refused to apply it or ignored it altogether, and the law ignored by the arbitrators was well-defined, explicit, and clearly applicable to the case.[148] Similarly, an arbitral award may be vacated for manifest disregard of the law when a party has actively encouraged the arbitrator to ignore applicable law.[149]

The burden is on the party seeking to vacate the award to show that the arbitrator was aware of the applicable legal standard.[150] Thus, the Second Circuit has enforced an arbitration award denying a prevailing ADEA claimant's attorney fees, which are mandatory under the Act, finding that the claimant's bare assertion that he was entitled to recover fees did not inform the arbitrators of the statute's requirement.[151]

In addition, an arbitrator's intentional disregard of applicable law may not be grounds for *vacatur* if the contract can be interpreted as showing the parties intended to opt out of applicable law.[152] Other courts have framed the inquiry in terms of a search for any basis in the record that could justify the arbitrator's award, and would only vacate arbitral awards that are wholly irrational.[153]

---

146 *See, e.g.*, P.R. Tel. Co. v. U.S. Phone Mfg. Corp., 427 F.3d 21, 32 (1st Cir. 2005) (rejecting manifest disregard argument as a "thinly veiled attempt to obtain appellate review of the arbitrator's factual and legal determinations regarding the contract dispute"); Biscanin v. Merrill Lynch & Co., 407 F.3d 905 (8th Cir. 2005) (size of arbitration award not sufficient proof that arbitrator manifestly disregarded the law); Brentwood Med. Associates v. United Mine Workers, 396 F.3d 237 (3d Cir. 2005) (arbitrator's reliance on language that was not in the agreement, while in error, did not constitute "manifest disregard of the agreement" sufficient to warrant *vacatur*); Montes v. Shearson Lehman Bros., Inc., 128 F.3d 1456, 1461 (11th Cir. 1997) ("An arbitration board that incorrectly interprets the law has not manifestly disregarded it."); Merrill Lynch, Pierce, Fenner & Smith, Inc. v. Jaros, 70 F.3d 418, 421 (6th Cir. 1995) ("[Manifest disregard is] a very narrow standard of review. A mere error in interpretation or application of the law is insufficient. Rather, the decision must fly in the face of clearly established legal precedent." (citations omitted)); PeopleSoft, Inc. v. Amherst, L.L.C., 369 F. Supp. 2d 1263 (D. Colo. 2005) (arbitrators' decision as to legal effect of interim settlements, even if wrong, did not indicate willful inattentiveness or manifest disregard of the law); Baize v. Eastridge Companies, 142 Cal. App. 4th 293, 47 Cal. Rptr. 3d 763 (2006) (contractual requirement that arbitrators apply California law did not support *vacatur* on grounds that arbitrator had failed to "correctly" apply California law); *cf.* Jones v. Humanscale Corp., 130 Cal. App. 4th 401, 29 Cal. Rptr. 3d 881 (2005) (trial court's finding that arbitrator exceeded authority by applying wrong law to enforceability question constituted improper examination of merits of arbitrator's decision).

147 George Watts & Son, Inc. v. Tiffany & Co., 248 F.3d 577 (7th Cir. 2001); *see also* Wise v. Wachovia Sec., L.L.C., 450 F.3d 265 (7th Cir. 2006); IDS Life Ins. Co. v. Royal Alliance Associates, Inc., 266 F.3d 645, 650 (7th Cir. 2001).

148 Porzig v. Dresdner, Kleinwort, Benson, N. Am. L.L.C., 2007 WL 2241592 (2d Cir. Aug. 7, 2007); Aldred v. Avis Rent-A-Car, 2007 WL 2110720 (11th Cir. July 24, 2007); Am. Laser Vision, Prof'l Ass'n v. The Laser Vision Inst., L.L.C., 487 F.3d 255 (5th Cir. 2007) (also requiring significant injustice to overturn an award); Lessin v. Merrill Lynch Pierce Fenner & Smith, Inc., 481 F.3d 813 (D.C. Cir. 2007); Three S Del., Inc. v. DataQuick Info. Sys., Inc., 2007 WL 2004454 (4th Cir. July 12, 2007); Elec. Data Sys. Corp. v. Donelson, 473 F.3d 684 (6th Cir. 2007); McCarthy v. Citigroup Global Markets, Inc., 463 F.3d 87 (1st Cir. 2006); B.L. Harbert Int'l, L.L.C., 441 F.3d 905 (11th Cir. 2006); St. John's Mercy Med. Ctr. v. Delfino, 414 F.3d 882 (8th Cir. 2005); Wallace v. Buttar, 378 F.3d 182, 195 (2d Cir. 2004);

Duferco Int'l Steel Trading v. T. Klaveness Shipping, 333 F.3d 383, 389 (2d Cir. 2003); Dawahare v. Spencer, 210 F.3d 666 (6th Cir. 2000); Halligan v. Piper Jaffray, Inc., 148 F.3d 197, 202 (2d Cir. 1998); Montes v. Shearson Lehman Bros., Inc., 128 F.3d 1456, 1461 (11th Cir. 1997); *see also* Dan J. Sheehan Co. v. McCrory Constr. Co., 643 S.E.2d 546 (Ga. Ct. App. 2007); RSG Caulking & Waterproofing, Inc. v. J.P. Morgan Chase & Co., 831 N.Y.S.2d 350 (Sup. Ct. 2006); Siemens Transp. P'ship P.R., S.E. v. Redondo Perini Joint Venture, 824 N.Y.S.2d 758 (Sup. Ct. 2006).

149 Montes v. Shearson Lehman Bros., Inc., 128 F.3d 1456, 1462 (11th Cir. 1997) ("[T]he arbitrators recognized that they were told to disregard the law . . . in a case where the evidence to support the award was marginal. Thus, there is nothing in the record to refute the suggestion that the law was disregarded.").

150 Wallace v. Buttar, 378 F.3d 182, 195 (2d Cir. 2004) (party that made no attempt to educate arbitrators about governing law cannot satisfy burden of showing manifest disregard of the law); Duferco Int'l Steel Trading v. T. Klaveness Shipping, 333 F.3d 383, 389 (2d Cir. 2003) ("A party seeking *vacatur* bears the burden of proving that the arbitrators were fully aware of the existence of a clearly defined governing legal principle, but refused to apply it, in effect, ignoring it."); Dawahare v. Spencer, 210 F.3d 666 (6th Cir. 2000); Halligan v. Piper Jaffray, Inc., 148 F.3d 197, 202 (2d Cir. 1998); Montes v. Shearson Lehman Bros., Inc., 128 F.3d 1456, 1460 (11th Cir. 1997);

151 DiRussa v. Dean Witter Reynolds, Inc., 121 F.3d 818, 822, 823 (2d Cir. 1997) (there is no persuasive evidence that the arbitrators knew of—and intentionally disregarded—the mandatory aspect of the ADEA's fee provision); *see also* Bear Stearns & Co. v. 1109580 Ontario, 409 F.3d 87 (2d Cir. 2005) (in securities arbitration, arbitrators did not manifestly disregard the law by refusing to give collateral estoppel effect to findings of previous arbitral panel).

152 *See, e.g.*, Long John Silver's Restaurants, Inc., 409 F. Supp. 2d 682 (D.S.C. 2006).

153 *See, e.g.*, Wise v. Wachovia Sec., Inc., 450 F.3d 265, 270 (7th Cir. 2006) (refusing to vacate award for manifest disregard when the court was unable to speculate as to how the award might have been reached under a theory "without [the arbitrators] taking leave of their senses"); Kurke v. Oscar Gruss & Son, Inc., 454 F.3d 350, 357–358 (D.C. Cir. 2006) ("In reviewing the decision of an arbitration panel, we do not decide

11.5.2.2 When Arbitrator Does Not Explain the Decision

It is even more difficult to prove manifest disregard of the law when arbitrators fail to provide an explanation for their awards. Courts have responded to this problem in a variety of ways. The California Supreme Court, recognizing the need for meaningful judicial review to provide effective enforcement of statutory rights, has construed the California Arbitration Act to require arbitrators hearing discrimination claims brought under state law to issue "a written... decision that will reveal, however briefly, the essential findings and conclusions on which the award is based."[154] The Sixth Circuit, however, has taken precisely the opposite approach under the FAA and held that review of the arbitration record is extremely deferential when there is no written explanation of the award for the court to examine.[155]

The Second Circuit has taken something of a middle ground on this issue by taking into account the arbitrator's failure to provide a written opinion when determining whether or not an award was issued in manifest disregard of the law.[156] Michigan courts make fine distinctions between cases in which employees waive the right to a trial as a condition of employment (and a written decision is required)[157] from cases in which parties agree to arbitrate after a dispute has arisen (and a written decision is not required).[158]

While a reviewing court can order that the arbitrator be deposed if there is clear evidence of bias or prejudice, the same is not the case when manifest disregard of the law is alleged.[159] The arbitrator's thought processes in reaching the award cannot be investigated.

11.5.2.3 A Different Standard for Statutory Claims?

While review for manifest disregard of the law is quite limited, a number of courts are willing to look more closely at an award responding to a party's statutory claim. This willingness is based on Supreme Court rulings that there is a fundamental requirement that arbitration allow parties to effectively vindicate their statutory rights.[160]

Furthermore, the Court has proclaimed repeatedly that judicial review is a guarantor of effective statutory enforcement when such claims are submitted to arbitration. In *Mitsubishi Motors Corp. v. Soler Chrysler-Plymouth, Inc.*,[161] for example, the Court held that a party's antitrust claim could be submitted to arbitration because "the national courts of the United States will have the opportunity at the award-enforcement stage to ensure that the legitimate

---

whether we would have assessed either the facts or the law in the same manner as the panel."); McGrann v. First Albany Corp., 424 F.3d 743 (8th Cir. 2005); Stark v. Sandberg, Phoenix & von Gontard, Prof'l Corp., 381 F.3d 793 (8th Cir. 2004), *cert. denied*, 125 S. Ct. 1973 (2005) (arbitrator's interpretation of clause as ambiguous not irrational when clause indicated claims were to be resolved in accordance with the FAA, which permits waiver of punitive damages, but choice-of-law provision stated claims would be resolved under Missouri law, which does not permit such waiver); Duferco Int'l Steel Trading v. T. Klaveness Shipping, 333 F.3d 383, 392 (2d Cir. 2003) (upholding award because it "was not irrational or inexplicable" even though it "only arguably conforms to legal standards"); Boise Cascade Corp. v. Paper Allied-Indus., Chem. & Energy Workers, 309 F.3d 1075, 1080 (8th Cir. 2002) (award is irrational when it "fails to draw its essence from the agreement"; the court found this to be true in a case in which the language of the contract was unambiguous and was not susceptible to the arbitrator's interpretation); Barnes v. Logan, 122 F.3d 820, 825 (9th Cir. 1997) ("An arbitrator's decision must be upheld unless it is 'completely irrational' or it constitutes a 'manifest disregard of law.'"); Willemijn Houdstermaatschappij, B.V. v. Standard Microsystems Corp., 103 F.3d 9, 14 (2d Cir. 1997) ("We need only decide whether there was any colorable justification for their decision."); Wein & Malkin L.L.P. v. Helmsley-Spear, Inc., 846 N.E.2d 1201 (N.Y. 2006).

154 Armendariz v. Found. Health Psychcare Services, Inc., 24 Cal. 4th 83, 99 Cal. Rptr. 2d 745, 6 P.3d 669, 685 (2000).

155 Merrill Lynch, Pierce, Fenner & Smith, Inc. v. Jaros, 70 F.3d 418, 421 (6th Cir. 1995) (when there is no explanatory opinion, "[i]f a court can find any line of argument that is legally plausible and supports the award then it must be confirmed. Only where no judge or group of judges could conceivably come to the same determination as the arbitrators must the award be set aside."); *see also* Univ. Commons-Urbana, Ltd. v. Universal Constructors Inc., 304 F.3d 1331 (11th Cir. 2002); H & S Homes v. McDonald, 910 So. 2d 79 (Ala. 2004) (in the absence of an explanation of damages awarded by arbitrator, court had no basis to determine whether arbitrator manifestly disregarded the law; arbitrator's failure to give reasons for the award did not itself constitute manifest disregard of the law; Fellus v. A.B. Whatley, Inc., 801 N.Y.S.2d 233 (Sup. Ct. 2005) (table) (text available at 2005 WL 975690) (in the absence of a reasoned decision supporting an arbitration award, there was no basis for court to decide whether arbitrator manifestly regarded the law); Stehli v. Action Custom Homes, Inc., 761 N.E.2d 129, 133 (Ohio Ct. App. 2001) (no requirement of written findings of fact and conclusions of law under Ohio arbitration statute absent contrary agreement by parties).

156 Halligan v. Piper Jaffray, Inc., 148 F.3d 197, 204 (2d Cir. 1998). *But see* Bear Stearns & Co. v. 1109580 Ontario, 409 F.3d 87, 91 (2d Cir. 2005) (giving arbitrator's failure to explain decision no weight and holding that the award "must be confirmed if there is any basis for upholding the decision and if there is even a barely colorable justification for the outcome reached" (internal quotations and citations omitted)).

157 Rembert v. Ryan's Family Steak Houses, Inc., 596 N.W.2d 208 (Mich. Ct. App. 1999).

158 Elec. Data Sys. Corp. v. Donelson, 473 F.3d 684 (6th Cir. 2007).

159 Hoeft v. MVL Group, Inc., 343 F.3d 57 (2d Cir. 2003); *In re* Nat'l Risk Underwriters, Inc., 884 F.2d 1389 (4th Cir. 1989).

160 Gilmer v. Interstate/Johnson Lane Corp., 500 U.S. 20, 26, 111 S. Ct. 1647, 114 L. Ed. 2d 26 (1991) ("by agreeing to arbitrate a statutory claim, a party does not forgo the substantive rights afforded by the statute"); *id.*, 500 U.S. at 28 ("[S]o long as the prospective litigant effectively may vindicate [his or her] statutory cause of action in the arbitral forum, the statute will continue to serve both its remedial and deterrent function.").

161 473 U.S. 614, 105 S. Ct. 3346, 87 L. Ed. 2d 444 (1985).

interest of the antitrust laws has been addressed."[162] Similarly, in *Shearson/American Express, Inc. v. McMahon*,[163] the Court permitted arbitration of Securities Act and Racketeer Influenced and Corrupt Organization Act claims because "there is no reason to assume at the outset that arbitrators will not follow the law; although judicial scrutiny of arbitration awards is necessarily limited, such review is sufficient to ensure that arbitrators comply with the requirements of the statute."[164]

The Court reiterated this sentiment in *Gilmer v. Interstate/Johnson Lane Corp.*, in which it held that an employee's claims under the Age Discrimination in Employment Act could be forced into arbitration,[165] and found that the function of judicial review in cases involving mandatory arbitration of statutory claims is to ensure that the parties' rights and the imperatives of public law are effectively vindicated. Arbitration does not require parties to forgo their statutory rights and judicial review must be sufficient to ensure statutory compliance: "[t]hese twin assumptions regarding the arbitration of statutory claims are valid only if judicial review under the 'manifest disregard of the law' standard is sufficiently rigorous to ensure that arbitrators have properly interpreted and applied statutory law" and that "[t]he value and finality of an employer's arbitration system will not be undermined by focused review of arbitral legal determinations."[166]

Thus a number of lower courts apply more searching review in cases involving statutory claims. In *Cole v. Burns International Security Services*, involving arbitration of employment discrimination claims under Title VII, the D.C. Circuit holds that review for manifest disregard of the law entails close judicial scrutiny of an arbitrator's statutory interpretations:

> [W]e believe that this type of review must be defined by reference to the assumptions underlying the [Supreme] Court's endorsement of arbitration. As discussed above, the strict deference accorded to arbitration decisions in the collective bargaining arena may not be appropriate in statutory cases in which an employee has been forced to resort to arbitration as a condition of employment. Rather, in this statutory context, the "manifest disregard of the law" standard must be defined in light of the bases underlying the Court's decisions in *Gilmer*-type cases.[167]

The Fifth and Seventh Circuits similarly have held that judicial review must be sufficiently exacting to ensure that arbitrators are complying with statutory directives.[168] These courts have recognized that searching review of an arbitrator's statutory interpretation is necessary to ensure that arbitration does not entail a sacrifice of the private rights and public values that are embodied in the public laws. Of course there must be a clear disregard of a statutory standard, and adopting one interpretation of a flexible standard may not be enough to show such a disregard.[169]

A federal court in *DeGaetano v. Smith Barney, Inc.*[170] vacated an arbitration award denying attorney fees to a successful Title VII claimant because the plaintiff had presented the arbitrators with the relevant statutory provision and case law making such an award mandatory and thereby rendered "nonsensical" the arbitration panel's finding that the defendant's discriminatory conduct did not rise to the level contemplated by Title VII for fee awards.[171] In the same vein, a state court has looked at a contract which required that the prevailing party be awarded costs and attorney fees, and then overturned an award that gave the party who appeared to prevail costs, but not attorney fees.[172]

11.5.3 Must Courts Insure Arbitration Decision Is Consistent with Public Policy?

In the context of collective bargaining agreement disputes, the Supreme Court has stated that a court's role in reviewing the merits of an arbitral award is to make sure that the arbitrator's interpretation of the private contract does not conflict with public policy.[173] This public policy review of

---

162 *Id.*, 473 U.S. at 638.
163 482 U.S. 220, 107 S. Ct. 2332, 96 L. Ed. 2d 185 (1987).
164 *Id.*, 482 U.S. at 232.
165 Gilmer v. Interstate/Johnson Lane Corp., 500 U.S. 20, 26, 111 S. Ct. 1647, 114 L. Ed. 2d 26 (1991).
166 *Id.*, 500 U.S. at 28.
167 Cole v. Burns Int'l Sec. Services, 105 F.3d 1465, 1487 (D.C. Cir. 1997).
168 Williams v. Cigna Fin. Advisors, Inc., 197 F.3d 752, 761 (5th Cir. 1999) ("The federal district courts and courts of appeals are charged with the obligation to exercise sufficient judicial scrutiny to ensure that arbitrators comply with their duties and the requirements of the statutes."; "the differences between collective bargaining contract arbitration under the LMRA [Labor Management Relations Act] and commercial arbitration under the FAA are too great for us to easily infer that the deferential standard once used with regard to the former is suitable as a judicial review standard with respect to the latter"); *see also* Koveleskie v. SBC Capital Markets, Inc., 167 F.3d 361, 366 (7th Cir. 1999), ("[W]e are convinced that judicial review of arbitration awards is sufficient to protect statutory rights.").
169 Braham v. A.G. Edwards & Sons, Inc., 376 F.3d 377 (5th Cir. 2004).
170 983 F. Supp. 459 (S.D.N.Y. 1997).
171 *Id.* at 461, 463.
172 Spencer v. The Ryland Group, Inc., 865 N.E.2d 301 (Ill. App. Ct. 2007).
173 E. Associated Coal Corp. v. United Mine Workers of Am. Dist. 17, 531 U.S. 57 (2000); United Paperworkers Int'l Union v. Misco, Inc., 484 U.S. 29 (1987) ("the public's interest in confining the scope of private agreements to which it is not a party will go unrepresented unless the judiciary takes account of those interests when it considers whether to enforce such agreements"); W.R. Grace & Co. v. Int'l Union of the United Rubber, Cork, Linoleum & Plastic Workers of Am. Local No. 759, 461

arbitral decisions is derived from the common law doctrine that a court may not enforce a contract that itself violates law or public policy.[174]

Still, the public policy consideration that would preclude judicial enforcement must be "well defined and dominant, and is to be ascertained by reference to the laws and legal precedents and not from general considerations of supposed public interests."[175] In *Eastern Associated Coal Corp.*, for example, the Supreme Court enforced an arbitrator's award interpreting a collective bargaining agreement's just cause provision to require reinstatement of a commercial vehicle driver who had twice tested positive for marijuana. The Court found the existence of a federal statute and a detailed regulatory scheme concerning drug use by safety sensitive employees to weigh *in favor of* enforcement, because neither explicit statement of federal policy on the general subject prohibited the specific relief that the arbitrator had awarded.[176]

Some cases involve challenges to arbitration awards for violation of public policy outside the context of collective bargaining agreements, in particular in the context of large damages awards. In general, these challenges have been squarely rejected.[177]

11.5.4 Arbitrary and Capricious Awards

There is uncertainty whether a court can also vacate an arbitration award for being arbitrary and capricious. The Fifth Circuit rejects such a ground,[178] while the Eleventh Circuit has recognized this as a ground to vacate an award.[179] The law is confused in other circuits.[180] A number of circuits have also stated that an award may be vacated as irrational, but it is not clear whether that is the same as arbitrary and capricious, or the same as made in manifest disregard of the law.[181]

11.5.5 Can the Court Re-Examine Evidence?

Although the presumption is that a reviewing court will not second guess an arbitrator's determination of the facts, there may be some room for the courts to re-examine the evidence that was presented to the arbitrator.[182] Whereas federal courts reviewing jury verdicts are restrained by the Seventh Amendment from engaging in independent fact finding,[183] there is no such explicit prohibition on judicial review of arbitral fact finding. Nonetheless, the Supreme Court's most recent discussion of judicial review of arbitral fact finding (in a labor relations case not involving the FAA) provides a reminder that such review is likely to be extremely narrow.[184]

U.S. 757 (1983) ("a court may not enforce any collective bargaining agreement that is contrary to public policy").

174 *Misco*, 484 U.S. at 42.
175 *Misco*, 484 U.S. at 43.
176 *E. Associated Coal Corp.*, 531 U.S. at 67 ("Neither Congress nor the Secretary has seen fit to mandate the discharge of a worker who twice tests positive for drugs. We hesitate to infer a public policy in this area that goes beyond the careful and detailed scheme Congress and the Secretary have created.").
177 *See, e.g.,* Sarofim v. Trust Co. of the W., 440 F.3d 213 (5th Cir. 2006); PeopleSoft, Inc. v. Amherst, L.L.C., 369 F. Supp. 2d 1263, 1270 (D. Colo. 2005) (in dispute between seller and purchaser of computer products, possible errors by arbitrators in applying law "did not rise to a public policy violation"); Praml v. Linsco/Private Ledger Corp., 2005 WL 2290943 (D. Minn. Sept. 20, 2005); Snyder v. Ben, 2005 WL 958413 (Cal. Ct. App. Apr. 27, 2005); Hadelman v. Deluca, 274 Conn. 442, 876 A.2d 1136 (2005); Medvalusa Health Programs, Inc. v. Memberworks, Inc., 273 Conn. 634 (2005).
178 Brabham v. A.G. Edwards & Sons Inc., 376 F.3d 377 (5th Cir. 2004); *see also* Birmingham News Co. v. Horn, 901 So. 2d 27 (Ala. 2004); Stephen L. Hayford, *A New Paradigm for Commercial Arbitration: Rethinking the Relationship Between Reasoned Awards and the Judicial Standards for Vacatur*, 66 Geo. Wash. L. Rev. 443 (1998).
179 Lifecare Int'l, Inc. v. CD Med., Inc., 68 F.3d 429 (11th Cir. 1995).
180 *See* George Watts & Son v. Tiffany Co., 248 F.3d 577 (7th Cir. 2001) (commenting that the law is confused).
181 *See* Schoch v. InfoUSA, Inc., 341 F.3d 785 (8th Cir. 2003); G.C. & K.B. Investments, Inc. v. Wilson, 326 F.3d 1096 (9th Cir. 2003); Roadway Package Sys., Inc. v. Kayser, 257 F.3d 287 (3d Cir. 2001).
182 *See, e.g.,* Halligan v. Piper Jaffray, Inc., 148 F.3d 197, 204 (2d Cir. 1998) (vacating arbitrator's ruling for employer on former employee's ADEA claim because "[i]n view of the strong evidence that Halligan was fired because of his age and the agreement of the parties that the arbitrators were correctly advised of the applicable legal principles, we are inclined to hold that they ignored the law or the evidence or both"); Mollison-Turner v. Lynch, 2002 WL 1046704, at *3 (N.D. Ill. May 23, 2002) (vacating award based on arbitrator's "significant mistaken assumption not about the facts of the case, but about the evidence [plaintiff] offered"). *But see* Wallace v. Buttar, 378 F.3d 182, 193 (2d Cir. 2004) ("[T]he Second Circuit does not recognize manifest disregard of the evidence as proper ground for vacating an arbitrator's award.... To the extent that a federal court may look upon the evidentiary record of an arbitration proceeding at all, it may do so only for the purpose of discerning whether a colorable basis exists for the panel's award so as to assure that the award can not be said to be the result of the panel's manifest disregard of the law.").
183 Gasperini v. Ctr. for Humanities, Inc., 518 U.S. 415, 432, 116 S. Ct. 2211, 135 L. Ed. 2d 659 (1996).
184 *See* Major League Baseball Players Ass'n v. Garvey, 532 U.S. 504, 509, 121 S. Ct. 1724, 149 L. Ed. 2d 740 (2001) (per curiam) ("When an arbitrator resolves disputes regarding the application of a contract, and no dishonesty is alleged, the arbitrator's 'improvident, even silly, factfinding' does not provide a basis for a reviewing court to refuse to enforce the award.") (quoting United Paperworkers Int'l Union v. Misco, Inc., 484 U.S. 29, 39, 108 S. Ct. 364, 98 L. Ed. 2d 286 (1987)); *see also* Coutee v. Barington Capital Group, Ltd. P'ship, 336 F.3d 1128 (9th Cir. 2003).

11.6 Arbitral Immunity

A party dissatisfied with the outcome of an arbitration proceeding may be tempted to sue the arbitrator or arbitration service provider. Arbitrators are shielded from civil liability for conduct in their quasi-judicial capacity by the doctrine of arbitral immunity, as long as they act within the scope of their jurisdiction.[185] The doctrine applies not only to arbitrators, but also to arbitration providers.[186]

The Tenth Circuit has recently stated that the doctrine of arbitral immunity does not protect arbitrators or their employing organizations from all claims asserted against them, but only those that arise out of a decisional act.[187] Other courts extend their immunity to the conduct of the proceedings and administrative tasks related to the proceedings.[188]

Although arbitral immunity should not apply to conduct by arbitrators acting outside the scope of their jurisdiction, the Seventh Circuit dismissed a claim that the American Arbitration Association (AAA) had violated state law by conducting an arbitration in the absence of a valid agreement to arbitrate.[189] The court reasoned that, although a court had later determined that the AAA lacked jurisdiction, "[j]udicial immunity applies ... unless there is a 'clear absence' of jurisdiction. We see no reason not to adopt the same parameter for arbitral immunity."[190]

Arbitrators are immune from claims alleging bias in the issuing of an arbitration award.[191] However, some courts have held that arbitral immunity does *not* bar breach-of-contract claims against an arbitrator and arbitration provider for failing to issue an award.[192] It would make sense that an arbitration service provider could be held liable, under a state deceptive practices statute, for deceptive advertising or related marketing practices.[193]

11.7 Protecting the Arbitrator's Punitive Damages Award

11.7.1 Introduction

Consumers can recover punitive damages in an arbitration proceeding unless the arbitration agreement or the arbitration service provider's rules explicitly restrict such recovery. Such restrictions are not common, and would serve as a basis to challenge the enforceability of the arbitration agreement.[194]

While consumer litigants are better off seeking such damages in front of a jury, the consumer may have no choice

---

185 *See, e.g.*, Hutchins v. Am. Arbitration Ass'n, 108 Fed. Appx. 647, 648 (1st Cir. 2004) ("The appellant fails to show that the negligence claim was not properly dismissed on the ground of arbitral immunity."); Caudle v. Am. Arbitration Ass'n, 230 F.3d 920, 922 (7th Cir. 2000) ("Like judges, arbitrators have no interest in the outcome of the dispute between the parties to the contract, and they should not be compelled to become parties to that dispute." (internal quotations and citations omitted)); Wasyl Inc. v. First Boston Corp., 813 F.2d 1579, 1582 (9th Cir.1987) ("arbitrators are immune from civil liability for acts within their jurisdiction arising out of their arbitral functions in contractually agreed upon arbitration hearings"); Corey v. N.Y. Stock Exch., 691 F.2d 1205, 1211 (6th Cir. 1982) ("The functional comparability of the arbitrators' decision-making process and judgments to those of judges and agency hearing examiners generates the same need for independent judgment, free from the threat of lawsuits. Immunity furthers this need. As with judicial and quasi-judicial immunity, arbitral immunity is essential to protect the decision-maker from undue influence and protect the decision-making process from reprisals by dissatisfied litigants."); Park v. Columbia Credit Services, Inc., 2007 WL 1847142 (W.D. Mo. June 25, 2007); Smith v. Shell Chem. Co., 333 F. Supp. 2d 579, 587 (M.D. La. 2004) ("[N]o cause of action can be asserted against an arbitrator based on the issuance of an unfavorable decision.");

186 Alexander v. Am. Arbitration Ass'n, 2001 WL 868823, at *2 (N.D. Cal. July 27, 2001) ("The doctrine of judicial immunity is applicable to the arbitration process and extends to arbitration associations such as the AAA."); Stasz v. Schwab, 121 Cal. App. 4th 420, 430 (2004) ("[T]he AAA enjoys common law immunity because, just as an arbitrator is immune from liability for bias or the failure to stay arbitration proceedings, so is the organization that sponsors the arbitration.").

187 Pfannenstiel v. Merrill Lynch Pierce Fenner & Smith, 477 F.3d 1155 (10th Cir. 2007).

188 New Eng. Cleaning Services, Inc. v. Am. Arbitration Ass'n, 199 F.3d 542, 545–546 (1st Cir. 1999) ("A sponsoring organization's immunity extends to the administrative tasks it performs, insofar as these are integrally related to the arbitration."); Olson v. Nat'l Ass'n of Sec. Dealers, 85 F.3d 381, 383 (8th Cir. 1996) (immunity protects "all acts within the scope of the arbitral process"); Austern v. Chicago Bd. Options Exch., Inc., 898 F.2d 882, 886 (2d Cir. 1990) (arbitral immunity barred claims arising from allegedly defective notice and improper selection of arbitration panel); Precision Mech., Inc. v. Karr, 2005 WL 3277966, at *8 (M.D. Fla. Dec. 2, 2005) (arbitral immunity bars claims that arbitration provider violated its own rules); Cort v. Am. Arbitration Ass'n, 795 F. Supp. 970, 972–973 (N.D. Cal. 1992) (arbitral immunity applies to selection of arbitrators).

189 New Eng. Cleaning Services, Inc. v. Am. Arbitration Ass'n, 199 F.3d 542 (1st Cir. 1999).

190 *Id.* at 545; *see also* Park v. Columbia Credit Services, Inc., 2007 WL 1847142 (W.D. Mo. June 25, 2007) (arbitrator has immunity even when consumer challenges authority of arbitrator to hear the proceeding).

191 *See, e.g.*, Pullara v. Am. Arbitration Ass'n, Inc., 191 S.W.3d 903, 907 (Tex. App. 2006) ("arbitrators and their sponsoring organizations are immune from civil liability for bias or the failure to disclose a possible source of bias"); Stasz v. Schwab, 121 Cal. App. 4th 420 (2004); Chia v. Narayan, 2003 WL 21007189 (Cal. Ct. App. May 6, 2003).

192 *See, e.g.*, Morgan Phillips, Inc. v. JAMS/Endispute, 140 Cal. App. 4th 795 (2006) (reasoning that "failure to render an arbitration award is not integral to the arbitration process; it is, rather, a breakdown of that process").

193 *Cf.* Garcia v. Wayne Homes, L.L.C., 2002 WL 628619, at *17 (Ohio Ct. App. Apr. 19, 2002) (dismissing as immature claims against AAA for failing to provide arbitration services as advertised).

194 *See* § 6.5.4.1, *supra*.

if the consumer's action is forced into arbitration. In that case the consumer should not give up on the possibility of punitive damages—a number of arbitrations in the securities context have resulted in sizeable punitive damages awards, and these awards and the size of the awards are almost always upheld during judicial review.[195]

Corporations hit with punitive damages awards in arbitration may seek every possible avenue to avoid paying, in part because of the amount of money at stake and in part because they assumed that the mandatory arbitration requirement would avoid this very result. Having chosen the procedure to resolve a dispute, they immediately will attack that procedure as flawed.

This section examines how to protect an arbitrator's punitive damages award from various attacks by the opposing corporation. In general, corporations will be surprised to discover that their ability to overturn an arbitrator's punitive damages award is quite limited.

11.7.2 Is a Challenge to a Punitive Damage Award Timely and Brought in the Correct Court?

Under the Federal Arbitration Act (FAA) and most state laws, a party must seek to vacate or modify an award within ninety days after receiving notice of the award.[196] On the other hand, the consumer typically has at least a year to confirm the award.[197] Consequently there are advantages to waiting ninety days to confirm the award to see if the opposing party forgoes its right to vacate or modify the award.[198]

If the merchant brings a timely action to vacate or modify the award, the first question is whether the action is brought in the proper court. The FAA does not provide an independent basis for federal jurisdiction.[199] If there is no diversity of citizenship between the parties, then there is no jurisdiction to bring an action to vacate the award in federal court.

11.7.3 Does the Award Exceed the Arbitrator's Powers?

11.7.3.1 Introduction

An award can be vacated if the arbitrator, in providing for punitive damages, exceeded the arbitrator's powers.[200] Thus a corporation may seek a court order vacating an award by arguing that the arbitrator exceeded his or her powers because the arbitration agreement, the rules of the arbitration service provider, or state law limits an arbitrator's power to award punitive damages.

11.7.3.2 Does the Arbitration Agreement Limit the Arbitrator's Authority to Award Punitive Damages?

The United States Supreme Court holds that punitive damages are available in an arbitration proceeding unless the arbitration agreement unambiguously limits them.[201] The Court finds a dual policy in allowing punitive damages whenever the language is unclear: ambiguities in the scope of an arbitration clause are to be resolved in favor of arbitration, and ambiguities in a contract are to be resolved against the party drafting the agreement.[202]

Thus courts find that punitive damages are available in arbitration unless the agreement unequivocally excludes them.[203] For example, if a clause states that punitive damages are waived to the fullest extent permitted by law, and state law does not clearly permit such a waiver, then the clause is not effective to waive that right.[204] A contract can also be ambiguous when one provision limits punitive damages, while another references the rules of the arbitration service provider which do not limit punitive damages.[205] When there is ambiguity as to whether the clause unequivocally excludes punitive damages, the determination can be

---

195 *See, e.g.,* Sarofim v. Trust Co. of the W., 440 F.3d 213 (5th Cir. 2006) ($2.9 million); Stark v. Sandberg, Phoenix & Von Gontard, Prof'l Corp., 381 F.3d 793 (8th Cir. 2004) ($6 million); Kostoff v. Fleet Sec., Inc., 2007 WL 1064217 (M.D. Fla. Apr. 5, 2007) ($343,000); Adams v. Sec. Am., Inc., 2006 WL 2631863 (E.D. La. Sept. 12, 2006) ($3.5 million); Citigroup Global Markets, Inc. v. Salerno, 445 F. Supp. 2d 124 (D. Mass. 2006) ($1.5 million); Praml v. Linsco/Private Ledger Corp., 2005 WL 2290943 (D. Minn. Sept. 20, 2005) ($247,000); Birmingham News Co. v. Horn, 901 So. 2d 27 (Ala. 2004) ($2.6 million); Snyder v. Ben, 2005 WL 958413 (Cal. Ct. App. Apr. 27, 2005) ($150,000); Hadelman v. Deluca, 274 Conn. 442, 876 A.2d 1136 (2005) ($300,000); Medvalusa Health Programs, Inc. v. Memberworks, Inc., 273 Conn. 634 (2005) ($5 million); Beatty v. Doctors' Co., 2007 WL 1732816 (Ill. App. Ct. June 12, 2007) ($4.5 million); Wallace v. Hayes, 124 P.3d 110 (Mont. 2005) (Wyo. law) ($2.5 million, primarily punitive damages); Pheng Investments, Inc. v. Rodriquez, 196 S.W.3d 322 (Tex. App. 2006) ($100,000).
196 *See* § 11.2.3.1, *supra*.
197 *See* § 11.2.3.2, *supra*.
198 *See* § 11.2.3.3, *supra*.
199 *See* § 11.2.1, *supra*.
200 9 U.S.C. § 10; Unif. Arbitration Act § 12(a) (1955); Unif. Arbitration Act § 23(a) (2000).
201 Mastrobuono v. Shearson Lehman Hutton, Inc., 514 U.S. 52, 115 S. Ct. 1212, 131 L. Ed. 2d 76 (1995).
202 *Id.*
203 Stark v. Sandberg, Phoenix & Von Gontard, Prof'l Corp., 381 F.3d 793 (8th Cir. 2004); Gateway Tech, Inc. v. MCI Telecommunications Corp., 64 F.3d 993 (5th Cir. 1995); Morton v. Polivchak, 931 So. 2d 935 (Fla. Dist. Ct. App. 2006).
204 Stark v. Sandberg, Phoenix & Von Gontard, Prof'l Corp., 381 F.3d 793 (8th Cir. 2004).
205 *See* Mastrobuono v. Shearson Lehman Hutton, Inc., 514 U.S. 52, 115 S. Ct. 1212, 131 L. Ed. 2d 76 (1995); Davis v. Prudential Sec., Inc., 59 F.3d 1186 (11th Cir. 1995).

made by the arbitrator.[206] Thus the arbitrator is not exceeding the arbitrator's powers by awarding punitive damages when there is doubt as to whether the arbitration clause unequivocally excludes punitive damages.

If an arbitration clause or the rules of the arbitration service provider do unequivocally exclude punitive damages, then there would be grounds to challenge the enforceability of the arbitration agreement in the first place.[207] Such a challenge could be made as a court challenge to the enforceability of the arbitration agreement,[208] or it could be made before the arbitrator, who could find the restriction on punitive damages to be unconscionable and thus severable.[209] Because the arbitrator has authority to determine if a contract provision is unconscionable, the only issue is whether the decision is in manifest disregard of the law. As a number of courts have struck down such clauses that limit punitive damages as unconscionable,[210] it is hard to see how such an arbitrator ruling could be in manifest disregard of the law.

An arbitrator may not have to explain the basis for including punitive damages in the award,[211] and it will be hard to argue that the arbitrator's decision is in manifest disregard of the law when it is unknown whether the arbitrator found the exclusion in the contract ambiguous or unconscionable. It should be even harder to vacate an award when the arbitrator explicitly states that the limitation on punitive damages is unconscionable and thus unenforceable.[212]

11.7.3.3 Do the Rules of the Arbitration Service Provider Limit The Arbitrator's Authority to Award Punitive Damages?

According to *Mastrobuono*, punitive damages are not limited unless the arbitration agreement unambiguously restricts them. The same standard should apply when evaluating arbitration service provider rules.

American Arbitration Association (AAA) rules state that "the arbitrator may grant any remedy or relief that the arbitrator deems just and equitable and within the scope of the agreement."[213] AAA's Supplementary Procedures for Consumer-Related Disputes state: "The arbitrator may grant any remedy, relief or outcome that the parties could have received in court."[214]

JAMS rules provide that: "The Arbitrator may grant any remedy or relief that is just and equitable and within the scope of the Parties' agreement."[215] JAMS' consumer arbitration standards state: "Remedies that would otherwise be available to the consumer under applicable federal, state or local laws must remain available under the arbitration clause, unless the consumer retains the right to pursue the unavailable remedies in court."[216]

The National Arbitration Forum (NAF) rules do not explicitly limit the arbitrator's ability to award punitive damages, but the rules state that awards cannot exceed the money requested in a claim or amended claim.[217] Thus the plaintiff will have to plead a specific amount of punitive damages in the original or an amended claim.[218] But NAF filing fees and other charges are linked to the size of the claim and therefore can become astronomical if the consumer includes a high amount of punitive damages in the claim.[219]

This problem may not be an immediate issue if the arbitration agreement specifies that the corporation initially pays all arbitration fees—in fact it may make the arbitration quite costly for the corporation. And the fees may also not be a problem for an indigent consumer if NAF waives the fees. But otherwise the fees may make the action impossible to bring economically. This difficulty may be grounds to challenge in court the enforceability of the award.[220]

11.7.3.4 Does State Law Limit the Arbitrator's Authority to Award Punitive Damages?

11.7.3.4.1 Few state laws limit punitive damages in arbitration

The Supreme Court in *Mastrobuono* ruled that the FAA authorizes punitive damages in arbitration awards.[221] Twelve states have enacted the revised Uniform Arbitration

---

206 Green Tree Fin. Corp. v. Bazzle, 539 U.S. 444, 123 S. Ct. 2402, 156 L. Ed. 2d 414 (2003); *see also* PacifiCare Health Sys., Inc. v. Book, 538 U.S. 401, 123 S. Ct. 1531, 155 L. Ed. 2d 578 (2003); WMS, Inc. v. Weaver, 602 S.E.2d 706 (N.C. Ct. App. 2004); Winkelman v. Kraft Foods, Inc., 693 N.W.2d 756 (Wis. Ct. App. 2005).
207 *See* § 6.5.4.1, *supra*.
208 *Id.*
209 *Cf.* Birmingham News Co. v. Horn, 901 So. 2d 27 (Ala. 2004).
210 *See* § 6.5.4.1, *supra*.
211 *See* § 11.5.2.2., *supra*.
212 *See* § 6.5.4.1, *supra*; *see also* Birmingham News Co. v. Horn, 901 So. 2d 27 (Ala. 2004).
213 Am. Arbitration Ass'n, Commercial Arbitration Rules and Mediation Procedures, Rule 43(a) (reprinted in Appx. B.1.1, *infra*).
214 Am. Arbitration Ass'n, Supplemental Procedures for the Resolution of Consumer-Related Disputes, Procedure C-7(c) (reprinted in Appx. B.1.2, *infra*).
215 JAMS, Comprehensive Arbitration Rules and Procedures, Rule 23(c) (reprinted in Appx. B.3.2, *infra*).
216 JAMS, Policy on Consumer Arbitrations Pursuant to Pre-Dispute Clauses, Minimum Standards of Procedural Fairness (reprinted in Appx. B.3.4.1, *infra*).
217 Nat'l Arbitration Forum, Code of Procedure, Rule 37(B) (reprinted in Appx. B.2.1, *infra*).
218 Nat'l Arbitration Forum, Code of Procedure, Rule 12(A)(1) (reprinted in Appx. B.2.1, *infra*).
219 Nat'l Arbitration Forum, Fee Schedule (reprinted in Appx. B.2.1, *infra*).
220 *See* § 6.5.2, *supra*.
221 Mastrobuono v. Shearson Lehman Hutton, Inc., 514 U.S. 52, 115 S. Ct. 1212, 131 L. Ed. 2d 76 (1995).

Act (UAA),[222] and the revised UAA specifically states: "An arbitrator may award punitive damages or other exemplary relief if such an award is authorized by law in a civil action involving the same claim and the evidence produced at the hearing justifies the award under the legal standards otherwise applicable to the claim."[223]

Most other states base their arbitration law on the older UAA, which is silent on the issue. Nevertheless, the comments to the revised UAA (by the same organization that drafted the UAA) state:

> In regard to punitive damages, it is now well established that arbitrators have authority to award punitive damages under the FAA. *Mastrobuono v. Shearson Lehman Hutton, Inc.*, 514 U.S. 52 (1995). Federal authority is in accord with the preponderance of decisions applying the UAA and state arbitration statutes. *See, e.g., Baker v. Sadick*, 162 Cal. App. 3d 618, 208 Cal. Rptr. 676 (1984); *Eychner v. Van Vleet*, 870 P.2d 486 (Colo. Ct. App. 1993); *Richardson Greenshields Sec., Inc. v. McFadden*, 509 So. 2d 1212 (Fla. Dist. Ct. App. 1987); *Bishop v. Holy Cross Hosp.*, 44 Md. App. 688, 410 A.2d 630 (1980); *Rodgers Builders, Inc. v. McQueen*, 76 N.C. App. 16, 331 S.E.2d 726 (1985), review denied, 315 N.C. 590, 341 N.E.2d 29 (1986); *Kline v. O'Quinn*, 874 S.W.2d 776 (Tex. Ct. App. 1994), cert. denied, 515 U.S. 1142 (1995); *Grissom v. Greener & Sumner Constr., Inc.*, 676 S.W.2d 709 (Tex. Ct. App. 1984); *Anderson v. Nichols*, 178 W. Va. 284, 359 S.E.2d 117 (1987); but see *Garrity v. Lyle Stuart, Inc.*, 40 N.Y.2d 354, 353 N.E.2d 793, 386 N.Y.S.2d 831 (1976); *Leroy v. Waller*, 21 Ark. App. 292, 731 S.W.2d 789 (1987); *School City of E. Chicago, Ind. v. East Chicago Fed. of Teachers*, 422 N.E.2d 656 (Ind. Ct. App. 1981); *Shaw v. Kuhnel & Assocs.*, 102 N.M. 607, 698 P.2d 880, 882 (1985).[224]

Since that comment was written, other courts have supported the availability of punitive damages under the Uniform Arbitration Act.[225]

11.7.3.4.2 FAA preempts state law limitations on punitive damages

In those few states where courts in the 1970s or 1980s found that a state arbitration statute limits punitive damages, the FAA should preempt that statute based on United States Supreme Court rulings from the 1990s and 2000s, including *Mastrobuono*. The argument is straightforward for the preemption of state law restrictions.[226] A state law that limits the full enforceability of an arbitration clause is preempted by the FAA,[227] and a law that specifies that certain types of damages cannot be awarded in arbitration limits the enforceability of that arbitration agreement. State law cannot single out arbitration for special treatment. If punitive damages are available in court, they must be available in arbitration.

11.7.3.4.3 Do general state law limits on punitive damages apply in arbitration?

A different issue is whether an arbitrator is bound by state law limiting or regulating punitive damages, when such a limitation applies to court actions and presumably to arbitration proceedings as well. First of all, an arbitrator probably need not comply with state *procedures* as to how the plaintiff seeks punitive damages in court, because arbitration is a different procedure entirely, and because such a state procedural law is not substantive.[228]

A number of states also have statutes that cap the amount of punitive damages that can be awarded. These statutes usually apply only to punitive damages and not to consequential damages, apply only to certain types of claims and not to others, and include exceptions for cases when the practice is particularly egregious.[229] Particularly when the arbitrator's award is silent as to whether the damages are punitive or consequential,[230] what claims form the basis of the award, or whether the practice is particularly egregious, the question then is whether the arbitrator could properly have found that the cap did not apply. Would it be manifest disregard of the law for an arbitrator to find that only a certain amount of the total award was for punitive damages, that recovery was had for certain claims which are not affected by the state statutory cap, or that the practice was particularly egregious, thereby increasing the statutory cap? In fact an award may not be reviewable at all, even if it clearly violates the state cap, when the parties never informed the arbitrator of that cap.[231]

---

222 Alaska, Colorado, Hawaii, Nevada, New Jersey, New Mexico, North Carolina, North Dakota, Oregon, Oklahoma, Utah, and Washington.
223 Unif. Arbitration Act § 21(a) (2000).
224 Unif. Arbitration Act § 21 cmt. 1 (2000).
225 *See, e.g., Beatty v. Doctors' Co.*, 2007 WL 1732816 (Ill. App. Ct. June 12, 2007); *Wallace v. Hayes*, 124 P.3d 110 (Mont. 2005) (Wyo. law); *Winkelman v. Kraft Foods, Inc.*, 693 N.W.2d 756 (Wis. Ct. App. 2005).
226 *Davis v. Prudential Sec., Inc.*, 59 F.3d 1186 (11th Cir. 1995).
227 *Allied-Bruce Terminix Companies, Inc. v. Dobson*, 513 U.S. 265, 115 S. Ct. 834, 130 L. Ed. 2d 753 (1995).
228 *See Praml v. Linsco/Private Ledger Corp.*, 2005 WL 2290943 (D. Minn. Sept. 20, 2005).
229 *See* National Consumer Law Center, Automobile Fraud § 7.10.5 (3d ed. 2007); *see also* National Consumer Law Center, Unfair and Deceptive Acts and Practices § 8.4.3.6.2 (6th ed. 2004 and Supp.).
230 *See H & S Homes, L.L.C. v. McDonald*, 910 So. 2d 79 (Ala. 2004) (arbitrator need not specify); *Snyder v. Ben*, 2005 WL 958413 (Cal. Ct. App. Apr. 27, 2005) (same).
231 *See Citigroup Global Markets, Inc. v. Salerno*, 445 F. Supp. 2d 124 (D. Mass. 2006).

11.7.4 Has the Arbitrator Disregarded the Law or Facts?

Although a party may attack a punitive damages award for manifest disregard of the law, as described in § 11.5.2, *supra*, this standard is very difficult to meet. Courts have overwhelmingly found that a punitive damages awards should not be vacated or modified based on manifest disregard of the law.[232]

Typically, an element of manifest disregard is that the arbitrator was informed of the controlling legal standard. In one recent case Massachusetts law clearly prohibited the award of punitive damages in a comparable court action. But when the defendant failed to adequately bring this basic principle to the arbitrator's attention, the court would not overturn a punitive damages award of $1.5 million.[233] It is not even clear that an arbitrator has to provide any rationale for her ruling,[234] so it will be particularly difficult to prove manifest disregard when an arbitrator does not issue a decision.

11.7.5 Does a Punitive Damages Award Violate Public Policy?

Some courts have found that arbitration decisions must be consistent with public policy.[235] But the policy in most states is in favor of punitive damages awards, some state statutes explicitly authorize punitive damages, and punitive damages are allowed in tort claims in virtually all states. Thus a punitive damages award is not inconsistent with public policy.[236] Nor is an award inconsistent with public policy because it does not follow Supreme Court due process rulings concerning punitive damages awards. As described in § 11.7.6, *infra*, due process does not apply to arbitration awards, and so an award cannot run afoul of these standards.[237]

11.7.6 Due Process Challenges to Punitive Damages Award

A series of United States Supreme Court decisions have established constitutional due process standards for court-issued punitive damages awards.[238] Corporations opposing an arbitrator's punitive damages award are likely to claim that the award does not meet these due process standards, and that the arbitration process itself does not provide sufficient due process to allow for a punitive damages award.

Courts generally reject this claim because the arbitration involves no state action, and thus there can be no due process violation.[239] It is clear that there is no state action in the arbitration proceeding itself.[240] Courts generally also find that court confirmation of a private arbitration proceeding is not sufficient state action to trigger due process considerations.[241]

---

232 *See* Sarofim v. Trust Co. of the W., 440 F.3d 213 (5th Cir. 2006) ($2.9 million punitive damages award); Rollins, Inc. v. Black, 2006 WL 355852 (11th Cir. Feb. 17, 2006); Stark v. Sandberg, Phoenix & Von Gontard, Prof'l Corp., 381 F.3d 793 (8th Cir. 2004); Wallace v. Buttar, 378 F.3d 182 (2d Cir. 2004) (upholding punitive damages award over challenge that arbitrator disregarded the law and facts; there was at least a barely colorable justification for the outcome reached, based on the law presented to the arbitrator, no error "so obvious that it would be instantly perceived as such by the average person qualified to serve as an arbitrator"); Kostoff v. Fleet Sec., Inc., 2007 WL 1064217 (M.D. Fla. Apr. 5, 2007); Adams v. Sec. Am., Inc., 2006 WL 2631863 (E.D. La. Sept. 12, 2006); Citigroup Global Markets, Inc. v. Salerno, 445 F. Supp. 2d 124 (D. Mass. 2006); Praml v. Linsco/Private Ledger Corp., 2005 WL 2290943 (D. Minn. Sept. 20, 2005); H & S Homes, L.L.C. v. McDonald, 910 So. 2d 79 (Ala. 2004); Birmingham News Co. v. Horn, 901 So. 2d 27 (Ala. 2004); Snyder v. Ben, 2005 WL 958413 (Cal. Ct. App. Apr. 27, 2005); Pheng Investments, Inc. v. Rodriquez, 196 S.W.3d 322 (Tex. App. 2006); *see also* Wallace v. Hayes, 124 P.3d 110 (Mont. 2005) (Wyo. law); Winkelman v. Kraft Foods, Inc., 693 N.W.2d 756 (Wis. Ct. App. 2005). *But see* Sawtelle v. Waddell & Reed Inc., 801 N.Y.S.2d 286 (App. Div. 2005).

233 Citigroup Global Markets, Inc. v. Salerno, 445 F. Supp. 2d 124 (D. Mass. 2006); *see also* Kostoff v. Fleet Sec., Inc., 2007 WL 1064217 (M.D. Fla. Apr. 5, 2007); Adams v. Sec. Am., Inc., 2006 WL 2631863 (E.D. La. Sept. 12, 2006) (upholding $3.5 million punitive damages award even though Louisiana law does not provide punitive damages for cases of that type).

234 *See* § 11.5.2.2, *supra*; *see also* Snyder v. Ben, 2005 WL 958413 (Cal. Ct. App. Apr. 27, 2005).

235 *See* § 11.5.3, *supra*.

236 Sarofim v. Trust Co. of the W., 440 F.3d 213 (5th Cir. 2006) ($2.9 million punitive damages award); Praml v. Linsco/Private Ledger Corp., 2005 WL 2290943 (D. Minn. Sept. 20, 2005); Snyder v. Ben, 2005 WL 958413 (Cal. Ct. App. Apr. 27, 2005); Hadelman v. Deluca, 274 Conn. 442, 876 A.2d 1136 (2005); Medvalusa Health Programs, Inc. v. Memberworks, Inc., 273 Conn. 634 (2005).

237 Hadelman v. Deluca, 274 Conn. 442, 876 A.2d 1136 (2005); Medvalusa Health Programs, Inc. v. Memberworks, Inc., 273 Conn. 634 (2005).

238 *See* National Consumer Law Center, Automobile Fraud § 7.10.6 (3d ed. 2007).

239 Davis v. Prudential Sec., Inc., 59 F.3d 1186 (11th Cir. 1995); Hadelman v. Deluca, 274 Conn. 442, 876 A.2d 1136 (2005); Medvalusa Health Programs, Inc. v. Memberworks, Inc., 273 Conn. 634 (2005).

240 Smith v. Am. Arbitration Ass'n, 233 F.3d 502 (7th Cir. 2000); Davis v. Prudential Sec., Inc., 59 F.3d 1186 (11th Cir. 1995); Fed. Deposit Ins. Corp. v. Air Fla. Sys., Inc., 822 F.2d 833 (9th Cir. 1987); Elmore v. Chicago & Ill. Midland Ry. Co., 782 F.2d 94 (7th Cir. 1986); Cremin v. Merrill Lynch Pierce Fenner & Smith, 957 F. Supp. 1460 (N.D. Ill. 1997); Int'l Ass'n of Heat & Frost Insulators & Asbestos Workers Local Union 42 v. Absolute Envtl. Services, Inc., 814 F. Supp. 392, 402 (D. Del. 1993); Medvalusa Health Programs, Inc. v. Memberworks, Inc., 273 Conn. 634 (2005).

241 Smith v. Am. Arbitration Ass'n, 233 F.3d 502 (7th Cir. 2000); Davis v. Prudential Sec., Inc., 59 F.3d 1186 (11th Cir. 1995); Medvalusa Health Programs, Inc. v. Memberworks, Inc., 273

In addition, even if state action were found, the arbitration proceeding is likely to meet due process standards. The arbitration avoids any issue of jury bias against large corporations or those without a presence in the local community.[242] Arbitrators issuing a punitive damages award will likely have good grounds for such an award, and it will be hard to prove that the arbitrator showed a manifest disregard for constitutional principles.[243] Finally, the merchant, having chosen the process to adjudicate a dispute, is not in any position to challenge the fairness of that process.[244]

11.8 Arbitration and Issue or Claim Preclusion

11.8.1 Introduction

The law of collateral estoppel and res judicata (also often called issue and claim preclusion) is well-developed, and typically deals with the preclusive effect of a prior court proceeding on a later court proceeding. Special issues are raised as to an arbitration proceeding's preclusive effect on a court proceeding or the preclusive effect of either an arbitration or court proceeding on a subsequent arbitration proceeding. For example, an arbitration proceeding may interpret a contract. Is that interpretation binding on a subsequent court action or arbitration proceeding that interprets the same contract?

11.8.2 Arbitration's Preclusive Effect on Subsequent Court Proceeding

In general courts apply the same collateral estoppel and res judicata standards to a prior arbitration decision as they would to a court ruling. If a prior court action would preclude a claim or issue being litigated in court, the same would apply to a prior arbitration proceeding.[245] This may be counter-intuitive because of the limited court review of an arbitration award and of the possibly limited legal expertise of the arbitrator. But courts are protective of their own resources, and do not want to litigate something that has already been determined, even by an arbitrator. Courts also want to prevent losing litigants from seeking a second bite at the apple by retrying their arbitration case in court under a different guise. Such a result would be inconsistent with the intent of the arbitration agreement.[246]

Of course, a holding that an arbitration proceeding is entitled to the same preclusive effect as a court proceeding does not resolve the effect of a prior arbitration in a particular case. A determination must still be made, under traditional standards, whether an earlier proceeding involves or should have involved the same issues as the later proceeding. It is not always easy to determine what issues that prior arbitration in fact resolved, particularly when an arbitrator does not provide a written decision.

11.8.3 Preclusive Effect of Arbitration or Court Ruling on Subsequent Arbitration

While an arbitration proceeding may have a preclusive effect on a subsequent court action, the same is not the case for either an arbitration or court proceeding's effect on a subsequent arbitration. There are few limits as to what an arbitrator can do in that subsequent arbitration. A challenge that the arbitrator, in failing to give preclusive effect to a prior decision, manifestly disregarded the law is unlikely to prevail.[247]

Of course an arbitrator may find a prior court ruling or arbitration award to be a compelling influence on the arbitrator's decision-making, but the arbitrator is also free to decide not to be influenced by that prior ruling or award.[248] Moreover the arbitrator can find a prior ruling to have a preclusive effect when a correct legal interpretation would not find such a preclusive effect.[249] There is very limited judicial review of an arbitrator' decision, whether or not the arbitrator finds a prior proceeding to have preclusive effect.

A party may argue that an arbitration award is violative of public policy (as enunciated in the doctrines of collateral estoppel and res judicata) when the arbitrator ignores the

---

Conn. 634 (2005); *see also* Cremin v. Merrill Lynch Pierce Fenner & Smith, 957 F. Supp. 1460 (N.D. Ill. 1997); United States v. Am. Soc'y of Composers, Authors & Publishers, 708 F. Supp. 95 (S.D.N.Y. 1989).

242 Davis v. Prudential Sec., Inc., 59 F.3d 1186 (11th Cir. 1995).
243 *See* Birmingham News Co. v. Horn, 901 So. 2d 27 (Ala. 2004).
244 Davis v. Prudential Sec., Inc., 59 F.3d 1186 (11th Cir. 1995).
245 *See* B-S Steel of Kan., Inc. v. Tex. Indus., Inc., 439 F.3d 653 (10th Cir. 2006); Sullivan v. Am. Airlines, Inc., 613 F. Supp. 226 (S.D.N.Y. 1985); Miles v. Aetna Cas. & Surety Co., 412 Mass. 424 (1992); Fulghum v. United Parcel Serv., Inc., 424 Mich. 89, 378 N.W.2d 472 (1985); Am. Ins. Co. v. Messinger, 43 N.Y.2d (1977); Martin v. Geico Direct Ins., 818 N.Y.S.2d 265 (App. Div. 2006); L.H. Morris Elec., Inc. v. Hyundai Semiconductor Am., 203 Or. App. 54, 125 P.3d 1 (2005); Robinson v. Hamed, 62 Wash. App. 92, 813 P.2d 171 (1991).

246 B-S Steel of Kan., Inc. v. Tex. Indus., Inc., 439 F.3d 653 (10th Cir. 2006).
247 *See* § 11.5.2, *supra*; *see also* Bear Stearns & Co. v. 1109580 Ontario, 409 F.3d 87 (2d Cir. 2005) (arbitrators did not manifestly disregard the law by refusing to give collateral estoppel effect to findings of previous arbitral panel); LaSalla v. Doctor's Associates, 278 Conn. 578, 898 A.2d 803 (2006).
248 Bear Stearns & Co. v. 1109580 Ontario, 409 F.3d 87 (2d Cir. 2005) (in securities arbitration, arbitrators did not manifestly disregard the law by refusing to give collateral estoppel effect to findings of previous arbitral panel).
249 *See* Hudson v. Conagra Poultry Co., 484 F.3d 496 (8th Cir. 2007).

preclusive effect of prior litigation.[250] But courts reviewing this argument have found a countervailing public policy in giving the arbitrator flexibility and independence.[251] Thus reviewing courts have found that arbitrators are free to attach to prior arbitration awards whatever precedential value they deem appropriate.[252]

Some courts have intimated that an arbitrator has to follow the preclusive effect of a prior court decision more than the arbitrator must a prior arbitration award.[253] But this runs contrary to the case law in the prior subsection that courts will recognize the preclusive effect of an arbitration award just as if it were a court ruling. State law typically indicates that an arbitration award, once confirmed, has the same force and effect as any other court judgment.[254] In any event it may be a distinction without a purpose, because whether a prior proceeding was before a court or arbitrator, there is little review over what weight an arbitrator gives it in a subsequent arbitration.

Of course, when a party elects to first proceed in court, it cannot then bring the same matter before an arbitrator. Participating in court litigation waives the right to arbitrate,[255] and thus there is no enforceable right to arbitrate.

---

250 *See* § 11.5.3, *supra*.

251 LaSalla v. Doctor's Associates, 278 Conn. 578, 898 A.2d 803 (2006) (first arbitration award is not res judicata as to a second award); Stratford v. Int'l Ass'n of Firefighters Local 998, 248 Conn. 108, 728 A.2d 1063 (1999) (no collateral estoppel of issues decided in first arbitration upon same issues in second arbitration).

252 Bear Stearns & Co. v. 1109580 Ontario, 409 F.3d 87 (2d Cir. 2005); LaSalla v. Doctor's Associates, 278 Conn. 578, 898 A.2d 803 (2006) (first arbitration award is not res judicata as to a second award); Stratford v. Int'l Ass'n of Firefighters Local 998, 248 Conn. 108, 728 A.2d 1063 (1999) (no collateral estoppel of issues decided in first arbitration upon same issues in second arbitration)

253 LaSalla v. Doctor's Associates, 278 Conn. 578, 898 A.2d 803 (2006).

254 Unif. Arbitration Act § 14 (1955); Unif. Arbitration Act § 25 (2000).

255 *See* Ch. 8, *supra*.

Chapter 12 Creditor's Use of Arbitration to Collect Consumer Debts

12.1 How Collection Using Arbitration Works

With astonishing frequency, creditors are placing mandatory arbitration clauses in their consumer agreements or stuffing in their billing envelopes notice of such a change of terms.[1] These clauses purport to force disputes between the consumer and the creditor into binding arbitration.

Until recently these clauses have been used primarily to compel arbitration of consumer class actions and other suits brought *against* the creditor. However some creditors, including MBNA[2] and buyers of MBNA debts, use arbitration clauses as a means of collecting consumer debts. Nonpayment of the debt is viewed as a dispute, and the arbitration clause allows a party to settle disputes through arbitration. While some credit card agreements permit the party initiating the action to choose between two or more arbitration service providers, most clauses specify a particular service provider. The service provider establishes procedural rules and fees for the arbitration proceeding and handles administrative tasks.

MBNA's credit card agreement provides that all disputes will be arbitrated by the National Arbitration Forum (NAF). NAF is widely recognized for handling a significant number of arbitrations on behalf of creditors against debtors.[3] More than half of all consumer arbitrations conducted by NAF in California are claims filed by MBNA or assignees of MBNA, and NAF typically conducts over 1000 arbitrations per quarter on behalf of MBNA in California.[4] NAF has advertised to creditors that requiring all disputes to be arbitrated by NAF not only avoids creditor exposure to class actions and punitive damages but also provides an efficient means to collect debts, saving the creditor up to 60% of collection costs.[5] In less than two years First USA Bank initiated over 40,000 collection actions through NAF, paying NAF $5.3 million.[6]

The most current data on NAF arbitration of MBNA and other collection actions is found in a September 2007 report by Public Citizen, *The Arbitration Trap, How Credit Card Companies Ensnare Consumers.*[7] Among the report's findings are that:

- 99.6% of NAF cases are brought by creditors, not consumers;
- 94.7% of awards were in favor of businesses;
- In California the top five NAF arbitrators handled an average of 1000 cases each, and ruled for businesses almost 97% of the time;
- The highest volume NAF arbitrator issued as many as sixty-eight awards in a single day—in which he awarded every penny the creditor sought in all sixty-eight cases; on his six busiest days, when he issued 332 awards, businesses sought $3,432,919 and he awarded them $3,432,919;
- Arbitrators ruling for consumers are blackballed;
- Excessive fees are charged for a written decision and

---

1 See §§ 5.2.3, 5.6.3, and 5.7, *supra*, for further discussion about when bill stuffers are sufficient to form an agreement to arbitrate.

2 According to a filing with the Securities and Exchange Commission by Bank of America: "[O]n January 1, 2006, MBNA Corporation merged with and into Bank of America Corporation. As a result of the merger, MBNA America Bank, National Association ('MBNA') became a wholly-owned subsidiary of Bank of America Corporation. On June 10, 2006, MBNA changed its name to FIA Card Services, National Association ('FIA').'' BA Credit Card Funding, L.L.C., Current Report (Form 8-K) (Oct. 20, 2006). Although it is doubtful that MBNA is still a proper claimant in any debt collection case, creditors and debt collectors attempting to enforce MBNA arbitration clauses are referred to in this manual as "MBNA" for the sake of simplicity.

3 *See* Caroline Mayer, *Win Some, Lose Rarely? Arbitration Forum's Rulings Called One-Sided*, Wash. Post. Mar. 1, 2000, at E1 (explaining that, of nearly 20,000 arbitration awards entered by the NAF in arbitrations filed by First USA between early 1998 and March 2000, "not only has the company sought arbitration far more often than consumers, it has also won in 99.6 percent of the cases that went all the way to an arbitrator").

4 Nat'l Arbitration Forum, California CCP 1281.96 Reports, *available at* www.adrforum.com/main.aspx?itemID=563&hideBar=False&navID=188&news=3.

5 *See* Plaintiff's Response to Defendant First USA's Motion to Dismiss and/or Stay Proceedings and to Compel Arbitration, Marsh v. First USA Bank, Clearinghouse No. 52,494 (N.D. Tex. Dec. 3, 1999) (text of this pleading is also available on the CD-Rom accompanying this manual).

6 *Id.*

7 Available on the CD-Rom accompanying this manual and also at www.citizen.org/documents/Final_wcover.pdf.

§ 12.2   *Consumer Arbitration Agreements*

for other aspects of the arbitration; and
- Consumer attorneys are frustrated by NAF's failure to follow its own procedures and its seeming pro-business bias in case administration.

Because NAF handles such a large number of debt collection cases for its creditor clients, much of the discussion in this chapter will focus on arbitration proceedings before the NAF.[8]

Often the first step in the collection using arbitration process is for the creditor, collector, or law firm hired by the creditor/collector to threaten that the matter will be turned over to arbitration. Then, when the creditor decides to go forward with arbitration, it files a claim with the NAF. NAF rules provide that the creditor may mail or even e-mail minimal paperwork to NAF to initiate the arbitration collection action.[9] Claims filed by creditors generally request an arbitration award in the amount of the principal allegedly owed, plus interest, arbitration fees, attorney fees, and other fees, such as "process of service" fees.

According to current NAF rules, the creditor is required to send notice of the proceeding to the consumer, giving the consumer thirty days to respond to the claim.[10] The notice must be substantially the same as set out in Appendix A of the NAF Code of Procedure. After the notice from the creditor is served, NAF is supposed to send a second notice, substantially the same as set out in Appendix B of the NAF Code of Procedure, giving the consumer up to fourteen more days to respond.[11] The notices are supposed to describe consumers' options, which include submitting a written response with supporting documents, demanding an in-person participatory hearing, or demanding a hearing online or by telephone. The notice does not typically indicate whether or not requests for hearings will be granted. In addition, in some cases, the consumer may never receive a copy of the claim filed by the creditor and may not learn that an arbitration was filed until she receives a notice of arbitration from NAF.

After an NAF employee determines the type of proceeding to be held, NAF assigns an arbitrator to the case. If either party has requested a participatory hearing, the arbitrator assigned must be available in the consumer's state. Either party may strike one arbitrator for any reason. If the consumer does not respond to the notice of arbitration, the arbitrator will reach a decision based solely on documentation provided by the creditor and will enter a default award against the consumer. The vast majority of NAF arbitrations in debt collection cases result in a default award.[12]

Once the arbitrator issues an award, a copy of the award is supposed to be delivered by the arbitrator to the consumer. The date of delivery determines the timeliness of future actions in court to vacate or confirm the award. Until and unless the creditor obtains judicial confirmation of the award, the award is not enforceable and the creditor has no right to garnish wages, place liens on the consumer's property, or subject the consumer to a debtor's examination.

The prevailing party generally has one year or even more to confirm the award. However, the losing party has only a very short time frame within which to challenge the award in court, usually ninety days (or even less in some states) from when the consumer receives notice of the arbitration award.

This chapter will explain some of the consumer's options for responding to a notice of arbitration, participating in an arbitration proceeding, challenging an arbitration award that has been entered against her, resisting confirmation of the award, and bringing an independent action for arbitration-related debt collection harassment.

12.2 Options After Receiving a Notice of Arbitration

12.2.1 Introduction

Many consumers do not seek legal advice until after an arbitration award has been entered against them on behalf of the creditor. But, in some cases, the consumer does contact an attorney soon after being served with notice of the arbitration proceeding. This section examines the advice that an attorney can give the consumer in this situation.

A consumer has several options upon receiving a notice of arbitration. Some consumer advocates in certain jurisdictions advise their clients to simply ignore the notice and then challenge the arbitration award later in court. However, as discussed in § 12.5.4, *infra*, this option may foreclose arguments against the enforcement of the award in some jurisdictions, and is therefore a risky strategy.

If the consumer has a valid argument that she is not bound by an arbitration clause (for example, she is a victim of identity theft or mistaken identity, she opted out of the arbitration clause, or she never received any bill stuffer containing an arbitration clause), she may respond by objecting that the arbitrator has no jurisdiction. This option is discussed in § 12.2.2, *infra*. After objecting, the consumer

---

8   For discussion of whether a creditor's selection of a particular arbitration service provider to handle thousands of collection actions, resulting in millions of dollars of business for that provider, could subject the arbitration service provider to a bias challenge, see § 6.5.7, *supra*.

9   Nat'l Arbitration Forum, Code of Procedure, Rules 2(M), 7 (reprinted in Appendix B.2.1, *infra*, and also available at www.arb-forum.com).

10   Nat'l Arbitration Forum, Code of Procedure, Rule 6(A) (reprinted in Appx. B.2.1, *infra*).

11   Nat'l Arbitration Forum, Code of Procedure, Rule 7(C) (reprinted in Appx. B.2.1, *infra*).

12   Nat'l Arbitration Forum, California CCP 1281.96 Reports, *available at* www.adrforum.com/main.aspx?itemID=563&hideBar=False&navID=188&news=3.

may either participate in the arbitration under protest or refuse to otherwise participate in the proceeding, and then later seek to vacate the award or oppose confirmation of the award. Alternatively, the consumer may also go to court to seek a stay of arbitration in order to challenge the validity of the arbitration clause. This option is discussed in § 12.2.3, *infra*.

Of course, the consumer may choose to participate in the arbitration while preserving any objections to the existence or enforceability of the arbitration agreement. This option is discussed in § 12.2.4, *infra*. The consumer may also file counterclaims against the creditor, either in arbitration or in court. This option is discussed in § 12.3, *infra*.

Whichever option is chosen, the consumer can send a complaint to the agency regulating the creditor, describing any unfair practices by the creditor, collector, collection attorney, arbitration service provider, or arbitrator. MBNA and virtually all credit card issuers are national banks regulated by the Office of the Comptroller of the Currency. Government enforcement is discussed in § 12.8, *infra*.

12.2.2 Objecting to Arbitration When No Agreement to Arbitrate Exists

Whether or not the consumer chooses to participate in the arbitration, many practitioners advise their clients to raise any objection to the enforceability of the arbitration agreement at the beginning of the arbitration proceeding.[13] While a consumer's objection to arbitration on the ground that no agreement exists is unlikely to have much impact on the arbitration itself, in some jurisdictions it is necessary to object at this stage in order to preserve the right to dispute the validity of the arbitration clause in a later court proceeding.[14]

In most jurisdictions raising this objection before the arbitrator should be sufficient to preserve the argument, and the consumer need not also raise this objection by seeking a stay of arbitration in a court proceeding.[15] In addition, some courts may treat a consumer's argument that she was a victim of identity theft as an objection that the consumer was not bound by an arbitration requirement.[16]

Because the arbitration is likely to move forward as if the consumer had not objected, many practitioners also find it advisable to file any other defenses or counterclaims in the arbitration, within the original time limits, in order to avoid a default award, being careful to make clear that the alleged debtor is participating only under protest and that she does not waive her argument that she is not bound by a valid arbitration clause.

12.2.3 Seeking a Stay of Arbitration

Federal and state law provide the consumer the right to go to court to seek a stay of an arbitration proceeding in order to determine whether there is a binding arbitration agreement between the parties. The Uniform Arbitration Act (UAA) (enacted in forty-nine states) provides that: "[O]n application, the court may stay an arbitration proceeding commenced or threatened on a showing that there is no agreement to arbitrate. Such an issue, when in substantial and bona fide dispute, shall be forthwith and summarily tried and the stay ordered if found for the moving party."[17] The application may be made in any state court of competent jurisdiction where venue is proper.[18] The UAA was revised in 2000, and twelve states have adopted this version, but the revised UAA provides the consumer similar rights to seek a court order staying the arbitration.[19] Jurisdiction is almost never appropriate in federal court.[20]

Thus, when a consumer receives notice of an arbitration action to collect on a credit card debt, one option many practitioners recommend is to file an action in state court seeking to stay the arbitration proceeding until the court resolves whether the consumer is bound by a valid arbitration agreement. These practitioners believe that a court is more likely than an arbitrator to require the creditor to produce the arbitration agreement and show that the consumer agreed to it. In addition there is some risk that, if the consumer does not seek a stay of arbitration, the creditor may argue in a subsequent confirmation proceeding that the consumer can no longer raise the issue of the existence or enforceability of the arbitration agreement.[21]

Such a court action may be frustrating for a collector seeking to use the arbitration proceeding as an inexpensive alternative to a court proceeding. In addition, creditors may have difficulty producing the credit agreement and arbitration clause agreed to by the particular consumer.[22] This requirement will be even more difficult for a debt buyer, who may even have difficulty providing evidence that the debt was in fact assigned to the debt buyer.[23] Without a proper

---

13 *See, e.g.*, Garner v. MBNA Am. Bank., 2006 WL 2354939 (N.D. Tex. Aug. 14, 2006) (confirming award against consumer who could not prove he had objected to arbitration, on grounds that he had participated in the proceeding); MBNA Am. Bank v. Felton, 2004 WL 2898632 (Conn. Super. Ct. Nov. 8, 2004).
14 *See* § 12.5.4, *infra*.
15 Holcim (Tex.) Ltd. P'ship v. Humboldt Wedag, Inc., 211 S.W.3d 796 (Tex. App. 2006). *But see* Garner v. MBNA Am. Bank., 2006 WL 2354939 (N.D. Tex. Aug. 14, 2006).
16 Boran v. Columbia Credit Services, Inc., 2006 WL 3388400 (D. Conn. Nov. 21, 2006).

17 Unif. Arbitration Act § 2(b) (1955).
18 Unif. Arbitration Act § 2(c) (1955); *see also* Unif. Arbitration Act § 18 (1955).
19 Unif. Arbitration Act § 7(b), (c), (e) (2000).
20 *See* § 11.2.1, *supra*.
21 *See* Garner v. MBNA Am. Bank., 2006 WL 2354939 (N.D. Tex. Aug. 14, 2006) (proper way to raise objection that no agreement to arbitrate exists is to move for a stay of arbitration).
22 *See* § 12.4.4.2, *infra*.
23 *Id.*

assignment, the debt buyer cannot utilize the arbitration clause and cannot seek to enforce the debt. And of course the consumer can raise all the issues, discussed elsewhere in this manual, why an arbitration agreement that was in fact entered into is still unenforceable.

12.2.4 Participating in the Arbitration Proceeding

12.2.4.1 Introduction

The consumer can, of course, participate in the arbitration proceeding that the creditor initiates to collect on the debt, and raise any defenses in arbitration. However, if the consumer contests the validity of the arbitration clause itself, it is essential to preserve this argument by making clear that the consumer did not agree to arbitration, does not concede that the arbitrator has authority to decide the dispute, and is participating in the arbitration only to make sure the consumer's rights are protected. The implications of participation on a later attempt to vacate or oppose confirmation of an award are discussed in § 12.5.4, *infra*. As described there, at least in Pennsylvania, Kansas, Kentucky, and Virginia, there may be advantages to *not* participating until ordered to do so by a court.

The nature of the consumer's participation will be shaped by the rules of the arbitration service provider selected by the creditor. NAF's rules may be found in Appendix B.2.1, *infra*, and at www.arb-forum.com. It is essential that an attorney representing a consumer in an NAF arbitration carefully read the NAF rules concerning document hearings, discovery, subpoenas, exchange of information before a participatory hearing, participatory hearing procedures, evidence, and so forth.

The NAF rules permit it to charge several different kinds of fees, including filing fees, commencement fees, and administrative fees; fees for hearings; penalties for late requests; fees for non-dispositive orders, discovery orders, and dispositive orders; and objection processing fees. In addition, a party wishing to request that the arbitrator issue "written findings" must pay a fee.

12.2.4.2 Filing a Response

Under present NAF rules, a consumer defending a debt collection claim is not required to pay a fee in order to simply submit a response to the creditor's claims. The response should include any documentation supporting the consumer's defenses. A sample response and counterclaim may be found in Appendix K, *infra*. In general, there are no up-front arbitration fees that the consumer must pay merely to submit documentation. A simple letter documenting identity theft or why certain charges were unauthorized may occasionally be enough for the consumer to prevail, if the consumer is fortunate with the choice of arbitrator.

12.2.4.3 Requesting a Hearing

Requesting a hearing may require certain up-front payments from the consumer. A consumer opting for an in-person or telephone hearing in response to a collection action must pay the fee for a participatory hearing, unless the arbitration agreement or state law require otherwise.[24] If the amount in dispute is $5000 or less, the hearing fee is $150 (and the consumer's portion would be $75) for each sixty-minute session. If the amount in dispute is over $5000 but under $15,000, the fee is $300 (and the consumer's portion would be $150) for each ninety-minute session. For larger disputes, the consumer pays $250 per session.[25] Some practitioners have reported that NAF hearing fees can be has high as $950 depending on the type of dispute. The NAF rules specify a procedure to request a waiver of hearing fees for indigent consumers.[26] As described in § 12.2.4.5, *infra*, it appears that, under the MBNA arbitration clause, a consumer can request that MBNA advance or reimburse these fees.

12.2.4.4 Risk That Consumer Will Be Ordered to Pay Creditor's Arbitration and Attorney Fees

If the consumer does not prevail, NAF rules allow the arbitrator to order the consumer to pay *all* of the creditor's arbitration fees and attorney fees, even if the consumer meets the federal poverty standards.[27] For starters this means that the arbitrator can require even an indigent consumer to pay the creditor's filing fees, which can amount to hundreds of dollars. Thus, even if the consumer received a waiver of hearing fees because of indigence, if the consumer loses the case the arbitrator can order the consumer to pay 100% of the hearing fees.

Non-prevailing consumers may also have to pay all other arbitration fees assessed to the creditor. On a $6000 debt, for example, when there are two hearing sessions and various objections to various requests by parties, the non-prevailing consumer may have to pay almost $2000 in arbitration costs. Nevertheless, as described in § 12.2.4.5, *infra*, at least the current version of the MBNA arbitration clause provides

---

24 Nat'l Arbitration Forum, Fee Schedule (reprinted in Appx. B.2.1, *infra*) (fees for common claims consumer respondents).
25 *Id.*; *see also* Nat'l Arbitration Forum, Code of Procedure, Rule 34(B) (reprinted in Appx. B.2.1, *infra*).
26 Nat'l Arbitration Forum, Code of Procedure, Rule 45 (reprinted in Appx. B.2.1, *infra*).
27 *See* Nat'l Arbitration Forum, Code of Procedure, Rule 44(A) (reprinted in Appx. B.2.1, *infra*).

that the consumer will not have to pay more than what he or she would have been required to pay in a state court action.

Perhaps more significantly, the arbitrator can award the creditor its attorney fees in almost any amount. The arbitrator also has discretion to decide if such attorney fees will be assessed in the same amount whether the consumer defaults, participates through a documentary hearing, or insists on a participatory hearing. Whatever the attorney fee award assessed, there are very narrow grounds for challenging an arbitration award, even when there is a clear error of law.[28] Consequently, one risk of contesting the creditor's collection action is that the arbitrator may assess a significant attorney fee against the consumer, and the consumer may have little recourse to challenge the size of that fee.

12.2.4.5 Can the Consumer Avoid Costs Under the MBNA Clause?

A great deal of collection using arbitration today, either in a collection action brought in MBNA's name or by a debt buyer purchasing an MBNA debt, involves the MBNA arbitration clause. MBNA's arbitration clause provides that in no case will the cost of arbitration to the consumer exceed what he or she would have had to pay if the action had been filed in state court.

The clause appears to limit the consumer's exposure to arbitration costs and fees. In particular the clause provides: "At [the consumer's] written request, [the creditor] will advance any arbitration filing fee, administrative and hearing fees which you are required to pay to pursue a claim in arbitration." When the consumer defends against a collection action brought before an arbitrator, the consumer must pay for the right to have a participatory hearing. This clause appears to allow the consumer to make a written request that the creditor advance those fees. "To pursue a claim in arbitration" should be interpreted as also applying to defending against the collection action.

The MBNA clause also provides that "[i]n no event will [the consumer] be required to reimburse [the creditor] for any arbitration filing, administrative or hearing fees in an amount greater than what [the consumer's] court costs would have been if the Claim had been resolved in a state court with jurisdiction." This unambiguously limits the amount an arbitrator can assess against the consumer. Left uncertain is whether the amount to be assessed is capped at a level established by the state court with jurisdiction that assesses the *highest* costs or by the state court with jurisdiction (such as a small claims court) that assesses the *lowest* costs. However, any ambiguities should be resolved in the consumer's favor, especially given that MBNA has used this provision of its arbitration clause to argue that the clause is not unconscionable.[29]

12.3 Filing Counterclaims Against the Creditor in Court or in Arbitration

One possible approach is to file counterclaims in the arbitration action. Filing the counterclaim may prevent the creditor or arbitrator from dismissing the case without prejudice, thus leaving the creditor free to initiate a lawsuit or an arbitration to collect the debt at a future date, when the consumer may not be able to seek or obtain legal representation.

Most practitioners prefer to raise substantive consumer claims in a separate court action rather than in a NAF arbitration proceeding. Filing the counterclaim in the arbitration would be most appropriate when collateral estoppel would prevent the consumer from raising the claim later in a separate court proceeding. While an arbitration proceeding may have as much of a preclusive effect as a court proceeding,[30] often an action to collect on a consumer debt does not preclude a separate action on consumer debt harassment claims.[31] Another factor in deciding whether to bring counterclaims in the arbitration or separately is whether that separate action could also be forced into arbitration.

Filing a counterclaim under NAF rules requires use of special forms that need be obtained from the NAF, which must then be delivered to the NAF and the creditor. NAF Rule 14 calls for a filing fee when making a counterclaim. Given that MBNA's arbitration agreement provides that the consumer will not be required to pay costs greater than she would in court, and that there is typically no fee to make a counterclaim, the consumer can request that the creditor pay all costs associated with filing the counterclaim.

12.4 Seeking to Vacate the Award

12.4.1 Introduction

The procedure and statutory grounds for seeking *vacatur* of an arbitration award are discussed in Chapter 11, *supra*. This section will highlight issues particularly relevant to *vacatur* of a debt collection arbitration award.

---

28 *See* § 11.5, *supra*.
29 *See* Jaimez v. MBNA Am. Bank, 2006 WL 470587 (D. Kan.

Feb. 27, 2006) (MBNA's clause not unconscionable based on unreasonable arbitration costs, given that it "provides that in no case will the cost of arbitration exceed the costs if the action were filed in state court").
30 *See* § 11.8, *supra*.
31 *See* National Consumer Law Center, Fair Debt Collection § 7.6.2 (5th ed. 2004 and Supp.).

12.4.2 Timeliness

A consumer may challenge an arbitration award by seeking a court order vacating or modifying the award. In many jurisdictions waiting for the creditor to seek confirmation of the award in court is not advisable, because some courts have held that they have no discretion to refuse to confirm an award unless a timely motion to vacate has been filed.[32]

In federal court and virtually all state courts, the consumer must seek to vacate or modify the award within ninety days of the consumer's receipt of that award,[33] but there are variations. Connecticut and Massachusetts provide only thirty days to vacate an award;[34] Michigan allows only twenty-one days.[35] On the other hand, Arizona law provides a ninety-day period to modify an award, but imposes no time limit to vacate the award, so that the consumer can seek to vacate the award at any time up through the confirmation proceeding.[36] California law provides for one-hundred days.[37]

Whatever the time period specified, equitable tolling may apply to extend this period,[38] and some states have rules that restart the time period if a case timely brought in federal court is dismissed because of a lack of federal jurisdiction.[39] The Uniform Arbitration Act (UAA) and revised UAA also extend the time period when the grounds are "predicated upon corruption, fraud, or other undue means." In that case the action to vacate "shall be made within ninety days after such grounds are known or should have been known."[40] Corruption, fraud, or undue means may be difficult to prove in the typical arbitration case.[41]

While there are generally strict time deadlines for the consumer to seek to vacate an award, the creditor typically has much longer to confirm an award. Thus creditors often wait to seek confirmation of an award until after the deadline for *vacatur* has passed. While many practitioners believe that every effort should be made to bring the action to vacate within the applicable time period, all is not lost if the consumer fails to do so. Section 12.5, *infra*, sets out a number of grounds on which to challenge the creditor's confirmation action even after the ninety-day or other applicable time period has expired.

Two of those grounds relate directly to the ability to vacate an award even beyond ninety days after an award is issued. As set out in § 12.5.3.3, *infra*, a growing number of courts find that the lack of a binding arbitration agreement can be raised as ground to vacate an award at a later date, in the confirmation proceeding. The lack of an arbitration agreement goes to the court's jurisdiction to confirm the award. In addition, as examined in § 12.5.3.2, *infra*, the time period to vacate an award does not begin to run until the consumer is properly notified of the award, and a number of questions can be raised concerning notice of an award relating to a debt collection arbitration.

12.4.3 Applicable Law, Jurisdiction, and Venue

Jurisdiction for the consumer's action to vacate or modify the award is almost always in state, not federal court.[42] Actions to vacate an award in state court will be governed by state law, not the FAA.[43] State law in forty-nine states concerning *vacatur* is patterned on the Uniform Arbitration Act (UAA),[44] but as of September 2007, twelve of these states have adopted the revised UAA.[45]

---

32 *See, e.g.*, MBNA v. Swartz, 2006 WL 1071523 (Del. Ch. Ct. Apr. 13, 2006) (confirming award despite "barely adequate paperwork provided by MBNA" on grounds that court was "without power to do otherwise"); MBNA Am. Bank v. Tackleson, 720 N.W.2d 192 (Iowa Ct. App. 2006) (table) (text available at 2006 WL 1229935) ("the court may deny confirmation of an arbitration award under the statute only if relief is granted under the accompanying vacation and correction statutes"); Asset Acceptance, L.L.C. v. Stancik, 2004 WL 2930997 (Ohio Ct. App. Dec. 16, 2004) (confirming award when no motion to vacate had been filed within state's ninety-day period, but holding that counterclaims are not subject to the same time limit); *see also* § 11.2.3, *supra*.

33 *See, e.g.*, Occidental Chem. Corp. v. Local 820, Int'l Chem. Workers Union, 614 F. Supp. 323 (W.D. Mich. 1985); Kutch v. State Farm Mut. Auto. Ins. Co., 960 P.2d 93 (Colo. 1998); MBNA Am. Bank v. Leslie, 2005 WL 2277252 (Conn. Super. Ct. Aug. 25, 2005); Walter A. Brown Inc. v. Moylan, 509 A.2d 98 (D.C. 1986); Broward County Paraprofessional Ass'n v. Sch. Bd. of Broward County, 406 So. 2d 1252 (Fla. Dist. Ct. App. 1981); Bingham County Comm'n v. Interstate Elec. Co., 105 Idaho 36 (Idaho 1983); MBNA Am. Bank v. Tackleson, 720 N.W.2d 192 (Iowa Ct. App. 2006) (table) (text available at 2006 WL 1229935); Local 589, Amalgamated Transit Union v. Mass. Bay Transp. Auth, 397 Mass. 426 (1986); MBNA Am. Bank v. Belleslie, 2005 Mont. Dist. LEXIS 1119 (Mont. Dist. Ct. Apr. 26, 2005); MBNA Am. Bank v. Hart, 710 N.W.2d 125 (N.D. 2006); MBNA Am. Bank v. McArdle, 2007 WL 1229214 (Ohio Ct. App. Apr. 27, 2007); CACV v. Kogler, 2006 WL 2790398 (Ohio Ct. App. Sept. 29, 2006); Garner v. MBNA Am. Bank, 2007 WL 499346 (Tex. App. Feb. 16, 2007); MBNA Am. Bank v. Miles, 2007 WL 1711803 (Wash Ct. App. June 14, 2007).

34 Conn. Gen, Stat. § 52-417; Mass. Gen. Laws ch. 251, § 12.

35 Mich. Ct. R. 3.602(J)(2).

36 Morgan v. Carillon Investments Inc., 207 Ariz. 547 (Ct. App. 2004).

37 Cal. Civ. Proc. Code § 1288 (West).

38 *See* Bauer v. Carty & Co., 2005 WL 948641, at *4 (W.D. Tenn. Mar. 9, 2005).

39 *See* Fischer v. MBNA, 2007 WL 779295 (Ky. Ct. App. Mar. 16, 2007).

40 Unif. Arbitration Act § 12(b) (1955).
  Revised Uniform Arbitration Act § 23(b) (2000) contains similar, but not identical language.

41 *See* MBNA v. Hart, 710 N.W.2d 125 (N.D. 2006).

42 *See* § 11.2.1, *supra*.

43 *See* § 11.2.2, *supra*.

44 Unif. Arbitration Act (1955), *available at* www.law.upenn.edu/bll/ulc/fnact99/1920_69/uaa55.pdf.

45 Unif. Arbitration Act (2000), *available at* www.law.upenn.edu/bll/ulc/uarba/arbitrat1213.pdf.

A state court action to vacate an award usually can be brought in any court of competent jurisdiction in the state.[46] There is no requirement to bring an action to vacate an award issued by NAF in Minnesota, despite the fact that the NAF is located in Minnesota and notices from the NAF contain a Minnesota address. If there had been an in-person proceeding, it would have been held near the consumer's residence.[47]

There is almost never federal court jurisdiction to bring a motion to vacate an arbitration collection award, because the Federal Arbitration Act (FAA) does not provide federal court jurisdiction and consumer collection actions rarely satisfy diversity or federal question jurisdictional requirements.[48] In the rare case in which a federal court has jurisdiction over a consumer's petition to vacate an award (or a creditor's petition to confirm an award),[49] the proceeding would be governed by the FAA. The FAA requires application in the court specified in the agreement, or if no court is specified, then in the federal district court for the district where the arbitration was held.[50] The Supreme Court has held that venue is proper under the FAA either in the district where the award was made or in any district proper under the general venue statute.[51]

12.4.4 Grounds for Vacating an Award in a Debt Collection Case

12.4.4.1 Introduction

Chapter 11, *supra*, examines generally the right of any party to seek to vacate, modify, or oppose confirmation of an award. This section focuses on the grounds to vacate an award and the applicability of these grounds to a creditor's arbitration collection award.

12.4.4.2 When Arbitration Award Not Binding on the Consumer

If the consumer never assented to the arbitration agreement, or for some other reason the arbitration agreement is not enforceable as to that consumer, then the arbitration award is not enforceable, unless the consumer participated in the arbitration without objection.[52] The UAA states that an award shall be vacated when there is no arbitration agreement unless a court had previously ruled that there was an arbitration agreement or the consumer participated in the arbitration proceeding without raising an objection.[53] The revised UAA has a similar provision.[54] The Supreme Court has stated: "Arbitration is a matter of contract and a party cannot be required to submit to arbitration any dispute that he has not agreed so to submit. This axiom recognizes the fact that arbitrators derive their authority to resolve disputes only because the parties have agreed in advance to submit such grievances to arbitration."[55]

The consumer should argue that the creditor or collector is required to produce evidence that the consumer agreed to arbitration. Creditors often cannot produce evidence that the particular consumer assented to or even was sent a particular arbitration agreement. If the company cannot produce evidence of an agreement, then it should not be allowed to enforce an arbitration award based on that purported agreement.[56] Debt buyers in particular will have difficulty showing the existence of a credit agreement, or an assignment from the creditor of the debt.[57] Of course a debt buyer cannot use arbitration to collect on a debt when it cannot

---

States adopting the revised UAA include Alaska, Colorado, Hawaii, Nevada, New Jersey, New Mexico, North Carolina, North Dakota, Oklahoma, Oregon, Utah, and Washington.

46 Unif. Arbitration Act § 17 (1955); Unif. Arbitration Act § 1(3) (2000).
See § 11.2.2, *supra*, for a discussion of these statutes.
47 See § 12.5.5.2, *infra*.
48 Fisher v. MBNA Am. Bank, 422 F. Supp. 2d 889 (S.D. Ohio 2006); Turner v. MBNA Am. Bank, 2006 W.L. 825991 (N.D. Ga. Mar. 29, 2006); Watson v. MBNA Am. Bank, 2005 WL 1875778 (W.D.N.C. Aug. 1, 2005); Garcia v. MBNA Am. Bank, 2005 WL 1653639 (D. Or. July 6, 2005); Stafford v. Chase Manhattan Bank U.S.A., 2005 WL 1330874 (M.D.N.C. June 3, 2005); Miles v. MBNA Am. Bank, 2005 WL 1220842 (E.D. Wash. May 23, 2005); Fischer v. MBNA Am. Bank, 2005 WL 1168388 (W.D. Ky. May 17, 2005); Mesdag v. MBNA Am. Bank, 2005 WL 418549 (D. Or. Feb. 17, 2005); Mellado v. MBNA Am. Bank, 2004 WL 2937224 (N.D. Tex. Dec. 17, 2004); Kearns v. MBNA Am. Bank, 2004 WL 2512742 (N.D. Tex. Nov. 5, 2004); MBNA Am. Bank v. Shnitzer, 2004 WL 1717670 (D. Or. July 30, 2004).
49 See § 11.2.1, *supra*; § 12.5.5.2, *infra*.
50 9 U.S.C. § 10.
51 Cortez Byrd Chips, Inc. v. Bill Harbert Constr. Co., 529 U.S. 193, 120 S. Ct. 1331, 146 L. Ed. 2d 171 (2000).

52 MBNA Am. Bank v. Felton, 2004 WL 2898632 (Conn. Super. Ct. Nov. 8, 2004); MBNA Am. Bank v. Phoenix, 2004 WL 2166955 (Conn. Super. Ct. Sept. 9, 2004); MBNA Am. Bank v. Credit, 132 P.3d 898 (Kan. 2006); MBNA Am. Bank v. Barben, 111 P.3d 663 (Kan. Ct. App. 2005) (table) (text available at 2005 WL 1214244); MBNA Am. Bank v. Cornock, No. 03-C-0018 (N.H. Super. Ct. Mar. 20, 2007), *available at* www.consumerlaw.org/unreported; MBNA Am. Bank v. Engen, 2005 WL 1754169 (Wash. Ct. App. July 25, 2005).
53 Unif. Arbitration Act § 12(5) (1955).
54 Unif. Arbitration Act § 23(5) (2000).
55 AT & T Technologies, Inc. v. Communications Workers of Am., 475 U.S. 643, 106 S. Ct. 1415, 89 L. Ed. 2d 648 (1986).
56 Acher v. Fujitsu Network Communications, 354 F. Supp. 2d 26 (D. Mass. 2005); Owen v. MBPXL Corp., 173 F. Supp. 2d 905, 922 (N.D. Iowa 2001); Alltell Corp. v. Sumner, 203 S.W.3d 77 (Ark. 2005); Am. Express Centurion Bank v. Frey, 2004 WL 1676465 (Mich. Ct. App. July 27, 2004). *But see* MBNA Am. Bank v. Tackleson, 720 N.W.2d 192 (Iowa Ct. App. 2006) (table) (text available at 2006 WL 1229935).
57 *See* Koch v. Compucredit Corp., 2007 WL 991070 (E.D. Ark. Mar. 29, 2007).

even present evidence that it has the right to enforce the credit agreement, including the arbitration clause.

A recent case in which MBNA sought to confirm an arbitration award discussed this problem in some detail:

> Petitioner must tender the *actual* provisions agreed to, including any and all amendments, and not simply a photocopy of general terms to which the credit issuer may currently demand debtors agree. For example, Petitioner's Exhibit A which is labeled "Credit Card Agreement and Additional Terms and Conditions" lacks Respondent's signature. Neither does it contain a date indicating when these terms were adopted by MBNA nor how the terms were amended or changed, if at all, over the years appear anywhere on the document. Furthermore, the contract does not contain any name, account number or other identifying statements which would connect the proffered agreement with the Respondent in this action. In fact, petitioners appear to have attached the exact same photocopy, which as noted is not specific to any particular consumer, to many of its confirmation petitions. While on its face there is nothing necessarily unusual about a large commercial entity such as MBNA providing a standard form contract that all credit card consumers agree to, the burden nevertheless remains with MBNA to tie the binding nature of its boiler-plate terms to the user at issue in each particular case and to show that those terms are binding on each Respondent it seeks to hold accountable (the Respondent's intent to be bound *after notice of terms is established* can be shown via card use. The fact that MBNA issues a particular agreement with particular terms with the majority of its customers is of little relevance in determining the actual terms of the alleged agreement before this Court, if not linked directly to respondent in some way shape or form. Just because a petitioner provides a photocopy of a document entitled "Additional Terms and Conditions," certainly does not mean those terms are binding on someone who could have theoretically signed a completely different agreement when they were extended credit. Whether the physical card itself or some solicitation agreement with Respondent's signature referenced the terms and conditions, or whether the terms were made readily accessible to Respondent by e-mail or the internet, and Respondent was in fact aware of this, may all be relevant to an inquiry into constructive notice but such notice must still be established. At bar, MBNA Bank has failed to establish that the provided terms and conditions were the actual terms and conditions agreed to by Nelson. As such, applying *Kaplan,* the Court does not find objective intent on the part of the Respondent to be bound to the contractual statements proffered by MBNA requiring the question of arbitrability to be decided by the arbitrator or that arbitration is the required forum for either party to bring claims against the other.
>
> While these deficiencies of proof are fatal to Petitioner's claim, such a problem is not without a solution. Since the credit card issuer is the party in the best position to maintain records of notification it may provide an affidavit from someone with knowledge of the policies, procedures and practices of its organization affirming (1) when and how the notification of the original terms and conditions was provided, including any solicitations or applications containing the Respondent's signature, (2) what those terms and conditions were *at the time of the notification,* (3) whether the mandatory arbitration clause, and any other additional provisions Petitioner now treats as binding, were included in the terms and conditions of card use at the time Respondent entered into the retail credit agreement, and if they were not, then when they were added, as well as a statement certifying that (a) such addition was made pursuant to the applicable law chosen by the parties to apply to the agreement, not limited to but especially including mandatory opt-out requirements, and (b) a statement indicating that upon reasonable and diligent inspection of the records maintained by the Petitioner, and to the best of Petitioners' knowledge Respondent never opted out of said clause, and the basis for this determination. The use of such affidavits to support confirmation of arbitration awards is not novel.[58]

Moreover, in many states, if an affidavit is used to support the company's evidence, additional requirements may exist if the affiant is out of state. In New York, the affidavit must be accompanied by a certificate of conformity, and a certificate of authority may also be required.[59]

Even if the collector does produce evidence of a binding arbitration agreement, the consumer can challenge the enforceability of the agreement on many bases. Chapter 5, *supra,* examines whether arbitration agreements sent in bill stuffers are enforceable. Chapter 6, *supra,* examines whether various aspects of the arbitration agreement are unconscionable. Other grounds are also examined throughout chapters 7 and 8, *supra.*

---

58 MBNA Am. Bank v. Nelson, 15 Misc. 3d 1148(A) (Civ. Ct. 2007) (table) (text available at 2007 WL 1704618) (footnotes omitted); *see also* Owen v. MBPXL Corp., 173 F. Supp. 2d 905, 922 (N.D. Iowa 2001) (rejecting affidavit as not sufficiently based on personal knowledge).

59 MBNA Am. Bank v. Nelson, 15 Misc. 3d 1148(A) (Civ. Ct. 2007) (table) (text available at 2007 WL 1704618).

12.4.4.3 Lack of Notice of the Arbitration Proceeding

Lack of notice of the arbitration proceeding is a sufficient basis for vacating or refusing to confirm an award.[60] The revised Uniform Arbitration Act (UAA) states that one basis on which to vacate an award is that "the arbitration was conducted without proper notice of the initiation of the arbitration ... so as to prejudice substantially the rights of a party to the arbitration proceeding."[61] The UAA, likewise, provides grounds for *vacatur* when the arbitrators failed to provide notice of the hearing, so as to prejudice substantially the rights of a party.[62] NAF rules require both the creditor and the NAF to send form notices of the proceeding. Failure to do so or sending the notice to the wrong address may be grounds to vacate the award.[63]

In addition, NAF arbitration may run afoul of the UAA and revised UAA if NAF notices are sent via regular mail. The UAA states that, "[u]nless otherwise provided by the agreement ... [t]he arbitrators shall appoint a time and place for the hearing and cause notification to the parties to be served personally or by registered mail."[64] Similarly, revised UAA section 9(a) requires notice "in the agreed manner between the parties or, in the absence of agreement, by certified or registered mail, return receipt requested and obtained, or by service as authorized for the commencement of a civil action." It is an open question whether notice by first class U.S. Mail is proper, when the arbitration agreement selects NAF, and NAF rules allow delivery via first class U.S. Mail.[65]

12.4.4.4 Lack of a Required In-Person Hearing

The consumer has a right under the UAA and revised UAA to an in-person hearing. UAA section 5 states that "the parties are entitled to be heard, to present evidence ... and to cross-examine witnesses," unless otherwise provided for by agreement.[66] Failure to provide such a hearing is grounds to vacate an award.[67]

The Supreme Court of Virginia, interpreting that state's version of the UAA, held that a trial court erred by failing to vacate an arbitration award issued without a hearing, when the arbitration clause did not specify that a hearing was not required.[68] At least one state trial court has interpreted the hearing requirement as barring confirmation of a creditor's action to confirm an arbitration award on behalf of an MBNA debt buyer, when the award was issued without a hearing.[69]

12.4.4.5 Failure to Follow the Arbitration Agreement or Arbitration Service Provider Rules

The arbitration agreement and the arbitration service provider will spell out rules for the conduct of its hearings, and violation of those rules may be grounds for *vacatur*.[70] For example, under NAF rules, even if the consumer fails to participate, the most an arbitrator can award is the amount initially sought by the creditor, plus fees and costs.[71] Awarding interest not sought in the original claim, for example, would violate this rule. The MBNA arbitration clause itself also appears to limit the amount of arbitration costs that may

---

60 Cas. Indem. Exch. v. Yother, 439 So. 2d 77 (Ala. 1983); CACV v. Miller, No. 845316 (Cal. Super. Ct. July 13, 2005) (petition to confirm NAF award denied when bank "failed to present sufficient, admissible evidence" that respondent was adequately served with notice of the arbitration proceedings); CACV v. Corda, 2005 WL 3664087 (Conn. Super. Ct. Dec. 16, 2005) (noting that NAF rules provide "no procedure by which the arbitrator makes any determination of whether the defendant has received actual notice of the demand for arbitration"); MBNA v. Nelson, 15 Misc. 3d 1148(A) (Civ. Ct. 2007) (table) (text available at 2007 WL 1704618) (denying without prejudice petition to confirm, when creditor failed to provide necessary evidence, including notice of arbitration and proof of service of notice of arbitration); MBNA Am. Bank v. Pacheco, 12 Misc. 3d 1194(A) (Civ. Ct. 2006) (table); MBNA v. Straub, 815 N.Y.S.2d 450 (Civ. Ct. 2006) (to confirm award creditor must show notice of arbitration was properly served, either as provided under state law or as provided in the arbitration agreement); Worldwide Asset Purchasing v. Karafotias, 801 N.Y.S.2d 721 (Civ. Ct. 2005) (explaining that a petition to confirm an arbitration award must be accompanied by proof of notice of arbitration); *cf.* Cavalry Investments, L.L.C. v. Grasson, 2005 WL 2981691 (Conn. Super. Ct. Oct. 19, 2005).
61 Unif. Arbitration Act § 23(a)(6) (2000).
62 Unif. Arbitration Act § 12(a)(4) (1955).
63 MBNA Am. Bank v. Pacheco, 12 Misc. 3d 1194(A) (Civ. Ct. 2006) (table).
64 Unif. Arbitration Act § 5 (1955); *cf.* Fodor v. MBNA, 34 A.D.3d 473 (2006) (when notice sent by certified mail, with a signed mail return receipt, this created presumption of proper notice).
65 Revised Uniform Arbitration Act § 9, comment 3, states that the NAF, AAA and other arbitration organizations allow service by regular mail, and this is acceptable if the parties agree.
66 Unif. Arbitration Act § 5 (1955).
67 Unif. Arbitration Act § 12(a)(4) (1955).
68 Bates v. McQueen, 270 Va. 95, 102–103, 613 S.E.2d 566, 569–570 (2005) ("In short, the failure to conduct 'the hearing' clearly intended by [the UAA], unless otherwise provided by an agreement, and by the provisions of [the UAA] was tantamount to no arbitration. Unless parties agree otherwise, a hearing is a fundamental part of the arbitration process because '[t]he arbitrators are the final judges of both law and fact, their award not being subject to reversal for a mistake of either.'" (citations omitted)).
69 CACV of Colo., L.L.C. v. Rubin, No. GV06-004208-00 (Va. Dist. Ct. Apr. 21, 2006), *reprinted at* www.consumerlaw.org/unreported.
70 *See* §§ 11.4.2, 11.5, *supra*.
71 Nat'l Arbitration Forum, Code of Procedure, Rules 37(B), 37(C) (reprinted in Appx. B.2.1, *infra*).

be assessed by the arbitrator.[72] Costs in excess of this amount should be sufficient grounds to vacate, or at least modify, the award.

12.4.4.6 Arbitrator Improperly Selected

Improper selection of the arbitrator should be a basis on which to vacate an award,[73] and the method of selection should be carefully reviewed, particularly when the consumer does not participate in the selection. State and federal arbitration law specify that, when the consumer does not participate, selection of the arbitrator must be referred to a court, unless the arbitration service provider has established a procedure in the absence of the consumer's participation.[74]

However, the NAF and American Arbitration Association (AAA) rules *do* provide procedures for the selection of an arbitrator when the consumer does not participate in the proceeding.[75] The arbitration service provider creates a list of arbitrators, and each side *that makes an appearance* has the right to strike arbitrators from the list, and then the arbitration service provider selects an arbitrator.

If an arbitration agreement does not provide that the AAA or NAF rules apply, and the arbitrator is neither chosen with the consumer's consent nor by the court, then the arbitration award should be void.[76] The award should be void even if the creditor selects the AAA or NAF to conduct the arbitration, because the consumer has not consented to use of this service provider or its method of selecting an arbitrator. The consumer's failure to participate in the arbitration does not waive the consumer's right to have an arbitrator selected properly.[77]

12.4.4.7 Arbitration Award Is Contrary to the Law or Facts

That an arbitration award is clearly contrary to the law or the facts is not listed in state or federal arbitration statutes as a basis on which to vacate an award. But the United States Supreme Court has recognized that there is some opportunity for courts to review the merits of an arbitrator's decision.[78] While great deference is paid to the arbitrator's decision, courts do have some role in reviewing the merits of that decision, although the exact nature of that role is still unsettled. For a more detailed discussion of when an award may be contrary to the law or facts, see § 11.5, *supra*.

12.4.4.8 Arbitrator Bias

Arbitrator bias, as described in § 11.4.3, *supra*, is another basis on which to vacate an award. It may be difficult to prove bias in a particular case, as discussed in §§ 6.5.7, 11.4.3, *supra*. Nevertheless, a California statute specifies that the court "shall" vacate an award if the arbitrator fails to make certain disclosures concerning relationships the arbitrator has to the parties.[79]

12.4.4.9 Inconvenient Venue

Consumer attorneys often focus on inconvenient venue of the arbitration proceeding itself as a possible basis on which to vacate an award, noting NAF's Minnesota address. It is important to understand that, while NAF is headquartered Minnesota, any in-person hearing should take place at a location near the consumer's residence, not in Minnesota. While a Minnesota venue would be inconvenient for an in-person hearing, a document hearing administered from Minnesota may not raise the same concerns.[80]

A venue challenge certainly makes sense when the consumer requested an in-person hearing, and that hearing was offered at a significant distance from the consumer's residence. NAF rules require that the hearing occur in the same federal judicial district where the consumer resides, and at "a reasonably convenient location."[81] In addition, to comply with the Fair Debt Collection Procedures Act (FDCPA), the Federal Trade Commission Act, and state deceptive

---

72 *See* § 12.2.4.5, *supra*.

73 Improper selection can be viewed as an award procured by undue means, or that the arbitrator exceeded his powers. *See* Brook v. Peak Int'l Ltd., 169 F. Supp. 2d 641, 645 (W.D. Tex. 2001) ("arbitrators are without power to arbitrate a dispute when they are not chosen in accordance with the parties' arbitration agreement"), *rev'd*, 294 F.3d 668 (5th Cir. 2002) (party failed to object properly and waived right to do so); Martinez v. Master Prot. Corp., 118 Cal. App. 4th 107 (2004); *see also* Alan v. Super. Ct., 111 Cal. App. 4th 217 (2003).

74 *See* 9 U.S.C. §§ 4, 5; Unif. Arbitration Act § 3 (1955); Unif. Arbitration Act § 11 (2000); *see also* Hugs & Kisses, Inc. v. Aguirre, 220 F.3d 890 (8th Cir. 2000).

75 Val-U Constr. Co. v. Rosebud Sioux Tribe, 146 F.3d 573 (8th Cir. 1998).

76 Hugs & Kisses, Inc. v. Aguirre, 220 F.3d 890 (8th Cir. 2000); *see also* R.J. O'Brien & Associates, Inc. v. Pipkin, 64 F.3d 257 (7th Cir. 1995); Cargill Rice, Inc. v. Empresa Nicaraguense Dealimentos Basicos, 25 F.3d 223 (4th Cir. 1994); Szuts v. Dean Witter Reynolds, Inc., 931 F.2d 830 (11th Cir. 1991); Avis Rent A Car Sys., Inc. v. Garage Employees Union Local 272, 791 F.2d 22 (2d Cir. 1986).

77 Hugs & Kisses, Inc. v. Aguirre, 220 F.3d 890 (8th Cir. 2000).

78 *See* First Options of Chicago, Inc. v. Kaplan, 514 U.S. 938, 942, 115 S. Ct. 1920, 131 L. Ed. 2d 985 (1995); Wilko v. Swan, 346 U.S. 427, 436, 745 S. Ct. 182, 98 L. Ed. 168 (1953).

79 Cal. Civ. Proc. Code § 1286.2(a)(6) (discussed in § 11.4.3.2, *supra*).

80 *See* Lamb v. Jovitch, Block & Rathbone, L.L.P., 2005 WL 4137778 (S.D. Ohio Jan. 24, 2005) (no Fair Debt Collection Practices Act violation when NAF administered the arbitration from Minnesota, but when consumer was entitled to an in-person hearing in a convenient location).

81 Nat'l Arbitration Forum, Code of Procedure, Rule 32(A) (reprinted in Appx. B.2.1, *infra*).

practices (UDAP) statutes, the location must be within the county where the consumer resides.[82] Consequently it should be improper to conduct an in-person hearing, even if it is within the federal judicial district where the consumer resides, if it is not also within the county where the consumer resides. There is no reason to establish a different standard as to venue for consumer collection actions utilizing arbitration proceedings than for those utilizing judicial actions. Courts will strike down an arbitration agreement if it requires an inconvenient venue to arbitrate the case,[83] and this should also provide grounds to vacate an award, particularly when the consumer did not participate in the arbitration.

12.5 Opposing Confirmation of the Award

12.5.1 Introduction

An arbitration award is not an enforceable judgment on the debt. The creditor cannot use the arbitration award to seize property or institute wage garnishment. Instead, the creditor must go to court to "confirm" the award, at which point the court enters a judgment that can be enforced like any other judgment in a civil action.[84] This allows the creditor to garnish wages, place liens on property, and conduct a debtor's examination.[85]

While it is traditionally thought that there are few grounds on which to resist confirmation of an award, particularly after the time to seek modification or vacation of the award has expired,[86] this section explores a number of promising approaches to challenging confirmation of an award on a debt. This is particularly important because consumers often do not participate in the arbitration process and only respond when they receive notice of a court proceeding to confirm the award.

In deciding whether an attorney should represent the consumer in a confirmation proceeding the availability of attorney fees paid by the other side will be a factor. At least in California a consumer successfully resisting a confirmation proceeding may recover attorney fees from the party seeking confirmation.[87]

12.5.2 The Confirmation Process

As described in § 11.2, *supra*, actions to confirm an arbitration award on a consumer collection matter will be brought in state court and governed by state law, patterned on either the Uniform Arbitration Act (UAA) or revised UAA. The confirmation process is generally governed by the Federal Arbitration Act (FAA) only when the action is brought in federal court. Despite this fact, state courts are often confused on this matter, and often refer to the FAA's provisions regarding confirmation.

This generally makes no difference because the UAA, revised UAA, and the FAA have similar provisions relating to award confirmation. The UAA and revised UAA provide that a court "shall" confirm the award unless "grounds are urged for vacating or modifying or correcting the award."[88] The FAA provides that a court "must" confirm an award upon a proper motion "unless the award is vacated, modified, or corrected" as provided in the statute.[89]

The court must give the consumer the opportunity to respond to a motion to confirm an award.[90] The deadline to file such an opposition to a motion to confirm varies by state and may be shorter than the deadline for responding to a regular civil complaint.[91]

The consumer should have a right to a hearing to oppose the motion.[92] The consumer must have received proper service concerning the confirmation proceeding,[93] and the

---

82 *See* National Consumer Law Center, Fair Debt Collection § 5.9 (5th ed. 2004 and Supp.).
   The Federal Trade Commission and numerous state unfair and deceptive practices (UDAP) cases have found it to be unfair and deceptive to bring consumer collection suits in inconvenient venues; also unfair are credit agreements that waive the consumer's right to a convenient venue. *See* National Consumer Law Center, Unfair and Deceptive Acts and Practices § 5.1 (6th ed. 2004 and Supp.).
83 *See* Patterson v. ITT Consumer Fin. Corp., 14 Cal. App. 4th 1659 (1993); Philyaw v. Platinum Enterprises, Inc., 54 Va. Cir. 364 (Va. Cir. Ct. 2001); *see also* Bailey v. Ameriquest Mortgage Co., 2002 WL 100391 (D. Minn. Jan. 23, 2002), *rev'd*, 346 F.3d 821 (8th Cir. 2003) (issues should first be presented to the arbitrator); Bolter v. Super. Ct., 87 Cal. App. 4th 900 (2001); Brower v. Gateway 2000, 246 A.D.2d 246, 676 N.Y.S.2d 569 (1998); *cf.* Bank v. Worldcom, Inc., 2002 N.Y. Misc. LEXIS 33 (Sup. Ct. Jan. 24, 2002).
84 Unif. Arbitration Act § 14 (1955); Unif. Arbitration Act § 25 (2000).
85 *See* Chauffers, Teamsters, Warehousemen and Helpers Local No. 135 v. Jefferson Trucking Co., 628 F.2d 1023 (7th Cir. 1980); MBNA Am. Bank v. Leslie, 2005 WL 2277252 (Conn. Super. Ct. Aug. 25, 2005); Bernstein v. Gramercy Mills, Inc., 452 N.E.2d 231 (Mass. App. Ct. 1983).

86 *See* Unif. Arbitration Act § 11 (1955); Unif. Arbitration Act § 22 (2000).
87 MBNA Am. Bank v. Gorman, 147 Cal. App. 4th Supp. 1 (2007).
88 Unif. Arbitration Act § 11 (1955); Unif. Arbitration Act § 22 (2000).
89 9 U.S.C. § 9.
90 *See, e.g.*, Vogt v. Liberty Mut. Fire Ins. Co., 900 A.2d 912 (Pa. Super. Ct. 2006).
91 *Compare* Cal. Civ. Proc. Code § 1290.6 (West) (providing ten days to respond to petition to confirm arbitration award) *with* Cal. Civ. Proc. Code § 412.20(3) (West) (providing thirty days to file answer to complaint).
92 MBNA Am. Bank v. McArdle, 2007 WL 1229214 (Ohio Ct. App. Apr. 27, 2007); MBNA Am. Bank v. Anthony, 2006 WL 1063752 (Ohio Ct. App. Apr. 18, 2005).
93 MBNA Am. Bank v. Dimario, 2006 WL 2349201 (Conn. Super.

§ 12.5.3   *Consumer Arbitration Agreements*

creditor must supply an affidavit that the debtor is not in the military[94] and must have also properly moved to seek confirmation. At least in some states it is not enough for the creditor to successfully resist the consumer's action to vacate the award—the creditor must also affirmatively move to confirm the award.[95]

12.5.3 Lack of Arbitration Agreement or Defective Arbitration Proceeding As Grounds to Oppose Confirmation

12.5.3.1 General

Important challenges to confirmation actions include whether there is a binding arbitration agreement allowing arbitration in the first place, and whether the arbitration proceeding was properly conducted. These are both grounds to vacate an award, as described in § 12.4.4, *supra*. As long as these challenges are timely brought, the consumer can raise either of these grounds for *vacatur* in response to the confirmation action. While one line of cases allows motions to vacate to be filed in response to a confirmation proceeding even after the time limits have expired,[96] most cases rule otherwise.[97] Because confirmation actions are invariably brought well over three months after the arbitration award, this is a significant impediment to bringing a motion to vacate in the confirmation proceeding.

The remainder of this subsection examines three ways in which the consumer can still raise, in the confirmation proceeding, substantive issues as to the existence or enforceability of an arbitration agreement or the nature of the arbitration proceeding and award, even well after the arbitration award is issued: (1) improper notice of the award means that the time period to vacate has not expired (thus allowing the consumer to raise the non-existence of an arbitration agreement or any other grounds to vacate); (2) lack of a binding arbitration agreement can be raised at any time because it goes to the court's jurisdiction; and (3) the creditor has not complied in the confirmation proceeding with state requirements including proof of the arbitration agreement and that the creditor owns the debt.

Section 12.5.4, *infra*, examines the effect on confirmation when the consumer objects to, or fails to participate in, the arbitration. Section 12.5.5, *infra*, considers certain defects in the confirmation application that may result in denial of that application.

12.5.3.2 Time Period to Vacate Does Not Start Running When Notice of Award Is Defective or Not Sent

Delivery to the consumer of the arbitration award triggers the running of the time period to move to vacate the award. Thus, a motion to vacate in a confirmation proceeding is timely if the consumer never received notice of the award. Furthermore, the burden is on the party claiming that *vacatur* is untimely to prove that the motion to vacate was not made within the ninety-day (or other applicable) time period, and therefore this party also has the burden of proving that notice of the award was delivered.[98]

The nature of the required notice is very different under the UAA (adopted in most states) than under the revised UAA (adopted in twelve states).[99] The UAA states: "[T]he award shall be in writing and signed by the arbitrators joining in the award. The arbitrators shall deliver a copy to each party personally or by registered mail, or as provided in the agreement."[100]

The UAA thus has two requirements, only the second of which can be altered "as provided in the agreement." The first requirement is that the arbitrator sign a written award and deliver a copy of the award to the consumer. (The "or as provided in the agreement" language modifies the mode of delivery and not the requirement that the arbitrator deliver the award.) The second requirement is that delivery be personally or by registered mail, or as provided in the agreement.

In the typical NAF documentary hearing, the arbitrator mails the award to the NAF director of arbitration. The NAF

Ct. Aug. 2, 2006); Cavalry Investments, L.L.C. v. Grasson, 2005 WL 2981691 (Conn. Super. Ct. Oct. 19, 2005); Vogt v. Liberty Mut. Fire Ins. Co., 900 A.2d 912 (Pa. Super. Ct. 2006).

94 MBNA Am. Bank v. Nelson, 15 Misc. 3d 1148(A) (Civ. Ct. 2007) (table).

95 MBNA Am. Bank v. Mackey, 343 F. Supp. 2d 966 (W.D. Wash. 2004). *But see, e.g.*, Mass. Gen. Laws ch. 251, § 12(d) (if application to vacate is denied, the court shall confirm the award).

96 *See* Paul Allison v. Minkin Storage of Omaha, Inc., 452 F. Supp. 573 (D. Neb. 1978); Riko Enterprises, Inc. v. Seattle Supersonics Corp., 357 F. Supp. 521 (S.D.N.Y. 1973); Milwaukee Police Ass'n v. City of Milwaukee, 285 N.W.2d 119 (Wis. 1979).

97 *See, e.g.*, MBNA Am. Bank v. Leslie, 2005 WL 2277252 (Conn. Super. Ct. Aug. 25, 2005); Kutch v. State Farm Mut. Auto. Ins. Co., 960 P.2d 93 (Colo. 1998); Walter A. Brown Inc. v. Moylan, 509 A.2d 98 (D.C. 1986); Broward County Paraprofessional Ass'n v. Sch. Bd. of Broward County, 406 So. 2d 1252, 1253 (Fla. Dist. Ct. App. 1981); MBNA Am. Bank v. Tackleson, 720 N.W.2d 192 (Iowa Ct. App. 2006) (table) (text available at 2006 WL 1229935); Local 589, Amalgamated Transit Union v. Mass. Bay Transp. Auth., 491 N.E.2d 1053 (Mass. App. Ct. 1986); MBNA Am. Bank v. Belleleslie, 2005 Mont. Dist. LEXIS 1119 (Mont. Dist. Ct. Apr. 26, 2005); MBNA Am. Bank v. Cooper, 2006 WL 1519640 (Ohio Ct. App. June 5, 2006); Burst v. MBNA Am. Bank, 2005 Tex. App. LEXIS 3461 (Tex. App. May 5, 2005).

98 MBNA Am. Bank v. Barben, 111 P.3d 663 (Kan. Ct. App. 2005) (table) (text available at 2005 WL 1214244); NCO Portfolio Mgmt. v. Williams, 2006 WL 2939712 (Ohio Ct. App. Oct. 13, 2006).

99 *See* § 11.2.2, *supra*.

100 Unif. Arbitration Act § 8(a) (1955).

then mails notice of the award to the parties. The notice also must include the actual award, not the NAF's summary or translation of the award.

It appears that the arbitrator must also deliver the award directly to the consumer, and not send the award to someone else, who then delivers the award to the consumer.[101] At least one court has noted that NAF's method of delivering awards to consumers may fall short of compliance with its own rules: "The award identifies Larry Rute as the arbitrator, but he makes no certification or acknowledgment of service in the form. We question whether delivery by the [NAF] Director of Arbitration fulfills the arbitrator's duty to deliver a copy of the Award."[102]

Moreover, NAF awards state that the award has been "duly entered and delivered to the parties on this date," followed by the date of the award. One court noted that such a statement is "patently false" in the case of a document hearing, because the consumer was not present on that date and the award was mailed to the director of arbitration and only then mailed to the consumer.[103] Thus any notice was delivered at some later date, not on the date of the award. If nothing else, the date an award is entered should not be considered evidence of when the NAF delivered it.

As for the form of delivery, in collection arbitrations, the award is almost never delivered personally or by registered mail. So the question is whether an alternative form of delivery is "provided in the agreement." Typical creditor arbitration agreements do not specify an alternative form of delivery but will specify that the arbitration will be administered by the NAF or pursuant to NAF rules, usually those in effect at the time of the arbitration. NAF rules permit delivery by U.S. mail,[104] and courts in other contexts have generally held that the rules of an arbitration provider specified in an agreement are deemed to be incorporated by reference into the contract.[105] A court may hold that incorporation of such rules in this context is sufficient. On the other hand, there is an argument that a reference to NAF rules is too attenuated and thus insufficient to show that the alternative form of delivery is "provided in the agreement."[106] This is especially true because a consumer would have to first note NAF Rule 39(D), which then refers the consumer to Rule 2(M).

The revised UAA dramatically loosens the UAA notice requirement, making it much more difficult to challenge the arbitrator's notice of the award. The revised UAA requires that the arbitrator or arbitration organization give notice of the award, including a copy of the award.[107] Notice is "taking action that is reasonably necessary to inform the other person in ordinary course, whether or not the other person acquires knowledge of the notice."[108] Even the signature requirement is loosened, allowing the arbitrator to make a "record" of an award, that is "signed or otherwise authenticated by an arbitrator who concurs with the award."[109]

12.5.3.3 Time Limits May Not Apply to Challenges to the Existence or Enforceability of the Arbitration Agreement

As § 12.4.4.2, *supra*, explains, lack of an enforceable arbitration agreement is a basis on which to vacate an award. But a growing number of courts have held that the consumer may seek to oppose confirmation of an award even if the deadline for seeking *vacatur* has passed.[110] According to the First Circuit:

---

101 MBNA Am. Bank v. Barben, 111 P.3d 663 (Kan. Ct. App. 2005) (table) (text available at 2005 WL 1214244).
102 *Id.*
103 *Id.*
104 Nat'l Arbitration Forum, Code of Procedure, Rules 39(D), 2(M) (reprinted in Appx. B.2.1, *infra*).
105 *See, e.g.*, Val-U Constr. Co. v. Rosebud Sioux Tribe, 146 F.3d 573 (8th Cir. 1998) (*ex parte* arbitration award enforceable when contract incorporated AAA rules that allow an arbitration hearing to proceed in a party's absence if that party is given notice of the hearing and an opportunity to have it postponed).
106 *See* MBNA Am. Bank v. Credit, 132 P.3d 898 (Kan. Ct. App. 2006); MBNA Am. Bank v. Barben, 111 P.3d 663 (Kan. Ct. App. 2005) (table) (text available at 2005 WL 1214244).
107 Unif. Arbitration Act § 19(a) (2000).
108 Unif. Arbitration Act § 2(a) (2000).
109 Unif. Arbitration Act § 19(a) (2000).
110 *See* MCI Telecommunications Corp. v. Exalon Indus., Inc., 138 F.3d 426 (1st Cir. 1998); Danner v. MBNA Am. Bank, 2007 WL 1219747 (Ark. Apr. 26, 2007); MBNA v. Boata, 2007 WL 2089678 (Conn. July 31, 2007); CACV of Colo., L.L.C. v. Corda, 2005 WL 3664087 (Conn. Super. Ct. Dec. 16, 2005) (in five related cases declining to confirm awards against consumers when the bank failed to present sufficient evidence that a valid agreement to arbitrate existed); MBNA Am. Bank v. Credit, 132 P.3d 898 (Kan. Ct. App. 2006); Arrow Overall Supply Co. v. Peloquin Enterprises, 323 N.W.2d 1 (Mich. 1982); MBNA v. Forsmark, 2005 WL 2401444 (Mich. Ct. App. Sept. 29, 2005); Bank of Am. v. Dahlquist, 2007 WL 404471 (Mont. Feb. 7, 2007); MBNA Am. Bank v. Cornock, No. 03-C-0018 (N.H. Super. Ct. Mar. 20, 2007), *available at* www.consumerlaw.org/unreported; *In re* Matarasso, 56 N.Y.2d 264 (1982); MBNA Am. Bank v. Nelson, 15 Misc. 3d 1148(A) (Civ. Ct. 2007) (table); MBNA Am. Bank v. Straub, 815 N.Y.S.2d 450 (Civ. Ct. 2006); Worldwide Asset Purchasing, L.L.C. v. Karafotias, 801 N.Y.S.2d 721 (Civ. Ct. 2005); MBNA Am. Bank v. Engen, 128 Wash. App. 1050 (2005) (allowing the consumer to contest an arbitration award after the award was confirmed when the consumer alleged no arbitration agreement); *see also* MBNA Am. Bank v. Gorman, 147 Cal. App. 4th Supp. 1 (2007) (while appellate court did not address the issue, the trial court had denied confirmation because no enforceable arbitration agreement existed, even though time to vacate the award had elapsed); *cf.* Dewitt v. Collins, 2004 WL 102514 (Mich. Ct. App. Jan. 22, 2004) (certain situations allow the consumer to challenge the confirmation beyond the time period, but not allowed in other situations). *But see* Webb v. MBNA Am. Bank, 2005 WL 2648019 (E.D. Ark. Oct. 13, 2005); MBNA Am. Bank v. Swartz, 2006 WL 1071523 (Del. Ch. Ct.

We find no indication that Congress intended for a party to be found to have waived the argument that there was no written agreement to arbitrate if that party failed to raise the argument within the time period established by section 12. . . . We thus conclude that, as a general matter, section 12, as well as section 2 and the other enforcement provisions of the FAA, do not come into play unless there is a written agreement to arbitrate. Thus, if there is no such agreement, the actions of the arbitrator have no legal validity. It follows that one is not required to mount a collateral challenge to such an ineffectual action, for if the agreement to arbitrate does not exist, there is no obligation to arbitrate—and a noncontracting person's failure to appear at the arbitration hearing does not create such an obligation. . . . A party that contends that it is not bound by an agreement to arbitrate can therefore simply abstain from participation in the proceedings, and raise the inexistence of a written contractual agreement to arbitrate as a defense to a proceeding seeking confirmation of the arbitration award, without the limitations contained in section 12, which are only applicable to those bound by a written agreement to arbitrate.[111]

One basis for arguing that the lack of a binding arbitration agreement can be raised in the confirmation proceeding irrespective of any time limits to seek to vacate is that this issue goes to the subject matter jurisdiction of the arbitrator, a defense that, under state law, can be raised at any time, even in the confirmation hearing after the deadline to vacate the award has passed.[112] In addition, some state arbitration statutes require the party seeking confirmation to file a copy of the arbitration agreement, the award, and other documents, implicitly conditioning confirmation on the existence of an enforceable agreement.[113] Failure to do so results in dismissal, although perhaps not dismissal with prejudice.[114]

Protecting the right to challenge the existence of the arbitration agreement at any time benefits creditors as well as alleged debtors. In several recent cases consumers have been persuaded by debt counselors that they should file arbitration proceedings with providers not specified in the creditor's arbitration agreement. These alternative providers charge the consumer a fee and typically issue an award on behalf of the consumer voiding the alleged debt. When the consumer seeks to confirm such an award in court, creditors have argued that the award is unenforceable, because the arbitrator had no jurisdiction to decide the dispute. For example, the Montana Supreme Court found that a credit card issuer could challenge confirmation of an award made by an arbitration service provider not specified in the arbitration agreement, even though the ninety-day period had lapsed for the card issuer to object.[115] The award was invalid *ab initio*.

There is another reason why consumers must be able to vacate an award in a confirmation proceeding after the time period to seek to vacate would appear to have elapsed. As explained in § 12.4.2, *supra*, the time period to seek to vacate an award begins when the consumer has proper notice of the award. The UAA provides for proper notice by delivery by the arbitrator personally or by registered mail or "as provided in the agreement."[116] NAF arbitration awards are typically not delivered personally or by registered mail, and instead rely on the "as provided in the agreement" language. To argue that notice can instead be provided by using a different method, as specified in the agreement, presupposes the existence of an agreement. A challenge to the enforceability of the arbitration agreement is challenging the very existence of an enforceable agreement to modify the notice requirement. Thus the enforceability challenge can be recast as simply arguing that the consumer did not receive proper notice of the award and thus still can seek to vacate the award. When notice was not delivered personally or by registered mail, a court thus must first determine if there is an enforceable agreement before it determines whether such a challenge is timely.[117] If it finds there is no

---

Apr. 13, 2006); MBNA Am. Bank v. Saleba, 69 Mass. App. Ct. 1102 (2007); MBNA Am. Bank v. Hart, 710 N.W.2d 125 (N.D. 2006); CACV v. Kogler, 2006 WL 2790398 (Ohio Ct. App. Sept. 29, 2006) (but Ohio also requires that the creditor file a copy of the arbitration agreement as a precondition to confirmation); Brust v. MBNA Am. Bank, 2005 WL 1047583 (Tex. App. June 2, 2005).

111 MCI Telecommunications Corp. v. Exalon Indus., Inc., 138 F.3d 426 (1st Cir. 1998).

112 MBNA v. Boata, 2007 WL 2089678 (Conn. July 31, 2007); MBNA Am. Bank v. Credit, 132 P.3d 898 (Kan. Ct. App. 2006); Bank of Am. v. Dahlquist, 2007 WL 404471 (Mont. Feb. 7, 2007).

113 *See* Ohio Rev. Code Ann. § 2711.14 (West).

114 *See, e.g.*, Worldwide Asset Purchasing, L.L.C. v. Karafotias, 801 N.Y.S.2d 721 (Civ. Ct. 2005) (denying motion to confirm arbitration award "in the absence of any evidentiary proof in admissible form to support confirmation of the award," but granting petitioner leave to renew); MBNA v. Berlin, 2005 WL 3193850, at *2 (Ohio Ct. App. Nov. 30, 2005) (trial court did not err by dismissing creditor's petition to confirm when credi-

tor failed to include appropriate documentation but did err in dismissing the application with prejudice).

115 Bank of Am. v. Dahlquist, 2007 WL 404471 (Mont. Feb. 7, 2007) (when procedure outlined in the parties' arbitration agreement for selecting an arbitrator is not followed, a party is not required to challenge the resulting arbitration award within the FAA's ninety-day time limitation because it is void *ab initio*); *see also* Buczek v. Trans Union L.L.C., 2006 WL 3666635, at *2 (S.D. Fla. Nov. 9, 2006) (dismissing consumer's argument that debt had been eliminated by arbitration award, when the agreement with the creditor had not provided for arbitration; award was "of no force and effect"); *cf.* MBNA v. Bodalia, 2006 WL 1793211 (Ala. Civ. App. June 30, 2006) (granting MBNA's motion to vacate award issued by alternative service provider). *But see* Citibank v. Wood, 862 N.E.2d 576 (Ohio Ct. App. 2006).

116 Unif. Arbitration Act §§ 8(a), 12(b) (1955).

117 MBNA Am. Bank v. Credit, 132 P.3d 898 (Kan. Ct. App. 2006).

enforceable agreement, then the challenge to the agreement's enforceability is not time-barred (because the award was never properly delivered), and the award must be vacated.[118]

12.5.3.4 Creditor's Failure to Produce Arbitration Agreement and Any Applicable Assignment

Some states or state courts require that the creditor produce the arbitration agreement as a precondition to confirmation. As this requirement is an affirmative one for the creditor, the consumer need not move to vacate and there is no issue as to the time period to seek to vacate expiring; the creditor must comply whenever it brings a confirmation action.

For example, Connecticut and Ohio require the party seeking confirmation of an award to file a copy of the arbitration agreement, the award, and other documents.[119] When the application for confirmation is not accompanied by all the required documentation, it must be dismissed, although perhaps not dismissed with prejudice.[120] On the other hand, if such documentation is presented, the burden may shift to the consumer to challenge that evidence.[121]

Courts should require the creditor to produce the contract, any applicable assignment of the contract, and the arbitration agreement,[122] or simply demand to see the documentation.[123] For example, a New York court has laid out the requirements that should be met before a court can confirm an MBNA/NAF award, under either New York law or the FAA:

(1) A written agreement to arbitrate must be included with the petition to confirm.
(2) The bank must establish that the credit card agreement—and the arbitration clause in it—are binding on the cardholder (an affidavit by a person with personal knowledge and the relevant supporting documents will suffice).
(3) The bank must show that the notice of arbitration was properly served, either as provided under state law or as provided in the arbitration agreement.
(4) The court must take into account issues such as whether the petition to confirm/vacate is timely and whether a court previously compelled the arbitration.[124]

Other courts have said it is not enough for the attorney to state on information and belief that the arbitration agreement exists.[125]

An assignee of the original creditor must provide proof of assignment of that particular account. It is not enough that the assignee show that there has been a general assignment; rather, a clear assignment chain for the particular account must be shown between the original creditor and the company seeking the confirmation. Furthermore it is not enough that the arbitrator issued the award to that party, thereby assuming a proper assignment.[126]

12.5.4 Effect on Confirmation When Consumer Objects to, or Fails to Participate in, Arbitration

The implications of participating in, objecting to, or simply ignoring arbitration proceedings need to be considered, and these effects vary by jurisdiction. A consumer who participates in an arbitration proceeding without objecting to the arbitrator's jurisdiction risks that a court will find that she has waived the right to argue, in opposing confirmation of an award, that she is not bound by the arbitration clause.[127] Thus if the consumer does participate in the arbitration proceeding, it is important to make it clear that the consumer is doing so only under protest, and that she disputes that she is bound by an agreement to arbitrate.[128] In

---

118 MBNA Am. Bank v. Credit, 132 P.3d 898 (Kan. Ct. App. 2006).
119 Conn. Gen. Stat. § 52-421(a); Ohio Rev. Code Ann. § 2711.14 (West).
120 MBNA Am. Bank v. Berlin, 2005 WL 3193850 (Ohio Ct. App. Nov. 30, 2005) (strict compliance is required as a matter of subject matter jurisdiction).
121 See MBNA Am. Bank v. O'Brien, 858 N.E.2d 1220 (Ohio Ct. App. 2006) (*pro se* consumer apparently did not present any evidence challenging documentation).
122 MBNA Am. Bank v. Straub, 815 N.Y.S.2d 450, 452–457 (Civ. Ct. 2006); Worldwide Asset Purchasing v. Karafotias, 801 N.Y.S.2d 721 (Civ. Ct. 2005). *But see* Parks v. MBNA, 204 S.W.3d 305 (Mo. Ct. App. 2006) (burden is on the consumer to first allege that there is no binding arbitration agreement).
123 See MBNA Am Bank v. Swartz, 2006 WL 1071523 (Del. Ch. Ct. Apr. 13, 2006); *cf.* MBNA Am. Bank v. Boyce, 723 N.W.2d 449 (Iowa Ct. App. 2006) (trial court had dismissed ten MBNA motions to confirm when MBNA had not produced a written agreement to arbitrate; the appellate court overturned these rulings when the consumers had never opposed the confirmation proceedings).

124 MBNA Am. Bank v. Straub, 815 N.Y.S.2d 450, 452–457 (Civ. Ct. 2006); *see also* MBNA Am. Bank v. Nelson, 15 Misc. 3d 1148(A) (Civ. Ct. 2007) (table); Citibank v. Martin, 807 N.Y.S.2d 284 (Civ. Ct. 2005) (setting forth the levels of proof required to support summary judgment on question of whether debtor owes debt).
125 Worldwide Asset Purchasing v. Karafotias, 801 N.Y.S.2d 721 (Civ. Ct. 2005).
126 *Id.*
127 *See, e.g.*, Garner v. MBNA, 2006 WL 2354939 (N.D. Tex. Aug. 14, 2006); Webb v. MBNA, 2006 WL 618186 (E.D. Ark. Mar. 10, 2006) (compelling arbitration of Fair Debt Collection Practices Act case when consumer had previously participated in arbitration of debt collection case initiated by a buyer of an MBNA debt); MBNA Am. Bank v. Saleba, 69 Mass. App. Ct. 1102 (2007).
128 *See, e.g.*, MBNA Am. Bank v. Felton, 2004 WL 2898632 (Conn. Super. Ct. Nov. 8, 2004); MBNA Am. Bank v. Barben,

most jurisdictions raising this objection before the arbitrator should be sufficient to preserve the argument, and the consumer need not also raise this objection by seeking a stay of arbitration in a court proceeding.[129]

Courts in some jurisdictions have held, in various ways, that an award obtained without the participation of the consumer cannot be confirmed. The UAA, revised UAA, and the FAA all provide that a party can go to court to compel the other party to submit to arbitration.[130] A number of courts find this procedure to be the proper one to follow when the consumer does not willingly participate in the collection using arbitration.

In Pennsylvania arbitration awards obtained without the consumer's participation cannot be judicially confirmed. In *Bank One Delaware v. Mitchell*, a Pennsylvania trial court held that, if a creditor proceeds to arbitration without the consumer's participation, and without a court's determination that the arbitration clause is valid, the creditor cannot later obtain judicial confirmation of the award.[131] Rather, if the consumer does not participate, the creditor must bring a court action to obtain an order that the arbitration clause applies to the dispute and that the consumer must arbitrate the dispute. The *Mitchell* court viewed the motion to compel arbitration as the proper procedure to follow if one party does not participate; the alternative procedure specified by the NAF rules, of going forward without both parties, was found to be invalid, because there was no jurisdiction to proceed.

After *Mitchell*, the Pennsylvania Supreme Court codified this requirement in the state's Rules of Civil Procedure.[132] A creditor can seek to confirm an award in Pennsylvania only if the consumer either attended a hearing before an arbitrator or signed a writing after the claim was filed agreeing to submit the claim to an arbitrator. If not, the creditor must have first obtained a court order compelling the consumer to proceed to arbitration, pursuant to procedures also spelled out in the rules.[133] The motion to confirm the award must contain factual allegations that the motion complies with these requirements.[134] In Virginia some courts have held that an award obtained without the consumer's participating in a hearing cannot be confirmed.[135]

Courts in other jurisdictions have held that, if the consumer *objects* to arbitration, the creditor must get a court order compelling arbitration if the consumer fails to participate. The Kansas Supreme Court and the Kentucky Court of Appeals have both held that, because any challenge to the existence of a valid agreement to arbitrate must be decided by a court, a cardholder's objection to arbitration triggers the creditor's responsibility to seek court intervention to compel arbitration.[136] On this basis, the courts refused to confirm an award issued in an arbitration proceeding that was conducted over the cardholder's objection.

12.5.5 Defects in the Form of the Confirmation Proceeding

12.5.5.1 Creditor's Petition to Confirm Is Untimely

There is much confusion as to when a creditor must file a confirmation action. Under the FAA[137] and several state statutes,[138] the deadline is one year from delivery of the award. California has a four-year limit.[139] Neither the revised UAA nor the UAA sets a time limit to confirm an award. An Indiana appellate court has decided to use the FAA's one-year time period when the Indiana arbitration procedures (based on the UAA) do not specify a time limit, even though the general limitations period to collect a debt in Indiana is much longer.[140] The revised UAA commentary states that states should use their general statute of limitations for the filing and execution of a judgment in a state.[141]

There is similar confusion as to the consequences of a creditor failing to meet the applicable deadline. It would appear in most states that the confirmation action will be dismissed as untimely.[142] Some states allow the creditor to bring a common law action to collect on the arbitration

---

128 111 P.3d 663 (Kan. Ct. App. 2005) (table) (text available at 2005 WL 1214244).
129 Holcim (Tex.) Ltd. P'ship v. Humboldt Wedag, Inc., 211 S.W.3d 796 (Tex. App. 2006). *But see* Garner v. MBNA Am. Bank., 2006 WL 2354939 (N.D. Tex. Aug. 14, 2006).
130 9 U.S.C. § 4; Unif. Arbitration Act UAA § 2 (1955); Unif. Arbitration Act § 7 (2000).
131 Bank One Del. v. Mitchell, 70 Pa. D. & C.4th 353 (C.P. 2005), *aff'd sub nom.* Bank One v. Mitchell, 897 A.2d 512 (Pa. 2006) (table).
132 Pa. R. Civ. P. 1326–1331.
133 Pa. R. Civ. P. 1327.
134 Pa. R. Civ. P. 1328(c).
135 *E.g.*, CACV v. Rubin, No. GV06-004208-00 (Va. Dist. Ct. Apr. 21, 2006).
136 MBNA Am. Bank v. Credit, 132 P.3d 898, 901 (Kan. 2006); Fischer v. MBNA, 2007 WL 779295 (Ky. Ct. App. Mar. 16, 2007).
137 9 U.S.C. § 9.
138 *See, e.g.*, Conn. Gen. Stat. § 52-417; N.Y. C.P.L.R. 7510 (McKinney); Ohio Rev. Code Ann. § 2711.09 (West); *see also* MBNA Am. Bank v. Terry, 2006 WL 513952 (Ohio Ct. App. Mar. 3, 2006).
139 Cal. Civ. Proc. Code § 1288 (West).
140 MBNA Am. Bank v. Rogers, 838 N.E.2d 475 (Ind. Ct. App. 2005).
141 Unif. Arbitration Act § 22 cmt. 2 (2000).
142 *See* MBNA Am. Bank v. Rogers, 838 N.E.2d 475 (Ind. Ct. App. 2005) (dismissing petition to confirm as untimely: "Having elected the benefits of the streamlined summary proceeding, MBNA may not complain that the limited time to preserve the arbitration award for later enforcement in a court of law deprives it of the applicable statute of limitations for the commencement of an action."); MBNA Am. Bank v. Terry, 2006 WL 513952 (Ohio Ct. App. Mar. 3, 2006). *See generally* § 11.2.3.2, *supra*.

award,[143] but in that case the consumer should be able to raise all available substantive defenses and counterclaims, and will not be limited to the statutory *vacatur* grounds.

12.5.5.2 Creditor Filed Petition to Confirm in the Wrong Court

The consumer can object to the creditor's choice of court and venue for the confirmation proceeding. As described in § 11.2.1, *supra*, there is almost never federal jurisdiction to confirm a consumer collection action. Any confirmation action brought in federal court without an independent basis for federal jurisdiction will be dismissed.[144] Moreover not all courts in a state will be authorized by the state to hear confirmation proceedings.[145]

The confirmation action should be brought in state court in the state of the consumer's residence. Any attempt to confirm the award other than in the state where the consumer resides will run afoul of the federal Fair Debt Collection Practices Act (FDCPA),[146] the Federal Trade Commission Act, and state deceptive practices (UDAP) law.[147] Consumer attorneys sometimes note NAF's address in Minnesota and question whether it is proper for an arbitration award in Minnesota to be confirmed in another state. But typically the arbitration proceeding is administered from Minnesota, but any in-person hearing will take place in the state of the consumer's residence.

The UAA and revised UAA allow creditors to seek to confirm awards in a court specified in the arbitration agreement, the court in the county where the award was made, or a court in the county where the consumer resides.[148] Because arbitration agreements will rarely specify a particular court, proper venue will generally be in the county where the consumer resides.

In addition, the FDCPA allows an attorney to bring an action to collect on a consumer debt only in the judicial district where the consumer signed the contract or presently resides.[149] If the case is brought elsewhere in the state, the attorney is liable under the FDCPA.[150] Even in cases brought when the FDCPA does not apply (such as when the creditor is the claimant), UDAP precedent indicates it is unfair to bring a consumer collection action in a distant venue.[151]

In the rare case in which federal court jurisdiction is proper, the FAA and FDCPA will determine venue. The FAA states that, if no court is specified in the agreement, then application to confirm the award must be sought in the federal district court where the award was made.[152] The United States Supreme Court has held that venue is proper either in the district where the award was made or in any district proper under the general venue statute.[153] But the FDCPA requires the action to be brought in the county where the consumer resides, and this more specific requirement should control.

12.5.5.3 Seeking an Amount in Excess of the Award

A confirmation application should only seek to confirm the exact amount of the arbitration award. There is no statutory authority for a court to confirm anything other than the award, such as interest that might accrue after the award. Any attempt to confirm a larger amount should be dismissed. If state procedure allows the creditor in the same proceeding to confirm the arbitration amount and seek additional recovery, then the consumer should have all available substantive defenses and counterclaims to that additional amount.

12.5.5.4 Other Requirements for Confirmation

In New York, a corporation seeking to confirm the award must plead that it is a corporation authorized to do business in New York, and provide proof to that effect.[154] Actions

---

143 *See* § 11.2.3.2, *supra*; *see also* MBNA Am. Bank v. Canfora, 2007 WL 2318095 (Ohio Ct. App. Aug. 15, 2007).

144 *See* Austin v. MBNA Am., 2006 WL 3496655 (M.D. Ala. Dec. 4, 2006); Watson v. MBNA Am. Bank, 2005 WL 1875778 (W.D.N.C. Aug. 1, 2005); Garcia v. MBNA Am. Bank, 2005 WL 1653639 (D. Or. July 6, 2005); Stafford v. Chase Manhattan Bank U.S.A., 2005 WL 1330874 (M.D.N.C. June 3, 2005); Miles v. MBNA Am. Bank, 2005 WL 1220842 (E.D. Wash. May 23, 2005); Fischer v. MBNA Am. Bank, 2005 WL 1168388 (W.D. Ky. May 17, 2005); Mesdag v. MBNA Am. Bank, 2005 WL 418549 (D. Or. Feb. 17, 2005); Mellado v. MBNA Am. Bank, 2004 WL 2937224 (N.D. Tex. Dec. 17, 2004); Kearns v. MBNA Am. Bank, 2004 WL 2512742 (N.D. Tex. Nov. 5, 2004); MBNA Am. Bank v. Shnitzer, 2004 WL 1717670 (D. Or. July 30, 2004).

145 *See* MBNA Am. Bank v. Bodalia, 949 So. 2d 935 (Ala. Civ. App. 2006); MBNA Am. Bank v. Torchia, Nos. 0442CV0163, 0442CV0164 (Mass. Dist. Ct. Jan. 14, 2005), *available at* www.consumerlaw.org/unreported; MBNA Am. Bank v. Coe, 770 N.Y.S.2d 588 (City Ct. 2003).

146 15 U.S.C. § 1692i.

147 National Consumer Law Center, Unfair and Deceptive Acts and Practices § 5.1.1.4 (6th ed. 2004 and Supp.).

148 Unif. Arbitration Act § 18 (1955); Unif. Arbitration Act § 27 (2000).

149 15 U.S.C. § 1692i.

150 *See* § 12.7.3, *infra*.

151 National Consumer Law Center, Unfair and Deceptive Acts and Practices § 5.1.1.4 (6th ed. 2004 and Supp.); *see also* Barquis v. Merchants Collection Ass'n, 7 Cal. 3d 94 (1972); Yu v. Signet Bank/Virginia, 69 Cal. App. 4th 1377 (1999).

152 9 U.S.C. § 9.

153 Cortez Byrd Chips, Inc. v. Bill Harbert Constr. Co., 529 U.S. 193, 120 S. Ct. 1331, 146 L. Ed. 2d 171 (2000).

154 MBNA Am. Bank v. Nelson, 15 Misc. 3d 1148(A) (Civ. Ct. 2007) (table); *cf.* MBNA Am. Bank v. McArdle, 2007 WL 1229214 (Ohio Ct. App. Apr. 27, 2007) (while a foreign cor-

brought in the name "MBNA" are suspect because on June 10, 2006, MBNA changed its name to FIA Card Services.[155] A New York court has also stated that the creditor must produce proof of timely notice to the consumer of the arbitration hearing.[156]

12.6 What If a Default Has Already Been Entered in the Confirmation Proceeding?

If the consumer has already defaulted in the confirmation proceeding, state rules similar to Federal Rule of Civil Procedure 60 allow the consumer to seek to re-open the confirmation proceeding even well after it has been held. The court can relieve the consumer of the judgment as long as the motion is made within a reasonable time, the consumer has a colorable defense, and the consumer has a good excuse for having failed to defend in a timely manner.

12.7 Affirmative Challenges to Debt Collection Practices Related to the Arbitration

12.7.1 Potential Defendants

Creditor use of arbitration to collect debts naturally leads to the question whether any conduct in connection with that arbitration process violates federal or state debt collection law. It is important to understand the status of various potential defendants, because available claims will vary depending on the nature of the defendant.

One type of party is the originating creditor, such as MBNA. That creditor can then sell the debt to a debt purchaser, who may purchase the debt before the consumer's default or, more commonly for credit card debt, after the default. The arbitration to collect on the debt can be in the name of any of these creditors, but the creditor can also hire various parties to handle the arbitration process, such as a collection law firm, collection agency, or process server.

The arbitration agreement will specify an arbitration service provider to administer the arbitration, such as the NAF, and the arbitration will be conducted by an arbitrator from the service provider's panel. In general there will be arbitral immunity for both the arbitrator and the arbitration service provider, at least as to their conduct of the arbitration proceeding.[157] They may face liability for breach of contract or for deceptive advertising, and the like, however.[158]

12.7.2 Practices Subject to Challenge

Almost any deceptive, unfair, or oppressive collection tactic in connection with a debt collection arbitration is potentially subject to challenge. Thus it should be actionable if a creditor or collector threaten to collect using an arbitration proceeding if there is no intent to follow through with that threat.[159] Nevertheless, filing for arbitration is relatively inexpensive and it may be difficult to prove that this threat is false. Of course, the threat is deceptive if the creditor has no right to proceed to arbitration, either because there is no agreement to arbitrate such disputes or because the agreement is not enforceable. In a recent case an action was allowed to proceed against MBNA's attorney, when that attorney brought an arbitration collection action on behalf of MBNA after MBNA had sold the debt to another creditor.[160] Similarly, the threat is deceptive if the creditor never proceeds to arbitration for that class of debts.

In addition, whether before or after the creditor or collector obtains an arbitration award, it is deceptive for a creditor or collector to imply that it can immediately seek to garnish wages or seize property based on the arbitration award.[161] Instead, the creditor must first confirm the award, and only then seek such post-judicial remedies based on the judgment obtained confirming the order. It should also be deceptive for a creditor or collector to imply that it will confirm any arbitration award resulting from an arbitration collection proceeding, if in fact it has no intent to confirm such an award.

A recent action certified in part as a class action alleges that the law firm Wolpoff & Abramson, as a collection attorney for MBNA, misrepresented the character, amount or legal status of debts, threatened action that cannot be taken or was not intended to be taken, and used deceptive representations to collect a debt.[162] The plaintiffs argued, among other things, that notices sent to consumers at least until 2005 stated that "unless you have agreed otherwise, an In-person Participatory Hearing will be held in the Judicial District where you reside," when in fact documentary hear-

---

poration in Ohio cannot seek confirmation of an award unless it has a license to transact business in the state, this requirement does not apply to a national bank).

155 See § 12.1, supra.
156 Worldwide Asset Purchasing v. Karafotias, 801 N.Y.S.2d 721 (Civ. Ct. 2005).
157 See § 11.6, supra; see also Park v. Columbia Credit Services, Inc., 2007 WL 1847142 (W.D. Mo. June 25, 2007) (arbitrator has immunity even when consumer challenges authority of arbitrator to hear the proceeding).
158 See § 11.6, supra.
159 National Consumer Law Center, Fair Debt Collection § 5.5.2.8 (5th ed. 2004 and Supp.).
160 Kelly v. Wolpoff & Abramson, L.L.P., 2007 WL 2381536 (D. Colo. Aug. 17, 2007).
161 See Worch v. Wolpoff & Abramson, L.L.P., 477 F. Supp. 2d 1015 (E.D. Mo. 2007) (allowing the allegation to go to trial).
162 Karnette v. Wolpoff & Abramson, L.L.P., 2007 WL 922288 (E.D. Va. Mar. 23, 2007).

ings were always held unless the consumer affirmatively requested a participatory hearing.

Another potential claim might involve arbitrations being brought by attorneys not admitted to practice in the state where the consumer resides. Although the parties to an arbitration do not have to be represented by attorneys, state law may prohibit attorneys from appearing if not admitted in that state.

12.7.3 The Federal Fair Debt Collection Practices Act

The FDCPA does not apply to creditors collecting their own debts, but only to collection agencies, collection attorneys, and those purchasing a debt after the consumer's default.[163] As such, the Act applies to threats or other deceptive conduct made by an attorney, collection agency, or credit card debt buyer.[164] But the Act does not apply to MBNA or other credit card issuers.[165] While abusive and harassing behavior of an individual hired to personally serve the arbitration notice to the consumer may be actionable under state law,[166] at least one court has found that that person is not covered by the FDCPA.[167]

The FDCPA prohibits unfair and deceptive conduct generally, enumerates a number of prohibited practices, and establishes a number of other requirements, such as notice of verification rights. If the potential defendant is within the scope of the Act, then the Act should be able to remedy most forms of collection abuse involved in the arbitration proceeding.

The FDCPA provides for actual damages, plus statutory damages of up to $1000 and attorney fees.[168] Class actions may be brought under the Act. A recent example is the partial class certification in *Karnette v. Wolpoff & Abramson, L.L.P.*,[169] an action brought on behalf of Virginia consumers against the law firm routinely utilized by MBNA in its collection using arbitration.

12.7.4 State Law Claims

Even if not covered by the FDCPA, deceptive collection practices by employees of the creditor initiating the debt (such as MBNA or another credit card issuer) should be actionable under state debt collection or deceptive practices laws, and perhaps even as a tort.[170] Even if the FDCPA applies to a potential defendant, it still may be preferable to bring only state law claims if state court is viewed as a more favorable forum than federal court. For example, when the consumer's collection harassment claim may be forced into arbitration, state courts are often more receptive to claims that the arbitration requirement is unconscionable.

12.7.5 Must the Consumer's Debt Harassment Claim Be Sent to Arbitration?

In response to a consumer's affirmative court action claiming debt collection abuse related to debt collection arbitration, the defendant may attempt to compel arbitration, arguing that it is included within the creditor's arbitration clause. A consumer may oppose arbitration of such a claim on several grounds.

First, the language of the arbitration clause may indicate that the clause is applicable only to certain parties, and thus not applicable to others, such as collection attorneys or collection agencies. Courts have interpreted MBNA's clause as not applying to collection attorneys and collectors unless the collector is named as a co-defendant with MBNA.[171] Likewise, it is unclear whether attorneys and third-party collection agencies are "agents" of MBNA (thus falling within the arbitration clause's language) or whether they are independent contractors not covered by the arbitration clause.[172]

If a debt buyer wishes to take advantage of its status as an assignee, a court should require that it provide documentation that it is in fact an assignee. Similarly, MBNA's clause provides that it covers actions "arising from or relating" to

---

163 *See* National Consumer Law Center, Fair Debt Collection § 4.2 (5th ed. 2004 and Supp.).
164 *See* Worch v. Wolpoff & Abramson, L.L.P., 2006 WL 1523240 (E.D. Mo. June 1, 2006); *see also* Karnette v. Wolpoff & Abramson, L.L.P., 444 F. Supp. 2d 640 (E.D. Va. 2006).
165 *See, e.g.*, Park v. Columbia Credit Services, Inc., 2007 WL 1847142 (W.D. Mo. June 25, 2007).
166 *See* § 12.7.4, *infra*.
167 Worch v. Wolpoff & Abramson, L.L.P., 477 F. Supp. 2d 1015 (E.D. Mo. 2007).
168 National Consumer Law Center, Fair Debt Collection (5th ed. 2004 and Supp.).
169 2007 WL 922288 (E.D. Va. Mar. 23, 2007).

170 *See* National Consumer Law Center, Fair Debt Collection (5th ed. 2004 and Supp.); *see also* Kelly v. Wolpoff & Abramson, L.L.P., 2007 WL 2381536 (D. Colo. Aug. 17, 2007) (state deceptive practices claim could proceed against MBNA's attorney).
171 Karnette v. Wolpoff & Abramson, L.L.P., 444 F. Supp. 2d 640 (E.D. Va. 2006); Bontempo v. Wolpoff & Abramson, 2006 WL 3040905 (W. D. Pa. Oct. 24, 2006). *But see* Nazar v. Wolpoff & Abramson, 2007 WL 528753 (D. Kan. Feb. 15, 2007) (arbitrator decides whether arbitration agreement applies to collector when agreement states that issues as to the applicability of the arbitration agreement are to be determined by the arbitrator).

It is important to carefully distinguish the nature of the parties, such as whether they are collectors or assignees. *See* Hoefs v. CACV of Colorado, L.L.C., 365 F. Supp. 2d 69 (D. Mass. 2005) (MBNA clause applies to assignees and collectors named as co-defendants with the assignee because the clause explicitly applies to "us" and also collectors named as co-defendants with "us," and "us" includes assignees).
172 *See* § 7.4, *supra*; *see also* Montgomery v. Fla. First Fin. Group, Inc., 2007 WL 1789115 (M.D. Fla. Apr. 19, 2007).

§ 12.7.6   *Consumer Arbitration Agreements*

the credit card agreement, and an action based on the tortious behavior of collectors may not arise from or relate to the credit card agreement.[173] In short, before a defendant can seek to take advantage of an arbitration clause, the defendant should have to demonstrate both that it is a party that can take advantage of the clause and that the debt collection harassment claim is covered by the clause.

In addition, even if the agreement applies to the creditor, collector, or attorney, the agreement may not be enforceable, for reasons discussed throughout this manual—for example, because the consumer never agreed to arbitration, or because the clause is unconscionable.[174]

If the action is brought on a classwide basis, the class can argue that any limitation on classwide arbitration procedure makes the clause unconscionable, and also that NAF's involvement in the case should preclude it from administering the action. The action becomes viable if the court throws out the arbitration agreement completely or only limits it so that classwide arbitration is available before an entity other than NAF.

12.7.6 Preclusive Effect of Creditor's Arbitration Action on Debt

If the consumer previously participated in an arbitration proceeding or other debt collection proceeding the collector may also attempt to argue, under the doctrines of claim preclusion, res judicata, or a similar theory, that the consumer was required to bring any counterclaims in that proceeding rather than in a separate case. While an arbitration proceeding may have the same preclusive effect as a court proceeding,[175] courts generally find that a consumer's debt harassment claims are not precluded by a collection lawsuit on the debt.[176] Thus a court has rejected a collection attorney's defense of claim preclusion based on a prior collection arbitration proceeding.[177]

12.8 Government Enforcement Action Against Using Arbitration for Collection

Challenges to collection using arbitration can be initiated through a private action, or through a government enforcement agency suing the creditor or the arbitration service provider. Such an action would avoid the practical problems of a private attorney realizing sufficient recovery from an action to justify the time and costs involved with such a major challenge. There is also no question that a government initiated action can remain in court, and need not be referred to arbitration pursuant to the creditor's arbitration clause with consumers.[178] Moreover, an action for injunctive relief, civil penalties, and perhaps even restitution will not be affected by the ninety-day period to vacate existing judgments.

The Federal Trade Commission (FTC) can bring enforcement actions against creditors and arbitration service providers to challenge unfair or deceptive acts or practices. The FTC has successfully issued rules and engaged in enforcement actions against overreaching creditor remedies found in consumer adhesion contracts,[179] and collecting on debts using arbitration is a similar practice. Nevertheless, Congress has explicitly denied the FTC the ability to bring enforcement actions against banks, credit unions, or savings and loans associations. Instead, authority to bring enforcement actions against these entities is reserved for federal banking agencies.

This exemption is significant because, at present, creditors using arbitration to collect on debts tend to be national banks, whose unfair practices are policed by the Office of the Comptroller of the Currency (OCC), not the FTC. Complaints about national banks' collecting on debts via arbitration should be addressed to the OCC. While the OCC states that it has the authority and willingness to stop any unfair practice by a national bank, critics are skeptical. The National Consumer Law Center would like to be kept informed of the OCC's responsiveness to complaints about national banks.

State attorneys general can also challenge unfair actions using arbitration to collect on debts. Unlike the FTC, state attorneys general typically are authorized to sue banks operating in their state and, like the FTC, are generally empowered to stop unfair or deceptive practices. A national bank sued by a state will claim that OCC regulation preempts state laws. The law in this area is only now developing,[180] but it is hard to see how a bank can avail itself of state laws to collect on its debts and to confirm its arbitration awards, but then claim that state law does not apply to determine if its arbitration procedures are unfair or deceptive.

---

173   *See* § 7.3.3, *supra*.
174   *See* Chs. 5, 6, *supra*.
175   *See* § 11.8, *supra*.
176   *See* National Consumer Law Center, Fair Debt Collection § 7.6.2 (5th ed. 2004 and Supp.); *see also* Kelly v. Wolpoff & Abramson, L.L.P., 2007 WL 2381536 (D. Colo. Aug. 17, 2007) (proceedings related to MBNA collection arbitration does not preclude FDCPA claim against MBNA's attorney).
177   Karnette v. Wolpoff & Abramson, L.L.P., 2007 WL 922288 (E.D. Va. Mar. 23, 2007).

178   *See* Equal Employment Opportunity Comm'n v. Waffle House, Inc., 534 U.S. 279, 122 S. Ct. 754, 151 L. Ed. 2d 755 (2002).
179   *See* Am. Fin. Services Ass'n v. Fed. Trade Comm'n, 767 F.2d 957 (D.C. Cir. 1985); *see also* National Consumer Law Center, Unfair and Deceptive Acts and Practices § 5.1.3 (6th ed. 2004 and Supp.).
180   *See* National Consumer Law Center, Unfair and Deceptive Acts and Practices § 2.5.3 (6th ed. 2004 and Supp.).

Appendix A Federal Statutes

A.1 The Federal Arbitration Act

9 U.S.C. §§ 1–16

[As enacted by Ch. 392, 61 Stat. 670 (1947), unless otherwise noted.]

TITLE 9—ARBITRATION
Chapter 1—General Provisions

§ 1. "Maritime transactions" and "commerce" defined; exceptions to operation of title

"Maritime transactions", as herein defined, means charter parties, bills of lading of water carriers, agreements relating to wharfage, supplies furnished vessels or repairs to vessels, collisions, or any other matters in foreign commerce which, if the subject of controversy, would be embraced within admiralty jurisdiction; "commerce", as herein defined, means commerce among the several States or with foreign nations, or in any Territory of the United States or in the District of Columbia, or between any such Territory and another, or between any such Territory and any State or foreign nation, or between the District of Columbia and any State or Territory or foreign nation, but nothing herein contained shall apply to contracts of employment of seamen, railroad employees, or any other class of workers engaged in foreign or interstate commerce.

§ 2. Validity, irrevocability, and enforcement of agreements to arbitrate

A written provision in any maritime transaction or a contract evidencing a transaction involving commerce to settle by arbitration a controversy thereafter arising out of such contract or transaction, or the refusal to perform the whole or any part thereof, or an agreement in writing to submit to arbitration an existing controversy arising out of such a contract, transaction, or refusal, shall be valid, irrevocable, and enforceable, save upon such grounds as exist at law or in equity for the revocation of any contract.

§ 3. Stay of proceedings where issue therein referable to arbitration

If any suit or proceeding be brought in any of the courts of the United States upon any issue referable to arbitration under an agreement in writing for such arbitration, the court in which such suit is pending, upon being satisfied that the issue involved in such suit or proceeding is referable to arbitration under such an agreement, shall on application of one of the parties stay the trial of the action until such arbitration has been had in accordance with the terms of the agreement, providing the applicant for the stay is not in default in proceeding with such arbitration.

§ 4. Failure to arbitrate under agreement; petition to United States court having jurisdiction for order to compel arbitration; notice and service thereof; hearing and determination

A party aggrieved by the alleged failure, neglect, or refusal of another to arbitrate under a written agreement for arbitration may petition any United States district court which, save for such agreement, would have jurisdiction under title 28, in a civil action or in admiralty of the subject matter of a suit arising out of the controversy between the parties, for an order directing that such arbitration proceed in the manner provided for in such agreement. Five days' notice in writing of such application shall be served upon the party in default. Service thereof shall be made in the manner provided by the Federal Rules of Civil Procedure. The court shall hear the parties, and upon being satisfied that the making of the agreement for arbitration or the failure to comply therewith is not in issue, the court shall make an order directing the parties to proceed to arbitration in accordance with the terms of the agreement. The hearing and proceedings, under such agreement, shall be within the district in which the petition for an order directing such arbitration is filed. If the making of the arbitration agreement or the failure, neglect, or refusal to perform the same be in issue, the court shall proceed summarily to the trial thereof. If no jury trial be demanded by the party alleged to be in default, or if the matter in dispute is within admiralty jurisdiction, the court shall hear and determine such issue. Where such an issue is raised, the party alleged to be in default may, except in cases of admiralty, on or before the return day of the notice of application, demand a jury trial of such issue, and upon such demand the court shall make an order referring the issue or issues to a jury in the manner provided by the Federal Rules of Civil Procedure, or may specially call a jury for that purpose. If the jury find that no agreement in writing for arbitration was made or that there is no default in proceeding thereunder, the proceeding shall be dismissed. If the jury find that an agreement for arbitration was made in writing and that there is a default in proceeding thereunder, the court shall make an order summarily directing the parties to proceed with the arbitration in accordance with the terms thereof.

[As amended by Ch. 1263, § 19, 68 Stat. 1233 (1954).]

§ 5. Appointment of arbitrators or umpire

If in the agreement provision be made for a method of naming or appointing an arbitrator or arbitrators or an umpire, such method shall be followed; but if no method be provided therein, or if a method be provided and any party thereto shall fail to avail himself of such method, or if for any other reason there shall be a lapse in the naming of an arbitrator or arbitrators or umpire, or in filling a vacancy, then upon the application of either party to the controversy the court shall designate and appoint an arbitrator or arbitrators or umpire, as the case may require, who shall act under the said agreement with the same force and effect as if he or they had been specifically named therein; and unless otherwise provided in the agreement the arbitration shall be by a single arbitrator.

§ 6. Application heard as motion

Any application to the court hereunder shall be made and heard in the manner provided by law for the making and hearing of motions, except as otherwise herein expressly provided.

§ 7. Witnesses before arbitrators; fees; compelling attendance

The arbitrators selected either as prescribed in this title or otherwise, or a majority of them, may summon in writing any person to attend before them or any of them as a witness and in a proper case to bring with him or them any book, record, document, or paper which may be deemed material as evidence in the case. The fees for such attendance shall be the same as the fees of witnesses before masters of the United States courts. Said summons shall issue in the name of the arbitrator or arbitrators, or a majority of them, and shall be signed by the arbitrators, or a majority of them, and shall be directed to the said person and shall be served in the same manner as subpoenas to appear and testify before the court; if any person or persons so summoned to testify shall refuse or neglect to obey said summons, upon petition the United States district court for the district in which such arbitrators, or a majority of them, are sitting may compel the attendance of such person or persons before said arbitrator or arbitrators, or punish said person or persons for contempt in the same manner provided by law for securing the attendance of witnesses or their punishment for neglect or refusal to attend in the courts of the United States.

[As amended by Ch. 655, § 14, 65 Stat. 715 (1951).]

§ 8. Proceedings begun by libel in admiralty and seizure of vessel or property

If the basis of jurisdiction be a cause of action otherwise justiciable in admiralty, then, notwithstanding anything herein to the contrary, the party claiming to be aggrieved may begin his proceeding hereunder by libel and seizure of the vessel or other property of the other party according to the usual course of admiralty proceedings, and the court shall then have jurisdiction to direct the parties to proceed with the arbitration and shall retain jurisdiction to enter its decree upon the award.

§ 9. Award of arbitrators; confirmation; jurisdiction; procedure

If the parties in their agreement have agreed that a judgment of the court shall be entered upon the award made pursuant to the arbitration, and shall specify the court, then at any time within one year after the award is made any party to the arbitration may apply to the court so specified for an order confirming the award, and thereupon the court must grant such an order unless the award is vacated, modified, or corrected as prescribed in sections 10 and 11 of this title. If no court is specified in the agreement of the parties, then such application may be made to the United States court in and for the district within which such award was made. Notice of the application shall be served upon the adverse party, and thereupon the court shall have jurisdiction of such party as though he had appeared generally in the proceeding. If the adverse party is a resident of the district within which the award was made, such service shall be made upon the adverse party or his attorney as prescribed by law for service of notice of motion in an action in the same court. If the adverse party shall be a nonresident, then the notice of the application shall be served by the marshal of any district within which the adverse party may be found in like manner as other process of the court.

§ 10. Same; vacation; grounds; rehearing

(a) In any of the following cases the United States court in and for the district wherein the award was made may make an order vacating the award upon the application of any party to the arbitration—
  (1) where the award was procured by corruption, fraud, or undue means;
  (2) where there was evident partiality or corruption in the arbitrators, or either of them;
  (3) where the arbitrators were guilty of misconduct in refusing to postpone the hearing, upon sufficient cause shown, or in refusing to hear evidence pertinent and material to the controversy; or of any other misbehavior by which the rights of any party have been prejudiced; or
  (4) where the arbitrators exceeded their powers, or so imperfectly executed them that a mutual, final, and definite award upon the subject matter submitted was not made.
(b) If an award is vacated and the time within which the agreement required the award to be made has not expired, the court may, in its discretion, direct a rehearing by the arbitrators.
(c) The United States district court for the district wherein an award was made that was issued pursuant to section 580 of title 5 may make an order vacating the award upon the application of a person, other than a party to the arbitration, who is adversely affected or aggrieved by the award, if the use of arbitration or the award is clearly inconsistent with the factors set forth in section 572 of title 5.

[As amended by Pub. L. No. 101-552, § 5, 104 Stat. 2745 (1990);

Pub. L. No. 102-354, § 5(b)(4), 106 Stat. 946 (1992); and Pub. L. No. 107-169, § 1, 116 Stat. 132 (2002).]

§ 11. Same; modification or correction; grounds; order

In either of the following cases the United States court in and for the district wherein the award was made may make an order modifying or correcting the award upon the application of any party to the arbitration—
 (a) Where there was an evident material miscalculation of figures or an evident material mistake in the description of any person, thing, or property referred to in the award.
 (b) Where the arbitrators have awarded upon a matter not submitted to them, unless it is a matter not affecting the merits of the decision upon the matter submitted.
 (c) Where the award is imperfect in matter of form not affecting the merits of the controversy.

The order may modify and correct the award, so as to effect the intent thereof and promote justice between the parties.

§ 12. Notice of motions to vacate or modify; service; stay of proceedings

Notice of a motion to vacate, modify, or correct an award must be served upon the adverse party or his attorney within three months after the award is filed or delivered. If the adverse party is a resident of the district within which the award was made, such service shall be made upon the adverse party or his attorney as prescribed by law for service of notice of motion in an action in the same court. If the adverse party shall be a nonresident then the notice of the application shall be served by the marshal of any district within which the adverse party may be found in like manner as other process of the court. For the purposes of the motion any judge who might make an order to stay the proceedings in an action brought in the same court may make an order, to be served with the notice of motion, staying the proceedings of the adverse party to enforce the award.

§ 13. Papers filed with order on motions; judgment; docketing; force and effect; enforcement

The party moving for an order confirming, modifying, or correcting an award shall, at the time such order is filed with the clerk for the entry of judgment thereon, also file the following papers with the clerk:
 (a) The agreement; the selection or appointment, if any, of an additional arbitrator or umpire; and each written extension of the time, if any, within which to make the award.
 (b) The award.
 (c) Each notice, affidavit, or other paper used upon an application to confirm, modify, or correct the award, and a copy of each order of the court upon such an application.

The judgment shall be docketed as if it was rendered in an action.

The judgment so entered shall have the same force and effect, in all respects, as, and be subject to all the provisions of law relating to, a judgment in an action; and it may be enforced as if it had been rendered in an action in the court in which it is entered.

§ 14. Contracts not affected

This title shall not apply to contracts made prior to January 1, 1926.

§ 15. Inapplicability of the Act of State doctrine

Enforcement of arbitral agreements, confirmation of arbitral awards, and execution upon judgments based on orders confirming such awards shall not be refused on the basis of the Act of State doctrine.

[Added by Pub. L. No. 100-669, § 1, 102 Stat. 3969 (1988).[1]]

§ 16. Appeals

 (a) An appeal may be taken from—
 (1) an order—
  (A) refusing a stay of any action under section 3 of this title,
  (B) denying a petition under section 4 of this title to order arbitration to proceed,
  (C) denying an application under section 206 of this title to compel arbitration,
  (D) confirming or denying confirmation of an award or partial award, or
  (E) modifying, correcting, or vacating an award;
 (2) an interlocutory order granting, continuing, or modifying an injunction against an arbitration that is subject to this title; or
 (3) a final decision with respect to an arbitration that is subject to this title.
 (b) Except as otherwise provided in section 1292(b) of title 28, an appeal may not be taken from an interlocutory order—
 (1) granting a stay of any action under section 3 of this title;
 (2) directing arbitration to proceed under section 4 of this title;
 (3) compelling arbitration under section 206 of this title; or
 (4) refusing to enjoin an arbitration that is subject to this title.

[Added by Pub. L. No. 100-702, § 1019(a), 102 Stat. 4671 (1988) as 9 U.S.C. § 15, renumbered by Pub. L. No. 101-650, § 325(a)(1), 104 Stat. 5120 (1990) as 9 U.S.C. § 16.]

---

1 [*Editor's Note: A second section 15 of this title enacted in November 1988 was subsequently renumbered as section 16 of this title.*]

A.2 Other Federal Statutes

A.2.1 Limits on Arbitration Involving Military Personnel

TITLE 10. ARMED FORCES

* * *

10 U.S.C. § 987. Terms of consumer credit extended to members and dependents: limitations

* * *

(e) Limitations.

It shall be unlawful for any creditor to extend consumer credit to a covered member or a dependent of such a member with respect to which—

* * *

(2) the borrower is required to waive the borrower's right to legal recourse under any otherwise applicable provision of State or Federal law, including any provision of the Servicemembers Civil Relief Act;

(3) the creditor requires the borrower to submit to arbitration or imposes onerous legal notice provisions in the case of a dispute;

* * *

(f) Penalties and remedies.
(1) Misdemeanor.

A creditor who knowingly violates this section shall be fined as provided in title 18, or imprisoned for not more than one year, or both.

(2) Preservation of other remedies.

The remedies and rights provided under this section are in addition to and do not preclude any remedy otherwise available under law to the person claiming relief under this section, including any award for consequential and punitive damages.

(3) Contract void.

Any credit agreement, promissory note, or other contract prohibited under this section is void from the inception of such contract.

(4) Arbitration.

Notwithstanding section 2 of title 9, or any other Federal or State law, rule, or regulation, no agreement to arbitrate any dispute involving the extension of consumer credit shall be enforceable against any covered member or dependent of such a member, or any person who was a covered member or dependent of that member when the agreement was made.

* * *

(h) Regulations.

(1) The Secretary of Defense shall prescribe regulations to carry out this section.

(2) Such regulations shall establish the following:

(A) Disclosures required of any creditor that extends consumer credit to a covered member or dependent of such a member.

(B) The method for calculating the applicable annual percentage rate of interest on such obligations, in accordance with the limit established under this section.

(C) A maximum allowable amount of all fees, and the types of fees, associated with any such extension of credit, to be expressed and disclosed to the borrower as a total amount and as a percentage of the principal amount of the obligation, at the time at which the transaction is entered into.

(D) Definitions of "creditor" under paragraph (5) and "consumer credit" under paragraph (6) of subsection (i), consistent with the provisions of this section.

(E) Such other criteria or limitations as the Secretary of Defense determines appropriate, consistent with the provisions of this section.

(3) In prescribing regulations under this subsection, the Secretary of Defense shall consult with the following:

(A) The Federal Trade Commission.
(B) The Board of Governors of the Federal Reserve System.
(C) The Office of the Comptroller of the Currency.
(D) The Federal Deposit Insurance Corporation.
(E) The Office of Thrift Supervision.
(F) The National Credit Union Administration.
(G) The Treasury Department.

(i) Definitions.

In this section:

(1) Covered member.

The term "covered member" means a member of the armed forces who is—

(A) on active duty under a call or order that does not specify a period of 30 days or less; or

(B) on active Guard and Reserve Duty.

(2) Dependent.

The term "dependent," with respect to a covered member, means—

(A) the member's spouse;

(B) the member's child (as defined in section 101(4) of title 38); or

(C) an individual for whom the member provided more than one-half of the individual's support for 180 days immediately preceding an extension of consumer credit covered by this section.

* * *

(5) Creditor.

The term "creditor" means a person—

(A) who—

(i) is engaged in the business of extending consumer credit; and

(ii) meets such additional criteria as are specified for such purpose in regulations prescribed under this section; or

(B) who is an assignee of a person described in subparagraph (A) with respect to any consumer credit extended.

(6) Consumer credit.

The term "consumer credit" has the meaning provided for such term in regulations prescribed under this section, except that such term does not include (A) a residential mortgage, or (B) a loan procured in the course of purchasing a car or other personal property, when that loan is offered for the express purpose of financing the purchase and is secured by the car or personal property procured.

[Pub. L. No. 109-364, § 670(a), 120 Stat. 2266 (2006) (effective date: Oct. 1, 2007 or on such earlier date as may be prescribed and published by the Secretary of Defense, and shall apply with respect to extensions of consumer credit on or after such effective date, except that subsection (h) is effective as of Oct. 17, 2006).]

A.2.2 Limits on Arbitration Involving Car Dealers and Their Franchisors

TITLE 15. COMMERCE AND TRADE

* * *

15 U.S.C. § 1226. Motor vehicle franchise contract dispute resolution process

(a) Election of arbitration.
(1) **Definitions.** For purposes of this subsection—
  (A) the term "motor vehicle" has the meaning given such term in section 30102(6) of title 49 of the United States Code; and
  (B) the term "motor vehicle franchise contract" means a contract under which a motor vehicle manufacturer, importer, or distributor sells motor vehicles to any other person for resale to an ultimate purchaser and authorizes such other person to repair and service the manufacturer's motor vehicles.
(2) **Consent required.** Notwithstanding any other provision of law, whenever a motor vehicle franchise contract provides for the use of arbitration to resolve a controversy arising out of or relating to such contract, arbitration may be used to settle such controversy only if after such controversy arises all parties to such controversy consent in writing to use arbitration to settle such controversy.
(3) **Explanation required.** Notwithstanding any other provision of law, whenever arbitration is elected to settle a dispute under a motor vehicle franchise contract, the arbitrator shall provide the parties to such contract with a written explanation of the factual and legal basis for the award.

(b) Application. Subsection (a) shall apply to contracts entered into, amended, altered, modified, renewed, or extended after the date of the enactment of this Act [enacted Nov. 2, 2002].

[Added by Pub. L. No. 107-273, § 11028, 116 Stat. 1835 (2002).]

Appendix B Arbitration Service Provider Rules

B.1 The American Arbitration Association[1]

B.1.1 Commercial Arbitration Rules and Mediation Procedures (Including Procedures for Large, Complex Commercial Disputes)

Amended and Effective September 15, 2005 (Fee Update)

TABLE OF CONTENTS

IMPORTANT NOTICE
INTRODUCTION
Standard Arbitration Clause
Administrative Fees

* * *

Large, Complex Cases

* * *

COMMERCIAL ARBITRATION RULES
R-1. Agreement of Parties
R-2. AAA and Delegation of Duties
R-3. National Roster of Arbitrators
R-4. Initiation under an Arbitration Provision in a Contract
R-5. Initiation under a Submission
R-6. Changes of Claim
R-7. Jurisdiction
R-8. Mediation
R-9. Administrative Conference
R-10. Fixing of Locale
R-11. Appointment from National Roster
R-12. Direct Appointment by a Party
R-13. Appointment of Chairperson by Party-Appointed Arbitrators or Parties
R-14. Nationality of Arbitrator
R-15. Number of Arbitrators
R-16. Disclosure
R-17. Disqualification of Arbitrator
R-18. Communication with Arbitrator
R-19. Vacancies
R-20. Preliminary Hearing
R-21. Exchange of Information
R-22. Date, Time, and Place of Hearing
R-23. Attendance at Hearings
R-24. Representation
R-25. Oaths
R-26. Stenographic Record
R-27. Interpreters
R-28. Postponements
R-29. Arbitration in the Absence of a Party or Representative
R-30. Conduct of Proceedings
R-31. Evidence
R-32. Evidence by Affidavit and Post-hearing Filing of Documents or Other Evidence
R-33. Inspection or Investigation
R-34. Interim Measures
R-35. Closing of Hearing
R-36. Reopening of Hearing
R-37. Waiver of Rules
R-38. Extensions of Time
R-39. Serving of Notice
R-40. Majority Decision
R-41. Time of Award
R-42. Form of Award
R-43. Scope of Award
R-44. Award upon Settlement
R-45. Delivery of Award to Parties
R-46. Modification of Award
R-47. Release of Documents for Judicial Proceedings
R-48. Applications to Court and Exclusion of Liability
R-49. Administrative Fees
R-50. Expenses
R-51. Neutral Arbitrator's Compensation
R-52. Deposits
R-53. Interpretation and Application of Rules
R-54. Suspension for Nonpayment

EXPEDITED PROCEDURES
E-1. Limitation on Extensions
E-2. Changes of Claim or Counterclaim
E-3. Serving of Notices
E-4. Appointment and Qualifications of Arbitrator
E-5. Exchange of Exhibits
E-6. Proceedings on Documents
E-7. Date, Time, and Place of Hearing
E-8. The Hearing

---

[1] © Copyright 2007 by the American Arbitration Association. Reprinted with permission of the American Arbitration Association.

E-9. Time of Award
E-10. Arbitrator's Compensation

PROCEDURES FOR LARGE, COMPLEX COMMERCIAL DISPUTES
L-1. Administrative Conference
L-2. Arbitrators
L-3. Preliminary Hearing
L-4. Management of Proceedings

OPTIONAL RULES FOR EMERGENCY MEASURES OF PROTECTION
O-1. Applicability
O-2. Appointment of Emergency Arbitrator
O-3. Schedule
O-4. Interim Award
O-5. Constitution of the Panel
O-6. Security
O-7. Special Master
O-8. Costs

ADMINISTRATIVE FEES
Fees
Refund Schedule
Hearing Room Rental

IMPORTANT NOTICE

These rules and any amendment of them shall apply in the form in effect at the time the administrative filing requirements are met for a demand for arbitration or submission agreement received by the AAA. To ensure that you have the most current information, see our Web Site at www.adr.org.

INTRODUCTION

Each year, many millions of business transactions take place. Occasionally, disagreements develop over these business transactions. Many of these disputes are resolved by arbitration, the voluntary submission of a dispute to an impartial person or persons for final and binding determination. Arbitration has proven to be an effective way to resolve these disputes privately, promptly, and economically.

The American Arbitration Association (AAA), a not-for-profit, public service organization, offers a broad range of dispute resolution services to business executives, attorneys, individuals, trade associations, unions, management, consumers, families, communities, and all levels of government. Services are available through AAA headquarters in New York and through offices located in major cities throughout the United States. Hearings may be held at locations convenient for the parties and are not limited to cities with AAA offices. In addition, the AAA serves as a center for education and training, issues specialized publications, and conducts research on all forms of out-of-court dispute settlement.

Standard Arbitration Clause

The parties can provide for arbitration of future disputes by inserting the following clause into their contracts:

> *Any controversy or claim arising out of or relating to this contract, or the breach thereof, shall be settled by arbitration administered by the American Arbitration Association under its Commercial Arbitration Rules, and judgment on the award rendered by the arbitrator(s) may be entered in any court having jurisdiction thereof.*

Arbitration of existing disputes may be accomplished by use of the following:

> *We, the undersigned parties, hereby agree to submit to arbitration administered by the American Arbitration Association under its Commercial Arbitration Rules the following controversy: (describe briefly) We further agree that the above controversy be submitted to (one) (three) arbitrator(s). We further agree that we will faithfully observe this agreement and the rules, that we will abide by and perform any award rendered by the arbitrator(s), and that a judgment of any court having jurisdiction may be entered on the award.*

In transactions likely to require emergency interim relief, the parties may wish to add to their clause the following language:

> *The parties also agree that the AAA Optional Rules for Emergency Measures of Protection shall apply to the proceedings.*

These Optional Rules may be found below.

The services of the AAA are generally concluded with the transmittal of the award. Although there is voluntary compliance with the majority of awards, judgment on the award can be entered in a court having appropriate jurisdiction if necessary.

Administrative Fees

The AAA charges a filing fee based on the amount of the claim or counterclaim. This fee information, which is included with these rules, allows the parties to exercise control over their administrative fees.

The fees cover AAA administrative services; they do not cover arbitrator compensation or expenses, if any, reporting services, or any post-award charges incurred by the parties in enforcing the award.

* * *

Large, Complex Cases

Unless the parties agree otherwise, the procedures for Large, Complex Commercial Disputes, which appear in this pamphlet, will be applied to all cases administered by the AAA under the Commercial Arbitration Rules in which the disclosed claim or counterclaim of any party is at least $500,000 exclusive of claimed interest, arbitration fees and costs.

The key features of these procedures include:

- a highly qualified, trained Roster of Neutrals;
- a mandatory preliminary hearing with the arbitrators, which may be conducted by teleconference;
- broad arbitrator authority to order and control discovery, including depositions;
- presumption that hearings will proceed on a consecutive or block basis.

* * *

COMMERCIAL ARBITRATION RULES

R-1. Agreement of Parties*+

(a) The parties shall be deemed to have made these rules a part of their arbitration agreement whenever they have provided for arbitration by the American Arbitration Association (hereinafter AAA) under its Commercial Arbitration Rules or for arbitration by the AAA of a domestic commercial dispute without specifying particular rules. These rules and any amendment of them shall apply in the form in effect at the time the administrative requirements are met for a demand for arbitration or submission agreement received by the AAA. The parties, by written agreement, may vary the procedures set forth in these rules. After appointment of the arbitrator, such modifications may be made only with the consent of the arbitrator.

(b) Unless the parties or the AAA determines otherwise, the Expedited Procedures shall apply in any case in which no disclosed claim or counterclaim exceeds $75,000, exclusive of interest and arbitration fees and costs. Parties may also agree to use these procedures in larger cases. Unless the parties agree otherwise, these procedures will not apply in cases involving more than two parties. The Expedited Procedures shall be applied as described in Sections E-1 through E-10 of these rules, in addition to any other portion of these rules that is not in conflict with the Expedited Procedures.

(c) Unless the parties agree otherwise, the Procedures for Large, Complex Commercial Disputes shall apply to all cases in which the disclosed claim or counterclaim of any party is at least $500,000, exclusive of claimed interest, arbitration fees and costs. Parties may also agree to use the Procedures in cases involving claims or counterclaims under $500,000, or in non-monetary cases. The Procedures for Large, Complex Commercial Disputes shall be applied as described in Sections L-1 through L-4 of these rules, in addition to any other portion of these rules that is not in conflict with the Procedures for Large, Complex Commercial Disputes.

(d) All other cases shall be administered in accordance with Sections R-1 through R-54 of these rules.

---

* The AAA applies the Supplementary Procedures for Consumer-Related Disputes to arbitration clauses in agreements between individual consumers and businesses where the business has a standardized, systematic application of arbitration clauses with customers and where the terms and conditions of the purchase of standardized, consumable goods or services are nonnegotiable or primarily non-negotiable in most or all of its terms, conditions, features, or choices. The product or service must be for personal or household use. The AAA will have the discretion to apply or not to apply the Supplementary Procedures and the parties will be able to bring any disputes concerning the application or non-application to the attention of the arbitrator. Consumers are not prohibited from seeking relief in a small claims court for disputes or claims within the scope of its jurisdiction, even in consumer arbitration cases filed by the business.

+ A dispute arising out of an employer promulgated plan will be administered under the AAA's National Rules for the Resolution of Employment Disputes.

R-2. AAA and Delegation of Duties

When parties agree to arbitrate under these rules, or when they provide for arbitration by the AAA and an arbitration is initiated under these rules, they thereby authorize the AAA to administer the arbitration. The authority and duties of the AAA are prescribed in the agreement of the parties and in these rules, and may be carried out through such of the AAA's representatives as it may direct. The AAA may, in its discretion, assign the administration of an arbitration to any of its offices.

R-3. National Roster of Arbitrators

The AAA shall establish and maintain a National Roster of Commercial Arbitrators ("National Roster") and shall appoint arbitrators as provided in these rules. The term "arbitrator" in these rules refers to the arbitration panel, constituted for a particular case, whether composed of one or more arbitrators, or to an individual arbitrator, as the context requires.

R-4. Initiation under an Arbitration Provision in a Contract

(a) Arbitration under an arbitration provision in a contract shall be initiated in the following manner:
  (i) The initiating party (the "claimant") shall, within the time period, if any, specified in the contract(s), give to the other party (the "respondent") written notice of its intention to arbitrate (the "demand"), which demand shall contain a statement setting forth the nature of the dispute, the names and addresses of all other parties, the amount involved, if any, the remedy sought, and the hearing locale requested.
  (ii) The claimant shall file at any office of the AAA two copies of the demand and two copies of the arbitration provisions of the contract, together with the appropriate filing fee as provided in the schedule included with these rules.
  (iii) The AAA shall confirm notice of such filing to the parties.

(b) A respondent may file an answering statement in duplicate with the AAA within 15 days after confirmation of notice of filing of the demand is sent by the AAA. The respondent shall, at the time of any such filing, send a copy of the answering statement to the claimant. If a counterclaim is asserted, it shall contain a statement setting forth the nature of the counterclaim, the amount involved, if any, and the remedy sought. If a counterclaim is made, the party making the counterclaim shall forward to the AAA with the answering statement the appropriate fee provided in the schedule included with these rules.

(c) If no answering statement is filed within the stated time, respondent will be deemed to deny the claim. Failure to file an answering statement shall not operate to delay the arbitration.

(d) When filing any statement pursuant to this section, the parties are encouraged to provide descriptions of their claims in sufficient detail to make the circumstances of the dispute clear to the arbitrator.

R-5. Initiation under a Submission

Parties to any existing dispute may commence an arbitration under these rules by filing at any office of the AAA two copies of a written submission to arbitrate under these rules, signed by the parties. It shall contain a statement of the nature of the dispute, the names and addresses of all parties, any claims and counterclaims, the amount involved, if any, the remedy sought, and the hearing locale requested, together with the appropriate filing fee as provided in the schedule included with these rules. Unless the parties state otherwise in the submission, all claims and counterclaims will be deemed to be denied by the other party.

R-6. Changes of Claim

After filing of a claim, if either party desires to make any new or different claim or counterclaim, it shall be made in writing and filed with the AAA. The party asserting such a claim or counterclaim shall provide a copy to the other party, who shall have 15 days from the date of such transmission within which to file an answering statement with the AAA. After the arbitrator is appointed, however, no new or different claim may be submitted except with the arbitrator's consent.

R-7. Jurisdiction

(a) The arbitrator shall have the power to rule on his or her own jurisdiction, including any objections with respect to the existence, scope or validity of the arbitration agreement.

(b) The arbitrator shall have the power to determine the existence or validity of a contract of which an arbitration clause forms a part. Such an arbitration clause shall be treated as an agreement independent of the other terms of the contract. A decision by the arbitrator that the contract is null and void shall not for that reason alone render invalid the arbitration clause.

(c) A party must object to the jurisdiction of the arbitrator or to the arbitrability of a claim or counterclaim no later than the filing of the answering statement to the claim or counterclaim that gives rise to the objection. The arbitrator may rule on such objections as a preliminary matter or as part of the final award.

R-8. Mediation

At any stage of the proceedings, the parties may agree to conduct a mediation conference under the Commercial Mediation Procedures in order to facilitate settlement. The mediator shall not be an arbitrator appointed to the case. Where the parties to a pending arbitration agree to mediate under the AAA's rules, no additional administrative fee is required to initiate the mediation.

R-9. Administrative Conference

At the request of any party or upon the AAA's own initiative, the AAA may conduct an administrative conference, in person or by telephone, with the parties and/or their representatives. The conference may address such issues as arbitrator selection, potential mediation of the dispute, potential exchange of information, a timetable for hearings and any other administrative matters.

R-10. Fixing of Locale

The parties may mutually agree on the locale where the arbitration is to be held. If any party requests that the hearing be held in a specific locale and the other party files no objection thereto within 15 days after notice of the request has been sent to it by the AAA, the locale shall be the one requested. If a party objects to the locale requested by the other party, the AAA shall have the power to determine the locale, and its decision shall be final and binding.

R-11. Appointment from National Roster

If the parties have not appointed an arbitrator and have not provided any other method of appointment, the arbitrator shall be appointed in the following manner:

(a) Immediately after the filing of the submission or the answering statement or the expiration of the time within which the answering statement is to be filed, the AAA shall send simultaneously to each party to the dispute an identical list of 10 (unless the AAA decides that a different number is appropriate) names of persons chosen from the National Roster. The parties are encouraged to agree to an arbitrator from the submitted list and to advise the AAA of their agreement.

(b) If the parties are unable to agree upon an arbitrator, each party to the dispute shall have 15 days from the transmittal date in which to strike names objected to, number the remaining names in order of preference, and return the list to the AAA. If a party does not return the list within the time specified, all persons named therein shall be deemed acceptable. From among the persons who have been approved on both lists, and in accordance with the designated order of mutual preference, the AAA shall invite the acceptance of an arbitrator to serve. If the parties fail to agree on any of the persons named, or if acceptable arbitrators are unable to act, or if for any other reason the appointment cannot be made from the submitted lists, the AAA shall have the power to make the appointment from among other members of the National Roster without the submission of additional lists.

(c) Unless the parties agree otherwise when there are two or more claimants or two or more respondents, the AAA may appoint all the arbitrators.

R-12. Direct Appointment by a Party

(a) If the agreement of the parties names an arbitrator or specifies a method of appointing an arbitrator, that designation or method shall be followed. The notice of appointment, with the name and address of the arbitrator, shall be filed with the AAA by the appointing party. Upon the request of any appointing party, the AAA shall submit a list of members of the National Roster from which the party may, if it so desires, make the appointment.

(b) Where the parties have agreed that each party is to name one arbitrator, the arbitrators so named must meet the standards of Section R-17 with respect to impartiality and independence unless the parties have specifically agreed pursuant to Section R-17(a) that the party-appointed arbitrators are to be non-neutral and need not meet those standards.

(c) If the agreement specifies a period of time within which an arbitrator shall be appointed and any party fails to make the appointment within that period, the AAA shall make the appointment.

(d) If no period of time is specified in the agreement, the AAA shall notify the party to make the appointment. If within 15 days after such notice has been sent, an arbitrator has not been appointed by a party, the AAA shall make the appointment.

R-13. Appointment of Chairperson by Party-Appointed Arbitrators or Parties

(a) If, pursuant to Section R-12, either the parties have directly appointed arbitrators, or the arbitrators have been appointed by the AAA, and the parties have authorized them to appoint a chairperson within a specified time and no appointment is made within that time or any agreed extension, the AAA may appoint the chairperson.

(b) If no period of time is specified for appointment of the chairperson and the party-appointed arbitrators or the parties do not make the appointment within 15 days from the date of the appointment of the last party-appointed arbitrator, the AAA may appoint the chairperson.

(c) If the parties have agreed that their party-appointed arbitrators shall appoint the chairperson from the National Roster, the AAA shall furnish to the party-appointed arbitrators, in the manner provided in Section R-11, a list selected from the National Roster, and the appointment of the chairperson shall be made as provided in that Section.

R-14. Nationality of Arbitrator

Where the parties are nationals of different countries, the AAA, at the request of any party or on its own initiative, may appoint as arbitrator a national of a country other than that of any of the parties. The request must be made before the time set for the appointment of the arbitrator as agreed by the parties or set by these rules.

R-15. Number of Arbitrators

If the arbitration agreement does not specify the number of arbitrators, the dispute shall be heard and determined by one arbitrator, unless the AAA, in its discretion, directs that three arbitrators be appointed. A party may request three arbitrators in the demand or answer, which request the AAA will consider in exercising its discretion regarding the number of arbitrators appointed to the dispute.

R-16. Disclosure

(a) Any person appointed or to be appointed as an arbitrator shall disclose to the AAA any circumstance likely to give rise to justifiable doubt as to the arbitrator's impartiality or independence, including any bias or any financial or personal interest in the result of the arbitration or any past or present relationship with the parties or their representatives. Such obligation shall remain in effect throughout the arbitration.

(b) Upon receipt of such information from the arbitrator or another source, the AAA shall communicate the information to the parties and, if it deems it appropriate to do so, to the arbitrator and others.

(c) In order to encourage disclosure by arbitrators, disclosure of information pursuant to this Section R-16 is not to be construed as an indication that the arbitrator considers that the disclosed circumstance is likely to affect impartiality or independence.

R-17. Disqualification of Arbitrator

(a) Any arbitrator shall be impartial and independent and shall perform his or her duties with diligence and in good faith, and shall be subject to disqualification for
  (i) partiality or lack of independence,
  (ii) inability or refusal to perform his or her duties with diligence and in good faith, and
  (iii) any grounds for disqualification provided by applicable law. The parties may agree in writing, however, that arbitrators directly appointed by a party pursuant to Section R-12 shall be nonneutral, in which case such arbitrators need not be impartial or independent and shall not be subject to disqualification for partiality or lack of independence.

(b) Upon objection of a party to the continued service of an arbitrator, or on its own initiative, the AAA shall determine whether the arbitrator should be disqualified under the grounds set out above, and shall inform the parties of its decision, which decision shall be conclusive.

R-18. Communication with Arbitrator

(a) No party and no one acting on behalf of any party shall communicate ex parte with an arbitrator or a candidate for arbitrator concerning the arbitration, except that a party, or someone acting on behalf of a party, may communicate ex parte with a candidate for direct appointment pursuant to Section R-12 in order to advise the candidate of the general nature of the controversy and of the anticipated proceedings and to discuss the candidate's qualifications, availability, or independence in relation to the parties or to discuss the suitability of candidates for selection as a third arbitrator where the parties or party-designated arbitrators are to participate in that selection.

(b) Section R-18(a) does not apply to arbitrators directly appointed by the parties who, pursuant to Section R-17(a), the parties have agreed in writing are non-neutral. Where the parties have so agreed under Section R-17(a), the AAA shall as an administrative practice suggest to the parties that they agree further that Section R-18(a) should nonetheless apply prospectively.

R-19. Vacancies

(a) If for any reason an arbitrator is unable to perform the duties of the office, the AAA may, on proof satisfactory to it, declare the office vacant. Vacancies shall be filled in accordance with the applicable provisions of these rules.

(b) In the event of a vacancy in a panel of neutral arbitrators after the hearings have commenced, the remaining arbitrator or arbitrators may continue with the hearing and determination of the controversy, unless the parties agree otherwise.

(c) In the event of the appointment of a substitute arbitrator, the panel of arbitrators shall determine in its sole discretion whether it is necessary to repeat all or part of any prior hearings.

R-20. Preliminary Hearing

(a) At the request of any party or at the discretion of the arbitrator or the AAA, the arbitrator may schedule as soon as practicable a preliminary hearing with the parties and/or their representatives. The preliminary hearing may be conducted by telephone at the arbitrator's discretion.

(b) During the preliminary hearing, the parties and the arbitrator should discuss the future conduct of the case, including clarification of the issues and claims, a schedule for the hearings and any other preliminary matters.

R-21. Exchange of Information

(a) At the request of any party or at the discretion of the arbitrator, consistent with the expedited nature of arbitration, the arbitrator may direct
  i) the production of documents and other information, and
  ii) the identification of any witnesses to be called.

(b) At least five business days prior to the hearing, the parties shall exchange copies of all exhibits they intend to submit at the hearing.

(c) The arbitrator is authorized to resolve any disputes concerning the exchange of information.

R-22. Date, Time, and Place of Hearing

The arbitrator shall set the date, time, and place for each hearing. The parties shall respond to requests for hearing dates in a timely manner, be cooperative in scheduling the earliest practicable date, and adhere to the established hearing schedule. The AAA shall send a notice of hearing to the parties at least 10 days in advance of the hearing date, unless otherwise agreed by the parties.

R-23. Attendance at Hearings

The arbitrator and the AAA shall maintain the privacy of the hearings unless the law provides to the contrary. Any person having a direct interest in the arbitration is entitled to attend hearings. The arbitrator shall otherwise have the power to require the exclusion of any witness, other than a party or other essential person, during the testimony of any other witness. It shall be discretionary with the arbitrator to determine the propriety of the attendance of any other person other than a party and its representatives.

R-24. Representation

Any party may be represented by counsel or other authorized representative. A party intending to be so represented shall notify the other party and the AAA of the name and address of the representative at least three days prior to the date set for the hearing at which that person is first to appear. When such a representative initiates an arbitration or responds for a party, notice is deemed to have been given.

R-25. Oaths

Before proceeding with the first hearing, each arbitrator may take an oath of office and, if required by law, shall do so. The arbitrator may require witnesses to testify under oath administered by any duly qualified person and, if it is required by law or requested by any party, shall do so.

R-26. Stenographic Record

Any party desiring a stenographic record shall make arrangements directly with a stenographer and shall notify the other parties of these arrangements at least three days in advance of the hearing. The requesting party or parties shall pay the cost of the record. If the transcript is agreed by the parties, or determined by the arbitrator to be the official record of the proceeding, it must be provided to the arbitrator and made available to the other parties for inspection, at a date, time, and place determined by the arbitrator.

R-27. Interpreters

Any party wishing an interpreter shall make all arrangements directly with the interpreter and shall assume the costs of the service.

R-28. Postponements

The arbitrator may postpone any hearing upon agreement of the parties, upon request of a party for good cause shown, or upon the arbitrator's own initiative.

R-29. Arbitration in the Absence of a Party or Representative

Unless the law provides to the contrary, the arbitration may proceed in the absence of any party or representative who, after due notice, fails to be present or fails to obtain a postponement. An award shall not be made solely on the default of a party. The arbitrator shall require the party who is present to submit such evidence as the arbitrator may require for the making of an award.

R-30. Conduct of Proceedings

(a) The claimant shall present evidence to support its claim. The respondent shall then present evidence to support its defense. Witnesses for each party shall also submit to questions from the arbitrator and the adverse party. The arbitrator has the discretion to vary this procedure, provided that the parties are treated with equality and that each party has the right to be heard and is given a fair opportunity to present its case.

(b) The arbitrator, exercising his or her discretion, shall conduct the proceedings with a view to expediting the resolution of the dispute and may direct the order of proof, bifurcate proceedings and direct the parties to focus their presentations on issues the decision of which could dispose of all or part of the case.

(c) The parties may agree to waive oral hearings in any case.

R-31. Evidence

(a) The parties may offer such evidence as is relevant and material to the dispute and shall produce such evidence as the arbitrator may deem necessary to an understanding and determination of the dispute. Conformity to legal rules of evidence shall not be necessary. All evidence shall be taken in the presence of all of the arbitrators and all of the parties, except where any of the parties is absent, in default or has waived the right to be present.

(b) The arbitrator shall determine the admissibility, relevance, and materiality of the evidence offered and may exclude evidence deemed by the arbitrator to be cumulative or irrelevant.

(c) The arbitrator shall take into account applicable principles of legal privilege, such as those involving the confidentiality of communications between a lawyer and client.

(d) An arbitrator or other person authorized by law to subpoena witnesses or documents may do so upon the request of any party or independently.

R-32. Evidence by Affidavit and Post-hearing Filing of Documents or Other Evidence

(a) The arbitrator may receive and consider the evidence of witnesses by declaration or affidavit, but shall give it only such weight as the arbitrator deems it entitled to after consideration of any objection made to its admission.

(b) If the parties agree or the arbitrator directs that documents or other evidence be submitted to the arbitrator after the hearing, the documents or other evidence shall be filed with the AAA for transmission to the arbitrator. All parties shall be afforded an opportunity to examine and respond to such documents or other evidence.

R-33. Inspection or Investigation

An arbitrator finding it necessary to make an inspection or investigation in connection with the arbitration shall direct the AAA to so advise the parties. The arbitrator shall set the date and time and the AAA shall notify the parties. Any party who so desires may be present at such an inspection or investigation. In the event that one or all parties are not present at the inspection or investigation, the arbitrator shall make an oral or written report to the parties and afford them an opportunity to comment.

R-34. Interim Measures**

(a) The arbitrator may take whatever interim measures he or she deems necessary, including injunctive relief and measures for the protection or conservation of property and disposition of perishable goods.

(b) Such interim measures may take the form of an interim award, and the arbitrator may require security for the costs of such measures.

(c) A request for interim measures addressed by a party to a

** The Optional Rules may be found below.

judicial authority shall not be deemed incompatible with the agreement to arbitrate or a waiver of the right to arbitrate.

R-35. Closing of Hearing

The arbitrator shall specifically inquire of all parties whether they have any further proofs to offer or witnesses to be heard. Upon receiving negative replies or if satisfied that the record is complete, the arbitrator shall declare the hearing closed. If briefs are to be filed, the hearing shall be declared closed as of the final date set by the arbitrator for the receipt of briefs. If documents are to be filed as provided in Section R-32 and the date set for their receipt is later than that set for the receipt of briefs, the later date shall be the closing date of the hearing. The time limit within which the arbitrator is required to make the award shall commence, in the absence of other agreements by the parties, upon the closing of the hearing.

R-36. Reopening of Hearing

The hearing may be reopened on the arbitrator's initiative, or upon application of a party, at any time before the award is made. If reopening the hearing would prevent the making of the award within the specific time agreed on by the parties in the contract(s) out of which the controversy has arisen, the matter may not be reopened unless the parties agree on an extension of time. When no specific date is fixed in the contract, the arbitrator may reopen the hearing and shall have 30 days from the closing of the reopened hearing within which to make an award.

R-37. Waiver of Rules

Any party who proceeds with the arbitration after knowledge that any provision or requirement of these rules has not been complied with and who fails to state an objection in writing shall be deemed to have waived the right to object.

R-38. Extensions of Time

The parties may modify any period of time by mutual agreement. The AAA or the arbitrator may for good cause extend any period of time established by these rules, except the time for making the award. The AAA shall notify the parties of any extension.

R-39. Serving of Notice

(a) Any papers, notices, or process necessary or proper for the initiation or continuation of an arbitration under these rules, for any court action in connection therewith, or for the entry of judgment on any award made under these rules may be served on a party by mail addressed to the party, or its representative at the last known address or by personal service, in or outside the state where the arbitration is to be held, provided that reasonable opportunity to be heard with regard to the dispute is or has been granted to the party.

(b) The AAA, the arbitrator and the parties may also use overnight delivery or electronic facsimile transmission (fax), to give the notices required by these rules. Where all parties and the arbitrator agree, notices may be transmitted by electronic mail (E-mail), or other methods of communication.

(c) Unless otherwise instructed by the AAA or by the arbitrator, any documents submitted by any party to the AAA or to the arbitrator shall simultaneously be provided to the other party or parties to the arbitration.

R-40. Majority Decision

When the panel consists of more than one arbitrator, unless required by law or by the arbitration agreement, a majority of the arbitrators must make all decisions.

R-41. Time of Award

The award shall be made promptly by the arbitrator and, unless otherwise agreed by the parties or specified by law, no later than 30 days from the date of closing the hearing, or, if oral hearings have been waived, from the date of the AAA's transmittal of the final statements and proofs to the arbitrator.

R-42. Form of Award

(a) Any award shall be in writing and signed by a majority of the arbitrators. It shall be executed in the manner required by law.

(b) The arbitrator need not render a reasoned award unless the parties request such an award in writing prior to appointment of the arbitrator or unless the arbitrator determines that a reasoned award is appropriate.

R-43. Scope of Award

(a) The arbitrator may grant any remedy or relief that the arbitrator deems just and equitable and within the scope of the agreement of the parties, including, but not limited to, specific performance of a contract.

(b) In addition to a final award, the arbitrator may make other decisions, including interim, interlocutory, or partial rulings, orders, and awards. In any interim, interlocutory, or partial award, the arbitrator may assess and apportion the fees, expenses, and compensation related to such award as the arbitrator determines is appropriate.

(c) In the final award, the arbitrator shall assess the fees, expenses, and compensation provided in Sections R-49, R-50, and R-51. The arbitrator may apportion such fees, expenses, and compensation among the parties in such amounts as the arbitrator determines is appropriate.

(d) The award of the arbitrator(s) may include:
  (i) interest at such rate and from such date as the arbitrator(s) may deem appropriate; and
  (ii) an award of attorneys' fees if all parties have requested such an award or it is authorized by law or their arbitration agreement.

R-44. Award upon Settlement

If the parties settle their dispute during the course of the arbitration and if the parties so request, the arbitrator may set forth the terms of the settlement in a "consent award." A consent award must include an allocation of arbitration costs, including administrative fees and expenses as well as arbitrator fees and expenses.

R-45. Delivery of Award to Parties

Parties shall accept as notice and delivery of the award the placing of the award or a true copy thereof in the mail addressed to the parties or their representatives at the last known addresses, personal or electronic service of the award, or the filing of the award in any other manner that is permitted by law.

R-46. Modification of Award

Within 20 days after the transmittal of an award, any party, upon notice to the other parties, may request the arbitrator, through the AAA, to correct any clerical, typographical, or computational errors in the award. The arbitrator is not empowered to redetermine the merits of any claim already decided. The other parties shall be given 10 days to respond to the request. The arbitrator shall dispose of the request within 20 days after transmittal by the AAA to the

R-47. Release of Documents for Judicial Proceedings

The AAA shall, upon the written request of a party, furnish to the party, at the party's expense, certified copies of any papers in the AAA's possession that may be required in judicial proceedings relating to the arbitration.

R-48. Applications to Court and Exclusion of Liability

(a) No judicial proceeding by a party relating to the subject matter of the arbitration shall be deemed a waiver of the party's right to arbitrate.

(b) Neither the AAA nor any arbitrator in a proceeding under these rules is a necessary or proper party in judicial proceedings relating to the arbitration.

(c) Parties to an arbitration under these rules shall be deemed to have consented that judgment upon the arbitration award may be entered in any federal or state court having jurisdiction thereof.

(d) Parties to an arbitration under these rules shall be deemed to have consented that neither the AAA nor any arbitrator shall be liable to any party in any action for damages or injunctive relief for any act or omission in connection with any arbitration under these rules.

R-49. Administrative Fees

As a not-for-profit organization, the AAA shall prescribe an initial filing fee and a case service fee to compensate it for the cost of providing administrative services. The fees in effect when the fee or charge is incurred shall be applicable. The filing fee shall be advanced by the party or parties making a claim or counterclaim, subject to final apportionment by the arbitrator in the award. The AAA may, in the event of extreme hardship on the part of any party, defer or reduce the administrative fees.

R-50. Expenses

The expenses of witnesses for either side shall be paid by the party producing such witnesses. All other expenses of the arbitration, including required travel and other expenses of the arbitrator, AAA representatives, and any witness and the cost of any proof produced at the direct request of the arbitrator, shall be borne equally by the parties, unless they agree otherwise or unless the arbitrator in the award assesses such expenses or any part thereof against any specified party or parties.

R-51. Neutral Arbitrator's Compensation

(a) Arbitrators shall be compensated at a rate consistent with the arbitrator's stated rate of compensation.

(b) If there is disagreement concerning the terms of compensation, an appropriate rate shall be established with the arbitrator by the AAA and confirmed to the parties.

(c) Any arrangement for the compensation of a neutral arbitrator shall be made through the AAA and not directly between the parties and the arbitrator.

R-52. Deposits

The AAA may require the parties to deposit in advance of any hearings such sums of money as it deems necessary to cover the expense of the arbitration, including the arbitrator's fee, if any, and shall render an accounting to the parties and return any unexpended balance at the conclusion of the case.

R-53. Interpretation and Application of Rules

The arbitrator shall interpret and apply these rules insofar as they relate to the arbitrator's powers and duties. When there is more than one arbitrator and a difference arises among them concerning the meaning or application of these rules, it shall be decided by a majority vote. If that is not possible, either an arbitrator or a party may refer the question to the AAA for final decision. All other rules shall be interpreted and applied by the AAA.

R-54. Suspension for Nonpayment

If arbitrator compensation or administrative charges have not been paid in full, the AAA may so inform the parties in order that one of them may advance the required payment. If such payments are not made, the arbitrator may order the suspension or termination of the proceedings. If no arbitrator has yet been appointed, the AAA may suspend the proceedings.

EXPEDITED PROCEDURES

E-1. Limitation on Extensions

Except in extraordinary circumstances, the AAA or the arbitrator may grant a party no more than one seven-day extension of time to respond to the demand for arbitration or counterclaim as provided in Section R-4.

E-2. Changes of Claim or Counterclaim

A claim or counterclaim may be increased in amount, or a new or different claim or counterclaim added, upon the agreement of the other party, or the consent of the arbitrator. After the arbitrator is appointed, however, no new or different claim or counterclaim may be submitted except with the arbitrator's consent. If an increased claim or counterclaim exceeds $75,000, the case will be administered under the regular procedures unless all parties and the arbitrator agree that the case may continue to be processed under the Expedited Procedures.

E-3. Serving of Notices

In addition to notice provided by Section R-39(b), the parties shall also accept notice by telephone. Telephonic notices by the AAA shall subsequently be confirmed in writing to the parties. Should there be a failure to confirm in writing any such oral notice, the proceeding shall nevertheless be valid if notice has, in fact, been given by telephone.

E-4. Appointment and Qualifications of Arbitrator

(a) The AAA shall simultaneously submit to each party an identical list of five proposed arbitrators drawn from its National Roster from which one arbitrator shall be appointed.

(b) The parties are encouraged to agree to an arbitrator from this list and to advise the AAA of their agreement. If the parties are unable to agree upon an arbitrator, each party may strike two names from the list and return it to the AAA within seven days from the date of the AAA's mailing to the parties. If for any reason the appointment of an arbitrator cannot be made from the list, the AAA may make the appointment from other members of the panel without the submission of additional lists.

(c) The parties will be given notice by the AAA of the appointment of the arbitrator, who shall be subject to disqualification for the reasons specified in Section R-17. The parties shall notify the AAA within seven days of any objection to the arbitrator appointed. Any such objection shall be for cause and shall be confirmed in writing to the AAA with a copy to the other party or parties.

E-5. Exchange of Exhibits

At least two business days prior to the hearing, the parties shall exchange copies of all exhibits they intend to submit at the hearing. The arbitrator shall resolve disputes concerning the exchange of exhibits.

E-6. Proceedings on Documents

Where no party's claim exceeds $10,000, exclusive of interest and arbitration costs, and other cases in which the parties agree, the dispute shall be resolved by submission of documents, unless any party requests an oral hearing, or the arbitrator determines that an oral hearing is necessary. The arbitrator shall establish a fair and equitable procedure for the submission of documents.

E-7. Date, Time, and Place of Hearing

In cases in which a hearing is to be held, the arbitrator shall set the date, time, and place of the hearing, to be scheduled to take place within 30 days of confirmation of the arbitrator's appointment. The AAA will notify the parties in advance of the hearing date.

E-8. The Hearing

(a) Generally, the hearing shall not exceed one day. Each party shall have equal opportunity to submit its proofs and complete its case. The arbitrator shall determine the order of the hearing, and may require further submission of documents within two days after the hearing. For good cause shown, the arbitrator may schedule additional hearings within seven business days after the initial day of hearings.

(b) Generally, there will be no stenographic record. Any party desiring a stenographic record may arrange for one pursuant to the provisions of Section R-26.

E-9. Time of Award

Unless otherwise agreed by the parties, the award shall be rendered not later than 14 days from the date of the closing of the hearing or, if oral hearings have been waived, from the date of the AAA's transmittal of the final statements and proofs to the arbitrator.

E-10. Arbitrator's Compensation

Arbitrators will receive compensation at a rate to be suggested by the AAA regional office.

PROCEDURES FOR LARGE, COMPLEX COMMERCIAL DISPUTES

L-1. Administrative Conference

Prior to the dissemination of a list of potential arbitrators, the AAA shall, unless the parties agree otherwise, conduct an administrative conference with the parties and/or their attorneys or other representatives by conference call. The conference will take place within 14 days after the commencement of the arbitration. In the event the parties are unable to agree on a mutually acceptable time for the conference, the AAA may contact the parties individually to discuss the issues contemplated herein. Such administrative conference shall be conducted for the following purposes and for such additional purposes as the parties or the AAA may deem appropriate:

(a) to obtain additional information about the nature and magnitude of the dispute and the anticipated length of hearing and scheduling;

(b) to discuss the views of the parties about the technical and other qualifications of the arbitrators;

(c) to obtain conflicts statements from the parties; and

(d) to consider, with the parties, whether mediation or other non-adjudicative methods of dispute resolution might be appropriate.

L-2. Arbitrators

(a) Large, Complex Commercial Cases shall be heard and determined by either one or three arbitrators, as may be agreed upon by the parties. If the parties are unable to agree upon the number of arbitrators and a claim or counterclaim involves at least $1,000,000, then three arbitrator(s) shall hear and determine the case. If the parties are unable to agree on the number of arbitrators and each claim and counterclaim is less than $1,000,000, then one arbitrator shall hear and determine the case.

(b) The AAA shall appoint arbitrator(s) as agreed by the parties. If they are unable to agree on a method of appointment, the AAA shall appoint arbitrators from the Large, Complex Commercial Case Panel, in the manner provided in the Regular Commercial Arbitration Rules. Absent agreement of the parties, the arbitrator(s) shall not have served as the mediator in the mediation phase of the instant proceeding.

L-3. Preliminary Hearing

As promptly as practicable after the selection of the arbitrator(s), a preliminary hearing shall be held among the parties and/or their attorneys or other representatives and the arbitrator(s). Unless the parties agree otherwise, the preliminary hearing will be conducted by telephone conference call rather than in person. At the preliminary hearing the matters to be considered shall include, without limitation:

(a) service of a detailed statement of claims, damages and defenses, a statement of the issues asserted by each party and positions with respect thereto, and any legal authorities the parties may wish to bring to the attention of the arbitrator(s);

(b) stipulations to uncontested facts;

(c) the extent to which discovery shall be conducted;

(d) exchange and premarking of those documents which each party believes may be offered at the hearing;

(e) the identification and availability of witnesses, including experts, and such matters with respect to witnesses including their biographies and expected testimony as may be appropriate;

(f) whether, and the extent to which, any sworn statements and/or depositions may be introduced;

(g) the extent to which hearings will proceed on consecutive days;

(h) whether a stenographic or other official record of the proceedings shall be maintained;

(i) the possibility of utilizing mediation or other non-adjudicative methods of dispute resolution; and

(j) the procedure for the issuance of subpoenas.

By agreement of the parties and/or order of the arbitrator(s), the pre-hearing activities and the hearing procedures that will govern the arbitration will be memorialized in a Scheduling and Procedure Order.

L-4. Management of Proceedings

(a) Arbitrator(s) shall take such steps as they may deem necessary or desirable to avoid delay and to achieve a just, speedy and cost-effective resolution of Large, Complex Commercial Cases.

(b) Parties shall cooperate in the exchange of documents, exhibits and information within such party's control if the arbitrator(s) consider such production to be consistent with the goal of achieving a just, speedy and cost-effective resolution of a Large, Complex Commercial Case.

(c) The parties may conduct such discovery as may be agreed to by all the parties provided, however, that the arbitrator(s) may place such limitations on the conduct of such discovery as the arbitrator(s) shall deem appropriate. If the parties cannot agree on production of documents and other information, the arbitrator(s), consistent with the expedited nature of arbitration, may establish the extent of the discovery.

(d) At the discretion of the arbitrator(s), upon good cause shown and consistent with the expedited nature of arbitration, the arbitrator(s) may order depositions of, or the propounding of interrogatories to, such persons who may possess information determined by the arbitrator(s) to be necessary to determination of the matter.

(e) The parties shall exchange copies of all exhibits they intend to submit at the hearing 10 business days prior to the hearing unless the arbitrator(s) determine otherwise.

(f) The exchange of information pursuant to this rule, as agreed by the parties and/or directed by the arbitrator(s), shall be included within the Scheduling and Procedure Order.

(g) The arbitrator is authorized to resolve any disputes concerning the exchange of information.

(h) Generally hearings will be scheduled on consecutive days or in blocks of consecutive days in order to maximize efficiency and minimize costs.

OPTIONAL RULES FOR EMERGENCY MEASURES OF PROTECTION

O-1. Applicability

Where parties by special agreement or in their arbitration clause have adopted these rules for emergency measures of protection, a party in need of emergency relief prior to the constitution of the panel shall notify the AAA and all other parties in writing of the nature of the relief sought and the reasons why such relief is required on an emergency basis. The application shall also set forth the reasons why the party is entitled to such relief. Such notice may be given by facsimile transmission, or other reliable means, but must include a statement certifying that all other parties have been notified or an explanation of the steps taken in good faith to notify other parties.

O-2. Appointment of Emergency Arbitrator

Within one business day of receipt of notice as provided in Section O-1, the AAA shall appoint a single emergency arbitrator from a special AAA panel of emergency arbitrators designated to rule on emergency applications. The emergency arbitrator shall immediately disclose any circumstance likely, on the basis of the facts disclosed in the application, to affect such arbitrator's impartiality or independence. Any challenge to the appointment of the emergency arbitrator must be made within one business day of the communication by the AAA to the parties of the appointment of the emergency arbitrator and the circumstances disclosed.

O-3. Schedule

The emergency arbitrator shall as soon as possible, but in any event within two business days of appointment, establish a schedule for consideration of the application for emergency relief. Such schedule shall provide a reasonable opportunity to all parties to be heard, but may provide for proceeding by telephone conference or on written submissions as alternatives to a formal hearing.

O-4. Interim Award

If after consideration the emergency arbitrator is satisfied that the party seeking the emergency relief has shown that immediate and irreparable loss or damage will result in the absence of emergency relief, and that such party is entitled to such relief, the emergency arbitrator may enter an interim award granting the relief and stating the reasons therefore.

O-5. Constitution of the Panel

Any application to modify an interim award of emergency relief must be based on changed circumstances and may be made to the emergency arbitrator until the panel is constituted; thereafter such a request shall be addressed to the panel. The emergency arbitrator shall have no further power to act after the panel is constituted unless the parties agree that the emergency arbitrator is named as a member of the panel.

O-6. Security

Any interim award of emergency relief may be conditioned on provision by the party seeking such relief of appropriate security.

O-7. Special Master

A request for interim measures addressed by a party to a judicial authority shall not be deemed incompatible with the agreement to arbitrate or a waiver of the right to arbitrate. If the AAA is directed by a judicial authority to nominate a special master to consider and report on an application for emergency relief, the AAA shall proceed as provided in Section O-1 of this article and the references to the emergency arbitrator shall be read to mean the special master, except that the special master shall issue a report rather than an interim award.

O-8. Costs

The costs associated with applications for emergency relief shall initially be apportioned by the emergency arbitrator or special master, subject to the power of the panel to determine finally the apportionment of such costs.

ADMINISTRATIVE FEES

The administrative fees of the AAA are based on the amount of the claim or counterclaim. Arbitrator compensation is not included in this schedule. Unless the parties agree otherwise, arbitrator compensation and administrative fees are subject to allocation by the arbitrator in the award.

In an effort to make arbitration costs reasonable for consumers, the AAA has a separate fee schedule for consumer-related disputes. Please refer to Section C-8 of the *Supplementary Procedures for Consumer-Related Disputes* when filing a consumer-related claim.

The AAA applies the *Supplementary Procedures for Consumer-Related Disputes* to arbitration clauses in agreements between individual consumers and businesses where the business has a standardized, systematic application of arbitration clauses with customers and where the terms and conditions of the purchase of standardized, consumable goods or services are non-negotiable or primarily non-negotiable in most or all of its terms, conditions, features, or choices. The product or service must be for personal or household use. The AAA will have the discretion to apply or not to apply the Supplementary Procedures and the parties will be able to bring any disputes concerning the application or non-application to the attention of the arbitrator. Consumers are not prohibited from seeking relief in a small claims court for disputes or claims within the scope of its jurisdiction, even in consumer arbitration cases filed by the business.

Fees

An initial filing fee is payable in full by a filing party when a claim, counterclaim or additional claim is filed. A case service fee will be incurred for all cases that proceed to their first hearing. This fee will be payable in advance at the time that the first hearing is scheduled. This fee will be refunded at the conclusion of the case if no hearings have occurred. However, if the Association is not notified at least 24 hours before the time of the scheduled hearing, the case service fee will remain due and will not be refunded.

These fees will be billed in accordance with the following schedule:

Amount of Claim	Initial Filing Fee	Case Service Fee
Above $0 to $10,000	$750	$200
Above $10,000 to $75,000	$950	$300
Above $75,000 to $150,000	$1,800	$750
Above $150,000 to $300,000	$2,750	$1,250
Above $300,000 to $500,000	$4,250	$1,750
Above $500,000 to $1,000,000	$6,000	$2,500
Above $1,000,000 to $5,000,000	$8,000	$3,250
Above $5,000,000 to $10,000,000	$10,000	$4,000
Above $10,000,000	*	*
Nonmonetary Claims**	$3,250	$1,250

Fee Schedule for Claims in Excess of $10 Million.

The following is the fee schedule for use in disputes involving claims in excess of $10 million. If you have any questions, please consult your local AAA office or case management center.

Claim Size	Fee	Case Service Fee
$10 million and above	Base fee of $12,500 plus .01% of the amount of claim above $10 million.	$6,000
	Filing fees capped at $65,000	

** This fee is applicable only when a claim or counterclaim is not for a monetary amount. Where a monetary claim amount is not known, parties will be required to state a range of claims or be subject to the highest possible filing fee.

Fees are subject to increase if the amount of a claim or counterclaim is modified after the initial filing date. Fees are subject to decrease if the amount of a claim or counterclaim is modified before the first hearing.

The minimum fees for any case having three or more arbitrators are $2,750 for the filing fee, plus a $1,250 case service fee. Expedited Procedures are applied in any case where no disclosed claim or counterclaim exceeds $75,000, exclusive of interest and arbitration costs.

Parties on cases held in abeyance for one year by agreement, will be assessed an annual abeyance fee of $300. If a party refuses to pay the assessed fee, the other party or parties may pay the entire fee on behalf of all parties, otherwise the matter will be closed.

Refund Schedule

The AAA offers a refund schedule on filing fees. For cases with claims up to $75,000, a minimum filing fee of $300 will not be refunded. For all other cases, a minimum fee of $500 will not be refunded. Subject to the minimum fee requirements, refunds will be calculated as follows:

- 100% of the filing fee, above the minimum fee, will be refunded if the case is settled or withdrawn within five calendar days of filing.
- 50% of the filing fee will be refunded if the case is settled or withdrawn between six and 30 calendar days of filing.
- 25% of the filing fee will be refunded if the case is settled or withdrawn between 31 and 60 calendar days of filing.

No refund will be made once an arbitrator has been appointed (this includes one arbitrator on a three-arbitrator panel). No refunds will be granted on awarded cases.

Note: the date of receipt of the demand for arbitration with the AAA will be used to calculate refunds of filing fees for both claims and counterclaims.

Hearing Room Rental

The fees described above do not cover the rental of hearing rooms, which are available on a rental basis. Check with the AAA for availability and rates.

B.1.2 Supplementary Procedures for Consumer-Related Disputes

Effective September 15, 2005

INTRODUCTION

Millions of consumer purchases take place each year. Occasionally, these transactions lead to disagreements between consumers and businesses. These disputes can be resolved by arbitration. Arbitration is usually faster and cheaper than going to court.

The AAA applies the Supplementary Procedures for Consumer-Related Disputes to arbitration clauses in agreements between individual consumers and businesses where the business has a standardized, systematic application of arbitration clauses with customers and where the terms and conditions of the purchase of standardized, consumable goods or services are non-negotiable or primarily non-negotiable in most or all of its terms, conditions, features, or choices. The product or service must be for personal or household use. The AAA will have the discretion to apply or not to apply the Supplementary Procedures and the parties will be able to bring any disputes concerning the application or non-application to the attention of the arbitrator. Consumers are not prohibited from seeking relief in a small claims court for disputes or claims within the scope of its jurisdiction, even in consumer arbitration cases filed by the business.

About the AAA

The American Arbitration Association (AAA) is a not-for-profit, private organization. We offer a broad range of conflict management services to businesses, organizations and individuals. We also provide education, training and publications focused on ways of settling disputes out of court.

The AAA's Consumer Rules

The AAA has developed the Supplementary Procedures for Consumer-Related Disputes for consumers and businesses that want to have their disagreements resolved by arbitrators. People throughout the world can make use of our services.

Availability of Mediation

Mediation is also available to help parties resolve their disputes. Mediations are handled under AAA's Commercial Mediation Procedures.

Administrative Fees

The Association charges a fee for its services under these rules. The costs to the consumer and business depend on the size and nature of the claims. A fee schedule is included at the end of this Supplement. In certain cases, fees paid by the consumer are fully refundable if the dispute is settled before the arbitrator takes any action.

Arbitrator's Fees

Arbitrators get paid for the time they spend resolving disputes. The arbitrator's fee depends on the type of proceeding that is used and the time it takes. The parties make deposits as outlined in the fee schedule at the end of this Supplement. Unused deposits are refunded at the end of the case.

GLOSSARY OF TERMS

Claimant

A Claimant is the party who files the claim or starts the arbitration. Either the consumer or the business may be the Claimant.

Respondent

A Respondent is the party against whom the claim is filed. If a Respondent states a claim in arbitration, it is called a counterclaim. Either the consumer or the business may be the Respondent.

ADR Process

An ADR (Alternative Dispute Resolution) Process is a method of resolving a dispute out of court. Mediation and Arbitration are the most widely used ADR processes.

Arbitration

In arbitration, the parties submit disputes to an impartial person (the arbitrator) for a decision. Each party can present evidence to the arbitrator. Arbitrators do not have to follow the Rules of Evidence used in court.

Arbitrators decide cases with written decisions or "awards." An award is usually binding on the parties. A court may enforce an arbitration award, but the court's review of arbitration awards is limited.

Desk Arbitration

In a Desk Arbitration, the parties submit their arguments and evidence to the arbitrator in writing. The arbitrator then makes an award based only on the documents. No hearing is held.

Telephone Hearing

In a Telephone Hearing, the parties have the opportunity to tell the arbitrator about their case during a conference call. Often this is done after the parties have sent in documents for the arbitrator to review. A Telephone Hearing can be cheaper and easier than an In Person Hearing.

In Person Hearing

During an In Person Hearing, the parties and the arbitrator meet in a conference room or office and the parties present their evidence in a process that is similar to going to court. However, an In Person Hearing is not as formal as going to court.

Mediation

In Mediation, an impartial person (the mediator) helps the parties try to settle their dispute by reaching an agreement together. A mediator's role is to help the parties come to an agreement. A mediator does not arbitrate or decide the outcome.

Neutral

A Neutral is a word that is used to describe someone who is a mediator, arbitrator, or other independent, impartial person selected to serve as the independent third party in an ADR process.

Case Manager

The Case Manager is the AAA's employee assigned to handle the administrative aspects of the case. He or she does not decide the case. He or she only manages the case's administrative steps, such as exchanging documents, matching schedules, and setting up hearings. The Case Manager is the parties' contact point for almost all aspects of the case outside of any hearings.

ADR Agreement

An ADR Agreement is an agreement between a business and a consumer to submit disputes to mediation, arbitration, or other ADR processes.

ADR Program

An ADR Program is any program or service set up or used by a business to resolve disputes out of court.

Independent ADR Institution

An Independent ADR Institution is an organization that provides independent and impartial administration of ADR programs for consumers and businesses. The American Arbitration Association is an Independent ADR Institution.

SUPPLEMENTARY PROCEDURES FOR THE RESOLUTION OF CONSUMER-RELATED DISPUTES

C-1. Agreement of Parties and Applicability

(a) The Commercial Dispute Resolution Procedures and these Supplementary Procedures for Consumer-Related Disputes shall apply whenever the American Arbitration Association (AAA) or its rules are used in an agreement between a consumer and a business where the business has a standardized, systematic application of arbitration clauses with customers and where the terms and conditions of the purchase of standardized, consumable goods or services are non-negotiable or primarily non-negotiable in most or all of its terms, conditions, features, or choices. The product or service must be for personal or household use. The AAA will have the discretion to apply or not to apply the Supplementary Procedures and the parties will be able to bring any disputes concerning the application or non-application to the attention of the arbitrator. The AAA's most current rules will be used when the arbitration is started. If there is a difference between the Commercial Dispute Resolution Procedures and the Supplementary Procedures, the Supplementary Procedures will be used. The Commercial Dispute Resolution Procedures may be found on our web site at www.adr.org. They may also be obtained from the Case Manager.

(b) The Expedited Procedures will be used unless there are three arbitrators. In such cases, the Commercial Dispute Resolution Procedures shall apply.

(c) The AAA may substitute another set of rules, such as the Real Estate or the Wireless Industry Arbitration Rules, for the Commercial Dispute Resolution Procedures in some cases.

(d) Parties can still take their claims to a small claims court.

C-2. Initiation Under an Arbitration Agreement

(a) The filing party (the "claimant") must notify the other party (the "respondent"), in writing, that it wishes to arbitrate a dispute. This notification is referred to as the "demand" for arbitration. The demand should:
  • briefly explain the dispute,
  • list the names and addresses of the consumer and the business,
  • specify the amount of money involved,
  • state what the claimant wants.

The claimant must also send two copies of the demand to the AAA at the time it sends the demand to the respondent. When sending a demand to the AAA, the claimant must attach a copy of the arbitration agreement from the consumer contract with the business. The claimant must also send the appropriate administrative fees and deposits. A fee schedule can be found in Section C-8 at the end of this Supplement.

(b) The AAA shall confirm receipt of the demand to the parties.

(c) The respondent may answer the demand and may also file a counterclaim. The answer must be sent to the AAA within ten calendar days after the AAA acknowledges receipt of claimant's demand. The answer must:
  • be in writing,
  • be sent, in duplicate, to the AAA,
  • be sent to the claimant at the same time.
  • If the respondent has a counterclaim, it must state the nature of the counterclaim, the amount involved, and the remedy sought.

(d) If no answer is filed within the stated time, the AAA will assume that the respondent denies the claim.

(e) The respondent must also send the appropriate administrative fees and deposits. A fee schedule can be found in Section C-8 at the end of this Supplement. Payment is due ten calendar days after the AAA acknowledges receipt of claimant's demand.

C-3. Initiation Under a Submission

Where no agreement to arbitrate exists in the contract between the consumer and the business, the parties may agree to arbitrate a dispute. To begin arbitration, the parties must send the AAA a submission agreement. The submission agreement must:

  • be in writing,
  • be signed by both parties,
  • briefly explain the dispute,
  • list the names and addresses of the consumer and the business,
  • specify the amount of money involved,
  • state the solution sought.

The parties should send two copies of the submission to the AAA. They must also send the administrative fees and deposits. A fee schedule can be found in Section C-8 at the end of this Supplement.

C-4. Appointment of Arbitrator

Immediately after the filing of the submission or the answer, or after the deadline for filing the answer, the AAA will appoint an arbitrator. The parties will have seven calendar days from the time the AAA notifies them, to submit any factual objections to that arbitrator's service.

C-5. Proceedings on Documents ("Desk Arbitration")

Where no claims or counterclaims exceed $10,000, the dispute shall be resolved by the submission of documents. Any party, however, may ask for a hearing. The arbitrator may also decide that a hearing is necessary.

The arbitrator will establish a fair process for submitting the documents. Documents must be sent to the AAA. These will be forwarded to the arbitrator.

C-6. Expedited Hearing Procedures

A party may request that the arbitrator hold a hearing. This hearing may be by telephone or in person. The hearing may occur even if the other party does not attend. A request for a hearing should be made in writing within ten calendar days after the AAA acknowledges receipt of a claimant's demand for arbitration. Requests received after that date will be allowed at the discretion of the arbitrator.

In a case where any party's claim exceeds $10,000, the arbitrator will conduct a hearing unless the parties agree not to have one.

Any hearings will be conducted in accordance with the Expedited Procedures of the Commercial Dispute Resolution Procedures. These procedures may be found on our web site at www.adr.org. They may also be obtained from the Case Manager.

C-7. The Award

(a) Unless the parties agree otherwise, the arbitrator must make his or her award within fourteen calendar days from the date of the closing of the hearing. For Desk Arbitrations, the arbitrator has fourteen calendar days from when the AAA sends the final documents to the arbitrator.

(b) Awards shall be in writing and shall be executed as required by law.

(c) In the award, the arbitrator should apply any identified pertinent contract terms, statutes, and legal precedents. The arbitrator may grant any remedy, relief or outcome that the parties could have received in court. The award shall be final and binding. The award is subject to review in accordance with applicable statutes governing arbitration awards.

C-8. Administrative Fees and Arbitrator Fees[*]

Administrative fees and arbitrator compensation deposits are due from the claimant at the time a case is filed. They are due from the respondent at the time the answer is due. The amounts paid by the consumer and the business are set forth below.

Administrative Fees

Administrative fees are based on the size of the claim and counterclaim in a dispute. They are based only on the actual damages and not on any additional damages, such as attorneys' fees or punitive damages. Portions of these fees are refundable pursuant to the Commercial Fee Schedule.

Arbitrator Fees

For cases in which no claim exceeds $75,000, arbitrators are paid based on the type of proceeding that is used. The parties make deposits as set forth below. Any unused deposits are returned at the end of the case.

Desk Arbitration or Telephone Hearing	$250 for service on the case
In Person Hearing	$750 per day of hearing

For cases in which a claim or counterclaim exceeds $75,000, arbitrators are compensated at the rates set forth on their panel biographies.

Fees and Deposits to be Paid by the Consumer:

If the consumer's claim or counterclaim does not exceed $10,000, then the consumer is responsible for one-half the arbitrator's fees up to a maximum of $125. This deposit is used to pay the arbitrator. It is refunded if not used.

If the consumer's claim or counterclaim is greater than $10,000, but does not exceed $75,000, then the consumer is responsible for one-half the arbitrator's fees up to a maximum of $375. This deposit is used to pay the arbitrator. It is refunded if not used.

If the consumer's claim or counterclaim exceeds $75,000, or if the consumer's claim or counterclaim is non-monetary, then the consumer must pay an Administrative Fee in accordance with the Commercial Fee Schedule. A portion of this fee is refundable pursuant to the Commercial Fee Schedule. The consumer must also deposit one-half of the arbitrator's compensation. This deposit is used to pay the arbitrator. This deposit is refunded if not used. The arbitrator's compensation rate is set forth on the panel biography provided to the parties when the arbitrator is appointed.

Fees and Deposits to be Paid by the Business:

Administrative Fees:

If neither party's claim or counterclaim exceeds $10,000, the business must pay $750 and a Case Service Fee of $200 if a hearing is held. A portion of this fee is refundable pursuant to the Commercial Fee Schedule.

If either party's claim or counterclaim exceeds $10,000, but does not exceed $75,000, the business must pay $950 and a Case Service Fee of $300 if a hearing is held. A portion of this fee is refundable pursuant to the Commercial Fee Schedule.

If the business's claim or counterclaim exceeds $75,000 or if the business's claim or counterclaim is non-monetary, the business must pay an Administrative Fee in accordance with the Commercial Fee Schedule. A portion of this fee is refundable pursuant to the Commercial Fee Schedule.

Arbitrator Fees:

The business must pay for all arbitrator compensation deposits beyond those that are the responsibility of the consumer. These deposits are refunded if not used.

If a party fails to pay its fees and share of the administrative fee or the arbitrator compensation deposit, the other party may advance such funds. The arbitrator may assess these costs in the award.

AAA Customer Service 1-800-778-7879
AAA Web site: www.adr.org

Rules, forms, procedures and guides are subject to periodic change and updating.

---

[*] Pursuant to Section 1284.3 of the California Code of Civil Procedure, consumers with a gross monthly income of less than 300% of the federal poverty guidelines are entitled to a waiver of arbitration fees and costs, exclusive of arbitrator fees. This law applies to all consumer agreements subject to the California Arbitration Act, and to all consumer arbitrations conducted in California. If you believe that you meet these requirements, you must submit to the AAA a declaration under of oath regarding your monthly income and the number of persons in your household. Please contact the AAA's Western Case Management Center at 1-877-528-0879, if you have any questions regarding the waiver of administrative fees. (Effective January 1, 2003)

B.1.3 Class Arbitrations

B.1.3.1 Policy on Class Arbitrations

July 14, 2005

On October 8, 2003, in response to the ruling of the United States Supreme Court in Green Tree Financial Corp. v. Bazzle, the American Arbitration Association issued its Supplementary Rules for Class Arbitrations to govern proceedings brought as class arbitrations. In Bazzle, the Court held that, where an arbitration agreement was silent regarding the availability of class-wide relief, an arbitrator, and not a court, must decide whether class relief is permitted. Accordingly, the American Arbitration Association will administer demands for class arbitration pursuant to its Supplementary Rules for Class Arbitrations if (1) the underlying agreement specifies that disputes arising out of the parties' agreement shall be resolved by arbitration in accordance with any of the Association's rules, and (2) the agreement is silent with respect to class claims, consolidation or joinder of claims.

The Association is not currently accepting for administration demands for class arbitration where the underlying agreement prohibits class claims, consolidation or joinder, unless an order of a court directs the parties to the underlying dispute to submit any aspect of their dispute involving class claims, consolidation, joinder or the enforceability of such provisions, to an arbitrator or to the Association.

Commentary to the American Arbitration Association's Class Arbitrations Policy

February 18, 2005

It has been the practice of the American Arbitration Association since its Supplementary Rules for Class Arbitrations were first enacted to require a party seeking to bring a class arbitration under an agreement that on its face prohibits class actions to first seek court guidance as to whether a class arbitration may be brought under such an agreement. The Association's practice has been neither to commence administration of a case nor to refer such a matter to an arbitrator until a court decides that it is appropriate to do so. The Association's determination not to administer class arbitrations where the underlying arbitration agreement explicitly precludes class procedures was made because the law on the enforceability of class action waivers was unsettled; the Association takes no position as to whether such clauses are or should be enforceable.

In a recent review of this practice by the Association's Executive Committee it was agreed that this practice should be maintained in light of the continued unsettled state of the law. Courts in different states and different federal circuits have reached differing conclusions concerning the preclusion of class actions by agreement and "gateway" issues generally. However, the courts that have confronted the question have generally concluded that the decision as to whether an agreement that prohibits class actions is enforceable is one for the courts to make, not the arbitrator. In fidelity to its Due Process Protocols, the Association will continue to require all proceedings brought to it for administration to meet the standards of fairness and due process set forth in those protocols, but the Association will not seek to make decisions concerning class action agreements that the courts appear to have reserved for themselves.

The Executive Committee also determined at the same meeting to proceed forthwith in the creation of a special committee to explore the possibility of identifying counsel who could assist parties who cannot afford to pay for an attorney in arbitral proceedings. This effort would supplement the Association's current ability to provide arbitrators who will serve pro bono, or for a reduced fee, in appropriate cases.

The Association will continue to monitor developments in this rapidly evolving intersection of arbitration and the courts.

B.1.3.2 Supplementary Rules for Class Arbitrations

Effective Date October 8, 2003

SUPPLEMENTARY RULES FOR CLASS ARBITRATIONS

1. Applicability

(a) These Supplementary Rules for Class Arbitrations ("Supplementary Rules") shall apply to any dispute arising out of an agreement that provides for arbitration pursuant to any of the rules of the American Arbitration Association ("AAA") where a party submits a dispute to arbitration on behalf of or against a class or purported class, and shall supplement any other applicable AAA rules. These Supplementary Rules shall also apply whenever a court refers a matter pleaded as a class action to the AAA for administration, or when a party to a pending AAA arbitration asserts new claims on behalf of or against a class or purported class.

(b) Where inconsistencies exist between these Supplementary Rules and other AAA rules that apply to the dispute, these Supplementary Rules will govern. The arbitrator shall have the authority to resolve any inconsistency between any agreement of the parties and these Supplementary Rules, and in doing so shall endeavor to avoid any prejudice to the interests of absent members of a class or purported class.

(c) Whenever a court has, by order, addressed and resolved any matter that would otherwise be decided by an arbitrator under these Supplementary Rules, the arbitrator shall follow the order of the court.

2. Class Arbitration Roster and Number of Arbitrators

(a) In any arbitration conducted pursuant to these Supplementary Rules, at least one of the arbitrators shall be appointed from the AAA's national roster of class arbitration arbitrators.

(b) If the parties cannot agree upon the number of arbitrators to be appointed, the dispute shall be heard by a sole arbitrator unless the AAA, in its discretion, directs that three arbitrators be appointed. As used in these Supplementary Rules, the term "arbitrator" includes both one and three arbitrators.

3. Construction of the Arbitration Clause

Upon appointment, the arbitrator shall determine as a threshold matter, in a reasoned, partial final award on the construction of the arbitration clause, whether the applicable arbitration clause permits the arbitration to proceed on behalf of or against a class (the "Clause Construction Award"). The arbitrator shall stay all proceedings following the issuance of the Clause Construction Award for a period of at least 30 days to permit any party to move a court of competent jurisdiction to confirm or to vacate the Clause Construction Award. Once all parties inform the arbitrator in writing during the period of the stay that they do not intend to seek judicial review of the Clause Construction Award, or once the requisite time period expires without any party having informed the arbitrator that it has done so, the arbitrator may proceed with the arbitration on the basis stated in the Clause Construction Award. If any party informs the arbitrator within the period provided that it has sought judicial review, the arbitrator may stay further proceedings, or some part of them, until the arbitrator is informed of the ruling of the court.

In construing the applicable arbitration clause, the arbitrator shall not consider the existence of these Supplementary Rules, or any other AAA rules, to be a factor either in favor of or against permitting the arbitration to proceed on a class basis.

4. Class Certification

(a) Prerequisites to a Class Arbitration

If the arbitrator is satisfied that the arbitration clause permits the arbitration to proceed as a class arbitration, as provided in Rule 3, or where a court has ordered that an arbitrator determine whether a class arbitration may be maintained, the arbitrator shall determine whether the arbitration should proceed as a class arbitration. For that purpose, the arbitrator shall consider the criteria enumerated in this Rule 4 and any law or agreement of the parties the arbitrator determines applies to the arbitration. In doing so, the arbitrator shall determine whether one or more members of a class may act in the arbitration as representative parties on behalf of all members of the class described. The arbitrator shall permit a representative to do so only if each of the following conditions is met:

(1) the class is so numerous that joinder of separate arbitrations on behalf of all members is impracticable;
(2) there are questions of law or fact common to the class;
(3) the claims or defenses of the representative parties are typical of the claims or defenses of the class;
(4) the representative parties will fairly and adequately protect the interests of the class;
(5) counsel selected to represent the class will fairly and adequately protect the interests of the class; and
(6) each class member has entered into an agreement containing an arbitration clause which is substantially similar to that signed by the class representative(s) and each of the other class members.

(b) Class Arbitrations Maintainable

An arbitration may be maintained as a class arbitration if the prerequisites of subdivision (a) are satisfied, and in addition, the arbitrator finds that the questions of law or fact common to the members of the class predominate over any questions affecting only individual members, and that a class arbitration is superior to other available methods for the fair and efficient adjudication of the controversy. The matters pertinent to the findings include:

(1) the interest of members of the class in individually controlling the prosecution or defense of separate arbitrations;
(2) the extent and nature of any other proceedings concerning the controversy already commenced by or against members of the class;
(3) the desirability or undesirability of concentrating the determination of the claims in a single arbitral forum; and
(4) the difficulties likely to be encountered in the management of a class arbitration.

5. Class Determination Award

(a) The arbitrator's determination concerning whether an arbitration should proceed as a class arbitration shall be set forth in a reasoned, partial final award (the "Class Determination Award"), which shall address each of the matters set forth in Rule 4.

(b) A Class Determination Award certifying a class arbitration shall define the class, identify the class representative(s) and counsel, and shall set forth the class claims, issues, or defenses. A copy of the proposed Notice of Class Determination (see Rule 6), specifying the intended mode of delivery of the Notice to the class members, shall be attached to the award.

(c) The Class Determination Award shall state when and how members of the class may be excluded from the class arbitration. If an arbitrator concludes that some exceptional circumstance, such as the need to resolve claims seeking injunctive relief or claims to a limited fund, makes it inappropriate to allow class members to request exclusion, the Class Determination Award shall explain the reasons for that conclusion.

(d) The arbitrator shall stay all proceedings following the issuance of the Class Determination Award for a period of at least 30 days to permit any party to move a court of competent jurisdiction to confirm or to vacate the Class Determination Award. Once all parties inform the arbitrator in writing during the period of the stay that they do not intend to seek judicial review of the Class Determination Award, or once the requisite time period expires without any party having informed the arbitrator that it has done so, the arbitrator may proceed with the arbitration on the basis stated in the Class Determination Award. If any party informs the arbitrator within the period provided that it has sought judicial review, the arbitrator may stay further proceedings, or some part of them, until the arbitrator is informed of the ruling of the court.

(e) A Class Determination Award may be altered or amended by the arbitrator before a final award is rendered.

6. Notice of Class Determination

(a) In any arbitration administered under these Supplementary Rules, the arbitrator shall, after expiration of the stay following the Class Determination Award, direct that class members be provided the best notice practicable under the circumstances (the "Notice of Class Determination"). The Notice of Class Determination shall be given to all members who can be identified through reasonable effort.

(b) The Notice of Class Determination must concisely and clearly state in plain, easily understood language:

(1) the nature of the action;
(2) the definition of the class certified;
(3) the class claims, issues, or defenses;
(4) that a class member may enter an appearance through counsel if the member so desires, and that any class member may attend the hearings;
(5) that the arbitrator will exclude from the class any member

who requests exclusion, stating when and how members may elect to be excluded;
(6) the binding effect of a class judgment on class members;
(7) the identity and biographical information about the arbitrator, the class representative(s) and class counsel that have been approved by the arbitrator to represent the class; and
(8) how and to whom a class member may communicate about the class arbitration, including information about the AAA Class Arbitration Docket (see Rule 9).

7. Final Award

The final award on the merits in a class arbitration, whether or not favorable to the class, shall be reasoned and shall define the class with specificity. The final award shall also specify or describe those to whom the notice provided in Rule 6 was directed, those the arbitrator finds to be members of the class, and those who have elected to opt out of the class.

8. Settlement, Voluntary Dismissal, or Compromise

(a)(1) Any settlement, voluntary dismissal, or compromise of the claims, issues, or defenses of an arbitration filed as a class arbitration shall not be effective unless approved by the arbitrator.
(2) The arbitrator must direct that notice be provided in a reasonable manner to all class members who would be bound by a proposed settlement, voluntary dismissal, or compromise.
(3) The arbitrator may approve a settlement, voluntary dismissal, or compromise that would bind class members only after a hearing and on finding that the settlement, voluntary dismissal, or compromise is fair, reasonable, and adequate.
(b) The parties seeking approval of a settlement, voluntary dismissal, or compromise under this Rule must submit to the arbitrator any agreement made in connection with the proposed settlement, voluntary dismissal, or compromise.
(c) The arbitrator may refuse to approve a settlement unless it affords a new opportunity to request exclusion to individual class members who had an earlier opportunity to request exclusion but did not do so.
(d) Any class member may object to a proposed settlement, voluntary dismissal, or compromise that requires approval under this Rule. Such an objection may be withdrawn only with the approval of the arbitrator.

9. Confidentiality; Class Arbitration Docket

(a) The presumption of privacy and confidentiality in arbitration proceedings shall not apply in class arbitrations. All class arbitration hearings and filings may be made public, subject to the authority of the arbitrator to provide otherwise in special circumstances. However, in no event shall class members, or their individual counsel, if any, be excluded from the arbitration hearings.
(b) The AAA shall maintain on its Web site a Class Arbitration Docket of arbitrations filed as class arbitrations. The Class Arbitration Docket will provide certain information about the arbitration to the extent known to the AAA, including:
(1) a copy of the demand for arbitration;
(2) the identities of the parties;
(3) the names and contact information of counsel for each party;
(4) a list of awards made in the arbitration by the arbitrator; and
(5) the date, time and place of any scheduled hearings.

10. Form and Publication of Awards

(a) Any award rendered under these Supplementary Rules shall be in writing, shall be signed by the arbitrator or a majority of the arbitrators, and shall provide reasons for the award.
(b) All awards rendered under these Supplementary Rules shall be publicly available, on a cost basis.

11. Administrative Fees and Suspension for Nonpayment

(a) A preliminary filing fee of $3,250 is payable in full by a party making a demand for treatment of a claim, counterclaim, or additional claim as a class arbitration. The preliminary filing fee shall cover all AAA administrative fees through the rendering of the Clause Construction Award. If the arbitrator determines that the arbitration shall proceed beyond the Clause Construction Award, a supplemental filing fee shall be paid by the requesting party. The supplemental filing fee shall be calculated based on the amount claimed in the class arbitration and in accordance with the fee schedule contained in the AAA's Commercial Arbitration Rules.
(b) Disputes regarding the parties' obligation to pay administrative fees or arbitrator's compensation pursuant to applicable law or the parties' agreement may be determined by the arbitrator. Upon the joint application of the parties, however, an arbitrator other than the arbitrator appointed to decide the merits of the arbitration, shall be appointed by the AAA to render a partial final award solely related to any disputes regarding the parties' obligations to pay administrative fees or arbitrator's compensation.
(c) If an invoice for arbitrator compensation or administrative charges has not been paid in full, the AAA may so inform the parties in order that one of them may advance the required deposit. If such payments are not made, the arbitrator may order the suspension or termination of the proceedings. If no arbitrator has yet been appointed, the AAA may suspend the proceedings.
(d) If an arbitration conducted pursuant to these Supplementary Rules is suspended for nonpayment, a notice that the case has been suspended shall be published on the AAA's Class Arbitration Docket.

12. Applications to Court and Exclusion of Liability

(a) No judicial proceeding initiated by a party relating to a class arbitration shall be deemed a waiver of the party's right to arbitrate.
(b) Neither the AAA nor any arbitrator in a class arbitration or potential class arbitration under these Supplementary Rules is a necessary or proper party in or to judicial proceedings relating to the arbitration. It is the policy of the AAA to comply with any order of a court directed to the parties to an arbitration or with respect to the conduct of an arbitration, whether or not the AAA is named as a party to the judicial proceeding in which the order is issued.
(c) Parties to a class arbitration under these Supplementary Rules shall be deemed to have consented that judgment upon each of the awards rendered in the arbitration may be entered in any federal or state court having jurisdiction thereof.
(d) Parties to an arbitration under these Supplementary Rules shall be deemed to have consented that neither the AAA nor any arbitrator shall be liable to any party in any action seeking damages or injunctive relief for any act or omission in connection with any arbitration under these Supplementary Rules.

Appx. B.1.4   *Consumer Arbitration Agreements*

B.1.4 Disclosures for California Consumer Cases

B.1.4.1 Consumer-Related Disputes Filing Form—California

AMERICAN ARBITRATION ASSOCIATION
SUPPLEMENTARY PROCEDURES FOR
CONSUMER-RELATED DISPUTES
(FOR USE ONLY IN CALIFORNIA)

Pursuant to Section 1284.3 of the California Code of Civil Procedure, consumers with a gross monthly income of less than 300% of the federal poverty guidelines are entitled to a waiver of arbitration fees and costs, exclusive of arbitrator fees. This law applies to all consumer agreements subject to the California Arbitration Act, and to all consumer arbitrations conducted in California. If you believe that you meet these requirements, you must submit to the AAA a declaration under oath regarding your monthly income and the number of persons in your household. Please contact the AAA's Western Case Management Center at 1-877-528-0879, if you have any questions regarding the waiver of administrative fees.

How to file a claim; consumers should:
- Fill out this form and retain one copy for your records.
- Mail two copies of this form and your check or money order made payable to the AAA, to the AAA Case Management Center nearest to you. Please consult Section C-8 of the *Supplementary Procedures for Consumer-Related Disputes* for the appropriate fee.
- Send a copy of this form to the business.

How to file a claim; businesses should:
- Fill out this form and retain one copy for your records.
- Mail two copies of this form and your check or money order made payable to the AAA, to the AAA Case Management Center nearest to you. Please consult Section C-8 of the *Supplementary Procedures for Consumer-Related Disputes* for the appropriate fee.
- Send a copy of this form to the consumer by registered mail return receipt requested.

---

1. How is this claim being filed? Check only one.
   [ ] By request of the consumer (A copy of the arbitration agreement **must** be attached. A copy of this form **must** also be sent to the business)

   [ ] By request of the business (A copy of the arbitration agreement **must** be attached. A copy of this form **must** also be sent to the consumer by registered mail return receipt requested)
   -or-
   [ ] By mutual agreement ("submission") of the parties (both parties **must** sign this form)

2. Briefly explain the dispute.

3. Do you believe there is any money owed to you? If yes, how much?

4. Is there any other outcome you want? [ ] Yes   [ ] No
   If yes, what is it?

5. Preferred hearing locale (if an in-person hearing is held) _____

6. Fill in the following information

Consumer
Name of Consumer _____
Address _____
City/State/Zip _____
Telephone _____
Fax _____
Signature of Consumer _____
Representative _____
Firm _____
Address _____
City/State/Zip _____
Telephone _____
Fax _____

Business
Name of Business _____
Address _____
City/State/Zip _____
Telephone _____
Fax _____
Signature of Business _____
Representative _____
Firm _____
Address _____
City/State/Zip _____
Telephone _____
Fax _____

B.1.4.2 Ethics Standards for Neutral Arbitrators in Contractual Arbitration in California: Fact Sheet

This fact sheet has been developed to provide information concerning the actions taken by the American Arbitration Association ("AAA") to comply with the California Ethics Standards for Neutral Arbitrators in Contractual Arbitration ("Standards") and provide the required disclosures. The AAA may amend this fact sheet periodically to update any changes to the AAA's procedures pursuant to these Standards or other changes implemented by the AAA. The AAA's Web site will contain the current fact sheet. For a hard copy of the most current fact sheet, please contact the Western Case Management Center at 1-877-528-0879.

The information provided in this fact sheet, and any disclosures made prior to or during an arbitration are pursuant to California Civil Code Section 1281.85. Parties participating in AAA administered dispute resolution services provide party information contained within the actual disclosures. The AAA has compiled the available information from parties. That information has not been reviewed, investigated, or evaluated for accuracy or completeness of the information received. The AAA makes no representations regarding the accuracy or completeness of this information.

The information provided in this document and any disclosures made pursuant to the Standards is on an "as is" basis without warranty of any kind, express or implied. To the fullest extent permissible, pursuant to applicable law, the AAA disclaims all warranties, express or implied, including, but not limited to, any implied warranties of merchantability or fitness for a particular purpose. You assume the entire risk related to your use of this information. In no event will the AAA be liable to you or any other person for any damages resulting from the use or misuse of the information provided, or any acts, omissions, and/or errors in the gathering, compiling and dissemination of this information.

1. **General Information Concerning the AAA's Gathering of Information for Disclosures**
   a. The AAA has made a reasonable effort to accurately comply with the reporting and disclosure requirements of the Standards. In gathering, compiling and reporting the information for a given arbitration, the AAA has relied upon the information provided by the parties to that arbitration. Any attempt to gather and compile information for a particular disclosure will be limited to a search based on the information provided by the parties to that particular arbitration.
   b. Regarding disclosures on lawyers for the parties, the AAA will rely solely on the information under "Name of Representative" contained in the original Demand for Arbitration unless advised otherwise by the parties prior to the AAA's gathering and compiling of information for possible disclosures. It is the responsibility of the parties to provide the AAA with additional information concerning any other relevant representatives if they wish the AAA to include in its gathering and compiling of information other representative information for possible disclosures. Under AAA rules, a party may be represented by an attorney or a non-attorney and therefore our disclosures will include both attorney and non-attorney representatives.
   c. Any attempt to gather and compile information concerning a specific company or organization is limited to the name of that particular company or organization as designated in the Demand Form, and will not include any parent organizations or subsidiaries of that company or organization. Specifically, the AAA will rely on the "Party" information contained in the original Demand for Arbitration unless advised otherwise by the parties prior to the AAA's gathering and compiling of possible disclosures. It is the responsibility of the parties to provide the AAA with information concerning any other relevant companies and organizations that they wish the AAA to include in its investigation for possible disclosures.
   d. By naming the AAA in an arbitration agreement, parties agree to arbitrate under the rules of the AAA. When participating in an AAA administered arbitration in accordance with the AAA's rules, the parties are expected to act in accordance with those rules. Any party who proceeds with the arbitration after knowledge that any provisions or requirement of the rules has not been complied with, and who fails to state objections thereto in writing, shall be deemed to have waived the right to object (see, for example, Rule 39 of the Commercial Dispute Resolution Procedures and Rule 31 of the National Rules for the Resolution of Employment Disputes).

2. **Relationship between provider organization and arbitrator**
The AAA administers cases. It does not determine the merits of a case: arbitrators decide cases. AAA staff members do not hear evidence, do not write awards, and do not review the reasoning of awards. AAA awards are only reviewed to ensure proper format.

Arbitrators and mediators at the AAA are independent contractors. Arbitrators that serve on the AAA panel are bound by the Code of Ethics for Arbitrators in Commercial Disputes. Mediators are bound by the Model Standards of Conduct for Mediators.

When an arbitrator or mediator is selected from a list of potential neutrals, (s)he is required to disclose the existence of interests or relationships that are likely to affect her/his impartiality or that might reasonably create an appearance that (s)he is biased against one party or favorable to another.

There is judicial oversight for arbitrator impartiality, as arbitrator bias is one of the grounds for vacating an award.

The AAA charges a $300 annual panel maintenance fee to Arbitrators to reimburse for the cost of maintaining and updating all Arbitrators' resumes. Not all Arbitrators pay this fee. Only those Arbitrators that serve on a case pay this fee, which is deducted from arbitrator compensation. Arbitrators must also pay for each of the training classes they are required to attend. The arbitrator training requirements are listed below.

3. **AAA Process and Criteria for Recruiting, Screening and Training of Neutrals**
Recruiting and Screening: The AAA is the nation's leading provider of alternative dispute resolution services. Openings on our National Roster of Neutrals are extremely limited, based primarily on caseload needs and user preferences. Consequently, even candidates with strong credentials may not be added to our roster.

Applicants for membership on the AAA National Roster of Arbitrators and Mediators must meet or exceed seven stringent requirements. Please visit our Web site at www.adr.org, in the

Resources page of the Roster of Neutrals section, to view these requirements and more information on our panel of neutrals.

Training: Arbitrators on our National Roster are required to complete the following training requirements to be considered for service:

a. Arbitrator I training—completed within 6 months of admission to the panel.
b. Arbitrator II training—completed within 1 year of completion of Arbitrator I.
c. Annual Arbitrator Update—completed within 1 year of Arbitrator II.
d. Arbitrator Continuing Education—upon completion of Arbitrator II, one class annually.

4. AAA Process for Identifying, Recommending, and Selecting Potential Neutrals for Specific Cases

For claims that exceed $75,000: The AAA encourages the parties to a dispute to provide their preference on the qualifications for arbitrators on specific cases, to assist in the identifying of potential neutrals. Using this information, the case manager will review our National Roster of Neutrals in the areas of expertise, locale and compensation ranges. Once a pool of candidates is identified, the AAA reviews the list to remove arbitrators with obvious conflicts to the parties or law firms to the dispute. In accordance with the Rules, the AAA sends simultaneously to each party to the dispute an identical list of names of persons recommended from the panel. It is the parties who select the neutral for a specific case. Parties are encouraged to agree on a neutral.

The specific procedures used to create a list for a particular case may vary depending on the type of case filed and the Rules under which that case is being administered. The AAA will also comply with the terms of any court order received regarding the arbitrator selection process, and unless the applicable administrative procedures state otherwise or the parties agree otherwise, the AAA will comply with any express contractual provisions.

Where appropriate and in accordance with AAA rules and procedures, the AAA will make direct appointments of neutral arbitrators without the submission of a list to the parties.

For claims that are $75,000 or less: If no claim in the arbitration exceeds $75,000, the AAA will appoint an arbitrator and notify the parties of the name and qualifications of the arbitrator. The AAA will appoint an arbitrator who is an attorney, unless the parties agree otherwise. After the appointment of the arbitrator, the parties may submit to the AAA any objections to that arbitrator's service.

5. AAA's Process in Ruling on Requests for Disqualification of Neutrals

In accordance with the applicable rules, upon objection of a party to the continued service of a neutral arbitrator, the AAA is empowered to determine, at its sole discretion, whether the arbitrator should be disqualified, which decision shall be conclusive. The AAA requests both parties input before making a decision on removal or confirmation.

The AAA will consider the requirements of any applicable statute or other controlling authority when making the determination to remove or reaffirm neutral arbitrators.

B.1.4.3 Business Advisory of Consumer Case Disclosures

Dear Businesses and Attorneys:

The purpose of this notice is to advise the users of our consumer, non-union employment and health care dispute resolution services that we will be required, by California law, to publicly post and disclose certain information regarding companies and attorneys who make use of American Arbitration Association ("AAA") services to resolve disputes involving consumers, employees and health care patients beginning January 1, 2003.

The AAA has been in the forefront in developing standards of fairness for disputes between consumers and businesses. In April 1998, the AAA developed the Consumer Due Process Protocol in cooperation with groups representing government agencies, consumer interest groups and educational institutions, as well as businesses. The goal of the Protocol, in concert with the Supplementary Procedures for Consumer-Related Disputes, is to ensure fairness and even-handedness in the resolution of disputes in arbitration. The Association also has issued other protocols dealing with fairness in disputes: A Due Process Protocol for Mediation and Arbitration of Statutory Disputes Arising out of the Employment Relationship (1995) and Health Care Due Process Protocol (1998).

As you may be aware, the California Legislature recently passed arbitration legislation, focusing on the provider organizations that administer consumer, non-union employment and healthcare arbitration cases and the arbitrators who serve in the decision-making role. Under the legislation, effective January 1, 2003, provider organizations will be required to collect certain statistical data and publish information regarding our users in consumer, employment and healthcare matters.

Specifically, California Code of Civil Procedure Section 1281.96, requires the collection and posting of the name of the non-consumer party; the type of dispute involved, i.e. the underlying subject matter of the dispute; the prevailing party; the number of previous occasions the non-consumer party has appeared in a case before the provider organization; whether the consumer was represented by an attorney; information regarding timelines; the disposition of the case; amount of claim and the award; name of the arbitrator; fee collected by the arbitrator for service on the case and allocation of the arbitrator's fee between the parties. Under this statute, the Association will be required to retain collected data for cases for 5 years. Other disclosures and publications may also be required. The Association does not anticipate that this will have a retroactive effect.

If you have any questions, please do not hesitate to refer to our Web site or call the Western Case Management Center at 1-877-528-0879.

B.1.4.4 Consumer Statistics

CLICK HERE TO VIEW THE PROVIDER ORGANIZATION REPORT.

[*Editor's Note: For the latest version of AAA's quarterly Provider Organization Report, please visit www.adr.org and click on the live weblink in the version of this document which may be found on that website.*]

Any "prevailing party" information contained within this Web site/document, has been provided solely by the arbitrator(s) to an arbitration. The AAA has not reviewed, investigated, or evaluated the accuracy or completeness of the arbitrator's/arbitrators' determination of the "prevailing party" and makes no representations on the accuracy or completeness of this information.

The information provided here is on an "as is" basis without warranty of any kind, express or implied. To the fullest extent permissible pursuant to applicable law, the AAA disclaims all warranties, express or implied, including, but not limited to, any implied warranties of merchantability or fitness for a particular purpose. You assume the entire risk related to your use of this information to the fullest extent permissible pursuant to applicable law. In no event will the AAA be liable to you or any other person for any damages resulting from the use or misuse of the information provided, or any acts, omissions, and/or errors in the gathering, compiling and dissemination of the information.

This report is pursuant to California Code of Civil Procedure Section 1281.96. If you wish to obtain a hard copy of the report or if you have questions regarding the report, please call the American Arbitration Association at 877-528-0879.

Searching the Report

To search the report, open the report, click on the "search" icon (binoculars) in the task bar in the upper left portion of the screen and enter the text you wish to find.

Report Legend

Non-Consumer Party—This is the business or employer involved in the dispute.

Type of Dispute—This is the general category of the dispute. Note that "Consumer Pre-Case" indicates an incomplete request for arbitration in which the filing requirements have not been met.

Salary Range—This is the salary range of the employee involved in the case, as provided by the filing party. This is reported only on employment cases.

Prevailing Party—If the arbitrator indicates a prevailing party in the award, that information is reflected here. This is reported only on awarded cases.

Consumer SelfRep'd—This indicates whether the consumer represented himself or herself in the arbitration proceeding.

Filing Date—This is the date the administrative case record was opened.

Disposition Date—This is the date the administrative case record was closed.

Type of Disposition—This is the manner in which the case was closed. Dispositions include:

Awarded—A case in which the arbitrator has rendered a decision

Settled—A case that was closed after the parties reached a mutual resolution of the dispute

Withdrawn—A case in which the moving party withdrew its claim prior to resolution

Amount of Claim—This is the monetary amount in dispute.

Total Fee—This is the full amount of arbitrator's fees and expenses charged on the case.

Fee Allocation—This is the percentage of the Total Fee borne by the consumer and non-consumer parties.

Arbitrator—This is the name of the arbitrator appointed to the case. The date immediately to the right of the arbitrator's name is the date of the arbitrator's appointment to the case.

Award Amount—This is the monetary amount awarded on the claim. This is reported only on awarded cases.

Other Relief—If there is a non-monetary component to the award, it is indicated here. This is reported only on awarded cases in which non-monetary relief is granted by the arbitrator.

The AAA provides information on consumer arbitrations in accordance with the California Code of Civil Procedure Section 1281.96. The information that is included in this website is based upon consumer cases filed after January 1, 2003, updated on a quarterly basis, as required by law. Further inquiries regarding this notice or the information in this section can be directed to Customer Service at the Western Case Management Center, at 877.528.0879.

B.1.4.5 Affidavit for Waiver of Fees—California

**American Arbitration Association Affidavit For Waiver of Fees
Notice
For Use By California Consumers Only**

Pursuant to section 1284.3 of the California Code of Civil Procedure, consumers with a gross monthly income of less than 300% of the federal poverty guidelines, are entitled to a waiver of all fees and costs, exclusive of arbitrator fees. This law applies to all consumer arbitration agreements subject to the California Arbitration Act, and to all consumer arbitrations conducted in California. If you believe that you meet these requirements, please complete this form and submit it with your demand for arbitration to the AAA's Western Case Management Center.

If (1) you are not a California consumer; or (2) your gross monthly income is more than 300% of the federal poverty guidelines, you may still apply for a reduction or deferral of AAA administrative fees by contacting the nearest AAA Case Management Center and requesting a hardship application form.

Name: _____
Address: _____
Number of Persons in Household _____
Gross Monthly Income _____

I hereby swear that the foregoing is a true and correct statement.

_____
Signature

Arbitration Service Provider Rules   Appx. B.1.4.6

B.1.4.6 Demand for Arbitration—California Employment-Related Disputes

AMERICAN ARBITRATION ASSOCIATION
EMPLOYMENT ARBITRATION RULES
DEMAND FOR ARBITRATION
(FOR USE ONLY IN CALIFORNIA)

Pursuant to Section 1284.3 of the California Code of Civil Procedure, consumers with a gross monthly income of less than 300% of the federal poverty guidelines are entitled to a waiver of arbitration fees and costs, exclusive of arbitrator fees. This law applies to all consumer agreements subject to the California Arbitration Act, and to all consumer arbitrations conducted in California. Only those disputes arising out of employer promulgated plans are included in the consumer definition. If you believe that you meet these requirements, you must submit to the AAA a declaration under oath regarding your monthly income and the number of persons in your household. Please contact the AAA's Western Case Management Center at 1-877-528-0879, if you have any questions regarding the waiver of administrative fees.

MEDIATION is a nonbinding process. The mediator assists the parties in working out a solution that is acceptable to them. If you would like the AAA to contact the other parties to determine whether they wish to mediate this matter, please check this box. ☐ There is no additional administrative fee for this service.

TO: Name	Name of Representative (if known)	Name of Firm (if applicable)
Address	Representative's Address	
City / State / Zip Code	City / State / Zip Code	
Phone No. / Fax No.	Phone No. / Fax No.	
E-Mail Address	E-Mail Address	

The named claimant, a party to an arbitration agreement or program which provides for arbitration under the Employment Arbitration Rules of the American Arbitration Association, hereby demands arbitration.

THE NATURE OF THE DISPUTE

THE CLAIM OR RELIEF SOUGHT (the amount, if any)

DOES THIS DISPUTE ARISE OUT OF AN EMPLOYMENT RELATIONSHIP?   Yes ☐   No ☐
DATE OF THE EMPLOYMENT AGREEMENT _____

WHAT WAS/IS THE EMPLOYEE'S ANNUAL WAGE RANGE? Note: this question is required by California law.
   ☐ Less than $100,000   ☐ $100,000 - $250,000   ☐ Over $250,000

Claimant   ☐ Employee   ☐ Employer
Respondent   ☐ Employee   ☐ Employer

HEARING LOCALE REQUESTED

You are hereby notified that copies of our arbitration agreement and this demand are being filed with the American Arbitration Association at its_____ office, with a request that it commence administration of the arbitration. Under the rules, you may file an answering statement within ten days after notice from the AAA.

Signature (may be signed by a representative)	Title	Date
Name of Claimant	Name of Representative	Name of Firm (if applicable)
Address (to be used in connection with this case)	Representative's Address	
City / State / Zip Code	City / State / Zip Code	
Phone No. / Fax No.	Phone No. / Fax No.	
E-Mail Address	E-Mail Address	

TO BEGIN PROCEEDINGS, PLEASE SEND TWO COPIES OF THIS DEMAND **AND THE ARBITRATION AGREEMENT**, WITH THE FILING FEE AS PROVIDED FOR IN THE RULES, TO THE AAA. SEND THE ORIGINAL DEMAND TO THE RESPONDENT.

Form E2-01/03

B.1.5 Consumer Due Process Protocol

Statement of Principles of the National Consumer Disputes Advisory Committee

Statement of Principles
Introduction: Genesis of the Advisory Committee
Scope of the Consumer Due Process Protocol
Glossary of Terms
Major Standards and Sources
Principle 1. Fundamentally-Fair Process
Principle 2. Access to Information Regarding ADR Program
Principle 3. Independent and Impartial Neutral; Independent Administration
Principle 4. Quality and Competence of Neutrals
Principle 5. Small Claims
Principle 6. Reasonable Cost
Principle 7. Reasonably Convenient Location
Principle 8. Reasonable Time Limits
Principle 9. Right to Representation
Principle 10. Mediation
Principle 11. Agreements to Arbitrate
Principle 12. Arbitration Hearings
Principle 13. Access to Information
Principle 14. Arbitral Remedies
Principle 15. Arbitration Awards
LIST OF SIGNATORIES

STATEMENT OF PRINCIPLES

PRINCIPLE 1. FUNDAMENTALLY-FAIR PROCESS

All parties are entitled to a fundamentally-fair ADR process. As embodiments of fundamental fairness, these Principles should be observed in structuring ADR Programs.

PRINCIPLE 2. ACCESS TO INFORMATION REGARDING ADR PROGRAM

Providers of goods or services should undertake reasonable measures to provide Consumers with full and accurate information regarding Consumer ADR Programs. At the time the Consumer contracts for goods or services, such measures should include (1) clear and adequate notice regarding the ADR provisions, including a statement indicating whether participation in the ADR Program is mandatory or optional, and (2) reasonable means by which Consumers may obtain additional information regarding the ADR Program. After a dispute arises, Consumers should have access to all information necessary for effective participation in ADR.

PRINCIPLE 3. INDEPENDENT AND IMPARTIAL NEUTRAL; INDEPENDENT ADMINISTRATION

1. **Independent and Impartial Neutral.** *All parties are entitled to a Neutral who is independent and impartial.*
2. **Independent Administration.** *If participation in mediation or arbitration is mandatory, the procedure should be administered by an Independent ADR Institution. Administrative services should include the maintenance of a panel of prospective Neutrals, facilitation of Neutral selection, collection and distribution of Neutral's fees and expenses, oversight and implementation of ADR rules and procedures, and monitoring of Neutral qualifications, performance, and adherence to pertinent rules, procedures and ethical standards.*
3. **Standards for Neutrals.** *The Independent ADR Institution should make reasonable efforts to ensure that Neutrals understand and conform to pertinent ADR rules, procedures and ethical standards.*
4. **Selection of Neutrals.** *The Consumer and Provider should have an equal voice in the selection of Neutrals in connection with a specific dispute.*
5. **Disclosure and Disqualification.** *Beginning at the time of appointment, Neutrals should be required to disclose to the Independent ADR Institution any circumstance likely to affect impartiality, including any bias or financial or personal interest which might affect the result of the ADR proceeding, or any past or present relationship or experience with the parties or their representatives, including past ADR experiences. The Independent ADR Institution should communicate any such information to the parties and other Neutrals, if any. Upon objection of a party to continued service of the Neutral, the Independent ADR Institution should determine whether the Neutral should be disqualified and should inform the parties of its decision. The disclosure obligation of the Neutral and procedure for disqualification should continue throughout the period of appointment.*

PRINCIPLE 4. QUALITY AND COMPETENCE OF NEUTRALS

All parties are entitled to competent, qualified Neutrals. Independent ADR Institutions are responsible for establishing and maintaining standards for Neutrals in ADR Programs they administer.

PRINCIPLE 5. SMALL CLAIMS

Consumer ADR Agreements should make it clear that all parties retain the right to seek relief in a small claims court for disputes or claims within the scope of its jurisdiction.

PRINCIPLE 6. REASONABLE COST

1. **Reasonable Cost.** *Providers of goods and services should develop ADR programs which entail reasonable cost to Consumers based on the circumstances of the dispute, including, among other things, the size and nature of the claim, the nature of goods or services provided, and the ability of the Consumer to pay. In some cases, this may require the Provider to subsidize the process.*
2. **Handling of Payment.** *In the interest of ensuring fair and independent Neutrals, the making of fee arrangements and the payment of fees should be administered on a rational, equitable and consistent basis by the Independent ADR Institution.*

PRINCIPLE 7. REASONABLY CONVENIENT LOCATION

In the case of face-to-face proceedings, the proceedings should be conducted at a location which is reasonably convenient to both parties with due consideration of their ability to travel and other pertinent circumstances. If the parties are unable to agree on a location, the determination should be made by the Independent ADR Institution or by the Neutral.

PRINCIPLE 8. REASONABLE TIME LIMITS

ADR proceedings should occur within a reasonable time, without undue delay. The rules governing ADR should establish specific reasonable time periods for each step in the ADR process and, where necessary, set forth default procedures in the event a party fails to participate in the process after reasonable notice.

PRINCIPLE 9. RIGHT TO REPRESENTATION

All parties participating in processes in ADR Programs have the right, at their own expense, to be represented by a spokesperson of their own choosing. The ADR rules and procedures should so specify.

PRINCIPLE 10. MEDIATION

The use of mediation is strongly encouraged as an informal means of assisting parties in resolving their own disputes.

PRINCIPLE 11. AGREEMENTS TO ARBITRATE

Consumers should be given:
  a. clear and adequate notice of the arbitration provision and its consequences, including a statement of its mandatory or optional character;
  b. reasonable access to information regarding the arbitration process, including basic distinctions between arbitration and court proceedings, related costs, and advice as to where they may obtain more complete information regarding arbitration procedures and arbitrator rosters;
  c. notice of the option to make use of applicable small claims court procedures as an alternative to binding arbitration in appropriate cases; and,
  d. a clear statement of the means by which the Consumer may exercise the option (if any) to submit disputes to arbitration or to court process.

PRINCIPLE 12. ARBITRATION HEARINGS

1. *Fundamentally-Fair Hearing.* All parties are entitled to a fundamentally-fair arbitration hearing. This requires adequate notice of hearings and an opportunity to be heard and to present relevant evidence to impartial decision-makers. In some cases, such as some small claims, the requirement of fundamental fairness may be met by hearings conducted by electronic or telephonic means or by a submission of documents. However, the Neutral should have discretionary authority to require a face-to-face hearing upon the request of a party.
2. *Confidentiality in Arbitration.* Consistent with general expectations of privacy in arbitration hearings, the arbitrator should make reasonable efforts to maintain the privacy of the hearing to the extent permitted by applicable law. The arbitrator should also carefully consider claims of privilege and confidentiality when addressing evidentiary issues.

PRINCIPLE 13. ACCESS TO INFORMATION

No party should ever be denied the right to a fundamentally-fair process due to an inability to obtain information material to a dispute. Consumer ADR agreements which provide for binding arbitration should establish procedures for arbitrator-supervised exchange of information prior to arbitration, bearing in mind the expedited nature of arbitration.

PRINCIPLE 14. ARBITRAL REMEDIES

The arbitrator should be empowered to grant whatever relief would be available in court under law or in equity.

PRINCIPLE 15. ARBITRATION AWARDS

1. *Final and Binding Award; Limited Scope of Review.* If provided in the agreement to arbitrate, the arbitrator's award should be final and binding, but subject to review in accordance with applicable statutes governing arbitration awards.
2. *Standards to Guide Arbitrator Decision-Making.* In making the award, the arbitrator should apply any identified, pertinent contract terms, statutes and legal precedents.
3. *Explanation of Award.* At the timely request of either party, the arbitrator should provide a brief written explanation of the basis for the award. To facilitate such requests, the arbitrator should discuss the matter with the parties prior to the arbitration hearing.

INTRODUCTION: GENESIS OF THE ADVISORY COMMITTEE

Recent years have seen a pronounced trend toward incorporation of out-of-court conflict resolution processes in standardized agreements presented to consumers of goods and services. Some of these processes (such as mediation and non-binding evaluation) involve third party intervention in settlement negotiations; others involve adjudication (binding arbitration). Such processes have the potential to be of significant value in making dispute resolution quicker, less costly, and more satisfying.[1]

Yet because consumer contracts often do not involve arm's length negotiation of terms, and frequently consist of boilerplate language presented on a take-it-or-leave it basis by suppliers of goods or services, there are legitimate concerns regarding the fairness of consumer conflict resolution mechanisms required by suppliers. This is particularly true in the realm of binding arbitration, where the courts are displaced by private adjudication systems. In such cases, consumers are often unaware of their procedural rights and obligations until the realities of out-of-court arbitration are revealed to them after disputes have arisen.[2] While the results may be entirely satisfactory, they may also fall short of consumers' reasonable expectations of fairness[3] and have a sig-

---

[1] See, *e.g.*, CPR Institute for Dispute Resolution, *ADR Cost Savings & Benefit Studies* (Catherine Cronin-Harris, ed. 1994) (summarizing some of the research findings on the relative advantages ADR may offer). See also, *e.g.*, *Madden v. Kaiser Foundation Hosp.*, 17 Cal. 3d 699, 711, 552 P.2d 1178, 1186 (1976) ("The speed and economy of arbitration, in contrast to the expense and delay of a jury trial, could prove helpful to all parties. . . .") [*Editor's Note*: Citations throughout Protocol as in original.]

[2] The arbitration agreement may be included in the "fine print" in a brochure of terms and conditions inside a box of goods. See, *e.g.*, *Hill v. Gateway 2000, Inc.*, 105 F.3d 1147 (7th Cir. 1997) (Customers agreed to computer company's contract terms, including arbitration agreement, by failing to return merchandise within 30 days). See *Age of Compelled Arbitration*, 1997, Wis. L. Rev. 33, 40–53 (Offering a "cautionary tale" regarding employment arbitration agreement.)

[3] See Mark E. Budnitz, *Arbitration of Disputes Between Consumers and Financial Institutions: A Serious Threat to Consumer Protection*, 10 Ohio St. J. On Disp. Res. 267 (1995) (discussing procedural limitations of arbitration in treating consumer disputes with banks and lenders); Schwartz, *supra* note 2 (discussing issues relating to adhesion contracts involving employees and consumers); Jean R. Sternlight, *Rethinking the Constitutionality of the Supreme Court's Preference for Binding Arbitration: A Fresh Assessment of Jury Trial, Separation of Powers, and Due Process Concerns*, 72 Tulane L. Rev. 1 (1997)

nificant impact on consumers' substantive rights and remedies./4

The use of mediation and other forms of alternative dispute resolution (ADR) by various state and federal courts has also raised concerns regarding quality, effectiveness and fairness. The response has been a number of national, state and local initiatives to establish standards for the guidance and information of courts. Until now, however, there has been no comparable national effort in the private consumer sphere.

In the spring of 1997, the American Arbitration Association (AAA) announced the establishment of a National Consumer Disputes Advisory Committee. The stated mission of the Advisory Committee is:

> To bring together a broad, diverse, representative national advisory committee to advise the American Arbitration Association in the development of standards and procedures for the equitable resolution of consumer disputes.

In light of its stated mission, the Advisory Committee's recommendations are likely to have a direct impact on the development of rules, procedures and policies for the resolution of consumer disputes under the auspices of the AAA.

The Advisory Committee's recommendations may also have a significant impact in the broader realm of consumer ADR. A Statement of Principles which is perceived as a broadly-based consensus regarding minimum requirements for mediation and arbitration programs for consumers of goods and services may influence the evolution of consumer rules generally and the development of state and federal laws governing consumer arbitration agreements. The standards may affect the drafting of statutes and influence judicial opinions addressing the enforceability of arbitration agreements pursuant to existing state or federal law./5

SCOPE OF THE CONSUMER DUE PROCESS PROTOCOL

The Consumer Due Process Protocol (Protocol) was developed to address the wide range of consumer transactions—those involving the purchase or lease of goods or services for personal, family or household use. These include, among other things, transactions involving: banking, credit cards, home loans and other financial services; health care services; brokerage services; home construction and improvements; insurance; communications; and the purchase and lease of motor vehicles and other personal property.

Across this broad spectrum of consumer transactions, the Protocol applies to all possible conflicts—from small claims to complex disputes. In light of these realities, the Advisory Committee sought to develop principles which would establish clear benchmarks for conflict resolution processes involving consumers, while recognizing that a process appropriate in one context may be inappropriate in another. Therefore, the Protocol embodies flexible standards which permit consideration of specific circumstances.

In some cases, the AAA is developing or has developed special dispute resolution policies and procedures governing particular transactional systems. A recent example is its current initiative with respect to ADR in contracts for health care services. Where the general principles set forth in this Protocol conflict with more specific standards developed under the auspices of the AAA or some other independent organization with relatively broad participation by affected parties, the latter should govern.

There are other transactions that share many of the features of consumer transactions, such as those involving small businesses and individual employment contracts. While the Protocol was not developed for specific application to such other transactions, there may be circumstances in which the Protocol might be applied by analogy to ADR in those venues. The Principles articulated here are likely to have an impact on minimum standards of due process for other ADR systems involving persons of disparate bargaining power.

Each section of this document is devoted to treatment of a discrete topic concerning consumer ADR. It begins with a basic Principle that embodies the fundamental reasonable expectation of consumers as defined by the Advisory Committee. Each Principle is accompanied by Reporter's Comments that explain the rationale of the Advisory Committee in the context of other emerging standards. In addition, some Principles are supplemented by Practical Suggestions for putting the Principles into practice.

The specific mention of mediation and binding arbitration reflects the current emphasis on these processes in consumer conflict resolution. The Advisory Committee recognizes that a number of other approaches are being employed to resolve commercial and consumer disputes, and encourages their use in accordance with the spirit of the Protocol.

The signatories to this Protocol were designated by their respective organizations, but the Protocol reflects their personal views and should not be construed as representing the policy of the designating organizations. Although the following Principles reflect a remarkable degree of consensus, achieved during the course of several meetings of the entire Advisory Committee, subcommittee deliberations, exchanges of numerous memoranda and of five drafts of the Protocol, Advisory Committee members at times accepted compromise in the interest of arriving at a common ground. As was the case with the task force which developed the *Employment Due Process Protocol*, opinions regarding the appro-

---

(discussing due process concerns with binding arbitration under employment and consumer contracts). See, e.g., *Engalla v. Permanente Med. Grp.*, 938 P.2d 903 (Cal. 1997) (medical group may not compel arbitration where it administers own arbitration program, fraudulently misrepresents speed of arbitrator selection process, and the forces delays); *Broemmer v. Abortion Serv. of Phoenix*, 840 P.2d 1013 (Az. 1992) (refusing to enforce agreement in "adhesion contract" where drafter inserted potentially self-serving term requiring sole arbitrator of medical malpractice claims to be licensed medical doctor).

/4 See Schwartz, *supra* note 2, at 60–61 (discussing perceptions regarding relative damages awards in court and in arbitration), 64–66 (summarizing some statistics on arbitration awards). See also William W. Park, *When and Why Arbitration Matters*, in The Commercial Way to Justice 73, 75 (G.M. Beresfort Hartwell ed., 1997) ("*Who* interprets an ... agreement will frequently be more significant than *what* the applicable law says about the agreement. . . .").

/5 See, e.g., *Cole v. Burns International Security Services*, 105 F.3d 1465 (D.C. Cir. 1997) (Citing Due Process Protocol for Employment Disputes). The consensus-based approach of the broadly constituted group reflects the "public interest" model espoused by Professor Speidel. See Richard E. Speidel, *Contract Theory and Securities Arbitration: Whither Consent?*, 62 Brook. L. Rev. 1335 (1996).

priateness of binding pre-dispute arbitration agreements in consumer contracts were never fully reconciled. Like that group, however, the Advisory Committee was able to address standards for ADR processes within the given context.

GLOSSARY OF TERMS

Consumer
Consumer refers to an individual who purchases or leases goods or services, or contracts to purchase or lease goods or services, intended primarily for personal, family or household use.

Provider
Provider refers to a seller or lessor of goods or services to Consumers for personal, family or household use.

ADR Process
An ADR (Alternative Dispute Resolution) Process is a method for out-of-court resolution of conflict through the intervention of third parties. Mediation and arbitration are two widely used ADR processes.

Mediation
Mediation refers to a range of processes in which an impartial person helps parties to a dispute to communicate and to make voluntary, informed choices in an effort to resolve their dispute. A mediator, unlike an arbitrator, does not issue a decision regarding the merits of the dispute, but instead facilitates a dialogue between the parties with the view of helping them arrive at a mutually agreeable settlement.

Arbitration
Arbitration is a process in which parties submit disputes to a neutral third person or persons for a decision on the merits. Each party has an opportunity to present evidence to the arbitrator(s) in writing or through witnesses. Arbitration proceedings tend to be more informal than court proceedings and adherence to judicial rules of evidence is not usually required. Arbitrators decide cases by issuing written decisions or "awards." An award may or may not be binding on the parties, depending on the agreement to arbitrate. A "binding" arbitration award may be enforced as a court judgment under the terms of federal or state statutes, but judicial review of arbitration awards is limited.

Neutral
A Neutral is a mediator, arbitrator, or other independent, impartial third party selected to intervene in a Consumer-Provider dispute.

ADR Agreement
An ADR Agreement is an agreement between a Provider and a Consumer to submit disputes to mediation, arbitration, or other ADR Processes. As used in this Statement, the term includes provisions (sometimes incorporated by reference) in standard contracts furnished by Providers which signify the assent of the Consumer and Provider to such processes (although the assent may only be the "generalized assent" typically given by Consumers to standard terms).

ADR Program
An ADR Program is any program or service established by or utilized by a Provider of goods and services for out-of-court resolution of Consumer disputes. The term includes ADR rules and procedures and implementation of administrative structures.

Independent ADR Institution
An Independent ADR Institution is an organization that provides independent and impartial administration of ADR Programs for Consumers and Providers, including, but not limited to, development and administration of ADR policies and procedures and the training and appointment of Neutrals.

MAJOR STANDARDS AND SOURCES

The Reporter's Comments accompanying these Principles cite a number of existing standards and sources relied upon by the Advisory Committee. The more frequently cited standards and sources are set forth below by their full title as well as the abbreviated title that appears in the Comments.

American Arbitration Association, *Commercial Arbitration Rules*, July 1, 1996 (AAA Commercial Rules)

American Arbitration Association, *Construction Industry Dispute Resolution Procedures*, Oct. 15, 1997 (AAA Construction Procedures)

American Arbitration Association, *Wireless Industry Arbitration Rules*, July 15, 1997 (AAA Wireless Rules)

American Arbitration Association & American Bar Association, *Code of Ethics for Arbitrators in Commercial Disputes* (1977) (Code of Ethics for Arbitrators)

Center for Dispute Settlement, Institute of Judicial Admin., *Standards for Court-Connected Mediation Programs* (Standards for Court-Connected Programs)

Council of Better Business Bureaus, Inc., *Arbitration (Binding)* (BBB Arbitration Rules)

CPR-Georgetown Commission on Ethics and Standards in ADR Working Group on Provider Organizations, *Principles for ADR Provider Organizations* (Draft of April 4, 1998) (Principles for ADR Provider Organizations)

Federal Arbitration Act, 9 U.S.C. §§ 1-16 (as amended and in effect July 1, 1992) (Federal Arbitration Act)

Blue-Ribbon Advisory Panel on Kaiser Permanente Arbitration, *The Kaiser Permanente Arbitration System: A Review and Recommendations for Improvement* 1 (1998) (Kaiser Permanente Review and Recommendations)

Joint Committee (American Arbitration Association, American Bar Association and Society of Professionals in Dispute Resolution) on Standards of Conduct, *Standards of Conduct for Mediators* (1994) (Joint Standards for Mediators)

Society of Professionals in Dispute Resolution (SPIDR) Commission on Qualifications, *Ensuring Competence and Quality in Dispute Resolution Practice* (Draft Report 1994) (SPIDR Report on Qualifications)

Society of Professionals in Dispute Resolution (SPIDR) Law and Public Policy Committee, *Mandated Participation and Settlement Coercion: Dispute Resolution as It Relates to the Courts* (1991) (SPIDR Report on Court-Mandated ADR)

Society of Professionals in Dispute Resolution (SPIDR) Commission on Qualifications, *Principles Concerning Qualifications* (1989) (SPIDR Principles)

Task Force on Alternative Dispute Resolution in Employment, *A Due Process Protocol for Mediation and Arbitration of Statutory Disputes Arising Out of the Employment Relationship* (1995) (Employment Due Process Protocol)

Uniform Arbitration Act, 7 U.A.A. 1 (1997) (Uniform Arbitration Act)

PRINCIPLE 1. FUNDAMENTALLY-FAIR PROCESS

All parties are entitled to a fundamentally-fair ADR process. As embodiments of fundamental fairness, these Principles should be observed in structuring ADR Programs.

Reporter's Comments

Users of ADR are entitled to a process that is fundamentally fair. Emerging standards governing consensual and court-connected ADR programs reflect pervasive concerns with fair process. *See, e.g.,* III Ian R. Macneil, Richard E. Speidel, & Thomas J. Stipanowich, *Federal Arbitration Law: Agreements, Awards & Remedies Under the Federal Arbitration Act* § 32.2.1 (1994) [hereinafter *Federal Arbitration Law*] (noting "universal agreement" that arbitrators must provide parties with fundamentally-fair hearing). *See also Kaiser Permanente Review and Recommendations 1* ("As the sponsor of a mandatory system of arbitration, Kaiser Permanente must assure a fair system to their members, physicians and staff.")

Where conflict resolution processes are defined by a written contract, that writing is often viewed by courts as the primary indicator of the "procedural fairness" for which the parties bargained. As the Advisory Committee recognized, however, ADR agreements in most Consumer contracts are "take-it-or-leave-it" contracts which are not products of negotiation by Consumers. *See* David S. Schwartz, *Enforcing Small Print to Protect Big Business: Employee and Consumer Rights Claims in an Age of Compelled Arbitration*, 1997 Wis. L. Rev. 33, 55–60 (discussing adhesion dimension of pre-dispute arbitration agreements in standardized contracts); *Kaiser Permanente Review and Recommendations 28* (noting that many members of a major HMO have no realistic alternative for medical care). It is possible, therefore, that contracts to which they have generally assented contain ADR Agreements which fall so far short of Consumers' reasonable expectations that they would not have entered into the agreement had they been aware of the provisions. Thus, although these Principles attempt to enhance the likelihood that Consumers will have specific knowledge of ADR provisions at the time of contracting, the Advisory Committee also believed it necessary to describe a baseline of reasonable expectations for ADR in Consumer transactions. These Principles identify specific minimum due process standards which embody the concept of fundamental fairness, including: informed consent; impartial and unbiased Neutrals; independent administration of ADR; qualified Neutrals; access to small claims court; reasonable costs (including, where appropriate, subsidized Provider-mandated procedures); convenient hearing locations; reasonable time limits; adequate representation; fair hearing procedures; access to sufficient information; confidentiality; availability of court remedies; application of legal principle and precedent by arbitrators; and the option to receive a statement of reasons for arbitration awards.

Where provisions in a standardized pre-dispute arbitration agreement fail to meet Consumers' reasonable expectations, there is authority for the principle that courts may properly refuse to enforce the arbitration agreement in whole or in part. *See Restatement (Second) of Contracts* § 211 (1981); *Broemmer v. Abortion Services of Phoenix, Ltd.*, 173 Ariz. 148, 840 P.2d 1013 (1992) (standardized arbitration agreement was unenforceable where its terms fell beyond patient's reasonable expectations); *Graham v. Scissor-Tail, Inc.*, 623 P.2d 165 (Cal. 1981) (arbitration clauses in adhesion contracts are unenforceable if they are contrary to the reasonable expectations of parties or unconscionable). *Cf. Cole v. Burns International Security Services*, 105 F.3d 1465 (D.C. Cir. 1997) (setting forth minimum due process standards for judicial enforcement of arbitration agreement in the context of a statutory employment discrimination claim where the employee was required to enter into the agreement as a condition of employment). Procedural fairness in Consumer arbitration agreements may also be policed under other principles. *See, e.g., Stirlen v. Supercuts*, 51 Cal. App. 4th Supp. 1519, 60 Cal. Rptr. 2d 138 (1997) (finding remedial limits in "adhesive" employment agreement unconscionable); *Engalla v. Permanente Med. Grp.*, 938 P.2d 903 (Cal. 1997) (arbitration agreement was unenforceable if there was substantial delay in arbitrator selection contrary to consumer's reasonable, fraudulently induced, contractual expectations).

Because the Principles in this Protocol represent a fundamental standard of fairness, waiver of any of these Principles in a pre-dispute agreement will naturally be subject to scrutiny as to conformity with the reasonable expectations of the parties and other judicial standards governing the enforceability of such contracts. Assuming they have sufficient specific knowledge and understanding of the rights they are waiving, however, Consumers may waive compliance with these Principles after a dispute has arisen.

PRINCIPLE 2. ACCESS TO INFORMATION REGARDING ADR PROGRAM

Providers of goods or services should undertake reasonable measures to provide Consumers with full and accurate information regarding Consumer ADR Programs. At the time the Consumer contracts for goods or services, such measures should include (1) clear and adequate notice regarding the ADR provisions, including a statement indicating whether participation in the ADR Program is mandatory or optional, and (2) reasonable means by which Consumers may obtain additional information regarding the ADR Program. After a dispute arises, Consumers should have access to all information necessary for effective participation in ADR.

Reporter's Comments

See SPIDR Report on Qualifications at 9 ("Consumers are entitled to know what tasks the neutral . . . may perform and what tasks they are expected to perform in the course of a particular dispute resolution service.") *Cf. SPIDR Principles* at 6–7 ("It is the responsibility of . . . private programs offering dispute resolution services to define clearly the services they provide . . . [and provide information about the program and Neutrals to the parties.]"); *Kaiser Permanente Review and Recommendations 28* (provider of medical services has duty to provide users with "enough information and facts to allow them to understand the actual operation of the arbitration system"); *Principles for ADR Provider Organizations 2*. At a minimum, Consumers should be provided with (or have prompt access to) written information to explain the process. This should include general information describing each ADR process used and its distinctive features, including:

*the nature and purpose of the process, including the scope of ADR provisions;
*an indication of whether or not the Consumer has a choice regarding use of the process;
*the role of parties and attorneys, if any;
*procedures for selection of Neutrals;
*rules of conduct for Neutrals, and complaint procedures;
*fees and expenses;
*information regarding ADR Program operation, including locations, times of operation, and case processing procedures;
*the availability of special services for non-English speakers, and persons with disabilities; and,
*the availability of alternatives to ADR, including small claims court.

See, e.g., BBB Arbitration Rules (defining arbitration and the roles of various participants; providing "checklist" for Consumers preparing for arbitration; setting forth procedural rules). *Cf. Standards for Court-Connected Programs* § 3.2.b. (listing information which courts sponsoring mediation should provide to program users). *See also SPIDR Principles* at 6–7 (listing information which private programs should offer to parties regarding the program and participating Neutrals). Consumers should also be able to obtain a copy of pertinent rules and procedures. In the case of binding arbitration provisions, there should also be a straightforward explanation of the differences between arbitration and court process. See Principle 11 "Agreements to Arbitrate." Although the Provider of goods or services is charged with the responsibility for making certain that Consumers have access to appropriate information regarding ADR, the Independent ADR Institution has an important role in this area. The Independent ADR Institution must be prepared to communicate to the parties all information necessary for effective use of the ADR process(es), particularly after a dispute arises.

All materials should be prepared in plain straightforward language. As a rule, such information should be in the same language as the principal contract for goods or services. *See, e.g., N.Y. Pers. Prop. Law* § 427 (McKinney 1997). *See also Standards for Court-Connected Programs* § 3.2.b., Commentary, at 3–4 (If a significant percentage of the population served is monolingual in a particular language, the material should be available in that language.)

Practical Suggestions

An example of a creative approach to providing information about Consumer ADR is provided by a major university medical center's Health Care Dispute Resolution Program. The medical center provides prospective patients with a written explanation of mediation and arbitration procedures for resolution of health care-related disputes one month before they visit the center to complete the remaining paperwork. As the written materials explain, the program is voluntary; patients are not required to opt for the procedures as a condition to receiving treatment. Patients may contact the center for additional information regarding the processes.

For purposes of allowing Consumers access to information about dispute resolution programs, the AAA makes available an 800 customer service telephone number. In addition, the AAA, like some other Independent ADR Institutions, also has a World Wide Web site; it posts its rules and an explanation of its mediation and arbitration procedures on the Web site.

A panel proposing reforms to a major HMO-sponsored arbitration system recommended the creation of an "ombudsperson program to assist members in navigating the system of dispute resolution." *Kaiser Permanente Review and Recommendations 2.43.*

PRINCIPLE 3. INDEPENDENT AND IMPARTIAL NEUTRAL; INDEPENDENT ADMINISTRATION

1. *Independent and Impartial Neutral. All parties are entitled to a Neutral who is independent and impartial.*
2. *Independent Administration. If participation in mediation or arbitration is mandatory, the procedure should be administered by an Independent ADR Institution. Administrative services should include the maintenance of a panel of prospective Neutrals, facilitation of Neutral selection, collection and distribution of Neutral's fees and expenses, oversight and implementation of ADR rules and procedures, and monitoring of Neutral qualifications, performance, and adherence to pertinent rules, procedures and ethical standards.*
3. *Standards for Neutrals. The Independent ADR Institution should make reasonable efforts to ensure that Neutrals understand and conform to pertinent ADR rules, procedures and ethical standards.*
4. *Selection of Neutrals. The Consumer and Provider should have an equal voice in the selection of Neutrals in connection with a specific dispute.*
5. *Disclosure and Disqualification. Beginning at the time of appointment, Neutrals should be required to disclose to the Independent ADR Institution any circumstance likely to affect impartiality, including any bias or financial or personal interest which might affect the result of the ADR proceeding, or any past or present relationship or experience with the parties or their representatives, including past ADR experiences. The Independent ADR Institution should communicate any such information to the parties and other Neutrals, if any. Upon objection of a party to continued service of the Neutral, the Independent ADR Institution should determine whether the Neutral should be disqualified and should inform the parties of its decision. The disclosure obligation of the Neutral and procedure for disqualification should continue throughout the period of appointment.*

Reporter's Comments

The concept of a fair, independent and impartial Neutral (or Neutral Panel) is enshrined in leading standards governing arbitration and mediation. *See Federal Arbitration Act* § 10(a)(2); *Uniform Arbitration Act* § 12(a)(2); *AAA Commercial Rules* 12, 13, 14, 19; *BBB Arbitration Rules* 6, 8. The *Joint Standards for Mediators* describe mediator impartiality as "central" to the mediation process and require mediators to conduct mediation in an impartial manner. *Joint Standards for Mediators*, Art. II; *Standards for Court-Connected Programs* § 8.1.a. Similar policies animate standards requiring mediators to disclose conflicts of interest and to conduct the mediation in a fair manner. *Joint Standards for Mediators*, Arts. III, VI; *SPIDR Principles*, Principles 4.b., c., f.; 6.d., e., i.; *Standards for Court-Connected Programs* § 8.1.b.

When Neutrals are appointed by a court or other organization, the appointing entity has an important obligation to ensure their impartiality. This obligation entails a reasonable level of oversight of Neutral performance. Comments to the *Joint Standards for Mediators* indicate that "[w]hen mediators are appointed by a court or institution, the appointing agency shall make reasonable efforts to ensure that mediators serve impartially." *Joint Standards for Mediators*, Art. II. The *Standards for Court-Connected Programs* therefore require courts to "adopt a code of ethical standards for mediators [covering, among other things, impartiality and conflict of interest], together with procedures to handle violations of the code." *Standards for Court-Connected Programs* § 8.1. For these and other reasons, the integrity and impartiality of the administrative organization is also important; the growing use of arbitration and mediation in the Consumer context has also raised issues regarding the administration of such processes. *See, e.g., Engalla v. Permanente Med. Grp.*, 928 P.2d 903 (Cal. 1997). *See generally* Edward Dauer, *Engalla's Legacy to Arbitration*, ADR Currents, Summer 1997, at 1; *Principles for ADR Provider Organizations* (setting forth general principles of responsible practice for ADR Provider Organizations, "entities which hold themselves out as offering, brokering or administering dispute resolution services").

In addition to appointing Neutrals, administering institutions often perform many functions which have a direct impact on the conduct of the dispute resolution process, including functions sometimes performed by Neutrals. The consensus of the Advisory Committee was that the reality and perception of impartiality and fairness was as essential in the case of Independent ADR Institutions as it was in the case of individual Neutrals. Thus, the Advisory Committee concluded that when an ADR Agreement mandates that parties resort to mediation or arbitration, the administering Independent ADR Institution should be independent of either party and impartial. *See, e.g., Kaiser Permanente Review and Recommendations* 31 (recommending, first and foremost, the "creation of an independent, accountable administrator" for the Kaiser Permanente arbitration system to counter "perception of bias" raised by "self-administration"). *See also Principles for ADR Provider Organizations* (draft standards for organizations providing ADR services). For this and other reasons, this Principle may be the single most significant contribution of the Protocol. In the long term, moreover, the independence of administering institutions may be the greatest challenge of Consumer ADR.

Broad disclosure of actual or potential conflicts of interest on the part of prospective Neutrals is critical to the real and perceived fairness of ADR. Although consenting parties have considerable freedom to choose Neutrals, including those with experience in a particular industry or profession, the key to informed consent is broad disclosure by prospective Neutrals. Therefore, a long line of authority under federal and state arbitration statutes establishes the principle that an arbitrator's failure to disclose certain relationships or other facts which raise issues of partiality may result in reversal of an arbitration award. *See generally* III *Federal Arbitration Law* Ch. 28 (discussing legal and ethical rules governing arbitrator impartiality). The principle of disclosure is embodied in leading arbitration rules and ethical standards. *See AAA Commercial Rule* 19, *NASD Code* § 10312; *BBB Arbitration Rules* 6, 8.

The *Joint Standards for Mediators* mandate disclosure of "all actual and potential conflicts of interest reasonably known to the mediator"—including any "dealing or relationship that might create an impression of possible bias." *Joint Standards for Mediators*, Art. III. Thereafter, the mediator must await the parties' agreement to proceed with mediation. The same concerns require mediators to identify and avoid conflicts during (and even after) mediation. *Id. Cf. Employment Due Process Protocol* § C.4. (mediators and arbitrators have a duty to disclose any relationship which might reasonably constitute or be perceived as a conflict of interest); *SPIDR Principles*, Principles 4.b., c., f.; 6.d., e., i.; *Standards for Court-Connected Programs* § 8.1.b.

Although they did not establish it as a requirement under these Principles, most members of the Advisory Committee endorsed the concept of a "list selection" process similar to that employed by the AAA. *See AAA Commercial Rule* 14. Under this process, the Independent ADR Institution provides each of the parties with lists of prospective Neutrals and invites the parties to identify and rank acceptable individuals. Mutually acceptable Neutrals are thereby identified. The AAA approach served as the model for other ADR standards. *See, e.g., Employment Due Process Protocol* § C.3.; Securities Industry Conference on Arbitration, *List Selection Rule* (Final Draft, Sept. 18, 1997) (proposed by SICA as modification to Section 8 of the *Uniform Code of Arbitration*); Proposed Rule Change by National Association of Securities Dealers, File No. SR-NASD097 (proposed by NASD as modification to Rules 10310 and 10311 of the NASD Code of Arbitration Procedure). The concern was expressed that the list selection approach may create a financial tie between Neutrals in the pool and Providers, who will be "repeat players" in the ADR Program. Such considerations may mandate, among other things, a larger panel of Neutrals, rotating assignments, or disclosure of past awards rendered by arbitrators.

In the interest of informed selection, the Advisory Committee recommends that parties be provided with or have access to some information regarding recent ADR proceedings conducted by prospective Neutrals. *Cf. Employment Due Process Protocol* § B.3 (recommending that parties be provided with names, addresses, and phone numbers of party representatives in a prospective arbitrator's six most recent cases to aid in selection).

The dictates of fairness also extend to the conduct of ADR sessions. Thus, for example, arbitrators generally are forbidden from communicating with parties outside of hearings. *See* III *Federal Arbitration Law* § 32.4. Similarly, standards for mediator conduct demand impartiality. *See, e.g., Standards for Court-Connected Programs* § 8.1.

Although the rules and procedures of an ADR Program and oversight by the Independent ADR Institution are important in assuring the impartiality of Neutrals, it is also essential that Neutrals be bound to perform in accordance with recognized ethical standards. In the case of arbitrators, the leading ethical standard is the *Code of Ethics for Arbitrators in Commercial Disputes* (current version). Similarly, ethical standards governing mediator eligibility also require impartiality. *See, e.g., Standards for Court-Connected Programs* § 8.1. It is the responsibility of the Independent ADR Institution to develop or adopt ethical standards for Neutrals and to ensure that Neutrals understand and conform to applicable standards.

Some arbitration procedures provide for a "tripartite" panel in which each party appoints its own "party-arbitrator," and the two party-arbitrators select a third arbitrator to complete the panel. *See generally* III *Federal Arbitration Law* § 28.4; *see also* Alan Scott Rau, *Integrity in Private Judging*, 38 S. Tex. L. Rev. 485, 505–08 (1997) (noting problems with party-arbitrator concept). For a number of reasons, the Advisory Committee believed such practices should be avoided in the Consumer sphere, and that all arbitrators should be neutral. *Cf. Kaiser Permanente Review and Recommendations* 42 (expressing serious concerns regarding tripartite panel approach).

Practical Suggestions

Independent ADR Institutions should develop procedures which are appropriate to each of the ADR Programs they administer. A helpful model for program administrators is the User Advisory Committee now being utilized by the AAA to establish procedures and policies for ADR in the areas of employment, construction, health care, and other transactional settings. *Cf. Kaiser Permanente Review and Recommendations* 32 (recommending "on-going, volunteer Advisory Committee" comprised of representatives of various interest groups, including "an appropriate consumer advocacy organization" to consult in development of arbitration program). Such entities should provide a forum in which representatives of Consumers and Providers cooperate in the development and implementation of policies and procedures governing an ADR program, including selection of Neutrals.

For selection of Neutrals, the Independent ADR Institution might utilize a list procedure similar to that used by the AAA. The list of prospective Neutrals should include pertinent biographical information, including the names of parties and representatives involved in recent arbitration proceedings handled by the prospective Neutral. *Cf. Employment Due Process Protocol* § B.3 (recommending that parties be provided with names, addresses, and phone numbers of party representatives in a prospective arbitrator's six most recent cases to aid in selection). Each party should be afforded discretion to reject any candidate with or without cause. Failing agreement on a Neutral or panel of Neutrals in this fashion, the Neutral should be appointed by the Independent ADR Institution, subject to objection for good cause.

PRINCIPLE 4. QUALITY AND COMPETENCE OF NEUTRALS

All parties are entitled to competent, qualified Neutrals. Independent ADR Institutions are responsible for establishing and maintaining standards for Neutrals in ADR Programs they administer.

Reporter's Comments

Organizations providing ADR services for Consumer transactions should have a continuing obligation to monitor the quality of the services they provide. This obligation requires that they establish and maintain standards for Neutrals within the program which are appropriate to the issues or disputes being addressed. The SPIDR Commission on Qualifications calls upon private as well as public programs offering ADR services to set and monitor program performance. *See SPIDR Principles*, Principle 6, at 3–4. Likewise, the *Standards for Court-Connected Programs* call upon courts to "ensure that the mediation programs to which they refer cases are monitored adequately . . . and evaluated [periodically]." *Standards for Court-Connected Programs* § 6.0.

The most critical element in ADR quality control is the establishment and maintenance of standards of competence for Neutrals within the program. "Competence" refers to "the acquisition of skills, knowledge and . . . other attributes" deemed necessary to assist others in resolving disputes in a particular setting. *See SPIDR Report on Qualifications* at 6. In 1989, the SPIDR Commission on Qualifications published a list of general skills and areas of knowledge that should be considered by groups establishing competency standards. *See SPIDR Principles*, Principle 11, at 4–7.

While ensuring the competence of Neutrals is always important, it is particularly "critical in contexts where party choice over the process, program or neutral is limited"—a reality of many Consumer ADR programs. *See SPIDR Report on Qualifications* at 5; *SPIDR Principles*, Principle 3 at 2 (extent to which Neutral qualifications are mandated should vary by degree of choice parties have over dispute resolution process, ADR Program, and Neutral). The SPIDR Commission on Qualifications requires private programs to, among other things, establish clear criteria for the selection and evaluation of Neutrals and conduct periodic performance evaluations. *SPIDR Principles* at 3. *See also SPIDR Report on Qualifications* at 6 (Neutrals, professional associations, programs and Consumers should all have responsibility for addressing and assessing Neutral performance); American Bar Ass'n Young Lawyers Div. & Special Comm. On Alternative Means of Dispute Resolution, *Resolving Disputes: An Alternative Approach, A Handbook for Establishment of Dispute Settlement Centers* 32 (1983) (noting importance of post-mediation evaluation by administering agency).

The Advisory Committee concluded that it would be inappropriate (and, probably, impossible) to set forth a set of universally applicable qualifications for Neutrals in Consumer disputes. The Advisory Committee's conclusions parallel those of other groups establishing broad standards for the conduct of ADR. *See, e.g., SPIDR Report on Qualifications; SPIDR Principles* at 1, 2. As the SPIDR Commission on Qualifications determined, Neutral qualifications are best established by joint efforts of concerned "stakeholders" in specific contexts. *See, e.g., Kaiser Permanente Review and Recommendations* 35–36 (recommending involvement of advisory committee in development of arbitrator qualifications).

It is important for Consumers to have a voice in establishing and maintaining standards of competence and quality in ADR programs. The SPIDR Commission on Qualifications recently observed that "consumers . . . share a responsibility with programs, [Neutrals] . . . and associations to join in evaluating and reporting on the performance of [Neutrals] . . . and programs and contributing to the development of policies and standards on qualifications." *SPIDR Report on Qualifications*, § G.2. at 9. *See also SPIDR Principles*, Principle 2 at 2 (private entities making judgments about neutral qualifications should be guided by groups that include representatives of consumers of services). Although Neutral expertise is traditionally a hallmark of arbitration, technical or professional experience often carries with it the perception if not the reality of bias. From the Consumer's perspective, therefore, an arbitrator who shares the professional or commercial background of a Provider may not be the ideal judge. *See, e.g., Broemmer v. Abortion Serv. of Phoenix*, 840 P.2d 1013 (Ariz. 1992) (adhesion arbitration agreement provided by abortion clinic which, among other things, required arbitrator to be a licensed obstetrician/gynecologist, was unenforceable as beyond reasonable expectations of patient).

An Independent ADR Institution's responsibility for the qualifications of Neutrals in a particular Consumer ADR program dictates the development of an appropriate training program. Ideally, the training should include a mentoring program with experienced Neutrals as well as coverage of applicable principles of Consumer law. *See* Mark E. Budnitz, *Arbitration of Disputes Between Consumers and Financial Institutions: A Serious Threat to Consumer Protection*, 10 Ohio St. J. on Disp. Res. 267, 315 (arbitrators need special legal expertise to address statutory issues respecting consumer claims against financial institutions). Successful completion of such training should be reflected in the information on prospective Neutrals furnished to the parties prior to selection. *Cf. Employment Due Process Protocol* § C.2.

The Advisory Committee generally supports the concept of broad choice in selection of Neutrals, and recognizes the right of Consumers and Providers to jointly select any Neutral in whom the parties have requisite trust, even one who does not possess all of the qualifications recommended by an ADR Program. *Cf. Employment Due Process Protocol* § C.1.; *Standards for Court-Connected Programs* § 13.4 ("Parties should have the widest possible latitude in selecting mediators, consistent with public policy."). This assumes, of course, that both parties have a true choice in the matter, that they are duly informed about the background and qualifications of the Neutrals proposed, and that all such Neutrals have made full disclosure of possible conflicts of interest in accordance with Principle 3.

Practical Suggestions

Elements of effective quality control include the establishment of standards for Neutrals, the development of a training program, and a program of ongoing performance evaluation and feedback. Because the requirements of parties will vary with the circumstances, it will be necessary to establish standards for Neutrals in an ADR Program with due regard for the specific needs of users of the program. As noted in connection with Principle 3, a helpful model for program administrators is the User Advisory Committee now being utilized by the AAA to establish procedures and policies for ADR in the areas of employment, construction, health care, and other transactional settings. Such entities could bring Consumer and Provider representatives together to assist in the development and implementation of programs to train, qualify and monitor the performance of Neutrals.

PRINCIPLE 5. SMALL CLAIMS

Consumer ADR Agreements should make it clear that all parties retain the right to seek relief in a small claims court for disputes or claims within the scope of its jurisdiction.

Reporter's Comments

Disputes arising out of Consumer transactions often involve relatively small amounts of money. Such disputes may be well-suited to resolution by informal ADR processes and judicial small claims procedures.

Within the judicial system, the least expensive and most efficient alternative for resolution of claims for minor amounts of money often lies in small claims courts. These courts typically provide a convenient, less formal and relatively expeditious judicial forum for handling such disputes, and afford the benefit, where necessary, of the coercive powers of the judicial system. The Advisory Committee concluded that access to small claims tribunals is an important right of Consumers which should not be waived by a pre-dispute ADR Agreement.

Practical Suggestions

Because, for cases involving small amounts of money, parties retain the option of an oral hearing in small claims court, it may be reasonable for the ADR Agreement to provide for arbitration of small claims without a face-to-face hearing. Such alternatives may include "desk arbitration," which involves the making of an arbitration award based on written submissions; proceedings conducted by telephone or electronic data transmission; and other options. *See* Principle 12.

Mediation conducted by telephone conference call has also proven effective in resolving Consumer disputes. At least one major auto manufacturer has successfully used this technique to resolve warranty claims.

PRINCIPLE 6. REASONABLE COST

1. *Reasonable Cost. Providers of goods and services should develop ADR programs which entail reasonable cost to Consumers based on the circumstances of the dispute, including, among other things, the size and nature of the claim, the nature of goods or services provided, and the ability of the Consumer to pay. In some cases, this may require the Provider to subsidize the process.*
2. *Handling of Payment. In the interest of ensuring fair and independent Neutrals, the making of fee arrangements and the payment of fees should be administered on a rational, equitable and consistent basis by the Independent ADR Institution.*

Reporter's Comments

A fundamental principle of our civil justice system is that a person should never be denied access to a court due to an inability to pay court costs. The reality is that the public justice system is heavily subsidized, and that users pay only a small fraction of the actual cost of trial and related procedures. Moreover, indigent litigants may be afforded relief from even these small fees. This principle has been extended in many cases to court-connected ADR programs, in which courts defray all or part of the expenses of mediation or court-connected arbitration. *See Standards for Court-Connected Programs*, §§ 5.1.a, 13.0 ("[c]ourts should impose mandatory attendance only when the cost of mediation is publicly funded"; "[c]ourts should make mediation available to parties regardless of the parties' ability to pay"). According to data from the National Center for State Courts' ADR database, approximately 60% of programs did not depend upon the parties to pay mediator fees for contract and tort cases; no programs charged user fees for mediation of small claims. *See Standards for Court-Connected Programs* § 13.2., Commentary, at 13-4.

Similar policies have prompted various private ADR tribunals to institute mechanisms for waiving filing fees and other administrative expenses in appropriate cases. *See, e.g., NASD Code* § 10332 (permitting Director of Arbitration to waive fees or deposits for parties in securities arbitration); *Nazon v. Shearson Lehman Bros., Inc.*, 832 F. Supp. 1540, 1543 (S.D. Fla. 1993) (employee, although required to bear expenses of pursuing civil rights claim in arbitration, might seek waiver of fees under NASD rules). One federal court of appeals recently concluded that to be enforceable with respect to actions under statutes governing employment discrimination, an arbitration agreement must not "require employees to pay either unreasonable costs or any arbitrators' fees or expenses as a condition of access to the arbitration forum." *Cole v. Burns Int'l Security Serv.*, 105 F.3d 1465, 1482–84 (D.C. Cir. 1997).

Due to the wide range of transactions and the equally broad spectrum of conflict in the Consumer arena, it is inappropriate to mandate bright-line rules regarding ADR costs. In determining what is reasonable, consideration should be given to the nature of the conflict (including the size of monetary claims, if any), and the nature of goods or services provided. In some cases, it may be possible to fulfill the principle of reasonable cost by the use of the Internet, the telephone, other electronic media, or through written submissions. *See, e.g.,* Michael F. Altschul & Elizabeth S. Stong,

AAA Develops New Arbitration Rules to Resolve Wireless Disputes, ADR Currents, Fall 1997, at 6. Abbreviated procedures may be particularly appropriate in the context of small monetary claims, where there is always the alternative of a face-to-face hearing in small claims court. *See* Principle 5.

In some cases, the need to ensure reasonable costs for the Consumer will require the Provider of goods or services to subsidize the costs of ADR which is mandated by the agreement. Indeed, many companies today deem it appropriate to pay most or all of the costs of ADR procedures for claims and disputes involving individual employees. *See* Mei L. Bickner, et al, *Developments in Employment Arbitration*, 52 Disp. Res. J. 8 (1997). The consensus of the Committee was that if participation in mediation is mandated by the ADR agreement, the Provider should pay the costs of the procedure, including mediator's fees and expenses. The Committee considered, and ultimately rejected, the alternative of establishing specific requirements for Provider subsidization of the cost of arbitration procedures, other than to conclude that the Provider of goods and services should ensure the consumer a basic minimum arbitration procedure appropriate to the circumstances.

In some cases, an arbitrator may find it appropriate to defray the cost of Consumer participation in arbitration by an award of costs. Some lemon laws provide for such relief. *See, e.g., Chrysler Corp. v. Maiocco*, 209 Conn. 579, 552 A.2d 1207 (1989) (applying Connecticut Lemon Law); *Walker v. General Motors Corp.*, 160 Misc. 2d 903, 611 N.Y.S.2d 741 (1994) (applying provision of New York Lemon Law permitting "prevailing consumer" to receive award of attorney's fees); *General Motors Corp. v. Fischer*, 140 Misc. 2d 243, 530 N.Y.S.2d 484 (1988) (same). In some cases, it may be appropriate for an arbitrator in a Consumer case to render an award of attorney's fees pursuant to statute or in other cases where a court might do so. Without such an award, however, the Committee does not support the proposition that Providers are required to subsidize Consumers' attorney's fees for ADR.

At the same time, there are legitimate concerns that having the Provider pay all or a substantial portion of neutral's fees and expenses may undermine the latter's impartiality. For this reason, as observed in the *Employment Due Process Protocol*, "[i]mpartiality is best assured by the parties sharing the fees and expenses of the mediator and arbitrator." *Employment Due Process Protocol* § 6. *See also* Stephen J. Ware, *Arbitration and Unconscionability After* Doctor's Associates, Inc. v. Casarotto, 31 Wake Forest L. Rev. 1001, 1023 (1996). *But see* Alan Scott Rau, *Integrity in Private Judging*, 38 S. Tex. L. Rev. 485, 528 (1997). Therefore, the Advisory Committee concludes that Consumers should have the option to share up to half of the Neutral's fees and expenses. In addition, unless the parties agree otherwise after a dispute arises, the handling of fee arrangements and the payment of fees should be conducted by the Independent ADR Institution. The latter, "by negotiating the parties' share of costs and collecting such fees, might be able to reduce the bias potential of disparate contributions by forwarding payment to the mediator and/or arbitrator without disclosing the parties' share therein." *Employment Due Process Protocol* § 6.

Some ADR Programs serving Consumers are staffed wholly or partly by unpaid volunteers. *See, e.g.,* BBB Arbitration Rules at 2. The use of such programs, including community dispute resolution centers, may be a satisfactory means of addressing cost concerns associated with Consumer ADR, particularly in cases involving low stakes. However, concerns have been expressed by some authorities regarding overdependence on volunteer Neutrals. *See Standards for Court-Connected Programs* § 13.1, Commentary, at 13-2 (warning of dangers of exclusive reliance on volunteers in ADR programs). Care must be taken by those responsible for overseeing such programs to make certain that lower cost does not come at the expense of adequately qualified Neutrals.

Practical Suggestions

In the event that an ADR procedure is mandated by the Provider of goods and services and the Consumer demonstrates an inability to pay all or part of the costs of the procedure, the Provider should front such costs subject to allocation in the arbitration award or mediation settlement.

In some cases, it may be possible to fulfill the principle of reasonable cost by the use of the Internet, the telephone, other electronic media, or through written submissions. See, e.g., Michael F. Altschul & Elizabeth S. Stong, *AAA Develops New Arbitration Rules to Resolve Wireless Disputes*, ADR Currents, Fall 1997, at 6.

PRINCIPLE 7. REASONABLY CONVENIENT LOCATION

In the case of face-to-face proceedings, the proceedings should be conducted at a location which is reasonably convenient to both parties with due consideration of their ability to travel and other pertinent circumstances. If the parties are unable to agree on a location, the determination should be made by the Independent ADR Institution or by the Neutral.

Reporter's Comments

The Advisory Committee concludes that ADR proceedings should take place at a location that is reasonably convenient to all parties.

Flexibility in choosing a hearing location is a theoretical advantage of consensual conflict resolution, permitting minimal cost and inconvenience to all parties. On the other hand, location terms may put one party at a great disadvantage, significantly increasing the cost and logistical complexity of dispute resolution. This is particularly true with regard to binding arbitration, which may involve the participation of multiple witnesses as well as the parties and their representatives. *See* III *Federal Arbitration Law* § 32.8.3.

Typically, contractual agreements which provide that arbitration hearings will be conducted in a particular place are honored by the courts. *See, e.g., Management Recruiters Int'l, Inc. v. Bloor*, 129 F.3d 851 (6th Cir. 1997) (under *Federal Arbitration Act*, forum expectations of parties in arbitration agreement are enforceable, and may not be upset by state law); *Bear Stearns & Co. v. Bennett*, 938 F.2d 31, 32 (2nd Cir. 1991) (noting "prima facie validity" of forum-selection clauses, including those in arbitration agreements); *Snyder v. Smith*, 736 F.2d 409, 419 (7th Cir.), cert. denied, 469 U.S. 1037, 105 S. Ct. 513, 83 L. Ed.2d 403 (1984) (courts must give effect to freely-negotiated arbitration clause in commercial agreement). *See* II *Federal Arbitration Law* § 24.2.3.4 (discussing *Federal Arbitration Act*). *Cf. Carnival Cruise Lines, Inc. v. Shute*, 449 U.S. 585, 111 S. Ct. 1522, 113 L. Ed. 2d 622 (1991) (judicial forum selection clause in terms on cruise ship passenger ticket enforceable); *M/S Bremen v. Zapata Off-Shore Co.*, 407 U.S. 1, 92 S. Ct. 1907. 32 L.Ed.2d (1972) (judicial forum selection clause is prima facie valid and should be enforced unless enforcement is shown by the resisting party to be unreasonable under the circumstances).

The same is true of cases where the parties agree to a process for selecting location, such as that provided by the *AAA Rules. See, e.g., AAA Commercial Rule* 11. There is authority for pre-award challenges to location selection mechanisms. *Aerojet-General Corp. v. AAA*, 478 F.2d 248 (9th Cir. 1973) (pre-award judicial review appropriate where choice of arbitration locale not made in good faith and one or more parties are faced with severe irreparable injury). Again, however, such action is likely to be deemed appropriate only in extreme cases. *See Seguro de Servicio de Salud v. McAuto Systems*, 878 F.2d 5, 9 n.6 (1st Cir. 1989); *S.J. Groves & Sons Co. v. AAA*, 452 F. Supp. 121, 124 (D. Minn. 1978).

Some courts, however, have identified limits on locational designations in judicial forum selection provisions. *See* Mark E. Budnitz, *Arbitration of Disputes Between Consumers and Financial Institutions: A Serious Threat to Consumer Protection*, 10 Ohio St. J. on Disp. Res. 267, 292; David S. Schwartz, *Enforcing Small Print to Protect Big Business: Employee and Consumer Rights Claims in an Age of Compelled Arbitration*, 1997 Wis. L. Rev. 36, 121 n.366. Forum selection clauses may be overcome if it can be demonstrated that their incorporation in the contract was the result of fraud, undue influence, or an extreme disparity in bargaining power, or if the selected forum is so inconvenient that it would effectively deprive a party of a day in court. *See, e.g., Kubis & Persyk Assoc., Inc. v. Sun Microsystems, Inc.*, 146 N.J. 176, 188–97, 680 A.2d 618, 624–29 (1996) (reviewing cases and recognizing limits on enforceability of forum selection clauses); *Moses v. Business Card Expr., Inc.*, 929 F.2d 1131, 1136–39 (6th Cir.), cert. denied, 502 U.S. 821, 112 S. Ct. 81, 116 L.Ed.2d 54 (1991) (in considering change of venue motion, forum selection clause must be considered along with convenience of parties and witnesses and overall fairness); *Hoffman v. Minuteman Press Int'l, Inc.*, 747 F. Supp. 552 (W.D. Mo. 1990) (denying venue change in accordance with forum selection agreement on basis of extreme hardship and alleged fraud in the inducement); *Cutter v. Scott & Fetzer Co.*, 510 F. Supp. 905, 908 (E.D. Wis. 1981) (refusing to enforce forum selection clause on basis of state Fair Dealership Law, and observing that clause was not the subject of negotiation). *See also Restatement (Second) of Conflict of Laws* § 80 (1969) (agreement regarding place of action will be given effect unless it is unfair or unreasonable); Benjamin Levin & Richard Morrison, *Kubis and the Changing Landscape of Forum Selection Clauses*, 16 Franchise. L.J. 97 (1997) (discussing trend to limit enforceability of forum selection clauses in franchise agreements by statute and case law); Donald B. Brenner, *There is a Developing Trend Among Courts of Making Choice of Forum Clauses in Franchise Agreements Presumptively Invalid*, 102 Com. L.J. 94 (1997) (same).

In the course of finding a judicial forum selection provision in a form franchise agreement presumptively invalid, the New Jersey Supreme Court recognized that the following factors may be relevant to enforceability: (1) whether the provision is the product of arm's length negotiations or is effectively imposed by a party with disproportionate bargaining power; and (2) whether the provision provides an "indirect benefit to . . . [the stronger party by making] litigation more costly and cumbersome for economically weaker . . . [parties] that often lack the sophistication and resources to litigate effectively a long distance from home." *Kubis*, 146 N.J. at 193–94, 680 A.2d at 626–27. *See also Model Choice of Forum Act* § 3(4) Comment (1968) ("A significant factor to be considered in determining whether there was an 'abuse of economic power or other unconscionable means' [sufficient to deny enforcement to a forum selection clause] is whether the choice of forum agreement was contained in an adhesion, or 'take-it-or-leave-it' contract.").

Such considerations may also affect the enforceability of an agreement to arbitrate. *See Patterson v. ITT Consumer Financial Corp.*, 14 Cal. App. 4th, 1659, 18 Cal. Rptr. 2d 563 (1993) (arbitration provisions in loan agreements requiring California consumers to arbitrate in Minnesota were unconscionable).

Similar concerns have led some states to enact laws placing geographical limitations on the situs of arbitration. *See, e.g., Hambell v. Alphagraphics Franchising Inc.*, 779 F. Supp. 910 (E.D. Mich. 1991) (provision in franchise agreement for arbitration to take place outside state is void and unenforceable under Mich. Stat. Ann. § 19.854(27)(f)(1984)); *Donmoor, Inc. v. Sturtevant*, 449 So.2d 869 (Fla. Ct. App. 1984) (clause in contract providing for arbitration in another state is unenforceable). Of course, such laws may be preempted by federal substantive law within the scope of the *Federal Arbitration Act. See* Levin & Morrison, *supra*, at 115–16.

In light of concerns such as the foregoing which are also relevant in the consumer arena, the Advisory Committee concluded that contractual ADR provisions should include a commitment to conduct ADR at a "reasonably convenient location." Some members of the Advisory Committee favored setting an arbitrary mileage limit (i.e. "no more than 50 miles from the place where the transaction occurred") while others advocated the nearest large city. Others pointed out that parties sometimes relocate. There was general agreement, however, that an agreed-upon process for independent determination of the locale if the parties fail to agree would be fair and equitable to both parties. *See, e.g., AAA Rule* 11; *Uniform Code of Arbitration* § 9; *NASD Code of Arbitration Procedure* § 10315. A similar function may be performed by the arbitrator or other duly appointed Neutral. (The *AAA Rules* already accord arbitrators the authority to set specific sites for arbitration hearings. *See AAA Rule* 21.)

In many cases, it may be possible to minimize the need for long distance travel and attendant expenses through the use of telephonic communications and submission of documents. An example of the application of such devices is the Expedited Procedures of the *AAA Rules*, which are generally applied to claims of $50,000 or less. *See AAA Rules* 9, 53–57. *See also Uniform Code of Arbitration* § 2. Telephonic mediation has long been a feature of some lemon law programs, and is currently being used in Consumer ADR by the National Futures Association (NFA). The National Association of Securities Dealers (NASD) is currently conducting a pilot program utilizing telephonic mediation.

Recent projects sponsored by the Better Business Bureau, the American Arbitration Association, and other organizations suggest the possibilities of online conflict resolution for online transactions as well as other kinds of disputes. *See generally* George H. Friedman, *Alternative Dispute Resolution and Emerging Online Technologies: Challenges and Opportunities*, 19 Hastings Comm. & Ent. L.J. 695 (1997).

If, as proposed, Consumers have the alternative of pursuing relief in a small claims court of competent jurisdiction, many concerns associated with long distance travel will be obviated with regard to small claims.

Practical Suggestions

Unless a convenient location can be specifically identified in the ADR agreement, the location should be left to the agreement of the parties after a dispute has arisen. The rules governing ADR under the agreement should establish a process for determination of the location by an independent party (such as a Neutral or the Independent ADR Institution) if the parties cannot agree on a location.

In some cases, it may be reasonable to conduct proceedings by telephone or electronic data transmission, with or without submission of documents. *See, e.g.,* Principle 12. Such options may be particularly desirable in the case of arbitration of small claims, since the parties have the choice of going to small claims court. *See* Principle 5.

PRINCIPLE 8. REASONABLE TIME LIMITS

ADR proceedings should occur within a reasonable time, without undue delay. The rules governing ADR should establish specific reasonable time periods for each step in the ADR process and, where necessary, set forth default procedures in the event a party fails to participate in the process after reasonable notice.

Reporter's Comments

A primary impetus for conflict resolution outside the court system is the potential for relatively speedy and efficient resolution of disputes. From the Consumer's perspective, moreover, the expectation of a reasonably prompt conclusion is likely to be, along with cost savings, the leading perceived advantage of consensual mediation or arbitration. *See Madden v. Kaiser Foundation Hospitals*, 17 Cal. 3d 699, 711, 131 Cal. Rptr. 882, 552 P.2d 1178 (1976) (speed and economy of arbitration, in contrast to the expense and delay of jury trial, could prove helpful to all parties).

The principle of relatively prompt, efficient conflict resolution underlies standards governing the conduct of Neutrals. Mediators are admonished that "[a] quality process requires a commitment by the mediator to diligence. . . ." *Joint Standards for Mediators*, Art. VI. The *Joint Standards for Mediators* also comment that "[m]ediators should only accept cases when they can satisfy the reasonable expectations of the parties concerning the timing of the process." *Id.*

A basic requirement is that the rules governing ADR establish and further the basic principle of conflict resolution within a reasonable time. This means not only that the rules should set forth specific time periods for various steps in the ADR process, but that default rules come into play if a party fails to participate in the manner required by the rules after due notice. This principle is embodied in leading ADR standards, including the *AAA Commercial Rules*. *See, e.g.,* Rules 6, 8, 11, 13, 14, 15, 21, 35, 36, 41. *See also BBB Arbitration Rule* 27 ("BBB shall make every effort to obtain a final resolution of your complaint within 60 days, unless state or federal law provides otherwise. This time period may be extended at the request of the customer.").

Of course, it is not enough that the agreement places strict time limitations on procedural steps if these limitations are not effectively enforced—a likely occurrence when an ADR Program is not independent of the Provider. Extreme disparity between stipulated time limits and actual practice under arbitration rules may render an arbitration agreement unenforceable, as discussed at length in a recent California Supreme Court decision. *See generally Engalla v. Permanente Med. Grp., Inc.*, 938 P.2d 903 (Cal. 1997). The court pointedly observed,

> [M]any large institutional users of arbitration, including most health maintenance organizations (HMO's), avoid the potential problems of delay in the selection of arbitrators by contracting with neutral third party organizations, such as the American Arbitration Association (AAA). These organizations will then assume responsibility for administering the claim from the time the arbitration demand is filed, and will ensure the arbitrator or arbitrators are chosen in a timely manner.

Id. at 975–76. In response to this decision, Kaiser appointed an advisory panel to propose reforms to its arbitration program. *See Kaiser Permanente Review and Recommendations* 33–34 (recommending establishment of and adherence to stated arbitration process deadlines). Similarly, courts interpreting state lemon laws have acknowledged the right of Consumers to forgo arbitration and sue in court when the statutory period for the lemon law remedy elapsed without a remedy through no fault of their own. *See, e.g., Harrison v. Nissan Motor Corp.*, 111 F.3d 343 (3rd Cir. 1997) (court suit permissible where BBB failed to conduct arbitration within stipulated period); *Ford Motor Co. v. Ward*, 577 So.2d 641 (1991) (Consumer not required to exhaust arbitration procedures before bringing suit where dealer made it impossible for Consumer to arbitrate).

Practical Suggestions

When a Consumer dispute involves a small amount of money and relatively straightforward issues, it is reasonable to assume that an out-of-court resolution of such issues should be relatively quick. In such cases, it may be appropriate to develop expedited procedures and to set outside time limits on ADR Processes. Thus, for example, "Fast Track" arbitration procedures for construction disputes provide that "[t]he arbitration shall be completed by settlement or award within sixty (60) days of confirmation of the arbitrator's appointment, unless all parties agree otherwise or the arbitrator extends this time in extraordinary cases. . . ." *AAA Construction Procedures*, § F-12. The rules also require the award to be rendered within seven days from the closing of the hearing. *See id.,* § F-11.

Similarly, the *AAA Wireless Rules* set forth Fast Track procedures for matters involving less than $2,000 in claims or counterclaims. The Fast Track contemplates a "desk" arbitration procedure involving a hearing on documents; a limit of one seven-day extension on the time to respond to a claim or counterclaim; notice by telephone, electronic mail and other forms of electronic communication and by overnight mail, shortened time limits to select an arbitrator; no discovery except in extraordinary cases; a shortened time limit for rendition of award; and a time standard which sets a goal of 45 days from appointment of the arbitrator to award.

PRINCIPLE 9. RIGHT TO REPRESENTATION

All parties participating in processes in ADR Programs have the right, at their own expense, to be represented by a spokesperson of their own choosing. The ADR rules and procedures should so specify.

Reporter's Comments

The right to be counseled by an attorney or other representative is an important one that is frequently reflected in standard rules governing ADR proceedings. *See, e.g., AAA Commercial Rule* 22; *NASD Code* § 10316; *BBB Arbitration Rule* 9.

The Advisory Committee adapted pertinent provisions of the *Employment Due Process Protocol*. *See Employment Due Process Protocol* § B.1.

In the interest of full disclosure of potential conflicts of interest on the part of Neutrals, the Advisory Committee recommends that the names and affiliations of lawyers and other representatives of each party be communicated to prospective Neutrals and to all parties prior to selection of Neutrals.

As previously noted, the Advisory Committee recognizes that the cost of legal services should be borne by the parties who are receiving the services, and Providers should not be expected to subsidize the cost of legal representation for Consumers. There may, however, be situations where an arbitrator awards attorney's fees in circumstances where they would be available in court. *See* Commentary to Principle 6.

The Advisory Committee recognizes that the involvement of non-attorney representatives in some forms of binding arbitration has raised issues respecting the unauthorized practice of law. The Committee takes no position regarding these issues.

Practical Suggestions

Although the cost of legal services should be borne by the parties who are receiving the services, Independent ADR Institutions should provide Consumers with information regarding referral services and other institutions which might offer assistance in locating and securing competent spokespersons, such as bar associations, legal service associations, and Consumer organizations.

PRINCIPLE 10. MEDIATION

The use of mediation is strongly encouraged as an informal means of assisting parties in resolving their own disputes.

Reporter's Comments

The increasing popularity of mediation has been a primary impetus for the revolution in conflict resolution approaches. Mediation describes a range of processes in which an impartial person helps disputing parties to communicate and to make voluntary, informed choices in an effort to resolve their dispute. The rapid growth of mediation may be attributed to its informality, flexibility, and emphasis on the particular needs of disputing parties. For this reason, mediation is uniquely adaptable to a wide spectrum of controversies.

The widespread use of mediation in court-connected programs inspired the development of a set of national standards for such endeavors. *See generally Standards for Court-Connected Programs.*

Parallel developments are occurring in the private sphere. Recently, the leading standard construction industry contract was modified to require mediation as an element in project conflict resolution, necessitating modification of related AAA rules. *See AAA Construction Procedures.*

Advisory Committee members agreed that mediation should be encouraged as a valuable intervention strategy, but differed as to the propriety and reasonableness of Provider-drafted ADR Agreements in Consumer contracts which require Consumers to participate in mediation. Those unopposed to such provisions, a majority of Advisory Committee members, noted that mediation offers significant potential advantages and relatively few risks to participants. Particularly where the Provider subsidizes mediation, they reasoned, the prospective benefits to Consumers far outweigh the costs. Those expressing concerns regarding "mandatory" mediation adhere to the view that the choice to participate in settlement discussions should be made voluntarily, and only after conflict arises. Other concerns relate to the cost of mediation, the quality of mediators, the likelihood that not all disputes will be appropriate for mediation, and the lack of understanding of mediation processes (including an understanding of the role of the neutral intervener) on the part of many Consumers. *Cf. Standards for Court-Connected Programs* § 5.0 (courts should impose mandatory attendance in court-connected mediation only when the cost of mediation is publicly funded, the mediation program is of high quality, and other requirements are met); *SPIDR Report on Court-Mandated ADR* at 2–3.

Encouragement of the use of mediation involves, among other things, educating Consumers and their attorneys about the process. *See* Principle 2 "Access to Information Regarding ADR Program." *See also SPIDR Principles* at 6 ("It is the responsibility of . . . private programs offering dispute resolution services to define clearly the services they provide . . . [and provide information about the program and neutrals to the parties.]"). At a minimum, Consumers should be provided with (or have immediate access to) written information to explain mediation. As a rule, such information should be in the same language as the principal contract for goods or services. *Cf. Standards for Court-Connected Programs* § 3.2.b., Commentary, at 3-4 (If a significant percentage of the population served is non-English-speaking, the material should be available in other languages as well.) *See* Principle 2.

Education of users should also include some treatment of the distinctive styles and strategies employed by mediators. Today, mediators handling commercial disputes sometimes employ a facilitative, non-directive approach to problem-solving; in other situations, a more directive approach may be employed. *See generally* Leonard L. Riskin, *Understanding Mediators' Orientations, Strategies, and Techniques: A Grid for the Perplexed*, 1 Harv. Negotiation L. Rev. 7 (1996) (providing a graphic tool for analyzing mediator approaches). Participants need to decide in advance of selection the approach they want a mediator to adopt. The Independent ADR Institution should advise the parties regarding the possibility of interviewing prospective mediators regarding qualifications and style, and help to arrange such interviews.

Practical Suggestions

As referenced in Principle 5, mediation conducted by telephone conference call has proven to be an effective, economical method of resolving Consumer disputes where in-person mediation may not be feasible.

SPECIAL PROVISIONS RELATING TO BINDING ARBITRATION

PRINCIPLE 11. AGREEMENTS TO ARBITRATE

Consumers should be given:

a. clear and adequate notice of the arbitration provision and its consequences, including a statement of its mandatory or optional character;

b. reasonable access to information regarding the arbitration process, including basic distinctions between arbitration and court proceedings, related costs, and advice as to where they may obtain more complete information regarding arbitration procedures and arbitrator rosters;

c. notice of the option to make use of applicable small claims court procedures as an alternative to binding arbitration in appropriate cases; and,

d. a clear statement of the means by which the Consumer may exercise the option (if any) to submit disputes to arbitration or to court process.

Reporter's Comments

In convening the Advisory Committee which developed this Protocol, the AAA requested that the Committee focus its attention upon due process standards for the conduct of Consumer ADR processes and not directly address the process of forming an agreement to mediate or to arbitrate. Committee deliberations revealed a range of opinions regarding the use of pre-dispute binding arbitration agreements in Consumer contracts. Without taking a position on the appropriateness of such agreements, the Committee developed Principle 11 with the intended purpose of providing guidance to the AAA and similar Independent ADR Institutions in the development of specific arbitration programs within the context of existing law enforcing pre-dispute arbitration agreements. Within this context, Principle 11 emphasizes the importance of knowing, informed assent to arbitration agreements.

Practical Suggestions

Consumers should have clear and adequate notice of the arbitration provision and basic information regarding the process at the time of assent. The appropriate method of giving notice and providing essential information will vary with the circumstances. For example, electronic transactions involving software licensure agreements require different notice procedures than face-to-face negotiations or paper transactions. In all cases, however, there should be some form of conspicuous notice of the agreement to arbitrate and its basic consequences (including comparison to court process, cost information, etc.). In addition, the Consumer should be given the opportunity to acquire additional information regarding the arbitration process. The latter might be obtainable through a mail or Web site address, an 800 number or other means for Consumers to obtain additional information regarding arbitration rules and procedures (such as a brochure available on request).

The following is an example of a possible notice. Ideally, the "notice box" would be sufficiently prominent in the contract document or electronic record so that a Consumer would readily notice it.

NOTICE OF ARBITRATION AGREEMENT:

This agreement provides that all disputes between you and [PROVIDER] will be resolved by <u>BINDING ARBITRATION</u>.

You thus GIVE UP YOUR RIGHT TO GO TO COURT to assert or defend your rights under this contract (EXCEPT for matters that may be taken to SMALL CLAIMS COURT).

*Your rights will be determined by a NEUTRAL ARBITRATOR and NOT a judge or jury.

* You are entitled to a <u>FAIR HEARING</u>, BUT the arbitration procedures are <u>SIMPLER AND MORE LIMITED</u> THAN RULES APPLICABLE IN COURT.

*Arbitrator decisions are as enforceable as any court order and are subject to <u>VERY LIMITED REVIEW</u> BY A COURT.

FOR MORE DETAILS,
* <u>Review Section 6.2 above</u>, OR
* Check our Arbitration Web Site @ ACMEADR.COM, OR
* Call 1-800-000-0000

Among other things, Consumers should have access to information regarding the initiation of the arbitration process. This may be accomplished, for example, by providing customers with a brochure outlining relevant arbitration procedures. If the Consumer has the option of choosing between arbitration or court process, either at the time of contracting or after disputes have arisen, the timing and means of electing the option should also be clearly stated in the notice.

PRINCIPLE 12. ARBITRATION HEARINGS

1. Fundamentally-Fair Hearing. All parties are entitled to a fundamentally-fair arbitration hearing. This requires adequate notice of hearings and an opportunity to be heard and to present relevant evidence to impartial decision- makers. In some cases, such as some small claims, the requirement of fundamental fairness may be met by hearings conducted by electronic or telephonic means or by a submission of documents. However, the Neutral should have discretionary authority to require a face-to-face hearing upon the request of a party.

2. Confidentiality in Arbitration. Consistent with general expectations of privacy in arbitration hearings, the arbitrator should make reasonable efforts to maintain the privacy of the hearing to the extent permitted by applicable law. The arbitrator should also carefully consider claims of privilege and confidentiality when addressing evidentiary issues.

Reporter's Comments

There is universal agreement that parties to arbitration are entitled to a "fundamentally-fair hearing." *See* III *Federal Arbitration Law* § 32.3.1.1. The language of subsection 1 closely follows the definition of a "fundamentally-fair hearing" set forth in *Bowles Financial Grp., Inc. v. Stifel, Nicolaus & Co.*, 22 F.3d 1010, 1013 (10th Cir. 1994) (applying the *Federal Arbitration Act*). Beyond these basic requirements, of course, "[a]rbitration need not follow all the niceties of . . . courts." *Grovner v. Georgia-Pacific Corp.*, 625 F.2d 1289, 1290 (5th Cir. 1980). Moreover, the arbitrators have great leeway in conducting hearings, within the bounds of the parties' agreement. *See Federal Arbitration Law, supra*, §§ 32.1., 32.3.1.1.

Although authority is split on whether or not parties are guaranteed a face-to-face hearing before the arbitrators, *see id.*, the Advisory Committee concluded that while in some circumstances fundamental fairness may require a face-to-face hearing, in other cases the requirement may be satisfied by telephonic or electronic communications or submissions of documents. *See, e.g., Construction Arbitration Procedures* § F-9. *See, e.g.,* Michael F. Altschul & Elizabeth S. Stong, *AAA Develops New Arbitration Rules to Resolve Wireless Disputes*, ADR Currents, Fall 1997, at 6. In small claims cases, the requirement of these Principles that parties retain the option of going to small claims court may make it reasonable for the ADR agreement to provide alternatives to a face-to-face hearing.

Although confidentiality of hearings may be considered an advantage of arbitration, there is no absolute guarantee of confidentiality. *See id.*, § 32.6.1. Unlike court proceedings, however, the general public has no right to attend arbitration proceedings; if the parties agree, moreover, attendance at hearings may be severely restricted. *See, e.g., AAA Commercial Rule* 25 (directing arbitrators to "maintain the privacy of the hearings unless the law provides to the contrary"). Likewise, arbitrators should be mindful of evidentiary privileges and confidentiality rights available to its parties under applicable law and have discretion to issue protective orders respecting such rights.

The Advisory Committee recognized the dilemma posed by the tension between the desire for confidentiality in arbitration and the need to provide Consumers access to information regarding arbitrators and sponsoring Independent ADR Institutions, including case statistics, data on recent arbitrations and other pertinent information. *See, e.g.,* Alan Scott Rau, *Integrity in Private Judging*, 38 S. Tex. L. Rev. 485, 524–26 (1997) (discussing concerns with "asymmetry of information" regarding arbitrators when one party is an institutional "repeat player," and suggesting need for increased disclosure of information regarding past decisions by an arbitrator); Mark E. Budnitz, *Arbitration of Disputes Between Consumers and Financial Institutions: A Serious Threat to Consumer Protection*, 10 Ohio St. J. on Disp. Res. 267, 293 (discussing disparity between "repeat players" and consumers with regard to knowledge of prospective arbitrators). Although the Advisory Committee did not address this issue, it recommends that the matter be the focus of serious study by the Committee or a similar advisory group, supported by appropriate independent research efforts.

Practical Suggestions

Because these Principles provide that parties should retain the option of an oral hearing in small claims court (Principle 5), it may be reasonable for the ADR agreement to provide other means for small claims arbitration. Such alternatives may include a "desk arbitration" involving a decision on written submissions, participation in proceedings by telephone or electronic data transmission, and other options.

As is generally the case in commercial arbitration, arbitrators may undertake reasonable means to protect the privacy of the hearing.

PRINCIPLE 13. ACCESS TO INFORMATION

No party should ever be denied the right to a fundamentally-fair process due to an inability to obtain information material to a dispute. Consumer ADR agreements which provide for binding arbitration should establish procedures for arbitrator-supervised exchange of information prior to arbitration, bearing in mind the expedited nature of arbitration.

Reporter's Comments

It is understood that ADR sometimes represents a tradeoff between the concept of full discovery associated with court procedures and the efficiencies associated with minimal pretrial process. A hallmark of binding arbitration is the avoidance of the cost and delay associated with extensive pre-hearing discovery. *See* III *Federal Arbitration Law* § 34.1. In recent years, however, the notion that arbitration means little or no discovery has moderated due to the widening range of cases submitted to arbitration and the increasing recognition that at least some pre-hearing exchange of information may be necessary and appropriate to meet the due process rights of participants—and may in some cases reduce the overall length of the process. *See id.*, Ch. 34. *See also* Mark E. Budnitz, *Arbitration of Disputes Between Consumers and Financial Institutions: A Serious Threat to Consumer Protection*, 10 Ohio St. J. on Disp. Res. 267, 283–84, 311, 314 (arguing that limits on discovery in arbitration hamper consumer claimants).

Addressing statutory disputes arising out of employment relationships, the *Employment Due Process Protocol* states that "[a]dequate but limited pre-trial discovery is to be encouraged and employees [and their representatives] should have access to all information reasonably relevant to mediation and/or arbitration of their claims." *Employment Due Process Protocol* § B.3. The Committee supports the concept of limiting the exchange of information as much as possible while ensuring that Consumers and Providers each have access to information that is legally obtainable and relevant to their case. In most cases, this means that pre-hearing information exchange will consist of an exchange of documents as directed by the arbitrator, identification of witnesses and a summary of their expected testimony. Arbitrators should have the authority to require additional discovery when necessary, such as requiring the deposition of witnesses unable to appear at the hearing in order to preserve their testimony.

Although information exchange issues which cannot be handled by the agreement of the parties should generally be left to the discretion of the arbitrator, it may be appropriate for advisory groups (including adequate consumer representation) to develop guidelines for information exchange in specific kinds of cases. *See, e.g.,* National Association of Securities Dealers, National Arbitration and Mediation Committee, *Report of the Drafting Subcommittee on The Discovery Guide*, Dec. 3, 1997 Draft.

Some Advisory Committee members also expressed concern about the forced production of privileged documents, and argued that arbitrators should be required to observe established privileges such as the attorney-client privilege and work-product privilege. *See* James H. Carter, *The Attorney-Client Privilege and Arbitration*, ADR Currents, Winter 1996–97, 1. As stated in Principle 12, arbitrators should "carefully consider claims of privilege and confidentiality when addressing evidentiary issues." Such protections may be addressed in the arbitration agreement (including incorporated arbitration procedures), and should be thoroughly treated, along with information exchange issues, in arbitrator training programs.

Practical Suggestions

In many cases, issues relating to information exchange may be addressed by the arbitrator(s) at a preliminary conference. *See, e.g., AAA Wireless Rules* §§ R-9, R-10. Some rules require that all exhibits be exchanged a certain number of days prior to hearings. *See id.,* R-10.

PRINCIPLE 14. ARBITRAL REMEDIES

The arbitrator should be empowered to grant whatever relief would be available in court under law or in equity.

Reporter's Comments

As a general rule, arbitrators have broad authority to fashion relief appropriate to the circumstances. *See* III *Federal Arbitration Law* § 36.1.1. Their discretion is limited only by the agreement of the parties and the scope of the submission to arbitration. *See id.,* § 36.1.2.

There are, however, a number of issues respecting the ability of arbitrators to award certain remedies which would be available in court. For example, although the trend under federal and state law is to acknowledge the authority of arbitrators to award punitive damages, a few state courts still take the opposing view. *See generally Federal Arbitration Law, supra,* § 36.3; Thomas J. Stipanowich, *Punitive Damages and the Consumerization of Arbitration,* 92 Nw. U. L. Rev. 1 (1998). And although courts may award attorney's fees where permitted by statute or by agreement of the parties, or where a party acts vexatiously or in bad faith, there is conflicting authority regarding the ability of arbitrators to take similar action. *See generally Federal Arbitration Law, supra,* § 36.8.

This provision incorporates language similar to that contained in the *Employment Due Process Protocol,* § C.5. The intent is to make clear that arbitrators deriving their authority from Consumer contracts should enjoy the same authority courts have to fashion relief, including awarding attorney's fees and punitive damages in appropriate cases.

Contractual limitations of damages may limit the authority of arbitrators in the same fashion that they limit judicial remedies. It is possible that an award of damages in excess of a contractual limit would be vacated under pertinent statutory standards or common law principles. *See, e.g.,* FAA § 10(a)(4). *But see* Stipanowich, *Punitive Damages, supra,* at 33–36 (discussing public policy limitations on pre-dispute caps on punitive damages).

PRINCIPLE 15. ARBITRATION AWARDS

1. *Final and Binding Award; Limited Scope of Review. If provided in the agreement to arbitrate, the arbitrator's award should be final and binding, but subject to review in accordance with applicable statutes governing arbitration awards.*
2. *Standards to Guide Arbitrator Decision-Making. In making the award, the arbitrator should apply any identified, pertinent contract terms, statutes and legal precedents.*
3. *Explanation of Award. At the timely request of either party, the arbitrator should provide a brief written explanation of the basis for the award. To facilitate such requests, the arbitrator should discuss the matter with the parties prior to the arbitration hearing.*

Reporter's Comments

Review of arbitration awards is very limited under modern arbitration statutes. Courts are very reluctant to vacate awards, or to second-guess the decisions of arbitrators on matters of procedure or substance. *See generally* IV *Federal Arbitration Law,* ch. 40. "Arbitrators can misconstrue contracts, make erroneous decisions of fact, and misapply law, all without having their awards vacated." *See id.,* § 40.6.1. While some members of the Advisory Committee expressed concerns regarding the current state of the law, it was generally agreed that finality was a primary objective of arbitration and that it would be inappropriate to recommend more rigorous judicial review for Consumer arbitration awards than for other arbitration awards. At the same time, however, the Advisory Committee concluded that the rules should specifically direct arbitrators to follow pertinent contract terms and legal principles. This requirement may have implications for qualifications and training of Neutrals pursuant to Principle 4.

Leading modern arbitration statutes do not require arbitrators to provide a written explanation or give reasons for their awards. *See generally* III *Federal Arbitration Law* § 37.4.1. Similarly, some leading commercial arbitration rules do not require findings of fact or conclusions of law. *See, e.g., AAA Commercial Rules.* Those supporting "bare" awards argue that a written rationale will make it more likely that courts will inquire into the merits of the award, contrary to policies of finality underlying modern statutes. They also observe that not being required to write an opinion simplifies the arbitral task and permits multi-member arbitration panels, like juries, to agree on a decision without concurring on a rationale. *See id.*

On the other hand, some other commercial arbitration rules call for a statement of the underlying rationale. *See, e.g., CPR Rules for Non-administered Arbitration of Business Disputes,* Rule 13.2. Those supporting awards with written rationales argue that a written rationale encourages more disciplined decision-making and enhances party satisfaction with the result. *See* Alan Scott Rau, *Integrity in Private Judging,* 38 S. Tex. L. Rev. 485, 529–39 (1997) (offering arguments in favor of "reasoned" awards). After considering the pros and cons of "reasoned" awards, the Advisory Committee concluded that arbitrators of Consumer disputes should provide at least a brief written explanation if requested to do so by any party.

As noted in the Comments accompanying Principle 12, the Advisory Committee recognized the dilemma posed by the tension between the desire for confidentiality in arbitration (including information regarding arbitration awards) and the need to provide Consumers access to information regarding arbitrators and sponsoring Independent ADR Institutions, including case statistics, data on recent arbitrations and other pertinent information. Although the Advisory Committee did not address this issue, it recommends that the matter be the focus of serious study by the Advisory Committee or a similar advisory group, supported by appropriate independent research efforts.

Practical Suggestions

To facilitate requests for reasoned awards, the arbitrator should raise the issue with the parties prior to the arbitration hearing. The matter should be addressed at the preliminary conference if one is conducted.

A DUE PROCESS PROTOCOL FOR MEDIATION AND ARBITRATION OF CONSUMER DISPUTES

Dated: April 17, 1998

Some of the signatories to this Protocol were designated by their respective organizations, but the Protocol reflects their personal views and should not be construed as representing the policy of the designating organizations.

The Honorable Winslow Christian
Co-chair
Justice (Retired)
California Court of Appeal

William N. Miller
Co-chair
Director of the ADR Unit Office of Consumer Affairs
Virginia Division of Consumer Protection
Designated by National Association of
Consumer Agency Administrators

David B. Adcock
Office of the University Counsel
Duke University

Steven G. Gallagher
Senior Vice President
American Arbitration Association

Michael F. Hoellering
General Counsel
American Arbitration Association

J. Clark Kelso
Director
Institute for Legislative Practice
University of the Pacific
McGeorge School of Law

Elaine Kolish
Associate Director
Division of Enforcement
Bureau of Consumer Protection
Federal Trade Commission

Robert Marotta
Wolcott, Rivers, Wheary, Basnight & Kelly, P.C.
Formerly Office of the General Counsel
General Motors Corporation

Robert E. Meade
Senior Vice President
American Arbitration Association

Ken McEldowney
Executive Director
Consumer Action

Michelle Meier
Former Counsel for Government Affairs
Consumers Union

Anita B. Metzen
Executive Director
American Council on Consumer Interests

James A. Newell
Associate General Counsel
Freddie Mac

Shirley F. Sarna
Assistant Attorney General-In-Charge
Consumer Frauds and Protection Bureau
Office of the Attorney General
State of New York
Designated by National Association of Attorneys General

Daniel C. Smith
Vice President and Deputy General Counsel
Fannie Mae

Terry L. Trantina
Member
Ravin, Sarasohn, Cook, Baumgarten, Fisch & Rosen, P.C.
Formerly General Attorney
AT&T Corp.

Deborah M. Zuckerman
Staff Attorney
Litigation Unit
American Association of Retired Persons

Thomas Stipanowich
Academic Reporter
W.L. Matthews Professor of Law
University of Kentucky College of Law

Arbitration Service Provider Rules   Appx. B.2.1

B.2 The National Arbitration Forum[2]

B.2.1 Code of Procedure and Fee Schedule

August 1, 2007

PART I—SCOPE

RULE 1 Arbitration Agreement
RULE 2 Definitions
RULE 3 Representation
RULE 4 Confidentiality

PART II—COMMENCEMENT OF ARBITRATION

RULE 5 Summary of Procedures
RULE 6 Service of Claims, Responses, Requests, and Documents
RULE 7 Filing
RULE 8 Notices and Conferences
RULE 9 Time Periods, Time Extensions, Adjournments, and Stays
RULE 10 Time Limitations

PART III—DOCUMENTS

RULE 11 Form and Parties
RULE 12 Initial Claim
RULE 13 Response
RULE 14 Counter Claim
RULE 15 Cross-claim
RULE 16 Third Party Claim
RULE 17 Amendment
RULE 18 Request to Arbitrator or Forum
RULE 19 Joinder, Intervention, Consolidation, and Separation

PART IV—ARBITRATORS

RULE 20 Authority of Arbitrators
RULE 21 Selection of Arbitrators
RULE 22 Number of Arbitrators
RULE 23 Disqualification of Arbitrator
RULE 24 Communications with Arbitrators

PART V—HEARING

RULE 25 Selection of a Document Hearing
RULE 26 Selection of a Participatory Hearing
RULE 27 Request for an Expedited Hearing
RULE 28 Document Hearing
RULE 29 Discovery
RULE 30 Subpoena for In-person Participatory Hearing
RULE 31 Exchange of Information Before a Participatory Hearing
RULE 32 Location of an In-person Participatory Hearing
RULE 33 Participatory Hearing
RULE 34 Participatory Hearing Proceedings
RULE 35 Evidence in a Participatory Hearing
RULE 36 Arbitration Proceedings in Absence of a Party

PART VI—AWARDS AND ORDERS

RULE 37 Awards
RULE 38 Orders
RULE 39 Entry and Service of Awards and Orders
RULE 40 Voluntary Dismissal
RULE 41 Involuntary Dismissal
RULE 42 Correction
RULE 43 Reopening and Reconsideration

PART VII—FEES

RULE 44 Fees
RULE 45 Waiver of Fees

PART VIII—CODE PROVISIONS

RULE 46 Compliance with Rules
RULE 47 Legal Proceedings
RULE 48 Interpretation and Application of Code

APPENDIX A

Notice of Arbitration

APPENDIX B

Second Notice of Arbitration

PART I

SCOPE

RULE 1. Arbitration Agreement.

A. Parties who contract for or agree to arbitration provided by the Forum or this Code of Procedure agree that this Code governs their arbitration proceedings, unless the Parties agree to other procedures. This Code shall be deemed incorporated by reference in every Arbitration Agreement, which refers to the National Arbitration Forum, the International Arbitration Forum, the Arbitration Forum, adrforum.com, Forum or this Code of Procedure, unless the Parties agree otherwise. This Code shall be administered only by the National Arbitration Forum or by any entity or individual providing administrative services by agreement with the National Arbitration Forum.

B. Parties may agree to submit any matter, including any Claim for legal or equitable relief, to arbitration unless prohibited by applicable law.

C. Arbitrations will be conducted in accord with the applicable Code of Procedure in effect at the time the Claim is filed, unless the law or the agreement of the Parties provides otherwise. A case that has been Stayed, extended or Adjourned for more than one hundred-eighty (180) days may be subject to the Code of Procedure and Fee Schedule in effect at the time the case proceeds.

D. Parties may modify or supplement these rules as permitted by law. Provisions of this Code govern arbitrations involving an appeal or a review de novo of an arbitration by other Arbitrators.

---

[2] © Copyright 1986–2007 by the National Arbitration Forum. Reprinted with the permission of the National Arbitration Forum.

RULE 2. Definitions.

For purposes of this Code, the following definitions apply:

A. Affidavit: A Written statement of a person who asserts the statement to be true under penalty of perjury or who makes the statement under oath before a notary public or other authorized individual.

B. Adjournment: A continuance or delay for a specific period of time requested after the appointment of an Arbitrator. See Time Extension and Stay.

C. Amendment: A change made to a Claim after it has been served on the Respondent and any change made to a Response after it has been filed and Delivered to all Parties.

D. Appearance: Any filing by a Party or Party's Representative under Rules 12, 13, 19B, 41A or 44H.

E. Arbitration Agreement: Any Written provision in any agreement between or among the Parties to submit any dispute, controversy or Claim to the Forum or to arbitration under this Code.

F. Arbitrator: An individual selected in accord with the Code or an Arbitration Agreement to render Orders and Awards, including a sole Arbitrator and all Arbitrators of an arbitration panel. No Arbitrator may be a director or officer of the Forum. A Party Arbitrator is an Arbitrator selected by a Party to serve as a member of a panel of Arbitrators in accord with the agreement of the Parties.

G. Award: Any Award establishing the final rights and obligations of the Parties or as otherwise provided by this Code or by law.

H. Claim: Any Claim submitted by any Party including an Initial Claim, Cross-claim, Counter Claim, and Third Party Claim.

I. Claimant: Any individual or Entity making any Claim under this Code.

J. Claim Amount: The total value of all relief sought. A Claimant seeking non-monetary relief states a monetary value for this relief for purposes of establishing the Claim Amount.

K. Common Claim: A Claim Amount less than $75,000.

L. Consumer: An individual, who is not a business or other Entity, whose Claim or Response against a business or other Entity arises:
   (1) From a transaction or event entered into primarily for personal, family or household purposes;
   (2) From an existing, past or prospective employment relationship with an employer Party; or
   (3) From a transaction or event involving any aspect of health care.

M. Delivery: Delivery to the address of a Party, the Forum or an Arbitrator by the postal service of the United States or any country, or by a reliable private service, or by facsimile, e-mail, electronic or computer transmission.

N. Director: The Director of Arbitration and the Forum staff administer arbitrations under this Code or under other rules agreed to by the Parties.

O. Document: Any Writing or data compilation containing information in any form, including an agreement, record, correspondence, summary, electronically stored information, tape, e-mail, video, audio, disk, computer file, electronic attachment, notice, memorandum or other Writings or data compilations.

P. E-commerce Transaction: All contracts and agreements entered into, in whole or in part, by electronic or computer communication and all transactions consummated through electronic or computer communication.

Q. Entity: Any association, business, company, cooperative, corporation, country, governmental unit, group, institution, organization, partnership, sole proprietorship, union or other establishment.

R. Fee Schedule: The Fee Schedule appears in a supplement to this Code.

S. Forum: The National Arbitration Forum, the International Arbitration Forum, the Arbitration Forum, arbitration-forum.com, and adrforum.com constitute the administrative organizations conducting arbitrations under this Code. The Forum or an entity or individual providing administrative services by agreement with the Forum administers arbitrations in accord with this Code.

T. Hearing: Hearings include:
   (1) Document Hearing: A proceeding in which an Arbitrator reviews documents or property to render an Order or Award and the Parties do not attend.
   (2) Participatory Hearing: Any proceeding in which an Arbitrator receives testimony or arguments and reviews documents or property to render an Order or Award. The types of Participatory Hearings include:
      a. In-person Hearing—A Hearing at which the participants may appear before the Arbitrator in person;
      b. Telephone Hearing—A Hearing at which the participants may appear before the Arbitrator by telephone; and,
      c. On-line Hearing—A Hearing at which the participants may appear before the Arbitrator on-line, by e-mail or by other electronic or computer communication.

U. Interim Order: Any Order providing temporary or preliminary relief pending a final Award.

V. Large Claim: A Claim Amount of $75,000 or more.

W. Order: Any Order establishing specific rights and obligations of the Parties.
   (1) A Dispositive Order results in a final Award or dismissal of any Claim or Response.
   (2) All other Orders are Non-dispositive.

X. Party: Any individual or Entity who makes a Claim or against whom a Claim is made including Claimants, Respondents, Cross-claimants, and Third Parties.

Y. Party Witness: Any person who is an individual Party or who is an employee of an entity Party at the time of the service of the subpoena.

Z. Proof of Service: An Affidavit stating how and where service was made.

AA. Receive or Receipt: The Delivery or other effective notice to the Forum, or to a Party at the address of the Party or Party Representative.

BB. Representative: Any individual, including an attorney, who makes an appearance on behalf of a Party.

CC. Request: Any Request by a Party directed to an Arbitrator or the Forum for an Order or other relief, including any motion, petition or other type of Request.

DD. Respondent: Any Party against whom a Claim is made.

EE. Response: Any Written Response by a Party or Representative to any Claim.

FF. Sanctions: Sanctions include dismissal of the arbitration or the Claims or Responses; preclusion of evidence; admission of facts; payment of costs; payment of fees including reasonable attorney fees, Arbitrator fees, and arbitration fees; the rendering of an Order or Award; and other Sanctions deemed appropriate. Sanctions may be imposed against a Party, a Representative or both.

GG. Signature or Signed: Any mark, symbol or device intended as an attestation, produced by any reliable means, including an electronic transcription intended as a Signature.

HH. Stay: A delay for an indefinite period of time requested by a Claimant before an Arbitrator is appointed. See Time Extension and Adjournment.

II. Time Extension: A continuance or delay for a specific period of time requested before the appointment of an Arbitrator. See Adjournment and Stay.

JJ. With Prejudice: The case cannot be brought again. The Claimant cannot subsequently bring the same Claim against the Respondent.

KK. Without Prejudice: The case may be brought again. The Claimant can subsequently file the same Claim against the same Respondent.

LL. Writing or Written: Any form intended to record information, including symbols on paper or other substance, recording tape, computer disk, electronic recording, and video recording and all other forms.

RULE 3. Representation.

A. Parties may act on their own behalf or may be represented by an attorney or by a person who makes an appearance on behalf of a Party.

B. Parties, their Representatives, and all participants shall act respectfully toward the Forum staff, the Arbitrator, other Parties, Representatives, witnesses, and participants in the arbitration.

RULE 4. Confidentiality.

Arbitration proceedings are confidential unless all Parties agree or the law requires arbitration information to be made public. Arbitration Orders and Awards are not confidential and may be disclosed by a Party. The Arbitrator and Forum may disclose case filings, case dispositions, and other case information filed with the Forum as required by a Court Order or the applicable law.

PART II

COMMENCEMENT OF ARBITRATION

RULE 5. Summary of Procedures.

A. Claim. A Party begins an arbitration by filing with the Forum a properly completed copy of the Initial Claim described in Rule 12, accompanied by the appropriate filing fee which appears in the Fee Schedule. The Forum reviews the Claim, opens a file, assigns a file number, and notifies the Claimant, who then serves the Respondent in accord with Rule 6.

B. Response. A Respondent may file a Response as explained in Rule 13 or respond otherwise as explained in these rules and the Notices of Arbitration, which appear in Appendices A and B. If there is no timely Response, the arbitration proceeds in accord with Rule 36.

C. After a Response. The arbitration proceeds in accord with a Scheduling Notice issued by the Forum or by action by the Parties.

D. Hearing. A Party may select a Document Hearing under Rule 25 or a Participatory Hearing under Rule 26 and pay the fee, if any, listed in the Fee Schedule. Parties have a full and equal right to present relevant and reliable direct and cross examination testimony, documents, exhibits, evidence, and arguments. A record may be made of Participatory Hearings.

E. Arbitrator. The Parties select an Arbitrator(s) by mutual agreement in accord with Rules 21, 22, and 23. Forum arbitrators are neutral, independent, experienced, and knowledgeable about the applicable law.

F. Arbitrator Qualifications. A neutral Arbitrator shall not serve if circumstances exist that create a conflict of interest or cause the Arbitrator to be unfair or biased in accord with Rules 21 and 23. A Forum Arbitrator may also be removed similar to the ways a judge or juror may be stricken.

G. Arbitrator Powers. An Arbitrator decides issues in a case including questions of fact and law. An Arbitrator follows the applicable substantive law and may grant any remedy or relief provided by law or equity, including monetary and injunctive relief, in accord with Rules 20, 27, 37, and 38.

H. Discovery. Before a Hearing is held, Parties shall cooperate in the discovery process and may exchange and obtain discovery in accord with Rule 29.

I. Requests. Parties may seek appropriate relief or remedies in accord with Rule 18.

J. Fee Schedules. The Fee Schedules appear in a supplement to this Code. The Forum Fee Schedules are a model of fair cost and fee allocation. The Common Claim Fee Schedule governs amounts under $75,000, and the Large Claim Fee Schedule governs all other Claim Amounts.

K. Consumers. See Rule 2L. Consumers include Consumers, employees, and patients. Consumers pay only reasonable arbitration fees as explained in these Rules and the Fee Schedule, and as required by the applicable law. Other Parties may have to pay fees for Consumers.

L. Indigent Parties. In accord with Rule 45, Consumers who meet the United States Federal poverty standards need not pay arbitration fees.

M. Substantive Law and Remedies. All types of legal and equitable remedies and relief available in court are available in arbitration. Claims, Responses, remedies or relief cannot be unlawfully restricted, and Parties may effectively pursue any remedy or relief in arbitration including statutory, common law, injunctive, equitable, and all other lawful remedies and relief.

N. Award or Order. After a Hearing, an Arbitrator shall promptly issue an Award or Order in accord with Rule 37 or 38. Reasons, findings of fact, and conclusions of law shall be in accord with Rule 37 or 38.

O. Review and Enforcement. An Award may be enforced in any court of competent jurisdiction, as provided by applicable law. An Award or Order may be reviewed by a court with jurisdiction to determine whether the Arbitrator properly applied the applicable substantive law and whether the arbitration complied with applicable arbitration laws.

P. Public Information. Arbitration information may be made public in accord with Rule 4 or as required by Court Order.

Q. Access to Justice. This Code shall be interpreted to provide all Parties with a fair and impartial arbitration and with reasonable access to civil justice. Arbitrations under the Code are governed by the Federal Arbitration Act in accord with Rule 48B.

RULE 6. Service of Claims, Responses, Requests, and Documents.

A. After being notified by the Forum that a Claim has been

accepted for filing in accord with Rules 7 and 12, and a file number has been provided, the Claimant shall promptly serve on each Respondent one (1) copy of the Initial Claim Documents, containing the Forum file number, together with a Notice of Arbitration substantially conforming to Appendix A of this Code, including notice that the Respondent may obtain a copy of the Code, without cost, from the Claimant or the Forum.

B. Service of Initial Claims and Third Party Claims shall be effective if done by:
   (1) United States Postal Service Certified Mail Signed return receipt or equivalent service by the national postal service of the country where the Respondent resides or does business;
   (2) Delivery by a private service with the Delivery receipt Signed by a person of suitable age and discretion who Received the Documents;
   (3) Delivery with a Written acknowledgment of Delivery by the Respondent or a Representative;
   (4) In accord with the Federal Rules of Civil Procedure of the United States or the rules of civil procedure of the jurisdiction where the Respondent entered into the Arbitration Agreement;
   (5) In accord with any agreement of the Party served;
   (6) For Claims related to or arising from an E-commerce Transaction, Delivery to the e-mail address of the Party served, Receipt confirmed; or
   (7) Service is complete upon Receipt by the Party served or the filing of a Response with the Forum by a Respondent.

C. Service of Responses, Counter Claims, Cross-claims, Requests, notices, and Documents shall be by Delivery, as defined in Rule 2M, to the address of all Parties or their Representatives at their addresses of record with the Forum, or by using service methods for an Initial Claim in Rule 6B. Amended Claims shall be served or Delivered as provided in Rule 17D.

D. The Party serving or Delivering a Claim, Response, Request, notice or Document shall timely Deliver copies to all Parties not required to be served. This rule does not apply to a Rule 45 Request.

E. Parties and Representatives shall immediately notify the Forum and all other Parties of their mail, facsimile and e-mail address and any changes in their addresses. If they fail to do so, Parties and their Representatives agree to Receive service at the previous address provided to the Forum.

RULE 7. Filing.

A. A Party who serves a Claim or Response shall timely file these and all other Documents and Proof of Service with the Forum. The filing of Proof of Service constitutes a certification that the service conforms to Rule 6. A Party who files paper Documents with the Forum shall file two (2) copies. A Party who files Documents online need only file one set of Documents.

B. Parties may file by Delivery as defined in Rule 2M, in person, or by other methods of filing authorized by the Forum at:

P.O. Box 50191
Minneapolis, Minnesota USA 55405-0191
or
www.adrforum.com
or
file@adrforum.com
or
Fax: 952-345-1160

C. Upon Proof of Service of an Initial Claim, where no Response has been filed, the Forum shall mail to Respondent the Second Notice of Arbitration, substantially conforming to Appendix B of this Code.

D. The Forum may distribute copies of Documents filed with the Forum to Parties or their Representatives who have entered an Appearance with the Forum.

E. Filing is complete upon Receipt by the Forum of all required Documents and fees. Claims, Responses, Requests, Notices, and all other Documents Received by the Forum are not considered filed until all required Documents are Received together with all applicable fees.

F. The effective date of filing is the business day the Forum Receives all required Documents and fees. A submission is due before Midnight, United States Central time, on its due date.

RULE 8. Notices and Conferences.

A. The Forum may notify and communicate with a Party or Parties by Writing, facsimile, e-mail, telex, telegram, telephone, in person or by other means of communication.

B. The Forum or Arbitrator may conduct a conference with a Party or Parties to discuss procedural matters on the initiative of the Forum or at the Request of a Party or Arbitrator.

C. The Forum may issue a Scheduling Notice regarding the Hearing process, including preliminary Hearings.

RULE 9. Time Periods, Time Extensions, Adjournments, and Stays.

A. **Time Periods.** In computing any period of time under this Code, the day of the act or event from which the designated period of time begins to run shall not be included.

B. **Holidays.** Saturdays, Sundays, and federal holidays of the United States are included in the computation of time, except when they fall on the last day of a period.

C. **Enforcement.** The time periods established in this Code are to be strictly enforced and a Party's untimely Claim, Response, Request, Notice, Document or submission may be denied solely because it is untimely.

D. **Time Extensions.** The Forum may extend time periods in this Code. A Request for a Time Extension must be filed with the Forum and delivered on all other Parties at least five (5) days before the time period ends or no later than a deadline established by a Scheduling Notice, whichever is earlier, and must be accompanied by a fee, if any, as provided in the Fee Schedule. A Request submitted after the time period has ended will not be considered unless extraordinary circumstances exist.

E. **Adjournments.** An Arbitrator may Adjourn the arbitration process or a Hearing to a later date. A Rule 18 Request for an Adjournment must be filed with the Forum and served on the other Parties at least seven (7) days before the scheduled event and must be accompanied by a fee, if any, as provided in the Fee Schedule. A Request submitted after the time period has ended will not be considered unless extraordinary circumstances exist. Any other Party may object to a Request by filing with the Forum and serving on all other Parties an objection within three (3) days of the Request being filed with the Forum.

F. **Stays**.
(1) A Claimant may obtain a Stay of a case for an indefinite period of time by filing with the Forum and serving on all other Parties a Stay Notice prior to the appointment of an Arbitrator. An opposing Party may end a Stay by filing with the Forum and serving on all Parties, within fifteen (15) days of the Notice being filed with the Forum, an objection which ends the Stay. Claimant may file only one (1) Stay Notice and may seek a subsequent Stay by submitting a Rule 18 Request. A Stay suspends the time when proceedings and hearings occur and when Documents and Fees are due.
(2) The Forum shall Stay a case if ordered by a court of competent jurisdiction, and may Stay a case when reasonably necessary.
G. **International**. For arbitration Hearings to be held outside of the United States, an additional thirty (30) days shall be added to the time periods in Rule 13 of this Code. Additional time for other proceedings will be made available at the determination of the Forum or at the Request of a Party.

RULE 10. Time Limitations.
A. No Claim may be commenced after the passage of time which would preclude a Claim regarding the same or similar subject matter being commenced in court. This time limitation shall be suspended for the period of time a court of competent jurisdiction exercises authority over the Claim or dispute. This rule shall not extend nor shorten statutes of limitation or time limits agreed to by the Parties, nor shall this rule apply to any case that is directed to arbitration by a court of competent jurisdiction.
B. An arbitration shall commence on the date the Respondent is served with the Initial Claim Documents or the date a Response is filed with the Forum, whichever is earlier.

PART III

DOCUMENTS

RULE 11. Form and Parties.
A. Every Claim, Response, Amendment, and Request shall be in Writing and Signed by a Party or Representative.
B. Parties and Representatives shall provide the Forum and all Parties with their names, current address, an address where service will be accepted, telephone numbers, and available facsimile numbers and e-mail addresses. Respondents shall provide the Forum with the address of their residence or business for determination of the proper location of the Hearing in accord with Rule 32.
C. Statements in Claims, Responses, Amendments, and Requests may be made in separate or numbered sentences, paragraphs or sections, and may refer to exhibits attached to Claims, Responses, Requests or Documents.
D. English is the language used in Forum proceedings unless the Parties agree to use another language. The Forum or Arbitrator may Order the Parties to provide translations at their own cost unless the Forum has agreed in advance to the use of another language.
E. A Party may be:
(1) An executor, administrator, guardian, bailee, trustee, or
(2) An assignee, a successor in interest, a recipient of a transfer of interest, or
(3) A guardian, conservator, fiduciary, or other legal Representative for an infant or incompetent person.
Proof of the status of a Party under this rule must be made by an Affidavit filed with the Forum. A Party who contests the status of another Party may file a Rule 18 Request for relief with the fee, if any, as provided in the Fee Schedule.

RULE 12. Initial Claim.
A. An Initial Claim, which begins an arbitration in accord with Rule 6 of this Code, shall include:
(1) A statement in plain language of the dispute or controversy, the facts and the law (if known) supporting the Claim, the specific relief requested and the reasons supporting the relief, the specific amount and computation of any money or damages, the specific value of non-monetary or other relief, the specific amount and computation of any interest, costs, and attorney fees under Rule 12B, and other relevant and reliable information supporting the Claim;
(2) A copy of the Arbitration Agreement, or, if not in the possession of the Claimant, notice of the location of a copy of the Arbitration Agreement;
(3) A copy of available Documents that support the Claim;
(4) An Affidavit asserting that the information in the Claim is accurate; and
(5) The appropriate Filing Fee as provided in the Fee Schedule.
B. A Claimant who seeks costs and attorney fees must include this statement in the Claim and may either:
(1) State the specific amount sought in the Claim; or
(2) Amend the Claim to state the specific amount sought:
  a. For Document Hearings no later than ten (10) days from the date of the Notice of the Selection of an Arbitrator; or
  b. For Participatory Hearings no later than seven (7) days from the close of the Hearing; or
  c. For prevailing Parties, by Order of the Arbitrator.
C. After service of the Initial Claim on the Respondent, the Claimant shall promptly file with the Forum Proof of Service of the Initial Claim on the Respondent. A Claim shall not proceed to arbitration until the Forum has received a copy of the Proof of Service of the Initial Claim or a Response has been filed with the Forum.
D. An Arbitrator may reject, in whole or in part, an Initial Claim that does not substantially conform to this rule.
E. A Claimant may seek any remedy or relief allowed by applicable substantive law.

RULE 13. Response.
A. Upon service of an Initial Claim, Counter Claim, Cross-claim, or Third Party Claim on a Respondent, the Respondent shall Deliver to the Claimant and file with the Forum, within thirty (30) days from Receipt of service or fourteen (14) days from the date of the Second Notice of Arbitration, whichever is later, a Response which shall include:
(1) A Written Document stating in plain language a Response to the Claim or stating the Respondent has insufficient information to affirm or deny a statement. A Response shall also include any defenses to each Claim made, the facts and the law (if known) supporting the defenses, including affirmative defenses and set offs;

Appx. B.2.1 *Consumer Arbitration Agreements*

(2) An objection to the arbitration of the Claim, if the Respondent so objects. A Response that does not assert this objection is an agreement to the arbitration of the Claim and a waiver of this objection which cannot be asserted in an Amendment;

(3) A copy of available Documents that support the Response;

(4) Any Counter Claim the Respondent has against the Claimant in accord with Rule 14 of this Code, including the Counter Claim filing fee;

(5) Proof of Delivery of the Response to all other Parties; and

(6) Any fees as provided in the Fee Schedule or as required by the agreement of the Parties.

B. A Party may obtain ten (10) additional days to respond to an Initial Claim by filing with the Forum and Delivering to all other Parties an extension Notice before the Response is due. Only one (1) extension by Notice is available.

C. A Respondent who responds but does not state available replies, defenses or Claims may be barred by the Arbitrator from presenting such replies, defenses or Claims at the Hearing. The failure of a Respondent to deny a statement in a Claim may be considered by the Arbitrator as an admission of that statement.

D. An Arbitrator may reject, in whole or in part, a Response that does not substantially conform to this rule.

RULE 14. Counter Claim.

A. A Respondent may assert a Counter Claim against a Claimant by Delivering to the Claimant, as part of the Response in accord with Rule 13, Counter Claim Documents which include:

(1) A Counter Claim stating in plain language the dispute or controversy, the facts and the law (if known) supporting the Counter Claim, the specific relief requested and the reasons supporting the relief, the specific amount and computation of any money or damages, the specific value of non-monetary or other relief, the specific amount and computation of any interest, costs, and attorney fees under Rule 12B, and other relevant and reliable information supporting the Counter Claim;

(2) A copy of available Documents that support the Counter Claim; and

(3) An Affidavit asserting that the information in the Counter Claim is accurate.

B. The Respondent shall also pay the filing fee for a Counter Claim as provided in the Fee Schedule at the time of filing the Counter Claim with the Forum.

C. An Arbitrator may reject, in whole or in part, Counter Claim Documents that do not substantially conform to this rule.

RULE 15. Cross-claim.

A. A Party may assert a Claim against a co-Party arising out of the same or related transaction or occurrence of the dispute or controversy by Delivering to the co-Party the Cross-claim Documents which include:

(1) A Cross-claim setting forth in plain language the dispute or controversy, the facts and the law (if known) supporting the Cross-claim, the specific relief requested and the reasons supporting the relief, the specific amount and computation of any money or damages, the specific value of non-monetary or other relief, the specific amount and computation of any interest, costs, and attorney fees under Rule 12B, and other relevant and reliable information supporting the Cross-claim;

(2) A copy of available Documents that support the Cross-claim; and

(3) An Affidavit asserting that the information in the Cross-claim is accurate.

B. A Party shall Deliver a Cross-claim on all Parties and shall file copies with the Forum within fifteen (15) days of the date of service of a Response.

C. The Cross-claimant shall file with the Forum, promptly after Delivery of the Cross-claim, the proof of Delivery of the Cross-claim on all Parties, with the fee for filing a Cross-claim, if any, and the fee for a Hearing, if selected, as provided in the Fee Schedule.

D. An Arbitrator may reject, in whole or in part, Cross-claim Documents that do not substantially conform to this Rule.

RULE 16. Third Party Claim.

A. If a Respondent asserts that a non-Party, who has entered into an Arbitration Agreement but was not served by the Claimant, is responsible for the Award demanded, the Respondent may serve a Third Party Claim on this Party, which shall include:

(1) All information required in an Initial Claim in Rule 12 of this Code, including a copy of the Claim Documents that gave rise to the Third Party Claim; and

(2) A copy of the Arbitration Agreement, or notice of the location of a copy of the Arbitration Agreement.

B. The Third Party Claim shall be Delivered to all other Parties and a copy shall be filed with the Forum within thirty (30) days of the date of service of the Initial Claim, as required by Rule 16A.

C. The Third Party Claimant shall file with the Forum, promptly after service of the Third Party Claim the Proof of Service of the Third Party Claim on Third Party Respondent and proof of Delivery on all other Parties, with the fee for a Third Party Claim, and the fee for a Hearing, if selected, as provided in the Fee Schedule.

D. An Arbitrator may reject, in whole or in part, Third Party Claim Documents that do not substantially conform to this rule.

RULE 17. Amendment.

A. A Claim or Response may be Amended:

(1) By agreement of the Parties at any time;

(2) By Request, not later than the Scheduling Notice deadline or ten (10) days from the date of the Notice of Selection of an Arbitrator for a Document Hearing or thirty (30) days before the earliest date set for a Participatory Hearing, if the Amendment does not delay the arbitration and promotes fairness, efficiency, or economy, which Request shall be promptly decided by an Arbitrator; or

(3) By Request during or within three (3) days following a Document or Participatory Hearing, if the Arbitrator finds the Amendment conforms to the evidence received.

B. An Amendment of a Claim or Response, or a Request for an Amendment, shall be designated as such and promptly served on all Parties and filed with the Forum. An amended Claim which increases the Claim Amount shall also be accompanied by the additional filing fee in the Fee Schedule. An amended Claim, excluding Amendments agreed to by all Parties, shall also be accompanied by the Amendment Request Fee as provided in the Fee Schedule.

C. A Respondent shall respond to an amended Claim within the time remaining for a Response to the Initial Claim or within fifteen (15) days after service of the amended Claim, whichever time is longer, unless the Parties agree or an Arbitrator orders otherwise.

D. After service of the Initial Claim, an Amendment of a Claim that increases the monetary amount of the value of relief sought in the Initial Claim must be served in accord with Rule 6B. All other Amendments may be Delivered in accord with Rule 2M.

E. Any change to the Claim before service is made on Respondent is not an Amendment. After service, a reduction of the Claim Amount, a change of address of a Party, and the substitution of a successor in interest are not Amendments.

F. An Amendment of a Claim shall relate back to the time the Initial Claim was commenced unless otherwise provided by applicable law.

RULE 18. Request to Arbitrator or Forum.

A. A Party may Request an Order or other relief from an Arbitrator or the Forum by filing with the Forum:
  (1) A Document stating in plain language:
    a. The Request;
    b. The specific rule, if any, relied on for an Order or other relief;
    c. The specific relief or Order sought;
    d. The facts and law supporting the Request; and
    e. Any other relevant and reliable information.
  (2) All Documents that support the Request, Order or relief;
  (3) Proof of Delivery of the Request Documents on all Parties; and
  (4) The fee, as provided in the Fee Schedule.

B. The Party shall Deliver the Rule 18A(1) and (2) Documents to all Parties at the time of filing.

C. Any other Party may object to a Request by filing with the Forum and Delivering to each other Party a Written objection(s) within ten (10) days of Delivery of the Request, unless another time is provided by rule or is necessary based on the relief requested.

D. Requests directed to the Forum are decided by the Forum as permitted by the Code. Requests directed to an Arbitrator are decided by an Arbitrator. Prior to the appointment of an Arbitrator, Requests may be granted by the Forum as permitted by this Code.

E. All Requests or motions made by a Party are Rule 18 Requests. A Party filing a Request or objection must pay the fee, if any, as provided in the Fee Schedule. A Request or motion to reconsider is usually not granted, unless the controlling law has changed. The Fee Schedule lists fees that may accompany Rule 18 Requests, objections, procedures, and proceedings.

F. No Request may be filed later than the Scheduling Notice deadline or fifteen (15) days before a Participatory Hearing or for Document Hearings later than ten (10) days from the date of the Notice of the Selection of an Arbitrator, unless another time is provided by rule or is necessary based on the relief requested.

RULE 19. Joinder, Intervention, Consolidation, and Separation.

A. Any individual or Entity may, as agreed to by the Parties or as required by applicable law, join any dispute, controversy, Claim or Response in an arbitration by filing a Claim Document stating the grounds. An Arbitrator has no authority to issue an Order or Award binding any individual or Entity not a Party, unless that individual or Entity agrees or as required by applicable law. The Forum may require a Party to pay a fee.

B. Any individual or Entity that entered into the Arbitration Agreement between Claimant and Respondent may intervene in an arbitration if a common question of fact or law arising from the same or related transaction or occurrence exists and such a proceeding promotes fairness, efficiency or economy. The Forum may require a Party to pay a fee.

C. Separate arbitrations involving the same named Parties and a common question of fact or law arising from the same or related transaction or occurrence shall be consolidated at the Request of a Party or at the determination of the Forum if the consolidation promotes fairness, efficiency or economy. A Party may challenge this consolidation by filing a Rule 18 Request for severance, and an Arbitrator shall promptly decide this Request by determining whether consolidation or severance promotes fairness, efficiency or economy. The Forum may require a Party to pay a fee.

D. An arbitration involving multiple Claims or Responses or Parties may be separated into individual Hearings if such proceedings promote fairness, efficiency or economy. The Forum may require the Party or Parties to pay Hearing fees for separate Hearings.

E. A Request by an individual or Entity to join or intervene or a Request by a Party for separation must be filed in accord with Rule 18.

F. An Arbitrator shall promptly decide Requests for joinder, intervention, severance or separation. Any decision by an arbitrator joining, consolidating or aggregating parties or claims is an Award under 9 U.S.C. Section 9.

PART IV

ARBITRATORS

RULE 20. Authority of Arbitrators.

A. Arbitrators have the powers provided by this Code, the agreement of the Parties, and the applicable law.

B. Arbitrators selected in accord with Rule 21A(3) shall take an oath prescribed by the Director and shall be neutral and independent.

C. Arbitrators shall decide all factual, legal, and other arbitrable issues submitted by the Parties and do not have the power to decide matters not properly submitted under this Code.

D. An Arbitrator shall follow the applicable substantive law and may grant any legal, equitable or other remedy or relief provided by law in deciding a Claim, Response or Request properly submitted by a Party under this Code. Claims, Responses, remedies or relief cannot be unlawfully restricted.

E. An Arbitrator shall have the power to rule on all issues, Claims, defenses, questions of arbitrability, and objections relating to the existence, scope, and validity of the contract, transaction, or relationship of the Parties.

F. An Arbitrator shall have the power to rule on all issues, Claims, Responses, questions of arbitrability, and objections regarding the existence, scope, and validity of the Arbitration Agreement including all objections relating to jurisdiction, unconscionability, contract law, and enforceability of the Arbitration Agreement.

RULE 21. Selection of Arbitrators.

A. Parties select an Arbitrator(s):
   (1) By selecting an Arbitrator or a panel of Arbitrators on mutually agreeable terms; or
   (2) By each Party selecting an Arbitrator and those Arbitrators selecting another Arbitrator for a panel of Arbitrators; or
   (3) In the absence of an election of Rule 21A(1) or (2), by using the selection process in Rules 21B through 23 of this Code.
   Parties must notify the Forum of their election of Rule 21A(1) or (2), or other agreement for Arbitrator selection, no later than thirty (30) days after the filing of a Response with the Forum.

B. For Large Claim Hearings, the Forum shall provide to each Party making an Appearance a list of Arbitrator candidates equal in number to the number of Parties plus the number of Arbitrators required under Rule 22. Each Party making an Appearance may strike one of the candidates and may Request disqualification of any candidate in accord with Rule 23C by notifying the Forum in Writing, within ten (10) days of the date of the strike list.

C. For Common Claim Hearings, the Forum shall submit one Arbitrator candidate to all Parties making an Appearance. A Party making an Appearance may remove one Arbitrator candidate by filing a notice of removal with the Forum within ten (10) days from the date of the notice of Arbitrator selection. A Party making an Appearance may request disqualification of any subsequent Arbitrator in accord with Rule 23.

D. Upon Request for an Expedited Hearing or if the need for an Arbitrator arises before an Arbitrator is designated in accord with Rule 21A, the Forum shall promptly designate an Arbitrator and the issues to be decided.

E. A Party is prohibited from striking or removing an Arbitrator or an Arbitrator candidate based on race, gender, nationality, ethnicity, religion, age, disability, marital status, family status, or sexual orientation.

F. A Party may request Receipt of the Notice of Arbitrator selection by notifying the Forum, in Writing, within ten (10) days from the date Claimant files Proof of Service of the Initial Claim. Notices related to Arbitrator selection need not be provided to a Party who has failed to respond to a Claim or otherwise appear or defend or pay fees as provided by this Code.

RULE 22. Number of Arbitrators.

Unless the Parties agree otherwise, for all Hearings, one (1) Arbitrator shall conduct the Hearing and issue an Award. Where the Parties have agreed to more than one (1) Arbitrator, that number of Arbitrators will serve and the Forum shall designate the chair of the panel, unless the Parties agree otherwise.

RULE 23. Disqualification of Arbitrator.

A. An Arbitrator shall be disqualified if circumstances exist that create a conflict of interest or cause the Arbitrator to be unfair or biased, including but not limited to the following:
   (1) The Arbitrator has a personal bias or prejudice concerning a Party, or personal knowledge of disputed evidentiary facts;
   (2) The Arbitrator has served as an attorney to any Party, the Arbitrator has been associated with an attorney who has represented a Party during that association, or the Arbitrator or an associated attorney is a material witness concerning the matter before the Arbitrator;
   (3) The Arbitrator, individually or as a fiduciary, or the Arbitrator's spouse or minor child residing in the Arbitrator's household, has a direct financial interest in a matter before the Arbitrator;
   (4) The Arbitrator, individually or as a fiduciary, or the Arbitrator's spouse or minor child residing in the Arbitrator's household, has a direct financial interest in a Party;
   (5) The Arbitrator or the Arbitrator's spouse or minor child residing in the Arbitrator's household has a significant personal relationship with any Party or a Representative for a Party; or
   (6) The Arbitrator or the Arbitrator's spouse:
      a. Is a Party to the proceeding, or an officer, director, or trustee of a Party; or,
      b. Is acting as a Representative in the proceeding.

B. An Arbitrator shall provide the Forum with a complete and accurate resume, a copy of which the Forum shall provide the Parties at the time of the selection process. An Arbitrator shall disclose to the Forum circumstances that create a conflict of interest or cause an Arbitrator to be unfair or biased. The Forum shall disqualify an Arbitrator or shall inform the Parties of information disclosed by the Arbitrator if the Arbitrator is not disqualified.

C. A Party making an Appearance may request that an Arbitrator be disqualified by filing with the Forum a Written Request stating the circumstances and specific material reasons for the disqualification. A Party who knows or has reason to know of circumstances disqualifying an Arbitrator must immediately disclose those circumstances to the Arbitrator, the Forum, and all other Parties. A Party who fails to timely and properly disclose disqualifying circumstances agrees to accept the Arbitrator and waives any subsequent objection to the Arbitrator in the pending arbitration or any other legal proceeding.

D. A Request to disqualify an Arbitrator must be filed with the Forum within ten (10) days from the date of the Notice of Arbitrator selection. The Forum shall promptly review the Request and shall disqualify the Arbitrator if there exist circumstances requiring disqualification in accord with Rule 23A or other material circumstances creating bias or the appearance of bias.

E. If an Arbitrator is disqualified or becomes unable to arbitrate before the issuance of an Award, the Forum shall designate a new Arbitrator or panel or re-schedule the hearing, unless the Parties agree otherwise.

RULE 24. Communications with Arbitrators.

A. No Party or Party Representative shall directly communicate with an Arbitrator except at a Participatory Hearing, by providing Documents in accord with this Code, or during a conference with the Arbitrator scheduled by the Forum.

B. No Party or Party Representative shall communicate with a Party Arbitrator after the complete panel of Arbitrators has been selected, except at a Participatory Hearing, by providing Documents in accord with this Code, or during a conference with the Arbitrator scheduled by the Forum.

PART V

HEARING

RULE 25. Selection of a Document Hearing.

A. In Common Claim cases, a Document Hearing shall be scheduled upon the filing of a Response and Receipt of the Administrative Fee.

B. In Large Claim cases, a Party may select a Document Hearing by filing a Written selection with the Forum, served on all other Parties by Delivery as defined in Rule 2M, and accompanied by a Written estimate of the number of hours or days required for the hearing and the fee for the Document Hearing provided in the Fee Schedule.

C. The Forum shall provide Written notice of a Document Hearing to all Parties not later than fifteen (15) days before the Document Hearing.

D. If another Party selects a Participatory Hearing, the Document Hearing shall be part of the Participatory Hearing.

E. For sufficient reason, the Forum or Arbitrator may postpone a Document Hearing at the Request of a Party or on the initiative of the Arbitrator or Forum.

RULE 26. Selection of a Participatory Hearing.

A. A Party may select a Participatory Hearing of any type by:
  (1) Filing a Written selection for a Participatory Hearing containing the information required in Rule 26B;
  (2) Designating the type of Participatory Hearing requested: In-person, Telephone, or On-line; and
  (3) Serving by Delivery, as defined by Rule 2M, the selection on all other Parties.
  (4) For Common Claim cases, a selection of a Participatory Hearing must be filed with the Forum not later than fifteen (15) days after the Delivery of a Response. A Request for a Participatory Hearing made after this time may be filed in accord with Rule 18.
  (5) The failure to timely select a Participatory Hearing is a waiver of the right to a Participatory Hearing.

B. Parties to a Participatory Hearing shall provide:
  (1) The Party's estimate of the number of hours or days required, taking into account the rights of all Parties under Rules 34B and 35A;
  (2) The names of witnesses proposed to offer evidence at the Hearing;
  (3) The number of exhibits to be offered at the Hearing and their description;
  (4) Any Request or requirement for a Written Award accompanied by the appropriate fee; and
  (5) The fee for the Hearing as provided in the Fee Schedule.
No selection for a Participatory Hearing session is effective without payment of the appropriate fee, unless a waiver under Rule 45 has been granted.

C. The Forum shall set the date, time, place, and length of the Participatory Hearing and notify all Parties of the Hearing at least thirty (30) days before the beginning of the Participatory Hearing.

D. Before or after the beginning of a Participatory Hearing, if it is determined that the Participatory Hearing requires additional sessions, the Forum or Arbitrator shall require that the responsible Party pay for additional sessions in accord with Rule 44, or may suspend the Hearing until the additional sessions are properly scheduled.

E. For sufficient reason, the Forum or Arbitrator may postpone a Participatory Hearing at the Request of a Party or on the initiative of the Arbitrator or Forum.

RULE 27. Request for an Expedited Hearing.

A. A Party may Request an Expedited hearing to obtain expedited relief in an Order or Award. A Request for an Expedited Hearing may be brought when the Respondent is served with Claim Documents or at any time before an Award becomes final and shall be accompanied by an explanation of the reasons for the expedited relief and the applicable law and by the fee as provided in the Fee Schedule.

B. An Arbitrator shall promptly decide the Request.

C. The requesting Party shall serve Notice of the Expedited Hearing on all Parties not less than forty-eight (48) hours before the time set for the Expedited Hearing. Proof of Service of this Notice shall be filed with the Forum before the Expedited Document Hearing or shall be presented at the Expedited Participatory Hearing.

D. A Party may seek a temporary restraining Order or a preliminary injunction to prevent irreparable injury by requesting an Expedited Hearing and filing with the Forum and serving on the Respondent and any other Parties the following:
  (1) An Initial Claim in accord with Rule 12 or a Counter Claim or Third Party Claim;
  (2) A Request that explains the irreparable injury and the specific reasons and Documents supporting the Request;
  (3) An Affidavit from a person with personal knowledge describing the irreparable injury and specific facts;
  (4) The proposed security for the relief sought;
  (5) A proposed Order stating the specific relief sought, including a Hearing for a preliminary injunction if a temporary restraining Order is sought; and
  (6) The fee as provided in the Fee Schedule.

E. Any Party may immediately file with the Forum and Deliver to all Parties an objection to the Request and a fee as provided in the Fee Schedule.

F. A temporary restraining Order may be granted without Written or oral notice to the Respondent or that Party's Representative only if:
  (1) It clearly appears from specific facts shown by Affidavit that immediate and irreparable injury, loss or damage will result to the Requesting Party before the Respondent or that Party's Representative can be heard in opposition; and
  (2) The Requesting Party or Representative of the Requesting Party certifies in writing the efforts, if any, which have been made to give the notice and the reasons supporting the claims that notice should not be required.
  (3) A temporary restraining Order granted without notice shall be immediately served on all Parties by the Requesting Party.

G. A preliminary injunction shall only be issued upon notice to all Parties.

H. An Expedited Telephone, Document or In-person Hearing shall be scheduled as soon as possible by the Forum. A Hearing for a temporary restraining Order shall be scheduled no later than forty-eight (48) hours from the time of filing or notice, whichever is later. If a temporary restraining Order is issued without notice, a Party may request that a Hearing with notice be held within forty-eight (48) hours of the issuance of the temporary restraining Order.

I. An Arbitrator will conduct the Hearing and issue an Order promptly, and the Forum will enter the Order promptly.

J. Every Order granting relief shall state the time and date of issuance, the reasons for the issuance including the irreparable injury, the specific conduct to be restrained, the duration of the Order, the security required, and, if applicable, the reason why it was issued without notice.

K. A temporary restraining Order shall expire within the time fixed in the Order, not to exceed ten (10) days, unless the Parties agree to a longer period of time or an Arbitrator issues a preliminary injunction.

L. If a Party who receives a temporary restraining Order fails to timely proceed with the Hearing for a preliminary injunction, the Arbitrator shall dissolve the temporary restraining Order.

M. A Hearing on a Request for a preliminary injunction may be consolidated by the Arbitrator with the final Hearing in the case upon a Request by a Party.

N. No temporary restraining Order or preliminary injunction shall be issued unless the Requesting Party provides security as deemed proper by the Arbitrator for the payment of costs and damages as may be incurred or suffered by a Party wrongfully restrained or enjoined.

O. Where security is given in the form of a bond, stipulation or other undertaking with a surety or sureties, each surety agrees to submit to the jurisdiction of the Forum and the arbitration and agrees to be bound by all Orders issued by the Arbitrator in the case including Orders affecting the liability of each surety on the bond, stipulation or undertaking.

RULE 28. Document Hearing.

A. A Party may submit any Document or property for consideration by the Arbitrator in a Document Hearing by filing with the Forum two (2) copies of the Document or property description and Delivering to all other Parties copies of the Document and property description.

B. Documents and property offered for consideration at a Document Hearing must be Received by the Forum and Delivered to all other Parties no later than ten (10) days from the date of the Notice of Selection of an Arbitrator as provided in Rule 21. Documents or property submitted after that date will be considered by Request of the submitting Party and granted by the Arbitrator for sufficient reason.

C. The Arbitrator shall determine the admissibility and weight of evidence and shall not be bound by rules of evidence.

D. During a Document Hearing, the Arbitrator may Request that the Parties submit additional information or Documents, including legal memoranda. Documents submitted in response to an Arbitrator's Request shall be filed with the Forum and Delivered to all other Parties no later than thirty (30) days after the date of the Request. A Party may obtain forty-five (45) additional days to respond to an Arbitrator's Request by filing with the Forum and Delivering to all other Parties an extension notice before the initial thirty (30) day time period expires. Only one (1) extension by notice is available.

E. The Arbitrator may visit a site to examine a matter relating to the arbitration.

F. The close of a Document Hearing occurs when the Arbitrator completes reviewing the Documents or property.

G. The presence or involvement of a Party in a Hearing results in the waiver of any objections to the notice of the Hearing.

RULE 29. Discovery.

A. Cooperative Discovery. After a Response is filed, Parties shall cooperate in the exchange of Documents and information. A Party seeking discovery shall contact other Parties and discuss discovery information and any objections and arrange for the exchange of Documents and information.

B. Seeking Discovery.
  (1) If the Parties are unable to resolve discovery matters under Rule 29A, a Party may seek the disclosure of Documents, sworn answers to not more than twenty-five (25) Written questions, and one or more depositions before a Hearing where:
    a. The information sought is relevant to a Claim or Response, reliable, and informative to the Arbitrator; and
    b. The production of the information sought is reasonable and not unduly burdensome and expensive.
  (2) The Party seeking discovery shall Deliver to all other Parties a Notice identifying the Documents to be produced, Written questions to be answered, or the Notice of deposition identifying the deponent, the proposed length of time for the deposition, and the scope of the deposition, no later than thirty (30) days before the date of a Participatory Hearing or for a Document Hearing ten (10) days from the date of the Notice of the Selection of an Arbitrator.
  (3) A Party may seek other discovery, including Requests for admissions and Requests for physical or mental examinations, before a Hearing, where:
    a. The information sought is relevant to a Claim or Response, reliable, and essential to a fair hearing of the matter; and
    b. The production of the information is reasonable and not unduly burdensome or expensive.
  (4) The Party seeking discovery shall Deliver to all other Parties a copy of the Notice identifying the discovery sought no later than thirty (30) days before the date of a Participatory Hearing or for a Document Hearing ten (10) days from the date of the Notice of Selection of an Arbitrator.

C. Responding to Discovery. A Party Receiving a Notice shall Deliver to the Requesting Party:
  (1) Within five (5) days after Receipt of the Notice of a deposition, a Written reply agreeing to the deposition or objecting to the deposition, including an explanation of the objections.
  (2) Within twenty (20) days of the Receipt of the Notice for other discovery, a copy of the Documents Requested or a statement permitting an examination of the original Documents or property at a convenient time and place, sworn answers to the Written questions, or a Written agreement to provide other Requested discovery, or a Written objection explaining why all or some of the Documents, property or other discovery has not been provided.

D. Request for Discovery. If a Party objects in accord with this Rule, the Requesting Party may file with the Forum and Deliver to all Parties, no later than the Scheduling Notice deadline or ten (10) days after Receiving the objection:
  (1) A Rule 18 Request for a Discovery Order;
  (2) A copy of the Written objections; and
  (3) A Written statement of reasons why the Requesting Party needs the discovery.

E. Decision. An Arbitrator shall promptly determine whether sufficient reason exists for the discovery and issue an Order.

F. Consequences. An Arbitrator may draw an unfavorable, adverse inference or presumption from the failure of a Party to provide discovery. An Arbitrator may impose Sanctions and costs and fees related to seeking or resisting discovery under Rule 29, including reasonable attorney fees, Arbitrator fees, and administrative fees against the non-prevailing Party.

RULE 30. Subpoena for In-person Participatory Hearing.
A. A Party may obtain a subpoena from an Arbitrator for a Participatory Hearing ordering a non-Party witness or other person permitted by law to produce Documents or property at the Hearing or ordering a witness to testify at the Hearing by filing with the Forum and serving on all other Parties a Rule 18 Request.
B. The Request shall state reasons for the relevancy and reliability of the Documents, property or testimony and shall identify the witness and describe the Documents or property.
C. A Request for a Rule 30 subpoena must be Received by the Forum no later than twenty (20) days before the In-person Participatory Hearing, unless the Scheduling Notice provides otherwise.
D. The subpoena shall be issued by an Arbitrator if the Request conforms to Rules 30A, 30B, and 30C and demonstrates the relevancy and reliability of the Documents, property or testimony. No Party, lawyer or Representative of a Party may issue a subpoena.
E. The subpoena shall be served:
  (1) By a person who is not a Party and is not less than eighteen (18) years of age if served upon a non-Party witness, or
  (2) By Delivery or personal service if served upon a Party witness or the Party. The subpoena must be Received by the person subpoenaed no later than five (5) days before the Hearing, unless the Arbitrator Orders otherwise.
F. A subpoena may be served on a non-Party witness at any place allowed by applicable law.
G. A subpoena served on a non-Party witness shall be accompanied by a witness fee of twenty-five dollars ($25) and reasonable travel reimbursement to and from the Hearing location and the residence or place of business of the non-Party. A subpoena for the production of Documents or property served on a non-Party witness shall also be accompanied by payment of the reasonable costs of producing the Documents and property.
H. Within five (5) days after being served with the subpoena or before the time specified in the subpoena to appear at the Hearing, if less than five (5) days, the witness or a Party may Request an Order that the subpoena be dismissed or modified. The Request shall conform to Rule 18 and shall state why the subpoena should be dismissed or modified.
I. If a witness or Party makes a Request under Rule 30H, an Arbitrator shall promptly determine whether sufficient reason exists for the Order, or enforce the subpoena.
J. The Party having the subpoena served shall provide the Arbitrator with the Proof of Service of the subpoena if the witness fails to appear at the Hearing.
K. Subpoenas issued under this Code may be enforced in accord with the applicable law. A subpoena not issued by an Arbitrator under this Rule is unenforceable.
L. An Arbitrator may draw an unfavorable, adverse inference or presumption from the failure of a Party to produce a Party witness, in addition to imposing any other Sanction.

RULE 31. Exchange of Information Before a Participatory Hearing.
A. Before all Participatory Hearings, each Party shall Deliver to all other Parties and file with the Forum two (2) copies of:
  (1) A list of all witnesses expected to testify and a summary of their testimony;
  (2) A list and description of all exhibits to be introduced;
  (3) A copy of all Documents and a detailed description of any property to be introduced at the Hearing;
  (4) An Affidavit establishing the authenticity of any Document proposed to be introduced at the Hearing; and
  (5) Any Request for additional Participatory Hearing sessions, accompanied by the fee as provided in the Fee Schedule.
B. All Parties and the Forum shall Receive the lists, Documents, and Affidavits provided for in Rule 31A no later than ten (10) days before the Participatory Hearing, unless a Notice from the Forum or Arbitrator provides otherwise. Lists, Documents, and Affidavits may be submitted after that date only by Request of the submitting Party. Such Requests may be granted by the Arbitrator for sufficient reason.
C. The Arbitrator may exclude witnesses, testimony or Documents sought to be introduced by a Party who fails to comply with Rules 31A and 31B.

RULE 32. Location of an In-person Participatory Hearing.
A. An In-person Participatory Hearing shall be held where the Arbitration Agreement designates or where the Parties agree or, in the absence of an agreement and for all Consumer cases, at a reasonably convenient location within the United States federal judicial district or other national judicial district where the Respondent to the Initial Claim resides or does business. A Respondent Entity does business where it has minimum contacts with a Consumer.
B. Unless the Parties agree otherwise, if there is more than one Respondent to an Initial Claim, an In-person Participatory Hearing shall be held in the United States federal judicial district or other national judicial district where the majority of the Respondents to the Initial Claim resides or does business. If there is no United States federal judicial district or other national judicial district where a majority of Respondents resides or does business, the Forum shall select a reasonably convenient location for the In-person Participatory Hearing.

RULE 33. Participatory Hearing.
A. A Participatory Hearing may include:
  (1) An introduction by the Arbitrator.
  (2) Opening statements by each of the Parties. The Respondent and other Parties have the option of reserving the opening statement until the presentation of their evidence.
  (3) Claimant's case. The Claimant may introduce evidence, examine witnesses, and submit exhibits. The Respondent and other Parties may also examine the witnesses and submit exhibits.
  (4) Respondent's case. The Respondent may introduce evidence, examine witnesses, and submit exhibits. The Claimant and other Parties may also examine the witnesses and submit exhibits.
  (5) Additional cases. Other Parties may present their case.
  (6) Rebuttal. A Party may introduce additional evidence, examine witnesses, and submit exhibits to rebut an opposing Party's case if the submissions are not repetitive, cumulative or otherwise inadmissible.
  (7) Summation. Each Party may present a closing statement.
  (8) Concluding remarks by the Arbitrator.

B. The close of a Participatory Hearing occurs when either the Arbitrator announces the Hearing closed or more than twenty (20) days elapse from the final session.

RULE 34. Participatory Hearing Proceedings.

A. A Participatory Hearing may consist of one or more sessions. A Hearing may be conducted on any business day, unless the Parties and Arbitrator agree otherwise.

B. Hearing Sessions: Parties shall select sufficient time and sessions for Participatory Hearings in accord with Rule 26B. For Common Claim cases, a Hearing session is scheduled for the following length of time, unless more time or sessions are selected and the fees are paid:

A one hundred eighty-minute (180) session is scheduled for cases in which the amount in controversy exceeds $30,000.

A one hundred twenty-minute (120) session is scheduled for cases in which the amount in controversy is between $15,001 and $30,000.

A ninety-minute (90) session is scheduled for cases in which the amount in controversy is between $5,001 and $15,000.

A sixty-minute (60) session is scheduled for cases in which the amount in controversy is $5,000 or less.

C. The Arbitrator shall conduct an arbitration in an orderly, efficient, and economic manner, and shall determine the order and presentation of evidence and oral arguments.

D. All Parties to the arbitration and their Representatives shall be entitled to attend or be involved in the Participatory Hearing. Other persons may not attend, unless the Parties agree or the Arbitrator Orders otherwise. The Arbitrator may sequester witnesses.

E. The Arbitrator may request Documents and information from the Parties and may question any witness or Party to clarify evidence or arguments.

F. An Arbitrator may Request Parties to submit additional information or Documents including legal memoranda, which the Forum, the Arbitrator, and the Parties shall Receive no later than thirty (30) days after the final Participatory Hearing session.

G. A Party may Request permission to submit a post-hearing memorandum, which may be granted by the Arbitrator. The responsible Party shall pay the fee provided by the Fee Schedule.

H. The presence or involvement of a Party in a Hearing results in the waiver of any objections to the Notice and scheduling of the Hearing.

RULE 35. Evidence in a Participatory Hearing.

A. Presentation. Parties shall have a full and equal opportunity to present relevant and reliable evidence and oral and written arguments in support of their positions. Parties may present evidence and arguments in any reasonable form and by any means of communication.

B. Oath. The Arbitrator shall administer an oath or affirmation before a witness testifies.

C. Admissibility. The Arbitrator shall determine the admissibility and weight of evidence and shall not be bound by rules of evidence.

D. Objections. A Party may object to the introduction of evidence by another Party or a Request or question by an Arbitrator, and the Arbitrator shall rule on the objection.

E. Site Examination. An Arbitrator may visit a site to examine a matter relating to the arbitration accompanied by the Parties or their Representatives if they so choose.

F. Record. No record of a Hearing shall be kept unless agreed by all Parties or Ordered by the Arbitrator. The responsible Party or Parties Requesting a record shall arrange and pay for the record, and promptly provide a copy of the transcript or recording to the Arbitrator and the Forum at no cost to the Arbitrator or the Forum, and, if Requested by another Party, to that Party, at that Party's expense.

G. Interpreter. A Party who requires an interpreter shall arrange and pay for the interpreter. An Arbitrator may have an interpreter present, with a fee assessed to a Party or Parties as determined by the Forum.

RULE 36. Arbitration Proceedings in Absence of a Party.

A. An Arbitrator may issue an Award or Order when any Party has failed to respond, appear, or proceed at a Hearing, or otherwise defend as provided in this Code.

B. If a Party does not respond to a Claim, an Arbitrator will timely review the merits of the Claim for purposes of issuing an Award or Order. The Claimant need not submit an additional Request for an Award.

C. An Arbitrator may require an Affidavit, information or Documents from Parties who have appeared or conduct a Hearing to Receive evidence necessary to issue an Award or Order. Documents submitted in Response to an Arbitrator's Request shall be filed with the Forum no later than thirty (30) days after the date of the Request. A Party may obtain forty-five (45) additional days to respond to an Arbitrator's Request by filing with the Forum and Delivering to all other Parties an extension notice before the initial thirty (30) day time period expires. Only one (1) extension by notice is available.

D. Each Party making an Appearance shall be provided notices relating to a Hearing.

E. No Award or Order shall be issued against a Party solely because that Party failed to respond, appear or defend.

PART VI

AWARDS AND ORDERS

RULE 37. Awards.

A. An Award or Dispositive Order establishes the rights and obligations of all Parties named in the Award or Order and is final and binding, unless those Parties agree otherwise.

B. An Award shall not exceed the money or relief requested in a Claim or amended Claim and any amount awarded under Rule 37C.

C. An Award may include fees and costs awarded by an Arbitrator in favor of any Party only as permitted by law. A Party with a Claim for attorney fees or costs may seek to recover those expenses by bringing a timely Request in accord with Rules 18 and 12B. An opposing Party may object in accord with Rule 18. The Arbitrator may include attorney fees and costs in the final Award or in a separate Award.

D. An Award may include arbitration fees awarded by an Arbitrator or in favor of the Forum for fees due.

E. An Arbitrator shall endeavor to render an Award within twenty (20) days after the date of the close of the Hearing.

F. All Awards and Orders shall be in Writing, dated, and Signed by the Arbitrator or by a majority of the panel, and filed with the Forum.

G. An Award of an arbitration panel shall be by a majority of the Arbitrators. The chair of an arbitration panel may issue Orders, make rulings, and conduct proceedings.

H. An Award is a summary Award unless: (1) a Written notice is filed by a Party seeking reasons, findings of fact or conclusions of law, or (2) a prior Written agreement of the Parties requires reasons, findings of fact or conclusions of law and at least one Party files a Written notice requesting reasons, findings or conclusions. This Written agreement or notice must be filed with the Forum within ten (10) days of the date of the Notice of Selection of an Arbitrator and must be accompanied by a fee, if any, as provided in the Fee Schedule.

I. Awards shall be based upon a preponderance of the evidence presented, unless an agreement of the Parties or the applicable law provides otherwise.

J. An Arbitrator or the Forum may issue an Award or Order based upon a Written settlement Signed by the Parties.

RULE 38. Orders.

A. An Arbitrator or the Forum, where permitted by the Code, may issue an Order at the Request of a Party or on the initiative of the Arbitrator or the Forum.

B. At any time following the filing of a Claim, upon a Request by a Party and after a Hearing, the Arbitrator may issue an Interim Order and may require security as a condition of the Interim Order.

C. An Arbitrator who dismisses a Claim because there was no Arbitration Agreement or because the Arbitrator does not have the power to decide a Claim shall state the reason in the dismissal Order.

RULE 39. Entry and Service of Awards and Orders.

A. An Award or Order shall be entered in the state, country, or other jurisdiction provided for a Hearing in Rule 32, which shall appear on the Award or Order.

B. An Award or Order becomes final when entered. An Award or Order may not be entered if fees required by the Fee Schedule remain unpaid.

C. The Forum shall Deliver a copy of the Award or Order to all Parties or their Representatives or as directed by any Party.

D. Parties consent to service of the Award or Order and of all Documents, notices, and Orders necessary to confirm an Award or Order or to enter a judgment based on an Award or Order by Delivery, as defined by Rule 2M, at any address of the Party or Representative of record with the Forum.

E. An Award or Order may be confirmed, entered or enforced as a judgment in any court of competent jurisdiction. The Forum may disclose necessary Award information in connection with the confirmation, entering, enforcement or challenge of an Award or Order or otherwise as required by law.

F. Parties may request a duplicate original of an Award or Order or a copy of other filed Documents and pay the fee as determined by the Forum.

RULE 40. Voluntary Dismissal.

A. A Claimant may dismiss a Claim after it is filed and before the Respondent is served with the Claim by filing with the Forum a notice of dismissal.

B. A Claimant may dismiss a Claim after it is served and before the Respondent Delivers a Response to Claimant by Delivering to all Parties and filing with the Forum a notice of dismissal.

C. A Claimant may dismiss a Claim after a Respondent Delivers a Response that contains no Counter Claim within forty-five (45) days of the date the Response has been delivered to the Claimant or no later than a deadline established by a Scheduling Notice, whichever is later, by delivering to all Parties and filing with the Forum a notice of dismissal.

D. Any other Claim may be dismissed at the Request of the Claimant in accord with Rule 18. Before the selection of an Arbitrator, the Forum may dismiss the Claim. After the selection of the Arbitrator, the Arbitrator may dismiss the Claim.

E. A Claim shall be dismissed upon agreement of the Parties filed with the Forum.

F. Unless stated otherwise, the first voluntary dismissal of a Claim is Without Prejudice, and the Claim may be brought again.

G. A Claim voluntarily dismissed more than once is dismissed With Prejudice, and cannot be brought again.

RULE 41. Involuntary Dismissal.

A. A Claim or Response may be dismissed by an Arbitrator at the Request of the Forum or a Party or on the initiative of the Arbitrator for one or more of the following reasons:
  (1) It is not supported by evidence.
  (2) It is not supported by existing law.
  (3) It is frivolous.
  (4) It has been presented or maintained for an improper purpose, such as to harass, cause unnecessary delay or needlessly increase the cost of arbitration.
  (5) It is brought by a Party who has been declared to be a vexatious litigant by a court or Arbitrator.
  (6) A Party has violated any provision of the Code, or any Order or notice from an Arbitrator or the Forum.

B. A Claim or Response may be dismissed by an Arbitrator or the Forum at the Request of a Party in accord with Rule 18 or on the initiative of the Arbitrator or the Forum for one or more of the following reasons:
  (1) A Party has failed to proceed with an arbitration or Claim.
  (2) A Party has failed to pay fees as provided in the Fee Schedule.
  (3) More than ninety (90) days have elapsed between the filing date of the Claim and the date the Forum receives a Response or Proof of Service of the Initial Claim.
  (4) More than sixty (60) days have elapsed since a Hearing has been postponed or an arbitration case has been placed on inactive status.

C. The Forum shall Deliver notice of an involuntary dismissal to all Parties who have made an Appearance.

D. Unless stated otherwise, an involuntary dismissal by an Arbitrator is With Prejudice and the Claim may not be brought again.

E. An involuntary dismissal by the Forum is Without Prejudice and the Claim may be brought again.

F. If a Claimant again brings a Claim against a Respondent that was dismissed Without Prejudice, the Forum or Arbitrator may Order the costs incurred by the Respondent in the previous case be paid to the Respondent and may Stay the proceedings of the arbitration until the Claimant has complied with this Order.

G. If a Request for an Involuntary Dismissal is the only Request for a dispositive Order, that Request may be determined at the Document or Participatory Hearing.

RULE 42. Correction.

The Forum or an Arbitrator may correct clerical or administrative mistakes or errors arising from oversight or omission in the administration of cases or in the issuance of an Order or Award.

RULE 43. Reopening and Reconsideration.

A. An Arbitrator may reopen a Hearing or reconsider an Order or Award within a reasonable time from the date the Order or Award is entered if:
  (1) Service of Process or Proof of Service of Process of a Claim was not complete as required by this Code;
  (2) The Order or Award is ambiguous or contains evident material mistakes; or
  (3) If all Parties agree.
B. An Arbitrator may reopen a Hearing or reconsider an Order or Award within forty-five (45) days from the date the Order or Award is entered if:
  (1) The Arbitrator failed to timely disclose material circumstances or material reasons for disqualification in accord with Rule 23A; or
  (2) The Arbitrator did not decide a submitted issue.
C. Otherwise, neither the Arbitrator nor the Forum has the power to vacate an Order or Award after the Order or Award becomes final, unless all Parties agree.
D. Requests that an Arbitrator reopen a Hearing or reconsider an Order or Award must be timely filed with the Forum in accord with Rule 18 and Delivered to all Parties. A Party cannot make a second Request.
E. An Order or Award is reviewable by a court of competent jurisdiction as provided by applicable law.

PART VII

FEES

RULE 44. Fees.

A. Fee Recovery. The prevailing Party may recover fees paid in the arbitration in accord with Rule 37C.
B. Prepaid Fees. All fees for the filing of a Claim, Response, Request, objection, and any other Document and Hearing fees must be paid at the time the Document is filed or the Hearing is selected. These fees include fees required by this Code, the Forum Fee Schedule, the Parties' contract, an Order of an Arbitrator, or as required by law.
C. Non-Monetary Relief Fees. A Respondent may file a Rule 18 Request to review the value of injunctive, declaratory or other non-monetary relief sought in a Claim. An Arbitrator shall promptly determine the value of the Claim, which value determines the amount of the fees to be paid in accord with the Fee Schedule.
D. Hearing Fees. The Party selecting the type of Hearing prepays the Hearing fee unless the agreement of the Parties, this Code or the applicable law provides otherwise. The Forum may proceed with an arbitration in a case involving a Consumer Party who Requests that the case proceed even after another Party required to pay the Hearing fee fails to pay. The Arbitrator may Award the Forum the amount of the unpaid Hearing fees.
E. Advance Fees. During the course of any Participatory Hearing, the Forum or an Arbitrator may require any Party, who is not a Consumer in a Common Claim case, to pay in advance a fee for necessary Participatory Hearing sessions in addition to those requested under Rules 26 and 27.
F. Arbitrators. Fees for Arbitrators selected in accord with Rules 21A(1) and (2) are paid by the Parties to the Forum. Fees for Arbitrators selected in accord with Rule 21A(3) are paid to the Forum by the Parties as provided for in the Forum Fee Schedule. In cases where the Parties select a number of Arbitrators in addition to those provided by the Code or select Arbitrators with qualifications different than those required by the Forum, a fee for each Arbitrator will be determined by the Forum to be paid by the responsible Party or Parties.
G. Consumer Request. A Consumer Claimant or a Consumer Respondent in a Large Claim who asserts that arbitration fees prevent the Consumer Party from effectively vindicating the Consumer's case in arbitration may, at the time of filing of the Consumer's Initial Claim or Consumer's Response to a Large Claim and prior to paying any filing fee, file a Request that another Party or Parties pay all or part of the arbitration fees or that the arbitration provision be declared unenforceable, permitting the Consumer to litigate the case instead of arbitrating the case. This Request shall be processed without a fee and must be filed with the Forum and Delivered to all Parties together with the Initial Claim or Response and proof of Delivery.
  (1) Within fifteen (15) days of the filing and Delivery of the Request, another Party may:
    a. Agree to pay all or part of the fees required of the Consumer, or
    b. Agree to litigate instead of arbitrate the case, or
    c. File an objection to the Request.
  (2) If there is no agreement by the Parties, an Arbitrator shall promptly decide the Request and objection, if any, based on the applicable law.
  (3) The arbitration is suspended during this process.
H. Respondent Request. In cases where a Consumer Claimant brings a Large Claim and a Respondent is obligated to pay the fees by agreement or by law, the Respondent may, before or reasonably after the time of filing a Response, file with the Forum and serve on all Parties a Rule 18 Request that an Arbitrator determine whether there is a prima facie Claim of $75,000 or more. If the Arbitrator determines the Claim is a Common Claim, the Common Claim Fee Schedule shall apply. Otherwise, the Large Claim Fee Schedule shall apply.
I. International Cases. The Forum may assess additional fees for arbitrations conducted outside the United States or involving Parties from more than one country.
J. United States Dollars. Forum Fee Schedule fees are listed in United States Dollars. Fees shall be paid to the Forum in United States Dollars, unless the Forum agrees to accept other currency based on the exchange rate in effect on the required date of the fee payment as determined by the Forum.
K. Refunds. Fees are not refundable, except as otherwise provided by the Code or Fee Schedule.
L. Other Fees. The Forum may establish reasonable fees for proceedings not covered by the Fee Schedule and may assess appropriate, additional fees for Code proceedings as permitted by law or in accord with this Code. Parties may obtain the amount of a fee by contacting the Forum.

RULE 45. Waiver of Fees.

A. An indigent Consumer Party may Request a waiver of Common Claim filing fees, Request Fees, Hearing Fees, or security for any arbitration, by filing with the Forum a Written Request for a waiver at the time payment is due. The Request for a waiver shall be accompanied by an Affidavit including:
   (1) The Party's family size;
   (2) All of the Party's income and sources, property and assets, expenses and costs, liabilities and debts;
   (3) A statement that there is no agreement providing for any other person or Entity to either pay the costs or share in the proceeds of the Claim or a copy of the agreement and the financial information described in Rule 45A(2) for any person or Entity that has agreed to pay the costs or share in the proceeds of the Claim; and
   (4) All other relevant information, including releases for credit information, as requested by the Forum.
   Neither the Request nor Affidavit need be sent to the other Parties.
B. The Forum shall promptly issue a full or partial waiver to a Consumer Party eligible under this Rule and under the United States federal poverty standards or the applicable law. The Forum may also Order another Party to pay all or part of the waived fees as permitted or required by law.
C. If another Party has agreed to pay fees, a Rule 45 Request is unnecessary and the fee paying Party is obligated to pay the fees.
D. The Consumer Party must file an amended Affidavit of Poverty within thirty (30) days of a material change in the financial condition or circumstances described in the Consumer Party's initial Affidavit of Poverty. A separate Request must be filed by the indigent Consumer Party for each subsequent fee waiver requested.
E. If the statements in the Rule 45 Affidavit are untrue or incomplete, or if the Consumer Party is later determined to be able to pay the fees, the Forum shall Order the Consumer Party to pay the fees waived.

PART VIII

CODE PROVISIONS

RULE 46. Compliance with Rules.

An Arbitrator may Sanction a Party or Representative, or both, for violating any Rule, notice, ruling, Order or for asserting an unsupportable Claim or Response. A Party may be Sanctioned on the initiative of the Arbitrator or at the Request of the Forum or a Party. An Arbitrator shall Sanction a Party who refuses to pay fees as required by agreement, these Rules, an Arbitrator Order, or the applicable law, unless the offending Party establishes reasonable neglect. A Sanction Order may require an offending Party to pay for fees and costs incurred by another Party, unpaid fees, and other appropriate monetary Sanctions, and may require payment to another Party or the Forum.

RULE 47. Legal Proceedings.

A. The Arbitrator, the Director, the Forum, and any individual or Entity associated with the Forum shall not be liable to any Party for any act or omission in connection with any arbitration conducted under this Code.
B. No Party or prospective Party, before or during the arbitration of any matter eligible for submission under this Code, shall commence or pursue any lawsuit, administrative proceeding, or other action against any other Party, prospective Party, the Forum, or individual or Entity associated with the Forum relating to any of the matters subject to arbitration under this Code or the agreement of the Parties. Any Party commencing or pursuing such a proceeding agrees to pay and indemnify all such Parties, the Forum, individuals, and Entities for all expenses and costs incurred, including attorney fees as permitted by applicable law.
C. No Arbitrator, Director or any individual associated with the Forum shall be a witness in any legal proceeding arising out of the arbitration.
D. Any Party commencing or pursuing any lawsuit, administrative proceeding, arbitration or other action against the Forum, an Arbitrator or individual or Entity associated with the Forum, after an Award is final, agrees to pay and indemnify the Forum, an Arbitrator, individuals and Entities for all expenses and costs incurred, including attorney fees.
E. Every Party to any arbitration administered by the Forum or to an Arbitration Agreement as described in Rules 1 or 2E and the Forum agree that any Claim or dispute of any nature against the Forum or any agent, officer, employee, or affiliate of the Forum or any Arbitrator shall be resolved by final, binding arbitration conducted by a panel of three (3) Arbitrators. The Party or Parties shall select one Arbitrator; the Forum shall select a second Arbitrator; and these two Arbitrators shall select a third Arbitrator who is neutral and independent and who shall be the chair of the panel. The Arbitrators shall conduct the arbitration pursuant to the Code of Procedure in effect at the time the arbitration is brought. The chair shall have the powers of the Forum and perform the responsibilities of the Director. All fees payable under the Fee Schedule shall be assessed by the chair and paid to the panel of Arbitrators. Neither the Forum, nor its Director, nor any employee or agent of the Forum shall administer the arbitration.

RULE 48. Interpretation and Application of Code.

A. This Code shall be interpreted in conformity with 9 U.S.C. §§ 1–16 and 9 U.S.C. §§ 201–208 in the United States or the applicable law of other countries in order to provide all participants in the arbitration with a fair and impartial proceeding and an enforceable Award or Order.
B. Unless the Parties agree otherwise, any Arbitration Agreement as described in Rules 1 and 2E and all arbitration proceedings, Hearings, Awards, and Orders are to be governed by the Federal Arbitration Act, 9 U.S.C. §§ 1–16.
C. In the event a court of competent jurisdiction shall find any portion of this Code or Fee Schedule to be in violation of the law or otherwise unenforceable, that portion shall not be effective and the remainder of the Code shall remain effective.
D. The Director or Arbitrator may decline the use of arbitration for any dispute, controversy, Claim, Response or Request that is not a proper or legal subject matter for arbitration or where the agreement of the Parties has substantially modified a material portion of the Code. If Parties are denied the opportunity to arbitrate a dispute, controversy or Claim before the Forum, the Parties may seek legal and other remedies in accord with applicable law.
E. In the event of a cancellation of this Code, any Party may seek legal and other remedies regarding any matter upon which an

Award or Order has not been entered.

F. The Forum Code Committee, appointed by the Board of Directors, shall have the power and authority to effectuate the purposes of this Code, including establishing appropriate rules and procedures governing arbitrations and altering, amending or modifying this Code in accord with the law.

APPENDIX A

NOTICE OF ARBITRATION

Dear Respondent:

AN ARBITRATION CLAIM HAS BEEN FILED AGAINST YOU.

Enclosed and served upon you is the Initial Claim. You may obtain a copy of the Code of Procedure, without cost, from the Claimant or from the Forum at www.adrforum.com or 800-474-2371.

IF YOU DO NOT DELIVER TO THE CLAIMANT AND FILE WITH THE FORUM A WRITTEN RESPONSE, AN AWARD MAY BE ENTERED AGAINST YOU. AN ARBITRATION AWARD MAY BE ENFORCED IN COURT AS A CIVIL JUDGMENT.

YOU HAVE THIRTY (30) DAYS TO RESPOND FROM RECEIPT OF SERVICE.

You have a number of options at this time. You may:

1. *Submit a written Response to the Claim*, stating your reply and defenses to the Claim, together with documents supporting your position. Your Response must be delivered to the Claimant and filed with the Forum. See National Arbitration Forum [NAF] Code of Procedure Rules 13 and 6C.

   Proof of delivery of the Response on the Claimant must also be filed with the Forum. See NAF Rules 2A, 2M, and 2Z. Proof of delivery can be a statement: "Respondent, under penalty of perjury, states that the Response was delivered to Claimant by [explain how delivered, such as mail or other methods in NAF Rule 6C]".

   A Counter Claim, Cross-claim or Third Party Claim must also be delivered and filed with the Forum, and accompanied by the fee as provided in the Fee Schedule. See NAF Rules 14, 15, and 16. Forms for such Response and Claims may be obtained from the Forum.

   If you fail to respond in writing to the Claim, an Award may be entered against you and in favor of the Claimant. See NAF Rule 36.

2. *Select a Document Hearing or a Participatory Hearing.* You may request a Hearing in your Response or in a separate writing. You may select a Document or Participatory Hearing, and you may also request a Hearing on-line or by telephone. If an In-person Participatory Hearing is selected, it will be held in the federal Judicial District where you reside or do business, unless you have agreed otherwise. Parties have a full and equal right to present relevant and reliable direct and cross examination testimony, documents, exhibits, evidence and arguments. Parties also have the right to subpoena witnesses. Your written Request for a Hearing must be filed with the Forum. You must also deliver a copy of your Request to the Claimant and any other Parties. See NAF Rules 5D, 25, 26, 29, 30, 31, and 33.

3. *Have other options.* You may seek the advice of an attorney or any person who may assist you regarding this arbitration. See NAF Rule 3. You should seek this advice promptly so that your Response can be delivered and filed within the time required by the Code of Procedure. Parties have the right to adjournment for good cause within the time period allowed in Rule 9E. See NAF Rule 5 for a Summary of Arbitration Procedures. If you have any questions about responding, you may contact the Forum.

The Forum is an independent and impartial arbitration organization, which does not give legal advice or represent parties. THIS SUMMARY IS NOT A SUBSTITUTE FOR READING AND UNDERSTANDING THE CODE OF PROCEDURE WHICH GOVERNS THIS ARBITRATION.

National Arbitration Forum
P.O. Box 50191, Minneapolis, MN USA 55405-0191
(800) 474-2371
info@adrforum.com
adrforum.com

APPENDIX B

SECOND NOTICE OF ARBITRATION

Date   Name of Case
    File Number

Dear Respondent,

We have received notice that you have been served with an Arbitration Claim in the above case. If you want to respond to the Claim, the Code of Procedure requires you to respond in writing.

If you have not yet responded, YOU MAY STILL SUBMIT A WRITTEN RESPONSE to the Claimant and the Forum. YOU HAVE THIRTY (30) DAYS FROM THE DATE OF SERVICE OR FOURTEEN (14) DAYS FROM THE DATE OF THIS NOTICE, whichever is later, to respond.

The First Notice of Arbitration you received with the Initial Claim documents stated that you could:

1. *Submit a written Response to the Claim, stating your reply and defenses to the Claim, together with documents supporting your position*. Proof of delivery of the Response on the Claimant must also be filed with the Forum. Proof of delivery can be a statement: "Respondent, under penalty of perjury, states that the Response was delivered to Claimant by [explain how delivered, such as by mail or other methods in NAF Rule 6C]".

2. *Request a Document Hearing, an In-Person Participatory Hearing where you reside or do business, or an On-Line or Telephone Hearing as provided in the Forum Code of Procedure*. Parties have a full and equal right to present relevant and reliable direct and cross examination testimony, documents, exhibits, evidence and arguments. Parties also have the right to subpoena witnesses. See NAF Rules 5, 25, 26, 29, 30, 31, and 33.

3. *Seek the advice of an attorney or any person who may assist*

you regarding this arbitration. See NAF Rule 3. You should seek this advice immediately. Parties have the right to adjournment for good cause within the time period allowed in NAF Rule 9. *You should also read the National Arbitration Forum Code of Procedure which explains what you must and can do.* See NAF Rules 5, 6C, 13, 14, 15, 16, 24, and 25.

You still have these options. If you have any questions or need a copy of the Initial Claim Documents or the Forum Code of Procedure, or have any questions about responding, you may contact the National Arbitration Forum:

P.O. Box 50191, Minneapolis, MN USA 55405-0191
(800) 474-2371; info@adrforum.com; www.adrforum.com

The Forum is an independent and impartial arbitration organization, which does not give legal advice or represent parties.

Notice of Proceeding

If you do not deliver to the Claimant and file with the Forum a written response, an Award may be entered against you in favor of the Claimant. An arbitration Award may be enforced in court as a civil judgment. NAF Rule 36B states in part: "If a Party does not respond to a Claim, an Arbitrator will timely review the merits of the Claim for purposes of issuing an Award or Order. . . ." This Notice informs you that an Arbitrator will conduct a Rule 36 Proceeding after the time has passed for you to submit a written response. If you do not respond, you will not receive any additional notice about this hearing.

THIS SUMMARY IS NOT A SUBSTITUTE FOR READING AND UNDERSTANDING THE FORUM CODE OF PROCEDURE WHICH GOVERNS THIS ARBITRATION.

FEE SCHEDULE
TO CODE OF PROCEDURE
August 1, 2007
National Arbitration Forum

This Fee Schedule governs Arbitrations filed with the Forum under the National Arbitration Forum [NAF] Code of Procedure. NAF Rules 44 and 45 and other NAF Rules govern fees.

Payment of Fees may be made by cash, personal or business check, bank credit (credit or debit card or other line of credit), or other payment arrangements made in advance of filing. The failure of payment may result in delays of a case or other sanctions as provided in the Code of Procedure.

There are two separate Fee Schedules:

COMMON CLAIM FEES: This Schedule governs all Arbitrations with a Claim Amount of less than $75,000.

LARGE CLAIM ARBITRATION FEES: This Schedule governs all Arbitrations with a Claim Amount of $75,000 or more.

Questions? Need help with the Fee Schedules?
Contact the Forum or your Case Coordinator:

P.O. Box 50191
Minneapolis, MN USA 55405-0191
800-474-2371

info@adrforum.com
www.adrforum.com

FEES FOR COMMON CLAIMS
(Claims less than $75,000)

Filing Fee: The fee paid by the Claimant for filing a Claim.

Commencement Fee: The fee assessed when the arbitration is commenced under Rule 10B.

Administrative Fee: The fee assessed by the Forum for its case work and the fee for a Document Hearing.

Participatory Hearing Fee: The fee for the Arbitrator(s) services in a Participatory Hearing.

The Administrative and Participatory Hearing Fees include the Arbitrator fees.

Claim Amount	Filing Fee	Commencement Fee	Administrative Fee	Participatory Hearing Session Fee*
$2,500 or less	$25	$25	$200	$150
$2501–5,000	$35	$35	$250	$150
$5,001–10,000	$35	$35	$350	$300
$10,001–15,000	$35	$35	$450	$300
$15,001–30,000	$60	$60	$650	$500
$30,001–50,000	$110	$110	$950	$750
$50,001–74,999	$240	$240	$1250	$950

***Participatory Hearing Sessions**: This fee is in addition to the Administrative Fee. Claim Amounts above $30,000 include a 180-minute session. For matters below $30,000, see NAF Rule 34 for the length of each session.

Multi-Party Hearing: The above fees include two-party Hearings involving one Claimant and one Respondent. Additional fees determined by the Forum may be assessed for each additional Party.

Non-Monetary, Injunctive and Declaratory Relief: The Fees for any Claim involving injunctive or declaratory relief valued up to $74,999 are the same as the fees for Claim Amounts valued at $74,999.

Consumer Claimants: A Consumer Claimant pays the Filing Fee and one-half the fee for a Participatory Hearing selected by the Consumer up to a total of $250 (two hundred fifty dollars), unless otherwise provided by agreement of the Parties or by applicable law. A Business Respondent pays the Commencement and Administrative Fees and the fee for a Participatory Hearing if selected by the Business Respondent, or if selected by the Consumer, the amount of the Participatory Hearing Fee that remains unpaid after the Consumer Claimant has paid the Consumer's portion of the Participatory Hearing Fee.

Consumer Respondents: A Consumer Respondent pays one-half of the fee for a Participatory Hearing if selected by the Consumer

Appx. B.2.1 *Consumer Arbitration Agreements*

Respondent up to a maximum of $250 (two hundred fifty dollars), unless otherwise provided by agreement of the Parties or by applicable law. A Business Claimant pays the amount of the Participatory Hearing Fee that remains unpaid after the Consumer Respondent has paid the Consumer's portion of the Participatory Hearing Fee.

Other Claimants and Respondents: A Claimant pays the Filing, Commencement, and Administrative Fees, and the fee for a Participatory Hearing selected by the Claimant. The Respondent pays the fee for a Participatory Hearing if selected by the Respondent.

Administrative Fee: Fifty dollars ($50) of the Administrative Fee is to be paid to the Forum at the time the Response is filed and the remaining amount is to be paid forty-five (45) days thereafter. The fee for a Document Hearing is included in the Administrative Fee.

Expedited Hearing Fee: There is a Fee of $500 (five hundred dollars) for an Expedited Document Hearing and $1,000 (one thousand dollars) for an Expedited Participatory Hearing in addition to applicable administrative and hearing fees.

Request Fees: There are no fees for Requests that are timely filed within the time period established in the Scheduling Notice. Any Request, excluding a Request for Expedited Relief or for a Dispositive Order, made by any Party during the case, within the time period established in the Scheduling Notice will be processed without the assessment of a Request Fee. A Party who files a Request after the time period established in the Scheduling Notice shall pay the late Request Fee as listed below.

Objection Fees: An Objection Fee is assessed if an Objection is filed to a Request. In Consumer cases, the Party other than a Consumer pays the Objection Fee; an Objecting Consumer Party pays a $20 Processing Fee and does not pay the Objection Fee. For all other cases, the objecting Party pays the Objection Fee. The Objection Fees are listed below. An Arbitrator, or the Forum, as provided by the Code of Procedure, will decide Requests without Objections.

Late Request Fees for Common Claims

These fees apply to late Requests filed after the time period established in the Scheduling Notice has ended. There is no fee for Non-Dispositive Requests filed within the time period established in the Scheduling Notice. The Requesting Party pays the late Request Fee.

$50 Fee
Request for Time Extension
Request for Stay
Request for Subpoena
Request for Amendment

$100 Fee
Request for Non-Dispositive Order

$250 Fee
Request for Discovery Order
Request for Dispositive Order
Request for Value of Non-Monetary Relief

Request Fees For Common Claims Applicable Anytime During a Case

These fees apply to the following requests filed anytime during a case.

$50 Fee
Request for Adjournment

$250 Fee
Request for Expedited Relief
Request for Reopening or Reconsideration

Objection Fees for Common Claims

These fees apply to all Objections.

$20 Processing Fee
Processing Fee Paid by Consumer Party filing an Objection (No other fee is paid by the Consumer)

$100 Fee
Objection to Time Extension Request
Objection to Stay Request
Objection to Adjournment Request
Objection to Amendment Request
Objection to Subpoena Request
Objection to Reopening or Reconsideration Request

$250 Fee
Objection to Non-Dispositive Request
Objection to Expedited Relief Request
Objection to Value of Non-Monetary Relief Request

$500 Fee
Objection to Discovery Order Request
Objection to Dispositive Request

Other Common Claim Fees

Request for Dispositive Order Fee: A fee may be assessed for a Dispositive Request made within the time period of the Scheduling Notice in an amount not greater than the Administrative Fee.

Post-Hearing Memorandum Fee: A Consumer Party who receives permission from the Arbitrator to submit a Post-Hearing Memorandum pays $100 (one hundred dollars). All other Parties who receive permission from the Arbitrator to submit a Post-Hearing Memorandum pay a $250 (two hundred fifty dollar) fee. See NAF Rule 34G.

Findings and Conclusions Fees: The fees for written findings of fact, conclusions of law or reasons for the Award in a Common Claim case are:

$2,500 or less	$200
$2,501–5,000	$250
$5,001–15,000	$300
$15,001–30,000	$400
$30,001–50, 000	$500
$50,001–74,999	$750

The above fees are paid as follows:

A Party obligated to pay fees for a Consumer pays the entire fee where an Arbitration Agreement with a Consumer Party requires written findings of fact, conclusions of law or reasons for an Award.

A Consumer Party pays $100 (one hundred dollars) and the Party obligated to pay fees for a Consumer pays the remaining portion where an Arbitration Agreement does not provide for written findings, conclusions or reasons and a Consumer Party requests such an Award.

A Non-Consumer Party pays the entire fee where such Party requests an Award with written findings, conclusions or reasons for the Award.

Determination of Other Fees: The Forum establishes all other fees. Parties may obtain the amount of a fee by contacting the Forum.

Cancelled or Rescheduled Hearings: A Party may seek a partial refund of a Participatory Hearing Fee if the Party withdraws the demand for the Hearing at least fifteen (15) days before the Hearing. Additional fees may be assessed for rescheduled Hearings.

Questions? Need Help? Any Party who has questions or needs help in filing or responding to a claim may contact the Forum:

P.O. Box 50191
Minneapolis, MN USA 55405-0191
800-474-2371
info@adrforum.com
www.adrforum.com

FEES FOR LARGE CLAIMS
(Claims $75,000 or more)

Filing Fee: The fee paid by the Claimant for filing a Claim.
Commencement Fee: The fee assessed when the arbitration is commenced under Rule 10B. The Claimant pays the Commencement Fee, unless otherwise provided by the agreement of the Parties or the law.
Administrative Fee: The fee assessed by the Forum for its case work.
Hearing Fee: The fee for the Arbitrator(s) services.

Claim Amount	Filing Fee	Commencement Fee	Administrative Fee
$75,000–125,000	$300	$300	$500
$125,001–250,000	$400	$400	$750
$250,001–500,00	$500	$500	$1,000
$500,001–1,000,000	$1,000	$1,000	$1,250
$1,000,001–5,000,000	$1,750	$1,750	$1,500

Above $5,000,000: Contact Forum for Fees.

Multi-Party Hearing: The above fees include two-party Hearings involving one Claimant and one Respondent. Additional fees determined by the Forum may be assessed for each additional party.

Hearing/Arbitrator Fees: The fee for the hearing and all other work done by an Arbitrator is billed at the hourly rate of the Arbitrator times the hours or portions of hours worked. A Party that Requests a Hearing shall pay the Fees associated with the Hearing, unless otherwise provided by agreement of the Parties or required by applicable law.

Expedited Hearing Fee:

For Claim Amounts of $75,000 to $999,999, there is a fee of $500 (five hundred dollars) for an Expedited Document Hearing and $1,000 (one thousand dollars) for an Expedited Participatory Hearing in addition to applicable administrative and hearing fees. The Forum may assess a higher fee.

For Claim Amounts of $1,000,000 and over, there is a fee of $2,000 (two thousand dollars) for an Expedited Document Hearing and $4,000 (four thousand dollars) for an Expedited Participatory Hearing in addition to applicable administrative and hearing fees. The Forum may assess a higher fee.

Requests to Forum: A Party who files a Request that is to be determined by the Forum as provided in the Code of Procedure pays a $150 Request Fee, and a Party who files an Objection to the Request pays $100 as an Objection Fee, unless otherwise provided by the Code of Procedure, the agreement of the Parties or applicable law. Requests include Requests for a Stay or Time Extension and all other requests decided by the Forum.

Requests to Arbitrator: A Party who files a Request for an Adjournment or Time Extension shall pay a fee of $100; and a Party who files an Objection to either of these two requests shall pay a fee of $50. The fees for other Requests shall be billed at the hourly rate of the Arbitrator times the hours or portions of hours worked plus any additional Forum administrative fees for work involved in submitting the matter to the Arbitrator. A Party that submits the Request shall pay the Fees associated with the matter unless otherwise provided by the agreement of the Parties or required by applicable law. A Party that submits an Objection may pay the fees associated with the Objection as determined by the Forum or Arbitrator.

Prepayment of Fees: The Forum may require a Party or Parties to pay in advance for Large Claim fees. This deposit shall be used for fees incurred by the Party in a case and any unused portion of the deposit shall be promptly refunded to the Party after the case is over. An arbitration may not proceed unless fees have been prepaid.

Findings and Conclusions: Where an Arbitration Agreement requires written findings of fact, conclusions of law or reasons for the Award, the Parties shall equally split the fee for this work. Where a Party requests written findings of fact, conclusions of law or reasons for the Award, the requesting Party shall pay the fee.

Determination of Other Fees: The Forum establishes all other fees. Parties may obtain the amount of a fee by contacting the Forum.

Cancelled or Rescheduled Hearings: A Party may seek a partial refund of a Hearing fee if the Party withdraws the demand for the Hearing at least fifteen (15) days before the Hearing. Additional fees may be assessed for rescheduled Hearings.

Consumer Party: A Consumer Party may not have to pay fees.

NAF Rule 44G allows a Consumer Party to request that another Party pay the fees or to seek another remedy.

Respondent Party: NAF Rule 44H allows a Respondent Party obligated to pay fees for a Consumer Party to challenge the Claim Amount.

Questions? Need help? Any Party who has questions or needs help in filing or responding to a Claim may contact the Forum:

P.O. Box 50191
Minneapolis, MN USA 55405-0191
800-474-2371
info@adrforum.com
www.adrforum.com

B.2.2 Consumer and Employee Arbitration Rights

You Have The Right To File A Claim.

Claim. You can file an arbitration Claim with the National Arbitration Forum by sending the Forum a completed Claim Form and a Filing Fee. You can ask the Forum for a Claim Form and also information on "How to File a Claim." You can complete the Claim Form and file it from your home by mail, fax, or e-mail at www.adrforum.com.

Fees. The amount of a fee depends upon the amount of the Claim. For Consumer Common Claims, the Filing Fee can be as low as $25. You can pay by check, credit card, or complete a credit application. If you are an indigent Consumer Party and cannot pay a fee, you can ask for a waiver of the fee, which may be granted by the Forum.

Response. If someone has filed a Claim against you, you have the right to Respond with a defense. You may also file a Counter Claim, Cross-claim or Third Party Claim at the same time; and a Filing Fee may be required. You can ask the Forum for a Response Form or for information on "How to File A Response."

You Have The Right To A Fair Hearing.

A Party in arbitration can choose the type of Hearing desired. You may choose from one of the following:

A **Document Hearing** allows you to present your case in Writing and provide supporting Documentation to an Arbitrator. No Party will personally appear at the Document Hearing.

A **Telephone Hearing** allows you to present your case, from a location of your choice, to the Arbitrator by way of a telephone conference call.

An **On-line Hearing** allows you to present your case, from a location of your choice, to the Arbitrator by way of on-line communication.

An **In-Person Hearing** allows you to appear in person at a place near where you live and present your case to an Arbitrator.

You Have The Right To An Expert And Neutral Arbitrator.

The Arbitrator who decides your case will be an experienced Arbitrator who is neutral and an expert in the law. You may select your own Arbitrator with the agreement of all Parties or use the selection process described in the Forum Code of Procedure. This independent Arbitrator will decide your case fairly, based on the law.

You Have The Right To Be Represented.

You can have an attorney represent you during the arbitration and at the Hearing, or you can represent yourself. You may also have a friend, family member or non-attorney assist you.

You Have More Rights And Responsibilities.

Our Code of Procedure explains your rights and obligations and the Forum arbitration procedures and rules.

You Have The Right To Have Your Questions Answered.

Our professional and helpful staff can answer your questions regarding the arbitration process and procedures and provide you with information. However, we cannot offer you legal advice or represent you.

This summary is not a substitute for reading and understanding the Code of Procedure which governs this arbitration.

B.3 JAMS[3]

B.3.1 Streamlined Arbitration Rules and Procedures

Revised March 26, 2007

TABLE OF CONTENTS

Rule 1. Scope of Rules
Rule 2. Party-Agreed Procedures
Rule 3. Amendment of Rules
Rule 4. Conflict with Law
Rule 5. Commencing an Arbitration
Rule 6. Preliminary and Administrative Matters
Rule 7. Notice of Claims
Rule 8. Interpretation of Rules and Jurisdiction Challenges
Rule 9. Representation

---

[3] Reprinted with permission. Copyright 2007 JAMS. All rights reserved.

Rule 10. Withdrawal from Arbitration
Rule 11. *Ex Parte* Communications
Rule 12. Arbitrator Selection and Replacement
Rule 13. Exchange of Information
Rule 14. Scheduling and Location of Hearing
Rule 15. Pre-Hearing Submissions
Rule 16. Securing Witnesses and Documents for the Arbitration Hearing
Rule 17. The Arbitration Hearing
Rule 18. Waiver of Hearing
Rule 19. Awards
Rule 20. Enforcement of the Award
Rule 21. Confidentiality and Privacy
Rule 22. Waiver
Rule 23. Settlement and Consent Award
Rule 24. Sanctions
Rule 25. Disqualification of the Arbitrator as a Witness or Party and Exclusion of Liability
Rule 26. Fees
Rule 27. Bracketed (or High-Low) Arbitration Option
Rule 28. Final Offer (or Baseball) Arbitration Option

Rule 1. Scope of Rules

(a) The JAMS Streamlined Arbitration Rules and Procedures ("Rules") govern binding Arbitrations of disputes or claims that are administered by JAMS and in which the Parties agree to use these Rules or, in the absence of such agreement, no disputed claim or counterclaim exceeds $250,000, not including interest or attorneys' fees, unless other Rules are prescribed.
(b) The Parties shall be deemed to have made these Rules a part of their Arbitration agreement whenever they have provided for Arbitration by JAMS under its Streamlined Rules or for Arbitration by JAMS without specifying any particular JAMS Rules and the disputes or claims meet the criteria of the first paragraph of this Rule.
(c) The authority and duties of JAMS are prescribed in the agreement of the Parties and in these Rules, and may be carried out through such representatives as it may direct.
(d) JAMS may, in its discretion, assign the administration of an Arbitration to any of its offices.
(e) The term "Party" as used in these Rules includes Parties to the Arbitration and their counsel or representatives.

Rule 2. Party-Agreed Procedures

The Parties may agree on any procedures not specified herein or in lieu of these Rules that are consistent with the applicable law and JAMS policies (including, without limitation, Rules 12(j), 25 and 26). The Parties shall promptly notify JAMS of any such Party-agreed procedures and shall confirm such procedures in writing. The Party-agreed procedures shall be enforceable as if contained in these Rules.

Rule 3. Amendment of Rules

JAMS may amend these Rules without notice. The Rules in effect on the date of the commencement of an Arbitration (as defined in Rule 5) shall apply to that Arbitration, unless the Parties have specified another version of the Rules.

Rule 4. Conflict with Law

If any of these Rules, or a modification of these Rules agreed on by the Parties, is determined to be in conflict with a provision of applicable law, the provision of law will govern, and no other Rule will be affected.

Rule 5. Commencing an Arbitration

(a) The Arbitration is deemed commenced when JAMS confirms in a Commencement Letter one of the following:
  (i) The submission to JAMS of a post-dispute Arbitration agreement fully executed by all Parties and that specifies JAMS administration or use of any JAMS Rules; or
  (ii) The submission to JAMS of a pre-dispute written contractual provision requiring the Parties to arbitrate the dispute or claim and which specifies JAMS administration or use of any JAMS Rules or which the Parties agree shall be administered by JAMS; or
  (iii) The oral agreement of all Parties to participate in an Arbitration administered by JAMS or conducted pursuant to any JAMS Rules, confirmed in writing by the Parties; or
  (iv) A court order compelling Arbitration at JAMS.
(b) The Commencement Letter shall confirm that one of the above requirements for commencement has been met, that JAMS has received all payments required under the applicable fee schedule, and that the claimant has provided JAMS with contact information for all Parties along with evidence that the Demand has been served on all Parties. The date of commencement of the Arbitration is the date of the Commencement Letter.
(c) If a Party that is obligated to arbitrate in accordance with subparagraph (a) of this Rule fails to agree to participate in the Arbitration process, JAMS shall confirm in writing that Party's failure to respond or participate and, pursuant to Rule 14, the Arbitrator shall schedule, and provide appropriate notice of, a Hearing or other opportunity for the Party demanding the Arbitration to demonstrate its entitlement to relief.
(d) The definition of "commencement" in these Rules is not intended to be applicable to any legal requirement, such as the statute of limitations or a contractual limitations period. The term "commencement" as used in this Rule is intended only to pertain to the operation of this and other rules (such as Rule 3, 7(a), 7(c), 10(a), 26(a).) The tolling of the statute of limitations or a contractual limitations period shall be regarded by JAMS to occur upon the date of service of a demand for arbitration; compliance with Rule 5(a) (i), (ii), (iii) or (iv) as appropriate; and payment of any fee required of that Party under the applicable fee schedule.
(e) Service by a Party under these Rules is effected by providing one signed copy of the document to each Party and two copies to JAMS. Service may be made by hand-delivery, overnight delivery service or U.S. Mail. Service by any of these means is considered effective upon the date of deposit of the document. Service by electronic mail or facsimile transmission is considered effective upon transmission, but only if followed within one week of delivery by service of an appropriate number of copies and originals by one of the other service methods. In computing any period of time prescribed or allowed by these Rules for a Party to do some act within a prescribed period after the service of a notice or other paper on the Party and the notice or paper is served on the Party only by U.S. Mail, three (3) calendar days shall be added to the prescribed period.

Rule 6. Preliminary and Administrative Matters

(a) JAMS may convene, or the Parties may request, administrative conferences to discuss any procedural matter relating to the administration of the Arbitration.

(b) At the request of a Party and in the absence of Party agreement, JAMS may determine the location of the Hearing, subject to Arbitrator review. In determining the location of the Hearing such factors as the subject matter of the dispute, the convenience of the Parties and witnesses and the relative resources of the Parties shall be considered.

(c) If, at any time, any Party has failed to pay fees or expenses in full, JAMS may order the suspension or termination of the proceedings. JAMS may so inform the Parties in order that one of them may advance the required payment. An administrative suspension shall toll any other time limits contained in these Rules, applicable statutes or the Parties' agreement.

(d) JAMS does not maintain a duplicate file of documents filed in the Arbitration. If the Parties wish to have any documents returned to them, they must advise JAMS in writing within 30 days of the conclusion of the Arbitration. If special arrangements are required regarding file maintenance or document retention, they must be agreed to in writing and JAMS reserves the right to impose an additional fee for such special arrangements.

(e) Unless the Parties' agreement or applicable law provides otherwise, JAMS may consolidate Arbitrations in the following instances:

   (i) If a Party files more than one Arbitration with JAMS, and if JAMS determines that the Arbitrations so filed have common issues of fact or law, JAMS may consolidate the Arbitrations and refer them to a single Arbitrator.

   (ii) Where a Demand or Demands for Arbitration is or are submitted naming Parties already involved in another Arbitration or Arbitrations pending under these Rules, JAMS may decide that the new case or cases will be consolidated into one or more of the pending proceedings and referred to one of the Arbitrators already appointed.

   (iii) Where a Demand or Demands for Arbitration is or are submitted naming parties that are not identical to the Parties in the existing Arbitration or Arbitrations, JAMS may decide that the new case or cases will be consolidated into one or more of the pending proceedings and referred to one of the Arbitrators already appointed.

When rendering its decision, JAMS will take into account all circumstances, including the links between the cases and the progress already made in the existing Arbitrations.

Where a third party seeks to participate in an Arbitration already pending under these Rules or where a Party to an Arbitration under these Rules seeks to compel a third party to participate in a pending Arbitration, the Arbitrator will decide on such request, taking into account all circumstances the Arbitrator deems relevant and applicable.

Unless applicable law provides otherwise, where JAMS decides to consolidate a proceeding into a pending Arbitration, the Parties to the consolidated case or cases will be deemed to have waived their right to designate an Arbitrator.

Rule 7. Notice of Claims

(a) If a matter has been submitted for Arbitration after litigation has been commenced in court regarding the same claim or dispute, the pleadings in the court case, including the complaint and answer (with affirmative defenses and counterclaims), may be filed with JAMS within seven (7) calendar days of the date of commencement, and if so filed, will be considered part of the record of the Arbitration. It will be assumed that the existence of such pleadings constitutes appropriate notice to the Parties of such claims, remedies sought, counterclaims and affirmative defenses. If necessary, such notice may be supplemented pursuant to Rule 7(b).

(b) If a matter has been submitted to JAMS prior to, or in lieu of, the filing of a case in court or prior to the filing of an answer, the Parties shall give each other notice of their respective claims, remedies sought, counterclaims and affirmative defenses (including jurisdictional challenges). Such notice may be served upon the other Parties and filed with JAMS, in the form of a Demand for Arbitration, response or answer to demand for Arbitration, counterclaim or answer or response to counterclaim. Any pleading shall include a short statement of its factual basis.

(c) Notice of claims, remedies sought, counterclaims and affirmative defenses may be served simultaneously, in which case they should be filed with JAMS within seven (7) calendar days of the date of commencement of the Arbitration, or by such other date as the Parties may agree. The responding Parties may, however, in their sole discretion, wait to receive the notice of claim before serving any response, including counterclaims or affirmative defenses. In this case, the response, including counterclaims and affirmative defenses, should be served on the other Parties and filed with JAMS within seven (7) calendar days of service of the notice of claim. If the notice of claim has been served on the responding Parties prior to the date of commencement, the response, including counterclaims and affirmative defenses, shall be served within seven (7) calendar days from the date of commencement.

(d) Any Party that is a recipient of a counterclaim may reply to such counterclaim, including asserting jurisdictional challenges. In such case, the reply must be served on the other Parties and filed with JAMS within seven (7) calendar days of having received the notice of counterclaim. No claim, remedy, counterclaim or affirmative defense will be considered by the Arbitrator in the absence of prior notice to the other Parties, unless all Parties agree that such consideration is appropriate notwithstanding the lack of prior notice.

Rule 8. Interpretation of Rules and Jurisdiction Challenges

(a) Once appointed, the Arbitrator shall resolve disputes about the interpretation and applicability of these Rules and conduct of the Arbitration Hearing. The resolution of the issue by the Arbitrator shall be final.

(b) Whenever in these Rules a matter is to be determined by "JAMS" (such as in Rules 6; 12(d), (e), (h) or (j); or 26(d)), such determination shall be made in accordance with JAMS administrative procedures.

(c) Jurisdictional and arbitrability disputes, including disputes over the existence, validity, interpretation or scope of the agreement under which Arbitration is sought, and who are proper Parties to the Arbitration, shall be submitted to and ruled on by the Arbitrator. The Arbitrator has the authority to determine jurisdiction and arbitrability issues as a preliminary matter.

(d) Disputes concerning the appointment of the Arbitrator shall be resolved by JAMS.

(e) The Arbitrator may upon a showing of good cause or *sua sponte,* when necessary to facilitate the Arbitration, extend any deadlines established in these Rules, provided that the time for rendering the Award may only be altered in accordance with Rule 19.

Rule 9. Representation

(a) The Parties may be represented by counsel or any other person of the Party's choice. Each Party shall give prompt written notice to JAMS and the other Parties of the name, address, telephone and fax numbers and email address of its representative. The representative of a Party may act on the Party's behalf in complying with these Rules.

(b) Changes in Representation. A Party shall give prompt written notice to the Case Manager and the other Parties of any change in its representation, including the name, address, telephone and fax numbers, and email address of the new representative. Such notice shall state that the written consent of the former representative, if any, and of the new representative, has been obtained and shall state the effective date of the new representation.

Rule 10. Withdrawal from Arbitration

(a) No Party may terminate or withdraw from an Arbitration after the issuance of the Commencement Letter (see Rule 5) except by written agreement of all Parties to the Arbitration.

(b) A Party that asserts a claim or counterclaim may unilaterally withdraw that claim or counterclaim without prejudice by serving written notice on the other Parties and on the Arbitrator. However, the opposing Parties may, within fourteen (14) calendar days of service of notice of the withdrawal of the claim or counterclaim, request that the Arbitrator order that the withdrawal be with prejudice. If such a request is made, it shall be determined by the Arbitrator.

Rule 11. *Ex Parte* Communications

No Party will have any *ex parte* communication with the Arbitrator regarding any issue related to the Arbitration. Any necessary *ex parte* communication with the Arbitrator, whether before or after the Arbitration Hearing, will be conducted through JAMS.

Rule 12. Arbitrator Selection and Replacement

(a) JAMS Streamlined Arbitrations will be conducted by one neutral Arbitrator.

(b) Unless the Arbitrator has been previously selected by agreement of the Parties, the Case Manager may attempt to facilitate agreement among the Parties regarding selection of the Arbitrator.

(c) If the Parties do not agree on an Arbitrator, JAMS shall send the Parties a list of at least three (3) Arbitrator candidates. JAMS shall also provide each Party with a brief description of the background and experience of each Arbitrator candidate. JAMS may replace any or all names on the list of Arbitrator candidates for reasonable cause at any time before the Parties have submitted their choice pursuant to subparagraph (d) below.

(d) Within seven (7) calendar days of service by the Parties of the list of names, each Party may strike one name and shall rank the remaining Arbitrator candidates in order of preference. The remaining Arbitrator candidate with the highest composite ranking shall be appointed the Arbitrator. JAMS may grant a reasonable extension of the time to strike and rank the Arbitrator candidates to any Party without the consent of the other Parties.

(e) If this process does not yield an Arbitrator, JAMS shall designate the Arbitrator.

(f) If a Party fails to respond to a list of Arbitrator candidates within seven (7) calendar days after its service, JAMS shall deem that Party to have accepted all of the Arbitrator candidates.

(g) Entities whose interests are not adverse with respect to the issues in dispute shall be treated as a single Party for purposes of the Arbitrator selection process. JAMS shall determine whether the interests between entities are adverse for purposes of Arbitrator selection, considering such factors as whether the entities are represented by the same attorney and whether the entities are presenting joint or separate positions at the Arbitration.

(h) If, for any reason, the Arbitrator who is selected is unable to fulfill the Arbitrator's duties, a successor Arbitrator shall be chosen in accordance with this Rule. JAMS will make the final determination as to whether an Arbitrator is unable to fulfill his or her duties, and that decision shall be final.

(i) Any disclosures regarding the selected Arbitrator shall be made as required by law or within ten (10) calendar days from the date of appointment. The obligation of the Arbitrator to make all required disclosures continues throughout the Arbitration process. Such disclosures may be provided in electronic format, provided that JAMS will produce a hard copy to any Party that requests it.

(j) At any time during the Arbitration process, a Party may challenge the continued service of an Arbitrator for cause. The challenge must be based upon information that was not available to the Parties at the time the Arbitrator was selected. A challenge for cause must be in writing and exchanged with opposing Parties who may respond within seven (7) days of service of the challenge. JAMS shall make the final determination as to such challenge. Such determination shall take into account the materiality of the facts and any prejudice to the Parties. That decision will be final.

Rule 13. Exchange of Information

(a) The Parties shall cooperate in good faith in the voluntary and informal exchange of all non-privileged documents and information relevant to the dispute or claim, including copies of all documents in their possession or control on which they rely in support of their positions or which they intend to introduce as exhibits at the Arbitration Hearing, the names of all individuals with knowledge about the dispute or claim and the names of all experts who may be called upon to testify or whose report may be introduced at the Arbitration Hearing. The Parties and the Arbitrator will make every effort to conclude the document and information exchange process within fourteen (14) calendar days after all pleadings or notices of claims have been received. The necessity of additional information exchange shall be determined by the Arbitrator based upon the reasonable need for the requested information, the availability of other discovery options and the burdensomeness of the request on the opposing Parties and the witness.

(b) As they become aware of new documents or information,

including experts who may be called upon to testify, all Parties continue to be obligated to provide relevant, non-privileged documents, to supplement their identification of witnesses and experts and to honor any informal agreements or understandings between the Parties regarding documents or information to be exchanged. Documents that were not previously exchanged, or witnesses and experts that were not previously identified, may not be considered by the Arbitrator at the Hearing, unless agreed by the Parties or upon a showing of good cause.

(c) The Parties shall promptly notify JAMS when a dispute exists regarding discovery issues. JAMS shall arrange a conference with the Arbitrator, either by telephone or in person, and the Arbitrator shall decide the dispute.

Rule 14. Scheduling and Location of Hearing

(a) The Arbitrator, after consulting with the Parties that have appeared, shall determine the date, time and location of the Hearing. The Arbitrator and the Parties shall attempt to schedule consecutive Hearing days if more than one day is necessary.

(b) If a Party has failed to participate in the Arbitration process, the Arbitrator may set the Hearing without consulting with that Party. The non-participating Party shall be served with a Notice of Hearing at least thirty (30) calendar days prior to the scheduled date unless the law of the relevant jurisdiction allows for or the Parties have agreed to shorter notice.

Rule 15. Pre-Hearing Submissions

(a) By at least seven (7) calendar days before the Arbitration Hearing, the Parties shall exchange a list of the witnesses they intend to call, including any experts, a short description of the anticipated testimony of each such witness, an estimate of the length of the witness's direct testimony, and a list of exhibits. In addition, at least seven (7) calendar days before the Arbitration Hearing, the Parties shall exchange copies of all exhibits intended to be used at the Hearing to the extent that any such exhibit has not been previously exchanged. The Parties should pre-mark exhibits and should attempt to resolve any disputes regarding the admissibility of exhibits prior to the Hearing. The list of witnesses with the description and estimate of length of their testimony and the copies of all exhibits that the Parties intend to use at the Hearing, in pre-marked form, should also be provided to JAMS for transmission to the Arbitrator, whether or not the Parties have stipulated to the admissibility of all such exhibits.

(b) The Arbitrator may require that each Party submit concise written statements of position, including summaries of the facts and evidence a Party intends to present, discussion of the applicable law and the basis for the requested Award or denial of relief sought. The statements, which may be in the form of a letter, shall be filed with JAMS and served upon the other Parties, at least seven (7) calendar days before the Hearing date. Rebuttal statements or other pre-Hearing written submissions may be permitted or required at the discretion of the Arbitrator.

Rule 16. Securing Witnesses and Documents for the Arbitration Hearing

(a) At the written request of a Party, all other Parties shall produce for the Arbitration Hearing all specified witnesses in their employ or under their control without need of subpoena. The Arbitrator may issue subpoenas for the attendance of witnesses or the production of documents either prior to or at the Hearing. Pre-issued subpoenas may be used in jurisdictions that permit them. In the event a Party or a subpoenaed person objects to the production of a witness or other evidence, the Party or subpoenaed person may file an objection with the Arbitrator, who will promptly rule on the objection, weighing both the burden on the producing Party and witness and the need of the proponent for the witness or other evidence. The Arbitrator, in order to hear a third party witness, or for the convenience of the Parties or the witnesses, may conduct the Hearing at any location unless the Arbitration agreement specifies a mandatory Hearing location.

(b) Any JAMS office may be designated a Hearing location for purposes of the issuance of a subpoena or subpoena *duces tecum* to a third party witness, unless the Arbitration agreement specifies a mandatory Hearing location. The subpoena or subpoena *duces tecum* shall be issued in accordance with the applicable law of the designated Hearing location and shall be deemed issued under that law. Objections to any subpoena or subpoena *duces tecum* shall be made and determined by the Arbitrator.

Rule 17. The Arbitration Hearing

(a) The Arbitrator will ordinarily conduct the Arbitration Hearing in the manner set forth in these Rules. The Arbitrator may vary these procedures if it is determined reasonable and appropriate to do so.

(b) The Arbitrator shall determine the order of proof, which will generally be similar to that of a court trial.

(c) The Arbitrator shall require witnesses to testify under oath if requested by any Party, or otherwise in the discretion of the Arbitrator.

(d) Strict conformity to the rules of evidence is not required, except that the Arbitrator shall apply applicable law relating to privileges and work product. The Arbitrator shall consider evidence that he or she finds relevant and material to the dispute, giving the evidence such weight as is appropriate. The Arbitrator may be guided in that determination by principles contained in the Federal Rules of Evidence or any other applicable rules of evidence. The Arbitrator may limit testimony to exclude evidence that would be immaterial or unduly repetitive, provided that all Parties are afforded the opportunity to present material and relevant evidence.

(e) The Arbitrator shall receive and consider relevant deposition testimony recorded by transcript or videotape, provided that the other Parties have had the opportunity to attend and cross-examine. The Arbitrator may in his or her discretion consider witness affidavits or other recorded testimony even if the other Parties have not had the opportunity to cross-examine, but will give that evidence only such weight as the Arbitrator deems appropriate.

(f) The Parties will not offer as evidence, and the Arbitrator shall neither admit into the record nor consider, prior settlement offers by the Parties or statements or recommendations made by a mediator or other person in connection with efforts to resolve the dispute being arbitrated, except to the extent that applicable law permits the admission of such evidence.

(g) The Hearing or any portion thereof may be conducted tele-

phonically with the agreement of the Parties or in the discretion of the Arbitrator.
(h) When the Arbitrator determines that all relevant and material evidence and arguments have been presented, the Arbitrator shall declare the Hearing closed. The Arbitrator may defer the closing of the Hearing until a date agreed upon by the Arbitrator and the Parties, to permit the Parties to submit post-Hearing briefs, which may be in the form of a letter. If post-Hearing briefs are to be submitted the Hearing shall be deemed closed upon receipt by the Arbitrator of such briefs.
(i) At any time before the Award is rendered, the Arbitrator may, *sua sponte* or upon the application of a Party for good cause shown, re-open the Hearing. If the Hearing is re-opened and the reopening prevents the rendering of the Award within the time limits specified by these Rules, the time limits will be extended until the reopened Hearing is declared closed by the Arbitrator.
(j) The Arbitrator may proceed with the Hearing in the absence of a Party that, after receiving notice of the Hearing pursuant to Rule 14, fails to attend. The Arbitrator may not render an Award solely on the basis of the default or absence of the Party, but shall require any Party seeking relief to submit such evidence as the Arbitrator may require for the rendering of an Award. If the Arbitrator reasonably believes that a Party will not attend the Hearing, the Arbitrator may schedule the Hearing as a telephonic Hearing and may receive the evidence necessary to render an Award by affidavit. The notice of Hearing shall specify if it will be in person or telephonic.
(k)(i) Any Party may arrange for a stenographic or other record to be made of the Hearing and shall inform the other Parties in advance of the Hearing. The requesting Party shall bear the cost of such stenographic record. If all other Parties agree to share the cost of the stenographic record, it shall be made available to the Arbitrator and may be used in the proceeding.
(ii) If there is no agreement to share the cost of the stenographic record, it may not be provided to the Arbitrator and may not be used in the proceeding unless the Party arranging for the stenographic record either agrees to provide access to the stenographic record at no charge or on terms that are acceptable to the Parties and the reporting service.
(iii) The Parties may agree that the cost of the stenographic record shall or shall not be allocated by the Arbitrator in the Award.

Rule 18. Waiver of Hearing

The Parties may agree to waive oral Hearing and submit the dispute to the Arbitrator for an Award based on written submissions and other evidence as the Parties may agree.

Rule 19. Awards

(a) The Arbitrator shall render a Final Award or Partial Final Award within thirty (30) calendar days after the date of the close of the Hearing as defined in Rule 17(h) or, if a Hearing has been waived, within thirty (30) calendar days after the receipt by the Arbitrator of all materials specified by the Parties, except (i) by the Agreement of the Parties, (ii) upon good cause for an extension of time to render the Award, or (iii) as provided in Rule 17(i). The Arbitrator shall provide the Final Award or Partial Final Award to JAMS for issuance in accordance with this Rule.
(b) In determining the merits of the dispute the Arbitrator shall be guided by the rules of law agreed upon by the Parties. In the absence of such agreement, the Arbitrator will be guided by the law or the rules of law that the Arbitrator deems to be most appropriate. The Arbitrator may grant any remedy or relief that is just and equitable and within the scope of the Parties' agreement, including but not limited to specific performance of a contract.
(c) In addition to a Final Award or Partial Final Award, the Arbitrator may make other decisions, including interim or partial rulings, orders and Awards.
(d) The Arbitrator may take whatever interim measures are deemed necessary, including injunctive relief and measures for the protection or conservation of property and disposition of disposable goods. Such interim measures may take the form of an interim Award, and the Arbitrator may require security for the costs of such measures. Any recourse by a Party to a court for interim or provisional relief shall not be deemed incompatible with the agreement to arbitrate or a waiver of the right to arbitrate.
(e) The Award of the Arbitrator may allocate Arbitration Fees and Arbitrator compensation and expenses unless such an allocation is expressly prohibited by the Parties' agreement. (Such a prohibition may not limit the power of the Arbitrator to allocate Arbitration fees and Arbitrator compensation and expenses pursuant to Rule 26(c).)
(f) The Award of the Arbitrator may allocate attorneys' fees and expenses and interest (at such rate and from such date as the Arbitrator may deem appropriate) if provided by the Parties' agreement or allowed by applicable law.
(g) The Award will consist of a written statement signed by the Arbitrator regarding the disposition of each claim and the relief, if any, as to each claim. Unless all Parties agree otherwise, the Award shall also contain a concise written statement of the reasons for the Award.
(h) After the Award has been rendered, and provided the Parties have complied with Rule 26, the Award shall be issued by serving copies on the Parties. Service may be made by U.S. Mail. It need not be sent certified or registered.
(i) Within seven (7) calendar days after issuance of the Award, any Party may serve upon the other Parties and on JAMS a request that the Arbitrator correct any computational, typographical or other similar error in an Award (including the reallocation of fees pursuant to Rule 26(c)), or the Arbitrator may *sua sponte* propose to correct such errors in an Award. A Party opposing such correction shall have seven (7) calendar days in which to file any objection. The Arbitrator may make any necessary and appropriate correction to the Award within fourteen (14) calendar days of receiving a request or seven (7) calendar days after the Arbitrator's proposal to do so. The corrected Award shall be served upon the Parties in the same manner as the Award.
(j) The Award is considered final, for purposes of judicial proceeding to enforce, modify or vacate the Award pursuant to Rule 20, fourteen (14) calendar days after service is deemed effective if no request for a correction is made, or as of the effective date of service of a corrected Award.

Rule 20. Enforcement of the Award

Proceedings to enforce, confirm, modify or vacate an Award will be controlled by and conducted in conformity with the Federal

Arbitration Act, 9 U.S.C. Sec 1 et. seq. or applicable state law.

Rule 21. Confidentiality and Privacy
(a) JAMS and the Arbitrator shall maintain the confidential nature of the Arbitration proceeding and the Award, including the Hearing, except as necessary in connection with a judicial challenge to or enforcement of an Award, or unless otherwise required by law or judicial decision.
(b) The Arbitrator may issue orders to protect the confidentiality of proprietary information, trade secrets or other sensitive information.
(c) Subject to the discretion of the Arbitrator or agreement of the Parties, any person having a direct interest in the Arbitration may attend the Arbitration Hearing. The Arbitrator may exclude any non-Party from any part of a Hearing.

Rule 22. Waiver
(a) If a Party becomes aware of a violation of or failure to comply with these Rules and fails promptly to object in writing, the objection will be deemed waived, unless the Arbitrator determines that waiver will cause substantial injustice or hardship.
(b) If any Party becomes aware of information that could be the basis of a challenge for cause to the continued service of the Arbitrator, such challenge must be made promptly, in writing, to the Arbitrator or JAMS. Failure to do so shall constitute a waiver of any objection to continued service by the Arbitrator.

Rule 23. Settlement and Consent Award
(a) The Parties may agree, at any stage of the Arbitration process, to submit the case to JAMS for mediation. The JAMS mediator assigned to the case may not be the Arbitrator, unless the Parties so agree pursuant to Rule 23(b).
(b) The Parties may agree to seek the assistance of the Arbitrator in reaching settlement. By their written agreement to submit the matter to the Arbitrator for settlement assistance, the Parties will be deemed to have agreed that the assistance of the Arbitrator in such settlement efforts will not disqualify the Arbitrator from continuing to serve as Arbitrator if settlement is not reached; nor shall such assistance be argued to a reviewing court as the basis for vacating or modifying an Award.
(c) If, at any stage of the Arbitration process, all Parties agree upon a settlement of the issues in dispute and request the Arbitrator to embody the agreement in a Consent Award, the Arbitrator shall comply with such request unless the Arbitrator believes the terms of the agreement are illegal or undermine the integrity of the Arbitration process. If the Arbitrator is concerned about the possible consequences of the proposed Consent Award, he or she shall inform the Parties of that concern and may request additional specific information from the Parties regarding the proposed Consent Award. The Arbitrator may refuse to enter the proposed Consent Award and may withdraw from the case.

Rule 24. Sanctions
The Arbitrator may order appropriate sanctions for failure of a Party to comply with its obligations under any of these Rules. These sanctions may include, but are not limited to, assessment of costs, exclusion of certain evidence, or in extreme cases determining an issue or issues submitted to Arbitration adversely to the Party that has failed to comply.

Rule 25. Disqualification of the Arbitrator as a Witness or Party and Exclusion of Liability
(a) The Parties may not call the Arbitrator, the Case Manager or any other JAMS employee or agent as a witness or as an expert in any pending or subsequent litigation or other proceeding involving the Parties and relating to the dispute that is the subject of the Arbitration. The Arbitrator, Case Manager and other JAMS employees and agents are also incompetent to testify as witnesses or experts in any such proceeding.
(b) The Parties shall defend and/or pay the cost (including any attorneys' fees) of defending the Arbitrator, Case Manager and/or JAMS from any subpoenas from outside Parties arising from the Arbitration.
(c) The Parties agree that neither the Arbitrator, Case Manager nor JAMS is a necessary Party in any litigation or other proceeding relating to the Arbitration or the subject matter of the Arbitration, and neither the Arbitrator, Case Manager nor JAMS, including its employees or agents, shall be liable to any Party for any act or omission in connection with any Arbitration conducted under these Rules, including but not limited to any disqualification of or recusal by the Arbitrator.

Rule 26. Fees
(a) Each Party shall pay its pro-rata share of JAMS fees and expenses as set forth in the JAMS fee schedule in effect at the time of the commencement of the Arbitration, unless the Parties agree on a different allocation of fees and expenses. JAMS agreement to render services is jointly with the Party and the attorney or other representative of the Party in the Arbitration. The non-payment of fees may result in an administrative suspension of the case in accordance with Rule 6(c).
(b) JAMS requires that the Parties deposit the fees and expenses for the Arbitration prior to the Hearing and the Arbitrator may preclude a Party that has failed to deposit its pro-rata or agreed-upon share of the fees and expenses from offering evidence of any affirmative claim at the Hearing. JAMS may waive the deposit requirement upon a showing of good cause.
(c) The Parties are jointly and severally liable for the payment of JAMS Arbitration fees and Arbitrator compensation and expenses. In the event that one Party has paid more than its share of such fees, compensation and expenses, the Arbitrator may Award against any Party any such fees, compensation and expenses that such Party owes with respect to the Arbitration.
(d) Entities whose interests are not adverse with respect to the issues in dispute shall be treated as a single Party for purposes of JAMS assessment of fees. JAMS shall determine whether the interests between entities are adverse for purpose of fees, considering such factors as whether the entities are represented by the same attorney and whether the entities are presenting joint or separate positions at the Arbitration.

Rule 27. Bracketed (or High-Low) Arbitration Option
(a) At any time before the issuance of the Arbitration Award, the Parties may agree, in writing, on minimum and maximum amounts of damages that may be awarded on each claim or on all claims in the aggregate. The Parties shall promptly notify JAMS, and provide to JAMS a copy of their written agreement setting forth the agreed-upon maximum and minimum amounts.
(b) JAMS shall not inform the Arbitrator of the agreement to proceed with this option or of the agreed-upon minimum and

maximum levels without the consent of the Parties.

(c) The Arbitrator shall render the Award in accordance with Rule 19.

(d) In the event that the Award of the Arbitrator is between the agreed-upon minimum and maximum amounts, the Award shall become final as is. In the event that the Award is below the agreed-upon minimum amount, the final Award issued shall be corrected to reflect the agreed-upon minimum amount. In the event that the Award is above the agreed-upon maximum amount, the final Award issued shall be corrected to reflect the agreed-upon maximum amount.

Rule 28. Final Offer (or Baseball) Arbitration Option

(a) Upon agreement of the Parties to use the option set forth in this Rule, at least seven (7) calendar days before the Arbitration Hearing, the Parties shall exchange and provide to JAMS written proposals for the amount of money damages they would offer or demand, as applicable, and that they believe to be appropriate based on the standard set forth in Rule 19(b). JAMS shall promptly provide a copy of the Parties' proposals to the Arbitrator, unless the Parties agree that they should not be provided to the Arbitrator. At any time prior to the close of the Arbitration Hearing, the Parties may exchange revised written proposals or demands, which shall supersede all prior proposals. The revised written proposals shall be provided to JAMS, which shall promptly provide them to the Arbitrator, unless the Parties agree otherwise.

(b) If the Arbitrator has been informed of the written proposals, in rendering the Award the Arbitrator shall choose between the Parties' last proposals, selecting the proposal that the Arbitrator finds most reasonable and appropriate in light of the standard set forth in Rule 19(b). This provision modifies Rule 19(f) in that no written statement of reasons shall accompany the Award.

(c) If the Arbitrator has not been informed of the written proposals, the Arbitrator shall render the Award as if pursuant to Rule 19, except that the Award shall thereafter be corrected to conform to the closest of the last proposals, and the closest of the last proposals will become the Award.

(d) Other than as provided herein, the provisions of Rule 19 shall be applicable.

B.3.2 Comprehensive Arbitration Rules and Procedures

Revised March 26, 2007

TABLE OF CONTENTS

Rule 1. Scope of Rules
Rule 2. Party-Agreed Procedures
Rule 3. Amendment of Rules
Rule 4. Conflict with Law
Rule 5. Commencing an Arbitration
Rule 6. Preliminary and Administrative Matters
Rule 7. Number of Arbitrators and Appointment of Chairperson
Rule 8. Service
Rule 9. Notice of Claims
Rule 10. Changes of Claims
Rule 11. Interpretation of Rules and Jurisdictional Challenges
Rule 12. Representation
Rule 13. Withdrawal from Arbitration
Rule 14. *Ex Parte* Communications
Rule 15. Arbitrator Selection and Replacement
Rule 16. Preliminary Conference
Rule 17. Exchange of Information
Rule 18. Summary Disposition of a Claim or Issue
Rule 19. Scheduling and Location of Hearing
Rule 20. Pre-Hearing Submissions
Rule 21. Securing Witnesses and Documents for the Arbitration Hearing
Rule 22. The Arbitration Hearing
Rule 23. Waiver of Hearing
Rule 24. Awards
Rule 25. Enforcement of the Award
Rule 26. Confidentiality and Privacy
Rule 27. Waiver
Rule 28. Settlement and Consent Award
Rule 29. Sanctions
Rule 30. Disqualification of the Arbitrator as a Witness or Party and Exclusion of Liability
Rule 31. Fees
Rule 32. Bracketed (or High-Low) Arbitration Option
Rule 33. Final Offer (or Baseball) Arbitration Option
Rule 34. Optional Arbitration Appeal Procedure

Rule 1. Scope of Rules

(a) The JAMS Comprehensive Arbitration Rules and Procedures ("Rules") govern binding Arbitrations of disputes or claims that are administered by JAMS and in which the Parties agree to use these Rules or, in the absence of such agreement, any disputed claim or counterclaim that exceeds $250,000, not including interest or attorneys' fees, unless other Rules are prescribed.

(b) The Parties shall be deemed to have made these Rules a part of their Arbitration agreement whenever they have provided for Arbitration by JAMS under its Comprehensive Rules or for Arbitration by JAMS without specifying any particular JAMS Rules and the disputes or claims meet the criteria of the first paragraph of this Rule.

(c) The authority and duties of JAMS are prescribed in the agreement of the Parties and in these Rules, and may be carried out through such representatives as it may direct.

(d) JAMS may, in its discretion, assign the administration of an Arbitration to any of its offices.

(e) The term "Party" as used in these Rules includes Parties to the Arbitration and their counsel or representatives.

Rule 2. Party-Agreed Procedures

The Parties may agree on any procedures not specified herein or in lieu of these Rules that are consistent with the applicable law and JAMS policies (including, without limitation, Rules 15(i), 30 and 31). The Parties shall promptly notify JAMS of any such Party-agreed procedures and shall confirm such procedures in writing. The Party-agreed procedures shall be enforceable as if contained in these Rules.

Rule 3. Amendment of Rules

JAMS may amend these Rules without notice. The Rules in effect on the date of the commencement of an Arbitration (as defined in Rule 5) shall apply to that Arbitration, unless the Parties have specified another version of the Rules.

Rule 4. Conflict with Law

If any of these Rules, or a modification of these Rules agreed on by the Parties, is determined to be in conflict with a provision of applicable law, the provision of law will govern, and no other Rule will be affected.

Rule 5. Commencing an Arbitration

(a) The Arbitration is deemed commenced when JAMS confirms in a Commencement Letter one of the following:
  (i) The submission to JAMS of a post-dispute Arbitration agreement fully executed by all Parties and that specifies JAMS administration or use of any JAMS Rules; or
  (ii) The submission to JAMS of a pre-dispute written contractual provision requiring the Parties to arbitrate the dispute or claim and which specifies JAMS administration or use of any JAMS Rules or which the Parties agree shall be administered by JAMS; or
  (iii) The oral agreement of all Parties to participate in an Arbitration administered by JAMS or conducted pursuant to any JAMS Rules, confirmed in writing by the Parties; or
  (iv) A court order compelling Arbitration at JAMS.

(b) The Commencement Letter shall confirm that one of the above requirements for commencement has been met, that JAMS has received all payments required under the applicable fee schedule, and that the claimant has provided JAMS with contact information for all Parties along with evidence that the Demand has been served on all Parties. The date of commencement of the Arbitration is the date of the Commencement Letter.

(c) If a Party that is obligated to arbitrate in accordance with subparagraph (a) of this Rule fails to agree to participate in the Arbitration process, JAMS shall confirm in writing that Party's failure to respond or participate and, pursuant to Rule 22(j), the Arbitrator, once appointed, shall schedule, and provide appropriate notice of a Hearing or other opportunity for the Party demanding the Arbitration to demonstrate its entitlement to relief.

(d) The definition of "commencement" in these Rules is not intended to be applicable to any legal requirement, such as the statute of limitations or a contractual limitations period. The term "commencement" as used in this Rule is intended only to pertain to the operation of this and other rules (such as Rule 3, 9(a), 9(c), 13(a), 17(a), 31(a).) The tolling of the statute of limitations or a contractual limitations period shall be regarded by JAMS to occur upon the date of service of a demand for arbitration; compliance with Rule 5(a) (i), (ii), (iii) or (iv) as appropriate; and payment of any fee required of that party under the applicable fee schedule.

Rule 6. Preliminary and Administrative Matters

(a) JAMS may convene, or the Parties may request, administrative conferences to discuss any procedural matter relating to the administration of the Arbitration.

(b) At the request of a Party and in the absence of Party agreement, JAMS may determine the location of the Hearing, subject to Arbitrator review. In determining the location of the Hearing such factors as the subject matter of the dispute, the convenience of the Parties and witnesses and the relative resources of the Parties shall be considered.

(c) If, at any time, any Party has failed to pay fees or expenses in full, JAMS may order the suspension or termination of the proceedings. JAMS may so inform the Parties in order that one of them may advance the required payment. An administrative suspension shall toll any other time limits contained in these Rules, applicable statutes or the Parties' agreement.

(d) JAMS does not maintain a duplicate file of documents filed in the Arbitration. If the Parties wish to have any documents returned to them, they must advise JAMS in writing within 30 days of the conclusion of the Arbitration. If special arrangements are required regarding file maintenance or document retention, they must be agreed to in writing and JAMS reserves the right to impose an additional fee for such special arrangements.

(e) Unless the Parties' agreement or applicable law provides otherwise, JAMS may consolidate Arbitrations in the following instances:
  (i) If a Party files more than one Arbitration with JAMS, and if JAMS determines that the Arbitrations so filed have common issues of fact or law, JAMS may consolidate the Arbitrations and refer them to a single Arbitrator.
  (ii) Where a Demand or Demands for Arbitration is or are submitted naming Parties already involved in another Arbitration or Arbitrations pending under these Rules, JAMS may decide that the new case or cases will be consolidated into one or more of the pending proceedings and referred to one of the Arbitrators already appointed.
  (iii) Where a Demand or Demands for Arbitration is or are submitted naming parties that are not identical to the Parties in the existing Arbitration or Arbitrations, JAMS may decide that the new case or cases will be consolidated into one or more of the pending proceedings and referred to one of the Arbitrators already appointed.

When rendering its decision, JAMS will take into account all circumstances, including the links between the cases and the progress already made in the existing Arbitrations.

Where a third party seeks to participate in an Arbitration already pending under these Rules or where a Party to an Arbitration under these Rules seeks to compel a third party to participate in a pending Arbitration, the Arbitrator will decide on such request, taking into account all circumstances the Arbitrator deems relevant and applicable.

Unless applicable law provides otherwise, where JAMS decides to consolidate a proceeding into a pending Arbitration, the Parties to the consolidated case or cases will be deemed to have waived their right to designate an Arbitrator.

Rule 7. Number of Arbitrators and Appointment of Chairperson

(a) The Arbitration shall be conducted by one neutral Arbitrator unless all Parties agree otherwise. In these Rules, the term "Arbitrator" shall mean, as the context requires, the Arbitrator or the panel of Arbitrators in a tripartite Arbitration.

(b) In cases involving more than one Arbitrator the Parties shall agree on, or in the absence of agreement JAMS shall designate, the Chairperson of the Arbitration Panel. If the Parties and the

Arbitrator agree, the Chairperson may, acting alone, decide discovery and procedural matters.

(c) Where the Parties have agreed that each Party is to name one Arbitrator, the Arbitrators so named shall be neutral and independent of the appointing Party unless the Parties have agreed that they shall be non-neutral.

Rule 8. Service

(a) Service by a Party under these Rules is effected by providing one signed copy of the document to each Party and two copies in the case of a sole Arbitrator and four copies in the case of a tripartite panel to JAMS. Service may be made by hand-delivery, overnight delivery service or U.S. mail. Service by any of these means is considered effective upon the date of deposit of the document. Service by electronic mail or facsimile transmission is considered effective upon transmission, but only if followed within one week of delivery by service of an appropriate number of copies and originals by one of the other service methods.

(b) In computing any period of time prescribed or allowed by these Rules for a Party to do some act within a prescribed period after the service of a notice or other paper on the Party and the notice or paper is served on the Party only by U.S. Mail, three (3) calendar days shall be added to the prescribed period.

Rule 9. Notice of Claims

(a) If a matter has been submitted for Arbitration after litigation has been commenced in court regarding the same claim or dispute, the pleadings in the court case, including the complaint and answer (with affirmative defenses and counterclaims), may be filed with JAMS within fourteen (14) calendar days of the date of commencement, and if so filed, will be considered part of the record of the Arbitration. It will be assumed that the existence of such pleadings constitutes appropriate notice to the Parties of such claims, remedies sought, counterclaims and affirmative defenses. If necessary, such notice may be supplemented pursuant to Rule 9(b).

(b) If a matter has been submitted to JAMS prior to or in lieu of the filing of a case in court or prior to the filing of an answer, the Parties shall give each other notice of their respective claims, remedies sought, counterclaims and affirmative defenses (including jurisdictional challenges). Such notice may be served upon the other Parties and filed with JAMS, in the form of a Demand for Arbitration, response or answer to demand for Arbitration, counterclaim or answer or response to counterclaim. Any pleading shall include a short statement of its factual basis.

(c) Notice of claims, remedies sought, counterclaims and affirmative defenses may be served simultaneously, in which case they should be filed with JAMS within fourteen (14) calendar days of the date of commencement of the Arbitration, or by such other date as the Parties may agree. The responding Parties may, however, in their sole discretion, wait to receive the notice of claim before serving any response, including counterclaims or affirmative defenses. In this case, the response, including counterclaims and affirmative defenses, should be served on the other Parties and filed with JAMS within fourteen (14) calendar days of service of the notice of claim. If the notice of claim has been served on the responding Parties prior to the date of commencement, the response, including counterclaims and affirmative defenses, shall be served within fourteen (14) calendar days from the date of commencement.

(d) Any Party that is a recipient of a counterclaim may reply to such counterclaim, including asserting jurisdictional challenges. In such case, the reply must be served on the other Parties and filed with JAMS within fourteen (14) calendar days of having received the notice of counterclaim. No claim, remedy, counterclaim or affirmative defense will be considered by the Arbitrator in the absence of prior notice to the other Parties, unless all Parties agree that such consideration is appropriate notwithstanding the lack of prior notice.

Rule 10. Changes of Claims

After the filing of a claim and before the Arbitrator is appointed, any Party may make a new or different claim against a Party or any third Party that is subject to Arbitration in the proceeding. Such claim shall be made in writing, filed with JAMS and served on the other Parties. Any response to the new claim shall be made within fourteen (14) calendar days after service of such claim. After the Arbitrator is appointed, no new or different claim may be submitted except with the Arbitrator's approval. A Party may request a Hearing on this issue. Each Party has the right to respond to any new claim in accordance with Rule 9(c).

Rule 11. Interpretation of Rules and Jurisdictional Challenges

(a) Once appointed, the Arbitrator shall resolve disputes about the interpretation and applicability of these Rules and conduct of the Arbitration Hearing. The resolution of the issue by the Arbitrator shall be final.

(b) Whenever in these Rules a matter is to be determined by "JAMS" (such as in Rules 6; 11(d); 15(d), (f) or (g); or 31(d)), such determination shall be made in accordance with JAMS administrative procedures.

(c) Jurisdictional and arbitrability disputes, including disputes over the existence, validity, interpretation or scope of the agreement under which Arbitration is sought, and who are proper Parties to the Arbitration, shall be submitted to and ruled on by the Arbitrator. The Arbitrator has the authority to determine jurisdiction and arbitrability issues as a preliminary matter.

(d) Disputes concerning the appointment of the Arbitrator shall be resolved by JAMS.

(e) The Arbitrator may upon a showing of good cause or *sua sponte*, when necessary to facilitate the Arbitration, extend any deadlines established in these Rules, provided that the time for rendering the Award may only be altered in accordance with Rules 22(i) or 24.

Rule 12. Representation

(a) The Parties may be represented by counsel or any other person of the Party's choice. Each Party shall give prompt written notice to the Case Manager and the other Parties of the name, address, telephone and fax numbers, and email address of its representative. The representative of a Party may act on the Party's behalf in complying with these Rules.

(b) Changes in Representation. A Party shall give prompt written notice to the Case Manager and the other Parties of any change in its representation, including the name, address, telephone and fax numbers, and email address of the new representative. Such notice shall state that the written consent of the former representative, if any, and of the new representative, has been obtained and shall state the effective date of the new representation.

Rule 13. Withdrawal from Arbitration

(a) No Party may terminate or withdraw from an Arbitration after the issuance of the Commencement Letter (see Rule 5) except by written agreement of all Parties to the Arbitration.

(b) A Party that asserts a claim or counterclaim may unilaterally withdraw that claim or counterclaim without prejudice by serving written notice on the other Parties and on the Arbitrator. However, the opposing Parties may, within fourteen (14) calendar days of service of notice of the withdrawal of the claim or counterclaim, request that the Arbitrator order that the withdrawal be with prejudice. If such a request is made, it shall be determined by the Arbitrator.

Rule 14. *Ex Parte* Communications

No Party may have any *ex parte* communication with a neutral Arbitrator regarding any issue related to the Arbitration. Any necessary *ex parte* communication with a neutral Arbitrator, whether before, during or after the Arbitration Hearing, shall be conducted through JAMS. The Parties may agree to permit *ex parte* communication between a Party and a non-neutral Arbitrator.

Rule 15. Arbitrator Selection and Replacement

(a) Unless the Arbitrator has been previously selected by agreement of the Parties, JAMS may attempt to facilitate agreement among the Parties regarding selection of the Arbitrator.

(b) If the Parties do not agree on an Arbitrator, JAMS shall send the Parties a list of at least five (5) Arbitrator candidates in the case of a sole Arbitrator and ten (10) Arbitrator candidates in the case of a tripartite panel. JAMS shall also provide each Party with a brief description of the background and experience of each Arbitrator candidate. JAMS may replace any or all names on the list of Arbitrator candidates for reasonable cause at any time before the Parties have submitted their choice pursuant to subparagraph (c) below.

(c) Within seven (7) calendar days of service upon the Parties of the list of names, each Party may strike two (2) names in the case of a sole Arbitrator and three (3) names in the case of a tripartite panel, and shall rank the remaining Arbitrator candidates in order of preference. The remaining Arbitrator candidate with the highest composite ranking shall be appointed the Arbitrator. JAMS may grant a reasonable extension of the time to strike and rank the Arbitrator candidates to any Party without the consent of the other Parties.

(d) If this process does not yield an Arbitrator or a complete panel, JAMS shall designate the sole Arbitrator or as many members of the tripartite panel as are necessary to complete the panel.

(e) If a Party fails to respond to a list of Arbitrator candidates within seven (7) calendar days after its service, JAMS shall deem that Party to have accepted all of the Arbitrator candidates.

(f) Entities whose interests are not adverse with respect to the issues in dispute shall be treated as a single Party for purposes of the Arbitrator selection process. JAMS shall determine whether the interests between entities are adverse for purposes of Arbitrator selection, considering such factors as whether the entities are represented by the same attorney and whether the entities are presenting joint or separate positions at the Arbitration.

(g) If, for any reason, the Arbitrator who is selected is unable to fulfill the Arbitrator's duties, a successor Arbitrator shall be chosen in accordance with this Rule. If a member of a panel of Arbitrators becomes unable to fulfill his or her duties after the beginning of a Hearing but before the issuance of an Award, a new Arbitrator will be chosen in accordance with this Rule unless, in the case of a tripartite panel, the Parties agree to proceed with the remaining two Arbitrators. JAMS will make the final determination as to whether an Arbitrator is unable to fulfill his or her duties, and that decision shall be final.

(h) Any disclosures regarding the selected Arbitrator shall be made as required by law or within ten (10) calendar days from the date of appointment. The obligation of the Arbitrator to make all required disclosures continues throughout the Arbitration process. Such disclosures may be provided in electronic format, provided that JAMS will produce a hard copy to any Party that requests it.

(i) At any time during the Arbitration process, a Party may challenge the continued service of an Arbitrator for cause. The challenge must be based upon information that was not available to the Parties at the time the Arbitrator was selected. A challenge for cause must be in writing and exchanged with opposing Parties who may respond within seven (7) days of service of the challenge. JAMS shall make the final determination as to such challenge. Such determination shall take into account the materiality of the facts and any prejudice to the Parties. That decision will be final.

(j) Where the Parties have agreed that a Party-appointed Arbitrator is to be non-neutral, that Party-appointed Arbitrator shall not be subject to disqualification.

Rule 16. Preliminary Conference

At the request of any Party or at the direction of the Arbitrator, a Preliminary Conference shall be conducted with the Parties or their counsel or representatives. The Preliminary Conference may address any or all of the following subjects:

(a) The exchange of information in accordance with Rule 17 or otherwise;

(b) The schedule for discovery as permitted by the Rules, as agreed by the Parties or as required or authorized by applicable law;

(c) The pleadings of the Parties and any agreement to clarify or narrow the issues or structure the Arbitration Hearing;

(d) The scheduling of the Hearing and any pre-Hearing exchanges of information, exhibits, motions or briefs;

(e) The attendance of witnesses as contemplated by Rule 21;

(f) The scheduling of any dispositive motion pursuant to Rule 18;

(g) The premarking of exhibits; preparation of joint exhibit lists and the resolution of the admissibility of exhibits;

(h) The form of the Award; and

(i) Such other matters as may be suggested by the Parties or the Arbitrator.

The Preliminary Conference may be conducted telephonically and may be resumed from time to time as warranted.

Rule 17. Exchange of Information

(a) The Parties shall cooperate in good faith in the voluntary and informal exchange of all non-privileged documents and other information relevant to the dispute or claim immediately after commencement of the Arbitration. They shall complete an initial exchange of all relevant, non-privileged documents, including, without limitation, copies of all documents in their possession or control on which they rely in support of their positions, names of individuals whom they may call as witnesses at the Arbitration Hearing, and names of all experts who may be called to testify at the Arbitration Hearing, together with each expert's report that may be introduced at the Arbitration Hearing, within twenty-one (21) calendar days after all pleadings or notice of claims have been received. The Arbitrator may modify these obligations at the Preliminary Conference.

(b) Each Party may take one deposition of an opposing Party or of one individual under the control of the opposing Party. The Parties shall attempt to agree on the time, location and duration of the deposition, and if the Parties do not agree these issues shall be determined by the Arbitrator. The necessity of additional depositions shall be determined by the Arbitrator based upon the reasonable need for the requested information, the availability of other discovery options and the burdensomeness of the request on the opposing Parties and the witness.

(c) As they become aware of new documents or information, including experts who may be called upon to testify, all Parties continue to be obligated to provide relevant, non-privileged documents, to supplement their identification of witnesses and experts and to honor any informal agreements or understandings between the Parties regarding documents or information to be exchanged. Documents that were not previously exchanged, or witnesses and experts that were not previously identified, may not be considered by the Arbitrator at the Hearing, unless agreed by the Parties or upon a showing of good cause.

(d) The Parties shall promptly notify JAMS when a dispute exists regarding discovery issues. JAMS shall arrange a conference with the Arbitrator, either by telephone or in person, and the Arbitrator shall decide the dispute. With the written consent of all Parties, and in accordance with an agreed written procedure, the Arbitrator may appoint a special master to assist in resolving a discovery dispute.

Rule 18. Summary Disposition of a Claim or Issue

(a) The Arbitrator may permit any Party to file a Motion for Summary Disposition of a particular claim or issue, either by agreement of all interested Parties or at the request of one Party, provided other interested Parties have reasonable notice to respond to the request.

(b) JAMS shall facilitate the Parties' agreement on a briefing schedule and record for the Motion. If no agreement is reached, the Arbitrator shall set the briefing and Hearing schedule and contents of the record.

Rule 19. Scheduling and Location of Hearing

(a) The Arbitrator, after consulting with the Parties that have appeared, shall determine the date, time and location of the Hearing. The Arbitrator and the Parties shall attempt to schedule consecutive Hearing days if more than one day is necessary.

(b) If a Party has failed to participate in the Arbitration process, the Arbitrator may set the Hearing without consulting with that Party. The non-participating Party shall be served with a Notice of Hearing at least thirty (30) calendar days prior to the scheduled date unless the law of the relevant jurisdiction allows for or the Parties have agreed to shorter notice.

Rule 20. Pre-Hearing Submissions

(a) Subject to any schedule adopted in the Preliminary Conference (Rule 16), at least fourteen (14) calendar days before the Arbitration Hearing, the Parties shall exchange a list of the witnesses they intend to call, including any experts, a short description of the anticipated testimony of each such witness, an estimate of the length of the witness's direct testimony, and a list of exhibits. In addition, at least fourteen (14) calendar days before the Arbitration Hearing, the Parties shall identify all exhibits intended to be used at the Hearing and exchange copies of such exhibits to the extent that any such exhibit has not been previously exchanged. The Parties should pre-mark exhibits and shall attempt to resolve any disputes regarding the admissibility of exhibits prior to the Hearing. The list of witnesses, with the description and estimate of the length of their testimony and the copies of all exhibits that the Parties intend to use at the Hearing, in pre-marked form, should also be provided to JAMS for transmission to the Arbitrator, whether or not the Parties have stipulated to the admissibility of all such exhibits.

(b) The Arbitrator may require that each Party submit concise written statements of position, including summaries of the facts and evidence a Party intends to present, discussion of the applicable law and the basis for the requested Award or denial of relief sought. The statements, which may be in the form of a letter, shall be filed with JAMS and served upon the other Parties, at least seven (7) calendar days before the Hearing date. Rebuttal statements or other pre-Hearing written submissions may be permitted or required at the discretion of the Arbitrator.

Rule 21. Securing Witnesses and Documents for the Arbitration Hearing

(a) At the written request of a Party, all other Parties shall produce for the Arbitration Hearing all specified witnesses in their employ or under their control without need of subpoena. The Arbitrator may issue subpoenas for the attendance of witnesses or the production of documents either prior to or at the Hearing. Pre-issued subpoenas may be used in jurisdictions that permit them. In the event a Party or a subpoenaed person objects to the production of a witness or other evidence, the Party or subpoenaed person may file an objection with the Arbitrator, who will promptly rule on the objection, weighing both the burden on the producing Party and witness and the need of the proponent for the witness or other evidence. The Arbitrator, in order to hear a third party witness, or for the convenience of the Parties or the witnesses, may conduct the Hearing at any location unless the Arbitration agreement specifies a mandatory Hearing location.

(b) Any JAMS office may be designated a Hearing location for purposes of the issuance of a subpoena or subpoena *duces tecum* to a third party witness, unless the Arbitration agreement specifies a mandatory Hearing location. The subpoena or subpoena *duces tecum* shall be issued in accordance with the applicable law of the designated Hearing location and shall be deemed issued under that law. Objections to any subpoena or subpoena *duces tecum* shall be made and determined by the Arbitrator.

Rule 22. The Arbitration Hearing

(a) The Arbitrator will ordinarily conduct the Arbitration Hearing in the manner set forth in these Rules. The Arbitrator may vary these procedures if it is determined reasonable and appropriate to do so.

(b) The Arbitrator shall determine the order of proof, which will generally be similar to that of a court trial.

(c) The Arbitrator shall require witnesses to testify under oath if requested by any Party, or otherwise in the discretion of the Arbitrator.

(d) Strict conformity to the rules of evidence is not required, except that the Arbitrator shall apply applicable law relating to privileges and work product. The Arbitrator shall consider evidence that he or she finds relevant and material to the dispute, giving the evidence such weight as is appropriate. The Arbitrator may be guided in that determination by principles contained in the Federal Rules of Evidence or any other applicable rules of evidence. The Arbitrator may limit testimony to exclude evidence that would be immaterial or unduly repetitive, provided that all Parties are afforded the opportunity to present material and relevant evidence.

(e) The Arbitrator shall receive and consider relevant deposition testimony recorded by transcript or videotape, provided that the other Parties have had the opportunity to attend and cross-examine. The Arbitrator may in his or her discretion consider witness affidavits or other recorded testimony even if the other Parties have not had the opportunity to cross-examine, but will give that evidence only such weight as the Arbitrator deems appropriate.

(f) The Parties will not offer as evidence, and the Arbitrator shall neither admit into the record nor consider, prior settlement offers by the Parties or statements or recommendations made by a mediator or other person in connection with efforts to resolve the dispute being arbitrated, except to the extent that applicable law permits the admission of such evidence.

(g) The Hearing or any portion thereof may be conducted telephonically with the agreement of the Parties or in the discretion of the Arbitrator.

(h) When the Arbitrator determines that all relevant and material evidence and arguments have been presented, the Arbitrator shall declare the Hearing closed. The Arbitrator may defer the closing of the Hearing until a date agreed upon by the Arbitrator and the Parties, to permit the Parties to submit post-Hearing briefs, which may be in the form of a letter, and/or to make closing arguments. If post-Hearing briefs are to be submitted, or closing arguments are to be made, the Hearing shall be deemed closed upon receipt by the Arbitrator of such briefs or at the conclusion of such closing arguments.

(i) At any time before the Award is rendered, the Arbitrator may *sua sponte* or on application of a Party for good cause shown, re-open the Hearing. If the Hearing is re-opened and the re-opening prevents the rendering of the Award within the time limits specified by these Rules, the time limits will be extended until the reopened Hearing is declared closed by the Arbitrator.

(j) The Arbitrator may proceed with the Hearing in the absence of a Party that, after receiving notice of the Hearing pursuant to Rule 19, fails to attend. The Arbitrator may not render an Award solely on the basis of the default or absence of the Party, but shall require any Party seeking relief to submit such evidence as the Arbitrator may require for the rendering of an Award. If the Arbitrator reasonably believes that a Party will not attend the Hearing, the Arbitrator may schedule the Hearing as a telephonic Hearing and may receive the evidence necessary to render an Award by affidavit. The notice of Hearing shall specify if it will be in person or telephonic.

(k)(i) Any Party may arrange for a stenographic or other record to be made of the Hearing and shall inform the other Parties in advance of the Hearing. The requesting Party shall bear the cost of such stenographic record. If all other Parties agree to share the cost of the stenographic record, it shall be made available to the Arbitrator and may be used in the proceeding.

(ii) If there is no agreement to share the cost of the stenographic record, it may not be provided to the Arbitrator and may not be used in the proceeding unless the Party arranging for the stenographic record either agrees to provide access to the stenographic record at no charge or on terms that are acceptable to the Parties and the reporting service.

(iii) If the Parties agree to an Optional Arbitration Appeal Procedure (see Rule 34), they shall ensure that a stenographic or other record is made of the Hearing and shall share the cost of that record.

(iv) The Parties may agree that the cost of the stenographic record shall or shall not be allocated by the Arbitrator in the Award.

Rule 23. Waiver of Hearing

The Parties may agree to waive the oral Hearing and submit the dispute to the Arbitrator for an Award based on written submissions and other evidence as the Parties may agree.

Rule 24. Awards

(a) The Arbitrator shall render a Final Award or a Partial Final Award within thirty (30) calendar days after the date of the close of the Hearing as defined in Rule 22(h) or, if a Hearing has been waived, within thirty (30) calendar days after the receipt by the Arbitrator of all materials specified by the Parties, except (i) by the agreement of the Parties, (ii) upon good cause for an extension of time to render the Award, or (iii) as provided in Rule 22(i). The Arbitrator shall provide the Final Award or the Partial Final Award to JAMS for issuance in accordance with this Rule.

(b) Where a panel of Arbitrators has heard the dispute, the decision and Award of a majority of the panel shall constitute the Arbitration Award.

(c) In determining the merits of the dispute the Arbitrator shall be guided by the rules of law and equity agreed upon by the Parties. In the absence of such agreement, the Arbitrator shall be guided by the rules of law and equity that the Arbitrator deems to be most appropriate. The Arbitrator may grant any remedy or relief that is just and equitable and within the scope of the Parties' agreement, including but not limited to specific performance of a contract.

(d) In addition to a Final Award or Partial Final Award, the Arbitrator may make other decisions, including interim or partial rulings, orders and Awards.

(e) Interim Measures. The Arbitrator may take whatever interim measures are deemed necessary, including injunctive relief and measures for the protection or conservation of property and disposition of disposable goods. Such interim measures may take the form of an interim Award, and the Arbitrator may require security for the costs of such measures. Any recourse by a Party to a court for interim or provisional relief shall not be deemed incompatible with the agreement to arbitrate or a

waiver of the right to arbitrate.
(f) The Award of the Arbitrator may allocate Arbitration fees and Arbitrator compensation and expenses unless such an allocation is expressly prohibited by the Parties' agreement. (Such a prohibition may not limit the power of the Arbitrator to allocate Arbitration fees and Arbitrator compensation and expenses pursuant to Rule 31(c).)
(g) The Award of the Arbitrator may allocate attorneys' fees and expenses and interest (at such rate and from such date as the Arbitrator may deem appropriate) if provided by the Parties' agreement or allowed by applicable law.
(h) The Award will consist of a written statement signed by the Arbitrator regarding the disposition of each claim and the relief, if any, as to each claim. Unless all Parties agree otherwise, the Award shall also contain a concise written statement of the reasons for the Award.
(i) After the Award has been rendered, and provided the Parties have complied with Rule 31, the Award shall be issued by serving copies on the Parties. Service may be made by U.S. Mail. It need not be sent certified or registered.
(j) Within seven (7) calendar days after issuance of the Award, any Party may serve upon the other Parties and on JAMS a request that the Arbitrator correct any computational, typographical or other similar error in an Award (including the reallocation of fees pursuant to Rule 31(c)), or the Arbitrator may *sua sponte* propose to correct such errors in an Award. A Party opposing such correction shall have seven (7) calendar days in which to file any objection. The Arbitrator may make any necessary and appropriate correction to the Award within fourteen (14) calendar days of receiving a request or seven (7) calendar days after the Arbitrator's proposal to do so. The corrected Award shall be served upon the Parties in the same manner as the Award.
(k) The Award is considered final, for purposes of either an Optional Arbitration Appeal Procedure pursuant to Rule 34 or a judicial proceeding to enforce, modify or vacate the Award pursuant to Rule 25, fourteen (14) calendar days after service is deemed effective if no request for a correction is made, or as of the effective date of service of a corrected Award.

Rule 25. Enforcement of the Award
Proceedings to enforce, confirm, modify or vacate an Award will be controlled by and conducted in conformity with the Federal Arbitration Act, 9 U.S.C. Sec 1 et seq. or applicable state law.

Rule 26. Confidentiality and Privacy
(a) JAMS and the Arbitrator shall maintain the confidential nature of the Arbitration proceeding and the Award, including the Hearing, except as necessary in connection with a judicial challenge to or enforcement of an Award, or unless otherwise required by law or judicial decision.
(b) The Arbitrator may issue orders to protect the confidentiality of proprietary information, trade secrets or other sensitive information.
(c) Subject to the discretion of the Arbitrator or agreement of the Parties, any person having a direct interest in the Arbitration may attend the Arbitration Hearing. The Arbitrator may exclude any non-Party from any part of a Hearing.

Rule 27. Waiver
(a) If a Party becomes aware of a violation of or failure to comply with these Rules and fails promptly to object in writing, the objection will be deemed waived, unless the Arbitrator determines that waiver will cause substantial injustice or hardship.
(b) If any Party becomes aware of information that could be the basis of a challenge for cause to the continued service of the Arbitrator, such challenge must be made promptly, in writing, to the Arbitrator or JAMS. Failure to do so shall constitute a waiver of any objection to continued service of the Arbitrator.

Rule 28. Settlement and Consent Award
(a) The Parties may agree, at any stage of the Arbitration process, to submit the case to JAMS for mediation. The JAMS mediator assigned to the case may not be the Arbitrator or a member of the Appeal Panel, unless the Parties so agree pursuant to Rule 28(b).
(b) The Parties may agree to seek the assistance of the Arbitrator in reaching settlement. By their written agreement to submit the matter to the Arbitrator for settlement assistance, the Parties will be deemed to have agreed that the assistance of the Arbitrator in such settlement efforts will not disqualify the Arbitrator from continuing to serve as Arbitrator if settlement is not reached; nor shall such assistance be argued to a reviewing court as the basis for vacating or modifying an Award.
(c) If, at any stage of the Arbitration process, all Parties agree upon a settlement of the issues in dispute and request the Arbitrator to embody the agreement in a Consent Award, the Arbitrator shall comply with such request unless the Arbitrator believes the terms of the agreement are illegal or undermine the integrity of the Arbitration process. If the Arbitrator is concerned about the possible consequences of the proposed Consent Award, he or she shall inform the Parties of that concern and may request additional specific information from the Parties regarding the proposed Consent Award. The Arbitrator may refuse to enter the proposed Consent Award and may withdraw from the case.

Rule 29. Sanctions
The Arbitrator may order appropriate sanctions for failure of a Party to comply with its obligations under any of these Rules. These sanctions may include, but are not limited to, assessment of costs, exclusion of certain evidence, or in extreme cases determining an issue or issues submitted to Arbitration adversely to the Party that has failed to comply.

Rule 30. Disqualification of the Arbitrator as a Witness or Party and Exclusion of Liability
(a) The Parties may not call the Arbitrator, the Case Manager or any other JAMS employee or agent as a witness or as an expert in any pending or subsequent litigation or other proceeding involving the Parties and relating to the dispute that is the subject of the Arbitration. The Arbitrator, Case Manager and other JAMS employees and agents are also incompetent to testify as witnesses or experts in any such proceeding.
(b) The Parties shall defend and/or pay the cost (including any attorneys' fees) of defending the Arbitrator, Case Manager and/or JAMS from any subpoenas from outside Parties arising from the Arbitration.
(c) The Parties agree that neither the Arbitrator, Case Manager nor JAMS is a necessary Party in any litigation or other proceeding relating to the Arbitration or the subject matter of the Arbitra-

tion, and neither the Arbitrator, Case Manager nor JAMS, including its employees or agents, shall be liable to any Party for any act or omission in connection with any Arbitration conducted under these Rules, including but not limited to any disqualification of or recusal by the Arbitrator.

Rule 31. Fees

(a) Each Party shall pay its pro-rata share of JAMS fees and expenses as set forth in the JAMS fee schedule in effect at the time of the commencement of the Arbitration, unless the Parties agree on a different allocation of fees and expenses. JAMS agreement to render services is jointly with the Party and the attorney or other representative of the Party in the Arbitration. The non-payment of fees may result in an administrative suspension of the case in accordance with Rule 6(c).

(b) JAMS requires that the Parties deposit the fees and expenses for the Arbitration prior to the Hearing and the Arbitrator may preclude a Party that has failed to deposit its pro-rata or agreed-upon share of the fees and expenses from offering evidence of any affirmative claim at the Hearing. JAMS may waive the deposit requirement upon a showing of good cause.

(c) The Parties are jointly and severally liable for the payment of JAMS Arbitration fees and Arbitrator compensation and expenses. In the event that one Party has paid more than its share of such fees, compensation and expenses, the Arbitrator may award against any other Party any such fees, compensation and expenses that such Party owes with respect to the Arbitration.

(d) Entities whose interests are not adverse with respect to the issues in dispute shall be treated as a single Party for purposes of JAMS assessment of fees. JAMS shall determine whether the interests between entities are adverse for purpose of fees, considering such factors as whether the entities are represented by the same attorney and whether the entities are presenting joint or separate positions at the Arbitration.

Rule 32. Bracketed (or High-Low) Arbitration Option

(a) At any time before the issuance of the Arbitration Award, the Parties may agree, in writing, on minimum and maximum amounts of damages that may be awarded on each claim or on all claims in the aggregate. The Parties shall promptly notify JAMS and provide to JAMS a copy of their written agreement setting forth the agreed-upon maximum and minimum amounts.

(b) JAMS shall not inform the Arbitrator of the agreement to proceed with this option or of the agreed-upon minimum and maximum levels without the consent of the Parties.

(c) The Arbitrator shall render the Award in accordance with Rule 24.

(d) In the event that the Award of the Arbitrator is between the agreed-upon minimum and maximum amounts, the Award shall become final as is. In the event that the Award is below the agreed-upon minimum amount, the final Award issued shall be corrected to reflect the agreed-upon minimum amount. In the event that the Award is above the agreed-upon maximum amount, the final Award issued shall be corrected to reflect the agreed-upon maximum amount.

Rule 33. Final Offer (or Baseball) Arbitration Option

(a) Upon agreement of the Parties to use the option set forth in this Rule, at least seven (7) calendar days before the Arbitration Hearing, the Parties shall exchange and provide to JAMS written proposals for the amount of money damages they would offer or demand, as applicable, and that they believe to be appropriate based on the standard set forth in Rule 24(c). JAMS shall promptly provide a copy of the Parties' proposals to the Arbitrator, unless the Parties agree that they should not be provided to the Arbitrator. At any time prior to the close of the Arbitration Hearing, the Parties may exchange revised written proposals or demands, which shall supersede all prior proposals. The revised written proposals shall be provided to JAMS, which shall promptly provide them to the Arbitrator, unless the Parties agree otherwise.

(b) If the Arbitrator has been informed of the written proposals, in rendering the Award the Arbitrator shall choose between the Parties' last proposals, selecting the proposal that the Arbitrator finds most reasonable and appropriate in light of the standard set forth in Rule 24(c). This provision modifies Rule 24(h) in that no written statement of reasons shall accompany the Award.

(c) If the Arbitrator has not been informed of the written proposals, the Arbitrator shall render the Award as if pursuant to Rule 24, except that the Award shall thereafter be corrected to conform to the closest of the last proposals, and the closest of the last proposals will become the Award.

(d) Other than as provided herein, the provisions of Rule 24 shall be applicable.

Rule 34. Optional Arbitration Appeal Procedure

At any time before the Award becomes final pursuant to Rule 24, the Parties may agree to the JAMS Optional Arbitration Appeal Procedure. All Parties must agree in writing for such procedure to be effective. Once a Party has agreed to the Optional Arbitration Appeal Procedure, it cannot unilaterally withdraw from it, unless it withdraws, pursuant to Rule 13, from the Arbitration.

B.3.3 Class Action Procedures

Revised February 2005

TABLE OF CONTENTS

Rule 1. Applicability
Rule 2. Construction of the Arbitration Clause
Rule 3. Class Certification
Rule 4. Notice of Class Determination
Rule 5. Final Award
Rule 6. Settlement, Voluntary Dismissal, or Compromise

Rule 1. Applicability

(a) These Class Action Procedures ("Procedures") shall apply to any dispute arising out of an agreement that provides for arbitration pursuant to any of the JAMS Arbitration Rules where a party submits a dispute to arbitration on behalf of or against a class or purported class, and shall supplement any other applicable JAMS Rules. These Procedures shall also apply whenever a court refers a matter pleaded as a class action to JAMS for administration, or when a party to a pending JAMS arbitration asserts new claims on behalf of or against a class or purported class.

(b) Where inconsistencies exist between these Procedures and other JAMS Rules that apply to any dispute, these Procedures shall control. The Arbitrator has the authority to resolve any inconsistency between any agreement of the parties and these Procedures and in doing so shall endeavor to avoid any prejudice to the interests of absent members of a class or purported class.

Rule 2. Construction of the Arbitration Clause

Once appointed, the Arbitrator shall determine as a threshold matter whether the applicable arbitration clause permits the arbitration to proceed on behalf of or against a class. In construing the applicable arbitration clause, the Arbitrator shall not consider the existence of these Supplementary Rules to be a factor either in favor of or against permitting the arbitration to proceed on a class basis.

The Arbitrator may set forth his or her determination in a partial final award subject to immediate court review.

Rule 3. Class Certification

(a) **Prerequisites to a Class Arbitration.**

The Arbitrator shall determine whether the arbitration should proceed as a class action, provided that:

(i) the Arbitrator is satisfied that the arbitration clause permits the arbitration to proceed as a class arbitration, as provided in rule 2; or

(ii) a court has ordered that an Arbitrator determine whether a class arbitration may be maintained.

In making that determination, the Arbitrator shall consider the criteria enumerated in this Rule 3 and any law or agreement of the parties that the Arbitrator determines applies to the arbitration. The Arbitrator also shall determine whether one or more members of a class may act in the arbitration as representative parties on behalf of all members of the class described. The Arbitrator shall permit a class member to serve as a representative only if all of the following conditions are met:

(1) the class is so numerous that joinder of all members is impracticable,

(2) there are questions of law or fact common to the class,

(3) the claims or defenses of the representative parties are typical of the claims or defenses of the class, and

(4) the representative parties will fairly and adequately protect the interests of the class.

(b) **Class Actions Maintainable.**

An action may be maintained as a class action if the prerequisites of subdivision (a) are satisfied, and in addition:

(1) the prosecution of separate actions by or against individual members of the class would create a risk of (A) inconsistent or varying adjudications with respect to individual members of the class which would establish incompatible standards of conduct for the party opposing the class, or (B) adjudications with respect to individual members of the class that would, as a practical matter, be dispositive of the interests of the other members not parties to the adjudications or substantially impair or impede their ability to protect their interests; or

(2) the party opposing the class has acted or refused to act on grounds generally applicable to the class, thereby making appropriate final injunctive relief or corresponding declaratory relief with respect to the class as a whole; or

(3) questions of law or fact common to the members of the class predominate over any questions affecting only individual members, and a class action is superior to other available methods for the fair and efficient adjudication of the controversy. The matters pertinent to the findings include: (A) the interest of members of the class in individually controlling the prosecution or defense of separate actions; (B) the extent and nature of any litigation concerning the controversy already commenced by or against members of the class; (C) the desirability or undesirability of concentrating the arbitration of the claims in a single forum; (D) the difficulties likely to be encountered in the management of a class action.

(c) In the discretion of the Arbitrator, his or her determinations with respect to the matter of Class Certification may be set forth in a partial final award subject to immediate court review.

Rule 4. Notice of Class Determination

The Arbitrator shall direct that class members be provided the best notice practicable under the circumstances (the "Notice of Class Determination"). The Notice of Class Determination shall be given to all members who can be identified through reasonable effort. The Notice of Class Determination must concisely and clearly state in plain, easily understood language:

(1) the nature of the action;

(2) the definition of the class certified;

(3) the class claims, issues, or defenses;

(4) that a class member may enter an appearance through counsel if the member so desires, and may attend the hearings;

(5) that the Arbitrator will exclude from the class any member who requests exclusion, with information about when and how members may elect to be excluded;

(6) the binding effect of a class award on class members; and

(7) the identities of, and biographical information about, the Arbitrator, and the class representative(s) and class counsel that have been approved by the Arbitrator to represent the class.

Rule 5. Final Award

The final award on the merits in a class arbitration, whether or not favorable to the class, shall be reasoned and shall define the class with specificity. The final award shall also specify or describe those to whom the notice provided in Rule 4 was directed, those whom the Arbitrator finds to be members of the class, and those who have elected to opt out of the class.

Rule 6. Settlement, Voluntary Dismissal, or Compromise

(a)(1) Any settlement, voluntary dismissal, or compromise of the claims, issues, or defenses of an arbitration filed as a class arbitration shall not be effective unless approved by the Arbitrator.

(2) The Arbitrator must direct that notice be provided in a reasonable manner to all class members who would be bound by a proposed settlement, voluntary dismissal, or compromise.

(3) The Arbitrator may approve a settlement, voluntary dismissal, or compromise that would bind class members only after a hearing and a finding that the settlement, voluntary dismissal, or compromise is fair, reasonable, and adequate.

(b) The parties seeking approval of a settlement, voluntary dismissal, or compromise under this Rule must submit to the Arbitrator any agreement made in connection with the proposed settlement, voluntary dismissal, or compromise.

(c) The Arbitrator may refuse to approve a settlement unless it affords a new opportunity to request exclusion to individual class members who had an earlier opportunity to request exclusion but did not do so.

(d) Any class member may object to a proposed settlement, voluntary dismissal, or compromise that requires approval under this Rule. Such an objection may be withdrawn only with the approval of the Arbitrator.

B.3.4 Policy on Consumer Arbitrations Pursuant to Pre-Dispute Clauses

B.3.4.1 Minimum Standards of Procedural Fairness

Revised January 1, 2007

JAMS will administer arbitrations pursuant to mandatory pre-dispute arbitration clauses between companies and consumers[1] only if the contract arbitration clause and specified applicable rules comply with the following minimum standards of fairness.

These minimum standards for arbitration procedures are:

1. The arbitration agreement must be reciprocally binding on all parties such that: A) if a consumer is required to arbitrate his or her claims or all claims of a certain type, the company is so bound; and, B) no party shall be precluded from seeking remedies in small claims court for disputes or claims within the scope of its jurisdiction.

2. The consumer must be given notice of the arbitration clause. Its existence, terms, conditions and implications must be clear.

3. Remedies that would otherwise be available to the consumer under applicable federal, state or local laws must remain available under the arbitration clause, unless the consumer retains the right to pursue the unavailable remedies in court.

4. The arbitrator(s) must be neutral and the consumer must have a reasonable opportunity to participate in the process of choosing the arbitrator(s).

5. The consumer must have a right to an in-person hearing in his or her hometown area.

6. The clause or procedures must not discourage the use of counsel.

7. With respect to the cost of the arbitration, when a consumer initiates arbitration against the company, the only fee required to be paid by the consumer is $250, which is approximately equivalent to current Court filing fees. All other costs must be borne by the company including any remaining JAMS Case Management Fee and all professional fees for the arbitrator's services. When the company is the claiming party initiating an arbitration against the consumer, the company will be required to pay all costs associated with the arbitration.

8. In California, the arbitration provision may not require the consumer to pay the fees and costs incurred by the opposing party if the consumer does not prevail.

9. The arbitration provision must allow for the discovery or exchange of non-privileged information relevant to the dispute.

10. An Arbitrator's Award will consist of a written statement stating the disposition of each claim. The award will also provide a concise written statement of the essential findings and conclusions on which the award is based.

---

[1] These standards are applicable where a company systematically places an arbitration clause in its agreements with individual consumers and there is minimal, if any, negotiation between the parties as to the procedures or other terms of the arbitration clause. A consumer is defined as an individual who seeks or acquires any goods or services, including financial services, primarily for personal family or household purposes. These standards do not apply to the use of arbitration in resolving disputes arising from commercial transactions between a lender and commercial borrowers or a company and commercial customers or to matters involving underinsured motorists. Nor do they apply if the agreement to arbitrate was negotiated by the individual consumer and the company.

B.3.4.2 Disclosures for California Consumer Arbitrations

Pursuant to Section 1281.96 of the California Code of Civil Procedure, JAMS provides information regarding consumer arbitrations administered in California. This information includes, among other things, the name of the non-consumer party, the result of the consumer arbitration and the number of past arbitrations and mediations JAMS has had with the non-consumer party beginning with the January 1, 2003 commencement date. The first report was made available April 1, 2003 for the preceding quarter and the website will be updated quarterly thereafter.

Download quarterly disclosures pursuant to CCP 1281.96

[*Editor's Note: For the latest version of JAMS's quarterly disclosure, please visit www.jamsadr.com and click on the live weblink in the version of this document which may be found on that website.*]

Pursuant to Standard 8(b)(1) of the California Judicial Council Standards of Ethics for Arbitrators in Commercial Arbitrations, consumer arbitration institutional disclosures are available for cases involving Kaiser Permanente and Related Entities.

Download summary report pursuant to Standard 8(b)(1)

Download detailed report pursuant to Standard 8(b)(1)

[*Editor's Note: For the latest version of JAMS's summary and detailed Standard 8(b)(1) reports, please visit www.jamsadr.com and click on the live weblink in the version of this document which may be found on that website.*]

If you have questions or comments, please email info@jamsadr.com.

Appendix C Sample Discovery

These documents are also available in Microsoft Word and Adobe Acrobat (PDF) format on the CD-Rom accompanying this volume.

C.1 Interrogatories and Document Requests Directed to Credit Card Issuer

IN THE CIRCUIT COURT FOR PRINCE GEORGE'S COUNTY, MARYLAND

[CONSUMERS],	)
Plaintiffs,	)
	)
v.	)
	)
CHEVY CHASE BANK,	)
F.S.B., a corporation, and	)
FIRST USA BANK, N.A., a	)
corporation,	)
Defendants.	)

INFORMATION TO BE SOUGHT THROUGH WRITTEN INTERROGATORIES

The following is a list of the types of information which Plaintiffs will seek, through written interrogatories, should this Court find that it needs additional factual information before it can decide the pending motion to compel arbitration:

1. Identity, including court, caption and civil number, of any case filed, and the current status of that case, in which Chevy Chase Bank, F.S.B. ("Chevy Chase Bank") or First USA Bank, N.A. ("First USA Bank") has been a party where a court has refused to enforce an arbitration clause included in their cardholder agreement.

2. Identity, including court, caption and civil number and current status of that case, in which Chevy Chase Bank or First USA Bank has been a party where a court has enforced an arbitration clause included in their cardholder agreement.

3. Identification of all communications between Chevy Chase Bank and/or First USA Bank and the American Arbitration Association ("AAA") since January 1, 1994.

4. Identification of all communications between Chevy Chase Bank, First USA Bank and any of its employees, agents, etc., and any arbitrators associated with the AAA, since January 1, 1994.

5. The names of every Chevy Chase Bank officer, director, employee and/or agent who has had any conversations with AAA employees or arbitrators together with an identification of all notes or memos, however recorded, referring or relating to those conversations.

6. Details of all business dealings and financial relationships between AAA or any arbitrators associated with AAA and Chevy Chase Bank and/or First USA Bank.

7. How many claims have been brought by cardholders against Chevy Chase Bank and/or First USA Bank in arbitration since the Virginia Document allegedly was made effective.

8. The identity of each arbitrator who heard one or more of those claims.

9. Information as to (a) how many claims that arbitrator heard; (b) how many of those claims did the arbitrator rule in favor of Chevy Chase Bank and/or First USA Bank; and (c) how many of those claims did the arbitrator rule for the cardholder?

10. Identification of any documents or memos relating to complaints or queries from cardholders concerning the arbitration clause in the Virginia Document or any other alleged agreement.

11. Identification of any documents, specifically including letters or memoranda however recorded, reflecting any cardholder complaints about the arbitration process after the cardholder had gone through an arbitration.

12. Identity of the individual or individuals at Chevy Chase Bank who made the decision for the Bank to adopt an arbitration clause and the reasons for that decision.

13. Identification of any and all documents, specifically including letters and internal memoranda however recorded, relating to the decision by the Bank to use AAA as the arbitrator and the reasons for that decision.

14. Identification of all documents relating to any attempts, or decisions to attempt, to change the provisions of the arbitration clause after the initial date when the Virginia Document was considered by the Bank to be effective.

15. Identification of any "readership surveys" or similar studies of which the Bank is aware which commented on the likelihood that cardholders would read material tucked in their billing envelopes, and when the Bank became aware of them.

16. Identification of any studies, memoranda however recorded, or in-house discussions among officers, directors, employees and/or agents of the Bank about the number or percentage of cardholders who actually read their stuffers and/or other types of communications to cardholders.

17. Identification of any and all documents, including statistical surveys, studies, correspondence and/or memoranda however re-

359

corded, discussing any relationships between AAA and/or its individual arbitrators and the banking industry.

18. Identification of all documents of any kind whatsoever which indicate any amount of income derived by AAA and/or its arbitrators from arbitration of credit card disputes between Chevy Chase Bank and/or First USA Bank since January 1, 1995, divided by year.

19. On a month-to-month basis with January 1, 1995, the total number of cardholders assessed over-limit fees.

20. On a month-to-month basis starting with January 1, 1995, the total number of cardholders assessed interest rates greater than 24%.

21. When did the Bank first attempt to amend the cardholder agreements to add an arbitration clause? If preferred, the Bank should produce complete and legible copies of any notices it used to notify cardholders of this amendment and state how that notice was provided to cardholders (e.g., as a "bill stuffer" or in a separate mailing.)

22. The identity of each and every lawsuit containing class action allegations filed against Chevy Chase Bank and/or First USA Bank from January 1, 1990 to date, including court, caption and case number.

23. The identity of each class action against Chevy Chase Bank and/or First USA Bank where a class has been certified. Be sure to identify the caption of the case, the court in which it was filed and the names of counsel or, in the Bank prefers, it may produce a complete and legible copy of any pleading providing this information.

24. Identification of any contracts, agreements or other arrangements between Chevy Chase Bank and/or First USA Bank and the American Arbitration Association ("AAA") and the identity of each person at the bank who has had contact with AAA since January 1, 1995.

25. The total number of the Bank's cardholders who have utilized arbitration through AAA since January 1, 1996.

26. The total number of the Bank's cardholders who refused to accept the amendment to the cardholder agreement which attempted to add the arbitration clause to the agreement and state the number of such cardholders whose accounts were thus terminated.

27. The total number of times Chevy Chase Bank and/or First USA Bank has initiated arbitration proceedings against any cardholders through AAA since January 1, 1998.

28. The identification of each and every lawsuit Chevy Chase Bank and/or First USA Bank has initiated against cardholders since January 1, 1995. NOTE: Be sure to include any accounts assigned to third parties for collection where litigation was initiated.

29. Identify each and every lawsuit filed since January 1, 1996 where Chevy Chase Bank and/or First USA Bank has invoked or attempted to invoke arbitration through AAA.

DOCUMENTS TO BE REQUESTED

The following is a list of the types of documents which Plaintiffs will seek, through a request for production of documents, should this Court find that it needs additional information before it can decide the pending motion to compel arbitration:

1. All documents identified in Answers to Interrogatories.

2. Complete and legible copies of each and every cardholder agreement version used by Chevy Chase Bank and/or First USA Bank from January 1, 1996 to date.

3. Complete and legible copies of each and every version of periodic statement form used by Chevy Chase Bank and/or First USA Bank from January 1, 1995 to date. NOTE: Be sure to indicate the time period during which each form was in use.

4. Complete copies of all documents in the Banks' files and archives relating to the named Plaintiffs for the time period January 1, 1995 to date.

5. Documents reflecting the total number of customer charged over-limit fees on a month-by-month basis during each month from January 1, 1995 to date.

6. Copies of any rejections by cardholders of the Virginia Document's attempted Amendments.

7. Copies of all rejections by cardholders of any attempted revision of any cardholder agreement since January 1, 1996.

[*Attorney for Plaintiff*]

C.2 Discovery Directed to Credit Card Issuers[1]

C.2.1 Interrogatories

IN THE CIRCUIT COURT OF
MONTGOMERY COUNTY, ALABAMA

————————————————)
[*CONSUMER*],   )
                            Plaintiff,)
)
v.   )
)
FIRST USA BANK, N.A.;   )
VISA U.S.A, INC.; et al.,   )
                            Defendants.)
————————————————)

**PLAINTIFF'S SECOND SET OF INTERROGATORIES
TO DEFENDANT FIRST USA BANK, N.A.**

Pursuant to Rule 33 of the Alabama Rules of Civil Procedure, Plaintiff propounds the following interrogatories to be answered by First USA Bank, N.A., in the manner and form prescribed by law:

1. State the full name, age, social security number, and address, including street, street number, city, state, zip code, and telephone number, job title, and job description of each person answering these interrogatories.

2. State the full name and last known address, including street, street number, city, state, zip code, and telephone number of each and every person known to Defendant or Defendant's attorneys who have any knowledge regarding the facts and circumstances surrounding the arbitration clause upon which Defendant has moved to compel arbitration, including, but not limited to, persons who participated in the decision to institute the use of said arbitration clause, persons who drafted the arbitration clause and/or

---

[1] This discovery was provided by Mark Englehart of Beasley, Allen, Crow, Methvin, Portis & Miles, Montgomery, Alabama. Mr. Englehart wishes to acknowledge that certain of this discovery is based on discovery drafted by Britton Monts, a private attorney in Dallas, Texas.

had input into its language, persons in charge of educating Defendant's employees with regard to the to the arbitration clause.

3. If any of the individuals listed above, or whom Defendant proposes to use at the trial of this matter, are employed by this Defendant, please describe the nature of such employment relationship, the present position of the individual, and how long the person has been in the employ of this Defendant.

4. Who made the decision to implement an arbitration in this Defendant's contracts?

5. Why does this Defendant utilize arbitration clauses?

6. Who drafted the arbitration clause relied upon by this Defendant in its claim that Plaintiff's claims are subject to arbitration?

7. Please state the date on which this Defendant began to include arbitration clauses in its contracts.

8. Have revisions been made to the arbitration clause since it was first utilized by this Defendant? If so, please provide the following information:
(a) On what dates were revisions made;
(b) The name and job title of the party(ies) who made the decision to revise the arbitration clause;
(c) The name and job title of the party(ies) who drafted the revision(s).

9. For the five (5) years prior to implementing the arbitration clause, please state the following:
(a) The number of lawsuits filed against this Defendant;
(b) The nature of the claim of each lawsuit; and
(c) In whose favor the claim was resolved and the amount.

10. For the five (5) years prior to implementing the arbitration clause, please state the following:
(a) The number of claims settled prior to litigation;
(b) The nature of each claim; and
(c) In whose favor the claim was resolved, the amount, and a description of any other relief.

11. State the number of disputes that have proceeded to arbitration.

12. As to each dispute that has proceeded to arbitration, state the following:
(a) The nature of the claim;
(b) In whose favor the claim was resolved and the amount;
(c) The name and address of the arbitrator; and
(d) The name and address of the arbitration association.

13. State the number of disputes in which you have invoked arbitration.

14. Fully describe each and every document or thing which this Defendant will rely upon or seek to introduce in defense of Plaintiffs' claims with regard to the arbitration clause.

15. State with particularity each and every document which discloses to customers or potential customers the fact that by transacting business with this Defendant the customer is subject to an alleged arbitration agreement.

16. Identify each and every fact and produce each and every document which supports your contention that the claims alleged in the Complaint are subject to arbitration.

17. Does this Defendant allow a customer to change or negotiate for change of any term in its card member agreement or contract? If so, please state with specificity the items a customer would be allowed to change on this Defendant's contract. If the answer is no, please state with specificity the reasons why a customer is not allowed to change or negotiate for terms in the contract.

18. Do any employees of this Defendant have the authority to change the language in the arbitration clause in negotiation with a customer? If so, please state the name, address, and title of the employee(s).

19. Can a customer negotiate concession in response to the arbitration clause used by this Defendant?

20. Can a customer negotiate removal of the arbitration clause used by this Defendant?

21. Would this Defendant transact business with a customer who refused to sign an arbitration clause? If not, why not?

22. How many customers have signed arbitration agreements with their contracts with this Defendant?

23. Is this Defendant aware of any competitor of this Defendant which does not require a customer to sign an arbitration agreement? If so, please state the name and address of the competitor.

24. Is this Defendant aware of any competitor of this Defendant which requires a customer to sign an arbitration agreement? If so, please state the name and address of the competitor.

25. Is this Defendant a member of any arbitration association? If so, which arbitration association?

26. Has this Defendant paid money to any arbitration association? If so, state how much and to which arbitration association.

[*Attorney for Plaintiff*]

C.2.2 Document Requests

IN THE CIRCUIT COURT OF
MONTGOMERY COUNTY, ALABAMA

```
_____  )
[CONSUMER],              )
              Plaintiff, )
                         )
v.                       )
                         )
FIRST USA BANK, N.A.;    )
VISA U.S.A., INC.; et al.,)
             Defendants. )
_____  )
```

PLAINTIFF'S SECOND REQUEST FOR PRODUCTION TO DEFENDANT FIRST USA BANK, N.A.

Pursuant to Rule 34 of the Alabama Rules of Civil Procedure, Plaintiff requests that Defendant First USA Bank, N.A. ("First USA") produce the following documents and things:

1. Each and every document, manual, memorandum, etc. used in educating this Defendant's employees or customers about arbitration.

2. A copy of the arbitration provision(s) utilized by First USA, and a copy of any and all revisions of the same since the original was put into use. (For each such original or revision, indicate the inclusive dates during which such version of that arbitration provision was in effect.)

3. All letters, memos, e-mails and other documents evidencing or reflecting communications between National Arbitration Forum (NAF) and First USA since January 1, 1995.

4. All brochures, circulars, advertisements and all other documents containing business solicitation directed to First USA by NAF since January 1, 1995. Any reference to First USA includes any predecessor in interest.

5. All documents provided to First USA by NAF informing First USA that if First USA chooses to use NAF for arbitration, First USA will not face consumer class actions.

6. Copies of any written contracts or other agreements entered into with NAF since January 1, 1995.

7. All studies, analysis or other documents prepared by NAF to show the benefits to financial institutions of arbitration before NAF as opposed to the American Arbitration Association.

8. Complete and legible copies of any and all contracts or business proposals submitted by NAF to First USA since January 1, 1995, soliciting First USA to use NAF for consumer arbitration.

9. Documents reflecting all officers and directors of First USA since January 1, 1997.

10. A **complete original** of each mailing sent by First USA (or any predecessor in interest) to [*Plaintiff*], in the exact format, manner, packaging, etc., as originally sent to plaintiff. For each such mailing, state the date (or best approximation of the date) on which First USA sent such mailing.

11. All documents evidencing, reflecting, referring to, or relating to any study, analysis, survey, research, etc., by, on behalf of, or used by First USA concerning how much, what parts, what format, what type, etc. of First USA mailings are read or are projected to be read by mail recipients, or are not read by mail recipients.

12. Any and all contracts or other agreements between NAF and First USA regarding the exclusive use of NAF for consumer disputes.

13. Documents showing the total number of arbitrations by NAF involving First USA since January 1, 1997.

14. Documents showing the total number of arbitrations involving First USA since January 1, 1997, in which the respondent or party opposing First USA did not respond, appear or otherwise defend against a notice of arbitration by First USA.

15. Documents showing the total number of arbitrations involving First USA since January 1, 1997, in which the notice of arbitration was served by a party against First USA, or was served by a party other than First USA.

16. Documents showing the awards or outcomes of all arbitrations involving First USA since January 1, 1997, in which the notice of arbitration was served by a party against First USA, or was served by a party other than First USA.

17. Documents showing the awards or outcomes of all arbitrations involving First USA since January 1, 1997, in which a party obtained relief against First USA through arbitration.

18. Documents showing the highest median, and mean monetary awards in all arbitrations involving First USA since January 1, 1997, in which a party obtained relief against First USA through arbitration.

19. Documents showing the awards or outcomes of all arbitrations involving First USA and a consumer or consumers since January 1, 1997, in which the notice of arbitration was served by a party against First USA, or was served by a party other than First USA.

20. Documents showing the awards or outcomes of all arbitrations involving First USA since January 1, 1997, in which a consumer or consumers obtained relief against First USA through arbitration.

21. Documents showing the highest, median, and mean monetary awards in all arbitrations involving First USA since January 1, 1997, in which a consumer or consumers obtained relief against First USA through arbitration.

22. Documents showing the total number of arbitrations involving First USA since January 1, 1997, in which the arbitrator awarded punitive damages to a consumer against First USA.

23. All documents showing the number of lawsuits filed against First USA by cardholders during the three (3) year period immediately before First USA sought to institute arbitration of cardholder disputes.

24. All documents showing the number of lawsuits filed against First USA by cardholders during the three (3) year period immediately before First USA sought to institute arbitration of cardholder disputes, in which plaintiff(s) obtained some monetary recovery from First USA.

25. All documents showing the amounts paid to plaintiffs or the outcomes of all lawsuits filed against First USA by cardholders during the three (3) year period immediately before First USA sought to institute arbitration of cardholder disputes.

26. All documents showing the highest, median, and mean monetary awards in all lawsuits filed by cardholders against First USA during the three (3) year period immediately before First USA sought to institute arbitration of cardholder disputes, in which plaintiff(s) obtained some monetary recovery from First USA.

27. All documents reflecting any punitive damage award (including the name to the case, case number, and jurisdiction) obtained by plaintiff(s) in lawsuits filed by cardholder(s) against First USA during the three (3) year period immediately before First USA sought to institute arbitration of cardholder disputes.

28. A copy of any documents pertaining to or reflecting claims that have proceeded to arbitration and/or the outcome.

29. Any documents received from any arbitration association in which First USA is a member.

30. Any documents received from any arbitration association.

31. Any documents, other than the arbitration agreement itself, available to explain to customers the meaning of the arbitration provision.

[*Attorney for Plaintiff*]

C.2.3 Additional Document Requests and Interrogatories

IN THE CIRCUIT COURT OF
MONTGOMERY COUNTY, ALABAMA

————————————)
[*CONSUMER*],)
                Plaintiff,)
)
v.)
)
FIRST USA BANK, N.A.;)
VISA U.S.A., INC.; et al.,)
             Defendants.)
————————————)

Sample Discovery

PLAINTIFF'S THIRD REQUEST FOR PRODUCTION AND INTERROGATORIES TO DEFENDANT FIRST USA BANK, N.A.

Pursuant to Rules 33 and 34 of the Alabama Rules of Civil Procedure, Plaintiff propounds the following interrogatories to be answered by Defendant First USA Bank, N.A. ("First USA"), in the manner and form prescribed by law, and requests that First USA produce the following documents and things:

INTERROGATORIES

1. Has First USA used any arbitration provider other than the National Arbitration Forum (NAF) to arbitrate any dispute with a cardmember? If so, please state for each such provider:
   (a) The name and address of the provider;
   (b) The number of arbitrations involving First USA handled by that provider;
   (c) The inclusive dates during which First USA used that provider;
   (d) All reasons why First USA used that particular provider rather than another provider; and
   (e) All reasons why First USA chose to use NAF instead of such other provider that had been used by First USA.

In addition, please produce all letters, memos, e-mails and other documents relating in any way to the decision by First USA to use that provider or the decision by First USA to use NAF instead of that provider.

2. Identify each current or former officer of First USA who serves or has served as an officer, shareholder, director, board member, advisory committee member, or arbitrator with NAF, is or has otherwise been affiliated with NAF, or has or has had any financial interest in NAF. For each such person, please state his/her name, position with First USA, business address, and position or other relationship (including the amount of any financial interest) with NAF.

3. From the date of First USA's implementation of an arbitration provision in cardmember agreements to the present, please state the following:
   (a) The number of lawsuits filed against First USA;
   (b) The nature of the claim(s) of each lawsuit; and
   (c) In whose favor the claim was resolved; and for each case,
   (d) The style, case number, and court in which it is or was pending; and
   (e) The manner in which it was resolved (e.g., jury verdict, settled, dismissed on summary judgment, arbitrated after motion to compel arbitration granted, dismissed after motion to compel arbitration granted, still pending), the amount, and, if identified, the amount of punitive damages and the amount of compensatory damages or other monetary relief.

4. Please state the number (or approximate number) of persons who were existing First USA cardmembers to whom the arbitration provision was mailed upon its implementation by First USA.

5. Please state the beginning and ending dates of each "round" of mailings by which First USA cardmembers were informed of First USA's implementation of an arbitration provision in its cardmember agreement.

6. Please state the number of cardmembers who have closed their accounts with First USA for the express reason that First USA had implemented an arbitration provision in its cardmember agreement.

REQUEST FOR PRODUCTION

1. All letters, memos, e-mails and other documents evidencing, referring to, or relating in any way to First USA's decision to adopt any arbitration provision in the cardmember agreement, or to any deliberations relating to such decision, including but not limited to:
   a. All letters, memos, e-mails and other documents considered by First USA in making such decision;
   b. All letters, memos, e-mails and other documents relating in any way to any proposed arbitration provision that was not adopted;
   c. All letters, memos, e-mails and other documents relating in any way to any cost projection, any cost-benefit analysis, or any anticipated (or realized) costs and/or benefits of the decision to adopt an arbitration provision;
   d. All letters, memos, e-mails and other documents relating in any way to any proposal to provide arbitration services solicited or received from any arbitration provider other than the National Arbitration Forum (NAF), or relating to the analysis of any such proposal;
   e. All letters, memos, e-mails and other documents relating in any way to First USA's decision to use NAF as First USA's sole arbitration provider;
   f. All letters, memos, e-mails and other documents relating in any way to communications with NAF regarding First USA's decision to use NAF as an arbitration provider.

2. All letters, memos, e-mails and other documents relating in any way to communications with NAF concerning the identity, qualifications or other characteristics of arbitrators used by NAF.

3. All letters, memos, e-mails and other documents relating in any way to communications with NAF regarding modification of NAF rules or proposed modification of NAF rules.

4. All documents relating to any arbitration involving First USA since January 1, 1997, in which the cardmember "prevailed," as that term was used by First USA in response to Plaintiff's second set of interrogatories and second request for production to First USA.

5. All documents relating to any arbitration involving First USA since January 1, 1997, in which the notice of arbitration was served by a party against First USA, or was served by a party other than First USA.

6. All documents relating to any arbitration involving First USA since January 1, 1997, in which the arbitrator awarded punitive damages to a party against First USA.

7. All documents relating to any arbitration involving First USA since January 1, 1997, in which a party adverse to First USA requested waiver or reduction of fees or any other expense or cost associated with the arbitration.

8. All documents relating to any arbitration involving First USA since January 1, 1997, in which the arbitrator granted the request of a party adverse to First USA for waiver or reduction of fees or any other expense or cost associated with the arbitration.

9. All documents relating to any arbitration involving First USA since January 1, 1997, in which the arbitrator, without request of a

party, granted to a party adverse to First USA a waiver or reduction of fees or any other expense or cost associated with the arbitration.

10. Documents reflecting the total number of arbitrations involving First USA since January 1, 1997, in which the final arbitration award assessed against the cardmember (or required the cardmember to pay) First USA's fees, expenses or costs associated with the arbitration.

11. All documents reflecting or relating to communications with NAF that do **not** relate to a specific arbitration proceeding.

12. All documents relating to any arbitration involving First USA since January 1, 1997, in which there was a "participatory hearing award," as that term was used by First USA in response to Plaintiff's second set of interrogatories and second request for production to First USA.

13. All documents reflecting **actual mailing** of the arbitration provision(s) at issue **to Plaintiff**, [*Plaintiff*].

14. All documents reflecting **actual receipt** of the arbitration provision(s) at issue **by Plaintiff**, [*Plaintiff*].

15. All scripting, question-and-answer formats, or other documents designed to inform, train, or be used by customer service representatives or other agents or employees of First USA in responding to customer inquiries about arbitration.

16. A copy of all information posted at any First USA-affiliated internet web site or at www.cardmember services.com since January 1, 1997, relating in any way to First USA's implementation of an arbitration provision in its cardmember agreement, or to arbitration.

17. All documents analyzing, reflecting or relating in any way to the nature, volume or frequency of questions or requests for information by First USA cardmembers relating to arbitration since First USA's implementation of an arbitration provision.

18. Documents reflecting the number of persons who were existing First USA cardmembers to whom the arbitration provision was mailed upon its implementation by First USA.

19. Documents reflecting the beginning and ending dates of each "round" of mailings by which First USA cardmembers were informed of First USA's implementation of an arbitration provision in its cardmember agreement.

20. Documents reflecting the number of cardmembers who have closed their accounts with First USA for the express reason that First USA had implemented an arbitration provision in its cardmember agreement.

21. All documents reflecting or relating to account closings or to any analysis of account closings by cardmembers for the stated reason that First USA had implemented an arbitration provision in its cardmember agreement.

22. Documents reflecting any increased rate of cardmembers closing their accounts after First USA implemented an arbitration provision in its cardmember agreement (as compared to the normal, usual or expected rate of account closings).

23. Documents reflecting statistics concerning the normal, usual or expected rate of account closings by First USA cardmembers.

24. All documents reflecting or relating to any analysis of any increased rate of account closings by cardmembers after First USA implemented an arbitration provision in its cardmember agreement (as compared to the normal, usual or expected rate of account closings).

25. A **complete original** sample or exemplar of each version of the mailing by which First USA informed existing cardmembers of First USA's implementation of an arbitration provision, in the exact size, format, manner, packaging, etc., as when mailed (including the outside envelope, the form of any billing statement, and any statement inserts).

26. If not included in your response to the preceding request, a **complete original** sample or exemplar of each version of the mailing by which First USA informed existing cardmembers who had no account balance of First USA's implementation of an arbitration provision, in the exact size, format, manner, packaging, etc., as when mailed (including the outside envelope, the form of any billing statement, and any statement inserts).

27. Any list maintained by First USA of individuals to serve as arbitrators.

28. The resume, curriculum vita and any other documents relating to the background and qualifications of persons who serve or have served as arbitrators in arbitrations involving First USA.

29. All documents relating to any arbitration involving First USA that proceeded as a classwide or class arbitration.

30. Please produce a privilege log that states, for each document withheld from disclosure on a claim of privilege, the date the document was created, the name and position of the author, the name and position of each recipient, the subject of the document, and a detailed summary of the contents of the document.

[*Attorney for Plaintiff*]

ITEMS FROM SECOND REQUEST FOR PRODUCTION TO FIRST USA

1. Each and every document, manual, memorandum, etc. used in educating this Defendant's employees or customers about arbitration.

2. A copy of the arbitration provision(s) utilized by First USA, and a copy of any and all revisions of the same since the original was put into use. (For each such original or revision, indicate the inclusive dates during which such version of that arbitration provision was in effect.)

3. All letters, memos, e-mails and other documents evidencing or reflecting communications between National Arbitration Forum (NAF) and First USA since January 1, 1995.

4. All brochures, circulars, advertisements and all other documents containing business solicitation directed to First USA by NAF since January 1, 1995. Any reference to First USA includes any predecessor in interest.

5. All documents provided to First USA by NAF informing First USA that if First USA chooses to use NAF for arbitration, First USA will not face consumer class actions.

6. Copies of any written contracts or other agreements entered into with NAF since January 1, 1995.

7. All studies, analysis or other documents prepared by NAF to show the benefits to financial institutions of arbitration before NAF as opposed to the American Arbitration Association.

8. Complete and legible copies of any and all contracts or business proposals submitted by NAF to First USA since January 1, 1995, soliciting First USA to use NAF for consumer arbitration.

9. Documents reflecting all officers and directors of First USA since January 1, 1997.

10. A **complete original** of each mailing sent by First USA (or any predecessor in interest) to Plaintiff [*Plaintiff*], in the exact format, manner, packaging, etc., as originally sent to Plaintiff. For each such mailing, state the date (or best approximation of the date) on which First USA sent such mailing.

11. All documents evidencing, reflecting, referring to, or relating to any study, analysis, survey, research, etc., by, on behalf of, or used by First USA concerning how much, what parts, what format, what type, etc. of First USA mailings are read or are projected to be read by mail recipients, or are not read by mail recipients.

12. Any and all contracts or other agreements between NAF and First USA regarding the exclusive use of NAF for consumer disputes.

13. Documents showing the total number of arbitrations by NAF involving First USA since January 1, 1997.

14. Documents showing the total number of arbitrations involving First USA since January 1, 1997, in which the respondent or party opposing First USA did not respond, appear or otherwise defend against a notice of arbitration by First USA.

15. Documents showing the total number of arbitrations involving First USA since January 1, 1997, in which the notice of arbitration was served by a party against First USA, or was served by a party other than First USA.

16. Documents showing the awards or outcomes of all arbitrations involving First USA since January 1, 1997, in which the notice of arbitration was served by a party against First USA, or was served by a party other than First USA.

17. Documents showing the awards or outcomes of all arbitrations involving First USA since January 1, 1997, in which a party obtained relief against First USA through arbitration.

18. Documents showing the highest median, and mean monetary awards in all arbitrations involving First USA since January 1, 1997, in which a party obtained relief against First USA through arbitration.

19. Documents showing the awards or outcomes of all arbitrations involving First USA and a consumer or consumers since January 1, 1997, in which the notice of arbitration was served by a party against First USA, or was served by a party other than First USA.

20. Documents showing the awards or outcomes of all arbitrations involving First USA since January 1, 1997, in which a consumer or consumers obtained relief against First USA through arbitration.

21. Documents showing the highest, median, and mean monetary awards in all arbitrations involving First USA since January 1, 1997, in which a consumer or consumers obtained relief against First USA through arbitration.

22. Documents showing the total number of arbitrations involving First USA since January 1, 1997, in which the arbitrator awarded punitive damages to a consumer against First USA.

23. All documents showing the number of lawsuits filed against First USA by cardholders during the three (3) year period immediately before First USA sought to institute arbitration of cardholder disputes.

24. All documents showing the number of lawsuits filed against First USA by cardholders during the three (3) year period immediately before First USA sought to institute arbitration of cardholder disputes, in which Plaintiff(s) obtained some monetary recovery from First USA.

25. All documents showing the amounts paid to Plaintiffs or the outcomes of all lawsuits filed against First USA by cardholders during the three (3) year period immediately before First USA sought to institute arbitration of cardholder disputes.

26. All documents showing the highest, median, and mean monetary awards in all lawsuits filed by cardholders against First USA during the three (3) year period immediately before First USA sought to institute arbitration of cardholder disputes, in which Plaintiff(s) obtained some monetary recovery from First USA.

27. All documents reflecting any punitive damage award (including the name to the case, case number, and jurisdiction) obtained by Plaintiff(s) in lawsuits filed by cardholder(s) against First USA during the three (3) year period immediately before First USA sought to institute arbitration of cardholder disputes.

28. A copy of any documents pertaining to or reflecting claims that have proceeded to arbitration and/or the outcome.

29. Any documents received from any arbitration association in which First USA is a member.

30. Any documents received from any arbitration association.

31. Any documents, other than the arbitration agreement itself, available to explain to customers the meaning of the arbitration provision.

[*Attorney for Plaintiff*]

C.2.4 *Notice of Deposition*

IN THE CIRCUIT COURT OF
MONTGOMERY COUNTY, ALABAMA

```
_____  )
[CONSUMER]               )
              Plaintiff, )
                         )
v.                       )
                         )
FIRST USA BANK, N.A.;    )
VISA U.S.A., INC.; et al.)
             Defendants. )
_____  )
```

PLAINTIFF'S NOTICE OF DEPOSITION

TO: First USA Bank, N.A., by and through its attorney of record,
[*Attorney for Defendant*],
[*address*].

PLEASE TAKE NOTICE that Plaintiff intends to take the oral depositions of 1) [*Deponent 1*], 2) [*Deponent 2*], and 3) First USA Bank, N.A. ("First USA"), in accordance with Rules 30(b)(1), (5) and (6), Alabama Rules of Civil Procedure. First USA is directed to designate the person or persons most knowledgeable about the following matters to testify on its behalf:

1. All communications between National Arbitration Forum and First USA since January 1, 1996.

2. All agreements between National Arbitration Forum and First USA since January 1, 1996.

3. All documents sent by National Arbitration Forum to First USA since January 1, 1996.

4. All documents sent by First USA to National Arbitration Forum since January 1, 1996.

5. Any relationship between First USA and National Arbitration Forum since January 1, 1996.

6. The number of First USA card members for each year since 1997.

7. The process by which First USA selected National Arbitration Forum to serve as arbitrator on all card member-related actions,

including the identity of all persons involved in selecting National Arbitration Forum and all actions taken by First USA to decide upon National Arbitration Forum as arbitrator.

8. The process by which First USA amended its card member agreement to implement an arbitration provision as to its card members, including but not limited to all notices sent to card members informing them of the arbitration provision, all corporate resolutions or other evidence of corporate decision making reflecting the decision to adopt the arbitration provision, and all steps taken to ensure compliance with applicable laws or regulations governing the adoption of amendments to card member agreements.

9. The planning, design, preparation and packaging of each version of the mailing by which First USA informed existing cardholders of First USA's implementation of an arbitration provision.

10. The planning, design, preparation and packaging of each version of the mailing by which First USA informed existing cardholders who had no account balance of First USA's implementation of an arbitration provision.

11. The actual mailing to Plaintiff, [*Plaintiff*], of the arbitration provision(s) made the subject of First USA's motion to compel arbitration.

12. The actual receipt by Plaintiff, [*Plaintiff*], of the arbitration provision(s) made the subject of First USA's motion to compel arbitration.

13. All documents relating in any way to the actual mailing to or receipt by Plaintiff, [*Plaintiff*], of the arbitration provision(s) made the subject of First USA's motion to compel arbitration.

14. All reasons for selecting National Arbitration Forum to serve as arbitrator, as well as the identity of all other arbitration providers considered by First USA and First USA's reasons for deciding against the use of any other provider.

15. All investigation, negotiations, discussions and considerations made or conducted by First USA with respect to National Arbitration Forum before amending the First USA card member agreement to implement an arbitration provision as to its card members.

16. All arbitrations between First USA and any card members in which National Arbitration Forum is or has served as arbitrator. This topic includes but is not limited to issues such as (a) the number of arbitrations initiated by First USA against card members as compared to the number of arbitrations initiated by card members against First USA, (b) the process or procedure by which a card member is notified of a demand or request for arbitration made by First USA, (c) all actual and potential costs associated with each arbitration, (d) the nature or type of relief sought or awarded in each arbitration, (e) the length of time used to resolve each arbitration, (f) frequency or number of requests for fee or expense waivers or reductions by card members in arbitrations with First USA, (g) decisions (including frequency or number of decisions) granting requests for fee or expense waivers or reductions by card members, or sua sponte waiving or reducing the fees or expenses of card members, in arbitrations with First USA, (h) decisions (including frequency or number of decisions) denying card member requests for waiver or reduction of fees or expenses in arbitrations with First USA, (i) decisions (including frequency or number of decisions) imposing First USA's costs, expenses and/or fees on card members in arbitrations with First USA, (j) requests by card members for punitive damages in arbitrations with First USA, (k) decisions (including frequency or number of decisions) awarding a card member punitive damages in arbitrations with First USA, (l) requests by card members for injunctive or other non-monetary/equitable relief in arbitrations with First USA, (m) requests by card members for injunctive or other non-monetary/equitable relief in lawsuits filed against First USA that were then compelled to arbitration, (n) decisions awarding a card member injunctive or other non-monetary/equitable relief in arbitrations with First USA, (o) decisions denying or failing to award a card member injunctive or other non-monetary/equitable relief in arbitrations with First USA, (p) arbitrations between any card member and First USA that was processed through National Arbitration Forum's class arbitration or class claim arbitration (or similar) procedure, (q) and any procedural mechanisms available to administer numerous consumer claims involving common questions of fact or law which would be similar or analogous to the mechanisms provided for by Rule 23 of the Federal Rules of Civil Procedure.

17. The number of card members who are not subject to the arbitration provision adopted by First USA as part of its card member agreement and the number of such card members of who have made balance transfers to a First USA Visa card from another card pursuant to a special or reduced introductory interest rate since January 1, 1997.

18. All costs incurred by First USA per year in connection with prosecuting or defending any arbitration before the National Arbitration Forum between First USA and any card member(s) (including any arbitral award or other amount assessed against First USA) since First USA's initial implementation of an arbitration provision.

19. All costs incurred by First USA per year in connection with prosecuting or defending litigation between First USA and any card member(s) (including any judgment against First USA or settlement amount paid or to be paid by First USA) since First USA's initial implementation of an arbitration provision.

20. All costs incurred by First USA per year in connection with prosecuting or defending litigation between First USA and any card member(s) (including any judgment against First USA or settlement amount paid or to be paid by First USA) from January 1, 1993 until First USA's initial implementation of an arbitration provision.

21. Class action complaints or claims filed in litigation by any card member(s) against First USA from January 1, 1993 until First USA's initial implementation of an arbitration provision. This topic includes but is not limited to (a) nature of claims, (b) nature of relief sought, (c) whether a class was certified, (d) outcome of each suit (e.g., whether dismissed before trial, settled, tried; amount and type of any relief awarded or agreed to).

22. Class action complaints or claims filed in litigation by any card member(s) against First USA from First USA's initial implementation of an arbitration provision to the present. This topic includes but is not limited to (a) nature of claims, (b) nature of relief sought, (c) whether a class was certified, (d) efforts by First USA to compel arbitration, (e) success of efforts by First USA to compel arbitration, (f) outcome of each suit (e.g., whether dismissed before trial, settled, tried, arbitrated; amount and type of any relief awarded or agreed to).

23. Complaints or claims filed in litigation by any card member(s) against First USA from January 1, 1993 until First USA's initial implementation of an arbitration provision. This topic includes but is not limited to (a) nature of claims, (b) nature of relief

sought, (c) outcome of each suit (e.g., whether dismissed, settled, tried; amount and type of any relief awarded or agreed to).

24. Complaints or claims filed in litigation by any card member(s) against First USA from First USA's initial implementation of an arbitration provision to the present. This topic includes but is not limited to (a) nature of claims, (b) nature of relief sought, (c) efforts by First USA to compel arbitration, (d) success of efforts by First USA to compel arbitration, (e) outcome of each suit (e.g., whether dismissed before trial, settled, tried, arbitrated; amount and type of any relief awarded or agreed to).

25. Complaints or claims filed in litigation by First USA against any person who or entity which is not a card member, from First USA's initial implementation of an arbitration provision to the present. This topic includes but is not limited to (a) nature of claims, (b) nature of relief sought, (c) efforts by any party to compel or pursue arbitration, (d) success of efforts by any party to compel or pursue arbitration, (e) outcome of each suit (e.g., whether dismissed before trial, settled, tried, arbitrated; amount and type of any relief awarded or agreed to).

26. Relationship between First USA in-house counsel and First USA outside counsel in litigation between card member(s) and First USA. This topic includes but is not limited to (a) administrative processing of litigation by in-house counsel, (b) maintenance of records relating to outcomes of litigation.

27. Any analysis by or for First USA relating to any difference(s) between (a) arbitrations involving card member(s) and First USA, and (b) litigation involving card member(s) and First USA (including but not limited to any comparative cost-benefit analysis, comparison of costs or outcomes, comparison between frequency and/or success of card member litigation (i) before First USA's initial implementation of an arbitration provision and (ii) after such implementation).

28. Any analysis of outcomes or results in cases involving card member(s) and First USA arbitrated before the National Arbitration Forum (including but not limited to outcomes or results in the aggregate, outcomes or results before individual arbitrators, number of arbitrations decided by individual arbitrators).

29. Communications between First USA and National Arbitration Forum concerning any proceeding in which challenge was made to the validity or enforceability of an arbitration provision or in which any party objected to arbitration (e.g., opposed a motion to compel arbitration).

30. Contracts between First USA and any person who or entity which is not a card member, specifically including but not limited to the presence of an arbitration provision, from January 1, 1997 to the present.

31. Documents that Plaintiff has requested be produced by First USA.

The depositions will be taken on [date], beginning at [time], and [date] beginning at [time] and continuing until concluded, at [location].

The deposition will be recorded and transcribed by a licensed court reporter in accordance with Rule 30 of the Alabama Rules of Civil Procedure. Please take further notice that this deposition may be taken by non-stenographic means (video).

C.2.5 Subpoena for Document Production to National Arbitration Forum

IN THE CIRCUIT COURT OF
MONTGOMERY COUNTY, ALABAMA

[CONSUMER]	)
Plaintiff,	)
	)
v.	)
	)
FIRST USA BANK, N.A.;	)
VISA U.S.A., INC.; et al.	)
Defendants.	)

CIVIL SUBPOENA FOR PRODUCTION OF DOCUMENTS, ETC., UNDER RULE 45

TO: National Arbitration Forum
    Custodian of Records
    [address]

You are hereby commanded to do each of the following acts at the instance of the Plaintiff within fifteen (15) days of the date after service of this Subpoena.

Produce for inspection at the office of [*Attorney for Plaintiff*], [*address*], the documents and things described in Exhibit "A" attached hereto.

Such productions and inspection is to take place at the place where the documents or things are regularly kept or at some other reasonable place designated by you.

You are further advised that other parties to the action in which this Subpoena have been issued have the right to be present at the time of such production or inspection.

You have the option to deliver or mail legible copies of the documents or things to [*Attorney for Plaintiff*], at the attorney for the party causing the issuance of this Subpoena, but you may condition such activity on your part upon the payment in advance by the party causing the issuance of this Subpoena of the reasonable costs of making such copies.

The Plaintiff agrees to pay all reasonable expenses incurred by you at the aforementioned time and place.

You have the right to object at any time prior to the date set forth in this Subpoena for compliance. Should you choose to object, you should communicate such objection in writing to the party causing the issuance of this Subpoena and stating, with respect to any item or category to which objection is made, your reasons for such objection.

[*date*]
[*Clerk*]

                                            [*Attorney for Plaintiff*]

EXHIBIT "A"

Definitions

As used herein, the following terms shall have the meanings indicated below.

1. "Person" shall mean and include a natural person, individual, partnership, firm, corporation or any kind of business or legal entity, its agents or employees.

2. As used herein, "identify" or "identity" used in reference to an individual person means to state his full name and present address, his present or last known position and business affiliation, and his position and business affiliation at the time in question. "Identify" or "identity" when used in reference to a document means to state the date and author, type of document (e.g., letter, memorandum, telegram, chart, etc.), or some other means of identifying it, and the present location or custodian of some or any copies thereof. "Identify" when used in reference to a verbal or oral communication means to state the date of the communication, the identity of the speaker and the person or persons to whom directed, the content of the communication, and the identity of any persons present when it occurred. The term "identify" when used in connection with any act, omission or other conduct means to specifically describe the act, omission, or conduct, to identify the individual who committed it, the date of its commission and the place of its commission.

3. "Defendant" refers to First USA Bank, N.A., and to each person who, with respect to the subject matter of the request, was or is acting on said Defendant's behalf, including any consultants, experts, investigators, agents (such as Bank One or First USA, Inc.) or other persons acting on said Defendant's behalf.

4. "You" or "your" refers to National Arbitration Forum.

5. "NAF" refers to National Arbitration Forum.

6. "AAA" refers to American Arbitration Association.

7. "Communication" shall mean any transmission of information, the information transmitted, and any process by which information is transmitted, and shall include written or recorded communications and oral communications.

8. As used herein, the term "document" shall mean every document or tangible thing which may be produced, inspected, copied, tested or sampled within the broadest scope of Rule 34(a), Ala. R. Civ. P, that is in your possession, control, custody and knowledge or obtainable through the exercise of reasonable diligence, which refers to or was prepared before, during, and after the events alleged in Plaintiff's complaint. The term "document" includes, but is not limited to, correspondence, memoranda, memoranda of agreements, assignments, meeting minutes, stenographic or handwritten notes, agendas, instructional materials, handouts, diaries, notebooks, reports, account books, checks, statements, studies, surveys, analyses, publications, books, pamphlets, periodicals, catalogues, brochures, schedules, circulars, bulletins, notices, instructions, manuals, journals, data sheets, work sheets, statistical compilations, data processing cards, microfilms, computer records (including electronic mail, printouts, floppy or magnetic storage media), maps, floor plans, blueprints, tapes, photographs (positive or negative prints), drawings, films, video tapes, pictures, voice recordings, and every copy of such writing or record when such copy contains any commentary or notation whatsoever that does not appear on the original. Plaintiff expressly intends for the term "document" to include any attachments or exhibits to the requested document or any other documents referred to in the requested document or incorporated into the document by reference.

9. "Relate to," "reflect," "discussing," "surrounding," "relevant" or "evidence" means any and all information which refers to, pertain to, reflect upon, are in any way logically or factually connected with or may afford any information regarding the matter discussed.

10. The singular form of a word used herein shall be construed to mean the plural and the plural to mean the singular when doing so would ensure the provision of additional information or more complete answers and to avoid the questions herein being considered ambiguous, inaccurate or confusing.

11. "And" and "or" as used herein shall be construed as conjunctive or disjunctive to ensure the provision of additional information or more complete answers and to avoid the questions herein being considered ambiguous, inaccurate or confusing.

Requested Documents

1. Documents reflecting all officers, directors and shareholders of NAF since January 1, 1997.

2. Copies of the articles of incorporation and bylaws of NAF.

3. All letters, memos, e-mails and other written documents evidencing or reflecting communications between NAF and First USA Bank, N.A. ("First USA") since January 1, 1995.

4. All brochures, circulars, advertisements and all other documents containing business solicitation directed to First USA and/or any other banks or credit providing entities since January 1, 1995.

5. All documents provided by you to financial institutions and other corporations informing them that if they choose to use NAF for arbitration, they will not face consumer class actions.

6. Complete copies of all rules of procedure governing arbitration before NAF since January 1, 1995. NOTE: If you have different rules for different types of disputes, please produce complete copies of rules for each and every type of dispute. For each set of rules of procedure, indicate the inclusive dates during which such set of rules was in effect.

7. Copies of any written contracts or other agreements entered into with First USA and/or Bank One since January 1, 1995.

8. All brochures, circulars, advertisements and all other documents containing business solicitation directed to Bank One and/or any other banks or credit providing entities since January 1, 1995.

9. All letter, memos, e-mails and other documents reflecting communications between NAF and Alan C. Kaplinsky since January 1, 1995 regarding the subject of arbitration of consumer disputes.

10. All studies, analyses or other documents prepared by NAF to show the benefits to financial institutions of arbitration before NAF as opposed to AAA.

11. Complete and legible copies of any and all business proposals submitted by NAF to any financial institution, included but not limited to First USA and Bank One since January 1, 1995, soliciting them to use NAF for consumer arbitrations.

12. Any and all contracts or other agreements between NAF and all other credit providers besides First USA regarding the exclusive use of NAF for consumer disputes.

13. Documents identifying any and all advertising agencies, marketing firms and printing companies used by NAF to create, and distribute marketing and advertising documents directed toward financial institutions and other corporations since January 1, 1995.

14. Documents showing the total number of arbitrations involving First USA since January 1, 1997.

Sample Discovery

15. Documents showing the total number of arbitrations involving First USA since January 1, 1997 in which the respondent or party opposing First USA did not respond, appear or otherwise defend against a notice of arbitration by First USA.

16. Documents showing the total number of arbitrations involving First USA since January 1, 1997, in which the notice of arbitration was served by a party against First USA, or was served by a party other than First USA.

17. Documents showing the awards or outcomes of all arbitrations involving First USA since January 1, 1997, in which the notice of arbitration was served by a party against First USA, or was served by a party other than First USA.

18. Documents showing the awards or outcomes of all arbitrations involving First USA since January 1, 1997, in which a party obtained relief against First USA through arbitration.

19. Documents showing the highest, median, and mean monetary awards in all arbitrations involving First USA since January 1, 1997, in which a party obtained relief against First USA through arbitration.

20. Documents showing the awards or outcomes of all arbitrations involving First USA and a consumer or consumers since January 1, 1997, in which the notice of arbitration was served by a party against First USA, or was served by a party other than First USA.

21. Documents showing the awards or outcomes of all arbitrations involving First USA since January 1, 1997, in which a consumer or consumers obtained relief against First USA through arbitration.

22. Documents showing the highest, median, and mean monetary awards in all arbitrations involving First USA since January 1, 1997, in which a consumer or consumers obtained relief against First USA through arbitration.

23. Documents showing all monies paid by First USA (or in its behalf) to NAF since January 1, 1995.

24. Documents showing all monies paid by Bank One to NAF since January 1, 1995.

25. Documents reflecting any monies paid to any officer, director and/or shareholder of NAF by First USA and/or Bank One since January 1, 1995.

26. Documents reflecting any monies paid to any affiliate of NAF by First USA and/or Bank One since January 1, 1995.

27. Documents showing total revenue by NAF for each calendar or fiscal year since January 1, 1995.

28. Complete financial statements for NAF for each calendar or fiscal year since January 1, 1995.

29. Complete list of all arbitrators currently used by the NAF throughout the United States, including any biographies, resumes, or curriculum vitae of each arbitrator.

C.2.6 Second Subpoena for Document Production to National Arbitration Forum

IN THE CIRCUIT COURT OF
MONTGOMERY COUNTY, ALABAMA

[CONSUMER]   )
        Plaintiff,)
)
v.   )
)
FIRST USA BANK, N.A.;)
VISA U.S.A., INC.; et al.)
        Defendants.)

SECOND CIVIL SUBPOENA FOR PRODUCTION OF DOCUMENTS ETC., UNDER RULE 45

TO: National Arbitration Forum
    Custodian of Records
    [address]

You are hereby commanded to do each of the following acts at the instance of the Plaintiff within fifteen (15) days of the date after service of this Subpoena.

Produce for inspection at the office of [*Attorney for Plaintiff*], the documents and things described in Exhibit "A" attached hereto.

Such productions and inspection is to take place at the place where the documents or things are regularly kept or at some other reasonable place designated by you.

You are further advised that other parties to the action in which this Subpoena have been issued have the right to be present at the time of such production or inspection.

You have the option to deliver or mail legible copies of the documents or things to [*Attorney for Plaintiff*], at the attorney for the party causing the issuance of this Subpoena, but you may condition such activity on your part upon the payment in advance by the party causing the issuance of this Subpoena of the reasonable costs of making such copies.

The Plaintiff agrees to pay all reasonable expenses incurred by you at the aforementioned time and place.

You have the right to object at any time prior to the date set forth in this Subpoena for compliance. Should you choose to object, you should communicate such objection in writing to the party causing the issuance of this Subpoena and stating, with respect to any item or category to which objection is made, your reasons for such objection.

[*date*]
[*Clerk*]

                                                                    [*Attorney for Plaintiff*]

EXHIBIT "A"

Definitions

As used herein, the following terms shall have the meanings indicated below.

1. "Person" shall mean and include a natural person, individual, partnership, firm, corporation or any kind of business or legal entity, its agents or employees.

2. As used herein, "identify" or "identity" used in reference to an individual person means to state his full name and present address, his present or last known position and business affiliation, and his position and business affiliation at the time in question. "Identify" or "identity" when used in reference to a document means to state the date and author, type of document (e.g., letter, memorandum, telegram, chart, etc.), or some other means of identifying it, and the present location or custodian of some or any copies thereof. "Identify" when used in reference to a verbal or oral communication means to state the date of the communication, the identity of the speaker and the person or persons to whom directed, the content of the communication, and the identity of any persons present when it occurred. The term "identify" when used in connection with any act, omission or other conduct means to specifically describe the act, omission, or conduct, to identify the individual who committed it, the date of its commission and the place of its commission.

3. "Defendant" refers to First USA Bank, N.A., and to each person who, with respect to the subject matter of the request, was or is acting on said Defendant's behalf, including any consultants, experts, investigators, agents (such as Bank One or First USA, Inc.) or other persons acting on said Defendant's behalf.

4. "You" or "your" refers to National Arbitration Forum.

5. "NAF" refers to National Arbitration Forum.

6. "AAA" refers to American Arbitration Association.

7. "Communication" shall mean any transmission of information, the information transmitted, and any process by which information is transmitted, and shall include written or recorded communications and oral communications.

8. As used herein, the term "document" shall mean every document or tangible thing which may be produced, inspected, copied, tested or sampled within the broadest scope of Rule 34(a), Ala. R. Civ. P., that is in your possession, control, custody and knowledge or obtainable through the exercise of reasonable diligence, which refers to or was prepared before, during, and after the events alleged in Plaintiff's complaint. The term "document" includes, but is not limited to, correspondence, memoranda, memoranda of agreements, assignments, meeting minutes, stenographic or handwritten notes, agendas, instructional materials, handouts, diaries, notebooks, reports, account books, checks, statements, studies, surveys, analyses, publications, books, pamphlets, periodicals, catalogues, brochures, schedules, circulars, bulletins, notices, instructions, manuals, journals, data sheets, work sheets, statistical compilations, data processing cards, microfilms, computer records (including electronic mail, printouts, floppy or magnetic storage media), maps, floor plans, blueprints, tapes, photographs (positive or negative prints), drawings, films, video tapes, pictures, voice recordings, and every copy of such writing or record when such copy contains any commentary or notation whatsoever that does not appear on the original. Plaintiff expressly intends for the term "document" to include any attachments or exhibits to the requested document or any other documents referred to in the requested document or incorporated into the document by reference.

9. "Relate to," "reflect," "discussing," "surrounding," "relevant" or "evidence" means any and all information which refers to, pertain to, reflect upon, are in any way logically or factually connected with or may afford any information regarding the matter discussed.

10. The singular form of a word used herein shall be construed to mean the plural and the plural to mean the singular when doing so would ensure the provision of additional information or more complete answers and to avoid the questions herein being considered ambiguous, inaccurate or confusing.

11. "And" and "or" as used herein shall be construed as conjunctive or disjunctive to ensure the provision of additional information or more complete answers and to avoid the questions herein being considered ambiguous, inaccurate or confusing.

Requested Documents

1. Documents reflecting the following (regardless of whether the information requested in the various subparts is contained in one document or in separate documents):
   a. The total number of arbitration proceedings initiated before NAF since January 1, 1997.
   b. The total number of arbitration proceedings initiated before NAF since the date of the first arbitration proceeding initiated with NAF by First USA Bank, N.A. ("First USA").
   c. The total number of awards in arbitration proceedings before NAF since January 1, 1997.
   d. The total number of awards in arbitration proceedings before NAF since the date of the first arbitration proceeding initiated with NAF by First USA.
   e. The total number of awards in arbitration proceedings before NAF involving First USA.

2. Lists of, or documents reflecting, the following (whether the information requested in the various subparts is contained in one document or in separate documents):
   a. All officers, directors and employees of NAF, by name, position/title with NAF, and business address.
   b. All current NAF arbitrators by name and business address.
   c. All former NAF arbitrators by name and last known business address.

3. A current or the most recent available resume or curriculum vitae for each current NAF arbitrator (including any NAF officer or director who issues orders or has entered awards in NAF arbitration proceedings), or, if unavailable, comparable documents identifying each such person's qualifications as an arbitrator.

4. A current or the most recent available resume or curriculum vitae for each former NAF arbitrator (including any NAF officer or director who has issued orders or entered awards in NAF arbitration proceedings), or, if unavailable, comparable documents identifying each such person's qualifications.

5. Documents reflecting the following (whether the information requested in the various subparts is contained in one document or separate documents):
   a. The number of arbitrations handled or processed by each NAF arbitrator (former or current) involving First USA.
   b. The number of arbitrations handled or processed by each NAF arbitrator (former or current), including arbitrations not involving First USA Bank, since the date of the first arbitration proceeding initiated with NAF by First USA.
   c. The number of awards entered by each NAF arbitrator (former or current) involving First USA.
   d. The number of awards entered by each NAF arbitrator (former or current) since the date of the first arbitration proceeding initiated with NAF by First USA.

6. All documents relating to any of the following:

a. Any arbitration proceeding involving First USA since January 1, 1997, in which the cardmember "prevailed," as that term was used by First USA in response to Plaintiff's second set of interrogatories and second request for production to First USA in this civil action.

b. Any arbitration proceeding involving First USA since January 1, 1997, in which the notice of arbitration was served by a party against First USA, or was served by a party other than First USA.

c. Any arbitration proceeding involving First USA since January 1, 1997, in which the arbitrator awarded punitive damages to a party against First USA.

d. Any arbitration proceeding involving First USA since January 1, 1997, in which a party adverse to First USA requested waiver or reduction of fees or any other expense or cost associated with the arbitration proceeding.

e. Any arbitration proceeding before NAF involving First USA since January 1, 1997, in which the arbitrator **granted** the request of a party adverse to First USA for waiver or reduction of fees or any other expense or cost associated with the arbitration.

f. Any arbitration proceeding before NAF involving First USA since January 1, 1997, in which the arbitrator, **without** request of a party, granted to a party adverse to First USA a waiver or reduction of fees or any other expense or cost associated with the arbitration.

g. Any arbitration proceeding before NAF involving First USA since January 1, 1997, in which there was a "participatory hearing award."

h. Any arbitration proceeding before NAF involving First USA that proceeded as a classwide or class arbitration.

i. Any arbitration proceeding before NAF that proceeded as a classwide or class arbitration.

7. Documents reflecting the total number of arbitrations before NAF involving First USA since January 1, 1997, in which the final arbitration award assessed against the cardmember (or required the cardmember to pay) First USA's fees expenses or costs associated with the arbitration.

8. All documents reflecting or relating to communications with First USA or Bank One that do **not** relate to a specific arbitration proceeding.

9. Documents reflecting the total amount of fees and other monies paid to NAF from all sources since the date of the first arbitration proceeding initiated with NAF by First USA.

10. All documents relating to any arbitration proceeding involving First USA in which the party adverse to First USA was awarded any relief against First USA.

11. All documents relating to training of arbitrators, and/or guidelines to arbitrators for the conduct of arbitrations or rendition of decisions (excluding the rules of procedure governing arbitration before NAF since January 1, 1995, which Plaintiff requested in item 6 in his first civil subpoena for production of documents). For each such document, indicate the inclusive dates during which it was in effect.

12. A list of, or documents reflecting, all entities that currently use NAF as an arbitration provider.

13. A list of, or documents reflecting, all entities that have used NAF (or any direct predecessor in interest) as an arbitration provider.

14. Documents reflecting, for each entity listed or identified in response to item 12 and 13 above, the number of arbitration proceedings involving that entity.

15. A list of, or documents reflecting, the twenty (20) entities which have been involved in the highest number of arbitration proceedings before NAF, and, for each such entity, the number of arbitration proceedings involving that entity.

16. A list of, or documents reflecting, each entity that identifies NAF as its arbitration provider in a form arbitration agreement or provision; and, if known, the number or estimated number of parties (whether persons or entities) to have entered into each such agreement or agreed to each such provision.

17. All documents relating to NAF's Class Claims Resolution Program, including but not limited to all documents relating to NAF's decision to adopt such a program, the start-up and frequency of use of such program, the advertising or marketing of such program (specifically including but not limited to advertising and marketing materials), the identity and qualifications of the arbitrators in such program, the rules or procedures governing arbitrations conducted under that program, or the fees and costs associated with arbitrations conducted under that program. (Plaintiff does **not** seek, in connection with this request, documents relating to the facts or outcomes of individual arbitrations that may have been conducted under that program.)

18. Copy of the questions asked in the Legal Dispute Study, conducted in approximately 1999 by Roper Starch Worldwide, on behalf of the Institute for Advanced Dispute Resolution, as referenced in a November 1999 press release that is attached hereto as Exhibit B [*omitted*].

19. Copy of the questions asked in any survey or poll relating to arbitration or alternative dispute resolution since January 1, 1997 commissioned by or conducted on behalf of NAF, the Institute for Advanced Dispute Resolution, or any predecessor in interest to or any organization affiliated with NAF.

20. Copy of all articles, papers, columns in newspapers or other periodicals, and other publications by Edward Anderson, Roger Haydock, or any other current or former director, officer, arbitrator or employee of NAF relating to arbitration or alternative dispute resolution since January 1, 1996.

21. Copy of all issues of the *Forum* or other newsletter or publication or periodical by NAF or any direct predecessor in interest.

22. Copy of any brief (including but not limited to any amicus brief), including all exhibits or attachments, filed by or on behalf of NAF in support of upholding the validity or enforceability of an arbitration provision or in support of a party seeking to enforce an arbitration provision.

23. Copy of any deposition, hearing testimony or trial testimony of any officer, director, agent, representative or employee of NAF, in any proceeding in which challenge was made to the validity or enforceability of an arbitration provision or in which any party objected to arbitration (e.g., opposed a motion to compel arbitration).

24. Copy of any affidavit, declaration or other sworn statement of any officer, director, agent, representative or employee of NAF, made in support of the validity or enforceability of an arbitration provision or in support of a party seeking to enforce an arbitration provision.

25. Copy of any survey or analysis of outcomes or results in cases arbitrated before NAF.

26. Copy of any survey or analysis of outcomes or results in cases arbitrated before NAF as compared to outcomes or results in litigated cases, including but not limited to the survey or analysis referenced in the article attached as Exhibit C hereto [*omitted*].

27. All documents relating in any way to each survey or analysis identified in response to the preceding two (2) items, including but not limited to methodology, raw data, the survey instrument, survey questions, the identity of the person(s) or entity(ies) performing such survey or analysis, any interim or preliminary findings or analyses, press releases, and marketing or related materials that reference such survey or analysis.

28. Copy of any survey or analysis of customer satisfaction with the services provided by NAF, and any documents relating in any way to such survey or analysis.

29. All documents reflecting or relating to the reasons for any decision to amend any rule or provision in NAF's rules or code of procedure, including but not limited to provisions for fees or costs.

30. A list of, or documents reflecting, all lawsuits known to you in which a party has opposed a motion to compel arbitration before NAF, Equilaw, or any predecessor in interest to NAF, or in which a provision calling for arbitration before NAF, Equilaw, or any predecessor in interest to NAF has been challenged as invalid or unenforceable, including for each lawsuit the style, case number, and court in which it is or was pending.

31. A list of, or documents reflecting, all lawsuits known to you in which a motion to compel arbitration before NAF, Equilaw, or any predecessor in interest to NAF has been denied (either in the trial court or on appeal), or in which a provision calling for arbitration before NAF, Equilaw, or any predecessor in interest to NAF has been held invalid or unenforceable (either in the trial court or on appeal), including for each lawsuit the style, case number, and court in which it is or was pending.

32. A list of, or documents reflecting, all lawsuits in which any party sought testimony or production of documents from NAF, or from any officer, director, agent, representative or employee of NAF, in connection with a dispute over the validity or enforceability of an arbitration provision, including for each lawsuit the style, case number, and court in which it is or was pending.

33. Copy of all press releases issued by NAF.

34. Copy of all advertisements (whether print or other media), letters or other mail solicitations, facsimile transmissions, e-mail solicitations, brochures, flyers, charts; recordings or transcripts of speeches, lectures, addresses, interviews or other presentations by any officer, director, agent, representative or employee of NAF, as well as any documents or tangible things (including but not limited to published/written seminar materials or handouts) distributed in connection with such speech, etc.; and any other documents or tangible things used to explain, promote or market NAF or its programs or services. (For any print advertisement, identify the publication(s) in which it appeared and the date of publication.)

35. Please produce a privilege log that states, for each document withheld from disclosure on a claim of privilege, the date the document was created, the name and position of the author, the name and position of each recipient, the subject of the document, and a detailed summary of the contents of the document.

Documents Requested in First NAF Subpoena

1. Documents reflecting all officers, directors and shareholders of NAF since January 1, 1997.

2. Copies of the articles of incorporation and bylaws of NAF.

3. All letters, memos, e-mails and other written documents evidencing or reflecting communications between NAF and First USA since January 1, 1995.

4. All brochures, circulars, advertisements and all other documents containing business solicitation directed to First USA and/or any other banks or credit providing entities since January 1, 1995.

5. All documents provided by you to financial institutions and other corporations informing them that if they choose to use NAF for arbitration, they will not face consumer class actions.

6. Complete copies of all rules of procedure governing arbitration before NAF since January 1, 1995. NOTE: If you have different rules for different types of disputes, please produce complete copies of rules for each and every type of dispute. For each set of rules of procedure, indicate the inclusive dates during which such set of rules was in effect.

7. Copies of any written contracts or other agreements entered into with First USA and/or Bank One since January 1, 1995.

8. All brochures, circulars, advertisements and all other documents containing business solicitation directed to Bank One and/or any other banks or credit providing entities since January 1, 1995.

9. All letter, memos, e-mails and other documents reflecting communications between NAF and Alan C. Kaplinsky since January 1, 1995 regarding the subject of arbitration of consumer disputes.

10. All studies, analyses or other documents prepared by NAF to show the benefits to financial institutions of arbitration before NAF as opposed to AAA.

11. Complete and legible copies of any and all business proposals submitted by NAF to any financial institution, included but not limited to First USA and Bank One since January 1, 1995, soliciting them to use NAF for consumer arbitrations.

12. Any and all contracts or other agreements between NAF and all other credit providers besides First USA regarding the exclusive use of NAF for consumer disputes.

13. Documents identifying any and all advertising agencies, marketing firms and printing companies used by NAF to create, and distribute marketing and advertising documents directed toward financial institutions and other corporations since January 1, 1995.

14. Documents showing the total number of arbitrations involving First USA since January 1, 1997.

15. Documents showing the total number of arbitrations involving First USA since January 1, 1997 in which the respondent or party opposing First USA did not respond, appear or otherwise defend against a notice of arbitration by First USA.

16. Documents showing the total number of arbitrations involving First USA since January 1, 1997, in which the notice of arbitration was served by a party against First USA, or was served by a party other than First USA.

17. Documents showing the awards or outcomes of all arbitrations involving First USA since January 1, 1997, in which the notice of arbitration was served by a party against First USA, or was served by a party other than First USA.

18. Documents showing the awards or outcomes of all arbitrations involving First USA since January 1, 1997, in which a party obtained relief against First USA through arbitration.

19. Documents showing the highest, median, and mean monetary awards in all arbitrations involving First USA since January 1, 1997, in which a party obtained relief against First USA through arbitration.

Sample Discovery

20. Documents showing the awards or outcomes of all arbitrations involving First USA and a consumer or consumers since January 1, 1997, in which the notice of arbitration was served by a party against First USA, or was served by a party other than First USA.

21. Documents showing the awards or outcomes of all arbitrations involving First USA since January 1, 1997, in which a consumer or consumers obtained relief against First USA through arbitration.

22. Documents showing the highest, median, and mean monetary awards in all arbitrations involving First USA since January 1, 1997, in which a consumer or consumers obtained relief against First USA through arbitration.

23. Documents showing all monies paid by First USA (or in its behalf) to NAF since January 1, 1995.

24. Documents showing all monies paid by Bank One to NAF since January 1, 1995.

25. Documents reflecting any monies paid to any officer, director and/or shareholder of NAF by First USA and/or Bank One since January 1, 1995.

26. Documents reflecting any monies paid to any affiliate of NAF by First USA and/or Bank One since January 1, 1995.

27. Documents showing total revenue by NAF for each calendar or fiscal year since January 1, 1995.

28. Complete financial statements for NAF for each calendar or fiscal year since January 1, 1995.

29. Complete list of all arbitrators currently used by the NAF throughout the United States, including any biographies, resumes, or curriculum vitae of each arbitrator.

C.3 Discovery Directed to Auto Financer[2]

C.3.1 Interrogatories

IN THE SUPERIOR COURT OF CONNECTICUT
J.D. OF NEW HAVEN

```
——————————————— )
[CONSUMER],              )
                Plaintiff, )
                         )
v.                       )
                         )
CHASE MANHATTAN          )
AUTOMOTIVE FINANCE       )
CORPORATION,             )
                Defendant. )
——————————————— )
```

PLAINTIFF'S INTERROGATORIES RELATING TO ARBITRATION

Plaintiff requests Defendant to respond to the following interrogatories under oath. The interrogatories must be signed by the person answering them, and be served upon the Plaintiff within 30 days hereof.

---

[2] This discovery was provided by Joanne Faulkner, a consumer attorney practicing in New Haven, Connecticut.

"Identify" or "identity" when used in reference to a natural person means to state his or her full name, present business and home addresses, present employer and position with employer, and the relationship, business or otherwise, between such person and the person answering he interrogatory.

"Document" means any written, recorded or graphic matter, whether produced, reproduced or stored on papers, cards, tapes, belts, or computer devices or any other medium in your possession, custody or control, or known by you to exist, and includes originals, all copies of originals, and all prior drafts.

These interrogatories shall be deemed continuing so as to require supplementary answers if you obtain further information between the time answers are served and the time of trial.

"Customer" means an individual who entered into a Retail Installment Contract with a Connecticut car dealer which was assigned to Defendant Chase.

1. Please set forth the text of the Plaintiff's arbitration clause in full, on a separate page.

2. Please set forth the text of the reverse of the Plaintiff's contract in full, on a separate page.

3. State when Chase first inserted an arbitration clause in Connecticut Retail Installment Contracts.

4. Identify each car dealer in Connecticut that has assigned to Chase any Chase Connecticut Retail Installment Contract which included an arbitration provision.

5. Set forth the number of persons who entered into the form of agreement CMB-Connecticut REV. 12/99.

6. List all persons by name and present home or business address, who provided disclosures to Plaintiff regarding the arbitration provisions purportedly applicable to the subject transaction.

7. List all Connecticut arbitrators associated with National Arbitration Forum (NAF).

8. List each arbitration in which Chase has participated relating to its consumer retail installment transactions and for each arbitration provide:
   (a) The name and last known addresses of the borrower and the borrower's lawyer, if any;
   (b) The respective costs to the parties relating to the process;
   (c) A description of the papers and documents filed by the parties;
   (d) The outcome of the arbitration;
   (e) The status of the possession of the motor vehicle which was the subject of the transaction during and after the arbitration process;
   (f) The names and addresses of any persons who served as an arbitrator in said proceeding(s).

9. Please list each contact, conversation or communication between agents and/or employees of the Defendant and National Arbitration Forum (NAF), concerning the arbitration clause purportedly included in the subject transaction and for each such contact, conversation or communication, state the date, nature of the contact, conversation or communication as closely to verbatim as possible. Please continue your response on a separate sheet of paper if necessary.

10. State the full name and last known address, including street, street number, city, state, zip code, and telephone number of each and every person known to Defendant or Defendant's attorneys who have any knowledge regarding the facts and circumstances surrounding the arbitration clause upon which Defendant relies, including, but not limited to, persons who participated in the

decision to institute the use of said arbitration clause, persons who drafted the arbitration clause and/or had input into its language, persons in charge of educating Defendant's employees with regard to the to the arbitration clause.

11. Why does this Defendant utilize arbitration clauses?

12. Did NAF participate in drafting the arbitration clause relied upon by this Defendant in its claim that Plaintiff's claims are subject to arbitration?

13. Please state all fees paid to NAF (a) for assistance in drafting and placement of the arbitration clause and (b) for arbitration fees.

14. Have revisions been made to the arbitration clause since it was first utilized by this Defendant? If so, please provide the following information:
 (a) On what dates were revisions made;
 (b) The name and job title of the party(ies) who made the decision to revise the arbitration clause;
 (c) The name and job title of the party(ies) who drafted the revision(s).

15. State the number of disputes that have proceeded to arbitration since Defendant began inserting an arbitration clause in its retail instalment contracts.

16. As to each dispute that has proceeded to arbitration, state the following:
 (a) The nature of the claim;
 (b) In whose favor the claim was resolved and the amount;
 (c) The name and address of the arbitrator;
 (d) The name and address of the arbitration association;
 (e) What fees the retail buyer had to pay that he or she would not have to pay in a judicial forum
 (f) What relief was not available in the arbitration forum, such as injunction, that is available in a judicial forum.

17. Have you used arbitration to recover a deficiency from a retail buyer? If so, provide the information requested in subsections (a)–(f) of the previous interrogatory.

18. As to each arbitrator used in connection with Connecticut retail instalment contracts, please set forth (a) how many claims that arbitrator heard; (b) how many of those claims did the arbitrator rule in favor of Defendant; and (c) how many of those claims did the arbitrator rule for the retail installment customer?

19. Set forth the total number of times Defendant has initiated arbitration proceedings against any retail installment customers through NAF since January 1, 1998.

20. Identify each and every lawsuit Defendant has initiated against retail installment customers since January 1, 1998.

21. State the number and percentage of disputes arising from a motor vehicle retail installment contract in which you have invoked arbitration.

22. Identify each and every lawsuit filed since January 1, 1998 where Defendant has invoked or attempted to invoke arbitration through NAF.

23. Identify each and every lawsuit filed since January 1, 1998 where Defendant has not invoked or attempted to invoke arbitration through NAF despite an arbitration clause.

24. State with particularity each and every document which discloses to customers or potential customers the fact that by transacting business with this Defendant the customer is subject to an alleged arbitration agreement.

25. Does this Defendant allow a customer to change or negotiate for change of any term in its retail instalment agreement? If so, please state with specificity the items a customer would be allowed to change on this Defendant's contract. If the answer is no, please state with specificity the reasons why a customer is not allowed to change or negotiate for terms in the contract.

26. Do any employees of this Defendant have the authority to change the language in the arbitration clause in negotiation with a customer? If so, please state the name, address, and title of the employee(s).

27. Can a customer negotiate concession in response to the arbitration clause used by this Defendant?

28. If your answer is yes, set forth the number and percentage of customers who have negotiated about the arbitration clause, and identify each such customer and the dealer involved.

29. Can a customer negotiate removal of the arbitration clause used by this Defendant?

30. If your answer is yes, set forth the number and percentage of customers who have negotiated removal of the arbitration clause, and identify each such customer and the dealer involved.

31. Would this Defendant transact business with a customer who refused to sign an arbitration clause? If not, why not?

32. Is this Defendant aware of any competitor of this Defendant which does not require a customer to sign an arbitration agreement? If so, please state the name and address of the competitor.

33. Is this Defendant aware of any competitor of this Defendant which requires a customer to sign an arbitration agreement? If so, please state the name and address of the competitor.

34. Is this Defendant a member of any arbitration association? If so, which arbitration association?

35. Has Chase used any arbitration provider other than the National Arbitration Forum (NAF) to arbitrate any dispute with a retail instalment customer? If so, please state for each such provider:
 (a) The name and address of the provider;
 (b) The number of arbitrations involving Chase handled by that provider;
 (c) The inclusive dates during which Chase used that provider;
 (d) All reasons why Chase used that particular provider rather than another provider; and
 (e) All reasons why Chase chose to use NAF instead of such other provider that had been used by Chase.

36. Identify each current or former officer of Chase who serves or has served as an officer, shareholder, director, board member, advisory committee member, or arbitrator with NAF, is or has otherwise been affiliated with NAF, or has or has had any financial interest in NAF. For each such person, please state his/her name, position with Chase, business address, and position or other relationship (including the amount of any financial interest) with NAF.

[*Attorney for Plaintiff*]

C.3.2 Document Requests

IN THE SUPERIOR COURT OF CONNECTICUT
J.D. OF NEW HAVEN

```
_____     )
[CONSUMER],             )
              Plaintiff,)
                        )
v.                      )
                        )
CHASE MANHATTAN         )
AUTOMOTIVE FINANCE      )
CORPORATION,            )
             Defendant. )
_____     )
```

PLAINTIFF'S REQUEST FOR PRODUCTION OF DOCUMENTS RELATING TO ARBITRATION

"Documents" or "Documentation" shall mean any kind of written, recorded or graphic matters, however produced or reproduced, of any kind or description whether sent or received, including originals, non-identical copies and drafts of both sides thereof, and including, but not limited to, papers, books, letters, correspondence, telegrams, bulletins, notices, announcements, instructions, charts, manuals, brochures, schedules, internal memoranda, notes, notations, transcripts, minutes, agendas, reports and recordings of telephonic or other conversations, interviews, conferences or other meetings, affidavits, statements, summaries, opinions, reports, studies, analyses, computer print-outs, data processing input/output, microfilms and all other records kept by electronic means, photographic or mechanical means, and other things similar to any of the foregoing.

1. Any and all agreements, contracts, memoranda and other correspondence between the Defendant and the National Arbitration Forum ("NAF") since Jan. 1, 1995.

2. Any and all manuals, memoranda, guidelines, instructions, and other documents setting forth the Defendant's policies and procedures relating to compliance with or enforcement of the form of arbitration clause which is contained in the Plaintiff's retail instalment contract.

3. Any and all documents relating to Defendant's experiences, policies, procedures or practices, relating to its arbitrations of consumer claims or disputes including but not limited to the following: contracts with individuals chosen to serve as arbitrators; invoices and check requests associated with arbitrations; correspondence relating to arbitrations actually commenced; and arbitrators' rulings.

4. Any and all documents that provide the following information relating to Defendant's arbitrations actually conducted in consumer transactions: the respective costs to the parties relating to the process; a description of the papers and documents filed by the parties; the outcome of the arbitration; the status of the possession of the motor vehicle that was the security for the retail installment during and after the arbitration process; and the names and addresses of any persons who served as an arbitrator in said proceeding(s).

5. Any and all documents relating to any proceeding (litigation or arbitration) to which Defendant has been a party where a court or arbitrator has refused to enforce an arbitration clause included in a retail installment contract.

6. All Defendant's communications from NAF since January 1, 1994, including letters, brochures, circulars, advertisements, and promotional material.

7. Documents showing details of all business dealings and financial relationships between NAF or any arbitrators associated with NAF and Defendant.

8. Each and every document, manual, memorandum, etc. used in educating or training this Defendant's employees or customers about arbitration.

9. A copy of the arbitration provision(s) utilized by Chase in retail instalment contracts, and a copy of any and all revisions of the same since the original was put into use. (For each such original or revision, indicate the inclusive dates during which such version of that arbitration provision was in effect.)

10. All documents provided to Chase by NAF informing Chase that if Chase chooses to use NAF for arbitration, Chase will not face consumer class actions.

11. All documents, specifically including letters and internal memoranda however recorded, relating to the decision by Chase to use NAF as the arbitrator and the reasons for that decision.

12. All "readership surveys" or similar studies of which Chase is aware which commented on the likelihood that retail installment customers would read the arbitration clause on the reverse of their contract, and when Chase became aware of them.

13. All studies, memoranda however recorded, or in-house discussions among officers, directors, employees and/or agents of Chase about the number or percentage of retail installment customers who actually read the arbitration clause.

14. All documents, including statistical surveys, studies, correspondence and/or memoranda however recorded, discussing any relationships between NAF and/or its individual arbitrators and Chase.

15. All documents of any kind whatsoever which indicate any amount of income derived by NAF and/or its arbitrators from arbitration of retail instalment contract disputes with Defendant since January 1, 1995, divided by year.

16. All studies, analysis or other documents prepared by NAF to show the benefits to financial institutions of arbitration before NAF as opposed to the American Arbitration Association.

17. Complete and legible copies of any and all contracts or business proposals submitted by NAF to Chase since January 1, 1995, soliciting Chase to use NAF for consumer arbitration.

18. Any and all contracts or other agreements between NAF and Chase regarding the exclusive use of NAF for consumer disputes.

19. Documents showing the total number of arbitrations by NAF involving Chase since January 1, 1997.

20. Documents showing the total number of arbitrations involving Chase since January 1, 1997, in which the respondent or party opposing Chase did not respond, appear or otherwise defend against a notice of arbitration by Chase.

21. Documents showing the total number of arbitrations involving Chase since January 1, 1997, in which the notice of arbitration was served by a party against Chase, or was served by a party other than Chase.

22. Documents showing the awards or outcomes of all arbitrations involving Chase since January 1, 1997, in which the notice of arbitration was served by a party against Chase, or was served by a party other than Chase.

23. Documents showing the awards or outcomes of all arbitrations involving Chase since January 1, 1997, in which a party obtained relief against Chase through arbitration.

24. Documents showing the highest median, and mean monetary awards in all arbitrations involving Chase since January 1, 1997, in which a party obtained relief against Chase through arbitration.

25. Documents showing the total number of arbitrations involving Chase since January 1, 1997, in which the arbitrator awarded punitive damages to a consumer against Chase.

26. All documents reflecting any punitive damage award (including the name to the case, case number, and jurisdiction) obtained by Plaintiff(s) in lawsuits filed by retail installment customer(s) against Chase during the three (3) year period immediately before Chase sought to institute arbitration of retail installment customer disputes.

27. Any documents received from any arbitration association other than NAF which were taken into account in selecting NAF instead of another arbitration forum.

28. Any documents, other than the arbitration agreement itself, available to explain to customers the meaning of the arbitration provision.

29. All documents relating to the print format, type size, color, contrast and other qualities of the retail instalment contract at issue, including those reflecting communications with the printer, billing, proofs and revision of proofs.

30. All letters, memos, e-mails and other documents evidencing, referring to, or relating in any way to Chase's decision to adopt any arbitration provision in the retail instalment agreement, or to any deliberations relating to such decision, including but not limited to:
   a. All letters, memos, e-mails and other documents considered by Chase in making such decision;
   b. All letters, memos, e-mails and other documents relating in any way to any proposed arbitration provision that was not adopted;
   c. All letters, memos, e-mails and other documents relating in any way to any cost projection, any cost-benefit analysis, or any anticipated (or realized) costs and/or benefits of the decision to adopt an arbitration provision;
   d. All letters, memos, e-mails and other documents relating in any way to any proposal to provide arbitration services solicited or received from any arbitration provider other than the National Arbitration Forum (NAF), or relating to the analysis of any such proposal;
   e. All letters, memos, e-mails and other documents relating in any way to Chase's decision to use NAF as Chase's sole arbitration provider;
   f. All letters, memos, e-mails and other documents relating in any way to communications with NAF regarding Chase's decision to use NAF as an arbitration provider.

31. All letters, memos, e-mails and other documents relating in any way to communications with NAF concerning the identity, qualifications or other characteristics of arbitrators used by NAF.

32. All letters, memos, e-mails and other documents relating in any way to communications with NAF regarding modification of NAF rules or proposed modification of NAF rules.

33. All documents relating to any arbitration involving Chase since January 1, 1997, in which the arbitrator granted the request of a party adverse to Chase for waiver or reduction of fees or any other expense or cost associated with the arbitration.

34. All documents relating to any arbitration involving Chase since January 1, 1997, in which the arbitrator, without request of a party, granted to a party adverse to Chase a waiver or reduction of fees or any other expense or cost associated with the arbitration.

35. Documents reflecting the total number of arbitrations involving Chase since January 1, 1997, in which the final arbitration award assessed against the retail buyer (or required the retail buyer to pay) Chase's fees, expenses or costs associated with the arbitration.

36. All documents reflecting or relating to communications with NAF that do **not** relate to a specific arbitration proceeding.

37. All documents relating to any arbitration involving Chase since January 1, 1997, in which there was a "participatory hearing award."

38. All scripting, question-and-answer formats, or other documents designed to inform, train, or be used by dealers, customer service representatives or other agents or employees of Chase in responding to customer inquiries about arbitration.

39. A copy of all information posted at any Chase-affiliated internet web site since January 1, 1997, relating in any way to Chase's implementation of an arbitration provision in its retail instalment contracts, or to arbitration.

40. Any list maintained by Chase of individuals chosen to serve as arbitrators.

41. The resume, curriculum vita and any other documents relating to the background and qualifications of persons who serve or have served as arbitrators in arbitrations involving Chase.

42. All documents relating to any arbitration involving Chase that proceeded as a classwide or class arbitration.

43. Please produce a privilege log that states, for each document withheld from disclosure on a claim of privilege, the date the document was created, the name and position of the author, the name and position of each recipient, the subject of the document, and a detailed summary of the contents of the document.

[*Attorney for Plaintiff*]

C.3.3 *Request for Admissions*

IN THE SUPERIOR COURT OF CONNECTICUT
J.D. OF NEW HAVEN

[CONSUMER],	)
Plaintiff,	)
	)
v.	)
	)
CHASE MANHATTAN	)
AUTOMOTIVE FINANCE	)
CORPORATION,	)
Defendant.	)

Sample Discovery   Appx. C.4

PLAINTIFF'S REQUESTS FOR ADMISSIONS RELATING TO ARBITRATION

1. This Defendant does not instruct its representatives or dealers to explain the arbitration provision to customers.

2. This Defendant does not instruct its representatives or dealers as to what arbitration means.

3. This Defendant requires customers to sign an arbitration agreement before transacting business with a customer.

4. More than fifty customers have signed an arbitration agreement with this Defendant.

5. More than one hundred customers have signed an arbitration agreement with this Defendant.

6. More than three hundred customers have signed an arbitration agreement with this Defendant.

7. More than five hundred customers have signed an arbitration agreement with this Defendant.

8. More than one thousand customers have signed an arbitration agreement with this Defendant.

9. More than five thousand customers have signed an arbitration agreement with this Defendant.

10. This Defendant will not transact business with a customer who refuses to sign an arbitration agreement.

11. This Defendant will not allow a customer to negotiate removal of the arbitration provision.

12. This Defendant will not allow a customer to negotiate for and obtain changes in the transaction agreement in return for agreeing to the arbitration provision.

13. Arbitration is more expensive for a consumer than a judicial proceedings due to fees which are not involved in judicial proceedings.

14. The National Arbitration Forum ("NAF") selects a small number of potential arbitrators who are likely to hear cases involving Chase on a repeat basis, but who are unlikely to hear cases involving an individual consumer on a repeat basis.

15. NAF has a loser pays rule to discourage consumers from commencing litigation.

16. NAF rules limit discovery.

17. NAF prohibits claimants from proceeding on a class action basis.

18. NAF puts an upper limit on recoveries.

19. Chase intentionally uses thin paper, and light ink which does not contrast with the background, for the arbitration clause.

[*Attorney for Plaintiff*]

C.4 Interrogatories Directed to Car Dealer[3]

IN THE CIRCUIT COURT, FOURTH JUDICIAL CIRCUIT, IN AND FOR DUVAL COUNTY, FLORIDA

[*CONSUMER*],
                Plaintiff,

v.

DUVAL MOTOR COMPANY and SCOTT-MCRAE AUTOMOTIVE GROUP, INC. d/b/a SCOTT-MCRAE GROUP, Florida corporations and GENERAL ELECTRIC CAPITAL AUTO FINANCIAL SERVICES, INC., a corporation.
                Defendants.

PLAINTIFF'S FIRST SET OF INTERROGATORIES RELATING TO ARBITRATION DIRECTED TO DEFENDANTS, DUVAL MOTOR COMPANY AND SCOTT-MCRAE AUTOMOTIVE GROUP

TO: Duval Motor Company and Scott-McRae Automotive Group, Inc. d/b/a Scott-McRae Group
c/o [*Attorney for Defendant*]
[*address*]

The Plaintiff, [*Plaintiff*], (hereinafter "Plaintiff"), submits the following interrogatories to be answered by Defendants, Duval Motor Company and Scott-McRae Automotive Group, Inc. d/b/a Scott-McRae Group (hereinafter "Duval Motors," "Scott-McRae" or "Defendants").

DEFINITIONS AND INSTRUCTIONS

1. If in furnishing answers to any of these interrogatories, you refer to any documents or consult with any person, please so specify in your answer, giving the name and address of the person consulted, or identifying the particular document to which you have referred with sufficient specificity to allow the proponent of these interrogatories to locate and to identify that document.

2. "Identify" with respect to a natural person means to give, to the extent known, the person's full name, present or last known address, telephone number, and the present or last known place of employment. Once a person has been identified in your response to these interrogatories, only the name of that person need to be listed in response to subsequent discovery requesting the identification of that person.

3. "Identify" with respect to corporations, partnerships, or other business entities, means to give the name of the entity, the present or last known address of its principal place of business, its place of

---

[3] This discovery was provided by Lynn Drysdale, Florida Legal Services, in Jacksonville, Florida.

incorporation or registration (including registration under any fictitious names), and the telephone number of its principal place of business.

4. "Identify" with respect to oral conversations means to give the date (or approximate date to the best of your knowledge) of the conversation; the parties to the conversation; the place where the conversation took place; and the substance of the conversation.

5. "Duval Motor Company," "Scott-McRae Automotive Group, Inc. d/b/a Scott-McRae Group" and "Defendants" means Duval Motor Company, Scott-McRae Automotive Group, Inc. d/b/a Scott-McRae Group, their parent, subsidiaries, branches, agents representatives and all person or entities reporting to act on behalf of the named Defendants.

6. "Relevant time period" means the period of time from August 18, 1995 to present.

7. "Relating to" or similar term means to make a statement about, discuss, described, identify, deal with, list, evidence, establish, comprise, consist of and include all matters and documentation that in any way pertains in whole or in part to the subject.

8. [*Plaintiff*]'s transaction with Duval Motors and the Scott-McRae Group shall be referred to as the subject transaction.

These interrogatories are, and shall be deemed to be, continuing and require supplementation to the full extent permitted and required under the Florida Rules of Civil Procedure.

INTERROGATORIES

1. State the full name and address, position and duties of the person answering these interrogatories.

2. State the full name, home and business address, position and duties of each and every person who is or was an agent or employee of the Defendants who participated in any phase of the subject transaction, including the negotiations for the transaction and the preparation, presentation and execution of any of the documents signed or purportedly signed by or provided to [*Plaintiff*].

3. List all persons by name and present home or business address, who provided disclosures to [*Plaintiff*] regarding the arbitration provisions purportedly applicable to the subject transaction.

4. Describe in detail your policy, procedure, or practice with respect to arbitrations of consumer claims or disputes including but not limited to:
   (a) Whether you maintain any lists of individuals you choose to serve as arbitrators;
   (b) Whether you maintain any contracts with individuals you choose to serve as arbitrators;
   (c) The respective costs to the parties associated with arbitrations;
   (d) The locations of the arbitrations;
   (e) Whether process is available to compel attendance of witnesses or the production of documents and whether testimony in person is received in the arbitration;
   (f) The average length of time between receipt of the initial demand for arbitration and the occurrence of an arbitration hearing;
   (g) Whether the rules of any professional arbitration association have been used as guidelines or benchmarks in the arbitrations;
   (h) Whether any in-house lawyers are employed who primarily work on arbitrations;
   (i) Whether any arbitrations have proceeded as class arbitrations and if not why not;
   (j) And whether you have ever failed to respond to a demand for arbitration within thirty (30) days of receiving that demand and, if so, the reason for such failure to respond.

5. Describe in complete detail the process Duval Motors contends is applicable to arbitration allegedly required and agreed to in the subject transaction. Specifically, what agreements were made as to:
   (a) Locale of the arbitration;
   (b) Rules which would govern the arbitration;
   (c) Selection of the arbitrator;
   (d) The parameters of discovery;
   (e) The payment of fees;
   (f) Enforceability of award;
   (g) Admissibility of evidence;
   (h) Measure of damages.

6. List each arbitration in which Duval Motors and Scott-McRae Group has participated relating to its motor vehicle transactions and for each arbitration provide:
   (a) The name, last known addresses and social security number of the borrower;
   (b) The respective costs to the parties relating to the process;
   (c) A description of the papers and documents filed by the parties;
   (d) The outcome of the arbitration;
   (e) The status of the possession of the motor vehicle which was the subject of the transaction during and after the arbitration process; and
   (f) The names and addresses of any persons who served as an arbitrator in said proceeding(s).

7. Identify, by name and business address, all persons presently employed by Duval Motors and Scott-McRae Group, its parent companies and subsidiaries who have had any responsibility for processing, working on, litigating or resolving consumer complaints or arbitrations from August, 1995 to present.

8. Identify by name, last known address and social security number, all persons who were but are not presently employed by Duval Motors and Scott-McRae Group, its parent companies and subsidiaries who had any responsibility for processing, working on, litigating or resolving consumer complaints or arbitrations from August, 1995 to present.

9. Please list each contact, conversation or communication between agents and/or employees of the Defendants and [*Plaintiff*], concerning the mediation and arbitration clause purportedly imposed upon [*Plaintiff*] in the subject transaction and for each such contact, conversation or communication, state the date, nature of the contact, conversation or communication as closely to verbatim as possible. Please continue your response on a separate sheet of paper if necessary.

[*Attorney for Plaintiff*]

C.5 Discovery Directed to Pay Day Loan Company

IN THE CIRCUIT COURT FOR
MONTGOMERY COUNTY, ALABAMA

[CONSUMER], individually and on behalf of similarly situated Alabama residents as defined herein,
    Plaintiff,

v.

A & B CHECK CASHING, INC., et al.,
    Defendant.

PLAINTIFF'S SECOND INTERROGATORIES AND REQUEST FOR PRODUCTION, AND FIRST REQUEST FOR ADMISSIONS, TO DEFENDANT A & B CHECK CASHING, INC.

INTERROGATORIES

Pursuant to Rule 33 of the Alabama Rules of Civil Procedure, Plaintiff propounds the following interrogatories to be answered by A & B Check Cashing, Inc., in the manner and form prescribed by law:

1. State the full name, age, social security number, and address, including street, street number, city, state, zip code, and telephone number, job title, and job description of each person answering these interrogatories.

2. State the full name and last known address, including street, street number, city, state, zip code, and telephone number of each and every person known to Defendant or Defendant's attorneys who have any knowledge regarding the facts and circumstances surrounding the arbitration provision(s) upon which Defendant has moved to compel arbitration, including, but not limited to, persons who participated in the decision to institute the use of said arbitration provision(s), persons who drafted the arbitration provision(s) and/or had input into its language, persons in charge of educating Defendant's employees with regard to the to the arbitration provision(s), and persons who participated in training Defendant's employees with regard to the arbitration provision.

3. If any of the individuals listed above, or whom Defendant proposes to use at the trial of this matter, are employed by this Defendant, please describe the nature of such employment relationship, the present position of the individual, and how long the person has been in the employ of this Defendant.

4. Who made the decision to implement an arbitration provision in this Defendant's contracts?

5. Why does this Defendant utilize arbitration provisions?

6. Who drafted the arbitration provision relied upon by this Defendant in its claim that Plaintiff's claims are subject to arbitration?

7. Please state the date on which this Defendant began to include arbitration provisions in its contracts.

8. Have revisions been made to the arbitration provision since this Defendant first utilized it? If so, please provide the following information:
   (a) On what dates were revisions made;
   (b) The name and job title of the party(ies) who made the decision to revise the arbitration provision;
   (c) The name and job title of the party(ies) who drafted the revision(s).

9. For the five (5) years prior to implementing the arbitration provision, please state the following:
   (a) The number of lawsuits filed against this Defendant;
   (b) The style, case number, and court/jurisdiction of each lawsuit;
   (c) The nature of the claim of each lawsuit; and
   (d) In whose favor the claim was resolved and the amount.

10. For the five (5) years prior to implementation of the arbitration provision, please state the following:
    (a) The number of claims settled prior to litigation;
    (b) The name, address and telephone number of each claimant;
    (c) The nature of each claim; and
    (d) In whose favor the claim was resolved, the amount, and a description of any other relief.

11. State the number of disputes that have proceeded to arbitration.

12. As to each dispute that has proceeded to arbitration, state the following:
    (a) The nature of the claim;
    (b) The name, address and telephone number of each party other than Defendant;
    (c) In whose favor the claim was resolved and the amount;
    (d) The name and address of the arbitrator; and
    (e) The name and address of the arbitration association.

13. State the number of disputes in which you have invoked arbitration, whether or not the dispute proceeded to arbitration.

14. Fully describe each and every document or thing that this Defendant will rely upon or seek to introduce in defense of Plaintiff's claims with regard to the arbitration provision.

15. State with particularity each and every document which discloses to customers or potential customers the fact that by transacting business with this Defendant the customer is subject to an alleged arbitration agreement.

16. Identify each and every fact and produce each and every document that supports your contention that the claims alleged in the Complaint are subject to arbitration.

17. Does this Defendant allow a customer to change or negotiate for change of any term in its transaction agreement or contract? If so, please state with specificity the items a customer would be allowed to change on this Defendant's contract. If the answer is no, please state with specificity the reasons why a customer is not allowed to change or negotiate for change of terms in the contract.

18. Do any employees of this Defendant have the authority to change the language in the arbitration provision in negotiation with a customer? If so, please state the name, address, and title of the employee(s).

19. Can a customer negotiate any concession relating to the transaction or the agreement in return for agreeing to the arbitration provision used by this Defendant?

20. Can a customer negotiate removal of the arbitration provision used by this Defendant?

21. Would this Defendant transact business with a customer who refused to agree to an arbitration provision? If not, why not?

22. How many customers have signed arbitration agreements with their contracts with this Defendant?

23. If different from number 22, how many customers have signed transaction agreements containing an arbitration provision with this Defendant?

24. Is this Defendant aware of any competitor of this Defendant that does not require a customer to agree to an arbitration provision? If so, please state the name and address of the competitor.

25. Is this Defendant aware of any competitor of this Defendant that requires a customer to agree to an arbitration provision? If so, please state the name and address of the competitor.

26. Is this Defendant a member of any arbitration association? If so, which arbitration association?

27. Has this Defendant paid money to any arbitration association? If so, state to which arbitration association, and for each such association, how much, and the beginning and ending dates of such payments.

REQUEST FOR PRODUCTION

Pursuant to Rule 34 of the Alabama Rules of Civil Procedure, Plaintiff requests that Defendant A & B Check Cashing, Inc. produce the following documents and things:

1. Each and every document, manual, memorandum, etc. used in educating this Defendant's employees about arbitration.

2. A copy of the arbitration provision utilized by this Defendant, and a copy of any and all revisions of the same since the original was put into use.

3. A copy of any audiotapes or videotapes of Plaintiff.

4. A copy of any and all material, whether in the form of printed material, letters, memoranda, newsletters, bulletins, audiotapes, or videotapes, provided to Defendant by the Alabama Check Cashers Association, which in any way touches or concerns the use of arbitration provisions.

5. The complete and entire file regarding Plaintiff.

REQUEST FOR ADMISSIONS

Pursuant to Rule 36 of the Alabama Rules of Civil Procedure, Plaintiff requests Defendant A & B Check Cashing, Inc., within 30 days after service of this request, to admit the truth of the following facts:

1. This Defendant does not instruct its representatives to explain the arbitration provision to customers.

2. This Defendant does not instruct its representatives as to what arbitration means.

3. This Defendant requires customers to sign an arbitration agreement before transacting business with a customer.

4. More than fifty customers have signed an arbitration agreement with this Defendant.

5. More than one hundred customers have signed an arbitration agreement with this Defendant.

6. More than three hundred customers have signed an arbitration agreement with this Defendant.

7. More than five hundred customers have signed an arbitration agreement with this Defendant.

8. More than one thousand customers have signed an arbitration agreement with this Defendant.

9. More than five thousand customers have signed an arbitration agreement with this Defendant.

10. More than ten thousand customers have signed an arbitration agreement with this Defendant.

11. This Defendant will not transact business with a customer who refuses to sign an arbitration agreement.

12. This Defendant will not allow a customer to negotiate removal of the arbitration provision.

13. This Defendant will not allow a customer to negotiate for and obtain changes in the transaction agreement in return for agreeing to the arbitration provision.

[*Attorney for Plaintiff*]

C.6 Discovery Directed to Payday Lender

C.6.1 First Set of Interrogatories and Document Requests

IN THE GENERAL COURT OF JUSTICE
SUPERIOR COURT DIVISION
NEW HANOVER COUNTY, NORTH CAROLINA

_____)
[CONSUMERS],)
on behalf of themselves and all)
other persons similarly situated,)
      Plaintiffs,)
)
v.   )
)
ADVANCE AMERICA,)
CHECK ADVANCE CENTERS)
OF NORTH CAROLINA, INC.;)
ADVANCE AMERICA, CASH)
ADVANCE CENTERS, INC.;)
and WILLIAM M. WEBSTER,)
IV,   )
      Defendants.)
_____)

PLAINTIFFS' FIRST SET OF INTERROGATORIES AND REQUEST FOR PRODUCTION OF DOCUMENTS TO CORPORATE DEFENDANTS

Pursuant to Rules 26, 33, and 34 of the North Carolina Rules of Civil Procedure, you are hereby served with the following Interrogatories and Requests for Production of Documents, to be answered under oath within thirty (30) days of service hereof or within forty-five (45) days of service of the Summons and Complaint, whichever is later.

In answering these interrogatories and requests for production of documents, you are required to furnish such information as is available to you, including information in the possession of your attorneys and investigators for your attorneys.

If either of you is unable to answer any of these interrogatories or requests for production of documents in full, after exercising due diligence to secure the information, then so state, and answer to the

Sample Discovery   Appx. C.6.1

fullest extent possible, specifying your inability to answer the remainder, and stating whatever information and knowledge you have concerning the unanswered portions. These interrogatories and requests for production of documents are continuing in nature and it is further requested that each of you seasonably supplement your answers to these interrogatories and requests for production of documents to include information acquired subsequent to the date of your original answers.

Each of you is hereby advised that you are under a duty to preserve documents and other information relevant to the pending litigation.

DEFINITIONS AND INSTRUCTIONS

A. "*Advance America locations*" means any offices or stores in which defendants have (or had) a direct or indirect ownership interest, and that do business (or that formerly did business) under the name "Advance America," "National Cash Advance" or "Advance America Cash Advance Centers."

B. "*Document*" means the original or any copy of a writing or other form of record preserving information, which is or may be in or subject to your possession, custody, or control. The term "document" also refers to any writing or other form of record of which you have knowledge, whether or not claimed to be privileged against discovery on any ground. "Document" includes, but is not limited to statements, correspondence, communications, emails, invoices, photographs, personal dairies, business diaries, calendars, contracts, deeds, drafts, minutes of meetings, books of account, summaries or records of telephone or personal conversations, interviews, computer data (including input, output and storage) and any and all other methods of preserving information.

C. "*Identify*" or "*identification*" when used in reference to an individual means to state the person's full name and last-known address, last-known telephone number and the person's last known title and business affiliation.

D. "*Identify*" or "*identification*" when used in reference to any writing or documents, means to state:
(1) The date of the document;
(2) The identity of the person(s) who prepared the document;
(3) A description of the contents of the document;
(4) The identity of each person to whom the document was addressed; and
(5) The location of the document.

E. "*Payday loan*" means a cash advance, delayed deposit transaction, and/or a deferred deposit transaction.

F. "*You*" or "*your*" refers to Advance America, Cash Advance Centers, Inc. and Advance America, Cash Advance Centers of North Carolina Inc., and to your representatives, employees, agents, servants, distributors, insurance carriers, and attorneys, or anyone else acting on your behalf, as appropriate within the context of the question.

G. If these interrogatories are addressed to more than one responding party, each party must sign the answers filed, or sign and file separate answers.

H. If you believe any of the following interrogatories or document requests are objectionable, answer as much of the interrogatory or document request as is not, in your view, objectionable, and separately state the portion of the interrogatory or document request to which you object and the grounds for your objection.

I. If you know that any document falling within the scope of a request for production has been destroyed or lost, or is unavailable for any reason, you are requested to identify each document so unavailable and set forth the reasons for its destruction or unavailability.

J. If you believe any of the information or documents sought are exempt from disclosure on grounds of privilege or otherwise, identify the information or document you contend is not subject to disclosure, and set out the basis for your claim of privilege.

K. Documents are to be produced at the offices of the [*Plaintiffs' Attorney*].

INTERROGATORIES

1. Identify all banks with which you have had a relationship or agreement under which Advance America, Cash Advance Centers, Inc., Advance America, Cash Advance Centers of North Carolina, Inc., or any of their affiliates has acted or purported to act as such bank's agent, marketer, servicer and/or contractor in connection with payday loans, including "agent-assisted bank loan" payday lending operations. For each bank:
   a. State the time during which such relationship existed;
   b. Describe the geographical scope of the relationship (i.e., which states it covered);
   c. Describe the business reasons for such relationship;
   d. Identify the agreements and other documents creating or describing the relationship; and
   e. Identify the executives at the bank and at Advance America, Cash Advance Centers, Inc. (or affiliates) charged with management of the relationship.

2. Describe all funds received from or on behalf of any individual who obtained a payday loan at any Advance America location in North Carolina and that have been transferred to or for the benefit of Advance America, Cash Advance Centers, Inc., Advance America, Cash Advance Centers of North Carolina, Inc. or any owner of either corporation at any time after August 31, 2001. Provide the dates, amounts, transferee and business reasons for each such transfer.

3. Provide the following for each individual who obtained a payday loan (or had a payday loan outstanding) at any Advance America location in North Carolina between August 31, 2001 and the present:
   a. Name, social security number and last known address of the individual;
   b. Amount financed for each loan obtained;
   c. Finance charge for each loan obtained;
   d. Date each loan was originated;
   e. Date each loan became due;
   f. Annual percentage rate of each loan;
   g. Amount and date paid by or on behalf of the individual towards repayment of principal on each loan;
   h. Amount and date paid by or on behalf of the individual towards interest or finance charge on each loan;
   i. Amount and date paid by or on behalf of the individual for late fees on each loan;
   j. Amount and date paid for bounced check, insufficient funds, or NSF charges on each loan;
   k. Amount and date paid in any other fees or charges for each loan; and
   l. Account number of each loan and/or individual.

4. If you store, process or maintain (or have done so in the past) any data concerning the information listed in the preceding interrogatory in a computer or other electronic processing format, please describe or specify to the fullest extent you can:
   a. The data that has been collected;
   b. The data that is currently stored or maintained;
   c. The software program(s) that is/are being used to store the data;
   d. The names of the fields used to store the data and a description of the data that each field contains;
   e. The file format used to store the data;
   f. The location of the computer(s) that store(s) the data;
   g. Your contention as to whether the data is in such a format so that it can be exported to a Microsoft Excel or Microsoft Access database, or as a comma-delimited file;
   h. If you contend that the data cannot be exported electronically into a Microsoft Excel or Access database, an explanation of your contention and the identity of all the formats available for exporting the data from your database or record sharing program(s); and
   i. The identity of the individual(s) who is charged with performing the technical support functions of maintaining such data.

5. Describe your ability to produce computer-generated reports or lists containing the information described in Interrogatory No. 3.

6. Identify all of your officers, directors and owners since January 1, 2001, and give the dates of service in each such office or directorship, and/or the dates of ownership.

REQUEST FOR PRODUCTION OF DOCUMENTS

You are requested to provide the following:

1. All standard forms that were created or used at any time from January 1, 2001 until the present that were used by you in connection with making, administering and collecting payday loans at Advance America locations in North Carolina. To the extent that such forms differ in various locations or have differed in different time periods, produce all documents that embody any such differences.

2. All documents that were created or used at any time from January 1, 2001 until the present that describe or discuss the underwriting criteria used in making payday loans at Advance America locations in North Carolina.

3. All documents that were created or used at any time from January 1, 2001 until the present that describe or discuss the policies and/or procedures for setting of interest rates or fees on payday loans made at Advance America locations in North Carolina.

4. All documents that were created or used at any time from January 1, 2001 until the present that describe or discuss policies and/or procedures regarding renewals or rollovers of payday loans made at Advance America locations in North Carolina.

5. All documents that were created or used at any time from January 1, 2001 until the present that describe or discuss the policies and/or procedures for determining the amount to be financed and setting the date the loan will become due for payday loans made at Advance America locations in North Carolina.

6. All materials that were created or used at any time from January 1, 2001 until the present that you have used in the marketing or advertising of payday loans, including brochures, solicitations and mailers.

7. All documents regarding the named plaintiffs' payday loans applied for and/or obtained at Advance America locations in North Carolina.

8. Your articles of incorporation, bylaws and corporate minutes since January 1, 1996, and all amendments thereto.

9. Organizational charts that reflect your supervisory and reporting structure at the national, regional and state levels, from January 1, 2001 until the present.

10. Financial statements showing the financial position (assets and liabilities) of Advance America, Cash Advance Centers of North Carolina Inc., at all times since January 1, 2001.

11. All documents that were created or used since January 1, 2001, that contain, describe or discuss your communications with the North Carolina Office of Commissioner of Banks and/or any other North Carolina governmental body or public official.

12. All documents that contain, describe or discuss communications with the Office of the Comptroller of the Currency, Federal Deposit Insurance Corporation, or any other federal governmental agency or federal public official, that concern your or your affiliates' relationships with banks in connection with payday lending.

13. All documents reflecting research or analysis on which you relied in concluding that it was lawful for you to conduct business at Advance America locations in North Carolina from and after the expiration of N.C. Gen. Stat. § 53-281 on August 31, 2001.

14. All documents that were created or used at any time from January 1, 2001 until the present that were used to instruct or train your employees about your marketing, administering, servicing, and/or collecting of payday loans in North Carolina. If said training materials have changed, been amended, or completely rewritten, please produce any such materials reflecting any such amended, altered or revised materials.

15. All documents that analyze or discuss your compliance or non-compliance with North Carolina laws governing usury, small loans, check-cashing, loan brokering, the collection of debt, or other consumer protection laws.

16. All agreements and other documents that describe or discuss your business relationship(s) with Peoples National Bank, Republic Bank and Trust Company, and/or any other banks whereby Advance America, Cash Advance Centers, Inc., Advance America, Cash Advance Centers of North Carolina, Inc., or any other affiliate purports or purported to act as such bank's agent, servicer, marketer or contractor, including any "bank agent-assisted lending" arrangements.

17. All budgets, forecasts, projections and other planning documents which describe, discuss, mention or otherwise concern the financial impact of the above-described bank relationships.

18. All documents that describe or discuss your document retention and/or document destruction policy that may apply to any of the documents or information pertaining to this lawsuit or requested in this discovery.

Respectfully submitted, this the _____ day of August, 2004.

[Attorney for Plaintiffs]

C.6.2 Second Set of Interrogatories and Document Requests

IN THE GENERAL COURT OF JUSTICE
SUPERIOR COURT DIVISION
NEW HANOVER COUNTY, NORTH CAROLINA

————————————————)
[CONSUMERS],)
on behalf of themselves and all)
other persons similarly situated,)
      Plaintiffs,)
)
v.)
)
ADVANCE AMERICA,)
CHECK ADVANCE CENTERS)
OF NORTH CAROLINA, INC.;)
ADVANCE AMERICA, CASH)
ADVANCE CENTERS, INC.;)
and WILLIAM M. WEBSTER,)
IV,)
      Defendants.)
————————————————)

PLAINTIFFS' SECOND SET OF INTERROGATORIES AND REQUEST FOR PRODUCTION OF DOCUMENTS TO CORPORATE DEFENDANTS

Pursuant to Rules 26, 33, and 34 of the North Carolina Rules of Civil Procedure, you are hereby served with the following Interrogatories and Requests for Production of Documents, to be answered under oath within thirty (30) days of service hereof.

In answering these interrogatories and requests for production of documents, you are required to furnish such information as is available to you, including information in the possession of your attorneys and investigators for your attorneys.

If either of you is unable to answer any of these interrogatories or requests for production of documents in full, after exercising due diligence to secure the information, then so state, and answer to the fullest extent possible, specifying your inability to answer the remainder, and stating whatever information and knowledge you have concerning the unanswered portions. These interrogatories and requests for production of documents are continuing in nature and it is further requested that each of you seasonably supplement your answers to these interrogatories and requests for production of documents to include information acquired subsequent to the date of your original answers.

DEFINITIONS AND INSTRUCTIONS

A. "*Advance America locations*" means any offices or stores in which defendants have (or had) a direct or indirect ownership interest, and that do business (or that formerly did business) under the name "Advance America," "National Cash Advance" or "Advance America Cash Advance Centers."

B. "*Document*" means the original or any copy of a writing or other form of record preserving information, which is or may be in or subject to your possession, custody, or control. The term "document" also refers to any writing or other form of record of which you have knowledge, whether or not claimed to be privileged against discovery on any ground. "Document" includes, but is not limited to statements, correspondence, communications, emails, invoices, photographs, personal dairies, business diaries, calendars, contracts, deeds, drafts, minutes of meetings, books of account, summaries or records of telephone or personal conversations, interviews, computer data (including input, output and storage) and any and all other methods of preserving information.

C. "*Identify*" or "*identification*" when used in reference to an individual means to state the person's full name and last-known address, last-known telephone number and the person's last known title and business affiliation.

D. "*Identify*" or "*identification*" when used in reference to any writing or documents, means to state:
(1) The date of the document;
(2) The identity of the person(s) who prepared the document;
(3) A description of the contents of the document;
(4) The identity of each person to whom the document was addressed; and
(5) The location of the document.

E. "*Payday loan*" means a cash advance, delayed deposit transaction, and/or a deferred deposit transaction.

F. "*Payday loan customer*" means any individual who has obtained a payday loan at an Advance America location in North Carolina, including any payday loan that was made, serviced, brokered, or otherwise administered by Advance America at its locations in North Carolina, specifically including but not limited to those transactions that purport to be made by Republic Bank or any other Bank.

G. "*You*" or "*your*" refers to Advance America, Cash Advance Centers, Inc. and Advance America, Cash Advance Centers of North Carolina Inc., and to your representatives, employees, agents, servants, distributors, insurance carriers, and attorneys, or anyone else acting on your behalf, as appropriate within the context of the question. "Affiliated corporation" means a corporation which is effectively controlled by another company, a corporation in which there is ownership (direct or indirect) of 5 percent or more of the voting stock, or corporations which are related as parent and subsidiary, characterized by identify of ownership of capital stock.

H. "*Affiliated corporation*" means a corporation which is effectively controlled by another company, a corporation in which there is ownership (direct or indirect) of 5 percent or more of the voting stock, or corporations which are related as parent and subsidiary, characterized by identify of ownership of capital stock.

I. If these interrogatories are addressed to more than one responding party, each party must sign the answers filed, or sign and file separate answers.

J. If you believe any of the following interrogatories or document requests are objectionable, answer as much of the interrogatory or document request as is not, in your view, objectionable, and separately state the portion of the interrogatory or document request to which you object and the grounds for your objection.

K. If you know that any document falling within the scope of a request for production has been destroyed or lost, or is unavailable for any reason, you are requested to identify each document so unavailable and set forth the reasons for its destruction or unavailability.

L. If you believe any of the information or documents sought are exempt from disclosure on grounds of privilege or otherwise, identify the information or document you contend is not subject to disclosure, and set out the basis for your claim of privilege.

M. Documents are to be produced at the offices of the [*Plaintiffs' Attorney*].

INTERROGATORIES

7. Identify each person who has knowledge regarding the facts and circumstances surrounding the arbitration provision(s) that form, are a part of, any contracts that are used or have been used in connection with the making, servicing, administering and/or collecting payday loans at Advance America locations in North Carolina, including, but not limited to, persons who participated in the decision to institute the use of arbitration provision(s), persons who drafted the arbitration provision(s) and/or had input into its language, persons in charge of educating Defendant's employees with regard to the arbitration provision(s), and persons who participated in training Defendant's employees with regard to the arbitration provision.

8. If any of the individuals listed above, or whom you proposes to use at the trial or hearing of this matter, are employed by you, please describe the nature of such employment relationship, the present position of the individual, and how long the person has been in your employ.

9. Please state the date on which an arbitration provision was first included in the form contracts used in connection with the making, servicing, administering and/or collecting payday loans at Advance America locations in North Carolina.

10. If revisions have been made to the arbitration provision(s) described in the preceding interrogatory, please provide the following information, to the greatest extent you can:
   (a) On what date each revision was made;
   (b) The name and job title of the party(ies) who made the decision to revise the arbitration provision;
   (c) The name and job title of the party(ies) who drafted the revision(s);
   (d) All reason(s) for the revision.

11. If the arbitration provision(s) that form, are a part of, any contracts that are used or have been used in connection with the making, servicing, administering and/or collecting payday loans at Advance America locations in North Carolina are different from those used by Advance America in other states, please describe the differences, and the reason for the differences.

12. For each year since 1997, please provide the following information:
   (a) The number of lawsuits filed in North Carolina against Advance America by your payday loan customers;
   (b) The number of lawsuits filed in North Carolina by Advance America against any of its payday loan customers;
   (c) The number of lawsuits filed in North Carolina against Republic Bank by any of your payday loan customers;
   (d) The number of lawsuits filed in North Carolina by Republic Bank against any of your payday loan customers;
   (e) The style, case number and court/jurisdiction of each lawsuit described in this interrogatory;
   (f) The nature of the claim of each lawsuit described in this interrogatory; and
   (g) In whose favor the claim described in this interrogatory was resolved and the amount of any monetary relief awarded.

13. List each arbitration in which you have participated in any way with any of your payday loan customers, and for each arbitration provide:
   (a) The identify of the payday loan customer;
   (b) A description of the papers and documents filed by the parties;
   (c) Whether it was filed by the customer or Advance America;
   (d) The nature of the claims raised;
   (e) The outcome of the arbitration;
   (f) The arbitration forum, if any, in which the arbitration was filed; and
   (g) The identity of the arbitrator(s) in said proceeding.

14. List each class action lawsuit that has ever been brought against you in any state by a payday loan customer(s), and provide the name of the parties to the lawsuit, the filing or case number, the court in which each such lawsuit was filed, resolved and/or remains pending, the nature of the claim(s) of each such lawsuit, whether and in whose favor the claims were resolved, and the current status of each such lawsuit.

15. Describe, to the fullest extent you can, any attempts by you or done on your behalf to assess, analyze, find out, or otherwise gain knowledge of the following demographic or other information about your payday loan customers or potential customers: the customer's education level, the customer's reading level, and/or whether the customer speaks a language other than English as their primary language. Include a description of the results of such assessment or analysis, if any.

16. Describe, to the fullest extent you can, any attempts by you or done on your behalf to assess, analyze, find out, or otherwise gain knowledge of, the extent to which your payday loan customers understand that they have signed an arbitration agreement, and/or the extent to which your payday loan customers understand the basic consequences of signing such an arbitration agreement. Include a description of the results of such assessment or analysis, if any.

17. Describe, to the fullest extent you can, any attempts by you or done on your behalf to assess, analyze, find out, or otherwise gain knowledge of information regarding how much and/or what parts of the form contracts used by you are actually read by the majority or any percentage of your payday loan customers. Include a description of the results of such assessment or analysis, if any.

18. Describe your policy with respect to how and what is communicated by your employees at Advance America store locations in North Carolina to your payday loan customers concerning the requirement of and/or existence of an arbitration agreement in contracts that are used or have been used in connection with the making, servicing, administering and/or collecting payday loans at Advance America locations in North Carolina, during the following situations or stages of a payday loan transaction:
   (a) During a telephone inquiry to your store locations about the process for obtaining a payday loan;
   (b) During an in-person inquiry at your store locations in North Carolina about obtaining a payday loan;
   (c) During the loan application process;
   (d) At the time the contract is entered into and/or signed by the payday loan customer;
   (e) During the collection process in cases where the customer has defaulted on a loan.

19. If you are aware of any other payday cash advance provider operating at or through one or more locations in North Carolina that DOES NOT require a customer to sign an arbitration agreement before obtaining a payday loan in, please identify this company or entity.

20. If you are aware of any other payday cash advance provider operating at or through one or more locations in North Carolina that DOES require a customer to sign an arbitration agreement before obtaining a payday loan, please identify this company or entity.

21. What is the highest amount that any payday loan customer currently owes on a payday loan that was made, marketed or serviced at an Advance America location in North Carolina.

22. Please describe your collection policy and procedures used at your locations in North Carolina for situations in which payday loan customers fail to repay the payday cash advance, including identifying all past-due collection efforts used by your employees, and a description of your collection targets and how these are set.

23. For each year from 1997 until the present, state how many of your payday loan customers in North Carolina have failed to repay the payday cash advance on the day it was purportedly due. Out of that number of defaulting loans, provide the following information:
   (a) State how many subsequently repaid the cash advance through collection efforts or otherwise;
   (b) State how many times you deposited or attempted to deposit the customers check held as security for the loan;
   (c) State how many times you collected the amount due through an arbitration proceeding.

24. Identify all of your affiliated corporations, and provide the following information for these affiliated corporations:
   (a) The identify of the officers and directors of each;
   (b) The shareholders of each;
   (c) The debt holders of each;
   (d) The identity of any individual(s) who has(ve) received any distribution of stock or other property from the affiliated corporations as a shareholder or creditor.

REQUEST FOR PRODUCTION OF DOCUMENTS

You are requested to provide the following:

19. All contracts containing an arbitration provision that was created or used by you in connection with making, administering and collecting payday loans at Advance America locations in North Carolina since January 1, 1997. To the extent that such contracts differ in various locations or have differed in different time periods, produce all documents that embody any such differences.

20. All documents that were created or used at any time from January 1, 1997 until the present that were used to educate, instruct or train your employees about the use of arbitration agreements in your contracts. If said training materials have changed, been amended, or completely rewritten, please produce any such materials reflecting any such amended, altered or revised materials.

21. All scripts or talking points created or used at any time from January 1, 1997 until the present by your employees to inform your customers of the existence of any arbitration provisions in your contracts and/or to explain to your customer of the consequences of any of these arbitration provisions. If said scripts or talking points have changed, been amended, or completely rewritten, please produce any materials reflecting any such amended, altered or revised script or talking points, including any materials that discuss the changes.

22. All manuals, memoranda, guidelines, instructions and other documents setting forth your policies and procedures relating to compliance with and/or enforcement of the arbitration clause which is or has been contained in your form contracts since January 1, 1997.

23. All documents that analyze or discuss any of the arbitration provision(s) created or used by you in connection with making, administering and collecting payday loans at Advance America locations in North Carolina.

24. All documents evidencing, referring to, or relating to your decision to adopt any arbitration provision in the customer agreement(s) used by you, or to any deliberations relating so such decision, including but not limited to:
   (a) All documents considered by you in making such a decision;
   (b) All documents relating to any proposed arbitration provision that was not adopted for use by you;
   (c) All studies, analysis or other documents relating to any cost-benefit analysis, or any anticipated (or realized) costs and/or benefits of the decision to adopt an arbitration provision;

25. All documents reflecting correspondence between you and any bank or other financial institution for whom you have acted, since January 1, 1997, as processing, marketing, and/or servicing agent, including Republic Bank & Trust Company, that relate to the arbitration provision(s) in the contracts used by you.

26. All documents that have been sent or provided to you by the Community Financial Services Association of America (CFSA) which relates to the use of arbitration provisions, including but not limited to, and document that discusses the benefits of arbitration.

27. All correspondence between you and the Community Financial Services Association of America (CFSA) which relates to the use of arbitration provisions, including but not limited to, and document that discusses the benefits of arbitration.

28. All documents that provide the following information relating to any arbitration proceedings that you have actually participated in with any of your North Carolina payday loan customers since January 1, 1997:
   (a) A description of the papers and documents filed by the parties;
   (b) The outcome of the arbitration;
   (c) The decision of the arbitrator;
   (d) The total number of arbitrations filed;
   (e) The total number of arbitrations initiated by you;
   (f) The total number of arbitrations initiated by a payday loan customer;
   (g) The total number of arbitrations initiated by you in which the payday loan customer did not respond, appear or otherwise defend against a notice of arbitration.

29. All documents evidencing or reflecting communications between you and the National Arbitration Forum (NAF) relating to the use of consumer arbitration agreements.

30. All documents evidencing or reflecting communications between you and the American Arbitration Association (AAA) relating to the use of consumer arbitration agreements.

31. All documents obtained at any trainings or conferences attended by your officers, directors and/or employees which relate to the use of arbitration agreements in consumer contracts.

32. All documents evidencing, reflecting, referring to, or relating to any study, analysis, survey, research, etc. by, on behalf of, or used by you concerning how much, what parts, what format, what type, etc. of your contracts are read or are projected to be read by your payday loan customers.

33. All documents evidencing, reflecting, referring to, or relating to any study, analysis, survey, research, etc. by, on behalf of, or used by you concerning how much, what parts, what format, what type, etc. of your contracts are understood or are projected to be understood by your payday loan customers.

34. All documents evidencing, reflecting, referring to, or relating to any study, analysis, survey, research, etc. by, on behalf of, or used by you concerning how many or what percentage or your payday loan customers or potential payday loan customers speak a language other than English as their primary language.

35. All documents, other than the arbitration agreement itself, available to explain to your payday loan customers the meaning of the arbitration provision(s) contained in your contract(s).

36. All documents evidencing queries or complaints from your payday loan customers concerning the arbitration provision(s) used by you.

37. All contracts containing arbitration provision(s) in which you are a party, other than contracts with your payday loan customers, including, but not limited to, any contracts between you and Republic Bank.

38. All manuals, memoranda, guidelines, instructions and other documents setting forth your policies and procedures relating to your collection procedure(s) for payday cash advances that are not returned or otherwise paid by your payday loan customers.

Respectfully submitted, this the _____ day of November, 2004.

[*Attorney for Plaintiffs*]

C.7 Document Request Directed to Auto Title Pawn Company[4]

IN THE CIRCUIT COURT, FOURTH JUDICIAL CIRCUIT, IN AND FOR DUVAL COUNTY, FLORIDA

[*CONSUMER*], on behalf of herself and others similarly situated,
    Plaintiff,

v.

FLORIDA TITLE LOAN, INC., successor by merger with CASH LOANS OF JACKSONVILLE II, INC.
    Defendant.

CLASS REPRESENTATION

---

4 This discovery was provided by Lynn Drysdale, Florida Legal Services, in Jacksonville, Florida.

PLAINTIFFS' REQUEST FOR PRODUCTION OF DOCUMENTS RELATING TO ARBITRATION DIRECTED TO DEFENDANT, FLORIDA TITLE LOAN, INC.

The Plaintiffs, [*Plaintiffs*] (hereinafter "the Plaintiffs"), on behalf of themselves and others similarly situated, pursuant to Rule 1.350, *Florida Rules of Civil Procedure* request the Defendant, Florida Title Loan, Inc., (hereinafter "FTL") to produce the following documents at the offices of Florida Legal Services, Inc., [*address*] or at such other location as is mutually agreeable, within the applicable time period provided by the Florida Rules of Civil Procedure. The title loan(s) which is(are) the subject of the above-styled lawsuit and these requests may be referred to as the "subject loan" in the singular.

I. DEFINITIONS

Unless otherwise stated, the following definitions apply to all of requests herein:

A. "*Documents*" or "*Documentation*" shall mean any kind of written, recorded or graphic matters, however produced or reproduced, of any kind or description whether sent or received, including originals, non-identical copies and drafts of both sides thereof, and including, but not limited to, papers, books, letters, correspondence, telegrams, bulletins, notices, announcements, instructions, charts, manuals, brochures, schedules, internal memoranda, notes, notations, transcripts, minutes, agendas, reports and recordings of telephonic or other conversations, interviews, conferences or other meetings, affidavits, statements, summaries, opinions, reports, studies, analyses, computer print-outs, data processing input/output, microfilms and all other records kept by electronic means, photographic or mechanical means, and other things similar to any of the foregoing.

B. "*Refer*" or "*Relate to*" shall mean to make a statement about, discuss, describe, reflect, constitute, identify, deal with, consist of, establish, comprise, list, evidence, substantiate or in any way pertain, in whole or in part, to the subject.

C. "*Defendants*" shall mean both Florida Title Loan, Inc. and Cash Loans of Jacksonville, II, Inc.

II. DOCUMENTS AND DOCUMENTATION REQUESTED

1. Any and all documents exchanged between the parties that are indexed, filed or retrievable under the Plaintiffs' names or any number, symbol, designation or code (such as a loan number or Social Security number) assigned to the Plaintiffs.

2. Defendants' entire file for the loan transactions for each of the named Plaintiffs.

3. Any and all agreements, contracts, memorandum and other correspondence between the Plaintiffs and FTL.

4. Any and all documents relating to FTL's policies, procedures or practices, relating to its arbitrations of consumer claims or disputes including but not limited to the following: contracts with individuals FTL chooses to serve as arbitrators; invoices and check requests associated with arbitrations; correspondence relating to arbitrations actually commenced; and rules of any professional arbitration association used as guidelines or benchmarks in the arbitrations in which FTL has participated in connection with consumer title loan transaction.

5. The names, including last known address and social security number of each of the borrowers who have participated in an arbitration proceeding with the Defendants concerning a title loan transaction.

6. Any and all documents that provide the following information relating to FTL's arbitrations actually conducted in consumer title loan transactions: the respective costs to the parties relating to the process; a description of the papers and documents filed by the parties; the outcome of the arbitration; the status of the possession of the motor vehicle that was the security for the title loan during and after the arbitration process; and the names and addresses of any persons who served as an arbitrator in said proceeding(s).

7. Any and all documents provided to the Florida Department of Motor Vehicles relating to or concerning the Plaintiffs' title loan transactions.

8. Any and all documents and disclosures provided to the Plaintiffs by the Defendants in an effort to comply with the federal Truth in Lending Act and Regulation Z.

9. Any and all assignments or other documents of transfer executed by the Defendants relating in any way to the transfer or assignment of the Plaintiffs' title loans.

10. Any and all manuals, memoranda, guidelines, instructions, and other documents setting forth the Defendants' policies and procedures relating to the origination or enforcement of arbitration clauses contained in their title loan contracts.

11. Any and all manuals, memoranda, guidelines, instructions, and other documents setting forth the Defendants' policies and procedures relating to compliance with or enforcement of the arbitration clause which is contained in the Plaintiffs' title loan contracts.

12. Any and all of the Defendants' files relating to the named Plaintiffs' title loan transactions.

13. Any and all telephone log sheets, internal memoranda, notes, and other documents concerning any communications relating to or reflecting activity in connection with the Plaintiffs' transactions.

14. Any and all check(s) issued by or to FTL, or any person acting on its behalf, to or from any person or entity, including but not limited to Title Loans of America, Inc. or Kingsland Auto Title Pawn in connection with the Plaintiffs' transactions.

15. Any and all documents in your possession relating to any judicial or administrative proceeding against FTL, Title Loans of America, Inc. and Kingsland Auto Title Loan relating to or arising out of arbitration.

16. Any and all documents, that were purportedly signed by the Plaintiffs and/or the Defendants, its employees, agents or officers concerning any aspect of the subject arbitration clause.

17. Any and all documents the Defendants, and/or employees and/or agents of the Defendants intend to introduce at the hearing referenced in the November 15, 1999 Order on Defendant's Motion to Stay Discovery.

18. A copy of any and all Powers of Attorney obtained from the Plaintiffs in connection with their title loan transactions.

19. Any and all non-privileged documents, materials or things referenced, received or relied upon by the Defendants, its agents or attorneys in preparation of its response to the Plaintiffs' First Set of Interrogatories Relating to Arbitration Directed to Defendant, Florida Title Loan, Inc.

[*Attorney for Plaintiff*]

Appendix D   Brief Requesting Discovery As to Arbitrability

This brief is also available in Microsoft Word and Adobe Acrobat (PDF) format on the CD-Rom accompanying this volume.

NORTH CAROLINA
NEW HANOVER COUNTY

IN THE GENERAL COURT OF JUSTICE
SUPERIOR COURT DIVISION

[PLAINTIFF 1], et al.,
    Plaintiffs,
v.
CHECK INTO CASH OF NORTH CAROLINA, INC., et al.,
    Defendants.

Case No. [No.]

[PLAINTIFF 2], et al.,
    Plaintiffs,
v.
ADVANCE AMERICA, CASH ADVANCE CENTERS OF NORTH CAROLINA, INC., et al.,
    Defendants.

Case No. [No.]

PLAINTIFFS' MOTION REQUESTING DISCOVERY AS TO ARBITRABILITY

Plaintiffs, by and through counsel, hereby request that this Court grant plaintiffs discovery regarding the enforceability of the arbitration agreements that defendants seek to impose upon them. Because the enforceability of defendants' arbitration agreements depends on the totality of facts surrounding their formation and requires this Court to make specific factual findings, this Court should allow the plaintiffs to conduct such discovery so that this Court may resolve the issue of arbitrability.

On July 27, 2004, plaintiffs filed these class actions on behalf of North Carolina consumers who have been victimized by the defendants' predatory lending practices. Defendants did not deny the allegations in plaintiffs' complaint but instead, on September 28, 2004, filed a Motion to Compel Arbitration and Stay Proceedings. Defendants contend that plaintiffs are bound by mandatory pre-dispute arbitration clauses and have sacrificed their rights to proceed in court. Defendants have refused to comply with any discovery pending this Court's ruling on the validity of defendants' arbitration clauses. *See* Defs.' Motion For Protective Order and To Stay Discovery of Oct. 12, 2004.

Although defendants have moved to compel arbitration, this Court cannot refer the case to arbitration unless it first determines that there exists a valid agreement to arbitrate. *See Sloan Fin. Group, Inc. v. Beckett*, 159 N.C. App. 470, 478, 583 S.E.2d 325, 330 (2003) (holding that under both the FAA and North Carolina law, "before a dispute can be ordered resolved through arbitration, there must be a valid agreement to arbitrate"); *see also* G.S. § 1-569.6 (stating that a court must decide if a valid agreement to arbitrate exists).[*] Plaintiffs contend that defendants' arbitration provisions are unenforceable because they are unconscionable and violate public policy. Under the Federal Arbitration Act (FAA), "generally applicable contract law defenses, such as fraud, duress, or unconscionability, may be applied to invalidate arbitration agreements." *Doctor's Assocs., Inc. v. Casarotto*, 517 U.S. 681, 687 (1996). Plaintiffs intend to argue that defendants' arbitration clauses violate public policy and are unenforceable because they reflect a vast disparity in knowledge, bargaining power and economic sophistication between the parties, and because the clauses are unreasonably one-sided in favor of defendants. *See, e.g., Fortson v. McClellan*, 113 N.C. 635, 508 S.E.2d 549 (1998). Plaintiffs' arguments on enforceability require some degree of factual development, and discovery will therefore substantially aid this Court in its task of determining the validity of defendants' arbitration clauses. *See Toppings v. Meritech Mortgage Servs.*, 140 F. Supp. 2d 683, 685 (S.D. W. Va. 2001) ("In order to discharge its obligation to assure there is a valid arbitration agreement, the Court agrees that discovery is necessary on the Toppings' challenges to the Agreement.").[1]

---

[*] [*Editor's Note: Citations throughout brief as in original.*]

[1] In Defendants' Motion For Protective Order and To Stay Discovery and Class Certification Proceedings (Oct. 28, 2004), defendants contend that they should not have to produce discovery on the merits because limited discovery obligations is one of the alleged "benefits" of arbitration. To the extent that this argument is correct (plaintiffs do not conceded that it is correct), it applies only merits discovery and not discovery as to

ARGUMENT

I. PLAINTIFFS ARE ENTITLED TO DISCOVERY ON THE ENFORCEABILITY OF DEFENDANTS' ARBITRATION CLAUSES.

"Under North Carolina discovery rules, subject only to limitation by court order, any party to a civil action is *entitled* to all information relevant to the subject matter of that action unless such information is privileged." *Stone v. Martin*, 56 N.C. App. 473, 476, 289 S.E.2d 898, 900 (1982) (emphasis added); *see* G.S. § 1A-1, Rule 26(b)(1). Plaintiffs' discovery rights are not limited to the underlying merits but also extend to all information relevant to defenses raised by opposing parties. G.S. § 1A-1, Rule 26(b)(1). Moreover, the discovery rules must be liberally construed in order to facilitate informed decision-making as well as a narrowing and sharpening of the issues in the case. *See Williams v. North Carolina Dep't of Corrections*, 120 N.C. App. 356, 359, 462 S.E.2d 545, 547 (1995).

Because the question of the validity of an arbitration agreement often depends on particularized facts, it is well recognized that plaintiffs may take discovery on the question of arbitrability. *See, e.g., Dun Shipping LTD v. Amareda Hess Shipping Corp.*, 234 F. Supp. 2d 291, 294 (S.D.N.Y. 2002) ("Discovery may be appropriate as to the question of arbitrability itself." (internal quotation and citation omitted)). Not only is discovery permissible, but because it is so crucial in the context of arbitration disputes, courts have held that it is an abuse of discretion for a trial court to deny discovery on arbitrability. For example, in *Wrightson v. ITT Fin. Servs., Inc.*, 617 So.2d 334, 336 (Fla. App. 1993), the Florida District Court of Appeal equated a motion to compel arbitration with a motion for summary judgment and found that the trial court should not have issued a ruling on arbitrability without first allowing the parties to engage in discovery. *See id.*; *see also Harrison v. Toyota Motor Sales, Inc.*, 2002 WL 533478 at *2 (Ohio App. Apr. 10, 2002) ("Consequently, we find that the trial court abused its discretion in granting Ganley's motion to stay the proceedings pending arbitration without affording Appellant an opportunity to conduct discovery as to the enforceability of the arbitration clause, and further, to present his findings on this issue."). Similarly, other courts have found that discovery must be allowed for a party alleging that an arbitration is unconscionable because it would be impossible for the party to make its case without it. *See, e.g., Blair v. Scott Specialty Gases*, 283 F.3d 585, 608–09 (3d Cir. 2002) ("Without some discovery, albeit limited to the narrow issue of the estimated costs of arbitration and the claimant's ability to pay, it is not clear how a claimant could present information on the costs of arbitration as required by *Green Tree* [*Fin. Corp. v. Randolph*, 531 U.S. 79, 92 (2000)]...."); *Livingston v. Assocs. Fin., Inc.*, 2001 WL 709465 at *2 (N.D. Ill. June 25, 2001) (allowing discovery on arbitrability because "it seems axiomatic that, if the Supreme Court places a burden of proof on a party, then that party must be given an opportunity to pursue discovery related to the issue that it has the burden to prove"). In fact, discovery on arbitrability is so important that even where plaintiffs have failed to conduct discovery as to unconscionability and consequently have failed to meet their burden, appellate courts, instead of ruling against those plaintiffs, have remanded the arbitration issue and have ordered trial courts to allow discovery. *See, e.g., Parilla v. IAP Worldwide Servs., VI, Inc.*, 368 F.3d 269, 284–85 (3d Cir. 2004) (noting that the plaintiff "submitted no evidence on the potential costs of arbitration or of her inability to pay those costs" to the trial court, but nonetheless remanding because "Parilla must be allowed limited discovery on remand in order to provide her with the means to show her inability to pay the anticipated costs of arbitration."); *Adler v. Fred Lind Manor*, 103 P.3d 773, 786 (Wash. 2004) (finding that plaintiff failed to meet his burden of demonstrating the unconscionability of the arbitration clause but remanding in order to allow discovery).

Discovery is particularly critical in this case because here the plaintiffs contend that defendants' arbitration clauses are unenforceable on unconscionability and public policy grounds. Although unconscionability is a question of law to be decided by a court, under general principles of North Carolina contract law, a court evaluating a claim that a contract is unconscionable or in violation of public policy "must consider all the facts and circumstances" surrounding the contract at issue. *Brenner v. Little Red Sch. House, Ltd.*, 302 N.C. 207, 213, 274 S.E.2d 206, 210 (1981); *Carlson v. Gen'l Motors Corp.*, 883 F.2d 287, 292–93 (4th Cir. 1989). In fact, it is an abuse of discretion for a trial court to rule on unconscionability without first affording the parties a full opportunity to present a detailed factual record. *See Garris v. Garris*, 92 N.C. App. 467, 471–72, 374 S.E.2d 638, 641 (1988) (district court abused its discretion in finding unconscionability as a matter of law without permitting the parties to present additional evidence); *Carlson*, 883 F.2d at 293 (finding that it was an abuse of discretion for a trial court to decide an unconscionability claim solely on the pleadings and instructing that "[t]rial courts obviously cannot apply these standards [of unconscionability] without carefully examining all relevant evidence of the setting in which the parties struck their bargain—and thus cannot resolve *bona fide* questions of unconscionability before the litigants have had an opportunity to present such evidence"). Plaintiffs in this case must be allowed to take discovery in order to develop a factual record on unconscionability. Without such discovery, this Court will not have sufficient information at its disposal to make a ruling on arbitrability.

Recognizing that unconscionability claims require a fully developed factual record, several courts have allowed discovery on arbitrability where, as here, parties challenge arbitration clauses as unconscionable. For example, in circumstances virtually identical to the present case, a New York court allowed a payday loan customer to take discovery as to whether the arbitration clause banning class actions in her payday loan contract was unconscionable. *See Hayes. v. County Bank*, 713 N.Y.S. 2d 267 (N.Y. Sup. Ct. 2000); *see also Toppings*, 140 F. Supp. 2d at 685 (allowing discovery with respect to unconscionability); *Hodge v. Equifirst Corp.*, 2000 WL 33775397 (S.D. W. Va. July 31, 2000) (same); *Ting v. AT&T*, 182 F. Supp. 902, 934 (N.D. Cal. 2002) (noting that much of the plaintiffs' evidence on unconscionability was "gleaned from discovery"), *aff'd in relevant part*, 319 F.3d 1126 (9th Cir. 2003).

Furthermore, the fact that evidence of the defendants' knowledge subjective motivations in fashioning and adopting their arbitration clauses is relevant in assessing unconscionability also demonstrates why discovery is necessary. *See Carlson*, 883 F.2d at

---

arbitrability. Defendants have a right to the "benefits" of arbitration only if there is a valid agreement to arbitrate. As explained in this motion, discovery on arbitrability is necessary for this Court to decide whether defendants' arbitration agreements are valid and enforceable.

295–96 ("Surveying the cases, one noted treatise observes that 'judicial finding[s] of lack of 'meaningful choice' . . . [are] usually founded upon a recipe consisting of one or more parts of assumed consumer ignorance and several parts of the seller's guile'; and it is at this level that court have necessarily case 'unconscionability' in largely *subjective* terms."). Plaintiffs are not mind readers. They cannot plumb the depths of defendants' knowledge, sophistication and motivation except through discovery.

Moreover, plaintiffs will suffer substantial prejudice if denied the opportunity to conduct discovery. As some scholars have noted, it is often impossible to develop the facts necessary to demonstrate unconscionability in the absence of discovery. *See* Jean R. Sternlight & Elizabeth J. Jensen, *Using Arbitration Clauses To Eliminate Consumer Class Actions: Efficient Business Practice or Unconscionable Clause?*, 67 Law & Contemp. Probs. 75, 100 (2004) ("For instance, in *Ting* [*v. AT&T*, 182 F. Supp. 2d 902 (N.D. Cal. 2002) (cited, *supra*)], the plaintiffs were able to convince the court to throw out the arbitration clause *only because they conducted extensive discovery* and presented large quantities of factual information at trial.") (emphasis added). Similarly, practitioners litigating arbitration questions have emphasized that their success in challenging unconscionable arbitration clauses has been due in large part to evidence obtained through discovery. *See* James C. Sturdevant, *The Critical Importance of Creating an Evidentiary Record To Prove that a Mandatory, Pre-Dispute Arbitration Clause is Unconscionable*, Forum, at 18 (Oct. 2002) [attached as Ex. ___, hereto] (describing how discovery evidence proved crucial in defeating arbitration clauses in two cases, and concluding "that the decisions in *Badie* [*v. Bank of America, N.A.*, 67 Cal. App. 4th 779 (Cal. App. 1998)] and *Ting* striking mandatory pre-dispute arbitration clauses for lack of consent and unconscionability, respectively, demonstrate the real difference substantial discovery can make to proving why the provisions in a particular clause are invalid under state law"). This Court's decision whether to allow discovery has the potential to make or break plaintiffs' case. Thus, because plaintiffs have asserted a colorable claim that the defendants' arbitration provisions are unenforceable on grounds of unconscionability and public policy, this Court should permit the plaintiffs to take discovery with respect to arbitrability.

II. PLAINTIFFS' DISCOVERY REQUESTS ARE RELEVANT TO THE UNCONSCIONABILITY OF DEFENDANTS' ARBITRATION CLAUSE.

Plaintiffs' discovery requests seek information that is relevant to the enforceability of defendants' arbitration clauses and that is not privileged, and therefore plaintiffs' requests should be granted. *See Stone*, 56 N.C. App. at 476. At the outset, although plaintiffs believe that every interrogatory and request for production of documents contained in Plaintiffs' Second Set of Interrogatories and Request for Product of Documents to Corporate Defendants is relevant to the question of arbitrability, in the interests of reducing the burden on the defendants in producing the discovery, and of facilitating a speedy but thorough resolution of the arbitration issue by this Court, plaintiffs have voluntarily narrowed their discovery requests. *See* Letter from Carlene McNulty, attached as Exhibit 1 hereto. Plaintiffs' actions, therefore, in no way constitute an admission concerning the relevance of any of the excluded discovery requests. Plaintiffs' remaining discovery requests can be broken down into several categories, each of which is relevant to the enforceability of the arbitration provisions, as is explained below.

A. Copies of Defendants' Arbitration Clauses.

Plaintiffs' Request for Production #19 seeks all contracts containing arbitration provisions that were created or used by defendants since 1997. It goes without saying that if defendants are going to attempt to bind plaintiffs to contracts containing arbitration clauses, that plaintiffs are entitled to see such clauses. The contracts themselves contain the relevant arbitration terms that this Court must analyze for the purpose of determining unconscionability. Moreover, plaintiffs are entitled to see past contracts containing arbitration clauses used by defendants because the manner in which the defendants have altered or modified their arbitration clauses over time sheds light on the defendants' motivation and purpose in imposing their current arbitration clause. *See Carlson*, 883 F.2d at 295–96 (a contracting party's subjective knowledge and motivation is relevant to unconscionability).

B. Arbitrator Bias

The alleged bias and partiality of a selected arbitration forum is relevant to the enforceability of an arbitration clause, and plaintiffs are entitled to discovery as to bias. In *Toppings v. Meritech Mortgage Servs., Inc.*, 140 F. Supp. 2d 683 (S.D. W. Va. 2001), the court stated:

> In order to discharge its obligation to assure that there is a valid arbitration agreement, the Court agrees that discovery is necessary on the Toppings' challenges to the Agreement. The Court believes additional factual development is warranted, particularly, *without limitation*, on both the issues of unconscionability *and the impartiality and other challenges to the* [*National Arbitration Forum*] *NAF as the chosen arbitral forum.*

Id. at 685 (emphasis added); *see also Hayes v. County Bank*, 713 N.Y.S.2d at 270 (allowing plaintiff challenging the enforceability of an arbitration agreement contained a payday loan contract to take discovery pertaining to alleged bias by the arbitrator).

Here, Interrogatory #13 and Request for Production #28 are relevant to bias because they seek information concerning how often defendants arbitrate disputes with their payday loan customers and how often they succeed. It stands to reason that the more frequently defendants prevail in arbitration, the greater likelihood there is of bias. For example, if defendants initiated 10,000 arbitrations against their payday loan customers in the same forum and won every single time, that fact certainly would give rise to an inference of bias. Defendants cannot credibly argue that plaintiffs would have no right to know that a defendant seeking to compel arbitration has a 100% success rate when appearing in the arbitral forum. These requests, therefore, are relevant.

C. Absence of Meaningful Choice

Another factor that is relevant in determining if defendants' arbitration clauses are unconscionable is the absence of meaningful choice on the part of plaintiffs to obtain a payday loan without having to agree to arbitration. *See Brenner*, 302 N.C. at 210 (holding that a contract is unconscionable if it is so one-sided so as to deprive a party of "meaningful choice"). For example, in *Ting v. AT&T*, 182 F. Supp. 2d 902, 914–15 (N.D. Cal. 2002), *aff'd in relevant part*, 319 F.3d 1126 (9th Cir. 2003), the court found that an arbitration clause contained in a contract for telephone service offered by a long-distance telephone company deprived consumers of meaningful choice and was procedurally unconscionable because there were very few other long-distance carriers in the area that did not require their customers to agree to arbitration. *See id.* ("Customers did not have any meaningful choice with respect to the Legal Remedies Provisions because the carriers who service 2/3 of the California market all include substantially similar dispute resolution provisions in their contracts."); *see also Am. Gen'l Fin. v. Branch*, 793 So.2d 738, 750–51 (Ala. 2000) (finding that a plaintiff seeking a loan lacked meaningful choice where "only 1 or 2 [lending] companies out of 16 might have allowed her to borrow money in November 1997 without agreeing to arbitrate").

Interrogatories #19 and #20 are relevant because they relate to the plaintiffs' ability to obtain a payday loan from other lenders without having to agree to arbitration. Whether or not other payday lenders in North Carolina require their customers to sign arbitration agreements is undoubtedly relevant to the plaintiffs' lack of meaningful choice.

D. Exculpatory Clauses Disclaiming Legal Liability

Under general principles of North Carolina contract law, a contract violates public policy and is unenforceable if it effectively immunizes one party to the agreement from legal liability. *See Fortson*, 113 N.C. 635; *Miller's Mutual Fire Ins. Ass'n v. Parker*, 234 N.C. 20, 24, 65 S.E.2d 341, 344 (1951). This basic principle of contract law was applied in the arbitration context in *Ting*, where the court found that the defendant AT&T's arbitration clause banning class actions was effectively exculpatory on the basis of evidence showing that before AT&T adopted a class action ban, consumers had prosecuted several successful class actions against it. *See Ting*, 182 F. Supp. 2d at 918. In one case, AT&T, paid out 100% of class members' claims, and in another agreed to an $88 million settlement. *See id.* The court held that those cases could not have been brought if an arbitration clause containing a class action ban had been in place, no attorney would have handled them on an individual basis. *See id.* Because the clause was exculpatory, the court found it to be unconscionable. *See id.* at 928–30.

Interrogatory #14(a–b), in which plaintiffs seek the name and case number of each class action brought against defendants by a payday loan customer, is relevant to whether the defendants' class action ban operates as an exculpatory clause. Like in *Ting*, evidence that payday loan customers, prior to the defendants' adoption of their current arbitration clauses, were able to successfully prosecute class claims that could not have been brought on an individual basis would be probative of the exculpatory nature of defendants' arbitration clause.

E. Unfair Surprise

Defendants' arbitration clause also may be unconscionable and unenforceable if it is written and presented in such a way that defendants' customers are unlikely to realize that they are signing an arbitration clause, or to understand its terms—i.e., where a contracting party is a victim of "unfair surprise." *See, e.g., King v. Owen*, 601 S.E.2d 326, 328 (N.C. App. 2004) ("Chicago Title offered no evidence that plaintiffs were aware of the arbitration clause in the policy at the time they closed the property, much less that the clause was the result of independent negotiations."); *Ting*, 182 F. Supp. 2d at 929–30 (finding a contract containing an arbitration clause unenforceable where it "possessed the 'surprise' necessary for a finding of procedural unconscionability"). A plaintiff can suffer unfair surprise in any number of ways, including (1) where the plaintiff does not speak English and is not given a translation of the agreement, *see Prevot v. Phillips Petroleum Co.*, 133 F. Supp. 2d 937, 940–41 (S.D. Tex. 2001); (2) where the arbitration clause is written in such a way that a typical consumer at a typical reading level would be unlikely to understand the clause's meaning and import, *see Geiger v. Ryan's Family Steak Houses, Inc.*, 134 F. Supp. 2d 985, 999 (S.D. Ind. 2001); (3) where the plaintiff is functionally illiterate and therefore could not comprehend the meaning of the arbitration clause, *see In re Turner Bros. Trucking Co., Inc.*, 8 S.W.3d 370, 376–77 (Tex. App. 1999); and (4) where the arbitration clause is purposely written in a way so as to discourage customers from reading it, *see Ting*, 182 F. Supp. 2d at 911–13, 929–30 (finding unfair surprise where it was unlikely that most customers read the contract containing the arbitration clause).

Several of plaintiffs discovery requests relate to unfair surprise. Specifically, Interrogatories #15–17, and Requests for Production # 20–21 and # 32–36 pertain to the likelihood that plaintiffs read and understood the arbitration clause, understood the rights they were forsaking by agreeing to arbitration and realized that they were in fact agreeing to arbitration, and the likelihood that defendants explained to their customers that they were signing an arbitration clause.

F. Defendants' Subjective Knowledge and Intent

Defendants' subjective knowledge and intent in adopting their arbitration provisions also is relevant in assessing unconscionability. Specifically, in seeking to demonstrate the unconscionability of defendants' arbitration clauses, plaintiffs are entitled to present evidence pertaining to, *inter alia*, defendants' knowledge concerning the effect of the arbitration clause, defendants' commercial sophistication and bargaining power, and defendants' ability to prey on consumer ignorance. *See Carlson*, 883 F.2d at 295–96. Requests for Production # 22–23, 25–27, 31 and 37 all relate to defendants' knowledge about the effects of their arbitration clauses as well as their motivations in adopting the arbitration clauses. Therefore, these discovery requests are relevant.

CONCLUSION

For the foregoing reasons, plaintiffs request that this Court allow plaintiffs to take discovery on the question of arbitrability and direct defendants to answer the specific discovery requests mentioned herein.

Appendix E Briefs on Arbitration Costs, Damage Limitations, and Unconscionability

These briefs are also available in Microsoft Word and Adobe Acrobat (PDF) format on the CD-Rom accompanying this volume.

E.1 Opening Brief Focusing on Unconscionability Based on Cost (Leeman)

IN THE SUPREME COURT OF ALABAMA

```
_____  )
                          )
GARY LEEMAN AND           )
KATHRYN LEEMAN,           )
              Appellants, )
                          )
v.                        )  No. 1022063
                          )
COOK'S PEST CONTROL,      )
INC., a corporation; et al, )
              Appellees.  )
_____  )
```

After an Order by the Circuit Court of Jefferson County, Civil Action No. CV-02-4976, Granting Appellee's Motion to Compel Arbitration and Stay Proceedings

APPELLANTS' OPENING BRIEF

ORAL ARGUMENT REQUESTED

STATEMENT REGARDING ORAL ARGUMENT

Appellants respectfully suggest that oral argument is appropriate and desirable in this case. The case poses important issues of public policy, and presents this Court with a well developed evidentiary record on the subject of arbitration costs in a consumer setting. While no one in this case disputes that the Federal Arbitration Act embodies a policy favoring the enforcement of valid arbitration agreements, this case raises the issue of whether generally applicable principles of Alabama contract law place an outer limit on the use of arbitration clauses in contracts of adhesion that are proven to impose enormous arbitration fees on persons bringing modest consumer claims.

TABLE OF CONTENTS

STATEMENT REGARDING ORAL ARGUMENT
TABLE OF CONTENTS
TABLE OF AUTHORITIES
STATEMENT OF JURISDICTION
STATEMENT OF THE CASE
STATEMENT OF THE ISSUE
STATEMENT OF THE FACTS
FACTS RELATING TO OVERWHELMING BARGAINING POWER
THE FACTUAL RECORD ON COSTS OF ARBITRATION UNDER COOK'S ARBITRATION CLAUSE
   1) The AAA's Commercial Rules Govern This Dispute
   2) Evidence of Arbitration Costs Imposed upon Consumers in Other Cases Against Cook's and Similar Pest Control Companies
   3) The Impossibility of Finding Counsel to Advance These Fees
STANDARD OF REVIEW
SUMMARY OF THE ARGUMENT
ARGUMENT
   I. This Court Should Apply Alabama Law to Determine Whether Cook's Arbitration Clause Is Unconscionable
      A. This Court must Determine Whether Cook's Arbitration Clause Is Unconscionable
      B. Alabama State Contract Law Governs the Question Of Whether This Arbitration Clause Is Unconscionable
   II. Cook's Arbitration Clause Is Unconscionable In This Case Because It Was Imposed Through Cook's Overwhelming Bargaining Power
      A. The Leemans Had No Meaningful Choice to Avoid Arbitration
      B. The Leemans Were Surprised, Given Cook's Failure to Disclose Information and the Impossibility of Determining the Costs of Arbitration
      C. Cook's Contract is Not Rendered Conscionable Merely Because the Leemans are Educated People
   III. The Arbitration Clause At Issue In This Case Contains Terms That Are Grossly Favorable To Cook's
      A. Cook's Arbitration Clause is So Broad As to Cover All Real and Potential Consumer Claims
      B. The Law is Clear that Arbitration Clauses that Impose

Prohibitive Costs on Consumers are Grossly Favorable to the Drafting Party
   1. The United States Supreme Court has declared that arbitral costs must not be so high as to deny claimants a forum to vindicate their rights
   2. Alabama law is consistent with the U.S. Supreme Court's prohibition on prohibitively costly arbitration clauses
C. The Record Here Demonstrates that Cook's Arbitration Clause is Prohibitively Expensive
D. The Circuit Court's Decision Relating to the Costs of Arbitration is Based on Two Major Mistakes of Fact and Law

CONCLUSION

APPENDIX [*omitted*]

TABLE OF AUTHORITIES

Case Authorities[*]

Alexander v. Anthony Int'l, 341 F.3d 256 (3d Cir. 2003)
American Gen. Fin., Inc. v. Branch, 793 So.2d 738 (Ala. 2000)
Anderson v. Ashby, 2003 WL 21125998 (Ala. May 16, 2003)
Armendariz v. Found. Health Psychcare Services, Inc., 24 Cal. 4th 83, 99 Cal. Rptr. 2d 745, 6 P.3d 669 (2000)
Arnold v. Goldstar Fin. Sys., Inc., 2002 WL 1941546 (N.D. Ill. Aug. 22, 2002)
Arnold v. United Companies Lending Corp., 204 W. Va. 229, 511 S.E.2d 854 (1998)
Ballard v. Southwest Detroit Hosp., 119 Mich. App. 814, 327 N.W. 2d 370 (1982)
BankAmerica Housing Services v. Lee, 833 So.2d 609 (Ala. 2002)
Bowen v. Security Pest Control, Inc., 2003 WL 22272915 (Ala. Oct. 3, 2003)
Brennan v. Bally Total Fitness, 198 F.Supp.3d 377 (S.D.N.Y. 2002)
Camancho v. Holiday Homes, Inc., 167 F.Supp.2d 892 (W.D. Va. 2001)
Circuit City Stores, Inc. v. Adams, 279 F.3d 889 (9th Cir. 2002), cert. denied, 535 U.S. 1112 (2002)
City of Mobile v. Jackson, 474 So.2d 644 (Ala. 1985)
Comb v. Paypal, Inc., 218 F.Supp.2d 1165 (N.D. Cal. 2002)
Cook's Pest Control v. Rebar, 852 So.2d 730 (Ala. 2002)
Cooper v. MRM Inv. Co., 199 F.Supp.2d 771 (M.D. Tenn. 2002)
Doctor's Assoc., Inc. v. Casarotto, 517 U.S. 681 (1996)
East Ford, Inc. v. Taylor, 826 So.2d 709 (Miss. 2002)
Ex parte Dan Tucker Auto Sales, Inc., 718 So.2d 33 (Ala. 1998)
Ex parte Roberson, 749 So.2d 441 (Ala. 1999)
Ex parte Thicklin, 824 So.2d 723 (Ala. 2002)
Faber v. Menard, Inc., 267 F.Supp.2d 961 (N.D. Iowa 2003)
Gayfer Montgomery Fair Co. v. Austin, 2003 WL 21480639 (Ala. July 27, 2003)
Geiger v. Ryan's Family Steak Houses, Inc., 134 F.Supp. 2d 985 (S.D. Ind. 2001)
Gilmer v. Interstate/Johnson Lane Corp., 500 U.S. 20 (1991)
Giordano v. Pep Boys–Manny, Moe & Jack, Inc., 2001 WL 484360 (E.D. Pa. Mar. 29, 2001)
Graham v. Scissor-Tail, 28 Cal. 3d 807, 171 Cal. Rptr. 604, 623 P.2d 165 (1981)
Green Tree Fin. Corp. v. Lewis, 813 So.2d 820 (Ala. 2001)
Green Tree Financial Corp. v. Randolph, 513 U.S. 79 (2000)
Green Tree Fin. Corp. V. Wampler, 749 So.2d 409 (Ala. 1999)
Harold Allen's Mobile Home Factory Outlet, Inc. v. Butler, 825 So.2d 799 (Ala. 2002)
Hutcherson v. Sears Roebuck & Co., 793 N.E.2d 886 (Ill. App. 2003)
In re Knepp, 229 B.R. 823 (Bankr. N.D. Ala. 1999)
In re Turner Bros. Trucking Co., 8 S.W.3d 370 (Tex. App. 1999)
Iwen v. U.S. W. Direct, 293 Mont. 512, 977 P.2d 989 (1999)
Layne v. Gardner, 612 So.2d 404 (Ala. 1992)
Leonard v. Terminix, 854 So.2d 529 (Ala. 2002)
Lozada v. Dale Baker Oldsmobile, Inc., 91 F.Supp.2d 1987 (W.D. Mich. 2000)
Luna Household Fin. Corp., 236 F.Supp.2d 1161 (W.D. Wash. 2002)
Mason v. Acceptance Loan Co., Inc., 850 So.2d 289 (Ala. 2002)
Maxwell v. Fidelity Fin. Servs., Inc., 907 P.2d 51 (Ariz. 1995)
Mendez v. Palm Harbor Homes, Inc., 45 P.3d 594 (Wash. Ct. App. 2002)
Mitisubishi Motors Corp. v. Soler Chrysler-Plymouth, Inc., 473 U.S. 614 (1985)
Morrison v. Circuit City Stores, Inc., 317 F.3d 646 (6th Cir. 2003)
Myers v. Terminix Int'l Co., 91 Ohio Misc. 2d 41, 497 N.E.2d 227 (Ct. Com. Pl. 1998)
Nicholson v. Labor Ready, Inc., 1997 U.S. Dist. LEXIS 23494 (N.D. Cal. May 23, 1997)
O'Donoghue v. Smythe, Cramer Co., 2002 WL 1454074 (Ohio Ct. App. July 3, 2002)
Perry v. Thomas, 482 U.S. 483 (1987)
Phillips v. Associates Home Equity Services, Inc., 179 F.Supp.2d 840 (N.D. Ill. 2001)
Plaskett v. Bechtel Int'l., 243 F.Supp.2d 334 (D.V.I. 2003)
Popovich v. McDonald's Corp., 2002 WL 47965 (N.D. Ill. Jan. 14, 2002)
Powertel, Inc. v. Bexley, 743 So.2d 570 (Fla. Dist. Ct. App. 1999)
Prevot v. Phillips Petroleum Co., 133 F.Supp. 2d 937 (S.D. Tex. 2001)
Prima Paint Corp. v. Flood & Conklin Mfg. Co., 388 U.S. 398 (1967)
Reece v. Finch, 562 SO.2d 195 (Ala. 1990)
Sears Termite & Pest Control, Inc. v. Robinson, 2003 WL 21205646 (Ala. May 23, 2003)
Shankle v. B-G Maint. Mgmt. Of Colo., Inc., 163 F.3d 1230 (10th Cir. 1999)
Sosa v. Paulos, 924 P.2d 357 (Utah 1996)
Stevens v. Phillips, 852 So.2d 123 (Ala. 2002)
Teleserv Sys., Inc. v. MCI Telecommunications Corp., 230 A.D. 2d 585, 659 N.Y.S.2d 659 (1997)
Ticknor v. Choice Hotels Int'l, Inc., 265 F.3d 931 (9th Cir. 2001)
Ting v. AT&T, 182 F.Supp.2d 902 (N.D. Cal. 2002) 319 F.3d 1126 (9th Cir. 2003), cert. denied, 2003 WL 1988529 (Oct. 6, 2003)
Toppings v. Meritech Mort., 569 S.E.2d 149 (W.Va. 2002)
Vann v. First Community Credit Corp., 834 So.2d 751 (Ala. 2002)
Williams v. Aetna Fin. Co., 83 Ohio St. 3d 464, 700 N.E.2d 859 (1998), cert. denied, 526 U.S. 1051 (1999)
Worldwide Ins. Group v. Klopp, 603 A.2d 788 (Del. Supr. 1992)
Zak v. Prudential Prop. & Cas. Ins. Co., 713 A.2d 681 (Pa. Super. Ct. 1998)

---

[*] [*Editor's Note: Citations throughout brief as in original.*]

Statutes Authorities

Ala. Admin. Code 80-10-9-.18
Alabama Code § 7-2-302
Ala. R. App. P.4(b)
9 U.S.C. § 2

Other Authorities

2 Law of Remedies 703, 706, Dan B. Dobbs (2nd ed. 1993)
American Arbitration Association, Commercial Arbitration Rules and Mediation Procedures website, http://www.adr.org/index2.1.jsp?JSPssis=15747
National Consumer Law Center, *Consumer Arbitration Agreements: Enforceability and Other Topics* (2d ed. 2002)
Public Citizen Congress Watch, *The Cost of Arbitration* (2002) http://www.citizen.org/documents/ACF110A.PDF

STATEMENT OF JURISDICTION

This Court has jurisdiction over this appeal under Ala. R. App. P. 4(d), "Appeals from Orders Granting or Denying Motions to Compel Arbitration." That rule provides that "an order granting or denying a motion to compel arbitration is appealable as a matter of right, and any appeal from such an order must be taken within 42 days. . . ."

The Circuit Court granted Appellee Cook's Pest Control's Motion to Compel Arbitration on July 23, 2003, and Appellants filed this appeal forty (40) days later on September 2, 2003. This appeal is thus timely and appropriate under Rule 4(d).

STATEMENT OF THE CASE

This case was originally filed in the Circuit Court of Jefferson County on August 19, 2002. In their Complaint, Gary and Kathryn Leeman ("the Leemans") alleged that defendants had failed to provide termite extermination services required by statute and the parties' contract, that defendants had negligently and recklessly failed to properly supervise inspectors and exterminators, and various other state and contract law violations related to termite inspection, prevention and eradication. Clerk's Record ("C") 1. The Complaint was filed against Cook's Pest Control, the extermination company, as well as three individuals: James Aycock, President of Cook's Pest Control; Harold R. Pinckard, a Certified Pest Operator, and Dennis Duggan, the Pest Control Representative from Cook's who signed the contract with the Leemans.

On September 19, 2002, Defendants ("Cook's") filed a Motion to Compel Arbitration and Stay Proceedings. C15. Cook's claimed that under the terms of the Leemans' contract, which they signed in May 2000, the Leemans claims could only be brought in arbitration before the American Arbitration Association ("AAA").

On Nov. 18, 2002, the Leemans filed a request for an extension of time in order to permit discovery regarding Cook's Motion to Compel. C46. Specifically, the Leemans asked to be able to gather evidence relating to the cost of prior arbitration proceedings against Cook's and other pest control companies. C43.

On June 4, 2003, Cook's filed a Supplemental Motion to Compel Arbitration. C59.[1]

On June 6, 2003, the Leemans filed their First Opposition to Defendants' Motion to Compel Arbitration. C79. In this Opposition, the Leemans argued that 1) the arbitration clause in the contract between Cook's and the Leemans was unconscionable and unenforceable because of its breadth, imposition of prohibitive costs, and lack of meaningful choice; and 2) the three individuals listed as defendants in the complaint were not parties to the contract and thus could not compel arbitration. C79. The Leemans' Opposition included extensive exhibits relating to the cost of arbitration. C86.

On June 17, 2003, Cook's filed a Reply to Plaintiffs' Opposition, C534, arguing that its arbitration clause was not unconscionable under Alabama law and that the clause could be invoked by the individual defendants, as the Leemans' claims against these individuals were "intertwined" with those against the company.

On June 20, 2003, the Leemans filed a Supplemental Opposition to the Motion to Compel. C602.

On June 30, Cook's filed a Reply to Plaintiffs' Supplemental Opposition. C644.

On July 1, 2003, the Leemans filed a Second Supplemental Opposition to the Motion to Compel Arbitration. C649. The Leemans attached trial exhibits from *Leonard v. Terminix*, 854 So.2d 529 (Ala. 2002), to this Supplemental Opposition, and asked the court to take judicial notice of these documents. C650.

On July 23, 2003, the Circuit Court entered its order granting Cook's Motion to Compel Arbitration. C794. The court held that the non-signatory defendants may enforce the arbitration clause so long as the clause is valid, and that the clause is not unconscionable because the cost of arbitration is not high enough in relation to the potential recovery in arbitration to make the cost truly prohibitive.

STATEMENT OF THE ISSUE

1. Where the party with greater economic power drafts an arbitration clause that is imposed upon a consumer without the possibility of negotiation, and all the other companies in that field require consumers to sign similar arbitration provisions, and the arbitration provision has an exceptionally broad scope, is the arbitration provision unconscionable when it requires consumers to pay undisclosed arbitration forum fees in the range of $12,000 to $16,000 to obtain any remedy for wrongs done to the consumers?

STATEMENT OF THE FACTS

On May 15, 2000, Gary Leeman, a public school principal, and his wife Kathryn, an elementary school teacher, entered into a Subterranean Termite Control Agreement Service Order and Retreatment Guarantee (the "Termite Control Contract") with Cook's Pest Control to cover termite inspections in their new home. C574. The Termite Control Contract was part of a packet of materials that the Leemans were given to sign at the closing on their home. C578.

No Cook's representative was present at the closing. C564. Instead, the Contract had the pretyped signature of Dennis Duggan, identified as "Cook's Pest Control Representative." C38. The Contract contained an extremely broad arbitration provision stating that "any dispute, controversy or claim arising out of or relating to the agreement and guarantee or the breach thereof, or arising out of any prior or future dealings between Cook's and customer, shall

---

[1] Cook's also filed a Supplement to its Motion to Compel Arbitration, on June 4, 2003. However, that document focused exclusively on whether the Termite Control Contract was a contract in interstate commerce, a question that is not at issue in this appeal.

be settled in arbitration. . . ." C17. The arbitration clause further stated that arbitration would proceed in accordance with the Commercial Rules of the American Arbitration Association ("AAA"). *Id.*

The Leemans believed that their contract with Cook's covered all termite inspection, annual reinspection and remediation. C576–77. With this understanding, they renewed the contract the following year. C583. However, in late 2001, just before Christmas, when Cook's arrived to do a retreatment of their property, the Leemans learned that their home was infested with termites. C585–86.

Because they believed that Cook's had not lived up to its agreement to protect their home from termite infestation, the Leemans brought the present suit in Circuit Court in Jefferson County on August 19, 2002. In their Complaint, the Leemans alleged that their home had not been adequately inspected and treated against termite infestation, and that Cook's had misrepresented that it would adequately inspect and treat the property. C5–6. The Leemans' specific claims against Cook's in the Complaint included: fraud, breach of warranty, negligence, breach of contract, and unjust enrichment. C9–12. The Leemans asked for unspecified damages including compensatory, incidental, consequential and punitive damages, as well as equitable relief against Cook's. C12. Damages were unspecified because the Leemans could not quantify the amount of damage that had been done to their home, or the extent of other compensable damage. C563, 592.

Cook's, on behalf of all defendants, responded to the Leemans' Complaint by filing a Motion to Compel Arbitration and Stay Proceedings. C15. Cook's stated that because Kathryn Leeman had signed the Termite Control Contract, and because the Leemans received the benefit of the contract in the form of the termite retreatment on December 7, 2001, the Leemans were bound to the contract and the arbitration clause found therein. C30–31.

The Leemans opposed arbitration of their claims against Cook's. They argued that the clause was the product of overwhelming bargaining power, and that it contained two major terms that were grossly favorable to Cook's: first, the breadth of the clause, which purported to cover all prior and future claims against the company, C80-81; and second, the excessive cost of arbitration under the AAA Commercial Rules. C81.

Facts Relating to Overwhelming Bargaining Power

The Leemans were presented with a contract as part of a stack of closing documents for their new home. No one pointed out the arbitration clause to the Leemans. There was no Cook's representative present to answer any questions they may have had about the contract or the arbitration clause. C564. No one explained to them the potential costs that they would have to incur if they brought future claims to arbitration under the AAA Commercial Rules. In fact, Cook's admits that it does not advise its employees how to answer questions about the arbitration clause. C421–422 ("[W]e are not the neighborhood advice givers . . . as far as how to interpret contracts. I think people can understand the terms themselves. And if they need more information about it, there are other sources to get that information than from us.").

Even if they had attempted to investigate the matter, the Leemans had no way to learn the full magnitude of costs of AAA arbitration. As this Statement of Facts will discuss in more detail below, the record contains extensive evidence of the costs imposed on consumers who brought other claims against Cook's to arbitration. In those other cases, AAA not only charged filing fees (money that goes to the AAA itself to administer cases and perform the types of functions handled by court clerks), but also charged very significant arbitrators' fees (money that goes to the for-profit AAA arbitrators themselves).[2] The hourly and/or daily rates of arbitrators are not posted on the AAA's website or otherwise made available to consumers such as the Leemans; indeed, the only way that a consumer can learn the magnitude of the costs that are likely to be imposed is to use the discovery process in litigation such as this to uncover what costs have been imposed upon other consumers in the past.

The record establishes that at the time the Leemans signed the Termite Control Contract, nearly every other pest control company in Alabama also required its consumers to agree to mandatory, binding, pre-dispute arbitration. The record includes standard form contracts, complete with arbitration provisions, from Orkin Exterminating Company, Vulcan Termite, Inc., Terminix Int'l, American Pest Control, and Alapestco. C703–735.[3] Cook's acknowledged in its interrogatory answers in this case that "Cook's is not aware of any particular competitor that does not include a provision for arbitration in its customer agreements, ..." C476. Cook's further stated that "Cook's is aware that many pest control operators in the State of Alabama do require its [sic] customers to agree to submit disputes to arbitration, . . ." *Id.*

The record establishes that the Leemans had no input into negotiating the terms of the Termite Control Contract, which was a standard form contract drafted by Cook's. Cook's General Counsel, Donald Sides, said in the company's Rule 30(b)(6) deposition testimony below that Cook's arbitration clauses "were part of the standard contract" used by Cook's, rather than being individually negotiated agreements. C342. In its answers to the Leemans' interrogatories, Cook's answered the question "Can a customer negotiate removal of the arbitration clause?" with the statement, "No, not as a general rule." C476. In answer to the next question, "Would this Defendant transact business with a customer who refused to sign the arbitration clause?" Cook's stated simply, "No." *Id.*[4]

---

2 This fact is also widely recognized in the case law. *See, e.g., Phillips v. Associates Home Equity Services, Inc.*, 179 F. Supp.2d 840, 846 (N.D. Ill. 2001) ("Furthermore, the initial filing fee is far from the only cost involved in the arbitration. The AAA's Commercial Rules provide that the arbitrator's fees (which range from $750 to $5,000 per day, with an average of $1,800 per day in the Chicago area), travel expenses, rental of a hearing room, and other costs are borne equally by the parties. . . ."); *Camacho v. Holiday Homes, Inc.*, 167 F. Supp.2d 892, 897 (W.D. Va. 2001) ("However, even if the initial $2,000 in administrative fees were waived or deferred, Mrs. Camacho has demonstrated that the additional costs of the arbitration process itself amount to an insurmountable financial burden to her.").

3 This Court already has notice of the fact that still other pest control companies also impose arbitration clauses upon their customers. This Court recently heard cases against Sears Termite & Pest Control and Security Pest Control that revolved around the arbitration clauses in those companies' standard contracts. *See Sears Termite & Pest Control, Inc. v. Robinson*, 2003 WL 21205646 (Ala. May 23, 2003); *Bowen v. Security Pest Control, Inc.*, 2003 WL 22272915 (Ala. Oct. 3, 2003).

4 This statement echoes a similar statement made by one of Cook's attorneys during the oral argument before this Court in

The Factual Record on Costs of Arbitration under Cook's Arbitration Clause

1. The AAA's Commercial Rules Govern this Dispute.

The undisputed record in this case establishes that the AAA's Commercial Rules apply to this dispute, not the less expensive AAA Consumer Rules. First, the arbitration clause itself specifies that disputes will be resolved under the AAA Commercial Rules. C38. Furthermore, as noted above, the Leemans have sought equitable and injunctive relief for their claims, a category of relief to which they are entitled under Alabama law should they prevail upon their claims.[5] In addition, the Leemans were not able to specify a dollar figure for their damages claims. Accordingly, the record establishes that these claims fall within the AAA's Commercial Rules.

In an e-mail to the Leemans' counsel that was put into evidence in this case, a AAA representative named Margaret Wilson of the AAA stated that any consumer bringing a claim in arbitration for unspecified damages or injunctive relief is automatically placed under the Commercial Arbitration Rules. C329.[6]

The Commercial Rules state that the consumer must pay a nonrefundable filing fee of $3250 and a nonrefundable administrative fee. C329.[7] The administrative fee, called a "Case Service Fee," was $750 in 2001, when the Leemans originally filed this claim; it has now gone up to $1250. Compare C166 with American Arbitration Association, Commercial Arbitration Rules and Mediation Procedures, available at http://www.adr.org/index2.1.jsp?JSPssid=15747 (last visited Nov. 6, 2003).

Furthermore, Ms. Wilson explained, "The consumer must also deposit one-half of the arbitrator's compensation. This deposit is used to pay the arbitrator. This deposit is refunded if not used." C329.[8]

[] *Cook's Pest Control v. Rebar*, Ala. Sup. Ct. No. 1010897, *opinion published at* 852 So.2d 730. During that argument, Cook's attorney stated at one point in regards to the Cook's standard contract that "[T]he consumer is not in a bargaining position to alter the terms and conditions. They make the payment, they accept what is offered to them. And if they don't like it, they go down the street." The relevant portion of this Transcript is attached as an Appendix.

5 Equitable relief is often appropriate in termite cases where facts establish that termite service providers have never applied the minimum chemical treatments required by law in Alabama. *See* Ala. Admin. Code 80-10-9-.18. Hence, specific performance injunctions are often warranted, and such remedies may require ongoing court supervision.

6 This fact is also recognized in the case law. *See, e.g., Luna v. Household Fin. Corp.*, 236 F. Supp.2d 1161, 1182, n. 7 (W.D. Wash. 2002) ("Because Plaintiffs seek equitable relief, the AAA consumer dispute provisions likely would not apply."). The reason that claims for any kind of injunctive relief must always be handled under AAA's Commercial Rules is that proceedings under AAA's Consumer Rules are sharply limited. Under the Consumer Rules, consumer claimants are not permitted to take any discovery whatsoever, to participate in a live hearing, or to file any briefs with the arbitrator. Under these circumstances, it is hardly surprising that persons with claims similar to the Leemans' are required to bring those claims under the Commercial Rules.

7 As noted below, consumers bringing similar claims under the Commercial Rules in the *Porter* and *Wunderlich* cases were required to pay precisely these initial fees.

8 Arbitrator compensation accrues for all time spent by the arbi-

2. Evidence of Arbitration Costs Imposed Upon Consumers in Other Cases Against Cook's and Similar Pest Control Companies.

The record contains undisputed evidence of the arbitration fees that were imposed upon consumers in five different cases brought against pest control companies under AAA's Commercial Rules. In each case, the consumers advanced claims that were nearly identical to the Leemans'. C326. In two of these cases, the defendant was Cook's Pest Control, the same defendant as in this case. Only one of these five cases, *Porter v. Cook's Pest Control*, actually went all the way through the AAA process to an arbitrator award, C475; the others all settled after proceeding in arbitration for some time.[9] As a result, the costs reflected in four of the five cases understate the arbitration costs that one would expect in a case that proceeds all the way through to an award.

In the *Porter* case, the plaintiffs were obligated to pay $12,950 in arbitration costs to the AAA in order to have their claims heard. C225–28. The Porter's arbitration costs broke down as follows:

- Initial Administration Fee: $3250
- Case Service Fee: $750
- Mediator Compensation: $1500
  (Plaintiff's share of 2 days hearing, 4 hours study at $1200/day)
- Arbitrator Compensation: $2450
  (Plaintiff's share of 10 hours study and 4 days hearing at $850/day)
- Arbitrator Compensation: $5000
  (Plaintiff's share of 5 days hearing, 5 days study at $850/day)

Id. In the *Porter* case, the arbitrator ultimately entered an award for the consumers in the amount of $16,000, plus just over $4800 in reimbursement for their share of the arbitrator's fees and costs. C230–231. Under the arbitrator's order, the consumers had to pay out more than $8,000 in arbitration fees that were not to be reimbursed in order to recover $16,000.

In *Wunderlich v. Cook's Pest Control*, the only other case ever brought against Cook's in arbitration, the consumer plaintiff's arbitration costs (half the total cost of arbitration) amounted to $13,750. C111–114. The Wunderlich's arbitration costs broke down as follows:

- Initial Administration Fee: $3200
- Case Service Fee: $750
- Mediator Compensation: $1750
  (Plaintiff's share of 2 days hearing, 4 hours study at $175/hour)
- Arbitrator Compensation: $900
  (Plaintiff's share of 2 day study and 1 day hearing at $1200/day)
- Arbitrator Compensation: $2100
  (Plaintiff's share of 12 hours study and 2 days hearing at $1200/day)

---

trator, including conducting discovery and other pretrial hearings, research, and the like. Arbitrators do not just bill for time spent in a hearing on the merits, as is commonly believed.

9 The record evidence cited is Cook's answer to Interrogatory number nine, dated February 2003. After the record below was filed, the *Wunderlich v. Cook's* matter was resolved through AAA arbitration in May 2003. A modest recovery was obtained by Ms. Wunderlich in that case.

- Arbitrator Compensation: $5000
  (Plaintiff's share of 2 days hearing, 12 hours study at $1200/day)

The three other cases taken to arbitration by consumers against pest control companies other than Cook's are *Plummer v. Sears Termite & Pest Control, Inc.*, *Barnard v. Orkin Exterminating Co., Inc.*, and *Travers v. Terminix Int'l*. Although, as noted above, all three cases settled before an arbitration award was entered, C168, the initial arbitration fees were similar. In *Plummer*, the plaintiffs paid $7425 in costs, including $4000 in initial costs and $3425 in additional arbitrator costs. C257. The *Plummer* case settled on the third day of the arbitration hearing. C168. In *Barnard*, Plaintiffs paid $11,500 altogether, including $4000 in initial costs, $7000 to cover four days of the arbitrator's study and hearing time, and $500 for the arbitrator's anticipated travel and hotel costs. C290, 292. The *Barnard* case settled prior to the commencement of a hearing. C168. And in *Travers*, plaintiffs paid $6425 in arbitration forum fees: $4000 in initial costs and an additional $2425 for two days of the arbitrator's study and hearing time. C320–21. The *Travers* case settled prior to commencement of a hearing. C168.[10]

In short, the initial Administrative and Case Service Fees in all five cases were $4,000. The average of additional costs (mostly arbitrators' fees) for the five cases was $6,560, and only two of these five cases ever went to the point of an evidentiary hearing.

The evidence also shows that if these five cases had been brought in the judicial system instead of arbitration, forum costs—that is, fees paid to a decisionmaking system in order to use that system—would be on average 51 times lower. C109. The *Porter* case, which was brought in a Circuit Court in Alabama before that court ordered parties to arbitrate, cost $211 to file. The *Wunderlich* case cost $229. The *Plummer*, *Barnard*, and *Travers* cases cost $221, 218, and $225.50, respectively. C109.

The record also shows that in *Morris v. Cook's Pest Control*, a consumer case against a pest control company with similar claims to those raised here, the court fees were about $300 altogether—$211 in initial filing fees, and $88 in additional costs. C126.[11] Hence, the cost of trying a similar case (*Morris*) to a civil jury to a conclusion was $300, whereas the cost of bringing a similar case (*Porter*) in arbitration to a conclusion was nearly $13,000.

3. The Impossibility of Finding Counsel to Advance These Fees.

The record contains sworn testimony from a number of Alabama attorneys that they would not take on consumer cases against companies incorporating the AAA Commercial Rules into their contracts, because the high forum costs make these cases financially infeasible, and from several Alabama consumers who attempted to find attorneys to represent them in arbitration, but were unable to do so. C680–96. One attorney testified that "consumers may not be able to find anyone to help them with their claim and may well be discouraged from pursuing meritorious claims on their own because of the high filing fees in arbitration and difficulty in obtaining counsel which regularly handles civil litigation." C689.

As noted above, there have been five cases against pest control companies raising allegations similar to those at issue here, that have proceeded to arbitration. The record establishes that all five of those cases were brought by the same counsel who represented the Leemans in the trial court here. The record contains unrebutted testimony that these counsel brought those cases not because it was economically justifiable to do so, but because it was the only way to establish an evidentiary record demonstrating the magnitude of the forum costs that consumers are required to bear in these types of cases. C652 ("Plaintiffs have built a record here, and their counsel have spent tens of thousands of dollars to build the record to show plainly and irrefutably that arbitration costs for typical single plaintiff cases are grossly unfair.").

STANDARD OF REVIEW

This Court's review of an order granting a motion to compel arbitration is *de novo. BankAmerica Housing Services v. Lee*, 833 So.2d 609, 617 (Ala. 2002). "Therefore, this Court must determine 'whether the trial judge erred on a factual or legal issue to the substantial prejudice of the party seeking review.' *Ex parte Roberson*, 749 So.2d 441, 446 (Ala.1999)." *Id.*; see also *Stevens v. Phillips*, 852 So.2d 123, 128 (Ala. 2002).

SUMMARY OF THE ARGUMENT

The record in this case establishes beyond serious contention that (a) Cook's arbitration clause is excessively broad, in the manner that this Court has found grossly favorable to the drafter in several previous cases; and (b) the Leemans had no meaningful choice with respect to Cook's arbitration clause because every other major pest control company in Alabama has the same sort of arbitration clause and because Cook's refuses to negotiate over the provision. The only issue that Cook's seriously disputes in this case is whether the Leemans have met their evidentiary burden of proving that Cook's arbitration clause imposes unconscionable costs upon its customers. They have.

In *Green Tree Financial Corp. v. Randolph*, 513 U.S. 79, 90 (2000), the U.S. Supreme Court recognized that if an arbitration clause imposes such heavy costs that a party would not be able to vindicate their rights, then the clause could not be enforced. The problem for the consumer plaintiff in *Randolph* was that she introduced no hard evidence to *prove* that the costs of arbitration were likely to be high. In the years that have followed, this Court has also rejected a number of challenges to arbitration clauses that

---

10   That the costs under AAA's Commercial Rules are often so high should not come as a surprise—there is extensive public documentation of the fact that the AAA's Commercial Rules frequently impose extremely hefty costs upon individuals with modest claims. One recent report collected invoices from a number of AAA arbitrations that involved similar costs. *See* Public Citizen Congress Watch, *The Cost of Arbitration* (April 2002) at 6–7, available at http://www.citizen.org/documents/ACF110A.PDF (last visited Nov. 5, 2003) (in *Betzler v. Ryland Corp.*, a case involving alleged construction defects in a home, AAA invoices document that the homeowners were required to advance $7,563.75), at 8–15 (in *Paul v. Allred*, a case involving legal malpractice claims, the claimant dropped her case upon receiving AAA's latest invoice for $37,500, after she had already spent $17,762 on fees to AAA); at 16–18 (in *Malkanis v. #1 Custom Homes*, AAA billed homeowners $13,068.67 to litigate a claim that resulted in an award of $18,818.93).

11   This fact is also consistent with the holdings of a number of courts. *See, e.g., Morrison v. Circuit City Stores, Inc.*, 317 F.3d 646 (6th Cir. 2003) ("Courts charge plaintiffs initial filing fees, but they do not charge extra for in-person hearings, discovery requests, routine motions, or written decisions, costs that are all common in the world of private arbitrators.").

were based on the cost of arbitrating, on the grounds that there was not enough evidence to prove that arbitration would be expensive in those cases.

This case is entirely different from those failed challenges; it is cut from a different cloth. In this case, the consumer plaintiffs have introduced admissible evidence that proved three propositions that were not proven in *Randolph* or in any previous case to come before this Court.

First, the plaintiffs conclusively proved which set of rules would govern any arbitration of their claims: the AAA's Commercial Rules. As this brief will establish, half a dozen federal and state courts have held that these rules impose such enormous forum costs that it is unconscionable for a corporation to require consumers to submit their claims to that system.

Second, the Leemans conclusively proved here how large the arbitration fees are going to be in a case of this sort, by introducing the very best evidence available on the subject. The plaintiffs established that in the only two consumer cases that have ever proceeded in arbitration against Cook's, the cost of arbitration was at least $12,000 and as much as $16,000. In five cases brought against Alabama pest control companies, the initial filing and administrative fees were $4,000 (in all five cases) and the other fees (mostly arbitrators' fees) averaged $6,560. In the only termite case where the case was tried to conclusion before the AAA, *Porter v. Cook's Pest Control*, the cost was nearly $13,000. These are shockingly high forum costs to impose on consumers bringing relatively modest claims. (In the only case to produce an award from the arbitrator, the award amounted to only $16,000.) The plaintiffs further proved that in similar cases that have been brought in Alabama against other pest control companies with essentially identical arbitration clauses, the arbitration fees were comparably large prior to those cases settling. This is not a case involving "speculation" about arbitration costs, and it is not a case involving generalities about arbitration in general. Instead, this Court has before it the irrefutable proof as to what arbitration under Cook's system has actually cost consumers with the same type of claims as the Leemans.

Finally, the record contains unrefuted proof that Alabama consumers can find no attorneys who are willing to advance such forum costs or pursue such claims under the AAA's Commercial Rules. The record establishes that the only reason that the five cases alluded to above proceeded in arbitration against pest control companies is that the counsel in those cases were willing to undergo those costs as the only way of establishing a evidentiary record on the subject of those costs.

In short, Cook's arbitration clause does not offer consumers such as the Leemans an alternative forum to the civil justice system, it offers them no forum at all. Cook's arbitration clause is, in reality, effectively an exculpatory provision, and a remedy-stripping clause. This Court has held that corporations may not impose upon their consumers contracts that state, in effect, that "you may never bring claims against us for punitive damages, even where those claims are provided for by state law." *See Ex parte Thicklin*, 824 So.2d 723, 733 (Ala. 2002). In this case, this Court should clarify that, by the same logic, a corporation may not impose upon its consumers contracts that effectively state "we will establish a system that is rigged to ensure that you may never bring any claims against us for any type of damages for wrongs that we may do to you, even where those claims are justified under state law."

The trial court disagreed for at least two clearly wrong reasons. First, the trial court disregarded the empirical evidence of the actual costs of arbitrating a case such as this, preferring to hazard a guess based upon a misunderstanding of how the AAA's Commercial Rules work. Second, the trial court concluded, in essence, that arbitration fees are never excessively high (even when they render a case prohibitive to any economically rational actor) if it is technically possible for a consumer to pay those fees.

As to the costs to be expected if the Leemans were to take this case to arbitration, the Circuit Court made an erroneous finding of fact about the magnitude of the arbitration costs in this case. The record in this case establishes that the AAA's Commercial Rules require claimants to pay two principal categories of fees: filing fee designed to cover AAA's administrative costs, and fees payable to the arbitrator himself. The record reflects that the arbitrator's fees tend to be far larger than the filing fees. Mistaking the visible tip for the entire iceberg, the trial court made a finding of fact that assumed that the entire cost of arbitration is found in the filing fee, and asserted that it was unimaginable that arbitration fees for a case such as the Leemans' could amount to sums such as $16,000. Given that this assertion is based upon a plainly wrong premise, and that the empirical experience of every case against a pest control company to actually proceed to arbitration in Alabama flatly contradicts the trial court's unsupported guess on the matter, this Court should hold that the Circuit Court's finding of fact on this point was erroneous.

As to the trial court's legal conclusion that a consumer's technical, conceivable ability to advance such costs is determinative, this Court has already rejected that notion in the context of arbitration clauses that require consumers to proceed on an individual, as opposed to a class action, basis. In *Leonard v. Terminix*, 854 So.2d 529 (Ala. 2002), this Court held that an arbitration clause that requires individuals to pay costs that are excessive relative to their expected recovery is unconscionable, without respect to whether all of those consumers are impoverished. The fact that the Leemans are a school principal and an elementary school teacher does not deprive them of any rights under Alabama law.

ARGUMENT

I. This Court Should Apply Alabama Law to Determine Whether Cook's Arbitration Clause is Unconscionable.

A. This Court Must Determine Whether Cook's Arbitration Clause is Unconscionable.

This Court, and not the arbitrator, should decide whether this arbitration agreement is unconscionable. *See Anderson v. Ashby*, 2003 WL 21125998 at *5 (Ala. May 16, 2003). As this Court pointed out in *Anderson*, the Federal Arbitration Act ("FAA") requires this Court to " 'faithfully apply general principles of Alabama contract law when considering a challenge to the validity of an arbitration agreement.' " *Id., quoting Green Tree Fin. Corp. v. Wampler*, 749 So.2d 409, 416 (Ala. 1999). The only time this validity analysis should be done by the arbitrator is where a party is challenging the entire contract as invalid, rather than the arbitration clause itself. *Id., citing Prima Paint Corp. v. Flood & Conklin Mfg. Co.*, 388 U.S. 398 (1967); *see also Ex parte Dan Tucker Auto Sales, Inc.*, 718 So.2d 33, 43 (Ala. 1998) ("While *Prima Paint* . . . relegates challenges to the validity of the contract as a whole to the arbitrator, a challenge to the arbitration clause only is properly determined by the court.") (Lyons, J. concurring) (citation omitted).

In this case, as in *Anderson*, the issue is the unconscionability of an arbitration clause, and therefore the court properly has jurisdiction over this question. *Anderson* at *6 ("Because Mrs. Ashby contends that the arbitration agreement included in the note and security agreement was itself unconscionable, the trial court did not err in holding that it had the authority to resolve that issue."); *see also American Gen. Fin., Inc. v. Branch*, 793 So.2d 738 (Ala. 2000) ("[T]he threshold 'issue of unconscionability of an *arbitration clause* is a question for the court and not the arbitrator.'") (citations omitted, emphasis in original).

If this Court were to reverse field and hold that arbitrators were to decide questions of unconscionability, it would have to overturn a number of its own recent decisions on the unconscionability of arbitration agreements. *See, e.g., Anderson* (arbitration clause held unconscionable on the basis of unusually broad language, lack of mutuality, limitation of damages and lack of meaningful choice)*; Branch* (same)*; Leonard v. Terminix*, 854 So.2d 529 (Ala. 2002) (arbitration clause held unconscionable based on class action ban and resulting prohibitive costs of arbitration for individual consumers); *Harold Allen's Mobile Home Factory Outlet, Inc. v. Butler*, 825 So.2d 779 (Ala. 2002) (arbitration clause held unconscionable based on the vendor's unilateral right to appoint the arbitrator).

As further evidence that courts are to decide unconscionability challenges, there are literally dozens of courts that have held that particular arbitration clauses had been drafted in a manner that rendered them unconscionable in particular cases.[12]

---

12 *Ting v. AT&T*, 319 F.3d 1126 (9th Cir. 2003), *cert. denied*, 2003 WL 1988529 (Oct. 6, 2003); *Alexander v. Anthony Int'l*, 341 F.3d 256 (3d Cir. 2003); *Circuit City Stores, Inc. v. Adams*, 279 F.3d 889 (9th Cir. 2002), *cert. denied*, 535 U.S. 1112 (2002); *Ticknor v. Choice Hotels Int'l, Inc.*, 265 F.3d 931 (9th Cir. 2001); *Shankle v. B-G Maint. Mgmt. of Colo., Inc.*, 163 F.3d 1230 (10th Cir. 1999); *Faber v. Menard, Inc.*, 267 F.Supp.2d 961 (N.D. Iowa 2003); *Plaskett v. Bechtel Int'l*, 243 F.Supp.2d 334 (D.V.I. 2003); *Luna v. Household Fin. Corp.*, 236 F.Supp.2d 1161 (W.D. Wash. 2002); *Comb v. Paypal, Inc.*, 218 F.Supp.2d 1165 N.D. Cal. 2002); *Cooper v. MRM Inv. Co.*, 199 F. Supp.2d 771 (M.D. Tenn. 2002); *Brennan v. Bally Total Fitness*, 198 F. Supp.3d 377(S.D.N.Y. 2002); *Geiger v. Ryan's Family Steak Houses, Inc.*, 134 F.Supp.2d 985 (S.D. Ind. 2001); *Prevot v. Phillips Petroleum Co.*, 133 F. Supp. 2d 937 (S.D. Tex. 2001); *Lozada v. Dale Baker Oldsmobile, Inc.*, 91 F. Supp. 2d 1087 (W.D. Mich. 2000); *In re Knepp*, 229 B.R. 821 (Bankr. N.D. Ala. 1999); *Nicholson v. Labor Ready, Inc.*, 1997 U.S. Dist. LEXIS 23494 (N.D. Cal. May 23, 1997); *Armendariz v. Found. Health Psychcare Services, Inc.*, 24 Cal. 4th 83, 99 Cal. Rptr. 2d 745, 6 P.3d 669 (2000); *Graham v. Scissor-Tail, Inc.*, 28 Cal. 3d 807, 171 Cal. Rptr. 604, 623 P.2d 165 (1981); *Worldwide Ins. Group v. Klopp*, 603 A.2d 788 (Del. Supr. 1992); *Powertel, Inc. v. Bexley*, 743 So. 2d 570 (Fla. Dist. Ct. App. 1999); *Ballard v. Southwest Detroit Hosp.*, 119 Mich. App. 814, 327 N.W.2d 370 (1982); *East Ford, Inc. v. Taylor*, 826 So.2d 709 (Miss. 2002); *Iwen v. U.S. W. Direct*, 293 Mont. 512, 977 P.2d 989 (1999); *Teleserve Sys., Inc. v. MCI Telecommunications Corp.*, 230 A.D.2d 585, 659 N.Y.S.2d 659 (1997); *Williams v. Aetna Fin. Co.*, 83 Ohio St. 3d 464, 700 N.E.2d 859 (1998), *cert. denied*, 526 U.S. 1051 (1999); *O'Donoghue v. Smythe, Cramer Co.*, 2002 WL 1454074 (Ohio Ct. App. July 3, 2002); *Myers v.*

B. Alabama State Contract Law Governs the Question of Whether this Arbitration Clause Is Unconscionable.

As discussed above, this Court has recognized that the FAA directs it to apply state contract law when addressing questions of the validity of an arbitration clause. The FAA incorporates a savings clause that provides that arbitration clauses will not be enforced if there are grounds under state contract law for invalidating the clause. 9 U.S.C. § 2. The U.S. Supreme Court has recognized that the defense of unconscionability is available to a party challenging an arbitration agreement. *Doctor's Assocs., Inc. v. Casarotto*, 517 U.S. 681, 687 (1996) ("[G]enerally applicable contract defenses, such as fraud, duress or unconscionability, may be applied to invalidate arbitration agreements without contravening [the F.A.A.]."). In other words, state contract law applies to arbitration clauses. This principle is incorporated into the federal substantive law of arbitration. *Perry v. Thomas* (1987) 482 U.S. 483, 492–93 ("An agreement to arbitrate is . . . enforceable, *as a matter of federal law*, 'save upon such grounds as exist at law or in equity for the revocation of *any* contract.' . . . Thus state law, whether of legislative or judicial origin, is applicable *if* that law arose to cover issues concerning the validity, revocability, and enforceability of contracts generally.") (emphasis in original, citations omitted).

In Alabama, the state law of unconscionability is most clearly set out in *American General Finance, Inc. v. Branch*, 793 So.2d 738 (Ala. 2000). There, this Court recognized an earlier four-part test to determine whether a contract is unconscionable under Alabama law: " '(1) whether there is an absence of meaningful choice on one party's part; (2) whether the contractual terms are unreasonably unfavorable to one party; (3) whether there was unequal bargaining power between the parties; and (4) whether the contract contained oppressive, one-sided, or patently unfair terms.' " *Branch*, 793 So.2d at 748, quoting *Layne v. Gardner*, 612 So.2d 404 (Ala. 1992). This Court then collapsed the test into two more comprehensive prongs: whether the clause contains grossly favorable terms, and whether there is an overwhelming disparity of bargaining power. *Id.; see also Anderson*, 2003 WL 21125998 at *8–9. Cook's arbitration clause clearly satisfies both prongs of this test, and is unconscionable.

II. Cook's Arbitration Clause Is Unconscionable In This Case Because It Was Imposed Through Cook's Overwhelming Bargaining Power.

A. The Leemans Had No Meaningful Choice to Avoid Arbitration.

In both *American General Finance v. Branch* and *Anderson v. Ashby*, this Court focused in on the question of whether the consumer had "meaningful choice" in contracting with a service provider with an arbitration clause in its contract. "A primary indicium of unconscionability in the modern consumer-transaction context," stated this Court in *Branch*, "is whether the consumer has the ability 'to obtain the product made the basis of [the] action'

Terminix Int'l Co., 91 Ohio Misc. 2d 41, 697 N.E.2d 227 (Ct. Com. Pl. 1998); *Zak v. Prudential Prop. & Cas. Ins. Co.*, 713 A.2d 681 (Pa. Super. Ct. 1998); *In re Turner Bros. Trucking Co.*, 8 S.W.3d 370 (Tex. App. 1999); *Sosa v. Paulos*, 924 P.2d 357 (Utah 1996); *Toppings v. Meritech Mort.*, 569 S.E.2d 149 (W.Va. 2002); *Arnold v. United Companies Lending Corp.*, 204 W. Va. 229, 511 S.E.2d 854 (1998); and *Mendez v. Palm Harbor Homes, Inc.*, 45 P.3d 594 (Wash. Ct. App. 2002).

without signing an arbitration clause." *Branch*, 793 So.2d at 750.

This Court made clear in *Anderson* that in order to show a lack of meaningful choice, a consumer does not have to show that she "actually shopped around for an arbitration-free [contract]." *Anderson* at *9. Instead, it is sufficient for the consumer to show that at the time the contract was signed, it was the practice of companies in same geographical area providing the same service to include arbitration provisions in their contracts. *Id.* at *10; *see also Branch*, 793 So.2d at 750–51 (basing the finding of overwhelming bargaining power on a record showing that every company listed in the City of Tuscaloosa phone book offering similar services to American General Finance, with the exception of one, also included an arbitration clause in its contract).

Finally, in *Leonard v. Terminix*, this Court found based on the record that "Terminix's competitors in Alabama also used arbitration provisions in their contracts at the time the Leonards bought their home." *Leonard*, 854 So.2d at 538.

The fact that this evidence is in the Leemans' record serves to distinguish this case from those in which this Court has refused to find a lack of meaningful choice because plaintiffs have presented no support for such a finding. *See, e.g., Vann v. First Community Credit Corp.*, 834 So.2d 751, 754 (Ala. 2002) (holding that the Vanns "have not put forth substantial evidence demonstrating that . . . First Community had overwhelming bargaining power.); *Green Tree Fin. Corp. v. Lewis*, 813 So.2d 820, 825 (Ala. 2001) ("The Lewises have made no showing that they lacked a meaningful choice in obtaining financing; the plaintiff in *Branch* did make such a showing."). As this Court noted in *Anderson*, both *Vann* and *Lewis* "turn[] on the utter failure of the plaintiffs to submit evidence of the scarcity of lenders that did not require arbitration agreements in the particular market in which the plaintiffs were seeking loans." *Anderson*, 2003 WL 21125998 at *11. The Leemans' case has no such failing; plaintiffs here have presented reams of evidence to this effect. Moreover, Cook's admits that it is unaware of any company which would issue termite bonds without an arbitration clause.

Another factor that this Court has considered in determining whether the non-drafter had meaningful choice when signing a contract is whether that party had any right to negotiate the terms of the contract. In *Anderson v. Ashby*, this Court found that "the Ashbys had no input into negotiating the terms of or drafting the arbitration agreement. This evidence establishes that the Ashbys had no meaningful choice in accepting the arbitration agreement and that American General Finance had overwhelming bargaining power in obtaining the arbitration agreement." *Anderson*, 2003 WL 21125998 at *11; *see also Leonard*, 854 So.2d at 538 (including in discussion of unconscionability the fact that "[t]he Leonards have shown that the Terminix contract is a contract of adhesion that has never been modified for any Alabama customer; they have also shown that they were not given any opportunity to accept or reject the arbitration provision.").

The upshot of these answers is that Cook's presents its consumers with a standard form contract on a take-it-or-leave-it basis. There is no way that the Leemans, or any Cook's customer, could have gotten out of this arbitration clause and still received any services from Cook's. Furthermore, the record also shows that the Leemans had no choice but to agree to arbitrate their pest control claims, as every conceivable local company providing these services included an arbitration clause similar to Cook's clause. Taken together, these facts alone support the conclusion that Cook's had overwhelming bargaining power in this transaction. *See Anderson*, 2003 WL 21125998 at *11 (holding that evidence that other lenders also used arbitration clauses combined with evidence that the borrowers here had no power to negotiate out of the arbitration clause "is sufficient to meet the second prong of the *Branch* unconscionability test.").

B. The Leemans Were Surprised, Given Cook's Failure to Disclose Information and the Impossibility of Determining the Costs of Arbitration.

Though this Court has not required a showing beyond lack of meaningful choice to meet the *Branch* test, it has indicated that more general principles, such as "the prevention of oppression and unfair surprise," are germane to the unconscionability analysis. *Stevens v. Phillips*, 852 So.2d 123, 134 (Ala. 2002), quoting Alabama Code § 7-2-302, comment 1.

The Alabama courts have not established a specific definition of the words "unfair surprise" in this section of the Alabama code. However, the Arizona Supreme Court, interpreting the same "oppression and unfair surprise" language in its own state law, has indicated that "unfair surprise" includes "fine print clauses, mistakes or *ignorance of important facts* or other things that mean bargaining did not proceed as it should." *Maxwell v. Fidelity Fin. Servs., Inc.*, 907 P.2d 51, 57–58 (Ariz. 1995); citing Dan B. Dobbs, 2 Law of Remedies 703, 706 (2nd ed. 1993) (emphasis added); *see also Hutcherson v. Sears Roebuck & Co.*, 793 N.E.2d 886, 891 (Ill. App. 2003) (same).

At the time they agreed to arbitrate their claims, the Leemans did not—and could not—learn of the magnitude of the costs that would be imposed on them if they ever brought claims to arbitration. As such, Cook's contract, and the circumstances surrounding the signing of that contract, certainly meet the general definition of "unfair surprise" set forth in the Alabama Code.

The element of surprise is enhanced by the fact that the AAA is not a transparent body whose fees, like those of courts, are easy to discern. While a schedule of filing fees can be obtained (with effort), the most significant element of the fees under the Commercial Rules—the arbitrator's fees—is not publicly available. For example, *see Ting v. AT&T*, 182 F.Supp.2d 902, 916–17 (N.D. Cal. 2002), *aff'd with respect to unconscionability*, 319 F.3d 1126 (9th Cir. 2003), *cert. denied*, 2003 WL 1988529 (Oct. 6, 2003):

> Different AAA arbitrators charge different hourly rates. To estimate the cost of an arbitration to be conducted under the AAA's Commercial Rules, a claimant must learn the hourly rate of the arbitrator who will hear the case. To determine . . . [this rate], a claimant must first initiate an arbitration with the AAA. . . . This makes it difficult for a class member before filing to meaningfully estimate the cost to have the case arbitrated under the Commercial Rules. Neither the AAA website or rules, nor the AT&T website, provides a class member with any information about likely arbitrator's fees.

See also Camacho, 167 F.Supp.2d at 897 n.4 ("It is impossible to establish the exact amount Camacho would have to pay because the arbitrator sets the amount after the arbitration has been initiated."). It is wrong to suggest that the Leemans could have readily determined the magnitude of these arbitration fees in advance of the dispute. The principal variable is the arbitrator's fees, and the rate that AAA arbitrators charge (much less the ultimate amount of fees that will be charged) cannot be determined until after one initiates the arbitration. However, in this record, there is evidence developed by extraordinary and unprecedented effort to establish the cost of AAA arbitration of termite cases.

C. Cook's Contract Is Not Rendered Conscionable Merely Because the Leemans Are Educated People.

Throughout this case, Cook's has attempted to argue that the fact that the Leemans are educated means that they cannot have signed an unconscionable arbitration clause. Cook's premise is apparently that no contract entered into by a school teacher could ever be unconscionable under Alabama law. As Cook's would have it, an arbitration clause in a contract of adhesion that required individual consumers to spend $1 million to vindicate a valid claim worth $41,000, or that would require consumers to travel enormous distances (perhaps to the deserts of New Zealand) to vindicate those claims, would still necessarily be enforceable if the consumers had college degrees and could read. Simply put, Cook's argument is preposterous. The law in Alabama (like other states) is *not* that "nothing done to a school teacher is ever unconscionable."

However, a finding that the consumer is uneducated or unsophisticated is not necessary to the unconscionability analysis in Alabama. In *Layne v. Gardner*, 612 So.2d 404 (Ala. 1992), where this Court first articulated the four-part unconscionability test later summarized and turned into a two-part test in *Branch*, this Court also mentioned the possibility that courts could look to whether one party was "unsophisticated and/or uneducated" in making a determination of unconscionability. *Layne*, 612 So.2d at 408. However, this specific question was never part of the four-part unconscionability test, and in fact it has dropped out completely in later renditions of that test. *See, e.g., Mason v. Acceptance Loan Co., Inc.*, 850 So.2d 289, 301 n.7 (Ala. 2002) (describing the four-part test, without mention of any "unsophisticated and/or uneducated" factor, as the "established—and still applicable" test for unconscionability in this state); *Gayfer Montgomery Fair Co. v. Austin*, 2003 WL 21480639 at *6, n.4 (Ala. July 27, 2003) (stating that the 2-part test of unconscionability used in *Branch* was created by "consolidating the four components of the test described in *Layne v. Gardner*," but not including any mention of the "unsophisticated and/or uneducated" factor).

As this Court made clear in *Leonard v. Terminix* and *Anderson v. Ashby*, it is not essential that a consumer be uneducated for a contract to be found unconscionable. In *Leonard*, as discussed above, this Court specifically did not rest its unconscionability holding on the Leonards' personal financial circumstances, arguing instead that disproportionately expensive arbitral forum costs will deter all consumers, rich and poor, from bringing claims in arbitration. *Leonard*, 854 So.2d at 537.

And in *Anderson*, the most recent case where this Court discussed the plaintiffs' education and sophistication level, this discussion was only in response to Justice Stuart's request in her special writing for evidence that the Ashbys actually shopped around for an arbitration-free loan. *Anderson*, 2003 WL 2125998 at *10. Though this Court specifically stated that such a finding was *not* required in order to find that the Ashbys had no meaningful choice, *id.*, it nonetheless went on to discuss the fact that the Ashbys could not read the contract containing the arbitration agreement, were not told about the arbitration agreement, and therefore had no compelling reason to think they needed to look around for another lender. *Id.* at *11. The context of this Court's discussion of the education/sophistication issue in *Anderson*, however, focused upon the meaningful choice issue. *Id.* ("[T]he facts of this case do not logically present an issue whether the Ashbys should have 'actually shopped around' for a lender that would not require that they execute an arbitration agreement."). Nor is it a dispositive issue in this case, where the Leemans have clearly shown that they could not have gone to another pest control company in the area and expect to find a contract without an arbitration clause, even had they tried to do so.[13]

III. The Arbitration Clause At Issue In This Case Contains Terms That are Grossly Favorable to Cook's.

This Court made clear in *Branch* that any provision in an arbitration clause that, as a practical matter, benefits only the stronger bargaining party, will satisfy the first prong of the Alabama unconscionability test. *Branch,* 793 So.2d at 749. Cook's arbitration clause contains two provisions that clearly benefit Cook's at the expense of consumers. The first provision requires arbitration for an extremely broad set of claims. The second designates the AAA Commercial Rules, which impose forum costs that are so prohibitive as to deter consumers from bringing claims against Cook's in arbitration.

A. Cook's Arbitration Clause is So Broad as to Cover all Real and Potential Consumer Claims.

The arbitration clause in the Leemans' contract applies to "any dispute, controversy or claim arising out of or relating to the agreement and guarantee or the breach thereof, or arising out of any prior or future dealings between Cook's and customer, shall be settled in arbitration. . . ." C17. Moreover, Cook's has argued in this case that the clause applies not only to signatories to the contract, but to nonsignatories as well. C547-49.

This extremely broad arbitration clause is strikingly similar to the clause found unconscionable in both *Branch* and *Anderson*. In both cases the defendant, American General Finance, had included in its contracts an arbitration clause applying to " 'every dispute[] or controversy[] relating to' every actual or potential transaction—whether past, present, or future—and to every person, whether signatory or nonsignatory to any document, involved in such a transaction between the parties." *Branch* at 748. This Court found that because "[t]he first indicium of unconscionability is the breadth of the clause," and that American General Finance's "unusually broad" arbitration clause was clearly unconscionable in that it "applie[d] to every cause of action that could conceivably arise in favor of Branch, and to every individual against whom a claim could conceivably be brought." *Id.*; *see also Anderson* at *9.

As in *Branch* and *Anderson*, the arbitration clause at issue here is so broad that it covers every conceivable claim that the Leemans ever had or ever could have, at any future date, against Cook's. In combination with the prohibitive costs imposed by Cook's chosen arbitration forum and the Leemans' lack of bargaining power or

---

13 The record reflects that the Leemans could not have obtained a bond without an arbitration clause if they had searched, and therefore that the search would have been futile. "The law is reasonable, and does not require the doing of useless or impossible things." *City of Mobile v. Jackson*, 474 So.2d 644, 650 (Ala. 1985).

ability to negotiate a more fair contract, the sheer scope of the clause renders it unconscionable.[14]

B. The Law Is Clear that Arbitration Clauses That Impose Prohibitive Costs on Consumers are Grossly Favorable to the Drafting Party.

1. The United States Supreme Court has Declared that Arbitral Costs Must Not be So High As to Deny Claimants a Forum to Vindicate Their Rights.

The U.S. Supreme Court has stated repeatedly that arbitration must allow a party to "effectively vindicate" its rights. *Mitsubishi Motors Corp. v. Soler Chrysler-Plymouth, Inc.*, 473 U.S. 614, 637 (1985); *Gilmer v. Interstate/Johnson Lane Corp.*, 500 U.S. 20, 28 (1991) (quoting *Mitsubishi*). That Court has also recognized that arbitration will not meet this standard if the parties' arbitration clause imposes excessive costs, thus preventing a party from even entering the arbitral forum. *Green Tree Financial Corp. v. Randolph*, 513 U.S. 79, 90 (2000).

In *Randolph*, the Supreme Court addressed the question of whether an arbitration clause that was silent as to the allocation of forum costs would undermine a plaintiff's ability to enforce her rights under the federal Truth In Lending Act. *Id.* at 91. The Court began by emphasizing that "[i]t may well be that the existence of large arbitration costs could preclude a litigant such as Randolph from effectively vindicating her federal statutory rights in the arbitral forum," but found that Randolph had not satisfied her burden of showing the likelihood of incurring such prohibitive costs because "the record contains hardly any information on the matter." *Id.*

2. Alabama Law Is Consistent with the U.S. Supreme Court's Prohibition on Prohibitively Costly Arbitration Clauses.

Notwithstanding the suggestions of Cook's, this Court has never held that an arbitration clause may impose such high costs upon consumers that the consumers are left with no effective remedy. Instead, this Court has held that arbitration clauses may not strip consumers of their legal rights under Alabama law. In the context of contractual bans on consumers' rights to bring class actions, this Court has held that arbitration clauses that have the predictable economic effect of stripping consumers of their legal rights cannot be enforced. Finally, while it is true that this Court has rejected a number of challenges to arbitration clauses based upon claims that they would impose excessive costs, it has always done so on the grounds that there was not adequate evidence to support those claims, grounds that are certainly not relevant here.

First, the U.S. Supreme Court's statement in *Randolph* that arbitration clauses may not impose prohibitive costs is consistent with this Court's repeated statements that contracts of adhesion may not eliminate substantive rights. *See, e.g., Ex parte Thicklin,* 824 So.2d 723, 733 (Ala. 2002) ("[I]t violates public policy for a party to contract away its liability for punitive damages, regardless whether the provision doing so was intended to operate in an arbitral or judicial forum. Thus, enforcement of this portion of the arbitration agreement violates public policy, and its enforcement would be unconscionable."). This body of Alabama law is applicable to all contracts, *see, e.g., Reece v. Finch,* 562 So.2d 195, 199 (Ala. 1990) ("[E]xculpatory agreements are not valid as to extreme forms of negligence or any conduct that constitutes an intentional tort."), and therefore is not preempted by the FAA.

Second, this Court has applied this principle not only to arbitration clauses that expressly stripped consumers of their rights, but also to clauses that effectively did so. In *Leonard v. Terminix*, this Court held that a pest control company's arbitration clause was unconscionable because that clause effectively banned class actions, with the result of keeping consumers with small claims out of arbitration altogether. *Leonard*, 854 So.2d at 539. This Court determined that if the Leonards were forced to arbitrate their claims on an individual basis, they would be placed in a position where their claims would actually be worth less than their filing fees, and that such a situation was clearly unconscionable:

> This arbitration agreement is unconscionable because it is a contract of adhesion that restricts the Leonards to a forum where the expense of pursuing their claim far exceeds the amount in controversy. The arbitration agreement achieves this result by foreclosing the Leonards from an attempt to seek practical redress through a class action and restricting them to a disproportionately expensive individual arbitration.

Id.

There have been a number of cases where this Court has not held high costs to be unconscionable, but the reason has almost uniformly been that claimants did not present enough evidence of those costs to this Court. Those cases are thus clearly distinguishable from the instant case, where the Leemans have presented an extensive and comprehensive record to show that their forum costs will be excessively high.

In *Ex Parte Thicklin*, for instance, the consumer plaintiff argued that the arbitration clause included in her contract with a mobile home seller and manufacturer, which required arbitration under the AAA Commercial Rules, was unconscionable. *Ex Parte Thicklin*, 824 So.2d at 734. Thicklin pointed to the filing fee under the AAA Commercial Rules, but introduced no evidence relating to any arbitrators' fees, or evidence to compare the costs of the combined arbitration fees to the value of the lawsuit.

This Court, citing *Randolph*, held that Thicklin had not met her burden of showing that her anticipated arbitration costs were more than speculative. *Id.* at 735. In fact, this Court noted that Thicklin had not presented "any evidence, such as her income, her family's expenses, or the estimated costs of the arbitration procedure, that would support an argument that the use of the Commercial Rules renders the arbitration clause unconscionable from a financial standpoint." *Id.* Here, in contrast, the Leemans have produced extensive evidence on the estimated costs of the arbitration procedure, which as we discussed above would deter anyone, regardless of income, from entering this arbitral forum for this type of claim.

In another case involving the AAA Commercial Rules, this Court similarly found that the consumer plaintiff had not presented adequate proof of prohibitive costs to warrant a finding of unconscionability. In *Stevens v. Phillips*, 852 So.2d 123 (Ala. 2002), this Court upheld a lower court opinion that an arbitration clause providing that claims would be arbitrated under the AAA's Commercial Rules was not unconscionable. There, the defendants had

---

14 Although the Leemans argued that Cook's Arbitration clause was unconscionably overbroad, C80–81, the Circuit Court below did not address this issue.

already paid the cost of the filing fee and the plaintiffs had not produced proof of any other prohibitive costs. *Id.* at 134–35. Without any evidence of such costs, the lower court had summarily stated in its opinion that " 'Plaintiff's other costs in prosecuting her claims should be no different in arbitration, if not less, than in civil litigation in the Circuit Court of Lee County, Alabama.' " *Id.* Because the plaintiff on appeal never disputed or even addressed this statement, this Court took the statement as true and upheld the clause. *Id.* at 135.

The case at bar could hardly be more different. Here, Cook's has not offered to pay any of the Leemans' costs in arbitration, and the Leemans have presented exhaustive evidence to show that the filing fee is only one fee among many forum costs that they would face in arbitration under the Commercial Rules. Finally, the Leemans have specifically shown that these arbitral forum costs would indeed be much greater than costs in civil litigation of the same claims—in fact, arbitration costs would be almost *51 times greater* than those court costs. C126, 168.

C. The Record Here Demonstrates that Cook's Arbitration Clause Is Prohibitively Expensive.

As discussed above in the Statement of Facts, the Leemans have assembled a comprehensive factual record to support their argument that the costs that will be imposed on them if they are forced into arbitration will be prohibitive, and thus unconscionable.

In this case, the Leemans have brought claims typical of claims by consumers against pest control companies. These same type of claims were at the heart of the only two cases ever brought in arbitration by a consumer against Cook's itself: *Porter v. Cook's Pest Control* and *Wunderlich v. Cook's Pest Control*. C326.

As the Statement of Facts demonstrates, the Leemans' claims—like the claims of the plaintiffs in the *Porter* and *Wunderlich* cases that proceeded through arbitration—would automatically be arbitrated under the AAA Commercial Rules. C329.

The record demonstrates that the AAA Commercial Rules require the consumer to pay an initial fee of $3250 as well as a case management fee, which under the rules in effect when the record was filed was $750, C148, but which has since been increased to $1250. *See* American Arbitration Association, Commercial Arbitration Rules and Mediation Procedures, *available at* http://www.adr.org/index2.1.jsp?JSPssid=15747 (last visited Nov. 6, 2003). Therefore the Leemans, to even get in the door of arbitration, will certainly have to pay at least $4000, and perhaps as much as $4500, to the AAA. Under the AAA's Commercial Rules, consumers must also pay half the anticipated arbitrator fee at the beginning of arbitration, simply in order to access the arbitral forum. C329. As Margaret Wilson of the AAA explained in her memo, this up-front arbitrator fee is based on the hourly rate of the arbitrator in any given case. *Id.* In *Porter*, this fee was $1500; in *Wunderlich*, $1750. In *Travers v. Terminix Int'l, Inc.,* the other case in which complete AAA invoices are available, this fee was $1600. The Leemans could therefore expect to have to pay at *least* $1500 in up-front arbitrator fees in order to access the arbitral forum.

The record further demonstrates that were the Leemans to actually litigate a case against Cook's to completion in arbitration, complete with witness testimony and argument, their forum costs would run much higher. The Porter case took 4 days to resolve in arbitration. The arbitrator's fees in that case, including study time and hearing time, came to $8,950. These costs were not paid to the witnesses or to any lawyers; these were forum costs paid to the AAA throughout the course of the arbitration. If the Porters had not been able to pay each AAA bill as it came in, their case could have been suspended or terminated, according to the AAA Rules. C146. Altogether, the Porters paid $12,950 in forum fees. C168.

The potential recovery in these cases may be quite low in some cases. As discussed above, the *Porter* case was the only one of these five cases against pest control companies that went all the way through the arbitration process to an award at the time the record evidence was assembled below. The arbitrator in that case ruled for the Porters and awarded them $16,000. He then granted them about $4800 more, which he claimed was to reimburse them for their share of the arbitrator fees. C230–31. In fact, this reimbursement covered only a small portion of their fees, which had amounted to $12,950.

The upshot of these facts is that for the Leemans to arbitrate their claims, they would certainly have to pay, at the bare minimum, either $5500 (using the old Case Filing Fee of $750) or $6000 (using the new Fee), in up-front forum fees. If Cook resisted and the Leemans were obliged to put on their substantive case in arbitration, they would certainly pay thousands of dollars more for the arbitrator's study and hearing time. All of this would be required for a case where the ultimate award could easily be less than $20,000. In contrast, filing these cases in court would result in forum fees between $211–$299, depending on which Alabama Circuit Court consumers happened to use and whether a jury is required. C109.

The prohibitive nature of these fees is proven with the sworn testimony of a number of Alabama lawyers, discussed in the Statement of Facts, that they would not (meaning that they could not afford to) bring cases such as this under the AAA's Commercial Rules.

The conclusion that these fees are prohibitive is hardly a new or radical one. Half a dozen courts across the country faced with similar factual records to that in this case have found the AAA's fees to be prohibitively high, even in cases where the fees imposed on the parties were expected to be far less than the over $12,000–$16,000 that would likely be demanded of the Leemans here.

In *Ting v. AT&T*, 182 F.Supp.2d 902 (N.D. Cal. 2002), *aff'd with respect to unconscionability*, 319 F.3d 1126 (2003), *cert. denied*, 2003 WL 1988529 (Oct. 6, 2003), for example, the district court examined an exhaustive evidentiary record on the average arbitration costs under the AAA's Commercial Rules. It found that the average daily rate for an arbitrator is nearly $2000, and that the AAA, though it offers the possibility of fee waivers, typically does not waive fees but instead defers them until the time of the hearing. *Id.* at 917.[15] The court held that these high costs, plus the additional case costs and service fees, would clearly "deter many potential litigants from proceeding" with arbitration. *Id.* at 934.

The *Ting* court's conclusions with respect to AAA's Commercial Rules are entirely consistent with the decisions of a host of other courts. *See also Camacho v. Holiday Homes, Inc.*, 167 F.Supp.2d 892 (W.D. Va. 2001) (arbitration clause precluded consumer from effectively vindicating her statutory rights because the fees under AAA's Commercial Rules were financially prohibitive); *Popovich v. McDonald's Corp.*, 2002 WL 47965 (N.D. Ill. Jan. 14, 2002)

---

15 In *Wunderlich v. Cook's Pest Control, Inc.*, the AAA arbitrator flatly refused to defer any payment of costs until after arbitration, and actually suspended the hearing pending both parties' payment of these costs. C497–98.

(refusing to enforce an arbitration clause on the grounds that under the AAA's Commercial Rules, "the costs of arbitration are likely to be staggering," and finding that the costs of arbitrating the consumer claims at issue in that case were likely to amount to $48,000 to $126,000); *Phillips v. Associates Home Equity Services*, 179 F.Supp.2d 840 (N.D. Ill. 2001) (arbitration clause not enforced in Truth in Lending Act suit because the costs of arbitration under AAA's Commercial Rules are prohibitive, noting that the filing fees alone would amount to $4,000); *Mendez v. Palm Harbor Homes, Inc.*, 45 P.3d 594, 605 (Wash. Ct. App. 2002) (arbitration clause requiring consumer bringing claims involving a defective home was unconscionable because the costs under the AAA's Commercial Rules were unconscionable; "Avoiding the public court system in a way that effectively denies citizens access to resolving everyday societal disputes is unconscionable"); *Arnold v. Goldstar Fin. Sys., Inc.*, 2002 WL 1941546 *10 (N.D. Ill. Aug. 22, 2002) (consumer cannot be required to arbitrate claims because of prohibitive costs under AAA's Commercial Rules); *Giordano v. Pep Boys–Manny, Moe & Jack, Inc.*, 2001 WL 484360 (E.D. Pa. Mar. 29, 2001) (fees under AAA rules would deter plaintiff's vindication of claims in arbitration).

It is important to note that the Leemans' challenge is not an attack on arbitration generally. In fact, a great many major corporations have moved to draft arbitration clauses contained in adhesive contracts that require the corporation to pay or at least advance nearly all of the costs of arbitration.[16] The issue in this case is not whether Cook's can require its customers to arbitrate their cases, but if it can require *them* to pay costs that are likely to be in the range of $12,000 to $16,000 to litigate claims likely to be modest in size.

D. The Circuit Court's Decision Relating to the Costs of Arbitration Is Based On Two Major Mistakes of Fact and Law.

Despite a wealth of evidence as to what arbitration fees actually have been in the real world in cases essentially identical to this one, the Circuit Court mis-analyzed the AAA Commercial Rules to come to the conclusion that the costs would necessarily be far lower. The court indicated that "in order for the arbitration fees to be in this range [from $12,000–$16,000], the fee schedule of the . . . [AAA Commercial Rules] specify a range of between $5,000,000 and $10,000,000 in the amount of the claim to require an initial fee of $10,000 and a case service fee of $4,000." C798–99.

---

16 *See, e.g.*, National Consumer Law Center, *Consumer Arbitration Agreements: Enforceability and Other Topics* (2d ed. 2002) (CD-Rom accompanying book) (contains copies of such arbitration clauses; a few illustrative examples are clauses from Advance America, Cash Advance Centers of Louisiana, Inc. ("If you demand arbitration, upon your written request to us, we will advance the arbitration organization's filing or hearing fees."); Associates Financial Services Co. of Texas ("If you start arbitration, you agree to pay the initial filing fee required by the American Arbitration Association up to a maximum of $125. We agree to pay for the filing fee and any deposit required by the American Arbitration Association in excess of $125."); MBNA America Bank, N.A. ("At your written request, we will advance any arbitration-filing fee, administrative and hearing fees, which you are required to pay to pursue a claim in arbitration.")).

It is evident from this passage that the Circuit Court was operating under the assumption that the only fees associated with arbitration under the AAA were the filing fees set forth in AAA's schedules. (There are no public schedules setting forth any information whatsoever about arbitrators' fees under the AAA Commercial Rules.) C150–166.

The Circuit Court's incorrect conclusion derives from its incorrect premise. As the evidence from cases such as *Porter* and *Wunderlich* demonstrates, forum fees include not only initial fees and case service fees, but also anticipated and actual arbitrator fees for both study time and hearing time. These fees, which are in the thousands of dollars, combine with the initial $4000 to bring forum costs into the tens of thousands of dollars, regardless of the amount of the potential recovery. This Court should hold that the Circuit Court's guess as to the likely arbitration fees is clearly erroneous and contrary to all of the evidence in this case.

The Circuit Court also concluded that the costs of arbitration were not unconscionable in this case, because there was no evidence that the Leemans were so impoverished that they unable to pay these sums. In so holding, the Circuit Court invented an extremely high hurdle that is contrary to Alabama law. Simply put, it is unconscionable to require any consumer to pay up front arbitration forum fees amounting to $12,000 to $16,000 to bring typical, comparatively modest claims for property damage to a home.

In *Leonard*, this Court compared the costs to proceed under the arbitration clause to the claimant's likely recovery. The Court did not require a showing that the claimant's income was too low to afford the arbitration. In *Leonard*, the consumer plaintiffs disclaimed any reliance on an economic hardship argument, since they could not claim poverty status. *Leonard*, 854 So.2d at 537 n.4. This Court deliberately did not base its decision on a financial hardship standard, instead holding: "That the expenses of arbitration would exceed the amount in controversy is not a problem personal or peculiar to any particular consumer but is, rather, a phenomenon inherent in the transaction itself." *Id.* at 537. Such is the case here: forum fees of up to $16,000 in cases where the amount in controversy may be less than $20,000 are disproportionate, regardless of the economic situation of the consumer faced with those fees.

As the Statement of Facts reflects, this case also presents a situation where an arbitration clause has been drafted in such a way as to be prohibitive—it requires individuals to pay costs that are disproportionate to their likely recovery.

The Leemans' evidence shows that such costs will deter consumers from bringing their claims in arbitration. Indeed, it demonstrates that no counsel can be found in Alabama to handle such cases under the AAA's Commercial Rules. As such, Cook's arbitration clause, imposing as it does enormously high forum costs that would surely deter any rational consumer from even attempting to arbitrate against Cook's, meets the Circuit Court's own definition of an unconscionable clause. As that court held, arbitration clauses are unenforceable "if they work to *deny the claimant a forum* in which to litigate or arbitrate their claim." C802 (emphasis added).

CONCLUSION

Cook's arbitration clause is the product of overwhelming economic bargaining power and contains terms that are grossly favorable to Cook's. This Court should hold that Cook's arbitration clause is unconscionable under generally applicable principles of Alabama contract law, and reverse the Circuit Court's order compelling the Leemans to arbitrate their claims.

Respectfully submitted,

[*Attorneys for Appellants*]

E.2 Reply Brief Focusing on Unconscionability Based on Cost (Leeman)

IN THE SUPREME COURT OF ALABAMA

```
_____    )
                            )
GARY LEEMAN AND             )
KATHRYN LEEMAN,             )
           Appellants,      )
                            )
v.                          )   No. 1022063
                            )
COOK'S PEST CONTROL,        )
INC., a corporation; et al, )
              Appellees.    )
_____    )
```

After an Order by the Circuit Court of Jefferson County, Civil Action No. CV-02-4976, Granting Appellee's Motion to Compel Arbitration and Stay Proceedings

APPELLANTS' REPLY BRIEF

ORAL ARGUMENT REQUESTED

TABLE OF CONTENTS

TABLE OF CONTENTS
TABLE OF AUTHORITIES
SUMMARY OF ARGUMENT
ARGUMENT
  I. The Proven High Cost of Arbitration Under Cook's Contract Render the Arbitration Clause Grossly Favorable to Cook's
    A. Notwithstanding Cook's Factual Quibbles, the Evidence Establishes the Leemans Face Costs of $12,000 to $16,000 Under the Terms of Cook's Arbitration Clause
    B. This Court Should Not Disregard the Proof that the Costs of Arbitrating Claims Against Cook's in the Past Have Been High, Simply Because Consumers Presented Strong Evidence and Witnesses in Those Proceedings
    C. Notwithstanding Cook's Claims, Plaintiffs Certainly Did Argue to the Trial Court that the Costs of Arbitration Include the Arbitrators' Fees, and Are not Merely Limited to the Filing Fees
    D. This Court Should Reject Cook's Request that it Re-write the Arbitration Clause to Rescue Defendants from the Consequences of Writing an Unconscionable Arbitration Clause that Imposes Prohibitive Costs
    E. The Enormous Costs Facing the Leemans Are Indeed Prohibitive Within the Meaning of the *Randolph* and *Leonard* Cases
  II. Cook's Arbitration Clause Is the Product of Overwhelming Bargaining Power
    A. Notwithstanding Cook's Misreading of the *Branch* Case, the Leemans Had No Meaningful Choice About this Arbitration Clause
    B. Notwithstanding Cook's Claims that the Issue of Surprise Is a New Argument on Appeal, the Leemans Have Consistently Argued that They Were Surprised by the High Costs of Arbitration under the AAA Commercial Rules
    C. The Protections of Alabama Contract Law Against Unconscionable Contracts Are Not Limited to the Uneducated
  III. Cook's Arbitration Clause Contains Still Another "Grossly Favorable Term"
CONCLUSION
CERTIFICATE OF SERVICE [*omitted*]

TABLE OF AUTHORITIES

Case Authorities**

American Gen. Fin., Inc. v. Branch, 793 So.2d 738 (Ala. 2000)
Anderson v. Ashby, 2003 WL 21125998 (Ala. May 16, 2003)
Browne v. Kline Tysons Imports, Inc., 190 F. Supp. 2d 827 (E.D. Va. 2002)
City of Mobile v. Jackson, 474 So.2d 644 (Ala. 1985)
Commercial Credit Corp. v. Leggett, 744 So.2d 890 (Ala. 1999)
Cooper v. MRM Inv. Co., 199 F. Supp. 2d 771 (2002)
EEOC v. Waffle House Corp., 534 U.S. 279 (2002)
Flores v. Transamerica Homefirst, Inc., 93 Cal. App. 4th 846 (2001)
Flyer Printing Co. v. Hill, 805 So. 2d 829 (Fla. Ct. App. 2001)
Gilmer v. Interstate/Johnson Lane Corp., 500 U.S. 20 (1991)
Green Tree Financial Corp. v. Randolph, 513 U.S. 79 (2000)
Gutierrez v. Autowest, Inc., 2003 WL 22890611 (Cal.App. Dec. 9, 2003)
Harold Allen's Mobile Home Factory Outlet, Inc. v. Butler, 825 So.2d 779 (Ala. 2002)
Layne v. Garner, 612 So.2d 404 (Ala. 1989)
Lelouis v. W. Directory Co., 2001 WL 34046279 (D. Or. Aug. 10, 2001)
Leonard v. Terminix, 854 So.2d 529 (Ala. 2002)
Phillips v. Associates Home Equity Services, Inc., 179 F. Supp.2d 840 (N.D. Ill. 2001)
Popovich v. McDonald's Corp., 189 F. Supp.2d 772 (N.D. Ill. 2002)
Stevens v. Phillips, 852 So.2d 123 (Ala. 2002)
Volt Info. Sciences, Inc. v. Bd. of Trustees, 489 U.S. 468 (1989)

Other Authorities

Restatement (Second) of Contracts § 184 cmt. b

SUMMARY OF ARGUMENT

It used to cost Alabamians around $200 to resolve termite cases. As this Court knows, homeowners with termite bonds must now go to AAA arbitration. For the first time, this Court now has unre-

---

** [*Editor's Note: Citations throughout brief as in original.*]

butted evidence that doing so costs around $16,000. This Court has clear discretion to rule that this cost is too unfair to be enforceable under generally applicable Alabama law. The Court should do so.

Defendant Cook's Pest Control ("Cook's") advances a vision of contract law with two remarkable features. Cook's first effectively suggests that the protections that Alabama contract law provides against unconscionable contracts are not available to literate middle class persons. It argues, for example, that since the Leemans are a teacher and a principal, they should have figured out the arbitration costs that would be imposed upon them in the event of a future dispute with Cook's. This argument conveniently ignores the facts that the majority of the costs of arbitration—the fees of the arbitrator—are not disclosed in the contract or in the rules of the American Arbitration Association ("AAA"), and can *only* be learned by discovering what consumers with similar disputes paid in the past, as the Leemans have done here. *See* Appellants' Opening Brief ("OB") at 36–39. Cook's similarly argues that since the Leemans are educated, they should have made a futile search for a termite bond including no or lower arbitration costs, even though Cook's itself doesn't know of such a bond. This Court should flatly reject Cook's notion that there is nothing that it can put into a contract of adhesion with a school teacher that would be unconscionable, and should make clear that Alabama contract law does not sanction forcing middle class Alabamians to pay undisclosed fees of $12,000–$16,000 to enforce their rights as citizens of this state.

Cook's also suggests that Alabama law provides no protection for middle class consumers by arguing that no arbitration clause may be deemed "prohibitively expensive" if it would be possible (even if completely economically irrational) for a consumer to pay the arbitration fees. Thus, according to Cook's, there is nothing unfair about requiring a middle class family to pay $16,000 up front to raise a claim that used to cost our citizens only $200, because the family might conceivably raise $16,000 by raiding its retirement accounts or borrowing money. In *Leonard v. Terminix*, 854 So.2d 529 (Ala. 2002), however, this Court rejected the idea that arbitration clauses are only prohibitively expensive as applied to the destitute. In *Leonard*, this Court recognized that where the costs of arbitration are very large relative to the likely value of a claim, those costs are prohibitive, even with respect to middle class people. Cook's suggests that the rationale behind *Leonard* only applies in cases where it can be proven to a "certainty" that the costs of arbitration will literally be greater than the highest possible recovery that consumers might recover, an impossibly high standard for which it cites no authority.

Cook's second proposal is for the Court to change Alabama contract law. Cook's would like this Court to hold that if the actual terms of a mandatory arbitration clause are unenforceable and the drafting party faces a challenge to those terms, the drafting party may just unilaterally replace those terms on the fly at any time before a state's high court reaches a decision.

This case involves a written contract that was drafted by Cook's. The unambiguous terms of this document required the Leemans (as persons with claims for injunctive relief) to pay arbitral fees in accordance with the AAA's Commercial Rules, just as all others who have arbitrated claims against Cook's have had to do. While the import of that requirement is not evident from the contract, the evidence shows that those fees, which a half a dozen federal courts have held to be unconscionably expensive, are typically $12,000 to $16,000 for persons with claims such as the Leemans'.\1 Throughout the trial court, and in every previous case that has actually gone through arbitration, Cook's stood on its rights under the language of its contract and insisted that the Leemans and its other customers pay these costs.

After receiving the Leemans' opening brief in this appeal, however, Cook's apparently recognized that it had been caught with its hand in the cookie jar, and that consequences might actually flow from its actions. Accordingly, on the day it filed its answering brief, Cook's for the first time offered to pay a small portion of the arbitral fees.\2

This Court should reject Cook's effort to evade judicial review and have this Court re-write its contract to render it enforceable. Cook's argument runs counter to the U.S. Supreme Court's direction that courts should enforce arbitration clauses "as written"; to the rule that courts should not re-write contracts of adhesion in favor of the drafting party; and to the rule that the conscionability of a contract is to be judged at the time of signing.

The timing of Cook's sudden ostensible generosity is transparent at best. Under the U.S. Supreme Court's decision in *Green Tree Financial Corp. v. Randolph*, 513 U.S. 79 (2000), consumers can only challenge an arbitration clause as prohibitively expensive *if* they put forth an extensive evidentiary record. As this Court's own cases in this area demonstrate, creating such a record is difficult, time-consuming, and rarely done. In this case, the record reflects that counsel have expended tens of thousands of dollars over a period of years actually arbitrating cases where the economics of the cases themselves did not justify that effort. Despite the creation of this record, Cook's did not make its offer to pay about a fourth of the Leemans' fees until the last possible moment before this Court. If this ploy works, then corporations can use prohibitively expensive arbitration clauses to bar any kind of legal challenge from being raised, and then in the handful of cases where consumers are actually about to have those clauses struck down, suddenly offer to pay. This Court should not permit, much less encourage, such gamesmanship.

\1 Cook's makes a few half-hearted arguments against this evidence. It suggests, for example, that the documentation of the exact fees in every known case in which a consumer has arbitrated claims against Cook's or any other pest control company in Alabama is merely "anecdotal" evidence. Appellee's Answering Brief ("AB") at 11.

\2 Specifically, Cook's offered to pay the AAA's Administrative Fees, but refused to pay the fees of the actual arbitrator. AB at 41. As the facts set forth in the Leemans' Opening Brief establish, the upshot of this is that Cook's is offering to amend its contract so that it will pay about one third or one fourth of the $12,000 to $16,000 costs of arbitration. Apparently, having confused the trial court into incorrectly imagining that the only cost of arbitration is the AAA's filing fees, and that the actual arbitration itself is free, Cook's is hoping that this Court will also overlook that Cook's 11th hour offer ungenerously ignores the far larger fees of the arbitrator himself.

ARGUMENT

I. The Proven High Cost of Arbitration Under Cook's Contract Renders the Arbitration Clause Grossly Favorable to Cook's.

A. Notwithstanding Cook's Factual Quibbles, the Evidence Establishes the Leemans Face Costs of $12,000 to $16,000 Under the Terms of Cook's Arbitration Clause.

Cook's misrepresents that the arbitration provision at issue in this case does not actually require the AAA to arbitrate this case, but only specifies that the AAA's Commercial Rules will be used in arbitration. AB at 49. Thus, Cook's argues, the high costs that are paid to AAA arbitrators themselves may not be relevant here. *Id.*

However, in the only two cases that have ever been brought against Cook's in arbitration, both involving claims identical to the Leemans' claims here, Cook's has indeed chosen to use AAA arbitrators. In *Porter v. Cook's Pest Control*, and *Wunderlich v. Cook's Pest Control*, these arbitrators billed $9,000 and $10,000 respectively. C111–14; 225–28. These costs were over and above the filing fees charged by the AAA. Throughout this case's pendency in the trial court, Cook's offered no evidence or reason to suppose that in this case, unlike all of the other cases that have gone forward in the past, they would suddenly be using new and cheaper arbitrators.

Furthermore, the AAA Commercial Rules themselves—Rules that Cook's admits would govern this dispute if it were sent to arbitration—require consumers to pay one-half the arbitrators' compensation up-front, whoever the arbitrator may be. There is no evidence to support Cook's apparent assumption that AAA arbitrators are paid considerably more than non-AAA arbitrators and no evidence identifying the cheap arbitrators Cook's now proposes to use.

The upshot of the AAA Commercial Rules is that the consumer must pay an enormous sum for arbitrator compensation up front. The Leemans presented unrebutted evidence that this sum runs to around $9000–$10,000 in cases involving claims identical to their own. The identity of the precise arbitrators who might hear the Leemans' case is not material.

B. This Court Should Not Disregard the Proof that the Costs of Arbitrating Claims Against Cook's in the Past Have Been High, Simply Because Consumers Presented Strong Evidence and Witnesses in Those Proceedings.

Cook's claims that the Leemans have not proved that arbitration of their claims under the AAA Commercial Rules will be prohibitively expensive. AB at 36–52. According to Cook's, the Leemans could easily avoid the kind of high arbitration costs assessed against plaintiffs in previous cases against pest control companies by 1) asking for only "modest" damages and no equitable relief, 2) not putting on a complete case, or 3) trusting the arbitrator to, at the conclusion of the case, allocate fees in such a way that the Leemans would recover some of their costs.

In arguing that the Leemans could have access to affordable arbitration if only they would curtail their own claims, Cook's has lost sight of the fundamental principle that arbitration clauses are only enforceable under the Federal Arbitration Act ("FAA") so long as they allow claimants to effectively vindicate their rights. *See, e.g., Gilmer v. Interstate/Johnson Lane Corp.*, 500 U.S. 20, 26 (1991) (citation omitted) ("[B]y agreeing to arbitrate a statutory claim, a party does not forgo the substantive rights afforded by the statute; it only submits to their resolution in an arbitral, rather than a judicial, forum."). The U.S. Supreme Court's decision in *Randolph* provides a good illustration of this principle, holding that "the existence of large arbitration costs may well preclude a litigant ... from effectively vindicating [its] rights." *Randolph*, 531 U.S. at 81. That decision underscores the fact that arbitration is only acceptable as an alternative to litigation in court because it is simply a "different forum"—one with somewhat different and simplified rules, but nonetheless one in which the basic mechanisms for obtaining justice permit a party to "effectively vindicate" his or her rights. *See, e.g., EEOC v. Waffle House Corp.* 534 U.S. 279, 295 n.10 (2002).

When they argue that the Leemans should have specified their monetary damages and dropped their claim for equitable relief (AB at 38), or that the Leemans could cut costs by putting on a drastically curtailed, potentially incomplete case in arbitration (AB at 42), Cook's ignores the above cases and asks this Court to require the Leemans to submit to an arbitration process in which they cannot effectively vindicate their rights.

For example, as we discussed in the Opening Brief, equitable relief is an important remedy in termite control cases, as these cases often require specific performance remedies. *See* OB at 11, n.5. The Leemans, like all the other consumers who have gone to AAA arbitration against Cook's and similar companies, included a prayer for equitable relief in their Complaint. C1–14. Asking the Leemans to drop this claim would not actually reduce the AAA filing fee, unless the Leemans also gave up the claim that the fact finder should use its full discretion to set the amount of damages. It would also require the Leemans to give up their substantive right to equitable relief merely in order to access affordable arbitration. Such a result is counter to everything the U.S. Supreme Court has said about the proper role of arbitration.

Furthermore, even if the Leemans were to drop their equitable relief claim, scale back their requested damages and reduce their Initial Filing and Case Management Fees, they would still be required to pay arbitrator compensation costs—costs that ran into the thousands of dollars in all five cases brought in arbitration in the record. Cook's argues that the amount of arbitrator compensation charged to the plaintiffs in those cases was a direct consequence of the kind of case that plaintiffs put forward. Specifically, Cook's argues without evidence that plaintiffs in the two earlier cases against Cook's itself, *Porter v. Cook's Pest Control* and *Wunderlich v. Cook's Pest Control*, "unnecessarily inflated" the costs by putting on extensive evidence in arbitrating their cases. AB at 44.

Cook's argument essentially boils down to a contention that the plaintiffs in these earlier cases against Cook's would have saved money had they put forward less evidence and fewer witnesses. The fact is that the plaintiffs won both cases after presenting that evidence and those witnesses. Nothing in this record provides factual support for Cook's implicit allegation that it would have lost both cases even if its customers had presented less evidence, or that plaintiffs in those cases threw money away in order to present deceptive evidence to this court on behalf of the Leemans. Cook's cites no authority which allows it to dictate what claims, evidence and witnesses its customers can present.

Cook's final attack on the Leemans' evidence relating to cost revolves around Cook's contention that the AAA Commercial Arbitration Rules allow the arbitrator to, at her discretion, shift costs from one party to another at the time of the award. AB at

40–41. This argument is spurious for two reasons. First, in order for the arbitrator to be in a position to shift costs away from the plaintiff, there has to be an arbitration proceeding in the first place. As the Leemans have shown through empirical evidence, lawyers throughout Alabama currently refuse to represent consumers in arbitration proceedings under the AAA Commercial Rules, precisely because the *up-front* cost of arbitration are so high. C680–96. If consumers are deterred from ever bringing these cases in the first place, the fact that an arbitrator might, after the plaintiff has already paid thousands of dollars to the AAA, agree to shift some of those costs back onto the defendant, is meaningless. *See Gutierrez v. Autowest, Inc.*, 2003 WL 22890611 at *6 (Cal.App. Dec. 9, 2003) (finding that the possibility that a plaintiff may recover AAA fees and costs at the conclusion of the arbitration under the Commercial Rules "provides little comfort to consumers like the plaintiffs here, who cannot afford to initiate the arbitration processes in the first place."). This sort of *speculation* about arbitration costs is exactly the guess work that courts have refused to engage in when considering prohibitive cost arguments.

Second, the arbitrator's ability to shift costs at the time of the award is completely discretionary under the AAA Rules. As one court has stated, in rejecting precisely the argument Cook's puts forward here, "[D]efendants note that the arbitrator at his or her discretion can assess all expenses to one party at the conclusion of the case. But that is nothing more than an argument that there exists some possibility that [the plaintiff] ultimately may not have to bear a prohibitively expensive portion of the arbitration costs." *Phillips v. Associates Home Equity Services, Inc.*, 179 F.Supp.2d 840, 846–47 (N.D. Ill. 2001).

C. Notwithstanding Cook's Claims, Plaintiffs Did Argue to the Trial Court that the Costs of Arbitration Include the Arbitrators' Fees, and Are not Merely Limited to the Filing Fees.

Cook's argues that plaintiffs have presented "for the first time on appeal" their argument that the trial court erred in imagining that the costs of arbitration include the arbitrators' fees. AB at 66. In fact, the plaintiffs put extensive evidence before the trial court of the exact quantum of the arbitrators' fees, and provided the trial court with detailed evidentiary breakdowns of fees that conclusively demonstrated that these fees represent the Lion's Share of the costs of arbitration under Cook's arbitration clause. OB at 13–18 (citing to the record).

Cook's says that there is no proof that the trial court's error caused the Leemans "substantial prejudice." AB at 66. This argument is somewhat bizarre. The Leemans' argument here is that Cook's arbitration clause is unduly favorable to Cook's because it imposes prohibitive costs. If this Court were to accept the trial court's confused and incorrect notion that the only fees in arbitration are the filing fees, this would have the effect of reducing the Court's estimate of the fees involved by about 66% to 75%. The trial court's error is like evaluating the cost of a meal by only looking at the tip. It is self-evident that it is prejudicial to the Leemans for this Court to ignore 75% of the actual costs of arbitration.

D. This Court Should Reject Cook's Request that it Rewrite the Arbitration Clause to Rescue Defendants from the Consequences of Writing an Unconscionable Arbitration Clause that Imposes Prohibitive Costs.

Cook's asks this Court to speculate that the costs of arbitration in this case will be lower than they were proven to be in all of the previous cases involving it and other similar companies, because two weeks ago Cook's offered to amend its contract with the Leemans. Cook's belated offer to pay a small portion of plaintiffs' costs of arbitration is merely a tactical ploy, allowing Cook's to preserve the advantages of an arbitration clause to itself at a moment when those advantages are threatened because of an effective challenge to that clause's unconscionable provisions. Cook's sudden change of heart is merely an effort to foil judicial scrutiny of a practice that it will repeat against the vast majority of its consumers who are not represented by counsel or who are otherwise unlikely to effectively challenge the costs imposed by its arbitration clause.

Cook's ploy represents an entirely new argument on appeal. Cook's last minute request that the Court rule in its favor based upon a letter written a few weeks ago and filed in court for the first time with its Answering Brief is totally inconsistent with Cook's own declaration in this case that "This Court does not consider matters outside the record." AB at 64. It is understandable that Cook's would wish to avoid the powerful record on costs developed in this case, but the rules of practice simply do not permit it to invent new arguments and construct new self-serving evidence for the first time halfway through an appeal to this Court.

Even if the argument had been made below, this Court should not re-write Cook's defectively drafted arbitration clause to render it legal. First, it is contrary to the FAA for courts to re-write an arbitration clause in such a way as to make it enforceable. The U.S. Supreme Court has said that arbitration agreements must be enforced "according to their terms." *Volt Info. Sciences, Inc. v. Bd. of Trustees*, 489 U.S. 468, 479 (1989). Accordingly, if a particular agreement to arbitrate cannot be enforced according to its terms because it falls afoul of generally applicable state contract law, a court should refuse to enforce it. If a court strikes illegal provisions or adds new provisions to an arbitration clause, this is not enforcing an agreement according to its terms, and thus violates the FAA.

Second, Cook's request to rewrite its arbitration clause is merely a unilateral offer to amend the contract, and need not be accepted. As a federal district court has explained, reviewing a similar offer:

> McDonald's has now offered to pay the arbitration fees to the extent they exceeded those provided for by the AAA's Consumer Rules, which were reasonable but which, we found, did not apply to Popovich's claim. This is not a basis for reconsideration of the Court's ruling. We agree with Popovich that McDonald's offer, which is inconsistent with the parties' contract, amounts to an offer for a new contract. Popovich is under no obligation to accept McDonald's offer, and the court is in no position to impose it. As a matter of elementary contract law, McDonald's cannot unilaterally modify the existing agreement.

Popovich v. McDonald's Corp., 189 F. Supp. 2d 772, 779 (N.D. Ill. 2002). *See also Flyer Printing Co. v. Hill*, 805 So. 2d 829, 833 (Fla. Ct. App. 2001) (ruling that corporation may not amend an unenforceable arbitration clause by offering during litigation to pay all costs, because this was "a unilateral offer to amend the agreement," and, "we are not authorized to remake the parties' contract."); *Lelouis v. W. Directory Co.*, 2001 WL 34046279 at *8 (D. Or. Aug. 10, 2001) (refusing to allow a defendant to "voluntarily pay" the costs of arbitration, noting that "the fairness of a contract must be viewed as of the time the contract was formed" and "this court may not re-write the contract for the parties.").

Third, it would be improper and unfair for this Court to interject itself into the parties' bargain and re-write Cook's adhesion contract to fix the unconscionable provisions in order to make the contract enforceable. *See* Restatement (Second) of Contracts § 184 cmt. b ("[A] court will not aid a party who has taken advantage of his dominant bargaining power to extract from the other party a promise that is clearly so broad as to offend public policy by redrafting the agreement so as to make a part of the promise enforceable.") As one court has stated, "[I]t strikes us as woefully unfair to allow Homefirst at this late date—after a dispute has arisen and after the reverse mortgage has terminated—to refute the unconscionable aspects of the arbitration agreement which Homefirst itself drafted and from which Homefirst stood to benefit over the life of the loan." *Flores v. Transamerica Homefirst, Inc.*, 93 Cal. App. 4th 846, 857 (2001). *See also Browne v. Kline Tysons Imports, Inc.*, 190 F. Supp. 2d 827 (E.D. Va. 2002).

Fourth, it is poor public policy for courts to step in to fix illegal contracts, thereby taking away any disincentive that corporations might have to drafting unfair and unconscionable contracts in the first place. *See Cooper v. MRM Inv. Co.*, 199 F. Supp. 2d 771, 782 (2002):

> The Defendants will not be allowed, at this point, to abandon a provision that KFC's attorneys carefully drafted, in order to "save" the Arbitration Agreement. If Defendants could sever invalid provisions from their contracts, the Court would create an incentive for employers to craft questionable arbitration agreements, require plaintiffs to jump through hoops in order to invalidate those agreements, and ultimately allow the defendants to jettison questionable provisions from the arbitration agreements. Allowing Defendants to do so at this point would be inequitable.

See also Lelouis, 2001 WL 34046279 at *8 (to the same effect).

Fifth, unconscionability is to be viewed at the time a contract is created, so subsequent changes to contract should not be considered in evaluating conscionability. The doctrine that unconscionability is to be judged at the outset is well established as a standard rule of contract law. *See Lelouis*, 2001 WL 34046279 at *8 (refusing to "re-write" an arbitration clause, in part, on the grounds that "the fairness of a contract must be viewed as of the time the contract was formed...."). Cook's admits this general principle of construction when it recognizes at page 20 of its brief that unconscionability should be judged "under the circumstances existing at the time of making the contract...."

Cook's incorrectly suggests later in its brief that this Court has already approved the practice of re-writing arbitration clauses on the fly, citing to *Stevens v. Phillips*, 852 So.2d 123 (Ala. 2002). In that case, this Court briefly mentioned that the defendant had paid all of the costs of arbitration and that the plaintiff had made no response to this fact. It is not clear from the case if the payment of costs was a modification of the parties' contract, or merely an action based upon an ambiguous contract. In *Stevens*, the defendant apparently paid all of the costs—not merely one-fourth of the costs, as Cook's offers here—up front, and the issue was not a new argument on appeal based on non-record evidence. And because the plaintiffs in *Stevens* made no response relating to the issue, that case includes no discussion of (and thus does not resolve) the arguments under the FAA and contract law set forth above.

E. The Enormous Costs Facing the Leemans Are Indeed Prohibitive Within the Meaning of the *Randolph* and *Leonard* Cases.

In *Green Tree Financial Corp. v. Randolph*, 513 U.S. 79 (2000), the U.S. Supreme Court stated that prohibitively expensive arbitration clauses should not be enforced. Because the plaintiff in that case had put forward no evidence relating to the cost of arbitration, her challenge was not successful. The Court gave little guidance as to what constitutes "prohibitive costs," however. Notwithstanding Cook's insinuation, AB at 30–31, the Court never suggested that arbitration costs are only "prohibitive" with respect to impoverished people.

In *Leonard v. Terminix*, 854 So.2d 529 (Ala. 2002), this Court held that an arbitration clause that prohibited class actions was unconscionable because consumers would be deterred from vindicating their rights by the prospect of arbitration costs that were likely to be quite high relative to the value of their claims. 854 So.2d at 539. Cook's suggests that *Leonard* does not apply here because this case is not a class action. AB at 34. This point is true, but it unreasonably confines the rationale of *Leonard* to its facts, and ignores the overall spirit of that case. If this Court concludes from the factual record the Leemans have compiled that the costs of arbitration here would likely preclude them from pursuing their claims, even if valid, then the rationale of *Leonard* dictates that this Court should hold the arbitration clause here invalid. The key point here is that *Leonard* undermines Cook's main argument, which is that no costs, no matter how large, can be found to be prohibitive with respect to the Leemans unless they prove themselves to be poor. In *Leonard*, this Court did not examine accounting records to determine if each class member was poor. Instead, this Court compared the cost of arbitration to the likely value of the claims at issue and held that those costs were prohibitive. In this case the record evidence is unrebutted that lawyers will not take cases with such high up-front costs.

Cook's argues that *Leonard* is irrelevant here because Cook's arbitration clause does not prohibit claims for consequential damages. It is true that this issue, which was one of several addressed in *Leonard*, is not present here. However, that point does not detract from the point for which the Leemans rely on *Leonard*.

Finally, Cook's argues that the comparative costs of arbitration to litigation were greater in *Leonard* than they are here, because the claims here are larger. Cook's argues that the only way that this Court can find that an arbitration clause is prohibitively expensive is if the consumer demonstrates that there is a "certainty" that the cost of arbitration will exceed the value of their claims. AB at 35. This ridiculous proposed standard could rarely be met, and would encourage corporations to use arbitration costs that are overwhelmingly likely to be prohibitive in the real world to eliminate claims against themselves. Cook's suggestion of a standard of proof amounting to "certainty" would make it easier to convict a criminal of murder (which only requires a showing beyond a reasonable doubt) than to demonstrate that an arbitration clause is unconscionable.

Cook's argument that costs are only effectively prohibitive when they actually exceed the exact value of the plaintiffs' claims ignores the facts here. The record establishes that the empirical reality in the market in Alabama is that no attorneys are willing to bring claims against pest control companies using the AAA Commercial Rules. OB at 18–19. Cook's never seriously controverted this evidence (it didn't even bother deposing these experts), and it certainly never identified any cases where consumers had pursued arbitration other than for the five cases brought by the Leemans' counsel as the only means possible of creating the evidentiary record in this case.

Before Cook's adopted this arbitration clause, it was accountable for its mistakes, like any other business in the United States. On those occasions where Cook's breached its duties to its customers under Alabama law and made significant errors that harmed its customers, they could and did hold Cook's liable in court. As the evidence in the record demonstrates, in the period since Cook's has adopted this arbitration clause that requires homeowners to put up more than $10,000 to have their claims heard, no claims have been brought against Cook's in arbitration whatsoever, with the two exceptions in the record here. Cook's might want this Court to imagine that no one has brought a claim in arbitration against it because at the same time that it adopted the clause, Cook's suddenly became a perfect and error-free company, but such an assumption would be credulous in the extreme. The actual empirical record of what has happened in the last several years proves the point that the Leemans are making here: the high fees imposed by Cook's arbitration clause are in fact keeping people in the real world from vindicating their rights against Cook's.

II. Cook's Arbitration Clause Is the Product of Overwhelming Bargaining Power.

A. Notwithstanding Cook's Misreading of the *Branch* case, the Leemans Had No Meaningful Choice About this Arbitration Clause.

Cook's maintains that the Leemans have not adequately demonstrated that they had no real choice but to enter into a pest control services contract containing an arbitration clause. AB at 53–54, AB at 59. The crux of Cook's argument is its contention, based on its reading of *American General Finance, Inc. v. Branch*, 793 So.2d 738 (Ala. 2000) and a number of decisions interpreting *Branch*, that a consumer must affirmatively show that she or he has actually "shopped around" to find other service providers and has found none that provide a contract without an arbitration clause. AB at 56–57.

However, as this Court recently clarified in *Anderson v. Ashby*, 2003 WL 21125998 (Ala. May 16, 2003)—decided after every one of the cases cited by Cook's on this point—the language in *Branch* does not actually require such "shopping around." Instead, this Court's decision in *Branch* rested on a number of "affidavits and stipulations regarding the practices of nearby lenders that were in the business of making loans comparable to the one Branch sought to obtain." *Anderson* at *10. These "sample responses" of nearby lenders led this Court to determine that enough lenders included arbitration clauses in their contract that Branch "*would have had* to expend considerable time and effort even to *find*" any company that did not require arbitration. *Id.*, emphasis in original.

Further clarifying its earlier position, this Court went on in *Anderson* to state:

Thus, our holding in *Branch* was not based upon evidence showing that Branch had actually gone out and traveled a particular geographical area of the state in an unsuccessful attempt to obtain a loan free from the restriction of an arbitration clause. We concluded that American General Finance possessed overwhelming bargaining power because 'Branch *would have had* to expend considerable effort even to *find*' the 1 or 2 of the 16 companies that would not have required arbitration.

Id., emphasis in original, *quoting Branch* at 751.

It is true that Justice Stuart, writing separately in *Anderson*, did argue that plaintiffs should prove that they actually searched for an alternate service provider. *Anderson* at *19 (Stuart, J. concurring in part and dissenting in part). However, the majority of this Court specifically rejected this position, noting that in the cases cited by Justice Stuart where this Court had required such a showing, this was due to the plaintiffs' utter failure to provide any evidence whatsoever of the business practices of other service providers in the area. *Id.* at *11. This Court's rejection of Justice Stuart's position is consistent with the view that the law does not require the doing of a useless thing. *City of Mobile v. Jackson*, 474 So.2d 644, 650 (Ala. 1985).

It is clear since *Anderson* that this Court requires only that consumers must show that the state of the market was such that any effort to "shop around" for a contract without arbitration would be timely, expensive, and potentially useless. The Leemans have met this requirement. First, the record below includes arbitration clauses from a number of major termite control companies in Alabama, all of which include arbitration clauses. Second, this Court's own case records show that at least two other companies providing pest control services when the Leemans contracted with Cook's, Sears and Security, also had arbitration clauses. *See* OB at 9, n.3. Third, this Court itself in the *Leonard* decision noted that the majority of "Terminix's competitors"—who are also Cook's competitors—include arbitration clauses in their contracts. And finally, Cook's itself has indicated that it cannot readily identify any of its competitors who have contracts without arbitration clauses. OB at 9 (citing record). If Cook's cannot identify any competitor whose contract does not contain an arbitration clause, surely its customers could not do so without expending a great deal of time and expense.

Cook's has also argued that its contract is not an adhesion contract, suggesting that perhaps the Leemans could have negotiated out of the arbitration clause if they had asked Cook's to explain or modify the clause. AB at 59–60. This contention is frankly amazing, given Cook's admissions in the record that 1) its employees are not given any training in how to explain the arbitration clause and thus would not be able to do so even if asked (C421–22); 2) Cook's does not "as a general rule" allow consumers to negotiate the removal of the arbitration clause (C476); and 3) Cook's would *flat-out refuse* to transact business with any consumer who refused to sign the arbitration clause (C426).\3 Cook's own statements amply demonstrate that there is no way that

---

\3 Cook's counsel also commented at oral argument in *Cook's Pest Control v. Rebar* that "the consumer is not in a bargaining position to alter the terms and conditions" of the Cook's contract. OB at 10, n.4.

the Leemans could have gotten out of this arbitration provision, even if a Cook's representative had been present at the time the contract was signed.

B. Notwithstanding Cook's Claims that the Issue of Surprise Is a New Argument on Appeal, The Leemans Have Consistently Argued that They Were Surprised by the High Costs of Arbitration under the AAA Commercial Rules.

The Leemans have argued that this Court's unconscionability analysis should include the question of whether the Leemans were unfairly surprised by the arbitration clause imposed by Cook's, due to their "ignorance of important facts" at the time they signed that clause. OB at 37. Cook's does not challenge the inclusion of surprise in the unconscionability analysis, but says only that the Leemans failed to include evidence in the record on this point, or to make this argument below. AB at 64.

In fact, this argument was squarely presented below. In their Supplemental Opposition to Defendants' Motion to Compel Arbitration, the Leemans stated: "no matter how sophisticated or educated [the Leemans] might have been, they could never have known about or foreseen the extremely high cost of arbitration unless Cook's disclosed this information to them. It is undisputed that Cook's made no such disclosures.... Even the sophisticated and educated can be tricked when they do not have all the facts upon which a knowing and intelligent decision regarding arbitration should be based." C604. The Leemans also argued that "Cook's never disclosed the actual and excessive cost of submitting their claims to arbitration pursuant to AAA rules, and this failure renders the entire agreement unconscionable." C604–605.\4

These arguments were based on specific facts in the record. The AAA Commercial Rules were not attached to Cook's arbitration clause. Even if they had been attached, the Rules do not actually indicate the full panoply of fees that must be paid to the arbitrator in any given case. *See* OB at 38. Furthermore, as Cook's has admitted, there was no Cook's representative present when the Leemans signed the contract, and therefore there was no way the Leemans could have even attempted to find out what kind of fees plaintiffs had paid in earlier arbitration proceedings against Cook's. The Leemans had not participated in any arbitration proceedings in the past (C559), and only became familiar with arbitration as a result of the instant dispute (C590).

Thus the issue of surprise, and the evidence supporting the Leemans' assertion that they had no notice of the thousands of dollars they would have to pay to participate in arbitration under the AAA Commercial Rules, is a part of the record below and may properly be considered by this Court now.

C. The Protections of Alabama Contract Law Against Unconscionable Contracts Are Not Limited to the Uneducated.

In its Answering Brief, Cook's attempts again to insert an "education/sophistication" prong into this state's unconscionability analysis. However, this factor simply is not part of the 2-part *Branch* test. In *Branch*, the trial court's discussion of unconscionability included this language from *Layne v. Garner*: " 'In addition to finding that one party was unsophisticated and/or uneducated, a court should ask [the following four questions]...' " *Branch,* 793 So.2d at 743, quoting *Layne v. Garner*, 612 So.2d 404, 408 (Ala. 1989). This Court, however, did not include any mention of education or sophistication in its own articulation of the four-factor *Layne v. Garner* test, and ultimately reduced the test to just two "essential elements": grossly favorable terms and overwhelming bargaining power. *Id.* at 748.

Thus the "education and/or sophistication" question was never actually part of the unconscionability test in *Branch*, nor has this Court included it as a factor in recent cases. In *Harold Allen's Mobile Home Factory Outlet, Inc. v. Butler*, 825 So.2d 779 (Ala. 2002), for instance, this Court found an arbitration clause unconscionable because it allowed one party to select the arbitrator. There is no mention of Mr. Butler's education or sophistication level anywhere in the opinion. The same is true for *Commercial Credit Corp. v. Leggett*, 744 So.2d 890 (Ala. 1999), where this Court focused its unconscionability analysis on the two "most relevant" elements of the *Layne v. Garner* test, " 'unreasonably favorable to [the defendants]' " and " 'oppressive, one-sided, or patently unfair.' " *Leggett* at 898 (citation omitted). This Court's decision in *Leggett* did not, as Cook's argues, anywhere state that a finding that the plaintiff is uneducated and/or unsophisticated is a "threshold matter" in determining unconscionability. AB at 62. That formulation is entirely an invention of Cook's.

Finally, in the only other case cited by Cook's on this point, *Anderson v. Ashby*, this Court found the arbitration clause to satisfy the "overwhelming bargaining power" test based on a lack of meaningful choice, not based on the Ashbys' education level. The Ashbys' illiteracy came up only during the Court's discussion of whether the Ashbys should have been required to "shop around" for another lender without an arbitration clause: the majority of the Court, after finding that there is no requirement that plaintiffs "shop around," noted that even if this were a requirement the Ashbys, due to their education level, were not in a good position to take such an affirmative step. *Anderson*, 2003 WL 21125998 at *11. The only other mention of the Ashbys' illiteracy was in this Court's discussion of the Ashbys' fraud claim, which was wholly separate from any question of unconscionability. *Id.* at *13–16.

III. Cook's Arbitration Clause Contains Still Another "Grossly Favorable Term."

As we argued in our Opening Brief, Cook's arbitration clause is unconscionably broad, covering as it does "any dispute, controversy or claim arising out of or relating to the agreement and guarantee or the breach thereof, or arising out of any prior or future dealings between Cook's and customer,...." OB at 43. Cook's claims that this clause is not overly broad, that overbreadth is not an indicator of unconscionability, and that even if it were, it is not a dispositive indicator. AB at 23–26.

In defending its clause, Cook's cites a number of cases in which courts have upheld clauses that are also broad. However, none of these clauses is as broad as the one at issue in this case. Here, the clause not only covers "any dispute, controversy or claim arising out of or relating to the agreement," as do the clauses that Cook's cites, it also covers disputes and controversies arising out of all "*past and future* dealings between Cook's and the customer."

\4 Addressing the same issue, one court, examining an arbitration clause specifying the AAA Commercial Rules in a very recent case, noted that "While arbitration may be within the reasonable expectation of consumers, a process that builds prohibitively expensive fees into the arbitration process is not." *Gutierrez v. Autowest, Inc.*, 2003 WL 22890611 at *5 (Cal. App. Dec. 9, 2003).

Furthermore, Cook's clause, according to Cook's itself, also covers non-signatories.

The broad scope of this clause echoes the arbitration clauses in *Branch* and *Anderson*—clauses that this Court did find to be unconscionably broad. The clause in *Branch* applied to "every 'dispute[] or controversy[] . . . relating to' every actual or potential transaction—whether past, present, or future—and to every person, whether signatory or nonsignatory to any document, involved in such a transaction between the parties." *Branch*, 793 So.2d at 748. This Court found such breadth to be an important "indicium of unconscionability." *Id.* The clause in *Anderson* was "identical to the arbitration agreement this Court found unconscionable in *Branch*," and this Court invalidated it on the same grounds—including the "breadth of the arbitration clause." *Anderson*, 2003 WL 21125998 at *9.\5

Cook's arbitration clause contains all of the elements that led this Court to find the clause in *Branch* and *Anderson* overly broad. In both cases, this Court indicated that overbreadth is just one indicator of unconscionability, not the dispositive indicator. The Leemans' argument is no different: they urge this Court to take the sheer breadth of Cook's clause, *along with all the other factors discussed in the Opening brief*, into consideration in the unconscionability analysis in this case.

CONCLUSION

For the above reasons, this Court should hold that Cook's arbitration clause is unconscionable.

Respectfully submitted,
[*Attorneys for Appellants*]

E.3 Brief Focusing on Unconscionability Based on Limitation of Remedies and Cost (Sanderson Farms)

IN THE SUPREME COURT OF THE STATE OF MISSISSIPPI

SANDERSON FARMS, INC.)
(PRODUCTION DIVISION),)
    Appellant)
)
v.)
) No. 2003-CA-02490-SCT
)
KENNY AUSTIN,)
CHAROLETT N. HATHORN)
AND LEROY SPRING,)
    Appellees)
)

\5 Cook's quotes extensively from Justice See's dissent in *Anderson* in support of its contention that overly broad arbitration clauses may be upheld. See AB at 24–25. However, the *majority* opinion in Anderson considers overbreadth to be an important part of the unconscionability analysis, and this Court should reaffirm that analysis.

On Appeal From the Chancery Court of Jefferson Davis County, Mississippi, Hon. Larry Buffington, Chancery Judge, in *Kenny Austin, et al. v. Sanderson Farms, Inc.*, No. 02-0225

SANDERSON FARMS, INC.)
(PRODUCTION DIVISION),)
    Appellant)
)
v.)
) No. 2002-IA-01938-SCT
)
TANYA BALLARD, RANN)
McCRAW AND WILLIE)
McINTOSH,)
    Appellees)

On Appeal From the Chancery Court of Lawrence County, Mississippi, Hon. Larry Buffington, Chancery Judge, in *Tanya Ballard, et al. v. Sanderson Farms, Inc.*, No. 2000-0246

TABLE OF CONTENTS

CERTIFICATE OF INTERESTED PERSONS [*omitted*]
TABLE OF CONTENTS
TABLE OF AUTHORITIES
STATEMENT OF ISSUES
STATEMENT OF THE CASE
STATEMENT OF THE FACTS
  A. The Plaintiffs' Relationship with Sanderson Farms
  B. Sanderson Farms' Binding Mandatory Arbitration Clause
    1. The Arbitration Clause's Express Terms
      a. Shortened Two-Day Limitations Period for Submitting Claims
      b. Restrictions on Legal and Equitable Relief
      c. Arbitration Cost Requirements
      d. Exemption for Sanderson Farms' Primary Remedies
    2. Contract Formation Process Regarding Arbitration Clause
  C. The Plaintiffs' Suits and the Proceedings Below
SUMMARY OF ARGUMENT
ARGUMENT
  I. Sanderson Farms' Arbitration Clause is Substantively Unconscionable
    A. The Clause's Two-Day and 14-Day Limitations Provisions are Unconscionable
    B. This Clause's Restrictions on Substantive Remedies are Unconscionable
    C. This Arbitration Clause's Cost-Shifting Provisions are Unconscionable
      1. The Clause's Terms Force Growers to Pay Enormous Fees to Arbitrate
      2. AAA Cannot and Will Not Waive the Arbitrators' Fees
      3. Sanderson Farms' Offer to Pay Costs Does Not Salvage the Arbitration Clause
    D. This Arbitration Clause is Also Substantively Unconscionable Because it Exempts Sanderson's Primary Remedies from Arbitration
  II. Sanderson Farms' Arbitration Clause is Procedurally Unconscionable

- III. The Arbitration Clause Does Not Cover Plaintiffs' Pre-Contract Claims
- IV. Jurisdiction and Venue in the Two Chancery Courts Were Proper
- V. The Appellees' Claims are Not Time-Barred by the Statute of Limitations
- VI. The Plaintiffs are Not Improperly Joined in These Actions
- VII. The Court Correctly Denied the Motion to Treat Plaintiffs' Complaint in *Ballard* as Dismissed
- VIII. The Chancery Court's Evidentiary Rulings in *Austin* Were Correct

CONCLUSION

CERTIFICATE OF SERVICE [*omitted*]

TABLE OF AUTHORITIES

Cases***

Adler v. Fred Lind Manor, 103 P.3d 773 (Wash. 2004)

Alexander v. Anthony Int'l, L.P., 341 F.3d 256 (3d Cir. 2003)

Al-Safin v. Circuit City Stores, Inc., 394 F.3d 1254 (9th Cir. 2005)

American Bankers Ins. Co. of Fla. v. Alexander, 818 So. 2d 1073 (Miss. 2001)

Anderson v. Ashby, 873 So. 2d 168 (Ala. 2003)

Armendariz v. Foundation Health Psychare Services, Inc., 6 P.3d 669 (Cal. 2000)

Arnold v. United Companies Lending Corp., 511 S.E.2d 854 (W. Va. 1998)

Banc One Acceptance Corp. v. Hill, 367 F.3d 426 (5th Cir. 2004)

Boswell v. Wheat, 37 Miss. 610 (1859)

Broughton v. CIGNA Healthplans, 988 P.2d 67 (Cal. 1999)

Camacho v. Holiday Homes, Inc., 167 F. Supp. 2d 892 (W.D. Va. 2001)

Cavalier Mfg., Inc. v. Jackson, 823 So. 2d 1237 (Ala. 2001)

Circuit City Stores, Inc. v. Adams, 279 F.3d 889 (9th Cir. 2002)

Cole v. Haynes, 62 So. 2d 779 (Miss. 1953)

Cooper v. MRM Inv. Co., 199 F. Supp. 2d 771 (M.D. Tenn. 2002)

Cooper v. MRM Inv. Co., 367 F.3d 493 (6th Cir. 2004)

Donald v. Holmes, 595 So. 2d 434 (Miss. 1992)

D.R. Horton, Inc. v. Green, 96 P.3d 1159 (Nev. 2004)

East Ford, Inc. v. Taylor, 826 So. 2d 709 (Miss. 2002)

Entergy Miss., Inc. v. Burdette Gin Co., 726 So. 2d 1202 (Miss. 1998)

Equal Employment Opportunity Comm'n v. Waffle House, Inc., 534 U.S. 279 (2002)

Ex Parte Thicklin, 824 So. 2d 723 (Ala. 2002)

Flores v. Transamerica Home First, Inc., 93 Cal. App. 4th 846 (2001)

Fortenberry v. Choctaw Maid Farms, Inc., Case No. 00-0284 (Chancery Court, Simpson County, Mississippi)

Green v. Winona Elevator Co., 319 So. 2d 224 (Miss. 1975)

Greenpoint Credit, LLC v. Reynolds, 151 S.W.3d 868 (Mo. Ct. App. 2005)

Graham Oil Co. v. ARCO Prod's Co., 43 F.3d 1244 (9th Cir. 1994)

Guice v. Mississippi Life Ins. Co., 836 So. 2d 756 (Miss. 2003)

Hadnot v. Bay, Ltd., 344 F.3d 474 (5th Cir. 2003)

Hentz v. State, 542 So. 2d 914 (Miss. 1989)

Iberia Credit Bureau, Inc. v. Cingular Wireless, LLC, 379 F.3d 159 (5th Cir. 2004)

In re Bankruptcy of Stephen Clyde Martin and Susan Gayle Martin, Case No. 03-61633 (Bankr. W.D. Tex.)

Jenkins v. First American Cash Adv. of Ga., LLC, 400 F.3d 868 (11th Cir. 2005)

Johnson v. Consol. Am. Life Ins. Co., 244 So. 2d 400 (Miss. 1971)

Koehring v. Hyde, 178 So. 2d 838 (Miss. 1965)

Kruger Clinic Orthopaedics, LLC v. Regence Bluesield, 98 P.3d 66 (Wash. App. 2004)

Lelouis v. Western Directory Co., 230 F. Supp. 2d 1214 (D. Or. 2001)

Leonard v. Terminix Int'l Co., L.P., 854 So. 2d 529 (Ala. 2002)

Longo v. AAA-Michigan, 569 N.E.2d 927 (Ill. App. 1990)

Lozada v. Dale Baker Oldsmobile, Inc., 91 F. Supp. 2d 1087 (W.D. Mich. 2000)

Martinez v. Master Protection Corp., 118 Cal. App. 4th 107 (2004)

McMillian v. Puckett, 678 So. 2d 652 (Miss. 1996)

Melena v. Anheuser-Busch, Inc., 816 N.E.2d 826 (Ill. App. 2004)

Mendez v. Palm Harbor Homes, Inc., 45 P.3d 594 (Wash. App. 2002)

O'Neil Steel, Inc. v. Millette, 797 So. 2d 869 (Miss. 2001)

Paladino v. Avnet Computer Technlolgies, Inc., 134 F.3d 1054 (11th Cir. 1998)

Parker v. Livingston, 817 So. 2d 554 (Miss. 2002)

Phillips v. Associates Home Equity Serv's, Inc., 179 F. Supp. 2d 840 (N.D. Ill. 2001)

Pilgrim Rest Missionary Baptist Church v. Wallace, 835 So. 2d 67 (Miss. 2003)

Pitts v. Watkins, __ So. 2d __, 2005 WL 851451 (Miss. April 14, 2005)

Pollard v. Phalen, 53 So. 453 (Miss. 1910)

Popovich v. McDonald's Corp., 189 F. Supp. 2d 772 (N.D. Ill. 2002)

Powertel, Inc. v. Bexley, 743 So. 2d 570 (Fla. Dist. Ct. App. 1999)

Robinson v. Cobb, 763 So. 2d 883 (Miss. 2000)

Royer Homes of Miss., Inc. v. Chandeleur Homes, Inc., 857 So. 2d 748 (Miss. 2003)

Salts v. Gulf Nat'l Life Ins., 743 So. 2d 371 (Miss. 1999)

Sanderson Farms, Inc. v. Gatlin, 848 So. 2d 828 (Miss. 2003)

Security Watch, Inc. v. Sentinel Systems, Inc., 176 F.3d 369 (6th Cir. 1999)

Smith v. Franklin Custodian Funds, Inc., 726 So. 2d 144 (Miss. 1998)

Spinetti v. Service Corp., Int'l, 341 F.3d 212 (3d Cir. 2003)

Taylor v. Butler, 142 S.W.3d 277 (Tenn. 2004)

Ting v. AT&T, 182 F. Supp. 2d 902 (N.D. Cal. 2002), *aff'd in part and rev'd in part*, 319 F.3d 1126 (9th Cir. 2003)

Travelers Indem. Co. v. Chappell, 246 So. 2d 498 (Miss. 1971)

Union Planters Bank, NA v. Rogers, __ So. 2d __, 2005 WL 976996 (Miss. April 28, 2005)

West Virginia ex rel Dunlap v. Berger, 567 S.E.2d 265 (W. Va. 2002)

Wisconsin Auto Title Loans, Inc. v. Jones, __ N.W.2d __, 2005 WL 674667 (Wis. App. March 24, 2005)

Zuver v. Airtouch Communications, Inc., 103 P.3d 753 (Wash. 2004)

Statutes

Federal Arbitration Act, 9 U.S.C. §§ 1 *et seq.*

Miss. Code Ann. § 11-5-1

Miss. Code Ann. § 15-1-5

Miss. Code Ann. § 15-1-49

*** [*Editor's Note: Citations throughout brief as in original.*]

Miss. Code Ann. § 75-2-302
Packers & Stockyards Act, 7 U.S.C. § 192

Rules

American Arbitration Association, Commercial Rule R-1
American Arbitration Association, Commercial Rule R-50
American Arbitration Association, Commercial Rule R-52
American Arbitration Association, Commercial Rule R-54
American Arbitration Association, Commercial Rule titled "Fees"
American Arbitration Association, Supplementary Procedures for Consumer-Related Disputes Rule C-8
Fed. R. Civ. Pr. 20
Miss. R. App. Pr. 15
Miss. R. Civ. Pr. 1
Miss. R. Civ. Pr. 20
Miss. R. Civ. Pr. 43
Miss. R. Civ. Pr. 82(c)

Other Authorities

20 Am. Jur. 2d § 81
Kris Christen, *Chickens, manure, and arsenic*, Policy News- March 22, 2001, Environmental Science and Technology
Mike Ewall, *Toxic Hazards Associated with Poultry Litter Incineration*, publication of Energy Justice Network, Sept. 2002
J.R. Garbino, *et al.*, *Degradation of Roxarsone in Poultry Litter*
V.A. Griffith, *Mississippi Chancery Practice*
Mississippi State Extension Service, *Broiler Production in Mississippi* (June 1997)
Restatement (Second) of Contracts § 184
John Vaniver, *Arsenic: Chicken Feed Effects Questioned: Researchers Study Health, Environmental Impact from Use of Arsenic*, Daily Times (Maryland), January 4, 2004
Wright, Miller and Kane, *Federal Practice & Procedure: Civil 2d*

STATEMENT OF ISSUES

1. Whether Sanderson Farms' binding mandatory arbitration clause is substantively unconscionable under applicable Mississippi contract law because it reduces the statutory limitations period for growers to submit claims to two working days, eliminates and sharply restricts the growers substantive remedies, forces growers to pay enormous up-front fees to arbitrate their claims, and exempts Sanderson's termination and repossession remedies from arbitration altogether.

2. Whether Sanderson Farms' binding mandatory arbitration clause is procedurally unconscionable under applicable Mississippi contract law because it is a non-negotiable contract of adhesion that growers were required to sign or else face termination of their relationships with Sanderson Farms after they had borrowed large sums of money to tailor their farms to Sanderson's plans and specifications.

3. Whether Plaintiffs' claims alleging fraudulent misrepresentation based on promises made by Sanderson Farms before the parties entered into an agreement with an arbitration clause fall outside the scope of that arbitration clause because it does not expressly apply backwards in time.

4. Whether jurisdiction lay with the Chancery Courts where Plaintiffs allege damage to real and personal property, where Plaintiffs assert class claims, and where Plaintiffs' claims predominate in injunctive relief.

5. Whether venue was permissible in the Jefferson Davis County and Lawrence County Chancery Courts when the real and personal property that is the subject of these cases is located in those counties.

6. Whether Sanderson Farms' concealment and misrepresentations to growers toll the statute of limitations applicable to the claims in these cases.

7. Whether Plaintiffs are properly joined where they assert claims arising from a common pattern of conduct involving Sanderson Farms' concealment and misrepresentations to them and where the only differences in the remedies they seek are based on the extent to which each Plaintiff was wronged.

8. Whether the complaint in *Ballard, et al. v. Sanderson Farms* was properly treated as not having been dismissed.

9. Whether the Chancery Court's evidentiary rulings in *Austin, et al. v. Sanderson Farms, Inc.* were correct and within that court's discretion.

STATEMENT OF THE CASE

These appeals are not about whether all arbitration is good or bad or whether companies can ever use private arbitration for resolving their disputes. Clearly they can. But what they cannot do is use mandatory arbitration clauses as a weapon to strip individual parties of their rights and shield themselves from liability. These appeals involve exactly this type of process, where a company that has overwhelming bargaining power over farmers because it can withhold the chicken flocks they depend on for their livelihood has exploited this power by imposing a binding mandatory arbitration clause whose express terms eliminate these farmers' legal and equitable remedies, and impose time limits and cost barriers that prevent them from vindicating their rights *in any forum*.

These two cases involve claims by hatching egg grower farmers (Kenny Austin, Charolett Hathorn, and Leroy Spring) and by broiler grower farmers (Tanya Ballard, Rann McCraw, and Willie McIntosh), alleging that Sanderson Farms, Inc. fraudulently or negligently induced them and other similarly situated growers to enter into contracts to raise chicken flocks by making false representations about their prospective incomes and the costs and requirements of raising these flocks. Sanderson Farms responded in both cases by moving to dismiss all claims, transfer jurisdiction, change venue, and compel the plaintiffs to arbitrate under the binding mandatory arbitration clause in its production contracts. The Chancery Courts of Jefferson Davis County and Lawrence County denied Sanderson Farms' motions, and both found this arbitration clause to be unconscionable. These appeals followed. For the reasons set forth herein, this Court should affirm the Chancery Courts' rulings and hold that Sanderson Farms' binding mandatory arbitration clause is both substantively and procedurally unconscionable or, alternatively, that the clause does not apply to the plaintiffs' pre-contract claims.

Since these binding mandatory arbitration clauses were imposed in 1997, no grower has ever been able to get a hearing on their claims against Sanderson Farms. Only two growers have even tried to arbitrate their claims, and both were thwarted because of this clause's disabling terms that:

- force growers to present all claims to Sanderson Farms within ***two (2) working days*** after discovering them, and then submit claims to binding arbitration within ***14 days*** after completing the company's Complaint Resolution process, thereby evis-

cerating the applicable statutory limitations periods;
- eliminate legal remedies available to growers in arbitration by **barring punitive or exemplary damages** awards; restricting damages for claims challenging Sanderson's failure or delay in performing its duties under the contract; and limiting growers' claims for consequential damages from Sanderson's breach by requiring arbitrators to apply a **clear and convincing evidence** standard to these claims;
- eliminate equitable remedies available to growers in arbitration by limiting the arbitrator's authority to award only actual money damages, specific performance, and temporary injunctive relief, thereby **barring claims for permanent injunctive relief**;
- force growers to bear their own attorneys' fees and expenses, regardless of any statutory or common law right to recover such costs if they prevail on claims;
- impose prohibitive cost obligations on growers by forcing them to pay half the cost of arbitrating before a three-arbitrator panel under the extremely expensive Commercial Arbitration Rules of the American Arbitration Association ("AAA");
- prohibit growers from defraying the costs of these arbitration proceedings by joining or aggregating their claims with one another unless Sanderson Farms affirmatively consents to such joinder.

While it imposes these prohibitive requirements against growers bringing claims against Sanderson Farms, this arbitration clause relieves Sanderson Farms of all of these obligations for its most important remedies by allowing the company to terminate the contract and repossess flocks from growers without having to go through these Complaint Resolution and Arbitration Processes.

Based on these one-sided and disabling terms and the record evidence showing that growers had to accept these terms under threat of losing their flocks and that growers could not switch to other suppliers without incurring significant new start-up costs, the Court should hold that Sanderson Farms' mandatory arbitration clause is both substantively and procedurally unconscionable.

STATEMENT OF FACTS

A. The Plaintiffs' Relationship with Sanderson Farms

Plaintiffs Kenny Austin, Charolett Hathorn, and Leroy Spring all began growing breeder chickens for Sanderson Farms between 1991 and 1994. Plaintiffs Tanya Ballard, Rann McCraw, and Willie McIntosh all began growing broiler chickens for Sanderson Farms between 1983 and 1994. At the time they began their growing operations, none of them was subject to an arbitration agreement with Sanderson Farms. *See* Austin R.(hereafter AR) 582–83; 588–89; 594–95; 564–65; 570–71; 576–77, Ballard R.(hereafter BR) 396–397.

When the plaintiffs began growing for Sanderson Farms, they had to make substantial financial investments to tailor their farms to Sanderson Farms' specifications. Sanderson Farms furnished precise plans and specifications for the construction of their houses and the type of equipment to be used therein, including such details as the spacing of light fixtures, the wattage of generators, and the water storage capacity of barns. *See, e.g.*, AR. 584–85; 590–591; 596–597; 566–67; 572–573; 578–579; Appellees Judicial Notice Ex. "J". As Sanderson Farms itself advertised, "[t]he growers finance, build and maintain poultry houses and equipment to Sanderson Farms' specifications," which include the precise dimensions of the houses, the types of foundation and roofing, and the use of feed bins, feed lines, heating equipment, ventilation and exhaust fans, environmental control equipment, generators, and alarm systems. AR.584–85; 590–591; 596–597; 566–67; 572–573; 578–579; Appellees' Judicial Notice Ex. "A" (Sanderson Farms Producer Prospectus Brochure at 3–4). The company also controlled the types of chicken feed and pesticides that plaintiffs had to use. Appellees' Judicial Notice Ex. "A" (Sanderson Farms Producer Prospectus Brochure at 3–4); AR.584–85; 590–591; 596–597; 566–67; 572–573; 578–579. To tailor their farms to these specifications, Plaintiffs had to borrow hundreds of thousands of dollars by taking out mortgages on their farms. Appellees' Judicial Notice Ex. "A" (Sanderson Farms Producer Prospectus Brochure at 6–8);("A hen farm contains two houses for a total cost of $310,000"); ("A Broiler farm contains four houses for a total cost of $432,000"); AR.568; 574; 580; 586; 592; 598; *see also* Austin-Tr. Cockrell 149 *see also* Appellees' Judicial Notice Ex. "B"(Gatlin transcript) at page 168 (trial testimony of broiler grower Roy Gatlin that he never considered changing companies because "each company has their own policy and procedure with their buildings, they're own equipment, and what they require in their houses and all. And if I had done that it would have probably cost me several more $100,000 to change over to their way of raising chickens. So I just couldn't see that that would be feasible to me. I couldn't afford it.")

B. Sanderson Farms' Binding Mandatory Arbitration Clause

1. The Arbitration Clause's Express Terms

In early 1997, approximately three to five years after the plaintiffs made these investments to start up their operations for Sanderson Farms, the company began using new 15-year contracts for its breeder and broiler growers. The 1997 contract contained new Complaint Resolution and binding Arbitration clauses governing all future legal claims by growers. Except for paragraph numbers, the wording of these provisions in the broiler and breeder contracts is identical. Austin-Cockrell Tr. 162. The new arbitration clause applied to:

> Any controversy or claim arising between the parties (and not resolved pursuant to Section 23 [Complaint Resolution and Mediation provisions] above), including, but not limited to, disputes relating to this Agreement, the arbitrability of any dispute relating to this Agreement, termination of this Agreement, or of any breach of this Agreement, whether such controversy or claim arises before, during or after termination of the agreement.

Hatching Egg Producer's Agreement (hereafter, "Contract") at 5, § 24; AR.32–37; Broiler Production Agreement (hereafter "Contract") at 6–7, § 27; BR.113–120.

a. Shortened Two-Day Limitations Period for Submitting Claims

This new binding arbitration clause includes multiple provisions that diminish the legal rights of growers. The arbitration clause incorporates as a prerequisite the contract's "Complaint Resolution" process for claims arising out of the contract. The Complaint

Resolution Clause covers all claims *by growers* (but not by Sanderson Farms) relating to the contract. For these grower claims, the Complaint Resolution clause requires that:

> The Grower must present his or her complaint orally or in writing to his or her Breeder/Hatchery Manager ***within two (2) working days*** after such complaint or grievance is discovered, or with reasonable care should have been discovered. ***Failure to present a complaint within this time limit will be conclusive evidence that the complaint or grievance has been abandoned.*** (emphasis added)

Contract at 4, § 23(a); AR. 32–37; Broiler Growers Agreement (hereafter, "Contract") at 6, § 26(a); BR.117–118 states 48 hours. If the grower and Breeder Manager are unable to resolve the dispute, the grower must submit his or her claim to the Division Manager within two working days of making the initial complaint. *Id.*, § 23(b); (§ 26(b) in Broiler Production Agreement). If the Division Manager does not resolve the dispute, the grower must submit a written request for mediation under AAA's Commercial Mediation Rules, again within two working days of the Division Manager's response or failure to respond. *Id.* at 5, § 23(c)(§ 26(c) in Broiler Production Agreement); AR. 32–37; § 26(b); BR.113–120. If disputes are not resolved in mediation, then growers trying to vindicate claims must submit them to binding arbitration *"within 14 calendar days of the conclusion of the mediation."* *Id.*, § 23(e) (emphasis added) (§ 26(e) in Broiler Production Agreement).

b. Restrictions on Legal and Equitable Relief

The arbitration clause further limits Plaintiffs' legal and equitable remedies. The clause restricts the remedies that arbitrators can award to "actual money damages as provided in Section 13 [titled "Limitation of Damages"] (§ 15 in Broiler Production Agr.)(with interest on unpaid amounts from the date due), specific performance, and temporary injunctive relief." *Id*, § 24. The clause specifies that "***arbitrators shall not have the authority to award exemplary or punitive damages***, and the parties expressly waive any claimed right to such damages." *Id.* (emphasis added). By incorporating these "Limitation of Damages" terms as restrictions on the arbitrators' authority, the arbitration clause limits Plaintiffs' consequential damages on contract claims by stating that "Sanderson will be liable only for contract damages and other damages relating directly to the breach, provided that *such other damages are proved by clear and convincing evidence*." *Id.* at 3, § 13; AR. 32–37, § 15; BR. 113–120 in Broiler Production Agr. For all other claims, the arbitrators can only award "actual damages proximately caused by any wrongful conduct." *Id.*

This arbitration clause thus prohibits growers from ever recovering punitive or exemplary damages, permanent injunctive relief, consequential damages not provable by clear and convincing evidence of causation, or any other legal remedies besides actual money damages, temporary injunctive relief, and specific performance. This clause also expressly requires growers to pay their own attorneys' fees and expenses, regardless of applicable law to the contrary. *Id.* at 5, § 24; AR.32–37 at 6 § 27; BR. 113–120 in Broiler Production Agreement.

c. Arbitration Cost Requirements

The arbitration clause also requires growers to pay thousands of dollars in fees and costs. The clause expressly provides that "[t]he cost of such arbitration will be divided equally among the parties to the arbitration." *Id.* at 5, § 24; AR.32–37; at 6 § 27; BR. 113–120 in Broiler Production Agreement. The clause also provides that arbitration will be conducted "in accordance with the Commercial Arbitration Rules of the [AAA] *by a panel of three arbitrators*." *Id.* (emphasis added). Under AAA's Commercial Rules, parties in disputes involving non-monetary claims must pay an Initial Filing Fee of $3,250 and an additional Case Service Fee of $1,250. Commercial Arbitration Rules (available at www.adr.org/sp.asp?id=22440), "Fees" schedule. Austin Tr. Ex 18 and 19, Appellees Judicial Notice Ex . "C" (pages 26 of 27 and 27 of 27 showing AAA Fees are missing from Tr. Ex 19). Thus, a grower would have to pay at least $2,250 to initiate such claims. In addition to the case filing and service fees, AAA also requires parties to pay all other non-witness-related expenses of the arbitration, including the arbitrators' fees and expenses, and may require parties to deposit their share of these expenses in advance of any hearing or else risk having the proceedings suspended or terminated. *See* AAA Commercial Rules R-50, R-52, and R-54; at pages 19–20, Austin Tr. Ex 19; at pages 23–24, Austin Tr. Ex 18; The arbitrators' fees alone can be at least $295 per hour, or $1,200 to $1,800 per day, for a single arbitrator. *See* Austin- Fisher Tr. 256; Appellees Judicial Notice Ex "D" Mike Cockrell Dep. at 41. These costs are tripled under Sanderson Farms' arbitration clause because it expressly requires a three-arbitrator panel, which results in arbitrators' fees of *over $5,000 per hearing day*. Finally, the arbitration clause prohibits growers from defraying these costs by joining or aggregating their claims in multi-party arbitration, unless Sanderson Farms affirmatively consents to it. Contract at 5, § 24; AR.32–37 at 6 § 27; BR. 113–120 in Broiler Production Agreement.

Under these cost-shifting terms, no grower has ever gotten his or her claims against Sanderson Farms to an arbitration hearing. Appellees Judicial Notice Ex "D" Cockrell Dep. at 39–40;("Q. Has Sanderson ever been involved in an arbitration, period? A. No.") Sanderson Farms' Chief Financial Officer, Mike Cockrell, testified to his knowledge of only two cases where growers tried to initiate the arbitration process for claims against the company. Austin-Cockrell Tr. 158. In one of these cases, Mississippi broiler grower Roy Gatlin was charged $11,000 in filing fees and up-front deposit costs by AAA as a condition for receiving a hearing on his wrongful termination claims, thus forcing him to turn to the court system and ultimately to this Court to save his claims. *See Sanderson Farms, Inc. v. Gatlin*, 848 So. 2d 828, 832 (Miss. 2003) (plurality opinion) (describing AAA's total charges to Gatlin); *see also* Appellees Judicial Notice Ex "D" Cockrell Dep. at 41 and 63,(describing deposit charges to each party in the *Gatlin* case);*see also* Austin-Tr. Ex. 20 R.E. 1 (this does not include filing fee and mediation fee paid by Gatlin).

In the other case, Texas breeder grower Susan Martin was billed over $22,000 by AAA as her share of the up-front costs, forcing her to abandon her arbitration against Sanderson Farms. *See* Appellees Judicial Notice Ex "E". After paying $6,700 towards these charges, Ms. Martin asked AAA to waive the remaining $15,800 balance. *See* Appellees Judicial Notice Ex "F". But AAA's Case Manager informed her that "***[t]he Association has no authority to defer arbitrator compensation and expenses or non-***

Association hearing room expenses." *See* Appellees Judicial Notice Ex "G" (emphasis added); *see also* AAA Supplementary Procedures for Consumer-Related Disputes (available at www.adr.org/sp.asp?id=22014), C-8 (describing provision for low-income consumers in California allowing waiver of arbitration fees and costs, "exclusive of arbitrator fees.")

d. Exemption for Sanderson Farms' Primary Remedies

While the arbitration clause imposes these requirements on all claims by growers, the clause expressly exempts from arbitration Sanderson Farms' most important remedies under the contract. The clause expressly provides that "[n]otwithstanding anything to the contrary, either party may terminate the Agreement prior to or without arbitration in accordance with Sections 19, 20 and 22 herein." Contract at 5, § 24; AR.32–37 at 6 § 27; BR. 113–120 in Broiler Production Agr.

Section 19 of the contract allows Sanderson Farms to terminate the contractual relationship upon *five days notice* to the grower for any of seven enumerated reasons, including material breach of any contractual term or condition or a material change in Sanderson's business operations, without resort to arbitration. *Id*. at 3–4, § 19; AR.32–37 at 6 § 27; BR. 113–120 in Broiler Production Agr.

Section 20 lets Sanderson Farms terminate the contract ***immediately*** for any of eight listed reasons, including a grower's use of abusive language or use of outside materials, again without resort to arbitration. *Id*. at 4, § 20; AR.32–37; at 6 § 27; BR. 113–120 in Broiler Production Agr.

In the event of a termination under Section 20, the arbitration clause lets Sanderson Farms repossess its flocks from the grower without resort to arbitration or a court for provisional remedies. *Id*. at 4; § 24 ("The seeking of any provisional remedy by either party shall be supplemental to, and not in place of, Sanderson's contractual right to repossess a Flock pursuant to Section 21.")[1]

2. Contract Formation Process Regarding Arbitration Clause

In the early to mid-1990s, discontent among poultry growers in Mississippi with the financial risks inherent in the industry's short-term growing contracts drew the attention of the Governor and the State legislature. Over the poultry companies' opposition, both houses of the legislature passed a growers' rights bill in 1996. Austin-McAlpin Tr. 24–26; R.E. 2. Governor Fordice vetoed that legislation, and instead created a Governor's Special Poultry Committee that consisted of industry executives and a single grower from each company to discuss some of the issues that the vetoed legislation covered. The Governor specifically excluded lawyers from participating in this committee's proceedings. *Id*. Austin-McAlpin Tr. 26; R.E. 2.

The Governor's Committee held a series of meetings in which the industry executives, including Joe F. Sanderson, Jr. representing Sanderson Farms, and one grower from each company participated. *Id*. Some of these growers were associated with the Mississippi Contract Poultry Growers Association (hereafter, "MCPGA"), *id*., and some with the Mississippi Farm Bureau, but neither these growers nor the MCPGA or any other entity had authority to negotiate contract terms on behalf of growers who were not present at these meetings. Austin-McKnight Tr. 341; *see also* Appellees Judicial Notice Ex "D" Cockrell Dep. at 70. When one assumed the role of President of MCPGA, his tenure as a poultry grower was short-lived. Then-MCPGA President Larry McKnight raised the issue of arbitration during these meetings, and was told by the company executives that arbitration clauses were going to be in the new long-term contracts that the companies would be using. Austin-McKnight Tr. 349–351.[2] There was no negotiation over the arbitration clauses. *Id*. at 350–351; AR 691–694; R.E. 3 ("No. There was no negotiation on our part in any way, shape, fashion or form.")

During the time when the growers' rights legislation was pending and the Governor's Committee was meeting, Sanderson Farms began drawing up the terms of its new 15-year contract for growers. The decision to add an arbitration clause to these new contracts was made by Sanderson Farms. Austin-Cockrell Tr. 129;("If we were going to have a long-term relationship, there were many things we wanted to include in the contract including an alternative dispute resolution process."). In October 1996, Sanderson Farms mailed a letter to growers informing them that the company was developing its new long-term contract that would address issues raised in the Governor's Committee meetings and in separate meetings the company had held with its own growers over the summer. *Id*. at 131.

On December 30, 1996, Sanderson Farms mailed copies of its new long-term contract to growers, along with letters inviting them to meetings to discuss the new contract. *Id*. at 131. There is no evidence that the plaintiffs attended any of these meetings. *See, e.g.*, Austin-Cockrell Tr. 133, 151–152; R.E. 4 ("We never sat down to my knowledge with them across the table. They were invited to the meetings and whether or not they came, I don't know.") *see also*, Austin-Rosa Tr. 95; R.E. 5. Although Sanderson Farms responded to comments on its arbitration clause from some other growers during this process, including then-MCPGA President Larry McKnight (who was *not* a Sanderson grower), *see* McKnight Tr. 353; the company never recognized MCPGA's or these growers' authority to bargain on behalf of the plaintiffs. *Id*. at 341; R.E. 6; *see also* Appellees Judicial Notice Ex "D" Cockrell Dep. At 70. Instead, Sanderson Farms said each grower's contract was private and confidential. *Id*.

The plaintiffs entered into the long-term contracts that contained the new arbitration clause in February 1997. The contracts were brought to the plaintiffs by Sanderson Farms' flock supervisors and presented for their signatures on a take-it-or-leave-it basis. Austin-Cockrell Tr.152–153;154–155; R.E. 7. By the time Sanderson Farms brought the contracts to the plaintiffs to sign, the company had made up its mind that it wanted the arbitration clause, and any grower who did not agree to it would have lost their flocks: "The answer is no. We would not deliver chickens to someone with whom we do not have a contractual relationship just [as] if they had not signed the flock-to-flock contract we would not have delivered chickens." *Id*. at 155, 158.[3]

---

[1] Although Section 22 also permits the grower to terminate the contract for any reason, the grower must provide notice of his or her intent to do so **at least 365 days prior to the termination date.** *Id*., § 22; AR.32–37.

[2] McKnight subsequently had his growing contract terminated, as has been done to every other MCPGA President of whom he is aware. Austin-McKnight Tr. 345.

[3] *See also* Appellees' Judicial Notice Ex. "B";(Roy Gatlin's trial testimony stating that "[I]t had been the policy of Sanderson ever since I been with them, if you don't sign the contract you don't get chickens. If you don't get chickens, you don't satisfy

C. The Plaintiffs' Suits and the Proceedings Below

The breeder-grower plaintiffs (Austin, *et al.*) filed suit in the Chancery Court of Jefferson Davis County on August 2, 2002, asserting claims on behalf of themselves and a class consisting of all Sanderson Farms breeder growers in Mississippi. Complaint ¶ 1. AR. 8–23. The broiler-grower plaintiffs (Ballard, *et al.*) filed suit in the Chancery Court of Lawrence County on September 26, 2002, asserting claims on behalf of themselves and a class consisting of all Sanderson Farms broiler growers in Mississippi. Second Amended-Complaint ¶ 1, Br 128–142.

Both sets of plaintiffs allege that Sanderson Farms fraudulently or negligently induced them into housing and tending to flocks and gathering and/or storing hatch eggs by knowingly making false representations about their future income, costs, expenses, equipment requirements, company policies, and working relationships. *Id.* ¶ 10. Plaintiffs also allege that Sanderson Farms concealed material facts and information relating to the method of payment and inequalities within the company's system for paying growers. Id. Plaintiffs further allege that their farm properties have been damaged from the application of chemicals required by Sanderson Farms, and from the by-products of housing and tending to the company's flocks. *Id.* Their complaint seeks predominantly equitable relief, including an injunction against the wrongful practices alleged and against retaliatory terminations, a full accounting of wrongfully retained funds, creation of a constructive trust and equitable lien for the plaintiffs, an award of common fund attorneys' fees and costs, and money damages, if any, that may flow from this equitable relief. *Id.* at ¶¶ 16, 21–26.

Sanderson Farms answered the suits by moving to dismiss, transfer jurisdiction, change venue, or compel arbitration. *See* Motion to Dismiss at 1, AR. 23–31. Sanderson Farms claimed that the Circuit Courts had exclusive jurisdiction because no aspect of the plaintiffs' claims fell within the Chancery Court's subject matter jurisdiction. *Id.* Sanderson Farms further alleged that venue in Jefferson Davis County and Lawrence County is improper because its principal place of business is in Jones County. *Id.* at ¶ 13, *see also* BR.338–352, Sanderson's First, Second and Thirteenth Defenses. Sanderson sought dismissal on the grounds that the plaintiffs cannot assert class claims, and that their claims are barred by the statute of limitations or the doctrine of laches. *Id.* at ¶¶ 15–17, *see also* BR.338–352, Sanderson's Third, Fourth, Fifth and Eleventh Defenses.

In the alternative to dismissal or transfer to another court, Sanderson Farms moved the Chancery Courts to stay proceedings and compel arbitration under its binding arbitration clause. *Id.* at ¶¶ 22, 24, BR.338–352, Sanderson's Third Defense. After a full hearing on this motion in *Austin*, where the Chancery Court heard extensive testimony from witnesses for both parties concerning the contract formation process relating to the arbitration clause and the effect of the clause's terms on growers, the court denied Sanderson Farms' motion. *See* Order on Motion to Dismiss at 3, AR. 858–860. The Chancery Court found that there was jurisdiction because the court has jurisdiction to hear matters involving property, and that venue was proper because the case involves real property in Jefferson Davis County. *Id.* at 1–2. With regard to arbitration, the Chancery Court relied on the testimony of Sanderson Farms' corporate representative, Mike Cockrell, in finding that (1) the

a note. If you don't satisfy a note, then you lose your— otherwise, if you didn't have clients you'd lose your practice.")

company would have terminated its relationship with any grower who rejected the arbitration clause, and (2) the growers had a significant disadvantage in sophistication relative to the company officials, as evidenced by the exclusion of attorneys from the Governor's Committee process. *Id.* at 2. The Chancery Court thus concluded that the arbitration clause was unconscionable because it was an adhesive contract where there was no arm's-length negotiation with each grower. *Id.* at 3.

In *Ballard*, the Chancery Court of Lawrence County also denied Sanderson Farms' motion. The court found that it had jurisdiction because the plaintiffs alleged damage to real and personal property, and that venue in Lawrence County was proper because the plaintiffs' property was located there, as were Sanderson Farms' flocks. BR. 570–572; Ballard Record Excerpts at 69–70. With regard to arbitration, the Chancery Court found that Plaintiffs' claims based on misrepresentations made before the contracts with the arbitration clause were made fell outside the scope of this clause. *Id.* at 70. The Chancery Court further found the arbitration clause unconscionable because Sanderson Farms controlled the contract formation process through its ability to terminate the existing grower operations of the plaintiffs, and because Sanderson Farms used this overwhelming bargaining power to impose excessive cost requirements:

> **Not only does the arbitration clause by its express terms close the courthouse doors to individual growers, it then imposes excessive costs that prohibit growers from obtaining relief through arbitration.**

Id. at 70–71 (emphasis added). These appeals followed.

SUMMARY OF ARGUMENT

The Chancery Courts correctly found that Sanderson Farms' mandatory arbitration clause is unconscionable. This arbitration clause is substantively unconscionable because it contains multiple terms that eliminate or severely restrict plaintiffs' substantive remedies, and impose insurmountable barriers that bar them from vindicating their claims, while it leaves Sanderson Farms free to exercise its primary contractual rights without having to arbitrate. This arbitration clause is also procedurally unconscionable because it was written by Sanderson Farms alone and was imposed on plaintiffs as a mandatory condition for continuing to receive flocks. Although this Court has only required a showing of *either* procedural *or* substantive unconscionability to invalidate a contract provision, *see East Ford, Inc. v. Taylor*, 826 So. 2d 709, 717 (Miss. 2002) (striking used car dealer's mandatory arbitration clause as procedurally unconscionable), there is abundant evidence of both in these cases. Therefore this arbitration clause should be struck on either or both of these grounds.

Sanderson Farms' arbitration clause is substantively unconscionable because it contains multiple terms that eliminate or severely diminish growers' legal and equitable remedies. The arbitration clause incorporates a ***two-business day limitations period*** for growers to notify Sanderson Farms of their claims and a ***14-day limitations period*** to file for binding arbitration. Both of these requirements are dwarfed even by the one-year contractual limitations provision this Court recently found to be unconscionable in *Pitts v. Watkins*, ___ So. 2d ___, 2005 WL 851451 at *5 (Miss. April 14, 2005). Likewise, this clause's ban on punitive or exemplary damages awards, permanent injunctive relief, and attorney fee awards, and its imposition of a heightened "clear and convincing evidence" standard for consequential damages, all run afoul of this Court's holdings in *Pitts*, 2005 WL 851451 at *4, and *Entergy Miss., Inc. v. Burdette Gin Co.*, 726 So. 2d 1202, 1206 (Miss. 1998), invalidating arbitration and indemnity clauses that restricted an individual litigant's remedies.

This arbitration clause's terms forcing growers to pay half the costs of arbitrating before a three-arbitrator panel under AAA's Commercial Arbitration Rules, and prohibiting growers from joining their claims to defray these costs, are also disabling because they prevent growers from vindicating their claims in *any* forum. In the only two cases known by Sanderson Farms officials where growers attempted to arbitrate their claims under this clause, the growers were billed $11,000 and $22,500 respectively in up-front costs by AAA, forcing them to abandon the arbitrations without ever receiving a hearing on their claims. These cost-shifting terms are unconscionable under the Court's cases striking exculpatory clauses described above, and also fail to heed the warning by members of this Court in *Sanderson Farms, Inc. v. Gatlin*, 848 So. 2d 828 (Miss. 2003), that this level of arbitration fees is shocking to the conscience. *Id.* at 849 (Cobb, J. dissenting).

Sanderson Farms' eleventh hour attempt to rewrite the arbitration clause by offering to pay all costs in *Austin* (though not in *Ballard* or any other case) cannot validate the clause because, under Mississippi law, a contract's validity is determined at the time it was made, and courts cannot aid in the later rewriting of a contract. *Id.* at 851–52 (Cobb, J., dissenting); *cf.* Miss. Code. Ann. § 75-2-302 (unconsiconability of contract for sale of goods is determined at time when contract was made). This offer made in court is also in contrast to Sanderson's artfully drafted addendum to its demand for arbitration, where it only agreed to cover all costs for the breach of contract claims Sanderson Farms itself was asserting, and said nothing about the costs of Austin, Hathorn, and Spring's claims. SF Jud. Notice Ex. A at page 2 of Addendum.

This arbitration clause is also unconscionable because, while it forces these disabling provisions on growers who assert claims, it lets Sanderson Farms exercise its most important contractual rights free and clear of these burdens. By allowing Sanderson Farms to terminate the growers' contracts and repossess their flocks without going through the complaint resolution process or arbitration, this clause creates precisely the type of one-sided obligation that this Court found unconscionable in *Pitts*. There, a home inspector's arbitration clause forced buyers to arbitrate all of their claims, but exempted the inspector's own claims for payment of fees. *Pitts*, 2005 WL 851451 at *2; *see also Taylor v. Butler*, 142 S.W.3d 277, 286 (Tenn. 2004) (striking used car dealer's arbitration clause for exempting dealer's repossession claims). Here, the one-sided effects of Sanderson Farms' arbitration clause are even worse because its multiple disabling terms will prevent the plaintiffs from vindicating their claims in any forum, while leaving Sanderson Farms free to terminate or repossess without restraint. For all these reasons, the arbitration clause should be struck as substantively unconscionable under established Mississippi law.

Finally, the arbitration clause should also be struck because it is procedurally unconscionable. After hearing hours of testimony from witnesses for both sides, the Chancery Court in *Austin* made findings of fact that this arbitration clause was a non-negotiable adhesion contract that growers had to accept at risk of Sanderson Farms terminating their existing relationships and repossessing their flocks. The factual findings of a chancelor are not to be disturbed on appeal unless they are "manifestly wrong," or "clearly erroneous." *Pilgrim Rest Missionary Baptist Church v. Wallace*, 835 So. 2d 67, 71 (Miss. 2003). Based on these findings, the Chancery Court concluded that the arbitration clause is procedurally unconscionable and cannot be enforced against the plaintiffs.

In *East Ford*, this Court struck a used car dealer's mandatory arbitration clause as procedurally unconscionable based on lack of *knowledge* because the clause appeared in small print that was obscured relative to the contract's other provisions. *See East Ford*, 826 So. 2d at 717; *see also Banc One Acceptance Corp. v. Hill*, 367 F.3d 426, 433 (5th Cir. 2004) (following *East Ford*). Here, the evidence of procedural unconscionability based on lack of *voluntariness* is even greater because Sanderson Farms introduced its arbitration clause years after the plaintiffs invested hundreds of thousands of dollars to start up their growing operations, and growers could not continue receiving birds if they refused the arbitration clause. Under these circumstances, the plaintiffs had no meaningful choice but to acquiesce to the arbitration clause. *See, e.g., Melena v. Anheuser-Busch, Inc.*, 816 N.E.2d 826, 833 (Ill. App. 2004) ("[I]n the instant case, the plaintiff had even less volition in the matter than the typical job applicant. Her 'choices' were to continue her employment, thereby automatically agreeing to the dispute resolution policy, or else resign.") Therefore, the Court should also affirm the Chancery Court's finding that the arbitration clause is procedurally unconscionable.

ARGUMENT

I. Sanderson Farms' Arbitration Clause is Substantively Unconscionable.

When Sanderson Farms imposed its binding mandatory arbitration clause upon the plaintiffs and other growers, it did not simply take away their right to go to court in favor of private arbitration. It also stripped them of their legal rights altogether by creating a system of arbitration where they would have next to no time to submit claims, their legal and equitable remedies would be severely diminished, and they would have to pay thousands of dollars in filing and arbitrators' fees before they could have a hearing on their claims.

This Court has correctly held in numerous cases involving mandatory arbitration and other types of clauses that contacts eliminating or diminishing an individual's legal remedies are substantively unconscionable. These decisions adhere to the U.S. Supreme Court's decisions applying the Federal Arbitration Act ("FAA"), 9 U.S.C. §§ 1, *et seq.*:

> We have held that federal statutory claims may be the subject of arbitration agreements that are enforceable pursuant to the FAA *because the agreement only determines the choice of forum*. In these cases, we recognized that *by agreeing to arbitrate a statutory claim, a party does not forgo the substantive rights afforded by the statute; it only submits to their resolution in an arbitral, rather than a judicial, forum.*

Equal Employment Opportunity Comm'n v. Waffle House, Inc., 534 U.S. 279, 295 n.10 (2002) (citation omitted) (emphasis added). This Court's decisions invalidating arbitration clauses and other contract terms that prevent parties from vindicating their rights in any forum should apply here to invalidate Sanderson Farms' exculpatory and one-sided arbitration clause.

A. The Clause's Two- and 14-Day Limitations Provisions are Unconscionable.

This arbitration clause's *two-business day* limitations period for growers to submit claims to Sanderson Farms, and its *14-day* limitations period for growers to file for binding arbitration, eviscerate Mississippi's three-year statute of limitations for fraud claims. *See* Miss. Code. Ann. § 15-1-49. This statutory limitations period cannot be altered by private agreement, so any contract purporting to do so is null and void under Mississippi law. Miss. Code Ann. § 15-1-5; *Pitts*, 2005 WL at *5. *Pitts* held that a home inspector's mandatory arbitration clause was unconscionable in part because it imposed a *one-year* limitations period, in contravention of these statutes:

> The attempt to create a private statute of limitations is further evidence of overreaching by Watkins, is oppressive, violates statutory law, and is likewise unconscionable.

Id. The only difference between the provision struck down in *Pitts* and the ones in Sanderson Farms' arbitration clause is that the ones here are *even more* oppressive and disabling because they give growers virtually no time in which to identify their claims, contact a lawyer, or determine whether a wrongful act is part of a broader pattern of illegal company conduct. These two-day and 14-day limitations provisions thus plainly render this arbitration clause unconscionable under *Pitts* and under Mississippi's blanket prohibition against contracts shortening the statute of limitations.

Even where courts apply a looser "reasonableness" standard to evaluate abridged contractual limitations periods, the two-day and 14-day periods for growers to initiate Sanderson Farms' complaint resolution and arbitration processes would be unconscionable. In *Alexander v. Anthony Int'l, L.P.*, 341 F.3d 256 (3d Cir. 2003), the court held that an employer's arbitration clause for oil refinery workers was unconscionable in part because of its 30-day limitations requirement for workers to notify the company of their claims. The court found that a provision limiting the time for filing claims was not *necessarily* invalid, so long as the time allowed was "reasonable." *Id*. at 266. In applying this standard to the 30-day notification requirement, however, the court found that:

> In addition to providing an apparently insufficient time to bring a well-supported claim, such an obligation prevents an employee from invoking the continuing violation and tolling doctrines. . . .
>
> Parties do generally benefit from the efficient resolution of disputes. But the requirement in this case inappropriately assists Anthony Crane by making it unnecessarily burdensome for an employee to seek relief from the company's illegal conduct.

Id. at 267. The court thus held that the arbitration clause provision shortening the statutory limitations period from either two or six years down to 30 days was unconscionable under applicable contract law. *Id*.^4 If the 30-day limitations period for employees in *Alexander* was unreasonable, then the *two-day* contractual limitations period for growers here is beyond question unreasonable.

Since this arbitration clause's two-day and 14-day limitations requirements eviscerate the three-year statute of limitations, make a shambles of Mississippi's ban on contractual limitations requirements, and leave growers with no means for vindicating their rights against Sanderson Farms in any forum, the Court should follow its recent decision in *Pitts* and hold that this arbitration clause is "overreaching, . . . oppressive, violates statutory law, and is likewise unconscionable."

B. This Clause's Restrictions on Substantive Remedies are Unconscionable.

As set forth herein, Sanderson Farms' arbitration clause also eliminates or severely restricts growers' legal and equitable remedies by barring arbitrators from awarding punitive or exemplary damages, permanent injunctive relief, attorneys' fees, consequential damages absent "clear and convincing evidence," or any other remedy besides contractual damages, temporary injunctive relief, and specific performance. These restrictions on Sanderson Farms' liability to growers further render this arbitration clause unconscionable.

In *Pitts*, this Court also held that the home inspector's arbitration clause was unconscionable in part because it limited the inspector's liability to home buyers for its own negligence to the amount of the fee they paid him for his work. The Court explained that:

> Again, like in *East Ford*, this clause precludes the plaintiff's ability to collect punitive damages, if otherwise warranted, but more importantly places an unreasonable restriction to collect compensatory damages in excess of $265. This Court has held that 'clauses that limit liability are given strict scrutiny unless the limitation is fairly and honestly negotiated and understood by both parties.'
>
> . . . The limitation of liability clause, when paired with the arbitration clause, effectively denies the plaintiff an adequate remedy and is further evidence of substantive unconscionability.

Pitts, 2005 WL 851451 at *3, 4 (quoting *Royer Homes of Miss., Inc. v. Chandeleur Homes, Inc.*, 857 So. 2d 748, 754 (Miss. 2003); *see also East Ford*, 826 So. 2d at 714 ("Substantively unconscionable clauses have been held to include waiver of choice of forum and waiver of certain remedies."); *Entergy Miss., Inc. v. Burdette Gin Co.*, 726 So. 2d 1202, 1206 (Miss. 1998) ("In contracts between the utility and its customers, where the utility's public duty to exercise a very high degree of care is invoked, we hold that

---

^4 *See also Al-Safin v. Circuit City Stores, Inc.*, 394 F.3d 1254, 1261 (9th Cir. 2005) (finding employer's arbitration clause unconscionable under Washington law based in part on one-year limitations provision); *Lelouis v. Western Directory Co.*, 230 F. Supp. 2d 1214, 1221 (D. Or. 2001) (same, under California law); *Adler v. Fred Lind Manor*, 103 P.3d 773, 787–88 (Wash. 2004) (striking 180 day provision under Washington law); *Martinez v. Master Protection Corp.*, 118 Cal. App. 4th 107, 117–18 (2004) (striking six-month provision under California law).

indemnity provisions protecting the utility from its own negligence are void as a matter of public policy.") The same assessment should apply here because Sanderson's arbitration clause, like the one in *Pitts*, bars growers from recovering punitive damages and limits their legal remedies to direct contractual damages, except upon a heightened proof standard of "clear and convincing evidence" for consequential damages. *Cf. Kruger Clinic Orthopaedics, LLC v. Regence Blueshield*, 98 P.3d 66, 74 (Wash. App. 2004) (arbitration clause applying contractual "arbitrary and capricious" standard to healthcare provider's determinations held unconscionable). These limitations on Plaintiffs' legal remedies further render this arbitration clause unconscionable.

Like this Court, other courts across the country have held that arbitration clauses like the one here that bar punitive damages awards and other legal and equitable remedies are unconscionable or otherwise invalid. In *Hadnot v. Bay, Ltd.*, 344 F.3d 474 (5th Cir. 2003), the Fifth Circuit affirmed a district court's holding that an employment arbitration clause's ban on punitive or exemplary damages awards in a Title VII case was unenforceable. *Id.* at 478 n. 14 (striking damages ban, enforcing clause). Similarly, the Alabama Supreme Court has struck down arbitration clauses that ban punitive damages awards as unconscionable and against state public policy:

> We hold that a predispute arbitration clause that forbids an arbitrator from awarding punitive damages is void as contrary to the public policy of this State—to protect its citizens in certain legislatively prescribed actions from wrongful behavior and to punish the wrongdoer. If parties to an arbitration agreement waive any arbitrator's ability to award punitive damages, the door will open wide to rampant fraudulent conduct with few, if any, legal repercussions.

Cavalier Mfg., Inc. v. Jackson, 823 So. 2d 1237, 1248 (Ala. 2001), *cert. denied*, 535 U.S. 986 (2002), *overruled in part on other grounds, Ex Parte Thicklin*, 824 So. 2d 723 (Ala. 2002).^5

The court's concern in *Jackson* about opening the door to rampant fraudulent conduct with no legal repercussions applies with special force here because Plaintiffs and other growers have 15-year contracts with Sanderson Farms. Sanderson tries to invert this problem by saying that the long-term relationship makes punitive damages allegations based on malicious or fraudulent conduct "**less than conducive to a productive ongoing relationship**." Brief at 34 (emphasis added). But this gets it exactly backwards. As the *Jackson* decision recognized, the real danger in a long-term relationship where a contract bars punitive damages is not the ***allegation*** of malicious or fraudulent conduct, but the ***actual*** malicious or fraudulent conduct that a party can commit without any repercussion.

Moreover, Sanderson's suggestion that the punitive damages ban is somehow even-handed because *both* parties bear risks in giving up this right, *see* Brief at 33, ignores the fact that the contract lets Sanderson Farms immediately terminate its relationship with growers who engage in almost any type of malicious or fraudulent conduct. *See* Contract, §§ 19, 20, and 22, AR. 32–37.^6 Under these types of circumstances, where a clause's ban on punitive damages awards and other remedies is both exculpatory and effectively one-sided, numerous courts have held consistent with *Pitts*, *Entergy Miss.*, *Hadnot*, and *Jackson*, that these clauses are unconscionable.^7

Sanderson Farms' arbitration clause also bans permanent injunctive relief like that sought by the plaintiffs here, attorneys' fee awards, and consequential damages unless proven by clear and convincing evidence. Like this Court did in *Pitts*, many other courts have struck arbitration clauses containing one or more of these types of provisions. For example, several courts have held that clauses banning forms of injunctive relief are unconscionable or unenforceable because they prevent plaintiffs from challenging and putting a stop to a defendant's systematic wrongdoing.^8 Likewise, courts have also found that arbitration clauses barring attorney fee awards by forcing parties to bear their own fees and costs in all cases are unconscionable because they prevent plaintiffs from vindicating their rights and are one-sided in favor of corporate defendants.^9

Since Sanderson Farms loaded up its binding mandatory arbitration clause with provisions stripping growers of legal and equitable remedies by prohibiting arbitrators from awarding these remedies, the Court should hold consistent with *Pitts* and all these other decisions from Mississippi and elsewhere that this arbitration clause is unconscionable.

---

^5 Although *Thicklin* overruled *Jackson* on other grounds, it strongly *re-affirmed Jackson* on the impropriety of arbitration clauses banning punitive damages: "[I]t violates public policy for a party to contract away its liability for punitive damages, regardless whether the provision doing so was intended to operate in an arbitral or judicial forum." *Thicklin*, 824 So. 2d at 733.

^6 Sanderson also claims that MCPGA President Larry McKnight okayed this punitive damages ban, Brief at 33, but neglects to mention that no company ever recognized McKnight's authority to negotiate for anyone but himself. *See* McKnight Tr.341; Appellees Judicial Notice Ex "D" Mike Cockrell Dep. at 70. In fact, Mr. McKnight *has never grown for Sanderson Farms*.

^7 *See, e.g., Alexander v. Anthony Int'l, L.P.*, 341 F.3d 256, 267 (3d Cir. 2003); *Zuver v. Airtouch Communications, Inc.*, 103 P.3d 753, 767 (Wash. 2004) ("The remedies limitation provision blatantly and excessively favors the employer in that it allows the employer alone access to a significant legal recourse."); *West Virginia ex rel Dunlap v. Berger*, 567 S.E.2d 265, 278 (W. Va. 2002); *Powertel, Inc. v. Bexley*, 743 So. 2d 570, 576 (Fla. Dist. Ct. App. 1999).

^8 *See, e.g., Lozada v. Dale Baker Oldsmobile, Inc.*, 91 F. Supp. 2d 1087, 1105 (W.D. Mich. 2000); *Broughton v. CIGNA Healthplans*, 988 P.2d 67, 76–77 (Cal. 1999); *Powertel*, 743 So. 2d at 576–77.

^9 *See, e.g., Alexander*, 341 F.3d at 267 (provision forcing refinery employees to bear own attorneys' fees is "one-sided in the extreme and unreasonably favorable to [the employer]"); *Adler*, 103 P.3d at 786 (employer's ban on attorney fee awards "helps the party with a substantially higher bargaining position and more resources, to the disadvantage of the employee needing to obtain legal assistance."); *cf. Jenkins v. First American Cash Advance of Ga., LLC*, 400 F.3d 868, 878 (11th Cir. 2005) (finding that payday lender's arbitration clause won't deter consumer enforcement because it "expressly permit[s] Jenkins and other consumers to recover attorneys' fees and expenses").

C. This Arbitration Clause's Cost-Shifting Provisions are Unconscionable.

1. The Clause's Terms Force Growers to Pay Enormous Fees to Arbitrate.

No grower has ever been able to obtain an arbitration hearing on his or her claims against Sanderson Farms under this arbitration clause. Appellees Judicial Notice Ex "D" Mike Cockrell Dep. at 39. The only two growers who have even tried to arbitrate under this clause, Roy Gatlin and Susan Martin, were billed $11,000 and $22,500 respectively in up-front costs by AAA and had to abandon arbitration before they could get hearings on their claims. When Mr. Gatlin's case came before this Court, several members of the Court found as follows:

> My conscience is shocked by a plaintiff's being billed $11,000 or more, simply to obtain a hearing (exclusive of attorney fees). A country in which legal redress was available only at such costs would deserve the criticism that Edward Gibbon directed at the Roman Empire's system of justice:
>
> > The expense of the pursuit sometimes exceeded the value of the prize, and the fairest rights were abandoned by the poverty or prudence of the claimants. **Such costly justice might tend to abate the spirit of litigation, but the unequal pressure serves only to increase the influence of the rich, and to aggravate the misery of the poor.**

Sanderson Farms, Inc. v. Gatlin, 848 So. 2d 828, 849–50 (Miss. 2003) (Cobb, J. dissenting) (emphasis in original).

The Gatlin and Martin cases were no aberration. The enormous arbitration fees billed to the growers in those cases were the direct result of the specific terms and rules regarding costs that Sanderson Farms loaded into its mandatory arbitration clause. As discussed herein, these terms explicitly require growers to proceed under AAA's Commercial Arbitration rules, arbitrate before a three arbitrator panel, and pay half the costs of this arbitration. Moreover, since this arbitration clause prohibits joinder or aggregation of claims except where Sanderson Farms consents to it, the plaintiffs cannot join together to defray these costs by filing jointly. *Cf. Leonard v. Terminix Int'l Co., L.P.*, 854 So. 2d 529, 537 (Ala. 2002) (where arbitration clause barred joinder and class claims and imposed heavy costs on consumers, finding that "the impracticality of pursuing a claim for a small amount of money at a cost in excess of the value of the claim is just as much an obstacle to the wealthiest member of society as it is to a pauper.") These are the very same terms that applied in the Gatlin and Martin cases, and they will lead to the same results here if this clause is enforced.

Under Sanderson Farms' cost-splitting provision and AAA's Commercial Rules, the plaintiffs would each have to pay $2,250 as their half share of the $3,250 case filing fee and $1,250 case service fee. AAA Commercial Arbitration Rules, Fees. Austin Tr. Ex.19; Austin Tr. Ex 18. The plaintiffs each then would have to pay half of the arbitrators' fees. Sanderson's own witnesses recognized that arbitrators charge parties fees of $300 per hour or $1,800 per day. *See* Austin-Fisher Tr. 256; Appellees Judicial Notice Ex "D" Mike Cockrell Dep. at 41. Moreover, since the clause expressly requires a three arbitrator panel, these arbitrator fees are tripled to over $5,000 per hearing day, an effect that Sanderon's Chief Financial Officer openly acknowledges. Appellees Judicial Notice Ex "D" Mike Cockrell Dep. at 69. ("I assume it would triple it. . . . You've still got to pay for the room and there's some fixed costs in there, but you pay for three arbitrators, yes.") Therefore, in addition to their $2,250 share of the filing and case service fees, each plaintiff would have to pay an additional $2,500 to $3,000 *per hearing day* as their half share of the arbitrators' fees. For a four-day hearing on their claims for fraud and misrepresentation, each plaintiff would have to pay a total of between $12,000 and $14,250 in up-front costs before they could have this hearing.

These expected costs are in line with the $22,000 that Susan Martin was billed by AAA as the up-front costs for a four-day hearing on her claims against Sanderson Farms, *see* Appellees Judicial Notice Ex "G", and the $11,000 in up-front costs Roy Gatlin was billed by AAA in his case against Sanderson Farms. *Gatlin*, 848 So. 2d at 832. This requirement that growers have to pay over $10,000 in up-front fees should be held unconscionable when applied as it is here to claimants working under a contract that pays them under $28,000 a year in pre-tax net income after expenses. *See* Appellees' Judicial Notice Ex. "A" (Sanderson Farms Producer Prospectus Brochure at 6–8); *see also* Austin Tr. Ex. 28.[10]

There is a sizable body of case law where courts have recognized, as members of this Court did in *Gatlin*, that arbitration clauses saddling individual parties with the enormous filing fees and arbitrators' fees under AAA Commercial Rules are shocking to the conscience and that these requirements should not be enforced. *See, e.g., Spinetti v. Service Corp. Int'l*, 341 F.3d 212, 217–18 (3d Cir. 2003) (striking employer's arbitration clause provision requiring losing claimant to pay $4,250 filing fee, $150 daily hearing fees, and half the arbitrator's $2,000 daily fees); *Alexander v. Anthony Int'l*, 341 F.3d 256, 269–70 (3d Cir. 2003) (finding employer's arbitration clause for refinery workers unconscionable based in part on provision requiring losing claimant to pay arbitrator's fees of approximately $800 to $1,000 per day); *Popovich v. McDonald's Corp.*, 189 F. Supp. 2d 772, 777–78 (N.D. Ill. 2002) (striking company's consumer arbitration clause, finding cost burden for consumer under AAA Commercial Rules of $48,000 to $126,000 to be "staggering").[11] In the case of *Mendez v. Palm Harbor Homes, Inc.*, 45 P.3d 594 (Wash. App. 2002), the court struck a mobile home seller's arbitration clause whose use of AAA's rules would have forced the buyer to "spend up front well

---

[10] It is important to clarify that Exhibit 28 does not include any deductions for operating expenses, as set out in Judicial Notice Exhibit "A."

[11] *See also Ting v. AT&T*, 182 F. Supp. 2d 902, 934 (N.D. Cal. 2002), *aff'd in relevant part*, 319 F.3d 1126 (9th Cir. 2003) (striking phone company's arbitration clause based in part on requirement of almost $6,000 in up-front deposits by consumer to arbitrate a $100,000 claim); *Phillips v. Associates Home Equity Serv's, Inc.*, 179 F. Supp. 2d 840, 846 (N.D. Ill. 2001) (striking mortgage lender's arbitration clause based on AAA Commercial Rules fees); *Camacho v. Holiday Homes, Inc.*, 167 F. Supp. 2d 892, 897 (W.D. Va. 2001) (striking manufactured home builder's arbitration clause based on AAA Commercial Rules fees); *cf. D.R. Horton, Inc. v. Green*, 96 P.3d 1159, 1165–66 (Nev. 2004) (striking property developer's arbitration clause because of cost-splitting provision and liquidated damages provision for failure to arbitrate).

over $2,000 to try to vindicate his rights under a contract to buy a $12,000 item in order to resolve a potential $1,500 dispute." *Id.* at 605. In striking this clause, the court found as follows:

> Avoiding the public court system to save time and money is a laudable societal goal. But avoiding the public court system in a way that effectively denies citizens access to resolving everyday societal disputes is unconscionable. Goals favoring arbitration of civil disputes must not be used to work oppression. ***When the goals given in support of contract clauses like this are used as a sword to strike down access to justice instead of as a shield against prohibitive costs, we must defer to the overriding principle of access to justice.***

Id. (emphasis added).

2. AAA Cannot and Will Not Waive The Arbitrators' Fees.

In the dissenting opinion in the *Gatlin* case, members of this Court concluded that there was insufficient evidence for the Court to determine whether Mr. Gatlin could not afford arbitration "in light of the potential for the arbitrator to make a finding of financial hardship on Mr. Gatlin's part," and would have remanded with instructions for Mr. Gatlin "to seek a diminution or waiver of fees from the AAA." *Gatlin*, 828 So. 2d 852 (Cobb, J. dissenting). The plaintiffs respectfully submit that the Court should not follow this course in this case because the evidence before the Court now demonstrates that AAA cannot and will not waive the arbitrators' fees that comprise the bulk of the costs Plaintiffs would have to bear if ordered to arbitrate.

First, AAA cannot waive the plaintiffs' share of these fees because Sanderson's arbitration clause specifies that "[t]he cost of such arbitration will be divided equally among the parties to the arbitration." Contract at 5, § 24;AR.32–37; at 6 § 27; BR. 113–120 in Broiler Production Agreement. Whatever provisions for fee waivers AAA might otherwise have, AAA's Commercial Arbitration Rule R-1 states that "[t]he parties, by written agreement, may vary the procedures set forth in these rules." AAA Commercial Arbitration Rules, Rule R-1, Austin Tr. Ex.19; Austin Tr. Ex 18; R.E. 8. Therefore, even if AAA could have waived the plaintiffs' fee obligations, Sanderson Farms' arbitration clause and Commercial Rule R-1 still would force the plaintiffs to pay their half-share.

Moreover, AAA's rules do not in fact allow any waiver of a party's obligation to pay arbitrators' fees. As an example, a footnote to AAA's Commercial Rule R-1 refers certain consumer cases to AAA's separate *Supplementary Procedures for Consumer-Related Disputes* ("Consumer Rules"). Although these Consumer Rules might reduce administrative costs for some consumers in some cases, they explicitly differentiate the arbitrators' fees as non-waivable: "[C]onsumers with a gross monthly income of less than 300% of the federal poverty guidelines are entitled to a waiver of arbitration fees, ***exclusive of arbitrator fees***." AAA Consumer Rule C-8, footnote (emphasis added). Therefore, the bulk of the costs Plaintiffs would encounter in the form of arbitrators' fees for the three-arbitrator panel required by Sanderson's contact are not waivable under AAA's rules.

Finally, if any doubt remained on this question, the record from Texas breeder grower Susan Martin's case against Sanderson Farms erases it. After Ms. Martin had already paid over $6,000 in case filing and service fees, AAA billed her for an additional $16,000+ for the arbitrators' compensation for the scheduled four-day hearing on her claims. *See* Appellees Judicial Notice Ex "E". Ms. Martin responded by telling the AAA Case Manager that she could not afford these up-front arbitrators' fees and asked AAA to waive these fees. *See* Appellees Judicial Notice Ex "F". In response, AAA's Case Manager for Ms. Martin's case denied her request for a waiver on the grounds that "***[t]he Association has no authority to defer arbitrator compensation and expenses or non-association hearing room expenses***. These charges will be due and payable when invoices are sent, in accordance with the Rules." Appellees Judicial Notice Ex "G".[^12]

Therefore, in light of (1) the express terms of Sanderson's arbitration clause, (2) the AAA Commercial Rules that the clause uses, and (3) the case of Susan Martin under this very arbitration clause, where AAA said it had no authority to defer arbitrator compensation, the plaintiffs submit that the Court should not require them to follow the course suggested by the *Gatlin* dissent and seek a fee-waiver that is not available. Instead, the Court should hold that the express fee-shifting provisions of this arbitration clause are substantively unconscionable because they would prevent Plaintiffs and other growers from vindicating their claims in any forum.

3. Sanderson Farms' Offer to Pay Costs Does Not Salvage the Arbitration Clause.

Sanderson Farms hinges much of its appeal to this Court in the *Austin* case (although not in *Ballard*) on its attempt to rewrite the arbitration clause by making a thirteenth-hour offer to pay for all the costs of arbitration. *See* Brief of Appellant at 35–37. Over five years after it imposed this arbitration clause and only after the plaintiffs filed suit in *Austin*, Sanderson Farms tried to unilaterally rewrite its contracts with these plaintiffs by amending the unconscionable arbitration clause provisions requiring them to pay half of the enormous costs of arbitrating individually before a three-arbitrator panel under AAA's Commercial Rules. *See* Appellant's Record Excerpts-Austin 28.[^13] The Court should not recognize this belated offer in assessing the unconscionability of Sanderson's arbitration clause because this would be contrary to Mississippi law. Moreover, this would also encourage Sanderson Farms and other companies to utilize overreaching contract terms secure in the knowledge that they could back off of them if challenged in court, while remaining free to enforce them against anyone who lacks the wherewithall to make such a challenge.

First, Sanderson Farms' belated offer to pay costs in contradiction of its own arbitration clause would violate Mississippi law barring a party or a court from unilaterally rewriting a contract. In

[^12]: Copies of the letters between AAA and Ms. Martin are in the court record in Ms. Martin and her husband's federal bankruptcy proceedings as exhibits to the "Motion by Trustee to Compromise Controversy With Sanderson Farms, Inc. Pursuant to bankruptcy Rule 9019." *See In re Bankruptcy of Stephen Clyde Martin and Susan Gayle Martin*, Case No. 03-61633 (Bankr. W.D Tex.), Docket No. 157 (filed 5/18/05). *See also* Appellees Judicial Notice Ex "H".

[^13]: *But, see* Appellant's Motion to Take Judicial Notice-Austin, Exhibit B (Sanderson Farms' Demand for Arbitration against Plaintiff Kenny Austin), in which Sanderson offers to pay the costs of arbitrating *its own claims against the plaintiffs* for breach of contract.

Gatlin, the dissenting members of this Court recognized that this arbitration clause is governed by several bedrock rules of Mississippi contract law. First, " 'this Court does not rewrite contracts when they are not illegal, immoral, or contrary to public policy.' " *Gatlin*, 848 So. 2d at 851 (Cobb, J. dissenting) (quoting *Travelers Indem. Co. v. Chappell*, 246 So. 2d 498, 510 (Miss. 1971)). Second, if a contract *is* illegal, immoral, or contrary to public policy, the Court only may rewrite it:

> [I]n light of the 'general rule in this state and elsewhere that reformation of a contract is justified only (1) if the mistake is a mutual one, or (2) where there is a mistake on the part of one party *and* fraud or inequitable conduct on the part of the other.'

Id. (quoting *Johnson v. Consol. Am. Life Ins. Co.*, 244 So. 2d 400, 402 (Miss. 1971)). Third, for a mistake to be the basis for rewriting a contract, it " 'must be in the drafting of the instrument, not in the making of the contract.' " *Id.* (quoting *Johnson*, 244 So. 2d at 402). Since no such drafting mistake was shown regarding this arbitration clause, the *Gatlin* dissent concluded that "the rule of *Johnson* will not permit us to rewrite the fee provision of the arbitration clause." *Id.* at 851–52. Since Sanderson Farms has never even alleged that there was any drafting error, the Court should not allow it to rewrite its arbitration clause here by substituting new provisions regarding payment of arbitration costs for this one case.

Authority outside Mississippi is in accord with the *Gatlin* dissent on this point. For example, the Second Restatement of Contracts advises that:

> [A] court will not aid a party who has taken advantage of his dominant bargaining power to extract from the other party a promise that is clearly so broad as to offend public policy by redrafting the agreement so as to make a part of the promise enforceable.

Restatement (Second) of Contracts § 184, Comment B. Similarly, the Fifth Circuit recently rejected a company's attempt to salvage its consumer arbitration clause by eliminating a provision exempting the company's own claims from arbitration, finding that "[s]aving the clause would require not that we excise a invalid excrescence and then send the pared-down contract to arbitration but that we redraft the contract to add new material—a duty on Centennial's part to arbitrate." *Iberia Credit Bureau, Inc. v. Cingular Wireless, LLC*, 379 F.3d 159, 171 (5th Cir. 2004). Even more on point, one court facing a company's last-minute offer to pay a consumer's arbitration costs found as follows:

> McDonald's has now offered to pay the arbitration fees.... We agree with Popovich that McDonald's offer, which is inconsistent with the parties' contract, amounts to an offer for a new contract. Popovich is under no obligation to accept McDonald's offer, and the court is in no position to impose it. As a matter of elementary contract law, McDonald's cannot unilaterally modify the existing agreement.

Popovich v. McDonald's, 189 F. Supp. 2d 772, 779 (N.D. Ill. 2002). Thus, under contract law principles recognized in Mississippi and elsewhere, Sanderson Farms' belated offer to pay the costs of arbitration is an impermissible attempt to rewrite the parties' contract.

More fundamentally, as the *Gatlin* dissent also observed, the Court should not let Sanderson Farms rewrite the disabling provisions of its arbitration clause for this one case because that would only encourage Sanderson and other companies to impose even more overreaching contracts since they would never face any consequence for doing so:

> Neither is it wise to allow companies to draft arbitration clauses with unconscionable provisions and then let them try them out in the marketplace, secure in the knowledge that the courts will at worst sever the offending cost allocation after plaintiffs have been forced 'to jump through hoops in order to invalidate those agreements.'

Id. at 852 (quoting *Cooper v. MRM Inv. Co.*, 199 F. Supp. 2d 771, 782 (M.D. Tenn. 2002)). Since rewriting the arbitration clause's cost-shifting provisions would put Sanderson Farms in exactly the same position it would have been in had it not imposed the unconscionable cost terms in the first place and would still leave the plaintiffs saddled with the numerous other unconscionable remedy-stripping provisions in this clause, the Court should heed the *Gatlin* dissent on this question and should hold that the arbitration clause is unconscionable.

Many other courts have held consistent with the *Gatlin* dissent that courts may not rewrite unconscionable cost-shifting terms of arbitration clauses under the FAA. For example, in the appeal of the *Cooper* case cited in *Gatlin*, the federal circuit court held that rejection of an employer's last-minute offer to pay arbitration costs was "sound as a matter of federal public policy," explaining that:

> To sever the costs and fees provision and force the employee to arbitrate a Title VII claim despite the employer's attempt to limit the remedies available would reward the employer for its actions and fail to deter similar conduct by others. Under the contrary approach, an employer will not be deterred from routinely inserting such a deliberately illegal clause into the illegal arbitration agreement it mandates for its employees if it knows that the worst penalty for such illegality is the severance of the clause after the employee has litigated the matter. Our *en banc* decision in *Morrison* [*v. Circuit City*, 317 F.3d 646, 676–77 (6th Cir. 2003) (*en banc*)] made clear that the district court's decision to reject MRM's offer to pay was the proper course.

Cooper v. MRM Investment Co., 367 F.3d 493, 512 (6th Cir. 2004) (citations omitted).^14 Thus, any applicable federal law concerning

---

^14 *See also Paladino v. Avnet Computer Technologies, Inc.*, 134 F.3d 1054, 1058 (11th Cir. 1998) ("[T]he presence of an unlawful provision in an arbitration agreement may serve to taint the entire arbitration agreement, rendering the agreement completely unenforceable, not just subject to judicial reforma-

arbitration clauses is consistent with the *Gatlin* dissent in rejecting last-minute offers to pay as invalid attempts to rewrite unconscionable clauses.

Finally, the Court should not indulge Sanderson Farms' attempt to rewrite the unconscionable cost-shifting terms because this arbitration clause contains numerous other unconscionable terms that taint the entire clause with impermissible purposes. In *Pitts*, this Court struck the home inspector's entire arbitration clause after finding that it contained at least three offending provisions limiting the plaintiffs' remedies, limiting the time in which they could file claims, and exempting the inspector's own claims from arbitration. *Pitts*, 2005 WL 851451 at *5. This holding striking the entire clause rather than just the multiple offending provisions also finds support from a wealth of authority elsewhere. In the *Alexander* case involving the oil refinery operator's mandatory arbitration clause for workers, the federal appeals court found as follows:

> In addition to the requirement to pay the arbitrator's fees and costs if unsuccessful, an employee must comply with an unreasonable time limitation, lose any right to attorney's fees, and give up the chance to receive any relief beyond either reinstatement of 'net pecuniary damages.' These draconian terms unreasonably favor Anthony Crane to the severe disadvantage of plaintiffs and other St. Croix employees. **The cumulative effect of so much illegality prevents us from enforcing the arbitration agreement. Because the sickness has infected the trunk, we must cut down the entire tree.**

Alexander, 341 F.3d at 271 (emphasis added).[15] Faced with an almost identical arbitration clause here under Sanderson Farms' contract, this Court should reach the same result and hold that the entire clause is unconscionable because of its multiple disabling provisions.

D. This Arbitration Clause is Also Unconscionable Because it Exempts Sanderson's Primary Remedies from Arbitration.

Finally, the Court should hold that Sanderson Farms' arbitration clause is substantively unconscionable because it creates a one-sided duty to arbitrate claims under the disabling terms described herein by exempting Sanderson's primary remedies from arbitration. This arbitration clause expressly permits Sanderson Farms to exercise its contractual rights to terminate a grower's contract and repossess the grower's flock without first resorting to arbitration, while forcing the plaintiffs and other growers to arbitrate all of their future legal and equitable claims. *See* Appellees Judicial Notice Ex "D," Mike Cockrell Dep. 44–46, (Q. So it's your position that you can terminate Ms. Hathorn without going to arbitration? A. The contract provides that either party may terminate the agreement without going to arbitration. Q. So the bottom line is—let's cut through the fat here and get to it. The bottom line is Sanderson Farms can terminate her without having to file a claim for arbitration? A. That's correct.)[16]

This is precisely the type of one-sided arbitration arrangement this Court recently found unconscionable in *Pitts*. There, the home inspector's arbitration clause applied broadly to all consumer claims, but carved out an exemption for the inspector's claims "based on payment of fee." *Pitts*, 2005 WL 851451 at *2. The Court found this one-sided obligation burdening the consumers alone to be oppressive and unconscionable:

> The language included in the clause, "(unless based on payment of fee)," maintains Watkins's ability to pursue a breach by Pitts in a court of law, while Pitts is required to arbitrate any alleged breach by Watkins. This arbitration clause is clearly one-sided, oppressive, and therefore, substantively unconscionable.

Id. The same finding should apply here with greater force since this one-sided arbitration clause is even more oppressive because of the severe time-limiting, remedy-stripping, and cost-shifting terms that would saddle the plaintiffs, but not Sanderson Farms in seeking its primary remedies.

Once again, this court is hardly alone in striking down such one-sided arbitration arrangements as unconscionable. Particularly where home mortgage or car lenders force individual consumers to arbitrate all claims and counter-claims while keeping for themselves the right to foreclose or repossess secured property without going through arbitration, numerous federal and state courts have struck down arbitration clauses as unconscionable. *See*, *e.g.*, *Iberia Credit Bureau, Inc. v. Cingular Wireless, Inc.*, 379 F.3d 159, 170 (5th Cir. 2004) (applying Louisiana contract law); *Taylor v. Butler*, 142 S.W.3d 277, 286 (Tenn. 2004) (striking used car dealer's arbitration clause for exempting repossession claims); *Greenpoint Credit, LLC v. Reynolds*, 151 S.W.3d 868, 875 (Mo. Ct. App. 2005) (striking mobile home mortgage lender's clause for exempting replevin actions from arbitration); *Wisconsin Auto Title Loans, Inc.*

---

tion."); *Graham Oil Co. v. ARCO Prod's Co.*, 43 F.3d 1244, 1249 (9th Cir. 1994) ("Our decision to strike the entire clause rests in part upon the fact that the offensive provisions clearly represent an attempt by ARCO to achieve through arbitration what Congress has expressly forbidden. ... Such a blatant misuse of the arbitration procedure serves to taint the entire clause."); *Lelouis v. Western Directory Co.*, 230 F. Supp. 2d 1214, 1225 (D. Or. 2001) ("[I]f I were to accept defendants' proposal, employers would have no incentive to ensure that a coerced arbitration agreement is fair to both sides. Instead, the employer could write a one-sided agrement that favors the employer, and then make the minimum modifications necessary to obtain the court's approval."); *Flores v. Transamerica Home First, Inc.*, 93 Cal. App. 4th 846, 857 (2001) ("[I]t strikes us as woefully unfair to allow HomeFirst at this late date—after a dispute has arisen and after the reverse mortgage has terminated—to refute the unconscionable aspect of the arbitration agreement **which HomeFirst itself drafted and from which HomeFirst stood to benefit over the life of the loan**.") (emphasis added).

[15] *See also Circuit City Stores, Inc. v. Adams*, 279 F.3d 889, 896 (9th Cir. 2002) (striking employer's arbitration clause with multiple unconscionable terms); *Anderson v. Ashby*, 873 So. 2d 168, 179 (Ala. 2003) (same, consumer arbitration clause); *Armendariz v. Foundation Health Psychare Services, Inc.*, 6 P.3d 669, 696–97 (Cal. 2000) (same, employment arbitration clause).

[16] In fact, Sanderson Farms did terminate Plaintiff Charolett Hathorn's contract in August 2003 without going through arbitration. *See* Jud. Notice Ex. "D," Cockrell Dep. 42–43.

v. Jones, __ N.W.2d __, 2005 WL 674667 at *4 (Wis. App. March 24, 2005) (striking used car lender's clause for allowing self-help repossession without arbitration). In *Arnold v. United Companies Lending Corp.*, 511 S.E.2d 854, 861 (W. Va. 1998), a case involving a one-sided arbitration clause between a national mortgage lender and two elderly homeowners with only elementary school educations, the West Virginia Supreme Court of Appeals held that this arrangement was unconscionable, finding that it was akin to a contract negotiated "between rabbits and foxes." The same finding should apply here.

Since Sanderson Farms' mandatory arbitration clause imposes illegal two- and 14-day limitations periods for growers to submit claims, eliminates or sharply restricts their legal and equitable remedies, forces them to pay enormous up-front costs while barring them from joining claims, and then lets Sanderson terminate or repossess flocks without arbitrating, the Court should hold that this clause is substantively unconscionable under well-established Mississippi law.

II. Sanderson Farms' Arbitration Clause is Procedurally Unconscionable.

Although the substantive unconscionability arguments are enough to invalidate Sanderson Farms' arbitration clause under *Pitts*, the Court should also strike this clause on the separate or additional grounds that it is procedurally unconscionable. The Record in these cases demonstrates that Sanderson Farms alone decided to use this arbitration clause, that Sanderson through its attorneys drafted this clause, that neither Plaintiffs nor any recognized bargaining agent negotiated this clause, and that growers who refused to agree to this arbitration clause when it was presented to them in 1997 would have been terminated and had their flocks repossessed. *See* Statement of Facts § B(3), *supra.*, and Record citations therein.^17 Moreover, the Record also shows that, when these clauses were introduced, the plaintiffs could not have found an alternative supplier of chickens without incurring enormous additional debt because of their pre-existing relationships with Sanderson Farms and their prior start-up investments of hundreds of thousands of dollars to meet Sanderson's specifications for their farms. *See id.* § A, and Record citations therein. Since this arbitration clause was given to Plaintiffs as a condition for continuing their relationships with Sanderson Farms and they could not avoid it except at enormous financial costs, the Court should hold that Sanderson's mandatory arbitration clause is also procedurally unconscionable.

Under Mississippi law, procedural unconscionability is a grounds for striking an arbitration clause or any other contract term. *See East Ford, Inc. v. Taylor*, 826 So. 2d 709, 717 (Miss. 2002) ("Because we find that the arbitration clause in this case is procedurally unconscionable, we find it unnecessary to address Taylor's lack of consideration argument, as well as his arguments regarding substantive unconscionability."); *see also Banc One Acceptance Corp. v. Hill*, 367 F.3d 426, 431 (5th Cir. 2004) (following *East Ford*). The Court has described procedural unconscionability as follows:

> The indicators of procedural unconscionability generally fall into two areas: (1) lack of knowledge, and (2) lack of voluntariness. A lack of knowledge is demonstrated by a lack of understanding of the contract terms arising from inconspicuous print or the use of complex legalistic language, disparity in sophistication of parties, and lack of opportunity to study the contract and inquire about contract terms. A lack of voluntariness is demonstrated in contracts of adhesion when there is a great imbalance in the parties' relative bargaining power, the stronger party's terms are unnegotiable, and the weaker party is prevented by market factors, timing or other pressures from being able to contract with another party on more favorable terms or to refrain from contracting at all.

East Ford, 826 So. 2d at 715–16 (quoting *Entergy Miss.*, 726 So. 2d at 1207) (internal citation omitted). Although *East Ford* itself turned primarily on lack of knowledge due to the presentation of the contract, here there is strong evidence of both lack of knowledge and particularly lack of voluntariness to support a finding that this arbitration clause is procedurally unconscionable.

Among the factors identified in *East Ford* as indicating lack of knowledge are a disparity in the sophistication of the parties, and the use of complex, legalistic language in the contract. *Id.* at 715–16. Here, the disparity in commercial sophistication between the parties is enormous. The plaintiffs are poultry growers with little or no commercial experience and no prior knowledge about arbitration. At 3; AR.584–85; 590–591; 596–597; 566–67; 572–573; 578–579. By contrast, Sanderson Farms is a large corporation that had previously negotiated contracts and arbitration clauses, and that employed the advice of legal counsel and the input of its own executive officers (some of whom themselves were lawyers) when it drafted and then introduced this contract. At 5–6, 8–10, Appellees Judicial Notice Ex "D". Moreover, Sanderson's arbitration clause incorporates extremely complex legalistic language, such as its limitations on the arbitrator's authority to award relief "as provided in Section 13," which is filled with subdivisions and legalistic terms of art such as "punitive and exemplary damages," "clear and convincing evidence," and "damages proximately caused by any wrongful conduct." Pages 3 and 5, AR. 32–37, pages 3 and 6, BR. 113–120 in Broiler Production Agreement. Sanderson Farms' use of such terminology to limit the legal and equitable remedies of unsophisticated chicken growers with no legal or business training demonstrates a lack of knowledge on their part that supports a finding of procedural unconscionability under *East Ford*.

There is even stronger evidence of a lack of voluntariness by the growers in entering into these arbitration agreements because of Sanderson Farms' overwhelming bargaining power. A knowing and voluntary waiver is necessary for an arbitration clause to be

---

^17 Sanderson Farms admits here that there was no one-on-one negotiation with growers, *see* Brief at 28–29, but attributes this lack of negotiation to its "obvious impracticality," and to the federal Packers & Stockyards Act ("PSA"), 7 U.S.C. § 192, which it claims forbids bargaining for different terms with different growers. Sanderson cites not authority whatsoever showing that the PSA overrides the Federal Arbitration Act, 9 U.S.C. §§ 1, *et seq.*, and prohibits negotiation over arbitration terms. Moreover, if the PSA did prevent Sanderson from offering different contract terms for different growers, then it would bar Sanderson's attempt here to rewrite these arbitration clauses by offering to pay the costs for the *Austin* plaintiffs **only**.

enforceable. *See Union Planters Bank, NA v. Rogers*, ___ So. 2d ___, 2005 WL 976996 at * (Miss. April 28, 2005) (rejecting argument for arbitration based on implicit waiver, finding "no evidence that either of the [plaintiffs] voluntarily and knowingly waived their right of access to the courts.") The record demonstrates that all of the plaintiffs had become deeply indebted to start up their growing operations and tailor their farms to Sanderson's specifications prior to 1997, when Sanderson introduced its binding arbitration clause. *See* Statement of Facts § A, and record citations therein; *see also* Mississippi State Extension Service, *Broiler Production in Mississippi* (June 1997) (noting that growers, "[t]o repay the loan during a ten year commitment, must pay about 60% of his gross income to the lending agency until the loan i[s] paid.") Moreover, Sanderson Farms would not continue delivering flocks to any grower who didn't agree to the contract with the arbitration clause. Austin-Cockrell Tr. 152, 155. Therefore, Plaintiffs had no meaningful choice but to accede to this arbitration clause because they could not service their debts or keep themselves afloat without their income from Sanderson's flocks, *see* At 3; AR.584–85; 590–591; 596–597; 566–67; 572–573; 578–579, and they could not turn to other poultry suppliers without incurring even greater debt to reconfigure their farms to another company's specifications. *See also* Appellees' Judicial Notice Ex. "B", Gatlin Tr. 168–169, ("[I]t would have probably cost me several more $100,000 to change over to their way of raising chickens[.]")

Under these circumstances where Sanderson Farms introduced the arbitration clause to growers who had already built up strong reliance and investment interests in receiving Sanderson birds and farming to Sanderson's specifications, the Court should find that the arbitration clause is procedurally unconscionable due to lack of voluntariness. In a case involving an employer's mandatory arbitration clause, one court recently explained why arbitration is not voluntary when it is imposed on an existing employee rather than at the point of hire:

> We have serious reservations regarding whether an agreement to arbitrate offered as a condition of employment is ever voluntary. When a job applicant is presented with an arbitration agreement as a condition of employment, the prospective employee is faced with a choice between accepting the arbitration agreement or continuing to search for a position that does not include such a requirement. That is a troubling enough scenario in its own right, but in the instant case, *the plaintiff had even less volition in the matter than the typical job applicant. Her 'choices' were to continue her employment, thereby automatically agreeing to the dispute resolution policy, or resign.* Counsel for the defendant admitted at oral argument that the *plaintiff would have been terminated had she refused to accept the policy. This left her with no viable options*. Unlike a job applicant, the plaintiff had not already begun a job search. She therefore did not have the benefit of having any other job leads, nor did she have the ability to wait for a firm offer of employment before resigning, an advantage many applicants have. *Moreover, being forced from her position with the defendant by refusing to agree to the dispute resolution likely would have made it quite difficult for her to obtain a new job*.

Melena v. Anheuser-Busch, Inc., 816 N.E.2d 826, 833 (Ill. App. 2004) (emphasis added).

Likewise, in the oil refinery workers case discussed elsewhere herein, the federal appeals court found that the employer "clearly possessed more bargaining power than two long-time equipment operators with limited educational backgrounds and, at best, very narrow options for other employment." *Alexander*, 341 F.3d at 266. There, the court concluded that these plaintiffs established procedural unconscionability because they were "presented with a 'take-it-or-leave-it' agreement to arbitrate by a multinational corporation," and "had no real choice but to accept these terms." *Id*. Based on the similar circumstances here, the Court should reach the same conclusion.

For all of the reasons stated herein, Sanderson Farms' binding mandatory arbitration clause is both substantively and procedurally unconscionable. Sanderson Farms exploited its overwhelming advantage in bargaining power and commercial sophistication not just by taking away Plaintiffs' right to go to court, but by forcing them to bring all their future claims in an arbitration system where they would have virtually no time to file, their legal and equitable remedies would be severely diminished, and they would have to pay enormous up-front costs, while Sanderson would be free to pursue its termination and repossession remedies without going through process. Under well-established Mississippi law, the Court should hold that this arbitration clause is unconscionable.

III. The Arbitration Clause Does Not Cover Plaintiffs' Pre-Contract Claims.

Even if this arbitration clause were enforceable (which it is not), it should not be applied to Plaintiffs' claims in these cases because they are based on misrepresentations that were made before the arbitration clauses were introduced. This arbitration clause applies to:

> [a]ny controversy or claim arising between the parties (and not resolved pursuant to Section 23 above), including, but not limited to, disputes relating to this Agreement, the arbitrability of any dispute relating to this Agreement, termination of this Agreement, or of any breach of this Agreement, whether such controversy or claim arises before, during or after termination of the Agreement . . .

Hatching Egg Producer's Agreement, AR.32–37; Broiler Production Agreement BR.113–120. On its face, this clause is forward looking, applying to claims arising during and after the duration of the contractual relationship. While the clause specifies that it applies to claims arising before *termination*, it nowhere addresses claims based on events taking place prior to contract *formation*. Here, the plaintiffs allege that Sanderson Farms "knowingly made materially false representations, both written and oral, about future income, costs, expenses, required equipment, company policies and working relationships to the plaintiffs," and that this was done "for the purpose of accomplishing the inducement of the Plaintiffs" into the contract and its surrounding obligations. AR. 8–22, Complaint pp. 5–6, ¶ 10, BR. 128–142. Complaint pp. 5–6, ¶ 10. These claims are thus based on actions by Sanderson Farms that predate the contract and arbitration clause. Since the arbitration clause does not encompass pre-contract claims, these claims are not subject to arbitration.

In *Security Watch, Inc. v. Sentinel Systems, Inc.*, 176 F.3d 369 (6th Cir. 1999), the federal appeals court held that an arbitration clause in a commercial contract did not apply to claims arising under earlier agreements between the parties that did not have arbitration clauses. Despite the later clause's general application to disputes "arising out of or relating to the Products furnished," the court found that "this breadth of scope does not extend over time." *Id.* at 372. The court rejected arguments for construing ambiguity as to the clause's scope in favor of compelling arbitration, finding that it was inappropriate to extend the arbitration clause to "previous time periods," unless the clause applied to them explicitly. *Id.* at 374. The same rule should apply here. Sanderson Farms' arbitration clause does not address claims based on actions taken before the contract was signed. Therefore, the clause should not apply to the plaintiffs' fraudulent misrepresentation claims.

IV. Jurisdiction and Venue in the Two Chancery Courts Were Proper.

Sanderson Farms argues that the Plaintiffs' lawsuit is about monetary damages. This could not be further from the truth. A companion case to these cases was filed in the Chancery Court of Simpson County Mississippi. (*Carl R. Fortenberry et al vs. Choctaw Maid Farms, Inc.,* Cause No. 00-0284, Chancery Court, Simpson County, Mississippi) The Complaint filed in that action is almost identical to the Complaints filed below in these cases. This is evidenced by a copy of the Complaint in the aforementioned case and the Complaints filed in the cases at hand. AR 695–702; R.E. 9. The Chancery Judge issued a previous order denying any right of transfer or change of venue on the part of the Defendant in *Carl R. Fortenberry vs. Choctaw Maid Farms, Inc.* AR 745–747; R.E. 10 , as well as similar orders in the cases before this Court. AR 829–832; BR 571–572; R.E. 11.

The Final Judgment, pursuant to a settlement between the parties, in *Fortenberry vs. Choctaw Maid Farms, Inc.* AR 751–755; R.E. 12, shows without question that the cases before this Court are about injunctive relief and righting the wrongs that are perpetrated upon growers by Sanderson Farms. Money damages, if any, would flow from this injunctive relief. In fact, a copy of the Choctaw Maid Farms, Inc. judgment was provided to Sanderson Farms as a template for settlement negotiations prior to the beginning of negotiations at the mediation in the Ballard case.

Sanderson Farms would have this Court believe that the Appellees are trying to destroy the poultry industry in Mississippi. Sanderson Farms would have the Court believe that an attack on the ranking system is an assault on *vertical integration*. Vertical integration consists of far more than a mere method of payment. First of all, some poultry companies pay by the square foot. That aside, what these poultry Growers have demanded is that they be treated fairly and that their system of payment be equitable and equitably administered. These are grass root farmers are salt of the earth people, not litigious zealots. They only ask to be treated fairly and seek to require Sanderson Farms to live up to its promises. They do not want to be treated like **sharecroppers** on their own land. This Court has the power to insure that this type of feudal system never resurfaces in Mississippi.

Further, these cases were filed as **class suits** AR 8–22; BR 128–142, predominating in injunctive relief. This type of action can *only* be filed in Chancery Court. Additionally, Sanderson Farms makes light of the property involved in these cases, but its argument is unfounded.

Mississippi Chancery Practice by V.A. Griffith, § 24 ("An enumeration of the subjects of equity jurisdiction"), lists actions within the Chancery Court's jurisdiction as follows:

> An approximate statement of the numerous subjects that have in the manner mentioned, become established as belonging within the jurisdiction of equity, or which have, at least as to some of their features, been added thereto by statue, may be conveniently consolidated into the following enumeration of original equity suits: . . .Suits based upon **fraud, actual and constructive**; . . .Suits based upon **trusts, express, resulting, and constructive**; . . . Suits for **accounting**; . . .Suits to prevent a multiplicity of suits at law; . . .Suits for **injunction**; (emphasis added)

Miss. Code An. § **11-5-1**, titled "**Venue Of Actions,**" states that:

> "other suits respecting real or personal property may be brought in the Chancery Court of the county in which the property, or some portion thereof, may be."

There is property, both real and personal, located in the counties where the farms of these Growers are located. These lawsuits deal with real and personal property which includes, but is not limited to, the poultry houses located on the Growers' farms, the poultry equipment located in said houses, as well as other real and personal property and damage related thereto from the mandated use of certain chemicals, vacines, antibiotics, as well as feed additives such as 3 Nitro 20 that contain arsenic. The use of these substances by Sanderson Farms was verified in the deposition of Bud West, Jr. taken on June 29, 2004 in the *Gatlin v. Sanderson Farms* case. Appellees Judicial Notice Ex "I" Bud West Dep. at 65–67. A large portion of this arsenic ends up in the excrement placed on the Growers' property. Sanderson Farms argues that we have not come forward with anything that shows an actual effect on the land. This is a matter that will be addressed during discovery as well as during the presentation of the merits of the case. However, it is well known in the poultry industry that the effects exist and in some cases are quite dangerous and extensive.^[18] The chicken and feed are an integral part of this suit and are located primarily on the Growers' farms. Under this Court's ruling in *Guice v. Mississippi*

---

^[18] *See, e.g.*, John Vandiver, *Arsenic: Chicken Feed Effects Questioned: Researchers Study Health, Environmental Impact from Use of Arsenic*, Daily Times (Maryland), Jan. 4, 2004; Mike Ewall, *Toxic Hazards Associated with Poultry Litter Incineration*, publication of Energy Justice Network, September 2002 (available at www.energyjustice.net/fibrowatch/toxics.html); Kris Christen, *Chickens, manure, and arsenic*, Policy News—March 22, 2001, Environmental Science and Technology (available at http://pubs.acs.org/subscribe/journals/esthag-w/2001/mar/ policy/kc_chicken.html); J.R. Garbarino, D.W. Rutherford, and R.L. Wershaw, *Degradation of Roxarsone in Poultry Litter* (available at http://www.brr.cr.usgs.gov/Arsenic/FinalAbsPDF/garbarino.pdf).

Life Ins. Co., 836 So. 2d 756 (Miss. 2003), where a suit concerns personal property, "venue is appropriate where the personal property is located." *Id.* at 760.[19]

This is not a cause of action wholly *in personam* as Sanderson Farms alleges, but is an action at least partially **in rem** or **quasi in rem**. Venue is therefore proper in the county where the property is located. In 20 Am. Jur. 2d § 81 *quasi- in- rem* is discussed and it is stated:

> [F]inally, *quasi- in- rem* action may be based on a claim for money begun by attachment or other seizure of property when the Court has no jurisdiction over the person of the Defendant but has jurisdiction over a thing belonging to the Defendant or over a person who either is indebted or owes a duty to the Defendant. *Longo v. AAA- Michigan*, 569 N.E.2d 927 (Ill. App. 1990)

This theory has been adopted in Mississippi. *See Koehring v. Hyde*, 179 So. 2d 838 (Miss. 1965).

Section 153 of *Mississippi Chancery Practice, by V.A. Griffith* entitled, "What are suits respecting property," states that:

> [A] decree however affects real or personal property not only when it is to declare some possessory interest in or lien upon the property but also when it in any substantial manner operates either against or in relief of the property. *Boswell v. Wheat*, 37 Miss. 610 (1859).

Section 154 also states:

> [B]ut in a later case, in a suit to establish a lien upon personal property by way of subrogation, it was held that the suit should have been brought in the county where the property is situated. In this state of decisions the safe rule to follow is to institute the suit in the county where property is situated. *Pollard v. Phalen*, 53 So. 453 (Miss. 1910).

The Growers' complaints ask that an equitable lien be issued which would attach any of the Defendant's property, therefore proper venue for this action would be where any of the Sanderson Farms property is located. *Cole v. Haynes*, 62 So. 2d 779 (Miss. 1953). Further, in *Green v. Winona Elevator Company*, 319 So. 2d 224 (Miss. 1975), this Court held as follows:

> Where soybeans located in Leflore County, venue in creditors suit brought by buyer of soybeans alleging that seller fraudulently conveyed soybeans to his wife and son in seeking writ of sequestration to detain portion of soybeans to protect buyers interest, was proper in Leflore County, rather than Choctaw County, which was seller's county of residence, under statue providing that suits respecting real or personal property may be brought in Chancery Court of county in which property or, some portion thereof, is located.

In Section 11-5-1, the term **"may"** is used in dealing with all other suits. This was done to eliminate conflicts involving concurrent jurisdiction. This Court is further aware, any claim within the complaint can establish proper venue. The Court in *Donald v. Holmes*, 595 So.2d 434 (Miss. 1992), recognized this proposition, stating that:

> [T]rial courts, both Chancery and Circuit, have full jurisdiction to adjudicate all claims in a single action without regard to whether they arise in equity or at law where suits involve several claims or several parties, venue is proper wherever it is proper to one such claim. Rules Civ.Proc., Rule82(c).

In *Mississippi Chancery Practice by V.A. Griffith,* section 516 entitled "Transfers not to be made in merely doubtful cases", the author pointed out that even if a case involves a question of law and not equity, **if it be of a technical or complicated nature which would exhaust the attention of, or confuse, the average jury** then the Chancellor should retain jurisdiction thereof. (Emphasis Added) The court has consistently held that the Plaintiff is entitled to select among proper venues. This was stated in *McMillian v. Puckett* 678 So.2d.652 (Miss. 1996) as follows:

> [I]f plaintiff selects among permissible venues, his choice must be sustained unless in end there is no creditable evidence supporting factional bases for claim of venue; otherwise, Plaintiff must be given benefit of reasonable doubt.

It would be hard to imagine anything more tedious and complicated than trying to decipher the **"ranking system"** scheme that Sanderson Farms uses to pay its growers.

The Court also stated in *Salts v. Gulf National Life Insurance*, 743 So. 2d 371 (Miss. 1999):

> Application for a change of venue is addressed to the discretion of the trial judge, and his ruling thereon will not be disturbed on appeal unless it clearly appears that there has been an abuse of discretion or that discretion has not been justly and properly exercised under the circumstances of the Plaintiffs' case.

The Growers' fraud claims can also be filed where they occurred, thereby establishing Lawrence County and Jefferson Davis County as the proper venues.

The aforementioned *Fortenberry* case, in which the Chancery Court retained jurisdiction, as well as the cases at hand, were filed in Simpson County, Jefferson Davis County, and Lawrence County where poultry farms are predominantly located. This Court should agree that it would enhance judicially economy, efficiency and consistency for one Chancellor to hear all of these cases.

---

[19] Moreover, *Guice* reaffirms that a chancellor's ruling on venue "will not be disturbed on appeal unless it clearly appears that there has been an abuse of discretion or that the discretion has not been justly and properly exercised under the circumstances of the case." *Id.* at 758. Here, the Chancellors in both cases held that venue was proper.

V. The Appellees' Claims are Not Time-Barred by the Statute of Limitations

There is no other industry in this country that has greater control of information and the ultimate continued concealment of same than the Poultry Industry. Sanderson Farms has complete control of all data and other information concerning the ranking system that is used to defraud the Plaintiffs. It has been long standing law in Mississippi that concealment and misrepresentation by a Defendant tolls the statue of limitations and therefore defeats its' use as an affirmative defense. This was stated by the Supreme Court in the case of *O'Neil Steel, Inc. v. Millette*, 797 So. 2d 869 (Miss. 2001), and *Robinson v. Cobb*, 763 So. 2d 883 (Miss. 2000), respectively:

> Rule of concealed fraud is exception to applicable statue of limitations, ... the fraudulent concealment doctrine, where by the statue of limitations is tolled, if a cause of action is fraudulently concealed, applies to any cause of action.

Also *Smith v. Franklin Custodian Funds, Inc.*, 726 So. 2d 144 (Miss. 1998), stated:

> Theory of equitable tolling provides that where a Plaintiff's delay in filing is caused by the Defendant's misrepresentation the statue is tolled.

Based on the foregoing it is obvious that the affirmative defense of Sanderson Farms that the Plaintiffs causes of action are barred by the statue of limitations is not well founded.

VI. The Plaintiffs are Not Improperly Joined in These Actions.

Rule 20 of the **MRCP**, entitled Permissive Joinder of parties, states as follows:

> All persons may join in one action as Plaintiffs if they assert any right to relief jointly, severely, or in the alternative in the respect of or arising out of the same transaction, occurrence or series of transactions and occurrences and if any question of law or fact common to all these persons will arise in the action.

The Growers are asserting rights jointly under the general equity powers of the Chancery Court, that there are similar series of transactions and occurrences and common questions of law and fact. To subscribe to the Sanderson Farm argument would seem to be in direct conflict with Rule 1 of the Mississippi Rules of Civil Procedure as evidenced in the footnote of said rule which states:

> The salient provision of Rule 1 is the statement that **"These rules shall be construed to secure the just, speedy, and inexpensive determination of every action."** There probably is no provision in these rules more important than this mandate: it reflects the sprit in which the rules were conceived and written and in which they should be interpreted.

Under *American Bankers Insurance Company Of Florida v. Alexander*, 818 So. 2d 1073 (Miss. 2001), joinder would be permissible in the cases at hand. Sanderson has used a common scheme to defraud these Growers. The *American Bankers* case states:

> The official comment to Rule 20 describes its purpose as: 'The general philosophy of the joinder provision of these Rules is to allow virtually unlimited joinder at the pleading stage but to give the court discretion to shape the trial to the necessities of the particular case.'
>
> Much like the state rule, **Fed. R. Civ. P. 20** imposes the same requirements for joinder of parties, i.e., the transaction or occurrence test and the common question of law or fact test. Similar to the approach adopted by the Official Comment to Miss. R. Civ. P. 20, the federal courts view the transaction or occurrence test on a case by case basis utilizing a liberal approach toward joinder. **7 Wright, Miller and Kane,** *Federal Practice & Procedure: Civil 2nd §* **1653** (1986). In fact, under the federal rule, if the transaction and occurrence test cannot be met, there is always a possibility that the cases can be consolidated solely on the existence of common issues. When reviewing common questions of law or fact, the existence of only a single common issue of law, or a single common issue of fact will support joinder.

In conclusion the Court further stated:

> It is clear that all of the plaintiffs' claims arise out of the same pattern of conduct, the same type of insurance, and involve interpretation of the same master policy. All of the Plaintiffs claims are similar with the exception of the actual dollar amount charged on premiums. Even considering a ridged application of Rule 20 as American Banker's suggest, this Court would find it hard to allow consolidation in these cases. In addition under an abusive discretion standard the course of conduct undertaken by the trial judges does not rise to such a level; and therefore we affirm the decision.

The complaints show that these matters involve a common scheme identical to each Plaintiff, the only differences among their recoveries being based on the extent to which each was wronged.

VII. The Court Correctly Denied the Motion to Treat Plaintiffs' Complaint in *Ballard* as Dismissed.

The Appellees' understanding was that lower Court did not take the arguments in the *Ballard* under advisement but held them in abeyance and in effect stayed any further proceeding, as has been done in other cases before that court, until the completion of the mediation process therefore, any running of time applicable in MRAP 15 would only begin to run upon the completion of the mediation process which was approximately one month ago. Further, any neglect on the part of the Plaintiffs to comply with MRAP 15 would constitute excusable neglect and further the granting of Sanderson Farms' motion would cause a manifest injustice to these Growers. This Court is aware that MRAP 15 has been amended and section (c) has been eliminated. Additionally, the Court is given discretion as shown in *Parker v. Livingston*, 817 So2d 554, (Miss. 2002).

Rule 15c does not apply here because an order granting any of Sanderson Farms' previous motions and affirmative defenses would not constitute a *Final Judgment*, being totally dispositive of all claims, thereby ending the litigation. Therefore, any such order would not be appealable.

VIII. The Chancery Court's Evidentiary Rulings in *Austin* Were Correct.

Sanderson Farms argues that the Chancery Judge made evidentiary errors in not allowing certain affidavits to be used as evidence when the witnesses were present to testify. They refer to MRCP 43 (e) but they disregard the wording of said rule which states in part "but the court may direct that the matter be heard wholly or partly on oral testimony or depositions". The rule clearly places within the discretion of the judge the right to determine the form of testimony to be allowed. Sanderson Farms further argues that the Court erred in not allowing other witness testimony and exhibits that the Court deemed inadmissable. These determinations are within the court's discretion as cited throughout the Mississippi Rules of Evidence. Relevancy and admissibility of evidence are within the discretion of the court. *Hentz v. State*, 542 So. 2d 914 (Miss. 1989). Therefore, Sanderson Farms must show an abuse of judicial discretion to prevail in its arguments.

CONCLUSION

For all the reasons set forth herein, the Chancery Court's decision denying Sanderson Farms' motions to dismiss, change venue, transfer jurisdiction, and/or to compel arbitration should be denied.

Respectfully Submitted,
[*Attorney for Appellees*]

E.4 Brief Focusing on Unconscionability Based on Lack of Mutuality, Limitation of Rights, and Cost (Scovill)

IN THE UNITED STATES COURT OF APPEALS
FOR THE SIXTH CIRCUIT

PETER SCOVILL,
    Plaintiff-Appellant,

v.   No. 04-3630, 04-3683

WSYX/ABC, *et al.*,
    Defendants-Appellees.

On Appeal from the United States District Court for the Eastern District of Ohio

PROOF BRIEF OF APPELLANTS

TABLE OF CONTENTS

TABLE OF AUTHORITIES
STATEMENT ON ORAL ARGUMENT
STATEMENT OF SUBJECT MATTER AND APPELLATE JURISDICTION
STATEMENT OF ISSUES PRESENTED
STATEMENT OF THE CASE
STATEMENT OF FACTS
SUMMARY OF ARGUMENT
ARGUMENT
  I. STANDARD OF REVIEW
  II. OHIO LAW AND FEDERAL POLICY PROHIBIT COURTS FROM REWRITING OTHERWISE ILLEGAL ARBITRATION CLAUSES
    A. Generally Applicable Rules of Ohio Contract Law Govern This Dispute
    B. Under Generally Applicable Principles of Ohio Contract Law, Courts Should Not Rewrite Contracts
    C. Ohio Courts Have Applied This General Principle to Arbitration Clauses, Consistently Striking Illegal Arbitration Clauses Rather Than Re-Writing Them
    D. Numerous Courts Applying the Laws of Other Jurisdictions Have Also Held That It would Be Unjust And Inappropriate to Fix Abusive Arbitration Clauses So As To Render Them Enforceable
  III. BY COMPLETELY REWRITING DEFENDANTS' ARBITRATION CLAUSE, THE DISTRICT COURT BELOW DISREGARDED OHIO LAW AND FEDERAL POLICY
  IV. THE DISTRICT COURT ERRED IN HOLDING THAT THE ARBITRATION CLAUSE WAS NOT UNCONSCIONABLE
    A. The Arbitration Clause Was Promulgated In This Case In A Manner That Was Procedurally Unconscionable
    B. The Arbitration Clause Is Substantively Unconscionable
      1. The Provisions Limiting Peter Scovill's Substantive Rights Are Substantively Unconscionable
      2. The Provisions Imposing Prohibitive Costs Are Substantively Unconscionable
      3. The One-Way Nature of the Clause is Unconscionable
CONCLUSION

TABLE OF AUTHORITIES

Cases:[****]

ACORN v. Household Int'l, Inc., 211 F. Supp. 2d 1160 (N.D. Cal. 2002)
Alexander v. Anthony Int'l, L.P., 341 F.3d 256 (3d Cir. 2003)
Anderson v. Ashyby, 873 So.2d 168 (Ala. 2003)
Armendariz v. Foundation Health Psychare Serv's, Inc., 6 P.3d 669 (Cal. 2000)
Arnold v. Goldstar Fin. Sys., Inc., 2002 WL 1941546 *10 (N.D.Ill. Aug. 22, 2002)
Aultman Hosp. Assn. v. Community Mutual Ins. Co., 544 N.E.2d 920 (Ohio 1989)
Banc One Acceptance Corp. v. Hill, 367 F.3d 426 (5th Cir. 2004)
Browne v. Kline Tysons Imports, Inc., 190 F. Supp. 2d 827 (E.D.

[****] [*Editor's Note: Citations throughout brief as in original.*]

Va. 2002)
Camacho v. Holiday Homes, Inc., 167 F. Supp.2d 892 (W.D. Va. 2001)
Carll v. Terminix Int'l Co., 793 A.2d 921 (Pa. Superior Ct. 2002)
Christiansburg Garment Co. v. EEOC, 434 U.S. 412 (1978)
Circuit City Stores, Inc. v. Adams, 279 F.3d 889 (9th Cir. 2002)
Collins v. Click Camera & Video, Inc., 621 N.E. 2d 1294 (Mont. Cty. 1993)
Comb v. Paypal, Inc., 218 F. Supp. 2d 1165 (N.D. Cal. 2002)
Cooper v. MRM Investment Co., 367 F.3d 493 (6th Cir. 2004)
D.R. Horton, Inc. v. Green, ___ P.3d ___, 2004 WL 2028999 (Nev. Sept. 13, 2004)
Doctor's Assocs., Inc. v. Casarotto, 517 U.S. 681 (1996)
Eagle v. Fred Martin Motors, 809 N.E.2d 1161 (Ohio Ct. App. 2004)
Ferguson v. Countrywide Credit Industries, Inc., 298 F.3d 778 (9th Cir. 2002)
First Options of Chicago, Inc. v. Kaplan, 514 U.S. 938 (1995)
Flores v. Transamerica Homefirst, Inc., 113 Cal. Rptr. 2d 376 (Cal. Ct. App. 2002)
Floss v. Ryan's Family Steak Houses, Inc., 211 F.3d 306 (6th Cir. 2000), *cert. denied*, 531 U.S. 1072 (2001)
Flyer Hill Printing Co. v. Hill, 805 So.2d 829 (Fla. Dist. Ct. App. 2001)
Foster Wheeler Envirespose, Inc. v. Franklin County Convention Facilities Authority, 678 N.E.2d 519 (Ohio 1997)
Garrett v. Hooters-Toledo, 295 F. Supp. 2d 774 (N.D. Ohio 2003)
Gibson v. Neighborhood Health Clinics, Inc., 121 F.3d 1126 (7th Cir. 1997)
Gilmer v. Interstate/Johnson Lane Corp., 500 U.S. 20 (1991)
Giordano v. Pep Boys—Manny, Moe & Jack, Inc., 2001 WL 484360 (E.D.Pa. Mar. 29, 2001)
Gourley v. Yellow Transp., L.L.C., 178 F. Supp. 2d 1196 (D. Colo. 2001)
Graham Oil Co. v. ARCO Products Co., 43 F.3d 1244 (9th Cir. 1994)
Hagedorn v. Veritas Software Corp., 250 F. Supp. 2d 857 (S.D. Ohio 2002)
Harper v. Ultimo, 7 Cal. Rptr.3d 418 (Cal. Ct. App. 2003)
Holt v. O'Brien, 862 So.2d 87 (Fla. Dist. Ct. App. 2003)
Hooters of Am., Inc. v. Phillips, 173 F.3d 933 (4th Cir. 1999)
Iberia Credit Bureau, Inc. v. Cingular Wireless LLC, 379 F.3d 159 (5th Cir. 2004)
Ingle v. Circuit City Stores, Inc., 328 F.3d 1165 (9th Cir. 2003)
Iwen v. U.S. West Direct, 977 P.2d 989 (Mont. 1999)
Lelouis v. Western Directory Co., 230 F. Supp. 2d 1214 (D. Or. 2001)
Luna v. Household Finance Corp., 236 F. Supp. 2d 1166 (W.D. Wash. Nov. 4, 2002)
Lytle v. Citifinancial Services, Inc., 810 A.2d 643 (Pa. Super. Ct. Oct. 24, 2002)
McMullen v. Meijer, Inc., 337 F.3d 697 (6th Cir. 2003)
McNulty v. H&R Block, Inc., 843 A.2d 1267 (Penn Super. Ct. 2004)
Medtronic v. Lohr, 518 U.S. 470 (1996)
Mendez v. Palm Harbor Homes, Inc., 45 P.3d 594 (Wash. Ct. App. 2002)
Miller v. Household Realty Corp., No 81968, 2003 WL 21469782 (Ohio Ct. App. June 26, 2003)
Mitsubishi Motors Corp. v. Soler Chrysler-Plymouth, Inc., 473 U.S. 614 (1985)

Morrison v. Circuit City Stores, Inc., 317 F.3d 646 (6th Cir. 2003)
Murphy v. Mid-West Nat'l Life Ins. Co. Of Tenn., 78 P.3d 766 (Idaho 2003)
Myers v. Terminex, 697 N.E. 2d 277 (Ohio Ct. Comm. Pleas 1998)
Paladino v. Avnet Computer Technologies., Inc., 134 F.3d 1054 (11th Cir. 1998)
Patterson v. ITT Consumer Fin. Corp., 14 Cal. App. 4th 1659 (1993)
Penn v. Ryan's Family Steakhouses, 269 F.3d 753 (7th Cir. 2001)
Perry v. Thomas, 482 U.S. 483 (1987)
Phillips v. Associates Home Equity Services, Inc., 179 F. Supp.2d 840 (N.D. Ill. 2001)
Plattner v. Edge Solutions, Inc., 2004 WL 1575557 (N.D. Ill. May 27, 2004)
Popovich v. McDonalds, 189 F. Supp. 2d 772 (N.D. Ill. 2002)
Schaefer v. Allstate v. Fallon-Murphy, 590 N.E. 2d 1242 (Ohio 1992)
Showmethemoney Check Cashers, Inc. v. Williams, 27 S.W.3d 361 (Ark. 2000)
State Farm v. Poyhanya, Nos. 92 AP-40, 93 AP-41, 1992 WL 249858 (Ohio App. 10 Dist. Sept. 29, 1992)
State of West Virginia ex rel. Dunlap v. Berger, 567 S.E.2d 265 (W. Va. 2002)
Stevens/Leinweber/ Sullens, Inc. v. Holm Development and Mgmt, Inc., 795 P.2d 1308 (Ariz. App. 1990)
Taylor v. Butler, ___ S.W.3d ___, 2004 WL 1925423 (Tenn. Aug. 31, 2004)
Ticknor v. Choice Hotels, Inc., 265 F.3d 931 (9th Cir. 2001)
Ting v. AT&T, 182 F.Supp.2d 902, 916–17 (N.D. Cal. 2002), *aff'd with respect to unconscionability*, 319 F.3d 1126 (9th Cir. 2003), *cert. denied*, 124 S. Ct. 53 (2003)
Ullmann v. May, 72 N.E.2d 63 (Ohio 1947)
Underwood v. Chef Francisco/Heinz, 200 F. Supp.2d 475 (E.D. Pa. 2002)
Volt Info. Sciences, Inc. v. Bd. of Trustees, 489 U.S. 468 (1989).
Wauseon Plaza Limited Partnership v. Wauseon Hardware Co., 807 N.E. 2d 953 (Ohio Ct. App. 2004)
Williams v. Aetna Finance Company, 700 N.E. 2d 859 (Ohio 1998)
Worldwide Insurance Group v. Klopp, 603 A.2d 788 (Del. 1992)

Other Authorities:

9 U.S.C. § 2
28 U.S.C. § 1291
28 U.S.C. §§ 1441 and 1446(b)
Age Discrimination in Employment Act, 29 U.S.C. § 621, et seq.
Older Workers Benefit Protection Act
Restatement (Second) of Contracts § 184 cmt. b.

STATEMENT ON ORAL ARGUMENT

Plaintiff Peter Scovill respectfully urges the Court to permit oral argument, because the issues raised in this appeal are important ones that recur regularly in employment disputes. A significant number of corporations continue to ignore this Court's directions that mandatory binding pre-dispute arbitration clauses may not contain provisions stripping employees of their substantive rights under the civil rights statutes, or imposing significant and prohibitive arbitration costs upon employees. This is one of the first cases to address the issues arising from this Court's en banc ruling in *Morrison v. Circuit City Stores, Inc.*, 317 F.3d 646 (6th Cir. 2003), and district courts need this Court's guidance as to how to respond to such abuses. Plaintiff respectfully suggests that permitting oral argument may help inform this Court's decision on this weighty matter.

STATEMENT OF SUBJECT MATTER AND APPELLATE JURISDICTION

This Court has subject matter jurisdiction of this case because the plaintiff brought claims in this action under the Age Discrimination in Employment Act, 29 U.S.C. § 621, et seq. This Court has jurisdiction under 28 U.S.C. § 1291 to review the final judgment of the District Court, filed by the clerk on March 29, 2004, which dismissed Mr. Scovill's case and disposed of all claims. R. 73, Apx. pg. ___. Plaintiff's Notice of Appeal to the clerk's order was timely filed on April 28, 2004, pursuant to Fed. R. App. P. 4(a)(4)(I). R. 77, Apx. pg. ___. Plaintiff moved for reconsideration. R. 74, Apx. pg. ___. The District Court denied the motion for reconsideration on June 7, 2004. R. 85, Apx. pg. ___. On September 10, 2004, this Court granted Mr. Scovill's unopposed motion for an extension to file this Opening Brief until October 4, 2004.

STATEMENT OF ISSUES PRESENTED

1. When an agreement to arbitrate contains several unenforceable provisions, is it improper and illegal for a court rewrite the agreement so as to render it enforceable?
Answer: YES.
2. When an employee quits his job and moves across the country with his family to take a new job pursuant to a written, signed agreement containing no reference to arbitration, and three weeks after he has begun his employer tells him that he must submit to a mandatory arbitration clause or he will be fired, is this procedurally unconscionable?
Answer: YES.

STATEMENT OF THE CASE

Plaintiff Peter B. Scovill filed this action in the court of Common Pleas for Franklin County, Ohio against Sinclair Broadcast Group, Inc., Sinclair Media II, Inc., WTTE/WSYX-TV, Columbus (WTTE-TV), Inc., WTTE, Channel 28, Inc., and David Silverstein ("Defendants"). He alleged that his employer, Defendant WSYX, discriminated against him on account of his age, in violation of the Age Discrimination in Employment Act (ADEA), 29 U.S.C. § 621, et. seq., and Ohio law. R. 1, Exh. B. Am. Compl., Apx. pg. ___. Defendants removed the case to the United States District Court for the Southern District of Ohio, Eastern Division, under 28 U.S.C. §§ 1441 and 1446(b). R. 1, Apx. pg. ___.

Defendants filed a Motion to Dismiss or Stay Pending Arbitration, arguing that Peter Scovill was required to submit his claims to arbitration according to the provisions found in his Employment Agreement. R. 6, Apx. pg. ___. Scovill countered that the arbitration clause was unenforceable because there was no meeting of the minds in entering the agreement; the clause is substantively and procedurally unconscionable; the arbitration clause is voidable under the doctrine of duress; the arbitration clause lacks mutuality; the clause violates the Older Workers Benefit Protection Act (OWBPA); ADEA claims are not subject to arbitration; and the arbitration clause lacks consideration. R. 43, Apx. pg. ___.

The District Court for the Southern District of Ohio found that several provisions of the arbitration clause were unenforceable. It held that the cost-shifting portion of the agreement, which burdened Peter Scovill with excessive arbitration fees if he were to pursue his claims in arbitration, was illegal and unenforceable. The district court also held unenforceable the portions of the arbitration agreement that attempted to restrict Peter Scovill's rights under the ADEA by changing the applicable legal and evidentiary standards for proving discrimination and stripping him of substantive remedies available under the civil rights laws.

The district court did not accept some of Peter Scovill's other arguments, however. It found that there was a meeting of the minds between Defendant and Mr. Scovill, for example, and that consideration existed for the arbitration clause. The district court also held that there was no duress, and that the agreement was not unconscionable. Finally, the court also found that neither the OWBPA nor the 1991 Civil Rights Amendment precluded arbitration of Mr. Scovill's claims.

Despite finding that a number of the provisions embedded in the language and structure of the arbitration clause were illegal, the district court did not strike the faulty arbitration clause. Rather, the court held that the parties must nonetheless proceed to arbitration. In order to facilitate this outcome, the court constructively altered its terms. First, having found that the allocation of arbitration fees set forth in the actual language of the arbitration agreement was illegal, the district court imposed a completely different scheme of its own creation. The Court stated:

> With respect to the costs of arbitration, this Court concludes that Plaintiff shall pay the initial filing fee, while the total costs shall be paid by the Defendants. Costs incurred, by either party, shall be apportioned by the arbitrator after the decision applying the same substantive law on costs which would be applicable had this case been tried under the ADEA in federal district court.

R. 72, Opinion at 36, Apx. pg. ___. The district court also added a new term to the "agreement" specifying that "Upon proceeding to arbitration, the parties shall be subject to the same substantive law and remedies regarding age discrimination that would apply in court." Id. None of these terms were included in the actual language of the agreement drafted by defendants (and supposedly agreed to by Peter Scovill).

The district court further rewrote the arbitration agreement by striking the provisions which imposed a heavier burden of proof on Peter Scovill than he would have faced under the civil rights laws. "[T]he cost-shifting provision, the remedies provision, and the evidentiary standard provision are all severable from the agreement." Id.

The district court granted Defendants' Motion to Dismiss and compelled arbitration on March 29, 2004. Peter Scovill filed this timely appeal with this Court.

STATEMENT OF FACTS

The Original Employment Agreement

Peter Scovill was hired and employed by Defendant Sinclair Media II, Inc. ("Sinclair") as an anchor/reporter for WSYX/WTTE-TV (Fox TV or Fox 28) from September 12, 1998 until May 17, 2002. R. 1, Exh. B., Am. Compl. at ¶¶ 2 and 12, Apx. pg.

___. At the time Peter Scovill entered the employment agreement with Defendants, he had for 11 years been a successful television anchor at a Cape Coral, Florida television station. Peter Scovill negotiated his new employment contract with Sinclair with Mike Hevel, the news director at Defendants' stations. The terms of employment were included in a letter of agreement ("original agreement") signed by both parties, dated July 31, 1998.

This original agreement provided that Sinclair would employ Peter Scovill for three years, specifying his compensation, designating his job title, and containing other applicable terms and conditions. This original agreement represented the understanding and meeting of the minds between Peter Scovill and Defendants, and included the following terms:

1. The contract would run from September 12, 1998 through September 11, 2001.

2. Peter Scovill's job position would be Anchor/Reporter.

3. Peter Scovill agreed to a 180 day non-compete agreement following termination of employment at WSYX/WTTE.

4. WSYX/WTTE could cancel the agreement on the yearly anniversary date of the contract by giving Peter Scovill 60 days prior written notice.

5. WSYX/WTTE would pay a clothing allowance to Peter Scovill, in trade or money, up to $2000 each year of the agreement, a salary of $90,000, $94,000, and $98,000 for each year of the contract, reasonable travel expenses from Florida to Ohio, and a yearly bonus based on the ratings of his 10:00 pm news broadcast, up to $4,500 per year of the contract. R. 43., Exh. 33, Apx. pg.___ .

This contract made no mention of arbitration, attorneys' fees, time limits, severability, or any of the other onerous terms later unilaterally imposed on Peter Scovill. In reliance on this original agreement, Peter Scovill gave up his employment in Florida, sold his home, and moved his family to Ohio. R. 43., Exh. 41, Apx. pg. ___.

It is undisputed in this case that no mention of or reference to arbitration or any related provisions occurred during the negotiations concerning Peter Scovill's employment prior to his signing the original agreement and relocating to Ohio. Although the original agreement refers to a "more comprehensive contract" to be generated by Sinclair's legal department, nothing was explained to Peter Scovill about what this meant. Hevel Dep. at 20. (No R. number), Apx. pg. ___.

The Unilateral Imposition of the Arbitration Agreement

At the time that he signed the original agreement, Peter Scovill understood that "the more comprehensive contract" would be a "fleshed out" version of the July 31, 1998 written agreement, rewritten in "legalese." Scovill Dep. at 54 (No R. number), Apx. pg. ___. Mr. Hevel testified that he sent a document to corporate headquarters that contained all of the terms under which Peter Scovill agreed to commence employment with Sinclair. Hevel Dep. at 22, Apx. pg. ___. The purpose of the form was to relay to the corporate lawyers the terms negotiated between the parties. *Id.* at 25, Apx. pg. ___. This form, like the original agreement, contained no mention of an arbitration clause, payment of Sinclair's attorney's fees, nor a severability clause.

It was not until two weeks *after* Peter Scovill had relocated his family to Ohio and assumed his duties at Defendants' station in Columbus that Mr. Scovill was presented with an employment agreement purportedly formalizing with more detail the terms of the previously negotiated contract. Scovill Dep. at 54–55, Apx. pg. ___. This new document included the arbitration clause at issue in this appeal. When, on or about September 30, 1998, the "more comprehensive" employment agreement appeared in his mailbox at work, Peter Scovill repeatedly voiced his objections to the unfair and one-sided terms in the agreement, which had not been negotiated or agreed upon before he left Florida, to his supervisor, Mike Hevel, and to Beulah Hatcher, Administrative Assistant. Scovill Dep. at 55–59, Apx. pg. ___. Mr. Scovill complained about the arbitration clause and the term requiring him to pay attorneys' fees and costs of defendants. *Id.* at 57–59, Apx. pg. ___. Mr. Scovill asked Hevel and Hatcher what would happen if he refused to sign the new agreement and was told that he had to sign it to keep his job. *Id.* at 56, Apx. pg. ___.

Hevel told Peter Scovill that the agreement was out of his hands, that it was a corporate document, and everyone had to sign it. *Id.* at 59, 66, Apx. pg. ___. In addition, both Hevel and Hatcher expressed that it was urgent that Mr. Scovill rapidly sign the agreement. *Id.* at 95, Apx. pg. ___. Mr. Scovill walked away from the conversations knowing that the agreement containing the arbitration and other objectionable clauses was non-negotiable. He had to sign it or leave. Peter Scovill testified that he was given no negotiating room, that he must take it or leave it, and that he had no choice, under the circumstances, but to sign it. *Id.* at 56, 60, Apx. pg. ___.

At the time he was presented with this one-sided agreement, Peter Scovill was the sole support for his three children and had no readily available comparable employment. R. 43, Exh. 41, Apx. pg. ___. In addition, the terms of the original agreement included a non-competition clause which prevented him from working for any of the defendants' competitors. Given his responsibility for his family, and the lack of any other alternatives, Mr. Scovill was forced to sign the new agreement on September 30, 1998. Scovill Dep. at 56–60, Apx. pg. ___.

The Unconscionable Terms of the Arbitration Clause

The new agreement contained the arbitration clause at issue. The identical arbitration clause was contained in employment agreements of all on-air employees working under contract hired by the defendants prior to January 2000. Faber Dep. at 21, 37–38, Apx. pg. ___. Different and less onerous arbitration clauses were used for employees in other job classifications, such as editors, producers, and managers.

The arbitration clause contained in Peter Scovill's contract[+1] included the following terms:

1. All Mr. Scovill's claims must be submitted to final and binding arbitration.

2. By contrast, the Defendants were not bound to arbitrate any breach of contract claims they might have against Peter Scovill.

3. If Mr. Scovill and Defendants were unable to agree on a neutral arbitrator, Defendants would obtain a list of arbitrators from an unidentified state or federal arbitration service.

4. The arbitrator would be bound by the qualifications and disclosures and procedures of the 1989 model employment arbitration procedures of the American Arbitration Association ("AAA").

[+1] R. 43, Exh. 21, Apx. pg. ___

5. The arbitrator would determine who was the prevailing party, and the costs of arbitration would be paid by the non-prevailing party.

6. Peter Scovill must deliver a written request for arbitration to the Defendants within three months of any event or occurrence giving rise to a claim. If a notice of a claim is not received within three months, Mr. Scovill the employee waives any such claim. This new three month statute of limitations, which is dramatically shorter than the six *year* limitations period provided by Ohio law for Peter Scovill's discharge claims, and 300 days under the ADEA, was not subject to equitable or other tolling.

7. The agreement contained a two-way "loser pays provision":

> In the event of any action, proceeding or litigation (collective, the "Action") between the parties arising out of or in relation to this Agreement, Employer, if the prevailing party in such litigation, shall be entitled to recover, in addition to any damages, injunctions, or other relief and without regard to whether the Action is prosecuted to final appeal, all of its costs and expenses including, without limitation, reasonable attorneys' fees, from the non-prevailing party.

Similarly, the employment agreement contained a second "loser pays provision" requiring that Peter Scovill pay the Defendants' attorneys' fees and costs if unsuccessful (Paragraph 14.8). Finally, the arbitration clause included a severability clause (Paragraph 14.7). These provisions are completely unlike the rule of law provided by the federal and state statutes on which Mr. Scovill relies.[+2]

8. Peter Scovill must pay significant costs to arbitrate his claim. While the magnitude of those costs was not discernable from the agreement itself, Mr. Scovill placed affidavits and documents before the district court that established that the costs of arbitrating his claims would be quite high:[+3]

> With respect to administrative fees, the Plaintiff pays an initial filing fee of, in general, either $3,250 for a claim with an unstated value, or $4,250 for a $300,000 claim. In addition, there is a case service fee of $1,250 for a claim valued at $300,000 or a case service fee of $750 if the claim does not state its value. Finally, there is a room rental fee of, in general, $150 per day. . . . In addition, the Plaintiff estimates the arbitrator's fees to range from $10,710 to $14,490, based on a four day arbitration hearing. In total, Plaintiff estimates the average of typical costs of arbitration as being between $15,310 to $20,590. . . . The range could be higher, however, depending on the length of the arbitration hearing and time spent by the arbitrator in rendering a decision. Nevertheless, it appears undisputed that the cost is, at a minimum, $15,310. (R. 72, Opinion at 19–20, Apx. pg. ___.)

The district court based these findings largely on the testimony of Neil Currie, an Assistant Vice President for Case Administration for the AAA. By contrast, as the district court found, "the initial costs of litigating [in court] are minimal, aside from the $150 filing fee in this Court. Furthermore, in contrast with the arbitral forum, a litigant never incurs a room rental fee or hourly fee from the judge when litigating." (R. 72, Opinion at 20, Apx. pg. ___.)

In light of these facts, and after weighing the evidence presented by each side, the district court held that "[i]n view of the forgoing, the court concludes that the costs of arbitration, viewed from the perspective of the Plaintiff and the relevant class of news anchors, is prohibitive in comparison to the costs of litigation." R. 72, Opinion at 23, Apx. pg. ___. The district court found that this was particularly true of Peter Scovill:

> Plaintiff has three children and a new business, all of which require a great deal of financial support. The costs of arbitration, which would be at minimum $15,000, are to be incurred at a time when Plaintiff's salary as a news anchor would not be forthcoming.

Id. at 24, Apx. pg. ___.

9. The arbitration clause also set forth that the "Arbitrator *must* uphold the action taken by the employer," R. 43, Exh. 21 at ¶ 15, Apx. pg. ___, if Defendants "reasonably believed" that the employee had not "command[ed] a high level of professionalism." The district court held that "[t]his standard alters the traditional burden-shifting method employed for proving an ADEA claim in this Court." R. 72, Opinion at 30, Apx. pg. ___.

Peter Scovill's Employment and Dismissal

During the time that Peter Scovill co-anchored the Fox TV 10:00 p.m. news program, the program's ratings rose consistently. R. 1, Exh. B, Am. Compl. at ¶ 17, Apx. pg. ___. Besides providing services to Defendants as an anchor, Peter Scovill also functioned as an investigative reporter and, at the station's request, engaged in numerous community services and public affairs activities. *Id.* at ¶ 18, Apx. pg. ___. At Defendants' encouragement and request, Mr. Scovill appeared on and worked with numerous radio stations in the central Ohio area. *Id.* at ¶ 20, Apx. pg. ___.

Throughout Peter Scovill's employment with Sinclair, Defendants' manager told Mr. Scovill that his contract would be renewed based on his performance and the show's ratings, and that he could expect a substantial increase in salary at the time of his contract renewal. *Id.* at ¶ 21, Apx. pg. ___. Relying on the manager's promises, Mr. Scovill refrained from looking for other employment and declined to pursue other employment opportunities. *Id.* at 22,

---

[+2] *See Christiansburg Garment Co. v. EEOC*, 434 U.S. 412, 422 (1978) ("To take the further step of assessing attorney's fees against plaintiffs simply because they do not prevail would substantially add to the risks inherent in most litigation and would undercut the efforts of Congress to promote the vigorous enforcement of the provisions of Title VII.").

[+3] Defendants pointed out that the costs of arbitration would be lower if the arbitration did not take place before the AAA. The District Court held that this point was of no relevance, as the arbitration clause specified that the arbitration should be conducted by the AAA. (R. 72, Opinion at p. 19, n. 7, Apx. pg. ___.) As this Court has noted, the inquiry into the costs of arbitration should be based on the "AAA rules prevailing on the date that [the employer] filed its motion in district court to compel [arbitration]." *Cooper v. MRM Investment Co.*, 367 F.3d 493, 513 (6th Cir. 2004).

Apx. pg. __. In the spring of 2001, Plaintiff applied for the position of News Director for WSYX/WTTE-TV. *Id.* at ¶ 23, Apx. pg. _. In July of 2001, Defendant David Silverstein was hired for the news director position instead of Peter Scovill. *Id.* at ¶ 24, Apx. pg. _. Mr. Scovill understood that age was a determining factor in the decision to hire Silverstein rather than him for the news director position. *Id.* at ¶ 25, Apx. pg. __.

In the summer of 2001, Peter Scovill was told that his employment agreement would not be renewed. He understood this to mean that he was no longer eligible for the clothing allowance or bonuses provided in his original agreement. Scovill Dep. at 8–9, Apx. pg. __. Silverstein instructed the older anchors to refrain from mentioning their names on the air and discontinued promotions featuring the older anchors. R. 1, Exh. B, Am. Compl. at ¶ 27c, Apx. pg. __. Silverstein told Mr. Scovill at the time that he had decided to promote the younger "more energetic" reporters on the staff to the key anchor positions, and that the "more mature" anchors would be placed on the less important day time news programs. Silverstein also informed Peter Scovill that these younger reporters would relate better to the station's target audience. R. 1, Exh. B, Am. Compl. at ¶ 27, Apx. pg. __.

In early January 2002, Peter Scovill was informed that he would no longer be an anchor/reporter on the 10:00 p.m. news, but instead would be assigned to the 5:00 p.m. and noon broadcasts as an anchor/reporter. Scovill Dep. at 93. Mr. Scovill testified that his move was damaging to his career. *Id.* The demotion, along with an unjustified disciplinary measure issued against him, triggered an extreme physical and emotional reaction in Mr. Scovill. His physicians advised him that his reaction to this stress jeopardized his health. R. 1, Exh. B, Am. Compl. at ¶ 31–32, Apx. pg. __.

In February 2002, Peter Scovill took a medical leave of absence due to the dangerous reactions he was having to the unjust measures being taken against him at work. *Id.* at 32, Apx. pg. __. Following Mr. Scovill's request for leave, Defendants instructed other employees to engage in surveillance and monitoring of Peter Scovill's personal activities away from work. *Id.* at ¶ 32, Apx. pg. __. In February 2002, Defendants informed Mr. Scovill's co-workers that he was not to be allowed on the station's premises and that if he appeared on the premises they were to call the police. *Id.* at ¶ 27g, Apx. pg. __.

Peter Scovill alleges that he was falsely accused by Defendants of violating obligations to the station and was notified that he would be disciplined upon his return to work following his medical leave of absence. *Id.* at ¶ 34, Apx. pg. __. On February 25, 2002, Mr. Scovill complained to Defendants of various unlawful discriminatory conduct and harassment to which he had been subjected. *Id.* at ¶ 35, Apx. pg. __. Eighty-one days after Mr. Scovill reported that he had been subjected to discrimination and harassment, Defendants notified him that his employment was terminated. *Id.* at ¶ 36, Apx. pg. __.

Following his termination, Peter Scovill looked for comparable work as an anchor, and there was nothing available. Scovill Dep. at 35, Apx. pg. __. Mr. Scovill testified that, at his age, moving to a new marketplace (since he was not allowed to seek work in the same market, under the non-compete clause) and obtaining comparable work was not a realistic option. *Id.* at 36, Apx. pg. __.

While he worked for the defendants and with their knowledge, Peter Scovill had formed a company called Scovill Outdoors, Inc. Following his termination, Mr. Scovill invested $30,000 in the business. Mr. Scovill has earned no income from the business. In fact, according to corporate tax returns, the business lost money in the year 2002. Mr. Scovill's personal tax return for 2002 showed minimal income, which was almost entirely unemployment compensation.

Mr. Scovill brought this action for age discrimination, invasion of privacy, promissory estoppel, and violation of public policy. R. 1, Exh. B, Apx. pg. __.

SUMMARY OF ARGUMENT

This Court should reverse the district court's order compelling Peter Scovill to arbitrate, and should make clear that district courts are not free to cure illegal contracts by drafting new contracts more to their liking. If courts will fix illegal contracts for corporations, nothing will deter corporations from filling their contracts with as many one-sided provisions as they can imagine, knowing that there will be no consequences to doing so. This strategy will benefit corporations because very few employees will have the temerity and ability to hire an attorney and risk their assets by challenging a threatening but illegal contract.

The arbitration clause written by Defendants contains several unenforceable provisions. The language of the arbitration clause burdens Mr. Scovill with arbitration fees and costs that are so large that they effectively make it impossible for him to pursue his claims. Defendants' arbitration clause was not limited to provisions spelling out the forum where Peter Scovill's claims would be heard: it also rewrote the substantive law that would govern any civil rights claims that Mr. Scovill might have. Under the civil rights laws, Mr. Scovill could not be held responsible for Defendants' attorneys' fees unless his action was frivolous. Under two separate provisions of Defendants' arbitration clause, however, Peter Scovill would be responsible for Defendants' attorneys' fees if he brought a well-founded claim but failed to prevail. Under the civil rights laws, Mr. Scovill had far longer to bring his claims. Under Defendants' arbitration clause, by contrast, Mr. Scovill is subject to an absurdly short three-month statute of limitations. Defendants' arbitration clause also alters the burdens of proof set forth in the civil rights laws. As the district court correctly held, all of these provisions are flatly illegal under the well-established law of this Circuit.

Faced with an arbitration clause that was illegal and unenforceable, the district court should have followed Ohio law applicable to all contracts and struck the entire arbitration clause. Instead, the district court chose to draft an entirely new arbitration clause of its own invention. The court not only struck some of the illegal terms that had been embedded and interwoven into Defendants' arbitration clause, but it also created from the ground up a whole new set of provisions that it believed would be legal. The district court's activist approach is flatly contrary to law.

Under the FAA, courts must apply generally applicable state contract law to questions governing arbitration agreements. In this case, this Court must apply Ohio contract law, unless that law somehow treats arbitration clauses less favorably than other contract terms. Generally applicable principles of Ohio contract law strictly forbid judicial intrusion into the terms of contracts. Even if the result of judicial modification of contract terms would be more equitable than enforcement or non-enforcement of the agreement without modification, a court must still not re-write the language of a contract. Rather than rewrite unenforceable contract provisions,

Ohio courts have consistently refused to enforce arbitration clauses that included unenforceable provisions.

It is not the province of judges to fix illegal arbitration clauses to achieve the end of compelling parties to arbitrate their claims. Not only is such judicial activism contrary to Ohio law, but it also contravenes the FAA. The FAA requires that arbitration agreements be enforced—if at all—"according to their terms," not according to new terms invented by courts. Ohio law is also consistent with a number of decisions by other courts holding that it would be unfair and unwise to permit courts to re-write illegal arbitration clauses to be enforceable. As this Court held in *Cooper v. MRM Investment Co.*, 367 F.3d 493 (6th Cir. 2004), parties writing illegal contract terms should not be rewarded by courts who affirmatively attempt to give such parties most of what they want. If illegal arbitration clauses are merely rewritten and not stricken, corporations drafting mandatory arbitration clauses in contracts of adhesion will have an incentive to lard them with every one-sided term they can think of, in the knowledge that the most that will happen is that illegal terms will be "fixed" by courts playing the role of corporate contract counsel. As this brief will establish, numerous courts have further held that it is particularly improper for courts to affirmatively craft new terms, or to re-write arbitration clauses containing multiple illegal provisions.

The district court also erred in finding that Defendants' arbitration clause was not unconscionable. Although the district court held that Defendants' arbitration clause contained many one-sided and illegal provisions, the court found that the contract was not promulgated in a manner that was procedurally unconscionable. That ruling ignored rules of Ohio contract law that are generally applicable to all contracts. Mr. Scovill was presented with this arbitration agreement after moving his family and career from Florida to Ohio, and after having begun work for Defendants. It was presented to him in non-negotiable, take-it-or-leave-it, sign-it-or-you're-fired situation. Peter Scovill, extremely dependent on his job, particularly after signing a non-compete agreement with Defendants, had no meaningful choice but to sign the agreement. Such is the making of a perfect case of procedural unconscionability. There is little question but that the one-sided and non-mutual clause, which imposed excessive costs of arbitration upon Mr. Scovill and re-wrote the substantive civil rights laws to his disadvantage, was substantively unconscionable.

In sum, the unenforceable and unconscionable arbitration agreement should be struck from the employment agreement. This Court should reverse the lower court's decision compelling arbitration and allow Peter Scovill to proceed with his age discrimination claim in court.

ARGUMENT

I. STANDARD OF REVIEW.

The Sixth Circuit Court of Appeals reviews *de novo* an order compelling arbitration. *Morrison v. Circuit City Stores, Inc.*, 317 F.3d 646, 665 (6th Cir. 2003); *see also Floss v. Ryan's Family Steak Houses, Inc.*, 211 F.3d 306, 311 (6th Cir. 2000), *cert. denied*, 531 U.S. 1072 (2001).

Also, to the extent that defendants argue that federal law preempts certain state principles of contract law, this Court should review those claims in light of the strong presumption against preemption. *See Medtronic v. Lohr*, 518 U.S. 470, 485 (1996) (a party seeking preemption of state law bears a heavy burden of overcoming the long-standing "presum[ption] that Congress does not cavalierly preempt state-law causes of action.").

II. OHIO LAW AND FEDERAL POLICY PROHIBIT COURTS FROM REWRITING OTHERWISE ILLEGAL ARBITRATION CLAUSES.

A. Generally Applicable Rules of Ohio Contract Law Govern This Dispute.

This Court has recognized that the FAA directs it to apply state contract law when addressing the validity of an arbitration clause: "We review the enforceability of an arbitration agreement according to the applicable state law of contract formation." *Morrison v. Circuit City*, 317 F.3d at 666 (citing *First Options of Chicago, Inc. v. Kaplan*, 514 U.S. 938, 943–44 (1995)). *See also Floss v. Ryan's Family Steak Houses,* 211 F.3d at 314 ("In deciding whether the [arbitration] agreements are enforceable, we examine applicable state-law contract principles.") (citation omitted). *Cf. Banc One Acceptance Corp. v. Hill*, 367 F.3d 426, 431 (5th Cir. 2004) ("the validity of an arbitration provision is a question of state law, . . . and this court recently reviewed under state law whether an arbitration clause was unconscionable.")

The FAA incorporates a savings clause that provides that arbitration clauses will not be enforced if there are grounds under state contract law for invalidating the clause. 9 U.S.C. § 2. The U.S. Supreme Court has recognized that common law contract defenses, such as unconscionability, are available to a party challenging an arbitration agreement. *Doctor's Assocs., Inc. v. Casarotto*, 517 U.S. 681, 687 (1996) ("[G]enerally applicable contract defenses, such as fraud, duress or unconscionability, may be applied to invalidate arbitration agreements without contravening [the F.A.A.].").

This principle that state contract law applies to arbitration clauses is also incorporated into the federal substantive law of arbitration. *Perry v. Thomas,* 482 U.S. 483, 492–93 (1987) ("An agreement to arbitrate is . . . enforceable, *as a matter of federal law*, 'save upon such grounds as exist at law or in equity for the revocation of *any* contract.' . . . Thus state law, whether of legislative or judicial origin, is applicable *if* that law arose to cover issues concerning the validity, revocability, and enforceability of contracts generally.") (emphasis in original, citations omitted).

Therefore, since the arbitration clause in this matter was signed in Ohio and its enforcement was attempted in Ohio, Ohio law governing all contracts should be applied by this Court.

B. Under Generally Applicable Principles of Ohio Contract Law, Courts Should Not Rewrite Contracts.

The common law of contracts in Ohio generally prohibits courts from rewriting contracts. Ohio courts have repeatedly held that it is not their province to modify the written agreement of contracting parties: "It is not the responsibility or function of this court to rewrite the parties' contract in order to provide for a more equitable result." *Wauseon Plaza Limited Partnership v. Wauseon Hardware Co.*, 807 N.E.2d 953 (Ohio Ct. App. 2004) (citing *Aultman Hosp. Assn. v. Community Mutual Ins. Co.*, 544 N.E.2d 920 (Ohio 1989) and *Ullmann v. May*, 72 N.E.2d 63 (Ohio 1947)).

Similarly, Ohio law does not permit courts to insert terms, implied or otherwise, into contracts. In *Ullmann v. May*, the Supreme Court of Ohio refused to interpret the terms of an employment contract to impute anything but their plain meaning. 72 N.E.2d 63. The court stated that, were it to construe the contract as urged by the appellant, the court would be "making . . . a new contract for the parties, which is not the function of a court." 72 N.E. 2d at 66. Again, in 1997, the Ohio high court stated: "It is not the responsibility or function of this court to rewrite the parties' contract in order to provide for a more equitable result." *Foster Wheeler Enviresponse, Inc. v. Franklin County Convention Facilities Authority*, 678 N.E.2d 519, 526 (Ohio 1997).

C. Ohio Courts Have Applied This General Principle to Arbitration Clauses, Consistently Striking Illegal Arbitration Clauses Rather Than Rewriting Them.

As mandatory arbitration clauses have spread rapidly in the last 10 years, certain businesses have experimented with particularly unfair and illegal clauses. In response, courts have repeatedly insisted that such clauses may not be abused, and must comport with basic standards of fairness. In case after case where courts have confronted abusive and illegal arbitration clauses, Ohio courts (and federal courts faithfully applying Ohio contract law) have struck the entire arbitration clause and have rejected requests that they rewrite or reform such clauses to make them legal.

The Supreme Court of Ohio applied the judicial prohibition against rewriting contract terms to arbitration clauses in *Schaefer v. Allstate v. Fallon-Murphy,* 590 N.E. 2d 1242 (Ohio 1992). The court heard a set of consolidated appeals concerning the inclusion in arbitration agreements of terms that rendered arbitration awards binding if under a certain dollar amount and non-binding if over that amount. The court reviewed the lower courts' holdings, some of which altered the terms of the contract to make all awards binding, some which made all awards non-binding, and decided that the proper remedy was not to attempt to fix the parties' invalid arbitration agreement, but strike it altogether from the contract. *Id.* at 1248. The court stated, "Given our conclusion that the provision is unenforceable . . . [the parties] are left with no valid alternative-dispute-resolution procedure and either party may seek access to the courts for the settlement of their disputes." *Id.* at 1249. The court refused to alter the agreement to correct the unenforceable clause.

The *Schaefer* decision has been interpreted by an Ohio appellate court in *State Farm v. Poyhanya* to stand for the proposition: "When an otherwise enforceable arbitration clause contains an invalid provision, the *entire* clause is invalid and unenforceable." Nos. 92 AP-40, 93 AP-41, 1992 WL 249858 at *3 (Ohio App. 10 Dist. Sept. 29, 1992) (emphasis added). In *Poyhanya*, the court considered a similar cap on binding arbitration awards, found it unfair, unconscionable, and unenforceable, and consequently struck the entire arbitration clause. *Id.* at *3–4. The parties were allowed to proceed to court. *Id.*

The Ohio Supreme Court likewise refused to enforce an arbitration clause that imposed prohibitive costs upon a consumer in a financing transaction, rather than rewrite the clause to make it enforceable. *See Williams v. Aetna Finance Company*, 700 N.E. 2d 859 (Ohio 1998).

In *Eagle v. Fred Martin Motors*, 809 N.E.2d 1161 (Ohio Ct. App. 2004), similarly, the court reviewed an arbitration clause in a car sales agreement of which the buyer was not provided a copy, that contained a confidentiality agreement and a negation of the buyer's right to assert her rights through a class action or as a private attorney general, and that shifted various arbitration costs to the buyer. Finding the arbitration clause at issue in the case both substantively and procedurally unconscionable, the court rendered the clause "unenforceable in its entirety." 809 N.E.2d at 1185. The court made no attempt to modify the clause or limit its unconscionable effects.

Federal courts faithfully applying Ohio law have reached the same results. In *Hagedorn v. Veritas Software Corp.*, 250 F. Supp. 2d 857 (S.D. Ohio 2002), the court rejected an ad-hoc attempt by a defendant to modify a faulty arbitration clause to avoid a finding of unenforceability. In *Hagedorn*, an arbitration clause in an employment agreement required the employee, a lifelong resident of Ohio, to participate in mandatory arbitration proceedings in San Francisco. As many other courts have done when faced with similar provisions in arbitration clauses, the court held that the clause was unduly burdensome and unenforceable. *Id.* at 862.

Having been caught with an abusive arbitration clause and facing the glare of judicial scrutiny, the defendant had a last-minute change of heart and informed the court in its reply brief that it was willing to conduct the arbitration in Ohio, instead of in California, as was required by the actual arbitration agreement. Applying Ohio law, the court properly based its review on the actual arbitration clause contained in the contract and disregarded the defendant's invitation to address a new agreement requiring arbitration in Ohio. *Id.* Accordingly, instead of altering the agreement to render it enforceable, the court properly severed the entire arbitration clause from the agreement and allowed the parties to proceed to court. *Id.* at 863.

Similarly, in *Garrett v. Hooters-Toledo*, 295 F. Supp. 2d 774, 777 (N.D. Ohio 2003), the court considered the claim of a female employee fired from Hooters because she became pregnant. The court found the arbitration clause in her employment agreement both procedurally and substantively unconscionable, due to its contents (a cost-splitting provision and pre-arbitration mediation requirement) and the situation in which it was presented to her (three months after she began working, and she was told that unless she returned it with her signature she could not work another shift). *Id.* at 780–84. Rather than simply striking the mediation requirement or shifting costs to the defendant (as did the district court in this case), the court concluded that the **entire** arbitration clause was unconscionable and unenforceable, and struck it from the contract. *Id.* at 783–84.

This body of Ohio law is entirely consistent with the approach required by the FAA. The U.S. Supreme Court has said that the enforcement of Arbitration agreements must be "according to their terms." *Volt Info. Sciences, Inc. v. Bd. of Trustees*, 489 U.S. 468, 479 (1989). Accordingly, if a particular agreement to arbitrate cannot be enforced according to its terms because it runs afoul of generally applicable state contract law, a court should refuse to enforce it. If a court strikes illegal provisions or adds other provisions to an arbitration clause, that is not enforcing an agreement according to its terms, and thus violates the FAA.

D. Numerous Courts Applying the Laws of Other Jurisdictions Have Also Held That It would Be Unjust And Inappropriate to Fix Abusive Arbitration Clauses So As To Render Them Enforceable.

Ohio's general law of contracts is hardly unusual. Indeed, a large number of federal and state courts throughout the United States have refused to re-write arbitration clauses that are unconscionable or otherwise unenforceable. The reason usually given is straightforward: if courts step in to fix illegal contracts, corporations will have no disincentive to drafting unfair and unconscionable contracts. This Court has recently held that there is a federal policy that courts should not rewrite or otherwise fix arbitration clauses containing illegal terms:

> To sever the costs and fees provision and force the employee to arbitrate a Title VII claim despite the employer's attempt to limit the remedies available would reward the employer for its actions and fail to deter similar conduct by others.... Under the contrary approach, an employer will not be deterred from routinely inserting such a deliberately illegal clause into the arbitration agreement it mandates for its employees if it knows that the worst penalty for such illegality is the severance of the clause after the employee has litigated the matter....

Cooper v. MRM Investment Co., 367 F.3d 493, 512 (6th Cir. 2004) (citations omitted). The *Cooper* case held that a district court decision that had refused to rewrite an arbitration "was also sound as a matter of federal policy." *Id.* The district court in this case violated that federal policy when it undertook to rewrite and fix Defendants' arbitration clause.

The concern expressed by this Court in *Cooper* has been voiced by numerous other courts. See *Lelouis v. Western Directory Co.*, 230 F. Supp. 2d 1214, 1225 (D. Or. 2001):

> [I]f I were to accept defendant's proposal [to pay the plaintiff's share of the costs of arbitration and to drop the provision of the clause shortening the period for limitations], employers would have no incentive to ensure that a coerced arbitration agreement is fair to both sides. Instead, the employer could write a one-sided agreement that favors the employer, and then make the bare minimum modifications necessary to obtain the court's approval.

See also Hooters of Am., Inc. v. Phillips, 173 F.3d 933, 940 (4th Cir. 1999) (where the improper provisions of an arbitration clause are "by no means insubstantial," the Court "therefore permit[ed the employee] to cancel the agreement and thus Hooters' suit to compel arbitration must fail."); *Paladino v. Avnet Computer Technologies, Inc.*, 134 F.3d 1054, 1058 (11th Cir. 1998) ("the presence of an unlawful provision in an arbitration agreement may serve to taint the entire arbitration agreement, rendering the agreement completely unenforceable, not just subject to judicial reformation"); *Graham Oil Co. v. ARCO Prods. Co.*, 43 F.3d 1244, 1249 (9th Cir. 1994) ("Our decision to strike the entire clause rests in part upon the fact that the offensive provisions clearly represent an attempt by ARCO to achieve through arbitration what Congress has expressly forbidden.... Such a blatant misuse of the arbitration procedure serves to taint the entire clause."); *Underwood v. Chef Francisco/Heinz*, 200 F. Supp.2d 475, 481 (E.D. Pa. 2002) ("When faced with situations similar to the one before us, other courts have declined to enforce the entire agreement rather than severing or reforming the offending clause."); *Browne v. Kline Tysons Imports, Inc.*, 190 F. Supp. 2d 827, 832 (E.D. Va. 2002) ("The Court finds [altering a provision in an arbitration clause] to be an impermissible attempt to rewrite the contract at issue."); *Flores v. Transamerica HomeFirst, Inc.*, 113 Cal. Rptr. 2d 376 (Cal. Ct. App. 2002) ("it strikes us as woefully unfair to allow HomeFirst at this late date—after a dispute has arisen and after the reverse mortgage has terminated—to refute the unconscionable aspect of the arbitration agreement which HomeFirst itself drafted and from which HomeFirst stood to benefit over the life of the loan.").

This concern is also strongly expressed in the Second Restatement of Contracts. It states, "[A] court will not aid a party who has taken advantage of his dominant bargaining power to extract from the other party a promise that is clearly so broad as to offend public policy by redrafting the agreement so as to make a part of the promise enforceable." Restatement (Second) of Contracts § 184 cmt. b.

Numerous courts around the country have also refused to rewrite arbitration clauses in a closely analogous situation. In a great many cases, corporate defendants facing judicial review of dubious arbitration clauses have volunteered to change the contract, to avoid having the clause struck down. In most cases, the change is that the defendant belatedly offers to pay the costs of arbitration. Just as these courts have refused to permit defendants to rewrite arbitration clauses, the district court below should have refused to rewrite the arbitration clause for both parties.

In *Popovich v. McDonalds*, 189 F. Supp. 2d 772, 779 (N.D. Ill. 2002), for example, the court explained:

> McDonald's has now offered to pay the arbitration fees.... This is not a basis for reconsideration of the Court's ruling. We agree with Popovich that McDonald's offer, which is inconsistent with the parties' contract, amounts to an offer for a new contract. Popovich is under no obligation to accept McDonald's offer, and the court is in no position to impose it. As a matter of elementary contract law, McDonald's cannot unilaterally modify the existing agreement.

See also Lelouis, 230 F. Supp. 2d at 1224–25 (refusing to allow a defendant to "voluntarily pay[]" the costs of arbitration, noting that "the fairness of a contract must be viewed as of the time the contract was formed" and that "this court may not re-write the contract for the parties"); *Cooper*, 367 F.3d at 512–13 ("MRM's offer was an impermissible attempt to vary the terms of a contract. There was neither a meeting of the minds nor consideration to support such a post hoc unilateral amendment of the agreement."); *Plattner v. Edge Solutions, Inc.*, 2004 WL 1575557 at *2 (N.D. Ill. May 27, 2004) (refusing to reconsider order denying arbitration when the defendant "fought tooth and nail on multiple fronts to preserve the arbitration clause as written and volunteered to pay only after the court ruled that the arbitration agreement was unenforceable.")

Even if this Court were to diverge from this general principle of law, this case falls cleanly into a category of cases where re-writing a contract is uniquely inappropriate. Courts have consistently refused to fix arbitration clauses that could only be made enforceable if the court were to affirmatively draft whole new terms, instead of merely striking out illegal terms. The U.S. Court of Appeals for the Fifth Circuit recently refused to compel arbitration in a similar situation:

> [T]he offensive provision here is the sentence in

which the customer, but not Centennial, is required to arbitrate. Saving the clause would require not that we exercise an invalid excrescence and then send the pared-down contract to arbitration but that we redraft the contract to add important new material—a duty on Centennial's part to arbitrate. The severability clause therefore cannot accomplish the needed repair. *Cf. Armendariz v. Found. Health Psychare Servs., Inc.*, 24 Cal. 4th 83, 99 (2000) (concluding that a severance could not save such an arbitration agreement.)

In conclusion, we hold that the district court did not err in denying Centennial's motion to compel arbitration.

Iberia Credit Bureau, Inc. v. Cingular Wireless LLC, 379 F.3d 159, 171 (5th Cir. 2004). *See also Ingle v. Circuit City Stores, Inc.*, 328 F.3d 1165, 1180 (9th Cir. 2003) ("Any earnest attempt to ameliorate the unconscionable aspects of Circuit City's arbitration agreement would require this court to assume the role of contract author rather than interpreter. Because that would extend far beyond the province of this court we are compelled to find the entire contract unenforceable."); *Plattner*, 2004 WL 1575557 at * 1 ("the court cannot rewrite the arbitration clause to compel arbitration in a forum not contemplated by the parties when the contract was executed.")

Moreover, even if it were possible to merely strike offending provisions to make an arbitration clause, courts have refused to do so when there were multiple offending provisions. In a case where an arbitration clause contained several unlawful provisions, the California Supreme Court held that it was "permeated" by unconscionability and must be struck in its entirety. *Armendariz v. Foundation Health Psychare Services, Inc.*, 24 Cal. 4th 83,126 (Cal. 2000); *see also Circuit City Stores, Inc. v. Adams*, 279 F.3d 889 (9th Cir. 2002) (adopting the *Armendariz* approach and striking an arbitration clause with multiple defects). The court noted that "Such multiple defects indicate a systematic effect to impose arbitration on an employee not simply as an alternative to litigation, but as an inferior forum that works to the employer's advantage. . . ." *Armendariz*, 24 Cal. 4th at 124.[+4] The Third Circuit, similarly, recently refused to rewrite an arbitration clause with multiple defects. *See Alexander v. Anthony Internat'l, L.P.*, 341 F.3d 256, 271 (3d Cir. 2003) ("The cumulative effect of so much illegality prevents us from enforcing the arbitration agreement. Because the sickness has infected the trunk, we must cut down the entire tree.") While the Alabama Supreme Court has been uniquely willing to rewrite arbitration clauses by striking unconscionable terms, it has drawn the line at cases in which there is only one such term. *See Anderson v. Ashyby*, 873 So.2d 168, 179 (Ala. 2003) ("However, the arbitration agreements considered in those cases [where the Court had struck the unconscionable terms] contained only one unconscionable provision; the arbitration agreement in this case is unconscionable in numerous respects. . . . The entire arbitration agreement is unconscionable and therefore unenforceable.")[+5]

III. BY COMPLETELY REWRITING DEFENDANTS' ARBITRATION CLAUSE, THE DISTRICT COURT BELOW DISREGARDED OHIO LAW AND FEDERAL POLICY.

As the Statement of the Case and the Statement of Facts make plain, the district court below completely rewrote Defendants' arbitration clause. Several different provisions were redrafted, replaced or excised. The end product bears little relationship to the actual contract that Defendants themselves had drafted and had originally attempted to enforce. This conduct plainly violates the legal standards of both Ohio law and federal policy, as set forth in the preceding section.

The district court recognized that the arbitration clause's provisions requiring Peter Scovill to pay enormous fees to arbitrate his claims was illegal, properly following this Court's ruling in *Morrison v. Circuit City Stores, Inc.*, 317 F.3d 646 (6th Cir. 2003). The district court ordered that this illegal provision be replaced with an entirely different fee provision, however, which would require Peter Scovill to pay the arbitration filing fees and then require Defendants to pay other costs of arbitration.

The district court recognized that arbitration clauses may not be used to effectively repeal civil rights statutes and strip employees of their substantive rights under those statutes. Accordingly, the district court acknowledged the illegality of the provisions of Defendants' arbitration clause which (a) replaced the statutory burdens of proof for employees asserting civil rights claims with a more restrictive burden of proof; (b) replaced the statutory scheme whereby losing plaintiffs are only responsible for Defendants' attorneys' fees if their claims are frivolous with a new loser pays rule that requires a non-prevailing employee to pay the employers' attorneys' fees. The district court failed to strike as illegal the provision shortening the statute of limitations period, however, on the grounds that the defendant offered in court not to enforce that provision.[+6]

This Court should re-affirm its holding in *Cooper* and follow Ohio precedent and the other consistent precedents cited above. First, this Court should make clear that Ohio law does not permit

---

[+4] California law is particularly relevant to this issue, because the Ohio Supreme Court has modeled its jurisprudence on the enforceability of arbitration clauses on the decisions of California courts. The leading Ohio case involving an unconscionability challenge to an arbitration clause is *Williams v. Aetna Fin. Co.*, 700 N.E.2d 859 (Ohio 1998). In *Williams*, the Ohio Supreme Court struck down as unconscionable an arbitration clause after noting that "[a] virtually identical arbitration clause was challenged as unenforceable in *Patterson v. ITT Consumer Fin. Corp.*, 14 Cal. App. 4th 1659 (1993)." 700 N.E.2d at 866. The Ohio Supreme Court went on to discuss and follow that California decision.

[+5] Similarly, where an arbitration clause (such as Defendants' clause here) gives the drafter great flexibility (Defendants may choose whether to arbitrate or go to court) but does not give similar flexibility to the individual (Peter Scovill must arbitrate his claims), courts have refused to rewrite such clauses. See *Gourley v. Yellow Transp., Ltd. Liab. Co.*, 178 F. Supp.2d 1196, 1205 (D. Colo. 2001) ("Yellow Cab's attempts [to have the court proceed to arbitration without the offending provisions] merely serve to underscore that the Handbook was written so as to provide unilateral flexibility to Yellow Cab regarding the Agreement's provisions, but no flexibility to its employees. I would therefore decline Yellow Cab's invitation to enforce the Arbitration Agreement absent the offending provisions.")

[+6] As Section II of this brief above establishes, this holding was in error: belated offers not to enforce illegal provisions do not curve the illegality of a contract.

the kind of contract rewriting engaged in by the district court. Accordingly, this Court should follow the lead of Ohio cases such as *Schaefer, Poyhanya, Hagedorn, Eagle, Garrett* and *Williams* and strike down the entire arbitration clause. Not one of these courts re-wrote the clause; each one invalidated the entire clause.

Second, this Court should follow cases such as *Iberia* and make clear that the district court erred by affirmatively drafting entirely new provisions not found in the original contract. The district court created from whole cloth a new set of rules for arbitrator compensation, drafting language and terms in a manner that is flatly improper.

Third, this Court should follow cases such as *Armendariz* and hold that the district court erred by rewriting *multiple* illegal provisions in the contract. It is particularly inappropriate for courts to intervene on behalf of a party and supply the legal acumen to create an enforceable contract, when it is clear from the existence of the numerous illegal provisions that the party was trying to draft a one-sided agreement. Courts should refuse to rewrite the "objectionable provisions [that] pervade the entire contract." *Adams*, 279 F.3d at 896.

Finally, this Court should refuse to rewrite this arbitration clause, because doing so will encourage future abuses. If the district court's decision is upheld, then corporate defendants who draft such agreements will not be held accountable for drafting illegal agreements, nor will they have any incentive to draft fair, legal arbitration clauses.

In short, the entire arbitration clause should fail, and the parties should proceed to court.

IV. THE DISTRICT COURT ERRED IN HOLDING THAT THE ARBITRATION CLAUSE WAS NOT UNCONSCIONABLE.

In Ohio, a contract is unconscionable if (1) there was an absence of meaningful choice or understanding of the terms on the part of one party (procedural unconscionability) and (2) the contract incorporated terms that were so unfair to one party that their enforcement would be unreasonable (substantive unconscionability). *See, e.g., Miller v. Household Realty Corp.*, No 81968, 2003 WL 21469782 at *7 (Ohio Ct. App. June 26, 2003) (citing *Collins v. Click Camera & Video, Inc.*, 621 N.E. 2d 1294, 1299 (Mont. Cty. 1993)).

As set forth in the Statement of the Case, while the district court held that several provisions of the arbitration clause were illegal, it held that the arbitration clause could not be unconscionable with respect to Peter Scovill because he was too sophisticated. R. 72, Opinion at 13, Apx. pg. __. The district court's decision on this point is in error.

A. The Arbitration Clause Was Promulgated In This Case In A Manner That Was Procedurally Unconscionable.

Procedural unconscionability is present where "there is an absence of meaningful choice for the contracting parties...." *Eagle v. Fred Martin Motors*, 809 N.E.2d 1161 (Ohio Ct. App. 2004) (citing *Collins*, 621 N.E. 2d 1294). In evaluating procedural unconscionability,

> [A] court will consider factors bearing on the relative bargaining position of the contracting parties, including age, education, intelligence, business acumen, experience in similar transactions, whether the terms were explained to the weaker party, and who drafted the contract.

Eagle, 809 N.E.2d at 1171.

The contract in this case is unconscionable under these factors. First, this is plainly a contract of adhesion. As set forth in the Statement of Facts, Peter Scovill had no choice but to sign this contract or be fired. In *Eagle*, the court discussed the adhesive nature of pre-printed form contracts, noted that they offer the consumer "no actual choice about the terms of arbitration" because they are offered on a "take it or leave it basis without affording [the] consumer realistic opportunity to bargain." *Id.* at 1179 (citation omitted).[+7] The Ohio Supreme Court has held that "the presumption in favor of arbitration should be substantially weaker in a case such as this, when there are strong indications that the contract at issue is an adhesion contract, and the arbitration clause itself appears to be adhesive in nature." *Williams v. Aetna Finance Co.*, 700 N.E.2d 859, 867 (Ohio 1998).[+8]

Second, Peter Scovill had no meaningful choice about entering the arbitration clause at issue here, because it was not possible for him to determine the costs of arbitration under Defendants' clause. While the record in this case contains extensive evidence of the costs imposed on employees by Defendants' arbitration clause, at the time that he was pressured to sign the contract Peter Scovill had no ready way to learn of those fees himself. Even if he had looked at AAA's website, he could only have learned of its filing fees (money that goes to the AAA itself to administer cases and perform the types of functions handled by court clerks), but not the far more important rates charged by the for-profit AAA arbitrators themselves.[+9] The hourly and/or daily rates of arbitrators are not posted

---

[+7] Many courts have held that non-negotiable arbitration clauses drafted by corporations and presented to consumers or employees on a take-it-or-leave-it basis are contracts of adhesion that are procedurally unconscionable. As the Third Circuit recently noted, procedural unconscionability "is generally satisfied if the agreement constitutes a contract of adhesion." *Alexander v. Anthony Int'l, L.P.*, 341 F.3d 256, 265 (3d Cir. 2003). *See also Ferguson v. Countrywide Credit Industries, Inc.*, 298 F.3d 778, 784 (9th Cir. 2002); *Circuit City Stores, Inc. v. Adams*, 279 F.3d 889, 893 (9th Cir. 2002); *ACORN v. Household Int'l, Inc.*, 211 F. Supp. 2d 1160, 1168 (N.D. Cal. 2002); *Flores v. Transamerica Homefirst, Inc.*, 113 Cal. Rptr. 2d 376, 382 (Cal. Ct. App. 2002); and *Comb v. Paypal, Inc.*, 218 F. Supp. 2d 1165, 1174–75 (N.D. Cal. 2002).

[+8] It is possible under Ohio law, however, for a contract to be unconscionable even if it is not a contract of adhesion. *See O'Donoghue v. Smythe, Cramer Co.*, 2002 WL 1454074 (Ohio Ct. App. July 3, 2002) (finding that there was no evidence that the contract was presented on a take-it-or-leave-it basis, but nonetheless holding that an arbitration clause which limited plaintiffs' remedies and imposed substantial arbitration costs was nonetheless unconscionable and unenforceable).

[+9] It is widely recognized in the case law that arbitrators' fees are separate from and generally much greater than the filing fees of the arbitration companies. *See, e.g., Phillips v. Associates Home Equity Services, Inc.*, 179 F. Supp.2d 840, 846 (N.D. Ill. 2001) ("Furthermore, the initial filing fee is far from the only cost involved in the arbitration. The AAA's Commercial Rules provide that the arbitrator's fees (which range from $750 to $5,000 per day, with an average of $1,800 per day in the Chicago area), travel expenses, rental of a hearing room, and other costs are borne equally by the parties...."); *Camacho v. Holiday Homes, Inc.*, 167 F. Supp.2d 892, 897 (W.D. Va. 2001) ("However, even

on the AAA's website or otherwise made available to employees such as Peter Scovill. Indeed, as a number of courts around the country have recognized, the only way that an employee can learn the magnitude of the costs that are likely to be imposed is to use the discovery process in litigation such as this to uncover what costs have been imposed upon other employees in the past. *See Ting v. AT&T*, 182 F.Supp.2d 902, 916–17 (N.D. Cal. 2002), *aff'd with respect to unconscionability*, 319 F.3d 1126 (9th Cir. 2003), *cert. denied*, 124 S. Ct. 53 (2003):

> Different AAA arbitrators charge different hourly rates. To estimate the cost of an arbitration to be conducted under the AAA's Commercial Rules, a claimant must learn the hourly rate of the arbitrator who will hear the case. To determine . . . [this rate], a claimant must first initiate an arbitration with the AAA. . . . This makes it difficult for a class member before filing to meaningfully estimate the cost to have the case arbitrated under the Commercial Rules. Neither the AAA website or rules, nor the AT&T website, provides a class member with any information about likely arbitrator's fees.

See also Camacho, 167 F.Supp.2d at 897 n.4 ("It is impossible to establish the exact amount Camacho would have to pay because the arbitrator sets the amount after the arbitration has been initiated."); *D.R. Horton, Inc. v. Green*, __ P.3d __, 2004 WL 2028999 (Nev. Sept. 13, 2004) ("the district court properly considered Horton's failure to disclose potential arbitration costs in examining the asymmetrical effects of the provision. We . . . conclude that the arbitration provision was also substantively unconscionable.").[+10] The only reason that this Court knows how much arbitration would have cost Peter Scovill is that after this litigation commenced, and facing a subpoena, the AAA reluctantly coughed up that data rather than have a witness appear at a deposition. The information was certainly not available to Peter Scovill when he was told, in effect, "agree to arbitration or be fired."

As set forth in Part II above, this Court should apply Ohio law to the question of whether this contract is unconscionable. Ohio courts have agreed that arbitration clauses that impose uncertain and undeterminable costs upon consumers are procedurally unconscionable. *See Eagle*, 809 N.E.2d at 1178 (finding, as one piece of evidence in favor of a finding of procedural unconscionability, that "even had Ms. Eagle read the arbitration clause thoroughly, nothing on the face of the clause could have put her on notice of excessive, prohibitive costs associated with the arbitration."); *Myers v. Terminex*, 697 N.E. 2d 277, 281 (Ohio Ct. Comm. Pleas 1998) ("[Plaintiff] was unaware of the undisclosed arbitration requirements. Such exorbitant filing fees [of $2000], "agreed to" unknowingly, would prevent a consumer of limited resources from having an impartial third party review his or her complaint against a business-savvy commercial entity. Therefore . . . the undisclosed filing fee requirement . . . is so one-sided as to oppress and unfairly surprise [the plaintiff].").

The district court did not focus upon the adhesive quality of the contract at issue, or the lack of information about the costs of arbitration. Instead, the totality of the district court's consideration of this issue was completed in two sentences: "Plaintiff, who is educated and experienced in his chosen profession, possessed a level of bargaining power sufficient to avoid any aspect of procedural unconscionability. Thus, the Court rejects any relief Plaintiff seeks on this ground." 312 F. Supp 2d at 964.

The district court's premise is apparently that no contract entered into by a television journalist could ever be unconscionable under Ohio law. As the district court would have it, an arbitration clause in a contract of adhesion that required individual employees to spend $1 million to vindicate a valid claim, or that would require consumers to travel enormous distances (perhaps to the deserts of New Zealand) to vindicate those claims, would still necessarily be enforceable if the employees were journalists who possessed college degrees. This argument is simply wrong. The law in Ohio (like other states) is *not* that "nothing done to a journalist is ever unconscionable."

While it is true that Peter Scovill was a journalist and capable of reading, that does not mean that he operates in a state of lawlessness where his employers are always free to impose whatever contract terms they wish. The Statement of Facts recited above reflects (a) that he had no particular education or training in legal or business issues; (b) that at the time he was presented the arbitration agreement, he was threatened with the loss of his job if he did not sign it; (c) that he had no readily available similar employment and was responsible for supporting his family and children; and (d) that after selling his home and moving his family to Ohio, and signing an agreement not to compete with the Defendant in Ohio, Peter Scovill truly had no realistic choice but to sign the agreement.

This case is thus remarkably similar to *Garrett v. Hooters-Toledo*, 295 F. Supp. 2d 774 (N.D. Ohio 2003). In *Garrett*, the employee had no opportunity to negotiate the terms of the agreement—it was presented to her three months after she began working; she was highly dependent on the job for her livelihood, and she was told that she must accept the agreement to be eligible for any job change, including promotions, bonuses, or transfers. *Id.* at 784. Like Ms. Garrett, Peter Scovill was presented with his arbitration clause weeks after starting his job. It was given to him after he had uprooted his family, sold his home, and relocated from Florida to Ohio in reliance on a written employment agreement that made no mention of arbitration at all. Like Ms. Garrett, he was also told, when he objected to the arbitration provisions, that they were non-negotiable and he must sign the agreement in order to keep his job. Scovill Dep. at 56–59, Apx. pg. __. Also like Ms. Garrett, he was highly dependent on this job for his livelihood: he was the only source of support for his three children, whom he had just moved to Ohio for the sole reason of beginning employment with Defendants. In addition, he had already signed a non-compete agreement,

---

if the initial $2,000 in administrative fees were waived or deferred, Mrs. Camacho has demonstrated that the additional costs of the arbitration process itself amount to an insurmountable financial burden to her.").

+10 Even when information is available on arbitration providers' websites, some courts have held that it is procedurally unconscionable to require individuals to go search out information about such systems. *See, e.g., Harper v. Ultimo*, 7 Cal. Rptr.3d 418, 422 (Cal. Ct. App. 2003) ("Here is the oppression: The inability to receive full relief is artfully hidden by merely referencing the Better Business Bureau rules, and not attaching those rules to the contract for the customer to sign. The customer is forced to go to another source to find out the full import of what he or she is about to sign—and must go to that effort prior to signing.")

which prevented him from seeking employment with any of Defendants' competitors. This Court should follow the persuasive reasoning of the *Garrett* case, and hold that Peter Scovill clearly lacked any meaningful choice but to sign the agreement.

B. The Arbitration Clause Is Substantively Unconscionable.

Defendants' arbitration clause is plainly substantively unconscionable. Indeed, numerous courts have struck down as substantively unconscionable arbitration clauses containing only a few of the dubious provisions contained in this clause.

1. The Provisions Limiting Peter Scovill's Substantive Rights Are Substantively Unconscionable.

As set forth in the Statement of Facts, the arbitration clause in this case did not merely force Peter Scovill to bring any claims that he might have under America's civil rights laws in a different forum. Instead, the "arbitration" clause also purported to alter the substance of those civil rights laws. The arbitration clause substituted a new burden of proof that was much heavier for Peter Scovill than the burden he would have under his statutory claims; the arbitration clause changed around the rules relating to attorneys' fees so that Peter Scovill faced a very different set of rules than he would have faced under the normal civil rights laws; the arbitration clause contained a new and dramatically shorter statute of limitations (a measly 90 days); and on and on. These contractual provisions, all drafted by defendants to tilt the playing field in their favor, not only violate the civil rights statutes themselves (as the district court held), they are also unconscionable as a matter of Ohio law.

The U.S. Supreme Court has stated repeatedly that arbitration must allow a party to "effectively vindicate" its rights. *Mitsubishi Motors Corp. v. Soler Chrysler-Plymouth, Inc.*, 473 U.S. 614, 637 (1985); *Gilmer v. Interstate/Johnson Lane Corp.*, 500 U.S. 20, 28 (1991) (quoting *Mitsubishi*). As this Court has noted, it is not permitted for arbitration clauses to strip individuals of their statutory rights:

> [E]ven if arbitration is generally a suitable forum for resolving a particular statutory claim, the specific arbitral forum provided under an arbitration agreement must nevertheless allow for the effective vindication of that claim. Otherwise, arbitration of the claim conflicts with the statute's purpose of both providing individual relief and generally deterring unlawful conduct through enforcement of its provisions.

Floss v. Ryan's Family Steak Houses, 211 F.3d at 313 (citation omitted). This Court has repeatedly reaffirmed its holding in *Floss* that arbitration clauses may not be enforced where they would bar parties from effectively vindicating their statutory rights. *See Morrison v. Circuit City Stores, Inc.*, 317 F.3d 646, 658–59 (6th Cir. 2003); and *McMullen v. Meijer, Inc.*, 337 F.3d 697, 703 (6th Cir. 2003).

Arbitration clauses that impose excessive costs not only violate the civil rights statutes, they also violate the state common law of contracts. A number of courts have also struck down as unconscionable arbitration clauses that stripped employees or consumers of their substantive statutory rights. *See, e.g., Circuit City Stores, Inc. v. Adams*, 279 F.3d 889, 894 (9th Cir. 2002); *Graham Oil Co. v. ARCO Products Co.*, 43 F.3d 1244, 1247 (9th Cir. 1994); *Paladino v. Avnet Computer Technologies., Inc.*, 134 F.3d 1054, 1062 (11th Cir. 1998) (Cox., J. concurring for majority of the panel); *Gourley v. Yellow Transp., L.L.C.*, 178 F. Supp. 2d 1196 (D. Colo. 2001); *Armendariz v. Foundation Health Psychare Services, Inc.*, 6 P.3d 669, 681 (Cal. 2000); *State of W. Va. ex rel. Dunlap v. Honorable Irene C. Berger*, 567 S.E.2d 265 (W. Va. 2002); *Holt v. O'Brien*, 862 So.2d 87 (Fla. Dist. Ct. App. 2003); *Flyer Hill Printing Co. v. Hill*, 805 So.2d 829 (Fla. Dist. Ct. App. 2001); and *Carll v. Terminix Int'l Co.*, 793 A.2d 921 (Pa. Superior Ct. 2002). This Court should apply this well established body of law to Defendants' clause here, and hold that it is substantively unconscionable.

2. The Provisions Imposing Prohibitive Costs Are Substantively Unconscionable.

As the Statement of Facts sets forth, and as the district court found, Defendants' arbitration clause imposed enormous and prohibitive costs upon Peter Scovill. To proceed with his claims arbitration, Peter Scovill would have been required to pay "a minimum" of $15,000 to the AAA and its arbitrator and probably quite a bit more.

Ohio courts have not hesitated to strike down arbitration clauses that imposed similarly excessive costs of arbitration on individuals. In *Eagle v. Fred Martin*, for example, the Ohio Court of Appeals noted that an arbitration clause that posed the possibility that a consumer might be required to pay substantial arbitration fees would deter the consumer from vindicating their rights. The court noted that where a consumer is not guaranteed a waiver of all fees that he or she would be required to pay in arbitration, the consumer will be " 'inclined to err on the side of caution, especially when the worst-case scenario would mean not only losing on their substantive claims but also the imposition of the costs of the arbitration.' " 809 N.E.2d at 1174 (citation omitted). Therefore the consumer "is caught between *scylla* and *charybdis*, potentially unable to obtain meaningful relief under the NAF terms and yet unable to proceed to the courts. *Id.* In *Eagle*, the Court found unconscionable fees that would require a consumer to pay somewhere between $4,200.00 and $6,000.00 in arbitration fees. "[T]hese arbitration costs and fees are prohibitive, unreasonable, and unfair as applied to Ms. Eagle. Therefore, we conclude, that, based on these prohibitive costs alone, the arbitration clause in general is substantively unconscionable." *Id.*, 809 N.E.2d at 1177.

The conclusion that requiring individuals to pay arbitration fees amounting to many thousands of dollars is unconscionable is hardly a new or radical idea. Half a dozen courts across the country faced with factual records similar to that in this case have found the AAA's fees to be prohibitively high.

In *Ting v. AT&T*, 182 F.Supp.2d 902 (N.D. Cal. 2002), *aff'd with respect to unconscionability*, 319 F.3d 1126 (2003), *cert. denied*, 124 S. Ct. 53 (2003), for example, the district court examined an exhaustive evidentiary record on the average arbitration costs under the AAA's Commercial Rules. It found that the average daily rate for an arbitrator is nearly $2000, and that the AAA, though it offers the possibility of fee waivers, typically does not waive fees but instead defers them until the time of the hearing. *Id.* at 917. The court held that these high costs, plus the additional case costs and service fees, would clearly "deter many potential litigants from proceeding" with arbitration. *Id.* at 934.

The *Ting* court's conclusions are entirely consistent with the decisions of a host of other courts. *See Alexander v. Anthony Int'l,*

L.P., 341 F.3d 256, 269–270 (3d Cir. 2003) (requiring employee to pay costs ranging from $800 to $1,000 a day for arbitration "effectively denied [the employee] recompense for [the employer's] alleged misconduct, resulting in an unfair advantage for their former employer.... We therefore must find that the 'loser pays' provision is unconscionable as to these particular plaintiffs."); *Camacho v. Holiday Homes, Inc.*, 167 F.Supp.2d 892 (W.D.Va. 2001) (arbitration clause precluding consumer from effectively vindicating her statutory rights because the fees under AAA's Rules were financially prohibitive was unenforceable); *Popovich v. McDonald's Corp.*, 189 F. Supp.2d 772 (N.D.Ill. 2002) (refusing to enforce an arbitration clause on the grounds that under the AAA's Rules, "the costs of arbitration are likely to be staggering," and finding that the costs of arbitrating the consumer claims at issue in that case were likely to amount to $48,000 to $126,000); *Phillips v. Associates Home Equity Services*, 179 F.Supp.2d 840 (N.D.Ill. 2001) (arbitration clause not enforced in Truth in Lending Act suit because the costs of arbitration under AAA's Rules are prohibitive, noting that the filing fees alone would amount to $4,000); *Murphy v. Mid-West Nat'l Life Ins. Co. Of Tenn.*, 78 P.3d 766 (Idaho 2003) (arbitration clause requiring insured to pay at least $2,500 to have a claim heard was unconscionable; it "is an expensive alternative to litigation that precludes the Murphys from pursuing the claim"); *McNulty v. H&R Block, Inc.*, 843 A.2d 1267 (Penn Super. Ct. 2004) (arbitration clause was unconscionable for imposing impermissible forum costs against consumers); *Mendez v. Palm Harbor Homes, Inc.*, 45 P.3d 594, 605 (Wash. Ct. App. 2002) (arbitration clause requiring consumer bringing claims involving a defective home was unconscionable because the costs under the AAA's Rules were unconscionable; "Avoiding the public court system in a way that effectively denies citizens access to resolving everyday societal disputes is unconscionable"); *Arnold v. Goldstar Fin. Sys., Inc.*, 2002 WL 1941546 *10 (N.D.Ill. Aug. 22, 2002) (consumer cannot be required to arbitrate claims because of prohibitive costs under AAA's Rules); *Giordano v. Pep Boys—Manny, Moe & Jack, Inc.*, 2001 WL 484360 (E.D.Pa. Mar. 29, 2001) (fees under AAA rules would deter plaintiff's vindication of claims in arbitration).

3. The One-Way Nature of the Clause is Unconscionable.

Defendants' arbitration clause is also substantively unconscionable because it is one-sided: Defendants retained their right to go to court, but required Peter Scovill to arbitrate any claims that he might have. Numerous state and federal courts have held that non-negotiable and one-sided arbitration clauses are unconscionable or otherwise unlawful under applicable state contract law. These courts recognize that it is unfair for businesses to maximize their advantage through adhesive contracts requiring unsophisticated and unsuspecting employees to resolve their legal claims through arbitration, while refusing to accept comparable limitations on their own rights. In Ohio, the leading case dealing with unconscionable arbitration clauses is the Ohio Supreme Court's decision in *Williams v. Aetna*, 700 N.E.2d 859, and in that case the Court noted with concern that the arbitration clause preserved for the finance company the judicial remedy of foreclosure on the debtor's mortgage but restricted the debtor's remedies solely to arbitration.

A leading decision addressing the issue in detail is *Armendariz v. Foundation Health Psychare Serv's, Inc.*, 6 P.3d 669 (Cal. 2000), which held that it is unconscionable for a business to require employees to submit to binding arbitration as a condition of employment while reserving the right to sue employees in court, absent some special justification for this disparity in rights. *Id.* at 692. Based on general standards of unconscionability, *id.* at 690, the California Supreme Court held that it was "unfairly one-sided for an employer with superior bargaining power to impose arbitration on the employee as plaintiff but not to accept such limitations when it seeks to prosecute a claim against the employee," absent some justification based on "business realities." *Id.* at 692.

In *Iwen v. U.S. West Direct*, 977 P.2d 989 (Mont. 1999), the court similarly held that a telephone company's arbitration clause applying to all claims by advertising customers but not to its own collection claims was unconscionable under Montana law:

> Drafted as such, the weaker bargaining party has no choice but to settle all claims arising out of the contract through final and binding arbitration, whereas the more powerful bargaining party has the unilateral right to settle a dispute for collection of fees pursuant to the agreement in a court of law.
>
> ...U.S. West pointedly protected itself by preserving its constitutional right of access to the judicial system while at the same time completely removing that right from the advertiser.

Id. at 994, 995–96. *Iwen* was recently quoted by the Tennessee Supreme Court in *Taylor v. Butler*, __ S.W.3d __, 2004 WL 1925423 (Tenn. Aug. 31, 2004), in the course of an opinion striking down as unconscionable a similarly one-way, non-mutual arbitration clause. *See also Gibson v. Neighborhood Health Clinics, Inc.*, 121 F.3d 1126 (7th Cir. 1997) (Indiana law voids one-sided clause for lack of mutual obligation); *Ticknor v. Choice Hotels, Inc.*, 265 F.3d 931 (9th Cir. 2001) (Montana law); *Circuit City Stores, Inc. v. Adams*, 279 F.3d 889 (9th Cir. 2002) (California law); *Luna v. Household Finance Corp.*, 236 F. Supp. 2d 1166 (W.D. Wash. Nov. 4, 2002) (Washington law); *Stevens/Leinweber/Sullens, Inc. v. Holm Development and Mgmt, Inc.*, 795 P.2d 1308 (Ariz. App. 1990); *Worldwide Insurance Group v. Klopp*, 603 A.2d 788 (Del. 1992) (one-sided arbitration appeal provision); *State of West Virginia ex rel. Dunlap v. Berger*, 567 S.E.2d 265 (W. Va. 2002); *Lytle v. Citifinancial Services, Inc.*, 810 A.2d 643 (Pa. Super. Ct. Oct. 24, 2002) (home equity lender's arbitration clause preserving judicial foreclosure and debt collection creates "presumption of unconscionability"); *cf. Penn v. Ryan's Family Steakhouses*, 269 F.3d 753, 760–61 (7th Cir. 2001) (contract between employee and third party arbitration service, required as condition of employment, held unenforceable for lack of mutual obligation under Indiana law); *Showmethemoney Check Cashers, Inc. v. Williams*, 27 S.W.3d 361, 367 (Ark. 2000) (payday lender's arbitration clause preserving judicial collection actions is void for lack of mutuality because arbitration clauses "should not be used as a shield against litigation by one party while simultaneously reserving solely to itself the sword of a court action.").

CONCLUSION

The district court erred when it redrafted a series of unenforceable provisions of the arbitration agreement to render them enforceable. Such judicial intrusion into the terms of contracts is not allowed under Ohio law. This court should properly apply Ohio law, reverse the district court's order compelling arbitration, and strike the unenforceable and unconscionable arbitration clause drafted by Defendants.

The district court also erred in finding that the arbitration clause was not unconscionable. The clause at issue is a classic contract of adhesion, that was imposed upon Peter Scovill on a take-it-or-leave-it basis, at a time when Defendants knew he would have no choice. The arbitration clause is also substantively unconscionable because it stripped Peter Scovill of numerous substantive statutory rights, imposed excessive costs of arbitration upon him, and was one-sided and non-mutual. This Court should hold that the arbitration was unconscionable, and therefore unenforceable.

If the lower court opinion is permitted to stand, it will reward corporate employers who include as many illegal provisions as possible in their arbitration provisions, knowing that the courts will rewrite or separate the provisions. At the same time, allowing the decision to stand will effectively prevent employees from vindicating their civil rights, as the onerous clauses will cause them to believe that they are jeopardizing their family's resources should they fail.

Date: October 4, 2004

[Attorneys for Plaintiff-Appellant]

Appendix F — Briefs on Unconscionability of Arbitration Clauses Restricting Class Actions

These briefs are also available in Microsoft Word and Adobe Acrobat (PDF) format on the CD-Rom accompanying this volume.

F.1 Opening Brief Focusing on Unconscionability Based on Class Action Ban (Insight)

IN THE COURT OF APPEALS
OF KENTUCKY

—————————————)
MICHAEL SCHNUERLE, AMY)
GILBERT, LANCE GILBERT,)
AND ROBIN WOLFF,)
              Appellants,)
)
v.)
) Civil No.
INSIGHT COMMUNICA-)
TIONS COMPANY, L.P. AND)
INSIGHT COMMUNICA-)
TIONS MIDWEST, L.L.C.,)
              Appellees.)
—————————————)

APPELLANTS' OPENING BRIEF

INTRODUCTION

This is a putative consumer class action alleging that a broadband internet provider breached its contract and violated various consumer protection statutes. Michael Schnuerle, Amy Gilbert, Lance Gilbert, and Robin Wolff (collectively, "Consumer Plaintiffs") appeal the trial court's order enforcing Insight Communications Company, L.P. and Insight Communications Midwest, LLC's (collectively, "Insight") mandatory arbitration clause, which bans customers from bringing or being a part of a class action.

STATEMENT CONCERNING ORAL ARGUMENT

Appellants believe that oral argument would be helpful to the Court in deciding the issues presented. In the last few years, numerous state and federal appellate courts around the country have addressed the enforceability of class action bans embedded in arbitration clauses, and this is an important and controversial issue that has divided the courts. This Court's decision in this case is likely to have enormous ramifications for the future of consumer protection law in this state.

While, as this brief will establish, two state supreme courts, intermediate appellate courts in four different states, and numerous federal courts have struck down class action bans as unconscionable and unenforceable within the last 12 months, this important issue is one of first impression in Kentucky, that has not yet been raised in this Court or the Kentucky Supreme Court.

TABLE OF CONTENTS

STATEMENT OF POINTS AND AUTHORITIES
INTRODUCTION
STATEMENT CONCERNING ORAL ARGUMENT
STATEMENT OF POINTS AND AUTHORITIES
STATEMENT OF THE CASE
   I. Underlying Facts About the Dispute.
   II. Facts Relating to the Enforceability of the Class Action Ban Embedded in Insight's Arbitration Clause.
   III. Procedural Facts.
KRS 367.110, *et seq.*[*]
ARGUMENT
   I. STANDARD OF REVIEW.
Conseco Finance Servicing Corp. v. Wilder, 47 S.W.3d 335 (Ky. App. 2001)
Louisville PeterBuilt, Inc. v. Cox, 132 S.W.3d 850 (Ky. 2004)
Stutler v. T.K. Constructors Inc., 448 F.3d 343 (6th Cir. 2006)
Muhammad v. Cnty. Bank of Rehobeth Beach, 912 A.2d 88 (N.J. 2006) *cert. denied*, ___ S. Ct. ___, 2007 WL 120665 (2007).
   II. THE PROVISION OF INSIGHT'S ARBITRATION CLAUSE THAT PROHIBITS CLASS PROCEEDINGS IS UNCONSCIONABLE AND UNENFORCEABLE.
     A. To the Extent that Plaintiffs Must Establish that the Class Action Ban Is Procedurally Unconscionable, They Have Done So.
Conseco Finance Servicing Corp. v. Wilder, 47 S.W.3d 335 (Ky. App. 2001)
Adler v. Fred Lind Manor, 103 P.3d 773 (Wash. 2004)
Vasquez-Lopez v. Beneficial Oregon, Inc., 152 P.3d 940 (Or. Ct. App. 2007)

---

* [*Editor's Note: Citations throughout brief as in original.*]

Appx. F.1   *Consumer Arbitration Agreements*

Wisconsin Auto Title Loans, Inc. v. Jones, 714 N.W.2d 155 (Wis. 2006)
Simpson v. MSA of Myrtle Beach, Inc., ___ S.E.2d ___, 2006 WL 4388016 (S.C. Mar. 26, 2007)
Williams v. Aetna Fin. Co., 700 N.E.2d 859 (Ohio 1998)
Jones v. Bituminous Casualty Corp., 821 S.W.2d 798 (Ky. 1991)
Coady v. Cross Country Bank, Inc., 729 N.W.2d 732 (Wis. App. 2007)
Kinkel v. Cingular Wireless, L.L.C., 828 N.E.2d 812 (Ill. Ct. App. 2005)
Powertel, Inc. v. Bexley, 743 So.2d 570 (Fla. Ct. App.1999)
Valley Constr. Co., Inc. v. Perry Host Mgmt. Co., 796 S.W.2d 365 (Ky. App. 1990)
Louisville Bear Safety Serv., Inc. v. South Central Bell Telephone Co., 571 S.W.2d 438 (Ky. App. 1978)
Discover Bank v. Superior Court (Boehr), 113 P.3d 1100 (Cal. 2005)
Schwartz v. Alltel Corp., 2006 WL 2243649, at *6 (Ohio Ct. App. 2006)
Forsythe v. BancBoston Mort. Corp., 135 F.3d 1069 (6th Cir. 1997)
Small v. HCF of Perrysburg, Inc., 823 N.E.2d 19 (Ohio Ct. App. 2004)
Ting v. AT&T, 182 F. Supp.2d 902 (N.D. Cal. 2002) *aff'd in relevant part*, 319 F.3d 1126 (9th Cir. 2003)
American Gen. Fin., Inc. v. Branch, 793 So.2d 738 (Ala. 2000)
Steinhardt v. Rudolph, 422 So.2d 884 (Fla. Ct. App. 1982)
Kloss v. Edward D. Jones & Co., 54 P.3d 1 (Mont. 2002)
Fairfield Leasing Corp. v. Techni-Graphics, Inc., 607 A.2d 703 (N.J. Super. 1992)
Skirchak v. Dynamics Research Corp., Inc., 432 F. Supp.2d 175 (D. Mass. 2006)
Muhammad v. Cnty. Bank of Rehobeth Beach, 912 A.2d 88 (N.J. 2006) *cert. denied*, ___ S. Ct. ___, 2007 WL 120665 (2007).

B. The Class Action Ban is Substantively Unconscionable.

Conseco Finance Servicing Corp. v. Wilder, 47 S.W.3d 335 (Ky. App. 2001)
Discover Bank v. Superior Court (Boehr), 113 P.3d 1100 (Cal. 2005)
Ting v. AT&T, 182 F. Supp.2d 902 (N.D. Cal. 2002) *aff'd in relevant part*, 319 F.3d 1126 (9th Cir. 2003)

   1. Kentucky Law Does Not Permit Exculpatory Clauses in Adhesive Contracts Between Parties of Differing Bargaining Strengths for Claims Brought Under Remedial Statutes.

Meiman v. Rehabilitation Center, Inc., 444 S.W.2d 78 (Ky. Ct. App. 1969).
Hargis v. Baize, 168 S.W.3d 36 (Ky. 2005)
Cumberland Valley Contractors, Inc., v. Bell Cnty Coal Corp., ___ S.W.3d ___, 2007 WL 188041, *4 (Ky. 2007)
Simpson v. MSA of Myrtle Beach, Inc., ___ S.E.2d ___, 2006 WL 4388016 (S.C. Mar. 26, 2007)
Floss v. Ryan's Family Steak Houses, 211 F.3d 306 (Ky. 2000)
Cowan v. Telcom Directories, Inc., 806 S.W.2d 638 (Ky. 1991)
Ford Motor Co. v. Mayes, 575 S.W.2d 480 (Ky. App. 1978)

   2. The Class Action Ban Embedded in Insight's Arbitration Clause Effectively Operates As An Exculpatory Clause.

Kristian v. Comcast Corp. 446 F.3d 25 (1st Cir. 2006)
Luna v. Household Fin. Corp. III, 236 F. Supp.2d 1166 (W.D. Wash. 2002)
Ting v. AT&T, 182 F. Supp.2d 902 (N.D. Cal. 2002) *aff'd in relevant part*, 319 F.3d 1126 (9th Cir. 2003)
Discover Bank v. Superior Court (Boehr), 113 P.3d 1100 (Cal. 2005)
Muhammad v. Cnty. Bank of Rehobeth Beach, 912 A.2d 88 (N.J. 2006) *cert. denied*, ___ S. Ct. ___, 2007 WL 120665 (2007).
Kinkel v. Cingular Wireless, L.L.C., 828 N.E.2d 812 (Ill. Ct. App. 2006)
Powertel, Inc. v. Bexley, 743 So.2d 570 (Fla. Ct. App.1999)
Reuter v. Davis, 2006 WL 3743016, *4 (Fla. Cir. Ct. 2006)
Eagle v. Fred Martin Motor Co., 809 N.E.2d 1161 (Ohio Ct. App. 2004)
Vasquez-Lopez v. Beneficial Oregon, Inc. 152 P.3d 940 (Or. Ct. App. 2007)
Thibodeau v. Comcast Corp. 912 A.2d 874 (Pa. Super. Ct. 2006)
Whitney v. Alltel Commn'cs., Inc., 173 S.W.3d 300 (Mo. Ct. App. 2005)
State ex rel. Dunlap v. Berger, 567 S.E.2d 265 (W. Va. 2002)
Amchem Products, Inc. v. Windsor, 521 U.S. 591 (1997)

   3. The Fact that Insight's Class Action Ban is Not Overtly Exculpatory, But Merely Exculpatory in Effect, Does Not Change Its Unconscionable Nature.

Gilmer v. Interstate/Johnson Lane Corp., 500 U.S. 20 (1991)
Mitsubishi Motors Corp. v. Soler Chrysler-Plymouth, Inc., 473 U.S. 614 (1985)
Rollins, Inc., Garrett, 176 Fed.Appx. 968 (11th Cir. 2006)
Carnegie v. Household Int'l, Inc., 376 F.3d 656 (7th Cir. 2004)
EEOC v. Waffle House, 534 U.S. 279 (2002)
Kristian v. Comcast Corp., 446 F.3d 25 (1st Cir. 2006)
Ting v. AT&T, 182 F. Supp.2d 902 (N.D. Cal. 2002) *aff'd in relevant part*, 319 F.3d 1126 (9th Cir. 2003)
Discover Bank v. Superior Court (Boehr), 113 P.3d 1100 (Cal. 2005)
Green Tree Fin. Corp. v. Randolph, 531 U.S. 79 (2000)
Swain v. Auto Servs., Inc., 128 S.W.3d 103 (Mo. App. 2003)

   4. The Possibility that Prevailing Consumers Might Receive Attorneys Fees Under Kentucky Consumer Rights Statutes Does Not Make It Likely that Many Consumers Could Find Competent Counsel to Bring Claims Such as these on an Individual Basis.

KRS 367.220(3) 20
Alexander v. S&M Motors, Inc., 28 S.W.3d 303 (Ky. 2000)
Hensley v. Eckerhart, 461 U.S. 424 (1983)
James v. Thermal Master, Inc., 563 N.E.2d 917 (Ohio Ct. App. 1988)
F.H. Krear & Co. v. Nineteen Named Trustees, 810 F.2d 1250 (2d Cir. 1987)

Muhammad v. Cnty. Bank of Rehobeth Beach, 912 A.2d 88 (N.J. 2006) *cert.denied*, ___ S. Ct. ___, 2007 WL 120665 (2007)

Kristian v. Comcast Corp., 446 F.3d 25 (1st Cir. 2006)

Discover Bank v. Superior Court (Boehr), 113 P.3d 1100 (Cal. 2005)

Kinkel v. Cingular Wireless, L.L.C., 828 N.E.2d 812 (Ill. Ct. App. 2006)

Szetela v. Discover Bank, 97 Cal.App. 4th 1094 (Cal.App. 2002)

C. The Secrecy Provision in Insight's Arbitration Clause Is Substantively Unconscionable.

Zuver v. Airtouch Communications, Inc., 103 P.3d 753 (Wash. 2004)

Kinkel v. Cingular Wireless, L.L.C., 828 N.E.2d 812 (Ill. Ct. App. 2006)

Ting v. AT&T, 182 F. Supp.2d 902 (N.D. Cal. 2002) *aff'd in relevant part*, 319 F.3d 1126 (9th Cir. 2003)

Torrance v. Aames Finding Corp., 242 F. Supp.2d 862 (D. Oregon 2002)

Luna v. Household Fin. Corp. III, 236 F. Supp.2d 1166 (W.D. Wash. 2002)

III. GENERALLY APPLICABLE PRINCIPLES OF KENTUCKY CONTRACT LAW ARE NOT PREEMPTED BY THE FEDERAL ARBITRATION ACT.

9 U.S.C. § 2

Doctor's Assocs., Inc. v. Casarotto, 517 U.S. 681 (1996)

Muhammad v. Cnty. Bank of Rehobeth Beach, 912 A.2d 88 (N.J. 2006) *cert.denied*, ___ S. Ct. ___, 2007 WL 120665 (2007).

Kinkel v. Cingular Wireless, L.L.C., 828 N.E.2d 812 (Ill. Ct. App. 2006)

Ky. Const., § 14

CONCLUSION

APPENDIX

STATEMENT OF THE CASE

I. Underlying Facts About the Dispute.

Beginning on or about April 18, 2006, Insight Communications Company, L.P. and Insight Communications Midwest, L.L.C. ("Insight") failed to provide continuous access to its Broadband Internet Service to Appellants, Michael Schnuerle, Amy Gilbert, Lance Gilbert, and Robin Wolff and the members of the putative class (the "Consumer Plaintiffs").[1] (Record ("R.") 6, Complaint, ¶ 26.)[2] Insight also failed to properly and promptly notify consumers of its failure to provide such services, failed to promptly remedy the lack of services, failed to provide an alternative high-speed Internet service, disseminated misleading or incorrect information to consumers who inquired about the failures, failed to protect consumers from deletion of information caused by the failure, and charged consumers for services it did not provide. (R. 6, Complaint, ¶ 28.)

In particular, the Consumer Plaintiffs presented sworn affidavits to the trial court. (*See* R. 585–602, Affidavits ("Aff.") of Michael Schnuerle, Lance Gilbert, David Johnson, Shawn Roddy, Clarissa Duvall, and Karen Straub.)[3] This sworn evidence establishes that for a period of time in April and May of 2006, the Consumer Plaintiffs were unable to access the Internet or send or receive e-mails. (Appendix ("App.") 3–8, ¶ 9; App. 4, ¶ 8.). In addition, the sworn evidence indicates that as consumers contacted Insight about their problems, they encountered long waits on the phone without actually reaching anyone (App. 3 & 8, Affs., ¶ 10); uninformative responses from Insight employees, (App. 6 & 8, Affs., ¶ 10; Gilbert., ¶ 9; Duvall, ¶ 11); and untrue responses from Insight that promised to but did not solve the problem. (*See id.*)

II. Facts Relating to the Enforceability of the Class Action Ban Embedded in Insight's Arbitration Clause.

Consumers in Louisville cannot obtain cable Internet broadband services without signing Insight's contract. Insight was and is the only provider of cable Internet broadband services in Louisville, Kentucky. (App. 3–8, ¶ 3.) Thus, if consumers wanted to receive high speed, cable broadband, Insight provided the only option. (*See id.*) In order to receive the service, Insight required its customers to sign a service agreement or check off on the Internet his or her approval to a service agreement. (*See* App. 10, Exhibit 8 to Pltfs' Response to Mot. to Dismiss, Service Agreement.) The service agreements are drafted and provided by Insight. These service agreements contain a mandatory arbitration clause that requires consumers to give up their right to a jury trial, and deprives consumers of the right to pursue a class action, either in court or in arbitration.

As a highly profitable and sophisticated corporation, Insight's bargaining power is far superior to that of individual, unrepresented, consumers. Headquartered in New York, Insight is one of the largest cable operators in the United States, and has 1.3 million customers in Illinois, Indiana, Kentucky, and Ohio. (R. 1, 3, Cplt., ¶¶ 2, 11, & 12.) It claims 514,800 Broadband Internet Service Customers. (R. 2, Cplt., ¶ 2; App. 9, Exhibit 1 to Plaintiffs' Response to Motion to Dismiss (excerpts from Insight's website).) Moreover, Insight boasts on its website of conducting "extensive, sophisticated research" on its customers. The Consumer Plaintiffs are less sophisticated and lack bargaining power relative to Insight. A number of consumers testified that they had not consulted with an attorney when they purchased broadband from Insight. (App. 3, 6–8, ¶ 7; App. 4, ¶ 6.)

The service agreement is a contract of adhesion, offered to Insight customers on a "take-it-or-leave-it" basis. The service agreements are standard form contracts, drafted entirely by Insight that customers may not alter. There is simply no negotiation as to the terms.

The agreement was communicated in a manner that ensured that few consumers would read and understand the arbitration clause. The testimony established, for example, that a number of consumers who signed up for Insight's broadband service on the Internet did not notice the arbitration clause and its ban on class actions because they were shown a box of text containing the terms of the agreement, and the class action ban and the arbitration clause did not appear within the viewing range in the text box. (App. 3, 8, ¶¶ 13 & 14; App. 4, ¶ 12.) In order to view the arbitration clause and

---

[1] Such service includes "all Software, downloadable materials, and other information that relates to Insight Broadband High Speed Internet Service, which may include Internet access, e-mail services, usage of portal or other Web site. . . ." (Record 5, Complaint, ¶ 19.)

[2] For the convenience of the Court, the pleadings cited herein are included in the Appendix.

[3] The consumer affidavits are included in the appendix at tabs 3 through 8.

its ban on class actions, consumers would have had to scroll down the screen. (*See id.*) A number of customers testified that no one at Insight pointed the arbitration provision out to them, or explained anything about the arbitration provision or its ban on class actions. (App. 3–8, Affs., ¶ 5.) Customers also testified that they did not understand that they had given up any rights to go to court or to have a jury trial when they signed the user agreement, and that they did not know what an arbitration agreement was. (App. 3–8, ¶¶ 6 & 7.)

The evidence before the trial court demonstrated that the Consumer Plaintiffs cannot effectively vindicate their legal rights on an individual basis. Six consumer witnesses signed sworn affidavits that because of the costs of arbitration or litigation and the relatively small amount of money in controversy, they would not pursue this matter on an individual basis, either through arbitration or small claims court. (App. 3–8,, ¶¶ 10, 11, & 12.) These consumers testified that they would not risk $125.00, the American Arbitration Association's fee for consumer disputes of this sort, to arbitrate their disputes with Insight on an individual basis. (*See id.*, ¶¶ 11, 12, & 13.) Even if they were to succeed in the arbitration, the consumers testified that it would not be worthwhile to them to pursue the matter on an individual basis because of the relatively small amount of money that would be recovered and the expenses incidental to arbitrating the dispute that they would incur, including but not limited to attorneys' fees and loss of time and effort. (*See id.*)

Moreover, even if they had wanted to pursue these claims on an individual basis, the consumer plaintiffs would almost certainly be unable to find an attorney willing to represent them in such an action. The Consumer Plaintiffs submitted expert affidavits from two Kentucky attorneys with extensive experience representing consumers in litigation over disputes with a wide range of businesses. (*See* App. 11, Affidavit of Ellen Friedman; App. 12, Affidavit of Scott Spiegel.) Both experts provided sworn affidavits that few if any attorneys would represent the Consumer Plaintiffs in individual actions, because the amount of money at stake in individual claims was too small relative to the time and expense required to pursue the matter for individual representation to be economically feasible. (*See id.*) The expert testimony further established that even if individual consumers prevailed, it would be very uncertain whether counsel would receive attorneys fees awards proportionate to the time required to prevail, and thus that it would be economically infeasible for attorneys to pursue cases such as this on an individual basis even though fee-shifting statutes were potentially applicable. (*See id.*)

III. Procedural Facts.

The Consumer Plaintiffs filed this Complaint on behalf of themselves and a putative class of Kentucky consumers who paid for broadband internet services on May 11, 2006, alleging that the actions and failures of Insight violated the Kentucky Consumer Protection Act, KRS 367.110 *et seq.*, resulted in a breach of contract, and provided Insight with unjust enrichment. Defendants moved to dismiss the action and to compel arbitration on June 12, 2006. The issue was fully briefed and oral arguments were heard on August 24, 2006. On October 6, 2006, Judge Roger Crittenden issued an "Opinion and Order" granting Defendants' motions to dismiss and to compel arbitration. (*See* R. 763–66, attached as Appendix 1.) Consumer Plaintiffs' Notice of Appeal was timely filed on October 6, 2006.

ARGUMENT

I. STANDARD OF REVIEW

This Court is to review the trial court's identification and application of legal principles in its decision that the ban on class actions was not unconscionable on a *de novo* basis. *See Conseco Finance Servicing Corp. v. Wilder*, 47 S.W.3d 335, 340 (Ky. App. 2001).

It is well-established that the court, not an arbitrator, must resolve the challenge to the lawfulness of the class-action ban embedded in Insight's arbitration clause, applying general principles of Kentucky contract law. *See Louisville PeterBuilt Inc. v. Cox*, 132 S.W.3d 850, 855–56 (Ky. 2004); *see also Stutler v. T.K. Constructors Inc.*, 448 F.3d 343, 345 (6th Cir. 2006); *Muhammad v. Cnty. Bank of Rehobeth Beach*, 912 A.2d 88, 96 (N.J. 2006) *cert. denied*, ___ S. Ct. ___, 2007 WL 120665 (2007).

II. THE PROVISION OF INSIGHT'S ARBITRATION CLAUSE THAT PROHIBITS CLASS PROCEEDINGS IS UNCONSCIONABLE AND UNENFORCEABLE.

A. To the Extent that Plaintiffs Must Establish that the Class Action Ban Is Procedurally Unconscionable, They Have Done So.

It is not entirely clear if the Consumer Plaintiffs must establish both procedural and substantive unconscionability in this case. The Kentucky Supreme Court has acknowledged that other jurisdictions distinguish between these two components,[4] but has not necessarily endorsed that approach itself. *Conseco*, 47 S.W.3d at 342. While the Court in *Conseco* discussed procedural unconscionability, it largely focused upon its holding that the contract terms at issue there were not substantively unconscionable. The Consumer Plaintiffs respectfully suggest that this Court hold that all the Consumer Plaintiffs are required to prove is substantive unconscionability, as several other states have held. *E.g., Adler v. Fred Lind Manor*, 103 P.2d 773 (Wash. 2004) ("[S]ubstantive unconscionability alone can support a finding of unconscionability."); *Vasquez-Lopez v. Beneficial Oregon, Inc.*, 152 P.3d 940, 948 (Or. Ct. App. 2007) ("both procedural and substantive unconscionability are relevant, although only substantive unconscionability is absolutely necessary.").

Alternatively, this Court should follow the lead of those states that hold that, there is a sliding scale relationship between procedural and substantive unconscionability, such that a party making a stronger showing on one factor need only make a modest showing on the other. *E.g., Wisconsin Auto Title Loans, Inc. v. Jones*, 714 N.W.2d 155, 171 (Wis. 2006) ("[t]he more substantive unconscionability present, the less procedural unconscionability is required, and vice versa."). In most states, all procedural unconscionability means is that the substantive terms of a contract between a corporation and a consumer may be viewed with "considerable skepticism." *Simpson v. MSA of Myrtle Beach, Inc.*,

---

4 As this Court in *Conseco* noted, in determining whether a contract term is unconscionable, most jurisdictions consider two related issues: procedural and substantive unconscionability. For a recent illustration of such an analysis, *see, e.g., Wisconsin Auto Title Loans, Inc. v. Jones,* 714 N.W.2d 155, 165 (Wis. 2006). Procedural unconscionability pertains to the process by which an agreement is reached, and substantive unconscionability relates to the fairness of the terms of the agreement.

___ S.E.2d ___, 2006 WL 4388016 (S.C. Mar. 26, 2007).[5]

To the extent that plaintiffs here are required to establish procedural unconscionability, they have done so. The class action ban embedded in Insight's arbitration clause is procedurally unconscionable because (1) it is contained within a contract of adhesion; (2) the Consumer Plaintiffs had significantly less bargaining power than Insight; and (3) the arbitration clause was communicated in a manner designed to deflect attention from it; and (4) Insight had a monopoly on broadband service, so class members had no meaningful choice to get this service without accepting the class action ban.

First, Insight's arbitration clause was a contract of adhesion. A contract of adhesion is defined as "a standardized contract, which, imposed and drafted by the party of superior bargaining strength, relegates to the subscribing party only the opportunity to adhere to the contract or reject it." *Conseco*, 47 S.W.3d at 342 n.20 (internal citation omitted). Contracts of adhesion are offered to the consumer on "essentially a 'take it or leave it' basis, without affording the consumer a realistic opportunity to bargain." *See Jones v. Bituminous Casualty Corp.*, 821 S.W.2d 798, 801 (Ky. 1991).

As explained in the statement of facts, all Insight customers must sign the service agreement in order to receive broadband Internet service, including the class action ban. The service agreements are standard form contracts, drafted entirely by Insight that customers may not alter.

Under Kentucky law, the fact that a contract is adhesive contributes to a finding of procedural unconscionability. *See Conseco*, 47 S.W.3d at 343 n.24 ("In consumer transactions in particular, courts have been willing to scrutinize such contracts and have refused to enforce egregiously abusive ones."). This approach is very similar to that of the South Carolina Supreme Court in *Simpson*, as quoted above, and is consistent with that of many other states. *See, e.g., Coady v. Cross Country Bank, Inc.*, 729 N.W.2d 732, 743 (Wis. App. 2007); *Kinkel v. Cingular Wireless*, LLC, 828 N.E.2d 812, 818–19 (Ill. Ct. App. 2005) (the fact that a contract is offered on an adhesive basis is not enough to render it procedurally unconscionable, but "it is an important factor to consider"), *aff'd*, *Kinkel*, 857 N.E.2d 250, 265 (Ill. 2006); *Powertel, Inc. v. Bexley*, 743 So.2d 570, 574 (Fla. Ct. App. 1999) ("we conclude that the arbitration clause at issue is procedurally unconscionable . . . [a]lthough not dispositive of this point, it is significant that the arbitration clause is an adhesion contract.").

Second, there is a disparity of bargaining power between the average, unrepresented consumer and Insight. Kentucky courts have cited uneven bargaining positions as a relevant factor weighing in favor of a finding of procedural unconscionability. *See Valley Constr. Co., Inc. v. Perry Host Mgmt. Co.*, 796 S.W.2d 365, 367 (Ky. App. 1990) (emphasizing that both parties were "sophisticated and knowledgeable businessmen" in enforcing the arbitration clause); *Louisville Bear Safety Serv., Inc. v. South Central Bell Telephone Co.*, 571 S.W.2d 438, 439–40 (Ky. App. 1978) (stressing that case did not involve unconscionability claim by an uninformed consumer against a business). Numerous other courts have held that a significant inequality of bargaining power supports a finding of procedural unconscionability. *See, e.g., Kinkel*, 857 N.E.2d at 265 ("Courts are more likely to find unconscionability when a consumer is involved, when there is a disparity in bargaining power. . . ."); *Discover Bank v. Superior Court (Boehr)*, 113 P.3d 1100, 1110 (Cal. 2005) (articulating that class action waivers embedded in arbitration clauses are unconscionable when a consumer contract of adhesion is involved and "the party with the superior bargaining power has carried out a scheme"); *Coady*, 729 N.W.2d at 742 (giving weight to the disproportionate relative bargaining power between credit card customers and multimillion dollar national credit card company defendant); *Schwartz v. Alltel Corp.*, 2006 WL 2243649 at *6 (Ohio Ct. App. 2006) ("Preliminarily we note the inherent disparity of the bargaining position of Schwartz and Alltel. Schwartz, a consumer, contracted with Alltel, a multi-billion dollar corporation, for the purchase of a cellular telephone and service. Though we are unaware of how often Schwartz engaged in contracts of this nature, it is clear that for Alltel, this was a common occurrence.")

The disparity of bargaining power was heightened by the fact that the consumers were unrepresented by counsel at the time of formation, or were unrepresented by counsel at the time of formation. *See Forsythe v. BancBoston Mort. Corp.*, 135 F.3d 1069, 1074 (6th Cir. 1997) (applying Kentucky law) (stressing that Ms. Forsythe was represented by counsel in finding that the terms were not unconscionable); *Small v. HCF of Perrysburg, Inc.*, 823 N.E.2d 19, 24 (Ohio Ct. App. 2004) ("we find procedural unconscionability . . . [w]hen Mrs. Small signed the agreement . . . she did not have an attorney present.").

Here, as the Statement of Facts establishes, Insight is a highly sophisticated and wealthy corporation, while its customers are normal, unrepresented consumers.

A third factor supporting a holding of procedural unconscionability is that the Consumer Plaintiffs could not receive this service without submitting to Insight's class action ban. This Court has recognized that the question of whether a consumer could obtain a product or service from any alternative source without being bound by an identical contract term is relevant to procedural unconscionability. *See Conseco*, 47 S.W.3d at n.24 (stressing that the plaintiffs did not allege that the service they sought from defendants was not reasonably available from other sources). A number of other courts throughout the country have held that a contract term is more likely to be unconscionable where it would be difficult for a consumer to receive the same good or service without agreeing to a similar contract term. *See, e.g., Ting v. AT&T*, 182 F. Supp. 2d 902, 929 (N.D. Cal. 2002) (finding consumer arbitration clause procedurally unconscionable when two-thirds of defendant's phone industry competitors imposed similar clauses), *aff'd in relevant part*, 319 F.3d 1126 (9th Cir. 2003); *American Gen. Fin., Inc. v. Branch*, 793 So.2d 738, 750–51 (Ala. 2000) (finding home lender's arbitration clause unconscionable where most local lenders used similar clauses); *Steinhardt v. Rudolph*, 422 So.2d 884, 892 (Fla. Ct. App. 1982) (the "scarcity" of housing units in Florida minimizes the meaningfulness of the choice to accept or reject a lease agreement); *Kloss v. Edward D. Jones & Co.*, 54 P.3d 1, 8 (Mont. 2002) (factor supporting finding of procedural unconscionability was that "the arbitration clause was found by Judge Johnson to be an industry-wide practice. Kloss would have been excluded from the securities market unless she accepted the agreement to arbitrate.").

Fourth, Insight imposed its arbitration clause in a manner that

---

5 *See also Williams v. Aetna Fin. Co.*, 700 N.E.2d 859, 866 (Ohio 1998) ("the presumption in favor of arbitration clauses is substantially weaker when there are strong indications that the contract at issue is an adhesion contract, and the arbitration clause itself appears to be adhesive in nature.").

predictably ensured that few consumers would read, notice or understand it. Under Kentucky law, courts look more closely at the enforceability of a contract that was communicated in "risk-shifting" terms which appear "in boilerplate." *Conseco*, 47 S.W.3d at 343, n. 22, or where consumers were unaware of the contract or did not understand it. *See Louisville Bear Safety*, 571 S.W.2d at 440. Insight's class action ban is a "classic example of a document which has been prepared with the intent that it be neither negotiated or read." *Fairfield Leasing Corp. v. Techni-Graphics, Inc.*, 607 A.2d 703, 704 (N.J. Super. 1992).

Kentucky courts are not alone in viewing this factor as significant to a finding of procedural unconscionability. *See, e.g., Skirchak v. Dynamics Research Corp., Inc.*, 432 F. Supp. 2d 175, 180 (D. Mass. 2006) (striking down class action ban as unconscionable where employer distributed contract term through process unlikely to alert employees); *Kinkel*, 857 N.E.2d at 264 (noting that terms that are "difficult to find" can often be procedurally unconscionable); *Muhammad*, 912 A.2d at 96 (procedural unconscionability includes situations in which a contract provision is "hidden"); *Coady*, 729 N.W.2d at 743 (citing fact that nobody from defendant credit card company reviewed any of the terms of the agreement with plaintiffs); *Schwartz*, 2006 WL 2243649, *6 ("The form itself contained small, hard-to-read print and contained margin-to-margin boilerplate, contractual language. . . . Alltel placed the arbitration provision at the very bottom of the back side of the agreement, without calling any attention to the provision."); *Simpson*, 2006 WL 4388016 at *6 (considering the "inconspicuous nature of the arbitration clause"). Courts also consider evidence that consumers lacked actual knowledge of the provision to be significant. *See, e.g., Skirchak*, 432 F. Supp. 2d at 180; *Kinkel*, 857 N.E.2d at 265 (noting that testimony of a plaintiff never seeing the clause is important to the analysis); *Coady*, 729 N.W.2d at 743 ("plaintiffs did not read or were not aware of the arbitration clause").

These factors are clearly present here. First, the Consumer Plaintiffs have submitted six affidavits stating that they were unaware of and did not understand the clause. *See Louisville Bear Safety*, 571 S.W.2d at 440. Second, the Consumer Plaintiffs were unable to read the arbitration clause and its ban on class proceedings because it did not appear within the viewing range in the text box; in order to view the arbitration clause and its ban on class actions, they had to scroll down the screen. (App. 3, ¶ 14; App. 4, ¶ 12; App. 8, ¶ 13.) Moreover, as further attested in each of the six submitted affidavits, nobody at Insight took any time to point out the arbitration clause to the Consumer Plaintiffs, or to explain anything about the clause or its ban on class proceedings. (*See id.*; App. 3–8, ¶¶ 6 & 7.)

These factors combine to make Insight's arbitration clause procedurally unconscionable. At minimum, they increase the risk that the clause, as an adhesion contract, is "subject to abuse." *Conseco*, 47 S.W.3d at n.20. Therefore, the Court must evaluate the fairness of the clause's terms with particular scrutiny.

B. The Class Action Ban is Substantively Unconscionable.

Where procedural unconscionability focuses on the circumstances under which the parties entered into the contract, substantive unconscionability is found where the contractual terms are "unreasonably or grossly favorable to one side. . . ." *Conseco*, 47 S.W.3d at n.22. Essentially, the doctrine of substantive unconscionability is concerned with "unfairly one-sided" contract terms, *see Discover Bank*, 113 P.3d at 1108; *Ting*, 319 F.3d at 1149.

The trial court ignored the effectively exculpatory nature of the class action ban embedded in Insight's arbitration clause, and erred in enforcing the class action ban.

1. Kentucky Law Does Not Permit Exculpatory Clauses In Adhesive Contracts Between Parties of Differing Bargaining Strengths For Claims Brought Under Remedial Statutes.

Kentucky law is clear that exculpatory contract terms will not be enforceable where they are imposed by stronger parties upon weaker parties, or where they would undermine statutes that are in place to protect the public:

> [I]n no event can such an exculpatory agreement be upheld where either (1) the interest of the public requires the performance of such duties, or (2) because the parties do not stand upon a footing of equality, the weaker party is compelled to submit to the stipulation.

Meiman v. Rehabilitation Center, Inc., 444 S.W.2d 78, 80 (Ky. Ct. App. 1969). In *Meiman*, this Court refused to enforce an exculpatory clause in a contract for physical therapy. While this case does not involve public safety, it does involve Kentucky's Consumer Protection Act, a remedial statute passed by the legislature for protection of the public. Just as no physician or physical therapist should be permitted to exempt themselves from Kentucky laws governing their actions, no Kentucky corporation should be free to engage in deceptive or unfair trade practices. The rule that "safety statutes" may not be the subject of exculpatory clauses was re-stated and reinforced by the Kentucky Supreme Court in *Hargis v. Baize*, 168 S.W.3d 36, 47–48 (Ky. 2005), and in *Cumberland Valley Contractors, Inc., v. Bell Cnty Coal Corp.*, ___ S.W.3d __, 2007 WL 188041, *4 (Ky. 2007). The Court also stressed, in *Hargis*, that exculpatory clauses are disfavored in Kentucky and are strictly construed against the parties relying upon them. In *Cumberland*, the Supreme Court went to great lengths to point out that it only permitted exculpatory clauses when there was neither a "significant disparity in bargaining power" between the parties nor any "public policy concerns" such as those that would arise from safety statutes.

Kentucky law on this point is in keeping with the law elsewhere in the country, as other jurisdictions do not permit contracts (including arbitration clauses) to include provisions that strip weaker parties of statutory rights. *E.g., Simpson*, 2006 WL 4388016 at *7 ("permitting the weaker party to waive these statutory remedies pursuant to an adhesion contract runs contrary to the underlying statutes' very purposes of punishing acts that adversely affect the public interest"); *Floss v. Ryan's Family Steak Houses,* 211 F.3d 306, 313 (Ky. 2000) (citation omitted) ("[E]ven if arbitration is generally a suitable forum for resolving a particular statutory claim, the specific arbitral forum provided under an arbitration agreement must nevertheless allow for the effective vindication of that claim. Otherwise, arbitration of the claim conflicts with the statute's purpose of both providing individual relief and generally deterring unlawful conduct through enforcement of its provisions.").

As the Kentucky Supreme Court and this Court have recognized, the General Assembly by enacting the Consumer Protection Act intended to "give Kentucky consumers the broadest possible protection for allegedly illegal acts." *Cowan v. Telcom Directories,*

Inc., 806 S.W.2d 638, 641 (Ky. 1991); *see also Ford Motor Co. v. Mayes*, 575 S.W.2d 480, 488 (Ky. App. 1978) (noting "legislative intent to protect the consumer public" and holding that "[p]ublic policy dictates that Ford not be permitted to limit the statutory remedy of consumers to recover 'actual damages' . . . for a violation of the Consumer Protection Act"). Thus, if the class action ban embedded in Insight's arbitration clause would effectively exculpate the company from liability for violations of the CPA, it cannot be enforced.

2. The Class Action Ban Embedded in Insight's Arbitration Clause Effectively Operates As An Exculpatory Clause.

As explained in the Statement of Facts above, the testimony of the Consumer Plaintiffs was that because of the costs of arbitration or litigation and the relatively small amount of money in controversy, they would not have been able pursue this matter individually through arbitration or small claims court. (App. 3 & 7, Affs., ¶ 12; App. 4 & 5, Aff., ¶ 10; App. 6 & 8, Aff., ¶ 11.) Similarly, the expert testimony from two Kentucky attorneys with extensive experience representing consumers in litigation over disputes with a wide range of businesses, was that few (if any) attorneys would represent the Consumer Plaintiffs in individual actions, because of the small stakes relative to the time and expense required to pursue the matter. (App. 11, ¶¶ 8, 14; App. 12, ¶¶ 8, 11.) Tellingly, Insight never offered any evidence to dispute the detailed factual testimony of either the consumers or of plaintiffs' experts. Putting aside the argument of counsel, the only admissible evidence on the question establishes that the ban on class actions is effectively exculpatory under the circumstances of the small claims involved in this case. The state of the evidence is exactly the same as in *Kristian*, 446 F.3d 25, 58 (1st Cir. 2006): "Plaintiffs have provided uncontested and unopposed expert affidavits demonstrating that without some form of class mechanism—be it class action or class arbitration—a consumer antitrust plaintiff will not sue at all."

The evidentiary record in this case is consistent with the holdings of courts in a variety of other cases. Numerous courts around the country have held that class action bans embedded in arbitration clauses are unconscionable in cases where these bans have the effect of making it impossible for individuals to effectively vindicate their legal rights. *See Luna v. Household Fin. Corp. III*, 236 F. Supp.2d 1166, 1178–79 (W.D. Wash. 2002) (arbitration clause substantively unconscionable where "prohibition of class actions would prevent borrowers from effectively vindicating their rights for certain categories of claims"); *Ting v. AT&T*, 182 F. Supp. 2d at 931 ("the prohibition on class action litigation functions as an effective deterrent to litigating many types of claims involving rates, services or billing practices and, ultimately . . . [serves] to shield AT&T from liability even in cases where it has violated the law"); *Discover Bank*, 113 P.3d at 1109; *Muhammad*, 912 A.2d at 99 ("[i]n most cases that involve a small amount of damages, "rational" consumers may decline to pursue individual consumer-fraud lawsuits because it may not be worth the time spent prosecuting the suit, even if competent counsel was willing to take the case); *id.* at 100 ("in addition to their impact on individual litigants, class-action waivers can functionally exculpate wrongful conduct by reducing the possibility of attracting competent counsel to advance the cause of action"); *Kinkel*, 857 N.E.2d at 820 (in context of individually pursued small damage claims, any potential recovery would be offset "by any costs incurred in presenting the claim and any lost wages for taking time from work to do so"), *aff'd, Kinkel*, 828 N.E.2d 250; *Powertel*, 743 So.2d at 576 ("Powertel has precluded the possibility that a group of its customers might join together to seek relief that would be impractical for any of them to obtain alone."); *Reuter v. Davis*, 2006 WL 3743016, *4 (Fla.Cir.Ct. 2006) (the evidence's "greater weight supports the proposition that it would be virtually impossible for Ms. Reuter, or anyone in a similar position, to obtain competent individual representation"); *Eagle v. Fred Martin Motor Co.*, 809 N.E.2d 1161, 1183 (Ohio Ct. App. 2004) ("by expressly eliminating a consumer's rights to proceed through a class action or as a private attorney general in arbitration, the arbitration clause directly hinders the consumer protection purposes" of the Ohio Consumer Protection Act); *Vasquez-Lopez*, 152 P.3d at 950–51 ("the opportunity that the class action ban denies to borrowers is, in many instances, a crucial one, without which many meritorious claims would simply not be filed"); *Thibodeau v. Comcast Corp.* 912 A.2d 874, 886 (Pa. Super. Ct. 2006); *Whitney v. Alltel Commn'cs., Inc.*, 173 S.W.3d 300, 309 (Mo. Ct. App. 2005) (striking class action ban as unconscionable where, "[b]y itself, such a claim would not be economically feasible to prosecute. However, when all of the customers are added together, large sums of money are at stake. Prohibiting class treatment of these claims would leave consumers with relatively small claims without a practical remedy."); *State ex rel. Dunlap v. Berger*, 567 S.E.2d 265, 278–79 (W. Va. 2002) (permitting class action ban in case involving small individual claims "would go a long way toward allowing those who commit illegal activity to go unpunished, undeterred, and unaccountable").[6]

This Court should follow this large body of persuasive authority and hold that the ban on class proceedings embedded in Insight's arbitration clause will deprive the Consumer Plaintiffs of any effective means of enforcing their statutory and contractual rights. Accordingly, this Court should find the ban on class actions embedded in Insight's arbitration provision is unconscionable, and therefore enforceable.

3. The Fact that Insight's Class Action Ban is Not Overtly Exculpatory, But Merely Exculpatory in Effect, Does Not Change Its Unconscionable Nature.

The trial court rejected the Consumer Plaintiffs' argument that Insight's class action ban was exculpatory, concluding that the clause ostensibly offered consumers a formal opportunity to vindicate their rights. The court stated that "the test should not be

---

[6] The U.S. Supreme Court, likewise, has repeatedly recognized the existence of such situations. *See, e.g., Amchem Products, Inc. v. Windsor*, 521 U.S. 591, 617 (1997) ("The policy at the very core of the class action mechanism is to overcome the problem that small recoveries do not provide the incentive for any individual to bring a solo action prosecuting his or her rights. A class action solves this problem by aggregating the relatively paltry potential recoveries into something worth someone's (usually an attorney's) labor.") (citation and quotation omitted). *Cf. Rollins, Inc., Garrett*, 176 Fed.Appx. 968, 968–69 (11th Cir. 2006) (affirming arbitrator's decision to permit an arbitration to proceed on a class action basis on grounds that, "[u]nder Florida law, a consumer contract that prohibits class arbitration is unconscionable because it preclude[s] the possibility that a group of its customers might join together to seek relief that would be impractical for any of them to obtain alone") (internal citations omitted); *Carnegie v. Household Int'l, Inc.*, 376 F.3d 656, 661 (7th Cir. 2004) (noting that "only a lunatic or a fanatic sues for $30").

whether someone will exercise these rights, but whether they are available." (Cite to Opinion and Order)

This Court should clarify that under Kentucky law, as elsewhere, the question of whether a contract term is exculpatory should be judged based upon its actual effect, not its formal appearance. The U.S. Supreme Court has repeatedly dictated that arbitration is permissible only where it permits parties to "effectively vindicate" their statutory rights. *E.g., Gilmer v. Interstate/Johnson Lane Corp.*, 500 U.S. 20, 28 (1991) (citing *Mitsubishi Motors Corp. v. Soler Chrysler-Plymouth, Inc.*, 473 U.S. 614, 637 (1985)); *EEOC v. Waffle House*, 534 U.S. 279, 295 n.10 (2002). The Supreme Court's approach rejects empty formalism—the high court has not said that arbitration agreements are enforceable where they pretend to permit individuals to vindicate their rights, but where they "effectively" do so.

Accordingly, in assessing the unconscionability of class action bans such as the one imbedded in Insight's service agreement, courts have looked past formalities to the actual real world effect of such terms. *See, e.g., Kristian*, 446 F.3d at 54 (while Comcast is correct that the class action device is procedural and not formally substantive, "we cannot ignore the substantive implications of this procedural mechanism."); *Ting*, 319 F.3d at 1149, n.14 (directing courts to "look beyond the facial neutrality and examine the actual effects," and criticizing a case that "ignores the obvious practical implications of the arbitration provision"); *Discover Bank*, 113 P.3d at 1109 ("[C]lass actions and arbitrations are, particularly in the consumer context, often inextricably linked to the vindication of substantive rights. Affixing the 'procedural' label on such devices understates their importance and is not helpful to resolving the unconscionability issue.").

Thus, numerous courts have acknowledged that contractual terms concerning procedural issues—such as arbitration costs or rules—are unenforceable if they prevent a party from vindicating substantive rights. *See, e.g., Green Tree Fin. Corp. v. Randolph*, 531 U.S. 79, 90 (2000) ("It may well be that the existence of large arbitration costs could preclude a litigant such as Randolph from effectively vindicating her federal statutory rights in an arbitral forum."); *Swain v. Auto Servs., Inc.*, 128 S.W.3d 103, 108 (Mo. App. 2003) (contractual venue provision requiring Missouri consumer to travel to Arkansas to resolve disputes was unconscionable).

4. The Possibility that Prevailing Consumers Might Receive Attorneys Fees Under Kentucky Consumer Rights Statutes Does Not Make It Likely that Many Consumers Could Find Competent Counsel to Bring Claims Such as These on an Individual Basis.

The availability of attorney's fees under the Kentucky consumer rights statutes fails to ameliorate the exculpatory effects of Insight's ban on class proceedings. Although the Kentucky Consumer Protection Act provides for the availability of attorneys' fees, an award of such attorneys' fees is left to the discretion of the court (or arbitrator). *See* KRS 367.220(3); *Alexander v. S&M Motors, Inc.*, 28 S.W.3d 303, 305 (Ky. 2000). Moreover, in cases such as this one, where the damages awarded may be small, courts throughout the country are wary of awarding attorneys fees in excess of those damages, often looking to the "proportionality" of the award. *See, e.g., Hensley v. Eckerhart*, 461 U.S. 424, 434–37 (1983) (a district court is vested with broad discretion to reduce a fee award based on the results obtained); *James v. Thermal Master, Inc.*, 563 N.E.2d 917, 919 (Ohio Ct. App. 1988) (affirming trial court's decision to reduce attorney's fee in light of small jury award); *F.H. Krear & Co. v. Nineteen Named Trustees*, 810 F.2d 1250, 1264 (2d Cir. 1987) ("New York courts have stated that, as a general rule, they will rarely find reasonable an award to a plaintiff that exceeds the amount involved in litigation."). The upshot of such decisions is that no wise attorney would form a business plan of supporting her or his family by bringing very small claims such as those involved here on an individual basis in the hopes that some future court (or arbitrator) might award attorneys' fees for the full amount of time it would take to prevail upon such claims.

The expert testimony submitted by the consumer plaintiffs in this case establishes that the chances of prevailing, the chances of receiving attorneys fees if they prevail, and the real risk that any granted fee request will be significantly reduced in any event—in light of the small damage award—are all too uncertain to convince an attorney to take the case. (*See* App. 11 & 12.) In the face of such evidence, courts have not hesitated to so hold. *See, e.g., Muhammad*, 912 A.2d at 100 ("The availability of attorney's fees is illusory if it is unlikely that counsel would be willing to undertake the representation."); *Kristian*, 446 F.3d 59 n.21 ("in any individual case, the disproportion between the damages awarded to an individual consumer antitrust plaintiff and the attorney's fees incurred to prevail on the claim would be so enormous that it is highly unlikely that an attorney could ever begin to justify being made whole by the court"); *Discover Bank*, 113 P.3d 1109–10 ("Nor are we persuaded by the rationale . . . that the potential availability of attorneys fees . . . ameliorates the problem.").

Based on the foregoing, it is clear that the existence of attorneys fees provisions under the Kentucky consumer rights laws does not save Insight's clause from being substantively unconscionable.[7]

C. The Secrecy Provision in Insight's Arbitration Clause Is Substantively Unconscionable.

In addition to the exculpatory effect of the class action ban, Insight's arbitration clause includes a confidentiality provision.

While no Kentucky court has yet passed upon the legality of such a gag order in an arbitration clause, numerous courts around the nation have held that similar secrecy terms in arbitration clauses are substantively unconscionable. *See, e.g., Zuver v. Airtouch Communications, Inc.*, 103 P.3d 753, 765 (Wash. 2004) (confidentiality provision substantively unconscionable because it "hampers [the] ability to prove a pattern of discrimination or to take advantage of findings in past arbitrations . . . [and] keeping past findings secret undermines an employee's confidence in the

---

[7] Appellees also argue that small claims court represents an adequate alternative for the vindication of the Consumer Plaintiffs' rights. Numerous courts disagree. *See, e.g., Kinkel*, 828 N.E.2d at 275–76, holding that the small claims forum had the same limitations as the arbitral forum, namely that pursuing such individual claims would still be economically irrational, in light of the plaintiff's low amount of actual damages and the fact that she would have to pay a filing fee and possibly hire an attorney to litigate her claim); *Szetela v. Discover Bank*, 97 Cal. App. 4th 1094, 1101 (Cal.App. 2002) (noting that defendant Discover was "fully aware that few customers will go to the time and trouble of using small claims court," when it employed the strategy of mandating arbitration and barring class actions but allowing for small claims actions); *Discover Bank*, 113 P.3d at 1110 ("nor do we agree . . . that small claims litigation . . . [is an] adequate substitute[].").

fairness and honesty of the arbitration process and thus, potentially discourages that employee from pursuing a valid discrimination claim"); *Kinkel*, 857 N.E.2d at 275 (confidentiality provision unconscionable where "Cingular . . . can accumulate experience defending these claims . . . while ensuring that none of [defendant's] potential opponents will have access to precedent") (citation omitted); *Ting*, 319 F.3d at 1152 (AT&T's confidentiality provision unconscionable because it placed AT&T in a "far superior legal posture" relative to aggrieved consumers); *Torrance v. Aames Finding Corp.*, 242 F. Supp. 2d 862, 875 (D. Oregon 2002) (confidentiality agreement in arbitration clause unconscionable); *Luna*, 236 F. Supp.2d at 1180–81 (confidentiality provision contributed substantive unconscionability because it "magnifies the effect of [the] advantages" that "repeat arbitration participants enjoy . . . over one-time participants"). Like the clauses struck down in each of these cases, Insight's arbitration provision requires all information to remain confidential including any finding that the company violated consumer protection laws.[8] (*See* App. 10.)

Accordingly, the Court should find the arbitration clause unconscionable based on its confidentiality requirement alone. If the court finds, however, that the offensiveness of the provision does not itself compel a finding of unconscionability, the court should find that the provision lends considerable support to such a finding.

II. GENERALLY APPLICABLE PRINCIPLES OF KENTUCKY CONTRACT LAW ARE NOT PREEMPTED BY THE FEDERAL ARBITRATION ACT.

Section 2 of the Federal Arbitration Act ("FAA") provides that contractual arbitration agreements are enforceable "save upon such grounds as exist at law or in equity for the revocation of any contract." 9 U.S.C. § 2. The U.S. Supreme Court has interpreted that provision to mean that "generally applicable contract defenses, such as fraud, duress or unconscionability, may be applied to invalidate arbitration agreements without contravening § 2." *Doctor's Assocs., Inc. v. Casarotto*, 517 U.S. 681, 687 (1996).

Thus, the vast majority of courts have held that the FAA does not preempt state laws finding that contractual bans on class actions embedded in arbitration clauses are unconscionable. *See Muhammad*, 912 A.2d at 94; *Kinkel*, 857 N.E.2d at 263 ("In sum, the FAA neither expressly nor impliedly preempts a state court from holding that an arbitration clause or a specific provision within an arbitration clause is unenforceable."). Because Kentucky law concerning exculpatory clauses would invalidate an unconscionable class action ban regardless of whether it is embedded in an arbitration clause, it is not preempted.

CONCLUSION

This Court should reverse the trial court's decision enforcing the arbitration clause as it is drafted. Because two provisions of the arbitration clause are substantively unconscionable, this Court should hold that the entire arbitration clause is unenforceable.

---

8 Section 14 of the Kentucky Constitution states that "[a]ll courts shall be open, and every person for an injury done him in his lands, goods, person or reputation, shall have remedy by due course of law, and right and justice administered without sale, denial, or delay." While this provision is not directly applicable to terms in private contracts, it should be noted that Insight's gag order is flatly contrary to the principles enshrined in this Constitutional guarantee.

Alternatively, this Court should hold that the ban on class actions and the secrecy provision are unconscionable, and should direct that the case proceed in arbitration with those two provisions stricken from the contract.

Respectfully Submitted,
[*Attorneys for Appellants*]

F.2 Briefs on Unconscionability of Class Action Ban (Scott)

F.2.1 *Plaintiffs' Opening Brief*

COURT OF APPEALS, DIVISION I
OF THE STATE OF WASHINGTON

DOUG SCOTT, LOREN TABASINKE, SANDRA TABASINSKE, PATRICK OISHI, JANET OISHI, et al.,
Appellants,

v.

CINGULAR WIRELESS,
Respondent.

APPEAL FROM THE SUPERIOR COURT FOR KING COUNTY

HONORABLE CATHERINE SHAFFER

APPELLANTS' OPENING BRIEF

TABLE OF CONTENTS

ASSIGNMENTS OF ERROR
ISSUES PERTAINING TO ASSIGNMENTS OF ERROR
STATEMENT OF THE CASE
SUMMARY OF ARGUMENT
ARGUMENT
 I. THE STANDARD OF REVIEW IS DE NOVO.
 II. EITHER PROCEDURAL OR SUBSTANTIVE UNCONSCIONABILITY IS SUFFICIENT TO MAKE CINGULAR'S ARBITRATION CLAUSE UNENFORCEABLE UNDER WASHINGTON LAW.
 III. CINGULAR'S ARBITRATION CLAUSE IS SUBSTANTIVELY UNCONSCIONABLE BECAUSE IT IS ONE-SIDED.
  A. One-Sided Arbitration Clauses, Regardless Of Whether They Are Nominally Mutual, Are Substantively Unconscionable Under Washington Law.
  B. By Banning Class Actions, Cingular's Arbitration Clause Is One-Sided.
 IV. CINGULAR'S ARBITRATION CLAUSE IS SUBSTANTIVELY UNCONSCIONABLE BECAUSE IT SERVES AS AN ABSOLUTE EXCULPATORY CLAUSE.
  A. Washington State Law Does Not Permit Corporations To Draft Adhesive Arbitration Clauses That Insulate The Corporations From Liability For Behavior That Violates The Law.
  B. By Banning Class Actions, Cingular's Arbitration Clause

Effectively Amounts To An Exculpatory Clause, Immunizing Cingular From Any Legal Responsibility Even If All Of Plaintiffs' Claims Are True and Correct.
1. The Undisputed Facts In This Case Establish That The Vast Majority, If Not All, Of Cingular's Customers Would Not Be Able To Bring Cases Such As This One On An Individual Basis.
2. Courts Throughout The United States Have Recognized That Contractual Bans On Class Actions Serve As Exculpatory Clauses, And For That Reason Violate Generally Applicable State Contract Laws.

V. BECAUSE THE CLASS-ACTION BAN CANNOT BE SEVERED FROM THE REST OF CINGULAR'S ARBITRATION CLAUSE, THE ENTIRE CLAUSE MUST BE INVALIDATED.

VI. WASHINGTON LAW OF SUBSTANTIVE UNCONSCIONABILITY IS CONSISTENT WITH THE FEDERAL ARBITRATION ACT.
  A. There Is A Heavy Presumption Against Federal Preemption Of State Law.
  B. Washington State Law Holding Cingular's Arbitration Clause Substantively Unconscionable Does Not Conflict With The Federal Arbitration Act.
  C. Washington State Law Recognizing The Value Of Class Actions Is Consistent With U.S. Supreme Court Jurisprudence.
  D. Cingular's Contract Provision Banning Class Actions Is Not Inherent To Or Necessary To Arbitration, But Is Merely An Unrelated Abusive Term That Cingular Has Chosen To Tack On To Its Arbitration Provision.

VII. CINGULAR'S ARBITRATION CLAUSE WAS FORMED IN A PROCEDURALLY UNCONSCIONABLE MANNER.

CONCLUSION

TABLE OF AUTHORITIES

Cases[**]

ACORN v. Household Int'l, Inc., 211 F. Supp. 2d 1160 (N.D. Cal. 2002)
Adler v. Fred Lind Manor, No. 74701-6, 2004 WL 3016302, *4 (Wash. Dec. 23, 2004)
Al-Safin v. Circuit City, No. 03-35297, 2005 WL 77145 (9th Cir. Jan. 14, 2005)
Amchem Products, Inc. v. Windsor, 521 U.S. 591 (1997)
Armendariz v. Foundation Health Psychare Services, Inc., 6 P.3d 669 (Cal. 2000)
Badie v. Bank of America, 79 Cal. Rptr. 2d 273 (1998)
Bowles v. Washington Dept. of Retirement Systems, 121 Wn. 2d 52, 847 P.2d 440 (1993)
Brown v. Brown, 6 Wn. App. 249, 492 P.2d 581 (Div. 2 1971)
California Div. of Labor Standards Enforcement v. Dillingham Construction, N.A., Inc., 519 U.S. 316 (1997)
California v. ARC America Corp., 490 U.S. 93 (1989)
Carll v. Terminix Int'l Co., 793 A.2d 921 (Pa. Super. Ct. 2002)
Circuit City Stores, Inc. v. Adams, 279 F.3d 889 (9th Cir. 2002)
Comb v. PayPal, 218 F. Supp. 2d 1165 (N.D. Cal. 2002)
Darling v. Champion Home Builders Co., 96 Wn. 2d 701, 638 P.2d 1249 (1982)
Deposit Guaranty Nat'l Bank v. Roper, 445 U.S. 326 (1980)
Dept of Labor Indus. v. Common Carriers, Inc., 111 Wn. 2d 586, 762 P.2d 348 (1988)
Discover Bank v. Shea, 827 A.2d 358, 366 (N.J. Super. Ct. 2001), *appeal dismissed*, 827 A.2d 292 (N.J. Super. A.D. 2003)
Dortch v. Straka, 59 Wn. App. 773, 801 P.2d 279 (Div. 1 1990)
Eagle v. Fred Martin Motor Co., 809 N.E.2d 1161 (Ohio Ct. App. 2004)
Eisen v. Carlisle & Jacquelin, 417 U.S. 156 (1974)
Equal Employment Opportunity Comm'n v. Waffle House, Inc., 534 U.S. 279 (2002)
Erie Railroad Co. v. Tompkins, 304 U.S. 64 (1983)
Flyer Hill Printing Co. v. Hill, 805 So.2d 829 (Fla. Dist. Ct. App. 2001)
Franks & Son, Inc. v. State, 136 Wn. 2d 737, 966 P.2d 1232 (1998)
Freightliner Corp. v. Myrick, 514 U.S. 280 (1995)
G.S. Rasmussen & Associates, Inc. v. Kalitta Flying Service, Inc., 958 F.2d 896 (9th Cir. 1992)
Gilmer v. Interstate/Johnson Lane Corp., 500 U.S. 20 (1991)
Gourley v. Yellow Transp., L.L.C., 178 F. Supp. 2d 1196 (D. Colo. 2001)
Graham Oil Co. v. ARCO Products Co., 43 F.3d 1244 (9th Cir. 1994)
Green Tree Financial Corp. v. Bazzle, 539 U.S. 444 (2003)
Green Tree Financial Corp. v. Randolph, 531 U.S. 79 (2000)
Hisle v. Todd Pacific Shipyards Corp., 151 Wn. 2d 853, 93 P.3d 108 (2004)
Holt v. O'Brien, 862 So.2d 87 (Fla. Dist. Ct. App. 2003)
In re Knepp, 229 B.R. 821 (N.D. Ala. 1999)
Ingle v. Circuit City Stores, Inc., 328 F.3d 1165 (9th Cir. 2003)
Jenkins v. First American Cash Advance of Georgia, LLC, 313 F. Supp. 2d 1370 (S.D. Ga. 2004)
Johnson v. Cash Store, 68 P.3d 1099 (Div. 3 2003)
Kruger Clinic Orthopaedics v. Regence Blushield, 123 Wn. App. 355, 98 P.3d 66 (Div. 1 2004)
Leonard v. Terminix Int'l Co., 854 So. 2d 529 (Ala. 2002) (petition for rehearing denied)
Luna v. Household Finance Corp. III, 236 F. Supp. 2d 1166 (W.D. Wash. 2002)
McCutcheon v. United Homes Corp., 79 Wn. 2d 443, 486 P.2d 1093 (1971)
Mitsubishi Motors Corp. v. Soler Chrysler-Plymouth, Inc., 473 U.S. 614 (1985)
Oda v. State, 111 Wn. App. 79, 44 P.3d 8 (Div. 1 2002)
Paladino v. Avnet Computer Technologies., Inc., 134 F.3d 1054 (11th Cir. 1998)
Powertel v. Bexley, 743 So. 2d 570 (Fla. App. 1 Dist. 1999)
Schroeder v. Fageol Motors, Inc., 86 Wn. 2d 256, 260, 544 P.2d 20, 23 (1975)
Smith v. Behr Process Corp., 113 Wn. App. 306, 54 P.3d 665 (Div. 2 2002)
Sporsem v. First Nat. Bank, 133 Wn. 199, 233 P. 641 (1925)
State v. Grimes, 111 Wn. App. 544, 46 P.3d 801 (Div. 1 2002)
Stevedoring Services of America, Inc. v. Eggert, 129 Wn. 2d 17, 914 P.2d 737 (1996)
Szetela v Discover Bank, 97 Cal. App. 4th 1094, 118 Cal. Rptr. 2d 862 (2002), *cert. denied*, 537 U.S. 1226 (2003)
Ticknor v. Choice Hotels Int'l, Inc., 265 F.3d 931 (9th Cir. 2001)
Ting v. AT&T, 182 F. Supp.2d 902 (N.D. Cal. 2002)

[**] [*Editor's Note:* Citations throughout brief as in original.]

Ting v. AT&T, 319 F.3d 1126 (9th Cir.), *cert. denied*, 540 U.S. 811 (2003)
Tjart v. Smith Barney, Inc., 107 Wn. App. 885, 28 P.3d 823 (Div. 1 2001), *review denied*, 145 Wn. 2d 1027, 42 P.3d 974 (2002), *cert. denied*, 537 U.S. 954 (2002)
Washington State Physicians Ins. Exchange & Ass'n v. Fisons Corp., 122 Wn.2d 299, 858 P.2d 1054 (1993)
West Virginia ex rel. Dunlap v. Berger, 567 S.E.2d 265 (W. Va. 2002), *cert. denied*, 537 U.S. 1087 (2002)
Zuver v. Airtouch Communications, Inc., No. 74156-5, 2004 WL 3016484 (Wash. Dec. 23, 2004)

ASSIGNMENTS OF ERROR

1. The trial court erred in granting Defendant Cingular Wireless' ("Cingular's") Motion to Compel Arbitration and Stay Proceedings by order entered on September 10, 2004. RP at 23; CP at 1870–71.

ISSUES PERTAINING TO ASSIGNMENTS OF ERROR

1. Did the trial court err in holding that Cingular's arbitration clause was not formed in a procedurally unconscionable manner and thus is enforceable as a matter of Washington contract law? (Yes.) (Error 1.)

2. Did the trial court err in holding that Cingular's arbitration clause is not substantively unconscionable and thus is enforceable as a matter of Washington contract law? (Yes.) (Error 1.)

STATEMENT OF THE CASE

Plaintiffs are residents of Washington State who purchased wireless phones and calling plans from Defendant Cingular Wireless ("Cingular") in 2001 and 2002. CP at 1139 ¶ 3; 1249 ¶ 3; 1257 ¶ 4. When Plaintiffs signed up for their wireless service plans, they were presented with a standard, pre-printed contract to sign. CP at 1139 ¶ 4; 1249 ¶¶ 4–5. The "terms and conditions" of these contracts were printed in tiny, single-spaced type on a legal-sized page with negligible margins.\1 CP at 339–49. The language on arbitration was not on the page Plaintiffs were told to sign, but rather was buried in the middle of a paragraph near the bottom of the page, just following a term concerning Cingular' right to terminate voicemail services. CP at 343; 345. Plaintiffs were not made aware that the contract included a mandatory arbitration provision. CP at 1139 ¶ 6; 1249 ¶ 5. The contract provided that if Plaintiffs changed their minds or wanted out of the contract, they must pay a $150 termination charge. CP at 343; 345. Cingular, however, retained power to unilaterally modify the agreement. CP at 343; 345.

According to the terms of the contracts, all local and long-distance calls made from the subscribers' local calling area were included in Plaintiffs' monthly service fee at no additional charge. CP at 845 ¶ 2.4.; 1139 ¶ 5; 1140 ¶ 16; 1250 ¶ 6; 1254; 1258 ¶ 9; 1259 ¶ 11. However, after having used Cingular's services for some time, Plaintiffs received bills which included charges for long-distance and/or out-of-network "roaming" calls. CP at 1140 ¶ 14; 1250; 1258 ¶ 9; 1259 ¶ 11. As a result of these billing practices, Cingular has allegedly overcharged Plaintiffs amounts ranging from less than $1.00 to over $45.00 per month. CP at 1140 ¶ 14; 1258 ¶ 7; 1258 ¶ 9; 1259 ¶ 11. Even if the individual claims of most putative class members are very low, if the alleged overbilling practices affect thousands of current Cingular wireless customers in Washington, the claims would amount to millions of dollars in the aggregate. CP at 845 ¶ 2.6.

Plaintiffs filed this putative class action in the Superior Court for the State of Washington, King County on February 23, 2004, and filed a Second Amended Complaint on June 25, 2004. CP at 3–11; 842–57.

On April 30, 2004, Cingular moved to compel Plaintiffs to arbitrate their claims individually. CP at 39. Cingular claims that the arbitration clause it seeks to enforce was part of a monthly bill-stuffer sent to all current subscribers in July 2003, months after Plaintiffs' original contracts were formed. CP at 42; 352 ¶ 3. The clause contains this term:

> You and Cingular agree that YOU AND CINGULAR MAY BRING CLAIMS AGAINST THE OTHER ONLY IN YOUR OR ITS INDIVIDUAL CAPACITY, and not as a plaintiff or class member in any purported class or representative proceeding. Further, you agree that the arbitrator may not consolidate proceedings or more than one person's claims, and may not otherwise preside over any form of a representative or class proceeding, and that is [sic] if this specific proviso is found to be unenforceable, then the entirety of this arbitration clause shall be null and void.

CP at 355–56. Plaintiffs opposed Cingular's Motion to Compel Arbitration on September 1, 2004, arguing that the provision prohibiting class actions is unconscionable under Washington law and that the arbitration clause is thus unenforceable. CP at 1114.

Plaintiffs put two important expert declarations before the trial court. The first was from Sally Gustafson Garratt, an attorney in private practice who focuses on litigation in consumer law and consults and lectures on consumer law issues. CP at 1568 ¶ 5. Ms. Garratt was the Division Chief for Consumer Protection in the Washington State Attorney General's office for eight years, supervising more than 100 employees who responded to more than a quarter of a million consumer inquiries or complaints each year. CP at 1568 ¶ 6–7. She testified that the Attorney General's office did not have the resources to respond to many individual cases, CP at 1568–69 ¶ 10, and often "relied on the private class action to correct the deceptive or unfair industry practice and to reimburse consumers for their losses." CP at 1569 ¶ 12.

Ms. Garratt's testimony made clear that the ban on class actions in Cingular's arbitration clause amounted to an exculpatory clause:

> [V]ery few private attorneys nationwide or in Washington State are able to handle consumer cases for individual consumers because of the costs involved. I have discussed the economies of consumer litigation scores of times with private attorneys who called me and tried to convince the

---

\1 The terms were apparently on the reverse side of the document, or on a separate page. For example, Mr. Tabasinske's contract provides, "I acknowledge that the Terms and Conditions are on the back of this page or that the Terms and Conditions version number _____ were separately provided to me." His initials appear after the provision; however, the space for insertion of a "version number" is left blank. CP at 1250 ¶¶ 4–5; 342.

Attorney General to pursue a case that they could not afford to handle. Because the loss to individual consumers is, in most cases, relatively small, and the cost of litigation so high, attorneys frequently cannot pursue worthy cases....

CP at 1570 ¶ 10.

> Another problem in pursuing consumer cases is that often times all of the consumers affected by deceptive practices are not aware that they have been deceived. Companies engaging in the deceptive practices can pay off the consumers who catch the problem while continuing to collect from consumers who don't notice the deception. I have found that in cases involving small amounts of money, individual consumers are more likely to not notice the problem or if they do notice it, to do nothing because the time, trouble, or expense involved is perceived by them to be too great for the potential benefit even if they win. The result is that if a company has many customers that are deceived by a practice that results in a small amount of loss for each customer, the practice could go unchecked indefinitely.

CP at 1570–71 ¶¶ 11–12.

Finally, Ms. Garratt's testimony contrasted the comparative real-world effect of this provision on Cingular to the effect on its customers: "Precluding class actions through a mandatory arbitration clause limits options available to harmed consumers, a result that benefits the company, not the consumer. This result has serious due process and public policy implications." CP at 1570 ¶ 13.

Plaintiffs also introduced a declaration from Peter Maier, a private Washington lawyer who has handled hundreds of consumer cases over a period of years. Mr. Maier chaired the subcommittee that wrote the first pattern jury instructions for the Consumer Protection Act, has edited for years the chapter on consumer law for the King County Bar Association Lawyers Practice Manual, chaired the Consumer Protection Committee of the Washington State Trial Lawyers Association, and has taught both lawyers and students on the subject of consumer law. CP at 1580 ¶ 4–5.

Mr. Maier's testimony also makes clear that Cingular's arbitration clause amounts to an exculpatory clause:

> The individual claims of the Cingular class members are too small and too complex factually and legally to be litigated by a private attorney representing an individual consumer or even by an individual consumer in Small Claims Court. As a result, these claims would not be litigated and remedied at all if the class process is unavailable to Cingular's consumers.

CP at 1582 ¶ 10. Mr. Maier testified that even if one makes extremely optimistic assumptions about the potential damages in this case,

> That amount would still be far too small for me to represent an individual consumer in an individual claim against Cingular. The reason is simple economics: the cost of litigation, especially against a large corporation in a case with a billing dispute arising out of a complicated agreement, is far too high to allow me or any other attorney in private practice to represent an individual consumer with a claim that small.

CP at 1582 ¶ 11. He concludes that, "Given these factors, not only would I be unwilling to take on such a claim for an individual consumer, but in my opinion it is very unlikely that any other private practice attorney would be willing to do so." CP at 1585 ¶ 14.

On September 10, 2004, the trial court ruled on Cingular's Motion to Compel Arbitration and Stay Proceedings and entered an order granting the motion. RP at 20; CP at 1870–71.

First, the court held that although Cingular's contract is a contract of adhesion, RP at 15, the contract is not sufficiently complex, illegible, or misleading to render it procedurally unconscionable. RP at 15–18.

Second, the court held that Cingular's arbitration clause is not substantively unconscionable. RP at 17–20. The court reasoned that as long as the costs of arbitration were not prohibitive, and Plaintiffs were not "financially strapped," arbitration was a viable and adequate forum. RP at 18–19. While acknowledging that Cingular would have no reason to want to file a class action against its customers, RP at 18, and that class actions provide an "incentive to litigate and correct consumer practices that would not otherwise be corrected," RP at 3–4, the court nonetheless declined to hold that Cingular's class-action ban was one-sided. RP at 19.

Finally, the court held that Cingular's arbitration clause is merely a limitation on remedies that is "fully supported by the Federal Arbitration Act." RP at 20.

Plaintiffs timely appealed on October 1, 2004. CP at 1872–73. This Court has appellate jurisdiction pursuant to Wash. Rev. Code § 2.06.030.

SUMMARY OF ARGUMENT

This appeal is not actually about arbitration. Instead, it's about whether a corporation can ban its customers from taking part in a class action, whether this device would be used in arbitration or in court. Cingular's own contract betrays that it is not interested in arbitration as a forum: Cingular would rather have the arbitration clause stricken entirely than face a class action in arbitration, even though arbitrators are regularly hearing class actions throughout the country. The point of Cingular's contract is to devise a system that effectively makes it impossible for its customers to bring legal actions against it for violations of law, and this flies in the fact of principles of Washington state law that apply to all contracts.

Cingular's arbitration clause is substantively unconscionable because it is one-sided. Under Washington law, contracts that are one-sided in favor of the stronger party with more resources are substantively unconscionable. In this case, Cingular's provision banning class actions unreasonably favors Cingular, as the provision eliminates the only meaningful remedy that Cingular's customers would have for claims that they might have against the corporation. By contrast, this provision in no way limits Cingular's ability to pursue any clams it may have against its customers, as Cingular does not bring and never has brought a class action against its own customers. Courts in a host of other jurisdictions have held that it is unconscionable for an arbitration clause to ban class actions, because such a provision is unreasonably one-sided.

Second, Washington law bars corporations from requiring individuals to submit to form contracts that immunize the corporation from liability if it violates state law. In this case, unrebutted expert testimony conclusively established that if the plaintiffs in this case were not permitted to pursue the case on a class-wide basis, they would be effectively barred from any meaningful opportunity to vindicate their claims. The Washington Supreme Court has struck down similar provisions in arbitration clauses that stripped individuals of their legal remedies, and a number of courts around the United States have struck down arbitration clauses that banned class actions on this ground.

Third, Cingular's arbitration clause was promulgated in a procedurally unconscionable manner. This adhesive contract was sent out in a way that predictably ensured that the overwhelming majority of Cingular's customers would never read it or grasp its meaning.

Finally, this brief will establish that the FAA does not protect any of Cingular's conduct from the principles of Washington law set forth above. The FAA incorporates and recognizes state contract law of general application, and as the Washington Supreme Court twice recognized at the end of 2004, Washington state law barring substantively and procedurally unconscionable contract provisions is a body of law that applies to all contracts, not merely arbitration clauses.

ARGUMENT

I. THE STANDARD OF REVIEW IS DE NOVO.

This Court reviews de novo a trial court's decision to grant a motion to compel arbitration. *Adler v. Fred Lind Manor*, No. 74701-6, 2004 WL 3016302, *4 (Wash. Dec. 23, 2004).

II. EITHER PROCEDURAL OR SUBSTANTIVE UNCONSCIONABILITY IS SUFFICIENT TO MAKE CINGULAR'S ARBITRATION CLAUSE UNENFORCEABLE UNDER WASHINGTON LAW.

Washington law recognizes two distinct classifications of unconscionability: substantive and procedural. *Zuver v. Airtouch Communications*, Inc., No. 74156-5, 2004 WL 3016484 at *3 (Wash. Dec. 23, 2004). Either kind of unconscionability alone is a sufficient basis for this Court to invalidate an arbitration clause. *Kruger Clinic Orthopaedics v. Regence Blushield*, 123 Wn. App. 355, 368, 98 P.3d 66, 74 (Div. 1 2004) ("Consumer transactions may be invalidated for procedural or substantive unconscionability.") (citing *Luna v. Household Finance Corp. III*, 236 F. Supp. 2d 1166, 1174 (W.D. Wash. 2002)).

Thus, in Washington, if a term is one-sided or otherwise substantively unconscionable, it is unenforceable regardless of whether the circumstances surrounding the formation of the contract indicate procedural unconscionability. *Adler*, 2004 WL 3016302 at *5 ("Substantive unconscionability alone can support a finding of unconscionability."); *see also Al-Safin v. Circuit City*, No. 03-35297, 2005 WL 77145 at *7 (9th Cir. Jan. 14, 2005) ("Although we have serious doubts about whether the agreement is procedurally unconscionable as well, we do not decide this issue because the agreement's substantive unconscionability alone renders it invalid under Washington law.").

This Court has likewise recognized that an arbitration clause may be unenforceable based on procedural unconscionability only.

Tjart v. Smith Barney, Inc., 107 Wn. App. 885, 898, 28 P.3d 823, 830 (Div. 1 2001), review denied, 145 Wn. 2d 1027, 42 P.3d 974 (2002), cert. denied, 537 U.S. 954 (2002) (engaging in unconscionability inquiry where plaintiff had alleged solely procedural unconscionability).

III. CINGULAR'S ARBITRATION CLAUSE IS SUBSTANTIVELY UNCONSCIONABLE BECAUSE IT IS ONE-SIDED.

A. One-Sided Arbitration Clauses, Regardless Of Whether They Are Nominally Mutual, Are Substantively Unconscionable Under Washington Law.

"Substantive unconscionability involves those cases where a clause or term in the contract is alleged to be one-sided or overly harsh." *Adler*, 2004 WL 3016302 at *4 (citation omitted); *Luna*, 236 F. Supp. 2d at 1177.

Thus, the Washington Supreme Court recently invalidated four terms in two different arbitration clauses on grounds that they were one-sided and therefore substantively unconscionable. In *Adler*, the court confronted an arbitration clause in an employment contract. The court first held that a term requiring each party to bear its own attorney fees was one-sided and substantively unconscionable because it "help[ed] the party with a substantially stronger bargaining position and more resources, to the disadvantage of [the party] needing to obtain legal assistance." 2004 WL 3016302 at *10 (citations and quotations omitted). Second, the court examined a contractual time bar that required the aggrieved party to notify the other party of its intent to seek arbitration within 180 days of the event first giving rise to the dispute, or waive its rights. *Id.* at *1. The court found that by shortening the time within which employees could bring claims under Washington's anti-discrimination laws, the corporation would obtain "unfair advantages" over its employees. *Id.* at *10–11. For example, in order to pursue arbitration within the time limit, employees might be forced to forgo filing a complaint with the EEOC or the Washington Human Rights Commission, and could be barred from seeking damages for a hostile work environment claim arising from illegal behavior that had begun outside the limitations period. *Id.* at *11. In light of these effects, the court held that the provision "unreasonably favor[ed]" the corporation over the employee and thus was substantively unconscionable. *Id.*

In *Zuver*, which also involved an employment contract, the Washington Supreme Court examined an arbitration clause provision that required that all arbitration proceedings be kept confidential, 2004 WL 3016484 at *1, and recognized that the provision benefited only one side:

> As written, the provision hampers an employee's ability to prove a pattern of discrimination or to take advantage of findings in past arbitrations. Moreover, keeping past findings secret undermines an employee's confidence in the fairness and honesty of the arbitration process and thus, potentially discourages that employee from pursuing a valid discrimination claim.

2004 WL 3016484 at *10. In holding that the provision was one-sided and thus substantively unconscionable, *id.*, the court drew from the Ninth Circuit's holding in *Ting v. AT&T*, 319 F.3d 1126 (9th Cir.), cert. denied, 540 U.S. 811 (2003), in which that court held that the confidentiality provision in AT&T's arbitration clause placed AT&T in a "far superior legal posture by ensuring that none of its potential opponents have access to precedent while, at the same time, AT&T accumulates a wealth of knowledge on how to negotiate the terms of its own unilaterally crafted contract." *Zuver*, 2004 WL 3016484 at *8 (quoting *Ting*, 319 F.3d at 1152). Finally, the court examined a provision that required employees to waive their rights to seek punitive or exemplary damages for common-law claims. *Id.* at *10. The clause left intact the employer's ability to pursue damages for "the only type of suit it would likely ever bring"—a claim for breach of the nondisclosure agreement. Accordingly, the court held that it was substantively unconscionable. *Id.* at *11.

In considering whether a term is one-sided, what matters is not whether the term "lacks mutuality" on its face," but whether the "*effect* of th[e] provision is so one-sided and harsh that it is substantively unconscionable." *Zuver*, 2004 WL 3016484 at *11 (emphasis added). In fact, three of the four terms the Washington Supreme Court struck down in the two cases were nominally mutual. *Adler*, 2004 WL 3016302 at *10 (attorney fees provision); *id.* at *10–11 (time limitation); *Zuver*, 2004 WL 3016484 at *11 (confidentiality provision).

This Court has been equally resolute in holding that one-sided terms in arbitration clauses are substantively unconscionable under Washington law—especially in the context of consumer contracts. In *Kruger*, the Court struck two provisions of arbitration clause as unfairly one-sided and thus substantively unconscionable, despite the fact that both parties were "reasonably sophisticated" and that "the policy considerations underlying an analysis of a consumer transaction are not at issue here." 123 Wn. App. at 371, 98 P.3d at 73. This is consistent with the U.S. district court's holding in *Luna*, in which Judge Lasnik emphasized that when evaluating whether an agreement is substantively unconscionable, courts must consider the terms of the agreement in light of the totality of the circumstances existing when the contract was made. 236 F. Supp. 2d at 1183. "A party's status as a consumer is one of those circumstances. Washington courts have recognized that the consumer or commercial nature of a contract should be considered in the substantive unconscionability inquiry." *Id.*

The basic principle that one-sided terms are substantively unconscionable is consistent with holdings in other jurisdictions as well. For example, the New Jersey Superior Court held:

> The provision against class-wide relief in Discover's amendment benefits only Discover, at the expense of individual cardholders. While Discover can use the provision to preclude class actions and therefore, effectively immunize itself completely from small claims, individual cardholders gain nothing, and in fact, are effectively deprived of their small individual claims. Discover can completely avoid accountability whenever the harm to each class member is small enough. Such a provision... is unconscionable under Delaware and New Jersey law.

Discover Bank v. Shea, 827 A.2d 358, 366 (N.J. Super. Ct. 2001), *appeal dismissed*, 827 A.2d 292 (N.J. Super. A.D. 2003).

In sum, Washington courts will not enforce contractual terms that operate only to the benefit of the more powerful party. If the class-action ban in Cingular's contract is one-sided, the term is substantively unconscionable and unenforceable under Washington law.

B. By Banning Class Actions, Cingular's Arbitration Clause Is One-Sided.

As set forth in part III.A, above, the law is clear in Washington that parties with superior bargaining power may not impose one-sided, non-mutual arbitration clauses upon weaker parties. In this case, it is abundantly clear that Cingular's contractual ban on class actions is a one-sided, non-mutual term. It will benefit only Cingular, and could not conceivably benefit even one of Cingular's customers. The well-understood reality is that without such a contract provision, it is foreseeable that Cingular consumers may from time to time bring class actions against the company. It is unimaginable, by contrast, that Cingular would ever sue its customers on a class action basis. Accordingly, the class action ban in Cingular's contract strips its customers of a remedy that they would be likely to invoke over time, but strips absolutely no remedy from Cingular that it might ever wish to pursue. This nearly self-evident fact was set out cogently in *Szetela v Discover Bank*:

> Although styled as a mutual prohibition on representative or class actions, it is difficult to envision the circumstances under which the provision might negatively impact Discover, because credit card companies typically do not sue their customers in class action lawsuits. This provision is clearly meant to prevent customers, such as Szetela and those he seeks to represent, from seeking redress for relatively small amounts of money, such as the $29 sought by Szetela. Fully aware that few customers will go to the time and trouble of suing in small claims court, Discover has instead sought to create for itself virtual immunity from class or representative actions despite their potential merit, while suffering no similar detriment to its own rights.

Szetela v Discover Bank, 97 Cal. App. 4th 1094, 1101, 118 Cal. Rptr. 2d 862, 867 (2002), *cert. denied*, 537 U.S. 1226 (2003).

A federal court applying Washington State law has held that a company's contract that prohibited class actions was effectively one-sided because it took away a remedy that only consumers would ever use. In *Luna*, the court held that:

> Although the Arbitration Rider's class action provision is nominally mutual, because there is no reasonable possibility that Household would institute a class action against its borrowers, the provision is effectively one-sided.

236 F. Supp. 2d at 1179. The court thus held that the arbitration clause was unconscionable under Washington law.

In *Ting*, similarly, the Ninth Circuit held that an identical term was one-sided and not bilateral because it limited the remedies available to consumers, but not AT&T. While a number of consumers have brought successful class actions against AT&T, the Ninth Circuit correctly observed that "[i]t is difficult to imagine AT&T bringing a class action against its own customers...." *Ting*, 319 F.3d at 1150.

The Ninth Circuit very recently confirmed that a class-action ban in an arbitration contract that is effectively one-sided is substantively unconscionable under Washington law. In *Al-Safin v. Circuit City Stores*, No. 03-35297, 2005 WL 77145 (9th Cir. Jan. 14, 2005), the court considered several provisions of Circuit City's employment contract, including a term banning class-wide arbitration. The court had previously held that the class-action ban, while nominally mutual, was simply an attempt by Circuit City "to seek to insulate itself from class proceedings while conferring no corresponding benefit" to employees. *Ingle v. Circuit City Stores, Inc.*, 328 F.3d 1165, 1176 (9th Cir. 2003). The court found that the class-action ban was "manifestly and shockingly one-sided" and thus substantively unconscionable under California law. *Id.* The *Al-Safin* court further held that "California applies virtually the same definition of substantive unconscionability as Washington." 2005 WL 77145 at *6.

The Ninth Circuit's decisions in *Ting* and *Al-Safin* are consistent with the Washington Supreme Court's decisions in *Zuver* and *Adler*—they are a logical extension of the holdings in those cases striking down one-sided arbitration clauses that disproportionately affect individuals while letting corporations retain all of the remedies that they desire. This Court should embrace and endorse the reasoning of these two decisions.

IV. CINGULAR'S ARBITRATION CLAUSE IS SUBSTANTIVELY UNCONSCIONABLE BECAUSE IT SERVES AS AN ABSOLUTE EXCULPATORY CLAUSE.

A. Washington State Law Does Not Permit Corporations To Draft Adhesive Arbitration Clauses That Insulate The Corporations From Liability For Behavior That Violates The Law.

In *Adler*, as discussed above, the Washington Supreme Court struck down as unconscionable and unenforceable a provision in an arbitration clause that shortened the limitations period for an employee to bring claims. In holding that the provision violated Washington law, the court emphasized that it "could be interpreted to insulate the employer from potential liability for violative behavior occurring outside the limitations period" and is thus substantively unconscionable. *Adler*, 2004 WL 3016302 at *11.

Washington state law on this topic is entirely in keeping with the law discussed in part III.A above, relating to one-sided contracts. In the *Zuver* case, the court noted that one-sided non-mutual terms are substantively unconscionable precisely when they effectively block one party from "access to a significant legal recourse." *Zuver*, 2004 WL 3016484 at *11. The point here is that a contract provision that strips individuals of legal recourse should be found to be substantively unconscionable. Accordingly, the Washington Supreme Court's guidance in *Zuver* that arbitration clauses may not bar consumers from "access to a significant legal resource" should apply both to contracts that openly strip consumers of such access and to contracts, such as Cingular's, that effectively do so.

Washington State law barring arbitration clauses from stripping individuals of substantive rights is entirely consistent with the law throughout the United States on this point. The U.S. Supreme Court has stated repeatedly that arbitration must allow a party to "effectively vindicate" its rights. *Mitsubishi Motors Corp. v. Soler Chrysler-Plymouth, Inc.*, 473 U.S. 614, 637 (1985); *Gilmer v. Interstate/Johnson Lane Corp.*, 500 U.S. 20, 28 (1991) (quoting Mitsubishi).\2

B. By Banning Class Actions, Cingular's Arbitration Clause Effectively Amounts To An Exculpatory Clause, Immunizing Cingular From Any Legal Responsibility Even If All Of Plaintiffs' Claims Are True and Correct.

1. The Undisputed Facts In This Case Establish That The Vast Majority, If Not All, Of Cingular's Customers Would Not Be Able To Bring Cases Such As This One On An Individual Basis.

The evidence below demonstrated that the ban on class actions in Cingular's contract effectively insulates it from any liability for claims such as those raised here, without respect to whether those claims are true and legally valid. Even if Plaintiffs are correct that Cingular broke its contract with the putative class members and cheated them out of money, they will still have no meaningful remedy if Cingular's arbitration clause is enforced.

Plaintiffs introduced expert testimony from Sally Gustafson Garratt and Peter Maier. As the Statement of the Case establishes, these two experts are probably the two best qualified persons in the state of Washington to speak to the practical effect of Cingular's ban on class actions. Each expert testified in detail that without the possibility of pursuing their claims on a class action basis, all or nearly all of Cingular's customers would be unable to obtain any legal remedy for the wrongs set forth in the complaint.

Cingular did not rebut this testimony with any evidence to suggest that any serious number of consumers would be able to find attorneys to help them bring claims of this size on an individual basis. In addition, the testimony of Plaintiffs' experts was strongly supported by a witness from the American Arbitration Association (Cingular's chosen arbitral forum), who acknowledged that *not one Cingular customer in at least the past six years had ever actually taken a claim against Cingular to arbitration.* CP at 1435 ¶ 8.

2. Courts Throughout The United States Have Recognized That Contractual Bans On Class Actions Serve As Exculpatory Clauses, And For That Reason Violate Generally Applicable State Contract Laws.

The factual record in this case is entirely consistent with the holdings and factual findings of courts in a number of cases brought throughout the United States. The leading case in this area is *Ting v. AT&T*, 319 F.3d 1126 (9th Cir.), *cert. denied*, 540 U.S. 811 (2003). In the *Ting* case, the U.S. district court held a trial over the question (among others) of whether it was unconscionable for AT&T's arbitration clause to ban class actions. Based on the district

---

\2 A number of courts have struck down as unconscionable arbitration clauses that explicitly stripped employees or consumers of their substantive statutory rights. *See, e.g., Circuit City Stores, Inc. v. Adams*, 279 F.3d 889, 894 (9th Cir. 2002); *Graham Oil Co. v. ARCO Products Co.*, 43 F.3d 1244, 1247 (9th Cir. 1994); *Paladino v. Avnet Computer Technologies., Inc.*, 134 F.3d 1054, 1062 (11th Cir. 1998) (Cox., J. concurring for majority of the panel); *Gourley v. Yellow Transp., L.L.C.*, 178 F. Supp. 2d 1196 (D. Colo. 2001); *Armendariz v. Foundation Health Psychare Services, Inc.*, 6 P.3d 669, 681 (Cal. 2000); *Holt v. O'Brien*, 862 So.2d 87 (Fla. Dist. Ct. App. 2003); *Flyer Hill Printing Co. v. Hill*, 805 So.2d 829 (Fla. Dist. Ct. App. 2001); *Carll v. Terminix Int'l Co.*, 793 A.2d 921 (Pa. Super. Ct. 2002). As set forth in Part IV.B.1, Cingular's contractual ban on class actions has the same impact as a provision that explicitly strips individuals of their rights.

court's extensive fact findings, the Ninth Circuit found that AT&T's prohibition on class actions was one-sided and non-mutual. Based upon extensive proof and testimony at the trial, the district court had also found, however, that the ban on class actions effectively would operate as an exculpatory clause. The district court found that the evidence in that case established that before AT&T had adopted its arbitration clause, consumers had successfully prosecuted a number of class actions against long distance phone carriers. *Ting v. AT&T*, 182 F. Supp. 2d 902, 915 (N.D. Cal. 2002). In one case, AT&T paid 100% of the class members' damages, *id.* at 918, and in another case a class recovered $88 million from a long distance carrier. *Id.* The parties in *Ting* stipulated that none of the lawyers in any of the identified earlier class actions could have brought those cases on an individual basis, whether in court or arbitration. *Id.* Based on these and other facts, the district court held that without the class action mechanism, "the potential reward would be insufficient to motivate private counsel to assume the risks of prosecuting the case just for an individual on a contingency basis." *Id.* Because of these realities, "the prohibition on class action litigation functions as an effective deterrent to litigating many types of claims involving rates, services or billing practices and, ultimately, . . . [serves] to shield AT&T from liability even in cases where it has violated the law." *Id.* Accordingly, the court found the ban on class actions in AT&T's arbitration clause to be substantively unconscionable. *Id.* at 931.

Applying Washington State law, a federal district court similarly held that a consumer contract that barred class actions effectively amounted to an exculpatory clause:

> The Arbitration Rider's prohibition of class actions would prevent borrowers from effectively vindicating their rights for certain categories of claims. Even if Household were correct in asserting that a borrower's arbitration costs are minimal . . ., some borrowers effectively may be prevented from vindicating their rights. This is a particular concern when, as alleged here, the plaintiffs are financially strapped. The Arbitration Rider's prohibition of class actions is likely to bar actions involving practices applicable to all potential class members, but for which an individual consumer has so little at stake that she is unlikely to pursue her claim.

Luna, 236 F. Supp.2d at 1178–79.

Another case looking into detail at how bans on class actions amount to unconscionable exculpatory clauses is *West Virginia ex rel. Dunlap v. Berger*, 567 S.E.2d 265 (W. Va. 2002), *cert. denied*, 537 U.S. 1087 (2002). In that case, the court's reasoning was rooted in that state's longstanding law prohibiting exculpatory clauses in contracts of adhesion:

> Based on all of the foregoing and in fidelity to the approach that we have taken in this area, we recognize and hold that exculpatory provisions in a contract of adhesion that if applied would prohibit or substantially limit a person from seeking and obtaining and vindicating rights and protections or from seeking and obtaining statutory or common law relief and remedies that are afforded by or arise under state law that exists for the benefit of the public are unconscionable; unless the court determines that exceptional circumstances exist that make the provisions conscionable.

567 S.E.2d at 275. In *Dunlap*, the court held that in light of the modest claims at issue, the defendant's contractual ban on class actions would insulate it from all liability:

> In Mr. Dunlap's case, the total of $8.46 in insurance charges that Friedman's added to his purchase price . . . is precisely the sort of small-dollar/high volume (alleged) illegality that class action claims and remedies are effective at addressing. In many cases, the availability of class action relief is a sine qua non to permit the adequate vindication of consumer rights. . . .
>
> [P]ermitting the proponent of such a[n adhesion] contract to include a provision that prevents an aggrieved party from pursuing class action relief would go a long way toward allowing those who commit illegal activity to go unpunished, undeterred, and unaccountable.

Id. at 278–79.

The Alabama Supreme Court has also held that a contract term banning class actions built into an arbitration clause was unconscionable for the same reasons. *See Leonard v. Terminix Int'l Co.*, 854 So. 2d 529 (Ala. 2002) (petition for rehearing denied).[3] The Court noted that such a ban forecloses all individual plaintiffs from bringing a claim where the expense of arbitrating is greater than the amount in controversy. "That the expenses of arbitration would exceed the amount in controversy is not a problem personal or peculiar to any particular consumer but is, rather, a phenomenon inherent in the transaction itself." *Leonard*, 854 So. 2d at 537. By "foreclosing the Leonards from an attempt to seek practical redress through a class action and restricting them to a disproportionately expensive individual arbitration," the court found that the defendants had closed the door of justice to these consumers. *Id.* at 539. Accordingly, the Court held that the arbitration clause was unconscionable.

A California Court of Appeals has also addressed in some detail the real-world impact on consumers of a ban on class actions. In *Szetela*, the court explained that contractual prohibitions on class actions would effectively act as a "get out of jail free" card for corporate defendants:

> It is the manner of arbitration, specifically, prohibiting class or representative actions, we take exception to here. The clause is not only harsh and unfair to Discover customers who might be owed a relatively small sum of money, but it also serves as a disincentive for Discover to avoid the type of conduct that might lead to class action litigation in the first place. By imposing this clause on its

---

\3 In *Leonard*, the arbitration clause was silent on whether the parties could pursue a class action, but the court found such a remedy barred because class action arbitration is not possible in Alabama. *Leonard*, 854 So. 2d at 535, n. 2.

customers, Discover has essentially granted itself a license to push the boundaries of good business practices to their furthest limits, fully aware that relatively few, if any, customers will seek legal remedies, and that any remedies obtained will only pertain to that single customer without collateral estoppel effect.... Therefore, the provision violates fundamental notions of fairness.

Szetela, 96 Cal. App.4th at 1101, 118 Cal. Rptr. 2d at 868.

A number of other courts have reached the same conclusion. *See Luna*, 236 F. Supp. 2d 1166, 1179 ("Here, the prohibition on class actions allows the Arbitration Rider to be 'used as a sword to strike down access to justice instead of a shield against prohibitive costs.' This finding weighs heavily in favor of a finding of substantive unconscionability.") (citations omitted); *Jenkins v. First American Cash Advance of Georgia*, LLC, 313 F. Supp. 2d 1370 (S.D. Ga. 2004) ("A class action is the only way that borrowers with claims as small as the individual loan transactions can obtain relief.... Here, prohibiting class actions and requiring arbitration pursuant to an adhesion clause would have the practical effect of providing Defendants immunity."); *Comb v. PayPal*, 218 F. Supp. 2d 1165, 1176–77 (N.D. Cal. 2002) (arbitration clause was unconscionable, in part because it prohibited collective actions); *ACORN v. Household Int'l, Inc.*, 211 F. Supp. 2d 1160, 1170–71 (N.D. Cal. 2002) (holding that an arbitration clause that prohibited class actions was unconscionable); *Powertel v. Bexley*, 743 So. 2d 570, 576 (Fla. App. 1 Dist. 1999) ("By requiring arbitration of all claims, Powertel has precluded the possibility that a group of its customers might join together to seek relief that would be impractical for any of them to obtain alone."); *Eagle v. Fred Martin Motor Co.*, 809 N.E.2d 1161, 1183 (Ohio Ct. App. 2004) ("by expressly eliminating a consumer's right to proceed through a class action or as a private attorney general in arbitration, the arbitration clause directly hinders the consumer protection purposes" of the Ohio Consumer Protection Act); *In re Knepp*, 229 B.R. 821, 827 (N.D. Ala. 1999) ("The pervasive use of arbitration agreements in consumer contracts could have the effect of eliminating class actions. If class actions are no longer an option, the vast majority of consumer claims involving relatively small sums of money on an individual basis will be left without a remedy.").

As the *Ting* district court found, the availability of arbitration for small consumer claims does not ameliorate the consumers' need for the class device. *See also* Jean R. Sternlight, *As Mandatory Binding Arbitration Meets the Class Action, Will the Class Action Survive?*, 42 Wm. & Mary L. Rev. 1, 90 n. 353 (2000) ("[W]here a class action is excluded from arbitration, it is likely that many if not most of the claimants will not be able to arbitrate their claims.").

The conclusions of plaintiffs' witnesses here, and the courts cited, are consistent with what corporate defense counsel regularly acknowledges. As one defense lawyer has written,

> [T]he franchisor with an arbitration clause should be able to require each franchisee in the potential class to pursue individual claims in a separate arbitration. Since many (and perhaps most) of the putative class members may never do that, and because arbitrators typically do not issue runaway awards, strict enforcement of an arbitration clause should enable the franchisor to dramatically reduce its aggregate exposure.

Edward Wood Dunham, *The Arbitration Clause as a Class Action Shield*, 16 Franchise L.J. 141, 141 (1997). Another defense lawyer has described arbitration clauses as a "defense" for banks against consumer claims, in part because they can be a "deterrent" to class actions. Alan Kaplinsky, *Excuse Me, But Who's the Predator: Banks Can Use Arbitration Clauses as a Defense*, Bus. Law. 24, 26 (May/June 1998).

The prohibition on exculpatory clauses in contracts of adhesion applies not only to contract terms that explicitly strip parties of public rights, but also apply to contract terms that effectively strip parties of their public rights. It would make no sense to say that a party may not write a contract that explicitly says "you may not bring an action under any state consumer protection law," while permitting the same party to write a contract that mandates procedures that effectively make it impossible to bring an action under state consumer protection laws.

V. BECAUSE THE CLASS-ACTION BAN CANNOT BE SEVERED FROM THE REST OF CINGULAR'S ARBITRATION CLAUSE, THE ENTIRE CLAUSE MUST BE INVALIDATED.

When presented with an arbitration clause containing only one or two substantively unconscionable clauses, Washington law permits courts to sever the unconscionable provisions and enforce the remainder.\4 For example, the *Zuver* court severed the offensive confidentiality and remedies provisions, while otherwise affirming the trial court's order to compel arbitration. 2004 WL 3016484 at *11.

In this case, however, such a resolution is explicitly barred by the language of Cingular's clause. The clause provides that "if [the class-action ban] is found to be unenforceable, then the entirety of this arbitration clause shall be null and void." CP at 355–56. Thus, any attempt by Cingular to salvage the unconscionable class-action ban by drawing the Court's attention to other terms in the arbitration clause is a red herring. If the Court finds that the provision banning class actions is unconscionable under Washington law, the Court has no choice but to hold that the entire arbitration clause is unenforceable.

VI. WASHINGTON LAW OF SUBSTANTIVE UNCONSCIONABILITY IS CONSISTENT WITH THE FEDERAL ARBITRATION ACT.

A. There Is A Heavy Presumption Against Federal Preemption Of State Law.

Cingular argued below that Washington State contract law should be lightly swept aside, on the grounds that the FAA supposedly federalizes this area of law. In considering the assertion that federal law requires states to enforce contract provisions banning class actions whenever those provisions are included in an arbitration clause, this Court should first consider core principles of federal preemption law.

Because preemption constitutes a radical intrusion on a state's power, the U.S. Supreme Court has long recognized a strong presumption against preemption of state laws. Particularly where

---

\4 However, courts will decline to enforce an arbitration clause if the unconscionable terms are so severe or numerous that they "pervade" the clause. *Zuver*, 2004 WL 3016484 at *11.

"'federal law is said to bar state action in fields of traditional state regulation, we have worked on the assumption that the historic police powers of the States were not to be superseded by the Federal Act unless that was the clear and manifest purpose of Congress.'" *California Div. of Labor Standards Enforcement v. Dillingham Construction, N.A., Inc.*, 519 U.S. 316, 325 (1997) (citation omitted). Washington's common law of contracts and unconscionability are an area of traditional and almost exclusive state regulation. *See, e.g., Erie Railroad Co. v. Tompkins*, 304 U.S. 64, 78 (1983) ("Congress has no power to declare substantive rules of common law applicable in a state . . ."); *California v. ARC America Corp.*, 490 U.S. 93, 101 (1989) (recognizing common-law remedies as an "area traditionally regulated by the States"); *G.S. Rasmussen & Associates, Inc. v. Kalitta Flying Service, Inc.*, 958 F.2d 896, 906 (9th Cir. 1992) ("[W]hen Congress legislates in a field traditionally occupied by the states, such as common law tort and contract remedies in business relationships, there is a presumption against finding preemption of state law.") (citation omitted).

Where a federal statute has no express preemption provision, and where a federal statute does not preempt an entire field, state law will only be preempted if there is an "actual conflict" between federal and state law, either because it is "impossible for a private party to comply with both . . . requirements" or because the state laws "stand[] as an obstacle to the accomplishment and execution of the full purposes of Congress." *Freightliner Corp. v. Myrick*, 514 U.S. 280, 287 (1995) (citations omitted). This standard is not easily met, and, in particular, there cannot be implied conflict preemption where there is no federal law standard addressing the subject of state law regulation.

Washington courts, likewise, could not be more clear on this point. As the Supreme Court of Washington recently declared, "Preemption is the exception, not the rule in Washington." *Hisle v. Todd Pacific Shipyards Corp.*, 151 Wn. 2d 853, 864, 93 P.3d 108, 113 (2004). The court has repeatedly recognized that "[i]n Washington, there is a strong presumption against finding preemption." *Dept of Labor Indus. v. Common Carriers, Inc.*, 111 Wn. 2d 586, 588, 762 P.2d 348, 349 (1988) (explaining that "[p]reemption may be found only if federal law clearly evinces a congressional intent to preempt state law, or there is such a direct and positive conflict that the two acts cannot be reconciled or consistently stand together.") (internal citations and quotations omitted). The burden of proof is on the party claiming preemption. *Washington State Physicians Ins. Exchange & Ass'n v. Fisons Corp.*, 122 Wn.2d 299, 327, 858 P.2d 1054, 1069 (1993). Further, the presumption against preemption is even more difficult to overcome when "the subject matter of the state statute is one within the state's traditional powers." *Franks & Son, Inc. v. State*, 136 Wn. 2d 737, 759, 966 P.2d 1232, 1243 (1998). In such cases, "the party arguing federal preemption must show that preemption was the 'clear and manifest purpose of Congress.'" *Id.* For example, the court held that state common-law claims were not preempted by federal law, when allowing the pursuit of state law remedies would "complement[] the purposes" of the federal law. *Stevedoring Services of America, Inc. v. Eggert*, 129 Wn. 2d 17, 39, 914 P.2d 737, 748 (1996). This Court has repeatedly agreed. *See, e.g., State v. Grimes*, 111 Wn. App. 544, 551, 46 P.3d 801, 804–05 (Div. 1 2002) ("There is a strong presumption against preemption. . . . The party asserting preemption has the burden of proof."); *Dortch v. Straka*, 59 Wn. App. 773, 777–78, 801 P.2d 279, 281 (Div. 1 1990) (federal preemption applies only where state law does "major damage" to "clear and substantial" federal interests) (citations omitted).

B. Washington State Law Holding Cingular's Arbitration Clause Substantively Unconscionable Does Not Conflict With The Federal Arbitration Act.

The Washington Supreme Court has twice reaffirmed within recent months that arbitration clauses are subject to "generally applicable contract defenses, such as . . . unconscionability. . . ." *Adler*, 2004 WL 3016302 at *3; *Zuver*, 2004 WL 3016484 at * 3.\5 This Court, likewise, has made clear that "general principles of state contract law, such as unconscionability, may be applied to invalidate arbitration agreements without contravening the FAA." *Kruger Clinic Orthopaedics v. Regence Blushield*, 123 Wn. App. 355, 368, 98 P.3d 66, 72 (Div. 1 2004). As set forth above, in both *Adler* and *Zuver*, the Washington Supreme Court applied Washington state contract law to strike down provisions in two arbitration clauses that were either one-sided or that had the effect of immunizing a party from liability for violating the law. In each case, the defendants strenuously argued that the provisions at issue were protected by the FAA. And in each case, the Supreme Court flatly rejected those arguments, finding that the FAA does not protect either one-sided contract terms or ones that provide immunity to law breakers.\6 These holdings are consistent with generally applicable Washington state contract law.

Since Washington law does not generally permit stronger parties to write one-sided contracts that immunize themselves even if they violate the law, to apply a lesser standard to Cingular's arbitration clause would contravene the FAA by applying different legal standards to arbitration clauses than are applied to other contracts. The FAA's goals are to "'reverse the longstanding judicial hostility to arbitration agreements . . . and to place arbitration agreements *upon the same footing as other contracts.*'" *EEOC v. Waffle House, Inc.*, 534 U.S. at 289 (emphasis added, citation omitted). Nothing in the FAA permits parties to launder otherwise illegal contract terms and make them legal merely by sticking them under the heading of "arbitration," however, and this Court has never so held. As the West Virginia Supreme Court held in the course of a decision striking down an arbitration clause that contained a contractual ban on class actions, the FAA does not allow for this

---

\5 In both cases, the court relied upon *Ticknor v. Choice Hotels Int'l, Inc.*, 265 F.3d 931 (9th Cir. 2001). In that case, the defendant argued (as does Cingular in this case) that the FAA preempts state laws of unconscionability as they relate to arbitration clauses containing one-sided provisions. The Ninth Circuit rejected that argument for reasons that apply here: "Montana law pertaining to the unconscionability of arbitration clauses was the result of 'the application of general principles that exist at law or in equity for the revocation of any contract.'" 265 F.3d at 941.

\6 For example, in cases outside the context of arbitration clauses, Washington courts have repeatedly struck down part or all of contracts that are one-sided or that effectively insulate one party from liability for wrongdoing. *See, e.g., Johnson v. Cash Store*, 68 P.3d 1099 (Div. 3 2003) (vacating default judgment against consumer where payday loan agreement was one-sided and thus unconscionable); *McCutcheon v. United Homes Corp.*, 79 Wn. 2d 443, 450, 486 P.2d 1093, 1097 (1971) (lease term making landlord immune from liability for common-law negligence against public policy); *Sporsem v. First Nat. Bank*, 133 Wn. 199, 204, 233 P. 641, 643 (1925) (bailee cannot by contract exempt himself from liability for his own negligence).

kind of escape from state contract liability "merely because the prohibiting or limiting provisions are part of or tied to provisions in the contract relating to arbitration." *Dunlap*, 567 S.E.2d at 280.

Another court holding that the FAA does not interfere with state laws that hold unconscionable provisions in arbitration clauses that ban class actions was the federal district court in *Comb*:

> [W]hile the FAA preempts any legislation "specifically aimed at arbitration agreements," "[I]n all situations where arbitration provisions are placed on the same footing as other contracts, state law applies." . . . Thus, while California's consumer protection statutes cannot prevent enforcement under the FAA of a prohibition on collection actions as such, a federal court properly may consider whether such a prohibition in combination with other provisions and circumstances renders an agreement substantively unconscionable as a matter of state law.

Comb, 218 F. Supp. 2d at 1175–76, citing *Ticknor v. Choice Hotels Int'l, Inc.*, 265 F.3d 931 (9th Cir. 2001).

C. Washington State Law Recognizing The Value Of Class Actions Is Consistent With U.S. Supreme Court Jurisprudence.

The Washington Supreme Court has recognized that class actions fill a critical need in the justice system by "establish[ing] effective procedures for redress of injuries for those whose economic position would not allow individual lawsuits." *Darling v. Champion Home Builders Co.*, 96 Wn. 2d 701, 706, 638 P.2d 1249, 1252 (1982). Individual consumers who would otherwise lack the means or ingenuity to pursue small damages claims can vindicate their rights through class actions. Indeed, Washington courts have consistently emphasized that "a primary function of the class suit is to provide a procedure for vindicating claims which, taken individually, are too small to justify individual legal action but which are of significant size and importance if taken as a group." *Brown v. Brown*, 6 Wn. App. 249, 253, 492 P.2d 581, 584 (Div. 2 1971); *see also Oda v. State*, 111 Wn. App. 79, 86, 44 P.3d 8, 12 (Div. 1 2002) (same); *Smith v. Behr Process Corp.*, 113 Wn. App. 306, 319, 54 P.3d 665, 673 (Div. 2 2002) (noting that "the interests of justice require that in a doubtful case . . . any error, if there is to be one, should be committed in favor of allowing the class action"); *cf. Bowles v. Washington Dept. of Retirement Systems*, 121 Wn. 2d 52, 71, 847 P.2d 440, 450 (1993) (making attorney fees available to prevailing class action plaintiffs "furthers important policy interests," because it means "plaintiffs will have less difficulty obtaining counsel and greater access to the judicial system. Little good comes from a system where justice is available only to those who can afford its price."). In short, the importance of class actions to preserving access to the courts for plaintiffs with individually small claims is a basic assumption of Washington law.

As set forth above, Washington law may only be found to be preempted by the FAA if the state law conflicts with Congress's purposes in enacting the FAA to such extent that Washington is an obstacle to the enforcement of federal law. In this case, plaintiffs are invoking two bodies of state law: (a) that Washington state contract law prohibits exculpatory clauses in contracts of adhesion; and (b) that Washington state law recognizes that in many settings class actions offer the only means whereby consumers asserting modest claims can get justice for those claims. Before this Court gives excessive credence to the idea that federal law preempts either of these propositions, it should recognize that both of these bodies of law are entirely consistent with a number of decisions of the U.S. Supreme Court.

First, the U.S. Supreme Court has directed that arbitration clauses are enforceable under the FAA only if they make proceedings accessible so that claimants can effectively enforce their rights. *See, e.g., Gilmer v. Interstate/Johnson Lane Corp.*, 500 U.S. 20, 26 (1991) ("[B]y agreeing to arbitrate a statutory claim, a party does not forgo the substantive rights afforded by the statute; it only submits to their resolution in an arbitral, rather than a judicial, forum.") (citation omitted). As an illustration of this principle, the U.S. Supreme Court has recognized that "the existence of large arbitration costs may well preclude a litigant . . . from effectively vindicating [its] rights," *Green Tree Financial Corp. v. Randolph*, 531 U.S. 79, 81 (2000). The Court further stated that arbitration is acceptable as an alternative to litigation in court because it is simply a "different forum" from court. While the Supreme Court has acknowledged that the arbitral forum has somewhat different and simplified rules, it is nonetheless a forum in which the basic mechanisms for obtaining justice permit a party to "effectively vindicate" his or her rights. *See, e.g., Equal Employment Opportunity Comm'n v. Waffle House, Inc.*, 534 U.S. 279, 295 n. 10 (2002). Where, as here, a corporation designs an arbitration system that fails to meet this promise, the underlying rationale for enforcing arbitration clauses disappears.

Washington law recognizing the importance of class actions for persons with small claims is also entirely consistent with the decisions of the U.S. Supreme Court on the point:

> A significant benefit to claimants who choose to litigate their individual claims in a class-action context is the prospect of reducing their costs obligation, particularly attorney's fees, by allocating such costs among all members of the class who benefit from any recovery. Typically, the attorney's fees of a named plaintiff proceeding without reliance on Rule 23 could exceed the value of the individual judgment in favor of any one plaintiff. Here the damages claimed by the two named plaintiffs totaled $1,006.00. *Such plaintiffs would be unlikely to obtain legal redress at an acceptable cost, unless counsel were motivated by the fee-spreading incentive and proceeded on a contingent-fee basis.* This, of course, is a central concept of Rule 23.

Deposit Guaranty Nat'l Bank v. Roper, 445 U.S. 326, 338 n. 9 (1980) (emphasis added). *See also Amchem Products, Inc. v. Windsor*, 521 U.S. 591, 617 (1997) ("The policy at the very core of the class action mechanism is to overcome the problem that small recoveries do not provide the incentive for any individual to bring a solo action prosecuting his or her rights. A class action solves this problem by aggregating the relatively paltry potential recoveries into something worth someone's (usually an attorney's) labor."); *Eisen v. Carlisle & Jacquelin*, 417 U.S. 156, 161 (1974) ("A critical fact . . . is that petitioner's individual stake . . . is only $70. No competent attorney would undertake this complex antitrust action to recover so inconsequential an amount. Economic reality dictates that petitioner's suit proceed as a class action or not at all.")

D. Cingular's Contract Provision Banning Class Actions Is Not Inherent To Or Necessary To Arbitration, But Is Merely An Unrelated Abusive Term That Cingular Has Chosen To Tack On To Its Arbitration Provision.

As set forth above, the FAA would preempt any state law that attempts to restrict or limit the use of arbitration. This raises an important question: if Washington state law were to limit the ability of a corporation to ban class actions, could that body of law be fairly characterized as "anti-arbitration"? Is it hostile to the idea of arbitration for a state to say that it is illegal for a corporation to put into its consumer contracts a provision that bars consumers from participating in class actions?

If one looks at the law of class actions, it becomes clear that the answer to these questions is unequivocally "no." If a corporation decides to try to bar its consumers from ever participating in a class action, that decision has nothing to do with any desire for arbitration. The reason is simple: there is nothing about arbitration that requires that it be conducted on an individual basis. Indeed, the U.S. Supreme Court has explicitly held that arbitrations may be conducted on a class action basis. *See Green Tree Financial Corp. v. Bazzle*, 539 U.S. 444, 447 (2003) (the question of whether arbitration may proceed on a class action basis in a case where the arbitration clause is silent on the question is "a matter of state law . . ."); *id.* at 450 (dissenting opinion advocating a particular reading of the arbitration clause suggests that "we should ignore the fact that state law, not federal law, normally governs such matters. . . ."). As further evidence that arbitrations may be handled on a class-wide basis, the American Arbitration Association has promulgated rules for handling class actions in arbitration, and has in fact handled quite a few cases on a class action basis. CP at 1441 ¶¶ 32–33.

As further evidence that it is anything but "anti-arbitration" for a state's contract law to bar a corporation from prohibiting its customers from participating in class actions, JAMS, one of the largest providers of alternative dispute resolution services in the United States, now takes the position that "it is inappropriate for a Company to restrict the right of a consumer to be a member of a class action arbitration or to initiate a class action arbitration." JAMS Policy Regarding Use of Class Action Preclusion Clauses, at www.jamsadr.com/images/PDF/JAMS-ClassActionPreclusion Policy.PDF. JAMS thus has instituted a policy of refusing to enforce class action bans in arbitration contracts:

> JAMS will not enforce [class action preclusion] clauses in class action arbitrations and will require that they be waived in individual cases. JAMS hopes that companies that utilize consumer arbitration will remove class action preclusion clauses from their arbitration clauses, understanding that the inclusion of such clauses is an unfair restriction on the rights of the consumer.

JAMS Press Release (Nov. 12, 2004), at http://www.jamsadr.com/press/show_release.asp?id=187. This policy, adopted by an undeniably pro-arbitration organization, further demonstrates that Cingular's ban on class actions has nothing to do with arbitration, and everything to do with preventing its customers from being able to join their small claims together and hold the corporation accountable for unlawful business practices.

At bottom, this appeal is not really about arbitration but about the right to class action relief. If this Court refuses to enforce this arbitration clause, Cingular will be able to write a new, legal contract and in the future hold all of its Washington customers to mandatory binding arbitration clauses if it so chooses. The one thing that Cingular can not do, however, is take away from customers the right to seek class-wide relief through class action proceedings—whether in arbitration or in court. No one denies that the drafter of any contract could both require arbitration and comply with the rule of law set forth in cases cited above such as *Ting* merely by expressly providing that arbitrations could proceed on a class-wide basis. This fact alone demonstrates that state law prohibiting contractual bans on class actions does not violate the FAA.

For Cingular to prevail that Washington State contract law is preempted by the FAA, Cingular must demonstrate that Washington law is hostile to arbitration. Cingular's own contract reveals that it is Cingular itself that is hostile to arbitration. Cingular's contract provides that if some court reviewing the contractual ban on class actions holds that "this specific proviso is . . . unenforceable, then the entirety of this arbitration clause shall be null and void." CP at 355–56. In other words, Cingular would rather have no arbitration at all than have a class action that takes place within the confines of arbitration. This provision emphasizes what this dispute is actually about: Cingular doesn't want to arbitrate disputes, Cingular wants to make sure that none of its consumers are able to bring any disputes in any forum.

VII. CINGULAR'S ARBITRATION CLAUSE WAS FORMED IN A PROCEDURALLY UNCONSCIONABLE MANNER.

Under Washington law, a contract is unenforceable for procedural unconscionability if one party lacked a "meaningful choice." *Adler*, 2004 WL 3016302 at *6; *Zuver*, 2004 WL 3016484 at *3. To determine whether a meaningful choice existed, courts look at a number of factors, such as the manner in which the contract was formed, whether the party had a reasonable opportunity to understand its terms, and whether important terms were hidden in fine print. *Adler*, 2004 WL 3016302 at *6; *see also Schroeder v. Fageol Motors, Inc.*, 86 Wn. 2d 256, 260, 544 P.2d 20, 23 (1975) (in analyzing limitation on liability, considering "conspicuousness" and "negotiations"). The court must consider "all the circumstances surrounding the transaction." *Adler*, 2004 WL 3016302 at *6.

First, an examination of the manner in which Cingular's original and revised arbitration clauses were formed supports a finding of procedural unconscionability. The trial court correctly held that Cingular's arbitration clause is a classic contract of adhesion. Washington uses three factors to determine whether a contract of adhesion exists: "(1) whether the contract is a standard form printed contract, (2) whether it was prepared by one party and submitted to the other on a take-it-or-leave-it basis, and (3) whether there was no true equality of bargaining power between the parties." *Zuver*, 2004 WL 3016484 at *4 (internal citations and quotations omitted). There is no dispute that Cingular's clause exemplifies these characteristics. While the fact that an arbitration agreement is a contract of adhesion does not end the inquiry, *id.*, it weighs in favor of finding procedural unconscionability.

In particular, the presence of one-sided terms, such as Cingular's class-action ban, in a contract of adhesion, such as Cingular's arbitration clause, is sufficient to render its formation void for procedural unconscionability. Where the terms of a contract of adhesion favor one party over the other such that the consumer has no meaningful choice, the contract is procedurally unconscionable. *Johnson v. Cash Store*, 116 Wn. App. 833, 68 P.3d 1099 (Div. 3 2003) (refusing to enforce payday loan contract that was one-sided and thus procedurally unconscionable).

Second, Plaintiffs have introduced uncontradicted evidence showing that the terms of the original arbitration clause were well-concealed in a "maze of fine print." *Schroeder*, 86 Wn. 2d at 260. As described in the Statement of the Case, the arbitration clause was buried in tiny print, in the middle of a paragraph near the bottom of a legal-sized page. CP at 340; 343. Consumer law expert Peter Maier testified that "[t]he agreement is very complex, hard to read and difficult to understand. Its fine print fills an entire legal-size page from margin to margin." CP at 1583 ¶ 13. Thus, while the trial court judge experienced relatively little difficulty comprehending the contract, RP at 16, the evidence presented in this case demonstrates that Plaintiffs lacked a "reasonable opportunity" to understand the terms of the clause.\7 CP at 1139 ¶ 6; 1249 ¶ 4–5.

Third, Cingular customers had no meaningful choice but to continue service with Cingular despite the arbitration clauses, given that the new clause was "effective immediately," CP at 355–56, and that nearly every other major wireless phone provider in Washington requires mandatory arbitration on nearly identical terms. CP at 1363–65 ¶¶ 3–13; 1366.\8 The U.S. district court in *Ting*, faced with virtually identical facts, found that AT&T subscribers "did not have any meaningful choice with respect to the [term] because the carriers who service 2/3 of the California market all include substantially similar dispute resolution provisions in their contracts." 182 F. Supp. 2d at 914. A meaningful choice would require that there were "reasonably available alternative sources of supply from which to obtain the desired goods and services *free of the terms claimed to be unconscionable.*" *Id.* at 929 (emphasis added). These facts supported the court's finding of procedural unconscionability. *Id.* at 930.

Fourth, Cingular's revised arbitration clause was sent to customers in the least conspicuous manner possible: inserted, together with a number of other papers and clauses, into a monthly bill. CP at 352 ¶ 3. This approach predictably guarantees that the overwhelming majority of consumers will never read the amendment. The reason is simple and intuitive: many corporations include all kinds of promotional invitations in the envelopes with bills (anyone who reads their mail can confirm that these promotions offer everything from "free computer printers if you buy another printer first" to "security" for your credit card to dance lessons), and the vast majority of consumers become inured to these solicitations. As a result, most consumers pull out the slip of paper that needs to be returned with the check, get the envelope in which the bill state-

---

\7 In fact, the terms of Cingular's contract in at least one instance were so garbled that they were unintelligible. CP at 1596 ¶¶ 5–6; 1598–99.

\8 For further evidence that a great many cellular service providers have adopted arbitration clauses that ban class actions, see National Consumer Law Center, Consumer Arbitration Agreements: Enforceability and Other Topics (4th ed. 2004) (CD-Rom accompanying book) (contains copies of arbitration clauses from, among others, Sprint and Verizon Wireless).

ment should be returned, and throw away the remainder of the junk mailing. In *Ting*, for example, after hearing extensive marketing evidence from the parties and reviewing documentation from AT&T's own in-house marketing team, the U.S. district court made the following findings about a notice sent out as a bill stuffer:

> The billing mailing was highly likely to be opened. However, a reasonable class member would not have expected the billing statement to contain a new contract, and therefore might well have discarded the [Consumer Service Agreement] as a stuffer.

Ting, 182 F. Supp. 2d at 912.

A number of commentators have addressed this phenomenon. *See, e.g.*, Senator Russell D. Feingold, *Mandatory Arbitration: What Process Is Due?*, 39 Harv. J. On Legis. 281, 295–96 (2002):

> Companies ... unilaterally insert mandatory, binding arbitration clauses into their agreements with consumers, often without the consumers' knowledge or consent. . . . [They] commonly do this through the advertisements and other materials they insert into envelopes with the customers' monthly statements, often called "bill stuffers." The arbitration provision is often buried in a lengthy legal document within these bill stuffers that most consumers do not so much as glance at, much less read carefully. . . . In one case involving Bank of America, the bank knew that no more than four percent of card holders would read the bill stuffers.

See also Alan M. White, Cathy Lesser Mansfield, *Literacy and Contract*, 13 Stan. L. & Pol'y Rev. 233, 233 (2002) ("Most consumers do not read contracts or disclosure forms. They routinely enter into contracts in an atmosphere that discourages them from reading the contract to be signed and, in any event, precludes negotiation of the terms of the writing."); *id.* at 249–50 ("Modern credit-card agreements routinely provide that the credit-card issuer will supply contract terms in writing later and that it unilaterally may change the terms of the credit-card agreement through future mailings of fine-print documents."). This research is consistent with Plaintiffs' uncontroverted testimony that, due to the large number of flyers and inserts in typical Cingular mailings, they ignore and discard Cingular's bill stuffers. CP at 1139 ¶ 7; 1250 ¶ 9.

As a consequence of these widely recognized facts, a number of courts around the country have recognized that arbitration clauses sent out on a take-it-or-leave-it basis in bill stuffers are procedurally unconscionable. *See Szetela*, 118 Cal. Rptr.2d at 867 ("Szetela received the amendment to the Cardholder Agreement in a bill stuffer. . . . His only option, if he did not wish to accept the amendment, was to close his account. [This] establishes the necessary element of procedural unconscionability."); *Powertel, Inc.*, 743 So.2d at 574–75 ("Powertel prepared the arbitration clause unilaterally and sent it along to its customers as an insert to their monthly telephone bill. The customers did not bargain for the arbitration clause, nor did they have the power to reject it. One of the hallmarks of procedural unconscionability is the absence of any meaningful choice on the part of the consumer. . . . Here, the customers had no choice but to agree to the new arbitration clause if they wished to continue to use the cellular telephone plans they had purchased from Powertel."); *Discover Bank v. Shea*, 827 A.2d at 365 ("The amendment to the agreement was included with a monthly statement, as a "bill stuffer" and not seen by Mr. Shea. . . . In the instant matter, the arbitration clause is contained in a contract of adhesion. There is clearly unequal bargaining power between the parties and the only purpose of the provision purporting to prevent class-wide litigation is to effectively remove the only legitimate remedy for cardholders with small claims."); *cf. Badie v. Bank of America*, 79 Cal. Rptr. 2d 273, 290 (1998) ("Nor do we find an unambiguous and unequivocal waiver . . . because . . . the notice contained in the 'bill stuffer' was 'not designed to achieve "knowing consent" ' to the ADR provision.").

This Court should join this consensus. The two-step process by which Cingular's class-action ban was imposed on its customers smacks of procedural unconscionability. First, Cingular buried an arbitration clause in a maze of fine print in a barely-legible document. Next, Cingular sent out a revised arbitration clause in a format that predictably ensured that only a tiny percentage of consumers would ever notice it, let alone read or understand it. If this sort of notice is not found to be procedurally unconscionable, consumers will be forced to await cases involving threats at gun point to meet that standard.

CONCLUSION

Because Cingular's class-action ban is unconscionable under Washington law and cannot be severed from the arbitration clause, this Court should hold the arbitration agreement unenforceable, reverse the decision of the superior court granting Cingular's motion to compel arbitration, and permit Plaintiffs to pursue their claims as a class in court.

Respectfully submitted this 21st January, 2005

[*Attorneys for Appellants*]

F.2.2 Plaintiffs' Reply Brief

COURT OF APPEALS, DIVISION I
OF THE STATE OF WASHINGTON

DOUG SCOTT, LOREN TABASINKE, SANDRA TABASINSKE, PATRICK OISHI, JANET OISHI, et al., Appellants,

v.

CINGULAR WIRELESS, Respondent.

APPEAL FROM THE SUPERIOR COURT FOR KING COUNTY HONORABLE CATHERINE SHAFFER

APPELLANTS' REPLY BRIEF ON THE MERITS

TABLE OF CONTENTS

TABLE OF AUTHORITIES
INTRODUCTION AND SUMMARY OF ARGUMENT

I. CINGULAR'S BAN ON CLASS-WIDE RELIEF IS SUBSTANTIVELY UNCONSCIONABLE.
  A. Cingular's Ban on Class-Wide Relief Violates Core Principles Laid Down in *Zuver* and *Adler*.
    1. The Ban On Class-Wide Relief Is One-Sided.
    2. The Ban On Class-Wide Relief Does Serve As An Exculpatory Clause.
    3. An Arbitration Clause With An Unseverable Unconscionable Term Is Not Rendered Enforceable By Other "Consumer-Friendly" Terms.
  B. The Cases Cited By Cingular In Which Courts Have Enforced Class-Action Bans Are Not Persuasive.
    1. The Stein Case Does Not Support Cingular's Position.
    2. The Cases from Other Jurisdictions Where Courts Permitted Arbitration Clauses That Banned Class Actions Are Inapplicable and Unhelpful.
  C. Cingular's Argument That This Court Should Rewrite Its Contract Law Because Its Customers Would Be Better Off Without Class Actions Is Not Persuasive.
II. THE FEDERAL ARBITRATION ACT DOES NOT PREVENT THIS COURT FROM APPLYING GENERALLY APPLICABLE PRINCIPLES OF WASHINGTON STATE CONTRACT LAW TO CINGULAR'S BAN ON CLASS-WIDE RELIEF.
CONCLUSION

TABLE OF AUTHORITIES

Cases[***]

Adler v. Fred Lind Manor, 153 Wn. 2d 331, 103 P.2d 773 (2004)
Al Safin v. Circuit City Stores, 394 F.3d 1254, 1262 (9th Cir. 2005)
Allen v. Marshall Field & Co., 93 F.R.D. 438 (N.D. Ill 1982)
American General Finance v. Branch, 793 So.2d 738 (Ala. 2000)
Armendariz v. Foundation Health Psychare Servs., Inc., 6 P.3d 669 (Cal. 2000)
Arnold v. United Companies Lending Corp., 511 S.E. 2d 854 (W. Va. 1998)
Crawford v. Results Oriented, Inc., 548 S.E. 2d 342 (Ga. 2001)
Dean Witter Reynolds v. Byrd, 470 U.S. 213, 221 (1985)
Dix v. ICT Group, Inc., ___ Wn. App. ___, 106 P.3d 841 (2005)
Eagle v. Fred Martin Motor Co., 809 N.E. 2d 1161 (Ohio Ct. App. 2004)
Gilman v. Wheat, First Securities, 692 A.2d 454 (Md. 1997)
Gilmer v. Interstate/Johnson Lane Corp., 500 U.S. 20 (1991)
Green Tree Financial Corp. v. Bazzle, 539 U.S. 444 (2003)
Harris v. Green Tree Fin. Corp., 183 F.3d 173 (3d Cir. 1999)
Heaphy v. State Farm Mutual Automobile Ins. Co., 117 Wn. App. 438, 72 P.3d 220 (Div. 2 2003)
Jenkins v. First Am. Cash Advance of Ga., LLC, 400 F.3d 868 (11th Cir. 2005)
Johnson v. W. Suburban Bank, 225 F.3d 366 (3d Cir. 2000)
Kruger Clinic Orthopaedics v. Regence Blueshield, 123 Wn. App. 355, 98 P. 3d 66 (Div. 1 2004)
Leonard v. Terminix Int'l Co., 854 So.2d 529 (Ala. 2002)
Luna v. Household Finance Corp. III, 236 F. Supp. 2d 1666 (W.D. Wash. 2002)
Patterson v. ITT Consumer Fin. Corp., 14 Cal. App. 4th 1659 (1993)
Randolph v. Green Tree, 244 F.3d 814 (11th Cir. 2001)

***
[***] [*Editor's Note: Citations throughout brief as in original.*]

Snowden v. CheckPoint Check Cashing, 290 F.3d 631 (4th Cir. 2002)
Stein v. Geonerco, Inc., 105 Wn. App. 41, 17 P.3d 1266 (2001)
Strand v. U.S. Nat'l Bank Ass'n ND, 693 N.W.2d 918 (N.D. 2005)
Ting v. AT&T, 182 F. Supp. 2d 902 (N.D. Cal. 2002), aff'd with respect to unconscionability, 319 F.3d 1126 (9th Cir.), *cert. denied*, 540 U.S. 811 (2003)
Ting v. AT&T, 319 F.3d 1126 (9th Cir.), *cert. denied*, 540 U.S. 811 (2003)
West Virginia ex rel. Dunlap v. Berger, 567 S.E.2d 265 (W. Va.), *cert. denied*, 537 U.S. 1087 (2002)
Williams v. Aetna Fin. Co., 700 N.E.2d 859 (Ohio 1998)
Zuver v. Airtouch Communications, Inc., 153 Wn. 2d 293, 103 P.2d 753 (2004)

Statutes

Federal Arbitration Act ("FAA"), 9 U.S.C. §§ 1–16

Other Authorities

Claudia L. Deutsch, Executive Pay: My Big Fat C.E.O. Paycheck, N. Y. TIMES, April 3, 2005, at 31

Public Citizen, Six Common Transactions That Cost Less Because of Class Actions (Aug. 20, 2003), at www.citizen.org/congress/civjus/class_action/articles.cfm?ID=10278

INTRODUCTION AND SUMMARY OF ARGUMENT

In *Zuver v. Airtouch Communications, Inc.*, 153 Wn. 2d 293, 103 P.2d 753 (2004), and *Adler v. Fred Lind Manor*, 153 Wn. 2d 331, 103 P.2d 773 (2004), the Washington Supreme Court set out and applied two principles: arbitration clauses are substantively unconscionable and thus unenforceable if they are either (a) one-sided in favor of the stronger party; or (b) effectively exculpatory clauses. While Cingular heaps praise on the window dressing it has draped around its arbitration clause, it remains clear that the central feature of that clause—the ban on class-wide relief—runs afoul of both of these principles.

The ban on class actions is one-sided in Cingular's favor. As a number of courts have recognized, consumers often sue large corporations such as Cingular on a class-action basis, but these corporations virtually never sue their own customers on such a basis. Moreover, as the record here establishes and as many courts have recognized, without the class-action mechanism, the vast majority of individuals with small dollar claims (such as Plaintiffs here) will not be able to vindicate those claims.

Cingular offers many meritless defenses of its arbitration clause, making much of the fact that its customers are permitted to go to small claims court. In the fantasy scenario Cingular offers this Court, even if Plaintiffs are correct that it has damaged many thousands of its customers for modest sums of money, all of those customers would (a) learn that they had been cheated; (b) formulate the proper legal theory to justify recovering those sums; and (c) affirmatively pursue Cingular in small claims court on an individual basis. This is simply implausible, given that the record demonstrates that virtually all of the individuals would have to do these three things without the aid of a lawyer, as there is no bar of consumer lawyers in Washington (or anywhere else) who handle such small cases on an individual basis.

Cingular relies heavily on *Stein v. Geonerco, Inc.*, 105 Wn. App. 41, 17 P.3d 1266 (2001) (which is *not* an unconscionability case), but that case is unpersuasive here. Among other things, *Stein* was decided without the aid of the principles set forth in *Zuver* and *Adler*, and prior to nearly all of the cases decided around the country that have struck down class-action bans. More recently, Division 3 of the Court of Appeals struck a consumer contract that bans class actions. *See Dix v. ICT Group, Inc.*, __ Wn. App. __, 106 P.3d 841 (2005).

Cingular cites to a number of cases from other jurisdictions that have held that it is acceptable for arbitration clauses to ban class actions, but those cases are also unpersuasive. Most of Cingular's cases are from jurisdictions which, unlike Washington, accept arbitration clauses that are one-sided in favor of the stronger party.

Finally, Cingular argues that the Federal Arbitration Act preempts any state law that would invalidate the contract provision barring class-wide relief. Cingular's preemption argument is cast as an alternative defense, but in fact it depends upon Cingular winning its arguments under Washington state contract law. In *Zuver* and *Adler*, the Washington Supreme Court rejected arguments that the FAA shields provisions in arbitration clauses that are either one-sided or effectively exculpatory clauses from generally applicable principles of state contract law.

I. CINGULAR'S BAN ON CLASS-WIDE RELIEF IS SUBSTANTIVELY UNCONSCIONABLE.[1]

A. *CINGULAR'S BAN ON CLASS-WIDE RELIEF VIOLATES CORE PRINCIPLES LAID DOWN IN* ZUVER *AND* ADLER.

1. The Ban On Class-Wide Relief Is One-Sided.

Cingular never disputes that under Washington law, a contract provision that is one-sided in favor the stronger party to the

---

[1] If Cingular's contract is substantively unconscionable, it may not be enforced. *Adler*, 153 Wn. 2d at 346–47 ("[S]ubstantive unconscionability alone can support a finding of unconscionability"). This Court should find that the same is true of procedural unconscionability. *Kruger Clinic Orthopaedics v. Regence Blueshield*, 123 Wn. App. 355, 371, 98 P. 3d 66 (Div. 1 2004) ("Consumer transactions may be invalidated for procedural or substantive unconscionability.") (citing *Luna v. Household Finance Corp. III*, 236 F. Supp. 2d 1666, 1174 (W.D. Wash. 2002). In this case, Cingular's arbitration clause was sent out on a take-it-or-leave-it basis in a bill stuffer, a notoriously ineffective means of communicating to consumers that they are waiving important legal rights. Appellants' Br. at 46–49. Cingular makes much of the fact that arbitration is referenced several times, but that was easy to do in a document that it knew few consumers would read because it was embedded in a bill stuffer. In addition, Cingular essentially acknowledges that the entire wireless industry requires similar arbitration clauses. Respondent's Br. at 47–48. While Cingular argues that this does not matter, numerous courts have recognized that an absence of meaningful choice is an important factor in procedural unconscionability. *See, e.g., Ting v. AT&T*, 182 F. Supp. 2d 902, 929 (N.D. Cal. 2002), *aff'd with respect to unconscionability*, 319 F.3d 1126 (9th Cir.), *cert. denied*, 540 U.S. 811 (2003) ("Finding a carrier who did not contain such a provision was not easy."); *American General Finance v. Branch*, 793 So.2d 738 (Ala. 2000). Cingular argues that because the revised arbitration clause was less draconian than its predecessor, it cannot be procedurally unconscionable. However, the Court must consider "all the circumstances surrounding the transaction," *Adler*, 153 Wn. 2d at 345. Even if this Court does not strike Cingular's clause solely because it is procedurally unconscionable, it should consider these facts in evaluating the clause's substantive unconscionability.

contract is substantively unconscionable. Instead, Cingular argues that its contract is not one-sided because it permits both sides to operate under the same rules. This formalistic argument is not credible.

By barring class-wide relief, Cingular strips its customers of rights that are often very important to them. By contrast, the provision takes nothing from Cingular. Throughout the U.S., consumers regularly sue major corporations—including cell phone companies—on a class-action basis. The obvious reality is that the converse never happens. One could search the case law for hours without finding a single instance where a cell phone company has ever sued its customers on a class-action basis. Simply put, Cingular is taking away a device that is predictably only used by one party. This point was strongly made in *Ting v. AT&T*, 319 F.3d 1126 (9th Cir.), *cert. denied*, 540 U.S. 811 (2003), which was cited by the Washington Supreme Court in *Zuver*. 153 Wn. 2d at 312. Moreover, Cingular's argument about apparent neutrality could have been made about the confidentiality clause at issue in *Zuver*—ostensibly that provision also involved "the same rules for both parties." The Washington Supreme Court was not fooled, however, and recognized that this provision actually affected the individual plaintiffs much more negatively than it affected the corporate defendant. The same is true here.

Cingular argues (Respondent's Br. at 33, 37) that Washington law does not recognize class actions as an important device for consumers. A similar claim was rejected in *Dix*. In *Dix*, the court held that a provision in a consumer contract that would operate as a class-action ban was not enforceable under Washington law. The plaintiffs in *Dix* were Washington customers of America Online ("AOL") who, like Plaintiffs here, filed a class action alleging Consumer Protection Act ("CPA") claims. AOL moved to dismiss based on the contract's forum-selection clause, which gave Virginia state courts exclusive jurisdiction over any disputes. The plaintiffs argued that this clause was unenforceable as applied to Washington consumers:

> [B]ecause class action suits are not available in Virginia and the amount of damages suffered by each individual is probably less than $250, Washington customers have little incentive to litigate in Virginia, thereby violating the CPA's public policy of protecting this state's policy of protecting this state's citizens from unfair and deceptive business practices.

106 P.3d at 844–45. If Cingular were right that class actions were not important, the court should have rejected this argument. It did not:

> [Plaintiffs] filed their purported class action alleging, among other claims, a violation of the CPA. The CPA provides that "[u]nfair methods of competition and unfair or deceptive acts or practices in the conduct of any trade or commerce are hereby declared unlawful." Because its purpose is "to protect the public and foster fair and honest competition," RCW 19.86.920, *the CPA does not exist merely for the purpose of benefiting an individual plaintiff*. Rather, the [statute's] purpose is to offer broad protection to the citizens of Washington from unfair or deceptive acts or practices. Requiring Ms. Dix and Mr. Smith to litigate their CPA claim in Virginia *without the benefit of a class action procedure* as is allowed in Washington therefore undermines the very purpose of the CPA, which is to offer broad protection to the citizens of Washington. The forum selection clause is unenforceable.

Id. at 845 (emphasis added; internal citations omitted).

2. The Ban On Class-Wide Relief Does Serve As An Exculpatory Clause

Under Washington law, if a provision in a contract of adhesion effectively serves as an exculpatory clause, then it is substantively unconscionable. Appellants' Br. at 19–20. Again, Cingular does not acknowledge this rule of law, but simply argues that its customers may readily pursue individual cases in small claims court. Cingular's position is implausible at best: it suggests that if it has cheated many thousands of customers out of small sums of money, that there is no need for the class-action mechanism because all of those persons will realize that they had been cheated; be able to pursue their legal claims in small claims court on an individual basis without the assistance of an attorney; and choose to devote the time and energy to this difficult task despite the small sum at issue. This same argument was made—and rejected—in the *Ting* case, as AT&T's arbitration clause, like Cingular's, permitted its customers to pursue their claims individually in small claims court. *Ting v. AT&T*, 182 F. Supp. 2d at 915, 935–36.

Tellingly, Cingular has never offered any evidence to dispute the detailed factual testimony presented by Plaintiffs' experts, who explained that the inevitable practical effect of making the class-action device unavailable to Cingular's customers with individually small claims would be to deprive the vast majority of them of *any viable remedy*. Appellants' Br. at 4–6. Instead of producing any factual testimony to support its claim that tens of thousands of customers would be likely to pursue individual cases without attorneys in small claims court, Cingular instead now urges this Court to dismiss the unrebutted record as "irrelevant" to the "legal" question of whether its customers are left without recourse. Respondent's Br. at 27. Cingular is attempting to turn a factual issue into a hypothetical one. While the question of whether a class-action ban that strips one party of its only meaningful remedy *is unconscionable* is surely a question of law, the question of whether Cingular's class-action ban indeed strips its customers of their only remedy is a question of fact, and one that has already been answered in the affirmative. Appellants' Br. at 4–6 and 21–22. The cases cited by Cingular are not to the contrary: without the benefit of an empirical record like that established here, the hypothetical availability of attorneys' fees in cases such as *Snowden v. CheckPoint Check Cashing*, 290 F.3d 631 (4th Cir. 2002), was apparently sufficient for that court to speculate that alternatives to class actions would provide sufficient redress as a matter of law. In this case, however, the factual record is clear, leaving this Court free to skip the speculation and go straight to addressing the critical legal question at stake.

Cingular's attempt to discredit Plaintiffs' experts' testimony as "self-interested" (Respondents' Br. at 27) is likewise unavailing. Sally Gustafson Garratt's testimony is based not on any personal interest in seeing this case proceed on a class-action basis, but on her eight years as Division Chief for Consumer Protection in the

Washington State Attorney General's office, during which her staff of over 100 employees handled more than 250,000 inquiries from consumers each year. CP at 1568–69 ¶¶ 6–7. And Cingular's baseless comments do nothing to rebut the testimony of Peter Maier, whose statement that the claims of Cingular's customers are "much too small . . . to consider litigating such a claim on behalf of an individual consumer," CP at 1582 ¶ 11, is based on his 24 years of experience as a Washington consumer lawyer, CP at 1579–80 ¶ 3.

3. An Arbitration Clause With An Unseverable Unconscionable Term Is Not Rendered Enforceable By Other "Consumer-Friendly" Terms.

Having stripped its customers of the one mechanism that would permit most of them to effectively vindicate their rights, Cingular congratulates itself for not stripping all of the other rights from the tiny minority of customers who might proceed on an individual (albeit unrepresented) basis against it. But there is no authority for Cingular's proposition (Respondent's Br. at 33) that its class-action ban is not unconscionable because *other* terms in its arbitration clause are not unconscionable. While it is true that many courts striking down class-action bans in arbitration clauses also strike down other terms (Respondents' Br. at 33 n.14), the presence of those other illegal terms does not determine whether the *class-action ban itself* is unconscionable, but rather goes to the question of whether the *clause as a whole* is so permeated by unconscionable provisions as to be unenforceable. See, e.g., *Al Safin v. Circuit City Stores*, 394 F.3d 1254, 1262 (9th Cir. 2005); *Ting*, 319 F.3d at 1149.^2 Cingular's argument here is tantamount to saying that if a company was found liable on three theories (breach of contract, fraud, and violation of the U.C.C.), the precedent relating to the U.C.C. would not apply in future cases that did not involve the other two theories.

Similarly, Cingular argues that the presence of other "consumer-friendly features" (Respondent's Br. at 15) permits this Court to enforce an arbitration clause containing an unconscionable term as long as the other terms in the clause are not unconscionable. Cingular even suggests (Respondent's Br. at 11) that *Adler* and *Zuver* support this contention because the court "refused to enforce only those aspects of the challenged arbitration provisions that . . . directly interfered with the plaintiffs' ability to obtain redress." In *Adler* and *Zuver*, however, the court could enforce the remainder of the terms because the unconscionable provisions in those cases could be severed. *Adler*, 153 Wn. 2d at 358; *Zuver*, 153 Wn. 2d. at 319–21. Cingular, on the other hand, specifically drafted its contract to make certain that its arbitration clause "*in its entirety*" is "*null and void*" if the class-action ban is found invalid, CP at 355–56, indicating in no uncertain terms that its interest lies not in arbitration, but in banning class actions.^3 In sum, the presence of enforceable terms in an arbitration clause neither absolves a class-action ban of unconscionability nor permits a court to enforce the clause despite the unconscionable term.

B. THE CASES CITED BY CINGULAR IN WHICH COURTS HAVE ENFORCED CLASS-ACTION BANS ARE NOT PERSUASIVE.

1. The *Stein* Case Does Not Support Cingular's Position.

Cingular's reliance on this Court's holding in *Stein v. Geonerco, Inc.*, 105 Wn. App. 41, 17 P.3d 1266 (2001), is misplaced. First, *Stein* was decided without the benefit of nearly all of the law that now governs this question. For example, when *Stein* was decided, it was not yet clear whether Washington would be one of the jurisdictions that refuse to enforce one-way, non-mutual arbitration clauses, or if Washington would join the jurisdictions that do enforce such clauses. The Washington Supreme Court's subsequent guidance in *Zuver* and *Adler* has changed the landscape fundamentally, however, as has the U.S. Supreme Court's decision in *Green Tree Financial Corp. v. Bazzle*, 539 U.S. 444 (2003).

Stein was also decided at a time when few if any courts had refused to enforce an arbitration clause that barred class actions. At the time this Court decided *Stein*, the Ninth Circuit had not yet decided *Ting v. AT&T*, 319 F.3d 1126, for example, the West Virginia Supreme Court of Appeals had not yet decided *West Virginia ex rel. Dunlap v. Berger*, 567 S.E.2d 265 (W. Va.), cert. denied, 537 U.S. 1087 (2002), the Alabama Supreme Court had not yet decided *Leonard v. Terminix Int'l Co.*, 854 So.2d 529 (Ala. 2002), and the Western District of Washington had not yet decided *Luna v. Household Fin. Corp. III*, 236 F. Supp.2d 1166 (W.D. Wash. 2002), among many other cases.

Furthermore, the state-law principles of unconscionability that govern this case were not before the Court in *Stein*. In *Stein*, the plaintiff argued that there was an "inherent conflict between arbitration and statutory provisions that encourage class participation," and thus that the contract at issue—which was *silent* on class actions—prevented him from filing a class action merely *by requiring arbitration*. 105 Wn. App. at 48. In light of the plaintiff's "fail[ure] to cite relevant statutory provisions that conflict with the arbitration of his claims," *id.* at 48–49, the Court found the arbitration clause enforceable.^4

Finally, *Stein* is distinguishable in that it did not involve a small-dollar consumer claim in a case with a factual record demonstrating that no attorneys would handle such claims on an individual basis. *Stein* concerned a dispute about a warranty that affected the purchase of a home—the kind of claim that can typically be pursued on an individual basis. There was no indication in the record in *Stein* that the factors that make Cingular's class-action ban function as an exculpatory clause in the context of small consumer claims like Plaintiffs' here were present there. See *Kruger Clinic Orthopaedics v. Regence Blueshield*, 123 Wn. App. 355, 371, 98 P. 3d 66 (Div. 1 2004) ("policy considerations underlying an analysis of a consumer transaction are not at issue"), *Luna*, 236 F. Supp. at 1183 (distinguishing consumer claims from

---

^2 Cingular's attempt (Respondent's Br. at 33) to distinguish *Ting* on grounds that the arbitration clause struck down there required the customer to split the arbitrator's fees is misleading. The provision in AT&T's clause required customers to pay the costs of arbitration only if their claims were for more than $10,000—so any difference evaporates in the context of small claims like those at issue here. 182 F. Supp. at 915, 933–34.

^3 It is also noteworthy that the class-action ban is the *only term* so essential to Cingular that it cannot be severed from the arbitration clause without invalidating the entire clause.

^4 The other question facing the Court in *Stein*—whether a conflict between arbitration and class actions prevents courts from compelling class arbitration where the clause is silent—has since been answered differently by the U.S. Supreme Court in *Bazzle*, 539 U.S. 444 (which held that depending on state contract law, arbitrators may proceed on a class-action basis when an arbitration clause is silent).

other types of claims in substantive unconscionability inquiry).

Finally, Plaintiffs do not argue, Cingular's gesticulations notwithstanding (Respondent's Br. at 15), that *all* class-action bans in *all* contracts are inherently unconscionable, but that a class-action ban in a consumer contract in a case involving small dollar claims that effectively insulates one party from liability cannot be enforced under Washington state law. *Stein* is not to the contrary, and Cingular's argument that it somehow has implications for this case should be dismissed.^5

2. The Cases from Other Jurisdictions Where Courts Permitted Arbitration Clauses That Banned Class Actions Are Inapplicable and Unhelpful.

Cingular cites (Respondent's Br. at 18) a list of cases where courts in other jurisdictions have enforced arbitration clauses that prohibit class-wide relief, insinuating that this Court should enforce its class-action ban because there are supposedly more courts for it than against it. If one looks closely at the cases cited by Cingular, however, it is clear that most of them are inapposite. First, many of these cases do not involve state unconscionability law. Cingular cites to *Randolph v. Green Tree*, 244 F.3d 814 (11th Cir. 2001) and *Johnson v. W. Suburban Bank*, 225 F.3d 366 (3d Cir. 2000), for example. The cases turn upon the language and legislative history of the federal Truth in Lending Act. They do not look at the contract law of Washington (or any other state), and say nothing about this state's law with respect to one-sided contracts.

Second, many of the cases cited by Cingular are decisions of state law that turn upon the contract law of states that—unlike this one—accept and enforce one-sided and non-mutual arbitration clauses. State laws relating to unconscionable contracts differ enormously from jurisdiction to jurisdiction. In this state, for example, it is unconscionable for an arbitration clause to be one-sided and non-mutual.

Washington State law in this respect is consistent with the law of many other jurisdictions. *See, e.g., Armendariz v. Foundation Health Psychare Servs., Inc.*, 6 P.3d 669, 692 (Cal. 2000) (unconscionable for business to require employees to submit to binding arbitration as a condition of employment while reserving right to sue employees in court, absent some special justification for disparity); Ohio, *Williams v. Aetna Fin. Co.*, 700 N.E.2d 859, 862 (Ohio 1998) (noting with concern that the arbitration clause preserved for the finance company the judicial remedy of foreclosure on the debtor's mortgage but restricted the debtor's remedies solely to arbitration); and West Virginia, *Arnold v. United Companies Lending Corp.*, 511 S.E.2d 854, 861 (W. Va. 1998) ("allowing such a one-sided agreement to stand would unfairly defeat the Arnolds' legitimate expectations").

It should not be surprising to learn that California, Ohio, and West Virginia are all states where appellate courts have struck down as unconscionable arbitration clauses that bar class actions (which, as set forth above, are a species of one-sided, non-mutual arbitration clause). *See, e.g., Ting*, 319 F.3d 1126 (California law); *Eagle v. Fred Martin Motor Co.*, 809 N.E. 2d 1161 (Ohio Ct. App. 2004) (Ohio law); *Dunlap*, 567 S.E. 2d 265 (West Virginia law).

The correlation here is strong, and it is hardly accidental. Jurisdictions (such as this one) that refuse to enforce arbitration clauses that are effectively one-sided consistently have also refused to enforce arbitration clauses that ban class actions. This fact helps explain the two-part holding of the federal district court in *Luna*, 236 F. Supp. 2d 1166. First, the court predicted (correctly, as it turns out) that the Washington Supreme Court would hold that it was unconscionable for a corporation to impose a one-sided arbitration clause upon a weaker party. Second, as a logical corollary, the *Luna* court held that the defendant's contractual ban on class-wide relief was one-sided and thus substantively unconscionable.

A number of other states have held that it is *not* substantively unconscionable for an arbitration clause to be either expressly or effectively one-sided. These courts would reject the holdings of *Zuver* and *Adler*. It should come as no surprise that most of the cases cited by Cingular come from courts applying the law of these jurisdictions. Cingular cites, for example (Respondent's Br. at 18, 26), *Johnson v. W. Suburban Bank*, 225 F.3d 366 (3d Cir. 2000). As one might predict, the Third Circuit is one of the jurisdictions that holds—unlike the Washington Supreme Court—that it is not substantively unconscionable for an arbitration clause to be one-sided and non-mutual *See Harris v. Green Tree Fin. Corp.*, 183 F.3d 173, 183 (3d Cir. 1999).

Similarly, Cingular (Respondent's Br. at 18, 24–25, 29–30, 33) cites *Jenkins v. First Am. Cash Advance of Ga., LLC*, 400 F.3d 868, (11th Cir. 2005). The *Jenkins* court was applying Georgia Law. *Id.* at 875. Georgia is another state in which the law—unlike the law here—permits one-sided arbitration clauses. *See Crawford v. Results Oriented, Inc.*, 548 S.E. 2d 342, 343 (Ga. 2001). Accordingly, if this Court is to follow *Zuver* and *Adler*, *Jenkins* is an untrustworthy guide.

Cingular also cites cases applying the law of jurisdictions that do not object to contractual terms that bar class actions outside of the arbitration setting. Cingular cites to *Snowden v. CheckPoint Check Cashing*, 290 F.3d 631 (4th Cir. 2002), for example, to argue that a prohibition on class actions is not unconscionable. This is consistent with Maryland law, which differs from the law set out in *Dix*. *See Gilman v. Wheat, First Securities*, 692 A.2d 454 (Md. 1997) (enforcing forum selection clause that required consumers to bring cases in Virginia (which does not permit class actions)).

Cingular also argues that the U.S. Supreme Court approved the use of arbitration clauses to ban class actions in *Gilmer v. Interstate Johnson Lane Corp.*, 500 U.S. 20 (1991). Respondent's Br. at 17. In *Gilmer*, however, the Court was interpreting the text and structure of the federal Age Discrimination in Employment Act, not a state law challenge to an arbitration clause such as those permitted under § 2 of the Federal Arbitration Act. The case contains no discussion of state law (much less state law limiting exculpatory clauses). *Gilmer* is also very different from this case because in *Gilmer* there was no reason to imagine that a ban on class actions would bar plaintiffs from effectively vindicating their substantive rights. Indeed, Congress was evidently aware that ADEA claims (typically claims that a person at the peak of her

---

^5 *Heaphy v. State Farm Mutual Automobile Ins. Co.*, 117 Wn. App. 438, 72 P.3d 220 (Div. 2 2003), a U.I.M. case, is equally inapposite. The issue in *Heaphy* was whether the plaintiff's claim—that the value of her automobile had diminished following an accident and repair—was a viable question of law or fact common to a class. The court concluded that, as a matter of law, the plaintiff's claim was not amenable to a class action. Thus, the court held that "[a]bsent any showing that the class action is appropriate for this case, the possibility of class certification cannot overcome the agreement to arbitrate the issue." 117 Wn. App. at 448. Here, in contrast, there is no question that Plaintiffs' claims are precisely the kind of claims for which a class action is appropriate.

earning power was wrongfully terminated) are unlike small consumer claims, and that class actions are generally not necessary to provide a remedy to such plaintiffs. This is demonstrated by the fact that class actions under the ADEA proceed on an "opt-in" basis rather than a normal opt-out process. *See, e.g., Allen v. Marshall Field & Co.,* 93 F.R.D. 438 (N.D. Ill 1982).

Finally, Cingular suggests (Respondent's Br. at 17–18) that class-action bans are never unconscionable because the class action is merely a "procedural" device, and arbitration clauses may enact any procedures imaginable without being unconscionable.^6 If Cingular's theory were the law, and corporations could impose upon consumers, in fine print adhesion contracts, any contract provision that can be characterized as "procedural," the Consumer Protection Act would be eviscerated. Drafters of adhesive contracts could evade limits on exculpatory clauses by, for example, requiring persons with small claims to travel to a completely inaccessible forum to arbitrate claims.

Fortunately for Cingular's customers and Washington consumers, the Washington Supreme Court has already flatly rejected Cingular's theory.^7 For example, a rule providing that the outcomes of all arbitration proceedings be kept confidential is clearly procedural, rather than substantive, in nature. But in *Zuver*, the court struck down this term as unconscionable, recognizing that such a term "hampers an employee's ability to prove a pattern of discrimination or to take advantage of findings in past arbitrations [and would] potentially discourage[] that employee from pursuing a valid discrimination claim." 153 Wn. App. at 315. Thus, if a procedural device (such as a class-action ban) would effectively bar individuals from vindicating their substantive rights, and would have the same impact as a more direct exculpatory clause, the procedural quality of this provision does not save it from violating state laws relating to unconscionable contracts. Cingular's argument that its class-action ban must be enforced because it is "procedural" thus essentially amounts to an argument that the court wrongly decided *Adler* and *Zuver*, and should be disregarded.

C. CINGULAR'S ARGUMENT THAT THIS COURT SHOULD REWRITE ITS CONTRACT LAW BECAUSE ITS CUSTOMERS WOULD BE BETTER OFF WITHOUT CLASS ACTIONS IS NOT PERSUASIVE.

Many of Cingular's arguments as to why its contract is not unconscionable are really policy arguments against the entire notion of enforcing consumer protection laws through the class-action device. According to Cingular, consumer protection class actions are bad because corporations are forced to raise their prices whenever they are held accountable for violating consumer protection laws. Respondent's Br. at 16. These sweeping notions—that the majority of consumer protection lawsuits should be wiped away and large corporations should be trusted to do what's right—would be better addressed to the legislature, but they certainly do not represent the law of Washington. As set forth in *Dix*, the policy of Washington State is to make the class-action device available to its citizens, to ensure that Washington consumers have a meaningful forum in which to bring their claims.

In any case, Cingular's self-serving explanations as to why there should be no effective legal checks upon its power are unpersuasive as a matter of policy. Cingular offers no proof that being held accountable under consumer protection laws will increase the costs of goods or services. In fact, a recent study has demonstrated that consumer class actions often reduce costs.

> [W]hen it comes to class action lawsuits to remedy fraudulent practices, there is no question that litigation reduces the prices that consumers pay.
>
> Most class actions are aimed at undisclosed fees, markups, kickbacks, and other over charges that chisel consumers in small quantities. Often obscured by complicated billing statements, these hidden costs enable businesses to advertise one price, but secretly charge a higher amount. This undermines consumers' ability to comparison shop, and benefits unscrupulous businesses at the expense of more honest competitors.

Public Citizen, *Six Common Transactions That Cost Less Because of Class Actions* (Aug. 20, 2003), at www.citizen.org/congress/civjus/class_action /articles.cfm?ID=10278. The study gives concrete illustrations of how consumer class actions have reduced the prices that consumers must pay for a range of goods and services. For example, FleetBoston Financial Corp. was charging $35 for a "No Annual Fee" credit card before a class action was brought against it, and $0 for such a card afterwards. Similarly, MCI was charging $2.87 a minute for phone calls on Sundays (despite an advertisement promising that calls could be made for five cents a minute) before a class action was filed against it, and then charged the promised five cents per minute after the class action.

In addition, the argument that enforcing consumer protection laws will drive up prices rests upon the faulty assumption that corporations pass on to their consumers all profits realized from breaking consumer protection laws. In fact, anyone familiar with today's economy will recognize that corporations do a great many things with such income other than pass it on to consumers. *See, e.g.,* Claudia L. Deutsch, *Executive Pay: My Big Fat C.E.O. Paycheck*, N. Y. Times, April 3, 2005, at 31 (C.E.O.'s at large companies paid average of $9.84 million in 2004, up 12 percent from 2003). There is no evidence—and no reason to suspect—that corporations who keep their ill-gotten gains when they break consumer protection laws will pass on those gains to their consumers.

---

^6 In making this argument, Cingular relies once again on decisions by jurisdictions with well-documented disagreements with the Washington Supreme Court on issues of unconscionability. *See* discussion of *Johnson* and *Jenkins, supra*. Cingular could find equally inapt support for its argument in *Strand v. U.S. Nat'l Bank Ass'n ND*, 693 N.W.2d 918 (N.D. 2005), in which the North Dakota Supreme Court found that a class-action ban was not unconscionable because "a class action is purely a procedural right . . . not a substantive remedy." *Id.* at 926 (citations omitted). As made clear below, Washington courts have emphatically rejected any such artificial distinction between substantive and procedural rights when it comes to a one-sided arbitration clause.

^7 In so doing, the Washington Supreme Court joined a number of courts that have refused to enforce illegal terms in arbitration clauses despite their supposed procedural character. *E.g., Patterson v. ITT Consumer Fin. Corp.*, 14 Cal. App. 4th 1659 (1993) (refusing to enforce arbitration clause that imposed excessive costs upon California consumers and required them to arbitrate their claims in Minnesota).

II. THE FEDERAL ARBITRATION ACT DOES NOT PREVENT THIS COURT FROM APPLYING GENERALLY APPLICABLE PRINCIPLES OF WASHINGTON STATE CONTRACT LAW TO CINGULAR'S BAN ON CLASS-WIDE RELIEF.

Cingular argues that even if its contractual ban on class-wide relief is unconscionable under Washington state contract law, the Federal Arbitration Act ("FAA"), 9 U.S.C. §§ 1–16, nonetheless preempts that law. First, Cingular asserts that "there is no general principle of Washington law precluding class-action waivers." Respondent's Br. at 12. Cingular's argument is wrong on several levels. There decidedly is a generally applicable principle of Washington state contract law that contracts of adhesion with one-sided provisions that favor the more powerful party are unconscionable and unenforceable. Appellants' Br. at 11–16. If this Court finds that a contract term barring consumers from pursuing class-wide relief is a one-sided provision that favors Cingular, this will be an application of a generally applicable rule of Washington state contract law and by Cingular's own logical admissions will not be preempted by the FAA.

Similarly, there is a generally applicable rule of Washington State contract law that contracts of adhesion that serve as exculpatory clauses are unconscionable and unenforceable. Appellants' Br. at 1920. If this Court credits the testimony from Mr. Maier and Ms. Garratt, and if this Court agrees with the numerous authorities discussed in Appellants' Brief at 20–29 and concludes that Cingular's contractual ban on class-wide relief does serve as an exculpatory clause, then a ruling for Plaintiffs will again be an application of a generally applicable rule of Washington State contract law. By acknowledging that the FAA does not preempt "general principle[s] of Washington law" (Respondent's Br. at 12), Cingular has hinged its FAA preemption argument on its weak factual arguments that banning class action has no effect on its customers. In addition, as discussed above, Cingular's assertion that no general principle of Washington law precludes class-action waivers is disproved by *Dix*.

Cingular's second preemption argument is that "even if there were such a general rule prohibiting class-action waivers, that rule would frustrate the purposes of the FAA," because class actions are supposedly neither speedy nor inexpensive. Respondent's Br. at 12, 38–45. This argument is entirely without authority. As Plaintiffs pointed out in our opening brief (at 33–34), this Court and the Washington Supreme Court have made abundantly clear that arbitration clauses are not to be enforced where they run afoul of generally applicable principles of state contract law. *Kruger*, 123 Wn. App. at 368; *Adler*, 153 Wn. 2d at 342. Cingular cites no case holding that a generally applicable principle of state law is overridden by some federal principle favoring "speedy and inexpensive" resolutions of cases. In *Dean Witter Reynolds v. Byrd*, 470 U.S. 213, 221 (1985), moreover, the Court held that the FAA permits the enforcement of arbitration clauses even where doing so would cause multiple proceedings, because saving time was not the overriding policy concern under the FAA.

Finally, Cingular's premise that a class-action ban leads to speedier and less expensive resolutions of cases is only imaginable if one presumes that the point of the class-action ban is to bar consumers from bringing cases at all. If one were to accept the premise in Cingular's brief that tens or hundreds of thousands of individual consumers would all bring individual actions in small claims court and/or arbitration, then it is clear that these duplicative adjudications of identical cases would hardly be speedier or less expensive than a class-wide proceeding. In short, with respect to FAA preemption, Cingular implicitly acknowledges that the point of its class-action ban is to save money by barring its consumers from bringing cases at all. This idea of "speedier and inexpensive resolutions"—not allowing cases to be pursued at all—is decidedly not consistent with the FAA's purpose. As Appellants' Opening Brief recounts (at 20, 37–38), numerous courts have recognized that arbitration is only favored under the FAA where it allows individuals to effectively vindicate their individual rights.

CONCLUSION

This Court should find that Cingular's unseverable class-action ban is unconscionable, hold the arbitration clause unenforceable, and reverse the superior court's decision.

Respectfully submitted this 22nd April, 2005

[*Attorneys for Appellants*]

F.2.3 Plaintiffs' Supplemental Brief

SUPREME COURT OF THE STATE OF WASHINGTON

DOUG SCOTT, LOREN TABASINKE, SANDRA TABASINSKE, PATRICK OISHI, JANET OISHI, et al.,
    Petitioners,

v.

CINGULAR WIRELESS,
    Respondent.

No. 77406-4

PETITIONERS' SUPPLEMENTAL BRIEF

TABLE OF CONTENTS

TABLE OF AUTHORITIES
INTRODUCTION AND SUMMARY OF ARGUMENT
ARGUMENT
  I. ADDITIONAL AUTHORITY SUPPORTS PETITIONERS' POSITION THAT CINGULAR'S CLAUSE IS SUBSTANTIVELY UNCONSCIONABLE.
  II. CINGULAR'S CITATION TO GILMER IS UNPERSUASIVE.
  III. CINGULAR'S CLASS ACTION BAN IS EFFECTIVELY EXCULPATORY REGARDLESS OF THE AVAILABILITY OF ATTORNEYS' FEES OR THE POSSIBILITY OF GOVERNMENT ENFORCEMENT ACTIONS.
    A. Prevailing Parties In Individual Cases Are Unlikely To Receive Full Fees.
    B. Individuals With Small Claims Have Little Incentive To Seek Out An Attorney Or Pursue Their Claims.
    C. Government Action Is Not An Adequate Alternative to Class Actions.
  IV. PETITIONERS' AUTHORITIES MAY NOT BE DISREGARDED MERELY BECAUSE SOME OF THOSE

CASES INVOLVED CONTRACTS WITH MULTIPLE UNFAIR PROVISIONS.
V. THE CONSTITUTIONAL PRESUMPTION AGAINST PREEMPTION IS PARTICULARLY POTENT HERE.
VI. THERE IS NOTHING RADICAL ABOUT BARRING CORPORATIONS FROM PROHIBITING THEIR CUSTOMERS FROM BRINGING OR PARTICIPATING IN CLASS ACTIONS.
CONCLUSION

TABLE OF AUTHORITIES

Cases[****]

Abels v. JBC Legal Group, P.C., 227 F.R.D. 541 (N.D. Cal. 2005)
Adler v. Fred Lind Manor, 153 Wn. 2d 331, 103 P.2d 773 (2004)
Aronson v. Quick Point Pencil Co., 440 U.S. 257 (1979)
Bates v. Dow Agrosciences, LLC, 125 S. Ct. 1788 (2005)
Carnegie v. Household Int'l, Inc., 376 F.3d 656 (7th Cir. 2004)
Deposit Guaranty Nat. Bank v. Roper, 445 U.S. 326 (1980)
Discover Bank v. Superior Court, 113 P.3d 1100 (Cal. 2005)
Eshagi v. Hanley Dawson Cadillac Co., 574 N.E.2d 760 (Ill. App. 1991)
Ethridge v. Hwang, 105 Wn. App. 447, 20 P.3d 958 (2001)
F.H. Krear & Co. v. Nineteen Named Trustees, 810 F.2d 1250 (2d Cir. 1987)
Geissal v. Moore Med. Corp., 338 F.3d 926 (8th Cir. 2003)
Gilmer v. Interstate/Johnson Lane Corp., 500 U.S. 20 (1991)
Hangman Ridge Training Stables, Inc. v. Safeco Title Ins. Co., 105 Wn. 2d 778, 719 P.2d 531 (1986)
In re Currency Conversion, 2005 WL 2364969 (S.D.N.Y. Sept. 27, 2005)
In re Taylor, 2003 WL 22282173 (Bankr. D. Vt. Oct. 1, 2003)
James v. Thermal Master, Inc., 563 N.E.2d 917 (Ohio App. 1988)
Jenkins v. First Am. Cash Advance of Ga., LLC, 400 F.3d 868 (11th Cir. 2005)
Johnson v. W. Suburban Bank, 255 F.3d 366 (3d Cir. 2000)
Northern Pipeline Constr. Co. v. Marathon Pipeline Co., 458 U.S. 50 (1982)
Nuttall v. Dowell, 31 Wn. App. 98, 639 P.2d 832 (1982)
Parrish v. Cingular Wireless, 28 Cal. Rptr. 3d 802 (2005), rev'd., 2005 WL 2420719 (Oct. 3, 2005)
Sheppard v. Riverview Nursing Center, Inc., 88 F.3d 1332 (4th Cir. 1996)
Sledge v. Sands, 182 F.R.D. 255 (N.D. Ill. 1998)
Snowden v. Checkpoint Check Cashing, 290 F.3d 631 (4th Cir. 2002)
Stewart Org., Inc. v. Ricoh Corp., 487 U.S. 22 (1988)
Strama v. Peterson, 689 F.2d 661 (7th Cir. 1982)
Szetela v. Discover Bank, 97 Cal. App. 4th 1094 (2002)
Ting v. AT&T, 319 F.3d 1126 (9th Cir. 2003)
Weiss v. Regal Collections, 385 F.3d 337 (3d Cir. 2004)
West Virginia ex rel. Dunlap v. Berger, 567 S.E.2d 265 (W. Va.), cert. denied, 537 U.S. 1087 (2002)
Whitney v. Alltel Communications, 173 S.W.3d 300 (Mo. App. 2005)
Zuver v. Airtouch Communications, Inc., 153 Wn. 2d 293, 103 P.3d 753 (2004)

[****] [*Editor's Note: Citations throughout brief as in original.*]

Statutes and Legislative Materials

28 U.S.C. § 1711 note, U.S. Pub. L. 109-2, § 2(a)(1), 119 Stat. 4 (Feb. 18, 2005)
S. Rep. 109-14, *reprinted at* 2005 U.S. Cong. Code and Admin. News 3 (Feb. 28, 2005)

Other Authorities

NASD Code of Arbitration Procedure, § 10301(d)(3)
Steven J. Cole, State Enforcement Efforts Directed Against Unfair or Deceptive Practices, 56 Antitrust L.J. 125 (1987)

INTRODUCTION AND SUMMARY OF ARGUMENT

This Court has already received extensive briefing on the merits of this appeal, and particularly how the issues posed here may be informed by cases from this Court's jurisprudence. This Supplemental Brief will avoid repeating the discussion set forth before the Court of Appeals. Nonetheless, because the issues raised in this appeal are of such exceptional significance, because two important decisions have come down from other courts, and because Respondent Cingular Wireless ("Cingular") has interposed a great number of arguments in support of its arbitration clause, Petitioners are grateful for the opportunity to expand upon some of their points in this Supplemental Brief.

First, since the close of the earlier briefing, two courts have decided cases that strongly support Petitioners' position in this matter. Of particular interest is *Discover Bank v. Superior Court*, 113 P.3d 1100 (Cal. 2005), where the California Supreme Court held that a contract provision barring class actions that is very similar to the provision at issue here was unconscionable under California law with respect to consumers with small claims. While there was a dissent relating to a choice-of-law issue not relevant here, every member of the court agreed that the Federal Arbitration Act did not preempt California state law barring class action bans. In addition, the Missouri Court of Appeals recently held that a class action ban in a wireless telephone contract is unconscionable. *Whitney v. Alltel Communications*, 173 S.W.3d 300 (Mo. App. 2005).

Second, Cingular has argued that the U.S. Supreme Court held in *Gilmer v. Interstate/Johnson Lane Corp.*, 500 U.S. 20 (1991), that corporations may insert class action bans in arbitration clauses. While Petitioners refuted this claim on several grounds in their earlier briefing, this Brief will offer additional reasons why Cingular's argument on this point is incorrect.

Third, Cingular has suggested that contractual provisions banning class actions are not exculpatory because individual consumers will be able to find lawyers willing to handle very small cases in the hopes of recovering attorneys' fees under Cingular's contract terms, and some of the cases cited by Cingular suggest that consumers will find lawyers willing to handle such cases in the hopes of recovering statutory attorneys' fees. But Cingular's arguments are based upon unrealistic assumptions about consumer protection that are sharply at odds with the actual state of the law and the practice in the field. This Brief will more thoroughly explain why attorneys' fees provisions are not an adequate replacement for the class action device in cases that involve small individual sums, and demonstrate that in this setting a provision banning class actions still operates as an exculpatory clause.

Fourth, Cingular has argued that the Court should disregard the portions of decisions that hold that bans on class actions are unconscionable if those cases concerned arbitration clauses with multiple unconscionable provisions. This Brief will establish that the holdings of cases such as *Ting v. AT&T*, 319 F.3d 1126 (9th Cir. 2003), striking down class action bans cannot be ignored merely because the contracts at issue suffered from other defects as well.

Fifth, this Brief will set forth additional authorities establishing that the presumption against the preemption of state law applies with particular force in this case.

Finally, this Brief will refute some of Cingular's "sky-is-falling" policy arguments, and will demonstrate that Cingular has no valid reliance interest in insulating itself from liability by banning class actions.

ARGUMENT

I. ADDITIONAL AUTHORITY SUPPORTS PETITIONERS' POSITION THAT CINGULAR'S CLAUSE IS SUBSTANTIVELY UNCONSCIONABLE.

Petitioners have consistently argued that Cingular's class action ban is unconscionable because it effectively serves as an exculpatory clause. In *Discover Bank v. Superior Court*, 113 P.3d 1100 (Cal. 2005), the California Supreme Court recently struck down a similar contractual waiver of class actions, where disputes typically involved small damages. *Id.* at 1110. While recognizing that class action waivers are not "in the abstract" exculpatory, the court found that they are exculpatory in effect for many consumers:

> [B]ecause . . . damages in consumer cases are often small and because a company which wrongfully exacts a dollar from each of millions of customers will reap a handsome profit, the class action is often the only effective way to halt and redress such exploitation.

Id. at 1108–09 (internal quotations and citation omitted). Based on this finding, the court held that class action waivers in adhesive consumer contracts were unconscionable applied to small-value claims. *Id.* at 1110.

Petitioners have further explained that Cingular's ban on classwide claims also is completely one-sided because it strips its customers of their claims, but leaves its own claims protected. In *Discover Bank*, the California Supreme Court described this one-sided arrangement as follows:

> Moreover, such class action or arbitration waivers are indisputably one-sided. 'Although styled as a mutual prohibition on representative or class actions, it is difficult to envision the circumstances under which the provision might negatively impact Discover Bank, because credit card companies typically do not sue their customers in class-action lawsuits.'

Id. at 1109 (quoting *Szetela v. Discover Bank*, 97 Cal. App. 4th 1094, 1101 (2002)).

Cingular has repeatedly suggested that the only important case law favoring Petitioner's position is from California, despite the many published favorable cases from non-California courts such as Florida, Ohio, West Virginia and Alabama cited in Petitioners' briefs to the Court of Appeals. Now, Petitioners respectfully urge the Court to closely consider yet another non-California opinion that is particularly thoughtful and persuasive: *Whitney v. Alltel Communications, Inc.*, 173 S.W.3d 300, 311 (Mo. App. 2005). In *Whitney*, the Missouri Court of Appeals refused to enforce a class action ban in a wireless telephone arbitration agreement, finding it to be "so prohibitive as to effectively deprive a party of his or her statutory rights." 173 S.W.3d at 311. While the court in *Whitney* considered additional limitations in that company's contract that are not present here, the essential exculpatory nature of the class action limitation alone is clear from the trial court's factual findings in that case:

> Here, plaintiff filed a putative class action challenging a charge of 88 cents per month. By itself, such a claim would not be economically feasible to prosecute. However, when all of the customers are added together, large sums of money are at stake. Prohibiting class treatment of these claims would leave consumers with relatively small claims without a practical remedy.

177 S.W.3d at 309. While the Missouri appellate court went beyond that finding and looked at even further evidence of unfairness, under Washington state law dealing with exculpatory and one-sided contracts, this Court should be informed by the *Whitney* court's citation to the factual finding that the ban on class actions alone rendered the small claims at issue infeasible to prosecute. In sum, after this Court's decisions in *Zuver v. Airtouch Communications, Inc.*, 153 Wn. 2d 293, 103 P.3d 753 (2004), and *Adler v. Fred Lind Manor*, 153 Wn. 2d 331, 103 P.2d 773 (2004), it was clear that Cingular's ban on class actions was of dubious legality in Washington. With the powerful new decisions in *Discover* and *Whitney*, however, the landscape has become considerably bleaker for Cingular.

Another recent case that provides analogous support to Petitioners' position is *Weiss v. Regal Collections*, 385 F.3d 337 (3d Cir. 2004). In that case, the court rejected an attempt by defendants to moot out a class action by offering the class representative the maximum recoverable statutory damages. The court recognized that if defendants could so easily avoid class actions, "meritorious FDCPA claims might go unredressed because the awards in an individual case might be too small to prosecute an individual action[,] . . . frustrating the goals and enforcement mechanism of the FDCPA." 85 F.3d at 345. While *Weiss* did not involve an unconscionability challenge to a class action waiver provision, it does underscore a fundamental flaw in Cingular's approach to this action. The upshot of Cingular's arguments is that the named plaintiffs in this case could abandon their obligation to the putative class members they undertook to represent, and seek recovery for their individual claims in an individual arbitration. Even if such an individual action made any economic sense (which it does not), Cingular's position amounts to a suggestion that it would be fair to require Petitioners to take their individual money and run. The *Weiss* case reveals the serious wrong suggested in this approach.

Finally, Cingular filed a supplemental authorities brief in the Court of Appeals that made much of *Parrish v. Cingular Wireless*, 28 Cal. Rptr. 3d 802 (2005). However, the California Court of Appeals has since reversed itself and held that Cingular's arbitration clause is unenforceable. 2005 WL 2420719 (Oct. 3, 2005).

II. CINGULAR'S CITATION TO GILMER IS UNPERSUASIVE.

Cingular has suggested that the U.S. Supreme Court's decision in *Gilmer v. Interstate/Johnson Lane Corp.*, 500 U.S. 20 (1991), supports its position that its class action ban is enforceable. Br. of Respondent at 17. While Petitioners' earlier briefing established that Cingular's argument is misguided, *Gilmer* is further distinguishable on several additional grounds. First, unlike the arbitration clause at issue here, the clause in *Gilmer* allowed for class arbitrations. *Id.* at 32 (noting that collective relief could be obtained in arbitration). Therefore, unlike the plaintiffs here, the *Gilmer* plaintiff would not be deprived of a class remedy if arbitration were compelled. Second, *Gilmer* was not a class action, but an individual civil rights action seeking damages substantially greater than the damages sought here. Thus, the availability of a class action was not necessary for the *Gilmer* plaintiff to obtain relief. Finally, *Gilmer* is inapposite because the Court there was interpreting the text and structure of the Age Discrimination in Employment Act, not whether the arbitration clause was unenforceable as a matter of generally applicable state contract law.[+1] For these reasons, *Gilmer* provides no ammunition to parties seeking to defend exculpatory arbitration clauses banning class actions against unconscionability challenges. *See Discover Bank*, 113 P.3d at 1113; *West Virginia ex rel. Dunlap v. Berger*, 567 S.E.2d 265, 279 (W. Va.), *cert. denied*, 537 U.S. 1087 (2002).

III. CINGULAR'S CLASS ACTION BAN IS EFFECTIVELY EXCULPATORY REGARDLESS OF THE AVAILABILITY OF ATTORNEYS' FEES OR THE POSSIBILITY OF GOVERNMENT ENFORCEMENT ACTIONS.

A. Prevailing Parties In Individual Cases Are Unlikely To Receive Full Fees.

Cingular defends its class action ban by asserting that its arbitration clause provides for the reimbursement of attorney fees in some cases. Br. of Respondent at 4. According to Cingular, this is sufficient to ensure that attorneys will represent its customers in arbitration on an individual basis despite their small claims, in the hope that they will receive a fee disproportionate to the underlying amount in controversy. However, this speculation is belied by the evidence in this case: Cingular's own arbitration provider testified that not one Cingular customer in Washington had filed a claim against Cingular in arbitration, even *after* the attorney fee provision was added to the contract. CP at 1435 ¶ 8.

This is unsurprising, given that Cingular's clause provides that an arbitrator need not award attorneys' fees unless the arbitrator awards the consumer at least 100% of the value of her claim. Thus, for example, a customer who prevails on her breach-of-contract claim will still recover no fees if the arbitrator determines she is entitled to even one dollar less than the amount in damages demanded.

In addition, Cingular need only reimburse attorney fees that the arbitrator decides are "reasonable." CP at 356. In determining what attorneys' fees are reasonable, courts and arbitrators may well be reluctant to award fees that are out of proportion to the plaintiff's damages, no matter how much time has been invested in the case. *See, e.g., Nuttall v. Dowell*, 31 Wn. App. 98, 113–14, 639 P.2d 832 (1982) (limiting attorney fee award to $1,400, the amount recoverable by the plaintiff for a CPA violation); *Ethridge v. Hwang*, 105 Wn. App. 447, 461, 20 P.3d 958 (2001) ("Ultimately, the fee award must be reasonable in relation to the results obtained.") (internal quotations omitted); *Sheppard v. Riverview Nursing Center, Inc.*, 88 F.3d 1332, 1335–36 (4th Cir. 1996) ("considerations of proportionality should guide the decision whether to award fees").[+2]

Thus, for small-dollar cases like those at issue here—each involving a few hundred dollars or less—a fee award tied to the amount at stake will make the case a money-loser for the attorney. Many attorneys simply cannot afford to take the risk that a court or arbitrator will sharply curtail a fee award, and thus will be deterred from representing aggrieved individuals with valid claims. As Plaintiffs' expert Peter Maier, a veteran Washington consumer attorney with 24 years of experience, explained:

> Even if there is a prospect of recovering attorney fees from the Defendant, the potential of recovering attorney fees does not provide a sufficient incentive for me to take the case if the amount of damages to be recovered is only a few hundred or even a few thousand dollars. The award of attorney fees is discretionary with the court or the arbitrator, and thus is inherently uncertain in its outcome, and, in my experience, a court or arbitrator is often unwilling to award full attorneys fees even if the consumer prevails if the amount of those fees far exceeds the amount of damages.

CP at 1583 ¶ 12.

In light of this, Cingular's rosy prediction concerning the eagerness of the private bar to handle small individual consumer claims rings hollow. Even where fee-shifting statutes or contract terms apply, small claims often translate into small fees, fees that likely represent just a fraction of the attorney's costs, time and labor. And even where a few private attorneys are willing to face the risk of receiving a substantially reduced fee, that same risk will deter many others from handling such cases, and while some

---

[+1] Cingular's reliance on *Johnson v. W. Suburban Bank*, 255 F.3d 366 (3d Cir. 2000), Br. of Respondent at 18, 26, is inapposite for the same reason. In that case, the court addressed whether class action bans are fundamentally inconsistent with federal law. However, whether a contractual term violates an entire statutory scheme is an entirely different question from whether the term is unconscionable under state contract law. *See, e.g. Discover Bank*, 113 P.3d at 1114 n.6.

[+2] Similarly, courts have found it unreasonable to award fees that exceed the amount at stake in the underlying litigation. *See, e.g., Geissal v. Moore Med. Corp.*, 338 F.3d 926, 932–33 (8th Cir. 2003) (instructing the district court "that any attorney's fee awarded for the proceedings on remand may not exceed one-third of the remaining amounts in controversy"); *James v. Thermal Master, Inc.*, 563 N.E.2d 917, 919 (Ohio App. 1988) (affirming trial court's decision to reduce attorney's fee in light of small jury award); *F.H. Krear & Co. v. Nineteen Named Trustees*, 810 F.2d 1250, 1264 (2d Cir. 1987) ("New York courts have stated that, as a general rule, they will rarely find reasonable an award to a plaintiff that exceeds the amount involved in litigation." (citation omitted)); *Strama v. Peterson*, 689 F.2d 661, 665 (7th Cir. 1982) ("usually attorneys' fees should not be granted greatly in excess of a client's recovery" (citation omitted)); *In re Taylor*, 2003 WL 22282173 at *5 (Bankr. D. Vt. Oct. 1, 2003) (holding that, under federal bankruptcy law, "attorney's fees in excess of the amount in controversy is prima facie unreasonable").

consumers may be able to obtain relief for their injuries, many others will not.[+3] Therefore, many aggrieved consumers will be left without recourse if class actions are disallowed. Cingular's contractual term offering to reimburse some winning plaintiffs for "reasonable" attorney fees does nothing to alter this reality.

B. Individuals With Small Claims Have Little Incentive To Seek Out An Attorney Or Pursue Their Claims.

The value of a class action is not only that it provides an incentive for an attorney to pursue claims that are otherwise economically infeasible, but also that it enables individual claimants to obtain relief that they otherwise would not be aware of or willing to pursue.

Small dollar claims will not be brought unless incentives exist for both attorneys *and* their potential clients. Even if fee-shifting provisions did provide an adequate incentive for attorneys to handle individual cases (which they do not), they fail to provide an adequate incentive for consumers to seek an attorney, because individual consumers suffering small injuries are unlikely to find it worthwhile to pursue small claims. Litigation or arbitration is a stressful and time-consuming endeavor for any plaintiff, and therefore the stakes of any case must be substantial enough so that a claimant will be willing to put up with the attendant burdens of fighting for her rights. *Cf. Carnegie v. Household Int'l, Inc.*, 376 F.3d 656, 661 (7th Cir. 2004) ("The realistic alternative to a class action is not 17 million individual suits, but zero individual suits, as only a lunatic or a fanatic sues for $30.").

Moreover, even if potential plaintiffs would be willing to fight to protect their rights, many claims still will go unremedied in the absence of a class action because, especially as to deceptive practices directed toward unwary consumers, "any plaintiffs may not know their rights are being violated." *Abels v. JBC Legal Group, P.C.*, 227 F.R.D. 541, 547 (N.D. Cal. 2005) (quoting *Sledge v. Sands*, 182 F.R.D. 255, 259 (N.D. Ill. 1998)). A primary benefit of class actions is that they provide relief to all victims of a defendant's misconduct, regardless of whether the defendant's illegal activities fly under the radar screens of many injured consumers. That broad relief cannot be replicated on an individual basis unless each potential class member knows that her rights were violated. Thus, prohibiting class actions and requiring individual actions inevitably would leave many consumers like the class members Petitioners represent with no recovery at all for violations of their rights, even if there would be attorneys willing to take their cases. Fee-shifting provisions, therefore, do not adequately substitute for class actions.

C. Government Action Is Not An Adequate Alternative to Class Actions.

Cingular and its *amici* are likely to argue that it is acceptable to strip consumers of the right to seek redress for their injuries because government agencies like the Attorney General's office and the Federal Trade Commission (FTC) can protect consumers through public enforcement actions. But an argument that it is permissible to effectively eliminate the Washington CPA's private right of action simply because there is a public right of action defies the Washington legislature's conclusion that public *and private* causes of action are necessary to effectuate the CPA's purpose of protecting consumers. *See Hangman Ridge Training Stables, Inc. v. Safeco Title Ins. Co.*, 105 Wn. 2d 778, 784, 719 P.2d 531 (1986) ("In apparent response to the escalating need for additional enforcement capabilities, the State Legislature in 1971 amended the CPA to provide for a private right of action whereby individual citizens would be encouraged to bring suit to enforce the CPA.").

It is well known that despite the good intentions of state and federal agencies, they simply do not have the capability to police all consumer protection violations without private help. The U.S. Supreme Court has recognized that class actions "evolved in response to injuries unremedied by the government," not the other way around. *Deposit Guaranty Nat. Bank v. Roper*, 445 U.S. 326, 339 (1980). Similarly, courts have held that "[t]he alternatives to the class action—private suits or government actions—have been so often found wanting in controlling consumer frauds that not even the ardent critics of class actions seriously contend that they are truly effective." *Eshagi v. Hanley Dawson Cadillac Co.*, 574 N.E.2d 760, 766 (Ill. App. 1991); *accord Discover Bank*, 113 P.3d at 1110 (rejecting the argument that government prosecution provides an adequate substitute to class actions).

Finally, federal and state agencies recognize that private rights of action are indispensable to effective consumer protection. *See* Steven J. Cole, *State Enforcement Efforts Directed Against Unfair or Deceptive Practices*, 56 ANTITRUST L.J. 125, 126 (1987) (FTC encouraged adoption of state consumer protection statutes because of "the unavailability of private enforcement of the Federal Trade Commission Act"). Sally Gustafson Garratt, former Division Chief for Consumer Protection, testified in this case that the Washington State Attorney General's office often "did not have the resources to pursue [consumer cases] and relied on the private class action to correct the deceptive or unfair industry practice and to reimburse consumers for their losses." CP at 1571 ¶ 12. In sum, class actions are necessary in order to fill the void in consumer protection created by the inherent limitations of government action.

IV. PETITIONERS' AUTHORITIES MAY NOT BE DISREGARDED MERELY BECAUSE SOME OF THOSE CASES INVOLVED CONTRACTS WITH MULTIPLE UNFAIR PROVISIONS.

Cingular repeatedly argues that decisions supporting Petitioners' argument should be accorded little weight because many of them involved contracts that not only banned consumers from bringing or participating in class actions, but that also explicitly stripped consumers of statutory remedies, imposed excessive arbitration costs on consumers, or the like. Cingular's argument is unpersuasive on several levels.

First, in a number of cases cited by Petitioners—*Discover Bank*, for example—the ban on class actions was the only flaw in the lender's contract that the plaintiffs challenged.

[+3] The cases cited by Cingular—*Snowden v. Checkpoint Check Cashing*, 290 F.3d 631 (4th Cir. 2002), and *Jenkins v. First Am. Cash Advance of Ga., LLC*, 400 F.3d 868 (11th Cir. 2005)—do not dictate otherwise. In those cases, the courts summarily concluded, with no evidence whatsoever and on the basis of nothing but their own conjecture, that the availability of attorneys' fees guaranteed that attorneys would handle small consumer claims on an individual basis. Additionally, in those cases there was no record evidence equivalent to the evidence here showing that not a single Washington consumer has filed an individual arbitration against Cingular, despite the availability of attorneys' fees. The California Supreme Court expressly criticized *Snowden* on this ground, holding that *Snowden*'s conclusion was based on "unsupported assertions" and concluding the fee-shifting statutes do not constitute an adequate substitute for class actions. *See Discover Bank*, 113 P.3d at 1110.

Second, while it is true that courts in some of Petitioners' cases considered more than one factor in determining unconscionability, in other cases the discussion of class action bans stands alone. In *Ting*, for example, it is true that the court struck down four separate elements of the arbitration clause as substantively unconscionable: the ban on class actions, the excessive costs of arbitration, the provisions stripping consumers of various substantive statutory rights, and the secrecy provision. 319 F.3d at 1126. However, there is no indication that any of these provisions would have been considered legal if only it had stood alone without the other three. Indeed, in *Zuver*, this Court relied on the *Ting* court's holding striking down the confidentiality provision without considering that term's relation to the other provisions in AT&T's contract. 153 Wn. 2d at 312–13. Like the Ninth Circuit in *Ting*, this Court examined each component of Airtouch's arbitration clause independently in evaluating unconscionability. It was only when discussing whether the unconscionable terms could be severed from the arbitration clause that the Court considered whether, when taken together, they rendered the clause unconscionable as a whole. *Id.* at 319–20.

V. THE CONSTITUTIONAL PRESUMPTION AGAINST PREEMPTION IS PARTICULARLY POTENT HERE.

In our briefing before the Court of Appeals, Petitioners argued that because preemption constitutes a radical intrusion on a state's power, the U.S. Supreme Court has recognized a strong presumption against preemption of state laws. In its most recent preemption decision, the Court greatly amplified and clarified the scope of this presumption:

> Because the States are independent sovereigns in our federal system, we have long presumed that Congress does not cavalierly pre-empt state law causes of action. In areas of traditional state regulation, we assume that a federal statute has not supplanted state law unless Congress has made such an intention clear and manifest.

Bates v. Dow Agrosciences, LLC, 125 S. Ct. 1788, 1801 (2005) (citations omitted). The Court further clarified that when there are two equally plausible readings of a federal statute, courts should adopt the reading that would find no preemption of state law. *Id.*

The presumption against preemption is particularly applicable here, because contract law is an area traditionally governed by the states, and the common law of unconscionability is an area of almost exclusive state regulation. While there is a body of federal common law governing contracts in certain narrow areas (such as in collective bargaining disputes governed by federal labor laws or in certain maritime settings), few areas of law have been more deeply entrusted to the states than contract law.[+4]

[+4] *See, e.g., Northern Pipeline Constr. Co. v. Marathon Pipeline Co.*, 458 U.S. 50, 84 (1982) ("the cases before us, which center upon appellant Northern's claim for damages for breach of contract..., involve a right created by *state* law...."), *id.* at 90 (Rehnquist, J. and O'Connor, J., concurring) ("the lawsuit... seeks damages for breach of contract... which are the stuff of traditional actions at common law.... There is apparently no federal rule of decision provided for any of the issues in the lawsuit; the claims... arise entirely under state law."); *Aronson v. Quick Point Pencil Co.*, 440 U.S. 257, 262 (1979) ("[C]ommercial agreements traditionally are the domain of state law.

Furthermore, if the Court finds that it is unconscionable for corporations to bar consumers with modest claims from bringing class actions, this holding could hardly be said to conflict with federal law, because just last year Congress made clear that federal law recognizes a necessary role for class actions in some circumstances. The findings that accompanied the Class Action Fairness Act ("CAFA"), for example, state:

> Class action lawsuits are an important and valuable part of the legal system when they permit the fair and efficient resolution of legitimate claims of numerous parties by allowing the claims to be aggregated into a single action against a defendant that has allegedly caused harm.

28 U.S.C. § 1711 note, U.S. Pub. L. 109-2, § 2(a)(1), 119 Stat. 4 (Feb. 18, 2005). Similarly, the Senate Report that accompanied CAFA stated:

> Class actions were designed to provide a mechanism by which persons, whose injuries are not large enough to make pursuing their individual claims in the court system cost efficient, are able to bind together with persons suffering the same harm and seek redress for their injuries. As such, class actions are a valuable tool in our jurisprudential system.

S. Rep. 109-14 at 4, *reprinted at* 2005 U.S. Cong. Code and Admin. News 3, 5 (Feb. 28, 2005).

VI. THERE IS NOTHING RADICAL ABOUT BARRING CORPORATIONS FROM PROHIBITING THEIR CUSTOMERS FROM BRINGING OR PARTICIPATING IN CLASS ACTIONS.

Cingular and its *amici* are likely to suggest that it will upset the settled expectations of the wireless industry if corporations can be held accountable for wrongdoing on a class action basis. In fact, the industry has no reasonable expectation that it should be permitted to insulate itself from class actions.

First, arbitration clauses that ban class actions are of very recent vintage. Prior to the detariffing of phone service on August 1, 2001, phone carriers' relations with their customers were governed by tariffs on file with the Federal Communication Commission. Few, if any, carriers attempted to ban class actions in these filings. Only in the wake of deregulation did companies in the industry decide to attempt to immunize themselves from effective enforcement of state consumer protection laws by banning class actions. *Cf. In re Currency Conversion*, 2005 WL 2364969 (S.D.N.Y. Sept. 27, 2005) (prior to 1999, only two major credit card issuers had adopted arbitration clauses banning class actions).

Second, the securities industry demonstrates that mandatory arbitration can be effectively integrated with class actions in court. Under the system adopted by the National Association of Security Dealers ("NASD"), investors with individual claims against bro-

---

State law is not displaced merely because the contract relates to intellectual property which may or may not be patentable"); *Stewart Org., Inc. v. Ricoh Corp.*, 487 U.S. 22, 40 (1988) (Scalia, J., dissenting) ("Nor can or should courts ignore that issues of contract validity are traditionally matters governed by state law.").

kers are required to bring those claims in private arbitration, but brokers may not bar investors from pursuing class action claims in court. *See* NASD Code of Arbitration Procedure, § 10301(d)(3) (prohibiting arbitration of class claims in favor of litigation of all such claims). There is certainly nothing "anti-arbitration" or "anti-business" about the way that the NASD conducts its arbitration system, and it would hardly be a radical step if the effect of this Court's decision is to replicate this core element of the NASD's system for cases involving small individual claims.

CONCLUSION

The Court should find that Cingular's unseverable class action ban is unconscionable, hold the arbitration clause unenforceable, and reverse the superior court's decision.

Respectfully submitted this 9th January, 2006.

[Attorneys for Appellant]

F.2.4 Plaintiff's Response to Industry Amicus Brief

SUPREME COURT OF THE STATE OF WASHINGTON

DOUG SCOTT, LOREN TABASINKE, SANDRA TABASINSKE, PATRICK OISHI, JANET OISHI, et al.,
  Petitioners,

v.

CINGULAR WIRELESS,
  Respondent.

No. 77406-4

PETITIONERS' RESPONSE TO *AMICUS* BRIEFS SUPPORTING RESPONDENT

TABLE OF CONTENTS

TABLE OF AUTHORITIES
INTRODUCTION AND SUMMARY OF ARGUMENT
I. THE POLICY ARGUMENTS OF CINGULAR'S AMICI ARE UNPERSUASIVE.
 A. This Court Should Place Little Weight on the Threat that Corporations Will Abandon All Arbitration Or Even Leave the State If They Are Not Permitted to Ban Class Actions.
 B. Occasional Abuses Do Not Justify Permitting Corporations to Self-Deregulate By Banning All Class Actions.
 C. A Ruling for Cingular's Customers Will Not Lead to Inflation.
 D. Notwithstanding the "Empirical" Defense of Mandatory Arbitration Offered By Cingular's Amici, Individual Arbitration Is Still Not an Effective Alternative to Class Action Proceedings.
II. THE LEGAL ARGUMENTS ADVANCED BY CINGULAR'S AMICI ARE UNPERSUASIVE.
 A. Many of the Legal Arguments Offered by Cingular's Amici Merely Repeat Unpersuasive Arguments Already Refuted in the Briefing in this Case.
 B. The Claim of Cingular's Amici that Class Actions Are Incompatible With Arbitration Has Been Rejected by the U.S. Supreme Court and Is Rooted in Hostility to Arbitration.
 C. The Miscellaneous Remaining Legal Arguments of Cingular's Amici Are Also Unpersuasive.
CONCLUSION

TABLE OF AUTHORITIES

Cases[*****]

Al Safin v. Circuit City Stores, 394 F.3d 1254 (9th Cir. 2005)
Discover Bank v. Superior Court, 113 P.3d 1100 (Cal. 2005)
EEOC v. Waffle House, Inc., 534 U.S. 279 (2002)
Green Tree Fin. Corp. v. Bazzle, 539 U.S. 444 (2003)
Heaphy v. State Farm Mutual Auto Ins. Co., 117 Wn. App. 438, 72 P.3d 220 (2003)
In re Worldcom, Inc. Securities Litig., 2005 WL 1048073 (S.D.N.Y. May 5, 2005)
Luna v. Household Fin. Corp. III, 236 F. Supp. 2d 1166 (W.D. Wash. 2002)
Motor Contract Co. v. Van Der Volgen, 162 Wn. 449, 298 P. 705 (1931)
Patterson v. ITT Consumer Financial Corp., 14 Cal. App. 4th 1659, 18 Cal. Rptr. 2d 563 (1993)
Stein v. Geonerco, Inc., 105 Wn. App. 41, 17 P.3d 1266 (2001)
Ting v. AT&T, 182 F. Supp. 2d 902 (N.D. Cal. 2002), *aff'd in relevant part*, 319 F.3d 1126 (9th Cir. 2003)
Ting v. AT&T, 319 F.3d 1126 (9th Cir. 2003)
Zuver v. Airtouch Communications, Inc., 153 Wn. 2d 293, 103 P.3d 753 (2004)

Statutes

9 U.S.C. § 2

Other Authorities

Alan Kaplinsky, *Excuse Me, But Who's the Predator: Banks Can Use Arbitration Clauses as a Defense*, BUS. LAW. 24 (May/June 1998)
Brief for American Bankers Association, American Financial Services Association, and Consumer Bankers Association as Amici Curiae in Support of Petitioner, Green Tree Corp v. Bazzle, 2003 WL 721688
Brief of the Chamber of Commerce of the United States as Amicus Curiae in Support of Petitioner, Green Tree Corp v. Bazzle, 2003 WL 721691
Caroline E. Mayer, *Win Some, Lose Rarely? Arbitration Forum's Rulings Called One-Sided*, Wash. Post, Mar. 1, 2000
Fee Objections Scuttle Settlement, The Daily Record, November 19, 2003, p. 1
Marcus Nieto and Margaret Hosel, Arbitration in California Managed Health Care Systems (2001)
New UDRP Study Finds Forum Shopping, Panel Problems, ADRWorld.com, March 26, 2002

[*****] [*Editor's Note: Citations throughout brief as in original.*]

INTRODUCTION AND SUMMARY OF ARGUMENT

A number of corporate entities and trade associations have filed *amicus* briefs in support of the position taken by Respondent Cingular Wireless LLC ("Cingular"). These entities are the Association of Washington Business ("AWB"); Amazon.com, Intel Corporation, Microsoft Corporation and Real Networks, Inc. ("The Computer Companies"); CTIA—The Wireless Association ("CTIA"); and the Chamber of Commerce of the United States ("Chamber"). Collectively, the organizations will be referred to as "Cingular's *Amici*."

Most of the arguments made by Cingular's *Amici* are broad tort reform arguments as to why class actions are generally undesirable and thus why consumers would benefit if corporations were free to completely eliminate class actions. A host of decisions of this Court and many other courts establish that these arguments go too far, however, and that if class actions are completely eliminated (as Cingular's contract does for its customers), large numbers of consumers with valid claims will realistically never have any opportunity to vindicate them.

Cingular's *Amici* also make a broad policy argument that, if corporations are not permitted to ban class actions (in court or in arbitration), they will abandon the use of arbitration. This thinly-veiled threat is not only demonstrably untrue, but it also supports a point that Petitioners have made throughout this appeal: Cingular and its *amici* are not genuinely interested in resolving disputes through arbitration, but are instead merely looking for a way to get rid of class actions.

One of Cingular's *Amici* even suggests that if this Court finds that generally-applicable Washington state contract law does not permit corporations to bar their customers from bringing or participating in class action lawsuits, some corporations will refuse to do business in this state. This threat is empty, however, for there is no evidence whatsoever that corporations have fled from any of the states where appellate courts have reached such holdings. Cingular's *Amici* point to no evidence to suggest that the economies of Alabama, California, Florida, Missouri, Ohio or West Virginia have suffered in any way merely because their courts have refused to permit corporations to gut their consumer protection laws.

In addition to these policy arguments, Cingular's *Amici* repeat the legal arguments already made by Cingular in its earlier briefing, adding only a few new points. For example, Cingular's *Amici* suggest that this Court should disregard decisions from California courts. This Court has already quoted from and adopted the reasoning of several important California decisions, however, and there is a significant overlap between the legal approach of California courts and this Court's own earlier cases.

Several of Cingular's *Amici* also make arguments to the effect that class actions are always inappropriate and unfair in arbitration, and thus suggest that it is necessary to ban class actions entirely in order for consumers to have access to the benefits of arbitration. Many of these arguments were made (sometimes by the same *amici*) to the U.S. Supreme Court in connection with the case of *Green Tree Fin. Corp. v. Bazzle*, 539 U.S. 444 (2003), however, and the Supreme Court flatly rejected them. *Bazzle* makes clear that there is no reason that class actions can't proceed in arbitration, and the retread of their earlier arguments by Cingular's *Amici* (without even citing to *Bazzle*) cannot change this fact. Moreover, these arguments demonstrate that it is Cingular's *Amici*—and not the state contract law of those states that refuse to allow corporations to bar their customers with very small dollar value claims from bringing class actions—that are hostile to arbitration.

I. THE POLICY ARGUMENTS OF CINGULAR'S AMICI ARE UNPERSUASIVE.

A. This Court Should Place Little Weight on the Threat that Corporations Will Abandon All Arbitration Or Even Leave the State If They Are Not Permitted to Ban Class Actions.

Several of Cingular's *Amici* suggest that if corporations are not permitted to bar their customers from bringing or participating in class actions, this will spell the end of arbitration in general. *See, e.g.*, AWB Brief at 1 (a ruling for the plaintiffs will amount to the state "turning its back" on arbitration); CTIA Brief at 3 (if corporations may not ban class actions, that will be the "death knell" of arbitration); Computer Companies' Brief at 9–14 (class actions are generally undesirable, and if corporations faced the possibility of class actions in arbitration, it would mean the end of mandatory arbitration). There is even a threat that if this Court does not rule as they wish, some corporations will refuse to do business in Washington. AWB Brief at 1 (if this Court holds that corporations may not bar their customers from bringing class actions, businesses may avoid this state).

These threats are unpersuasive on a number of levels. First, as noted in our earlier briefing, quite a few jurisdictions have adopted the same position as that urged by Petitioners here. *See, e.g.*, Appellants' Opening Brief in the Court of Appeals ("Opening Brief") at 22–27; Petitioners' Supplemental Brief at 3–7. If the threats made by Cingular's *Amici* were real, and not merely scare tactics, then many corporations should have abandoned all arbitration in Alabama, California, Florida, Missouri, Ohio, and West Virginia. There is no evidence that this is the case, however.

Second, this threat is also belied by the experience of the securities industry. As Petitioners have previously explained, the National Association of Securities Dealers has permitted brokers to require their customers and employees to submit to mandatory arbitration on an individual basis, but has explicitly refused to permit brokers to prohibit their customers from bringing or participating in class actions. Supplemental Brief at 20. Under the theory of the Computer Companies' Brief (at 5), for example, all securities brokers should have elected to "simply avoid arbitration." As it turns out, however, the securities industry happily arbitrates many thousands of individual cases every year, while still being held accountable in class actions for major missteps. *See In re Worldcom, Inc. Securities Litig.*, 2005 WL 1048073 (S.D.N.Y. May 5, 2005), at *5 ("Thousands of individuals are currently pursuing arbitration cases against the Citigroup defendants.").

Third, the federal courts that have addressed this issue have consistently held that Washington state law prohibits arbitration clauses that bar consumers and employees with small claims from bringing class actions. *E.g.*, *Al Safin v. Circuit City Stores*, 394 F.3d 1254, 1262 (9th Cir. 2005); *Luna v. Household Fin. Corp. III*, 236 F. Supp. 2d 1166 (W.D. Wash. 2002). If Cingular's *Amici* are correct that a ruling for Cingular's customers here would "wreak havoc with countless arbitration provisions in contracts," Chamber Brief at 2, then the Ninth Circuit and Western District's decisions should have already triggered this disaster. Of course, nothing of the sort has occurred.

Fourth, as this Brief will further establish in Part II-B below, there is no inherent inconsistency between arbitration and class actions. The U.S. Supreme Court has held that arbitrations can be held on a class action basis, and numerous class actions are proceeding before the American Arbitration Association at this moment. The whole approach of Cingular's *Amici*—"Give us our way, or we will take our arbitration ball and go home"—is unworthy of serious consideration by this Court.

B. Occasional Abuses Do Not Justify Permitting Corporations to Self-Deregulate By Banning All Class Actions.

Several of Cingular's *Amici* are critical generally of class actions, complaining that class actions "accomplish[] little or nothing for consumers" (CTIA Brief at 3), and that class actions are often abused (Chamber Brief at 9).

These arguments are unpersuasive here for several reasons. First, the U.S. Supreme Court, this Court, and Washington courts of appeal have repeatedly noted that there are many circumstances in which class actions are necessary for individuals with small dollar value claims to effectively vindicate their legal rights. *See* Opening Brief at 22–27, 36–37; Brief of *Amicus Curiae* Attorney General of Washington ("A.G. Brief") at 6–7. The Brief of *Amicus Curiae* Washington State Trial Lawyers Association Foundation (at 9–11) also includes a thoughtful discussion of this Court's case law setting forth the powerful public policy of this state in support of class actions, and explains why this Court's consistent jurisprudence (and particularly this Court's decision in *Motor Contract Co. v. Van Der Volgen*, 162 Wn. 449, 298 P. 705 (1931)) does not permit private contracts to flout the state's public policy.

Second, the factual record in this case belies the general policy assertions of Cingular's *Amici* here, establishing that, in this case, individual actions do not offer a meaningful alternative to class actions. Opening Brief at 4–6, 20–22; Appellants' Reply Brief on the Merits in the Court of Appeals ("Reply") at 6–8.

Cingular's *Amici* speak of "abuses" of the class action process, CTIA Brief at 15, and Petitioners acknowledge that there have been circumstances in which some class actions have been abused. Indeed, undersigned counsel for Petitioners have objected to a number of abusive class actions over time.[1] Plainly, courts already possess ample powers to address such abuses, however, and many courts have dismissed class actions that should not have been filed or have rejected settlements that should not have been reached. Thus, while abuses of class actions may have occurred in some occasions, this in no way justifies eliminating them entirely—Cingular's *Amici* propose to throw out a great deal of baby along with a small amount of bath water. Similarly, it is true that Congress expressed concern about abuse when it passed the Class Action Fairness Act of 2005. Chamber Brief at 9. However, because Congress recognized that there are many instances in which class actions offer consumers their only meaningful chance for justice, Congress responded to these concerns not by banning class actions entirely, but by implementing reforms aimed at correcting those abuses. *See* Supplemental Brief at 18–19.

C. A Ruling for Cingular's Customers Will Not Lead to Inflation.

Several of Cingular's *Amici* argue that consumers will suffer if corporations are not permitted to strip their customers of the right to bring class actions, because corporations will be forced to pay out too much money when they violate consumer protection laws and thus will be forced to raise the cost of their goods and services. *E.g.*, Chamber Brief at 17; CTIA Brief at 6. As Petitioners have previously explained, however, there is ample reason to believe the opposite is true. *See* Reply at 19–22.

Indeed, this case illustrates that the inflation concern raised by Cingular's *Amici* is not plausible. In this case, Cingular is accused of deceiving its customers and breaking its contract with them, by promising certain services for free and then charging for those services. If Cingular wins this appeal, and is effectively insulated from any meaningful accountability for charging its customers for services it promised would have no charge, it is hard to see how Cingular's *Amici* could be correct that this result would lead to *lower* prices for consumers in Washington.

Finally, the entire premise of the "class actions lead to higher prices" argument is inimical to the purpose of consumer protection laws. *See Ting v. AT&T*, 182 F. Supp. 2d 902, 931 n.16 (N.D. Cal. 2002), *aff'd in relevant part*, 319 F.3d 1126 (9th Cir. 2003) ("the notion that it is to the public's advantage that companies be relieved of legal liability for their wrongdoing so that they can lower their cost of doing business is contrary to a century of consumer protection laws.") (citations omitted).

D. Notwithstanding the "Empirical" Defense of Mandatory Arbitration Offered By Cingular's *Amici*, Individual Arbitration Is Still Not an Effective Alternative to Class Action Proceedings.

As Petitioners have previously explained, the problem with Cingular's ban on class actions is not that arbitration is a bad process when compared with court, but that it is (a) one-sided and (b) effectively exculpatory for Cingular to require its customers with small claims to proceed solely on an individual basis. Several of Cingular's *Amici* seek to rebut these points by offering arguments about how individual arbitration is very fair to consumers. *See* Chamber Brief at 11; Computer Companies' Brief at 7–9. These arguments are unpersuasive.

First, no matter how strenuously Cingular and its *amici* defend the supposed fairness of its individual arbitration process,[2] this argument does nothing to change the fact that most if not all customers—even if they were aware they had been cheated—would be unable to pursue their claims on an individual basis no matter how reasonable those individual proceedings might be. *See* Reply at 6–8; Reply in Support of Discretionary Review at 6–9.

---

[1] *See, e.g., Fee Objections Scuttle Settlement,* The Daily Record, November 19, 2003, p. 1 (Trial Lawyers for Public Justice, counsel for Petitioners here, represented objectors in a case where the court rejected a settlement agreement that would have given disproportionate fees to class counsel and not helped the class).

[2] It is ironic that the Computer Companies (Brief at 8) cite a study of NASD arbitration that does not appear to be publicly available, for the proposition that many investors are supposedly satisfied with the NASD process. Even if the Computer Companies are correct that NASD arbitration offers individual investors a fine process, the NASD explicitly forbids the corporations subject to its rules to bar their customers from bringing class actions. *See* Supplemental Brief at 21. The fact that the NASD has insisted that investors with small claims be provided a meaningful remedy through class actions may go a long way to explain why NASD arbitration is supposedly favored by those who participate in it.

Second, many of the sources cited by Cingular's *Amici* for their conclusions that individual arbitration is fair are, with respect, quite dubious. The Computer Companies, for example, cite a law review article by Roger Haydock for the proposition that consumers supposedly prefer to be compelled to arbitrate claims rather than be given the option of going the court. Brief at 8. What these *amici* do not disclose is that Mr. Haydock is a principal in the notorious National Arbitration Forum ("NAF").~3 While Mr. Haydock may publish studies claiming that arbitration is very fair, the evidence that has emerged suggests that his own company hardly meets the fine claims that he makes. *See* Caroline E. Mayer, *Win Some, Lose Rarely? Arbitration Forum's Rulings Called One-Sided*, Wash. Post, Mar. 1, 2000 (in 19,618 cases arbitrated by NAF between consumers and First USA Bank, the cardholder had prevailed in 87 cases, which works out to a success rate for the lender of 99.6%).~4

In fact, the empirical record relating to the fairness of arbitration in consumer cases is still very much an open question. A study of the results of arbitration in HMOs by the California Research Bureau found, for example, that in every instance where an arbitrator awarded a plaintiff (generally raising medical malpractice claims) over $1 million, "the arbitrator was only employed in that case." Marcus Nieto and Margaret Hosel, *Arbitration in California Managed Health Care Systems* at 22–23 (2001). The study went on to find that arbitrators selected by this system were 20 times more likely to enter summary judgment for HMOs than were courts, and that arbitrator awards to plaintiffs were lower than court awards. *Id.*

II. THE LEGAL ARGUMENTS ADVANCED BY CINGULAR'S AMICI ARE UNPERSUASIVE.

A. Many of the Legal Arguments Offered by Cingular's *Amici* Merely Repeat Unpersuasive Arguments Already Refuted in the Briefing in this Case.

Several of the legal arguments set forth by Cingular's *Amici* simply repeat arguments already thoroughly explored in the briefing in this case. For example, several of Cingular's *Amici* suggest that this Court should be guided by the rulings in *Stein v. Geonerco,*

~3 The first of a number of decisions striking down arbitration clauses that required consumers to submit their claims to the NAF was *Patterson v. ITT Consumer Financial Corp.*, 14 Cal. App. 4th 1659, 18 Cal. Rptr. 2d 563 (1993). In the *Patterson* case, the court of appeals held that "the likely effect of these procedures [NAF's rules] is to deny a borrower against whom a claim has been brought any opportunity to a hearing. . . ." 14 Cal. App. 4th at 1666.

~4 An academic study also concluded that NAF's rules permit it to manipulate results so as to favor more powerful parties. Michael Geist, a Professor at the University of Ottowa Law School, found that NAF arbitrators rule for the complainant in the internet domain name dispute resolution system far more often than arbitrators from other providers, because of NAF's practice of "granting an ever-larger share of its caseload to a small group of panelists." *New UDRP Study Finds Forum Shopping, Panel Problems*, ADRWorld.com, March 26, 2002. The study found that "three of NAF's busiest panelists have decided 324 out of 324 cases in favor of complainants in default cases," and explains that default cases in this setting are not automatic wins in front of non-NAF arbitrators because of UDRP's proof requirements. *Id.*

Inc., 105 Wn. App. 41, 17 P.3d 1266 (2001) and *Heaphy v. State Farm Mutual Auto Ins. Co.*, 117 Wn. App. 438, 72 P.3d 220 (2003). *E.g.*, CTIA Brief at 12; AWB Brief at 7–9. As Petitioners have previously made clear, those two cases cannot govern the issues here under any plausible legal theory. *See* Reply at 10–13, Reply in Support of Petition for Discretionary Review at 1–4.

Similarly, several of Cingular's *Amici* repeat the argument that this Court cannot find the ban on class actions to be unconscionable, because the class action is merely a "procedural" device and is not substantive. *E.g.*, CTIA Brief at 3, 12; Chamber Brief at 7–8. But as Petitioners have consistently pointed out, this Court—and many other courts—have repeatedly held that arbitration clauses that incorporate one-sided or exculpatory procedures are unconscionable. *E.g.*, Reply at 18–19. *See also Discover Bank v. Superior Court*, 113 P.3d 1100, 1109 (Cal. 2005) ("[C]lass actions and arbitrations are, particularly in the consumer context, often inextricably linked to the vindication of substantive rights. Affixing the 'procedural' label on such devices understates their importance and is not helpful to resolving the unconscionability issue.").

B. The Claim of Cingular's *Amici* that Class Actions Are Incompatible With Arbitration Has Been Rejected by the U.S. Supreme Court and Is Rooted in Hostility to Arbitration.

Several of Cingular's *Amici* argue that class actions are incompatible with arbitration. *See* Chamber Brief at 15–18 (class arbitration is unacceptable); CTIA Brief at 2 (class actions are "completely at odds" with arbitration), *id.* at 18 (class actions are antithetical to arbitration); AWB Brief at 11 (ruling for plaintiffs would "defeat the entire body of public policy supporting arbitration").

This is puzzling, given that the same arguments were made by business *amici* in *Green Tree Corp. v. Bazzle*—and rejected by the U.S. Supreme Court. In *Bazzle*, as here, the Chamber urged the U.S. Supreme Court to find that the effect of permitting class actions to proceed in arbitration would be to cause corporations to abandon arbitration entirely:

> Many of the Chamber's members . . . have adopted as standard features of their business contracts provisions that mandate the arbitration of disputes arising from or related to those agreements. They utilize arbitration because it is a prompt, fair, inexpensive, and effective method of resolving disputes with consumers and other contracting parties. Many of those advantages would be forfeited if, as the court below held, the class action device may be superimposed on arbitration.

Brief of the Chamber of Commerce of the United States as *Amicus Curiae* in Support of Petitioner, *Green Tree Corp v. Bazzle*, 2003 WL 721691, at 1. Similarly, the American Bankers Association argued that "class arbitration cannot possibly provide the full protections for absent parties that are afforded by the painstakingly worked out procedures for judicial class actions." Brief for American Bankers Association, American Financial Services Association, and Consumer Bankers Association as *Amici Curiae* in Support of Petitioner, *Green Tree Corp v. Bazzle*, 2003 WL 721688 at 18.

In short, the same argument that Cingular's *Amici* make to this Court was made to the U.S. Supreme Court in support of the proposition that the Court should hold that arbitration was incompatible with class actions. And despite these arguments, the U.S. Supreme Court held that the question of whether a class action can be brought in arbitration depends upon state law. *Bazzle,* 539 U.S. at 447. Having lost in their effort to persuade the U.S. Supreme Court to find that a class action could never proceed in arbitration, and that permitting a state court to find that this might happen would undermine the FAA and arbitration, the Chamber and Cingular's other *amici* are trying for a second bite at the apple by asking this Court to come to a different conclusion.

Finally, given that the American Arbitration Association is currently handling quite a few cases on a class action basis (*see* Opening Brief at 41), Cingular's *Amici*'s argument that permitting class actions to proceed in arbitration would undermine the FAA and arbitration in general falls flat.

C. The Miscellaneous Remaining Legal Arguments of Cingular's *Amici* Are Also Unpersuasive.

In addition to the foregoing, Cingular's *Amici* have set forth a hodge-podge of unrelated legal arguments.

First, several of Cingular's *Amici* argue that this Court should disregard *Discover Bank* and *Ting,* as well as any other cases applying California law to arbitration clauses. The Computer Companies argue, for example, that California law has been "singled out for critical commentary," and point to an article by Alan Kaplinsky. Brief at 19.~5 This argument is unpersuasive on a number of levels. First, this Court has already cited California law, as it was enunciated in *Ting v. AT&T,* 319 F.3d 1126 (9th Cir. 2003), with approval in *Zuver v. Airtouch Communications, Inc.,* 153 Wn. 2d 293, 103 P.3d 753 (2004). In addition, California law on non-mutual arbitration clauses that require individuals to arbitrate their claims while permitting the corporate drafters of the clause to go to court is consistent with the law in this state, unlike the law in most of the jurisdictions that have adopted Cingular's position. *See* Reply at 13–17. In any case, Petitioners' arguments are supported by courts applying the law of many other states as well, and are rooted in basic principles of Washington state contract law on one-sided and exculpatory contracts.

A more unusual argument comes from the Computer Companies, who cite Justice Thomas' dissent in *EEOC v. Waffle House, Inc.,* 534 U.S. 279, 310 (2002), for the proposition that "a rule requiring the provision of class procedures would clash with the fundamental policies of the FAA." Brief at 14. This citation to a dissent contravenes the principle of that case, however, which was that arbitration clauses are not exempt from the laws that govern other contracts. In *Waffle House,* the U.S. Supreme Court refused to enforce an arbitration provision in an employment contract in a case where claims were asserted by a federal agency that was not a party to that contract. The Court reversed the lower court's decision, which had effectively treated arbitration clauses as some sort of super contract especially favored under federal law. The argument of Cingular's *Amici* is essentially that, when dealing with arbitration clauses, this Court must put aside the normal rules against one-sided and exculpatory contract provisions, because otherwise corporations will no longer like arbitration and won't use it. By a 6–3 vote, however, the U.S. Supreme Court rejected this notion, and held the FAA requires courts to place arbitration agreements on "equal footing" with other contracts. *Id.* at 293.

Several of Cingular's *Amici* also echo Cingular's argument that class actions are not necessary, because consumers can count on government agencies to enforce their rights under the consumer protection laws. *E.g.,* CTIA Brief at 3. This argument was refuted in Petitioners' earlier briefing. *See, e.g.,* Supplemental Brief at 13–15. Moreover, this generic argument is particularly weak in this case, given that the Washington Attorney General has filed a strong *amicus* brief arguing that corporations should not be permitted to immunize themselves from class actions because (1) private suits are instrumental to the enforcement of the Consumer Protection Act, and (2) class actions are often the only cost-effective means for private parties for enforce the CPA. A.G. Brief at 4–7.

The Chamber's suggestion that the Federal Communications Commission ("FCC") is an adequate substitute for private class actions is equally unavailing. Chamber Brief at 12–13. This precise argument was raised by the defendant in *Ting v. AT&T,* 182 F. Supp. 2d 902 (N.D. Cal. 2002), *aff'd in relevant part,* 319 F.3d 1126 (9th Cir. 2003), and rejected by the district court in a detailed opinion:

> It was largely undisputed at trial that it took the FCC approximately seventeen years before it effectively responded to "slamming" complaints.... [T]he FCC does not appear to have concerned itself with obtaining individual relief for... complainants, even in situations where the FCC has concluded the carrier committed an "egregious" practice.... Under all these circumstances, I find that the FCC is not a forum before which a class member can effectively vindicate her right to recover damages from AT&T in a variety of contexts.... Presumably, it was recognition of factors such as these that caused Congress in enacting the [Federal Communications Act] to give parties wronged by a carrier a choice of fora—the FCC or the courts. See 47 U.S.C. 207.

182 F. Supp. 2d at 919–20. This Court likewise should give no weight to the argument from the Chamber that it is acceptable to gut Washington's state consumer protection laws in favor of FCC enforcement, just as it should give no weight to Cingular's arguments for gutting those laws in favor of enforcement from state law enforcement officials.

Finally, the AWB argues that this Court may not strike down the contractual class action ban in Cingular's contract without some sort of new legislative authorization. AWB Brief at 13. This argument is flatly wrong, and misunderstands this Court's existing authority under federal and state law. Under the express language of the FAA, 9 U.S.C. § 2, arbitration clauses are subject to the same laws as all other contracts. This Court has the longstanding au-

---

~5 In evaluating Mr. Kaplinsky's views about the California Supreme Court, it should not be overlooked that he is a noted defense attorney for lenders who has appeared as counsel for defendants or *amici* for defendants in a series of cases raising the same issue as this one. Citing Mr. Kaplinsky's opinions as legal authority would be like plaintiffs' counsel citing themselves. Mr. Kaplinsky has described arbitration clauses as a "defense" for banks against consumer claims, in part because they can be a "deterrent" to class actions. Alan Kaplinsky, *Excuse Me, But Who's the Predator: Banks Can Use Arbitration Clauses as a Defense,* Bus. Law. 24, 26 (May/June 1998).

thority and power to set forth the generally applicable contract law of this state. Thus, just as this Court had ample authority under existing law to reach its decisions in *Zuver* and *Adler*, it requires no new legislative authority to make the decision sought by Petitioners in this case.

CONCLUSION

For the foregoing reasons, this Court should reject the arguments of Cingular's *Amici*, and strike down Cingular's ban on class actions.

Respectfully submitted this 14th February, 2006.

[*Attorneys for Appellants*]

Appendix G

Brief on Magnuson-Moss Warranty Act's Prohibition of Predispute Binding Arbitration Clauses

This brief is also available in Microsoft Word and Adobe Acrobat (PDF) format on the CD-Rom accompanying this volume.

SUPREME COURT OF THE UNITED STATES

JOHN AND BARBARA ABELA,)
                  Petitioners,)
)
v.   )
)
GENERAL MOTORS)
CORPORATION, A DELAWARE)
CORPORATION,)
                  Respondents.)

On Petition for a Writ of Certiorari to the Michigan Supreme Court

PETITION FOR A WRIT OF CERTIORARI

QUESTION PRESENTED

The Magnuson-Moss Warranty Act, 15 U.S.C. §§ 2301–2312, allows warrantors to include in their written warranties a requirement that consumers submit claims to "informal dispute settlement procedure[s]," 15 U.S.C. § 2310(a)(3), but also preserves a consumer's right to commence a civil action after he or she "initially resorts to such procedure." *Id.* The Federal Trade Commission interprets this statutory provision to make all private dispute resolution procedures related to a written warranty to be nonbinding (16 C.F.R. § 703.5(j)), and therefore to prohibit warrantors from enforcing pre-dispute agreements for binding arbitration with respect to claims arising from a written warranty (64 Fed. Reg. 19700, 19708 (1999)).

The question presented is whether the Magnuson-Moss Warranty Act and the Federal Trade Commission's regulations and interpretive guidelines issued pursuant to the Act prohibit warrantors from enforcing pre-dispute binding arbitration clauses against consumers raising claims related to a written warranty.

PARTIES TO THE PROCEEDING

The parties to the proceedings below were petitioners John and Barbara Abela (as appellants) and respondent General Motors Corporation (as appellee).

TABLE OF CONTENTS

QUESTION PRESENTED
PARTIES TO THE PROCEEDING
TABLE OF AUTHORITIES
OPINIONS BELOW
JURISDICTION
STATUTORY AND REGULATORY PROVISIONS INVOLVED
STATEMENT OF THE CASE
    A. The Federal Statutory and Regulatory Framework
        1. The Magnuson-Moss Warranty Act
        2. The FTC's Long-Standing Interpretation of the Act
    B. The Proceedings Below
        1. GM's Mandatory Binding Arbitration Program
        2. The Lower State Court Decisions
        3. The Michigan Supreme Court's Decision
REASONS FOR GRANTING THE WRIT
    I. REVIEW IS WARRANTED BECAUSE THERE IS A DIRECT SPLIT OF AUTHORITY OVER WHETHER THE MMWA PROHIBITS ENFORCEMENT OF PREDISPUTE BINDING ARBITRATION CLAUSES
        A. Substantial Authority Holds that the MMWA Prohibits Pre-Dispute Binding Arbitration Clauses
        B. There is Also Confusion Among the Courts Holding that the MMWA Allows Enforcement of Pre-Dispute Binding Arbitration Clauses
        C. Review is Warranted Because This Case Presents an Important and Recurring Issue of Federal Law
    II. THE HOLDING BELOW IS CONTRARY TO THE LANGUAGE AND INTENT OF THE MMWA, AND TO THE INTERPRETATION OF THE AGENCY CHARGED WITH ADMINISTERING THE ACT
        A. The MMWA's Language and Intent Establish that Warrantors May Not Force Consumers to Submit Claims Under the Act to Binding "Informal Dispute Settlement Mechanisms."
        B. The 1974 Congress Reasonably Understood the Phrase "Informal Dispute Settlement Mechanisms" to Include Pre-dispute Binding Arbitration
        C. This Court Should Defer to the FTC's Authoritative Determination
CONCLUSION

TABLE OF AUTHORITIES

*Cases**

Abela v. General Motors Corp., 677 N.W.2d 325 (Mich. 2004)
Andrews v. Louisville & Nashville R.R. Co., 406 U.S. 320 (1972)
Borowiec v. Gateway 2000, Inc., 808 N.E.2d 957 (Ill. 2004)
Browne v. Kline Tyson's Imports, Inc., 190 F. Supp. 2d 827 (E.D. Va. 2002)
Chevron U.S.A., Inc. v. Natural Resources Defense Council, Inc., 467 U.S. 837 (1984)
Cunningham v. Fleetwood Homes of Georgia, Inc., 253 F.3d 611 (11th Cir. 2001)
Daimlerchrysler Corp. v. Matthews, 848 A.2d 577 (Del. Ch. 2004)
Davis v. Southern Energy Homes, Inc., 305 F.3d 1268 (11th Cir. 2002)
In re American Homestar of Lancaster, Inc., 50 S.W.3d 480 (Tex. 2001)
Mitsubishi Motors Corp. v. Soler Chrysler-Plymouth, 473 U.S. 614 105 S Ct 3346 (1985)
NLRB v. Bell Aerospace Co., 416 U.S. 267 (1974)
Parkerson v. Smith, 817 So. 2d 529 (Miss. 2002)
Pitchford v. Oakwood Mobile Homes, Inc., 124 F. Supp. 2d 958 (W.D. Va. 2000)
Rickard v. Teynor's Homes, Inc., 279 F. Supp. 2d 910 (N.D. Ohio 2003)
Smiley v. Citibank, 517 U.S. 735, 116 S Ct 1730 (1996)
Southern Energy Homes, Inc. v. Ard, 772 So. 2d 1131 (Ala. 2000)
Southern Energy Homes, Inc. v. Lee, 732 So. 2d 994 (Ala. 1999)
United States v. Mead Corp., 533 U.S. 218, 121 S. Ct. 2164 (2001)
Walton v. Rose Mobile Homes, 298 F.3d 470 (5th Cir. 2002)
Wilson v. Waverlee Homes, Inc., 954 F. Supp. 1530 (M.D. Ala. 1997), *aff'd*, 127 F.3d 40 (11th Cir. 1997), *abrogated by Davis v. Southern Energy Homes, Inc.*, 305 F.3d 1268 (11th Cir. 2002)
Zenith Radio Corp. v. United States, 437 U.S. 443 (1978)

Statutes and Legislative Materials

117 Cong. Rec. 39626 (Nov. 5, 1971)
15 U.S.C. § 2302
15 U.S.C. § 2310
28 U.S.C. § 1257
93 Cong., 2d Sess. 41, *reprinted in* 1974 U.S.C.C.A.N. 7702
Consumer Class Actions: Hearings on S. 984, S. 1222, and S. 1378 before the Consumer Subcomm. of the Sen. Comm. on Commerce, 92nd Cong., 1st Sess. 163 (1971)
Consumer Products Guaranty Act: Hearings on S. 3074 Before the Consumer Subcomm. of the Senate Comm. on Commerce, 91st Cong., 2d Sess. 259 (1970)
Federal Arbitration Act, 9 U.S.C. §§ 1–16
H.R. Rep. No. 93-1107, at 22–28 (1974), reprinted in 1994 U.S.C.C.A.N. 7702, 7705–10
Magnuson-Moss Warranty Act of 1975, 15 U.S.C. § 2310
N.J. Rev. Stat. § 56-12-30
S. Rep. No. 92-269 (1971)
Warranties and Guaranties: Hearings on H.R. 18056, H.R. 106090, H.R. 12656, H.R. 16782, H.R. 13390, H.R. 18758, H.R. 19293, and S. 3074, Before the Subcomm. On Commerce and Finance of the House Comm. On Interstate and Foreign Commerce, 91st Cong., 2d Sess. 64 (1970)

---

* [*Editor's Note: Citations throughout brief as in original.*]

Regulations

119 Cong. Rec. 972
16 C.F.R. § 700.8
16 C.F.R. § 703.5
40 Fed. Reg. 60168
64 Fed. Reg. 19700

Other Authorities

Blumrosen, *Labor Arbitration, EEOC Conciliation and Discrimination in Employment*, 24 Arb. J. 88 (1969)
Domke, The Law and Practice of Commercial Arbitration 5 (1968)

OPINIONS BELOW

The opinion of the Michigan Supreme Court (App. 1–4) is reported at 677 N.W.2d 325 (Mich. 2004). The opinion of the appellate court (App. 5–21) is reported at 669 N.W.2d 271 (Mich. Ct. App. 2003). The unreported order of the trial court (App. 22–25) was entered on August 9, 2000.

JURISDICTION

The decision of the Michigan Supreme Court was filed on April 7, 2004. This Court has jurisdiction under 28 U.S.C. § 1257.

STATUTORY AND REGULATORY PROVISIONS INVOLVED

The "Remedies in consumer disputes" provision of the Magnuson-Moss Warranty Act of 1975, 15 U.S.C. § 2310, addresses informal dispute resolution and a consumer's right to commence a civil action as follows:

(a) Informal dispute settlement procedures; establishment; rules setting forth minimum requirements; effect of compliance by warrantor; review of informal procedures or implementation by Commission; application to existing informal procedures;

(1) Congress hereby declares it to be its policy to encourage warrantors to establish procedures whereby consumer disputes are fairly and expeditiously settled through informal dispute settlement mechanisms.

(2) The [Federal Trade] Commission shall prescribe rules setting forth minimum requirements for any informal dispute settlement procedure which is incorporated into the terms of a written warranty to which any provision of this title applies. Such rules shall provide for participation in such procedure by independent or governmental entities.

(3) One or more warrantors may establish an informal dispute settlement procedure which meets the requirements of the Commission's rules under paragraph (2). If—

(A) a warrantor establishes such a procedure,

(B) such procedure, and its implementation, meets the requirements of such rules, and

(C) he incorporates in a written warranty a requirement that the consumer resort to such procedure before pursuing any legal remedy under this section respecting such warranty,

then (i) the consumer may not commence a civil action (other than a class action) under subsection (d) of this section unless he initially resorts to such procedure . . .

. . .

(d) Civil action by consumer for damages, etc.; jurisdiction; recovery of costs and expenses; cognizable claims.

(1) Subject to subsections (a)(3) and (e), a consumer who is damaged by the failure of a supplier, warrantor, or service contractor to comply with any obligation under this title or under a written warranty, implied warranty, or service contract, may bring suit for damages and other legal and equitable relief—

(A) in any court of competent jurisdiction in any State or the District of Columbia; or

(B) in an appropriate district court of the United States, subject to paragraph (3) of this subsection.

. . .

The Federal Trade Commission's regulations addressing informal dispute settlement procedures for consumer claims under the Act provide in relevant part as follows:

[16 C.F.R.] § 700.8 Warrantor's decision as final

A warrantor shall not indicate in any written warranty or service contract either directly or indirectly that the decision of the warrantor, service contractor, or any designated third party is final or binding in any dispute concerning the warranty or service contract. . . .

[16 C.F.R.] § 703.5 Operation of the Mechanism

. . .

(j) Decisions of the Mechanism shall not be legally binding on any person. However, the warrantor shall act in good faith, as provided in § 703.2(g) of this part. In any civil action arising out of a warranty obligation and relating to a matter considered by the Mechanism, any decision of the Mechanism shall be admissible in evidence, as provided in section 110(a)(3) of the Act.

The Commission's Final Agency Action Interpreting the Act and Regulations, 40 Fed. Reg. 60168, 60210 (1975), provided in relevant part as follows:

The Rule [of 16 C.F.R. § 703.5] does not allow (binding arbitration) for two reasons. First, . . . Congressional intent was that decisions of section 110 Mechanisms not be legally binding. Second, even if binding Mechanisms were contemplated by section 110 of the Act, the Commission is not prepared, at this point in time, to develop guidelines for a system in which consumers would commit themselves, at the time of product purchase, to resolve any difficulties in a binding, but nonjudicial proceeding. The Commission is not now convinced that any guidelines which it set out could ensure sufficient protection for consumers.

The Commission's Final Agency Action reaffirming this interpretation, 64 Fed. Reg. 19700, 19708 (1999), provides in relevant part as follows:

The Commission believes that this interpretation continues to be correct. Therefore, the Commission has determined not to amend § 703.5(j) to allow for binding arbitration. Rule 703 will continue to prohibit warrantors from including binding arbitration clauses in their contracts with consumers that would require consumers to submit warranty disputes to binding arbitration.

STATEMENT OF THE CASE

This case presents the question of whether the Magnuson-Moss Warranty Act of 1975, 15 U.S.C. § 2301–2312 (1996) ("MMWA" or "Act"), and regulations and interpretive guidelines issued by the Federal Trade Commission ("FTC") prohibit warrantors from enforcing pre-dispute binding arbitration clauses against consumers raising claims pursuant to a written warranty. The Michigan Supreme Court rejected the FTC's interpretation of the Act and held that the Act permits enforcement of these arbitration clauses. In so holding, the court below disregarded not only the FTC's long-standing interpretation of the Act, but also this Court's teaching that "considerable weight should be accorded to an executive department's construction of a statutory scheme it is entrusted to administer." *Chevron USA, Inc. v. Natural Resources Defense Council*, 467 U.S. 837, 844 (1984). The Michigan Supreme Court's decision, which is in direct conflict with the Mississippi Supreme Court's holding in *Parkerson v. Smith*, 817 So. 2d 529 (Miss. 2002), is the subject of this petition.

A. The Federal Statutory and Regulatory Framework

1. The Magnuson-Moss Warranty Act

The MMWA was enacted to "improve the adequacy of information available to consumers, prevent deception, and improve competition in the marketing of consumer products. . . ." 15 U.S.C. § 2302(a). To realize these goals, the Act gives consumers a statutory right of action in federal or state court when they have been "damaged by the failure of a supplier, warrantor, or service contractor to comply with any obligation under this chapter or under a written warranty, implied warranty, or service contract. . . ." 15 U.S.C. § 2310(d)(1).

While the MMWA provides consumers with a cause of action in court to enforce their statutory rights, the Act also permits warrantors to require consumers to submit claims to "informal dispute settlement procedures" before commencing a civil action. 15 U.S.C. § 2310(a)(3). The Act states that warrantors may incorporate into their warranties the requirement that a consumer "resort to such procedure before pursuing any legal remedy," 15 U.S.C. § 2310(a)(3)(C), and that the consumer "may not commence a civil action . . . unless he initially resorts to such procedure. . . ." 15 U.S.C. § 2310(a)(3). The MMWA thus treats informal dispute resolution procedures as a prerequisite, not an alternative, to adjudication through the public court system for claims arising from a written warranty. The Act also delegates authority to the FTC to "prescribe rules setting forth minimum requirements for any informal dispute settlement procedure which is incorporated into the terms of a written warranty" covered by the Act. 15 U.S.C. § 2310(a)(2).

2. The FTC's Long-Standing Interpretation of the Act

Pursuant to the MMWA's express delegation of authority, the FTC has issued regulations setting out the requirements for informal dispute settlement procedures used by warrantors. The FTC's regulations mandate that "[d]ecisions of the Mechanism shall not be legally binding on any person," 16 C.F.R. § 703.5(j), and that the warranty shall not state that the decision of any third party is final or binding in any dispute concerning the warranty. 16 C.F.R. § 700.8.

In 1975, shortly after the MMWA was enacted into law, the FTC clarified that the statutory and regulatory prohibitions against binding dispute settlement procedures applied to a warrantor's use of arbitration so that warrantors were prohibited from enforcing pre-dispute binding arbitration clauses against consumers. 40 Fed. Reg. 60,168, 60,211. The FTC's interpretive regulation drew a distinction between pre-dispute and post-dispute uses of arbitration, finding that "nothing in the Rule . . . precludes the use of any other remedies by the parties *following* a Mechanism decision," but that "reference within the written warranty to any binding, non-judicial remedy is prohibited by the Rule and the Act." *Id.*

In 1999, the FTC reaffirmed its position that the MMWA prohibits enforcement of pre-dispute binding arbitration clauses. The FTC noted that its earlier decision had been based on both the plain language of 15 U.S.C. § 2310 and on concerns for protecting consumers against waivers of their right of access to courts at the time of purchasing a product. 64 Fed. Reg. 19,700, 19,708. The FTC found that this earlier interpretation "continues to be correct," and therefore rejected requests from industry groups to amend 16 C.F.R. § 703.5(j) to permit binding arbitration clauses in written warranties. *Id.* at 19,708–09.

B. The Proceedings Below

1. GM's Mandatory Binding Arbitration Program

General Motors ("GM") imposes an arbitration clause requiring consumers to submit their claims for breach of express warranty under the MMWA to binding arbitration. GM's Arbitration Program reserves for the company (but not for its employee/consumers) the absolute right to "unilaterally modify, change, or withdraw the program at any time." The contractual "agreement" before this Court is one that gives a single party the power to design, change, and/or revoke its own dispute resolution procedures.

GM's standard practice has been to provide its arbitration clause to an employee/consumer after she or he had selected a vehicle and taken delivery of it. Upon receiving the arbitration clause (and other papers related to the Arbitration Program), the employee/consumer was then told to either sign the agreement and waive her or his rights to bring a suit in court, or pay several thousand dollars more for the car. She or he could not return the car, however; it was already titled in their name and the car could no longer be sold as a new vehicle. This is the "choice" that Plaintiffs had when they obtained GM's written warranty and binding arbitration clause.

2. The Lower State Court Decisions

On August 10, 2000, the Michigan Circuit Court for the County of Oakland concluded that Plaintiffs' claims for breach of express warranty under MMWA may not be forced into binding arbitration. The trial court looked to the Act's plain language, its legislative history, and to the FTC's regulations in determining that the MMWA bars enforcement of GM's mandatory pre-dispute binding arbitration clause. App. 23–24.

The Michigan Court of Appeals reversed, noting that two U.S. Courts of Appeal have held that claims for breach of express warranty under the MMWA may be compelled into arbitration. *See Walton v. Rose Mobile Homes*, 298 F.3d 470 (5th Cir. 2002), and *Davis v. Southern Energy Homes, Inc.*, 305 F.3d 1268 (11th Cir. 2002). The Court of Appeals stated that "[w]here there is no conflict among the circuits of the federal court of appeals on a question of federal law, we are bound by the authoritative holdings of the federal circuit courts on federal questions." App. 14. The Court of Appeals reached this decision despite acknowledging that its conclusion was contrary to that of the Federal Trade Commission, and even though "there is a split of authority in the federal district courts and in the state courts that have addressed the issue." App. 15 n.5.

Court of Appeals Judge Murphy concurred in the court's opinion, but wrote separately to voice his disagreement with the federal circuit court rulings in *Walton* and *Davis* and to embrace Fifth Circuit Chief Judge King's dissent in *Walton*. App. 20 (quoting *Walton*, 298 F.3d at 492 (King, C.J. dissenting)). Judge Murphy also noted the split of authority among federal district courts and state courts, App. 19, and declared that, "[i]f I were not obligated to apply the majority opinion from *Walton* and the holding in *Davis*, I would conclude that the MMWA as reasonably interpreted by the FTC, precludes the application of binding arbitration agreements to claims arising under the MMWA for the reasons set forth by Chief Judge King in *Walton*." App. 20–21 (citation omitted).

3. The Michigan Supreme Court's Decision

The Michigan Supreme Court granted review and issued a memorandum opinion deciding the case without merits briefing or oral argument. The court held that the MMWA permits binding arbitration not because the federal circuit court opinions in *Walton* and *Davis* were binding on Michigan courts, but because their reasoning was persuasive. App. 3–4. The court stated that *Walton* and *Davis* both examined the text, legislative history, and purposes of the MMWA and concluded that Congress did not intend to bar binding arbitration under this statute. App. 3. Based on this analysis, the court held that the plaintiffs' claims in this case are subject to binding arbitration.[1]

---

[1] Two Justices wrote separately to express disagreement with the decision to decide the case by memorandum opinion without merits briefing or oral argument. App. 4.

REASONS FOR GRANTING THE WRIT

There is a direct split of authority on the question presented. Federal and state courts have been divided both among and within themselves over whether the FTC's interpretation of the MMWA as prohibiting pre-dispute binding arbitration clauses for disputes arising from a written warranty is permissible. In contrast with the Michigan Supreme Court below, the Mississippi Supreme Court and a number of other courts have found that the FTC's interpretation of the Act *is* reasonable and should be accorded deference.[2]

Furthermore, the Michigan Supreme Court erred in declining to follow the FTC's considered judgment in interpreting the MMWA. The MMWA authorizes the FTC to issue rules governing informal dispute resolution, and for nearly 30 years the Commission has consistently interpreted the Act to prohibit pre-dispute binding arbitration for disputes arising from a written warranty. The FTC's judgment is entirely reasonable, as the language of the MMWA explicitly provides that manufacturers may require consumers to submit disputes to informal dispute settlement mechanisms only as a pre-requisite, not a substitute, for the consumer's right to file a civil action in court. The MMWA's legislative history also reveals that, when the Act was adopted, Congress reasonably understood the phrase "informal dispute settlement mechanism" to encompass private arbitration mechanisms.

In light of the sharp split of federal and state court authority over the question presented and in light of the Michigan Supreme Court's erroneous determination below, this Court should grant review to resolve this issue and hold that the FTC permissibly interpreted the MMWA to prohibit enforcement of pre-dispute binding arbitration clauses.

I. REVIEW IS WARRANTED BECAUSE THERE IS A DIRECT SPLIT OF AUTHORITY OVER WHETHER THE MMWA PROHIBITS ENFORCEMENT OF PREDISPUTE BINDING ARBITRATION CLAUSES.

There is a direct split of authority between the Michigan Supreme Court's ruling below (along with decisions of two federal circuit courts and three other state high courts) and decisions by the Mississippi Supreme Court and other federal courts over whether the MMWA and FTC regulations bar enforcement of pre-dispute binding arbitration clauses in consumer product warranties.

Courts addressing this question agree on a few basic propositions. First, they agree that § 2310(a)(3) of the MMWA allows warrantors to include in their warranties a requirement that consumers submit claims to an informal dispute settlement procedure as a prerequisite to initiating a civil action in court. *See, e.g., Davis v. Southern Energy Homes, Inc.*, 305 F.3d 1268, 1272 (11th Cir. 2002); *Walton v. Rose Mobile Homes, LLC*, 298 F.3d 470, 475 (5th Cir. 2002); *id.* at 480–81 (King, C.J. dissenting). These courts also agree that the Act authorizes the FTC to make rules governing these out-of-court procedures, and that the FTC has declared both that all such procedures must be non-binding and that this requirement covers private arbitration procedures. *Davis*, 305 F.3d at 1277; *Walton*, 298 F.3d at 475; *Parkerson v. Smith*, 817 So. 2d 529, 533 (Miss. 2002). All courts thus recognize that the FTC construes the Act to bar enforcement of pre-dispute binding arbitration clauses.

But these courts sharply disagree over whether the FTC had authority to so interpret the MMWA and over whether this interpretation is reasonable so as to be accorded deference under *Chevron USA, Inc. v. Natural Res. Defense Council, Inc.*, 467 U.S. 837 (1984). The courts that have deferred to the FTC have found that the Commission's interpretation is consistent with the Act's plain language and therefore is reasonable and entitled to deference under *Chevron. See, e.g., Parkerson*, 817 So. 2d at 533–34 (finding both that the MMWA's plain language evinces Congress's intent to preserve a consumer's access to court, and that FTC's interpretation is reasonable). By contrast, most federal circuit courts and state courts that have addressed this issue, including the Michigan Supreme Court below, rejected the FTC's interpretation and allowed enforcement of pre-dispute binding arbitration clauses. *See, e.g.,* App. 3–4 (and cases cited therein). Moreover, these courts that rejected the FTC's interpretation of the Act have done so using conflicting rationales. *Compare Walton*, 298 F.3d at 475 (rejecting FTC interpretation as contrary to Congress's intent in the Federal Arbitration Act ("FAA"), 9 U.S.C. §§ 1 *et seq.*, to make arbitration agreements generally enforceable); *with Davis*, 305 F.3d at 1278–79 (finding Congress's intent unclear, but holding that FTC's interpretation of MMWA is unreasonable in light of its text and legislative history). In light of the confusion this issue has generated among lower courts, this Court should grant review to resolve the question presented.

A. Substantial Authority Holds that the MMWA Prohibits Pre-Dispute Binding Arbitration Clauses.

The decision below is in direct conflict with the Mississippi Supreme Court's holding in *Parkerson v. Smith*, 817 So. 2d 529 (Miss. 2002), that the MMWA bars enforcement of pre-dispute binding arbitration clauses for disputes arising from a written warranty. In *Parkerson*, the court found that "the plain language of the statute indicates that it intends to preserve the right of any consumer to bring a lawsuit for breach of written or implied warranties." *Id.* at 533. *Parkerson* also examined the MMWA's legislative history and concluded that "[t]his history reflects that it was Congress's intent that any nonjudicial dispute resolution procedures would be nonbinding, and consumers would always retain the right of final access to court." *Id.* at 533–34 (quoting *Wilson v. Waverlee Homes, Inc.*, 954 F. Supp. 1530, 1538 (M.D. Ala. 1997), *aff'd*, 127 F.3d 40 (11th Cir. 1997), *abrogated by Davis v. Southern Energy Homes, Inc.*, 305 F.3d 1268 (11th Cir. 2002)). Parkerson concluded that the FTC's interpretation of the MMWA as prohibiting binding arbitration is reasonable and therefore entitled to deference under Chevron. *Id.* at 534.

Although *Parkerson* is the only state high court or federal circuit court opinion to hold that the MMWA prohibits predispute binding arbitration clauses, the disagreement and confusion among and within the lower federal and state courts is widespread. For example, numerous federal district courts continue to hold that the

---

2 Compare *Abela v. General Motors Corp.*, 677 N.W.2d 325, 327 (Mich. 2004) (App. 3–4); *Davis v. Southern Energy Homes, Inc.*, 305 F.3d 1268, 1272 (11th Cir. 2002); *Walton v. Rose Mobile Homes, LLC*, 298 F.3d 470, 475 (5th Cir. 2002); *Southern Energy Homes, Inc. v. Ard*, 772 So. 2d 1131, 1135 (Ala. 2000); *Borowiec v. Gateway 2000, Inc.*, 808 N.E.2d 957 (Ill. 2004); *In re American Homestar of Lancaster, Inc.*, 50 S.W.3d 480, 490 (Tex. 2001); *with Parkerson v. Smith*, 817 So. 2d 529, 533 (Miss. 2002); *Rickard v. Teynor's Homes, Inc.*, 279 F. Supp. 2d 910, 921 (N.D. Ohio 2003); *Browne v. Kline Tyson's Imports, Inc.*, 190 F. Supp. 2d 827, 831 (E.D. Va. 2002); *Pitchford v. Oakwood Mobile Homes, Inc.*, 124 F. Supp. 2d 958, 964 (W.D. Va. 2000).

MMWA prohibits pre-dispute binding arbitration clauses for claims arising from a written warranty based on the Act's plain language addressing "informal dispute settlement procedures," and on the FTC's interpretation of this language. *See Rickard v. Teynor's Homes, Inc.*, 279 F. Supp. 2d 910, 921 (N.D. Ohio 2003) ("[T]he FTC's expressed rationales for its interpretation of the MMWA indicate that the FTC's reading is based on a reasonable construction of the statute."); *Browne v. Kline Tyson's Imports, Inc.*, 190 F. Supp. 2d 827, 831 (E.D. Va. 2002) ("The FTC's regulations mirror the MMWA's statutory language to encourage dispute resolution, yet mandate that consumers have full and final access to the courts for resolution of their written warranty disputes."); *Pitchford v. Oakwood Mobile Homes, Inc.*, 124 F. Supp. 2d 958, 964 (W.D. Va. 2000) ("The clear intent of Magnuson-Moss, as explicitly detailed in the attendant regulations, is to encourage alternative dispute settlement mechanisms, but to not deprive any party of their right to have their warranty dispute adjudicated in a judicial forum."). Notably, *Rickard* discussed the federal circuit court opinions in *Walton and Davis*, but rejected both courts' analyses. *See* 279 F. Supp. 2d at 920–21. Given this growing split of authority among federal and state courts, this Court should step in to resolve the question presented in this case.

In addition to these courts holding that the MMWA prohibits binding arbitration for claims arising from a written warranty, there have also been several pointed dissenting opinions in the cases where appellate courts allowed binding arbitration under the Act. Perhaps most notably, Chief Judge King dissented from the Fifth Circuit's holding in *Walton* and issued a lengthy opinion in which she concluded that "[t]he case before us is, in essence, a classic *Chevron* case." *Walton*, 298 F.3d at 480 (King, C.J. dissenting). The *Walton* dissent noted that the MMWA's provisions addressing non-binding informal dispute settlement procedures contain neither a definition nor a clarification as to whether they were meant to address arbitration. *Id.* at 480–81.[3] After finding that the MMWA is unclear regarding any intention to limit the Federal Arbitration Act ("FAA"), 9 U.S.C. §§ 1–16, by prohibiting binding arbitration, the dissent rejected the Fifth Circuit majority's holding that the FAA itself is controlling on this question as "circular logic." *Id.* at 484; *see also Borowiec*, 808 N.E.2d at 972 (Kilbride, J. dissenting) (describing *Walton's* FAA holding as a "mistaken conclusion").

Instead, the *Walton* dissent found that the key statutory provision is the MMWA's express delegation of authority to the FTC to "prescribe rules setting forth minimum requirements for any informal dispute settlement procedure which is incorporated into the terms of a written warranty." *Walton*, 298 F.3d at 481 (quoting 15 U.S.C. § 2310(a)(2)). Based on this delegation and the Act's ambiguity about binding arbitration, the *Walton* dissent asked whether the FTC's interpretation of the Act is reasonable and thus entitled to deference under *Chevron*. Here, the *Walton* dissent departs from the Eleventh Circuit's holding in *Davis* by finding the FTC's interpretation reasonable because it was based on the Commission's independent examination of the MMWA's text and legislative history, and not (as *Davis* found) on presumptions drawn from now discarded case law barring all arbitration of statutory claims. *Id.* at 486–88; *see also Borowiec*, 808 N.E.2d at 985

(Rarick, J. dissenting) (finding that FTC's interpretation is entitled to "controlling weight" because it is not arbitrary, capricious, or contrary to the statute). The *Walton* and *Borowiec* dissents thus squarely rejected the result and rationales of both the Fifth Circuit majority's holding in *Walton* and the Eleventh Circuit's holding in *Davis*.

In light of these cases and opinions conflicting with the decision below and with rulings of numerous other federal and state courts, this Court should grant review to resolve the question presented in this petition.

B. There is Also Confusion Among the Courts Holding that the MMWA Allows Enforcement of Pre-Dispute Binding Arbitration Clauses.

In addition to the split of authority over whether the FTC's interpretation of the MMWA is permissible, courts that rejected the FTC's interpretation have done so based on conflicting rationales. Several courts holding that the MMWA does not bar enforcement of pre-dispute binding arbitration clauses purported to follow the Fifth Circuit's split-panel decision in *Walton v. Rose Mobile Homes, LLC*, 298 F.3d 470 (5th Cir. 2002). In *Walton*, the Fifth Circuit found that "Congress has expressed a clear intention in favor of arbitration for contractual claims" in the FAA. *Id.* at 475. *Walton* examined whether, in light of the FAA, "Congress expressed any contrary intent" to regulate arbitration of claims under the MMWA. *Id. Walton* found that the MMWA does not evince Congress's intent to restrict binding arbitration because its text does not mention arbitration by name, its legislative history is inconclusive, and because there is no conflict between binding arbitration and the Act's underlying consumer protection goals. *Id.* at 475–78.

Walton further held that the FTC's interpretation of the MMWA as limiting uses of binding arbitration is directly contrary to Congress's clear statement in the FAA allowing arbitration, and therefore should not be given any deference under the first prong of *Chevron*:

> It is improper to use the FTC regulations themselves to determine congressional intent here. As noted previously, we must consider the statute's text, legislative history, and whether its purpose conflicts with another statute, to determine congressional intent. An agency's regulations, promulgated pursuant to a statute, are not part of this test.

Id. at 479; *but, see id.* at 480 (King, C.J. dissenting) (finding no clear indicia of Congress's intent, and that FTC's interpretation is reasonable). Having found that Congress spoke clearly to this issue in the FAA, the Fifth Circuit majority concluded that the FTC lacked authority to construe the MMWA as prohibiting pre-dispute binding arbitration clauses.

Shortly after *Walton* was decided, the Eleventh Circuit also rejected the FTC's interpretation of the MMWA as barring pre-dispute binding arbitration clauses, but did so on different grounds. In *Davis v. Southern Energy Homes, Inc.*, 305 F.3d 1268 (11th Cir. 2002), the court similarly found that Congress did not express a clear intent to restrict uses of binding arbitration in the MMWA's text or legislative history and that there was no inherent conflict between binding arbitration and the Act's primary purposes. *Id.* at 1274–77. After finding that the MMWA is unclear about binding

---

3 As the dissent noted, Congress's failure to mention arbitration or the FAA by name is hardly surprising since the FAA was widely held to be inapplicable to statutory claims at the time of the MMWA's enactment. *Id.* at 480 n.2.

arbitration, however, *Davis* did not conclude as the Fifth Circuit did in *Walton* that the FTC's interpretation was impermissible due to a lack of authority to address the issue. *Id.* at 1278 n.6 (noting that *Walton* never reached question of whether FTC's interpretation was reasonable). Instead, *Davis* applied the second prong of *Chevron* and addressed whether the FTC's interpretation of the Act was reasonable. In deciding this issue, *Davis* examined the FTC's rationale for its interpretation, which was based largely on the Act's legislative history, and concluded that the interpretation was not reasonable because the MMWA's legislative history paralleled that of other statutes that this Court has construed to allow arbitration. *Id.* at 1278–79; *see also In re American Homestar of Lancaster, Inc.*, 50 S.W.3d 480, 490 (Tex. 2001) (finding FTC's interpretation of MMWA's legislative history unreasonable). The Eleventh Circuit thus held that "the FTC's interpretation of the MMWA is unreasonable," *id.* at 1280, and that claims under the Act can be subject to binding arbitration.[4]

Despite the divergent analyses of the Fifth and Eleventh Circuits, the Michigan Supreme Court below and the Illinois Supreme Court have purported to follow *both* circuit court opinions in rejecting the FTC's interpretation and holding that the MMWA permits enforcement of pre-dispute binding arbitration clauses. *See* App. 3 ("We have examined the decisions in [*Walton*] and [*Davis*] and find their analyses and conclusions persuasive."); *Borowiec v. Gateway 2000, Inc.*, 808 N.E.2d 957, 970 (Ill. 2004) (finding that "the federal circuit courts of appeals are in agreement in their interpretation of this federal statute"). By failing to distinguish and choose between the two circuit courts' conflicting rationales for rejecting the FTC's interpretation, these opinions add to the confusion on this question of federal law by failing to set forth a coherent rationale. As one of the dissents in *Borowiec* explained:

> [T]he purported uniformity of the federal circuit courts of appeals relied on here by the majority is illusory. Regrettably, the majority opinion does not adopt a single rationale based on either of these cases, appearing instead to apply both. Without any explanation of the specific rationale used to decide this case, the majority's opinion fails to provide any guidance for future cases. I cannot countenance such an open-ended approach to setting precedent in this state.

---

4 *Davis*'s holding that the MMWA's provisions regulating "informal dispute settlement procedures" cannot reasonably be construed by the FTC to cover arbitration also conflicts with an earlier decision by the Eleventh Circuit itself that embraced this very interpretation of identical statutory language in a different section of the MMWA governing warranty disclosures. *See Cunningham v. Fleetwood Homes of Georgia, Inc.*, 253 F.3d 611, 622 (11th Cir. 2001) (discussing disclosure requirements of 15 U.S.C. § 2302(a)(7), and holding that warrantor cannot compel arbitration because it "failed to disclose in the warranty a term or clause requiring the Cunninghams to utilize *an informal dispute resolution mechanism*") (emphasis added); *see also Ex Parte Thicklin*, 824 So. 2d 723, 730 (Ala. 2002) (following *Cunningham*); *cf. Damlerchrysler Corp. v. Matthews*, 848 A.2d 577, 587 (Del. Ch. 2004) ("[T]here admittedly is some tension between *Cunningham*, on the one hand, and *Walton* and *Davis* on the other.").

Borowiec, 808 N.E.2d at 974 (Kilbride, J. dissenting). The divergence in reasoning among these courts rejecting the FTC's interpretation of the MMWA thus further demonstrates the need for this Court's review.

The confusion and disagreement both among and within federal and state courts over the question presented is perhaps best illustrated by the Alabama Supreme Court's rulings on this issue. In *Southern Energy Homes, Inc. v. Lee*, 732 So. 2d 994 (Ala. 1999), the court held by a 5–4 vote that the MMWA prohibits enforcement of pre-dispute binding arbitration clauses based on the Act's text and legislative history addressing informal dispute settlement procedures as non-binding and based on the FTC's interpretation of the Act. *Id.* at 999. Less than 18 months later, however, the Alabama Supreme Court reversed course. In *Southern Energy Homes, Inc. v. Ard*, 772 So. 2d 1131 (Ala. 2000), the court by another 5–4 vote issued a *per curiam* opinion adopting the dissenting opinion from Lee and held that the Act permits pre-dispute binding arbitration clauses. *Id.* at 1135 ("On the rationale of Justice See's dissent in *Lee*, we hereby hold that the Magnuson-Moss Act does not invalidate arbitration provisions in a written warranty."). The Alabama Supreme Court's history of reversal and divisions over this issue illustrate the need for this Court's review.

In light of the confusion that the question presented has generated among and within federal and state courts across the country, this Court should grant review to provide a definitive resolution of this important question of federal law.

C. Review is Warranted Because This Case Presents an Important and Recurring Issue of Federal Law.

Review also is warranted because the question presented in this case implicates the right of virtually every adult consumer in the country to have access to the civil justice system. The cases creating the split of authority discussed above involve some of the most critical economic transactions in the lives of most adult Americans. For example, many of these cases arose from purchases of manufactured homes that turned out to be defective. *See, e.g., Walton v. Rose Mobile Homes, LLC*, 298 F.3d 470, 472 (5th Cir. 2002); *Davis v. Southern Energy Homes, Inc.*, 305 F.3d 1268, 1270 (11th Cir. 2002); *Cunningham v. Fleetwood Homes of Georgia, Inc.*, 253 F.3d 611, 613 (11th Cir. 2001); *Rickard v. Teynor's Homes, Inc.*, 279 F. Supp. 2d 910, 911–12 (N.D. Ohio 2003); *Pitchford v. Oakwood Mobile Homes, Inc.*, 124 F. Supp. 2d 958, 960 (W.D. Va. 2000); *Southern Energy Homes, Inc. v. Ard*, 772 So. 2d 1131, 1132 (Ala. 2000) (overruling *Southern Energy Homes, Inc. v. Lee*, 732 So. 2d 994 (Ala. 1999)); *Parkerson v. Smith*, 817 So. 2d 529, 531–32 (Miss. 2002); *In re American Homestar of Lancaster, Inc.*, 50 S.W.3d 480, 482 (Tex. 2001). The issue is also arising in cases like this one involving the purchase of automobiles, *see, e.g.*, App. 1–2; *Browne v. Kline Tyson's Imports, Inc.*, 190 F. Supp. 2d 827, 828 (E.D. Va. 2002); *Daimlerchrysler Corp. v. Matthews*, 848 A.2d 577, 578–79 (Del. Ch. 2004), or other products such as home computers. *See Borowiec v. Gateway 2000, Inc.*, 808 N.E.2d 957, 959 (Ill. 2004). The question presented is thus a recurring one because it is continually arising out of the types of transactions to which most adult Americans are a party. Moreover, this question of federal law is important because its resolution will determine whether homeowners, automobile drivers, and other consumers can enter into these types of transactions while preserving their right of access to the public court system.

Federal and state courts are deeply divided over whether the

Magnuson-Moss Warranty Act and agency regulations promulgated to further the Act's consumer protection goals can and do protect consumers who are entering into the most important of economic transactions against mandatory pre-dispute waivers of their right of access to public courts. This Court should grant review to provide a definitive resolution of this important and recurring question of federal law.

II. THE HOLDING BELOW IS CONTRARY TO THE LANGUAGE AND INTENT OF THE MMWA, AND TO THE INTERPRETATION OF THE AGENCY CHARGED WITH ADMINISTERING THE ACT.

The Court below erred in concluding that GM could insist that its employee-customers be subject to pre-dispute binding arbitration clauses covering claims for breach of a written warranty under the MMWA as a condition of purchasing a GM vehicle. The MMWA requires that all informal dispute settlement procedures established by warrantors be non-binding so that consumers retain the right to bring an action in court after they exhaust such procedures. In light of extensive legislative history establishing that Congress understood the phrase "informal dispute settlement mechanisms" to include private arbitration, and in light of Congress's broad grant of discretion to the FTC to implement the MMWA, the Court below departed from principles of law established by this Court by substituting its own judgment for that of the expert agency. *See, e.g., Mitsubishi Motors Corp. v. Soler Chrysler-Plymouth*, 473 U.S. 614, 628, 105 S Ct 3346 (1985) (congressional intent to restrict or prohibit arbitration of statutory claims may be "deducible" from a statute's text, legislative history or underlying purposes).

A. The MMWA's Language and Intent Establish that Warrantors May Not Force Consumers to Submit Claims Under the Act to Binding "Informal Dispute Settlement Mechanisms."

The MMWA, enacted in 1974, sets out specific requirements for disclosures, duties, remedies, and procedures relating to warranties on consumer products, creating an unqualified right of access to court for consumers who are injured by a breach of warranty. "[A] consumer who is damaged by the failure of a supplier, warrantor, or service contractor to comply with an obligation under this title or under a written warranty, implied warranty, or service contract, may bring suit for damages and other legal and equitable relief." 15 U.S.C. § 2310(d)(1). While the MMWA allows warrantors to use informal dispute resolution procedures like arbitration, the Act makes these procedures a non-binding exhaustion requirement for claims arising from a written warranty, and not a substitute for litigation. *See* 15 U.S.C. § 2310(c)(3) (emphasis added). The MMWA thus only permits warrantors to establish informal dispute resolution procedures that are disclosed in their warranties, that preserve consumers' right of access to court, and whose decisions are deemed no more than relevant in judicial proceedings on the merits of a consumer's claim.

The legislative history of the MMWA confirms that Congress intended to ban the use of binding "informal dispute settlement mechanisms" in warranties. Congressman Moss, the named sponsor of the Act, explained to his colleagues in floor remarks that these provisions allow an opportunity for alternative dispute resolution, without limiting a warranty claimant's ultimate right to a judicial resolution:

First, the bill provides the consumer with an economically feasible private right of action so that when a warrantor breaches his warranty or service contract obligations, the consumer can have effective redress. Reasonable attorney's fees and expenses are provided for the successful consumer litigant, and the bill is further refined so as to place a minimum extra burden on the courts by requiring as *a prerequisite to suit* that the purchaser give the [warrantor] reasonable opportunity to settle the dispute out of court, including the use of a fair and formal dispute settlement mechanism....

119 Cong. Rec. 972 (Jan. 12, 1973). The word "pre-requisite" here is key—the dispute mechanism was intended to be something a consumer could be required to use *before* going to court, but not *instead* of going to court. The House report accompanying this legislation further states that "[a]n adverse decision in any informal dispute settlement proceeding would not be a bar to a civil action on the warranty involved in the proceeding." H.R. Rep. 93-1107, 93 Cong., 2d Sess. 41, *reprinted* in 1974 U.S.C.C.A.N. 7702, 7723. The MMWA's legislative history thus accords with the Act's plain language in making out-of-court proceedings a non-binding exhaustion prerequisite and not a complete substitution for the judicial resolution of express warranty claims.

B. The 1974 Congress Reasonably Understood the Phrase "Informal Dispute Settlement Mechanisms" to Include Pre-dispute Binding Arbitration.

As set forth above, a number of the courts that have held that claims under the MMWA may be compelled into arbitration have done so based upon the premise that "arbitration" is something very different than "informal dispute settlement mechanisms." The legislative history of the MMWA plainly demonstrates that arbitration was seen as one illustration of an informal dispute settlement mechanism.

In the Congress before the Congress which passed the MMWA, the predecessor bill to the MMWA became tied up in large part over a dispute over non-judicial proceedings. The resolution that Congress reached at that time was to authorize the National Institute for Consumer Justice to perform a study of informal dispute settlement mechanisms. Sen. Cook, the author of the floor amendment authorizing this study, said that the study should address "existing and potential voluntary settlement procedures, *including arbitration*." S. Rep. No. 92-269 at 63 (1971) (emph. added). Sen. Dole, similarly, said that this study was needed because Congress wanted more data on "private dispute settlement techniques, including arbitration in resolving consumer grievances." 117 Cong. Rec. 39,626 (Nov. 5, 1971). For courts more than 30 years later to simply assume that arbitration could not be a type of informal dispute settlement mechanism is flatly at odds with the way these terms were used by the Congress that passed the MMWA.

In 1970, similarly, Miles W. Kirkpatrick, the Chairman of the FTC, equated an earlier draft of the MMWA's provision relating to "informal dispute settlement mechanisms" with "arbitration." Warranties and Guaranties: Hearings on H.R. 18056, H.R. 106090, H.R. 12656, H.R. 16782, H.R. 13390, H.R. 18758, H.R. 19293, and S. 3074, Before the Subcomm. On Commerce and Finance of the House Comm. On Interstate and Foreign Commerce, 91st

Cong., 2d Sess. 64 (1970). Business advocates also linked these terms. *See* Eugene Keeney, Pres. American Retail Fed., *Consumer Class Action: Hearings on S. 984, S. 1222, and S. 1378 before the Consumer Subcomm. of the Sen. Comm. on Commerce*, 92nd Cong., 1st Sess. 163–66 (1971) (speaking of American Arbitration Association's "National Center for Dispute Settlement"). Consumer advocates also treated the terms the same way. *See* David Swankin, Consumers Union, *Consumer Products Guaranty Act: Hearings on S. 3074 Before the Consumer Subcomm. of the Senate Comm. on Commerce*, 91st Cong., 2d Sess. 259 (1970) (with respect to bill's provision relating to informal dispute settlement procedure, "we put so much importance in mandating a system of negotiation and arbitration").

The fact that the legislative history of the MMWA and its predecessor bills is replete with references to "arbitration" as one illustration of "informal dispute settlement mechanisms" is consistent with the way those terms were regularly used throughout the legal world at that time. Indeed, this very Court described the Railway Labor Act's procedures, including its arbitration mechanism, as "dispute settlement procedures." *Andrews v. Louisville & Nashville R.R. Co.*, 406 U.S. 320, 325 (1972). The leading treatise on arbitration at the time also described arbitration as a type of dispute settlement. *See* Martin Domke, The Law and Practice of Commercial Arbitration 5 (1968) ("nobody should be bound to resort to arbitration unless he has previously agreed to that method of *dispute settlement*.") (emph. added). Government officials used the same terminology. *E.g.*, Alfred Blumrosen, *Labor Arbitration, EEOC Conciliation and Discrimination in Employment*, 24 Arb. J. 88, 90 (1969) (arbitration listed as one "informal dispute settlement mechanism."). In subsequent years, state legislatures have also frequently conjoined these terms. *E.g.* N.J. Rev. Stat. § 56-12-30 ("Manufacturer's informal dispute settlement procedure' means an arbitration process or procedure by which the manufacturer attempts to resolve disputes. . . .").

The facts of this case further demonstrate that there can be no serious dispute that GM's arbitration clause is "informal," within the meaning of the MMWA's requirement in § 2310(a)(3) that warrantors' "informal dispute settlement procedure[s]" be non-binding. GM's arbitration program reserves for GM a unilateral right to "modify, change, or withdraw the program at any time." This is hardly a model of procedural formality from which to argue that the MMWA does not apply.

C. This Court Should Defer to the FTC's Authoritative Determination.

The Court below erred in substituting its own judgment for that of the FTC. As set forth above, the FTC determined that the MMWA prohibits the use of mandatory pre-dispute binding arbitration for claims under the statute in 1975, and then after extensive reconsideration re-affirmed this conclusion in 1999. The Court below erred in ignoring this longstanding and consistent interpretation of the expert agency charged with implementing the Act. The agency regulation should be given "controlling weight" unless it is "arbitrary, capricious, or manifestly contrary to the statute." *Chevron U.S.A., Inc. v. Natural Resources Defense Council, Inc.*, 467 U.S. 837, 843–44 (1984).

The FTC's interpretation of the phrase "informal dispute settlement mechanisms" in the MMWA is entitled to particularly deferential treatment for several reasons. First, the MMWA delegates broad direction to the FTC in a number of respects. The Act directs the FTC to determine the extent of the disclosures to be made under the MMWA, for example. 15 U.S.C. § 2302(a). The Act also requires that all informal dispute settlement mechanisms must comply with regulations to be promulgated by the FTC. *See* 15 U.S.C. § 2310(a)(2) ("The Commission shall prescribe rules setting forth minimum requirements for any informal dispute settlement procedure which is incorporated into the terms of a written warranty to which any provision of this title applies"); 15 U.S.C. § 2310(a)(3)(A)–(C). This statutory authorization highlights the importance of deference here. *See United States v. Mead Corp.*, 533 U.S. 218, 121 S. Ct. 2164, 2172 (2001) ("We have recognized a very good indicator of delegation meriting *Chevron* treatment in express congressional authorizations to engage in the process of rulemaking or adjudication that produces regulations for which deference is claimed."); *Smiley v. Citibank*, 517 U.S. 735, 739, 116 S Ct 1730 (1996) ("It is our practice to defer to the reasonable judgments of agencies with regard to the meaning of ambiguous terms in statutes that they are charged with administering.").

Second, contemporaneous interpretations of administrative agencies deserve "peculiar weight" and deference. *See Zenith Radio Corp. v. United States*, 437 U.S. 443, 450 (1978) (citation omitted). The FTC's 1975 interpretation of the Act is of particular importance, because the FTC was intimately involved in the debates that led to the passage of the Act. As noted above, the FTC Chairman was a lead witness in the hearings that led to the passage of the MMWA. Indeed, Congress noted that MMWA was a response to a "rising tide of complaints" received by the FTC, among others. H.R. Rep. No. 93-1107, at 22–28 (1974), reprinted in 1994 U.S.C.C.A.N. 7702, 7705–10.

Third, longstanding and consistent agency interpretations also deserve particular deference. *NLRB v. Bell Aerospace Co.*, 416 U.S. 267, 274–75 (1974). When the FTC re-considered the issue in 1999 and reached the same conclusion that it had reached in 1975, it displayed a consistency that is entitled to be given serious weight.

CONCLUSION

This petition for a writ of *certiorari* should be granted.

Respectfully submitted,

[*Attorneys for the Petitioners*]

Appendix H Brief on Arbitration Service Provider Bias

This brief is also available in Microsoft Word and Adobe Acrobat (PDF) format on the CD-Rom accompanying this volume.

IN THE GENERAL COURT OF JUSTICE
SUPERIOR COURT DIVISION
NEW HANOVER COUNTY, NORTH CAROLINA

_____)
ADRIANA MCQUILLAN and)
SANDRA K. MATTHIS, on)
behalf of themselves and all)
other persons similarly situated,)
                   Plaintiffs,)
)
v.   )
) 04-CVS-2858
CHECK 'N GO OF NORTH)
CAROLINA, INC.; CNG)
FINANCIAL CORPORATION;)
JARED A. DAVIS and A.)
DAVID DAVIS,)
                   Defendants.)
_____)

PLAINTIFFS' MEMORANDUM OF LAW IN OPPOSITION TO DEFENDANTS' MOTION TO COMPEL ARBITRATION AND STAY PROCEEDINGS

INTRODUCTION AND SUMMARY OF ARGUMENT

Adriana McQuillan and Sandra K. Matthis (collectively "Plaintiffs") bring this case on behalf of themselves and a putative class of North Carolina consumers who paid exorbitant interest charges on short-term "payday loans." Plaintiffs allege that defendants Check 'N Go of North Carolina, Inc., CNG Financial Corporation, Jared A. Davis and A. David Davis (collectively "Defendants" or "Check 'N Go") operated an illegal lending business in North Carolina in violation of the Consumer Finance Act, G.S. § 53-166(a)–(b); the Check Cashing Statute, G.S. § 53-276; and the Unfair Trade Practice Statute, G.S. § 75-1.1.* Check 'N Go responded to these allegations by moving the Court to enforce provisions in its payday loan contracts prohibiting Plaintiffs from asserting their class-wide claims and instead requiring them to arbitrate only their *individual* claims.

Plaintiffs hereby oppose Check 'N Go's motion to compel individual arbitrations for two separate and independent reasons.

    * [*Editor's Note: Citations throughout brief as in original. All relevant exhibits cited below are not reproduced herein but may be found on the CD-Rom accompanying this volume.*]

First, the company's mandatory arbitration clause, by barring their class-wide claims, is an illegal exculpatory clause that violates public policy and is unconscionable under North Carolina contract law. Second, this arbitration clause also is unenforceable because it is part of an illegal payday lending contract that is void *ab initio*, and whose terms therefore never created binding obligations under North Carolina law. Third, the arbitration agreement forces customers to appear before a biased forum. Since Check 'N Go's arbitration clause is unenforceable on any or all of these grounds, the Court should deny its motion to compel individual arbitrations.

Check 'N Go's mandatory individual arbitration clause is governed by the same rules of North Carolina contract law that apply to all of the terms in these payday loan contracts. Under the Federal Arbitration Act ("FAA"), 9 U.S.C. §§ 1 *et seq.*, and North Carolina law, the law of contracts governs whether there exists a valid arbitration agreement. *King v. Owen*, 601 S.E.2d 326, 327, 106 N.C.App. 246, 249 (2004). North Carolina law prohibits enforcement of exculpatory contracts that are gained through unequal bargaining power or are contrary to substantial public interests. *See Fortson v. McClellan*, 131 N.C. App. 635, 636, 508 S.E.2d 549, 551 (1998). Likewise, North Carolina law also prohibits enforcement of contracts that are unconscionable because of a lack of meaningful choice by one party together with terms that are unreasonably favorable to the other. *See State Farm Mutual Automobile Ins. Co. v. Atlantic Indemnity Co.*, 122 N.C. App. 67, 73, 468 S.E.2d 570, 573 (1996). Check 'N Go's mandatory individual arbitration clause runs afoul of both of these prohibitions because it was imposed against Plaintiffs and payday loan borrowers without any opportunity for negotiation and strips them of their only economically viable legal remedy by prohibiting class-wide claims, but leaves Check 'N Go free to vindicate all of its legal claims.

Moreover, under North Carolina law, contracts made for an illegal purpose in violation of controlling statutes are void as against public policy, and therefore can never be given legal effect. As a matter of North Carolina law, parties cannot give assent to contracts entered into for an illegal purpose. Here, these high-interest payday loan contracts are illegal under several North Carolina statutes, including the Consumer Finance Act and Unfair Trade Practice Statute. If these payday loan contracts are illegal and void, then none of their terms—including their arbitration clauses—can ever have legal effect because neither plaintiffs nor Check 'N Go could have assented to Check 'N Go's illegal purpose. Therefore, the illegality of Check 'N Go's entire payday loan contract is an additional basis for this Court to deny the motion to compel individual arbitration.

Check 'N Go's arbitration clause is unenforceable for a third reason. In North Carolina, it is unconstitutional for a decision maker to have a substantial financial interest in the outcomes of her or his decisions. Many courts looking at analogous cases have held that if it would be unconstitutional for a government to impose a biased decision maker upon individuals, it should also be unconscionable for a company to impose a similar system upon an individual consumer. Unlike most other lenders, who give consumers a choice among arbitration companies, Check 'N Go has elected to force its customers to submit all of their claims to a single bad actor firm—the National Arbitration Forum ("NAF"). NAF, as set forth in dozens of documents from its own files, as well as a large number of sworn declarations attached to this brief, is severely biased in favor of lenders and against consumers.

Finally, there is nothing in federal arbitration law under the FAA that preempts these principles of North Carolina contract law and compels a contrary result. First, the FAA contains an express "savings clause" that subjects arbitration clauses to generally applicable state laws governing the formation and revocation of contracts. *See First Options of Chicago, Inc. v. Kaplan*, 514 U.S. 938, 944 (1995); *Doctor's Associates, Inc. v. Casarotto*, 517 U.S. 681, 687 (1996). Second, the FAA's preemption of state laws was enacted for the purpose of singling out arbitration clauses and subjecting them to less favored treatment than other contracts, *see id.* at 686–87, has no application here because North Carolina's public policy rule against exculpatory clauses, its doctrine of unconscionability, and its prohibition against enforcing terms in illegal contracts are all generally applicable rules. Finally, U.S. Supreme Court cases applying the FAA are consistent with North Carolina law against exculpation in holding that the arbitral forum must allow parties to effectively vindicate their claims. *See, e.g., Gilmer v. Interstate/Johnson Lane Corp.*, 500 U.S. 20, 26 (1991).

Therefore, under these generally applicable rules of North Carolina contract law, Check 'N Go's mandatory individual arbitration clause is unenforceable. The motion to compel individual arbitrations should be denied.

STATEMENT OF FACTS

I. BACKGROUND ON PAYDAY LENDING

A. Check 'N Go's Payday Lending Business Model

Plaintiffs are borrowers of payday loans from Check 'N Go offices in North Carolina. Payday loans are short-term loans provided for a set fee that translates into an extremely high interest rate. Under Check 'N Go's form of payday lending as practiced in North Carolina, a customer in need of a loan writes a personal check for an amount of $500 or less, and obtains a promise that the check will not be presented for payment until a short time in the future, typically 14–30 days. Compl., ¶ 15. The customer is then given the amount of the check, minus a substantial finance charge. For example, if a customer wants a loan for $400, the customer writes a check for $472, with the extra $72 representing the finance charge. When calculated out over the course of a year, the finance charge typically works out to an annual percentage rate of interest of 400% or more. At the end of the short-term loan period, the customer then must pay back the total amount of the loan to get the check back, or, if they cannot pay it back, "roll over" the loan into a new loan by paying an additional finance charge. *Id.* Thus, a customer borrowing $200 can end up paying many times that amount in interest charges without ever paying off the original loan principal.

Check 'N Go's entire payday lending business is based on a uniform practice of getting borrowers to write checks that Check 'N Go has reasonable grounds to believe are not covered, at the time of the making of the check, by adequate funds in the maker's checking account. This practice violates N.C. Gen. Stat. § 14-107(b) which makes it unlawful:

> or any person, firm or corporation to *solicit* or to *aid and abet* any other person . . . to draw, make, utter or issue and deliver to any person, firm or corporation, any check or draft on any bank or depository for the payment of money or its equivalent, being informed, knowing *or having reasonable grounds for believing* at the time of the soliciting or the aiding and abetting that the maker or the drawer of the check or draft has not sufficient funds on deposit in, or credit with, the bank or depository with which to pay the check or draft upon presentation.

(emphasis added).

The effect of the consumer not having funds in the checking account to keep the check from bouncing if deposited, gives rise to one of the worst evils of payday lending—rollovers. Payday lenders make most of their profits through particular borrowers' repeated borrowings. Consumers become fearful of criminal prosecution if they do not pay back the loan (*See* McQuillan Affidavit, Exhibit 1A and Matthis Affidavit, Exhibit 1B), and become trapped in a rollover debt cycle when they must continue renewing or repeating the loan transaction. Check 'N Go's practice of requiring its borrowers to write checks "knowing or having reasonable grounds for believing" there are insufficient funds to cover the checks has additional negative and perverse effects. Failure to repay the loan (or roll over the loan) leads to bounced check fees from the consumer's bank, negative credit ratings on specialized databases, possible loss of a bank account, and difficulty in opening a new bank account if the borrower has a record of bouncing checks. Taking the borrower's personal check in connection with the payday loan deprives the customer of any effective opportunity to present defenses to the loan. This practice gives Check 'N Go enormous leverage over the consumer in collecting the payday debt.

The named plaintiffs have obtained payday loans of $500 or less from Check 'N Go. The loan were for periods of 14–30 days. Compl., ¶ 38. The plaintiffs were required to pay hefty finance charges as part of the loan agreement. For instance, Andrea McQuillan paid $501.50 to obtain a $425 loan, and paid $354 to obtain a $300 loan. *Id.*, ¶ 40. To obtain a loan of $200 dollars, Ms. Matthis was instructed to write a personal check for $236. To obtain a loan of $225, Ms. Matthis was instructed to write a personal check for $265.50. The charges on such loans ranged translated into an annual percentage ranged from 199% to 469.29%. *See id*, ¶ 49.

B. The Illegality of Payday Lending

Prior to 1997, payday lending was illegal in North Carolina. A 1992 North Carolina Attorney General's opinion made it clear to

Check 'N Go and other payday lenders that payday lending violates the North Carolina Consumer Finance Act, N.C. Gen. Stat. § 53-164 et seq., and North Carolina criminal law, N.C. Gen. Stat. § 14-107(b). *See* 60 N.C.A.G. 86 (1992). In 1997, the North Carolina General Assembly acted to temporarily legalize payday lending, while at the same time heavily regulating the activities of the industry. Act of Aug. 18, 1997, 1997 N.C. Sess. Laws 391 (codified as amended at N.C. Gen. Stat. §§ 53-275–53-289 (1999) (repealed 2001)). The purpose of the law was to prevent some of the industry's most abusive lending practices, such as excessive fees and "rollovers" that turned a short-term loan into a revolving line of credit, while at the same time providing access to small amounts of short-term credit for emergencies. Scott A. Schaaf, *From Checks to Cash: The Regulation of the Payday Lending Industry*, 5 N.C. Banking Inst. 339, 359–62 (2001).

The statute included a sunset provision, which allowed the law to expire on July 31, 2001. § 3, 1997 N.C. Sess. Laws 391. However, the General Assembly also indicated its intent to remove the sunset once the industry demonstrated its good faith willingness to comply with the regulations and provided there was "no evidence of excessive complaints by consumers or unfair and deceptive trade practices" by lenders. § 2, 1997 N.C. Sess. Laws 391; Schaaf, 5 N.C. Banking Inst. at 360–61.

Payday lenders failed their probationary period. Numerous lenders ignored the prohibitions against rollovers and excessive fees. Schaaf, 5 N.C. Banking Inst. at 362. Lenders also found ways to circumvent the 31-day limit imposed by the statute. *Id*. Ultimately, the General Assembly determined that payday lenders were unwilling to cooperate with reasonable regulations. After initially extending the sunset by one month, the General Assembly refused to renew authorization for payday lending. Legal authority for payday lending expired on August 31, 2001.

Check 'N Go had ample warning of the law's sunset date, as on July 31, 2001 and again on August 30, 2001, the North Carolina Commissioner of Banks informed all payday lending businesses in the state that the law was set to expire and no legal authority would exist for payday lending to continue in the state. *See* Banking Commissioner Hal D. Lingerfelt's Memo of July 31, 2001 and August 30, 2001, attached as Exhibits 2 and 3. Nevertheless, Check 'N Go has continued to operate its payday loan business and to offer payday loans to North Carolina residents after August 31, 2001, notwithstanding the statute's expiration.

In order to evade the requirements of North Carolina law, Check 'N Go adopted an "agency model" for its payday lending operations in North Carolina. Under this model, Check 'N Go entered into an arrangement to a series of "rent a charter" arrangements, including with Brickyard Bank and County Bank of Rehoboth Beach, an FDIC insured, state-chartered bank, whereby Check 'N Go purports to act as an agent of the banks. Check 'N Go believes that by entering into this arrangement, it is no longer subject to North Carolina law and can offer payday loans free and clear of any state regulation.

C. Check 'N Go's Arbitration Clause

The entire payday loan model is composed of usurious interest terms and an exculpatory arbitration provision. As stated above, Check 'N Go charges triple digit interest rates on its payday loans. A second essential characteristic of Check 'N Go's business model is the inclusion in its loan agreements of a binding mandatory arbitration clause that deprives borrowers of the right to pursue a class action remedy, either in court or in arbitration, and that requires all arbitrations to be conducted by the National Arbitration Forum (NAF). In order to obtain a payday loan, plaintiffs were required to sign loan agreements drafted and provided by Check 'N Go as a condition of obtaining the loan. Included in those loan agreements were clauses requiring plaintiffs to give up their right to a jury trial and to submit any disputes with Check 'N Go to binding mandatory arbitration. *See* McQuillan Arbitration Agreement, attached as Exhibit 4. The arbitration clause written by Check 'N Go forbids plaintiffs from acting as a representative, private attorney general or as a member of a class action. *See id*. Check 'N Go's arbitration clause prohibits anything other than arbitration on an individual basis, and specifically prohibits class proceedings of any kind, either in court or in arbitration. Check 'N Go also designated the National Arbitration Forum ("NAF") as the exclusive arbitrator for all disputes. *See id*. Under the terms of the loan agreement, the plaintiffs cannot choose, or in any way participate in the choosing of the company that will arbitrate future disputes.

II. FACTS RELATING TO THE ENFORCEABILITY OF DEFENDANTS' ARBITRATION CLAUSES

A. There is a Vast Disparity of Bargaining Power Between the Wealthy and Sophisticated Defendants and the Economically Desperate Plaintiffs

Check 'N Go is a highly profitable and sophisticated corporation. It operates more than 1,100 stores in 29 states, including 64 stores in North Carolina alone. *See* excerpts from Check 'N Go website, attached at Exhibit 5. Check 'N Go's annual revenues have exceeded $12.9 million. See Affidavit of Robert E. Kassner in Support of Defendants' Notice or Removal, attached as Exhibit 6. Check 'N Go has retained the services of some of the most prominent attorneys in both North Carolina and the nation, it is advised by prominent accountants and is represented by numerous well-heeled lobbyists. Check 'N Go prides itself as an industry leader. *See id*., ¶ 5.

The Plaintiffs, by contrast, are far from economically powerful. In fact, for the times they were borrowing from Check 'N Go at an exorbitant interest rate, they are most accurately described as economically desperate. *See* McQuillan and Matthis Affidavits, Exhibit 1A and 1B. Studies of payday lending consumers confirm the circumstances of the named plaintiffs here, showing that most payday borrowers face severe financial pressure that make payday loans an economic necessity. *See, e.g.*, Jean Ann Fox, *"A Portrait of the Small Loan Consumer": A Review of Existing Research on Payday Loan Customers*, May 17, 2003, at 13 (attached); *see also Smith v. Steinkamp*, 318 F.3d 775, 776 (7th Cir. 2003) (noting that a payday borrowers are "poor or improvident borrowers who have no savings or credit and run out of living expenses before they receive their weekly or biweekly paycheck," and that they "*must* be desperate" if they are willing to agree to such high interest rates).

B. Check 'N Go's Arbitration Clause Is A Contract of Adhesion

Check 'N Go's arbitration clause is a standard form document that was drafted by Check 'N Go. It was presented to each of the plaintiffs as part of an agreement that they were required to sign as a condition of obtaining a payday loan. No employee of Check 'N Go explained to them that the loan agreements contained an arbitration clause, that the arbitration clause required them to give up their right to go to court, or that the arbitration clause prohibited plaintiffs from pursuing their claims on a classwide basis. *See* McQuillan and Matthis Affidavits, Exhibits 1A and 1B. The plaintiffs were not given any opportunity to negotiate different terms, and were hurried through the loan process so quickly that they did not have time to read the loan agreements thoroughly before signing them. *Id.* In short, the arbitration clause was presented on a "take-it-or-leave-it" basis.

C. All of the Other Payday Lenders in North Carolina Also Require Borrowers to Submit to Mandatory Pre-Dispute Binding Arbitration Clauses that Ban Class Actions

Check 'N Go is not unique among North Carolina payday lenders in requiring its customers to submit their claims to individual arbitration. Indeed, as shown in Exhibit 7, these clauses are ubiquitous throughout this industry in North Carolina, and they all prohibit consumers from proceeding on a class action basis. *See also* Robert W. Snarr, Jr., Supervising Examiner, Federal Reserve Bank of Philadelphia, *Compliance Corner*, Spring 2002, at CC2 <*available at* http://www.phil.frb.org/src/srcinsights/pdf/ccq1.pdf> ("The inclusion of mandatory arbitration clauses within payday loan contracts appears to be standard operating procedure among payday lenders and banks that partner with payday lenders to originate payday loans.") (Attached). In response to discovery requests, Check 'N Go was unable to identify any payday lender which does not use an arbitration clause in connection with their loans. See Defendants' Responses and Objections to Plaintiffs' Second Set of Interrogatories, ¶ 19, 8. The bottom line is that it would be extremely difficult, if not impossible, for a North Carolina consumer to obtain a payday loan without signing a contract that contains a pre-dispute binding mandatory arbitration clause prohibiting class actions.

D. Check 'N Go Presented Its Arbitration Clause to Plaintiffs In A Manner that Made It Very Difficult to Understand

Check 'N Go's arbitration clause was drafted in a manner that makes it unreadable for individuals seeking payday loans. Ms. Beth Weir, an expert on readability, conducted an analysis of the arbitration clause that Adriana McQuillan was required to sign in order to obtain a payday loan from Check 'N Go. Affidavit of Beth Weir., ¶ 4 (Exhibit 9). In her attached expert affidavit Weir concluded that "the vast majority of Americans would have difficulty comprehending the arbitration agreements I assessed." *Id.*, ¶ 38. Based on her analysis, Weir stated that only an individual with the ability "to read well beyond the high school level" would be able to comprehend Check 'N Go's arbitration clause. *Id.*, ¶ 6. Weir found certain sentences of the arbitration clause, such as the 168-word first sentence of the Check 'N Go's arbitration clause, to be so long and complex so as to render them "essentially not comprehensible." *Id.*, ¶ 15 (concluding also that one would have to read at a "69th" grade level to understand the sentence). Weir found that the arbitration clause registered a score of "very difficult" and would require a 16th grade reading level for comprehension. Unfortunately, the average American only reads at between a seventh and ninth grade level, and fewer than one in five North Carolinians and only one in five Americans can read at a high school level or beyond. *Id.*, ¶¶ 6, 40–41.

Not only does Check 'N Go's arbitration clause include a number of difficult words, but several important terms in the arbitration clause, such as the term "servicer" (apparently referring to Check 'N Go) are undefined and do not appear in conventional dictionaries. *Id.*, ¶ 31. Factors like this, as well as the cramming of multiple complex ideas into a single sentence, *see id.*, ¶¶ 32–34, caused Weir to conclude that "a reader is likely to have even more difficulty in comprehending the arbitration agreements than the readability formula scores would indicate." *Id.*, ¶ 30.

By contrast, Weir found that the text contained on Check 'N Go's website that it uses to market its loan products to potential customers is written at a much simpler level than the arbitration clause. *Id.*, ¶¶ 17–18. Accordingly, Check 'N Go knows how to make itself understood when it wants to acquire a customer's business, and how to prevent itself from being understood when it does not want its customers to know the rights they are being forced to sacrifice.

E. Plaintiffs' Claims May Not Realistically Be Pursued on An Individual Basis

The class action ban in Check 'N Go's arbitration clause operates as an exculpatory provision because payday borrowers will not be able to pursue their claims on an individual basis. Because the stakes of an individual arbitration on behalf of a payday borrower are so small, no attorney will represent a payday borrower absent the availability of classwide relief. In his attached expert affidavit, Stuart Rossman, the Director of Litigation at the National Consumer Law Center, opined that an aggrieved consumer bringing these actions as an individual would not be able to obtain private legal counsel, and would be very unlikely to obtain representation from a legal aid program. He reasoned that:

> The costs associated with preparing and litigating the claims asserted in the Complaints, particularly against defendants commanding significant resources, could not be recovered through a contingency fee. The cost of representation based upon an hourly fee, similarly, would be greater than any potential recovery the individual Plaintiff might seek. Because of the dramatic cuts in funding, few legal aid programs have the resources to address this type of case.

Rossman Affidavit, Exhibit 10, ¶ 16. Also atttached hereto are affidavits from seventeen different private attorneys practicing throughout North Carolina, with experience representing consumers, and one attorney from Georgia with significant experience litigating claims involving payday lending. *See* Exhibits 11 (A-R). All eighteen private attorneys stated that they would not have represented the named Plaintiffs in individual actions, either in court or in arbitration, because the small stakes relative to the time and expense required to pursue the case made it a financially infeasible alternative. *See id.* Those attorneys also attested that they would not take the named Plaintiffs' cases on an individual basis notwithstanding the availability of statutory attorneys fees, because the chance of prevailing in the dispute, along with the chance of actually receiving attorneys fees if they prevail, is too uncertain to justify taking the case. *See id.* Thus, the attorneys concluded that even if the named Plaintiffs had valid claims, if they were required to proceed on an individual basis, either in arbitration or in court, "it is overwhelmingly likely that few, if any, of the people in the proposed class would be able to find an attorney to represent them on a contingency basis, and that it would be foolhardy for any consumer to retain counsel to pursue the relatively small amounts on an hourly basis. If those claims can only be pursued on an individual basis, my opinion is that very few—and probably, none—of the people in the proposed class have any realistic chance of obtaining a remedy for the conduct described in the complaints, no matter how strong their claims are." *Id.*

Not only would the named Plaintiffs find themselves unable to retain a private attorney to represent them on an individual basis, they also would not be able to obtain representation from legal aid and legal services attorneys. Affidavits from four legal aid and legal services attorneys state that legal aid offices are woefully understaffed and underfunded, and that they simply do not have the time or resources to be able to represent aggrieved payday borrowers. *See* Exhibits.12-A–D. While the likelihood that any consumer will be able to receive legal assistance from a legal aid office in North Carolina is small, it is downright minuscule for payday borrowers, who occupy a lower case intake priority than many other consumers, particularly those facing home foreclosures. *See* Affidavit of Andrea Bebber, ¶¶ 13–18; Hausen Affidavit, ¶ 10. Moreover, most payday borrowers have a level of income that makes them ineligible for traditional legal assistance programs. *See* Affidavit of George Hausen ¶ 10. Furthermore, there is no formalized system of *pro bono* representation in North Carolina for individuals above the legal aid income guidelines, making it highly unlikely that payday lending borrowers will be able to obtain representation. *See* Hausen Affidavit ¶ 16 Therefore, absent the opportunity to pursue a class action, the named Plaintiffs have no legal recourse at all for their injuries.

Check 'N Go's attempt to use its arbitration clause banning class actions as an exculpatory device has been successful. Since 1997, not a single Check Into Cash customer has initiated an individual arbitration against it. *See* Defendants CNG Financial Corporation and Check 'N Go of North Carolina, Inc.'s Objections and Responses to Plaintiffs' Second Set of Interrogatories and Request for Production of Documents, ¶ 20.

F. Plaintiffs Allege that the Single Purpose Contract At Issue Here is Illegal and Violates a Number of North Carolina Statutes

The sole purpose of Defendants' contracts with Plaintiffs was to provide for payday lending transactions. Plaintiffs allege that these transactions violate a number of North Carolina statutes including the North Carolina Consumer Finance Act, G.S. § 53-166(a) and (b); the North Carolina Unfair Trade Practice Statute, G.S. § 75-1.1; and the North Carolina Check Casher Act, G.S. § 53-276. Because these contracts are alleged to have solely an illegal purpose, they are thus alleged to be void *ab initio* under North Carolina contract law. Accordingly, defendants' payday loan contracts are not contracts at all, and no legally cognizable or binding contractual relationship (including any supposed agreement to arbitrate) ever came into existence in the first place.

G. The Payday Lending Industry Is a Heavily Regulated Industry

In North Carolina, a number of laws promoting the state's interest in protecting consumers regulate payday lenders. In fact, former N.C. Gen. Stat. 53-275 is only the latest chapter in North Carolina's nearly 80-year struggle to control payday lending. "Payday lending" is the same practice formerly known as "wage buying" or "salary buying." Christopher L. Peterson, *Truth, Understanding, and High-Costs Consumer Credit: The Historical Context of the Truth in Lending Act*, 55 Fla. L. Rev. 807, 810, 850–55 (2003). Early payday lenders acquired the nickname of "wagebuyers" or "salary buyers" because they sought to evade usury laws by claiming to be "buying wages" or salaries. *Id.* at 810, 852; Schaaf, 5 N.C. Banking Inst. at n.3. The term "loan shark" was originally coined to describe these early payday lenders. *Id.*

The North Carolina General Assembly first acted to restrain the practice of "wage buying" in 1927, when it amended the state's usury statute to clarify that loans "upon any assignment or sale of wages earned or to be earned" were subject to North Carolina's usury law prohibiting interest in excess of 6%. 1927 N.C. Public Laws, c. 72. (current version at N. C. Gen. Stat. § 14-391 (2003), amended by N.C. Gen. Stat. §§ 53-164 et. seq. (2003) (exempting persons licensed under Consumer Finance Act)). Furthermore, though the penalties for usury normally entailed only the forfeiture of interest charged, North Carolina imposed criminal penalties for wage-buying. *Id.*

However, due to payday lenders' practice of withholding promissory notes, receipts or other evidence that could prove usury, *see* William Hays Simpson, *The Loan Shark Problem in the Southeastern States*, 19 Law & Contemp. Probs. 68, 69 (1954), the clarification did little to curb the practice of wage buying, *Proposals for Legislation in N.C.*, 11 N.C. L. Rev. 51, 74 (1932). Payday lenders also evaded usury laws by cashing checks that were given solely as evidence of a loan. *See Melton v. Rickman*, 225 N.C. 700 (1945). When the check bounced, as the lender knew it would, the lender used the threat of criminal prosecution to force collection of usurious interest. *Id.* Justice Seawell referred to the payday lending industry as "a nefarious business" employing "vicious small loan practices." *Id.*, (Seawell, J., dissenting).

As a result, the General Assembly passed a law in 1935 prohibiting the assignment of future wages without the express, written agreement of the employer. 1935 N.C. Public Laws, Ch. 410; *Morris v. Holshouser*, 220 N.C. 293, 298, 17 S.E.2d 115, 119 (1941) (statute limiting the assignment of unearned wages was enacted "to restrain the activities of those ... engaged in the business of buying at a discount the unearned wages of employees.")

When this regulation too failed to restrain payday lenders from evading the usury laws—in 1940, the average annual interest rate on small loans ranged from 279% to 444%, Simpson, 19 Law & Contemp. Probs. at 74—the General Assembly, "seeking a solution to the loan shark problem enacted a law [in 1945] which placed the loan agencies under the supervision of the Commission of Banks and provided that a fee of $2.50 could be charged in addition to 6 per cent interest per annum on installment loans of $50 or less." *Id.* at 75.

The new law specifically included wage buyers in the definition of loan agencies and brokers, N.C. Gen. Stat. §§ 53-164 (1950), and prohibited the "rollover" fees that typically chained borrowers to a treadmill of debt, § 53-165 (1950); Simpson, 19 Law & Contemp. Probs. at 75. The State Banking Commission issued regulations pursuant to its new authority that required loan agencies and brokers to maintain certain records, report regularly to the Banking Commission and "prohibited the dividing of loans and the charging of excessive fees." Simpson, Law & Contemp. Probs. at 75.

Rather than comply with the law, payday lenders responded by instituting what the Commissioner of Banks, Gurney P. Hood called "a legalized accident and health insurance racket." *Id.* at 76.

Loan agencies began to require life insurance on each loan. *Id.* at 75. Eventually, payday lenders required borrowers to purchase health insurance and accident insurance as well, *id.*, and it became "almost impossible to obtain a loan at the vast majority of the [loan] agencies without buying insurance," *id.* at 77.

Often, the insurance premiums equaled or even exceeded the full amount of the loan. *Id.* at 76. According to a report by the State Banking Commissioner, in 1951, 43% of small loan agencies' total income came from insurance commissions. *Id.* at 77. Frequently, the company never even wrote the insurance policy once it collected the premium. *Id.* at 78. Furthermore, because the Banking Commission's authority did not extend to the regulation of insurance, there was little the Commission could do to curb these abusive practices. *Id.* at 78.

In response to payday lenders' flagrant violation of the law, the General Assembly passed the North Carolina Small Loans Act in 1955 "to provide additional protection to borrowers from small loan agencies." Small Loans Act, 1955 N.C. Sess. Laws c. 1279 (codified at N.C. Gen. Stat. § 53-164 et. seq. (1960) (repealed)). The Small Loans Act specifically prohibited the industry's abusive insurance practices and provided that any insurance activity was subject to the Commissioner of Insurance. N.C. Gen. Stat. § 53-166 (1960) (repealed).

By the end of the 1950s, it had become clear that the attempt to control payday lending through legislation and regulation was a failure. The lenders simply would not obey the law. Each regulation met with a new attempt to evade the law. 33 Op. Att'y Gen. 24 (1955) (small loan agencies may not charge fees, directly or indirectly, by entering into "kickback" arrangements with notary publics); 34 Op. Att'y Gen. 20 (1958) (small loan agencies may not repeatedly refinance loans such that interest is "pyramided" and the same lender is charged the 6% interest limit multiple times in the same borrowing period on the same loan).

Ultimately, the General Assembly decided to start from scratch. It scrapped all existing small loan laws and passed the significantly more comprehensive North Carolina Consumer Finance Act in 1961. 1961 Session Laws, c. 1053 (codified as amended at N.C. Gen. Stat. §§ 53-164 et. seq. (2003)); *see also Usury Law in North Carolina*, 47 N.C. L. Rev. 761, 767 (1969). The Consumer Finance Act exempted loans under $600 (now $3000) from the state's usury limits, provided the lenders are licensed and comply with provisions of the Act and any regulations promulgated by the Commissioner of Banks. N.C. Gen. Stat. § 53-166 (1965), *amended by* § 53-166 (2003). Given payday lenders' history of evading the law, the Act further specified that its provisions apply to "any person who seeks to avoid its application by any device, subterfuge or pretense whatsoever." N.C. Gen. Stat. § 53-166(b) (1965).

Under the Consumer Finance Act, payday lending remained illegal in North Carolina. Despite the industry's resurgence in the 1990s, payday lending is illegal today. The Commissioner of Banks recently instituted a contested case proceeding against Advance America, one of Check 'N Go's counterparts. *See In re Advance America*, Amended Notice of Hearing, Exhibit 13.

H. Facts Pertaining to the National Arbitration Forum

NAF is a very secretive company, resisting discovery and insisting upon sweeping secrecy orders whenever it can. In a companion case to this one, for example, also brought before this Court, NAF has vigorously resisted all discovery, including refusing to appear for a properly scheduled deposition. *See* Affidavit of Richard Fisher, Exhibit 14 hereto. Nonetheless, from documents produced in other cases (generally after extensive stonewalling and lengthy delays, and only after getting court orders in Minnesota requiring the organization to appear), and from plaintiffs' own investigation, some important facts have come to light about this secretive organization that would replace the civil justice system.

NAF is a for-profit organization. As of a few years ago, it operated with twenty-six employees all employed out of a small office in Minnesota. *See* Dep. of Edward C. Anderson taken in the case of *Toppings v. Meritech*, excerpts from which are attached as Exhibit 15 hereto, at 16–17. Pursuant to NAF rules, arbitrators are paid on a fee-per-case basis. That is to say, arbitrators only get paid if they hear a case, and they get paid more if they handle more cases. *See* id. at 19–20. Under the NAF Code of Procedure, parties must select an arbitrator from a list of individuals approved and pre-selected by NAF, *see* Anderson Depo. in *Toppings*, Exhibit 15 at 24, unless both parties agree to depart from the NAF list.[1] In the "vast majority" of cases, the NAF's director ends up selecting the candidates for arbitrators in NAF cases. *See* Anderson Depo. in *Hubbert*, Exhibit 16 hereto, at 56–57.

1. Facts Relating to NAF's Statements to Lenders

NAF has written a series of letters and published a series of advertisements soliciting business from lenders, promising to conduct arbitrations under a variety of rules that differ from the practice in court and from those of other arbitration service providers. A number of these promises favor the lenders' interests and place consumers at a disadvantage. In the interests of space this brief will merely forth an illustrative sample of such statements.

a) One NAF advertisement urging corporations and lenders to draft mandatory arbitration clauses naming the NAF as the arbitrator promises that NAF is "the alternative to the million dollar lawsuit."[2] Before an NAF arbitrator actually hears the facts of any dispute, NAF is apparently proclaiming that its mission is to make sure that no claimant will receive $1 million for their legal claims.

b) In another advertisement, NAF promises potential corporate clients that it will "make a positive impact on [their] bottom line." Exhibit 18.

c) In an article written for in house corporate lawyers, NAF's Director Ed Anderson has boasted that NAF has a "loser pays" rule that requires any consumer who does not win his case to pay the finance company's attorney's fees. See *ADR—Organizations; Do An LRA: Implement Your Own Civil Justice Reform Program NOW*, The Metropolitan Corporate Counsel (Aug. 2001) ("The rules of the National Arbitration Forum allow the arbitrator to award the prevail-

---

1 On another occasion, Mr. Anderson was asked "If [arbitrators] don't get selected [to hear a case], they don't get paid; correct?," and he answered "That's correct." *See* Dep. Edward C. Anderson, taken in the case of *Hubbert v. Dell*, excerpts of which are attached as Exhibit 16 hereto.

2 This document is one of many that NAF produced in the *Toppings* case pursuant to a subpoena, from its own files, and that were admitted into evidence and made part of the court record in that case. They were also part of the record on appeal, where the state supreme court struck down an NAF clause as unconscionable. *Toppings v. Meritech Mortgage Services, Inc.*, 569 S.E.2d 149 (W. Va. 2002). The document is attachment 1 to Exhibit 17 hereto.

ing party the cost of the arbitration, including attorneys' fees. . . . There is no such thing as a 'no risk' arbitration for either side.").

d) In one letter, an NAF executive promises a lawyer who specializes in defending finance companies that if the lawyer's clients will require their consumers to submit to NAF arbitration, that his clients will not need to worry about the plaintiffs' "class action bar" in lawsuits arising out of the Y2K computer issue. *See* Letter from Roger Haydock to Alan Kaplinsky, Exhibit 19 hereto. Consider the approach embodied in this letter. The letter characterizes an area of litigation as a battle between "the class action bar" and lenders. The letter—written by the top person in the NAF—clearly takes the lenders' side in this battle, and urges defense counsel for lenders to use the NAF as a means of foiling "the class action bar."

e) In correspondence from NAF's Director of Development, Curtis D. Brown, to a potential NAF client, NAF promised that "By adding arbitration language to your contracts, the [NAF's] national system of arbitration lets you minimize lawsuits, and the threat of lender liability jury verdicts." Exhibit 17 hereto, Attachment 2. The correspondence also included a "starter kit," to help the lender draft an arbitration clause that would be particularly likely to be enforced and help limit its liability. This was then followed by another solicitation promising to limit arbitration awards to the amount claimed. *Id.*

f) In another letter, Leif Stennes, a policy analyst for NAF, wrote a lender's in-house counsel that "There is no reason for Saxon Mortgage, Inc. to be exposed to the costs and the risks of the jury system." Exhibit 17 hereto, Attachment 3.

g) A memo attached to a letter from Mr. Anderson to a client explained to NAF's potential clients why its rules banning class actions are important: "In the court system, financing transactions are always at risk for Class Action treatment. . . ." It went on: "Most often, the claims of class action plaintiffs' lawyers are based on printed or computer-generated documents or standard procedure manuals, which leave little room to argue against 'commonality' or 'typicality.' " Exhibit 17, Attachment 4. In other words, even where any court would recognize that class action treatment was appropriate and superior to individual actions, the NAF was assuring the lender that it would not permit such handling.

h) NAF issues a publication entitled "Domain News: that touts when its arbitrators rule for famous people in disputes over internet domain names. *E.g., Johnny Unitas Wins Another One.* 2 Domain News, Vol. 4 at 2; *Master of Domains: metallica org*, 1 Domain News, Vol. 7 at 1. Exhibit 17, attachment 5. Plaintiffs know, of no other arbitrator, and certainly no court, that affirmatively publicizes decision favoring one party over the other.[3]

i) In another article, Mr. Anderson revealed the extent of his zealotry for using arbitration as "tort reform." In this article, he criticized the Congress for not enacting "civil justice reform," i.e., limits on damages in medical malpractice suits, and argued that in the mean time all hospitals, medical professionals and airlines should adopt binding arbitration clauses to help with "the war on terrorism." Edward C. Anderson, "Civil Justice Reform—Legal Service Providers; Civil Justice Reform and Homeland Security," Metropolitan Corporate Counsel, November 2002, at 54.

2. Facts Relating to NAF's Relationship With Lenders

NAF has a symbiotic relationship with lenders, upon whom it depends for its financial survival. One piece of evidence for this fact comes from NAF's own advertisements and letters. One NAF advertisement labeled "Professionals and the National Arbitration Forum," consists of a list of favorable quotes, all of which come from attorneys or officials affiliated with lenders. Exhibit 21 hereto. Another NAF News Release lists "Lenders Adopting Forum Agreements," and also provides the names of twenty-one individuals who specialize in representing financial institutions and banks as "Information Resources." Exhibit 22 hereto. There are no consumer advocates, or lawyers who specialize in representing consumers, included among the persons endorsing or serving as "Information Resources" for the NAF.

One of the persons worth noting on this list of "resources" is Alan Kaplinsky, the "Partner-in-charge" of the Consumer Financial Services Group with the law firm Ballard, Spahr, Andrews & Ingersoll. Mr. Kaplinsky has a deep relationship with NAF. In addition to serving as a resource for the NAF, and speaking out repeatedly and filing amicus briefs on their behalf, Mr. Kaplinsky has advised lenders to hire NAF as its arbitration service provider. *See, e.g.,* excerpts of Deposition of Clinton Walker (formerly general counsel of First USA Bank), Exhibit 23 hereto, at 220–21. Mr. Kaplinsky is also the person who received the letter from Mr. Haydock referenced in subpart III-A of the Statement of Facts above, advising him on how his clients could best defeat a certain category of lawsuits. In addition, NAF's top executive and shareholder, Ed Anderson, has testified that he has met with Mr. Kaplinsky "maybe 20" times, or "maybe 12." Anderson Depo. in *Hubbert v. Dell*, Exhibit 16, at 86.

So why the emphasis on Mr. Kaplinsky? According to his firm's website, its "Consumer Financial Services Group has developed one of the pre-eminent and largest consumer financial services litigation defense practices in the country, defending banks and other financial institutions throughout the United States in class actions and other complex litigation." <www.ballardspahr.com/home.htm>. In an article entitled "Excuse me, but who's the predator: Banks can use arbitration clauses as a defense," *Bus. Law.* 24 (May/June 1998), Kaplinsky wrote that "Consumers have been ganging up on banks. But now the institutions have found a way to defend themselves." *Id.* at 24. The article makes clear that mandatory arbitration is this "defense" for financial institutions against consumer claims, and notes that "Arbitration is a powerful deterrent to class action lawsuits. . . ." *Id.* 24–26. See also Kaplinsky, "Alternative to Litigation Attracting Consumer Financial Services Companies," *Consumer Financial Services L. Report* (1997) ("[i]n an attempt to eliminate the risks inherent in litigation *and discourage future lawsuits*, many consumer financial services companies have implemented arbitration programs.") (emphasis added). Consumers looking for truly neutral, independent decision makers might well ask if Mr. Kaplinsky would recommend NAF to

---

3 *See also* Affidavit of Michael Geist, Exhibit 20 hereto, at ¶ 14 ("During my research, I was on NAF's media distribution list. Unlike the WIPO and eResolution, the NAF regularly distributed press releases heralding recent decisions. From May through August 2001, for example, I received several press releases, all but one of which promoted a complainant win.").

clients such as First USA, if he did not feel that NAF would serve his twice-published objective of "defending" lenders against consumer lawsuits.

Another link between NAF and lenders comes from its principal, Edward C. Anderson. Immediately prior to becoming the head of a "neutral" organization, Mr. Anderson worked as in-house litigation counsel at ITT Financial Services. *See* Anderson Depo. in *Toppings*, Exhibit 15, at 11. At that time, ITT Financial was a lender beset with consumer lawsuits for financial wrongdoing. *See Patterson v. ITT Consumer Fin. Corp.*, 14 Cal. App.4th 1659, 18 Cal. Rptr.2d 563 (1993). In other words, when Mr. Anderson left one job on a Friday, he was charged with defending a particular lender against consumer cases against it. The following Monday, he was supposedly the head of a "neutral" firm choosing the arbitrators of cases involving that company.

As one indication of the favoritism that NAF offered to ITT Financial after Mr. Anderson left that company and became the head of NAF, this Court could look to two documents that came out of the attachments to the 1994 deposition of Mr. Anderson in *ITT Commercial Finance Corp. v. Wagerin*. In a letter attached as Exhibit 6 to Mr. Anderson's 1994 deposition, an official of Equilaw (Equilaw was NAF's corporate parent in of 1994, *see* Anderson Depo. in *Toppings*, Exhibit 15, at 10), proposed an arbitrator for an ITT Commercial Finance Corp. case despite the fact that the arbitrator's law firm represented three other ITT corporations. In Exhibit 7 to Mr. Anderson's 1994 deposition, Equilaw official proposed an arbitrator for another ITT case, even though the arbitrator then represented the law firm that represented ITT in that case, albeit "in an unrelated case." See Exhibit 23 hereto.

As another indication of the depth of NAF's relationship with lenders, and as the previous section indicates, NAF also routinely sends letters and "information packages" to lenders that offer legal advice to lenders on the issue of how best to defeat consumers' challenges to mandatory arbitration clauses.

As another indication of NAF's closeness to lenders, it is worth noting that NAF regularly engages in ex parte contacts with defense lawyers who represent lenders, while not extending this same courtesy to consumer plaintiffs or to counsel who represent such plaintiffs. *See, e.g.,* Exhibits 24, 25, and 26 hereto (affidavits of Richard Fisher, Gregory Duhl, and Bren Pomponio).

NAF has also displayed its close ties to lenders by repeatedly entering into litigation between lenders and against consumers as an *amicus*. While NAF's briefs always state that it is officially taking neither party's side, in fact the positions and arguments that it advances in each and every one of these briefs supports the positions that the defendant lenders were taking in the litigation and opposed the positions being taken by the individual consumers. *See, e.g.,* Brief of *Amicus Curiae* National Arbitration Forum, appeal from *Mitchell v. Banc One Delaware*, 2004 WL 1362010, 70 Pa. D & C 4th 353 (Pa. Comm. Pl. Jan. 27, 2005); Brief of *Amicus Curiae* National Arbitration Forum, *Marsh v. First USA Bank, N.A.*, No. 00-10648 (5th Cir Dec. 12, 2000), Brief of National Arbitration Forum as *Amicus Curiae*, *Green Tree Financial Corp. v. Randolph*, 531 U.S. 79 (2000); Brief of *Amicus Curiae* National Arbitration Forum, *Baron v. Best Buy Co., Inc.*, No-14028-E (11th Cir. Dec. 15, 1999). NAF also unsuccessfully petitioned the California Supreme Court to depublish a California Court of Appeals decision holding that an arbitration clause was unconscionable, in part, because of repeat-player bias on the part of NAF. *Mercuro v. Superior Court*, 116 Cal. Rptr.2d 671 (Cal. Ct. App. 2002). Plaintiffs know of no case in which the NAF filed one of its many *amicus* briefs in support of the factual or legal position taken by plaintiffs in a case.

3. Facts Relating to NAF's Handling of Consumer Claims

NAF's handling of consumer claims raises concerns in a great many areas. One overarching piece of evidence came in the sworn interrogatory answers of a credit card issuer, First USA Bank (whose business has since been bought and sold several times). According to First USA's own analysis of the results of NAF arbitrations between First USA and its consumers, out of a sample of nearly 20,000 arbitrations, NAF prevailed an astonishing 99.6% of the time. *See* Exhibit 17, hereto, as Attachment 6.[4]

Perhaps in response to this data, at the hearing on March 10, 2005 on discovery issues, counsel for Advance America offered to this Court a press release put out by a banking industry trade group prepared by the accounting firm of Ernst & Young, that praises the results that the NAF has reached in consumer cases. As plaintiffs pointed out at the hearing, this document was prepared by consultants paid by the banking industry, and is about as credible as old Tobacco Institute "studies" purportedly showing that cigarette smoking was good for children's health.

The Ernst & Young "study" supposedly shows that consumers fare well in about 250 selected cases taken to arbitration before the NAF. Perhaps the most obvious flaw of this bankers-paid-for press release is acknowledged at page 6: it does not compare the results in NAF arbitration with the results consumers would get in court. That consumers win some share of the cases they bring with the NAF says little if consumers would have done better in court.

Another obvious flaw with the Ernst & Young "study" is that it assumes that a consumer who wins *any money at all* before the NAF has "prevailed."[5] If a consumer has lost their home due to mortgage fraud, however, and has a claim worth over $100,000 and they are awarded $1 by NAF no one (besides Ernst & Young) could fairly claim that they had "prevailed."[6]

The "study" assumes, at page 9, that consumers were satisfied in every case that they dismissed. In light of NAF's declared "loser

---

4 This result is not surprising. At that time, First USA had been a major repeat client for NAF. In 1999, Clinton Walker, General Counsel of First USA, testified in a deposition that First USA had then paid at least $2 million to NAF in fees. Exhibit 23. This is a great deal of money to NAF, whose corporate parent Equilaw went bankrupt in 1994.

5 NAF's own Ed Anderson himself has acknowledged that NAF's records are set up to support claims of such an unrealistic result:

> Q. For example, if that person from Granite City had a $1400 dispute with Dell and ended up getting $100 from Dell, would that be listed in your system as a victory for the consumer?
> A. It captures who gets the award.

Anderson Depo. in *Hubbert v. Dell*, Exhibit 16, at 37–38.

6 When this factor is considered, the evidence shows that the monetary awards to individuals suing corporations in court are higher than those awarded in BMA. *See Armendariz v. Armendariz v. Found. Health Psychcare Services, Inc.*, 24 Cal. 4th 83, 99 Cal. Rptr. 2d 745, 6 P.3d 669 (2000) ("the amount awarded [in arbitration] is on average smaller"). As set forth above, NAF itself has stressed this fact to potential corporate clients, advertising itself as a way of "minimizing . . . the threat of lender liability jury verdicts," and as "the alternative to the million dollar lawsuit."

pays" policy, as set forth in the prior section, of threatening consumers who do not prevail before the NAF with paying the banks' attorneys' fees, however, it is likely that consumers who encounter an arbitrator who is favorable to the bank and then decide to drop a case are just trying to avoid retaliation rather than expressing "satisfaction."

The Ernst & Young telephone survey results of customer satisfaction are meaningless, similarly, because the sample is so tiny. There were only 29 respondents.

The Ernst & Young "study" unintentionally dramatizes the extent to which NAF arbitration is favored by corporations and not consumers. NAF's Executive Director testified in 2004 that NAF handles 50,000 cases per year brought by corporations against individual consumers. Exhibit 28 hereto. The Ernst & Young "study" shows that consumers brought only 256 cases before NAF in a period of four *years*, however. The Bankers' Association's own press release thus establishes the extent to which the NAF is a corporate service: in a single year it handled almost 200 cases by corporations against consumers for every one case it had handled over a four year period that was brought by consumers against corporations.

Finally, the Ernst & Young press release demonstrates NAF's close relationship with lenders. Unlike its competitors such as the American Arbitration Association and JAMS, the NAF has largely refused to comply with a California statute, C.C.P. § 1281.96, that requires private arbitration companies to disclose certain information about consumer disputes that they handle.[7] This statute requires arbitration companies to publicly disclose includes the number of cases the arbitration firm has handled for various corporations (so consumers can tell if a given arbitration firm has an ongoing and recurring relationship with a given company), the disposition of those cases (so consumers can ascertain if a given arbitration company tends to favor a given corporation), and the total costs imposed on consumers who have had their cases handled by that arbitration firm. While NAF has posted a few cases (unlike AAA and JAMS, that have posted information on hundreds of cases), it has refused to post the results of cases where it NAF has posted a statement that it believes that this statute is preempted by federal law.

In addition to broad statistics, however, there is a wealth of other troubling facts about the way that NAF handles consumer cases. In one infamous case, for example, a state appellate court found that the NAF was requiring consumers living in California to travel to Minnesota to pursue small predatory lending claims. Accordingly, the court held that a lender's arbitration clause that required consumers to bring their claims before the NAF was unconscionable. *See Patterson v. ITT Consumer Fin. Corp.*, 14 Cal. App.4th 1659, 18 Cal. Rptr.2d 563 (1993). (NAF subsequently changed that particular rule. It can hardly win many lender clients if it persists in insisting upon such extreme rules that its clauses cannot be enforced.)

In another case, a consumer responded to a notice of arbitration by arguing that the NAF had no jurisdiction over her. The NAF directed a consumer to elaborate on her claims that it had no jurisdiction, and she did so. Then, the NAF entered an award against her in the full amount sought by the lender, *without giving her a chance to even present her argument on the merits*. (NAF's characteristic decision to refuse to permit this consumer to even present her argument on the merits was significant—she had already paid the full amount that the lender had agreed would satisfy her debt.) *See* Affidavits of Justin Baxter and Laurie Raymond, Exhibit 30 hereto.

In another case, a consumer documented that NAF violated its own rules repeatedly to favor a corporate defendant over a consumer. The NAF accepted late filings from the defendant, engaged in ex parte communications with the defendant, required the consumer (but not the defendant) to hand write a lengthy case number on every page of documents, and refused to even accept pleadings relating to certain procedural issues from the consumer. This well educated consumer concluded that "it was impossible for me to get a fair result through arbitration before the NAF." Affidavit of Gregory Duhl, Exhibit 25 hereto.

In another case, a consumer was given an option of refusing arbitration when a credit card company adopted its arbitration clause, and she did so. Later, the credit card company nonetheless brought a claim against her with NAF. She sent an affidavit to NAF proving that she had never agreed to arbitration, and received no response. Later, she learned from a debt collector (having heard nothing from the NAF itself) that NAF had issued an award against her for the full amount claimed by the lender. Affidavit of Eve Curtis, Exhibit 31 hereto.

Another consumer who opted out of an arbitration agreement through certified mail (as that agreement supposedly permitted), and who fully documented that fact to the NAF, received the same pro forma result: a judgment for the lender for everything it wanted, in a case where NAF had no jurisdiction at all, with no explanation:

> 10. On or about August 1, 2005, I received a notice from NAF indicating that it was going forward with the arbitration in Minnesota. A copy of this notice is attached hereto as Exhibit F. NAF has not responded to my letter of July 23, 2005 or the fact that Mr. Marchand and MBNA agreed that the arbitration provision was not effective as to Mr. Marchand and the fact that Mr. Marchand has objected to arbitration of his rights under his agreement with MBNA.

Affidavit of Lester A. Perry, Exhibit 32 hereto.

Roughly the same story was told by another identity theft victim, in whose name someone else had opened a credit card account:

---

7 For example, despite handling tens of thousands of MBNA consumer cases, NAF has not posted the results of its MBNA cases on its website. And in general, NAF's most prominent posting on the subject is an assertion that it is not require to comply with this consumer protection statute (a position not taken by AAA or JAMS) because it is supposedly exempted by federal law. One California court has specifically noted that NAF has not complied with this law. See Superior Court decision in *Klussman v. Cross-Country Bank*, Exhibit 29 hereto, at 9 ("By way of dicta, the Court notes that the arbitration provision may also not be enforceable because NAF does not comply with C.C.P. 1291.96.") In any case, it is extremely hard for a normal person to find the few cases that NAF has posted, as one must click upon about half a dozen links, the last of which is not even highlighted.

5. In late 2002 and early 2003, I received three notices of Arbitration from the NAF. In each case, I responded by sending a letter explaining that the accounts were not mine, that I had never agreed to any arbitration provision, and that the credit card company had never provided the requested debt verification. True and correct copies of my letters are attached as Exhibits A, B, and C.

6. The NAF never required the credit card company to prove that I was responsible for the debt or that I was bound by an arbitration agreement. Despite the fact that I was not responsible for the debt and was never a party to an arbitration agreement, and that I informed the NAF of these facts, the NAF entered three arbitration awards against me.

Affidavit of Patricia Meisse, Exhibit 33 hereto.

Similarly, another consumer who was the victim of an identity theft got the same short shrift from the NAF. In this case, a consumer not only documented that he had never opened a credit card with a lender (much less agreed to arbitration of claims with that lender), but the bank acknowledged in writing that it had made an error about the account number involved. Nonetheless, the NAF produced its usual result:

8. On November 24, 2004, despite the fact that MBNA's own evidence established conclusively that the account submitted to NAF arbitration was not my client's account, the NAF entered an award for MBNA on the original claim.

Affidavit of Joanne Faulkner, Exhibit 34 hereto.

NAF's pro-lender handling of consumer claims is also evidenced by a practice that it widely promotes to lenders as being more favorable to them than the rules of its competitors, such as the non-profit American Arbitration Association: NAF's rules limit awards to "the amount of the claim." *See* NAF Code of Procedure, Rule 37.B. This practice prohibits the recovery of damages based on new evidence discovered during the litigation. The nature of lending litigation, however, is that the full extent of a lender's wrongdoing (and thus the damages that would be appropriate to award the plaintiff) often cannot be known until the plaintiff has had an opportunity to pursue reasonable discovery. Complex fraud schemes, for example, can generally only be identified after layers of deceit and obfuscation are peeled away and the true facts are made known. NAF's rule capping awards is particularly pernicious, because NAF's rules pressure consumers to reduce the amount of their claim at the outset of a case. By forcing claimants to place a dollar figure on their claim, not only must a consumer sacrifice her or his right to access the courts, the consumer also waives relief he or she would be entitled to under the law.

In a similar vein, NAF boasts to lenders that its rules provide for "[v]ery little, if any, discovery." Exhibit 17, attachment 7. The consequence of this rule for consumers is obvious. Consumers have the burden or proof, but few borrowers with valid legal claims have independent access to a lender's documents. As NAF knows well, all pertinent paper and loan documents are typically held by the lender. By denying the consumer access to discovery, NAF rules effectively prohibit consumers from proving their case. In *Armendariz v. Foundation Health Psychare Services, Inc.*, 24 Cal. 4th 83, 104 (2002), for example, the California Supreme Court held that "adequate discovery is indispensable for the vindication of FEHA claims."

Another indication of NAF's approach to consumers is found in the fact that several courts have refused to enforce NAF arbitration clauses on the grounds that NAF often imposes unreasonable fees on consumers who wish to bring claims. While Check 'N Go here offers to pay most of plaintiffs' arbitration fees, NAF's practice of imposing large (and largely hidden) costs on consumers where possible says much about its approach to consumer claims. *See, e.g., Eagle v. Fred Martin Motor Co.*, 809 N.E.2d 1161, 1177 (Ohio Ct. App. 2004) ("Practically speaking, such arbitration costs would serve to deter even low-income persons who do not qualify for indigent status, as well. That a consumer such as Ms. Eagle, a primary caregiver for one child and who recently made approximately $20,000 per year, would be willing and able to expend on a conservative scale between $4,000 and $6,000 on arbitration fees and costs, is highly doubtful."); *Licitra v. Gateway, Inc.*, 189 Misc. 2d 721, 734 N.Y.S.2d 389 (N.Y. Civ. Ct. 2001) ("outlining the NAF's fees and concluding that "[i]t is obvious that these costs can make arbitration not a viable alternative for many consumers."); *Ferguson v. Countrywide Credit Indus., Inc.*, 298 F.3d 778 (9th Cir. 2002) (arbitration clause was unconscionable, in part, because of NAF's fees); *Tamayo v. Brainstorm USA*, Case No. 01-20386 JF (N.D. Cal. March 29, 2002), on appeal, No. 02-51721 (arbitration clause unconscionable, in part, because NAF's fees were prohibitive).

4. Facts Relating to NAF's Power to Influence the Outcomes of Arbitrations

In a number of other cases where consumer plaintiffs have challenged the NAF, lender defendants have made some variant of this argument: "it doesn't matter whether the people who run the NAF are biased in favor of lenders and against consumers, or have financial incentives to favor lenders, because the only thing that matters is the arbitrators themselves. Unless the plaintiffs can prove that each of the arbitrators themselves is biased, the court must reject the challenge." A few courts have even accepted this argument.

In fact, NAF wields enormous power in these cases. The mechanics of selecting an arbitrator involve a system of strikes that inevitably results in an arbitrator who ultimately is selected solely by the NAF Director. "The parties are provided with a list of names that is one more than the number of parties." *See* Dep. of Anderson in *Toppings*, Exhibit 15 hereto, at 78. Each party then gets to make one strike. In cases such as this, the plaintiffs would strike one arbitrator from the list and the lender defendant would strike one. Left after the strikes would be the one extra arbitrator selected by the NAF. If NAF were to submit a list of arbitrators in which two had strong ties to corporate lenders, one of those two would almost certainly end up as the decision maker replacing the courts and the jury system for the case.

This fact is nailed down by the sworn testimony of Michael Geist, a law professor who studied every single decision entered in an Internet domain name dispute between the program's inception in 1999 and February of 2002 (4,332 cases), where the more powerful party and the party selecting the arbitrator is the Complainant (unlike lending disputes, where that party is typically the defendant):

> 7. I concluded that the NAF disproportionately assigned arbitrators who issued pro-Complainant rulings, and thus exerted influence over the outcomes of arbitrations in the UDRP system in order to market itself favorably to Complainants, who have the exclusive power to choose whether the NAF or a different provider will earn their business.
>
> ...
>
> 12. Fourth, the study found that case allocation by the NAF appeared to be heavily biased toward ensuring that a majority of cases were steered toward Complainant-friendly panels. Most troubling was data that suggested that, despite claims of impartial random case allocation as well as a large panel of panelists, the majority of NAF single panel cases were actually assigned to little more than a handful of panelists. Of the 1,379 NAF cases decided by a single NAF-assigned arbitrator through February 18, 2002, 778 of them—56.4%—were decided by only six arbitrators. (In comparison, the six busiest single panelists at the two other providers accounted for approximately 17% of those providers' single panel caseloads.
>
> ...
>
> 15. By assigning the majority of cases to the subset of arbitrators who ruled most consistently for its clients, the Complainants, the NAF exerted a great deal of influence over case outcome. When combined with the fact that outcome was the most decisive factor among Complainants choosing arbitration providers, and evidence that the NAF aggressively marketed its services to potential claimants by promoting Complainant wins, this data supports the conclusion that the NAF used its control over the selection of arbitrators in single panel cases to achieve outcomes that would enable it to attract the business of future UDRP Complainants.

Geist Affidavit, Ex. 20 hereto.

In addition to the power to select the arbitrator, the NAF rules extend all sorts of other crucial powers to NAF's director and staff, refuting the claim that it does not matter whether the NAF is structured in an inherently biased manner. The Rules give the Director the ability to grant extensions (Rule 9.D), hear motions (Rule 18), alter fees for intervention and hearings (Rule 19.B, 19.D), set the length of hearings (Rule 26), issue orders, including at his own initiative (Rule 38), request involuntary dismissal of a claim (Rule 41), waive fees (Rule 45), request sanctions (Rule 46), interpret the code (Rule 48.A), and change the code (Rule 48.F). See Rules of the National Arbitration Forum attached hereto as Exhibit 35.

5. Facts Relating to NAF's Propensity Towards Dishonesty

NAF and its principles have shown a disturbing propensity to say things that are simply untrue, where they think that doing so will induce a court to enforce an arbitration clause. Perhaps the best known example came from the case of *Toppings v. Meritech Mortgage Services, Inc.*, 569 S.E.2d 149 (W. Va. 2002), where the West Virginia Supreme Court of Appeals struck down a lender's arbitration clause as unconscionable. As will be discussed below, there, as here, the lender required its consumers to take all claims to the NAF, and the *Toppings* court held that this created impermissible structural incentives to bias.

When the plaintiffs first challenged the NAF as being biased in the *Toppings* case, NAF rushed to provide the defendant lenders with the names of well-regarded members of the State Bar, including a respected former Justice of the Supreme Court of Appeals of West Virginia, a Professor from West Virginia University College of Law, and well respected local attorneys it claimed would be arbitrators for arbitration proceedings in West Virginia. The problem is, NAF's representations were Completely false: not one of the arbitrators listed who was contacted had agreed to serve as an arbitrator for NAF at that time. *See* Affidavit of Bren Pomponio, Exhibit 26 hereto, at ¶ 6 ("Each of the people whom our office contacted replied that they had never agreed to work for the NAF as an arbitrator. At our request, some of these individuals subsequently wrote letters to the court and/or the NAF stating that they were not NAF arbitrators and that they objected to the NAF's false statement to the contrary.") *See also* Affidavit of Charles Disalvo, Exhibit 36 hereto. NAF evidently attempted to bolster the defendant lenders' argument that NAF was a neutral forum, and arbitration ought to be compelled by falsely including the names of respected attorneys from West Virginia.

NAF is also prone to attempting to deceive the general public. *See* Affidavit of Sally Greenberg, Senior Product Safety Counsel of Consumers Union, Exhibit 37 hereto at ¶ 6 ("I believe then, and continue to believe today, that the NAF solicitation letter badly misrepresented Consumers Union's position on mandatory arbitration."); and at ¶ 8 ("the NAF letter distorts the content of an article in Consumer Reports and misquotes and distorts the content of a book published by Consumers Union. Indeed, no honest reader of either Consumers Union publication could have drawn from them the conclusion claimed by NAF.")

Similarly, in a deposition in the *Toppings* case, NAF's principal Ed Anderson flatly testified that NAF had never promised to improve the "bottom lines" of its corporate clients. See Exhibit 15 at 69. This statement was untrue. See also letter from Curtis Brown to Robert S. Banks, Jan. 14, 1999, Exhibit 18 hereto. It is understandable that Mr. Anderson would wish to deny some of NAF's most inappropriate statements, but it is troubling that he would falsely do so in a deposition.

Also along these lines, Mr. Anderson has testified under oath that NAF had not represented to lenders that it would reduce their collection costs. See Exhibit 15 at 69. The truth, again, is quite different. See Exhibit 17, Attachment 8 (full page NAF advertisement asserting that "Arbitration can save up to 66% of your collection costs.")

The plaintiffs and the other parties to this litigation have a right to a neutral decision maker, not one who will say anything, regardless of the truth, to a court in order to ensure arbitration occurs and its financial interests are protected.

ARGUMENT

I. CHECK 'N GO'S MANDATORY INDIVIDUAL ARBITRATION CLAUSE VIOLATES NORTH CAROLINA PUBLIC POLICY AGAINST EXCULPATORY CLAUSES AND IS UNCONSCIONABLE

Despite the existence of federal and state policy favoring arbitration as a means of resolving disputes, "this public policy does not come into play unless a court first finds that the parties entered into an enforceable agreement to arbitrate." *Sears Roebuck and Co. v. Avery*, 163 N.C. App. 207, 211m 593 S.E.2d 424, 428 (2002). Accordingly, "before a dispute can be settled in this manner, there must first exist a valid agreement to arbitrate." *King v. Owen*, 166 N.C. App. at 248, 601 S.E.2d at 327. "The law of contracts governs the issue of whether there exists an agreement to arbitrate." *Id.* (quoting *Routh v. Snap-On Tools Corp.*, 108 N.C. App. 268, 271, 423 S.E.2d 791, 794 (1992)). Here, Check 'N Go cannot satisfy this threshold requirement because its mandatory individual arbitration clause violates North Carolina contract law prohibiting adhesive, exculpatory clauses in contracts affecting public interests, and is also procedurally and substantively unconscionable.

A. Check 'N Go's Arbitration Clause is Governed by North Carolina Law

As a threshold matter, Check 'N Go's footnoted assertion, <u>Brief at 13 n.6</u>, that Delaware (not North Carolina) law governs this arbitration clause because of its choice-of-law provision should be rejected. Under North Carolina's choice-of-law rules, a contractual choice of law clause cannot be enforced if *either* of the following conditions is met:

> (a) the chosen state has no substantial relationship to the parties or the transaction and there is no other reasonable basis for the parties' choice, or
>
> (b) application of the law of the chosen state would be contrary to a fundamental policy of a state which has a materially greater interest than the chosen state in the determination of the particular issue and which . . . would be the state of applicable law in the absence of an effective choice of law by the parties.

Cable Tel Services, Inc. v. Overland Contracting, Inc., 154 N.C. App. 639, 643, 574 S.E.2d 31, 33–34 (2002). Here, both of these conditions barring enforcement of a choice-of-law clause are present.

First, this case is between North Carolina consumers and North Carolina lenders over payday loan transactions that all took place within North Carolina. Therefore, this dispute between these North Carolina parties over these loans made in North Carolina can only reasonably be governed by North Carolina law. *See Bundy v. Commercial Credit Co.*, 200 N.C. 511, 516, 157 S.E. 860, 863 (1931) (finding parties' Delaware choice of law clause "immaterial" based on trial record that "[did] not disclose that any transaction took place in Delaware or that the parties even contemplated either the making or the performance of the contract in said State.")

Second, Plaintiffs' challenges to Check 'N Go's arbitration clause allege that the clause is an illegal exculpatory clause that violates North Carolina public policy, that it is unconscionable, and that it is unenforceable because the entire payday loan contract is illegal and void under numerous North Carolina consumer protection statutes. *See*, *infra* at §§ IB and C and III. To the extent Check 'N Go argues that Delaware law compels a contrary result on *all* of these questions, this result would violate the fundamental policies of North Carolina discussed herein. Therefore, the Delaware choice-of-law clause is invalid, and the case should be governed by the law of North Carolina, where all of the underlying payday loan transactions occurred and where all of the named parties reside.

B. The Mandatory Individual Arbitration Clause is an Illegal Exculpatory Clause

It is well-established law in North Carolina that "[c]ontracts which seek to exculpate one of the parties from liability for his own negligence are not favored by the law." *Hill v. Carolina Freight Carriers Corp.*, 235 N.C. 705, 71 S.E. 2d 133 (1952) (citation omitted). While exculpatory contracts are not prohibited *per se*, such a contract will not be enforced if "it violates a statute, is gained through inequality of bargaining power, or is contrary to a substantial public interest." *Fortson v. McClellan*, 131 N.C. App. 635, 636, 508 S.E.2d 549, 550 (1998) (quoting *Jordan v. Eastern Transit & Storage Co.*, 266 N.C. 156, 146 S.E.2d 43 (1966)).[8] Furthermore, the North Carolina Constitution provides that "every person for an injury done him in his lands, goods, person, or reputation shall have remedy by due course of law; and right and justice shall be administered without favor, denial, or delay." N.C. Const., Art. I, 18.[9]

Therefore, under North Carolina's public policy rule against enforcing adhesive, exculpatory contracts, the validity of Check 'N Go's mandatory individual arbitration clause turns on two factors: (1) whether it is *either* (a) an adhesion contract that is the result of unequal bargaining power between the company and its payday loan-borrowing customers, *or* (b) part of a contract whose subject matter is regulated therefore deemed to affect public interests; *and* (2) whether the arbitration clause's terms are exculpatory. As is demonstrated below, *all* of these conditions are easily established here. The arbitration clause therefore is contrary to public policy and unenforceable.

---

[8] *See also Tatham v. Hoke*, 469 F. Supp. 914, 917 (M.D.N.C. 1979) (liability-limiting contracts are "void as contrary to public policy . . . when they relate to transactions affected with a substantial public interest or colored by inequality of bargaining power."); *Hall v. Sinclair Refining Co., Inc.*, 242 N.C. 707, 710, 89 S.E.2d 396, 398 (1955) ("[C]losely related to the public policy test of determining the validity of these exemption clauses is the factor . . . of giving consideration to the comparable positions which the contracting parties occupy in regard to their bargaining strength."); *Miller's Mutual Fire Ins. Ass'n of Alton, Ill. v. Parker*, 234 N.C. 20, 22, 65 S.E.2d 341, 342 (1951) ("A provision in a contact seeking to relieve a party to the contract from liability for his own negligence may or may not be enforceable. It depends upon the nature and the subject matter of the contract, the relation of the parties, the presence or absence of equality of bargaining power and the attendant circumstances."); *cf. Fortson*, 131 N.C. App. at 638 (distinguishing case upholding liability waiver on grounds that earlier court "did not characterize the release as an adhesion contract involving unequal bargaining power and did not hold that such contracts involved a public interest.") (citation omitted).

[9] *See also*, N.C. Const., Art. I, 35 ("A frequent recurrence to fundamental principles is absolutely necessary to preserve the blessings of liberty.")

1. The Clause Resulted from Severely Unequal Bargaining Power.

It is clear beyond serious dispute that Check 'N Go's mandatory individual arbitration clauses here are products of extreme inequalities in bargaining power and commercial sophistication between the company and plaintiffs. As set forth in the statement of facts, Check 'N Go is a large, multi-state lending company, with over 1,000 store locations in 29 states, with annual revenues in excess of $12 million. *Supra* at § IIA. Plaintiffs, by contrast, are financially pressed consumers who were forced by their limited credit options into seeking out these high-interest payday loans to meet their basic living expenses. *Id.* It is hard to imagine a situation involving a greater disparity of bargaining power unless Microsoft Corporation begins to contract with homeless people.

In contrast to Check 'N Go's superior bargaining position, the Plaintiffs' lack of bargaining power is apparent. First, plaintiffs lacked any meaningful choice to obtain a loan without agreeing to arbitration, as almost every payday lender with an office in North Carolina requires prospective borrowers to sign arbitration clauses specifically prohibiting class actions. *Supra*, at § IIC. Second, the arbitration clauses imposed by Check 'N Go, like the other provisions in these payday loan contracts, were non-negotiable adhesive provisions. Plaintiffs were given no opportunity to negotiate over these arbitration clauses, but instead were hurried into signing them without any explanation given, while other customers were waiting behind them. *Supra* at § IIB. Third, even if plaintiffs could have negotiated with Check 'N Go, it would have been a hollow exercise because plaintiffs would not have known what it was they were negotiating. As Beth Weir explains in her affidavit, Check 'N Go's arbitration clause was so Complex that few if any payday loan customers could have understood it. *Supra*, at § IID. Therefore, Plaintiffs and the putative class members could not have obtained these loans anywhere in North Carolina without first agreeing to exempt their lender from class-wide liability.

Under North Carolina law, adhesive contract provisions resulting from unequal bargaining power are closely scrutinized, and will not be enforced if they relieve the stronger party from liability. *Fortson*, 131 N.C. App. at 637, 508 S.E.2d at 551, ("[A]n exculpatory contract will be enforced unless it . . . is gained through inequality of bargaining power."). This requirement for close scrutiny applies as well to adhesive arbitration clauses. *See Sciolino v. TD Waterhouse Investor Serv's, Inc.*, 149 N.C. App. 642, 645, 562 S.E.2d 64, 66 (2002) ("This apparent requirement for independent negotiation underscores the importance of an arbitration provision and militates against its inclusion in contracts of adhesion.") (citations omitted). Thus, North Carolina courts have struck down as against public policy exculpatory clauses in adhesive consumer contracts that resulted from disparities in bargaining power. *See, e.g., Gore v. Ball*, 279 N.C. 192, 202–03, 182 S.E.2d 389, 395 (1971) (striking warranty waiver in seed manufacturer's sale to farmers, noting that "[i]f such practice is sufficiently widespread among seed vendors and is sufficient to limit the vendor's liability, the farmer will find it virtually impossible to purchase seed with an effective right of recourse . . ."); *Jordan v. Eastern Transit & Storage Co.*, 266 N.C. 156, 163, 146 S.E.2d 43, 49–50 (1966) (striking liability limiting clause in warehouse storage contract).

Check 'N Go does not (and cannot) seriously dispute the record evidence showing that as a major provider of payday loans in a market where arbitration clauses are universal, it could impose these adhesive, non-negotiable, and incomprehensible arbitration clauses without having to worry about any opposition from its financially-strapped customers. Therefore, the Court should find that these clauses are the product of a severe inequality in bargaining power.

2. Check 'N Go's Payday Loans are Heavily Regulated and Affect Important Public Interests.

North Carolina's general prohibition against exculpatory clauses in adhesive contracts has been applied most frequently to contracts imposed by defendants in regulated industries. For example, in *Tatham v. Hoke*, 469 F. Supp. 914 (W.D.N.C. 1979), the district court, applying state law, invalidated a liability cap in a doctor-patient contract as contrary to public policy, finding in relevant part that "the contract is a contract for exculpation from liability of an enterprise that is heavily regulated by state authorities who have demonstrated the public interest in the activity and stated a desire to leave the regulated entities amendable to private suit as well as public review." *Id.* at 919.[10] *Tatham* held that, while "a clear and significant inequality of bargaining power must be demonstrated to support invalidation of a limitation of liability clause in the private sector, . . . a much lesser showing, if any, is required when the entity seeking exculpation is heavily infected with a public interest." *Id.* (citations omitted).

Similarly, in the present case, North Carolina has a "powerful public interest" in protecting North Carolina citizens against actors who violate the Consumer Finance Act. *See New Bern Pool & Supply Co. v. Graubart*, 94 N.C. App. 619, 625, 381 S.E.2d 156, 160 (1989) ("The interest of the State of North Carolina in providing consumer protection for its citizens and corporate entities and a forum for the adjudication of controversies involving them is substantial.")

Here, it is also beyond serious dispute that the payday lending industry is heavily regulated in North Carolina by various laws—such as the Consumer Finance Act, the Deceptive Trade Practices Act, the Check Casher Act, and state usury provisions—that are designed to protect consumers and the public from unscrupulous financial practices. The North Carolina General Assembly has attempted to regulate this industry for more than 80 years. This fact of heavy industry regulation is particularly true in North Carolina, where payday lending has been made illegal on at least two separate occasions and where one of Check 'N Go's biggest rivals, Advance America, has been the subject of State regulatory investigations concerning the legality of its operations. *Supra* at § IIG.

Since the record evidence plainly demonstrates *both* that there was severe inequality in bargaining power between Plaintiffs and Check 'N Go *and* that payday lending is heavily regulated out of a public concern for protecting consumers (though only one of the above need be shown), any provision in these payday loan contracts found to be exculpatory is contrary to public policy and cannot be enforced.

---

10 *See also Gore v. Ball*, 279 N.C. at 202–03, 182 S.E.2d at 294–396 (striking liability limitation in seed manufacturer's contract with farmers); *Jordan v. Eastern Transit*, 266 N.C. at 162–63, 146 S.E.2d at 48–49 (treating warehouse storage contract as subject to regulation of common carriers); *Fortson*, 131 N.C. App. at 638, 508 S.E.2d at 551 (motorcycle training course found to implicate public safety interests).

3. The Arbitration Clause's Class Action Ban is Effectively Exculpatory.

North Carolina's prohibition on exculpatory clauses in adhesive contracts that affect the public interest applies not only to clauses that explicitly strip parties of legal remedies, but also to terms that effectively strip them of these remedies by making it prohibitively burdensome to vindicate their claims.

As the Statement of Facts demonstrates, *supra* at § IIE, Check 'N Go's mandatory individual arbitration clause acts as an exculpatory clause for the types of claims Plaintiffs have here by prohibiting them from bringing these claims on a class-wide basis. Simply put, the Plaintiffs' claims are individually too small to be viable unless they can be aggregated into a class action. A host of fact and expert witnesses, including 18 private consumer lawyers and four North Carolina legal services lawyers who represent consumers, all testified that Check 'N Go's contractual ban on class actions will, if enforced, shield the company from liability to virtually all of its borrowers *without regard to the validity of these consumers' claims*.

Moreover, as an empirical matter, the exculpatory effect of Check 'N Go's class action ban is irrefutable. No Advance America customer has initiated an individual claim in arbitration against the company in the last eight years. *See supra* at § IIE. If the class action ban had no effect on a borrower's substantive rights, one would expect that Check 'N Go would face at least *some* individual arbitrations over eight years. The fact is, however, that these claims simply are not brought on an individual basis.

This unrebutted record evidence is consistent with decades of findings by the U.S. Supreme Court and other courts on the necessity of class actions for vindicating small-value consumer claims. In *Eisen v. Carlisle & Jacqueline*, 417 U.S. 156 (1974), the Supreme Court reversed a denial of class certification in an antitrust case based in part on its finding that:

> A critical fact in this litigation is that petitioner's individual stake in the damages award is only $70. No competent attorney would undertake this Complex antitrust action to recover so inconsequential an amount. Economic reality dictates that petitioner's suit proceed as a class action or not at all.

Id. at 161. More recently, the Supreme Court reiterated in addressing standards for class action settlements that "[t]he policy at the very core of the class action mechanism is to overcome the problem that small recoveries do not provide the incentive for any individual to bring a solo action prosecuting his or her rights." *Amchem Products, Inc. v. Windsor*, 521 U.S. 591, 617 (1997).[11]

These conclusions also are consistent with those reached by courts across the country in holding that provisions in consumer contracts banning class actions are exculpatory and therefore against public policy or unconscionable. In *Szetela v. Discover Bank*, 118 Cal. Rptr. 2d 862 (Cal. App. 2002), the court cogently set out the argument for why a provision banning class actions turns an ordinary arbitration clause into an exculpatory one, effectively acting as a "get out of jail free" card for corporate defendants:

> It is the manner of arbitration, specifically, prohibiting class or representative actions, we take exception to here. The clause is not only harsh and unfair to Discover customers who might be owed a relatively small sum of money, but it also serves as a disincentive for Discover to avoid the type of conduct that might lead to class action litigation in the first place. By imposing this clause on its customers, Discover has essentially granted itself a license to push the boundaries of good business practices to their furthest limits, fully aware that relatively few, if any, customers will seek legal remedies, and that any remedies obtained will only pertain to that single customer without collateral estoppel effect.... Therefore, the provisions violates fundamental notions of fairness.

Szetela, 96 Cal. App.4th at 1101, 118 Cal.Rptr.2d at 868.

Perhaps the leading case supporting this finding that a class action ban in a consumer contract covering small-money transactions is exculpatory is *Ting v. AT&T*, 182 F. Supp. 2d 902 (N.D. Cal. 2002), *aff'd in relevant part and reversed in part on other grounds*, 319 F.3d 1126 (9th Cir. 2003). In *Ting*, the federal district court conducted a trial over several questions concerning whether several provisions, including a class action ban, in the phone company's mandatory arbitration clause were unconscionable. Based upon extensive proof and testimony at trial, the district court found that the ban on class actions would operate as an exculpatory clause. This evidence showed that before AT&T adopted its arbitration clause, consumers had successfully prosecuted several class

---

11 *See also Deposit Guaranty Nat'l Bank v. Roper*, 445 U.S. 326, 338 n.9 (1980) ("Here, the damages claimed by the two named plaintiffs totaled $1,006.00. Such plaintiffs would be unlikely to obtain legal redress at an acceptable cost, unless counsel were motivated by the fee-spreading incentive and proceed on a contingent-fee basis. This, of course, is a central concept of Rule 23."); *Weiss v. Regal Collections*, 385 F.3d 337, 345 (3d Cir. 2004) ("Representative actions appear to be fundamental to the statutory structure of the [Fair Debt Collection Practices Act]," so that "lacking this procedural mechanism, meritorious FDCPA claims might go unredressed because the awards in an individual case might be too small to prosecute an individual action."); *Linder v. Thrifty Oil Co.*, 2 P.3d 27, 30–31 (Cal. 2000) ("Courts have long acknowledged the importance of class actions as a means to prevent a failure of justice in our judicial system."); *Riley v. New Rapids Carpet Center*, 294 A.2d 7, 10 (N.J. 1972) ("If each victim were remitted to an individual suit, the remedy could be illusory, for the individual loss may be too small to warrant a suit or the victim too disadvantaged to seek relief. Thus the wrongs would go without redress, and there would be no deterrence to further aggressions. If there is to be relief, a class action should lie unless it is clearly infeasible."); *Friar v. Vanguard Holding Corp.*, 434 N.Y.S.2d 698, 706 (App. Div. 1980) ("By construing the availability of class action relief narrowly, the judiciary is seen as denying access to the courts to thousands of individuals whose minimal damages are greatly outweighed by the prohibitive costs involved in prosecuting a lawsuit against a wealthy opponent."); *Cruz v. All Saints Healthcare Sys., Inc.*, 625 N.W.2d 344, 348–49 (Wis. App. 2001) ("[G]iven the economic realities of this case, class action may be the only effective means to implement the legislature's intent to provide redress for unreasonable charges... The individual amounts at issue are small and not likely to justify individual suits.")

actions against long distance phone carriers, including one where AT&T paid 100% of the class's damages and another where a rival carrier paid $88 million to consumers. *Id.* at 915. AT&T stipulated to the fact that none of the plaintiffs in those earlier cases could have brought them individually, whether in court or in arbitration. *Id.* Based on these and other facts in the record, the district court held that without the class action mechanism, "the potential reward would be insufficient to motivate private counsel to assume the risks of prosecuting the case just for an individual on a contingency fee basis." *Id.* Because of these economic realities, "the prohibition on class action litigation functions as an effective deterrent to litigating many types of claims involving rates, services or billing practices and, ultimately, . . . [serves] to shield AT&T from liability even in cases where it has violated the law." *Id.* Accordingly, the court found the ban on class actions unconscionable, *id.* at 931, and the U.S. Court of Appeals for the Ninth Circuit affirmed this holding.

A host of other federal and state courts have likewise held—all in cases where the factual record did not approach the record in this case—that consumer contracts that ban class actions amount to exculpatory clauses, and therefore are not enforceable.[12]

As the *Ting* district court found, it is clear that the availability or imposition of arbitration for small consumer claims does not ameliorate the consumers' need for the class device. Often, the same consumer claims that prove too expensive to *litigate* individually are also too expensive to *arbitrate* individually. *See* Jean R. Sternlight, *As Mandatory Binding Arbitration Meets the Class Action, Will the Class Action Survive?*, 42 Wm. & Mary L. Rev. 1, 90 n. 353 (2000) ("[W]here a class action is excluded from arbitration, it is likely that many if not most of the claimants will not be able to arbitrate their claims.").

The conclusions of plaintiffs' witnesses here, and the decisions cited above, are consistent with what corporate defense counsel regularly proclaim outside of court. As one defense lawyer admits, "the franchisor with an arbitration clause should be able to require each franchisee in the potential class to pursue individual claims in a separate arbitration. *Since many (and perhaps most) of the putative class members may never do that*, and because arbitrators typically do not issue runaway awards, *strict enforcement of an arbitration clause should enable the franchisor to dramatically reduce its aggregate exposure*." Edward Wood Dunham, *The Arbitration Clause as a Class Action Shield*, 16 Franchise L.J. 141, 141 (1997) (emphasis added). Another defense lawyer has described arbitration clauses as a "defense" for banks against consumer claims, in part because they can be a "deterrent" to class actions. Alan Kaplinsky, *Excuse Me, But Who's the Predator: Banks Can Use Arbitration Clauses as a Defense*, Bus. Law. 24, 26 (May/June 1998). *See also* Sternlight, *supra*, at 5 n. 2 ("Several commentators have urged companies in various industries to adopt mandatory binding arbitration, at least in part to avoid class actions.") (citing Dunham article and four others).[13]

Therefore, the overwhelming record evidence in this case and a considerable body of judicial and secondary authority establishes the following: (1) that Check 'N Go's mandatory individual arbitration clause is the product of extreme inequality in bargaining power between this payday lending giant and its financially-pressed borrowers; (2) that payday lending is a heavily regulated industry because of the significant public interest in protecting consumers; and (3) that the arbitration clause's explicit ban on class actions makes this an exculpatory clause that will effectively prevent Plaintiffs and other borrowers from vindicating their legal claims against Check 'N Go. For all of these reasons, the Court should hold that this mandatory individual arbitration clause is an illegal exculpatory clause that is contrary to public policy under North Carolina contract law.

C. The Mandatory Individual Arbitration Clause is Unconscionable

For many of the same reasons that Check 'N Go's arbitration clause violates public policy, it also is unconscionable. Under North Carolina contract law, "to find unconscionability there must be an absence of meaningful choice on part of one of the parties [procedural unconscionability] *together with* contract terms unreasonably favorable to the other [substantive unconscionability]." *State Farm Mutual Automobile Ins. Co. v. Atlantic Indemnity Co.*, 122 N.C. App. 67, 73, 468 S.E.2d 570, 573 (1996) (citations omitted) (emphasis in original). Here, there is abundant record

---

12 *See, e.g., Luna v. Household Fin. Corp. III*, 236 F. Supp. 2d 1166, 1178–79 (W.D. Wash. 2002) ("The Arbitration Rider's prohibition of class actions would prevent borrowers from effectively vindicating their rights for certain categories of claims."); *Kinkel v. Cingular Wireless, LLC*, 828 N.E.2d 812, 820–21 (Ill. App. 2005) ("[T]he ban on class-wide arbitration in a different version of Cingular's clause is substantively unconscionable because it effectively precludes consumers with small claims from seeking remedies."); *Whitney v. Alltell Communications, Inc.*, __ S.W.3d __, 2005 WL 1544777 at *5 (Mo. Ct. App. July 5, 2005) ("Here, plaintiff filed a putative class action challenging a charge of 88 cents per month. By itself, such a claim would not be economically feasible to prosecute. However, when all of the customers are added together, large sums of money are at stake. Prohibiting class treatment of these claims would leave consumers with relatively small claims without a practical remedy . . ."); *West Virginia ex rel. Dunlap v. Berger*, 567 S.E.2d 265, 278 (W.Va. 2002) ("In many cases, the availability of class action relief is a sine qua non to permit the adequate vindication of consumer rights."); *Discover Bank v. Superior Court*, 30 Cal. Rptr. 3d 76 (Cal. 2005); *Leonard v. Terminix Int'l Co.*, 854 So. 2d 529, 537 (Ala. 2002); *Eagle v. Fred Martin Motor Co.*, 809 N.E.2d 1161, 1183 (Ohio Ct. App. 2004); *In re Knepp*, 229 B.R. 821, 827 (N.D. Ala. 1999).

13 Check 'N Go argues, without reference to *any* record evidence, that the arbitration clause's class action ban is not exculpatory because awards of attorneys' fees are available to Plaintiffs under North Carolina's consumer protection statutes, and because other courts have upheld class action bans. Brief at 11, 16–17. With no supporting evidence showing that Plaintiffs' claims *in this case* would actually be brought, however, this is no answer to Plaintiffs' more than 20 affidavits from consumer lawyers saying they would *not* bring the Plaintiffs' claims here on an individual basis *despite the availability of fee-shifting awards*. *Supra* at 10; *cf. Discover Bank v. Superior Court*, 30 Cal. Rptr. 3d at 87 ("There is no indication other than these courts' unsupported assertions that, in the case of small individual recovery, attorney fees are an adequate substitute for the class action or arbitration mechanism. Nor do we agree with the concurring and dissenting opinion that small claims litigation, government prosecution, or informal resolution are adequate substitutes.") Nor is this an answer to the record evidence in this case showing that no consumer has ever brought an individual case against Check 'N Go to arbitration in the eight years its mandatory individual arbitration clause has been in effect.

evidence and case authority supporting findings of both procedural and substantive unconscionability.

As set forth in the statement of facts, the record in this case shows at least four different ways in which plaintiffs lacked meaningful choice over the arbitration clause: (1) there was an extreme imbalance in bargaining power and commercial sophistication between this payday lending giant and these financially-pressed consumers, *supra* at 6–7; (2) these arbitration clauses were non-negotiable adhesive provisions that were never explained to them and that they were hurried to sign, *id.* at 7–8; (3) every payday lender in North Carolina also requires borrowers sign arbitration clauses waiving class action rights and requiring arbitration only on an individual basis, *id.* at 8; and (4) the arbitration clause, as explained by readability expert Beth Weir, was drafted in such a Complex and incomprehensible way that few if any payday customers could have understood the meaning of its terms, *id.* at 8–9. Check 'N Go offers no evidence to the contrary.

Taken together, this evidence shows conclusively that Plaintiffs and the putative class of payday loan borrowers had no meaningful choice over these arbitration clause terms because they did not and could not understand their effect, they could not negotiate with Check 'N Go over them, and they could not obtain this type of short-term consumer credit from any other source except by acquiescing to nearly identical requirements for individual, non-class arbitration. Because of this lack of meaningful consumer choice over these exculpatory contract terms, the Court should find that this mandatory individual arbitration clause is procedurally unconscionable.[14]

This mandatory individual arbitration clause is also substantively unconscionable both because of its exculpatory effects discussed herein, *supra* at 17–22, and because these exculpatory effects are wholly one-sided, falling entirely upon consumers without burdening any of Check 'N Go's rights. Not only is this effectively exculpatory for the reasons discussed herein, but also because the exculpatory effects are wholly one-sided, falling entirely upon consumers without burdening any of Check 'N Go's rights. While the arbitration clause's ban on class actions effectively extinguishes plaintiffs' claims, it has no impact on Check 'N Go's legal rights because lending companies never bring class actions *against* consumers. The California Supreme Court recently described the unfairness of this one-sided waiver of rights as follows:

> Although styled as a mutual prohibition on representative or class actions, it is difficult to envision the circumstances under which the provision might negatively impact Discover Bank, because credit card companies typically do not sue their customers in class-action lawsuits.

Discover Bank v. Superior Court, 30 Cal. Rptr. 3d at 85 (quoting *Szetela*, 118 Cal. Rptr. 2d at 867).[15] Since North Carolina courts determine substantive unconscionability based on whether non-negotiable contract terms are "unreasonably favorable" to the party that dictated them, *State Farm*, 122 N.C. App. at 73, 468 S.E.2d at 573,[16] the Court should find here that Check 'N Go's one-sided arbitration clause stripping small-loan borrowers of the right to bring class-wide claims while preserving all of Advance America's own foreseeable claims is substantively unconscionable.[17]

Thus, plaintiffs' lack of meaningful choice over the terms of this arbitration clause, combined with the clause's one-sided class action ban extinguishing their small dollar claims while preserving all of Check 'N Go's legal rights, renders this arbitration clause unconscionable.

Check 'N Go's mandatory individual arbitration clause therefore is unenforceable for two separate and independent reasons: (1) It violates North Carolina public policy against adhesive, exculpatory

---

14 For cases finding that the presence or absence of market alternatives is relevant to determining procedural unconscionability, *see Brenner v. Little Red School House, Ltd.*, 302 N.C. 207, 213, 274 S.E.2d 206, 211 (1981) ("Plaintiff was not forced to accept defendant's terms, for there were other private and public schools available to educate the child."); *Ting v. AT&T*, 182 F. Supp. 2d at 929; *American General Finance v. Branch*, 793 So. 2d 738 (Ala. 2000); *Kloss v. Edward D. Jones & Co.*, 54 P.3d 1 (Mont. 2002) (finding lack of choice concerning arbitration in investment brokerage community in Montana); *cf. Alexander v. Anthony Int'l, LP*, 341 F.3d 256, 266 (3d Cir. 2003) (noting limited alternatives for employment among Virgin Islands oil refinery workers whose employer imposed mandatory arbitration clause). For cases finding that arbitration clauses promulgated in similar form contracts on a take-it-or-leave-it basis are procedurally unconscionable, *see Szetela*, 118 Cal. Rptr. 2d at 867; *Discover Bank v. Shea*, 827 A.2d at 365; *Powertel v. Bexley*, 743 So. 2d at 574–75; *cf. Luna*, 236 F. Supp. 2d at 1183 ("A party's status as a consumer is one of those circumstances. Washington courts have recognized that the consumer or commercial nature of a contract should be considered in the unconscionability inquiry.")

15 *See also Ting v. AT&T*, 319 F.3d at 1150 ("It is difficult to imagine AT&T bringing a class action against its own customers . . ."); *Luna*, 236 F. Supp. 2d at 1179 ("Although the Arbitration Rider's class action provision is nominally mutual, because there is no reasonable possibility that Household would institute a class action against its borrowers, the provision is effectively one-sided."); *Discover Bank v. Shea*, 827 A.2d 358, 366 (N.J. Super. Ct. 2001) ("The provision against class-wide relief in Discover's amendment benefits only discover, at the expense of individual cardholders. While Discover can use the provision to preclude class actions and, therefore, immunize itself completely from small claims, individual cardholders gain nothing, and in fact, are effectively deprived of their individual small claims.")

16 *See also Crowder Construction Co. v. Kiser*, 134 N.C. App. 190, 207, 517 S.E.2d 178, 190 (1999) ("[I]f the provisions are then viewed as so one-sided that the contracting party is denied any opportunity for a meaningful choice, the contract should be found unconscionable.") (citation omitted).

17 In the unlikely event the Court finds that Delaware law applies here (which it does not), the Delaware Supreme Court has struck down a similarly one-sided consumer arbitration clause as unconscionable and against public policy in *Worldwide Ins. Group v. Klopp*, 603 A.2d 788 (Del. 1992). In *Klopp*, the Delaware Supreme Court noted state policy favoring arbitration, but cautioned that arbitration cannot be required where it is "unfairly structured in that its effect is to allow the [company] to avoid a high award whether or not it is fair and just." *Id.* at 790 (citation omitted). The court then struck down the insurer's arbitration system that allowed for de novo appellate review *only* where an award exceeded $15,000 because it was unreasonably favorable to the insurer. *Id.* at 791 ("While high awards may be appealed by either party, common experience suggests that it is unlikely that an insured would appeal such an award.")

clauses; and (2) it is unconscionable. Therefore, Check 'N Go's motion to compel individual arbitrations should be denied.

II. THE FAA DOES NOT PREEMPT NORTH CAROLINA LAW PROHIBITING ENFORCEMENT OF EXCULPATORY CLAUSES AND CONTRACT TERMS FOUND TO BE UNCONSCIONABLE.

Check 'N Go spends much of its brief arguing that the FAA applies to its mandatory individual arbitration clause and that its application compels enforcement of this clause without regard to whether the clause comports with North Carolina contract law. But this heavy reliance on federal law is misguided because the FAA expressly preserves the application of state contract law, does not preempt any of the arbitration-neutral North Carolina contract law rules discussed herein, and is perfectly consistent with general principles of North Carolina contract law in prohibiting uses of arbitration that are exculpatory. Therefore, the FAA's application to this case does not alter the conclusion that Check 'N Go's mandatory individual arbitration clause violates public policy against exculpatory clauses and is unconscionable under North Carolina contract law.

A. There Is a Strong Presumption Against Finding Federal Preemption of State Contract Law

Because preemption constitutes a radical intrusion on a state's power, the U.S. Supreme Court has long recognized a strong presumption against preemption of state laws. In its most recent decision addressing federal preemption questions, the Court explained that:

> Because the States are independent sovereigns in our federal system, we have long presumed that Congress does not cavalierly pre-empt state law causes of action. In areas of traditional state regulation, we assume that a federal statute has not supplanted state law unless Congress has made such an intention clear and manifest.

Bates v. Dow Agrosciences, LLC, 125 S. Ct. 1788, 1801 (2005). North Carolina's common law of contracts and unconscionability are areas of traditional and almost exclusive state regulation. *See, e.g., Erie Railroad Co. v. Tompkins* 304 U.S. 64, 78 (1938) ("Congress has no power to declare substantive rules of common law applicable in a state . . .").

Where a federal statute has no express preemption provision and does not preempt an entire field of regulation, it only preempts state law if there is an "actual conflict," either because it is "impossible for a private party to comply with both . . . requirements," or because the state laws "stand[] as an obstacle to the accomplishment and execution of the full purposes of Congress." *Freightliner Corp. v. Myrick*, 514 U.S. 280, 287 (1995) (citations omitted). But this type of "implied conflict preemption" has no possible application where, as here, there is no federal law standard addressing the subject the state is regulating. *See id.* at 284–85 (holding that state tort law standard calling for antilock brakes on 18-wheel trucks was not preempted, finding that "it is not impossible . . . to comply with both federal and state law because there is simply no federal standard for a private party to comply with."); *id.* at 289–90 ("[a] finding of liability against petitioners would undermine no objectives or purposes with respect to ABS devices, since none exist."); *see also Sprietsma v. Mercury Marine*, 537 U.S. 51, 63–64 (2002) (finding no implied conflict preemption of common law tort claims in the absence of governing federal regulation).

B. The FAA Preempts Only Those State Laws That Frustrate its Purposes, and Expressly *Saves* General State Contract Law from Preemption

The FAA has no express preemption provision and does not reflect a congressional intent to occupy the entire field of arbitration or contract law. *Volt Info. Sciences, Inc. v. Bd. of Trustees of Leland Stanford Junior Univ.*, 489 U.S. 468, 477 (1989). Therefore, the FAA only preempts state laws whose application would frustrate the will of Congress by undermining the Act's policy goals by singling out arbitration agreements from other contracts for disfavored treatment. *Id.* at 477–78.

In addition, the FAA contains a savings clause which expressly provides that arbitration clauses will not be enforced if there are grounds under state contract law for invalidating the clause. 9 U.S.C. § 2. The U.S. Supreme Court has recognized that the defense of unconscionability under state contract law is available to a party challenging an arbitration agreement. *Doctor's Assocs., Inc. v. Casarotto* 517 U.S. 681, 687 (1996) ("[G]enerally applicable contract defenses, such as fraud, duress or unconscionability, may be applied to invalidate arbitration agreements without contravening [the F.A.A.].").[18] In other words, state contract law applies to arbitration clauses. *Perry v. Thomas* 482 U.S. 483, 492–93 (1987) ("An agreement to arbitrate is . . . enforceable, *as a matter of federal law*, 'save upon such grounds as exist at law or in equity for the revocation of any contract.' . . . Thus state law, whether of legislative or judicial origin, is applicable if that law arose to cover issues concerning the validity, revocability, and enforceability of contracts generally.") (emphasis in original, citations omitted).[19] *See also Discover Bank*, 113 P.3d 1100 (holding that the FAA does not preempt state unconscionability law).

State and federal courts across the country routinely apply these doctrines to strike down arbitration clauses with abusive terms inserted by companies that strip consumers and workers of their rights. While these decisions do not (and cannot) invalidate *all* arbitration clauses, these courts have used equitable principles of state contract law in dozens of cases to draw a line between valid uses of arbitration *as an alternative forum to court* and unconscionable uses of arbitration clauses *as effectively denying individuals*

---

18 *Cf. Allied-Bruce Terminix Cox., Inc. v. Dobson* (1995) 513 U.S. 265, 281 ("States may regulate contracts, including arbitration clauses, under general contract law principles."); *First Options of Chicago, Inc. v. Kaplan*, 514 U.S. 938, 944 (1995) (state law of contract formation determines existence of agreement to arbitrate).

19 Because the FAA expressly preserves application of generally applicable state contract law, Check 'N Go's heavy reliance on the Fourth Circuit's decision in *Snowden v. CheckPoint Check Cashing*, 290 F.3d 631 (4th Cir. 2002), Brief at 11, 16–17 , as support for its class action ban is misplaced. In *Snowden*, the Fourth Circuit held that an arbitration clause banning consumer class actions was *not* unconscionable, a holding that reflects the state of the law in Maryland, the state in which the claims in that case arose. *See, e.g., Gilman v. Wheat First Securities*, 692 A.2d 454 (Md. 1997) (upholding Virginia forum selection clause that would bar class actions). This rule of Maryland contract law that was decisive in *Gilman* and *Snowden* has no application here because this case is governed by North Carolina's rather than Maryland's contract law.

of any forum. An illustrative list of these decisions is enclosed as Exhibit 39.

C. North Carolina Contract Law Prohibiting Exculpatory Class Action Bans Does Not Conflict with the FAA's Policy of Placing Arbitration Clauses on the Same Footing as Other Contracts

While the FAA generally allows parties to enforce agreements providing for arbitration, federal law says nothing about whether Check 'N Go can include in an arbitration agreement a term barring consumer class actions. Check 'N Go argues to this Court as though federal policy allowing arbitration somehow also allows companies to exempt themselves from class actions whenever they want. But federal law says nothing of the sort.

There is nothing in the FAA requiring that arbitration be conducted on an individual basis. Indeed, the U.S. Supreme Court has held that arbitrations may be conducted on a class action basis. *See Green Tree Fin. Corp. v. Bazzle*, 125 S. Ct. 2402, 2405 (2003) (question of whether arbitration clause allows class actions is "a matter of state law"); *id.* at 2406 ("state law, not federal law, normally governs such matters") (Stevens, J. concurring in the judgment); *see also Discover Bank v. Superior Court*, 113 P.3d 1100, 30 Cal. Rptr. 3d 76, 91 (Cal. 2005) ("[T]here is nothing to indicate that class action and arbitration are inherently incompatible."). As further evidence that arbitrations may be handled on a class-wide basis, the American Arbitration Association has promulgated rules for handling class actions in arbitration, and has in fact handled quite a few cases on a class action basis. *See* American Arbitration Association, Supplementary Rules for Class Arbitrations (available at http://www.adr.org/sp.asp?id=21936).

Likewise, the many cases discussed herein where courts have found arbitration clauses barring consumer class actions unconscionable were pro- rather than anti-arbitration because they created a rule that *encouraged* arbitration of consumer claims that would not be brought under contracts requiring arbitration on an individual basis. *See Discover Bank v. Superior Court*, 30 Cal. Rptr. 3d at 90–91 (criticizing lower court opinion upholding class action ban as reflecting "the very mistrust of arbitration that has been repudiated by the United States Supreme Court.") (citation omitted). Moreover, the lack of any anti-arbitration bias by those courts that struck down class action bans is shown conclusively by the fact that they applied the same rule that other courts have applied in cases having *nothing to do with arbitration. See, e.g., America Online, Inc. v. Superior Court*, 90 Cal. App. 4th 1, 17–18 (2001) (striking down judicial forum selection and choice of law clause as unconscionable for barring class claims by consumers);[20] *cf. Weiss v. Regal Collections*, 385 F.3d 337, 345 (3d Cir. 2004) (barring defendant from "picking off" named plaintiff in class action with Rule 68 offer of judgment because practice would prevent consumers from bringing class-wide claims).

At bottom, Check 'N Go's motion to compel individual arbitrations isn't about arbitration at all, but about exculpation. If the Court refuses to enforce this arbitration clause, Check 'N Go would be able to write a new, legal contract and in the future hold all of their North Carolina customers to mandatory binding arbitration clauses if it so desires. The one thing that Check 'N Go cannot do, however, whether in court or arbitration, is take away from customers the ability to vindicate substantive rights by seeking class-wide relief through class action proceedings (whether in arbitration or in court). No one denies that the drafter of any contract could both require arbitration *and* Comply with the rule of law set forth in cases such as *Szetela*, *Ting* and *AOL*, merely by expressly providing that arbitrations could proceed on a class-wide basis. This fact alone demonstrates that state law prohibiting contractual bans on class actions withstands the FAA.

D. North Carolina Contract Law Prohibiting Exculpatory Contracts is Consistent with U.S. Supreme Court Cases Disallowing Exculpation Under the FAA

As set forth above, North Carolina law may only be found to be preempted by the FAA if it conflicts with Congress' purposes in enacting the FAA to such an extent that North Carolina law is an obstacle to the enforcement of federal law. In fact, North Carolina's law prohibiting exculpatory clauses is entirely consistent with the purposes of the FAA, as articulated by the U.S. Supreme Court. The Court has directed that arbitration clauses are enforceable under the FAA only if they make proceedings accessible so that claimants can effectively enforce their rights. *See, e.g., Gilmer v. Interstate/Johnson Lane Corp.* 500 U.S. 20, 26 (1991) (citation omitted) ("[B]y agreeing to arbitrate a statutory claim, a party does not forgo the substantive rights afforded by the statute; it only submits to their resolution in an arbitral, rather than a judicial, forum."). As an illustration of this principle, the Court has recognized that "the existence of large arbitration costs may well preclude a litigant... from effectively vindicating [its] rights," *Green Tree Financial Corp. v. Randolph* 531 U.S. 79, 81 (2000). The Court also has stated that arbitration is acceptable as an alternative to courts because it is simply a "different forum"—one with somewhat different and simplified rules—but nonetheless one where the basic mechanisms for obtaining justice permit a party to "effectively vindicate" his or her rights. *See, e.g., Equal Employment Opportunity Comm'n v. Waffle House, Inc.* 534 U.S. 279, 295 n.10 (2002).

Numerous other federal and state courts have held that particularly unfair or exculpatory arbitration clauses may be struck down without violating the FAA. In *Ting*, for example, the U.S. Court of Appeals for the Ninth Circuit flatly stated that "[w]e recognize, ... that the FAA preempts state laws of limited applicability, ... but we follow well settled Supreme Court precedent in rejecting the proposition that unconscionability is one of those laws." *Ting*, 319 F.3d at 1150, n. 15. In *Ticknor v. Choice Hotels Int'l, Inc.* 265 F.3d 931 (9th Cir. 2001), similarly, the defendant argued that the FAA preempts state laws of unconscionability as they relate to arbitration clauses. The Ninth Circuit rejected that argument for reasons that apply here: "Montana law pertaining to the unconscionability of arbitration clauses was the result of 'the application of general principles that exist at law or in equity for the revocation of any contract.'" *Ticknor*, 265 F.3d at 941, citing *Iwen*, 977 P.2d at 996.

These cases thus demonstrate that, notwithstanding the FAA, the anti-exculpatory and unconscionability principles of North Carolina law apply with full force to Check 'N Go's mandatory individual arbitration clause. The arbitration clause is therefore

---

20 *See also America Online, Inc. v. Pasieka*, 870 So. 2d 170, 171–72 (Fla. Dist. Ct. App. 2004) (following California *AOL* case); *Dix v. ICT Group, Inc.*, 106 P.3d 841, 845 (Wash. App. 2005) ("Requiring Ms. Dix and Mr. Smith to litigate their [Consumer Protection Act] claim in Virginia without the benefit of a class action procedure as is allowed in Washington... undermines the very purpose of the CFA, which is to offer broad protection to the citizens of Washington.")

unenforceable, and the motion to compel individual arbitrations should be denied.

III. CHECK 'N GO'S ARBITRATION CLAUSE IS UNENFORCEABLE BECAUSE IT IS PART OF AN ILLEGAL CONTRACT THAT IS VOID *AB INITIO* AND NEVER CAME INTO EXISTENCE

Additionally, there is no valid agreement to arbitrate because the arbitration clause at issue is part of an illegal contract that is void *ab initio*, and therefore none of its provisions—including the arbitration clause—ever came into existence.

A. Under General Principles of North Carolina Contract Law, Illegal Contracts Are Void *Ab Initio* and Unenforceable

It is a longstanding rule of general North Carolina contract law that contracts entered into for an illegal purpose and in violation of state statutes are void *ab initio* and cannot be enforced. *See Cauble v. Trexler*, 227 N.C. 307, 311, 42 S.E.2d 77, 80 (1947) ("Hence an agreement which violates a provision of a statute or which cannot be performed without a violation of such a provision is illegal and void."); *Pierce v. Cobb*, 161 N.C. 300, 77 S.E. 350, 350–51 (N.C. 1913). This principle continues to be applied today. *See, e.g., Carolina Water Serv., Inc. v. Town of Pine Knoll Shores*, 145 N.C. App. 686, 689, 551 S.E.2d 558, 560 (2001)

The reason that a void *ab initio* contract cannot be enforced is because it is non-existent: a contract that is void *ab initio* is considered not to have any legal force. "A void contract is no contract at all; it binds no one and is a mere nullity." *Bryan Builders Supply v. Midyette*, 274 N.C. 264, 270, 162 S.E.2d 507, 511 (1968) (quoting *Am. Jur. 2d Contracts*, § 7); *see also Sphere Drake Ins. Ltd. v. Clarendon Nat'l Ins. Co.*, 263 F.3d 26, 31 (2d Cir. 2001) (noting that the term "void contract" is a misnomer, "for '[i]f an agreement is void, it cannot be a contract.'" quoting 1 Samuel Williston & Richard A. Lord, *A Treatise on the Law of Contracts*, § 1:20, at 49 (4th ed. 1990)). Because an agreement that is illegal and void does not exist, no part of it can be carried out, as no party should be permitted to benefit from an illegal act. *See Lamm v. Crumpler*, 242 N.C. 438, 442, 88 S.E. 2d 83, 86 (1955).[21] Moreover, a court will not lend its assistance to any party to an illegal transaction. *See id.* at 443; *Cobb*, 161 N.C. 300 at 302, 77 S.E.2d 350.

It stands to reason that, just as every other provision of a contract that is illegal and void *ab initio* is unenforceable, an arbitration clause included in an illegal contract is void and unenforceable. Several courts have refused to enforce arbitration clauses contained in contracts alleged to be illegal. In *Cardegna v. Buckeye Check Cashing, Inc.*, 894 So.2d 860 (Fla. 2005), *cert. granted*, 125 S.Ct. 2937 (2005),[22] for example, the Florida Supreme Court refused to enforce in arbitration clause in a payday lending contract that was illegal under Florida law, holding that "an arbitration provision contained in a contract which is void under Florida law cannot be separately enforced while there is a claim pending in a Florida trial court that the arbitration clause containing the arbitration provision is itself illegal and void *ab initio*." *Id.*; *see also Alabama Catalog Sales v. Harris*, 794 So.2d 312, 317 (Ala. 2000) (holding that, in a case challenging the legality of payday loan contracts with arbitration clauses, "if the contracts are void and unenforceable, no claims arising out of or relating to the contracts are subject to arbitration"); *Sandvik v. Advent Int'l Group*, 220 F.2d 99, 108 (3d Cir. 2000); *Onvoy, Inc. v. Shal, LLC*, 669 N.W.2d 344, 354 (Minn. 2003). The reason for this is simple: arbitration is a creature of contract, and without a valid contract, there is no authority for an arbitrator to act. *See EEOC v. Waffle House, Inc.*, 534 U.S. 279, 293–94 (2002). As the Seventh Circuit succinctly stated with respect to arbitration: "No contract, no power." *Sphere Drake Ins., Ltd. v. All American Ins. Co.*, 256 F.3d 587, 591 (7th Cir. 2001); *see I.S. Joseph Co., Inc. v. Mich. Sugar Co.*, 803 F.2d 396, 399 (8th Cir. 1986) (noting that arbitrator has no source of authority outside the agreement of the parties). Thus, without a valid contract, there is no valid agreement to arbitrate, and plaintiffs' claims cannot be forced into arbitration.

B. Plaintiffs Have Alleged Colorable Claims That The Payday Loan Agreements At Issue Are Illegal and Void Ab Initio

In this case, defendants cannot enforce their illegal contract's arbitration clause because the entire contract is illegal and void. The arbitration clauses at issue are contained in plaintiffs' payday loan contracts. These contracts are illegal and void. Since at least 1992, when the North Carolina Attorney General issued an opinion declaring that payday lending violates the North Carolina Consumer Finance Act, G.S. § 53-166 as well as G.S. § 14-107, defendants have known that their payday loan contracts have an illegal purpose. *See* 60 N.C. Op. Atty. Gen. 86 (Jan. 24, 1992). Moreover, the State Commissioner of Banks currently is considering whether industry rival Check 'N Go's payday loan contracts violate the Consumer Finance Act, and is set to rule on that question next month. Thus, the forthcoming ruling from the Commissioner of Banks will determine whether defendants' payday loan contracts are illegal and void.

Additionally, plaintiffs have specifically alleged in the Complaint that defendants' loan contracts were made for an illegal purpose and violate various North Carolina statutes, including § 53-166 and the North Carolina Unfair Trade Practices Act, § 75-1.1. Plaintiffs have alleged colorable claims that Check 'N Go's loans run afoul of these statutes and thus are illegal and void. Because plaintiffs allege that their payday loan agreements are illegal and void *ab initio*, Check 'N Go's efforts to compel arbitration arising from those agreements must be rejected.

C. Refusing To Enforce Defendants' Arbitration Clauses Comports With Federal Law

Finally, no principle of federal law overrides this rule of North Carolina contract law that illegal contracts are void to require

---

21 Although the general rule is that no part of an illegal contract will be enforced, the non-offending provisions of an illegal contract can be enforced if the illegal part of the contract "does not constitute the main or essential feature or purpose of the agreement." *Rose v. Vulcan Materials Co.*, 282 N.C. 643, 658 (N.C. 1973). That exception is inapplicable here, however, because the main purpose of the agreement—the payday loan transaction—is precisely the part of the agreement plaintiffs allege to be illegal.

22 On June 20, 2005, the United States Supreme Court granted *certiorari* in *Cardegna* in order to determine whether, as a matter of federal law, an arbitration clause in an illegal and void *ab initio* contract can be enforced. 125 S.Ct. 2937. Because of the factual similarity between this case and *Cardegna*, in that both cases involve the enforceability of arbitration clauses in illegal payday loan contracts, the Court's ruling may provide instruction as to the enforceability of the arbitration clauses at issue here.

enforcement of an arbitration clause contained in a void contract. Plaintiffs' position that the arbitration clauses here are part of an illegal contract and cannot be enforced is consistent with the United States Supreme Court's decision in *Prima Paint Corp. v. Flood & Conklin Mfg. Co.*, 388 U.S. 395 (1967). In that case, the Court held that when a party alleges that an arbitration clause is unenforceable because it is contained in a contract that was fraudulently induced, the argument as to whether the contract is fraudulently induced must be decided by an arbitrator rather than by a court. *See id.* at 403–04. The Court established what is now known as the "separability" doctrine, holding that with respect to validly-created contracts, challenges directed at the contract as a whole are decided by an arbitrator while challenges directed specifically at the arbitration clause are decided by a court. *See id.*

The *Prima Paint* rule is inapplicable here because it applies only to voidable contracts, not contracts that are void *ab initio*. *Prima Paint* involved a contract alleged to be voidable on the ground that it was fraudulently induced. Unlike a contract that is void *ab initio*, a voidable contract exists as an enforceable contract subject to ratification or rejection by one of the parties to the agreement. *See, e.g.*, Restatement (Second) Contracts, § 7. Therefore, because an arbitration clause embedded in a voidable contract has come into existence, disputes as to the enforceability of the contract as a whole can be sent to arbitration. A void *ab initio* contract, by contrast, never came into being and therefore no basis exists for enforcing the arbitration agreement contained within it. Consequently, a number of courts have held that the *Prima Paint* separability rule applies only to voidable contracts, and not to contracts that are void *ab initio*. *See, e.g.*, *Cardegna*, 894 So.2d 860 (holding that *Prima Paint* does not apply to a challenge to the legality of a payday loan contract); *Onvoy, Inc.*, 669 N.W.2d 344; *Harris*, 794 So.2d at 316–17 (refusing to apply *Prima Paint* rule to challenge to the legality of a payday loan contract).[23] Thus, *Prima Paint* does not require this case to be sent to arbitration.[24]

---

23 *Weis Builders, Inc. v. Kay S. Brown Living Trust*, 236 F. Supp. 2d 1197, 1203–04 (D. Colo. 2002); *Sandvik v. Advent Int'l Group*, 220 F.3d 99 (3d Cir. 2000); *Sphere Drake*, 263 F.3d at 31–32; *Sphere Drake*, 256 F.3d at 589–91; *Three Valleys Municipal Water Dist. v. E.F. Hutton & Co.*, 925 F.2d 1136, 1140–41 (9th Cir. 1991); *I.S. Joseph*, 803 F.2d at 399–400; *Pittsfield Weaving Co., Inc. v. Grove Textiles, Inc.*, 430 A.2d 638 (N.H. 1981); *cf. Hotels Nevada v. Bridge Banc, LLC*, ___ Cal.Rptr.3d ___, 2005 WL 1595278 (Cal. App. July 8, 2005) (holding that in a case governed by the FAA, "[u]nder California law, the question whether the contract as a whole is illegal is one for the court to decide").

24 A few courts, including the Fourth Circuit, have held that *Prima Paint* requires that claims alleging that a contract as a whole is illegal and void *ab initio* be decided by an arbitrator. *See, e.g.*, *Snowden v. Checkpoint Check Cashing*, 290 F.3d 631, 637–38 (4th Cir. 2002); *Bess v. Check Express*, 294 F.3d 1298, 1305–06 (11th Cir. 2002); *Burden v. Check Into Cash*, 267 F.3d 483 (6th Cir. 2001); *cf. Keel v. Private Business, Inc.*, 594 S.E.2d 796, 798–99 (N.C. App. 2004) (acknowledging the separability doctrine). These courts have distinguished between contracts that are void because a party never assented to the agreement in the first place, and contracts that are void because they violate a statutory provision. Under North Carolina law, both contracts that lack assent and contracts that violate a voiding statute are "void." *See Marriott Financial Services v. Capitol Funds, Inc.*, 288 N.C. 122, 128, 217 S.E.2d 551, 555 (1975) ("The general

---

Indeed, to apply *Prima Paint* here would disrupt general principles of North Carolina contract law by creating a special rule making arbitration clauses enforceable in situations where no other contractual provision would be enforced. Such a rule is improper for two reasons. First, it would allow the defendants unfairly to benefit from their illegal activities by enforcing the arbitration clause in an illegal contract. *See Lamm*, 242 N.C. at 442–43. Under defendants' interpretation, a person who included an arbitration clause in a contract to sell crack cocaine or to carry out a murder would be allowed to demand that any question over the contract's legality be decided in accordance with that contract's arbitration clause. Second, carving out a unique exception for arbitration clauses turns on its head the cardinal purpose of the Federal Arbitration Act which is to "make arbitration agreements as enforceable as other contracts, but not more so." *Prima Paint*, 388 U.S. at 404 n.12.

The separability rule of *Prima Paint* also does not apply here because the rule only governs proceedings in federal court, not in state court. In determining the ultimate question at issue in *Prima Paint*—whether the arbitration clause was severable from the rest of the contract—the Court held that the separability doctrine derives from § 4 of the FAA, which requires a court to order a dispute into arbitration, if "the making of the agreement for arbitration or the failure to Comply (with the arbitration agreement) is not in issue." *Prima Paint*, 388 U.S. at 403. The Court determined that because a challenge to the contract as a whole rather than just to the arbitration agreement does not put in issue the making of the arbitration agreement, Section 4 requires the challenge to be sent to arbitration. *See id.* at 403–04 ("But the statutory language [of § 4] does not permit the *federal court* to consider claims of fraud in the inducement of the contract generally." (emphasis added)). The Court never indicated that its decision rested on § 2 of the Act, or any of the other of the Act's substantive provisions.

Section 4 of the FAA, by its own terms, is a procedural rule that applies only to actions brought in federal court, and therefore the *Prima Paint* rule, which is an interpretation of Section 4, does not apply here. Section 4 states that a party aggrieved by a failure to arbitrate may petition to compel arbitration in "any United States district court" that would otherwise have jurisdiction, and that service of the petition shall be governed by the Federal Rules of Civil Procedure. 9 U.S.C. § 4. The statutory language clearly limits

---

rule is that an agreement which violates a constitutional statute or municipal ordinance is illegal and void."); *Mazda Motors of America, Inc. v. Southwestern Motors, Inc.*, 36 N.C. App. 1, 14, 243 S.E.2d 793, 802 (1978), *reversed* 296 N.C. 357, 250 S.E.2d 250 (1979) on ground of legislative intent as to meaning and effect of N.C.G.S. § 20-305(6) ("As failure to give the required notice to the Commissioner was unlawful, the "voluntary agreement" without such notice was contrary to the statutory provisions and, thereby, to public policy. It was therefore illegal and void ab initio. 3 Strong, N.C. Index 3d, Contracts, s 6, pp. 374–5."). In contrast, N.C.G.S. § 53-166(d) is clear and unambiguous: contracts in violation "shall be void." In fact, the reasoning of those courts distinguishing between lack of assent and illegality does not appear to be grounded in any recognized principle of contract law, and has received criticism for that very reason. *See Match-E-Be-Nash-She-Wish Band of Pottawatomi Indians v. Kean-Argovitz Resorts*, 383 F.3d 512, 518–21 (6th Cir. 2004) (Cleland, J., concurring).

its application to federal court, and the Supreme Court has emphasized that "we have never held that §§ 3 and 4 [of the FAA], which by their terms appear to apply only to proceedings in federal court, are nonetheless applicable in state court." *Volt Info. Sciences, Inc. v. Bd. of Trustees of Leland Stanford Junior Univ.*, 489 U.S. 468, 476 n.6 (1989). Building on both the plain language and the Supreme Court's interpretation of the Act, other courts have also held that the reach of § 4 does not extend to state courts. *See Wells v. Chevy Chase Bank*, 768 A.2d 620, 625–26 (Md. 2001).

This conclusion that the *Prima Paint* rule applies only in federal courts is confirmed by *Prima Paint* itself. There, the Court emphasized that its holding was directed toward federal courts, stating that it was merely deciding "whether Congress may prescribe how *federal courts* are to conduct themselves with respect to subject matter over which Congress plainly has the power to legislate." *Prima Paint*, 388 U.S. at 405 (emphasis added). Since *Prima Paint* does not apply in state court, it does not overturn well-settled principles of North Carolina contract law that illegal contracts are void *ab initio* and unenforceable.[25] Because the contracts containing the arbitration clauses at issue here never came into existence, plaintiffs' claims cannot be sent into arbitration.

IV. CNG'S ARBITRATION CLAUSE IS UNCONSCIONABLE BECAUSE IT REQUIRES ITS CUSTOMERS TO SUBMIT ALL OF THEIR CLAIMS TO NAF

A. Federal and North Carolina Constitutional Law Recognize a Right to a System Designed to Produce a Neutral Decision Maker

The North Carolina State Constitution requires "remedy by due process of law" for all injured parties, as well as the administration of justice "without favor." N.C.G.S.A. Art. I, § 18. The Supreme Court of North Carolina has interpreted this due process guarantee, citing the United States Constitution, as requiring an impartial decision-maker. *County of Lancaster v. Mecklenburg County*, 334 N.C. 496, 511 (1993). In that case, the Court articulated a test for impartiality, holding that "an elected official with a direct and substantial financial interest in a zoning decision may not participate in making that decision." *Id.* Further, "[w]here there is a specific, substantial, and readily identifiable financial impact on a member, nonparticipation is required." *Id.*

In *County of Lancaster*, the court considered a scenario in which a request for a zoning permit was submitted to the Zoning Administrator, whose job security was alleged to be dependent upon the good graces of the Board of Commissions, the party making the request for a zoning permit. *Id.* at 500. In *County of Lancaster*, however, the court found no due process violation because the decision-maker's job security was "protected by certain personnel policies and regulations, which would prohibit the termination or demotion of Mr. Brandon by his supervisors except for cause." *Id.*

The United States Supreme Court has embraced the fundamental principle that decision makers should not be tainted by a financial interest in *Ward v. Village of Monroeville*, 409 U.S. 57 (1972). That case involved a mayor who had overall authority over the village affairs; the village's income derived, in large part, upon "the fines, forfeitures, costs and fees imposed by him in his mayor's court." 409 U.S. at 58. Even though the mayor did not personally profit from fines levied against alleged violators, the Court found that " 'possible temptation' may also exist when the mayor's executive responsibilities for village finances may make him partisan to maintain the high level of contribution from the mayor's court." *Id.* at 60. Similarly, in this case, Check 'N Go's arbitration system makes the officials running the NAF (who select the arbitrators and operate the system), and the arbitrators themselves, dependent upon Check 'N Go's continued good will for continued income.

In California, similarly, a fee-per-case systems for judicial decision makers violate due process. In *Haas v. County of San Bernadino*, the California Supreme Court recognized the fundamental concept that " '[a] fair trial in a fair tribunal is a basic requirement of due process.' " 27 Cal.4th 1017, 1025 (2002) (citation omitted). Consistent with this fundamental right, the Court held unconstitutional a system that allowed counties to select temporary administrative hearing officers on an *ad hoc* basis, paying them according to the number and duration of their cases:

> The requirements of due process are flexible, especially where administrative procedure is concerned, but they are strict in condemning the risk of bias that arises when an adjudicator's future income from judging depends on the goodwill of frequent litigants who pay the adjudicator's fee.

Id. at 1037. The court in *Haas* made clear that "The risk of bias caused by financial interest need not manifest itself in overtly prejudiced, automatic rulings in favor of the party who selects the arbitrator." 27 Cal.4th at 1030. However, "that such a temptation can arise from the hope of future employment as an adjudicator is easy to understand and impossible in good faith to deny." *Id.*

B. North Carolina State Contract Law Should Find Unconscionable Any Contract of Adhesion that Requires a Consumer to Submit His or Her Claims to A Decision Maker With an Incentive to Favor the Stronger Party

Ward and *Haas* both involved state actors, and thus the cases turned on a finding of unconstitutionality, not unconscionability. However, it should be beyond argument that an adjudicative system that is so biased as to be unconstitutional when imposed by powerful state actors must also be unconscionable when imposed by powerful corporations against individual litigants. This was the crux of a recent opinion from the West Virginia Supreme Court, which cited *Haas* for the proposition that "an impermissible structural unfairness in a tribunal, *be it judicial or arbitral*, would be presumed where the decision-maker is designated by one of the parties to a dispute and where the person making the decisions is compensated on a fee-per-case." *State ex rel Dunlap v. Berger*, 567 S.E.2d 265 (W.Va. 2002) (emphasis added); *see also Toppings v. Meritech Mortgage Servs. Inc.*, 569 S.E.2d 149 (2002) (extending the reasoning in a West Virginia case involving the unconstitutionality of a statute giving judicial officials a pecuniary interest in their cases to the context of private arbitration, and holding that an arbitration system in which disputes were submitted to an arbitration service provider compensated on a per-case basis "so im-

---

25 Although some North Carolina courts have referred to the severability doctrine of *Prima Paint*, *see Keel v. Private Business, Inc.*, 163 N.C. App. 703, 705–06 (N.C. App. 2004); *Eddings v. S. Orthopaedic & Musculoskeletal Assocs.*, 605 S.E.2d 680, 684 (N.C. App. 2004), in neither case did the court address the question of whether the doctrine is binding on state courts in addition to federal courts. Specifically, neither court considered whether the *Prima Paint* rule derived from FAA § 4 and therefore was limited only to federal courts.

pinges on neutrality and fundamental fairness that it is unconscionable and unenforceable under West Virginia law."). Accordingly, plaintiffs urge this Court to apply the principles of *County of Lancaster*, *Ward* and *Haas* in the way that the West Virginia Supreme Court did in *Toppings*, and hold that just as such a system would be unconstitutional if imposed by state actors, it is unconscionable when imposed by private actors such as Check 'N Go, and it must not be enforced under North Carolina law.

While there are no North Carolina cases on the point, it is well established in other jurisdictions that arbitration clauses which require arbitration by non-neutral arbitrators are unconscionable. In *Graham v. Scissor-Tail*, for example, the California Supreme Court held a person cannot serve as an arbitrator if "his interests are so allied with those of [a] party that, for all practical purposes, he is subject to the same disabilities which prevent the party [to the contract] himself from serving." 28 Cal.3d. 807, 827 (1981). The court concluded the designated arbitrator in that case could not be expected to arbitrate with the required degree of "disinterestedness and impartiality," and refused to enforce the arbitration clause before it. *Id.* at 828.

Many other courts have refused to compel arbitration in settings where the arbitrators' neutrality were compromised. In *Hooters of America, Inc. v. Phillips*, 173 F.3d 933 (4th Cir. 1999), the Fourth Circuit refused to compel arbitration in a case where an employer's arbitration rules were "crafted to ensure a biased decisionmaker." *Id.* at 938. Noting that the employer had complete control over the selection of two of the three arbitrators on a panel, to the point where even managers of the employer could be on the list of arbitrators, the court noted that "the selection of an impartial decisionmaker would be a surprising result." *Id.* at 939. Accordingly, the court (which in general expressed fervent admiration for arbitration) held that the employer had created "a sham system unworthy even of the name of arbitration," and thus held that the employer had breached its contractual obligation to provide an impartial arbitral forum. *See also Hudson v. Chicago Teachers Union Local No. 1*, 743 F.2d 1187 (7th Cir. 1984), *aff'd*, 475 U.S. 292 (1986) (arbitrator not independent where she or he was to be picked by and paid by union); *Cheng-Canindan v. Renaissance Hotel Assocs.*, 57 Cal. Rptr. 2d 867 (Ct. App. 1996), *rev. denied*, 1997 Cal. LEXIS 817 (1997) (procedure was so dominated by an employer that it did not even qualify as arbitration and would not be compelled); *Ditto v. Re/Max Preferred Properties, Inc.*, 861 P.2d 1000 (Okla. Ct. App. 1993) (where only one party had a voice in selection of arbitrator, clause would not be enforced); *In re Cross & Brown Co.*, 167 N.Y.S.2d 573, 575 (App. Div. 1957) (not enforcing an arbitration agreement between a real estate broker and his employer because it appointed the employer's Board of Directors as arbitrator. This contravened the "well-recognized principle of 'natural justice' that a man may not be a judge in his own cause.").

It is important to note that these courts have struck down these arbitration clauses due to concerns with structural bias, and did not require a showing that a particular arbitrator was corrupt. According to many lender defendants who have defended against arbitrator bias challenges, it is not enough that an arbitration system is structured in an unfair way, instead a consumer must prove that the arbitrator appointed to a given case is personally corrupt. In fact, as the prior illustrations establish, many courts have not held themselves to such an impossible standard of specificity. One example brings this conclusion home with particular force, however. When the Fourth Circuit held it was not legal for Hooters Restaurant's arbitration clause to make it possible for a Hooters manager to decide a sexual harassment case against Hooters, the court did not initiate an inquiry into the purity of heart and good intentions of each Hooters manager. Instead, the Court flatly declared that Hooters's system had a basic level of unfairness built into the system and declared it to be illegal. *See Hooters*, 173 F.3d at 938–40.

C. Check 'N Go's Arbitration Clause Requires Consumers to Submit their Claims to An Arbitration Company With An Incentive to Favor Check 'N Go

As set forth above, NAF and its arbitrators only get paid if the corporations who write arbitration clauses—and particularly the lenders on whom NAF relies for most of its income—continue to bring cases to it. Accordingly, Check 'N Go's system—which unlike Advance America or Check Into Cash, requires consumers to submit their claims to the NAF alone—makes the NAF directly dependent upon repeat business from a lender. If Check 'N Go is unhappy with NAF's results, it can simply name another arbitration corporation who wants its business even more desperately (if that can be imagined). Accordingly, NAF is a decision-maker "with a direct and substantial interest" in the outcome of a decision in a dispute. As a result, it should be prohibited from participation in making that decision, for the same reasons that the court in *County of Lancaster* delineated in considering the role of an elected official. In any case involving the resolution of disputes between parties, there is a state interest in the administration of justice "without favor," under the North Carolina State Constitution. N.C.G.S.A. Art. I, § 18. An arbitration company whose livelihood is directly linked to its making lender-favorable decisions betrays "a specific, substantial, and readily identifiable financial impact" on the arbitration company, as a result of its decisions, and it should therefore fail the tests of impartiality both under the North Carolina Supreme Court's test for impartiality in *County of Lancaster* and the due process requirement of the State Constitution.

Where, as here, the neutrality of an arbitration service provider is likely compromised because of the incentive inherent in a system whereby a powerful corporate party imposes its own chosen arbitration service that is paid on a fee-per-case basis, arbitration does not operate as a fair substitute to a judicial forum. An arbitration clause that compels arbitration before an arbitrator who is designated by one party and who is paid under a fee-per-case system is substantively unfair and therefore unconscionable under North Carolina law.

A number of authorities have noted that the generally applicable principles set forth in *Ward*, *County of Lancaster* and *Haas* apply commentators are equally true with respect to arbitrators. NAF is only one of several large arbitration service providers, all competing for the same business. In this competitive marketplace, an obvious implication hangs over NAF's business like a cloud: were it to rule against a large company, such as a franchisor, too often (from the franchisor's viewpoint), or in too great an amount, then franchisors could easily take their business to other arbitration service providers. As one commentator has written:

> [A]rbitrators may be consciously or unconsciously influenced by the fact that the company, rather than the consumer, is a potential source of repeat business. An arbitrator who issues a large

punitive damages award against a company may not get chosen again by that company or others who hear of the award.

Jean Sternlight, *Panacea or Corporation Tool? Debunking the Supreme Court's Preference for Binding Arbitration*, 74 Wash. U.L.Q. 637, 685 (1996) (footnote omitted).

One court recognized this "repeat player" problem in an arbitration clause that, like the one here, allowed the stronger party to pick the arbitration forum, and the arbitral forum to select a closed list of arbitrators for any dispute taken to that forum. In *Mercuro v. Superior Court*, 96 Cal. App. 4th 167 (2002), the court examined an employment contract that required arbitration before the NAF, which then provided parties with a list of its arbitrators from which they could choose one. The plaintiff argued that this system did not guarantee a neutral arbitrator, given the size of the defendant's business and the likelihood that it would enlist the NAF in multiple arbitration proceedings, whereas the employee himself would only participate in this one arbitration. *Id.* at 178. The Court there agreed that "The fact an employer repeatedly appears before the same group of arbitrators conveys distinct advantages over the individual employee. These advantages include knowledge of the arbitrators' temperaments, procedural preferences, styles and the like and the arbitrators' cultivation of further business by taking a 'split the difference' approach to damages." *Id.* The court found that this factor, in combination with the general lack of mutuality in the arbitration provision, rendered the provision substantively unconscionable. *Id.* at 179

The Equal Employment Opportunity Commission, similarly has stated in the employment context, "results cannot but be influenced by the fact that the employer, and not the employee, is a potential source of future business for the arbitration." Gilbert F. Caselias, *Policy Statement on Mandatory Binding Arbitration of Employment Discrimination Disputes as a Condition of Employment*, 11 EEOC Compliance Manual at 8 (July 10, 1997); *see also* Richard C. Rueben, *The Dark Side of ADR*, Cal. Law. 53, 54 (Feb. 1994) (quoting an attorney experienced in litigating arbitration claims as stating, "Anytime you are paying someone by the hour to decide the rights and liabilities of litigants, and that person is dependent for future business on maintaining good will with those who will bring him business, you've got a system that is corrupt at its core"); David Schwartz, *Enforcing Small Print to Protect Big Business: Employee and Consumer Rights Claims in an Age of Compelled Arbitration*, 1997 Wisc. L. Rev. 33, 61 ("[T]he independent arbitration companies have an economic interest in being looked on kindly by large institutional corporate defendants who can bring repeat business.").[26]

It is important to note that this "repeat player" problem is not endemic to arbitration, but rather occurs as a result of arbitration clauses that single out one arbitration provider as the sole provider for all adjudicative services for a particular company. Thus plaintiffs' argument here is not a generalized attack on arbitration, but rather an argument that a specific system—one that operates on a fee-per-case compensation basis and where one party selects the arbitral forum—is inherently biased and unconscionable under North Carolina law.

D. The Bias Issue Here Is Not Inherent to Arbitration, But Arises From Check 'N Go's Misuse and Abuse of the Arbitration Forum

It would have been easy for Check 'N Go to draft an arbitration clause that gave the parties a choice among, for example, the three largest arbitration providers in the country: the AAA, the National Arbitration Forum, and JAMS. Such a clause would take away any incentive for one provider to curry favor with the contract drafter, since the other party would likely not then select that provider to arbitrate her dispute. Such clauses are used by several other defendants in companion cases to this one, including Advance America and Check Into Cash. They are also used by a number of other companies across the U.S.[27]

However, Check 'N Go did not include such a clause, and instead drafted an agreement in which the arbitration provider, NAF, is designated by only one party, and NAF then provides a closed list of arbitrators for the parties to select. This is precisely the systematic flaw identified in cases such as *Toppings* and *Mercuro*: NAF and its arbitrators have a pecuniary interest in the cases they hear, and if they rule against the corporations very often, they will risk losing that business to one of the other large arbitration providers such as AAA or JAMS. In short, Check 'N Go's arbitration system encourages arbitrators to rule in favor of lenders, rather than "bite the hand that feeds them."

An arbitration system like the one at issue here—in which arbitrators are compensated through a fee-per-case system and one party selects the decision maker forum—is inherently biased on its face, making the facts concerning any individual such system unnecessary to the ultimate question. But the practical importance of this legal question becomes clear from the factual record, which contains substantial evidence that the arbitration service provider at issue in this case—the for-profit NAF—has been profoundly influenced by the market reality that its business depends upon referrals from and the good favor of lenders.

E. NAF's Conduct Demonstrates the Pitfalls Inherent in a Biased Arbitration System that Has a Built-in Incentive to Favor One Party

There is an inherent bias in the fee-per-case system, creating an incentive for NAF arbitrators to rule for lenders in order to garner repeat business. In addition to employing a system with this general structural defect, NAF's behavior exemplifies the concerns highlighted in cases such as *Ward* and *County of Landcaster*. As the Statement of Facts sets forth in great detail, in a series of improper communications, NAF has repeatedly made clear that it sees its role as one of helping corporate lenders reduce and resist legitimate

---

26 A study of the results of arbitration in HMOs supports this concern. The study found that with respect to "repeat player" bias issue, in every instance where an arbitrator awarded a plaintiff (generally raising medical malpractice claims) over $1 million "the arbitrator was only employed in that case." Marcus Nieto and Margaret Hosel, Arbitration in California Managed Health Care Systems at 22–23 (2000).

27 For evidence that a great many companies have adopted arbitration clauses that give consumers a choice of multiple arbitration service providers, see, e.g., National Consumer Law Center, Consumer Arbitration Agreements: Enforceability and Other Topics (2d ed. 2002) (CD rom accompanying book) (contains copies of arbitration clauses with a choice of several providers by companies such as Beneficial Mississippi (second agreement), Capital One, Chase Manhattan, Citibank, Citifinancial, Discover Financial Services, Fleet, Household, JC Penney Card, MCI, Monogram Credit Card Bank of Georgia, Sears National Bank, Shell Credit, Universal Bank).

claims brought by their consumers. The NAF's recurring approach is not that of an entity committed to even-handed judging of disputes, but instead that of a for-profit vendor soliciting lucrative work by advising lenders how it can help them reduce their liabilities (*i.e.*, avoid the "risks of the jury system"). NAF's solicitation letters and advertisements are frankly inappropriate. If this Court were to solicit parties to bring their cases before it with promises that it would "improve their bottom line" and discourage its opponents, this Court would quickly run afoul of North Carolina's ethics rules. If this Court were to issue press relies crowing when it ruled for famous parties and against smaller concerns, the same would occur. The documents described in the Statement of Facts and attached hereto establish that the NAF operates without any concern to such ethical rules, however. Check 'N Go seeks to have NAF replace the civil justice system for any disputes involving the lender defendants. But while NAF would supplant the publicly accountable system of courts and juries, it has not held itself to the same ethical standards imposed upon courts and juries.

NAF's pro-lender litigation activities also support an inference as to its bias. It is scarcely a coincidence that dozens of lenders would endorse NAF, or that lenders and their counsel would line up to give testimonials of NAF for use in its solicitations to still other lenders. What lender would not? As set forth in the Statement of Facts, NAF's system is structured in a manner not to provide a fair and equitable forum to resolve legal disputes without the expense of a lawsuit, but rather in a manner that serves as a thinly veiled attempt to ensure an end result favorable to NAF's clients, the financial service industry. NAF features its rules—and results—prominently in its literature soliciting business from the financial industry, creating an appearance of impropriety so blatant it undermines any confidence a consumer would have in the fairness of NAF arbitration.

Similarly, as set forth in the Statement of Facts, NAF advertises to corporate counsel that it has a Loser Pays Rule for attorneys' fees. Applying a Loser Pays Rule undermines remedial statutes, such as those aimed at protecting consumers and the civil rights of workers. *See Christiansburg Garment Co. v. EEOC*, 434 U.S. 412, 418 (1978). One state Supreme Court has held that a similar Loser Pays Rule in an arbitration agreement rendered the agreement substantively unconscionable. *See Sosa v. Paulos*, 924 P.2d 357, 362 (Utah 1996) (an arbitration provision requiring a medical malpractice plaintiff to pay the litigation costs of the doctor if the patient "wins less than half the amount of damages sought in arbitration" was unconscionable).

Check 'N Go can certainly produce a number of cases where courts have said positive things about the NAF. Unlike this case, however, none of the handful of cases in which courts have approved arbitration clauses forcing consumers to take their claims to the NAF or even in the few cases where courts have praised the NAF have the factual records that remotely compare to this one. None of these cases make reference to documents establishing that NAF made inappropriate promises to lenders, NAF made false and self-serving statements to courts, NAF ruled for lenders in 99.6% of cases, or to any of the other pieces of evidence in the record here. Simply put, the conclusions reached by other courts based upon records bereft of the powerful undisputed evidence present in this case are unpersuasive.

CONCLUSION

For the foregoing reasons, the Court should deny Check 'N Go's motion to compel individual arbitrations.

Respectfully submitted, this the _____ day of August, 2005.

[*Attorneys for Plaintiffs*]

Appendix I **Brief on Waiver and on Bankruptcy Court Discretion to Deny Arbitration**

This brief is also available in Microsoft Word and Adobe Acrobat (PDF) format on the CD-Rom accompanying this volume.

IN THE UNITED STATES COURT OF APPEALS
FOR THE EIGHTH CIRCUIT

RHONDA J. LEWALLEN,
    Plaintiff-Appellee,

v.

    Case No.: 06-1925

GREEN TREE SERVICING,
LLC., and U.S. BANK TRUST
NATIONAL ASSOCIATION,
    Defendants-Appellants.

APPEAL FROM THE UNITED STATES DISTRICT COURT OF THE WESTERN DISTRICT OF MISSOURI

THE HONORABLE FERNANDO GAITAN

BRIEF OF APPELLEE RHONDA J. LEWALLEN

SUMMARY AND REQUEST FOR ORAL ARGUMENT

This is an interlocutory appeal from a district court order affirming a bankruptcy court's denial of a motion to compel arbitration of core bankruptcy claims that was filed after more than a year of litigation in the bankruptcy court.

Plaintiff-Appellee Rhonda J. Lewallen ("Lewallen") filed for bankruptcy on February 23, 2004. Defendant-Appellant Green Tree Servicing, LLC ("Green Tree") filed proof of claims on March 16, 2004, claiming money owed and a security interest in her home. Lewallen objected based in part on Green Tree's violation of consumer protection statutes. Green Tree demanded that Lewallen assert these objections in an adversary bankruptcy proceeding. After several hearings, the bankruptcy court granted Green Tree's demand. Lewallen then filed the adversary action challenging Green Tree's proof of claims. Green Tree responded by serving discovery, then moving to dismiss Lewallen's claims on the merits and asserting for the first time after over a year of judicial proceedings that her claims were subject to arbitration.

The bankruptcy and district courts held that Lewallen's core claims should not be split out from the pending bankruptcy for arbitration and that Green Tree waived any right to compel arbitration by demanding and then participating in litigation for over a year before asserting this right. These decisions should be affirmed.

Appellee respectfully requests 20 minutes for oral argument.

TABLE OF CONTENTS

SUMMARY AND REQUEST FOR ORAL ARGUMENT
TABLE OF CONTENTS
TABLE OF AUTHORITIES
JURISDICTIONAL STATEMENT
STATEMENT OF ISSUES PRESENTED
STANDARD OF REVIEW
STATEMENT OF CASE
STATEMENT OF FACTS
    A. The Underlying Mortgage Loan and Transactional History
    B. Ms. Lewallen's Bankruptcy
    C. Green Tree's First Appeal and the District Court's Affirmance
SUMMARY OF ARGUMENT
ARGUMENT
I. THE BANKRUPTCY COURT PROPERLY EXERCISED ITS DISCRETION TO DENY ARBITRATION OF LEWALLEN'S CORE CLAIMS TO AVOID DISRUPTING THE BANKRUPTCY PROCESS.
    A. Lewallen Raises Core Bankruptcy Claims.
    B. A Bankruptcy Court Has Discretion to Deny Arbitration of Core Claims Where it Would Disrupt the Underlying Bankruptcy.
    C. The Bankruptcy Court Properly Denied Arbitration.
II. BOTH COURTS BELOW CORRECTLY FOUND THAT GREEN TREE WAIVED ANY RIGHT TO DEMAND ARBITRATION.
    A. A Court, Not an Arbitrator, Decides if a Party's Conduct in Judicial Proceedings Results in Waiver of the Right to Demand Arbitration.
    B. Green Tree Waived Any Right to Demand Arbitration.
CONCLUSION
CERTIFICATE OF SERVICE
CERTIFICATE OF COMPLIANCE

TABLE OF AUTHORITIES

*Cases**[*]

Abromowitz v. Palmer, 999 F.2d 1274 (8th cir. 1993)

---

[*] *[Editor's Note: Citations throughout brief as in original.]*

Cabinetree of Wis., Inc. v. Kraftmaid Cabinetry, Inc., 50 F.3d 388 (7th Cir. 1995)
Com-Tech Assoc. v. Computer Assoc. Int'l, Inc., 938 F.2d 1574 (2d Cir. 1991)
Doctor's Associates, Inc. v. Casarotto, 517 U.S. 681 (1996)
First Nat'l Bank v. Allen, 118 F.3d 1289 (8th Cir. 1997)
Getz Recycling, Inc. v. Watts, 71 S.W.3d 224 (Mo. Ct. App. 2002)
Howsam v. Dean Witter Reynolds, Inc., 537 U.S. 79 (2002)
In re Brown, 311 B.R. 702 (Bankr. E.D. Pa. 2004)
In re Cassidy Land and Cattle Co., Inc., 836 F.2d 1130 (8th Cir. 1988)
In re Dogpatch USA, Inc., 810 F.2d 782 (8th Cir. 1987)
In re Gandy, 299 F.3d 489 (5th Cir. 2002)
In re Hemphill Bus Sales, Inc., 259 B.R. 865 (Bankr. E.D. Tex. 2001)
In re Hicks, 285 B.R. 317 (Bankr. W.D. Ok. 2002)
In re Larocque, 283 B.R. 640 (Bankr. D.R.I. 2002)
In re Merrill, ___ B.R. ___, 2006 WL 1669758 (Bankr. D. Me. June 16, 2006)
In re Mintze, 434 F.3d 222 (3d Cir. 2006)
In re O'Brien, 351 F.3d 832 (8th Cir. 2004)
In re Pate, 198 B.R. 841 (Bankr. S.D. Ga. 1996)
In re Spectrum Info. Technologies, Inc., 183 B.R. 360 (Bankr. E.D.N.Y. 1995)
In re Tatge, 212 B.R. 604 (8th Cir. B.A.P. 1997)
In re United States Lines, Inc., 197 F.3d 631 (2d Cir. 1999)
In re United States Lines I, 169 B.R. 804 (Bankr. S.D.N.Y. 1994)
In re White Mountain Mining Co., LLC, 403 F.3d 164 (4th Cir. 2005)
Kelly v. Golden, 352 F.3d 344 (8th Cir. 2003)
Lewallen v. Green Tree Servicing, LLC, ___ B.R. ___, 2006 WL 744285 (W.D. Mo. March 22, 2006)
Marie v. Allied Home Mortgage Corp., 402 F.3d 1 (1st Cir. 2005)
MBNA America Bank, N.A. v. Hill, 436 F.3d 104 (2d Cir. 2006)
National American Ins. Co. v. Transamerica Occidental Life Ins. Co., 328 F.3d 462 (8th Cir. 2003)
N&D Fashions, Inc. v. DHJ Industries, Inc., 548 F.2d 722 (8th Cir. 1976)
Pro Tech Industries, Inc. v. URS Corp., 377 F.3d 868 (8th Cir. 2004)
Reis v. Peabody Coal Co., 935 S.W.2d 625 (Mo. Ct. App. 1997)
Shearson/Am. Express, Inc. v. McMahon, 482 U.S. 220 (1987)
Shugre v. Air Line Pilots Ass'n Int'l, 922 F.2d 984 (2d Cir. 1990)
Triarch Industries, Inc. v. Crabtree, 158 S.W.3d 772 (Mo. 2005)

Statutes

9 U.S.C. §§ 1, *et seq.*
9 U.S.C. § 2
9 U.S.C. § 3
9 U.S.C. § 4
9 U.S.C. § 16
11 U.S.C. §§ 101, *et seq.*
12 U.S.C. §§ 2601, *et seq.*
15 U.S.C. §§ 1601, *et seq.*
15 U.S.C. §§ 1692, *et seq.*
28 U.S.C. § 157
Mo. Rev. Stat. §§ 470.010, *et seq.*

Miscellaneous

Jacob Aaron Esher, *Arbitration and Judicial Discretion: Circuits are Split*, Norton Bankr. L. Advisor, May 2006, 6

JURISDICTIONAL STATEMENT

The Court has jurisdiction pursuant to 9 U.S.C. § 16(a)(1) over this interlocutory appeal of the district court's order affirming the bankruptcy court's denial of Green Tree's motion to compel arbitration.

STATEMENT OF ISSUES PRESENTED

1. Whether the bankruptcy court abused its discretion in denying Green Tree's motion to compel Lewallen to arbitrate her core claims challenging Green Tree's filed proof of claims against the bankrupt estate after finding that splitting these claims out would prejudice her and the other parties to the underlying bankruptcy.
   1. *In re United States Lines, Inc.*, 197 F.3d 631 (2d Cir. 1999);
   2. *In re White Mountain Mining Co., LLC*, 403 F.3d 164 (4th Cir. 2005);
   3. *In re Gandy*, 299 F.3d 489 (5th Cir. 2002);
   4. *In re Larocque*, 283 B.R. 640 (Bankr. D.R.I. 2002).
2. Whether the bankruptcy court and district court clearly erred in finding that Green Tree waived any right to compel arbitration by failing to assert this right for more than 16 months, during which Green Tree demanded that Lewallen initiate an adversary bankruptcy action, both parties served extensive discovery, the bankruptcy court held multiple hearings, and Green Tree sought a judicial determination on the merits of the claims at issue.
   1. *Kelly v. Golden*, 352 F.3d 344 (8th Cir. 2003);
   2. *Triarch Industries, Inc. v. Crabtree*, 158 S.W.3d 772 (Mo. 2005);
   3. *Getz Recycling, Inc. v. Watts*, 71 S.W.3d 224 (Mo. Ct. App. 2002);
   4. *Reis v. Peabody Coal Co.*, 935 S.W.2d 625 (Mo. Ct. App. 1997).

STANDARD OF REVIEW

This Court applies the same standard of review that a district court applies in reviewing a bankruptcy court's determinations. *In re O'Brien*, 351 F.3d 832, 836 (8th Cir. 2004). A bankruptcy court's legal conclusions are reviewed *de novo*, while its findings of fact are reviewed for clear error. *Id.*; *MBNA America Bank, N.A. v. Hill*, 436 F.3d 104, 107 (2d Cir. 2006).

A bankruptcy court's conclusions respecting enforcement of an arbitration clause raise mixed questions of law and fact. *Id.* "If the bankruptcy court 'has properly considered the conflicting [statutory] policies in accordance with law, we acknowledge its exercise of discretion and show due deference to its determination that arbitration will seriously jeopardize a particular core bankruptcy proceeding.'" *Id.* (quoting *In re United States Lines, Inc.*, 197 F.3d 631, 641 (2d Cir. 1999)).

Whether a party waived a pre-existing right is a question of fact concerning a party's intent. *First Nat'l Bank v. Allen*, 118 F.3d 1289, 1294 (8th Cir. 1997); *In re Tatge*, 212 B.R. 604, 609 (8th Cir. B.A.P. 1997). This Court thus reviews a bankruptcy court's waiver determinations for clear error. *Allen*, 118 F.3d at 1294–95 ("The bankruptcy court concluded that the Banks intended to waive their unsecured claims, and we do not find this factual finding to be clearly erroneous."); *Tatge*, 212 B.R. at 609 (reviewing bankruptcy court's waiver determination for clear error).

STATEMENT OF CASE

Ms. Lewallen filed for bankruptcy on February 23, 2004. Green Tree filed proofs of claim against the estate on March 16 and July 28, 2004 based on money owed on its mortgage on Lewallen's home. Lewallen asserted multiple objections to Green Tree's proofs of claim, including challenges to the amount owed based on violations of consumer protection statutes. Green Tree demanded that Lewallen file an adversary action to resolve her objections. The bankruptcy court granted Green Tree's demand that Lewallen proceed in bankruptcy court in a hearing on March 22, 2005, dismissing her objections without prejudice to her right to file an adversary bankruptcy action. Lewallen then filed the adversary action re-asserting her statutory claims objecting to Green Tree's proof of claim. Green Tree responded by serving discovery, and later moving to dismiss Lewallen's claims on the merits and moving for the first time after 16 months of judicial proceedings to compel arbitration.

The bankruptcy court denied Green Tree's motion for arbitration. The district court affirmed, holding that (1) the bankruptcy court acted within its discretion to deny arbitration of Lewallen's core bankruptcy claims challenging Green Tree's proof of claim; and (2) the bankruptcy court's finding that Green Tree waived any right to compel arbitration was supported by the factual record showing over a year of affirmative litigation conduct by Green Tree, and thus was not clearly erroneous.

STATEMENT OF FACTS

A. The Underlying Mortgage Loan and Transactional History

Ms. Lewallen refinanced her family home in Kidder, Missouri in May 2000 with a $50,300 mortgage loan from Conseco Finance Servicing Corp. ("Conseco"). Appellants' Appendix ("App.") at 11. The terms of this loan required her to make monthly payments of $524.76 for 20 years, and then make a single "balloon payment" of $36,822.85. *Id.* Conseco never explained this required balloon payment to Lewallen. *Id.* Shortly after originating the mortgage loan, Conseco transferred its interest in it to a securitization trust over which U.S. Bank served as trustee, while Conseco retained servicing rights. *Id.* at 11–12. Conseco filed for Chapter 11 bankruptcy in December 2002. *Id.* at 12. On or about June 23, 2003, a bankruptcy-approved asset sale resulted in the transfer of servicing rights on Lewallen's loan from Conseco to Green Tree. *Id.* at 12.

In 2001, Conseco began sending Lewallen inaccurate and inconsistent billing statements that inflated the amounts due on her mortgage. *Id.* at 12. Lewallen repeatedly contacted Conseco, and later Green Tree, to resolve the amounts owed on her account, but neither ever corrected its billing errors. *Id.* at 12–13. In January 2004, facing the prospect of Green Tree foreclosing on her home, Lewallen tried to refinance her mortgage. *Id.* at 13. When her prospective new lender contacted Green Tree to determine her payoff amount, Green Tree gave an amount significantly greater than what Lewallen actually owed. *Id.* The prospective lender then declined to provide her the refinance. *Id.* At the time Lewallen was seeking to refinance her home, her primary sources of annual income (Social Security Disability and child support) totaled less than $10,000. Appellees' Appendix ("EE App.") at 42.

B. Ms. Lewallen's Bankruptcy

To stop Green Tree from foreclosing on her home, Lewallen petitioned for Chapter 13 bankruptcy on February 23, 2004 with the United States Bankruptcy Court for the Western District of Missouri. App. at 13. Apart from her home, valued at $51,800, Lewallen listed personal assets totaling $6,727.68 in value. EE App. at 12. She also listed liabilities to eight creditors totaling $55,830.25, of which Green Tree's secured interest in her mortgage was approximately 90% ($49,793). *Id.* at 12, 18–22. Lewallen's home and mortgage thus were the single largest asset and liability of the bankrupt estate, and represented the vast majority of the economic value being allocated through the bankruptcy process.

Green Tree filed Claim No. 2 in Lewallen's bankruptcy case on March 16, 2004, asserting that she owed it a secured claim of $54,502.99, with an arrearage of $4,652.84. App. at 14. Lewallen objected to Green Tree's proof of claim on various grounds. *Id.* Green Tree answered Lewallen's objections on July 28, 2004 without mentioning any duty or right to arbitrate the claims at issue. EE App. at 44.

On the same day, Green Tree filed an Amended Proof of Claim against Lewallen, representing that "Green Tree Financial Servicing, LLC" (not "Green Tree Servicing, LLC") was her creditor, and asserting that she owed it $54,471.25. App. at 14. Lewallen again objected, alleging that Green Tree's claims were inflated and that its inadequate responses to her prior requests for clarification of amounts owed violated the Real Estate Settlement Practices Act ("RESPA"), 12 U.S.C. § 2601, *et seq.* EE App. at 48. In support of these objections, Lewallen served discovery on Green Tree. *Id.* at 50. The bankruptcy court held a hearing on these objections on March 22, 2005, during which counsel for Green Tree reiterated its position that the claims forming the basis for Lewallen's objections had to be resolved through an adversary bankruptcy proceeding (*without ever mentioning arbitration*). App. at 353. The bankruptcy court granted Green Tree's request and dismissed Lewallen's objections to the Amended Proof of Claim without prejudice to her right to re-assert her objections as claims in an adversary bankruptcy proceeding. App. at 354–56.

Lewallen filed her adversary bankruptcy complaint against Green Tree on May 24, 2005, reasserting her objections to Green Tree's secured claim in the bankruptcy action by making affirmative claims challenging Green Tree's overcharges and collection practices under RESPA, the Fair Debt Collection Practices Act ("FDCPA") (15 U.S.C. §§ 1692, *et seq.*), and the Missouri Merchandising Practices Act ("MMPA") (Mo. Rev. Stat. §§ 470.010, *et seq.*). See App. at 09–22. Among Green Tree's actions she challenged were its filing of two Proofs of Claim in the bankruptcy that misrepresented the nature of the relationship between the parties. *Id.* at 20. In support of the adversary complaint, Lewallen again served discovery. *Id.* at 27–28.

Green Tree also initiated discovery, serving interrogatories and requests for document production on Lewallen on July 1, 2005 after obtaining an extension of time to answer the adversary complaint. *Id.* at 29–30. On July 28, 2005, Green Tree for the first time invoked the arbitration clause in Lewallen's mortgage loan contract as part of a motion to compel her to arbitrate her claims. *Id.* at 42–46. Three days after asserting that Lewallen had to arbitrate, Green Tree moved for the bankruptcy court to decide the merits of her claims and dismiss them, arguing that she was judicially estopped from asserting her statutory claims, that U.S. Bank was not a real party in interest, that the FDCPA and MMPA were inapplicable, and that she had missed various statutes of limitations. *Id.* at 49–56.

The bankruptcy court held a hearing on Green Tree's motions on

August 23, 2005. During this hearing, Green Tree again argued that the bankruptcy court should dismiss Lewallen's claims on the merits. This required Lewallen to answer these merits arguments in order to preserve her objections to Green Tree's proof of claim. App. at 129–33. After hearing merits arguments by both sides, the bankruptcy court issued a decision from the bench denying Green Tree's motions to dismiss and/or compel arbitration. *Id.* at 134. With regard to arbitration, the bankruptcy court found that Lewallen's adversary claims arose from her objections to Green Tree's proof of claim. *Id.* The court then found that it would be "inequitable to" and would "disadvantage" Lewallen in the underlying bankruptcy to send these claims to arbitration when "Bankruptcy Courts are here to take care of claims like this." *Id.* Finally, the court found that Green Tree had "waived any claim to arbitration" by participating in the litigation, demanding that Lewallen assert her claims in an adversary bankruptcy action, and serving extensive discovery on her. *Id.* The court also denied Green Tree's motion to dismiss on the merits, finding that its judicial estoppel argument was misplaced. *Id.*

C. Green Tree's First Appeal and the District Court's Affirmance

Green Tree noted an appeal of the bankruptcy court's denial of its motion to compel arbitration to the United States District Court for the Western District of Missouri. *Id.* at 149–52. In the district court, Green Tree engaged in extensive motions practice and briefing addressed to designations in the appellate record. *Id.* at 166–73, 309–15, 317–20, 328–31.

The district court affirmed the bankruptcy court's order denying Green Tree's motion to compel arbitration. *See Lewallen v. Green Tree Servicing, LLC*, ___ B.R. ___ 2006 WL 744285 (W.D. Mo. March 22, 2006); App. at 332–45. The district court first noted that the bankruptcy court's exercise of the discretion given it by law to determine if arbitration would jeopardize core bankruptcy proceedings should be accorded "due deference." App. at 334–35 (citation omitted). The district court then held that Lewallen's adversary claims were core bankruptcy matters because she raised and asserted them to contest Green Tree's proof of claim against the bankrupt estate. *Id.* at 338–41. The district court next held that the bankruptcy court did not abuse its discretion in denying arbitration of these core claims based on the latter's finding that the separation of claims involving Green Tree would "be a great disadvantage" to Lewallen, which the district court held would "seriously jeopardize the core bankruptcy proceedings." *Id.* at 342. Finally, the district court affirmed the bankruptcy court's finding that Green Tree waived any right to compel arbitration. The district court held that waiver of arbitration based on litigation conduct is for a court to decide, and then held that the bankruptcy court's finding based on Green Tree's invocation of and substantial participation in litigation, including its filing of dispositive motions and discovery, was not clearly erroneous. *Id.* at 343–45.

The notice of this appeal followed. *Id.* at 347.

SUMMARY OF ARGUMENT

The district court's decision affirming the bankruptcy court's denial of Green Tree's motion to compel arbitration should be affirmed for both of the primary reasons given by those courts.

First, the bankruptcy court properly exercised its discretion to deny arbitration of Lewallen's core claims based on the prejudicial effect that splitting out these claims would have on Lewallen and other creditors in the underlying bankruptcy. Lewallen's statutory claims raised and asserted as objections to Green Tree's filed proof of claim are core bankruptcy matters under 28 U.S.C. § 157(b)(2) because they directly affect the allowance or disallowance of claims by and against the estate and would determine the validity and extent of liens asserted by creditors. *See generally* 28 U.S.C. § 157(b)(2)(A), (B), (C), and (K); *In re White Mountain Mining Co., LLC*, 403 F.3d 164, 169 (4th Cir. 2005) (citing § 157's examples of core proceedings in affirming denial of arbitration). Moreover, the bankruptcy court properly exercised its discretion to deny arbitration based on its finding that splitting out these core claims, which involve the estate's sole substantial asset, from the bankruptcy would work a "great disadvantage" upon Lewallen's and other creditors' interests in her pursuit of a Chapter 13 Plan. *See, e.g., In re United States Lines, Inc.*, 197 F.3d 631, 638 (2d Cir. 1999) (finding adverse impact on other core proceedings where claims involving estate's "most important asset" would be arbitrated); *In re Gandy*, 299 F.3d 489, 498 (5th Cir. 2002) (claims representing "very nearly the entirety of Debtor's bankruptcy estate" implicate matters central to Bankruptcy Code's purposes).

Second, the bankruptcy and district courts correctly found that Green Tree waived any right to compel arbitration through its demand for and prolonged participation in the bankruptcy litigation. The bankruptcy court found that Green Tree's demand for an adversary bankruptcy action to resolve Lewallen's statutory claims, coupled with its active litigation on the merits and participation in discovery over these claims for over a year, demonstrated an intention to litigate that is inconsistent with the right to arbitrate, thus compelling a finding of waiver. This finding is consistent with Circuit and Missouri case law finding waiver of arbitration where a party's invocation of and/or prolonged participation in judicial proceedings results in delay and duplication that prejudice the opposing party. *See, e.g., Kelly v. Golden*, 352 F.3d 344, 349–50 (8th Cir. 2004) (finding waiver of arbitration based on party's initiation of suit and merits-based litigation); *Getz Recycling, Inc. v. Watts*, 71 S.W.3d 224, 229 (Mo. Ct. App. 2002) (same). Thus, the bankruptcy court's finding of waiver based on Green Tree's gamesmanship in invoking and participating in merits-based litigation before seeking arbitration was not clearly erroneous. The decisions below should be affirmed.

ARGUMENT

I. THE BANKRUPTCY COURT PROPERLY EXERCISED ITS DISCRETION TO DENY ARBITRATION OF LEWALLEN'S CORE CLAIMS TO AVOID DISRUPTING THE BANKRUPTCY PROCESS.

A. Lewallen Raises Core Bankruptcy Claims.

Lewallen's claims raised in objection to and for the purpose of substantially reducing Green Tree's proof of claims against the estate are core bankruptcy claims. Under 28 U.S.C. § 157(b), a bankruptcy court has *exclusive* jurisdiction over the following types of matters defined as "core bankruptcy proceedings":

(A) matters concerning the administration of the estate;

(B) allowance or disallowance of claims against the estate or exemption from property of the estate, and estimation of claims or interests for the purposes of confirming a plan under chapter . . . 13, . . .

(C) counterclaims by the estate against persons filing claims against the estate;

. . .

(K) determinations of the validity, extent, or priority of liens[.] 28 U.S.C. § 157(b)(2). Adversary actions raising claims covered under § 157(b)(2) constitute core proceedings within the bankruptcy court's exclusive jurisdiction. *See, e.g., Abromowitz v. Palmer*, 999 F.2d 1274, 1276 (8th Cir. 1993) (adversary action by creditor to determine non-dischargeability of debt is core proceeding under 28 U.S.C. § 157(b)(2)(I)). Lewallen's adversary claims challenging the validity and amount of Green Tree's proof of claims against the estate fall within each of these types of core bankruptcy proceedings.

This Court also has found that the centrality of a particular asset to the bankrupt estate is relevant to whether claims involving that asset are "core" under § 157(b)(2)(A) because of their effect on the entire bankruptcy process. *See, e.g., In re Cassidy Land and Cattle Co., Inc.*, 836 F.2d 1130, 1133 (8th Cir. 1988) ("[T]he two million dollar note secured by the mortgage constitutes the sole asset of the bankrupt estate. Although this fact alone is not determinative of a core proceeding, we note that the prompt collection of these assets is essential to the expeditious administration of the bankruptcy proceeding.") (citation omitted); *In re Dogpatch USA, Inc.*, 810 F.2d 782, 785–86 (8th Cir. 1987) (finding that claims relating to "the principal asset of the bankruptcy estate" could be deemed core). Here, the statutory claims in Lewallen's adversary complaint contest Green Tree's proof of a secured claim on her family home, which constitutes approximately 90% of the value of the bankrupt estate's assets. These are thus core claims under § 157.

The fact that Lewallen's claims allege violations of statutes other than the Bankruptcy Code, 11 U.S.C. §§ 101, *et seq.*, does not alter their status as core bankruptcy claims. A substantial body of circuit and bankruptcy court authority holds that a party's claims challenging a proof of claim or substantially affecting the equitable distribution of estate assets constitute core proceedings under § 157 whether or not they arise from the Bankruptcy Code itself. In *In re U.S. Lines*, for example, the Second Circuit held that a debtor's claims seeking a declaration of an insurer's obligations under a pre-bankruptcy liability policy were core because of the impact of these claims involving what "may well be the most important asset of the debtor's estate" on the whole bankruptcy. *U.S. Lines*, 197 F.3d at 638 (citation omitted). Specifically, the Second Circuit found that the policy was the "only potential source of cash available" to personal injury claimants, so that any other arrangement for paying them risked an inequitable distribution among all creditors. *Id.* at 638–39.

Similarly, in *In re White Mountain*, the Fourth Circuit held that a creditor's adversary action seeking a determination of whether a *pre-bankruptcy* cash advance was a loan or capital contribution was core without regard to the legal basis for this claim because it sought " 'a determination that he is owed money by the Debtor.' " *White Mountain*, 403 F.3d at 167 (quoting 28 U.S.C. § 157(b)(2)(B)). The Fourth Circuit further relied on the bankruptcy court's finding that the proposed arbitration of these claims sought " 'a determination of the extent of equity holders in the [bankrupt] entity.' " *Id.* (quoting bankruptcy court opinion). The Fourth Circuit thus took it as given that these claims were core, *id.* at 169, without ever addressing whether they arose under the Bankruptcy Code (which they did not).

Numerous bankruptcy courts likewise have held that individual debtors' claims under consumer protection statutes that are raised in objection to creditors' proofs of claims, as Lewallen's are here, are core bankruptcy matters. In *In re Larocque*, 283 B.R. 640 (Bankr. D.R.I. 2002), for example, the bankruptcy court held that a debtor's claim under the Truth In Lending Act ("TILA"), 15 U.S.C. §1601, *et seq.*, asserted as an objection to a mortgage lender's proof of claim were core claims. *Larocque* held that the debtor's TILA claim was core because "the resolution of this dispute will establish whether CitiFinancial is a secured or unsecured creditor in the bankruptcy case, thereby affecting how creditors will share in the Debtor's assets, and in what priority." *Larocque*, 283 B.R. at 642; *see also In re Pate*, 198 B.R. 841, 842–43 (Bankr. S.D. Ga. 1996) ("The claims asserted by the Debtor are core proceedings. (Bankruptcy Courts have jurisdiction to decide a Truth In Lending Act claim against a secured creditor that has filed a claim in the bankruptcy case.)") (citation omitted); *In re Hicks*, 285 B.R. 317, 322 (Bankr. W.D. Ok. 2002) ("Conversely, the Court does believe that Debtor's objection to Homeq's secured claim is a core proceeding that 'arises in' Debtor's bankruptcy proceeding.").[1] Since Lewallen raised her claims here in objection to Green Tree's filed proof of claim, they are core matters under § 157(b)(2) even though they allege violations of non-bankruptcy statutes.

B. A Bankruptcy Court Has Discretion to Deny Arbitration of Core Claims Where it Would Disrupt the Underlying Bankruptcy.

Although neither the U.S. Supreme Court nor this Court has squarely addressed the issue, other federal circuits facing motions for arbitration of core bankruptcy matters have held that a bankruptcy court has discretion to deny such a motion if it finds that splitting these claims out would disrupt the underlying bankruptcy. *See, e.g., In re United States Lines*, 197 F.3d at 640 ("In exercising its discretion over whether, in core proceedings, arbitration provisions ought to be denied effect, the bankruptcy court must still carefully determine whether any underlying purpose of the Bankruptcy Code would be adversely affected by enforcing an arbitration clause."). These decisions heed the Supreme Court's finding that Congress can override its general provision for enforcing arbitration clauses in the Federal Arbitration Act ("FAA"), 9 U.S.C. §§ 1, *et seq.*, with a separate statutory command, and that:

> If Congress did intend to limit or prohibit waiver of a judicial forum for a particular claim, such an intent will be deducible from [a statute's] text or legislative history, or from an inherent conflict between arbitration and the statute's underlying purposes.

Shearson/Am. Express, Inc. v. McMahon, 482 U.S. 220, 227 (1987).

The circuits recognizing a bankruptcy court's discretion to deny arbitration of core claims have found that Congress's provision for exclusive bankruptcy court jurisdiction over core claims allows those courts to preclude a party's resort to an arbitral forum where it finds that arbitration would frustrate the Bankruptcy Code's purposes. Foremost among these purposes is to " 'allow the bankruptcy court to centralize all disputes concerning property of

---

1 *Cf. In re Brown*, 311 B.R. 702, 711 (Bankr. E.D. Pa. 2004) (finding debtor's TILA claims to be core when asserted against lender that filed proof of claim, but non-core when filed against lender that did not file proof of claim).

the debtor's estate so that reorganization can proceed efficiently, unimpeded by uncoordinated proceedings in other areas.' " *U.S. Lines*, 197 F.3d at 640 (quoting *Shugrue v. Air Line Pilots Ass'n Int'l*, 922 F.2d 984, 989 (2d Cir. 1990)); *see also In re White Mountain*, 403 F.3d at 169 ("Congress intended to centralize disputes about a debtor's assets and legal obligations in the bankruptcy courts."). Another of the Bankruptcy Code's purposes with which arbitration of core claims can conflict is the need "to protect creditors and reorganizing debtors" against adverse effects from piecemeal dispute resolution. *In re Gandy*, 299 F.3d at 500; *In re White Mountain*, 403 F.3d at 169–70 (identifying preservation of debtor-creditor rights as one of Code's purposes potentially undermined by arbitration).[2] In light of the adverse effect that splitting core claims out for arbitration can have on these unique Congressional purposes embodied in the Bankruptcy Code, these courts have held that a bankruptcy court has discretion to deny arbitration of these claims where it finds that separate proceedings would disrupt the underlying bankruptcy.

As discussed herein, *supra* at 14–15, these decisions recognizing a bankruptcy court's discretion to deny arbitration of core claims logically focus on the effect that splitting these claims out would have on the underlying bankruptcy, and *not* on whether the claims arise under the Bankruptcy Code or some other law. A recent decision by the Third Circuit (which Green Tree did not cite in its opening brief), however, rejects this approach in favor of a more formalistic test of whether the claims at issue arose under the Bankruptcy Code itself. In *In re Mintze*, 434 F.3d 222 (3d Cir. 2006), the Third Circuit held that a bankruptcy court lacked discretion to deny arbitration of core claims raised in objection to a filed proof of claim because these claims did not arise under the Bankruptcy Code. Specifically, *Mintze* held that "[w]ith no bankruptcy issue to be decided by the Bankruptcy Court, we cannot find an inherent conflict between arbitration . . . and the underlying purposes of the Bankruptcy Code." Respectfully, this Court should reject *Mintze's* formalistic test as inadequate to protect the Bankruptcy Code's *underlying purposes*.

In holding that bankruptcy courts have discretion to deny arbitration of core claims asserting *pre-bankruptcy* contract rights, the Second and Fourth Circuits in *U.S. Lines* and *White Mountain* focused on how splitting out these core claims involving the estates' primary assets would undermine the Bankruptcy Code's purposes to (1) centralize claims by and against the estate; and (2) protect debtors *and other creditors'* interests in an equitable distribution of the estate's assets. *U.S. Lines*, 187 F.3d at 638–39; *White Mountain*, 403 F.3d at 169–70. The Third Circuit's "Bankruptcy Code claims-only" test adopted in *Mintze* ignores the fact that arbitration of core claims can undercut these statutory purposes *regardless* of whether these claims concerning an estate's primary assets arise under the Bankruptcy Code itself or any other law. Under the *Mintze* test, a single creditor could gain advantage over other creditors with competing claims involving an estate's primary assets by using an arbitration clause to have its own claims decided separately from *and without regard to* their competing interests. This is exactly why *Mintze's* analysis is already drawing criticism from courts and elsewhere:

> In reversing the district court, the Third Circuit held that the debtor's causes of action failed to raise any 'bankruptcy issue' at all, but instead raised only statutory issues of state and federal consumer protection laws. The statement is arguably a somewhat strained interpretation of 'bankruptcy issue' given the context of the ongoing Chapter 13 plan, *see e.g.*, Jacob Aaron Esher, *Arbitration and Judicial Discretion: Circuits Are Split*, Norton Bankr. L. Advisor, May 2006, 6, at 9–10 (criticizing *Mintze's* finding of no 'bankruptcy issue' as 'overly simplistic') . . .

In re Merrill, ___ B.R. ___, 2006 WL 1669758 at *8 (Bankr. D. Me. June 16, 2006). Given the merit of this criticism and the abuses the *Mintze* test invites by encouraging a "race to arbitration" among competing creditors, this Court should reject *Mintze* and affirm the decisions below holding that a bankruptcy court has discretion to deny arbitration of *any* core claim where it would disrupt an underlying bankruptcy.

C. The Bankruptcy Court Properly Denied Arbitration.

The bankruptcy court did not abuse its discretion in denying arbitration of Lewallen's core claims involving her family home. The bankruptcy court found that "it would be inequitable to at this stage push this over to arbitration where it would be to a great disadvantage to the debtor." App. at 134. In affirming, the district court found that "[Bankruptcy] Judge Venters properly considered the conflicting policies and determined that granting the defendants' Motion to Compel Arbitration in this instance would seriously jeopardize the core bankruptcy proceedings." App. at 342. These findings that arbitration of Lewallen's core claims against Green Tree involving the estate's sole substantial asset would disrupt the underlying bankruptcy by prejudicing Lewallen's and the other creditors' interests are consistent with findings of bankruptcy and appellate courts in a considerable number of cases.

At least three different federal circuits have affirmed bankruptcy court rulings denying motions for arbitration of core claims involving an estate's primary assets. In *U.S. Lines*, the Second Circuit affirmed an order denying arbitration of claims over the debtor company's primary liability insurance policy and embraced the bankruptcy court's findings that these proceedings "are integral to the bankruptcy court's ability to preserve and equitably distribute the Trust's assets," and that " 'arbitration of the disputes raised in the Complaint would prejudice the Trust's efforts to preserve the Trust as a means to compensate claimants.' " *U.S. Lines*, 197 F.3d at 641 (quoting *In re U.S. Lines I*, 169 B.R. 804, 825 (Bankr. S.D.N.Y. 1994)). Similarly, in *White Mountain*, the Fourth Circuit affirmed an order denying arbitration of core claims based on the bankruptcy court's findings that a separate arbitration of the largest claim against the estate would "undermine creditor confidence," "impose additional costs on the estate," and thereby "substantially interfere[] with the debtor's efforts to reorganize." *White Mountain*, 403 F.3d at 170. Finally, in *In re Gandy*, 299 F.3d 489 (5th Cir. 2002), the Fifth Circuit affirmed an order denying arbitration of claims found to "represent very nearly the entirety of Debtor's bankruptcy estate," where the defendants' actions in transferring

---

[2] *See also MBNA America Bank, N.A. v. Hill*, 436 F.3d 104, 108 (2d Cir. 2006) ("The objectives of the Bankruptcy Code relevant to this inquiry include the goal of centralized resolution of purely bankruptcy issues, the need to protect creditors and reorganizing debtors from piecemeal litigation, and the undisputed power of a bankruptcy court to enforce its own orders.") (citation omitted).

debtor funds off-shore threatened to undermine "the expeditious and equitable distribution of the assets of Debtor's estate." *Id.* at 498–99. Consistent with this appellate authority, this Court should hold that the findings of the courts below addressing the same factors merit affirmance of the orders denying Green Tree's motion to compel arbitration of Lewallen's core claims involving her family home.

Likewise, numerous bankruptcy courts have exercised their discretion to deny arbitration of core claims based on circumstances similar to those here. In *In re Larocque*, the bankruptcy court denied arbitration of the debtor's adversary claims objecting to a creditor's secured claim in his family home, finding that "the resolution of this dispute will establish whether CitiFinancial is a secured or unsecured creditor in the bankruptcy case, thereby affecting how creditors will share in the Debtor's assets and in what priority." *Larocque*, 283 B.R. at 642.[3] Similarly, in *In re Hicks*, the bankruptcy court denied arbitration of a debtor's TILA claims raised as objections to a creditor's secured claim, finding that the costs of separate proceedings could either deter her pursuit of these claims or else "have a significant impact on the estate and its creditors." *Hicks*, 285 B.R. at 323.

Finally, in *In re Spectrum Info. Technologies, Inc.*, 183 B.R. 360 (Bankr. E.D.N.Y. 1995), the bankruptcy court considered the factor of whether a decision-maker's "special expertise" would favor a particular forum in exercising its discretion to deny arbitration. *Id.* at 364–65. Here, consideration of this expertise factor likewise weighs in favor of bankruptcy court adjudication because of that court's familiarity with Lewallen's objections to Green Tree's proof of claim, which were pending before the court for over a year, and its effect on the interests of the other creditors that have filed claims before it.

The bankruptcy and district courts' decisions denying Green Tree's motion to compel arbitration of Lewallen's core claims should be affirmed. Both lower courts carefully considered the need for centralized resolution of these core claims to protect the interests of *all parties* in the underlying bankruptcy, and accordingly exercised their discretion to deny arbitration of these claims. In light of the substantial body of appellate and bankruptcy case law deciding motions for arbitration of core bankruptcy claims based on identical considerations, the courts below did not abuse their discretion in denying arbitration. The decisions below thus should be affirmed.

II. BOTH COURTS BELOW CORRECTLY FOUND THAT GREEN TREE WAIVED ANY RIGHT TO DEMAND ARBITRATION.

The bankruptcy and district courts' findings that Green Tree waived any right to compel arbitration by demanding that Lewallen file an adversary bankruptcy action and engaging in extensive litigation for over a year also should be affirmed. Whether a party has waived a pre-existing right is a fact-bound determination focusing on the party's intent. *First Nat'l Bank v. Allen*, 118 F.3d 1289, 1294 (8th Cir. 1997); *In re Tatge*, 212 B.R. 604, 609 (8th Cir. B.A.P. 1997). Accordingly, a trial or bankruptcy court's finding of waiver is reviewed for clear error. *Allen*, 118 F.3d at 1295 ("The bankruptcy court concluded that the Banks intended to waive their unsecured claims, and we do not find this factual finding to be clearly erroneous."); *Tatge*, 212 B.R. at 609 ("Th[e bankruptcy court's] finding regarding intent was not clearly erroneous."). Here, the bankruptcy and district courts' findings in support of waiver were not clearly erroneous.

A. A Court, Not an Arbitrator, Decides if a Party's Conduct in Judicial Proceedings Results in Waiver of the Right to Demand Arbitration.

As a threshold matter, the bankruptcy court had authority to determine whether Green Tree's litigation conduct before it gave rise to waiver of any right to compel arbitration. Under the FAA, a federal court is authorized to stay litigation and enforce an arbitration agreement, "providing the applicant for the stay is not in default in proceeding with such arbitration." 9 U.S.C. § 3; *see also* 9 U.S.C. § 4 (federal court may order arbitration "upon being satisfied that the making of the agreement *or the failure to comply therewith* is not in issue") (emphasis added).[4] The FAA thus directs courts to address questions of default or waiver of an arbitration agreement before they can enforce any such agreement. *See, e.g., N&D Fashions, Inc. v. DHJ Industries, Inc.*, 548 F.2d 722, 728–29 (8th Cir. 1976) (" '[W]aiver' can mean that the party proceeding with such arbitration under § 3 is . . . in default . . . and so under the terms of the Arbitration Act is not entitled to a stay. This is a question for determination by the courts . . .").

The U.S. Supreme Court's decision in *Howsam v. Dean Witter Reynolds, Inc.*, 537 U.S. 79 (2002), and this Court's subsequent ruling in *Pro Tech Industries, Inc. v. URS Corp.*, 377 F.3d 868 (8th Cir. 2004), are not to the contrary. In *Howsam*, the Supreme Court granted review to resolve whether a court or an arbitrator decides if an arbitrated claim is timely under the arbitration service's rule creating a six-year limitations period for filing claims. 537 U.S. at 81. In holding that an arbitrator decides this issue, *Howsam* found that (1) a dispute over the timeliness of an arbitration filing "seems an aspect of the controversy which called the grievance procedures into play;" and (2) the "arbitrators, comparatively more expert about the meaning of their own rule, are comparatively better able to interpret and to apply it." *Id.* at 85 (citation omitted). *Howsam* also stated more generally that "the arbitrator should decide allegations of waiver, delay, or a like defense to arbitrability." *Id.* at 84 (citation omitted). In *Pro-Tech*, this Court followed *Howsam* in holding that an arbitrator, not a court, decides a defendant's allegation that the plaintiff waived its claims by filing a deficient demand for arbitration with the American Arbitration Association. *Pro-Tech*, 377 F.3d at 870, 871–72. *Pro-Tech* held that this challenge to the plaintiff's arbitration filing "involve[s] issues of procedural arbitrability, matters presumptively for the arbitrator, not for the judge." *Id.* at 872. *Pro-Tech*'s holding that an arbitrator decides if conduct *in arbitration* results in a waiver of claims is

---

3 *See also In re Hemphill Bus Sales, Inc.*, 259 B.R. 865, 871–72 (Bankr. E.D. Tex. 2001) ("[T]he arbitration issue of the Distribution Contract will determine which creditors are entitled to share in the debtor's assets and in what priority. . . .[This] agreement results in 90% of Hemphill's business and . . . without the Distribution Contract, the estate is eviscerated and reorganization would be impossible.").

4 Moreover, Section 2 of the FAA allows courts to revoke arbitration clauses "upon such grounds as exist at law or in equity for the revocation of any contract." 9 U.S.C. § 2. Since waiver is a potential defense to any contract, it falls within this "savings clause" for generally applicable state contract law defenses. *See generally Doctor's Associates, Inc. v. Casrotto*, 517 U.S. 681, 687 (1996).

doubtless a correct application of *Howsam*.[5]

Neither of these cases, however, involves the distinct issue here of who decides whether a party's extensive conduct in *judicial* proceedings results in a waiver of the right to demand the arbitral *forum*. This Court and others in cases decided pre- and post-*Howsam* have held that a court (not an arbitrator) decides allegations of waiver of the arbitral forum based on a party's conduct in court proceedings. *See, e.g., N&D Fashions*, 548 F.2d at 728–29 (default based on active litigation "is a question for determination by the courts"); *Kelly v. Golden*, 352 F.3d 344, 349 (8th Cir. 2003) ("[T]he district court did not err in finding that Kelly had waived his right to arbitration."); *Marie v. Allied Home Mortgage Corp.*, 402 F.3d 1, 14 (1st Cir. 2005) ("We hold that the Supreme Court in *Howsam* . . . did not intend to disturb the traditional rule that waiver by conduct, at least where due to litigation-related activity, is presumptively an issue for the court to decide.").

Moreover, as the First Circuit found in *Marie*, a court's determination of whether conduct in judicial proceedings constitutes waiver adheres to *Howsam*'s "comparative expertise" analysis for identifying appropriate decision-makers since the court is deciding the effect of party conduct that took place before it. *Marie*, 402 F.3d at 13. Finally, as the First Circuit also found in *Marie*, it would be "exceptionally inefficient" to send waiver claims based on judicial conduct to an arbitrator, whose finding of waiver would just put the case back in court "without making any progress." *Id.* at 13–14. This process of bouncing back and forth between fora would create endless opportunities for delay and abuse by litigants who grow dissatisfied with the course of judicial litigation that is well under way, as were the proceedings below in this case. The district court below thus correctly held that the waiver question here based on Green Tree's extensive litigation conduct is for a court, not an arbitrator, to decide.

B. Green Tree Waived Any Right to Demand Arbitration.

Under well-established Missouri law, a party is found to waive a pre-existing legal right where it (1) has knowledge of the right; (2) acts inconsistently with the right; and (3) as a result, causes prejudice to the opposing party. *See, e.g., Reis v. Peabody Coal Co.*, 935 S.W.2d 625, 630 (Mo. Ct. App. 1997); *see also Kelly v. Golden*, 352 F.3d at 349 (citing federal case law in applying same standard to arbitration clause). Here, the two courts below correctly found that Green Tree's conduct in the proceedings before them evidenced waiver of any right to arbitrate.

First, knowledge of a contractual right to arbitrate is imputed to the contract's drafter. *Getz Recycling, Inc. v. Watts*, 71 S.W.3d 224, 229 (Mo. Ct. App. 2002); *see also Kelly v. Golden*, 352 F.3d at 349 (finding knowledge element of waiver satisfied where "Kelly, a lawyer, negotiated the terms of the [contract], including the arbitration clause."). Here, there is no serious question but that Green Tree's predecessor in interest, Conseco Finance, drafted the standard-form arbitration clause at issue and made it a term of Lewallen's mortgage contract that Green Tree assumed. Thus, Green Tree is presumed to have prior knowledge of any rights created by this arbitration clause. Nothing in the record even suggests a contrary conclusion.

Second, the bankruptcy and district courts correctly found that Green Tree's extensive and prolonged litigation activity in the bankruptcy proceedings was inconsistent with its later-asserted right to compel arbitration. The bankruptcy court found that Green Tree's demand for and participation in judicial proceedings demonstrated an intent to litigate Lewallen's claims in that court:

> I think you waived [arbitration] basically by participating in the action and by filing extensive discovery requests, et cetera, and this went on for some time. I believe that this all arose out of the objection to the claim. And it was perhaps your suggestion, I believe, that the matter ought to be an adversary proceeding. And then the adversary proceeding went forward and you served extensive discovery, it appears from the papers. And so I think you waived any claim to arbitration.

App. at 134. These findings that Green Tree's demand for litigation and its prolonged and extensive participation in judicial proceedings are inconsistent with the later-asserted right to compel arbitration are well-supported by federal and state case law.

This Court and Missouri's appellate courts have repeatedly found that a party's invocation of the litigation process is inconsistent with a later-asserted right to demand arbitration. In *Kelly v. Golden*, for example, this Court found that a party acted inconsistently with his right to arbitrate by "litigating the merits of his self-initiated lawsuit," when he "consistently encouraged the district court to resolve the entire dispute . . ." 352 F.3d at 349–50. Likewise, the Missouri Court of Appeals has affirmed a finding that a company acted inconsistently with the right to arbitrate when it "first initiated suit for breach of contract, replevin, etc." in court. *Getz Recycling*, 71 S.W.3d at 229; *see also Triarch Industries, Inc. v. Crabtree*, 158 S.W.3d 772, 777 (Mo. 2005) (party that initiated litigation cannot later move for arbitration under contract requiring it to choose one or the other forum). In the bankruptcy proceedings below, Green Tree twice affirmatively invoked the litigation process without even mentioning arbitration: first, in filing its proof of claims against the bankrupt estate; and second in answering Lewallen's objections by demanding that she assert an adversary bankruptcy action. These invocations of the bankruptcy litigation process alone would be sufficient to affirm the bankruptcy court's finding that Green Tree acted inconsistently with its later-asserted right to arbitrate.[6]

Likewise, this Court and Missouri's courts have found that a

---

5 Nor is *National American Ins. Co. v. Transamerica Occidental Life Ins. Co.*, 328 F.3d 462 (8th Cir. 2003), to the contrary. There, this Court held consistent with *Howsam* that the arbitrators in an on-going arbitration proceeding should decide whether the *merits claims* before it were waived based on a party's participation in prior proceedings. *Id.* at 466. It is not clear whether those prior proceedings were arbitral, *see id.* at 463–64, or judicial, *see id.* at 466. In either event, the waiver allegation concerned waiver of claims on the merits rather than waiver of the right to have those claims decided in a particular forum.

6 *Cf. Cabinetree of Wisconsin, Inc. v. Kraftmaild Cabinetry, Inc.*, 50 F.3d 388, 390 (7th Cir. 1995) (holding that *defendant's* invocation of judicial forum by removing state court case to federal court "without at the same time asking the district court for an order to arbitrate . . . manifested an intention to resolve the dispute through the processes of the federal court."). This is directly analogous to what Green Tree did here in demanding that Lewallen file an adversary bankruptcy action and only later, after she did so, asserting the right to arbitrate.

party's prolonged and extensive litigation conduct like Green Tree's below shows an intention to litigate in court that is inconsistent with any right to arbitrate. Again in *Kelly v. Golden*, in addition to finding that the party seeking arbitration had initiated the litigation, this Court also found that he had "consistently encouraged the district court to resolve the entire dispute and failed to object or move to compel arbitration throughout a year of court proceedings," and had "vigorously pursued discovery." 352 F.3d at 350; *see also Reis*, 935 S.W.2d at 630–31 (finding two-year delay in which party twice moved for dismissal or summary judgment by court was inconsistent with later-asserted right to arbitrate). Here, Green Tree waited for over a year after filing a proof of claim and then demanding that Lewallen file an adversary action before it asserted the right to arbitrate her claims. Moreover, Green Tree also asked the bankruptcy court to decide and dismiss Lewallen's claims on the merits, served discovery on Lewallen, put Lewallen in the position of having to serve discovery twice, and participated in six hearings on non-arbitration matters. The bankruptcy and district court's findings that this prolonged and extensive litigation conduct by Green Tree was inconsistent with any right to arbitrate these same claims were not clearly erroneous.

Finally, Lewallen was prejudiced by Green Tree's active litigation and delay that forced her to expend resources to actively litigate for over a year while her bankruptcy plan was on hold. The bankruptcy court found that "it would be inequitable to at this stage push this over to arbitration where it would be to a great disadvantage to the debtor." App. 134. This finding too is well-supported by federal and state case law. In *Kelly v. Golden*, this Court held that a party was prejudiced by his opponent's delay in seeking arbitration where he "incurred expense and experienced substantial delay as a result of the extensive litigation and would be required to extensively duplicate his efforts" if ordered to arbitrate. 352 F.3d at 350; *see also Getz Recycling*, 71 S.W.3d at 229 ("[D]elay and the moving party's trial-oriented activity are material factors in assessing prejudice. Prejudice may also result from . . . duplication of efforts, use of discovery methods unavailable in arbitration, or litigation of substantial issues going to the merits.") (citation omitted); *Reis*, 935 S.W.2d at 631 (citing same factors). Lewallen faces the same prejudice here, where Green Tree's conduct forced her to wait for over a year and litigate the merits of her claims before receiving the company's demand to do it all over again in arbitration.

In assessing the prejudicial effect of a party's pre-trial maneuvers and delay like those here, the appeals court in *Reis* found that:

> [T]he parties have been deprived of arbitration's main purpose: efficient and low-cost resolution of disputes. . . . 'To permit litigants to exercise their contractual rights to arbitrate at such a late date, after they have deliberately chosen to participate in costly and extended litigation would defeat the purpose of arbitration: that disputes be resolved with dispatch and with minimum expense.'

Reis, 935 S.W.2d at 631–32 (quoting *Com-Tech Assoc. v. Computer Assoc. Int'l, Inc.*, 938 F.3d 1574, 1578 (2d Cir. 1991)). The delay and expense of duplicate proceedings due to a party's dilatory tactics are especially prejudicial in bankruptcy cases like this where an estate's limited resources must be allocated among multiple creditors. *See, e.g., MBNA America*, 436 F.3d at 108 ("The objectives of the Bankruptcy Code . . . include . . . the need to protect creditors and reorganizing debtors from piecemeal litigation."); *In re Hicks*, 285 B.R. at 323 ("[T]he potential liability arising from the cost structure of the Arbitration Agreement would have a significant impact on the estate and its creditors."). For all of these reasons, the decisions below finding that Green Tree waived any right to demand arbitration was not clearly erroneous, and thus should be affirmed.

CONCLUSION

For all of the reasons stated herein, the decisions of the Bankruptcy Court and the U.S. District Court below denying Defendants' belated motion to compel arbitration of Plaintiff's core bankruptcy claims should be affirmed.

Respectfully submitted,

[*Counsel for Plaintiff-Appellee*]
[*Attorney for Plaintiff-Appellee*]

Appendix J

Brief Advocating Switching to Service Provider Capable of Administering Class Arbitration

This brief is also available in Microsoft Word and Adobe Acrobat (PDF) format on the CD-Rom accompanying this volume.

IN THE CIRCUIT COURT OF THE NINTH JUDICIAL CIRCUIT
IN AND FOR ORANGE COUNTY, FLORIDA

WENDY BETTS,
    Plaintiff,

v.

FASTFUNDING THE
COMPANY, INC., et al.,
    Defendants.

Case No. C10-99-3457

PLAINTIFF'S MOTION UNDER FLORIDA STATUTE 682.04 FOR APPOINTMENT OF ARBITRATOR CAPABLE OF FULFILLING THE COURT OF APPEAL'S MANDATE

INTRODUCTION

On March 16, 2007, the Fifth District Court of Appeal remanded this case with instructions that the case proceed in arbitration, and specifically mandated that "the arbitrator **must determine** whether, under Florida law, the arbitration may proceed as a class action." *FastFunding the Co., Inc. v. Betts*, 951 So.2d 116, 116 (Fla. 5th DCA 2007) (emphasis added).* Soon after, this Court entered an order staying the proceedings and compelling the parties to arbitration. (Order Staying Action Pending Arbitration, May 3, 2007.)

While plaintiff does not challenge the order compelling the parties to arbitration, plaintiff has learned that the designated arbitrator, the National Arbitration Forum ("NAF"), is unwilling and/or incapable of following the Fifth DCA's mandate that the arbitrator must consider and determine whether, under Florida law, the case may proceed as a class action in arbitration. Instead, without respect to any facts relating to this case or the Fifth DCA's mandate, a very recent federal decision and a very recent posting on the NAF's website make clear that the NAF cannot, and will not, conduct a class arbitration.[1]

Because the contract does not provide for an alternative arbitral forum in the event that the NAF is unable or unwilling to arbitrate the parties' dispute, this method of designating an arbitrator has failed. As such, this Court should exercise its authority under section 682.04, Florida Statutes, and designate an alternative arbitral forum that is capable and willing to obey and give effect to the Fifth DCA's mandate that the arbitrator in this case must determine whether, under Florida law, the arbitration may proceed as a class action.

STATEMENT OF FACTS

A. Events Leading to Litigation.

The Plaintiff, Wendy Betts, began doing business with the Defendants, FastFunding the Company, Inc., et al., in 1998, when she obtained three $100 loans from one of the Defendants' stores. (*See* Ex. 1.) In exchange for these loans, the Plaintiff wrote three personal checks, each for $125, that the Defendants agreed to hold until the Plaintiff's next payday, which was two weeks away. *Id.* On the date of the Plaintiff's next payday, she was given the option to either pay the pay the amount of money due on her checks to redeem them, or she could roll-over her loans into new loans by writing three new $125 checks. *FastFunding the Co., Inc. v. Betts*, 758 So.2d 1143 (Fla. 5th DCA 2000), *rev'd*, 852 So.2d 353 (Fla. 5th DCA 2003). During an eight month period, the Plaintiff rolled over her debt every two to three weeks, eventually incurring $900 in interest on a principal loan amount of $300. *Id.* Each time she obtained a new "payday loan," as these loans are commonly called, she signed a loan agreement that contained an arbitration clause. (*See* Ex. 1.) The arbitration clause required the parties to arbitrate any dispute regarding the terms of the loan agreement with the NAF. *Id.*

The Defendants ultimately deposited the Plaintiff's checks after she was unable to pay a $75 fee to roll her debt over into a new loan once more. *FastFunding*, 758 So.2d at 1143. The checks were returned to the Defendants due to insufficient funds, at which time the Defendants demanded payment from the Plaintiff. *Id.* The

---

* [*Editor's Note: Citations throughout brief as in original.*]
1 As this brief will make clear, there have been some indications from the NAF in the past that it refused to handle class actions in any situation. Other arbitration forums used to have similar policies, but abandoned them after the U.S. Supreme Court held in 2003 that cases could proceed on a class action basis in arbitration. Unfortunately, two brand new developments demonstrate that the NAF stubbornly refuses to permit its arbitrators to even consider the issue of whether an arbitration may proceed as a class action.

Plaintiff then filed suit against the Defendants, citing violations of Florida's Lending Practices Act, Florida's Consumer Finance Act, Florida's Deceptive and Unfair Trade Practices Act, Florida's Civil Remedies for Criminal Practices Act, and the complaint additionally set forth a claim for fraud. (Third Am. Compl. and Demand for Jury Trial at 2, June 7, 2001.) In short, the complaint alleged that the Defendants had compelled the Plaintiff and those similarly situated to pay unconscionable, usurious interest rates on the Defendants' loans. *FastFunding*, 758 So.2d at 1143.

B. Procedural History.

In response to the Plaintiff's complaint, the Defendants moved to compel arbitration of the dispute pursuant to the arbitration clause contained in the Defendants' loan contract. *Id.* The trial court ruled that the arbitration clause was unconscionable, and therefore unenforceable, and the Fifth District Court of Appeal affirmed. *Id.* The Fifth DCA also opined that if the Defendants' loan contracts were illegal because the transactions involved usurious loans, then "an arbitrator could not require [the Plaintiff] to perform under the contract." *Id.* On remand, the trial court ultimately found that the Defendants had indeed charged usurious interest rates on their loans, and therefore once again denied the Defendants' motion to compel arbitration. *See FastFunding the Co., Inc. v. Betts*, 852 So.2d 353, 354 (Fla. 5th DCA 2003).

While *FastFunding* was on remand, the Fifth DCA decided another case involving similar claims against a different payday lending company, Ace Cash Express ("Ace"). *Betts v. Ace Cash Express, Inc.*, 827 So.2d 294 (Fla. 5th DCA 2002). There, the Fifth DCA held that the loans offered by Ace did not violate Florida's usury laws. *Id.* at 354. In light of this decision, coupled with the Fourth District Court of Appeal's decision in *Buckeye Check Cashing, Inc. v. Cardegna*, 824 So.2d 228 (Fla. 4th DCA 2002) (finding that an arbitration clause identical to the one at issue in *FastFunding* was enforceable), the Fifth DCA reversed the order of the trial court and certified the question of whether the arbitration clause was enforceable to the Florida Supreme Court. *FastFunding*, 852 So.2d at 354.

On May 24, 2005, the Florida Supreme Court stayed proceedings in *FastFunding,* and eventually remanded the case on October 26, 2006, to the Fifth DCA for reconsideration in light of two cases: *Buckeye Check Cashing, Inc. v. Cardegna*, 546 U.S. 440 (2006); and *McKenzie Check Advance of Florida, L.L.C. v. Betts*, 928 So.2d 1204 (Fla. 2006). *See Betts v. FastFunding the Company, Inc.,* 950 So.2d 379 (Fla. 2006). The Fifth DCA then remanded the case to this Court with directions that the case be referred to arbitration. *FastFunding*, 951 So.2d at 116.

Most importantly, for the purposes of this Motion, the District Court of Appeal also directed this Court to order the arbitrator to "***determine, whether, under Florida law, the arbitration may proceed as a class action***." *Id.* (emphasis added). On May 3, 2007, this Court ordered the parties to arbitration, and this motion followed. (Order Staying Action Pending Arbitration, May 3, 2007.)

C. Facts Relating to the Availability of Class Arbitration in the NAF.

At the time the Plaintiff and putative class members obtained their loans from the Defendants, the Defendants' loan agreements contained an arbitration clause that required "binding arbitration by and under the Code of Procedure of the [NAF]" of all disputes arising from the terms of the loan agreement. (*See* Ex. 1.) As noted above, the Fifth DCA has ordered the Plaintiff to arbitrate her claims against the Defendants, but also ordered that the arbitrator must consider whether the arbitration may proceed as a class action.

Two brand new developments make clear, however, that the NAF has a bright-line policy of refusing to conduct class arbitrations in any setting. Plaintiffs' counsel have just learned of a decision issued by the U.S. District Court for the Western District of Kentucky a few weeks ago. *See Lockman v. J.K. Harris & Co., LLC*, 2007 WL 734951, at *2, n.1 (W.D. Ky. March 6, 2007). While plaintiff does not believe that *Lockman*'s legal conclusions are consistent with those of either the U.S. Supreme Court or the District Court of Appeals' mandate in this very case, *Lockman* does reveal ***facts*** that are crucial to this motion. In short, the *Lockman* decision reveals that the NAF, unlike other arbitral forums, continues to prohibit class arbitration in all cases. *Lockman* makes clear that the NAF will not entertain the directions of the Fifth DCA to consider whether this case may proceed, under Florida law, on a class-wide basis, but instead the NAF has already categorically resolved this question for all cases.

In *Lockman*, a plaintiff sought to amend a claim to provide for class action treatment in arbitration. The Court noted that "The arbitrator denied that request on the grounds that the National Arbitration Forum's procedural rules do not provide jurisdiction over unnamed persons...." 2007 WL 734951 at *2. In other words, *Lockman* makes clear that the actual practice of NAF arbitrators is to look first and only at NAF's own rules, and then to decide questions about the possibility of class action treatment automatically in favor of the defendant. The *Lockman* court further noted that NAF's policy in this respect is not uniform among arbitration firms: "Unlike the American Arbitration Association, which apparently amended its rules in response to the [U.S. Supreme Court's holding in *Green Tree Financial Corp. v. Bazzle*, 539 U.S. 444, 451–52 (2003) that an arbitrator must decide whether the parties' contract permits class arbitration], **the National Arbitration Forum does not permit class arbitration** and advertises that fact." *Lockman*, 2007 WL 734951, at *2, n.1 (citing Robert S. Safi, *Beyond Unconscionability: Preserving the Class Mechanism Under State Law in the Era of Consumer Arbitration*, 83 Tex. L. Rev. 1715, 1737 (2005)) (emphasis added).

In addition to the Lockman case, on May 30, 2007, the NAF posted on its website its latest declaration that in its view, its anti-class action tort-reform ideology governs over any state laws that might favor or provide for class actions in a given case. The NAF stated just a few weeks ago the flat rule that "[g]iven the affordability and accessibility of consumer arbitration, there is no need for class-wide proceedings." National Arbitration Forum, *Class Action Waiver Upheld Under D.C. Law* (May 30, 2007), available at www.arb-forum.com/adr_CaseDetails.aspx?caseid= 969 (attached at Ex. 7).

These two recent events indicate that the NAF is simply adhering to its long-term policy of opposing class arbitration in all settings, notwithstanding changes in the law or court orders that are not congenial to its tort-reform viewpoint, and will continue to do so regardless of the Fifth DCA's order that the arbitrator in this case "must determine whether, under Florida law, the arbitration may proceed as a class action." *FastFunding*, 951 So.2d at 116. As early as 1997, the Forum Counsel for the NAF announced its position that "[a]rbitrations may *not* be consolidated into class actions unless all parties consent." Forum Counsel for the NAF,

Arbitration & Class Actions in Financing (Oct. 1, 1997) (emphasis in original) (attached at Ex. 2). Furthermore, the Director of Arbitration stated in 1998 that "the *only* thing which will prevent 'Year 2000' class actions is an arbitration clause in every contract, note, and security agreement." Letter from Roger S. Haydock, Director of Arbitration, to Alan Kaplinsky (Apr. 16, 1998) (emphasis in original) (attached at Ex. 3). These sentiments were echoed by the Vice President and General Counsel for the NAF, when he stated that "a properly-drafted arbitration clause in credit applications and agreements *eliminates class actions*...." Letter from Curtis D. Brown, V.P. and General Counsel, to Robert S. Banks (Jan. 14, 1999) (emphasis in original) (attached at Ex. 4). Likewise, an interview with the Managing Director of the NAF in 2001 revealed the NAF's position that "if the dispute is governed by an arbitration clause, neither party can participate in a class action nor bring a class arbitration." The Metropolitan Corporate Counsel, *Do An LRA: Implement Your Own Civil Justice Reform Program NOW*, Northeast Edition, Aug. 2001, at 30 (attached at Ex. 6).

Even if the NAF were to depart from its over ten years of steadfast refusal to conduct class-wide arbitrations and agree to arbitrate the plaintiff's class-wide claims, the NAF has no capacity to adequately guide its arbitrators through a class arbitration. Notably absent from the NAF's *Code of Procedure* are any rules of procedures governing the arbitration of claims on a class-wide basis. *See National Arbitration Forum Code of Procedure* (May 1, 2006) (hereinafter "*Code of Procedure*") (attached at Ex. 5). Thus, the NAF does not have an established set of rules and procedures to guide its arbitrators and parties through the class arbitration process.

In short, the NAF is simply unwilling to conducting arbitration on a class-wide basis, and its *Code of Procedure* demonstrates that the NAF lacks any means of arbitrating the present dispute. The NAF is thus incapable of serving as the arbitral forum to resolve the Plaintiff's claims.

D. Facts Relating to the Availability of Class Arbitration in Other Arbitral Forums.

In stark contrast to the NAF, at least two other prominent arbitral forums have created specific procedures governing class action claims in arbitration. For one, JAMS utilizes its *Class Action Procedures* "whenever a court refers a matter pleaded as a class action to JAMS for administration." *JAMS Class Action Procedures* (Feb. 2005), *available at* http://www.jamsadr.com/rules/class_action.asp, Rule 1(a) (hereinafter "*JAMS Procedures*") (attached at Ex. 8). The *JAMS Procedures* establish criteria for class certification, *id.* at Rule 3, and also give arbitrators the authority to direct class notice, *id.* at Rule 4. The *JAMS Procedures* also explicitly address the settlement or compromise of class action claims in arbitration, and require settling parties to obtain approval of their settlement by the arbitrator, provide notice to class members, and also permit class members to object to any proposed settlement. *Id.* at Rule 6.

Likewise, the American Arbitration Association ("AAA") adopted the *Supplementary Rules for Class Arbitrations* (Oct. 2003), *available at* http://www.adr.org/sp.asp?id=21936 (hereinafter "*AAA Rules*") (attached as Ex. 9). As with JAMS, the *AAA Rules* apply "whenever a court refers a matter pleaded as a class action to the AAA for administration." *Id.* at Rule 1(a). AAA also has designated a national roster of arbitrators for class action cases. *Id.* at Rule 2(a). Notably, the *AAA Rules* create an express presumption against confidentiality in class action proceedings, *id.* at Rule 9, and require all class action award determinations to be made publicly available, *id.* at Rule 10. Since the AAA enacted its class action rules in 2003, its public class action docket has grown to include more than 100 cases. *See* Searchable Class Action Docket, *available at* http://www.adr.org/sp.asp?id=25563 (last visited Jun. 28, 2007) (attached at Ex. 10).

ARGUMENT

This Court must appoint a new arbitrator who is capable of and willing to comply with the District Court of Appeal's mandate, because the parties' contractual designation of the NAF as the arbitral forum for all disputes involving the Defendants' loan agreements, as well as their designation of the NAF's *Code of Procedure* to govern all arbitrations, fail as applied to the Plaintiff's class action claims within the meaning of Florida's arbitration act. The NAF has consistently stated that it will not arbitrate class-wide claims, and it lacks any sort of procedure or mechanism to handle class arbitration. As explained in greater detail below, the inability of the NAF to conduct class arbitrations renders it incapable of following the Fifth DCA's order in this case. Even if the NAF were to come in to this Court in support of the Defendants (it has some history in the past of having ex parte communications with counsel for lender defendants and producing last-minute affidavits supporting those defendants), and profess (for the first time) a willingness to consider the Plaintiff's claims on a class-wide basis, it lacks the procedural safeguards necessary to protect the interests of absent class members. For both of these reasons, this Court should appoint an arbitrator that can resolve this class action dispute in a manner that is consistent with court orders, and that adequately protects the interests of absent class members.

I. THIS COURT SHOULD EXERCISE ITS AUTHORITY TO APPOINT AN ARBITRATOR BECAUSE THE PARTIES' CONTRACTUAL METHOD OF APPOINTING AN ARBITRATOR HAS FAILED.

Although the loan agreement between the Plaintiff and the Defendants designates the NAF as the arbitral forum for disputes involving the terms of the Defendants' loans, this method of designating an arbitrator has failed in the present case because (as the statement of facts makes clear), the NAF is unwilling to follow the Fifth DCA's order to "determine whether, under Florida law, the arbitration may proceed as a class action." *FastFunding*, 951 So.2d at 116. Accordingly, this Court should therefore exercise its authority to appoint an arbitrator that is capable of conducting a class arbitration consistent with the mandate from the Fifth DCA.

The Florida Arbitration Act gives courts the authority to appoint an arbitrator whenever the parties' method of designating one fails. Section 682.04 of the Act provides, in relevant part:

> If an agreement or provision for arbitration subject to this law provides a method for the appointment of arbitrator or an umpire, this method shall be followed. In the absence thereof, or if the agreed method fails or for any reason cannot be followed, or if an arbitrator or umpire who has been appointed fails to act and his or her successor has not been duly appointed, the court, on application of a party to such agreement or provision shall appoint one or more arbitrators or an umpire.

§ 682.04 Fla. Stat. This provision recognizes that a contractually designated method for initiating arbitration may fail, and enables courts in these situations to appoint an arbitrator capable of carrying out the parties' intent for their disputes to be arbitrated.

Federal Courts have interpreted Section 5 of the Federal Arbitration Act, on which the Florida Arbitration Act is modeled, *Seretta Constr., Inc. v. Great Am. Ins. Co.*, 869 So. 2d 676, 680 (Fla. 5th DCA 2004), to grant them power to appoint an arbitrator when contractual methods have failed.[2] For example, in *Brown v. ITT Consumer Financial Corp.*, 211 F.3d 1217, 1222 (11th Cir. 2000), the Eleventh Circuit upheld the district court's appointment of a different arbitration company when the company designated by the parties' contract had dissolved. In doing so, the court stated that "[w]here the chosen forum is unavailable ... or has failed for some reason, § 5 applies and a substitute arbitrator may be named." *Id.*

Likewise, the district court in *McGuire v. Grider*, 771 F. Supp. 319, 320 (D.C. Colo. 1991), appointed a replacement arbitrator after evidence established that the contractually designated arbitrator was unwilling to arbitrate some or all of the parties' disputes. According to the *McGuire* court, this unwillingness on the part of the arbitrator to arbitrate the parties' disputes constituted a failure of the method of naming an arbitrator under Section 5 of the Federal Arbitration Act. *Id.* at 320. The court thus remedied the failure by appointing a new arbitrator. *Id.*

Numerous state courts have applied their analogous state arbitration acts in a manner identical to federal courts, and have exercised their judicial authority to appoint a new arbitrator when the contractually designated arbitrator failed. In *Deeds v. Regence Blueshield of Idaho*, 141 P.3d 1079, 1081 (Idaho 2006), for example, the court addressed a case where the parties' health insurance contract designated the AAA to arbitrate claims, but the AAA subsequently announced a policy whereby it refused to conduct arbitrations of healthcare disputes absent a *post-dispute* agreement to arbitrate. The court stated that " '[o]nly if the choice of forum is an integral part of the agreement to arbitrate, rather than an 'ancillary logistical concern,' will the failure of the chosen forum preclude arbitration.' " *Id.* at 1082 (quoting *Brown*, 211 F.3d at 1222). The court then found that because the AAA's services were not specialized or unique when compared to other arbitration companies, it was not an integral part of the arbitration agreement.

Deeds, 141 P.3d at 1082. The court therefore appointed a non-AAA arbitrator to arbitrate the parties' dispute pursuant to its authority under Idaho's Uniform Arbitration Act. *Id.*[3]

Similarly, both the Missouri and California Supreme Courts ordered their respective trial courts to appoint an arbitrator after finding that the arbitrator designated by the parties' contract in each case was impermissibly biased. In *State ex rel. Vincent v. Schneider*, 194 S.W.3d 853, 859 (Mo. 2006), the court concluded that "[t]he method of appointment of an arbitrator in the agreement has failed" because the arbitrator was found to be biased. The court therefore exercised its authority under Missouri's Uniform Arbitration Act to appoint a neutral arbitrator. *Id.*[4] Likewise, the California Supreme Court in *Graham v. Scissor-Tail, Inc.*, 623 P.2d 165 (Cal. 1981), found that the parties' named arbitrator was biased, and directed the trial court to consider its authority to appoint a new arbitrator if the parties were unable to agree to a new one on their own:

> The parties have indeed agreed to arbitrate, but in doing so they have named as sole and exclusive arbitrator an entity which we cannot permit to serve in that broad capacity. In these circumstances we do not believe that the parties should now be precluded from attempting to agree on an arbitrator who is not subject to the disabilities we have discussed. We therefore conclude that upon remand the trial court should afford the parties a reasonable opportunity to agree on a suitable arbitrator and, *failing such agreement, the court should on petition of either party appoint the arbitrator.*

Id. at 180 (emphasis added); *see also* Cal. Code Civ. Proc. § 1281.6.[5] Thus, whether the arbitrator is biased, unwilling, or simply unable to arbitrate the parties' disputes, courts around the

---

2　Section 5 of the Federal Arbitration Act provides:

> If in the agreement provision be made for a method of naming or appointing an arbitrator or arbitrators or an umpire, such method shall be followed; but if no method be provided therein, or if a method be provided and any party thereto shall fail to avail himself of such method, or if for any other reason there shall be a lapse in the naming of an arbitrator or arbitrators or umpire, or in filling a vacancy, then upon the application of either party to the controversy the court shall designate and appoint an arbitrator or arbitrators or umpire, as the case may require, who shall act under the said agreement with the same force and effect as if he or they had been specifically named therein; and unless otherwise provided in the agreement the arbitration shall be by a single arbitrator.

9 U.S.C. § 5.

3　Idaho's Uniform Arbitration Act, Idaho Code § 7-903, states in relevant part: "If the arbitration agreement provides a method of appointment of arbitrators, this method shall be followed. In the absence thereof, or if the agreed method fails or for any reason cannot be followed, or when an arbitrator appointed fails or is unable to act and his successor has not been duly appointed, the court on application of a party shall appoint one or more arbitrators."

4　Mo. Stat. § 435.360 states in relevant part: "If the arbitration agreement provides a method of appointment of arbitrators, this method shall be followed. In the absence thereof, or if the agreed method fails or for any reason cannot be followed, or when an arbitrator appointed fails or is unable to act and his successor has not been duly appointed, the court on application of a party shall appoint one or more arbitrators."

5　Cal. Code Civ. Proc. § 1281.6 states in relevant part: "If the arbitration agreement provides a method of appointing an arbitrator, that method shall be followed. If the arbitration agreement does not provide a method for appointing an arbitrator, the parties to the agreement who seek arbitration and against whom arbitration is sought may agree on a method of appointing an arbitrator and that method shall be followed. In the absence of an agreed method, or if the agreed method fails or for any reason cannot be followed, or when an arbitrator appointed fails to act and his or her successor has not been appointed, the court, on petition of a party to the arbitration agreement, shall appoint the arbitrator."

nation have exercised their statutory authority to appoint a new arbitrator to effectuate the parties' underlying intent to have their disputes arbitrated.

This Court should exercise its authority under section 682.04, Florida Statutes, and appoint a new arbitrator in the present case. Here, the Fifth District Court of Appeal determined that the parties were to arbitrate their claims, and mandated that the arbitrator "determine, whether, under Florida law, the arbitration may proceed as a class action." *FastFunding*, 951 So.2d at 116. This mandate would be rendered meaningless if the arbitrator applied the procedures of his or her arbitration forum to determine that class arbitration is not permitted, rather than conducting an analysis of and basing his or her decision on Florida law. Yet this is exactly what will occur in the present case, because the NAF has made it clear that it is incapable and unwilling to conduct class arbitrations.

As explained above, a U.S. District Court recently exposed the fact that the NAF has made no effort to accommodate class arbitration in light of the U.S. Supreme Court's finding in *Bazzle*, 539 U.S. at 451–52, regarding the permissibility of class-wide arbitration. *Lockman*, 2007 WL 734951, at *2, n.1. Indeed, the *Lockman* court explained that unlike its competitor, the AAA, the NAF has failed to amend its rules in response to *Bazzle*, and continues to stand staunchly opposed to class arbitration under any circumstance. *Id.* This case brings to light the fact that the NAF's blanket rejection of class arbitration has not changed in the years following *Bazzle*, and there is no indication that the NAF plans to embrace class arbitration in the future. The NAF has no procedures in place to govern the arbitration of class-wide claims, *see Code of Procedure* (Ex. 5), and it specifically markets itself as a venue that will "eliminate class actions" against defendant credit companies. (Ex. 4); *see also* (Ex. 7) (noting that "there is no need for class-wide proceedings"); (Ex. 6) (stating that "neither party can participate in a class action nor bring a class arbitration" if the dispute is governed by an arbitration clause); (Ex. 3) (explaining that arbitration clauses are the "*only*" thing" that prevent class actions) (emphasis in original); (Ex. 2) (noting that arbitrations may not be consolidated unless all parties consent).

As was the case in *McGuire* and *Deeds*, the unwillingness and inability of NAF to conduct class arbitrations constitutes a failure of the parties' contractual method of choosing an arbitrator, because it would result in the frustration of the Court of Appeal's directive that the arbitrator consider whether the case will proceed as a class action. This Court, therefore, can remedy this failure by exercising its authority under section 682.04, Florida Statutes, and appoint an arbitrator capable of arbitrating this dispute on a class-wide basis.

II. THIS COURT SHOULD APPOINT AN ARBITRATOR THAT HAS ESTABLISHED PROCEDURES TO GOVERN THE ARBITRATION OF CLASS-WIDE DISPUTES.

Even if the NAF agreed to consider arbitrating this dispute on a class-action basis, the fact that the NAF lacks any rules or procedures to govern class arbitration warrants the appointment of a new arbitrator to protect the constitutional due process rights of absent class members. As explained below, this Court should exercise its authority under section 682.04 and appoint a new arbitrator because the NAF is simply not equipped with methodology to ensure due process requirements would be met if it decided to arbitrate the Plaintiff's class-wide claims.

Where class actions are concerned, courts require strict compliance with procedural safeguards to ensure "protection of the interests of absent parties who are to be bound" by the outcome of the class litigation. *Paulino v. Hardister*, 306 So.2d 125, 128 (Fla. 2d DCA 1974) (quoting *Hansberry v. Lee*, 311 U.S. 32, 42 (1940)). For example, the Florida Supreme Court has stated that due process requires "that individual notice be given to those class members who can be identified through reasonable effort." *Nat'l Lake Dev., Inc. v. Lake Tippecanoe Owners Ass'n, Inc.*, 417 So.2d 655, 657 (Fla. 1982). Similarly, due process "requires that the class representative adequately represent the interests of the other class members." *Marco Island Civic Ass'n, Inc. v. Mazzini*, 805 So.2d 928, 931 (Fla. 2001). These due process requirements, along with other procedural safeguards that function to adequately protect the interests of the class, are embodied in Rule 1.220 of the Florida Rules of Civil Procedure, and its federal counterpart, Rule 23 of the Federal Rules of Civil Procedure.[6]

To satisfy constitutional due process, other arbitration forums, including JAMS and the AAA, have adopted procedures to govern class arbitration that are substantially equivalent to those embodied in Rule 23. For example, both JAMS and the AAA have established rules for certifying a plaintiff class, *JAMS Procedures* at Rule 3; *AAA Rules* at Rule 4, and for issuing notice of class certification to absent class members, *JAMS Procedures* at Rule 4; *AAA Rules* at Rule 5. With regard to the settlement of class actions in arbitration, JAMS and the AAA safeguard the interests of absent class members by: (1) requiring the settling parties to obtain the arbitrator's approval; (2) directing the parties to issue notice of the settlement to absent class members; (3) permitting class members to object to the proposed class action settlement; and (4) requiring the arbitrator to determine whether the proposed settlement is fair, adequate, and reasonable. *JAMS Procedures* at Rule 6; *AAA Rules* at Rule 8. To further ensure the integrity of class action proceedings in arbitration, both JAMS and the AAA require arbitrators to issue reasoned final awards on the merits of class action claims. *JAMS Procedures* at Rule 5; *AAA Rules* at Rule 7.

The NAF has not incorporated *any* rule or guideline into its *Code of Procedure* that even resembles what its competitors have adopted and utilized in order to adequately protect the due process rights of the putative class in arbitration. This absence of formal procedures for making class action determinations is fatal to the ability of the NAF to safeguard the interests of absent class members. As such, this Court should exercise its authority under Florida Statute § 682.04, and appoint an arbitrator that is capable of meeting constitutional due process requirements.

CONCLUSION

The Fifth District Court of Appeal remanded this case with instructions that the case proceed in arbitration, and specifically mandated that "the arbitrator **must determine** whether, under Florida law, the arbitration may proceed as a class action." *FastFunding*, 951 So.2d at 116 (emphasis added). However, the NAF

---

6 *See Barnhill v. Florida Microsoft Anti-Trust Litigation*, 905 So.2d 195, 198 (Fla. 3d DCA 2005) (noting that Florida's class action rules are based on the federal class action Rule 23, and thus Florida courts look to federal cases as persuasive authority in their interpretation of the state rule); *Chase Manhattan Mortg. Corp. v. Porcher*, 898 So.2d 153, 156–57 (Fla. 4th DCA 2005) (same).

has made it clear that it is unwilling to conduct any class arbitrations, regardless of state law, and the NAF is clearly procedurally incapable of handling a class arbitration. This Court should therefore grant the Plaintiff's Motion Under Florida Statute 682.04 for Appointment of Arbitrator Capable of Fulfilling Court of Appeal's Mandate.

Appendix K — Sample Response and Counterclaim in Arbitration Action to Collect a Consumer Debt

This response and counterclaim is also available in Microsoft Word and Adobe Acrobat (PDF) format on the CD-Rom accompanying this volume.

IN THE NATIONAL ARBITRATION FORUM

```
_____        )
                               )
CREDIT CARD DEBT               )
PURCHASER                      )
CLAIMANT                       )
                               )
    RE:        [Case Name]     )
    Forum File Number:   xxx   )
    Account Number:            )
        xxxx-xxxx-xxxx-xxx     )
                               )
CONSUMER VICTIM                )
RESPONDENT                     )
_____        )
```

RESPONSE AND COUNTERCLAIM

Now comes Respondent and Counterclaimant Consumer Victim and for his Response and Counterclaim alleges and says as follows:

FIRST RESPONSE
(Objection to Arbitration of Claim Because No Agreement to Arbitrate Exists)

Mr. Consumer objects to arbitration of this Claim. Mr. Consumer denies that he executed any agreement to arbitrate this controversy with MBNA America Bank ("MBNA") or Credit Card Debt Purchaser ("Collector" or "Claimant"), or that any purported agreement to arbitrate this controversy ever became binding upon him. *See* Exhibit 1 hereto (Affidavit of Mr. Consumer). [*Editor's Note: Not reprinted herein.*] All further proceedings by Mr. Consumer before the National Arbitration Forum ("NAF") or any arbitration forum are made under protest.

This Honorable Arbitrator may only hear this Claim if a valid agreement exists. *See AT&T Technologies, Inc. v. Commc'ns Workers of America*, 475 U.S. 643, 648–49 (1986)[1] ("Arbitration is a matter of contract and a party cannot be required to submit to arbitration any dispute which he has not agreed so to submit. This axiom recognizes the fact that arbitrators derive their authority to resolve disputes only because the parties have agreed in advance to submit such grievances to arbitration.") (citations omitted). The burden is upon Claimant to establish with actual evidence (as opposed to unsworn assertions of counsel made without any established foundation) that Mr. Consumer agreed to arbitrate disputes with it. *See, e.g., Novecon Ltd. v. Bulgarian-American Enterprise Fund*, 190 F.3d 556 (D.C. 1999) (under D.C. law, the party asserting the existence of an enforceable contract bears the burden of proof on the issue of contract formation).

Claimant has quoted excerpts from an undated and unauthenticated MBNA cardholder agreement and has argued that this generic agreement binds Mr. Consumer to arbitrate disputes. However, Claimant has not put forward any evidence that this particular agreement was ever sent to Mr. Consumer, much less that he agreed to it. Claimant has not offered any evidence that any agreement to arbitrate was in place for cardholders during the brief and long-ago period when Mr. Consumer's MBNA account was active.

Accordingly, Mr. Consumer demands that this claim be dismissed with prejudice. *See, e.g., MBNA v. Credit*, 132 P.3d 898 (Kan. 2006) (affirming vacatur of arbitration award issued by NAF where MBNA failed to provide sufficient evidence that alleged debtor had agreed to arbitrate); *MBNA v. Engen*, 128 Wash. App. 1050 (2005) (reversing award that NAF arbitrator had entered against consumer who had never used MBNA card after receiving arbitration clause, and thus who had never become bound by arbitration clause); *MBNA v. Nelson*, 2007 WL 1704618 (NY Civ. Ct. May 24, 2007) (refusing to "rubber stamp" MBNA's motion to confirm NAF award where MBNA had failed to provide any evidence connecting the generic agreements it submitted to the specific alleged cardholder).

SECOND RESPONSE
(Objection to Arbitration: Claimant Has Violated Its Own Purported Arbitration Agreement)

Claimant asserts rights under a standard form MBNA arbitration agreement that provides: "In no event will you be required to reimburse us for arbitration filing, administrative or hearing fees in an amount greater than what your court costs would have been if the Claim had been resolved in a state court with jurisdiction." (Mr. Consumer denies that he is bound by any such agreement, but for the purposes of this response presumes that this Honorable Arbitrator will find otherwise. Accordingly, since Claimant is seeking benefits under the portions of the boilerplate arbitration clause MBNA has used with many other cardholders, it should also be bound to the terms of that agreement that benefit cardholders.)

---

1 [*Editor's Note: Citations throughout response and counterclaim as in original.*]

In light of this language in the contract upon which it relies, Claimant's demand in paragraph 5 of its claim for the "fees and expenses of Arbitration" is unjustified.

The standard MBNA contract relied upon by Claimant further provides: "At your written request, we will advance any arbitration filing fee, administrative and hearing fees which you are required to pay to pursue a claim in arbitration." This very language is quoted in paragraph 6 of the Claim.

In this case, Mr. Consumer would be charged $120 to pursue his claims in D.C. Superior Court. In this arbitration, however, Mr. Consumer is required to pay (and has paid with the mailed filing of this Response and Counterclaim) the following initial fees: $150.00 for a participatory hearing, $60 for the filing fee for his counterclaim, and $400 for written findings and conclusions. (These figures, which are based upon the NAF's rules, were all confirmed in a telephone call on [date] between counsel for Mr. Consumer and _____, an NAF employee.) Accordingly, Mr. Consumer's fees to date already exceed the filing fee for a claim of this size in D.C. Superior Court, and under the MBNA contract upon which Claimant relies, Claimant should have advanced to Mr. Consumer the sum of $490.00.

On [date], a letter was faxed to Claimant demanding that Claimant agree to pay Mr. Consumer's fees to the NAF. See Exhibit 2 hereto. [Editor's Note: Not reprinted herein.] Claimant has made no written response to Mr. Consumer, and has simply ignored the demand. In the face of Claimant's refusal to respond, undersigned counsel for Mr. Consumer telephoned Claimant's counsel on [date], urging Claimant's counsel to read Mr. Consumer's faxed demand that Claimant advance arbitration fees, and comply with the MBNA contract's promise to do so. Despite acknowledging the receipt of Mr. Consumer's [date] letter, counsel for Claimant declined to advance arbitration fees. In short, Claimant has flagrantly breached the written promise to advance all arbitration fees.

By refusing to pay the arbitration fees that it is required to pay under the contract which it claims gives it the right to arbitrate, Claimant has breached its own contract and thus waived and lost its right to invoke the arbitration clause. *See Sanderson Farms v. Gatlin*, 848 So.2d 828 (Miss. 2003); *Sink v. Aden Enterprises, Inc.*, 352 F.3d 1197 (9th Cir. 2003). These cases establish that a party that breaches its own arbitration clause loses the right to compel arbitration based on that agreement.

Accordingly, Mr. Consumer demands that Claimant's claim and this arbitration be dismissed with prejudice.

THIRD RESPONSE
(Objection to Arbitration: Claimant Violated Its Own Purported Arbitration Agreement and NAF Rules by Failing to Serve the Claim)

Both the MBNA Agreement upon which Claimant relies and the NAF rules require Claimant to serve its claim upon Mr. Consumer.

Claimant did not serve the Claim upon Mr. Consumer. See Exhibit 1, Consumer Affidavit. [*Editor's Note: Not reprinted herein.*] On [date], Mr. Consumer faxed Claimant and demanded that it serve him with the Claim. See Exhibit 2. [*Editor's Note: Not reprinted herein.*] Claimant ignored this request. Mr. Consumer did not receive a copy of the Claim until a PDF file was forwarded by NAF on [date].

Again, claimant has breached the very arbitration clause under which it makes claims. Under the authorities cited in the Second Response, Claimant has lost its right to pursue arbitration. In addition, Claimant's claim that it deserves expenses for "serving the Respondent with this Claim," Claim at Paragraph 5(B), is fanciful in light of this failure.

Accordingly, Mr. Consumer demands that Claimant's claim and this arbitration be dismissed with prejudice.

FOURTH RESPONSE
(Defense of Statute of Limitations)

This claim is barred by the relevant statute of limitations. The relevant statute of limitations for claims on this account is three years. Claimant asserts rights under an MBNA arbitration clause that includes a Delaware choice-of-law provision. Paragraph 7 of the Claim acknowledges that the agreement is governed by Delaware law, estopping Claimant from denying that it is bound by Delaware's statute of limitations.

The statute of limitations in Delaware is three (3) years. *See Fike v. Ruger*, 754 A.2d 254 (Del. Ch. 1999). As Mr. Consumer's affidavit makes clear, the account was closed more than six years ago, and no payment has been on the account made for over four years. Exhibit 1. [*Editor's Note: Not reprinted herein.*] In addition, an employee of Claimant, _____, verbally acknowledged to counsel for Mr. Consumer on [date], that the last payment date on the account was more than four years ago.

Accordingly, Mr. Consumer demands that Claimant's Claim upon a debt that is well past the limitations period be dismissed with prejudice.

FIFTH RESPONSE
(No Sum Owed to Claimant)

Mr. Consumer denies that he is indebted to Claimant for any amount. Claimant has failed to meet its burden of proving with actual evidence that it is the assignee of MBNA.

As the First Response established, Claimant has the burden of establishing the existence of an agreement entitling it to make any claim whatsoever against Mr. Consumer, and it has failed to do so.

Accordingly, Mr. Consumer demands that the Claim be dismissed with prejudice.

SIXTH RESPONSE
(Claimant Relies Upon Unsubstantiated and Apparently Made Up Numbers)

The Claim somberly intones that the demand for the sum of $_____ is "reflected in the attached account summary." The actual "summary" does not include any breakdown of the supposed claim as to dates, to principle, interest, or fees, and does not include any figure for arbitration fees claimed by Claimant.

This Claim is a classic illustration of a debt collector that buys time-barred debt for pennies on the dollar, inflates the claimed debt with made-up and imaginary fees and sums, and hopes to obtain a quick default award in the arbitration and intimidate individuals such as Mr. Consumer into paying some portion of the time-barred and illegal debt. *E.g., MBNA v. Nelson*, 2007 WL 1704618 (NY Civ. Ct. May 24, 2007) ("[i]t is almost never apparent, from the filings [in confirmations of NAF awards for MBNA] . . ., what evidence, if any, the arbitrator considered, what claims the arbitrator ruled upon, and what figures the arbitrator used in calculating each award.'').

Because Claimant has not substantiated the amounts it claims with any sort of evidence (merely a fanciful one-line conclusory figure set forward without enumeration or foundation), Mr. Consumer demands that the Claim be dismissed with prejudice.

SEVENTH RESPONSE AND COUNTERCLAIM
(Violation of Fair Debt Collection Practices Act—
Attempt to Recover Alleged Debt That Is
Plainly Beyond the Relevant Limitations Period)

As set forth in the Fourth Response above, Claimant's claim is plainly barred by the relevant limitations period, and Claimant is aware of this fact.

Claimant is indisputably covered by the Fair Debt Collection Practices Act, having allegedly purchased the debt after the consumer's alleged default.

Accordingly, Claimant's filing of this arbitration claim violates the Fair Debt Collection Practices Act, 15 U.S.C. § 1692f. *See Kimber v. Federal Fin. Corp.*, 668 F. Supp. 1480, 1487 (M.D. Ala. 1987):

> [A] debt collector's filing of a lawsuit on a debt that appears to be time-barred, without the debt collector having first determined after a reasonable inquiry that that limitations period has been or should be tolled, is an unfair and unconscionable means of collecting the debt.

See also 15 U.S.C. § 1692f(1) (collecting any amount not permitted by law is prohibited).

Accordingly, Mr. Consumer demands statutory damages pursuant to 15 U.S.C. § 1692k in the sum of $1,000.00.

Mr. Consumer further demands costs and reasonable attorney's fees pursuant to 15 U.S.C. § 1692k. He currently estimates that his total attorney's fees to pursue this FDCPA claim will amount to $10,000.00.

EIGHTH RESPONSE AND COUNTERCLAIM
(Violation of Fair Debt Collection Practices Act—
Attempt to Impose Costs of Arbitration
Not Permitted by Contract)

As set forth in the Second Response above, Claimant's claim is based upon a contract that requires it to advance all costs of arbitration exceeding $120, but Claimant has refused to do so, breaching its own contractual promise.

Claimant's refusal to pay the costs of arbitration as it is obligated under the contract upon which it relies constitutes a violation of the Fair Debt Collection Practices Act. *E.g., Patzka v. Viterbo College*, 917 F. Supp. 654 (W.D. Wis. 1996) (by charging a collection fee and interest not allowed by the contract or state law, debt collector violated the FDCPA).

Accordingly, Mr. Consumer demands additional statutory damages pursuant to 15 U.S.C. § 1692k in the sum of $1,000.00.

Mr. Consumer further demands costs and reasonable attorney's fees pursuant to 15 U.S.C. § 1692k. He estimates that his total attorney's fees to pursue this FDCPA claim will amount to $10,000.00.

PRAYER FOR RELIEF

If this Honorable Arbitrator finds, despite Responses 1 through 4, that he has jurisdiction to decide this dispute, Respondent and Counterclaimant demands $11,000 for Response/Counterclaim 7 ($1,000 in statutory damages under the FDCPA, and $10,000 in attorneys' fees). Respondent and Counterclaimant further demands $11,000 for Response/Counterclaim 8 ($1,000 in statutory damages under the FDCPA, and $10,000 in attorneys' fees). Respondent and Counterclaimant's total demand is $22,000.

CONCLUSION

WHEREFORE, in light of the foregoing eight responses and two counterclaims, Mr. Consumer demands that the claim be dismissed with prejudice and that Claimant have and recover nothing, that an award be entered against Claimant in favor of Mr. Consumer for $2,000 plus the sum of Mr. Consumer's attorneys' fees.

This _____ day of _____, 2007.

Attorney for Respondent

I swear under the penalties of perjury that all allegations in the foregoing Response and Counterclaim are accurate.

Attorney for Respondent

Date: _____

Appendix L — Brief Opposing Confirmation of Collector's Arbitration Award

This brief is also available in Microsoft Word and Adobe Acrobat (PDF) format on the CD-Rom accompanying this volume.

STATE OF MICHIGAN
IN THE COURT OF APPEALS

[CONSUMER],
    Appellant,

v.

MBNA America Bank, N.A.,
    Appellee

No. 270540

Appeal from the Circuit Court for the County of Macomb Honorable Richard L. Caretti

APPELLANT'S BRIEF ON APPEAL
ORAL ARGUMENT REQUESTED
TABLE OF CONTENTS

TABLE OF AUTHORITIES
STATEMENT OF JURISDICTION
STATEMENT OF QUESTIONS PRESENTED
STATEMENT OF FACTS
SUMMARY OF ARGUMENT
ARGUMENT
I. THE STANDARD OF REVIEW IS DE NOVO.
II. UNDER MICHIGAN LAW AND THE FAA, A PARTY CANNOT JUDICIALLY CONFIRM AN ARBITRATION AWARD WITHOUT PROVING THAT AN AGREEMENT TO ARBITRATE EXISTS.
  A. Under the FAA, Michigan Contract Law Governs the Question of Whether An Agreement to Arbitrate Was Formed.
  B. Under Michigan Law, the Party Seeking to Enforce Arbitration Bears the Burden of Proving the Existence of An Agreement to Arbitrate.
  C. This Court and Numerous Courts in Other Jurisdictions Have Refused to Confirm Arbitration Awards or Compel Arbitration Where the Party Seeking to Enforce Arbitration Failed to Prove the Existence of an Agreement to Arbitrate.
III. BECAUSE MBNA FAILED TO MEET ITS BURDEN OF PROVING THE EXISTENCE OF AN AGREEMENT TO ARBITRATE, MBNA WAS NOT ENTITLED TO SUMMARY DISPOSITION UNDER RULE 2.116(C)(10).
  A. MBNA Failed to Satisfy Its Initial Burden of Establishing that [Consumer] Assented to Arbitration.
  B. Even if MBNA Had Met Its Initial Burden, [Consumer] Presented Evidence Sufficient to Raise a Disputed Fact.
IV. BECAUSE THE LACK OF AN AGREEMENT TO ARBITRATE IS A VALID DEFENSE AGAINST CONFIRMATION OF AN ARBITRATION AWARD, MBNA WAS NOT ENTITLED TO SUMMARY DISPOSITION UNDER RULE 2.116(C)(9).
CONCLUSION

TABLE OF AUTHORITIES

Cases*

Acher v. Fujitsu Network Commc'ns., Inc., 354 F. Supp. 2d 26 (D. Mass. 2005)

Allied-Bruce Terminix Cos., Inc. v. Dobson, 513 U.S. 265 (1995)

Alltel Corp. v. Sumner, 360 Ark 573, 2005 WL 318679 (Feb. 10, 2005)

American Express Centurion Bank v. Frey, 2004 WL 1676465 (Mich. Ct. App. July 27, 2004)

Arrow Overall Supply Co. v. Peloquin Enterprises, 414 Mich. 95 (1982)

AT & T Technologies, Inc. v. Commc'ns. Workers of America, 475 U.S. 643 (1986)

Blackburne & Brown Mortgage Co. v. Ziomek, 264 Mich. App. 615 (2004)

Buckeye Check Cashing, Inc. v. Cardegna, 126 S. Ct. 1204 (2006)

CACV of Colorado, LLC v. Acevedo, 2005 WL 2981673 (Conn. Super. Ct. Oct. 19, 2005)

CACV of Colorado, LLC v. Cassidy, 2005 WL 2981680 (Conn. Super. Ct. Oct. 19, 2005)

CACV of Colorado, LLC v. Corda, 2005 WL 3664087 (Conn. Super. Ct. Dec. 16, 2005)

CACV of Colorado, LLC v. McNeil, 2005 WL 2981676 (Conn. Super. Ct. Oct. 19, 2005)

CACV of Colorado, LLC v. Werner, 2005 WL 2981677 (Conn. Super. Ct. Oct. 19, 2005)

Case v. Beech Lanes, 338 Mich. 631 (1954)

City of Ferndale v. Florence Cement Co., 269 Mich. App. 452 (2006)

Clairol, Inc. v. Enertrac Corp., 44 Conn. App. 506, 690 A2d 418 (1997)

Cruz v. State Farm Mut. Auto. Ins. Co., 241 Mich. App. 159 (2000)

---

* [*Editor's Note*: Citations throughout brief as in original.]

Davis v. Prudential Securities, Inc., 59 F.3d 1186 (11th Cir. 1995)
E.R. Zeiler Excavating, Inc. v. Valenti, Trobec & Chandler, Inc., 270 Mich. App. 639 (2006)
Eerdmans v. Maki, 226 Mich. App. 360 (1997)
Equal Employment Opportunity Comm'n v. Waffle House, Inc., 534 U.S. 279 (2002)
First Options of Chicago v. Kaplan, 514 U.S. 938 (1995)
Flanary v. Carl Gregory Dodge of Johnson City, LLC, 2005 WL 1277850 (Tenn. Ct. App. May 31, 2005)
Fleetwood Enterprises, Inc. v. Gaskamp, 280 F.3d 1069 (5th Cir. 2003)
Gerben v. Northville Downs, 1998 WL 1989834 (Mich. Ct. App. Sept. 25, 1998)
Green Tree v. Randolph, 531 U.S. 79 (2000)
Hammel v. Foor, 359 Mich. 392 (1960)
Horn v. Cooke, 118 Mich. App. 740 (1982)
In re Matarasso, 56 NY2d 264, 436 NE2d 1305 (N.Y. 1982)
Kamalnath v. Mercy Memorial Hosp. Corp., 194 Mich. App. 543 (1992)
Lockridge v. State Farm Mut. Auto. Ins. Co., 240 Mich. App. 507 (2000)
Madison Dist. Pub. Schools v. Myers, 247 Mich. App. 583 (2001)
Maiden v. Rozwood, 461 Mich. 109 (1999)
MBNA America Bank, N.A. v. Boata, 94 Conn. App. 559, 893 A.2d 479 (Mar. 28, 2006)
MBNA America Bank, N.A. v. Credit, 132 P.3d 898 (Kan. 2006)
MBNA America Bank, N.A. v. Forsmark, 2005 WL 2401444 (Mich. Ct. App. Sept. 29, 2005)
MBNA America Bank, N.A. v. Straub, 815 NYS2d 450 (N.Y. Civ. Ct. 2006)
Miller v. Miller, 474 Mich. 27 (2005)
Milwaukee Police Ass'n v. Milwaukee, 92 Wis. 2d 145, 285 NW2d 119 (1979)
Morales v. Auto-Owners Ins. Co., 458 Mich. 288 (1998)
Morris & Doherty, P.C. v. Lockwood, 259 Mich. App. 38 (2003)
Neubacher v. Globe Furniture Rentals, Inc., 205 Mich. App. 418 (1994)
Newton & Assocs., Inc. v. Furgal, 2006 WL 1479906 (Mich. Ct. App. May 30, 2006)
Offerdahl v. Silverstein, 224 Mich. App. 417 (1997)
Owen v. MBPXL Corp., 173 F. Supp. 2d 905 (N.D. Iowa 2001)
Paul Allison, Inc. v. Minkin Storage of Omaha, 452 F. Supp. 573 (D. Neb. 1978)
People v. Washington, 468 Mich. 667 (2003)
Poulson v. Trans Union LLC, 406 F. Supp. 2d 744 (E.D. Tex. 2005)
Quinto v. Cross and Peters Co., 451 Mich. 358 (1996)
Riley Manufacturing Co. v. Anchor Glass Container Corp., 157 F.3d 775 (10th Cir. 1998)
Saint George Greek Orthodox Church of Southgate v. Laupmanis Assocs., 204 Mich. App. 278 (1994)
Specht v. Netscape Commc'ns. Corp., 306 F.3d 17 (2d Cir. 2002)
SSC Assocs. Ltd. P'ship v. General Retirement System, 192 Mich. App. 360 (1991)
Strong v. Hercules Life Ins. Co., 284 Mich. 573 (1938)
Tokar v. Albery, 258 Mich. App. 350 (2003)
Tomkowski v. Ish, 2001 WL 682235 (Mich. Ct. App. Apr. 20, 2001)
Volt Information Sciences, Inc. v. Bd. of Trustees of Leland Sanford Jr. Univ., 489 U.S. 468 (1989)
Wood v. Unison Corp., 1997 WL 33330681 (Mich. Ct. App. 1997)
Worldwide Asset Purchasing, LLC v. Karafotias, 9 Misc 3d 390, 801 NYS2d 721 (Civ. Ct. 2005)
Young & Assocs. v. Rocar Precision, Inc., 2001 WL 637405 (Mich. Ct. App. May 25, 2001)
Zine v. Chrysler Corp., 236 Mich. App. 261 (1999)

Statutes

9 U.S.C. § 2
MCR 2.116(C)(10)
MCR 2.116(C)(9)
MCR 2.116(G)(3)
MCR 2.116(G)(5)
MCR 2.116(G)(6)
MCR 2.116(I)(2)
MCR 7.203(A)(1)
Mich. R. Ev. 901

Other Authorities

Caroline Mayer, Win Some, *Lose Rarely? Arbitration Forum's Rulings Called One-Sided*, Wash. Post. Mar. 1, 2000, at E1
National Arbitration Forum, California Consumer Arbitrations, 2005 Fourth Quarter, http://www.arb-forum.com/rcontrol/documents/FocusAreas/CAConsumerArbitrations2005Q4.pdf
National Arbitration Forum, Company Fact Sheet, http://www.arb-forum.com/resource.aspx?id=568

STATEMENT OF JURISDICTION

This is an appeal as of right under Michigan Court Rule ("MCR") 7.203(A)(1) from an Order of Judgment of the Circuit Court entered May 1, 2006 granting summary disposition in favor of Plaintiff-Appellee MBNA America Bank, N.A. ("MBNA") against Defendant-Appellant [*Consumer*] ("[*Consumer*]"). [*Consumer*] timely appealed on May 19, 2006.

STATEMENT OF QUESTIONS PRESENTED

1. Does the party seeking to confirm an arbitration award bear the burden of proving, with sufficient admissible evidence, the existence of a valid agreement to arbitrate, regardless of whether the party opposing confirmation has moved to vacate the award? (Yes.)

2. Did MBNA fail to satisfy its burden of proving the existence of a valid agreement to arbitrate? (Yes.)

3. In the absence of sufficient proof of the existence of a valid agreement to arbitrate, and given [*Consumer's*] uncontroverted testimony that she did not agree to arbitration, did the trial court err by granting summary disposition in favor of MBNA, whether under MCR 2.116(C)(9) or MCR 2.116(C)(10)? (Yes.)

STATEMENT OF FACTS

MBNA, alleging that [*Consumer*] owed money on a credit card account, commenced arbitration proceedings against her before the National Arbitration Forum (the "NAF"). The NAF is a private firm headquartered in Minneapolis, Minnesota. *See* National Arbitration Forum, Company Fact Sheet, http://www.arb-forum.com/resource.aspx?id=568.[1]

---

[1] The NAF is widely recognized for handling a significant number of arbitrations on behalf of creditors against debtors. *See* Caroline Mayer, *Win Some, Lose Rarely? Arbitration Forum's*

On March 9, 2005, an NAF arbitrator issued an award on behalf of MBNA against [*Consumer*] in the amount of $27,327.02. Pl.'s Mot. Summ. Disposition ("MBNA Mot.") Ex. B.

On October 31, 2005, MBNA filed this action in the 16th Judicial Circuit Court in Macomb County to confirm the arbitration award. Summons and Compl.

On March 16, 2006, MBNA filed a Motion for Summary Disposition, arguing that it was "entitled" to confirmation of the arbitration award under MCR 2.116(C)(9) and (C)(10). MBNA Mot. 2, Br. Supp. Pl.'s Mot. Summ. Disposition ("MBNA Br.") 1–2. MBNA alleged that [*Consumer*] opened an MBNA account on or about August 17, 1995; that MBNA amended its cardholder agreement in January 2000 to include a binding arbitration clause with an opt-out provision; that [*Consumer*] "failed to submit written objections to the arbitration provision to Plaintiff after the amendment notice was received by him [sic]"; and that [*Consumer*] "continued to use the account." MBNA Br. 1–2.

Attached to MBNA's motion were two exhibits: the arbitration award, and a photocopy of generic, unsigned, undated, unauthenticated credit card account document that contains an arbitration provision. MBNA Mot. ¶¶ 2, 8 & Exs. A, B. MBNA's motion stated: "Attached hereto and incorporated by reference is MBNA's credit card agreement, which sets forth the terms and conditions of the Defendant's account." MBNA Mot. ¶ 2. No affidavits or other evidence were submitted by MBNA.

[*Consumer*] opposed summary disposition, stating that she had never entered into an arbitration agreement with MBNA. Resp. Pl.'s Mot. Summ. Disp. ("[*Consumer*] Response"); Br. Opp. Pl.'s Mot. Summ. Disp. ("[*Consumer*] Br."). In support of this defense, [*Consumer*] submitted to the trial court an affidavit in which she swore, under oath, that she never agreed to arbitration when she signed up for an MBNA account; that she never received any agreement containing an arbitration clause; that she never received any document that gave her the opportunity to opt out of any changes to the MBNA account; that she reads all of her mail, including all inserts to bills; and that she would never have agreed to arbitration. [*Consumer*] Aff. ¶¶ 2–7. [*Consumer*] based these sworn statements on her personal knowledge. [*Consumer*] Aff. ¶ 11.

On May 1, 2006, a hearing was held on MBNA's Motion for Summary Disposition. At the hearing, counsel for MBNA made the following assertions:

> Just to quickly fill you in on the facts of this. The Defendant opened up a retail charge account with plaintiff, breached that account after MBNA properly amended the cardholder agreement whereby all disputes would go to arbitration. . . .
>
> [I]n 2000 MBNA properly amended the cardholder agreement. [*Consumer*] was given an opportunity to opt out of arbitration. She did not. She continued using the card. She continued receiving statements. And use of the card without objecting within 30 days is deem[ed] acceptance of the terms and conditions of the cardholder agreement.

Tr. 3–4, 10. Counsel for MBNA was not under oath while making these statements, and did not purport to be testifying as a witness. Counsel for MBNA did not introduce any witnesses at the hearing to testify in support of these factual assertions, and did not cite any evidence in the record in support of these statements. Tr. 3–4, 10.

Counsel for [*Consumer*] pointed out that, on a motion for summary disposition, "the standard of review requires the Court to look at the evidence, the record evidence in the light most favorable to the nonmoving party, [*Consumer*]." Tr. 7. Counsel for [*Consumer*] further stated that MBNA had introduced no evidence to support its claim that [*Consumer*] was bound by an arbitration agreement:

> [T]he record indicates that, number one, she never received the document claimed to be the agreement.
>
> Number two, she never got the opt out agreement, which is referenced in the plaintiff's agreement that they claim was made.
>
> [*Consumer*] in her affidavit indicates she does read all her mail, and she would have noticed changes to her credit card agreement and never agreed to those changes. . . .
>
> There is no person who, from MBNA who submitted any record evidence that, in fact, this particular agreement was sent out or the, whatever opt [out] agreement that they haven't produced, that is referred to was sent out.

Tr. 7–9. Notwithstanding this, the circuit court concluded:

> The Court believes that the agreement was properly amended. The Defendant didn't opt out of the agreement. The arbitration clause is valid. . . . The award is proper in all respects. I will confirm it.

Tr. 11. The court identified no facts in the record to support these conclusions. Tr. 11. The court then entered an order granting summary disposition for MBNA in the amount of $27,784.02.[2] Order of J. May 1, 2006. The court did not specify under which standard it was entering summary disposition for MBNA. Tr. 11; Order of J. May 1, 2006.

Rulings Called One-Sided, WASH. POST. Mar. 1, 2000, at E1 (explaining that, of nearly 20,000 arbitration awards entered by the NAF in arbitrations filed by First USA between early 1998 and March 2000, "not only has the company sought arbitration far more often than consumers, it has also won in 99.6 percent of the cases that went all the way to an arbitrator"). In California, in the fourth quarter of 2005 alone, the NAF conducted 1,119 debt collection arbitrations on behalf of MBNA. National Arbitration Forum, California Consumer Arbitrations, 2005 Fourth Quarter, www.arb-forum.com/rcontrol/documents/FocusAreas/CAConsumerArbitrations2005Q4.pdf. Statistical information about arbitrations conducted nationwide is not available on NAF's web site.

2 The court did not explain why it entered judgment against [*Consumer*] in the amount of $27,784.02 (the amount requested by MBNA in its complaint plus costs and fees), instead of $27,607.82 (the amount of the arbitration award plus costs and fees, and the amount requested by MBNA in its motion for summary disposition). MBNA Mot. 2 & Ex. B; Summons & Compl.; Order of J. May 1, 2006.

SUMMARY OF ARGUMENT

This case poses a simple question, but one of great consequence to Michigan consumers: Before a creditor is entitled to judicially confirm an arbitration award against an alleged debtor, must the creditor introduce evidence sufficient to prove that a valid agreement to arbitrate exists? Under basic principles of contract law, the Federal Arbitration Act ("FAA"), and Michigan's summary disposition rules, the answer is the same: yes.

First, arbitration is a matter of contract. An arbitrator has no authority to decide a dispute unless he or she is given jurisdiction by agreement of the parties. Thus, absent a contractual agreement between MBNA and [*Consumer*] to arbitrate their disputes, any award issued by an arbitrator is a nullity. For this reason, a court cannot confirm an arbitration award without first determining that a valid arbitration agreement exists.

Second, under ordinary principles of Michigan contract law, the party relying on the existence of a contract bears the burden of proving its existence. Likewise, under Michigan court rules, the party moving for summary disposition on grounds that no disputed fact exists bears the initial burden of supporting its claim with sufficient evidence. Thus, under any applicable standard, MBNA bore the burden of proving that a valid agreement to arbitrate existed.

MBNA failed to meet this burden. Unsworn assertions of counsel, such as those made by MBNA's counsel at the hearing on MBNA's motion, have no evidentiary value. [*Consumer*], in contrast, submitted a sworn affidavit stating unequivocally that she never agreed to arbitrate any disputes with MBNA. MBNA offered no evidence or testimony to rebut this evidence. Nonetheless, the circuit court decided by summary judgment that [*Consumer*] had agreed to waive her constitutional right to a trial on the merits, apparently based upon an unsworn assertion by the MBNA's counsel unsupported by any evidence, and in the face of her sworn testimony to the contrary. This was error under MCR 2.116(C)(10), and it should be reversed.

Likewise, any argument that [*Consumer*] did not present a valid defense to confirmation is entirely without merit. Under Michigan law, as in jurisdictions across the country, a party may validly oppose confirmation of an arbitration award on grounds that no valid agreement to arbitrate exists. Thus, summary disposition on MBNA's claim under MCR 2.116(C)(9) was erroneous and should be reversed.

ARGUMENT

I. THE STANDARD OF REVIEW IS DE NOVO.

This Court reviews *de novo* a trial court's confirmation of an arbitration award. *Tokar v. Albery*, 258 Mich. App. 350, 352 (2003). Review of a trial court's order granting summary disposition is also *de novo*. *Lockridge v. State Farm Mut. Auto. Ins. Co.*, 240 Mich. App. 507, 511 (2000). In determining whether the moving party was entitled to judgment as a matter of law, this Court "must review the record in the same manner as must the circuit court." *Morris & Doherty, P.C. v. Lockwood*, 259 Mich. App. 38, 41 (2003). Lastly, this Court reviews a trial court's interpretation of court rules *de novo*. *Saint George Greek Orthodox Church of Southgate v. Laupmanis Assocs.*, 204 Mich. App. 278, 282 (1994).

II. UNDER MICHIGAN LAW AND THE FAA, A PARTY CANNOT JUDICIALLY CONFIRM AN ARBITRATION AWARD WITHOUT PROVING THAT AN AGREEMENT TO ARBITRATE EXISTS.

Arbitration is purely a matter of contract. Under the Federal Arbitration Act ("FAA"), arbitration agreements are governed by generally-applicable rules of state contract law. In particular, state contract law principles govern the threshold determination of whether an arbitration agreement exists. *First Options of Chicago v. Kaplan*, 514 U.S. 938, 944 (1995). Because an arbitrator derives jurisdiction to decide disputes solely from an agreement between the parties, the question of whether the parties agreed to arbitrate a dispute is one that a court—not an arbitrator—must decide. Thus, until and unless a court has determined that a valid agreement to arbitrate exists under state contract law, it cannot confirm an arbitration award.

Under ordinary principles of Michigan contract law, the party asserting a contractual right bears the burden of proving that the contract exists. Therefore, unless MBNA presented sufficient evidence to prove that a valid arbitration agreement existed between MBNA and [*Consumer*], it was not entitled to confirm its arbitration award in court.

Courts in numerous jurisdictions have reached the same conclusion, refusing to confirm arbitration awards (or to compel arbitration) where the party seeking to enforce an arbitration clause fails to present sufficient evidence that an agreement to arbitrate was formed. The principles underlying these decisions—that arbitration is purely a matter of contract, and that no party can be forced to arbitrate without her consent—require reversal of the circuit court's decision in this case.

A. Under the FAA, Michigan Contract Law Governs the Question of Whether An Agreement to Arbitrate Was Formed.

As the Michigan Supreme Court recently reaffirmed, "[A]rbitration is a matter of contract. It is the agreement that dictates the authority of the arbitrators." *Miller v. Miller*, 474 Mich. 27, 32 (2005) (quotations omitted). The same basic principle was articulated by the U.S. Supreme Court two decades ago:

> Arbitration is a matter of contract and a party cannot be required to submit to arbitration any dispute which he has not agreed so to submit. This axiom recognizes the fact that arbitrators derive their authority to resolve disputes only because the parties have agreed in advance to submit such grievances to arbitration.

AT & T Technologies, Inc. v. Commc'ns. Workers of America, 475 U.S. 643, 648–49 (1986) (citations and quotations omitted).

Consistent with this, the primary substantive provision of the Federal Arbitration Act ("FAA") expressly incorporates contract law, providing in relevant part that "[a] written provision in . . . a contract evidencing a transaction involving commerce to settle by arbitration a controversy thereafter arising . . . shall be valid, irrevocable, and enforceable, save upon such grounds as exist at law or in equity for the revocation of any contract." 9 U.S.C. § 2. The FAA's grounding in contract principles ensures that "[a]rbitration under the Act is a matter of consent, not coercion." *Volt Information Sciences, Inc. v. Bd. of Trustees of Leland Sanford Jr. Univ.*, 489 U.S. 468, 479 (1989); *see also Allied-Bruce Terminix Cos., Inc. v. Dobson*, 513 U.S. 265, 281 (1995) ("[FAA] § 2 gives States a method for protecting consumers against unfair pressure to agree to a contract with an unwanted arbitration provision. States may regulate contracts, including arbitration provisions, under general contract law principles...."). Thus, an arbitration clause, to be enforceable, must be valid as a matter of state contract law.

Because "arbitrators derive their authority to resolve disputes only because the parties have agreed in advance to submit such grievances to arbitration," *AT & T Technologies*, 475 U.S. at 648–49, the threshold determination of whether an agreement to arbitrate *exists* is one that a court—not an arbitrator—must make. As the Michigan Supreme Court, the U.S. Supreme Court, and this Court have all made clear, "[t]he existence of a contract to arbitrate . . . is a judicial question which cannot be determined by an arbitrator." *Arrow Overall Supply Co. v. Peloquin Enterprises*, 414 Mich. 95, 99 (1982); *see also Buckeye Check Cashing, Inc. v. Cardegna*, 126 S. Ct. 1204, 1208 n. 1 (2006) (rule that arbitrators may decide validity of contract does not apply to question of whether an agreement was formed in the first instance); *Madison Dist. Pub. Schools v. Myers*, 247 Mich. App. 583, 590 (2001) ("The first inquiry into the arbitrability of a dispute is to determine whether an arbitration agreement has been reached by the parties. . . . The determination of whether an arbitration contract exists is for the courts to decide, applying general contract principles.") (internal quotations and citations omitted).

The reason for this rule is simple. As this Court has explained, "in the context of arbitration, the threshold issue [of whether a particular party is subject to an arbitration agreement] is not governed by the terms of the arbitration agreement, which would be a circular proposition, but by the court." *Offerdahl v. Silverstein*, 224 Mich. App. 417, 419–20 (1997).

Likewise, because arbitration is a matter of contract, and thus consent, there is no presumption that an arbitration agreement was formed, and no policy in favor of enforcing arbitration, until and unless a court finds that there is an agreement to arbitrate. Indeed, the U.S. Supreme Court explicitly rejected the argument that the FAA's pro-arbitration policy should be considered in determining whether an agreement to arbitrate exists. *Equal Employment Opportunity Comm'n v. Waffle House, Inc.*, 534 U.S. 279, 294 (2002) ("[W]e look first to whether the parties agreed to arbitrate a dispute, not to general policy goals, to determine the scope of the agreement."); *see also Fleetwood Enterprises, Inc. v. Gaskamp*, 280 F.3d 1069, 1073 (5th Cir. 2003) ("federal policy favoring arbitration does not apply to the determination of whether there is a valid agreement to arbitrate between the parties; instead '[o]rdinary contract principles determine who is bound' ") (citation omitted); *Riley Manufacturing Co. v. Anchor Glass Container Corp.*, 157 F.3d 775, 779 (10th Cir. 1998) ("[W]hen the dispute is whether there is a valid and enforceable arbitration agreement in the first place, the presumption of arbitrability falls away.").

Thus, before a court may enforce an arbitration clause by compelling arbitration or confirming an award, it must first determine that a valid agreement to arbitrate was formed under the generally-applicable contract law of the state whose law governs the question. *First Options*, 514 U.S. at 944 ("When deciding whether the parties agreed to arbitrate a certain matter (including arbitrability), courts generally . . . should apply ordinary state-law principles that govern the formation of contracts."). Here, the question of whether an agreement to arbitrate was formed between the parties must be determined under Michigan law.

B. Under Michigan Law, the Party Seeking to Enforce Arbitration Bears the Burden of Proving the Existence of An Agreement to Arbitrate.

As the Michigan Supreme Court has made clear, "[t]he burden is ordinarily on the party relying on a contract to prove that it came into existence." *Strong v. Hercules Life Ins. Co.*, 284 Mich. 573, 578 (1938); *see also Kamalnath v. Mercy Memorial Hosp. Corp.*, 194 Mich. App. 543, 549 (1992) ("The burden is on plaintiffs to show the existence of the contract sought to be enforced, and no presumption will be indulged in favor of the execution of a contract since, regardless of the equities in a case, the court cannot make a contract for the parties when none exists.") (quoting *Hammel v. Foor*, 359 Mich. 392, 400 (1960)).

It follows that a party claiming a right under a contract cannot prevail without establishing, through sufficient evidence, that the contract exists. *See Case v. Beech Lanes*, 338 Mich. 631, 636–37 (1954) (reversing with instructions to enter judgment for defendants, where, "[u]nder the record before us it must be said that plaintiff failed to establish a contract. . . . The proofs clearly preponderate against plaintiff's right to recover."); *see also Young & Assocs. v. Rocar Precision, Inc.*, 2001 WL 637405 at *4 (Mich. Ct. App. May 25, 2001) ("plaintiff, as the moving party, has the burden of proof with respect to establishing its alleged contract").[3]

The same principles apply in the case at hand. It is bedrock Michigan contract law that "[a] valid contract requires mutual assent on all essential terms." *Eerdmans v. Maki*, 226 Mich. App. 360, 364 (1997). As with any other kind of contract, the party seeking to enforce an arbitration clause bears the burden of proving that the other party assented to arbitration. *See Horn v. Cooke*, 118 Mich. App. 740, 744 (1982) ("No contract to arbitrate can arise except on the expressed mutual assent of the parties."); *Specht v. Netscape Commc'ns. Corp.*, 306 F.3d 17, 30 (2d Cir. 2002) ("Arbitration agreements are no exception to the requirement of manifestation of assent."). MBNA bore that burden here. Thus, unless MBNA met its burden of proving that [*Consumer*] assented to arbitration, the circuit court erred by confirming MBNA's arbitration award.

C. This Court and Numerous Courts in Other Jurisdictions Have Refused to Confirm Arbitration Awards or Compel Arbitration Where the Party Seeking to Enforce Arbitration Failed to Prove the Existence of an Agreement to Arbitrate.

This Court recently affirmed that, absent evidence of a valid arbitration agreement giving the arbitrator power to decide a dispute, an arbitration award cannot be confirmed in court. In *Blackburne & Brown Mortgage Co. v. Ziomek*, 264 Mich. App. 615 (2004), the plaintiff sought to enforce a California court's judgment confirming an arbitration award against the defendant. The trial court had quashed the judgment, concluding that "a valid contract never existed between the parties," that "the alleged agreement was the only basis for requiring arbitration," and that, "[b]ecause a valid contract never arose, defendants could not be required to arbitrate." 264 Mich. App. at 619. This Court affirmed both the trial court's inquiry into the existence of the alleged contract and its determination that no valid contract had been formed.

Unsurprisingly, a large number of courts have consistently declined to confirm awards obtained by creditors such as MBNA, where the creditor fails to prove that an agreement to arbitrate was

---

3 Pursuant to MCR 7.203, all unpublished cases cited herein are attached as an Appendix to this brief. Cases are in alphabetical order without regard to jurisdiction.

formed. For example, in *MBNA America Bank, N.A. v. Credit*, 132 P.3d 898 (Kan. 2006), the Kansas Supreme Court affirmed the trial court's vacatur of an arbitration award issued by the NAF based on its finding that "there is no existing agreement between the parties to arbitrate and therefore the award entered against Defendant is null and void." 132 P.3d at 900. In *Credit*, as here, MBNA asserted that it was entitled to judicial confirmation of its award simply because the defendant had not filed a timely motion to vacate. *Id.*; MBNA Br. 2–3. Rejecting MBNA's argument, the court explained: "MBNA cannot rely on Credit's tardiness in challenging the award if the arbitrator never had jurisdiction to arbitrate and enter an award. An agreement to arbitrate bestows such jurisdiction." 132 P.3d at 900.

Likewise, in *CACV of Colorado, LLC v. Corda*, 2005 WL 3664087 (Conn. Super. Ct. Dec. 16, 2005), the plaintiff, who had allegedly purchased a credit card debt from MBNA, sought to confirm an arbitration award issued by the NAF. The court declined to confirm the award, explaining:

> In support of [its claim for confirmation] the plaintiff has appended to its papers what appears to be a copy (and a poor quality copy at that) of a brochure containing an arbitration clause, with no dates and no signatures. The plaintiff alleges that the arbitration clause in this brochure is one to which the defendant consented. But there is *no evidence, aside from the plaintiff's assertion*, that the defendant ever agreed to any such thing, orally or in writing or by conduct. The signature of the defendant appears nowhere in any of the supporting documents as having entered into any contract of any kind with MBNA or as having made or authorized any charges to a credit card in the defendant's name. Under these circumstances the court cannot make a finding that the defendant agreed to arbitrate this billing dispute.

2005 WL 3664087 at *1 (emphasis added).[4]

In *MBNA America Bank, N.A. v. Straub*, 815 NYS2d 450 (N.Y. Civ. Ct. 2006), the court likewise refused to confirm an award entered on behalf of MBNA, where MBNA failed to submit evidence sufficient to permit the court to conclude that a binding credit card agreement with an arbitration provision existed. The court explained that, under either state law or the FAA, submission of the alleged agreement was necessary—but *not sufficient*—for confirmation. Rather, if a credit card contract is not signed by the cardholder, the bank must provide evidence, in the form of an "affidavit of a person with personal knowledge" presenting "the relevant documents and supporting proof" to demonstrate how the agreement became binding. *Id.* at 453; *see also Worldwide Asset Purchasing, LLC v. Karafotias*, 9 Misc 3d 390, 391, 801 NYS2d 721 (Civ. Ct. 2005) (denying petition to confirm award where moving party "failed to make a prima facie case that the award is entitled to confirmation").

For the same reasons, a court will not compel arbitration until it has determined that a valid arbitration agreement exists. In *Specht*, 306 F.3d 17, for example, the U.S. Court of Appeals for the Second Circuit held that the district court had properly denied Netscape's motion to compel arbitration, where the company failed to prove that the plaintiffs had agreed to arbitration. At issue was whether individuals who had downloaded software from a web site had become bound by a software licensing agreement that contained an arbitration clause. The individuals opposing arbitration submitted affidavits swearing that they had never seen, let alone accepted, any arbitration agreement. 306 F.3d at 23, 27. The court concluded that, "upon the record assembled, a fact-finder could not reasonably find that [Netscape] prevailed in showing that any of the user plaintiffs had entered into an agreement on defendants' license terms." *Id.* at 28. Given that Netscape had urged the court to decide the contract formation issue as a matter of law based on the "uncontroverted facts" before it, the Court of Appeals declined to remand the case for further factfinding, and simply affirmed the district court's holding that no contract had been formed. *Id.* at 27–28.

Likewise, in *Alltel Corp. v. Sumner*, 360 Ark 573, 2005 WL 318679 (Feb. 10, 2005), the Supreme Court of Arkansas refused to enforce a wireless company's arbitration clause, where the company had failed to provide sufficient proof that subscribers had received notice of the arbitration term. The company, unlike MBNA here, had submitted an affidavit in support of its motion. Nonetheless, the court declined to compel arbitration:

> Alltel relies on the Chapman affidavit to suggest that because its practice and procedure is to provide copies of the terms and conditions prior to the initiation of service, notice was established. . . . However, . . . the affidavit provided by Chapman solely confirms Alltel's practices and procedures without any information regarding whether those practices and procedures were followed at the time [Plaintiffs] subscribed to Alltel's service. We have found no case law suggesting that notice can simply be inferred from a company's statement of its practices and procedures. . . . [R]ather, there must be specific evidence that the company implemented those practices and procedures such that notice to the affected party can be reasonably inferred from the circumstances. . . .
>
> Accordingly, we affirm the circuit court's finding that there is insufficient proof that [Plaintiffs] were given a contract which provided for the requirement of arbitration.

2005 WL 318679 at *3–4.

In *Acher v. Fujitsu Network Commc'ns., Inc.*, 354 F. Supp. 2d 26 (D. Mass. 2005), similarly, the court refused to compel an employee to arbitrate his wrongful termination claim against his former employer, where the employer failed to produce evidence that the employee had been informed of the arbitration clause. The court explained:

> Mr. Acher, on the other hand, has submitted two affidavits, signed under the pains and penalties of perjury, averring that . . . [he] was not aware that the [arbitration] Policy existed until after his termination.

---

4 *See also CACV of Colorado, L.L.C. v. Acevedo*, 2005 WL 2981673 (Conn. Super. Ct. Oct. 19, 2005); *CACV of Colorado, L.L.C. v. Cassidy*, 2005 WL 2981680 (Conn. Super. Ct. Oct. 19, 2005); *CACV of Colorado, L.L.C. v. McNeil*, 2005 WL 2981676 (Conn. Super. Ct. Oct. 19, 2005); *CACV of Colorado, L.L.C. v. Werner*, 2005 WL 2981677 (Conn. Super. Ct. Oct. 19, 2005).

FNC, which bears the burden of proof on this issue, has not proffered: any evidence, such as a signed acknowledgment, that Mr. Acher actually received the Policy . . . ; any evidence, such as a sign in sheet, that Mr. Acher attended any meeting(s) at which the Policy was distributed and/or discussed; or any evidence either that Mr. Acher was advised that the Policy could be found on FNC's internal web site, or that he had accessed the Policy on the web site. . . .

Under these circumstances, I cannot find that Mr. Acher ever received notice of the Policy and therefore, FNC has failed to meet its burden to establish that there was an 'agreement' to arbitrate between the parties.

354 F. Supp. 2d at 37; *see also Poulson v. Trans Union LLC*, 406 F. Supp. 2d 744 (E.D. Tex. 2005) (refusing to compel arbitration where credit card issuer failed to prove that original contract gave issuer right to make arbitration provision binding by sending notice and requiring opt-out); *Owen v. MBPXL Corp.*, 173 F. Supp. 2d 905, 921–25 (N.D. Iowa 2001) (refusing to compel arbitration where employer failed to carry its burden of proving that arbitration clause had been distributed to employee); *Flanary v. Carl Gregory Dodge of Johnson City, LLC*, 2005 WL 1277850 (Tenn. Ct. App. May 31, 2005) (holding that party seeking to compel arbitration was not entitled to summary judgment, where genuine issue of material fact existed as to whether there was mutual agreement). The rule of these cases is straightforward: a party that does not present sufficient evidence of an agreement to arbitrate cannot expect a court to enforce that purported agreement.

The rationale for the rule that the party seeking to enforce an arbitration agreement must provide proof that the parties agreed to arbitration is plain. One of the acknowledged benefits of arbitration is that it is inherently streamlined, without the formal procedures and protections of a court proceeding. *See Davis v. Prudential Securities, Inc.*, 59 F.3d 1186, 1190 (11th Cir. 1995) ("In the arbitration setting . . . [t]he rules of evidence are employed, if at all, in a very relaxed manner.") (internal citations and quotations omitted); *Clairol, Inc. v. Enertrac Corp.*, 44 Conn. App. 506, 514, 690 A2d 418 (1997) ("This relaxation of strict evidentiary rules is both necessary and desirable because arbitration is an informal proceeding designed, in part, to avoid the complexities of litigation.") (citation omitted). However, the determination of whether an agreement to arbitrate exists is unique: unlike a typical factual finding, it goes to the heart of the arbitrator's power to decide a dispute. See *Arrow Overall*, 414 Mich. at 98; *Offerdahl*, 224 Mich. App. at 420. Particularly given the high volume of debt collection arbitrations conducted by the NAF on behalf of creditors such as MBNA,[5] and particularly in situations in which an arbitration award has been entered without the participation of one party, it is essential that courts require some proof that the defendant in a confirmation proceeding is bound by an arbitration agreement before confirming an award.

In sum, under the FAA and generally-applicable rules of Michigan contract law, a valid agreement to arbitrate is a precondition for confirmation of an arbitration award. The party seeking to confirm an arbitration award bears the burden of proving that an agreement to arbitrate exists. Unless MBNA provided sufficient evidence the [*Consumer*] agreed to arbitration, it was not entitled to confirmation of its arbitration award.

III. BECAUSE MBNA FAILED TO MEET ITS BURDEN OF PROVING THE EXISTENCE OF AN AGREEMENT TO ARBITRATE, MBNA WAS NOT ENTITLED TO SUMMARY DISPOSITION UNDER RULE 2.116(C)(10).

In this case, MBNA claimed that it was entitled to confirmation of its arbitration award against [*Consumer*], and sought summary disposition on grounds that [*Consumer*] had not raised an issue of disputed fact as to this claim under MCR 2.116(C)(10).[6] The circuit court erred in granting MBNA's motion under this standard for two reasons. First, MBNA failed to meet its burden of demonstrating, through sufficient admissible evidence, that [*Consumer*] is bound by a valid arbitration agreement. Second, even if MBNA *had* met its initial burden, [*Consumer*] submitted sworn testimony that she did not agree to arbitrate disputes with MBNA. This testimony was more than sufficient to establish a genuine issue of disputed fact as to whether an arbitration agreement had ever been formed. The circuit court was required to consider all the evidence in the light most favorable to [*Consumer*], the non-moving party. By granting summary disposition to the moving party in the face of clear, uncontested evidence presented by the nonmoving party, the circuit court turned Rule 2.116(C)(10) on its head. This was error.

A. MBNA Failed to Satisfy Its Initial Burden of Establishing that [*Consumer*] Assented to Arbitration.

A motion for summary disposition under MCR 2.116(C)(10) "tests whether there is factual support for a claim." *Neubacher v. Globe Furniture Rentals, Inc.*, 205 Mich. App. 418, 419 (1994); *see also Maiden v. Rozwood*, 461 Mich. 109, 119–20 (1999). As the Michigan Supreme Court has explained, "the initial burden of production is on the moving party." *Quinto v. Cross and Peters Co.*, 451 Mich. 358, 360 (1996). The moving party must satisfy this initial burden by submitting "affidavits, depositions, admissions, or other documentary evidence." MCR 2.116(G)(3)(b); *see also E.R. Zeiler Excavating, Inc. v. Valenti, Trobec & Chandler, Inc.*, 270 Mich. App. 639 (2006) ("The moving party must specifically identify the undisputed factual issues and has the initial burden of supporting its position with documentary evidence."). Furthermore, the moving party's evidence can only be considered to the extent that it would be admissible. MCR 2.116(G)(6).

The fact that the moving party is seeking confirmation of an arbitration award in no way alters the burden of proof. *See City of Ferndale v. Florence Cement Co.*, 269 Mich. App. 452, 456–57 (2006) (applying standard under MCR 2.116(C)(10) in analyzing disputed arbitration award); *Cruz v. State Farm Mut. Auto. Ins. Co.*, 241 Mich. App. 159, 163–64 (2000) (applying standard under MCR 2.116(C)(10) in appeal of trial court decision denying confirmation of arbitration award).

Therefore, MBNA bore the initial burden of establishing, through sufficient admissible evidence, the existence of the alleged

---

5 For example, MBNA instituted 1,119 debt collection arbitrations against alleged cardholder before the NAF in three months of 2005 in a single state. *See* note 1, *supra*.

6 MBNA moved for summary disposition under both MCR 2.116(C)(9) and MCR 2.116(C)(10). MBNA Br. 1. The circuit court did not specify under which standard it granted MBNA's motion. Tr. 1–11; Order of J. May 1, 2006. Therefore, both standards are addressed on appeal (*see* Section IV, *infra*).

arbitration agreement it sought to enforce. *See Young & Assocs.*, 2001 WL 637405 at *4 ("plaintiff, as the moving party, has the burden of proof with respect to establishing its alleged contract"). MBNA did not satisfy that burden here.

Rather, in support of its claim that it was entitled to a judgment of over $27,000 against [*Consumer*], MBNA provided the trial court with only two documents: (1) a copy of the arbitration award, and (2) a copy of a generic, unsigned, undated, unauthenticated credit card account document that contains an arbitration provision. MBNA Mot. Exs. A, B. These documents were wholly insufficient to demonstrate that [*Consumer*] was bound by an arbitration agreement.

First, an arbitration award is not evidence of a contract. The mere fact that an arbitration award has been entered against a person cannot suffice to establish that the person agreed to arbitration. As explained in Section II.A, *supra*, the threshold question of whether an agreement to arbitrate exists is a question for the court, not an arbitrator. This Court has pointed out that to permit an arbitrator to make the final determination of whether an arbitration agreement exists—when the arbitrator has no jurisdiction *unless an arbitration agreement exists*—would be a "circular proposition." *Offerdahl*, 224 Mich. App. at 420. It follows that an arbitrator's determination, particularly in an uncontested proceeding, that an arbitration agreement exists is entitled to no deference by a court of law. In short, the arbitration award attached to MBNA's motion indicates merely that an award was entered against [*Consumer*], and cannot itself constitute evidence of a valid arbitration agreement.

Nor does the generic credit card account document suffice to establish an agreement to arbitrate. For starters, the purported contract was not authenticated. MBNA put no evidence or testimony into the record to demonstrate that the document attached as Exhibit B to its motion in fact "sets forth the terms and conditions of the Defendant's account." MBNA Mot. ¶ 2. An unauthenticated document may not be considered by a court in support of a motion for summary disposition. *See Gerben v. Northville Downs*, 1998 WL 1989834, *1 (Mich. Ct. App. Sept. 25, 1998) (refusing to consider documents submitted in support of motion for summary disposition "because the unsworn and unauthenticated documents were not admissible evidence"); *see also* Mich. R. Ev. 901.

Likewise, no representative of MBNA ever testified that the purported contract is binding on [*Consumer*], let alone *how* it supposedly became binding on her. Rather, there is no evidence in the record that "MBNA properly amended the cardholder agreement whereby all disputes would go to arbitration," Tr. 3–4; that [*Consumer*] received any such amendment, MBNA Br. 1–2; that [*Consumer*] "was given an opportunity to opt out of arbitration," Tr. 10; that "[s]he did not," Tr. 10; or that by "use of the card and receiving statements without objecting within 30 days" [*Consumer*] became bound by the agreement. Tr. 10. MBNA's counsel at no time pointed to any evidence in the record to support these factual allegations, because there is no such evidence.

Thus, the statements by MBNA's counsel are nothing more than unsworn opinions with no evidentiary value. *See People v. Washington*, 468 Mich. 667, 673–74 (2003) ("unsubstantiated assertions of defense counsel are not substantive evidence"). As this Court has explained, "[o]pinions, conclusionary denials, unsworn averments, and inadmissible hearsay do not satisfy the court rule; disputed fact (or the lack of it) must be established by admissible evidence." *SSC Assocs. Ltd. P'ship v. General Retirement System*, 192 Mich. App. 360, 363–64 (1991); *see also* MCR 2.116(G)(3). Thus, MBNA's counsel's bald assertions that [*Consumer*] is bound by the arbitration clause do nothing to change the fact that MBNA failed to present *any evidence* sufficient to show that a valid agreement to arbitrate exists. Therefore, MBNA failed to meet its initial burden, and it was not entitled to confirm its award against [*Consumer*]. On this basis, the circuit court's decision granting summary disposition for MBNA must be reversed.

This Court does not hesitate to reverse grants of summary judgment where the moving party failed to meet its burden. For example, in *Newton & Assocs., Inc. v. Furgal*, 2006 WL 1479906 (Mich. Ct. App. May 30, 2006), the Court reversed the circuit court's grant of summary disposition under MCR 2.116(C)(10), where the moving party failed to submit evidence sufficient to prove the existence of a contract. Despite the fact that the defendant in *Newton* (unlike [*Consumer*]) had not filed a response to the plaintiff's motion, the Court made clear that, because the moving party had failed to satisfy its initial burden, the burden *never shifted* to the non-moving party to establish a genuine issue of material fact:

> Plaintiff has failed to present a written contract, testimony of people who allegedly entered into or witnessed an agreement, or any other evidence showing that a definite agreement actually existed. . . . Based upon the only evidence properly before the court, plaintiff clearly failed to meet its initial burden to support its claim that there was an actual agreement between the parties. . . . Accordingly, the trial court erred in granting plaintiff's motion for summary disposition under MCR 2.116(C)(10).

2006 WL 1479906 at *2; *see also Tomkowski v. Ish*, 2001 WL 682235, *1 (Mich. Ct. App. Apr. 20, 2001) (reversing trial court order granting plaintiff's motion for summary disposition where "there was no documentary evidence submitted to support the allegations"). Likewise, in *Wood v. Unison Corp.*, 1997 WL 33330681, *2 (Mich. Ct. App. 1997), the Court affirmed summary dismissal of a plaintiff's claims where, as here, the "lower court record [did] not include evidence (only unsupported statements of counsel)."

Only if the moving party satisfies its initial burden does the burden *then* shift to the opposing party to present evidence that a genuine issue of disputed fact exists. *See SSC Assocs.*, 192 Mich. App. at 364 ("[T]he party opposing a motion for summary disposition has no obligation to submit any affidavit until the moving party submits a proper affidavit regarding a dispositive fact.").

In this case, the two documents offered by MBNA no more prove the existence of an agreement to arbitrate between MBNA and [*Consumer*] than they prove the existence of an agreement to arbitrate between MBNA and any randomly-chosen individual. Moreover, MBNA's counsel's unsworn statements do nothing to support the bank's claims, because they have no evidentiary value whatsoever. As such, MBNA failed to meet its initial burden of proving that a valid agreement to arbitrate existed, and the burden never shifted to [*Consumer*] to demonstrate the existence of a genuine issue of material fact. Thus, even if [*Consumer*] had offered *no* evidence whatsoever in support of her argument that she had never agreed to arbitration, MBNA was not entitled to summary disposition. Of course, that was anything but the case here.

B. Even if MBNA Had Met Its Initial Burden, [*Consumer*] Presented Evidence Sufficient to Raise a Disputed Fact.

As demonstrated above, MBNA failed to meet its burden of proving, by sufficient admissible evidence, the existence of an agreement to arbitrate. This alone mandated denial of MBNA's motion for summary disposition.

However, in this case, the circuit court did not need to rely merely on MBNA's lack of evidence. [*Consumer*] presented sworn testimony that she never agreed to arbitration when she signed up for an MBNA account; that she never received any arbitration clause, nor any document allowing her to opt out of an arbitration clause; that she reads her mail, including bill-stuffers; and that she would never have agreed to an arbitration clause. [*Consumer*] Aff. ¶¶ 2–7. MBNA did not present any evidence or testimony to contest [*Consumer*]'s sworn statements. Nor did MBNA ever challenge [*Consumer*]'s statements through cross-examination or discovery. Thus, even if MBNA *had* made a prima facie case that an arbitration agreement existed—which it did not—[*Consumer*]'s testimony was more than sufficient to raise an issue of material fact. *See City of Ferndale*, 269 Mich. App. at 458 ("A genuine issue of material fact exists when the record, giving the benefit of reasonable doubt to the opposing party, leaves open an issue on which reasonable minds could differ.").

As this Court has made clear, in deciding whether to grant a motion for summary disposition under MCR 2.116(C)(10), the court "*must* consider not only the pleadings, but also depositions, affidavits, admissions, and other documentary evidence, MCR 2.116(G)(5), and *must* give the benefit of any reasonable doubt to the nonmoving party and *must* be liberal in finding a genuine issue of material fact." *Zine v. Chrysler Corp.*, 236 Mich. App. 261, 270 (1999); *see also Morales v. Auto-Owners Ins. Co.*, 458 Mich. 288, 294 (1998).

In *American Express Centurion Bank v. Frey*, 2004 WL 1676465 (Mich. Ct. App. July 27, 2004), the Court confronted a case in which the plaintiff credit card company—like MBNA here—claimed rights based on an alleged contract. The circuit court had granted the creditor's motion for summary disposition. Reversing, the Court explained:

> Plaintiff's complaint alleged breach of contract, and its motion for summary disposition argued there was no genuine issue of fact that defendant had breached the contract and was indebted to plaintiff, yet at no time did plaintiff submit a copy of the contract it alleged defendant had breached. The contract not being before us, the parties' obligations thereunder in the event of unauthorized charges are unknown to us, beyond the cursory explanation provided on the back of monthly account statements.... Nor did plaintiff submit below the application that defendant signed. The affidavit plaintiff submitted below states only broad, conclusory statements [and] is unsupported by pertinent documentation...
>
> The circuit court did not view the facts in a light most favorable to defendant, the non-movant, and erroneously concluded that plaintiff had met its burden to show entitlement to judgment as a matter of law by mere allegations.... Under these circumstances, summary disposition under MCR 2.116(C)(10) was improper.
>
> Even assuming that plaintiff did meet its initial burden of production under MCR 2.116(C)(10), we conclude that the pleadings and documentary evidence submitted below, viewed in a light most favorable to defendant, raised a genuine issue of fact whether the disputed charges could be legitimately charged to defendant ... given that defendant maintains he did not authorize the disputed charges.

Id. at *3–4.

Here, likewise, there is no evidence in the record connecting any alleged arbitration clause to [*Consumer*]. MBNA did not meet its burden of showing it was entitled to judgment as a matter of law by "mere allegations." *Frey*, 2004 WL 1676465 at *4. Thus, viewing the evidence in the light most favorable to the non-moving party, it is clear that MBNA was not entitled to summary disposition. Indeed, the record demonstrates that [*Consumer*] never assented to arbitration with MBNA.[7]

Furthermore, given that MBNA failed to meet its burden of proof despite ample opportunity to put forth evidence before the trial court, MBNA's complaint should now simply be dismissed with prejudice. *See Specht*, 306 F.3d at 27–28 (affirming district court's holding that no agreement to arbitrate had been formed and declining to remand for further factfinding); *cf. Green Tree v. Randolph*, 531 U.S. 79, 91–92 (2000) ("[W]here, as here, a party seeks to invalidate an arbitration agreement on the ground that arbitration would be prohibitively expensive, that party bears the burden of showing the likelihood of incurring such costs. Randolph did not meet that burden. How detailed the showing of prohibitive expense must be before the party seeking arbitration must come forward with contrary evidence is a matter we need not discuss; for in this case neither during discovery nor when the case was presented on the merits was there any timely showing at all on the point.").

IV. BECAUSE THE LACK OF AN AGREEMENT TO ARBITRATE IS A VALID DEFENSE AGAINST CONFIRMATION OF AN ARBITRATION AWARD, MBNA WAS NOT ENTITLED TO SUMMARY DISPOSITION UNDER RULE 2.116(C)(9).

Michigan Court Rule 2.116(C)(9) provides that a motion for summary disposition may be based on the grounds that "[t]he opposing party has failed to state a valid defense to the claim asserted against him or her." MCR 2.116(C)(9).[8] Under this subrule, summary disposition is appropriate only if "the defenses are

---

7 On this basis, [*Consumer*]—rather MBNA—was entitled to summary disposition. *See* MCR 2.116(I)(2) ("If it appears that the party opposing summary judgment, rather than the moving party, is entitled to judgment, the court may render judgment in favor of the opposing party.").

8 As explained in note 6, *supra*, MBNA moved for summary disposition under both MCR 2.116(C)(9) and MCR 2.116(C)(10). A court considering whether to grant summary disposition under MCR 2.116(C)(9) may consider only the pleadings. MCR 2.116(G)(5).

so clearly untenable as a matter of law that no factual development could possibly deny the plaintiff's right to recovery." *Morris & Doherty,* 259 Mich. App. at 42 n.4. Here, MBNA claimed that it was entitled to confirm an arbitration award against [*Consumer*]. [*Consumer*]'s defense to this claim was, simply, that no agreement to arbitrate was ever formed between the parties. Under settled Michigan law, the lack of an agreement to arbitrate is a valid defense to confirmation of an arbitration award. Thus, MBNA was not entitled to summary disposition under MCR 2.116(C)(9).

The Michigan Supreme Court decided this issue in [*Consumer*]'s favor over two decades ago in *Arrow Overall,* 414 Mich. 95. In *Arrow Overall,* as in the present case, an arbitration award had been entered against the defendant, and the plaintiff brought an action in circuit court to confirm the award. 414 Mich. at 97. Like [*Consumer*], the defendant—who had not participated in the arbitration—raised the argument that there was no agreement to arbitrate for the first time in opposition to the plaintiff's motion to confirm. *Id*; [*Consumer*] Aff. ¶ 10; Tr. 10. The court confirmed the award without determining that a binding arbitration agreement existed, and the Court of Appeals affirmed, holding that the defendant had not timely raised the argument. Reversing, the high court held that "the defense of 'no valid agreement to arbitrate' may be raised in an action to confirm or enforce an arbitration award." *Id.* at 98. The court explained:

> The defense of "no valid agreement to arbitrate" is a direct attack on the exercise of jurisdiction of both the arbitrator and the circuit court. The decision to submit disputes to arbitration is a consensual one. Arbitration is a matter of contract and a party cannot be required to submit to arbitration any dispute which he has not agreed so to submit.... It follows that a valid agreement must exist for arbitration to be binding.

Id. (citations omitted). In holding that the defense was valid, the court also made clear that a party may oppose confirmation of an arbitration award on grounds that no agreement to arbitrate exists regardless of whether a motion to vacate the award has been filed, and regardless of whether such a motion would be timely. As the court explained, "Whenever the jurisdiction of an arbitrator is questioned, it must be determined in order to make an award on arbitration binding." *Id.* at 98–99; *see also id.* at 100 ("[T]he defendant is not seeking to vacate the award, but simply opposes its confirmation. Since the rule prescribes no time limitation on the interposition of defenses, it would appear proper to allow it whenever it be sought to confirm the award.").[9] Thus, [*Consumer*]'s defense that no valid agreement to arbitrate exists is both valid *and* timely.

Consistently with this, this Court recently refused to affirm a trial court's confirmation of an MBNA arbitration award where the trial court had failed to determine that a valid agreement to arbitrate existed. *MBNA America Bank, N.A. v. Forsmark,* 2005 WL 2401444 (Mich. Ct. App. Sept. 29, 2005). MBNA's argument in *Forsmark* mirrored its argument in this case:

> Plaintiff argues that, on the merits, it was entitled to summary disposition because the asserted defense rested solely on a challenge to the validity of the agreement to arbitrate, but defendant failed to take the necessary action to vacate, correct, or modify the arbitration award.

2005 WL 2401444 at *1. Applying *Arrow Overall,* the Court rejected MBNA's argument and held that "the defendant was not precluded from challenging the existence of an arbitration agreement as a defense to plaintiff's action to confirm the arbitration award." *Id.* at *2.

A myriad of courts in other jurisdictions have likewise held that a motion to confirm an arbitration award may be denied on grounds that no agreement to arbitrate exists, regardless of whether a timely motion to vacate the award was filed. *See, e.g., MBNA America Bank, N.A. v. Boata,* 94 Conn. App. 559, 893 A.2d 479 (Mar. 28, 2006), *review granted,* 2006 WL 1623360 (Conn. May 16, 2006) (reversing confirmation on grounds that defendant's argument that no agreement to arbitrate existed was relevant to subject matter jurisdiction, and thus could be raised outside time limit for moving to vacate); *Corda,* 2005 WL 3664087 at *1 (declining to confirm award where creditor failed to present sufficient evidence that agreement to arbitrate existed); *Credit,* 132 P.3d 898 (vacating MBNA/NAF arbitration award on grounds that MBNA had failed to prove that a valid agreement to arbitrate existed); *Straub,* 815 NYS2d 450 (denying motion to confirm where MBNA failed to provide adequate documentation to prove existence of arbitration agreement); *Karafotias,* 801 NYS2d 721 (denying petition to confirm where moving party included only assertions of counsel and copy of arbitration award); *Milwaukee Police Ass'n v. Milwaukee,* 92 Wis. 2d 145, 285 NW2d 119 (1979) (holding that party may object to confirmation outside time limit for moving to vacate); *cf. Paul Allison, Inc. v. Minkin Storage of Omaha,* 452 F. Supp. 573, 575 (D. Neb. 1978) (FAA's time limit for moving to vacate award "is inapplicable when the party who prevails at arbitration moves to confirm the award and the defendant desires to raise objections in response to that motion"); *In re Matarasso,* 56 NY2d 264, 267, 436 NE2d 1305 (N.Y. 1982) (stay of arbitration may be granted on grounds that no agreement to arbitrate exists, regardless of untimeliness).

In sum, an agreement to arbitrate is a precondition to judicial enforcement of arbitration. Absent an agreement, there is simply no basis on which a court may compel arbitration or confirm an arbitration award. As such, [*Consumer*]'s argument that no agreement to arbitrate exists is by definition a "valid defense" to MBNA's motion to confirm its award. Thus, MBNA was not entitled to summary disposition under MCR 2.116(C)(9), and the circuit court's decision must be reversed.

CONCLUSION

For the reasons stated above, the decision of the circuit court should be reversed, and MBNA's complaint should be dismissed.

Respectfully submitted this [*Date*]

[*Attorneys for Defendant-Appellant*]

---

9 Although the plaintiff in *Arrow Overall* sought confirmation pursuant to the precursor to MRC 3.602, rather than seeking summary disposition under MRC 2.116, the court's reasoning applies with equal force regardless of the procedure by which a plaintiff seeks to confirm an award. Like MRC 3.602, Michigan's summary disposition rules certainly "prescribe[] no time limitation on the interposition of defenses." 414 Mich. at 100.

Appendix M — AAA and NAF Documents, Additional Briefs, Other Resources Found Only on the CD-Rom

M.1 Introduction

This appendix summarizes key documents found on the CD-Rom accompanying this volume that are not found in the volume's appendices. These documents can be searched using key words and Internet-style navigation, and pasted into a word processing program.

M.2 American Arbitration Association Materials

A commonly used arbitration service provider in consumer cases is the American Arbitration Association (AAA). The AAA's Rules are reprinted with permission in Appendix B, *supra*, and are found on the CD-Rom accompanying this volume. The CD-Rom also includes a series of AAA documents relevant to establishing AAA arbitration costs, the availability of fee waivers, the AAA's relationship to companies that specify arbitration by the AAA in their consumer contracts, and the AAA's financial status. The AAA has changed some of its rules for certain categories of cases since many of these documents were created, so practitioners need to verify the continuing accuracy of much of this information.

A number of these documents are affidavits from AAA personnel filed in individual lawsuits, and the affidavits include attachments that are *not* included on the CD-Rom, as they are not germane. The attachments are outdated copies of AAA rules and pleadings in the cases in which the affidavits were filed. Many of the documents are numbered, for example as AAA000100, and these numbers are listed below. These documents were obtained through discovery in a case, and the pages were numbered during that process.

- *Affidavit of Christine Newhall, Vice President, Case Administration of the AAA, on April 18, 2001 (AAA 000309–311)*: In commercial cases, arbitrators shall be compensated at a rate consistent with the arbitrator's stated rate of compensation, established by the arbitrator. A random sample of twenty-six arbitrators from the commercial panel in Indiana found daily rates ranging from $700 to $1800, the mean rate being $1308 and the median rate being $1225. Administrative fees can be waived, but the AAA has no authority to defer or reduce the arbitrator's compensation.
- *Affidavit of Frank Zotto, Vice President, Case Administration of the AAA, on June 25, 2001 (AAA 000452–454)*: In an employment case, the filing fee before a single arbitrator is $500 payable in full, in advance, by the filing party, and there is an administrative fee of $150 for each hearing day payable by each party. The filing and administrative fee can be waived, deferred, or reduced upon filing of a hardship affidavit.
- *Affidavit of Frank Zotto, Vice President, Case Administration of the AAA, on June 28, 2001 (AAA 000387–389)*: Notwithstanding what is specified in the agreement, if a claim is for less than $10,000, it will be administered using the AAA's consumer claims rules, unless the parties agree otherwise after commencement of the arbitration. A random sampling of thirty-eight arbitrators on the commercial panel in Denver found compensation ranging from $600 to $2500 a day, with a mean rate of $1442 and median rate of $1500.
- *Affidavit of Frank Zotto, Vice President, Case Administration of the AAA, on June 28, 2001 (AAA 000119–122)*: Regardless of the arbitration agreement, if a case fits within the scope of the AAA's consumer rules, it will be decided under those rules. The arbitrator has authority to apportion fees in any manner in the award. A random sampling of sixty arbitrators on the Chicago commercial panel found a range of daily rates from $750 to $5000, with a mean rate of $1800 and a median rate of $1698. The AAA can not change, modify or waive arbitrator compensation. The affidavit also refers to other arbitrator expenses, including travel. The consumer rules apply if the amount in dispute is less than $10,000. The total charge for this type of arbitration is $125 to the consumer and $625 to the business. Such arbitration involves reviewing documents and an optional telephone hearing. If an in-person hearing is requested, it must be administered under the commercial rules.
- *Affidavit of Chris Heelan, Vice President of Finance of the AAA, on August 1, 2001 (AAA 000116–118)*: The consumer rules do not provide for financial hardship

551

requests. The consumer pays $125 solely for arbitrator compensation and the AAA can not seek deferral or reduction of this amount. In commercial cases the AAA will waive all administrative fees only in the case of extreme financial hardship. More commonly, the consumer would pay a small percentage of the fee and the balance would be apportioned between the parties by the arbitrator in the award. The AAA has no authority to defer or reduce the arbitrator's compensation.

- *Affidavit of Frank Zotto, Vice President, Case Administration of the AAA, on August 15, 2001 (AAA 000188, 000189)*: The party making the claim must advance the filing fee. The parties can agree to another arrangement. A sampling of thirty-one arbitrators on the commercial panel in Hamilton County, Ohio found arbitrator compensation to range from $600 to $2100 a day, with a mean rate of $1468 and a median rate of $1400. The AAA has no authority to change, modify or waive arbitrator compensation.

- *Affidavit of Chris Heelan, Vice President of Finance of the AAA, on August 28, 2001 (AAA 000218, 000219)*: Discusses fee waiver procedure, but finds no authority to defer, reduce, or waive arbitrator compensation.

- *Affidavit of Chris Heelan, Vice President of Finance of the AAA, on September 18, 2001 (AAA 000220–222)*: No waiver or deferral of $125 fee in arbitration under consumer rules because fee is used to pay arbitrator. As to waiver of the administrative fee, commonly the consumer would pay a small percentage of the fee and the balance would be apportioned between the parties by the arbitrator in the award. He receives approximately two to three financial hardship requests a week and, since July 1, 2001, has not denied a request for deferment or reduction of administrative fees. [*Editor's Note: He does not mention requests for a full waiver, and these deferments apply only to administrative fees.*]

- *Affidavit of Frank Zotto, Vice President, Case Administration of the AAA, on August 15, 2001 (AAA 000223, 000224)*: Administrative fees were deferred or reduced in approximately ninety-five percent of cases.

- *Affidavit of Frank Zotto, Vice President, Case Administration of the AAA, on September 4, 2001 (AAA 000225–228)*: Cases meeting the AAA's criteria will be administered pursuant to the consumer rules despite language to the contrary in the agreement. Arbitrators can apportion fees in any way in the award and the parties can agree to an alternate division. The default is that each side pays half. Arbitrators are to be compensated at a rate consistent with a rate of compensation set by the arbitrator. A sampling of sixty arbitrators on the commercial panel in Chicago found compensation to range from $750 to $5000 per day, with a mean rate of $1800 and a median rate of $1698. The AAA has no authority to modify, defer, or waive this compensation. If the amount in dispute is less than $10,000, the consumer rules apply and the consumer pays $125 and the business pays $625. The case is resolved by reviewing documents, with an optional phone call costing $100 to be paid by the business. In-person hearings must proceed under the commercial rules.

- *Affidavit of Frank Zotto, Vice President, Case Administration of the AAA, on October 4, 2001 (AAA 000478–480)*: In an employment case, the filing fee before a single arbitrator is $500, there is an administrative fee of $150 for each hearing day payable by each party, and arbitrators are paid consistent with their stated rate of compensation, established by the arbitrator. A sampling of fifteen arbitrators on the employment panel in Virginia, North Carolina, Maryland, and the District of Columbia found daily rates ranging from $700 to $2000, the mean rate being $1403 and the median rate being $1500. Estimated arbitrator compensation is to be deposited before the hearing. The daily rate is generally applied to hearing time, and also to study and research time and to time spent writing the award.

- *Affidavit of Chris Heelan, Vice President of Finance of the AAA, on October 5, 2001 (AAA 000517–519)*: The AAA in cases of extreme hardship can reduce or defer the administrative fee. The more common action would be a requirement that a party pay a small percentage of the fee, and the arbitrator will then apportion the remainder of the administrative fee between the parties upon resolution of the case. The fee waiver only applies to AAA administrative fees and in no way relates to arbitrator compensation—the AAA has no authority to and can not waive, defer, or reduce arbitrator compensation.

- Information regarding sample AAA (and National Arbitration Forum) arbitration dollar costs, based on (1) a confidential AAA affidavit; (2) the affidavit of Donald Cox, on February 27, 2004; (3) the affidavit of Donald Cox, affiliated with NAF, on February 25, 2004, discussing his hourly rates and the number of hours required for a typical employment discrimination case; and (4) the affidavit of David Patterson, an experienced arbitrator in employment discrimination cases, on February 24, 2004, indicating his hourly rates and the time required for a typical employment discrimination case.

- *AAA Documents in Its AT & T File (AAA000001–115)*: The CD-Rom includes approximately one hundred pages of correspondence between AT & T and the AAA, and notes by AAA employees relating to their relationship with AT & T. While AT & T charged the AAA with conducting neutral arbitration, it simultaneously hired the AAA to help set up its arbitration program. Document AAA000018 states that the AAA was charging $2400 per day for "Senior Advisors" providing advice to AT & T on how to implement AT & T's arbitration program. Document AAA000088 recites how AT & T was "upset with us over a $150 million case that they believe was mishandled" but that AAA representatives had met with an AT & T official and "mended the relationship. . . . They are a substantial customer."

- *Depositions of Frank Zotto and Chris Heelan, October 4, 2001*: The content of these depositions can be summarized by the following from the court's opinion in *Ting v. AT & T*:

  > 60. No AAA rule governs when it will or will not waive or defer its administrative fee. No publicly available documents describe the criteria used for determining what constitutes extreme hardship. There are no internal AAA documents that define or discuss how waivers or deferrals should be granted. The last two people responsible for evaluating such requests received no training or instruction in how to evaluate such requests.
  >
  > 61. Although AAA frequently grants requests for administrative fee reductions, waivers, or deferrals, it rarely waives or defers its fees entirely. Instead, AAA more typically defers a portion of its fees to a later date in the proceeding, such as the hearing.

[*Editor's Note: AAA has amended its rules in the wake of the Zotto and Heelan depositions. Explicit criteria are provided as to what constitutes "extreme hardship": income below 200% of the federal poverty guidelines.*]

- *Deposition of Christine Newhall, October 4, 2001*: Deals with what information is available on AAA's computers and in its files to track cases.
- *AAA Federal Tax Return Form 990 for the Year 2000*: Includes gain from sale of securities and schedule of investments, schedule of depreciation expense, list of officers, trustees, key employees, and board of directors, relationship of activities to accomplishment of exempt purposes, schedule of other functional expenses and other assets, statement of program service accomplishment, change in fund balance explanation, reason for difference of expenses, and reason for nonprofit status.
- *Affidavit of Adam Bushman, former AAA Case Administrator, on September 26, 2002, and October 16, 2002*: Alleges AAA bias towards businesses and that AAA was in violation of its own ethical standards.
- *Deposition of Molly Bargenquest, Vice President of Case Management for the AAA, on December 16, 2003 (Vol. 1)*: Describes the potential arbitration costs involved in a complex arbitration involving numerous home owners.
- Transcript of telephone conference in *In re Wireless Telephone Services Antitrust Litigation*, Southern District of New York, November 18, 2004, relating to a motion to compel the AAA to provide certain information and discussing, among other topics, the number and background of arbitrators, how AAA keeps their records, the nature of the AAA's due process protocols, and how AAA is complying with the California disclosure requirements.
- Affidavit of Gerald Strathmann, AAA Assistant Vice President for consumer arbitrations, describing AAA rules and procedures, including the fact that AAA will not administer loser pay rules for non-prevailing consumers, that there are seventy-six class actions currently pending before the AAA and fourteen have been completed, AAA knows of no case in which an arbitrator has handled a class action on a pro bono basis, and AAA will not accept class claims unless a court orders the parties to submit a dispute to arbitration.
- Letter from AAA to Paul Mengedoth stating that Household Finance and related companies have not complied with AAA's Consumer Rules and/or Consumer Due Process Protocol and that AAA will not administer any consumer-related claims involving that business.
- Letter from AAA to Melissa Sherman stating that Household Finance had not complied with AAA's Consumer Rules and/or Consumer Due Process Protocol and that AAA will not administer any consumer-related claims involving that business.
- Letter from AAA regarding calculation of administrative fees.

M.3 National Arbitration Forum Materials

The CD-Rom contains a number of materials relating to the National Arbitration Forum (NAF), another major provider of arbitration services to resolve disputes involving consumers. The documents were either filed as exhibits in litigation or otherwise collected by lawyers around the country in an attempt to demonstrate that NAF is biased in favor of corporations and other repeat users of its services. Another document contains a complaint filed against NAF for violating California's disclosure law relating to arbitration service providers. Perhaps the most current and comprehensive document is a report (reprinted with permission from Public Citizen) focusing on NAF arbitrations, and consumer collection arbitrations in particular.

- Public Citizen, *How Credit Card Companies Ensnare Consumers* (Sept. 2007), analyzing NAF data on California arbitrations disclosed pursuant to California statute, and also including case studies and other information about NAF arbitrations.
- *Corbett & Consumer Action v. National Arbitration Forum* (Cal. Super. Court, San Francisco, Case No. 04-431430), Complaint, filed May 17, 2004. Trial Lawyers for Public Justice's lawsuit charging the National Arbitration Forum with violating California disclosure law.

- Information regarding sample NAF (and American Arbitration Association) arbitration dollar costs, based on (1) a confidential AAA affidavit; (2) the affidavit of Donald Cox, on February 27, 2004; (3) the affidavit of Donald Cox, affiliated with NAF, on February 25, 2004, discussing his hourly rates and the number of hours required for a typical employment discrimination case; and (4) the affidavit of David Patterson, an experienced arbitrator in employment discrimination cases, on February 24, 2004, indicating his hourly rates and the time required for a typical employment discrimination case.
- Deposition of Edward Anderson, General Manager of the NAF, on September 29, 2003, including over one-hundred pages discussing various aspects of the NAF, including its history, clients, methods of operation, and the nature of its arbitrations.
- NAF solicitation including "Lenders Adopting Forum Agreements" and "Information Resources," a list of lenders and lender counsel considered by NAF to be its clients.
- A letter from Curtis Brown, Director of Development of the NAF, encouraging Richard Shephard, General Counsel of Saxon Mortgage (a subsidiary of Meritech), to add arbitration language to Saxon's contracts.
- A letter from Leif Stennes of the NAF to Richard Shephard, General Counsel of Saxon Mortgage, encouraging him to use the NAF as his arbitration provider.
- A letter from Ed Anderson, Managing Director of the NAF, to Richard Shephard, General Counsel of Saxon Mortgage, chastising him for invoking the rules of "the other guys" (referring to the American Arbitration Association) in his arbitration agreement, and encouraging him to redraft the agreement.
- The NAF Fee Schedule (in effect on March 1, 1996).
- The NAF "Starter Kit." This pamphlet is sent to companies by the NAF, which encourages them to "plan now [and ensure] no lawsuits, no exorbitant legal fees, no court delays, no irrational jury verdicts" by including "a simple clause—an arbitration clause—in every contract." The kit includes sample arbitration clauses for standard business, employment, and credit contracts, as well as consumer credit contracts.
- An NAF marketing document entitled "All Arbitration is Not the Same," indicating the differences between arbitration by the NAF and by the American Arbitration Association (AAA)—for instance, in NAF proceedings "consolidation [is] permitted only with agreement of all parties" whereas the rules in other forums are silent as to consolidation, and in NAF proceedings the failure of a party to respond to a claim results in admission of the claim whereas in other forums there is a mandatory hearing even if the other party does not respond.
- An NAF marketing document that begins by describing the NAF as "[t]he Alternative to the Million Dollar Lawsuit."
- A letter from Curtis Brown, Vice President and General Counsel of the NAF, to Robert Banks, encouraging him to use arbitration because it eliminates class actions and "will make a positive impact on the bottom line."
- A letter from Roger Haydock, Director of Arbitration of the NAF, to Alan Kaplinsky, encouraging him to use arbitration to resolve Y2K class actions, and characterizing the plaintiff's bar as the "class action" bar.
- Advertisement in Corporate Counsel stating that: "Arbitration can save up to 66% of your collection costs."
- Letters from Charles DiSalvo, Martin Glasser, and the Hon. Thomas McHugh, indicating that they have become aware that they are listed by the NAF in a federal court filing as neutral arbitrators for the NAF, but that NAF's representations to the court are not true—that in fact they have never agreed to arbitrate for the NAF.
- Answers to interrogatories from First U.S.A. Bank in the case *Bownes v. First USA Bank*, in the Circuit Court of Montgomery County, Alabama, indicating in a chart on the final page that First USA prevailed in 98% of almost 20,000 bank/card member arbitrations that had proceeded to a final resolution.
- An NAF marketing document summarizing the NAF Code of Procedure and stating benefits of the NAF such as limited awards, cost control, "little or no discovery," confidentiality, and loser pays provisions requiring consumers to pay the corporation's attorney fees.
- Interview with Ed Anderson, Managing Director of the NAF, in *Metropolitan Corporate Counsel*, including observations by Anderson that arbitration can reduce the possibility of punitive damages and extensive discovery; also that arbitration agreements can include "loser pays" provisions.
- July 16, 2001 deposition of Ed Anderson, Managing Director of the NAF, in *Toppings v. Meritech*. Deposition includes information about Anderson's previous involvement as a shareholder of Equilaw, a wholly-owned subsidiary of NAF, at the same time he was counsel for ITT Financial, a company that used NAF arbitration. Deposition also discusses arbitrator selection, arbitration fees, and the Code of Procedure. [*Editor's Note: PDF file.*]
- Letter dated October 20, 1997, from Ed Anderson, Managing Director of the NAF, to an undisclosed recipient, urging this person to put arbitration agreements in all contracts and stating that "there is no reason for your clients to be exposed to the costs and risks of the jury system."
- Article by Alan Kaplinsky, entitled "Excuse Me, but Who's the Predator?," discussing ways in which "banks can use arbitration clauses as a defense." Kaplinsky is listed by the NAF as one of its "Information Resources" on a document it sends to corporate counsel (listed above).
- A legal memorandum from NAF counsel to undis-

AAA and NAF Documents   Appx. M.3

closed recipients, regarding "Arbitration and Class Actions in Financing," concluding that: "Forum Arbitrations may not be consolidated into class actions unless all parties consent."
- Professor Michael Giest's study of NAF arbitrator bias in the Internet Corporation for Assigned Names and Numbers (ICANN) process, entitled "Fair.com? An Examination of the Allegations of Systematic Unfairness in the ICANN UDRP" (UDRP is the Uniform Domain Name Dispute Resolution Policy). Study finds that complainants win in arbitration before the NAF nearly 83% of the time, due primarily to the fact that "despite claims of impartial random case allocation as well as a large roster of 131 panelists, the majority of NAF single panel cases are actually assigned to little more than a handful of panelists." The study also mentions the NAF's marketing strategy of sending out a newsletter highlighting cases in which complainants have won in arbitration (see DomainNews articles referenced below).
- Articles from DomainNews, the news service of the National Arbitration Forum, highlighting cases in which a high-profile complainant won a domain name dispute in arbitration. Examples include "Master of Domains: metallica.org," "Rose Bowl Kicks out Squatter," and "Johnny Unitas Wins Another One."
- Letter brief from Trial Lawyers for Public Justice to the California Supreme Court in *Mercuro v. Superior Court*, opposing NAF's request for depublication of that case on the grounds that the case involves an issue of continuing public interest, and that the court in *Mercuro* correctly characterized the NAF as being subject to repeat-player bias.
- *Amicus* brief filed by NAF in the federal District Court for the Northern District of Texas in *Marsh v. First USA Bank*. The NAF brief is filed on behalf of neither side, but makes the same arguments as the defendant in that case: namely, that "arbitration is pro-consumer," that arbitration is important in the modern economy, that arbitration provisions should be enforced, and that the NAF is not a biased forum. [*Editor's Note: PDF file.*]
- June 1, 1994 deposition of Ed Anderson in *ITT Commercial Finance v. Wangerin*, demonstrating the connection between the NAF and Equilaw, Inc., the decision of ITT (where Anderson was employed) to use Equilaw for arbitration, and Mr. Anderson's involvement as a shareholder of Equilaw.
- Declaration Concerning Debtor's Schedules filed in U.S. Bankruptcy Court in 1994 by Ed Anderson on behalf of Equilaw, and indicating that at that time Mr. Anderson was Director, officer, and major shareholder of Equilaw.
- November 27, 2002 deposition of Ed Anderson, Managing Director of the NAF, in *Ebarle v. Household Retail Services*. Deposition includes discussion of NAF's solicitations comparing NAF and AAA, NAF's arbitrator selection process, the application of NAF rules when they conflict with the language in the parties' contract, and NAF's relationship with Household.
- Memorandum of Law in Opposition to Defendants' Motion to Compel Arbitration in *McQuillan v. Check 'N Go of North Carolina, Inc.*, North Carolina Superior Court, arguing, among other things, that the arbitration requirement forces consumers to appear before a biased forum (NAF arbitration). The brief refers to a number of exhibits that are listed below which relate to NAF bias.
- *Affidavit of Richard Fisher on August 5, 2005*, indicating NAF's failure to appear for a deposition (*McQuillan* Exh. 14).
- *Deposition of Edward Anderson, Managing Director of the NAF, on September 29, 2003*, taken in *Hubbert v. Dell*, concerning the workings of NAF (*McQuillan* Exh. 16).
- *Affidavit of Paul Bland on August 8, 2005*, with exhibits, concerning NAF marketing to corporations and other aspects of NAF (*McQuillan* Exh. 17).
- *Affidavit of Professor Michael Geist on August 3, 2005*, concerning NAF marketing to corporations (*McQuillan* Exh. 20).
- NAF advertisement labeled "Professionals and the National Arbitration Forum" (*McQuillan* Exh. 21).
- NAF News Release listing "Lenders Adopting Forum Agreements" (*McQuillan* Exh. 22).
- Excerpts from deposition of Clinton Walker discussing NAF marketing to corporations (*McQuillan* Exh. 27).
- *Affidavit of Gregory Duhl* discussing NAF bias (*McQuillan* Exh. 25).
- *Affidavit of Bren Pomponio* discussing NAF bias (*McQuillan* Exh. 26).
- California Superior Court decision in *Klussman v. Cross-Country Bank*, discussing NAF's lack of compliance with California law requiring NAF to make certain disclosures (*McQuillan* Exh. 29).
- *Affidavit of Justin Baxter on May 26, 2005, and of Laurie Raymond on March 18, 2005*, discussing questionable NAF procedures (*McQuillan* Exh. 30).
- *Affidavit of Eve Curtis on August 4, 2005*, discussing questionable NAF procedures (*McQuillan* Exh. 31).
- *Affidavit of Lester Perry on August 3, 2005*, discussing questionable NAF procedures (*McQuillan* Exh. 32).
- *Affidavit of Patricia Meisse on August 3, 2005*, discussing questionable NAF procedures (*McQuillan* Exh. 33).
- *Affidavit of Joanne Faulkner on August 5, 2005*, discussing questionable NAF procedures (*McQuillan* Exh. 34).
- *Affidavit of Charles DeSalvo on August 2, 2005*, discussing questionable NAF procedures (*McQuillan* Exh. 36).
- *Affidavit of Sally Greenberg* discussing questionable NAF procedures (*McQuillan* Exh. 37).

M.4 Reprints of Arbitration Agreements

The CD-Rom contains over 150 arbitration agreements found in standard form contracts. Approximately half are included in consumer credit agreements with various credit card issuers and other creditors, such as Bank One, Citibank, Associates Financial Services, Fleet Bank, First USA, Provident Bank, Wells Fargo, Crestar, Monogram Credit Card Bank, Discover, Conseco, and Toyota Motor Credit. The other half are from merchants, insurers, utilities, and employers.

Such sample arbitration agreements may be helpful in comparing a particular agreement with that found in other contracts, or they may be helpful in demonstrating that it is becoming more and more difficult for a consumer to find a creditor or other merchant which offers an agreement without an arbitration clause.

M.5 Statutes and Standards Concerning Arbitration

The CD-Rom reprints the full text of the California Ethics Standards for Arbitrators (Apr. 16, 2002), issued by the Judicial Council of California as an appendix to the California Rules of Court, pursuant to Cal. Civ. Proc. Code § 1281.85 (West). These detailed rules establish standards to ensure arbitrator neutrality, including the relationship of the arbitrator to companies involved in the arbitration.

The CD-Rom also reprints selected provisions recently enacted in California concerning the conduct of arbitration proceedings. Cal. Civ. Code § 1281.9 (West) deals with neutral arbitrators, disclosure of information, disqualification, and waiver. Cal. Civ. Code § 1281.92 (West) deals with restrictions against private arbitration companies from administering consumer arbitration or related services. Cal. Civ. Code § 1281.96 (West) deals with private arbitration companies, quarterly or biannual publication of consumer arbitration information, and liability.

The CD-Rom contains a series of National Consumer Law Center model state acts relating to arbitration. NCLC believes that these acts would allow states to effectively regulate or limit various aspects of arbitration in ways that would not be preempted by the FAA.

Also included is the text of New Mexico's version of the Revised Uniform Arbitration Act, N.M. Stat. Ann. § 44-7A (Michie), enacted in 2001. It is instructive because it contains a significant departure from the uniform act, by limiting "disabling civil dispute clauses" in consumer transactions, such as clauses which require a forum that is less convenient, more costly, or more dilatory than a court action, that limit the consumer's ability to discover evidence, and that limit the consumer's ability to pursue a claim as a class. The New Mexico statute is influenced in part by a model statute entitled the Fair Bargain Act, which is also found on the CD-Rom.

The CD-Rom contains a letter from the National Automobile Dealers Association to Congress indicating support for a voluntary arbitration act.

M.6 Pleadings

Appendices C–L, *supra*, contain discovery, briefs, and other pleadings related to arbitration. The CD-Rom contains over fifty additional briefs concerning arbitration clauses, divided into the following categories:

- Requesting Discovery on Arbitration Clause's Enforceability;
- Relationship of FAA to Bankruptcy Code;
- Relationship of FAA to Magnuson-Moss Act;
- California Disclosure Requirements and the FAA;
- Method of Arbitration Clause Consummation;
- Who Decides Unconscionability—Court or Arbitrator;
- Bias of Designated Arbitrator or Arbitration Service Provider;
- Cost;
- Limits on Remedies and Non-Mutuality;
- Limits on Classwide Arbitration;
- Distant Venue;
- Unconscionability—General;
- Waiver;
- Arbitration As a Creditor Collection Device;
- Other.

M.7 Materials Regarding Impact on Consumers of Arbitration Requirement

- *Sullivan v. QC Financial Servicers, Inc.*, Affidavit of Edward F. Sherman, concerning the importance of the class action remedy in certain cases, which is of relevance to claims that arbitration's limitations on class actions make the clause unenforceable.
- Letter to Mr. Phil Goldsmith from opposing counsel representing Beneficial, indicating that Beneficial will opt for AAA arbitration, and suggesting a resolution of the dispute, which Beneficial counsel indicates would be in the consumer's best interest because "in my experience that arbitration through the AAA can be quite expensive, especially for your client."
- November 7, 2002 H & R Block conference call discussing judicial ruling's effect on H & R Block, indicating, for years after arbitration agreement went into effect, that exposure to liability would be largely eliminated.
- *McQuillan v. Check 'N Go of North Carolina, Inc.*,

Memorandum of Law in Opposition to Defendants' Motion to Compel Arbitration, North Carolina Superior Court, arguing, among other things, that the arbitration clause prevents consumers from having a practical remedy for illegal conduct. The brief refers to a number of relevant exhibits which are listed below.

- Compilation of payday lending contracts showing consumer lack of choice (*McQuillan* Exh. 7).
- *Affidavit of Beth Weir on August 5, 2005*, detailing the readability of the arbitration clause (*McQuillan* Exh. 9).
- *Affidavit of Stuart Rossman on July 15, 2005*, indicating the impact of the arbitration clause limiting class actions (*McQuillan* Exh. 10).
- Series of affidavits from private attorneys indicating that arbitration clause and requirement for individual appearance before an arbitrator makes litigation impractical (*McQuillan* Exhs. 11A–11I).
- Series of affidavits from legal aid attorneys indicating that it would not be practical for legal aid offices to handle the consumer's dispute (*McQuillan* Exhs. 12A–12D).
- Illustrative list of arbitration court decisions (*McQuillan* Exh. 38).
- *Woods v. JK Harris Financial Recovery Systems, LLC*, Case No. C04-1836C (W.D. Wash. Jan. 24, 2005) (finding arbitration clause unconscionable based on limitation on remedies and cost).

Index

ACTIONS
see CLAIMS; CLASS ACTIONS; LITIGATION

ADHESION CONTRACTS
defined, 6.4.1
procedural unconscionability, 6.4.1

ADMINISTRATIVE AGENCIES
consumer arbitration agreements, binding effect, 7.4.8
debt collection abuses, regulation, 12.8

AFFINITY GROUPS
arbitration agreements, 7.4.6

AGENTS
arbitration agreements
    debt collectors, enforcement, 7.4.7.3
    enforcement by or against, 7.4.4
    nursing home signatories, 7.4.7.2
debt collectors as, 12.7.5

AGREEMENTS
adhesion contracts, *see* ADHESION CONTRACTS
arbitrability, *see* ARBITRABILITY
binding arbitration, *see* MANDATORY ARBITRATION AGREEMENTS
canceled sales, 6.7.4.2
change-in-terms provisions, 5.7.2
choice of law clauses, 3.3.3
    class action bans, 6.5.5.1
condition precedent contracts, 6.7.4.1
contract defenses, *see* CONTRACT DEFENSES
credit agreements, *see* CREDIT AGREEMENTS
electronic agreements, *see* ELECTRONIC AGREEMENTS
exculpatory clauses, 6.5.5.2, 6.5.5.3
existence of agreement, *see* CONTRACT DEFENSES
fraud in the factum, 5.2.2.2
fraud in the inducement, 6.7.1
illusory agreements
    unconscionable, 6.5.3.3
    unenforceable, 5.3, 6.5.3.2
integration clauses, 6.7.4.3
post-termination disputes, 5.3.5
sales agreements, *see* SALES AGREEMENTS
standard form agreements, 6.3, 6.4.1
state regulation, 6.7.3
superseded agreements, 6.7.4.3, 7.3.5
unconscionability, *see* UNCONSCIONABILITY
unilateral additions, 5.6, 5.7
unlawful provisions, validity determinations, 3.4.1, 3.4.5
void agreements, determination in court or arbitration, 3.4.5

AMERICAN ARBITRATION ASSOCIATION (AAA)
see also ARBITRATION SERVICE PROVIDERS
fee schedule, unconscionability, 6.5.2.2
rules not binding on court, 8.6
rules of procedure, Appx. B.1
    California disclosures, Appx. B.1.4
    class arbitration rules, Appx. B.1.3
    commercial rules, Appx. B.1.1
    consumer due process protocol, Appx. B.1.5
    consumer rules, Appx. B.1.2
status as private body, 9.2
summary of resources found on CD-Rom, Appx. M

APPEALS
arbitration decisions, *see* JUDICIAL REVIEW
FAA limitations, 1.3.7
judicial orders, 2.6
    motions to compel arbitration, 2.6.1, 2.6.2, 3.2.2.1
    pendent jurisdiction, 2.6.3
    state court orders, 2.6.4
    trial court review of award, 11.2.5
non-mutual appeal rights in arbitration clauses, 6.5.3.6

ARBITRABILITY
arbitration re, 3.4.4, 7.2, 7.3.2
bankrupt debtors, claims against, 4.2.3
burden of proof, 5.1
contempt proceedings, 7.4.8
debt harassment claims, 12.7.5
determinations
    ambiguous language, 7.2
    class proceedings, 10.2.1
    jurisdiction, 2.2, 3.4.3, 3.4.4, 7.3.2, 5.1, 7.2, 7.3.2, 8.2
    jury determination, 2.5
    language of clause determinative, 7.2
    removal to federal court, 2.3.1
    scope of arbitration clause, 7.3
discovery rights, 2.4
    sample brief, Appx. D
earlier agreements, 7.3.6
earlier conduct, 7.3.5
fraud claims, 7.3.3
intent of parties, 7.2
later agreements, 7.3.6
Magnuson-Moss claims, 4.2.2.1, 5.6.3
    sample brief, Appx. G
non-arbitrable claims, 7.3.7
non-signatory issues, 7.4
nursing home claims, 7.4.7.2
post-termination disputes, 7.3.5
self-help actions, 7.3.4
state law, 7.3.3
statutory claims, 4.1, 7.3.3, 11.5.2.3
tort claims, 7.3.3

559

ARBITRABILITY (cont.)
vacating award based on lack of, 11.4.2
   debt collection actions, 12.4.4.2, 12.5.3.3
waiver, *see* WAIVER
wrongful death claims, 7.4.7.1

ARBITRAL IMMUNITY
doctrine of, 11.6

ARBITRATION
see also ARBITRABILITY
arbitrators, *see* ARBITRATORS
awards, *see* ARBITRATION AWARDS; ARBITRATION DECISIONS
bias, *see* BIAS
binding, *see* MANDATORY ARBITRATION AGREEMENTS
class arbitrations, 10
clauses, *see* MANDATORY ARBITRATION AGREEMENTS
compelling
   motion to compel, *see* MOTION TO COMPEL ARBITRATION
   necessity to invoke arbitration clause, 7.3.3
   waiver of rights, *see under* WAIVER
consolidation of claims, 7.3.7, 10.3.4
constitutional issues, *see* CONSTITUTIONAL RIGHTS
contract provisions, 3.4.1, 3.4.5
debt collection via, 12
   see also DEBT COLLECTION
decisions, *see* ARBITRATION DECISIONS
disadvantages
   consumers, 1.3
   corporations, 1.4
   flaws with studies showing benefits, 1.5
discovery rights, *see* DISCOVERY
due process challenges, 9.4
fees, *see* FEES
hearings, *see* ARBITRATION PROCEEDINGS
impact on consumers, 1.3
   studies of, 1.5
   summary of resources found on CD-Rom, Appx. M
informal nature, 4.2.2.6
jurisdiction, *see* JURISDICTION
litigation alternative, *see* LITIGATION
mechanisms, *see* ARBITRATION SERVICE PROVIDERS
mediation distinguished, 1.2
NCLC manual, overview, 1.1
   summary of CD-Rom resources, Appx. M
   web-based text searching, 1.1
nonbinding, 11.1.2
notice, *see* NOTICE
preclusive effect, 11.8
   debt harassment claims, 12.7.6
predispute agreements, *see* MANDATORY ARBITRATION AGREEMENTS
presumption favoring, 7.2
procedures, *see* PROCEDURES
proceedings, *see* ARBITRATION PROCEEDINGS
right to
   see also ARBITRABILITY
   compelling, *see* MOTION TO COMPEL ARBITRATION
   scope issues, 7
service providers, *see* ARBITRATION SERVICE PROVIDERS
statutory law
   see also STATUTORY CLAIMS

federal arbitration law, *see* FEDERAL ARBITRATION ACT (FAA)
limitations periods, shortening, 4.3.2.7, 6.5.4.4
state law, *see* STATE LAW
stay of proceedings, *see* STAY OF PROCEEDINGS
"unless prohibited by applicable law," 3.3.3
venue, *see* VENUE
waiver of rights, *see* WAIVER

ARBITRATION AGREEMENTS
see MANDATORY ARBITRATION AGREEMENTS

ARBITRATION AWARDS
see also ARBITRATION DECISIONS
amounts in excess, 12.5.5.3
appeals, *see* JUDICIAL REVIEW
arbitrary and capricious awards, 11.5.4
biased, *see* BIAS
contrary to law or facts, 11.5.2, 11.7.4, 12.4.4.7
effect, 11.1.1
enforcement, 11.1, 12.5.1
   nonbinding awards, 11.1.2
exceeding powers, 11.4.2, 11.7.3
injunctive relief, appropriateness, 6.5.4.3
notice, defective or lack thereof, 12.5.3.2
procured by corruption, fraud or undue means, 11.4.5
public policy considerations, 11.5.3, 11.7.5
punitive damages, 11.7
statutory rights, affecting, 11.5.2.3
vacating, modifying, or confirming, *see* JUDICIAL REVIEW

ARBITRATION CLAUSES
see MANDATORY ARBITRATION AGREEMENTS

ARBITRATION COSTS
see FEES

ARBITRATION DECISIONS
see also ARBITRATION AWARDS; ARBITRATORS
arbitrary and capricious, 11.5.4
biased, *see* BIAS
contrary to facts, 12.4.4.7
explanation, failure to provide, 11.5.2.2
incomplete or indefinite, 11.4.2
judicial review, *see* JUDICIAL REVIEW
manifest disregard of the law, 11.5.2, 11.7.4, 12.4.4.7
preclusive effect, 11.8
   debt harassment claims, 12.7.6
procured by corruption, fraud or undue means, 11.4.5
public policy conflicts, 11.5.3
ultra vires, 11.4.2
written opinions, 11.5.2.2

ARBITRATION HEARINGS
see ARBITRATION PROCEEDINGS

ARBITRATION MECHANISMS
see ARBITRATION SERVICE PROVIDERS

ARBITRATION PROCEEDINGS
see also PROCEDURES
adjournment refusal, judicial review, 11.4.4
consumer participation, 12.2.4
   effect on confirmation, 12.2.4.1, 12.5.4
counterclaims, raising, 12.3
fees, *see* FEES
filing a response, 12.2.4.2
informal nature, 4.2.2.6

ARBITRATION PROCEEDINGS (*cont.*)
in-person hearings, 12.4.4.4
mechanisms, *see* ARBITRATION SERVICE PROVIDERS
non-prevailing consumers, 4.4.4, 12.2.4.4, 12.2.4.5
notice
   consumer options after receiving, 12.2
   lack of notice, 11.4.1, 12.4.4.3
requesting a hearing, 12.2.4.3
rules, *see* ARBITRATION SERVICE PROVIDERS; PROCEDURES
stay of proceedings, 12.2.3

ARBITRATION SERVICE PROVIDERS
see also ARBITRATORS
AAA, *see* AMERICAN ARBITRATION ASSOCIATION (AAA)
bias, 1.3.3, 6.5.7
   defenses to allegations of, 6.5.7.3
   National Arbitration Forum, 6.5.7.2, 12.1
   repeat player bias, 11.4.3.1, 12.1
   sample brief, Appx. H
   unconscionability, 6.5.7.1
debt collection via, 12.1
designated forum not possible, effect, 6.6.2
fees, *see* FEES
JAMS, *see* JAMS
NAF, *see* NATIONAL ARBITRATION FORUM (NAF)
rules, Appx. B
   American Arbitration Association, Appx. B.1
   failure to follow, 12.4.4.5
   JAMS, Appx. B.3
   National Arbitration Forum, Appx. B.2
   punitive damages restrictions, 11.7.3.2, 11.7.3.3
   statute of limitations, shortened, 4.3.2.7, 6.5.4.4
sample briefs
   bias, Appx. H
   class arbitrations, switching, Appx. J
state law regulation, federal preemption, 3.2.4
warranty arbitrations, designation in agreement, 4.2.2.8.5

ARBITRATORS
see also ARBITRATION SERVICE PROVIDERS
acting outside powers, 11.4.2, 11.7.3
bias, *see* BIAS
blackballing of, 1.3.3
corruption, 11.4.3, 11.4.5
decisions, *see* ARBITRATION DECISIONS
deposing for judicial review purposes, 11.5.2.2
disclosure requirements
   business relationships, 11.4.3.1
   California statute, 11.4.3.2
   ex parte communications, 11.4.3.3
disregard of law, 11.5.2, 11.7.4
evident partiality, 11.4.3
   see also BIAS
   ex parte communications, 11.4.3.3
   generally, 11.4.3.1
failure to explain decision, 11.5.2.2
fees, *see* FEES
immunity, 11.6
impartiality concerns, 1.3.3
   see also BIAS
   evident partiality, 11.4.3
   unconscionability, 6.5.7
improper selection, 12.4.4.6

jurisdiction, 2.1
   arbitrability determinations, 3.4.4
   class proceedings determinations, 10.2.1
   injunctive relief, 6.5.4.3
   procedural issues, 8.2
   punitive damages, 11.7.3
   scope determinations, 7.3.2
   unconscionability determinations, 6.1
   waiver determinations, 8.2
misconduct, 11.4.4, 11.4.5
misinterpretation of law, 11.5.2.1
pro bono arbitrators, 6.5.2.2
punitive damages awards
   challenges to arbitrator's authority, 11.7.3
   public policy violations, 11.7.5
refusal to hear evidence or grant adjournment, 11.4.4
state law regulation, federal preemption, 3.2.4

ASSENT
arbitration agreements, 5.2
   bill stuffers, 5.2.3.2, 5.2.3.3
   electronic assent, 5.2.2.3
   express assent, 5.2.2
   implied assent, 5.2.3
   signature, by, 5.2.2.1

ASSIGNEES
arbitration agreements, application, 6.7.4.3, 7.4.5
debt collection, 12.7.5

ATTORNEY FEES AND COSTS
debt collection via arbitration, 12.2.4.4
limitations on, 4.3.1.1, 4.3.2.2, 6.5.4.2
loser pays rules, 4.3.2.3, 6.5.9

AUTOMOBILE SALES
see also DEALERS; MANUFACTURERS
arbitration agreement, enforcement by manufacturer, 7.3.5
arbitration restrictions, federal statute, text, Appx. A.2.2
sample discovery
   directed to dealer, Appx. C.4
   directed to financer, Appx. C.3
   directed to title pawn company, Appx. C.7

AWARDS
see ARBITRATION AWARDS

BAD FAITH
arbitration awards, vacating, 11.4.5
breach of good faith covenant as waiver, 8.4.2
contract law defense, 6.7.2

BANKRUPTCY PROCEEDINGS
binding arbitration and, 4.2.1.3, 4.2.3
   sample brief, Appx. I
core proceedings, 4.2.3.4, 4.2.3.5
non-core proceedings, 4.2.3.6
rescission claims, 6.7.4.2

BIAS
arbitration service provider, 1.3.3
   defenses, 6.5.7.3
   National Arbitration Forum, 1.3.3, 6.5.7.2, 12.1
   repeat player bias, 1.3.3, 11.4.3.1, 12.1
   sample brief, Appx. H
   unconscionability, 6.5.7
arbitrators
   evident partiality, 11.4.3

BIAS (*cont.*)
arbitrators (*cont.*)
   grounds to vacate order, 6.5.7.1, 11.4.3, 12.4.4.8
   immunity, 11.6
   impartiality concerns, 1.3.3
   unconscionability, 6.5.7
discovery, right to, 2.4.2
judicial review grounds, 6.5.7.1, 11.4.3, 12.4.4.8
repeat player bias, 1.3.3
   debt collection via arbitration, 12.1
   evident partiality, 11.4.3.1

BILL STUFFERS
arbitration clauses, enforceability, 5.7
   implied assent, 5.2.3
   notice, 5.2.3.2
change-in-terms, as, 5.7.2

BINDING ARBITRATION CLAUSES
see MANDATORY ARBITRATION AGREEMENTS

BRIEFS
see PLEADINGS

BURDEN OF PROOF
see also EVIDENCE
arbitration agreement, validity, 5.1
arbitration award, delivery, 11.2.3.1
arbitration clauses
   notice, 5.2.3.2
   retroactivity, 7.3.5
arbitration fees, excessiveness, 2.4.2, 4.4.2
corruption, fraud, or undue means, 11.4.5
diversity jurisdiction, 2.3.1.2
FAA applicability, 3.3.2.1
FAA preemption by federal statute, 4.2.1.1
manifest disregard of law, 11.5.2.1
waiver of arbitration, 8.3.2.1

CASE LAW
bill stuffer change in terms, 5.7.2.1
class action bans
   exculpatory nature, 6.5.5.2, 6.5.5.3
   FAA application, 6.5.5.7
   unconscionability, 6.5.5.4
   upholding bans, 6.5.5.5
class claims when arbitration agreement silent
   Bazzle decision, 10.2
   Champ decision, 10.3
   post-*Bazzle* cases, 10.2.4
   pre-*Bazzle* cases, 10.3
confidentiality provisions
   finding unconscionable, 6.5.8.2
   not finding unconscionable, 6.5.8.3
delay as waiver, 8.3.2.2, 8.3.2.3, 8.3.2.4
excessive fees as unconscionable, 6.5.2.5
knowing and voluntary waiver of rights
   examples of doctrine, 5.5.3
   rejection of doctrine, 5.5.5
Magnuson-Moss and arbitration, 4.2.2.5
non-mutuality
   as unconscionable, 6.5.3.3
   not unconscionable, 6.5.3.4
research aids, 1.1

CHOICE OF LAW
class action bans, 6.5.5.1

contractual provisions, 3.3.3

CIVIL RIGHTS CLAIMS
see also CONSTITUTIONAL RIGHTS
mandatory arbitration of, 4.2.1.3

CLAIMS
see also LITIGATION; PLEADINGS
arbitration clauses, application, 7.3
class actions, *see* CLASS ACTIONS
consolidation of claims, 10.3.4
counterclaims, *see* COUNTERCLAIMS
employment-related, *see* EMPLOYMENT-RELATED CLAIMS
enforcement agencies, 7.4.8
   debt collection abuses, 12.8
public injunctive relief, 6.5.4.3
   arbitrability, 7.4.8
   FAA preemption, 3.2.1.4.1
statutory claims, *see* STATUTORY CLAIMS
tort claims, *see* TORT CLAIMS
UDAP claims, *see* UDAP CLAIMS
warranty claims, *see* WARRANTY CLAIMS

CLASS ACTIONS
Bazzle decision, 10.2
Champ decision, 10.3
class arbitrations, 10
   AAA rules, Appx. B.1.3
   arbitrability determinations, 10.2.1
   JAMS rules, Appx. B.3.3
   sample brief regarding service provider switch, Appx. J
   state law determination, 10.2.2
consolidation of claims distinguished, 10.3.4
debt harassment claims, 12.7.5
diversity jurisdiction, 2.3.1.2
limitations on, 1.3.2, 4.3.2.5, 6.5.5, 10.1
   express prohibitions, 6.5.5, 10.5
   federal court view, 10.3.3
   sample briefs challenging, Appx. F
   state court view, 10.4
   unconscionability, 6.5.5, Appx. F

CLEARINGHOUSE NUMBERS
see also SARGENT SHRIVER NATIONAL CENTER ON POVERTY LAW
documents and unpublished cases, 1.1

COLLATERAL ESTOPPEL
arbitration decisions, effect, 11.8

COLLECTION ACTIVITIES
see DEBT COLLECTION

COMMON LAW DEFENSES
see CONTRACT DEFENSES

COMPELLING ARBITRATION
see MOTION TO COMPEL ARBITRATION

COMPLAINTS
see CLAIMS; PLEADINGS

CONFIDENTIALITY PROVISIONS
unconscionability of, 6.5.8

CONFIRMATION HEARINGS
see JUDICIAL REVIEW

CONSENT
see ASSENT

CONSOLIDATION OF CLAIMS
class action distinguished, 10.3.4
non-arbitrable and arbitrable claims, 7.3.7

CONSTITUTIONAL RIGHTS
civil rights claims, 4.2.1.3
due process, 9.4, 11.7.6
equal protection rights, 9.2
FAA preemption and, 3.2.1.1
improper delegation of power, 9.3
jury trial rights, 9.1
   waiver must be clear and unambiguous, 5.4
   waiver must be knowing and voluntary, 5.5
waiver
   clear and unambiguous, 5.4
   jury trial, 5.5, 9.1
   state laws requiring, 9.1.2
   voluntary and knowing, 5.5

CONSUMER CONTRACTS
see ADHESION CONTRACTS; AGREEMENTS; CREDIT AGREEMENTS; SALES AGREEMENTS

CONSUMER DEBTS
see DEBT COLLECTION

CONSUMER PROTECTION LAWS
see also STATUTORY CLAIMS
FAA preemption, 3.2.3.3

CONSUMER REMEDIES
see STATUTORY CLAIMS

CONTEMPT PROCEEDINGS
arbitrability, 7.4.8

CONTRACT DEFENSES
bad faith, 6.7.2
canceled contracts, 6.7.4.2
condition precedent contracts, 6.7.4.1
duress, 6.7.2
formation of agreement, 3.4.2, 5
   assent to agreement, 5.2
   bill stuffers, 5.2.3.2, 5.7
   clear and unambiguous, 5.4, 7.2
   consideration, 5.3
   electronic agreements, 5.2.2.3
   illusory agreements, 5.3, 6.5.3.2, 6.5.3.3
   incapacity, 5.2.4
   incorporation by reference, 5.2.2.1
   integration clauses, 6.7.4.3
   judicial determination, 3.4.3, 3.4.4, 5.1
   judicial review, 11.4.2, 12.4.4.2, 12.5.3.3
   lack of assent, 5.2
   mutuality, 5.3, 6.5.3.2
   no presumption, 5.1
   notice, 5.2.3.2
   raising, 12.2.2
   signature, 5.2.2.1
   state law application, 3.4.2
   stay of arbitration pending determination, 12.2.3
   superseded agreements, 6.7.4.3, 7.3.5
   unilateral clauses, 5.6, 5.7
   voluntary and knowing doctrine, 5.5
fraud in the factum, 5.2.2.2
fraud in the inducement, 6.7.1
frustration, 6.7.2
impossibility, 6.7.2
incapacity, 5.2.4, 6.7.2
interpretation of agreement, 7.2
judicial determination, 3.4.4
lack of assent, 5.2
lack of consideration, 5.3
lack of mutuality, 5.3, 6.5.3
misrepresentations, 6.7.1
mistake, 6.7.2
state law determination, 3.2.3.2, 3.4, 7.2
state law regulation, 6.7.3
unconscionability, 6.1–6.6
   general standards, 6.2
   partial unconscionability, 6.6
   procedural unconscionability, 6.4
   relationship between procedural and substantive, 6.3
   state law application, 3.4.3
   substantive unconscionability, 6.5
undue influence, 6.7.2
waiver of arbitration rights, 8.1, 8.5, 8.6

CONTRACTS
see AGREEMENTS; CONTRACT DEFENSES

COOLING-OFF PERIODS
effect on arbitration clauses, 6.7.4.2

CORPORATIONS
avoidance of arbitration, 1.4

CORRUPTION
arbitrators, 11.4.3
awards procured by, 11.4.5

COSTS
see ATTORNEY FEES AND COSTS; FEES

COUNTERCLAIMS
filing, 12.3
   sample counterclaim, Appx. K

COURT ORDERS
see also JURISDICTION; MOTION TO COMPEL ARBITRATION
appeals, 2.6
   pendent jurisdiction, 2.6.3
   state court orders, 2.6.4
judicial review of arbitration decision, *see* JUDICIAL REVIEW
violations, arbitrability, 7.4.8

CREDIT AGREEMENTS
see also AGREEMENTS; CREDIT CARDS
affinity groups, 7.4.6
arbitration clauses, *see* MANDATORY ARBITRATION AGREEMENTS
contract defenses, *see* CONTRACT DEFENSES
debt collection under, *see* DEBT COLLECTION
state regulation, 6.7.3
TIL remedies, *see* TIL REMEDIES

CREDIT CARDS
see also CREDIT AGREEMENTS
affinity cards, 7.4.6
bill stuffer arbitration clauses, 5.7
   notice sufficiency, 5.2.3.2
   use of card as assent, 5.2.3.3
change-in-terms provisions, 5.7.2
sample discovery pleadings, Appx. C.1, Appx. C.2

CREDIT REPAIR ORGANIZATIONS ACT
claims under, mandatory arbitration of, 4.2.1.3

CREDITORS
debt collection, *see* DEBT COLLECTION
FDCPA, application, 12.7.3
sample discovery directed to auto financer, Appx. C.3

DAMAGES
FDCPA, 12.7.3
limitations on, 4.3.1.1
   punitive damages, 4.3.2.4, 11.7.3, 11.7.5
   sample briefs, Appx. E.3, Appx. E.4
   unconscionability, 6.5.4.1

DEALERS
arbitration agreements, enforcement by manufacturer, 7.4.5
auto dealers, disputes with manufacturers, limits on mandatory arbitration, 4.2.1.1
sample interrogatories, Appx. C.4

DEBT COLLECTION
affirmative challenges to collection practices, 12.7
   claim preclusion, 12.7.6
   compelling arbitration of, 12.7.5
   FDCPA, 12.7.3
   government enforcement agencies, by, 12.8
   knowing the parties, 12.7.1
   practices subject to challenge, 12.7.2
   state law, 12.7.4
arbitration as a collection technique, 12
   affirmative challenges, 12.7, 12.8
   consumer options after notice, 12.2
   fees, 12.2.4
   filing counterclaim, 12.3, Appx. K
   judicial review of award, 12.4
   national banks, 12.8
   non-signatories to credit agreement, 7.4.7.3
   objecting to arbitration, 12.2.2
   opposing confirmation, 12.5, Appx. L
   overview, 12.1
   participating in the proceeding, 12.2.4
   preclusive effect, 12.7.6
   sample response, Appx. K
   stay of arbitration, 12.2.3
   vacating awards, 12.4
venue, 12.5.5.2

DECEPTIVE PRACTICES
see UDAP CLAIMS

DEFAMATION CLAIMS
arbitrability, 7.3.3

DEFENSES
see CONTRACT DEFENSES

DEFINITIONS
binding arbitration, 1.2
contract of adhesion, 6.4.1
predispute arbitration agreement, 1.2
predispute binding arbitration agreement, 1.2

DEPOSITIONS
see also DISCOVERY
arbitrators for judicial review purposes, 11.5.2.2
sample notice, Appx. C.2.4

DISCLOSURE
arbitrators
   business relationships, 11.4.3.1
   California statute, 11.4.3.2
   ex parte communications, 11.4.3.3
California disclosures, 11.4.3.2
   AAA rules of procedure, Appx. B.1.4
   JAMS rules of procedure, Appx. B.3.4.2
   summary of resources found on CD-Rom, Appx. M
warranty arbitration, 4.2.2.8
   service contracts, 4.2.2.8.4
   written warranties, 4.2.2.8.2

DISCOVERY
arbitrability issues, 2.4
   precedent upholding, 2.4.2
   sample brief requesting, Appx. D
deposition of arbitrator, 11.5.2.2
limitations on, 1.3.5
public policy goals, 2.4.3
sample pleadings, Appx. C, Appx. D

DOCUMENT REQUESTS
see also DISCOVERY
sample pleadings, Appx. C
   auto financer, Appx. C.3.2
   auto title pawn company, Appx. C.7
   credit card issuer, Appx. C.1, Appx. C.2.2, Appx. C.2.3
   payday loan company, Appx. C.5, Appx. C.6

DUE PROCESS
see also CONSTITUTIONAL RIGHTS
mandatory arbitration, 9.4
punitive damages, 11.7.6

DURESS
contract law defense, 6.7.2

ELECTRONIC AGREEMENTS
assent, 5.2.2.3
"browse-wrap" agreements, 5.2.2.3
"click-wrap" agreements, 5.2.2.3
formation, 5.2.2.3

ELECTRONIC DELIVERY
notice, 5.2.3.2

EMPLOYMENT-RELATED CLAIMS
arbitrability, 7.3.3
mandatory arbitration, 4.2.1.3, 4.3.1.1
   excessive charges, 4.4.3.1
   limits on class actions, 4.3.2.5
   one-sided control by employer, 4.5

ENFORCEMENT AGENCIES
see GOVERNMENT ENFORCEMENT AGENCIES

EQUITABLE ESTOPPEL
arbitration agreements, enforcement, 7.4.2
   non-signatory, against, 7.4.2.3
   non-signatory, by, 7.4.2.2

EQUITABLE RELIEF
see also INJUNCTIVE RELIEF
arbitration forum, restrictions, 4.3.2.6, 6.5.4.3

EVIDENCE
see also BURDEN OF PROOF
arbitration agreement, existence, 12.4.4.2

EVIDENCE (cont.)
false evidence, judicial review, 11.4.5
re-examination on judicial review, 11.5.5
refusal to hear, judicial review, 11.4.4

EXTENDED WARRANTIES
see also WARRANTIES
binding arbitration clauses, disclosure requirements, 4.2.2.8.4

FAIR DEBT COLLECTION PRACTICES ACT
overview, 12.7.3
venue provisions, 12.5.5.2

FEDERAL ARBITRATION ACT (FAA)
appeal rules, 2.6.1
class actions, application, 6.5.5.7
conflicts with other federal statutes, 4
    Bankruptcy Code, 4.2.3.2
    explicit conflicts, 4.3
    generally, 4.1
    high arbitration fees as, 4.4
    Magnuson-Moss Warranty Act, 4.2.2
    one-sided control of arbitration process as, 4.5
    per se inconsistency, 4.2
insurance disputes, application, 3.3.4
judicial review procedures
    application, 11.1.2, 11.2.2
    grounds to modify or correct award, 11.3
    grounds to vacate award, 11.4.1
    proper court, 11.2.1
    timing requirements, 11.2.3.1, 11.2.3.2
    venue, 12.5.5.2
jurisdiction to compel arbitration, 2.3.1.1
limited applicability, 3.3
    burden of proof, 3.3.2.1
    contractual displacement, 3.3.3
    enforceability determinations, 3.4
    interstate commerce, 3.3.2
policy favoring arbitration agreements, 3.1
    application to particular disputes, 7.2
    clarification of, 3.1.3
    limits on, 3.1.2
    presumption against waiver, 8.1
procedural provisions, 3.2.2
    judicial review, 11.2
    jury trials, 2.5
punitive damages
    authorization, 11.7.3.4.1
    state restrictions, preemption, 11.7.3.4.2
severability determinations, application, 3.4.5
state law preemption, see FEDERAL PREEMPTION
text, Appx. A.1

FEDERAL JURISDICTION
diversity jurisdiction, 2.3.1.2
federal question jurisdiction, 2.3.1.3
judicial review, 11.2.1
motion to compel arbitration, 2.3.1

FEDERAL PREEMPTION
FAA by other federal statutes, 4.2
implied conflict preemption, 3.2.3.3.1
presumption against preemption, 3.2.3.3.1
public injunctive relief claims, 3.2.1.4.1
state arbitration law, 3.2
    judicial review of award, 11.2.2
    laws regulating arbitrators and services, 3.2.4
    laws that limit enforceability, 3.2.1
    procedural provisions, 2.5, 3.2.2
    punitive damages restrictions, 11.7.3.4.2
state non-arbitration law, 3.2.3
    consumer protection law, 3.2.3.3
    contract law, 3.2.3.2, 3.4.3
    laws applying only to certain contracts, 3.2.3.3
    laws effectively prohibiting arbitration, 3.2.1.3, 3.2.1.4
    unconscionability laws, 3.4.3, 6.1, 6.5.5.7
statutory claims, 3.2.1.4.2
voluntary and knowing doctrine, 5.5.2

FEDERAL TRADE COMMISSION (FTC)
see GOVERNMENT ENFORCEMENT AGENCIES

FEES
American Arbitration Association, 6.5.2.2
attorney fees, see ATTORNEY FEES AND COSTS
breach of contractual obligation as waiver, 8.4.3
consumer disadvantage, 1.3.6
    loser pay rules, 1.3.7
debt collection via arbitration, 12.2.4
excessive as limitation on remedies, 4.4, 6.5.4.5
    arbitration charges exceeding court fees, 4.4.3.1
    burden of proof, 2.4.2, 4.4.2
    charges deterring pursuit of claims, 4.4.3.2
    loser pays rules, 4.3.2.3
    reimbursement of fees, effect, 4.4.4
excessive as unconscionable, 6.5.2
    hardship reduction, 6.5.2.2
    loser pays rules, 6.5.9
    modification of agreement to avoid, 6.6.2
    precedent, 6.5.2.5
    sample briefs, Appx. E
filing a response, 12.2.4.2
hearing requests, 12.2.4.3
National Arbitration Forum, 6.5.2.3
who pays, 6.5.2.4
    loser pays rules, 4.3.2.3, 6.5.9
    MBNA clause, 12.2.4.5
    non-prevailing consumer, 4.4.4, 12.2.4.4
    service provider rules, 12.4.4.5

FORUM
see ARBITRATION SERVICE PROVIDERS; VENUE

FRAUD
awards procured by, 11.4.5
claims re, arbitrability, 7.3.3
forged signatures, 5.2.2.2
fraud in the factum, 5.2.2.2
fraud in the inducement, 6.7.1
    arbitrability, 7.3.3

GOVERNMENT ENFORCEMENT AGENCIES
consumer arbitration agreements, binding effect, 7.4.8
debt collection abuses, regulation, 12.8

GUARANTORS
arbitration agreements, application, 7.4.5

HEARINGS
see ARBITRATION PROCEEDINGS

IMMUNITY
arbitrators, 11.6

IMPOSSIBILITY
contract law defense, 6.7.2

INCAPACITY
contract law defense, 5.2.4, 6.7.2

INJUNCTIVE RELIEF
arbitration forum, restrictions, 4.3.2.6, 6.5.4.3
  rescission remedy, effect, 6.7.4.2
public injunctive relief claims
  appropriate forum, 6.5.4.3
  arbitrability, 7.4.8
  FAA preemption, 3.2.1.4.1

INSTALLMENT SALES CONTRACTS
arbitration and integration clauses, 6.7.4.3

INSURANCE DISPUTES
applicable law, 3.3.4
arbitrability, 7.4.5

INTEGRATION CLAUSES
side documents, effect, 6.7.4.3

INTERNET CORPORATION FOR THE ASSIGNED NAMES AND NUMBERS (ICANN)
arbitration awards by, 11.1.2

INTERNET RESOURCES
see WEB RESOURCES

INTERROGATORIES
see also DISCOVERY
sample pleadings, Appx. C
  auto financer, Appx. C.3.1
  car dealer, Appx. C.4
  credit card issuer, Appx. C.1, Appx. C.2.1
  payday loan company, Appx. C.4, Appx. C.5

INTERSTATE COMMERCE
FAA applicability, 3.3.2.1

JAMS
see also ARBITRATION SERVICE PROVIDERS
rules of procedure, Appx. B.3
  California disclosures, Appx. B.3.4.2
  comprehensive rules, Appx. B.3.2
  consumer arbitration policies, Appx. B.3.4
  procedural fairness standards, Appx. B.3.4.1
  streamlined rules, Appx. B.3.1

JUDICIAL REVIEW
appeals of trial court review, 11.2.5
applicable law, 3.2.2.4, 11.2.2, 12.4.3
challenging arbitration clause through, 2.1
confirmation process, 12.5.2
  procedures, 12.5.5
  production of agreement, 12.5.3.4
  re-opening after default, 12.6
  vacating awards during, 11.2.3.3, 12.5.3.1, 12.5.3.3
contractual modification of review, 11.2.4
  increase in scope, 11.2.4.2
  limits on review, 11.2.4.1
debt collection orders, 12.4, 12.5
  grounds to vacate, 12.4.4
deposing of arbitrator, 11.5.2.2
grounds to modify or correct award, 11.3
grounds to oppose confirmation, 12.5
  defective arbitration proceeding, 12.5.3
  defective confirmation proceedings, 12.5.5
  sample brief, Appx. L
grounds to vacate based on merit, 11.5
  arbitrary and capricious awards, 11.5.4
  contractually created standards, 11.2.4.2
  contrary to facts, 12.4.4.7
  failure to explain decision, 11.5.2.2
  manifest disregard of the law, 11.5.2, 11.7.4, 12.4.4.7
  public policy conflicts, 11.5.3, 11.7.5
  re-examination of evidence, 11.5.5
  statutory claims, 11.5.2.3
grounds to vacate based on process, 11.4, 12.4
  arbitration agreement unenforceable, 11.4.2, 12.4.4.2, 12.5.3.3
  arbitrator exceeding powers, 11.4.2, 11.7.3, 12.4.4.5
  arbitrator improperly selected, 12.4.4.6
  arbitrator misconduct, 11.4.4, 11.4.5
  arbitrator partiality or corruption, 11.4.3, 12.4.4.8
  bias in arbitration mechanism, 6.5.7.1
  breach of agreement, 8.4.2
  contrary to law or facts, 12.4.4.7
  corruption, fraud, or undue means, 11.4.5
  debt collection actions, 12.4.4
  failure to follow rules, 11.7.3.3, 12.4.4.5
  generally, 11.4.1
  incomplete or indefinite awards, 11.4.2
  inconvenient venue, 12.4.4.9
  lack of hearing, 12.4.4.4
  lack of notice, 11.4.1, 12.4.4.3
  manifest disregard of law, 11.5.2, 11.7.4
  merits of award, 11.5
  refusal to postpone hearing or hear evidence, 11.4.4
jurisdiction, 11.2.1, 12.4.3
  diversity jurisdiction, 2.3.1.2
overview, 11.1.1
participation in arbitration proceedings, effect, 12.2.4.1, 12.5.4
procedures, 11.2, 12.5.2, 12.5.5
  application, 11.1.2
punitive damages awards, 11.7
re-examination of evidence, 11.5.5
state versus federal court, 11.2.1
statutory rights, awards affecting, 11.5.2.3
timing requirements, 11.2.3
  confirming award, 11.2.3.2, 12.5.5.1
  extending time for vacating, 11.2.3.3, 12.5.3.2
  punitive damages, 11.7.2
  vacating or modifying award, 11.2.3.1, 12.4.2, 12.5.3.3
venue, 11.2.1, 12.4.3, 12.4.4.9

JURISDICTION
arbitrability issues, 2.1, 2.3, 3.4, 5.1, 7.2, 7.3.2
  appellate courts, 2.6.3
  jury determination, 2.5
  removal to federal court, 2.3.1
arbitration agreement existence, determinations, 5.1
bankruptcy court, 4.2.3
class actions, 2.3.1.2
combined arbitrable and non-arbitrable claims, 7.3.7
contract validity determinations, 3.4.1, 3.4.5
diversity jurisdiction, 2.3.1.2, 11.2.1
federal question jurisdiction, 2.3.1.3
judicial review of arbitration decision, 11.2
  applicable law, 11.2.2, 12.4.3
  confirmation actions, 12.5.5.2
  proper court, 11.2.1, 12.4.3

566

JURISDICTION (*cont.*)
motion to compel, 2.3
    appeals, 2.6
    pendent jurisdiction, 2.6.3
    right to jury trial, 2.5
    waiver of right determinations, 8.2
motion to vacate, 2.3.1.2
overview, 2.2
parallel proceedings in state and federal courts, 2.3.2
pendent jurisdiction, 2.6.3
procedural questions, 8.2
unconscionability determinations, 2.5, 6.1
    class action bans, 6.5.5.1
venue, 2.3.3, 11.2.1
waiver issues, 8.2

JURY TRIALS
right to
    see also CONSTITUTIONAL RIGHTS
    assent issues, 5.2.1
    enforceability issues, 2.5
    FAA preemption, 3.2.1.3
    waiver, 5.5, 9.1

KNOWING AND VOLUNTARY DOCTRINE
see VOLUNTARY AND KNOWING DOCTRINE

LANGUAGE
clear and unambiguous, 5.4
    interpreting ambiguous language, 7.2
inability to read English, 6.4.2
interpretation of arbitration clauses, 7.3.1
    ambiguous language, 7.2

LEMON LAW CLAIMS
see also STATUTORY CLAIMS
informal dispute procedures, 11.1.2

LIMITATIONS
see STATUTE OF LIMITATIONS

LITIGATION
see also CLAIMS
class actions, *see* CLASS ACTIONS
consolidation of claims
    class action distinguished, 10.3.4
    non-arbitrable and arbitrable claims, 7.3.7
jury trials, *see* JURY TRIALS
statutory claims, *see* STATUTORY CLAIMS
stay of proceedings, *see* STAY OF PROCEEDINGS
waiver of arbitration rights, as, 8.3, 8.6
    delay enforcing arbitration, 8.3.2
    filing suit, 8.3.1
    jurisdiction to decide, 8.2

LOSER PAYS RULES
see also FEES
arbitration concern, 1.3.7
enforceability, 4.3.2.3
    unconscionability, 6.5.9

MAGNUSON-MOSS CLAIMS
see also STATUTORY CLAIMS
binding arbitration, 4.2.2
    case law, 4.2.2.5
    disclosure requirement, 4.2.2.8
    enforceability, 4.2.1.3, 4.2.2.1, 5.6.3
    sample brief, Appx. G
    tie-in restrictions, 4.2.2.8.5
informal dispute settlement procedures, 4.2.2.2
    enforcement, 11.1.2
service contracts, 4.2.2.8.4

MAILBOX RULE
notice delivery, 5.2.3.2

MANDATORY ARBITRATION AGREEMENTS
see also AGREEMENTS; ARBITRATION
adhesion contracts, 6.4.1
affinity groups, 7.4.6
agents, application, 7.4.4
ambiguous language, 5.4, 7.2
assent, 5.2
    electronic assent, 5.2.2.3
    express assent, 5.2.2
    implied assent, 5.2.3
    lack of capacity, 5.2.4
assignees, application, 7.4.5
bad faith, 6.7.2
bankruptcy proceedings, effect, 4.2.3, 6.7.4.2
bill stuffers, 5.7
    as change-in-terms, 5.7.2
    notice sufficiency, 5.2.3.2
breach of provisions as waiver, 8.4
    good faith covenant, 8.4.2
    payment provisions, 8.4.3
"browse-wrap" agreements, 5.2.2.3
canceled agreements, 6.7.4.2, 6.7.4.3
choice-of-law provisions, 3.3.3
    class action bans, 6.5.5.1
class action bans, 6.5.5, 10.5
    exculpatory clause, as, 6.5.5.2, 6.5.5.3
    unconscionability, 6.5.5
class action issues, 10
clear and unambiguous requirement, 5.4
"click-wrap" agreements, 5.2.2.3
concealment, 6.7.1
conspicuousness, 6.4.2
constitutional challenges, 9
    equal protection rights, 9.2
    improper delegation of power, 9.3
    jury trial rights, 9.1
contempt proceedings, application, 7.4.8
contract defenses, *see* CONTRACT DEFENSES
corporate avoidance, 1.4
courts, application, 7.4.8, 11.8
debt harassment claims, application, 12.7.5
defined, 1.2
disadvantages, 1.3
    class action limitations, 1.3.2, 10.1
    discovery limitations, 1.3.5
    fees, 1.3.6
    flaws with studies showing benefits, 1.5
    generally, 1.3.1
    impartiality concerns, 1.3.3
    other concerns, 1.3.7
    secrecy, 1.3.4
disclosure, *see* DISCLOSURE
duress, 6.7.2
earlier contracts, application, 7.3.6
electronic agreements, 5.2.2.3
enforceability, 3.1, 3.4, 5, 6
    see also ARBITRABILITY

MANDATORY ARBITRATION AGREEMENTS (*cont.*)
enforceability (*cont.*)
   agents, 7.4.4
   assent requirement, 5.2
   assignees, 7.4.5
   auto manufacturers against dealers, 4.2.1.1
   bill stuffers, 5.2.3.2, 5.7
   breach of agreement, effect, 8.4.1
   burden of proof, 5.1
   challenging, 2.1, 12.2.2
   class action bans, 6.5.5
   consideration requirement, 5.3, 6.5.3.2
   constitutional challenges, 9
   contract law defenses, 3.4, 6
   delay, effect, 8.3.2
   discovery rights, 2.4
   earlier agreements, 7.3.6
   electronic agreements, 5.2.2.3
   employment matters, 4.2.1.3, 7.3.3
   equitable estoppel, 7.4.2
   existence of agreement, 3.4.2, 5
   FAA policy, clarification, 3.1.3
   FAA preemption by federal law, 4.2
   FAA preemption of state law, 3.2.1
   federal law claims, 4
   judicial determination, 2.2, 3.4.3, 3.4.4, 5.1, 7.2, 8.2
   judicial review based on, 11.4.2, 12.4.4.2, 12.5.3.3
   jury determination, 2.5
   later agreements, 7.3.6
   limits on, 3.1.2, 4.2.1
   military personnel, 4.2.1.1
   motion to compel, *see* MOTION TO COMPEL ARBITRATION
   no presumption, 5.1
   non-mutual agreements, 5.3, 6.5.3
   non-signatories, 7.4
   objecting to, 12.2.2
   public injunctive relief claims, 3.2.1.4.1, 7.4.8
   removal to federal court, 2.3.1
   side documents, 5.2.2.1
   specific claims, 7.4.7
   state law application, 3.4, 6.1
   state law enforcement, 3.3.2.2
   state law preemption, 3.2
   state law restrictions, 3.3.2.2, 6.7.3
   statutory claims, 3.2.3, 4
   terms unsatisfiable, 7.5
   third parties, general rule, 7.4.5
   third party beneficiaries, 7.4.3
   unconscionable agreements, 3.4.3, 4.3, 6
   unilateral addition, 5.6, 5.7
   waiver of rights, *see* WAIVER
   warranty claims, 4.2.2, 5.6.3, Appx. G
enforcement agencies, application, 7.4.8
FAA application, 3.2, 3.3, 4.2
FAA policy towards, 3.1, 7.2
   clarification of, 3.1.3
   limits on, 3.1.2
fraud in the factum, 5.2.2.2
fraud in the inducement, 6.7.1
future contracts, application, 7.3.6
illusory agreements, 5.3, 6.5.3.3
impossibility, 6.7.2
incapacity, 5.2.4, 6.7.2

incorporation by reference, 5.2.2.1
integration clauses, 6.7.4.3
interpretation, 7.3.1
   arbitrability issues, 7.3.2
judicial review provisions, validity, 11.2.4
language considerations, 6.4.2
later contracts, application, 7.3.6
Magnuson-Moss Warranty Act, application, 4.2.2, 5.6.3
   sample brief, Appx. G
material contract term, 5.6.2
meaningful choice, 6.4.3
merits, flaws with studies, 1.5
misrepresentations, 6.7.1
non-mutual clauses, 5.3, 6.5.3
   mutual appearance, 6.5.3.5
non-signatories, application, 7.4
one-way clauses, 6.5.3
oppression, 10.1
opt-out provisions, 6.3
post-termination conduct, application, 7.3.5
producing at confirmation hearing, 12.5.3.4
public injunctive relief, application, 3.2.1.4.1, 7.4.8
punitive damages, limits on, 11.7.3.2
retroactivity, 7.3.5
rewriting, 6.6.2
sample agreements, summary of CD-Rom resources, Appx. M
scope, 7
   see also ARBITRABILITY
   ambiguous language, interpreting, 7.2
   applicable law, 7.2
   arbitrability issues, 7.3.2
   generally, 7.3.1
   jurisdiction, 7.2
   language and intent determinative, 7.2
   non-arbitrable claims, 7.3.7
   non-signatories, 7.4
   other agreements, 7.3.6
   particular claims, 7.3
   self-help remedies, 7.3.4
   statutory claims, 7.3.3
   temporal scope, 7.3.5, 7.3.6
   tort claims, 7.3.3
secrecy provisions, 6.5.8
severance, 3.4.1, 4.3.2.4, 6.6.3
side documents, 5.2.2.1
signature requirements, 5.2.2.1
   electronic agreements, 5.2.2.3
   forged signatures, 5.2.2.2
spot delivery sales, 6.7.4.1
standard form contracts, 6.3, 6.4.1
state law application, 3.3, 3.4
state regulation, 6.7.3
statutory claims, 4, 6.5.4, 7.3.3
superseded agreements, 6.7.4.3, 7.3.5
termination of contract, survival after, 6.7.4.3, 7.3.5
terms, satisfaction of, 7.5
UDAP complaints attacking, 6.7.3
unconscionability, *see* UNCONSCIONABILITY
undue influence, 6.7.2
unilateral presentation, 5.6
   bill stuffers, 5.7
"unless prohibited by applicable law," 3.3.3
validity, *see* ARBITRABILITY
venue provisions, 2.3.3

MANDATORY ARBITRATION AGREEMENTS (cont.)
voiding, 6.1
    vacating award, 11.4.2, 12.4.4.2, 12.5.3.3
voluntary and knowing doctrine, 5.5
waiver of arbitration rights
    see also WAIVER
    breach of provisions as, 8.4
    "no waiver" clauses, 8.6
warranties, 4.2.2, 5.6.3
    sample brief, Appx. G
wrongful death claims, application, 7.4.7.1
yo-yo sales, 6.7.4.1

MANUFACTURERS
dealer's arbitration agreement, enforcement, 7.4.5
dealer disputes, arbitration, 4.2.1.1

MEDIATION
arbitration distinguished, 1.2

MILITARY PERSONNEL
mandatory arbitration, restrictions
    credit matters, 4.2.1.1
    employment matters, 4.2.1.3
    federal statute, text, Appx. A.2.1

MISREPRESENTATIONS
fraud in the factum, 5.2.2.2
fraud in the inducement, 6.7.1

MISTAKE
contract law defense, 6.7.2

MOTION TO COMPEL ARBITRATION
appeals, 2.6, 3.2.2.1
challenging arbitrability at, 2.1
class action issues, 10
debt harassment claims, 12.7.5
delay in filing, effect, 8.3.2
discovery rights, 2.4
jurisdiction, 2.3
    jury trial, 2.5
non-signatory to agreement, 7.4.2.1
removal to federal court, 2.3.1.2
stay pending state court proceedings, 2.3.2
venue, 2.3.3
waiver of right, *see* WAIVER

MOTION TO VACATE
see JUDICIAL REVIEW

MULTIPLE DAMAGES
punitive damages distinguished, 4.3.2.4

NATIONAL ARBITRATION FORUM (NAF)
see also ARBITRATION SERVICE PROVIDERS
bias challenges, 6.5.7.2
blackballing of arbitrators, 1.3.3
code of procedure, Appx. B.2.1
debt collection via, 12.1
fee schedule, unconscionability, 6.5.2.3
sample discovery pleadings
    second subpoena for document production, Appx. C.2.6
    subpoena for document production, Appx. C.2.5
summary of resources found on CD-Rom, Appx. M

NATIONAL BANKS
collection via arbitration, 12.8

NATIONAL CLEARINGHOUSE FOR LEGAL SERVICES
see SARGENT SHRIVER NATIONAL CENTER ON POVERTY LAW

NOTICE
arbitration award, 12.5.3.2
arbitration clauses, prerequisite to implied assent, 5.2.3.2
arbitration proceedings
    consumer options after receiving, 12.2
    judicial review based on lack thereof, 11.4.1, 12.4.4.3
bill stuffer arbitration clauses, 5.2.3.2
"mailbox rule," 5.2.3.2
sample notice of deposition, Appx. C.2.4

NURSING HOMES
arbitration of claims, 7.4.7.2

OFFICE OF THE COMPTROLLER OF THE CURRENCY (OCC)
enforcement actions against national banks, 12.8

PARTIALITY
see BIAS

PAYDAY LOAN COMPANIES
sample discovery, Appx. C.5, Appx. C.6

PLEADINGS
sample pleadings
    arbitration costs, Appx. E
    arbitration mechanism bias, Appx. H
    bankruptcy proceedings, Appx. I
    class action, Appx. F, Appx. J
    confirmation, opposing, Appx. L
    damage limitations, Appx. E
    debt collection arbitrations, Appx. K
    discovery, Appx. C, Appx. D
    Magnuson-Moss prohibition on arbitration, Appx. G
    unconscionability, Appx. E, Appx. F
    waiver, Appx. I
summary of resources found on CD-Rom, Appx. M

PRECEDENT
see CASE LAW

PREDISPUTE BINDING ARBITRATION AGREEMENTS
see MANDATORY ARBITRATION AGREEMENTS

PREEMPTION
see FEDERAL PREEMPTION

PRESUMPTIONS
arbitration, favoring, 7.2
arbitration agreement, no presumption of formation, 5.1
arbitration rights, against waiver, 8.1
federal preemption of state law, against, 3.2.3.3.1

PROCEDURES
appeal procedures, *see* APPEALS; JUDICIAL REVIEW
applicable law, 3.2.2
arbitration proceedings, *see* ARBITRATION PROCEEDINGS
arbitration service provider rules, *see under* ARBITRATION SERVICE PROVIDERS
arbitrator selection, 12.4.4.6
class actions, *see* CLASS ACTIONS
confirmation process, 12.5.2, 12.5.5
discovery, *see* DISCOVERY
errors in, judicial review, 11.4.5
FAA provisions not preemptory, 2.5, 3.2.2

PROCEDURES (cont.)
judicial review procedures, see JUDICIAL REVIEW
jury trials, see JURY TRIALS
procedural unconscionability, 6.4
removal to federal court, 2.3.1
    judicial review of award, 11.2.1

PRODUCTION REQUESTS
see also DISCOVERY
sample pleadings, Appx. C

PUBLIC POLICY CONSIDERATIONS
arbitration awards, 11.5.3
    preclusive effect, 11.8.3
    punitive damages, 11.7.5
discovery, 2.4.3

PUNITIVE DAMAGES
see also DAMAGES
availability, 11.7.3.2, 11.7.3.4.1
due process challenges to, 9.4, 11.7.6
limitations on, 4.3.1.1, 4.3.2.4
    arbitration agreements, 11.7.3.2
    arbitration rules, 11.7.3.3
    challenging, 11.7.3.2
    state law, 11.7.3.4
    unconscionability, 6.5.4.1
protecting arbitrator's award of, 11.7

REPEAT PLAYER BIAS
see also BIAS
concerns, 1.3.3
debt collection via arbitration, 12.1
evident partiality, 11.4.3.1

REPOSSESSIONS
waiver of arbitration, as, 8.3.1

REQUESTS FOR ADMISSIONS
sample pleadings, Appx. C
    auto financer, Appx. C.3.3
    payday loan company, Appx. C.5

REQUESTS FOR DOCUMENTS
see DISCOVERY; DOCUMENT REQUESTS

RESCISSION
effect on arbitration clause, 6.7.4.2, 7.3.4
TIL, see TIL REMEDIES

RESEARCH AIDS
see also CASE LAW
arbitration cases, 1.1

RES JUDICATA
arbitration decisions, effect, 11.8
    debt harassment claims, on, 12.7.6

RICO CLAIMS
see also STATUTORY CLAIMS
binding arbitration, 4.1
    limitations on damages, 4.3.2.4

***ROOKER-FELDMAN* DOCTRINE**
federal court review of state court rulings, 2.3.2

SALES AGREEMENTS
see also AGREEMENTS
arbitration clauses, see MANDATORY ARBITRATION AGREEMENTS

contract defenses, see CONTRACT DEFENSES
state regulation, 6.7.3
warranty claims, 4.2.2
    implied warranties, 4.2.2.7

SARGENT SHRIVER NATIONAL CENTER ON POVERTY LAW
see also CLEARINGHOUSE NUMBERS
documents and cases, obtaining, 1.1

SECRECY PROVISIONS
see CONFIDENTIALITY PROVISIONS

SELF-HELP REMEDIES
arbitration clauses
    applicability, 7.3.4
    effect, 6.7.4.2
waiver of arbitration rights, as, 8.3.1

SERVICE CONTRACTS
binding arbitration clauses, disclosure requirements, 4.2.2.8.4

SERVICEMEMBERS
see MILITARY PERSONNEL

SEVERABILITY
arbitration clauses, 4.3.2.4, 6.6.3
    FAA, application, 3.4.5
    from other unlawful provisions, 3.4.1, 3.4.5

SIGNATURES
contract law requirements, 5.2.2.1
electronic agreements, 5.2.2.3
forged signatures, 5.2.2.2
non-signatories, arbitration enforcement, 7.4

SPOT DELIVERY SALES
void agreements, effect, 6.7.4.1

STATE ENFORCEMENT AGENCIES
see GOVERNMENT ENFORCEMENT AGENCIES

STATE LAW
arbitration awards, vacating and confirming, 3.2.2.4
arbitration clauses
    application, 3.2.1.1, 3.3.2.2, 3.3.3, 3.4, 10.2.3
    class arbitrations, 10.2.2, 10.2.3
    enforceability, 3.3.2.2, 3.4, 5.1
    FAA preemption, 3.2
    FAA's policy and, 3.1.3
    restrictions on, 3.3.2.2
    scope restrictions, 7.3.3
    statutory regulation, 6.7.3
    voiding under, 6.1
choice-of-law provisions, 3.3.3
claims, see STATUTORY CLAIMS
consumer protection laws, 3.2.3.3
contract law principles, application, 3.2.3.2, 3.4, 5, 6
debt collection practices, 12.7.4
federal preemption, 3.2
    see also FEDERAL PREEMPTION
    FAA displacement by agreement, 3.3.3
    laws regulating arbitrators and services, 3.2.4
    limits on enforceability, 3.2.1
    nonspecific arbitration laws, 3.2.3
    procedural laws, 3.2.2
insurance disputes, application, 3.3.4
judicial review of arbitration award, application, 11.2.2
jury trial, waiver of rights, constitutionality, 9.1.2

References are to sections

STATE LAW (*cont.*)
national banks collecting via arbitration, application, 12.8
procedural laws, application, 3.2.2
punitive damages, limit on, 11.7.3.4
summary of resources found on CD-Rom, Appx. M
UDAP claims, *see* UDAP CLAIMS
unconscionability, *see* UNCONSCIONABILITY

STATUTE OF LIMITATIONS
judicial review of arbitration award
    confirmation, 11.2.3.2
    punitive damages, 11.7.2
    vacating or modifying, 11.2.3.1, 11.2.3.3
shortening, enforceability, 4.3.2.7, 6.5.4.4

STATUTORY CLAIMS
arbitration of
    bankruptcy, claims asserted in, 4.2.3
    federal claims, generally, 4.1
    federal claims, restrictions, 4.2.1
    judicial review, 11.5.2.3
    Magnuson-Moss claims, 4.2.2
    scope determinations, 7.3.3
    state consumer law, 3.2.3.3
    state law claims generally, 3.2.1.4.2
Bankruptcy Code, *see* BANKRUPTCY CLAIMS
Civil Rights Act, *see* CIVIL RIGHTS CLAIMS
class actions, *see* CLASS ACTIONS
consolidation of claims, 10.3.4
excessive fees thwarting, 4.4, 6.5.4.5
    arbitration charges exceeding court fees, 4.4.3.1
    charges deterring pursuit of claims, 4.4.3.2
    loser pays rules, 4.3.2.3
    reimbursement of fees, effect, 4.4.4
    sample briefs, Appx. E
FAA preemption
    federal law claims, 4.2
    public injunctive relief, 3.2.1.4.1
    state consumer law, 3.2.3.3
    state law claims generally, 3.2.1.4.2
federal claims, 4
judicial review of awards affecting, 11.5.2.3
limits on, 1.3.7, 4.3
Magnuson-Moss Warranty Act, *see* MAGNUSON-MOSS CLAIMS
one-sided control of arbitration process effectively nullifying, 4.5
RICO claims, *see* RICO CLAIMS
UDAP claims, *see* UDAP CLAIMS
waiver of remedies, 4.3, 6.5.4
    attorney fees, 4.3.2.2, 6.5.4.2
    class action rights, *see* CLASS ACTIONS
    damages, 4.3.2.4, 6.5.4.1
    excessive fees as, 4.4, 6.5.4.5
    federal remedies, 4.2.1
    injunctive and equitable relief, 4.3.2.6, 6.5.4.3
    knowing and voluntary waiver, 5.5.4

STAY OF PROCEEDINGS
arbitration proceedings, 12.2.3
pending arbitration
    appeals, 2.6.1, 2.6.2
    dismissal of claims, 2.6.2
    state court proceedings, 2.3.2
pending bankruptcy proceedings, 4.2.3

SUBPOENA
sample pleadings, Appx. C.2.5, Appx. C.2.6

SUITS
see CLAIMS; LITIGATION

SURETIES
arbitration agreements, application, 7.4.5

THIRD PARTIES
arbitration agreements, application
    affinity group members, 7.4.6
    agents, 7.4.4
    assignees, 7.4.5
    common third party relationships, 7.4.5
    debt collectors, 7.3.7.3
    enforcement officials, 7.4.8
    generally, 7.4.1
    nursing home patients, 7.4.7.2
    third party beneficiaries, 7.4.3
    wrongful death claimants, 7.4.7.1

THREATS
debt collection via arbitration, 12.7.2

TIE-INS
Magnuson-Moss restrictions, 4.2.2.8.5

TIL REMEDIES
see also STATUTORY CLAIMS
bankruptcy proceedings, 4.2.3.5
binding arbitration, 4.1
effect on arbitration clause, 6.7.4.2
limits on class action rights, 4.3.2.5

TORT CLAIMS
arbitration clauses, applicability, 7.3.3
    limitations on damages, 4.3.2.4

TREBLE DAMAGES
see MULTIPLE DAMAGES

UDAP CLAIMS
see also STATUTORY CLAIMS
arbitration clauses
    application, 7.3.3
    attacking, 6.7.3
collection via arbitration
    deceptive threats, 12.7.2
    government enforcement actions re, 12.8

UNCONSCIONABILITY
arbitration clauses, 3.4.3, 6.1–6.6
    adhesive, 6.4.1
    general standards, 6.2
    incorporation by reference, 6.4.2
    jurisdiction to determine, 2.5, 6.1
    language considerations, 6.4.2
    non-mutual clauses, 6.5.3
    opt-out provisions, 6.3
    punitive damages restrictions, 11.7.3.2
    re-drafting or severing, 6.6
    right to compel discovery, 2.4.2
    shortened statute of limitations, 6.5.4.4
    standard form agreements, 6.3, 6.4.1
bias of arbitrator or mechanism, 6.5.7
    sample brief, Appx. H
class action restrictions, 6.5.5
    sample briefs, Appx. F

UNCONSCIONABILITY (cont.)
confidentiality provisions, 6.5.8
contract as a whole, 6.1
   adhesion contracts, 6.4.1
determination, time, 6.2, 6.5.4.4
equitable relief limitations, 6.5.4.3
excessive fees and costs, 6.5.2, 6.6.2
   AAA fees, 6.5.2.2
   limitation on remedies, as, 6.5.4.5
   NAF fees, 6.5.2.3
   sample briefs, Appx. E
general standards, 6.2
inconvenient venue, 6.5.6
loser pays rules, 4.3.2.3, 6.5.9
non-mutual clauses, 6.5.3
partial unconscionability, 6.6
procedural unconscionability, 6.4
   adhesion contracts, 6.4.1
   meaningful choice as a factor, 6.4.3
   relationship to substantive, 6.3
   surprise as a factor, 6.4.2
sample briefs, Appx. E
secrecy provisions, 6.5.8
statutory remedies limitations, 6.5.4
   attorney fees, 6.5.4.2
   damages, 6.5.4.1
   high fees as, 6.5.4.5
   injunctive and equitable relief, 6.5.4.3
   sample briefs, Appx. E.3, Appx. E.4
   shortened limitations period, 6.5.4.4
substantive unconscionability, 6.5
   relationship to procedural, 6.3
UCC doctrine, application, 6.2

UNDUE INFLUENCE
contract law defense, 6.7.2

UNFAIR AND DECEPTIVE ACTS AND PRACTICES
see UDAP CLAIMS

UNIFORM ARBITRATION ACT (UAA)
insurance exemption, effect, 3.3.4.2, 3.3.4.3
judicial review procedures, 11.2.2
   grounds to modify or correct award, 11.3
   grounds to vacate award, 11.4.1
   timing requirements, 11.2.3.1, 11.2.3.2
   venue, 12.5.5.2
notice of award, 12.5.3.2
punitive damages, authorization, 11.7.3.4.1
stay of arbitration proceedings, 12.2.3

UNIFORM COMMERCIAL CODE (UCC)
self-help remedies, application, 7.3.4
unconscionability doctrine, application, 6.2

USED GOODS
warranty claims, 4.2.2.7

VACATING AWARD
see JUDICIAL REVIEW

VENUE
collection actions, 12.5.5.2
inconvenient venue, 1.3.7
   as grounds for judicial review, 12.4.4.9
   as unconscionable, 6.5.6
judicial review of arbitration decision, 11.2.1, 12.4.3

confirmation proceedings, 12.5.5.2
motions to compel, 2.3.3

VOLUNTARY AND KNOWING DOCTRINE
arbitration clauses, requirement, 5.5
cases rejecting, 5.5.5
constitutional waivers, 5.5.1
examples, 5.5.3
FAA preemption and, 5.5.2
statutory rights, waiver, 5.5.4

WAIVER
class action rights, 6.5.5
constitutional rights
   jury trial, 5.5, 9.1
   voluntary and knowing doctrine, 5.5
FAA application, 3.3.3
right to compel arbitration, 8
   actions found to constitute, 8.3.2.2
   actions not constituting, 8.3.2.3
   actions not defenses to waiver, 8.3.2.4
   arbitration rules not determinative, 8.6
   breach of arbitration clause as, 8.4
   burden of proof, 8.3.2.1
   delay as, 8.3.2
   filing suit as, 8.3.1
   jurisdiction to decide, 8.2
   litigation as, 8.3
   non-legal proceedings as, 8.3.1
   "no-waiver" clauses, 8.6
   prejudice requirement, 8.5
   presumption against, 8.1
sample brief, Appx. I
statutory remedies, 4, 6.5.4
   attorney fees, 6.5.4.2
   damages, 6.5.4.1
   excessive fees as, 4.4, 6.5.4.5
   federal remedies, 4
   injunctive and equitable relief, 6.5.4.3
   military personnel, 4.2.1.3
   unconscionability, 6.5.4
   voluntary and knowing doctrine, 5.5.4

WARRANTY CLAIMS
binding arbitration clauses, 4.2.2
   see also MANDATORY ARBITRATION AGREEMENTS
   designation of service provider, 4.2.2.8.5
   disclosure requirements, 4.2.2.8
   implied warranties, 4.2.2.7
   restrictions on, 4.2.2.1, 4.2.2.5, 5.6.3, Appx. G
   written warranties, 4.2.2.4
class actions, see CLASS ACTIONS
consolidation, 10.3.4
extended warranties, 4.2.2.8.4
Magnuson-Moss Warranty Act, see MAGNUSON-MOSS CLAIMS

WEB RESOURCES
Clearinghouse cases and documents, 1.1
NCLC manuals, web-based text searching, 1.1

WRONGFUL DEATH CLAIMS
arbitrability, 7.4.7.1

YO-YO SALES
void agreements, effect, 6.7.4.1

Quick Reference to the Consumer Credit and Sales Legal Practice Series

References are to sections in *all* manuals in NCLC's Consumer Credit and Sales Legal Practice Series. References followed by "S" appear only in a Supplement.

Readers should also consider another search option available at *www.consumerlaw.org/keyword*. There, users can search all seventeen NCLC manuals for a case name, party name, statutory or regulatory citation, or *any* other word, phrase, or combination of terms. The search engine provides the title, page number and context of every occurrence of that word or phrase within each of the NCLC manuals. Further search instructions and tips are provided on the web site.

The Quick Reference to the Consumer Credit and Sales Legal Practice Series pinpoints where to find specific topics analyzed in the NCLC manuals. References are to individual manual or supplement sections. For more information on these volumes, see *What Your Library Should Contain* at the beginning of this volume, or go to www.consumerlaw.org.

This Quick Reference is a speedy means to locate key terms in the appropriate NCLC manual. More detailed indexes are found at the end of the individual NCLC volumes. Both the detailed contents pages and the detailed indexes for each manual are also available on NCLC's web site, www.consumerlaw.org.

NCLC *strongly recommends*, when searching for PLEADINGS on a particular subject, that users refer to the *Index Guide* accompanying *Consumer Law Pleadings on CD-Rom*, and *not* to this *Quick Reference*. Another option is to search for pleadings directly on the *Consumer Law Pleadings* CD-Rom or on the *Consumer Law in a Box* CD-Rom, using the finding tools that are provided on the CD-Roms themselves.

The finding tools found on *Consumer Law in a Box* are also an effective means to find statutes, regulations, agency interpretations, legislative history, and other primary source material found on NCLC's CD-Roms. Other search options are detailed in *Finding Aids and Search Tips*, included in the front matter, *supra*.

Abbreviations

AUS	=	Access to Utility Service (3d ed. 2004 and 2007 Supp.)
Auto	=	Automobile Fraud (3d ed. 2007)
Arbit	=	Consumer Arbitration Agreements (5th ed. 2007)
CBPL	=	Consumer Banking and Payments Law (3d ed. 2005 and 2007 Supp.)
Bankr	=	Consumer Bankruptcy Law and Practice (8th ed. 2006 and 2007 Supp.)
CCA	=	Consumer Class Actions (6th ed. 2006 and 2007 Supp.)
CLP	=	Consumer Law Pleadings, Numbers One Through Thirteen (2007)
COC	=	The Cost of Credit (3d ed. 2005 and 2007 Supp.)
CD	=	Credit Discrimination (4th ed. 2005 and 2007 Supp.)
FCR	=	Fair Credit Reporting (6th ed. 2006 and 2007 Supp.)
FDC	=	Fair Debt Collection (5th ed. 2004 and 2007 Supp.)
Fore	=	Foreclosures (2d ed. 2007)
Repo	=	Repossessions (6th ed. and 2007 Supp.)
Stud	=	Student Loan Law (3d ed. 2006 and 2007 Supp.)
TIL	=	Truth in Lending (6th ed. 2007)
UDAP	=	Unfair and Deceptive Acts and Practices (6th ed. 2004 and 2007 Supp.)
Warr	=	Consumer Warranty Law (3d ed. 2006 and 2007 Supp.)

Quick Reference to the Consumer Credit and Sales Legal Practice Series

References are to sections in *all* manuals in NCLC's Consumer Credit and Sales Legal Practice Series

Abandonment of Apartment Building in Bankruptcy—Bankr § 17.8.2
Abbreviations Commonly Used by Debt Collectors—FDC App G.4
Abuse of Process—UDAP § 5.1.1.4; FDC § 10.6
Acceleration—COC §§ 5.6.2, 5.7.1; Repo § 4.1
Accessions—Repo § 3.5.3.2
Accord and Satisfaction—CBPL §§ 2.7, 9.3.1
Account Aggregation—CBPL § 3.12
Accountants—UDAP § 5.12.8
Accrediting Agencies, Student Loans—Stud § 9.4.1.2
Accurate Information in Consumer Reports—FCR Ch. 4
ACH—*See* NACHA
Actual Damages—*See* Damages
Actuarial Rebates—COC § 5.6.3.4
Adhesion Contracts—UDAP § 5.2.3
Adjustable Rate Mortgages—TIL § 4.6.4; COC § 4.3.6
Administration of Lawsuit, Class Action—CCA Ch 13
Admissibility of Other Bad Acts—Auto § 9.8.1
Admissions, Requests for—CCA § 7.1.3; Repo App E.5; Fore App. J.2.3; CLP; COC App L; FDC App I.3; Auto App F.1.4
Advertisements as Warranties—Warr § 3.2.2.5
Advertising Credit Terms—TIL §§ 5.4, 10.4
Affordability Programs, Utilities—AUS Ch 9, App F
After-Acquired Property—Repo § 3.4.5.2
Age Discrimination re Credit—CD § 3.4.2
Airbags—AF §§ 2.8S, 6.3bS
Airline Fare Advertising—UDAP §§ 2.5, 5.4.13.1
Alteration of Checks—CBPL § 2.3.1.4
Alimony Discharged in Bankruptcy—Bankr § 14.4.3.5
Alimony, Protected Source under ECOA—CD §§ 3.4.1, 5.5.5.3
Alternative Dispute Mechanisms—Arbit; FDC § 15.4
American Arbitration Association—Arbit App B.1
Americans With Disabilities Act—CD § 1.6
Amortization Explained—COC § 4.3.1
Amortization Negative—COC § 4.3.1.2
Amount Financed—TIL § 4.6.2
Annual Percentage Rate—TIL §§ 4.6.4, 5.6.9; COC § 4.4
Answer and Counterclaims—Repo Apps D.1, D.2; Fore App. J.2; COC App L; CLP
Antecedent Debt Clauses—Repo § 3.9
Anti-Competitive Conduct as UDAP Violation—UDAP § 4.10
Anti-Deficiency Statutes—Repo § 12.6.3
Apartment Buildings Abandoned in Bankruptcy—Bankr § 17.8.2
Apartment Leases—Bankr § 12.9; UDAP §§ 2.2.6, 5.5.2
Appeal of Order Requiring Arbitration—Arbit § 2.6
Applications for Credit—CD § 5.4
Appraisal Fraud—COC § 11.5.6
Appraisals, Right to a Copy—CD § 10.11
APR—*See* Annual Percentage Rate
Arbitration—Arbit; Bankr § 13.3.2.5; COC § 10.6.11; FDC § 15.4; TIL § 7.7; Warr § 13.4
Arbitration and Class Actions—Arbit ch. 10; CCA Ch 2;
Arbitration & Collection Actions—Arbit Ch. 12
Arbitration Fees—Arbit §§ 4.4, 6.5.2
As Is—Warr Ch 5; Auto § 7.8.2
Assignee Liability—UDAP § 6.6; TIL § 7.3
Assignment of Tax Refunds—COC § 7.5.4
Assistance for the Payment of Utility Service—AUS Ch 16
Assisted Living Facilities—UDAP § 5.11.4
Assistive Device Lemon Laws—Warr Ch 16
ATM Cards—CBPL Ch 3
ATM Machines, Bank Liability for Robberies at—CBPL § 3.5.4
ATM Machine Payments—CBPL Ch 3
ATM Machines, Access for Disabled—CBPL Ch 8

Attorney as Debt Collector—FDC §§ 4.2.7, 11.5.3
Attorney Fees—TIL § 8.9; Bankr Ch 15; Auto §§ 5.8.4, 9.12; CD § 11.7.6; FCR § 11.14; FDC §§ 6.8, 11.2.5, 11.3.5; UDAP § 8.8; Warr §§ 2.7.6, 10.7
Attorney Fees, Class Actions—CCA Ch 15, App E
Attorney Fees for Creditors—COC § 7.3.3; FDC § 15.2
Attorney Fees, Pleadings—Auto App L; FDC App K
Attorney General Enforcement—UDAP Ch 10
Attorneys Liable Under FDCPA—FDC §§ 4.2.7, 4.6.3
Attorneys Liable Under UDAP—UDAP §§ 2.3.9, 5.12.1
Auctions—Repo §§ 10.7.2, 10.10.6; Auto §§ 2.5.4, 2.6.4
Authorization to Represent—CCA App E
Authorization to Sue—CCA § 1.2.4
Automated Clearing House for Electronic Transfer—CBPL Ch3
Automatic Stay—Bankr Ch 9
Automobile Accessories—UDAP § 5.4.11
Automobile Auctions—*See* Auctions
Automobile Dealer Files—UDAP § 5.4.2
Automobile Dealer Licensing—Auto § 6.4, Appx. F
Automobile Dealers, Bonding Requirement—Auto § 9.13.4, App C
Automobile Dealers, Registration with Auction—Auto Appx. E.3
Automobile Fraud—Auto
Automobile Insurance, Force-Placed—*See* Force-Placed Auto Insurance
Automobile Leases, Article 9 Coverage—Repo § 14.2.1
Automobile Leases, Default and Early Termination—TIL Ch 10; UDAP § 5.4.8.3; Repo § 14.2
Automobile Leases, Misrepresentation—UDAP § 5.4.8
Automobile Leases, Odometer Rollbacks—Auto §§ 4.6.6.5, 5.2.6
Automobile Leases, Sublease Scams—UDAP § 5.4.10
Automobile Leases, Unconscionability—UDAP § 5.4.8.5
Automobile Manufacturers, List—Warr App N
Automobile Pawn Transactions—Bankr § 11.9; COC § 7.5.2.3; Repo § 3.5.5
Automobile Rentals—UDAP § 5.4.9
Automobile Repairs—Warr Ch 19; UDAP § 5.4.1
Automobile Repossession—*See* Repossessions
Automobile Safety Inspection Laws—Warr § 15.4.6
Automobile Sales—Warr Chs 14, 15; UDAP §§ 5.4.2, 5.4.6, 5.4.7
Automobile Service—Warr § 19.8; UDAP § 5.3.5
Automobile Sublease Scams—UDAP § 5.4.10
Automobile, Theft Prevention, Federal Statutes & Regulations—Auto App B.2
Automobile Title—Auto §§ 2.3, 2.4, Apps. D, E; UDAP § 5.4.5; Warr § 15.2
Automobile Valuation—Bankr § 11.2.2.3.2
Automobile Yo-Yo Abuses—UDAP § 5.4.5; Repo § 4.5; TIL §§ 4.4.5, 4.4.6
Bad Checks—FDC §§ 5.6.4, 15.3
Bail (i.e. replevin)—Repo Ch 5
Bait and Switch—UDAP § 4.6.1
Balance Billing—FDC § 14.3.6.S
Balloon Payments—COC § 4.6.2, Ch 5; TIL § 2.2.4.2.3
Bank Accounts, Attachment—FDC Ch 12, CBPL § 4.2
Bank Accounts, Closing—CBPL § 2.6.3
Bank Account Garnishment—CBPL § 4.2, FDC Ch 12
Bank Accounts, Joint—FDC § 12.7
Bank Accounts, Set-Off—FDC § 12.6.7, CBPL § 4.3
Bank Fees—CBPL § 4.5
Bank Accounts, Unfair Practices—UDAP §§ 4.4.9, 5.1.10
Bankruptcy Abuse Prevention and Consumer Protection Act—Bankr; Stud § 7.2.2
Bankruptcy and Debt Collection—FDC §§ 2.2, 9.10; Bankr § 9.4.3
Bankruptcy and Security Interests—Repo Ch 8

Quick Reference to the Consumer Credit and Sales Legal Practice Series
References are to sections in *all* manuals in NCLC's Consumer Credit and Sales Legal Practice Series

Bankruptcy and Utility Service—AUS §§ 4.5, 12.1; Bankr § 9.8
Bankruptcy, Claims Against Landlords in—Bankr § 17.8
Bankruptcy, Claims Against Creditors, Merchants in—Bankr Ch 17; UDAP § 6.8
Bankruptcy Code, Text—Bankr App A
Bankruptcy, Consumer Reports of—FCR Chs 4, §§ 5.2.3.7, 12.6.8
Bankruptcy Court as Litigation Forum—Bankr Ch 13
Bankruptcy Discharge of Student Loans—Stud Ch 7
Bankruptcy Forms—Bankr Apps D, E, G
Bankruptcy Petition Preparers—Bankr § 15.6
Benefit Overpayments and Bankruptcy—Bankr § 14.5.5.4
Bibliography—Bankr
Billing Errors—FDC § 5.7; Fore § 8.2.2
Billing Error Procedures, Credit Cards—CBPL § 6.5; TIL § 5.8
Bill Stuffers—Arbit § 5.7
Binding Arbitration—Arbit
Blanket Security Interests—Repo § 3.4.5.2.2
Bond, Claims Against Seller's—UDAP § 6.8; Auto § 9.13.4, App C
Bonding Statutes—Auto App C
Book-of-the-Month Clubs—UDAP § 5.8.5
Bounced Checks—CBPL § 2.5
Bounce Loans—TIL § 3.9.3.3, COC § 7.5.6
Breach of Contract—UDAP § 5.2.5
Breach of the Peace and Repossession—Repo § 6.4
Breach of Warranties—Warr; UDAP § 5.2.7.1
Briefs, Class Action—CCA Ch 9
Broker Fees—COC §§ 7.4.2, 11.5.4
Brokers, Auto—UDAP § 5.4.10
Brokers, Loan—*See* Loan Brokers
Brokers, Real Estate—*See* Real Estate Brokers
Budget Payment Plans—AUS § 6.4
Burglar Alarm Systems—UDAP § 5.6.2
Business Credit, Discrimination re—CD § 2.2.6.4
Business Opportunities—UDAP §§ 2.2.9.2, 5.13.1
Buy Here, Pay Here Car Sales—UDAP § 5.4.6.13
Buy Rate—UDAP § 5.4.7.6
Buying Clubs—UDAP § 5.10.6
Calculating Interest Rates—COC Ch 4
Campground Resort Memberships—UDAP §§ 2.2.8, 5.10.5
Cancellation Rights—TIL Ch 6; UDAP §§ 5.2.6, 5.8.2, 9.5
Cardholders' Defenses—TIL § 5.9.5
Carfax—Auto § 2.3.2, Appx. E.2
Cars—*See* Automobile
Case Selection—CCA § 1.2
Case Summaries, FDCPA—FDC App L
Cash Discounts—TIL § 5.9.6.4
Cashier's Checks—CBPL § Ch 5
Chapter 7 Bankruptcy—Bankr Ch 3
Chapter 11 Bankruptcy—Bankr §§ 6.3.4, 17.7
Chapter 12 Bankruptcy—Bankr Ch 16
Chapter 13 Bankruptcy—Bankr Ch 4
Charge Cards—TIL § 5.2.4.2
Charitable Contributions—Bankr § 1.1.2.6
Charitable Solicitations—UDAP § 5.13.5
Check 21—CBPL §§ 2.2, 2.4, App B
Check Advancement Loans—*See* Payday Loans
Check Approval Companies—FCR § 2.6.2.2
Check Cards—CBPL § 4.1.4.2
Check Cashing Services—UDAP §§ 5.1.10
Check Cashing Regulation—CBPL § 1.14
Check Collection Agencies Working for DA's—FDC § 1.4.3.10S
Check Guarantee Companies—FDC § 4.2.3
Checklist, Automobile Fraud Litigation—Auto § 1.4
Checklist, Debt Collection—FDC App G

Checklist, Truth in Lending—TIL §§ 1.6, 3.11
Checklist, Usury—COC § 1.6
Checks—CBPL Ch 2
Checks, Bad—FDC §§ 5.6.4, 15.3, CBPL § 2.5
Checks, Preauthorized Draft—UDAP §§ 5.1.10, CBPL § 2.3.5
Child Support, Credit Reports—FCR § 7.4.2
Child Support Discharged in Bankruptcy—Bankr § 14.4.3.5
Children in Household, Discrimination Based On—CD § 3.5.1
Choice of Laws—COC § 9.2.9; Repo § 2.6
Churning Repossession Schemes—Repo § 10.11
Civil Rights Act—CD § 1.5
Class Actions Fairness Act of 2005—CCA §§ 2.4, 11.5, 11.6
Class Actions—CCA; Auto § 9.7, App H; FCR § 11.2.2; FDC §§ 6.2.1.3, 6.3.5, 6.6; TIL §§ 6.9.9, 8.8; UDAP § 8.5
Class Actions and Arbitration—Arbit ch 10; CCA Ch 2
Class Actions and Diversity Jurisdiction—CCA §§ 2.3, 2.4
Class Actions Guidelines for Settlement, NACA—CCA App D
Class Actions in Bankruptcy Court—Bankr §§ 13.7, 17.4.2
Class Actions, Removal to Federal Court—CCA § 2.5
Class Certification Motions, Sample—CCA App N; CLP
Class Definitions—CCA Ch 3
Class Notices—CCA Ch 10, App Q
Client Authorization to Represent—CCA App E
Client Authorization to Sue—CCA § 1.2.4
Client Contacts with Other Parties—CCA §§ 1.2.6, 5.3
Client Handout on Bankruptcy—Bankr App K
Client Handout on Credit Discrimination—CD App I
Client Handout on Credit Reporting—FCR App L
Client Interview Checklist, Bankruptcy—Bankr App F
Client Interview Checklist, Debt Collection Harassment—FDC App G
Client Interview Sheet, Warranties—Warr App I
Client Retainer Forms, Sample—CLP
Closed-End Auto Leases—TIL Ch 10; Repo § 14.2
Closed-End Credit—TIL Ch 4
Closed School Discharge—Stud § 6.2
Closing Arguments, Sample—Auto App I
Coercive Sales Techniques—UDAP § 4.8
Collateral—Repo
Collection Agency Collection of Federal Taxes—FDC § 4.2.8S
Collection Fees—FDC § 15.2; Stud § 4.4
Collection of Student Loans—Stud Ch 4
Collection via Arbitration—Arbit Ch 12
College Cost Reduction and Access Act of 2007—Stud ch. SA.S
College Transcripts and Bankruptcy—Bankr §§ 9.4.3, 14.5.5.2
Collision Damage Waiver (CDW)—UDAP § 5.4.9
Common Law Contract Defenses—UDAP § 9.5
Common Law Fraud, Misrepresentation—Warr § 11.4; UDAP § 9.6.3; Auto Ch 7
Common Law Right to Utility Service—AUS § 3.1
Common Law Violations and Credit Reporting—FCR § 10.4
Common Law Warranties—Warr § 19.4
Communications to Client from Other Attorney—CCA § 5.3; FDC § 5.3.3
Community Reinvestment Act—CD § 1.9
Compensating Balances—COC § 7.4.4
Complaint Drafting, Class Actions—CCA Ch 4
Complaints—Auto App G; CD App G; CCA App F; COC App L; FCR App J.2; FDC App H; Repo Apps D.3, D.4; Fore App J; Warr App K; TIL Apps D, E; CLP
Compound Interest—COC § 4.6.1
Computers, Sale of—UDAP § 5.7.6
Condominiums—UDAP § 5.5.4.5
Condominium Warranties—Warr Ch 18

Quick Reference to the Consumer Credit and Sales Legal Practice Series
References are to sections in *all* manuals in NCLC's Consumer Credit and Sales Legal Practice Series

Consignment—Repo § 9.6.3.3
Consolidation Loan—Stud § 8.2
Conspiracy in Odometer Case—Auto § 4.7
Constitutionality of Arbitration Agreement—Arbit Ch 9
Contract Formation of Arbitration Agreement—Arbit Ch 5
Constructive Strict Foreclosure—Repo §§ 10.5.2, 12.5
Consumer Class Actions—CCA
Consumer Complaints to Government Agencies—UDAP § 9.8
Consumer Credit Reporting Reform Act of 1996—FCR § 1.4.6
Consumer Guide to Credit Reporting—FCR App L
Consumer Leasing Act—TIL Ch 10, App I.1
Consumer Recovery Funds—Auto § 9.13.5
Consumer Reporting Agencies—FCR
Consumer Reporting Agency List and Addresses—FCR App NS
Consumer Reporting Agencies, Enforcement Agreements—FCR App K
Consumer Reports, Disputing—FCR Ch 4
Consumer Reports, Keeping Credit Disputes Out of—FCR § 12.4
Consumer Reports for Business Transactions—FCR §§ 2.3.6.2, 2.3.6.8, 7.2.8
Consumer Reports for Employment Purposes—FCR §§ 2.3.6.4, 7.2.4
Consumer Reports for Government Benefits—FCR §§ 2.3.6.6, 7.2.6
Consumer Reports for Insurance Purposes—FCR §§ 2.3.6.5, 7.2.5
Consumer Reports from Non-Reporting Agencies—FCR § 8.2.18
Consumer/Seller Liability under Odometer Act—Auto § 4.8.13
Contests—UDAP §§ 4.6.6, 5.13.4
Contract Defenses—UDAP § 9.5
Contractual Misrepresentations—UDAP § 5.2.4
Cooling Off Periods—*See* Cancellation
Correspondence Schools—Stud Ch 9
Cosigners—Bankr § 9.4.4; CD § 5.4; Repo § 12.9; TIL §§ 2.2.2.2, 8.2; UDAP § 5.1.1.2.9
Counseling the Debtor—Bankr Ch 6
Coupon Settlement, Class Actions—CCA § 11.6
Cramming—AUS § 2.7.5
Credit Abuses—COC; UDAP §§ 2.2.1, 5.1
Credit Accident and Health Insurance—COC § 8.3.1.3; TIL §§ 3.7.9, 3.9.4
Credit Balances—TIL § 5.6; UDAP § 5.1.9.4
Credit Card Finders—UDAP § 5.1.9.2
Credit Card Issuers, Raising Seller-Related Claims Against—UDAP § 6.6, TIL § 5.9.5; CBPL § 6.4
Credit Card Issuer's Security Interest in Goods Purchased—Repo § 3.6
Credit Card Surcharges—TIL § 5.9.6.4
Credit Card Unauthorized Use—TIL § 5.9.4
Credit Cards—TIL Ch 5; CBPL Ch 6; UDAP § 5.1; FDC § 4.2.3
Credit Cards, Reporting Services for Lost—UDAP § 5.1.5.5
Credit Charges—COC Ch 5; UDAP § 5.1.6
Credit Denial, Notice—CD § 10.5; FCR § 8.2.6
Credit Disability Insurance—COC §§ 8.3.1.3, 8.5.2.3; Fore § 5.3.3; TIL §§ 3.7.9, 3.9.4
Credit Evaluation—CD §§ 6.2, 6.3
Credit File, Disputing and Right to See—FCR Chs 3, 4
Credit Insurance—COC Ch 8; TIL §§ 3.7.9, 3.9.4; Repo § 4.4; UDAP § 5.3.10
Credit Life Insurance—COC §§ 8.3.1.2, 8.5.3.1.2; TIL §§ 3.7.9, 3.9.4
Credit Math—COC Ch 4
Credit Property Insurance—COC §§ 8.3.1.5, 8.5.3.1.4, 8.5.3.4, 8.5.4.4; TIL §§ 3.9.4.4, 3.9.4.6, 4.9.8

Credit Rating, Injury to—FCR § 1110.2.3; FDC §§ 5.5.2.9, 8.3.8; UDAP § 8.3.3.6
Credit Regulation, History of—COC Ch 2
Credit Repair Organizations—FCR Ch 15; UDAP § 5.1.2.2
Credit Reporting Agencies, Contacting—FCR Ch. 3
Credit Reporting Sample Forms—FCR App I
Credit Reports—FCR; TIL § 5.9.4.7
Credit Reports, Affiliate Sharing—FCR §§ 2.4.3, 3.3.1.5, 8.2.18
Credit Reports, Furnishers of Information Obligations—FCR Ch 6
Credit Reports, Keeping Credit Disputes Out of—FCR § 12.4
Credit Reports from Non-Reporting Agencies—FCR § 8.2.18
Credit Scams—UDAP §§ 5.1.2; 5.1.3; 5.1.8
Credit Scoring—CD § 6.4; FCR Ch. 14
Credit Terms—COC; UDAP § 5.1.5; 5.1.7
Creditor Remedies—FDC Chs 12, 13, 15; UDAP § 5.1.1; 5.1.1
Creditors, Types of—COC Chs 2, 9
Creditors Filing Bankruptcy—Bankr Ch 17
Creditworthiness—Bankr § 6.2.2.3
Criminal Prosecution Threats—FDC § 15.3
Cross-Collateral—Repo § 3.7.2
Cross Metering, Utility Service—AUS § 5.2
Cruise Line Port Charges—UDAP § 5.4.13.2
Cure of Default—Repo §§ 4.8, 13.2.4.4
Cy Pres—CCA § 11.7
Daily Accrual Accounting—COC § 4.6.8
Damages—FDC §§ 2.5.2, 6.3, Ch 10; FCR Ch 11; Repo Ch 13; TIL Ch 8; UDAP § 8.3; Warr §§ 10.3–10.5
Damage to Credit Rating—UDAP § 8.3.3.6
Dance Studios—UDAP § 5.10.4
Daubert Doctrine—Warr § 13.8.4
Dealer's Only Auto Auctions—Repo § 10.10.6
Debit Cards—CBPL Ch 3
Debt Buyers—FDC § 1.4.3.7S
Debt Cancellation Agreements—TIL §§ 3.7.10, 3.9.4.7
Debt Collection—FDC; UDAP §§ 2.2.2, 5.1.1
Debt Collection and Bankruptcy—FDC § 2.2.5
Debt Collection by Arbitration—FDC § 15.4; Arbit Ch. 12
Debt Collection Case Preparation—FDC Ch 2
Debt Collection Procedures Act—FDC § 13.2.1.1
Debt Collectors—FDC § 1.2, Ch 4
Debt Collector's Common Abbreviations—FDC App G.4
Debt Harassment, How to Stop—FDC § 2.3
Debtor in Possession under Chapter 12—Bankr § 16.3
Debt Pooling—FDC § 1.5.5
Deceit—Warr § 11.4; UDAP § 9.6.3
Deception—UDAP § 4.2; FDC § 5.5
Deceptive Practices Statutes—*See* UDAP
Deceptive Pricing—UDAP § 4.6.3
Defamation—FDC § 10.5; FCR § 10.5.2
Deeds-in-Lieu of Foreclosure—Fore § 2.4.5
Defamatory Use of Mail—FDC § 9.1
Default—Repo Ch 4
Default Insurance—TIL § 3.7.7
Defective Automobile Title—Auto
Defenses as Grounds for Nonpayment—Repo § 4.6
Defenses to Credit Card Charges—CBPL § 6.4; TIL § 5.9.5; UDAP § 6.6
Deferment of Student Loan—Stud § 3.2
Deferral Charges—COC § 4.8.2
Deferred Payment Plans—AUS § 6.6
Deficiency Actions—Repo Ch 12, App C.1
Deficiency Judgments—Fore § 14.3
Delay—UDAP § 4.9.2
Delaying Tactics, Opposing—CCA Ch 6

Quick Reference to the Consumer Credit and Sales Legal Practice Series

References are to sections in *all* manuals in NCLC's Consumer Credit and Sales Legal Practice Series

Delinquency Charges—*See* Late Charges
Deliverable Fuels—AUS § 1.6
Demonstrator Vehicles—Auto §§ 1.4.9, 2.1.7
Denial of Credit, Notice—FCR § 8.2.6
Department of Housing and Urban Development (HUD)—CD § 12.3.1, App D; Fore Chs 2, 4, § 3.2
Department of Motor Vehicles—Auto Appx. D
Deposit, Consumer's Right to Return When Seller Files Bankruptcy—Bankr § 17.5
Depositions in Class Actions—CCA § 7.1.2.4, Ch 8
Deposition Notice, Sample—CLP
Deposition Questions, Sample—Auto § 9.5.6; CLP
Deposition Questions and Answers, Sample—CLP
Depository Creditors—COC Ch 2; FDC Ch 12
Deregulation of Utilities—AUS Ch 1
Detinue—Repo Ch 5
Digital Divide—CD § 3.8.2
Direct Deposits—CBPL Ch 10
Disabilities, Discrimination Based On—CD § 3.5.2
Disability Discharge—Stud § 6.6
Disabled Access to ATM machines—CBPL Ch 8
Discharge in Bankruptcy—Bankr Ch 14
Discharge of Indebtedness Income—Fore § 14.7.3
Discharging Student Loan Obligations—Stud Ch 6, § 7.2.3
Disclaimers, Warranties—Warr Ch 5
Disclosure and UDAP—UDAP § 4.2.14
Disclosure of Credit Terms—TIL
Disconnection of Utility Service—AUS Chs 11, 12
Discovery—Auto § 9.5, App H; *see also* Interrogatories; Document Requests
Discovery, Arbitration—Arbit § 2.4, App C
Discovery, Class Actions—CCA Ch 7, App H
Discovery, Motions to Compel—CCA Apps I, J
Discrimination in Collection Tactics—FDC § 9.8
Discrimination re Credit—CD
Disposition of Repo Collateral—Repo Chs 9, 10
Dispute Resolution Mechanisms—Warr §§ 2.8, 14.2.9
Disputing Information in Consumer Report—FCR Ch. 4
District Attorneys Hiring Check Collection Agencies—FDC § 1.4.3.10S
Document Preparation Fees—TIL § 3.9.6; UDAP § 5.4.3.8
Document Production Requests, Sample—Arbit App C; Auto App F; CCA App H; CD App H; FDC App I.2; Repo Apps E.2; Fore App. J.2.3; TIL App F.3; Warr App L.3; CLP
Document Requests, Sample Objection to—CCA App M
D'Oench, Duhme Doctrine—COC § 10.7; Repo § 12.10; Fore § 5.12.3; UDAP § 6.7.5
Door-to-Door Sales—UDAP § 5.8.2
Dragnet Clauses—Repo § 3.9
Driver Privacy Protection Act—Auto § 2.2.4, App A.2
Driver's Licenses and Bankruptcy—Bankr §§ 14.5.4, 14.5.5.1
Drunk Driving Debts in Bankruptcy—Bankr § 14.4.3.9
Due on Sale Clauses—Fore § 4.6.5
Due Process—Fore § 3.1.2.2, 4.4
Dunning, How to Stop with Sample Letters—FDC § 2.3
Duress—UDAP § 9.5.12; AUS § 6.1.9
Duty of Good Faith and Fair Dealing—COC § 12.8
Early Termination Penalties in Auto Leases—TIL § 10.5
Earned Income Tax Credit—Bankr § 2.5.5
EBT—CBPL Ch 8
E-Commerce, Jurisdiction—COC § 9.2.9.4
Educational Loans—*See* Student Loans
EFT 99—CBPL Ch 10
Election of Remedy Statutes—Repo § 12.4

Electric Service—AUS § 1.2.2; UDAP § 5.6.9
Electric Industry Restructuring—AUS § 1.4
Electronic Banking—CBPL Ch 3; FDC § 12.6.6
Electronic Benefit Transfers—CBPL Ch 8
Electronic Check Conversion—CBPL Ch 3
Electronic Credit Transactions—COC § 9.2.10
Electronic Disclosure—TIL §§ 4.2.9, 5.3.6, 9.3.9; UDAP § 4.2.14.3.9
Electronic Fund Transfers—CBPL Chs 3, 10
Electronic Repossession—Repo § 6.6
Electronic Check Representment—CBPL Ch 2
Electronic Signatures and Records—CBPL Ch 11
Electronic Transaction Fraud—UDAP § 5.9.4; CBPL Ch 3
Electronic Transfer Account (ETA)—CBPL Ch 10
Employer Bankruptcy—Bankr § 17.7.12
Employment Agencies—UDAP § 5.13.2
Encyclopedia Sales—UDAP § 5.7.1
Endorsements—UDAP § 4.7.7
Energy Savings Claims—UDAP § 5.6.7
Enforceability of Arbitration Clause—Arbit
Equal Credit Opportunity Act—CD; AUS § 3.7.2
Equal Credit Opportunity Act Regulations—CD App B
E-Sign—CBPL Ch 11; COC § 9.2.10, 11.3.1.8a
ETAs (Electronic Transfer Accounts)—CBPL Ch 10
Ethnic Discrimination—CD § 3.3.3
Evictions—AUS § 12.4; UDAP § 5.5.2.10; FDC § 1.5.2
Evidence Spoilation—Warr § 13.2.5
Evidentiary Issues in Automobile Litigation—Auto § 9.8
Exempt Benefits and Bankruptcy—Bankr § 10.2.2.11
Exempting Interest Rates—COC Ch 3
Exemption Laws, Liberal Construction—FDC § 12.2
Exemption Planning—Bankr § 10.4.1
Exemptions, Benefits, Earnings, Due Process Protections—FDC Ch 12
Expert Inspection—Warr § 13.6.1
Experts, Attorney Fee Award for—UDAP § 8.8.7.3
Expert Witnesses—FDC § 2.4.14; Warr § 13.8
Expert Witnesses, Sample Questions—Auto App I
Exportation of Interest Rates—COC Ch 3
Express Warranties—Warr Ch 3
Expressio Unius Est Exclusio Alterius—COC § 9.3.1.2
Extended Warranties—*See* Service Contracts
Extortionate Collection—FDC § 9.5
FACT Act—FCR
FACT Act Regulations—FCR Appx. B
Fair Credit Billing Act—CBPL § 6.5; TIL § 5.8; FCR § 12.4.2.; AUS § 11.3.5
Fair Credit Reporting Act—FCR; FDC § 9.6
Fair Debt Collection Practices Act—FDC Chs 3–7, Apps A, B, L
Fair Housing Act—CD
Fair Housing Act Regulations—CD App D
False Certification Discharge—Stud § 6.3
False Pretenses, Obtaining Consumer Reports—FCR § 7.7
Family Expense Laws—FDC § 14.6; CD § 9.3
Farm Reorganizations, Bankruptcy—Bankr Ch 16
Farmworker Camps—UDAP §§ 2.2.7, 5.5.4
Faxes, Junk—UDAP § 5.9.2.2
Federal Agency Collection Actions—FDC Ch 13
Federal Arbitration Act—Arbit Ch 3, App A
Federal Benefit Payments, Electronic—CBPL Ch 10
Federal Civil Rights Acts—CD; AUS § 3.7.1
Federal Direct Deposit of Benefits—CBPL Ch 10
Federal Direct Student Loans—Stud
Federal Energy Regulatory Commission (FERC)—AUS § 1.2.2.2

Quick Reference to the Consumer Credit and Sales Legal Practice Series

References are to sections in *all* manuals in NCLC's Consumer Credit and Sales Legal Practice Series

Federal False Claims Act—UDAP § 9.4.13
Federal Family Education Loans—Stud
Federal Preemption—FDC §§ 2.2, 6.14; UDAP § 2.5
Federal Preemption of State Usury Laws—COC Ch 3
Federal Racketeering Statute—*See* RICO
Federal Reserve Board—*See* FRB
Federal Tax Collections and Collection Agencies—FDC § 4.2.8S
Federal Trade Commission—*See* FTC
Fees—TIL § 3.7; COC § 7.2.1; FDC § 15.2
FHA Mortgage Foreclosure—Fore Ch 3
Fiduciary Duty—COC §§ 8.7.2, 12.9
Fifth Amendment Privilege—Auto § 9.8.6.7
Filed Rate Doctrine—UDAP § 5.6.10.1
Film Developing Packages—UDAP § 5.7.10
Finance Charge—TIL Ch 3; COC § 4.4
Finance Charges, Hidden—COC Ch 7; TIL § 3.10
Finance Companies—COC Ch 2; UDAP §§ 2.2.1, 5.1.5
Flipping—COC § 6.1; UDAP § 5.1.5
Flipping of Property—COC 11.5.6
Flood Damage to Vehicle—Auto § 2.1.3
Food Advertising—UDAP § 5.11.2
Food Stamps, Electronic Payment—CBPL Ch 8
Forbearance of Student Loans—Stud § 3.3
Forbearance Plans, Mortgage Loans—Fore § 2.3.4.3
Force-Placed Auto Insurance—UDAP § 5.3.11; COC § 8.3.1.4; TIL § 3.9.4.4.2
Foreclosure—Fore
Foreclosure, False Threat—Repo Ch 6
Foreclosure, Government-Held Mortgages—Fore Ch 3
Foreclosure, Preventing Through Bankruptcy—Bankr Ch 9, §§ 10.4.2.6.4, 11.5, 11.6; Fore Ch 9
Foreclosure, Preventing Through Refinancing—COC § 6.5; Fore § 2.11.2
Foreclosure, Preventing Through Rescission—TIL Ch 6; Fore § 5.5.1
Foreclosure, Preventing Through Workouts—Fore Ch 2
Foreclosure, Rescue Scams—Fore ch 15; TIL §§ 6.8.5, 9.2.5.6, 9.2.6.3.8
Foreclosure, Setting Aside—Fore § 14.1
Foreclosure, Summary of State Laws—Fore App C
Foreclosures and UDAP—UDAP § 5.1.1.5; Fore § 5.12.1
Forged Signatures, Indorsements—CBPL § 2.3.1.3
Franchises—UDAP §§ 2.2.9.2, 5.13.1
Fraud—UDAP; Warr § 11.4
Fraud and Arbitration—Arbit Ch 6
FRB Official Staff Commentary on Reg. B—CD App C
FRB Official Staff Commentary on Reg. M—TIL App I.3
FRB Official Staff Commentary on Reg. Z—TIL App C
Free Offers—UDAP § 4.6.4
Freezer Meats—UDAP § 5.7.2
FTC (Federal Trade Commission)—UDAP
FTC Act, No Private Action Under—UDAP § 9.1
FTC Cooling Off Period Rule—UDAP § 5.8.2, App B.3
FTC Credit Practices Rule—Repo § 3.4.2; UDAP § 5.1.1.2, App B.1; FDC § 8.4.2
FTC Debt Collection Law—FDC Ch 8
FTC FCR Enforcement Actions—FCR App K
FTC FCR Official Staff Commentary—FCR App D
FTC FDCPA Official Staff Commentary—FDC § 3.2.6, App C
FTC Funeral Rule—UDAP § 5.11.5, App B.5
FTC Holder Rule—UDAP § 6.6, App B.2
FTC Mail or Telephone Order Merchandise Rule—UDAP § 5.8.1.1, App B.4
FTC Staff Letters on FCR—FCR App E

FTC Staff Letters on FDCPA—FDC § 3.2.5, App B
FTC Telemarketing Sales Rule—UDAP App D.2.1
FTC Telephone and Dispute Resolution Rule—UDAP App D.2.2
FTC Used Car Rule—UDAP § 5.4.3.2, App B.6; Warr § 15.8, App D
Funds Availability—CBPL § 9.4
Funerals—UDAP § 5.11.5
Furniture Sales—UDAP § 5.7.3
Future Advance Clauses—Repo § 3.9
Future Service Contracts—UDAP § 5.10
GAP Insurance—TIL §§ 3.7.10, 3.9.4.7
Garnishment—FDC § 5.5.7, Ch 12, App D
Garnishment of Bank Account—CBPL § 4.2
Garnishment to Repay Student Loans—Stud § 5.3, App B.1.3
Gas Service—AUS § 1.2.1; UDAP § 5.6.9
Gasoline, Price Gouging—UDAP § 5.6.8.5
Gift Cards—UDAP § 5.1.10.6S
Government Benefits—FCR §§ 2.3.6.6, 7.2.6
Government Checks—CBPL Ch 9
Government Collection Practices—FDC Ch 13; Stud Ch 4
GPS Devices—UDAP § 5.4.9.5S
Gramm-Leach-Bliley Act—COC §§ 3.9, 8.4.1.5.2; FCR § 16.4.1
Gray Market Sales—Auto § 1.4.12; Warr § 14.7
Guaranteed Student Loans—Stud
Guarantees—UDAP § 5.2.7.3
Guarantors—*See* Cosigners
Handguns—UDAP § 5.7.9
Handicapped, Discrimination Against—CD § 3.5.2
Handouts for Client—*See* Client Handouts
Health Care Bills—FDC Ch 14; Bankr § 6.2.2.4.1
Health Care Plans, Misrepresentations—UDAP § 5.11.6
Health Care Treatment, Discrimination In—CD § 2.2.2.6
Health Cures, Misrepresentations—UDAP § 5.11
Health Spas—UDAP § 5.10.3
Hearing Aids—UDAP § 5.11.1
Heating Fuel—AUS §§ 1.2, 1.6; UDAP § 5.6.8
HELC—TIL § 5.10
Hidden Interest—COC Ch 7; TIL § 3.10
High Cost Loans, State Laws—COC Ch 7
High Pressure Sales—UDAP § 4.8
Hill-Burton Act Compliance—UDAP § 5.11.5
Holder in Due Course—UDAP § 6.6; COC §§ 10.6.1
Home Builders—UDAP § 5.5.5.2
Home Equity Lines of Credit—TIL § 5.10
Home Equity Loans—TIL Ch 9
Home Foreclosure—*See* Foreclosure
Home Heating Fuel—AUS §§ 1.2, 1.6; UDAP § 5.6.8
Home Improvement Practices—TIL § 6.5.3; UDAP § 5.6.1; Warr § 19.7, Apps I.3, K.4
Home Mortgage Disclosure Act—CD § 4.4.5
Home Mortgage, Rescission of—TIL Ch 6, App E.3
Home Owners' Loan Act—COC § 3.5
Home Owners Warranty Program—UDAP § 5.5.5.2
Home Ownership & Equity Protection Act—TIL Ch 9, App E.2.3; Fore § 5.6.1
Homes and UDAP—UDAP §§ 2.2.5, 5.5.5
Homes, Warranties—Warr Ch. 18
Homestead Exemptions, Bankruptcy—Bankr § 10.2.2.2
Horizontal Privity—Warr § 6.3
Hospital Bills—FDC Ch 14
House Warranties—Warr Ch 18
Household Goods, Bankruptcy Exemption—Bankr §§ 10.2.2.4, 10.4.2.4
Household Goods Security Interest—Repo § 3.4; UDAP §§ 5.1.1.2; 5.1.1.5; TIL § 4.6.7

Quick Reference to the Consumer Credit and Sales Legal Practice Series
References are to sections in *all* manuals in NCLC's Consumer Credit and Sales Legal Practice Series

Household Goods Security Interest, Credit Property Insurance on—COC § 8.5.4.4
Houses and UDAP—UDAP §§ 2.2.5, 5.5
HOW Program—UDAP § 5.5.5.5.2
HUD—*See* Department of Housing and Urban Development
Identity Theft—FCR Ch. 9
Illegal Conduct—UDAP §§ 4.3.9, 9.5.8
Illegality as Contract Defense—UDAP § 9.5.8
Immigrant Consultants, Deceptive Practices—UDAP § 5.12.2
Immigrant Status, Discrimination Based On—CD § 3.3.3.3
Implied Warranties—Warr Ch 4
Improvident Extension of Credit—UDAP § 5.1.4
Incomplete Information in Consumer Reports—FCR Ch 4
Inconvenient Venue—*See* Venue
Indian Tribal Law, Bankruptcy Exemptions—Bankr § 10.2.3.1
Industrial Loan Laws—COC Ch 2
Infancy—*See* Minority
Infliction of Emotional Distress—FDC § 10.2
In Forma Pauperis Filings in Bankruptcy—Bankr §§ 13.6, 17.6
Informal Dispute Resolution—Warr § 2.8
Injunctions—UDAP § 8.6; FDC §§ 6.12, 12.6.2, 13.3
Insecurity Clauses—Repo § 4.1.6
Inspection by Experts—Warr § 13.6.1
Installment Sales Laws—COC §§ 2.3.3.4, 9.3.1.1
Insurance and Arbitration—Arbit § 3.3.4
Insurance and UDAP—UDAP §§ 2.3.1, 5.3
Insurance Consumer Reports—FCR §§ 2.3.6.5, 2.6.8, 7.2.5
Insurance, Credit—COC Ch 8; TIL §§ 3.7.9, 3.9.4; UDAP § 5.3.10
Insurance, Illusory Coverage—UDAP § 5.3.6
Insurance Packing—COC § 8.5.4; UDAP § 5.3.12
Insurance Redlining—CD § 7.3
Insurance, Refusal to Pay Claim—UDAP § 5.3.3
Intentional Infliction of Emotional Distress—FDC § 10.2
Intentional Interference with Employment Relationships—FDC § 10.4
Interest Calculations—COC §§ 4.2, 4.3
Interest, Hidden—COC Ch 7; TIL § 3.10
Interest Rates, Federal Preemption of—COC Ch 3
Interference with Employment Relationships—FDC § 10.4
Interim Bankruptcy Rules—Bankr App B
International Driving Permits—UDAP § 5.4.13.5S
International Money Orders and Wires—CBPL Ch 5
Internet Banking—CBPL Ch 3
Internet, Fraudulent Schemes—UDAP § 5.9
Internet, Invasion of Privacy—UDAP § 4.11
Internet Service Providers—UDAP § 5.6.10.7
Interrogatories—Arbit App C; Auto App F; CCA App E; CD App H; COC App L; FCR App J.3; FDC App I.1; Repo App E; Fore Apps J.2.3, J.3.4, J.3.5; Warr App L; TIL App F.2; CLP
Interstate Banking and Rate Exportation—COC § 3.4.5
Intervenor Funding—AUS § 9.5
Interview Checklist for Debt Collection—FDC App G
Interview Form, Bankruptcy—Bankr App F
Interview Form for Clients, Warranties—Warr App I
Invasion of Privacy—FCR §§ 10.5.3, 16.3; FDC § 10.3
Investigative Reports—FCR Ch 13
Investments—UDAP §§ 2.2.9, 5.13
Involuntary Bankruptcy Cases—Bankr §§ 13.8, 16.1.2
JAMS—Arbit App B.3
Joint Bank Accounts, Seizure—FDC § 12.7
Joint Checking Accounts—CBPL §§ 2.6.3, 4.2, 4.3
Judicial Liens, Avoiding in Bankruptcy—Bankr § 10.4.2.3
Jury, Disclosure to, that Damages Will Be Trebled—UDAP § 8.4.2.8; Auto § 9.9.10

Jury Instructions, Sample—CCA Ch 14; Auto App G; FDC App J.2; FCR App J.8; TIL App G
Jury Trial, Class Action—CCA Ch 14
Jury Trial, Preparing FDCPA Case—FDC § 2.5.7
Land Installment Sales Contract (aka "Contract for Deed")—Fore Ch. 12
Land Sales—UDAP §§ 2.2.5, 5.5.4.7
Land Trusts—TIL §§ 2.2.1.1, 2.4.3
Landlord Evictions—FDC § 1.5.2.2
Landlord's Removal of Evicted Tenant's Property—Repo § 15.7.4; FDC § 1.5.2.4
Landlord's Requested Disconnection of Utility Service—AUS § 12.4
Landlord's Termination of Utility Service—AUS Ch 4
Landlord-Tenant—Bankr §§ 12.9, 17.8; UDAP §§ 2.2.6, 5.5.2; FDC § 1.5.2
Landownership, Utility Service Conditioned on—AUS Ch 4
Late Charges—COC §§ 4.8, 7.2.4; TIL §§ 3.9.3, 4.7.7; UDAP §§ 5.1.1.2.8; 5.1.6
Late Charges, Utility Bills—AUS §§ 6.2, 6.3
Late Posting of Payments and Interest Calculation—COC § 4.6.3.5
Law, Unauthorized Practice of—FDC §§ 4.2.7.7.3, 11.5; Bankr § 15.6
Lawyer—*See* Attorney
Layaway Plans—UDAP § 4.9.1
Lease-Back of Home—COC § 7.5.2.1; TIL § 6.2.4.1
Leases—Repo Ch 14; TIL § 2.2.4.2, Ch 10; UDAP §§ 2.2.6, 5.4.8, 5.5.2; Warr Ch 21; Auto §§ 4.6.2.3, 4.6.6.5, 5.2.6; Bankr § 12.9; CD § 2.2.2.2; COC § 7.5.3; *see also* Rent to Own
Lease Terms for Residence—UDAP §§ 5.5.2.2, 5.5.2.3
Leased Vehicle Damages—Auto § 9.10.4
Legal Rights, Misrepresentation of—UDAP § 5.2.8
Lemon Cars Being Resold—Auto §§ 1.4.7, 2.1.6, 2.4.5.5, 6.3, App C; Warr § 15.7.3; UDAP § 5.4.6.7
Lemon Laws—Warr § 14.2, App F
Lender Liability—UDAP Ch 6
Letter to Debt Collector, Sample—FDC § 2.3
Liability of Agents, Principals, Owners—UDAP Ch 6; FDC § 2.8
Licenses to Drive and Bankruptcy—Bankr § 14.5.5.1
Liens—Repo Ch 15
Life Care Homes—UDAP § 5.11.3
Life Insurance, Excessive Premiums for—UDAP § 5.3.9
Lifeline Assistance Programs—AUS § 2.3.2
LIHEAP—AUS Ch 7, App D
Limitation of Remedies Clauses—Warr Ch 9
Live Check Solicitations—UDAP § 5.1.10.5S
Living Trusts—UDAP § 5.12.3
Loan Brokers—UDAP §§ 2.2.1, 5.1.3; COC § 7.3.2
Loan Flipping—*See* Flipping
Loan Rehabilitation—Stud § 8.4
Loans, High Cost—COC Ch7
Long Arm Jurisdiction—COC § 9.2.9.6; UDAP § 7.6.2
Loss Mitigation, Foreclosures—Fore Ch 2
Lost Checks—CBPL §§ 2.8, 9.2
Lost Credit Card Reporting Services—UDAP § 5.1.5.5
Low Balling—UDAP § 4.6.5
Low Income Home Energy Assistance Program—AUS Ch 7, App D
Magazine Sales—UDAP § 5.7.1
Magnuson-Moss Warranty Act—Warr Ch 2, Apps A, B; Auto § 8.2.11.2
Magnuson-Moss Warranty Act Relation to Federal Arbitration Act—Arbit § 4.2.2, App G
Mail Fraud—UDAP § 9.2.4; FDC § 9.1
Mail Order Sales—UDAP § 5.8.1

579

Quick Reference to the Consumer Credit and Sales Legal Practice Series
References are to sections in *all* manuals in NCLC's Consumer Credit and Sales Legal Practice Series

Malicious Prosecution—FDC § 10.6.2
Managed Care, Misrepresentations—UDAP § 5.11.6
Manufacturer Rebates—UDAP § 4.6.3
Marital Status Discrimination—CD § 3.4.1
Mass Action—CCA § 2.4.5
Master Metering—AUS § 5.5
Math, Credit—COC Ch 4
MBNA Use of Collection via NAF Arbitration—Arbit Ch 12
McCarran-Ferguson Act—Arbit § 3.3.4; COC § 8.5.2.7; TIL § 2.4.9.5
Means Testing—Bankr
Mechanical Breakdown Insurance—*See* Service Contracts
Mediation—Auto § 9.11.1.3
Medical—*See* Health Care
Mental Anguish Damages—FDC §§ 2.5, 6.3, 10.2
Mental Incompetence—UDAP § 9.5.7.3
Meter Tampering—AUS Ch 5
Migrant Farmworker Camps—UDAP §§ 2.2.7, 5.5.4
Mileage Disclosure—Auto §§ 2.4.5.8, 4.6.6
Military Personnel and Credit Protection—FDC § 9.12; FCR § 5.5.1; Repo § 6.3.5.1; Fore § 4.9
Mini-FTC Laws—*See* UDAP
Minority—UDAP § 9.5.7
Misrepresentation—UDAP § 4.2; Warr § 11.4; Auto § 8.4
Mistaken Undercharges, Utility Bills—AUS § 5.1.2
Mobile Home Defects—Warr § 17.1.3
Mobile Home Foreclosure—Fore Ch 11
Mobile Home Parks—UDAP §§ 2.2.6, 5.5.1
Mobile Homes, Federal Statutes—Warr App C
Mobile Homes and Interstate Rate Deregulation—COC Ch 3
Mobile Homes and Repossession—Repo §§ 2.4.1, 3.5, 4.8.3, 5.2, 6.3.3, 7.1
Mobile Homes, Sale by Consumer—Repo § 9.6.3
Mobile Homes and UDAP—UDAP §§ 2.2.5, 5.4.12
Mobile Homes, Utility Service—AUS § 5.6
Mobile Homes, Warranties—Warr Ch 17
Model Pleadings—*See* Complaints, Interrogatories, Document Requests, etc.
Modification of Mortgage Loans—Fore § 2.3.4.6
Money Orders—CBPL Ch 5
Moratorium on Foreclosures—Fore § 2.13.1
Mortgage Assistance Scams—UDAP § 5.1.2.1; Fore Ch. 15
Mortgage Assistance, State Programs—Fore § 2.11.3
Mortgage Electronic Registration System (MERS)—Fore § 4.3.4.3
Mortgage Fees—TIL § 3.9.6; COC Ch 7
Mortgage Loans—UDAP § 5.1.5
Mortgage Servicers—Fore § 2.2.5.3, Chs 4AS, 5
Mortgage Servicing, Summary of State Laws—Fore App E
Most Favored Lender—COC § 3.4.3
Motion in Limine, Sample—Auto App I; FDC App J.5
Motions for Class Certification—*See* Class Certification Motions
Motor Homes—Warr § 14.8.5
Motor Vehicle Information and Cost Savings Act—Auto Chs 4, 5, App A.1
Motor Vehicle Installment Sales Act—COC § 2.3.3.5; Repo § 2.2
Multiple Damages—UDAP § 8.4.2; Auto § 5.8.1
Municipal Utilities (MUNIs)—AUS §§ 1.5, 12.2
NACA Class Actions Guidelines for Settlement—CCA App D
NACHA—CBPL Ch 3
National Arbitration Forum—Arbit App B.2, App H
National Origin Discrimination—CD § 3.3.3
"Nationwide" Reporting Agencies—FCR § 2.6.1
Native Americans and Repossession—Repo § 6.3.5.2
Natural Disasters—Fore § 2.13

Necessities Laws—FDC § 14.6; CD § 9.3
Negative Equity—COC § 11.6.3
Negative Option Plans—UDAP § 5.8.5
Negligence—Warr Ch 12; FCR § 10.5.4; FDC §§ 10.2, 10.7
Negotiations, Class Actions—CCA Ch 11
New Car Lemon Laws—Warr § 14.2, App F
New Cars, Sales—Warr Ch 14; UDAP § 5.4.7
New Cars, Undisclosed Damage to—Auto §§ 1.4.6, 6.2.3
New House Warranties—Warr Ch 18
900 Numbers—UDAP §§ 5.9.3, 6.10, Apps D, E
Nonattorney Legal Service Providers, Deceptive Practices—UDAP § 5.12.2
Nondisclosure and UDAP—UDAP § 4.2.14
Non-English Speaking—UDAP § 5.2.1
Nonfiling Insurance—COC § 8.5.4.5
Nonpayment of Loans, When Excused—Repo § 4.6
Non-Signatories Rights and Obligations—Arbit § 7.4
Notario Fraud—UDAP § 5.12.2
Notice Consumer Deducting Damages From Outstanding Balance—*See* Warr App J.3
Notice of Rescission—*See* Rescission Notice
Notice of Revocation—Warr App J.2
Notice to Class—CCA Ch 10
Notice to Quit, Deceptive—UDAP § 5.5.2.9
Not Sufficient Funds (NSF) Checks—CBPL § 2.5
Nursing Homes, Deceptive Practices—UDAP § 5.11.3
Obsolete Information in Consumer Reports—FCR § 5.2
Odometers—Auto; Warr § 15.7.2; UDAP § 5.4.6.5
Odometer Tampering—Auto §§ 4.3, 4.4
Offer of Judgment—FDC § 2.4.13; CCA § 6.3.2
Official Bankruptcy Forms—Bankr App D
Oil, Home Heating—AUS § 1.6; UDAP § 5.6.8
On-Line Fraud—UDAP § 5.9.4
On-Line Disclosures—UDAP § 4.2.14.3.9
On Us Checks—CBPL § 1.3.1.4
Open-End Credit—TIL Ch 5; COC § 2.3.2.3
Open-End Credit, Spurious—TIL § 5.2.3
Opening Statement, Sample—Auto App I
Outdated Information in Consumer Reports—FCR § 5.2
Overcharges by Creditor in Bankruptcy—Bankr § 13.4.3.3
Pain and Suffering Damages—FDC § 2.5; UDAP § 8.3.3.9
Paralegals, Attorney Fees for—UDAP §§ 8.6.11.6, 8.8.7.2
Parol Evidence—UDAP § 4.2.15.3; Warr § 3.7
Partial Prepayment—COC § 8.2
Pattern and Practice Evidence—Auto § 9.8
Payroll Cards—CBPL Ch 7
Pawnbrokers—COC §§ 2.3.3.9, 7.5.2.3; UDAP § 5.1.1.5.5
Payday Loans—COC § 7.5.5, App L
Payment Holidays for Interest-Bearing Loans—COC § 4.8.3
Payment Packing—COC § 11.6.4
Payment Plans, Utility Bills—AUS Ch 6
Pay Phones—AUS § 2.6
Pensions in Bankruptcy—Bankr §§ 2.5.2, 10.2.2.11
Percentage of Income Payment Plans—AUS § 9.2.3
Perkins Loans—Stud
Personal Injury Suits—UDAP § 2.2.11
Personal Property Seized with Repo—Repo Ch 7
Pest Control Services—UDAP § 5.6.3
Petroleum Products, Price Gouging—UDAP § 5.6.8.5
Photoprocessing Packages—UDAP § 5.7.10
Plain English—UDAP § 5.2.2
Pleadings—*See* Complaints, Interrogatories, Document Requests, etc.
Point of Sale (POS) Electronic Transfers—CBPL Ch 3

Quick Reference to the Consumer Credit and Sales Legal Practice Series
References are to sections in *all* manuals in NCLC's Consumer Credit and Sales Legal Practice Series

Points—COC §§ 4.7, 6.4.1.3, 7.2.1, 8.3.1.2; TIL § 3.7.5
Postal Money Order—CBPL Ch 5
Postdated Checks—CBPL § 2.6.1
Preauthorized Drafts—CBPL § 2.3.5
Precomputed Interest—COC § 4.5
Precut Housing—UDAP § 5.5.5.8
Preemption of State Usury Laws—COC Ch 3
Preemption and State Chartered Banks—COC Ch3
Preexisting Debt Clauses—Repo § 3.9
Prepayment—TIL § 4.7.6; COC Ch 5
Prepayment Penalties—COC § 5.8
Prescreening Lists—FCR § 7.3
Preservation of Documents, Class Actions—CCA § 5.2
Price Gouging in an Emergency—UDAP § 4.3.11
Pricing—UDAP § 4.6
Privacy, Invasion of—FCR §§ 10.5.3, 16.3; FDC § 10.3
Privacy, Restrictions on Use of Consumer Reports—FCR § Ch 7, § 12.2
Private Mortgage Insurance (PMI)—COC § 8.3.2.1; UDAP § 5.3.13
Private Sale of Collateral—Repo § 10.5.7
Privity—Warr Ch 6; UDAP § 4.2.15.3
Prizes—UDAP § 5.13.4
Procedural Unconscionability—Warr § 11.2; COC § 12.7
Proceeds—Repo § 3.3.2
Progress Payments—COC § 4.9
Propane—AUS § 1.6; UDAP § 5.6.8
Property Flipping—COC § 11.5.6; Fore § 5.3.4
Protective Orders—CCA § 5.2, App K
Public Assistance Status, Discrimination Based on—CD § 3.4.3
Public Housing, UDAP Coverage—UDAP §§ 2.3.3.3, 2.3.6
Public Housing, Utility Service—AUS Ch 8
Public Records—FCR
Public Sale of Collateral—Repo § 10.7
Public Utilities—AUS
Public Utility Credit—TIL § 2.4.6
Punitive Damages—Auto § 7.10; CD § 11.7.4; FCR § 11.12; FDC § 2.6, Ch 10; UDAP § 8.4.3
Punitive Damages & Arbitration—Arb § 11.7
Pyramid Sales—UDAP § 5.13.3
Pyramiding Late Charges—COC § 7.2.4.3; AUS § 6.2.6
Qualified Written Request—Fore App G
Race Discrimination re Credit—CD § 3.3.1
Racketeering Statute—*See* RICO
Reachback Periods—Bankr § 6.5.3.4
Reaffirmations and Bankruptcy—Bankr § 14.5.2
Real Estate—UDAP §§ 2.2.5, 5.5.5
Real Estate Settlement Procedures Act—*See* RESPA
Real Estate Tax Abatement Laws—Fore App H
Real Party in Interest—Fore § 4.3.4
Reassembled Cars from Parts—Auto §§ 1.4.3, 2.1.4; UDAP § 5.4.6.6
Rebates from Manufacturer—UDAP § 4.6.3.2; TIL § 3.7.5.2
Rebates of Interest—COC Ch 5, §§ 6.3, 6.4; TIL §§ 2.7, 3.7.2.2
Recoupment Claims—TIL §§ 6.3.3, 7.2.5; Bankr § 13.3.2.4
Redemption and Repo—Repo § 9.3
Redemption, Foreclosures—Fore §§ 4.2.6, 14.2
Redlining—CD §§ 7.1, 7.2
Referral Sales—UDAP § 5.8.3
Refinancings—COC Ch 6; Repo § 3.8; TIL § 4.9; UDAP § 5.1.5
Refund Anticipation Loans—COC § 7.5.4
Refunds—UDAP § 5.2.6
Regulation B, Text—CD App B
Regulation E—CBPL Ch 3, App D

Regulation M, Text—TIL App I.2
Regulation Z, Text—TIL App B
Regulation CC—CBPL § 9.4
Regulation DD—CBPL § 4.5
Rejection—Warr Ch 8
Reliance—TIL §§ 8.5.3.2, 8.5.4.7; UDAP § 4.2.12
Religious Discrimination re Credit—CD § 3.3.2
Remittances—UDAP § 5.1.10.4S
Rent and Bankruptcy—Bankr §§ 12.9, 14.5.5.3, 17.8
Rent to Own—UDAP § 5.7.4; Bankr § 11.8; COC § 7.5.3; Repo § 14.3
Rent, Utility Service—AUS Chs 4, 8
Rental Cars—UDAP § 5.4.9; Auto § 2.4.5.6
Rental Housing, Substandard—UDAP §§ 5.5.2.4, 5.5.2.5
Repairs—UDAP § 4.9.7
Repairs, Automobile—Warr § 19.8; UDAP § 5.4.1
Repayment Plan for Student Loans—Stud § 8.3
Replevin—Repo Ch 5
Reporting Agencies—FCR
Repossessions—Repo; UDAP § 5.1.1.5; FDC § 4.2.5
Repossessions, Stopping—Bankr Ch 9
Resale of Utility Service—AUS §§ 5.5, 5.6
Rescission—TIL Ch 6, App E.2.2; Auto § 7.11; Fore § 5.5.1; UDAP §§ 8.7, 9.5.2
Rescission by Recoupment—TIL § 6.3.3
Rescission Notice, Sample—TIL App D
Resisting Repossession, Liability for—Repo § 6.2.4.3
RESPA—COC § 12.2.2; Fore §§ 2.2.4.6, 2.2.5.3, Ch 8; TIL §§ 4.1.1, 4.3.4
Retail Installment Sales Acts (RISA)—COC § 2.3.3.5; Repo § 2.5.2
Retail Sellers—COC §§ 2.3.1.3.2, 9.2.3.2
Retaliation for Exercise of TIL, CCPA Rights—CD § 3.4.4
Retroactive Statutes—UDAP § 7.4; COC § 9.3.2
Reverse Metering—AUS § 5.1
Reverse Mortgages—Fore § 5.3.7.2
Reverse Redlining—CD §§ 8.2, 8.3
Review of Arbitration Decision—Arbit Ch 11
Revised Uniform Arbitration Act—Arbit Ch. 11
Revocation of Acceptance—Warr Ch 8
Revolving Repossessions—Repo § 10.11
RHS—*See* Rural Housing Service
RICO—UDAP §§ 9.2, 9.3, App C.1.1; COC § 12.6; FDC § 9.5; Auto § 8.5
Right to Cure Default—Repo § 4.8, App B; Bankr § 11.6.2
Right to See Consumer Reports—FCR § 3.3
Right to Utility Service—AUS Ch 3
RISA—COC § 2.3.3.5; Repo § 2.5.2
Rooker Feldman—FDC § 7.6.4
RTO Contracts—*See* Rent to Own
Rule of 78—COC § 5.6.3.3; TIL § 3.7.2.2.3; Repo § 11.3.2.2.2
Rural Electric Cooperatives (RECs)—AUS §§ 1.5, 12.2
RHS—*See* Rural Housing Service
Rural Housing Service—Fore § 2.7.3
Rustproofing—UDAP § 5.4.3.3
Safety—UDAP § 4.7.4
Sale and Lease-Back—COC § 7.5.2.1; TIL § 6.2.5
Sale of Collateral—Repo Ch 10
Salvage Auctions—Auto § 2.6.4.2
Salvage Vehicles, Sale of—Auto §§ 1.4.3, 2.1.4, 2.4.5.4, 6.2.1; Warr § 15.7.4
Salvaged Parts—UDAP § 5.4.6.6
Sample Answer and Counterclaims—*See* Answer and Counterclaims

Quick Reference to the Consumer Credit and Sales Legal Practice Series
References are to sections in *all* manuals in NCLC's Consumer Credit and Sales Legal Practice Series

Sample Attorney Fee Pleadings—*See* Attorney Fee Pleadings
Sample Client Retainer Forms— *See* Client Retainer Forms
Sample Closing Arguments—*See* Closing Arguments
Sample Complaints—*See* Complaints
Sample Deposition Questions—*See* Deposition Questions
Sample Discovery—*See* Interrogatories; Document Requests
Sample Document Production Requests—*See* Document Production Requests
Sample Forms, Bankruptcy—*See* Bankruptcy Forms
Sample Interrogatories—*See* Interrogatories
Sample Jury Instructions—*See* Jury Instructions
Sample Motion in Limine—*See* Motion in Limine Auto App I; FDC App J.5
Sample Motions for Class Certification—*See* Class Certification Motions
Sample Notice for Rescission—*See* Rescission Notice
Sample Notice of Deposition—*See* Deposition Notice
Sample Notice of Revocation—*See* Notice of Revocation
Sample Objection to Document Requests—*See* Document Requests, Sample Objection to
Sample Opening and Closing Statement—*See* Opening Statement; Closing Argument
Sample Pleadings—*See* Complaint, Interrogatories, Document Requests, etc.
Sample Requests for Admissions—*See* Admission Requests
Sample Trial Brief—*See* Trial Brief
Sample Trial Documents—*See* Trial Documents
Sample Voir Dire—*See* Voir Dire
School-Related Defenses to Student Loans—Stud § 9.6
Schools, Vocational—Stud Ch 9
Scope of Arbitration Agreement—Arbit Ch 7
Scrip Settlements, Class Actions—CCA § 11.6; CLP
Second Mortgage, Rescission of—TIL Ch 6
Secret Warranties—UDAP § 5.4.7.10.2; Warr § 14.5.3.2
Securities Law—UDAP § 9.4.10
Securitization of Consumer Paper—COC § 2.4.2
Security Deposits, Consumer's Rights to Reform Where Seller in Bankruptcy—Bankr § 17.8.4
Security Deposits, Tenant's—UDAP §§ 5.5.2.2, 5.5.2.3; FDC § 1.5.2.5
Security Deposits, Utility § 3.7
Security Interest Charges—TIL § 3.9
Security Interests—Repo Ch 3; TIL § 4.6.7
Security Interests, Avoiding in Bankruptcy—Bankr § 10.4.2.4, Ch 11
Security Systems—UDAP § 5.6.2
Seizure of Collateral—Repo
Self-Help Repossession—Repo Ch 6
Service Contracts—Warr Ch 20, App G; UDAP §§ 5.2.7.2, 5.4.3.5; Auto §§ 2.5.11, 2.6.2.11
Service Contracts, When Hidden Interest—COC §§ 7.2.3, 7.3.1; TIL § 3.6.5
Servicemembers Civil Relief Act—FDC § 9.12; Fore § 4.7; FCR 5.5.1; Repo 6.3.5.1
Servicer Abuses—Fore Ch 8
Services and Warranties—Warr Ch 19
Set Off, Banker's—CBPL Ch 4.3
Set-Offs—TIL §§ 5.9.3, 8.4; FDC § 12.6.7
Settlement, Auto Case—Auto § 9.11; Warr § 13.7
Settlement, Class Actions—CCA Chs 11, 12, Apps R, S, T
Settlement, Class Actions, Objections—CCA § 12.10, App U
Settlement, Individual Prior to Class Action—CCA § 1.2
Settlements and Consumer Reports—FCR § 12.6.4
Sewer Service—AUS § 1.2.3

Sex Discrimination re Credit—CD § 3.3.4
Sexual Orientation, Discrimination Based On—CD § 3.7
Shell Homes—UDAP § 5.5.5.8
Single Document Rule—COC § 11.6.8
Slamming, Telephone Service—AUS § 2.7.5.1; UDAP § 5.6.11
Small Loan Laws—COC § 2.3.3.2
Smart Cards—CBPL § Ch 7
Social Security Benefit Offset to Repay Student Loan—Stud § 5.4
Social Security Payments, Electronic—CBPL Ch 10
Soldiers' and Sailors' Civil Relief Act—*See* Servicemembers' Civil Relief Act
Spendthrift Trusts in Bankruptcy—Bankr § 2.5.2
Spoilation of Evidence—Warr § 13.2.5
Spot Delivery of Automobiles—UDAP § 5.4.5; Repo § 4.5; TIL §§ 4.4.5, 4.4.6; COC § 11.6.5
Spouses, Consumer Reports on—FCR § 5.6.1
Spreader Clauses—TIL § 4.6.7.6
Spurious Open-End Credit—TIL § 5.2.3
Stafford Loans—Stud
Standard Form Contracts, Unfair—UDAP § 5.2.3
State Arbitration Law—Arbit Ch 3
State Bonding Laws—Auto App C
State Chartered Banks and Preemption—COC Ch 3
State Cosigner Statutes—Repo § 12.9.6.2
State Credit Discrimination Laws—CD § 1.6, App E
State Credit Repair Laws—FCR App H
State Credit Reporting Laws—FCR § 10.6, App H
State Debt Collection Statutes—FDC § 11.2, App E
State Foreclosure Laws—Fore App C
State High Cost Loan Laws—COC Ch 7
State Home Improvement Statutes and Regs—Warr § 19.7.4
State Leasing Disclosure Statutes—TIL § 10.5.2.2
State Lemon Buyback Disclosure Laws—Auto App C
State Lemon Laws—Warr § 14.2, App F
State Lending Statutes—COC App A
State 900 Number Laws—UDAP App E
State Odometer Statutes—Auto App C
State Real Estate Tax Abatement Laws—Fore App H
State RICO Statutes—UDAP § 9.3, App C.2
State Right to Cure, Reinstate and Redeem Statutes—Repo App B
State Salvage Laws—Auto App C
State Service Contract Laws—Warr App G
State Telemarketing Laws—UDAP App E
State TIL Laws—TIL § 2.6
State Title Transfer Laws—Auto § 6.7, App C
State UDAP Statutes—UDAP App A
State Usury Statutes—COC App A
Statute of Limitations—TIL § 7.2
Statute of Limitations as Consumer Defense to Collection Action—Repo § 12.7
Statutory Damages—TIL § 8.6; FDC §§ 6.4, 11.2; Repo § 13.2; UDAP § 8.4.1
Statutory Liens—Repo Ch 15
Statutory Liens, Avoiding in Bankruptcy—Bankr § 10.4.2.6.3
Staying Foreclosure—Bankr Ch 9
Stolen Checks—CBPL §§ 2.8, 9.2
Stolen Vehicles—Auto §§ 1.4.11, 2.1.8, 8.2.2
Stop Payment on Checks, Credit and Debit Cards—CBPL §§ 2.6.2, 6.4, Ch3
Storage of Evicted Tenant's Property—Repo § 15.7.4; UDAP § 5.5.2.5
Stored Value Cards—CBPL Ch 7, App F
Straight Bankruptcy—Bankr Ch 3
Strict Liability in Tort—Warr Ch 12

582

Quick Reference to the Consumer Credit and Sales Legal Practice Series

References are to sections in *all* manuals in NCLC's Consumer Credit and Sales Legal Practice Series

Student Loan Collection Abuse—Stud Ch 4
Student Loan Repayment Plans—Stud Ch 8
Student Loan Regulations—Stud App B
Student Loans—Bankr § 14.4.3.8; FCR § 12.6.5; Stud; TIL § 2.4.5
Student Loans and Bankruptcy—Stud Ch 7
Student Loans, Reinstating Eligibility—Stud Ch 8
Summary Judgment Briefs, Sample—FDC App J.1; CLP
Surety for Consumer Debtor—Repo § 12.9
Surety Liability for Seller's Actions—Auto § 9.13.4
Survey Evidence—FDC § 2.9.3
Surveys, Use in Litigation—CCA § 7.1.2.2.3
Target Marketing Lists—FCR § 7.3.4
Tax Abatement Laws, State Property, Summaries—Fore App H
Tax Collections—FDC §§ 4.2.8S, 13.2
Tax Consequences, Bankruptcy Discharge—Bankr § 14.6
Tax Form 1099-C—CCA § 12.5.2.3.6
Tax Implications of Damage Award—CCA § 12.5.2.3
Tax Implications to Client of Attorney Fees—CCA § 15.5
Tax Intercept—Bankr § 9.4.3
Tax Liens—Fore Ch 13
Tax Refund Intercepts—Stud § 5.2; FDC § 13.2
Tax Refunds—COC § 7.5.4
Tax Refunds in Bankruptcy—Bankr § 2.5.5
Tax Sales—Fore Ch 13
Taxis, Undisclosed Sale of—Auto § 2.4.5.6
Telechecks—UDAP §§ 5.1.10
Telecommunications Act of 1996—AUS Ch 2, App C
Telemarketing, Payment—CBPL §§ 2.3.5, 3.8
Telemarketing Fraud—UDAP § 5.9; FCR § 15.4
Telemarketing Fraud, Federal Statutes—UDAP App D
Telephone Cards, Prepaid—CBPL Ch 7
Telephone Companies as Credit Reporting Agencies—FCR § 2.7.9
Telephone Harassment—FDC § 9.3
Telephone Inside Wiring Maintenance Agreements—UDAP §§ 5.2.7.2, 5.6.10
Telephone Rates, Service—AUS Ch 2, App C
Telephone Service Contracts—UDAP §§ 5.2.7.2, 5.6.10
Telephone Slamming—AUS § 2.7.5.1; UDAP § 5.6.10
Teller's Checks—CBPL Ch 5
Tenant Approval Companies—FCR §§ 2.6.2.2, 3.2.4
Tenant Ownership in Chapter 7 Liquidation—Bankr § 17.8.2
Tenant's Property Removed with Eviction—Repo § 15.7.4
Tenant's Rights When Landlord Files Bankruptcy—Bankr § 17.8; AUS § 4.5
Termination of Utility Service—AUS Chs 11, 12
Termite Control Services—UDAP § 5.6.3
Testers, Fair Housing—CD §§ 4.4.4, 11.2.2
Theft at ATM Machines, Bank Liability—CBPL § 3.5.4
Theft of Identity—FCR § 9.2
Third Party Liability Issues—AUS §§ 11.4, 11.5
Threats of Criminal Prosecution—FDC § 15.3
Tie-In Sale Between Mobile Home and Park Space—UDAP § 5.5.1.2
TIL—*See* Truth in Lending
Time Shares—UDAP § 5.5.5.10
Tire Identification—Auto § 2.2.3
Title, Automobile—Auto §§ 2.3, 2.4, Ch 3, Apps. D, E; UDAP § 5.4.5; Warr § 15.4.4
Tobacco—UDAP § 5.11.7
Tort Liability—FDC Ch 12
Tort Liability, Strict—Warr Ch 12
Tort Remedies, Unlawful Disconnections—AUS § 11.7.2
Tort Remedies, Wrongful Repossessions—Repo § 13.6
Towing—UDAP § 5.4.1.8; Repo Ch 15

Trade-in Cars—UDAP § 5.4.4.4
Trade Schools—Stud Ch 9; UDAP § 5.10.7
Trading Posts—UDAP § 5.1.1.5.5
Transcripts and Bankruptcy—Bankr § 14.5.5.2
Traveler's Checks—CBPL Ch 5, UDAP § 2.2.1.3
Travel Fraud—UDAP § 5.4.13
Treble Damages—UDAP § 8.4.2
Trebled, Disclosure to Jury that Damages Will Be—UDAP § 8.4.2.7.3
Trial Brief, Sample—FDC App J.4
Trial Documents, Sample—*See* Auto App I; FDC App J; Warr App M
Trustees in Bankruptcy—Bankr §§ 2.6, 2.7, 16.4.1, 17.7
Truth in Lending—TIL; COC §§ 2.3.4, 4.4.1; FDC § 9.4
Truth in Mileage Act—Auto Chs 3, 4, 5
Truth in Savings—CBPL § 4.5
Tuition Recovery Funds—Stud § 9.8
Typing Services—Bankr § 15.6
UCC Article 2—Warr
UCC Article 2 and Comments Reprinted—Warr App E
UCC Article 2A—Repo §§ 2.5.1.1, 14.1.3.1; Warr Ch 21, App E.5; UDAP § 5.4.8.5
UCC Articles 3 and 4—CBPL Chs 1, 2, App A
UCC Article 9—Repo
UCC Article 9, Revised—Repo App A
UCC Article 9 and Comments Reprinted—Repo App A
UDAP—UDAP; AUS § 1.7.2; Auto § 8.4; COC §§ 8.5.2.6, 12.5; FDC § 11.3; FCR § 10.6.2; Repo §§ 2.5.3.1, 13.4.3; Warr § 11.1
Unauthorized Card Use—TIL § 5.9.4
Unauthorized Practice of Law—FDC §§ 4.2.7.7, 5.6.2, 11.5; Bankr § 15.6; UDAP § 5.12.2
Unauthorized Use of Checks, Credit and Debit Cards—CBPL §§ 2.3, 3.3, 6.3
Unauthorized Use of Utility Service—AUS § 5.3
Unavailability of Advertised Items—UDAP § 4.6.2
Unconscionability—Warr §§ 11.2, 21.2.6; COC §§ 8.7.5, 12.7; UDAP §§ 4.4, 5.4.6.5; Auto § 8.7
Unconscionability of Arbitration Clauses—Arbit ch. 6
Unearned Interest—COC Ch 5
Unemployment Insurance—COC § 8.3.1.4
Unfair Insurance Practices Statutes—UDAP § 5.3; COC § 8.4.1.4
Unfair Practices Statutes—*See* UDAP
Unfairness—UDAP § 4.3
Uniform Arbitration Act—Arbit. Ch. 11
Uniform Commercial Code—*See* UCC
United States Trustee—Bankr §§ 2.7, 17.7.2
Universal Telephone Service—AUS Ch 2
Unlicensed Activities—COC § 9.2.4.5
Unpaid Refund Discharge of Student Loan—Stud § 6.4
Unsolicited Credit Cards—TIL § 5.9.2
Unsolicited Goods—UDAP § 5.8.4; FDC § 9.2
Unsubstantiated Claims—UDAP § 4.5
Used as New—UDAP § 4.9.4
Used Car Lemon Laws—Warr § 15.4.5
Used Car Rule—Warr § 15.8, App D; UDAP § 5.4.6.2, App B.6
Used Cars—Auto; Warr Ch 15, App K.3, App L.4; UDAP § 5.4.6
Used Cars, Assembled from Salvaged Parts—Auto §§ 1.4.3, 2.1.4
Used Cars, Financing—COC § 11.6
Used Cars, Undisclosed Sale of Wrecked Cars—Auto §§ 1.4.5, 2.1.4
Users of Consumer and Credit Reports—FCR Ch 7
Usury, Trying a Case—COC Ch 10
Utilities—AUS; CD §§ 2.2.2.3, 2.2.6.2; TIL § 2.4.6; UDAP §§ 2.3.2, 5.6.9

Quick Reference to the Consumer Credit and Sales Legal Practice Series
References are to sections in *all* manuals in NCLC's Consumer Credit and Sales Legal Practice Series

Utilities and Bankruptcy—AUS §§ 4.5, 12.1; Bankr § 9.8
Utilities as Credit Reporting Agencies—FCR § 2.7.9
Utility Commission Regulation—AUS § 1.3, App A
Utility Service Terminated by a Landlord—AUS § 12.4
Utility Subsidies in Subsidized Housing—AUS Ch 8
Utility Termination, Remedies—AUS § 11.7; UDAP § 5.6.9.1; FDC § 1.5.6
Utility Terminations, Stopping—AUS Chs 11, 12; Bankr Ch 9
VA Mortgage Foreclosures and Workouts—Fore §§ 2.7.2, 3.3
Variable Rate Disclosures—TIL § 4.8
Variable Rates, Calculation—COC § 4.3.6
Vehicle Identification Number—Auto § 2.2.4
Venue, Inconvenient—FDC §§ 6.12.2, 8.3.7, 10.6.3, 11.7; UDAP § 5.1.1.4
Vertical Privity—Warr § 6.2
Vocational Schools—Stud Ch 9
Voir Dire, Sample Questions—FDC App J.2
Voluntary Payment Doctrine—UDAP § 4.2.15.5; COC § 10.6.5
Wage Earner Plans—Bankr Ch 4
Wage Garnishment—FDC Ch 12, App D
Waiver of Default—Repo § 4.3
Waiver of Right to Enforce Arbitration Clause—Arbit Ch 8
Wage Garnishment of Student Loans—Stud § 5.3, App B.1.3
Warehouseman's Lien—Repo § 15.7.4
Warranties—Warr; Auto § 8.2; UDAP § 5.2.7

Warranties, Secret—Warr § 14.5.3.2; UDAP § 5.4.7.10.2
Warranty Disclaimers—Warr Ch 5
Warranty of Habitability, Utility Service—AUS § 4.4.1
Water Quality Improvement Systems—UDAP § 5.6.5
Water Service—AUS § 1.2.3, App I; UDAP § 5.6.11
Weatherization Assistance—AUS Ch 10
Web Sites, Consumer Advocacy—UDAP § 1.3
Welfare Benefits, Bankruptcy—Bankr §§ 10.2.2.11, 14.5.5
Welfare Benefits, Credit Discrimination—CD §§ 3.4.3, 5.5.2.5
Welfare Benefits, Credit Reporting—FCR §§ 2.3.6.6, 7.2.2
Welfare Benefits, Exemptions—FDC § 12.5
"Wheelchair" Lemon Laws—Warr Ch 16a
Wire Fraud—UDAP § 9.2.4.4
Wires—CBPL Ch 5
Withholding Credit Payments—Repo § 4.6.3; Warr § 8.5
Women's Business Ownership Act of 1988—CD § 1.3.2.4
Workers Compensation and Bankruptcy—Bankr § 10.2.2.1
Workout Agreements—TIL § 4.9.7
Workout Agreements, Foreclosures—Fore Ch 2
Wraparound Mortgages—COC § 7.4.3
Writ of Replevin—Repo Ch 5
Yield Spread Premiums—CD § 8.4; COC §§ 4.7.2, 7.3.2, 11.2.1.4.3, 11.2.2.6; UDAP §§ 5.1.3.3, 5.4.3.4
Yo-Yo Delivery of Automobiles—UDAP § 5.4.5; Repo § 4.5; TIL §§ 4.4.5, 4.4.6; COC § 11.2.2.5; CD § 10.4.2

NOTES

NOTES

NOTES

NOTES

About the Companion CD-Rom

CD-Rom Supersedes All Prior CD-Roms

This CD-Rom supersedes the CDs accompanying *Consumer Arbitration Agreements* (4th ed. 2004) and its supplements. Discard all prior CDs. The 2007 CD-Rom contains everything found on earlier CD-Roms and much additional material.

What Is on the CD-Rom

For a detailed listing of the CD's contents, see the CD-Rom Contents section on page xxiii of this book. Highlights and new additions include:

- The Federal Arbitration Act and federal statutes on limitations of arbitration involving military personnel and car dealers; California arbitration legislation, California ethics standards for arbitrators; a New Mexico statute restricting disabling civil dispute clauses; and NCLC's model state arbitration act;
- AAA, NAF and JAMS rules and procedures, newly updated for 2007;
- 15 sets of discovery in cases involving enforceability of arbitration clauses;
- Affidavit on importance of class action remedy;
- Over 50 sample briefs challenging enforceability of arbitration clauses on various grounds;
- AAA tax returns and documents in its file with major corporation seeking its services;
- 19 affidavits and depositions of AAA personnel on arbitration costs, fee waivers, and procedures;
- Over 30 documents related to the NAF's potential lack of impartiality, including an all-new report from Public Citizen and a brief and numerous related exhibits in *McQuillan v. Check 'N' Go of North Carolina* regarding NAF and arbitration's impact on consumers;
- Reprints of numerous arbitration agreements; and
- The full text of unreported case law cited in the text.

How to Use the CD-Rom

The CD's pop-up menu quickly allows you to use the CD—just place the CD into its drive and click on the "Start NCLC CD" button that will pop up in the middle of the screen. You can also access the CD by clicking on a desktop icon that you can create using the pop-up menu.[1] For detailed installation instructions, see *One-Time Installation* below.

All the CD-Rom's information is available in PDF (Acrobat) format, making the information:

- Highly readable (identical to the printed pages in the book);
- Easily navigated (with bookmarks, "buttons," and Internet-style forward and backward searches);
- Easy to locate with keyword searches and other quick-search techniques across the whole CD-Rom; and
- Easy to paste into a word processor.

While much of the material is also found on the CD-Rom in word processing format, we strongly recommend you use the material in PDF format—not only because it is easiest to use, contains the most features, and includes more material, but also because you can easily switch back to a word processing format when you prefer.

The CD-Rom includes a link to the Adobe web site to download the free Adobe Reader. **We strongly recommend that new Acrobat users read the Acrobat tutorial on the Home Page. It takes two minutes and will really pay off.**

How to Find Documents in Word Processing Format

Most pleadings and other practice aids are also available in Microsoft Word format to make them more easily adaptable for individual use. (Current versions of WordPerfect are able to convert the Word documents upon opening them.) The CD-Rom offers several ways to find those word processing documents. One option is simply to browse to the folder on the CD-Rom containing all the word processing files and open the desired document from your standard word processing program, such as Word or WordPerfect. All word processing documents are in the D:\WP_Files folder,

---

1 Alternatively, click on the D:\Start.pdf file on "My Computer" or open that file in Acrobat—always assuming "D:" is the CD-Rom drive on your computer.

if "D:" is the CD-Rom drive,[2] and are further organized by book title. Documents that appear in the book are named after the corresponding appendix; other documents have descriptive file names.

Another option is to navigate the CD in PDF format, and, when a particular document is on the screen, click on the corresponding bookmark for the "Word version of . . ." This will automatically run Word, WordPerfect for Windows, or *any other word processor* that is associated with the ".DOC" extension, and then open the word processing file that corresponds to the Acrobat document.[3]

Important Information Before Opening the CD-Rom Package

Before opening the CD-Rom package, please read this information. Opening the package constitutes acceptance of the following described terms. In addition, the *book* is not returnable once the seal to the *CD-Rom* has been broken.

The CD-Rom is copyrighted and all rights are reserved by the National Consumer Law Center, Inc. No copyright is claimed to the text of statutes, regulations, excerpts from court opinions, or any part of an original work prepared by a United States Government employee.

You may not commercially distribute the CD-Rom or otherwise reproduce, publish, distribute or use the disk in any manner that may infringe on any copyright or other proprietary right of the National Consumer Law Center. Nor may you otherwise transfer the CD-Rom or this agreement to any other party unless that party agrees to accept the terms and conditions of this agreement. You may use the CD-Rom on only one computer and by one user at a time.

The CD-Rom is warranted to be free of defects in materials and faulty workmanship under normal use for a period of ninety days after purchase. If a defect is discovered in the CD-Rom during this warranty period, a replacement disk can be obtained at no charge by sending the defective disk, postage prepaid, with information identifying the purchaser, to National Consumer Law Center, Publications Department, 77 Summer Street, 10th Floor, Boston, MA 02110.

---

[2] The CD-Rom drive could be any letter following "D:" depending on your computer's configuration.

[3] For instructions on how to associate WordPerfect to the ".DOC" extension, go to the CD-Rom's home page and click on "How to Use/Help," then "Word Files."

After the ninety-day period, a replacement will be available on the same terms, but will also require a $20 prepayment.

The National Consumer Law Center makes no other warranty or representation, either express or implied, with respect to this disk, its quality, performance, merchantability, or fitness for a particular purpose. In no event will the National Consumer Law Center be liable for direct, indirect, special, incidental, or consequential damages arising out of the use or inability to use the disk. The exclusion of implied warranties is not effective in some states, and thus this exclusion may not apply to you.

System Requirements

Use of this CD-Rom requires a Windows-based PC with a CD-Rom drive. (Macintosh users report success using NCLC CDs, but the CD has been tested only on Windows-based PCs.) The CD-Rom's features are optimized with Acrobat Reader 5 or later. If you do not have Adobe Acrobat or Adobe Reader, please visit www.adobe.com/reader to download the current version suitable for your computer and operating system. If you already have Adobe Reader 6.0, we *highly* recommend you install the 6.0.1 update from the Adobe web site at www.adobe.com because a bug in version 6.0 interferes with optimum use of this CD-Rom. The Microsoft Word versions of pleadings and practice aids can be used with any reasonably current word processor (1995 or later).

One-Time Installation

When the CD-Rom is inserted in its drive, a menu will pop up automatically. (Please be patient if you have a slow CD-Rom drive; this will only take a few moments.) If you do not already have Acrobat Reader 5 or later, first click the "Download Acrobat Reader" button. Do not reboot, but then click on the "Make Shortcut Icon" button. (You need not make another shortcut icon if you already have done so for another NCLC CD.) Then reboot and follow the *How to Use the CD-Rom* instructions above.

[*Note*: If the pop-up menu fails to appear, go to "My Computer," right-click "D:" if that is the CD-Rom drive, and select "Open." Then double-click on "Read_Me.txt" for alternate installation and use instructions.]